PENGUIN BOOKS

GUIDE TO AMERICAN GRADUATE SCHOOLS

Harold R. Doughty is currently a Management and Educational Consultant. He was formerly a Human Resource Staffing Specialist and Recruiter for J.P. Morgan Chase & Company; Executive Vice President and Chief Operating Officer at American Commonwealth University; Vice President for Admissions, Financial Aid, and Enrollment Services at United States International University; Director of Admissions and Summer Sessions at New York University; and Director of Admissions and Freshmen Development at Adelphi University. He is also the author of *The Penguin Guide to American Business Schools, The Penguin Guide to American Law Schools,* and *The Penguin Guide to American Medical and Dental Schools.*

TENTH EDITION, COMPLETELY REVISED

GUIDE TO AMERICAN GRADUATE SCHOOLS

Harold R. Doughty

PENGUIN BOOKS

PENGUIN BOOKS

Published by the Penguin Group
Penguin Group (USA) Inc., 375 Hudson Street,
New York, New York 10014, U.S.A.
Penguin Books (Canada), 90 Eglinton Avenue East, Suite 700,
Toronto, Ontario, Canada M4P 2Y3
(a division of Pearson Penguin Canada Inc.)
Penguin Books Ltd, 80 Strand,
London WC2R 0RL, England
Penguin Ireland, 25 St Stephen's Green, Dublin 2, Ireland
(a division of Penguin Books Ltd)
Penguin Group (Australia), 250 Camberwell Road, Camberwell,
Victoria 3124, Australia
(a division of Pearson Australia Group Pty Ltd)
Penguin Books India Pvt Ltd, 11 Community Centre,
Panchsheel Park, New Delhi – 110 017, India
Penguin Group (NZ), 67 Apollo Drive, Rosedale, North Shore 0632,
New Zealand (a division of Pearson New Zealand Ltd)
Penguin Books (South Africa) (Pty) Ltd, 24 Sturdee Avenue,
Rosebank, Johannesburg 2196, South Africa

Penguin Books Ltd, Registered Offices:
80 Strand, London WC2R 0RL, England

First edition published in the United States of America by
The Viking Press 1967
Published in a Viking Compass edition 1967
Second edition published 1970
Third edition published 1975
Published in Penguin Books 1976
Fourth edition published 1982
This tenth edition published 2009

1 3 5 7 9 10 8 6 4 2

ISBN 978-0-14-311468-0

Printed in the United States of America
Set in Times Roman

CONTENTS

PREFACE TO THE TENTH EDITION

"Crisis" is a word grown impotent from overuse.

That sentence has opened every edition of this *Guide* since it was first published in 1967. Many of the traumata that inspired the remark are now so dated as to seem almost quaint. Some remain, festering. And still others, thought to be in remission, have returned to haunt us. The original observation continues to be valid, then, both for the American educational system and the larger society that supports it and receives its benefits.

Yet, despite a lingering propensity to react to challenges, rather than to anticipate them, our colleges and universities have managed to transform themselves in meaningful ways. This is specially true of the postbaccalaureate. From 1995 to 2006 the number of women graduating with either a master's or doctoral degree has increased 150 percent and minority group registrations have doubled. In 2007, the number of doctorates awarded reached an all-time high of 55,300 with women earning almost 50 percent of those conferred. In addition, it is projected that by 2016 women will represent 56 percent of all doctorates awarded and that minority enrollment will level.

Problems persist, of course. Task forces of educators doggedly debate overproduction of doctorates, although the much-bemoaned "Ph.D. glut" is still confined primarily to the humanities and social sciences, and demand is still high for the products of most other disciplines. Complicating the anxieties of those same graduate faculties is the slowdown in the rate of increase of students pursuing advanced study. There is no *decline* in graduate enrollments, it must be understood. But after doubling every ten years since the turn of the century and tripling in the 1960s, graduate enrollments increased "only" from 1,031,000 in 1970 to 1,309,000 in 1979, to 1,742,000 in 1996 and is projected, over the next several years, to increase only slightly from the 2006 level of 2,250,000. The rush to advanced education has cooled, it is true, but it long threatened to boil over, so the results are not entirely negative. Unrestricted growth has been curtailed, costs are being contained, and some marginal academic operations are being eliminated or absorbed by those in which demand remains high. Under such circumstances—which should prevail throughout this decade—the quality of facilities and instruction should improve as universities learn to live within their means and focus on those areas in which they can best serve their client students.

Despite these contractions, applications for admission in most fields have remained constant. As education beyond high school has become a commonplace expectation, the demand for further training intensifies, if only to give a competitive edge in an ever-more-credentialed and specialized marketplace now being governed by consumer-oriented licensure requirements and regulations. That this is true is exemplified by the marked upswing in candidates for the master's degree, especially in business administration, computer application, and other narrowly defined and specialized programs. In spite of this, the current graduate student is being torn between the perceived need for graduate study and the immediate desire for career or job and instant financial gratification. The burdensome overabundance of applications of the past, which swamped understaffed administrative offices, has been greatly reduced. Higher application fees, earlier and earlier deadlines, and more stringent entrance standards, long a hallmark of the oversubscribed, have given way to the need for many graduate schools to market and offer programs via the Internet, use direct mail solicitations, and actively recruit students in order to maintain an adequate applicant pool. Full-time study has given way to part-time. Indeed, full-time faculty has in many cases had to give way to more specialized part-time or adjunct associates. It is fair to say that only a few prestigious institutions can hold to and enforce the high academic requirements of just a few years ago.

Those full-time applicants who gain entrance to the fabled colleges of their choice are now confronted by financial difficulties substantially greater than those experienced in their undergraduate years. The belief that ample financial aid funds await the use of every graduate student is quickly dispelled. Inflation, tight money, and parents who often are unable or just unwilling to subsidize further education force many students to assume staggering financial burdens just when he or she is least able to afford them. This may be the first confrontation with the practical reality that graduate students must have alternative financial means in order to afford the graduate education they desire. This scenario further reinforces the belief that to find employment now will give the needed direction to pursue graduate study on one's own, the direction that is so often missing in undergraduate study.

Although college guidance is fully developed at the high-school level, no equivalent counseling structure exists for the potential graduate student. Such advisement as is available is provided by a small number of placement officers and faculty members concerned that able students realize their full potential. Unfortunately, no single individual can keep abreast of current offerings at even the major institutions. Indeed, it is difficult to keep track of developments within a single large university. Despite these obstacles, it remains true that most students who hold bachelor's degrees can gain admission to some graduate school in any section of the country.

This volume is designed to provide the kind of basic information students need to reach sound decisions in the selection of appropriate institutions at which to continue their education. It describes more than thirteen hundred institutions throughout the United States providing graduate and professional study. All have been reviewed once again for this tenth edition of the *Guide to American Graduate Schools,* and still more complete information has been sought from their Web sites.

Listed are programs in all areas of the liberal arts and sciences, education, medicine, dentistry, veterinary medicine, pharmacy, nursing, law, social work, agriculture, theology, the applied arts, engineering, and business. Admission and degree requirements, standards, enrollment and faculty figures, tuition charges, financial aid opportunities, and research and housing facilities are given whenever possible. While this book has been prepared with the student in mind, it is hoped that counselors, faculty, and administrative officers will find it of value, as well.

It should be noted that the *Guide to American Graduate Schools* is intended only as a first source of information. Careful use of the data summarized should enable the student to become more fully aware of the opportunities available and then to narrow selections to the geographical area and then the institutions he or she is likely to find most suitable. The student is encouraged to seek the advice of undergraduate faculty, especially those who teach in the proposed field of graduate study. Catalogues, bulletins, departmental brochures, and Web sites should be used when possible. Most important, the applicant must be brutally frank in self-appraisal of his or her ability, objectives, and motives for undertaking graduate study.

The author wishes to express his indebtedness to the graduate deans, admission officers, their assistants, and the Web masters in the nation's colleges and universities who provided the information presented. Further revisions of this volume are planned, and corrections and suggestions are welcomed.

H.R.D.

INTRODUCTION

The Graduate School

Many students believe graduate study to be essentially an extension of undergraduate work, "only harder." On the contrary, the basic character and objectives of graduate and undergraduate study differ in many important particulars. The doctorate, and to a certain extent the master's degree, signifies the attainment of a high level of expertise in a given academic or professional field as well as the mastery of the investigative techniques of the scholar. Achievement of these goals relies upon the cultivation of habits of rigorous self-discipline and diligent thoroughness of mind.

The ensuing pages attempt to outline in forthright terms what a student can anticipate in graduate school, what will be demanded of him or her, and what he or she can expect in return. Since graduate education in the United States is simultaneously the target of severe criticism and the recipient of bountiful favor, the following remarks attempt to offer a balanced view of both the strengths and deficiencies of the system. This is not meant to suggest that these words constitute a complete analysis of graduate study. It is hoped, however, that these notes will help the student approach the decisions that face him or her with realism and some precision.

THE FIRST ONE HUNDRED TWENTY-FIVE YEARS

Graduate education in the United States is barely seven generations old. The attitudes and social conditions that characterized this predominantly rural young nation in the first half of the nineteenth century simply were not favorable to the extension of education beyond the college years. Despite the encouragement of many leaders, among them George Washington and Thomas Jefferson, several attempts to establish graduate education failed. The start of a tragic war sped the development of national maturity, and with it the first formal graduate program. Yale awarded three doctorates to students of its Scientific School in 1861.

Resistance to the founding of graduate programs dwindled as concern mounted over the numbers of American students flocking to German universities for postbaccalaureate study. Harvard announced in 1872 the availability of work leading to the Master of Arts, Doctor of Science, and Doctor of Philosophy. With the establishment of Johns Hopkins in 1876, and that university's avowed mission to bring its substantial resources to bear upon its graduate programs, higher education made its first firm commitment to advanced study beyond the baccalaureate.

With this recognition of responsibility, graduate education grew rapidly. By the end of the century, dozens of public and private universities enrolled graduate students. Soon the American penchant for standardization led quite naturally to the formation of the Association of American Universities. Harvard, Princeton, Columbia, Chicago, Johns Hopkins, California, Catholic, Pennsylvania, Michigan, Wisconsin, Clark, Cornell, and Yale were the charter members. As conceived, the organization was to encourage greater uniformity of conditions for successful work leading to higher degrees, to make representations to foreign universities regarding their admission of American students, and to improve European opinion of American degrees. Inevitably, since its membership included many of the most highly regarded universities, the Association became a prestigious organization into which invitation was eagerly sought. By World War I, ten additional institutions had been admitted.

After a period of stabilization in enrollment, during which acceptable standards for graduate study were defined, rapid growth resumed. Graduate enrollments, more than doubling every decade, went from 5800 in 1900 to 106,000 in 1940. World War II brought the demands for trained scientists and attendant governmental support that remain with us today, and the booming college enrollments of the 1950s intensified the need for college teachers. As a result of these and other pressures, graduate enrollment had surpassed the one-million mark by the mid-seventies and now the two-million mark.

Although the prestige of the Ph.D. and the other badges of completion of programs of graduate study has grown steadily over the last century, the increase in stature has been accompanied by rising criticism. The graduate school is often named as the assassin of the liberal arts college, and is said to have promoted professional proficiency at the expense of scholarship. Many critics feel that the value of the Ph.D. is demeaned by the practice of conferring this degree in fields other than those traditionally felt to be worthy of serious study. The graduate school is also accused, with justice, of enforcing archaic degree requirements simply because they have become the "keys to the club" of scholars.

Others have attacked graduate schools for emphasizing research over the training of college teachers (and vice versa), for promoting academic snobbery, and for adopting allegedly second-rate "professional" or "specialized" master's and doctoral degrees. Undoubtedly, debate will continue in the years to come, and along essentially the same lines as in the past. Witness this warning from the North Central Association: "The crowding of graduate schools has become so great as to raise some question as to the quality of work done and the value of the degree." This statement was issued in 1926.

Criticism notwithstanding, it is evident that increasing proportions of college graduates will seek the prestige of graduate degrees and the advantages, both intellectual and material, which accrue to those fortunate enough to be able to add those magic letters to their names.

SELECTING A GRADUATE SCHOOL

Once the student decides that graduate study will be of sufficient value to justify one or more years of hard work, major expenses, and the possible delay of personal plans or obligations, he or she must begin the often torturous task of making a choice of schools and opportunities. Once the choice of the proposed field of study is made, a number of considerations assume importance.

COST, SIZE, LOCATION. Contrary to widely held beliefs, financial aid for graduate students is by no means ample. Most students have to manage their support through means other than fellowships or similar awards. The most common solution is part-time study while employed full-time outside the graduate school. Whatever the method, the cost of attending graduate school is a primary factor in most students' deliberations. Fortunately, at least half of the most highly regarded institutions are publicly supported. Tuition costs therefore remain affordable, although usually somewhat higher than on the undergraduate level. Even the substantially higher charges normally set for out-of-state students at public universities are customarily less than the charges at private institutions. Furthermore, some public institutions are permitted to waive tuition and fees for nonresident graduate students under certain circumstances, or a student can establish residency in a relatively short period of time, thereby reducing tuition enormously, and these features should be checked.

Annual fees or tuition for residents in public institutions range from about $2200 to $7500, and from about $4000 to $21,000 for nonresidents. At most private colleges and universities the student can expect tuition charges from $6000 to $31,000, although some church-related schools may be less expensive. Private institutions rarely make distinctions between resident and nonresident students. Housing expenses vary widely, of course, depending upon sections of the country, rural or urban location, and the student's accustomed standard of living. Very roughly, married students can anticipate rents from $3500 to $17,000 annually, while single students will usually be charged between $3300 and $7400 for institutional housing, exclusive of board.

Size of a graduate school is an important factor, but caution must be observed in weighing this consideration.

Even in a graduate school with a very large enrollment, students in many fields can enjoy the advantages of small classes and close faculty–student rapport. Since graduate study is pursued primarily in a single field of study, the size of the major department may determine the closeness of faculty–student relationships as well as class enrollments. This is not meant to suggest that departments with large enrollments do not offer these benefits, but rather to warn against the assumption that large enrollments mean an impersonal, factory-like atmosphere in contrast to the presumed warmth and individual attention of smaller schools. It must be remembered, too, that larger institutions generally offer the extensive facilities required for many fields of study, while smaller institutions are more likely to specialize in fewer areas to permit them to provide equivalent research opportunities. In either case, care must be exercised in selecting not only a graduate school, but also the individual department in question.

Geographical location and type of environment can significantly influence choice of school. Institutions in urban centers offer distinct advantages, including cultural resources and greater research and employment opportunities than may customarily be found in rural locations. On the other hand, students who have spent most of their lives in nonurban environments may well find the tensions of the city too difficult, living costs too high, and distractions too numerous. The study of many fields is enhanced in obvious ways by the environment and by the availability of raw material for research. Sociology can have either an urban or rural emphasis, but other fields, such as public administration and art history, or animal husbandry and geology, are clearly oriented to specific environments. The student must weigh both his own background and preferences. Graduate study is demanding enough without the additional stress of unfamiliar surroundings or inadequate research opportunities.

THE QUESTION OF QUALITY. By the time a student is ready to consider graduate study, he or she knows that no thoroughly reliable measure of quality in education has been devised, including the latest attempts by *U.S. News & World Report.* Viewed through this screen of healthy cynicism, the selection of a graduate school can prove to be a less agonizing task than one might imagine. Recognizing that no two students can be equally served by one institution or program, the potential graduate student is nevertheless in a position to make certain basic judgments that will strengthen his or her chances for a satisfactory experience in graduate school.

The five factors most likely to influence estimations of quality are faculty resources, facilities, student body, reputation, and placement success. The question of reputation is most subject to challenge and yet apparently is most unshakable as it is assigned to particular institutions. This fact is evidenced in several evaluations of quality in graduate education dating from 1925 to the most recent in 2007. In these compilations of academic opinion, the same twenty to twenty-five graduate schools have appeared consistently as the most distinguished institutions. While schools within this group shift position somewhat in each new study, and occasionally a newer school makes the grade, this cluster of top-rated schools varies only slightly.

A relationship clearly exists between *perceived* quality and prestige. For many reasons, however, these listings of academic departments in order of presumed merit inevitably favor the older institutions. Most of the individuals queried in these surveys of opinion are senior professors or deans, for the quite logical reason that they possess sufficient experience to enable them to draw distinctions between departments. On the other hand, it must be remembered that until 1970 only twenty-five graduate schools gave over half the doctorates awarded annually. Since it can be assumed that most faculty members participating in these studies received their doctorates from these same twenty-five schools, some narrowness in scope of representation persists as a result of institutional background and loyalties.

Despite these and other limitations, these studies, undertaken by reputable agencies, serve as valuable guides to students seeking strong programs in certain fields. Other criteria for assessing quality are available, however. School catalogues, departmental brochures, or Web sites are valuable sources of information. Many graduate schools list the institutions that awarded the highest degrees held by each member of the faculty. It is often possible to discover the number and kind of publications produced and the professional honors and awards received by a professor by referring to such volumes as *Who's Who in America,* the *Directory of American Scholars,* and reports provided by the professional associations representing each academic field. Since the most distinguished members of every faculty are eagerly sought by industry, government, and other institutions, the catalogue often states whether professors are on leave or sabbatical, and, of course, whether they are still employed by the university. Since graduate students often seek the opportunity to study under noted scholars, it should be determined whether particular faculty members are to be available during the student's period of attendance. This is particularly true of students taking only the master's degree.

Examination of the catalogue or Web site also reveals the number of courses in each department that are open to undergraduate as well as graduate students. While course requirements often differ in such cases, depending upon the status of each student, effectiveness and content of a course may be impaired because of disparities in student backgrounds. Further, the number of courses and breadth of material covered can be important, allowing for the tendency to offer too many courses that might overlap.

Reports in general and academic news media are additional sources of information. These list the institutions attended by the recipients of the many prestigious fellowships, such as the National Science Foundation Fellowship program, as well as the grants of federal and state governments. Since the competition for these awards is keen, the institutions selected by these honored few can be assumed to offer well-regarded programs in specific fields. The simple fact that clusters of fellowship recipients attend specific schools at the very least reflects favorably upon the composition of their student bodies.

Most graduate students agree that the capability of their colleagues is very important in their assessments of the effectiveness of their programs. In fact, many observers suggest that it is difficult to determine whether a school or department is good because the training is better than elsewhere or because the students enrolled are stronger. This suggests a relationship between competitiveness of admission standards and quality of program. The potential graduate student can indeed reach valid conclusions about the makeup of a school's student body by determining the levels of competition resulting from admission policies.

It must be emphasized, however, that difficulty of admission *cannot be equated* with quality of program. As observed elsewhere, students exercise self-selection in applying to the more prestigious institutions, but often little restraint is evident in applications to more lightly regarded schools. This may result in the former group of schools accepting more than two-thirds of their applicants, while the latter rejects a much larger percentage. Also, small departments with excellent faculties and facilities sometimes find they must employ "soft" admission policies to build their enrollments, and thus their contribution to institutional budgets, while larger departments in more popular fields often must restrict admission because of limited faculties and facilities.

Availability and scope of research facilities provide another clue to the quality of individual schools. The nature and breadth of facilities can be indicative of a school's commitment to serious research and of its ability to attract support. The manner in which funds are allocated suggests something of the priorities established by an institution. Elaborate stadia and athletic arenas casting shadows across aging classroom buildings may not only be symptoms of the enthusiasms of misguided alumni, but the situation may also be evidence of misplaced emphasis by the administration.

The size of an institution's library holdings and the manner in which these resources are made available to students can be assumed to have considerable bearing upon quality. Virtually all of the highly regarded universities have library holdings well in excess of three million volumes, and several have more than five million. The only significant exceptions are a few leading technological institutions. Large numbers of volumes, microforms, and periodicals do not in themselves insure the quality of library resources, of course. A major portion of the collections should be on open stacks, or at least permission for access should be easily obtainable. Ideally, individual alcoves or carrels and research databases and Internet access are made available to graduate students. Students are wise to seek information about the nature of specialized collections in their particular fields of interest. Older institutions with large libraries may have weaker collections in the modern disciplines, while newer universities often possess holdings of less breadth and more internal access. Institutional resources are often supplemented by nearby public libraries and research institutes, and this is to be borne in mind when considering graduate schools. Finally, some groups of institutions have arrangements pooling their libraries for the common use of their combined student bodies.

Other criteria are useful in assessing quality, though perhaps not as important as those discussed above. Among these are faculty salaries, eminence of alumni, number of recipients of major fellowships among both the graduate students and the faculty, number of Nobel Prize winners on the faculty, and institutional rank in production of doctorates and in size of annual gifts. Most of these factors are weighted in favor of the larger institutions, which makes it again necessary to stress the importance of investigating individual departments within graduate schools as well as the schools themselves.

GUIDANCE. Counseling services for prospective graduate students are largely informal and unorganized at most undergraduate colleges, with the exception of a few institutions that send large percentages of their graduates on to advanced study. Some universities have established regular series of interviews for those undergraduates who have demonstrated particular promise for graduate work. In addition, representatives of professional schools, especially those offering study in law and business administration, often visit colleges and universities as part of recruitment efforts. Unfortunately, this practice is rare on the part of graduate schools.

The best sources of specialized information about graduate study continue to be the members of the faculty in the student's proposed field of graduate study or current graduate students. Most professors can readily list the five to ten graduate schools offering what they believe to be the strongest programs in their disciplines. They can also aid the student in planning for financial aid and in discussing career opportunities. If the student is able to obtain some consensus on these matters from several faculty members, so much the better.

Some college placement offices make efforts to gather material about opportunities for graduate study and financial aid, and libraries and admissions offices generally keep files of graduate catalogues.

ADMISSION

It may be reassuring to know at the outset that most college graduates can gain admission to some graduate school somewhere in the section of the country they prefer. There are, of course, exceptions to this rule in some fields of specialization, but the statement remains valid for the vast majority of applicants. The reason this is true is the tendency on the part of most graduate schools to screen students more vigorously *following* entrance rather than before. This results in the common distinction made between probationary admission, admission to study, and admission to candidacy. The latter procedure is typical on the doctoral level, and preliminary or qualifying examinations are usually employed to determine eligibility for continuance toward the degree. Applicants for the master's degree are not often expected to meet requirements for formal candidacy, but the practice is less standard at this level.

Although admission policies and procedures vary widely from school to school and between departments, there are general requirements that have become fairly standard.

PREPARATION. Graduate schools of arts and science, education, business, and the like nearly always expect applicants to possess an appropriate bachelor's degree at the time of entrance. Although it is occasionally possible to gain admission without this degree, compensatory strength in previous academic performance or experience is customarily demanded.

The specific kind of undergraduate preparation necessary for individual fields of graduate study is much less subject to uniformity. Some social science departments are willing to consider applicants who do not present undergraduate majors in a particular social science discipline, but who have accumulated course work in several social science fields. While sociology departments are often liberal on this point, economics departments generally demand full undergraduate preparation. Because of the often greater-than-usual curricular requirements on the graduate level in psychology, many psychology departments accept applications from students with as few as twelve semester hours of undergraduate study in psychology, assuming substantial work was completed in the natural and social sciences or statistics. While it is not possible to note all these variations here, it is usually true that natural and physical science departments demand extensive undergraduate preparation in the proposed field of graduate study, and departments of business, political science, sociology, and education place less emphasis on specific training at the college level. The humanities and older social sciences are likely to fall somewhere in the middle range in this regard.

CREDENTIALS. Every graduate institution requires that at least one official transcript of the undergraduate record be provided in support of the application for admission. If a student has attended more than one college or university, a single official transcript from the institution conferring the baccalaureate, showing courses accepted in transfer, is often adequate. More often, graduate schools request submission of transcripts from *each* undergraduate institution attended. Since admission procedures on the graduate level are often coordinated efforts between the offices of the dean, the departments, and/or admissions, it is not unusual for two or even three copies of each transcript to be required. Applicants are of course expected to provide official transcripts of any graduate study completed elsewhere, in addition to undergraduate records.

Letters of recommendation are typically required, usually from one to three persons, but often from as many as four or five. Generally, the letters are to be provided by members of the applicant's faculty who are in a position to assess his aptitude and motivation for graduate study. In the case of elementary and secondary teachers seeking further study, references may be required from a school supervisor. While potential for graduate study is customarily the basis for the letter of recommendation, some graduate schools desire evaluations of the character of the applicant as well.

Special departmental applications must be submitted on occasion if it is felt that a particular area of specialization is not adequately served by the general graduate school application. This is characteristically true of departments or schools offering programs of a more professional nature within larger graduate divisions empowered to grant all or most graduate degrees. This might include majors in social work, business administration, education, urban planning, or architecture, among others.

ENTRANCE EXAMINATIONS. Contrary to widely held opinion, the submission of results of entrance examinations is by no means a standard graduate school admission requirement. Accordingly, a student should ascertain whether he or she must meet this entrance requirement for the specific department of the particular graduate school in which he or she is interested. Those who intend to apply for national fellowships must also determine whether an examination is required for consideration.

Very few graduate schools have flat, divisionwide entrance exam requirements. Individual departments may specify single parts of exams, such as the general or appropriate subject test of the Graduate Record Examination. Others accept either the GRE or the Miller Analogies Test or require both. Many departments have no stated exam requirement but *strongly recommend* submission of test results. (In this case, the prudent applicant will take the suggested exams.) In still other schools, there is a minimum test requirement for all applicants, with the departments stipulating additional exams when felt to be appropriate.

It must be noted that the reason for this lack of uniformity in entrance exam requirements is the divergence of opinion on the relative value of these tests as predictors of success in graduate study. Many graduate schools and departments use the tests essentially as a screening device when confronted with the problem of selecting a limited number of students from a much larger group of highly qualified applicants. It is further suspected that some schools utilize the tests more to satisfy notions of status or prestige than to measure aptitude.

The examinations most commonly used are the Graduate Record Examination (referred to here as the GRE), the Miller Analogies Test (MAT), and the Graduate Management Admissions Test (GMAT). On occasion, individual schools supplement or replace these exams with tests of their own creation. Arrangements often can be made to take the exam at the applicant's present institution if it is inconvenient to travel to the school requiring the special exam.

The Graduate Record Examination has a general test plus subject tests in eight fields of graduate study. The general test has verbal, quantitative, and analytical writing sections, scored separately, and is designed to determine scholastic ability in those three general areas. The general test is two and one-half hours long, the subject test in each field takes three hours. While there is no minimum "passing" score, scores below 450 on the 200 to 800 scale and 500 on the 200 to 990 scale for the subject test are rarely considered adequate by most graduate schools with this requirement.

The Miller Analogies Test attempts to measure verbal and reasoning ability and takes only fifty minutes to complete.

The Graduate Management Admissions Test measures abilities and skills developed over a long period of time. It requires you to think clearly and systematically.

Information about these examinations may be obtained from most graduate admissions offices, their Web sites, or from the Psychological Corporation, 7500 Old Oak Blvd., Cleveland, Ohio 44130 (MAT), the Educational Testing Service in Princeton, N.J., or Los Angeles, Calif. (GRE), and www.mba.com (GMAT). The examinations are given at colleges and universities across the country.

OTHER REQUIREMENTS. Some departments offering certain forms of advanced study set additional admission requirements. Applicants for graduate study in music are usually expected to audition for performance and music education programs or to provide samples of work for composition programs. Creative art majors typically are asked to supply either portfolios or photographs of finished work. Other departments or schools require statements of purpose for graduate study, which may include projected plans for the thesis or final project. Interviews are often requested, either for students with marginal records or for entrance to certain departments.

STANDARDS. Although graduate schools commonly specify a minimum "B–" average for entrance, the manner in which this standard is interpreted or applied varies substantially. It may refer to the cumulative grade average of all four years of undergraduate study, or to just the junior and senior years. The school may have in mind the average for all study completed, or only the courses in the proposed field of graduate study. Still another distinction is in the degree of rigidity with which the stated minimum average is observed. Some schools make no exceptions to the minimum, others regard the average as simply a point of guidance and regularly admit students whose records fall below it.

Further, some schools interpret the "B" as "B–." In other words, "B" to one school may be a 3.0 average on the customary four-point scale (A = 4, B = 3, C = 2), while another school might regard a 2.75 as essentially a "B" average. In practice, therefore, the "B" average stipulation can mean either the admission of virtually any college graduate or of a limited number of superior applicants. Despite the elusive manner in which this standard is interpreted, specific minimum grade point averages are listed, when available, for each graduate institution in this revised *Guide*. Due caution should be exercised in interpreting this information.

Most schools give greatest weight to the undergraduate performance in the proposed field of graduate study, assuming the total average is not significantly out of line with that in the courses in the major area of concentration.

The reputation of the undergraduate college undeniably has some bearing upon admission to the more highly selective graduate schools. It is not unusual for departments to offer admission more readily to graduates of institutions of substantial national prestige than to students applying from little-known colleges. Unhappy experiences with graduates of particular colleges often cause departmental suspicion of subsequent applicants. Some graduate departments are known to deny admission even to honors graduates of colleges they view with disfavor. Generally, however, applicants are judged upon the merits of their individual records. Among the students of the most highly regarded graduate schools are found many alumni of obscure colleges.

DEADLINES. Students are urged to make their inquiries about admission and financial aid at least a year in advance of the date of anticipated enrollment. While closing dates for receipt of applications for admission are rarely as early as for undergraduate colleges, the deadlines for financial aid applications for the more selective institutions are generally set for midwinter, and some fall as early as December 1. Schools state their closing dates in different ways. Some of the highly selective schools simply give the date by which applications for financial aid *and* admission must be filed, indicating that applications solely for admission are considered after that date as long as spaces continue to exist. Most graduate schools give separate closing dates for each type of application, noting that those applying for particular forms of aid must file both applications by the same stated deadline.

Since the award of most assistantships and some service fellowships depends upon vacancies created by the anticipated graduation of present recipients, departments may accept applications later in the spring for these particular awards than for scholarships and most fellowships.

The fragmented organizational structure of graduate schools often makes it difficult to determine to which office inquiries should be directed. Most often, requests for information are answered by the office of the dean of the graduate school or by the admissions office of the school or university. Sometimes the head of the proposed major department is the proper person to query about assistantships as well as admission. Students are advised to contact the specific individuals or offices noted in the institutional entries of this book as an initial resource or visit the individual school's Web site to obtain current information.

FINANCIAL ASSISTANCE

Many types of financial assistance are available through federal and state governmental agencies, private foundations, and civic organizations. While space does not permit a listing here of specific grants and awards, the following paragraphs should enable students to identify sources for further exploration.

The customary distinction drawn between fellowships and scholarships is that the former type of grant often requires some service in exchange for a stipend, while the latter carries no obligation other than satisfactory academic performance. Increasingly, however, graduate schools use the term "fellowship" to cover both outright awards and service grants, since "fellowships" are more readily associated with graduate study. Whatever label is used, it is worth noting that grants that require no service function are tax-free, while those demanding some form of work must be reported on income tax forms. However, IRS regulations and the interpretation of the regulations sometimes change the way income is reported and therefore all students receiving some type of stipend should verify how this remuneration will be reported for tax purposes.

Traineeships, assistantships, and internships provide stipends for performance of a variety of tasks. These include classroom teaching, proctoring in residence halls, laboratory research, and duties of a more or less clerical nature, such as grading undergraduate test papers or gathering and filing research materials.

An aura of status often surrounds the fellowship, and this characteristic may be enhanced by larger stipends and perhaps more engaging tasks than are normally associated with assistantships. Fellowship stipends range on the average from $15,000 to $20,000, and in private institutions carry tuition remission privileges as well. Allowances for dependents of married fellows may range from $1500 to $3500. Assistantships normally carry grants on a somewhat lower scale than fellowships, from perhaps $6000 to $12,000 plus free tuition or tuition waivers. Stipends for some fellowships and/or for married students with two or more dependents occasionally reach highs of more than $45,000. At the other end of the scale, awards of an essentially honorary nature may pay as little as $500. Fellowships, assistantships, traineeships, and similar grants are available through the graduate schools or through individual departments, either from their own funds or from outside funds administered by them.

Although fellowships traditionally were reserved for doctoral candidates, many of those mentioned above and those available from other sources are open to students seeking the master's degree. Further information can be obtained through the office of the dean of the graduate school or designated members of the faculty representing various agencies. Students should also note the announcements of fellowships and other forms of assistance customarily posted on bulletin boards at central points in most colleges.

Students should not forget the possibility of full-time employment in the administrative offices of the institution in which they wish to study. Clerical positions are usually available in the offices of the Registrar, Dean of Admissions, Student Housing, Personnel, and others, and often carry a limited tuition remission privilege for part-time graduate study.

Most students must continue to find their solutions in combinations of outside employment, part-time study, loans, and support by parents or working spouses. This situation continues to run counter to the generally accepted conviction that graduate work is best accomplished through full-time study, but it does recognize the practical reality that graduate students must have alternative financial means in order to afford the graduate education they desire.

A note should be made at this point: the Internet has become a potential graduate student's best source of information for both university and nonuniversity financial assistance. Among the most noteworthy nonuniversity Web sites are the Council of Graduate Schools site (www.cgsnet.org) and the National Association of Graduate Professional Students site (www.nagps.org). Obviously one should consider that the best source for institutional financial assistance is always the individual College's or University's financial aid site. However, one word of caution: always check for the date the Web site was last modified to ensure you are getting the most current information. The author found that some institutional sites were quite out of date; in fact, some sites observed had not been updated in the last three years.

THE STRUCTURE OF GRADUATE STUDY

Anxiety and doubt often attend a student's embarkation on the path to the master's and doctoral degrees. The candidate is confronted by a maze of course options, language and research tool requirements, oral and written examinations, thesis proposals and faculty committees, and academic standards. While no one is likely to suggest that successful negotiation of these obstacles can be accomplished with ease, certain patterns of expected performance can be anticipated prior to entrance.

THE PROGRAMS. Perhaps the first surprise for the beginning student is the realization that graduate study, especially on the master's level, is not necessarily a series of intimate seminars conducted by brilliant scholars and famous professors. In many universities, a number of courses are open to both graduate and undergraduate students, and these are likely to be conducted as lectures rather than discussion groups. In the more popular majors or in classes taught by senior members of the faculty, more than half the courses for the master's may have enrollments in excess of one hundred students. Even courses billed as seminars may have twenty or thirty students, which makes the free-discussion format difficult, or the professor may simply choose to conduct the class on a lecture basis.

For most master's degrees, the customary course requirement is the equivalent of two semesters (or three quarters) of full-time study. In some cases, however, the professional master's extends over two academic years; this is true of the Master of Fine Arts and the Master of Business Administration, for example. In the data disciplines, the necessary time for the master's often includes a full year of course work plus up to one additional year for research for the thesis. A great many graduate schools have two plans for the master's degree, one including the thesis or final project, the other without a thesis.

The candidate planning to continue to the doctorate is wise to make his preliminary decision for his doctoral dissertation early in the master's program. The exercise of this foresight may permit him to accomplish basic research for the dissertation while working on the master's thesis.

Although some cross-disciplinary programs are available for both the master's and doctorate, permitting some flexibility in course work, the graduate student must realize that he or she is subject to what might be described as "instant commitment"; that is, all or nearly all of his or her courses will be in one area of specialization or in fields bearing directly upon his or her major field of study. Interdepartmental programs such as American Studies or biochemistry allow somewhat more latitude in course work, but a common objective serves to emphasize a particular aspect of even the broadest interdisciplinary study. Students cannot expect, therefore, to make decisions about their majors following entrance, as may have been the case when they began undergraduate study.

In the second or third years of study, course work becomes more advanced than in the first year of essentially introductory work. Seminars in more specialized areas are increasingly the rule, and large lecture classes are generally less common. The doctoral candidate can expect to be required to complete a minimum of two years of course work beyond the master's, in full-time attendance or the equivalent in part-time study.

EXAMINATIONS, CANDIDACY, AND RESIDENCE. Some departments conduct placement exams at the time of initial registration for the master's program. This is characteristic of chemistry and music departments, among others, and the test is used essentially for guidance purposes. Others set the exam later in the first semester of registration and use it for the dual purpose of placement and formal matriculation. In either case, the test varies greatly in duration, content, and format from school to school. It may measure general English usage, or knowledge in specific areas of the major field, or simply aptitude for graduate study. The requirement is often waived altogether if the student presents acceptable results of the GRE, MAT, or GMAT taken prior to entrance. Only a few departments or schools make this requirement for the master's, however.

An exam after the initial stages of doctoral study is much more common, although not universal. Again, the test may simply determine the student's acceptability for advanced doctoral study, in which case it is usually referred to as a "preliminary" examination. An exam more comprehensive in content is generally required following completion of a majority of formal course work for the doctorate. Satisfactory performance on this test often precedes admission to doctoral candidacy. At many schools, these tests are combined in a variety of ways, and in form they can be written, oral, or both. Terminology is also mixed, even between departments within schools. As a result, exams may be labeled as "qualifying," "candidacy," or "comprehensive."

In any event, a student can anticipate at least one examination before he or she is admitted to formal candidacy for the doctorate. Less standard is an exam for master's degree candidacy. Candidacy may be withheld further, especially on the doctoral level, until satisfaction of the language or research tool requirements, submission of an acceptable dissertation proposal, and/or appointment of a dissertation advisory committee.

Finally, presentation of the master's thesis or doctoral dissertation is usually followed by an oral and/or written examination, the oral portion of which is customarily a defense of the thesis or dissertation itself. A final written exam is typically required if the "candidacy" or "comprehensive" was oral in form.

Potential students should determine prior to entrance the graduate school's interpretation of the term "residence." At minimum, it refers to the number of semester or quarter hours which must be completed at the school itself, exclusive of advanced standing awarded for work completed at other graduate schools. However, "residence" is sometimes interpreted to mean only work completed while in *full-time* attendance at the institution awarding the degree. Graduate schools are often rather obscure in their explanations of this requirement. An impression may be given in their catalogues that only full-time study is permitted, but the qualification "or its equivalent" may be found tucked away in the text.

Most master's programs demand that at least 24 semester hours of a 30-hour requirement (or 36 *quarter* hours of a 45-hour total) be completed at the institution granting the degree. If the thesis or final project is included in the total credit-hour requirement, the stated residence still applies. Some schools expect only one summer session in full-time attendance, so the attendance and residence requirements obviously differ. Schools or departments requiring full-time residence for the master's during the regular academic year are in the minority. Periods of full-time attendance are increasingly expected for the Ph.D., less commonly for "professional" doctorates such as the Ed.D., Psy.D., and D.B.A.

It is difficult to make definitive statements regarding residence requirements for the doctorate. However, while the trend toward increased full-time residence is clear in the most prestigious schools, most graduate schools still permit students to complete most or all course work while in attendance as part-time students. A number of schools refuse to make flat statements about the doctoral credit-hour requirement, preferring instead to state this in terms of total semesters, quarters, term units, or years. In general, students are expected to complete at least three years of full-time study or its equivalent beyond the bachelor's, including course work applied toward the master's. Time needed for the writing of the dissertation usually extends beyond this minimum period of course work. Indeed, the average total period of work for recipients of the Ph.D. is estimated to be well over six years. This includes, of course, time for the master's degree, research for the dissertation, and interruptions in attendance. It might be noted that this "Ph.D. stretch-out" is a subject of much academic controversy, since lingering students tie up faculty and facilities, cause substantial administrative problems, and contribute to the oversupply of ABDs.

THE LANGUAGE REQUIREMENT. Perhaps five percent of the nation's graduate schools require some sort of ability in at least one foreign language for the master's degree. A diminishing number of schools, however, demand knowledge of at least one language, and sometimes two, for the doctorate. The language requirement has evolved from the traditional French, German, and/or Russian of the early years of graduate study in the United States to a variety of present forms.

For the master's degree, the language requirement is generally stated as a "reading knowledge of one modern foreign language, usually French, German, or Russian." The requirement is usually not schoolwide, but some departments may stipulate a reading knowledge when their schools do not. On the doctoral level, two of the above-named languages may be specified. Several variations of this customary requirement for the doctorate have cropped up in recent years, however. These include (1) a reading, speaking, and writing knowledge of one foreign language, *or* reading knowledge only of two languages; (2) a proficiency in one foreign language or in two languages; (3) a reading knowledge of one language plus proven ability to use another appropriate research tool such as statistical methods; and (4) reading knowledge of only one language.

Although some graduate schools adhere to the traditional French, German, or Russian requirement for the doctorate, most now permit substitution of another language deemed appropriate for a particular area of specialization for at least one of the two languages. A substantial number of graduate schools, responding to the criticism that the language requirement is no longer justifiable as a research tool in most fields, have either eliminated the language requirement altogether or have reduced it for the

doctorate to one language, permitting individual departments to set additional requirements as they feel appropriate. This trend appears to be accelerating. Thus, three or more languages may be stipulated for the Ph.D. in the art history or comparative literature departments, while only one language may be mandatory for the history department; or appropriate languages may be required for particular specializations within a single academic discipline and not for others.

While the language requirement, in its various forms, remains a part of most Ph.D. programs in the arts and sciences, other doctoral programs, notably in education, business, and psychology, have reduced or eliminated the requirement. In these cases, additional course work and a research tool/computer literacy have become acceptable substitutes.

Criticisms of the foreign language requirement are many—that it is no longer a functional tool, that the "general culture" justification is out-of-date, that it serves to discourage able students—and modifications will continue to be made. The admonition to examine departmental rather than institutional standards thus gains strength.

THE THESIS, PROJECT, AND DISSERTATION. When a thesis is required for the master's degree, its purpose is often described as a "comprehensive survey of a specific area of knowledge." The doctoral thesis or dissertation, on the other hand, is typically expected to be the result of substantial research in an area of interest providing an "original contribution to the advancement of knowledge" in a given discipline. The distinction is essentially in the "original contribution" stipulation of the dissertation as compared to the "survey" nature of the master's thesis.

As with all other graduate degree requirements, however, variety abounds. The master's thesis may actually be an essay or an essay-length report of a research or creative project, or a recital, or an exhibition of art works, or a musical composition, or a combination of almost any of these. Schools which use the terms "essay," "paper," or "report" are generally implying a more limited length or depth of content than suggested by the term "thesis." As indicated above, the thesis or similar requirement is made only by some schools and departments, and nonthesis options of additional course work are usually available. As a rule, the thesis is included in total credit-hour requirements; that is, three to six semester hours (or the equivalent in quarter hours) are given for the completed thesis toward the thirty-two hours customarily required. Exceptions are theses or projects for the two-year professional master's degrees, where more credit is typically assigned toward the total semester or quarter-hour requirement.

The length of a master's thesis may be anywhere from fifty to three hundred and fifty pages, but the average is probably around one hundred pages. The doctoral dissertation is rarely less than one hundred pages and ranges up to five hundred pages or more. Although some professors are fond of relating stories about superb dissertations ten pages long, the student is advised not to cling to such fragile hopes.

With diligence and careful planning, the dissertation can be written in less than a year, especially if research material is gathered and sorted while the candidate is still engaged in course work. Unfortunately, the temptation to delay commencement of research or writing until completion of other degree requirements is strong, obviously resulting in increased difficulty when the project is finally begun.

The "contribution to knowledge" aspect of the doctoral dissertation has been increasingly diluted in favor of "significance and relevance." This trend is intended to counter the tendency to seek novelty of concept or subject matter, a practice that often leads to dissertations that are "islands of minutiae in a sea of trivia." To compensate for the peripheral quality of many dissertation topics, departments may emphasize the interpretive and critical approach in preference to pure research.

Whatever the faults or virtues of the master's thesis and doctoral dissertation, there is little doubt that it is for most students the single most satisfying experience in graduate study.

SIXTH-YEAR PROGRAMS. Some mention must be made of the certificates of advanced study available in certain professional fields, notably education and engineering, but occasionally in other areas. These programs fill the need for refresher training beyond the master's, and, it must be said, salary increments often reward those who complete this additional work.

The sixth-year certificate/diploma customarily requires at least one year of full-time study in residence, or the equivalent in part-time attendance. There is usually no language or thesis requirement, but a final project of a type promoting professional proficiency in specific areas is often required. The certificate of advanced study does not attempt to replace the doctorate, but is instead an intermediate program of graduate training.

The Professional School

All study beyond the undergraduate college is essentially "professional" in nature. The graduate school of arts and science was created primarily to train college teachers and scholars, even though most of those who hold master's and doctoral degrees do not enter higher education. But graduate training in fields other than the humanities and sciences is clearly designed for readily identifiable occupations.

Although there are no agreed demarcations, it can be fairly stated that some sixteen disciplines are the predominant arenas of postbaccalaureate professional study: architecture, business, dentistry, education, engineering, forestry, law, library science, medicine, nursing, optometry, pharmacy, public health, social work, theology, and veterinary medicine. Cases can be made for including under this label such fields as journalism and physical therapy, but for the purposes at hand these sixteen are most relevant.

Even this list could be winnowed further. The origins of formal education for just three professions predate those of all others by many decades. Training for these—law, medicine, theology—has developed independently of most forms of graduate study. Indeed, law schools still speak of work for the first law degree as "undergraduate," as if candidates could enter directly from high school. Many of the other programs still struggle for acceptance to fully recognized professional status for themselves, but remain as mere departments of larger divisions.

And make no mistake—the designation of an academic subdivision as a department or institute or school or college is a distinction important beyond simple academic snobbery. Professional "schools" within broader institutions have more stature than departments. They have more independent administrations and faculties, sometimes even their own boards of trustees. Often, they are able to detach their fund-raising activities from their parent institutions and thus have greater latitude in distribution of moneys separated from contributors. There is greater unity of purpose in, say, a graduate school of business administration than in a graduate school of arts and science, which is more often a collection of thirty or more mini-colleges pulling in separate directions. Faculties of *schools* are typically better paid than those of *departments* in the same fields. There is less jockeying for internal political advantage, because academic apples are not thrown together with professional oranges.

And in the current atmosphere of student specialization and vocationalism, professional schools have the upper hand in determining the direction of their institutions, while many liberal arts programs struggle with enrollment and fiscal problems. The following pages outline these schools and programs and briefly survey factors to be considered in selection, admission, degree requirements, and sources of financial aid. Much of the descriptive material contained in the previous section applies to professional schools as well, so these remarks are concerned only with the distinctive characteristics of these programs.

SELECTING A PROFESSIONAL SCHOOL

Professional schools often have been accused of unduly restricting enrollments at times of expanding need. Now, having rushed to meet urgently expressed national needs, educational institutions find themselves the targets of the reverse criticism: they went too far in some professions, but not far enough in health related professions.

There are now oversupplies of teachers in some areas of the country; some say two for every job. New members of the bar are encountering stiffer competition. According to

AAMC data, there will be five new allopathic schools opening between 2007–08 and 2015–16 and the aggregate enrollment increase in 2010–2011 will be an additional 360 new M.D. candidates. Even with this increase, the results of retirement and those leaving the profession will leave the medical profession sadly understaffed. According to the Journal of Dental Education, between 1986–1993 five dental schools closed because of their belief that there would be an oversupply of dentists and Northwestern's Dental

School closed in 2001. Since 1997, three new schools have been added. Even with these modest improvements, it is still estimated that there will be a shortage of dentists in many parts of the country, especially in those states that do not have in-state dental education opportunities.

The result of these trends will be to make some professional study more difficult to undertake than it is already. Medical schools, for example, are talking tentatively about charging tuition that actually covers instructional expenses, meaning annual tuition could soon reach as high as $43,500 at some private institutions! This, not even counting living expenses, and when financial aid is far from munificent and federal cutbacks can be anticipated. Admission standards, too, may escalate still further, putting even the least glossy law and medical schools out of reach of all but the most capable applicants.

In the very short-lived meantime, students of above-average, if unspectacular, aptitude and credentials have reason to be hopeful about gaining entrance to some school in their chosen fields—as long as they are not unrealistically fussy about location and "image."

COST, SIZE, LOCATION. As with graduate schools of arts and science, costs for professional study vary widely, depending principally upon the field and the type of institutional or state support. Nearly all schools of veterinary medicine and forestry are affiliated with public institutions, so tuition expenses are correspondingly lower for state residents in those majors. The other professional schools are as likely to be under private sponsorship as public, so

costs can differ substantially. Annual tuition ranges from about $7676 to $32,800 at publicly supported schools, from $24,000 to $43,500 at private schools, all escalating at an average rate of nearly 5 percent a year. The exceptions are the theological seminaries and schools of divinity. These are all privately controlled, yet tuitions may be as little as $3500 or as much as $11,000. In general, tuition has been increasing by 6 to 7 percent each year. Always check with the institution in question regarding current tuition charges.

Student bodies of professional schools are customarily in the 200 to 500 range, but some exceed 1300 in enrollment and some seminaries have as few as 25 students. The great majority of professional schools are affiliated with universities, but divinity schools are more frequently parts of colleges or are autonomous. Increasingly, formerly independent law and medical schools are being absorbed into larger institutions or are joining with other institutions to form new entities.

Only the most populous states have schools offering all sixteen types of professional study. There are law schools in forty-nine states, medical, dental, and osteopathic schools in forty-six, and veterinary schools in twenty-seven. On the other hand, there is at least one school of business, one graduate school of education, and one theological school in every state. Under the circumstances, most full-time professional students can expect to enroll at institutions at much greater distance from their homes than their undergraduate colleges.

ADMISSION

The professional schools of law, medicine, dentistry, and veterinary medicine set rigorous entrance requirements and thus avoid the separate step of "admission to candidacy," not to mention the high attrition rate, of most graduate schools. It is not possible, therefore, to suggest that *any* college graduate can gain admission to some professional school in his or her chosen field. Nevertheless, admission is not always as difficult as is commonly supposed, if students are willing to consider professional schools without regard to location or to presumed reputation. (Since most types of professional schools must meet fairly high minimum criteria to retain accreditation by appropriate professional associations, it is probably safe to say that few truly "bad" schools exist.) Several factors influence the decisions of admission committees, and these should be understood by the potential applicant.

PREPARATION. Some professional schools are willing to consider applicants who do not hold a bachelor's degree certifying completion of a four-year undergraduate program. Schools of veterinary medicine and dentistry, for example, sometimes admit students with as little as two years of undergraduate study, though nearly all medical and law schools now require the bachelor's degree.

Undergraduate preparation need not have followed the curricula laid down in preprofessional programs. However, applicants to schools of medicine, dentistry, public health, engineering, nursing, osteopathy, pharmacy, and veterinary medicine should have completed programs that permitted substantial emphasis upon the natural and/or

physical sciences. This does not mean, of course, that the diversity of background provided by study in the humanities and social sciences is to be minimized. In fact, basic work in English, humanities, and the social sciences are required for medical school admission nearly as often as biology, chemistry, and physics.

Schools of law, business, social work, and theology are less likely to require specific undergraduate preparation. These schools emphasize in their catalogues that general liberal arts studies are more important for their students than specialized majors in fields thought to be closely related to the professions in question. Applicants to a law school, for example, might hold majors in economics, history, English, sociology, or even business administration.

CREDENTIALS. In addition to transcripts of undergraduate study completed, applicants to the types of professional schools discussed here are nearly always expected to provide one to four letters of recommendation and the scores on the standard tests available for each professional field (except theology). In many cases, the letters of recommendation may be replaced totally or in part by the recommendations of the undergraduate preprofessional faculty committees. Professional schools, particularly those in theology, often request character references as well as estimations of potential for study in the particular field.

Nearly all schools of dentistry, medicine, law, business, nursing, osteopathy, and veterinary medicine demand the results of the appropriate entrance examinations prepared and/or administered by the professional associations. These are as follows:

Dental Aptitude Test (DAT)—applications available from either the chosen dental school or from the Department of Testing Services, American Dental Association, 211 East Chicago Avenue, Suite 1840, Chicago, IL 60611-2678; (312)440-2500. Web site: www.ada.org.

Graduate Management Admission Test (GMAT)—applications available and registration information available from mba.com. For customer service call: 1-800-717-GMAT (4628).

Graduate Record Examination (GRE)—application available from Graduate Record Examination Testing Service, P.O. Box 6000, Princeton, NJ 08541-6000; (609)771-7670. Web site: www.gre.org.

Law School Admission Test (LSAT)—applications available from Law School Admission Council, Box 2000, Newtown, PA 18940; (215)968-1001. Web site: www.lsac.org.

Medical College Admission Test (MCAT)—applications available from AAMC, 2450 N Street, NW, Washington, DC 20037; (202)828-0690. Web site: www.aamc.org.

Miller Analogies Test (MAT)—applications available from Harcourt Assessment, Inc., 19500 Bulverde Road, San Antonio, TX 78259. Web site: www.harcourtassessment.com.

Optometry Admission Test (OAT)—applications available from Optometry Admission Testing program, 211 East Chicago Avenue, Suite 600, Chicago, IL 60611-2678; (800) 232-2159. Web site: www.opted.org.

Pharmacy College Admission Test (PCAT)—applications available from Harcourt Assessment, Inc., 19500 Bulverde Road, San Antonio, TX 78259. Web site: www.harcourtassessment.com

Praxis Series Tests—applications available from the Praxis Series, P.O. Box 6051, Educational Testing Service, Princeton, NJ 08541-6051; (800)772-9476 or (609)771-7395. Web site: www.ets.org/praxis.

Test of English as a Foreign Language, Test of Written English, Test of Spoken English (TOEFL, TWE, TSE)—applications available from TOEFL, P.O. Box 6151, Princeton, NJ 08541-6151; (609)771-7100. Web site: www.toefl.org.

A majority of professional schools required a qualifying interview by invitation for the semifinalist applicants, but this is not universal. For dental, medical, and osteopathy school, the interview usually follows preliminary screening of applications.

DEADLINES. Medical and dental schools customarily accept applications for admission starting in June of the year preceding the proposed term of entrance. Most medical schools set closing dates for receipt of completed applications in October or November, although these dates are now often flexible. Some dental schools accept applications as late as May. Preliminary applications are sometimes required, followed by formal applications from those who pass the initial screening.

The other types of professional schools generally accept applications well into the summer preceding the term of entrance, although some of the more prestigious law and business schools have deadlines in January. It is to be remembered that most professional schools restrict entrance for beginning full-time students to the Fall term, or occasionally to the Summer and Fall terms.

COMMON APPLICATION SERVICES. In an effort to ease the burden on students intent on applying for admission—and to cut their own clerical cost—most law, medical, osteopathic, and dental schools have subscribed to the services of centralized processing agencies. These offices accept academic credentials and other data from applicants, summarizing them in uniform formats and passing them on to the designated schools. The clearinghouses do not offer advisement and do not make admission decisions; that remains the province of the schools themselves. After ascertaining whether the schools in which the student is interested employ the relevant service, he or she should write to it as follows:

American Association of Colleges of Osteopathic Medicine Application Service (AACOMAS)—for application information contact AACOMAS, 5550 Friendship Blvd., Suite 310, Chevy Chase, MD 20815; (301)968-4190. Web site: www.aacom.org.

American Association of Dental Schools Applications Service (AADSAS)—for application information contact AADSAS, 1625 Massachusetts Avenue, NW, Suite 600, Washington, DC 20036; (202)667-9433. Web site: www.adea.org.

American Medical College Application Service (AMCAS)—for application information contact AMCAS, Section for Student Service, AAMC, 2501 "M" Street, NW, Washington, DC 20037-1306; (202)828-0600. Web site: www.aamc.org.

Law School Data Assembly Service (LSDAS)—for application information contact the Law School Admissions Council, Box 2000-M, 661 Penn Street, Newtown, PA 18940-0993; (215)968-1314. Web site: www.lsac.org.

Veterinary Medical College Application Service (VMCAS)—for application information contact VMCAS, 1101 Vermont Avenue, NW, Suite 411, Washington, DC 20005-3521; (202)682-0750. Web site: www.AAVMC.org.

There is a fee associated with these applications, usually escalating with the number of schools to which the materials are to be sent. Some of the schools require supplementary materials and/or an interview. A few expect payment of additional application fees.

STANDARDS. It is probably safe to say that at least between 40% and 50% of the applicants to professional schools are accepted for admission, a little less than that for law, medicine, dentistry, and veterinary medicine, and higher for the other professional schools. Allowing for duplication of applications, available statistics suggest that an even larger percentage of students eventually gain entrance to some school, perhaps as many as two-thirds of all applicants.

Most professional schools seek students with undergraduate grade point averages of "B." Depending on the degree of competition created by numbers of applicants, this may be interpreted to mean an average as low as "C plus" or as high as "A minus." It is generally agreed, in any event, that the grade average is the single most reliable predictor of success in postbaccalaureate professional studies. While the scores on the various entrance exams are undeniably important in the deliberations of admissions committees, students should not expect strong scores to outweigh mediocre grades in undergraduate course work, even if the degree is from a prestigious institution.

FINANCIAL ASSISTANCE

Professional study is expensive and although various forms of aid are available, most students must plan to meet their costs through loans or their own resources. Most financial assistance is based on demonstrated and documented need. Some schools provide limited numbers of scholarships, fellowships, grants, and tuition waivers from institutional funds; the size of these awards is generally tied to the student's academic achievement. However, the basic component in all financial aid packages will be loans. In addition to the loan resources of the schools themselves, low-cost loans are widely available through government agencies, some banks, private lending groups, professional associations, and private or community groups.

Students apply for the Government sponsored loans and scholarships through the individual schools to which they seek admission or through the parent institution's financial aid office. In general, all financial aid applicants must use FAFSA (Free Application for Federal Student Aid). For some schools the GAPS-FAS, CSS, or NEED ACCESS may be required also.

Most professional schools assist the spouses of their students in obtaining local or institutional employment. Although part-time employment is usually discouraged for first-year students, this possibility should still be explored. Finally, some schools have teaching or research assistantships or fellowships for advanced students.

THE STRUCTURE OF PROFESSIONAL STUDY

Programs leading to first degrees require four years of full-time study for the medical, osteopathy, veterinary, and dental professions, three years of full-time study or the equivalent in part-time attendance (when permitted) for law, and usually two years for the other fields.

Since practice in the medical/osteopathy/veterinary/dental professions demands both clinical skills and thorough understanding of the physical and natural sciences, students in these fields can expect balanced study in both these aspects of training. For most institutions the first two years are spent in work in the basic and preclinical sciences, while the last two are devoted largely to clinical work. There are no language or thesis requirements as in the graduate school, and summers may not be free.

Law students can anticipate a beginning year of introductory work, usually conducted in lecture classes. The following two years permit more latitude in course selection, and seminars are more commonly available. Course work is generally supplemented by tutorial work emphasizing training in research and various forms of legal writing. First professional degrees in religion usually follow this same pattern, but variations are many.

In the other professions, a full-time two-year program (or its equivalent) is the norm, with the exception of those fields in which graduate study is primarily a continuation of undergraduate work, as in architecture and pharmacy. In many areas, undergraduate study in the field will reduce credit requirements for the graduate degree.

Most medical, osteopathy, dental, and veterinary schools offer advanced study beyond the first degree in both clinical and research specializations. Graduate study in law and religion is also available, though proportionally less common. Such programs are generally administered by the graduate schools of the institutions with which the professional schools are affiliated, and students usually must meet admission and degree requirements established by both the graduate and professional divisions. Sometimes graduate work is given through the professional school itself, especially if the school is located at a medical center separated from the main campus of the institution.

Programs leading to professional degrees are demanding, and standards of performance are rigorous, but the rewards are substantial. If the potential student is realistic in selecting a school consistent with his or her interests and aptitudes, the experience will test his or her mind and spirit and lead to the kind of lifelong fulfillment few others are fortunate to enjoy.

UNDERSTANDING
THE ENTRIES

The information on the following pages describes the structure and content of the institutional entries that make up the main portion of this volume. For the entries to be of maximum value, it is important that the reader properly interpret the data provided.

The entries contain the kinds of basic information a potential applicant is likely to seek in choosing a graduate school. Careful examination of the school descriptions should aid the student in reaching realistic preliminary decisions. Since admission standards and requirements, course offerings, and financial aid opportunities are subject to frequent revision, it is not to be assumed that the entries can replace individual school bulletins or their Web sites.

All institutions in this *Guide* are accredited by the appropriate national, regional, and/or professional accrediting associations. Although no agency is specifically charged with the accreditation of graduate schools, those schools which are part of properly approved colleges and universities are all included. Among the associations that assign

accreditation of independent professional schools as well as those affiliated with larger institutions are the Liaison Committee on Medical Association, the Commission on Accreditation of the Council on Social Work Education, the American Dental Association, Commission on Osteopathic College Accreditation, and the American Veterinary Medical Association.

Every effort has been made to render these data understandable without reference to elaborate indexes of codes and abbreviations. However, one symbol, other than abbreviations for degrees and commonly required entrance examinations, has been used throughout this book: the "diagonal" or "slash" mark, as in "teaching/research." As employed here, the slash means *only* "and/or."

The following pages describe in detail the kinds of information to be found under each entry, in the same order. The items listed below are not included in every entry, either because they are not relevant or because specific data were not available.

GENERAL CHARACTERISTICS OF THE INSTITUTION

Name of the institution. The colleges and universities are arranged in alphabetical order according to the most important word in the title. Separate institutional entries are provided for individual university centers that are either autonomously administered or distinct in character or offerings. An institutional index for further assistance is at the back of the book.

Mailing address of the main campus. The name of the city and state in which the main campus offering graduate study is located, plus the zip code. When individual graduate or professional departments or schools are located in other towns or cities, that fact is noted in the body of the text. Internet Web sites are also included when available.

Founding date. Usually this is the year the institution was chartered, but sometimes the year classes were started or the year of the opening of another institution from which the present one developed.

Location in direction and miles from nearest major city.

Direction from nearest major city is given in appropriate capital letters (NW, SE). The mileage given is approximate road distance. Often the city named is relatively small but sufficiently well known, and is given only to establish the location of the main campus.

Institutional membership. There are many prestigious organizations that institutions can join or are invited to join. Two of the more important ones are Council of Graduate Schools and the Association of American Universities, and if the institution holds membership in either, it is noted in this section.

Coed, men only, or women only. Relatively few institutions limit their graduate enrollments to students of one sex. When the undergraduate program is thus restricted, and the graduate programs are not, it is stated: "Coed on the graduate level."

Type of control. If the institution is supported primarily by public funds, the level of government is specified, whether state, county, or municipal. Occasionally, institutions receive substantial amounts of financial support from the state or city government but decision-making powers are retained by the board of trustees. In other cases, individual divisions of universities are totally or mostly supported by public funds. In these instances, control is often shared. When appropriate, these situations are noted.

Many private institutions are sponsored by religious denominations, and this affiliation is mentioned. Although few such colleges and universities restrict their enrollments to members of the sponsoring churches, students may be expected to adhere to certain basic social or curricular requirements. Institutions that are open only to members of particular denominations or to the clergy are not listed in this book unless they are divisions of larger institutions that are not otherwise restricted. This is also true of colleges offering training only for the clergy of particular churches.

Semester, quarter, or trimester system. The semester system provides study during two terms of a nine-month academic year and, usually, during one or more summer sessions. The quarter system divides the calendar year into four equal terms, the trimester into three. Under all three systems, students typically attend classes for about nine months. For no apparent historical reason, Western colleges and universities most often operate on the quarter system, those in the East on the semester. The trimester is still relatively uncommon but has met favor in some sections.

Major research facilities. Special institutes, laboratories, interdepartmental and interinstitutional programs and resources are mentioned. The list is not intended to be exhaustive, but only to note distinctive offerings or equipment and to suggest their scope. Since this information is not always available, its absence does not necessarily mean that special facilities do not exist at any given institution.

Library. This figure is the total number of bound volumes in the institution's collections; current periodicals are also included when available. When special collections or several libraries at different centers are available, the figure represents the combined number of volumes. If the term "capacity" is used, it can be assumed that fewer volumes are actually in stock and that this figure is not available. If "items" is used instead of "volumes," the figure includes periodicals and similar materials in addition to books.

National Institutes of Health and other rankings (when available). NIH ranking information was obtained from NIH web site and it includes the top 200 institutions/organizations receiving awards or grants in the year 2005–2006. Total Federal Research funding, total Institutional expenditures, University endowments, number of doctorates awarded and national honor academies membership information was obtained from *TheCenter*, at the University of Florida. This resource has changed its physical location to: The Center for Measuring University Performance, P.O. Box 877805, Tempe, AZ; Web site: www.mup.asu.edu. This information gives a potential applicant an indication of the recognized quality of the research being undertaken at the institution he or she may be considering, as well as the probability for doctoral funding available at the institution.

Annual tuition charges for full-time students. Many public institutions use the term "fees" rather than "tuition," often with additional "tuition" for out-of-state students. This semantic distinction is often employed to maintain the illusion of tuition-free institutions. As used here, "fees" refers only to basic expense of course work and does not include the additional charges for use of laboratory and similar facilities. Generally, the cost of tuition and/or fees at public institutions is greater for nonresidents than for residents, while there is usually no such distinction at private colleges and universities. On occasion, still a third level of tuition is charged foreign students. When no flat-rate tuition is set for full-time students, the per hour charge is given.

Throughout this book, "annual" refers to the academic, not the calendar, year. It also should be remembered that tuition charges are constantly on the rise, increasing at a 5 percent annual rate at most institutions. This fact has been anticipated when possible, and the charges indicated are customarily for the 2006–07 year.

Part-time tuition charges. Schedules of charges are either per credit (or semester or quarter) hour, or according to varying ranges of hours, *i.e.,* $100 for 1–4 hours, $200 for 5–8 hours, and so on. As above, charges are indicated for both resident and nonresident students, when appropriate. Charges indicated are for graduate or professional students only. Tuition scales for undergraduate students sometimes differ and are not listed. If charges are mainly the same for most divisions of a university, any specific difference is noted under this heading *or* under the divisional heading. Unless so indicated, the tuition stated in the general institutional paragraph applies to all divisions.

On-campus housing available. Many institutions are unable to provide separate statistics for housing available to graduate students only. Therefore, unless noted as "for 100 graduate men," the figures given are for all students, both undergraduate and graduate. In this event, it may be assumed that graduate students are eligible for such housing. The figure given for married student housing should be interpreted as family units, while the figure for men and women refers to individual spaces only. "On-campus housing" means institutionally owned or controlled housing and does not include private accommodations. Only one or two colleges indicate that nearby privately owned, off-campus housing is *not* available. Graduate students who choose to live in institutional housing must remember that they are usually expected to observe the restrictions in force for all residents.

Average academic year housing cost. This is for the academic year only. When housing is available to graduate students only during the summer, the summer housing cost is provided. These figures relate only to the cost of university-owned or operated housing, not to private accommodations. The cost described is generally for the middle range, and variations depend upon the nature of accommodations. Unless otherwise specified, figures are for rent or room charges only, not board.

Title of housing officer. This notes the titles of the officers or office to contact for on- and off-campus housing information. If only one officer or office is named, he or she provides information for both institutional and private accommodations unless otherwise indicated.

GRADUATE AND PROFESSIONAL DIVISION REQUIREMENTS AND OFFERINGS

Name of division. The full proper name is usually given. If there is no separate graduate or professional school within the institution, this section is simply headed "Graduate Study" or "Graduate Program."

Founding date. The year graduate study began or when the division was established or affiliated may be given.

Location if other than main campus. In the case of professional schools, graduate study may be offered at two or more centers or in a different city.

Tuition and housing. These are given only if they are different from those indicated in the general institutional paragraph. This is most often true of professional schools.

Enrollment. Figures are for graduate or postbaccalaureate students only, if the division offers undergraduate courses as well. In rare cases, the statistics are for all enrolled students in the division, both graduate and undergraduate. If so, this fact is noted. The figures are usually broken down into full- and part-time enrollments, and the percentages of men and women for the combined total. On occasion, the latter figures refer either to the full- or part-time figure.

Faculty. This is the total number of faculty teaching graduate courses on a full- and/or part-time basis. This is often the least reliable statistic of all, for it is not always possible for institutions to make cut-and-dried distinctions between faculty members teaching primarily graduate or undergraduate students. Where possible, some clarification has been noted.

Types of degrees conferred. All master's, sixth-year, and doctoral level degrees are listed. Abbreviations often differ for the same degree, as in M.A. or A.M., D.Sc. or Sc.D. In the engineering master's degree, the subject field is often part of the formal title, such as "M.S. in Chemical Engineering." To conserve space when many such master's degrees are offered, the subject field has been deleted. Abbreviations have been used wherever possible, such as C.A.S. (Certificate of Advanced Standing); consult the list beginning on page xxvii.

ADMISSION REQUIREMENTS

Credentials required in support of application. This paragraph lists all documents, entrance examinations, interviews, and other requirements for admission to all programs and degrees. Since virtually all graduate schools expect applicants to hold a bachelor's degree, only exceptions to this normal requirement are mentioned. Professional schools, on the other hand, may admit students with fewer than four years of undergraduate study. The minimum number of preprofessional years is usually indicated in law, medical, dental, osteopathy, and veterinary school entries. Transcripts of previous undergraduate and graduate study (when applicable) are always required in support of applications for admission. Generally, applicants must submit one transcript from each college or university attended. In some cases, however, transcripts must be provided in duplicate. The opening words "Two official transcripts . . ." refer to this requirement.

Almost all schools/colleges/universities have an online or electronic application available on its Web site. In some cases you must use the online application and not a paper one. In the majority of cases, you can use either application process, but the online process is preferred. A few institutions will waive or reduce the application fee for online applicants.

Many schools request one or more letters of recommendation. Ordinarily, the applicant is asked to have the letters sent directly to the school. In other cases, the names of the persons willing to send recommendations are requested in the application, and the school takes the responsibility of obtaining the letters.

When the Graduate Record Examination (GRE) is required, the specific test, whether General and/or Subject, is noted wherever possible.

Many graduate schools accept students in special or nonmatriculant categories without prior submission of these credentials. In this *Guide,* degree and admission requirements refer only to those students intending to seek degrees.

Additional requirements for admission. Individual programs, schools, or departments sometimes request supplementary credentials in addition to those mentioned above. This is generally due to the professional nature of the program in question or to the need to have more data available. Entrance examinations such as the Miller Analogies Test (MAT) or the Graduate Management Admissions Test (GMAT) are typical of these extra requirements. Potential art majors often must submit portfolios of their work, and music majors may have to audition. Mention is made of additional requirements only if they pertain to two or more departments. Otherwise, special notice is made in the appropriate departmental listing under the *Fields of Study* section.

Transfer applicants. Most graduate and professional schools accept transfer applicants from similar institutions. Generally speaking, no more than 20 to 25 percent of the total course work for the master's degree is allowed for work completed at other graduate schools. The amount of advanced standing permitted toward the doctorate varies widely, but usually at least the equivalent of the master's degree is granted as transfer credit. Some schools are willing to consider transfer applicants, but not with advanced standing. Graduate schools often give advanced standing only after a student has completed study in residence.

Graduates of unaccredited institutions. Most graduate schools are willing to consider applicants from colleges or universities that do not hold approval from one of the six regional accrediting associations. Therefore, *only* those graduate schools that do *not* consider such applicants have statements to that effect. Special testing is often demanded of graduates of unaccredited colleges, or formal admission may be conditional upon satisfactory performance in residence.

Restrictions upon terms of entrance. Individual departments of graduate schools may restrict entrance to only the Fall semester, or to the Fall and Summer terms. Medical and dental schools nearly always admit only for the Fall, whereas some law schools permit initial entrance to other terms as well. It is usually preferable to begin in the Fall, whether or not such restrictions are set.

Title of admitting officer or office and dates of application. This refers to the officer or office of the college from which application forms can be obtained. The completed forms and supporting documents are customarily returned to the same officer or office. Closing dates for filing applications follow, and should be carefully observed. These dates are generally final, and all supporting credentials must be received with the application by these deadlines for the terms indicated. In some cases, no firm deadlines are set

but *preferred* dates are suggested. The applicant is advised to apply well in advance in any event, and both the applications for admission *and* financial aid should be submitted by the date indicated in the *Financial Aid* section. Information on closing dates for all terms is not always available, so it should not be implied that no summer term exists simply because no closing date is mentioned for that term.

Application fee. This information is not always available. Its absence here does not necessarily mean that no fee is required.

Telephone and fax numbers and e-mail addresses. The number listed in both the Admission Requirements and the Financial Aid sections is a general contact number and is being supplied for a preliminary applicant's convenience only. The reader should be aware that e-mail addresses at most institutions are in a constant state of flux and therefore the address listed may not be the most appropriate address at this time.

ADMISSION STANDARDS, RANKINGS, AND RECOGNITION

A college's/school's/university's quality, strengths, and academic position may be assessed or interpreted in a variety of ways. Accrediting bodies fiercely resist any rating/ranking of their accredited programs beyond a simple statement of accreditation. Qualities that make a graduate/professional school desirable to one student may not be as important to another student. The quality of credentials of the groups of applicants to different institutions varies widely and the degree of difficulty of admission must be interpreted accordingly. In other words, the most highly regarded institutions naturally attract applications from superior students in greater numbers than the less favored colleges/schools.

Therefore, prospective students should consider a variety of factors in making their choice among schools/universities. This section attempts to present factors that may assist the reader in determining the appropriate institutional fit. Among these factors are the selectivity level (very competitive, competitive, very selective, selective, or relatively open); the usual minimum required UGPA and test score; mean UGPA and mean test scores of entering class; and several rating or ranking sources.

Since selectivity may vary from department to department within a graduate school, this item may be stated, for example, "Very competitive for some departments, competitive for the others," or some similarly appropriate combination. Some institutions overestimate their selectivity; others receive most applications from colleges with very difficult grading systems. Thus, it is possible to be

described as "Selective" (accepting up to 75% of all applicants) and have a 3.0 minimum grade point average, or be "Competitive" with a 2.25 required grade point average.

The UGPA minimum averages were converted to the most widely used 4-point system (A = 4.0, B = 3.0, C = 2.0, D = 1.0). Normally, graduate departments expect somewhat higher averages in the proposed field of graduate study. It must be remembered that grade point average stated here is not necessarily the absolute "Floor" but that typically required for unconditional matriculation. Many schools offer limited matriculation to students below the reported grade point average. As with the characterization of admissions policy above, this information is offered merely as a guide.

Mean UGPAs and test score information should be viewed with a discriminating eye as well. It is not a cutoff score but should be viewed as roughly the middle of the class with half the scores below that number.

The rating/ranking sources may include the *U.S. News & World Report's America's Best Graduate Schools,* which also ranks a number of programs and professional schools, and *BusinessWeek's Guide to the Best Business Schools.* There are other rating/ranking guides available online and in book form. The above information—along with the data in the institution's entry with reference to NIH Grants, Federal & Institutional funding, Endowments, number of doctorates awarded, National Academies membership—is included to give an applicant the opportunity to form some sense of institutional perspective.

FINANCIAL AID

Types of aid other than loans. Scholarships, fellowships, internships, assistantships, tuition waivers, grants, and traineeships are the most common forms of aid available. As given here, they are grants offered from institutional funds or from aid programs administered by the college or university in question. This line also specifies the type of service

required of the recipient, when appropriate. Scholarships rarely have service requirements, and the term "fellowship" is often used in lieu of "scholarship." Thus, an entry reading "Scholarships, fellowships, teaching/research assistantships" means that no service is required in exchange for the first two forms of aid, while those who hold assistantships are expected to assume either teaching or research responsibilities, or both. Duties may involve direct assistance in research to a particular faculty member, or general responsibilities within a department, such as grading papers or assisting in laboratory experiments or demonstrations. Fellowships and assistantships typically carry a tuition remission privilege plus an annual stipend. Since fellowships are generally regarded as the more prestigious of the two types of award, the stipend is often larger than for assistantships and the tasks assigned may be more challenging in nature. This is subject to broad variations between departments and schools, however. In medical and dental schools, scholarships are usually the only form of aid other than loans available during the academic year. Many of these schools also award research fellowships for intervening summer sessions when regular classes are not in session.

To whom to apply, and the closing date. It is often necessary to apply to different persons or offices for the kinds of aid available. If no deadline date is set, it is wise to apply by February 1 or earlier to receive maximum consideration. Scholarships and fellowships are often awarded through a central committee of a graduate school, while assistantships are typically granted by the department offering study in the proposed major field. As a result, it may be necessary to contact as many as three or four persons or offices to obtain information about various forms of aid. All graduate and professional schools require interested students to apply for financial aid using the Free Application for Federal Student Aid (FAFSA).

Percentage of students receiving aid other than loans. The percentage given here relates to the number of students awarded scholarships, fellowships, assistantships, and other grants (but not loans) from *both* internal *and* external sources. The latter includes grants provided by private and governmental agencies. Unfortunately, it is not always possible to determine whether the percentages refer to the total graduate enrollment, both full- and part-time, or solely to the full-time student body. Normally, however, the figures are for the entire student group, regardless of full- or part-time status. In any event, this factor changes so rapidly from year to year that the percentages must be considered only as rough estimates.

Aid available to part-time students. It is by no means universal practice to make aid, even loans, available to part-time students. This line states whether or not such aid, including loans, is offered.

DEGREE REQUIREMENTS

For master's degrees. This section begins with the minimum total number of credit (or semester or quarter) hours that must be completed for the master's, followed by the minimum number of hours to be completed in residence at the institution granting the degree. As used here, and throughout this book, "residence" refers to *credit hours completed while in full- or part-time attendance at the institution granting the degree.* Therefore, the difference in credit hour requirements between the minimum number for the degree and the number to be completed "in residence" is the number of hours accepted in transfer from other graduate or professional schools. In those cases where residence credit hours must be completed while in attendance as a full-time student, the entry reads "at least 24 in full-time residence." If the residence and full-time attendance requirements differ, this is normally stated as "at least 24 in residence and 18 in full-time attendance."

If a student may elect whether or not to complete a thesis in partial fulfillment of degree requirements, both options are stated in terms of minimum total and residence credit hours. For example: "24 credit hours plus thesis, at least 18 in residence, *or* 30 hours without thesis, at least 24 in residence." These options are stated in different ways, generally in accordance with the terminology of the school being reported.

Listed next are additional degree requirements: qualifying, candidacy, or final exams; thesis or final projects; language or other research tools. If any of these requirements are only for particular majors or departments, this fact is noted: "thesis for most departments; final oral exam for some departments," etc. Most graduate schools stress that the requirements specified are minimums only, and that additional credit hours, exams, or the like may be stipulated, depending upon the candidate's previous background, his or her performance in, or the special nature of, a particular program. In practice, such variations are more likely to occur at the doctoral rather than the master's level.

Schools always point out that admission to study does not imply automatic admission to candidacy. Advancement to formal candidacy for the degree depends upon successful completion of a variety of requirements, such as the filing of an acceptable thesis plan, appointment of a faculty thesis committee, and/or language tests or candidacy exams. This is true for both the master's and doctoral degrees.

For sixth-year degrees or certificates. The number of credit hours required is generally given as a minimum total "beyond the bachelor's" *or* "beyond the master's." Ordinarily, there are relatively few requirements other than course work, but a thesis or project and/or final exam may be expected. Sixth-year certificates are given primarily in the fields of dentistry, education, music, and engineering.

For doctoral degrees. As with the sixth-year certificate, the number of hours is given as a minimum total beyond the bachelor's or master's. However, many institutions do not specify a set number of credits for the doctorate, choosing instead to state the residence requirements in terms of semesters or years. (This is occasionally true of the master's as well.) In this case, it can be assumed that the years or semesters of residence required may be completed in equivalent part-time attendance, unless otherwise specified. As mentioned above, "residence" refers to hours completed while in full- *or* part-time attendance at the institution granting the degree. In those cases where residence credit must be completed while in full-time attendance, the entry specifies "in full-time residence." Further, the number of hours (or semesters or years) to be completed in residence is the total required for the doctorate minus maximum possible transfer credit beyond the master's or bachelor's, as indicated.

The nature and scope of the doctoral dissertation and/or project vary for each type of degree. The dissertation for the Ph.D. is normally expected to show technical mastery of the major field and to offer an original contribution to the existing body of knowledge in the field. For the Ed.D. and other professional doctorates, the dissertation is likely to be based upon a specific project designed to fully develop research skills and to contribute new knowledge to the professional field.

FIELDS OF STUDY

Areas of concentration or academic departments. These are arranged alphabetically, usually in the manner listed in the school bulletin; that is, if several divisions contribute programs to the graduate school, the fields of study are noted under each division. Since titles of major fields or departments vary from school to school, the reader should look carefully for the programs that interest him or her. For instance, various engineering majors are listed *either* individually *or* under one department heading. This is often true of education programs as well. To take another example, a biological sciences department may include majors in biochemistry, microbiology, zoology, or these may be in a variety of other combinations. "Art history" is sometimes called "history of art" or "fine arts"; "political science" might be "government" or simply "politics." Further, the Ph.D. in a particular field might be offered by one division while the master's in the same field is offered by another school within the university. Still another complication is the fact that some majors are offered by more than one school or department or even at two or more centers of an institution.

Special majors. Following each departmental listing, if necessary, is a clarification of available majors. The name of the department may not be self-explanatory, so it might be stated, for example: *"Art.* Includes studio art, art history, art education," or *"Modern Languages.* Includes French,

German, Spanish." In other cases, special notice is made of unusual majors or of majors not ordinarily found under a particular departmental heading. This is then stated: *"English.* Includes creative writing." The "includes" gives notice that the other more common majors of the field are available. It is important to remember that only fields which offer programs leading to at least one degree are listed. Departments that simply contribute courses to degrees are not mentioned.

Special degree or admission requirements. Notation is made of degree or admission requirements which deviate from those outlined in the general paragraphs, whether in addition to, or in lieu of, those stated above. This can include special entrance examinations, such as the MAT, or extra credit hours for the degree. If no such mention is made, it can be assumed that the general requirements apply.

Types of degrees awarded. This is stated only if appropriate degrees are not awarded in particular departments on all levels conferred by the school. For example, if both master's and doctoral degrees are granted by the school, but the Music Department offers only the M.F.A., the listing reads *"Music.* M.F.A. only." Without this notation, it can be assumed the department offers all the degrees appropriate to the field in question. Occasionally, an additional degree not listed under the general headings is mentioned here, but only if of a special nature.

KEY TO ABBREVIATIONS

MASTER'S DEGREES

A.M.	Master of Arts
Ed.M.	Master of Education
E.M.B.A.	Executive Master of Business Administration
LL.C.M.	Master of Comparative Law
LL.M.	Master of Law
M.A.	Master of Arts, Master of Administration
M.A.A.	Master of Applied Art, Master of Administrative Arts, Master of Aeronautics and Astronautics, Master of Applied Anthropology
M.A.A.A.	Master of Arts in Arts Administration
M.A.A.B.S.	Master of Arts in Applied Behavioral Sciences
M.A.A.E.	Master of Arts in Applied Economics, Master of Aeronautical and Astronautical Engineering, Master of Arts in Art Education
M.A.Am.St.	Master of Arts in American Studies
M.A.A.O.M.	Master of Arts in Applied Organizational Management
M.A.A.T.	Master of Arts in Art Therapy
M.Acc.	Master of Accounting
M.Accy.	Master of Accountancy
M.A.B.S.	Master of Arts in Behavior Science
M.A.C.	Master of Arts in Communications, Master of Arts in Counseling
M.A.C.A.	Master of Arts in Computer Applications
M.A.C.C.S.	Master of Arts in Cross-Cultural Studies
M.A.C.E.	Master of Arts in Computer Education
M.A.C.P.	Master of Arts in Community Psychology, Master of Arts in Counseling Psychology
M.A.C.C.T.	Master of Arts in Community College Teaching
M.A.C.T.A.	Master of Arts in Computer Teaching Applications
M.Ad.	Master of Administration
M.A.Ad.Ed.	Master of Arts in Adult Education
M.A.C.P.	Master of Arts in Counseling Psychology
M.A.C.T.	Master of Arts in College Teaching, Master of Arts in Communications and Technology
M.A.D.R.	Master of Arts in Dispute Resolution
M.A.E.	Master of Agricultural Extension, Master of Agricultural Engineering, Master of Aerospace Engineering, Master of Architectural Engineering, Master of Arts in Economics
M.A.Ed.	Master of Arts in Education
M.A.E.L.	Master of Arts in Educational Leadership
M.A.E.S.	Master of Arts in Environmental Sciences
M.Ag.	Master of Agriculture
M.Ag.Ed.	Master of Agricultural Education
M.Ag.Ext.	Master of Agricultural Extension
M.Aq.	Master of Aquacultures
M.A.F.	Master of Arts in Finance
M.A.F.C.	Master of Arts in Family Counseling
M.A.H.	Master of Arts in Humanities
M.A.H.E.	Master of Arts in Human Ecology
M.A.H.E.& F.E.	Master of Arts in Home Economics and Family Ecology
M.A.H.R.M.	Master of Arts in Human Resource Management
M.A.H.S.	Master of Arts in Human Services
M.A.H.S.M.	Master of Arts in Human Service Management
M.A.I.A.	Master of Arts in International Affairs, Master of Arts in International Administration
M.A.I.B.	Master of Arts in International Business
M.A.I.C.	Master of Arts in International Communication
M.A.I.D.	Master of Arts in International Diplomacy, Master of Arts in Interior Design
M.A.I.R.	Master of Arts in Industrial Relations, Master of Arts in International Relations
M.A.I.S.	Master of Arts in International Studies, Master of Arts in Interdisciplinary Studies, Master of Accounting and Information Systems
M.A.J.	Master of Arts in Journalism
M.A.L.A.	Master of Arts in Liberal Arts
M.A.L.A.S.	Master of Arts in Latin American Studies
M.A.L.D.	Master of Arts in Law and Diplomacy
M.A.L.S.	Master of Arts in Library Science, Master of Arts in Liberal Studies
M.A.L.T.	Master of Arts in Language Teaching, Master of Arts in Learning and Teaching
M.A.M.	Master of Arts Management, Master of Animal Medicine, Master of Aviation Management, Master of Arts in Management, Master of Agriculture and Management, Master of Acquisition Management, Master of Applied Mathematics
M.A.M.B.	Master of Arts in Molecular Biology
M.A.M.C.	Master of Arts in Mass Communication
M.A.M.F.C.	Master of Arts in Marriage and Family Counseling
M.A.M.F.C.C.	Master of Arts in Marriage, Family, and Child Counseling
M.A.M.F.T.	Master of Arts in Marriage and Family Therapy

M.A.M.R.D.	Master of Agricultural Management and Resource Development
M.A.M.S.	Master of Applied Mathematical Sciences
M.A.N.M.	Master of Arts in Nonprofit Management
M.A.O.M.	Master of Aerospace Operations Management, Master of Arts in Organizational Management
M.A.P.A.	Master of Arts in Public Administration, Master of Arts in Public Affairs
M.A.P.E.	Master of Arts in Physical Education, Master of Arts in Political Economy
M.Appl.M.	Master of Applied Mathematics
M.Ap.Sc.	Master of Applied Science
M.A.P.P.	Master of Arts in Public Policy
M.A.P.R.S.	Master of Arts in Pacific Rim Studies
M.A.P.S.	Master of Arts in Pastoral Studies
M.A.Psych.	Master of Arts in Psychology
M.A.R.	Master of Arts in Religion, Master of Arts in Research
M.Arch.	Master of Architecture
M.Arch.E.	Master of Architectural Engineering
M.Arch.H.	Master of Architectural History
M.Arch.U.D.	Master of Architecture in Urban Design
M.A.S.	Master of Accounting Science, Master of Actuarial Science, Master of Aeronautical Science, Master of American Studies, Master of Applied Statistics, Master of Archival Studies
M.A.S.A.C.	Master of Arts in Substance Abuse Counseling
M.A.S.L.	Master of Arts in School Leadership
M.A.S.P.	Master of Applied Social Psychology, Master of Arts in School Psychology
M.A.T.	Master of Arts in Teaching, Master of Athletic Training
M.A.T.M.	Master of Arts in Teaching Mathematics
M.A.U.A.	Master of Arts in Urban Affairs
M.A.U.D.	Master of Arts in Urban Design
M.A.U.R.P	Master of Arts in Urban and Regional Planning
M.A.W.	Master of Arts in Writing
M.B.	Master of Bioninformatics
M.B.A.	Master of Business Administration
M.B.A.I.B.	Master of Business Administration in International Business
M.B.A.I.M.	Master of Business Administration in International Management
M.B.C.	Master of Building Construction
M.B.E.	Master of Bilingual Education, Master of Biomedical Engineering, Master of Business Education, Master of Business Economics
M.B.I.	Master of Biological Illustration
M.Biorad.	Master of Bioradiology
M.B.M.	Master of Brand Management
M.B.S.	Master of Basic Science, Master of Behavioral Science, Master of Building Science, Master of Biological Science, Master of Biomedical Sciences
M.B.T.	Master of Business Taxation, Master of Biomedical Technology
M.C.	Master of Counseling, Master of Communication, Master of Cybersecurity
M.C.A.M.	Master of Computational and Applied Mathematics
M.C.D.	Master of Communication Disorders, Master of Community Development
M.C.E.	Master of Chemical Engineering, Master of Civil Engineering, Master of Computer Engineering
M.C.H.	Master of Community Health
M.C.H.S.	Master of Clinical Health Sciences
M.C.I.S.	Master of Communication and Information Studies, Master of Computer Information Systems
M.C.J.	Master of Comparative Jurisprudence, Master of Criminal Justice
M.C.J.A.	Master of Criminal Justice Administration
M.C.L.	Master of Comparative Law, Master of Civil Law
M.C.M.	Master of Church Music, Master of Construction Management
M.C.M.S.	Master of Clinical Medical Science
M.C.P.	Master of City Planning, Master of Community Planning, Master of Counseling Psychology
M.C.R.	Master of Clinical Research
M.C.R.P.	Master of City and Regional Planning
M.C.S.	Master of Computer Science
M.C.S.E.	Master of Computer Science and Engineering
M.Des.	Master of Design
M.Des.S.	Master of Design Studies
M.Div.	Master of Divinity
M.D.R.	Master of Dispute Resolution
M.D.S.	Master of Dental Science, Master of Decision Sciences, Master of Defense Studies
M.E.	Master of Engineering
M.E.A.	Master of Engineering Administration, Master of Engineering Architecture
M.E.C.	Master of Electronic Commerce
M.E.C.E.	Master of Electrical and Computer Engineering
M.Ed.	Master of Education
M.E.D.	Master of Environmental Design, Master of Education of the Deaf
M.E.D.S.	Master of Environmental Design Studies
M.E.E.	Master of Electrical Engineering, Master of Environmental Engineering
M.E.H.W.E.	Master of Engineering in Hazardous Waste Engineering
M.E.M.	Master of Engineering Management, Master of Ecosystem Management
M.E.M.S.	Master of Engineering in Manufacturing Systems
M.Eng.	Master of Engineering
M.E.P.	Master of Environmental Planning, Master of Engineering Physics
M.E.P.C.	Master of Environmental Pollution Control
M.E.R.	Master of Energy Resources
M.E.S.	Master of Engineering Science, Master of Environmental Science, Master of Environmental Studies
M.E.T.	Master of Education in Teaching, Master of Engineering Technology, Master of Environmental Toxicology
M.Ex.St.	Master of Experimental Statistics
M.Ext.Ed.	Master of Extension Education
M.F.	Master of Forestry, Master of Finance
M.F.A.	Master of Fine Arts
M.F.C.S.	Master of Family and Consumer Sciences
M.F.E.	Master of Forest Engineering
M.F.M.	Master of Financial Mathematics
M.F.R.	Master of Forest Resources
M.F.S.	Master of Family Studies, Master of Foreign Service, Master of Forest Science, Master of Forensic Science
M.F.T.	Master of Family Therapy
M.G.	Master of Genetics
M.G.A.	Master of Government Administration
M.G.E.	Master of Geological Engineering, Master of Geotechnical Engineering
M.G.S.	Master of Gerontological Studies, Master of Global Studies

M.G.T.	Master of Gas Technology
M.H.	Master of Humanities
M.H.A.	Master of Health Administration, Master of Healthcare Administration, Master of Hospital Administration
M.H.A.M.S.	Master of Historical Administration and Museum Studies
M.H.C.A.	Master of Health Care Administration
M.H.E.	Master of Health Education, Master of Higher Education, Master of Home Economics
M.H.E.Ed.	Master of Home Economics Education
M.H.H.S.	Master of Health and Human Service
M.H.C.M.	Master of Health Care Management
M.H.K.	Master of Human Kinetics
M.H.M.	Master of Hospitality Management
M.H.P.	Master of Heritage Preservation, Master of Historical Preservation
M.H.R.	Master of Human Resources
M.H.R.D.	Master of Human Resource Development
M.H.S.	Master of Health Services, Master of Human Services, Master of Hispanic Studies
M.H.S.A.	Master of Health Services Administration, Master of Human Services Administration
M.I.A.	Master of International Affairs
M.I.B.	Master of International Business
M.I.B.A.	Master of International Business Administration
M.I.D.	Master of Industrial Design, Master of Interior Design, Master of International Development
M.I.E.	Master of Industrial Engineering
M.I.L.R.	Master of Industrial and Labor Relations
M.I.L.S.	Master of Information and Library Science
M.I.M.	Master of Industrial Management, Master of International Management
M.I.P.	Master of Intellectual Property
M.I.P.A.	Master of International Public Administration
M.I.P.P.	Master of International Public Policy
M.I.R.	Master of Industrial Relations, Master of International Relations
M.I.S.	Master of Individualized Studies, Master of Information Services, Master of Interdisciplinary Studies
M.I.T.	Master of Industrial Technology, Master of Information Technology, Master of Internet Technology
M.J.	Master of Journalism
M.J.A.	Master of Justice Administration
M.J.N.M.M.	Master of Journalism in New Media Management
M.J.S.	Master of Judicial Science
M.L.A.	Master of Landscape Architecture, Master of Liberal Arts
M.L.A.U.D.	Master of Landscape Architecture in Urban Development
M.L.H.R.	Master of Labor and Human Resources
M.L.I.R.	Master of Labor and Industrial Relations
M.L.I.S.	Master of Library and Information Science
M.Lit.M.	Master of Liturgical Music
M.L.L.	Master of Law Librarianship
M.L.S.	Master of Legal Studies, Master of Liberal Studies, Master of Library Science, Master of Life Science
M.L.S.P.	Master of Law and Social Policy
M.L.&T.	Master of Law and Taxation
M.M.	Master of Music, Master of Mathematics
M.M.A.	Master of Marine Affairs, Master of Media Art, Master of Musical Art

M.M.B.	Master of Medical Biochemistry
M.M.C.	Master of Mass Communication
M.M.E.	Master of Manufacturing Engineering, Master of Material Engineering, Master of Mechanical Engineering, Master of Mineral Engineering
M.M.Ed.	Master of Music Education
M.M.F.C.C.	Master of Marriage, Family, and Child Counseling
M.M.F.T.	Master of Marriage and Family Therapy
M.M.I.S.	Master of Management Information Systems
M.M.M.	Master of Manufacturing Management, Master of Marine Management
M.M.M.E.	Master of Metallurgical and Materials Engineering
M.M.P.	Master of Marine Policy, Master of Museum Practice
M.M.R.	Master of Marketing Research
M.M.S.	Master of Management Science, Master of Marine Science, Master of Materials Science, Master of Medieval Studies, Master of Medical Science
M.M.T	Master of Music Therapy, Master of Music Teaching
M.Mu.	Master of Music
M.Mus.	Master of Music
M.N.	Master of Nursing
M.N.A.	Master of Nursing Administration, Master of Nonprofit Administration, Master of Nurse Anesthesia
M.Nat.Sci.	Master of Natural Science
M.N.E.	Master of Nuclear Engineering, Master of Networking Engineering
M.N.Ed.	Master of Nursing Education
M.N.S.	Master of Nursing Science, Master of Nutritional Sciences, Master of Natural Sciences, Master of Nuclear Science
M.Nuc.Sc.	Master of Nuclear Science
M.O.	Master of Oceanography
M.O.B.	Master of Organizational Behavior
M.Oc.E.	Master of Oceanographic Engineering
M.Opt.	Master of Optometry
M.O.D.	Master of Organizational Development
M.O.E.	Master of Ocean Engineering
M.O.H.	Master of Organizational Health, Master of Occupational Health
M.O.T.	Master of Occupational Therapy
M.P.	Master of Planning
M.P.A.	Master of Physician Assistant, Master of Public Administration, Master of Public Affairs, Master of Professional Accounting
M.P.Acc.	Master of Public Accounting
M.P.A.S.	Master of Physician Assistant Science, Master of Physician Assistant Studies
M.P.C.	Master of Professional Counseling, Master of Professional Communication
M.P.D.	Master of Product Design, Master of Product Development
M.P.D.S.	Master of Planning and Development Studies
M.P.E.	Master of Physical Education
M.P.E.M.	Master of Project Engineering and Management
M.P.E.R.	Master of Personnel and Employee Relations
M.Pet.E.	Master of Petroleum Engineering
M.P.H.	Master of Public Health
M.P.H.Ed.	Master of Public Health Education
M.P.H.T.M.	Master of Public Health and Tropical Medicine
M.Pharm.	Master of Pharmacy
M.Phil.	Master of Philosophy
M.P.I.A.	Master of Public and International Affairs, Master of Pacific International Affairs
M.P.M.	Master of Personnel Management, Master of

	Project Management, Master of Public Management
M.P.M.&P.H.	Master of Preventive Medicine and Public Health
M.P.N.A.	Master of Public and Nonprofit Administration
M.P.O.T.	Master in Psychiatric Occupational Therapy
M.P.P.	Master of Public Policy
M.P.P.A.	Master of Public Policy Administration
M.Prof.Acc.	Master of Professional Accounting
M.P.P.P.M.	Master of Plant Protection and Pest Management
M.Pr.Met.	Master of Professional Meteorology
M.P.R.T.M.	Master of Park, Recreation, and Tourism Management
M.Ps.Sc.	Master of Psychological Science
M.P.S.	Master of Perfusion Science, Master of Political Science, Master of Policy Studies, Master of Preservation Studies, Master of Public Service
M.P.S.L.	Master of Public Safety Leadership
M.P.T.	Master of Physical Therapy
M.P.V.M.	Master of Preventive Veterinary Medicine
M.Q.F.	Master of Quantitative Finance
M.Q.M.	Master of Quality Management
M.Q.S.	Master of Quantitative Systems, Master of Quality Systems
M.R.A.	Master of Recreation Administration, Master of Rehabilitation Administration, Master of Resource Administration
M.R.C.	Master of Rehabilitation Counseling
M.R.C.P.	Master of Regional and Community Planning
M.R.D.	Master of Rural Development
M.R.E.	Master of Religious Education
M.R.Ed.	Master of Recreation Education
M.Rel.Ed.	Master of Religious Education
M.R.E.C.M.	Master of Real Estate and Construction Management
M.R.E.D.	Master of Real Estate Development
M.R.M.	Master of Rehabilitation Medicine, Master of Resource Management
M.R.P.	Master of Regional Planning
M.R.P.A.	Master of Recreation and Parks Administration
M.R.T.P.	Master of Rural and Town Planning
M.S.	Master of Science
M.S.A.	Master of Science in Accounting, Master of Science in Administration, Master of Sport Administration
M.S.A.A.E.	Master of Science in Aeronautical and Astronautical Engineering
M.S.A.E.	Master of Science in Aerospace Engineering
M.S.Ag.	Master of Science in Agriculture
M.S.A.I.	Master of Science in Artificial Intelligence
M.S.Ap.Sc.	Master of Science in Applied Science
M.S.Arch.	Master of Science in Architecture
M.S.A.S.	Master of Science in Architectural Studies
M.S.B.A.	Master of Science in Business Administration
M.S.B.E.	Master of Science in Biomedical Engineering
M.S.C.	Master of Speech Communication, Master of Science in Counseling, Master of Science in Criminology
M.Sc.A.	Master of Social Administration
M.S.Ch.E.	Master of Science in Chemical Engineering
M.S.Chem.	Master of Science in Chemistry
M.S.C.E.	Master of Science in Civil Engineering, Master of Science in Computer Engineering
M.Sc.D.	Master of Science in Dentistry, Master of Science in Design
M.S.C.Ed.	Master of Science in Continuing Education
M.S.Cer.E.	Master of Science in Ceramic Engineering
M.S.C.F.	Master of Science in Computational Finance
M.S.C.J.	Master of Science in Criminal Justice
M.S.Econ.	Master of Science in Economics
M.Sc.T.	Master of Science Teaching, Master of Science in Teaching
M.S.D.	Master of Science in Dentistry
M.S.E.	Master of Science Education, Master of Science in Education, Master of Science in Engineering, Master of Software Engineering
M.Sec.Sch.Sci.	Master of Secondary School Science
M.S.Ed.	Master of Science Education, Master of Science in Education
M.S. in Ed.	Master of Science in Education
M.S.E.E.	Master of Science in Electrical Engineering, Master of Science in Environmental Engineering
M.S.Eng.	Master of Science in Engineering
M.S.Engr.	Master of Science in Engineering
M.S.E.M.	Master of Science in Engineering and Mining
M.S.E.Mgt.	Master of Science in Engineering Management
M.S.E.R.	Master of Science in Energy Resources
M.S.Envr.E.	Master of Science in Environmental Engineering
M.S.E.S.S.	Master of Science in Exercise and Sport Studies
M.S.F.	Master of Science in Finance, Master of Science in Forestry
M.S.F.S.	Master of Science in Financial Services, Master of Science in Forensic Science, Master of Science in Foreign Service
M.S.G.	Master of Science in Gerontology
M.S.G.C.	Master of Science in Genetic Counseling
M.S.G.L.	Master of Science in Global Leadership
M.S.H.A.	Master of Science in Health Administration
M.S.H.C.A.	Master of Science in Health Care Administration
M.S.H.E.	Master of Science in Health Education
M.S.H.R.	Master of Science in Human Resources
M.S.I.A.	Master of Institutional Administration, Master of Science in International Affairs
M.S.I.E.	Master of Science in Industrial Engineering
M.S.I.E.O.R.	Master of Science in Industrial Engineering and Operations Research
M.S.I.M.	Master of Science in Information Management, Master of Science in Investment Management
M.S.I.M.C.	Master of Science in Information Management and Communication, Master of Science in Integrated Marketing Communication
M.S.I.R.	Master of Science in Industrial Relations
M.S.I.S.	Master of Science in Information Science, Master of Science in Information Systems, Master of Science in Interdisciplinary Studies
M.S.I.T.	Master of Science in Information Technology
M.S.J.	Master of Science in Journalism
M.S.J.A.	Master of Science in Judicial Administration
M.S.J.P.S.	Master of Science in Justice and Public Safety
M.S.K.	Master of Science in Kinesiology
M.S.L.	Master of Science in Limnology, Master of Studies in Law
M.S.L.S.	Master of Science in Library Science, Master of Science in Logistic Systems
M.S.M	Master of Sacred Music, Master of Science in Management
M.S.Mat.S.E.	Master of Science in Materials Science Engineering
M.S.M.C.	Master of Science in Mass Communication, Master of Science in Marketing Communication
M.S.M.E.	Master of Science in Mechanical Engineering
M.S.Met.E.	Master of Science in Metallurgical Engineering
M.S.Mgt.	Master of Science in Management
M.S.M.I.	Master of Science in Medical Illustration

M.S.M.O.T.	Master of Science in Management of Technology		Master of Science in Technology, Master of Science in Tourism, Master of Speech Therapy, Master of Science in Telecommunication
M.S.M.S.Ed.	Master of Science in Mathematics and Science Education		
M.S.M.T.	Master of Science in Medical Technology	M.S.T.E.	Master of Science in Technical Education, Master of Science in Transportation Engineering
M.S.N.	Master of Science in Nursing		
M.S.N.A.	Master of Science in Nursing Administration, Master of Science in Nurse Anesthesia		
		M.S.T.Ed.	Master of Science in Technical Education
M.S.N.E.	Master of Science in Nuclear Engineering	M.S.Text.	Master of Science in Textiles
M.S.N.S.	Master of Science in Natural Science	M.S.T.M.	Master of Science in Technology Management, Master of Science in Technical Management
M.S.O.	Master of Science in Orthodontics		
M.S.O.D.	Master of Science in Organizational Development		
		M.S.T.S.L.	Master of Science in Teaching a Second Language
M.S.O.M.	Master of Science in Organization and Management		
		M.S.U.D.	Master of Science in Urban Design
M.S.O.R.	Master of Science in Operations Research	M.S.V.C.	Master of Vocational Counseling
M.S.O.T.	Master of Science in Occupational Therapy, Master of Science in Occupational Technology	M.S.W.	Master of Social Work
		M.T.	Master of Taxation, Master of Teaching, Master of Technology
M.S.P.	Master of Science in Planning, Master of Speech Pathology	M.T.A.	Master of Tax Accounting, Master of Teaching Arts, Master of Tourism Administration
M.S.P.A.	Master of Science in Public Administration, Master of Science in Professional Accounting, Master of Science in Physician Assistant		
		M.Tech.	Master of Technology
		M.Th.	Master of Theology
		M.T.H.M.	Master of Tourism and Hospitality Management
M.S.Pet.E.	Master of Science in Petroleum Engineering		
M.S.P.Ex.	Master of Science in Physiology of Exercise	M.T.M.	Master of Tourism Management
M.S.P.H.	Master of Science in Public Health	M.T.M.H.	Master of Tropical Medicine & Hygiene
M.S.P.H.N.	Master of Science in Public Health Nursing	M.T.P.W.	Master of Technical and Professional Writing
M.S.P.N.G.E.	Master of Science in Petroleum and Natural Gas Engineering	M.T.S.	Master of Teaching of Science
		M.T.S.C.	Master of Teaching Speech Communication, Master of Technical and Scientific Communication
M.S.Poly.	Master of Science in Polymers		
M.S.P.S.	Master of Science in Pharmaceutical Science, Master of Science in Psychological Services		
		M.Tx.	Master of Taxation
M.S.P.T.	Master of Science in Physical Therapy	M.U.A.	Master of Urban Affairs, Master of Urban Architecture
M.S.Psy.	Master of Science in Psychology		
M.S.R.E.D.	Master of Science in Real Estate Development	M.U.D.	Master of Urban Design
M.S.R.S.	Master of Science in Rehabilitation Sciences	M.U.P.	Master of Urban Planning
M.S.R.T.M.	Master of Science in Resort and Tourism Management	M.U.P.P.	Master of Urban Planning and Policy
		M.U.R.P.	Master of Urban and Regional Planning, Master of Urban and Rural Planning
M.S.S.	Master of Science in Software, Master of Social Service, Master of Sport Science, Master of Stategic Studies		
		M.U.S.	Master of Urban Studies
		M.Vet.Sc.	Master of Veterinary Science
M.S.S.A.	Master of Science in Social Administration	M.V.T.E.	Master of Vocational Technical Education
M.S.S.E.	Master of Science in Software Engineering	M.W.P.S.	Master of Wood and Paper Science
M.S.S.P.A.	Master of Speech Pathology and Audiology, Master of Student Personnel Administration	M.W.R.	Master of Water Resources
		M.W.S.	Master of Women's Studies
		Phil.M.	Master of Philosophy
M.S.Stat.	Master of Science in Statistics	P.M.B.A.	Professional Master of Business Adminstration
M.S.S.T.	Master of Science in Science Teaching, Master of Science in Systems Technology	S.M.	Master of Science
		S.T.M.	Master of Sacred Theology
M.S.S.W	Master of Science in Social Work	Th.M.	Master of Theology
M.S.T.	Master of Sacred Theology, Master of Secondary Teaching, Master of Science in Taxation, Master of Science in Teaching,	W.E.M.B.A.	Weekend Executive Master of Business Administration
		X.M.B.A.	Executive Master of Business Administration

SIXTH-YEAR DEGREES

A.C.	Advanced Certificate	Ed.S.	Specialist in Education
A.D.	Artist's Diploma	Eng.	Engineer
A.G.C.	Advanced Graduate Certificate	Engr.	Engineer
A.G.S.C.	Advanced Graduate Specialist Certificate	G.D.M.	Graduate Diploma in Management
C.A.G.S.	Certificate of Advanced Graduate Studies	G.D.P.A.	Graduate Diploma in Public Administration
C.A.G.S.B.	Certificate in Advanced Study in Business	G.D.T.	Graduate Diploma in Taxation
C.A.M.S.	Certificate of Advanced Management Studies	G.P.D.	Graduate Performance Diploma
C.A.P.S.	Certificate of Advanced Professional Studies	P.D.	Professional Diploma
C.A.S.	Certificate of Advanced Study	Psy.S.	Specialist in Psychology
C.E.	Civil Engineer	S.C.C.T.	Specialist in Community College Teaching
Ch.E.	Chemical Engineer	S.C.G.	Specialist Certificate in Gerontology
E.E.	Electrical Engineer	S.L.S.	Specialist in Library Science

Sp.C.	Specialist in Counseling	S.S.A.	Specialist in School Administration
Sp.Ed.	Specialist in Education	S.S.P.	Specialist in School Psychology
S.P.A.	Specialist in Public Administration	S.T.L.	Licentiate in Sacred Theology

DOCTORAL DEGREES

A.Mus.D.	Doctor of Musical Arts	D.M.Sc.	Doctor of Medical Science
Au.D.	Doctor of Audiology	D.M.L.	Doctor of Modern Languages
D.A.	Doctor of Arts	D.Mus.	Doctor of Music
D.A.I.S.	Doctor of Arts in Information Science	D.Mus.Ed.	Doctor of Music Education
D.Arch.	Doctor of Architecture	D.N.	Doctor of Nursing
D.B.A.	Doctor of Business Administration	D.N.P.	Doctor of Nursing Practice
D.C.L.	Doctor of Comparative Law, Doctor of Civil Law	D.N.Sc.	Doctor of Nursing Science
		D.O.	Doctor of Osteopathy
D.C.S.	Doctor of Computer Science	D.P.A.	Doctor of Public Administration
D.Chem.	Doctor of Chemistry	D.P.D.S.	Doctor of Planning and Development Studies
D.D.S.	Doctor of Dental Surgery	D.P.E.	Doctor of Physical Education
D.E.	Doctor of Engineering	D.P.H.	Doctor of Public Health
D.Eng.	Doctor of Engineering	Dr.P.H.	Doctor of Public Health
D.E.D.	Doctor of Environmental Design	D.P.T.	Doctor of Physical Therapy
D.Ed.	Doctor of Education	D.R.E.	Doctor of Recreation Education
D.Eng.Sc.	Doctor of Engineering Science	D.Sc.	Doctor of Science
D.Env.Des.	Doctor of Environmental Design	D.Sc.D.	Doctor of Science in Dentistry
D.E.S.	Doctor of Engineering Science	D.Sc.V.M.	Doctor of Science in Veterinary Medicine
D.F.	Doctor of Forestry	D.S.L.	Doctor of Strategic Leadership
D.F.A.	Doctor of Fine Arts	D.S.M.	Doctor of Sacred Music, Doctor of Sport Management
D.F.E.S.	Doctor of Forestry and Environmental Studies		
		D.S.Sc.	Doctor of Social Science
D.H.S.	Doctor of Health Services, Doctor of Human Services	D.S.W.	Doctor of Social Work
		D.Th.	Doctor of Theology
D.I.B.A.	Doctor of International Business Administration	D.V.M.	Doctor of Veterinary Medicine
		Ed.D.	Doctor of Education
D.I.T.	Doctor of Industrial Technology	J.D.	Doctor of Jurisprudence
D.L.I.S.	Doctor of Library and Information Sciences	J.S.D.	Doctor of Judicial Science
D.L.S.	Doctor of Library Science	L.L.D.	Doctor of Laws
D.M.	Doctor of Management, Doctor of Music	Ph.D.	Doctor of Philosophy
D.M.A.	Doctor of Musical Arts	Pharm.D.	Doctor of Pharmacy
D.M.D.	Doctor of Medical Dentistry, Doctor of Dental Medicine	Psy.D.	Doctor of Psychology
		Re.D.	Doctor of Recreation
D.M.Ed.	Doctor of Music Education	Rh.D.	Doctor of Rehabilitation
D.M.F.T.	Doctor of Marriage and Family Therapy	Sc.D.	Doctor of Science
D.Min.	Doctor of Ministry	S.J.D.	Doctor of Judicial Science

EXAMINATIONS AND OTHER ABBREVIATIONS

AACOMAS	American Association of Colleges of Osteopathic Medicine Application Service	FAF	Financial Aid Form
		FAFSA	Free Application for Federal Student Aid
AACSB	American Assembly of Collegiate Schools of Business—The American Association of Management Education	FAT	Financial Aid Transcript
		FWS	Federal Work-Study
		GMAC	Graduate Management Admission Council
AADSAS	American Association of Dental Schools Application Service	GMAT	Graduate Management Admissions Test
		GPA	Grade Point Average
AAU	Association of American Universities	GRE	Graduate Record Exam
AAUW	American Association of University Women	HEAL	Health Education Assistance Loan
ABA	American Bar Association	IELTS	International English Language Testing Systems
AMCAS	American Medical College Application Service		
AOA	American Optometric Association	IIE	Institute of International Education
CGS	Council of Graduate Schools	LSAC	Law School Admission Council
COPA	Council on Postsecondary Accreditation	LSAT	Law School Aptitude Test
DAT	Dental Aptitude Test	LSDAS	Law School Data Assembly Service
DSTP	Dental Scientist Training Program	MAT	Miller Analogies Test
ED	Education Department	MCAT	Medical College Admissions Test
EDP	Early Decision Program	MELAB	Michigan English Language Assessment Battery
EMSAP	Early Medical School Acceptance Program		
ETS	Educational Testing Service	MMPI	Minnesota Multiphasic Personality Inventory

MSTP	Medical Scientist Training Program	SAAC	Student Aid Application for California
NCATE	National Council for Accreditation of Teacher Education	SAR	Student Aid Report
		SREB	Southern Regional Education Board
NIH	National Institutes of Health	TOEFL	Test of English as a Foreign Language
NLNGNE	National League of Nursing Graduate Nursing Examination	TSE	Test of Spoken English
		TWE	Test of Written English
NSF	National Science Foundation	UGPA	Undergraduate Grade Point Average
NTE	National Teaching Examination	USMLE	U.S. Medical Licensing Examination
OAT	Optometry Admissions Test	VA	Veterans Administration
PAEG	Prueba de Admisiones para Estudios Graduados	VMAT	Veterinary Medicine Aptitude Test
		WAMI	Wyoming, Alaska, Montana, Idaho
PAT	Perceptual Ability Test	WES	World Education Service
PCAT	Pharmacy College Admissions Test	WICHE	Western Interstate Commission for Higher Education
PHEAA	Pennsylvania Higher Education Assistance Agency		
		WWAMI	Washington, Wyoming, Alaska, Montana, Idaho

GUIDE TO
AMERICAN GRADUATE SCHOOLS

ABILENE CHRISTIAN UNIVERSITY
Abilene, Texas 89699
Web site: www.acu.edu

Founded 1906. Coed. Independent/religious. Semester system. CGS member. Library: more than 550,000 volumes. Special facilities: Center for Conflict Resolution, Center for Restoration Studies, Center for Aging, Center for Adolescent Studies. More than 700 computers on campus for student use. Total University enrollment: 4700.

Tuition: per credit $487. On-campus rooms and apartments available. Annual room and board expenses: single students $5670, married students $8000 (room only). Apply to the Graduate Housing Office by May 11. Phone: (325)674-2066. Day-care facilities available.

Graduate School
E-mail: gradinfo@acu.edu

Enrollment: full- and part-time 565. University faculty teaching graduate students: full- and part-time 131. Degrees conferred: M.A., M.Acc., M.A.C.H., M.A.M.I., M.Div., M.Ed., M.L.A., M.M.F.T., M.P.A., M.S., M.S.N., D.Min.

ADMISSION REQUIREMENTS. Transcripts, GRE/MAT/GMAT, personal interview, three letters of recommendation (license to practice nursing in Texas for nursing) required in support of application. TOEFL or other evidence of English ability required of foreign students. Accepts transfer applicants. Apply to Office of University Admission by June 1 (Fall), April 1 (Summer), November 1 (Spring). Application fee $40, $45 for international students. Phone: (325)674-2355.

ADMISSION STANDARDS. Selective for most departments. Usual minimum average: 2.75 (A = 4).

FINANCIAL AID. Annual awards from institutional funds: scholarships, research/teaching assistantships, internships, Federal W/S, loans. Apply to the University of Financial Aid by April 1. Use FAFSA. Aid available for part-time students.

DEGREE REQUIREMENTS. For M.A., M.Acc., M.S., M.L.A.: 30–42 credit hours depending upon program; thesis/nonthesis option/professional paper/synthesis project, depending upon major; comprehensive exam; reading knowledge of one foreign language for some majors; practicum (M.S.). For M.A. (Psychology), M.M.F.T.: 45 credit program; practicum; thesis. For M.A.C.H., M.A.M.I.: 54 credit programs; advancement to candidacy; thesis optional. For M.P.A.: 42 credit hour program; internship; comprehensive exam. For D.Min.: 45–72 credit hours beyond master's depending upon program; reading knowledge of at least two foreign languages; preliminary exam; dissertation; final oral/written exam.

FIELDS OF GRADUATE STUDY.
Accounting. M.Acc.
Christian Ministry. M.A.C.M.
Communication.
Communication Sciences and Disorders.
Conflict Resolution.
Divinity. M.Div.
Education.
English.
Family Studies.
Gerontology.
Higher Education.
History and Theology. M.A.
Liberal Arts. M.L.A.
Marriage and Family Therapy.
Ministry. 84 credit program, nonthesis. D.Min.
Missions. 54 credit program. M.A.M.I.

New Testament. M.A.
Nursing.
Old Testament. M.A.
Organizational and Human Resource Development.
Psychology.
Social Work.

ADAMS STATE COLLEGE
Alamosa, Colorado 81102
Web site: www.adams.edu

Founded 1921. Located 220 miles SW of Denver. Coed. State control. Semester system. CGS member. Special facilities: Luther Bean Historical Museum, Hatfield Art Gallery, Zachers Observatory. Library: 493,581 volumes, 614 subscriptions. More than 350 computers on campus for student use. Total University enrollment: 5578.

Tuition: per credit resident $169, nonresident $503. On-campus housing for both single and married students. Average annual housing cost: $4000 for married students, $6500 (including board) for single students. Apply to Director of Housing by May 1. Phone: (719)587-7227.

Graduate School

Enrollment: full-time 46, part-time 426. Faculty: full- and part-time 42. Degree conferred: M.A.

ADMISSION REQUIREMENTS. Transcripts, GRE/MAT, a letter of intent required in support of application. TOEFL required for international applicants. Accepts transfer applicants. Apply to Office of the Dean by May 15 (Fall), October 15 (Spring). Application fee $30. Phone: (719)587-8152; (866)407-0013.

ADMISSION STANDARDS. Selective. Usual minimum average: 2.75 (A = 4), MAT score: 37, GRE combined score: 1250.

FINANCIAL AID. Annual awards from institutional funds: graduate assistantships, internship, Federal W/S, loans. Approved for VA benefits. Apply by March 1 to Dean for assistantships; to Financial Aid Office for all other programs. Use FAFSA. Phone: (800)824-6494 or (719)587-7306. About 10% of students receive aid other than loans from College and outside sources.

DEGREE REQUIREMENTS. For M.A.: 30–36 semester hours, at least 24–30 in residence; thesis/nonthesis option/creative project; final comprehensive exam; no language requirement.

FIELDS OF GRADUATE STUDY.
Art. Includes ceramics, drawing, fiber, metalsmithing, open media, painting, photography, printmaking, sculpture.
Community Counseling.
Education. Includes curriculum, educational leadership, literacy, language and culture (teacher of the linguistically diverse, reading teacher).
Humanities. Includes emphasis in U.S. history.
School Counseling.
Special Education. Includes generalist, generalist (literacy, language and culture).

ADELPHI UNIVERSITY
Garden City, New York 11530-0701
Web site: www.adelphi.com

Founded 1896. Located 20 miles E of New York City. Coed. Private control. Semester system. Library: 630,000 volumes, 1750 subscriptions. Special facilities: Hy Weinberg Center for Communicative Disorders, Adelphi Institute for Prevention of Drug Abuse, Center for Social Policy. More than 540 computers available on campus, 100 in library. Total University enrollment: 8000.

Tuition: per credit $690. No on-campus housing. Annual room and board expenses: $7450. Apply to Director of Housing for off-campus housing information. Phone: (516)877-3650. Daycare facilities available.

Graduate School of Arts and Sciences

Enrollment: full- and part-time 75 (men 30%, women 70%). University faculty teaching graduate students: full- and part-time 19. Degrees conferred: M.A., M.S., D.A.

ADMISSION REQUIREMENTS. Transcripts, two letters of recommendation required in support of application. GRE required by some departments. TOEFL (score of 550/213 or better) required of foreign students. Interview by invitation. Accepts transfer applicants. Apply to Graduate Office of Admission at least two months prior to registration. Foreign students must apply by February 1 (Fall admission only). Rolling admission process. Application fee $50. Phone: (516)877-3050; (800)233-5744.

ADMISSION STANDARDS. Selective for most departments. Usual minimum average: 2.75 (A = 4).

FINANCIAL AID. Annual awards from institutional funds: partial scholarships, research/teaching assistantships, internships, Federal W/S, loans. Apply to the University Office of Financial Aid by February 15. Use FAFSA. About 50% of full-time students receive aid other than loans from University and outside sources.

DEGREE REQUIREMENTS. For M.A., M.S.: 30–36 credit hours depending upon program; thesis optional, depending upon major; reading knowledge of one foreign language for some M.S. majors. For D.A.: 45–72 credit hours beyond master's depending upon program; reading knowledge of at least two foreign languages for mathematics and language majors, one language or knowledge of computer programming for psychology majors; preliminary exam; dissertation; final oral/written exam.

FIELDS OF STUDY.
Art, Studio. 33 credits for M.A.
Art History.
Biology. 33 hours for M.S.
Creative Writing.
Environmental Studies.
Physics. M.S. only.

Gorden F. Derner Institute of Advanced Psychological Studies

Founded 1951. Annual tuition: $28,500.
Enrollment: full- and part-time 365 (men 30%, women 70%). Institute faculty teaching graduate students: about 25 full- and part-time. Degrees conferred: M.A., Ph.D.

ADMISSION REQUIREMENTS: Transcripts, GRE, two letters of recommendation required in support of application. TOEFL (minimum scores of 550/213) required of foreign students. Interview by invitation. Accepts transfer applicants. For M.A.: rolling admissions, apply to Office of Graduate Admission at least two months prior to registration. Admits Fall, Spring, and Summer. For Ph.D: Apply by January 15; admits Fall only. Foreign students must apply by February 1 (Fall admission only). Application fee $50. Phone: (516)877-3050.

ADMISSION STANDARDS. Selective. Usual minimum average: 3.0 (A = 4).

FINANCIAL AID. Annual awards from institutional funds: scholarships and fellowships (New York State residents), clinical/research/teaching assistantships, internships, paid field placements, Federal W/S, loans. Apply to the University Financial Aid Office by February 15. Use FAFSA. About 70% of full-time students receive aid other than loans from University and outside sources.

DEGREE REQUIREMENTS. For M.A.: 36 credit hours program, no thesis, or 18 core credits and thesis. For Ph.D: five-year program, four years in full-time study on campus; weekly colloquia, clinical practicum; second-year research project; clerkship; internship in fifth year; dissertation; final oral exam.

FIELDS OF STUDY.
Clinical Psychology. Ph.D. only.
General Psychology. M.A. only.
Mental Health Counseling. M.A.
Postdoctoral Diplomas.
School Psychology. M.A.

School of Business and Management

Tuition: per credit $690.
Enrollment: full-time 74, part-time 200 (men 50%, women 50%). Graduate faculty: full-time 20, part-time 14. Degrees conferred: M.B.A., M.S.

ADMISSION REQUIREMENTS. Transcripts, three recommendations, GMAT required in support of application. TOEFL required for foreign applicants. Accepts transfer applicants. Admits Fall and Spring semester. Apply to the University's Office of Graduate Admissions at least one month prior to semester of registration. Application fee $50. Phone: (516)877-3050.

ADMISSION STANDARDS. Selective. Usual minimum average: 2.75 (A = 4).

FINANCIAL AID. Annual awards from institutional funds: assistantships, Federal W/S, loans. Apply to the Financial Aid Office by March 1 (Fall and Spring). Use FAFSA. Phone: (516)877-3364. About 5% of students receive aid other than loans from School and outside sources.

DEGREE REQUIREMENTS. For M.B.A.: 33–66 credit hour program. For M.S.: 30–51 credit hour program. For M.B.A.-M.S. (Nursing): 72–74 credit hour program.

FIELDS OF STUDY.
Accounting.
Business Administration.
Finance.
Human Resource Management. Certificate only.
Information Systems.
Management.
Marketing/E-Commerce.

School of Education

Tuition: per credit $690.
Enrollment: full- and part-time 1350 (men 20%, women 80%). University faculty teaching graduate students: full- and part-time 60. Degrees conferred: M.A., M.S., P.D., D.A.

ADMISSION REQUIREMENTS. Transcripts, three letters of recommendation required in support of School's application. MAT required by some departments. TOEFL required of international applicants. Interviews encouraged. Accepts transfer applicants. Apply to Office of Graduate Admission at least two months prior to registration. Foreign students must apply by February 1 (Fall admission only). Application fee $50. Phone: (516)877-3050.

ADMISSION STANDARDS. Selective for most departments. Usual minimum average: 2.75 (A = 4).

FINANCIAL AID. Annual awards from institutional funds: fellowships, tuition waivers, partial scholarships, research/teaching assistantships, Federal W/S, loans. Apply to the Office of Financial Aid by February 15. Use FAFSA. About 20% of full-time students receive aid other than loans from University and outside sources. Aid available for part-time students.

DEGREE REQUIREMENTS. For M.A., M.S.: 30–36 credit hours depending upon program; thesis/nonthesis option, depending upon the program. For M.S. (Communication Disorders): 53–56 credit program; clinical practica; departmental final comprehensive exam. For D.A.: 60 credit hours beyond master's; candidacy; preliminary exam; dissertation; final oral exam.

FIELDS OF GRADUATE STUDY.
Art Education. M.A.
Audiology. Au.D.
Bilingual Education/TESOL. M.A.
Childhood Education. M.A.
Childhood Special Education. M.S.
Communication Sciences and Disorders. M.S., D.A.
Community Health Education. M.A.
Early Childhood Education. M.A.
Early Childhood Special Education. M.A.
Educational Leadership and Technology. M.A.
English Education. M.A.
Health Education. M.A.
Literacy. M.S.
Mathematics Education. M.A.
Physical Education Studies. M.A.
Science Education. M.A.
Social Studies Education. M.A.

School of Nursing—Graduate Division

Graduate study since 1949. Tuition: per credit $650. On-campus housing available. Enrollment: full- and part-time 110. Graduate Faculty: full- and part-time 22. Degrees conferred: M.S., M.S.-M.B.A.

ADMISSION REQUIREMENTS. Transcripts, two years experience in nursing, GRE, letters of reference required in support of application. TOEFL required for foreign applicants. Accepts transfer applicants. Apply to Office of Graduate Admissions by May 1 (Fall), November 1 (Spring); for Ph.D. apply by February 15. Rolling admission process. Application fee $50. Phone: (516)877-3050.

ADMISSION STANDARDS. Selective. Usual minimum average: 3.0 (A = 4).

FINANCIAL AID. Annual awards from institutional funds: Federal Nursing traineeships, Federal W/S, loans. Apply to Director, Graduate Studies by February 15. Use FAFSA. Phone: (516)877-4545. About 75–90% of students receive aid other than loans from all sources.

DEGREE REQUIREMENTS. For M.S.: 45–48 credit hours minimum; master's project. For M.S.-M.B.A.: 69–71 credit hours minimum. For Ph.D.: 54 credit minimum; dissertation.

FIELDS OF GRADUATE STUDY.
Adult Health Nurse Practitioner. M.S.
Emergency Nursing and Disaster Management. M.S.
Nursing. Ph.D.
Nursing Administration. M.S.
Nursing Education. M.S.

POST-MASTER'S CERTIFICATE PROGRAMS:
Adult Health Nurse Practitioner.
Emergency Nursing and Disaster Management.
Nursing Administration.

School of Social Work

Founded 1949. Annual tuition: $22,800; per credit $650. On-campus housing available. Contact Director of Housing. Phone: (516)877-3650.

Enrollment: full-time 218, part-time 652. Faculty: full-time 28, part-time 35. Degrees conferred: M.S.W., D.S.W.

ADMISSION REQUIREMENTS. Transcript, three professional references, minimum of twenty semester hours in social sciences required in support of application. Interview sometimes required. TOEFL score of 585 required for foreign applicants. Accepts transfer applicants. Apply to Director of Admissions. Rolling admissions process. Application fee $50. Phone: (516)877-3050; fax: (516)877-3039.

ADMISSION STANDARDS. Competitive. Usual minimum average: 3.0 (A = 4).

FINANCIAL AID. Annual awards from institutional funds: assistantships, Federal W/S, loans. Apply to Director of Admissions by February 15. Phone: (516)877-3080; fax: (516)877-3380. Use FAFSA. About 20% of students receive aid other than loans from School and outside sources.

DEGREE REQUIREMENTS. For M.S.W.: 64 credit hours minimum, at least one year in full-time residence; internship; capstone seminar. For D.S.W.: 48 doctoral-level credits beyond master's degree; candidacy exam; dissertation; oral exam.
Note: Accelerated one-year program available for qualified applicants with undergraduate Social Work degree; 16-month accelerated M.S.W. also available.

FIELDS OF STUDY.
Social Welfare. D.S.W. only.
Social Work. M.S.W. only.

AIR FORCE INSTITUTE OF TECHNOLOGY
Dayton, Ohio 45433-7765
Web site: www.afit.edu

Founded 1919 as the Air School of Application to provide education and research to meet Air Force requirements. Located adjacent to Dayton. Coed. Federal control. Graduate only. Quarter system. Library: 110,000 volumes, 1600 subscriptions. More than 200 computers available.

Tuition paid by U.S. Government. Air Base has facilities for limited number of single and married students.

Enrollment: full- and part-time 1029. Participation in Institute by military personnel and Federal Civil Service employees is on a voluntary basis. Faculty: full-time 132, part-time 16. Degrees conferred: M.S., Ph.D.

ADMISSION REQUIREMENTS. Transcripts, GRE/GMAT required in support of application. Apply to the Director of Admission/Registrar by March 1. Application fee: none. Applications processed on a rolling basis. Phone: (937)255-7168.

ADMISSION STANDARDS. Very selective for most majors, competitive for others. Usual minimum average: for M.S. in management programs: 2.5, for M.S. in engineering/technical: 3.0, for Ph.D.: 3.5 (A = 4).

FINANCIAL AID. All students are military officers or Federal or Civil Service employees drawing full pay.

DEGREE REQUIREMENTS. For M.S.: 48 quarter hours, 36 in residence; thesis. For Ph.D.: 3 consecutive quarters of full-time course work, 48 quarter hours residence; dissertation; final oral exam.

FIELDS OF STUDY.
Aeronautical Engineering. M.S., Ph.D.
Applied Mathematics.
Applied Physics. M.S., Ph.D.
Astronautical Engineering. M.S., Ph.D.
Computer Engineering. M.S., Ph.D.
Computer Systems.
Cost Analysis.
Electrical Engineering. Ph.D.
Electro Optics.
Engineering Management.
Environmental Engineering & Science.
Financial Analysis.
Industrial Hygiene.
Information Resource Management.
Logistics Management.
Materials Science. Ph.D.
Mobility Management.
Nuclear Engineering.
Operations Research. Ph.D.
Research & Development.
Systems Engineering. M.S., Ph.D.

UNIVERSITY OF AKRON
Akron, Ohio 44325-0001
Web site: www.uakron.edu

Founded 1870 by the Unitarians. Located about 45 miles S of Cleveland, Ohio. CGS member. Coed. State supported. Semester system. Special facilities: Akron Polymer Training Center, Ray C. Bliss Institute of Applied Politics, Institute for Biomedical Engineering Research, Center for Economic Education, Center for Environmental Studies, Center for Family Business, Institute for Health and Social Policy, Center for Nursing, Center for Conflict Management, Center for Small Business, Center for Urban Studies, Fisher Institute for Professional Selling, William and Rita Fitzgerald Institute for Entrepreneurial Studies, Institute for Future Studies, Institute for Global Business, Institute for Life-Span Development and Gerontology, Center for Organizational Research, Center for Policy Studies, Institute for Polymer Engineering, The Maurice Morton Institute of Polymer Science, Microscale Physiochemical Engineering Center, Training Center for Fire and Hazardous Materials, Institute for Teaching and Learning. According to The Center at the University of Florida, the University of Akron has had two of its faculty members elected to National Honor Academics and this ranks it 117th among all U.S. institutions. The library: about 1,200,000 volumes, 13,000 subscriptions. There are 2450 computers on campus for student use. Total University enrollment: 21,000.

Tuition: per credit, resident $342, nonresident $611. Limited on-campus housing available. Annual housing costs: $7208 (including board). For off-campus housing contact the Off-Campus Housing Office. Phone: (330)972-6936.

Graduate School

First graduate degree conferred 1880. Enrollment: full-time 1676, part-time 1703. University faculty teaching graduate students: full-time 495, part-time 124. Degrees conferred: M.A., M.A.Ed., M.A.H.E.&F.E., M.P.A., M.S., M.S.Ed., M.S.A.,

M.S.M., M.B.A., M.T., M.S.T.Ed., M.S.E., M.S.E.E., M.S.C.E., M.S.M.E., M.S.Ch.E., M.S.N., M.M., Ed.D., Ph.D.

ADMISSION REQUIREMENTS. Transcripts, departmental exam may be required in support of application. TOEFL (scores of 550/213 preferred) for foreign students. Accepts transfer applicants. Graduates of unaccredited institutions not considered. Apply to Graduate School at least six weeks prior to registration. Rolling admissions process. Application fee $30, international application fee $40. Phone: (330)972-7663; fax: (330)972-7663; International Students: (330)972-6349.

ADMISSION STANDARDS. Selective for most departments. Usual minimum average: 2.75 (A = 4).

FINANCIAL AID. Annual awards from institutional funds: fellowships, research assistantships, teaching assistantships, Federal W/S, loans. Approved for V.A. benefits. Apply to Office of Student Financial Aid by March 1. Phone: (330)972-7032. About 60% of full-time students receive aid other than loans from both University and outside sources.

DEGREE REQUIREMENTS. For master's: 30–36 semester hours minimum; thesis required by some departments; advancement to candidacy; final/cumulative exams for most departments. For M.B.A.: 58 credit hour program; some foundation courses may be waived. For M.P.A.: 40 credit hour program. For Ph.D.: at least two academic years beyond the master's; one year minimum in full-time residence; reading knowledge of two languages or comprehensive knowledge of one language; or language option in selected departments; preliminary/cumulative exams for many departments; advancement to candidacy; dissertation; final oral exam. For Ed.D.: essentially the same as for Ph.D. except no language requirement.

FIELDS OF STUDY.

BUCHTEL COLLEGE OF ARTS AND SCIENCES:
Applied Mathematics. Thesis optional. Master's only.
Applied Politics.
Biology. Thesis for master's.
Chemistry. Includes analytical, inorganic, organic, physical. Thesis for master's.
Computer Science. M.S. only.
Counseling Psychology.
Creative Writing. M.F.A.
Economics. M.A. only.
English. Thesis or two essays for master's. Master's only.
French. Thesis/nonthesis options for master's. Master's only.
Geography/Urban Planning. Thesis for M.A. Master's only.
Geology. Includes earth science, geophysics engineering, geology. Thesis. Master's only.
Geophysics. Thesis. Master's only.
History. Master's, Ph.D.
Industrial/Organizational Psychology.
Mathematical Sciences. Thesis optional. Master's only.
Physics. Thesis optional. Master's only.
Political Science. Thesis for master's. Master's only.
Psychology. Includes industrial, general; M.A., Ph.D.
Public Administration.
Sociology. Thesis for master's.
Spanish. Thesis/nonthesis option for master's. Master's only.
Statistics. Final paper of thesis for master's. Master's only.
Urban Planning.
Urban Studies. M.A., Ph.D.
Urban Studies and Public Affairs. Ph.D.

COLLEGE OF BUSINESS ADMINISTRATION:
Accounting. Master's only.
Accounting Information Systems. M.S.
Business Administration. Master's only.

Business Administration/Law. J.D./M.B.A.
Electronic Business.
Entrepreneurship.
Finance. Master's only.
Global Sales Management.
International Business.
Management. Master's only.
Management-Human Resources.
Management Information Systems.
Management of Technology.
Marketing. Master's only.
Quality Management.
Taxation. Master's only.
Taxation/Law. J.D.-M.Tax.

COLLEGE OF EDUCATION:
Classroom Guidance for Teachers.
Community Counseling.
Counseling Psychology. Ed.D.
Counselor Education and Supervision. Ed.D.
Curriculum and Instruction.
Educational Administration. Ed.D.
Educational Administration-Administrative Specialist.
Educational Foundations. Includes educational psychology,
   instructional technology, social/philosophy foundations of
   education.
Elementary Education. Includes literacy. M.A., M.S., Ph.D.
Higher Educational Administration.
Marriage and Family Counseling/Therapy.
Physical Education. Includes physiology/adult fitness, sport
   science/coaching.
Postsecondary Technical Education. Includes postsecondary
   teaching, training.
Principalship Education. Includes literacy.
School Counseling.
Secondary Education. Ed.D.
Special Education.

COLLEGE OF ENGINEERING:
Biomedical Engineering.
Chemical Engineering.
Civil Engineering.
Computer Engineering. Ph.D. only.
Electrical Engineering.
Engineering. Includes specializations in management, polymer.
   M.S. only.
Engineering-Applied Mathematics. Ph.D. only.
Mechanical Engineering.

COLLEGE OF FINE AND APPLIED ARTS:
Audiology. Joint degree with Kent State University and Cleveland
   Clinic Foundation. Au.D. only
Clothing, Textiles and Interiors.
Communication.
Family and Consumer Sciences. Includes child and family devel-
   opment, child life specialist.
Music. Includes accompanying, composition, history and literature,
   performance, technology, theory.
Music Education. Includes choral.
Nutrition/Dietetics.
Social Work.
Speech-Language Pathology.
Theater Arts. Includes arts administration.

COLLEGE OF NURSING:
Adult Gerontological Health Nursing Clinical Nurse Specialist.
Adult Gerontological Health Nursing Nurse Practitioner.
Behavioral Health Nursing Clinical Nurse Specialist.
Behavioral Health Nursing Nurse Practitioner.
Child and Adolescent Health Clinical Nurse Specialist.
Child and Adolescent Health Nurse Practitioner.

Nursing. M.S.N., Ph.D.
Nursing Anesthesia.
Nursing Service Administration.
Public Health.

COLLEGE OF POLYMER SCIENCE AND POLYMER ENGINEERING:
Polymer Engineering.
Polymer Science.

C. Blake McDowell Law Center (44325-2901)

Founded 1921. Merged with University of Akron 1959. Located in downtown Akron. ABA approved 1961. AALS member.
Semester system. Full- and part-time study; both day and evening
available. Special facility: Center for Intellectual Property Law
and Technology. Law library: 288,287 volumes; 3325 periodicals/
subscriptions; has LEXIS, NEXIS, WESTLAW, OhioLINK; is a
Federal Government Depository. The law student's microcomputer network has 66 workstations with complete Internet access.

Annual tuition: resident full-time $14,292, part-time $9051;
nonresident full-time $23,883, part-time $15,126. Limited on-
campus housing for single students, none for married students.
Affordable housing opportunities within walking distance of
campus available. Annual room and board expenses: single students $13,648.

Enrollment: first-year class 182 day and evening; total day and
evening 525 (men 60%, women 40%).

Faculty: full- and part-time 52; 40% female; 10% minority;
student to faculty ratio 14 to 1.

Degrees conferred: J.D., J.D.-M.A.P., J.D.-M.B.A., J.D.-M.P.A.,
J.D.-M.S.M.H.R., J.D.-M.TAX., LL.M. (Intellectual Property).

ADMISSION REQUIREMENTS FOR FIRST-YEAR APPLI-
CANTS. LSDAS Law School report, LSAT, two recommendations, bachelor's degree from accredited institution, personal
statement required with application. Applicants must have received bachelor's degree prior to enrollment. In addition, international applicants must submit TOEFL and TSE before application
can be considered. Interview not required. Apply to Admission
Director as early as possible after September 1, before April 1
(priority deadline). Applicants admitted Fall semester only (mid-
August). Rolling admissions process; notification begins in late
November/early December. Application fee $35; online applica-
tion fee: none. Phone: (800)425-7668; fax: (330)258-2343. Acceptance of offer and first deposit due in April.

ADMISSION REQUIREMENTS FOR TRANSFER APPLI-
CANTS. Accepts transfer applicants from other ABA accredited
schools on a space available basis. At least one year of enrollment, letter from current Dean indicating applicant is in good
standing, LSAT, LSDAS report (photocopy of original acceptable), personal statement, current Law School transcript required
in support of School's application. Submit course descriptions/
syllabi for all courses taken at current law school. Apply to Admission Director by May 1 (decision made by mid-July). Application fee $35. Will consider visiting/transient students.

ADMISSION STANDARDS. Number of full-time applicants
1164, part-time 400; number accepted 489 full-time, 193 part-time;
enrolled 115 full-time, 67 part-time. LSAT: 151 (75% of full-time
students have a score at or above 151 and 75% of part-time students
have a score at or above 156); GPA: 3.37 (A = 4) (75% of full-
time students have a GPA at or above 3.25, 75% of part-time students have a score at or above 3.10). *U.S. News & World Report*
ranking is in the third tier of all U.S. law schools.

FINANCIAL AID. Scholarships, need- and merit-based loans.
Assistantships available for upper divisional joint degree candidates. Apply after January 1, but prior to May 1 (priority deadline)
to the University's Office of Student Financial Aid. Phone:
(800)621-3847 or (330)972-7332. Use FAFSA (School code:

003123). Information from the College Scholarship Service regarding the applicant's financial need must be received before a Financial Aid offer can be extended. About 60% of students receive full or partial scholarships; merit- and need-based loans available. Financial assistance available for part-time students. Average grant full-time $9550, part-time $3300.

DEGREE REQUIREMENTS. For J.D.: 88 credits (44 required credits) with a 2.0 (A = 4) GPA, plus an upper divisional writing requirement; three-year day program, four-year evening program; accelerated J.D. program available. On-campus summer sessions available. Upper divisional students may attend an ABA accredited law school's "Summer Abroad Program" as long as it does not effect the J.D. degree residency requirements. For J.D.-M.B.A.: total 103 credits (J.D. 78 credits, M.B.A. 25 credits). For J.D.-M.P.A., J.D.-M.S.M.H.R., J.D.-M.A.P.: total 109 credits (J.D. 77 credits, M.P.A., M.S.M.H.R., M.A.P. 32 credits). For J.D.-M.Tax.: total 98 (J.D. 78 credits, M.Tax. 20 credits). For LL.M. (Intellectual Property): one-year program beyond the J.D.

ALABAMA AGRICULTURAL AND MECHANICAL UNIVERSITY
Normal, Alabama 35762
Web site: www.aamu.edu

Founded 1875. Located in Huntsville. CGS member. Coed. State control. Semester system. Library: 396,000 volumes, 528,000 microforms. Special facilities: Optics Center, Agriculture Research Center, Biological Research Center, Remote Sensor Center.

Annual tuition: residents $2736, nonresidents $5112. Limited on-campus housing available for single graduate students, none for married students. Average annual housing cost: $4770 (including board) for single students. Apply to Director of Housing. Phone: (256)851-5797.

Graduate School

Enrollment: full- and part-time 1300. Graduate faculty: full- and part-time 200. Degrees conferred: M.S., M.Ed., M.B.A., Ed.S., Ph.D.

ADMISSION REQUIREMENTS. Two transcripts, evaluation or recommendations, GRE, GMAT (business) required in support of application. TOEFL and statement of financial support required for international applicants. Admits Spring, Fall, Summer. Apply three months prior to registration. International students must apply six months in advance. Application fee $40. Phone: (256)372-5266.

ADMISSION STANDARDS. Selective. Usual minimum average: 2.5 (A = 4); minimum GRE 800, GMAT 350.

FINANCIAL AID. Annual awards from institutional funds: research fellowships, internships, Federal W/S, loans. Apply to Office of Financial Aid by February 15. Use FAFSA. Phone: (256)851-5400; fax: (256)851-5407. About 10% of students receive aid other than loans from University and outside sources.

DEGREE REQUIREMENTS. For master's: 39–48 semester hours minimum; thesis, or 6 additional hours and research paper; comprehensive exam for some programs. For Ed.S.: 30 semester hours beyond the master's; thesis. For M.S.W.: 60 semester hour program. For Ph.D.: at least 45 credits beyond the master's degree; preliminary exam; reading knowledge of two foreign languages or one language and approved appropriate research technique substitution; dissertation; final oral exam.

FIELDS OF STUDY.
Accounting.

Agribusiness. Includes agribusiness management. M.S. only.
Agriscience Education.
Apparel, Merchandising and Design.
Applied Physics. Includes optics, materials science.
Art Education.
Biology. Includes biology education.
Clinical Psychology.
Communicative Sciences and Disorders.
Computer Science.
Counseling Psychology.
Curriculum and Instruction.
Early Childhood (P–3).
Economics.
Educational Administration and Supervision.
Elementary Education (K–6).
Finance.
Fine Arts.
Food Science. M.S., Ph.D.
Foundations of Education.
Higher Education Administration.
Human Development and Family Studies.
Human Resources Management.
Industrial Technology. Includes civil infrastructure system technology, electrical engineering technology, manufacturing technology management, mechanical engineering technology, industrial technology education.
Management and Marketing.
Music Education.
Nutrition and Hospitality Management.
Office Systems Management.
Physical Education and Recreation.
Physics. Includes physics education.
Plant and Soil Science. M.S., Ph.D.
Psychology.
Reading/Literacy. Ph.D.
Rehabilitation Counseling.
School Psychometry.
Secondary Education. Includes agriscience technology, biology, business education, chemistry, English language arts, family and consumer science, general science, general social science, mathematics, physics, technical education, technology education.
Social Work. M.S.W.
Special Education.
Urban and Regional Planning. M.U.R.P.

ALABAMA STATE UNIVERSITY
Montgomery, Alabama 36101-0271
Web site: www.alasu.edu

Founded 1867. State control. Semester system. Library 267,000 volumes, 1299 subscriptions. 350 computer stations on campus. Total University enrollment: 5000.

Annual tuition: residents $3456, nonresidents $6912–$8516. On-campus housing available on a first-come, first-served basis for single graduate students, none for married students. Average annual housing cost: $4050 (including board) for single students. Apply to Director of Housing by July 15.

School of Graduate Studies

Enrollment: full- and part-time 911. Graduate faculty: full- and part-time 56. Degrees conferred: M.A., M.Ed., M.M.E., M.S., Ed.S.

ADMISSION REQUIREMENTS. Transcripts, GRE, MAT required in support of application. TOEFL, financial statement and all foreign transcripts (must be translated/interpreted course-by-course by WES or AACRAO) required for foreign applicants. Admits Spring, Fall, Summer. Apply at least two months prior to registration. International students must apply six months in advance. Applications fee $10. Phone: (334)229-4275, fax: (334)229-4928.

ADMISSION STANDARDS. Selective. Usual minimum average: 2.5, 3.25 (Ed.S.) (A = 4).

FINANCIAL AID. Annual awards from institutional funds: research assistantships, Federal W/S, grants, loans. Apply to Office of Financial Aid. Use FAFSA. Aid available for part-time students.

DEGREE REQUIREMENTS. For master's: 30 semester hours minimum; foreign language proficiency for most degrees, a computer language may be substituted in some programs; thesis, or 6 additional hours and research paper. For Ed.S.: 30 semester hours beyond the master's; thesis.

FIELDS OF STUDY.
Accountancy. M.S.
Administration and Supervision. M.Ed., Ed.S.
Biology. M.Ed., M.S., Ed.S.
Biology Education. M.Ed., Ed.S.
Collaborative Teacher (Special Education). M.Ed.
Early Childhood Education. M.Ed., Ed.S.
Elementary Education. M.Ed., Ed.S.
English Language Arts. M.Ed.
General Counseling. M.A.
Health Education. M.Ed.
History. M.A., M.Ed., Ed.S.
History Education. M.Ed., Ed.S.
Library Education Media. M.Ed., Ed.S.
Mathematics. M.S., M.Ed., Ed.S.
Music—Instrumental. M.M.E.
Music—Vocal/Choral. M.M.E.
Physical Education. M.Ed.
Physical Therapy. M.S.
School Counseling. M.Ed., Ed.S.
Secondary Education. M.Ed.
Social Sciences. M.Ed., Ed.S.

UNIVERSITY OF ALABAMA
Tuscaloosa, Alabama 35487
Web site: www.ua.edu

Founded 1831. Main campus located 50 miles SW of Birmingham. Coed. State control. Semester system. CGS member. 2000 computers for campus use. Special facilities: Alabama Business Research Council, Alabama Law Institute, Alabama Museum of Natural History, Alabama Oil and Gas Board, Belser-Parton Reading Laboratory, Brewer-Porch Children's Center, Bureau of Education Services and Research, Bureau of Engineering, Research Bureau of Legal Research, Capstone International Program Center, Cartographic Laboratory Center for Administrative and Policy Studies, Center for Alcohol and Drug Education, Center for Business and Economic Research, Center for Communication Research and Service, Center for Developmental and Learning Disorders, Center for Economic Education, Center for Government and Public Service, Center for Law and Public Policy, Center for Southern Regional Folk Life Studies, Center for the Study of Aging, Center for the Study of Southern History and Culture, Child Development Laboratories, Computer Center, Early Childhood Day Care Center, Electron Microscope Laboratory, Evaluation and Assessment Laboratory, Geological Survey of Alabama, Herbarium, Human Development Laboratory, Human Resources Institute, Institute of Higher Education Research and Services, Inter-University Consortium for Political

Research, J. Nicholene Bishop Biological Station, Legal Aid Clinic, Marine Environmental Services Consortium Incorporated, Mineral Resources Institute—State Mine Experimental Station, Minority Culture Archives, Mound State Monument, Museum of Natural History, Natural Resources Center, Office for Archeological Research, Office of Education Media, Psychological Clinic, Remote Sensing Laboratory, Research Laboratory of Human Nutrition, Ridgecrest Center, Rochester Products Applied Research Facility, Rose Tower Learning Center, School of Mines and Energy Development, Speech and Hearing Center, Teaching and Learning Center, Transportation Research Group, Tuscaloosa Metallurgical Laboratory, U.S. Bureau of Mines, University of Alabama Arboretum, University of Alabama Art Gallery, University of Alabama Icthyological Collection, University of Alabama Press, University of Alabama Theatre, University of Alabama Television Service, William B. Bennett International Trade Center. Library: 3,400,000 volumes, 31,199 subscriptions, plus access to online retrievals services. Total University enrollment: approximately 21,835.

Annual tuition: full-time, resident $4864, nonresident $13,516. On-campus housing for 300 married students, 500 men, 500 women. Average housing cost: $550 monthly for married students, $3000 per semester for single students. Apply to Director of Housing by March 1. Phone: (205)348-6676. Day-care facilities available.

Graduate School

Organized 1924. Enrollment: full-time 2543, part-time 1302. Graduate faculty: full-time 676, part-time 274. Degrees conferred: M.A., M.S., M.B.A., M.C.R., M.F.A., M.L.S., M.P.A., M.S.W., Ed.S., D.M.A., D.P.A., Ed.D., D.S.W., Ph.D.

ADMISSION REQUIREMENTS. Two transcripts, references, GRE required in support of application. GRE Subject Test required by many departments. GMAT required for Manderson Graduate School of Business. GRE or MAT or NTE for College of Education. GRE or MAT for School of Human Environmental Sciences. GRE for College of Engineering. Interview sometimes required. Accepts transfer applicants. TOEFL, financial statement, and all foreign transcripts (must be translated/interpreted course-by-course by WES or AACRAO) required for international applicants. Apply to Dean of the Graduate School six weeks prior to registration. Application fee $25. Phone: (205)348-5921.

ADMISSION STANDARDS. Very selective for some departments, selective for the others. Usual minimum average: 3.0 (A = 4). Usual minimum test score, 50th percentile.

FINANCIAL AID. Annual awards from institutional funds; graduate council fellowships, departmental teaching and research assistantships, Federal W/S, loans, tuition waivers. All full-time fellowships and departmental assistantships accompanied by full-tuition scholarships. Apply to Dean of the Graduate School by March 1. Phone: (205)348-6756. Use FAFSA. About 30% of the students receive aid other than loans from University and outside sources.

DEGREE REQUIREMENTS. For master's: Plan I—24 semester hours minimum; reading knowledge of one foreign language for some departments; thesis; final written/oral exam. Plan II—30 semester hours minimum; reading knowledge of one foreign language for some departments; no thesis; final written/oral exam. For Ed.S.: 30 semester hours minimum beyond master's. For Ph.D.: 48 semester hours minimum beyond the bachelor's, at least 18 in full-time residence; preliminary exam; dissertation; reading knowledge of two foreign languages or one language and appropriate research technique/tool or other approved substitution; final written/oral exam. For other doctoral programs: 90 semester hours minimum beyond the bachelor's, at least 45 in residence; preliminary exam; final oral exam; no language requirement; dissertation.

FIELDS OF STUDY.

COLLEGE OF ARTS AND SCIENCES:
American Studies. M.A.
Anthropology. M.A.
Applied Math. Ph.D.
Art History. M.A.
Audiology. M.S.
Biology. Includes ecology and systematics, molecular and cellular biology. M.S., Ph.D.
Chemistry. M.S., Ph.D.
Communicative Disorders. M.S.
Creative Writing. M.F.A.
Criminal Justice. M.C.J.
English. M.A., Ph.D.
French. M.A.
Geography. M.S.
Geological Sciences. M.S., Ph.D.
German. M.A.
History. M.A., Ph.D.
Mathematics. M.A., Ph.D.
Music. M.M., D.M.A.
Physics and Astronomy. M.S., Ph.D.
Political Science. M.S., Ph.D.
Psychology. M.A., Ph.D., Psychological Spec.
Public Administration. M.P.A.
Romance Languages. M.A., Ph.D.
Spanish. M.A.
Theatre. M.F.A.
Women's Studies. M.A.

COLLEGE OF COMMERCE AND BUSINESS ADMINISTRATION:
Accounting. M.A., Ph.D.
Applied Statistics. M.A., Ph.D.
Business Administration. M.B.A.
Economics. M.A., Ph.D.
Finance. M.A., Ph.D.
Human Resource Management. M.S., M.S.C., Ph.D.
Management. M.A., Ph.D.
Marketing. M.A., M.S.C., Ph.D.
Operations Management. M.S., Ph.D.
Tax Accounting. M.T.A.

COLLEGE OF COMMUNICATION AND INFORMATION SCIENCES:
Advertising and Public Relations. M.A.
Communication Studies. M.A.
Journalism. M.A.
Library and Information Studies. M.A., M.F.A., M.L.I.S.
Telecommunications. M.A.

COLLEGE OF EDUCATION:
Art Education. M.A.
Business Education. M.A.
Counselor Education. M.A. in community, elementary, rehabilitation, secondary, student personnel counseling. Ed.D., Ph.D., Ed.S.
Early Childhood Education. M.A.
Educational Administration. Ed.D., Ph.D.
Educational Leadership. M.A., Ed.S.
Educational Psychology. M.A., Ed.D., Ph.D., Ed.S.
Educational Research. Ph.D., Ed.S.
Elementary Education. M.A., Ed.D., Ph.D., Ed.S.
Higher Education Administration. M.A., Ed.D., Ph.D.
Human Performance. M.A., Ph.D.
Instructional Leadership. Ed.D., Ph.D.
Middle School Education. Includes biology, chemistry, earth and space science, economics, English, French, general science, geography, history, language arts, mathematics, physics, political science, sociology, Spanish, speech communication/theater. M.A., Ed.S.
Music Education. M.A., Ed.D., Ph.D., Ed.S.
School Psychology. M.A., Ed.D., Ph.D., Ed.S.

Secondary Education. M.A., Ed.D., Ph.D., Ed.S. offered in all areas except as indicated: anthropology, M.A. only; art, Ed D., Ph.D., Ed.S.; biology, business education, Ed.D., Ph.D., Ed.S.; chemistry, earth science, M.A., Ed.S.; economics, English, French, geography, German, M.A. only; history, home economics, Ed.D., Ph.D., Ed.S.; language arts, M.A., Ed.S.; Latin American studies, mathematics, music, Ed.D., Ph.D., Ed.S.; physics, political science, psychology, M.A., Ed.S.; social science, sociology, Spanish, rhetoric and speech communication.
Special Education. Ed.D., Ed.S.; M.A. in emotional conflict, gifted and talented, learning disabilities, mental retardation, multiple disabilities, special education administration.
Sport Management. M.A., Ed.S.
Teaching of Reading. M.A., Ed.S.
Trade and Industrial Education. M.A.

COLLEGE OF ENGINEERING:
Aerospace Engineering and Mechanics. M.A.E.
Chemical and Biological Engineering. M.C.E., Ph.D.
Civil, Construction & Environmental Engineering. M.C.V., Ph.D.
Computer Science. M.C.S., Ph.D.
Electrical & Computer Engineering. M.E.E., Ph.D.
Engineering Science & Mechanics. M.E.S., Ph.D.
Environmental Engineering. M.E.V.
Materials Science. Ph.D.
Mechanical Engineering. M.M.E., Ph.D.
Metallurgical/Materials Engineering. Ph.D.
Metallurgical Engineering. M.M.L.

COLLEGE OF HUMAN ENVIRONMENTAL SCIENCES:
Clothing, Textiles, Interior Design. M.H.S.
Consumer Science. M.H.S.
Health Education/Promotion. Ph.D.
Health Studies. M.A.
Human Development and Family Studies. M.H.S.
Human Environmental Sciences. M.H.S.
Human Nutrition. M.H.S.

CAPSTONE COLLEGE OF NURSING:
Nurse Case Management. M.S.

SCHOOL OF SOCIAL WORK:
Social Work. M.S.W., Ph.D.

INTERDISCIPLINARY PROGRAMS:
Interdisciplinary Studies. Ph.D.
Materials Science. Ph.D.

School of Law (35487-0382)
Web site: www.law.ua.edu

Established 1872. Located at Tuscaloosa. ABA approved since 1926. AALS member. Semester system. Full-time, day study only. Special facility: Public Interest Institute. Law library: 381,559 volumes; 3368 subscriptions; has LEXIS, NEXIS, WESTLAW, DIALOG, OCLC, Dialog; is a Federal Government Depository. Special programs: summer study abroad at University of Fribourg, Switzerland, and Australia National University in Camberra, Australia.

Annual tuition: resident $9736, nonresident $19,902. On-campus housing available for both single and married students. Annual on-campus housing cost: $12,500. Law students tend to live off-campus. Off-campus housing cost: approximately $13,000.

Enrollment: first-year class 177; total full-time 484 (men 63%, women 37%); no part-time students.

Faculty: full- and part-time 84; 29% female; 14% minority; student to faculty ratio 11.3 to 1.

Degrees conferred: J.D., J.D.-M.B.A., LL.M. (Tax), LL.M. (International Lawyers for persons who have completed a basic legal education and received a university degree in law in another country).

ADMISSION REQUIREMENTS FOR FIRST-YEAR APPLI-CANTS. LSDAS report, LSAT (not later than December test date; if more than one LSAT, highest is used), bachelor's degree from an accredited institution, transcripts (must show all schools attended and at least three years of study), two essays required in support of application. Applicants must have received bachelor's degree prior to entrance. Interview not required but may be requested by School. In addition, international applicants must submit TOEFL (not older than two years). Apply to Admission Coordinator after September 1, before March 1. First-year students admitted Fall only. Rolling admissions process, notification starts in November and is finished by late April. Acceptance of offer and first deposit deadline May 1. School does maintain a waiting list. Application fee $35. Phone: (205)348-5440; e-mail: admissions@law.ua.edu. Admission deadline for LL.M. February 1.

ADMISSION REQUIREMENTS FOR TRANSFER APPLI-CANTS. Accepts transfers from other ABA accredited schools. Admission limited to space available. At least one year of enrollment, in good standing, prefer applicants in the top quarter of first-year class, LSAT, LSDAS, personal statement regarding reason for transfer request. Apply to Admission coordinator by June 1. Application fee $25.

ADMISSION STANDARDS. Number of full-time applicants 1071; number of accepted 344; number enrolled 171; LSAT (75% of class have a score at or above 159); GPA (75% of class have a GPA at or above 3.29). *U.S. News & World Report* ranking is in the top tier, tied for 36th.

FINANCIAL AID. Scholarships, merit scholarships; loans and Federal W/S offered through University's Financial Aid Office. For scholarships (selection criteria places heavy reliance on LSAT and undergraduate GPA) apply to Assistant Dean of School after January 1, before May 1; phone: (205)348-4508; use School's FAF. For all other programs apply to Director of Student Financial Services, University of Alabama, P.O. Box 870162, phone: (205)348-6756. Use FAFSA (School code: 001051). Approximately 41% receive grant. Average scholarship grant $2000.

DEGREE REQUIREMENTS. For J.D.: 90 credits (36 credits required) with a GPA of at least 2.0 (A = 4), plus completion of upper divisional writing course; three-year program. Accelerated J.D. with one summer of course work. For J.D.-M.B.A.: total 118 credits (J.D. approximately 80 credits, M.B.A. approximately 38). For LL.M. (Tax): 24 credits. For LL.M. (International Lawyers): 24 credits; at least two semesters in residence; a GPA of 2.5 (A = 4) required.

UNIVERSITY OF ALABAMA AT BIRMINGHAM

Birmingham, Alabama 35294-1203
Web site: www.uab.edu

Founded 1966. Coed. Semester system. CGS member. 500 computers on campus for general use. Special facilities: Center for Urban Affairs, Small Business Development Center. The University's ranking by NIH is 23rd with 518 awards/grants worth $228,687,941. According to The Center at University of Florida, University of Alabama at Birmingham is ranked 24th in receipt of Federal Research funds with $245,217,000 and it ranks 44th for total University expenditures with $284,497,000. Seven of the University's faculty members have been elected to National Honor Academies and this ranks it 78th among all U.S. institutions. The library: 1,450,000 volumes, 2520 subscriptions. Total University enrollment: 16,572.

Tuition: per credit hour, residents $170, nonresidents $425. Limited on-campus housing for married and single students. Average housing cost: single students $6471 (including board); married students $2536. Contact UAB Student Housing Office, 1604 Ninth Ave., South Birmingham, AL 35294-1230. Phone: (205)934-2092. Day-care facilities available.

Graduate School (35294-1150)

Enrollment: full-time 3110, part-time 886. Faculty: full- and part-time 1200. Degrees conferred: M.S.N.A., M.P.A., M.S.O.T., M.S.H.A., M.S.F.S., M.A., M.Ac., Ph.D., M.S., M.B.A., M.S.C.L.S., M.S.C.J., M.A.Ed., Ed.S., Ed.D., M.S.B.E., M.S.C.E., M.S.E.E., M.S.Mte., M.S.M.E., M.S.H.I., D.S.N., M.S.N.

ADMISSION REQUIREMENTS. Two transcripts, three evaluations, GRE (some UAB graduate programs require, or are willing to accept, other recognized national tests) required in support of application. TOEFL and TWE required of foreign students. Interview required for some departments. Accepts transfer applicants. Apply to Dean of the Graduate School at least six weeks prior to registration; some graduate programs admit only at certain times of the year and have specific deadlines. Application fee $35, international applicants $60. Phone: (205)934-8227, or (800)975-GRAD.

ADMISSION STANDARDS. Competitive for most departments.

FINANCIAL AID. Partial tuition waivers, assistantships, fellowships, Federal W/S, loans. Financial Aid Office administers loan, grant, and work-study programs, students in certain programs may participate in UAB's Coop Ed program. Contact Office of Student Financial Aid. Phone: (205)934-8223; fax: (205)934-8941. Apply to the specific graduate program director for assistantships and fellowships.

DEGREE REQUIREMENTS. For master's: Plan I—24 hours minimum, at least 18 in major and 6 in related minor; thesis; reading knowledge of one foreign language for some departments; candidacy; final written/oral exam. Plan II—30 hours minimum, at least 18 in major; no thesis; reading knowledge of one foreign language for some departments; candidacy; final written/oral exam for some programs. For Ed.S.: 30 hours beyond the master's; final oral/written exam. For doctoral programs: preliminary exam; candidacy; dissertation; reading knowledge of one language, a research tool, or computer technique; research project for some programs; final oral exam.

FIELDS OF STUDY.

ARTS AND HUMANITIES:
Art History. M.A.
Communication Management. M.A.
English. M.A.

BIOLOGICAL/BIOMEDICAL SCIENCE:
Biochemistry and Molecular Genetics. Ph.D.
Cell Biology. Ph.D.
Cellular and Molecular Biology. Ph.D.
Cellular and Molecular Physiology. Ph.D.
Genetics. Ph.D.
Integrative Biomedical Sciences. Ph.D.
Microbiology. Ph.D.
Neurobiology. Ph.D.
Neuroscience Training Program. Ph.D.
Pathology. Ph.D.
Pharmacology and Toxicology. Ph.D.
Toxicology Training Program. Ph.D.
Vision Science. M.S., Ph.D.

BUSINESS:
Accounting. M.Ac.
Business Administration. M.B.A.

COORDINATED DEGREES:
D.M.D.-Ph.D.
M.S.-M.D. & Ph.D.-M.D.
O.D.-M.S. & O.D.-Ph.D.
M.D.-M.S.B.M.S.
M.B.A.-M.P.H.
M.S.H.A.-M.B.A.
M.P.A.-M.P.H.
M.P.A.-J.D.
Ph.D.-M.B.A.

DENTISTRY:
Dentistry. M.S.

EDUCATION:
Curriculum and Instruction. Includes early childhood, elementary, high school, art education, music education, English as a second language. M.A.E.
Educational Leadership. M.A.Ed., Ed.D., Ph.D., Ed.S.
Human Studies. Includes counseling (E.D.S.), health (M.A.E.), health education and health promotion (Ph.D.), physical (M.A.E.), school psychology.
Special Education. M.A.Ed., Ed.S.

ENGINEERING:
Biomedical Engineering. M.S.B.M.E., Ph.D.
Civil Engineering. M.S.C.E., Ph.D.
Computer Engineering. Ph.D.
Electrical Engineering. M.S.E.E., Ph.D.
Environmental Health Engineering. Ph.D.
Materials Science. Ph.D.
Mechanical Engineering. M.S.M.E., Ph.D.

HEALTH PROFESSIONS:
Clinical Laboratory Sciences. M.S.
Health Administration. M.S.H.A.
Health Services Administration. Ph.D.
Health Informatics. M.S.H.I.
Nurse Anesthesia. M.N.A.
Nutrition Sciences. M.S., Ph.D.
Occupational Therapy. M.S.
Physical Therapy. D.Sc.PT., D.P.T.
Physician Assistant Studies. M.S.P.A.S.

MEDICINE:
Medical Scientist Training Program. M.D., Ph.D.

NATURAL SCIENCES AND MATHEMATICS:
Applied Mathematics. Ph.D.
Biology. M.S., Ph.D.
Chemistry. M.S., Ph.D.
Computer and Information Sciences. M.S., Ph.D.
Mathematics. M.S.
Physics. M.S., Ph.D.

NURSING:
Nursing. M.S.N., Ph.D.

PUBLIC HEALTH:
Biostatistics. M.P.H., M.S., Ph.D.
Environmental Health Sciences. Ph.D.
Epidemiology. Ph.D.
Health Education/Health Promotion. Ph.D.
Public Health. M.P.H., M.S.P.H., Dr.P.H.

SOCIAL AND BEHAVIORAL SCIENCES:
Anthropology. M.A.

Criminal Justice. M.S.C.J.
Forensic Science. M.S.F.S.
History. M.A.
Medical Sociology. Ph.D.
Psychology. Ph.D.
Public Administration. M.P.A.
Sociology. M.A.

School of Dentistry (SDB Box 125)
Web site: www.dental.uab.edu

Established 1945. Located in Birmingham (35294-0007) at the Medical Center. Quarter system. Special facility: Research Center for Oral Biology. Library: (combined with School of Medicine) 250,000 volumes, 2800 subscriptions.

Tuition: resident $12,678, nonresident $34,632. Housing: very limited. Total average cost for all other first-year expenses: $12,000.

Enrollment: first-year class 56, total full-time 225 (men 57%, women 43%, minorities 20%, state resident 87%). Faculty: full-time 76, part-time 78. Degrees conferred: D.M.D., M.S. (Oral Biology), D.M.D.-M.P.H., D.M.D.-Ph.D.

ADMISSION REQUIREMENTS. For D.M.D.: AADSAS transcripts showing completion of at least three years of undergraduate study, DAT, four recommendations required in support of School's application. A supplemental application is sent to all applicants under serious consideration. Interview by invitation only. Accepts transfer applicants for second and third years only. Preference given to Alabama and SREB residents. Graduates of unaccredited colleges not considered. For M.S., M.P.H., Ph.D.: students may apply after completion of second year of program. Apply to AADSAS after June 1 and before December 1. Acceptance fee $50. Phone: (205)934-3387; fax: (205)934-0209.

ADMISSION STANDARDS. Competitive. Admits 40% of total annual applicants. Mean DAT: 19; mean GPA: 3.60 (A = 4). Approximately 90% are state residents.

FINANCIAL AID. Scholarships, minority scholarships, grants, HEAL, DEAL, HPSL, loans. Apply to School's Office of Financial Aid; no specified closing date. For need based programs use FAFSA (School code: 001052). About 79% of students receive aid other than loans from School.

DEGREE REQUIREMENTS. For D.M.D.: satisfactory completion of four-year program. For M.S., M.P.H., Ph.D.: see Graduate School listing above.

FIELDS OF GRADUATE STUDY.
Biomaterials.
Endodontics.
Maxillofacial Prosthetics.
Oral Biology.
Oral & Maxillofacial Surgery.
Orthodontics.
Pediatric Dentistry.
Periodontology.
Prosthodontics.
Public Health.

School of Medicine
(Box 100-UAB Station)
Web site: www.uab.edu/uasom

Founded 1859 in Mobile; located in Birmingham (35294) since 1945. Branch campuses created in 1969 at Huntsville and Tuscaloosa. Medical Library: 240,000 volumes. The University's NIH ranking is 23rd among all U.S. institutions with 518 awards/grants worth $228,338,684.

Annual tuition: resident $16,539, nonresident $40,861; student fees $2924. Very limited on-campus housing available. Room & board expenses: approximately $10,879. Contact Admission office for both on- and off-campus housing availability.

Enrollment: first year class 160 (8 were M.D.-Ph.D., approximately 10 EDP); total full-time 700 (men 59%, women 41%, minorities 23%, in-state residents 92%). Faculty: full-time 500, part-time 200. Degrees conferred: M.D., M.D.-Ph.D., M.S.T.P. funded program. The Ph.D. conferred through the Graduate School.

ADMISSION REQUIREMENTS. AMCAS report, transcripts, MCAT, recommendations, interview required in support of application. Has EDP for Alabama residents only. Graduates of unaccredited institutions not considered. For EDP, apply to Director of Admissions after June 1, before November 1. Secondary applications sent to all residents and selected nonresidents. Dual degree candidates must be accepted by both schools. Application fee $70. Phone: (205)934-2330; fax: (205)934-8724; e-mail: medschool@uab.edu.

ADMISSION STANDARDS. Competitive. Accepts about 12% of all applicants. Number of applications 1734 (1298 out-of-state); number interviewed 346 (75 out-of-state); number of acceptance 213 (33 out-of-state); number enrolled 160 (16 out-of-state). Mean Composite MCAT 10.1; mean UGPA 3.73. *U.S. News & World Report* ranking is in the top 27 of all medical schools and top 34 of all primary care medical schools.

FINANCIAL AID. Scholarships, summer stipends, summer fellowships, loans, grants, HEAL, NIH stipends. Assistantship may be available for dual degree candidates. Apply to Director of Financial Aid after acceptance; no specified closing date. Phone: (205)934-8223. 79% of students receive financial aid. Has loan forgiveness program for Doctors who will practice in rural areas in Alabama.

DEGREE REQUIREMENTS. For M.D.: satisfactory completion of four-year program; must pass Step 1 and Step 2 of USMLE.

FIELDS OF GRADUATE STUDY.
Biochemistry and Molecular Genetics.
Cellular and Molecular Biology.
Genetics.
Integrative Biomedical Sciences.
Neuroscience.
Toxicology.

UNIVERSITY OF ALABAMA IN HUNTSVILLE

Huntsville, Alabama 35899
Web site: www.uah.edu

Established 1950. Coed. Public control. Semester system. CGS member. There are 1091 computers available on campus for student use. Special facilities: Alabama Solar Research Center, Center for Applied Optics, Johnson Research Center, Center for Microgravity and Materials Research, Center for Robotics, Center for Space Plasma and Aeronomic Research. Library: 627,000 volumes, 2677 subscriptions. Total University enrollment: 7084.

Annual tuition: resident $5866, nonresident $12,060. On-campus housing available for 160 married students, for 700 single graduate students. Average academic year housing costs: $4375 (including board) for single students, $7000 for married students. Contact Director of University Housing for both on- and off-campus housing information. Phone: (205)895-6108. Day-care facilities available.

School of Graduate Studies

Enrollment: full-time 482, part-time 766. Faculty: full-time 189, part-time 50. Degrees conferred: M.A., M.Acc., M.S., M.S.E., M.S.M.I.S., M.S.M., M.S.N., M.S.O.R., Ph.D.

ADMISSION REQUIREMENTS. Two official transcripts, bachelor's degree, GRE (subject for some departments)/GMAT/MAT, three recommendations required in support of School's application. TOEFL required for international applicants. Accepts transfer applicants. Graduates of unaccredited institutions not considered. Apply to Graduate Office by July 1 (Fall), December 1 (Spring); international students must apply three months prior to registration. Rolling admissions process. Application fee $40. Dean's office: (256)824-6199; fax: (256)824-6405; e-mail: deangrad@uah.edu. Admissions office: (256)824-6198.

ADMISSION STANDARDS. Selective. Usual minimum average: 3.0 (A = 4).

FINANCIAL AID. Annual awards from institutional funds: scholarships, tuition waivers, fellowships, research assistantships, teaching assistantships, Federal W/S, loans. Approved for VA benefits. Apply to the Office of Financial Aid by February 15. Phone: (256)824-6241. Use FAFSA. About 36% of students receive aid other than loans from both University and outside sources.

DEGREE REQUIREMENTS. For master's: 24 semester hours minimum plus thesis; or 36 semester hours without thesis; final comprehensive exam. For Ph.D.: three years of study beyond the bachelor's, at least one year in full-time residence; qualifying exam; dissertation; final exam; additional requirements determined by appropriate department adviser.

FIELDS OF STUDY.

COLLEGE OF ADMINISTRATIVE SCIENCE:
Accounting. M.Acc.
Management. M.S.M.
Management of Information Systems. M.S.M.I.S.

COLLEGE OF ENGINEERING:
Aerospace Engineering. M.S.E.
Chemical and Material Engineering. M.S.E.
Civil and Environmental Engineering. M.S.E.
Computer Engineering. M.S.E., Ph.D.
Electrical Engineering. M.S.E., Ph.D.
Industrial and Systems Engineering. M.S.E., Ph.D.
Mechanical Engineering. M.S.E., Ph.D.
Operations Research. M.S.O.R.
Software Engineering. M.S.E., M.S.S.E.

COLLEGE OF LIBERAL ARTS:
English. M.A.
History. M.A.
Psychology. M.A.
Public Affairs. M.A.

COLLEGE OF NURSING:
Nursing. M.S.N.

COLLEGE OF SCIENCE:
Applied Mathematics. Ph.D.
Atmospheric Science. M.S., Ph.D.
Biological Sciences. M.S.
Chemistry. M.S.
Computer Science. M.S., Ph.D.
Mathematics. M.A., M.S.
Physics. M.A., Ph.D.

INTERDISCIPLINARY PROGRAMS:
Biotechnology Science and Engineering. Ph.D.
Materials Science. M.S., Ph.D.
Optical Science and Engineering. Ph.D.

FIFTH-YEAR PROGRAMS–EDUCATION:
Biology.
Chemistry.
English.
History.
Mathematics.
Physics.

UNIVERSITY OF ALASKA FAIRBANKS
Fairbanks, Alaska 99775-7480
Web site: www.uaf.edu

Founded 1917. Located 4 miles NW of Fairbanks. Coed. State control. Semester system. CGS member. More than 500 computers on campus. Special research units: Alaska Cooperative Wildlife Research Unit, Alaska Coop Fisheries Research Unit; Center for Cross-Cultural Studies, Institute of Arctic Biology, Geophysics Institute, Marine Science, Water Resources, and Institute of Northern Engineering; Mineral Industry Research Laboratory, Petroleum Development Laboratory. State and federal agencies on campus include the Branch of Alaskan Geology of the U.S. Geological Survey, Alaska Division of Geological and Geophysical Survey, Institute of Northern Forestry (U.S. Forest Service), and College Observatory (U.S. Dept. of Commerce). Library: 616,456 volumes, 8377 subscriptions, plus access to on-line data retrieval services. Total University enrollment: 8230.

Semester tuition/fees: full-time, resident $5811, nonresident $11,204. On-campus housing for 180 married students, housing available as needed for single graduate students. Average academic-year housing cost: $7750 for married students, $5780 for single students. Apply to Director of Housing by March 15. Phone: (907)474-7247. Day-care facilities available.

Graduate School

Graduate study since 1950. Enrollment: full-time 672, part-time 410. Faculty teaching graduate students: full-time 300, part-time 111. Degrees conferred: M.A., M.A.T., M.B.A., M.F.A., M.Ed., M.M.E., M.C.E., M.E.E., M.S., Ph.D.

ADMISSION REQUIREMENTS. Transcripts, résumé/vitae, Statement of Academic Goals, three letters of recommendation required in support of application. GRE/GMAT required. TOEFL required for all foreign students; TSE and TWE may be requested. Interview not required. Accepts transfer applicants. Apply to Director of Admissions and Records; apply by June 1 (Fall), October 1 (Spring). Application fee $50. Phone: (907)474-7500; fax: (907)474-5379; e-mail: fygrads@uaf.edu.

ADMISSION STANDARDS. Selective for most departments. Usual minimum average: 3.0 (A = 4).

FINANCIAL AID. Annual awards from institutional funds: scholarships, fellowships, assistantships, grants, Federal W/S, loans. Apply to Dean of the appropriate College for assistantships; closing date early Spring; for all other aid apply by February 15 for Fall semester. Phone: (907)474-7256. Use FAFSA (University code: 001063) and institutional FAF. About 50% of students receive aid other than loans from University and outside sources. Aid sometimes available for part-time students.

DEGREE REQUIREMENTS. For master's: 30–33 semester credits minimum, at least 21 in residence; candidacy; thesis or project for most departments; final written/oral exam. For Ph.D.: number of credits determined by the advisory committee, but usually at least two years beyond the master's; minimum 18 credit thesis; written comprehensive exam; reading knowledge of one foreign language or other research-tool competence for most programs; dissertation; final oral exam.

FIELDS OF STUDY.
Administration of Justice. M.A.
Anthropology. M.A., Ph.D.
Arctic Engineering. M.S.
Art. M.F.A.
Atmospheric Sciences. M.S., Ph.D.
Biochemistry/Molecular Biology. M.S., Ph.D.
Biological Sciences. Ph.D.
Biology. M.S.
Botany. M.S.
Business Administration. M.B.A.
Chemistry. M.A., M.S.
Civil Engineering. M.C.E., M.S.
Community Psychology. M.A.
Computational Physics. M.S.
Computer Science. M.S.
Counseling. M.Ed.
Creative Writing. M.F.A.
Cross-Cultural Studies. M.A.
Economics, Resources and Applied Economics. M.S.
Education. Includes cross-cultural, curriculum and instruction, educational leadership, language and literacy. M.Ed.
Electrical Engineering. M.E.E., M.S.
Engineer of Mines. E.M.
Engineering. Includes arctic, civil, electrical, engineering management, environmental, mechanical. Ph.D.
Engineering Management. M.S.
English. M.A.
Environmental Chemistry. M.S., Ph.D.
Environmental Engineering and Environmental Quality Science. M.S.
Fisheries. M.S., Ph.D.
General Science. M.S.
Geological Engineering. M.S.
Geology. Includes economic, general, petroleum, quaternary, remote sensing, volcanology. M.S., Ph.D.
Geophysics. Includes remote sensing, snow, ice and permafrost, solid-earth. M.S., Ph.D.
Interdisciplinary Studies. M.A., M.S., Ph.D.
Marine Biology. M.S., Ph.D.
Mathematics. M.S., Ph.D.
Mechanical Engineering. M.S.
Mineral Preparation Engineering. M.S.
Mining Engineering. M.S.
Music. Includes conducting, music education, music history, performance, theory/composition. M.A.
Natural Resource Management. M.S.
Northern Studies. M.A.
Oceanography. Includes biological, chemical, fisheries, geological, physical. M.S., Ph.D.
Petroleum Engineering. M.S.
Physics. M.S., M.A.T., Ph.D.
Professional Communication. Includes communication, journalism. M.A.
Psychology. Includes clinical, community. Ph.D.
Resource & Applied Economics. M.S.
Rural Development. M.A.
Science Management. M.S.
Software Engineering. M.S.E.
Space Physics. M.S., Ph.D.
Statistics. M.S.
Wildlife Biology. M.S.

ALBANY LAW SCHOOL OF UNION UNIVERSITY

Albany, NY 12208-3494
Web site: www.albanylaw.edu

Founded 1851. Semester system. There are more than 800 network connections available on campus for student use. Special facilities: Government Law Center, Law Clinic and Justice Center, Science and Technology Center. Library: 660,000 volumes, 3061 subscriptions; has LEXUS, NEXIS, WESTLAW, DIALOG, VU TEST, WILSONLINE.

Annual tuition: full-time $37,400, part-time $28,050. No on-campus housing available. Off-campus cost approximately $6000.

Enrollment: first-year class full-time 247, part-time 37; full-time 702 (men 50%, women 50%, 19% minority). Faculty: full-time 42, part-time 35. Degrees conferred: J.D., J.D.-M.B.A. (Union College, R.P.I., St. Rose College), J.D.-M.P.A. (University at Albany), J.D.-M.R.P. (University at Albany).

ADMISSION REQUIREMENTS. LSDAS report, Bachelor's degree, transcripts, LSAT (prior to March 15), two letters of recommendation required in support of application. In some cases the GRE or GMAT may be required for Joint Degree Programs. Interview not required. Accepts transfer applicants on a space-available basis. Graduates of unaccredited colleges not considered. Apply to School by March 15. Fall admission only. Application fee $60. Phone: (518)445-2326; fax: (518)445-2369; e-mail: admissions@mail.als.edu.

ADMISSION REQUIREMENTS FOR TRANSFER APPLICANTS. Accepts transfer applications from other ABA accredited schools on a space available basis. The applicant must have completed at least two semesters and be eligible to return. In addition, the applicant must submit an Albany Law School application and $60 application fee, an official transcript from their current Law School and their rank in class, a letter indicating they are in good academic standing, an LSDAS report, and two letters of recommendation. There is no application filing deadline and applications are considered between July 15 and August 10. At least 55 credits of the total of 87 required for the degree must be completed at Albany.

ADMISSION STANDARDS. Selective. Number of full-time applicants 2175, number of accepted 876, number enrolled 247; LSAT (75% of class have a score at or above 153); GPA (75% of class have a GPA at or above 2.89). *U.S. News & World Report* ranking is in the third tier of all U.S. Law Schools.

FINANCIAL AID. Scholarships, partial tuition waiver, assistantships, Federal W/S, loans. Apply to Financial Aid Director by April 15. Phone: (518)445-2357. Use FAFSA and institutional request for Financial Assistance form. Aid available for part-time students. About 85% of students receive aid other than loans from School.

DEGREE REQUIREMENTS. For J.D.: satisfactory completion of either the three-year or four-year program. For J.D.-M.B.A., J.D.-M.P.A., J.D.-M.R.P.: Satisfactory completion of the required four-year program instead of the usual five-year program.

ALBANY MEDICAL COLLEGE

47 New Scotland Avenue
Albany, New York 12208-3479
Web site: www.amc.edu

Founded 1839. College is part of Union University, one of the oldest medical schools in the country. Medical college is attached to Albany Medical Center Hospital. Private control. Special facilities: Cell and Molecular Biology Center, Cardiovascular Sciences Center, Immunology & Microbial Disease Center, Neuropharmocology & Neuroscience Center, Alden March Bioethics Institute, Heart Institute, Neurosciences Institute, Vascular Institute. Library: 111,300 volumes, 1250 subscriptions.

Annual tuition: M.D. program resident $41,224, graduate study, full-time $17,400. Limited on-campus housing available. Total average figure for all other expenses: $7500.

Enrollment: M.D. program, first-year class 135; total 538 (men 46%, women 54%, minorities 8%, state residents 44%); graduate study, full-time 136, part-time 3. Faculty: M.D., full-time 54, part-time 35; Graduate Study, full-time 631, part-time 39. Degrees conferred: B.A.-M.D., B.S.-M.D. (with Union College, Siena College, and RPI), M.D., M.D.-Ph.D., Ph.D.

ADMISSION REQUIREMENTS. For M.D. program: AMCAS report, transcripts, MCAT, letters of recommendation required in support of application. Interview by invitation only. Applicants must complete at least three years of college study. Does not have EDP. Apply to Secretary of Admission after June 1, before November 15 (Fall). Application fee $100. Phone: (518)262-5521; fax: (518)262-5887. For graduate study: transcripts, two letters of recommendation, GRE required in support of application. TOEFL required for international applicants. Accepts transfer applicants. Apply to Office of Admissions at least forty-five days prior to registration. Phone: (518)262-5824. Application fee $100.

ADMISSION STANDARDS. Competitive. Accepts about 12% of all applicants. Number of applications 6834; number interviewed 663; number enrolled 135. Mean Composite MCAT 9.8; mean UGPA 3.50. *U.S. News and World Report* ranked only the top 50 medical schools and, therefore, did not rank Albany Medical College. Approximately 56% are state residents.

FINANCIAL AID. For M.D. program: scholarships. Apply to Financial Aid Committee on Scholarships and Loans by January 15. Phone: (518)262-5435. For graduate study: research fellowships/ assistantships, grants, loans. Apply to Office of Admissions, Graduate School; no specified closing date. Use FAFSA. About 85% of medical students, 35% of graduate students receive some aid from College.

DEGREE REQUIREMENTS. For M.D.: satisfactory completion of four-year program; must take steps 1 and 2 of USMLE. For M.D.-Ph.D.: Completion of 6-year program. For Ph.D.: 90 hours minimum beyond the bachelor's; preliminary exam; dissertation; final oral/written exam.

FIELDS OF GRADUATE STUDY.
Cardiovascular Sciences. M.S., Ph.D.
Cell Biology and Cancer Research. M.S., Ph.D.
Immunology and Microbial Disease. M.S., Ph.D.
Neuropharmacology and Neurosciences. M.S., Ph.D.

UNIVERSITY AT ALBANY, STATE UNIVERSITY OF NEW YORK

Albany, New York 12222-0001
Web site: www.albany.edu

Founded 1844. Coed. State control. Semester system. CGS member. More than 500 computers on campus for general use. Special facilities: Albany Center for Learning Disabilities, Atmospheric Sciences Research Center, Center for Biological Macromolecules, Child Research and Study Center, Hindelang Criminal Justice Center, Center for Molecular Genetics, Center for Neuro-Biological Research, Center for Executive Development, Instructional Resources Center, Local Government Studies Center, New York State Writer's Institute, Performing Arts Center, Center for Social and Demography Analysis, Center for

Stress and Anxiety Disorders, Dudly Observatory, Wadsworth Center for Laboratories and Research. Library: 2,100,000 volumes, 39,240 subscriptions. Total university enrollment: 17,000.

Annual tuition; resident full-time $6900, per credit $288; nonresident full-time $10,920, per credit $455. On-campus housing for 100 graduate men, 100 graduate women; none for married students. Average annual housing cost: $10,500 (including board). Contact Housing Office for both on- and off-campus housing information. Phone: (518)442-5875. Day-care facilities available.

School of Graduate Studies

Graduate study since 1913. Enrollment: full-time 2190, part-time 2220 (men 45%, women 55%). University faculty: full-time 631, part-time 530. Degrees conferred: M.A., M.S., M.B.A., M.L.S., M.P.A., M.P.H., M.F.A., M.R.P., M.S.W., C.A.S., Dr.P.H., D.A., Ed.D., D.P.A., Ph.D., Psy.D.

ADMISSION REQUIREMENTS. Official transcripts, three letters of recommendation, statement of background and goals required in support of School's application. GRE General/Subject Tests required for University Certificate and doctoral applicants, GMAT for business applicants. Interview required by some departments. TOEFL required for international applicants. Accepts transfer applicants. Graduates of unaccredited institutions not considered. Master's applicants apply to appropriate School or College by August 15 (Fall), January 1 (Spring), April 15 (Summer). Doctoral and University Certificate applicants apply to Office of Graduate Studies by April 30 (Fall), November 15 (Spring), March 1 (Summer). International applicants apply to Office of Graduate Admission and Academic Services by February 1 (Fall). Application fee $75. Phone: (518)442-3980; fax: (518)442-3922; e-mail: graduate@uamail.albany.edu.

ADMISSION STANDARDS. Competitive for most departments, selective for the others. Usual minimum average: 3.0 (A = 4).

FINANCIAL AID. Annual awards from institutional funds: external assistantships, internal assistantships, internal fellows, external fellows, Federal W/S, loans. Approved for VA benefits. Apply by February 15 to appropriate department chair for fellowships, assistantships; to Financial Aid Office for all other programs. Phone: (518)442-5757. Use FAFSA. About 35% of students receive aid other than loans from School and outside sources. No aid for part-time students.

DEGREE REQUIREMENTS. For M.A., M.S.: 30 semester hours minimum, at least 24 in residence; reading knowledge of one foreign language required by some departments; thesis/nonthesis option for some departments; comprehensive exam required by some departments. For M.B.A.: 30–60 semester hours, depending on previous preparation. For M.L.S.: 36 semester hours minimum. For M.F.A.: 48 credits minimum, at least 40 in residence. For M.P.H.: 51 semester hours, at least 30 in residence; two internships required. For M.P.A.: 12 graduate courses minimum; comprehensive exam. For M.S.W.: 60 semester hours minimum, at least 30 in residence, one year in full-time attendance; research project. For C.A.S.: 48 semester hours minimum, at least 30 in residence, one semester or equivalent in full-time attendance; comprehensive exam. For Ed.D.: 75 semester hours minimum, at least 38 in residence, one year in full-time attendance; qualifying exam; dissertation. For D.P.A.: 60 credit hours minimum beyond the bachelor's; dissertation. For Ph.D.: 60 semester hours minimum, at least 30 in residence, one year in full-time attendance; competency in one or two research tools; qualifying exam; dissertation. For D.A.: 60 semester hours minimum, at least 30 in residence; research project; supervised college teaching internship; research tool; written/oral comprehensive exam.

FIELDS OF STUDY.

COLLEGE OF ARTS AND SCIENCE:
Africana Studies.
Anthropology.
Art Studio.
Atmospheric Sciences.
Biopsychology.
Cellular and Developmental Biology.
Chemistry.
Classics.
Clinical Psychology.
Cognitive Psychology.
Communication.
Computer Science.
Demography.
Ecology and Animal Science.
Economics.
English.
Evolution and Behavior.
Forensic Molecular Biology.
French Studies.
General/Experimental Psychology.
Geography.
Geological Sciences.
History.
Humanistic Studies.
Industrial/Organizational Psychology.
Italian.
Latin American and Caribbean Studies.
Liberal Studies.
Mathematics.
Molecular Biology.
Neural Biology.
Philosophy.
Physics.
Public History.
Regional Planning.
Russian.
Social Psychology.
Sociology.
Spanish.
Statistics.
Theater.
Urban Policy.
Women's Studies.

COLLEGE OF NANOSCALE SCIENCE & ENGINEERING:
Nanoscale Engineering. M.S., M.S.-M.B.A., Ph.D.
Nanoscale Science. M.S., M.S.-M.B.A., Ph.D.

SCHOOL OF BUSINESS:
Accounting.
Business Administration. Weekend program in Saratoga, NY.
Finance.
Human Resources Information Systems.
Management.
Management Information Systems.
Organizational Studies.
Taxation.

SCHOOL OF CRIMINAL JUSTICE:
Criminal Justice. Includes nature of crime, law and social justice, administration, planned change.

SCHOOL OF EDUCATION:
Counseling Psychology.
Curriculum and Instruction.
Curriculum Planning and Development.
Educational Administration.
Educational Communication.
Educational Psychology.

Educational Psychology and Statistics.
Measurement and Evaluation.
Reading.
Rehabilitation Counseling.
School Psychology.
Special Education.
Statistic and Research Design.

COLLEGE OF COMPUTING AND INFORMATION:
Computer Science.
Information Science.
Information Science and Policy.
Library Science.

NELSON A. ROCKEFELLER COLLEGE OF PUBLIC AFFAIRS AND POLICY:
Administrative Behavior.
Comparative and Development Administration.
Human Resources.
Information Science and Policy.
Legislative Administration.
Nonprofit Leadership and Management.
Planning and Policy Analysis.
Political Science.
Program Analysis and Evaluation.
Public Administration.
Public Affairs and Policy.
Public Finance.
Public Management.

SCHOOL OF PUBLIC HEALTH:
Behavior Science.
Biochemistry, Molecular and Genetics.
Biostatistics.
Cell and Molecular Structure.
Environmental Chemistry.
Environmental Health.
Epidemiology.
Health Administration.
Immunobiology and Immunochemistry.
Molecular Pathogenesis.
Neurosciences.
Public Health.
Toxicology.

SCHOOL OF SOCIAL WELFARE:
Social Welfare.

ALFRED UNIVERSITY
Alfred, New York 14802-1232
Web site: www.alfred.edu

Founded 1836. Located 70 miles S of Rochester. Coed. Private control. CGS members. There are 390 computers on campus for student use. The New York College of Ceramics in located on campus. Special facilities: Powell Institute for Children and Families, Center for Rural School Psychology, NSF Industry/University Center for Biosurfaces, the Whiteware Research Center, NYS Center for Advanced Ceramic Technology, the Center for Family Business, Institute for Electronic Arts, Center for Glass Research. Library: 350,000 volumes, 1500 subscriptions. Total University enrollment: 2335.

Annual tuition: full-time $28,450. For College of Ceramics, annual tuition: $17,530. On-campus housing available on a first-come, first-served basis. Contact Assistant Dean for Student Life for on- and off-campus housing information. Phone: (607)871-2186. Total annual average housing costs: $9900.

Graduate School

Graduate study since 1947. Enrollment: full-time 173, part-time 101. University faculty teaching graduate students: full-time 87, part-time 7. Degrees conferred: M.A., M.S. in Ed., M.P.S., M.S., M.F.A., Ph.D.

ADMISSION REQUIREMENTS. Transcripts, GRE/GMAT, personal statement of objectives, two letters of recommendation required in support of application. Art portfolio required for M.F.A. and M.S.Ed. (Art). TOEFL required of foreign students. Interview required for some Programs. Accepts transfer applicants. Apply to Office of Graduate Admissions, rolling admissions process. Application fee $50. Phone: (607)871-2115, (800)541-9229; fax: (607)871-2198.

ADMISSION STANDARDS. Very selective for some departments, selective for the others. Usual minimum average: 3.0 (A = 4).

FINANCIAL AID. Annual awards from institutional funds: scholarships, full and partial tuition grants, research assistantship, teaching assistantships, Federal W/S, loans. Apply to the Graduate Admissions Office. Phone: (607)871-2159. Use FAFSA. About 80% of students receive aid from University and outside sources.

DEGREE REQUIREMENTS. For M.A. (Psychology): 52 hours minimum; oral/written qualifying exam, thesis. For M.B.A.: 55 hours minimum. For M.S. in Ed., M.P.S.: 30–36 hours minimum; thesis or master's project or final oral/written comprehensive exam.

College of Ceramics. For M.S.: 30 hours minimum; thesis; comprehensive exam. For M.F.A.: 60 hours minimum, at least two years in residence; thesis. For Ph.D.: 90 hours minimum beyond the bachelor's, at least two years in residence (105 hours for Psy.D.); qualifying exam; doctoral thesis; final oral exam.

FIELDS OF STUDY.
Art. M.F.A., M.S. in Ed.
Biomedical Materials Engineering Science. M.S.
Business Administration. M.B.A.
Ceramic Art. M.F.A.
Ceramic Engineering. M.S.
Ceramics. Ph.D.
Community Services Administration. M.P.S.
Counseling. M.S. in Ed.
Electrical Engineering. M.S.
Electronic Integrated Arts. M.F.A.
Elementary Education. M.S. in Ed.
Glass Art. M.F.A.
Glass Science. M.S., Ph.D.
Industrial Engineering. M.S.
Literacy Teacher. M.S. in Ed.
Materials Science and Engineering. M.S.
Mechanical Engineering. M.E.
School Psychology. M.A., Psy.D.
Sculpture. M.F.A.
Secondary Education. Includes art, biology, business, chemistry, earth science, English, mathematics, physics, social studies. M.S. in Ed.

ALLIANT INTERNATIONAL UNIVERSITY
San Diego, California 92131-1799
Web site: www.alliant.edu

Founded 1924. Private control. Quarter system. Multicampus institution: graduate study at Fresno, Irvine, Los Angeles, San Diego, San Francisco, Nairobi, Kenya, Mexico City, Mexico campuses. Library in San Diego about 205,000 volumes, 1200 subscriptions. Total University enrollment: 6,200.

Tuition: per unit $500–$865 depending on program and location. On-campus housing available in San Diego. Average academic year housing costs: $11,700 (private room), $15,480 (double occupancy). Contact Director of Housing for both on- and off-campus housing information. Phone: (858)635-4592.

Graduate Programs

Enrollment (San Diego): full-time 487, part-time 336. University faculty teaching graduate students: full-time 53, part-time 69. Degrees conferred: M.A., M.A.O.B., M.A.O.P., M.B.A., M.I.B.A., D.B.A., Ed.D., Psy.D.

ADMISSION REQUIREMENTS. Official transcripts, references, personal essay, GRE or MAT or GMAT required in support of School's application. Online application available. Interview not required. International applicants must also submit evidence of proficiency in English or TOEFL and a financial statement. Accepts transfer applicants. Graduates of unaccredited institutions not considered. Apply to Director of Admissions at least six weeks prior to registration. Application fee $55. Phone: (858)635-4772; fax (858)635-4739.

ADMISSION STANDARDS. Selective. Usual minimum average: 3.0 master's; 3.2 doctorate (A = 4). TOEFL minimum score: 500.

FINANCIAL AID. Scholarships, research assistantships, internships, Federal W/S, loans. Apply to individual schools for fellowships, assistantships; to Financial Aid Office for federal programs. Phone: (858)635-4558. Use FAFSA and institutional FAF.

DEGREE REQUIREMENTS. For master's: 45 quarter units minimum, at least 35 in residence; thesis; final written exam. For D.B.A., Ed.D., Psy.D.: at least 105 quarter units beyond the master's; dissertation; final oral exam.

FIELDS OF STUDY.

MARSHALL GOLDSMITH SCHOOL OF MANAGEMENT:
Business Administration. M.B.A., D.B.A.
Consulting Psychology. Ph.D.
Industrial-Organizational Psychology. M.A., M.S.
International Business Administration. M.I.B.A.
International Relations, M.A.

CALIFORNIA SCHOOL OF PROFESSIONAL PSYCHOLOGY
Clinical Psychology. Psy.D., Ph.D.
Marital and Family Therapy. M.A., Psy.D.

GRADUATE SCHOOL OF EDUCATION
Educational Administration K–12. M.A.
Educational Administration Higher Education. M.A.
Educational Leadership and Management. Ed.D.
Higher Educational Administration. Ed.D.
School Psychology. M.A., Psy.D.
TESOL. M.A., Ed.D.

THE AMERICAN UNIVERSITY
Washington, D.C. 20016-8111
Web site: www.american.edu

Founded 1893 by an act of Congress. Located 3 miles W of downtown. CGS member. More than 760 computers on campus for student use. Coed. Private control, Methodist affiliation. University participates in Joint Graduate Consortium with Catholic, Georgetown, George Washington, Howard Universities. Special

facilities: American University of Sharjah, Center for Asian Studies, Center for Congressional and Presidential Studies, Center for Global Peace, Center for the Global South, Center for Islamic Peace, Center of Slavic and Related Studies, Graduate Research Center in Europe, Intercultural Management Institute, International Institute for Health Promotion, Kogod's Center for Information, Technology and Economy, National Center for Health and Fitness. Transnational Crime and Corruption Center, Women and Politics Institute. Library: 850,000 volumes, 4466 subscriptions, plus access to online data retrieval services. Total enrollment: 11,279.

On-campus housing available for single and married students. Average annual cost: $7000–$11,000. Apply to Housing Office. Phone: (202)885-3370. Day-care facilities available.

College of Arts and Sciences—Graduate Division

Annual tuition: $17,802, part-time $989 per credit. Enrollment: full-time 463, part-time 793. Faculty: full-time and part-time 375. Degrees conferred: M.A., M.S., M.F.A., Ph.D.

ADMISSION REQUIREMENTS. Transcripts, two letters of recommendation required in support of application. GRE, interview for some departments. TOEFL required of foreign students. Accepts transfer applicants. Apply to Office of Graduate Admissions by February 1 (Fall), October 1 (Spring), April 15 (Summer). Application fee $50. Phone: (202)885-3621, (202)885-6000; fax: (202)885-1505.

ADMISSION STANDARDS. Selective for most departments. Usual minimum average: 3.0 (A = 4). Accepts about 60% of applicant pool.

FINANCIAL AID. Annual awards from institutional funds: scholarships, fellowships, assistantships, grants, tuition waivers, Federal W/S, loans. Apply by January 15 to Financial Aid Office. Phone: (202)885-1098. About 60% of students receive aid other than loans from College and outside sources.

DEGREE REQUIREMENTS. For master's: 30 hours minimum, at least 24 in residence; reading knowledge of one foreign language for some departments; thesis or nonthesis option for some departments; written comprehensive exam. For Ph.D.: 72 hours minimum beyond the bachelor's, at least 42 in residence; two languages or one language and statistical or computer analysis as a research tool; three to four written comprehensives; one oral comprehensive; dissertation; final oral defense.

FIELDS OF STUDY.
Applied Computing. Interdisciplinary. M.S.A.S.
Anthropology. Includes public anthropology. M.A., Ph.D.
Art (Studio). Includes drawing, multimedia, painting, printmaking, sculpture. M.F.A.
Art History.
Arts Management. M.A.
Biology. M.A., M.S.
Biotechnology. Interdisciplinary. M.S.A.S.
Chemistry. M.S.
Computer Science. M.S.
Creative Writing. M.F.A.
Curriculum and Instruction. Includes literacy, educational leadership, global literacy, technology. M.Ed.
Economics. Includes development finance, financial economic policy. M.A.
Environmental Assessment. Interdisciplinary. M.S.A.S.
Environmental Science. M.S.
Ethics, Peace and Global Affairs. Interdisciplinary. M.A.
Health Promotion Management. M.S.
History. M.A.
International Training and Education. M.A.
Literature. M.A.

Mathematics. M.A.
Philosophy. M.A.
Psychology. M.A.
Sociology. M.A.
Spanish and Latin American Studies. M.A.
Special Education for Learning Disabilities. M.A.
Statistics. M.S.
Teaching. Includes elementary, secondary, ESOL. M.A.T.
TESOL. M.A.

Kogod School of Business
Web site: www.kogod.american.edu

Established 1955. Special programs: foreign study Tokyo Keizai University, the Netherlands International Institute of Management, Université Paris Dauphine, École Supérieure de Commerce de Nantes. Enrollment: full-time 179, part-time 284. Graduate faculty: full-time 57, part-time 17.

Tuition: $1048 per credit. Housing is available for single and married students. Degrees conferred: M.A., M.B.A., M.S. (Acc.), M.S.T., M.B.A.-J.D., M.B.A.-M.A.I.A., M.B.A.-M.S.

ADMISSION REQUIREMENTS. Transcripts, GMAT, personal statement, two letters of recommendation, interview required in support of application. TOEFL recommended for international students. Graduates of unaccredited institutions not considered. Apply to the Director of Graduate Admissions and Financial Aid by February 1. Rolling admission process. Application fee $75. Phone: (202)885-1319; fax: (202)885-1078.

ADMISSION STANDARDS. Selective. Accepts about 60% of total annual applicant pool.

FINANCIAL AID. Annual awards from institutional funds: research assistantships, scholarships, fellowships, internships, partial tuition waivers, Federal W/S, loans. Apply to the Director of Financial Aid by February 1. Phone: (202)985-6000; fax: (202)885-6014. Use FAFSA. Aid available for part-time students. About 40% of students receive aid other than loans from School and outside sources.

DEGREE REQUIREMENTS. For M.B.A.: 54 semester hour program. For M.A., M.S., M.S.T.: 30–33 semester hour programs.

FIELDS OF STUDY.
Accounting. M.S.
Business Administration. Includes career tracks in accounting, asset management, commercial banking, corporate financial management, entrepreneurship, global emerging markets (finance, information technology), international business consulting, international trade and global supply chain management, information technology consulting, investment banking, leadership, management consulting, marketing management, marketing research, money management, real estate, taxation.
Information Technology Management. M.S.
Taxation. M.S.

School of Communication

Special programs: Center for Social Media, Film and Video Institute, Center for Environmental Film Making. Annual tuition: $19,998.

Enrollment: full- and part-time 331. Faculty: full-time 45, part-time 50. Degrees conferred: M.A., M.F.A.

ADMISSION REQUIREMENTS. Offical transcripts, GRE, 1000-word Statement of Purpose, résumé, two letters of recommendation, 3.0 GPA (A = 4), in last 60 credits required in support of application. TOEFL (minimum score 600, or 250 on computer-based version) required of international students. Accepts transfer applicants. Graduates of unaccredited institutions not considered. Apply to the Office of Admissions by November 15 (Spring), June 1 (Fall). Application fee $75. Phone: (202)885-1098.

ADMISSION STANDARDS. Selective. Usual minimum average: 2.75, 3.0 average last 60 credits (A = 4).

FINANCIAL AID. Merit-based financial aid awards available including fellowships, scholarships, assistantships; Federal W/S, loans. Approved for VA benefits. Apply by February 1 to School for merit-based aid, assistantships, fellowships; to Financial Aid Office for all other programs. Phone: (202)885-6100. Use FAFSA for all need based programs. Aid available for part-time students.

DEGREE REQUIREMENTS. For M.A.: 30–33 semester hours minimum, at least 24 in residence; written general communication and journalism comprehensive exams; thesis or two research papers.

FIELDS OF STUDY.
Broadcast Journalism.
Communication.
Film and Electronic Media.
Film and Video Production.
Interactive Journalism.
Multimedia Development.
News Media Studies.
Print Journalism.
Public Communication.

School of International Service

Established 1958. Annual tuition: $19,998. On-campus housing available. Contact Director, Residential Life. Phone: (202)885-3370. Day-care facilities available.

Enrollment: full-time 540, part-time 367. Faculty: full-time 66, part-time 34. Degrees conferred: M.A., M.S., Ph.D., M.A.-M.B.A., M.A.-J.D., M.A.-M.T.S. (Wesley Theological Seminary).

ADMISSION REQUIREMENTS. Transcripts, two letters of recommendation, GRE required in support of application. TOEFL required for non-English-speaking foreign students. Graduates of unaccredited institutions not considered. Apply to the Office of Admissions by January 15 (Fall), September 15 (Spring). Rolling admissions process. Application fee $75. Phone: (202)885-6000; fax: (202)885-6014.

ADMISSION STANDARDS. Selective. Usual minimum average: 3.45, 3.0 average last 60 credits (A = 4).

FINANCIAL AID. Scholarships, fellowships, research and teaching assistantships, all federal financial aid programs. Apply to Dean of the School before January 15 for all non-Federal programs; to the Financial Aid Office before April 1 for all Federal programs. Use FAFSA. No aid for part-time students.

DEGREE REQUIREMENTS. For master's: 36–42 semester hours minimum, at least 24 in residence; proficiency in one foreign language; written comprehensive exams; thesis or two research papers. For Ph.D.: 72 semester hours, at least 30 in residence; proficiency in one foreign language; oral and written exams; dissertation; final oral exam. For M.B.A., M.T.S., J.D.: see degree requirements listed in the other graduate schools.

FIELDS OF STUDY.
Comparative & Regional Studies. M.A.
Development Management. M.S.
Ethics, Peace and Global Affairs. Interdisciplinary. M.A.
Global Environmental Policy. M.A.
International Affairs. M.A.

International Communication. M.A.
International Development. M.A.
International Economic Relations. M.A.
International Media. M.A.
International Peace & Conflict Resolution. M.A.
International Politics. M.A.
International Relations. Ph.D.
U.S. Foreign Policy.

School of Public Affairs

Established 1958. Annual Tuition: $19,998. Enrollment: full-time 221, part-time 305. Faculty: full-time 61, part-time 57. Degrees conferred: M.A., M.P.A., M.P.P., Ph.D.

ADMISSION REQUIREMENTS. Official transcripts, GRE, two letters of recommendation (three letters for Ph.D. applicants) required in support of application. TOEFL required of international students. GRE General/Subject Tests recommended for those who desire consideration for financial aid. Accepts transfer applicants. Graduates of unaccredited institutions not considered. Apply to the Office of Admissions by February 1 (Fall), November 1 (Spring). Application fee $55. Phone: (202)885-6230. School Contact: Phone: (202)885-6202.

ADMISSION STANDARDS. Selective. Usual minimum average: 2.75, 3.0 average last 60 credits (A = 4).

FINANCIAL AID. Fellowships, scholarships, research and teaching assistantships, tuition waivers, Federal W/S, loans. Approved for VA benefits. Apply by February 1 to School for assistantships, fellowships; to Financial Aid Office for all other programs. Phone: (202)885-6100. No aid for part-time students.

DEGREE REQUIREMENTS. For M.A.: 33 semester hours minimum, at least 24 in residence; written comprehensive exams; thesis or two research papers. For M.P.A.: 42 semester hours minimum, at least 33 in residence; written comprehensive exam. For M.P.P.: 36 credit hour program; written comprehensive exam; thesis/nonthesis option. For Ph.D.: 60–72 semester hours, at least 30 in residence; proficiency in one foreign language or proficiency in statistics, computer science; written exam; dissertation; final oral exam.

FIELDS OF STUDY.
Justice, Law and Society. M.S., Ph.D.
Political Science. M.A., Ph.D.
Public Administration. Ph.D.
Public Policy. M.P.P.

Washington College of Law
Web site: www.wcl.american.edu

Founded 1896. ABA approved since 1940. AALS member. Semester system. Full- and part-time study. Special facilities: Academy on Human Rights and Humanitarian Law, Center for Human Rights and Humanitarian Law, National Institute of Military Justice, National Institute of Corrections/WCL Project on Addressing Prison Rape. Law Library: 568,391 volumes, 6736 subscriptions; Library has LEXIS, WESTLAW, and access to on-line data retrieval systems. Special summer programs in Chile, Argentina, London, Paris, Geneva, and Istanbul.

Annual tuition: full-time $36,464, part-time $25,650. On-campus housing limited. Total annual additional expenses: $20,000.

Enrollment: first-year full-time 365, part-time 99; total full-time 1128, part-time 276 (men 48%, women 52%, minority 33%).

Faculty: full-time 87, part-time 190 (men 52%, women 48%); student to faculty ratio 14 to 1.

Degrees conferred: J.D., J.D.-M.A. (International Service), J.D.-M.B.A. (Kogod College), J.D.-M.S. (Justice, Law and Society), LL.M. (International Legal Studies and Law and Government, a one year program for both U.S. and internationally trained attorneys), LL.M. (Law and Government). Dual Degrees: J.D./LL.B. WCL and the University of Ottawa, Canada; J.D./Licenciatura en Derecho, WCL and the University Alfonso X El Sabio (UAX), Madrid, Spain; J.D./Master I/Master II, WCL and the University of Paris X-Nanterre (UPX), Paris, France.

ADMISSION REQUIREMENTS. LSDAS Law School report, transcripts, LSAT, bachelor's degree required in support of application. Interview not required. Accepts transfer applications. Graduates of unaccredited colleges not considered. Apply to Director of Admission of the College after October 1, before March 1. International apply by January 15. Fall admission only. Application fee $65. Phone (202)274-4101; fax: (202)274-4107; e-mail: wcladmit@wcl.american.edu.

ADMISSION REQUIREMENTS FOR TRANSFER APPLICANTS. Accepts transfer applications from other ABA accredited schools on a space available basis. The applicant must have completed at least two semesters. In addition, the applicant must submit a Transfer/Visitor application and $60 application fee, an official transcript from their current Law School and their rank in class, an LSDAS report and a letter from the Dean stating that you are in good academic standing and eligible to return. Application deadline Fall Semester June 15, Spring Semester November 1, and Summer Semester May 1.

ADMISSION STANDARDS. Selective. Number of full-time applicants 7710, part-time 1154; number of full-time acceptance 1849, part-time 350; number of full-time enrolled 365, part-time 99; LSAT (75% of class have a score at or above 160); GPA (75% of class have a GPA at or above 3.20). *U.S. News & World Report* ranking is in the first tier of all Law Schools with a rank of 47th.

FINANCIAL AID. Scholarships, fellowships, loans. Apply to Director of Financial Aid by March 1. Phone: (202)274-4040. Use FAFSA. About 5% of students receive aid other than loans from College. Aid available for part-time students.

DEGREE REQUIREMENTS. For J.D.: 86 semester hours minimum, at least 28 in residence. Transfer credit individually considered. For LL.M.: at least 24 graduate credits beyond J.D. For M.A., M.B.A., M.S.: see Graduate School listing above.

ANDREWS UNIVERSITY
Berrien Springs, Michigan 49104
Web site: www.andrews.edu

Founded 1874. Located 25 miles N of South Bend, Indiana. CGS member. Coed. Private control. Seventh-Day Adventist. Semester system. Special facilities: Center for Caring, Center for College Faith, Center for Global Urban Mission, Global Church Growth Research Center, Greek Manuscript Research Center, Horn Archaeological Museum, Institute for Prevention of Addictions, Institute of Archaeology, Institute of Church Ministry, Institute of Hispanic Ministry. Library: about 684,600 volumes, 3000 subscriptions. Total University enrollment: 3000.

Tuition: per hour $728 (master's), $849 (doctoral and Ed.S.). On-campus housing for 460 married students, 100 graduate men,

100 graduate women. Annual housing costs: $5700. Efficiency and one-bedroom apartments for single students only. Apply to Housing Manager. Phone: (269)471-6979. Day-care facilities available.

School of Graduate Studies

Coordinates programs for College of Arts and Sciences, College of Technology, School of Business, School of Education, and SDA Theological Seminary. Enrollment: full-time 544, part-time 675. University faculty teaching graduate: full-time 162, part-time 20. Degrees conferred: M.A., M.Mus., M.S., M.S.C.L.S., M.S.M.T., M.S.P.T., M.A.T., M.B.A., M.Div., Ed.S., Ed.D., Ph.D., D.Min., Th.D.

ADMISSION REQUIREMENTS. Transcripts, GRE, recommendations required in support of application. GMAT required for business programs. TOEFL/MELAB required for foreign applicants. Accepts transfer applicants. Apply to Supervisor of Admissions at least one month prior to registration. Application fee $45. Phone: (269)471-3490 or (800)253-2874; fax: (269)471-3228; e-mail: graduate@andrews.edu.

ADMISSION STANDARDS. Selective. Usual minimum average: 2.6 (A = 4); doctoral: 3.5 (A = 4).

FINANCIAL AID. Annual awards from institutional funds: scholarships, research/teaching fellowships, Federal W/S, loans. Apply to Office of Financial Aid; no specified closing date. Phone: (269)471-3334. Use FAFSA and institutional FAF.

DEGREE REQUIREMENTS. For master's: 30–48 quarter credits minimum, at least 35 in residence; candidacy; thesis; comprehensive exam/project paper, depending upon major and degree. For doctoral degrees: 64-credit program, at least three years of study beyond bachelor's, at least three semesters in residence; candidacy; appropriate research tool; comprehensive exam; dissertation; final oral defense.

FIELDS OF STUDY.
Architecture. M.Arch.
Biology. M.S.
Business Administration. M.B.A.
Church Administration. M.S.A.
Clinical Laboratory Science. M.S.C.L.S.
Communication: Interdisciplinary Studies. M.A.
Community Counseling. M.A.
Community and International Development. M.S.A.
Counseling Psychology. Ph.D.
Curriculum and Instruction. M.A., Ed.S., Ed.D., Ph.D.
Divinity. M.Div.
Educational Administration & Leadership. M.A., Ed.S., Ed.D., Ph.D.
Educational and Developmental Psychology. M.A., Ed.D., Ph.D.
Elementary Education. M.A.T.
English. M.A.
International Development. M.S.A.
Leadership. M.A., Ed.D., Ph.D.
Mathematics. M.S.
Ministry. M.Div., D.Min.
Music. M.A., M.Mus.
Music Education. M.Mus.
Nursing. M.S.
Nutrition. M.S.
Pastoral Ministry. M.A.
Physical Therapy. M.S.P.T., M.P.T.
Religion. M.A., Ph.D., Th.D.
Religious Education. M.A., Ph.D.
School Counseling. M.A.
School Psychology. Ed.S.
Secondary Education. M.A.T.
Social Work. M.S.W.
Software Engineering. M.S.
Special Education/Learning Disabilities. M.S.
TESOL. M.A.
Theology. M.Th., Th.D.
Youth Ministry. M.A.

ANGELO STATE UNIVERSITY
San Angelo, Texas 76909-1025
Web site: www.angelo.edu

Formerly Angelo State College, created in 1963. A member of Texas Tech University system. CGS member. Coed. Semester system. Special facilities: Management, Instruction and Research Center, Small Business Development Center, International Trade Office. Library: 481,826 volumes, 1850 subscriptions. 600 computers on campus for student use. Total University enrollment: 6200.

Annual tuition: resident $3112, nonresident $8080. Housing available for 82 married, single graduate students. Annual housing cost: $7144 (including board). Apply by July 15. Phone: (325)942-2035. Some day-care facilities available.

College of Graduate Studies
Web site: www.angelo.edu/gradschool

Graduate study since 1970. Enrollment: full- and part-time 450. Faculty: full-time 109, part-time 18. Degrees conferred: M.A., M.A.T., M.B.A., M.Ed., M.M.Ed., M.M.E., M.P.A., M.P.T., M.S., M.S.N.

ADMISSION REQUIREMENTS. Official transcripts, GRE/GMAT required in support of School's application. Nursing students can substitute MAT for GRE. TOEFL required for international applicants. Accepts transfer applicants. Graduates of unaccredited institutions not considered. Apply to Coordinator of Graduate Admissions by July 15 (Fall), December 15 (Spring). Application fee, $45; $50 for international applicants. Phone: (325)942-2169; fax: (325)942-2194.

ADMISSION STANDARDS. Selective. Usual minimum average: 2.5 (A = 4); or 3.0 for last 60 semester hours.

FINANCIAL AID. Fellowships, research and teaching assistantships, tuition waivers, Federal W/S, loans. Approved for VA benefits. Apply by July 15 to Dean of Graduate School for fellowships, assistantships; to Financial Aid Office for all other programs. Phone: (325)942-2246. Use FAFSA and University's FAF. Aid available for part-time students.

DEGREE REQUIREMENTS. For master's: 30–36 semester hours minimum; written/oral comprehensive exam; thesis/nonthesis option in some programs. For M.B.A.: Plan I—39 semester hours minimum; capstone course; Plan II—36 semester hours (accounting concentration).

FIELDS OF STUDY.
Accounting. M.B.A., M.P.A.
Animal Science. M.S.
Biology. M.S.
Biology: Science Education. M.S.
Business Administration. M.B.A.
Communication Systems Management. M.A.
Educational Diagnostics. M.Ed.

English. M.A.
Guidance and Counseling. M.Ed.
History. M.A.
Interdisciplinary Studies. M.A., M.S.
Kinesiology. M.S.
Medical-Surgical Clinical Nurse Specialist. M.S.N.
Nurse Education. M.S.N.
Nursing. M.S.N.
Physical Therapy. M.P.T.
Psychology. M.S.
Psychology: Counseling. M.S.
Psychology: Industrial/Organizational. M.S.
Public Administration. M.P.A.
Reading Specialist. M.Ed.
School Administration. M.Ed.
Student Development & Leadership in Higher Education. M.Ed.

ANTIOCH UNIVERSITY MCGREGOR
Yellow Springs, Ohio 45387
Web site: www.mcgregor.edu

Founded 1852. Located 20 miles E of Dayton. Coed. Private control. Quarter system. Library: over 285,000 volumes, 1000 subscriptions. University has graduate campuses in Keene, New Hampshire; Los Angeles and Santa Barbara, California; Seattle, Washington.

Tuition: full-time per quarter: liberal studies $2980, per credit $423; conflict resolution $2980; per credit, management $393, leadership $380. No campus housing available.

Graduate Programs

Graduate study since 1964. Enrollment: full- and part-time 543. Graduate faculty: full-time 22, part-time 31. Degrees conferred: M.A., M.Ed.

ADMISSION REQUIREMENTS. Two transcripts, three letters of recommendation, goal statement, résumé, interview required in support of application. Apply to Director of Admissions at least one month prior to quarter of registration. Admits to Fall (September 1), Winter (December 1), and Summer (June 1) quarters. Application fee $45. Phone: (937)769-1818; fax: (937)769-1805; e-mail: admiss@mcgregor.edu.

ADMISSION STANDARDS. Selective. Usual minimum average: 2.5 (A = 4).

FINANCIAL AID. Scholarships, assistantships, Federal W/S, loans. Apply to Director of Admissions and Financial Aid: no specified closing date. Use FAFSA.

DEGREE REQUIREMENTS. For M.A. (Management): two years in full-time residence; program offered on Saturdays only. For other M.A.: 45–60 quarter hours; residency requirements vary by program. For M.Ed.: 45 quarter hours; internship; professional portfolio.

FIELDS OF STUDY.
Community Change and Civil Leadership. M.A.
Community College Management. M.A.
Conflict Resolution. M.A.
Educational Leadership. M.Ed.
Individualized Study. M.A.
Intercultural Relations. M.A.
Liberal and Professional Studies. M.A.
Liberal Studies. M.A.
Management. M.A.

ANTIOCH LOS ANGELES
Culver City, California 90230
Web site: www.antiochla.edu

Established 1972. Coed. Private control. Semester and quarter system. Library: access to online bibliographic databases, union catalogs, and interlibrary loan networks. The main University campus is located in Yellow Springs, Ohio. It also has graduate campuses in Keene, New Hampshire; Santa Barbara, California; Seattle, Washington.

Tuition: Education, full-time per semester $5146, part-time $3050, per unit $517; psychology per unit $556.50; organizational Management per unit $649.50; Creative Writing per semester full-time $6235. Off-campus housing only.

Graduate School

Enrollment: full-time 270, part-time 153. Graduate faculty: full-time 14, part-time 76. Degrees conferred: M.A.E., M.F.A., M.A.O.M., M.A.P.

ADMISSION REQUIREMENTS. Transcripts, two letters of recommendation, goal statement, interview (except Creative Writing) required in support of application. GRE/MAT may be submitted. Passing CBEST required for M.A.E. TOEFL required for all international applicants. Apply to Director of Admissions by August 4 (Fall); rolling for other quarters. Admits Fall, Winter, Spring, and Summer. Application fee $60. Phone: (310)578-1080, ext. 411; fax: (310)822-4824.

ADMISSION STANDARDS. Selective. Usual minimum average: 2.5 (A = 4).

FINANCIAL AID. Scholarships, Federal W/S, loans. Apply to Director of Financial Aid by August 4. Phone: (310)578-1080; fax: (310)822-4824. Use FAFSA.

DEGREE REQUIREMENTS. For M.A.E.: 45 quarter hour program. For M.A.P.: 72 quarter units; thesis/nonthesis option or special project. For M.A.O.M.: 60-credit program; field study project. For M.F.A.: 48–60 semester units; five-month project; teaching; final manuscript.

FIELDS OF STUDY.
Creative Writing. M.F.A.
Education Leadership and Change. M.A.
Organizational Management. Includes specializations in organizational development, human resources management, leadership. M.A.O.M.
Psychology. Includes specializations in applied community psychology, child studies. M.A.P.

ANTIOCH NEW ENGLAND GRADUATE SCHOOL
Keene, New Hampshire 03431-3552
Web site: www.antiochne.ed

Coed. Private control. Three semester system. Graduate only institution. Library: 30,864 volumes, 1100 subscriptions, 23 PCs, and access to online bibliographic databases, union catalogs, and interlibrary loan networks. The main University campus is located in Yellow Springs, Ohio. It also has graduate campuses in Los Angeles and Santa Barbara, California; Seattle, Washington.

Tuition (Master's programs): Dance/Movement Therapy, full-time per semester $9375; Clinical Mental Health Counseling, full-time per semester $7175–$8725; Marriage and Family Therapy, full-time per semester $3425; Education per semester, full-time $3000–$6550; Environmental Studies, Interdisciplinary

Studies, full-time $6750; Organization & Management, full-time per semester $5200–$6750. Doctoral program: Clinical Psychology, full-time per semester $12,325; Environmental Studies full-time per semester $8950. Off-campus housing only.

Graduate School

Enrollment: full- and part-time 820. Graduate faculty: full-time 36, part-time 89. Degrees conferred: M.A., M.B.A., M.Ed., M.S.H.A., M.S., Psy.D.

ADMISSION REQUIREMENTS. Two transcripts, three letters of recommendation, goal statement, interview required in support of application. Accepts transfer applicants. Graduates of unaccredited institutions not considered. Apply to Director of Admissions by December 31 (Winter), August 31 (Fall); January 15 for doctoral programs. Admits Winter, Summer, Fall for master's; Fall only for doctoral programs. Application fee $40. Phone: (800)553-8902, ext. 287; fax: (603)357-0718; e-mail: admissions@antiochne.edu.

ADMISSION STANDARDS. Selective. Usual minimum average: 2.5 (A = 4).

FINANCIAL AID. Annual awards from institutional funds: fellowships, research and teaching assistantships, traineeships, scholarships for ethnic and racial groups which are historically underrepresented, Federal W/S, loans, institutional interest-free loans. Apply to Director of Financial Aid by March 1. Phone: (603)357-7563. Use FAFSA (School code: E00557). Aid available for part-time students.

DEGREE REQUIREMENTS. For master's: 40–60 credits, at least 30 in residence; thesis/nonthesis option or special project. For Psy.D.: 60 credits beyond an approved master's; qualifying exam; advancement to candidacy; dissertation; final oral exam.

FIELDS OF STUDY.
Administration and Supervision. M.Ed.
Clinical Mental Health Counseling. M.A.
Clinical Psychology. Psy.D.
Dance/Movement Therapy. M.A.
Elementary/Early Childhood Education. Includes integrated day, Waldorf education. M.Ed.
Environmental Studies. M.S., Ph.D.
Foundation of Education for Experience Educators. M.Ed.
Interdisciplinary Studies. M.A.
Marriage and Family Therapy. M.A.
Organizational and Environmental Sustainability. M.B.A.
Organizational Leadership and Management. M.S.
Resource Management and Conservation. M.S.

ANTIOCH SANTA BARBARA

Santa Barbara, California 93101
Web site: www.antiochsb.edu

Coed. Private control. Quarter system. Library: access to on-line bibliographic databases, union catalogs, and interlibrary loan networks. The main University campus is located in Yellow Springs, Ohio. It also has graduate campuses in Keene, New Hampshire; Los Angeles, California; and Seattle, Washington.
Tuition: full-time $5405–$6360, half-time $3245 per quarter, $530–$545 per credit. Only off-campus housing is available.

Graduate School

Enrollment: full-time 152, part-time 68. Graduate faculty: full-time 14, part-time 19. Degrees conferred: M.A.C.L., M.A.E., M.A.O.M., M.A.P., Psy.D.

ADMISSION REQUIREMENTS. Transcripts, two letters of recommendation, admissions dialogue, interview required in support of application. TOEFL (minimum score 600) required of international applicants. Accepts transfer applicants. Apply to Director of Admissions for M.A.C.L. August 1 (Fall), November 12 (Winter); for M.A.E. April 1 (Summer); for M.A.O.M. September 1 (Fall), December 1 (Winter), March 1 (Spring), June 1 (Summer); for M.A.P. in Professional Development and Career Counseling November 12 (Winter), for M.A.P. in Family and Child Studies August 1 (Fall), November 12 (Winter); rolling admissions process. Application fee $60. Phone: (805)962-8179; fax: (805)962-4786; e-mail: admissions@antiochsb.edu.

ADMISSION STANDARDS. Selective. Usual minimum average: 2.5 (A = 4).

FINANCIAL AID. Scholarship, tuition grants, Federal W/S, loans. Approved for VA benefits. Apply to Director of Financial Aid by August 1. Use FAFSA (School code: E00556). About 70% of students receive some sort of financial assistance.

DEGREE REQUIREMENTS. For M.A.E.: 45-credit program. For M.A.O.M.: 56–60 quarter units; thesis/nonthesis option, or special project. For M.A.C.L.: 72 quarter units; internship. For M.A.P.: 60-credit program; project. For Psy.D.: 4–5 year program; internship; dissertation; professional competence evaluation.

FIELDS OF STUDY.
Clinical Psychology. M.A.C.L., Psy.D.
Education. Includes emphasis in social justice and educational leadership. Teaching credential or equivalent required for admission. M.A.E.
Organizational Management. M.A.O.M.
Psychology. Includes professional development, career counseling, family and child studies. M.A.P.

ANTIOCH UNIVERSITY SEATTLE

Seattle, Washington 98121-1814
Web site: www.antiochsea.edu

Established 1997. Coed. Private control. Quarter system. Library: 6000 volumes, 150 subscriptions. Special facilities: Center for Creative Change, Center for Native Education. Special program: study abroad in Egypt, Bali. The main University campus is located in Yellow Springs, Ohio. It also has graduate campuses in Keene, New Hampshire, Los Angeles and Santa Barbara, California.
Tuition: per credit $450–$625. Off-campus housing only.

Graduate Programs

Enrollment: full-time 341, part-time 296. Graduate faculty: full-time 36, part-time 79. Degrees conferred: M.A., M.A.Ed., M.S.

ADMISSION REQUIREMENTS. Two transcripts, three letters of recommendation, goal statement, interview required in support of application. TOEFL (minimum score 600 or 250 on computer-based version) required for all international applicants. Accepts transfer applicants. Apply to Director of Admissions by August 16 (Fall); rolling for other semesters. Admits Winter, Spring, Summer, Fall. Application fee $60. Phone: (206)268-4202; e-mail: admissions@antiochsea.edu.

ADMISSION STANDARDS. Selective. Usual minimum average: 2.5 (A = 4).

FINANCIAL AID. Limited to Federal W/S, loans. Apply by June 15 to Director of Financial Aid. Phone: (206)268-4004. Use FAFSA (School code: E00555).

DEGREE REQUIREMENTS. For master's: 48–70 credits, at least 30 in residence; thesis/nonthesis option or special project. For M.S.: two-year program; personal excellence project.

FIELDS OF STUDY.
Education. M.A.Ed. 48-credit program.
Environment and Community. M.A. 66 credits for degree.
Management. M.S.
Organizational Psychology. M.A. 62-credit program.
Psychology. M.A. 62-credit program.
Strategic Communication. M.A. 66-credit program.
Whole System Design. Includes individualized degree. M.A. 70-credit minimum for degree.

APPALACHIAN STATE UNIVERSITY
Boone, North Carolina 28608
Web site: www.appstate.edu

Founded 1899. Located 120 miles NW of Charlotte. CGS member. Coed. State control. Semester system. More than 500 computers on-campus for student use. Special facilities: Dark Sky Observatory, Center for Appalachian Studies, Early Childhood Learning Center, Center for Management Development, Western Carolina Research Center. Library: 904,597 volumes, 5000 subscriptions. Total University enrollment: 14,653.

Tuition: resident per semester full-time $1295, nonresident per semester full-time $6085. On-campus housing available for both single and married students. Average academic year housing cost $2340–$3100. Contact Director of Residential Life for both on- and off-campus housing information. Phone: (828)262-2160.

Cratis D. Williams Graduate School

Graduate study since 1948. Enrollment: full-time 700, part-time 1000. Graduate faculty: full-time 530. Degrees conferred: M.A., M.S., M.M., M.L.S., M.B.A., M.P.A., Ed.S., Ed.D.

ADMISSION REQUIREMENTS. Transcripts, three letters of recommendation, GRE/GMAT/MAT required in support of the School's application. Interview required by some departments. TOEFL required for international applicants. Accepts transfer applicants. Graduates of unaccredited institutions not considered. Apply to the Office of the Dean of Graduate Studies by July 1 (Fall), November 1 (Spring); international applicants apply by April 1 (Fall). Rolling admission process. Application fee $45. Phone: (828)262-2130; fax: (828)262-2709.

ADMISSION STANDARDS. Selective. Use 2,000 point formula (Undergraduate GPA × 400)+GRE – V + GRE – Q = 2000. Use 1050 point formula for M.B.A. (Undergraduate GPA × 200) + GMAT=Total. MAT minimum score is 41. TOEFL minimum score 550 or 233 for computer-based score.

FINANCIAL AID. Scholarships, fellowships, assistantships, grants, Federal W/S, loans. Approved for VA benefits. Apply by March 31 (Fall); October 31 (Spring) to Office of the Dean of Graduate Studies for fellowships, assistantships; to Director of Student Financial Aid for all other programs. Phone: (825)262-2190. Use FAFSA. About 60% of students receive aid other than loans from University and outside sources.

DEGREE REQUIREMENTS. For M.A.: 30–37 semester hours, exclusive of the thesis, 24 in residence; thesis/nonthesis option; written and oral comprehensive exam. For M.B.A., M.P.A.: 36 semester hour program. For M.L.S.: 37–42 credit program. For M.S.: 30 credit hours minimum with thesis. For Ed.S.: 30–36 hours beyond the master's degree. For Ed.D.: 60 hours beyond

master's, one year of full-time study; comprehensive exam; internship; dissertation; oral/written exam.

FIELDS OF STUDY.
Accounting. M.S.
Appalachian Studies. M.A.
Applied Physics. M.S.
Biology. M.A.
Biology Education. M.A.
Business Administration. M.B.A.
Child Development, Birth through Kindergarten. M.A.
College Student Development. M.A.
Communication Disorders. M.A.
Community Counseling. M.A.
Computer Science. M.S.
Counseling. M.A.
Criminal Justice. M.S.
Curriculum Specialist. M.A.
Educational Leadership. Ed.D.
Educational Media. M.A.
Elementary Education. M.A.
English. M.A.
English Education. M.A.
Exercise Science. M.A.
Family and Consumer Sciences. M.A.
Family and Consumer Sciences Education. M.A.
French. M.A.
Geography. M.A.
Gerontology. M.A.
Higher Education. M.A., Ed.S.
History. M.A.
History Education. M.A.
Industrial Technology. M.A.
Library Science. M.L.S.
Marriage and Family Therapy. M.A.
Mathematics. M.A.
Mathematics Education. M.A.
Media Literacy. M.A.
Middle Grades Education. M.A.
Music. Includes music composition, music performance. M.M.
Music Education. M.M.
Music Therapy. M.M.I.
Physical Education. M.A.
Physical Engineering. M.S.
Political Science. M.A.
Psychology. Includes clinical, general experimental, health, industrial/organizational and human resource management, school, social. Admits Fall only. M.A.
Public Administration. M.P.A.
Public History. M.A.
Reading Education. M.A.
Romance Languages. M.A.
School Administration. M.S.A.
School Counseling. M.A.
Social Science. M.S.
Social Work. M.S.W.
Spanish. M.A.
Special Education. M.A.
Sports Management. M.A.
Technology Education. M.A.

ARIZONA STATE UNIVERSITY
Tempe, Arizona 85287-1003
Web site: www.asu.edu

Founded 1885. Located 10 miles E of Phoenix. CGS member. Coed. State control. Semester system. Special facilities: Architecture Library, Bureau of Broadcasting with Public Broadcasting Station KAET, Center for Asian Studies, Center for Executive Development, Center for Latin American Studies, Center for Medieval and Renaissance Studies, Institute for Studies in the Arts, Cancer Research Institute, Center for Research in Engineering and Applied Sciences, Center for Environmental Studies, Exercise and Sport Research Center, Center for Meteorite Studies with Miniger Meteorite Collection, Center for Solid State Science, Fine Arts Center, Grady Gammage Center for the Performing Arts, Law Library, Music Library, Research Park, University Art Collection. According to The Center at the University of Florida, Arizona State University ranks 94th for total University research expenditures with $145,591,000. In 2004, the University awarded 335 doctorates and ranked 35th among all U.S. institutions eligible to award that degree. Seven of the University's faculty members have been elected to National Honors Academies and ranked 78th among U.S. institutions. The Library: approximately 3,000,000 volumes, 28,100 subscriptions. Total University enrollment: 43,000.

Tuition: per credit resident $326, nonresident $747. On-campus housing for 98 graduate men and 98 graduate women; none for married students. Housing cost: per semester $2750–$4600. Apply to Residential Life. Phone: (480)965-3515.

Graduate College

Organized 1937. Enrollment: full-time 4801, part-time 2132. Faculty: full-time 1831, part-time 134. Degrees conferred: M.A., M.S., M.Acc., M.Arch., M.Ed., M.E.P., M.T., M.B.A., M.C., M.C.S., M.F.A., M.H.S.A., LL.M., M.M., M.M.C., M.N.S., M.P.A., M.S.D., M.S.E., M.S.W., M.Tax., M.T.E.S.L., Au.D., Ed.D., Ph.D., D.M.A., D.P.A.

ADMISSION REQUIREMENTS. Official application, two official transcripts, letters of recommendation required in support of application. Some academic departments may require additional information, e.g., GRE, GMAT, MAT. TOEFL and Financial Guarantee form required for international applicants. Accepts transfer students. Apply to the Admissions Office, Graduate College at least two months prior to registration, earlier for international applicants. Deadlines vary by degree program. Application fee $65, $80 international applicants. Phone: (480)965-6113; fax: (480)965-5158; e-mail: asugrad@asu.edu.

ADMISSION STANDARDS. Selective to very competitive. Generally students must have a minimum junior/senior average: 3.0 (A = 4). Some academic departments may require higher averages. TOEFL minimum score 550 or 213 on computer-based version required.

FINANCIAL AID. Annual awards from institutional funds: scholarships, fellowships, assistantships, grants, tuition waivers, Federal W/S, loans. Approved for VA benefits. Apply to Director of Financial Aid by July 15. Phone: (480)965-3355. Use FAFSA.

DEGREE REQUIREMENTS. For most master's: 30 semester hours minimum, at least 24 in residence; reading knowledge of one foreign language for some departments; thesis often required; final written/oral exam. For Ph.D.: normally 84 hours minimum beyond the bachelor's, at least 30 in residence, plus 24 hours dissertation and two semesters in continuous full-time attendance; comprehensive oral/written exams; dissertation; final oral exam.

FIELDS OF STUDY.
Accountancy and Information Systems. M.A.I.S.
Aerospace Engineering. M.S., M.S.E., Ph.D.
Agribusiness. Includes agribusiness management and marketing, food quality assurance. M.S. only. (Courses offered at ASU East Site.)
Anthropology. Includes archaeology, bioarchaeology, linguistic, medical anthropology, museum studies, physical anthropology, social-cultural anthropology. M.A., Ph.D.

Architecture. M.Arch. only.
Art. Includes art education, art history, ceramics, digital technology, drawing, fibers, intermedia, painting, photography, printmaking, sculpture, wood. M.A., M.F.A.
Asian Languages and Civilization—Chinese/Japanese. M.A.
Astrophysics. M.S.
Audiology. Au.D.
Bioengineering. M.S., Ph.D.
Biological Sciences. M.S. only.
Building Design. Includes computer-aided design, energy performance of buildings, facilities development and management, solar architecture. M.S. only.
Business Administration. M.B.A., Ph.D.
Chemical Engineering. Includes biomedical and clinical, chemical processing, chemical reactor, energy and material conversion, environmental control, solid state processing, transport phenomena. M.S., M.S.E., Ph.D.
Chemistry. Includes analytical, biochemistry, geochemistry, inorganic, organic, physical, solid state. M.S., M.N.S., Ph.D.
Civil Engineering. Includes environmental/sanitary, geotechnical/soil mechanics, structure, transportation, water resources/hydraulics. M.S., M.S.E., Ph.D.
Communication. M.A., Ph.D.
Communication Disorders. M.S. only.
Computer Science. M.C.S., M.S., Ph.D.
Construction. Includes facilities, management. M.S. only.
Counseling. M.C. only.
Counseling Psychology. Ph.D. only.
Counselor Education. M.Ed., Ed.D. only.
Creative Writing. M.F.A. only.
Curriculum and Instruction. M.A., M.Ed., Ed.D., Ph.D.
Dance. M.F.A. only.
Design. Includes graphics, industrial, interior. M.S.D. only.
Economics. M.S., Ph.D. only.
Educational Administration and Supervision. M.Ed., Ed.D.
Educational Leadership and Policy Studies. Ph.D. only.
Educational Psychology. M.A., M.Ed., Ph.D.
Educational Technology. Ph.D.
Electrical Engineering. M.S., M.S.E., Ph.D.
Elementary Education. Includes bilingual, educational media and computers, ESL, reading. M.Ed.
Engineering Sciences. M.S., M.S.E., Ph.D.
English. Includes comparative literature, English linguistics, literature and language, rhetoric and composition. M.A., Ph.D.
Environmental Design and Planning. Ph.D. only.
Environmental Planning. Includes landscape ecological planning, urban and regional development. M.E.P. only.
Environmental Resources. M.S. only.
Exercise Science. Includes biomechanics, physiology of exercise, psychology of exercise and sport. Ph.D. only.
Exercise Science/Physical Education. M.S. only.
Family and Human Development. M.S. only.
Family Science. Ph.D. only.
French. Includes comparative literature, language and culture, literature. M.A. only.
Geography. M.A., Ph.D.
Geological Sciences. M.S., M.N.S., Ph.D.
German. M.A. only.
Health Sector Management. M.H.S.M. only.
Higher and Postsecondary Education. M.Ed., Ed.D. only.
History. Includes Asian, British, European, Latin, Public, United States, U.S./Western. M.A., Ph.D.
History and Theory of Art. Ph.D. only.
Humanities. M.A. only.
Industrial Engineering. Includes human factor, information systems, operations research, organization control, quality control/reliability. M.S., M.S.E., Ph.D.
Information Management. M.S.
Justice Studies. M.S., Ph.D.
Kinesiology. M.S.
Learning and Instructional Technology. M.A., M.Ed., Ed.D., Ph.D.

Liberal Studies. M.L.S.

Mass Communication. M.M.C. only.

Materials Engineering. M.S., M.S.E.

Materials Science. M.S.

Mathematics. M.A., M.N.S., Ph.D.

Mechanical Engineering. M.S., M.S.E., Ph.D.

Microbiology. M.S., M.N.S., Ph.D.

Molecular and Cellular Biology. M.S., Ph.D.

Music. Includes education, ethnomusicology, history, choral, instrumental, performance, theory and composition. M.A., M.M., D.M.A.

Natural Science. Includes biology, chemistry, geological sciences, microbiology, physics, plant biology. M.N.S.

Nursing. Includes administration, adult health, community health, community mental health/psychiatric, parent–child nursing, women's health. M.S. only.

Philosophy. M.A., Ph.D.

Physical Education. M.P.E.

Physics. M.S., M.N.S., Ph.D.

Plant Biology. Includes ecology, photosynthesis. M.S.

Political Science. Includes American politics, comparative politics, international relations, political theory. M.A., Ph.D.

Psychology. Includes behavior neuroscience, clinical, developmental, experimental, social. Ph.D. only.

Public Administration. M.P.A., D.P.A.

Public Health. M.P.H.

Real Estate Development. M.R.E.D.

Recreation. Includes outdoor, administration, social/psychological aspects of leisure, tourism, and commercial. M.S. only.

Religious Studies. M.A. only.

School Library Sciences. M.A., M.Ed.

Science and Engineering of Materials. Ph.D.

Secondary Education. Includes educational media and computers. M.Ed.

Social and Philosophical Foundations of Education. M.A. only.

Social Work. Includes advanced direct practice, planning, administration, community practice. M.S.W., Ph.D.

Sociology. M.A., Ph.D.

Spanish. Includes comparative literature, language and culture, linguistics, literature. M.A., Ph.D.

Special Education. Includes gifted, mildly disabled, multicultural exceptional, severely, multiply disabled. M.Ed. only.

Speech and Hearing Sciences. Includes developmental neurolinguistic disorders, neuroauditory processes, neurogerontologic communication disorders. Ph.D. only.

Statistics. M.S. only.

Taxation. M.Tax. only.

Teaching English as a Second Language. M.TESL only.

Technology. Includes aeronautical engineering, aeronautical management, electronics engineering, graphic communication, industrial management and supervision, manufacturing engineering, mechanical engineering, welding engineering. M.S.T. only. (Courses offered at ASU East site.)

Theater. Includes directing, performance, scenography, theater for youth. M.A., M.F.A., Ph.D.

Urban and Environmental Planning. M.A.E.P.

Zoology. M.S., M.N.S., Ph.D.

CONCURRENT AND DUAL DEGREE PROGRAMS:

M.B.A.-M.A.I.S, M.B.A.-M.Arch., M.B.A.-M.S.A., M.B.A.-M.I.M., M.B.A.-M.S. (Economics), M.B.A.-M.S. (Information Management), M.B.A.-M.Tax., M.S.E.-M.I.M.T. (Thunderbird), M.S. (Justice)-M.A. (Anthropology), M.S.N.-M.H.S.A.

Sandra Day O'Connor College of Law (85287-7906)

Web site: www.law.asu.edu

Established 1969. ABA approved since 1974. AALS member since 1969. Semester system. Full-time day only. Special facilities: Center for the Study of Law, Science and Technology; Indian Legal

Program. Library: 413,877 volumes, 4031 subscriptions. Library has LEXIS, WESTLAW.

Annual tuition: resident $14,628, nonresident $26,320. Off-campus housing available for married students, on- and off-campus housing available for single students. Total annual costs for all other expenses: approximately $17,000.

Enrollment: first year 256, total full-time 650 (men 56%, women 44%, minority 36%).

Faculty: full-time 32, part-time 33; student to faculty ratio 11 to 1. Degrees conferred: J.D., J.D.-M.B.A., J.D.-M.D. (with Mayo Medical School, MN), J.D.-M.H.S.A. (Health Services Administration), J.D.-M.S. (Economics), J.D.-Ph.D. (Justice Studies, Law and Psychology), LL.M. (Biotechnology and Genomics), LL.M. (Tribal Policy, Law and Government), M.L.S.

ADMISSION REQUIREMENTS. LSDAS report, transcripts, LSAT, personal statement, résumé, bachelor's degree required in support of application. Interview not required. Preference given to state residents. Accepts transfer applicants on a space-available basis. Graduates of unaccredited colleges not considered. Apply to Office of Admissions after September 1, before February 15. Applicants admitted Fall only. Application fee state residents none, $35 for nonresidents. Phone: (480)965-1474; fax: (480)965-7930.

ADMISSION REQUIREMENTS FOR LL.M., M.L.S. APPLICANTS. For LL.M.: All applicants must have obtained a J.D. (or equivalent) from a U.S. law school or terminal law degree from a foreign law school, official transcripts, two letters of recommendation, personal statement required in support of application. For M.L.S.: proof of a 4-year degree (either an accredited college or university in the United States or a comparable degree from a foreign institution approved by either the government or the relevant accrediting authority of the nation where the school is located); official transcripts of all undergraduate and graduate degrees, personal statement, a résumé, a writing sample, two letters of recommendation, completed M.L.S. application. Admits Fall only. Apply by May 1. Application fee $50.

ADMISSION STANDARDS. Selective. Number of applicants 3039; number of acceptance 831; number enrolled 256; LSAT (75% of class have a score at or above 154); GPA (75% of class have a GPA at or above 3.10). *U.S. News & World Report* ranking is in the second tier of all Law Schools with a rank of 51st.

FINANCIAL AID. Scholarships, grants, fellowships, assistantship, Federal W/S, state grants, loans. Median grant $3000. About 40% of students receive aid other than loans from College funds. Apply to Financial Aid Office by March 1. Phone: (480)965-1474.

DEGREE REQUIREMENTS. For J.D.: 87 semester hours minimum; transfer credit individually considered. For LL.M.: 24 credit program, full-time. For M.L.S.: 30 credit program; either one or two years in duration. For M.B.A., M.H.S.A., Ph.D.: see Graduate College listing above.

ARIZONA STATE UNIVERSITY WEST

Box 37100
Phoenix, Arizona 85069-7100
Web site: www.west.asu.edu

Founded 1984. Located in northwest Phoenix. Coed. State control. Semester system. Library: 397,987 volumes, 2481 subscriptions; has links to all other ASU libraries. Over 400 computers on campus for student use. Total University enrollment: 7734.

Annual tuition: full-time resident $3114, nonresident $8960; per credit resident $326, nonresident $747. No on-campus housing available. Average cost for off-campus housing: $5839.

Graduate College

Enrollment: full-time 304, part-time 595. University faculty: full-time 81, part-time 40. Degrees conferred: M.A., M.B.A., M.Ed.

ADMISSION REQUIREMENTS. Official application, two official transcripts. GRE/GMAT required for some departments. TOEFL and Financial Guarantee form required for international applicants. Accepts transfer students. Apply to the Admissions Office, Graduate College at least two months prior to registration, earlier for international applicants. Application fee $65. Phone: (602)543-4567; fax: (602)543-4561; e-mail: asuwgrad@asu.edu.

ADMISSION STANDARDS. Selective. Generally students must have a minimum junior/senior average: 2.75 (A = 4). Some departments may require higher averages.

FINANCIAL AID. Annual awards from institutional funds: scholarships, assistantships, full and partial tuition waivers, Federal W/S, loans. Apply to Financial Aid Services Office by July 15. Phone: (602)543-8178. Use FAFSA.

DEGREE REQUIREMENTS. For M.A., M.Ed.: 30–36 semester hours minimum, at least 24 in residence; thesis/nonthesis option; final written/oral exam. For M.B.A.: 45 semester hour program.

FIELDS OF STUDY.
Business Administration. M.B.A.
Communication Studies. M.A.
Criminal Justice. M.A.
Educational Administration. M.Ed.
Elementary Education. Includes bilingual, educational media and computers, ESL, reading. M.Ed.
Gerontology. M.S.
Global Management and Leadership. M.B.A.
Interdisciplinary Studies. M.A.
Secondary Education. Includes educational media and computers. M.Ed.
Social Work. M.S.W.
Special Education. M.A.

THE UNIVERSITY OF ARIZONA
Tucson, Arizona 95721
Web site: www.arizona.edu

Founded 1885. Located 100 miles SW of Phoenix. CGS and AAU member. Coed. State control. Semester system. Special facilities: Agricultural Experiment Station, Arizona Arthritis Center, Arizona Cancer Center, Arizona Center on Aging, Arizona Center for Mathematical Sciences, Arizona Cooperative Fish and Wildlife Research Unit, Arizona Cooperative National Park Resources Studies Unit, Arizona Emergency Medicine Research Center, Arizona Institute for Neurogenic Communication Disorders, Arizona Poison and Drug Information Center, Arizona Remote Sensing Center, Arizona Research Laboratories, Arizona State Museum, Arizona Transportation and Traffic Institute, Arizona Veterinary Diagnostic Laboratory, Boyce Thompson Southwestern Arboretum, Bureau of Applied Research in Anthropology, Bureau of Mineral Technology, Center for Computing and Information Technology, Center for Creative Photography, Center for Electronic Packaging Research, Center for Insect Science, Center for Microcontamination Control, Center for Middle Eastern Studies, Center for Pharmaceutical Economics, Center

for the Management of Information, Center for the Study of Complex Systems, Center for the Study of Higher Education, Center for Toxicology, Cooperative Extension System, Division of Economic and Business Research, Division of Neural Systems, Memory and Aging, Division of Neurobiology, Division of Social Perspectives in Medicine, Economic Science Laboratory, Engineering Experiment Station, Flandrau Science Center and Planetarium, Institute for the Study of Planet Earth, Institute of Atmospheric Physics, Jeffrey M. Golding Clinical Research Unit, Karl Eller Center for the Study of the Private Market Economy, KUAT Communications Group, Laboratory of Tree-Ring Research, Latin American Area Center, Lunar and Planetary Laboratory, Mexican American Studies and Research Center, Mineral Museum, Office of Arid Land Studies, Optical Sciences Center, Respiratory Sciences Center, Ruth E. Golding Clinical Pharmacokinetics Laboratory, Sematech Center of Excellence for Contamination/Defect Control and Assessment, Social and Behavioral Sciences Research Institute, Southwest Center, Southwest Institute for Research on Women, Southwest Retail Center, Steele Memorial Children's Research Center, Steward Observatory, USDA Forest Service Cooperative Research Unit, University Animal Care, University Heart Center, University of Arizona Museum of Art, University of Arizona Press, Water Resources Research Center, Extended University, Summer Sessions, Guadalajara Summer School in Mexico. The University's NIH ranking is 59th among U.S. institutions with 293 awards/grants valued at $108,596,865. According to The Center at University of Florida, the University of Arizona is ranked 23rd in receipt of Federal Research funds worth $259,074,000 and it ranks 21st for total University research expenditures with $454,941,000. In 2004, the University awarded 398 doctorates which ranked them 27th among all U.S. institutions eligible to award that degree. Twenty-nine of the University's faculty members have been elected to National Honor Academies and this ranks it 32nd among U.S. institutions. The library system: approximately 7,000,000 volumes, 26,900 subscriptions. Total University enrollment: 37,500.

Tuition: resident $290 per unit; nonresident $681 per unit. On-campus housing for a limited number of graduate students, some housing for married students. Average annual (9 month) housing cost: $4400–$7000 for married students or single students. Apply to Director of Resident Life. Phone: (520)621-5859.

Graduate College

Graduate study since 1898. Enrollment: full-time 4681, part-time 1269. Graduate faculty, teaching and research: 1402. Degrees conferred: M.A., M.S., M.Acc., M.Ag.Ed., M.H.E.Ed., M.Arch., M.B.A., M.Ed., M.F.A., M.L.S., M.M., M.P.A., M.T., Ed.S., Ed.D., Ph.D.

ADMISSION REQUIREMENTS. One transcript from each institution attended required in support of application. GRE General/Subject Tests/GMAT, interview required for some majors. TOEFL required of all non-English-speaking international applicants. Graduates of unaccredited colleges not considered. Accepts transfer applicants. Apply to the Dean of Graduate College at least by June 1 (Fall), considerably earlier for most departments. Application fee for degree program $35, nondegree status $10. Phone: (520)621-3132; fax: (520)621-7112; e-mail: gradadm@lorax.admin.arizona.edu.

ADMISSION STANDARDS. Selective. Usual minimum average: 3.0 (A = 4).

FINANCIAL AID. Annual awards from institutional funds: academic scholarships, teaching assistantships, research assistantships, unspecified assistantship, Federal W/S, loans. Approved for VA benefits. Apply to appropriate department head by February 1. Phone: (520)621-1858. Use FAFSA and University FAF. About 33% of students receive aid other than loans from University and outside sources. Aid sometimes available for part-time students.

DEGREE REQUIREMENTS. For M.A., M.S.: 30 units minimum, at least 15 in residence; thesis required by many departments; reading knowledge of one or more foreign language(s) in some departments (options available in lieu of second language in some cases); final exam. For M.Acc.: 30 units minimum, at least 15 in residence; thesis optional; GMAT required. For M.Ag.Ed., M.H.E.Ed.: 32 units minimum; final research problem. For M.Arch.: 32 units minimum; three-part thesis; final oral exam. For M.B.A.: 60 units minimum, at least 30 units in residence; research project instead of thesis. Prerequisites are Mathematics 119 (Finite Mathematics) and Mathematics 123 (Elements of Calculus) or the equivalent. For M.Ed.: 32 units minimum; final exam may be written, oral, or both. For M.F.A.: major in Art—60 units minimum; thesis or original work or group of such work presented to the public. For major in Creative Writing—36 units minimum; original book-length work of fiction or poetry; final exam. For major in Drama—60 units minimum, in lieu of thesis, monograph/rehearsal, performance journal/original designer production project; final oral exam. For M.L.Arch.: 30 units minimum; thesis. For M.P.H.: a minimum of 33 units including a minimum of 3 units of internships. For M.M.: 30 units minimum; public recital for Applied Music Majors only; reading knowledge of German or French for Music History majors. For M.P.A.: 54 units minimum; optional internship or thesis. For M.T.: 32 units minimum; final written exam. For Ph.D.: 6 semesters minimum beyond bachelor's; at least 2 semesters and 30 units in full-time residence; qualifying exam; language requirement varies; preliminary and oral exam; dissertation; final oral exam. For Ed.D.: essentially the same as for the Ph.D.; reading knowledge of one foreign language is required only when deemed necessary. For A.Mus.D.: essentially the same as for the Ed.D. For Ed.S.: 60 units minimum; GRE General required.

FIELDS OF STUDY.

Accounting. GMAT for admission. M.Acc., Ph.D. (Management).

Acute Care Nurse Practitioner. M.S.

Adult Nurse Practitioner. M.S.

Aerospace Engineering. Thesis optional for M.S.

Agricultural and Biosystems Engineering.

Agricultural and Resource Economics. Thesis for M.S. M.S. only.

Agricultural Education. One year's teaching experience for admission. M.S., M.Ag.Ed. only.

American Indian Studies. M.S., Ph.D.

Animal Science. Thesis for M.S. M.S. only.

Anthropology. GRE for admission.

Applied and Industrial Physics. M.S.P.

Applied Biosciences. M.S.B.

Applied Mathematics.

Architecture. Bachelor's degree in architecture for admission; three-part thesis for M.Arch. M.Arch. only.

Arid Lands Resource Sciences. Ph.D. only.

Art. Portfolio for admission; thesis optional. M.A. only.

Art Education. Portfolio for admission; thesis optional. M.A. only.

Art History. One language for M.A. M.A. only.

Astronomy. GRE/Subject (Physics) for admission; written document for M.S.

Atmospheric Sciences. GRE admission. Thesis for M.S.

Bilingual/Bicultural Education. M.A., M.Ed.

Biochemistry and Molecular and Cellular Biology. Ph.D.

Biochemistry and Molecular Biophysics. Ph.D.

Biomedical Engineering.

Business Administration. GMAT or GRE for admission.

Cancer Biology.

Cell Biology and Anatomy. M.S., Ph.D.

Chemical Engineering. Thesis for M.S.

Chemistry. Thesis for M.S.; reading knowledge of one foreign language and thesis for M.S.

Civil Engineering. Thesis or Engineering Report for M.S.

Classics. M.A. only.

Clinical Nurse Leader. M.S.

Communication. GRE for admission.

Computer Science.

Creative Writing. M.F.A.

Dance. M.A., M.F.A.

Drama. Thesis for theater history and criticism. M.A., M.F.A.

East Asian Studies.

Ecology and Evolutionary Biology. GRE/Subject for admission.

Economics. GRE/Subject for admission.

Educational Administration/Leadership. Thesis for M.A.; GRE General/ Subject for Ph.D., Ed.D., Ed.S.

Educational Psychology. GRE for admission.

Educational Technology. M.S.

Electrical and Computer Engineering. Thesis option for M.S. M.S., M.S.E., Ph.D.

Elementary Education. M.T.

Engineering Mechanics. Thesis or Engineering Report for M.S.

English. GRE/Subject for admission.

English as a Second Language. Language proficiency required for admission. M.A. only.

Entomology. GRE/Subject for admission. Thesis for M.S.

Environmental Engineering.

Epidemiology. M.S., Ph.D.

Family and Consumer Resources. M.S., Ph.D. only.

Finance. GMAT for admission; thesis or report for M.S. M.S. only.

French. GRE/Subject for admission.

Genetic Counseling. M.S.

Genetics. Thesis for M.S.

Geography. GRE/Subject for admission; thesis option for M.S.

Geosciences. GRE/Subject for admission; thesis/nonthesis optional for M.A.

German Studies. M.A., M.Ed. only.

Higher Education. MAT or GRE for admission to doctoral programs.

History. GRE Subject for admission; one language; thesis optional for M.A.

History and Theory Arts. Ph.D.

Human Language Technology. M.S.

Hydrology. Thesis for M.S.

Immunology. M.S., Ph.D.

Industrial Engineering. M.S. only.

Information Resources and Library Science. M.A. only.

Insect Science. Interdisciplinary. Ph.D. only.

Journalism. M.A. only.

Landscape Architecture. Thesis for M.L.Arch. M.L.Arch. only.

Latin American Studies. GRE Subject for admission; oral and written proficiency in Spanish/Portuguese. M.A. only.

Management. Ph.D.

Management Information Systems. GMAT or GRE for admission; proficiency in programming language.

Marketing. GMAT for admission.

Materials Science and Engineering.

Mathematical Sciences.

Mathematics. Computer programming exam for master's.

Mechanical Engineering. Thesis optional for M.S.

Media Arts. M.A. only.

Mexican American Studies. M.S.

Microbiology. GRE for admission; thesis for M.S.

Mining, Geological and Geophysical Engineering. GRE/Subject (Engineering); thesis for M.S.

Molecular and Cellular Biology. GRE/Subject for admission.

Music. Includes applied music, theory, music education, musicology, composition; conducting large-scale composition for A.Mus.D. in composition; three years' experience for admission to A.Mus.D. in music education; four recitals in lieu of dissertation for A.Mus.D. in performance and conducting.

Natural Resources. M.S.

Near Eastern Studies. M.A., Ph.D.

Neuroscience. M.S., Ph.D. only.

Nursing. GRE for admission.
Nutritional Sciences. M.S. only.
Optical Sciences. GRE for admission; thesis for M.S.
Pathobiology.
Pharmaceutical Sciences.
Pharmacology. GRE for admission; thesis for M.S.
Philosophy. GRE/Subject for admission.
Physics. GRE/Subject for admission; thesis for M.S.
Physiological Sciences. GRE for admission.
Planetary Sciences. GRE/Subject for admission; thesis for M.S.
Planning. M.S. only.
Plant Pathology. Thesis for M.S.
Plant Sciences.
Political Science. GRE for admission.
Psychology. GRE for admission.
Public Administration. GRE for admission; thesis or internship for M.P.A. M.P.A. only.
Public Health. Interuniversity and interdisciplinary. M.P.H.
Rangeland Science and Management. GRE for admission.
Reliability and Quality Engineering. M.S. only.
Renewable Natural Resources.
Russian. M.A., M.Ed. only.
School Psychology.
Second Language Acquisition and Teaching.
Sociology. GRE/Subject for admission.
Soil, Water and Environmental Science. Thesis for M.S.
Spanish. GRE/Subject for admission.
Special Education and Rehabilitation. GRE/Subject for Ph.D., Ed.D., Ed.S.; thesis for M.A.
Speech, Language and Hearing Sciences. GRE for admission.
Statistics.
Systems and Industrial Engineering. Ph.D. only.
Systems Engineering. Thesis for M.S. M.S. only.
Teaching and Teacher Education.
Theatre. Includes theatre studies, education (M.A.); acting, directing, design/technical (M.F.A.).
Toxicology. GRE for admission; thesis for M.S. M.S. only.
Water Resources Administration. Thesis for M.S.
Wildlife and Fisheries Science. GRE/Subject for admission; thesis or professional paper for M.S. M.S., Ph.D.
Women's Studies. M.A. only.

James E. Rogers College of Law (P.O. Box 210176)
Web site: www.law.arizona.edu

Law instruction since 1914. ABA approved since 1930. AALS member since 1931. Semester system. Full-time study only. Special facility: Rehnquist Center on the Constitutional Structures of Government. Library: 422,660 volumes, 4435 subscriptions; has LEXIS, NEXIS, WESTLAW, DIALOG, OCLC.

Annual tuition: resident $16,201, nonresident $25,991. On-campus housing available for single graduate students. Total annual cost for all other expenses: single students $10,000, married students $17,706.

Enrollment: first-year 154; full-time 463 (men 50%, women 50%, minorities 28%). Faculty: full-time 36, part-time 33. Student to faculty ratio 12.7 to 1. Degrees conferred: J.D., J.D.-M.A. (Economics, American Indian Studies, Latin American Studies, Women's Studies), J.D.-M.B.A., J.D.-M.P.A., J.D.-M.M.F., J.D.-Ph.D. (Philosophy, Psychology, Economics), LL.M., S.J.D.

ADMISSION REQUIREMENTS. LSDAS Law School report, transcripts, LSAT, bachelor's degree, personal statement, two letters of recommendation, a domicile affidavit required in support of application. Interview not required. Preference given to state residents. Accepts transfer applicants. Graduates of unaccredited colleges not considered. Apply to Admissions Office after September 1, before February 15. Beginning and nonresident applicants admitted Fall only. Application fee $50. Phone (520)621-3477; fax: (520)621-9140; e-mail: admissions@law.arizona.edu.

ADMISSION STANDARDS. Selective. Accepts 25–27% of total annual applicants. Number of applicants 2194; number of acceptance 517; number enrolled 151; LSAT (75% of class have a score at or above 159); GPA (75% of class have a GPA at or above 3.28). *U.S. News & World Report* ranking is in the top 44 of all law schools.

FINANCIAL AID. Scholarships, cash awards, fellowships, research assistantships, partial tuition waivers, loans. Apply to Financial Aid Office by March 1. Phone: (520)626-8101. Use FAFSA (College code: 001083). Some preference given to minority group students. About 84% of students receive aid other than loans from College funds.

DEGREE REQUIREMENTS. For J.D.: 6 semester minimum, at least the final 2 semesters in residence; 85 units. For LL.M.: at least 24 units beyond J.D. For S.J.D.: at least one or two years of clinical and applied research; writing a significant document which will contribute to legal scholarship. For M.A., M.B.A., M.P.A., Ph.D.: see Graduate School listing above.

FIELDS OF GRADUATE STUDY.
Banking Law. S.J.D.
Commercial Law. S.J.D.
Customs Law. S.J.D.
International Trade Law. LL.M., S.J.D.
Indigenous People Law and Policy. LL.M.
Transportation Law. S.J.D.

College of Medicine
P.O. Box 245075
Web site: www.medicine.arizona.edu

First class entered 1967. University Medical Center completed 1971. Located on main campus. Special facilities: Arizona Arthritis Center, Arizona Cancer Center, Arizona Center on Aging, Arizona Emergency Medicine Research Center, Arizona Hispanic Center of Excellence, Arizona Respiratory Center, Steele Children's Research Center, The University of Arizona Sarver Heart Center, Valley Fever Center of Excellence. Library: 176,000 volumes. The University's NIH ranking was 59th among all U.S. institutions with 293 awards/grants worth $108,596,865.

Annual tuition: state resident and WICHE resident $15,956. Medical students must assume the responsibility for making their own living arrangements. Average figure for all other expenses $10,500–$13,000 depending on location.

Enrollment: first-year class 100; total 479 (men 49%, women 51%, minorities 30%). Faculty: full-time 834, part-time 35. Degrees conferred: M.D., M.D.-M.P.H., M.D.-Ph.D.

ADMISSION REQUIREMENTS. AMCAS report, transcripts, MCAT, Preprofessional committee evaluation, personal statement, letters of recommendation, interview required in support of application. Medical students should be conversant in Spanish. Applicants must have completed at least ninety semester units of college study. All candidates must be residents of Arizona or WICHE certified residents. Graduates of unaccredited institutions not considered. Does not have EDP. Apply to College Admissions Office after June 1, before November 1. Application fee, $75. Phone: (520)626-6214; fax: (520)626-3777.

ADMISSION STANDARDS. Competitive. Accepts about 28% of all applicants. Number of applications 538 (13 out-of-state); number interviewed 538 (13 out-of-state); number of acceptance 153 (4 out-of-state); number enrolled 110 (1 out-of-state). Mean Composite MCAT 9.9; mean UGPA 3.67. *U.S. News & World Report* ranked only the top 50 medical schools and, therefore, did not rank University of Arizona College of Medicine.

FINANCIAL AID. Scholarships, minority scholarships, loans; assistantships may be available for dual degree programs. About

87% of students receive aid other than loans from College. Apply after acceptance, before May 15, to Financial Aid Office. Phone: (520)626-7145. Use FAFSA (College code: 001083). 79% of students receive financial aid.

DEGREE REQUIREMENTS. For M.D.: satisfactory completion of four-year program. Must receive a passing score on both Steps 1 and 2 of USMLE. For Ph.D., M.P.H.: see degree requirements above.

FIELDS OF GRADUATE STUDY.
Cell Biology and Anatomy.
Immunology.
Medical Pharmacology.

INTERDISCIPLINARY PROGRAMS:
Cancer Biology.
Cognitive Science.
Genetics.
Neuroscience
Physiological Sciences.

ARKANSAS STATE UNIVERSITY
Jonesboro, State University, Arkansas 72467
Web site: www.astate.edu

Founded 1909. CGS member. Located 60 miles NW of Memphis, Tennessee. Coed. State control. Semester system. Library: 596,300 volumes; 1775 subscriptions. There are 500 computers on campus for student use. Total University enrollment: 10,400.

Annual tuition: resident $3232, per credit $180, nonresident $8164, per credit $454. On-campus housing for 217 married students, 1000 men, 1000 women. Average annual housing cost: $4185 for married students, $4185 for single students (including board). Apply to Director of Housing. Phone: (870)972-2042.

Graduate School

Graduate study since 1995. Enrollment: full-time 367, part-time 909. College faculty: full-time 242, part-time 9. Degrees conferred: M.A., M.S.A., M.S.E., M.M.E., M.M., M.R.C., M.B.A., M.P.A., M.S.Agric., M.S.M.C., M.S.N., M.C.D., S.C.C.T., Ed.S., Ed.D., Ph.D.

ADMISSION REQUIREMENTS. Transcripts required in support of application. MAT/GRE/GMAT required by some departments or programs. Interview required for Specialist and Doctoral programs. TOEFL required for international applicants. Accepts transfer applicants. Apply to Graduate Dean at least six weeks prior to registration. Rolling admission process. Application fees: $15, for international applicants $25, for doctoral applicants $35. Phone: (870)972-3209, (877)278-4723.

ADMISSION STANDARDS. Selective. Usual minimum average: 2.5 overall or 2.75 last 60 hours.

FINANCIAL AID. Annual awards from institutional funds: fellowships, research and teaching assistantships, internships, Federal W/S, loans. Apply to Dean six weeks prior to registration. Use FAFSA. Phone: (870)972-2310. About 60% of full-time students receive aid loans from other than University funds. Aid available for part-time students.

DEGREE REQUIREMENTS. For M.A.: 30 semester hours minimum, at least 24 in residence; thesis for 6 semester hours; reading knowledge of one foreign language; comprehensive exam. For M.S.M.C.: same as M.A., except no language requirement. For M.S.: 30–36 semester hours minimum including thesis; reading knowledge of one foreign language or research tool; final written/ oral exam. For M.B.A.; M.M., M.M.E., M.S.A., M.S.E., M.S.N.,

M.C.D.: 30–39 hours minimum, at least 24 in residence; thesis optional; no language requirement. For M.R.C.: 48–54 hours. For M.P.A.: 42 hours. For Ed.S., S.C.C.T.: 30 hours beyond the master's including internship or field study; admission to candidacy; final written comprehensive. For Ed.D.: 99-credit program beyond bachelor's; comprehensive exam; admission to candicacy; dissertation; oral defense. For Ph.D.: 90-credit program beyond bachelor's; one year full-time residency; qualifying exam; admission to candidacy; comprehensive exam; dissertation; oral defense.

FIELDS OF STUDY.
Accounting.
Adult Health Nursing.
Agriculture.
Agriculture Education.
Art.
Biology.
Business Administration.
Business Technology.
Chemistry.
College Student Personnel Services.
Communication Disorders.
Community College Teaching. Includes agricultural education, biology, business administration, business education, chemistry, community college administration, English, history, music education, physical education, political science, reading, sociology, speech communication and theater, vocational-technical administration. Ed.S. only
Computer Science.
Counselor Education.
Curriculum and Instruction.
Early Childhood Education.
Early Childhood Services.
Educational Leadership. M.S.E., Ed.D.
Education Theory and Practice.
Elementary Education.
English.
Environmental Science. M.S., Ph.D.
Family Nurse Practitioner.
Health Science.
Heritage Studies. Ph.D. only.
History.
Information Systems & eCommerce.
Journalism.
Mathematics.
Molecular Biosciences. Ph.D. only.
Music Performance.
Music Education.
Nursing. Includes adult health nursing, family nurse practitioner.
Physical Education. Includes exercise science, sports studies.
Physical Therapy.
Political Science.
Public Administration.
Radio-Television.
Reading.
Rehabilitation Counseling.
Sociology.
Special Education Gifted and Talented.
Special Education Emotionally Disturbed.
Speech Communication.
Theater Arts.
Vocational-Technical Administration.

UNIVERSITY OF ARKANSAS
Fayetteville, Arkansas 72701-1201
Web site: www.uark.edu

Founded 1871. Main campus at Fayetteville, 200 miles NW of Little Rock. In Little Rock (72201): University of Arkansas for

Medical Sciences, includes College of Health-Related Professions, Medicine, Nursing, Pharmacy, Graduate Institute of Technology (72203). CGS member. Coed. State control. Semester system. Special facilities: Agricultural Experiment Station, Engineering Experiment Station, Bureau of Business and Economic Research, Water Resources Research Center. Sponsoring University of the Oak Ridge Institute of Nuclear Studies in Tennessee. According to The Center at University of Florida, the University's endowment asset ranks it 64th, $566,544,000. In 2004, 2 of the University's faculty members were elected to National Honor Academies and this ranks it 117th among all U.S. institutions. Library: approximately 1,500,000 volumes, 14,170 subscriptions. Total University enrollment: 17,800.

Tuition: per credit, resident $269, nonresident $638. On-campus housing for 334 married students, unlimited for single graduate students. Average annual housing cost: $4258 (including board) for single students, $3000 for married students. Contact the Residence Life and Dining services for both on- and off-campus housing information. Phone: (479)575-3951.

Graduate School
Web site: www.uark.edu/depts/gradinfo

Graduate study since 1927. Enrollment: full- and part-time 3328. University faculty: full-time 844, part-time 137. Degrees conferred: M.A., M.Acc., M.A.T., M.B.A., M.F.A., M.M., M.Ed., M.S., M.S.C.E., M.S.Ch.E., M.S.E.E., M.S.I.E., M.S.M.E., M.P.A., M.T.L.M., Ed.S., Ed.D., Ph.D.

ADMISSION REQUIREMENTS. Two official transcripts, three letters of recommendation, GRE/GMAT/MAT required in support of School's application. GRE for marginal applicants. Interview not required. TOEFL required for international applicants. Accepts transfer applicants. Graduates of unaccredited institutions not considered. Apply to Office of Graduate Admissions; no specified closing dates. Rolling admission process. Application fee $40; $50 for international applicants. Phone: (479)575-4401; fax: (479)575-5908; e-mail: gradinfo@cavern.uark.edu.

ADMISSION STANDARDS. Selective for most departments. Usual minimum average: 2.75 (A = 4).

FINANCIAL AID. Annual awards from institutional funds: scholarships, fellowships, teaching/research assistantships, Federal W/S, loans. Approved for VA benefits. Apply to appropriate department head, normally before April 1 for assistantships; to Financial Aid Office for all other programs. Phone: (479)575-3806; fax: (479) 575-7790. Use FAFSA. About 35% of students receive aid other than loans from University and outside sources. Aid available for part-time students.

DEGREE REQUIREMENTS. For M.A., M.S., M.M.: 24 semester hours minimum and thesis, or 30 hours minimum, without thesis, at least 30 weeks in residence; final written/oral exam; no language requirement in most cases. For M.B.A.: 30 hours minimum, at least 30 weeks in residence, final exam. For M.Ed.: 33 hours minimum, at least 30 weeks in residence, final exam. For M.F.A.: 60 hours minimum in residence; thesis and creative project; final written/oral exam. For Ed.S.: 60 hours minimum beyond bachelor's, 30 weeks in residence. For Ed.D.: at least three years of full-time residence beyond bachelor's or the equivalent; preliminary written/oral exam; dissertation; final oral exam. For Ph.D.: same as for Ed.D., except reading knowledge of two foreign languages required by some departments.

FIELDS OF STUDY.
Accounting. M.Acc. only.
Adult Education. Ed.D. only.
Agricultural and Extension Education. M.S. only.
Agricultural Economics. M.S. only.
Agricultural Education. M.A.T. only.

Agricultural Food and Life Sciences. M.S.
Agronomy. M.S., Ph.D. only.
Anatomy. At U. of A. M.S., Ph.D.
Animal Science. M.S., Ph.D.
Anthropology. M.A. only.
Applied Physics. M.S. only.
Art. M.F.A.
Biological Engineering. M.S., Ph.D.
Biology. M.A., M.S., Ph.D.
Biomedical Engineering. M.S.B.E.
Business Administration. M.B.A., Ph.D. (finance, management).
Cell and Molecular Biology. M.S., Ph.D.
Chemical Engineering. M.S., Ph.D.
Chemistry. M.S., Ph.D.
Childhood Education. M.A.T. only.
Civil Engineering. M.S., Ph.D.
Communication. M.A. only.
Communicative Disorders. M.S. only.
Comparative Literature. M.A., Ph.D.
Computer Science. M.S., Ph.D.
Computer Systems Engineering. M.S., Ph.D.
Counseling. M.S.
Counselor Education. Ph.D. only.
Creative Writing. M.F.A. only.
Crop, Soil and Environmental Sciences. M.S., Ph.D.
Curriculum and Instruction. Ph.D. only.
Drama. M.A., M.F.A.
Economics. M.A. only.
Educational Administration. M.Ed. only.
Educational Technology. M.Ed. only.
Electrical Engineering. M.S., Ph.D.
Elementary Education. M.Ed., Ed.S. only.
Engineering. M.S.E., Ph.D.
English. M.A., Ph.D.
Entomology. M.A., Ph.D.
Environmental Dynamics. Ph.D.
Environmental Engineering. M.S.
Food Science. M.S., Ph.D.
Foreign Languages and Literature. Includes French, German, Spanish. M.A. only.
Geography. M.A. only.
Geology. M.S. only.
Health Science. M.S., Ph.D.
Higher Education. M.Ed., Ed.S., Ed.D.
History. M.A., Ph.D.
Horticulture. M.S. only.
Human Environmental Sciences. M.S.
Industrial Engineering. M.S., Ph.D.
Information Systems. M.I.S.
Journalism. M.A.
Kinesiology. M.S., Ph.D.
Mathematics. M.A., M.S., Ph.D.
Mechanical Engineering. M.S., Ph.D.
Microelectronics-Photonics. M.S., Ph.D.
Music. M.M. only.
Nursing. M.S.N.
Operational Research. M.S. only.
Operations Management. M.S. only.
Philosophy. M.A., Ph.D.
Physical Education. M.A.T. only.
Physics. M.A., M.S., Ph.D.
Plant Pathology. M.S. only.
Plant Science. Ph.D. only.
Political Science. M.A. only.
Poultry Science. M.S., Ph.D.
Psychology. M.A., Ph.D.
Public Administration. M.P.A. only.
Public Policy. Ph.D. only.
Recreation. M.Ed., Ed.D.
Rehabilitation Counseling. M.S. only.
Secondary Education. M.Ed. only.

Social Work. M.S.W.
Sociology. M.A. only.
Space and Planetary Sciences. M.S., Ph.D.
Special Education. M.A.T., M.Ed.
Statistics. M.S. only.
Telecommunications Engineering. M.S.Tc.E.
Translation. M.F.A. only.
Transportation and Logistics Management. M.T.L.M.
Transportation Engineering. M.S. only.
Vocational Education. M.A.T., Ed.D.

Robert A. Leflar Law Center
Web site: www.law.uark.edu

Established in 1924. Located on main campus. ABA approved since 1928. AALS member since 1927. Semester system. Full-time day only. Special programs: Summer study in Cambridge, England, and St. Petersburg, Russia. Special facility: National Center for Agricultural Law Research and Information. Library: 299,494 volumes, 3574 subscriptions; has LEXIS, WESTLAW.

Annual tuition: resident $5752, nonresident $11,536. On- and off-campus housing available. Total annual cost for all other expenses: $13,752.

Enrollment: first-year 113; full-time 426 (men 56%, women 44%, minorities 26%). Faculty: full-time 30, part-time 8; student to faculty ratio 13.2 to 1. Degrees conferred: J.D., J.D.-M.B.A., J.D.-M.P.A., LL.M. (Agricultural Law).

ADMISSION REQUIREMENTS. LSDAS Law School report, transcripts, current résumé, two letters of recommendation, personal statement, LSAT (no later than February) required in support of application. Interview not required. International applicants submit TOEFL. Preference given to state residents. Accepts transfer applicants. Graduates of unaccredited colleges not considered. Apply to Director of Admissions after September 1, before April 1. Applicants admitted Fall only. Application fee: none. Phone: (479) 575-3102. For LL.M.: Apply to Director of Graduate Programs.

ADMISSION STANDARDS. Selective. Accepts 24% of total annual applicants. Number of applicants 1494; number of acceptance 354; number enrolled 143; LSAT (75% of class have a score at or above 152); GPA (75% of class have a GPA at or above 3.09). *U.S. News & World Report* ranking is in the third tier of all U.S. law schools.

FINANCIAL AID. Scholarships, minority scholarships, grants, Federal W/S, loans. Apply by April 1 to the University's Office of Student Financial Aid. Phone: (479)575-3806. Use FAFSA. About 70% of students receive aid other than loans from School.

DEGREE REQUIREMENTS. For J.D.: satisfactory completion of three-year program: 90 semester hours; transfer credit individually considered. For LL.M.: at least 24 credits beyond the J.D. For M.B.A., M.P.A.: see Graduate School listing above.

William H. Bowen School of Law (72202-5142)
Web site: www.law.ualr.edu

Established 1966. Located in Little Rock. ABA approved since 1969. AALS member since 1970. Semester system. Full- and part-time study. Law library: 289,993 volumes, 3593 subscriptions; has LEXIS, WESTLAW, DIALOG.

Annual tuition: resident $9817, nonresident $19,747; per credit resident $287, nonresident $618. No on-campus housing available.

Enrollment: first-year full-time 89, part-time 54; total full- and part-time 444 (men 51%, women 49%, minorities 15%). Faculty: full-time 21, part-time 11; student to faculty ratio 16.9 to 1. Degrees conferred: J.D., M.D.-M.B.A., J.D.-M.D., J.D., M.P.H.

ADMISSION REQUIREMENTS. LSDAS Law School report, LSAT, transcripts, bachelor's degree, three recommendations, personal statement required in support of application. Preference given to state residents. Accepts transfer applicants. Graduates of unaccredited colleges not considered. Apply to the Director of Admissions by April 15. Admits to Fall semester only. Application fee: none. Phone: (501)324-9439; fax: (501)324-9433.

ADMISSION STANDARDS. Selective. Accepts approximately 16% of full-time and 54% of part-time students. Number of full-time applicants 929, part-time 148; number of full-time acceptance 153, part-time 80; number full-time enrolled 89, part-time 54; LSAT (75% of full-time students have a score at or above 151, part-time 146); GPA (75% of full-time students have a GPA at or above 3.20, part-time 2.90). *U.S. News & World Report* ranking is in the third tier of all U.S. law schools.

FINANCIAL AID. Scholarships available to second- and third-year students, Federal W/S, loans. Apply to Director of Financial Aid by March 1. Phone: (501)569-3035. Use FAFSA. About 58% of full-time and 35% of part-time students receive some financial assistance.

DEGREE REQUIREMENTS. For J.D.: 87 semester hours, at least two years in residence. For M.B.A., M.P.A.: see Graduate School listing above.

College of Medicine
Web site: www.uams.edu

Established 1879. Located in Little Rock (72205-7199) and is part of the University of Arkansas for Medical Sciences. Library: 183,000 volumes, 1500 subscriptions. The University's NIH ranking is 96th among U.S. institutions with 132 awards/grants worth $55,177,142.

Annual tuition: residents $15,565, nonresidents $30,357. On-campus housing available. Phone: (501)686-5850. All single first-year students housed on-campus; 35 apartments for married students. Average figure for all other expenses: $10,000.

Enrollment: first-year class 144; total full-time 593 (men 57%, women 42%, minorities 8%, state residents 94%). Faculty: full-time 190, part-time 190. Degrees conferred: M.D., M.D.-M.S., M.D.-Ph.D. The M.S. and Ph.D. are offered through the Graduate School.

ADMISSION REQUIREMENTS. AMCAS, transcripts, MCAT, interview (all state residents), recommendations required in support of application. Interview by invitation only. Admission to first-year class given almost exclusively to state residents. Apply to the Dean or AMCAS after June 1, before November 1. Does not have EDP. Application fee $50. Phone: (501)686-5354; fax: (501)686-5873.

ADMISSION STANDARDS. Competitive. Accepts about 25% of all applicants. Number of applications 694 (432 out-of-state); number interviewed 315 (66 out-of-state); number of acceptance 173 (18 out-of-state); number enrolled 150 (9 out-of-state). Mean Composite MCAT 9.3; mean UGPA 3.63. *U.S. News & World Report* ranks only the top 50 medical schools for Research and, therefore, did not rank College of Medicine, but did rank it 45th for Primary Care.

FINANCIAL AID. Scholarships, minority scholarships, loans, grants. Assistantships may be available for dual degree applicants. Apply to Dean after notification of acceptance. Phone: (501)686-5813. Use FAFSA (School code: E00600). About 46% of students receive aid other than loans from School.

DEGREE REQUIREMENTS. For M.D.: satisfactory completion of four-year program, a passing grade on Step 1 of USMLE for promotion to third year. For M.S., Ph.D.: see Graduate School listing above.

FIELDS OF GRADUATE STUDY.
Biochemistry and Molecular Biology. M.S., Ph.D.
Clinical Nutrition. M.S.
Communication Sciences and Disorders. Ph.D.
Communicative Disorders. M.S.
Genetic Counseling. M.S.
Health Systems Research. Ph.D.
Interdisciplinary Biomedical Sciences. M.S., Ph.D.
Interdisciplinary Toxicology. M.S., Ph.D.
Microbiology and Immunology. M.S., Ph.D.
Neurobiology and Developmental Sciences. M.S., Ph.D.
Nursing Science. M.N.Sc., Ph.D.
Occupational and Environment Health. M.S.
Pathology. M.S.
Pharmacology. M.S., Ph.D.
Pharmaceutical Sciences. M.S.
Physiology and Biophysics. M.S., Ph.D.

ARMSTRONG ATLANTIC STATE UNIVERSITY

Savannah, Georgia 31419-1997
Web site: www.armstrong.edu

Founded 1935. CGS member. Public control. Semester system. Coed. Library: 187,000 volumes, 1043 subscriptions. About 160 PCs on campus for student use.

Annual tuition: full-time resident $3198, nonresident $11,558; per credit, resident $118, nonresident $350. On-campus housing available for single graduate students. Average academic year housing costs: $5220–$6600 (includes board). Contact Office of Student Affairs for both on- and off-campus housing information. Phone: (912)927-5271. Total University enrollment: 6710.

School of Graduate Studies

Graduate study since 1971. Enrollment: full-time 218, part-time 570. College faculty: full- and part-time 148. Degrees conferred: M.A., M.Ed., M.S.C.J., M.H.S.A., M.S.N., M.S.N.-M.H.S.A., M.S.P.T.

ADMISSION REQUIREMENTS. Two official transcripts, GRE/MAT/GMAT, letter of intent required in support of application. TOEFL required for international applicants. Accepts transfer applicants. Graduates of unaccredited institutions not considered. Apply to Admissions Office at least one month prior to registration. Application fee $15. Phone: (912)927-5377; fax: (912)921-5586; e-mail: graduate@mail.armstrong.edu.

ADMISSION STANDARDS. Relatively open. Usual minimum average: 2.5 (A = 4). Minimum scores GRE 900, MAT 44, GMAT 450.

FINANCIAL AID. Regent's Opportunity grants, fellowships, assistantships, grants, out-of-state tuition waivers, Federal W/S, loans. Approved for VA benefits. Apply to the Dean's Office for assistantships; to Financial Aid Office for all other programs. Use FAFSA. Phone: (912)927-5272; fax: (912)921-7357.

DEGREE REQUIREMENTS. For master's: 30–45 semester hours minimum; at least 24–36 in residence; candidacy; thesis; comprehensive exam. For M.S.N.-M.H.S.A.: 54 credit program.

FIELDS OF STUDY.

COLLEGE OF ARTS AND SCIENCES:
Criminal Justice.
History.
Liberal and Professional Studies.

COLLEGE OF EDUCATION
Adult Education.
Curriculum and Instruction.
Early Childhood Education.
English Education.
Middle Grades Education.
Secondary Education.
Special Education. Includes behavior disorders, learning disabilities.

COLLEGE OF HEALTH PROFESSION:
Communication Sciences and Disorders.
Health Services Administration.
Nursing.
Nursing/Health Services Administration.
Physical Therapy.
Public Health.
Speech/Language Pathology.
Sports Medicine.

SCHOOL OF COMPUTING:
Computer Science.

THE SCHOOL OF THE ART INSTITUTE OF CHICAGO

Chicago, Illinois 60603-3103
Web site: www.saic.edu

Founded 1866. Coed. Private control. Semester system. Associated with The Art Institute of Chicago, the Ryerson and Burnham libraries. Special facilities: Museum of the Art Institute, Center for Advanced Studies in Art and Technology. Library: 216,000 volumes, 2225 current periodicals.

Tuition: per credit $1140. Limited on-campus housing available for single students only, average cost from $8500–$10,500. Contact the Student Affairs Office for off-campus housing information. Phone: (312)345-3527.

Graduate Program

Enrollment: full- and part-time 580 (men 34%, women 66%). School faculty: full-time 16, part-time 40. Degrees conferred: M.F.A., M.A.A.H., M.A.A.T., M.A.T., P.B.C., M.A.A.E., M.S.H.P., M.A.A.A.

ADMISSION REQUIREMENTS. Official transcripts, three letters of recommendation, portfolio (preferably 20 pieces, on slides), statement of purpose required in support of application. GRE required for Art History applicants. Photographs, videocassette, film for Time Arts, Video and Filmmaking. Interview and résumé required for several programs. TOEFL (TWE is required for several degree programs) required for international applicants. Apply to Office of Admission by March 1 for M.F.A. (Studio); at least two months prior to registrations for all other programs. Application fee $80, $100 international applicants. Phone: (800)232-7242.

ADMISSION STANDARDS. Very selective. Decision based primarily on general creativity and visual perception displayed in portfolio.

FINANCIAL AID. Scholarship, grants, Federal W/S, loans. Approved for VA benefits. Apply to the Director of Financial Aid by March 15. Phone: (312)899-5106; e-mail: finaid@artic.edu. Use FAFSA. About 65% of students receive aid other than loans from Institute.

DEGREE REQUIREMENTS. For the M.F.A., M.A.A.T., M.S.H.P.: 60 semester hours minimum, at least 30 in full-time residence (programs worked out with adviser); 48 semester hours in studio work, and 12 semester hours in advanced art history;

thesis for M.S.H.P. For M.A.A.H., M.A.A.E.: 36 semester hours. For M.A.A.A., M.A.T.: 48 semester hours; thesis for M.A.T. For P.B.C.: 30 semester hours.

FIELDS OF STUDY.
Architecture. M.Arch.
Art Education. M.A.
Art Therapy.
Arts Administration and Policy.
Design Object. M.Des.
Historic Preservation. M.S.
Interior Architecture. M.I.A.
Modern Art History, Theory and Criticism.
Studio. Includes painting, drawing, photography, fiber and material studies, sculpture. M.F.A.
Teaching. M.A.T.
Visual and Critical Studies.
Writing. M.F.A.

ASSUMPTION COLLEGE
Worcester, Massachusetts 01615-1296
Web site: www.assumption.edu.

Established 1904. Private control. Roman Catholic. Semester system. More than 190 computers on campus for student use. Library: 240,000 volumes, 1119 subscriptions. Total College enrollment: 2451.

Tuition: per credit $450. No on-campus housing available. Apply to Director of Residential Life for off-campus housing information. Phone: (508)767-7505.

Graduate School

Established 1951. Enrollment: full-time 101, part-time 223. Graduate faculty: full-time 13, part-time 23. Degrees conferred: M.A., M.B.A., C.A.G.S.

ADMISSION REQUIREMENTS. Transcripts, three letters of recommendation, personal essay required in support of application. TOEFL (minimum score 500) required for international applicants. Graduates of unaccredited colleges not considered. Accepts transfer applicants. Rolling admissions policy. Apply to Director of Graduate Enrollment by March 1; Rehabilitation Counseling March 29. Rolling admission process. Application fee $30, Phone: (508)767-7365; fax: (508)767-7387.

ADMISSION STANDARDS. Selective. Usual minimum average: 2.75 overall, 3.0 for Psychology Program, last 60 credits 3.0 (A = 4).

FINANCIAL AID. Fellowships, traineeships, assistantships, loans. Approved for VA benefits. Use FAFSA. Apply for assistantships to the department chair by July 1. Phone: (508)767-7387.

DEGREE REQUIREMENTS. For M.A. (Counseling Psychology): 60 credit program; internship; oral exam. For M.A. (Special Education): 30 credit program. For M.A. (Rehabilitation Counseling): 62–68 credit program; internship. For M.B.A.: 36 credits minimum, with undergraduate degree in business. For C.A.G.S., C.A.P.S.: 30 credits beyond the master's. For C.P.S.: 15 credits beyond master's.

FIELDS OF STUDY.
Business Administration. GMAT for admission. M.B.A., C.A.G.S.
Counseling Psychology. M.A., C.A.G.S.
Rehabilitation Counseling. Includes substance abuse, guidance, psychiatric rehabilitation, supervision of rehabilitation personnel and programs. M.A., C.A.G.S.

School Counseling. M.A., C.A.G.S.
Special Education. M.A., C.A.G.S.

A.T. STILL UNIVERSITY
5850 E. Still Circle
Mesa, Arizona 85206
Web site: www.atsu.edu

ATSU began with the founding of Kirksville College of Osteopathic Medicine in 1892. A School of Health Sciences was established in Mesa, Arizona, in 1995, a School of Health Management in 1999, a School of Dentistry & Oral Health in 2003, and a second Osteopathic Medical School on the Mesa Campus in 2006.

Kirksville College of Osteopathic Medicine
Kirksville Campus
800 W. Jefferson Street
Kirksville, Missouri 63501-1497

Established 1892 by Andrew Taylor Still, the Founder of Osteopathic Medicine, as the first school of Osteopathic Medicine in the U.S. The College is located next to the Kirksville Osteopathic Medical Center and Diagnostic and Treatment. Private control. Semester system. Special facility: Rea Cancer Treatment Center. Library: 87,000 volumes, 906 subscriptions.

Limited on-campus rooms and apartments available for both single and married students. Annual on-campus housing costs: single student $4440, married students $4980. Contact Office of Student Affairs for both on- and off-campus housing information. Phone: (660)626-2788. Medical students tend to live off-campus. Off-campus housing and personal expenses: approximately $16,000.

Annual tuition: $38,000.

Enrollment: first-year class 172, total 683 (men 59%, women 41%, minorities 16%, state residents 18%). Faculty: full- and part-time 90. Degrees conferred: D.O., D.O.-M.B.A., D.O.-M.H.A., D.O.-M.P.H., D.O.-M.S. , D.O.-Ph.D.

ADMISSION REQUIREMENTS. AACOMAS report, supplemental school application, bachelor's degree preferred, transcripts, MCAT, two letters of recommendation from premed advisory committee required in support of application. Interview by invitation only. Graduates of unaccredited college not considered. Apply by February 1. Admits first-year students Fall only. Application fee $60. Phone: (660)626-2237; fax: (660)626-2969; e-mail: admissions@kcom.edu.

ADMISSION STANDARDS. Selective. Accepts about 15% of all applicants. Number of applications 2634 (2517 out-of-state); number interviewed 538 (488 out-of-state); number of acceptance 388 (340 out-of-state); number enrolled 172 (144 out-of-state). Mean Composite MCAT 8.4, mean UGPA 3.47.

FINANCAIL AID. Institutional scholarships, National Health Services Corps Scholarships, Federal W/S, loans including HEAL. Special loan programs for minorities and rural students. Apply by May 1 to Students Affairs Office. Phone: (660)626-2529. Use FAFSA (University code: G02477). About 87% of students receive some form of financial assistance.

DEGREE REQUIREMENTS. For D.O.: satisfactory completion of four-year program. All students must take the National Board of Osteopathic Medical Examination Level I and II prior to the awarding of D.O.

AUBURN UNIVERSITY
Auburn University, Alabama 36849-5122
Web site: www.auburn.edu

Founded 1856. Located 60 miles NE of Montgomery. CGS member. Coed. State control. Semester system. Special facilities: Alabama Microelectronics Science and Technology Center, Advanced Manufacturing Technology Center, Scott-Ritchey Small Animal Research Facility, The Center for the Arts and Humanities, Center for Aging Studies, Detection and Food Safety Center, National Center for Asphalt Technology, National Textile Center, Space Power Institute, Truman Pierce Institute for the Advancement of Teacher Education, Institute for Biological Detection Systems, Pulp and Paper Research and Education Center, Dauphin Island Sea and Gulf Coast Research Laboratories, International Center for Aquaculture. According to The Center at the University of Florida, Auburn in 2004 awarded 161 doctorates which ranked it 90th among all U.S. institutions eligible to award that degree. Library: 2,500,000 volumes, 23,121 subscriptions. Total University enrollment: 24,000.

Annual tuition: full-time resident $4800, nonresident $14,400. On-campus housing for 384 married students, 700 men, 2500 women. Average annual housing cost: $6000 for married students, $4000 ($6500 including board) for single students. Apply to Director of Housing. Phone: (334)844-4580.

Graduate School

Graduate study since 1870. Enrollment: full-time 2391, part-time 1641. Graduate faculty: 920. Degrees conferred: M.S., M.A., M.Acc., M.Ag., M.A.C.T., M.A.E., M.B.A., M.B.C., M.C., M.C.D., M.Ch.E., M.C.E., M.C.P., M.Ed., M.E.E., M.F.A., M.F., M.F.S., M.H.S., M.I.D., M.I.E., M.Mat.E., M.M.E., M.M.I.S., M.Mu., M.P.S., M.Z.S., Au.D., Ed.S., Ed.D., Ph.D.

ADMISSION REQUIREMENTS. Transcripts, GRE required in support of application. GRE Subject Test required for some master's applicants, for most doctoral applicants. GMAT required for M.B.A. Letters of recommendation required by some departments. Accepts transfer applicants. Apply to Graduate School at least six weeks prior to first day of class. Rolling admission process. Application fee $25, $50 for international applicants. Phone: (334) 844-4700; fax: (334)844-4348; e-mail: gradadm@auburn.edu.

ADMISSION STANDARDS. Selective; competitive for some departments.

FINANCIAL AID. Scholarships, fellowships, teaching assistantships, research assistantships, Federal W/S, loans. Apply by February 15 to Dean of the Graduate School for fellowships, to appropriate department head for assistantships. Use FAFSA. About 50% of students receive aid other than loans from University and outside sources. Aid available for part-time students.

DEGREE REQUIREMENTS. For master's: 30–45 hours, at least one semester in residence; thesis/final paper/nonthesis option; final written/oral exam. For Ed.D.: 90 hours beyond the bachelor's, at least two semesters full-time residence; preliminary exam; dissertation; final written/oral exam. For Ph.D.: 60–90 hours beyond the bachelor's, at least two semesters in full-time residence; preliminary exam; dissertation; final written/oral exam; reading knowledge of foreign language required by some departments.

FIELDS OF STUDY.
Accountancy. M.Acc.
Aerospace Engineering. M.A.E., M.S., Ph.D.
Agricultural Economics. M.Ag., M.S., Ph.D.
Agricultural Engineering. M.S., Ph.D.
Agronomy and Soils. M.Ag., M.S., Ph.D.

Anatomy, Physiology and Pharmacology. M.S., Ph.D.
Animal Sciences. Includes behavior, biochemistry and molecular biology, breeding and genetics, growth biology, microbiology, muscle foods, nutrition, reproductive biology. M.Ag., M.S., Ph.D.
Biological Sciences. Includes animal, botany, cell biology, conservation biology, developmental biology, ecology, herpetology, ichthyology, microbiology, molecular biology, neurobiology, ornithology, parasitology, physiology, population genetics, stream biology, systematics evolution, wetland biology. M.S., Ph.D.
Biomedical Sciences. Includes anatomy and histology, animal genetic disease, animal parasitology, cardiovascular physiology, cell and molecular pathobiology, cell and molecular physiology, endocrinology, hermatology, infectious disease, membrane biophysics, neurophysiology, oncology, pathobiology, pharmacology, reproduction, large animal surgery and medicine, toxicology.
Building Science. M.B.C.
Business Administration. M.B.A., M.S.
Chemical Engineering. M.Ch.E., M.S., Ph.D.
Chemistry and Biochemistry. M.S., Ph.D.
Civil Engineering. M.C.E., M.S., Ph.D.
Communication. M.A., M.Com.
Communication Disorders. M.C.D., M.S., Au.D.
Community Planning. M.C.P.
Computer Science and Software Engineering. M.C.W.E., M.S., Ph.D.
Consumer Affairs. M.S.
Counseling and Counseling Psychology. Includes community agency counseling, counselor education supervision, school counseling, school psychology, school psychometry. M.Ed., M.S., Ed.S., Ed.D., Ph.D.
Curriculum and Teaching. Includes agriscience, business, early childhood, elementary, music education (vocal and instrumental), secondary science (biology, chemistry, physics), secondary mathematics, English language arts, history, French, Spanish, reading, social science studies. M.Ed., M.S., Ed.S., Ph.D.
Economics. M.S.
Educational Foundations, Leadership and Technology. Includes administration and supervision of curriculum, adult education, educational administration, educational psychology, higher education administration, library media. M.Ed., M.S., Ed.S., Ed.D., Ph.D.
Electrical and Computer Engineering. M.E.E., M.S., Ph.D.
English. M.A., Ph.D.
Entomology. M.Ag., M.S., Ph.D.
Finance. M.S.
Fisheries and Allied Aquacultures. M.Ag., M.S., Ph.D.
Forestry and Wildlife Sciences. Includes economics, forestry, wildlife sciences. M.F., M.S., Ph.D.
Geology. M.S.
Health and Human Performance. Includes exercise science, health promotion, physical education. M.Ed., M.S., Ed.S., Ed.D., Ph.D.
History. M.A., Ph.D.
Horticulture. M.Ag., M.S., Ph.D.
Human Development and Family Studies. M.S., Ph.D.
Industrial and Systems Engineering. M.I.S.E., M.S., Ph.D.
Industrial Design. M.I.D.
Integrated Textile and Apparel Science. Ph.D.
Large Animal Surgery and Medicine. M.S., Ph.D.
Management. Includes human resource, management information systems, management information technology and innovation, organizational analysis and change. M.M.I.S., M.S., Ph.D.
Marketing and Transportation. M.S.
Materials Engineering. M.Mtl.E., M.S., Ph.D.
Mathematics and Statistics. M.A.M., M.S., Ph.D.
Mechanical Engineering. M.M.E., M.S., Ph.D.
Nursing. M.S.
Nutrition and Food Science. M.S., Ph.D.

Pathobiology. M.S., Ph.D.
Pharmacal Science. M.S., Ph.D.
Pharmaceutical Sciences. Includes medicinal chemistry, pharmaceutics, pharmacology. Ph.D.
Pharmacy Care System. M.S., Ph.D.
Physics. M.S., Ph.D.
Physiology and Pharmacology. M.S., interdepartmental Ph.D.
Plant Pathology. M.Ag., M.S., Ph.D.
Political Science. M.A.
Polymer and Fiber Engineering. M.S., Ph.D.
Poultry Science. M.Ag., M.S., Ph.D.
Psychology. M.S., Ph.D.
Public Administration. M.P.A., Ph.D.
Radiology. M.S., Ph.D.
Rehabilitation and Special Education. Includes early childhood, special education, emotional conflict, learning disability, MR transition, rehabilitation.
Rural Sociology. M.S.
Small Animal Surgery and Medicine. M.S., Ph.D.
Sociology. M.A., M.S.
Spanish. M.A., M.H.S.
Sport Management. M.A., M.S.
Statistics. M.S., M.H.S.
Technical and Professional Communication. M.A., M.S.
Textile Science. M.A., M.H.S.
Urban Forestry. M.A., M.S.
Vocational and Adult Education. M.A., M.H.S.
Wildlife Sciences. M.A., M.S.
Zoology. M.A., M.H.S.

College of Veterinary Medicine (36949-5536)

Web site: www.vetmed.auburn.edu

College began as a department in 1892, became a college in 1907. Special facilities: Canine & Detection Research Institute, Southeastern Raptor Center, Scott-Richey Research Center.

Annual tuition: full-time resident and nonresident contract $11,204, nonresident $32,924. Total other expenses: $15,000.

Enrollment: first-time 94, total 380 (men 28%, women 72%, minorities 2%, state residents 50%). Faculty: full-time 76, part-time 10. Degrees conferred: D.V.M., D.V.M.-M.S., D.V.M.-Ph.D. The M.S. and Ph.D. are offered through the Graduate School.

ADMISSION REQUIREMENTS. VMCAS report, two transcripts (prerequisite courses must be completed by June 1), letters of recommendation, GRE (October Test), narrative statement of purpose required in support of application. Supplemental application required. Interview by invitation only. Does not accept transfer applicants. Applicants must have completed at least three years of college study. Preference given to Kentucky and state residents. Apply to the Dean after August 1, but before October 1. Application fee $25, $50 for international applicants. Phone: (334)844-2685; e-mail: admiss@vetmed.auburn.edu.

ADMISSION STANDARDS. Competitive. Accepts about 10–15% of all applicants. Number of applications 891 (102 Kentucky resident, 641 out-of-state); number enrolled 60 (34 Kentucky resident, 15 out-of-state). Usual minimum UGPA: 3.0 (A = 4). GRE mean score (V + Q) 1130; mean UGPA 3.56.

FINANCIAL AID. Scholarships, fellowships, assistantships, Federal W/S, loans. Apply to Office of Student Financial Aid by March 15. Use FAFSA. About 20% of students receive aid other than loans.

DEGREE REQUIREMENTS. For D.V.M.: satisfactory completion of four-year program. For M.S. and Ph.D.: see Graduate School listing above.

FIELDS OF GRADUATE STUDY.
Anatomy, Physiology & Pharmacology.
Equine Surgery & Medicine.

Food Animal Surgery & Medicine.
Pathobiology.
Radiology.
Small Animal Medicine.
Small Animal Surgery.
Sport Medicine.

AUBURN UNIVERSITY AT MONTGOMERY

Montgomery, Alabama 36124-4023
Web site: www.aum.edu

Founded 1969. Coed. State control. Semester system. More than 285 computers on campus for student use. Library: 675,000 volumes, 790,000 microforms, 5800 current periodicals, 50 PCs. Total campus enrollment: 5100.

Tuition: resident per credit $217, nonresident per credit $575. On-campus housing available. Annual housing cost: $2500–$2850 (room only) for single student; $4500 for married students. Phone: (334)244-3572. Day-care facilities available.

Graduate Studies

Enrollment: full-time 212, part-time 616. Faculty: full-time 139, part-time 26. Degrees conferred: M.B.A., M.P.A., M.Ed., M.P.S., M.S.J.P.S., M.P.G., Ed.S., M.L.A. (Master of Liberal Arts). Joint Ph.D. with Auburn main campus in Public Administration.

ADMISSION REQUIREMENTS. Official transcripts, GRE/MAT/GMAT required in support of application. Interview sometimes required. Accepts transfer applicants. Graduates of unaccredited institutions not considered. Apply to Director of Admissions at least three weeks prior to registration. Application fee: $25. Phone: (334)244-3614; fax: (334)244-3762.

ADMISSION STANDARDS. Selective. Usual minimum average: 2.75 (A = 4).

FINANCIAL AID. Fellowships, assistantships, Federal W/S, loans. Approved for VA benefits. Apply to appropriate department for fellowships, assistantships; to Financial Aid for all other programs. No specified closing date. Phone: (334)244-3564. Use FAFSA.

DEGREE REQUIREMENTS. For M.B.A.: 46–49 credit hours program. For M.Ed.: 30 credit hour program. For M.L.A.: 30 credit hour program; thesis. For M.S.J.P.S.: 30–36 credit hour program; thesis/comprehensive exam option. For M.P.S.: 30 credit hour program; comprehensive exam. For M.S.P.: 50–52 credit hour program; practicum. For M.P.A.: 36 credit hour program; comprehensive exam. For Ed.S.: 30 credits program beyond the master's; comprehensive exam. For Ph.D.: 39 credit program beyond master's (M.P.A.); written and oral exam; dissertation; oral defense.

FIELDS OF STUDY.

SCHOOL OF BUSINESS:
Business Administration. M.B.A.

SCHOOL OF EDUCATION:
Art Education. M.Ed.
Counseling (N–12). Includes counseling and development, school counseling.
Early Childhood Education (P–3). M.Ed., Ed.S.
Educational Leadership. Includes nonschool, educational administrator (N–12). M.Ed.
Elementary Education. (K–6). M.Ed., Ed.S.
Physical Education. Includes exercise science, general physical education (N–12). M.Ed., Ed.S.

Reading Education. Includes reading teacher. M.Ed.
Secondary Education. Includes biology, history, language arts, mathematics, social studies. M.Ed.
Special Education. Includes early childhood special education (B–6), collaborative teacher (K–6), collaborative teacher (6–12). M.Ed., Ed.S.

SCHOOL OF LIBERAL ARTS:
Audiology. D.Au.
Liberal Arts. M.L.A.
Sociology. M.A.S., M.S.S.

SCHOOL OF NURSING:
Nursing. M.S.N.

SCHOOL OF SCIENCES:
International Relations. M.I.R.
Justice and Public Safety. M.S.J.P.S.
Political Science. M.P.S.
Psychology. M.S.P.
Public Administration. M.P.A., Ph.D.

AUGUSTA STATE UNIVERSITY
Augusta, Georgia 30904-2200
Web site: www.aug.edu

Established in 1783 as the Academy of Richmond County, became Augusta College in 1958 and Augusta University in 1996. Public control. Semester system. Library: 454,590 volumes, 3379 subscriptions. About 325 computers on campus for student use. Total University enrollment: 6312.

Annual tuition: per credit resident $122, nonresident $488. No on-campus housing available. For off-campus housing information contact the Office of Student Affairs. Phone: (888)327-8291.

Graduate Studies

Graduate study since 1971. Enrollment: full-time 168, part-time 320. Faculty: full-time 43, part-time 8. Degrees conferred: M.Ed., M.B.A., M.P.A., M.S., Ed.S.

ADMISSION REQUIREMENTS. Transcripts, NTE/WCET/GRE/MAT (Education, Psychology), GMAT (Business Administration), Statement of Goals (Psychology) required in support of application. TOEFL required for international applicants. Accepts transfer applicants. Graduates of unaccredited institutions not considered. Apply to Admissions Office at least four weeks prior to beginning of semester. Application fee $30. Phone: (706)737-1632; fax: (706)667-4355.

ADMISSION STANDARDS. Selective. Usual minimum average: 2.5 (A = 4).

FINANCIAL AID. Scholarships, research assistantships, partial tuition waivers, Federal W/S, loans. Approved for VA benefits. Apply to the Office of Financial Aid. No specified closing date. Phone: (706)737-1431; fax: (706)737-1777. Use FAFSA. About 3% of students receive aid other than loans from College and outside sources.

DEGREE REQUIREMENTS. For M.B.A.: 30–33 credit hour program. For M.Ed.: 36–48 credit hour program; candidacy. For M.P.A.: 30–33 credits; internship option; candidacy; thesis/capstone paper; oral comprehensive exam. For M.S.: two year program; candidacy; internship. Ed.S.: 30 credits beyond the master's.

FIELDS OF STUDY.
Business Administration. M.B.A.
Educational Leadership. M.Ed.
Elementary Education. M.Ed., Ed.S.
Health and Physical Education. M.Ed.
Middle Grades Education. M.Ed., Ed.S.
Political Science. M.P.A.
Psychology. GRE for admission. Fall admission only. M.S.
Public Administration. M.P.A.
School Counseling. M.Ed.
Seconary Education. Includes English, history, mathematics, social studies. M.Ed., Ed.S.
Special Education. Includes behavior disabilities, intellectual disorders, interrelated learning disabilities. M.Ed.

AUSTIN PEAY STATE UNIVERSITY
Clarksville, Tennessee 37040-0001
Web site: www.apsu.edu

Founded 1927. CGS member. Coed. State control. Semester system. Library: 400,000 volumes, 1790 subscriptions. More than 400 computers on campus for student use. Total University enrollment: 8800.

Annual tuition: full-time resident $4936, nonresident $14,248; per credit, resident $340, nonresident $744. On-campus housing available for both married and single graduate students. Average academic year housing costs: $6550 for married students, $2900–$4800 for single students. Apply by May 1. Contact Director of Housing for both on- and off-campus housing information. Phone: (931)221-7444. Day-care facilities available.

Graduate School

Graduate study since 1952. Enrollment: full-time 200, part-time 376. Faculty: full-time 93, part-time 21. Degrees conferred: M.A., M.S., M.A.Ed., M.M., Ed.S.

ADMISSION REQUIREMENTS. Two official transcripts, GRE required in support of School's application. Interview not required. TOEFL required of international students. Accepts transfer applicants. Graduates of unaccredited institutions not considered. Apply to Dean of Graduate School by July 31 (Fall), December 1 (Spring), May 15 (Summer). Rolling admission process. Application fee $25. Phone: (931)221-7414; fax: (931)221-7641.

ADMISSION STANDARDS. Relatively open. Usual minimum average: 2.5 (A = 4).

FINANCIAL AID. Annual awards from institutional funds: minority scholarships, assistantships, Federal W/S, loans. Approved for VA benefits. Apply by April 1 to Dean of Graduate School and appropriate chair for assistantships. Phone: (931)221-7907; fax: (931)221-6305. Use FAFSA. About 20% of students receive aid from University and outside sources. Aid available for part-time students.

DEGREE REQUIREMENTS. For master's: 32–37 semester hours minimum, at least 24 in residence and one semester full-time attendance; research course; recital, performance, comprehensive exam for some programs; thesis or research paper, literacy paper, or field study report; final written/oral exam. For Ed.S.: 30 semester hours minimum beyond the master's; special project.

FIELDS OF STUDY.
Administration and Supervision. Ed.S.
Biology. M.S.
Clinical Laboratory Science. M.S.
Communication Arts. Includes general, corporate. M.A.

Community Counseling. M.A.
Curriculum and Instruction. Includes instructional technology, leadership, mathematics. M.A.Ed.
Educational Leadership Studies. M.A.Ed.
Elementary Education. M.A.Ed., Ed.S.
English. M.A.
Guidance and Counseling. M.S., Ed.S.
Health and Human Performance. Includes exercise science, gerontology, health services, sport administration. M.S.
Management. M.S.
Music. Includes education, performance. M.M.
Nursing. M.S.
Psychology. Includes clinical, industrial/organizational, psychological science, school. M.A., Ed.S (School).
Radiologic Science. M.S.
Reading. M.A.Ed.
Secondary Education. Ed.S.

AZUSA PACIFIC UNIVERSITY

Azusa, California 91702-7000
Web site: www.apu.edu

Founded 1899. Located 25 miles E of Los Angeles. CGS member. Coed. Private control. Library: 185,000 volumes, 1400 current periodicals, 10 PCs. More than 500 computers on campus for student use. Total University enrollment: 8100.

Tuition: per credit hour $440–$750. No on-campus housing for graduate students. Average monthly off-campus housing costs: $700.

Graduate Center

Enrollment: full-time 676, part-time 3000. College faculty teaching graduate students: full-time 206, part-time 135. Degrees conferred: M.A., M.Ed., M.M., M.S., M.A.M.F.T., M.A.H.O.D., M.A.O.M., M.Div., M.H.R.D., M.P.H., M.S., M.A.P.S., M.B.A., Ed.D., Psy.D.

ADMISSION REQUIREMENTS. Official transcripts, references required in support of application. Interviews may be requested by some departments. TOEFL (550 minimum) required for international applicants. Accepts transfer applicants. Graduates of unaccredited institutions not considered. Apply to the Graduate Admissions Office at least two months prior to registration. Application fee $45 (domestic), $65 (international). Phone: (626) 815-4570; fax: (626)815-4545.

ADMISSION STANDARDS. Selective. Usual minimum average for full admission: 3.0 (A = 4) ; 2.5–2.9 needed for provisional admission.

FINANCIAL AID. Fellowships, assistantships, grants, loans. Contact the Office of Student Financial Services for further information. Use FAFSA.

DEGREE REQUIREMENTS. For master's: 32–48 semester hours, at least 26–42 hours in residence; thesis/nonthesis option; final written/oral exam, varies according to program. For Ed.D.: 60 semester hours minimum beyond the master's, at least one year in full-time residence; qualifying exam; dissertation; final oral exam. For Psy.D.: 89 credit program; practicum; dissertation; oral defense.

FIELDS OF STUDY.
Applied Computer Science and Technology. Includes client/server technology, computer information systems, end-user support, technical programming, telecommunications. M.S.
Business Administration. Includes strategic, international, general.

Christian Business and Professional Leaders. M.B.A.
Christian Education. Includes youth ministries. M.A.
College Student Affairs. M.A.Ed.
Curriculum and Instruction in Multicultural Contexts. M.A.Ed.
Divinity. M.Div.
Educational Counseling. M.A.
Educational Leadership and Administration. Includes educational administration, higher education, teaching and learning. Ed.D.
Educational Technology. M.A.
Human and Organizational Development. M.A.H.O.M.
Human Resource Development. M.H.R.D.
International Business. M.B.A.
Language Development. M.A.
Marital and Family Therapy. M.A.M.F.T.
Music. Includes education, performance (conducting, instrumental, piano, vocal). M.M.
Nonprofit Leadership and Theology. M.A.
Nursing. Includes family nurse practitioner, high-risk home health nursing, nursing education, parent/child, parish nursing. M.S.
Organizational Management. M.A.O.M.
Pastoral Studies. Includes urban and intercultural ministries, church development. M.A.
Physical Education. M.Ed.
Pupil Personnel Services. M.A.
School Administration. M.A.Ed.
School Librarianship. M.A.Ed.
Social Science. Includes leadership studies. M.A.
Special Education. M.A.Ed.
Strategic Management. M.B.A.
Teaching. M.A.Ed.
TESOL. M.A., Certificate.

BABSON COLLEGE

Babson Park, Massachusetts 02457-0310
Web site: www.babson.edu

Founded 1919. Located 12 miles from Boston. Coed. Small independent college. Semester system. Library: 130,000 volumes, 1500 subscriptions. About 290 computers on campus for student use. Total enrollment on main campus: 3210.

Tuition: per credit $953. On-campus housing for married and single students. Total average housing costs: $13,000–$20,000. Contact the Office of Campus Life for both on- and off-campus housing information. Phone: (781)239-4438. Apply by June 15.

F.W. Olin Graduate School of Business

Enrollment: full time 451, part-time 1033. Faculty: full-time 91, part-time 65. Degree conferred: M.B.A. (one-year program, two-year program, evening program).

ADMISSION REQUIREMENTS. Official transcripts, undergraduate degree, GMAT, résumé, reference, essays, interview required in support of School's application. TOEFL and official English translation of all pertinent academic documents required of international applicants. Apply to M.B.A. Admissions Office by January 15 (Spring), April 15 (Fall). Rolling admissions process. Application fee $100. Phone: (800)488-4512; fax: (781)239-4194; e-mail: mbaadmission@babson.edu.

ADMISSION STANDARDS. Selective. Usual minimum average: 3.0 (A = 4). GMAT median score: 622. *U.S. News & World Report* ranks Babson in the top 5 of all business schools for part-time study.

FINANCIAL AID. Several forms of financial assistance for full-time M.B.A. students who are U.S. citizens or permanent residents. These awards include Babson Fellows, grants, graduate assistantships, scholarships, Federal W/S, loans. Apply to the Office of Financial Aid by April 15. Phone: (781)239-4219. Use FAFSA (College code: 002121).

DEGREE REQUIREMENTS. For M.B.A.: 45–60 credit hours, depending on previous degree, experience. Advanced standing may be granted for prior business course work. Program can be completed on a full- or part-time basis.

FIELD OF STUDY.
Business Administration.

BALL STATE UNIVERSITY
Muncie, Indiana 47306-1099
Web site: www.bsu.edu

Founded 1918. Located 55 miles NE of Indianapolis. CGS member. Coed. State control. Semester system. Library: 1.4 million volumes, 2937 subscriptions, plus access to online data retrieval services. About 1500 computers on campus for student use. Total University enrollment: 20,300.

Annual tuition: full-time resident $6246, nonresident $16,000; per credit resident $130, nonresident $785. On-campus housing for 600 married students, about 2700 men, 4300 women. Average annual housing cost: $6500 for married students, $6500 (including board) for single student. Apply to Director of Housing. Phone: (765)285-1678. Day-care facilities available.

Graduate School

Graduate study since 1932. Enrollment: full-time 1004, part-time 1633. Graduate faculty: full- and part-time 712. Degrees conferred: M.A., M.A. in Ed., M.S., M.P.A., M.Arch., M.L.A., M.U.R.P., M.B.A., M.M., Ed.S., D.A., Ed.D., Ph.D.

ADMISSION REQUIREMENTS. Transcripts required in support of application. For Ed.S. and doctoral Programs: GRE, letters of recommendation required. TOEFL required for foreign applicants. Accepts transfer applicants. Graduates of unaccredited colleges not considered. Apply to Graduate School's Office of Admissions at least one month prior to registration. Application fee $35 ($40 for international students). Phone (765)285-1300; e-mail: gradschool@bsu.edu.

ADMISSION STANDARDS. Selective. Usual minimum average: 2.8 (A = 4).

FINANCIAL AID. Annual awards from institutional funds: doctoral fellowships, master's graduate assistantships for teaching, research, or appropriate assignment, Federal W/S, loans. Apply to Dean of Graduate School by March 1. Phone: (765)285-5600; fax: (765)285-2173. Use FAFSA. About 10–15% of students receive aid other than loans from University and outside sources. No aid other than loans for part-time students.

DEGREE REQUIREMENTS. For master's: 30–55 semester hours minimum (counseling 48, clinical psychology 45, TESOL 32, historical preservation 55); thesis (required for M.S., except computer science, management, information and communication sciences), research paper, creative project or departmental designated research course included in most majors. For Ed.S.: 30 semester hours minimum beyond the master's, at least 24 in residence and one semester in full-time attendance; thesis included in 30 hours; final written/oral exams. For Ed.D., Ph.D.: 55–65 semester hours beyond the master's, at least 48 in residence and two consecutive semesters, in full-time attendance; internship (counseling psychology); dissertation included in 90 hours; preliminary, final written/oral exam. For D.A.: 90 credits beyond the bachelor's; teaching internship/externship; dissertation; oral exam.

FIELDS OF STUDY.
Accounting. M.S.
Actuarial Science. M.A.
Adult and Community Education. M.A., Ed.D.
Anthropology. M.A.
Applied Gerontology. M.A.
Architecture. M.Arch.
Art. Includes studio, art education, art history. M.A.
Audiology. M.A., Au.D.
Biology. M.A. M.S.
Biomechanics. M.S.
Business Administration. M.B.A.
Business Education. M.A.Ed.
Chemistry. M.A., M.S.
Clinical Exercise Physiology. M.S.
Clinical Psychology. M.A.
Cognitive and Social Processes. M.A.
Communication Studies. M.A.
Computer Science. M.S.
Counseling Psychology. Ph.D.
Creative Writing. M.A.
Criminal Justice. M.A.
Curriculum. M.A.Ed., Ed.S.
Dietetics. M.S.
Educational Administration and Supervision. M.A.Ed., Ed.D.
Educational Psychology. M.A.
Elementary Education. M.A.Ed., Ed.D., Ph.D.
English. M.A., Ph.D.
Executive Development for Public Services. M.A.
Exercise Science. M.A., M.S.
Family and Consumer Sciences. M.A.
Geography. M.S.
Geology. M.A., M.S.
Health Science. M.A., M.S.
Historical Preservation. M.S.
History. M.A.
Human Bioenergetics. Ph.D.
Information and Communication Sciences. M.S.
Journalism. M.A.
Junior High/Middle School Education. M.A.Ed.
Landscape Architecture. M.L.A. only.
Linguistics. M.A.
Management. M.S.
Mathematical Statistics. M.A.
Mathematics. M.A., M.S.
Mathematics Education. M.A.Ed.
Music. Includes conducting, history and musicology, literature, music education, performance, theory and composition. M.A., M.M., D.A.
Natural Resources and Environmental Management. M.A., M.S.
Nursing. M.S.
Physical Education. M.A., M.S.
Physics and Astronomy. M.S.
Physiology. M.A., M.S.
Political Science. M.A.
Public Administration. M.P.A. only.
Public Relations. M.A.
School Psychology. M.A., Ph.D.
School Superintendency. Ed.S.
Science and Science Education. Ed.D.
Secondary Education. M.A.
Social Psychology. M.A.
Sociology. M.A.
Special Education. M.A., M.A.Ed., Ed.D.
Speech Pathology. M.A.
Sports Administration. M.A.
Sports Management. M.A.

Teaching English to Speakers of Other Language (TESOL). M.A.
Technology Education. M.A.
Urban and Regional Planning. M.U.R.P. only.
Wellness Management. M.A., M.S.

UNIVERSITY OF BALTIMORE

Baltimore, Maryland 21201-5779
Web site: www.ubalt.edu

Founded 1925. Coed. Public. Semester system. Special facilities: Hoffberger Center for Professional Ethics, Institute for Publication Design, William Donald Schaefer Center for Public Policy Studies. Library: 389,000 volumes, 8000 subscriptions. Total University enrollment: 4600.

Tuition: per credit hour, resident $498, business $510, doctoral $656, tax $885; nonresident $751, business $770, doctoral $1123, tax $1349. No on-campus housing available.

Graduate School

Enrollment: full-time 516, part-time 960. Faculty: full- and part-time 212. Degrees conferred: M.A., M.B.A., M.P.A., M.S., Certificate, D.C.D., Psy.D., D.P.A. (offered in Washington, D.C.).

ADMISSION REQUIREMENTS. Official transcripts, three letters of recommendation, GMAT (Business), GRE (for some programs) required in support of School's application. TOEFL required for international applicants. Accepts transfer applicants. Graduates of unaccredited schools not considered. Apply to the Office of Graduate Admission by July 15 (Fall), November 15 (Spring). Application fee $30 online, $45 paper, $60 after deadline. Phone: (410)837-4777; fax: (410)837-4793.

ADMISSION STANDARDS. Selective for most departments. Usual minimum average: 3.0 (A = 4).

FINANCIAL AID. Fellowships, assistantships, scholarships, Federal W/S, loans. Approved for VA benefits. Apply by April 1 to Director of Financial Aid. Use FAFSA (School code: 002102). Aid available for part-time students.

DEGREE REQUIREMENTS. For M.A., M.P.A., M.S.: 30–42 credits minimum, at least 24 in residence; thesis/research paper/field experience; final written exam. For M.B.A.: 30 credits minimum, at least 24 in residence. For Certificate: at least 30 credits beyond master's. For D.C.D.: 48 credits beyond master's minimum; written/oral qualifying exam; satisfy competency requirement; major project. For Psy.D.: 42 credits beyond master's minimum; comprehensive exam; doctoral project; practicum. For D.P.A.: 42 credits beyond master's; qualifying exam; final project.

FIELDS OF STUDY.

COLLEGE OF LIBERAL ARTS GRADUATE PROGRAMS:
Applied Psychology. M.S.
Communications Design. D.C.D.
Creative Writing and Publishing Arts. M.F.A.
Criminal Justice. M.S.
Health System Management. M.S.
Human Services Administration. M.S.
Integrated Design. M.F.A.
Interaction Design and Imformation Architecture. M.S.
Legal and Ethical Studies. M.A.
Negotiations and Conflict Management. M.S.
Public Administration. M.P.A., D.P.A.
Publications Design. M.A.

MERRICK SCHOOL OF BUSINESS:
Accounting and Advisory Services. M.S.

Business Administration. M.B.A.
Taxation. M.S.

School of Law (21201-5779)

Web site: www.law.ubalt.edu

Full-time day division established 1969. Semester system. Public control. Special facilities: Center for International and Cooperative Law, Center for Litigation Skills, Center for Children, Families and the Court. Library has LEXIS, CARL, and WESTLAW.

Annual tuition: full-time resident $19,235, nonresident $31,151: part-time resident $8410, nonresident $13,810. On-campus housing only. Total annual cost for all other expenses: $15,394.

Enrollment: first-year class, day 229, evening 94. Total enrollment: day division 726, evening 306. Faculty: full-time 35, part-time 87. Student to faculty ratio 21.9 to 1. Degrees conferred: J.D., J.D.-M.B.A., J.D.-M.P.A., J.D.-M.S. (Criminal Justice), J.D.-LL.M. (Taxation), LL.M. (Taxation), LL.M. (Law of the U.S., for international lawyers), J.D.-Ph.D. (Policy Science).

ADMISSION REQUIREMENTS. LSDAS Law School report, transcripts, LSAT, at least three years of college work, two letters of recommendation, personal statement, résumé required in support of application. Interview not required. Accepts transfer applications. Graduates of unaccredited colleges not considered. Apply to Director of Admission of the School after September 1, before April 1. Admits Fall only. Rolling admission process. Application fee $40. Phone: (410)837-4459; fax: (410)837-4450; e-mail: lwadmiss@ ubmail.ubalt.edu. For LL.M., Phone: (410)837-4200.

ADMISSION STANDARDS. Accepts approximately 30% of full-time and 22% of part-time students. Number of full-time applicants 2417, part-time 673; number of full-time acceptance 727, part-time 146; number full-time enrolled 229, part-time 94; LSAT (75% of full-time students have a score at or above 152, part-time 150); GPA (75% of full-time students have a GPA at or above 2.98, part-time 2.83). *U.S. News & World Report* ranking is in the fourth tier of all U.S. law schools.

FINANCIAL AID. Scholarships, assistantships, Federal W/S, loans. Apply to Office of Financial Aid by April 1; submit copies to Law School Admissions Office. Phone: (410)837-4763. Use FAFSA. About 10% of students receive some form of aid.

DEGREE REQUIREMENTS. For J.D.: satisfactory completion of three-year (day) or four-year (evening) program; 90 semester hours. Transfer credit individually considered. For LL.M.: at least 24 graduate hours beyond J.D. For other master's degrees, see Graduate School listing above. For LL.M. (foreign lawyer): 30-credit, one full-year program.

BANK STREET COLLEGE OF EDUCATION

New York, New York 10025-1120
Web site: www.bankstreet.edu

Founded 1916. Private control. Semester system. More than 50 computers on campus for student use. Special facilities: Early Childhood Four-College Consortium, Infancy Institute, Leadership Center, Midtown West School, The Principals Institute. Library: 128,500 volumes, 1794 subscriptions.

Tuition: per credit, $960. No on-campus housing. For off-campus housing information: contact Dean's Office. Phone: (212)875-4404.

Graduate School

Graduate study since 1930. Enrollment: full- and part-time 966. Faculty: full-time 78, part-time 54. Degrees conferred: M.S. in Ed.,

Ed.M. Dual degrees with Hunter and Columbia schools of Social Work, Parsons School of Design.

ADMISSION REQUIREMENTS. Transcripts, references, personal essay, interview required in support of application. TOEFL required for foreign applicants. Accepts transfer applicants. Apply to Director of Admissions by March 1 (Fall), November 1 (Spring). Application fee $50. Phone: (212)875-4404; fax: (212)875-4678; e-mail: gradcourse@bankstreet.edu.

ADMISSION STANDARDS. Selective. Usual minimum average: 3.0 (A = 4).

FINANCIAL AID. Scholarships, grants, internships, Federal W/S, loans. Apply to the Director of Financial Aid by March 1. Phone: (212)875-4404; fax: (212)875-4678. Use FAFSA (School code: GO2669). About 60% of students receive aid other than loans from College and outside sources.

DEGREE REQUIREMENTS. For M.S. in Ed.: 36–57 credit hours in graduate courses and seminars; 12 credit hours in supervised fieldwork; integrative master's study. For Ed.M.: 36 credits beyond the master's.

FIELDS OF STUDY.
Bilingual Education. Includes early childhood, early childhood special and general, childhood general, middle school general and special.
Child Life.
Childhood Education. Includes general education, special education, bilingual education, museum education, literacy and childhood general education.
Early Childhood. Includes general education, special education, bilingual education.
Educational Leadership. Includes early childhood, mathematical education, museum education, supervision and administration in the visual arts (with Parsons School of Design).
Infant and Parent Development.
Literacy. Includes reading and literacy, teaching literacy, literacy and childhood general education.
Middle School Education (Grades 5–9). Includes general education, special education, bilingual education, museum education.
Museum Education. Includes childhood (1–6), middle school (5–9).
Special Education. Includes infant and parent development, early childhood, bilingual early childhood, middle school, bilingual middle school.

BARRY UNIVERSITY
Miami, Florida 33161-6695
Web site: www.barry.edu

Founded 1940. Coed. Private control. Roman Catholic. Semester system. Library: 233,938 volumes, 2880 subscriptions. More than 368 computers on campus for student use. Total University enrollment: 9200.

Tuition: per credit hour $765, Ph.D. $875. On-campus housing for single students only. Apply to Director, Residential Life. Phone (305)899-3875, or (800)756-6000, ext. 3875. Annual housing cost: $7500–$8500.

Graduate Programs

Enrollment: full- and part-time 3265. Faculty: full- and part-time 295. Degrees conferred: M.A., M.S., M.S.E.C., M.S.N., M.S.W., M.B.A., or M.B.A.-M.S.N., Ed.S., Ph.D.

ADMISSION REQUIREMENTS. Transcripts, GRE/MAT/MCAT/GMAT, three letters of recommendation required in support of University's application. No admission test required for Social Work. TOEFL required for foreign applicants. Interview may be required. Accepts transfer applicants. Apply to Graduate Admissions Office by August 1 (Fall), December 1 (Spring), May 1 (Summer). Application fee $30. Phone: (800)695-2279, (305)899-3100; fax: (305)899-2471; e-mail: admissions@mail.barry.edu.

ADMISSION STANDARDS. Selective. Usual minimum average 3.0 (A = 4).

FINANCIAL AID. Limited to scholarships (M.S.W.), Federal W/S, loans. Approved for VA benefits. Apply to Director of Financial Aid by May 1. Phone: (305)899-3673; fax: (305)899-3104. Use FAFSA. Aid available for part-time students.

DEGREE REQUIREMENTS. For M.A., M.S., M.S.N., M.B.A.: 30–60 semester hours minimum; final comprehensive exam for some programs. For M.S.W.: 60 semester hours, at least 30 in residence; thesis optional. For Ph.D. in Education: 62 semester hours beyond master's; dissertation; final oral/written exam. For Ph.D. in Social Work: essentially the same as for Education except 45 semester hours.

FIELDS OF STUDY.

SCHOOL OF ADULT CONTINUING EDUCATION:
Information Technology. M.S.
Liberal Studies. M.A.

SCHOOL OF ARTS AND SCIENCE:
Clinical Psychology. M.S.
Communication. M.A.
Communication, Executive. M.S.
Communication, Organizational. M.S.
Ministry. D.Min.
Pastoral Ministry for Hispanics. M.A.
Pastoral Theology. M.A.
Photography. M.A., M.F.A.
Psychology. M.S.
School Psychology. M.S.
Theology. M.A.

D. INEZ ANDREAS SCHOOL OF BUSINESS:
Business Administration. Includes concentrations in accounting, finance, health service administration, international business, management, management information systems, marketing.
E-Commerce. M.S.E.C.

ADRIAN DOMINICAN SCHOOL OF EDUCATION:
Counseling. M.S., Ed.S.
Counseling—Leadership and Education. Ph.D.
Culture, Language and Literacy. Ph.D.
Curriculum and Instruction. Ed.S.
Educational Computing and Technology. M.S., Ed.S.
Educational Leadership. M.S., Ed.S., Ed.D.
Educational Technology—Leadership and Education. Ph.D.
Elementary Education. M.S.
Exceptional Student Education. M.S., Ed.S., Ph.D.
Guidance and Counseling. M.S., Ed.S.
Hearing Impairment Education. M.S.
Higher Education Administration—Leadership and Education. M.S., Ph.D.
Human Resources Development and Administration. Includes leadership of not-for-profit/religious organizations. M.S.
Marital, Couple and Family Counseling/Therapy. M.S., Ed.S.
Mental Health Counseling. M.S., Ed.S.
Montessori Early Childhood and Elementary Education. M.S., Ed.S.
PreK/Primary Education. M.S.
Reading. M.S., Ed.S.
Rehabilitation Counseling. M.S., Ed.S.

SCHOOL OF GRADUATE MEDICAL SCIENCES:
Anatomy. M.S.
Physician Assistant—Clinical Medical Science. M.C.M.Sc.
Podiatric Medicine and Surgery. D.P.M.
Public Health. M.P.H.

SCHOOL OF HUMAN PERFORMANCE AND LEISURE SCIENCES:
Movement Science. Includes athletic training, biomechanics, exercise science, sport and exercise psychology. M.S.
Sport Management. M.S., M.S.S.M.-M.B.A.

SCHOOL OF NATURAL AND HEALTH SCIENCES:
Anesthesiology. M.S.
Biology. M.S.
Biomedical Sciences. M.S.
Health Services Administration. M.S.
Occupational Therapy. M.S.

SCHOOL OF NURSING:
Nursing. Includes acute care nurse practitioner, family nurse practitioner, nursing administration, nursing education. M.S.N., M.S.N.-M.B.A.

SCHOOL OF SOCIAL WORK:
Social Work. M.S.W., Ph.D.

Dwayne O. Andreas School of Law
Web site: www.barry.edu/law

Founded 1995. Located in Orlando. ABA approved since 2005. Semester system. Law library: 259,018 volumes, 1723 subscriptions. Library has LEXIS, WESTLAW, DIALOG, OCLC.

Tuition: full-time $27,560, part-time $20,776. Off-campus housing only available. Check Web site for housing information. Annual housing costs approximately $17,600.

Enrollment: full- and part-time 167; total full-time 407, part-time 156 (men 49%, women 51%, minority 29%).

Faculty: Total full- and part-time 31 (men 68%, women 32%, minority 22%). Student to faculty ratio 18 to 1. Degrees conferred: J.D., J.D.-M.A. (Human Resource Development).

ADMISSION REQUIREMENTS. LSDAS Law School report, official transcript, LSAT, two letters of recommendation required in support of application. Interview not required. TOEFL required for all international applicants. Accepts transfer applications. Graduates of unaccredited colleges not considered. Apply to Director of Admission by April 1. Application fee $50. Phone: (866)532-2779.

ADMISSION STANDARDS. Selective. Accepts approximately 35% of full-time and 57% of part-time students. Number of full-time applicants 1960, part-time 138; number of acceptance full-time 681, part-time 78; number enrolled full-time 167, part-time 37; LSAT (75% of full- and part-time students have a score at or above 149); GPA (75% of full-time students have a GPA at or above 2.73, part-time 2.71). The School of Law is unranked by *U.S. News & World Report.*

FINANCIAL AID. Scholarships, grants, Federal W/S, loans. Approximately 75% of full-time and 52% of part-time students received aid other than loans from school funds. For all financial aid apply by April 1 to the Office of Financial Aid. Phone: (321)206-5621. Use FAFSA.

DEGREE REQUIREMENTS. For J.D.: satisfactory completion of three (full-time) or four (part-time) year program, at least 55 credits in residence. For master's, see Graduate School listing above.

BERNARD M. BARUCH COLLEGE OF THE CITY UNIVERSITY OF NEW YORK
New York, New York 10010-5585
Web site: www.baruch.cuny.edu

Established 1919. Formerly a branch of City College, became independent unit in 1968. Municipal control. Semester system. Special facilities: Bert W. and Sandra Wasserman Trading Floor/Subotnick Financial Services Center, Lawrence N. Field Center for Entrepreneurship and Small Business, Weisman Center for International Business, Steven L. New Real Estate Institute, Baruch Survey Research Unit, Center for Innovation and Leadership in Government, Center for the Study of Business and Government, Center on Equality, Pluralism and Policy, Center for Educational Leadership, Robert Zicklin Center for Corporate Integrity, Direct and Interactive Marketing Center. Library: more than 410,000 volumes, 4167 subscriptions. More than 1500 computers on campus for student use. Total University enrollment: 15,756.

Tuition: per credit, city resident $270, non-city resident $500. No on-campus housing.

Graduate Study

Graduate study since 1920. Enrollment: full-time 829, part-time 2083. College faculty: full-time 271, part-time about 259. Degrees conferred: M.B.A., M.P.A., M.S.Ed., M.S.Ed. in H.E.A., M.S. in Business, Ph.D., M.B.A.-J.D. (with New York Law or Brooklyn Law).

ADMISSION REQUIREMENTS. Transcripts, two letters of recommendation, essay, GMAT (M.B.A.), GRE (M.P.A.) required in support of application. TOEFL required for international applicants. Accepts transfer applicants. Apply to Office of Graduate Admissions by July 1 (Fall), December 1 (Spring). Application fee $65. Phone: (646)312-1300; fax: (646)312-1301. E-mail for Zichlin: zichlingradadmissions@baruch.cuny.edu; for Wiessman School of Arts and Science: wsas_graduate_studies@baruch.cuny.edu; for Public Affairs: spa_admissions@baruch.cuny.edu.

ADMISSION STANDARDS. Very selective. Usual minimum average: 3.0 (A = 4). Average GMAT: 540.

FINANCIAL AID. Annual awards from institutional funds: scholarships, assistantships, fellowships, tuition waivers, Federal W/S, loans. Approved for VA benefits. Apply to Office of Financial Aid by May 15 (Fall), December 20 (Spring). Use FAFSA. Phone: (646)312-1360; fax: (646)312-1361. Aid available for part-time students.

DEGREE REQUIREMENTS. For M.B.A.: 54 semester hours minimum, depending on previous academic work. For M.P.A.: 42–45 semester hours minimum, depending on previous academic work; capstone seminar; internship. M.S.: 30–36 semester hours, including specialization courses; thesis/nonthesis option. For Ph.D.: 60 semester hours minimum, at least 38 in residence and two consecutive semesters in full-time residence, one may be required in some departments; written exam; oral/written exam; research methodology; dissertation; final exam.

FIELDS OF STUDY.
Accountancy. M.B.A., M.S.
Business Computer Information Systems. M.S.
Computer Information Systems. M.B.A.
Corporate Communication. M.A.
Decision Sciences. M.B.A.
Economics. M.B.A.
Educational Leadership. M.S.Ed.
Finance. M.S.
Finance and Investments. M.B.A.

Financial Engineering. M.S.
Health Care Administration. M.B.A.
Higher Education Administration. M.S.Ed.
Industrial and Labor Relations. M.S.
Industrial/Organizational Psychology. M.B.A., M.S.
International Auditing: Risk Assessment and Assurance. M.S.
International Business. M.B.A.
Management/Entrepreneurship and Small Business Management. M.B.A.
Management/Operations Management. M.B.A.
Management/Organizational Behavior–Human Resource Management. M.B.A.
Marketing. M.B.A., M.S.
Public Administration. Includes specializations in nonprofit administration, public management, health care policy, policy analysis and evaluation. M.P.A.
Quantitative Methods and Modeling. M.S.
Real Estate. M.B.A., M.S.
Statistics. M.B.A., M.S.
Taxation. M.B.A., M.S.

BAYLOR COLLEGE OF MEDICINE
Houston, Texas 77030
Web site: www.bcm.edu

Founded 1903. Private control. Quarter system. Special facilities: DeBakey Heart Center, Huffington Center on Aging, Center for Medical Ethics and Health Policy. On-campus housing available for married and single students at Texas Medical Center. Total average figure for other expenses $19,718. The College NIH ranking is 21st among U.S. institutions with 585 awards/grants worth $256,809,346. According to The Center at University of Florida, Baylor College of Medicine is ranked 19th in receipt of Federal Research funds with $461,769,000 and is ranked 16th for total College research expenditures with $302,764,000. The College's endowment assets ranks it 50th with a value of $972,351,000. In 2004, 15 of the College's faculty members have been elected to National Honor Academies and this ranks it 56th. The Library: 180,000 volumes, 4500 current subscriptions.

Graduate School of Biomedical Science

Annual tuition: $15,975. For Ph.D. tuition: none, tuition paid for by graduate School, plus a $23,000 annual stipend.

Enrollment: full-time 533 (men 50%, women 50%), postdoctoral fellows 100. Degrees conferred: Ph.D.

ADMISSION REQUIREMENTS. Official transcripts, three letters of recommendation, GRE, résumé, personal statement, research statement essay, interview required in support of application. GRE Advanced test is strongly recommended. TOEFL required for international applicants whose native language is not English. Accepts transfer applicants. Graduates of unaccredited colleges not considered. Apply to the Office of Admissions by January 1 (Fall). Application fee $35.

ADMISSION STANDARDS. Selective. Received approximately 1300 applications, enrolled 100. Average GPA 3.5; GRE scores were greater than the 70th percentile.

FINANCIAL AID. Fellowships, teaching/research assistantships, stipends; apply to appropriate chair after acceptance.

DEGREE REQUIREMENTS. For Ph.D.: 108 quarter hours minimum; preliminary exam; thesis; final oral exam.

FIELDS OF STUDY.
Biochemistry and Molecular Biology.

Bioengineering. In conjunction with Rice University.
Immunology.
Molecular and Cellular Biology.
Molecular and Human Genetics.
Molecular Physiology & Biophysics.
Molecular Virology & Microbiology.
Neuroscience.
Pharmacology.
Structural and Computational Biology and Molecular Biophysics Program. In conjunction with Rice University and the University of Houston.

INTERDEPARTMENTAL PROGRAMS
Cardiovascular Sciences.
Cell and Molecular Biology.
Developmental Biology.
Structural and Computational Biology and Molecular Biophysics.
Translational Biology & Molecular Medicine

Baylor College of Medicine
Web site: www.bcm.edu

Established in Dallas in 1900 as the University of Dallas Medical Department; affiliated with Baylor University in 1903. Located in Houston in 1943. Separated from Baylor University in 1969. Quarter system. Affiliated hospitals: Harris County Hospital District, The Methodist Hospital, St. Luke's Episcopal Hospital, Texas Children's Hospital, Veterans Affairs Medical Center.

Annual tuition and fees: resident $12,752, nonresident $25,882. Near-campus housing available; one residency hall. Medical students tend to live off-campus. Off-campus housing and personal expenses: approximately $14,000–$16,000.

Enrollment: first-year class 168 (EDP 5, M.D.-Ph.D. approximately 10–12 yearly); total full-time 678 (men 53%, women 47%, minorities 36%, state residents 85). Faculty: full-time 1774, part-time/volunteers 357. Degrees conferred: M.D., B.S.-M.D. (with Rice University), M.D.-M.P.H., M.D.-Ph.D., M.S.T.P.

ADMISSION REQUIREMENTS. AMCAS Report, official transcripts, MCAT, a personal statement, three letters of recommendation (one from pre-professional committee) required in support of application. Preference given to state residents. Accepts transfer applicants from both U.S. and foreign schools. Graduates of unaccredited colleges not considered. Has EDP; apply after June 1, before September 1. Interviews are by invitation only and generally for final selection. A second interview is required for M.S.T.P. Dual Degree applicants must apply to and be accepted by both Schools, contact the admissions office for current information and specific admissions requirements. First-year students admitted Fall only. Rolling admission process. Application fee $60. Apply to Office of Admission after June 1, before November 1. School does maintain an alternate list. Phone: (713)798-4842; fax: (713)798-5563. M.S.T.P. contact: (713)798-5264.

ADMISSION STANDARDS. Competitive. Accepts about 6.7% of all applicants. Number of applications 4285 (2909 out-of-state); number interviewed 664 (265 out-of-state); number of acceptance 285 (100 out-of-state); number enrolled 168 (39 out-of-state). Mean Composite MCAT 11.3; mean UGPA 3.80. *U.S. News & World Report* ranking is in the top 20 of all medical schools and top 11 of all primary care medical schools.

FINANCIAL AID. Scholarships, merit scholarship, minority scholarships, Grants-in-Aid, institutional and state loans, HEAL, Alternative loan programs, NIH stipends; Federal Perkins loans, Stafford Subsidized and Unsubsidized, Federal W/S, Service Commitment Scholarships programs are available. Assistantships/fellowships may be available for Dual Degree candidates.

Contact the Financial Aid Office for current information; phone: (713)798-4603. Use FAFSA (Title IV School code #015170), also submit Financial Aid Transcript, Federal Income Tax forms. Approximately 50% of current students receive some form of financial assistance.

DEGREE REQUIREMENTS. For M.D.: satisfactory completion of 4-year program; step 1 and 2 of USMLE optional. For M.D.-Ph.D., M.S.T.P.: generally a seven- or eight-year program. See Graduate listing above.

BAYLOR UNIVERSITY
Waco, Texas 76798
Web site: www.baylor.edu

Founded 1845. CGS member. Located 90 miles S of Dallas/Fort Worth. Coed. Private control. Semester system. Special facilities: Glassock Energy Center, Institute of Environmental Studies, Institute for Famine Research and Alternative Agriculture, Van de Graaff accelerator laboratory. Library: 2,000,000 volumes, 9100 subscriptions. More than 1500 computers on campus for student use. Total University enrollment: 13,975.

Annual tuition: full-time $16,650, per credit $855. On-campus housing available for graduate students. Average academic year housing costs: $3500–$5500 (including board) for single students, $4500–$5500 for married students. Contact Office of the Dean for Campus Life for both on- and off-campus housing. Phone: (254)710-3642, (254)710-1761.

Graduate School

Enrollment: full-time 1076, part-time 247. Faculty: full-time 350, part-time 0. Degrees conferred: M.A., M.B.A., M.B.A.-M.I.M., M.C.G., M.E.S., M.F.A., M.H.A., M.M., M.S., M.S.Ed., M.S.E.C., M.S.S.P.A., M.T., M.P.P.A., M.P.T., M.I.J., Ed.S., Ed.D., Psy.D., Ph.D.

ADMISSION REQUIREMENTS. Official transcripts required in support of School's application. GRE required for many departments, GRE Subject Test for some departments, GMAT for business. Interview required for some departments. TOEFL (minimum score 550, 213 for computer-based version; 600, 250 for Business) required for international students. Accepts transfer students. Graduates of unaccredited institutions not considered. Apply to Graduate School Admission by February 15 for most programs (Fall), December 1 for most programs (Spring). Rolling admissions process. Application fee $40, $50 for Business. Phone: (254)710-3588; fax: (254)710-3870; e-mail: graduate_school@baylor.edu.

ADMISSION STANDARDS. Selective to very competitive. Usual minimum average: 2.75 (A = 4); minimum GRE combined score 1000.

FINANCIAL AID. Annual awards from institutional funds: fellowships, teaching assistantships, research assistantships, general duties assistantships, full and partial tuition waivers, Federal W/S, loans. Approved for VA benefits. Apply to appropriate department chair for fellowships, assistantships; to Director of Student Financial Aid for all other programs. No specified closing date. Phone: (254)710-2611. Use FAFSA. About 70% of students receive aid from School and outside sources.

DEGREE REQUIREMENTS. For M.A., M.M., M.S.: 30 credit hours minimum, at least 24 in residence; thesis/nonthesis option, comprehensive oral exam; reading knowledge of one foreign language for some programs. For M.S. in professional fields: 30

credit hours minimum, at least 24 in residence; thesis/nonthesis option; comprehensive exam. For M.B.A.: 36 credit hours minimum, at least 30 in residence. For Ed.S.: 30 credit hours minimum beyond master's. For Ph.D.: 78 credit hours minimum beyond the bachelor's, at least 48 in residence and two consecutive semesters in full-time attendance; reading knowledge of one foreign language; preliminary exam; dissertation; final oral exam. For Ed.D.: 60 credit hours minimum beyond the master's, at least two consecutive semesters in full-time residence; preliminary exam; dissertation; final oral exam. For Psy.D.: 107 credit hours minimum beyond the bachelor's, plus one year of internship; at least nine consecutive semesters of residence study; no foreign language or dissertation; comprehensive written and oral exam at end of third year to qualify for internship.

FIELDS OF STUDY.
Accountancy. M.Acc.
American Studies. M.A. only.
Anthropology. M.A. only.
Applied Sociology. Ph.D. only.
Behavioral Science. Ph.D.
Biology. M.A., M.S., Ph.D.
Biomedical Engineering. M.S., B.E.
Biomedical Studies. M.S., Ph.D.
Business Administration. GMAT for admission. Includes information systems management, international management. M.B.A., M.B.A.-I.M.
Chemistry. Includes biochemistry. M.S., Ph.D.
Church-State Studies. M.A., Ph.D.
Clinical Psychology. M.S., Psy.D.
Communication Disorders. M.A., M.S.
Communication Studies. M.A. only.
Computer Science. M.S.
Curriculum and Instruction. M.A., M.S.Ed., Ed.D.
Earth Science. M.A.
Economics. Includes international. M.A., M.S.
Education. Includes administration, curriculum and instruction, educational psychology, health, human performance, recreation. M.S., M.A., Ed.S., Ph.D.
English. M.A., Ph.D.
Electrical and Computer Engineering. M.S.E.C.E.
Environmental Biology. M.S.
Environmental Chemistry. M.S.
Environmental Studies. M.S., M.E.S. only.
Exercise, Nutrition and Preventive Health. Ph.D.
Fine Arts (Theater Arts). M.F.A.
Geology. M.S., Ph.D.
Health Care Administration. M.H.A. only. For military personnel only. Offered in San Antonio.
Health, Human Performance, Recreation. M.S.
History. M.A. only.
Information Systems. M.S.
International Economics. M.A., M.S.
International Journalism. M.I.J. only.
International Management. M.I.M.
International Relations. M.A.
Journalism. M.A.
Limnology. M.S.L.
Mathematics. M.A., M.S. only.
Mechanical Engineering. M.S.M.E.
Museum Studies. M.A.
Music. Includes church music, composition, conduction, education, history and literature, theory, performance, piano pedagogy, string pedagogy; qualifying exam. M.M. only.
Nursing. Includes family, patient care management, administration and management, neonatal, nursing leadership.
Philosophy. M.A., Ph.D.
Physical Therapy. M.P.T. only. For military personnel only. Offered in San Antonio.
Physics. M.S., Ph.D.

Political Science. Includes international relations, public policy and administration. M.A., M.P.P.A.
Psychology. M.A., Psy.D., Ph.D. only.
Religion. M.A., Ph.D.
Social Work. M.S.W.
Sociology. M.A. only.
Spanish. M.A.
Statistics. M.A., Ph.D.
Taxation. M.T.

School of Law
Web site: law.baylor.edu

Founded 1857, the oldest law school in Texas. ABA approved since 1931. AALS member since 1932. Quarter system. Law library 224,929 volumes, 2456 subscriptions. Library has LEXIS, WESTLAW, DIALOG, OCLC.

Annual tuition: $31,246. On-campus housing available. Apply to Baylor Rental properties.

Enrollment: first-year class 63 (Fall), 77 (Spring); total full-time 435 (men 55%, women 45%, minorities 14%), part-time 8. Faculty: full-time 22, part-time 38. Student to faculty ratio 17 to 1. Degrees conferred: J.D., J.D.-M.B.A., J.D.-M.P.P.A., J.D.-M.Tax.

ADMISSION REQUIREMENTS. LSDAS Law School report, transcripts indicating at least 90 semester hours of college study. LSAT required in support of application. TOEFL required for all international applicants. Interview not required. Accepts transfer applications. Graduates of unaccredited colleges not considered. Apply to Director of Admissions and Scholarship Coordinator by November 1 (Spring), February 1 (Summer), March 1 (Fall). Application fee $40. Phone: (254)710-7617; fax: (254)710-2316.

ADMISSION STANDARDS. Selective. Accepts 20–25% of total annual applicants. Number of applicants 2437; number of acceptance 520; number enrolled 80; LSAT (75% of class have a score at or above 161); GPA (75% of class have a GPA at or above 3.510). *U.S. News & World Report* ranking is in the second tier of all Law Schools with a rank of 53rd.

FINANCIAL AID. Scholarships (one-third full tuition), Texas Tuition Equalization grants, Federal W/S, loans. About 80% of students receive aid other than loans from school funds. For all financial aid, apply by May 1 to the Director of Admissions and Scholarship Coordinator. Phone: (254)710-2611. Use FAFSA (School code: 003545).

DEGREE REQUIREMENTS. For J.D.: satisfactory completion of three-year program, at least 120 quarter hours minimum. Transfer credit individually considered. For other master's: see Graduate School listing above.

BEMIDJI STATE UNIVERSITY
Bemidji, Minnesota 56601-2699
Web site: www.bemidjistate.edu

Founded 1919. Located 230 miles NW of Minneapolis. Coed. State control. Semester system. Library: 250,000 volumes, 900 subscriptions. More than 400 computers on campus for student use. 721,000 microforms. Special facilities: Freshwater Aquatics Laboratory, Center for Environmental Studies.

Tuition: per credit, resident $295, nonresident $315. On-campus housing for 40 men, 32 women; none for married students. Average annual housing cost: $3880 (including board). Apply to Director of Housing by April 25. Phone: (218)755-3750. Day-care facilities available.

Graduate Studies
Enrollment: full-time 36, part-time 204 (men 30%, women 70%). Graduate faculty: full- and part-time 62. Degrees conferred: M.A., M.S., M.S.Ed., M.Sp.Ed.

ADMISSION REQUIREMENTS. Transcripts, GRE, two letters of recommendation required in support of application. TOEFL required for foreign applicants. Interview not required. Accepts transfer applicants. Apply to Director of Graduate Studies by May 1. Application fee $20. Phone: (218)755-2027; fax: (218)755-3788.

ADMISSION STANDARDS. Selective for some departments, relatively open for most. Usual minimum average: 3.0, 2.75 for provisional status (A = 4).

FINANCIAL AID. Annual awards from institutional funds: teaching, research assistantships, Federal W/S, loans. Apply to department chair; no specified closing date. Use FAFSA. Phone: (218)755-2034. Less than 10% of students receive aid other than loans from University and outside sources. No aid for part-time students.

DEGREE REQUIREMENTS. For master's: 30–32 credit hours minimum, at least 30 in residence; competency requirement; research paper or thesis; final oral exam.

FIELDS OF STUDY.
Biology. M.A.
Counseling Psychology. M.S.
Education. Includes elementary, curriculum and instruction, mathematics, music, special. M.S.Ed.
English. M.A., M.S.
Environmental Studies. M.S.
Industrial Technology. M.S.
Mathematics. M.S.
Physical Education. M.S.
Science. M.S.
Special Education. M.S., M.Sp.Ed.
Sports Studies. Includes physical education. M.S.
Teacher Education. M.S.

BENNINGTON COLLEGE
Bennington, Vermont 05201-9993
Web site: www.bennington.edu

Founded 1932. Located 40 miles E of Albany, New York. Coed. Private control. Semester system. Special facilities: Regional Center for Language and Culture, Visual and Performing Arts Center. Library: 128,413 volumes, 500 subscriptions. About 60 computers on campus for student use. Total College enrollment: 725.

Annual tuition: $20,640. On-campus housing available. Average academic year housing costs: approximately $6330 (including board) for single student; $3500 for married students. Contact Director of Residential Life for both on- and off-campus housing information. Phone: (802)442-5401.

Graduate Programs
Enrollment: full-time 138, part-time 18. Faculty: full-time 41, part-time 11. Degree conferred: M.A.L.S., M.A.T., M.F.A.

ADMISSION REQUIREMENTS. Official transcript, references, interview/audition in support of application. Accepts transfer applicants. Apply to Assistant Director of Admission by February 1 (M.F.A.), March 1 (M.A.T.), July 1 (M.A.L.S.). Application fee $60. Phone: (800)833-6845 or (802)440-4312; fax: (802)440-4320; e-mail: admission@bennington.edu.

ADMISSION STANDARDS. Selective. Usual minimum average: 2.75 (A = 4).

FINANCIAL AID. Teaching assistantships, Federal W/S, loans. Apply to the appropriate department for assistantships; to Financial Aid office for all other programs. Apply by April 1. Use FAFSA.

DEGREE REQUIREMENTS. For master's: four semesters of study, master's project.

FIELDS OF STUDY.
Art.
Creative Writing.
Dance.
Drama.
Liberal Arts.
Literature.
Music.
Teaching a Second Language. Includes French, Spanish.
Visual Arts.
Writing.

BENTLEY COLLEGE
Waltham, Massachusetts 02154-4705
Web site: www.bentley.edu

Founded 1917. Located 9 miles W of Boston. Private control. Semester system. Special facilities: Center for Excellence in Teaching, Center for Business Ethics, New England Heritage Center, Center for Financial Analysis and Risk. Library: 208,000 volumes, 9300 subscriptions; more than 2500 computers on campus for student use.

On-campus rooms and apartments available for both single and married students. Annual on-campus housing cost: single students $7830 (room only), $13,500 (room and board); married students $13,000. Contact Graduate Housing Office for both on- and off-campus housing information; phone: (781)891-2348. Estimated annual budget for tuition, room and board, and personal expenses: approximately $30,065. Total College enrollment: approximately 5565.

McCallum Graduate School of Business

Established 1974. Semester system. Special programs: foreign exchange programs (Estonia, Japan, the Netherlands); internships. Annual tuition: full-time $27,330, part-time per three credit course $2733; evening full-time $18,640.

Enrollment: total full-time 235, part-time 1057. Faculty: 270 full-time, 205 part-time. Degrees conferred: M.B.A. (full-time, part-time, day, evening), M.S.A., M.S.A.I.S. (Accounting Information Systems), M.S.C.F. (Corporate Finance), M.S.F.P. (Financial Planning), M.S.G.F.A. (Global Financial Analysis), M.S.H.F.I.D. (Human Factors in Information Design), M.S.I.A.M. (Information Age Marketing), M.S.I.T. (Information Technology), M.S.T. (Taxation).

ADMISSION REQUIREMENTS. Bachelor's degree from a recognized institution of higher education required. Submit an M.B.A. application (electronic application available), GMAT results (will accept GMAT test results from the last five years, latest acceptable date is August), two official transcripts from each undergraduate/graduate school attended, two letters of recommendation, three essays, current résumé (prefers at least four years of work experience), and an application fee of $50 to the Admissions office. In addition, international students (whose native language is other than English) should submit a TOEFL report (minimum score 580), certified translations and evaluations of all official transcripts; recommendation should be in English or with certified translations and proof of sufficient financial resources for two years of academic study. Students are admitted Fall, Spring, and Summer. Both U.S. citizens and International applicants apply by March 15 (Fall), November 1 (Spring), March 1 (Summer). On-campus visits and interviews encouraged prior to the admissions committee reviewing completed application; interview required for Information Age Marketing. Admissions Committee will consider applicants with some academic course work deficiencies. Rolling admissions process, notification is made within three weeks of receipt of completed application and supporting documents. Admissions Office phone: (781)891-2108; fax: (781)891-2464; e-mail: gradadm@bentley.edu.

ADMISSION STANDARDS. For M.B.A.: number of applicants 1268; number accepted 918; number enrolled 490; median GMAT: 545; median GPA: 3.2 (A = 4).

FINANCIAL AID. Scholarships, International Grants, graduate and departmental assistantships, Federal Perkins loans, Stafford Subsidized and Unsubsidized loans, Federal W/S available. Financial aid is available for part-time study. Financial aid may be available for international students. Financial Aid applications and information are generally available at the on-campus visit/interview or after January 1; apply by June 1. Submit Graduate Assistantship application, résumé, two letters of reference directly to Graduate School of Business. Contact the College's Financial Aid Office for current need-based financial aid information. Phone: (781)891-3168. For most financial assistance and all Federal programs submit FAFSA (College code: 002124) or CSS profile. Approximately 13% of students receive some form of financial assistance.

DEGREE REQUIREMENTS. For M.B.A.: 36–59 credit program (10–19 courses, up to 9 courses may be waived); Internship; degree program must be completed in seven years. For M.S. degrees: 30-credit program; internship option for some programs.

FIELDS OF STUDY.
Accounting. M.S.A.
Accounting Information System. M.S.A.I.S.
Business Administration. Includes concentrations in accountancy, business communication, business data analysis, business economics, business ethics, entrepreneurial studies, environmental management, finance, international business, management, management information systems, management of technology, marketing, operations management, taxation. M.B.A.
Business Ethics. M.B.A.
Corporate Finance. M.S.C.F.
Finance. M.S.F.
Financial Planning. M.S.F.P.
Global Financial Analysis. M.S.G.F.A.
Human Factors in Information Design. M.S.H.F.I.D.
Information Age Marketing. M.S.I.A.M.
Information Technology. M.S.I.T.
Marketing Analysis. M.S.M.A.
Real Estate Management. M.S.R.E.M.
Taxation. M.S.T.

BERRY COLLEGE
Mount Berry, Georgia 30149-0159
Web site: www.berry.edu

Founded 1902. Coed. Semester system. Library: 321,335 volumes, 1792 subscriptions. More than 134 computers on campus for student use. Total College enrollment: 1970.

Tuition: per credit $318. No on-campus housing available for graduate students. Contact Director of Residence Life for off-campus housing information.

Graduate Studies

Enrollment: full-time 17, part-time 125. Faculty: full-time 1, part-time 24. Degrees conferred: M.B.A., M.Ed.

ADMISSION REQUIREMENTS. Official transcript, bachelor's degree, two letters of reference, GMAT (Business) required in support of application. TOEFL required for international applicants. Accept transfer applicants. Graduates of unaccredited institutions not considered. Apply to Dean of Admissions by May 1 (Fall), October 1 (Spring), February 1 (Summer). Rolling admission process. Application fee $25 (international applicants $30). Phone: (706)236-2215; fax: (706)236-2178.

ADMISSION STANDARDS. Selective. Usual minimum average: 3.0 (A = 4), with above average scores.

FINANCIAL AID. Assistantships, loans. Apply to Office of Financial Aid by April 1. Phone: (706)236-2276.

DEGREE REQUIREMENTS. For M.B.A.: 33 semester hours minimum; thesis not required. For M.Ed.: 33 semester hours minimum; thesis/nonthesis option.

FIELDS OF STUDY.
Administrative Leadership.
Business Administration.
Early Childhood Education.
Middle Grades Education.
Reading.
Secondary Education.
Teacher-Research.

BLOOMSBURG UNIVERSITY OF PENNSYLVANIA
Bloomsburg, Pennsylvania 17815-1301
Web site: www.bloomu.edu

Founded 1839. Located 70 miles N of Harrisburg. CGS member. Coed. State control. Semester system. Special facilities: Institute for Comparative and International Management Studies, Institute for Interactive Technologies, Reading Clinic, Speech and Hearing Clinic. Library: 406,647 volumes, 2402 subscriptions. More than 1250 computers on campus for student use. Total University enrollment: 8570.

Tuition: per hour, resident $327, nonresident $523. Limited on-campus housing for graduate students. Average academic year housing costs: $5376 (including board). Contact Office of Residence Life for both on- and off-campus housing information. Phone: (570)389-4088.

School of Graduate Studies
Web site: www.bloomu.edu/gradschool

Graduate study since 1960. Enrollment: full-time 327, part-time 351. College faculty teaching graduate students: full-time 178. Degrees conferred: M.A., M.B.A., M.Ed., M.S., M.S.N. Supervisory Certificates are also granted.

ADMISSION REQUIREMENTS. Transcripts, MAT, GRE, NTE, GMAT (Business Administration), interview required in support of School's application. TOEFL required for international applicants. Accepts transfer applicants. Graduates of unaccredited institutions not considered. Apply to Office of Graduate Studies and Research at least six weeks prior to registration. Application fee $30. Phone: (570)389-4015; fax: (570)389-3054.

ADMISSION STANDARDS. Relatively open. Usual minimum average 2.5 for admission, 3.0 for degree candidacy (A = 4).

FINANCIAL AID. Scholarships, research assistantships, teaching assistantships, Federal W/S, loans. Apply to Assistant Vice President Graduate Studies and Research at least one month prior to registration for assistantships; contact the Financial Aid Office for all other programs. Use FAFSA. Phone: (570)389-4498; fax: (570)389-4795. About 15% of students receive aid other than loans from College and outside sources. Aid available for part-time students.

DEGREE REQUIREMENTS. For M.A., M.Ed., M.S.: 30 credits minimum; thesis or research project; final oral/written exam. For M.S.N.: 39 credits minimum; thesis. For M.B.A.: 36 credits minimum.

FIELDS OF STUDY.
Accounting. M.A.C.
Art. Includes art studio, art history. M.A.
Audiology. M.S.
Biology. M.Ed., M.S.
Business Administration. M.B.A.
Business Education. M.Ed.
Curriculum and Instruction. M.Ed.
Early Childhood Education. M.Ed.
Education of the Deaf/Hard of Hearing. M.S.
Elementary Education. M.Ed.
Exercise Science and Adult Fitness. M.S.
Guidance Counseling and Student Affairs. M.Ed.
Instructional Technology. M.S.
Nursing. M.S.N.
Radiologist Assistant. M.S.
Reading. M.Ed.
Special Education. Includes mentally retarded, learning disabilities, behavioral disorders, and exceptional persons. M.S.
Speech Pathology. M.S.

BOISE STATE UNIVERSITY
Boise, Idaho 83725-0399
Web site: www.idbsu.edu

Established 1932. Coed. Public control. CGS member. Semester system. Library: 505,000 volumes, 4800 subscriptions. More than 900 computers on campus for student use.

Annual tuition: resident $5240; nonresident $13,408; per credit for both $272. There are 170 units available for full-time married students. Apply by August 1. Annual housing cost for single students: $5938 (including board). Monthly housing cost for married students: $450–$525. Phone: (208)447-1001.

Graduate College

Graduate study since 1969. Enrollment: full-time 306; part-time 942. Graduate faculty: full-time 265, part-time 99. Degrees conferred: M.A., M.B.A., M.H.S., M.S., M.M., M.P.A., M.S.W., Ed.D., Ph.D.

ADMISSION REQUIREMENTS. Transcripts, GMAT/GRE/MAT required in support of application. TOEFL required for foreign applicants. Accepts transfer applicants. Graduates of unaccredited institutions not considered. Apply to Graduate Admissions Office at least two months prior to registration. Application fee $20. Phone: (800)824-7017 or (208)426-2789.

ADMISSION STANDARDS. Selective. Usual minimum average: 2.75 (3.0 last two years) (A = 4).

FINANCIAL AID. Graduate assistantships, Federal W/S, loans. Apply to Dean, Graduate College, phone: (208)426-3647, or Department Chair for assistantships; to Director of Financial Aid for W/S, loans; no specified closing date. Phone: (208)422-3085. Use FAFSA.

DEGREE REQUIREMENTS. For master's: 30 semester hours minimum, at least 21 in residence; thesis/project; final oral written exam. For M.S.F.: 30 semester hours, at least 24 in residence; thesis/project option. For M.S.W.: full-time two-year program. For Ed.D.: six semesters minimum beyond the bachelor's, at least two in residence; qualifying exam; dissertation; final oral exam.

FIELDS OF STUDY.

COLLEGE OF ARTS ANDS SCIENCES:
Art. Includes visual Arts. M.F.A.
Art Education. M.A.
Biology. Includes raptor biology. M.A., M.S.
Creative Writing. M.F.A.
Earth Sciences. M.S.
English. Includes education, rhetoric and composition. M.A.
Geology. M.S.
Geophysics. M.S., Ph.D.
Geosciences. Ph.D.
Hydrologic Sciences. M.S.
Interdisciplinary Studies. M.A., M.S.
Mathematics. Includes mathematics education. M.S.
Music. Includes education, pedagogy, performance. M.M.
Technical Communication. M.A.

COLLEGE OF BUSINESS AND ECONOMICS:
Accountancy. Includes taxation. M.S.
Business Administration, Includes Information Technology Management. M.B.A.

COLLEGE OF EDUCATION:
Athletic Administration. M.P.E.
Bilingual Education. M.Ed.
Counseling. M.A.
Curriculum & Instruction. Includes physical education pedagogy. M.A., Ed.D.
Early Childhood Studies. M.A. Ed., M.Ed.
Educational Leadership. M.Ed.
Educational Technology. M.E.T., M.S.
English as a Second Language. M.Ed.
Exercise & Sport Studies. Includes behavioral studies, biophysical, socio-historical studies. M.S.
Reading. M.A. Ed
Special Education. M.Ed.

COLLEGE OF ENGINEERING:
Civil Engineering. M.Engr., M.S.
Computer Engineering. M.Engr., M.S.
Computer Science. M.S.
Electrical and Computer Engineering. Ph.D.
Electrical Engineering. M.Engr., M.S.
Instructional & Performance Technology. M.S.
Materials Science and Engineering. M.Engr., M.S.
Mechanical Engineering. M.S.

COLLEGE OF HEALTH SCIENCE:
Environmental Health. M.H.S.
General Research. M.H.S.
Health Policy. M.H.S.
Health Promotion. M.H.S.
Health Services Leadership. M.H.S.
Nursing. M.N., M.S.N.

COLLEGE OF SOCIAL SCIENCES AND PUBLIC AFFAIRS:
Anthropology. M.A.
Applied Anthropology. M.A.A.
Applied Historical Research. M.A.H.R.
Communication. M.A.

Criminal Justice Administration. M.A.
Environmental and Natural Resources Administration. M.P.A.
General Public Administration. M.P.A.
History. M.A.
State and Local Government Policy and Administration. M.P.A.
Social Work. M.S.W.

BOSTON COLLEGE
Chestnut Hill, Massachusetts 02467-3800
Web site: www.bc.edu

Founded 1863. CGS member. Located 6 miles from downtown Boston. Private control. Catholic affiliation. Semester system. Special facilities: Center for the Child, Family and Community Partnerships, Center for International Higher Education, Center for Corporate Community Relations, Center for East Europe, Russia and Asia, Center for Irish Management, Center for Educational Policy, Center for Work and Family, Institute for Medieval Philosophy and Theology, Institute for Scientific Research, Jesuit Institute, Lonergan Center, Management Center, Mathematics Institute, National Urban League Education Division, Small Business Development Center, Social Welfare Research Institute, Weston Observatory. More than 1000 computers on campus for student use. According to The Center at University of Florida, the College's endowment assets ranks it 40th with a value of $1,150,148,000. In 2004, 2 of the University's faculty members have been elected to National Honor Academies and this ranks it 117th among all U.S. institutions. The Library: approximately 2,200,000 volumes, 22,266 subscriptions. Total University enrollment: 13,755.

Tuition: per hour $736. No on-campus housing for graduate students. Apply to Housing Office for off-campus housing information. Phone: (617)552-3075.

Graduate School of Arts and Sciences

Enrollment: full-time 363, part-time 736. Faculty: full- and part-time 404. Degrees conferred: M.A., M.S., M.A.T., M.S.T., C.A.G.S., Ph.D.

ADMISSION REQUIREMENTS. Transcripts, two letters of recommendation required in support of application. GRE General/Subject Tests, MAT required by some departments. Interview not required. TOEFL required for international applicants. Accepts transfer applicants. Apply to the Graduate Office by February 15, contact departments for Spring admissions deadlines. Application fee $70. Phone: (617)552-3265; fax: (617)552-3700.

ADMISSION STANDARDS. Selective for most departments, relatively open to very competitive for the others. Usual minimum average: 3.0 (A = 4).

FINANCIAL AID. Scholarships, teaching fellowships, assistantships, tuition waivers, Federal W/S, loans. Apply to the University Financial Aid Office by March 1. Phone: (617)552-4987. Use FAFSA. About 30% of students receive aid other than loans from School and outside sources. No aid for part-time students.

DEGREE REQUIREMENTS. For master's: 30 semester hours minimum, at least 24 in residence; language requirement varies by department; final oral/written exam. For C.A.G.S.: 30 credits beyond the master's; final exam. For Ph.D.: 60 hours minimum beyond bachelor's, at least one year in full-time residence; comprehensive exam; dissertation; final oral exam.

FIELDS OF STUDY.
American Politics. M.A., Ph.D.
Biblical Studies. M.A.

Biology. M.S., M.S.T., Ph.D.
Chemistry. M.S., M.S.T., Ph.D.
Classics. M.A.
Comparative Politics. M.A., Ph.D.
Comparative Theology. Ph.D.
Developmental Psychology. M.A., PH.D.
Economics. M.A., Ph.D.
English. M.A., M.A.T., Ph.D.
European National Studies. M.A.
French Literature and Culture. M.A., M.A.T., Ph.D., M.A.-
    M.B.A.
Geology. M.S., M.S.T., M.S.-M.B.A.
Geophysics. M.S., M.S.-M.B.A.
Greek. M.A.
Hispanic Literature and Culture. M.A., M.A.T., Ph.D., M.A.-
    M.B.A.
History. M.A., M.A.T.
History of Christian Life and Thought. Ph.D.
International Relations. M.A., Ph.D.
Irish Studies. M.A.
Italian Literature and Culture. M.A., M.A.-M.B.A.
Latin. M.A., M.A.T.
Linguistics. M.A., M.A.-M.B.A.
Mathematics. M.A., M.S.T., M.A.-M.B.A.
Medieval Studies. M.A.
Medieval Studies/Romance Languages. Ph.D.
Pastoral Ministry. M.A., M.A.-M.S.W., M.A.-M.S.
Philosophy. M.A., Ph.D.
Physics. M.S., M.S.T., Ph.D.
Political Science. M.A., Ph.D., M.A.-M.B.A.
Psychology. Ph.D.
Religion and Education. Ph.D.
Romance Literature. Ph.D.
Russian. M.A., M.A.-M.B.A.
Slavic Studies. M.A., M.A.-M.B.A.
Social and Cultural Psychology. M.A., Ph.D.
Sociology. M.A., Ph.D., M.A.-M.B.A., Ph.D.-M.B.A.
Systematic Theology. Ph.D.
Theological Ethics. Ph.D.
Theology. M.A., Ph.D.

Lynch Graduate School of Education

Enrollment: full-time 608, part-time 350. Faculty: full-time 58, part-time 47. Degrees conferred: M.A., M.Ed., M.A.T., M.S.T., M.A.-J.D., M.A.-M.Ed. (Pastoral Ministry and Educational Administration), M.Ed.-J.D., M.A.-M.A. (Counseling and Pastoral Ministry), Ph.D.

ADMISSION REQUIREMENTS. Official transcripts, GRE for M.S.T. and Ph.D. candidates, GRE or MAT for all other programs, three letters of reference, statement of purpose required in support of School's application. Résumé and writing sample required for all doctoral candidates. Interview is by invitation for Ph.D. TOEFL required for international applicants. Two applications required for all joint degree programs and observe deadlines for both schools. Apply to Office of Admissions by February 1, most programs. Exceptions are Higher Education, Counseling, Educational Psychology, January 1; Counseling Psychology, December 15. Application fee $70. Phone: (617)552-4214; fax: (617)552-0812; e-mail: gsoe@bc.edu

ADMISSION STANDARDS. Selective. Accepts about 50% of all applicants. *U.S. News & World Report* ranking was 21st in all Schools of Education.

FINANCIAL AID. Scholarships, fellowships, assistantships, Federal W/S, loans. Apply by March 1 to the School's Financial Aid Office for School-sponsored funds, to the College's Financial Aid Office for all Federal programs. Phone: (800)294-0294. Use FAFSA and College's FAF.

DEGREE REQUIREMENTS. For M.A. (Counseling Psychology): 60 credit hour program; practicum. For all other M.A.s: 30 credit hour programs. For M.Ed.: 30 credit hour program; comprehensive exam. For M.A.T., M.S.T.: 37–46 credit hours; practicum; comprehensive exam. For Ph.D.: 84 credit hour program; comprehensive exam; candidacy, dissertation; oral exam.

FIELDS OF STUDY.
Applied Development and Educational Psychology. Includes Early childhood specialist. M.A., Ph.D.
Counseling Psychology. Ph.D.
Counseling Psychology/Mental Health Counselor. Includes school counseling. M.A.
Curriculum & Instruction. M.Ed.
Early Childhood Education. M.Ed.
Education (G8–12). Includes biology, earth science, English, geosciences, history, mathematics, Spanish, teaching English language. M.A.T., M.S.T.
Educational Administration. M.Ed, Ed.D., Ph.D.
Educational Research, Measurement and Evaluation. M.A., Ph.D.
Elementary Education (G1–8). M.A.T., M.Ed.
Higher Education Administration. M.A., Ph.D.
Reading. Includes literacy education. M.A.T., M.Ed.
Teachers of Students with Moderate Disabilities. M.Ed.
Teachers of Students with Severe and Multiple Disabilities. M.Ed.

Law School
Web site: www.bc.edu/lawschool

Established 1929. Located at Newton (02459-1163). Semester system. ABA approved since 1932. AALS member. Law library 450,833 volumes, 3386 subscriptions. Library has LEXIS-NEXIS, WESTLAW, DIALOG, 25 Macintosh computers.

Annual tuition: full-time $34,846. No housing on-campus. Total average annual expenses: $17,675. Enrollment: first-year class 276; total full-time 800 (men 50%, women 50%, minority 36%). Faculty: full-time 48, part-time 26. Student to faculty ratio is 14 to 1. Degrees conferred: J.D., J.D.-M.B.A., J.D.-M.A., J.D.-M.Ed., J.D.-M.S.W., LL.M. (for lawyers from countries other than the U.S.).

ADMISSION REQUIREMENTS. LSDAS Law School report, transcripts, LSAT, recommendation, bachelor's degree required in support of application. Interview not required. Accepts transfer applicants. Graduates of unaccredited colleges not considered. Apply to the Director of Admissions; closing date March 1. Application fee $75. Phone: (617)552-4351; e-mail: bclawadm@bc.edu. For LL.M.: All applicants must have either (a) graduated from a U.S. law school that is approved by the American Bar Association, (b) obtained the basic degree in law from a non-U.S. university or (c) be admitted to practice law in a country other than the U.S. Submit Official transcripts with certified English translation from all of your law and/or graduate schools, a résumé, two letters of recommendation, statement of purpose, TOEFL (if an international applicant), a writing sample required in support of application. Apply to the LL.M. office. See Web site: www.bc.edu/llm. Admits Fall only. Apply by March 1. Application fee $75.

ADMISSION STANDARDS. Selective. Accepts 20–25% of total annual applicants. Number of applicants 6769; number of acceptance 1372; number enrolled 275; LSAT (75% of class have a score at or above 161); GPA (75% of class have a GPA at or above 3.44). *U.S. News & World Report* ranking is 28th of all law schools.

FINANCIAL AID. Scholarships, resident assistantships, Federal W/S, loans. About 75% receive aid other than loans from School funds. Apply by March 15 to the Boston College Office of Financial Aid. Phone: (617)552-4243. Use FAFSA.

DEGREE REQUIREMENTS. For J.D.: 85 credit hours minimum, at least the last four semesters in residence. For LL.M.: satisfactory completion of one year full-time program. For other master's degrees: see Graduate School listing above.
Note: Semester-abroad program (University of London) available.

Wallace E. Carroll School of Management
Web site: www.bc.edu

Graduate study since 1957. Semester system. Tuition: per course $1938.

Enrollment: full-time 221, part-time 713. Faculty: full-time 45, part-time 25. Degrees conferred: M.B.A., M.S.A., M.S.F., M.B.A.-Ph.D. (Sociology, Finance, Organization Studies), Ph.D.

ADMISSION REQUIREMENTS. Transcripts, GMAT, two letters of recommendation required in support of college's application. TOEFL, TSE, TWE required for foreign applicants. Interview recommended. Accepts transfer students. Graduates of unaccredited institutions not considered. Apply to the Director of Admissions by April 15 (Fall), December 1 (Spring). Application fee $100. Phone: (617)552-3920; fax: (617)552-8078.

ADMISSION STANDARDS. Selective. Usual minimum average: 3.39 (A = 4). Median GMAT: 645. *U.S. News & World Report* ranking: 39th for M.B.A.s, 17th for part-time M.B.A. programs.

FINANCIAL AID. Annual awards from School funds: academic scholarships, AHANA scholarships, and research assistantships, fellowships, tuition waivers, Federal W/S, loans. Apply to the Director of Financial Aid by March 1. Phone: (617)552-3320. Use FAFSA. About 25% of students receive aid other than loans from School and outside sources. Aid available for part-time students.

DEGREE REQUIREMENTS. For M.B.A.: 62 semester hours, 21 courses including 15 required courses in the common body of knowledge and 8 electives; consulting project. For M.S.A., M.S.F.: 30 semester hours, either a one-year full-time or 21-month part-time program. For Ph.D.: four-year full-time program; doctoral seminar in teaching; comprehensive exam, dissertation; oral defense.

FIELDS OF STUDY.
Accounting. M.S.A.
Business Administration. Includes asset management, change leadership, competitive service delivery, corporate finance, entrepreneurial management, financial reporting and controls, global management, marketing informatics, product and brand management. M.B.A.
Finance. M.S.F., Ph.D.
Organizational Studies. Ph.D. only.
Note: International exchange program in France, Spain, Ireland, New Zealand.

William F. Connell School of Nursing
Enrollment: full-time 146, part-time 53. Faculty: full- and part-time 76. Degrees conferred: M.S., M.S.-M.A. (Pastoral Ministry), M.S.-M.B.A., Ph.D.

ADMISSION REQUIREMENTS. Official B.S.N. transcripts from an NLN accredited program, three letters of reference, goal statement, GRE required in support of School's application. In addition, RN license and one year experience as an RN required. Interview is by invitation for Ph.D. TOEFL required for international applicants. Apply to Office of Admissions by March 31. Application fee $50. Phone: (617)552-4059.

ADMISSION STANDARDS. Selective.

FINANCIAL AID. College-administered Federal W/S, loans. School-administered traineeships, scholarships, VA stipends, graduate assistantships, minority scholarships, and various grants on funds-available basis. Apply by March 15 to School's Financial Aid Office for School-sponsored funds, to the College's Financial Aid Office for all Federal programs. Phone: (800)294-0294. Use FAFSA and College's FAF.

DEGREE REQUIREMENTS. For M.S.: 30–33 semester hours; comprehensive exam; thesis. For Ph.D.: 46 semester hours beyond master's; comprehensive exam; colloquium, dissertation; oral exam.

FIELDS OF STUDY.
Nurse Anesthesia. M.N.A.
Nursing. Entry level program. M.S.N.
Palliative Care. Includes adult and older adult patients and their families undergoing treatment for life-threatening illness, adult and older adult patients and families facing death, adult and older adult patients and families with chronic illness requiring quality of life interventions. A.P.N.

Graduate School of Social Work

Established 1936. Tuition: per credit $1040. Enrollment: full-time 388, part-time 117. Faculty: full-time 22, part-time 34. Degrees conferred: M.S.W., Ph.D., M.S.W.-M.B.A., M.S.W.-J.D., M.S.W.-M.A. (Pastoral Counseling, Social Ministry), M.S.W.-Ph.D.

ADMISSION REQUIREMENTS. Official transcripts, three letters of reference, GRE or MAT required in support of School's application. TOEFL required for international applicants. Interview not required. For Ph.D. candidates: M.S.W. degree, transcripts, essay, three references, MAT or GRE. Apply to Office of Admissions by March 1. Application fee $40. Phone: (617)552-4024; e-mail: swadmit@bc.edu.

ADMISSION STANDARDS. Multidimensional: MAT/GRE or UG content and GPA, related experience, references, and statement of purpose weighted.

FINANCIAL AID. College-administered Federal W/S, loans. School-administered work-study internships, VA stipends, Forensic grant, graduate assistantships, minority scholarships, and various grants on funds-available basis. Apply to School's Director of Financial Aid; no specified closing date. Phone: (617)552-4982. Use FAFSA.

DEGREE REQUIREMENTS. For M.S.W.: 81 semester hours, including field practicum; thesis. For Ph.D.: 14 courses beyond master's; qualifying exam; dissertation; oral exam.

FIELDS OF STUDY.
Social Welfare. Ph.D.
Social Work. Includes either clinical or macro practice with concentrations in children, youth and families, global practice, health and mental health, older adults and families. M.S.W.

BOSTON UNIVERSITY
Boston, Massachusetts 02215
Web site: www.bu.edu

Founded 1839. CGS member. Coed. Private control. Methodist affiliation. Semester system. Special facilities: Institute for Accounting Research and Education, Center for Advanced Biotechnology, African Studies Center, Center for Applied Research in

Language, Asian Management Center, Center for Astrophysical Research, Center for BioDynamics, BioMolecular Engineering Research Center, Cancer Research Center, Institute for the Classical Tradition, Center for Communication and Deafness, Communication Research Center, Center for Computational Science, Center for Defense Journalism, International Center for East Asian Archaeology, Institute for Economic Development, Center for Einstein Studies, Center for Energy and Environmental Studies, Center for Enterprise Leadership, Center for Families, Communities, Schools and Children's Learning, Gerontology Center, Center for Human Genetics, Human Resources Policy Institute, Center for International Health, International History Institute, Center for Judaic Studies, Center for Law and Health Sciences, Center for Law and Technology, Institute for Literacy and Language, Center for Molecular Engineering, Design and Analysis, Morin Center for Banking and Financial Law, NeuroMuscular Research Center, Opera Institute, Center for Philosophy and History of Science, Institute for Philosophy and Religion, Photonics Center, Center for Polymer Studies, Institute for Religion and World Affairs, Center for Remote Sensing, Center for Space Physics, Institute for the Study of Conflict, Ideology and Policy, Institute for Study of Economic Culture, Institute for Television, Film and Radio Production, Theatre Institute, Center for Transportation Studies, United States Strategic Institute, Visual Arts Institute, Whitaker Cardiovascular Institute, Center on Work and Family. The University's NIH ranking is 42nd among all U.S. Institutions with 398 awards/grants valued at $155,050,412. According to The Center at University of Florida, Boston University is ranked 34th in receipt of Federal Research funds with $203,947,000 and it ranks 57th for total University research expenditures with $224,841,000. The University's endowment assets ranks it 69th, valued at $694,051,000. In 2004, the University awarded 267 doctorates which ranked it 54th among all U.S. institutions eligible to award that degree. Fourteen of the University's faculty members have been elected to National Honor Academies and this ranks it 57th among all U.S. institutions. The Library: approximately 2,300,000 volumes, 31,000 subscriptions. Total University enrollment: 30,000.

Annual tuition: full-time $33,330; per credit $1042. Limited on-campus housing. Average annual housing cost: $850–$1200 per month. Contact off-campus housing office. Phone (617)353-3523.

Graduate School of Arts and Sciences

Graduate study since 1874. Enrollment: full-time 1704, part-time 257. Arts and Science faculty: 600. Degrees conferred: M.A., Ph.D.

ADMISSION REQUIREMENTS. Official transcripts, two to three letters of recommendation required in support of application. GRE/Subject Tests for most departments, GMAT/MAT for some departments. TOEFL and statement of financial support required for foreign applicants. Interviews may be requested. Graduates of unaccredited institutions not considered. Apply to Office of Admissions by January 15 (Fall), October 15 (Spring). Application fee $65. Phone: (617)353-2693; fax:(617) 358-0540; e-mail: grartsci@bu.edu.

ADMISSION STANDARDS. Selective for most departments. Usual minimum average: 3.0 (A = 4).

FINANCIAL AID. Annual awards from institutional funds: research scholarships, graduate assistantships, fellowships, traineeships, Federal W/S, loans. Apply to Director of Financial Aid by March 1. Phone: (617)353-2697. Use FAFSA. About 65% of full-time students receive aid from School. Aid available for part-time students.

DEGREE REQUIREMENTS. For most M.A. programs: eight semester courses; thesis or final comprehensive exam; students who have not completed two years of undergraduate language study must make up deficiency. For most Ph.D. programs: eight semester courses beyond the master's; residency requirements of a minimum of two consecutive regular semesters of full-time study; qualifying exam; dissertation; candidacy; final oral exam; reading knowledge of one or more foreign languages.

FIELDS OF STUDY.
African-American Studies. M.A. only.
American and New England Studies. Ph.D. only.
Anthropology.
Applied Linguistics. Ph.D. only.
Archaeological Studies.
Art History.
Astronomy.
Bioinformatics.
Biology.
Biostatistics.
Cellular Biophysics.
Chemistry.
Classical Studies.
Cognitive and Neural Systems.
Computer Science.
Creative Writing.
Earth Sciences.
Economics.
Editorial Studies.
Energy and Environmental Studies. Includes Environmental Remote Sensing and Geographic Information. M.A. only.
English. Includes English and American literature, creative writing. M.A. only.
Geography.
History.
International Relations. Includes joint programs in international relations and international communication, and international relations and resource environmental management.
Mathematics.
Modern Foreign Languages and Literatures. Includes French, Hispanics.
Molecular Biology. Includes cell, biochemistry.
Music. Includes musicology; 12 semester courses for Ph.D.
Neuroscience.
Philosophy.
Physics.
Political Science.
Preservation Studies.
Psychology. Includes clinical, community, developmental, experimental, social.
Religion and Theological Studies.
Sociology. Includes joint Ph.D. in Sociology/Social Work.
Statistics.

College of Communication

Graduate study since 1947. Special facilities: Washington Journalism Center. Annual tuition: $34,930. Graduate enrollment: full-time 340, part-time 39. Faculty: full-time 57, part-time 81. Degrees conferred: M.F.A., M.S., J.D.-M.S., M.B.A.-M.S.

ADMISSION REQUIREMENTS. Official transcripts, three letters of recommendation, MAT/GMAT/GRE/LSAT and program-related writing requirement required in support of College's application. Interview not required. TOEFL/ TSE/TWE required for international applicants. Transfer students not accepted. Graduates of unaccredited institutions not considered. Apply to Admissions Officer, preferably by February 1 (admits Fall only). Application fee $70 for paper application, $60 for online application. Phone: (617)353-3481; fax: (617)358-0399; e-mail: comgrad@bu.edu.

ADMISSION STANDARDS. Very selective to competitive. Usual minimum average: 3.0 (A = 4).

FINANCIAL AID. Annual awards from institutional funds: scholarships, grants, tuition waivers, research assistantships, administrative assistantships, teaching assistantships, internships, Federal W/S, loans. Approved for VA benefits. Apply by April 30 to Graduate Financial Aid Coordinator. Phone: (617)353-4658. Use FAFSA. About 75% of students receive aid other than loans from School and outside sources. Aid available for part-time students.

DEGREE REQUIREMENTS, For M.S.: 32–48 credits minimum; thesis, creative project, analytical project or comprehensive exam. For M.F.A.: 64 credit program; thesis/project.

FIELDS OF STUDY.
Advertising. M.S.
Broadcast Journalism. M.S.
Business and Economics Journalism. M.S.
Film. M.F.A.
Journalism. Includes print, photo. M.S.
Mass Communication. Includes applied communication research, communications studies.
Public Relations. Includes public relations for the nonprofit sector, corporate. M.S.
Science Journalism. M.S.
Television. M.S.
Television Management. M.S.

DUAL DEGREE PROGRAMS:
J.D.-M.S. in Mass Communications and Law.
M.B.A.-M.S. in Television Management.

College of Engineering
110 Cummington Street
Annual tuition: $34,930.
Enrollment: full-time 446, part-time 44. Faculty: full- and part-time 117. Degrees conferred: M.S., M.S.-M.B.A., Ph.D.

ADMISSION REQUIREMENTS: Transcripts, GRE, two letters of recommendation, statement of personal and research goals required in support of application. TOEFL required for international applicants. Accepts transfer applicants. Graduates of unaccredited institutions not considered. Apply to Graduate Admission Office by April 1 (Fall), October 1 (Spring). Application fee $70. Phone: (617)353-9760; fax: (617)353-0259; e-mail: enggrad@bu.edu.

ADMISSION STANDARDS. Competitive for most departments, selective for the others. Usual minimum average: 2.75 (A = 4).

FINANCIAL AID. Annual awards from institutional funds: scholarships, fellowships, research assistantships, teaching assistantships, tuition waivers, Federal W/S, loans. Approved for VA benefits. Apply to Dean by January 15. Phone: (617)353-8970. Use FAFSA and University's FAF. More than 70% of students receive some form of financial aid.

DEGREE REQUIREMENTS. For M.S.: 32–36 semester hours minimum, at least 24 in residence; project, thesis, or laboratory course. For Ph.D.: a minimum of 32 credits beyond M.S. degree; qualifying exam; candidacy; dissertation; final oral exam.

FIELDS OF STUDY.
Aerospace Engineering.
Biomedical Engineering.
Computer Engineering.
Computer Systems Engineering.
Electrical Engineering.
Engineering Sciences.
General Engineering.
Global Manufacturing.

Manufacturing Engineering.
Mechanical Engineering.
Photonics.
Systems Engineering. Interdepartmental Ph.D. Includes software engineering.
Note: Joint Program is with School of Management and Manufacturing Department. M.S.-M.B.A.; with the Medical School, Ph.D.-M.D.

College of Fine Arts
Annual tuition: $34,930. Graduate enrollment: full-time 482, part-time 49. Graduate faculty: full-time 68, part-time 34. Degrees conferred: M.F.A., Mus.M., Mus.A.D., Diploma.

ADMISSION REQUIREMENTS: Transcripts, two–three letters of recommendation required in support of College's application. Audition, interview, or portfolio required depending upon major. GRE required for History and Literature of Music applicants. Curriculum vitae required for doctoral candidates. TOEFL and statement of financial support required for international applicants. Accepts transfer applicants. Applications should be filed by February 1 (for most programs) with the Office of Graduate Admissions of the College. Application fee $65. Phone: (617)353-3350; e-mail: arts@bu.edu. For audition information call (617)353-3341.

ADMISSION STANDARDS. Competitive for most departments. Usual minimum average of 3.0 (A = 4) in undergraduate studies.

FINANCIAL AID. More than 200 annual awards, including teaching fellowships, graduate assistantships, Director's Awards, Federal W/S, loans. Application for aid should be submitted with application for admission but before March 1. Use FAFSA (University code: 002130).

DEGREE REQUIREMENTS. For Mus.M.: 32–36 credits minimum; recitals, thesis, or terminal project. For M.F.A.: 32–42 credits minimum; project. For Mus. A.D.: 48 credits minimum beyond the master's, at least two semesters in full-time residence; qualifying examinations; reading knowledge of French and German; dissertation/terminal project; final oral examination. For the Diploma/Certificate programs: usually it represents about two years of study beyond the master's degree.

FIELDS OF STUDY.

SCHOOL OF MUSIC:
Collaborative Piano. Mus.M., Mus.A.D.
Composition. Mus.M., Mus.A.D.
Conducting. Includes orchestral and choral. Mus.M., Mus.A.D.
History and Literature of Music. Mus.M.
Historical Performance. Mus.M, Mus.A.D.
Music Education. Mus.M., Mus.A.D.
Performance. Mus.M., Mus.A.D.
Theory. Mus.M.

SCHOOL OF THEATRE:
Costume Design & Production. M.F.A.
Directing. M.F.A.
Scene Design.
Technical Production.
Theatre Education. M.F.A.

SCHOOL OF VISUAL ARTS:
Art Education. M.F.A.
Graphic Design. M.F.A.
Painting. M.F.A.
Sculpture. M.F.A.

Sargent College of Health and Rehabilitation Science

Annual tuition: $34,930. Graduate enrollment: full-time 377, part-time 364. Faculty: full-time 54, part-time 44. Degrees conferred: M.S., M.S.O.T., M.S.P.T., D.P.T., D.Sc.

ADMISSION REQUIREMENTS. Official transcripts, three letters of recommendation, MAT/GRE required in support of College's application (electronic application available). Interview required for doctoral candidates. TOEFL required for international applicants. Transfer students accepted. Graduates of unaccredited institutions not considered. Apply to Graduate Admissions Office for Communication Disorders February 1 (Fall), Health Sciences March 1, Occupational Therapy February 15, Physical Therapy January 5, Rehabilitation Counseling rolling admissions. Application fee $65. Phone: (617)353-2713; e-mail: sargrad@bu.edu.

ADMISSION STANDARDS. Selective to competitive. Usual minimum average 3.0 (A = 4).

FINANCIAL AID. Annual awards from institutional funds: scholarships, grants, research assistantships, teaching assistantships, traineeships, Federal W/S, loans. Approved for VA benefits. Apply by April 1 to Sargent College Financial Aid Office. Use FAFSA. Phone: (617)353-2714. Limited aid other than loans for part-time students.

DEGREE REQUIREMENTS. For M.S.: 32–64 credits minimum depending on program; thesis or comprehensive exam. For M.S.O.T.: two-year entry-level program; internship. For D.P.T.: 98 credit full-time program; preliminary exam; clinical experience; dissertation; final oral exam. For D.Sc.: 48 credit program beyond the master's degree; one year in full-time study (two consecutive semesters); qualifying tasks; dissertation; final oral exam.

FIELDS OF STUDY.
Applied Anatomy and Physiology. M.S., Ph.D.
Audiology. M.S.
Communication Disorders. M.S.
Dietetic Internship. M.S.
Movement and Rehabilitation Sciences. D.Sc.
Nutrition. M.S.
Occupational Therapy. M.S.O.T., M.S., D.Sc.
Physical Therapy. M.S.P.T., D.P.T.
Rehabilitation Counseling. M.S.
Rehabilitation Sciences. D.Sc.
Speech-Language Pathology. M.S.
Therapeutic Studies. M.S.

Henry M. Goldman School of Dental Medicine
Web site: dentalschool.bu.edu

Established 1963. Located at the Medical Center. Semester system. Special facilities: Clinical Research Center, Northeast Center for Research to Evaluate and Eliminate Dental Disparities; Center for Advanced Biomedical Research, Joan and Herbert Schilder Endodontics Research Center. Library: electronic library.

Annual tuition: $49,514. Housing: very limited. Total average cost for all other first-year expenses: $25,000.

Enrollment: first-year class 115, total full-time 761 (men 52%, women 48%, minorities 13%, state resident 20%). Faculty: full- and part-time 575. Degrees conferred: D.M.D., M.Sc., C.A.G.S., D.Sc.

ADMISSION REQUIREMENTS. AADSAS application, transcripts, DAT (no later than October), two letters of reference required in support of School's application. Interview by invitation only. Applicants must have completed at least three years of undergraduate study for D.M.D. Graduates of unaccredited colleges not considered. TOEFL required of international applicants. Does not have EDP. Apply to Admissions Committee after

June 1 and before March 1 for all programs. Rolling admission process. Application fee $65. Phone: (617)638-4787, (617)638-4798.

ADMISSION STANDARDS. Competitive. Accepts 25% of total applicants. Mean UGPA: 3.4 (A = 4), mean DAT Academic: 19; PAT: 18. Approximately 10% are state residents. Gourman rating: 4.31; this places school in top 30 schools of dentistry.

FINANCIAL AID. Scholarships, grants, tuition waivers, APEX, DEAL, HEAL, loans. Apply by April 15 to the Dean for scholarships; to Office of Financial Management, Medical Center for all other programs. Phone: (617)638-5130; e-mail: OSFM@bu.edu. Use FAFSA or CSS profile. About 75% of students receive aid other than loans from School and outside sources.

DEGREE REQUIREMENTS. For D.M.D.: satisfactory completion of 4-year program; externship. For M.S., M.Sc.: 36 credits minimum in residence; final oral exam; research project. For C.A.G.S.: same as M.S., except no research project. For D.Sc.: 54 credits minimum, at least three years in residence; research project; final written/oral exam.

FIELDS OF STUDY.
Advanced Education in General Dentistry.
Dental Care Management. C.A.G.S. only.
Dental Materials.
Dental Public Health.
Endodontics.
Implantology.
Molecular and Cell Biology.
Operative Dentistry.
Oral and Maxillofacial Pathology.
Oral and Maxillofacial Surgery.
Oral Biology.
Orthodontics.
Pediatric Dentistry.
Pedodontics.
Periodontology.
Prosthodontics.
Note: Ph.D. programs available through the Department of Medical and Dental Sciences, School of Medicine.

School of Education

Tuition: full-time $34,930; per credit $985. Graduate enrollment: full-time 244, part-time 294. Faculty: full-time 44, part-time 57. Degrees conferred: Ed.M., M.A.T., C.A.G.S., Ed.D.

ADMISSION REQUIREMENTS. Transcripts, MAT/GRE, three letters of recommendation required in support of School's application. Interview not required. TOEFL required for international applicants. Accepts transfer applicants. Graduates of unaccredited institutions not considered. Apply by February 15 (Fall), October 15 (Spring) to Office of Graduate Admissions. Rolling admissions process. Application fee $65. Phone: (617)353-4237; fax: (617)353-8937.

ADMISSION STANDARDS. Selective for most departments.

FINANCIAL AID. Scholarships, fellowships, teaching/research assistantships, partial tuition waivers, Federal W/S, loans. Approved for VA benefits. Apply by February 15 (Fall), October 15 (Spring) to Graduate School for fellowships, assistantships; to the Office of Graduate Financial Assistance for all other programs. Phone: (617)353-4238. Use FAFSA. About 45% of full-time students receive aid from School and outside sources. No aid for part-time students.

DEGREE REQUIREMENTS. For Ed.M.: 32 credits minimum. For C.A.G.S.: 30 credits minimum beyond the master's, at least

24 in residence; final written/oral exam; no language requirement. For M.A.T.: twelve-month, 46 credit program. For Ed.D.: 60 credits minimum beyond the master's, at least 45 in residence and 24 in full-time attendance; preliminary exam; dissertation; no language requirement.

FIELDS OF STUDY.
Administration, Training, and Policy Studies.
Bilingual Education.
Counseling.
Counseling Psychology.
Curriculum and Instruction.
Early Childhood Education.
Educational Media and Technology.
Education of Deaf.
Elementary Education.
English and Language Arts Education.
English Education.
Health Education.
Higher Educational Administration.
Human Movement.
Human Resource Education.
International Educational Development.
Latin and Classical Humanities.
Leisure Education.
Mathematics Education.
Modern Foreign Language Education.
Physical Education and Coaching.
Policy, Planning, and Administration.
Reading Education.
Science Education.
Social Studies Education.
Special Education.
TESOL (Teaching English to Speakers of Other Languages).
Therapeutic Recreation.

School of Law
Web site: bu.edu/law

Founded 1872. ABA approved since 1925. AALS member. Semester system. Special facilities: Morin Co. for Banking Law Studies, Center for Law and Health, Center for Law and Technology. Library: 661,828 volumes, 4630 subscriptions; has LEXIS, NEXIS, WESTLAW, DIALOG.

Annual tuition: $35,398. On-campus housing available. Apply to Office of Housing. Total average annual expenses: $16,400.

Enrollment: first-year class 294; total full-time 821 (men 50%, women 50%, minorities 25%). Faculty: full-time 58, part-time 27; student to faculty ratio 12.2 to 1. Degrees conferred: J.D., J.D.-M.B.A. (Management, Health Care Management), J.D.-M.A. (Historic Preservation, International Relations, Philosophy), J.D.-M.P.H., J.D.-M.S. (Mass Communication), LL.M. (Banking and Financial Law, Intellectual Property Law, Taxation), J.D.-LL.M.

ADMISSION REQUIREMENTS. LSDAS Law School report, transcripts, LSAT, letter of recommendation required in support of application. Interview not required, but visits encouraged. Accepts transfer applicants. In addition, international candidates submit TOEFL, unless the undergraduate degree was awarded by a U.S. institution. Graduates of unaccredited colleges not considered. Apply to the Office of Admissions after September 15, before March 1. Admits to Fall semester only. Application fee $75. Phone: (617)353-3100; fax: (617)353-0578; e-mail: bulawadm@bu.edu.

ADMISSION STANDARDS. Selective. Accepts 24% of total annual applicants. Number of applicants 6219; number of acceptance 1521; number enrolled 294; LSAT (75% of class have a score at or above 163); GPA (75% of class have a GPA at or above 3.48). *U.S. News & World Report* ranking is 20th of all law schools.

FINANCIAL AID. Partial tuition grants, MLK fellowships, scholarships, Federal W/S, loans. Apply by March 1 to the Assistant Dean. Phone: (617)353-3160. Use FAFSA. About 48% of students receive aid including loans from School funds.

DEGREE REQUIREMENTS. For J.D.: satisfactory completion of 3-year program; 84 semester units. For LL.M.: at least 24 credits beyond the J.D.; one year in full-time residence.
Note: Study abroad available at University of Buenos Aires (Argentina), Université Jean Moulin Lyon 3 (France), Université Panthéon-Assas (Paris II) (France), St. Catherine's College, University of Oxford (U.K.), Leiden University (The Netherlands), Tel Aviv University (Israel), National University of Singapore (Republic of Singapore), University of Hong Kong (Hong Kong).

School of Management
Web site: management.bu.edu

Established 1913. Graduate study since 1974. Located on main campus. Library: 80,000 volumes, 350 subscriptions. Special program: Accelerated M.B.A. Special facilities: Asian Management Center, Center for Enterprise Leadership, Entrepreneurial Management, Human Resources Policy Institute, Institute for Accounting Research and Education, Leadership Institute. Annual tuition: full-time, M.B.A., M.S.I.S., D.B.A. $34,930; M.S.I.M. $44,000 (includes board, books, and fees).

Enrollment: full-time 544, part-time 578 (men 60%, women 40%). Faculty: full-time 106, part-time 72. Degrees conferred: M.B.A., A.M.B.A., E.M.B.A, M.S.I.M., M.S.I.S., M.B.A.-J.D., M.B.A.-M.S., M.B.A.-M.P.H., D.B.A.

ADMISSION REQUIREMENTS. Transcripts, two letters of recommendation, essays, résumé, GMAT required in support of School's application. Interview not required. TOEFL (minimum score 600) and Statement of Financial Support required for foreign applicants. Accepts transfer applicants. Graduates of unaccredited institutions not considered. Apply to Office of Admissions by April 1 (international applicants), May 1 (full-time, begins Fall semester only), July 15 (part-time), December 1 (January admissions), January 5 (D.B.A. admission). Application fee $60, $95 for doctoral candidates. Phone: (617)353-2670: fax: (617)353-7368; e-mail: mba@bu.edu, dba@bu.edu.

ADMISSION STANDARDS. Competitive. Usual minimum average: 3.0 (A = 4) median GMAT: 581.

FINANCIAL AID. Scholarships, merit scholarships, fellowships, assistantships, Federal W/S, loans. Apply to Financial Aid Office by March 15. Phone: (617)353-2670. Use FAFSA. Approximately 25% of students receive some form of aid.

DEGREE REQUIREMENTS. For A.M.B.A., E.M.B.A., M.B.A.: 64 semester hours maximum; advanced standing for previous academic background is possible; program must be completed in six years. For M.S.I.S.: one-year full-time (Summer and two semesters); field project. For M.S.I.M.: seventeen-month program. For D.B.A.: 14 courses minimum, at least eight in residence; curriculum paper; qualifying exam; teaching/applied research internships; dissertation.

FIELDS OF STUDY.
Accelerated Executive. M.B.A.
Executive. M.B.A.
Health Sector Management. M.B.A.
Information System. M.S.I.S.
International Management. M.B.A.
Investment Management. M.S.I.M.
Public and Nonprofit Management. M.B.A.

D.B.A. CONCENTRATIONS:
Accounting.
Finance and Economics.
Information Systems.
Marketing.
Operations Management.
Organizational Behavior.
Strategy and Policy.
Note: Dual degrees offered are M.B.A.-M.A. (Economics, International Relations, Medical Sciences), M.B.A.-M.S. (Television Administration, Management Information Sciences, Manufacturing Engineering), M.B.A.-J.D., M.B.A.-M.P.H.

Division of Graduate Medical Sciences
Web site: www.bumc.bu.edu

Annual tuition: $28,512.
Enrollment: First-year full-time (Fall only) 10–15; total 50–60. Degrees conferred: Ph.D., M.D.-Ph.D.

ADMISSION REQUIREMENTS. Official transcripts, personal statement, three letters of recommendation, GRE required in support of application (electronic application available). TOEFL required for international applicants whose native language is not English. Accepts transfer applicants. Graduates of unaccredited college not considered. Apply to Office of Admission by January 1 (Fall), masters' candidates apply by March 31 (Fall), December 1 (Spring). Application fee $50, $60 for online applications. Phone: (617)638-5120; fax: (617)638-4842.

ADMISSION STANDARDS. Selective.

FINANCIAL AID. Fellowships, teaching/research assistantships, Federal W/S, Federal and Private loans; apply to appropriate department chair by January 31 (Fall), October 31 (Spring). Use FAFSA.

DEGREE REQUIREMENTS. For M.A., M.S.: 32–36 credit programs; thesis/nonthesis option. For Ph.D.: eight semesters beyond master's; residence requirement of two consecutive semesters in full-time study; reading knowledge of at least one foreign language; qualifying exam; final oral exam.

FIELDS OF STUDY.
Anatomy and Neurobiology.
Behavior Neuroscience.
Biochemistry.
Bioimaging. M.A. only.
Biomedical Forensics. M.S. only.
Biophysics.
Cell and Molecular Biology.
Clinical Investigation. M.A. only.
Genetics and Genomics.
Genetic Counseling. M.S. only.
Immunology.
Medical Nutrition Sciences.
Medical Sciences. M.A. only.
Mental Health and Behavioral Medicine. M.S. only.
Microbiology.
Molecular Medicine.
Oral Biology.
Pathology.
Pharmacology.
Physiology.

School of Medicine
Web site: www.bumc.bu.edu

Established 1848. Located in Boston (02118). Acquired by Boston University in 1873. The Boston Medical Center is composed of the School of Medicine, School of Dental Medicine, School of Public Health, Center for Advancement in Health and Medicine and the University Hospital. Special facility: BioSquare Research Park. Library: 100,000 volumes. The University's NIH ranking is 42nd among U.S. institutions with 398 awards/grants worth $155,228,278.

Annual tuition: $42,540. Off-campus housing only. Total average figure for all other expenses: $13,500.

Enrollment: first year class 135 (3 EDP); total full-time 629 (men 58%, women 42%, minorities 46%, state residents 18%). Faculty: full-time 1183, part-time 1213. Degrees conferred: M.D., M.D.-M.B.A., M.D.-Ph.D., M.D.-M.P.H.

ADMISSION REQUIREMENTS. AMCAS, transcripts, MCAT (oldest score considered 2000), interview (by invitation), three letters of recommendation, and bachelor's degree from an approved college of arts and science required in support of application. Candidates of unusual ability sometimes accepted after three years in undergraduate school (90 semester hours required). Does have EDP. Accepts transfer candidates on a space available basis. Apply to School Office of Admissions after June 15, before November 1. Application fee $100. Phone: (617)638-4630; fax: (617)638-4718.

ADMISSION STANDARDS. Very competitive. Accepts about 4.7% of all applicants. Number of applications 9589 (8936 out-of-state); number interviewed 1038 (890 out-of-state); number of acceptance 454 (372 out-of-state); number enrolled 155 (132 out-of-state). Mean Composite MCAT 10.1; mean UGPA 3.66. *U.S. News & World Report* ranking is in the top 34 of all medical schools.

FINANCIAL AID. Scholarships, grants, Federal and private loans available for accepted students. Apply to Financial Aid Office after acceptance. Phone: (617)638-5130. Approximately 40% receive aid other than loans from institutional funds.

DEGREE REQUIREMENTS. For M.D.: satisfactory completion of four-year program; must pass Step 1 of USMLE for graduation. For M.B.A., M.P.H., Ph.D.: see Graduate Schools listings.

School of Public Health

Annual tuition: $34,930. Graduate enrollment: full-time 286, part-time 386. Faculty: full-time 90, part-time 223. Degrees conferred: M.P.H., M.Sc., D.Sc., J.D.-M.P.H., M.A. (Medical Sciences)-M.P.H., M.B.A.-M.P.H., M.D.-M.P.H., M.S.W.-M.P.H.

ADMISSION REQUIREMENTS. All applicants should hold a baccalaureate degree. Official transcripts, three letters of recommendation, GRE required in support of College's application. GMAT/LSAT/MCAT can be submitted in lieu of GRE. Interview not required. TOEFL or IELTS required for international applicants. Transfer students not accepted. Graduates of unaccredited institutions not considered. Apply to the School's Office of Admissions. For M.P.H. and D.Sc. (Environmental Health Science) Fall applications completed by March 15 will be notified by April 15, those completed by April 15 will be notified by May 31. Spring applications completed by October 25 will be notified by November 25, applications completed after October 25 will be reviewed on a space available basis. For M.Sc., D.Sc. (Epidemiology) admits Fall only, apply by April 15. Application fee $60. Phone: (617)638-4640; fax: (717)638-5299; e-mail: sphadmis@bu.edu.

ADMISSION STANDARDS. Selective. Usual minimum average: 3.0 (A = 4).

FINANCIAL AID. Annual awards from institutional funds: Dean's scholarships, grants, traineeships, private loan programs, Federal W/S, loans. Approved for VA benefits. Apply by April 15 to Office of Student Financial Management. Phone: (617)638-5115; e-mail: osfmspj@bumc.bu.edu. Use FAFSA. 25% of students receive aid other than loans from School and outside sources. Aid available for part-time students.

DEGREE REQUIREMENTS. For M.P.H.: 48 credit program, at least 32 credits in residence. For Dr.P.H.: 40 credit program beyond master's degree; doctoral seminar; Field Practice placement; dissertation; final oral exam. For D.Sc.: 48 credit program beyond master's degree; one year of full-time study (two consecutive semesters); comprehensive; dissertation; final oral exam.

FIELDS OF STUDY.
Biostatistics. M.A, Ph.D. Both degrees are offered jointly with the Department of Mathematics, Graduate School of Arts and Science and with collaboration with the Division of Graduate Medical Sciences.
Environmental Health Sciences. D.Sc. only.
Epidemiology. M.Sc., D.Sc.
Public Health. Includes environmental health, epidemiology & biostatistics, health law, health services, international health, maternal and child health, social and behavioral sciences. M.P.H., Dr.P.H.

School of Social Work

Annual tuition: $22,902. On-campus housing available. Contact Housing Office. Phone: (617)353-3511. Day-care facilities available.

Enrollment: full-time 183, part-time 184. School faculty: full-time 22, part-time 93. Degrees conferred: M.S.W., M.S.W.-J.D., M.S.W.-M.P.H., M.S.W.-M.T.S., M.S.W.-Ed.M., Ph.D. (Social Work and Sociology).

ADMISSION REQUIREMENTS. Transcripts, references, MAT/GRE, personal statement required in support of School's application. TOEFL required for international applicants. Interview not required. Accepts transfer applicants. Graduates of unaccredited colleges not considered. Apply to the School's Admissions Office by March 1. Application fee $65. Phone: (617)353-3765; fax: (617)353-5612; e-mail: busswad@bu.edu.

ADMISSION STANDARDS. Selective. Usual minimum GPA: 2.7. Average GPA: 3.2 (A = 4).

FINANCIAL AID. Annual awards from institutional funds: Scholarships, internships, grants, Federal W/S, loans. Apply to School's Financial Aid Office by March 1. Phone: (617)353-3765. Use FAFSA and School's application. About 50% of students receive aid other than loans from School and outside sources. Aid available for part-time students.

DEGREE REQUIREMENTS. For M.S.W.: 65 credit programs, advance standing may be awarded for candidates with a bachelor's degree in Social Work; field education. For Ph.D.: at least 48 credits beyond the master's; reading proficiency in one foreign language; qualifying exam; critical essay; dissertation; final oral exam.

FIELDS OF STUDY.
Social Work. Includes major in either clinical social work practice with individuals, families, and groups, or Macro practice, which includes community organizing, management, and planning.

School of Theology

Graduate study since 1839. Coed. Semester system. Annual tuition: $14,560. Graduate enrollment: full-time 248, part-time 36. Faculty: full-time 24, part-time 18. On-campus housing available. Day care facilities available. Degrees conferred: M.Div., M.T.S., D.Min., S.T.M., M.S.M., Th.D., M.T.S.-M.S.W., M.Div.-M.S.W., M.Div.-M.S.M. The A.M. and Ph.D. are offered through the Graduate School.

ADMISSION REQUIREMENTS. Official transcripts, four letters of recommendation required in support of application. GRE required for some degrees. TOEFL, TWE required for international applicants. Interview not required. Accepts transfer applicants. Apply to Director of Admissions by February 15 (Fall), October 15 (Spring). For A.M. or Ph.D., apply by November 1 (Fall), February 1 (Spring). Application fee $60. Phone: (617)353-3036; fax: (617)353-0140; e-mail: sthadmis@bu.edu.

ADMISSION STANDARDS. Very selective. Usual minimum average: 3.0 M.Div.; 3.3 D.Min; 3.3 Th.D. (A = 4).

FINANCIAL AID. Annual awards from institutional funds: fellowships, scholarships, research, teaching assistantships, Federal W/S, loans. Approved for VA benefits. Apply by July 15 to the Director of Financial Aid. Phone: (617)353-3053; fax: (617)353-3061. Use FAFSA. All D.Min. students and 50% of Ph.D. students receive aid other than loans from School; 80% of all students receive some form of financial aid. Aid available for part-time students.

DEGREE REQUIREMENTS. For M.Div.: 96 credits minimum, at least 32 in residence and two semesters in full-time attendance; functional competence in one Biblical language for Biblical Studies majors. For M.T.S.: 64 credits minimum, at least 32 in residence. For S.T.M.: 32 credits minimum beyond the M.Div., at least 24 in residence and two semesters in full-time attendance; final comprehensive exam or thesis. For M.S.M.: 60 credits minimum, at least 32 in residence and two semesters in full-time attendance; thesis or research project or composition or two recitals. For D.Min.: 40 credits minimum beyond the M.Div., at least two semesters in full-time residence. For Th.D.: 48 credits minimum; language and/or research competence; qualifying exam; dissertation; final oral exam.

FIELDS OF STUDY:
Biblical & Historical Studies. S.T.M., M.Div., M.T.S., D.Min., Th.D.
Ministry in Church & Society. S.T.M., M.Div., M.T.S., D.Min., Th.D.
Philosophy, Theology & Ethics. S.T.M., M.Div., M.T.S., D.Min., Th.D.
Religion, Culture & Personality. S.T.M., M.Div., M.T.S., D.Min., Th.D.
Religious Music. M.S.M.
Theological Studies. S.T.M., M.Div., M.T.S., D.Min.

BOWIE STATE UNIVERSITY
Bowie, Maryland 20715-9465
Web site: www.bowiestate.edu

Established 1865. CGS member. Located 25 miles N of Washington, D.C. Coed. Public control. Semester system. Evening session only. Library: 331,640 volumes, 3152 current periodicals.

Tuition: per credit, resident $293, nonresident $587. On-campus housing for single student only. Average academic year housing costs: $6132 (including board). Contact Housing Department for both on- and off-campus housing information. Phone (301)464-7135.

Division of Graduate Studies

Graduate study since 1970. Enrollment: full-time 269, part-time 1025. Faculty: full-time 48, part-time 32. Degrees conferred: M.A., M.B.A., M.P.A., M.S., M.Ed., Ed.D., M.M.I.S., M.S.N.

ADMISSION REQUIREMENTS. Official transcripts, three letters of recommendation required in support of application. Written essay required for Nursing. TOEFL required for international applicants. Accepts transfer applicants. Graduates of unaccredited institutions not considered. Apply to Graduate Office by April 1

(Fall), November 7 (Spring). Rolling admissions process. Application fee $40. Phone: (877)772-6943, (301)860-3448; e-mail: admissions@bowiestate.edu.

ADMISSION STANDARDS. Selective. Usual minimum average: 2.5 (A = 4).

FINANCIAL AID. Fellowships, assistantships, tuition waivers, Federal W/S, loans. Approved for VA benefits. Apply to Dean's Office for fellowships, assistantships; to Financial Aid Office for all other programs. No specified closing date. Phone: (301)464-6544. Use FAFSA.

DEGREE REQUIREMENTS. For most master's: 36–39 semester hours minimum; advancement to candidacy; seminar paper; comprehensive exam. For M.B.A.: 45 semester hours minimum. For M.S. in Nursing: 42–37 semester hours minimum; practicum; comprehensive exam; thesis. For Ed.D.: 60 credit program beyond the master's degree; qualifying exam; internship; dissertation; final order exam.

FIELDS OF STUDY.

SCHOOL OF ARTS AND SCIENCES:
Applied and Computational Mathematics. M.S.
Computer Science. M.S.
English. M.A.
Organizational Communications. M.A.

SCHOOL OF EDUCATION:
Counseling Psychology. M.S.
Educational Leadershp. Ed.D.
Elementary Education. M.Ed.
Guidance and Counseling. M.Ed.
Mental Health Counseling. M.S.
Reading Education. M.Ed.
School Administration and Supervision. M.Ed.
Secondary Education. M.Ed.
Special Education. M.Ed.
Teaching. M.A.T.

SCHOOL OF PROFESSIONAL STUDIES:
Administrative Management. M.A.
Business Administration. Includes concentrations in accounting, finance, management, marketing management. M.B.A.
Human Resources Development. M.A.
Management Information Systems. M.M.I.S.
Nursing. M.S.N.
Public Administration. Includes concentrations in public administration, public policy & management, human resource management. M.P.A.

BOWLING GREEN STATE UNIVERSITY
Bowling Green, Ohio 43403-0180
Web site: www.bgsu.edu

Founded 1910. CGS member. Located 23 miles S of Toledo. Coed. State assisted. Semester system. Special facilities: Center for Archival Collections, Center for Biomolecular Sciences, Center for the Study of Popular Culture, Center for Photo Chemical Sciences, Center for Microscopy and Microanalysis, Institute for Great Lakes Research, Environmental Study Center, Laboratory of Marine Studies, Population and Society Research Center, Center for Governmental Research, Public Service Management Center, Institute for Psychological Research and Application, Social Philosophy and Policy Center. Library: 2,500,000 volumes, 9500 current periodicals. Total University enrollment: 19,000.

Tuition: per credit, resident $505, nonresident $854. On-campus housing available for graduate students. Average academic year housing costs: $3320–$4732; meal plans cost $2000–$3000. Contact Director of Student Housing and Residential Programs for both on- and off-campus housing information. Phone: (419)372-2458.

Graduate College

Enrollment: full-time 1550, part-time 1018. University faculty: full-time 571, part-time 421. Degrees conferred: M.A., M.A.T., M.M., M.B.A., M.O.D., M.P.A., M.R.C., M.S., M.F.A., M.Ed., M.A.H.E., M.I.T., Specialist, Ed.S., Ph.D.

ADMISSION REQUIREMENTS. Two official transcripts, GRE/GMAT, three letters of recommendation to department required in support of College's application. TOEFL/MELAB required of international applicants. Accepts transfer students. Apply at least six months prior to semester of registration (Ph.D.), three months prior to semester of registration (Masters). Application fee $35. Phone: (419)372-2791; fax: (419)372-8569; e-mail: gradweb@bgnet.bgsu.edu.

ADMISSION STANDARDS. Competitive. Usual minimum average: 2.6 (A = 4).

FINANCIAL AID. Annual awards from institutional funds: Ph.D. fellowships, research assistantships, teaching assistantships, internships and externships, Federal W/S, loans. Approved for VA benefits. Admission process must be completed by January 15. Apply by February 15 to appropriate department chair for fellowships, assistantships; to Financial Aid Office for all other programs. Phone: (419)372-2651. Use FAFSA and submit as soon as possible after January 1. About 60% of students receive aid from Institution in the form of assistantships or fellowships.

DEGREE REQUIREMENTS. General requirements for master's: Plan I—30 hours minimum, minimum of 24 hours in residence; thesis; final written/oral exam. Plan II—30 hours minimum, minimum of 24 hours in residence; final comprehensive exam. For M.A.: Plan I or II available. For M.Ed.: 30 hours minimum; thesis or written exam; 33 hours minimum; comprehensive exam. For M.A.T.: 35 hours minimum; final written comprehensive. For M.M.: 34 hours minimum; option of thesis, recital and research document or composition. For M.B.A.: Phase I—for students with little or no previous work in business administration or economics; required work must be completed, but not to exceed the 30 hours of Phase II courses. For M.I.T.: 33 hours minimum; thesis or major project. For M.S.: 30 hours minimum; Plan I or Plan II available. For M.F.A.: in Art, 62 hours; thesis; exhibition; in Creative Writing, 40 hours minimum; thesis. For M.A.H.E.: 33 hours minimum; applied or research option. For M.O.D.: 33 hours minimum; thesis. For M.P.A.: 42 hours minimum; thesis; final written/oral exam. For M.R.C.; 48 hours minimum; thesis; final comprehensive exam. For Specialist: 30 hours minimum beyond the master's; comprehensive oral exam. For Ph.D.: 90 hours minimum beyond the bachelor's; proficiency in one foreign language, proficiency in computer research applications; preliminary exam; dissertation; final/oral written exam.

FIELDS OF STUDY.
Accounting. M.Acc.
American Culture Studies. M.A., M.A.T., Ph.D.
Applied Human Ecology. Includes human development, family studies, food and nutrition, textile and clothing. M.A.H.E.
Applied Philosophy. M.A.
Applied Statistics and Operation Research. M.S.
Art. M.A., M.F.A.
Biological Sciences. M.A., Ph.D.
Business Administration. M.B.A.

Business Education. M.Ed.
Career and Technology Education. M.Ed.
Chemistry. M.S., M.A.T.
Classroom Technology. M.Ed.
College Student Personnel. M.A., M.Ed.
Communication Disorders. M.S., Ph.D.
Communications Studies. M.A., Ph.D.
Computer Science. M.S.
Creative Writing. M.F.A.
Criminal Justice. M.S.C.J.
Cross-Cultural and International Education. M.A.
Curriculum and Teaching. Includes elementary, library and educational media, mathematics supervision, secondary, reading.
Economics. M.A.
Education. Includes elementary, secondary. M.Ed., Ph.D.
Educational Administration and Supervision. M.Ed., Ed.S., Ph.D.
Educational Teaching and Learning. M.Ed., Ed.S.
English. Includes creative, interpersonal, technical writing, teaching. M.A., Ph.D.
Family and Consumer Sciences. M.F.C.S.
French. M.A.
Geology. M.S., M.A.T.
German. M.A., M.A.T.
Guidance and Counseling. M.A., M.Ed.
History. M.A., M.A.T., Ph.D.
Human Movement, Sport, and Leisure Studies. M.Ed.
Industrial Technology. M.I.T.
Interdisciplinary Studies. M.A., Ph.D.
Leadership Studies. Ed.D.
Mathematics and Statistics. Includes pure mathematics, mathematical statistics, scientific computation. M.A., M.A.T., Ph.D.
Mathematics Supervision. Ed.S.
Music. Includes performance, music education, instrumental specialist, music composition, music theory, music history. M.M.
Organizational Development. M.O.D.
Philosophy. Ph.D.
Photochemical Sciences. Ph.D.
Physics. Includes astrophysics, computational physics, theoretical physics, solid state, material science. M.A.T., M.S.
Political Science. M.A., M.A.T.
Popular Culture. M.A., Ph.D.
Psychology. Includes clinical, developmental, experimental, industrial, social. M.A., Ph.D.
Public Administration. M.P.A.
Public Health. M.P.H. Joint degree composed of Medical College of Ohio, University of Toledo, and BGSU.
Reading. M.Ed.
Rehabilitation Counseling. M.R.C.
School Psychology. M.Ed.
Sociology. M.A., Ph.D.
Spanish. M.A.
Special Education. Includes educable mentally retarded, trainable mentally retarded, learning/behavioral disorders. M.Ed.
Technology Management. Ph.D.
Theater. M.A., Ph.D.

BRADLEY UNIVERSITY
Peoria, Illinois 61625-0602
Web site: www.bradley.edu

Founded 1897. CGS member. Located 163 miles SW of Chicago. Coed. Private control. Semester system. Special facilities: Center for Learning Resources (includes on-campus CCTV and satellite, teleproduction capacity, computer center), Caterpillar Global Communications Center, Materials Testing and Research Lab, Turner Center for Entrepreneurship, Institute for Urban Affairs and Business Research. Library: 650,000 volumes, 2500 subscriptions. More than 2000 computers on campus for student use, 112 PCs in all libraries. Total University enrollment: 6154.

Annual tuition: per credit 1–7 hours $550, 7½–11½ hours $565; Master of Liberal Studies $208 per hour. No on-campus housing available. Average academic year housing costs: $750 per month. Contact Director of Housing for off-campus housing information. Phone: (309)677-3218.

Graduate School

Enrollment: full-time 205, part-time 452. Graduate faculty: full- and part-time 251. Degrees conferred: M.A.. M.S., M.F.A., M.B.A., M.M.E., M.M., M.S.C.E., M.S.E.E., M.S.I.E., M.S.M.E., M.L.S., M.S.N., M.N.S.

ADMISSION REQUIREMENTS. Two official transcripts, two references required in support of School's application. Interview, GRE required by some departments. GMAT for M.B.A. applicants, MAT or GRE for all Education and Nursing programs. Portfolio for Art program. TOEFL and evidence of financial resources required of international applicants. Accepts transfer applicants. Graduates of unaccredited institutions not considered. Apply to Dean of the Graduate School by May 15 (Fall), October 15 (Spring). Rolling admission process. Application fee $40, $50 for international candidates. Phone: (309)677-2375; fax: (309) 677-3343; e-mail: bugrad@bradley.edu.

ADMISSION STANDARDS. Selective. Usual minimum average: 2.5 (2.75 major areas) (A = 4). Nondegree students permitted.

FINANCIAL AID. Scholarships, fellowships, assistantships, full and partial tuition waivers, Federal W/S, loans. Approved for VA benefits. Apply by April 1 to Dean of the Graduate School for assistantships; to Financial Aid Office for all other programs. Phone: (309)677-3215. Use FAFSA. Aid available for part-time students.

DEGREE REQUIREMENTS. For master's: 30 semester hours minimum; thesis/nonthesis option; final comprehensive exam.

FIELDS OF STUDY.

FOSTER COLLEGE OF BUSINESS ADMINISTRATION:
Accounting. M.S.A.
Business Administration. Includes concentrations in finance, management, marketing. M.B.A.
Executive Master of Business Administration. E.M.B.A.

SLANE COLLEGE OF COMMUNICATIONS AND FINE ARTS:
Art. Includes ceramics, drawing/illustration, painting, photography, printmaking, sculpture, visual communication & design. M.A., M.F.A.

COLLEGE OF EDUCATION AND HEALTH SCIENCES:
Curriculum and Instruction. M.A.
Leadership in Educational Administration. M.A.
Human Development Counseling. M.A.
Human Service Administration. M.A.
Nurse Administered Anesthesia. M.S.N.
Nurse Administration. M.S.N.
Physical Therapy. D.P.T.

COLLEGE OF ENGINEERING AND TECHNOLOGY:
Civil Engineering. M.S.C.E.
Electrical Engineering. M.S.E.E.
Industrial Engineering. M.S.I.E.

Manufacturing Engineering. M.S.Mf.E.
Mechanical Engineering. M.S.M.E.

COLLEGE OF LIBERAL ARTS AND SCIENCES:
Biology. M.S.
Chemistry. M.S.
Computer Information System. M.S.
Computer Science. M.S.
English. M.A.
Liberal Studies. M.L.S.

BRANDEIS UNIVERSITY
Waltham, Massachusetts 02454-9110
Web site: www.brandeis.edu

Founded 1948. CGS and AAU member. Located 8 miles NW of Boston. Coed. Private control. Semester system. Special facilities: research centers for biology, biochemistry, chemistry, mathematics, social sciences, physics; Judaic Center, American Civilization Center, Humanities Center, Rose Art Museum, music center, Rosenstiel Basic Medical Sciences Research Center, Center for Health Policy Analysis and Research, Levinson Policy Institute, Center for Employment and Income Studies, Center for Aging and Income Maintenance, theater arts center. Library: 938,835 volumes, 15,835 subscriptions. Total University enrollment: 5200.

Annual tuition: full-time $31,532, per course $3942. Some on-campus housing for graduate students. Housing costs: $500–$950 per month. Apply by June 1. Contact Graduate Student Services for off-campus housing information. Phone: (781)736-3550.

Graduate School of Arts and Sciences

Graduate study since 1953. Enrollment: full- and part-time 1578. Faculty: full-time 348, part-time 153. Degrees conferred: M.A., M.F.A., Ph.D.

ADMISSION REQUIREMENTS. Transcripts, statement of purpose, two letters of recommendation required in support of application (electronic application available). GRE, interview required for some departments. Writing samples, portfolio, or audition for theater and studio programs. GRE recommended for all departments. TOEFL (600 minimum score) required of all foreign applicants. Accepts transfer applicants. Graduates of unaccredited colleges not considered. Apply to the Associate Dean of the School by January 15, earliest deadline (Fall). Application fee $60, electronic fee $55. Phone: (781)736-3410; fax: (781) 736-3412; e-mail: gradschool@brandeis.edu.

ADMISSION STANDARDS. Very competitive. Usual minimum average: 3.0 (A = 4).

FINANCIAL AID. Scholarships, fellowships, assistantships for teaching/research, tuition waivers, Federal W/S, loans. Apply to the Associate Dean of the School by February 1. Phone: (781) 736-3410. Use FAFSA. Aid available for part-time students.

DEGREE REQUIREMENTS. For M.A.: 24 semester hours minimum in residence; reading knowledge of one foreign language; thesis sometimes required; final written/oral exam. For M.F.A. in Music: 36 hours minimum in residence; reading knowledge of one or two foreign languages; moderate instrumental proficiency; general exams; composition for composers, thesis for music history or theory majors. For M.F.A. in Theater Arts: acting and dramatic writing; 48 semester hours in residence; thesis play for dramatic writing; design-technical, 54 semester hours in residence; thesis. For Ph.D.: 48 hours minimum beyond the bachelor's, at least one year in residence; reading knowledge of at least one foreign language for most departments; qualifying exams; dissertation; final oral exam.

FIELDS OF STUDY.
American and Comparative History. M.A., Ph.D.
Anthropology. GRE for admission; apply by February 16. M.A., Ph.D.
Biochemistry. GRE, three letters of recommendation for admission. Apply by January 15, rolling admissions. M.S., Ph.D.
Biology. GRE, three letters of recommendation for admission. Rolling admission. M.S., Ph.D.
Biophysics and Structural Biology. GRE, three letters of recommendation for admission. Rolling admission. M.S., Ph.D.
Chemistry. GRE for admission. Apply by March 15. M.S., Ph.D.
Classical Studies. M.A.
Computer Science. GRE, three letters of recommendation. Apply by March 1. M.A., Ph.D.
English and American Literature. GRE/Subject, writing sample. Apply by February 15. Ph.D.
Genetic Counseling. GRE, three letters of recommendation. Apply by February 15. M.S
History of American Civilization. For M.A.: GRE, writing sample for admission. Apply by July 30.
Jewish Communal Services. GRE or GMAT, interview, writing sample for admission. Apply by February 15. M.A.
Literary Studies. Writing sample for admission. Apply by March 15.
Mathematics. GRE/Subject. Apply by February 15. M.A., Ph.D.
Molecular and Cell Biology. Ph.D. only.
Music. For musicology, GRE and writing sample for admission; Composition, sample of work. Apply by January 31. M.A., M.F.A., Ph.D.
Near Eastern and Judaic Studies. GRE suggested. Apply by February 1. M.A., Ph.D.
Neuroscience. M.S., Ph.D.
Physics. GRE/Subject Test for admission. Apply by February 15. M.A., Ph.D.
Politics. GRE, writing sample, three letters of recommendation for admission. M.A., Ph.D.
Psychology and Cognitive Science. GRE/Subject Test for admission. For Ph.D.: apply by February 15; for M.S., apply by June 1. M.A., M.S., Ph.D.
Software Engineering. M.S.E.
Sociology. Writing sample for admission. Apply by February 15. M.A., Ph.D.
Theater Arts. For admission: designers, portfolio; actors, audition; writers, sample of work. M.F.A.
Women's Studies. Joint degree with anthropology, English, Near Eastern and Judaic studies, or sociology.

International Business School

Special program: a semester abroad at Partner Universities in twelve countries. Affiliated institutions are Copenhagen Business School (Denmark), Ecole Superieure des Sciences Economiques et Commerciales (France), Eramus University (The Netherlands), Escuela Superior de Administracion y Direccion de Empresas (Spain), Fundacao Getulio Vargas (Brazil), Instituto Tecnologico Autonomo de Mexico (Mexico), International University of Japan, Keio University (Japan), WHU Koblenz (Germany), Luigi Bocconi University (Italy), National University of Singapore, Tel Aviv University (Israel), Univeersiteit Maastricht (The Netherlands), University of Paris (France), Yonsei University (Korea).

Annual tuition: $34,200.

Graduate enrollment: full-time 183, part-time 55. Faculty: full-time 21, part-time 35. Degrees conferred: M.A.eif, M.B.A.i., M.S.F., Ph.D.

ADMISSION REQUIREMENTS. Official transcripts, three letters of recommendation, résumé, GMAT required in support of College's application. Interview encouraged. TOEFL (minimum score 600, 250 on computer-based test) and official translations of all academic documents required for international applicants. Transfer students not accepted. Graduates of unaccredited institutions not considered. Apply to Admissions Office, preferably by February 15 (Fall). Phone: (781)736-2252. Application fee $55.

ADMISSION STANDARDS. Very selective. Usual minimum average: 3.3 (A = 4), GRE range: 510–660.

FINANCIAL AID. Scholarships, grants, assistantships, internships, Federal W/S, loans. Approved for VA benefits. Apply by March 1 to Financial Aid. Use FAFSA (School code: 002133). Phone: (781)736-2250.

DEGREE REQUIREMENTS. For M.A., M.B.A.i.: two-year program, 16 courses; basic knowledge of one foreign language other than English; semester of study at Partner University; capstone. For M.S.F.: 18–20 month program (full- or part-time), 10 courses; capstone. For Ph.D.: three- to four-year program; preliminary exam; two areas of specialization; research papers; thesis; final oral exam.

FIELDS OF STUDY.
Finance. M.S.F.
International Business. M.B.A.i.
International Economics and Finance. M.A., Ph.D.
International Finance/International Economics. M.B.A.i.

The Heller School for Social Policy and Management
Web site: www.heller.brandeis.edu

Organized for training in social policy and health, and human services management, 1959. Semester system. Annual tuition master's: full-time $32,951. For Ph.D.: $34,566 per year. On-campus housing available. Day-care facilities available.

Enrollment: full-time 125, part-time 54. Faculty: full-time 44, part-time 15. Degrees conferred: M.A., M.M., M.B.A. (Human Services), M.P.P., Ph.D.

ADMISSION REQUIREMENTS. Transcripts, successful academic and professional experience, writing sample, statement of purpose, two letters of recommendation, résumé, GMAT/GRE required in support of application. Interviews suggested. Apply no later than December 15 (Ph.D.), March 15 (Master's, Fall), November 1 (Master's, Spring), June 1 (Master's, part-time, Fall), priority given to early applicants. Application process on a rolling basis. Master's academic year starts in June. Application fee $50. Phone (781)736-3835; fax: (781)736-3881; e-mail: HellerAdmissions@brandeis.edu.

ADMISSION STANDARDS. Competitive. Usual minimum average: 3.0 (A = 4).

FINANCIAL AID. Scholarships, grants, fellowships, teaching assistantships, traineeships, tuition waivers, loans. Apply to Director of Financial Aid by February 15. Phone: (781)736-3820. Use FAFSA and CSSFA profile.

DEGREE REQUIREMENTS. For M.B.A, M.M.: (day) 17 semester courses; internship; (evening) program 17 semester courses; team consulting project. For M.A., M.P.P.: two-year program; one-year residence; practical training; fieldwork; project/thesis. For Ph.D.: 14–18 semester courses minimum; qualifying exam; dissertation; final oral exam.

FIELDS OF STUDY.
Health Care Administration. M.B.A.
Human Services. M.B.A.
International Health Policy and Management. M.S.
Public Policy. M.P.P.
Social Policy. Ph.D.
Sustainable International Development. M.A.

UNIVERSITY OF BRIDGEPORT
Bridgeport, Connecticut 06601
Web site: www.bridgeport.edu

Founded 1927. CGS member. Located 60 miles NE of New York. Coed. Private control. Semester system. Special facilities: Bernhard Center for Arts and Humanities, Carlson Art Gallery, Connecticut Technology Institute, Center for Venture Management and Entrepreneurial Studies. Library: 310,000 volumes, 2117 subscriptions. Total University enrollment: 3626.

Tuition: per credit School of Education and Human Resources $505, School of Business $575, School of Engineering and Design $575. On-campus housing for single students, none for married students. Average academic year housing costs: $6400 ($10,600 including board). Contact Office of Residential Life for both on- and off-campus housing information. Phone: (203)576-4461.

Graduate Studies

Enrollment: full-time 1082, part-time 868. Faculty: full-time 92, part-time 232. Degrees conferred: M.S., M.B.A., Sixth Year Professional Diplomas, Ed.D.

ADMISSION REQUIREMENTS. Official transcripts, three letters of recommendation required in support of application (electronic application available). GRE/GMAT/MAT required by some departments. Supplemental application, personal statement, and/or an interview may be requested. TOEFL required for international applicants. Accepts transfer applicants. Apply to Office of Admissions at least 30 days (60 days for Business) prior to registration. Admits Fall, Spring, and Summer. Application fee $25, $35 for international applicants. Phone: (800)898-8278, (203)576-4552; fax: (203)576-4941. E-mail: admit@bridgeport.edu.

ADMISSION STANDARDS. Selective. Usual minimum average: 2.5 (A = 4).

FINANCIAL AID. Assistantships, endowed scholarships, internships, co-op, residence hall directors, Federal W/S, loans. Approved for VA benefits. For assistantship contact department, for all other aid apply to Financial Aid Office; no specified closing date. Phone: (203)576-4568. Use FAFSA.

DEGREE REQUIREMENTS. For master's: 30–33 credits minimum, at least 27 in residence; thesis/nonthesis options. For Sixth-Year Professional Certificate: 30 credits beyond master's, at least 24 in residence. For Ed.D.: at least two years in residence; qualifying exam; dissertation; final oral exam. For D.C.: Successful completion of the three phases of basic sciences, clinical sciences, and clinical services; clinical competency exam. For N.D.: Successful completion of four year program; 1296 hours of clinical service.

FIELDS OF STUDY.

COLLEGE OF CHIROPRACTIC:
Chiropractic. D.C.

COLLEGE OF NATUROPATHIC MEDICINE:
Naturopathic. N.D.

NUTRITION INSTITUTE:
Human Nutrition. M.S.

SCHOOL OF BUSINESS:
Business Administration. Includes concentrations in accounting, computer applications & information systems, finance, global marketing, management & operations. M.B.A.

FONES SCHOOL OF DENTAL HYGIENE:
Dental Hygiene. M.S.

SCHOOL OF EDUCATION & HUMAN RESOURCES:
Counseling. Includes college student personnel, community counseling, human resource development. M.S.
Education. M.S.
Educational Leadership. Ed.D.
Instructional Technology. M.S.I.T.

SCHOOL OF ENGINEERING:
Computer Engineering. M.S.
Computer Science. M.S.
Computer Science and Engineering. Ph.D.
Electrical Engineering. M.S.
Mechanical Engineering. M.S.
Technology Management. M.S.

BRIDGEWATER STATE COLLEGE
Bridgewater, Massachusetts 02325-0001
Web site: www.bridgew.edu

Founded 1840. CGS member. Located 35 miles S of Boston. Coed. State control. Semester system. Library: 326,000 volumes, 1100 subscriptions. Approximately 780 computers on campus for student use. Total College enrollment: 9649.

Tuition and fees: per hour, resident $278, nonresident $278. No on-campus housing available.

School of Graduate Studies

Enrollment: approximately 1900 full- and part-time. Graduate faculty: approximately 140. Degrees conferred: M.A., M.A.T., M.Ed., M.P.A., M.S., M.S.M., C.A.G.S.

ADMISSION REQUIREMENTS. Official transcripts, three letters of reference, GRE required in support of College's application (GRE Subject Test for M.A. Only). Interview required for some programs. TOEFL required for international applicants. Accepts transfer applicants. Apply to the Graduate Office by October 1 for November admission, December 1 for February admission, March 1 for May admission, June 1 for August admission. Application fee $50. Phone (508)531-2919; fax: (508) 531-6162.

ADMISSION STANDARDS. Selective for most departments. Usual minimum average: 2.5 (A = 4).

FINANCIAL AID. Assistantships, scholarships, tuition waivers, grants, Federal W/S, loans. Apply by March 1 to Graduate School Dean for assistantships; to Financial Aid for all other programs. Phone: (508)531-1341. Use FAFSA.

DEGREE REQUIREMENTS. For M.A.: 30 semester hours minimum; research proficiency test; comprehensive exam; thesis. For M.A.T., M.S., M.S.M., M.Ed., M.P.A.: 30–36 semester hours minimum; thesis/nonthesis option; comprehensive exam. For C.A.G.S.: 30 semester hours beyond the master's degree; special project.

FIELDS OF STUDY.
Accounting. M.S.M.
Biology. M.A.T.
Business. M.S.M.
Chemistry. M.A.T.
Computer Science. M.S.
Counseling. M.Ed., C.A.G.S.
Creative Arts. M.A.T.
Criminal Justice. M.S.

Early Childhood Education. M.Ed.
Earth Sciences. M.A.T.
Educational Leadership. M.Ed., C.A.G.S.
Elementary Education. M.Ed.
English. M.A., M.A.T.
Global Electronic Commerce. M.S.M.
Health Education. M.A.T.
Health Promotion. M.Ed.
History. M.A.T.
Instructional Technology. M.Ed.
Library Media Studies. M.Ed.
Management. M.S.M.
Marketing. M.S.M.
Mathematics. M.A.T.
Organizational Development. M.S.M.
Physical Education. M.A.T., M.S.
Physical Sciences. M.A.T.
Physics. M.A.T.
Psychology. M.A.
Public Administration. Includes financial and personnel administration, municipal development and management, public safety administration, nonprofit and human services administration. M.P.A.
Reading. M.Ed., C.A.G.S.
Social Studies. M.A.T.
Special Education. M.Ed.

BRIGHAM YOUNG UNIVERSITY
Provo, Utah 84602-1001
Web site: www.byu.edu

Founded 1875. CGS member. Located 50 miles S of Salt Lake City. Coed. Private control; Church of Jesus Christ of Latter-day Saints. Trimester system. Library: 3,500,000 volumes, 27,000 subscriptions. Total University enrollment: approximately 34,000.

Annual tuition and fees: full-time, LDS church members $4860, nonchurch members $9720; for Marriott School of Management, LDS church members $8700, nonchurch members $17,400. On-campus housing for 1048 married students, 2210 for men, 2950 for women. Average annual housing cost: $4500 for single students (includes room and board); $6500 for married students. For both on- and off-campus housing information, contact Off-Campus Housing Manager. Phone: (801)422-1513.

Graduate Studies

Graduate study since 1918. Enrollment: full-time 2470, part-time 655. Graduate faculty: full-time 1064, part-time 165. Degrees conferred: M.A., M.S., M.P.A., M.Acc., M.B.A., M.Ed., M.E.A., M.E.M., M.M., M.T.M., Ed.Spec. Cert., Ed.D., Ph.D., TESOL Certificate.

ADMISSION REQUIREMENTS. Two transcripts, three letters of recommendation required in support of application. GRE/GMAT/MAT required by some departments. TOEFL required of foreign applicants. Interview required by some departments. Accepts transfer applicants. Graduates of unaccredited colleges not considered. Usual deadline February 1 (Fall), June 30 (Winter), February 1 (Spring), March 15 (Summer); some programs have earlier deadlines. Apply to Office of Graduate Studies, B-356 ASB by published department deadlines. Application fee $50. Phone: (801)422-4091; fax: (801)422-0270; e-mail: gradstudies@byu.edu.

ADMISSION STANDARDS. Selective for most departments. Usual minimum average: 3.0 (A = 4).

FINANCIAL AID. Scholarships, internships, teaching/research assistantships, Federal W/S, loans. Apply by application deadline to department of specialization for scholarships and assistantships; to Office of Financial Aid for all other aid. Phone: (801)378-4104; fax: (801)378-4264. Use FAFSA.

DEGREE REQUIREMENTS. For master's: 30 semester hours minimum, at least 20 in residence for most programs; thesis/nonthesis option; final oral/written exam. For Certificate, Ed.Spec.Cert.: 30 semester hours beyond master's. For Ed.D.: three years minimum of full-time study or its equivalent beyond the bachelor's, two consecutive semesters in residence; qualifying exam; research project; final oral/written exam. For Ph.D.: ordinarily two years of full-time course work or research or its equivalent to be taken in residence; language/research tool; comprehensive exam; dissertation; final oral exam.

FIELDS OF STUDY.

COLLEGE OF BIOLOGY AND AGRICULTURAL SCIENCES:
Agronomy. M.S.
Animal Science. M.S.
Botany and Range Science. Includes biological science education, botany, range science, wildlife and range resources. M.S., Ph.D. (Botany)
Food Science. M.S.
Genetics and Biotechnology. M.S.
Horticulture. M.S.
Microbiology. M.S., Ph.D.
Molecular Biology. M.S., Ph.D.
Neuroscience. M.S., Ph.D.
Nutrition. M.S.
Physiology and Developmental Biology. M.S., Ph.D.

COLLEGE OF ENGINEERING AND TECHNOLOGY:
Chemical Engineering. M.S., Ph.D.
Civil Engineering. M.S., Ph.D.
Construction Engineering. M.S.
Electrical Engineering. M.S., Ph.D.
Engineering Technology. M.S.
Information Technology. M.S.
Manufacturing Systems. M.S.
Mechanical Engineering. M.S., Ph.D.
Technology Education. M.S.

COLLEGE OF FAMILY, HOME AND SOCIAL SCIENCES:
Anthropology. M.A.
Clinical Psychology. P.h.D.
Geography. M.A.
History. M.A.
Marriage and Family Therapy. M.S., Ph.D.
Marriage, Family, and Human Development. M.S., Ph.D.
Psychology. M.S., Ph.D.
Social Work. M.S.W.
Sociology. M.S., Ph.D.

COLLEGE OF FINE ARTS AND COMMUNICATIONS:
Mass Communication. M.A.
Music. Includes composition, conducting music education, musicology, pedagogy, performance. M.A., M.M.
Theater and Media Arts. M.A.
Theater Design and Technology. M.F.A.
Visual Arts. Includes art education, art history, curatorial studies, studio art. M.A., M.F.A.

COLLEGE OF HUMANITIES:
Comparative Literature. M.A.
English. M.A.
French Studies. M.A.
German Literature. M.A.
Humanities. M.A.
Language Acquisition. Includes Arabic, Chinese, French, German, Japanese, Russian. M.A.

Linguistics. M.A.
Portuguese. M.A.
Spanish. M.A.
Spanish/Latin American Literature. M.A.
TESOL. M.A.

COLLEGE OF NURSING:
Nursing. Includes nursing administration, family nurse practitioner, pediatric nurse practitioner. M.S.

COLLEGE OF PHYSICAL AND MATHEMATICAL SCIENCES:
Biochemistry. M.S., Ph.D.
Chemistry. Includes inorganic, organic, physical. M.S., Ph.D.
Computer Science. M.S., Ph.D.
Geology. M.S.
Mathematics. Includes mathematics education. M.A., M.S., Ph.D.
Physics. M.S., Ph.D.
Physics and Astronomy. Ph.D.
Statistics. M.S.

COLLEGE OF HEALTH AND HUMAN PERFORMANCE:
Athletic Training. M.S.
Curriculum and Instruction in Physical Education. Ph.D.
Exercise Science. Ph.D.
Health and Human Performance. M.P.H., M.S.
Health Promotion. M.S., Ph.D.
Physical Education. M.S.
Public Health. M.P.H.
Sports Pedagogy. M.S.
Youth and Family Recreation. M.S.

DAVID O. MCKAY SCHOOL OF EDUCATION:
Counseling Psychology. Ph.D.
Educational Leadership. M.Ed., Ph.D., Ed.D.
Instructional Psychology and Technology. M.S., Ph.D.
Reading. Ed.D.
School Psychology. M.S.
Special Education. M.S.
Speech-Language Pathology. M.S.
Teaching and Learning. M.A., M.Ed.

THE J. WILLARD AND ALICE S. MARRIOTT SCHOOL OF MANAGEMENT:
Accountancy. Includes professional accountancy, accounting information systems, tax. M.Acc.
Business Administration. M.B.A.
Information Systems Management. M.I.S.M.
Organizational Behavior. M.O.B.
Public Management. M.P.A.

J. Reuben Clark Law School
Web site: www.law.byu.edu

Established 1971. ABA approved since 1974. AALS member. Semester system. Full-time study only. Exchange program with Central European University, Budapest, Hungary, and a clerkship with T. C. Beirne School of Law, University of Queensland, Australia. Law library 477,601 volumes, 4447 subscriptions. Library has LEXIS, NEXIS, RLIN, and WESTLAW.

Annual tuition: church members $8200, nonmembers $16,400. On-campus housing available, contact University Housing Office. Total average cost of all other expenses: $11,300.

Enrollment: first-year class 160; total 487 (men 67%, women 33%). Faculty: full-time 26, part-time 41. Student to faculty ratio 19.2 to 1. Degrees conferred: J.D., J.D.-Ed.D., J.D.-M.A., J.D.-M.B.A., J.D.-M.P.A., J.D.-M.Acc., J.D.-M.O.B., LL.M. (American and Comparative Legal Studies; for persons who have completed a basic legal education and received a degree in law in another country).

ADMISSION REQUIREMENTS. LSDAS Law School report, transcripts, LSAT, three recommendations, interview with a clergyman or bishop required in support of application. Accepts transfer applicants. Apply to Director of Admissions by March 1. Fall admission only. Application fee $50. Phone: (801)422-7871; fax: (801)422-5897.

ADMISSION STANDARDS. Selective. Accepts 27% of total annual applicants. Number of applicants 940; number of acceptance 254; number enrolled 153; LSAT (75% of class have a score at or above 161); GPA (75% of class have a GPA at or above 3.52). *U.S. News & World Report* ranking is 44th of all law schools.

FINANCIAL AID. Scholarships, assistantships, Federal W/S, loans, church loans. Apply to Student Financial Aid Office; no specified closing date. Phone: (801)422-6386. Use FAFSA. About 53% of students receive some form of financial assistance.

DEGREE REQUIREMENTS. For J.D.: satisfactory completion of three-year program; 90 semester credits. For LL.M.: at least 24 credits and two semesters in residence. For other master's and Ed.D. degrees: see Graduate listing above.

BROOKLYN COLLEGE OF THE CITY UNIVERSITY OF NEW YORK

Brooklyn, New York 11210-2889
Web site: www.brooklyn.cuny.edu

Founded 1930. CGS member. Coed. Municipal control. Semester system. Special facilities: Africana Research Institute, Applied Science Institute, Archaeological Research Institute, Computer Center, Dynamitron, Electronic Music Studio, Graduate Center for Worker Education, Center for Health Promotion, Center for Human Relations Training, Wolfe Institute for the Humanities, Infant Studies Center, Center for Italian-American Studies, Center for Puerto Rican Studies, Center for Nuclear Theory, Institute for Studies in American Music, Center for the Study of World Television, Speech and Hearing Clinic. Library: 1,300,000 volumes, 13,500 subscriptions. Approximately 800 computers on campus for student use. Total College enrollment: 15,300.

Tuition: per semester, State residents $6400, non-State residents $12,000; per credit, State resident $270, non-State $500. No on-campus housing available.

Division of Graduate Studies

Graduate study since 1935. Enrollment: full-time 397, part-time 3040. Faculty: full-time 187, part-time 140. Degrees conferred: M.A., M.F.A., M.S., M.S. in Ed., Advanced Certificate.

ADMISSION REQUIREMENTS. Official transcripts, two letters of reference required in support of application. GRE/Subject Tests, interview required by some departments. Accepts transfer applicants. Graduates of unaccredited colleges not considered. Apply to Office of Admissions by March 1 (Summer and Fall), November 1 (Spring), March 1 for selected teacher-education programs. Application fee $125. Phone: (718)951-5902; e-mail: adminqry@brooklyn.cuny.edu.

ADMISSION STANDARDS. Competitive. Usual minimum average: 2.75 overall, 3.0 in the major (A = 4).

FINANCIAL AID. Teaching/research fellowships, assistantships, lectureships, internships, tuition waivers, Federal W/S, loans. Approved for VA benefits. Apply by April 1 to appropriate department for fellowships and internships; to Office of Financial Aid for all other programs. Use FAFSA (College code: 002687) and City University's FAF.

DEGREE REQUIREMENTS. For all master's: 30 credits minimum, at least 24 in residence; thesis/nonthesis option; comprehensive exam. For liberal arts and science majors: thesis/written comprehensive exam; reading knowledge of one foreign language required in some programs. For Advanced Certificate: 30 credits beyond the master's degree; special project.

FIELDS OF STUDY.

Art. Portfolio required for admission. Includes drawing and painting, graphics, photography, sculpture. M.A., M.F.A.

Art History. Two languages for master's. M.A.

Audiology. Includes speech-language pathology. M.S.

Biology. One language for master's. M.A.

Chemistry. One language for master's. M.A.

Community Health. M.A.

Computer and Information Science. M.A.

Computer Science and Health Science. M.S.

Creative Writing. Includes fiction, playwriting, poetry. M.F.A.

Earth and Environmental Sciences. M.S.

Economics. M.A.

Education.
  Elementary. Special concentrations in early childhood, home economics, comparative and industrial education art, bilingual teaching, social science, mathematics, music, reading, science, teaching of Spanish-speaking children. M.S.Ed.
  Secondary. All junior and senior high-school subjects. M.S.Ed.
  Special Education. Education of children with retarded mental development/emotional handicaps/neuropsychological learning disabilities; bilingual special education; education of the speech and hearing handicapped; speech improvement. M.S.Ed.
  Sixth-Year Certificate Program. Includes administration and supervision, guidance and counseling, school psychologist, educational use of computers.

English. One language for master's. M.A.

Exercise Science and Rehabilitation. M.S.

French. M.A.

General Science. M.A.

Geology. M.A.

Graphics/Multimedia. M.A.

Guidance and Counseling. M.S.Ed.

Health and Nutrition Sciences. M.S.Ed.

Health Care Management. M.P.H.

History. M.A.

Information Systems. M.S.

Judaic Studies. M.A.

Liberal Studies. M.A.

Mathematics. M.A.

Music. One language for master's. Includes musicology, performance. M.A., M.M.

Nutrition. M.S.

Physical Education. Includes psychosocial aspects of physical activities, sports management. M.S.

Physics. M.A.

Political Economy. M.A.

Political Science. One language for master's. Includes urban policy and administration. M.A.

Psychology. Includes experimental, industrial and organizational. M.A.

School Counseling. M.S.Ed.

School Psychologist. M.S.Ed.

Social Studies. M.A.

Sociology. M.A.

Spanish. M.A.

Speech. Includes public communication (M.A.); audiology, pathology, speech and hearing science (M.S.).

Theater. Includes criticism, history (M.A.); acting, design, technical production, directing, performing arts management (M.F.A.).

TV/Radio. Includes television production. M.F.A., M.S.

Urban Policy and Administration. M.A.

BROOKLYN LAW SCHOOL

250 Joralemon Street
Brooklyn, New York 11201-3798
Web site: www.brooklaw.edu

Established 1901. ABA approved since 1937, AALS member. Private control. Semester system. Special facilities: Center for the Study of International Business Law, Center for Health, Science and Public Policy, Center for Law Language and Cognition. Library: 544,380 volumes, 2237 subscriptions. Library has LEXIS, WESTLAW, DIALOG.

Annual tuition: full-time $37,525, part-time $28,233. Total average cost for all other expenses: $12,000–$15,000. Enrollment: first-year class full-time 280, part-time 185; total full- and part-time 1499 (men 50%, women 50%, minorities 26%). Faculty: full-time 74, part-time 122. Student to faculty ratio 20 to 1. No on-campus housing, but six Law School residence halls in close proximity to campus. Degrees conferred: J.D., combined J.D.-Master's program with Baruch College, Hunter College, Brooklyn College, and Pratt Institute.

ADMISSION REQUIREMENTS. LSDAS Law School report, transcripts, LSAT, bachelor's degree required in support of application. Interview not required. Graduates from unaccredited colleges not considered. Apply to the Office of Admissions after October 15, before April 1. Admits Fall only. Rolling admission process. Application fee $60. Phone: (718)780-7906; fax: (718) 780-0395.

ADMISSION STANDARDS. Selective. Accepts 25% of total annual applicants. Number of applicants 4100; number of acceptance 1041; number enrolled 503; LSAT (75% of class have a score at or above 161); GPA (75% of class have a GPA at or above 3.15). *U.S. News & World Report* ranking is in the second tier of all law schools with a rank of 60th.

FINANCIAL AID. Scholarships, fellowships, assistantships, Federal W/S, loans. Apply to the Financial Aid Office by April 15. Phone: (718)780-7915. Use FAFSA (School code: E00057). About 68% of full-time students receive aid other than loans from school.

DEGREE REQUIREMENTS. For J.D.: three-year program (full-time), four-year program (part-time), 84 semester hours minimum. For master's program: see other institutional listings.

BROWN UNIVERSITY

Providence, Rhode Island 02912
Web site: www.brown.edu

Founded in 1764. CGS and AAU member. Coed. Private control. Semester system. Special facilities: Biomedical Center, Computing Laboratory, East Asia Language and Area Center, Geology-Chemistry research centers, Graduate Center (dormitories and administrative offices), Haffenreffer Museum of Anthropology, herbarium, Hunter Psychological Laboratory, Institute of Life Sciences, Ladd Observatory, Lefschetz Center for Dynamic Systems, Population Studies and Training Center, Prince Engineering Laboratory, University Library (2,225,000 items), John Carter Brown Library (Americana, 40,000 volumes), Annmary Brown Memorial Library (Renaissance and Medieval culture). The University's NIH ranking is 99th among all U.S. institutions with 155 awards/grants valued at $52,592,893. According to The Center at University of Florida, Brown University is ranked 96th in receipt of Federal Research funds with $81,445,000. The University's endowment assets ranks it 26th, $1,647,295,000. Fourteen of the University's faculty members have been elected to National Honor Academies and this ranks it 56th among all U.S. institutions. The Library: approximately 2,200,000 volumes, 30,000 subscriptions.

Annual tuition: full-time $35,584. On-campus housing available for single students, none for married students. Average annual housing cost: $675–$900 per month. Apply to Housing Office, Box 1864. Phone: (401)863-3500.

Graduate School

Graduate study since 1887. Enrollment: full-time 1800, part-time 200. Faculty: full-time 500, part-time 30. Degrees conferred: A.M., Sc.M., M.A.T., M.F.A., M.M.Sc., Ph.D., M.D.-Ph.D.

ADMISSION REQUIREMENTS. Transcripts, three letters of recommendation required in support of application (electronic application accepted) and letter from the student stating plans for graduate study. GRE/Subject required for biochemistry, biology and medical science, comparative literature, computer science, English, French studies, Hispanic and Italian studies, mathematics, psychology. GRE for most other departments. TOEFL required of foreign applicants. Accepts transfer applicants. Graduates of unaccredited colleges not considered. Apply to Graduate School by January 2. Application fee $70. Phone: (401)863-2600.

ADMISSION STANDARDS. Competitive. Usual minimum average: 3.0 (A = 4).

FINANCIAL AID. Scholarships, fellowships, research assistantships, teaching assistantships, proctorships, grants, endowed awards, Federal W/S, loans. Apply to the Office of Financial Aid by January 15. Use FAFSA. About 75% of students receive aid other than loans from school and outside sources. No aid for part-time students.

DEGREE REQUIREMENTS. For master's: 8 semester courses minimum, additional courses required by some programs; thesis, special projects, special exams required by some departments. For Ph.D.: three years of full-time study or equivalent beyond master's, at least two semesters in residence; oral preliminary exam; final exam; dissertation.

FIELDS OF STUDY.
American Civilization. A.M., Ph.D.
Anthropology. Ph.D.
Applied Mathematics. Ph.D.
Archaeology and the Ancient World. Ph.D.
Artificial Organs, Biomaterials and Cellular Technology. Sc.M.
Biomedical Engineering. Sc.M., Ph.D.
Biostatistics. Sc.M., Ph.D.
Brain Science. Ph.D.
Brazilian Studies. A.M.
Chemistry. Ph.D.
Classics. A.M., Ph.D.
Cognitive Science. Ph.D.
Comparative Literature. Ph.D.
Computer Music and Multimedia. Ph.D.
Computer Science. Sc.M.
Development Studies. A.M.
Ecological and Evolutionary Biology. Ph.D.
Economics. Ph.D.
Egyptology and Ancient Western Studies. Ph.D.
Elementary Education. M.A.T.
Engineering. Sc.M., Ph.D.
Environmental Studies. A.M.
Epidemiology. Ph.D.
Ethnomusicology. Ph.D.
French Studies. Ph.D.
Geological Sciences. Ph.D.

Health Services Research. Ph.D.
Hispanic Studies. Ph.D.
History. A.M., Ph.D.
History of Art and Architecture. Ph.D.
Innnovation Management and Entrepreneurship Engineering. Sc.M.
Italian Studies. Ph.D.
Linguistics. Ph.D.
Literary Arts. A.M.
Mathematics. Ph.D.
Modern Culture and Media. Ph.D.
Molecular Biology, Cell Biology and Biochemistry. Ph.D.
Molecular Pharmacology and Physiology. Ph.D.
Neuroscience. Ph.D.
Pathobiology. Ph.D.
Philosophy. Ph.D.
Physics. Ph.D.
Political Science. Ph.D.
Portuguese and Brazilian Studies. A.M., Ph.D.
Public Affairs and Public Policy. M.P.P.
Public Health. M.P.H.
Public Humanities. A.M.
Psychology. Ph.D.
Religious Studies. Ph.D.
Slavic Studies. Ph.D.
Sociology. Ph.D.
Theater and Performance Studies. M.F.A., Ph.D.
Urban Education Policy. A.M.

Warren Alpert Medical School (Box G-A212)
Web site: bms.brown.edu

Four- year program in medicine leading to the M.D. was accredited in 1975. Special program: Program in Liberal Medical Education (an eight-year program combining undergraduate education at Brown and the M.D. degree. Apply through the College's admissions Office). The University's NIH ranking is 99th among U.S. institutions with 155 awards/grants worth $52,592,893.

Annual tuition: $39,350. On-campus housing available. Total average figure for all other expenses: $16,172.

Enrollment: first year class 73, total 360 (men 43%, women 57%, minorities 47%, state residents 15%). Faculty: full-time 700. Degrees conferred: M.D., M.D.-M.M.Sc., M.D.-Ph.D.

ADMISSION REQUIREMENTS. Entry into the first year of the Medical School is available to students enrolled in post-baccalaureate premedical study at Brown University, Bryn Mawr College, Columbia University, and Goucher College; to students enrolled in the Early Identification Program at Providence College, Rhode Island College, Tougaloo College and University of Rhode Island; and to graduates of Brown University Program in Liberal Medical Education. AMCAS report, MCAT, transcripts, three letters of recommendation, supplemental Medical School application required in support of application. Accepts transfer applicants. Apply to Office of Admissions, Box G-A212 after June 1, before December 31. Application fee $95. Phone: (401)863-2149; fax: (401)863-3801; e-mail: medschool_admissions@brown.edu

ADMISSION STANDARDS. Competitive. Accepts about 4% of all applicants. Number of applications 4324 (4247 out-of-state); number interviewed 294 (279 out-of-state); number of acceptance 184 (73 out-of-state); number enrolled 73 (64 out-of-state). Approximately 45% of class is PLME. Mean Composite MCAT 11.3; mean UGPA 3.12. *U.S. News & World Report* ranking is in the top 34 of all medical schools in Research, 27th in primary care.

FINANCIAL AID. Scholarship, awards, Federal and private loans. No qualified student will be denied admission solely because of financial disability. About 55% of students receive financial assistance. Apply to Dean; no specified closing date. Phone: (401) 863-1142. Use FAFSA and Need Access Form.

DEGREE REQUIREMENTS. For PLME M.D.: satisfactory completion of eight-year PLME; passing Objective Structural Clinical Exam. For traditional M.D.: Satisfactory completion of 4-year program; passing Objective Structural Clinical Exam.

FIELDS OF GRADUATE STUDY.
Artificial Organs, Biomaterials and Cellular Technology.
Ecology and Evolutionary Biology.
Epidemiology.
Molecular Biology, Cell Biology and Biochemistry.
Molecular Pharmacology and Physiology.
Neuroscience.
Pathobiology.

BRYANT UNIVERSITY
Smithfield, Rhode Island 02917-1284
Web site: www.bryant.edu

Located 12 miles N of Providence. Coed. Private control. Semester system. Day and evening programs. Special facility: Center for International Business and Economic Development. Library: 133,000 volumes, 1500 subscriptions. Approximately 460 computers on campus for general student use. Total University enrollment: 3642.

Tuition: per credit $650. On-campus housing for single students. Average academic year housing costs: $6400–$8378 ($10,400–$12,500 including board); off-campus housing costs: $600–$900 per month. Contact housing office for both on- and off-campus housing information. Phone: (401)232-6140.

Graduate School
Enrollment: full-time 39, part-time 391. Faculty: full-time 30, part-time 8. Degrees conferred: M.B.A., M.S.A., M.S.I.S., M.S.T.

ADMISSION REQUIREMENTS. Official transcripts, GMAT, statement of objectives, three letters of recommendation required in support of School's application. Accepts transfer applicants. Apply by July 15 (Fall), November 15 (Spring) to Director of Graduate Programs. Rolling admissions process. Application fee $80. Phone: (401)232-6230; fax: (401)232-6494; e-mail: gradprog@bryant.edu.

ADMISSION STANDARDS. Selective. Usual minimum average: 2.5 (2.75 last two years) (A = 4).

FINANCIAL AID. Research assistantships, fellowships, tuition waivers, Federal W/S, loans. Approved for VA benefits. Apply by August 1 to Director of Financial Aid. Phone: (401)232-6020. Use FAFSA.

DEGREE REQUIREMENTS. For master's: 30–61 semester hours; no thesis or foreign language requirement.

FIELDS OF STUDY.
Accounting. M.S.A.
Business Administration. Concentration in accounting, computer information systems, e-strategy, finance, general business, management, marketing, operations management, taxation.
Information Systems. M.S.I.S.
Taxation. M.S.T.

BRYN MAWR COLLEGE
Bryn Mawr, Pennsylvania 19010-2899
Web site: www.brynmawr.edu

Founded 1885. Located 11 miles W of Philadelphia. CGS member. Coed on graduate level. Private control. Semester system. Special facilities: Ella Riegel Museum of Classical Archaeology, Visual Resources Center. Library: 1,100,000 volumes, 4400 subscriptions. Total College enrollment: 1799.

Annual tuition: full-time $27,600, per course $4660. Campus housing available at Glenmede Graduate Residence Center for men and women. Average annual housing cost: $700–$1050 per month. Contact Director of Graduate Housing for both on- and off-campus housing information. Phone: (610)526-7331.

Graduate School of Arts and Sciences
Web site: www.brynmawr.edu/gsas

Graduate study since 1885. Enrollment: full-time 71, part-time 98. College faculty: full-time 116, part-time 40. Degrees conferred: M.A., Ph.D.

ADMISSION REQUIREMENTS. Official transcripts, three letters of recommendation (including at least one from a professor in applicant's major field), GRE (Subject for Biology, Chemistry, Physics, Psychology, and Russian), a writing sample required in support of School's application. TOEFL required for international applicants. Applicants for financial aid should apply by January 1 (Science programs), January 25 (Humanities), February 1 (Clinical Development), January 25 for foreign applicants, all others must be completed by June 30. Application fee $25. Phone: (610)526-5072; e-mail: gsas@brynmawr.edu.

ADMISSION STANDARDS. Competitive. Usual minimum average: 3.0 (A = 4).

FINANCIAL AID. Annual awards from institutional funds: scholarships, research fellowships, teaching assistantships, tuition awards, loans. Apply by January 2 (January 25 for foreign applicants) to the Dean of the School for fellowships, assistantships; to Financial Aid Office for all other programs. Phone: (610)526-5245. Aid available for part-time study.

DEGREE REQUIREMENTS. For M.A.: one year minimum in full-time residence; thesis; final oral/written exam. For Ph.D.: three years minimum, at least two in full-time residence; reading knowledge of foreign languages/computer languages/special techniques as required by individual departments; preliminary exam; dissertation; final oral exam.

FIELDS OF STUDY.
Biochemistry.
Biology.
Chemistry.
Classical and Near Eastern Archaeology.
Classical Studies.
Clinical Developmental Psychology. Apply by February 1; admits Fall only.
French. M.A. only.
Geology.
Greek.
History of Art.
Latin.
Mathematics.
Neural and Behavioral Sciences. Interdisciplinary.
Physics.
Russian.

Graduate School of Social Work and Social Research (19010-1697)
Web site: www.brynmawr.edu/socialwork

Founded as the Graduate Department of Social Economy and Social Research in 1915. Semester system. Special facilities: Center for Child and Family Well-being, the Nonprofit Executive Leadership Institute.

Tuition: $2800 (Master's), $3500 (Doctoral). Enrollment: full-time 174, part-time 107. Faculty: full-time 15, part-time 31. Degrees conferred: M.L.S.P., M.S.S., Ph.D.

ADMISSION REQUIREMENTS. Official transcripts, three letters of recommendation required in support of School's application. TOEFL required for international applications. Accepts transfer applicants. Graduates of unaccredited institutions not considered. Apply to Assistant Dean and Director of Admission. Applications must be completed by March 1. Rolling admissions process. Application fee $50. Phone: (610)520-2601; fax: (610)520-2655.

ADMISSION STANDARDS. Competitive. Usual minimum average: 2.75 (A = 4), 3.0 (Doctoral programs).

FINANCIAL AID. Annual awards from institutional fund; fellowships, grants, research assistantships, teaching assistantships, full and partial tuition waivers, Federal W/S, loans. Approved for VA benefits. Apply by March 1 to Assistant Dean for fellowships, assistantships; to Financial Aid Office for all other programs. Phone: (610)527-5403. Use FAFSA. Aid available for part-time students.

DEGREE REQUIREMENTS. For master's: 45–60 credits minimum, at least one year in full-time residence; field placement; thesis/special project; final exam. For Ph.D.: three years minimum, at least two in full-time residence; advance practice internship; dissertation; final oral exam.

FIELDS OF STUDY.
Law and Social Policy. M.L.S.P.
Social Services. Includes concentrations in clinical practice, management, policy practice and advocacy. M.S.S.
Social Work. Ph.D.

BUCKNELL UNIVERSITY
Lewisburg, Pennsylvania 17837
Web site: www.bucknell.edu

Founded 1846. Located 155 miles NW of Philadelphia. Coed. Private control. Semester system. Library: 432,700 volumes, 2789 subscriptions. More than 350 computers on campus for general student use.

Tuition: per course $4165. Limited on-campus housing available for single students, none for married students. Average annual housing cost: $3784–$5200. Apply to Residential Life Director. Phone: (570)577-1195.

Graduate Studies

Enrollment: full-time 78, part-time 40, total 116 (men 30%, women 70%). University faculty teaching graduate students: full-time 16, part-time 0. Degrees conferred: M.A., M.S., M.S.Ed., M.S.Che., M.S.C.E., M.S.E.E., M.S.M.E.

ADMISSION REQUIREMENTS. Transcripts, GRE/Subject Tests, GMAT (Business), two letters of recommendation required in support of application. TOEFL required for international applicants. Accepts transfer applicants. Graduates of unaccredited colleges not considered. Apply to Director of Graduate Studies by March 1 (Fall), December 1 (Spring), April 15 (Summer).

Application fee $25. Phone: (570)577-1304; fax: (570)577-3760; e-mail: gradstds@bucknell.edu.

ADMISSION STANDARDS. Selective for most departments, very selective for some. Usual minimum average: 2.8 (A = 4).

FINANCIAL AID. Annual awards from institutional funds: scholarships, fellowships, assistantships, tuition waivers, Federal W/S, loans. Apply by March 1 to Graduate Office. Phone: (570)577-1304. Use FAFSA and University's FAF. About 50% of students receive aid other than loans from University and outside sources. Aid sometimes available for part-time students.

DEGREE REQUIREMENTS. For master's: 28 credit hours minimum, at least 22 in residence; thesis; final exam; reading knowledge of one foreign language required for M.A. (English).

FIELDS OF STUDY.
Animal Behavior.
Biology.
Chemical Engineering.
Chemistry.
Civil and Environmental Engineering.
Classroom Teaching.
Educational Research.
Electrical Engineering.
English.
Management.
Mathematics.
Mechanical Engineering.
Psychology.
Reading.
School Administration and Supervision.
School Psychology.

UNIVERSITY AT BUFFALO, STATE UNIVERSITY OF NEW YORK

Buffalo, New York 14260-1608
Web site: www.buffalo.edu

Founded 1846. CGS and AAU member. Coed. State control. Semester system. Special facilities: Canada-United States Trade Center, Center for Studies in American Culture, Center for Advanced Photonic and Electronic Materials, Center for Advanced Molecular Biology and Immunology, Center for Assistive Technology, Center for Comparative and Global Studies in Education, Center for Computational Research, Center for Critical Languages, Center for Curriculum Planning, Center for the Study of Psychoanalysis and Culture, National Center for Earthquake Engineering Research, National Center for Geographic Information and Analysis, Center for Electronic and Electro-optic Materials, Center for Applied Molecular Biology and Immunology, Center for Research in Special Environments, New York Center for Hazardous Waste Management, Center for Study of Aging, Baldy Center for Law and Social Policy, Center for Research on Urban Social Work Practice, Center for Behavioral and Social Aspects of Health, Center for Cognitive Sciences, Center for Research in Special Environments, Center for Hearing and Deafness, Center for Structural Biology, Research Center for Law and Jurisprudence, Center of Excellence for Document Analysis and Recognition, Comprehensive Oral Health Research Center, Research Institute on Addiction, Toxicology Research Center, Environment and Society Institute, Institute for Research and Education on Women and Gender, New York State Center for Engineering Design and Industrial Innovation. The University's NIH ranking is 95th among all U.S. institutions with 181 awards/grants valued at $55,508,124. According to The Center at University of Florida, the University at Buffalo is ranked 57th in receipt of Federal Research funds with $129,794,000 and it ranks 55th for total University research expenditures with $240,180,000. In 2004, the University awarded 299 doctorates which ranked it 44th among all U.S. institutions eligible to award that degree. Five of the University's faculty members have been elected to National Honor Academies and this ranks it 90th among all U.S. institutions. The Library: approximately 3,400,000 volumes, 34,126 subscriptions. Total University enrollment: 27,220.

Annual tuition: full-time, resident $8288, nonresident, $10,920. Unlimited on-campus housing available for single graduate students. Average academic year housing costs: $10,700 (including board); $12,500 for married students. Contact Director of Residence Life for on-campus housing information, phone: (716) 645-2171; for off-campus housing, phone: (716)829-2224. Daycare facilities available.

Graduate School

Graduate study since 1923. Enrollment: full-time 6737, part-time 2099. Graduate faculty: full- and part-time 2200. Degrees conferred: M.A., M.B.A., M.S., M.Arch., M.U.P., M.M., M.F.A., M.E., Ed.M., Ed.D., Ph.D., M.D., D.D.S., Pharm.D., D.N.S.

ADMISSION REQUIREMENTS. Transcripts required in support of application. Online application available. GRE/MAT, letters of recommendation required by some departments. Interview not required. TOEFL (minimum score 550) required for foreign applicants. Accepts transfer applicants. Graduates of unaccredited institutions not considered. Contact individual program regarding deadlines for admission. Rolling admissions process. Application fee $35. Phone: (716)645-6968; or (716)645-6998, ask for individual department chair.

ADMISSION STANDARDS. Relatively open to very competitive. Usual minimum average varies by department.

FINANCIAL AID. Annual awards from institutional funds: fellowships, teaching assistantships, graduate assistantships, research assistantships, grants, Federal W/S, loans. Approved for VA benefits. Apply to the appropriate department chair for fellowships, assistantships; to the Financial Aid Office for all other programs. Phone: (716)645-3724. Use FAFSA (School code: 002837). About 55% of full-time students receive aid other than loans from School and outside sources. Aid available for part-time students.

DEGREE REQUIREMENTS. For most master's: 30 semester hours minimum, at least 24 in residence; comprehensive exam; thesis/nonthesis option/special project; oral exam requirements vary by department. For Ph.D.: three years minimum, at least one year in full-time residence; preliminary exam; dissertation; final oral exam. Contact individual programs for other requirements.

FIELDS OF STUDY.
American Studies. M.A., Ph.D.
Anthropology. M.A., Ph.D.
Art. M.F.A. only.
Art History. M.A. only.
Biological Sciences. M.A., Ph.D.
Chemistry. M.A., Ph.D.
Classics. M.A., Ph.D.
Clinical Psychology. Ph.D.
Cognitive Psychology. Ph.D.
Communication. M.A., Ph.D.
Communicative Disorders and Sciences. M.A., Ph.D.
Comparative Literature. M.A., Ph.D.
Economics. M.A., Ph.D.
English. M.A., Ph.D.

Fine Arts. M.F.A.
French. M.A., Ph.D.
Geography. M.A., Ph.D.
Geology. M.A., Ph.D.
History. M.A., Ph.D.
Humanities. Interdisciplinary. M.A. only.
Linguistics. M.A., Ph.D.
Mathematics. M.A., Ph.D.
Medicinal Chemistry. M.S., Ph.D.
Music. Includes music history, music composition, performance. M.A., M.M., Ph.D.
Natural Sciences. Interdisciplinary. M.S. only.
Philosophy. M.A., Ph.D.
Physics. M.A., Ph.D.
Political Science. M.A., Ph.D.
Psychology. M.A., Ph.D.
Social Sciences. Interdisciplinary. M.A., Ph.D.
Sociology. Includes medical sociology. M.A., Ph.D.
Spanish. M.A., Ph.D.
Women's Studies. M.A.

School of Architecture and Planning

Web site: www.ap.buffalo.edu

Tuition: per credit, resident $288, nonresident $455. Enrollment full-time 194, part-time 25. Faculty: full-time 30, part-time 29. Degree conferred: M.U.P., M.Arch.

ADMISSION REQUIREMENTS. Official transcripts, three letters of recommendation, 500-word personal statement, résumé required in support of School's application. Online application available. TOEFL (minimum score 550) and Financial Statement Form required for international applicants. Does not consider transfer applicants. Apply to Office of Academic Programs Administration in the School. Application fee $35 (online application), $50 fee for paper application. Phone: (716)829-3485, ext. 105; fax: (716)829-3256.

ADMISSION STANDARDS. Selective. Usual minimum average: 3.0 (A = 4).

FINANCIAL AID. Research/teaching assistantships, internships, traineeships, tuition waivers, Federal W/S, loans. Approved for VA benefits. Apply as early as possible to the Dean's Office for assistantships; to Financial Aid Office for all other programs. Phone: (716)645-2450. Use FAFSA. About 20% of full-time students receive some form of financial aid. Aid available for part-time students.

DEGREE REQUIREMENTS. For M.Arch., M.U.P.: 52 credit full-time, two-year program; planning practicum; thesis or professional planning project.

FIELDS OF STUDY.
Architecture. M.Arch.
Urban Planning. M.U.P.

School of Dental Medicine

Web site: www.sdm.buffalo.edu

Organized 1892. Joined SUNY system in 1962. Located at Health Science Center.

Annual tuition: resident $16,200, nonresident $32,000. On-campus housing available. Average academic year housing and personal expenses: $14,410. For housing apply to SUNYAB, Housing Office. Phone: (716)636-2181. Total cost for all other first-year expenses: $15,260.

Enrollment: first-year class 89, total full-time 354 (men 69%, women 31%, minorities 20%, state resident 60%). Faculty: full-time 65, part-time 112. Degrees conferred: D.D.S, D.D.S.-M.S., D.D.S.-Ph.D., Certificate.

ADMISSION REQUIREMENTS. AADSAS report, transcripts, DAT, three letters of recommendation required in support of School's application. Interviews by invitation only. Applicants must have completed at least three years of college, prefer four years of college. Accepts transfer students from U.S. and Canadian dental schools. Graduates of unaccredited colleges not considered. Apply to Admissions Office after July 1, before January 1. Application fee $50. Phone: (716)829-2839, or (716)829-3517.

ADMISSION STANDARDS. Selective. Usual minimum average: 2.8 (A = 4). Mean DAT: Academic 19.54, PAT 19.12, Mean UGPA: 3.34 (A = 4). Accepts 12% of total annual applicants. Approximately 90% are state residents.

FINANCIAL AID. Scholarships, fellowships, grants, loans. Apply to the Financial Aid Office by June 1. Phone: (716)829-2839. Use FAFSA (School code: 002837). About 96% of students receive some aid from School.

DEGREE REQUIREMENTS. For D.D.S.: satisfactory completion of forty-five-month program.

FIELDS OF GRADUATE STUDY.
Advanced Education in General Dentistry Program.
Biomaterials. M.S.
Endodontics. Certificate.
Oral and Maxillofacial Pathology.
Oral and Maxillofacial Surgery.
Oral Biology. Ph.D.
Oral Sciences. M.S.
Orthododontics. M.S., Certificate.
Pediatric Dentistry. Certificate.
Periodontics. Certificate.
Prosthodontics. Certificate.
TMD and Orofacial Pain Program.

Graduate School of Education

Graduate study since 1931. Tuition: per credit, resident $288, nonresident $455. Graduate housing available. Apply to Office of Housing Services, 106 Spaulding Quad, Ellicott Housing. Phone: (716)645-2171. For off-campus housing, apply to Off-Campus Housing, 100 Allen. Phone: (716)829-2224.

Enrollment: full- and part-time 1283. Faculty: full-time 71, part-time 77. Degrees conferred: Ed.M., Ed.D. The M.A., M.S., and Ph.D. are offered through the Graduate School.

ADMISSION REQUIREMENTS. Transcripts, GRE/MAT, letters of reference required in support of all doctoral applications. Consult departments for additional requirements. TOEFL required for international applicants. Accepts transfer applicants. Graduates of unaccredited institutions not considered. Deadlines vary with department. Application fee $50. Phone: (716)645-2110, ext. 1209.

ADMISSION STANDARDS. Competitive. Usual minimum average: 3.0 (A = 4).

FINANCIAL AID. Teaching assistantships, graduate assistantships, internships, Federal W/S, loans. Approved for VA benefits. Apply to Director of Financial Aid; no specified closing date. Phone: (716)829-3724. Use FAFSA and TAP.

DEGREE REQUIREMENTS. For master's: 32 semester hours minimum; comprehensive exam. For Certificate: 30 credits beyond the master's. For Ed.D., Ph.D.: 72 semester hours minimum, at least two semesters in continuous full-time residence; preliminary exams; dissertation; final oral exam.

FIELDS OF STUDY.
Biology: Adolescence (7–12 or 5–12).
Chemistry: Adolescence (7–12 or 5–12).

Childhood (Grade 1–6). Includes bilingual extension (1–6).
Counseling Psychology.
Counselor Education.
Early Childhood (Birth–grade 2).
Early Childhood/Childhood (Birth–6).
Earth Science: Adolescence (7–12 or 5–12).
Education In and through the Arts.
Educational Administration.
Educational Psychology.
Elementary Education.
English Education.
English for Speakers of Other Languages.
English: Adolescence (7–12 or 5–12).
Foreign and Second Language.
Higher Education.
Languages. Includes teaching French, German, Italian, Latin, Spanish: adolescence (7–12 or 5–12).
Library Media.
Mathematics: Adolescence (7–12 or 5–12)
Mental Health Counseling.
Music.
Physics: Adolescence (7–12 or 5–12).
Reading.
Rehabilitation Counseling.
School Counseling.
School Psychology.
Science.
Science and the Public–Distance Learning.
Social and Philosophical Foundations.
Social Studies: Adolescence (7–12 or 5–12).
Special Education.
Teaching English to Speakers of Other Languages.

School of Engineering and Applied Sciences
Web site: www.eng.buffalo.edu

Tuition: per credit, resident $288, nonresident $455. Enrollment full-time 755, part-time 150. Faculty: full-time 124, part-time 37. Degrees conferred: M.Eng., M.S., Ph.D.

ADMISSION REQUIREMENTS. Official transcripts, GRE required in support of School's application. Online application available. TOEFL (minimum score 550) and Financial Statement Form required for international applicants. Will consider transfer applicants. Apply to Office of Academic Programs Administration in the School. Application fee $35 fee for online application, $50 fee for paper application. Phone: (716)645-2771, ext. 1105, fax: (716)645-2495.

ADMISSION STANDARDS. Selective. Usual minimum average: 3.0 (A = 4).

FINANCIAL AID. Fellowships, research/teaching assistantships, grants, internships, tuition waivers, Federal W/S, loans. Approved for VA benefits. Apply as early as possible to the Dean's Office for assistantships; to Financial Aid Office for all other programs. Phone: (716)645-2450. Use FAFSA. About 40% of full-time students receive some form of financial aid. Aid available for part-time students.

DEGREE REQUIREMENTS. For Master's: 30 credit program, at least 24 credits in residence; comprehensive exam; admission to candidacy; thesis/nonthesis option/project. For Ph.D.: three-year program; qualifying exam; admission to candidacy; dissertation; final oral exam.

FIELDS OF STUDY.
Aerospace Engineering
Chemical Engineering
Civil Engineering. Includes computational engineering mechanics, geomechanics, geoenvironmental and foundation engineering.

Computer Science and Engineering.
Electrical Engineering. Includes communication and signal processing, energy systems, microelectronics, photonics and materials.
Engineering Management. Includes production management.
Engineering Science.
Environmental Engineering. Includes environmental engineering and science, water resources and environmental fluid mechanics.
Human Factors Engineering/Ergonomics.
Industrial Engineering.
Mechanical Engineering.
Operations Research.
Production Systems Engineering.
Structural Engineering. Includes construction engineering and management, structural and earthquake engineering.

School of Informatics

Annual tuition: resident $8288, nonresident $10,920. Enrollment: full-time 216, part-time 181. Faculty: full-time 23, part-time 18. Degrees conferred: M.A., M.L.S., Ph.D.

ADMISSION REQUIREMENTS. Transcripts, bachelor's degree, GRE, computer skills required in support of School's application. TOEFL required for international applicants. Accepts transfer applicants. Graduates of unaccredited institutions not considered. Apply to School by September 15 (Spring), February 1 (Summer), April 1 (Fall). Application fee $35. Phone: (716)645-3162; fax: (716)645-3775.

ADMISSION STANDARDS. Selective. Usual minimum average: 3.0 (A = 4).

FINANCIAL AID. Annual awards from institutional funds: scholarships, fellowships, internships, Federal W/S, loans. Apply to Director of Financial Aid; no specified closing date. Phone: (716)645-2412. Use FAFSA.

DEGREE REQUIREMENTS. For M.A.: 36 credit program, at least 24 credits in residence; thesis. For M.L.S.: 36 credit hours minimum, at least 30 credits in residence. For Ph.D.: 72 credit program, at least 44 credits in residence; preliminary exam; dissertation; oral defense.

FIELDS OF STUDY.
Communications. Includes information and library science. M.A., Ph.D.
Informatics. M.A.
Library Studies. Includes music librarianship. M.L.S.

School of Law
Web site: www.law.buffalo.edu

Established 1887. Located on Amherst campus. ABA approved since 1936. AALS member. Semester system. Full-time, day study only. Special facilities: Baldy Center for Law and Social Policy, Buffalo Criminal Law Center, Buffalo Human Rights Center, Center for the Study of Business Transactions, Center for State and Local Democracy. Special programs: Government Law Program (Public Service), Public Service summer internships, externships in Public Interest. Law library: 567,785 volumes, 6651 subscriptions; has LEXIS, WESTLAW, RLIN, LRS, QUICKLAW (Canadian Database); is a Federal Government Depository.

Annual tuition: resident $13,532, nonresident $19,632. On-campus housing available for both single and married students. Annual on-campus housing cost: $14,444. Housing deadline May 1. Contact University Residence Hall for on-campus information. Phone: (716)645-2171. Law students tend to live off-campus. For off-campus housing information contact the office of Off-campus Housing (a student-run organization); phone: (716)829-2224. Off-campus housing and personal expenses: approximately $9529.

Enrollment: first-year class 247, full-time 728 (men 51%, women 49%, minorities 18%). Faculty: full-time 38, part-time 93. Student to faculty ratio 13.2 to 1. Degrees conferred: J.D., J.D.-M.A., J.D.-M.B.A., J.D.-M.S.W., J.D.-M.P.A., LL.M. (General, Criminal Law), J.D.-Ph.D.

ADMISSION REQUIREMENTS. LSDAS Law School report, bachelor's degree, transcript, LSAT, three recommendations required in support of application. Interview not required. Transfer applicants considered. Apply to Admissions Office after September 1, before April 1. Admits Fall only. Application fee $50. Phone: (716)645-2907.

ADMISSION STANDARDS. Selective. Accepts approximately 36% of total applicants. Number of applicants 1544; number of acceptance 560; number enrolled 247; LSAT (75% of students have a score at or above 152); GPA (75% of students have a GPA at or above 3.15). *U.S. News & World Report* ranking is in the second tier tied at 77th of all U.S. law schools.

FINANCIAL AID. TAP, SUSTA (New York State residents only), fellowships, assistantships, Federal W/S, loans. Apply to Financial Aid Office by March 1. Phone: (716)645-7324. Use FAFSA (School code: 002837). Approximately 70% of students receive some financial assistance.

DEGREE REQUIREMENTS. For J.D.: satisfactory completion of six-semester program, or five semesters plus two summer sessions; 82 credit hour program. For master's, Ph.D. degrees: see Graduate School listing above. For LL.M.: a full-time, 224 credit program; successfully complete three courses—Criminal Law (U.S.), Criminal Procedures (U.S.), and Evidence; two written papers or master's thesis.

School of Management
Web site: www.mgt.buffalo.edu

Established 1927. Tuition: per credit, resident $288, nonresident $455. Enrollment: full-time 454, part-time 176. Faculty: full-time 61, part-time 2. Degrees conferred: M.B.A., M.S., Ph.D.

ADMISSION REQUIREMENTS. Transcripts, GMAT required in support of School's application. Online applications available. TOEFL required for international applicants. Does not consider transfer applicants. Apply to Office of Academic Programs Administration in the School by June 1, March 1 for international applicants. Rolling admission process. Application fee $50. Phone: (716)645-3204; fax: (716)645-2341.

ADMISSION STANDARDS. Selective. Usual minimum average: 3.2 (A = 4); GMAT 575 (M.B.A.), 645 (Ph.D.).

FINANCIAL AID. Fellowships, assistantships, internships, Federal W/S, loans. Approved for VA benefits. Apply as early as possible to the Dean's Office for assistantships but not later than March 1; to Financial Aid Office for all other programs. Phone: (716)829-3724; fax: (716)829-2022. Use FAFSA. About 41% of full-time students receive some form of financial aid.

DEGREE REQUIREMENTS. For M.B.A.: 60-hour program, 30 hours in residence. For M.S.: one-year, full-time program. For Ph.D.: formal requirements are primarily qualitative; qualifying exam; second-year research paper; admission to candidacy; dissertation; final oral exam.

FIELDS OF STUDY.
Accounting. M.S.
Business Administration. Includes accounting, corporate financial management, financial analysis, information systems and e-business, international management, management consulting, marketing management, supply chains and operations management. M.B.A. program (full-time).
Business Management. Includes accounting, financial managerial economics, management science and systems, marketing, organization and human resources. Ph.D. program.
Finance. M.S.
International M.B.A.
Management. Ph.D.
Management Information Systems. M.S.
Supply Chains and Operations Management. M.S.

School of Medicine and Biomedical Sciences
Web site: www.smbs.buffalo.edu

Established 1846. Located in Buffalo (14214-3013). Library: 200,000 volumes, 3100 subscriptions. NIH ranking is 95th with 181 awards/grants worth $55,508,124.

Annual tuition: resident $20,148, nonresident $34,848. Limited on-campus housing for single students only. Total average figure for all other expenses: $14,000.

Enrollment: first-year class 136, total 557 (men 47%, women 53%, minorities 33%, state residents 100%). Faculty: full-time 440, part-time 200. Degrees conferred: M.D., M.D.-M.B.A., M.D.-M.P.H., M.D.-Ph.D. (Medical Scientist Training Program).

ADMISSION REQUIREMENTS. AMCAS report, transcripts, MCAT, letters of recommendation, interview required in support of application. Interview by invitation only. Applicants must have completed at least three years of college study. Preference given to state residents. Has EDP; apply between June 1 and August 1. Accepts very few transfer applicants. Supplement application for MSTP. Apply to AMCAS after June 1, before November 15. Application fee $65. Phone: (716)829-3466.

ADMISSION STANDARDS. Competitive. Accepts about 13% of all applicants. Number of applications 2772 (1134 out-of-state); number interviewed 548 (125 out-of-state); number of acceptance 358 (63 out-of-state); number enrolled 136 (22 out-of-state). Mean Composite MCAT 9.9; mean UGPA 3.60.

FINANCIAL AID. Scholarships, fellowships, assistantships, loans. Apply to Office of Financial Aid after acceptance, but prior to May 15. Phone: (716)645-2450. Use FAFSA (School code: 002837). About 90% of students receive some form of financial assistance.

DEGREE REQUIREMENTS. For M.D.: satisfactory completion of four-year program; all students must take and pass Step 1 of USMLE for promotion to third year; take Step 2 prior to graduation. For Ph.D. requirements refer to Graduate School listing above.

FIELDS OF GRADUATE STUDY.
Anatomical Sciences. M.A., Ph.D.
Biochemistry. M.A., Ph.D.
Biophysics. M.S., Ph.D.
Biotechnology. M.S.
Chemical and Biological Engineering. Ph.D.
Clinical Laboratory Sciences. M.S.
Epidemiology and Community Health. Ph.D.
Microbiology. M.A.
Microbiology and Immunology. Ph.D.
Neuroscience. Ph.D.
Oral Biology. Ph.D.
Pathology. M.A., Ph.D.
Pharmacology. M.A., Ph.D.
Physiology. M.A.
Structural Biology. M.S., Ph.D.
Toxicology. M.A., Ph.D.

School of Nursing

Tuition: per credit, resident $288, nonresident $455. Enrollment: full-time 115, part-time 63. Faculty: full-time 39, part-time 10. Degrees conferred: M.S., D.N.S.

ADMISSION REQUIREMENTS. Official transcripts, baccalaureate degree in nursing, three references required in support of School's application. GRE may be required for applicants with less than a 3.0 GPA (A = 4). Online application available. TOEFL (minimum score 550) and Financial Statement Form required for international applicants. Will consider transfer applicants. D.N.S. applicants admitted Fall and Spring. Apply by May 1 (Fall), October 15 (Spring) to Office of Academic Programs Administration in the School. Rolling admission process. Application fee $35 for online application, $50 for paper application. Phone: (716)829-3314, fax: (716)829-2021.

ADMISSION STANDARDS. Selective. Usual minimum average: 3.0 (A = 4).

FINANCIAL AID. Fellowships, scholarships, research/ teaching assistantships, grants, tuition waivers, Federal W/S, loans. Approved for VA benefits. Apply as early as possible, but not later than March 15, to the Dean's office for fellowships, scholarships, assistantships; to Financial Aid Office for all other programs. Phone: (716)645-2450. Use FAFSA (School code: 002837). About 25% of full-time students receive some form of financial aid. Aid available for part-time students.

DEGREE REQUIREMENTS. For master's: 42–53 credit program; comprehensive clinical training experience; admission to candidacy; research project. For D.N.S.: 48-credit program beyond master's; qualifying exam; admission to candidacy; dissertation; final oral exam.

FIELDS OF STUDY.
Acute Care Nurse Practitioner.
Adult Health Nursing.
Child Health Nursing.
Family Nurse Practitioner.
Geriatric Nurse Practitioner.
Maternal and Women's Health Nurse Practitioner.
Neonatal Nurse Practitioner.
Nurse Anesthetist. 27-month, full-time program.
Pediatric Nurse Practitioner.
Psychiatric/Mental Health Nursing.

School of Pharmacy and Pharmaceutical Sciences

Established 1886. Annual tuition: full-time resident $13,700, nonresident $23,700; per credit resident $571, nonresident $988. Graduate enrollment: full-time 336, part-time 10. Faculty: full-time 37; part-time 8. Degrees conferred: M.S., Ph.D., Pharm.D.

ADMISSION REQUIREMENTS. Transcripts, GRE required in support of School's application. Online application available. TOEFL (minimum score 550) required for international applicants. Accepts transfer applicants. Graduates of unaccredited institutions not considered. Apply by March 1 to appropriate department. Pharm.D. admits Fall only. Rolling admission process. Application fee $35. Phone: (716)645-2825; fax: (716)645-3688.

ADMISSION STANDARDS. Competitive. Usual minimum average: 3.0 (A = 4).

FINANCIAL AID. Fellowships, assistantships, tuition waivers, Federal W/S, loans. Apply by February 28 to appropriate department chair for assistantships; to Office of Financial Aid for all other programs. Use FAFSA.

DEGREE REQUIREMENTS. For M.S.: 30 semester hours minimum, at least 24 in residence; thesis, oral exam required by some

departments. For Ph.D.: three years minimum, at least one year in full-time residence; preliminary exam; dissertation; final oral exam. For Pharm.D.: essentially the same as for Ph.D., except no foreign language requirement.

FIELDS OF STUDY.
Chemical and Pharmaceutical Sciences. Interdisciplinary.
Drug Discovery and Experimental Therapeutics. Interdisciplinary.
Pharmaceutical Sciences. Includes clinical research, drug formulation/delivery/development, drug metabolism/transport, drug analysis, experimental pharmacokinetics and pharmacodynamics, pharmacogenetics/pharmacogenomics, pharmacometrics. M.S.

Roswell Park Cancer Institute
Graduate Division (14263)

Web site: www.roswellpark.org

Founded 1898. The Institute's NIH ranking is 125th among all U.S. instiutions with 83 awards/grants worth $37,982,961.
Annual tuition: resident $8288, nonresident $10,920.
Enrollment: full-time 180, part-time 90. Faculty: full-time 130. Degrees offered through the graduate school: M.A., M.S., Ph.D.

ADMISSION REQUIREMENTS. Transcripts, GRE, recommendations required in support of application. Online application available. TOEFL required for foreign applicants. Apply by February 1. Application fee $50. Phone: (716)845-2339; fax: (716)845-8178; e-mail: gradapp@roswellpark.org.

ADMISSION STANDARDS. Usual minimum average: 3.0 (A = 4). TOEFL (minimum score 600) required.

FINANCIAL AID. Annual awards from insititutional funds: tuition scholarships, research fellowships, research assistantships, NIH stipends, Federal W/S, loans. Apply after acceptance to appropriate department. Use FAFSA. Phone: (716)831-3724. About 66% of students receive aid other than loans from Institute and outside sources.

DEGREE REQUIREMENTS. For M.A., M.S.: 30 semester hours minimum, at least 24 in residence; thesis, oral exam required by some departments. For Ph.D.: three years minimum, at least one year in full-time residence; preliminary exam; dissertation; final oral exam.

FIELDS OF STUDY.
Cancer Pathology and Prevention.
Cellular-Molecular Biology.
Immunology.
Interdisciplinary program in Biomedical and Natural Sciences.
Molecular & Cellular Biophysics and Biochemistry.
Molecular Pharmacology and Cancer Therapeutics.

School of Social Work

Established 1934. Annual tuition: resident $8288, nonresident $10,920; per credit, resident $288, nonresident $455. On-campus housing available. Day care facilities available.
Enrollment: full-time 231, part-time 243. Faculty: full-time 18, part-time 32. Degrees conferred: M.S.W., Ph.D.

ADMISSION REQUIREMENTS. Transcripts, GRE, three letters of reference, personal statement required in support of School's application. Online application available. TOEFL required for international applicants. Accepts transfer applicants and advanced-standing applicants. Graduates of unaccredited institutions not considered for advanced standing. Apply to Director of Admissions by March 1. Admits Fall only, for both full- and part-time programs. Rolling admission process. Application fee $50. Phone: (716)645-3381, ext. 262; fax: (716)645-3456.

ADMISSION STANDARDS. Selective. Usual minimum average: 3.0 (A = 4).

FINANCIAL AID. Scholarships, assistantships, tuition waivers, Federal W/S, loans. Apply by February 1. Phone: (716)829-3724. Use FAFSA. Aid available for part-time students.

DEGREE REQUIREMENTS. For M.S.W.: 60 credit hours minimum, for full-time at least two years in residence, for part-time one year in residence with advanced standing. For Ph.D.: a minimum of 47 credits beyond M.S.W.; pro-seminar; research internship; comprehensive exam; candidacy; dissertation; oral defense.

FIELDS OF STUDY.
Social Work. Includes alcohol and other drug problems, health, mental health and disability, children and youth, community, individualized. M.S.W.
Social Welfare. Ph.D.

BUTLER UNIVERSITY
Indianapolis, IN 46208-3485
Web site: www.butler.edu

Founded 1855. Coed. Private control. Semester system. Special facility: Holcomb Observatory and Planetarium. Library: 345,400 volumes, 2200 subscriptions. Approximately 430 computers on campus for student use. Total University enrollment: 4384.

Tuition: $320 per credit. On-campus housing available for graduate students. Average academic year housing costs: $8170 (including board). Contact Director of Residential Life for both on- and off-campus housing information. Phone: (317)283-9570. Day-care facilities available.

Division of Graduate Studies

Graduate study since 1932. Enrollment: full-time 279, part-time 347. University faculty: full-time 68, part-time 43. Degrees conferred: M.A., M.S., M.M., M.B.A., Ed.S.

ADMISSION REQUIREMENTS. Two official transcripts, GRE/GMAT required in support of application (electronic application available). Interview not required. TOEFL (minimum score 550) required for international applicants. Accepts transfer applicants. Graduates of unaccredited institutions not considered. Apply to Office of Graduate Admissions by August 15. Application fee $35. Phone: (800)972-2882, (317)940-8100; fax: (317)940-8250.

ADMISSION STANDARDS. Selective. Usual minimum average: 2.75 (A = 4).

FINANCIAL AID. Scholarships, teaching fellowships, teaching assistantships, music awards, Federal W/S, loans. Apply to the Office of Graduate Studies for fellowships, assistantships; to Financial Aid Office for all other programs. No specified closing date. Phone: (800)972-2882. Use FAFSA.

DEGREE REQUIREMENTS. For master's; 30–36 hours for most programs; final written/oral exam for some majors; comprehensive exam. For Specialist: 30 credits beyond the master's; special project.

FIELDS OF STUDY.

COLLEGE OF BUSINESS ADMINISTRATION:
Business Administration. Up to 12 additional prerequisite hours for M.B.A., depending upon previous preparation; GMAT for admission. Concentrations in finance, leadership, marketing.

COLLEGE OF EDUCATION:
Educational Administration. M.S., Ed.S.
Effective Teaching. Includes elementary, institutional technology, middle level, secondary, reading, special. M.S.
School Counseling. M.S.

COLLEGE OF LIBERAL ARTS AND SCIENCES:
English. M.A.
History. M.A.

JORDAN COLLEGE OF FINE ARTS:
Composition.
Conducting.
Music Education.
Music History.
Organ.
Performance.
Piano Pedagogy.
Theory.

COLLEGE OF PHARMACY:
Pharmacy. Pharm.D.

CALIFORNIA COLLEGE OF THE ARTS
San Francisco, California 94102-2247
Web site: www.cca.edu

Founded 1907. Graduate programs located in San Francisco; housing located at Oakland campus. Private control. Semester system. Special facilities: Graduate Center Gallery; MFA Student Gallery. Library: 57,000 volumes, 320 subscriptions. Total College enrollment: 1616.

Tuition: per credit $1017. No on-campus housing. Off-campus room and board average $10,500. For off-campus housing information, contact Student Services Office. Phone: (510)420-2000.

Graduate Division

Graduate study since 1956. Enrollment: full-time 296. Faculty: full- and part-time 58. Degrees conferred: M.A., M.Arch., M.F.A.

ADMISSION REQUIREMENTS. Transcripts, statement/personal essay, résumé, portfolio, slides/photographs of artwork required in support of College's application. TOEFL required of foreign applicants. Interview not required. Graduates of unaccredited colleges not considered. Apply to Office of Enrollment Services (San Francisco campus) by January 15 (Fall). Application fee $50. Phone: (415)703-9523; fax: (415)703-9539.

ADMISSION STANDARDS. Selective. Admission based on talent.

FINANCIAL AID. Annual awards from institutional funds: scholarships, Federal W/S, loans. Apply to Director of Graduate Division by March 1 (Fall), October 1 (Spring). Phone: (415)703-9528. Use FAFSA and institutional FAF. About 63% of students receive aid other than loans from College and outside sources. No institutional aid for part-time students.

DEGREE REQUIREMENTS. For M.A., M.Arch.: 36 credit program; master's project. For M.F.A.: 60 units minimum, at least 48 in residence; thesis; final oral exam.

FIELDS OF STUDY.
Architecture. M.Arch.
Curatorial Practice. M.A.
Design. M.F.A.
Design Strategy. M.F.A.
Film.

Fine Arts.
Visual and Critical Studies. M.A.
Writing. M.F.A.

CALIFORNIA INSTITUTE OF TECHNOLOGY
Pasadena, California 91125-0001
Web site: www.caltech.edu

Founded 1891. CGS and AAU member. Coed. Private control. Quarter system. Special facilities: well-equipped laboratories in fields of specialization, computing center (computing support services for IBM, DEC, Apple, Sun, NeXT; INTEL Touchstone Delta, Cray Y-MP), large telescopes at Big Bear Solar, Caltech Submillimeter (Mauna Kea, Hawaii) and Palomar Observatories, radio telescopes at Bishop and Palomar Observatories, seismological laboratory at Pasadena, Kerckhoff Marine Laboratory at Corona del Mar, Environmental Quality Laboratory, Kellog Radiation Laboratory, Graduate Aeronautics Laboratory, Jet Propulsion Lab at Pasadena. According to The Center at University of Florida, Cal Tech is ranked 29th in receipt of Federal Research funds with $219,097,000 and it ranks 54th for total University research expenditures with $240,644,000. The University's endowment assets ranks it 36th, $1,261,122,000. In 2004, the University awarded 166 doctorates which ranked it 87th among all U.S. institutions eligible to award that degree. Seven of the University's faculty members have been elected to National Honor Academies and this ranks it 87th among all U.S. institutions. The Library: approximately 1,000,000 volumes, 3200 subscriptions.

Annual tuition: full-time $31,020. On- and off-campus housing available for single and married students. Average academic year housing costs: $5400–$10,150. Apply to Graduate Housing Office before May 1. Phone: (626)356-6178. Day-care facilities available.

Graduate Studies

Graduate study since 1916. Enrollment: full-time 1100 (men 80%, women 20%); no part-time study except in unusual cases. Institute faculty, research and teaching: full-time 339, part-time 56. Degrees conferred: M.S., Engineer, Ph.D.

ADMISSION REQUIREMENTS. Transcripts, three letters of recommendation required in support of application. GRE/Subject Tests required by some divisions, strongly recommended by all. Interview not required. TOEFL (minimum score 600, 250 on computer-based test) or IELTS (minimum score 7) required for international applicants, TSE and TWE strongly recommended. Graduates of unaccredited institutions not considered. Apply to Dean of Graduate Studies by January 15; applications received later considered as long as vacancies exist. Admits September only. Application fee, none. Phone: (626)395-6346; fax: (626) 577-9246; e-mail: gradoffice@caltech.edu.

ADMISSION STANDARDS. Very competitive. Usual minimum average: 3.5 (A = 4).

FINANCIAL AID. Research fellowships, teaching assistantships, full and partial scholarships, loans. Most scholarships and fellowships have no teaching or research requirements. Apply to Graduate Office by January 15. Phone: (626)356-3811. Use FAFSA and University's FAF. Most students receive aid other than loans from Institute and outside sources.

DEGREE REQUIREMENTS. For M.S.: at least three terms in full-time residence; candidacy; thesis required by some divisions. For Engineer: at least six terms in full-time residence beyond the bachelor's; candidacy; thesis; final exam for some divisions. For Ph.D.: at least nine terms in full-time residence beyond the bachelor's; candidacy; foreign languages proficiency required by some programs; thesis; final oral exam.

FIELDS OF STUDY.

BIOLOGY DIVISION:
Biology. Ph.D.
Biochemistry. Ph.D.
Cell Biology. Ph.D.
Computation and Neural Systems (Interdisciplinary). Ph.D.
Developmental Biology. Ph.D.
Genetics. Ph.D.
Immunology. Ph.D.
Molecular Biophysics. Ph.D.
Neurosciencs. Ph.D.
Structural Biology. Ph.D.

CHEMISTRY AND CHEMICAL ENGINEERING DIVISION:
Chemical Engineering. M.S., Ph.D.
Chemistry. Ph.D.

ENGINEERING AND APPLIED SCIENCE DIVISION:
Aeronautics. M.S., Engr., Ph.D.
Applied and Computation Mathematics. M.S, Ph.D.
Applied Mechanics. M.S., Ph.D.
Applied Physics. M.S., Ph.D.
Astrophysics. M.S., Ph.D.
Bioengineering (Interdisciplinary). Ph.D. only.
Civil Engineering. M.S., Ph.D.
Computation and Neural Systems (Interdisciplinary). M.S., Ph.D.
Computer Science. M.S., Ph.D.
Control and Dynamical Systems. M.S., Ph.D.
Electrical Engineering. M.S., Ph.D.
Environmental Science and Engineering. M.S., Ph.D.
Materials Sciences. M.S., Ph.D.
Mechanical Engineering. M.S., Ph.D.

HUMANITIES DIVISION:
Social Sciences. Ph.D.

GEOLOGICAL AND PLANETARY SCIENCES DIVISION:
Geobiology. Ph.D.
Geochemistry. M.S., Ph.D.
Geology. M.S., Ph.D.
Geophysics. M.S., Ph.D.
Planetary Sciences. M.S., Ph.D.

PHYSICS, MATHEMATICS AND ASTRONOMY:
Astronomy. Ph.D.
Mathematics. Ph.D.
Physics. Ph.D.

CALIFORNIA INSTITUTE OF THE ARTS
Valencia, California 91355-2340
Web site: www.calarts.edu

CalArts was established as a result of the merger of Los Angeles Conservatory of Music (founded in 1883) and the Chouinard Arts Institute (founded in 1921) and the generosity of Walt and Roy Disney and Lulu May Von Hagen and was incorporated in 1961. Private control. Semester system. Library: 98,000 volumes, 613 subscriptions. More than 40 computers on campus for general student use. Total Institute enrollment: 1327.

Annual tuition: full-time $27,260. On-campus housing available for single students only on a first-come, first-served basis. Average annual housing cost: $7700 (including board). For off-campus housing information, contact Student Services Office.

Graduate Studies

Enrollment: full-time 499. Institute faculty: full-time 197, part-time 140. Degree conferred: M.F.A.

ADMISSION REQUIREMENTS. Transcripts, portfolio, slides/photographs of artwork, three recent works (music composition), interview (directing), personal statement, three letters of recommendation required in support of College's application. TOEFL required of foreign applicants. Apply to Director of Admissions by January 15 (Fall, priority deadline), November 11 (Spring). Application fee $65. Phone: (661)255-1050; fax: (661) 253-7710.

ADMISSION STANDARDS. Selective. Admission based on talent.

FINANCIAL AID. Annual awards from institutional funds: scholarships, grants, assistantships, Federal W/S, loans. Apply to Financial Aid Office by March 1. Use FAFSA.

DEGREE REQUIREMENTS. For M.F.A.: 60 units minimum, at least 48 in residence; final oral exam; projects.

FIELDS OF STUDY.

SCHOOL OF ARTS:
Arts.
Graphic Design.
Photography.

SCHOOL OF CRITICAL STUDIES:
Writing.

SCHOOL OF DANCE:
Dance.

SCHOOL OF FILM/VIDEO:
Experimental Animation.
Film and Video.
Film Directing.

SCHOOL OF MUSIC:
African Music.
Composition.
Composition/New Media.
Jazz.
Music Technology.
Performer/Composer.

SCHOOL OF THEATER:
Acting.
Design and Production.
Directing.
Performing Art Design and Technology.
Producing.
Theater Management.
Writing for Performance.

CALIFORNIA LUTHERAN UNIVERSITY

Thousand Oaks, California 91360
Web site: www.callutheran.edu

Founded in 1959. Located 50 miles NW of Los Angeles. Church related—Lutheran. Semester system. Special facilities: California Institute of Finance, Center for Leadership and Values, Center for Equality and Justice, Segerhammar Center for Faith and Culture. Library: 125,032 volumes, 586 subscriptions. About 250 computers on campus for student use.

Tuition: per credit M.B.A. $570, computer sciences $635, Ed.D. $695, all other programs $505. No on-campus housing available. For information contact Housing Office. Phone: (805)493-3220.

Graduate Studies

Graduate study since 1970. Enrollment: full- and part-time 1095. Faculty: full-time 26, part-time 89. Degrees conferred: M.A., M.Ed., M.S., M.B.A., M.B.A.F.P., M.P.P.A., Ed.D.

ADMISSION REQUIREMENTS. Transcripts, GRE/GMAT, three letters of recommendation, personal statement, interview required in support of application. TOEFL required for foreign applicants. Apply to Graduate Enrollment Services Office six weeks prior to registration. Application fee $50. Phone: (805)493-3335; fax: (805)493-3542.

ADMISSION STANDARDS. Selective. Usual minimum average 3.0 (A = 4).

FINANCIAL AID. Limited to scholarships, graduate assistantships, Lutheran Teacher awards, Federal W/S, loans. Apply to the Office of Financial Aid; no specified closing date. Phone: (805)493-3115; fax: (805)493-3114. Use FAFSA and Institutional FAF.

DEGREE REQUIREMENTS. For master's: 30–48 credits minimum; thesis/nonthesis option. For Ed.D.: 60-credit program beyond master's degree; dissertation; final oral exam.

FIELDS OF STUDY.
Business Administration. Includes finance, information technology, management, international business, management and organization behavior, marketing tracks. M.B.A.
Clinical Psychology. M.S.
Computer Science. M.S.
Counseling and Guidance. M.S.
Counseling Psychology. M.F.T., M.S.
Curriculum and Instruction. Includes specializations in cross-cultural language and academic development, curriculum coordination, educational technology, elementary education, reading, subject areas. M.A.
Educational Leadership. M.A., Ed.D.
Financial Planning. M.B.A.F.P.
Public Policy Administration. M.P.P.A.
Special Education. M.S.
Teacher Preparation. M.Ed.

CALIFORNIA POLYTECHNIC STATE UNIVERSITY

San Luis Obispo, California 93407
Web site: www.calpoly.edu

Founded 1901. Located 200 miles N of Los Angeles. Coed. Public control. Quarter system. Special facilities: Agricultural Safety Institute, Applied Research and Development facilities, Brock Center for Agricultural Communication, Center for Practical Politics, Coastal Resource Institute, Computer-Integrated Manufacturing Center, Dairy Products Technology Center, Design and Construction Institute, Electric Power Institute, Irrigation Training and Research Center, Small Business Institute. Library: 1,200,000 volumes, 5529 subscriptions. About 1900 computers on campus for general student use. Total University enrollment: 18,475.

Annual fees/tuition: residents $5238, non-residents pay fees plus $226 per unit out-of-state tuition. No on-campus housing available. For off-campus housing information: Phone: (805) 756-1226.

Research and Graduate Program

Enrollment: full-time 616, part-time 172. Faculty: full-time 125, part-time 56. Degrees conferred: M.A., M.S., M.B.A., M.C.R.P., M.S.I.T.S. teacher credential.

ADMISSION REQUIREMENTS. Transcripts required in support of application. GRE/GMAT required for some programs. TOEFL (minimum score 550), TWE (minimum score 4.5), and confidential financial certification required for foreign applicants. Accepts transfer applicants. Apply to Office of Admissions by July 1 (Fall), November 1 (Winter), March 1 (Spring), April 1 (Summer). Application fee $55. Phone: (805)756-2311; fax: (805) 756-5400; e-mail: admissions@polymail.calpoly.edu.

ADMISSION STANDARDS. Selective. Minimum average: 2.5 (A = 4).

FINANCIAL AID. Annual awards from institutional funds: graduate fellowships, equity fellowships, scholarships, Federal W/S, loans. Apply by March 1 to Financial Aid Office. Phone: (805) 756-2927; fax: (805)756-7243. Use FAFSA.

DEGREE REQUIREMENTS. For master's: 45 quarter units minimum except for M.C.R.P. (72 units), English (48), Psychology (90), Business (48–96), at least 32 in residence; advancement to candidacy; thesis, project or culminating exam.

FIELDS OF STUDY.
Accounting. M.S.
Aeronautical Engineering. M.S.
Agribusiness. M.S.
Agriculture. Includes agricultural education, animal science, crop science, dairy products technology, engineering technology, environmental horticultural science, food science and nutrition, irrigation, plant protection science, soil science. M.S.
Architecture. M.S.
Biological Sciences. M.S.
Business Administration. M.B.A.
City and Regional Planning. M.C.R.P.
Civil and Environmental Engineering. M.S.
Computer Science. M.S.
Credentials Programs. Include single subject, multiple subject, educational specialist, pupil personnel.
Education. Includes counseling and guidance, curriculum and instruction, education administration, literacy and reading, special education. M.A.
Educational Leadership. Ed.D.
Electrical Engineering. Includes computer engineering, electronic. M.S.
Engineering. Includes biochemical, bioengineering, biomedical, integrated technology management, materials, water. M.S.
Engineering Management. M.B.A.-M.S.
English. M.A.
Forestry Sciences. M.S.
History. M.A.
Industrial and Technical Studies. M.S.I.T.S.
Kinesiology. M.S.
Mathematics. M.S.
Mechanical Engineering. M.S.
Polymers and Coating. M.S.
Psychology. M.S.
Public Policy. M.P.P.
Transportation Planning. M.C.R.P.-M.S.

CALIFORNIA STATE POLYTECHNIC UNIVERSITY
Pomona, California 91768-2557
Web site: www.csupomona.edu

Established 1938. Located 30 miles from Los Angeles. CGS member. Coed. Public control. Quarter system. Special facilities: W. K. Kellogg Arabian Horse Center, Center for Advanced Computer Technology, Institute for Cellular and Molecular Biology, Center for Regenerative Studies, Center for Community Affairs, Center for Geographic Information Research, Center for Entrepreneurship and Innovation, Center for Economic Education and Research, Equine Research Center, Institute for Ethics and Public Policy, Reproductive Physiology Center, Center for Science and Mathematics Education, Small Business Institute. Library: 592,000 volumes, 5100 subscriptions. More than 1800 computers on campus for general student use. Total University enrollment: 19,885.

Annual fees: residents $3414 plus $506 mandatory University fees for most programs; teaching credential residents $3216 plus $506 mandatory fees. On-campus housing for single graduate students: $7900 (including board). Apply by May 1. Contact Director of Marketing for both on- and off-campus housing information. Phone: (909)569-3308.

Graduate School

Graduate study since 1968. Enrollment: full-time 625, part-time 596. Faculty: full- and part-time 659. Degrees conferred: M.A., M.S., M.Arch., M.B.A., M.L.A., M.S.E., M.S.E.E., M.S.B.A., M.U.R.P.

ADMISSION REQUIREMENTS. Transcripts, GRE/Subject Tests, GMAT (business) required in support of School's application. Interview required for Architecture, Urban and Regional Planning, and Landscape Architecture. TOEFL required of international applicants. Accepts transfer applicants. Graduates of unaccredited colleges not considered. Apply to Admissions Office by December 1 (Winter), March 1 (Spring), May 15 (Summer), August 1 (Fall). Application fee $55. Phone: (909)869-3532; fax: (909)869-4529.

ADMISSION STANDARDS. Selective. Usual minimum average: 3.0 (A = 4).

FINANCIAL AID. Graduate presidential fellowships, teaching assistantships, internships, Federal W/S, loans. Apply by March 1 to Dean's Office for fellowships, assistantships; to Financial Aid Office for all other programs. Phone: (909)869-3700; fax: (909)869-4757. Use FAFSA (University code: 001144).

DEGREE REQUIREMENTS. For master's: 45 units minimum, at least 32 units residence; reading knowledge of one foreign language may be required; thesis, project, or comprehensive examination, varies by program.

FIELDS OF STUDY.

COLLEGE OF AGRICULTURE:
Agricultural Sciences. M.S.
Animal Science. M.S.
Irrigation Science. M.S.
Nutrition and Food Science. M.S.
Plant Sciences. M.S.
Sports Nutrition. M.S.

COLLEGE OF BUSINESS:
Business Administration. M.B.A.
Business Administration. Includes entrepreneurship, creativity and innovation management, information systems auditing. M.S.B.A.

COLLEGE OF EDUCATION AND INTEGRATIVE STUDIES:
Bilingual Crosscultural Education. M.A.Ed.
Curriculum and Instruction. M.A.Ed.
Educational Leadership. M.A.Ed.
Educational Multimedia. M.A.Ed.
Heritage Languages: Literacy & Leadership. M.A.Ed.
Special Education. M.A.Ed.

COLLEGE OF ENGINEERING:
Engineering. M.S.
Electrical Engineering. Includes computer systems, communication and microwave, control systems and robotics. M.S.
Mechanical Engineering. M.S.
Structural Engineering. M.S.

COLLEGE OF ENVIRONMENTAL DESIGN:
Architecture. M.Arch.
Landscape Architecture. M.L.A.
Regenerative Studies. M.S.
Urban and Regional Planning. M.U.R.P.

COLLEGE OF LETTERS, ARTS, AND SOCIAL SCIENCES:
Economics. Includes financial economics, environmental and natural resources economics, economic analysis, economic education. M.S.
English. Includes literature, rhetoric and composition, teaching English as a second language. M.A.
History. M.A.
Kinesiology. Includes sports nutrition. M.S.
Psychology. M.S.
Public Administration. M.P.A.

COLLEGE OF SCIENCE:
Biological Sciences. M.S.
Chemistry. M.S.
Computer Science. M.S.
Mathematics. M.S.

CALIFORNIA STATE UNIVERSITY, BAKERSFIELD

Bakersfield, California 93311-1022
Web site: www.csubak.edu

Established 1970. Located 125 miles N of Los Angeles. CGS member. Coed. Public control. Quarter system. Special facilities: Applied Research Center, Archaeological Information Center, Business Research and Education Center, California Well Sample Repository, Center for Research in Agriculture and Biology, Center for the Study of Classical Economics, Direct Marketing Institute, Center for International Studies, Center for Environmental Studies, Center for Living and Learning, Center for Mathematical and Statistical Studies, Center for Physiological Research, Kegley Institute of Ethics, Politics Research Center, Small Business Institute. Library: 354,000 volumes, 2260 subscriptions. Total University enrollment: 7449.

Fees/nonresident tuition: resident 0–6 credits $660 per quarter, over 6 credits $1138; nonresident 0–6 $660 plus $226 per unit, over 6 credits $1138 plus $226 per unit. On-campus housing for single and married students. Average academic year housing costs: $6000 (including board). Apply by August 1. Contact Director of Housing for both on- and off-campus housing information. Phone: (661)664-3014.

Division of Graduate Studies and Research

Web site: www.csubak.edu/on_campus.html

Enrollment: full-time 906, part-time 886. Faculty: full-time 165, part-time 100. Degrees conferred: M.A., M.S., M.B.A., M.H.A., M.P.A., M.S.W.

ADMISSION REQUIREMENTS. Transcripts, GRE/GMAT/MAT required in support of School's application. GRE Subject Test, letters of recommendation, interview required by some departments. TOEFL required for international applicants. Accepts transfer applicants. Graduates of unaccredited institutions not considered. Apply to Admissions Office by March 1 (Fall), November 1 (Spring). Late admission will be considered. Application fee $55. Phone: (661)664-2161; fax: (661)664-3342.

ADMISSION STANDARDS. Selective. Usual minimum average: 2.75 (A = 4).

FINANCIAL AID. Scholarships, teaching assistantships, Graduate Equity Fellowships, Federal W/S, loans. Approved for VA benefits. Apply by March 1 to Dean, School of Graduate Studies for assistantships, fellowships; to Office of Financial Aid for all other programs. Phone: (661)664-2231. Use FAFSA. About 10% of students receive aid other than loans from College, 21% from all sources. Aid sometimes available for part-time students.

DEGREE REQUIREMENTS. For master's: 60–90 units minimum, at least 45 in residence; candidacy; final written/oral exam for most majors; reading knowledge of one foreign language for some majors; thesis/creative/research project.

FIELDS OF STUDY.
Administration. M.S.
Anthropology. M.A.
Bilingual/Multicultural Education. M.A.
Biology. M.S.
Business Administration. M.B.A.
Counseling. M.S.
Counseling Psychology. M.S.
Curriculum and Instruction. M.A.
Educational Administration. M.A.
English. M.A.
Geology. M.S.
Health Care Management. M.H.A.
History. M.A.
Interdisciplinary Studies. M.A.
Nursing. M.S.
Psychology. M.S.
Public Administration. M.P.A.
Reading Literacy. M.A.
School Counseling. M.S.
Social Work. M.S.W.
Sociology. M.A.
Spanish. M.A.
Special Education. M.A.
Teaching Mathematics. M.A.

CALIFORNIA STATE UNIVERSITY, CHICO

Chico, California 95929-0875
Web site: www.csuchico.edu

Founded 1887. Located 100 miles N of Sacramento. CGS member. Coed. State control. Semester system. Special facilities: Eagle Lake Biological Field Station, Instructional Media Center, Survey Research Center, Vertebrate Museum. Library: 1,365,000 volumes, 927,000 microforms, 13,000 subscriptions.

Fees/nonresident tuition: resident 0–6 credits $1449 per semester, over 6 credits $2166; nonresident 0–6 $1449 plus $339 per unit, over 6 credits $2166 plus $339 per unit. On-campus housing for single students only. Average academic year housing costs: $6000 (including board); average off-campus housing costs: $350 per month. Contact Director of University Housing and Food Service for both on- and off-campus housing information. Phone: (530)898-6325.

School of Graduate, International, and Interdisciplinary Studies

Enrollment: full-time 628, part-time 321. University faculty: full-time 589, part-time 215. Degrees conferred: M.A., M.S., M.B.A., M.P.A., M.R.T.P., M.S.A., M.S.W.

ADMISSION REQUIREMENTS. Two official transcripts, GRE, two letters of recommendation required in support of application. GRE Subject/MAT/GMAT required for some departments. Interview not required. TOEFL required for international students. Accepts transfer applicants. Graduates of unaccredited institutions not considered. Apply to Graduate School by March 1 (Fall), September 15 (Spring), June 15 (Summer). Rolling admissions process. Application fee $55. Phone: (530)898-6880; fax: (530) 898-6804.

ADMISSION STANDARDS. Selective. Usual minimum average: 2.5 in last 60 units. 3.0 in last 30 units (A = 4).

FINANCIAL AID. Annual awards from institutional funds: scholarships, equity fellowships, teaching assistantships, Federal W/S, loans. Approved for VA benefits. Apply by February 15 to the Dean's Office for fellowships, assistantships; to the Office of Financial Aid for all other programs. About 50% of students receive aid other than loans from College and outside sources.

DEGREE REQUIREMENTS. For most master's: 30 semester units minimum, at least 24 in residence; thesis/nonthesis option for most majors; final written/oral exam. For M.S.W.: 36–61 semester units depending on baccalaureate degree; thesis/special project/comprehensive exam.

FIELDS OF STUDY.
Accountancy. GMAT for admission.
Anthropology. Admits Fall only. Statement of purpose/intent for admission. Includes Museum Studies.
Art/Fine Arts. Portfolio for admission.
Biological Sciences. GRE for admission.
Botany. GRE for admission.
Business Administration. GMAT, three letters of recommendation, written statement of purpose for admission.
Communication Studies. Three letters of recommendation, one page personal statement for admission.
Computer Science.
Creative Writing. GRE, portfolio of original writings, critical paper, personal statement for admission. M.F.A.
Education. Includes curriculum and instruction, linguistically and culturally diverse learners, reading/language arts, special.
Electrical Engineering. GRE or MAT for admission. Includes computer engineering, electronic engineering.
English. GRE, writing sample for admission.
Environmental Science. GRE, statement of intent for admission.
Geography. GRE, written statement of interest for admission. Includes rural town planning.
Geosciencs. GRE, statement of interest for admission. Includes earth science, hydrology/hydrogeology.
History. GRE, statement of purpose, writing sample for admission.
Instructional Design and Technology. GRE or MAT, three letters of recommendation, personal statement for admission.
Interdisciplinary Studies.
Kinesiology. GRE for admission.
Mathematical Education.
Music. Includes education, performance; GRE General, Subject Test, audition for admission.
Nursing. MAT for admission.
Nutritional Science. GRE, statement of purpose for admission. Includes nutrition education.
Physical Education. Written statement of purpose for admission.
Political Science. Written statement of purpose for admission.
Psychology. GRE, three letters of recommendation (on departmental form) for admission. Includes psychological science, applied psychology. M.A., M.S.
Public Administration. Includes health administration, local government management.
Recreation Administration. GRE, three letters of recommendation, statement of intent, résumé for admission.
Social Science. GRE, written statement of interest and goals.
Social Work. Three letters of recommendation (on departmental form), personal statement for admission.
Speech-Language Pathology and Audiology. MAT or GRE, three letters of recommendation, written statement of interest, résumé for admission. Admits Fall semester only, apply by March 1.
Teaching of International Languages.

CALIFORNIA STATE UNIVERSITY, DOMINGUEZ HILLS
Carson, California 90747-0001
Web site: www.csudh.edu

Founded 1965. Located in Los Angeles County. CGS member. Coed. Public control. Semester system. Special facilities: Center for Urban Research and Learning, Desert Studies Center, Social Systems Research Center, Southern California Ocean Studies Center; art gallery. Library: 440,000 volumes, 2300 subscriptions. Total University enrollment 12,500.

Fees/nonresident tuition: resident 0–6 credits $990 per semester, over 6 credits $1707; nonresident 0–6 $990 plus $339 per unit, over 6 credits $1707 plus $339 per unit. On-campus housing for married or graduate students. Apply by April 15. Average academic year housing costs: $4000–$6000 (room only) for single students; $7500 for married students. Average off-campus housing cost: $600–$1000 per month. Contact Office of Dean of Student Affairs for both on- and off-campus housing information. Phone: (310)243-2228.

Division of Graduate Studies and Research

Graduate enrollment: full- and part-time 5100. University faculty teaching graduate students: full-time 292, part-time 243. Degrees conferred: M.A., M.S., M.B.A., M.H.S., M.P.A., M.S.W.

ADMISSION REQUIREMENTS. Two official transcripts required in support of application. Electronic application available. GRE may be required by some departments. TOEFL required for international applicants. Graduates of unaccredited institutions not considered. Accepts transfer applicants. Apply to Office of Admission and Records by June 1 (Fall), November 30 (Spring). Application fee $55. Phone: (310)243-3693.

ADMISSION STANDARDS. Selective. Usual minimum average: 2.5 overall, 2.75 in last two years (A = 4).

FINANCIAL AID. Scholarships, teaching/research assistantships, graduate equity fellowships, Federal W/S, loans. Apply to Financial Aid Office; no specified closing dates. Phone: (310)516-3647; e-mail: finaid@csudh.edu. Use FAFSA (University code: 001240). About 30% of students receive aid from University and outside sources. Aid sometimes available for part-time students.

DEGREE REQUIREMENTS. For master's: 30–48 semester hours minimum, at least 21 in residence; thesis/nonthesis option; final written/oral exam or project.

FIELDS OF STUDY.

Behavior Sciences. Includes gerontology, negotiation and conflict managment. M.A.

Biology. M.A.

Clinical Science. Includes cytotechnology, medical technology, nuclear medicine technology. M.S.

Business Administration. Includes general management, international. M.B.A.

Education. Includes technology-based, counseling, educational administration, multicultural, physical, teaching/curriculum. M.A.

English. Includes literature, rhetoric, and composition, TESL. M.A.

Health Sciences. Includes physician's assistant, professional studies. M.H.S.

Humanities. M.A.

Interdisciplinary Studies. M.A., M.S.

Marital and Family Therapy. M.S.

Nursing. Includes nurse educator, nurse administration, parent–child clinical nurse specialist, gerontology clinical nurse specialist, family nurse practitioner. M.S.

Quality Assurance. M.S.

Psychology. Includes clinical. M.A.

Public Administration. M.P.A.

Rhetoric and Composition. M.A.

Social Work. M.S.W.

Sociology. Includes general, research skills. M.A.

Special Education. Includes learning handicapped, severely handicapped. M.A.

Teaching English as a Second Language. M.A.

Teaching Mathematics. M.A.

CALIFORNIA STATE UNIVERSITY, EAST BAY

Hayward, California 94542-3000
Web site: www.csuhayward.edu

Founded 1957. Located in San Francisco Bay Area, 12 miles SE of Oakland. CGS member. Coed. State control. Quarter system. Special facilities: Institute of Mental Illness and Wellness Education, Microscope and Graphic Imaging Center, Moss Landing Marine Laboratory, C. F. Smith Museum of Anthropology. Library: 908,500 volumes, 2200 subscriptions. More than 700 computers on campus for general student use. Total enrollment: 12,500.

Fees/nonresident tuition: resident $1329 per quarter; nonresident $1329 plus $226 per unit. On-campus apartments available. Apply by March 1. Annual housing cost: on-campus $8739, off-campus $10,000. No on-campus housing for married students. Contact Director of Housing and Residential Life for off-campus housing information. Phone: (510)885-7444. Day-care facilities available.

Graduate Study

Enrollment: full-time 2353, part-time 1161. College faculty teaching graduate students: approximately 368. Degrees conferred: M.A., M.B.A., M.P.A., M.S.

ADMISSION REQUIREMENTS. Transcripts required in support of application. GRE, GMAT, or MAT required by some departments. TOEFL required of foreign students. Interview required by some departments. Accepts transfer applicants. Graduates of unaccredited institutions not considered. Apply by June 15 (Fall), October 15 (Winter), January 15 (Spring) to the Office of Admissions. Application fee $55. Phone: (510)885-3286; fax: (510)885-4777; e-mail: gradprograms@csuhayward.edu.

ADMISSION STANDARDS. Competitive. Minimum undergraduate GPA for postbaccalaureate status is 2.5 in last 90 quarter units (A = 4).

FINANCIAL AID. Scholarships, grants, fellowships, assistantships, internships, Federal W/S, loans. Apply to Director of Financial Aid by March 1. Phone: (510)885-3616. Use FAFSA and institution FAF. Aid available for part-time students. About 10% of students receive aid other than loans from University and outside sources.

DEGREE REQUIREMENTS. For master's: 45 quarter hours minimum, at least 32 in residence; thesis, project, or comprehensive exam; foreign language for several majors.

FIELDS OF STUDY.

Anthropology. M.A.

Biological Science. M.S.

Biostatistics. M.S.

Business Administration. Includes options in accounting, business economics, computer information systems, e-business, entrepreneurship, finance, human resources management, marketing management, operations and materials management, strategic management, supply chain management, taxation, telecommunications management. M.B.A.

Business Administration. Includes options in computer information systems/quantitative, business methods. M.S.

Chemistry. Includes option in biochemistry. M.S.

Computer Science. M.S.

Counseling. Includes options in clinical child/school psychology, marriage and family therapy. M.S.

Economics. Includes options in comparative economic systems, international economics, labor economics, monetary economics, public sector economics. M.A.

Education. Includes options in curriculum, educational technology leadership, online teaching and learning, reading instruction. M.S.

Educational Leadership. Includes option in urban teacher leadership. M.S.

Engineering Management. M.S.

English. Includes option in teaching English as a second language. M.A.

Geography. M.S.

Geology. Includes option in environmental geology. M.S.

Health Care Administration. Includes options in administration of healthy communities, management and change in health care. M.S.

History. Includes options in public history, teaching. M.A.

Interdisciplinary Studies. M.A., M.S.

Kinesiology. Includes options in exercise physiology, professional perspective, skill acquisition and sport psychology, sports humanities. M.S.

Marine Science. M.A.

Mathematics. Includes options in teaching, applied mathematics. M.S.

Multimedia. M.A.

Music. M.A.

Public Administration. Includes options in health care administration, organizational change, public human resource management, public management, public policy development. M.P.A.

Social Work. M.S.W.

Special Education. M.S.

Speech Communication. M.A.

Speech Pathology and Audiology. M.S.

Statistics. Includes options in actuarial statistics, biostatistics, computational statistics, mathematical statistics, theoretical and applied statistics. M.S.

Taxation. M.S.

Telecommunication Systems. Includes options in computer technologies of telecommunications, telecommunications management. M.S.

CALIFORNIA STATE UNIVERSITY, FRESNO

Fresno, California 93740-0051
Web site: www.csufresno.edu

Founded 1911. Located 185 miles SE of San Francisco. CGS member. Coed. Public control. Semester system. Special facilities: California Agricultural Technology Institute, Center for Agricultural Business, Center for Irrigation Technology, Center for Korean Studies, Central California Futures Institute, Computer Integrated Manufacturing Center, Digital Economy Center, Institute for Family Business, Moss Landing Marine Laboratory (shared by five state colleges), Small Business Development Center, University Business Center, Viticulture and Enology Research Center. Library: 977,100 volumes, 2500 subscriptions. More than 850 computers on campus for student use.

Fees/nonresident tuition: resident 0–6 units $1253, more than 7 units $1871; nonresident 0–6 units 1253 plus $339 per unit, more than 7 units $1871 plus $339 per unit. On-campus housing for 555 men, 660 women; none for married students. Average annual housing cost: $6500 (including board). Off-campus moderately priced housing is also available. Apply by June 1 to Director of Housing. Phone: (559)278-2345.

Division of Graduate Studies

Graduate study since 1946. Enrollment: full-time 941, part-time 919. Faculty: full-time 429, part-time 133. Degrees conferred: M.A., M.S., M.B.A., M.F.A. M.S.W., M.P.A., M.P.T., M.P.H.

ADMISSION REQUIREMENTS. Transcripts, GRE required in support of University's application. Letters of recommendation, GMAT, interview required by some departments. TOEFL (minimum score 550) required for foreign applicants. Accepts transfer applicants. Apply to Admissions Office by March 1 (Fall), November 1 (Spring). Late admission will be considered. Application fee $55. Phone: (559)278-2261; fax: (559)278-4658.

ADMISSION STANDARDS. Selective. Usual minimum average: 2.75 (A = 4).

FINANCIAL AID. Scholarships, fellowships, teaching assistantships, traineeships, tuition waivers, Federal W/S, loans. Approved for VA benefits. Apply to Office of Financial Aid by March 1 for scholarships, to Department Chairperson for assistantships. Phone: (559)278-2183. Use FAFSA. About 20% of students receive aid other than loans from University. Aid sometimes available for part-time students.

DEGREE REQUIREMENTS. For master's: 30 units minimum, at least 21 in residence; GRE or GMAT for M.P.A., and M.B.A.; advancement to candidacy; final written/oral exam for most majors; reading knowledge of one foreign language for some majors; thesis/creative/research project.

FIELDS OF STUDY.
Accountancy. M.S.
Agriculture. Includes agricultural chemistry, animal science, food science, nutrition.
Art. Includes art history, theory; thesis or project for master's. M.A.
Biology. Includes marine, microbiology. M.S.
Biotechnology. M.S.
Business Administration. M.B.A.
Chemistry. GRE Subject; thesis for master's. M.S.
Civil Engineering. M.S.
Communication. M.A.
Communicative Disorders. Includes speech-language pathology, education of the deaf. M.A.
Computer Science. M.S.
Counseling. M.S.
Creative Writing. M.F.A.
Criminology. Includes law enforcement, corrections. M.S.
Education. Includes early childhood, elementary, secondary, curriculum and instruction, educational theory, administration, counselor, health, home economics, music, physical, reading, special. M.A.
Educational Leadership. Ed.D.
Engineering. Includes electrical, mechanical. M.A.
English. Includes creative writing; thesis or project for master's. M.A.
Food and Nutritional Sciences. M.S.
Forensic Science. M.S.
Geology. M.S.
History. One language; GRE Subject, thesis for master's. M.A.
Industrial Technology. M.S.
International Relations. Includes government; one language, GRE Subject, project for master's. M.A.
Kinesiology. M.A.
Linguistics. Includes English as a second language. M.A.
Marine Science. M.S.
Mass Communication and Journalism. M.A.
Mathematics. GRE Subject, thesis for master's. M.A.
Music. Includes performance, music education. M.A.
Nursing. Includes clinical, primary nurse practitioner. M.S.
Physical Therapy. M.P.T.
Physics. GRE Subject, thesis or project for master's. M.S.
Plant Science. M.S.
Psychology. GRE Subject, qualifying exam, thesis or project for master's. M.A., M.S.
Public Administration. M.P.A.
Public Health. M.P.H.
Rehabilitation Counseling. M.S.
Social Work. Admits Fall only; two years full-time, thesis for master's. M.S.W.
Spanish. M.A.
Special Education. M.A.
Viticulture and Enology. M.S.

CALIFORNIA STATE UNIVERSITY, FULLERTON

Fullerton, California 92634-9480
Web site: www.fullerton.edu

Founded 1957. Located 35 miles SE of Los Angeles. CGS member. Coed. Public control. Semester system. Special facilities: Desert Studies Consortium, Center for Economic Education, Institute for Economics and Environmental Studies, Center for Governmental Studies, Center for International Business, Ruby Gerontology Center, Social Science Research Center, Twins Study Center. Library: 1,200,000 volumes, 10,827 subscriptions. More than 1000 computers on campus for student use. Total University enrollment: 35,000.

Fees/nonresident tuition: resident 0–6 units $900, more than 7 units $1551; nonresident 0–6 units $900 plus $339 per unit, more than 7 units $1551 plus $339 per unit. On-campus housing available for single students only. Average annual housing cost: $5800 (including board). Contact the Housing Office for both on- and off-campus housing information. Phone: (714)278-2168.

Graduate Studies

Graduate study since 1960. Enrollment: full-time 1316, part-time 2844. College faculty; full-time 608, part-time 614. Degrees conferred: M.A., M.S., M.B.A., M.P.A., M.M., M.F.A., M.A.T.

ADMISSION REQUIREMENTS. Two official transcripts required with application. GRE required for some programs; GMAT for M.B.A., Accountancy, Taxation, Management Science. TOEFL required for international applicants. Accepts transfer applicants. Graduates of unaccredited institutions not considered. Apply to Office of Admissions and Records by July 1 (Fall), November 1 (Spring); earlier deadlines exist for some programs. Application fee $55. Phone: (714)278-7788.

ADMISSION STANDARDS. Selective. Usual minimum average: 2.5 (A = 4) in last 60 credits (90 Quarter) units.

FINANCIAL AID. Annual awards from institutional funds: equity fellowships, scholarships, assistantships, internships, grants, Federal W/S, loans. Approved for VA benefits. Apply by March 1 to appropriate department chair for assistantships; to Financial Aid Office for all other programs. Phone: (714)278-3125. Use FAFSA. Aid available for part-time students

DEGREE REQUIREMENTS. For master's: 30–51 units minimum, at least 21 in residence; advancement to candidacy; capstone, thesis, project, or comprehensive exam required for all programs.

FIELDS OF STUDY.
Accountancy. Project for M.S.
American Studies. Thesis or final exam for M.A.
Anthropology. Thesis or project for M.A.
Art. Includes studio and art history programs; thesis or project for M.A., M.F.A.
Biology. GRE General/Subject for admission; thesis for M.S.
Business Administration. Final exam or thesis for M.B.A.
Chemistry. Departmental exams for classified standing; thesis for M.S.
Civil Engineering. M.S.
Communications. GRE for admission; thesis or project for M.A.
Communicative Disorders. Thesis option; comprehensive exam required for M.A.
Computer Science. GRE for admission; project or thesis for M.S.
Counseling. Project required for M.S.
Economics. GRE for classified standing; thesis for M.A.
Education. Includes bilingual/bicultural education (Spanish/ English), elementary curriculum/instruction, reading, special education, administration, TESOL; teaching experience required for classified standing; project/thesis/final exam as determined by concentration for M.S.
Educational Leadership. Ed.D.
Engineering. Includes electrical, mechanical, civil, engineering mechanics systems, engineering science; thesis/project option; final exam for M.S.
English. Project option; final exam for M.A.
Environmental Studies. Thesis for M.S.
Foreign Languages. Includes French, German, Spanish; thesis option; final exam for M.A.
Geography. Project or thesis for M.A.
Geology. M.S.
Gerontology. M.S.
History. Thesis/project/final exam option for M.A.
Information Systems. M.S.
Interdisciplinary Studies. M.A. only.
Instructional Design and Technology (online only). M.S.
Kinesiology. Thesis or project; final exam for M.S.
Linguistics. Thesis option; final exam for M.A.
Mathematics. Includes applied, teaching. Final exam for M.A.
Music. Includes history and literature, performance, theory-composition, music education, proficiency exams for classified standing; thesis or project for M.M., M.A. Admits Fall only.
Physics. Final exam or thesis for M.S.
Political Science. Project, final exam for M.A.
Psychology. Includes clinical, experimental. Admits Fall only. GRE/Subject Test for admission; thesis for M.A.; final exam for M.S.
Public Administration. GRE for classified standing; project/thesis/ final exam option for M.P.A.

Public Health. M.P.H.
Radio, TV, and Film.
Science. Thesis or project for M.A.T.
Social Work. M.S.W.
Sociology. Thesis for M.A.
Speech Communication. Thesis option; final exam for M.A.
Taxation. Project for M.S.
Theater Arts. Includes acting, directing, technical theater and design. Thesis/project and final exam for M.A.; two projects for M.F.A. (technical theater and design, theater for children, acting). Admits Fall only.

CALIFORNIA STATE UNIVERSITY, LONG BEACH

Long Beach, California 90840-0118
Web site: www.csulb.edu

Founded 1949. Located between Los Angeles and Orange County. CGS member. Coed. Public control. Semester system. Special facilities: Center for Asian Pacific American Studies, Center for Behavioral Research and Studies, Center for Collaboration in Education, Center for Commercial Deployment of Transportation Technology, Center for Criminal Justice Research and Training, Center for Educational Applications of Brain-Hemisphere Research, Center for Entrepreneurship, Center for European Studies, Center for First Amendment Studies, Center for Health Care Innovation, Center for Humanities, Center for Information Systems Technologies, Center for International Trade and Transportation, Center for Language Minority Education and Research, Molecular Ecology Institute, Center for the Preservation of Jazz, Center for Study of Southeast Asia, Center for Study of Judeo-Christian Origins, Center for Successful Aging. Library: 1,500,000 volumes, 18,000 subscriptions. More than 2000 computers on campus for general student use. Total University enrollment: 34,500.

Fees/nonresident tuition: resident 0–6 units $990, more than 7 units $1707; nonresident 0–6 units $990 plus $339 per unit, more than 7 units $1707 plus $339 per unit. On-campus housing for 725 men, 1075 women; none for married students. Average annual housing cost: $6791–$7529 (including board). Apply by April 1 to Director of Housing. Dance Center. Day-care facilities available.

Graduate Studies

Enrollment: full-time 1828, part-time 2874. University faculty: full- and part-time 1200. Degrees conferred: M.A., M.S., M.F.A., M.P.A., Ph.D. (Engineering Mathematics with Claremont Graduate School).

ADMISSION REQUIREMENTS. Transcripts, GRE/GMAT required in support of University's application. A business college application required in addition to University's. Electronic application available. TOEFL required for foreign applicants. Accepts transfer applicants. Graduates of unaccredited institutions not considered. Apply to Office of Admissions and Records by August 1 (Fall), December 1 (Spring). Application fee $55. Phone: (562) 985-8476; fax: (562)985-7786.

ADMISSION STANDARDS. Very selective for some departments, relatively open for others. Minimum average: 2.75 in last 60 units attempted (A = 4).

FINANCIAL AID. Annual awards from institutional funds; scholarships, fellowships, grants, assistantships, Federal W/S, loans. Apply to the Office of Financial Aid between February 1 and March 1 for scholarships, loans, W/S; to appropriate department chair for assistantships. Phone: (562)985-4641. Use FAFSA. Aid available for part-time students.

DEGREE REQUIREMENTS. For master's: 30 units minimum, at least 24 in residence; reading knowledge of one foreign language for some majors; candidacy exam; thesis/project or final written/oral exam. For Ph.D.: see degree requirements in Claremont Graduate School listing.

FIELDS OF STUDY.

COLLEGE OF BUSINESS ADMINISTRATION:
Business Administration. Includes self-paced evening M.B.A., fully employed M.B.A. and one-year accelerated M.B.A.

COLLEGE OF EDUCATION:
Administrative Services.
Elementary Education. Includes curriculum & instruction, dual language development, early childhood education, reading and language arts.
Educational Administration.
Educational Technology.
Educational Psychology.
Librarianship.
Library Media Services.
School Psychology.
Secondary Education. Includes curriculum & instruction, reading and language arts.
Social & Multicultural Foundations

COLLEGE OF ENGINEERING:
Aerospace Engineering. M.S.
Chemical Engineering. M.S.E.
Civil Engineering. M.S.C.E.
Computer Engineering. M.S.
Computer Science. M.S.
Electrical Engineering. M.S.
Engineering. M.S.E.
Mechanical Engineering. M.S.

CALIFORNIA STATE UNIVERSITY, LOS ANGELES

Los Angeles, California 90032-8350
Web site: www.calstatela.edu

Founded 1947. CGS member. Public control. Quarter system. Special facilities: Center for the Study of Business in Society, Chinese Studies Center, Center for Korean-American Studies, Center for Armament and Disarmament, Desert Studies Center. Library: 1,700,000 volumes, 2700 subscriptions. More than 1500 computers on campus for general student use. Total University enrollment: 20,000.

Fees/nonresident tuition: resident 0–6 units $785, more than 6 units $1219; nonresident 0–6 units $785 plus $226 per unit, more than 6 units $1219 plus $226 per unit. On-campus housing available. Total annual cost: $7353 (including board). For off-campus housing, contact Housing and Residence Life. Phone: (323)343-4800. Day-care facilities available.

Graduate Studies

Enrollment: full-time 1982, part-time 2640. Faculty: full-time 313, part-time 192. Degrees conferred: M.A., M.F.A., M.S., M.B.A., M.S.W., Ph.D. (Special Education) offered jointly with UCLA.

ADMISSION REQUIREMENTS. Two transcripts, two letters of recommendation required in support of University's application. GRE and interview required by some departments. TOEFL required for international applicants. Accepts transfer applicants. Graduates of unaccredited institutions not considered. Apply by June 30 (Fall), October 1 (Winter), February 1 (Spring), April 1 (Summer) to Office of Admissions and Records. Application fee $55. Phone: (323)343-3901.

ADMISSION STANDARDS. Relatively open. Usual minimum average: 2.5 (A = 4).

FINANCIAL AID. Fellowships, assistantships, grants, internships, Federal W/S, loans. Approved for VA benefits. Apply by March 1 to Office of Student Financial Services. Phone: (323)343-3240. Use FAFSA. Aid available for part-time students.

DEGREE REQUIREMENTS. For master's: 45 quarter units minimum, at least 32 in residence; foreign language competency for some departments; thesis for some majors; advancement to candidacy; comprehensive; oral/written exam for some majors. For Ph.D.: 32 quarter units in residence; for additional Ph.D. requirements, see UCLA listing.

FIELDS OF STUDY.
Accountancy. M.S.
Anthropology. M.A.
Art. Includes education, history, design, studio. M.A., M.F.A.
Biology. M.S.
Business Administration. Includes accounting, business economics, business education, finance, health care management, information systems, international, management, marketing. M.B.A., M.S.
Chemistry. M.S.
Child Development. M.A., M.Ed.
Communication Studies. Includes speech, telecommunications and film. M.A.
Communicative Disorders. M.A.
Computer Science. M.S.
Counseling. Includes school counseling and school psychology, rehabilitation counseling, community college counseling, applied behavior analysis.
Criminal Justice. M.S.
Criminalistics. M.S.
Economics. M.A.
Education. Includes early childhood, elementary, secondary, computer education, educational foundation, reading, special interests. M.A.
Educational Administration. M.A.
Engineering. Includes civil, electrical, mechanical. M.S.
English. Includes composition, literature, creative writing. M.A.
Environmental Science. M.S.
French. M.A.
Geography. M.A.
Geology. Offered jointly with California State University, Long Beach, California State University, Northridge. M.S.
Health Care Management. M.S.
Health Science. M.A.
History. M.A.
Industrial and Technical Studies. M.A.
Information Systems. M.S.
Interdisciplinary Studies. M.A.
Kinesiology. M.A.
Latin-American Studies. M.A.
Mathematics. Includes applied and pure. M.S.
Mexican-American Studies. M.A.
Music. Includes music composition, commercial music, performance, musicology. M.A., M.Mus.
Music Education.
Nursing. Includes acute care nurse practitioner, administrator. M.S.
Nutritional Science. M.S.
Philosophy. M.A.
Physics. M.S.
Political Science. M.A.
Psychology. M.A., M.S.
Public Administration. M.S.

Social Work. M.S.W.
Sociology. M.A.
Spanish. M.A.
Special Education. Includes early childhood, gifted, mild/moderate disabilities, moderate/severe disabilities, multicultural/multilingual, resource specialist. M.A., Ph.D. offered jointly with UCLA.
Speech Communication. M.A.
TESOL. M.A.
Theater Arts. M.A.

CALIFORNIA STATE UNIVERSITY, NORTHRIDGE

Northridge, California 91330
Web site: www.csun.edu

Founded 1958. Located near Los Angeles. CGS member. Coed. Public control. Semester system. Special facilities: California African American Political Institute, Central American Studies, China Institute, Entertainment Industry Institute, Institute for the Advancement of Educational Studies and Programs, Institute for Business and Economics, Institute for Health and Human Development, Institute for Social and Behavioral Sciences, Center for Achievement for the Physically Disabled, Center for Cancer and Developmental Biology, Center for Earthquake Studies, Center for Ethics and Values, Center for Finance and Business Research, Center for Family Business Education and Research, Center for the Humanities, Center for Management and Organizational Development, Center for Partnerships for Educational Reform, Center for Real Estate, Center for Research and Services, Center for Sex Research, Center for Southern California Studies, Center for Supramolecular Studies, Center for the Study of the San Fernando Valley Economy, Center for the Study of Biodiversity, Center for Study of Peoples of the Americas, Center for Small Business and Entrepreneurship, Center for the Visual and Performing Arts. Library: 1,200,000 volumes, 2754 subscriptions.

Fees/nonresident tuition: resident 7 units plus $1970; nonresident 7 units $1970 plus $339 per unit, more than 6 units $1219 plus $226 per unit. On-campus housing for single students only. Average academic year housing costs: $4336–$5413; $9350 (including board). Contact Housing Office for both on- and off-campus housing information. Phone: (818)667-2160.

Graduate Studies

Enrollment: full-time 1226, part-time 1759. Faculty: full-time 829, part-time 632. Degrees conferred: M.A., M.B.A., M.P.A., M.P.H., M.S.

ADMISSION REQUIREMENTS. Two official transcripts, GRE/MAT/GMAT required in support of School's application. Departmental applications required for some programs. TOEFL required for international applicants. Interview required for some departments. Separate departmental applications required in some departments. Accepts transfer applicants. Apply to Admissions Office by August 1 (Fall), January 1 (Spring). Application fee $55. Phone: (818)677-2138; fax: (818)677-4691; e-mail: graduatestudies@csun.edu.

ADMISSION STANDARDS. Selective for most departments. Usual minimum average: 2.5 (A = 4).

FINANCIAL AID. Annual awards from institutional funds: scholarships, fellowships, assistantships, partial tuition waivers, internships, Federal W/S, loans. Approved for VA benefits. Apply by March 1 to the Office of Student Assistance. Phone: (818)677-2085. Use FAFSA (School code: 001153). About 5% of students receive aid from University and outside sources. Aid available for part-time students.

DEGREE REQUIREMENTS. For master's: 30 units minimum, at least 21 in residence; thesis/project; comprehensive exam; reading knowledge of one foreign language for some departments. For M.B.A.: 33 units.

FIELDS OF STUDY.
Anthropology. Includes public archaeology. M.A.
Art. Includes art education, art history, studio art, visual communication, M.A.; studio arts, visual communication, M.F.A.
Biochemistry. M.S.
Biology. M.S.
Business Administration. M.B.A.
Chemistry. M.S.
Chicano/a Studies. M.A.
Cinema and Television Arts—Screenwriting. M.A.
Communication Disorders and Sciences. Includes speech language and pathology, audiology. M.S.
Communication Studies. M.A.
Computer Science. M.S.
Counseling. Includes career counseling, college counseling and student services, marriage and family therapy, school counseling, school psychology. M.S.
Education. Includes educational psychology, elementary education, secondary education. M.A.
Education—Special. Includes deaf and hard of hearing, early childhood educational therapy, mild/moderate disabilities, moderate/severe disabilities. M.A.
Educational Administration. M.A.
Electrical Engineering. M.S.
Engineering. Includes structural. M.S.
Engineering—Management. M.S.
Engineering—Manufacturing Systems. M.S.
Engineering—Materials. M.S.
Engineering—Mechanical. M.S.
English. M.A.
Environmental and Occupational Health. Includes industrial hygiene. M.S.
Family and Consumer Science. M.S.
Genetic Counseling. M.S.
Geography. M.A.
Geology. M.S.
Health Administration. M.S.
History. M.A.
Interdisciplinary Studies. M.A., M.S.
Kinesiology. M.S.
Knowledge Management. M.K.M.
Linguistics. M.A.
Mass Communications. Includes journalism. M.A.
Mathematics. Includes mathematics for educational careers, applied mathematics. M.S.
Music. Includes conducting, composition, music education, performance. M.A., M.S.
Physical Therapy. M.P.T.
Physics. M.S.
Political Science. M.A.
Psychology. Includes clinical, general-experimental, human factors and applied experimental. M.A.
Public Administration. M.P.A.
Public Health. M.P.H.
Recreation Administration. M.S.
Sociology. M.A.
Social Work. M.S.W.
Spanish. M.A.
Theatre. M.A.

CALIFORNIA STATE UNIVERSITY, SACRAMENTO

Sacramento, California 95819-6048

Web site: www.csus.edu

Founded 1947. CGS member. Coed. Public control. Semester system. Special facilities: California Center for Public Dispute Resolution, Center for California Studies, Real Estate and Land Use Institute. Library: 1,300,000 volumes, 3761 subscriptions, more than 800 computers on-campus for general student use. Total University enrollment: 27,900.

Fees/nonresident tuition: resident 0–6 units $900, more than 6 units $1551; nonresident 0–6 units $900 plus $339 per unit, more than 6 units $1551 plus $339 per unit. On-campus housing for single students. Average academic year housing costs: $7052 (including board). Contact Office of Residence Hall Life for both on- and off-campus housing information. Phone: (916)278-6655.

Graduate Studies

Enrollment: full-time 1670, part-time 1922. Graduate faculty: full-time 399, part-time 222. Degrees conferred: M.A., M.S., M.S.B.A., M.B.A., M.P.P.A., M.S.W.

ADMISSION REQUIREMENTS. Two official transcripts required in support of application. GRE/GMAT required by some departments. Interview may be requested. TOEFL required for international applicants. Accepts transfer applicants. Graduates of unaccredited institutions not considered. Apply by March 15 (Fall), November 1 (Spring) to Office of Graduate Admissions. Application fee $55. Phone: (916)278-6470; fax: (916)278-5669; e-mail: gradctr@csus.edu.

ADMISSION STANDARDS. Selective. Usual minimum average: 2.5 (A = 4).

FINANCIAL AID. Assistantships, internships, Federal W/S, loans. Apply by March 1 to the Dean for assistantships; to Financial Aid Office for all other programs. Phone: (916)278-6554. Use FAFSA. Aid available for part-time students.

DEGREE REQUIREMENTS. For most master's: 30 semester hours minimum, at least 21 in residence; thesis/nonthesis option for many majors; final written/oral exam for some majors. For M.B.A., M.P.A.: 30–57 hours, depending upon previous preparation. For M.S.W.: satisfactory completion of two-year program, at least one year in residence.

FIELDS OF STUDY.
Accounting. M.S.
Anthropology. M.A.
Art. Includes fine arts, art history. M.A.
Biological Sciences. M.A., M.S.
Business Administration. M.B.A.
Business Administration. Includes management information systems. M.S.B.A.
Chemistry. M.S.
Childhood Development. M.A.
Civil Engineering. M.S.
Communication Studies. M.A.
Computer Science. Includes software engineering, scientific and engineering applications, computer systems. M.S.
Counseling. Includes career counseling, generic counseling, school counseling, school psychology, marriage, family, and child counseling, rehabilitation counseling. M.S.
Criminal Justice. Includes forensic science. M.A.
Economics. M.A.
Education. Includes behavioral sciences in education, art, bilingual/cross-cultural education, curriculum and instruction, early child-hood education, educational administration, English language development, gifted/talented education, guidance, reading specialist, special education. M.A.
Electrical and Electronic Engineering. M.S.
English. Includes creative writing, teaching English to speakers of other languages. M.A.
Geology. M.S.
Government. M.A.
History. Includes public history. M.A.
International Affairs. M.A.
Kinesiology. Includes exercise physiology, sport performance, strength/conditioning.
Liberal Arts. M.A.
Marine Science. M.S.
Mathematics. M.A.
Mechanical Engineering. M.S.
Music. M.M.
Nursing. Includes family nurse practitioner. M.S.
Psychology. Includes counseling, industrial organizational. M.A.
Public Policy and Administration. M.P.P.A.
Recreation, Parks and Tourism Administration. M.S.
Social Work. Includes family and children's services, health care, mental health, social justice and corrections. M.S.W.
Sociology. M.A.
Software Engineering. M.S.
Spanish. M.A.
Special Major. M.A., M.S.
Speech Pathology. M.S.
TESOL. M.A.
Theater. M.A.
Urban Development. M.S.

CALIFORNIA STATE UNIVERSITY, SAN BERNARDINO

San Bernardino, California 92407-2397

Web site: www.csusb.edu

Established 1965. Located 60 miles NE of Los Angeles. CGS member. Coed. Public control. Quarter system. Special facilities: Center for Equity in Education, Center for Global Management, Center for the Study of Hate and Extremism, Desert Research Center, Institute for Social and Public Policy Research, Water Resource Institute. Library: 731,000 volumes, 2080 subscriptions. More than 1300 computers on campus for student use. Total University enrollment: 16,400.

Fees/nonresident tuition: resident 0–6 units $660, more than 6 units $1138; nonresident 0–6 units $660 plus $226 per unit, more than 6 units $1138 plus $226 per unit. On-campus housing for single students only. Average academic year housing costs including board $4506–$5390. Contact Housing Director for both on- and off-campus housing information. Phone: (909)573-7800. Day-care facilities available.

Graduate Studies

Graduate study since 1972. Enrollment: full-time 1522, part-time 956. Graduate faculty: full-time 431, part-time 120. Degrees conferred: M.A., M.S., M.B.A., M.P.A., M.S.W.

ADMISSION REQUIREMENTS. Transcripts GRE/GMAT required in support of application. TOEFL, TWE required for international applicants. Accepts transfer applicants. Graduates of unaccredited institutions not considered. Apply to the Office of Admissions by September 15 (Fall), December 15 (Winter), March 15 (Spring). Application fee $55. Phone: (909)537-5058.

ADMISSION STANDARDS. Selective. Usual minimum average: 2.5 in last 90 quarter/60 semester credits (A = 4).

FINANCIAL AID. Annual awards from institutional funds: scholarships, fellowships, assistantships, grants, Federal W/S, loans. Approved for VA benefits. Apply to Director of Financial Aid by July 1. Phone: (909)537-5227; fax: (909)537-7024. Use FAFSA. Aid available for part-time students.

DEGREE REQUIREMENTS. For master's: 45 quarter hours minimum, 36 in residence; thesis/nonthesis option; 3.0 GPA required.

FIELDS OF STUDY.
Art. M.A.
Biology. M.S.
Business Administration. Includes concentrations in accounting, corporate management, entrepreneurship, finance, information management, management of conflict, management and human resources, marketing management, operations management. M.B.A.
Communication Studies. M.A.
Computer Science. M.S.
Counseling and Guidance. M.S.
Criminal Justice. M.A.
Education. Includes bilingual/cross-cultural career and technical, curriculum and instruction, environmental, health instructional technology, kinesiology, language literacy and culture, middle grades, reading, secondary (English, history, Spanish), special, TESOL.
Educational Administration. M.A.
English Composition. Includes ESL, literature. M.A.
Environmental Sciences. M.S.
Health Services Administration. M.S.
Interdisciplinary Studies. M.A.
Mathematics. M.A.
National Security Studies. M.A.
Nursing. M.S.
Psychology. Includes child development, general, industrial-organizational, lifespan. M.A., M.S.
Public Administration. M.P.A.
Public Health. M.P.H.
Rehabilitational Counseling. M.A.
Science. M.A.T.
Social Science. M.A.
Social Work. M.S.W.
Spanish. M.A.
Teaching Mathematics. M.A.
Theater Arts. M.A.

CALIFORNIA STATE UNIVERSITY, SAN MARCOS
San Marcos, California 92096-0001
Web site: www.csusm.edu

Founded 1965. Located in San Diego County. CGS member. Coed. Public control. Semester system. Library 233,445 volumes, 2043 subscriptions. More than 1300 computers on campus for general student use. Total University enrollment: 6956.

Fees/nonresident tuition: resident 0–6 units $990, more than 6 units $1707; nonresident 0–6 units $990 plus $339 per unit, more than 6 units $1707 plus $339 per unit. On-campus housing for married or graduate students. Average academic year housing costs: $6800 (room only) for single students; $9500 for married students. Contact Office of Dean of Student Affairs for both on- and off-campus housing information.

Graduate Studies

Graduate enrollment: full-time 183, part-time 446. University faculty teaching graduate students: full-time 201, part-time 18. Degrees conferred: M.A., M.S., M.B.A.

ADMISSION REQUIREMENTS. Two official transcripts, two letters of recommendation required in support of application. GRE and a departmental application may be required by some departments. Two essays, three recommendations, résumé, GMAT (or GRE) required for Business applicants. Interview required for Education applicants. TOEFL (minimum score 550, computer-based score 213), TWE required for international applicants. Accepts transfer applicants. Graduates of unaccredited institutions not considered. Apply to Office of Admission by April 15 (Fall), October 15 (Spring). Application fee $55. Phone: (760)750-4848; fax: (760)750-3248.

ADMISSION STANDARDS. Selective. Usual minimum average: 2.5 overall, 2.75 in last two years (A = 4).

FINANCIAL AID. Scholarships, assistantships, graduate equity fellowships, traineeships, internships, Federal W/S, loans. Apply to Financial Aid Office; no specified closing dates. Use FAFSA. Aid available for part-time students.

DEGREE REQUIREMENTS. For master's: 30–36 semester hours minimum, at least 21 in residence; foreign language requirement for some programs; comprehensive thesis/nonthesis option or project; final written/oral exam.

FIELDS OF STUDY.

COLLEGE OF ARTS AND SCIENCES:
Biological Sciences. M.S.
Computer Sciences. M.S.
Literature and Writing Studies. M.A.
Mathematics. M.S.
Psychology. M.A.
Sociological Practice. M.A.
Spanish. M.A.

COLLEGE OF BUSINESS ADMINISTRATION:
Business Administration. M.B.A.

COLLEGE OF EDUCATION:
Biliteracy, Language and Culture. M.A.
Educational Administration. M.A.
Learning and Instruction. M.A.
Science, Mathematics and Educational Technology for Diverse Populations. M.A.
Special Education. M.A.

CALIFORNIA STATE UNIVERSITY, STANISLAUS
Turlock, California 95382
Web site: www.csustan.edu

Founded 1965. Located 13 miles S of Modesto. CGS member. Coed. Public control. 4-1-4 system. Special facility: Moss Landing Marine Laboratories. Library: 338,700 volumes, 1980 subscriptions. More than 200 computers on campus for general student use. Total University enrollment: 8100.

Fees/nonresident tuition: resident 0–6 units $905, more than 6 units $1622; nonresident 0–6 units $905 plus $339 per unit, more than 6 units $1622 plus $339 per unit. On-campus housing for single graduate students only. Annual room and board cost: $7300. Apply to Director of Housing. Phone: (209)667-3675. Day-care facilities available.

Graduate Studies

Enrollment: full-and part-time 700. Faculty: full-time 82, part-time 30. Degrees conferred: M.A., M.S., M.B.A., M.P.A.

ADMISSION REQUIREMENTS. Two transcripts, GRE Subject Test (History, Education, Psychology, Marine Science, English), GRE (International Relations, Interdisciplinary Studies), GMAT (Business) required in support of University's application. Electronic application available. TOEFL required for foreign applicants. Accepts transfer applicants. Apply by May 30 (Fall), November 30 (Winter), January 30 (Spring) to Admissions and Records Office. Application fee $55. Phone: (209)667-3129; fax: (209)667-7025.

ADMISSION STANDARDS. Selective. Usual minimum average: 3.0 (A = 4).

FINANCIAL AID. Scholarships, fellowships, research assistantships, Federal W/S, loans. Approved VA benefits. Apply by March 1 to Office of Financial Aid. Phone: (209)667-3063. Use FAFSA and University's FAF. Aid available for part-time students.

DEGREE REQUIREMENTS. For master's: 30 units minimum, at least 24 in residence; thesis/project or final written/oral exam.

FIELDS OF STUDY.
Business Administration. Includes international finance.
Childhood Development. M.A.
Criminal Justice.
Ecology and Sustainability. M.S.
Education. Includes administration and supervision, school counseling, curriculum and instruction (elementary, secondary, reading, special education), physical education.
English.
Genetic Counseling. M.S.
History.
Interdisciplinary Studies.
International Relations. (Concentration in M.A., History)
Marine Science.
Psychology.
Public Administration.
Social Work.

CALIFORNIA UNIVERSITY OF PENNSYLVANIA
California, Pennsylvania 15419-1394
Web site: www.cup.edu

Founded 1852. Located 35 miles S of Pittsburgh. CGS member. Coed. Public control. Semester system and two 5-week Summer terms. Library: 437,000 volumes, 880 subscriptions. More than 1200 computers on campus for general student use. Total University enrollment: 8200.

Tuition: full-time, resident $6214, per credit $345; nonresident $9944, per credit $552. On-campus housing for single students only. Average academic year housing cost: $8500 (including board). Contact Director of Housing for both on- and off-campus housing information. Phone: (724)938-4439. Day-care facilities available.

School of Graduate Studies and Research

Enrollment: full-time 663, part-time 578. Faculty: full-time 53, part-time 40. Degrees conferred: M.A., M.A.T., M.S., M.Ed., M.S.W.

ADMISSION REQUIREMENTS. Transcripts, teacher certification for M.Ed. programs, MAT/GRE/GMAT, interview required for some programs in support of application. TOEFL, statement of financial support required for foreign applicants. Accepts transfer applicants. Graduates of unaccredited colleges not con-

sidered. Apply by August 23 (Fall), January 10 (Spring), April 27 (Summer). Application fee $25. Phone: (724)938-4187; fax: (724)938-5712; e-mail: gradschool@cup.edu.

ADMISSION STANDARDS. Selective. Usual minimum average: 2.50 (A = 4), some programs are higher.

FINANCIAL AID. Annual awards from institutional funds: assistantships, tuition waivers, internships, Federal W/S, loans. Apply to the Graduate Dean for assistantships; to Financial Aid Office for all other programs. No specified closing date. Phone: (724)938-4415. Use FAFSA. About 5% of students receive aid other than loans from College and outside sources.

DEGREE REQUIREMENTS. For master's: 30–36 credits minimum, 24 in residence; thesis/nonthesis option; final oral/written exam.

FIELDS OF STUDY.
Athletic Training. M.S. only.
Biology. M.Ed., M.S. only.
Business Administration. M.S.
Chemistry. M.A.T.
Communication. M.A. only.
Communication Disorders. M.S.
Community and Agency Counseling. M.S.
Computer Science. M.Ed.
Counselor Education. Includes elementary, secondary guidance; M.Ed. only; business and industry counseling, M.S. only.
Early Childhood Education. M.Ed. only.
Earth Science. M.S. only.
Educational Administration. Includes elementary, secondary principal, superintendent's letter of eligibility.
Elementary Education. M.Ed. only.
English. M.A., M.Ed. only.
French. M.A.T.
Geography and Regional Planning. M.A., M.Ed. only.
Mathematics. M.A.
Mathematics Education. M.Ed. only.
Mentally and Physically Handicapped. M.Ed.
Multimedia Technology. M.S.
Physics. M.A.T.
Reading Specialist. M.Ed. only.
School Counseling. M.Ed.
School Psychology. M.S. only.
Science Education. M.Ed., M.A.
Social Sciences–Criminal Justice. M.A.
Social Work. M.S.W.
Spanish. M.A.T.
Special Education. M.Ed.
Technology Education. M.Ed. only.

UNIVERSITY OF CALIFORNIA AT BERKELEY
Berkeley, California 94720
Web site: www.berkeley.edu

Founded 1868. Located 12 miles E of San Francisco. CGS and AAU member. Coed. Public control. Semester system. Special facilities: Lawrence Berkeley and Livermore National Laboratories, Bodega Marine Laboratory, Center for Pure and Applied Mathematics, Mathematical Sciences Research Institute, Space Sciences Laboratory, Virus Laboratory, Naval Biomedical Laboratory, International House, Low-Density Wind-Tunnel Facility; Laboratories for Electronics Research, Hydraulic Engineering, Sea Water Conversion, Structural and Sanitary Engineering; Institutes of Transportation, Traffic Engineering, Personality Assessment and Research, Business and Economic Research,

Governmental Studies, Human Development, Human Learning, Industrial Relations, International Studies, Library Research, Marine Resources, Basic Research in Science, Urban and Rural Development; Operations Research Center, White Mountain Research Station, Lick Observatory; centers for study of Law and Society, Study of Higher Education, Research in Management Science, Survey Research; Chinese Studies, Japanese and Korean Studies, Latin American Studies, Planning Development and Research; computer facilities. The University's NIH ranking is 62nd among all U.S. institutions with 322 awards/grants valued at $98,048,910. According to The Center at University of Florida, U.C. Berkeley is ranked 25th in receipt of Federal Research funds with $238,206,000 and it ranks 12th for total University research expenditures with $507,186,000. The University's endowment assets rank it 24th, $2,037,297,000. In 2004, the University awarded 775 doctorates, which ranked it number one among all U.S. institutions eligible to award that degree. 209 of the University's faculty members have been elected to National Honor Academies and this ranks it 4th among all U.S. institutions. The 26 Berkeley libraries house more than 7,000,000 volumes, 50,000 subscriptions. Total University enrollment: 32,000.

Annual fees/tuition: full-time, resident $4789, nonresident $24,639. Fifteen residence halls for graduate and upper division students. Rooms are double occupancy. 994 apartments for married and single students. Average annual housing cost for both on- and off-campus $18,500. Apply to Housing Services. Phone: (510)642-7781. For off-campus information, phone (510)643-6544.

Graduate Division

Graduate study since 1868. Enrollment: 8454 (men 4870, women 3584). Faculty: full-time 1790, part-time 0. Degrees conferred: M.A., M.S., M.A.T., M.Arch., M.B.A., M.C.P., M.Eng., M.F., M.J., M.F.A., LL.M., M.L.A., M.P.A., M.P.P., M.S.W., Ed.D., D.Eng., LL.M., J.S.D., Dr.P.H., Ph.D.

ADMISSION REQUIREMENTS. Transcripts, GRE/GMAT, three letters of recommendation (Form G) required in support of University's application. Interview normally not required. GRE Subject test for some departments. TOEFL (minimum score 570, 230 on computer-based test) or IELTS required for all non-English speaking applicants. Graduates of unaccredited colleges not considered. Request application materials directly from department. Deadline range: December 15–February 10 (Fall); September 1 (Spring). Many departments admit for the Fall only. Application fee $60, $80 international applicants. Phone: (510)642-7405; fax: (510)643-1524; e-mail: gradadm@uclink4.berkeley.edu.

ADMISSION STANDARDS. Very selective for most departments.

FINANCIAL AID. Fellowships, research assistantships, teaching assistantships, readers, Federal W/S, loans. Apply to appropriate department; no specified closing date. For Federal programs apply to Financial Aid Office. Phone: (510)642-0485. Use FAFSA.

DEGREE REQUIREMENTS. For M.A. and M.S.: Plan I—20 semester units minimum plus thesis, at least two semesters (one year) in residence. Plan II—24 semester units minimum without thesis, at least two semesters (one year) in residence, comprehensive exam. For other master's: the same requisites outlined above normally apply. For Ph.D.: normally at least two years minimum in residence beyond the bachelor's degree; reading knowledge of at least one foreign language required by most departments; qualifying exams; dissertation; final oral exam. For other doctorates: essentially the same minimum requisites as for Ph.D., except no foreign language requirement.

FIELDS OF STUDY.
African American Studies. M.A., Ph.D.
Agricultural and Environmental Chemistry. M.S., Ph.D.

Agricultural and Resource Economics and Policy. M.S., Ph.D.
Ancient History and Mediterranean Archaeology.
Anthropology.
Applied Mathematics. Ph.D. only.
Applied Science and Technology.
Architecture. M.S., M.Arch., Ph.D.
Art. Studio; portfolio for admission; M.F.A. only.
Asian Studies. Emphasis on East Asia, Southeast Asia, South Asia, Northeast Asia studies for M.A.
Astrophysics. M.A., Ph.D.
Bioengineering (with UCSF).
Biophysics. Ph.D. only.
Biostatistics.
Buddhist Studies. Ph.D. only.
Business Administration. GMAT for admission; M.B.A. normally two-year program. M.B.A., M.F.E., Ph.D.
Chemical Engineering.
Chemistry.
City and Regional Planning. M.C.P., Ph.D.
Civil and Environmental Engineering.
Classical Archaeology.
Classics.
Comparative Biochemistry.
Comparative Literature.
Computer Science.
Demography.
Design (Visual). M.A. only.
Earth and Planetary Science.
East Asian Languages. Includes Chinese, Japanese.
Economics.
Education.
Electrical Engineering and Computer Science.
Endocrinology.
Energy and Resources.
English.
Environmental Health Sciences.
Environmental Science Policy and Management.
Epidemiology.
Ethnic Studies.
Financial Engineering. M.F.E.
Folklore. M.A. only.
Forestry. M.F. only.
French.
Geography.
Geology.
Geophysics.
German.
Greek. M.A. only.
Health and Medical Sciences. Dual degree option; genetic counseling, M.S.; medical program (with UCSF), M.S., M.D.
Health Services and Policy Analysis. Ph.D. only.
Hispanic Languages and Literatures.
History.
History of Art.
Industrial Engineering and Operations Research.
Infectious Diseases and Immunity.
Information Management and Systems. M.I.M.S., Ph.D.
Integrative Biology.
Italian Studies.
Jewish Studies. Joint program with Graduate Theological Union. Ph.D. only.
Journalism. M.J. only.
Jurisprudence and Social Policy. Ph.D. only.
Landscape Architecture. M.L.A., Ph.D.
Latin. M.A. only.
Latin American Studies. M.A. only.
Law. LL.M., J.S.D.
Linguistics.
Logic and the Methodology of Science. Ph.D. only.
Materials Science and Engineering.
Mathematics.

Mechanical Engineering.
Medical Anthropology (with UCSF). Ph.D. only.
Microbiology.
Molecular and Biochemical Nutrition.
Molecular and Cell Biology.
Molecular Toxicology.
Music. Includes performance, musicology.
Near Eastern Religions. Joint program with Graduate Theological Union. Ph.D. only.
Near Eastern Studies.
Neuroscience. Ph.D. only.
Nuclear Engineering.
Ocean Engineering.
Optometry. O.D., Certificate.
Performance Studies.
Philosophy.
Physics.
Plant Biology.
Political Science.
Psychology.
Public Health. M.P.H., Dr.P.H.
Public Policy. M.P.P., Ph.D.
Range Management. M.S. only.
Rhetoric.
Romance Languages and Literatures. Includes French, Italian, Spanish.
Scandinavian Languages and Literatures. Includes Danish, Norwegian, Old Norse, Swedish.
Science and Mathematics Education. Ph.D. only.
Slavic Languages and Literatures. Includes Russian, Polish, Czech, Serbo-Croatian.
Social Welfare. M.S.W., Ph.D., M.S.W.-Ph.D.
Sociology.
Sociology and Demography. Ph.D. only.
South and Southeast Asian Studies. Includes Hindu-Urdu, Malay-Indonesian Sanscrit, South Asian Archaeology.
Statistics.
Urban Design. M.U.D.
Visual Science.

Boalt Hall School of Law (94720-7200)

Web site: www.law.berkeley.edu

Established 1912. ABA approved since 1923. AALS member. Special facilities: Berkeley Center for Criminal Justice, Berkeley Center for Law and Technology, Berkeley Center for Environmental Law and Policy, Thelton E. Henderson Center for Social Justice, Center for Clinical Education, Center for the Study of Law and Society, Chief Justice Earl Warren Institute on Race, Ethnicity and Diversity, Institute for Legal Research, Kadish Center for Morality Law and Public Affairs, Robert D. Burch Center for Tax Policy and Public Finance. Law Library: 865,801 volumes; 7923 subscriptions. Library has LEXIS, NEXIS, WESTLAW, INNOPAC, MELVYL; is a Federal Government Depository; has more than 100 network connections.

Annual tuition: resident $25,476, nonresident $37,721; for LL.M. $37,000. On-campus housing available. Average housing and personal expenses: $20,851.

Enrollment: first-year class 170; full-time 879 (men 41%, women 59%, minorities 30%); post-graduates approximately 50. Faculty: full-time 45, part-time 54. Student to faculty ratio 14.2 to 1.

ADMISSION REQUIREMENTS. LSDAS Law School report, transcripts, LSAT (no later than December), personal statement, two references recommended in support of application. Applicants must have received the bachelor's prior to entrance. Accepts transfer applicants. Preference given to state residents. Graduates of unaccredited colleges not considered. Apply to Admissions Office after September, before February 1; early filing strongly recommended; transfer deadline July 1. Admission on full-time ba-

sis only; admits Fall only. Application fee $75. Phone: (510)642-2274; e-mail: admissions@law.berkeley.edu.

ADMISSION STANDARDS. Selective. Accepts approximately 10% of total applicants. Number of applicants 7535; number of acceptance 778; number enrolled 246; LSAT (75% of students have a score at or above 164); GPA (75% of students have a GPA at or above 3.67). *U.S. News & World Report* ranking is in the top eight of all U.S. law schools.

FINANCIAL AID. Scholarships, fellowships, research assistantships, grants, Federal W/S, loans. All financial aid based on need. Apply to Office of Financial Aid by March 1. Phone: (510)642-1563. Use FAFSA. About 75% of students receive aid other than loans from institution and outside sources.

DEGREE REQUIREMENTS. For J.D.: six terms minimum, at least two terms in full-time residence; 81 units. For LL.M.: 24 units minimum in full-time residence; final research project. For J.S.D.: At least two semesters beyond LL.M.; approved dissertation; dissertation must be completed within three years of receipt of LL.M. For other master's, Ph.D. programs: see Graduate School listing above or other institutional programs.

UNIVERSITY OF CALIFORNIA, DAVIS

Davis, California 95616
Web site: www.ucdavis.edu

Founded 1906. Located 15 miles W of Sacramento. CGS and AAU member. Coed. State control. Quarter system. Special facilities: Arboretum and Natural Reserve System, Agricultural Experiment Stations, Agricultural History Center, Agricultural Issues Center. Adult Fitness Laboratory, Bodega Marine Laboratory (off-campus), Botany Department Herbarium, California Regional Primate Research Center, Center for Consumer Research, Center for Image Processing and Integrated Computing Research (CIPICR), Computer Center, Crocker Nuclear Laboratory, Embryological Collection from Carnegie Institution, Facility for Advanced Instrumentation, Institute for Environment Health Research, Institute of Governmental Affairs, Humanities Institute, Institute of Marine Resources, Lawrence Livermore Laboratory, Nuclear Magnetic Resonance Facility, Plant Growth Laboratory, Serology Laboratory, Institute of Transportation Studies. The University's NIH ranking is 46th among all U.S. institutions with 362 awards/grants valued at $141,677,930. According to The Center at University of Florida, U.C. Davis is ranked 31st in receipt of Federal Research funds with $208,327,000 and it ranks 16th for total University research expenditures with $482,145,000. In 2004, the University awarded 375 doctorates, which ranked it 31st among all U.S. institutions eligible to award that degree. Thirty-three of the University's faculty members have been elected to National Honor Academies and this ranks it 28th among all U.S. institutions. Libraries house more than 4,400,000 volumes, 44,000 subscriptions. Total University enrollment: 28,800.

Annual fees/tuition: full-time, resident $9651, nonresident $24,639. On-campus housing for 476 married students, 180 single students. Average annual housing cost: $17,000 for married students, $17,200 (including board) for single students. Contact Housing Office for both on- and off-campus housing information. Phone: (530)752-2033. Day-care facilities available.

Graduate Studies

Graduate study since 1924. Enrollment: full- and part-time 4624. University faculty teaching graduate students: full-time 1371, part-time 231. Degrees conferred: M.A., M.A.T., M.B.A., M.Ed., M.E., M.F.A., M.S., M.A.M., M.Admin., D.Engr., Ed.D., Ph.D.

ADMISSION REQUIREMENTS. Transcripts, three letters of recommendation required in support of application. Electronic application available. GRE/Subject Tests, GMAT required by most departments. TOEFL required for international applicants. Interview not required. Accepts transfer applicants. Graduates of unaccredited institutions not considered. Apply to the Office of Graduate Studies by April 1 (Fall). Rolling admission process. Application fee $60. Phone: (530)752-0650; fax: (530)752-6222.

ADMISSION STANDARDS. Selective. Usual minimum average: 3.0 (A = 4).

FINANCIAL AID. Annual awards from institutional funds: scholarships, research assistantships, teaching assistantships, nonresident tuition fellowships, Federal W/S, loans. Approved for VA benefits. Apply by January 15 to appropriate department for fellowships, assistantships; apply by March 1 to Graduate Financial Aid Office for all other programs. Phone: (530)752-2390. Use FAFSA. About 35–45% of students receive aid other than loans from University and outside sources.

DEGREE REQUIREMENTS. For master's: Plan I—30 units minimum in residence plus thesis, reading knowledge of one foreign language for some departments; Plan II—36 units minimum in residence, reading knowledge of one foreign language for some departments, final comprehensive exam. For Ph.D.: two years minimum in residence; dissertation; preliminary, final oral exams; reading knowledge of two foreign languages for some departments. For Ed.D., D.Eng.: essentially the same as for the Ph.D., except no foreign language requirement.

FIELDS OF STUDY.
Agricultural and Environmental Chemistry. M.S., Ph.D.
Agricultural and Resource Economics. M.S., Ph.D.
Animal Behavior. M.S., Ph.D.
Animal Biology. M.S., M.A.M.
Anthropology. M.A., Ph.D.
Applied Linguistics. M.A., Ph.D.
Applied Mathematics. M.S., Ph.D.
Applied Science. M.S., Ph.D.
Art. Includes art only; portfolio for admission; M.F.A. only.
Art History. M.A. only.
Atmospheric Science. M.S., Ph.D.
Avian Sciences. M.S. only.
Biochemistry and Molecular Biology. M.S., Ph. D.
Biological Systems Engineering. M.S., Ph.D.
Biomedical Engineering. M.S., Ph.D.
Biophysics. M.S., Ph.D.
Biostatistics. M.S., Ph.D.
Cell and Developmental Biology. Ph.D.
Chemistry. M.S., Ph.D.
Child Development. M.S. only.
Community Development. M.S. only.
Comparative Literature. M.A., Ph.D.
Comparative Pathology. M.S., Ph.D.
Computer Science. M.S., Ph.D.
Creative Writing. M.A.
Cultural Studies. M.A., Ph.D.
Dramatic Art. Production; M.A.; M.F.A., Ph.D.
Ecology. M.S., Ph.D.
Economics. M.A., Ph.D.
Education. M.A., M.Ed., Ph.D.
English. M.A., Ph.D.
Entomology. M.S., Ph.D.
Epidemiology. M.S., Ph.D.
Exercise Science. M.S. only.
Food Science. M.S., Ph.D.
Forensic Science. M.S. only.
French. M.A., Ph.D.
Genetics. M.S., Ph.D.
Geography. M.A., Ph.D.

Geology. M.S., Ph.D.
German. M.A., Ph.D.
Health Informatics. M.S.
History. M.A., Ph.D.
Horticulture. M.S. only
Human Development. Ph.D. only.
Hydrologic Sciences. M.S., Ph.D.
Immunology. M.S., Ph.D.
International Agricultural Development. M.S. only.
Linguistics. Interdepartmental; M.A. only.
Mathematics. M.A., M.A.T., Ph.D.
Microbiology. M.S., Ph.D.
Molecular, Cellular and Integrative Physiology. M.S., Ph.D.
Music. Includes composition, conducting, musicology; M.A., M.A.T., Ph.D.
Native American Studies. M.A., Ph.D.
Neuroscience. Ph.D.
Nutrition. M.S., Ph.D.
Pharmacology and Toxicology. M.A., Ph.D.
Philosophy. M.A., Ph.D.
Physics. M.A., Ph.D.
Plant Biology. M.S., Ph.D.
Plant Pathology. M.S., Ph.D.
Plant Protection and Pest Management. M.S. only.
Political Science. M.A., Ph.D.
Population Biology. M.S., Ph.D.
Psychology. Ph.D.
Sociology. M.A., Ph.D.
Soil and Biogeochemistry. M.S., Ph.D.
Spanish. M.A., Ph.D.
Statistics. M.S., Ph.D.
Textile Arts and Costume Design. M.S. only.
Textiles. M.S. only.
Viticulture and Enology. M.S., Ph.D.

School of Law (King Hall) (95616-5201)
Web site: www.law.ucdavis.edu

Opened 1965. ABA approved since 1968. AALS member. Library: 437,445 volumes; 4208 Subscriptions; has LEXIS, NEXIS, WESTLAW, MELVYL; is both a Federal and State Depository.

Annual Tuition: resident $24,358, nonresident $36,603, LL.M. $26,000. On-campus housing available. Apply well in advance of April 1 deadline. Total average annual additional expenses: $14,787.

Enrollment: first-year class 194; total full-time 582 (men 45%, women 55%, minorities 33%); no part-time study. Faculty: full-time 40, part-time 35. Student to faculty ratio 12.9 to 1. Degrees conferred: J.D., J.D.-M.A., J.D.-M.B.A., J.D.-M.C.P., J.D.-M.S., LL.M. (foreign law students only).

ADMISSION REQUIREMENTS. LSDSA report, transcripts indicating award of bachelor's degree, two letters of recommendation, personal statement, LSAT (no later than December) required in support of application. TOEFL required of all international applicants educated outside the U.S. Graduates of unaccredited college not considered. Apply to Admission Office of School by February 1. Fall admission only. Application fee $75. Phone: (530)752-6477; e-mail: admission@law.ucdavis.edu. LL.M. candidates apply by January 10th.

ADMISSION STANDARDS. Selective. Accepts approximately 23% of total applicants. Number of applicants 3768; number of acceptance 877; number enrolled 194; LSAT (75% of students have a score at or above 158); GPA (75% of students have a GPA at or above 3.46). *U.S. News & World Report* ranking is in the top 34 of all U.S. law schools.

FINANCIAL AID. Fellowships, grants, Federal W/S, loans. Apply to Financial Aid office by March 1. Phone: (530)752-6573. Use FAFSA. About 75% of students receive aid other than loans from School.

DEGREE REQUIREMENTS. For J.D.: 88 credit minimum; three years in full-time residence. For LL.M.: 20 credit full-time program. For master's programs: see Graduate School listing above.

Graduate School of Management

Established 1981. Public control. Quarter system. Accredited program: M.B.A.

Annual tuition and fees: resident full-time $24,069, nonresident full-time $36,314.

Enrollment: total full-time 125, part-time 314. Faculty: 24 full-time, 26 part-time; all have either a Ph.D. or D.B.A.

Degrees conferred: M.B.A. (Concentrations in Accounting, Agricultural Management, E-Commerce, Environmental and Natural Resource Management, Finance, Information Systems, International Management, Management Science, Marketing, Not-for-Profit Management, Technology Management; individually designed concentration), M.B.A. for Working Professionals, M.B.A.-J.D., M.B.A.-A.E. (Agricultural and Resource Economics), M.B.A.-M.E. (Engineering), M.B.A.-M.D.

ADMISSION REQUIREMENTS. All applicants should have a bachelor's degree from a recognized institution of higher education and a strong mathematics background. Submit a Graduate application, GMAT results (will accept GMAT test results from the last five years; latest acceptable date is March), official transcripts from each undergraduate/graduate school attended, three letters of recommendation, a writing sample, work history (prefers at least four years of work experience), and an application fee of $150 to the Office of Admission, Graduate School of Management. Electronic applications available. Beginning students are admitted Fall only. U.S. citizens apply by March 15 (Fall), international students apply by March 15 (Fall). In addition, international students (whose native language is other than English) should submit a TOEFL (minimum score 600) report taken by March 1, certified translations and evaluations of all official transcripts; recommendation should be in English or with certified translations, and proof of sufficient financial resources for one year of academic study. For current information and/or modification in admission requirements the international applicant's contact telephone number is: (530)752-0864. On-campus visits are encouraged prior to the admissions committee reviewing completed applications. Joint degree applicants must apply to and be accepted to both schools/programs; contact the admissions office for current information and specific admissions requirements. Rolling admission process, notification is made as soon as possible after the receipt of completed application and all supporting documents, but no later than June 1. Admissions Office phone: (530)754-5476; fax: (530)754-9355.

ADMISSION STANDARDS. Selective. Mean GMAT 671; mean GPA 3.4 (A = 4). *U.S. News & World Report* ranked UC Davis in the top 46 of all U.S. business schools.

FINANCIAL AID. Special stipend for minorities, Graduate Opportunity Fellowships, State Grants, graduate assistantships, Federal W/S, loans. Financial aid is available for part-time study. Financial aid may be available for international students after the first year. Assistantships/fellowships may be available for joint degree candidates. Request scholarship, assistantship information from the Graduate School of Management. Apply by March 1 for all financial assistance. Contact the University's Financial Aid Office for current need-based financial aid information. Phone: (530)752-9246. For most financial assistance and all Federal programs submit FAFSA (School code: 001313); also submit Financial Aid Transcript, Federal Income Tax forms. Approximately 52% of students receive some form of financial assistance.

DEGREE REQUIREMENTS. For M.B.A.: 72 quarter hours for full-time program, including 33 elective hours; degree program must be completed in three years. For M.B.A.-Master's: generally a three- to four-year program. For M.B.A.-J.D.: four- to five-and-one-half-year program.

School of Medicine

Web site: www.ucdmc.ucdavis.edu/medschool

Founded 1968. First class entered 1968. Public control. Quarter system. Library: 142,000 volumes, 3700 subscriptions. The University's NIH ranking is 46th among all U.S. institutions with 362 awards/grants worth $141,377,930.

Annual tuition: resident $25,565, nonresident $37,810. On-campus housing available for both single and married students. Average figure for all other expenses: $21,638.

Enrollment: first-year class 91; total full-time 400 (men 44%, women 56%, minorities 54%, state residents 99%). Faculty: full-time approximately 500, part-time 82. Degrees conferred: M.D., M.D.-M.B.A., M.D.-Ph.D., M.D.-M.P.H.

ADMISSION REQUIREMENTS. AMCAS report, transcripts, MCAT, essay questions, three letters of recommendation required in support of application. Interview by invitation. Usually, bachelor's degree from an accredited U.S. or Canadian school required for admission. Preference given to state and WICHE residents. Interview required for all accepted candidates. Transfer applicants may be considered. Does not have EDP. Apply through AMCAS after June 1, before November 1. Application fee $60. Phone: (530)752-2717; e-mail: medadmisinfo@ucdavis.edu.

ADMISSION STANDARDS. Very competitive. Accepts about 5% of all applicants. Number of applications 4109 (775 out-of-state); number interviewed 392 (15 out-of-state); number of acceptance 202 (11 out-of-state); number enrolled 91 (3 out-of-state). Mean Composite MCAT 10.3; mean UGPA 3.61. *U.S. News & World Report* ranking is in the top 49 of all medical research schools, 30th in Primary Care.

FINANCIAL AID. Scholarships, fellowships, grants, federal and private loans. Apply to Financial Aid Office following admission. Phone: (530)752-6618; e-mail: medfinancialaid@ucdavis.edu. About 85% of students receive aid other than loans from institutional funds.

DEGREE REQUIREMENTS. For M.D.: satisfactory completion of four-year program. For M.B.A., M.P.H., Ph.D., see graduate listing above.

FIELDS OF GRADUATE STUDY.
Biochemistry & Molecular Biology.
Biomedical Engineering.
Biophysics.
Cancer Biology.
Cell and Developmental Biology.
Comparative Medicine.
Comparative Pathology.
Genetics.
Human Genetics.
Immunology.
Microbiology.
Mouse Biology.
Neurosciences.
Neurodevelopmental Disorders.
Pharmacology and Toxicology.
Physiology.
Population Biology.

School of Veterinary Medicine (95616-8734)
Web site: www.vetmed.ucdavis.edu

Established 1949. Quarter system. Special facilities: California Raptor Center, CA National Primate Research Center, Center for

Children's Environmental Health, Center for Companion Animal Behavior, Center for Companion Animal Health, Center for Equine Health, Center for Food Animals Health, Center for Laboratory Animal Science, Center for Vector Borne Diseases, Wildlife Health Center.

Annual tuition: full-time resident $22,418, nonresident $34,663. On-campus housing available. Total other expenses: $16,500.

Enrollment: first-year 131, total 535 (men 20%, women 80%, minorities 20%, state residents 15%). Faculty: full- and part-time 242. Degrees conferred: D.V.M., M.P.V.M., D.V.M.-M.P.V.M., D.V.M.-Ph.D. (Veterinary Scientist Training Program). The Ph.D. is offered through the Graduate School.

ADMISSION REQUIREMENTS. VMCAS report, transcripts, GRE, GRE in biology (October test), three letters of evaluation, personal statement, essay, Veterinary/Animal experience required in support of application. Electronic application available. Accepts transfer applicants if openings exist (priority to state and WICHE residents). Interviews by invitation only. Applicants must have completed at least three years of college study. Apply to the Admissions Office after July 1, before October 1. Application fee $40. Phone: (530)752-1324.

ADMISSION STANDARDS. Competitive. Accepts about 10–15 % of all applicants. Number of applications 1120 (90 WICHE resident, 482 out-of-state); number of acceptance 141 (4 WICHE residents, 15 out-of-state); number enrolled 119 (3 WICHE resident, 9 out-of-state). Usual minimum UGPA: 2.50 (A = 4). GRE mean score (V + Q) 1276; mean UGPA 3.47.

FINANCIAL AID. Scholarships, fellowships, teaching assistantships, loans. Apply to UCD Financial Aid office. Use FAFSA. About 8% of students receive aid other than loans from School funds.

DEGREE REQUIREMENTS. For D.V.M.: satisfactory completion of four-year programs. For M.P.V.M.: 50 quarter hour, full-time program; research project which culminates in a written and oral presentation.

FIELDS OF GRADUATE STUDY.
Animal Behavior.
Biochemistry and Molecular Biology.
Biophysics.
Cell and Developmental Biology.
Ecosystem Health. M.P.V.H.
Exercise Science.
Food Safety. M.P.V.M.
Genetics.
International Health. A Peace Corps International program. M.P.V.M.
Molecular, Cellular and Integrative Physiology.
Neuroscience.
Plant Biology.
Population Biology.
Population Health. M.P.V.M.
Public Health and Zoonoses. M.P.V.M.
Wildlife & Disease Ecology. M.P.V.M.

UNIVERSITY OF CALIFORNIA, HASTINGS COLLEGE OF THE LAW
San Francisco, California 94102-4978
Web site: www.uchastings.edu

Established 1878 as the University of California's first law school. ABA approved since 1937. Is now the Law Department of the University of California. Semester system. Special facilities: State and Local Government Center, Center for Gender & Refugee Studies, Center of Negotiation and Mediation, Center for Human Rights and International Justice, Public Law Research Institute, The Center for Worklife Law. Special programs: international study at the University of London, University of New South Wales, the University of the Netherlands, the University of Heidelberg, University of Copenhagen, University of Buenos Aires, Wuhan University, China, Bucerius School of Law, Hamburg, Bocconi University of Milan. Library: 707,052 volumes, 7961 subscriptions. Library has LEXIS, NEXIS, WESTLAW, DIALOG, INFORTRAC, DATATIMES, LEGITECH, FIRST SEARCH, EPIC; has more than 400 network connections.

Annual tuition: resident $22,190, nonresident $33,415, LL.M. $33,415. On-campus housing available for 480 students. Estimated housing cost: $19,341. Enrollment: first-year class 418; total 1262 (men 47%, women 53%, minorities 33%). Faculty: full-time 48, part-time 81. Student to faculty ratio 20.5 to 1. Degrees conferred: J.D., J.D.-M.A. with Berkeley (Asian Studies, Business Administration, City and Regional Planning, Economics, History, Journalism, and Public Policy), J.D.-M.B.A., LL.M. (foreign lawyers).

ADMISSION REQUIREMENTS. LSDAS Law School report, bachelor's degree, LSAT (no later than December), transcripts required in support of application. Personal statements and recommendations are considered. Graduates of unaccredited colleges not considered. Apply to Office of Admissions before March 1. Application fee $75. Phone: (415)565-4623; fax: (415)565-4863; e-mail: admiss@uchastings.edu.

ADMISSION STANDARDS. Selective. Accepts approximately 24% of total applicants. Number of applicants 6189; number of acceptance 1470; number enrolled 419; LSAT (75% of students have a score at or above 160); GPA (75% of students have a GPA at or above 3.38). *U.S. News & World Report* ranking is in the top 36 of all U.S. law schools.

FINANCIAL AID. Scholarships, full and partial tuition waivers, Federal W/S, loans. Apply by March 1 to Office of Admissions. Phone: (415)565-4624. Use FAFSA and Student Financial Aid Supplement. About 75% of students receive some form of aid.

DEGREE REQUIREMENTS. For J.D.: satisfactory completion of three-year, 86 credit program. For LL.M.: one-year, full-time program.
Note: Exchange programs with Nihon University, Leiden University, University of British Columbia, Vermont Law School.

UNIVERSITY OF CALIFORNIA, IRVINE
Irvine, California 92697
Web site: www.uci.edu

Opened 1965. Located 40 miles S of Los Angeles. CGS and AAU member. Coed. Public control. Quarter system. Special facilities: Advanced Power and Energy Center, Beckman Laser Institute, Cancer Research Institute, Center for Arts Research in Education, Center for Asian Studies, Center for Community Health Research, Center for Decision Analysis, Center for Immunology, Center for Research in Educational Assessment and Measurement, Center for Research on Immigration, Population Dynamics and Public Policy, Center for Research on Latinos in a Global Society, Center for the Study of Democracy, Center for Virus Research, Critical Theory Institute, Developmental Biology Center, Epilepsy Research Center, Institute for Brain Aging and Dementia, Institute for Genomics and Bioinformatics, Institute of Geophysics and Planetary Physics, Institute for Mathematical Behavioral Sciences, Institute for Software Research, Institute of Transportation Studies, Newkirk Center for Science and Society, Reeve-Irvine Research Center, Urban Water Research Center. The University's NIH ranking is 50th among all U.S. institutions with 350 awards/grants valued at $126,040,602.

According to The Center at University of Florida, U.C. Irvine is ranked 55th in receipt of Federal Research funds with $133,873,000 and it ranks 56th for total University research expenditures with $234,656,000. In 2004, the University awarded 187 doctorates, which ranked it 79th among all U.S. institutions eligible to award that degree. Thirty-two of the University's faculty members have been elected to National Honor Academies and this ranks it 29th among all U.S. institutions. Libraries house more than 2,400,000 volumes, 19,000 subscriptions. Total University enrollment: 22,000.

Annual fees/tuition: full-time, resident $9481, nonresident $24,469. On-campus housing includes 862 one-, two-, and three-bedroom apartments for married and single graduate students; 203-unit complex for full-time graduate, medical, and postdoctoral students; residence hall for 60 single graduate students. Average annual housing cost: $9500 (excluding board). Apply to Housing Office. Phone: (949)824-6811. Day-care facilities available.

Office of Graduate Studies

Enrollment: approximately 3100. Faculty: full- and part-time 1624. Degrees conferred: M.A., M.S., M.B.A., M.F.A., M.A.T., M.U.R.P., Ed.D., Ph.D.

ADMISSION REQUIREMENTS. Transcripts, three letters of recommendation required in support of University's application. Electronic application available. GRE required for most majors. TOEFL required of foreign applicants. Interview not required. Accepts transfer applicants. Graduates of unaccredited institutions not considered. Apply to Office of Graduate Studies by January 15 (Fall), October 15 (Winter), January 15 (Spring). Application fee $60, $80 for international applicants. Phone. (949)824-4611; fax: (949)824-2095.

ADMISSION STANDARDS. Very competitive to relatively open. Usual minimum average: 3.0 (A = 4)

FINANCIAL AID. Annual awards include fellowships, teaching and research assistantships, need-based grants, Federal W/S, loans. Approved for VA benefits. Apply by February 1 on Graduate Application form to appropriate academic unit. Apply to the Financial Aid Office for Federal programs. Phone: (949)824-6261. Use FAFSA. Most students receive aid other than loans from University and outside sources.

DEGREE REQUIREMENTS. For most master's: three quarters minimum, at least 80% of courses in residence; full-time attendance is normally expected, but part-time study is possible; thesis or final comprehensive exam. For M.F.A. (Creative Writing): six quarters minimum in residence; book-length thesis in recognized genre (poetry, short stories, plays, novel); final comprehensive exam. For Ph.D.: normally six quarters minimum in residence; one foreign language for some departments; qualifying exam and advancement to candidacy; dissertation; final oral exam. For Ed.D.: at least six quarters in residence; qualifying exam and advancement to candidacy; dissertation; final oral exam.

FIELDS OF STUDY.
Anthropology. M.A., Ph.D.
Biological Sciences. M.S., Ph.D.
Biomedical Engineering. M.S., Ph.D.
Business Administration. M.B.A.
Chemical and Biochemical Engineering. M.S., Ph.D.
Chemistry. M.S., Ph.D.
Civil Engineering. M.S., Ph.D.
Classics. M.A., Ph.D.
Comparative Literature. M.A., Ph.D.
Criminology, Law, and Society. M.A., Ph.D.
Culture and Ethics. M.S., Ph.D.
Dance. M.F.A.
Drama. M.F.A.
Drama and Theatre. Ph.D.
Earth System Science. M.S., Ph.D.
East Asian Languages and Literatures. M.A., Ph.D.
Economics.
Education. Includes administrative services, bilingual/cross-cultural specialist, early childhood education specialist, multiple-subject instruction (elementary), pupil personnel service, single-subject instruction (secondary), special education (learning handicapped, physically handicapped, severely handicapped). State credential, M.A.T.
Electrical and Computer Engineering. M.S., Ph.D.
Engineering. M.S., Ph.D.
English. M.A., M.F.A., Ph.D.
Environmental Toxicology. M.S., Ph.D.
French. M.A., Ph.D.
Genetic Counseling. M.S.
German. M.A., Ph.D.
History. M.A., Ph.D.
Humanities. M.A., Ph.D.
Information and Computer Science. M.S., Ph.D.
Management. Ph.D.
Materials Science and Engineering. M.S., Ph.D.
Mathematics. M.S., Ph.D.
Mechanical and Aerospace Engineering. M.S., Ph.D.
Music. M.F.A.
Network Systems. M.S., Ph.D.
Nursing. M.S.N.
Pharmacology and Toxicology. M.S., Ph.D.
Philosophy. M.A., Ph.D.
Physics. M.S., Ph.D.
Planning, Policy and Design. Ph.D.
Political Science. Ph.D.
Psychology. Ph.D.
Psychology and Social Behavior. Ph.D.
Social Ecology. Ph.D.
Social Science. M.A., Ph.D.
Sociology. M.A., Ph.D.
Spanish. M.A., M.A.T., Ph.D.
Statistics. M.S., Ph.D.
Studio Art. M.F.A.
Transportation Science. Ph.D.
Urban and Regional Planning. M.U.R.P., Ph.D.
Visual Studies. M.A., Ph.D.

College of Medicine (92697-4089)
Web site: www.ucihs.uci.edu/som

Founded 1967. Public control. Quarter system. Library: 100,000 volumes, 2000 subscriptions. The University's NIH ranking is 50th among all U.S. institutions with 350 awards/grants worth $126,040,602.

Annual tuition: resident $23,445 nonresident $35,690. No on-campus housing available. Average figure for all other expenses: $13,490.

Enrollment: first-year class 103; total full-time 400 (men 52%, women 48%, minorities 32%, state residents 100%). Faculty: full-time approximately 500, part-time 108. Degrees conferred: M.D., M.D.-M.B.A., M.D.-Ph.D.

ADMISSION REQUIREMENTS. AMCAS report, transcripts, letters of recommendation, MCAT required in support of U.C. application. Applicants must have completed at least three years of college study. Interview required for all final candidates. Preference given to California residents. Does not have EDP. Does not consider transfer applicants. Apply to the Director of Admissions after June 15, before November 1. Application fee $60. Phone: (949)824-5388; fax: (949)824-2485.

ADMISSION STANDARDS. Very competitive. Accepts about 7% of all applicants. Number of applications 3798 (475 out-of-state); number interviewed 455 (8 out-of-state); number of acceptance 277 (3 out-of-state); number enrolled 103 (0 out-of-state). Mean

Composite MCAT 10.7; mean UGPA 3.70. *U.S. News & World Report* ranking is in the top 41 of all medical research schools, 50th in Primary Care.

FINANCIAL AID. Scholarships, fellowships, grants, loans, summer research fellowships. Apply to the Office of Medical Student Financial Aid; no closing date. About 74% of students receive aid of some type. Phone: (949)824-6476.

DEGREE REQUIREMENTS. For M.D.: satisfactory completion of four-year program; must pass Steps 1 and 2 of USMLE and pass Clinical Practice Exam. For Ph.D.: see Graduate Division listing above for degree requirements.

FIELDS OF GRADUATE STUDY.
Anatomy.
Biochemistry.
Community and Environmental Toxicology.
Genetic Counseling. M.S. only.
Microbiology.
Molecular Genetics.
Neurobiology.
Pharmacology.
Physiology.

UNIVERSITY OF CALIFORNIA, LOS ANGELES
Los Angeles, California 90025-1301
Web site: www.ucla.edu

Founded 1919. CGS and AAU member. Coed. State control. Quarter system. Special facilities: Center for the Study of Comparative Folklore and Mythology, Center for Medieval and Renaissance Studies, Center for African Studies, Institute of Archaeology, Center for Latin American Studies, Gustave E. Von Grunebaum Center for Near Eastern Studies, Institute of Social Science Research, Dental Research Institute, Jules Stein Eye Institute, Mental Retardation Center, Brain Research Institute, Institute of American Cultures, Afro-American Studies Center, Asian American Studies Center, Chicano Studies Research Center, Institute of Geophysics and Planetary Physics, Institute of Industrial Relations, Laboratory of Biomedical and Environmental Sciences, Molecular Biology Institute, Institute of Medical Engineering, University Elementary School, Grunwald Center for the Graphic Arts, Frederick S. Wight Art Gallery, Mildred E. Mathias Botanical Gardens, Fernald School, Center for Plasma Physics and Fusion Technology, Dental Clinic, Cancer Research Center, Cardiovascular Research Laboratory, Reed Neurological Research Center, Committee on International and Comparative Studies, Neuropsychiatric Institute, Museum of Cultural History, UCLA Hospital and Clinics. The University's NIH ranking is 8th among all U.S. institutions with 914 awards/grants valued at $385,788,286. According to The Center at University of Florida, U.C.L.A. is ranked 5th in receipt of Federal Research funds with $421,174,000 and it ranks 2nd for total University research expenditures with $849,357,000. The University's endowment assets ranks it 79th with a value of $586,839,000. In 2004, the University awarded 666 doctorates which ranked it 5th among all U.S. institutions eligible to award that degree. Sixty-six of the University's faculty members have been elected to National Honor Academies and this ranks it 16th among all U.S. institutions. The libraries house more than 7,500,000 volumes, 51,000 subscriptions. Total University enrollment: 32,900.

Annual fees/tuition: full-time, resident $8967, nonresident $23,955. University maintains 1183 units for married graduate students five miles from campus, one residence hall on campus to house 334 single graduate students. Average academic year housing costs: $13,575 (including board) for single students; $12,000 for single students off-campus; $17,575–$19,375 for married students. Apply by May 15. Contact the Office of Residential Life for both on- (310-398-4692) and off-campus (310-390-1274) housing information. Day-care facilities available.

Graduate Division

Graduate study since 1933. Enrollment: full-time 7454 (men 50%, women 50%). Faculty: full-time 1526. Degrees conferred: M.A., M.S., M.B.A., M.A.T., M.Ed., M.Engr., M.F.A., M.P.H., M.S.W., M.Arch., M.L.S., M.M., M.N., Ed.D., C.Phil., D.M.A., D.N.Sc., Dr.P.H., D.Env., Engr.

ADMISSION REQUIREMENTS. Two transcripts, statement of purpose, required in support of application. Electronic application available. Additional application, supplementary information form, three letters of recommendation, GRE/GRE Subject/MAT required by some departments. Interview sometimes required. TOEFL (minimum score 560, 220 on computer-based test) or IELTS (overall band score of at least 7.0) required for international applicants. Accepts transfer applicants. Apply to Graduate Admissions/Student and Academic Affairs by December 15 (Fall), October 1 (Winter), December 31 (Spring). Application fee $60, $80 for international applicants. Phone: (310) 825-1711; fax: (310)206-4627.

ADMISSION STANDARDS. Selective for most departments, very competitive or competitive for the others.

FINANCIAL AID. Annual awards from institutional funds: fellowships and grants, research assistantships, teaching assistantships, Federal W/S, loans. Approved for VA benefits. Apply by March 1 to the appropriate department for assistantships, fellowships; to Financial Aid Office for all Federal programs. Use FAFSA and University's Supplemental FAF. Phone: (310)206-0400. About 52% of students receive aid other than loans from University and outside sources.

DEGREE REQUIREMENTS. For M.A., M.S.: nine graduate courses, at least seven in residence and three in full-time attendance; advancement to candidacy; thesis or final written/oral exam; reading knowledge of one foreign language for some majors. For other master's: the same minimum requisites outlined normally apply. For Ph.D.: normally three years minimum in residence beyond the bachelor's; preliminary exam; reading knowledge of one or two foreign languages; written/oral qualifying exam; advancement to candidacy; dissertation; final oral exam. For other doctorates: essentially the same minimum requisites as for the Ph.D., except no foreign language requirement.

FIELDS OF STUDY.
Aerospace Engineering. GRE/Subject in engineering, mathematics or related area, departmental application for admissions; M.S., Ph.D.; admits Fall only; offered by School of Engineering and Applied Science.
African Studies. Interdepartmental. GRE, research paper for admission; one language (African) for M.A. M.A. only.
Afro-American Studies. Interdepartmental. GRE, writing sample for admission; one language for M.A. M.A. only; admits Fall only.
American Indian Studies. Interdepartmental. GRE recommended, not required. M.A. only; admits Fall only.
Anatomy and Cell Biology. GRE for admission. M.S., Ph.D.
Anthropology. GRE for admission; one language for M.A., one language special proficiency for Ph.D.; admits Fall only.

Applied Linguistics. Interdepartmental. GRE for admission; two languages or one language special proficiency for Ph.D. Ph.D. only; admits Fall only.

Archaeology. Interdepartmental. GRE, three research papers for admission; one language for M.A., two languages for Ph.D. M.A., Ph.D. only; admits Fall only.

Architecture. Portfolio, GRE (Ph.D.) for admission; M.Arch. I and II, M.A., Ph.D.; urban design program; offered by Graduate School of Architecture and Urban Planning.

Art. Twenty slides due January 15 for admission. M.A., M.F.A.; admits Fall only; offered by School of the Arts.

Art History. GRE, thesis or three research papers for admission; two languages for M.A. and Ph.D.

Asian American Studies. Interdepartmental. Writing sample for admission; one language or research tool for M.A. M.A. only; admits Fall only.

Asian Languages and Culture. GRE for admission; admits Fall only. M.A., Ph.D.

Astronomy. GRE/Subject in physics for admission. M.S., Ph.D.; admits Fall only.

Atmospheric Sciences. GRE for admission. M.S., Ph.D.

Biochemistry and Molecular Biology. GRE/Subject in chemistry for admission. M.S., Ph.D.; admits Fall only; offered by Department of Chemistry and Biochemistry.

Biological Chemistry. GRE/Subject, three letters of recommendation for admission; admits Fall only. M.S., Ph.D.

Biology. Includes ecology and evolutionary biology. Admits Fall only. M.A., Ph.D.

Biomathematics. GRE/Subject for admission. M.S., Ph.D.

Biomedical Engineering. GRE/Subject, three letters of recommendation for admission; admits Fall and Spring. M.S., Ph.D.

Biomedical Physics. GRE for admission. M.S., Ph.D.; usually admits in Fall; offered by Department of Radiological Sciences.

Biostatistics. GRE for admission. M.S., Ph.D.; offered by School of Public Health.

Cellular and Molecular Pathology. GRE/Subject, three letters of recommendation for admission; admits Fall only. Ph.D. only.

Chemical Engineering. GRE/Subject in engineering, mathematics or related area, Departmental application for admission. M.S., Ph.D.; admits Fall only; offered by School of Engineering and Applied Science.

Chemistry. Apply by January 15; GRE/Subject for admission; one language for M.S. and Ph.D. M.S., Ph.D. only. Ph.D.; admits Fall only.

Civil and Environmental Engineering. GRE/Subject in engineering or mathematics or related area, departmental application for admission. M.S., Ph.D.; admits Fall only; offered by School of Engineering and Applied Science.

Classics. Apply by January 15; GRE, term paper for admission; one language for M.A., two languages for Ph.D., M.A., Ph.D.

Comparative Literature. Interdepartmental. Apply by January 15; GRE, writing sample for admission; two languages for M.A. and Ph.D. M.A., Ph.D.

Computer Science. Apply by January 15; GRE/Subject in mathematics or computer science for admission; M.S., Ph.D.; admits Fall only; offered by School of Engineering and Applied Science.

Conservation of Archaeological and Ethnographic Materials. M.A.

Culture and Performance. GRE, three letters of recommendation, writing sample, statement of purpose for admission; admits Fall only. M.A., Ph.D.

Dance. Audition, interview for admission. M.A., M.F.A.; admits Fall only; offered by School of the Arts.

Design Media. Twenty slides for admission, due January 15; admits Fall only. M.A., M.F.A.

East Asian Languages and Cultures. GRE, writing sample for admission; one year Japanese (Chinese majors) or one year Chinese (Japanese majors) for M.A., two languages for Ph.D. M.A., Ph.D.

East Asian Studies. GRE, three letters of recommendation for admission; admits Fall only. M.A. only.

Economics. GRE General for admission; one language for Ph.D. M.A., Ph.D.; admits Fall only.

Education. GRE, departmental application for admission; M.Ed., M.A., Ed.D., Ph.D.; Ph.D. in Special Education with CSULA, certificate (credential) program; admits Fall only for credential; offered by Graduate School of Education.

Educational Leadership. GRE, three letters of recommendation, essay, résumé, departmental application for admission; admits Fall only. Ed.D. only.

Electrical Engineering. GRE/Subject in engineering, mathematics or related area, departmental application for admission. M.S., Ph.D.; admits Fall only; offered by School of Engineering and Applied Science.

English. GRE General/Subject in literature for admission; one language for M.A., two languages for Ph.D. M.A., Ph.D.

Environmental Health Sciences. GRE for admission. M.S., Ph.D.; offered by School of Public Health.

Environmental Science and Engineering. Interdepartmental. GRE/Subject for admission. D.Env. only.

Epidemiology. GRE for admission. M.S., Ph.D; offered by School of Public Health.

Ethnomusicology. Biographical/purpose statement, sample work for admission; apply by December 30. M.A., Ph.D., offered by School of the Arts.

Film, Television, and Digital Media. GRE for admission. M.A., M.F.A., Ph.D.; offered by School of Theater, Film and Television.

Folklore and Mythology. Interdepartmental. GRE recommended; one language for M.A., two languages for Ph.D.

French and Francophone Studies. GRE, research paper or thesis for admission; one language for M.A., two languages for Ph.D. M.A., Ph.D.

Geochemistry. GRE/Subject for admission. M.S., Ph.D.; offered by Department of Earth and Space Sciences.

Geography. GRE for admission; research tool for M.A. and Ph.D. M.A., Ph.D.

Geology. GRE for admission; M.S., C.Phil., Ph.D.; offered by Department of Earth and Space Sciences.

Geophysics and Space Physics. GRE/Subject in physics for admission. M.S., Ph.D.; offered by Department of Earth and Space Sciences.

Germanic Languages. GRE, writing sample for admission; one language for Ph.D. Ph.D.; offered by Department of Germanic Languages.

Greek. GRE, term paper for admission; one language for M.A. M.A. only; offered by Department of Classics.

Health Services. GRE for admission. M.S., Ph.D.; offered by School of Public Health.

Hispanic Languages and Literatures. GRE, term paper for admission; two languages for Ph.D. Ph.D.; offered by the Department of Spanish and Portuguese.

History. GRE for admission; one language for M.A., two languages for Ph.D. M.A., Ph.D.; admits Fall only.

Human Genetics. GRE/Subject, three letters of recommendation, statement of purpose for admission; admits Fall only. M.S., Ph.D.

Indo-European Studies. Interdepartmental. Two languages for Ph.D. Ph.D.

Information Studies. GRE, three letters of recommendation, statement of purpose for admission; admits Fall only. M.L.I.S., Ph.D.

Islamic Studies. Interdepartmental. GRE for admission, recommended for international applicants; one language for M.A.; two languages for Ph.D.

Italian. GRE for admission, recommended for international applicants; one language for M.A., two languages for Ph.D. M.A., Ph.D.

Latin. GRE, term paper for admission, one language for M.A. M.A. only.

Latin American Studies. Interdepartmental. GRE for admission; two languages for M.A. M.A. only.

Library and Information Science. GRE for admission. M.L.I.S.

Linguistics. GRE, sample of work for admission; one language for M.A., two languages or one language special proficiency for Ph.D. M.A., Ph.D.; admits Fall only.

Management. GMAT (M.B.A.), GMAT or GRE (M.S., Ph.D.) for admission. M.B.A., M.S., Ph.D.; admits Fall only.

Manufacturing Engineering. GRE/Subject in engineering, mathematics or related area, departmental application for admission; M.S. only; admits Fall only; offered by School of Engineering and Applied Science.

Material Science and Engineering. GRE for admission. M.A., Ph.D.; admits Fall only; offered by School of Engineering and Applied Science.

Mathematics. GRE/Subject, departmental application for admission; two languages for Ph.D. M.A., M.A.T., Ph.D.; admits Fall only.

Mechanical and Aerospace Engineering. GRE/Subject in engineering, mathematics or related area, departmental application for admission. M.A., Ph.D.; admits Fall only; offered by the School of Engineering and Applied Science.

Microbiology and Immunology. GRE/Subject in biology for admission; apply by January 15. Ph.D. only; admits Fall only.

Microbiology and Molecular Genetics. GRE/Subject in biology or chemistry for admission. M.A., Ph.D.; admits Fall usually.

Molecular Biology. Interdepartmental. GRE for admission. Ph.D. only.

Molecular, Cell, and Development Biology. GRE, three letters of recommendation, personal statement for admission; admits Fall only. Ph.D. only.

Molecular, Cellular, and Integrative Physiology. GRE/Subject, three letters of recommendation, personal statement for admission; admits Fall only. Ph.D. only.

Molecular and Medical Pharmacology. GRE, personal statement for admission; admits Fall only. Ph.D. only.

Molecular Toxicology. GRE, departmental application, statement of purpose for admission. Ph.D. only.

Music. Departmental exam, sample work, biographical/purpose statement for admission; apply by December 30; one language for M.A. and M.F.A., two languages for Ph.D. M.A., M.F.A., M.M., D.M.A., Ph.D.; admits Fall only; offered by the School of Arts.

Musicology. Department exam, sample work, biographical/purpose statement for admission; apply by December 30. M.A., Ph.D.

Near Eastern Languages and Cultures. GRE, recent term paper for admission; one language for M.A., two languages for Ph.D. M.A., Ph.D.

Neurobiology. GRE, three letters of recommendation for admission; admits Fall only. M.S., Ph.D.

Neuroscience. Interdepartmental. GRE for admission; apply by January 5. Ph.D. only; admits Fall only.

Nursing. GRE (D.N.Sc.), CGFNS exam for admission. M.N.-P.h.D.; admits Fall only.

Oral Biology. Apply by January 15. M.S., Ph.D.; offered by School of Dentistry.

Pharmacology. GRE, personal statement for admission. Ph.D. only; admits Fall only.

Philosophy. GRE sample work, departmental application for admission; apply by January 10; one language for M.A., one language special proficiency for Ph.D. M.A., Ph.D.; admits Fall only.

Physics. GRE/Subject for admission. M.A.T., Ph.D.; admits Fall usually.

Physiological Science. GRE for admission. M.S., Ph.D.

Physiology. GRE/Subject for admission. M.S., Ph.D.; admits Fall only for Ph.D.

Political Science. GRE, sample work for admission; one language for Ph.D. (or substitute program). M.A., Ph.D.; admits Fall only.

Portuguese. GRE, personal statement, recent term paper for admission; one language for M.A. M.A. only.

Psychology. GRE/Subject, personal statement for admission. M.A., M.A.T., Ph.D.; admits Fall only to Ph.D.

Public Health. GRE for admission. M.P.H., M.S., Dr.P.H., Ph.D.; admits Fall only; offered by School of Public Health.

Public Policy. GRE, three letters of recommendation, departmental statement of purpose for admission; admits Fall only. M.P.P. only.

Romance Linguistics and Literature. Interdepartmental. GRE, writing sample, one language (M.A.), two languages (Ph.D.) for admission. M.A, Ph.D.

Scandinavian. One language for M.A. M.A., Ph.D.; offered by Department of Germanic Languages.

Slavic Languages and Literatures. GRE, personal statement for admission; one language for M.A., two languages for Ph.D. M.A., Ph.D.

Social Welfare. GRE, personal statement for admission. M.S.W., Ph.D.; admits Fall only.

Sociology. GRE, writing sample for admission; one language for Ph.D. M.A., Ph.D.; admits Fall only.

Spanish. GRE, personal statement, recent term paper for admission; one language for admission. M.A. only.

Special Education. GRE, three letters of recommendation, departmental application, statement of purpose; admits Fall only. Ph.D. only.

Statistics. GRE/Subject, three letters of recommendation, departmental application, statement of purpose; admits Fall only. M.S., Ph.D.

Teaching English as a Second Language. GRE, research paper for admission. M.A., Certificate only; admits Fall only.

Theater. GRE for admission; apply by December 1; one language for Ph.D. M.A., M.F.A., Ph.D.; admits Fall only.

Urban Planning. Departmental application for admission. M.A., Ph.D.; admits only; offered by Graduate School of Architecture and Urban Planning.

Women's Studies. GRE, three letters of recommendation, personal statement, departmental application, writing sample for admission; admits Fall only. M.A., Ph.D.

School of Dentistry (90095-1762)

Web site: www.uclasod.dent.ucla.edu

Founded in 1960. Located at Center for Health Sciences. Special facility: Dental Research Institute.

Annual tuition: resident $26,000, nonresident $38,245. Limited on-campus housing available. Average academic year housing and personal expenses: approximately $20,000. For housing information contact UCLA Community Housing Office. Phone: (310)825-4491. Total cost for all other first-year expenses: $15,000.

Enrollment: first-year class 88, total full-time 391 (men 51%, women 49%, minorities 35%, state resident 85%). Faculty: full-time 72, part-time 168. Degrees conferred: D.D.S., D.D.S.-M.B.A., D.D.S.-M.S. (Oral Biology), D.D.S.-Ph.D. (Oral Biology), Certificate.

ADMISSION REQUIREMENTS. AADSAS, transcripts, DAT, substantive letters of recommendation, comprehensive bibliography and personal statement required in support of application. Interviews by invitation only. Applicants must have completed at least three years of college study. Preference given to state and WICHE residents. Graduates of unaccredited colleges not considered. Apply to Office of Admissions or AADSAS after June 1, before January 1. Application fee $60. Phone: (310)794-7971.

ADMISSION STANDARDS. Competitive. Mean DAT: Academic 22; PAT 20; mean GPA: 3.6 (A = 4); science GPA: 3.7. Accepts about 20% of total annual applicants. Approximately 95% are state residents.

FINANCIAL AID. Limited number of scholarships, fellowships, loans, summer work study. Apply to Financial Aid Office by May 1. Phone: (310)825-6994. Use FAFSA. About 92% of students receive some aid from School.

DEGREE REQUIREMENTS. For D.D.S.: satisfactory completion of forty-five-month program. For D.D.S.-M.S.: Satisfactory completion of fifth-year program. For D.D.S.-Ph.D.: Satisfactory completion of six- to seven-year program; research project.

FIELDS OF GRADUATE STUDY.

Advanced Dental Anesthesiology. Certificate.
Advanced Education in General Dentistry. Certificate.
Advanced Prosthodontics. Certificate.
Endodontics. Certificate.
Maxillofacial Prosthetics. Certificate.
Oral and Maxillofacial Surgery. Certificate.
Oral Biology. Includes cancer cell biology, bacterial and fungal pathogenesis, calcified tissue biology, developmental biology, immunology, neuroscience, pain research, pharmacology, and virology. M.S., Ph.D.
Orofacial Pain and Dysfunction. Certificate.
Orthodontics. Certificate.
Pediatric Dentistry. Certificate.
Periodontics. Certificate.

School of Law (90095-1445)

Web site: www.law.ucla.edu

Established 1947. ABA approved since 1950. AALS member. Semester system. Special facilities: Environmental Law Center, International Law Center, Center for Law and Economics, Center for the Study of Mergers and Acquisitions, Native Nations Law & Policy Center, Richard S. Ziman Center for Real Estate at UCLA, Williams Institute on Sexual Orientation Law and Public Policy. Library: 630,825 volumes, 8482 subscriptions. Library has LEXIS, NEXIS, WESTLAW, DIALOG, INFORTRAC; has more than 1100 network connections.

Annual fees: residents $25,457, nonresidents $36,381, LL.M. $37,750. Both on- and off-campus housing available. Total average of all other expenses: $19,053.

Enrollment: first year class 317, total full-time 1019 (men 53%, women 47%, minorities 32%); no part-time study. Faculty: full-time 70, part-time 21. Student to faculty ratio 11.8 to 1. Degrees conferred: J.D., J.D.-M.A. (African American Studies, American Indian Studies, Urban Planning), J. D.-M.B.A., J.D.-M.P.H., J.D.-M.P.P., J.D.-M.S.W., LL.M. (Comparative Law), S.J.D.

ADMISSION REQUIREMENTS. LSDAS Law School report, transcripts, LSAT (no later than December) required in support of application. Interview not required. Accepts transfer applicants. Graduates of unaccredited colleges not considered. Apply to Admissions and Records Office after October 1, before February 1, transfer applicants July 1. First-year students admitted Fall only. Application fee $75. Phone: (310)825-2080; e-mail: admissions@law.ucla.edu. For both LL.M. and S.J.D. apply by February 1.

ADMISSION STANDARDS. Selective. Accepts approximately 16% of total applicants. Number of applicants 6319; number of acceptance 1015; number enrolled 317; LSAT (75% of students have a score at or above 162); GPA (75% of students have a GPA at or above 3.51). *U.S. News & World Report* ranking is in the top 15 of all U.S. law schools.

FINANCIAL AID. Scholarships, grants, Federal W/S, loans available. All financial aid, except for second- and third-year students, is administered by the campus-wide Office of Financial Aid. Apply by March 1. Phone: (310)825-2459. Use FAFSA. The Supplemental Financial Aid Application should be submitted to law school before February 1. About 60% of all students receive some form of financial aid.

DEGREE REQUIREMENTS. For J.D.: satisfactory completion of three-year program. For LL.M.: at least 24 credits beyond J.D.: one year in full-time residence. For S.J.D.: At least two semesters

beyond LL.M. in full-time study; 20 credits of graded coursework; candidacy; dissertation. For M.A.: Course work divided in second and third year between both schools. M.A. awarded after fourth year in school of Architecture and upon acceptance of thesis. For M.B.A., M.P.P., M.P.H., M.S.: see Graduate School listing above.

John E. Anderson Graduate School of Management (Box 951481)

Web site: www.anderson.ucla.edu

Established 1935. Public control. Accredited programs: M.B.A.; recognized Ph.D. Quarter system. Special facilities: Center for Corporate Renewal, Center for Digital Media, Center for Finance and Investments, Center for Healthcare Management, Center for International Business Education and Research, Center for Real Estate, Center for Operations and Technology Management, John M. Olin Center for Public Policy, Harold Price Center for Entrepreneurial Studies, Western Management Science Institute. Library: 147,000 volumes.

Annual tuition/fees: M.B.A. resident full-time $28,446; nonresident full-time $37,286. E.M.B.A. tuition: $35,000; F.E.M.B.A. tuition: $24,000. Ph.D. annual tuition/fee: resident $8967, nonresident $23,955. On-campus rooms and apartments available for both single and married students. Annual on-campus housing cost: $12,000 (room and board). Contact Graduate Housing Office for both on- and off-campus housing information; phone: (310)825-4491. Estimated annual budget for tuition, room and board and personal expenses: residents approximately $31,000, nonresidents $39,500.

Enrollment: total full-time 640, part-time 534 (men 70%, women 30%). Faculty: 92 full-time, 50 part-time; 94% with Ph.D/D.B.A. Degrees conferred: M.B.A. (Concentrations in Accounting, Business Economics, Decision Science, Finance, Human Resource and Organizational Behavior, Information Systems, Marketing, Operations and Technology Management, Strategic and Organization), E.M.B.A. (weekends only, alternating Fridays, Saturdays), F.E.M.B.A., M.B.A.-J.D., M.B.A.-M.D., M.B.A.-M.A. (Latin American Studies, Urban Planning), M.B.A.-M.L.I.S. (Library and Information Science), M.B.A.-M.S. (Computer Science), M.B.A.-M.S.N. (Nursing), M.B.A.-M.U.P., M.S.M., Ph.D. in Management (concentrations in Accounting, Business Economics, Decision Sciences, Finance, Human Resources and Organizational Behavior, Information Systems, International Business and Comparative Management, Marketing, Operations and Technology, Strategy and Organization).

ADMISSION REQUIREMENTS. Students are required to have their own personal computer. Early applications are encouraged for both admission and financial aid consideration. U.S. citizens apply by April 1 (Fall), international students apply by February 28 (Fall). Submit an application, GMAT results (will accept GMAT test results from the last five years, if GMAT is retaken highest score is used), two offical transcripts from each undergraduate/graduate school attended, two letters of recommendation, Data Form, employment history (prefers at least four years of work experience), and an application fee of $125 to the Director of M.B.A. Admission. Applications can be downloaded from School's Web site. Accepts MBA Multi-App electronic application in lieu of institutional application. Admits Fall only. In addition, international students (whose native language is other than English) should submit a TOEFL (minimum score 600) report, two certified translations and evaluations of all official transcripts, recommendation should be in English or with certified translations, proof of health/immunization certificate, and proof of sufficent financial resources for one year of academic study. For current information and/or modification in admission requirements the international applicant's contact telephone number is: (310)825-6944. On-campus visits are strongly encouraged. Interviews are by invitation. Joint degree applicants must apply to and be accepted to both schools (LSAT required for Law, MCAT for Medicine), contact the admissions office for current information and specific admissions requirements. There are five decision rounds, notification is made on January 28, March 4, April 28, May 27, June 19. Admissions Office phone: (310)825-6944; fax: (310)825-8582; e-mail: mba.admissions@anderson.ucla.edu.

ADMISSION REQUIREMENTS FOR DOCTORAL CANDIDATES. Contact Ph.D. Program Office at (310)825-2824; e-mail: ms.phdadmissions@anderson.ucls.edu for application material and information. Beginning students are admitted Fall Only. Both U.S. citizens and international application apply by January 1 (Fall). Submit an application, a GMAT/GRE (will accept GMAT/GRE test results from the last five years), two official transcripts from each undergraduate/graduate school attended, two letters of recommendation, statement of purpose, and application fee of $40 to the Office of Graduate Admission. In addition, international students (whose native language is other than English) should submit a TOEFL (minimum score 600) report; two certified translations and evaluations of all offical transcripts, recommendation should be in English or with certified translations, proof of health/ immunization certificate. International students' contact: (310)825-2824. Interviews strongly encouraged. Doctoral applicants must be accepted by both the Anderson School and the Graduate Division. Notifications are generally completed by mid-April.

ADMISSION STANDARDS. For M.B.A.: Very selective. Median GMAT 670; median GPA 3.5 (A = 4). *U.S. News & World Report* ranked Anderson in the top 8 for E.M.B.A. programs, and top 16 for M.B.A. programs of all U.S. business schools. *BusinessWeek* listed Anderson in the top 16 American business schools.

FINANCIAL AID. For M.B.A.: Scholarships, merit scholarships, special stipends for minority students, state grants, merit-based fellowships, graduate assistantships, Federal Perkins loans, Stafford Subsidized and Unsubsidized loans, Federal W/S available. Apply by March 1. Financial aid is available for part-time study. Financial aid may be available for international students after first year. Assistantships/fellowships may be available for joint degree candidates. For assistantships, fellowships, scholarships the selection criteria places heavy reliance on GMAT and undergraduate GPA. Contact the University's Financial Aid Office for current need-based financial aid information; phone: (310)825-0629. For most financial assistance and all Federal programs, submit FAFSA to a federal processor (School code: #001315), also submit Financial Aid Transcript, Federal Income Tax forms. Approximately 65% of students receive some form of financial assistance.

For Ph.D.: fee waiver, nonresident fee waiver, Anderson School fellowships and stipends, research and teaching assistantships and UCLA graduate fellowships. For all need-based financial aid information, contact the university's Office of Financial Aid.

DEGREE REQUIREMENTS. For M.B.A.: 24 courses including 14 elective courses, two-year program; degree program must be completed in three years. For F.E.M.B.A.: 84 credits, a three-year program. For E.M.B.A.: 66-credit, twenty-three-month program. For M.S. (Decision Sciences): 9 courses; thesis. For M.B.A.-M.A. (Latin American Studies, Urban Planning): 129–144 quarter hours, three- to four-year program. For M.B.A.-J.D.: 185 quarter hours, four- to five-year program. M.B.A.-M.P.H.: 132 quarter hours, generally a three- to four-year program. For M.B.A.-M.L.I.S.: 124 quarter hours, three- to four-year program. For M.B.A.-M.S. (Computer Science): 96 quarter hours, two- to three-year program. For M.B.A.-M.S.N.: 96 quarter hour program. For Ph.D.: three- to five-year program; specialization; research and

breadth requirement; oral qualifying exam; dissertation proposal and oral presentation; dissertation; final oral defense.

David Geffen School of Medicine (90095-7035)
Web site: www.medsch.ucla.edu

Founded 1951. Public control. Quarter system. Library: 200,000 volumes, 3500 subscriptions. The University's NIH ranking is 8th among all U.S. institutions with 914 awards/grants worth $385,788,286.

Annual tuition: resident $23,445, nonresident $35,690. On-campus housing is comprised of 840 units containing studio apartments, two-bedroom/two-bath apartments, and two-bedroom/two-bath townhouses. All units are unfurnished. Average figure for all other expenses: $10,490.

Enrollment: first-year class 122; total full-time 693 (men 48%, women 52%, minorities 52%, state residents 100%). Faculty: full-time approximately 2102, part-time 217. Degrees conferred: M.D., M.D.-M.B.A., M.D.-M.P.H., M.D.-Ph.D., M.S.T.P. Graduate study (M.S.T.P.) in preclinical departments, M.S., Ph.D. degrees offered through UCLA Graduate Division.

ADMISSION REQUIREMENTS. AMCAS report, transcripts, MCAT, letters of recommendation, personal essay, interview required in support of application. Bachelor's is ordinarily required, but students who have completed three academic years may be admitted. Supplemental application required of those who pass first screening review. Preference given to state residents. Graduates of unaccredited colleges not considered. Does not have EDP. Apply to Office of Student Affairs Division of Admissions after June 1, before November 1, transfer applicants by January 1. Fall admission only. Screening fee $60. Phone: (310)825-6081.

ADMISSION STANDARDS. Very competitive. Accepts about 4.5% of all applicants. Number of applications 5465 (2115 out-of-state); number interviewed 698 (212 out-of-state); number of acceptance 245 (65 out-of-state); number enrolled 122 (23 out-of-state). Mean Composite MCAT 11.1; mean UGPA 3.76. *U.S. News & World Report* ranking is in the top 13 of all medical research schools, 18th in Primary Care.

FINANCIAL AID. Scholarships, fellowships, research assistantships, loans. Apply after acceptance to Office of Student Affairs before March 1. Phone: (310)825-4181. Use FAFSA.

DEGREE REQUIREMENTS. For M.D.: 12 quarters minimum, at least the last 6 in residence; satisfactory completion of Steps 1 and 2 of USMLE. Candidates must be 21 years old. For M.S., Ph.D.: see Graduate Division listing above for degree requirements.

FIELDS OF GRADUATE STUDY.
Bioinformatics.
Biological Chemistry.
Biochemistry and Molecular Biology.
Biomathematics.
Biomedical Physics (Interdepartmental).
Cellular and Molecular Pathology.
Experimental Pathology.
Gene Regulation.
Human Genetics.
Microbiology, Immunology and Molecular Genetics.
Molecular and Medical Pharmacology.
Molecular Biology (Interdepartmental).
Molecular, Cellular, and Integrative Physiology.
Molecular Toxicology.
Neurobiology.
Neuroscience (Interdepartmental).
Oral Biology (School of Dentistry).

UNIVERSITY OF CALIFORNIA, RIVERSIDE

Riverside, California 92521-0102
Web site: www.ucr.edu

Founded 1954. Located 60 miles E of Los Angeles. CGS member. Coed. State control. Quarter system. Special facilities: California Museum of Photography, Centers for agricultural research, air pollution research, bibliographic studies, citrus research, dry lands research, geophysics and planetary physics, social and behavioral science research, extensive botanic gardens and natural area reserve system; entomological teaching and research collection, and academic computing center, laboratory for historic research. Library: 2,000,000 volumes, 26,000 subscriptions. More than 800 computers on campus for general student use. Total University enrollment: 16,622.

Annual tuition/fees: resident $9813, nonresident $24,802; there is an additional charge of $15,000 for M.B.A. program. University housing for 268 married students, 600 men, 600 women. Additionally, there are 316 University-owned apartments available for either married students without children or single students. Phone: (951)827-6350. For off-campus information: Phone (951) 827-6350. Day-care facilities available.

Graduate Division

Established 1960. Enrollment: full-time 1886, part-time 38. University faculty: full-time 592. Degrees conferred: M.A., M.S., M.B.A., Ph.D.

ADMISSION REQUIREMENTS. Two transcripts, GRE/Subject Test, GMAT, three letters of recommendation, statement of purpose required in support of University's application. Interview required for some departments. TOEFL (minimum score 550, 213 on computer-based test) required for foreign applicants. Graduates of unaccredited colleges not considered. Apply to Graduate Division by May 1 (Fall), September 1 (Winter), December 1 (Spring); international applicants apply by February 1 (Fall), July 1 (Winter), October 1 (Spring). Application fee $60, $80 international applicants. Phone: (951)827-3313; fax: (951)827-2238.

ADMISSION STANDARDS. Selective. Usual minimum average: 3.2 (A = 4).

FINANCIAL AID. Annual awards from institutional funds: scholarships, fellowships, teaching assistantships, research assistantships, tuition waivers, grants, Federal W/S, loans. Approved for VA benefits. GRE Test is required of all fellowship applicants. Apply to appropriate departments and Financial Aid Office by February 1. Phone: (951)827-3878. Use FAFSA. About 60% of students receive aid other than loans from University and outside sources. Aid available for part-time students.

DEGREE REQUIREMENTS. For M.A., M.Ed., M.S.: 36 quarter units minimum; thesis or comprehensive exam. For M.B.A.: 92 quarter units; capstone course; internship; thesis or case project. For Ph.D.: two years minimum beyond the bachelor's; written and qualifying exams; dissertation, final oral defense of dissertation.

FIELDS OF STUDY.

COLLEGE OF NATURAL AND AGRICULTURAL SCIENCES:
Applied Statistics. Ph.D.
Biochemistry and Molecular Biology. M.S., Ph.D.
Cell, Molecular, and Developmental Biology. M.S., Ph.D.
Chemistry. M.S., Ph.D.
Entomology. M.S., Ph.D.
Environmental Sciences. M.S., Ph.D.
Environmental Toxicology. M.S., Ph.D.
Evolution, Ecology and Organismal Biology. M.S., Ph.D.

Genetics. M.S., Ph.D.
Geological Sciences. M.S., Ph.D.
Mathematics. M.A., M.S., Ph.D.
Neuroscience. Ph.D.
Physics. M.A., M.S., Ph.D.
Plant Biology. M.S., Ph.D.
Plant Pathology. M.S., Ph.D.
Plant Science. M.S.
Soil and Water Sciences. M.S., Ph.D.
Statistics. M.S.

COLLEGE OF HUMANITIES, ARTS, AND SOCIAL SCIENCES:
Anthropology. M.A., M.S., Ph.D.
Art History. M.A.
Comparative Literature. M.A., Ph.D.
Creative Writing. M.F.A.
Dance. M.F.A.
Dance History and Theory. Ph.D.
Economics. M.A., Ph.D.
English. M.A., Ph.D.
History. M.A., Ph.D.
Music. M.A.
Philosophy. M.A., Ph.D.
Political Science. M.A., Ph.D.
Psychology. Ph.D.
Religious Studies. M.A., Ph.D.
Sociology. Ph.D.
Southeast Asian Studies. M.A.
Spanish. M.A., Ph.D.
Visual Arts. M.F.A.

DIVISION OF BIOMEDICAL SCIENCES:
Biomedical Sciences. Ph.D.

THE MARIAN AND ROSEMARY BOURNS COLLEGE OF ENGINEERING:
Bioengineering. M.S., Ph.D.
Chemical and Environmental Engineering. M.S., Ph.D.
Computer Science. M.S., Ph.D.
Electrical Engineering. M.S., Ph.D.
Mechanical Engineering. M.S., Ph.D.

A. GARRY ANDERSON GRADUATE SCHOOL OF MANAGEMENT:
Management. M.B.A.

SCHOOL OF EDUCATION:
Curriculum and Instruction. M.A., Ph.D.
Educational Administration. M.A., Ph.D.
Educational Psychology. M.A., Ph.D.
School Psychology. Ph.D.
Special Education. M.A., Ph.D.

UNIVERSITY OF CALIFORNIA, SAN DIEGO

La Jolla, California 92093-5003
Web site: www.ucsd.edu

Founded in 1964. CGS and AAU member. Coed. State control. Quarter system. Special facilities: California Space Institute, Cancer Center, Center for Astrophysics and Space Sciences, Center for Energy and Combustion Research, Center for Human Information Processing, Center for Iberian and Latin American Studies, Center for Magnetic Recording Research, Center for Research in Computing and the Arts, Center for Molecular Genetics, Center for Research in Language, Center for United States–Mexican Studies, Cray C90, Intel paragon supercomputer, Thinking Machine CM-Z, DEC Alpha Fany, Institute for Biomedical Engineering, Institute on Global Conflict and Cooperation, Institute for Geophysics and Planetary Physics, Institute for Neural Computation, Institute for

Nonlinear Science, Institute for Pure and Applied Physical Sciences, Institute for Research on Aging, Intercampus Institute for Research and Particle Accelerators, Laboratory for Comparative Human Cognition, Laboratory for Mathematics and Statistics, Scripps Institution of Oceanography, International House, San Diego Supercomputer Center. The University's NIH ranking is 14th among all U.S. institutions with 681 awards/grants valued at $309,416,840. According to The Center at University of Florida, U.C. San Diego is ranked 7th in receipt of Federal Research funds with $400,100,000 and it ranks 7th for total University research expenditures with $646,508,000. In 2004, the University awarded 372 doctorates, which ranked it 41st among all U.S. institutions eligible to award that degree. Five of the University's faculty members have been elected to National Honor Academies and this ranks it 101st among all U.S. institutions. Libraries house more than 2,900,000 volumes, 29,000 subscriptions. Total University enrollment: 25,000.

Annual tuition/fees: resident $9376, nonresident $24,364. On-campus housing for about 500 graduate students. Average annual housing cost: $11,000 (including board) for single students. Apply to Housing Office. Phone: (858)824-0850. For off-campus information call (858)534-3670. Limited day-care facilities available.

Graduate Studies and Research

Graduate study since 1965. Enrollment: full-time 2750, part-time 200. University faculty: 1100. Degrees conferred: M.A., M.S., M.F.A., M.P.I.A., C.Phil., Ph.D.

ADMISSION REQUIREMENTS. Transcripts, GRE (for all programs except M.F.A. programs and Leadership of Health Care Organizations), three letters of recommendation, statement of purpose required in support of University's application. Electronic application available. GRE Subject Test recommended for many degree programs. TOEFL required, TWE strongly recommended for foreign applicants. Interview not required. Accepts transfer applicants. Graduates of unaccredited institutions not considered. Apply to the prospective major department and Office of Graduate Admission; note program deadlines in Fields of Study below. Application fee $60, $80 for international applicants. Phone: (858) 534-1193; fax: (858)534-4722.

ADMISSION STANDARDS. Selective. Minimum average: 3.0 (A = 4).

FINANCIAL AID. Annual awards from institutional funds: fellowships, research assistantships/fellowships, teaching assistantships/fellowships, traineeships, Federal W/S, loans. Fellowship and assistantships applicants must take GRE no later than December. Apply to appropriate department and Financial Aid Office; no specified closing date. Phone: (858)534-4480. Use FAFSA. (University code 001317). About 80% of students receive aid from University and outside sources. Aid available for part-time students. Phone: (858)534-3807.

DEGREE REQUIREMENTS. For master's: requirements vary but normally include one year of course work; thesis or comprehensive exam; one year in residence. For Ph.D.: requirements vary but normally includes a minimum of two years beyond the master's; preliminary exam; dissertation; final oral exam.

FIELDS OF STUDY.
Aerospace Engineering. International applicants apply by January 31, U.S. citizens apply by May 31. M.S., Ph.D.
Anthropology. Apply by January 10. Ph.D.
Applied Mathematics. Appy by March 1. GRE Subject for admission. M.A. only.
Applied Mechanics. International applicants apply by January 31, U.S. citizens apply by May 31. Joint Ph.D. program with S.D.S.U. M.S., Ph.D.

Applied Ocean Science. Apply by January 11. GRE for admission. M.S., Ph.D.
Applied Physics. Apply by January 11. GRE for admission. M.S., Ph.D.
Art History. Includes theory and criticism. Writing sample for admission. Ph.D.
Biochemistry. Apply by January 4. GRE Subject recommended for admissions. Ph.D.
Bioengineering. Apply by January 16. M.Eng., M.S., Ph.D.
Bioinformatics. Apply by January 18. Ph.D.
Biology. Apply by January 4. GRE Subject recommended for admission. Ph.D.
Biomedical Sciences. Apply January 7. Ph.D.
Biophysics. Apply by January 15. GRE Subject for admission. Ph.D.
Business Administration. M.B.A.
Chemical Engineering. Apply by January 16. M.S., Ph.D.
Chemistry and Biochemistry. Apply by January 18. GRE Subject for admission. Ph.D.
Clinical Research. M.A.S.
Cognitive Science. Apply by January 11.
Communication. Apply by January 18. Ph.D.
Communication Theory and Systems. Apply by January 11. GRE for admission. M.S., Ph.D.
Comparative Literature. Apply by January 16. M.A. only.
Computational Neurobiology. Apply by January 4. GRE Subject recommended for admission. Ph.D.
Computer Sciences. Apply by January 7. Statement of purpose, GRE Subject recommended for admission. M.S., Ph.D.
Computer Engineering. Apply by January 7. Statement of purpose required, GRE Subject recommended for admission. M.S., Ph.D.
Economics. Apply by January 18. GRE Subject recommended for admission. Ph.D.
Education Studies. Apply by February 1. CBEST for admission. M.Ed.
Educational Leadership. Joint Ed.D. program with CSU San Marcos.
Electronic Circuits and Systems. Apply by January 11. GRE for admission. M.S., Ph.D.
Engineering. Apply by January 11. GRE for admission. M.Eng.
Engineering Physics. International applicants apply by January 31, U.S. citizens apply by May 31. M.S., Ph.D.
Ethnic Studies. Apply by January 15. Ph.D.
French Literature. Apply by January 16. M.A. only.
German Literature. Apply by January 16. M.A. only.
History. Apply by January 18. Writing sample for admission.
Intelligence Systems, Robotics, and Control. Apply by January 11. GRE required for admission. M.S., Ph.D.
Judaic Studies. Apply by January 18. M.A. only.
Latin American Studies. Apply by January 18. M.A. only.
Leadership of Health Care Organizations. Admits Fall, Winter, Spring. M.A.S.
Linguistics. Apply by January 18. Ph.D.
Literature. Apply by January 16. Ph.D.
Literature in English. Apply by January 16. M.A. only.
Marine Biodiversity and Conservation. Apply by January 6. GRE Subject for admission. Ph.D.
Materials Science and Engineering. Admits Fall, Winter, Spring. M.S., Ph.D.
Mathematics. Apply by March 1. GRE Subject for admission. M.A., Ph.D.
Mechanical and Aerospace Engineering. International applicants apply by January 31, U.S. citizens apply by May 31. M.S., Ph.D.
Molecular Pathology. Apply January 15. GRE Subject for admission. Ph.D.
Music. Apply by January 12. M.A., Ph.D., D.M.A.
Nanoscale Devices and Systems. Apply by January 5. M.S., Ph.D.
Neuroscience. Apply by December 17. GRE Subject for admission. Ph.D.
Oceanography. Apply by January 6. Ph.D.

Pacific and International Affairs. Apply by February 15. Departmental application required, GMAT may be substituted for GRE for admission. M.P.I.A.

Philosophy. Apply by January 18. Writing sample for admission. Ph.D.

Photonics. Apply by January 11. GRE for admission. M.S., Ph.D.

Physics. Apply by January 15. GRE Subject for admission. M.S., Ph.D.

Political Science. Apply by January 5. Departmental application required for admission. Ph.D.

Political Science and International Affairs. Apply by January 5. Departmental application required for admission. Ph.D.

Psychology. Apply by January 5. Ph.D.

Signal and Image Processing. Apply by January 11. GRE for admission. M.S., Ph.D.

Sociology. Apply by January 2. Writing sample for admission. Ph.D.

Spanish Literature. Apply by January 16. M.A. only.

Statistics. Apply by February 15. GRE Subject for admission. M.S. only.

Structural Engineering. International applicants apply by January 31, U.S. citizens apply by May 31. M.S., Ph.D.

Teaching and Learning (Curriculum Design). Admits Summer only. Apply by February 15. M.A.

Teaching and Learning (Bilingual Education/ASL). Admits Summer only. Apply by February 1. CBEST for admission. M.A.

Theatre. Apply by January 4. Audition and/or interview, GRE (acting, dance, design, directing, playwriting, stage management) for admission. M.F.A.

Visual Arts. Apply by February 1. Portfolio for admission. M.F.A.

School of Medicine (92093-0621)

Web site: meded.ucsd.edu

Founded 1968. Public control. Quarter system. Library: 200,000 volumes, 2000 subscriptions. The University's NIH ranking is 14th among all U.S. institutions with 681 awards/grants worth $309,416,840.

Annual tuition: resident $23,445, nonresident $35,690. On- and off-campus housing available. Average figure for all other expenses: $12,046.

Enrollment: first-year class 122; total full-time 502 (men 51%, women 49%, minorities 49%, state residents 92%). Faculty: full-time approximately 797, part-time 34. Degrees conferred: M.D., M.D.-M.P.H. (with San Diego State University School of Health), M.D.-Ph.D., M.S.T.P.

ADMISSION REQUIREMENTS. AMCAS report, transcripts, MCAT, letters of recommendation, personal autobiography, interview required in support of application. Applicants must have completed at least three years of college study. Interviews are by invitation. Graduates of unaccredited colleges not considered. Preference given to state and WICHE residents. Does not have EDP. Apply to Director of Admissions after June 1 and before November 1. Application fee $60. Phone: (858)534-3880; fax: (858) 534-8282.

ADMISSION STANDARDS. Very competitive. Accepts about 4% of all applicants. Number of applications 5018 (1769 out-of-state); number interviewed 629 (107 out-of-state); number of acceptance 301 (40 out-of-state); number enrolled 122 (9 out-of-state). Mean Composite MCAT 11.2; mean UGPA 3.73. *U.S. News & World Report* ranking is in the top 14 of all medical research schools, 38th in Primary Care.

FINANCIAL AID. Scholarships, fellowships, grants, loans. About 63% of students receive aid other than loans from School funds. Apply to Financial Aid Officer as soon as possible after acceptance. Phone: (858)534-4664.

DEGREE REQUIREMENTS. For M.D.: satisfactory completion of four-year program. Senior thesis or equivalent required. For M.D.-Ph.D.: seven- to eight-year program.

FIELDS OF STUDY.
Biochemistry.
Bioengineering.
Biology.
Biophysics.
Marine Biomedical Science.
Neurosciences.
Pathology.
Pharmacology.
Physiology.
Public Health.

UNIVERSITY OF CALIFORNIA, SAN FRANCISCO

San Francisco, California 94143
Web site: www.ucsf.edu

Founded 1864. CGS member. Coed. State control. Quarter system. Graduate study only. Special facilities: Cardiovascular Research Institute, Cancer Research Institute, Francis I. Proctor Foundation for Research in Ophthalmology, Hormone Research Laboratory, Institute for Health and Aging, Institute of Health Policy Studies, Laboratory of Radiobiology, Langley Porter Psychiatric Institute, Metabolic Research Unit, Reproductive Endocrinology Center, George Williams Hooper Foundation for Medical Research. The University's NIH ranking is 4th among all U.S. Institutions with 988 awards/grants valued at $452,165,301. According to The Center at University of Florida, U.C. San Francisco is ranked 10th in receipt of Federal Research funds with $371,697,000 and it ranks 10th for total University research expenditures with $676,443,000. Eight of the University's faculty members have been elected to National Honor Academies and this ranks it 92nd among all U.S. institutions. Library: 691,041 volumes, 3000 subscriptions.

Tuition/fees: full-time, resident $9813, nonresident $24,802. On-campus housing for 165 married students. Average monthly housing cost: $1300 per month for single students; $2850 per month married students. Apply to Housing Officer. Phone: (415)476-2211.

Graduate Division

Established 1961. Enrollment: full-time 1047. Faculty: full-time 1200, part-time 30. Degrees conferred: M.S., M.A., M.P.T. (Physical Therapy), Ph.D.

ADMISSION REQUIREMENTS. Transcripts, GRE, letters of recommendation required in support of application. Electronic application available. Interview required by some programs. TOEFL (minimum score 550, 213 on computer-based test) required of all international applicants. Accepts transfer applicants. Graduates of unaccredited colleges not considered. Apply to graduate program by the deadline established by each department. Admits Fall only. Application fee $60, $80 for international applicants. Phone: (415)476-2310.

ADMISSION STANDARDS. Very selective for most departments. Minimum average: 3.0 (A = 4).

FINANCIAL AID. Annual awards from institutional funds: fellowships, scholarships, traineeships, grants, teaching/research assistantships, Federal W/S, loans. Application for fellowships and assistantships should be filed with the application for admission, but prior to January 10. For all other aid apply to Office of Financial Aid: no specified closing date. Phone: (415)476-4181. Use FAFSA.

DEGREE REQUIREMENTS. For master's: Plan I—30 quarter units minimum; thesis; Plan II—36 quarter units minimum; advancement to candidacy; no thesis; final comprehensive exam. For Ph.D.: at least six quarters in full-time residence; foreign language requirement determined by department; advancement to candidacy; qualifying exams; dissertation; final oral exam.

FIELDS OF GRADUATE STUDY.
Biochemistry and Molecular Biology.
Bioengineering.
Biological and Medical Informatics.
Biomedical Sciences. Includes anatomy, endocrinology, immunology, microbiology, experimental pathology, physiology.
Biophysics.
Cell Biology.
Chemistry and Chemical Biology.
Clinical Research.
Genetics.
History of Health Sciences. One language for M.S.
Medical Anthropology.
Neurosciences.
Nursing. M.S., Ph.D.
Oral and Craniofacial Sciences. M.S., Ph.D.
Pharmaceutical Sciences and Pharmacogenomics.
Physical Therapy.
Sociology.

School of Dentistry (94143-0430)
Web site: dentistry.ucsf.edu

Established 1881. Located at Medical Center. School has ranked number one in Dental research from NIH since 1992. Quarter system. Special facilities: Research Center in Oral Biology, Oral Cancer Research Center, Oral AIDS Center, Center to Address Disparities in Children's Oral Health (CAN DO), Center for Craniofacial and Mesenchymal Biology, Comprehensive Oral Health Research Center of Discovery, Center for Health Professions.

Annual tuition: resident $26,001, nonresident $38,245. Off-campus housing only. Some apartments are University owned. Average academic year housing and personal expenses: approximately $20,000. For housing information contact Housing Office. Total cost for all other first-year expenses: $15,000.

Enrollment: first-year class 80, International Dentist Program 24, total full-time 391 (men 51%, women 49%, minorities 35%, state resident 85%). Faculty: full-time 105, part-time 200. Degrees conferred: D.D.S, D.D.S.-M.B.A., D.D.S.-M.D. (Oral and Maxillofacial), D.D.S.-M.S., D.D.S.-Ph.D. (D.S.T.P.).

ADMISSION REQUIREMENTS. AADSAS report, two official transcripts, DAT, three recommendations required in support of School's application. Supplemental application required by November 1. Interview by invitation only. Applicants must have completed at least three years of college study. Preference given to state and WICHE residents. Does not accept transfer applicants. Does not have EDP. Apply after June 1, before October 15, to Dental Admissions Office, Room S-630. Application fee $60, $80 for international applicants. Phone: (415)476-2737; fax: (415)476-4226.

ADMISSION STANDARDS. Competitive. Mean GPA 3.5; mean DAT academic average: 20, PAT: 18. Accepts about 15% to 20% of total annual applicants.

FINANCIAL AID. Scholarships, grant, Federal W/S, loans. Apply to Financial Aid Office after acceptance. Phone: (415)476-4181. About 52% of first-year students receive some aid from School.

DEGREE REQUIREMENTS. For D.D.S.: satisfactory completion of forty-eight-month program. For M.S., Ph.D.: see Graduate Division listing above.

FIELDS OF GRADUATE STUDY.
Dental Public Health.
Craniofacial and Mesenchymal Biology.
Bioengineering.
Endodontics.
General Practice.
Oral and Craniofacial Sciences. M.S., Ph.D.
Oral and Maxillofacial Surgery.
Orthodontics.
Pediatric Dentistry.
Periodontology.
Prosthodontics.

School of Medicine
Web site: medschool.ucsf.edu

Established as Toland Medical College in 1864, affiliated with UCSF 1873. Public control. Quarter system. Library: 800,000 volumes, 9000 subscriptions. The University's NIH ranking is 4th among all U.S. institutions with 988 awards/grants worth $452,165,301.

Annual tuition: resident $22,678, nonresident $34,923. Off-campus housing available. Average figure for all other expenses: $18,447.

Enrollment: first-year class 141 (12 MSTP); total full-time 603 (men 44%, women 56%, minorities 50%, state residents 96%). Faculty: full-time approximately 1604, part-time 59. Degrees conferred: M.D., M.D.-M.P.H., M.D.-M.S., M.D.-Ph.D., M.S.T.P.

ADMISSION REQUIREMENTS. AMCAS report, transcripts, MCAT, three recommendations required in support of application. A second application is sent out after initial screening. Interview by invitation. Preference given to state and WICHE residents. Graduates of unaccredited colleges not considered. Does not have EDP. Apply to Admissions Office after June 15, before October 1. Application fee $60. Phone: (415)476-4044; e-mail: admissions@medsch.ucsf.edu.

ADMISSION STANDARDS. Very competitive. Accepts about 4% of all applicants. Number of applications 5298 (2520 out-of-state); number interviewed 538; number of acceptance 257 (73 out-of-state); number enrolled 141 (24 out-of-state). Mean Composite MCAT 11.1; mean UGPA 3.75. *U.S. News & World Report* ranking is in the top 5 of all medical research schools, 10th in Primary Care.

FINANCIAL AID. Limited scholarships, grants, loans (all need-based). Apply after acceptance to Financial Aid Office. Phone: (415)476-4044. Use FAFSA.

DEGREE REQUIREMENTS. For M.D.: satisfactory completion of four-year program; must pass Step 1 of USMLE for promotion to third year, Step 2 taken only to record a score. For M.D.-M.S.: satisfactory completion of five-year programs. For M.D.-Ph.D.: satisfactory completion of six- to seven-year program.

FIELDS OF STUDY.
Biochemistry.
Biophysics.
Cancer Biology and Cell Signaling.
Cellular Biology.
Chemistry and Chemical Biology.
Developmental and Stem Cell Biology.
Genetics.
Human Genetics.
Neurobiology.
Neurosciences.
Tissue/Organ Biology & Endocrinology.
Vascular & Cardiac Biology.

School of Nursing
Web site: nurseweb.ucsf.edu

Annual tuition/fees: $12,245 resident; $24,668 nonresident.
Enrollment: 175 full-time, part-time 18. School's faculty: full-time 42, part-time 5. Degrees conferred: M.S.N., Ph.D.

ADMISSION REQUIREMENTS. Two transcripts, GRE (doctoral candidate), four letters of recommendation, evidence of licensure as a RN required in support of application. Personal interview is optional. Accepts graduates of accredited colleges only. TOEFL, TWE required for international applicants. Submit all documents by December 31 (doctoral candidates), February 28 (master's candidates) to both the School of Nursing and the Graduate division. Admits Fall only. Application fee $60. Phone (415)476-1435; fax: (415)476-9707.

ADMISSION STANDARDS. Selective. Usual minimum average: 3.0 (A = 4.0).

FINANCIAL AID. Scholarships, nonresident tuition scholarships, traineeships, nursing loans, Federal W/S, loans. Approved for VA benefits. Apply to the Financial Aid Office by February 1 for priority consideration. Phone: (415)476-4181. Use FAFSA for all Federal programs.

DEGREE REQUIREMENTS. For MSN: two-year, full-time 36 credit, six academic quarter program; area of specialization; comprehensive exam. For Ph.D.: four-year, full-time program; qualifying exam; two-year research residency; advancement to candidacy; dissertation; final oral exam.

FIELDS OF STUDY.
Acute Care Pediatric Nurse Practitioner.
Acute Care Nurse Practitioner.
Adult Nurse Practitioner.
Advance Community Health and International Nursing.
Cardiovascular Nursing.
Critical Care/Trauma Nursing.
Family Nurse Practitioner.
Gerontological Nursing.
Health Policy Nursing.
Midwifery/Women's Health Nurse Practitioner.
Neonatal Nurse Practitioner.
Nursing Administration.
Occupational & Environmental Health Nursing.
Oncology Nursing.
Pediatric Nurse Practitioner.
Perinatal Advanced Practice Nursing.
Psychiatric/Mental Health Nursing.

School of Pharmacy

Founded 1872.
Tuition/fees: full-time resident $20,877, nonresident $33,122. On-campus housing available for single and married students. Average annual housing cost: $12,500. Apply to Housing office. Phone: (415)476-2231.
Enrollment: Full-time 154, part-time 83. Faculty: full-time 10, volunteers 700. Degrees conferred: M.S. Ph.D.

ADMISSION REQUIREMENTS. Transcripts, GRE, three letters of recommendation, statement of purpose, résumé/curriculum vitae required in support of School's application. TOEFL required for foreign applicants. Graduates of unaccredited institutions not considered. Apply to the Department of Pharmaceutical Chemistry by January 15. Admits Fall quarter only. Application fee $60, $80 for international applicants. Phone: (415)476-2732.

ADMISSION STANDARDS. Competitive. Usual minimum average: 3.0 (A = 4).

FINANCIAL AID. Teaching assistantships, research assistantships, supplemental fellowships, tuition waivers, Federal W/S, loans. Apply to Department; no specified closing date. Use FAFSA. Most doctoral candidates receive funding at the standardized level of $15,200. No aid for M.S. students.

DEGREE REQUIREMENTS. For M.S.: 36 unit program; research project. For Ph.D.: curriculum is individualized to meet student's needs; at least two years in residence; oral qualifying exam; full-time dissertation research; one-year teaching experience as teaching assistant; proficiency in biostatistics for pharmaceutics pathway, and toxicology pathway; dissertation; final oral exam.

FIELDS OF GRADUATE STUDY.
Biological and Medical Informatics. M.S., Ph.D.
Biophysics. Ph.D.
Chemistry and Chemical Biology. Ph.D.
Medicinal Chemistry.
Pharmaceutical Sciences and Pharmacogenics. Ph.D.
Pharmaceutics.
Quantitative Biology. Ph.D.
Toxicology.

UNIVERSITY OF CALIFORNIA, SANTA BARBARA
Santa Barbara, California 93106
Web site: www.ucsb.edu

Founded 1891. Located 100 miles NW of Los Angeles. CGS and AAU member. Coed. State control. Quarter system. Special facilities: Federally Funded Research Centers: Center for Quantized Electronic Structures, Institute for Theoretical Physics, Materials Research Laboratory, National Center for Ecological Analysis & Synthesis, National Center for Geographic Information and Analysis, National Nanofabrication Users Network, Southern California Earthquake Center, Optoelectronics Technology Center; Other Federally Funded Research Centers: ARPA Center for Optical Communications, Center for Computational Modeling & Systems, Center for Non-Stoichiometric Semiconductors, High Performance Composites Center, Multidisciplinary Optical Switching Technology, Long-Term Ecological Research on the Antarctic Marine Ecosystem, Research Project on Forty Gigabit Per Second WDM Fiber Optic Components and Architecture for Telecommunication and Supercomputing, Robust Nonlinear Control of Stall and Flutter in Aeroengines; Organized Research Units: Center for Chicano Studies, Community and Organization Research Institute, Institute for Computational Earth Systems Science, Institute for Crustal Studies, Institute for Polymers and Organic Solids, Marine Science Institute, Neuroscience Research Institute, Quantum Institute; Multi-Campus Research Units: Linguistic Minority Research Institute, Institute for Nuclear Particle Astrophysics & Cosmology; Engineering Research Centers: Center for Computational Modeling & Systems, Center for Control Engineering & Computation, Center for High-Speed Image Processing, Center for Information Processing Research, Center for Macro-Molecular Science & Engineering, Center for Risk Studies and Safety, Compound Semiconductor Research Center, Ocean Engineering Laboratory, other Research Groups: Center for Black Studies, Interdisciplinary Humanities Center, The Writings of Henry D. Thoreau, Five Natural Land and Water Reserves. According to The Center at University of Florida, U.C. Santa Barbara has 100 of its University's faculty members that have been elected to National Honor Academies and this ranks it 20th among all U.S. institutions. In 2004, the University awarded 253 doctorates, which ranks it 58th among all U.S. institutions eligible to award that degree. Library: 2,800,000 volumes, 22,000 subscriptions. Total University enrollment: 21,000.

Annual fees/tuition: full-time, resident $8074, nonresident $23,062. On-campus housing available, average academic year room and board cost: $8500–$13,500. Apply to Housing Office for University housing. Phone: (805)893-4501 (on-campus apartment living), (805)893-4371 (off-campus housing). Day-care facilities available.

Graduate Division

Web site: www.graddiv.uscb.edu

Graduate study since 1954. Enrollment: full-time 2900, part-time 102. Faculty: full-time 650. Degrees conferred: M.A., M.Ed., M.E.S.M., M.S., M.F.A., M.M., Certificate Programs, D.M.A., Ph.D.

ADMISSION REQUIREMENTS. Transcripts, three letters of recommendation required in support of application. Electronic application available. GRE/MAT required for most departments. GRE required of all fellowship applicants. TOEFL required for foreign applicants. Interview not required. Graduates of unaccredited colleges not considered. Apply by May 1 (Fall), November 1 (Winter), February 1 (Spring), May 1 (Summer—earlier deadline for some majors and fellowships consideration, see Fields of Study below for early deadlines). Application fee $60. Phone: (805)893-2881; fax: (805)893-8259; e-mail: admissions @graddiv.uscb.edu.

ADMISSION STANDARDS. Selective for all departments. Usual minimum average: 3.0 (A = 4).

FINANCIAL AID. Annual awards from institutional funds: scholarships, teaching assistantships, research fellowships, nonresident waivers, Federal W/S, loans. Approved for VA benefits. Apply by mid-January to Graduate Division for scholarships, to appropriate department chair for assistantships and fellowships; apply by March 1 to Financial Aid Office for all other programs. Phone: (805)893-2432; e-mail: financial@graddiv.uscb.edu. Use FAFSA.

DEGREE REQUIREMENTS. For master's: Plan I—30 units minimum, at least 3 quarters in residence; thesis; final written exam; Plan II—36 units minimum, comprehensive exam; reading knowledge of one foreign language for some majors. For Ph.D.: two years (48–72 credits) minimum, at least 6 quarters in residence, including three consecutive quarters; qualifying exam; advancement to candidacy; dissertation or thesis; preliminary, final oral exams; reading knowledge of one or two foreign languages.

FIELDS OF STUDY.
Anthropology. Writing sample for admission. Apply by December 1. Includes Archaeology (M.A. only.) M.A., Ph.D.
Applied Mathematics. GRE Subject for admission. Apply by January 1. M.A., Ph.D.
Art History. Writing sample for admission. Apply by January 15. Ph.D.
Art Studio. Portfolio for admissions. Apply by January 1 for Financial support, April 1 for admission only. M.F.A.
Asian Studies. Apply by May 1. Includes East Asian Languages and Cultural Studies. M.A. only.
Biochemistry and Molecular Biology. GRE Subject recommended for admission. Apply by December 15. Includes bioengineering and biomaterials. Ph.D.
Chemical Engineering. Apply by January 31. Includes computational science and engineering. M.S., Ph.D.
Chemistry. Admits Fall, Winter, Spring. M.A., M.S., Ph.D.
Chicana and Chicano Studies. M.A.-Ph.D. only.
Classics. Writing sample for admission. Includes ancient history, literature and theory. Admits Fall, Winter, Spring. M.A., Ph.D.

Communication. Includes human development, quantitative methods in the social sciences. Apply by January 15. Ph.D.
Comparative Literature. Writing sample for admission. Admits Fall, Winter, Spring. M.A., Ph.D.
Computer Science. Includes computational science and engineering. Apply by January 15 for financial support; by April 1 for admissions only. M.S., Ph.D.
Counseling, Clinical, School Psychology. GRE or MAT, writing sample, background questionnaire for admission. Apply by December 10. M.Ed., Ph.D.
Dramatic Art. Writing sample for admission. Includes European medieval studies. Apply by January 15 (Ph.D.), April 1 (M.A.). M.A., Ph.D.
Ecology, Evolution, and Marine Biology. Apply by December 15. M.A., Ph.D.
Economics. Includes business economics (M.A. only). Apply by December 15. M.A., Ph.D.
Education. Includes cultural perspectives, developmental studies, educational leadership, research methodology, special education, disabilities and risk studies, teaching and learning, administrative services. Apply by December 15 for financial support, May 1 for admission only. M.A., M.Ed., Credential Certificate, Ph.D.
Electrical and Computer Engineering. Includes computer engineering, communications, control and signal processing, electronic and photonics. Admits Fall (Ph.D. only), Winter, Spring. M.S., Ph.D.
English. GRE Subject, writing sample for admission. Includes European medieval studies, women's studies. M.A., Ph.D.
Environmental Science and Management. Admits December 15 for financial support, May 1 for admission only. M.E.S.M., Ph.D.
French. Writing sample, tape of spoken French for admission. Admits Fall, Winter, Spring. M.A., Ph.D.
Geography. Apply by January 15. M.A., Ph.D.
Geological Science. Includes geophysics (M.S.). Admits Fall, Winter, Spring. M.S., Ph.D.
Geophysics. M.S. only.
Germanic Languages and Literatures. Writing sample, tape of spoken German and English, research paper in German or English for admission. Admits Fall, Winter, Spring. M.A., Ph.D.
Global and International Studies. M.A.
Hispanic Languages and Literatures. Two writing samples for admission. Apply by January 5 (Fall) for financial support; admits Fall, Winter, Spring. M.A., Ph.D.
History. Two writing sample for admission. Includes public historical studies. Apply by December 15 for financial support, January 15 for admission only. Ph.D.
Latin American and Iberian Studies. Writing sample for admission. Apply Fall, Winter, Spring. M.A. only.
Linguistic. Copy of publications or professional papers. Apply by January 4. Ph.D.
Marine Science. Apply by December 15. M.S., Ph.D.
Materials. Admits Fall, Winter, Spring. M.S., Ph.D.
Mathematics. GRE Subject for admission. Apply January 1. M.A., Ph.D.
Mechanical Engineering. Apply by January 15 for financial support (Fall), May 1 for admission only. Admits Fall, Winter, Spring. M.S., Ph.D.
Media Arts and Technology. Includes multimedia engineering (M.S.), music and sound design (M.A.), visual and spatial arts (M.A.). Apply by January 15. M.A., M.S.
Molecular, Cellular and Developmental Biology. GRE Subject for admission. Apply by January 7. M.A., Ph.D.
Music. Writing sample, videotape, or audition for admission. Includes composition, ethnomusicology, musicology, theory (M.A., Ph.D.), conducting, keyboard, strings, voice (M.M., D.M.A), woodwinds/brass, piano accompanying (M.M.). M.A., M.M., D.M.A., Ph.D.
Philosophy. Writing sample for admission. Apply by December 15 for financial support, May 1 for admission. Admits Fall, Winter, Spring. Ph.D.

Physics. GRE Subject for admission. Apply by January 15. Ph.D.
Political Science. Writing sample for admission. Apply by January 1. M.A., Ph.D.
Portuguese. Two writing samples for admission. Apply by January 5 for financial support, April 15 for admission only. Admits Fall, Winter, Spring. M.A.
Psychology. GRE Subject suggested, GRE writing recommended for admission. Apply for December 15. M.A., Ph.D.
Religious Studies. Apply by December 15. M.A., Ph.D.
Sociology. Writing sample required, GRE Subject optional for admission. Apply by December 31. Ph.D.
Spanish. Two writing samples for admission. Apply by January 5 for financial support, April 15 for admission only (Fall). Admits Fall, Winter, Spring. M.A., Ph.D.
Spanish and Portuguese. Two writing samples for admission. Apply by January 5 for financial support, April 15 for admission only (Fall). Admits Fall, Winter, Spring. M.A.
Statistics and Applied Probability. Includes mathematical and empirical finance. Admits Fall, Winter, Spring. M.A.
Statistics and Applied Probability. Ph.D.
Theater Studies. M.A., Ph.D.

UNIVERSITY OF CALIFORNIA, SANTA CRUZ
Santa Cruz, California 95064
Web site: www.ucsc.edu

Opened 1965. Located in the redwoods of California's central coast, 75 miles S of San Francisco. CGS member. Coed. Public control. Quarter system. Special facilities: Syntax Research Center, Lick Observatory, forest ecology and marine environments, Center for Non-Linear Science, Santa Cruz Institute for Particle Physics, Tectonics Institute, Third World Teaching Resource Center. Library: 1,500,000 volumes, more than 21,000 current periodicals. Total University enrollment: 15,000.

Annual tuition/fees: residents $8074, nonresidents $23,062. On-campus housing consists of 199 apartments for graduate men and women with priority given to married couples. Average academic year housing cost: $11,000 (includes board), $7800–$8000 for married students. Phone: (831)459-2394. For family student housing: phone: (831)459-2549.

Graduate Studies

Graduate study initiated in 1966. Enrollment: full- and part-time 1450. University faculty for graduate students: full-time 500. Degrees conferred: M.A., M.S., Professional Certificate, Ph.D.

ADMISSION REQUIREMENTS. Transcripts, GRE, three letters of recommendation, statement of purpose required in support of application. GRE/Subject recommended for most programs. TOEFL (minimum score 550, 220 for computer-based test) required for international applicants. Interview not required. Accepts transfer applicants. Graduate program deadlines vary: December 1–February 1. Fall admission only. Rolling admissions process. Application fee $60. Phone: (831)459-5906; fax: (831)459-4843.

ADMISSION STANDARDS. Very selective or competitive for most departments. Usual minimum average: 3.0 (A = 4).

FINANCIAL AID. Annual awards from institutional funds: scholarships, teaching assistantships, research assistantships, grants, loans. Apply by February 1 to Graduate Office for assistantships; to the Financial Aid Office for all other programs. Phone: (831)459-2335. Use FAFSA (University code: 001321). About 65% of students receive aid other than loans from University and outside sources.

DEGREE REQUIREMENTS. For master's: requirements vary, but normally include one year of course work; thesis/nonthesis option; final written exam. Some programs require reading knowledge of one foreign language. For Certificates: varies by program. For Ph.D.: requirements vary, but normally include two years of course work beyond the master's; preliminary exam; reading knowledge of one foreign language; dissertation; final written/oral exam.

FIELDS OF STUDY.
Anthropology. Ph.D. only.
Astronomy and Astrophysics. Ph.D. only.
Bioinformatics. M.S., Ph.D.
Biology. M.A., Ph.D.
Chemistry and Biochemistry. M.S., Ph.D.
Computer Engineering. M.S., Ph.D.
Computer Sciences. M.S., Ph.D.
Earth and Planetary Sciences. M.S., Ph.D.
Economics. Includes applied, international. M.S., Ph.D.
Education. M.A. only.
Electrical Engineering. M.S., Ph.D.
Environmental Studies. Ph.D. only
History. Ph.D. only.
History of Consciousness. Ph.D. only.
Linguistics. M.A., Ph.D.
Literature. M.A., Ph.D.
Marine Sciences. M.S. only.
Mathematics. M.A., Ph.D.
Music. M.A. only.
Network Engineering. M.S.N.E.
Ocean Sciences. Ph.D. only.
Philosophy. M.A., Ph.D.
Physics. M.S., Ph.D.
Politics. Ph.D.
Psychology. Includes developmental, experimental, social. Ph.D. only.
Science Communication. Application deadline April 1. Certificate only.
Sociology. Ph.D. only.
Statistics and Stochastic Modeling. M.S., Ph.D.
Theater Arts. Application deadline March 1. Certificate only.

CALIFORNIA WESTERN SCHOOL OF LAW
225 Cedar Street
San Diego, California 92101-3046
Web site: www.cwsl.edu

Chartered in 1924. Located in downtown San Diego. ABA approved since 1962. AALS member since 1967. Private control. Trimester system. Special facilities: Center for Creative Problem Solving, National Center for Preventive Law, the Telecommunications and Intellectual Property Law Center. Library: 319,819 volumes, 3905 subscriptions; has LEXIS, NEXIS, WESTLAW, DIALOG. 515 computers in library.

Annual tuition: $32,380, part-time $22,900. No on-campus housing available. Total average annual additional expenses: $19,700.

Enrollment: first-year class full-time 325, part-time 22; total full-time 735, part-time 87 (men 48%, women 52%, minorities 40%). Faculty: full-time 37, part-time 31. Student to faculty ratio 18 to 1. Degrees conferred: J.D., J.D.-M.B.A., J.D.-M.S.W., J.D.-Ph.D. (History, Political Science), LL.M. (Trial Advocacy), LL.M. (for foreign lawyers), M.C.L. (for foreign lawyers).

ADMISSION REQUIREMENTS. LSDAS Law School report, transcripts, LSAT, three recommendations, bachelor's degree required in support of application. Interview granted on request. Accepts transfer applicants from ABA accredited law schools only. Apply to Director of Admissions after September 1, before June 1 (Fall), November 1 (Spring). Application fee $45. Phone: (800) 255-4252, ext. 1401; fax: (619)525-1401; e-mail: admissions@cwsl.edu.

ADMISSION STANDARDS. Selective. Accepts 37% of total annual applicants. Number of applicants 3652; number of acceptance 1353; number enrolled 325; LSAT (75% of class have a score at or above 151); GPA (75% of class have a GPA at or above 2.98). *U.S. News & World Report* ranking is in the fourth tier of all law schools.

FINANCIAL AID. Scholarships, full and partial tuition grants, Federal W/S, loans. Apply to Director of Financial Aid after acceptance but before March 15. Phone: (614)525-7060. Use FAFSA. About 35% of students receive some aid from School.

DEGREE REQUIREMENTS. For J.D.: 89 semester hours minimum, at least forty-five hours and three semesters in residence. Optional two-year program is also available. For LL.M., M.C.L.: twenty-four credit, full-time programs. For master's degrees: see San Diego State University's institutional listing. For Ph.D. degree: see University of California at San Diego listing.

CAMPBELL UNIVERSITY
Buies Creek, North Carolina 27506
Web site: www.campbell.edu

Founded in 1887. Located 30 miles south of Raleigh. Coed. Private control. Southern Baptist. Semester system. Library: 218,000 volumes, 1700 subscriptions. More than 250 computers on campus for general student use. Total University enrollment: 3645.

Tuition: per semester hour $285 (Education), $420 (Business), $496 (M.S.C.R., M.S.P.S.), $295 (Divinity). On-campus housing for single and married students. Annual housing cost: $3200. Apply by July 1 to Director of Housing. Phone: (910)893-1200, ext. 2226. Day-care facilities available.

Graduate Studies

Enrollment: full- and part-time 1650. Faculty: full- and part-time 139. Degrees conferred: M.B.A., M.S., M.Ed., M.Div., M.A.C.E., M.S.C.R., M.S.P.S.

ADMISSION REQUIREMENTS. Transcripts, GRE/MAT, letters of recommendation required in support of University's application. GMAT required for business programs. TOEFL (minimum score 580) required for international applicants. Graduates of unaccredited colleges not considered. Apply to the Director of Graduate Admissions at least forty-five days prior to expected semester of entrance. Application fee $55. Phone: (910)893-1200, ext. 1318; fax: (910)893-4718.

ADMISSION STANDARDS. Relatively open. Usual minimum average: 2.5 (A = 4).

FINANCIAL AID. Scholarships, assistantships, internships, Federal W/S, loans. Apply to the Director of Financial Aid; no specified closing date. Phone: (800)334-4111, ext. 1310. Use FAFSA. Aid available for part-time students.

DEGREE REQUIREMENTS. For M.A., M.Ed., M.S.A.: 33–48 credits minimum, at least 24 in residence; thesis/research paper/field experience/final written exam. For M.S.C.R., M.S.P.S.: 46 credit program; research project. For M.B.A.: 33 credits minimum; comprehensive oral exam. For M.Div.: 90 semester hour, three-year, full-time program; supervised ministry. For M.A.C.E.: 60 semester hour, two-year, full-time program; concentration; supervised ministry.

FIELDS OF STUDY.

FUNDY-FETTERMAN SCHOOL OF BUSINESS:
Business Administration. M.B.A.

SCHOOL OF DIVINITY:
Christian Education. M.Div.
Christian Social Ministries. M.A.C.E.
Church Staff Ministries. M.A.C.E.
Counseling and Chaplaincy. M.Div.
Education and Music Ministries. M.A.C.E.
Lay and Marketplace Ministries. M.A.C.E.
Missions and Evangelism. M.Div.
Music and Worship. M.Div.
Pastoral Ministries. M.Div.

SCHOOL OF EDUCATION:
Administration. M.S.A.
Community Counseling. M.A.
Elementary Education. M.Ed.
English Education. M.Ed.
Mathematics Education. M.Ed.
Middle Grades Education. M.Ed.
Physical Education. M.Ed.
School Counseling. M.Ed.
Science Education. M.Ed.

SCHOOL OF PHARMACY:
Clinical Research. M.S.C.R.
Pharmaceutical Science. Includes concentrations in bioprocessing/biotechnology, industrial pharmacology, pharmaceutical analysis, pharmacology. M.S.P.S.

Norman Adrian Wiggins School of Law
P.O. Box 158
Web site: www.law.campbell.edu

Established 1976. ABA approved since 1979. Private control. Semester system. Library: 196,000 volumes, 2668 subscriptions; has LEXIS, NEXIS, WESTLAW.

Annual tuition: resident $24,700. Enrollment: first-year class 120; total 340 (men 51%, women 49%, minorities 1%). Faculty: full-time 16, part-time 8. Student to faculty ratio 17 to 1. Degrees conferred: J.D., J.D.-M.B.A.

ADMISSION REQUIREMENTS. LSDAS Law School report, transcripts, bachelor's degree, LSAT, recommendations required in support of application. Interview by invitation. Graduates of unaccredited colleges not considered. Apply by March 31 (priority deadline) to Director of Admissions. Rolling admission process. Application fee $50. Phone: (800)334-4111, ext. 1754; (910)893-1754; fax: (910)893-1780; e-mail: culaw@webster.campbell.edu.

ADMISSION STANDARDS. Selective. Accepts 20% of total annual applicants. Number of applicants 1118; number of acceptance 229; number enrolled 120; LSAT (75% of students have a score at or above 153); GPA (75% of students have a GPA at or above 3.03). *U.S. News & World Report* ranking is in the fourth tier of all law schools.

FINANCIAL AID. Full and partial scholarships, grants, Federal W/S, loans. Apply by April 15 to Director of Admissions. Phone: (910)893-1310. Use FAFSA. About 43% of students receive some aid from School.

DEGREE REQUIREMENTS. For J.D.: satisfactory completion of 90 semester hour program. For M.B.A.: see Graduate Studies listing.

CANISIUS COLLEGE

Buffalo, New York 14208-1098
Web site: www.canisius.edu

Founded 1870. Coed. Private control. Roman Catholic Jesuit. Semester system. Library: 328,278 volumes, 1637 current periodicals, 68 PCs in all libraries. Total College enrollment: 4975.

Tuition: per credit, $639. On-campus housing for 100 graduate students. Average academic year housing costs: $10,070 (including board). Contact Office of Residence Life for both on- and off-campus housing information. Phone: (716)888-2220.

Graduate Division

Graduate study since 1919. Enrollment: full-time 696, part-time 697. Faculty teaching graduate students: full-time 67, part-time 113. Degrees conferred: M.S., M.B.A., M.B.A.P.A., M.S., M.S.O.C.D.

ADMISSION REQUIREMENTS. Two official transcripts, GRE, two letters of recommendation required in support of application. For Education program, two transcripts for admission. TOEFL required for international applicants. Accepts transfer applicants. Graduates of unaccredited institutions not considered. Apply to Director of Admissions by July 1 (Fall), November 1 (Spring), April 15 (Summer). Application fee $25. Phone: Education (800)950-2505 or (716)888-2200; fax: (716)888-3230; Business (800)543-7906.

ADMISSION STANDARDS. Selective. Usual minimum average: 2.5 (A = 4).

FINANCIAL AID. Scholarships, assistantships, Federal W/S, loans. Apply to Office of Financial Aid; no specified closing date. Use FAFSA (College code: 002681). Phone: (716)888-2300.

DEGREE REQUIREMENTS. For M.B.A.: 48-credit program; internship. For M.B.A.P.A.: 61-credit program; capstone. For M.S. (Education): 33–45 credits for most majors; thesis/nonthesis options for all majors. For M.S. (Telecommunications): 37-credit program; capstone. For M.S.O.C.D.: 36 credit program; 15 credits are taken in School of Business.

FIELDS OF STUDY.

COLLEGE OF ARTS AND SCIENCES:
Communication and Leadership. M.S.C.+L.

RICHARD J. WEHLE SCHOOL OF BUSINESS:
Business Administration. One-year, full-time. M.B.A.
Business Administration. Evening, part-time. M.B.A.
Professional Accounting. M.B.A.P.A.

SCHOOL OF EDUCATION AND HUMAN SERVICES:
Adolescence Education (grades 7–12).
Childhood Education (grades 1–6).
College Student Personnel Administration.
Counseling and Human Services. Includes agency counseling, rehabilitation counseling, school counseling, substance abuse counseling.
Deaf Education.
Differential Instruction.
Educational Administration and Supervision.
Health and Human Performance.
Physical Education.
Special Education.
Sport Administration.

CAPITAL UNIVERSITY

2199 E. Main Street
Columbus, Ohio 43209-2394
Web site: www.capital.edu

Founded 1830. Coed. Lutheran. Semester system. Library: 376,000 volumes, 90,000 microforms, 55 PC workstations; OHIONET.

Annual tuition: per credit hour, M.B.A. $500, Nursing $410, Music $345. Evening program only. No on-campus housing.

Graduate School of Management

Enrollment: part-time 300 (men 150, women 150). Faculty: full-time 7, part-time 18. Degree conferred: M.B.A.

ADMISSION REQUIREMENTS. Transcripts, GMAT (minimum score 550), interview required in support of application. Accepts transfer applicants and graduates of accredited colleges. Applicants must have two years' work experience and be employed full-time. Preference given to Central Ohio residents. TOEFL (minimum score 550, 213 on computer-based test) required for international applicants. Apply to Director of Admissions; no specified closing date. Admits Fall and Spring. Application fee $25. Phone: (614)236-6101; fax: (614)236-6926.

ADMISSION STANDARDS. Selective. Usual minimum average. 3.0 (A = 4).

FINANCIAL AID. Federal W/S, loans only. Apply to Financial Aid Office; no specified closing date. Use FAFSA. Phone: (614)236-6511; e-mail: finaid@capital.edu.

DEGREE REQUIREMENTS. For M.B.A.: 40 credits in residence; research paper option.

Law School (43215)

Web site: www.law.capital.edu

Established 1903 as Columbus College of Law, affiliated with Capital University in 1966. Located downtown in the Discovery district, adjacent to German Village. ABA approved since 1950. AALS member. Private control. Semester system. Special facilities: Center for Dispute Resolution, Institute for International Education, National Center for Adoption Law & Policy, Tobacco Public Policy Center. Library: 267,750 volumes, 2585 subscriptions; has LEXIS, NEXIS, WESTLAW, INFOTRAC. Special programs: Summer study in Germany and Greece. Sister-institutional agreements with the Center for International and European Economic Law in Greece, Demokritus University of Thrace (Greece), The University of Saskatchewan (Canada), The University of Glasgow (Scotland), the University of Passau (Germany).

Annual tuition: full-time $28,275, part-time $18,525. Limited off-campus housing available. Total average annual additional expense: $12,125.

Enrollment: first-year class 168 (day), 86 (evening); total full- and part-time 695 (men 56%, women 44%, minorities 11%).

Faculty: full-time 33, part-time 44. Student to faculty ratio 16.3 to 1. Degrees conferred: J.D., J.D.-M.B.A., J.D.-M.S.(Nursing), J.D.-M.S.A.(Sport Administration with Ohio University), J.D.-M.T.S., J.D.-LL.M.(Taxation), LL.M. (Taxation, Business and Taxation).

ADMISSION REQUIREMENTS. LSDAS Law School report, transcripts, LSAT, essay required in support of application. Interview by invitation only. Preference is given to state residents. Accepts transfer applicants. Graduates of unaccredited colleges not considered. Apply to Director of Admissions by May 1. Rolling admission process. Application fee $40. Phone: (614)236-6310; fax: (614)236-6972; e-mail: admissions@law.capital.edu.

ADMISSION STANDARDS. Selective. Accepts 43% of total annual applicants. Number of full-time applicants 1274, part-time 301; number of full-time acceptance 486, part-time 138; number enrolled full-time 168, part-time 87; LSAT (75% of full-time class have a score at or above 151, part-time 150); GPA (75% of full-time class have a GPA at or above 2.96, part-time 2.90). Approximately 45% of enrolled students are nonresident. *U.S. News & World Report* ranking is in the fourth tier of all law schools.

FINANCIAL AID. Scholarships, research and teaching assistantships, Federal W/S, loans. Apply as early as possible after application has been filed to Director of Admissions before April 1. Phone: (614)236-6350. Use FAFSA. About 63% of students receive some aid from School.

DEGREE REQUIREMENTS. For J.D.: satisfactory completion of 86-semester hour program. For LL.M.: satisfactory completion of one-year program beyond J.D. For master's degree: see Graduate School listing above and Ohio University listings.

School of Nursing

Established in 1950, graduate study since 1994.
Enrollment: full-time 22, part-time 18. School's Faculty: full-time 11, part-time 5. Degrees conferred: M.S.N., M.S.N.-M.B.A., M.S.N.-J.D.

ADMISSION REQUIREMENTS. Transcripts, writing sample, résumé, GRE, three professional references, interview required in support of application. Accepts transfer applicants and graduates of accredited colleges. Preference given to Central Ohio residents. TOEFL (minimum score 550) required for international applicants. Apply to Director of Admissions; no specified closing date. Admits Fall and Spring. Application fee $25. Phone: (614)236-6361; fax: (614)236-6157.

ADMISSION STANDARDS. Selective. Usual minimum average. 3.0 (A = 4).

FINANCIAL AID. Scholarships, Federal W/S, loans only. Apply to Financial Aid Office; no specified closing date. Phone: (614)236-6115. Use FAFSA.

DEGREE REQUIREMENTS. For M.S.N.: at least 36–42 credits in residence; thesis or project.

FIELDS OF STUDY.
Administration.
Family and Community Health Nursing.
Occupational Health Nursing.
Parish Nursing.
School Health Nursing.

CARDINAL STRITCH COLLEGE
Milwaukee, Wisconsin 53217-3985
Web site: www.stritch.edu

Chartered 1937. Coed. Private control. Roman Catholic. Semester system. Library: 139,000 volumes, 700 subscriptions. More than 250 computers on campus for general student use. Total College enrollment: 7000.
Tuition: per credit $395–$582. On-campus single housing limited to a space-available basis; none for married students. Average academic year housing costs: $4680–$5850 (including board). Phone: (414)352-5400, ext. 347. Day-care facilities available.

Graduate Division

Graduate study since 1956. Enrollment: full- and part-time 3800. Graduate faculty: full-time 57, part-time 212. Degrees conferred: M.A., M.B.A., M.Ed, M.S.

ADMISSION REQUIREMENTS. Official transcripts, GMAT (Business), MAT (Education) required in support of application. TOEFL required for international applicants. Interview not required. Accepts transfer applicants. Graduates of unaccredited colleges not considered. Apply to Graduate Admission Office at least three weeks prior to registration. Application fee $25. Phone: (414)410-4042.

ADMISSION STANDARDS. Relatively open. Usual minimum average: 2.75 (A = 4).

FINANCIAL AID. Annual awards from College funds: assistantships, Federal W/S, loans. Approved for VA benefits. Apply by May 1 to Chair of the Graduate Committee for assistantships; to Financial Aid Office for all other programs. Phone: (800)347-8822, ext. 4048. Use FAFSA. About 5% of students receive aid other than loans from College and outside sources.

DEGREE REQUIREMENTS. For M.B.A.: 33–36 credits minimum, at least 24 in residence; thesis, research paper/field experience; final written exam. For M.A.: 35 credits minimum; practice/research option. For M.Ed., M.S.: 30–31 credits minimum; thesis/nonthesis option; comprehensive exam.

FIELDS OF STUDY.

COLLEGE OF ARTS AND SCIENCE:
Clinical Psychology. M.A.
History. M.A.
Lay Ministry. M.A.
Ministry. M.A.
Piano. M.M.
Religious Studies. M.A.
Visual Studies. M.A.

COLLEGE OF BUSINESS AND MANAGEMENT:
Business Administration. M.B.A.
Management. M.S.M.

COLLEGE OF EDUCATION AND LEADERSHIP:
Educational Leadership. M.S.
Instructional Technology. M.Ed., M.S.
Leadership for the Advancement of Learning and Service. M.Ed.
Reading/Language Arts. M.A.
Reading/Learning Disability. M.A.
Special Education. M.A.
Teaching. M.A.
Urban Education. M.A.

COLLEGE OF NURSING:
Nursing. M.S.

CARNEGIE MELLON UNIVERSITY
Pittsburgh, Pennsylvania 15213-3891
Web site: www.cmu.edu

Founded 1900. Coed. CGS and AAU member. Private control. Semester system. Special facilities: Center for the Materials of the Artist and Conservator, Center for Building Performance and Diagnostics, Center for Machine Translation, Center for the Management of Technology, Center for Molecular Genetics, Center for the Study of Public Policy, Communications Design Center, Engineering Design Center, Laboratory for Computational Linguistics, Mellon Institute, National Center for the Study of Writing, Robotics Institute, Software Engineering Institute, Statistical Center for Quality Improvement. According to The Center at University of Florida, the University is ranked 51st in receipt of Federal Research funds with $157,583,000 and it ranks 76th for total University research expenditures with $186,351,000. The University's endowment assets ranks it 60th with a value of $768,990,000. In 2004, the University awarded 195 doctorates, which ranked it 74th among all U.S. institutions eligible to award that degree. Twenty-three of the University's faculty members have been elected to National Honor Academies and this ranks it 42nd among all U.S. institutions. The Library: approximately 950,000 volumes, 5700 subscriptions. Total University enrollment: 8000.

Annual tuition; full time $32,400. No on- campus housing available. Average annual housing cost: $14,700. For off-campus housing: phone (412)268-2139. Day-care facilities available.

Carnegie Institute of Technology
Graduate Engineering
Web site: www.cit.cmu.edu

Tuition: full-time $32,400. No on-campus housing available. Enrollment: full-time 541, part-time 64. Faculty: full-time 190. Degrees conferred: M.S., M.Ch.E., M.E., M.P.D., Ph.D.

ADMISSION REQUIREMENTS. Transcripts, three letters of recommendation, GRE/Subject tests required in support of Institute's application. TOEFL required of foreign applicants. Interview not required. Accepts transfer applicants. Graduates of unaccredited institutions not considered. Apply to department of interest by February 1, January 15 for Electrical and Computer Engineering (Fall), October 15 (Spring). Application fee $75. Phone: (412)268-2482.

ADMISSION STANDARDS. Selective. Usual minimum average: 3.0 (A = 4). *U.S. News & World Report* ranked engineering program 10, computer engineering 10.

FINANCIAL AID. Teaching assistantships, fellowships, research assistantships/fellowships, tuition waivers, Federal W/S, loans. Approved for VA benefits. Apply by February 1 (preferably) to department of interest for scholarships, fellowships, and assistantships; to Financial Aid Office for Federal Funds, for priority consideration by February 1. Phone: (412)269-2478. Use FAFSA and CMU FAF.

DEGREE REQUIREMENTS. For M.S.: one-year, full-time study beyond bachelor's degree; comprehensive final oral/written exam; thesis for some departments. For M.E., M.P.D.: two-year, full-time study beyond bachelor's; comprehensive exam; project. For Ph.D.: three years minimum beyond the bachelor's degree, at least one in full-time residence; qualifying exam; dissertation; final oral public exam.

FIELDS OF STUDY.
Air Quality Engineering. Interdisciplinary. M.S.
Biomedical Engineering. M.S., Ph.D.
Chemical Engineering. M.S., M.Ch.E., Ph.D.
Civil and Environmental Engineering. M.S., Ph.D.
Colloids, Polymer and Surfaces. Interdisciplinary. M.S.
Electrical and Computer Engineering. M.S., Ph.D.
Engineering and Public Policy. Ph.D.
Engineering and Technology Innovation Management. Interdisciplinary. M.S.
Information Networking. M.S.I.N.
Information Security Technology and Management. M.S.I.S.T.M.
M.B.A.—Engineering Integrated 5-year program. B.S.E.-M.B.A.
Materials Science & Engineering. M.E., Ph.D.
Mechanical Engineering. M.S., Ph.D.
Product Development. Interdisciplinary. M.P.D.

College of Fine Arts Graduate Division
Web site: www.cmu.edu/cfa

Annual tuition: $30,950 (Architecture), $31,500 (School of Design). Enrollment: full-time 181, part-time 23. College faculty teaching graduate students: full-time 66, part-time 7. Degrees conferred: M.S., M.A.M., M.Des., M.F.A., M.M., M.M.M.Ed., Ph.D.

ADMISSION REQUIREMENTS. Transcripts, three letters of reference, statement of purpose, portfolio/audition required in support of application. Interview for most departments. TOEFL required for all students whose native language is not English. Accepts transfer applicants. Apply to the School by February 1, January 1 Drama. Fall admission only. Application fee $75. Phone: (412)268-2349.

ADMISSION STANDARDS. Very competitive.

FINANCIAL AID. Annual awards from institutional funds: scholarships, fellowships and half-tuition fellowships, research assistantships, internships, tuition remission, Federal W/S, loans. Apply by April 1 to appropriate department chair for fellowships, assistantships; to Financial Aid Office for all other programs. Phone: (412)268-8186. Use FAFSA. About 50% of students receive aid other than loans from College and outside sources.

DEGREE REQUIREMENTS. For M.Arch: nine-month, full-time program; final project; thesis/nonthesis option; final written/oral exam. For M.F.A.: three-year, full-time program; M.F.A. project/thesis. For M.S., M.Des.: two-year, full-time programs. For M.M.: two-year, full-time program; recital. For M.M.M.Ed.: one-year, full-time program, candidacy; thesis/recital; comprehensive exam. For Ph.D.: two years minimum in residence; qualifying exam; dissertation; final oral exam.

FIELDS OF STUDY.

SCHOOL OF ARCHITECTURE:
Architecture. M.S.A.
Architecture Engineering Construction Management. M.S.A.E.C.M.
Design or Building Performance and Diagnostics. M.Sc., Ph.D.
Sustainable Design. M.S.
Urban Design. M.U.D.

SCHOOL OF ART:
Art. M.F.A.
Arts Management. Joint degree with School of Public Policy and Management. M.A.M.

SCHOOL OF DESIGN:
Design Theory, Interaction Design, Typography and Information Design. M.Des.
Interactive Design, Communication Planning and Information Design. M.Des.
New Product Development. Ph.D.

SCHOOL OF DRAMA:
Design. M.F.A.
Directing. M.F.A.
Drama. M.F.A.
Dramatic Writing. M.F.A.
Production Technology and Management. Includes costumes, lighting, scenery. M.F.A.

SCHOOL OF MUSIC:
Composition. M.M.
Conducting. M.M.
Education. M.M.M.Ed.
Performance. M.M.

College of Humanities and Social Sciences

Enrollment: full-time 142, part-time 81. Faculty: full-time 180, part-time 37. Degrees conferred: M.A., M.S., Ph.D.

ADMISSION REQUIREMENTS. Transcripts, additional application form, three letters of recommendation, GRE required in support of College's application. TOEFL required for foreign applicants; TSE and TOEFL required for foreign applicants in psychology. Interview not required. Accepts transfer applicants. Apply to individual departmental chairs by April 15 (Fall) in History: February; in English: March 1; prior to registration for other sessions. Application fee: generally $35, but varies by department. Dean's Phone: (412)268-2830.

ADMISSION STANDARDS. Selective to very selective. Usual minimum average: 3.0 (A = 4).

FINANCIAL AID. Annual awards from institutional funds: scholarships, teaching fellowships, research fellowships, research assistantships, teaching assistantships, tuition waivers, Federal W/S, loans. Apply to the appropriate departmental chairman and to Financial Aid Office by March 15. Phone: (412)268-2068. Use FAFSA. About 100% of students receive aid other than loans from College and outside sources.

DEGREE REQUIREMENTS. For M.A., M.S.: two-year, full-time program; thesis. For Ph.D.: flexible individualized programs and varies by department.

FIELDS OF STUDY.
Economics. Provided by faculty of the Graduate School of Industrial Administration. Ph.D.
English. Includes rhetoric, literary and cultural studies, professional writing, creative writing. M.A., Ph.D.
History. Includes history and policy, social and cultural history. Ph.D.
Information System. M.S.
Philosophy. Includes logic and computation (M.S.), logic, computation and logic (Ph.D.). M.A., M.S., Ph.D.
Psychology. Includes cognitive psychology, social psychology, developmental psychology, cognitive neuroscience.
Second Language Acquisition. Ph.D.
Social and Decision Sciences. Includes behavioral decision research, organizational behavior, organizational science, technological change and industrial evaluation, political psychology and economy.
Statistics. M.S., Ph.D.

Mellon College of Science

Annual tuition: $33,300 full-time, $366 per unit part-time.
Enrollment: full-time 192, part-time 6. Faculty full-time 196, part-time 3. Degrees conferred: M.S., Ph.D.

ADMISSION REQUIREMENTS. Transcripts, additional application form, three letters of recommendation, GRE required in support of departmental application. TOEFL (minimum score 600–620) required for all foreign applicants. Accepts transfer applicants. Apply to individual departmental chairs by January 1. Admits Fall only. Application fee: none, $50 for international applicants. Dean's phone: (412)268-6400.

ADMISSION STANDARDS. Selective. Usual minimum average: 3.0 (A = 4).

FINANCIAL AID. Scholarships, fellowships, research/teaching assistantships, traineeships, tuition waiver, Federal W/S, loans. Apply to appropriate department chairman and to Financial Aid Office by April 15. Phone: (412)268-2086. Use FAFSA. 100% of students receive aid other than loans from College and outside sources.

DEGREE REQUIREMENTS. Determined by each department and varies by program.

FIELDS OF STUDY.
Biological Sciences. Ph.D.
Chemistry. Includes organic, bioorganics and materials chemistry, bioorganic and organometallic chemistry, biophysical

chemistry and spectroscopy, chemical physics, green and environmental chemistry, nuclear chemistry, polymer science, theoretical and computational chemistry.
Computational Biology. M.S.
Mathematics. Includes algorithms, combinatorics and optimization, computational finance, mathematical finance, mathematical sciences, pure and applied logic.
Physics. Includes astrophysics, biological physics, computational physics, experimental condensed matter physics, experimental high energy physics, experimental medium energy physics, quantum theory, theoretical condensed matter physics, theoretical high energy physics, theoretical nuclear/medium energy physics.
Note: Interdisciplinary programs available in Biomedical and Health Engineering, Colloids, Polymers and Surfaces, Merck Computational Biology and Computational Chemistry.

School of Computer Science
Web site: www.sc.cmu.edu

Department of Computer Science established in 1965, became School 1988.
Annual tuition: full-time $33,300, part-time $366 per unit.
Enrollment: 398 total (261 doctoral candidates, 137 master's candidates; men 85%, women 15%). Faculty: 197 full-time, 1 part-time. Degree conferred: Ph.D. School does not offer a master of Computer Science but does participate in many master's degrees jointly with related programs or disciplines of other CMU Schools/Colleges.

ADMISSION REQUIREMENTS. Transcripts, GRE, statement of purpose, résumé, three letters of recommendation required in support of application. GRE Subject recommended for most programs. TOEFL (minimum score 600–620) required for foreign applicants. Apply to School by January 5. Application fee $75. Dean's phone: (412)268-2592.

ADMISSION STANDARDS. Selective. Usual minimum average: 3.0 GPA (A = 4).

FINANCIAL AID. Scholarships, fellowships, research/teaching assistantships, grants, tuition waivers, Federal W/S, loans. Apply February 1 to appropriate departmental chair for fellowships, assistantships, by March 15 to Financial Aid Office for all need-based programs. Phone: (412)268-2086. Use FAFSA. About 100% of doctoral candidate's receive aid other than loans from School and outside sources.

DEGREE REQUIREMENTS. Determined by each department and varies by program.

FIELDS FOR DOCTORAL STUDY.
Computational and Statistical Learning.
Computer Science. Includes specializations in algorithms, combinatorics and optimization, neural basis of cognition, pure and applied logic.
Human-Computer Interaction.
Language and Information Technologies.
Robotics. Includes specialization in neural basis of cognition.
Software Engineering.

FIELDS FOR MASTER'S STUDY.
Computational Finance.
Computer-Assisted Language Learning.
Computer Science.
Distance Education.
Electronic Commerce.
Entertainment Technology.
Human–Computer Interaction.
Information Networking.
Information Technology.

Knowledge Discovery and Data Mining.
Language and Information Technologies.
Machine Learning.
Robotics.
Software Engineering.

Tepper School of Business
Web site: www.tepper.cmu.edu

Established 1949. Private control. Accredited programs: M.B.A.; recognized Ph.D. Located on main campus and in New York City; suburban environment. Six mini-semesters per year. Special programs: foreign exchange programs (Austria, France, Germany, Japan, United Kingdom), internships, cooperative program.

Annual M.B.A., Ph.D. tuition: full-time $45,250; for M.S.C.F.: $45,250 Pittsburgh, $45,250 New York City. No on-campus housing available. Estimated annual budget for tuition, room and board and personal expenses: approximately $72,700.

Enrollment: total full-time 442, part-time 165 (men 80%, women 20%). Faculty: 90 full-time, 32 part-time; 95% with Ph.D./D.B.A. Degrees conferred: M.B.A. (Concentrations in Accounting, Decision Sciences, Economics, Entrepreneurship, Finance, Health Care Management, Human Resource Management, International Business/Management, Management, Management Information Systems, Marketing, Production and Operations Management and Information Management/Systems, Organizational Behavior, Quantitative Analysis, Real Estate, Strategic Planning), M.S.C.F. (Computational Finance), M.B.A.-J.D. (University of Pittsburgh), Ph.D.

ADMISSION REQUIREMENTS. All applicants should have a bachelor's degree from a recognized institution of higher education and a strong mathematics background. Early applications are encouraged for both admission and financial aid consideration. Does not accept transfer students. Submit an application, GMAT results (will accept GMAT test results from the last five years, latest acceptable date is January), official transcripts from each undergraduate/graduate school attended, three letters of evaluation, two essays, current résumé/work history, and a one-page cover letter highlighting objectives and qualifications (prefers at least four years of work experience), and an application fee of $100 to the Director of Admissions. In addition, international students (whose native language is other than English) should submit a TOEFL score, certified translations and evaluations of all official transcripts, recommendation should be in English or with certified translations, proof of health certificate, and proof of sufficient financial resources for two years of academic study. For current information and/or modification in admission requirements the international applicant's contact telephone number is (412)268-7055. Interviews are strongly encouraged either on campus, a field interview or a telephone interview prior to the admissions committee reviewing completed application. Application timetable: completed applications received by November 13 are notified by December 18, applications received by January 15, notification by February 19, applications received by March 12, notification by April 19, applications received after March 12 are notified on a rolling basis. Admits Fall only. Admissions Office phone: (800)850-GSIA; (412)268-2273; fax: (412)268-4209.

ADMISSION REQUIREMENTS FOR DOCTORAL CANDIDATES. Beginning students are admitted Fall Only. Contact the GSIA Doctoral Office at (412)268-2301 for application material and information. Submit the doctoral application, a GMAT/GRE (will accept GMAT/GRE test results from the last five years), official transcripts from each undergraduate/graduate school attended, three letters of evaluation, current résumé, statement of objectives and purpose, and application fee of $40 ($30 for online application) to the Doctoral Admission Office. In addition, international students (whose native language is other than English) should submit TOEFL scores; certified translations and evaluations of all official transcripts, recommendation should be in English or with certified translations, proof of health/immunization certificate. International students' contact: (412)268-7055. Interviews are strongly recommended. Notifications are generally completed by mid-April.

ADMISSION STANDARDS AND RANKINGS. Very selective. Median GMAT 696; median GPA 3.4 (A = 4.0). *U.S. News & World Report* ranked Tepper in the top 17 of all U.S. business schools. *BusinessWeek* listed Tepper in the top 20 of American business schools.

FINANCIAL AID. Scholarships, merit scholarship, special stipends programs for minorities, grants, fellowships, graduate assistantships, tuition waivers, internships, Federal Perkins loans, Stafford Subsidized and Unsubsidized loans, Federal W/S available. Financial aid is available for part-time study. Financial aid may be available for international students. Assistantships/fellowships may be available for joint degree candidates. Request scholarship, fellowship, assistantship information from the Graduate School. Contact the University's Financial Aid Office for current need-based financial aid information; phone: (412) 268-1242. For most financial assistance and all Federal programs submit FAFSA by February 15 (School code: E00074), also submit a NEED ACCESS form, Financial Aid Transcript, Federal Income Tax forms. Approximately 80% of students receive some form of financial assistance.

DEGREE REQUIREMENTS. For M.B.A.: 204 units (3 units equal 1 semester hour of credit), two-year full-time program, three-year part-time program; degree program must be completed in thirty-six months. For M.S.C.F.: 144 units. For M.B.A.-J.D.: four-year program. For Ph.D.: four- to five-year program; a first and a second summer research papers; qualifying exam; dissertation proposal and oral presentation, dissertation; oral defense; degree programs must be completed within seven years; students who leave at the end of the second year may receive an M.B.A.

FIELDS OF STUDY.
Accounting. Ph.D.
Business Administration. M.B.A.
Computational Finance. M.S.C.F.
Economics. Ph.D.
Finance. Ph.D.
Manufacturing and Operating Systems. Ph.D.
Marketing. Ph.D.
Operations Research. Ph.D.
Organizational Behavior and Theory. Ph.D.
Note: The following joint Ph.D. programs are available: Algorithms, Combinatorics and Optimization (with Mathematics and Computer Science Department), Mathematical Finance (with the Mathematics Department), Management of Manufacturing and Automation (with the Robotics Institute).

H. John Heinz III School of Public Policy and Management
Web site: www.heinz.cmu.edu

Annual tuition: full-time $34,600, part-time $384 per unit.
Enrollment: total full-time 237, part-time 258 (men 45%, women 55%). Faculty: 48 full-time, 30 part-time. Degrees conferred: M.S.P.P.M., M.A.M., M.P.M., M.M.M., M.S.H.C.P.M., M.S.E.T.M., Ph.D.

ADMISSION REQUIREMENTS. All applicants should have a bachelor's degree from a recognized institution of higher education. Accepts transfer students. Submit an application, GMAT or GRE, official transcripts from each undergraduate/graduate school attended, three letters of recommendation, essays, current résumé to the Director of Admission. Apply by February 1. Electronic application available. In addition, international students (whose native language is other than English) should submit a TOEFL score, certified translations and evaluations of all official transcripts, recommendations should be in English or with certified translations. Admits Fall only. Admissions Office phone: (800) 877-3498; (415)268-2164; fax: (412)268-7036; e-mail: hnzadmitt @andrew.cmu.edu.

ADMISSIONS STANDARDS. Selective. Usual minimum average: 3.0 GPA (A = 4).

FINANCIAL AID. Scholarships, full and partial fellowships, graduate assistantships, tuition waivers, internships, Federal W/S, loans. Financial aid is available for part-time study. Financial aid may be available for international students. Request scholarship, fellowship, assistantship information from the Heinz School. Contact the University's Financial Aid Office for current need-based financial aid information; phone: (412)368-7581. For most financial assistance and all Federal programs submit FAFSA by February 15 (School code: E00074). Approximately 80% of master's candidates receive some form of financial assistance. All Ph.D. candidates receive a full-tuition scholarship as long as they are in good academic standing.

DEGREE REQUIREMENTS. For master's: individualized degrees and varies by program. For Ph.D.: four- to five-year program; two interdisciplinary research papers; qualifying exam; dissertation proposal and oral presentation; dissertation; final oral defense; degree programs must be completed within seven years.

FIELDS OF STUDY.
Arts Management. Joint degree with the College of Fine Arts. M.A.M.
Entertainment Industry Management. M.E.I.M.
Health Care Policy and Management. M.S.H.C.P.M.
Medical Management. M.M.M.
Public Management. Includes specializations in management, organizational behavior, analytic techniques and communication skills. M.P.M.
Public Policy and Management. Includes concentrations in financial management and analysis, information systems, policy analysis, urban and regional economic development management. M.S.P.P.M., Ph.D.

CASE WESTERN RESERVE UNIVERSITY
Cleveland, Ohio 44106
Web site: www.cwru.edu

University formed with merger in 1967 of Case Institute of Technology (founded 1880) and Western Reserve University (1826). CGS and AAU member. Coed. Private control. Semester system. Special facilities: Alzheimer Center, Center on Aging and Health, Center for Applied Polymer Research, Center for Automation and Intelligent Systems Research, Biology Field Station, Center for Biomedical Ethics, Cancer Research Center, Case Center for Adhesives, Sealants & Coatings, Case Center for Electrochemical Sciences, Center for Management Development and Research, Center for International Health, Mental Development Center, Institute of Pathology, Cleveland Hearing and Speech Center, Electronics Design Center, Genetics Center, Health Systems Management Center, Mandel Center for Nonprofit Organizations, Center for Urban Poverty and Social Change. Joint programs with Cleveland Museum of Art, Institute of Art, Institute of Music, Cleveland Playhouse. The University's NIH ranking is 18th among all U.S. institutions with 673 awards/grants valued at $278,820,079. According to The Center at University of Florida, the University is ranked 33rd in receipt of Federal Research funds with $205,452,000 and it ranks 49th for total Uni-

versity research expenditures with $250,674,000. The University's endowment assets ranks it 29th, $1,441,819,000. In 2004, the University awarded 203 doctorates, which ranked it 72nd among all U.S. institutions eligible to award that degree. Twenty of the University's faculty members have been elected to National Honor Academies and this ranks it 45th among all U.S. institutions. The Library: approximately 2,000,000 volumes, 18,000 subscriptions. Total University enrollment: 10,000.

Tuition: per credit $1242. On-campus housing for single students only; 120 coed units. Average annual housing cost: $6000–$8500. Married students, contact University Off-Campus Housing Bureau. Phone: (216)368-3780. Day-care facilities available near campus.

School of Graduate Studies

Graduate study since 1926. Enrollment: full- and part-time 2090. University faculty teaching graduate students: full-time 1800, part-time 79. Degrees conferred; M.A., M.S., M.F.A., D.M.A., Ph.D., M.A.-J.D., M.A.-M.S.N., M.D.-Ph.D., M.A.-Ph.D., M.S.-Ph.D.

ADMISSION REQUIREMENTS. Transcripts, three letters of recommendation, statement of objectives required in support of application. GRE/MAT/GMAT required for some departments. Interview generally not required. TOEFL (minimum score 550) and affidavit of support required for international applicants. Accepts transfer applicants. Graduates of unaccredited institutions not considered. Submit both A and B Applications to Office of Graduate Studies Admissions and appropriate department at least one month prior to registration. Application fee $50. Phone: (216) 368-4390; fax: (216)368-4250.

ADMISSION STANDARDS. Very selective to very competitive. Usual minimum average: 3.0 (A = 4).

FINANCIAL AID. Fellowships, assistantships for teaching/research, partial tuition reimbursement, internships, Federal W/S, loans. Apply by March 1 (Fall), November 1 (Spring) to Office of Graduate Studies Admissions. Phone: (216)368-4530. Use FAFSA; program FAFs may be requested. About 45% of students receive aid other than loans from University and outside sources. Limited aid for part-time students.

DEGREE REQUIREMENTS. For M.A., M.S.: 27 semester hours minimum, at least 21 semester hours in residence; thesis/oral comprehensive exam (Plan A–thesis, Plan B–comprehensive exam). For M.F.A.: 60 semester hours minimum; thesis; oral and written exam. For D.M.A., Ph.D.: three years minimum beyond the bachelor's, at least one year in full-time residence; reading knowledge of one or two foreign languages and statistics for some departments; general/qualifying exam; advancement to candidacy dissertation; final oral defense.

FIELDS OF STUDY.
Accounting. Ph.D. only.
American Studies. GRE for admission.
Anatomy. GRE/Subject for admission.
Anesthesiologist Assistant. GRE for admission. M.S. only.
Anthropology. GRE for admission.
Applied Anatomy. M.S. only.
Applied Mathematics.
Art Education. M.A. only.
Art History.
Astronomy. GRE for admission. Thesis required for M.S., two languages for Ph.D.
Biochemical Research. M.S. only.
Biochemistry. GRE for admissions.
Bioethics. GRE for admission. M.A. only.
Biology. Includes zoology; GRE/Subject for admission.
Biomedical Sciences (BSTP). Ph.D. only.
Biophysics and Bioengineering. Ph.D. only.

Cell Biology. Ph.D. only.
Cell Physiology. Ph.D. only.
Ceramics and Materials Sciences.
Chemistry. GRE/Subject for admission.
Clinical Psychology (Adult). Ph.D. only.
Clinical Psychology (Child). Ph.D. only.
Communication Sciences. Includes speech-language, pathology, and audiology. GRE for admission.
Comparative Literature. M.A. only.
Computer and Information Sciences.
Contemporary Dance. M.F.A.
Developmental Psychology. Ph.D. only.
Early Music Performance. M.A., D.M.A.
Economics. Ph.D. only.
Engineering. M.E. only.
Engineering. Includes aerospace, biomedical, chemical, civil computer, electrical, engineering mechanics, fluid and thermal, macromolecular science, materials science and engineering, mechanical, system & control. GRE for admission. M.S., Ph.D.
English. GRE for admission.
Entrepreneurship. Ph.D. only.
Environmental Health Sciences. GRE for admission.
Epidemiology. M.P.H. only.
Epidemiology and Biostatistics. GRE for Admission.
Experimental Psychology. GRE for admission. Ph.D. only.
Genetics. GRE General/Subject for admission. Ph.D. only.
Genetic Counseling. M.S. only.
Geological Sciences. GRE/Subject for admission.
Health Systems Management. Ph.D. only.
History. Includes history of science and technology. GRE for admission.
Information Systems. Ph.D. only.
Labor and Human Resource Policy. Ph.D.
Management Policy. Ph.D. only.
Marketing. Ph.D. only.
Mathematics. GRE/Subject for Admission.
Medical Scientist (MSTP). M.D.-Ph.D. only.
Molecular Biology and Microbiology. GRE/Subject for admission. Ph.D. only.
Molecular Medicine. Ph.D. only.
Molecular Virology. GRE/Subject for admission. Ph.D. only.
Music. Include music history and research, Ph.D. in Musicology, D.M.A. in performance or composition.
Music Education. M.A., Ph.D.
Neurosciences. GRE/Subject for admission. Ph.D. only.
Nursing. GRE for admission. Ph.D. only.
Nutrition. Includes dietetic internship program.
Operations. GRE for admission. Ph.D. only.
Organizational Behavior. Ph.D. only.
Pathology. GRE for admission. Ph.D. only.
Pharmacology. GRE for admission. Ph.D. only.
Physics.
Physiology and Biophysics. GRE for admission. Ph.D. only.
Political Science. GRE for admission.
Psychology. GRE for admission.
Public Health. M.P.H.
Public Health Nutrition. M.S. only.
Social Welfare. M.S.W. required; MAT or GRE for admission. Ph.D. only.
Sociology. GRE/Subject for admission. Ph.D. only.
Statistics. GRE for admission.
Systems Physiology. Ph.D. only.
Theater Arts. Includes acting, contemporary dance. M.F.A. only.
World Literature. M.A.

Mandel School of Applied Social Sciences
Web site: www.mass.case.edu

Established 1916. Graduate study only. Semester system. Tuition: per credit $994. On-campus housing available for single students. Apply to Director of Residence Life. Phone: (216)368-3780.

Enrollment: full-time 347, part-time 12. Faculty: full-time 35, part-time 40. Degrees conferred: M.S.S.A., Ph.D., M.S.S.A.-M.A.

ADMISSION REQUIREMENTS. Transcripts, letters of reference required in support of School's application. GRE/MAT required for Ph.D. and applicants with G.P.A. below 2.7 (A = 4). Interview optional. TOEFL required of foreign students. Accepts transfer applicants. Graduates of unaccredited institutions not considered. Apply to Mandel School of Applied Social Sciences at least two months prior to registration. Fall admission only. Application fee $50 (not required of foreign students). Phone: (800)863-6772, ext. 2280; fax: (216)368-5065; e-mail: msassadmit@po.cwru.edu.

ADMISSION STANDARDS. Usual minimum average: 2.7 (A = 4). Personal suitability for human services and experience evaluated.

FINANCIAL AID. Annual awards from institutional fund: scholarships, MSASS grants, Federal W/S, loans. Apply to Admissions Office of the School by April 27. Phone: (216)368-22103; fax: (216)368-5065. Use FAFSA. About 60% of students receive aid other than loans from School and outside sources.

DEGREE REQUIREMENTS. For M.S.S.A. (Master of Science in Social Administration): 60 credits minimum. For Ph.D.: 54 credits minimum beyond the master's; general/qualifying exam; advancement to candidacy; dissertation; final oral exam.

FIELDS OF STUDY.
Adult Mental Health Specialization.
Aging Specialization.
Alcohol and Other Drug Abuse Specialization.
Child/Adolescent Mental Health Specialization.
Children, Youth and Families Specialization.
Community and Social Development Concentration.
Health Specialization.
School Social Work. Cooperative program with Baldwin-Wallace College. Concentration in children, youth and families only. M.S.S.A. only.

School of Dental Medicine
Web site: dental.case.edu

Organized in 1892. Located in the Health Science Center since 1969.

Annual tuition: $45,265. On-campus housing available. Average academic year housing and personal expenses: approximately $15,786. Contact Director of Housing for more information. Phone: (216)368-3780. Total cost for all other first-year expenses: $13,000.

Enrollment: first-year class 75, total full-time 337 (men 77%, women 23%, minorities 19%, state resident 25%). Faculty: full-time 49, part-time 230. Degrees conferred: D.D.S., M.S.D., D.D.S.-M.D. (Oral and Maxillofacial Surgery), D.D.S.-M.S.D., Certificate.

ADMISSION REQUIREMENTS. AADSAS report, transcripts, DAT, letters of recommendation required in support of application. Interview by invitation only. Applicants must have completed at least two years of college study, prefer four years of college work. TOEFL required of international students. Accepts transfer applicants. Apply to Committee on Admissions after June 1, before February 1. Rolling admission process. Fall admission only. Application fee $45 (not required of foreign students). Phone: (216)368-2460; fax: (216)368-3204.

ADMISSION STANDARDS. Competitive. Mean UGPA: 3.4 (A = 4), mean DAT Academic: 18.6; PAT: 18.0. Accepts 10–15% of total annual applicants. Approximately 20% are state residents.

FINANCIAL AID. Scholarships, grants, tuition waivers, Federal W/S, loans. Students should not depend on aid from School for first semester of attendance. Apply by April 30 to Financial Aid

Office. Phone: (216)368-3256. Use FAFSA. About 85% of students receive some aid from school and outside sources.

DEGREE REQUIREMENTS. For D.D.S.: satisfactory completion of 46-month program, at least 36 months in residence. For M.S.: see Graduate School listing above.

FIELDS OF GRADUATE STUDY.
Advanced Education in General Dentistry. Certificate.
Endodontics. M.S.D.
Oral and Maxillofacial Surgery.
Orthodontics. M.S.D.
Periodontics. M.S.D.

School of Law
Web site: www.law.cwru.edu

Established 1892. ABA approved since 1923. AALS Charter member. Private control. Semester system. Special Facilities: Frederick K. Cox International Law Center, Institute for Global Security Law and Policy, Canada–United States Law Institute, Center for Business Law and Regulation, The Center For Professional Ethics, Center for the Interdisciplinary Study of Conflict and Dispute Resolution, Center for Law, Technology, and the Arts, The Law-Medicine Center, Milton A. Kramer Law Clinic Center. Library 402,678 volumes, 5241 subscriptions; has LEXIS and access to more than 700 databases.

Annual tuition: $33,384, part-time $1288 per credit; LL.M. $34,700. No on-campus housing available. Total average cost for off-campus living: $16,240. Contact Director of Housing for off-campus information.

Enrollment: first-year class 220; total full-time 673 (men 59%, women 41%, minorities 17%). Faculty: full-time 75, part-time 130. Student to faculty ratio 14.7 to 1. Degrees conferred: J.D., J.D.-M.B.A. (Management), J.D.-M.S.S.A. (Social Work), J.D.-M.A. (Bioethics, Legal History), J.D.-M.D., J.D-M.N.O. (Nonprofit Organizations), J.D.-M.P.H., LL.M. (Taxation), LL.M. (U.S. Legal Studies–only for persons who have completed basic legal education and received a university level law degree in another country).

ADMISSION REQUIREMENTS. LSDAS report, transcripts, LSAT (no later than December) required in support of application. Early Decision single choice available (apply by November 1). Electronic application available. Interviews not required. Accepts transfer applicants on a space-available basis only. Graduates of unaccredited colleges not considered. Apply to Director of Admissions after July, before February 1. Fall admission only. Application fee $40. Phone: (800)756-0036; fax: (216)368-1042; e-mail: lawadmissions@case.edu.

ADMISSION STANDARDS. Selective. Accepts 25% of total annual applicants. Number of applicants 2768; number of acceptance 699; number enrolled 200; LSAT (75% of class have a score at or above 157); GPA (75% of class have a GPA at or above 3.13). *U.S. News & World Report* ranking is tied for 53rd of all law schools.

FINANCIAL AID. Scholarships, grants, loans. Apply by May I to Director of Admissions. Phone: (877)889-4279. Use FAFSA (School code: E00082). School has a Loan Repayment Assistance program. About 48% of students receive aid other than School loans.

DEGREE REQUIREMENTS. For J.D.: satisfactory completion of three-year, 88 semester hour program. For LL.M. (Taxation): satisfactory completion of one-year, 24-credit program. For LL.M. (U.S. Legal Studies): satisfactory completion of 30-credit program, at least two semesters in residence, mentorship with a Cleveland law firm or corporation.

Weatherhead School of Management
Web site: www.weatherhead.cwru.edu

School established with the federation of the Division of Organizational Sciences and School of Business in 1967. Accredited programs: M.B.A., Accounting; recognized Ph.D. Semester system. Special programs: foreign exchange programs, Foreign Study at International Management Center, Budapest, Hungary.

Annual tuition: full-time $26,460, part-time $1102.50 per credit. On-campus rooms and apartments available for single students only. Estimated annual budget for tuition, room, board and personal expenses: approximately $35,500.

Enrollment: total full-time 536, part-time 671 (men 65%, women 35%). Faculty: 85 full-time, 20 part-time; 15% women; 97% with Ph.D./D.B.A. Degrees conferred: (full-time, part-time, day, evening) (Concentrations in Accounting, Economics, Entrepreneurship, Finance, Health Care Management, Human Resource Management, International Management, Management, Management Information Systems, Marketing, Nonprofit Management, Operations Management, Organizational Behavior/Development, Technology Management), E.M.B.A. (weekends only, alternating Fridays, Saturdays), M.S.M.I.S., M.N.O. (Nonprofit Organizations), M.B.A.-J.D., M.B.A.-M.D., M.B.A.-M.I.M. (with Thunderbird, the American Graduate School of International Management), M.B.A.-M.S., M.B.A.-M.S.M.S. (Management Science), M.B.A.-M.S.N. (Nursing), M.Acc., Ph.D. (Concentrations in Accountancy, Banking and Finance, Economics, Labor and Human Resource Policy, Management Information Systems, Management Policy, Marketing, Operations Research, Organizational Management), E.D.M. (Executive Doctorate in Management).

ADMISSION REQUIREMENTS. All applicants should have a bachelor's degree from a recognized institution of higher education, a strong mathematics background required. Beginning students are admitted Fall and Spring. U.S. citizens apply by February 1 (Fall), December 15 (Spring), international students apply by April (Fall). Submit an application, GMAT results, official transcripts from each undergraduate/graduate school attended, two letters of recommendation, essays, current employment résumé (prefers at least four years of work experience), and an application fee of $55 to the Director of Admission. In addition, international students (whose native language is other than English) should submit a TOEFL (minimum score 580) report, certified translations and evaluations of all official transcripts, recommendation should be in English or with certified translations. For current information and/or modification in admission requirements the international applicant's contact telephone number is: (216)368-2069. On-campus visits are encouraged; interviews are required for all full-time applicants prior to the admissions committee reviewing completed application. Joint degree applicants must apply to and be accepted to both schools/programs; contact the admissions office for current information and specific admissions requirements. Rolling admission process, notification is made within 6 weeks of receipt of completed application and supporting documents. Admissions Office phone: M.B.A. (216)368-2030; fax: (216)368-5548; Accounting (216)368-2065.

ADMISSION REQUIREMENTS FOR DOCTORAL CANDIDATES. Contact the Ph.D. Program coordinator for an application and current information. A master's degree in applicant's intended major required. Beginning students are admitted Fall only. U.S. citizens apply by February 1 (Fall), international students apply by January 1. Submit a Ph.D. application, a GMAT (will accept GMAT test results from the last five years), official transcripts from each undergraduate/graduate school attended, three letters of recommendation, essays, current résumé, statement of purpose, and application fee of $55 to the Director of Admissions. In addition, international students (whose native language is other than English) should submit a TOEFL (minimum score 600) report; certified translations and evaluations of all official transcripts, recommendation should be in English or with certified translations, proof of health/immunization certificate. International student contact: (216)368-2069. Interviews strongly encouraged prior to the admissions committee reviewing completed application. Notifications are generally completed by mid-April.

ADMISSION STANDARDS. Selective. Median GMAT: 603; median GPA: 3.2 (A = 4.0). *BusinessWeek* listed School in the top 50 American business schools.

FINANCIAL AID. Scholarships, Enterprise Scholars, grants, fellowships, assistantships, Federal W/S, loans. Financial aid is available for part-time study. Assistantships/fellowships may be available for joint degree candidates. Apply by April 1. Request scholarship, fellowship, assistantship information from the School of Management. Contact the University's Financial Aid Office for current need-based financial aid information; phone: (216) 368-2030. Submit FAFSA (School code: 003137), also submit Financial Aid Transcript, Federal Income Tax forms. Approximately 90% of current students receive some form of financial assistance.

DEGREE REQUIREMENTS. For M.B.A. (nonbusiness majors): 64 credit program including 18 elective credits, two-year program; degree program must be completed in six years. For M.B.A. (recent business majors): 48 credit program; degree program must be completed in six years. For E.M.B.A.: 45 credit two-year program. For M.Acc.: 36 credit program. For M.S.M.I.S., M.N.O.: 42 credit program. For M.B.A.-M.I.M.: 68–78 credit program. For M.B.A.-M.S.N.: 78–104 credit program. For M.B.A.-J.D.: 107 credit program; generally three-and-one-half- to five-year program. For Ph.D.: three- to five-year program; general exam; candidacy; teaching apprenticeship; dissertation proposal and oral defense; dissertation; oral defense.

School of Medicine
Web site: casemed.case.edu

Organized in 1843; affiliated with the Cleveland Clinic Lerner College of Medicine in 2004. Private control. Semester system. Library: 150,000 volumes, 3000 subscriptions. The University's NIH ranking is 18th among all U.S. institutions with 673 awards/grants worth $278,820,079.

Annual tuition: $40,752. Off-campus housing available. Average figure for all other expenses: $17,760.

Enrollment: first-year class 167 (12 MSTP); total full-time 652 (men 55%, women 45%, minorities 13%, state residents 52%). Faculty: full-time approximately 1780, part-time 700. Degrees conferred: M.D., M.D.-M.B.A. M.D.-M.S., M.D.-Ph.D., M.S.T.P.

ADMISSION REQUIREMENTS. AMCAS report, transcripts, MCAT, interview (at the discretion of Admission Committee), three letters of recommendation, a secondary application required in support of application. Applicants must have completed at least three years of college study. At least 50% are residents of Ohio. Accepts transfer applicants. Does have EDP; approximately 20–25 per year. Apply to AMCAS after June 1, before November 1. Application fee $85. Phone: (216)368-3450; fax: (216)368-6011.

ADMISSION STANDARDS. Very competitive. Accepts about 9% of all applicants. Number of applications 4975 (4241 out-of-state); number interviewed 1027 (811 out-of-state); number of acceptance 427 (347 out-of-state); number enrolled 167 (123 out-of-state). Mean Composite MCAT 11.0; mean UGPA 3.69. *U.S. News & World Report* ranking is in the top 21 of all medical research schools, 28th in Primary Care.

FINANCIAL AID. Scholarships, research fellowships, loans. Submit data for an analysis of need by NEED ACCESS to Office of the Dean of the School before May 1. Phone: (216)368-3666.

Use FAFSA (school code 000079). About 30% of students receive aid other than loans from School, 75% from all sources.

DEGREE REQUIREMENTS. For M.D.: satisfactory completion of either four-year program or five-year program at Cleveland Clinic, at least three years in residence; must take Step 2 of USMLE and obtain a passing score on Step 2 of USMLE to graduate. Combined M.D.-M.S., M.D.-Ph.D. programs offered in most basic science departments. See Graduate School and School of Management listings above for master's or Ph.D. requirements.

FIELDS OF GRADUATE STUDY.
Biochemistry.
Biology.
Biomedical Engineering.
Cell Biology.
Chemistry.
Genetics and Molecular Epidemiology.
Genetics: Molecular and Developmental and Human Genetics.
Neurosciences.
Nutritional Sciences.
Pathology (Tracks in Cancer Biology, Immunology, Molecular and Cellular Basis of Disease).
Pharmacological Sciences.
Physiology and Biophysics.

Frances Payne Bolton School of Nursing (44106-4804)
Web site: www.fpb.cwru.edu

Established 1898. Semester system.
Tuition: per credit $1330.
Graduate enrollment: full-time 261, part-time 220. Faculty: full-time 87, part-time 14. Degrees conferred: M.S.N., M.S.N.-M.A. (Bioethics, Anthropology), M.S.N.-M.B.A., M.S.N.-M.P.H., N.D.

ADMISSION REQUIREMENTS. Transcripts, eligible for RN license in Ohio, three letters of reference, résumé, essay, MAT or GRE for M.S.N., GRE for N.D., Ph.D. required in support of School's application. Interview strongly recommended; required for N.D. applicants. TOEFL required for international applicants. Accepts transfer applicants. Graduates of unaccredited institutions not considered. Apply to Assistant Dean by June 1 (Fall), October 1 (Spring), March 1 (Summer). Application fee $75. Phone: (216)368-2529; e-mail: admissions@fpb.case.edu.

ADMISSION STANDARDS. Selective. Usual minimum average: 3.0 (A = 4).

FINANCIAL AID. Scholarships, grants, fellowships, research assistantships, traineeships, teaching assistantships, partial tuition waivers, Federal W/S, loans. Approved for VA benefits. Apply when requesting admission but prior to June 30. Phone: (216)368-2183; e-mail: cfq@po.case.edu. Use FAFSA. About 85% of students receive financial assistance. Aid available for part-time students.

DEGREE REQUIREMENTS. For M.S.N.: 36 semester hours minimum; thesis or research project. For N.D.: completion of four levels of program; Licensure exam; thesis. For M.S.N.-M.A.: 45 credit hours, a minimum of 18 credits in each school. For M.S.N.-M.B.A.: 72 credits, a minimum of 30 credits in each school.

FIELDS OF STUDY.
Acute Care Nurse Practitioner. Includes flight nursing, cardiovascular nursing.
Adult Nurse Practitioner. Includes infection control.
Community Health Nursing. Includes infection control.
Family Nurse Practitioner.
Gerontological Nurse Practitioner.
Medical Surgical Clinical Specialist.
Neonatal Nurse Practitioner.

Nurse Anesthesia.
Nurse Midwifery.
Nursing Informatics.
Pediatric Nurse Practitioner.
Psychiatric Mental Health Nurse.
Women's Health Nurse Practitioner.

THE CATHOLIC UNIVERSITY OF AMERICA

Washington, D.C. 20064
Web site: www.cua.edu

Founded 1887. CGS and AAU member. Coed. Private control. Semester system. University participates in Joint Graduate Consortium with American, Georgetown, George Washington, Howard Universities. Special facilities: Center for Advanced Training in Cell and Molecular Biology, Center for Global Standard Analysis, Latin American Center for Graduate Studies in Music, Life Cycle Institute; Center for the Study of Youth Development, Computer Center—VT320 terminals at various campus locations; fiber optics network; two VAX 4000 computers; laboratories for fluid mechanics, solid state, solid mechanics, acoustics, member Folger Institute of Renaissance and Eighteenth-Century Studies, Institute of Christian Oriental Research, Center for Service-Learning. Library: more than 1,600,000 volumes, 12,000 subscriptions. More than 1000 computers on campus for general student use. Total University enrollment: 6130.

Annual tuition: full-time $24,800, part-time $940 per credit. On-campus housing for single graduate students. Annual cost: $9838 (including board). Contact Director of Housing for both on- and off-campus housing information. Phone: (202)319-5615; e-mail: housing@cua.edu/och.

School of Arts and Sciences

Graduate study since 1895. Enrollment: full-time 163, part-time 377. School faculty teaching graduate students: full-time 167, part-time 87. Degrees conferred: M.A., M.F.A., M.S., Ph.D.

ADMISSION REQUIREMENTS. Transcripts, GRE, two letters of recommendation required in support of application. GRE Subject/MAT/interviews required by some departments. TOEFL required of international applicants. Accepts transfer applicants. Apply to Office of Graduate Admissions at least two months prior to registration. Priority deadline is February 1. Application fee $55. Phone: (202)319-5305.

ADMISSION STANDARDS. Competitive for most departments, selective for others. Usual minimum average: 3.0 (A = 4).

FINANCIAL AID. Annual awards from institutional funds: scholarships, fellowships, teaching assistantships, research assistantships, Federal W/S, loans. Apply by February 1 to Committee on Fellowships and Scholarships, to appropriate department head for assistantships; to Office of Financial Aid for all other programs. Phone: (202)319-5185. Use FAFSA. About 50% of students receive aid other than loans from University and outside sources.

DEGREE REQUIREMENTS. For master's: 30–36 semester hours, 24 credits in residence; thesis/nonthesis/two research papers option; reading knowledge of one language for some majors; final comprehensive exam. For M.F.A.: same as above except no language and creative project instead of thesis. For Ph.D.: 53 credits minimum including the master's, at least 4 full-time semesters in residence; comprehensive exam; candidacy; reading knowledge of one foreign language; dissertation; final oral exam.

FIELDS OF STUDY.
Accounting. M.S.

Anthropology. Includes cultural and archaeological. M.A., Ph.D.
Biology. Includes cell and microbial, clinical laboratory science. M.S., Ph.D.
Chemistry. Includes chemical education. M.A.
Comparative Literature. M.A., Ph.D.
Drama. Includes acting. directing, playwriting, theater history and criticism. M.A., M.F.A.
Early Christian Studies. M.A., Ph.D.
Economics. Includes financial, industrial organization/regulation of business, international, international political, public. M.A.
Education. Includes administration, curriculum, foundation and policy studies, Catholic leadership, counseling, ESL, learning and instruction, special (M.A.); administration and policy studies, clinical administration and policy studies, educational psychology (Ph.D.).
English Language and Literature. M.A., Ph.D.
Financial Management. M.A.
Greek and Latin. Includes classics. M.A.
History. M.A.
Human Resource Management. M.A.
Irish Studies. M.A.
Medieval and Byzantine Studies. M.A., Ph.D.
Microbiology. M.S., Ph.D.
Modern Languages and Literature. Includes French, Italian, Spanish, romance languages and literature, romance philology (M.A.); French, Spanish, romance languages and literature (Ph.D.).
Physics. Includes astrophysics, condensed matter, material science, nuclear, statistical, vitreous state. M.S., Ph.D.
Politics. Includes American government, congressional studies, international affairs, international political economics, political theory, world politics (M.A.); American government, political theory, world politics (Ph.D.).
Psychology. Includes general, human factors (M.A.); applied-experimental, clinical, human development (Ph.D.).
Rhetoric Program. M.A., Ph.D.
Semitic and Egyptian Languages and Literature. M.A.
Sociology. M.A., Ph.D.

School of Engineering

Web site: www.ee.cua.edu

Graduate study since 1896. Semester system. Annual tuition: $24,800, per credit hour $1090. On-campus housing available. For costs: See University listing above.

Enrollment: full-time 22, part-time 131. School faculty: full-time 26, part-time 23. Degrees conferred: M.S.E., D.Arch., D.Eng., Ph.D.

ADMISSION REQUIREMENTS. Transcripts, two letters of recommendation required in support of School's application. GRE strongly recommended; required by some departments. TOEFL required of international applicants. Interview not required. Accepts transfer applicants. Graduates of unaccredited colleges not considered. Apply to Office of Graduate Admissions by February 1. Fall admission only. Application fee $55. Phone: (202) 319-5305; fax: (202)319-6533.

ADMISSION STANDARDS. Selective. Usual minimum average: 2.5 (A = 4).

FINANCIAL AID. Annual awards from institutional funds: scholarships, teaching assistantships, research assistantships, Federal W/S, loans. Apply by March 1 to the Registrar for scholarships, to the Dean for assistantships, to Financial Aid Office for all other programs. Phone: (202)319-5185. Use FAFSA. About 50% of full-time students receive aid other than loans from School and outside sources. No aid other than loans for part-time students.

DEGREE REQUIREMENTS. For master's: 30 semester hours minimum, at least 18 in residence; thesis/nonthesis option. For D.Eng., Ph.D.: 54 hours minimum beyond the bachelor's, at least four semesters in residence; qualifying exam; comprehensive exam; candidacy; dissertation; final written/oral exams.

FIELDS OF STUDY

Biomedical Engineering. Includes cell/tissue engineering, biomechanics, biosignal processing and medical imaging, home care technologies, rehabilitation engineering, telemedicine. M.B.E., M.S.E., D.Eng., Ph.D.

Civil Engineering. Includes environmental engineering and management, fluid and solid mechanics, geotechnical, management of construction, structures and structural mechanics, systems. M.C.E., D.Eng., Ph.D.

Electrical Engineering and Computer Science. Includes communication systems and networks, microwave, optics and materials, robotics and intelligent control, signal and image processing, software engineering, computer graphics. M.E.E., M.S.C.S., D.Eng, Ph.D.

Engineering Management. M.S.E.

Mechanical Engineering. Includes applied energy systems, biomechanics, controls and applied mechanics, dynamics, control and mechanics, environmental engineering, mechanical design and structural mechanics, thermal and fluid sciences (M.M.E., M.S.E.); controls and applied mechanics, thermal and fluid sciences (D.Eng., Ph.D.).

Columbus School of Law

Founded 1897. ABA approved since 1925. AALS member since 1921. Semester system. Special facilities: Center for Law, Philosophy and Culture, Institute for Communication Law, the Comparative and International Law Institute. Law library: 402,845 volumes, 5276 subscriptions; has LEXIS, NEXIS, WESTLAW, DIALOG.

Tuition: full-time $32,555, part-time $24,820. Total cost for all other expenses: $23,395.

Enrollment: first-year class 242 (day), 87 (night); total full-time 604, part-time 302 (men 52%, women 48%, minorities 18%). Faculty: full-time 42, part-time 66. Student to faculty ratio 16.3 to 1. Degrees conferred: J.D., J.D.-M.A., J.D.-M.L.S., J.D.-M.S.W.

ADMISSION REQUIREMENTS. LSDAS Law School report, transcripts, two character references, LSAT (not later than December), two letters of recommendation, bachelor's degree required in support of application. Interview not required. TOEFL required for all international applicants. Accepts transfer applicants. Applicants from unaccredited institutions not considered. Apply to the Dean after October 1, before March 1. Admits first-year students Fall only. Application fee $65. Phone: (202)319-5151; e-mail: admissions@law.edu.

ADMISSION STANDARDS. Selective. Accepts 32% of total annual applicants. Number of full-time applicants 2716, part-time 786; number of full-time acceptance 860, part-time 200; number enrolled full-time 242, part-time 87; LSAT (75% of full-time class have a score at or above 156, part-time 154); GPA (75% of full-time class have a GPA at or above 3.06, part-time 2.99). *U.S. News & World Report* ranking is tied for 97th of all law schools.

FINANCIAL AID. Scholarships, grants, Federal W/S, loans. Apply to the Financial Aid Office by March 15. Phone: (202)319-5143. Use FAFSA. About 37% of full-time students receive aid other than loans from School.

DEGREE REQUIREMENTS. For J.D.: 84 semester hours in residence. Advanced standing from other law schools will be considered. Combined programs available in economics, accounting, history, management, philosophy, psychology, politics, social work, library science. For degree requirements: see Graduate School listing above.

School of Library and Information Science

Web site: slis.cua.edu

Annual tuition: full-time $24,800, per credit $1092. On-campus housing available. See University listing above.

Enrollment: full-time 29, part-time 218. Graduate faculty: full-time 6, part-time 15. Degrees conferred: M.L.S., M.L.S.-J.D., M.L.S.-M.A.

ADMISSION REQUIREMENTS. Transcripts, GRE, two letters of recommendation, statement of purpose required in support of School's application. TOEFL (minimum score 550) required for international applicants. Interviews may be requested. Apply to Office of Graduate Admissions, attention SLIS Admissions at least forty-five days prior to beginning of semester. Application fee $65. Phone: (202)319-5057; fax (202)319-5199.

ADMISSION STANDARDS. Competitive. Usual minimum average: 3.0 (A = 4).

FINANCIAL AID. Scholarships (awarded for Fall admission only), research assistantships, teaching assistantships, Federal W/S, loans. Apply to Graduate Financial Aid Office by February 1. Phone: (202)319-5307. Use FAFSA. Aid is available for part-time study.

DEGREE REQUIREMENTS. For M.L.S.: 36 credit program, at least 30 credits in residence; computer competency; comprehensive exam.

FIELDS OF STUDY

Archives and Records Management.
Biomedical Information.
Book Arts.
Information Management.
Information Systems.
Law Librarianship.
Library and Information Services.
Music Librarianship.
School Library Media Services.
Services for Children and Young Adults.
Special Collections.

The Benjamin T. Rome School of Music

Web site: www.cua.edu

Graduate study since 1887. School established 1950. Annual tuition: full-time $24,800, per credit $1090. On-campus housing available. See University listing above.

Enrollment: full-time 54, part-time 82. Graduate faculty: full-time 16, part-time 18. Degrees conferred: M.A., M.M., M.L.M., Ph.D., D.M.A., M.A.-M.S.L.S.

ADMISSION REQUIREMENTS. Transcripts, two letters of recommendation required in support of School's application. Additional requirements vary by program (performance proficiency, recital, original composition, research paper). TOEFL required for international applicants. GRE and interview recommended for some programs. GRE required for University scholarship consideration. Apply to the Office of Graduate Admission at least forty-five days prior to beginning of semester. Application fee $65. Phone: (202)319-5305; fax: (202)319-6533.

ADMISSION STANDARDS. Competitive. Usual minimum average: 3.0 (A = 4).

FINANCIAL AID. Scholarships, research assistantships, teaching assistantships, performance awards, Federal W/S, loans. Apply to Dean and Financial Aid Office by February 1. Phone: (202)319-5185. Use FAFSA and University's FAF.

DEGREE REQUIREMENTS. For master's: 30–36 credits, at least one year in residence; language and thesis for M.A.; thesis optional for M.S.Mus.Ed.; performance for M.M. For D.M.A. (degree individualized): 54 credits beyond master's, at least two years in residence; comprehensive exam; candidacy; dissertation; composition/recital. For Ph.D.: 54 credits minimum, at least three years in residence; two foreign languages; comprehensive exam in both a major and minor field; candidacy; dissertation; written/oral exam.

FIELDS OF STUDY
Liturgical Music. M.L.M.
Music. Includes accompanying and chamber music (piano), composition, instrumental conducting, orchestral instruments (violin, viola, cello, string bass, solo woodwinds and bass instruments, percussion, harp, classical guitar), organ, harpsichord, piano, piano pedagogy, vocal pedagogy, vocal performance. M.M., D.M.A.
Music Education. M.M.
Music History. Ph.D.
Music Performance. Ph.D.
Music Theory, Ph.D.
Musicology. Includes history, theory. M.A.
Note: A concentration in Latin American Music is available in cooperation with the School's Latin American Center for Graduate Studies in Music.

School of Nursing

Graduate study since 1951. Semester system. Annual tuition: full-time $24,800, per credit $1090.

Enrollment: full-time 25, part-time 57. School faculty: full-time 26, part-time 5. Degrees conferred: M.S.N., M.S.N.-M.A. (Health Services Management with George Washington University), D.N.P., Ph.D. Certificates.

ADMISSION REQUIREMENTS. Transcripts, a license to practice nursing in a state or jurisdiction of the U.S., three letters of recommendation, GRE required in support of School's application. TOEFL (minimum score 550) required for international applicants. Interview for some majors. Accepts transfer applicants. Graduates of unaccredited institutions not considered. Apply to School's Admissions Office by February 1 (Fall); November 1 (Spring), April 1 (Summer). Application fee $65. Phone: (202) 319-5305; fax: (202)319-6533.

ADMISSION STANDARDS. Selective. Usual minimum average: 3.0 (A = 4).

FINANCIAL AID. Partial scholarships, internships, Federal traineeships, Federal W/S, loans. Apply to Dean and Financial Aid Office by April 1. Use FAFSA. Phone: (202)319-5307; fax: (202)319-5573.

DEGREE REQUIREMENTS. For M.S.N.: 30 semester hours; candidacy; thesis/nonthesis option; comprehensive exam. For M.S.N.-M.A.: 61 semester hours required. For certificates: varies by program, at least 18 semester hours. For Ph.D.: 70-credit program, full- or part-time study; comprehensive exam; dissertation. For D.N.P.: 34–37 credits beyond the master's, full- or part-time study.

FIELDS OF STUDY.
Adult Health Clinical Nurse Specialist/Nurse Educator.
Adult Nurse Practitioner.
Community/Public Health Nurse Specialist Educator.
Family Nurse Practitioner.
Geriatric Nurse Practitioner.
Immigrant, Refugee and Global Health Clinical Nurse Specialist.
Pediatric Nurse Practitioner.
Psychiatric-Mental Health Clinical Nurse Specialist.

School of Philosophy

Founded 1895. Annual tuition: $24,800. Off-campus housing available.

Graduate enrollment: full-time 47, part-time 81. School faculty: full-time 17, part-time 10. Degrees conferred: M.A., Ph.L., Ph.D.

ADMISSION REQUIREMENTS. Transcripts, statement of intent, three letters of recommendation, GRE required in support of School's application. TOEFL required for foreign applicants. Interview not required. Accepts transfer applicants. Apply to Office of Graduate Admission, at least one month in advance of registration day. Application fee $65. Phone: (202)319-5305.

ADMISSION STANDARDS. Very competitive. Usual minimum average: 3.0 (A = 4).

FINANCIAL AID. Scholarships, research fellowships, teaching assistantships, Federal W/S, loans. Apply by February 1 to the Dean for scholarships fellowships and assistantships, to the Financial Aid Office for all other programs. Phone: (202)319-5307; fax: (202)319-5573. Use FAFSA. About 50% of students receive aid other than loans from School and outside sources. Aid other than loans sometimes available for part-time students.

DEGREE REQUIREMENTS. For M.A., Ph.L.: 24 semester hours in full-time residence; transfer credit not accepted for M.A.; thesis and reading knowledge of one foreign language; final written/oral exam. For Ph.D.: 60 semester hours minimum beyond the bachelor's, at least 36 in residence; three Graduate Reading Program exams; preliminary exam; candidacy; reading knowledge of two foreign languages; dissertation, final oral exam.

FIELDS OF STUDY.
Ancient Philosophy.
Aquinas.
Husserl; Heidegger.
Logic and Epistemology.
Medieval Philosophy.
Metaphysics.
Modern Philosophy.
Moral Philosophy.
Phenomenology.
Philosophical Anthropology.
Philosophy of Science.

School of Theology and Religious Studies

Formal study since 1931. Annual tuition: full-time $27,700, per credit hour $1090.

Enrollment: full-time 132, part-time 173. Faculty: full-time 40, part-time 15. Degrees conferred: M.Div., M.A., M.A.-Lit., M.R.E., D.Min., Ph.D., S.T.B., S.T.L., S.T.D.

ADMISSION REQUIREMENTS. Transcripts, bachelor's degree, two letters of recommendation, GRE/MAT required in support of application. Reading knowledge of Latin for some programs. TOEFL required for foreign applicants. Admission open to all qualified applicants. Apply by August 1 (Fall), December 1 (Spring) to the Office of Graduate Admissions. Application fee $65. Phone: (202)319-5305.

ADMISSION STANDARDS. Selective. Usual minimum average: 2.75 (A = 4).

FINANCIAL AID. Annual awards from institutional funds: scholarships, teaching assistantships, fellowships, Burses, Federal W/S, loans. Use FAFSA and institutional FAF. Apply to the Dean and Graduate Financial Aid Office by February 1. Phone: (202)319-5185.

DEGREE REQUIREMENTS. For M.Div: 90-credit program; demonstrated knowledge of Latin; three ministry seminars; supervised ministry. For D.Min.: 36 credits beyond M.Div., at least four semesters in full-time residence; two areas of specialization; D.Min. project; candidacy; dissertation; final oral exam. For S.T.B., S.T.L., S.T.D.: individualized programs, contact Dean for program specifics. For M.A., Ph.D.: requirements same as for School of Arts and Sciences, above.

FIELDS OF STUDY.
Adult Spiritual Formation.
Biblical Studies.
Catholic Theology and Hispanic Ministry.
Church History.
Historical and Systematic Theology.
Historical Theology. Ph.D. only.
Liturgical Studies and Sacramental Theology.
Moral Theology/Ethics.
Pastoral Care & Counseling.
Religion and Culture.
Religious Education/Catechetics.
Spirituality.
Systematic Theology.

The National Catholic School of Social Service

Established 1918. Annual tuition: full-time $24,800, per credit $1090. On-campus housing available. See University listing above.
Enrollment: full-time 111, part-time 117. Faculty: full-time 17, part-time 27. Degrees conferred: M.S.W. (full- and part-time study), Ph.D.

ADMISSION REQUIREMENTS. Transcripts, GRE or MAT, three letters of recommendation, personal statement, résumé required in support of School's application. TOEFL required for foreign applicants. Accepts advanced standing and M.S.W. transfer students. Interview sometimes required. Graduates of unaccredited institutions not considered. Apply to Office of Graduate Admissions by February 1. Fall admission only for M.S.W.; Ph.D. admits both Fall and Spring. Application fee $65. Phone: (202) 319-5305; fax: (202)319-6533.

ADMISSION STANDARDS. Selective. Usual minimum average: 3.0 (A = 4).

FINANCIAL AID. Limited assistance available. Scholarships, fellowships, graduate assistantships (Ph.D.), loans. Approved for VA benefits. Apply by March 1 to Director of Admissions. Use FAFSA. About 35% of students receive aid other than loans.

DEGREE REQUIREMENTS. For M.S.W.: 60 credits and four semesters minimum, at least two semesters in full-time residence; thesis or major paper; two field placements. For Ph.D.: 45 credits beyond the master's minimum, at least four semesters in residence and two semesters in full-time attendance; qualifying exam; reading knowledge of one foreign language; written/oral comprehensive exams; dissertation; final oral exam.

FIELDS OF DOCTORAL STUDY.
Individual Educational Contract.
Theory and Research in Clinical Social Work.
Theory and Research in Policy and Administration in Social Work.

UNIVERSITY OF CENTRAL ARKANSAS
Conway, Arkansas 72035-0001
Web site: www.uca.edu

Founded 1907. CGS member. Located 30 miles NW of Little Rock. Coed. State control. Semester system. Library: 505,000 volumes, 2500 subscriptions. More than 1500 computers on campus for general student use. Total University enrollment: 11,375.

Tuition: per hour, resident $190, nonresident $380. Limited on-campus housing graduate students. Annual housing cost $3920 (including board) for single students; $5850 (including board) for married students. Apply to Director of Housing. Phone: (501)450-3124.

Graduate School

Graduate study since 1955. Enrollment: full-time 547; part-time 839. College faculty teaching graduate students: full-time 216; part-time 22. Degrees conferred: M.A., M.S. in Ed., M.S., M.S.N., M.M.E., M.M., M.B.A., Ed.S.

ADMISSION REQUIREMENTS. Transcripts, GRE/MAT, three references required in support of application. TOEFL required for foreign applicants. Accept transfer applicants. Graduates of unaccredited institutions not considered. Apply to Office of Graduate Dean by March 1 (priority deadline for Summer and Fall), October 1 (priority deadline for Spring). Phone: (501)450-3128; fax: (501)450-5678.

ADMISSION STANDARDS. Selective. Usual minimum average: 2.7 (A = 4).

FINANCIAL AID. Annual awards from institutional funds: fellowships, grants, traineeships, assistantships, tuition waivers, Federal W/S, loans. Apply to Dean of Graduate School for assistantship information; February 15 (Fall), October 1 (Spring). Use FAFSA. Phone: (501)450-3140. About 10% of students receive aid other than loans from School and outside sources.

DEGREE REQUIREMENTS. For master's: 30 semester hours minimum (48 for counseling, 60 for counseling psychology, 60 for school psychology), at least 24 in residence; thesis/nonthesis options; final written and/or oral exam. For Ed.S.: 33 semester hours beyond master's; project.

FIELDS OF STUDY.

COLLEGE OF BUSINESS:
Accounting.
Business Administration.
International Business.

COLLEGE OF EDUCATION:
Counseling Psychology.
Library Media and Information Technology.
Physical Education.
Reading.
School Counseling.
School Psychology.
Spanish Education.
Special Education.
Training Systems.

COLLEGE OF FINE ARTS & COMMUNICATION:
Music.

COLLEGE OF HEALTH AND APPLIED SCIENCES:
Family and Consumer Sciences.
Health Education.
Health Sciences.
Kinesiology.
Nursing.
Occupational Therapy.
Physical Therapy.
Speech-Language Pathology.

COLLEGE OF LIBERAL ARTS:
English.
History.
Sociology.
Spanish.

COLLEGE OF NATURAL SCIENCE AND MATHEMATICS:
Applied Computing.
Biology.
Mathematics Education.

GRADUATE SCHOOL OF MANAGEMENT, LEADERSHIP &
ADMINISTRATION:
College Student Personnel Services.
Community and Economic Development.
Elementary School Leadership.
Health Systems.
Secondary School Leadership.

CENTRAL CONNECTICUT STATE UNIVERSITY

New Britain, Connecticut 06050-4010
Web site: www.ccsu.edu

Founded 1849. CGS member. Located 13 miles SW of Hartford. Coed. State control. Semester system. Library: 639,000 volumes, 2800 subscriptions. More than 880 computers on campus for general student use. Total University enrollment: 12,300.

Annual tuition/fees: resident $7490, nonresident $16,170. Limited on-campus housing. Average annual housing cost: $7312 per year. Apply by May 1. Contact the Director of Residence Life for on- and off-campus accommodations. Phone: (860)832-1660. Limited day-care facilities available.

School of Graduate Studies

Graduate study since 1954. Enrollment: full-time 505, part-time 1637. Graduate faculty: full-time 309, part-time 265. Degrees conferred: M.A., M.S., M.B.A., sixth-year certificate (Reading and Educational Leadership).

ADMISSION REQUIREMENTS. Transcripts, GMAT (International Business only) required in support of University's application. References, TOEFL, and proof of financial support required for international applicants. Apply to Assistant Director of Recruitment and Admission by June 1 (Fall), December 1 (Spring). Rolling admissions process. Application fee $40. Phone: (860)832-2350; fax: (860)832-2362.

ADMISSION STANDARDS. Moderately selective. Minimum average: 2.7 (A = 4).

FINANCIAL AID. Annual awards from institutional funds: scholarships, assistantships, internships, tuition waivers, Federal W/S, loans. Apply to Dean and Director of Financial Aid by March 15 (Fall), October 1 (Spring). Phone: (860)832-2200. Use FAFSA. Aid available for part-time students.

DEGREE REQUIREMENTS. For master's: 30–36 semester hours minimum, at least 21 in residence; thesis or final written exam or special project/capstone; no language requirement in most programs. For sixth-year program: 30 credits beyond master's, at least 21 in residence. Some programs require capstone project.

FIELDS OF STUDY.

SCHOOL OF ARTS AND SCIENCES:
Anesthesia. M.S.
Art Education. M.S.
Biological Sciences. M.A., M.S.
Communication. M.S.
Criminal Justice. M.S.
Data Mining. M.S.

English. M.A.
Geography. M.S.
History. M.A.
Information Design. M.A.
International Studies. M.S.
Mathematics. M.A., M.S.
Modern Languages. M.A.
Music Education. M.S.
Natural Sciences. M.S.
Psychology. M.A.
Public History. M.A.
Spanish. M.S.
TESOL. M.S.

SCHOOL OF BUSINESS:
Business Administration. M.B.A.
Business Education. M.S.

SCHOOL OF EDUCATION AND PROFESSIONAL STUDIES:
Counselor Education. M.S.
Early Childhood Education. M.S.
Educational Foundations. M.S.
Educational Leadership. M.S.
Educational Technology. M.S.
Elementary Education. M.S.
Marriage and Family Therapy. M.S.
Physical Education. M.S.
Reading. M.S.
Special Education. M.S.

SCHOOL OF TECHNOLOGY:
Biomolecular Sciences. M.A.
Computer Information Technology. Interdisciplinary. M.S.
Engineering Technology. M.S.
Technology Education. M.S.
Technology Management. M.S.

UNIVERSITY OF CENTRAL FLORIDA

Box 160112
Orlando, Florida 32816-0112
Web site: www.ucf.edu

Founded 1963. CGS member. Located 15 miles from downtown. Coed. Public control. Semester system. Library: 1,200,000 volumes, 9800 subscriptions. More than 2400 computers on campus for student use. Total University enrollment: 45,000.

Annual tuition: residents $5788, nonresidents $21,927; per credit, resident $241, nonresident $913. On-campus housing available for single students only. Average academic year housing costs: $450 per month one-bedroom, $780 per month two-bedroom. Apply by March 1. Contact Housing Office for both on- and off-campus housing.

Graduate Studies

Web site: www.graduate.ucf.edu

Enrollment: full-time 3163, part-time 3160. Graduate faculty: full- and part-time 1500. Degrees conferred: M.A., M.S., M.Ed., M.S.A., M.B.A., M.A.A.E., M.P.H., M.S.T., M.S.W., M.C.E., M.S.E., M.S.I.E., M.S.M.E., M.S.Mfg.E., Ed.S., Ed.D., Ph.D.

ADMISSION REQUIREMENTS. Transcripts, GRE, GMAT (for business programs) required in support of application. Three letters of recommendation for most programs. TOEFL required for international students. Accepts transfer applicants. Graduates of unaccredited institutions not considered. Apply to the Office of Graduate Studies at least six months prior to the date of registration.

Rolling admissions process. Application fee $30. Phone: (407)823-2766; fax: (407)823-3299; e-mail: graduate@mail.ucf.edu.

ADMISSION STANDARDS. Selective. Usual minimum average: 2.75 (A = 4).

FINANCIAL AID. Scholarships, fellowships, assistantships, internships, partial tuition waivers, Federal W/S, loans. Approved for VA benefits. Apply by March 1 to appropriate Dean's Office for fellowships, assistantships, to Financial Aid Office for all other programs. Use FAFSA. About 20% students receive aid from University and outside sources. Aid available for part-time students.

DEGREE REQUIREMENTS. For most master's: 30–48 semester hours minimum, at least one year in residence for most departments; however some departments require two or more years of full-time study; thesis/nonthesis option; reading knowledge of one foreign language for some departments; written/oral exam; completion of degree no later than five years from date of entrance. For M.B.A.: 39–51 credit program; core course must be completed in four consecutive years. For Ed.S.: 30 semester credits minimum beyond the master's degree; special project. For Ed.D.: 90 semester hours, at least three years minimum in residence; written comprehensive exam; dissertation; final oral exam; completion of all requirements no later than seven years from date of entrance. For Ph.D.: 60–67 semester hours minimum beyond the bachelor's, and three years of full-time study or equivalent in residence; written comprehensive exam; advancement to candidacy; internship for some programs; dissertation; final oral exam; completion of all requirements no later than seven years from date of entrance.

FIELDS OF STUDY.
Accounting. M.S.A.
Aerospace Engineering. Includes space systems, design and engineering, thermofluid aerodynamics systems design and engineering. M.S.A.E.
Anthropology. Includes archaeological investigations in forensics and human adaptation, cultural competence in the professions, Maya studies. M.A.
Applied Sociology. Includes domestic violence. M.A.
Art Education. Includes community college teaching. M.A., M.Ed.
Biology. M.S.
Biomedical Sciences. Ph.D.
Business Administration. M.B.A., Ph.D.
Career and Technical Education. M.A.
Chemistry. Ph.D.
Civil Engineering. Includes structural and geotechnical engineering, transportation systems engineering, water resources engineering. M.S., M.S.C.E., Ph.D.
Clinical Psychology. M.A.
Communication. Includes mass communication. M.A.
Communication Sciences and Disorders. M.A.
Computer Engineering. Includes computer networking, digital systems, intelligent systems, software engineering. M.S.Cp.E., Ph.D.
Computer Science. M.S., Ph.D.
Conservation Biology. Includes applied conservation biology, ecology and organismal biology. Ph.D.
Counselor Education. Includes mental health counseling, school counseling., M.A., M.Ed.
Creative Writing. M.F.A.
Criminal Justice. M.S.
Curriculum and Instruction. M.A., M.Ed.
Early Childhood Development & Education. M.A.
Early Childhood Education. Includes early literacy, educational leadership, family, school and community. M.Ed.
Economics. M.S., Ph.D.
Education. Ed.S., Ed.D., Ph.D.
Education. Includes communication sciences and disorders, counselor education, elementary education, exceptional education, hospitality education, instructional technology, mathematics technology, science education. Ph.D.
Education Media—Instruction Technology. M.Ed.
Educational Leadership. M.A., M.Ed., Ed.S., Ed.D.
E-Learning—Instructional Technology. M.A.
Electrical Engineering. Includes communication, controls and robotics, digital signal processing, photonics, electro-optics, electromagnetics, power electronics and electronics, solid state and microelectronics, VLSI design. M.S.E.E., Ph.D.
Elementary Education. M.A., M.Ed.
English Language Arts. M.Ed.
English. Includes literature, rhetoric and composition, technical writing. M.A.
Environmental Engineering. M.S.Env.E., Ph.D.
Environmental Science. M.S.
Exceptional Education. Includes varying exceptionalities. M.A., M.Ed.
Film and Digital Media. Includes entrepreneurial digital cinema, visual language and interactive media. M.F.A.
Forensic Science. Includes forensic analysis, forensic biochemistry. M.S.
Health Sciences. Includes clinical and lifestyle sciences, health services administration. M.S.
History. Includes public history. M.A.
Hospitality and Tourism Management. M.S.
Industrial Chemistry. M.S.
Industrial Engineering. Includes engineering management, human engineering/ergonomics, interactive simulation and training systems, operations research, quality engineering, simulation modeling and analysis. M.S., M.S.I.S., Ph.D.
Industrial Organization Psychology. M.S.
Interactive Entertainment. M.S.
Interdisciplinary Studies. M.A., M.S.
K-8 Math and Science. M.Ed.
Management Information System. M.S., M.I.S.
Marriage and Family Therapy. M.A.
Material Science & Engineering. M.S.M.S.E.
Mathematical Science. Includes industrial mathematics. M.S.
Mathematics Education. M.Ed.
Mechanical Engineering. Includes computer-aided mechanical engineering, mechanical systems, miniature engineering systems, thermofluids. M.S.M.E., Ph.D.
Modeling and Simulation. M.S., Ph.D.
Molecular Biology and Microbiology. M.S.
Music. M.A.
Nonprofit Management. M.N.M.
Nursing. Includes adult nurse practitioner, clinical nurse leader, clinical nurse specialist, family nurse practitioner, leadership and management, nurse educator, pediatric nurse practitioner. M.S., Ph.D.
Nursing Practice. D.N.P.
Optics. M.S., Ph.D.
Physical Education. Includes sports and fitness. M.A.
Physical Therapy. D.P.T.
Physics. M.S., Ph.D.
Political Science. Includes environmental politics, international studies, political and policy. M.A.
Psychology. Includes applied experimental and human factors psychology, clinical psychology, industrial and organizational psychology. Ph.D.
Public Administration. M.P.A.
Public Affairs. Ph.D.
Reading Education. M.Ed.
School Psychology. Includes school counseling. Ed.S.
Science Education. Includes community college teaching, middle school science, biology, chemistry, physics. M.A., M.Ed.
Social Science Education. Includes community college teaching. M.A., M.Ed.
Social Work. M.S.W.
Sociology. Ph.D.
Spanish. M.A.

Sport Business Management. M.S.B.M.

Statistical Computing. Includes actuarial science, data mining. M.S.

Studio Art and the Computer. M.F.A.

Taxation. M.S.T.

Teaching English (TESOL). M.A.

Texts and Technology. Ph.D.

Theatre. Includes acting, design, musical theatre, theatre for young audiences. M.F.A.

CENTRAL MICHIGAN UNIVERSITY

Mount Pleasant, Michigan 48859
Web site: www.cmich.edu

Founded 1892. CGS member. Located 70 miles N of Lansing. Coed. State control. Semester system. Special facilities: Beaver Island Neckercut Wood, Center for Computer Vision and Robotics, Center for Polymer Chemistry, Michigan Geographic Alliance. Library: 1,000,000 volumes, 4500 subscriptions. More than 1500 computers on campus for general student use. Total University enrollment: 27,200.

Tuition: per credit, resident $325, nonresident $603. On-campus housing for married and single students. Annual cost for single students $8500–$10,100 (including board), for married students $460–$525 per month (room only). Apply to Director of Housing. Phone: (989)774-3112. Day-care facilities available.

College of Graduate Studies

Graduate study since 1939. Enrollment: full-time 800, part-time 1052. Faculty: full- and part-time 707. Degrees conferred: M.A., M.S., M.B.A., M.F.A., M.M., M.S.A., Specialist, Psy.D., Au.D., Certificates.

ADMISSION REQUIREMENTS. Transcripts, GRE/GMAT (for some programs) required in support of College's application. TOEFL required for foreign applicants; TWE required for some programs. Interview required for some programs. Accepts transfer applicants. Graduates of unaccredited institutions not considered. Apply to Graduate Office by July 15 (Fall), December 1 (Spring). International applicants should apply at least six months prior to preferred time of enrollment. Application fee $30. Phone: (989)774-1059; fax: (989)774-1587; E-Mail:grad@cmich.edu.

ADMISSION STANDARDS. Selective. Usual minimum average: 2.5 (A = 4).

FINANCIAL AID. Annual awards from University funds: fellowships, research assistantships, teaching assistantships, internships, Federal W/S, loans. Apply by March 1 to Dean of College of Graduate Studies for fellowships, to appropriate department chair for assistantships, to Financial Aid Office for all other programs. Phone: (989)774-3674. Use FAFSA. About 30% of students receive aid other than loans from University. Aid available for part-time students.

DEGREE REQUIREMENTS. For most master's: 30–36 semester hours minimum; comprehensive exam for some programs; thesis/nonthesis option or two research papers. For M.S.P.T.: three-year full-time 110 credit program; thesis. For Specialist: 30 semester hours beyond the master's; thesis or field study; final oral exam. No language requirements. For Psy.D.: at least 60 credit hours beyond the master's; two years in full-time residence; qualifying exam; full-year internship; case study; final exam.

FIELDS OF STUDY.

Administration. Includes general, health services, human resources, information resource, international, leadership, organizational communication, public, recreation and parks, sport. M.S.A.

Art. M.A.

Audiology. Au.D.

Biology. Includes conservation biology. M.S.

Broadcast and Cinematic Arts. M.A.

Business Administration. Includes accounting, business economics, finance, human resources management, international business, management, marketing; GMAT for admission. M.B.A.

Business Education. M.B.E.

Chemistry. Includes teaching high school chemistry (M.A.), teaching college chemistry (M.A.). M.S.

Communication Disorders. M.A.

Computer Science. M.S.

Counseling. Includes school counseling, professional counseling. M.A.

Creative Writing. M.A.

Economics. M.A.

Educational Administration. Includes general educational administration (M.A., Ed.S), community leadership (M.A.), school principalship (M.A.), educational leadership (Ed.D).

English Language and Literature. Includes composition and communication, creative writing, teaching English to speakers for other languages. M.A.

Fine Arts. M.F.A.

Geographic Information Sciences. M.S.

Health Promotion and Program Management. M.A.

History. M.A.

Human Development and Family Studies. M.A.

Humanities. M.A.

Industrial and Engineering Technology. Includes industrial education, industrial management and technology. M.A.

Information Systems. M.S.I.S.

Mathematics. M.A., M.A.T., Ph.D.

Music. Includes composition, conducting, performance, music education supervision. M.M.

Nutrition and Dietetics. M.S.

Oral Interpretation. M.A.

Physical Education and Sport. Includes teaching, athletic administration, exercise science, coaching, sport administration. M.A.

Physical Therapy. M.S.

Physician Assistant. M.S.

Physics. M.S.

Political Science. M.A.

Psychology. Includes applied experimental (Ph.D), clinical (Ph.D.), general (M.S.), experimental (M.S.), industrial/organizational (M.A., Ph.D.), school (Ph.D).

Public Administration. M.P.A.

Recreation, Park, and Leisure Services Administration. Includes therapeutic recreation. M.A.

Sociology. M.A.

Spanish. M.A.

Special Education. Includes counseling and special education. M.A.

Speech Language Pathology. M.A.

Teacher Education and Professional Development. Includes middle level, educational technology, elementary, classroom teaching, early childhood, reading in elementary school, secondary education, teaching in the senior high. M.A.

TESOL. M.A.

Theater. M.A.

CENTRAL MISSOURI STATE UNIVERSITY

Warrensburg, Missouri 64093
Web site: www.cmsu.edu

Founded 1871. CGS member. Located 50 miles SE of Kansas City. Coed. State control. Semester system. Library 1,300,000 vol-

University of Central Oklahoma *119*

umes, 3550 subscriptions. More than 1220 computers on campus for general student use. Total University enrollment: 10,604.

Tuition per credit: resident $215, nonresident $430. On-campus housing for about 200 married students, 3000 men, 3000 women. Housing cost: $450–$600 per month for married students, $5180 (including board) for single students. Apply to Director of Residential Life. Phone: (660)543-4515.

Graduate Studies

Graduate study since 1947. Enrollment: full-time 276, part-time 1290. Graduate faculty: full-time 294, part-time 25. Degrees conferred: M.A., M.S., M.S.Ed. M.B.A., Ed.Specialist. Ph.D. (Technology awarded by Indiana State University; Educational Leadership awarded by University of Missouri–Columbia).

ADMISSION REQUIREMENTS. Transcripts, bachelor's degree required in support of University's application. Electronic application available. GRE/GMAT/MAT may be required by some departments. Accepts transfer applicants. Interview not required. Graduates from unaccredited institutions not considered. Application fee $25 ($50 for international applicants). Apply to Admissions Office by August 15 (Fall), January 5 (Spring), June 1 (Summer). Phone: (660)543-4328; e-mail: gradinfo@cmsu1.cmsu.edu.

ADMISSION STANDARDS. Relatively open. Usual minimum average 2.0 (A = 4).

FINANCIAL AID. Annual awards from institutional funds: scholarships, grants, fellowships, administrative assistantships, research assistantships, teaching assistantships, Federal W/S, loans. Apply by March 1 to chair of proposed major for assistantships, fellowships; to financial aid office for W/S, loans. Phone: (660)543-4040; fax: (660)543-8080. Use FAFSA. About 10% of students receive aid other than loans from College funds. Aid available for part-time students.

DEGREE REQUIREMENTS. For master's: 32 credits minimum; qualifying/comprehensive exam; some departments require thesis. For Ed.Specialist: 30 credits minimum beyond the master's; thesis or research project.

FIELDS OF STUDY.
Accountancy.
Administration. Includes elementary school princpalship, secondary school principalship, superintendancy.
Agriculture Technology.
Aviation Safety.
Biology.
Business Administration.
Business/Office Education.
Communication.
Communication Disorders.
Counseling.
Criminal Justice.
Curriculum and Instruction.
Economics.
Educational Technology.
English.
Environmental Studies.
Guidance and Counseling.
Higher Education.
History.
Human Services.
Industrial Hygiene.
Industrial Management.
Industrial Technology.
Information Technology.
Learning Resources.
Library Information Technology.
Library Science and Information Services.

Literary Education.
Mass Communication.
Mathematics.
Music.
Occupational Safety Management.
Physical Education, Exercise, and Sports Science.
Psychology.
Public Services.
Rural Family Nursing.
School Administration.
School Counseling.
Social Gerontology.
Social Studies.
Sociology.
Special Education.
Speech-Language Pathology.
Student Personnel Administration.
Teaching English as a Second Language.
Technology and Occupational Education.
Theater.
Note: Ed. Specialist available in most education-related programs.

UNIVERSITY OF CENTRAL OKLAHOMA
Edmond, Oklahoma 73034-5209
Web site: www.ucok.edu

Founded 1800. CGS member. Located 12 miles N of Oklahoma City. Coed. State control. Semester system. Library: 250,000 volumes, 3700 subscriptions. Total University enrollment: 16,000.

Tuition: per hour, resident $125, nonresident $197. On-campus housing for 158 married students, 592 men, 716 women. Average annual housing cost: $3200 for married students, $4476 (including board) for single students. Apply by July 1 to Director of Housing for on-campus housing; to Vice President, Student Services for off-Campus housing information. Phone: (405)974-3368.

Dr. Joe C. Jackson College of Graduate Studies and Research

Graduate study since 1954. Enrollment: full-time 448, part-time 877. Faculty: full-time 249, part-time 100. Degrees conferred: M.A., M.S., M.F.A., M.B.A., M.Ed., M.M.

ADMISSION REQUIREMENTS. Transcripts, GRE, GMAT (for business) required in support of College's application. Online application available. TOEFL required for international applicants. Interview not required. Accepts transfer applicants. Graduates of unaccredited colleges not considered. Apply to Dean of the Graduate College at least one month prior to registration. Application fee, $25. Phone: (405)974-3341; fax: (405)974-3852.

ADMISSION STANDARDS. Relatively open. Usual minimum average: 2.5 (2.5, last 60 hours) (A = 4).

FINANCIAL AID. Scholarships, grants, assistantships, internships, Federal W/S, loans. Apply by March 15 to appropriate department chair for assistantships. For W/S, loans apply by March 31 to Office of Student Financial Aid. Phone: (405)974-3336. Use FAFSA. Aid available for part-time students.

DEGREE REQUIREMENTS. For master's: 32–34 semester hours minimum, at least 24 in residence; comprehensive exam for some programs; thesis/nonthesis option/projects.

FIELDS OF STUDY.

COLLEGE OF ARTS, MEDIA & DESIGN:
Design. M.F.A.
Jazz Studies. M.M.
Music. M.M.

COLLEGE OF BUSINESS ADMINISTRATION:
Business Administration. M.B.A.

COLLEGE OF EDUCATION & PROFESSIONAL STUDIES:
Adult Education. Includes training, gerontology. M.Ed.
Bilingual/TESL/Multicultural Education.
Business Education. M.Ed.
Early Childhood Education. M.Ed.
Elementary Education. M.Ed.
Family and Child Studies. Includes family life educator, family support specialist. M.S.
General Physical Education. M.Ed.
Guidance and Counseling. M.Ed.
Instructional Media Education. Includes applied technology, library information. M.Ed.
Marketing Education. M.Ed.
Nutrition and Food Management. M.S.
Professional Health Occupations. M.Ed.
Psychology. M.A.
Reading Education. M.Ed.
Safety Education. M.Ed.
School Administration. M.Ed.
Secondary Education. M.Ed.
Secondary Physical Education. M.Ed.
Special Education. M.Ed.
Speech-Language Pathology. M.S.
Wellness Management. Includes health studies, exercise science. M.S.

COLLEGE OF LIBERAL ARTS:
Criminal Justice Management and Administration. M.A.
English. Includes composition and rhetoric, creative writing, 20th and 21st century studies, traditional studies, TESL. M.A.
History. Includes museum studies, social studies teaching. M.A.
Political Science. Includes international affairs, public administration. M.S.

COLLEGE OF MATHEMATICS & SCIENCES:
Applied Mathematics. Includes mathematics, computer science, statistics and mathematics teaching. M.S.
Biology. M.S.
Forensic Sciences. Includes criminalistics, technical investigations, forensic nursing. M.S.
Physics. M.S.

CENTRAL WASHINGTON UNIVERSITY
Ellensburg, Washington 98926-7510
Web site: www.cwu.edu

Founded 1890. CGS member. Located 36 miles N of Yakima and 100 miles E of Seattle. Coed. State control. Quarter system. Special facilities: educational television in conjunction with Ellensburg public schools, computer center, Geographic Information System Lab, Chimpanzee and Human Communication Institute. Library: 537,700 volumes, 1450 subscriptions. More than 700 computers on campus for general student use. Total University enrollment: 10,200.

Annual tuition: full-time resident $5904, nonresident $12,960; per credits resident $196, nonresident $441. On-campus housing for married, single students. Average annual housing cost: $5031 (including board) for single students, $3195 for married students. Apply to Housing Office. Phone: (509)963-1831.

Graduate Studies and Research

Graduate study since 1947. Enrollment: full-time 270, part-time 166. Graduate faculty: full- and part-time 293. Degrees conferred: M.A., M.Ed., M.S., M.A.T., M.M., M.F.A. M.P.A.

ADMISSION REQUIREMENTS. Transcripts, GRE (for some programs) required in support of University's application. TOEFL (minimum score 550, 213 on computer-based test) required for foreign applicants. Accepts transfer applicants. Apply to Office of Graduate Admissions by April 1 (Fall), October 1 (Winter), January 1 (Spring). Application fee $35. Phone: (509)963-3103; fax: (509)963-1799; e-mail: masters@cwu.edu.

ADMISSION STANDARDS. Relatively open. Required minimum average: 3.0 (A = 4).

FINANCIAL AID. Annual awards from College funds: graduate assistantships, minority fellowships, internships, Federal W/S, loans. Apply by March 1 to Dean of Graduate School. Use FAFSA. Phone: (509)963-1611. About 30% of students receive aid other than loans from College and outside sources.

DEGREE REQUIREMENTS. For M.A., M.Ed., M.S., M.A.T., M.M.: 45 credit hours minimum; thesis or project; advancement to candidacy: final oral/written exam. For M.F.A.: 90 credit hours minimum; at least three quarters in residence.

FIELDS OF STUDY.
Accountancy.
Administration.
Art.
Biological Sciences.
Business and Marketing Education.
Chemistry.
Counseling Psychology.
Educational Administration.
Engineering Technology.
English. Includes literature, TESOL.
English Language Learning.
Exercise Science.
Experimental Psychology.
Family and Consumer Sciences.
Geology.
History.
Human Performance.
Master Teacher.
Mathematics.
Mental Health Counseling.
Music.
Organization Development.
Physical Education, Health Education, and Leisure Studies.
Reading Specialist.
Resource Management.
School Counseling.
School Psychology.
Special Education.
Supervision and Curriculum.
Theater Production.

CHADRON STATE COLLEGE
Chadron, Nebraska 69337
Web site: www.csc.edu

Founded 1911. Located 300 miles NE of Denver, Colorado. Coed. State control. Semester system. Library: 593,100 volumes, 1200 subscriptions. Total College enrollment: 2636

Tuition: per hour, resident $124, nonresident $248. On-campus housing for 62 married students, 800 single students. Annual housing cost (including board): $4800. Apply by June 1 to Director of Housing. Phone: (800)CHA-DRON. Day-care facilities available.

School of Professional and Graduate Studies

Graduate study since 1955. Average enrollment per year: full-time 48, part-time 272. Graduate faculty: full-time 49, part-time 15. Degrees conferred: M.B.A., M.S. in Ed., M.A. in Ed., Specialist in Education.

ADMISSION REQUIREMENTS. Two transcripts, references, GRE or MAT required in support of College's application. TOEFL required for foreign applicants. Interview required for Specialist Degree only. Accepts transfer applicants. Graduates of unaccredited institutions not considered. Apply to Chair of the Graduate Council. Application fee $15. Phone: (800)CHA-DRON; fax: (308)432-6454.

ADMISSION STANDARDS. Selective. Usual minimum average: 2.75 (A = 4).

FINANCIAL AID. Scholarships, teaching assistantships, internships, Federal W/S, loans. Apply by June 1 to Financial Aid Officer for scholarships, Federal W/S, loans, to Chair of the Graduate Council for assistantships. Phone: (800)CHA-DRON. Use FAFSA. About 5% of students receive aid other than loans from College, 20% from all sources. Aid available for part-time students.

DEGREE REQUIREMENTS. For M.B.A., M.S., M.A. in Ed.: 36 credits minimum, at least 12 in residence; thesis/nonthesis option; final oral exam. For Specialist in Education Degree: 30 credits minimum, at least 15 in residence; thesis or field study option; final oral/written exams.

FIELDS OF STUDY.
Business Administration.
Education. Includes elementary, secondary teaching, administration; computer education, fine arts, history, language arts, mathematics, physical education, reading, science, social studies, guidance, supervision, reading.

CHAPMAN UNIVERSITY

Orange, California 92666-1011
Web site: www.chapman.edu

Founded 1861. Located 35 miles SE of Los Angeles. Coed. Private control. Disciples of Christ affiliation. Semester system. Special facilities: Center for Economic Research, Center for International Business. Library: 210,000 volumes, 2200 subscriptions. More than 450 computers on campus for general student use. Total University enrollment: 5752.

Tuition: per credit $720, M.P.T. $840, Education $505, all other programs $495–$665. On-campus housing for both single and married students. Average academic year housing cost: $8000–$11,000 (including board) for single students; $700–$1000 per month for married students. Contact Director of Resident Life for both on- and off-campus housing information. Phone: (714) 997-6604.

Division of Graduate Studies

Enrollment: full- and part-time 1700. Faculty teaching graduate students: full- and part-time 248. Degrees conferred: M.A., M.B.A., M.F.A., M.H.A., M.P.T., M.S.

ADMISSION REQUIREMENTS. Official transcripts, GRE, two letters of recommendation required in support of application.

GRE Subject/GMAT/MAT/NTE required for some programs. TOEFL or Institutionally administered TOEFL required for international applicants. Accepts transfer applicants. Graduates of unaccredited institutions not considered. Apply to Office of Graduate Admissions. Application fee $50. Phone: (888)CUAPPLY or (714)997-6786; fax: (714)997-6713.

ADMISSION STANDARDS. Competitive. Usual minimum average: 3.0 (A = 4).

FINANCIAL AID. Graduate assistantships, fellowships, internships, tuition awards, Federal W/S, loans. Approved for VA benefits. Apply by March 1 to Graduate Dean for fellowships, assistantships; to Financial Aid Office for all other programs. Phone: (714)997-6741. Use FAFSA (University code: 001167) and complete the Supplemental Application for Graduate Students.

DEGREE REQUIREMENTS. For master's: 33–60 credits at least 24 credits in residence; candidacy; thesis/nonthesis/project option; comprehensive exam; internship for most programs.

FIELDS OF STUDY.

ARGYROS SCHOOL OF BUSINESS AND ECONOMICS:
Business Administration. M.B.A., E.M.B.A.

SCHOOL OF EDUCATION:
Counseling and Pupil Personnel Services. M.A.
Education. Includes curriculum and instruction, reading. M.A.
Educational Leadership and Administration. M.A.
Educational Psychology and Pupil Personnel Services. M.A.
Elementary Education. M.A. Teaching.
School Psychology. Ed.S.
Secondary Education. M.A. Teaching.
Special Education. Includes mild/moderate, moderate/severe. M.A.

SCHOOL OF FILM AND TELEVISION:
Film and Television Production. M.F.A.
Film Production. M.F.A.
Film Studies. M.F.A.
Screen Writing. M.F.A.

WILKINSON COLLEGE OF LETTERS AND SCIENCES:
English. M.A.
Creative Writing. M.F.A.
Food Science. M.S.
Physical Therapy. D.P.T., Transitional D.P.T.
Psychology. M.A.

School of Law

Web site: www.chapman.edu/law

Founded 1995. ABA approved since 1998. AALS member. Semester system. Law library: 279,673 volumes, 3050 subscriptions. Library has LEXIS, WESTLAW, DIALOG, OCLC.

Tuition: full-time $32,834, part-time $22,604, LL.M. $1070 per credit. Off-campus housing only available. Check website for housing information. Annual housing costs approximately $17,600.

Enrollment: full- and part-time 194; total full-time 515, part-time 41 (men 50%, women 50%, minority 45%).

Faculty: Total full- and part-time 54 (men 59%, women 41%, minority 8%). Student to faculty ratio 17.1 to 1. Degrees conferred: J.D., J.D.-M.B.A., LL.M. (Taxation), LL.M. (Prosecutorial Science).

ADMISSION REQUIREMENTS. LSDAS Law School report, official transcript, LSAT, two letters of recommendation, personal statement required in support of application. Interview not required. TOEFL required for all international applicants. Accepts transfer applications. Graduates of unaccredited colleges not considered. Apply to Director of Admission after November 1, by June 1. Rolling admission process. Application fee $50. Phone: (714)628-2500.

ADMISSION STANDARDS. Selective. Accepts approximately 30% of full-time and 100% of part-time students. Number of full-time applicants 2210, part-time 9; number of acceptance full-time 668, part-time 9; number enrolled full-time 187, part-time 7; LSAT (75% of full-time students have a score at or above 154, part-time 151); GPA (75% of full-time students have a GPA at or above 3.01, part-time 2.98). *U.S. News & World Report* ranking is in the fourth tier of all U.S. law schools.

FINANCIAL AID. Scholarships, grants, Federal W/S, loans. Approximately 35% of students received aid other than loans from school funds. Apply to the Office of Financial Aid; for financial aid the priority deadline is March 2, for scholarship consideration the priority deadline is April 1. Phone: (714)628-2510. Use FAFSA.

DEGREE REQUIREMENTS. For J.D.: satisfactory completion of three (full-time) or four (part-time) year program. For LL.M.: Satisfactory completion of 24 credit program. For master's: see Graduate School listing above.

CHICAGO STATE UNIVERSITY
Chicago, Illinois 60628
Web site: www.csu.edu

Founded 1867. Coed. State control. Semester system. Library: 323,000 volumes, 1500 subscriptions.

Annual tuition: full-time per hour, resident $201, nonresident $374. Limited on-campus housing available for single graduate students. Average academic year housing cost: $8200 (includes board). Contact Student Housing Director for on-campus housing information. Phone: (773)995-DORM. Day-care facilities available.

School of Graduate and Professional Studies

Graduate study since 1938. Enrollment: full-time 312, part-time 1540. Graduate faculty: full-time 133, part-time 87. Degrees conferred: M.A., M.A.T., M.O.T., M.S., M.S. in Ed., M.S.W.

ADMISSION REQUIREMENTS. Official transcripts, statement of goals and objectives required in support of School's application. Online application available. Interview recommended by some departments. TOEFL, financial statement, certificate of sponsorship, two transcripts with credential evaluation required for international applicants. Accepts transfer applicants. Graduates of unaccredited institutions not considered. Apply to the Admissions and Records Office by March 15 (Fall), October 15 (Spring). Rolling admissions process. Students may enroll on a nondegree basis pending formal admission. Application fee $25. Phone: (773)995-2404; fax: (773)995-3671.

ADMISSION STANDARDS. Selective. Usual minimum average: 2.75 (A = 4).

FINANCIAL AID. Scholarships, research fellowships, research/teaching assistantships, tuition waivers, Federal W/S, loans. Approved for VA benefits. Apply to the Director of Financial Aid; no specified closing date. Phone: (773)995-2304. Use FAFSA. Aid available for part-time students.

DEGREE REQUIREMENTS. For master's: 30–36 semester hours minimum, at least 21–27 in residence; thesis optional; final written/oral exam. For M.A. in Ed.: same as above, except 32 hours minimum.

FIELDS OF STUDY.

COLLEGE OF ARTS AND SCIENCE:
Biological Sciences. M.S.
Computer Science. M.S.
Creative Writing. M.F.A.
Criminal Justice. M.S.
English. M.A.
Geography and Economic Development. M.A.
History. M.A.
Mathematics. M.S.
Social Work. M.S.W.

COLLEGE OF EDUCATION:
Bilingual Education. M.S.Ed.
Early Childhood Education. M.A.T.
Educational Leadership and Administration. Ed.D.
Elementary Education. M.A.T.
General Administration. M.A.
Higher Education Administration. M.A.
Instructional Foundations. M.S.Ed.
Library Science. M.S.
Middle School Education. M.A.T.
Physical Education. M.S.Ed.
Secondary Education. M.A.T.
Special Education. M.S.Ed.
Technology and Education. M.S.Ed.

COLLEGE OF HEALTH AND SCIENCES:
Occupation Therapy. M.O.T.

THE UNIVERSITY OF CHICAGO
Chicago, Illinois 60637-1513
Web site: www.uchicago.edu

Founded 1890, CGS and AAU member. Coed. Private control. Quarter system. Special facilities: ASCI/Alliances Center for Astrophysical Thermonuclear Flashes, the Bell May Institute, Brain Research Imaging Center, the Cancer Research Center, the Center for Cosmological Physics, Center for East Asian Studies, Center for East European and Russian/Eurasian Studies, Center for Gender Studies, Center for International Studies, Center for Middle Eastern Studies, Center for School Improvement, Center for the Study of Race, Politics and Culture, the Computation Institute, Center for Computational Psychology, Cultural Policy Center, Enrico Fermi Institute, Film Studies Center, James Franck Institute, Franke Institute for the Humanities, Franklin McLean Memorial Research Institute, the Center for Health Administration Studies, Institute for Biophysical Dynamics, Institute for Mind and Biology, Center for Magnetic Resonance Imaging, Materials Research Science and Engineering Center, Oriental Institute, South Asia Language and Area Center. The University's NIH ranking is 28th among all U.S. institutions with 444 awards/grants valued at $194,716,584. According to The Center at University of Florida, the University is ranked 36th in receipt of Federal Research funds with $201,129,000 and it ranks 51st for total University research expenditures with $247,322,000. The University's endowment assets ranks it 13th, with a value of $3,620,228,000. In 2004, the University awarded 331 doctorates, which ranked it 40th among all U.S. institutions eligible to award that degree. Fifty-one of the University's faculty members have been elected to National Honor Academies and this ranks it 20th among all U.S. institutions. The Libraries: approximately 5,710,000 volumes, 40,000 subscriptions. Total University enrollment: 13,620.

On-campus housing available for graduate students. Approximately 1300 apartments and more than 500 single rooms are available. Average monthly housing cost: $600–$1250 for married, $475–$900 for single students. For specific Graduate Student Housing information, contact the Assignments Office, phone: (773)753-2218. For International House information, contact the Housing Office, phone: (773)753-2270

Division of the Biological Sciences

Graduate study since 1892. Tuition: per course $3883.

Graduate enrollment: full- and part-time 437. Graduate faculty: full-time 458; no part-time faculty. Degrees conferred: S.M., Ph.D., M.D.-Ph.D.

ADMISSION REQUIREMENTS. Transcripts, GRE, three letters of recommendation required in support of application. TOEFL required for foreign applicants. Interview recommended. Accepts transfer applicants. Apply to Associate Dean for Graduate Affairs by December 28 (Fall quarter). Application fee $50, $55 for foreign applicants. Phone: (773)834-2105; fax: (773)834-1618.

ADMISSION STANDARDS. Very selective for most departments, competitive to very competitive for the others. Usual minimum average 3.0 (A = 4).

FINANCIAL AID. Scholarships, research assistantships, fellowships, grants, traineeships, Federal W/S, loans. Apply to Associate Dean for Graduate Affairs; no specified closing date. Use FAFSA. 100% of students receive aid other than loans from University and outside sources.

DEGREE REQUIREMENTS. For S.M.: Individual degree granting units set requirements; thesis; final written/oral exam. For Ph.D.: six quarters in residence and completion of Research Residency; preliminary exam; teach twice in credit-approved positions; take the course Scientific Integrity and the Ethical Conduct of Research; dissertation; final written/oral exam. For M.D.: see School of Medicine listing below.

FIELDS OF STUDY.
Biochemistry and Molecular Biology.
Biophysical Sciences.
Cancer Biology.
Cell Physiology.
Cellular and Molecular Physiology.
Computational Neuroscience.
Developmental Biology.
Ecology and Evolution.
Evolutionary Biology.
Genetics.
Health Studies.
Human Genetics.
Human Nutrition and Nutritional Biology.
Immunology.
Medical Physics (Radiology).
Microbiology.
Molecular Genetics and Cell Biology.
Neurobiology.
Ophthalmology and Visual Science.
Organismal Biology and Anatomy.
Pathology.
Pharmacology.
Physiology.
Virology.

Division of the Humanities

Graduate study since 1892.

Tuition: per course $4075. Graduate enrollment: full-time 1152. Division faculty: full-time 188, part-time 10. Degrees conferred: A.M., M.A.P.H., M.F.A., Ph.D.

ADMISSION REQUIREMENTS. Transcripts, GRE/Subject Test, three letters of recommendation, evidence of satisfactory training in one foreign language required in support of application. Writing sample required by some departments. TOEFL (minimum score 550) required for foreign applicants. Interview not required. Graduates of unaccredited institutions not considered. Apply to the Dean of Students, Division of the Humanities by January 5. Application fee $50, $55 for foreign applicants. Phone: (773)702-1552; fax: (773)702-9861.

ADMISSION STANDARDS. Competitive for most departments, very competitive for others. Usual minimum average: 3.5 (A = 4).

FINANCIAL AID. Scholarships, fellowships, tuition waivers, Federal W/S, loans. Apply by January 5 to the Dean of Students. Use FAFSA. About 70% of students receive aid other than loans from University and outside sources.

DEGREE REQUIREMENTS. For A.M., M.A.P.H.: 3 quarters minimum in residence; thesis/essay/similar project; final written/oral exam. For M.F.A.: 18 courses, final creative project and paper instead of thesis. For Ph.D.: 12 quarters minimum beyond the bachelor's, at least 3 quarters in residence; qualifying exam; reading knowledge of foreign languages set by individual departments; admission to candidacy; dissertation; final written/oral exam.

FIELDS OF STUDY.
Ancient Mediterranean World. Interdisciplinary. A.M. only.
Anthropology. Ph.D.
Art. Includes history and theory; one language for A.M.; two languages for Ph.D.
Cinema and Media Studies. Ph.D.
Classical Languages and Literature. Greek, Latin, classical archaeology; reading knowledge of Greek, Latin, one other language for A.M., two other languages for Ph.D.
Comparative Literature. A.M., Ph.D.
Conceptual and Historical Studies of Science. A.M., Ph.D.
East Asian Languages and Civilizations. GRE for admission.
English Language and Literature. Includes creative writing program; GRE/Subject for admission; samples of work for admission to creative writing. A.M., Ph.D.
General Studies in the Humanities. A.M. only.
Germanic Studies. Includes German, Scandinavian; one language in addition to major for A.M.; specialization available in medieval studies.
History of Culture. Includes study of cultures of various geographic areas and historical periods. Interdisciplinary. A.M., Ph.D.
History and Theory of Art. A.M., Ph.D.
Humanities. Master of Arts in Humanities program; M.A.P.H. only.
Jewish Studies. A.M., Ph.D.
Latin American Studies. A.M. only.
Linguistics. Includes Indo-European and Balkan studies. A.M., Ph.D.
Middle Eastern Studies. A.M. only.
Music. Includes composition, ethnomusicology, theory, history; term essay for admission; apply for fellowships before January 1; two languages (German required) for A.M.; 3 languages (German required) for Ph.D. in theory and history. A.M., Ph.D.
Near Eastern Languages and Civilizations. Includes Western Asia, Egypt, Judaic, Islam. A.M., Ph.D.
New Testament and Early Christian Literature. Competence in Greek for A.M., Greek and Hebrew for Ph.D.
Philosophy. A.M., Ph.D.
Romance Languages and Literatures. Includes French, Spanish, Italian; GRE for admission; one language in addition to major for A.M., two in addition to major for Ph.D.
Slavic Languages and Literatures. Includes Russian, Polish, Czech, and Slovak literatures, Slavic linguistics. A.M., Ph.D.
South Asian Languages and Civilization. Includes Bangla, Hindi, Malayalam, Maruthi, Pali, Sanskrit, Tamil, Urdu languages, lit-

eratures, and cultures; French and German in addition to major for A.M. and Ph.D.
Social Thought and Classics. Joint Ph.D.
Visual Arts. A.M., Ph.D.

Division of the Physical Sciences

Graduate study since 1892.
Tuition: per course $4658. Enrollment: full-time 544, part-time 60. Faculty: full-time 173, part-time 9. Degrees conferred: S.M., Ph.D.

ADMISSION REQUIREMENTS. Transcripts, GRE/Subject Test, three letters of recommendation required in support of application. TOEFL required for foreign applicants. Interview not required. Accepts transfer applicants. Apply to Department Chair before January 15 (priority date for Fall). Application fee $50, $55 for international applicants. Phone: (773)702-8789.

ADMISSION STANDARDS. Competitive. Usual minimum average: 3.0 (A = 4).

FINANCIAL AID. Scholarships, fellowships, assistantships, training grants, tuition waivers, Federal W/S, loans. Apply to department chair for scholarships, fellowships, assistantships, to Office of Financial Aid for federal programs; priority application date February 15. About 99% of students receive aid other than loans from University and outside sources. Aid available for part-time students.

DEGREE REQUIREMENTS. For S.M.: 9 courses and 3 quarters minimum in residence; full-time attendance normally expected. For Ph.D.: course requirements vary by department; candidacy qualifying exam sometimes required; two quarters of teaching; reading knowledge of foreign languages in some departments; dissertation; final dissertation defense.

FIELDS OF STUDY.
Applied Mathematics.
Astronomy and Astrophysics.
Atmospheric Sciences.
Chemistry. Ph.D. only.
Computer Sciences. Includes Conversion Master's Program.
Divisional Master's Program.
Earth Sciences.
Environmental Science and Policy. Interdisciplinary.
Financial Mathematics. Master's only.
Geophysical Sciences. Interdisciplinary.
Mathematics.
Physics.
Planetary and Space Sciences.
Statistics. Includes biostatistics.

Division of Social Sciences.

Graduate study since 1992.
Tuition: per course $4074. Graduate enrollment: full- and part-time 1265. Division faculty: full-time 225. Degrees conferred: A.M., M.A.P.S.S., Ph.D.

ADMISSION REQUIREMENTS. Transcripts, three letters of recommendation, personal statement required in support of application. TOEFL required for international applicants. GRE General/Subject Tests and foreign language proficiency required for most departments. Interview not required. Accepts transfer applicants. Graduates of unaccredited institutions not considered. Application deadline for U.S. citizens and nationals is January 5, for international citizens January 1. Application fee $50, international applicants $55. Phone: (773)702-8414; fax: (773)834-3509.

ADMISSION STANDARDS. Competitive for most departments, very competitive for others.

FINANCIAL AID. Scholarships, teaching assistantships, fellowships, tuition waivers, Federal W/S, loans. Apply by January 1 to Dean for fellowships, assistantships; to the University's Financial Aid Office for all other programs. Use FAFSA. About 70% of students receive aid from both Division and outside sources.

DEGREE REQUIREMENTS. For A.M.: 9 courses and 3 quarters minimum in residences, thesis or research paper, final comprehensive exam. For M.A.P.S.S.: nine graduate level courses; master's paper. For Ph.D.: 18 courses or 6 quarters in full-time residence; reading knowledge of at least one foreign language; preliminary oral exam; candidacy; internship for some departments; dissertations; final oral exam.

FIELDS OF STUDY.
Anthropology. GRE for admission. Joint Ph.D. in Anthropology and Linguistics available; social, cultural, and psychological anthropology, archaeology, linguistic anthropology, physical anthropology, and museology. Ph.D. only.
Comparative Human Development. GRE for Admission. Includes comparative life course, clinical ethnography and mental health, cultural psychology and psychological anthropology, comparative behavioral biology, language, communication and cognition, professional education in clinical psychology.
Conceptual and Historical Studies of Science. GRE for admission. Interdisciplinary program. Includes a history option, philosophy option and science option. A.M., Ph.D.
Economics. GRE for admission; A.M. through divisional master's; joint degree in law and economics; price theory, theory of income, employment, and price level, mathematical economic theory, monetary theory and banking, economic history, econometrics and statistics, history of economic thought, labor economics, agricultural economics, public finance, international economic relations, urban economics, industrial organization, economic development. Ph.D. only.
History. GRE for admission. High competence in reading either German or French required for admission; United States history, ancient history, medieval history, Byzantine history, Russian history, Renaissance and Reformation history, modern European history, British history, history of science and/or medicine, and the histories of the Chinese, Indian and Islamic civilizations. Ph.D. only.
International Relations. GRE for admission. Interdepartmental: includes international politics, organization, economics; American foreign policy; international theory; economic development; strategic studies; international law and communism; and political geography. A.M. only.
Latin American and Caribbean Studies. Five-quarter A.M. program leads to competency in one of the Latin American or Caribbean languages in addition to studying history, culture, civilization, and current problems of the area. A.M. only.
Middle Eastern Studies. Five-quarter A.M. program leads to competency in one of the Middle Eastern languages in addition to studying history, culture, civilization, and current problems of the area. A.M. only.
Political Science. GRE for admission. Includes political theory; international relations; comparative politics.
Psychology. Includes biopsychology, cognition, developmental psychology, perception program, social psychology program; joint Ph.D. in Psychology–Linguistics. Ph.D. only.
Social Thought. GRE for admission. Interdepartmental; application deadline is January 1. Ph.D. only.
Sociology. GRE for admission. Includes community structure; demography; human ecology; deviance; economic and work institutions; family and socialization; formal organization; educational institutions; mathematical sociology; medical sociology; methodology; modernization; personality and social structure;

political organization; race and ethnic relations; small groups; social change and social movements; social psychology; social stratification; and urban sociology. Ph.D. only.

Graduate School of Business
Web site: www.chicago-gsb.edu

Established 1898. Private control. Accredited programs: M.B.A.; recognized Ph.D. Located at New Hyde Park Center and offers programs in downtown Chicago (M.B.A. part-time, evening and weekends; E.M.B.A.). Quarter system. Special Programs: International Business Exchange programs (in Australia, Austria, Belgium, Brazil, Chile, France, Germany, Hong Kong, Israel, Italy, Japan, Mexico, the Netherlands, People's Republic of China, Spain, South Africa, Sweden, Switzerland, United Kingdom); foreign Study in Barcelona, Singapore, Spain. Special facilities: Center for International Business Education and Research, Center for Decision Research, Center for Population Economics, Center for Research in Security Prices, Center for Statistics Research, Center for the Study of the Economy and the State.

Annual tuition: full-time $41,600, part-time $4425 per course. On-campus rooms and apartments available for both single and married students. Enrollment: total full-time 1093, part-time 995. Faculty: full-time 139, part-time 42; all have Ph.D./D.B.A. Degrees conferred: Campus M.B.A. (full-time, day), Evening M.B.A. (evening, weekends, located at Graduate School of Business's Gleacher Center), I.E.M.B.A. (International Executive M.B.A. in London, Singapore), I.M.B.A. (International), M.B.A.-J.D., M.B.A.-M.D., M.B.A.-A.M. (Area Studies: East Asian, Latin American, Middle Eastern and South Asian; International Relations and Business; Social Services Administration and Business), M.B.A.-M.P.P., M.B.A.-S.M. (Physical Sciences and Business), Ph.D. (Dissertation areas in Behavior Science, Econometrics and Statistics Economics, Finance, Management Science, Marketing, Organizations and Markets, Production).

ADMISSION REQUIREMENTS. All applicants should have a bachelor's degree from a recognized institution of higher education. Accepts MBA Multi-App and Computer Edge electronic applications in lieu of institutional application. Early applications are encouraged for both admission and financial aid consideration. Full-time students are admitted Summer, Fall only; part-time evening applicants may enter any quarter, part-time weekend applicants are admitted Fall only; International M.B.A. applicants begin Summer only. There are three deadlines for Fall and both U.S. citizens and international applicants should observe the following deadlines: November 15, January 1, March 15 (applicants who file after February are generally at a disadvantage); scholarship applicants should apply by January 1. Applicants to international M.B.A. should apply by January 15. Part-time applicants should apply at least six weeks in advance of quarter for which they are seeking admission. Submit an application, a GMAT result (will accept GMAT test results from the last five years, latest acceptable date is March), official transcripts from each undergraduate/graduate school attended, two letters of recommendation, personal statement, current résumé (prefers at least four years of work experience), and an application fee of $200 to the Director of Admissions. Phone: campus M.B.A. (773)702-7369; evening, weekend, phone: (773)464-8700. Applicants for I.M.B.A. whose native language is not English must submit a foreign language assessment. In addition, international students (whose native language is other than English) should submit a TOEFL (will not consider scores taken more than two years ago, minimum score 600), certified translations and evaluations of all official transcripts, recommendation should be in English or with certified translations and proof of sufficient financial resources for two years of academic study. In some cases full-time day applicants may be invited to an on-campus interview. Joint degree applicants must apply to and be accepted to both schools/programs, contact the admissions office for current information and specific admissions requirements.

ADMISSION REQUIREMENTS FOR DOCTORAL CANDIDATES. Contact the Office of Doctoral Programs for application material and current information. Applications may be downloaded from Web site. Beginning students are admitted Fall quarter only. Both U.S. citizens and international applicants apply by January 15. Submit an application, a GMAT/GRE (will accept GMAT/GRE test results from the last five years), two official transcripts from each undergraduate/graduate school attended, three letters of recommendation, essays, current résumé, statement of purpose, and application fee of $200 to the Graduate School of Business. In addition, international students (whose native language is other than English and have completed at least two years of study in the U.S.) should submit TOEFL (minimum score 600), TSE scores, certified translations and evaluations of all official transcripts, recommendation should be in English or with certified translations. International student's contact: (773)702-7438. Interviews are strongly encouraged.

ADMISSION STANDARDS. Very selective. Median GMAT: 701; median GPA: 3.5 (A = 4). *U.S. News & World Report* ranked Graduate School in the top two for part-time M.B.A., top four for Accounting, top two in Finance, top six for E.M.B.A., top seven M.B.A. of all U.S. business schools. *BusinessWeek* listed Graduate School in the top six American business schools.

FINANCIAL AID. Scholarships, minority stipend programs, corporate-sponsored fellowships, graduate assistantships, Federal W/S, loans available. Financial aid is available for part-time study. Financial aid may be available for international students. Assistantships/fellowships available for joint degree candidates. Apply by March 1 for most financial assistance, by January 1 for scholarships, fellowships, and assistantships. Request both need- and merit-based financial aid information from the Graduate School of Business; phone: (773)702-3694. For most financial assistance and all Federal programs submit FAFSA (School code: E00512). Approximately 65% of current students receive some form of financial assistance. For Ph.D. applicants the financial assistance is primarily merit-based. Full support is provided through tuition waivers or tuition waivers plus stipends for four years if all academic conditions are met. International applicants must be able to provide full financial support for the first year of doctoral study.

DEGREE REQUIREMENTS. For M.B.A. (both full- and part-time programs): 20-course program including 11 elective courses; a Leadership, Exploration and Development (LEAD) course for campus M.B.A.; two-year full-time program or two-and-one-half- to three-and-one-half-year program (part-time), degree program must be completed in five years. For M.B.A.-Master's: generally from three-and-one-half- to five-year programs. For M.B.A.-J.D.: four-and-one-half- to five-and-one-half-year program. For M.B.A.-M.D.: five-and-one-half- to seven-year program. For Ph.D.: 6–12 quarter program in residence depending on a student's prior degree; general exam; successfully complete both Breadth (4 courses) and Support (3 courses) courses; complete a curriculum paper; dissertation; oral defense.

M.B.A. AREAS OF CONCENTRATION.
Accounting.
Analytic Finance.
Econometrics and Statistics.
Economics.
Entrepreneurship.
Finance.
General Management.
Human Resource Management.
International Business.
Managerial and Organization Behavior.
Marketing Management.
Operations Management.
Strategic Management.

PH.D. DISSERTATION AREAS:
Accounting.
Finance.
Econometrics & Statistics.
Economics.
Managerial & Organizational Behavior.
Management Science/Operations.
Marketing.
Organizations & Market.

Divinity School

All study at the graduate level. Tuition: per course $2334. Enrollment: full-time 330. Faculty: full-time 30. Degrees conferred: A.M., A.M.R.S., Ph.D., M.Div.

ADMISSION REQUIREMENTS. Transcripts, four letters of recommendation, GRE, essay required in support of application. TOEFL required for foreign applicants. Interview not required. Apply to Dean of Students of the School, preferably by January 1 (A.M., A.M.R.S., and Ph.D. applicants), March 1 (M.Div.). Application fee $45, $50 international applicant. Phone: (773)702-8217; fax: (773)834-4581.

ADMISSION STANDARDS. Very competitive. Usual minimum average: 3.25 (A = 4).

FINANCIAL AID. Scholarships, fellowships, assistantships, field education/fieldwork stipends, Federal W/S, loans. Apply to Dean of Students of the School by January 1. Phone: (773)702-8217. Use FAFSA. About 90% of students receive aid other than loans from School.

DEGREE REQUIREMENTS. For A.M.: Two years of full-time residence; reading knowledge of French or German; three course sequence on the Modern Study of Religion. For A.M.R.S.: 1- to 2-year program in full-time residence; reading competency in one foreign language; oral exam. For Ph.D.: four years of full-time residence; reading knowledge of French and German; qualifying exams; research paper and oral exam; dissertation; oral defense. For M.Div.: three years of full-time residence beyond B.A. (27 courses); one Biblical language (either New Testament Greek or biblical Hebrew); M.Div. paper/essay.

FIELDS OF STUDY.
Anthropology and Sociology of Religion.
Biblical Studies.
History of Christianity.
History of Judaism.
History of Religions.
Islamic Studies.
Philosophy of Religion.
Religion and Literature.
Religious Ethics.
Theology.
Note: Dual degrees available: M.Div.-A.M. (School of Social Science Administration), M.Div.-A.M. (Harris School of Public Policy), M.Div.-Ph.D. (Divinity School), A.M.-J.D., A.M.R.S.-J.D., Ph.D.-J.D., M.Div.-J.D. (Law School).

Law School
Web site: www.law.uchicago.edu

Opened 1902. ABA approved since 1923. AALS charter member. Private control. Quarter system. Special facilities: Center for Studies in Criminal Justice, Center for Constitutionalism and Eastern Europe. Law library: 718,749 volumes, 8878 subscriptions; has LEXIS, NEXIS, WESTLAW, DIALOG; more than 1000 network connections.

Annual tuition: $37,945. Off-campus housing available two blocks from School. Total average cost for all other expenses: $22,560.

Enrollment: first-year 196, total 600 (men 55%, women 45%, minorities 30%). No part-time students. Postgraduate: 12. Faculty: full-time 60, part-time 42. Student to faculty ratio 9.5 to 1. Degrees conferred: J.D., J.D.-M.A. (Economics, History, International relations), J.D.-M.B.A., J.D.-M.P.P., J.D.-Ph.D. (Business, Economics, History), LL.M., J.S.D., M.C.L.

ADMISSION REQUIREMENTS. LSDAS Law School report, LSAT (not later than December), letters of recommendation, personal statement, résumé required in support of application. Interview used in a number of cases; by invitation only. LSAT recommended but not required of graduate law applicants. Applicants must hold a bachelor's degree. Accepts about 10 transfer applicants annually. Graduates of unaccredited colleges not considered. Apply to Law School Admissions office after September 1 and preferably by February 1. For early decision program, apply by December 1. Beginning students admitted Fall only. Application fee $75. Phone: (773)702-9484; fax: (773)702-0942.

ADMISSION STANDARDS. Selective. Accepts approximately 15% of total applicants. Number of applicants 4800; number of acceptance 705; number enrolled 190; LSAT (75% of students have a score at or above 168); GPA (75% of students have a GPA at or above 3.46). *U.S. News & World Report* ranking is in the top six of all U.S. law schools.

FINANCIAL AID. Scholarships, tutorial and research fellowships. Apply to Admissions Office by April 1 for scholarships. Phone: (773)702-9484. No closing date for loans. Use FAFSA. About 95% of students receive aid other than loans from School.

DEGREE REQUIREMENTS. For J.D.: 9 full quarters and 140 credit hours minimum. For LL.M.: 3 consecutive quarters in full-time residence; final research paper. For J.S.D.: at least 3 consecutive quarters in full-time residence; dissertation; final oral exam. For M.C.L.: 3 consecutive quarters in full-time residence. For D.C.L.: at least 3 consecutive quarters in full-time residence; dissertation. The M.C.L. program available to law graduates primarily from foreign legal institutions.

Pritzker School of Medicine (60637-5416)
Web site: pritzker.bsd.uchicago.edu

Established 1927 and is part of the Division of Biological Sciences. Private control. Semester system. Library: 996,000 volumes, 7000 subscriptions. The University's NIH ranking is 28th among all U.S. institutions with 444 awards/grants worth $194,716,584.

Annual tuition: $36,401. On-campus apartments available. Average figure for all other expenses: $15,018.

Enrollment: first-year class 104 (2 MSTP); total full-time 422 (men 51%, women 49%, minorities 28%, state residents 31%). Faculty: same as for the Division of Biological Sciences. Degrees conferred: M.D., M.D.-A.M. (Public Policy), M.D.-M.B.A., M.D.-M.H.A., M.D.-Ph.D., MSTP.

ADMISSION REQUIREMENTS. AMCAS report, transcripts, three letters of recommendation, MCAT, interview required in support of application. Applicants must have completed at least three years of college study. Has EDP (apply between June 15–August 1). Will consider transfers on a space available basis. Apply to University Director of Admissions after June 1, before October 15. Application fee $75. Phone: (773)702-1937; fax: (773)834-5412.

ADMISSION STANDARDS. Very competitive. Accepts about 7% of all applicants. Number of applications 3830 (3269 out-of-state); number interviewed 599 (469 out-of-state); number of acceptance 277 (216 out-of-state); number enrolled 104 (66 out-of-state). Mean Composite MCAT 11.3; mean UGPA 3.75. *U.S. News & World Report* ranking is in the top 11 of all medical research schools.

FINANCIAL AID. Scholarships, tuition awards, loans. Apply by February 1 to Dean of Students of the School of Medicine. Use FAFSA (School code: G10141). About 82% of medical students receive aid other than loans from School.

DEGREE REQUIREMENTS. For M.D.: satisfactory completion of four-year program, or a three-year program for students who already have Ph.D. For Master's, Ph.D.: see Graduate Schools listings above.

FIELDS OF GRADUATE STUDY.
Biomedical Sciences.
Biophysics and Synthetic Biology.
Cell Physiology.
Darwinian Sciences.
Health Studies.
Integrative Science Training.
Medical Physics.
Molecular Biosciences.
Neurosciences.
Ophthalmology and Visual Sciences.

The Irving B. Harris Graduate School of Public Policy

Established 1987.
Annual tuition: full-time $30,000, per course $4280. On-campus housing available.
Enrollment: full-time 165, part-time 10. Faculty: full-time 20, part-time none. Degrees conferred: A.M. (one-year program open to only those students who have completed at least one year (nine courses with quality grades) of graduate work at the University of Chicago), M.P.P., S.M.(with the Division of the Physical Sciences), Ph.D.

ADMISSION REQUIREMENTS. Official transcripts, three letters of recommendation, GRE or GMAT required in support of School's application. TOEFL required for international applicants. Accepts transfer applicants. Graduates of unaccredited colleges may not be considered. Application deadline: Ph.D. January 3, Master's priority deadline January 3. Rolling admission process. Early application encouraged. Application fee $50. Phone: (773)702-8401; fax: (773)702-0926.

ADMISSION STANDARDS. Selective. Usual minimum average: 2.75 (A = 4), 3.0 in major field of undergraduate study.

FINANCIAL AID. Fellowships, assistantships, Federal W/S, loans. Apply by February 1 to appropriate department chair for fellowships, assistantships; to Office of Financial Aid for all other programs. Phone: (773)702-6062. Use FAFSA.

DEGREE REQUIREMENTS. For A.M.: 6–7 courses and 3 quarters minimum in residence; candidacy; thesis or essay, reading knowledge of one foreign language usually required; final written/oral exam. For M.P.P.: two-year full-time program; LEAD. For Ph.D.: 27 courses and 9 quarters minimum beyond the bachelor's, at least 3 quarters in residence; qualifying paper and exam; reading knowledge of at least one foreign language; dissertation; final oral defense. For S.M.: 18 course program; dissertation proposal and oral defense.

FIELDS OF STUDY.
Environmental Science and Policy. Joint degree. S.M.
Public Policy. Includes concentrations in child and family policy, education policy, environmental policy, finance and public finance, health policy, international policy, organizations, institutions and management, poverty and inequality. M.P.P., Ph.D.
Public Policy Studies. A.M.only.
Note: Joint degrees available: M.P.P.-A.M. (Center for Middle Eastern Studies), M.P.P.-M.Div. (Divinity School), M.P.P.-M.B.A.

(Graduate School of Business), M.P.P.-J.D. (Law School), M.P.P.-A.M. (School of Social Science Administration).

School of Social Service Administration

Chartered 1908.
Tuition: per course $4365. Graduate enrollment: full-time 421, part-time 62. Faculty: full-time 33, part-time 48. Degrees conferred: A.M., Ph.D.

ADMISSION REQUIREMENTS. Transcripts required in support of School's application. TOEFL required for international applicants. Interview not required. Accepts transfer applicants. Graduates of unaccredited institutions not considered. Apply to the School by February 1 (priority date). Fall admission only. Rolling admission process. Application fee $60, $70 for international applicants. Phone: (773)702-1492; fax: (773)834-4751.

ADMISSIONS STANDARDS. Selective. Usual minimum average: 2.8 (A = 4) UGPA from a liberal arts program.

FINANCIAL AID. Annual awards from School funds: scholarships, teaching assistantships, fieldwork, Federal W/S, loans. Apply by April 15 to Dean's Office for assistantships; to Financial Office for all other programs. Phone: (773)702-1126. Use FAFSA. About 80% of students receive aid from School and outside sources. Aid available for part-time students.

DEGREE REQUIREMENTS. For A.M.: 18 courses, at least 3–6 quarters in full-time residence; field placement. For Ph.D.: minimum of 13 courses beyond the master's; evidence of research and statistics competency; qualifying exam; research project; dissertation; final oral exam.

FIELDS OF STUDY.
Clinical Practice. Includes social and psychological services to individuals, families, and groups. A.M.
Social Administration. Includes advocacy, community organizations, management, planning, policy development and implementation, evaluation. A.M., Ph.D.
Note: Joint degree programs available with Business School, Divinity School, and Harris Graduate School of Public Policy.

UNIVERSITY OF CINCINNATI
Cincinnati, Ohio 45221
Web site: www.uc.edu

Founded 1819. CGS member. Coed. Public control. Quarter system. Cooperative graduate program in social work with Ohio State University. Special facilities: Biomedical Chemistry Research Center, Center for Computational Fluid Dynamics, Center for Cultural Resources, Center for Hazardous Waste Research, Center for Economic Education, Environmental Health Center, Center for Geographic Informational Systems and Spatial Analysis, Center for Neighborhood and Community Studies, Institute of Policy Research, Center for Women's Studies. The University's NIH ranking is 60th among all U.S. Institutions with 260 awards/grants valued at $104,425,887. According to The Center at University of Florida, the University is ranked 42nd in receipt of Federal Research funds with $185,261,000 and it ranks 48th for total University research expenditures with $255,083,000. The University's endowment assets ranks it 49th, $987,785,000. In 2004, the University awarded 212 doctorates which ranked it 69th among all U.S. institutions eligible to award that degree. 6 of the University's faculty members have been elected to National Honor Academies and this ranks it 86th among all U.S. institutions. The Library: approximately 2,600,000 volumes, 27,000 subscriptions. Total University enrollment: 34,000.

Tuition: full-time Cincinnati residents $4037, per quarter; non-residents $7315 per quarter. On-campus housing for 656 single men or women. Average per month housing cost: $525–$750. Apply by July 1 to Housing Office. Phone: (513)556-0682; for off-campus information (513)556-7375.

Graduate School

Established 1906. Enrollment: full-time 3660, part-time 2276. Graduate faculty: full- and part-time 750. Degrees Conferred: M.A., M.S., M.Ed., M.A.T., M.B.A., M.C.P., M.Des., M.F.A., M.S.Arch., M.S.N., Ed.D., D.M.A., M.M., Pharm.D., Ph.D.

ADMISSION REQUIREMENTS. Transcripts, three letters of recommendation (two for engineering) required in support of application. Interview, GRE, GMAT, writing samples, portfolios, statement of purpose required by some departments. Accepts transfer applicants. TOEFL, TWE required for all international students; TSE optional. Graduates of unaccredited institutions not considered. Apply to appropriate Dean at least seven months prior to registration. Foreign students apply to Foreign Students Office. Application fee $40. Phone: (513)556-4335; (513)556-0128.

ADMISSION STANDARDS. Selective. Usual minimum average: 3.0 (A = 4).

FINANCIAL AID. Scholarships, fellowships, research assistantships, teaching assistantships, internships, Federal W/S, loans. Graduate tuition reciprocity with surrounding counties in Ohio and Kentucky. Apply by February 15 to appropriate Dean for scholarships and fellowships, to appropriate department chair for assistantships, to the Office of Financial Aid for all other programs. Phone: (513)556-6982; fax: (513)556-9171; e-mail: financeaid@uc.edu. Use FAFSA. About 90% of full-time students receive aid other than loans from School and outside sources. No aid for part-time students.

DEGREE REQUIREMENTS. For master's: 45–90 quarter hours minimum, at least one year in residence for some departments; however some departments require two or more years of full-time study; thesis; reading knowledge of one foreign language for some departments; completion of degree no later than seven years from date of entrance; written/oral exam. For Ed.D.: three years minimum in residence; written comprehensive exam; dissertation. For Ph.D.: 135 quarter hours minimum and three years of full-time study or equivalent in residence; written comprehensive exam; advancement to candidacy; dissertation; final oral exam; completion of all requirements no later than nine years from date of entrance.

FIELDS OF STUDY.
Accounting. M.S.
Aerospace Engineering. M.S., Ph.D.
Anthropology. M.A.
Applied Economics. M.A.
Architecture. M.S. Arch., M.Arch.
Art Education. M.A.
Art History. M.A.
Audiology. Au.D.
Biological Sciences. M.S., Ph.D.
Biomedical Engineering. M.S., Ph.D.
Biostatistics. M.S., Ph.D.
Business Administration. Ph.D.
Cell and Molecular Biology. Ph.D.
Chemical Engineering. M.S., Ph.D.
Chemistry. M.S., Ph.D.
Civil Engineering. M.S., Ph.D.
Classics. M.A., Ph.D.
Communication. M.A.
Communication Sciences and Disorders. M.A., Ph.D.

Community Counseling. M.A.
Community Planning. M.C.P.
Computer Engineering. M.S.
Computer Science. M.S.
Computer Science and Engineering. Ph.D.
Counselor Education. Ed.D.
Criminal Justice. M.S., Ph.D.
Curriculum and Instruction. M.Ed., Ed.D.
Early Childhood Education. M.Ed.
Educational Administration. M.Ed., Ed.S.
Educational Leadership. M.Ed.
Educational Studies. M.A., Ph.D.
Electrical Engineering. M.S., Ph.D.
Elementary/Middle Education. M.Ed.
Economics. M.A., Ph.D.
Engineering Mechanics. M.S., Ph.D.
English and Comparative Literature. M.A., Ph.D.
Environmental Engineering. M.S., Ph.D.
Environmental Health. M.S., Ph.D.
Environmental Science. M.S., Ph.D.
Finance. M.S.
Fine Arts. M.F.A.
French. M.A.
Genetic Counseling. M.S.
Geography. M.A., Ph.D.
Geology. M.S., Ph.D.
Germanic Languages and Literature. M.A., Ph.D.
Health Education. M.Ed., M.S., Ph.D.
Health Physics. M.S.
Health Promotion and Education. M.Ed.
History. M.A., M.A.T., Ph.D.
Immunobiology. M.S., Ph.D.
Information Systems. M.S.
International Business. M.B.A.
Labor and Employment Relations. M.A.
Literacy. M.Ed., Ed.D.
Management. M.S.
Management of Advanced Technology and Innovation. M.B.A.
Marketing. M.S.
Materials Science. M.S., Ph.D.
Mathematics. M.S., M.A.T., Ph.D.
Mechanical Engineering. M.S., Ph.D.
Metallurgical Engineering. M.S., Ph.D.
Molecular and Cellular Pathophysiology. D.Sc.
Molecular and Cellular Physiology. Ph.D.
Molecular & Developmental Biology. M.S., Ph.D.
Molecular, Cellular, and Biochemical Pharmacology. M.S., Ph.D.
Molecular Genetics, Biochemistry, and Microbiology. M.S., Ph.D.
Neuroscience. Ph.D.
Nuclear and Radiological Engineering. M.S., Ph.D.
Nursing. Includes adult health, community health, critical care trauma, family nurse practitioner, neonatal, nurse anesthesia, nurse midwifery, nurse service administration, occupational health, pediatric nurse practitioner, perinatal health, psychiatric, women's health. M.S.N., Ph.D.
Nutrition. M.S.
Operations Management. M.S.
Pathobiology and Molecular Medicine. M.S., Ph.D.
Pharmaceutical Sciences. M.S., Ph.D.
Pharmacy Practice. Pharm.D.
Philosophy. M.A., Ph.D.
Physical Therapy. D.P.T.
Physics. M.S., Ph.D.
Political Science. M.A., Ph.D.
Psychology. Ph.D.
Quantitative Analysis. M.S.
Radiology—Radiological Sciences. Includes medical physics. M.S.
Regional Development Planning. Ph.D.
School Counseling. M.Ed.
School Psychology. M.Ed., Ph.D.
Secondary Education. M.Ed.

Social Work. M.S.W.
Sociology. M.A., Ph.D.
Spanish. M.A., Ph.D.
Special Education. M.Ed., Ed.D.
System Biology and Physiology. Ph.D.
Taxation. M.S.
Teaching English and Language Arts. M.A.T.
Teaching Science. M.T.S.
Theater Design and Production. M.F.A
Theater Performance. M.F.A.
Toxicology. M.S., Ph.D.
Transfusion and Transplantation Sciences. M.S.
Urban Educational Leadership. Ed.D.
Women Studies. M.A.

College of Law (45221-0040)

Web site: www.law.uc.edu

Opened 1833. Fourth oldest law school in U.S., ABA approved since 1923. AALS charter member. Public control. Semester system. Special facilities: Center for Corporate Law, Center for Dispute Resolution, Morgan Institute for Human Rights, Weaver Institute for Law and Psychiatry. Law library: 422,146 volumes, 8367 subscriptions; has LEXIS, NEXIS, WESTLAW, ICLIO, OHIOLINK, OCLC, DIALOG, EPIC, DATATIMES.

Annual tuition: full-time resident $18,032, nonresident $32,152. Limited on-campus housing available. Apply to University Office for Resident Living for both on- and off-campus housing. Total average cost for all other expenses: $14,687.

Enrollment: first-year 140, total 392 (men 51%, women 49%, minorities 18%). Faculty: full-time 31, part-time 26. Student to faculty ratio 11.8 to 1. Degrees conferred: J.D., J.D.-M.A. (Women's Studies), J.D.-M.B.A., J.D.-M.C.P. (Community Planning), J.D.-M.S. (Economics, Political Science), J.D.-M.S.W., J.D.-Ph.D.

ADMISSION REQUIREMENTS. LSDAS Law School report, transcripts, bachelor's degree, two letters of recommendation, LSAT, personal statement required in support of application. Interview not required. TOEFL required of international applicants. Accepts transfer applicants. Applicants from unaccredited colleges not considered. Apply to College after September 1, before April 1. For early decision apply by December 1. Fall admission. Application fee $35. Phone: (513)556-6805; fax: (513)556-2391; e-mail: admissions@law.cu.edu.

ADMISSION STANDARDS. Selective. Accepts approximately 37% of total applicants. Number of applicants 1186; number of acceptance 435; number enrolled 133; LSAT (75% of students have a score at or above 156); GPA (75% of students have a GPA at or above 3.29). *U.S. News & World Report* ranking is in the second tier tied at 57th of all U.S. law schools.

FINANCIAL AID. Scholarships, fellowships, assistantships, Federal W/S, loans. Apply by April 1. Phone: (513)556-6805. Use FAFSA. About 50% of students receive aid other than loans from College.

DEGREE REQUIREMENTS. For J.D.: 90 semester hours minimum, at least one year in full-time residence; upper divisional writing course and professional responsibility course.

College of Medicine (45267-0552)

Web site: www.med.uc.edu

Established 1819. Library: 270,000 volumes, 3000 subscriptions. NIH ranking is 60 among all U.S. institutions with 260 awards/grants worth $104,425,887.

Annual tuition: residents $27,272, nonresidents $46,438. On-campus housing is limited. Total average figure for all other expense $16,000.

Enrollment: first-year class 160, total full-time 621 (men 56%, women 44%, minorities 29%, state residents 93%). Faculty: full-time 1000, part-time 160. Degrees conferred: M.D., M.D.-M.B.A., M.D.-M.S., M.D.-Ph.D. (M.S.T.P., P.S.T.P.).

ADMISSION REQUIREMENTS. AMCAS, transcripts, letters of recommendation, MCAT, supplementary application required in support of application. Preference given to state resident. Applicants must have completed at least three years of college study. Interview required of final candidates. Has EDP; apply between June 15 and August 1. Accepts transfer applicants. Graduates of unaccredited colleges not considered. Apply to Admissions Committee of the College after June 15, before November 15. Application fee $25. Phone: (513)558-7314; fax: (513)558-1165.

ADMISSION STANDARDS. Competitive. Accepts about 11% of all applicants. Number of applications 2971 (2017 out-of-state); number interviewed 627 (279 out-of-state); number of acceptance 343 (109 out-of-state); number enrolled 160 (40 out-of-state). Mean Composite MCAT 10.1; mean UGPA 3.59. *U.S. News & World Report* ranking is in the top 41 of all medical schools.

FINANCIAL AID. Scholarships, Federal and private loans. Apply by May 1 to the Associate Dean. Phone: (513)558-6797. Use FAFSA, NEED ACCESS program. About 80% of students receive some aid from College.

DEGREE REQUIREMENTS. For M.D.: satisfactory completion of four-year program; must pass Step 1 of USMLE to advance to third year; must pass Step 2 to graduate. For Master's, Ph.D.: see Graduate School listing above.

FIELDS OF GRADUATE STUDY.
Biomedical Engineering.
Biomedical Sciences.
Cell and Cancer Biology.
Environmental Health.
Immunobiology.
Medical Physics.
Molecular and Developmental Biology.
Molecular, Cellular & Biochemical Pharmacology.
Molecular Genetics, Biochemistry & Microbiology.
Neuroscience.
Pathobiology and Molecular Medicine.
Systems Biology and Physiology.

College-Conservatory of Music, Graduate Division

Graduate study since 1929, doctoral study since 1971. Coed. Quarter system.

Tuition; resident $4037 per quarter, nonresident $7315 per quarter.

Enrollment: full-time 400, part-time 175. Total college faculty: full-time 90, part-time 30. Degrees conferred: M.A., M.F.A., Artist Diploma, M.M., D.M.A., D.M.E., Ph.D.

ADMISSION REQUIREMENTS. Official transcripts, three letters of recommendation, audition/interview, GRE required in support of College's application. GMAT required for Art Administration. TOEFL (520 minimum score) and verification of available funding required for international applicants. Accepts transfer applicants. Apply to Assistant Dean for Admissions and Student Services by February 1 for priority consideration. Application fee $100. Phone: (513)556-6638; fax: (513)556-1028.

ADMISSION STANDARDS. Selective on basis of demonstrated talent and academic background. Usual minimum average: 3.0 (A = 4).

FINANCIAL AID. Annual awards from institutional funds: scholarships, awards, prizes, teaching assistantships, Federal W/S, loans. Approved for VA benefits. Apply by February 15 to Assistant Dean for Admissions and Student Services. Phone: (513)556-6982; fax: (513)556-9171. Use FAFSA.

DEGREE REQUIREMENTS. For M.M.: 51–56 quarter hours minimum (theory 66 quarter hours, music history 65 quarter hours, orchestral conducting 68 quarter hours, accompanying 62 quarter hours, jazz studies 64 quarter hours, woodwinds 69 quarter hours); at least one year in residence; comprehensive review; recitals where appropriate; final oral exam; knowledge of one foreign language for some programs. For M.A.: 84 quarter hour program; research project; internship. For M.F.A.: 144–154 quarter hours, at least seven quarters in residence; thesis/thesis production/two professional internships. For D.M.A., D.M.E.: 90 quarter hours minimum beyond master's (135 quarter hours for D.M.E.); preliminary exam; final document; reading knowledge of one foreign language for D.M.A. For Ph.D.: 90 quarter hours, minimum beyond the master's; reading knowledge of two foreign languages; outside-of-field cognate; preliminary exam; dissertation; final oral exam.

FIELDS OF STUDY.
Accompanying. M.M.
Arts Administration. M.A.
Bassoon. M.M., D.M.A.
Choral Conducting. M.M., D.M.A.
Clarinet. M.M., D.M.A.
Classical Guitar. M.M.
Composition. M.M., D.M.A.
Conducting. Includes choral, orchestral, wind ensemble. M.M., D.M.A.
Double Bass. M.M., D.M.A.
Euphonium. M.M.
Flute. M.M., D.M.A.
French Horn. M.M., D.M.A., A.D.
Harp. M.M.
Harpsichord. M.M., D.M.A., A.D.
Jazz Studies. M.M.
Music. Includes theory, musicology. Ph.D. only.
Music Education. M.M.
Music History. M.M.
Oboe. M.M., D.M.A.
Opera. A.D. only.
Organ. M.M., D.M.A.
Percussion. M.M., D.M.A., A.D.
Piano. M.M., D.M.A., A.D.
Saxophone. M.M., D.M.A.
Theater Design and Production. Includes costume, makeup, sound, stage, stage lighting, stage management, technical production. M.F.A.
Theater Directing. M.F.A.
Theater Performance. M.F.A.
Theory. M.M., Ph.D.
Trombone. M.M., D.M.A.
Trumpet. M.M., D.M.A.
Tuba. M.M., D.M.A.
Viola. M.M., D.M.A.
Violin. M.M., D.M.A.
Violoncello. M.M., D.M.A.
Voice. M.M., D.M.A., A.D.
Woodwinds. M.M., A.D.

THE CITADEL
Charleston, South Carolina 29409
Web site: www.citadel.edu

Founded 1842. Located 100 miles S of Columbia. Coed on graduate level. State control. Semester system. Library: 233,745 volumes, 1300 subscriptions. Total University enrollment: 3386.

Tuition: per credit hour, resident $235, nonresident $438. No on-campus housing for graduate students.

College of Graduate and Professional Studies

Graduate study since 1968. Enrollment: full-time 160, part-time 645. Faculty teaching graduate students: full- and part-time 130. Degrees conferred: M.A., M.A. Ed., M.A.T., M.B.A., M.Ed., Ed.S.

ADMISSION REQUIREMENTS. Transcripts, interview, MAT/GRE/GMAT, two letters of recommendation required in support of application. TOEFL required for international applicants. Accepts transfer applicants. Graduates of unaccredited institutions not considered. Apply to Dean of Graduate Studies or Director of M.B.A. Program at least one month prior to registration. Application fee for Graduate Education and M.B.A. is $30. Phone: (843)953-5089; fax: (843)953-7630.

ADMISSION STANDARDS. Selective. Usual minimum average: 2.75 (A = 4).

FINANCIAL AID. Limited to graduate assistantships, Federal W/S, loans. Apply to Graduate Office for assistantship, to Financial Aid Office for all Federal programs; no specified closing date. Phone: (843)953-5187; fax: (843)953-6759. Use FAFSA.

DEGREE REQUIREMENTS. For M.A., M.A. Ed., M.A.T., M.Ed.: 39–45 semester hours minimum, at least 24 in residence; comprehensive exam; no language or thesis requirements. For M.B.A.: 30 semester hours minimum, at least 24 in residence; no language or thesis requirements; comprehensive exam. For Ed.S.: 39 semester hours beyond the master's.

FIELDS OF STUDY.
Biology. M.A.Ed.
Business Administration. M.B.A.
Clinical Counseling. M.A.
Computer Science. M.S.
Counselor Education. M.Ed.
Educational Leadership. Includes elementary, secondary (M.Ed.); superintendency, school psychology (Ed.S.).
English. M.A.
Guidance and Counseling. M.Ed.
History. M.A.
Mathematics. M.A.Ed.
Physical Education. M.Ed.
Psychology. M.A.
Reading. M.Ed.
Secondary Education. Includes math, English, biology, social studies. M.A.T.
Social Sciences. M.A.Ed.
Special Education. Joint program with University of Charleston.
Sport Management. M.B.A.

CITY COLLEGE OF THE CITY UNIVERSITY OF NEW YORK
New York, New York 10031-6977
Web site: www.ccny.cuny.edu

Founded 1847. Coed. Municipal control. Semester system. Special facilities: Benjamin Levich Institute, Center for Worker Education, Center for Analysis of Structures and Interfaces/CASI, Center for Biomedical Engineering, Center for Teaching and Learning, Dominican Institute, Earthquake Engineering Center, International Center for Environmental Resources and Development, Institute for Municipal Waste Research, Institute for Research on the African Diaspora in the Americas and the Caribbean, Institute for Transportation Systems, Max E. &

Filomen M. Greenberg Center for Legal Education and Urban Policy, Rifkind Center for the Humanities, Robinson Center for Graphic Arts and Communication Design, Sonic Arts Center. Library: 1,400,000 volumes; designated as a Federal depository in 1884. Total College enrollment: 12,440.

Tuition: New York City and State residents $270 per credit, nonresidents $500. No on-campus housing.

College of Liberal Arts and Sciences— Graduate Division

Graduate study since 1944. Enrollment: full- and part-time 1045. College faculty: full- and part-time 205. Degrees conferred: M.A., M.S., M.F.A., Ph.D. (offered through CUNY Graduate).

ADMISSION REQUIREMENTS. Transcripts, GRE, three letters of recommendation required in support of application. Some programs require writing samples, portfolios, or auditions. TOEFL or evidence of proficiency in English required of international students. Interview not required. Accepts transfer applicants. Apply to Office of Admissions, Room 100 by May 1 (Fall). December 1 (Spring). Application fee $40. Phone: (212)650-6977; fax: (212)650-6417.

ADMISSION STANDARDS. Relatively open for some departments, selective for others. Usual minimum average: 2.75 (A = 4).

FINANCIAL AID. Annual awards from institutional funds: scholarships, assistantships, full and partial tuition waivers, Federal W/S, loans. Apply by February 1 to University's Financial Aid Office for scholarships, fellowships, Federal funds; by March 1 to appropriate department chair for assistantships. Phone: (212)650-5819. Use FAFSA and CUNY's FAF. About 5–10% of students receive aid other than loans from University and outside sources. Aid available for part-time students.

DEGREE REQUIREMENTS. For master's: 30–48 credit hours minimum, at least two semesters in residence (24 credits); foreign language proficiency for some programs; thesis or comprehensive exam in many fields. For Ph.D.: two years minimum, at least one year in residence; preliminary exam; reading knowledge of one or two foreign languages; and proficiency in one research tool; dissertation; final oral exam.

FIELDS OF STUDY.
Art. M.F.A.
Art History. M.A.
Biochemistry. M.A.
Biology. M.A.
Chemistry. M.A.
Clinical Psychology. M.A.
Creative Writing. M.A.
Earth and Environmental Science. Includes oceanography. M.A.
Economics. M.A.
English Literature—Language and Literacy. M.A.
History. M.A.
International Relations. M.A.
Mathematics. M.A.
Media Arts Production. M.F.A.
Music. M.A.
Physics. M.A.
Psychology. M.A.
Sociology. M.A.
Spanish. M.A.

School of Architecture, Urban Design and Landscape Architecture

Tuition: New York State resident $315 per credit, nonresident $555.

Enrollment: full-time 18, part-time 10. Faculty: full-time 12, part-time 10. Degrees conferred: M.Arch. I, M.Arch II, M.U.P.

ADMISSION REQUIREMENTS. Transcripts, three letters of reference, curriculum vitae, 500-word essay required in support of application. Interview not required, but encouraged. TOEFL required for international applicants. Apply to Admissions Office of the School by January 1. Application fee $40. Phone: (212)650-7284.

ADMISSION STANDARDS. Selective. Usual minimum average 2.75 (A = 4.0).

FINANCIAL AID. Scholarships, research/teaching assistantships, Federal W/S, loans. Apply to Dean for scholarships, assistantships, to Financial Aid Office for all other aid by May 1. Phone: (212)650-5819 or (212)650-6656. Use FAFSA.

DEGREE REQUIREMENTS. For M.Arch. I.: 108 credit full-time program; thesis. For M.Arch. II; 51 credit full-time program; thesis optional. For M.U.P.: 32 credit full-time program.

FIELDS OF STUDY.
Architecture.
Landscape Architecture
Urban Design.

School of Education—Graduate Division
Web site: www.ccny.cuny.edu

Graduate study since 1921. Semester system.
Tuition: per credit, New York State resident $270, nonresident and international $500. Enrollment: full- and part-time 1587. Faculty: full-time 84, part-time 75. Degrees conferred: M.A., M.S., Advanced Certificate.

ADMISSION REQUIREMENTS. Transcripts, two letters of recommendation required in support of School's application. TOEFL required for international applicants. Interview required by some departments. Accepts transfer applicants. Graduates of unaccredited institutions not considered. Apply to Graduate Admissions Office of the School by April 15 (Summer, Fall), November 15 (Spring). Application fee $40. Phone: (212)650-6296; fax: (212)650-6970.

ADMISSION STANDARDS. Selective. Usual minimum average: 2.5, 3.0 for Administration and Supervision, School Psychology (A = 4).

FINANCIAL AID. Graduate assistantships, research/teaching assistantships, Federal W/S, loans. Approved for VA benefits. Apply to Financial Aid Office. Phone: (212)650-6656. Use FAFSA and University's FAF. Aid available for part-time students.

DEGREE REQUIREMENTS. For M.A., M.S.: 30 credit hours minimum, at least 19 in residence; qualifying exam may be required based on GPA; thesis optional. For Advanced Certificate: 30 credit hours beyond master's.

FIELDS OF STUDY.
Administration and Supervision. A.C.
Art. Includes K–12. M.A.
Bilingual Childhood Education. M.S.Ed.
Bilingual Special Education. M.S.Ed.
Childhood Education. M.S.Ed.
Curriculum and Teaching in the Elementary School. M.S.Ed.
Developmental and Remedial Reading. M.S.Ed.
Early Childhood Education. M.S.Ed.
Elementary Education. M.S.Ed.
English. M.A., A.C.
Environmental Studies. Includes science and social studies.
Literacy. Includes Birth–6, 5–12. M.S.Ed.
Mathematics. M.A., A.C.
Reading. M.S.Ed.
Secondary Science Education. Includes biology, chemistry, Earth science, physic. M.A., A.C.

Social Studies. M.A., A.C.

Teaching Students with Disabilities in Childhood Education. M.S.Ed.

Teaching Students with Disabilities in Middle Childhood Education. M.S.Ed.

TESOL. M.S.

School of Engineering—Graduate Division

Tuition: New York State resident $315 per credit; nonresident (including foreign students) $555 per credit.

Enrollment: full- and part-time 453. Graduate faculty: full-time 72, part-time 24. Degrees conferred: M.E., M.S., Ph.D. (doctoral programs are administered by the Graduate School and University Center of CUNY).

ADMISSION REQUIREMENTS. Transcripts, letters of recommendation, GRE (for Ph.D.) required in support of application. Interview not required. TOEFL (500 minimum score) required for international applicants; GRE/Advanced test may also be required. Accepts transfer applicants. Apply to Admission Office of the School by May 15 (Fall), December 15 for Spring. Application fee $125. Phone: (212)650-6977, 642-2812 (Ph.D.).

ADMISSION STANDARDS. Selective. Usual minimum average 2.75 (A = 4).

FINANCIAL AID. For Ph.D. students only: Scholarships, fellowships, assistantships for teaching/research. Minority fellowships, Federal W/S, loans for both master's and Ph.D. candidates. Apply by May 1 to Dean for scholarship, fellowships, assistantships, to Financial Aid Office for all other aid. Use FAFSA. Aid sometimes available for part-time students.

DEGREE REQUIREMENTS. For M.E., M.S.: 30 credit hours minimum, at least 24 in residence; thesis/project/report/seminar. For Ph.D.: 60 credit hours minimum, at least 30 in residence; knowledge of tools of research; field of specialization; first and second exams; candidacy; dissertation; final oral exam.

FIELDS OF STUDY.

Biomedical Engineering. Interdepartmental and interdisciplinary. M.S., Ph.D.

Chemical Engineering. Includes solid processing, polymers and materials, systems engineering, process operations. M.E., Ph.D.

Civil Engineering. Includes structures, environmental engineering, water resources, transportation planning, traffic engineering, highway engineering, network analysis. M.E., Ph.D.

Computer Science. Includes networks and multimedia, database management, computer systems, computer-based modeling. Ph.D.

Computer Science Engineering. M.S.

Electrical Engineering. Includes computer engineering, systems engineering, telecommunications engineering, photonics engineering. M.E., Ph.D.

Mechanical Engineering. Includes mechanical systems and design, energy systems and design, biomedical engineering. M.E., Ph.D.

CLAREMONT GRADUATE SCHOOL

Claremont, California 91711-6160

Web site: www.cgu.edu

Established 1925. CGS member. Located 35 miles E of Los Angeles. Coed. Private control. Semester system. Special facilities: Ancient Biblical Manuscript Center, Blaisdell Programs in World Religions and Cultures, California Institute of Public Affairs, Center for Process Studies, Claremont Information and

Technology Institute, Claremont Institute for Economic Policy Studies, Claremont Research Institute of Applied Mathematical Sciences, Institute for Advanced Studies in Leadership, Institute for Antiquity and Christianity, Rancho Santa Ana Botanic Garden, Tomas Rivera Policy Institute, U.S./Japan Institute, Venture Finance Institute. Library: 3,400,000 volumes, 6000 subscriptions. Total School enrollment: 2195.

Annual tuition: full-time $27,900, per credit $1214. Limited on-campus housing for married students, men, and women. Average annual living expenses: $17,000. Apply to Housing Office. Phone: (909)621-8036.

Graduate School

Enrollment: full-time 1152, part-time 812 (men 54%, women 46%), Faculty: full-time 85, part-time 85. Degrees conferred: M.A., M.B.A., M.F.A., M.S., D.C.M., M.Phil., Ph.D., D.M.A.

ADMISSIONS REQUIREMENTS. Transcripts, GRE/GMAT (not required for Art and Teacher Education), three letters of recommendation required in support of School's application. Electronic application available. TOEFL (550 minimum score), affidavit of financial support, certified English translation of all official transcripts required for foreign applicants. Accepts transfer applicants. Graduates of unaccredited institutions not considered. Apply to Office of Admissions by February 15 (priority consideration date), November 1 (Spring), April 1 (Summer). Rolling admissions process. Application fee $50. Phone: (909) 627-0434; fax: (909)607-7285; e-mail: admiss@cgu.edu.

STANDARDS. Very competitive for most programs. Usual minimum average: 3.0 (A = 4).

FINANCIAL AID. Fellowships, scholarships, assistantships, grants, tuition waivers, Federal W/S, loans. Apply to Office of Financial Aid by March 31 for fellowships, assistantships; for other aid April 16 (Fall), November 15 (Spring). Phone: (909)621-8337; fax: (909)607-7285; e-mail: finaid@cgu.edu. Use FAFSA and institution's FAF. Aid available for part-time students.

DEGREE REQUIREMENTS. For M.A., M.S.: 30 credits minimum, at least one semester of 12 credits for residence; thesis or critique; qualifying or final exam. For M.B.A., M.F.A.: 60 credits program; advancement to candidacy (M.F.A.). For Ph.D.: 3 years of full-time enrollment, or equivalent beyond the bachelor's (72 units); at least one year of full-time study for residence requirement; reading knowledge of two foreign languages or two optional research tools required; advancement to candidacy; oral/written qualifying exam; dissertation; final oral exam.

FIELDS OF STUDY.

SCHOOL OF THE ARTS AND HUMANITIES:

Applied Women's Studies. M.A.

Art. M.A., M.F.A.

Art and Cultural Management. Joint program with Graduate School of Management. M.A.

Cultural Studies. M.A., Ph.D.

English. M.A., M. Phil., Ph.D.

History. M.A., Ph.D.

Music. M.A., D.C.M., D.M.A., Ph.D.

Philosophy. M.A., Ph.D.

PETER F. DRUCKER AND MASATOSHI ITO GRADUATE SCHOOL OF MANAGEMENT:

Arts and Cultural Management. Joint program with Arts & Humanities. M.A.

Executive Management. M.A., E.M.B.A., M.S., Ph.D.

Financial Engineering. Joint program with School of Mathematical Sciences. M.S., Ph.D.

Management. M.B.A.
Politics, Economics and Business. Joint program with School of Politics and Economics. M.A.

SCHOOL OF BEHAVIORAL AND ORGANIZATIONAL SCIENCES:
Human Resources Design. M.S.
Psychology. M.A., Ph.D.

SCHOOL OF EDUCATIONAL STUDIES:
Education. Joint Ph.D. with SDSU. M.A., Ph.D.
Teacher Education. M.A.

SCHOOL OF INFORMATION SYSTEMS AND TECHNOLOGY:
Information Systems and Technology. M.S., Ph.D.

SCHOOL OF MATHEMATICAL SCIENCES:
Computational and Systems Biology. Ph.D.
Computational Science. Joint program with SDSU. Ph.D.
Engineering and Industrial Applied Mathematics. Joint program with CSULB. Ph.D.
Financial Engineering. Joint program with Graduate School of Management. M.S., Ph.D.
Mathematics. M.A., M.S., Ph.D.

SCHOOL OF POLITICS AND ECONOMICS:
Economics. M.A., Ph.D.
Politics and Policy. M.A., Ph.D.

SCHOOL OF RELIGION:
Religion. M.A., Ph.D.

INDEPENDENT PROGRAM:
Botany. Program in conjunction with Rancho Santa Ana Botanic Garden. M.S., Ph.D.

CLARION UNIVERSITY OF PENNSYLVANIA

Clarion, Pennsylvania 16214-1232
Web site: www.clarion.edu

Founded 1867. CGS member. Located 85 miles N of Pittsburgh. Coed. State control. Semester system. Library: 540,000 volumes, 12,198 subscriptions. Total University enrollment: 5600.

Tuition: per credit hour resident $345, nonresident $552; M.B.A. full-time resident $7623, nonresident $11,316. On-campus housing for 30 graduate men, 40 graduate women, none for married students. Average annual housing cost: $2445–$4890 (room only), $1258–$2196 (board). Apply to Student Affairs Housing Office. Phone: (814) 226-2352.

College of Graduate Studies

Enrollment: full-time 174, part-time 204. Faculty: part-time 144. Degrees conferred: M.A., M.B.A., M.Ed., M.S., M.S. in L.S., M.S.N. (Joint program with Slippery Rock University of PA).

ADMISSION REQUIREMENTS. Transcripts, three current recommendations required in support of application. Interview recommended. TOEFL, proof of financial support required for foreign applicants. GRE required of graduates of unaccredited institutions and for Biology, English, Speech Pathology, and Nursing programs. GMAT required for Business program. Accepts transfer applicants. Apply to Dean of Graduate College by August 1 (Fall), December 1 (Spring), June 1 (Summer). Application fee $30. Phone: (814)393-2337; fax: (814)393-2722.

ADMISSION STANDARDS. Selective to relatively open. Usual minimum average: 2.75 (A = 4). S.P.A., Reading and Library Science require a minimum of 3.0.

FINANCIAL AID. Annual awards from institutional funds: graduate assistantships, loans. Apply to Graduate College by March 1. Phone: (814)226-2315.

DEGREE REQUIREMENTS. For master's: 30–45 semester hours minimum, 21–27 hours in residence (depending upon program); written comprehensive exam; qualifying papers for some programs; thesis optional in some programs.

FIELDS OF STUDY.
Biology. Includes biological sciences, environmental science. M.S.
Business Administration. M.B.A.
Education. Includes concentrations in curriculum & instruction, early childhood, English, history, literacy, mathematics, principalship preparation, reading specialist, science, science education, technology, world cultures. M.Ed.
English. M.A.
Library Science. M.S.L.S.
Mass Media Arts & Journalism. M.S.
Nursing. M.S.
Rehabilitative Sciences. M.S.
Special Education. M.S.
Speech Language Pathology. M.S.

CLARK ATLANTA UNIVERSITY

Atlanta, Georgia 30314-4389
Web site: www.cau.edu

Founded 1865. Name change 1988. CGS member. It is one of two historically black universities. Coed. Private control. Semester system. Special facilities: Biotechnology Research Center, Resource Center for Science and Engineering, Center for Computational Science, Center for Polymer and Material Research, Center for International Business, Institute for Community Development, Center on Aging, Criminal Justice Institute, Institute for International Affairs, Center for Afro-American Studies. Library: 800,000 items, 1300 subscriptions. Total University enrollment: 4464.

Tuition: per credit $648. On-campus housing for 400 graduate men and women; none for married students. Annual housing cost: $3900–$4984 (room only). Apply by June 1 to Director of Graduate Residential Complex. Phone: (404)880-8072.

Graduate Programs

Graduate study since 1929. Enrollment: full- and part-time 1333. Graduate faculty: full- and part-time 290. Degrees conferred: M.A., M.S., M.B.A., M.S.L.S., M.S.W., Specialist in Ed., Ph.D.

ADMISSION REQUIREMENTS. Transcripts, GRE/GMAT, three letters of recommendation required in support of application. TOEFL (minimum score 500) required for foreign applicants. Supplemental documents required for some degree programs. Interview not required. Graduates of unaccredited institutions not considered. Accepts transfer applicants. Admits September (Fall), January (Winter), June (Summer). Apply to Office of Graduate Admissions at least three months prior to registration. Application fee $40 ($55 international applicants). Phone: (800)688-3228, (404)880-8765.

ADMISSION STANDARDS. Selective for most departments. Usual minimum average: 2.75 (A = 4).

FINANCIAL AID. Scholarships, grants, fellowships, assistantships, stipends, tuition waivers, Federal W/S, loans. Apply to the Office of Financial Aid by March 1 (Fall), November 1 (Spring). Phone: (404)880-8992. Use FAFSA (University code: 001559). About 20% of students receive aid other than loans from University and outside sources.

DEGREE REQUIREMENTS. For M.A., M.S.: 24–36 semester hours, at least 24 in residence; reading knowledge of one foreign language for some degree programs; thesis; final written/oral exam. For M.B.A.: 60 semester hours; no language requirement. For M.S.L.S.: same as for M.A., except thesis is optional. For M.S.W.: 53 semester hours minimum, at least 24 in full-time residence, including fieldwork experience; thesis; final exam. For M.A. in Ed.: 30–48 semester hours; final exam. For Specialist: 30 semester hours beyond the master's; research project; final oral exam. For Ph.D.: 72 semester hours minimum beyond the bachelor's, at least one year in full-time residence; qualifying exam; candidacy; reading knowledge of two foreign languages; dissertation; final written/oral exam.

FIELDS OF STUDY.

SCHOOL OF ARTS AND SCIENCES:
African Women's Studies. M.A.
African and African American Studies. M.A., D.A.
Biology. M.S., Ph.D.
Chemistry. M.S., Ph.D.
Computer and Information Sciences. M.S. only.
English. M.A. only.
Foreign Languages. M.A. only.
History. M.A. only.
International Affairs and Development. M.I.A.D., Ph.D.
Mathematics Sciences. M.S. only.
Physics. M.S. only.
Political Sciences. M.A., Ph.D.
Public Administration. M.P.A. only.
Sociology and Criminal Justice. M.A.

SCHOOL OF BUSINESS ADMINISTRATION:
Accounting. M.B.A.
Finance. M.B.A.
Marketing. M.B.A.
Operations Research/Supply Chain Management. M.B.A.

SCHOOL OF EDUCATION:
Community Counseling. M.A.
Counseling Psychology. M.A.
Curriculum. Includes early childhood, middle grades, reading, secondary education. M.A., Ed.S.
Educational Leadership. M.A., Ed.S., Ed.D.
Exceptional Education. M.A.
Interrelated. Includes children and youth with mild disabilities. M.A.

WHITNEY M. YOUNG, JR., SCHOOL OF SOCIAL WORK:
Social Work. Includes child and family, health/mental health. M.S.W.
Social Work Policy. Ph.D.

CLARK UNIVERSITY
Worcester, Massachusetts 01610-1477
Web site: www.clarku.edu

Founded 1887. Located 40 miles W of Boston. CGS member. Coed. Private control. Semester system. Special facilities: American Language and Culture Institute, Computer Career Institute, George Perkins Marsh Institute, Jacob Hiatt Center for Urban Education, Heinz Werner Institute for Development Analysis, Institute for Economic Studies, Arthur M. Sackler Science Center, Teachers Center for Global Studies. Library: 500,000 volumes, 4600 subscriptions. Total University enrollment: 3118

Annual tuition: full-time $32,600, part-time $4075 per course. No on-campus housing. Apply to Off-campus Housing Office for housing information. Phone: (508)793-7453.

Graduate School

Graduate study since 1887. Enrollment; full- and part-time 810. Faculty: full-time 176, part-time 80. Degrees conferred: M.A., M.A. in Ed., M.B.A., M.H.A., Ph.D.

ADMISSION REQUIREMENTS. Transcripts, three letters of recommendation required in support of University's application. TOEFL required for foreign applicants. Some departments require, the others recommend GRE Subject Tests/GMAT. Interview usually not required. Accepts transfer applicants. Apply to chair of proposed major department by February 15 (Fall), January 15 (Spring). Application fee $50. Phone: (508)793-7676; fax: (508)793-8834.

ADMISSION STANDARDS. Competitive for most departments. Usual minimum average: 2.75 (A = 4).

FINANCIAL AID. Annual awards from institutional funds: scholarships, teaching assistantships, full and partial tuition remission, grants, tuition waivers, Federal W/S, loans. Apply to chair of proposed major department by February 15. Use FAFSA and institutional FAF. About 60% of students receive aid other than loans from University and outside sources. Aid available for part-time students.

DEGREE REQUIREMENTS. For M.A., M.B.A., M.H.A.: 30 semester hours minimum, at least 24 in full-time residence; reading knowledge of one foreign language for some programs; thesis; final oral exam. For M.A. in Ed.: same as above, except thesis may be replaced by six additional hours or by election of double seminar. For Ph.D.: 48 semester hours minimum beyond the bachelor's, at least 24 in full-time residence; reading knowledge of foreign language is set by department; preliminary written/oral exam; dissertation; final oral exam.

FIELDS OF STUDY.
Biology. GRE Subject for admission; M.A. usually requires three or four semesters.
Biomedical Sciences.
Business Administration. Includes accounting, finance, global business, health care, information technology, management, marketing. M.B.A.
Chemistry. Includes inorganic, organic, physical.
Community Development.
Economics.
Education. Includes elementary, secondary, counseling, one- or two-year M.A. program, interview usually required for admission.
English. M.A.
Environmental Science and Policy. M.A.
Finance. M.S.F.
Geographic Information Sciences. M.A.
Geography. GRE for admission; full-time only.
History.
International Development and Social Change.
Liberal Studies.
Mathematics. Two languages for Ph.D.
Physics.
Psychology. GRE Subject, interview for admission; admits Fall only; full-time only. Includes clinical, developmental, social-evolutionary-cultural. M.A.
Women's Studies.

CLARKSON UNIVERSITY
Potsdam, New York 13699
Web site: www.clarkson.edu

Founded 1896. CGS member. Located 150 miles NE of Syracuse. Coed. Private control. Semester system. Special facilities:

Center for Advanced Materials Processing, New York State Center for Advanced Technology, Center for the Environment, Clarkson Space Grant Program (with Cornell University), Institute for Nonlinear Studies, Institute for Statistical Physics, computer center. Library: 257,900 volumes, 1806 subscriptions. Total University enrollment: 3045.

Annual tuition: per credit hour $840. Very limited on-campus housing. Average annual off-campus housing cost: $5900–$7500 (includes room and board). Apply to Residence Life Office. Phone: (315)268-6442.

Graduate Division

Enrollment: full-time 358, part-time 35. College teaching faculty: full-time 122, part-time 21. Degrees conferred: M.E., M.S., M.B.A., M.P.T., Ph.D.

ADMISSION REQUIREMENTS. Transcripts, GRE, three references required in support of University's application. GMAT required for business programs. TOEFL (minimum score 550, 213 on computer-based test) required for foreign applicants. Interview not required. Accepts transfer applicants. Apply to Dean of Graduate School, preferably by April 15 (Fall), prior to registration for other terms. D.P.T. admits Spring only. Application fee $25; $35 for application sent from outside the U.S. Phone: (315) 268-6442; fax: (315)268-7994. Engineering (315)268-7929, fax: (315)268-3841; Arts & Science (315)268-3802, fax: (315)268-6670; D.P.T. (315)268-3786, fax: (315)208-1539.

ADMISSION STANDARDS. Selective in some departments, competitive in others. Usual minimum average: 3.0 (A = 4).

FINANCIAL AID. Annual awards from institutional funds: fellowships, scholarships, teaching assistantships, research assistantships, graduate assistantships, industrial fellowships, tuition waivers, Federal W/S, loans. Apply to the Dean of the Graduate School by March 1. Use FAFSA. About 80% of students receive aid other than loans from University and outside sources.

DEGREE REQUIREMENTS. For M.S., M.E.: 30 credit hours minimum, at least 20 in residence; qualifying exam; thesis (6–10 credit hours); nonthesis option in some departments. For M.B.A.: 32 credit hours beyond foundation requirements. For D.P.T.: Seven semester full-time program; three clinical experiences. For Ph.D.: 90 credit hours minimum beyond the bachelor's, at least two years in residence; language/research tool may be required; comprehensive exam (physics); dissertation; comprehensive exam; final oral exam.

FIELDS OF STUDY.

SCHOOL OF ARTS AND SCIENCES:
Biology.
Chemistry.
Computer Science. M.S. only.
Environmental Science and Engineering.
Information Technology. Interdisciplinary. M.S. only.
Mathematics.
Physics.

SCHOOL OF BUSINESS:
Business Administration. M.B.A.
Engineering & Global Operations Management. Interdisciplinary. M.S.
Information Technology. Interdisciplinary. M.S.

SCHOOL OF ENGINEERING:
Chemical Engineering.
Civil and Environmental Engineering.
Electrical and Computer Engineering.
Engineering Science. Interdisciplinary. M.S., Ph.D.

Engineering and Global Operations Management. Interdisciplinary. M.S.
Environmental Science and Engineering.
Information Technology. Interdisciplinary. M.S.
Mechanical and Aeronautical Engineering.

CENTER FOR HEALTH SCIENCES:
Physical Therapy. D.P.T

CLEMSON UNIVERSITY
Clemson, South Carolina 29634
Web site: www.clemson.edu

Founded 1889. CGS member. Located 25 miles SW of Greenville. Coed. Land grant, state assisted. Semester system. Special facilities: Archbold Tropical Research Center (Dominica), Belle W. Baruch Forest Science Institute, Center for Advanced Engineering Fibers, Center for Advanced Manufacturing, Center for Computer Communication, Center for Engineering Ceramic Manufacturing, Center for International Trade, Center for Semiconductor Device Reliability Research, Division of Computing and Information Technology, Electron Microscope, Institute of Wildlife and Environment Toxicology, Lee Hall Art Gallery, Daniel Center (Genoa, Italy), Nursing and Wellness Center, Recreation, Travel and Tourism Center, South Carolina Energy Research and Development Center, South Carolina Water Resources Research Institute, Strom Thurman Institute of Government and Public Policy. Library: 1,637,000 volumes, 5978 subscriptions. More than 1000 computers for general student use. Total University enrollment: 17,100.

Annual tuition: resident full-time $9286; per credit $535; nonresident $18,510, per credit $918. On-campus housing for 100 married students, 200 graduate men, 200 graduate women. Average annual housing cost: $1710–$2500 (room only) for single students; $2150–$2550 (apartment rent only) for married students. Apply to Housing Office. Phone: (803)656-2295.

Graduate Division

Enrollment: full-time 2047, part-time 745. University faculty teaching graduate students: full-time 856, part-time 127. Degrees conferred: M.A., M.S., M.B.A., M.Ed., M.Ag.Ed., M.Arch., M.C.R.P., M.C.S.M., M.E.Com., M.F.A., M.E.R., M.P.Acc., M.H.R.D., M.P.R.T.M., M.of.Ed., M.N.S., M.Engr., M.Ag., Ed.S., Ed.D., Ph.D.

ADMISSION REQUIREMENTS. Transcripts required in support of University's application. Electronic application available. GRE required for M.A,, M.S., Ed.D., Ph.D, GMAT required for M.B.A., M.P.Acc. and M.S. in Industrial Management, MAT for some programs in the College of Health, Education, and Human Development. TOEFL required for non-English-speaking international applicants. Interview not required. Graduates of unaccredited institutions not considered. Accepts transfer applicants. Apply to Graduate School Office by July 1 (Fall); for international applicants all application materials must arrive by April 15 (Fall), September 15 (Spring). Application fee $50. Phone: (803) 656-3195; fax: (803)656-5344.

ADMISSION STANDARDS. Very competitive for some departments, competitive or selective for the others. Usual minimum average: 2.75 (A = 4).

FINANCIAL AID. Annual awards from institutional funds: scholarships, grants, fellowships, traineeships, teaching assistantships, research assistantships, internships, Federal W/S, loans. Apply by April 1 to appropriate Department for fellowships, assistantships, to Office of Student Aid for need based programs. Aid may be available for international students. Use FAFSA. About 90% of full-time students receive aid other than loans from University and outside sources. Aid available for part-time students.

DEGREE REQUIREMENTS. For professional master's: 30 credit hours minimum; final oral/written exam. For M.A., M.S.: 30 hours may include 6 in research; knowledge of one foreign language for some programs; thesis/nonthesis option. For Ed.S.: 30 credit program beyond master's. For Ed.D., Ph. D.: 3 years minimum beyond the bachelor's, at least 2 consecutive semesters in residence; preliminary/qualifying exam for some programs; comprehensive written/oral exam; reading knowledge of foreign language required for some departments; admission to candidacy; dissertation; final oral defense of dissertation.

FIELDS OF STUDY.

COLLEGE OF AGRICULTURAL, FORESTRY, AND LIFE SCIENCES:
Agricultural and Applied Economics. M.S.
Agricultural Education. M.Ag.Ed.
Animal and Food Industries. M.S.
Animal Physiology. M.S., Ph.D.
Applied Economics. M.S., Ph.D.
Aquaculture, Fish, and Wildlife Biology. M.S., Ph.D.
Biosystems Engineering. M.Engr., M.S., Ph.D.
Biochemistry. M.S., Ph.D.
Botany. M.S.
Entomology. M.S., Ph.D.
Environmental Toxicology. M.S., Ph.D.
Food Technology. Ph.D. only.
Forest Resources. M.F.R., M.S., Ph.D.
Genetics. M.S., Ph.D.
Microbiology. M.S., Ph.D.
Packaging Science. M.S.
Plant and Environmental Sciences. M.S., Ph.D.
Wildlife and Fisheries Biology. M.S., Ph.D.
Zoology. M.S., Ph.D.

COLLEGE OF ARCHITECTURE, ARTS, AND HUMANITIES:
Architecture. M.Arch., M.S.
City and Regional Planning. M.C.R.P.
Construction Science and Management. M.C.S.M.
Development Planning. M.C.R.P.
English. M.A.
Historic Preservation. M.S.
History. M.A.
Landscape Architecture. M.L.A.
Professional Communication. M.A.
Real Estate. M.S.
Visual Studies. M.F.A.

COLLEGE OF BUSINESS AND BEHAVIORAL SCIENCE:
Accounting. M.P.Acc.
Applied Economics. Ph.D.
Applied Psychology. M.S.
Applied Sociology. M.S.
Business Administration. M.B.A.
Economics. M.A.
Electronic Commerce. M.E.Com.
Graphic Communication. M.S.
Human Factors Psychology. Ph.D.
Industrial Management. M.S., Ph.D.
Industrial/Organizational Psychology. Ph.D.
Management Science. Ph.D.
Marketing. M.S.
Public Administration. M.P.A.

COLLEGE OF ENGINEERING AND SCIENCE:
Astronomy and Astrophysics. M.S., Ph.D.
Bioengineering. M.S., Ph.D.
Biosystems Engineering. M.Engr., M.S., Ph.D.

Ceramic and Materials Engineering. M.S., Ph.D.
Chemical Engineering. M.S., Ph.D.
Chemistry. M.S., Ph.D.
Civil Engineering. M.Engr., M.S., Ph.D.
Computer Engineering. M.S., Ph.D.
Computer Science. M.S., Ph.D.
Electrical Engineering. M.Engr., M.S., Ph.D.
Environmental Engineering and Science. M.Engr., M.S., Ph.D.
Hydrogeology. M.S.
Industrial Engineering. M.S., Ph.D.
Materials Science and Engineering. M.S., Ph.D.
Mathematical Sciences. M.S., Ph.D.
Mechanical Engineering. M.Engr., M.S., Ph.D.
Management Science. Ph.D.
Operations Research. M.S., Ph.D.
Physics. M.S., Ph.D.
Polymer and Fiber Science. M.S., Ph.D.
Statistics. M.S., Ph.D.

COLLEGE OF HEALTH, EDUCATION, AND HUMAN DEVELOPMENT:
Administration and Supervision. M.Ed., Ed.S.
Career and Technology Education. M.C.T.E.
Counseling and Guidance Services. M.Ed.
Curriculum and Instruction. Ph.D.
Educational Leadership. Ph.D.
Elementary Education. M.Ed.
English. M.Ed.
Health Administration. M.H.A.
History and Government. M.Ed.
Human Resource Development. M.H.R.D.
Nursing. M.S.
Parks, Recreation, and Tourism Management. M.P.R.T.M.
Reading. M.Ed.
School Counseling. M.Ed.
Secondary Education. Includes English, history, mathematics, natural science. M.Ed.
Special Education. M. Ed.
Student Affairs. M. Ed.
Vocational/Technical Education. Ed.D.

INTERDISCIPLINARY PROGRAMS:
Fine Arts in Computing. M.F.A.C.
Policy Studies. Ph.D.

CLEVELAND STATE UNIVERSITY
Cleveland, Ohio 44115-2440
Web site: www.csuohio.edu

Formerly private, Fenn College became state university in 1965. CGS member. Coed. Semester system. Special facilities: Advanced Manufacturing Center, Biomedical and Health Institute, Center for Economic Development, Center for Environmental Science, Technology, and Policy, Center for Housing Research and Policy, Center for Public Management, Center for Nonprofit Practice and Policy, Center for Public Management, Center for Sacred Landmarks, Cleveland Health Institute, Great Lakes Environmental Center, Labor-Management Relations Center, Cleveland Center for Mass Spectrometry, Ohio Center for the Advancement of Women in Public Service, Center for the Study of Real Estate Brokerage and Markets, Real Estate Research Center, Unger Croatia Center for Local Government Leaders, the Urban Center, Urban Child Research Center. Library: 900,000 volumes, 6500 subscriptions. More than 600 computers on campus for general student use. University enrollment: 16,000.

Tuition: per quarter hour, resident $439, nonresident $834. Limited on-campus housing. Average academic housing costs: $7800 (three quarters). Contact Residence Life Office for both on- and off-campus housing information. Phone: (216)697-7330.

College of Graduate Studies

Enrollment: full-time 1728, part-time 4216. Faculty: full- and part-time 637. Degrees conferred: M.A., M.Ed., M.S., M.B.A., M.M., M.C.I.S., M.L.R.H.R., M.P.A., M.S.U.S., M.S.W., M.U.P.D.D., Ed.S., D.B.A., D. Engr., Ph.D.

ADMISSION REQUIREMENTS. Transcripts, two letters of recommendation required in support of College's application. GRE for arts, sciences, and engineering applicants; GMAT for business applicants; MAT for education applicants. TOEFL/IELTS/MELAB and proof of financial support required for international applicants. Accepts transfer applicants. Apply to College of Graduate Studies at least six weeks prior to registration. Some programs have early deadline. International applicants apply by July 15 (Fall), December 1 (Spring), April 1 (Summer). Application fee: $30. Phone: (216)687-5599.

ADMISSION STANDARDS. Selective for most majors. Usual minimum average: 2.75 (A = 4)

FINANCIAL AID. Tuition grants, graduate assistantships, Federal W/S, loans. Approved for VA benefits. Apply by May 15 to appropriate department chair for assistantships; to Financial Aid for all other programs. Use FAFSA. Phone: (216)687-3764.

DEGREE REQUIREMENTS. For master's: 32 semester hours minimum, at least 24 in residence; thesis (for up to 6 credits) or final comprehensive exam. No language requirement. For D.B.A.: 60 semester hours beyond master's; oral/written qualifying exam; dissertation; final oral exam. For Ph.D.: 60–75 semester hours beyond the master's; oral/written qualifying exam; dissertation; final oral exam.

FIELDS OF STUDY.

COLLEGE OF LIBERAL ARTS AND SOCIAL SCIENCES:
Applied Communication Theory and Methodology.
Economics.
English. Includes creative writing, literature.
Fine Arts in Creative Writing.
History. Includes art history, museum studies, social studies.
Music. Includes composition, music education, performance.
Philosophy. Includes bioethics.
Social Work.
Sociology.
Spanish.

NANCE COLLEGE OF BUSINESS ADMINISTRATION:
Accounting. M.Acct. only.
Business Administration. Includes accounting, business economics, finance, health care administration, information systems, management and labor relations, marketing, operations management and business statistics. M.B.A.
Business Administration. Includes finance, information systems, marketing, operations management. D.B.A.
Computer and Information Science. M.C.I.S. only.
Labor Relations and Human Resources. M.L.R.H.R. only.

COLLEGE OF EDUCATION AND HUMAN SERVICES:
Administration. M.Ed.
Administration with Curriculum, Instructional and Professional Development. Ed.S.
Administration with Education Staff Personnel Administration. Ed.S.
Administration with Pupil Services Administration. Ed.S.
Administration with Principalship. Ed.S.
Administration with Superintendent. Ed.S.
Adult Learning and Development. M.Ed.
Community Agency Counseling. M.Ed.
Community Health Education. M.Ed.

Counseling. Ed.S.
Counselor Education. M.Ed.
Curriculum & Instruction. All the usual concentrations. M.Ed.
Exercise Science. M.Ed.
Nursing. Includes clinical nurse leader, forensic, nursing education, nursing executive. M.S.N. only.
Organizational Leadership. M.Ed.
Public Health. M.P.H.
School Counseling. M.Ed.
Sports & Exercise Psychology. M.Ed.
Sports Management. M.Ed.
Urban Education. Includes counseling, counseling psychology, leadership and lifelong learning, learning and development, policy studies, school administration. Ph.D. only.

FENN COLLEGE OF ENGINEERING:
Applied Biomedical Engineering. Ph.D. only.
Chemical Engineering.
Civil Engineering. Includes structure and foundations, transportation, water resources.
Electrical Engineering.
Engineering. Ph.D. only.
Engineering Mechanics. Includes structural mechanics, mechanics and materials.
Environmental Engineering.
Industrial Engineering. Includes advanced industrial engineering, engineering management, manufacturing engineering, quality engineering.
Mechanical Engineering. Includes dynamics and control, mechanical systems and design, mechatronics. Thermal-fluid mechanics and energy systems.
Software Engineering.

COLLEGE OF SCIENCE:
Biology.
Clinical-Bioanalytical Chemistry. Includes clinical chemistry, molecular medicine. Ph.D. only.
Chemistry.
Environmental Science. Includes environmental biology, environmental chemistry, environmental earth sciences.
Health Sciences. Includes physician assistant science.
Mathematic. M.A., M.S.
Occupational Therapy.
Physics. Includes medical physics, optics and medical imaging.
Physical Therapy. Ph.D. only.
Psychology. Includes clinical, consumer industrial research, diversity management, experimental research, school psychology.
Regulatory Biology. Includes molecular medicine. Ph.D. only.
Speech Pathology and Audiology.

MAXINE GOODMAN LEVIN COLLEGE OF URBAN AFFAIRS:
Environmental Studies. Includes environmental nonprofit management, environmental planning policy and administration. M.A. only.
Nonprofit Administration and Leadership. M.N.A.L.
Public Administration. Includes economic development, health care administration, public management. M.P.A.
Urban Planning Design and Development. Includes economic development, environmental sustainability, geographic information systems, housing and neighborhood development, real estate development and finance. M.U.P.D.D.
Urban Studies. Includes community and neighborhood development, economic development, public finance, urban policy analysis, urban real estate development. M.A. only.
Urban Studies and Public Affairs. Includes communication, environmental policy and administration, housing and neighborhood development, public administration, urban economic development, urban human services administration. Ph.D. only.

Cleveland-Marshall College of Law
Web site: www.law.csuohio.edu

Cleveland Law School established 1887. John Marshall Law school established 1996. Merged into University 1969. ABA approved. AALS member. Public control. Semester system. Law library: 519,176 volumes, 3243 subscriptions; has LEXIS, NEXIS WESTLAW.

Tuition: full-time resident $14,982, nonresident $20,525; part-time resident per credit $576, nonresident $789.

Enrollment: full-time 170, part-time 66. Total full-and part-time 702 (men 53%, women 47%, minority 18%).

Faculty: Total full-time 46, part-time 46 (men 59%, women 41%, minority 7%). Student to faculty ratio 12.1 to 1. Degrees conferred: J.D., J.D.-M.A.E.S., J.D.-M.B.A., J.D.-M.P.A., J.S.-M.S.E.S., J.D.-M.U.P.D.D., LL.M.

ADMISSION REQUIREMENTS. LSDAS Law School report, transcripts, bachelor's degree, LSAT (no later than December), two letters of recommendation, personal statement required in support of application. Applicants must have completed at least four years of college study. TOEFL required of all international applicants. Apply to the Assistant Dean after September 1, before May 1. Application fee $40. Phone: (216)687-2304; fax: (216) 687-6881.

ADMISSION STANDARDS. Selective. Accepts approximately 31% of all students. Number of full-time applicants 1403, part-time 351; number of acceptance full-time 431, part-time 110; number enrolled full-time 170, part-time 66; LSAT (75% of full-time students have a score at or above 151, part-time 151); GPA (75% of full-time students have a GPA at or above 3.14, part-time 2.87). *U.S. News & World Report* ranking is in the fourth tier of all U.S. law schools.

FINANCIAL AID. Scholarships, grants, loans. Apply to the Dean by May 1; use FAFSA (College code: 003032). Phone: (216)687-2317. About 55% of students receive aid other than loans from College funds. Aid available for part-time students.

DEGREE REQUIREMENTS. For J.D.: Three academic years minimum (day), or four years minimum (evening), at least one year or equivalent in residence; 87 semester hours. For LL.M.: 20 credits for graduates of American law schools; thesis; 24 credits for graduates of foreign law schools. One year minimum in residence; final essay.

COLORADO SCHOOL OF MINES
Golden, Colorado 80401-1887
Web site: www.mines.edu

Founded 1874. CGS member. Located 10 miles W of Denver. Coed. State control. Semester system. Special facilities: Colorado Advanced Materials Institute, Advanced Steel Processing and Products Center, Center for Ground Water Research, Center for Research on Hydrates and Other Solids, Center for Wave Phenomena, Center for Waste Management, Center for Directional Drilling, Energy and Mineral Field Institute, Excavation Engineering and Earth Mechanics Institute, Kroll Institute for Extractive Metallurgy, Center for Welding and Joining Research, Colorado Center for Advanced Ceramics. Library 150,000 volumes, 2500 subscriptions. Total enrollment: 3921.

Annual tuition: full-time, resident $7240, nonresident $19,840; part-time, per credit, resident $362, nonresident $992. On-campus housing for married students and for single graduate students. Average annual housing cost: $5400 for single students; $530–$600 per month for married students. Apply to Director of Student Housing. Phone: (303)273-3351.

Graduate School
Enrollment: full-time 552 (men 70%, women 30%), part-time 199. Faculty: full-time 225, part-time 129. Degrees conferred: M.Eng., M.S., Ph.D., Professional Engr.

ADMISSION REQUIREMENTS. Two transcripts, three letters of recommendations, GRE, GRE Subject Test in some departments required in support of School's application. Electronic application available. TOEFL (minimum score 550) required for foreign applicants. Interview not required. Accepts transfer applicants. Graduates of unaccredited colleges not considered. Apply to Graduate Office preferably by December 1 (Fall), September 1 (Spring). Rolling admissions process. Application fee $50. Phone: (800)245-1064 (toll-free in state), (800)446-9488 (toll-free outside state), (303)273-3249; fax: (303)273-3244; e-mail: grad-school @mines.edu.

ADMISSION STANDARDS. Very selective. Usual minimum average: 3.0 (A = 4).

FINANCIAL AID. Annual awards from institutional funds: scholarships, fellowships, research assistantships, teaching assistantships, internships, Federal W/S, loans. Apply by February 1 (Fall), August 1 (Spring) to the Financial Aid Office. Use FAFSA. About 75% of students receive aid other than loans from School and outside sources. No aid for part-time students.

DEGREE REQUIREMENTS. For M.Eng., M.S.: 24 semester hours minimum plus 12 hours of research, at least 14 in residence; qualifying exam; thesis; final oral exam. For M.S. (nonthesis): at least 36 credits. For Ph.D.: 72 hours minimum beyond the bachelor's, at least 30 in residence and two semesters in full-time attendance; minor field requirement; preliminary exam; foreign language is a department option; comprehensive exams; dissertation; final written/oral exam.

FIELDS OF STUDY.
Applied Chemistry.
Applied Physics.
Chemical and Petroleum Refining Engineering.
Chemistry. Includes geochemistry.
Engineering and Technology Management.
Engineering Geology.
Engineering Systems.
Environmental Sciences and Engineering.
Geochemistry.
Geological Engineering.
Geology.
Geophysical Engineering.
Geophysics.
Hydrogeology.
Materials Science.
Mathematics and Computer Science.
Metallurgical and Materials Engineering.
Mineral Economics.
Mineral/Petroleum Exploration and Development.
Mining Engineering.
Petroleum Engineering.
Physics.

COLORADO STATE UNIVERSITY
Fort Collins, Colorado 80523-0015
Web site: www.colostate.edu

Founded 1879. CGS member. Located 65 miles N of Denver. Coed. Public control. Semester system. Special facilities: Archaeomagnetic Laboratory, Engineering Research Center, Electron Microscope, Radiological Health Lab, National Seed

Storage Lab, Colorado Water Resource Center, Rocky Mountain Forest and Range Experimental Station. The University's NIH ranking is 97th among all U.S. Institutions with 118 awards/grants valued at $53,307,839. According to The Center at University of Florida, the University is ranked 64th in receipt of Federal Research funds with $117,151,000 and it ranks 75th for total University research expenditures with $187,054,000. In 2004, the University awarded 160 doctorates which ranked it 91st among all U.S. institutions eligible to award that degree. Seven of the University's faculty members have been elected to National Honor Academies and this ranks it 78th among all U.S. institutions. The Library: approximately 1,900,000 volumes, 21,000 subscriptions. Total University enrollment: 27,133.

Annual tuition: full-time, resident $3690, nonresident $14,958, part-time, per credit, resident $205, nonresident $831. On-campus housing for 700 married students, 200 graduate men or women. Average academic year housing costs: $6316 single, $9500 married. Apply to Office of Housing and Food Service for both on- (970-491-6511) and off-campus (970-491-2248) housing information. Day-care facilities available.

Graduate School
Web site: www.colostate.edu/depts/grad

Graduate study since 1893. Enrollment: full-time 2471, part-time 3100. University faculty: full-time 870, part-time 31. Degrees conferred: M.A., M.Ag., M.A.T., M.B.A., M.Ed., M.F., M.F.A., M.M., M.S., M.S.W., Ph.D.

ADMISSION REQUIREMENTS. Two official transcripts, GRE, GMAT, three letters of recommendation required in support of School's application. Interview not required. TOEFL required for international applicants. Accepts transfer applicants. Graduates of unaccredited institutions not considered. Apply to proposed major department and Graduate School by March 1 (Fall), October 1 (Spring), March 1 (Summer); some departments may have earlier deadlines. Application fee $50. Phone: (970)491-6817; fax: (970)491-2194; e-mail: gschool@grad.colostate.edu.

ADMISSION STANDARDS. Very competitive for some departments, competitive or selective for the others. Usual minimum average: 3.0 (A = 4).

FINANCIAL AID. Annual awards from institutional funds: scholarships, teaching assistantships, research assistantships, traineeships, fellowships, tuition waivers, Federal W/S, loans. Apply by February 1 to appropriate department for fellowships, internships, assistantship; to Student Financial Services for all other aid. Phone: (970)491-6321. Use FAFSA (University code: 001350) and University's FAF. About 55% of students receive aid other than loans from University and outside sources. Aid available for part-time students.

DEGREE REQUIREMENTS. For most master's: 30–36 credits minimum, at least 24 in residence; thesis required for many majors, optional for others; reading knowledge of one foreign language for some majors; final written/oral exam. For M.M.: 33 credits minimum; thesis may be required. For M.S.W.: 40–63 credits minimum; thesis optional. For M.F.A.: 48–60 credits minimum, at least three years of full-time study; M.F.A. thesis; final written/oral exam. For Ph.D.: 72 credits minimum beyond the bachelor's, at least 32 in residence or thesis; preliminary exam; dissertation or thesis; final written/oral exam.

FIELDS OF STUDY.
Accounting. M.S.
Agricultural and Resource Economics. M.S., Ph.D.
Agricultural Sciences. M.Ag.
Anatomy. M.S., Ph.D.
Animal Sciences. M.S., Ph.D.
Anthropology. M.A.
Art. M.F.A.
Atmospheric Science. M.S., Ph.D.
Bioagricultural Sciences and Pest Management. M.S.
Biochemistry. M.S., Ph.D.
Bioengineering. M.E., M.S., Ph.D.
Biomedical Engineering. M.E.
Bioresource and Agricultural Engineering. M.S., Ph.D.
Botany. M.S., Ph.D.
Business Administration. M.B.A., M.S.
Cell and Molecular Biology. M.S., Ph.D.
Chemical Engineering. M.E., M.S., Ph.D.
Chemistry. M.S., Ph.D.
Civil Engineering. M.E., M.S., Ph.D.
Clinical Sciences. M.S., Ph.D.
Computer Science. M.S., Ph.D.
Construction Management. M.S.
Creative Writing. M.F.A.
Design and Merchandising. M.A., M.S.
Earth Resources. M.S., Ph.D.
Ecology. M.S., Ph.D.
Economics. M.A., Ph.D.
Education and Human Resources Studies. M.Ed., Ph.D.
Electrical and Computer Engineering. M.E.E., M.S., Ph.D.
English. M.A.
Entomology. M.S., Ph.D.
Environmental Health. M.S., Ph.D.
Fish, Wildlife and Conservation Biology. M.S., Ph.D.
Food Science and Nutrition. M.S., Ph.D.
Foreign Languages and Literatures. M.A.
Forest Sciences. M.F., M.S., Ph.D.
Geology. M.S.
Global Social and Sustainable Enterprise. M.S.
Health and Exercise Science. M.S.
History. M.A.
Horticulture and Landscape Architecture. M.S., Ph.D.
Human Development and Family Studies. M.S.
Human Dimensions of Natural Resources. M.S., Ph.D.
Journalism and Technical Communication. M.S.
Mathematics. M.S., Ph.D.
Mechanical Engineering. M.S., Ph.D.
Microbiology. M.S., Ph.D.
Music. M.M.
Occupational Therapy. M.S.
Pathology. M.S., Ph.D.
Philosophy. M.A.
Physics. M.S., Ph.D.
Plant Pathology and Weed Science. M.S., Ph.D.
Political Science. M.A., Ph.D.
Psychology. M.S., Ph.D.
Radiological Health Sciences. M.S., Ph.D.
Social Work. M.S.W.
Sociology. M.A., Ph.D.
Soil and Crop Sciences. M.S., Ph.D.
Speech Communication. M.A.
Statistics. M.S., Ph.D.
Student Affairs in Higher Education. M.S.
Technical Communication. M.S.
Zoology. M.S., Ph.D.

College of Veterinary Medicine and Biomedical Sciences
Web site: www.cvmbs.colostate.edu

Semester system. Special facilities: Equine Orthopaedic Center, Animal Population Health Institute, Center for Complimentary Medicine and Natural Healing, Center for Veterinary Epidemiology and Animal Disease Surveillance Systems, Center of Economically Important Infectious Animal Diseases, Flint Animal Cancer Center.

Annual tuition and fees: full-time resident $14,626, nonresident $40,926. On- and off-campus housing available for both married and single students. Total of other expenses: $13,500–$17,000.

Enrollment: first-time 138, total 550 (men 28%, women 72%, minorities 20%, state residents 55%). Faculty: full-time 137, part-time 6. Degrees conferred: D.V.M., D.V.M.-M.B.A., D.V.M.-M.S.P.H., D.V.M.-Ph.D.

ADMISSION REQUIREMENTS. VMCAS report, transcripts, GRE, three letters of recommendation, essay, animal/veterinary experience required in support of application. Electronic application available. Will consider international applicants. Interview by invitation only. Applicants must have completed at least three years of college study. State residents and WICHE residents given preference. Accepts transfer applicants if opening exists. Has EAP, applicants must have at least 68 credits, G.P.A. 3.8, GRE combined score of 1750. Apply to the Office of the Dean of the College after August before October 1. Transfer applicants apply by May 1. Application deadlines for M.S. and Ph.D.: January 1 (Fall), October 1 (Spring). Application fee $50. Phone: (970)491-7051; fax: (970)491-2250.

ADMISSION STANDARDS. Competitive. Accepts about 10–15% of all applicants. Number of applications 1604 (187 WICHE resident, 1168 out-of-state); number enrolled 138 (44 WICHE resident, 19 out-of-state). Usual minimum UGPA: 3.2 (A = 4). GRE mean score (V + Q) 1183; mean UGPA 3.70.

FINANCIAL AID. Scholarships, assistantships, fellowships, traineeships, tuition waivers, Federal W/S, loans. Apply to the Office of Financial Aid following admission.

DEGREE REQUIREMENTS. For D.V.M.: Satisfactory completion of four-year program. For M.S. Plan A—30-credit program, thesis/comprehensive exam, Plan B—40-credit program, professional paper/departmental report; internship. For Ph.D.: 72-credit program beyond the bachelor's, written and oral preliminary exam; advancement to candidacy; dissertation; final oral exam.

FIELDS OF GRADUATE STUDY.
Anatomy.
Cellular and Molecular Radiobiology.
Critical Care/Emergency Medicine.
Environmental Health.
Epidemiology.
Equine Medicine.
Equine Reproduction.
Experimental Radiation Oncology.
Food Animal Medicine.
Health Physics/Radiation Protection.
Industrial Hygiene.
Interdisciplinary Programs. Includes cell and molecular biology, molecular, cellular and integrative neurosciences, anthropod-borne and infectious diseases, mycobacteria research, integrated livestock management.
Large and Small Animal Surgery.
Microbiology.
Neurobiology.
Pathology.
Radioecology.
Reproductive Biology.
Small Animal Medicine.
Veterinary Neurology.
Veterinary Oncology.
Veterinary Ophthalmology.
Veterinary Radiology.

UNIVERSITY OF COLORADO, BOULDER
Boulder, Colorado 80309
Web site: www.colorado.edu

Founded 1876. CGS and AAU member. Located 28 miles NW of Denver. Public control. Semester system. Special facilities: Center for Advanced Decision Support for Water and Environmental Systems, Center for Advanced Manufacturing and Packaging of Microwave, Optical, and Digital Electronics, Center for Applied Mathematics, Center for Asian Studies, Center for Astrophysics and Space Astronomy, Center for Computer Research in the Humanities, Center for Geography Education, Center for Integrated Plasma Studies, Center for Limnology, Center for Physical Activity, Disease Prevention, and Aging, Center for Separations using Thin Film, Center for Space and Geosciences Policy, Center for Study of Ethnicity and Race in America, Center for Values and Social Policy, Center for the Study of the Native Languages of the Plains and Southwest, Colorado Center for Astrodynamics Research, Colorado Center for Chaos and Complexity, Cooperative Institute for Research in Environmental Sciences, Ferro-Electric Liquid Crystal Materials Research Science and Engineering Center, Institute for Behavioral Genetics, Institute of Arctic and Alpine Research, Institute of Behavioral Science, the Institute of Cognitive Science, Natural Hazards Center. The University's NIH ranking is 116th among all U.S. Institutions with 167 awards/grants valued at $41,539,275. According to The Center at University of Florida, the University is ranked 41st in receipt of Federal Research funds with $192,750,000 and it ranks 62nd for total University research expenditures with $214,013,000. In 2004, the University awarded 286 doctorates which ranked it 47th among all U.S. institutions eligible to award that degree. Twenty-eight of the University's faculty members have been elected to National Honor Academies and this ranks it 36th among all U.S. institutions. The Library: approximately 3,100,000 volumes, 20,000 subscriptions. More than 1800 computers on campus for student use. Total University enrollment: 31,068.

Tuition: 1–3 credits resident A & S $1172, M.B.A. 1746, Engineering $1479, Journalism/Music $1172; 1–3 credits nonresident A &S $3657, M.B.A. $4106, Engineering $3929, Journalism/Music $3700. Limited on-campus housing available. Annual average housing costs: $9500. Off-campus Housing Office: phone: (303) 492-7053. Family Housing Office: phone: (303)492-6384. Day-care facilities available.

Graduate School

Graduate study since 1892. Enrollment: full-time 3606, part-time 1345. University faculty: approx. 950. Degrees conferred: M.A., M.S., M.F.A., M.E., M.Mus., M.Mus.Ed., M.B.S., D.Mus.A., Ph.D.

ADMISSION REQUIREMENTS. Two transcripts, four letters of reference required in support of School's application. GRE/GMAT, three letters of recommendation required for many departments. Contact Departments for the supplemental materials required. TOEFL required for international applicants. Interview not required. Accepts transfer applicants. Graduates of unaccredited colleges not considered. Apply to office of the major department at least 120 days before term admission is sought. Application fee $50, $60 for international. Phone: (303)492-2890.

ADMISSION STANDARDS. Selective to competitive. Usual minimum average: 2.75 (A = 4), 3.0 in some departments.

FINANCIAL AID. Annual awards from institutional funds: scholarships, fellowships, teaching/research assistantships, traineeships, Federal W/S, loans. Number of awards varies. Apply by January 15 through appropriate department, to the Financial Aid Office for all Federal programs. Phone: (303)492-5091; e-mail:

finaid@colorado.edu. Use FAFSA (University code: 001370). Aid sometimes available for part-time students.

DEGREE REQUIREMENTS. For most master's: 24 semester hours minimum with thesis or 30 semester hours minimum without thesis, at least two semesters in residence; qualifying exam; up to 9 semester hours in transfer; final written/oral exam. For M.F.A.: 48 hours minimum; written, creative thesis. For M.Mus.: same as for the master's, except final creative or performance project. Some departments require foreign languages for master's. For Ph.D., D.Mus.A.: 30 hours minimum beyond the master's, at least 6 semesters in residence; preliminary exam; final written/oral exam; dissertation. Some departments require foreign language for Ph.D.

FIELDS OF STUDY.

COLLEGE OF ARTS AND SCIENCES:
Anthropology. M.A., Ph.D.
Applied Mathematics. M.S., Ph.D.
Art History. M.A.
Astrophysical and Planetary Sciences. M.S., Ph.D.
Atmospheric and Ocean Sciences. M.S., Ph.D.
Biochemistry. Ph.D.
Biology. Includes environmental, population and organismic, molecular, cellular and developmental. M.A., Ph.D.
Chemical Physics. Ph.D.
Classics. M.A., Ph.D.
Cognitive Science. Ph.D.
Communication. M.S., Ph.D.
Comparative Literature. M.A., Ph.D.
Dance. M.F.A.
East Asian Languages and Civilizations. M.A.
Economics. M.A., Ph.D.
English. M.A., Ph.D.
Environmental Studies. M.S., Ph.D.
Fine Arts. M.A., M.F.A.
French. M.A., Ph.D.
Geography. M.A., Ph.D.
Geological Sciences. M.S., Ph.D.
Geophysics. Ph.D.
German and Slavic Languages and Literature. M.A.
History. M.A., Ph.D.
International Affairs. M.A.
Kinesiology. M.S., Ph.D.
Linguistics. M.A., Ph.D.
Mathematics. M.A., Ph.D.
Museum and Field Studies. M.S.
Neurobiology. M.A.
Neuroscience. Ph.D.
Philosophy. M.A., Ph.D.
Physics. M.A., Ph.D.
Political Science. M.A., Ph.D.
Psychology. M.A., Ph.D.
Religious Studies. M.A.
Sociology. M.A., Ph.D.
Spanish. M.A., Ph.D.
Speech, Language, and Hearing Sciences. M.A., Ph.D.
Theatre. M.A., Ph.D.

COLLEGE OF ENGINEERING:
Aerospace Engineering. M.S., Ph.D.
Building Systems. M.S., Ph.D.
Chemical Engineering. M.S., Ph.D.
Civil, Environmental and Architectural Engineering. M.S., Ph.D.
Computer Engineering. M.S., Ph.D.
Construction Engineering Management. M.S., Ph.D.
Electrical and Computer Engineering. M.S., Ph.D.
Environmental Engineering. M.S., Ph.D.
Engineering Management. M.E.
Mechanical Engineering. M.S., Ph.D.

Structural Engineering. M.S., Ph.D.
Telecommunications. Interdisciplinary. M.S.
Water Resources Engineering. M.S., Ph.D.

SCHOOL OF EDUCATION:
Educational and Psychological Studies. M.A., Ph.D.
Instruction and Curriculum. M.A., Ph.D.
Research and Evaluation Methodology. Ph.D.
Social, Multicultural, and Bilingual Foundations. M.A., Ph.D.

SCHOOL OF JOURNALISM:
Journalism. M.A., Ph.D.
Mass Communication. M.A.
Media Studies. Ph.D.
News Gathering. M.A.

SCHOOL OF MUSIC:
Music. M.Mus., Ph.D.
Music Education. M.Mus.Ed.
Musical Arts. D.M.A.

Graduate School of Business Administration

Graduate study since 1965. Accredited programs: M.B.A.; recognized Ph.D. Semester system. Special facilities: Burridge Center for Financial Analysis, Center for Sustainable Tourism, Deming Center for Entrepreneurship, Real Estate Center. Library: 69,000 volumes, 1200 subscriptions.

Annual tuition: resident M.B.A. full-time $5239, M.S. $5046, part-time $1746 per semester; nonresident M.B.A. full-time $12,317, M.S. $12,317, part-time $4160 per semester.

Enrollment: total full-time 178, part-time 103. Faculty: 51 full-time, 10 part-time; 97% with Ph.D./D.B.A. Degrees conferred: M.B.A. (FT, PT, days), M.S.Acct., M.S.Actx., M.B.A.-J.D., M.B.A.-M.S. (Telecommunications), Ph.D.

ADMISSION REQUIREMENTS. All applicants should have a bachelor's degree from a recognized institution of higher education, a strong mathematics background, a 3.0 GPA (A = 4), and a GMAT score of 550. Submit two official transcripts from each undergraduate/graduate school attended, GMAT, three letters of recommendation, essay, résumé (prefers at least four years of work experience), and an application fee of $40 ($60 international applicants) to the Director of Graduate Student Services. In addition, international students (whose native language is other than English) should submit a TOEFL (minimum score 550) report, certified translations and evaluations of all official transcripts, recommendation should be in English or with certified translations, and proof of sufficient financial resources for two years of academic study. On-campus visits and interviews are required. Beginning students are admitted Fall only. U.S. citizens apply by December 15 round-one deadline, February 15 round-two deadline, May 1 late deadline (Fall), international students apply by December 1 round-one deadline, February 1 round-two deadline. Joint degree applicants must apply to and be accepted to both schools/programs, contact the admissions office for current information and specific admissions requirements. Rolling admissions process, notification is made two weeks after receipt of completed application and supporting documents. Admissions Office phone: (303)492-1809; fax: (303)492-1727; e-mail: busgrad@colorado.edu.

ADMISSION REQUIREMENTS FOR DOCTORAL CANDIDATES. Contact the Application Request Service at (303) 492-7662 for applications and current information. Beginning students are admitted Fall Only. Both U.S. citizens and international applicants apply by January 1 (Fall). Submit an application, a GMAT (will accept GMAT test results from the last five years), two official transcripts from each undergraduate/graduate school attended, four letters of recommendation, résumé, statement of purpose, and application fee of $40 ($60 international applicants) to the Graduate Admission Office. In addition, international student (whose native language is other than English) should submit TOEFL (minimum score 590) report, certified translations and evaluations of all official transcripts, recommendation should be in English or with certified translations, proof of health/immunization certificate. International students' contact: (303)492-7536. Interviews encouraged. Notification is made by mid-April.

ADMISSION STANDARDS. Competitive. Mean GMAT: 647; mean GPA: 3.11 (A = 4).

FINANCIAL AID. Minority scholarships, grants, fellowships, graduate assistantships, Federal W/S, loans. Financial aid is available for part-time study. Financial aid may be available for international students. Assistantships/fellowships may be available in the second year for joint degree candidates. Request scholarship, fellowship, assistantship information from the Graduate School of Business. Contact the University's Financial Aid Office for current need-based financial aid information. Phone: (303)492-5091. Submit FAFSA (School code: 001370), also submit Financial Aid Transcript, Federal Income Tax forms. Approximately 75% of students receive some form of financial assistance.

DEGREE REQUIREMENTS. For M.B.A.: 51-credit program including 27 elective credits, two-year program; degree program must be completed in five years. For M.S.Acct., M.S.Actx.: 32-credit program. For M.B.A.-M.S. (Telecommunications): 60-credit program, a two-and-one-half- to five-year program. For M.B.A.-J.D.: 141 credit program, four-and-one-half- to six-year program. For Ph.D.: 60 credit, three- to five-year program; comprehensive (written, oral, or both) exam; teaching experience; research internship; dissertation proposal and oral defense, dissertation; oral defense.

FIELDS OF STUDY.
Accounting. M.S.Acct., M.S.Actx., Ph.D.
Business Strategy. Ph.D.
Entrepreneurship. Ph.D.
Finance. M.B.A., Ph.D.
Information Systems. Ph.D.
Management. Ph.D.
Marketing. M.B.A., Ph.D.
Operations Research. Ph.D.
Organizational Management. M.B.A., Ph.D.
Self-Designed Option. M.B.A. only.
Technology and Innovation Management. M.B.A. only.

School of Law (90309-0401)
Web site: www.colorado.edu/law

Organized 1892. ABA approved since 1923. AALS member. Semester system. Special facilities: Natural Resources Law Center, Indian Law Clinic, Bryon White Center for the Study of American Constitutional Law, Entrepreneurial Law Center, National Wildlife Federation's Natural Resource Litigation Clinic. Library: 523,473 volumes, 4037 subscriptions; has LEXIS, NEXIS, WESTLAW, LEGISLATE.

Annual tuition: resident $16,738, nonresident $30,814. On-campus housing available for single and married students. Apply to University Housing Office. Total average cost for all other expenses: $12,814.

Enrollment: first-year class 167, total 511 (men 49%, women 51%, minorities 23%); no part-time study. Faculty; full-time 37, part-time 20. Student to faculty ratio 12.5 to1. Degrees conferred: J.D., J.D.-M.B.A., J.D.-M.A.I.A., J.D.-M.P.A., J.D.-M.S. (Telecommunications, Environmental Law), J.D.-M.D.

ADMISSION REQUIREMENTS. LSDAS Law School report, two transcripts, LSAT, recommendations, personal statement required in support of application. 55% of students must be state residents. Applicants must have received bachelor's prior to ad-

mission. Accepts 5–10 transfer applicants each year. Graduates of unaccredited colleges not considered. Apply to School by February 15. Entering students admitted Fall only. Application fee $65. Phone: (303)492-7203; fax: (303)492-2542.

ADMISSION STANDARDS. Selective. Accepts approximately 25% of total applicants. Number of applicants 2537; number of acceptance 646; number enrolled 168; LSAT (75% of students have a score at or above 160); GPA (75% of students have a GPA at or above 3.43). *U.S. News & World Report* ranking is in the top 36 of all U.S. law schools.

FINANCIAL AID. Scholarships, grants-in-aid, Federal W/S, loans; research assistantships for advanced students only. For best aid packages apply by January 1. Financial Aid deadline, March 1. Phone: (303)492-8223. Use FAFSA (School code: 001370). About 62% of students receive aid other than loans from School. Priority given to state residents.

DEGREE REQUIREMENTS. For J.D.: 6 semesters minimum; 89 semester hours; advanced standing for work completed at other approved law schools. For M.B.A., M.A.I.A., M.P.A.: see Graduate School listing above.

UNIVERSITY OF COLORADO, COLORADO SPRINGS
Colorado Springs, Colorado 80918
Web site: www.uccs.edu

Established 1965. Public control. Semester system. Library: 380,900 volumes, 2171 subscriptions. More than 600 computers on campus for student use. Total University enrollment: 8450.

Annual tuition: resident $4068, per credit $312; nonresident $11,570, per credit $890. On-campus housing for single students only. Average on-campus housing costs: $6500 (including board). Day-care facilities available.

Graduate School

Enrollment: full-time 743, part-time 494. Faculty: full-time 197, part-time 38. Degrees conferred: M.A., M.B.A., M.B.S., M.C.J., M.E., M.P.A., M.S., M.S.N., Ph.D.

ADMISSION REQUIREMENTS. Two transcripts, three letters of recommendation, statement of purpose required in support of Part I and Part II of School's application. GRE, GMAT (minimum score 400), writing sample required for some departments. Online application available. TOEFL required for international applicants. Accepts transfer applicants. Graduates of unaccredited colleges not considered. Apply to the appropriate program office at least 60 days prior to the beginning of anticipated semester of entrance. Application fee $60, $75 for international applicants. General information phone number: (719)262-3417; fax: (719)262-3045.

ADMISSION STANDARDS Selective. Usual minimum average: 2.75 (A = 4), 3.0 in some programs.

FINANCIAL AID. Annual awards from institutional funds: scholarships, fellowships, teaching/research assistantships, grants, Federal W/S, loans. Apply by March 1 through appropriate program for fellowships, assistantships, to the Office of Student Aid for all other programs. Phone: (800)990-UCCS; e-mail: finaidse@uccs.edu. Use FAFSA. Aid available for part-time students.

DEGREE REQUIREMENTS. For master's: Plan I—30 semester credit program, at least two semesters in residence; comprehensive exam; admission to candidacy; thesis, Plan II (nonthesis option)—30 semester credit program, at least two semesters in residence; comprehensive exam; admission to candidacy; final written/oral exam or special project/report. For Ph.D.: 75 credit hour program, at least three semesters in residence;. foreign language proficiency; preliminary exam; specialty exam; comprehensive exam; admission to candidacy; dissertation proposal; dissertation; public defense.

FIELDS OF STUDY

BETH-EL COLLEGE OF NURSING & HEALTH SCIENCES:
Forensic Science. M.Sc.
Nursing. M.S.N.
Nursing Practice. D.N.P.
Sports Medicine. M.Sc.

COLLEGE OF EDUCATION:
Counseling and Human Services. Includes community counseling, school counseling, student affairs in higher education. M.A.
Curriculum and Instruction. Includes instructional technology, reading, science education. M.A.
Educational Leadership. Ph.D.
Principal Licensure. M.A.
Special Education. M.A.

COLLEGE OF ENGINEERING AND APPLIED SCIENCE:
Computer Science. M.S.
Electrical Engineering. Includes circuit design, communications, computer engineering, controls, electromagnetics, microelectronics. M.S.
Engineering. Includes computer science, mechanical & aerospace engineering. Ph.D.
Engineering Management. Includes computer science/software systems, electrical and computer engineering, mathematics, manufacturing, mechanical engineering & space systems. M.E.
Information Assurance. M.E.
Mechanical Engineering. Includes manufacturing, remote sensing, space systems. M.S.
Software Engineering. M.S.
Space Operations. M.E.
System Engineering. M.E.

COLLEGE OF LETTERS, ARTS & SCIENCES:
Applied Geography. M.A.
Applied Mathematics. M.S.
Biology. M.Sc.
Communication. M.A.
History. M.A.
Mathematics. M.Sc.
Physics. M.Sc.
Psychology. M.A.
Science Teaching. M.Sc.
Sociology. M.A.

GRADUATE SCHOOL OF BUSINESS ADMINISTRATION:
Business Administration. Includes accounting, finance, general business, health care administration (online only), homeland defense, information systems (online only), international business, management, marketing, operations management, project management (online only), service management, technology management. M.B.A.
Distance M.B.A. Includes finance, general business, health care administration, homeland defense, information systems, international business, management, project management, technology management. M.B.A.
Health Care Administration. M.B.A.

SCHOOL OF PUBLIC AFFAIRS:
Criminal Justice. M.C.J.
Public Administration. Includes criminal justice, homeland defense, nonprofit management, public management. M.P.A.

UNIVERSITY OF COLORADO, DENVER
Denver, Colorado 80202
Web site: www.cudenver.edu

CGS member. Public control. Semester system. Library: 588,582 volumes, 4346 subscriptions. More than 750 computers on campus for student use. Total University enrollment: approximately 19,755.

Tuition: per credit resident $406 Architecture, $470 Business, $340 Education, $410 Engineering, Arts & Media, $468 Public Affairs, $337 Liberal Arts; nonresident $1099 Architecture, $1118 Business, $1099 Education, $1099 Engineering, Arts & Media, $1099 Public Affairs, $1029 Liberal Arts. No on-campus housing available. Day-care facilities available.

Graduate Programs

Enrollment: full-time 1434, part-time 2667. Faculty: full- and part-time approximately 350. Degrees conferred: M.A., M.Arch., M.B.A., M.B.S., M.C.J., M.Eng., M.H., M.L.A., M.P.A., M.S., M.S.I.B., M.S.S., M.U.D., M.U.R.P., Ed.S., Ph.D.

ADMISSION REQUIREMENTS. Two transcripts, three letters of reference, statement of purpose required in support of School's application. GRE, GMAT (minimum score 400), interview, portfolios, writing sample required for some departments. TOEFL (minimum score range 500–575 depending on program) required for international applicants. Accepts transfer applicants. Graduates of unaccredited colleges not considered. Apply to office of the major department at least 120 days before term admission is sought. Application fee $50, $75 for international. General information phone number: (303)556-6536.

ADMISSION STANDARDS. Selective to competitive. Usual minimum average GPA: 2.75 (A = 4), 3.0 in some schools.

FINANCIAL AID. Annual awards from institutional funds: scholarships, fellowships, teaching/research assistantships, Federal W/S, loans. Number of awards varies. Apply by February 1 through appropriate department for fellowships, assistantships, to Office of Student Aid for all other programs. Use FAFSA. Aid available for part-time students.

DEGREE REQUIREMENTS. For most master's: 24 semester hours minimum with thesis or 30 semester hours minimum without thesis, at least 2 semesters in residence; comprehensive (written or oral or both) exam; up to 9 semester hours in transfer; admission to candidacy; final written/oral exam; project/report. For Ph.D.: 30–46 hours minimum beyond the master's, at least 3 semesters in residence; foreign language proficiency; preliminary review/annual review; comprehensive exam; final written/oral exam; admission to candidacy; dissertation; public defense/dissertation colloquium.

FIELDS OF STUDY.

COLLEGE OF ARCHITECTURE AND PLANNING:
Architecture. M.Arch.
Design and Planning. Ph.D.
Landscape Architecture. M.L.A.
Urban and Regional Planning. M.U.R.P.
Urban Design. M.U.D.

GRADUATE SCHOOL OF BUSINESS ADMINISTRATION:
Accounting. M.S.
Business Administration. M.B.A., E.M.B.A.
Finance. M.S.
Health Administration. M.S.
Information Systems. M.S.
International Business. M.S.I.B.
Management and Organization. M.S.

Marketing. M.S.
Pharmaceutical Management. M.B.A.

SCHOOL OF EDUCATION:
Administrative Leadership and Policy Studies. M.A., Ed.S., Ph.D.
Counseling Psychology and Counselor Education. M.A.
Curriculum and Instruction. M.A.
Early Childhood Education. M.A.
Educational Psychology. M.A., Ed.S.
Information and Learning Technologies. M.A.
School Psychology. Ed.S.
Special Education. M.A.

COLLEGE OF ENGINEERING:
Civil Engineering. M.S., Ph.D.
Computer Science and Engineering. M.S.
Electrical Engineering. M.S.
Engineering and Applied Science. M.Eng., M.S., Ph.D.
Mechanical Engineering. M.S.

COLLEGE OF ARTS AND SCIENCES:
Anthropology. M.A.
Applied Mathematics. M.S., Ph.D.
Applied Science. M.S.
Biology. M.A.
Chemistry. M.S.
Communication. M.A.
Economics. M.A.
English. M.A.
Environmental Studies. M.S.
Health and Behavioral Science. Ph.D.
History. M.A.
Humanities. M.H.
Literature. M.A.
Political Science. M.A.
Psychology. M.A.
Social Science. M.S.S.
Sociology. M.A.
Technical Communication. M.S.

GRADUATE SCHOOL OF PUBLIC AFFAIRS:
Criminal Justice. M.C.J.
Public Administration. M.P.A., E.M.P.A.
Public Affairs. Ph.D.

UNIVERSITY OF COLORADO HEALTH SCIENCES CENTER

Denver, Colorado 80262
Web site: www.uchsc.edu

Established 1965. CGS member. Coed Public control. Quarter system. Special facilities: Alcohol Research Center, Barbara Davis Center for Childhood Diabetes, Center for Computational Biology, Center for Aging and Division of Geriatrics, Center of Excellence in Molecular Biology, Center for Health Services and Policy Research, Center for Human Caring and Caring Science, Center for Human Nutrition, Center for Nursing Research, Center for Pharmaceutical Biotechnology, Center for Schizophrenia Research, Clinical Investigation Center, Colorado Emergency Medicine Research Center, Colorado Prevention Center, Colorado Sickle Cell Treatment and Research Center, Denver Institute for Psychoanalysis, Eleanor Roosevelt Institute for Cancer Research, Hepatobiliary Research Center, John F. Kennedy Center for Developmental Disabilities, Mental Retardation Research Center, National Center for American Indian and Alaska Native Mental Health Research, National Resource Center for Health and Safety in Child Care, Native Elder Health Care Resource Center, Pediatric General Clinical Research Center, Rocky

Mountain Center for Sensor Technology, University of Colorado Cardiovascular Institute, Webb-Waring Institute for Cancer, Aging and Antioxidant Research. The Health Center's NIH ranking is 30th among all U.S. Institutions with 466 awards/grants valued at $181,939,144. According to The Center at University of Florida, the Center is ranked 44th in receipt of Federal Research fund with $181,412,000 and it ranks 59th for total University research expenditures with $218,381,000. 11 of the University's faculty members have been elected to National Honor Academies and this ranks it 64th among all U.S. institutions. The Library: approximately 250,000 volumes, 1750 subscriptions. Total Health Center enrollment: 2500.

No on-campus housing available. Average annual off-campus housing costs: $12,000–$13,500. Contact Student Assistance Office for off-campus housing information. Phone: (303)315-7620.

Graduate School

Tuition: per credit resident $125 Clinical and Basic Sciences, $415 Genetic Counseling, $441 Public Health, $278 Child Health Associates, $375 Nursing, $125 Pharmacy; nonresident $575 Clinical and Basic Sciences, $812 Genetic Counseling, $798 Public Health, $600 Child Health Associates, $979 Nursing, $575 Pharmacy.

Enrollment: full-time 751, part-time 102, Faculty: full- and part-time 900. Degrees conferred M.S., M.S.P.H., Ph.D.

ADMISSION REQUIREMENTS. Two official transcripts, GRE, four letters of recommendation required in support of Part I and Part II of School's application. TOEFL (minimum score 550) required for all international applicants. Apply by January 31 to the Graduate School. Application fee $65. Phone: (303)315-7929; fax: (303)315-6932.

ADMISSION STANDARDS. Selective for most programs, very selective for some programs. Usual minimum average GPA: 3.0 (master's programs), 3.2 (doctoral programs) (A = 4).

FINANCIAL AID. Fellowships, traineeships, research/teaching assistantships, grants, Federal W/S, loans. Apply to Student Financial Aid Office by March 15. Use FAFSA. Aid available for part-time students.

DEGREE REQUIREMENTS. For master's: 45 quarter credit hour programs; comprehensive exam; admission to candidacy; thesis/nonthesis option. For Ph.D.: 90 quarter credit hour program, preliminary exam; foreign language proficiency; comprehensive exam; admission to candidacy; dissertation; oral defense.

FIELDS OF STUDY.
Biochemistry and Molecular Genetics. Ph.D.
Bioinformatics. Ph.D.
Biomedical Sciences. Ph.D.
Biometrics. M.S., Ph.D.
Biomolecular Structure. Ph.D.
Biostatistics. M.S., Ph.D.
Cancer Biology. Ph.D.
Cell and Developmental Biology. Ph.D.
Child Health Associate/Physician Assistant Program. M.S.
Clinical Science. Ph.D.
Epidemiology. Ph.D.
Experimental Pathology. Ph.D.
Genetic Counseling. M.S.
Human Medical Genetics. Ph.D.
Immunology. Ph.D.
Microbiology. Ph.D.
Molecular Biology. Ph.D.
Neuroscience. Ph.D.
Nursing. M.S., Ph.D.
Pharmaceutical Sciences. Ph.D.
Pharmacology. Ph.D.

Physical Therapy. M.S.
Physiology and Biophysics. Ph.D.
Public Health. M.S.P.H.
Toxicology. Ph.D.

School of Dentistry
Web site: www.uchsc.edu/sod

Organized in 1973. Located at the new Anschutz Medical Campus, Aurora, Colorado, 80045. Special facility: Lazzara Center for Oral Facial Health.

Annual tuition: resident $15,785, nonresident $38,919. Off-campus housing only. Average academic year housing and personal expenses: approximately $11,000. Contact Community Housing Services, Inc. for more information. Phone: (303)831-1935. Total cost for all other first-year expenses: $13,000.

Enrollment: first-year class 50, postgraduates 16, total full-time 182 (men 52%, women 48%, minorities 18%, state resident 64%). Faculty: full-time 49, part-time 230. Degrees conferred: D.D.S., Certificate (Orthodontics).

ADMISSION REQUIREMENTS. AADSAS report, official transcripts, DAT (no later than October), personal essay, two letters of recommendation required in support of School's application. Applicants must have completed at least three years of study; prefers four years of study. Submit supplemental application only when requested. Interview by invitation. Accepts transfer applicants. Preference given to state residents and WICHE participating states. Graduates of unaccredited colleges not considered. Apply after June 1, before January 1 (WICHE certification deadline October 15), to Admission Committee. Application fee $50, $125 for international applicants. Phone: (303)724-6900.

ADMISSION STANDARDS. Competitive. Mean DAT Academic: 19.8, PAT: 18; mean GPA: 3.5 (A = 4). Admits about 5–10% of total annual applications. Approximately 65% are state residents.

FINANCIAL AID. Scholarships, grants, tuition waivers, loans. Apply to Director, Student Financial Aid Office of Medical Center after acceptance. Phone: (303)315-8364. Use FAFSA (School code: 004508). About 92% of students receive some aid from School and outside sources. Reduced tuition for residents who will upon graduation practice in underserved areas of Colorado.

DEGREE REQUIREMENTS. For D.D.S: satisfactory completion of forty-five-month program. For Certificate programs: 27-month full-time program.

School of Medicine (PO Box C290)
Web site: www.uchsc.edu/som

Established 1833. Located at the University Health Sciences Center along with the School of Dentistry, School of Nursing and Graduate School. Library: 150,000 volumes, 2100 subscriptions. NIH ranking is 30th among all U.S. institutions with 460 awards/grants worth $188,939,144.

Annual tuition: residents $24,038, nonresidents $46,455. No on-campus housing available. Total average figure for all other expenses: $11,700.

Enrollment: first-year class 143, total full-time 586 (men 52%, women 48%, minorities 20%, state residents 91%). Faculty: full-time 1200, part-time 2000. Degrees conferred: M.D., M.D.-M.B.A., M.D.-M.S., M.D.-Ph.D.

ADMISSION REQUIREMENTS. AMCAS report, transcripts, MCAT, letters of recommendation requires in support of application. Interviews for final selections. Applicants must have completed 120 semester hours of college study. Accepts transfer applicants into the sophomore year only. Preference given to

residents of Colorado, Wyoming, and Montana. Apply to Office of Admissions and Records of School after June 1, before November 1. Application fee $100. Phone: (303)315-7361; fax: (303)315-1614.

ADMISSION STANDARDS. Competitive. Accepts about 10% of all applicants. Number of applications 2526 (1943 out-of-state); number interviewed 558 (228 out-of-state); number of acceptance 246 (105 out-of-state); number enrolled 143 (35 out-of-state). Mean Composite MCAT 11.0; mean UGPA 3.67. *U.S. News & World Report* ranking is in the top 27 of all medical schools.

FINANCIAL AID. Scholarships, grants, Federal and private loans. Apply by May 31 to the Associate Dean. Phone: (303)556-2866. Use FAFSA (School code: 004508). About 50% of students receive aid other than loans from School.

DEGREE REQUIREMENTS. For M.D.: satisfactory completion of four-year program. For M.S., Ph.D: see Graduate School listing above.

FIELDS OF GRADUATE STUDY.
Biochemistry and Molecular Genetics.
Bioinformatics.
Biomedical Sciences.
Biostatistics. M.S., Ph.D
Biomolecular Structure.
Cancer Biology.
Cell and Developmental Biology.
Clinical Science. M.S.C.S., Ph.D.
Epidemiology.
Genetic Counseling.
Human Medical Genetics.
Immunology.
Medical Scientist Training Program. M.D./Ph.D.
Microbiology.
Molecular Biology.
Neuroscience.
Pharmaceutical Sciences.
Pharmacology.
Physiology and Biophysics.
Reproductive Sciences.
Toxicology.

COLUMBIA UNIVERSITY
New York, New York 10027
Web site: www.columbia.edu

Founded 1754. CGS and AAU member. Coed. Private control, Semester system. Special facilities: Institute of Nutrition Sciences, Lamont Geological Observatory, Russian Institute, East Asian Institute, Institute on Western Europe, Middle East Institute, Institute on East Central Europe, Institute of African Studies, Institute of Latin American and Iberian Studies, Nevis Synchrocyclotron Laboratory, Armstrong Field Laboratories for Microwave Research, Cooperative Industrial Reactor Laboratories, Institute of Administrative Research, Institute of Field Studies, Institute of Psychological Research, Horace Mann-Lincoln Institute of School Experimentation, Institute of Research and Service in Nursing Education, Institute of Language Arts, Curriculum Service Center, Evaluation and Measurement Service Center, Institute of Higher Education, Institute of Educational Technology, Institute of Philosophy and Politics of Education, Institute of the Education of the Handicapped, Nevis Biological Station, Columbia Radiation Laboratory. The University's NIH ranking is 11th among all U.S. Institutions with 763 awards/grants valued at $330,754,949. According to The Center at University of Florida, the University is ranked 9th in receipt of Federal Research funds with $385,529,000 and it ranks 22nd for total University research expenditures with $437,669,000. The University's endowment asset ranks it 7th, $4,493,085,000. In 2004, the University awarded 495 doctorates which ranked it 17th among all U.S. institutions eligible to award that degree. 9 of the University's faculty members have been elected to National Honor Academies and this ranks it 91st among all U.S. institutions. The Library: approximately 4,000,000 volumes, 41,000 subscriptions. Total University enrollment: 23,500.

On-campus housing for married students, 611 graduate men, 391 graduate women. Average annual housing cost: $10,000–$13,000 for married students, $9000 for single students. Apply to Livingston Hall (on-campus housing for single and married students), to Housing Office for off-campus housing information. Phone: (212)854-3923.

Graduate School of Arts and Sciences

Graduate study since 1880. Annual tuition: full-time $33,364. Enrollment: full- and part-time 3250. Faculty: full- and part-time 700. Degrees conferred: M.A., Liberal Studies M.A. (Interdisciplinary), M.A.-M.P.A., M.A.-M.S., M.Phil., J.D.-Ph.D., M.D.-Ph.D., Ph.D.

ADMISSION REQUIREMENTS. Transcripts, GRE, three letters of recommendation required in support of School's application. GRE Subject Test recommended for all applicants. TOEFL (minimum score 600, 250 on computer-based test) required for international applicants from non-English-speaking countries. Interview not required. Accepts transfer applicants. Graduates of unaccredited institutions not considered. Apply to Graduate School of Arts and Sciences Office of Admissions by January 3 (for priority consideration for both admissions and Financial Aid), April 30 for regular consideration (Fall). Application fee $85. Phone: (212)854-4737; fax: (212)854-2863.

ADMISSION STANDARDS. Very competitive for some departments, competitive or very selective for the others. Usual minimum average: 3.0 (A = 4).

FINANCIAL AID. Annual awards from institutional funds: scholarships, fellowships, teaching assistantships, research assistantships, Federal W/S, loans. Apply by the first Monday in January (for priority consideration) to Office of Student Affairs for scholarships and fellowships. Phone: (212)854-3808. Use FAFSA. About 90% of students receive aid other than loans from University and outside sources. Aid usually not available for part-time students.

DEGREE REQUIREMENTS. For M.A.: Two semesters minimum in full-time residence; reading knowledge of one foreign language for some departments; essay required by many departments. For Liberal Studies M.A.: 36-credit program; final paper. For M.Phil.: essentially the same as Ph.D., except no dissertation requirement. For Ph.D.: six semesters minimum beyond the master's in full-time residence; reading knowledge of two foreign languages; qualifying exam; dissertation; final oral exam.

FIELDS OF STUDY.
African-American Studies. M.A. only.
American Studies. Liberal Studies M.A.
Anatomy and Cell Biology.
Anthropology. Includes museum anthropology.
Applied Mathematics. Interdepartmental. Ph.D. only.
Applied Physics and Applied Mathematics. M.Phil., Ph.D.
Architecture (History and Theory). Ph.D. only.
Art History and Archaeology.
Astronomy.
Atmospheric and Planetary Science. Interdepartmental. Ph.D. only.
Biochemistry and Molecular Biophysics. M.Phil., Ph.D.

Biological Sciences.
Biomedical Engineering. M.Phil., Ph.D.
Biomedical Informatics.
Biostatistics. M.Phil., Ph.D.
Biotechnology. M.A. only.
Buddhist Studies. Ph.D. only.
Business. M.Phil., Ph.D.
Cellular, Molecular and Biophysical Studies.
Chemical Engineering. M.Phil., Ph.D.
Chemical Physics.
Civil Engineering. M.Phil., Ph.D.
Classical Studies.
Classics.
Climate and Society. M.A. only.
Communication.
Computer Science. M.Phil., Ph.D.
Conservation Biology. M.A. only.
Dental Sciences. M.A. only.
Earth and Environmental Science Journalism. Dual degree program, M.S. Journalism, Earth and Environmental Science. M.A.
Earth and Environmental Sciences.
East Asian Language and Cultures.
East Asian Studies. Liberal Studies M.A.
Ecology, Evolution, and Environmental Biology. Includes evolutionary primatology.
Economics.
Education. M.Phil., Ph.D.
English and Comparative Literature.
Environmental Health Sciences.
Epidemiology. M.Phil., Ph.D.
French and Romance Philology.
French Cultural Studies in a Global Context. M.A. only.
Genetics and Development.
Germanic Languages.
History.
Human Rights Studies. Liberal Studies M.A.
Industrial Engineering & Operations Research. M.Phil., Ph.D.
Islamic Studies. Liberal Studies M.A.
Italian.
Japanese Pedagogy. Summer only. M.A. only.
Jewish Studies. Liberal Studies M.A.
Materials Science and Engineering/Solid State Science and Engineering. Ph.D. only.
Mathematical Structures for Environmental and Social Sciences. Interdepartmental. Ph.D.
Mathematics.
Mathematics of Finance. M.A. only.
Mechanical Engineering. M.Phil., Ph.D.
Medieval Studies. Liberal Studies M.A.
Microbiology.
Middle East and Asian Languages and Cultures.
Modern Art: Critical and Curatorial Studies. M.A. only.
Modern European Studies. Liberal Studies M.A.
Music. Includes Musicology (M.A., M.Phil. Ph.D.), Composition (M.A., D.M.A.).
Neurobiology and Behavior. M.Phil., Ph.D.
Nutrition. M.Phil., Ph.D.
Operations Research. Interdepartmental. Ph.D. only.
Pathology and Cell Biology.
Pharmacology.
Philosophical Foundations of Physics. M.A. only.
Philosophy.
Physics.
Physiology and Cellular Biophysics.
Political Science.
Psychology.
Quantitative Methods in the Social Sciences. M.A., M.A.-M.P.A. only.
Religion.
Religion—Journalism. M.A.-M.S.

Russia, Eurasia and East Europe. Regional Studies M.A.
Russian Translation. M.A. only.
Slavic Cultures. M.A. only.
Slavic Languages.
Social Work. M.Phil., Ph.D.
Sociology.
Sociomedical Sciences.
South Asian Studies. Liberal Arts M.A.
Spanish and Portuguese.
Statistics.
Sustainable Development.
Theatre.
Urban Planning. M.Phil., Ph.D.
Yiddish Studies. Interdepartmental.

School of the Arts
Web site: www.columbia.edu/cu/arts

Established 1965. Special facility: LeRoy Neiman Center for Print Studies, Oscar Hammerstein Center for Theatre Studies, Fritz Reiner Center for Contemporary Music, Computer Music Center, Digital Media Center. Annual tuition: full-time M.F.A. \$38,812, film studies \$33,364. Enrollment: full-time 740. Faculty: full-time 44, part-time 156. Degrees conferred: M.F.A., D.M.A.

ADMISSION REQUIREMENTS. Transcripts, three letters of recommendation, statement of intent, portfolio or samples of work, audition/interview (depending upon major), at least three years of relevant professional experience required in support of application. Electronic application available. TOEFL required for international applicants. Accepts transfer applicants. Apply to Office of the Dean for Admission and Financial Aid. Application deadlines vary, depending on field of study. Fall and Spring admissions, except in Painting and Sculpture (Fall only). Application fee \$120. Phone: (212)854-2134; e-mail: admission-arts@columbia.edu.

ADMISSION STANDARDS. Competitive or very competitive. Usual minimum average: 3.25 (A = 4).

FINANCIAL AID. Scholarships, tuition waivers, research assistantships, teaching assistantships, Federal W/S, loans. Apply by February 7. Phone: (212)854-2875. Use FAFSA. About 80% of students receive aid other than loans from School and outside sources.

DEGREE REQUIREMENTS. For M.F.A.: 60-credit program, four semesters in full-time residence; program by advisement; knowledge of at least one foreign language; final project or thesis project. For D.M.A.: usually six semesters beyond the bachelor's or 30 credits beyond the M.F.A., at least four semesters in residence; final project/dissertation.

FIELDS OF STUDY.
Acting.
Digital Media.
Directing.
Dramaturgy/Script Analysis.
Fiction.
Film Production.
Film Screenwriting.
Nonfiction.
Painting.
Photography.
Playwriting.
Poetry.
Producing.
Printmaking.
Sculpture.
Stage Management.
Theatre Directing.

Theatre Management and Producing.
Theatre Playwriting.
Visual Arts.
Writing.
Note: Joint J.D.-M.F.A. program in Entertainment Law.

Graduate School of Business
Web site: www.gsb.columbia.edu

Established 1916. Accredited programs: M.B.A.; recognized Ph.D. Semester system. Special Programs: foreign exchange programs (Australia, Austria, Belgium, Brazil, Finland, Germany, Hong Kong, Israel, Italy, the Netherlands, the Philippines, Republic of Singapore, Spain, Sweden, Switzerland, United Kingdom), foreign study, global studies. Special facilities: Center for Chinese Business Studies, Center for Human Resource Management, Center for Japanese Economy and Business, Center for Research in the Marketing Financial Services, Center for Global Consumers, Brands and Communication, Columbia Institute for Tele-Information, Institute for Marketing Studies, Center for the Studies of Futures Marketing, Center for International Business Education, Deming Center for Quality, Productivity, and Competitiveness. Library: 360,000 volumes, 3000 subscriptions.

Annual tuition: full-time \$43,436.

Enrollment: new students 485 (Fall), 184 (Spring); total full- and part-time 1683. Faculty: 118 full-time, 85 part-time; 99% with Ph.D./D.B.A. Degrees conferred: M.B.A. (FT, PT, day, evening), E.M.B.A. (Company Sponsored), M.B.A.-D.D.S., M.B.A.-J.D., M.B.A.-M.I.A. (International Affairs), M.B.A.-M.P.H. (Public Health), M.B.A.-M.S. (Engineering and Applied Science, Journalism, Nursing, Social Work, Urban Planning), M.B.A.-Ed.D. (Educational Administration and Higher Education with Teachers College), Ph.D.

ADMISSION REQUIREMENTS. A bachelor's degree from a recognized institution of higher education and a strong mathematics background are required for consideration. Submit an application, GMAT results (will accept GMAT test results from the last five years, latest acceptable date is April 15), official transcripts from each undergraduate/graduate school attended, two letters of recommendation, résumé (prefers at least four years of work experience), and an application fee of \$180 to the Office of Admission and Financial Aid. Online application available. Beginning students are admitted Fall and Spring. U.S. citizens apply by April 20 (Fall), October 1 (Spring); international applicants apply by March 1 (Fall), October 1 (Spring). In addition, international students (whose native language is other than English) should submit a TOEFL (minimum score 610) report, certified translations and evaluations of all official transcripts, recommendation should be in English or with certified translations, proof of health/immunization certificate, and proof of sufficient financial resources for one year of academic study. On-campus visits are encouraged. Interviews are by invitation of the Admissions Committee. Joint degree applicants must apply to and be accepted to both schools/programs, contact the admissions office for current information and specific admissions requirements. Rolling admissions process, notification is made within 8–10 weeks of receipt of completed application and supporting documents. Admissions Office phone: (212)854-1961; fax: (212)662-6754.

ADMISSION REQUIREMENTS FOR DOCTORAL CANDIDATES. All applicants should have a bachelor's degree from a recognized institution of higher education, master's degree is optional. Strong mathematics background required. Contact the Ph.D. Programs, Graduate School of Business at (212)854-2836 for application material and information. Beginning students are admitted Fall only. Both U.S. citizens and international applicants apply by February 1 (Fall). Submit an application, a GMAT/GRE (will accept GMAT/GRE test results from the last five years, scores must arrive at admissions office prior to February 1), GRE including writing assessment required for Finance and Economics, official transcripts from each undergraduate/graduate schools attended, two letters of recommendation, 500-word essay, résumé, Statistical Information Sheet, and application fee of $60 to the Office of Admission and Financial Aid. Online application encouraged. In addition, international students (whose native language is other than English) should submit a TOEFL (minimum score 610) report; certified translations and evaluations of all official transcripts, recommendation should be in English or with certified translations, proof of health/immunization certificate. Interviews are not required, but can be arranged. Phone: (212)854-2836. Notification is made by mid-April.

ADMISSION STANDARDS. Competitive. Mean GMAT: 660; mean GPA: 3.45 (A = 4). *U.S. News & World Report* ranked Columbia in the top nine (M.B.A.), top five (E.M.B.A.), top four (Finance), top four (International Business), top four (Marketing) of all U.S. business schools. *BusinessWeek* listed Columbia in the top six of American business schools.

FINANCIAL AID. Need-based scholarships, international fellowships, minority fellowships, graduate assistantships, State Grants, Federal W/S, loans. Financial aid is available for part-time study. Financial aid may be available for international students. Assistantships/fellowships may be available for joint degree candidates. Request scholarship, fellowship, assistantship information as well as current need-based financial aid information from the School of Business. Phone: (212)854-4057. For most financial assistance and all Federal programs submit FAFSA (School code: E00116), also submit Financial Aid Transcript, Federal Income Tax forms. Approximately 65% of current students receive some form of financial assistance. Financial Aid for doctoral students: fellowships, assistantships, tuition exemptions, dissertation research support, loans. Apply for Financial Aid at the same time as admissions by submitting the Financial Assistance Application.

DEGREE REQUIREMENTS. For M.B.A.: 21-course program including 10 elective courses, two-year program; degree program must be completed in five years. For E.M.B.A.: 60-credit program. For M.B.A.-M.S.: 75–90-credit programs (Computer Science 75 credits, Industrial Engineering 75 credits, Journalism 78 credits, Mining Engineering 75 credits, Nursing 75 credits, Operations Research 75 credits, Social Work 90 credits, Urban Planning 90 credits). For M.B.A.-M.I.A.: 90-credit program. For M.B.A.-M.P.H.: 80-credit program. For M.B.A.-Ed.D.: 90-credit program. For M.B.A.-J.D.: 118 credit program, four- to five-year program. For Ph.D.: 20-course minimum, three- to five-year program; comprehensive exam; field exam; oral major field exam; at least two teaching assignments; dissertation proposal and oral defense; dissertation; oral defense.

FIELDS OF STUDY.
Accounting.
Decision, Risk Operations. Ph.D.
Entrepreneurship.
Finance and Economics. Ph.D.
Global Business Administration.
Healthcare and Pharmaceutical Management.
Human Resource Management.
International Business.
Management. Ph.D.
Marketing. M.B.A., Ph.D.
Operations Management.
Public and Nonprofit Management.
Real Estate.
Social Enterprise.

College of Dental Medicine
Web site: dental.columbia.edu

Established 1852. Semester system. Special facilities: Center to Study and Address Oral Health Disparities, Center for Oral, Facial and Head Pain, Dental Implant/Specialty Consultation Center, Center for Clinical Research in Dentistry, Center for Craniofacial Reconstruction and Rehabilitation, Center for Maxillofacial Prosthodontics, Center for Skin and Mucosal Biology.

Annual tuition: $44,200. On-campus housing available. Contact Office of Housing Services at Medical Center for both on- and off campus housing. Phone: (212)304-7000 Average academic year housing and personal expenses: approximately $15,900. Total cost for all other first-year expenses: $8,500.

Enrollment: D.D.S. program, first-year class 75, total full-time 260 (men 74%, women 26%, minorities 10%, state resident 25%), postgraduate program, full-time 48, part-time 4. Faculty: full-time 75, part-time 130. Degrees conferred: D.D.S., D.D.S.-M.B.A., D.D.S.-M.P.H., D.D.S.-M.S. (Health Care Management), D.D.S.-M.A. (Education), Certificate.

ADMISSION REQUIREMENTS. AADSAS report, official transcripts, three letters of recommendation, DAT required in support of School's application. Interview by invitation only. Applicants must have completed at least three years of college study. Graduates of unaccredited institutions not considered. Does not have EDP. Apply to Director of Student Affairs of the School after July 1, before February 15. Application fee $70. Phone: (212) 305-3478; fax: (212)305-1034.

ADMISSION STANDARDS. Competitive. Accepts about 15% of all applicants. Number of applications 1360; number interviewed 256; number of acceptance n/a (n/a out-of-state); number enrolled 75 (n/a out-of-state). Mean DAT: academic 21, PAT 19; mean UGPA 3.40.

FINANCIAL AID. Scholarships, grants, tuition waivers, loans. Apply to Office of Student Financial Planning. Phone: (212)305-4100. Use FAFSA (School code: E00119). No specified closing date. About 95% of students receive aid other than loans from School and outside sources.

DEGREE REQUIREMENTS. For D.D.S.: satisfactory completion of forty-five-month program.

FIELDS OF POSTGRADUATE STUDY.
Advanced Education in General Dentistry.
Dental Informatics.
Endodontics.
Orthodontics.
Periodontics.
Prostodontics.

Fu Foundation School of Engineering and Applied Science—Graduate Division
Web site: www.engineering.columbia.edu

Special facilities: Center for Advanced Technology, Center for Applied Probability, Center for Computational Biology and Bioinformatics, Center for Computational Learning Systems, Center for Integrated Science Engineering, Columbia Center for Electron Transport in Molecular Nanostructures, Computational Optimization Research Center, Earth Engineering Center, Environmental Molecular Science Institute.

Annual tuition: full-time $35,800. On-campus housing available. See housing information above. Enrollment: full-time 830, part-time 390. Faculty: full-time 172, part-time 80. Degrees conferred: M.S., Eng., Sc.D., Ph.D., Prof. Engr., M.B.A.-M.S.

ADMISSION REQUIREMENTS. Official transcripts, GRE, two letters of recommendation required in support of School's application. Electronic application available. GRE Subject required for Computer Science. TOEFL required for international applicants. Accept transfer applicants. Graduates of unaccredited institutions not considered. Apply to Office of Graduate Student Services by January 1 (Fall, for both admission and financial aid), February 15 (Fall, M.S. only and professional degree), October 1 (Spring). Application fee $60, $45 if you apply online. Phone: (212)854-6438.

ADMISSION STANDARDS. Very selective. Usual minimum average: 3.0 (A = 4). *U.S. News & World Report* ranking is in the top 26 of all U.S. schools.

FINANCIAL AID. Annual awards from institutional funds: scholarships, fellowships, research assistantships, teaching assistantships, Federal W/S, loans. Approved for VA benefits. Apply by January 15 (Fall) to Office of Graduate Student Services of the School for scholarships, fellowships, assistantships; to the Office of Financial Aid for all other programs. Phone: (212) 854-3711; e-mail: engradfinaid@columbia.edu. Use FAFSA (School code: E00120). Aid available for international applicants.

DEGREE REQUIREMENTS. For master's: 30 semester hours of approved graduate courses beyond the bachelor's; thesis at discretion of department or division program. For Eng., Sc.D.: 30 semester hours of approved graduate courses beyond the master's, or 60 residence units beyond the bachelor's; foreign language proficiency at discretion of department/division; departmental qualifying exam; thesis and research required; final exam; degree completion within seven years. For Ph.D.: see Graduate School of Arts and Sciences listing above.

FIELDS OF STUDY.
Applied Chemistry.
Applied Mathematics.
Applied Physics.
Biomechanics.
Biomedical Engineering.
Chemical Engineering.
Civil Engineering.
Computer Engineering.
Computer Science.
Earth and Environmental Engineering.
Electrical Engineering. Includes multimedia networking, telecommunications engineering, new media engineering, lightwave (photonics) engineering, wireless and mobile communications, microelectronic circuits, microelectronic devices.
Engineering Mechanics. Includes continuum mechanics, vibration, random processes and reliability, fluid mechanics, computational mechanics.
Environmental Control Engineering.
Financial Engineering.
Genomics Science and Technology.
Industrial Engineering. Includes engineering and management systems, production and operations management, industrial regulations studies, manufacturing, financial engineering.
Manufacturing Engineering.
Materials Science and Engineering.
Mechanical Engineering.
Medical Physics.
Operations Research.
Optical Physics.
Plasma Physics.
Process Engineering.
Solid-State Physics.
Solid-State Science and Engineering.
Telecommunication.

School of International and Public Affairs and the Regional Institutes
Web site: www.sipa.columbia.edu

Established 1946. Graduate study only. Annual tuition: full-time $35,316.

Enrollment: full- and part-time 1150. Faculty: full-time 88. Degrees conferred: M.I.A., M.P.A., E.M.P.A., Ph.D.

ADMISSION REQUIREMENTS. Transcripts, personal statement, CV or résumé, GRE, three letters of recommendation required in support of School's application. Interviews are encouraged. TOEFL (minimum score 600, 250 on computer-based test) required for international applicants. Graduates of unaccredited institutions not considered. Apply to Office of University Admission, Low Memorial Library, by March 15 (Fall), October 15 (Spring). Application fee $75. Phone: (212)854-6216.

ADMISSION STANDARDS. Competitive. Usual minimum average: 3.0 (A = 4). Accepts about 35% of annual applicants.

FINANCIAL AID. Annual awards from institutional funds: fellowships, grants, assistantships, Federal W/S, career-related internships, loans. Apply by January 5 for fellowships, assistantships to Director of Admissions of the School. Phone: (212)854-6216. Use FAFSA (School code: 00128). About 35% of students receive aid other than loans from School. Financial assistance is available for international students.

DEGREE REQUIREMENTS. For M.I.A., M.P.A.: 54 credits minimum, full-time four-semester program, at least 30 in residence; functional or regional concentration for M.I.A.; proficiency in one foreign language (M.I.A.); internships; thesis. For Ph.D.: see Graduate School of Arts and Sciences above.

PROGRAMS OF STUDY.
Economic Policy Management. M.P.A.
Environmental Science and Policy. M.P.A.
International Affairs. M.I.A.
Public Administration. M.P.A.
Public Policy and Administration. E.M.P.A.
Sustainable Development. Ph.D.

M.I.A. FUNCTIONAL CONCENTRATION AND M.P.A. CONCENTRATIONS:
Advanced Policy and Economic Analysis.
Economic and Political Development.
Environmental Policy Studies.
Human Rights.
International Economic Policy.
International Energy Management and Policy.
International Finance and Policy.
International Media and Communications.
International Security Policy.
Management and Institutional Analysis.
Social Policy.
Urban Policy

M.I.A. REGIONAL CONCENTRATION:
Africa.
East Asia.
East Central Europe.
Latin America.
Russia and Former Soviet States.
Southern Asia.
The Middle East.
Western Europe.

Graduate School of Journalism

Established 1912. Annual tuition: $37,600. Graduate study only. Enrollment: full-time 180, part-time 15. Faculty: full-time 19, part-time 78. Degree conferred: M.A., M.S., Ph.D.

ADMISSION REQUIREMENTS. Official transcripts, up to three letters of recommendation, two essays, résumé, writing test required in support of School's application. Online application available. TOEFL (minimum score 600, 270 on computer-based test) required for international applicants. Transfer applicants not considered. Graduates of unaccredited institutions not considered. Apply to Office of Journalism Admissions by December 15 (Fall, full-time), May 1 (Fall, part-time), November 1 (Spring, part-time). Application fee $75. Phone: (212)854-8608; e-mail: admissions@jrn.columbia.edu.

ADMISSION STANDARDS. Competitive. Decisions based on professional promise, academic excellence, and writing test.

FINANCIAL AID. Annual awards from institutional funds: fellowships, grants, scholarships, loans, on- and off-campus employment. Apply to Office of Journalism Admissions. Phone: (212)854-3829. Use FAFSA (School code: E00122). Aid available for international students through the School's International Division (ID). About 80% of students receive aid from School and outside sources.

DEGREE REQUIREMENTS. For M.A., M.S.: 30–34 credits minimum; master's project (major paper or tape of publishable or broadcast quality). For Ph.D.: see Graduate School of Arts and Sciences above.

FIELDS OF STUDY.
Communication. Ph.D.
Journalism. Includes concentrations in arts & culture, business & economics, politics, science. M.A.
Journalism. Includes concentrations in broadcast, magazine, new media, newspaper. M.S.

School of Law
Web site: www.law.columbia.edu

Established 1858. ABA approved since 1923. AALS member. Private control. Semester system. Special facilities: Center for Chinese Legal Studies, Center for Contract and Economic Organization, Center for Japanese Legal Studies, Center for Korean Legal Studies, Center for Law & Philosophy, Center for Law and Economic Studies, Center for Public Interest Law, Center for the Study of Law and Culture, Center on Corporate Governance, Center on Crime, Community and Law, Center on Global Legal Problems, European Legal Studies Center, Kernochan Center for Law, Media and the Arts. Law library: 1,092,534 volumes, 6472 subscriptions; a federal Government Depository.

Annual tuition: full-time $41,226. Total average cost for all other expenses: $18,798.

Enrollment: first-year class 378; total 1230 (men 57%, women 43%, minorities 29%). Faculty: full-time 110, part-time 130. Student faculty ratio 11.7 to 1. Degrees conferred: J.D., J.D.-Maitrise en Droit, J.D.-D.E.S.S., LL.M., J.S.D.

ADMISSION REQUIREMENTS. For J.D. program: LSDAS report, transcript, biographical information sheet, personal profile sheet, personal statement/essay, two letters of recommendation, résumé, LSAT required in support of application. Interview not required. Accepts transfer applicants. Apply to Law Admission Office after September 1, before February 15. Application fee $70. Phone: (212)854-2670. For LL.M.: transcripts, written statement, résumé, two letters of recommendation required in support of application. For J.S.D.: in addition to the above must also submit a dissertation proposal and bibliography. Apply to Office of Graduate Legal Studies of the School by December 15. International applicants for all programs must submit TOEFL (not older than two years), TSE and TWE. Fall admission only. Accepts full-time students only. Application fee $70. Phone: (212)854-2655.

ADMISSION STANDARDS. Selective. Accepts approximately 15% of all students. Number of applicants 8020; number of acceptance 1169; number enrolled 378; LSAT (75% of students have a score at or above 168); GPA (75% of students have a GPA at or above 3.50). *U.S. News & World Report* ranking is in the top 5 of all U.S. law schools.

FINANCIAL AID. For J.D. program: scholarships, fellowships, assistantships, Federal W/S, apply for financial aid at time of application for admission, but before March 1. Phone: (212)854-7730. Use FAFSA (School code: E00488). For graduate program: apply for fellowships by March 1 to Office of Graduate Legal Studies of the School. About 48% of students receive aid other than loans from School.

DEGREE REQUIREMENTS. For J.D.: satisfactory completion of three-year program; 83 credits. For LL.M.: 24 credits minimum, at least one year in residence; essay; up to six credits may be taken in other Columbia University Graduate Schools. For J.S.D.: at least one year in residence; publishable dissertation; oral exam.

FIELDS OF GRADUATE STUDY.
Civil Procedure.
Commercial Law.
Constitutional Law.
Corporation Securities Law.
Criminal Law.
Government Service.
Human Rights Law.
International Law.
Labor Law.
Legal History.
Legal Philosophy.
Property.
Taxation.
Note: School has joint degree programs with the Graduate Schools of the Arts, Arts and Sciences, Business, Journalism, International Affairs, Physicians & Surgeons, Social Work; programs in Public Affairs, Urban Planning, with Princeton University's Woodrow Wilson School of Public and International Affairs.

School of Nursing
Web site: www.nursing.columbia.edu

Founded 1892, graduate study since 1956. Semester system. Special facilities: Center for AIDS Research, Center for Health Policy, World Health Organization Center for the International Nursing Development in Advanced Practice, Center for Evidence-Based Practice in the Underserved.

Tuition: per credit $1322 master's, doctoral programs per credit $1420.

Enrollment: full- and part-time 415. Faculty: full-time 42, part-time 26. Degrees conferred; M.S., D.N.Sc., Dr.N.P.

ADMISSION REQUIREMENTS. Official transcripts, personal statement, three letters of recommendation, GRE, MAT or another appropriate objective test, copy of nursing license required in support of School's application. Interview sometimes required. TOEFL required for international applicants. Graduates of unaccredited institutions not considered. Apply to Office of Student Services of the School at least three months prior to preferred date of enrollment. Admits Fall, Spring, and Summer. Application fee $70, $100 for D.N.Sc. applicants. Phone: (212)305-5756; e-mail: nursing@columbia.edu.

ADMISSION STANDARDS. Competitive. Usual minimum average: 3.0 (A = 4).

FINANCIAL AID. Scholarships, grants, assistantships, Federal W/S, Federal Nursing loans, loans. Apply by March 1 to Student Service Office. Phone: (212) 305-8147; fax: (212)305-6937. Use FAFSA (School code: E00124). About 50% of students receive aid from all sources. Aid sometimes available for part-time students.

DEGREE REQUIREMENTS. For M.S.: see credit requirements in Fields of Study below, at least one year in full-time residence. For D.N.Sc., Dr.N.P.: 45–75 credit program (depending on preparation), at least one semester in full-time residence; comprehensive written and oral exam; research and speciality practicum experience; dissertation proposal defense, dissertation; final exam.

FIELDS OF SPECIALIZATION.
Acute Care Nursing Practitioner. 47-credit M.S. program.
Adult/Geriatric Nurse Practitioner. 55-credit M.S. program.
Adult Nurse Practitioner. 46-credit M.S. program.
Advanced Clinical Management. 45-credit M.S. program.
Family Nurse Practitioner. 46–48-credit M.S. program.
Geriatric Nurse Practitioner. 49-credit M.S. Program.
HIV Nursing. 44-credit M.S. program.
Neonatal Nurse Practitioner. 46-credit M.S. program.
Nurse Anesthesia. 59-credit M.S. program.
Nurse Midwifery. 49-credit M.S. program.
Oncology Nurse Practitioner. 54–56 credit M.S. program.
Pediatric Nurse Practitioner. 46-credit M.S. program.
Psychiatric Mental Health Nurse Practitioner. 46-credit M.S. program.
Women's Health Nurse Practitioner. 48–52-credit M.S. program.

College of Physicians and Surgeons (10032)
Web site: www.cumc.columbia.edu

Established 1767. The first school to award an M.D. in the American colonies. Library: 450,000 volumes, 4000 subscriptions. NIH ranking is 11th among all U.S. institutions with 763 awards/grants worth $330,754,949.

Annual tuition: $43,700. On- and off-campus housing available. Total average figure for all other expenses: $18,000.

Enrollment: first-year class 150, total full-time 624 (men 53%, women 47%, minorities 38%, state residents 35%). Faculty: full-time 1778, part-time 1500. Degrees conferred: M.D., M.D.-M.B.A., M.D.-M.P.H., M.D.-Ph.D.

ADMISSION REQUIREMENTS. AMCAS report, transcripts, MCAT, recommendations required in support of application. Interview by invitation only. Supplemental application required. Applicants must have completed at least three years of college study. Does not have EDP. Apply to Office of the Dean of the College after June 1, before October 15. Application fee $75. Phone: (212)305-3595; fax: (212)305-3601.

ADMISSION STANDARDS. Very Competitive. Accepts about 5% of all applicants. Number of applications 5768 (n/a out-of-state); number interviewed 1247 (1095 out-of-state); number of acceptance 307 (256 out-of-state); number enrolled 150 (117 out-of-state). Mean Composite MCAT 11.8; mean UGPA 3.79. *U.S. News & World Report* ranking is in the top 10 of all medical schools.

FINANCIAL AID. Scholarships, grants, assistantships, fellowships, Federal and institutional loans. Apply after acceptance. Phone: (212)305-4100. Use FAFSA (College code: E00117). About 68% of students receive some aid from institutional funds.

DEGREE REQUIREMENTS. For M.D.: satisfactory completion of four-year program. For M.B.A., M.P.H., Ph.D.: see Graduate School listing above.

FIELDS OF GRADUATE AND POSTGRADUATE STUDY.
Biochemistry and Molecular Biophysics.
Biological Sciences.
Biomedical Engineering.
Biomedical Informatics.
Cell Biology and Pathology.
Cellular, Molecular and Biophysical Studies.

Chemistry.
Computational Biology.
Epidemiology.
Genetics and Development.
Immunology.
Microbiology.
Neurobiology and Behavior.
Pharmacology.
Physiology and Cellular Biophysics.

Joseph L. Mailman School of Public Health
Web site: www.publichealth.columbia.edu

Graduate study since 1921. Semester system. Special facilities: Center for Applied Public Health, Columbia Center for Children's Environmental Health, Center for Community Health and Education, Center for Environmental Health in Northern Manhattan, Harlem Health Promotion Center, Harlem Lung Center, Center for the History and Ethics of Public Health, Center for Infectious Disease Epidemiology Research, Center for Lesbian, Gay, Bisexual, and Transgender Health, National Center for Children in Poverty, Center for Psychosocial Study of Health and Illness, Center for Public Health Preparedness, Statistical Analysis Center for Clinical Trials, Center for Violence Research and Prevention.

Tuition: per credit $1155.

Enrollment: full- and part-time 740 (men 30%, women 70%). Faculty: full-time 86, part-time 206. Degrees conferred: M.P.H., Executive M.P.H., M.S., Dr.P.H. The Ph.D. is administered by the Graduate School of Arts and Sciences.

ADMISSION REQUIREMENTS. Official transcripts, GRE or another appropriate objective test, personal statement, three letters of reference required in support of School's application. Interview sometimes required. M.P.H. or equivalent master's, internship required for Dr.P.H. applicants. TOEFL required for international applicants. Accepts transfer applicants. Graduates of unaccredited institutions not considered. Apply to Office of Admissions of the School before January 15 (Fall), October 1 (Spring), February 1 (Summer). Application fee $100. Phone: (212) 305-3927, Fax: (212)305-6450.

ADMISSION STANDARDS. Competitive. Usual minimum average: 3.0 (A = 4).

FINANCIAL AID. Assistantships, traineeships, Federal W/S, loans. Apply to Financial Aid Office; no specified closing date. Phone: (212)305-4113; fax: (212)305-1861. Use FAFSA. About 50% of students receive aid from all sources.

DEGREE REQUIREMENTS. For M.P.H.: 45 credits minimum, at least one year in full-time residence; practicum; master's essay or culminating experience. For M.S.: 30-credit program, at least one year in residence; master's essay. For Dr.P.H.: two-year, 40-credit minimum program, at least one year in residence; qualifying exam; dissertation; final oral exam. Fo Ph.D.: see Graduate School of Arts and Sciences listing above.

FIELDS OF STUDY.
Biostatistics. M.P.H., M.S., Ph.D., Dr.P.H.
Environmental Health Sciences. Includes environmental and molecular epidemiology, environmental and molecular toxicology, environmental policy, global health, medical/health physics. M.P.H., Ph.D., Dr.P.H.
Epidemiology. M.P.H., M.S., Ph.D., Dr.P.H.
General Public Health. Interdisciplinary School-wide program. M.P.H.
Global Health. Interdisciplinary School-wide program. M.P.H.
Health Policy and Management. Includes management, policy, effectiveness and outcomes research. M.P.H.

Population and Family Health. Includes forced migration and health, reproductive and family health, sexuality and health. M.P.H. only.

Sociomedical Sciences. Includes aging & public health, history of public health & medicine, health promotion, sexuality & health, social science research in public health, urban & the built environment. M.P.H., Ph.D., Dr.P.H.

Note: Dual degree programs are available with the Architecture School, Business School, Dental College, International Affairs & Public Administration School, Medical School, Nursing School, Social Work School.

School of Social Work

Web site: www.socialwork.columbia.edu

Annual tuition: Full-time $33,004. On-campus housing available. See Housing listing above. Enrollment: full-time 595, part-time 139 (men 15%, women 85%). Faculty: full-time 44, part-time 53. Degrees conferred: M.S.S.W., Ph.D.

ADMISSION REQUIREMENTS. Official transcripts, three letters of reference, personal statement required in support of School's application. Electronic application available. Interviews sometimes requested by School. GRE required for doctoral applicants. TOEFL (minimum score 575), TWE, TSE required for international applicants. Accepts transfer applicants. Especially interested in minority group applicants. Apply to Office of Admissions by March 15 (Fall) for full-time; November 1 (Spring). Application fee: online $65, paper $225. Phone: (212)954-2856; fax: (212)854-2975.

ADMISSION STANDARDS. Selective. Usual minimum average: 3.0 (A = 4).

FINANCIAL AID. Annual awards from institutional funds: scholarships, merit scholarships, teaching assistantships, internships, Federal W/S, loans. Apply by June 15 (Fall) to Office of Student Financial Planning. Phone: (212)851-2293. Use FAFSA. About 90% of students receive aid from School and outside sources.

DEGREE REQUIREMENTS. For M.S.S.W: 60 credits full-time, two-year or 17-month (accelerated) minimum. For Ph.D.: see Graduate School of Arts and Sciences listing above.

FIELDS OF STUDY.
Social Work. Includes concentrations in advanced clinical social work practice, advanced generalist practice and programming, policy practice, social enterprise administration, research. M.S.S.W.
Social Work. Ph.D.

Teachers College

Web site: www.tc.columbia.edu

Founded 1887. Graduate study only. Affiliated with the University since 1898 and is designated the Graduate Faculty of Education. Semester system. Special facilities: Center for Health Promotion, Center for Infants and Parents, Institute for Urban and Minority Education, Institute of Higher Education, Institute of Philosophy and Politics of Education, Institute for Learning Technologies, Institute for Education and Economy, International Center for Cooperation and Conflict Resolution, Center for the Study and Education of the Gifted, Institute of International Education, Center for Community Colleges, Microcomputer Center, Center for Nursing Leadership Development, National Center for Restructuring Education, Schools and Teaching, Institute of Research and Service in Nursing Education. Milbank Library houses the largest American collection on education, psychology, and health services. Library: 1,100,000 volumes, 2700 subscriptions.

Annual tuition: $22,400, per credit $935.

Enrollment: full- and part-time 5100. Faculty: full-time 152, part-time 260. Degrees conferred: M.A., M.S., Ed.M., Sixth-Year Professional Diploma, Ed.D., Ph.D.

ADMISSION REQUIREMENTS. Official transcripts, personal statement, two letters of recommendation required in support of application. Interview, GRE/MAT required by some departments. TOEFL required for international applicants. Accepts transfer applicants. Graduates of unaccredited institutions not considered. Apply to Teachers College Admissions Office by February 1 (Fall, for some programs and scholarships), July 1 (Fall), December 15 (Spring), April 15 (Summer). Application fee $50. Phone: (212)678-3710; fax: (212)678-4171.

ADMISSION STANDARDS. Competitive for most departments, very competitive for the others. Usual minimum average: 3.0 (A = 4).

FINANCIAL AID. Annual awards from institutional funds: scholarships, teaching fellowships, research assistantships, grants, Tuition Assistance Awards, Federal W/S, loans. Apply by December 15 (Fall, all Ph.D., Psychology), January 1 (Fall, all Ed.D. programs), January 15 (Fall, all master's programs), November 1 (Spring) to appropriate department chair for assistantships, scholarships, fellowships; to Director of Student Aid of the College for all other programs. Phone: (212)678-3714; fax: (212)678-4089. Use FAFSA (College code: G03979). About 25% of students receive aid other than loans from College and outside sources.

DEGREE REQUIREMENTS. For M.A., M.S.: 30 credits minimum, at least one year in residence; thesis or essay. For Ed.M.: 60 credits minimum, at least 30 in residence. For Ed.D.: 90 credits minimum beyond the bachelor's, at least 45 in residence; certification exam; dissertation; final oral/written exam. For Sixth-Year Diploma: 60 semester hours beyond bachelor's; research project. For Ph.D.: 75 credits minimum beyond the bachelor's, at least 45 in residence; certification exam; Proficiency in foreign languages for some programs; dissertation; final oral/written exam.

FIELDS OF STUDY.
Administration of Special Education.
Adult Education.
Adult Learning and Leadership.
Anthropology and Education.
Applied Anthropology.
Applied Behavior Analysis.
Applied Linguistics.
Applied Physiology.
Applied Physiology and Nutrition.
Applied Statistics.
Art and Art Education.
Arts Administration.
Bilingual/Bicultural Education.
Blindness and Visual Impairment.
Clinical Psychology.
Cognitive Studies in Education.
College Teaching of Biological Science.
College Teaching of Earth Science.
College Teaching of Physical Science.
Communication and Education.
Communication, Computing, and Technology in Education.
Community Nutrition Education.
Comparative and International Education.
Computing and Education.
Conflict Resolution.
Counseling Psychology.
Cross-Categorical Studies.
Curriculum and Teaching.

Curriculum and Teaching in Physical Education.
Deaf or Hard of Hearing.
Developmental Psychology.
Early Childhood Special Education.
Economics and Education.
Education Leadership. Includes private school leadership.
Education Leadership and Management. With the Business School.
Education of Teacher of Science.
Educational Policy.
Elementary/Childhood Education—Preservice.
English Education.
Gifted Education.
Guidance and Habilitation.
Healthcare Human Resources.
Higher and Postsecondary Education.
History and Education.
Humanities.
Instructional Practice.
Instructional Technology and Media.
Interdisciplinary Studies in Education.
International Educational Development.
Kinesiology.
Learning Disabilities.
Mathematics Education.
Measurement and Evaluation.
Mental Retardation.
Motor Learning and Control.
Music and Music Education.
Neurosciences and Education.
Nurse Executive.
Nursing Education.
Nutrition Education.
Philosophy and Education.
Physical Disabilities.
Physical Education.
Politics and Education.
Psychological Counseling.
Psychology in Education.
Reading and Learning Disabilities.
Reading Specialist.
School Psychology.
Science Education.
Secondary School Science Education.
Social Studies.
Social-Organizational Psychology.
Sociology and Education.
Speech and Language Pathology.
Supervision of Special Education.
Teaching of American Sign Language as a Foreign Language.
Teaching of English and English Education.

COLUMBUS STATE UNIVERSITY
Columbus, Georgia 31907-5645
Web site: www.colstate.edu

Founded in 1958. Public control. Coed. Semester system. Special facilities: McCullers Center for Writers and Musicians, Child Care Resource and Referral Center, Coca Cola Space Science Center, College of Education Center for Quality Teaching and Learning, Oxbow Meadows Environmental Learning Center. Library: 250,000 volumes, 1400 subscriptions. University enrollment: 7475.

Annual tuition: full-time resident $4056, nonresident $14,820; per credit, resident $143, nonresident $842. Limited on-campus housing for single students only. Average academic year housing costs: $4570–$6720 (includes a limited board plan). Contact Office of Residential Life for both on- and off-campus housing information. Phone: (706)568-1480.

Graduate Studies

Graduate program since 1973. Enrollment: full-time 293, part-time 541. Faculty: full-time 59, part-time 23. Degrees Conferred: M.B.A., M.Ed., M.M., M.S., Ed.S.

ADMISSION REQUIREMENTS. Transcripts, GRE/MAT/GMAT required in support of application. Audition required for M.M. TOEFL/MTELP (minimum TOEFL 550, MTELP 75) required for international applicants. Accepts transfer applicants. Graduates of unaccredited institutions not considered. Apply to Admissions Office before May 1 (Fall), November 1 (Spring). Application fee $25. Phone: (706)568-2035; fax: (706)568-2462.

ADMISSION STANDARDS. Selective. Usual minimum average: 2.75 (A = 4).

FINANCIAL AID. Scholarships, graduate assistantships, internships, grants, tuition waivers, Federal W/S, loans. Approved for VA benefits. Apply to Director of Financial Aid before May 1. Phone: (706)568-2036, fax: (706)568-2230; e-mail: financial_aid@colstate.edu. Use FAFSA. About 10% of students receive aid other than loans from University and outside sources.

DEGREE REQUIREMENTS. For M.Ed., M.M., M.P.A.: 36–37 credit hours minimum, at least 30 in residence. For M.B.A.: 30–55 credit hours minimum, depending upon previous preparation; at least 30 hours in residence. For M.S..: 36 credit hours minimum, at least 30 in residence. For Ed.S.: at least 30 hours beyond master's.

FIELDS OF STUDY.
Applied Computer Science. M.S.
Art Education. M.Ed.
Business Administration. M.B.A.
Community Counseling. M.S.
Early Childhood Education. M.Ed.
Educational Leadership. M.Ed.
Environmental Science. M.S.
General Government Administration. M.P.A.
Health and Physical Education. M.Ed.
Health Services Administration. M.P.A.
Instructional Technology. M.S.
Justice Administration. M.P.A.
Middle Grades Education. M.Ed.
Music Education. M.M.
School Counseling. M.Ed.
Secondary Education. Includes English language arts, mathematics, science, social sciences. M.Ed.
Special Education. Includes behavioral disorders, mental retardation. M.Ed.

CONCORDIA UNIVERSITY
Seward, Nebraska 68434-1599
Web site: www.cune.edu

Founded 1894. Located 20 miles NW of Lincoln. Coed. Private control. Lutheran-Missouri Synod. Semester system. Library: 232,000 volumes.

Tuition: per credit hour $215. On-campus housing for 200 graduate men, 200 graduate women, 30 married students. Housing cost: (2½-week session) $120. Apply to Student Life Office for on-campus information. Phone: (402)643-7411, for off-campus information (402)643-7239.

College of Graduate Studies

Enrollment: full-time 36, part-time 197. College faculty: full-time 40, part-time 8. Degrees conferred: M.Ed., M.S., M.P.Ed., D.C.E.SP.

ADMISSION REQUIREMENTS. Transcripts, three letters of recommendations, MAT required in support of College's application. TOEFL required for international applicants. Interview not required. Accepts transfer applicants. Graduates of unaccredited institutions not considered. Apply to Director of Admissions by June 1 (Summer), August 1 (Fall). Application fee $25. Phone: (800)535-5494, ext. 7464 or (402)643-4073; admiss@ seward.cune.edu.

ADMISSION STANDARDS. Selective. Usual minimum average: 3.0 (last two years) (A = 4).

FINANCIAL AID. Scholarships, Federal W/S, loans. Apply to Financial Aid Officer by April 15. Phone: (402)643-7270; fax: (402)643-4073. Use FAFSA and College's FAF.

DEGREE REQUIREMENTS. For master's: 36 credit hours minimum, at least 24 residence; thesis option; final written/oral exam.

FIELDS OF STUDY.
Director of Christian Education. D.C.E.Sp.
Elementary Education. M.Ed.
Elementary School Administration. M.Ed.
Family Life Ministry. M.S.
Parish Education. M.P.E.
Secondary Education. M.Ed.
Secondary School Administration. M.Ed.
Special Education. M.Ed.

CONCORDIA UNIVERSITY CHICAGO
River Forest, Illinois 60305-1499
Web site: www.cuchicago.edu

Founded 1864. CGS member. Located 10 miles W of Chicago. Coed. Private control. Lutheran-Missouri Synod. Semester system. Library: 165,000 volumes, 470 subscriptions.
Tuition: per hour $555; doctoral programs $617. On-campus housing available. Annual housing cost: $6992 (includes board). Apply to Director of Housing for on- and off-campus housing information. Phone: (708)209-3006. Day-care facilities available.

School of Graduate Studies

Graduate study since 1957. Enrollment: full- and part-time 620. College faculty: full-time 48, part-time 30. Degrees conferred: M.A., M.A.T., M.C.M., C.A.S., Ed.D.

ADMISSION REQUIREMENTS. Transcripts, two letters of recommendation, GRE/MAT required in support of University's application. TOEFL and proof of financial support required for international applicants. Interview not required. Accepts transfer applicants. Graduates of unaccredited institutions not considered. Apply to Office of Graduate Admission; no specified closing dates. Rolling admissions process. Application fee, none. Phone: (708)209-4093; fax: (708)209-3454.

ADMISSION STANDARDS. Selective. Usual minimum average 2.85 (A = 4).

FINANCIAL AID. Annual awards from institutional funds: scholarships, assistantships, tuition waivers, Federal W/S, loans. Apply by April 1 to Dean of Graduate Studies. Use FAFSA (School code: 001666). About 45% of students receive aid other than loans from School and outside sources. Aid sometimes available for part-time students.

DEGREE REQUIREMENTS. For M.A., M.A.T.: 33–37 hours minimum, at least 24 in residence; candidacy; capstone experi-

ence (written/oral exam, thesis, independent research project). For M.C.M.: 36 credit program. For C.A.S.: at least 30 credits beyond master's. For Ed.D.: 60–63 credit program, at least 30 in residence; fieldwork component, admission to candidacy; dissertation; final oral exam.

FIELDS OF STUDY.
Christian Education. M.A.
Church Music. M.C.M.
Community Counseling. M.A.
Curriculum & Instruction. M.A.
Early Childhood Education. M.A., M.A.T., Ed.D.
Elementary Education. M.A.T.
Gerontology. M.A.
Human Services. Includes administration, exercise science. M.A.
Liberal Studies. M.A.
Music. M.A.
Psychology. M.A.
Religion. M.A.
School Counseling. M.A.
School Leadership. M.A., Ed.D.
Secondary Education. M.A.T.

UNIVERSITY OF CONNECTICUT
Box U-6-A
Storrs, Connecticut 06269
Web site: www.uconn.edu

Founded 1881. Located 30 miles E of Hartford. The Schools of Law and Social Work are located in West Hartford; the Schools of Dental Medicine and Medicine are located at the University's Health Center in Farmington. Part-time evening M.B.A. programs offered at off-campus centers in Hartford and Stamford. CGS member. Coed. State control. Semester system. Special facilities: Institute of Materials Science, Marine Science Institute, Institute of Water Resources, Institute of Social Inquiry. The University's NIH ranking is 76th among all U.S. Institutions with 235 awards/ grants valued at $76,935,853. According to The Center at University of Florida, 3 of the University's faculty members have been elected to National Honor Academies and this ranks it 105th among all U.S. institutions. Library: 3,000,000 volumes, 17,300 subscriptions. Total University enrollment: 23,000.
Annual tuition/fees: maximum per semester, resident $8442, nonresident $21,924; per credit resident $769, nonresident $1218. On-campus housing limited. Average annual housing cost: $5700, board charges $3064. Apply to Division of Housing and Food Services, Housing Services Officer. Phone: (860)486-2926.

Graduate School

Graduate study since 1920. Enrollment: full-time 3332, part-time 2244. University faculty: full-time 1242, part-time 48. Degrees conferred: M.A., M.S., M.B.A., M.M., M.P.A., M.F.A., M.P.H., M.Dent.Sc., M.S.W., D.M.A., Ph.D.

ADMISSION REQUIREMENTS. Transcripts, two or three letters of recommendation, personal letter required in support of School's application. GRE/MAT required by some departments, recommended for all. Audition required for music programs. TOEFL (minimum score 550) required for international students. Interview required by some departments. Accepts transfer applicants. Graduates of unaccredited institutions not considered. Apply to the Graduate Admissions Office by February 1 (Fall), November 1 (Spring); international applicants by February 1 (Fall), October 1 (Spring). Apply directly to professional schools, Application fee $55. Phone: (860)486-3617; fax: (860)486-8739.

ADMISSION STANDARDS. Selective for most departments. Usual minimum average: 3.0 (last 2 years) (A = 4).

FINANCIAL AID. Annual awards from institutional funds: scholarships, fellowships, research assistantships, Federal W/S, loans. Apply by February 1 to appropriate department head on forms available from Office of Student Financial Aid Services; phone: (860)486-2819. Use FAFSA and institutional FAF. About 50% of students at Storrs receive aid other than loans from University and outside sources. Aid sometimes available for part-time and international students.

DEGREE REQUIREMENTS. For M.A., M.S.: 15 credits minimum plus thesis or 24 credits minimum without thesis; final (written, oral, or both) exam. For M.B.A.: 57 credits, which may be reduced depending upon previous registration, at least 24 credits in residence; final written/oral exam. For M.S.W.: 60 credits minimum, at least one year in full-time residence; final paper and group project; final written/oral exam. For M.F.A.: two years full-time study minimum; final project. For D.M.A.: two years full-time study beyond master's, at least 43 credits; general exam; foreign language proficiency; dissertation proposal; candidacy; recital; dissertation; final oral exam. For Ph.D.: three years minimum beyond the bachelor's, at least one year in full-time residence; general exam.; reading knowledge of one foreign language or 6 credits of advanced work in a related or supporting area; candidacy; dissertation; oral defense.

FIELDS OF STUDY.

Accounting. M.S.

Adult Learning. Ph.D. only.

Agricultural and Resource Economics. M.S., Ph.D.

Allied Health. M.S.

Animal Science. Includes physiology of reproduction. M.S., Ph.D.

Anthropology. Includes social science and health care (Ph.D. only). M.A., Ph.D.

Applied Financial Mathematics. M.S.

Applied Genomics. M.S.

Art. M.F.A.

Art History. M.A.

Biochemistry. M.S., Ph.D.

Biological Engineering. Interdisciplinary. M.S., Ph.D.

Biomedical Science. Ph.D.

Botany. Includes morphology, natural products chemistry, paleobotany, phycology, plant cell and molecular biology, plant physiology, plant systematics.

Business Administration. Full-time M.B.A. program at Storrs includes finance, health care management, information technology, interactive marketing, management consulting; part-time evening M.B.A. programs at Hartford and Stamford include accounting, finance, general, health care management, international business, management; Ph.D. programs include accounting, finance, management, marketing, operations and information management. GMAT for admission; September admission only; apply by March 15. M.B.A., Ph.D.

Cell Biology. Includes cytology, development biology, plant cell and molecular biology, plant physiology.

Chemical Engineering. M.S., Ph.D.

Chemistry. M.S., Ph.D.

Civil Engineering. Includes applied mechanics, environmental engineering, fluid dynamics, geotechnical engineering, structural engineering, transportation and urban engineering. M.A., Ph.D.

Clinical and Translational Research. M.S.

Communication Science. Includes communication, communication process and marketing communication (Ph.D. only), speech, language, and hearing. M.A., Ph.D.

Comparative Literary and Cultural Studies. Interdisciplinary. M.A., Ph.D.

Computer Science and Engineering. M.S., Ph.D.

Curriculum and Instruction. Includes bilingual and bicultural education, elementary, secondary. Ph.D. only.

Dental Science. M.Dent.S.

Dramatic Arts. Includes acting, design, directing, performance/production, puppetry, technical direction, theater history and criticism. M.A., M.F.A.

Ecology. Includes ecology and biological control, plant ecology. M.S., Ph.D.

Economics. M.A., Ph.D.

Education. M.A.

Educational Administration. Ph.D. only.

Educational Leadership. Ed.D. only

Educational Psychology. Includes cognition/instruction, counseling psychology, evaluation and measurement, gifted and talented education, school psychology. Ph.D. only.

Educational Studies. Includes history and philosophy of education, social foundations of education. Ph.D. only.

Educational Technology. Ph.D.

Electrical Engineering. Includes control and communication systems, electromagnetics and physical electronics, fluid dynamics. M.S., Ph.D.

Engineering. Includes civil and environmental, chemical, computer science and engineering, electrical and systems, mechanical, metallurgy, and materials. M. Eng.

English. Includes American studies (interdisciplinary). GRE Subject for admission; apply by May 1 (Fall), December 1 (Spring). M.A., Ph.D.

Entomology. Includes morphology and physiology, systematics. M.S., Ph.D.

Environmental Engineering. Interdisciplinary. M.S., Ph.D.

French. M.A., Ph.D.

Genetics. M.S., Ph.D.

Geography. M.A., Ph.D.

Geological Sciences. Includes geology, geophysics. M.S., Ph.D.

German. M.A., Ph.D.

History. Includes American studies (interdisciplinary), Latin American, medieval European, modern European, United States. M.A., Ph.D.

Homeland Security Leadership. M.P.S.

Human Development and Family Relations. M.A., Ph.D.

International Studies. Includes African studies, European studies, Italian history and culture, Latin American studies. M.A. only.

Instructional Media and Technology. Ph.D. only.

Italian. M.A., Ph.D.

Judaic Studies. Interdisciplinary. M.A.

Kinesiology. Includes exercise science, social science of sport and leisure. Ph.D.

Linguistics. M.A., Ph.D.

Materials Science. Includes alloy science, biomaterials, corrosion science, crystal science, dental materials, metallurgy, polymer science. Interdisciplinary. M.S., Ph.D.

Mathematics. Includes actuarial science. M.S., Ph.D.

Mechanical Engineering. Includes applied mechanics, design, dynamics and control, energy and thermal science, fluid dynamics, manufacturing. M.S., Ph.D.

Medieval Studies. Interdisciplinary. M.A., Ph.D.

Metallurgy and Material Engineering. M.S., Ph.D.

Microbial Systems Analysis. M.S.

Microbiology. M.S., Ph.D.

Music. Audition during first semester of enrollment. Includes conducting, historical musicology, music education, music theory and history, performance, theory. M.Mus., M.A., D.M.A., Ph.D.

Natural Resources: Land, Water, and Air. M.S., Ph.D.

Nursing. M.S., Ph.D.

Nutritional Science. M.S., Ph.D.

Oceanography. M.S., Ph.D.

Pathobiology. D.V.M. for admission to comparative pathology major. Includes bacteriology, pathology, virology. M.S., Ph.D.

Pharmaceutical Sciences. Includes medicinal and natural products chemistry, neurosciences, pharmaceutics, pharmacology and toxicology. M.S., Ph.D.

Philosophy. M.A., Ph.D.

Physics. M.S., Ph.D.

Physiology and Neurobiology. Includes comparative physiology, endocrinology, neurobiology, neurosciences. M.S., Ph.D.

Plant Science. Includes agronomy, horticulture, landscape, plant breeding, plant environment, soil science. M.S., Ph.D.

Political Science. Includes American studies (interdisciplinary), survey research. M.A., Ph.D.

Polymer Science. M.S., Ph.D.

Professional Higher Education Administration. M.A.

Psychology. GRE General/Subject, MAT for admission. Includes behavioral neuroscience, clinical, cognition/instruction, development, ecological psychology, general experimental, industrial/organizational, language, neurosciences, social. M.A., Ph.D.

Public Administration. M.P.A., Ph.D.

Public Health. M.P.H. only.

Social work. Interviews required; offered in Hartford. M.S.W., Ph.D.

Sociology. Includes social science and health care, survey research. M.A., Ph.D.

Spanish. M.A., Ph.D.

Special Education. Ph.D. only.

Structural Biology and Biophysics. M.S., Ph.D.

Survey Research. M.A. only.

Statistics. Includes industrial statistics. M.S., Ph.D.

Zoology. Includes biological/anthropology, parasitology, systematics and evolution. M.S., Ph.D.

School of Law

Web site: www.law.uconn.edu

Founded in 1921. ABA approved since 1933. AALS member Semester system. Located in Hartford (06105-2296). Special facilities: Connecticut Urban Legal Initiative, Center for Children's Advocacy, Insurance Law Center. Special programs: student/faculty exchange programs with University of Exeter (United Kingdom), University of Puerto Rico, the University of International Business and Economics (People's Republic of China), Trinity College (Dublin, Ireland), Aix-en-Provence (France). Library: 527,337 volumes, 5006 subscriptions; has LEXIS, NEXIS, WESTLAW; has more than 800 network connections.

Annual tuition and fees: full-time, resident $17,280, nonresident $35,692; part-time resident $12,086, nonresident $19,000; per credit resident $692, nonresident NEHEC $1038, nonresident $1459. No on-campus housing available. Contact School for off-campus accommodations. Total average cost for all other expenses: $16,900.

Enrollment: first-year class 126, evening 73; total full- and part-time 497 (men 49%, women 51%, minorities 15%). Faculty: full-time 54, part-time 36. Student to faculty ratio 11.2 to 1. Degrees conferred: J.D., J.D.-M.A. (with Trinity College), J.D.-M.L.S. (with Southern Connecticut State University), J.D.-M.P.A., J.D.-M.P.H., J.D.-M.S.W., LL.M. (Insurance Law), LL.M. (U.S.-Legal Studies).

ADMISSION REQUIREMENTS. LSDAS Law School report, bachelor's degree, transcript, LSAT, two letters of recommendation, residency affidavit, résumé required in support of application. Interview not required. Accepts transfer applicants. Graduates of unaccredited colleges not considered. Apply to the Dean of Admissions after October 1, before March 1. Application fee: day or evening $30; day and evening $45. Phone: (860)570-5100; fax: (860)570-5153. For LL.M.: Submit three letters of recommendation, personal statement, writing sample (in English) required in support of application. TOEFL, Financial Declaration Form, Immigration Biographic Information Form required for applicants to LL.M. (US Legal Studies). Apply by June 1 (Fall), November 1 (Spring). Application fee $40.

ADMISSION STANDARDS. Selective. Accepts approximately 17% of total applicants. Number of full-time applicants 2311, part-time 1068; number of full-time acceptance 395, part-time

183; number full-time enrolled 126, part-time 73; LSAT (75% of full-time students have a score at or above 159, part-time 155); GPA (75% of full-time students have a GPA at or above 3.23, part-time 3.20). *U.S. News & World Report* ranking is in the top 47 of all U.S. law schools.

FINANCIAL AID. Scholarships, tuition remission, grants, loans. About 70% of students receive aid other than loans from School funds. Apply by March 15. Phone: (860)570-5147. Use FAFSA (School code: E00387) and school forms. Aid available for part-time students.

DEGREE REQUIREMENTS. For J.D.: 84 semester hours minimum; advanced standing for work completed at other law school individually considered. For LL.M.: 24–30 credits beyond the J.D; at least 2 semesters in residence.

UNIVERSITY OF CONNECTICUT HEALTH CENTER
Farmington, Connecticut 06030-3906

Coed. State control. Semester system. No on-campus housing available.

Graduate School

Annual tuition: full-time $8442, nonresident $21,924; per credit, resident $469, nonresident $1218. Enrollment: full- and part-time 400. Faculty: full-time 20, part-time 141. Degrees conferred: M.P.H., M.D.S., Ph.D., M.D.-Ph.D., D.M.D.-Ph.D., M.D.-M.P.H., M.D.S.-Ph.D.

ADMISSION REQUIREMENTS. Official transcripts, three letters of recommendation, GRE required in support of College's application. TOEFL required for international applicants. Interviews may be arranged. Accepts transfer applicants. Graduates of unaccredited institutions not considered. Combined degree candidates must be accepted by both schools. Apply to Office of Graduate Admissions by January 1, March 1 (M.P.H.). Rolling admissions process. Application fee $40, $45 for international applicants. Phone: (860)679-4306.

ADMISSION STANDARDS. Competitive. Usual minimum average: 3.0 (A = 4).

FINANCIAL AID. Fellowships, research assistantships, teaching assistantships, tuition waivers, Federal W/S, loans. Approved for VA benefits. Apply by April 1 to the office of the Graduate School for fellowships, assistantships; to the Financial Aid Office at Storrs for all other programs. Use FAFSA. Aid available for part-time students.

DEGREE REQUIREMENTS. For M.D.S.: 30 credit hours, at least 24 in residence; thesis/nonthesis option. For M.P.H.: 48 credit hours minimum, at least 30 in residence; thesis. For Ph.D.: 60 credit hours minimum beyond the bachelor's, 30 credit hours in full-time residency; qualifying exam; dissertation defense.

FIELDS OF STUDY.

AREAS OF CONCENTRATION:

Cell Biology.

Biomedical Scholars program. Includes concentrations in microbial pathogenesis, oncology, vascular biology, immunology, neuroscience. Ph.D.

Cellular and Molecular Pharmacology. Ph.D.

Clinical and Translational Research. M.S.

Dental Science. M.D.S.
Genetics and Development Biology. Ph.D.
Immunology. Ph.D.
Molecular Biology and Biochemistry. Ph.D.
Neuroscience. Ph.D.
Public Health. M.P.H.
Skeletal, Craniofacial and Oral Biology. Ph.D.

THEMATIC RESEARCH AREAS:
Biomaterials and Bioengineering.
Brain and Behavior.
Cancer Biology and Molecular Medicine.
Cell Biology, Cell Signaling, and Pharmacology.
Development and Differentiation.
Genetics and Genomics.
Host-Pathogen Interactions and Immunology.
Quantitative Cell Biology.
Stem Cells.
Structural Biology and Biophysics.

School of Dental Medicine
Web site: sdm.uchc.edu

First class entered September 1968. Located in Farmington (06030) at the Health Center. Public control. Semester system. Special facilities: Center for Biomaterials, Center for Regenerative Medicine and Skeletal Development, Center for Research and Education in Technology Evaluation, Center for Neurosciences.

Annual tuition: resident $16,674, New England resident $29,180, other nonresident $40,519. No on-campus housing available. Average academic year housing and personal expenses: approximately $22,000. Total cost for all other first-year expenses: $7,500.

Enrollment: D.D.S. program, first-year class 70, total full-time 260 (men 63%, women 37%, minorities 29%, state resident 21%), postgraduates 55. Faculty: full-time 37, part-time and volunteers 100. Degrees conferred: B.A./B.S.-D.M.D (with University of Connecticut)., D.M.D., D.M.D.-M.D.., D.M.D.-M.D.S., D.M.D.-M.P.H., D.M.D.-Ph.D.

ADMISSION REQUIREMENTS. AADSAS report, transcripts, DAT (not later than October), three letters of recommendation required in support of School's application. Interview by invitation only. Applicants must have completed at least three years of college study. Preference given to state residents. Accepts transfer students. Has EDP for state and New England residents only. Apply to the Associate Dean, Student Affairs, after June 1, before February 1. Application fee $75. Phone: (860)679-2175; fax: (860) 679-1899.

ADMISSION STANDARDS. Competitive. Accepts about 15% of all applicants. Number of applications 1550; number interviewed 186; number enrolled 70. Minimum science UGPA 3.2; mean DAT: academic 21, PAT 18.6; mean UGPA 3.50.

FINANCIAL AID. Scholarships, grants, tuition waivers, DEAL, HEAL, loans. Apply by April 1 to Office Financial Aid Office. Phone: (860)679-3873. Use FAFSA (School code: G11215) and institutional application. About 80% of students receive some aid from School funds.

DEGREE REQUIREMENTS. For D.M.D.: satisfactory completion of four-year program. For D.M.D.-Ph.D.: a minimum of three additional years.

FIELDS OF GRADUATE STUDY.
Biomedical Science. Ph.D.
Dental Science. M.D.S.
Public Health. M.P.H.

School of Medicine
Web site: www.uchc.edu

Established 1968. Located at the Health Center in Farmington, Connecticut (06030-1905) along with the Dental School and Biomedical Science programs. Library: 160,000 volumes, 1500 subscriptions. NIH ranking is 76th among all U.S. institutions with 235 awards/grants worth $76,935,853.

Annual tuition/fees: resident $25,920, nonresident $49,195. For off-campus housing, apply to Student Affairs Office. Total average figure for all other expenses: $12,000.

Enrollment: first-year class 79 (EDP 5), total full-time 328 (men 37%, women 63%, minorities 34%, state residents 91%). Faculty: full-time 403, part-time 117. Degrees conferred: M.D., M.D.-M.B.A., M.D.-M.P.H., M.D.-Ph.D.

ADMISSION REQUIREMENTS. AMCAS report, transcripts, MCAT, recommendations required in support of application. Interview by invitation. Supplemental application required. Accepts transfer applicants. Preference given to state residents. Has EDP; apply between June 1 and August 1. Apply to Admissions Office after June 1, before December 15. Application fee $75. Phone: (860)679-3874; fax: (860)679-1282.

ADMISSION STANDARDS. Competitive. Accepts about 6% of all applicants. Number of applications 2685 (2289 out-of-state); number interviewed 400 (170 out-of-state); number of acceptance 193 (85 out-of-state); number enrolled 79 (19 out-of-state). Mean Composite MCAT 10.3; mean UGPA 3.65. *U.S. News & World Report* ranking is in the top 34 of all medical schools.

FINANCIAL AID. Scholarships, Federal W/S, loans. Information regarding financial aid applications provided following admission from Director of Financial Aid. Phone: (860)679-3574. Use FAFSA (School code: G09867). About 45% of students receive some aid from School funds.

DEGREE REQUIREMENTS. For M.D.: satisfactory completion of four-year program. For master's, Ph.D., see Graduate School listing above.

FIELDS OF GRADUATE STUDY.

AREAS OF CONCENTRATION:
Cell Biology.
Cellular and Molecular Pharmacology.
Genetics and Developmental Biology.
Molecular Biology and Biochemistry.
Immunology.
Neuroscience.
Skeletal, Craniofacial, and Oral Biology.

THEMATIC RESEARCH AREAS:
Biomaterials and Bioengineering.
Brain and Behavior.
Cancer Biology and Molecular Medicine.
Cell Biology, Cell Signaling, and Pharmacology.
Development and Differentiation.
Genetics and Genomics.
Host-Pathogen Interactions and Immunology.
Quantitative Cell Biology.
Stem Cells.
Structural Biology and Biophysics.

CONVERSE COLLEGE
Spartanburg, South Carolina 29301-1931
Web site: www.converse.edu

Established 1889. Located 70 miles SW of Charlotte, North Carolina. Coed on graduate level. Private independent. Semester system. Library: 139,360 volumes, 1467 subscriptions. More than 75 computers available for general student use.

Tuition: per credit hour $320. No on-campus housing for graduate students.

Graduate Division

Enrollment: full-time 169, part-time 590. College faculty: full-time 76, part-time 11. Degrees conferred: M.A.T., M.M., M.Ed., Ed.S.

ADMISSION REQUIREMENTS. Official transcripts, GRE/NTE, research paper required in support of application. Audition/composition required for some programs. Accepts transfer applicants. Apply to the Director of the Graduate Education by May 1 (Fall), January 30 (Spring). Phone: (864)596-9021 (Music); (864)596-9082 (Education). Rolling admissions process. Application fee $40.

ADMISSION STANDARDS. Selective. Usual minimum average: 2.75 (A = 4).

FINANCIAL AID. Annual awards from institutional funds: assistantships, grants, Federal W/S, loans. Approved for VA benefits. Apply by March 1 to Graduate Office or appropriate programs for assistantships, grants; to Director of Financial Aid for all other need-based programs. Phone: (864)596-9019. Use FAFSA.

DEGREE REQUIREMENTS. For M.A.T., M.Ed.: 36 semester hours minimum, at least two summer sessions in residence. For M.M.: 30 semester hours minimum, at least two semesters in residence; thesis/final project, or performance in music. For Ed.S.: 36 semester hours minimum, at least two summer sessions in residence.

FIELDS OF STUDY.
Art Education. M.Ed.
Curriculum and Instruction. Ed.S.
Early Childhood Education. M.A.T.
Educable Mental Disabilities. M.A.T.
Elementary Administration. Ed.S.
Elementary Education. M.A.T., M.Ed.
English. M.L.A.
Gifted Education. M.Ed.
History. M.L.A.
Learning Disabilities. M.A.T.
Middle Level Education. Includes language arts, mathematics, science, social studies. M.A.T.
Music. Includes composition, education, musicology, performance, piano pedagogy, theory. M.M.
Political Science. M.L.A.
Secondary Administration. Ed.S.
Secondary Education. Includes biology, chemistry, English, mathematics, social science. M.A.T., M.Ed.
Special Education. M.Ed.

CORNELL UNIVERSITY
Ithaca, New York 14850
Web site: www.cornell.edu

Founded 1865. Located 220 miles NW of New York City. CGS and AAU member. Coed. Private control. Some graduate divisions are statutory colleges of the State University of New York. Semester system. Special facilities: Africana Studies and Research Center; American Indian Program; American Studies; Center for Applied Mathematics; Full-Year Asian Language Concentration (FALCON); Laboratory of Atomic and Solid State Physics; James A. Baker Institute for Animal Health; Biophysics Program; Boyce Thompson Institute for Plant Research; Bronfenbrenner Life

Course Center; Community and Rural Development Institute; Institute for Comparative and Environmental Toxicology; Program of Computer Graphics; Institute for the Study of Continents; Cornell Institute for Social and Economics Research; Cornell International Institute for Food, Agriculture and Development; East Asia Program; Mario Einaudi Center for International Studies; Center for the Environment; Program on Ethics and Public Life; Institute for European Studies; Exchange Scholar Program; International Network for Graduate Student Exchange; Family Life Development Center; Farming Alternatives Programs; Center for High-Energy Synchrotron Studies; Society for the Humanities; Program in International Nutrition; Latin American Studies Program; Latino Studies Program; Center for Manufacturing Enterprise; Materials Science Center; National Nanofabriction Facility (NNF); New York State Agricultural Experiment Stations; Floyd R. Newman Laboratory of Nuclear Studies; Northeast Regional Climate Center; Peace Studies Program; Laboratory of Plasma Studies; Center for Radiophysics and Space Research; Renaissance Studies; Rural Development; South Asia Program; Southeast Asia Program; Center for Statistics; Center for Theory and Simulation in Science and Engineering; Ward Laboratory of Nuclear Engineering. The University's NIH ranking is 29th among all U.S. institutions with 497 awards/grants valued at $192,563,168. According to The Center at University of Florida, the University is ranked 30th in receipt of Federal Research funds with $212,991,000 and it ranks 30th for total University research expenditures with $356,049,000. The University's endowment asset ranks it 18th, $2,654,312,000. In 2004, the University awarded 412 doctorates which ranked it 24th among all U.S. institutions eligible to award that degree. Seventeen of the University's faculty members have been elected to National Honor Academies and this ranks it 64th among all U.S. institutions. The Library: approximately 6,300,000 volumes, 61,000 subscriptions. Total University enrollment: 19,500.

Annual tuition: for endowed research degree programs $32,800, endowed professional degree programs, for contract college research degree program $20,800, contract college professional degree programs $22,600. On-campus housing for 411 married students and 262 single students. Average annual cost: $16,100–$23,500. Inquire at Campus Life Office. Phone: (607)255-5368; e-mail: gpsh@cornell.edu.

Graduate School
Web site: www.gradschool.cornell.edu

Enrollment: full-time 4638 (men 60%, women 40%). University faculty teaching graduate students: full-time 1511, part-time 71. Degrees conferred: M.A., M.S., M.Arch., M.L.A., M.A.T., M.F.A., M.F.S., M.H.A., M.I.L.R., M.M.H., M.P.A., M.P.S., M.R.P., M.S.T., M.Eng., LL.M., D.M.A., Ph.D., J.S.D.

ADMISSION REQUIREMENTS. Transcripts, two or three letters of recommendation (depending on the field), statement of purpose required in support of School's application. GRE required by most fields, GMAT for Hotel Administration. TOEFL (minimum score 550, 213 on computer-based test) required for international applicants unless he or she (1) has received a degree from a college or a university in a country where the native language is English or (2) has studied for two or more years in an undergraduate or graduate program in a country where the native language is English. Accepts transfer students. Graduate of unaccredited institutions not considered. Apply to the Graduate School by January 10 for Fall admission (some fields have later deadlines). Application fee $70. Phone: (607)255-4884.

ADMISSION STANDARDS. Very competitive to very selective. Usual minimum average: 3.0 (A = 4).

FINANCIAL AID. Annual awards from institutional funds: merit-based fellowships, fellowships, teaching assistantships, research assistantships, graduate assistantships, Federal W/S, loans. Apply by January 10 for Fellowships, assistantships; most programs use this deadline date, some are later. Apply to Financial Aid Office for all federal programs. Phone: (607)255-5820; e-mail: gfao@cornell. edu. Use FAFSA. About 75% of students receive primary support from University and outside sources; 97% of all doctoral students receive primary support from Cornell or outside sources.

DEGREE REQUIREMENTS. For master's: 2-semester minimum in full-time residence; for research master's degrees, thesis and final oral/written exam; for professional master's degrees, usual course requirements, no thesis. Additional requirements may vary by field. For doctorate: 6-semester minimum in full-time residence; admission to candidacy examination; dissertation; final oral exam. Additional requirements vary by field.

FIELDS OF STUDY.
Aerospace Engineering. M.Eng., M.S., Ph.D.
Africana Studies. M.P.S.
Agricultural and Biological Engineering. M.Eng., M.P.S. (Agr.), M.S., Ph.D.
Animal Breeding. M.S., Ph.D.
Animal Science. M.P.S. (Agr.), M.S., Ph.D.
Anthropology. M.A., Ph.D.
Applied Economics and Management. M.P.S., M.S., Ph.D.
Applied Mathematics. Ph.D.
Applied Physics. M.Eng., M.S., Ph.D.
Archaeology. M.A.
Architecture. M.S., M.A., M.Arch., Ph.D.
Art. M.F.A.
Asian Religion. M.A.
Asian Studies. M.A.
Astronomy and Space Sciences. M.S., Ph.D.
Atmospheric Science. M.S., Ph.D.
Biochemistry, Molecular, and Cell Biology. Ph.D.
Biomedical Engineering. Ph.D.
Biometry. M.S., Ph.D.
Biophysics. Ph.D.
Chemical Engineering. M.Eng., M.S., Ph.D.
Chemistry and Chemical Biology. M.S., Ph.D.
City and Regional Planning. M.A., M.R.P., Ph.D.
Civil and Environmental Engineering. M.Eng., M.S., Ph.D.
Classics. M.A., Ph.D.
Communication. M.A.
Community and Rural Development. M.A., M.R.P., Ph.D.
Comparative Literature. Ph.D.
Computational Biology. Ph.D.
Computer Science. M.Eng., Ph.D.
Design and Environmental Analysis. M.A., M.P.S. (Hu.Ec.), M.S.
Developmental Sociology. M.P.S. (Agr.), M.S., Ph.D.
East Asian Literature. M.A., Ph.D.
Ecology and Evolutionary Biology. M.S., Ph.D.
Economics. Ph.D.
Education. M.A.T., M.P.S. (Agr.), M.S., Ph.D.
Electrical and Computer Engineering. M.Eng., M.S., Ph.D.
English Language and Literature. M.A., M.F.A., Ph.D.
Entomology. M.S., Ph.D.
Environmental Toxicology. M.S., Ph.D.
Food Science and Technology. M.E.S., M.P.S. (Agr.), M.S., Ph.D.
Genetics and Development. Ph.D.
Geological Sciences. M.Eng., M.S., Ph.D.
Germanic Studies. M.A., Ph.D.
Government. Ph.D.
Health Administration. M.H.A.
History. M.A., Ph.D.
History of Art and Archaeology. Ph.D.
Horticulture. M.P.S. (Agr.), M.S., Ph.D.
Hotel Administration. M.P.S. (H.Ad.), M.H.A., M.S., Ph.D.
Human Development. M.A., Ph.D.
Immunology. M.S., Ph.D.

Industrial and Labor Relations. M.I.L.R., M.P.S. (I.L.P), M.S., Ph.D.
Information Science. Ph.D.
International Agriculture and Rural Development. M.P.S. (Agr.).
International Development. M.P.S. (I.P.).
Landscape Architecture. M.L.A.
Law. LL.M., J.S.D.
Linguistics. M.A., Ph.D.
Management. Ph.D.
Materials Science and Engineering. M.Eng., M.S., Ph.D.
Mathematics. Ph.D.
Mechanical Engineering. M.Eng., M.S., Ph.D.
Medieval Studies. Ph.D.
Microbiology. Ph.D.
Molecular and Integrative Physiology. M.S., Ph.D.
Music. M.A., M.F.A., D.M.A., Ph.D.
Natural Resources. M.P.S. (Agr.)., M.S., Ph.D.
Near Eastern Studies. M.A., Ph.D.
Neurobiology and Behavior. Ph.D.
Nutrition. M.P.S. (Hu.Ec.), M.S., Ph.D.
Operations Research. M.Eng., Ph.D.
Pharmacology. M.S., Ph.D.
Philosophy. M.A., Ph.D.
Physics. M.S., Ph.D.
Physiology. M.S., Ph.D.
Plant Biology. Ph.D.
Plant Breeding. M.P.S. (Agr.), M.S., Ph.D.
Plant Pathology. M.P.S. (Agr.), M.S., Ph.D.
Plant Protection. M.P.S. (Agr.)
Policy Analysis and Management. Ph.D.
Psychology. Ph.D.
Public Affairs. M.P.A.
Real Estate. M.P.S.
Regional Science. M.A., M.S., Ph.D.
Romance Studies. M.A., Ph.D.
Science and Technology Studies. M.A., Ph.D.
Slavic Studies. M.A., Ph.D.
Sociology. M.A., Ph.D.
Soil and Crop Sciences. M.P.S. (Agr.), M.S., Ph.D.
Statistics. M.S., Ph.D.
System Engineering. M.S., Ph.D.
Textiles. M.A., M.P.S. (Hu.Ec.), M.S., Ph.D.
Theatre Arts. M.A., Ph.D.
Theoretical and Applied Mechanics. M.Eng., M.S., Ph.D.
Veterinary Medicine. M.S., Ph.D.
Zoology. M.S., Ph.D.

College of Human Ecology

Special facilities: Bronfenbrenner Life Course Center, Community and Rural Development Institute, Cornell Applied Gerontology Research Institute, Cornell Employment and Family Careers Institute, Cornell Institute for Research on Children, Family Life Development Center. The Division of Nutrition was established in 1974 and is a union of the Graduate School and the Department of Food and Nutrition in the College of Human Ecology and the College of Agriculture and Life Science.

Tuition: $22,800. Enrollment: full-time 200. Faculty: full-time 102, part-time 0. Degrees conferred: M.A., M.N.S., M.S., M.P.S.; Ph.D. offered in conjunction with Graduate School.

ADMISSION REQUIREMENTS. Transcripts, GRE (except for interior design), statement of purpose, three letters of recommendation required in support of College's application. Portfolio required for Interior Design. TOEFL (minimum score 550) required of all international applicants. Interview not usually required. Accepts transfer applicants. Graduates of unaccredited colleges not considered. Apply to Cornell Graduate School by January 10 (for fellowship consideration), May 1 (Fall). Application fee $70. Phone: (607)255-2138.

ADMISSION STANDARDS. Very competitive in some departments, selective to competitive in others. Usual minimum average: 3.0 (A = 4).

FINANCIAL AID. Annual awards from institutional funds: teaching/research assistantships, fellowships, traineeships, tuition waiver, Federal W/S, loans. Applications received by January 10 will receive consideration for all financial aid; final deadline February 15. Use FAFSA. About 80% of students receive aid other than loans from College and outside sources.

DEGREE REQUIREMENTS. For master's: 2 residence units minimum; thesis; final exam. For M.P.S., M.N.S.: 30 credits beyond master's. For Ph.D.: 6 residence units minimum; qualifying exam; dissertation; final exam.

FIELDS OF STUDY.
Design and Environmental Analysis.
Fiber Science & Apparel Design.
Human Development.
Nutritional Sciences.
Policy Analysis and Management.

School of Law

Web site: www.lawschool.cornell.edu

Established 1887. ABA approved since 1923. AALS member. Semester system. Special facilities: Clark Center for International and Comparative Legal Studies, the Legal Information Institute. Law library: 708,899 volumes, 6632 subscriptions. Library has LEXIS, NEXIS, WESTLAW, DIALOG. Special programs: Sumner Institute at University of Paris I; formal international exchange programs with Bucerius University, Hamburg, Germany, the Central University, Budapest, Hungary, ESADE, Barcelona, Spain, Heidelberg University, Germany, University of Paris I, France, Waseda University Graduate School of Law, Tokyo, The University of Sydney, Australia.

Annual tuition: $43,620, LL.M. $45,690. On-campus housing available. Total annual housing costs approximately $17,275 single, married $21,000.

Enrollment: first year class 193; total full-time 580 (men 52%, women 48%, minority 25%).

Faculty: Total full-time 42, part-time 22. Student to faculty ratio 10.1 to 1. Degrees conferred: J.D., J.D.-M.A., J.D.-Maitrise en Droit, J.D.-D.E.S.S. (Humbolt Universitat zu Berlin), J.D.-M.B.A., J.D.-M.P.A., J.D.-M.I.L.R., J.D.-Ph.D., J.D.-LL.M. (International Legal Studies), LL.M., J.S.D.

ADMISSION REQUIREMENTS. LSDAS Law School report, bachelor's degree, official transcript, LSAT (not later than December), two faculty recommendations, personal statement required in support of application. Interview not required. TOEFL required for all international applicants. Accepts transfer applications from other accredited law schools. Graduates of unaccredited colleges not considered. Apply to Director of Admission after September 1 before February 1 (Early Action program by November 1). Application fee $70. Phone: (607)255-5141; e-mail: lawadmit@postoffice.law.cornell.edu. For LL.M.: Official transcripts or LSAC LL.M. Credential Assembly Service School Report, personal statement, two letters of recommendation. TOEFL (550 minimum) required of all international applicants. Apply by January 10. Application fee $70. For J.S.D.: Official Certification of all degrees received, personal statement, detailed and footnoted research proposal. TOEFL (550 minimum) required of all international applicants. Apply by May 1. Application fee $70. All non-U.S. applicants must submit evidence of full financial support.

ADMISSION STANDARDS. Selective. Accepts approximately 23% of total applicants. Number of applicants 4177; number of acceptance 862; number enrolled 193; LSAT (75% of students have a score at or above 165); GPA (75% of students have a GPA at or above 3.50). *U.S. News & World Report* ranking is 13th of all U.S. law schools.

FINANCIAL AID. Scholarships, grants-in-aid, fellowships, assistantships, Federal W/S, loans. Approximately 43% of students received aid other than loans from school funds. Apply to the Director of Admissions of School by March 15. Phone: (602)255-5141. Use FAFSA (School code: 002711). Has a Public Interest Low-Income Protection Plan.

DEGREE REQUIREMENTS. For J.D.: satisfactory completion of three-year program. For LL.M.: 2 semesters beyond J.D.: oral exam. For J.S.D.: 4 semesters beyond J.D.: thesis; final exam. For Joint degree requirements: see Graduate School listing above.

Johnson Graduate School of Management

Web site: www.johnson.cornell.edu

Established 1946. Private control. Accredited programs: M.B.A.; recognized Ph.D. Semester system. Special programs: twelve-month M.B.A. program for individuals with an advanced scientific or technological degree; foreign exchange programs (in Australia, Belgium, China, France, Italy, the Netherlands, Norway, Spain, Sweden, Switzerland, Venezuela, Thailand, United Kingdom). Library: 140,000 volumes, 1900 subscriptions.

Annual tuition: full-time $38,800. Enrollment: first-year M.B.A. 252; total full-time 552 (men 75%, women 25%). Faculty: M.B.A. 60 full-time, 20 part-time; 96% with Ph.D./D.B.A. Degrees conferred: M.B.A. (FT day only), M.B.A.-M.A. (Asian Studies), M.B.A.-M.E. (Engineering), M.B.A.-J.D., M.B.A.-M.I.L.R. (Industrial and Labor Management), Ph.D.

ADMISSION REQUIREMENTS. All applicants should have a bachelor's degree from a recognized institution of higher education and a strong mathematics background. Submit an application, a GMAT, two official transcripts from each undergraduate/graduate school attended, two evaluations, two essays, résumé (prefers at least four years of work experience), and an application fee of $180 to the Director of Admission. In addition, international students (whose native language is other than English) should submit a TOEFL (minimum score 600) report, certified translations and evaluations of all official transcripts, recommendation should be in English or with certified translations, proof of health/immunization certificate, and proof of sufficient financial resources for two years of academic study. On-campus visits and interviews are encouraged. Beginning students are admitted Fall only. U.S. citizens apply by October 1 (first read period), November 1 (second read period), December 1 (third read period), January 1 (fourth read period), international students apply by January 1 (Fall). Joint degree applicants must apply to and be accepted to both schools/programs, contact the admissions office for current information and specific admissions requirements. Decisions are mailed by November 30 (first read), January 25 (second read), March 15 (third read), April 15 (fourth read). Admissions Office phone: (607)254-2082; fax: (607)254-8886; e-mail: mba@johnson.cornell.edu.

ADMISSION REQUIREMENTS FOR DOCTORAL CANDIDATES. Contact either the Graduate School at (607)255-4884 or the Doctoral Programs Office, Johnson Graduate School, at (800) 847-2082, for application material and information. Beginning students are admitted Fall Only. Both U.S. citizens and international applicants apply by January 15 (Fall). Submit a Graduate School application, a GMAT or GRE (will accept GMAT or GRE test results from the last five years), official transcripts from each undergraduate/graduate schools attended, two letters of recommendation, résumé, statement of purpose, and application fee of $75 to the Graduate School. In addition, international students (whose native language is other than English and have not studied at least one year in the U.S.) should submit TOEFL (minimum score 600), certified translations and evaluations of all official transcripts, recommendation should be in English or with certified translations, proof of health/immunization certificate. Interviews may be requested by doctoral committee. Notification is generally made by early April. E-mail contact: phd@johnson.cornell.edu.

ADMISSION STANDARDS. For M.B.A.: median GMAT: 677; median GPA: 3.3 (A = 4). *U.S. News & World Report* ranked the Johnson School in the top 14 of all U.S. business schools. *BusinessWeek* listed Johnson School in the top 22 of all American business schools. For the Ph.D.: median GMAT: 700; acceptance rate is approximately 5%.

FINANCIAL AID. Scholarships, merit-based scholarships (for both U.S. and international applicants), minority scholarships, Park Fellowships (U.S. students only), graduate, research, teaching assistantships, State Grants, Federal W/S, loans. Financial assistance is available for international students. Assistantships/fellowships may be available for joint degree candidates. Apply by March 1, deadline for Park Fellowships is January 15. Request scholarship, fellowship, assistantship information from the Johnson School. For most financial assistance and all Federal programs submit FAFSA (School code: 002711), also submit Financial Aid Transcript, Federal Income Tax forms. Approximately 65% of current students receive some form of financial assistance. For Ph.D.: The Johnson School offers both fellowships and assistantships, which cover tuition, fees, and include a stipend.

DEGREE REQUIREMENTS. For M.B.A.: 60-credit program including 37 elective credits and a strategy course; two-year program; a twelve-month M.P.A. option available. For M.B.A.-M.A.: six- to seven-semester program. For M.B.A.-M.I.L.R., M.Eng.: five-semester program. For M.B.A.-J.D.: four- to five-year program. For Ph.D.: three- to four-year program, at least six semesters in full-time residence; qualifying written and oral exam; admission to candidacy; research paper; dissertation; oral defense.

DOCTORAL AREAS OF STUDY.
Accounting.
Behavioral Sciences.
Finance.
Management and Organizations.
Marketing.
Production and Operations Management.
Quantitative Analysis for Administration.

Weill Medical College of Cornell University
Web site: www.med.cornell.edu

Established 1898. Name changed from Cornell University Medical School in 1998. Located on the Upper East side of New York City (10021). NIH ranking is 29th among all U.S. institutions with 497 awards/grants worth $192,563,068. Library: 1,322,000 volumes, 1830 subscriptions. Affiliated hospitals for clinical instruction: Memorial Sloan-Kettering Cancer Center, the Hospital for Special Surgery, the New York Hospital Medical Center of Queens, the New York Methodist Hospital, the New York Community Hospital of Brooklyn, St. Barnabas Hospital, the Burke Rehabilitation Center in White Plains, United Hospital Medical Center in Port Chester, Cayuga Medical Center in Ithaca.

Annual tuition: $35,125. Medical College residences are available for both single and married students. All housing is subsidized by the College. Housing and personal expenses per year: approximately $12,000.

Enrollment: first-year class 101 (EDP 2); total full-time 405 (men 50%, women 50%, minorities 45%, state residents 50%). Faculty: full-time/part-time 3000. Degrees conferred: M.D., J.D.-M.D., M.D.-Ph.D., M.S.T.P. (in conjunction with Rockefeller University and Memorial Sloan-Kettering Cancer Center).

ADMISSION REQUIREMENTS. AMCAS report, transcripts, letters of recommendation required in support of application. Interview by invitation. Supplemental application required. MCAT recommended. Has EDP; apply between June 1 and August 1. Apply to Chair of the Admissions Committee after June 1, before October 15. Application fee $75. Phone: (212)746-1067. Phone for M.D.-Ph.D. program: (212)746-6023.

ADMISSION STANDARDS. Very competitive. Accepts about 4% of all applicants. Number of applications 5177 (3974 out-of-state); number interviewed 759 (597 out-of-state); number of acceptance 225 (166 out-of-state); number enrolled 101 (65 out-of-state). Mean Composite MCAT 11.4; mean UGPA 3.72. *U.S. News & World Report* ranking is in the top 15 of all medical schools.

FINANCIAL AID. Grants, loans. Apply upon notification of acceptance to Committee on Financial Aid of the College. Phone: (212)746-1066. No closing date. About 80% receive aid other than loans from School funds.

DEGREE REQUIREMENTS. For M.D.: satisfactory completion of four-year program.

FIELDS OF GRADUATE STUDY.
Biochemistry, Cell and Molecular Biology.
Biochemistry and Structural Biology.
Cancer Biology.
Chemical Biology.
Clinical Investigation.
Clinical Epidemiology and Health Services Research.
Computational Biology.
Development Biology.
Immunology and Microbial Pathogenesis.
Microbiology.
Molecular Biology.
Neurosciences.
Pharmacology.
Physiology, Biophysics and System Biology.

New York State School of Industrial and Labor Relations
Web site: www.ilr.cornell.edu

Graduate study since 1945. Annual tuition: $20,800. On-campus housing for married, single students. Average academic year housing costs: $13,000–$20,000. Contact Housing Office. Phone: (607) 255-5511.

Graduate enrollment: first-year class 30–40, full-time 150 (men 50%, women 50%). Faculty: full-time 50. Degrees conferred: M.I.L.R., M.I.L.R.-M.B.A., M.P.S., M.S., Ph.D.

ADMISSION REQUIREMENTS. Official transcripts, three letters of recommendation, GRE/GMAT (if degree is from English-speaking institution) required in support of School's application. Interview not required. TOEFL required for international applicants. Graduates of unaccredited institutions not considered. Apply to Graduate School by February 15 (Fall), November 15 (Spring). Application fee $70. Phone: (607)225-2227; fax: (607) 255-7774.

ADMISSION STANDARDS. Competitive. Usual minimum average: 3.0 (A = 4). Accepts 25% of total applicants.

FINANCIAL AID. Annual awards from institutional funds: scholarships, fellowships, research assistantships, teaching assistantships, loans. Approved for VA benefits. Apply by January 15 (Fall), November 1 (Spring), to Graduate department for fellowships, assistantships; to Director of Financial Aid for all other programs. Phone: (607)255-4884, Fax: (607)255-1816. Use FAFSA. About 70% of students receive aid other than loans from University/School and outside sources.

DEGREE REQUIREMENTS. For M.I.L.R.: 13 courses (48 credit hours), one year minimum in full-time residence; qualifying exam; admission to candidacy. For M.P.S.: 30 credits, minimum; one year minimum in full-time residence. For M.S.: one year minimum in full-time residence; thesis; final oral/written exam. For Ph.D.: four semesters minimum in full-time residence; thesis; qualifying and candidacy exams; final exam.

FIELDS OF STUDY.
Collective Representation.
Dispute Resolution.
Human Resources and Organizations.
International and Comparative Labor.
Labor Market Policy.

New York State College of Veterinary Medicine

Web site: www.vet.cornell.edu

Professional graduate study since 1894. Coed. State supported. Special facilities: On-campus Teaching Hospital, Regional Veterinary Laboratories for Poultry Disease Diagnosis, New York State Mastitis Control Program Laboratories, James A. Baker Institute for Animal Health, Equine Research Park. Library: 90,000 volumes. 800 subscriptions..

Annual tuition: resident $24,000, nonresident $35,000. For housing information contact the Campus Life Office. Living expenses: $15,000.

Enrollment: first-year class 80, total 320 (men 20%, women 80%, minorities 21%, state residents 75%), graduate students 100. Faculty: full- and part-time 265. Degrees conferred: D.V.M., D.V.M.-M.S., D.V.M.-Ph.D. The M.S. and Ph.D. are offered through the Graduate School.

ADMISSION REQUIREMENTS. VMCAS report, transcripts, prerequisite course work: English composition, 6 credits; Biology (with laboratory), 6 credits; Inorganic Chemistry (with laboratory), 6 credits; Organic Chemistry (with laboratory), 6 credits; Biochemistry, 4 credits; Physics (with laboratory), 6 credits; GRE/MCAT (test older than five years will not be considered), experience with animals and the veterinary profession, essay, three recommendations (one from an academic advisor), required in support of application. At least three years of undergraduate college study leading to a bachelor's degree. Interview by invitation. Preference given to state or contract state residents. Accepts transfers only if vacancies exist. Apply to the Office of Admissions beginning August 15 for an application, deadline of October 1. For transfer April 1. Fall admission only. Application fee $70. Phone: (607)253-3700.

ADMISSION STANDARDS. Competitive. Accepts about 10–15% of all applicants. Usual minimum UGPA: 3.0 (A = 4). GRE mean score (V + Q) 1380; mean UGPA 3.70.

FINANCIAL AID. Loans, grants, scholarships, fellowships, assistantships, Federal W/S, loans. Apply to College Financial Aid Office. Use FAFSA or CSS PROFILE. Apply by March 15.

DEGREE REQUIREMENTS. Satisfactory completion of four-year D.V.M. program. For Ph.D.: see Graduate School listing.

FIELDS OF GRADUATE STUDY.
Biochemistry and Cellular and Molecular Biology. M.S., Ph.D.
Comparative Biomedical Sciences. Ph.D.
Immunology. M.S., Ph.D.
Microbiology. M.S., Ph.D.
Pharmacology. Ph.D.
Physiology. Ph.D.
Zoology. M.S., Ph.D.

CRANBROOK ACADEMY OF ART
Box 801
Bloomfield Hills, Michigan 48303-0801
Web site: www.cranbrook.edu/art

Founded 1932. Located 20 miles from Detroit. Coed. Private control. Semester system. Special facility: semiprivate studios in most. Library: 30,000 volumes, 95 subscriptions.

Annual tuition: full-time $21,500. Limited on-campus housing for 95 students; none for married students. Average annual housing cost: $6850 for single students. Estimated cost for 9 months: meals $3800, supplies $2700, personal expenses $1600, transportation $1400. Apply to the Dean of Admission for housing information. Phone: (248)645-3300.

Graduate Program

Enrollment: full-time 155 (men 75, women 80); no part-time students. Academy faculty: full-time 10, part-time 0. Degrees conferred: M.F.A., M.Arch.

ADMISSION REQUIREMENTS. Transcripts, references, statement of purpose, portfolio required in support of application. Electronic application available. TOEFL required for foreign applicants. Interview not required. Accepts transfer applicants, but two years' residence still required for degree. Apply to Dean of Admission by February 1 (Fall), November 1 (Spring). Application fee $50. Phone: (248)645-3360, (248)646-0046; e-mail: caaadmission@cranbrook.edu.

ADMISSION STANDARDS. Competitive.

FINANCIAL AID. Scholarships, grants, assistantships, Federal W/S, loans. Apply by February 1 to the Registrar. Phone: (248)645-3303. Use FAFSA (Academy code: G02248). Assistantships reserved for second-year students. About 70% of students receive aid from the Academy.

DEGREE REQUIREMENTS. For M.F.A., M.Arch.: 60 semester hours minimum in full-time residence; thesis including photographic record of work.

FIELDS OF STUDY.
Architecture.
Ceramics.
Design. Includes 2-D, 3-D.
Fiber Arts.
Metalsmithing.
Painting.
Photography.
Printmaking.
Sculpture.

THE CREIGHTON UNIVERSITY
Omaha, Nebraska 68178-0001
Web site: www.creighton.edu

Founded 1878. CGS member. Coed. Private control, Roman Catholic affiliation. Semester system. Library: 481,800 volumes, 1666 subscriptions. Total University enrollment: 6800.

Tuition: per credit: business $595, all other programs $607. On-campus housing for both married and single students. Average annual housing cost: $12,000. Apply to Housing Office. Phone: (402)280-3016.

Graduate School

Enrollment: full-time 185, part-time 288. Faculty; full- and part-time 251. Degrees conferred: M.A., M.B.A., M.S., M.C.S., M.C.S.M., Ph.D.

ADMISSION REQUIREMENTS. Transcripts, GRE/GMAT, three letters of reference required in support of School's application. TOEFL required for international applicants. Interview varies by department. Apply to Graduate School Office by March 1 (Fall), December 15 (Spring), May 15 (Summer). Application fee $40. Phone: (402)280-2870; fax: (402)280-5762; e-mail: gradsch@creighton.edu.

ADMISSION STANDARDS. Selective. Usual minimum average: 3.0 (A = 4).

FINANCIAL AID. Scholarships, research assistantships, teaching assistantships, tuition waivers, grants, Federal W/S, loans. Apply by March 15 to Dean of the Graduate School. Phone: (402) 280-2731; e-mail: gpfinaid@creighton.edu. Use FAFSA (School code: 002542). About 15% of students receive aid other than loans from University and outside sources. Aid available for part-time students.

DEGREE REQUIREMENTS. For most master's: 30–38 credit hours minimum; thesis; reading knowledge of one foreign language; comprehensive oral/written exam; or 33 credit hours minimum; written comprehensive exam. For M.B.A.: 33 credit hours minimum. For Ph.D.: 90 credits beyond the bachelor's, one year in full-time study; two foreign languages or one language and alternative tool for some departments; comprehensive exam; dissertation.

FIELDS OF STUDY.
Atmospheric Sciences.
Biomedical Sciences.
Business Administration. GMAT for admission: M.B.A. only.
Christian Spirituality.
Clinical Anatomy.
Counseling.
Educational Leadership.
English.
Health Services Administration.
Information Technology.
International Relations.
Liberal Studies.
Medical Microbiology. 2 years minimum in full-time residence for M.S.
Ministry.
Negotiation and Dispute Resolution.
Nursing.
Pharmaceutical Sciences.
Pharmacology.
Physics.
Secondary School Teaching.
Security Analysis and Portfolio Management.
Special Populations in Education.
Theology.

School of Dentistry
Web site: cudental.creighton.edu

Founded 1905. Semester system.
Annual tuition: $39,570. Some on-campus housing available. Average academic year housing costs: $10,160–$12,160 (apartment living). Contact Student Personnel Office for housing information. Phone: (402)280-3016. Total cost for all other first-year expenses: $7,500.
Enrollment: D.D.S. program, first-year class 85 (men 53, women 32), total full-time 340 (men 62%, women 38%, minorities 6%, state resident 13%). Faculty: full-time 51, part-time 78. Degrees conferred: D.D.S.

ADMISSION REQUIREMENTS. AADSAS, official transcripts, three letters of recommendation, DAT required in support of application. Applicants must have completed at least three years

of college study; prefer four years of study. Interview not required. Graduates of unaccredited colleges not considered. Preference given to educational compact states of Idaho, New Mexico, Nevada, North Dakota, Utah, and Wyoming. Accepts transfer applicants. Apply to Director of Admissions after July 15, before March 1. Application fee $45. Phone: (402)280-2695, (800)544-5094.

ADMISSION STANDARDS. Competitive. Median DAT: Academic 18.5, PAT 18.7; median GPA: 3.0 (A = 4). Accepts about 15–20% of total annual applicants. Approximately 15% are state residents.

FINANCIAL AID. Scholarships, grants, tuition waivers, loans. Apply by June 1 to the Director of Financial Aid. Phone: (402)280-2731, (800)282-5835. Use FAFSA. About 90% of students receive some aid from School.

DEGREE REQUIREMENTS. For D.D.S.: satisfactory completion of four-year program.

School of Law (68178-0140)
Web site: culaw2.creighton.edu

Organized 1904. ABA approved since 1924. AALS member since 1907. Private control. Semester system. Law library: 345,458 volumes, 4627 subscriptions; has LEXIS, NEXIS, WESTLAW.
Annual tuition: full-time $24,828, part-time $14,486. On-campus housing available. Total average annual additional expenses: $16,530.
Enrollment: first-year class 155; total full-time 456 (men 57%, women 43%, minorities 10%). Faculty: full-time 20, part-time 19. Student to faculty ratio 15.4 to 1. Degrees conferred: J.D., J.D.-M.B.A., J.D.-M.S. (E-Commerce).

ADMISSION REQUIREMENTS. LSDAS Law School report, transcripts, LSAT, two letters of recommendation, bachelor's degree required in support of application. Accepts transfer applicants. Graduates of unaccredited colleges not considered. Admits Fall only. Apply to University Admissions Office after August 31, before May 1. Application fee $45. Phone: (800)282-5835; fax: (402)280-3161.

ADMISSION STANDARDS. Selective. Accepts 36% of total annual applicants. Number of applicants 1402; number of acceptance 505; number enrolled 155; LSAT (75% of class have a score at or above 150); GPA (75% of class have a GPA at or above 3.21). *U.S. News & World Report* ranking is in the third tier of all law schools.

FINANCIAL AID. Scholarships, fellowships, assistantship, partial tuition waiver, Federal W/S, loans. Apply by March 1 to Dean of the School. Phone: (402)280-2352. Use FAFSA (School code: 002542). About 43% of students receive aid other than loans from School. Has a loan repayment assistance plan for those who work in a public interest legal setting.

DEGREE REQUIREMENTS. For J.D.: 94 hours minimum, at least final two semesters in residence.

School of Medicine
Web site: medicine.creighton.edu

Established 1892. Clinical instruction at St. Joseph Hospital, Children's Memorial, Veteran's Administration, Alegent Health System Hospital. Library: 200,000 volumes, 1000 subscriptions.
Annual tuition: $40,972 Limited on-campus housing. Total average figure for all other expenses: $13,500.
Enrollment: first-year class 125, total full-time 498 (men 53%, women 47%, minorities 14%, state residents 13%). Faculty: full-

time 289, part-time 21. Degrees conferred: M.D., M.D.-M.S., M.D.-Ph.D.

ADMISSION REQUIREMENTS. AMCAS report, transcripts, MCAT, interview required in support of application. Supplemental application required. Applicants must have completed at least three years of college study. Preference given to residents of midwestern states. Accepts transfer applicants on a space available basis. Has EDP; apply between June 15 and August 1. For regular admission apply between June 15 and December 1. Application fee $75. Phone: (402)280-2799; fax: (402)280-1241.

ADMISSION STANDARDS. Competitive. Accepts about 13% of all applicants. Number of applications 4962; number interviewed 578; number of acceptance 310; number enrolled 125 (108 out-of-state). Mean Composite MCAT 9.6; mean UGPA 3.67.

FINANCIAL AID. Scholarships, grants, fellowships, assistantships, loans. Apply to Office of the Dean, preferably before January 15. Phone: (402)280-2666. About 95% of students receive some aid from School.

DEGREE REQUIREMENTS. For M.D.: satisfactory completion of four-year program; must pass Step 1 of USMLE before promotion to clinical years. For M.S., Ph.D.: see Graduate School listing above.

FIELDS OF GRADUATE STUDY.
Biomedical Sciences. Includes Anatomy, Molecular and Cellular Biology, Biological Chemistry, Physiology.
Medical Microbiology and Immunology.
Pharmacology.

UNIVERSITY OF DALLAS
Irving, Texas 75062-4799
Web site: www.udallas.edu

Founded 1956. Coed. Located 8 miles from downtown Dallas and 25 miles from Forth Worth. Private control. Roman Catholic. Semester for Braniff Graduate School. Trimester for Graduate School of Management. Library: 300,000 volumes, 800 subscriptions. Total University enrollment: 3020.

Tuition: per credit $600 (LA), $522 (GSM). On-campus housing is limited. Average annual off-campus housing cost: $600–$900 per month, plus board. Apply by April 1 to Director of Housing. Phone: (972)721-5113.

Graduate Divisions

Enrollment: full-time 446, part-time 1400. Graduate faculty: full- and part-time 148. Degrees conferred: M.A., M.B.A., M.F.A., M. Pol., M.R.E., M.Eng., M.H., M.Mgt., M.Th., M.T.S., Ph.D.

ADMISSION REQUIREMENTS. Transcripts, letter of intent, two letters of recommendation, résumé, portfolio for art programs required in support of University's applications. GMAT required for Business. TOEFL required for foreign applicants. GRE Subject Test recommended. Accepts transfer applicants. Graduates of unaccredited institutions not considered. Apply to Graduate Office by February 1 (doctoral programs), February 15–June 15 (master's programs). Application fee $50. Phone: (972)721-5106; e-mail: graduate@acad.udallas.edu. Graduate School of Management: (972)714-5198; fax: (972)721-4009.

ADMISSION STANDARDS. Selective. Usual minimum average: 3.0 (A = 4).

FINANCIAL AID. Scholarships, assistantships, Federal W/S, loans. Apply by August 5 to Graduate Dean. For all need-based programs apply to the Financial Aid Office. Phone: (972)721-5384. Use FAFSA.

DEGREE REQUIREMENTS. For master's: 30 semester hours, minimum, at least 24 in residence and 12 in full-time attendance; language requirement for some programs; thesis; final oral exam. For M.B.A.: 37–49 credit hours and attendance at 10 lectures in GSM's Ethics & Management Lecture series. For M. Mgt.: 25 credit hours (8 courses and attendance at 10 lectures in GSM's Ethics & Management Lecture series). Ph.D.: 84 Semester hours, at least 40 in full-time residence; qualifying exam; dissertation; final written/oral exam.

FIELDS OF STUDY.

BRANIFF GRADUATE SCHOOL OF LIBERAL ARTS:
American Studies.
Art. M.A., M.F.A.
Education.
English. M.A., M.Eng.
Humanities. M.A.
Literature. M.A., Ph.D.
Pastoral Ministries.
Philosophy. M.A., Ph.D.
Politics. M.A., M. Pol., Ph.D.
Psychology. M.A.
Theology. M.A., M.S.T., M.R.E., M.Th.

GRADUATE SCHOOL OF MANAGEMENT:
Accounting.
Business Management.
Corporate Finance.
Engineering Management.
Entrepeneurship.
Financial Services.
Global Business.
Health Services Management.
Human Resource Management.
Information Assurance.
Information Technology.
Marketing.
Not-for-Profit Management.
Organizational Development.
Project Management.
Sport and Entertainment Management.
Strategic Leadership.
Supply Chain Management and Market Logistics.
Telecommunications Management.

DARTMOUTH COLLEGE
Hanover, New Hampshire 03755-3526
Web site: www.dartmouth.edu

Founded 1769. CGS member. Located 135 miles NW of Boston. Coed. Private control. Year-round operation. Special facilities: Fairchild Science Center, Gilman Biomedical Center, Murdough Center. The College's NIH ranking is 15th among all U.S. institutions with 219 awards/grants valued at $91,527,923. According to The Center at University of Florida, Dartmouth is ranked 72nd in receipt of Federal Research fund with $106,034,000 and it ranks 85th for total research expenditures with $155,795,000. The College's endowment assets ranks it 19th, with a value of $454,293,000. Eleven of the College's faculty members have been elected to National Honor Academies and this ranks it 64th among all U.S. institutions. The Library: approximately 2,400,000 volumes, 20,600 subscriptions. There are approximately 500 computers on campus for student use. Total College enrollment: 5780.

On-campus housing for 136 married students, a few available rooms for single students. Average housing cost: $18,500 for married students, $13,800 for single students. Apply to Director of Rental Housing. Phone: (603)646-2170.

School of Arts and Sciences

Graduate study since 1960. Tuition per year: $31,770. Enrollment: full-time 608, part-time 76. Faculty teaching graduate students: full-time 246. Degrees conferred: A.M., M.S., M.A.L.S., Ph.D.

ADMISSION REQUIREMENTS. Transcripts, three letters of recommendation, GRE required in support of School's application. TOEFL required of foreign students. Interview not required. Accepts transfer applicants. Graduates of unaccredited institutions not considered. Apply by February 1 to department of study. Application fee, varies by field of study. General information number: Phone: (603)646-2107; fax: (603)646-3488.

ADMISSION STANDARDS. Competitive for most departments, very competitive for others. Usual minimum average: 3.0 (A = 4).

FINANCIAL AID. Annual awards from institutional funds: tuition scholarships, fellowships, research assistantships, grants, Federal W/S, loans. Apply to Financial Aid Office by February 15. Phone: (603)646-2451. Use FAFSA. All applicants for graduate program simultaneously considered for financial aid and all financial resources available at College. Most Ph.D. students received financial assistance from College funds.

DEGREE REQUIREMENTS. Vary by department, but generally for A.M., M.S.: eight courses minimum, at least three terms in residence; thesis; final oral exam. For M.A.L.S.: two to three summers in residence. For Ph.D.: eight courses minimum, at least six terms in residence; language requirement established by department; qualifying exam; dissertation; final oral exam.

FIELDS OF STUDY.
Biochemistry. Ph.D.
Biology. Ph.D.
Chemistry. Ph.D.
Comparative Literature. A.M.
Computer Science. Ph.D.
Earth Sciences. M.S., Ph.D.
Electro-Acoustic Music. A.M.
Engineering Sciences. Ph.D.
Environmental Sciences. Ph.D.
Evaluative Clinical Sciences. M.S., Ph.D.
Genetics. Ph.D.
Immunology and Microbiology. M.S.
Liberal Studies. M.A.L.S.
Mathematics. Ph.D.
Molecular and Cell Biology. Cross-disciplinary program with Medical School and Thayer. Ph.D.
Pharmacology and Toxicology. Ph.D.
Physics and Astronomy. M.S., Ph.D.
Physiology. Ph.D.
Psychological and Brain Sciences. Ph.D.

Amos Tuck School of Business Administration
Web site: www.tuck.dartmouth.edu

Established 1900, the oldest graduate school of business in world. Private control. Accredited programs: M.B.A. Trimester system. Library: 115,000 volumes, 3000 subscriptions. Special Programs: foreign exchange programs (France, Germany, Japan, Spain, United Kingdom), internships. Special facilities: Center for Asia and the Emerging Economics.

Annual tuition: full-time $38,400. On-campus rooms available during first year.

Enrollment: total full-time 504. Faculty: 44 full-time, 22 part-time, all have Ph.D./D.B.A. Degrees conferred: M.B.A. (full-time only), M.B.A.-M.D., M.B.A.-M.A.L.D. (Law and Diplomacy with Fletcher School at Tufts University), M.B.A.-M.E., M.B.A.-M.P.A. (Kennedy School of Government, Harvard University).

ADMISSION REQUIREMENTS. All applicants should have a bachelor's degree from a recognized institution of higher education and a strong mathematics background. Students are required to have their own personal computer. Submit an application, a GMAT (will accept GMAT test results from the last five years, latest acceptable date is March), two official transcripts from each undergraduate/graduate school attended, two letters of recommendation, three or four essays, résumé (prefers at least four years of work experience), and an application fee of $220 to the Office of Admission. In addition, international students (whose native language is other than English) should submit a TOEFL (may be waived under special conditions, contact Admissions Officer for current information), certified translations and evaluations of all official transcripts, recommendation should be in English or with certified translations, proof of health/immunization certificate, and proof of sufficient financial resources for two years of academic study. On-campus interviews are strongly recommended; appointment phone: (603)646-3162. Beginning students are admitted Fall only. U.S. citizens have four deadlines: October 15, December 1, January 15, April 15, international students apply by April 10 (Fall). Joint degree applicants must apply to and be accepted to both schools/programs, contact the admissions office for current information and specific admissions requirements. Notification is made within 4–6 weeks of application deadlines if application is complete and all supporting documents have been received. Admissions Office phone: (603)646-3162; fax: (603)646-1441; e-mail: tuck.admissions@dartmouth.edu.

ADMISSION STANDARDS. Very selective. Median GMAT: 699; median GPA: 3.4 (A = 4). *U.S. News & World Report* ranked Tuck School in the top seven of all U.S. business schools; ranked 6th in Management, 9th for Nonprofit Management. *Business-Week* listed Tuck in the top ten of all American business schools.

FINANCIAL AID. Scholarships, minority scholarships, fellowships, low-interest Tuck Loans, Federal W/S, loans. Financial aid may be available for international students. Assistantships/fellowships may be available for joint degree candidates. Request scholarship, assistantship as well as need-based information from the School of Business. Apply by March 1. For most financial assistance and all Federal programs submit FAFSA (School code: 002573), also submit Financial Aid Transcript, Federal Income Tax forms. Approximately 70% of students receive some form of financial assistance.

DEGREE REQUIREMENTS. For M.B.A.: 26-course program including 12 elective courses all in second year, two-year program. For M.B.A.-Masters: generally a three- to four-year program, For M.B.A.-M.D.: five- to six-year program.

Thayer School of Engineering—Graduate Division
Web site: www.dartmouth.edu/thayer

Established 1871. Tuition: $34,965 for three terms. Enrollment: full-time 133. Faculty: full-time 43, part-time 29. Degrees conferred: B.E., M.E.M., M.E.M.-M.B.A., M.S., Ph.D., M.D.-Ph.D.

ADMISSION REQUIREMENTS. Transcripts, two letters of reference, GRE required in support of School's application. Joint degree applicants must be accepted by both programs. TOEFL required for foreign applicants. Graduates of unaccredited institutions not considered. Apply to Graduate Admission by January 1. Application fee $40, $50 for application originating out of the U.S. Phone: (888)842-9376; (603)646-2606; fax: (603)646-3856; e-mail: engg.admissions@dartmouth.edu.

ADMISSION STANDARDS. Competitive. Usual minimum average 3.0 (A = 4).

FINANCIAL AID. Fellowships and teaching assistantships are available from institutional funds; research assistantships are available from contract research. Such support normally covers tuition plus a monthly stipend. Approved for VA benefits. Apply to Director of Financial Aid by January 15. Phone: (603)646-3844; fax: (603)646-3856. Use FAFSA and CSS PROFILE.

DEGREE REQUIREMENTS. For B.E.: 9 courses, proficiency in design, analytical and experimental work, and economic analysis of engineering problems. For M.E.M.: nonthesis option requires 13–18 courses with distribution in engineering, design and manufacturing, and management; internship. For M.S.: 6–10 courses minimum, at least three consecutive terms in residence; thesis; oral defense. For Ph.D.: two-year minimum in residence; candidacy; oral exam; thesis.

FIELDS OF STUDY.
Biomedical Engineering.
Biotechnology/Biochemical Engineering.
Computer Engineering.
Electrical Engineering.
Engineering Management.
Engineering Physics.
Environmental Engineering.
Manufacturing Engineering.
Materials Science and Engineering.
Mechanical Engineering.

Medical School
Web site: www.dartmouth.edu/dms

Founded 1979. The fourth oldest medical school in U.S. Clinical instruction at Brattleboro Retreat (VT), Family Medical Institute (ME), Hartford Hospital (CT), Tuba City Indian Health Service Hospital (AZ), Mary Hitchcock Memorial Hospital (NH). NIH ranking is 15 among all U.S. institutions with 219 awards/grants worth $91,527,923.

Annual tuition: $38,625. Limited on-campus housing available. Most students live in off-campus housing. Total average figure for all other expenses: $9750.

Enrollment: first-year class 82, total full-time 316 (men 52%, women 47%, minorities 22%, state residents 9%). Faculty: full-time 410, part-time 500. Degrees conferred: M.D., M.D.-M.B.A., M.D.-M.P.H., M.D.-Ph.D.

ADMISSION REQUIREMENTS. AMCAS report, transcripts indicating completion of three years of college work, letters of recommendation, MCAT, interview required in support of application. Does not have EDP. Transfer applicants considered on a space available basis. Graduates of unaccredited colleges not considered. Has a commitment to residents of New Hampshire and Maine. Apply to Admissions Office of the School after June 15, before November 1. Application fee $75. Phone: (603)650-1505; fax: (603)650-1560.

ADMISSION STANDARDS. Competitive. Accepts about 7% of all applicants. Number of applications 3599 (3549 out-of-state); number interviewed 669 (640 out-of-state); number of acceptance 259 (248 out-of-state); number enrolled 82 (74 out-of-state). Mean Composite MCAT 10.7; mean UGPA 3.70. *U.S. News & World Report* ranking is in the top 32 of all medical research schools, in top 18 in primary care.

FINANCIAL AID. Scholarships, part-time jobs, loans. Apply to Office of Financial Aid of the School after acceptance. Phone: (603)650-1919. Use FAFSA, the Needs Access form, and MS financial aid application. About 87% of students receive some aid from School.

DEGREE REQUIREMENTS. For M.D.: completion of four-year program; must take Steps 1 and 2 of USMLE required; passing is not.

FIELDS OF GRADUATE STUDY.
Chemistry.
Computational Biology.
Earth Sciences.
Ecology and Evolutionary Biology.
Engineering.
Evaluative Clinical Sciences. Includes outcomes research, health policy, decision making, and improvement.
Mathematics.
Molecular and Cellular Biology. Includes Biochemistry, Biological Sciences, Genetics, Microbiology/Immunology.
Molecular, Cellular and Systems Physiology.
Pharmacology and Toxicology.
Physics and Astronomy.
Physiology (See PEMM).
Program in Experimental and Molecular Medicine (PEMM). Includes Cancer Biology and Molecular Therapeutics, Molecular Pharmacology, Toxicology and Experimental Therapeutics, Neuroscience, Systems Biology, Vascular Biology.
Psychological and Brain Sciences.

UNIVERSITY OF DAYTON
Dayton, Ohio 45469-1620
Web site: www.udayton.edu

Founded 1850. CGS member. Coed. Private control. Roman Catholic affiliation. Trimester system. Library: about 1,150,463 volumes, 7554 subscriptions. Total University enrollment: 10,500.

No on-campus housing for graduate students. Contact Residents Services for off-campus information. Phone: (937)229-3317. Day-care facilities available.

Graduate School

Tuition: College of Arts and Science and Engineering $637 (Master's), $724 (Ph.D.), M.B.A. $694, M.P.A. $435, Education $435 (Master's), $544 (Ed.S.), $587 (Ed.D), D.P.T. $23,175 (academic year).

Enrollment: full-time 1232, part-time 1168. Graduate faculty: full-time 172, part-time 121. Degrees conferred: M.A., M.B.A., M.C.L.T., M.C.S., M.P.A., M.S., M.S.Ed., M.S.T., Ed.S., Ed.D., Ph.D., D.P.T., J.D.-M.B.A.

ADMISSION REQUIREMENTS. Transcripts, three letters of recommendation, personal statement, GMAT for M.B.A., GRE/MAT for Psychology, Biology, and Clinical Psychology required in support of School's application. Online application available. TOEFL or evidence of proficiency in English required of international students. Accepts transfer applicants. Graduates of unaccredited colleges not considered. Apply to the Graduate School by March 1 priority date (Fall), December 1 (Spring), April 1 (Third Term). Application fee $30. Phone: (937)229-3065; fax: (937)229-4729.

ADMISSION STANDARDS. Varies for each program, usually 3.0 in areas desired for graduate study (A = 4).

FINANCIAL AID. Fellowships, scholarships, teaching/research assistantships, traineeships, Federal W/S, loans. Apply by March 1 for assistantships, for all other programs apply to Graduate School at time of application. Use FAFSA. Aid available for part-time students.

DEGREE REQUIREMENTS. For master's: 30–36 semester hours minimum (includes 6 in research if thesis required), at least 24 in residence; thesis/comprehensive oral/written exam/internship or project required by some departments. For Ed.S.: at least 30 semester hours beyond the master's. For Ph.D.: 60 semester hours minimum, at least two years in residence; preliminary exam; qualifying exam; candidacy exam; dissertation; research tool. For Ed.D., D.P.T.: essentially the same as for the Ph.D., except one-year internship.

FIELDS OF STUDY.

COLLEGE OF ARTS AND SCIENCES:
Applied Mathematics.
Biology.
Chemistry.
Clinical Psychology.
Communication.
Computer Science.
English.
Experimental Factors.
History.
Mathematics.
Pastoral Ministries.
Philosophy.
Political Science.
Psychology. Includes clinical, experimental, general, human factors.
Public Administration.
Theological Studies.

SCHOOL OF BUSINESS ADMINISTRATION:
Business Administration. Includes accounting, finance, international business, MIS, marketing, operations management. M.B.A.

SCHOOL OF EDUCATION AND ALLIED PROFESSIONS:
Adolescence to Young Adult. M.S.E.
Art Education. M.S.E.
College Student Personnel. M.S.E.
Community Counseling. M.S.E.
Early Childhood Education. M.S.E.
Educational Leadership. M.S.E., Ed.S., Ph.D.
Exercise Science. M.S.E.
Higher Education Administration. M.S.E.
Interdisciplinary Education. M.S.E.
Intervention Specialist. M.S.E.
Middle Childhood Education. M.S.E.
Multi-Age Education. M.S.E.
Music Education. M.S.E.
Physical Therapy. D.P.T.
School Counseling. M.S.E.
School Psychology. M.S.E., Ed.D.
Teacher as Child/Youth Development Specialist. M.S.E.
Teacher as Leader. M.S.E.
Technology-Enhanced Learning. M.S.E.

SCHOOL OF ENGINEERING:
Aerospace Engineering.
Chemical Engineering.
Civil Engineering.
Electrical and Computer Engineering.
Electro-Optics.
Engineering.
Engineering Management.
Engineering Mechanics.
Environmental Engineering.
Management Science.
Materials Engineering.
Mechanical Engineering.
Transport Engineering.

School of Law (45469-2272)

Web site: www.law.udayton.edu

Reopened 1974. ABA approved since 1975. AALS member. Semester system. Library: 307,600 volumes, 4778 subscriptions.

Annual tuition: $32,360, per credit $910. Limited on-campus housing available. Total average annual additional expenses: $11,100.

Enrollment: first-year class 119; total 458 (men 57%, women 43%, minorities 12%). Faculty: full-time 26, part-time 21. Student to faculty ratio 15.4 to 1. Degrees conferred: J.D., J.D.-M.B.A., J.D.-M.S. (Education).

ADMISSION REQUIREMENTS. LSDAS Law School report, bachelor's degree, transcripts, LSAT, recommendations, personal statement required in support of application. Accepts transfers from other ABA approved School. Graduates of unaccredited colleges not considered. Apply to Admissions Office by May 1. Rolling admission process. Application fee $50; online application fee none. Phone: (937)229-3555; fax: (937)229-4194.

ADMISSION STANDARDS. Selective. Accepts approximately 27% of total applicants. Number of applicants 2117; number of acceptance 580; number enrolled 119; LSAT (75% of students have a score at or above 152); GPA (75% of student have a GPA at or above 2.87). *U.S. News & World Report* ranking is in the fourth tier of all U.S. law schools.

FINANCIAL AID. Full and partial scholarships, grants, Federal W/S, loans. Apply by March 1 to Financial Aid Office. Phone: (937)229-3555. Use FAFSA. About 53% of students receive some aid from School.

DEGREE REQUIREMENTS. For J.D.: Satisfactory completion of three-year program. For master's degrees: see Graduate School listing above.

UNIVERSITY OF DELAWARE

Newark, Delaware 19716-1501
Web site: www.udel.edu

Established 1743, degree granting since 1834. CGS member. Located 15 miles SW of Wilmington. Coed. State-related. Semester system. Special facilities: Institute of Applied Mathematics, Center for the Study of Catalysts, Center for the Study of Composite Materials, University Computing Center, Agricultural Experiment Station, Bartol Research Institute, Institute for Energy Conversion, Science Teaching Center, Mathematics, Teaching Center, Mt. Cuba Astronomical Observatory, Marine Biology Field Station; cooperative program in American Studies and related fields with the Henry Francis du Pont Winterthur Museum and in American technological, business and Labor History with the Hagley Museum. Library: 2,600,000 volumes, 12,600 subscriptions. Total University enrollment: 20,373.

Annual tuition: full-time, resident $6210, nonresident $15,728; per credits, resident $388, nonresident $983; for M.B.A./E.M.B.A. resident $476, nonresident $983. On-campus housing for both married and single students. Average academic year housing costs: $8000 (including board) single students; $9500 for married students. Contact Office of Housing and Residence Life for both on- and off-campus housing information. Phone: (302)831-6573.

Graduate Studies

Graduate study since 1900. Enrollment: full-time 2586, part-time 971. University faculty teaching graduate students: full-time 1077, part-time 33. Degrees conferred: M.A., M.S., M.B.A., M.Ed., M.C.E., M.E.E., M.M.S., M.M.E., M.A.S., M.P.A., M.C., M.F.A., M.M., M.P.T., M.M.P., M.I., M.S.N., Ph.D., Ed.D.

ADMISSION REQUIREMENTS. Transcripts, GRE, GMAT (Business), three letters of recommendation required in support of application. TOEFL required of international applicants. Accepts transfer applicants. Graduates of unaccredited institutions not considered. Apply to the Office of Graduate Studies before July 1 (Fall), December 1 (Spring), April 1 (Summer). Application fee $60. Phone: (302)831-2129; fax: (302)831-8745.

ADMISSION STANDARDS. Selective to very competitive.

FINANCIAL AID. Annual awards from institutional funds: scholarships, University fellowships, teaching assistantships, research assistantships, traineeships, tuition waivers, Federal W/S, loans. Approved for VA benefits. Apply by March 1 to appropriate department chair in each Graduate College for assistantships, fellowships; to the Financial Aid Office for all other programs. Phone: (302)931-9761. Use FAFSA. About 70% of students receive aid from University.

DEGREE REQUIREMENTS. For master's: 30–48 semester hours minimum; proficiency in one language for some departments thesis/nonthesis option/special project. For Ph.D.: three years minimum beyond the bachelor's, at least one year in continuous residence; language proficiency for some programs; oral/written qualifying exam; dissertation; final oral exam.

FIELDS OF STUDY.

COLLEGE OF AGRICULTURE AND NATURAL RESOURCES:
Agricultural and Resource Economics.
Agricultural and Technology Education.
Animal and Food Science. Ph.D.
Biosciences Engineering. M.S.
Entomology and Wildlife Ecology.
Food Science. M.S. only.
Operations Research.
Plant and Soil Science. M.S., Ph.D.
Public Horticulture. M.S.

COLLEGE OF ARTS AND SCIENCE:
Art. M.F.A. only.
Art Conservation. M.S.
Art History. M.A., Ph.D.
Biological Sciences. Interdepartmental; includes marine biology, morphology, ichthyology, botany, zoology, microbiology; one language for master's. M.S., Ph.D.
Biomechanics and Movement Science. Interdisciplinary.
Chemistry and Biochemistry. M.A., M.S., Ph.D.
Communication.
Computer and Information Science. M.S., Ph.D.
Early American Culture. Two-year program; M.A. only.
English. One language; general qualifying exam for M.A.
Foreign Languages and Literatures. Includes French, German, Spanish. M.A.
Foreign Languages and Pedagogy.
Geography and Climatology. M.A., M.S., Ph.D.
History. M.A., Ph.D.
Liberal Studies. M.A.
Linguistics. M.A., Ph.D.
Mathematical Sciences. M.A., M.S., Ph.D.
Music. Includes performance, teaching. M.M. only.
Physical Therapy. D.P.T.
Physics. Oral exam for M.S.
Political Science and International Relations. M.A. only.
Preservation Studies. M.A.
Psychology. Includes clinical, cognitive, social, neuroscience. Ph.D. only.
Sociology and Criminology. M.A., Ph.D.
Theatre. Includes acting, stage management, technical production. M.F.A. only.

ALFRED LERNER COLLEGE OF BUSINESS AND ECONOMICS:
Accounting. M.S. only.
Business Administration. GMAT for admission. M.B.A. only.
Economics. M.A., M.S., Ph.D.

Economics-Business Administration. M.A.-M.B.A.
Information Systems and Technology Management. M.S.
Organization Effectiveness, Development and Change. M.S.

COLLEGE OF HUMAN SERVICES, EDUCATION AND PUBLIC POLICY:
Education. Ph.D.
Educational Leadership. M.Ed.
Counseling in Higher Education. M.A.
Curriculum and Instruction. M.Ed.
Educational Technology. M.Ed.
Environmental and Energy Policy. M.E.E.P., Ph.D.
Exceptional Children and Youth. M.Ed.
Hotel, Restaurant and Institutional Management. M.S.
Human Development and Family Studies. M.S., Ph.D.
Instruction. M.I.
Public Administration. M.P.A.
Reading. M.Ed.
School Psychology. M.A., Ed.S.
Teaching English as a Second Language. M.A.
Urban Affairs and Public Policy. M.A., Ph.D.

COLLEGE OF ENGINEERING:
Biomechanics and Movement Science. Interdisciplinary. M.S., Ph.D.
Chemical Engineering. M.CH.E., Ph.D.
Civil and Environmental Engineering. M.C.E., Ph.D.
Electrical and Computer Engineering. M.E.E., Ph.D.
Materials Science and Engineering. M.M.S.E., Ph.D.
Mechanical Engineering. M.M.E., Ph.D.
Ocean Engineering. M.S., Ph.D.

COLLEGE OF HEALTH SCIENCES:
Biomechanics and Movement Science. Interdisciplinary.
Exercise Science. M.S.
Health Promotion. M.S.
Health Services Administration.
Human Nutrition. M.S.
Nursing.

COLLEGE OF MARINE AND EARTH STUDIES:
Geological Sciences.
Marine Management. M.M.M.
Marine Policy. M.P.P.
Marine Studies.
Ocean Engineering. Interdisciplinary.
Oceanography. Ph.D.

DELTA STATE UNIVERSITY
Cleveland, Mississippi 38733-0001
Web site: www.deltastate.edu

Founded 1924. Located 100 miles S of Memphis, Tennessee. Coed. State control. Semester system. Library: 345,565 volumes, 1337 subscriptions. Total University enrollment: 4000.

Annual tuition: resident $3726; nonresident $8702; per credit resident $205, nonresident $490. On- and off-campus housing available. Annual on-campus housing cost: $4000 (including board). Phone: (662) 846-4151. Day-care facilities available.

Graduate Studies

Graduate study since 1964. Enrollment: full-time 246, part-time 494. Faculty: full-time 112, part-time 18. Degrees conferred: M.B.A., M.C.A., M.Ed., M.S., M.M.E., M.S.N., M.P.A., M.S.C.J., Ed.S., Ed.D.

ADMISSION REQUIREMENTS. Two transcripts, GRE/GMAT/MAT required in support of application. TOEFL required for international applicants. Graduates of unaccredited colleges not considered. Accepts transfer applicants. Apply to Coordinator of Admissions at least forty-five days prior to registration. Application fee: none. Phone: (662)846-4875; fax: (662)846-4313.

ADMISSION STANDARDS. Selective. Usual minimum average: 2.5 (A = 4).

FINANCIAL AID. Scholarships, grants, graduate assistantships, Federal W/S, loans. Apply to the Office of Student Financial Assistance: no specified closing date. Phone: (662)846-4670. Use FAFSA and institutional FAF. About 80% of students receive aid from all sources.

DEGREE REQUIREMENTS. For master's: 33 semester hours minimum, at least 27 in residence and one semester in full-time attendance; thesis optional; final oral/written exam. For Ed.S.: 30 semester hours beyond the master's; paper, final oral/written exam. For Ed.D.: 90 semester hours beyond the bachelor's degree; dissertation and residency requirement.

FIELDS OF STUDY.
Accountancy. M.P.A.
Biological Science. M.S.
Business Administration. M.B.A.
Commercial Aviation. M.C.A.
Community Development. M.C.D.
Counseling. M.Ed.
Criminal Justice. M.C.J.
Educational Administration and Supervision. Ed.S.
Elementary Education. M.Ed., Ed.S.
English Education. M.Ed.
Health, Physical Education, and Recreation. M.Ed.
History Education. M.Ed.
Mathematical Education. M.Ed.
Music Education. M.M.
Natural Science. M.S.
Nursing. M.S.N.
Physical Science. M.S.
Professional Studies. Ed.D.
Secondary Education. M.Ed., Ed.S.
Social Science Education. M.Ed.
Special Education. M.Ed.
Teaching. M.A.T.

UNIVERSITY OF DENVER
Denver, Colorado 80208
Web site: www.du.edu

Founded 1864. CGS member. Coed. Private. Quarter system. Special Facilities: Humanities Institute, Echo Lake Lab, Mount Evans Observatory, Denver Research Institute, Child Study Center, Center of Marital Studies, Center for Policy and Contemporary Issues. Library: 2,900,00 volumes, 6283 subscriptions; a U.S. government document depository. Total University enrollment: 10,400.

Tuition: per credit $771. On-campus housing for single and married students. Housing cost: One bedroom $6852 (9-month academic year); meal plan available: $2200 (9-month academic year). Two-bedroom units and suites available; monthly costs $650–$725. Contact Graduate Housing Office. Phone: (303)871-2246, fax: (303)871-4064.

Division of Arts, Humanities and Social Sciences

Enrollment: full- and part-time graduate students: 324 (men 45%, women 55%). Faculty: full-time 86. Degrees Conferred: M.A., M.M., M.F.A., Ph.D.

ADMISSION REQUIREMENTS. Two transcripts, GRE (Subject Test for some programs) required in support of application. Contact department for additional requirements. TOEFL required for international students. TSE required for some programs. TSE is required for all international graduate teaching assistants. The TWE required by Communications. Application fee: $45. Phone: Graduate Admissions (303)871-2706, or request application materials directly from Web site: www.du.edu.

ADMISSION STANDARDS. Selective to competitive for most departments. Usual minimum average: 2.75 (A = 4).

FINANCIAL AID: Annual awards from institutional funds: scholarships, fellowships, minority student fellowships, teaching assistantships, grants, Federal W/S, loans. Apply by March 1 to departments for scholarships and assistantships, to Financial Aid Office for all other programs. Phone: (303)871-2681. Use FAFSA.

DEGREE REQUIREMENTS. For M.A., M.M.: 45–75 quarter hours; qualifying exam; reading knowledge of one foreign language for some departments; comprehensive exam; thesis required by many departments, optional in others, final oral/written exam required by some programs. For M.F.A.: 90 quarter hours, at least two years in residence; qualifying exam, advancement to candidacy, thesis, oral exam; gallery exhibition. For Ph.D.: 135 quarter hours minimum beyond bachelor's degree or 90 quarter hours beyond master's; at least six quarters in residence, including two consecutive quarters of full-time attendance; reading knowledge of two foreign languages or advanced proficiency in one language; preliminary exam; advancement to candidacy; dissertation; final oral exam.

FIELDS OF STUDY.
Anthropology. M.A.
Art History. Includes museum studies. M.A.
Composition (Music). M.M.
Conducting (Music). M.M.
Digital Media Studies. M.A.
Economics. M.A.
Electronic Media and Design. M.F.A.
English. Includes literary studies, creative writing. M.A., Ph.D.
French. M.A.
German. M.A.
History. M.A.
Human Communication Studies. M.A., Ph.D.
International and Intercultural Communication. M.A.
Judaic Studies. M.A., M.A.-M.S.W.
Mass Communications and Journalism Studies. M.A.
Music History and Literature. M.A.
Music Theory. M.A.
Orff-Schulwerk. M.M.
Philosophy. M.A.
Piano Pedagogy. M.M.
Piano Performance. M.M.
Psychology. Includes child, clinical, experimental, developmental. Ph.D.
Public Policy. M.P.P.
Public Relations. M.S.
Religious Studies. M.A. (Joint Ph.D. program with Iliff School of Theology.)
Russian. M.A.
Sociology. M.A.
Spanish. M.A.
Studio Art. M.F.A.
Suzuki Pedagogy. M.M.
Video Production. M.A.
Note: University offers Flexible Dual Degrees; students design their own programs.

Division of Natural Sciences and Mathematics

Enrollment: full- and part-time graduate students: 125 (men 45%, women 55%). Faculty: full-time 47. Degrees Conferred: M.A., M.S., Ph.D.

ADMISSION REQUIREMENTS. Two transcripts, GRE (Subject Test for some programs) required in support of application. Contact department for additional requirements. TOEFL required for international students. TSE required for some programs. TSE is required for all international graduate teaching assistants. Application fee: $45. Phone: Graduate Admissions (303)871-3119, or request application materials directly from Web site: www.du.edu.

ADMISSION STANDARDS. Selective to competitive for most departments. Usual minimum average: 2.75 (A = 4).

FINANCIAL AID. Annual awards from institutional funds: scholarships, fellowships, minority student fellowships, teaching assistantships, grants, Federal W/S, loans. Apply by March 1 to departments for scholarships and assistantships, to Financial Aid Office for all other programs. Phone: (303)871-2681. Use FAFSA.

DEGREE REQUIREMENTS. For M.A., M.S., M.S.M.: 45–75 quarter hours; qualifying exam; reading knowledge of one foreign language for some departments; comprehensive exam; thesis required by many departments, optional in others, final oral/written exam required by some programs. For Ph.D.: 135 quarter hours minimum beyond bachelor's degree or 90 quarter hours beyond master's; at least six quarters in residence, including two consecutive quarters of full-time attendance; reading knowledge of two foreign languages or advanced proficiency in one language; preliminary exam; advancement to candidacy; dissertation; final oral exam.

FIELDS OF STUDY.
Applied Mathematics. M.A., M.S.
Biological Sciences. M.A., Ph.D.
Chemistry and Biochemistry. M.A., M.S., Ph.D.
Computer Science. M.S.
Geography. Includes geographic information science (M.S.). M.A., M.S., Ph.D.
Natural Science and Mathematics. M.S., Ph.D.
Physics and Astronomy. M.S., Ph.D.

Daniels College of Business—Graduate Studies

Web site: www.dcb.du.edu

Established 1908. Private control. Accredited programs: M.B.A. (accredited since 1923), Accounting. Quarter system. Special Programs: foreign exchange program in Denmark. Special facilities: Center for Management and Development.

Annual tuition: full-time $27,756 (three quarters), part-time $14,733.

Enrollment: total full-time 429, part-time 473. Faculty: 83 full-time, 15 part-time; 90% with Ph.D./D.B.A. Degrees conferred: M.B.A. (full-time, part-time, day, evening) (General Business Concepts), E.M.B.A. (weekends only), M.Acc., M.I.M. (International Management), M.S.F. (Finance) M.S.M. (Management), M.S.R.T.M. (Resort and Tourism Management), M.T. (Taxation), M.B.A.-J.D., M.I.M.-J.D.

ADMISSION REQUIREMENTS. All applicants should have a bachelor's degree from a recognized institution of higher education and a strong mathematics background. Submit application, GMAT (will accept GMAT test results from the last five years, latest acceptable date is March; will accept GRE), official transcripts from each undergraduate/graduate school attended, two letters of recommendation, essays, résumé, and work history (prefers at least four years of work experience), and an applica-

tion fee of $50 to the College's Office of Admission. In addition, international students (whose native language is other than English) should submit a TOEFL (minimum score 600) report, certified translations and evaluations of all official transcripts, recommendation should be in English or with certified translations, proof of health/immunization certificate, and proof of sufficient financial resources for nine months of academic study On-campus visits are encouraged. Admissions Committee will consider applicants with some academic course work deficiencies. Joint degree applicants must apply to and be accepted by both schools, contact the admissions office for current information and specific admissions requirements. Beginning students are admitted Fall, Spring only. U.S. citizens apply by March 1 (Fall), January 1 (Spring), international students apply by March 1 (Fall only). Rolling admissions process. Admissions Office phone: (303) 871-3416; fax: (303) 871-4466; e-mail: dcb@du.edu.

ADMISSION STANDARDS. Competitive for most programs. For M.B.A.: median GMAT: 581; median GPA: 3.28 (A = 4).

FINANCIAL AID. Scholarships, Colorado Resident Grants, international assistantships, research and teaching assistantships, Federal W/S, loans. Financial aid is available for part-time study. Financial assistance is available for international students. Assistantships/fellowships may be available for joint degree candidates. Apply by February 1 for scholarship, fellowship, assistantship from the Daniels College of Business. Contact the University's Financial Aid Office for current need-based financial aid information; phone: (303)871-3416. For most financial assistance and all Federal programs submit FAFSA (School code: 001371), also submit Financial Aid Transcript, Federal Income Tax forms. Approximately 50% of current students receive some form of financial assistance.

DEGREE REQUIREMENTS. For M.B.A., M.I.M.: 72 quarter hours including 16 elective hours, one- to two-year program; degree program must be completed in five years. For E.M.B.A.: 70 quarter hour eighteen-month program. For M.Acc., 56 quarter hour program. For M.S.F.: 64 quarter hour program. For M.R.C.M.: 64 quarter hour program. M.S.T.: 60 quarter hour program. For M.T., LL.M.: 45 quarter hour program. For M.B.A.-Masters: generally a two- to five-year program. For M.B.A., M.I.M.-J.D.: four- to five-and-one-half-year program.

FIELDS OF STUDY.
Accountancy. M.Acc.
Business Administration. M.B.A.
Construction Management. M.S.
Data Mining. M.S.
Finance. M.S.F.
Information Technology. Includes business information technology, electronic commerce. M.S.M.
InternationalManagement. Joint degree with the Graduate School of International Studies. M.I.M.
Management. Includes education, healthcare systems, public health, sport and entertainment. M.S.M.
Management and Cable/Telecommunication. Joint degree with the School of Communications. M.S.M.
Management and Engineering. Joint degree with the department of Engineering. M.S.M.
Marketing. M.S.
Real Estate and Construction Management. M.R.C.M.
Taxation. Interdisciplinary degree with the College of Law. M.Tax., LL.M.

Morgridge College of Education

Enrollment: full-time 273, part-time 484. Faculty teaching graduate students: full-time 25, part-time 10. Degrees conferred: M.A., Ph.D.

ADMISSION REQUIREMENTS. Transcripts, letters of recommendation required in support of application. Online application available. TOEFL required for international applicants. Accepts transfer applicants. Graduates of unaccredited colleges not considered. Apply to Office of Admission by January 1 (priority date). Rolling admissions process. Application fee $45. Phone: (303) 871-2509, Fax: (303)871-4566.

ADMISSION STANDARDS. Competitive. Usual minimum average 2.75 (A = 4).

FINANCIAL AID. Annual awards from institutional funds: Scholarships, fellowships, research assistantships, teaching assistantships, Federal W/S, loans. Apply by March 1 to the Financial Aid Office. Phone: (303)871-2681. Use FAFSA. About 30% of students receive aid other than loans from University and outside sources. Aid available for part-time students.

DEGREE REQUIREMENTS. For M.A.: 45 quarter hours minimum, at least 35 in residence; thesis or extra credit required for some departments; final written/oral exam. For Ph.D.: 135 quarter hours minimum beyond the bachelor's degree, at least 90 quarter hours in full-time study; qualifying exam; comprehensive exam; advancement to candidacy; research tool; dissertation; final oral exam.

FIELDS OF STUDY.
Child and Family Studies. M.A., Ph.D.
Counseling Psychology. Ph.D.
Curriculum Leadership. M.A., Ph.D.
Educational Leadership and Policy Studies. M.A., Ph.D.
Educational Psychology. M.A., Ph.D.
Higher Education and Adult Studies. M.A., Ph.D.
International Studies. M.A.
Library and Information Sciences. M.L.I.S.
Management and Education. M.S.M. with concentration in Education.
Mental Health Counseling. M.A.
School Administration. Ph.D.
School Psychology. Ed.S., Ph.D.

College of Law (80208)

Web site: www.law.du.edu

Establish 1864. ABA approved since 1975. AALS member. Located in downtown Denver. Private control. Semester system. Special facilities: Earth Justice Clinic, National Center for Preventive Law, Rocky Mountain Mineral Law Foundation, Rocky Mountain Land Use Institute. Library: 358,464 volumes, 5804 subscriptions; has LEXIS, NEXIS, WESTLAY, DIALOG, INFOTRAC; has more than 1500 network connections.

Annual tuition: $30,960, part-time $22,264. Total average annual additional expenses: $14,337.

Enrollment: first-year class, full-time 212, part-time 87; total enrollment 1129 (men 53%, women 47%, minorities 19%). Faculty: full-time 49, part-time 60. Student to faculty ratio 14 to 1. Degrees conferred: J.D., J.D.-M.A (History, Psychology, Sociology), J.D.-M.B.A., J.D.-M.I.M., J.D.-M.M.P., J.D.-M.S.W., LL.M. (Environmental and Natural Resources, American and Comparative Law), M.S.L.A., M.T.

ADMISSION REQUIREMENTS. LSDAS Law School report, bachelor's degree, transcripts, LSAT, résumé, personal statement, two letters of recommendation required in support of application. Interview discouraged. Accepts transfer applicants. Graduates of unaccredited colleges n-ot considered. Apply to Admissions Committee after November 1, before May 1 (flexible). Admits Fall only. Rolling admission process. Application fee $60. Phone: (303)871-6135; e-mail: admissions@law.du.edu.

ADMISSION STANDARDS. Selective. Accepts approximately 24% of full-time and 28% of part-time applicants. Number of full-time applicants 3115, part-time 440; number of full-time acceptance 749, part-time 123; number full-time enrolled 262, part-time 87; LSAT (75% of full-time students have a score at or above 155, part-time 148); GPA (75% of full-time student have a GPA at or above 3.10, part-time 2.80). *U.S. News & World Report* ranking is in the second tier tied at 77th of all U.S. law schools.

FINANCIAL AID. Scholarships, fellowships, Federal W/S, loans, internships, externships. Apply by February 15 to Scholarship Committee Use FAFSA. Phone: (303)871-6136. About 40% of students receive aid other than loans from College.

DEGREE REQUIREMENTS. For J.D.: satisfactory completion of three-year program (day), four-year program (evening). For dual degrees in History, International Studies, International Management, Mineral Economics, Psychology, Social Work, Sociology: the J.D. is reduced by 10 credits; the other degree is reduced by 9–12 quarter hours. For LL.M., M.S.L.A., M.T.: satisfactory completion of two-semester program.

Graduate School of International Studies

Graduate study since 1929. Tuition: per credit $771. Graduate housing available. Enrollment: full- and part-time 336. Faculty teaching graduate students: full-time 19, part-time 6. Degrees conferred: M.A., M.I.M., M.P.P., M.A.–M.S.W., M.A.–J.D., Ph.D.

ADMISSION REQUIREMENTS. Transcripts, 3 letters of recommendation, GRE (GMAT or LSAT may be substituted), statement of purpose required in support of the school's application. TOEFL (minimum score 550) required for international applicants. Accepts transfer applicants. Graduates of unaccredited institutions not considered. Apply to the Office of Admission by January 15 (priority date). Application fee $50, $45 for international applicants. Phone: (303)871-2544; fax: (303)871-2456; e-mail: gsisadm@du.edu.

ADMISSION STANDARDS. Competitive. Mean GPA: 3.3 (A = 4.0). Mean GRE: 500–530 (Verbal), 570–590 (Quant.), 590–610 (Analytical). Usual minimum average: 3.0 (A = 4).

FINANCIAL AID. Annual awards from institutional funds: fellowships (includes Foreign Language and Area Studies Fellowships), graduate research/teaching assistantships, grants, Federal W/S, loans. Apply to department chair by February 15 for all non-Federal programs; to Student Financial Services for all Federal programs. Phone: (303)871-2681. Use FAFSA (School code: 001371) and Departmental FAF.

DEGREE REQUIREMENTS. For M.A.: 90 quarter hour program (must include the core, one field, one concentration, and two methodology courses); thesis; foreign language proficiency. For M.P.P.: 90 quarter hour program (must include the core, one policy analysis area, one policy issue area, and a participant-observer experience). For Ph.D.: 135 quarter hour beyond bachelor's, at least three consecutive quarters in residence; most programs include the core, two fields, one concentration, three methodology courses; research tool; advancement to candidacy; one foreign language proficiency; written/oral comprehensive exam; dissertation.

FIELDS OF STUDY.
Global Finance, Trade and Economic Integration. M.A.
Global Studies. M.G.S.
Homeland Security. M.A. in H.S.
International Administration. M.A.
International Development.
International Human Rights. M.A.
International Security. M.A.
International Studies. M.A., Ph.D.

Graduate School of Professional Psychology

Graduate study since 1976. Tuition: per credit $771. Enrollment: full- and part-time 185. Faculty teaching graduate students; full-time 6, part-time 31. Degree conferred: Psy.D.

ADMISSION REQUIREMENTS. Transcripts, GRE Subject Test, four letters of recommendation required in support of School's application. TOEFL, TSE required for international applicants. Accepts transfer applicants. Graduates of unaccredited colleges not considered. Apply to Office of Admission by January 1. Application fee $45. Phone: (303)871-3873; fax: (303)871-4220.

ADMISSION STANDARDS. Competitive. Usual minimum average 3.0 (A = 4). Mean GRE: 550; mean GPA: 3.5 (A = 4).

FINANCIAL AID. Annual awards from institutional funds: fellowship, research/teaching assistantships, Federal W/S loans. Apply by March 1 to the Financial Aid Office. Phone: (303)871-2681. Use FAFSA. About 20% of students receive aid other than loans from University and outside. Aid available for part-time students.

DEGREE REQUIREMENTS. For M.A.: 72 quarter hours, two years in full-time residency; supervised field placement; competency exam/thesis. For Psy.D.: 135 quarter hours minimum beyond the bachelor's degree, at least two years minimum in full-time study; clinical experience; advancement to candidacy; research tool; practicum; twelve-month clinical psychology internship; doctoral paper.

FIELDS OF STUDY.
Clinical Psychology. Psy.D.
Forensic Psychology. M.A.
International Disaster Psychology. M.A.
Sport and Performance Psychology. M.A.

Graduate School of Social Work

Tuition: per credit $771. Enrollment: full- and part-time 370. Faculty teaching graduate students: full-time 23, part-time 0. Degrees conferred: M.S.W., Ph.D.

ADMISSION REQUIREMENTS. Official transcripts, three letters of recommendation required in support of School's application. A personal interview may be requested by School. TOEFL, TSE required for international applicants. Accepts transfer applicants. Graduates of unaccredited colleges not considered. Apply to Office of Admissions by May 31. Rolling admission process. Application fee $50. Phone: (303)871-2841; fax: (303)871-2845.

ADMISSION STANDARDS. Competitive. Usual minimum average: 2.75 (A = 4).

FINANCIAL AID. Annual awards from institutional funds: fellowships, scholarships, teaching/research assistantship, Federal W/S, loans. Apply by February 1 to the Financial Aid Office. Phone: (303)871-2841. Use FAFSA. About 10% of students receive aid from School and outside sources. Aid available for part-time students.

DEGREE REQUIREMENTS. For M.S.W.: 90 quarter hours minimum, at least three quarters in full-time study; advancement to candidacy; six quarters of field practicum. For Ph.D.: 135 quarter hours minimum beyond the bachelor's degree, at least 75 quarter hours in full-time study; preliminary exam; advancement to candidacy; research tool; dissertation; final oral exam.

FIELDS OF STUDY.
Advanced Clinical Practice. Includes social work with individuals, couples, families, small groups.
Advanced Community Practice. Includes social work in organizations and communities in the policy arena.

DEPAUL UNIVERSITY
Chicago, Illinois 60604-2287
Web site: www.depaul.edu

Founded 1898. CGS member. The largest Catholic University in the country. Coed. Private control. Roman Catholic affiliation. Quarter system. Graduate study at Loop, Lincoln Park, O'Hare, and Oakbrook campuses. Special facilities: Institute for Applied Artificial Intelligence, Chicago Area Studies Center, Center for Church/State Studies, DePaul Performance Center, Hispanic Research Center, Center for the Studies of Values, Institute for Business Ethics, Kellstadt Center for Marketing Analysis and Planning, Learning Disabilities Center, Mental Health Clinic, Blackstone Theatre, Psychological Testing Center. Library: 1,200,000 volumes, 18,000 subscriptions. Total University enrollment: 23,100.

Tuition: per credit $478 (Communication, Liberal Arts and Science, Education), $598 (Computer Science), $609 (Music, Theatre), $749 (Business). No on-campus housing available. Average academic year off-campus housing costs: $9000–$12,000.

Graduate Study

Enrollment: full-time 4397, part-time 3715. Faculty teaching graduate students: full-time 390, part-time 251. Degrees conferred: M.A., M.S., M.M., M.F.A., M.B.A., M.Ed., M.S.A., M.S.T., M.Acc., M.S.-M.I.S., Ph.D.

ADMISSION REQUIREMENTS. Official transcripts, written statement of purpose required in support of application. Letters of recommendation, GRE/GMAT interview required for some departments. TOEFL required for international applicants. Accepts transfer applicants. Graduates of unaccredited colleges not considered. Apply to appropriate Graduate College/School at least one month prior to registration. For some programs there are earlier deadlines. Rolling admission process. Application fee $25, $40 (Psychology). Phone: Business (312)362-8810; Liberal Arts and Sciences (312)362-8300; Computer Science (312)362-8381; Education (773)325-7582; Music (773)325-7444; School for New Learning (312)362-8512; Theater School (773)325-7999.

ADMISSION STANDARDS. Selective to competitive for most departments. Usual minimum average 2.75 (A = 4).

FINANCIAL AID. Annual awards from institutional funds: scholarships, research assistantships, teaching assistantships, tuition waivers, Federal W/S, loans. Approved for VA benefits. Apply by May 1 to head of appropriate department for scholarships, assistantships; to Financial Aid Office for all other programs. Phone: (312)362-8526. Use FAFSA and institutional FAF. About 20% of students receive aid other than loans from University and outside sources. Aid available for part-time students.

DEGREE REQUIREMENTS. For master's: 44–60 quarter hours minimum, at least three quarters in residence for full-time students, five quarters in residence for part-time student; reading knowledge of one or two foreign languages for some department; thesis required by many departments, optional in others; final oral/written exam required by some programs. For Ph.D.: 90 quarter hours minimum, at least six quarters in residence; comprehensive exam; advance to candidacy; dissertation; final oral exam.

FIELDS OF STUDY.

COLLEGE OF LIBERAL ARTS AND SCIENCES:
Applied Physics.
Biochemistry.
Biological Sciences.
Chemistry. Includes polymer chemistry.
Communications. Includes multicultural, organizational.
Economics.
English.
Health Law and Policy.
History.
Interdisciplinary Studies.
International Studies.
Liberal Studies.
Mathematical Sciences.
Mathematics Education.
Nursing.
Philosophy. M.A., Ph.D.
Physics.
Public Administration.
Public Service Management.
Psychology. Includes clinical, experimental, general, industrial organizational school. GRE/Subject for admission; additional departmental application for admission. M.A., Ph.D.
Sociology.
Writing.

CHARLES H. KELLSTADT GRADUATE SCHOOL OF BUSINESS:
Accountancy. M.Acc., M.S.
Applied Economics. M.B.A.
Behavioral Finance. M.B.A.
Brand Management. M.B.A.
Business Information Technology. M.S.
Computational Finance. M.S.
Customer Relationship Management. M.B.A.
E-Business. M.B.A., M.S.
Entrepreneurship. M.B.A.
Finance. M.B.A., M.S.
Financial Analysis. M.B.A.
Financial Management and Control. M.B.A.
Health Sector Management. M.B.A.
Human Resource Management. M.B.A.
Human Resources. M.S.
Integrated Marketing Communications. M.B.A.
International Business. M.B.A.
Leadership/Change Management. M.B.A.
Management Accounting. M.B.A.
Management Information Systems. M.B.A.
Managerial Finance. (Weekend M.B.A. Program.)
Marketing Analysis. M.S.
Marketing Management. M.B.A.
Marketing Research and Analysis. M.B.A.
Marketing Strategy and Planning. M.B.A.
New Product Management. M.B.A.
Operations Management. M.B.A.
Real Estate. M.S.
Real Estate Finance and Investment. M.B.A.
Sales Leadership. M.B.A.
Strategy, Execution and Valuation. M.B.A.
Taxation. M.S.

SCHOOL OF COMPUTER SCIENCE TELECOMMUNICATION AND INFORMATION SYSTEMS:
Computer Information and Network Security.
Computer Science. Includes artificial intelligence, data analysis, data communication, database systems, systems foundations, computer graphics, computer vision.
Distributed Systems.
E-Commerce Technology.
Human–Computer Interaction.

Information Systems. Includes computer supported collaborative work, data warehousing, e-commerce, IT project management, networking, systems development.
Information Technology.
Management of Information Systems.
Software Engineering. Includes project management, software development, software systems.
Telecommunication Systems. Includes computer science, standard telecommunication.

SCHOOL OF EDUCATION:
Bilingual/Bicultural Education.
Curriculum Studies. Includes middle school mathematics program. Ed.D.
Educational Leadership. Ed.D.
Human Development and Learning.
Human Services and Counseling.
Language, Literacy, and Special Instruction. Includes reading and learning disabilities.
Social and Cultural Foundations in Education. Includes early childhood education, elementary education, secondary education.
Teaching and Learning. Includes early childhood, elementary, secondary. M.A., M.Ed.

SCHOOL OF MUSIC:
Composition.
Jazz Studies.
Music Education.
Performance.

SCHOOL FOR NEW LEARNING:
Customized Adult Master's Program. M.A.

THEATRE SCHOOL:
Acting.
Directing.

College of Law
Web site: www.law.depaul.edu

Founded 1912. ABA approved since 1925. AALS member. Private control. Semester system. Located at Loop Campus. Special facilities: Center for Intellectual Property Law & Information Technology, International Human Rights Law Institute, Schiller, DuCanto and Fleck Family Law Center, Health Law Institute, Center for Justice in Capital Cases, International Aviation Law Institute, Center for Public Interest Law, Center for the Study of Race & Bioethics, Center for Law Science, Center for Church-State Studies. Library: 378,493 volumes, 5297 subscriptions; has LEXIS, NEXIS, WESTLAW, DIALOG, ILLLINET, 120 PCs.

Tuition: $30,670 (day), $19,960 (evening). On-campus housing limited. Contact Director of Housing. Total average annual additional expense: $21,184.

Enrollment: first-year class day 234, evening 96. Total day and evening 1070 (men 51%, women 49%, minority 23%).

Faculty: Total full-time 34, part-time 44 (men 49%, women 51%, minority 23%). Student to faculty ratio 17.1 to 1. Degrees conferred: J.D., J.D.-M.B.A., J.D.-M.A. (International Studies, Computer Science), J.D.-M.S.(Computer Science, Public Service), LL.M.(Taxation, Health Law, Intellectual Property).

ADMISSION REQUIREMENTS. LSDAS Law School Report, transcripts, one letter of recommendation, personal statement, résumé required in support of application. TOEFL required of international applicants. Accepts transfer students. Graduates of unaccredited colleges not considered. Apply to Director of Admissions after October 1, before March 1. Rolling admission process. Application fee $60. Phone: (312)632-6831, outside Illinois (800)428-7453; fax: (312)362-5280. For LL.M.: Official transcripts, résumé, personal statement, two letters of reference required in support of application. TOEFL required of international applicants. Apply to Law Graduate Program, Room 948 at least six week in advance of semester of entrance. Phone: (312) 362-8185. Application fee $40.

ADMISSION STANDARDS. Selective. Accepts approximately 26% of all students. Number of full-time applicants 4198, part-time 830; number of full-time acceptance 1081, part-time 330; number full-time enrolled 234, part-time 96; LSAT (75% of full-time students have a score at or above 158, part-time 154); GPA (75% of full-time student have a GPA at or above 3.12, part-time 3.02). *U.S. News & World Report* ranking is in the third tier of all U.S. law schools.

FINANCIAL AID. Scholarships, Federal W/S, loans. Apply to Office of Financial Aid by March 1. Phone: (312)362-8091. Use FAFSA. Aid available for part-time students. Approximately 62% of students receive aid other than loans from the College.

DEGREE REQUIREMENTS. For J.D.: 86 semester hours, 6 semesters (day) or 8 semesters (evening) in residence; acceleration possible through attendance at two summer sessions; "C" average required. For LL.M.: at least 24 credits (with a 2.5 GPA [A = 4]) beyond J.D.

DES MOINES UNIVERSITY

3200 Grand Avenue
Des Moines, Iowa 50312-4198
Web site: www.dmu.edu

Gained University status in 1980. Private control. Semester system. Graduate study only. Special facilities: the University operates five clinics; an on-campus Medical Center opened in 1987 and the University added the College of Podiatric Medicine and Surgery and the College of Health Sciences.

College of Osteopathic Medicine and Surgery

Established 1898 as the Dr. S.S. Still College of Osteopathic Medicine/Second oldest and second largest osteopathic School in U.S. Affiliated with Des Moines General Hospital and twelve other hospitals throughout the East and Midwest.

Annual tuition: $32,830. No on-campus housing available. Contact Off-Campus Housing Office for housing information. Off-campus housing and personal expenses: approximately $17,500.

Enrollment: first-year class 215, total 814 (men 51%, women 49%, minorities 16%, state residents 23%). Faculty: full-time 68, part-time 22. Degrees conferred: D.O., D.O.-M.H.A., D.O.-M.P.H.

ADMISSION REQUIREMENTS. Preference given to State residents, U.S. citizens and permanent residents only. Bachelor's degree from an accredited institution required. All applicants have bachelor's degree awarded prior to enrollment. Apply through AACOMAS (file after June 1, before February 1), submit MCAT (will accept test results from last two years: one year is recommended), official transcripts for each school attended (should show at least 90 semester credits/135 quarter credits), service processing fee. After a review of the AACOMAS application and supporting documents a decision is made concerning which candidates should receive supplemental materials. The supplementary application, an application fee of $50, a statement of purpose, and three recommendations (one from a premed adviser and two from science faculty members) should be returned to Office of Admission by March 15. Interviews are by invitation only and generally for final selection. Accepts transfer applicants on a space available basis. First-year students admitted Fall only. Rolling admissions process, notification starts in January and is finished when class is filled. Priority deadline February 1. College does main-

tain an alternate list. Phone: (515)271-1450, (800)240-2767, ext. 1450; fax: (515)271-1578.

ADMISSION STANDARDS. Selective. Accepts about 18% of all applicants. Number of applications 2387 (2227 out-of-state); number interviewed 579 (468 out-of-state); number of acceptance 446 (353 out-of-state); number enrolled 215 (156 out-of-state). Usual minimum UGPA: 3.0 (A = 4). Mean Composite MCAT 8.6, mean UGPA 3.56.

FINANCIAL AID. Scholarships, merit scholarships, minority scholarships, Grants-in-Aid, institutional loans, NOF, HEAL, alternative loan programs, NIH stipends; Federal Perkins loans, Stafford Subsidized and Unsubsidized loans, Service Obligation Scholarships programs, Military and National Health Service programs are available. Financial Aid applications and information are given out at the on-campus by invitation interview. Contact the Financial Aid Office for current information. Phone: (515) 271-1470. Use FAFSA (School code: 015616), also submit Financial Aid Transcript, Federal Income Tax forms. Approximately 85% of students receive some form of financial assistance.

DEGREE REQUIREMENTS. For D.O.: satisfactory completion of four-year program.

UNIVERSITY OF DETROIT MERCY

Detroit, Michigan 48221-3038
Web site: www.udmercy.edu

Founded 1877. In 1990 the University of Detroit and Mercy College consolidated to form a new university. Private control. Roman Catholic affiliation. Coed. Semester system. The Colleges of Business Administration, Engineering and Sciences, and Liberal Arts are at the McNichols Campus; the Colleges of Health Services, and Education and Human Services, and Housing are at Outer Drive Campus. Special facilities: Center for the Study of Development and Aging, Manufacturing Institute, Institute for Business and Community Services, Kellstadt Consumer Research Center, Polymer Institute, Center for Excellence in Environmental Engineering and Science. Library: 645,000 volumes, 777,000 microforms, 5500 current periodicals. Total University enrollment: 6000.

Tuition: full-time $13,340–$20,040; per credit $565–$955. On-campus housing for 200 single students, 30 married student accommodations. Annual room and board costs: $7800. Apply to Director of Residential Life for on-campus housing, to Director of Students Activities for off-campus housing information. Phone: (313)993-1230.

Graduate Studies

Graduate study since 1885. Enrollment: full-time 1279, part-time 1591 (men 55%, women 45%). Graduate faculty: full-time 165, part-time 32. Degrees conferred: M.A., M.S., M.B.A., S.Sec., M.A.T.M., M.P.A., M.Engr.Mgt., M.A.C.S., Ed.S., M.E., M.C.S., Ph.D., D.E.

ADMISSION REQUIREMENTS. Official transcripts, GRE/GMAT required in support of application. Proof of English proficiency required for international applicants. Interview not required. Accepts transfer applicants. Graduates of unaccredited institutions not considered. Apply to Graduate Office of the College or School listed below at least six weeks prior to registration. Application fee $25, $35 for international applicants. Phone: (800)635-5020; E-mail: admission@udmercy.edu.

ADMISSION STANDARDS. Selective to competitive. Usual minimum average: 3.0 (A = 4).

FINANCIAL AID. Annual awards from institutional funds: scholarships, teaching fellowships, graduate assistantships, residence assistantships, coaching assistantship, internships, Federal W/S, loans. Approved for VA benefits. Apply by April 1 to appropriate department chair for fellowships, assistantships; to Scholarships and Financial Aid Office for all other programs. Phone: (313)993-3350. Use FAFSA (University code: 002323).

DEGREE REQUIREMENTS. For master's: 30–36 semester hours minimum (counseling master's: 48–54 credit program), at least 18 in residence; six hours for thesis when required or elected; final written/oral exam in some programs. For Ed.S.: 30 semester hours minimum beyond master's. For D.E.: two-year minimum beyond master's (total of 51 hours including dissertation), usually at least 30 hours in full-time residence, must be in residence in the trimester in which the final qualifying exam is taken; dissertation; oral exam. For Ph.D.: about 60–65 hours beyond the master's, at least 30 in full-time residence; language proficiency for some departments; preliminary exam; dissertation; final oral exam.

FIELDS OF STUDY.

COLLEGE OF BUSINESS ADMINISTRATION:
Business Administration. M.B.A.
Business Turnaround Management. B.T.M.
Computer Information Systems. M.S.C.I.S.
Global Entrepreneurial M.B.A. Joint program with Fu Jen Catholic University. G.E.M.B.A.
Information Assurance. M.S.
Product Development. Joint program with Engineering school. M.P.D.

COLLEGE OF ENGINEERING AND SCIENCE:
Chemistry. M.S.
Civil Engineering. M.E., D.E.
Computer and Information Systems/Software Management. M.S.
Computer Science. M.A.
Electrical and Computer Engineering. M.E., D.E.
Engineering Management. M.E.M.
Mechanical Engineering. M.E., D.E.
Product Development. Joint program with Business College.
Teaching of Mathematics. M.A.

COLLEGE OF HEALTH PROFESSIONS:
Family Nurse Practitioner.
Health Services Administration.
Health Systems Management.
Nurse Anesthesia.
Nursing Education.
Physician Assistant.

COLLEGE OF LIBERAL ARTS AND EDUCATION:
Clinical Psychology.
Counseling. Includes addictions, community, school counseling.
Criminal Justice.
Curriculum and Instruction.
Economics.
Financial Economics.
Educational Administration.
Industrial/Organizational Psychology.
Intelligence Analysis.
Liberal Studies.
Psychology.
Religious Studies.
School Psychology.
Security Administration.
Special Education. Includes emotional impaired, learning disabled.

SCHOOL OF ARCHITECTURE:
Architecture. M. Arch.
Community Development. M.C.D.

MCAULEY SCHOOL OF NURSING:
Nurse Anesthesia. M.S.N.
Family Nurse Practitioner. M.S.N.
Health Systems Management. M.S.N.

School of Dentistry (48219-0900)
Web site: www.udmercy.edu/dental

Established 1932. School relocated in 1997 to a facility in NW Detroit. Private control. Annual tuition: $39,722. Contact Office of Student Affairs for housing information. Phone: (313)446-1825. Total average cost for all other first-year expenses: $14,850.

Enrollment: first-year class 78; total 264 (men 68%, women 32%, minorities 23%, state residents 75%); postgraduates 7. Faculty: full-time 52; part-time 120. Degree conferred: D.D.S. Certificate.

ADMISSION REQUIREMENTS. AADSAS report, official transcripts, DAT (October date preferred), three letters of recommendation required in support of School's application. Interview by invitation only. Applicants must have completed at least three years of college study. Accepts transfer applicants. Preference given to state residents. Apply to Director of Admissions after June 1, before March 1 Fall admission only. Application fee $50. Phone: (313)494-6650; fax: (313)494-6659; e-mail: dental@udmercy.edu.

ADMISSION STANDARDS. Competitive. Median DAT: Academic 19.0, PAT 18.0; median GPA: 3.5 (A = 4.0). Accepts about 20–25% of total annual applicants. Approximately 95% are state residents.

FINANCIAL AID. Scholarships, grants, tuition waivers, DEAL, HEAL, loans. Apply after acceptance to the University Financial Aid office. Use FAFSA, (School code: E00635). Phone: (313)993-1405. About 83% of Michigan students receive some aid from School and outside sources.

DEGREE REQUIREMENTS. For D.D.S.: satisfactory completion of forty-five-month program.

FIELDS OF POSTGRADUATE STUDY.
Advance Education in General Dentistry.
Endodontics.
Orthodontics.
Periodontics.

School of Law (48226)
Web site: www.law.udmercy.edu

Established 1912. ABA approve since 1933. AALS member. Private control. Semester system. Special facility: Intellectual Property Law Institute. Law library: 356,891 volumes, 3000 subscriptions; has NEXIS, WESTLAW.

Tuition: full-time $26,880, part-time $16,128. Limited on-campus housing for single and married students available. Total average annual additional expense: $18,085.

Enrollment: first-year class full-time 196, part-time 58; total full- and part-time 729 (men 53%, women 47%, minorities 11%). Faculty: full-time 12, part-time 23. Student to faculty ratio 20.6 to 1. Degrees conferred: J.D., J.D.-M.B.A., J.D.-LL.B. (with University of Windsor, Canada).

ADMISSION REQUIREMENTS. LSDAS Law School report, bachelor's degree, transcripts, personal statement, two letters of recommendation, LSAT, required in support of application. Interview not required. Accepts transfer applicants. Apply to Director of Admissions after September 1, before April 15. Fall admissions only. Application fee $50. Phone: (313)596-0264; e-mail: admlawao@udmercy.edu.

ADMISSION STANDARDS. Selective. Accepts approximately 46% of full-time and 43% of part-time applicants. Number of full-time applicants 1438, part-time 221; number of full-time acceptance 664, part-time 94; number full-time enrolled 196, part-time 58; LSAT (75% of full-time students have a score at or above 147, part-time 145); GPA (75% of full-time student have a GPA at or above 3.00, part-time 2.92). *U.S. News & World Report* ranking is in the fourth tier of all U.S. law schools.

FINANCIAL AID. Scholarships, grants, Federal W/S, loans. Apply to Director of Financial Aid before April 1 (flexible). Phone: (313)596-0214. Use FAFSA. About 15% of students receive aid other than loans from institutional funds.

DEGREE REQUIREMENTS. For J.D.: 86 hours required. For J.D.-M.B.A.: 108–111 hours required, 72 hours of law, 36–39 boom of M.B.A. For J.D.-LL.B.: 104-credit full-time program; receive both an American and Canadian Law Degree. *Note:* Study-abroad programs available.

UNIVERSITY OF THE DISTRICT OF COLUMBIA
Washington, D.C. 20008-1175
Web site: www.udc.edu

Founded in 1976 by the merger of District of Columbia Teachers College, Federal City College, and Washington Technical Institute. Located in NW Washington. Coed. Public control. Semester system. Library: 540,000 volumes, 1500 subscriptions.

The University's other Graduate Colleges/Schools: School of Arts and Science, College of Professional Studies.

David A. Clarke School of Law
Web site: www.law.udc.edu

Founded 1986, merged with the University in 1996. Name changed in 1998. ABA approved since 1998. AALS member. Semester system. Full-time, day study only. Law library: 243,651 volumes, 1603 subscriptions; has LEXIS, WESTLAW, DIALOG, CALI.

Annual tuition: resident $7350, nonresident $14,700. No on-campus housing available. Apply to Housing Office. Contact Law School's Orientation Committee for off-campus information. Off-campus housing and personal expenses: approximately $20,000.

Enrollment: first-year class 81; total full-time 232 (men 39%, women 61%, minorities 44%). Faculty: full-time 29, part-time 8. Student to faculty ratio 11.1 to 1. Degree conferred: J.D.

ADMISSION REQUIREMENTS. LSDAS Law School report, LSAT (not later than December test date, if more than one LSAT, highest is used), bachelor's degree from an accredited institution, personal statement, two recommendations, essay, transcripts (must show all schools attended and at least three years of study) required in support of application. Applicants must have received bachelor's degree prior to enrollment. Accepts transfer applicants. Interview not required but may be requested by School. In addition, international applicants whose native language is not English must submit TOEFL (not older than two years). Apply to Office of Admission after September 30, before April 15. First-year students admitted Fall only. The rolling admissions process is finished when the class is filled. Application fee $35. Phone: (202)274-7341; fax: (202)274-5583.

ADMISSION STANDARDS. Selective. Accepts approximately 20% of all students. Number of applicants 1373; number of acceptance 316; number enrolled 81; LSAT (75% of students have a score at or above 149; GPA (75% of students have a GPA at or above 2.80. *U.S. News & World Report* ranking is in the fourth tier of all U.S. law schools.

FINANCIAL AID. Need-based scholarships, merit scholarships, legal scholar awards, grants, fellowships, private and institutional loans, Federal loans and Federal W/S available. Apply as soon as possible after January 1, but before April 1 deadline. Phone: (202) 274-7337. For all Federal programs submit FAFSA (School code: B08083), also submit Financial Aid Transcript, Federal Income Tax forms. Approximately 78% of students receive some form of financial assistance.

DEGREE REQUIREMENTS. For J.D.: 85 (61 required) credits with a GPA of at least 2.0 (A = 4), plus completion of upper divisional writing course; three-year program. No accelerated J.D. program; limited number of summer courses available.

DOMINICAN UNIVERSITY
River Forest, Illinois 60305-1099
Web site: www.dom.edu

Founded 1901. Located 10 miles W of the Chicago Loop. Coed. Private control. Roman Catholic. Semester system. Library: 280,475 volumes, 4000 subscriptions. Total University enrollment: 3250.

Tuition: per three-credit course $1950. On-campus housing available for single students only. Annual housing cost: $7750 (including board). Apply to Housing Office. Phone: (708)524-6237. Day-care facilities available.

Edward A. and Lois L. Brennan School of Business

Enrollment: full-time 138, part-time 180. Faculty: full-time 12, part-time 28. Degrees conferred: M.B.A., M.S.A., M.B.A.-M.L.I.S., M.S./C.I.S., M.S./M.I.S., M.S.O.M., M.B.A.-J.D. (with John Marshall Law School).

ADMISSION REQUIREMENTS. Transcripts, three letters of recommendation, GMAT required in support of School's application. Online application available. TOEFL required for international applicants. Accepts transfer applicants. Apply to School at least one month prior to registration. Application fee $25. Phone: (708)524-6507; fax: (708)522-6939.

ADMISSION STANDARDS. Selective. Usual minimum average: 2.5 (A = 4).

FINANCIAL AID. Scholarships, assistantships, tuition waivers, Federal W/S, loans. Approved for VA benefits. Apply by April 15 to Dean for scholarships, assistantships; to the Director of Financial Aid for all other programs. Phone: (708)524-6809. Use FAFSA. Aid available for part-time students.

DEGREE REQUIREMENTS. For master's: 30–51 semester hours minimum, at least 24 in residence; practicum (for some programs); computer proficiency for M.B.A.

FIELDS OF STUDY.
Accounting. M.S.A.
Business Administration. Concentrations in accounting, entrepreneurship, finance, general management, health care administration, human resource management, international business administration, management information systems, marketing.
Computer Information Systems. M.S./C.I.S.
Management Information Systems. M.S./M.I.S.
Organizational Management. M.S.O.M.

Graduate School of Education

Tuition: per credit $650. On-campus housing available.
Enrollment: full-time 8, part-time 499. Faculty: full-time 15, part-time 44. Degrees conferred: M.A.E.A., M.A.Ed., M.S.Ed., M.S.Sp.Ed., M.A.T.

ADMISSION REQUIREMENTS. Transcripts, three letters of recommendation, required in support of School's application. TOEFL required for international applicants. Accepts transfer applicants. Apply to School by August 15 (Fall), January 10 (Spring). Rolling admissions process. Application fee $25. Phone: (708)524-6921; fax (708)524-6665.

ADMISSION STANDARDS, Selective. Usual minimum average: 3.0 (A = 4).

FINANCIAL AID. Fellowships, assistantships, internships, grants. Federal W/S, loans. Approved for VA benefits. Apply by August 15 to Dean for fellowships, assistantships; to the Director of Financial Aid for all other programs. Phone: (708)524-6809. Use FAFSA. Aid available for part-time students.

DEGREE REQUIREMENTS. For master's: 32–40 semester hours minimum, at least 24 in residence; thesis/nonthesis option.

FIELDS OF STUDY.
Curriculum and Instruction. M.A.
Early Childhood Education. M.S.
Education. M.A.Ed., M.S.Ed.
Education Administration. M.A.E.A.
Literacy. M.S.
Special Education. M.S.Sp.Ed.
Teaching. M.A.T.

Graduate School of Library and Information Science

Graduate study since 1949. Tuition: per 3-credit course $1950. Enrollment full-time 157, part-time 595. Faculty: full-time 17, part-time 53. Degrees conferred: M.L.I.S., several Certificates of Special Studies.

ADMISSION REQUIREMENTS. Transcripts of all postsecondary study, two letters of recommendation required in support of School's application. GRE required for some applicants. TOEFL required for international applications. Accepts transfer applicants. Graduates of unaccredited institutions not considered. Apply to the Graduate School at least one month prior to registration. Application fee $25. Phone: (708)524-6848.

ADMISSION STANDARDS, Selective. Usual minimum average: 3.0 (A = 4).

FINANCIAL AID. Annual awards from institutional funds: scholarships, assistantships, internships, tuition waivers, Federal W/S, loans. Approved for VA benefits. Apply to Director of Financial Aid by April 15. Phone: (708)524-6845. Use FAFSA. Aid available for part-time students.

DEGREE REQUIREMENTS. For M.L.I.S.: 36 semester hours minimum; thesis. Degree must be completed within 5 years or 6 summers.

FIELDS OF STUDY.
Library Information Science. Includes library media specialist.
Management Information System. Combined program with School of Business.
Note: Collaborative programs with College of St. Catherine in St. Paul, MN. Requires courses at Dominican University as well as at CSC.

DOMINICAN UNIVERSITY OF CALIFORNIA
San Rafael, California 94901-2298
Web site: www.dominican.edu

Founded 1890. Coed. Private control, Roman Catholic. Semester system. Library: 103,000 volumes, 508 subscriptions. Total University enrollment: 1631.

Annual tuition: full-time $16,680, part-time $695 per credit. On-campus housing for single students only. Average academic year housing cost: $9000 (including board); off-campus housing costs: $1200 per month. Contact the Dean of Student Services. Phone: (415)485-3277.

Graduate Division

Graduate study since 1950. Enrollment: full-time 307, part-time 236. Faculty: full-time 48, part-time 84. Degrees conferred: M.A., M.B.A., M.S.

ADMISSION REQUIREMENTS. Official transcripts, three letters of recommendation, interview required in support of application. TOEFL required for international applicants. Accepts transfer applicants. Graduates of unaccredited institutions not considered. Apply to chair of appropriate department. Admissions deadlines vary by departments. Applications processed on a rolling basis. Application fee $40. Phone: (415)485-3246; fax: (415)485-3214.

ADMISSION STANDARDS. Selective. Usual minimum average: 2.75 (A = 4).

FINANCIAL AID. Annual awards from institutional funds: scholarships, fellowships, grants, assistantships, Federal W/S, loans. Approved for VA benefits. Apply by March 2 to Financial Aid Office. Phone: (415)485-3204; fax: (415)485-3205. Use FAFSA. About 20% of students receive aid other than loans from College and outside sources. Aid available for part-time students.

DEGREE REQUIREMENTS. For master's: 30–43 units depending on degree, at least 24 in residence; reading knowledge of one foreign language for some programs; thesis for M.S. in Education; thesis option for M.A. Humanities; final comprehensive exam or internship.

FIELDS OF STUDY.
Counseling Psychology. M.S.
Education. M.S.
Geriatric CNS/Nurse Educator. M.S.N.
Global Strategic Management. M.B.A.
Humanities. M.A.
Integrated Health Practices. M.S.N.
Occupational Therapy. M.S.
Strategic Leadership. M.B.A.
Sustainable Enterprise. M.B.A.

DRAKE UNIVERSITY
Des Moines, Iowa 50311-4516
Web site: www.drake.edu

Founded 1881. Coed. Private control. Semester system. Special facilities: Agricultural Law Center, Center for Hypertension Research, Health Issues Research Center, Information System Research Center, Insurance Research and Professional Development Center, Center for the Study of Urban Problems, Library 550,000 volumes, 4000 subscriptions. Total University enrollment: 5275.

Tuition: per credit $340–$430. On-campus housing available for both single and married students. Average academic year housing costs: $315–350 per month; off-campus $400–$650 per month. Apply by August 1, housing is based on first-come, first-served basis. Contact Housing Office for both on- and off-campus housing information. Phone: (515)271-2196.

Graduate Programs

Graduate study since 1881. Enrollment full- and part-time 2138. Faculty: full-time 66, part-time 56. Degrees conferred: M.A., M.S., M.S.T., M.A.T., M.S. in Education, M.S.N., Ed.S., Ed.D., Doctor of Pharmacy. Joint programs: M.B.A.-J.D., M.P.A.-J.D., M.A.(Mass Communication)-J.D., M.B.A.-Pharmacy.

ADMISSION REQUIREMENTS. Official transcripts, GRE or MAT required in support of application. Online application available. GMAT is required for M.B.A. degree program. Interview usually not required. TOEFL required for international applicants. Accepts transfer applicants. Graduates of unaccredited institutions not considered. Apply to the Office of Graduate Admissions at least six weeks prior to registration; Doctoral applicants apply by February 1. Application fee $30. Phone: (515)271-3871 or toll-free (800)44-DRAKE; fax: (515)271-2831; e-mail: gradadmit@acad.drake.edu

ADMISSION STANDARDS. Competitive for some departments, selective for the others. Usual minimum average: 2.5 (3.0 last two years in major) (A = 4).

FINANCIAL AID. Assistantships, fellowships, Federal W/S, loans. Approved for VA benefits. Apply by March 1 to appropriate department chair for assistantships, fellowships; to Office of Student Financial Planning for all other aid. Priority deadline March 1. Phone: (515)271-2905. Use FAFSA. Aid available for part-time students.

DEGREE REQUIREMENTS. For master's: 30–36 semester hours minimum, at least two-thirds of the course work in residence; 3–8 hours are given for graduate project, usually a thesis, field report, or creative project; final written/oral exam. For Ed.S.: 30 hours minimum beyond the master's. For Ed.D.: 60 hours minimum beyond master's, at least 2 semesters in residence; written/oral exam; dissertation; internship experience.

FIELDS OF STUDY.

COLLEGE OF BUSINESS AND PUBLIC ADMINISTRATION:
Accounting. M.Acc.
Business Administration. M.B.A.
Public Administration. M.P.A.

COLLEGE OF EDUCATION:
Adult Development. M.S.
American History. M.A.T.
Art. M.A.T.
Biology. M.A.T.
Business. M.A.T.
Chemistry. M.A.T.
Community and Agency Counseling. M.S.Ed.
Counselor Education. Includes rehabilitation administration, rehabilitation counseling, rehabilitation placement. M.S
Early Childhood Education. M.S. Ed.
Educational Leadership. Includes elementary and secondary. M.S.Ed., Ed.S., Ed.D.
Effective Teaching, Learning, and Leadership. M.S.Ed.
Elementary Education. M.S.T.
English. M.A.T.
Foreign Language. M.A.T.
General Science. M.A.T.
Journalism. M.A.T.

Mathematics. M.A.T.
Physical Science. M.A.T.
Physics. M.A.T.
Rehabilitation. M.S.
Rhetoric and Communication Studies/Theater. M.A.T.
School Counseling. Includes elementary, secondary. M.S.Ed.
Sociology. M.A.T.
Special Education. M.S.Ed.
Speech Communication. M.S.
World History. M.A.T.

COLLEGE OF PHARMACY AND HEALTH SCIENCES:
Pharmacy. D. Pharm.

Law School
Web site: www.law.drake.edu

Founded 1881. ABA approved since 1923. AALS charter member. Private control. Semester system. Special facilities: Children's Rights Center, Constitutional Law Center, Agricultural Law Center, Center for Legislative Practice. Special programs at Robert Gordon University, Aberdeen Scotland, University of Nantes, Clermont-Ferrand, France. Library: 319,959 volumes, 3241 subscriptions; 160 network connections.

Annual tuition: full-time $26,206, per credit $900. Limited on-campus housing available. Total average annual additional expense: $12,500.

Enrollment: first-year class 156, total full-time 429 (men 53%, women 47%, minorities 15%). Faculty: full-time 23, part-time 24. Student to faculty ratio 17.8 to 1.

ADMISSION REQUIREMENTS. LSDAS Law School report, bachelor's degree, transcripts, letters of recommendation, LSAT, personal statement required in support of application. TOEFL required of international applicants. Interview not required. Accepts transfer applicants. Graduates of unaccredited colleges not considered. Apply to Admissions Director after September 1, before April 1 (Fall admission). Fall and Summer admission (Conditional Admission programs only). Application fee $50. Phone: (800)44-DRAKE, ext. 2782, (515)271-2782; e-mail: lawadmit@drake.edu.

ADMISSION STANDARDS. Selective. Accepts approximately 46% of all students. Number of applicants 1158; number of acceptance 490; number enrolled 134; LSAT (75% of students have a score at or above 153); GPA (75% of student have a GPA at or above 3.14). *U.S. News & World Report* ranking is in the third tier of all U.S. law schools.

FINANCIAL AID. Scholarships, merit awards, fellowships, Federal W/S, loans. Apply by March 1 to Director, Financial Aid Office. Phone: (515)271-2905. Use FAFSA (School code: 001860). About 65% of students receive aid other than loans from School funds.

DEGREE REQUIREMENTS. For J.D.: 90 hours minimum, at least three semesters in residence.

DREW UNIVERSITY
Madison, New Jersey 07940-1493
Web site: www.drew.edu

Founded 1867. CGS member. Located 25 miles W of New York City. Coed. Private control. Semester system. Special facilities: Center for Holocaust Studies, United Methodist Archive and History Center. Library: about 500,00 volumes, 800 subscriptions; depository for both Federal government and New Jersey documents. Total University enrollment: 2627.

Annual tuition: full-time $30,744; per credit $790, reduced rates for senior citizens. Limited on-campus housing for single and married students. Average academic year housing cost: $6000–$12,000 (including board). Apply by July 1 to University Housing Office. Phone: (973)408-3037. Day-care facilities available.

Caspersen School of Graduate Studies

Graduate study 1912. Enrollment: full- and part-time 615. Graduate faculty: full- and part-time 117. Degrees conferred: M.A., C.M.H., M.M.H., M.Litt., Ph.D.

ADMISSION REQUIREMENTS. Transcripts, GRE (for U.S. and Canadian citizens), three letters of reference, writing sample required in support of School's application. TOEFL, TWE required for international applicants. Interview encouraged. Accepts transfer applicants. Graduates of Unaccredited Institutions not considered. Apply to Office of Graduate Admissions by February 1 (M.A., Ph.D. candidates). For Spring application deadline contact Admissions Office. Application fee $35. Phone: (973)408-3110; fax: (973)408-3242; e-mail: gradm@drew.edu.

ADMISSION STANDARDS. Selective. Usual minimum average: 3.3 (A = 4).

FINANCIAL AID. Scholarships, fellowships, merit awards, Federal W/S, loans. Apply to the Financial Aid Office by February 15. Phone: (973)408-3112; fax: (973)408-3188. Use FAFSA. About 70% of students receive aid other than loans from University and outside sources. Aid available for part-time students.

DEGREE REQUIREMENTS. For master's: one year minimum in residence; reading knowledge of French or German or substitute; thesis. For Ph.D.: three years in full-time residence beyond the bachelor's; reading knowledge of French and German or substitute for one; final comprehensive; dissertation.

FIELDS OF STUDY.
Arts and Letters. Interdisciplinary. M.Litt., D. Litt.
Biblical Studies and Early Christianity. M.A., Ph.D.
English Literature. Includes British and American. M.A., Ph.D.
Historical Studies. M.A., Ph.D.
Liturgical Studies. M.A., Ph.D.
Medical Humanities. C.M.H., M.M.H., D.M.H.
Modern History and Literature. Interdisciplinary. M.A., Ph.D.
New Testament. M.A., Ph.D.
Religion and Society. Includes Christian social ethics; sociology and anthropology of religion; psychology and religion. M.A., Ph.D.
Religion of Ancient Israel. M.A., Ph.D.
Theological and Religious Studies. Includes philosophic, theology, historical, theology and church history, theological studies, Methodist and Wesley studies, American religious studies, contemporary theology. M.A., Ph.D.
Wesleyan and Methodist Studies. M.A., Ph.D.
Women's Studies. M.A., Ph.D.

DREXEL UNIVERSITY
Philadelphia, Pennsylvania 19104-2875
Web site: www.drexel.edu

Founded 1891. CGS member. Coed. Private control. Quarter system. Special facilities: Art Museum, Center for Applied Neurogerontology, Image Processing Center, Bioelectrode Research Laboratory, Center for Multidisciplinary Study and Research, Biomedical Engineering and Science Institute, Environmental Studies Institute, Survey Research Center. Library: 450,000 volumes, 7000 subscriptions. More than 6500 computers on campus for student use. Total University enrollment: 18,000.

No on-campus housing available. For off-campus information contact Dean of Students Office. Average academic year expenses: $13,500–$18,500. Phone: (215)895-3507.

College of Arts and Sciences

Tuition: per credit $835. Enrollment: full-time 67, part-time 241. College faculty: full-time 58, part-time 89. Degrees conferred: M.S., Ph.D.

ADMISSION REQUIREMENTS. Transcripts, at least two letters of recommendation required in support of application. Online application available. GRE General/Subject Test suggested for some departments. TOEFL (score must be two years old or less) required for international applicants. Accepts transfer applicants. Graduates of unaccredited institutions not considered. Apply to University Office of Admissions by August 20 (Fall), November 2 (Winter), March 1 (Spring), May 31 (Summer); International students June 20 (Fall), September 25 (Winter), January 3 (Spring), March 31 (Summer). Application fee $50. Phone: (215)895-6700; fax: (215)895-5939; e-mail: enroll@drexel.edu.

ADMISSIONS STANDARDS. Selective for most departments. Usual minimum average: 3.0 (A = 4) for last two years, 2.75 (A = 4) may be admitted on a probationary basis, departmental approval required.

FINANCIAL AID. Annual awards from institutional funds, research assistantships, teaching assistantships, research fellowships, tuition waivers, Federal W/S, loans. Use FAFSA (School code: 003256). Phone: (215)895-1021. Apply to appropriate department chair by February 1. About 50% of full-time students receive aid from University and outside sources. Aid available for part-time students.

DEGREE REQUIREMENTS. For M.S.: 45 quarter credits minimum, at least 30 in residence; comprehensive exam. For Ph.D.: three-year minimum beyond the bachelor's, at least one year in full-time residence; preliminary exam; advancement to candidacy; dissertation; final oral exam.

FIELDS OF STUDY.
Biological Sciences. M.S., Ph.D.
Chemistry. M.S., Ph.D.
Clinical Psychology. Ph.D.
Communication. M.S.
Environmental Policy. M.S.
Environmental Science. M.S., Ph.D.
Human Nutrition. M.S.
Mathematics. M.S., Ph.D.
Physics. M.S., Ph.D.
Publication Management. M.S.
Science, Technology and Society. M.S.

Bennett S. Lebow College of Business
Web site: www.lebow.drexel.edu

Private control. Accredited programs: M.B.A., Accounting; recognized Ph.D. Quarter system.

Tuition: $1050 per credit. Estimated annual budget for room and board and personal expenses: approximately $12,500.

Enrollment: total full-time 294, part-time 483 (men 65%, women 35%). Faculty: 85 full-time, 23 part-time; 85% with Ph.D./D.B.A. Degrees conferred: M.B.A. (full-time, part-time, day, evening), M.S.Acc., M.S.D.S. (Decision Sciences), M.S.F. (Finance), M.S.M. (Marketing), M.S.T. (Taxation), Ph.D.

ADMISSION REQUIREMENTS. All applicants should have a bachelor's degree from a recognized institution of higher education, a strong mathematics background and a 3.0 (A = 4) GPA. Submit Application, GMAT (will accept GMAT test results from the last five years, latest acceptable date is June), two official transcripts from each undergraduate/graduate school attended, two letters of recommendation, essays, résumé (prefers at least four years of work experience), and an application fee of $50 to the Graduate Admissions Office of the College of Business. In addition, international students (whose native language is other than English) should submit TOEFL (scores not older than two years, minimum score 600), certified translations and evaluations of all official transcripts, recommendation should be in English or with certified translations, proof of health/immunization certificate, and proof of sufficient financial resources for two years of academic study. Beginning students are admitted Fall, Winter, Spring, Summer. U.S. citizens apply by August 1 (Fall), December 1 (Winter), March 1 (Spring), May 1 (Summer), international students apply by June 15 (Fall), September 20 (Winter), January 1 (Spring), June 1 (Summer). Application fee: $50. On-campus visits are encouraged. Admissions Office phone: (215) 895-0592; e-mail: enroll@drexel.edu.

ADMISSION REQUIREMENTS FOR DOCTORAL CANDIDATES. University has adopted an alternate year approach to doctoral study and will admit doctoral candidates in odd-number years only. Contact Doctoral Programs in Business for application material and information; phone: (215)895-2131; fax: (215) 895-1745. For serious consideration an applicant should have at least a 3.0 (A = 4) UGPA and a 3.3 (A = 4) Graduate GPA. Beginning students are admitted Fall Only. Both U.S. citizens and international applicants should apply by February 1 (Fall). Submit application, GMAT/GRE (will accept GMAT/GRE test results from the last five years), official transcripts from each undergraduate/graduate schools attended, two letters of recommendation, personal statement, résumé, statement of purpose, and application fee of $35 to the Office of Graduate Admission. In addition, international students (whose native language is other than English) should submit a TOEFL (score not older than two years, minimum score 600) report; certified translations and evaluations of all official transcripts, recommendation should be in English or with certified translations, proof of health/immunization certificate. Graduate Admissions Office phone: (215)895-6704; Doctoral Programs office phone: (215)895-1745.

ADMISSION STANDARDS. Selective. Mean GMAT: 577; mean GPA: 3.24 (A = 4). Accepts about 37% of total annual applicant pool.

FINANCIAL AID. State grants, fellowships, graduate assistantships, Federal W/S, loans. Request fellowship and assistantships information from the College of Business. Financial Aid applications should be completed by March 1. Contact the University's Financial Aid Office for current need-based financial aid information; phone: (215)895-2537. For most financial assistance and all Federal programs submit FAFSA (College code: 003256), also submit Financial Aid Transcript, Federal Income Tax forms. Approximately 20% of students receive some form of financial assistance. Aid available for part-time study.

DEGREE REQUIREMENTS. For M.B.A.: 84 quarter hour program including 12 elective hours, two-year program; degree program must be completed in seven years. For M.S.Acc., M.S.F., M.S.D.S., M.S.M., M.S.T.: 48 quarter hour program. For Ph.D.: 57 quarter hours beyond masters, at least three consecutive terms in full-time study, generally a three- to five-year program; comprehensive exam in major and minor field; written and oral candidacy exam, Core exams, Specialization exams; dissertation proposal and oral defense; dissertation; oral defense.

FIELDS OF STUDY.
Accounting. M.S.Acc., Ph.D.
Business Administration. Ph.D.
Decision Sciences. M.S.D.S., Ph.D.
Economics. M.B.A., Ph.D.

Finance. M.S.F., Ph.D.
Legal Studies. M.B.A.
Management. M.B.A.
Marketing. M.S.M., Ph.D.
Organizational Sciences. Ph.D.
Quantitative Methods. M.S.
Statistics. Ph.D.
Strategic Management. Ph.D.
Taxation. M.S.T.

College of Engineering

Tuition: per credit $835. Enrollment: full-time 300, part-time 644 (men 80%, women 20%). Faculty: full-time 100, part-time 20. Degrees conferred: M.S., Ph.D.

ADMISSION REQUIREMENTS. Transcripts, two letters of recommendation required in support of College's application. GRE strongly recommended for applicants requesting assistantships. TOEFL (scores must be two years old or less) required for international applicants. Accepts transfer applicants. Graduates of unaccredited institutions not considered. Apply to University Office of Admissions by August 20 (Fall), November 2 (Winter), March 1 (Spring), May 30 (Summer); international students June 20 (Fall), September 25 (Winter), January 3 (Spring), March 31 (Summer). Application fee $50. Phone: (215)895-6700; fax: (215)895-5939; e-mail: enroll@drexel.edu.

ADMISSION STANDARDS. Selective for most departments. Usual minimum average: 3.0 (A = 4) for last two years; 2.75 may be admitted on a probationary basis; departmental approval required.

FINANCIAL AID. Annual awards from institutional funds: research assistantships, teaching assistantships, fellowships, tuition waivers, Federal W/S, loans. Approved for VA benefits. Apply by February 1 to appropriate department chair for fellowships, assistantship; to Financial Aid Office for all other programs. Phone: (215)895-2964. Use FAFSA (School code: 003256). About 50% of full-time students receive aid from University and outside sources. Aid available for part-time students.

DEGREE REQUIREMENTS. For M.S.: 45 credit hours minimum, at least 30 in residence; comprehensive exam. For Ph.D.: 90 credits, three-year minimum beyond the bachelor's, at least one year in residence (requirement varies by Department); qualifying exam; candidacy; dissertation; final oral exam.

FIELDS OF STUDY.
Biochemical Engineering.
Biomedical Engineering and Sciences. Multidisciplinary.
Chemical Engineering.
Civil Engineering.
Computer Engineering. M.S. only.
Computer Science.
Electrical Engineering.
Engineering Geology. M.S. only.
Engineering Management. M.S. only.
Environmental Engineering.
Manufacturing Engineering.
Materials Engineering.
Mechanical Engineering.
Software Engineering. Multidisciplinary.
Telecommunications Engineering.

College of Information Science and Technology

Founded 1892. Tuition: per credit $835. Enrollment: full-time 81, part-time 480. Faculty: full-time 27, part-time 25. Degrees conferred: M.S., M.S.I.S., Ph.D.

ADMISSION REQUIREMENTS. Official transcripts, two letters of recommendation, résumé, GRE required in support of College's application. TOEFL (scores must be two years old or less) required for international applicants. Interview not required. Accepts transfer applicants. Graduates of unaccredited institutions not considered. Apply to Office of Graduate Admissions of the College at least one month prior to registration. Application fee $50. Phone: (215)895-6700; fax: (215)895-5939; e-mail: enroll@drexel.edu.

ADMISSION STANDARDS. Competitive. Usual minimum average: 3.0 (A = 4).

FINANCIAL AID. Annual awards from institutional funds: scholarships, research/teaching assistantships, Federal W/S, loans. Apply by February 1 to Office of the Dean for assistantships; to Financial Aid Office for all other programs. Phone: (215)895-2474. Use FAFSA (School code: 003256). About 20% of students receive aid other than loans from School and outside sources. Aid available for part-time students.

DEGREE REQUIREMENTS. For M.S., M.S.I.S.; 60 quarter hours minimum, at least 30 in residence. For Ph.D.: one year, full-time residence; approved plan of study; dissertation; final oral exam.

FIELDS OF STUDY.
Information Studies. Ph.D. only.
Information Systems. M.S.I.S. only.
Information Technology/Leadership. M.S.
Library and Information Science. M.S. only.

Westphal College of Media Arts and Design

Graduate study since 1952. Tuition: per credit $670 (Interior Design), $835 (all other programs). Enrollment: full-time 72, part-time 90. Graduate faculty: full-time 35, part-time 90. Degrees conferred: M.S., M.Arch.

ADMISSION REQUIREMENTS. Transcripts, two letters of recommendation required in support of application. TOEFL (scores must be no more than two years old) required for international applicants. Interview recommended. Accepts transfer applicants and a limited number of nonmatriculants. Graduates of unaccredited institutions not considered. Apply to Dean of Graduate Admissions. Application fee $50. Phone: (215)895-6700; fax: (215)895-5939.

ADMISSION STANDARDS. Very selective. Usual minimum average: 3.0 (A = 4).

FINANCIAL AID. Research assistantships, teaching assistantships, Federal W/S, loans. graduate assistantships for second-year students. Apply by February 1 to Office of the Dean for assistantships; to Financial Aid Office for all other programs; no specified closing date. Phone: (215)895-2474. Use FAFSA (School code: 003256).

DEGREE REQUIREMENTS. For M.S.: 45 quarter credits minimum, at least 30 in residence; major comprehensive project. For M.Arch.: 48 credits, two- to three-year evening program.

FIELDS OF STUDY.
Architecture. M.Arch.
Arts Administration. M.S.
Digital Media. M.S.
Fashion Design. M.S.
Interior Design. M.S.
Media Arts.
Television Management. M.S.

School of Biomedical Engineering, Science and Health Systems

Founded 1961 as the Biomedical Engineering Institute. Tuition: per credit $835. Enrollment: full-time 21, part-time 52. Faculty: full-time 17, part-time 45. Degrees conferred; M.S., Ph.D.

ADMISSION REQUIREMENTS. Transcripts, two letters of recommendation, essay, résumé required in support of School's application. GRE required for applicants requesting assistantships. TOEFL (minimum score 550) required for international applicants. Accepts transfer applicants. Graduates of unaccredited institutions not considered. Apply to University Office of Admissions by August 15 (Fall), November 15 (Winter), February 15 (Spring), May 15 (Summer); international students June 15 (Fall), September 15 (Winter), December 15 (Spring), March 15 (Summer). Application fee $50. Phone: (215)895-6700, fax(215)895-5939; e-mail: enroll@drexel.edu.

ADMISSION STANDARDS. Selective for most departments. Usual minimum average: 3.0 (A = 4) for last two years; applicants with 2.75 may be admitted on a nonmatriculated basis; departmental approval required.

FINANCIAL AID. Annual awards from institutional funds: research assistantships, teaching assistantships, fellowships, tuition waivers, Federal W/S, loans. Career Integrated Education is available. Approved for VA benefits. Apply by February 28 to appropriate department chair for fellowships, assistantship; to Financial Aid Office for all other programs. Phone: (215) 895-2964. Use FAFSA (School code: 003256). About 50% of full-time students receive aid from University and outside sources. Aid available for part-time students.

DEGREE REQUIREMENTS. For M.S.: 45 credit hours minimum, at least 30 in residence; comprehensive exam. For Ph.D.: 90 credit minimum, three-year program beyond the bachelor's, at least one year in full-time residence (requirement varies by Department); qualifying exam; candidacy exam; dissertation; oral defense.

FIELDS OF STUDY
Biomedical Engineering. Includes biomaterials and tissue engineering, biomechanics and human performance engineering, biosensors and biomedical imaging. Genome sciences and bioinformatics, functional bioinformatics, neuroengineering. M.S., Ph.D.
Biomedical Sciences. Includes biomaterials and tissue engineering, bioinformatics. M.S., Ph.D.

School of Education

Tuition: per credit $835. Enrollment: full- and part-time 500. School faculty: full-time 18, part-time 26. Degrees conferred: M.S., Ph.D.

ADMISSION REQUIREMENTS. Transcripts, two letters of recommendation, essay required in support of School's application. TOEFL (minimum score 550) required for international applicants. Accepts transfer applicants. Graduates of unaccredited institutions not considered. Apply to University Office of Admission by August 1 (Fall), October 1 (Spring), March 1 (Summer). Application fee $50. Phone: (215)895-6700; fax (215)895-5939; e-mail: enroll@drexel.edu.

ADMISSION STANDARDS. Usual minimum average: 3.0 (A = 4).

FINANCIAL AID. Annual awards from institutional funds: assistantships, fellowships, tuition waivers Federal W/S, loans. Career Integrated Education available. Approved for VA benefits. Apply by February 15 to appropriate department chair for fellowships, assistantships; to Financial Aid Office for all other programs.

Phone: (215)895-2964. Use FAFSA (School code: 003256). About 35% of full-time students receive aid from University and outside sources. Aid available for part-time students.

DEGREE REQUIREMENTS. For M.S.: 45–48 credit hours minimum, at least 30 in residence; thesis/nonthesis option. For Ph.D.: 90 credit minimum, three-year program beyond the bachelor; at least one year in full-time residence (requirements vary by department); qualifying exam; candidacy exam; dissertation; oral defense.

FIELDS OF STUDY.
Educational Administration. M.S.
Educational Leadership Development and Learning Technologies. Ph.D.
Higher Education. M.S.
Human Resource Development. M.S.
Learning Technologies. M.S.
Mathematics Learning and Teaching. M.S.
Science of Instruction. M.S.
Teaching, Learning and Curriculum. M.S.

DREXEL UNIVERSITY HEALTH SCIENCES

Established 2002. Located at the Hahneman Center City campus. On-campus housing available. Housing costs $500–$800 per month.

College of Nursing and Health Professions
Web site: cnhp.drexel.edu

Established 2002. Tuition: $20,200, Nursing $18,675.

Enrollment full- and part-time 1425. Faculty: full- and part-time more than 450. Degrees conferred M.F.T., M.H.S., M.S., M.S.N., D.P.T., Ph.D., J.D.-Ph.D. (Psychology).

ADMISSION REQUIREMENTS. Official transcripts, three letters of recommendation required in support of application. GRE/MAT, interview, essays, résumés required for some programs. Online application available. TOEFL (minimum score 550) required for international applicants. Accepts transfer applicants in some programs. Admits Fall only. Apply to the Office of Enrollment Services by December 1 (Physician Assistant entry-level), December 15 (D.P.T. entry-level), January 15 (Clinical Psychology—Ph.D.), February 1 (Couple and Family Therapy), February 15 (Clinical Psychology—M.A., M.S., J.D.-Ph.D.), March 15 (Rehabilitation Sciences), April 1 (Family Therapy), June 1 (Art Therapy, Dance Therapy), July 1 (Music Therapy), 16–24 months in advance of January start date (M.S.N. in Anesthesia). Phone: (800)2-DREXEL, ext. 6333.

ADMISSION STANDARDS. Selective. Usual minimum average: 2.75 (A = 4).

FINANCIAL AID. Scholarships, fellowships, research/teaching assistantships, internships, traineeships, grants. Federal W/S, loans. Apply to Office of University Student Financial Affairs by January 1 for assistantships, fellowships; March 1 for all other programs. Phone: (215)762-7739; fax (215)762-4261. Use FAFSA (School code: 003271). About 40% of students receive some financial assistance from school; about 95% of doctoral students receive aid from School.

DEGREE REQUIREMENTS. For M.F.T., M.S.: usually a two-year full-time program; supervised practica/internships. For M.H.S.: 119 semester hour, 27-month program; graduate project. For M.S.N.: 39–48 credit program, practicum/clinical practicum. For M.S.N. in Anesthesia program: 27-month, 66-credit full-time program; clinical practicum. For D.P.T. three-year full-time, 8 academic semester program; research project.

FIELDS OF STUDY.
Art Therapy. M.A.
Clinical Nurse Leader. Includes adult health, pediatric health, women's health. M.S.N.
Clinical Trials Research. M.S.N.
Contemporary Nursing Faculty. M.S.N.
Couple and Family Therapy. Ph.D.
Dance/Movement Therapy. M.A.
Family Therapy. M.F.T.
Innovative and Intra/Entrepreneurship in Advanced Nursing Practices. M.S.N.
Nurse Anesthesia. M.S.N.
Nurse Practitioner. Includes acute care, family, pediatrics, psychiatric mental health, women's health. M.S.N.
Nursing Leadership in Health System Management. M.S.N.
Nursing Practice. Dr.N.P.
Physical Therapy and Rehabilitation Sciences. D.P.T., M.H.S., Ph.D.
Physician Assistant Studies. M.H.S.

College of Medicine
Web site: www.drexelmed.edu

Medical College of Pennsylvania founded 1850, Hanemann University School of Medicine founded 1848, merged with Drexel University and name was changed 2002. Private control. Library: 50,000 volumes, 1050 subscriptions. NIH ranking is 149 among all U.S. institutions with 86 awards/grants worth $26,900,388.

Annual tuition: $40,800. No on-campus housing available. All students live in off-campus housing. Total average figure for all other expenses: $15,700.

Enrollment: first-year class 250, total full-time 1025 (men 50%, women 50%, minorities 43%, state residents 30%). Faculty: full-time 510, part-time 59. Degrees conferred: M.D., M.D.-M.B.A., M.D.-M.P.H., M.D.-Ph.D.

ADMISSION REQUIREMENTS. AMCAS report, transcripts, MCAT, letters of recommendation required in support of application. Supplemental application will be sent 4–6 weeks after applying to AMCAS. Interviews are by invitation. Will consider transfer applicants on a space-available basis. Has EDP: apply between June 1 and August 1. The combined degree programs require acceptance to both the College of Medicine and the respective University program. Apply to AMCAS by December 1; to M.D.-Ph.D. by November 15. Application fee $75. Phone: (215) 991-8202.

ADMISSION STANDARDS. Competitive. Accepts about 16% of all applicants. Number of applications 6475 (5795 out-of-state); number interviewed 1523 (1260 out-of-state); number of acceptance 858 (698 out-of-state); number enrolled 231 (167 out-of-state). Mean Composite MCAT 10.2; mean UGPA 3.51.

FINANCIAL AID Merit scholarships, Federal W/S, Federal and private loans. Apply to the Office of Student Financial Affairs after acceptance, before May 31. Phone: (215)991-8210. Use PHEAA and FAFSA (School code: 003256). About 85% of students receive aid from School.

DEGREE REQUIREMENTS. For M.D.: satisfactory completion of four-year program. Accelerated M.D. available. All students must pass USMLE Step 1 prior to entering third year and must pass USMLE Step 2 prior to awarding of M.D.

FIELDS OF GRADUATE STUDY.
Biochemistry.
Clinical Research. M.S. only.
Forensic Science. M.S. only.
Molecular Biology and Genetics.
Molecular Medicine.
Microbiology and Immunology.
Neuroengineering

Neuroscience.
Pathologists' Assistant. M.S. only.
Pathology.
Pharmacology and Physiology.
Physical Cell Biology.

Biomedical Graduate Studies

Annual tuition $19,150, per credit $1065; Certificate programs $10,000–$17,876. Enrollment in degree programs: full-time 75, part-time 90, total 245. Faculty: 75, part-time 25. Degrees conferred: M.S., Ph.D., M.D.-Ph.D.

ADMISSION REQUIREMENTS. Official transcripts, GRE, three letters of recommendation, personal statement of research interest required in support of application. VCAT can be used in lieu of GRE for Certificate programs; MCAT can be used in lieu of GRE. Online application available. Interviews required for some programs. TOEFL required for international applicants. Accepts transfer applicants. Graduates of unaccredited institutions not considered. Apply by November 1 (M.D.-Ph.D.), March 1 (all other programs) to Office of Enrollment Services. Phone: (866)-6BIOMED. Application fee $50.

ADMISSIONS STANDARDS. Selective. Usual minimum average 3.0 (A = 4).

FINANCIAL AID. Scholarships, stipends, research/teaching assistantships, Federal W/S, loans. Apply May 1 to the Biomedical Graduate Studies Office for scholarships, assistantships, to the Office of Student Financial Services for all other programs. Phone: (215)762-7739. Use FAFSA (School code: 003256). About 70% of students receive some form of financial assistance.

DEGREE REQUIREMENTS. For M.S.: 39–48 credit programs, comprehensive exam, thesis/nonthesis option. For Ph.D.: 60 semester hours program; preliminary exam after one year; qualifying exam; dissertation; final oral defense. For Certificates: generally two semesters in full-time study.

FIELDS OF GRADUATE STUDY.
Biochemistry.
Molecular Biology.
Molecular Medicine.
Microbiology and Immunology.
Neuroengineering.
Neuroscience.
Pathology.
Pharmacology and Physiology.
Physical Cell Biology.

School of Public Health

Established 1996. Semester system. Tuition: per credit $790 (Dr.P.H.), $770 (all other programs). Enrollment: full- and part-time 75 (men 25%, women 75%). Faculty: full- and part-time 21. Degrees conferred, M.P.H., M.D.-M.P.H.

ADMISSION REQUIREMENTS. Official transcripts, three letters of recommendation, essay, résumé, interview required in support of application. Will accept GRE, MCAT, LSAT, GMAT. Online application available. TOEFL (minimum score 550) required for international applicants. Admits Fall only. Apply by August 1 to the Office of Enrollment Management. Phone: (215) 762-8785. Application fee $50.

ADMISSION STANDARDS. Selective. Usual minimum average: 2.75 (A = 4).

FINANCIAL AID. Scholarships, assistantships, traineeships, Federal W/S, loans. Apply by April 1 to the office of University Student Financial Affairs. Phone: (215)762-7739; fax: (215)762-4261. Use FAFSA (School code: 003271).

DEGREE REQUIREMENTS. For M.P.H.: satisfactory completion of 52-credit, four- to twelve-week interdisciplinary blocks; community-based master's project. For M.D.-M.P.H.: five-year program; the third year is spent in full-time study in the School of Public Health.

FIELDS OF STUDY.
Community Health and Prevention.
Environmental and Occupation Health.
Epidemiology.
Health Management and Policy.

DRURY UNIVERSITY
Springfield, Missouri 65802-3791
Web site: www.drury.edu

Founded 1873. Located 180 miles SE of Kansas City. Coed. Private control, United Church of Christ Congregational Church. Semester system. Library: 244,000 volumes, 800 subscriptions.

Tuition; M.B.A., per semester hour $550; M.Ed., per semester hour $265; Criminal Justice $350. On-campus housing for single students only. Average annual housing cost: single student $4000 (including board), married students $3500 (room only). During Summer terms (two 5-week terms): single person $295 per term. Apply to Dean of Students. Phone: (417)873-7215.

College of Graduate and Continuing Studies

Enrollment: 300, most are part-time. College faculty teaching graduate students: full-time 25, part-time 20. Degrees conferred: M.B.A., M.Ed.

ADMISSION REQUIREMENTS: Transcripts, MAT or GMAT (depending on major) required in support of application. Online application available. TOEFL required for international applicants. Accepts transfer applicants. Graduates of unaccredited institutions not considered. Apply to Director of appropriate program well in advance of registration. Application fee $25. Phone: (417)873-7271; fax: (417)873-7269.

ADMISSION STANDARDS. Selective. Usual minimum average: 2.75 (A = 4).

FINANCIAL AID. Fellowships, teaching assistantships, Federal W/S, loans. Apply by May 15 to Director of appropriate program for fellowships, assistantships; to Financial Aid Office for federal programs. Phone: (417)873-7312. Use FAFSA.

DEGREE REQUIREMENTS. For M.Ed.: 36 semester hours for degree. For M.B.A.: 31 semester hours required, 25 in residence plus 24 hours of undergraduate prerequisite courses.

FIELDS OF STUDY.
Business Administration. M.B.A.
Communication. M.A.
Criminal Justice. M.S.C.J.
Criminology. M.A.C.
Education. Includes elementary, gifted, human services, instructional mathematics K–8, instructional technology, middle school, secondary, special education, special reading. M.Ed.

UNIVERSITY OF DUBUQUE
Dubuque, Iowa 52001-5099
Web site: www.dbq.edu

Founded 1852. Located 185 miles W of Chicago. Coed. Private control. Affiliated with the Presbyterian Church (U.S.A.). Semester system. Library: 165,000 volumes, 700 subscriptions.

Tuition: per semester credit $485. On-campus housing available for single students, but limited for married students. Average academic year housing costs: single students $7900 (including board). Contact the Director of Housing for both on- and off-campus housing information. Phone: (563)589-3583.

Graduate Studies

Graduate study since 1964. Enrollment: full-time 192, part-time 120. College faculty teaching graduate students: full-time 21, part-time 12. Degrees conferred: M.A., M.A.R., M.B.A., M.Div., D.Min. (pastoral leadership, congregational revitalization).

ADMISSION REQUIREMENTS. Transcripts, two letters of recommendation, personal statement, eligibility for School Certification (Education), GRE/MAT/GMAT required in support of application. TOEFL (minimum score 550) required for international applicants. Accepts transfer applicants. Apply to Graduate Studies at least one month prior to registration. Application fee $25. Phone: (563)589-3300, (800)722-5583.

ADMISSION STANDARDS. Selective. Usual minimum average: 2.5 (A = 4).

FINANCIAL AID. Limited to assistantships, Federal W/S, loans, and area Professional Development Grants. Apply by May 1 to the Office of Financial Aid. Phone: (563)589-3170; e-mail: finaid@duq.edu. Use FAFSA.

DEGREE REQUIREMENTS. For master's: 36–45 semester hours minimum, at least 30 in residence; thesis/nonthesis option. For M.Div.: three-year program of full-time study. For M.A.R.: two-year program of full-time study. For D.Min.: three- to five-year part-time weekend and summer program for full-time clerical workers.

FIELDS OF STUDY.
Business Administration M.B.A.
Communication. Includes global public relations management, leadership and management communication, strategic and corporate communication. M.A.C.
Divinity. M.Div., D.Min.
Education. M.A.Ed.
Religion. Includes specializations in biblical studies, history and theology, pastoral theology and counseling, rural ministry, spiritual foundation. M.A.R.

DUKE UNIVERSITY
Durham, North Carolina 27708-0065
Web site: www.duke.edu

Founded 1838. CGS and AAU member. Private control. Semester system. Special facilities: Animal Behavior Station, Asian-Pacific Institute, Botanical and Zoological Laboratories, Canadian Studies program, Center for Demographic Studies, Center for Documentary Studies, Center on East-West Trade Investments and Communications, Center for Emerging Cardiovascular Technologies, Center for Health Policy Research and Education, Center for International Development Research, Center for International Studies, Center for Mathematics and Computation in Life Sciences and Medicine, Center for the Study of Aging and Human Development, Center for Tropical Conservation, Center for Research on Women, Duke Forest with 7700 acres, Marine Laboratory, Morphometrics Laboratory, Oak Ridges National Laboratory, Organization for Tropical Studies, Phytotron, Primate Facilities, Program in Integrative Biology, Program in Latin-American Studies, Program in Political Economy, Program in Russian and East European Studies. The University's NIH rank-ing is 6th among all U.S. institutions with 795 awards/grants valued at $391,196,272. According to The Center at University of Florida, the University is ranked 15th in receipt of Federal Research fund with $306,864,000, and it ranks 10th for total University research expenditures with $520,191,000. The University's endowment assets rank it 14th, with a value of $3,313,859,000. In 2004, the University awarded 259 doctorates which ranked it 55th among all U.S. institutions eligible to award that degree. 21 of the University's faculty members have been elected to National Honor Academies and this ranks it 48th among all U.S. institutions. The Library: approximately 5,500,000 volumes, 36,900 subscriptions. Total University enrollment: 14,075.

Annual tuition: full-time $29,340 (Ph.D. students); per unit $978 (master's students). On-campus apartments: 206 available for single students. Average cost per academic year of an on-campus single room $5350, married housing $10,700. Contact Office of Housing Administration for both on- and off-campus housing information. Phone: (919)684-4304.

Graduate School

Enrollment: full- and part-time 2791. Faculty: full-time 800, part-time 267. Degrees conferred: A.M., M.S., M.A.T., Ph.D.

ADMISSION REQUIREMENTS. Two copies of official transcript from each college, university, or seminary attended, three letters of recommendation, GRE required in support of School's application. Online application available. GRE Subject Test required for some programs. International applicants must submit a TOEFL (minimum score 550, 213 on computer-based test) report and a financial statement. Accepts transfer applicants. Graduates of unaccredited colleges not considered. Apply to the Graduate School Office of Enrollment Services by December 31 (Fall), November 1 (Spring). For Summer Session apply to the Dean of the Graduate School and to the Director of the Summer Session by April 15 (Summer Session I), May 15 (Summer Session II). Application fee $75. Phone: (919)684-3913; E-mail: grad-admission @duke.edu.

ADMISSION STANDARDS. Competitive for most departments, very competitive for the other. Usual minimum average: 3.0 (A = 4).

FINANCIAL AID. Annual awards: Scholarships, fellowships, teaching assistantships, traineeships, research assistantships, Federal W/S, loans. Apply to the Dean of the Graduate School for fellowships, assistantships. The application form for admission is also the application for financial aid, and should be completed by December 31. Use FAFSA (School code: E00165). About 80% of full-time students receive aid other than loans from University and outside sources.

DEGREE REQUIREMENTS. For A.M., M.S., M.A.T.: 30 credits minimum; thesis; final oral exam; nonthesis option in some departments. For Ph.D.: 60 credits minimum beyond the bachelor's, at least one year full-time in residence; language requirements vary by department; preliminary exam; dissertation; final oral exam.

FIELDS OF STUDY.
Art, Architecture and Visual Culture. Ph.D.
Biochemistry. Ph.D. only.
Biological Anthropology and Anatomy. Ph.D.
Biological Chemistry. Ph.D.
Biology. Ph.D.
Biomedical Engineering. Ph.D.
Business Administration. Ph.D.
Cell and Molecular Biology. Ph.D.
Cell Biology. Ph.D.
Chemistry. Ph.D.
Civil and Environmental Engineering. M.S., Ph.D.
Classical Studies. Ph.D.

Computational Biology and Bioinformatics. Ph.D.
Computer Science. Ph.D.
Cultural Anthropology. Ph.D.
Earth and Ocean Sciences (Geology). M.S., Ph.D.
East Asian Studies. A.M.
Ecology. Ph.D.
Economics. A.M., Ph.D.
Electrical and Computer Engineering. M.S., Ph.D.
English. Ph.D.
Environment. A.M., Ph.D.
Genetics and Genomics. Ph.D.
Germanic Studies. Ph.D.
History. Ph.D.
Humanities Program. A.M.
Immunology. Ph.D.
International Development Policy. A.M.
Liberal Studies. A.M.
Literature. Ph.D.
Marine Science. A.M., M.S., Ph.D.
Mathematics. Ph.D.
Mechanical Engineering and Materials Science. M.S., Ph.D.
Medical Physics. M.S., Ph.D.
Molecular Cancer Biology.
Molecular Genetics and Microbiology. Ph.D.
Music. A.M., Ph.D.
Neurobiology. Ph.D.
Pathology. Ph.D.
Pharmacology. Ph.D.
Philosophy. Ph.D.
Physics. Ph.D.
Political Science. A.M., Ph.D.
Psychology. Includes experimental, social and health science. Ph.D. only.
Public Policy Studies. A.M. only.
Religion. Ph.D.
Romance Studies. Ph.D.
Slavic and Eurasian Studies. A.M.
Sociology. A.M., Ph.D.
Statistics. Ph.D.

Fuqua School of Business
Web site: www.fuqua.duke.edu

Established 1969. Accredited programs: M.B.A.; recognized Ph.D. Semester/term system. Library: 22,000 volumes, 1200 subscriptions. Special programs: foreign exchange programs (Australia, Belgium, Costa Rica, Denmark, France, Italy, the Netherlands, Norway, South Africa, Spain, Sweden, Switzerland, Thailand, United Kingdom). Special facilities: Center for the Advancement of Social Entrepreneurship, Center for Entrepreneurship and Innovation, Center for International Business Education and Research, Duke Global Capital Markets Center, Center for Customer Relationship Management, Fuqua/Coach K Center of Leadership and Ethics.

Annual tuition: M.B.A. full-time $41,670, M.B.A.—Cross-Continent $101,900, W.E.M.B.A. $97,500, G.E.M.B.A. $123,500 (total program includes laptop, printer, tuition, books, room and board).

Enrollment: total full-time 800; 78 in doctoral programs. Faculty: 64 full-time, 25 part-time; 75% with Ph.D./D.B.A. Degrees conferred: M.B.A., G.E.M.B.A. (Global Executive), W.E.M.B.A. (Weekend Executive), M.B.A.-J.D., M.B.A.-M.D., M.B.A.-M.F. (Forestry), M.B.A.-M.E.M. (Environmental Management), M.B.A.-M.P.P. (Public Policy), M.B.A.-M.S. (Engineering, Nursing), Ph.D.

ADMISSION REQUIREMENTS. All applicants should have a bachelor's degree from a recognized institution of higher education and a strong mathematics background. Students are required to have their own personal computer. Will accept institutional on-line application. Submit application, GMAT (will accept GMAT test results from the last five years, latest acceptable date is Janu-

ary), official transcripts from each undergraduate/graduate school attended, three letters of recommendation, two essays, résumé (prefers at least four years of work experience), and an application fee of $150 to the Admission Office. In addition, international students (whose native language is other than English) should submit a TOEFL (minimum score 600) report, certified translations and evaluations of all official transcripts, recommendation should be in English or with certified translations, proof of health/immunization certificate, and proof of sufficient financial resources for two years of academic study. On-campus interviews are strongly recommended prior to the admissions committee reviewing completed application. To arrange an interview call: (919)660-7705. Joint degree applicants must apply to and be accepted to both schools/programs, contact the admissions office for current information and specific admissions requirements. Beginning students are admitted Fall only. Both U.S. citizens and international applicants apply by April 1 (Fall, final deadline). Applications received and interview completed by November 15 will be notified by December 18; applications received and interview completed by December 18 will be notified by January 29; applications received and interview completed by February 6 will be notified by April 7; applications received and interview completed by March 19 will be notified by April 23; applications received and interview completed by April 16 will be notified by May 21. Admissions Office phone: (919)660-7805; G.E.M.B.A. and W.E.M.B.A. phone: (919)660-7705; e-mail: fuqua-wemba@mail.duke.edu.

ADMISSION REQUIREMENTS FOR DOCTORAL CANDIDATES. Contact Ph.D. Programs at (919)660-7862 for application material and information. Beginning students are admitted Fall Only. Both U.S. citizens and international applicants apply by February 1. Submit Graduate School application (online preferred), a GMAT/GRE (will accept GMAT/GRE test results from the last five years), official transcripts from each undergraduate/graduate school attended, three letters of recommendation, résumé, statement of purpose, and application fee of $75 to the Graduate School's Director of Admission, 127 Allen Building. In addition, international students (whose native language is other than English) should submit a TOEFL (minimum score 600) report; certified translations and evaluations of all official transcripts, recommendation should be in English or with certified translations, proof of health/immunization certificate. International student's contact: (919)660-7807. Interviews encouraged. Notification is generally completed by mid-April. Graduate School phone: (919)684-3913.

ADMISSION STANDARDS. For M.B.A.: median GMAT: 700; median GPA: 3.5 (A = 4). For Ph.D: average GPA range: 3.5–3.7; average GMAT range: 520–795. *U.S. News & World Report* ranked Fuqua (M.B.A.) in the top 12 of all U.S. business schools; in Management ranked 8th, Marketing 3rd, Nonprofit 7th. *BusinessWeek* listed Fuqua in the top 11 of all American business schools.

FINANCIAL AID. Scholarships, merit scholarship, school funded minority scholarships, full tuition grants, fellowship, graduate assistantships, Federal W/S, loans. Financial aid is available for part-time study and aid may be available for international students. Assistantships/fellowships may be available for joint degree candidates. Financial Aid applications and information are generally available at the on-campus visit/interview or after January 1; apply by February 1. Request scholarship, fellowship, assistantship information from the Fuqua School of Business. Contact the University's Financial Aid Office for current need-based financial aid information; phone: (919)660-7934; fax: (919)681-6243. Use FAFSA (School code: E00160), also submit Financial Aid Transcript, Federal Income Tax forms. Approximately 65% of current students receive some form of financial assistance.

DEGREE REQUIREMENTS. For M.B.A.: at least 79 units including 39 elective term credits, two-year program; degree program must be completed in two years. For M.B.A. Cross-Continent: 20-month program. For G.E.M.B.A.: 19-month program. For W.E.M.B.A.: 20-month program. For M.B.A.-Master's: generally a two-and-one-half- to three-and-one-half-year programs. For M.B.A.-J.D.: four-and-one-half- to five-and-one-half-year program. For M.B.A.-M.D.: five-and-one-half- to six-and-one-half-year program. For Ph.D.: four- to five-year program; comprehensive exam; candidacy, dissertation proposal and oral defense; dissertation; oral defense.

FIELDS OF DOCTORAL STUDY (Through the Graduate School).
Accounting.
Decision Sciences.
Finance.
Management.
Marketing.
Operations Management.
Strategy.

Divinity School

Web site: www.divinity.duke.edu

Founded 1926. Annual tuition: $15,860 (M.Div., M.T.S., M.C.M.), $17,600 (Th.M.), $24,910 (Th.D.).

Enrollment: full-time 250, part-time 50. Faculty: full-time 36, part-time 22. Degrees conferred: M.Div., M.T.S., Th.M., Th.D.

ADMISSION REQUIREMENTS. Transcripts, five letters of recommendations, required in support of School's application. TOEFL, TSE required for international applicants. Interview not required. Accepts transfer applicants. Apply to Director of Admissions by April 1 (Fall), February 1 (Fall M.T.S.), December 1 (January). Application fee $25. Phone: (919)660-3436; fax: (919)660-3535; e-mail: divinity.info@duke.edu.

ADMISSION STANDARDS. Selective. Usual minimum average: 2.7 (A = 4); for M.T.S.: 3.0; for Th.M.: 3.25.

FINANCIAL AID. Tuition grants, field education grants, scholarships, Federal W/S, loans. Apply to Financial Aid Office by May 1. Phone: (919)660-3442; fax: (919)660-3473. Use FAFSA. No aid for nondegree candidates.

DEGREE REQUIREMENTS. For M.Div.: 24-course units plus 2 field education credits. For M.C.M.: 16-course units plus 1 field education credit. For M.T.S.: 16-course units with a 2.5 GPA average. For Th.M.: 8-course units with a B average. For Th.D.: 12-course program, at least two academic years in residency; core seminar; demonstrated competence in two modern languages; preliminary exam; oral preliminary exam; dissertation; oral dissertation exam.

FIELDS OF STUDY.
Christian Education. M.Div.
Theological Studies. M.T.S.
Theology. Th.M., Th.D.

Nicholas School of the Environmental and Earth Sciences

P.O. Box 90330
Web site: www.nicholas.duke.edu

Graduate study since 1938. School moved into a new Research Center (Levine Science Research Center) in 1994. Special facility: marine laboratory. Annual tuition: $26,600; per credit $1100. Graduate enrollment: full-time 218, part-time 2 (men 48%, women 52%). Faculty: full-time 60 (includes Durham at Marine Laboratory), part-time 12. Degrees conferred: M.F., M.E.M., M.S., A.M., Ph.D. through the Graduate School.

ADMISSION REQUIREMENTS. Transcripts, three letters of recommendation, personal statement, GRE required in support of School's application. TOEFL required for international applicants. Interview not required. Graduates of unaccredited institutions not considered. Apply to Office of Enrollment Services by December 31 for M.S., A.M., Ph.D.; February 1 for M.F., M.E.M. Application fee $65 before January 1, $75 after January 1. Phone: (919)613-8070; fax: (919)684-8741; e-mail: envadm@duke.edu.

ADMISSION STANDARDS. Average of all accepted applicants: 3.4 (A = 4), 650 score on each section of GRE.

FINANCIAL AID. Scholarships, fellowships, assistantship, Federal W/S, loans. Apply by February 1 to Office of Enrollment Services. Phone: (919)613-8070. Use FAFSA.

DEGREE REQUIREMENTS. For M.F., M.E.M.: 48 semester credits (with a possible exception for professionals in the field), at least four semesters in residence; master's project. For A.M., M.S., Ph.D.: see Graduate School listing above.

FIELDS OF STUDY.
Coastal Environmental Management. M.E.M.
Ecosystems Science and Conservation. M.E.M.
Energy and Environment. M.E.M.
Environmental Economics and Policy. M.E.M., Ph.D.
Environmental Management. M.E.M.
Forest Resource Management. M.E.M., M.F.
Global Environmental Change. M.E.M.
Water and Air Resources. M.E.M.

School of Law (Box 90393)

Web site: www.law.duke.edu

Founded 1904. ABA approved since 1931. AALS member. Private control. Semester system. Located at Loop Campus. Special facilities: Center for International and Comparative Law, Center on Law, Ethics and National Security, Center for the Study of the Public Domain, Center for Genome Ethics, Law and Policy, Global Capital Markets Center; Institute for Environmental Policy Solutions, Public Interest and Pro Bono Programs, International Programs, Program in Intellectual Property. Library: 622,400 volumes, 7016 subscriptions; has LEXIS, NEXIS, WESTLAW, DIALOG, more than 800 network connections.

Annual tuition: $38,739. On-campus housing available. Contact Director of Housing for available. Total average annual additional expense: $16,000.

Enrollment: first-year class 200. Total full-time 712 (men 52%, women 48%, minorities 21%). Faculty: Total full-time 50, part-time 56 (men 78%, women 22%, minorities 9%). Student to faculty ratio 12.6 to 1. Degrees conferred: J.D., LL.M. (International and Comparative Law), LL.M (American Law for foreign lawyers), J.S.D. The School offers joint degree programs in Cultural Anthropology, Business Administration, Classical Studies, East Asian Studies, Electonics/Computer Engineering, Environmental Management, Environmental Science/Policy, Economics, History, Humanities, Mechanical Engineering, Medicine, Philosophy, Political Science, Public Policy Studies, Political Science, Psychology, Romance Studies, Sociology, Religion, Theological Studies.

ADMISSION REQUIREMENTS. LSDAS Law School report, bachelor's degree, transcripts, LSAT (no later than December), two recommendations, personal statement, résumé required in support of application. Interview not required. Transfer applicants considered. Graduates of unaccredited colleges not considered. Applications should be completed by February 15. Fall admission only. Application fee $70. Phone: (919)613-7020; fax: (919) 613-7257.

ADMISSION STANDARDS. Selective. Accepts approximately 15% of all students. Number of applicants 4486; number of acceptance 960; number enrolled 200; LSAT (75% of students have a score at or above 165); GPA (75% of students have a GPA at or above 3.54). *U.S. News & World Report* ranking is in the top 10 of all U.S. law schools.

FINANCIAL AID. Scholarships, Federal W/S, loans. Submit financial aid application with admission application. Phone: (919) 613-7026. Use FAFSA. About 30% of students receive aid other than loans from School, 80% from all sources. A loan forgiveness plan is available.

DEGREE REQUIREMENTS. For J.D.: 84 semester hours minimum, at least four semesters in residence. For LL.M: program is normally completed in one year beyond J.D.; U.S. and international students take almost all their classes together. For S.J.D.: programs arranged on an individual basis, usually requires two to three years to complete; at least one semester beyond LL.M.; thesis.

School of Medicine (27710)
Web site: www.dukemed.duke.edu

Established 1930. Located in Durham at Medical Center. Private control. Semester system. Library: 200,000 volumes, 5000 subscriptions. The University's NIH ranking is 6th among all U.S. institutions with 795 awards/grants worth $391,196,272.

Annual tuition: $41,215. Off-campus housing only. Average figure for all other expenses: $13,872.

Enrollment: first-year class 101; total full-time 408 (men 51%, women 49%, minorities 45%, state residents 16%). Faculty: full-time 1500, part-time 18. Degrees conferred: M.D., M.D.-J.D., M.D.-M.A.L.S., M.D.-M.B.A., M.D.-M.P.H., M.D.-M.P.P., M.D.-Ph.D., MSTP.

ADMISSION REQUIREMENTS. AMCAS report, transcripts, MCAT, interview required in support of application. Supplemental application required. Applicants must have completed at least three years of college study. Interviews are by invitation only. Graduates of unaccredited colleges not considered. Special consideration given to North Carolina residents. Does not have EDP. Apply to Committee on Admissions after June 1, before November 15. Application fee $80. Phone: (919)877-2985; fax: (919) 684-8893.

ADMISSION STANDARDS. Very competitive. Accepts about 4.4% of all applicants. Number of applications 5042 (4675 out-of-state); number interviewed 1024 (801 out-of-state); number of acceptance 222 (201 out-of-state); number enrolled 101 (84 out-of-state). Mean Composite MCAT 11.1; mean UGPA 3.74. *U.S. News & World Report* ranking is in the top 8 of all medical research schools, 34th in primary care.

FINANCIAL AID. Scholarships, grants, Federal and Private loans, summer research fellowships. Apply to Coordinator, Financial Aid after acceptance, before April 1. Phone: (919)684-6649. Use FAFSA and NEED ACCESS Form. About 72% of students receive some aid from School.

DEGREE REQUIREMENTS. For M.D.: satisfactory completion of four-year program. For all joint degree programs: there is usually an additional year needed to complete both degrees.

FIELDS OF GRADUATE STUDY.
Anatomy.
Biochemistry.
Biomedical Engineering.
Cell Biology.
Genetics.
Immunology.
Medical Historian Training Program.
Microbiology.
Molecular Biology.
Neurosciences.
Pathology.
Pharmacology.
Physiology.

School of Nursing
Web site: www.nursing.duke.edu

Founded 1931. Tuition: per credit $785. Graduate enrollment: full-time 123, part-time 195. Faculty: full-time 45, part-time 6. Degree conferred: M.S.

ADMISSION REQUIREMENTS. Two transcripts, three letters of recommendation, GRE or MAT, personal interview, licensure or eligibility for licensure in North Carolina required in support of School's application. TOEFL required for international applicants. Graduates of unaccredited institutions not considered. Apply to Office of Admission by July 1 (Fall), November 15 (Spring). Application fee $75. Phone: (877)415-3853; fax: (919) 684-3786.

ADMISSION STANDARDS. Usual minimum average: 3.0 (A = 4).

FINANCIAL AID. Merit scholarships, Federal W/S, loans. Apply by March 1 (Fall), October 1 (Spring) to the Office of Financial Aid. Phone: (919)613-8070. Use FAFSA (School code: E00162).

DEGREE REQUIREMENTS. For M.N.: 39–60 credit program; research option (thesis, research project, or a course in research utilization); capstone residency course.

FIELDS OF STUDY.
Clinical Nurse Specialist.
Clinical Research Management.
Nurse Anesthesia.
Nurse Practitioner.
Nursing. Ph.D.
Nursing and Healthcare Leadership.
Nursing Education.
Nursing Informatics.

DUQUESNE UNIVERSITY
Pittsburgh, Pennsylvania 15282-0001
Web site: www.duq.edu

Founded 1878. CGS member. Coed. Private control. Roman Catholic affiliation. Semester system. Library: 723,919 volumes, 3400 subscriptions. Total University enrollment: 9900. Tuition: per credit $692. On-campus housing for single students only. Average annual housing cost: $8054 (including board). Contact Housing Director for both on- and off-campus housing information. Phone: (412)396-5028 or (412)396-6660.

McAnulty Graduate School of Liberal Arts

Enrollment: full-time 442, part-time 270. Faculty: full-time 117, part-time 60. Degrees conferred: M.A., M.L.S., M.S., Ph.D.

ADMISSION REQUIREMENTS. Official transcripts, GRE/MAT, three letters of recommendation required in support of School's application. TOEFL required for international applicants. Interview required by some departments. Accepts transfer applicants. Graduates of unaccredited institutions not considered. Apply to Office of Graduate School by May 1 (Fall), January 1 (Spring). Application fee $40. Phone: (412)396-6400; fax: (412)396-5265.

ADMISSION STANDARDS. Selective to very competitive. Usual minimum average: 3.0 (A = 4).

FINANCIAL AID. Annual awards from institutional funds: scholarships, research assistantships, teaching assistantships, Federal W/S, loans. Apply by May 1 to Dean of School for assistantships, scholarships; to Financial Aid Office for all other programs. Phone: (412)396-6607. Use FAFSA. About 25% of students receive aid other than loans from School and outside sources.

DEGREE REQUIREMENTS. For master's: 24 credit hours minimum, at least one year in residence; reading knowledge of one foreign language in some departments; thesis; comprehensive exam; or 30 credit hours minimum, at least one year in residence; reading knowledge of one foreign language in some departments; comprehensive exam. For Ph.D.: 56 credits hours minimum, at least one year in residence; preliminary exam; reading knowledge of two foreign languages or one language and one language equivalency; dissertation; final oral/written exam.

FIELDS OF STUDY.
Archival, Museum, and Editing Studies. M.A.
Church Administration and Canon Law. M.A.
Clinical Psychology. Ph.D.
Computational Mathematics. M.A.
Conflict Resolution. M.A.
Corporate Communications. M.A.
English. M.A., Ph.D.
Health-Care Ethics. M.A., Ph.D.
History. M.A.
Liberal Studies. M.L.S.
Multimedia Technology. M.A.
Pastoral Ministry. M.A.
Philosophy. M.A., Ph.D.
Psychology. Essay, two letters of recommendation for admission; 30 hours minimum; thesis for M.A.; 48 hours minimum beyond the master's for Ph.D. Admits Fall semester only.
Religious Education. M.A.
Rhetoric and Philosophy of Communication. M.A., Ph.D.
Social and Public Policy. M.A.
Systematic Theology. Ph.D.
Theology. M.A., Ph.D.

John F. Donahue Graduate School of Business
Web site: www.bus.duq.edu

Established 1958. Private control. Accredited programs: M.B.A., Accounting. Semester system. Special Programs: Foreign Study (U.S./China M.B.A.). Special facilities: Small Business Development Center, Center for Corporate and Executive Education, Beard Center for Leadership in Ethics.

Tuition: $692 per credit. On-campus rooms and apartments available for single students only.

Enrollment: total full-time 88, part-time 262. Faculty: 46 full-time, 12 part-time; 87% with Ph.D./D.B.A. Degrees conferred: M.B.A. (FT, PT, day, evening), M.S.I.S.M. (Information Systems Management), M.B.A.-J.D., M.B.A.-M.L.S. (Liberal Studies), M.B.A.-M.Pharm. (Pharmacy), M.B.A.-M.S. (Environmental Sciences, Health Management Systems, Industrial Pharmacy, Informational Systems, Nursing), M.S.T. (Taxation).

ADMISSION REQUIREMENTS. All applicants should have a bachelor's degree from a recognized institution of higher education, a strong mathematics background, and a 3.0 (A = 4) GPA. Submit application, GMAT (will accept test results from the last five years, latest acceptable date is June), official transcripts from each undergraduate/graduate school attended, three letters of recommendation, one comprehensive essays, résumé (prefers at least four years of work experience), and an application fee of $40 to the Office of Graduate Admission. In addition, international students (whose native language is other than En-

glish) should submit a TOEFL (minimum score 550) report, TSE (recommended) score, certified translations and evaluations of all official transcripts, recommendation should be in English or with certified translations, proof of health/immunization certificate, and proof of sufficient financial resources to complete the academic program. Beginning students are admitted Fall and Spring. Both U.S. citizens and international applicants apply by June 1 (Fall), November 1 (Spring). On-campus interviews may be requested by the Admissions Committee. Admissions Committee will consider applicants with some academic course work deficiencies. Joint degree applicants must apply to and be accepted to both schools/programs, contact the admissions office for current information and specific admissions requirements. Rolling admissions process, notification is made within 4-6 weeks of receipt of completed application and supporting documents. Admissions Office phone: (412)396-6276; fax: (412) 396-1726.

ADMISSION STANDARDS. Selective. For M.B.A.: median GMAT: 510; median GPA: 3.1 (A = 4).

FINANCIAL AID. Scholarships, research assistantships, Federal W/S, loans. Financial aid is available for part-time study. Assistantships/fellowships may be available for joint degree candidates. Request assistantship information from the Graduate School of Business; phone: (412)396-6976. Contact the University's Financial Aid Office for current need-based financial aid information; phone: (412)396-6607. Apply by May 1 for most financial assistance and all Federal programs; use FAFSA (School code: 003258), also submit Financial Aid Transcript, Federal Income Tax forms. Approximately 5% of students receive some form of financial assistance.

DEGREE REQUIREMENTS. For M.B.A.: 56-credit program including 21 elective credits, two-year program; research project; degree program must be completed in six years. For U.S./China M.B.A.: one year at Duquesne, one year at Northern Jiatong University, P.R.C. For M.S.T.: 30-credit program. For M.B.A.-M.S.I.S.M.: 80-credit program. For M.B.A.-M.L.S.: 68 credit program. For M.B.A.-M.S. 64–75-credit programs. For M.B.A.-M.Pharm.: 75-credit program. For M.B.A.-J.D.: 126-credit four-and-one-half- to six-year program.

FIELDS OF STUDY.
Accountancy. M.S.
Business Administration. Concentrations in business ethics, environmental management, finance, health care management, information systems management, international business, marketing, management, supply chain management, taxation. M.B.A.
Information Systems Management. M.S.
Sustainability. M.B.A.
Taxation. M.S.

School of Education—Graduate Division

School established 1929. Enrollment: full- and part-time 962. Graduate faculty: full-time 58, part-time 50. Degrees conferred: M.S.Ed., C.A.G.S., Ed.D.

ADMISSION REQUIREMENTS. Official transcripts required in support of School's application. MAT, three letters of recommendation, interviews sometimes required. TOEFL required for international applicants. Accepts transfer applicants. Graduates of unaccredited institutions not considered. Apply to the School by August 1 (Fall), January 1 (Spring), June 1 (Summer). Application fee $50. Phone: (412)396-5193; fax: (412)396- 5585.

ADMISSION STANDARDS. Selective. Usual minimum average: 2.50 (A = 4).

FINANCIAL AID. Assistantships, tuition waivers, Federal W/S, loans. Approved for VA benefits. Apply to Dean's Office for assistantships; to Financial Aid Office for all other programs. No specified closing date. Phone: (412)396-6607; fax: (412)396-5284. Use FAFSA and institution's FAF. Aid available for part-time students.

DEGREE REQUIREMENTS. For master's: 30 credit hours minimum, at least 24 in residence; comprehensive exam in some programs; thesis option. For C.A.G.S.: 30 credit hour minimum beyond master's. For Ed.D.: 60 credit hours minimum beyond the master's; qualifying exam; candidacy; dissertation; final oral exam.

FIELDS OF STUDY.
Child Psychology.
Community Counseling.
Counselor Education.
Early Childhood Education.
Educational Studies. Interdisciplinary Doctoral Program for Educational Leaders (IDPEL).
Elementary Education.
English as a Second Language.
Instructional Leadership.
Instructional Technology.
Marriage and Family Therapy.
Reading and Language Arts.
Religious Education/CCO.
School Administration. Includes elementary and secondary.
School Psychology.
School Supervision.
Secondary Education.
Secondary Mathematics.
Special Education. Includes mentally/physically handicapped.

Rangos School of Health Science

Enrollment: full- and part-time 267. Faculty: full-time 37, part-time 23. Degrees conferred: M.H.M.S., M.O.T., M.P.T., M.S., Ph.D., D.P.T.

ADMISSION REQUIREMENTS. Official transcripts, GRE, three letters of recommendation, curriculum vitae, evidence of computer literacy, statement of personal goals required in support of School's application. GRE or GMAT for Health Management Systems. 250 hours experience at two separate clinical site required for Physical Therapy program. TOEFL required for international applicants. Accepts transfer applicants. Graduates of unaccredited institutions not considered. Apply to the School by May 1 (Fall). Application fee $50. Phone: (412)396-5653; fax: (412)396-5554.

ADMISSION STANDARDS. Selective. Usual minimum average: 3.0 (A = 4).

FINANCIAL AID. Assistantships, tuition waivers, Federal W/S, loans. Approved for VA benefits. Apply by May 31 to appropriate department for assistantships; to Financial Office for all other programs. Phone: (412)396-6607; fax (412)396-5284. Use FAFSA. Aid available for part-time students.

DEGREE REQUIREMENT, For M.S.H.S., M.S.: 36 credit hour minimum, at least 30 credits in residence; comprehensive exam. For M.O.T.: two-year 78–82 credit program; fieldwork experience, For M.P.T.: three-year 114-credit full-time program; clinical experience. For M.S.P.: two-year program; practicum. For M.P.T.: three-year 111-credit full-time program; 8-week clinical experience. For Ph.D.: 60 credit hour minimum, at least one-year of full-time residence; qualifying exam; thesis proposal and defense; candidacy; dissertation; final oral exam.

FIELDS OF STUDY.
Health Management System. M.H.M.S.
Occupational Therapy. M.O.T.
Physical Therapy. M.P.T., D.P.T.

Rehabilitation Science. M.S., Ph.D.
Speech-Language Pathology. M.S.P.

School of Law
Web site: www.law.duq.edu

Established 1911. ABA approved since 1960. AALS member. Semester system. Special programs: ABA approved summer program as the European Union at University College, Dublin, Ireland; Vatican City, Italy; Beijing, China. Law library: 294,108 volumes, 3942 subscriptions, has LEXIS, WESTLAW; has about 50 network connections.

Annual tuition: full-time $25,785, evening $19,968. On-campus housing available. Total average annual additional expense: $14,142.

Enrollment: first-year class day 162, evening 31; total full- and part-time 1126 (men 52%, women 48%, minorities 12%). Faculty: full-time 26, part-time 20. Student to faculty ratio is 26 to 1. Degrees conferred: J.D., J.D.-M.B.A., J.D.-M.Div., J.D.-M.S. (Environmental Science and Management), J.D.-M.S.T. (Taxation), LL.M. (Foreign Lawyers).

ADMISSION REQUIREMENTS. LSDAS Law School report, bachelor's degree, transcripts, LSAT, two letters of recommendation, personal statement required in support of application. Interview sometimes required. Transfer applicants considered. Apply to Office of Admissions after September 1, before April 1 (Day), June 1 (part-time day), May 1 (Evening). Fall admission only. Application fee $60. Phone: (412)396-6296.

ADMISSION STANDARDS. Selective. Accepts approximately 44% of all students. Number of full-time applicants 915, part-time 181; number of full-time acceptance 406, part-time 35; number of full-time enrolled 162, part-time 31; LSAT (75% of full-time students have a score at or above 153, part-time 153); GPA (75% of full-time students have a GPA at or above 3.23, part-time 3.11). *U.S. News & World Report* ranking is in the fourth tier of all U.S. law schools.

FINANCIAL AID. Scholarships, grants-in-aid, Federal W/S, loan. Apply to University's Financial Aid Office by May 1. Phone: (412)396-6607. Use FAFSA or PHEAA. About 12% of students receive aid other than loans from School funds.

DEGREE REQUIREMENTS. For J.D.: satisfactory completion of three-year (day), or four-year (evening) program; 86 credit hours minimum. For LL.M.: one year full-time program. For other programs see Graduate School listings above for degree requirements.

Bayer School of Natural and Environmental Sciences

Tuition: per credit $570. Enrollment: full-and part-time 600. Graduate faculty: full-time 40, part-time 20. Degrees conferred: M.S., Ph.D.

ADMISSION REQUIREMENTS. Official transcripts, GRE, two or three letters of recommendation, personal interview required in support of School's application. Online application available. GRE subject required for several programs. TOEFL (TSE required for assistantship consideration) required for international applicants. Accepts transfer applicants. Graduates of unaccredited institutions not considered. International applicants apply to School by February 15 (Fall), October 1 (Spring). Domestic students recommended dates April 1 (Fall), November 1 (Spring); contact appropriate department for final application deadlines. Application fee $40. Phone (412)396-6091; fax: (412)396-5585.

ADMISSIONS STANDARDS. Selective. Usual minimum average: 2.8 (A = 4).

FINANCIAL AID. Assistantships, tuition waivers, Federal W/S, loans. Approved for VA benefits. Apply by May 31 to appropriate departments for assistantships; to Financial Aid Office for all other programs. Phone: (412)396-6339; fax: (412)396-4881. Use FAFSA. Aid available for part-time students.

DEGREE REQUIREMENTS. For M.S. Plan A (thesis): 32–42 credit hours minimum, at least 24–36 in residence; thesis. For M.S. Plan B (nonthesis): 32–42 credit hours minimum, at least 24–36 in residence; comprehensive exam. For Ph.D.: 46–56 credit hours beyond the bachelor's; comprehensive exam, candidacy, dissertation; final defense.

FIELDS OF STUDY.
Biochemistry.
Biology.
Chemistry.
Environmental Science and Management.
Forensic Science.
Health and Safety Management.

EAST CAROLINA UNIVERSITY
Greenville, North Carolina 27858-4353
Web site: www.ecu.edu

Founded 1907. CGS member. Located 80 miles E of Raleigh. State control. Semester system. Special facilities: Center on Aging, Center for Coastal and Marine Resources, Mental Health Training Institute, East Carolina Development Institute. Library: 1,500,000 volumes, 27,000 subscriptions. Total University enrollment: 23,100.

Annual tuition: full-time resident $4000, nonresident $14,516. On-campus housing for single students. Average academic year housing costs: $6840 (including board) for single students. Contact the Housing office for both on- and off-campus housing information. Phone: (919)328-6012.

Graduate School

Graduate study since 1929. Enrollment: full-time 1750, part-time 2192. Graduate faculty: full-time 526, part-time 67. Degrees conferred: M.A., M.A.Ed., M.B.A., M.S.A., M.P.A., M.S.E.H., M.F.A., M.M., M.S., M.Physics, Ed.S., C.A.S., Ph.D. (Medical Sciences), Ed.D. (Educational Leadership).

ADMISSION REQUIREMENTS. Two official transcripts, GRE/GMAT (Business) required in support of School's application. MAT/GRE Subject Tests, interviews, letters of reference sometimes required. TOEFL required for international applicants. Accepts transfer applicants. Graduates of unaccredited institutions not considered. Apply to Graduate School June 1 (Fall), October 15 (Spring); some programs have earlier deadlines. Rolling admission process. Application fee $50. Phone: (919)329-6012; fax: (919)328-6071; e-mail: gradschool@mail.ecu.edu.

ADMISSION STANDARDS. Selective for most departments. Usual minimum average: 2.5 (3.0 in major or senior year) (A = 4).

FINANCIAL AID. Annual awards from institutional funds: assistantships, fellowships, Federal W/S, loans. Approved for VA benefits. Apply by April 15 to appropriate department chair for assistantships, fellowships; to Financial Aid Office for all other programs. Use FAFSA. Phone: (919)328-6610. About 20% of students receive aid other than loans from University and outside sources.

DEGREE REQUIREMENTS. For M.A., M.S., M.F.A.: 30 semester hours minimum; reading knowledge of one foreign language or other research skill; thesis for most programs; final oral/written exam. For M.A. in Ed., M.B.A., M.M., M.S.H.E., M.Physics: same as for M.A., except no thesis or language requirement. For C.A.S., Ed.S.: 30 credits minimum beyond the master's; comprehensive exam. For Ed.D.: 60 semester hours beyond the master's, at least one year in full-time residency; internships, candidacy exam; dissertation. For Ph.D.: 58 semester hours, one calendar year of full-time study; candidacy exam; dissertation; final oral exam.

FIELDS OF STUDY.
Accounting. M.S.A.
Adult Education. M.A.Ed.
Anatomy and Cell Biology. Ph.D.
Anthropology. M.A.
Art. Includes art education. M.A., M.F.A., M.A.Ed.
Athletic Training. M.S.
Biochemistry. Ph.D.
Bioenergetics. Ph.D.
Biological Sciences. Ph.D.
Biology. Includes molecular/biotechnology. M.S.
Biomedical Physics. Ph.D.
Business Administration. M.B.A.
Chemistry. M.S.
Child Development and Family Relations. M.S.
Coastal Resource Management. Ph.D.
Communication Sciences and Disorders. Ph.D.
Computer Science. M.S.
Construction Management. M.C.M.
Counselor Education. M.S., Ed.S.
Criminal Justice. M.S.
Economics. M.S.
Educational Leadership—Educational Administration and Supervision. Ed.S.
Educational Leadership—Higher Education. Ph.D.
Educational Leadership—K–12. Ed.D.
Educational Leadership—Supervision and School Administration. M.A.Ed., M.S.A.
Elementary Education. M.A.Ed.
English. M.A., M.A.Ed.
Environmental Health. M.S.E.H.
Exercise and Sport Science. M.A., M.A.Ed.
Geography. M.A.
Geology. M.S.
Health Education. M.A., M.A.Ed.
Health Psychology. Ph.D.
History. Includes maritime history. M.A., M.A.Ed.
Industrial Technology. M.S.I.T.
Instructional Technology Education. M.A.Ed., M.S.
Instructional Technology Specialist—Computers. M.A.Ed., M.S.
International Studies. M.A.I.S.
Library Science. M.L.S., C.A.S.
Maritime Studies. M.A.
Marriage and Family Therapy. M.F.T.
Mathematics. M.A., M.A.Ed.
Medical Family Therapy. Ph.D.
Microbiology and Immunology. Ph.D.
Middle Grades Education. M.A.Ed.
Molecular Biology and Biotechnology. M.S.
Music. Includes theory/composition, education, therapy, performance. M.M.
Nursing. M.S.N., Ph.D.
Nutrition and Dietetics. M.S.
Occupational Safety. M.S.
Occupational Therapy. M.S., M.S.O.T.
Pharmacology. Ph.D.
Physical Therapy. M.P.T., Ph.D.
Physical Education. M.A., M.A.Ed.
Physician Assistant Studies. M.S.
Physics. M.S., Ph.D.
Physiology. Ph.D.

Psychology. Includes clinical, general and theoretic, school. M.A., C.A.S.

Public Administration. M.P.A.

Public Health. M.P.H.

Reading Education. M.A.Ed.

Recreation and Leisure Facilities and Service Administration. M.S.

Recreational Therapy Administration. M.S.

Rehabilitation Counseling and Administration. Ph.D.

Rehabilitation Studies. Includes rehabilitation counseling, substance abuse and clinical counseling, vocational evaluation. M.S.

Science Education. M.A., M.A.Ed.

Social Work. M.S.W.

Sociology. M.A.

Software Engineering. M.S.

Special Education. Includes learning disabilities, low incidence disabilities, mental retardation, M.S.

Speech-Language Pathology and Audiology. M.S.

Technology Management (Consortium Program). Ph.D.

Vocational Education. M.S.

Brody School of Medicine (27858-4354)

Web site: www.ecu.edu/med

Four-year program established 1977. Library: 138,000 volumes, 1800 subscriptions.

Annual tuition: resident $9036, nonresident $33,834. Average expense for all other costs: $10,346.

Enrollment: first-year class 72 (EDP 9); total 286 (men 51%, women 49%, minorities 31%, state resident 100%). Faculty: full-time 400, part-time 47. Degrees conferred: M.D., M.D.-M.B.A., M.D.-Ph.D.

ADMISSION REQUIREMENTS. AMCAS report, transcripts, MCAT, three letters of recommendation, essay required in support of application. Supplemental application required. Interview by invitation only. No out-of-state student has been admitted in over 20 years. Accepts transfer students. Has EDP; apply between June 15 and August 1. For regular admission apply to Office of Admission after June 15, before November 15. Application fee $60. Phone: (252)744-2202.

ADMISSION STANDARDS. Selective. Accepts about 14.9% of all applicants. Number of applications 745 (0 out-of-state); number interviewed 400 (0 out-of-state); number of acceptance 111 (0 out-of-state); number enrolled 72 (0 out-of-state). Mean Composite MCAT 9.0; mean UGPA 3.60. *U.S. News & World Report* ranking is in the top 34th in primary care.

FINANCIAL AID. Scholarships, grants, assistantships, Federal and private loans. Apply after acceptance to Financial Aid Office. Phone: (252)744-2278. About 90% of student receive some financial assistance.

DEGREE REQUIREMENTS. For M.D.: satisfactory completion of four-year program; must pass Step 1 of USMLE and take Step 2.

FIELDS OF GRADUATE STUDY.

Anatomy and Cell Biology.

Biochemistry.

Biological Sciences. Interdisciplinary.

Microbiology and Immunology.

Pathology.

Pharmacology.

Physiology.

EAST CENTRAL UNIVERSITY

Ada, Oklahoma 74820-6999

Web site: www.ecok.edu

Established 1909. CGS member. Located 90 miles SE of Oklahoma City. Coed. state control. Semester system. Special facilities: Center for Advancement of American History, Center for Excellence in Teaching and Learning, Center for Oklahoma Studies, Hayes Native American Studies Center, Institute for Environmental Science Education and Research.. Library 221,000 volumes, 793,000 microforms, 12 PC workstations.

Tuition: per semester hour resident $116, nonresident $218. On-campus housing for 95 married students, 418 single men, 558 single women. Academic year housing cost: $3800. Apply to Director of Housing. Phone: married housing information (580) 332-8000, ext. 226; single housing information (580)332-8000, ext. 208. Day-care facilities available.

School of Graduate Studies

Enrollment: full-time 50, part-time 485 (academic year), about 575 (Summer). College faculty teaching graduate students: full-time 50, part-time 10. Degrees conferred: M.Ed., M.S. in Psychological Services, M.S. in Human Resources.

ADMISSION REQUIREMENTS. Transcripts, GRE/MAT required in support of application. Departmental writing exam for Education. TOEFL required for foreign applicants. Accepts transfer applicants. Apply to Graduate School at least 30 days prior to registration. Phone: (580)332-8000, ext. 5234; fax: (580) 559-5432.

ADMISSION STANDARDS. Selective. Usual minimum average: 2.5 (A = 4); 2.75 in last 60 credits.

FINANCIAL AID. Awards from institutional funds: scholarships, assistantships, Federal W/S, loans; no specified closing date. Phone: (580)322-8000, ext. 242. Use FAFSA.

DEGREE REQUIREMENTS. For M.Ed.: 32 semester hours minimum, at least 24 in residence; thesis optional. For M.S.P.S.: 60 semester hours minimum; thesis optional. For M.S.H.R.: 36 semester hours minimum; rehabilitation counselor option 60 semester hours.

FIELDS OF STUDY.

Criminal Justice.

Elementary Education.

Elementary School Principal.

Human Resources.

Human Resources Counselor.

Human Resources Rehabilitation Counseling.

Library Media Specialist.

Psychological Services.

Reading Specialist.

School Counselor. Includes elementary, secondary.

Secondary Education. Includes educational technology, sports administration.

Secondary School Principal.

Special Education.

EAST STROUDSBURG UNIVERSITY OF PENNSYLVANIA

East Stroudsburg, Pennsylvania 18301

Web site: www.esu.edu

Founded 1893. Located 75 miles W of New York City. Coed. State control. Semester system. Library: 411,000 volumes, 1800 subscriptions. Total University enrollment: 5500.

Tuition: full-time resident $6214, nonresident $9944. Limited on-campus housing for graduate students. Average academic year cost: $3788–$5259. On-campus housing in Summer only for single students. Average Summer cost: $125 per week (including board). Apply to director of Housing. Phone: (570)422-3461.

Graduate Studies

Enrollment: full-time 225, part-time 800 (men 30%, women 70%). Faculty: full-time 111, part-time 10. Degrees conferred: M.A., M.S., M.Ed., M P.H.

ADMISSION REQUIREMENTS. Two official transcripts required in support of School's application. GRE required for some programs. TOEFL required for international applicants. Interview required by some departments. Accepts transfer applicants. Apply to Dean of Graduate Studies at least six weeks prior to registration. Admits to Fall and Spring semesters. Application fee $50. Phone: (570)424-3536; fax: (570)422-3506.

ADMISSION STANDARDS. Selective. Usual minimum average: 2.5, 3.0 major field (A = 4).

FINANCIAL AID. Annual awards from institutional funds: graduate assistantships, tuition waivers, grants, Federal W/S, loans. Apply to the Graduate School by March 1. Phone: (570)422-3340. Use FAFSA (School code: 003320). About 95% of full-time students receive aid other than loans from College and outside sources. Aid available for part-time students, sometimes available for international students.

DEGREE REQUIREMENTS. For M.A.: 30 credit hours minimum, at least 24 in residence; thesis. For M.Ed. or M.S.: 30–51 credit programs, at least 24 in residence, plus thesis; or 34–51 credits, at least 28 in residence, and research project; written comprehensive exam; final oral exam. For M.P.H.: 48 credit hours, at least 32 credits in residence; thesis.

FIELDS OF STUDY.
Administration and Leadership Studies. Ed.D.
Athletic Training. Includes an advanced clinical practice track. M.Ed.
Biology. M.Ed., M.S.
Clinical Exercise Physiology. M.S.
Computer Science. M.S.
Elementary Education. Includes early childhood, middle school. M.Ed.
Exercise Science. M.S.
Health Education. M.S.
Health and Physical Education. M.Ed.
History. M.A., M.Ed.
Instructional Technology. Joint degree program with Kutztown University. M.Ed.
Management and Leadership. Includes hotel, restaurant and tourism management, public administration, sports management, M.S.
Political Science. M.A., M.Ed.
Public Health. M.P.H.
Reading. M.Ed.
Secondary Education. M.Ed.
Special Education. M.Ed.
Speech-Language Pathology. M.Ed.
Sport Management. M.S.

EAST TENNESSEE STATE UNIVERSITY
Johnson City, Tennessee 37614-0054
Web site: www.etsu.edu

Founded 1911. CGS member. Located 100 miles E of Knoxville. Coed. State control. Semester system. Library: 1,100,000 volumes, 3400 subscriptions. Total University enrollment: 12,000.

Graduate tuition fees: per semester hour, resident $261, nonresident $404. On-campus housing available for both single and married students. Average academic year cost: single $4100 (including board), married $5200 (including board). Apply to Director of Housing. Phone: (423)439-4446. Day-care facilities available.

School of Graduate Studies

Enrollment: full-time 1253, part-time 813. University faculty: full-time 463, part-time 42. Degrees conferred: M.A., M.A.L.S., M.B.A., M.S., M.S.N., M.S.E.H., M.F.A., M.A.T., M.P.M., M.P.H., M.P.T., Ed.S., Ed.D., Ph.D.

ADMISSION REQUIREMENTS. Transcripts, personal essay required in support of School's application. GRE/GMAT, letters of recommendation required in some departments. Interview sometimes required. TOEFL required for international applicants. Accepts transfer applicants. Graduates of unaccredited institutions not considered. Apply to Dean, School of Graduate Studies by August 1 (Fall), December 1 (Winter), March 1 (Spring), May 1 (Summer). International applicants should apply at least 12 weeks prior to expected date of enrollment. Application fee $25, $35 for international applicants. Phone: (423)439-4221; fax: (423)439-5624; e-mail: gradsch@etsu.edu.

ADMISSION STANDARDS. Selective. Usual minimum average: 2.5 (A = 4).

FINANCIAL AID. Annual awards from institutional funds: scholarships, fellowships, graduate assistantships, research assistantships, grants, Federal W/S, loans. Approved for VA benefits. Apply by May 1 to appropriate department chair. Use FAFSA and University's FAF. About 50% of students receive aid other than loans from School and outside sources. Aid available for part-time students.

DEGREE REQUIREMENTS. For all master's: 30 semester hours minimum; thesis, final oral/written exam; or 36 semester hours minimum, final oral exam. For Ed. S.: 30 semester hours beyond the master's; dissertation. For Ed.D.: 90 semester hours minimum, at least one year in full-time study; preliminary exam; qualifying exam; final exam; dissertation. For Ph.D.: 60 semester hours beyond the master's; preliminary and qualifying exam; language/computer option; final exam; dissertation.

FIELDS OF STUDY.

COLLEGE OF ARTS AND SCIENCES:
Art and Design. Includes art history (M.A.), studio art (M.A., M.F.A.).
Biological Sciences. Includes biology, microbiology, paleontology. M.S.
Chemistry. M.S.
Communication. M.A,
Criminal Justices. M.A.
English. M.A.
History. M.A.
Mathematics. M.S.
Psychology. Includes clinical (M.A., Ph.D.), general (M.A.).
Social Work. M.S.W.
Sociology. Includes applied, general. M.A.

COLLEGE OF BUSINESS AND TECHNOLOGY:
Accounting. M.Acc.
Business Administration. M.B.A.
Clinical Nutrition. M.S.
Computer and Information Science. Includes applied computer science, information technology. M.S.
Public Administration. M.P.A.
Technology. Includes digital media technology, engineering technology, geoscience. M.S.

COLLEGE OF EDUCATION:

Counseling. Includes community agency, elementary and secondary school, higher education, marriage and family therapy. M.A.

Early Childhood Education. M.A., M.Ed.

Educational Media and Educational Technology. Includes educational communication and technology, school library media. M.Ed.

Educational Leadership. M.Ed.

Elementary Education. M.Ed.

Kinesiology and Sport Studies. Includes exercise physiology and performance, physical education K–12, sport management. M.A.

Reading. Includes reading education, storytelling. M.A.

Secondary Education. Includes classroom technology. M.Ed.

Special Education. M.Ed.

SCHOOL OF NURSING:

Nursing. M.S.N., D.S.N.

COLLEGE OF PUBLIC AND ALLIED HEALTH:

Allied Health. M.S.A.H.

Audiology. Au.D.

Communicative Disorders. M.S.

Environmental Health. M.S.E.H.

Microbiology. M.S.

Physical Therapy. D.P.T.

Public Health. Includes biostatistics, community health, epidemiology, health services administration. M.P.H., D.P.H.

James H. Quillen College of Medicine (P.O. Box 70694)

Web site: www.qcom.etsu.edu

Established 1978. Annual tuition: resident $20,131; nonresident $39,895. Total average cost of all other expenses: $12,900. Enrollment: first-year class 60 (EDP 6); total 234 (men 54%, women 46%, minorities 15%, state residents 94%). Faculty: full-time 250; part-time, 38. Degrees conferred: M.D., M.D.-Ph.D.

ADMISSION REQUIREMENTS. AMCAS report, transcripts, MCAT, recommendations required in support of application. Supplemental application required. Interview by invitation. Preference given to state residents and veterans of U.S. military service. Graduates of unaccredited colleges not considered. Has EDP; apply between June 15 and August 1. Apply to Admissions Office/Registrar after June 15, before November 15. Application fee, $50. Phone. (423)439-2033; fax: (423)439-2110.

ADMISSION STANDARDS. Selective. Accepts about 12% of all applicants. Number of applications 1187 (715 out-of-state); number interviewed 197 (34 out-of-state); number of acceptance 142 (20 out-of-state); number enrolled 60 (7 out-of-state). Mean Composite MCAT 9.3; mean UGPA 3.57.

FINANCIAL AID. Scholarships, fellowships, tuition waivers, grants, loans. Apply after acceptance to Financial Aid Office. Phone: (423)439-2035. Use FAFSA.

DEGREE REQUIREMENTS. For M.D.: satisfactory completion of four-year program.

FIELDS OF GRADUATE STUDY.

Anatomy and Cell Biology.

Biochemistry and Molecular Biology.

Biophysics.

Microbiology.

Pharmacology.

Physiology.

EASTERN CONNECTICUT STATE UNIVERSITY

Willimantic, Connecticut 06226-2295

Web site: www.csu.ctstateu.edu

Founded 1889. Located 30 miles E of Hartford. Coed. State control. Semester system.

Tuition: full-time resident $3750, nonresident $10,449. No on-campus housing for married or single graduate students. Apply to Student Affairs office for off-campus housing information. Phone: (860)465-5369.

School of Education and Professional Studies

Enrollment: full-time 20, part-time 165. College faculty teaching graduate courses: full-time 16, part-time 4. Degree conferred: M.S.

ADMISSION REQUIREMENTS. Transcripts, two recommendations, personal statement, GMAT (for Accounting) required in support of application. TOEFL required for international applicants. Accepts transfer applicants. Apply to appropriate department. No specified closing date. Admits Fall, Spring. Application fee $50. Phone: (860)465-5292; fax: (860)465-4543.

ADMISSION STANDARDS. Selective. Usual minimum average: 2.7 (A = 4).

FINANCIAL AID, Annual awards from institutional funds: assistantships, grants, Federal W/S, loans. Apply to appropriate department by March 15. Phone: (860)456-5205. Use FAFSA and institutional FAF.

DEGREE REQUIREMENTS. For M.S.: 36 semester hours minimum, at least 21 in residence; thesis or comprehensive exam.

FIELDS OF STUDY.

Accounting. Includes financial reporting, international operations, taxation, accountancy for nonprofit/governmental units.

Education. Includes early childhood, educational technology, elementary, language arts, reading, science.

Organizational Management. Includes individual behavior, group dynamics, organizational processes and structure.

EASTERN ILLINOIS UNIVERSITY

Charleston, Illinois 61920-3099

Web site: www.eiu.edu

Founded 1895. CGS member. Located 180 miles S of Chicago. Coed. State control. Semester system. Library: 1,110,000 volumes, 12,000 subscriptions. Total University enrollment: 12,100.

Tuition/fees: per credit resident $189, nonresident $569. On-campus housing for 100 married students, 600 graduate men, 600 graduate women. Average academic year housing costs: $3770 for married students, $3356 for single graduate students. Contact Director, University Housing for both on- and off-campus housing information. Phone: (217)581-3923.

Graduate Studies

Enrollment: full- and part-time 1754. University faculty teaching graduate students: full-time 425, part-time 25. Degrees conferred: M.A., M.A.M., M.A.P.S., M.S., M.S.C., M.S.C.D.S., M.S.N.S., M.S. in Ed., M.B.A., Ed.S., S.S.P.

ADMISSION REQUIREMENTS. Transcripts, GRE, MAT, GMAT may be required in support of application. Interview not required. TOEFL (minimum score 550) required for international applicants. Accepts transfer applicants. Graduates of unaccredited institutions not considered. Apply to Graduate School's Admissions Office at least 30 days prior to registration. Application fee $30. Phone: (217)581-7489, Fax: (217)581-6020.

ADMISSION STANDARDS. Relatively open. Usual minimum average: 2.75 (A = 4); higher in some programs.

FINANCIAL AID. Annual awards from institutional funds: tuition waiver scholarships, research assistantships, teaching assistantships, residence hall assistantships, Federal W/S, loans. Approved for VA benefits. Apply by February 15 to appropriate department for assistantships; to the Financial Aid Office for all need-based programs. Phone: (217)581-3713. Use FAFSA. About 25% of students receive aid other than loans from University and outside sources. Scholarships for international students available.

DEGREE REQUIREMENTS. For master's: 30–32 semester hours; final oral/written exam. For Ed.S., S.S.P.: 64 semester hours minimum beyond the bachelor's; final oral/written exam/special project.

FIELDS OF STUDY.

COLLEGE OF ARTS AND HUMANITIES:
Art. M.A.
Art Education. M.A.
English. M.A.
History. Includes historical administration. M.A.
Music. M.A.
Speech Communication. M.A.

LUMPKIN COLLEGE OF BUSINESS AND APPLIED SCIENCES:
Business Administration. Includes accountancy. M.B.A.
Family and Consumer Sciences. Includes dietetics. M.S.
General Business. M.B.A.
Gerontology. M.A.
Technology. M.S.

COLLEGE OF EDUCATION AND PROFESSIONAL STUDIES:
College Student Affairs. M.S.
Community Counseling. M.S.
Educational Administration. M.S.Ed., Ed.S.
Elementary Education. M.S.Ed.
Physical Education. M.S.
School Counseling. M.S.
Special Education. M.S.Ed.

COLLEGE OF SCIENCES:
Chemistry. M.S.C.
Communication Disorders and Sciences. M.S.C.D.S.
Economics. M.A.
Mathematics. Includes education. M.A.M.
Natural Sciences (for Teachers of Science). Includes biological sciences, chemistry, earth science, physics. M.S.N.S.
Political Science. Includes American government and politics, comparative and international relations, and public administration and public policy. M.A.P.S.
Psychology. Includes clinical, school. M.A.C.P., S.S.P.

EASTERN KENTUCKY UNIVERSITY
Richmond, Kentucky 40475-3101
Web site: www.eku.edu

Founded 1906. CGS member. Located 26 miles SE of Lexington. Coed. State control. Semester system. Library: about 811,000 volumes, 1,151,000 microforms, 4000 current periodicals. Special facilities: Hummel Planetarium, Lilley Cornett Woods, Oral History Center, Spenser Morton Preserves.

Annual tuition: full-time, resident $5682, nonresident $14,382; per hour, resident $237, nonresident $641. On-campus housing for married students: 292 units, single on-campus housing available for about 3000 men, 4000 women. Average academic year housing costs: $900–$1400 per semester for single students, about $1100 per semester for married students. Contact Director of Housing for both on- and off-campus housing information. Phone: (859)622-1575.

Graduate School

Graduate study since 1935. Enrollment: full-time 446, part-time 1521. Graduate faculty: full-time 350, part-time 10. Degrees conferred: M.A., M.A.C., M.A.Ed., M.S., M.B.A., M.I.O.P., M.P.A., M.M., M.S.N., Ed.S., joint doctoral programs available.

ADMISSION REQUIREMENTS. Official transcripts, statement of personal and professional objectives, GRE/MAT, GMAT (Business) required in support of application. Online application available. Interview required for some programs. TOEFL required for international applicants. Accepts transfer applicants. Graduates of unaccredited institutions not considered. Apply to Graduate Office at least two weeks prior to registration. Foreign students must be clearly admitted at least 60 days prior to the beginning of the semester of attendance. Application fee $35. Phone: (859)622-1742; e-mail: graduate@eku.edu.

ADMISSION STANDARDS. Selective. Usual minimum average: 2.5 (A = 4).

FINANCIAL AID. Annual awards from institutional funds: scholarships, fellowships, teaching/research assistantships, Federal W/S, loans. Approved for VA benefits. Apply by March 15 to Graduate Office for assistantships; to Financial Aid Office for all other programs. Use FAFSA (School code: 001963). About 50% of full-time students receive aid other than loans from University and outside sources. Aid available for part-time students.

DEGREE REQUIREMENTS. For most master's: 24 semester hours plus thesis, or 30 semester hours without thesis; final oral/comprehensive exam. For M.A.Ed.: same as for M.A., except candidates are required to hold the teaching certificate. For Ed.S.: 30–39 semester hours beyond the master's; special project.

FIELDS OF STUDY.
Administration and Supervision. Ed.S., joint Ed.D. with University of Kentucky.
Applied Computing—Bioinformatics. M.S.
Applied Computing—Business Computing. M.S.
Applied Computing—Industrial Computing. M.S.
Applied Computing—Software Engineering. M.S.
Applied Computing—Statistical Computing. M.S.
Biology. Includes bioinformatics, ecology. M.S. Joint Ph.D. with University of Kentucky.
Business Administration. M.B.A.
Business Computing. M.A.C.
Chemistry. M.S.
Clinical Psychology. M.S.
Communication Disorders. M.A.Ed.
Community Nutrition. M.S.
Creative Writing. M.F.A.
Criminal Justice. Includes corrections and juvenile justice studies, police administration. M.S.
Educational Psychology. Joint Ed.D. with University of Kentucky.
Educational Policies, Studies, and Evaluation. Joint Ed.D. with University of Kentucky.
Elementary Education. Includes early elementary, gifted, middle grades, reading. M.A., M.A.Ed.
English. M.A., M.A.Ed.

Geology. M.S. Joint Ph.D. with the University of Kentucky.

Geosciences. M.S.

Health, Physical Education, and Recreation. Joint Ed.D. with University of Kentucky.

History. M.A., M.A.Ed.

Human Services—Student Personnel Services. M.A.

Human Services—Community Agencies. M.A.

Industrial Computing. M.A.C.

Industrial Education. Includes occupational training/development, technology, vocational administration. M.S.

Industrial Organizational Psychology. M.I.O.P., M.S.

Instructional Leadership. M.A.Ed. Joint Ed.D. with the University of Kentucky.

Library Science. Includes K–12. M.A.Ed.

Mathematical Sciences. Includes computer science, statistics. M.S.

Mental Health Counseling. M.A.

Music. Includes choral/instrumental conducting, general, performance, theory/composition. M.M.

Nursing. Includes rural health family nurse practitioner, rural community health care nursing. M.S.N.

Occupational Training/Development. M.A.Ed.

Occupational Therapy. M.S.

Physical Education. Includes exercise/sport science, exercise/wellness, sports administration. M.S.

Political Science. M.A., M.A.Ed.

Psychology. Includes clinical, education, school. Psy.S. Joint Ph.D. with University of Kentucky.

Public Administration. Includes community development, community health administration, environmental health. M.P.A.

Public Health. Includes chemical abuse, community health, environmental health science, wellness. M.P.H., M.S.

Recreation and Park Administration. M.S.

Safety, Security and Emergency Management. M.S.

School Counseling. M.A.Ed.

Secondary Education. Includes agriculture, art, biology, business, English, family and consumer sciences, mathematics, music, physical education, physical science, social studies (geography, history), technology. M.A., M.A.Ed.

Software Engineering. M.A.C.

Special Education. Includes deaf and hard of hearing, early childhood, early childhood (nonteaching), LBD, moderate and severe. M.A.Ed. Joint Ed.D. with the University of Kentucky (LBD, TMH, hearing impaired).

Student Personnel Services. Ed.S.

Technology Education. M.S.

Vocational Education. Joint Ed.D. with University of Kentucky.

EASTERN MICHIGAN UNIVERSITY

Ypsilanti, Michigan 48197

Web site: www.emich.edu

Founded 1849. CGS member. Located 30 miles W of Detroit. Coed. State control. Semester system. Special facilities: Center for Environmental Information Technologies and Applications, the Center for Research Support, Center for Coating Research, Institute for Community and Regional Development, Institute for Diversity and Business Services, Institute for the Study of Children, Families and Communities, National Institute for Consumer Education, Textile Research and Training Institute, Urban Water Research Consortium. Library: 600,000 volumes, 4300 subscriptions. Total University enrollment: 23,400.

Tuition: per hour, resident $327, nonresident $657. On-campus housing for married students, graduate men and women. Average academic year housing cost: $5597 per academic year (including board) for single students. Apply to Director of Auxiliary Services. Phone: (734)487-0445. Day-care facilities available.

Graduate School

Graduate study since 1953. Enrollment: full-time 807, part-time 2959. University faculty: full- and part-time 618. Degrees conferred: M.A., M.S., M.S.A. M.B.A., M.L.S., M.O.T., M.P.A., M.B.E., M.F.A., M.S.E.S., M.S.N., M.S.W., Sp.A., C.A.S., Ed.D.

ADMISSION REQUIREMENTS. Transcripts, GRE/MAT/ GMAT, letters of recommendation required in support of School's application. Interview not required. TOEFL required for international applicants. Accepts transfer applicants. Graduates of unaccredited institutions not considered. Apply to Graduate School Office at least 60 days before registration; priority deadlines May 15 (Fall), November 1 (Spring). Application fee $30. Phone: (734) 487-3400; fax: (734)487-6559; e-mail: graduate.admission@ emich.edu.

ADMISSION STANDARDS. Selective. Usual minimum average: 2.75 (A = 4).

FINANCIAL AID. Annual awards from institutional funds: fellowships, assistantships, tuition waivers, Federal W/S, loans. Apply to appropriate department head; no specified closing date. Apply by March 15 (Spring), February 15 (Fall) to Financial Aid Officer for federal funds. Phone: (734)487-0455. Use FAFSA. Aid sometimes available for part-time students.

DEGREE REQUIREMENTS. For master's: 30 semester hours minimum (maximum varies by department), at least 6 in residence; thesis/nonthesis option; research paper may be included; final written/oral exam may be required. For Sp.A., C.A.S.: normally 32 hours beyond the master's, at least 16 in residence. For Ed.D.: 28 hours beyond University's specialist degree; all in residence; major project; written/oral exam.

FIELDS OF STUDY.

COLLEGE OF ARTS AND SCIENCES:

Applied Statistics. M.A.

Applied Economics. M.A.

Art Education. M.A.

Arts Administration. M.A.

Biology. Includes general biology, community college teaching, molecular/cellular, physiology. M.S.

Chemistry. M.S.

Children's Literature. M.A.

Clinical Behavior Psychology. M.S.

Clinical Psychology. M.S., Ph.D.

Communication. M.A.

Computer Science. Includes artificial intelligence. M.S.

Creative Writing. M.A.

Criminology and Criminal Justice. M.A.

Drama/Theatre for the Young. M.A., M.F.A.

Economics. M.A.

Economics/Health Economics. M.A.

Economics/International Economics and Development. M.A.

English Linguistics. M.A.

Foreign Language—French. M.A.

Foreign Language—German. M.A.

Foreign Language—Spanish. M.A.

General Science. M.S.

Geographic Information Systems. M.S.

Geography. M.S.

Historic Preservation. M.S.

Historic Preservation Administration. M.S.

Historic Preservation Planning. M.S.

History. M.A.

Interdisciplinary Studies. M.S.

Literature. M.A.

Math–Computer Science. M.A.

Math Education. M.A.

Mathematics. M.A.
Music. Includes choral music, education, theory/literature, performance, pedagogy. M.A.
Physics. M.S.
Physics Education. M.S.
Psychology. M.S.
Public Administration. M.P.A.
School Psychology. M.A.
Social Science. M.A.
Social Science and American Culture. M.L.S.
Sociology. M.A.
Sociology—Family Specialty. M.A.
Spanish Bilingual/Bicultural. M.A.
Statistics. M.S.
Teaching English to Speakers of Other Languages. M.A.
Theatre Arts. M.A.
Trade and Development. M.A.
Urban and Regional Planning. M.S.
Women's Studies. M.A.
Written Communication. M.A.

COLLEGE OF BUSINESS:
Accounting. M.S.
Accounting Information Systems. M.S.
Business Administration. Includes accounting/financial and operational controls, accounting/taxation, management information systems, finance, international business, management/human resource, marketing, organizational development, strategic quality. M.B.A.
Computer Information Systems. M.S.I.S.
Human Resource and Organizational Development. M.S.
Information Systems. M.S.

COLLEGE OF EDUCATION:
Adapted Physical Education. M.S.A.
College Student Personnel. M.A.
Community Counseling. M.A.
Curriculum and Instruction. M.A.
Development and Personality. M.A.
Early Childhood Education. M.A.
Educational Media and Technology. M.A.
Educational Psychology Research and Evaluation. M.A.
Elementary Education. M.A.
Leadership. M.A., Ed.D.
Middle School Education. M.A.
Physical Education—Pedagogy. M.S.
Reading. M.A.
School Counseling. M.A.
Secondary Education. M.A.
Social Foundations. M.A.
Special Education. Includes emotionally impaired, hearing impaired, learning disabilities, mentally impaired, visually impaired, speech and language impaired, physically and otherwise health impaired. M.A.
Speech and Language Pathology. M.A.
Sports Medicine—Biomechanics. M.S.
Sports Medicine—Corporate/Adult Fitness. M.S.
Sports Medicine—Exercise Physiology. M.S.
Teaching for Diversity. M.A.

COLLEGE OF HEALTH AND HUMAN SERVICES:
Health Promotion and Human Performance. M.S.
Human Nutrition. M.S.
Mental Health and Chemical Dependency. M.S.W.
Nursing. M.S.N.
Occupational Therapy. M.O.T., M.S.
Social Work. M.S.W.

COLLEGE OF TECHNOLOGY:
Information Security. M.L.S.
Industrial Technology. Includes CAD/CAM, construction, quality. M.S.
Interdisciplinary Technology. M.L.S.
Polymer and Coating Technology. M.S.
Technology Education. M.S.

EASTERN NEW MEXICO UNIVERSITY
Portales, New Mexico 88130
Web site: www.enmu.edu

Founded 1927. CGS member. Coed. State control. Branches located in Roswell, Ruidoso. Semester system. Library: 500,000 volumes, 8795 subscriptions. Total University enrollment: 4000.

Annual tuition: full-time, resident $2316, nonresident $7872; per credit, resident $97, nonresident $328. On-campus housing for 181 married students, 540 graduate men, 918 graduate women. Average academic year housing costs: $2000–$4480 for single students; $400–$550 per month for married students. Contact Director of Housing for both on- and off-campus housing information. Phone: (505)562-2631. Day-care facilities available.

Graduate School

Enrollment: full-time 26, part-time 531. University faculty: full-time 78, part-time 9. Degrees conferred: M.A., M.B.A., M.Ed., M.M., M.S., M.S.Ed.

ADMISSION REQUIREMENTS. One official transcript, GRE/GMAT (business) required in support of School's application. Online application available. Interview not required. TOEFL required for international applicants. Accepts transfer applicants. Graduates of unaccredited institutions not considered. Apply to Dean of Graduate School at least 30 days prior to registration. Rolling admission process. Application fee $10. Phone: (505) 562-2147; fax: (505)562-2168.

ADMISSION STANDARDS. Relatively open. Usual minimum average: 3.0 (regular), 2.5 (provisional) (A = 4).

FINANCIAL AID. Annual awards from institutional funds; research assistantships, teaching assistantships, fellowships for minorities, women and handicapped, tuition waivers, Federal W/S, loans. Approved for VA benefits. Apply by March 1 to appropriate department chair for assistantships; to the Financial Aid Office for all other programs. Use FAFSA and University's FAF. Phone: (505)562-2147. About 85% of students receive aid from University and outside sources. No aid for part-time students.

DEGREE REQUIREMENTS. For master's: 30 credit hours minimum, at least 24 in residence; thesis; final oral exam; or 32 credit hours minimum, at least 16 in residence; final oral written exam.

FIELDS OF STUDY.

COLLEGE OF BUSINESS:
Business Administration. M.B.A.

COLLEGE OF EDUCATION AND TECHNOLOGY:
Bilingual Education. M.Ed.
Counseling. M.Ed.
Educational Administration. M.Ed.
Educational Technology. M.Ed.
Elementary Education. M.Ed.
Pedagogy and Learning. M.Ed.

School Counseling. M.Ed.
Secondary Education. M.Ed.
Special Education. M.Ed.
Sport Administration. M.S.
Sport Science. M.S.
Teaching English to Speakers of Other Languages. M.Ed.

COLLEGE OF LIBERAL ARTS AND SCIENCES:
Anthropology. M.A.
Biology. Includes applied ecology, botany, education, microbiology, cell, molecular biology and biotechnology, zoology. M.S.
Chemistry. Includes analytical, biochemistry, inorganic, physical. M.S.
Communication. Includes mass communication, speech communication. M.A.
Communicative Disorders. Includes speech-language pathology. M.S.
English. M.A.
History. M.A.

EASTERN OREGON UNIVERSITY

La Grande, Oregon 97850-2899
Web site: www.eou.edu

Founded 1929. Located 265 miles E of Portland. Coed. State control. Quarter system. Library: 329,000 volumes, 1000 subscriptions.

Annual tuition: per credit, resident $227, nonresident $227. On-campus housing for married and single students. Average academic year housing costs: $8475 (including board) for single students. Contact Director of Residence Life for both on- and off-campus housing information. Phone: (541)962-3553.

Graduate Studies

Established 1952. Enrollment: full-time 66, part-time 118. Faculty: full-time 0, part-time 20. Degrees conferred: M.B.A., M.S., M.T.E. for Interns, M.T.E. for Practitioners.

ADMISSION REQUIREMENTS. Transcripts, two letters of reference, GRE required in support of application. TOEFL required for international applicants. Accepts transfer applicants. Apply to Office of Admission well in advance of registration. Application fee $50. Phone: (541)962-3772; fax: (541)962-3701.

ADMISSION STANDARDS. Relatively open. Usual minimum average: 3.0 (A = 4) last 60 credits.

FINANCIAL AID. Scholarships, tuition waivers, Federal W/S, loans. Approved for VA benefits. Apply to Financial Aid Office with admission application. Phone: (541)962-3393. Use FAFSA.

DEGREE REQUIREMENTS. For M.B.A., M.S.: 45 quarter hours minimum, at least 30 in residence; qualifying exam; written/oral comprehensive exam. M.T.E. Intern, during academic year; M.T.E. Practitioner, primarily summers.

FIELDS OF STUDY.
Business Administration. M.B.A.
Education.
Elementary Education—Fifth Year.
Reading.
Secondary Education—Fifth Year.
Special Education.

Teacher Education. Includes early childhood, elementary, middle school, secondary.

EASTERN VIRGINIA MEDICAL SCHOOL OF THE MEDICAL COLLEGE OF HAMPTON ROADS

Norfolk, Virginia 23501-1980
Web site: www.evms.edu

Established 1973. Private control. Semester system. Special facilities: Center for the Comprehensive Care of Immune Deficiency, Center for Pediatric Research, The Voice Center at EVMS, Virginia Prostate Center, The Virginia Center for Breast Cancer Awareness, Leonard R. Strelitz Diabetes Institutes, Sleep Disorders Center, Thomas R. Lee Center for Ocular Pharmacology, Howard and Georgeanna Jones Institute for Reproductive Medicine, Hearing and Balance Center, Glennan Center for Geriatrics and Gerontology, Center for Pediatric Research. Library: 86,000 volumes, 1800 subscriptions.

Annual tuition: full-time $22,087, nonresident $34,499. No on-campus housing available, call for information on off-campus housing. Phone: (757)446-5812. Total average figure for all other expenses $11,000.

Enrollment: first-year class 110 (5 EDP); total 436 (men 47%, women 53%, minorities 19%, state residents 70%). Degrees conferred: M.D., M.D.-Ph.D., M.D. Psy.D., M.P.A., M.P.H., M.S.

ADMISSION REQUIREMENTS. AMCAS report, transcripts, MCAT, two letters of recommendation, interview required in support of application. Preference given to residents of Tidewater area. Transfer applicants accepted on a space available basis. Graduates of unaccredited colleges not considered. Has EDP; apply between June 15 and August 1. Apply to Chair of Admissions Committee after June 15, before November 15. Application fee $95. Phone: (757)446-5812; fax: (757)446-5896.

ADMISSION STANDARDS. Selective. Accepts about 7.5% of all applicants. Number of applications 3424 (n/a out-of-state); number interviewed n/a (n/a out-of-state); number of acceptance 256 (n/a out-of-state); number enrolled 110 (37 out-of-state). Mean Composite MCAT 10.1; mean UGPA 3.45.

FINANCIAL AID. Scholarships, loans available. Apply to Financial Aid Office after acceptance, before March 15. Phone: (757) 446-5814. Use FAFSA. About 90% of students receive financial assistance.

DEGREE REQUIREMENTS. For M.D.: satisfactory completion of four-year program. For M.S.: 30-credit program with a thesis and nonthesis track. For M.P.A. 60-credit, two-year full-time program; nine clinical experiences.

FIELDS OF GRADUATE STUDY.
Art Therapy. M.S.
Biomedical Sciences. Includes molecular and integrative biosciences. Ph.D. only.
Biomedical Sciences. Includes applied biotechnology. M.S. Thesis, nonthesis option.
Clinical Embryology and Andrology. M.S. (Distance Learning).
Clinical Psychology. Psy.D. (with College of William and Mary, Eastern Virginia Medical School, Norfolk State University, and Old Dominion University).
Health Care and Public Health.
Medical Master's. M.S. (Post-Baccalaureate Program)
Master of Physician Assistant. M.P.A.
Master of Public Health. M.P.H. (with Old Dominion University).

EASTERN WASHINGTON UNIVERSITY
Cheney, Washington 99004-2431
Web site: www.ewu.edu

Founded 1882. CGS member. Located 16 miles SW of Spokane. Coed. State control. Quarter system. Library: 1,000,000 volumes, 6240 subscriptions.

Tuition: part-time resident $2160 per quarter, nonresident $5771 per quarter. On-campus housing for 143 married students, 1749 single students. Average academic year housing cost: $2364 married students, $4828 (including board) for single students. Apply to Director of Residential Life. Phone: (509)359-2451. Day-care facilities available.

Graduate School

Graduate study since 1947. Enrollment: full-time 589, part-time 440. College faculty teaching graduate students: full-time 230, part-time 30. Degrees conferred: M.A., M.S., M.Ed., M.B.A., M.F.A., M.N., M.P.A., D.P.T., M.S.W., M.U.R.P.

ADMISSION REQUIREMENTS. Two official transcripts, letters of recommendation required in support of application. GRE, interview for some programs, GMAT for business. TOEFL required for international applicants. Accepts transfer applicants. Apply to Graduate Program Office at least one month prior to beginning of quarter; some programs have earlier deadlines. Application fee $50. Phone: (509)359-6297; fax: (509)359-6044; e-mail: gradprogram@mail.ewu.edu.

ADMISSION STANDARDS. Selective. Minimum average: 3.0 (A = 4) in the last three years.

FINANCIAL AID. Annual awards from institutional funds: Scholarships, waiver scholarships, assistantships, Federal W/S, loans. Apply by February 1 to appropriate department for assistantships, to Financial Aid Office for federal programs. Phone: (509) 359-2314. Use FAFSA. Aid available for part-time students. About 45% of students receive aid from University and outside sources.

DEGREE REQUIREMENTS. For M.A., M.S.: 45 quarter hours minimum, at least 34 credits in residence; final comprehensive exam; thesis, reading knowledge of one foreign language sometimes required. For M.Ed., M.B.A.: 49 quarter hours minimum, at least 36 credits in residence; final comprehensive exam; thesis or research paper. For M.P.A.: 60 quarter hours minimum, at least 45 in residence; final comprehensive exam; thesis or research paper. For D.P.T.: 127 quarter hours minimum, at least 100 credits in residence: final comprehensive exam. For M.S.W.: 84 quarter hours minimum, 63 in residence; final comprehensive exam; thesis or research paper. For M.F.A., M.U.R.P.: 72 quarter hours minimum, 54 in residence; thesis (M.F.A.); final comprehensive exam. For M.N.: 59 quarter hours minimum, 44 in residence; thesis; final comprehensive exam.

FIELDS OF STUDY.
Adult Education. M.Ed.
Applied Psychology. M.S.
Biology. M.S.
Biology-Medical Technology Option.
Business Administration. M.B.A.
College Instruction. M.A., M.S.
Communication. M.S.
Communications Disorders. M.S.
Computer Science. M.S.
Counseling. Includes mental, health, school. M.S.
Creative Writing. M.F.A.
Curriculum and Instruction. M.Ed.
Early Childhood Education. M.Ed.
Educational Leadership. M.Ed.
Elementary Teaching. M.Ed.

English. Includes English in the public school, literature, rhetoric and composition, teaching English as a second language, technical and professional writing. M.A.
Foundations of Education. M.Ed.
French Education. M.Ed.
History. M.A.
Instructional Media and Technology. M.Ed.
Interdisciplinary. M.A., M.S.
Literacy Specialist Studies. M.Ed.
Mathematics. M.Ed., M.S.
Music. Includes composition, music education, performance. M.A.
Nursing. M.N.
Occupational Therapy. M.O.T.
Physical Education. M.S.
Physical Therapy. D.P.T.
Psychology. Includes clinical, developmental, experimental, school. M.S.
Public Administration. M.P.A.
School Library Media Administration. M.Ed.
Science Education. M.Ed.
Social Science Education. M.Ed.
Social Work. M.S.W.
Special Education. M.Ed.
Supervising (Clinic) Teaching. M.Ed.
Urban and Regional Planning. M.U.R.P.

EDINBORO UNIVERSITY OF PENNSYLVANIA
Edinboro, Pennsylvania 16444
Web site: www.edinboro.edu

Founded 1857. Located 20 miles S of Erie. State control. Semester system. Library: 468,900 volumes, 1829 subscriptions. Total University enrollment: 7700.

Tuition: per credit, resident $327, nonresident $523. On-campus housing available for single and married graduate students. Average academic year housing costs: $5518 (including board) for single students; $6000 for married students. Off-campus housing cost: $600 per month. Contact Housing Office for both on- and off-campus housing information. Phone: (814)732-2818. Day-care facilities available.

Graduate Studies and Research

Graduate study since 1957. Enrollment: full-time 498, part-time 670. College faculty teaching graduate students: full-time 88. Degrees conferred: M.Ed., M.A., M.S., M.F.A., M.I.T., M.S.N., M.S.W.

ADMISSION REQUIREMENTS. Transcripts, interview required in support of application. Online application available. MAT/GRE required for some departments. TOEFL required for international applicants. Accepts transfer applicants. Graduates of unaccredited institutions not considered. Apply to Coordinator of Graduate Studies Admissions at least one month prior to registration. Rolling admission process. Application fee $30. Phone: (814)732-2856; fax: (814)732-2611.

ADMISSION STANDARDS. Relatively open. Usual minimum average: 2.5 (A = 4).

FINANCIAL AID. Annual awards from institutional funds: Scholarships, assistantships, Federal W/S, loans. Apply by May 1 to Financial Aid Office. Phone: (814)732-2821. Use FAFSA and institutional FAF for graduate assistantship. Aid available for part-time students.

DEGREE REQUIREMENTS. For M.A., M.S., M.Ed., M.I.T.: 30 semester hours minimum, at least 21 in residence; thesis/nonthesis option. For M.F.A., M.S.W.: 60 semester hours, at least 45 in residence. For M.S.N.: 42 semester hours, at least 30 in residence.

FIELDS OF STUDY.
Art. M.A.
Biology. M.S.
Ceramics. M.F.A.
Clinical Psychology. M.A.
Communication Studies. M.A.
Community Counseling. M.A.
Educational Leadership. M.Ed.
Educational Psychology. M.Ed.
Elementary Education. M.Ed.
Elementary School Administration. M.Ed.
Information Technology. M.I.T.
Jewelry/Metalsmithing. M.F.A.
Middle and Secondary Education. M.Ed.
Nursing. Includes family nurse practitioner. M.S.N.
Painting. M.F.A.
Printmaking. M.F.A.
Reading. M.Ed.
Rehabilitation Counseling. M.A.
School Counseling. M.A.
Scuplture. M.F.A.
Secondary School Administration. M.Ed.
Social Science. M.A.
Social Work. M.S.W.
Special Education. M.Ed.
Speech-Language Pathology. M.A.
Student Personnel Services. M.A.
Studio Art. Includes ceramics, painting, printmaking, sculpture. M.F.A.

ELMIRA COLLEGE

Elmira, New York 14901
Web site: www.elmira.edu

Founded 1855. Located 54 miles SW of Binghamton, New York. Coed. Private control. 12-12-6-6 term. Special facility: off-campus graduate centers at Oswego, Bath, Corning, Ithaca, Rome, Watkins Glen, N.Y.; multimedia learning center, Center for Mark Twain Studies at Quarry Farms. Library: 389,000 volumes, 1755 subscriptions. Total College enrollment: 1200.

Graduate tuition: per credit Education $465, Management $520. Limited on-campus housing available for single students only. Annual housing cost: $8200 (including board). Apply to Coordinator of Housing.

Graduate Studies

Enrollment: about 618 (evening and summer sessions only). College faculty teaching graduate students: about 25. Degrees conferred: M.S.Ed.

ADMISSION REQUIREMENTS. Transcripts, three letters of recommendation, interview required in support of College's application. Online application available. Accepts transfer applicants. Apply to Dean of Continuing Education and Graduate Studies at least two weeks prior to registration. Application fee $100. Phone: (607)735-1825; fax: (607)735-1758; e-mail: graduate @elmira.edu.

ADMISSION STANDARDS. Relatively open. Usual minimum average 2.7 (A = 4).

FINANCIAL AID. Limited to Federal W/S, loans. Approved for VA benefits. Apply to Financial Aid Office at time of application. Use FAFSA.

DEGREE REQUIREMENTS. For master's: 36 semester hours, at least 30 on campus; research experience required.

FIELDS OF STUDY.
Childhood Education. M.S. Ed.
Emergency-Disaster Preparedness Management. M.S.M.
General Management. M.S.M.
Health Services Management. M.S.M.
Information Technology Management. M.S.M.
Literacy (Birth–12). M.S.Ed.

EMERSON COLLEGE

Boston, Massachusetts 02116-4624
Web site: www.emerson.edu

Founded 1880. CGS member. Located in downtown Boston. Coed. Private control. Semester system. Special facilities: one television and two radio stations, speech clinic, theater facilities, Center for Acquired Communication Disorders, Early Childhood Communication Center, Robbins Speech, Language, and Hearing Center. Library: 193,000 volumes, 7400 subscriptions. Total College enrollment: 4325.

Annual tuition: per credit $840. No on-campus housing available for graduate students. Average academic year housing costs: $7782 (including board). Off-campus housing costs: $600–$800 per month shared living accommodations. Contact Office of Off-Campus Students Services for off-campus housing information. Phone: (617)824-7863.

Graduate Division

Enrollment: full-time 754, part-time 171. Faculty: full-time 138, part-time 55. Degrees conferred: M.A., M.F.A., M.S.

ADMISSION REQUIREMENTS. Official transcripts, three letters of recommendation, GRE/GMAT, portfolio or writing sample required in support of application. Interview required by some departments. TOEFL required for international applicants. Accepts transfer applicants. Graduates of unaccredited institutions not considered. Apply to Director of Graduate Admission by June 1 (Fall, priority deadline March 1), November 1 (Spring, priority deadline November 1). Application fee $45, $75 for international students. Phone: (617)824-8610; fax: (617)824-8614; e-mail: gradapp@emerson.edu.

ADMISSION STANDARDS. Selective. Usual minimum average: 3.0 (A = 4), 2.7 for provisional admission.

FINANCIAL AID. Annual awards from institutional funds: fellowships, assistantships, scholarships, Federal W/S, loans. Approved for VA benefits. Apply by April 1 (Fall), December 1 (Spring), to the appropriate department for assistantships; to Office of Financial Aid for all other programs. Phone: (617)578-8655. Use FAFSA. Aid available for part-time students.

DEGREE REQUIREMENTS. For M.A.: 36–40 credits: thesis/nonthesis program; final written/oral exam. For M.S.: 51 credits. For M.F.A.: 52 credits; thesis/nonthesis program; final written/oral exam.

FIELDS OF STUDY.
Communication Management. M.A.
Creative Writing. M.F.A.
Global Marketing Communication and Advertising. M.A.
Health Communication. M.A.
Integrated Marketing Communication. M.A.
Journalism. M.A.
Media Arts. M.A.

Publishing and Writing. M.A.
Speech Communication & Disorder. M.S.
Theatre Education. M.A.

EMORY UNIVERSITY
Atlanta, Georgia 30322-1100
Web site: www.emory.edu

Founded 1836. Located in a suburban area 6 miles NE of downtown Atlanta. CGS and AAU member. Private control. Methodist affiliation. Semester system. Special facilities: Carter Center of Emory University, Center for Public Health Practice, Emerson Center for Scientific Computation, Emory Fertility Center, Institute for Women's Studies, Institute for African Studies, National Institute of Church Finance and Administration, Nutrition and Health Science Center, Vascular Surgery Center, Institute of the Liberal Arts, Yerkes Regional Primate Research Center, Michael C. Carlos Museum, Winship Cancer Center, Center for Research in Social Change. Library: 2,300,000 volumes, 24,600 subscriptions. The University's NIH ranking is 25th among all U.S. institutions with 574 awards/grants valued at $221,790,571. According to The Center at University of Florida, the University is ranked 27th in receipt of Federal Research funds with $228,255,000 and it ranks 32nd for total University research expenditures with $323,224,000. The University's endowment assets rank it 6th with $4,535,587,000. In 2004, the University awarded 164 doctorates, which ranked it 88th among all U.S. institutions eligible to award that degree. Seventeen of the University's faculty members have been elected to National Honor Academies and this ranks it 51st among all U.S. institutions. The Library: approximately 2,500,000 volumes, 24,600 subscriptions. Total University enrollment: 12,134.

Annual tuition: full-time $30,246, per credit $1260. On-campus graduate housing: approximately 272 units. Average academic year housing cost: $8000–$10,000. Apply to Graduate and Family Housing Office. Phone: (404)727-8960.

Graduate School of Arts and Sciences

Graduate study since 1919. Enrollment: full- and part-time 1647. Faculty: 655. Degrees conferred: M.A., M.S., M.A.T., M.Ed., M.M., M.S.M., Ph.D.

ADMISSION REQUIREMENTS. Two copies of transcripts, three letters of recommendation, essay, GRE required in support of School's application. International applicants whose native language is not English must demonstrate proficiency in English as specified by the individual department. Accepts transfer applicants. Graduates of unaccredited institutions not considered. Apply to Graduate School by January 1. (To be considered for Financial Aid in the Fall, apply by January 15; some departments have earlier deadlines.) Application fee $50. Phone: (404)727-0184; fax: (404)727-4990.

ADMISSION STANDARDS. Competitive to selective for most departments. Usual minimum average: 3.0 in major (A = 4).

FINANCIAL AID. Annual awards from institutional funds: tuition scholarships, graduate assistantships, teaching assistants, nonservice fellowships, tuition waivers, Federal W/S, loans. Apply by January 20 to the Financial Aid Office. Phone: (404)727-1141. Use FAFSA. About 60% of students receive aid. These awards available on a competitive basis. Aid available for part-time students.

DEGREE REQUIREMENTS. For M.A., M.S.: 24 semester hours minimum, two semesters in residence; thesis, final oral/written exam. For M.A.T., M.Ed., M.M., M.S.M.: 40 semester hours minimum, three semesters in residence; no thesis or language requirement. For Ph.D.: 48 semester hours beyond the master's; comprehensive exam; reading knowledge of one or more foreign languages in some departments; dissertation; final oral exam.

FIELDS OF STUDY.
Anthropology. Ph.D.
Art History. Ph.D.
Behavioral Sciences and Health Education. Ph.D.
Biological and Biomedical Sciences. Includes biochemistry, cell and development biology, genetics and molecular biology, immunology and molecular pathogenesis, microbiology and molecular genetics, molecular and systems pharmacology, neuroscience, nutrition and health sciences, population biology, ecology and evolution. Ph.D.
Biomedical Engineering. Ph.D.
Biostatistics. Ph.D.
Business. Includes accounting, finance, information systems, marketing, organizational management. Ph.D.
Chemistry. Ph.D.
Clinical Research. M.S. only.
Comparative Literature. Ph.D.
Computer Science and Informatics. Ph.D.
Economics. Ph.D.
Educational Studies. M.A., M.A.T., M.Ed., Ph.D.
English. Ph.D.
Epidemiology. Ph.D.
Film Studies. M.A. only.
French. Ph.D.
Health Services Research and Health Policy. Ph.D.
History. Ph.D.
Jewish Studies. M.A. only.
Liberal Arts. Graduate Institute of the Liberal Arts. Comparative and Interdisciplinary Studies. Ph.D.
Mathematics. M.S., Ph.D.
Music. Includes conducting, organ performance, sacred music. M.M., M.S.M.
Nursing. Ph.D.
Philosophy. Ph.D.
Physics. Includes computational sciences (M.S.). M.S.,Ph.D.
Political Science. Ph.D.
Psychology. Includes clinical, cognition and development, neuroscience and animal behavior. Ph.D.
Religion. Includes American religious cultures, comparative literature and religion, ethnics and society, Hebrew Bible, historical studies in theology and religion, new testament, person, community and religious life, theological studies, west and south Asian religions. Ph.D.
Sociology. Ph.D.
Spanish. Ph.D.
Women's Studies. Ph.D.

Roberto C. Goizueta Business School
Web site: www.goizueta.emory.edu

Established 1954. Public control. Accredited programs: M.B.A., E.M.B.A. offered in Buckhead and in downtown Atlanta; suburban environment. Semester system. Special Programs: accelerated M.B.A. program; foreign exchange programs (in Austria, Chile, Costa Rica, Finland, France, Germany, Hungary, Italy, Korea, Mexico, People's Republic of China, Republic of Singapore, Russia, Spain, United Kingdom, Venezuela); internships; Scholar Partnership Program with Spelman College. Special facilities: Center for Leadership and Career Studies, Center for Relationship Marketing.

Annual tuition: full-time $32,100. Enrollment: total full-time 462, part-time 190 (men 60%, women 40%). Faculty 72 full-time, 8 part-time; 99% with Ph.D./D.B.A. Degrees conferred: M.B.A. (full-time, part-time, day, evening), E.M.B.A. (weekends only, alternating Fridays, Saturdays), M.B.A.-J.D., M.B.A.-M.Div., M.B.A.-M.N., M.B.A.-M.P.H.

ADMISSION REQUIREMENTS. All applicants should have a bachelor's degree from a recognized institution of higher education and a strong mathematics background. Students are required to have their own personal computer. Submit application, GMAT (will accept GMAT test results from the last five years, latest acceptable date is March), official transcripts from each undergraduate/graduate school attended, three letters of recommendation, four essays, résumé (prefers at least four years of work experience), and an application fee of $140 to the Office of Admission and Student Services. Interview strongly recommended. Accepts electronic applications. In addition, international students (whose native language is other than English) should submit a TOEFL (minimum score 600) report, certified translations and evaluations of all official transcripts; recommendation should be in English or with certified translations, proof of health/immunization certificate, and proof of sufficient financial resources for two years of academic study. Beginning students are admitted Fall only. U.S. citizens apply by March 15 (Fall), international students apply by February 15 (Fall). On-campus interviews are strongly encouraged. Joint degree applicants must apply to and be accepted to both schools, contact the Admissions Office for current information and specific admissions requirements. Completed applications received by December 31 will be notified by January 31, after December 31 a rolling admissions process is used, notification is made within 4–6 weeks of receipt of completed application and supporting documents, Admissions Office phone: (404) 727-6311; fax: (404)727-4612; e-mail: admissions@bus.emory.edu.

ADMISSION STANDARDS. Highly selective. Median GMAT: 680; median GPA: 3.4 (A = 4). *U.S. News & World Report* ranking is in the top 20 of all U.S. business schools. *BusinessWeek* listed Business School in the top 50 American business schools.

FINANCIAL AID. Scholarships, Dean's Scholar Awards, minority scholarships, grants, Woodruff Fellowships, teaching assistantships, Dietz Loan Fund, Federal W/S, loans. Financial aid is available for part-time study. Financial aid may be available for international students. Assistantships may be available for joint degree candidates. Financial Aid applications and information are generally available at the on-campus visit/interview or after January 1; apply by March 1. Request scholarship, fellowship, assistantship information from the Business School; phone: (404)727-6039. Contact the University's Financial Aid Office for current need-based financial aid information. Phone: (404)727-1141. Use FAFSA (School code: 001564), also submit Financial Aid Transcript, Federal Income Tax forms. Approximately 45% of students receive some form of financial assistance.

DEGREE REQUIREMENTS. For M.B.A.: 63-credit program including 27 elective credits, two-year program; degree program must be completed in 9 semesters. For E.M.B.A.: sixteen-month program; International Business Colloquium (ten days abroad). For M.B.A.-M.N.: 6-semester program. For M.B.A.-M.Div.: Four-year program. For M.B.A.-M.P.H: 5-semester program. For M.B.A.-J.D.: four-year program.

M.B.A. AREAS OF CONCENTRATION:
Accounting.
Brand Marketing.
Capital Markets and Real Estate.
Corporate Finance.
Customer Relationship Management.
Decision Analysis/Operations Management.
Entrepreneurship and Global Management.
Finance.
Financial Analysis.
Global Financial Reporting & Analysis.
Healthcare Management.
Leadership.
Management Consulting.
Marketing.
Marketing Consulting.

Organization and Management.
Real Estate.
Sports, Media & Entertainment.
Strategy.

PH.D. AREAS OF CONCENTRATION:
Accounting.
Finance.
Information Systems.
Marketing.
Organizational Management.

School of Law
Web site: www.law.emory.edu

Founded 1916. ABA approved since 1923. AALS member. Semester system. Law library: 400,929 volumes, 4053 subscriptions; has LEXIS, NEXIS, WESTLAW, DOBIS; has more than 123 network connections.

Annual tuition: $38,176. Limited on-campus housing available. Contact housing office for availability. Phone: (404)727-8830.

Enrollment: first-year class 235, total full-time 701 (men 53%, women 47%, minorities 26%); postgraduates 60. Faculty: full-time 43, part-time 37. Student to faculty ratio 13.3 to 1. Degrees conferred: J.D., J.D.-M.A., J.D.-M.B.A., J.D.-M.P.H., J.D.-M.Div., J.D.-M.T.S., J.D. R.E.E.S., J.D.-Ph.D., LL.M. (Litigation, Taxation), LOL.M. (for foreign law students and professionals).

ADMISSION REQUIREMENTS. LSDAS report, transcripts, two letters of recommendation, LSAT (not later than December), personal statement, bachelor's degree required in support of application. Interview not required, but visits are encouraged. TOEFL required for international applicants. Accepts transfer applicants. Apply to Director of Admissions after September 1, before March 1. Beginning students admitted Fall only. Application fee $70. Phone: (404)727-6802; fax: (404)727-2477; e-mail: lawinfo@law.emory.edu.

ADMISSION REQUIREMENTS FOR BOTH AMERICAN AND INTERNATIONAL LL.M. APPLICANTS. Submit official application form (online), a curriculum vitae (résumé), official transcripts (for international applicants transcripts translated, if need be, through World Education Services, Inc. (312)966-6311 or info@wes.org, or visit their Web site at www.wes.org); the Law School Admission Council (LSAC) also offers a credential assembly service for our international applicants. For more information you can visit www.llm.lsac.org., TOEFL score (if needed), personal statement, at least two letters of recommendation. Apply by April 15. Application fee $70.

ADMISSION STANDARDS. Selective. Accepts approximately 36% of all students. Number of applicants 3659; number of acceptance 1064; number enrolled 235; LSAT (75% of students have a score at or above 161); GPA (75% of students have a GPA at or above 3.28). *U.S. News & World Report* ranking is in the top 22 of all U.S. law schools.

FINANCIAL AID Scholarships, fellowships (advanced students only), assistantships, Federal W/S, loans. Apply to Director of Admissions by March 1. Use FAFSA. Phone:(404)727-6039. About 36% of students receive aid other than loans from School funds.

DEGREE REQUIREMENTS, For J.D.: 88 semester hours minimum. For LL.M.: 24 semesters beyond the J.D.; one-year minimum in residence. For the master's and doctoral degrees: see Graduate School listing above.

School of Medicine (30322-1053)
Web site: www.med.emory.edu

Founded as Atlanta Medical College in 1854. Name changed to School of Medicine in 1915. Library: 220,000 volumes, 3000 subscriptions. NIH ranking is in top 25 of all U.S. institutions with 574 awards/grants worth $221,790,571.

Annual tuition: $38,346. On-campus housing for married students only. Apply to University Housing Office. Total average costs for all other expenses: $16,000.

Enrollment: first-year class 114; total full-time 462 (men 49%, women 51%, minorities 12%, state residents 33%); postgraduates 650; fellows 95. Faculty: approximately 1800 full-time, 516 part-time and volunteers. Degree conferred: M.D.; M.M.Sc., M.D.-M.P.H. are offered through Division of Allied Health Professions. The combined degree programs, M.S. and Ph.D. (Medical Scientist Training Program) are offered through the Graduate School of Arts and Sciences.

ADMISSION REQUIREMENTS. AMCAS report, transcripts, letters of reference, MCAT (preferably in Spring), supplemental application, interview required in support of application. Interview by invitation only. Applicants must have completed at least three years of college study. Accepts transfer applicants. Does not have EDP. Apply to Office of the Dean, School of Medicine, after June 15, before October 15. Application fee $80. Phone: (404)727-5660; fax: (404)727-5456; e-mail: medschadmiss@medadm.emory.edu.

ADMISSION STANDARDS. Very competitive. Accepts about 8.2% of all applicants. Number of applications 3759 (3359 out-of-state); number interviewed 752 (613 out-of-state); number of acceptance 308 (248 out-of-state); number enrolled 114 (79 out-of-state). Mean Composite MCAT 11.1; mean UGPA 3.64. *U.S. News & World Report* ranking is in the top 23 of all medical schools; ranked 38th in primary care. Approximately 33% are state residents.

FINANCIAL AID. Scholarships (merit and minority), fellowships, assistantships, NIH stipends, Federal W/S, loans. Apply to Financial Aid Office. Phone: (800)727-6039. Use FAFSA (school code: 001564). About 52% of students receive aid other than loans from School funds.

DEGREE REQUIREMENTS. For M.D.: satisfactory completion of four-year program; must pass Step 1 of USMLE for promotion to third year; pass Step 2 for graduation. For M.P.H. see Division of Allied Health Professions listing below. For M.S., Ph.D., see Graduate School of Arts and Sciences listing above.

FIELDS OF GRADUATE STUDY.
Biochemistry, Cell and Developmental Biology.
Genetics and Molecular Biology.
Immunology and Molecular Pathogenesis.
Microbiology and Molecular Genetics.
Molecular and Systems Pharmacology.
Neuroscience.
Nutrition and Health Sciences.
Population Biology, Ecology and Evolution.

Nell Hodgson Woodruff School of Nursing
Web site: www.nursing.emory.edu

Annual tuition: $30,200, per credit $1258. Enrollment: full-time 74, part-time 41. School faculty: full-time 34, part-time 21. Degrees conferred: M.S.N., M.S.N.-M.P.H., M.S.N.-M.B.A., Ph.D.

ADMISSION REQUIREMENTS. Transcripts, B.S.N., MAT or GRE, résumé, statement of purpose, three letters of recommendation, one year experience in a clinical area required in support of School's application. Online application available. TOEFL required for international applicants. Accepts transfer applicants. Graduates of unaccredited institutions not considered. Apply by January 15 (Fall), October 1 (Spring) to Office of Student Affairs. Application fee $50. Phone: (404)727-7980 or (800)222-3879; fax: (404)727-8509; e-mail: admit@nursing.emory.edu.

ADMISSION STANDARDS. Selective. Usual minimum overall average: 3.0; average for nursing courses: 3.3 (A = 4).

FINANCIAL AID. Scholarships, fellowships, assistantships, Federal W/S, loans. Approved for VA benefits. Apply by February 15 to the Programs Director for scholarships, fellowships, assistantships; to the Financial Aid Office for all other programs. Phone: (404)727-6039. Use FAFSA (School code: 005187) and CSS Profile. Aid available for part-time students.

DEGREE REQUIREMENTS. For M.S.N.: 48 semester hours minimum, all in residence; thesis option.

FIELDS OF STUDY.
Acute Care Nurse Practitioner.
Adult Nurse Practitioner.
Adult Oncology Nurse Practitioner.
Emergency Nurse Practitioner.
Family Nurse Practitioner.
Family Nurse-Midwife.
Gerontological Nurse Practitioner.
International Health. M.S.N.-M.P.H. only.
Nurse-Midwifery.
Pediatrics Nurse Practitioner—Acute Care.
Pediatrics Nurse Practitioner—Primary Care.
Public Health Nursing Leadership.
Women's Health/Adult Health Nurse Practitioner.
Women's Health Nurse Practitioner.
Women's Health Care.

Rollins School of Public Health
Web site: www.sph.emory.edu

Semester system. Annual tuition: $30,200, per credit $1258. On-campus housing available. Apply to University Housing Office. Phone: (404)727-5481; fax: (404)727-3996.

Enrollment: full-time 557, part-time 148. Faculty: full-time 160, part-time 233. Degrees conferred: M.P.H., M.S.P.H., M.B.A.-M.P.H., M.D.-M.P.H., M.S.N.-M.P.H., J.D.-M.P.H.

ADMISSION REQUIREMENTS. Transcript, GRE, bachelor's degree required in support of School's application. TOEFL (minimum score 550) required for foreign applicants. Graduates of unaccredited institutions not considered. Apply to School by January 15. Application fee $75. Phone: (404)727-3317; fax: (404) 727-3996; e-mail: admit@sph.emory.edu.

ADMISSION STANDARDS. Selective. Usual minimum average: 3.0 (A = 4).

FINANCIAL AID. Scholarships, grants, fellowships, teaching assistantships, Federal W/S, loans. Apply by February 15 to the Financial Aid Office and to Program Director. Phone: (404)727-3958. Use FAFSA.

DEGREE REQUIREMENTS. For M.P.H., M.S.P.H.: 42–48 semester hours minimum, at least two in residence; comprehensive written exam or thesis. For Ph.D.: for degree requirements, please consult Graduate School of Arts and Sciences listing above.

FIELDS OF STUDY.
Behavioral Sciences and Health Education.
Biostatistics.
Environmental and Occupational Health.
Epidemiology.
Global Health.
Health Policy and Management.

EMPORIA STATE UNIVERSITY

Emporia, Kansas 66801-5087
Web site: www.emporia.edu

Founded 1863. CGS member. Located 55 miles SW of Topeka. Coed. State control. Semester system. Special facilities: Ross Natural History Reservation, Butcher Laboratory School, Charles Coughlen Tall Grass Preserve, Reading Woods. Library: 733,000 volumes, 1405 subscriptions. Total University enrollment: 6288.

Tuition: per semester, full-time resident $3300, nonresident $10,796, per credit resident $173, nonresident $463. On-campus housing for 93 married students, unlimited for single students. Average academic year housing cost: $2160 for married students, $2363–$4800 for single students. Apply to Residential Life and Housing Coordinator. Phone: (620)341-5264, (620)341-5909. Day-care facilities available.

Graduate Division

Enrollment: full-time 277, part-time 1285. College faculty teaching graduate students: full-time 198, part-time 21. Degrees conferred: M.A., M.A.T., M.B.A., M.M., M.L.S., M.L.I.M., M.S., Ed.S., Ph.D.

ADMISSION REQUIREMENTS. Transcript, letters of recommendation required in support of University's application. Online application available. GRE/GMAT/MAT required by some departments. TOEFL required for international applicants. Interview required for library science major. Accepts transfer applicants. Graduates of unaccredited institutions not considered. Apply to Graduate Office at least 30 days before the first day of enrollment period. Application fee $30, $75 for international applicants. Phone: (800)950-GRAD; fax: (620)341-5909.

ADMISSION STANDARDS. Relatively open. Usual minimum average: 2.5 (A = 4), 2.75 in last 60 credits.

FINANCIAL AID. Annual awards from institutional funds: fellowships, research assistantships, teaching assistantships, graduate aides, special graduate assistantships, grants, Federal W/S, loans. Approved for VA benefits. Apply to Graduate Office by March 15. Phone: (620)341-5457. Use FAFSA. About 30% of students receive aid other than loans from University and outside sources. Aid available for part-time students.

DEGREE REQUIREMENTS. For M.A., M.B.A., M.M., M.S.: 30 semester hours with thesis, or 32–38 hours without thesis, at least 22 in residence and one semester in full-time attendance; final written/oral exams. For M.A.T.: 36 semester hours minimum, at least 22 in residence and one semester in full-time attendance; thesis/nonthesis option; final written/oral exam. For M.L.S., M.L.I.M.: 42 specified hours; thesis/nonthesis option; final written/oral exam. For Ed.S.: 22 hours minimum in residence beyond the master's, thesis included, at least one semester in full-time attendance; GRE for candidacy; final written/oral exam. For Ph.D.: 60 semester hours beyond master's minimum, at least 42 in full-time residence; advancement to candidacy; research tool; comprehensive exam; dissertation; final oral exam.

FIELDS OF STUDY.
Accounting. M.B.A.
Art Therapy. M.S.
Biology. M.A., M.S.
Business Administration. M.B.A.
Business Education. M.S.
Education. Includes art, early childhood, education of the gifted, elementary, reading, secondary, counselor education, rehabilitation counseling, curriculum and instruction, school counseling. M.S.
Educational Administration. M.S.
English. M.A.

Health, Physical Education and Recreation. M.S.
History. Includes American and world. M.A.
Legal Information Management. M.L.I.M.
Library and Information Management. M.L.S., Ph.D.
Mathematics. M.S.
Mental Health Counseling. M.S.
Music. Includes music education, performance; recital for performance majors. M.M.
Physical Science. Includes chemistry, earth science, physics, physical sciences. M.S.
Psychology. Includes clinical, organizational, school psychology. M.S., Ed.S.
Rehabilitation Counseling. M.S.
School Counseling. M.S.
School Psychology. M.S.
Social Science. M.A.T.
Special Education. M.S.

FAIRFIELD UNIVERSITY

Fairfield, Connecticut 06430-5195
Web site: www.fairfield.edu

Founded 1942. Located 50 miles NE of New York City. Coed on graduate level. Private control. Roman Catholic. Semester system. Library: 325,166 volumes, 1790 subscriptions. Total University enrollment 5100.

No on-campus housing available for graduate students.

Graduate School of Education and Allied Professions

Graduate study since 1950. Tuition: per credit hour $585. Enrollment: full-time 167, part-time 402. University faculty teaching graduate students: full-time 17, part-time 25. Degrees conferred: M.A., C.A.S.

ADMISSION REQUIREMENTS. Transcripts, two letters of recommendation, PRAXIS I CBT or waiver required in support of School's application. TOEFL required for international applicants. Graduates of unaccredited institutions not considered. Apply to Graduate School Office; no specified closing date except for MMTP and Counselor Education program. Rolling admission process. Application fee $55. Phone: (203)254-4184; fax: (203)254-4073.

ADMISSION STANDARDS. Relatively open. Usual minimum average: 2.67 (A = 4).

FINANCIAL AID. Annual awards from institutional funds: scholarships, fellowships, tuition waivers, grants, graduate assistantships, Federal W/S, loans. Apply to Dean by May 1 (Fall) December 15 (Spring). Phone: (203)254-4125. Use FAFSA and University's FAF. Loans available for part-time students.

DEGREE REQUIREMENTS. For M.A.: 33–54 credits; comprehensive examination or thesis. For C.A.S.: 30 credits minimum beyond the master's, at least 24 in residence. No thesis or language requirement.

FIELDS OF STUDY.
Applied Psychology. Includes human services, foundations of advanced psychology, industrial/organizational/personal. M.A.
Bilingual Education. M.A., C.A.S.
Community Counseling. M.A., C.A.S.
Computers in Education. M.A., C.A.S.
Curriculum and Instruction. Includes curriculum and teaching, elementary education, secondary education. M.A., C.A.S.
Educational Technology. M.A., C.A.S.
Marriage and Family Therapy. M.A.

School Counseling. M.A., C.A.S.
School Media Specialist. M.A., C.A.S.
School Psychology. M.A., C.A.S.
Secondary Education. M.A.
Special Education. M.A., C.A.S.
TESOL Foreign Languages and Bilingual/Multicultural Education. M.A., C.A.S.

Charles F. Dolan School of Business

Graduate study since 1978. Accredited program: M.B.A. Tuition: per credit $585. Enrollment: full-time 36, part-time 148. University faculty teaching graduate students: full-time 43, part-time 3. Degrees conferred: E.M.B.A., M.B.A., M.B.A.P.A. (Public Accounting), M.S.F.

ADMISSION REQUIREMENTS. Transcripts, statement of self-evaluation, two references, GMAT required in support of School's application. Online application available. For M.B.A.P.A. a Statement of Certification is required. In addition, a sponsorship by a public accounting firm required for practicum. TOEFL (minimum score 550) required for international applicants. Graduates of unaccredited institutions not considered. Apply to School Office by July 15 (Fall), November 15 (Spring). Rolling admissions process. Application fee $55. Phone: (203)254-4184.

ADMISSION STANDARDS. Admission formula: 200 × GPA + GMAT must equal 1100 or better.

FINANCIAL AID. Annual awards from institutional funds: grants, assistantships, Federal W/S, loans. Approved for VA benefits. Apply to Dean by May 1 (Fall), December 15 (Spring). Phone: (203)254-4000. Use FAFSA (School code: 001385) and University's FAF. Loans available for part-time students.

DEGREE REQUIREMENTS. For M.B.A.: 62 credits, at least 35 in residence. For M.B.A.P.A.: 12–15 month program (includes 150 hour criterion to sit for Uniform CPA Exam); practicum. For M.S.F.: 30 credits program, at least 24 in residence.

FIELDS OF STUDY.
Accounting. M.S.
Business Administration. Includes concentrations in accounting, e-business, finance, health care management, human resource management, information systems and operations, international business, marketing, taxation. M.B.A.
Finance. M.S.F.
Public Accounting. Includes concentrations in finance, information systems and operations management, taxation. M.B.A.P.A.
Taxation. M.S.

FAIRLEIGH DICKINSON UNIVERSITY
College at Florham
Madison, New Jersey 07940-1099
Web site: www.fdu.edu

Established 1942. Private control. Coed. Semester system. Special facilities: Contemporary Center for Advanced Psychoanalytic Studies, Corporate Communication Institute, Florham Center for University Women's Issues, Institute for Global Commerce, Center for Global Teaching and Learning, Center for Human Resource Management Studies, New York/New Jersey Economic Research Center, Public Administrations Institute, Regional Center for College Students with Learning Disabilities, Rothman Institute of Entrepreneurial Studies, Center for Service Professionals. Library: 182,000 volumes, 1259 subscriptions. Daycare facilities available. Total University enrollment: 11,000.

Tuition: $767 per graduate credit. Contact Office of Student Life for off-campus housing. Phone: (973)443-8570.

Graduate Studies

Enrollment: full- and part-time 891. Faculty: full-time 62, part-time 84. Degrees conferred: M.A., M.A.T., M.B.A., M.P.A., M.S., M.S.T.

ADMISSION REQUIREMENTS. Official transcripts required in support of application. Three letters of recommendation, GRE/GMAT/MAT/PRAXIS required for some programs. TOEFL required for international applicants. Accepts transfer applicants. Graduates of unaccredited institutions may not be considered. Rolling admissions process. Early application encouraged. Application fee $40. Phone: (973)442-8905; fax: (973)443-8088.

ADMISSION STANDARDS. Selective. Usual minimum average: 2.5, 3.0 in major field of undergraduate study (A = 4).

FINANCIAL AID. Limited to fellowships, loans. Approved for VA benefits. Apply to appropriate department chair for fellowships; to Office of Financial Aid for loans. Phone: (973)443-8700. Use FAFSA.

DEGREE REQUIREMENTS. For master's: 32–60 semester credits minimum, at least 26 in residence; final written exam: thesis/nonthesis option; other requirements vary by department.

FIELDS OF STUDY.

MAXWELL BECTON COLLEGE OF ARTS AND SCIENCES:
Addictions Counseling. M.A.
Applied Social and Community Psychology. M.A.
Biology. M.S.
Chemistry. M.S.
Clinical/Counseling Psychology. M.A.
Computer Science. M.S.
Corporate and Organizational Communications. M.A.
Creative Writing. M.F.A.
English Language and Literature. M.A.T.
General Experimental Psychology. M.A.
Industrial/Organizational Psychology. M.A.
Mathematics. M.S.
Organizational Behavior. M.A.
Physical Science. M.A.T.
Teaching. Includes elementary education, English as a second language, English language and literacy, secondary education, social studies education, world languages. M.A.T.

SAMUEL J. SILBERMAN COLLEGE OF BUSINESS ADMINISTRATION:
Accounting.
Accounting (for Non-Accountants).
Business Administration.
Corporate and Organizational Communication.
Entrepreneurial Studies.
Finance.
Hospitality Management Studies.
Human Resource Management.
International Business.
Management. Includes corporate and organizational communication, corporate communication.
Marketing.
Pharmaceutical-Chemical Studies.
Public Administration. M.P.A.
Taxation. M.S.T.

FAIRLEIGH DICKINSON UNIVERSITY

Metropolitan Campus
Teaneck, New Jersey 07666-1914
Web site: www.fdu.edu

Established 1942. Private control. Coed. Semester system. Library: 435,700 volumes, 15,000 subscriptions. Total Campus enrollment: 7930.

Tuition: per credit $767. No on-campus housing available. Contact the Office of Student Life for off-campus housing information. Phone: (201)692-2231.

Graduate Studies

Enrollment: full- and part-time 2500. Faculty: full-time 148, part-time 67. Degrees conferred: M.A., M.A.T., M.B.A., M.S., M.P.A., M.S., M.S.E.E., M.S.N., M.S.T., Ph.D. (Clinical Psychology).

ADMISSION REQUIREMENTS. Transcripts, three letters of recommendation, GRE/GMAT/MAT/PRAXIS required in support of applications. TOEFL required for international applicants. Accepts transfer applicants. Graduates of unaccredited institutions may not be considered. Rolling admissions process. Early application encouraged. Application fee $40. Phone: (201)692-2560.

ADMISSION STANDARDS. Selective. Usual minimum average: 2.5 (A = 4), 3.0 in major field of undergraduate study.

FINANCIAL AID. Scholarships, research fellowships, teaching fellowships, M.P.A., M.A.T. paid internships, loans. Approved for VA benefits. Apply to appropriate department chair for fellowships; to Office of Financial Aid for all other programs. Phone: (201)692-2362. Use FAFSA.

DEGREE REQUIREMENTS. For master's: 32–60 semester credits minimum, at least 26 in residence; final written exam; thesis/nonthesis option; other requirements vary by department. For Ph.D.: 60 semester credits beyond the master's; qualifying exam; internship; dissertation; final exam.

FIELDS OF STUDY.

UNIVERSITY COLLEGE:
Biological Sciences. M.A.T.
Biology. M.S.
Clinical Psychology. M.A., Ph.D.
Computer Engineering. M.S.
Computer Science. M.S.
E-Commerce. M.S.
Educational Leadership. M.A.
Electrical Engineering. M.S.E.E.
English and Comparative Literature. M.A.
General-Theoretical Psychology. M.A.
History. M.A.
International Studies. M.A.
Learning Disabilities. M.A.
Management Information Systems. M.S.
Medical Technology. M.S.
Multilingual Education. M.A.
Nursing. M.S.N.
Physical Sciences. M.A.T.
Physics. Includes photonics. M.S.
Political Science. M.A.
Science. Includes science education, elementary science, cosmetic science. M.A.
School Psychology. M.A., Psy.D.
System Science. Includes environmental studies. M.S.
Teaching. Includes elementary education, English as a second language, secondary education. M.A.T.

SAMUEL J. SILBERMAN COLLEGE OF BUSINESS ADMINISTRATION:
Accounting.
Accounting (for Non-Accountants).
Administrative Science.
Economics.
Entrepreneurial Studies.
Finance.
Financial Economics. M.A.
Global Management.
Hospitality Management Studies.
Health Systems Management. E.M.B.A.
Human Resource Management.
International Business.
Management. Includes corporate communication, health systems management, information systems.
Marketing.
Pharmaceutical-Chemical Studies.
Public Administration. M.P.A.
Taxation. M.S.T.

FITCHBURG STATE COLLEGE

160 Pearl Street
Fitchburg, Massachusetts 01420-2697
Web site: www.fsc.edu

Founded 1894. CGS member. Located 26 miles N of Worcester. Coed. State control. Semester system. Library: 236,743 volumes, 2039 subscriptions. Total Campus enrollment: 5340.

Tuition: per credit, resident $150, nonresident $150. Limited on-campus housing available. Average academic year housing costs: $4680 (including board). Contact Office of Residence Life for both on- and off-campus housing information. Phone: (978)665-3219. Day care facilities available.

Division of Graduate and Continuing Education

Enrollment: full-time 200, part-time 721. Graduate faculty: part-time 150. Degrees conferred: M.A.T., M.B.A., M.Ed. M.S., C.A.G.S.

ADMISSION REQUIREMENTS. Transcripts, GRE/MAT/GMAT required in support of application. TOEFL required for international applicants. Accepts transfer applicants. Graduates of unaccredited institutions not considered. Apply to Director of Admission at least one month prior to entrance. Rolling admissions process. Application fee $25, $50 for international applicants. Phone: (978)665-3144; fax: (978)665-4540; e-mail: admissions@fsc.edu.

ADMISSION STANDARDS. Selective. Usual minimum average: 2.8 (A = 4). Minimum GMAT score 400, MAT 50th percentile.

FINANCIAL AID. Scholarships, research and graduate assistantships, loans. Apply to the Graduate Office by September 15 (Fall), January 15 (Spring) for scholarships; by May 15 (Fall) for assistantships; to Financial Aid Office for all other programs. Phone: (978)665-3185. Use FAFSA.

DEGREE REQUIREMENTS. For master's: 33–36 semester hours minimum, at least 30 in residence; no language requirement; thesis/nonthesis option. For C.A.G.S.: 30 semester hours beyond the master's; special project/final exam.

FIELDS OF STUDY.
Accounting. M.B.A.
Arts Education. M.Ed.
Biology. M.A., M.A.T.

Business Administration and Management. M.B.A.
Communication and Media Management. M.S.
Computer Science. M.S.
Consultation and Peer Leadership. C.A.G.S.
Counseling. Includes psychological, school. M.S.
Criminal Justice. M.S.
Earth Science. M.A., M.A.T.
Early Childhood Education. M.Ed.
Educational Leadership and Management. C.A.G.S.
Educational Staff Development. C.A.G.S.
Elementary Education. M.Ed.
English. M.A., M.A.T.
Forensic Nursing. M.S.
History. M.A., M.A.T.
Interdisciplinary Studies. C.A.G.S.
Mathematics. M.A., M.A.T.
Middle School Education. M.Ed.
Nursing. M.S.
Occupational Education. M.Ed.
Science Education. M.Ed.
Secondary Education. M.Ed.
Special Education. M.Ed.
Teacher Leadership. C.A.G.S.
Technology Education. M.Ed.

FLORIDA AGRICULTURAL AND MECHANICAL UNIVERSITY

Tallahassee, Florida 32307
Web site: www.famu.edu

Founded 1887. CGS member. Coed. State control. Semester system. Special facilities: Community Development and Research Center, Environmental Technology Transfer Center, Center for Water Quality, Small Business Development Center, Viticulture and Small Farm Development Center, Environmental Sciences Institute, Cooperative Institute for Internal Policy Research and Education, Institute for Building Sciences, Institute on Urban Policy and Commerce. Library: 466,000 volumes, 2200 subscriptions.

Tuition: full-time resident $1969, nonresident $6855; per hour, resident $164, nonresident $571. On-campus housing for 85 married students. Average per semester housing cost: $2800–$3900 per single occupancy. Apply to Business Manager for on-campus housing; to Dean of Men or Dean of Women for off-campus housing information. Phone: (850)599-3992.

School of Graduate Studies and Research

Graduate study since 1945. Enrollment: full-time 800, part-time 1,591. Graduate faculty: full-time 200, part-time 20. Degrees conferred: M.Arch., M.S., M.Ed., M.B.A., M.A.S.S., M.L.A., M.P.T., M.P.H., M.S.S.C.P., M.S.W., Pharm.D., Ph.D.

ADMISSION REQUIREMENTS. Transcripts, GRE/GMAT required in support of School's application. Online application available. TOEFL (minimum score 550) required for international applicants. Interview not required. Accepts transfer applicants. Graduates of unaccredited colleges not considered. Apply by July 22 (Fall), April 2 (Summer), November 30 (Spring). Application fee $20. Phone: (850)599-3796.

ADMISSION STANDARDS. Selective. Usual minimum average: 2.5 (A = 4). For Business the admission formula is 200 × GPA + GMAT must be 1000 or above.

FINANCIAL AID. Scholarships, fellowships, Federal W/S, loans. Apply to Graduate Dean by March 1 for fellowships and scholarships; to Financial Aid Office for Federal programs. Phone: (850) 599-3730. Use FAFSA (University code: 001480). About 20% of students receive aid other than loans from School and outside sources. No aid other than loans for part-time students.

DEGREE REQUIREMENTS. For master's: 36 hours minimum including thesis, at least 30 in residence; final written/oral exam. For Pharm. D.: series of clinical clerkships, covering approximately 2000 hours; written comprehensive exam; clinical research project. For Ph.D.: 90 semester hours minimum beyond bachelor's; one foreign language or research tool; qualifying exam; dissertation; final oral exam.

FIELDS OF STUDY.

COLLEGE OF ARTS AND SCIENCES:
African American History. M.A.S.S.
Biology. M.S.
Chemistry. M.S.
Criminal Justice. M.A.S.S.
Economics. M.A.S.S.
History. M.A.S.S.
Physics. M.S., Ph.D.
Political Sciences. M.A.S.S.
Psychology. Includes community, (M.S.), school (M.S.). M.A.S.S. M.S.
Public Administration. M.A.S.S.
Public Management. M.A.S.S.
Sociology. M.A.S.S.
Social Work. M.A.S.S., M.S.W.
Software Engineering. M.S.

COLLEGE OF EDUCATION:
Adult Education. M.Ed., M.S.
Business Education. M.Ed., M.S.
Counselor Education. M.Ed., M.S.
Educational Leadership. M.Ed., M.S., Ph.D.
Elementary Education. M.Ed., M.S.
Physical Education. Includes sport and leisure management. M.Ed., M.S.
Secondary Education. Includes biology, chemistry, English, history, mathematics, physics. M.Ed., M.S.
Vocational Education. M.Ed., M.S.

COLLEGE OF PHARMACY AND PHARMACEUTICAL SCIENCES:
Pharmaceutical Sciences. Includes medicinal chemistry (M.S., Ph.D.), pharmacology and toxicology (M.S., Ph.D.), environmental toxicology (M.S., Ph.D.), pharmacoeconomics (M.S.), pharmacoepidemiology (M.S.), pharmaceutics (M.S., Ph.D.), pharmacy administration (M.S.).

COLLEGE OF ENGINEERING SCIENCES, TECHNOLOGY, AND AGRICULTURE:
Agricultural Sciences. Include agribusiness, animal science, engineering tech, international program, entomology, biotechnology, plant science. M.S.
Entomology. Includes aquatic entomology, biological control. Ph.D. in cooperation with the University of Florida.
Food Science. M.S.

COLLEGE OF ENGINEERING:
Biomedical Engineering. M.S., Ph.D.
Chemical Engineering. M.S., Ph.D.
Civil Engineering. M.S., Ph.D.
Electrical Engineering. M.S., Ph.D.
Environmental Engineering. M.S., Ph.D.
Industrial Engineering. Includes engineering management. M.S., Ph.D.
Mechanical Engineering. M.S., Ph.D.
Note: Engineering is administered by Florida State University.

ENVIRONMENTAL SCIENCES INSTITUTE:

Environmental Science. Includes environmental restoration and waste management, marine and estuarine science, environmental policy and management, environmental biotechnology, radiation protection. M.S.

Environmental Science. Includes aquatic and terrestrial ecology, environmental chemistry, biomolecular science, environmental policy and management. Ph.D.

SCHOOL OF ALLIED HEALTH SCIENCES:

Health Administration. M.S.
Health Care Administration. M.S.
Physical Therapy. M.P.T.

SCHOOL OF ARCHITECTURE:

Architecture. M.Arch.
Architectural Studies. M.S.
Landscape Architecture. M.L.A.

SCHOOL OF BUSINESS AND INDUSTRY:

Business Administration. M.B.A.

SCHOOL OF JOURNALISM AND GRAPHIC COMMUNICATION:

Journalism. M.S.
Professional Development Track. Includes broadcast journalism, copy editing, newspaper journalism.

SCHOOL OF NURSING:

Nursing. Includes adult/gerontology nursing. M.S.

FLORIDA ATLANTIC UNIVERSITY

P.O. Box 3091
Boca Raton, Florida 33431-0991
Web site: www.fau.edu

Opened 1964. CGS member. Main campus located midway between Ft. Lauderdale and West Palm Beach just off I-95, other campus in Broward County. Coed. State control. Semester system. Library: 1,400,000 volumes, 8500 subscriptions. Total University enrollment: 25,700.

Tuition: per semester hour, resident $244, nonresident $912. On-campus housing for graduate single men and women; none for married students. Annual housing cost: $7993 (including board). Apply to Director of Housing. Phone: (561)297-2880; e-mail: housing@fau.edu.

Graduate Studies

Enrollment: degree-seeking students full-time 1456, part-time 1984. University faculty teaching graduate students: full-time and part-time 1057. Degrees conferred: M.Ed., M.S., M.A., M.Acc., M.A.T., M.F.A., M.J.P.M., M.N.M., M.S.T., M.P.A., M.B.A., M.B.S., M.Tax., M.U.R.P., M.S.W., Ed.S., M.S.N., Ed.D., Ph.D., D.N.S.

ADMISSION REQUIREMENTS. Transcripts, letters of recommendation, GRE Subject Tests/GMAT required in support of application. Online application available. TOEFL required for foreign applicants. Accepts transfer applicants. Graduates from unaccredited institutions not considered. Apply to Director of Admissions at least ninety days prior to registration. Application fee $20. Phone: (561)297-3624; e-mail: gradadm@fau.edu.

ADMISSION STANDARDS. Selective. Usual minimum average: 3.0 (A = 4), and combined score of 1000 on GRE, 450 GMAT.

FINANCIAL AID. Scholarships, assistantships, fellowships, teaching/research assistantships, nonresident tuition waivers, Federal W/S, loans. Apply to appropriate department chair for assistantship, fellowships; to Office of Student Financial Aid for all other programs. No specified closing date. Phone: (561)297-3530. Use FAFSA.

DEGREE REQUIREMENTS. For master's: 30–40 semester hours minimum, thesis/nonthesis option. For Ed.D.: 90 semester hours minimum beyond the bachelor's degree; essentially the same as for the Ph.D., except no language requirement. For Ph.D.: 40–80 semester hours minimum beyond master's; one foreign language or research tool; qualifying exam; admission to candidacy; dissertation; final oral exam.

FIELDS OF STUDY.

Accounting.
Anthropology.
Applied Mathematics and Statistics.
Art.
Biological Sciences.
Biomedical Science.
Business Administration.
Chemistry.
Civil Engineering.
Communication.
Comparative Literature.
Comparative Studies.
Complex Systems and Brain Sciences.
Computer Arts.
Computer Engineering.
Computer Science.
Counselor Education. Includes mental health, rehabilitation.
Criminology and Criminal Justice.
Crises and Emergency Management.
Curriculum and Instruction.
Economics.
Educational Leadership.
Electrical Engineering.
Elementary Education.
English.
Environmental M.B.A.
Environmental Science.
Exceptional Student Education.
Exercise and Health Promotion.
Finance.
French.
Geography.
Geology.
German.
Global Entrepreneurship.
Graphic Design.
Health Administration.
History.
International Business.
Languages and Linguistics.
Liberal Studies.
Manufacturing Systems Engineering.
Marketing.
Mathematics.
Mechanical Engineering.
Music.
Non-Profit Management.
Nursing.
Ocean Engineering.
Physics.
Political Science.
Psychology.
Public Administration.
Reading.
Real Estate.
School Counseling.

Social Foundations. Includes educational psychology, educational research, education technology, multicultural education.
Social Work.
Sociology.
Spanish.
Speech-Language Pathology.
Sport Management.
Taxation.
Teacher Education.
Theatre.
Urban and Regional Planning.
Women's Studies.

FLORIDA COASTAL SCHOOL OF LAW

7555 Beach Boulevard
Jacksonsonville, FL 32216
Web site: www.fcsl.edu

Founded 1996. ABA approved since 1998. AALS member. Private control. Semester system. Special facilities: Center for Sports and Law, Center for Law and Public Policy. Law library: 220,091 volumes, 3175 subscriptions. Library has LEXIS, WESTLAW, DIALOG, OCLC.

Tuition: full-time $27,088, part-time $21,910. Off-campus housing available only. Check Web site for housing information. Annual housing costs approximately $17,670.

Enrollment: full- and part-time 449; total full-time 834, part-time 214 (men 55%, women 45%, minorities 39%).

Faculty: Total full- and part-time 102 (men 43%, women 57%, minorities 20%). Student to faculty ratio 17.8 to 1. Degree conferred: J.D.

ADMISSION REQUIREMENTS. LSDAS Law School report, official transcript, LSAT, two letters of recommendation, personal statement required in support of application. Interview not required. International applicant must present adequate evidence of his or her knowledge and usage of the English language. Accepts transfer applications. Graduates of unaccredited colleges not considered. Apply to Director of Admission after November 1, by June 1. Rolling admission process. Application fee $50. Phone: (904)680-7710.

ADMISSION STANDARDS. Selective. Accepts approximately 37% of full-time and 67% of part-time students. Number of full-time applicants 4659, part-time 60; number of acceptance full-time 1715, part-time 40; number enrolled full-time 431, part-time 18; LSAT (75% of full-time students have a score at or above 150, part-time 147); GPA (75% of full-time students have a GPA at or above 2.88, part-time 2.71). *U.S. News & World Report* ranking is in the 4th tier of all U.S. law schools.

FINANCIAL AID. Scholarships, grants, Federal W/S, loans. Approximately 35% of students received aid other than loans from school funds. Apply to the Financial Aid Office by April 1. Phone: (904)680.7717. Use FAFSA.

DEGREE REQUIREMENTS. For J.D.: satisfactory completion of 90-credit, three (full-time) or four (part-time) year program.

FLORIDA INSTITUTE OF TECHNOLOGY

Melbourne, Florida 32901-6975
Web site: www.fit.edu

Founded 1958. Located within an hour's drive of Kennedy Space Center and Disney World. CGS member. Coed. Private control. Semester system. Special facilities: Vero Beach Marine Research Center, Center of Electronics Manufacturability, Center for Energy Alternatives, Claude Pepper Institute for Aging and Therapeutic Research, Infectious Diseases Laboratory. Library: 281,800 volumes, 6000 subscriptions. Total Institute enrollment: 4745.

Tuition: per credit $900. Limited on-campus housing for married and single graduate students. Average academic year housing cost: $6800 (includes board). Apply to Assistant Dean of Students. Phone: (321)674-8080.

Graduate School

Enrollment: full-time 625, part-time 1640. Faculty teaching graduate students: full-time 116, part-time 176. Degrees conferred: M.B.A., M.S., Ed.S., Psy.D., Ph.D.

ADMISSION REQUIREMENTS. Transcripts required in support of School's application. Online application available. GRE/GMAT required for some majors. TOEFL required for international applicants. Accepts transfer students. Graduates of unaccredited institutions not considered. Apply to Graduate Admissions office by March 1, some programs have earlier deadlines. Rolling admission process. Application fee $40, for international applicants $50. Phone: (321)674-7118 or (800)944-4348; fax: (321) 674-9468.

ADMISSION STANDARDS. Usual master's level minimum average: 3.0 (A = 4).

FINANCIAL AID. Annual awards from institutional funds: fellowships, research/teaching assistantships, tuition waivers, Federal W/S, loans. Apply to Graduate School Admissions Office by March 1; February 15 for assistantships. Phone: (321)674-8070. Use FAFSA. About 80% of students receive aid other than loans from institute and outside sources. Aid available for part-time students.

DEGREE REQUIREMENTS. For master's: 32–48 credits minimum, at least 24–36 credits in residence; thesis option; final written/oral exam in some programs. For Ph.D.: 60 credits minimum, at least 32 credits, in full-time study; preliminary exam; advancement to candidacy; one foreign language or research tool; dissertation; final oral exam. For Psy.D.: essentially the same as Ph.D., except no foreign language requirement; special project may be substituted for dissertation.

FIELDS OF STUDY.
Aeronautics. Includes airport development, management, aviation safety.
Aerospace Engineering.
Applied Behavior Analysis.
Applied Mathematics.
Aviation Human Factors.
Aviation Safety.
Biological Sciences.
Business Administration.
Chemical Engineering.
Chemistry.
Civil Engineering.
Clinical Psychology.
Coastal Resource Management.
Communication.
Computer Education.
Computer Engineering.
Computer Information Systems.
Computer Science.
Contract and Acquisition Management.
Electrical Engineering.
Engineering Management.
Environmental Engineering.

Environmental Resources Management.
Industrial/Organizational Psychology.
Interdisciplinary Science.
Management of Technology.
Mathematics Education.
Mechanical Engineering.
Meteorology.
Ocean Engineering.
Oceanography. Includes bio-environmental, chemical, geological, physical-environments.
Operations Research.
Personnel Psychology.
Physics.
Science Education.
Software Engineering.
Space Sciences.
Systems Engineering.
Technical and Professional Communication.

FLORIDA INTERNATIONAL UNIVERSITY

Miami, Florida 33199
Web site: www.fiu.edu

Founded 1969. CGS member. State control. Semester system. Special facilities: Academy for the Art of Teaching, High Performance Database Research Center, the Hemispheric Center for Environmental Technology, the International Hurricane Center, Latin American and Caribbean Center, Southeast Florida Center for Aging. Library: 1,800,000 volumes, 9300 subscriptions.

Annual tuition: full-time resident $4294, nonresident $15,641; per credit resident $239, nonresident $869. On-campus housing available for both single and married students. Annual housing cost for single students: $5900 (including board). Phone: University Park (305)348-4190; Biscayne Bay (305)919-5587.

Graduate School

Web site: www.gradschool.fiu.edu

Graduate study since 1979. Enrollment: full- and part-time 6500. Graduate faculty: full- and part-time 450. Degrees conferred: M.A., M.Acc., M.B.A., M.F.A., M.H.S.A., M.I.B., M.M., M.P.H., M.S., M.S.F., M.S.N., M.S.T., M.S.W., D.P.T., Ed.D., Ed.S., Ph.D.

ADMISSION REQUIREMENTS. Official transcripts, diplomas, certificates (documents in a language other than English must be translated by an official translation agency), GRE or GMAT required in support of applications. TOEFL required for applicants whose native language is not English. Interviews not required. Accepts transfer applicants. Graduates of unaccredited institutions not considered. Apply to Graduate Admissions Office (P.O. Box 659004) by June 1 (Fall), October 1 (Spring), March 1 (Summer); international applicants April 1 (Fall), September 1 (Spring), February 1 (Summer). Some programs have earlier deadlines. Application fee $30. Phone: (305)348-7442; fax: (305)348-7441.

ADMISSION STANDARDS. Competitive for most departments, selective for others. Usual minimum average: 2.75 (A = 4) for most departments, 2.5 for conditional admission to most departments.

FINANCIAL AID. Annual awards from institutional funds: Scholarships, fellowship, assistantships, nonresident fee waivers, Federal W/S, loans. Approved for VA benefits. Apply by April 1 to appropriate department chair for fellowship, assistantship; to Financial Aid Office for all other programs. Use FAFSA. About 20% of students receive aid from University and outside sources. Aid available for part-time students.

DEGREE REQUIREMENTS. For master's: 30–45 semester hours minimum, thesis/nonthesis options. For Ed.S.: 30 semester hours beyond master's. For Ed.D.: 90 semester hours minimum beyond bachelors degree; essential the same as for the Ph.D. except no language requirement. For Ph.D.: 40–80 semester hours minimum beyond master's; one language or research tool; qualifying exam; admission to candidacy; dissertation; final oral exam.

FIELDS OF STUDY.

COLLEGE OF ARCHITECTURE AND THE ARTS:

School of Architecture:
Architecture. Includes advanced design, urban development. M.Arch., M.A.A.
Interior Design. M.I.D., M.A.I.D.
Landscape Architecture. M.L.A.

School of Art and History:
Studio Art. Includes ceramics, drawing, painting, sculpture. M.F.A.

School of Music:
Composition. M.M.
Jazz Arranging. M.M.
Jazz Vocal Performance. M.M.
Music Education. M.S.
Music Technology. M.M.
Orchestral Conducting. M.M.
Organ Performance. M.M.
Percussion Performance. M.M.
Performing Arts Management. M.M.
Piano Performance. M.M.
String Performance. M.M.
Vocal Performance. M.M.
Wind Conducting. M.M.
Wind/Brass Performance. M.M.

COLLEGE OF ARTS AND SCIENCES:
African–New World Studies. M.A.
Asian Studies. M.A.
Biological Sciences. Includes marine biology. M.S., Ph.D.
Chemistry and Biochemistry. M.S., Ph.D.
Creative Writing. M.F.A.
Economics. M.A. Ph.D.
English. M.A.
Environmental Studies. M.S.
Geology. M.S., Ph.D.
History. M.A., Ph.D.
International Relations. M.A., Ph.D.
Latin America and Caribbean. M.A.
Liberal Studies. M.A.
Linguistics. M.A.
Mathematics. M.S.
Physics. M.S., Ph.D.
Political Science. M.A., Ph.D.
Psychology. M.S., Ph.D.
Sociology/Anthropology. M.A., Ph.D.
Spanish. M.A., Ph.D.
Statistics. M.S.

COLLEGE OF BUSINESS ADMINISTRATION:
Accounting. M.Acct.
Business Administration. M.B.A., Ph.D.
Finance. M.S.
Human Resource Management. M.S.
International Business. M.I.B
International Real Estate. M.S.
Management Information Systems. M.S.
Public Managers. M.B.A.

COLLEGE OF EDUCATION:
Adult Education. M.S.
Adult Education and Human Resource Development. Ed.D.
Art Education (K–12). M.A.T., M.S.
Counselor Education. Includes mental health counseling, rehabilitation counseling, school counseling. M.S.
Curriculum and Instruction. Includes curriculum development, elementary education, English education, learning technologies, mathematics education, modern language education, physical education, science education, social studies education, special education. M.S., Ed.S., Ed.D., Ph.D.
Early Childhood Education. M.S.
Educational Administration and Supervision. Ed.D.
Educational Leadership. M.S., Ed.S.
English Education/ESOL (6–12). M.A.T.
Exceptional Student Education/ESOL. M.A.T., Ed.D.
Exercise and Sport Sciences. Includes exercise physiology. M.S.
Foreign Language Education. Includes TESOL. M.S.
French Education (6–12). M.A.T.
Higher Educational Administration. M.S., Ed.D.
Human Resource Development. M.S.
International and Intercultural Development Education. M.S.
Mathematics Education (6–12). M.A.T.
Park and Recreation Management. Includes leisure services management, therapeutic recreation. M.S.
Physical Education. Includes sport management. M.S.
Reading Education. M.S.
School Psychology. Ed.S.
Science Education (6–12). M.A.T.
Social Studies Education (6–12). M.A.T.
Spanish Education (6–12). M.A.T.
Urban Education. Includes multicultural/bilingual education, multicultural/TESOL. M.S.

COLLEGE OF ENGINEERING AND COMPUTING:
Biomedical Engineering. M.S., Ph.D.
Civil Engineering. M.S., Ph.D.
Computer Engineering. M.S., Ph.D.
Computer Science. Ph.D.
Construction Engineering. M.S.
Digital Signal Processing. Ph.D.
Electrical Engineering. M.S., Ph.D.
Electronics and Electronic Material. Ph.D.
Environmental Engineering. M.S.
Environmental and Urban Systems. M.S.
Environmental and Water Resource Engineering. Ph.D.
Industrial and Systems Engineering. M.S., Ph.D.
Material Science and Engineering. M.S., Ph.D.
Mechanical Engineering. M.S., Ph.D.
Structural and Geotechnical Engineering. Ph.D.
Technology Management. M.S.
Telecommunication and Networking. M.S., Ph.D.
Transportation Engineering. Ph.D.

COLLEGE OF NURSING AND HEALTH SCIENCES:
Athletic Training. M.S.
Speech-Language Pathology. M.S.
Nursing. Includes the following specialty tracks: adult health nursing, anesthesiology nursing, child health nursing, family health nursing, nursing administration, psychiatric/mental health nursing. M.S.N.
Nursing. Ph.D.
Occupational Therapy. M.S., M.O.T.
Physical Therapy. D.P.T.

COLLEGE OF SOCIAL WORK, JUSTICS AND PUBLIC AFFAIRS:
Criminal Justice. M.S.
Public Administration. M.P.A.
Public Management. Ph.D.
Social Welfare. Ph.D.
Social Work. M.S.W.

SCHOOL OF HOSPITALITY AND TOURISM MANAGEMENT:
Business Administration. Includes specialization in hospitality and tourism management. Ph.D.
Hospitality Management. Includes an executive program. M.S.
Tourism Studies. M.S.

SCHOOL OF JOURNALISM AND MASS COMMUNICATION:
Business Journalism. M.S.
Integrated Communication. Includes advertising and public relations, advertising and public relations (creative track). M.S.
Spanish-Language Journalism. Includes investigative reporting. M.S.
Student Media Advising. M.S.

ROBERT STEMPEL SCHOOL OF PUBLIC HEALTH:
Dietetics and Nutrition. M.S., Ph.D.
Public Health. Includes specializations in biostatistics, community nutrition, environmental and occupational health, epidemiology, health policy and management, health promotion and disease prevention (M.P.H.); specializations in community nutrition, environmental and occupational health, epidemiology, health promotion and disease prevention (Ph.D.). M.P.H., Ph.D.

College of Law
Web site: www.law.fiu.edu

Founded 2002. ABA approved since 2006. Public control. Semester system. Law library: 190,649 volumes, 1135 subscriptions. Library has LEXIS, WESTLAW, DIALOG. Summer programs in Beijing, China; Rio de Janeiro, Brazil.

Tuition: per credit resident $292, nonresident $751. On-campus housing available only. Check Web site for housing information. Annual housing costs approximately $14,244.

Enrollment: first-year full- and part-time 439; total full-time 176, part-time 156 (men 54%, women 46%, minorities 47%).

Faculty: Total full- and part-time 43 (men 60%, women 40%, minorities 52%). Student to faculty ratio 13.3 to 1. Degrees conferred: J.D., J.D.-M.B.A., J.D.-M.I.B., J.D.-M.L.A.C.S., J.D.-M.P.A., J.D.-M.S. (Criminal Justice, Psychology), J.D., M.S.W.

ADMISSION REQUIREMENTS. LSDAS Law School report, official transcript, LSAT, three letters of recommendation, personal statement required in support of application. Interview not required. International applicants must present adequate evidence of his or her knowledge and usage of the English language. TOEFL required of candidates for whom English is not their first language. Documents in a language other than English must be translated by an official translation agency. Accepts transfer applications. Graduates of unaccredited colleges not considered. Apply to Director of Admission after November 1, by May 1. Rolling admission process. Application fee $20. Phone: (305)348-8006; e-mail: lawadmit@fiu.edu.

ADMISSION STANDARDS. Selective. Accepts approximately 14% of full-time and 20% of part-time students. Number of full-time applicants 1064, part-time 432; number of acceptance full-time 150, part-time 88; number enrolled full-time 64, part-time 56; LSAT (75% of full-time students have a score at or above 153, part-time 515); GPA (75% of full-time students have a GPA at or above 3.11, part-time 2.88). *U.S. News & World Report* ranking is in the third tier of all U.S. law schools.

FINANCIAL AID. Scholarships, grants, Federal W/S, loans. Approximately 38% of students receive aid other than loans from school funds. Apply to the Financial Aid Office by May 1. Phone: (305)348-8006. Use FAFSA.

DEGREE REQUIREMENTS. For J.D.: satisfactory completion of 90-credit, three (full-time) or four (part-time) year program. For joint degree programs see Graduate listing above.

FLORIDA STATE UNIVERSITY

Tallahassee, Florida 32306
Web site: www.fsu.edu

Founded 1857. CGS member. Coed. State control. Semester system. Special facilities: The National High Magnetic Field Laboratory, The Center for Materials Research and Technology (MARTECH), 9 Mev Super FN tandem Van de Graaff accelerator, Florida State University Marine Laboratory, Center for Music Research, Antarctic Research Facility, Two Supercomputers: The Cray Y-MP and a Connection Machine, FSU Proton-Induced X-Ray Emission (PIXE) Laboratory, Supercomputer Computations Research Institute (SCRI), Institute of Science and Public Affairs, Institute for Social Research, Geophysical Fluid Dynamics Institute, Institute of Molecular Biophysics, Creative Writing Program, Educational Research Center for Child Development, Center for Information Systems Research, Beaches and Shores Resource Center. According to The Center at University of Florida, the University is ranked 86th in receipt of Federal Research funds with $88,422,000 and it ranks 88th for total University research expenditures with $152,277,000. In 2004, the University awarded 271 doctorates, which ranked it 53rd among all U.S. institutions eligible to award that degree. Four of the University's faculty members have been elected to National Honor Academies and this ranks it 97th among all U.S. institutions. The Library: approximately 2,700,000 volumes, 42,000 subscriptions. Total University enrollment: 39,100.

Tuition: per credit, resident $236, nonresident $868. Capacity for on-campus housing for graduate students is 791. Average academic year housing costs: $12,220 for married students, $8220 (includes board) for single students. Contact Office of Resident Student Development for both on- (850)644-0089 and off-campus (850)644-2860 housing information. Day-care facilities available.

Graduate School

Enrollment: full-time 4251, part-time 2682. Graduate faculty: full-time 1142, part-time 136. Degrees conferred: M.A., M.S., M.Acc., M.B.A., M.M., M.M.Ed., M.S.N., M.S.P., M.S.W., Adv.M., Ed.Sp., Ad.M.L.S., M.F.A., M.P.A., Ed.D., D.Mus., Ph.D.

ADMISSION REQUIREMENTS. Two transcripts, GRE/GMAT required in support of School's application. Online application available. TOEFL (minimum score 550) required for international applicants. Interview, GRE Subject Test, auditions, personal interviews, departmental applications, letters of recommendation required for some departments. Accepts transfer applicants. Graduates of unaccredited institutions not considered. Apply to Office of Admissions by May 1 (Fall), November 25 (Spring), April 2 (Summer), some programs have earlier deadlines. Application fee $30. Phone: (850)644-3420; fax: (850)644-0197.

ADMISSION STANDARDS. Competitive or very selective for some departments, selective for most. Usual minimum average: 3.0 (A = 4); GRE total: 1000.

FINANCIAL AID. Annual awards from institutional funds that meet the minimum University requirements for tuition waivers: graduate fellowships, research and service assistantships, assistantships with instructional responsibility, assistantships assisting faculty with instruction, scholarships, Federal W/S, loans. Approved for VA benefits. Apply by March 1 to appropriate department chair for fellowships, assistantships; to University's Office of Financial Aid for all other programs. Phone: (850)644-5871; fax: (850)644-6404. Use FAFSA. About 45% of students receive aid other than loans from University and outside sources. Aid available for part-time students.

DEGREE REQUIREMENTS. For M.A., M.S.: 30 semester hours minimum including thesis or 32 hours minimum without thesis, reading knowledge of one language for M.A. sometimes required for M.S.; final written/oral exams required by some departments. For M.Acc.: 33 hours minimum. For M.B.A., M.P.A.: 39 hours minimum. For M.M., M.M.Ed., M.P.: 30 hours minimum, including thesis, recital, or composition, or 36 hours minimum without thesis. For M.S.W.: 4 semesters (Fall and Spring consecutively), 60 hours minimum; 36 hours on-campus instruction, 24 hours field instruction. For M.F.A.: 75 hours minimum in Creative Art; 60 hours minimum in Theater; includes creative project and final exhibition; final written/oral exams sometimes required. For Ph.D.: at least 24 hours during any one-year period after completion of 30 hours or master's degree, additional hours may be required by departments; a minimum of 24 hours of dissertation credit; preliminary exam; dissertation; final oral exam. For D.Mus.: 80 hours minimum beyond the bachelor's; diagnostic exam; five recitals: two public, one studio, two chamber works; one performance with a large ensemble for performance majors: for theory/composition majors, 70 hours minimum beyond the bachelor's, diagnostic exam, public performance of original chamber works, dissertation (which must be a major work for composition majors); final written/oral exams.

FIELDS OF STUDY.

COLLEGE OF ARTS AND SCIENCES:
American and Florida Studies.
Anthropology.
Aquatic Environmental Science.
Biological Sciences.
Biomedical Mathematics.
Biostatistics.
Chemical Physics.
Chemistry.
Classics.
Computational Science.
Computer Science.
Creative Writing.
English.
French.
French and Francophone Studies.
Geology.
Geographic Information Sciences.
Geophysical Fluid Dynamics. Ph.D. only.
German.
Greek.
History.
History and Philosophy of Science.
Humanities.
Italian Studies.
Latin.
Mathematics.
Meteorology.
Molecular Biophysics. Ph.D. only.
Neuroscience. Ph.D. only.
Oceanography.
Philosophy.
Physics.
Psychology.
Religion.
Science Teaching.
Secondary Science/Mathematical Teaching.
Slavic.
Spanish.
Statistics.

COLLEGE OF BUSINESS:
Accounting.
Business Administration.
Finance.
Management.

Management Information Systems.
Marketing.

COLLEGE OF COMMUNICATION:
Communication.
Communication Sciences and Disorders.

COLLEGE OF CRIMINOLOGY AND CRIMINAL JUSTICE:
Criminology.

COLLEGE OF EDUCATION:
Adult Education.
Comprehensive Vocational Education.
Counseling and Human Systems. Master's only.
Counseling Psychology and Human Systems. Ed.D. only.
Curriculum and Instruction.
Early Childhood Education.
Educational Leadership and Policy Standards.
Educational Psychology.
Educational Research.
Educational Theory and Practice.
Elementary Education.
Emotional Disturbances and Learning Disabled. Master's only.
English Education.
Foundations of Education.
Health Education.
Higher Education.
History and Philosophy of Education.
Human Services and Studies.
International and Intercultural Development.
Leisure Services and Studies. Master's only.
Mathematics Education.
Measurement and Statistics.
Mental Retardation. Master's only.
Multilingual and Multicultural Education.
Physical Education.
Psychological Services.
Reading Education.
Recreation and Leisure Services Administration.
Rehabilitation Counseling.
Science Education.
Social Studies Education.
Special Education.
Sport Management.
Sport Psychology.

FAMU–FSU COLLEGE OF ENGINEERING:
Biomedical Engineering.
Chemical Engineering.
Civil Engineering.
Electrical Engineering.
Industrial Engineering.
Mechanical Engineering.

COLLEGE OF HUMAN SCIENCES:
Clothing, Textiles and Merchandising.
Exercise Science.
Family and Child Sciences.
Family and Consumer Sciences Education.
Food and Nutrition.
Human Sciences. Ph.D. only.
Marriage and Family Therapy. Ph.D.

COLLEGE OF INFORMATION:
Library and Information Studies.

COLLEGE OF MOTION PICTURE, TELEVISION AND RECORDING ARTS:
Motion Picture, Television and Recording Arts.

COLLEGE OF MUSIC:
Arts Administration.
Music Composition.
Music Education.

Musicology.
Music Performance.
Music Theatre.
Music Theory.
Music Therapy.
Opera Production.

SCHOOL OF NURSING:
Adult Nurse Practitioner.
Family Nurse Practitioner.
Nurse Case Manager.
Nurse Educator.

COLLEGE OF SOCIAL SCIENCES:
Aging Studies.
Applied Social Research.
Asian Studies.
Demography.
Economics.
Geography.
International Affairs.
Political Science.
Public Administration.
Public Health.
Russian and East European Studies.
Social Science. Interdisciplinary.
Sociology.
Urban and Regional Planning.

COLLEGE OF SOCIAL WORK:
Social Work. Includes clinical social work, social policy, and administration.

COLLEGE OF VISUAL ARTS, THEATRE AND DANCE:
American Dance Studies.
Art Education.
Art Therapy.
Dance.
History and Criticism of Art.
Interior Design.
Studio Art.
Theatre.

College of Law (32306-1601)
Web site: www.law.fsu.edu

Established 1966. ABA approved since 1968. AALS member. Semester system. Special facilities: Children's Advocacy Center, Florida Dispute Resolution Center. Library: 485,342 volumes, 3602 subscriptions; has LEXIS, NEXIS, WESTLAW, OCLC.

Tuition: per credit resident $328, nonresident $995. On-campus housing available. Apply to Director of Housing. Total average additional expenses: $16,500.

Enrollment: first-year class 245; total full-time 765 (men 60%, women 40%, minorities 19%). Faculty: full-time 50, part-time 64 (men 56%, women 44%, minorities 11%). Student to faculty ratio 13.8 to 1. Degrees conferred: J.D., J.D.-M.B.A., J.D.-M.L.S., J.D.-M.P.A., J.D.-M.S. (International Affairs, Economics, Urban Regional Planning), J.D.-M.S.W.

ADMISSION REQUIREMENTS. LSDAS Law School report, bachelor's degree, transcripts, LSAT, personal statement, letters of recommendation, residency form required in support of application. TOEFL required for international applicants. Accepts transfer applicants. Graduates of unaccredited colleges not considered. Apply to Office of Admissions after September 1, before February 15. Admits first-year students, Fall only; transfers Fall and Summer. Application fee $30, Phone: (850)644-3787; fax: (850) 644-7284.

ADMISSION STANDARDS. Selective. Accepts approximately 23% of all students. Number of applicants 3877; number of acceptance 873; number enrolled 284; LSAT (75% of students have a score at or above 158); GPA (75% of students have a GPA at or above 3.21). *U.S. News & World Report* ranking is in a tie for 53rd of all U.S. law schools.

FINANCIAL AID. Scholarships, fellowships, Federal W/S, loans. Apply to University Office of Financial Aid by March 1. Use FAFSA. Phone: (850)644-5716. About 34% of students receive aid other than loans from College and outside sources.

DEGREE REQUIREMENTS. For J.D.: satisfactory completion of three-year program; 88 semester hours. J.D.-M.B.A. offered with School of Business, J.D.-M.A./M.S. with the departments of Economics, International Affairs, Public Affairs, Urban and Regional Planning, Graduate School of Arts and Science. The J.D.-M.P.A. with the School of Criminology and Criminal Justice.

UNIVERSITY OF FLORIDA
Gainesville, Florida 32611-8140
Web site: www.ufl.edu

Founded 1953. CGS and AAU member. Located 75 miles SW of Jacksonville. Coed. State control. Semester system. Sponsoring University of Oak Ridge associated universities. Special facilities: Agricultural Research Center, Cancer Center, Florida Engineering and Experiment Station, Center for Applied Optimization, Center for Applied Thermodynamics and Corrosion, Center for Aquatic Sciences, Engineering Research Center for Particle Science and Technology, Clinical Research Center, Center for Gerontological Studies, Human Development Center, Center for Information Research, Center for Intelligent Machines and Robotics, Center for International Studies, Center for Latin American Studies, Center for Research on Human Prosthesis, Florida Museum of Natural History, Florida Water Resources Research Center. The University's NIH ranking is 52nd among all U.S. institutions with 377 awards/grants valued at $124,982,809. According to The Center at University of Florida, the University is ranked 40th in receipt of Federal Research funds with $194,958,000 and it ranks 23rd for total University research expenditures with $429,734,000. The University's endowment assets rank it 63rd, with a value of $738,299,000. In 2004, the University awarded 694 doctorates, which ranked it 4th among all U.S. institutions eligible to award that degree. Seventeen of the University's faculty members have been elected to National Honor Academies and this ranks it 51st among all U.S. institutions. The Library: approximately 5,000,000 volumes, 28,100 subscriptions. Total University enrollment: 49,600.

Annual tuition: resident, per credit hour $236, nonresident $868. On-campus housing for 980 married students, graduate men, women. Annual housing cost: $2650–$5600. On-campus one-bedroom apartments rent for about $475 per month. Apply to Division of On-Campus Housing; to Division of Off-Campus Housing for information. Phone: (352)392-2161. Child-care facilities available.

Graduate School

Graduate study since 1906. Enrollment: full-time and part-time 9000. University faculty: full- and part-time 3000. Degrees conferred: M.A., M.S., M.A.T., M.S.T., M.Ag., M.Arch., M.Acc., M.A.E., M.H.S.E., M.S.H.S.E., M.A.M.C., M.A.M.R.D., M.A.U.R.P., M.ER.C., M.S.R.S., M.H.S., M.Nsg., M.S.B.C., M.S.Nsg., M.S.P., M.Stat., M.S.Stat., M.B.C., M.E., M.Ed., M.B.A., M.F.A., Ed.S., Engr., M.S.A.S., M.C.E., M.S.E.S.S., M.E.S.S., M.L.A., M.M., LL.M., D.Aud., Ed.D., Ph.D.

ADMISSION REQUIREMENTS. Two transcripts, letters of recommendation, GRE/GMAT/LSAT required in support of School's application. Online application available. GRE Subject Test recommended. Interview required by some departments. TOEFL (minimum score 550) required for international applicants. Accepts transfer applicants. Graduates of unaccredited institutions not considered. Apply to Director of Admissions by June 9 (Fall), November 1 (Spring), March 1 (Summer). Anthropology, Architecture, Business Administration, Clinical Health Psychology, Counseling Education, Counseling Psychology, History Programs have earlier deadline dates. Application fee $30. Phone: (352)392-1365; fax: (352)392-3987.

ADMISSION STANDARDS. Very selective for most departments. Usual minimum G.P.A.: 3.0 (A = 4).

FINANCIAL AID. Annual awards from institutional funds: fellowships, research fellowships, assistantships, Federal W/S, loans. Approved for VA benefits. Apply by February 15 to appropriate department chair for fellowships, assistantships; to Office of Student Aid for all other aid. Use FAFSA. Phone: (352)392-1275. About 44% of students receive aid other than loans from University and outside sources. Aid available for part-time students.

DEGREE REQUIREMENTS. For master's: 30 credits minimum, thesis, final written/oral exam; 32 minimum nonthesis option, written comprehensive exam; reading knowledge of one foreign language required for many majors. Exceptions to the above include: LL.M. in Tax: 24 credits; M.Acc.: 34 credits; M.Ag.: 32 credits; M.Arch.: 52 credits; M.A.M.R.D.: 32 credits; M.A.T.: 36 credits; M.A.U.R.P.: 52 credits; M.B.A.: 48 credits; M.B.C.: 33 credits; M.Ed.: 36 credits; M.E.S.S.: 34 credits; M.F.A.: 60 credits for art and theater; 48 credits for English; M.F.R.C.: 32 credits; M.H.S.: 36 credits for occupational therapy, 43 credits for rehabilitation counseling; M.H.S.E.: 36 credits; M.L.A.: 48 credits; M.M.: 32 credits; M.S.R.S.: 34 credits; M.Nsg. and M.S.Nsg.: 48 credits; M.S.T.: 36 credits; M.Stat.: 36 credits; Engr.: 30 credits beyond the master's; Ed.S.: 36 credits beyond the master's. For Ph.D. and Ed.D.: 90 credits beyond the bachelor's, 30 credits in one calendar year, qualifying written and oral exam, dissertation, final written/oral exam.

FIELDS OF STUDY.

COLLEGE OF AGRICULTURE AND LIFE SCIENCE:
Agricultural and Biological Engineering.
Agricultural Education and Communication.
Agronomy.
Animal Science.
Biochemistry and Molecular Biology.
Breeding and Genetics.
Ecology.
Entomology and Nematology.
Environmental Horticulture.
Family, Youth, and Community Science.
Fisheries and Aquatic Sciences.
Food and Resource Economics.
Food Science and Human Nutrition.
Forest Resources and Conservation.
Horticultural Science. Includes fruit crops, vegetable crops.
Microbiology and Cell Science.
Plant Molecular and Cellular Biology.
Plant Pathology.
Soil and Water Science.
Statistics.
Sustainable/Organic Practices.
Weed Science.
Wildlife Ecology and Conservation.

COLLEGE OF DESIGN, CONSTRUCTION, AND PLANNING:
Architecture.
Architectural Studies.
Building Construction and International Construction.
Interior Design.

Landscape Architecture.
Urban and Regional Planning.

COLLEGE OF LIBERAL ARTS AND SCIENCES:
Anthropology.
Astronomy.
Botany.
Chemistry.
Classics.
Communication Sciences and Disorders.
Creative Writing.
English.
Geography.
Geological Sciences.
German.
History.
International Relations.
Latin.
Latin American Studies.
Linguistics.
Mathematics.
Philosophy.
Physics.
Political Science.
Psychology.
Public Affairs.
Religion.
Romance Languages and Literatures—French.
Romance Languages and Literatures—Spanish.
Sociology.
Statistics.
Women's Studies.
Zoology.

WARRINGTON COLLEGE OF BUSINESS:
Accounting.
Business Administration. Includes decision and information sciences, finance and insurance, management, marketing, real estate.
Economics.
Finance.
International Business.
Real Estate and Urban Analysis.

COLLEGE OF EDUCATION:
Curriculum and Instruction.
Educational Leadership.
Educational Psychology.
Educational Technology.
Elementary Education.
English Education.
English to Speakers of Other Languages (ESOL).
Foreign Language Education.
Higher Education Administration.
Marriage and Family Counseling.
Mathematics Education.
Mental Health Counseling.
Reading Education.
Research and Evaluation Methodology.
School Counseling and Guidance.
School Psychology.
Science Education.
Social Studies Education.
Special Education.
Speech Pathology.
Student Personnel in Higher Education.

COLLEGE OF ENGINEERING:
Aerospace Engineering.
Agricultural and Biological Engineering.
Biomedical Engineering.
Chemical Engineering.

Civil Engineering. Includes geomatics.
Coastal and Oceanographic Engineering.
Computer and Information and Engineering.
Computer Sciences.
Electrical and Computer Engineering.
Engineering Mechanics.
Engineering Science.
Environmental Engineering Sciences.
Industrial and Systems Engineering.
Materials Science and Engineering.
Mechanical Engineering.
Nuclear Engineering Sciences.

COLLEGE OF DENTISTRY:
Endodontic.
Oral Biology.
Orthodontics.
Periodontics.
Prosthodontics.

COLLEGE OF FINE ARTS:
Art.
Art Education.
Art History.
Digital Arts and Sciences.
Museum Studies.
Music.
Music Education.
Studio Art.
Theater.

COLLEGE OF PUBLIC HEALTH PROFESSIONS:
Audiology.
Biostatistics.
Clinical Psychology.
Epidemiology.
General Health Psychology.
Health Services Administration. Includes health service research. E.M.H.A.
Occupational Therapy.
Physical Therapy.
Public Health Management and Policy.
Rehabilitation Counseling.
Rehabilitation Sciences.

COLLEGE OF JOURNALISM AND COMMUNICATIONS:
Advertising.
International Communication.
Journalism—Print.
Mass Communication.
News and Documentary.
Public Relations.
Science-Health Communication.
Telecommunication.

COLLEGE OF LAW:
Comparative Law.
International Taxation.
Taxation.

COLLEGE OF MEDICINE:
Biochemistry and Molecular Biology.
Medical Sciences. Includes anatomical sciences, molecular genetics and microbiology, neuroscience, oral biology, pathology, pharmacology, physiology.

COLLEGE OF NURSING:
Nursing.
Nursing Sciences.

COLLEGE OF PHARMACY:
Medicinal Chemistry.
Pharmaceutics.
Pharmacodynamics.
Pharmacology.
Pharmacy Health Care Administration.

COLLEGE OF HEALTH AND HUMAN PERFORMANCE:
Biomechanics.
Exercise and Sport Sciences.
Health and Human Performance.
Health Behavior.
Health Science Education.
Human Performance.
Public Health.
Recreation, Studies.
Sport and Exercise Psychology.

COLLEGE OF VETERINARY MEDICINE:
Large Animal Clinical Sciences.
Pathobiology.
Physiological Sciences/VM.
Small Animal Clinical Sciences.

INTERDISCIPLINARY PROGRAMS:
Animal Molecular and Cellular Biology.
Hydrologic Sciences.
Jewish Studies.
Mammalian Genetics.
Toxicology.
Women's/Gender Studies.
Note: The Graduate Catalog, Graduate Coordinators for each program are listed on the University's home page noted above.

College of Dentistry (32610-0445)
Web site: www.dental.ufl.edu

Established 1972. Semester system. Special facilities: Center for Comprehensive Pain Research, Center for Dental Biomaterials, Center for Implant Dentistry, Claude Denson Pepper Center for Oral Health in Aging, Craniofacial Center, Lorenz Center for Pediatric Facial Disorders, Periodontal Disease Research Center.

Annual tuition: resident $19,276, nonresident $48,082. On-campus housing available. Contact Housing Office for both on- and off-campus housing information. Phone: (352)392-2161. Average academic year living expenses: $11,000. Total cost for all other first-year expenses: $8622.

Enrollment: first-year class 82 , total full-time 340 (men 51%, women 49%, minorities 39%, state residents 94%), postgraduate 105. Faculty: full-time 50, part-time 82. Degrees conferred: D.M.D., M.S., Certificates.

ADMISSION REQUIREMENTS. AADSAS report, official transcripts, DAT (not later than October), three letters of recommendation, at least three years of college required in support of application. TOEFL required for international applicants. Accepts transfer applicants on a space available basis. Interview by invitation only. Preference given to state residents. Graduates of unaccredited colleges not considered. Apply after June 1, before October 15 to Director of Admissions. Application fee $30. Phone: (352)392-4866; fax: (352)846-0311.

ADMISSION STANDARDS. Selective. Mean DAT: Academic 19, PAT 18; mean GPA: 3.5 (A = 4). Accepts about 10–15% of total annual applicants. Approximately 99% are state residents.

FINANCIAL AID. Scholarships, grants, loans. Apply to Office of Dental Admissions after acceptance; no specified closing date. Phone: (352)846-1384. Use FAFSA (College code: 001535). Approximately 89% of class receives some financial assistance from College.

DEGREE REQUIREMENTS. For D.M.D.: satisfactory completion of 11-semester program. For M.S.: 24–36 month full-time program.

FIELDS OF GRADUATE STUDY.
Advance Education in General Dentistry. M.S.
Dental Biomaterials.
Endodontics. M.S.
Oral Biology.
Oral and Maxillofacial Pathology.
Oral and Maxillofacial Surgery.
Orthodontics. M.S.
Pediatric Dentistry
Periodontics. M.S.
Prosthodontics.

Fredric G. Levin College of Law (P.O. Box 117620)
Web site: www.law.ufl.edu

Founded 1909. ABA approved since 1925. AALS member since 1920. Semester system. Law library: 584,564 volumes, 7838 subscriptions; has LEXIS, WESTLAW, DIALOG, PLATO.

Tuition: resident $9861, nonresidents $29,227. Total average annual additional expense: $12,260. Enrollment: first-year class 213 (Fall), 209 (Spring), total full-time 1364 (men 53%, women 47%, minorities 20%); no part-time study. Faculty: full-time 51, part-time 22. Student to faculty ratio 18.7 to 1. Degrees conferred: J.D., J.D.-M.B.A., J.D.-M.A. (Accounting, Political Science, Sociology, Urban and Regional Planning), J.D.-Ph.D. (History), LL.M. (Tax), LL.M. (for persons who have completed a basic legal education and received a university degree in law in another country).

ADMISSION REQUIREMENTS. LSDAS Law School report, transcript showing bachelor's degree completion, LSAT (no later than December) required in support of application. Interview not required. Accepts transfer applicants. Graduates of unaccredited colleges not considered. Apply to Assistant Dean for Admission and Financial Aid by February 1 (Fall), May 15 (Spring). Application fee $30. Phone: (352)392-0890; e-mail: patrick@law.ufl.edu.

ADMISSION STANDARDS. Selective. Mean LSAT: 158 (Fall), 155 (Spring); mean GPA: 3.45 (Fall), 3.35 (Spring). *U.S. News & World Report* ranking is tied at 47th of all U.S. law schools.

FINANCIAL AID. Limited scholarship, loans available; most funds directed toward loans. Apply to Office of Financial Aid. Phone: (352)392-0620. Use FAFSA and College's Financial Aid form. Applications should be completed no later than March 1. About 18% of students receive aid other than loans.

DEGREE REQUIREMENTS. For J.D.: 88 hours minimum; transfer credit from other law school considered. For LL.M.: 24–30 credits of study beyond J.D.

College of Medicine (32610-0215)
Web site: www.med.ufl.edu

Established 1930. Public control. Semester system. Library: 193,000 volumes, 1000 subscriptions. The University's NIH ranking is 52nd among all U.S. institutions with 377 awards/grants worth $124,982,809.

Annual tuition: full-time resident $21,117, nonresident $48,965. Limited on-campus housing. Average cost for all other expenses: $10,000.

Enrollment: first-year class 131; total full-time 500 (men 49%, women 51%, minorities 35%, state residents 72%). Faculty: full-time 1097, part-time 101. Degrees conferred: B.S.-M.D. (junior honors program and bachelor's completion program with FSU and FAMU), M.D., M.D.-M.B.A., M.D.-J.D., M.D.-M.S., M.D.-Ph.D. (Medical Scientist Training Program). The M.S. and Ph.D are offered through the Graduate School.

ADMISSION REQUIREMENTS. AMCAS report, transcripts, MCAT, recommendations, interview required in support of application. Supplemental application required of competitive applicants. Florida residents given preference. Graduates of unaccredited colleges not considered. Bachelor's normally required for admission. Does not have EDP. Apply to Chairman, Medical Selection Committee after June 15, before December 1 (flexible). Admits Fall only. Application fee: $30. Phone: (352)392-4569; fax: (352)392-1307.

ADMISSION STANDARDS. Competitive. Accepts about 10.4% of all applicants. Number of applications 2048 (800 out-of-state); number interviewed 362 (30 out-of-state); number of acceptance 212 (11 out-of-state); number enrolled 131 (3 out-of-state). Mean Composite MCAT 10.5; mean UGPA 3.80. *U.S. News & World Report* ranking is in the top 48 of all medical research schools, 45th in primary care.

FINANCIAL AID. Scholarships, summer fellowships, assistantships, NIH stipends, loans. Apply to Office for Student Financial Aid after acceptance and prior to June 1. Phone: (352)392-7800. Use FAFSA (School code: 001535). About 73% of students receive aid other than loans from College.

DEGREE REQUIREMENTS. For B.S.-M.D.: satisfactory completion of either a six-year or seven-year program. For M.D.: satisfactory completion of four-year program; must pass Step 1 of USMLE and take Step 2 prior to graduation. Advanced standing for work completed in another school will be considered. For M.S., Ph.D.: see Graduate School listing above.

FIELDS OF GRADUATE STUDY.
Anatomy and Cell Biology.
Biochemistry and Molecular Biology.
Molecular Genetics and Microbiology.
Genetics. Interdisciplinary
Immunology and Microbiology. Interdisciplinary.
Molecular Cell Biology. Interdisciplinary.
Neuroscience. Interdisciplinary.
Pharmacology.
Physiology and Functional Genomics. Interdisciplinary.

College of Veterinary Medicine (32610-0125)
Web site: www.vetmed.ufl.edu

Established 1976. Semester system. Special facilities: Biotechnology Institute, the Horse Research Center.

Annual tuition: resident $18,400, nonresident $39,376. For housing information contact the Division of Housing. Living expenses: $12,000–$15,000.

Enrollment: first-year class 88, total 365 (men 20%, women 80%, minorities 15%, state residents 82%). Faculty: full- and part-time 108. Degrees conferred: D.V.M., D.V.M.-M.S., D.V.M.-Ph.D., Certificates. The M.S. and Ph.D. are offered through the Graduate School.

ADMISSION REQUIREMENTS. VMCAS report, two transcripts, animal/veterinary experience, GRE, essay, three letters of recommendation (one from an academic adviser), supplemental application required in support of application. Interview by invitation only. Transfer applicants for second-year class rarely considered. Applicants must have completed at least three years of college study. Preference given to state residents. Apply to the Dean after July 1, before October 1. Application fee $30. Phone: (352)392-4700, ext. 5100; fax: (352)392-8351.

ADMISSION STANDARDS. Competitive. Accepts about 10–15% of all applicants. Number of applications 896 (582 out-of-state); number interviewed 234 (69 out-of-state); number of acceptance n/a (n/a out-of-state); number enrolled 88 (16 out-of-state). Usual minimum UGPA: 2.75 (A = 4). Mean GRE (V + Q) 1192; mean UGPA 3.60.

FINANCIAL AID. Scholarships, fellowships, assistantships, Federal W/S, loans. Apply to Office of Financial Aid by February 15. Use FAFSA. About 20% of students receive aid other than loans.

DEGREE REQUIREMENTS, For D.V.M.: satisfactory completion of 9-semester program. For M.S. and Ph.D.: see Graduate School listing above.

FIELDS OF GRADUATE STUDY.
Biochemistry and Molecular Biology.
Comparative Anatomy and Physiology.
Comparative Toxicology.
Epidemiology and Infectious Diseases.
Forensic Toxicology. Certificate only.
Immunology.
Pathology.
Parasitology.
Pharmacology.

FORDHAM UNIVERSITY
Rose Hill Campus
Bronx, New York 10458
Web site: www.fordham.edu

Founded in 1841. CGS member. Coed. Independent institution in the Jesuit tradition. Semester system. Library: 2,500,000 volumes, 15,000 subscriptions. Total University enrollment: 14,600.

Tuition: per credit $995. Limited on-campus housing for single graduate students only. Annual housing cost: $6500; shared rental units $600–$800 per month. Apply to Director of Residential Life. Phone: (718)817-3080.

Graduate School of Arts and Sciences

Established in 1916. Enrollment: full-time 424, part-time 315. Graduate faculty: full-time 220, part-time 6. Degrees conferred: M.A., M.S., Ph.D.

ADMISSION REQUIREMENTS. Transcripts, three letters of recommendation, GRE, résumé, statement of intent required in support of School's application. MAT required in Psychology. Evidence of Proficiency in English or TOEFL required of all international applicants. Interview not required. Accepts transfer applicants. Graduates of unaccredited institutions not considered. Apply to Office of Graduate Admission by April 1 (Summer), May 1 (Fall), December 1 (Spring). Psychology applications must be completed by January 15. Application fee $65. Phone: (718) 817-4420; fax: (718)817-3566.

ADMISSION STANDARDS. Very competitive for some departments, competitive or selective for others. Usual minimum average: 3.0 (A = 4).

FINANCIAL AID. Awards from institutional funds: scholarships, teaching fellowships, research assistantships, tuition waivers, Federal W/S, loans. Apply to Office of Graduate Admissions by January 30 for most departments. Phone: (718)817-3800. No aid for part-time students.

DEGREE REQUIREMENTS. For master's: 30–36 credits minimum, up to six transfer credits accepted; thesis optional in some departments; comprehensive exam required; reading knowledge of one foreign language or demonstrated computer/research skill required. For Ph.D.: 60–72 credits minimum; at least two years in residence; reading knowledge of two foreign languages or one computer/research skill and one language; comprehensive exam; dissertation required; final oral exam.

FIELDS OF STUDY.
Biological Sciences. M.S., Ph.D.
Classical Languages and Literatures. M.A., Ph.D.
Clinical Psychology. Ph.D.
Communication. M.A.
Computer Science. M.S.
Economics. M.A., Ph.D.
English Language and Literature. M.A., Ph.D.
History. M.A., Ph.D.
Humanities and Sciences. M.A.; interdisciplinary.
International Political Economy and Development. M.A.; interdisciplinary.
Medieval Studies Program. M.A., Ph.D.; interdisciplinary.
Philosophy. M.A., Ph.D.
Political Science. M.A., Ph.D. only.
Psychology. M.A., Ph.D.
Psychometrics. Ph.D.
Sociology. M.A., Ph.D.
Theology. M.A., Ph.D.

Graduate School of Business Administration

113 West 60th Street
New York, New York 10023
Web site: www.bnet.fordham.edu

Established 1969. Private control, Accredited programs: M.B.A., Accounting. Located on Manhattan campus near Lincoln Center, courses also offered in Tarrytown; urban environment. Trimester system. Special programs: foreign exchange programs (in Belgium, Finland, France, Spain).

Tuition: per credit $950. Enrollment: total full- and part-time 1575. Faculty: full-time 91, part-time 94; 96% with Ph.D./D.B.A. Degrees conferred: M.B.A. (full-time, part-time, day, evening, weekends), M.B.A. in Accounting and Taxation, M.B.A. in Professional Accounting, M.B.A. in Quality Management, G.P.M.B.A. (Global Professional), T.M.B.A. (Transnational), M.B.A.-J.D., M.S.T. (Taxation).

ADMISSION REQUIREMENTS. All applicants should have a bachelor's degree from a recognized institution of higher education and a strong mathematics background. Submit application, GMAT (will accept GMAT test results from the last five years, latest acceptable date is March), official transcripts from each undergraduate/graduate school attended, two letters of recommendation, two personal statements, résumé (prefers at least four years of work experience), and an application fee of $65 to the Office of Admission and Financial Aid. In addition, international students (whose native language is other than English) should submit a TOEFL report (minimum score 600), certified translations and evaluations of all official transcripts; recommendation should be in English or with certified translations, proof of health/immunization certificate, and proof of sufficient financial resources for two years of academic study. Beginning students admitted Fall, Winter, Spring. U.S. citizens apply by June 1 (Fall), November 1 (Winter), March 1 (Spring), international students apply by May 1 (Fall), October 1 (Winter), February 1 (Summer). Interviews are encouraged. Admissions Committee will consider applicants with some academic course work deficiencies. Joint degree applicants must apply to and be accepted to both schools/programs; contact the Admissions Office for current information and specific admissions requirements. Rolling admissions process; notification is made within 4–6 weeks of receipt of completed application and supporting documents. Admissions Office phone: (212)636-6200; fax: (212)636-7076; e-mail: admissionsgb@school.fordham.edu.

ADMISSION STANDARDS. Selective. Median GMAT: full-time 580, part-time 570; median GPA: 3.15 (A = 4). *U.S. News & World Report* ranked Fordham in the top 15 of all U.S. business schools for part-time M.B.A. programs.

FINANCIAL AID. Scholarships, merit scholarships, minority fellowships, fellowships/graduate assistantships, Federal W/S, loans. Financial aid is available for part-time study. Assistantships/fellowships may be available for joint degree candidates. Request scholarship, fellowship, assistantship information from the Graduate School of Business. Contact the Assistant Dean, Admissions and Financial Aid for current need-based financial aid information. Phone: (212)636-6200. Apply by April 1. Use FAFSA (School code: 002722), also submit Financial Aid Transcript, Federal Income Tax forms.

DEGREE REQUIREMENTS. For M.B.A.: 60-credit program including 36 elective credits, two-year program; degree program must be completed in six years. For G.P.M.B.A., T.M.B.A.: 69-credit programs. For M.S.T.: 54 credit program. For M.B.A. in Accounting and Taxation: 90 credit program. For Deming Scholars M.B.A. in Quality Management: eighteen-month program. For M.B.A.-J.D.: four-and-one-half- to five-and-one-half-year program.

FIELDS OF CONCENTRATION FOR M.B.A.:
Accounting.
Communication and Media Management.
Finance.
Information Systems.
Management.
Marketing.
Taxation.

Graduate School of Education

Located at Lincoln Center Campus, New York City (10023). Special facilities: Early Childhood Center, Center for Non-Public Education, Center for Technology in Education, Intensive Teacher Institute in Bilingual Education.

Tuition: per credit $875. On-campus housing available. Average academic year housing cost: $6500–$7500. Contact University's Residential Life Office for both on- and off-campus housing information. Phone: (212)579-2327.

Enrollment: full-time 201, part-time 1406. Graduate faculty: full-time 53, part-time 72. Degrees conferred: M.S.Ed., M.A.T., Advance Certificate, Ed.D., Ph.D.,

ADMISSION REQUIREMENTS. Official transcripts required in support of School's application. GRE required for Ed.D. and Ph.D. applicants. Evidence of proficiency in English required of international students. Accepts transfer applicants. Graduates of unaccredited institutions not considered. Apply to Office of Admissions by May 15 (Fall), October 15 (Spring), March 15 (Summer). Rolling admissions process. Application fee $65. Phone: (212)636-6400; fax: (212)636-7826.

ADMISSION STANDARDS. Selective. Usual minimum average: 2.75 (A = 4).

FINANCIAL AID. Annual awards from institutional funds: scholarships, fellowships, assistantships, Federal W/S, loans. Approved for VA benefits. Apply by February 1 to Dean's Office for assistantships; to the Financial Aid Office for all other programs. Phone: (212)636-6700. Use FAFSA. About 20% of students receive aid other than loans from School and outside sources. Aid available for part-time students.

DEGREE REQUIREMENTS. For master's: 30–36 credits minimum; thesis/nonthesis option; comprehensive exam. For Professional Diploma: 30 credits beyond the master's; comprehensive exam. For Ph.D.: 39–57 credits minimum beyond the master's; matriculation exam; reading knowledge of one foreign language or proficiency in a computer language and statistics; written comprehensive exam; dissertation; final oral exam. For Ed.D.: 66 credits minimum beyond the master's; requirements essentially the same as Ph.D. except no foreign language requirement.

FIELDS OF STUDY.

Administration and Supervision.

Administration and Supervision—Catholic Educational Leadership Administration and Supervision—Executive Leadership Program. Ed.D. only.

Adult Education. Includes adult literacy, continuing and higher educational administration, human relations skills, human resource development, resource enhancement and leadership, TESOL, technology learning, workforce development.

Bilingual Special Education.

Bilingual Teacher Education.

Church and Non-Public School Leadership. Ph.D. only.

Counseling Psychology. Fall admission only. Ph.D. only.

Curriculum and Teaching. Includes elementary and secondary.

Early Childhood Education.

Early Childhood Special Education.

Educational Psychology. Includes psychology of bilingual students, preschool psychology, bilingual school psychology.

Elementary Education.

Human Resource Program.

Language, Literacy and Learning. Ph.D. only.

Leadership for Learning Organization. Ph.D. only.

Reading Education.

School District Administration.

School Psychology. Includes urban bilingual.

Secondary Education.

Special Education.

Teaching. Includes English 7–12, social studies 7–12, biology 7–12.

Teaching English as a Second Language.

School of Law (10023-7485)

Web site: www.law.fordham.edu

Founded 1905. ABA approved since 1936. AALS member since 1936. Private control. Semester system. Full- and part-time study. Located at Lincoln Center Campus. Special facilities: Center for Corporate, Securities and Financial Law, Center on European Community Law and International Antitrust, Brendan Moore Advocacy Center, Crowley Institute for International Human Rights, Stein Institute on Law and Ethics. Law library: 626,231 volumes, 4880 subscriptions; has LEXIS, NEXIS, WESTLAW, DIALOG; has more that 448 network connections.

Annual tuition: $39,220 (day), $29,976 (evening). Limited on-campus housing. Estimated living expenses: $21,200.

Enrollment: first-year class 323 (day), 160 (evening); total day and evening 1516 (men 52%, women 48%, minorities 38%). Faculty: full-time 75, part-time 200. Student to faculty ratio 15.9 to 1. Degrees conferred: J.D., J.D.-M.A., J.D.-M.B.A., J.D.-M.S.W., LL.M. (Banking, Corporate and Finance Law, International Business).

ADMISSION REQUIREMENTS. LSDAS Law School report, bachelor's degree, transcripts, LSAT, personal statement required in support of application. Interview not required. Accepts transfer applicants. Graduates of unaccredited colleges not considered. Apply to Office of Admissions of School after September 1, before March 1. Application fee $65. Phone: (212)636-6810; e-mail: Lawadmissions@law.fordham.edu. For LL.M.: submit official transcripts, résumé, letters of reference, personal statement in support of application. Admits Fall only. Apply by February 28 to the Office of Graduate Studies. Application fee $100.

ADMISSION STANDARDS. Selective. Accepts approximately 21% of full-time and 24% of part-time students. Number of full-time applicants 5823, part-time 1043; number of acceptance full-time 1244, part-time 249; number enrolled full-time 323, part-time 160; LSAT (75% of full-time students have a score at or above 164, part-time 160); GPA (75% of full-time students have a GPA at or above 3.37, part-time 3.24). *U.S. News & World Report* ranking is in the top 25 of all U.S. law schools.

FINANCIAL AID. Scholarships, grants, loans. Apply by April 1 to Financial Aid Office of School. Phone: (212)636-6815. Use FAFSA (School code: 002722). About 29% of full-time, 22% of part-time students receive aid other than loans from School. A Public Service loan forgiveness program available.

DEGREE REQUIREMENTS. For J.D.: three-year program for day students; four-year program for evening students; 83 credits minimum. For LL.M.: 24-credit, 2-semester program beyond J.D.

Graduate School of Social Service

Established 1916. Located at Lincoln Center Campus. Special facility: Langenfeld Research and Demonstration Center. Tuition: per credit $685. On-campus housing for single students only. Enrollment: full-time 600, part-time 450. Faculty: full-time 47, part-time 6. Degrees conferred: M.S.W., Ph.D.

ADMISSION REQUIREMENTS. Transcripts, three letters of recommendation, autobiographical statement, interview required in support of School's application. Online application available. GRE required for Ph.D. program. TOEFL required for international applicants. Accepts transfer applicants. Graduates of unaccredited institutions not considered. Apply to Office of Admissions by June 1 (Fall), December 1 (Spring). Full-time students admitted Fall only. Application fee $50. Phone: (212)636-6600; fax: (212)636-6613.

ADMISSION STANDARDS. Competitive. Usual minimum average: 3.0 (A = 4).

FINANCIAL AID. Scholarships, fellowships, assistantships, grants, loans. Approved for VA benefits. Apply to Financial Aid Office by April 1. Phone: (212)636-6700. Use FAFSA. About 5% of students receive aid other than loans from School, 98% from all sources. Aid available for part-time students.

DEGREE REQUIREMENTS. For M.S.W.: 60 credits minimum, at least one year in full-time residence; two-semester internship; thesis optional. For Ph.D.: 48 credits minimum beyond M.S.W., at least two semesters in residence; oral and written exam; dissertation; final oral/written exam.

FORT HAYS STATE UNIVERSITY

Hays, Kansas 67601

Web site: www.fhsu.edu

Founded 1902. CGS member. Located 300 miles W of Kansas City. Coed. State control. Semester system. Library: 624,637 volumes, 3400 subscriptions.

Tuition: per credit, resident $141, nonresident $371. On-campus housing for 92 married students, unlimited for single graduate students. Annual academic year average cost: $5100 (including board). Apply to Housing Director. Phone: (785)628-4245.

Graduate School

Graduate study since 1929. Enrollment: full-time 186, part-time 651; about 1500 students during Summer session. Faculty: full-time 126, part-time 26. Degrees conferred: M.A., M.S., M.A.T., M.B.A., M.S.N., M.F.A., Ed.S.

ADMISSION REQUIREMENTS. Official transcripts, personal statement, three letters of recommendation, GRE Subject Tests (Psychology, Counseling, Speech Language, and Pathology), MAT (Administration, Education, Nursing, Specialist in Educ. Ed.S.), GMAT (M.B.A.) required in support of

School's application. Online application available. Interview not required. Accepts transfer applicants. Graduates of unaccredited institutions not considered. Apply to Dean of Graduate School; no specified closing dates. Application fee $30, $35 for international applicants. Phone: (785)628-4236.

ADMISSION STANDARDS. Selective for most departments. Usual minimum average. 2.5 (A = 4). Some departments require 3.0 G.P.A. minimum.

FINANCIAL AID. Annual awards from institutional funds: scholarships, grants, teaching assistantships, research assistantships, administrative assistantships, Federal W/S, loans. Apply to Dean of Graduate School for scholarships, assistantships; for all other aid apply to the Office of Financial Aid; no specified closing date. Phone: (785)628-4408; fax: (785)628-4014. Use FAFSA. Aid available for part-time students.

DEGREE REQUIREMENTS. For M.A., M.F.A., M.S.: 30 semester hours minimum; thesis or research paper for most majors; final written exam; final oral exam for thesis writers. For Ed.S.: 30 semester hours minimum beyond the master's; field study or research project; final written/oral exams.

FIELDS OF STUDY.
Accounting.
Art. M.F.A.
Biology.
Business.
Communication.
Counseling.
Education Administration.
Elementary Education.
English.
Geology.
Health and Human Performance.
History.
Instructional Technology.
Liberal Studies.
Management.
Mathematics.
Nursing.
Psychology.
School Psychology.
Secondary Education.
Special Education.
Speech-Language Pathology.

FORT VALLEY STATE UNIVERSITY
Fort Valley, Georgia 31030-3262
Web site: www.fvsu.edu

Founded 1895. Located 25 miles from Macon, Georgia. Coed. State control. Semester system. Library: 190,000 volumes, 880 subscriptions. Total University enrollment: 2561.

Tuition: per hour, resident $135, nonresident $538. On-campus housing for single students only. Average academic year housing cost: $6160–$6260 (including board); off-campus room and board charges: $800 per month. Contact Dean of Students for both on- and off-campus housing information. Phone: (478)825-6293. Day-care facilities available.

Graduate Studies

Graduate study since 1957. Enrollment: full- and part-time 195. Faculty: full-time 7, part-time 15. Degrees conferred: M.S., M.P.H.

ADMISSION REQUIREMENTS. Official transcripts, three letters of recommendation, personal statement, MAT or GRE required

in support of application. Online application available. TOEFL required for international applicants. Accepts transfer applicants. Apply to Admissions Office in month prior to beginning of registration. Application fee: none. Phone: (478) 825-6307.

ADMISSION STANDARDS. Selective. Usual minimum average: 2.5 (A = 4).

FINANCIAL AID. Annual awards from institutional funds: assistantships, Federal W/S, loans. Apply to Graduate Dean; no specified closing date. Phone: (478)825-6351. Use FAFSA and institutional form. Aid available for part-time students.

DEGREE REQUIREMENTS. For M.S.: 30 semester hours minimum, at least 24 in residence: thesis/nonthesis option; written exam/oral exam. For M.P.H.: 48 semester hours, at least 42 in residence; thesis/nonthesis option; field experience.

FIELDS OF STUDY.
Animal Science. M.S.
Business Administration. Joint degree with Albany State University. M.B.A.
Environmental Health. M.P.H.
Mental Health Counseling. M.S.

FRAMINGHAM STATE COLLEGE
Framingham, Massachusetts 01701-9101
Web site: www.framingham.edu

Founded 1839. Located 20 miles W of Boston. Coed. State control. Semester system. Library: 198,250 volumes, 1123 subscriptions.

Tuition: per course resident and nonresident $799. Limited on-campus housing available for single students only. Contact Housing Office for both on- and off-campus housing information. Phone: (508)626-4636.

Division of Graduate and Continuing Education

Graduate study since 1961. Enrollment: full-time 52, part-time 815 (men 40%, women 60%). Graduate faculty: full-time 24, part-time 39. Degrees conferred: M.A., M.A.A., M.S., M.Ed.

ADMISSION REQUIREMENTS. Two transcripts, two letters of recommendation, MAT or GRE required in support of application. Interview not required. Accepts transfer applicants. Graduates of unaccredited colleges not considered. Apply to Graduate Office by April 1 (Fall), October 1 (Spring). Application fee $50. Phone: (508)626-4550, ext. 9.

ADMISSION STANDARDS. Selective. Usual minimum average: 3.0 (A = 4).

FINANCIAL AID. Limited to loans. Apply to Financial Aid Office by March 1. Use FAFSA. Phone: (508)626-4534. About 5% of students receive aid other than loans from College and outside sources.

DEGREE REQUIREMENTS. For master's: ten courses or seminars minimum; final oral exam; no thesis or language requirement.

FIELDS OF STUDY.
Art.
Biology.
Business Administration.
Counseling Psychology. Includes alcohol, substance abuse, community, families.

Criminal Justice. In cooperation with Westfield State College.
Curriculum and Administration.
Early Childhood Education.
Educational Leadership.
Elementary Education. Includes mathematics, reading and language arts. M.Ed. only.
English.
Food and Nutrition. Includes dietetics, food science, nutrition science, human nutrition. M.S. only.
Health Care Administration.
History.
Home Economics.
Human Resources Administration.
Literacy and Language.
Mathematics.
Nursing.
Public Administration.
Spanish.
Special Education.
Teaching English as a Second Language.

FRANKLIN PIERCE LAW CENTER

2 White Street
Concord, New Hampshire 03301
Web site: www.piercelaw.edu

Established 1973. ABA approved since 1974. AALS member. Private control. Semester system. Special facilities: Germeshauser Center for the Law of Innovation and Entrepreneurship, Institute for Health Law and Ethics, Social Justice Institute, the Patent, Trademark and Copyright Research Foundation. Special programs: Summer programs in Beijing, China; Cork, Ireland. Library: 260,165 volumes, 4600 subscriptions; has LEXIS, NEXIS, WESTLAW, DIALOG.

Annual tuition: $30,700. No on-campus housing. Total Average annual additional expense: $15,600.

Enrollment: first-year class 134; total 423 (men 62%, women 38%, minorities 17%). Faculty: full-time 20, part-time 43 (men 74%, women 26%, minorities 11%). Student to faculty ratio 19.6 to 1. Degrees Conferred: J.D., J.D.-M.E.L.(Education Law), J.D.-M.I.P. (Intellectual Property).

ADMISSION REQUIREMENTS. LSDAS Law School report, bachelor's degree, transcripts, LSAT, two letters of recommendation, personal statement, résumé required in support of application. Accepts transfer applicants. TOEFL required of foreign students whose education was taken outside U.S. Apply to Admissions Office by April 1 (flexible), rolling admissions process. Application fee $55. Phone: (603)228-9217; fax: (603)228-4661; e-mail: admission@piercelaw.edu.

ADMISSION STANDARDS. Selective. Accepts 38% of total annual applicants. Number of applicants 1536; number of acceptance 577; number enrolled 142; LSAT (75% of students have a score at or above 150); GPA (75% of students have a GPA at or above 3.00). *U.S. News & World Report* ranking is in the third tier of all U.S. law schools.

FINANCIAL AID. Merit and Diversity scholarships, Federal W/S, loans. Apply to Financial Aid office by March 15. Phone: (603) 228-1541. Use FAFSA (FPLC code: G20979) and FPLC Financial Aid Application. About 71% of students receive some aid from School.

DEGREE REQUIREMENTS. For J.D.: satisfactory completion of three-year program. For J.D.-M.I.P., J.D.-M.E.L.: satisfactory completion of three- or four-year program.

FROSTBURG STATE UNIVERSITY

Frostburg, Maryland 21532-1099
Web site: www.frostburg.edu

Founded 1898. Located 110 miles S of Pittsburgh and 150 miles from both Baltimore and Washington, D.C. Coed. State control. Semester system. Library: 510,000 volumes, 3353 subscriptions. Total University enrollment: 5041.

Tuition: per credit resident $294, nonresident $332. On-campus housing for limited number of graduate students, none for married students. Average academic year housing cost: $6442 (board included). Apply to Director of Residence Life. Phone: (301)687-4121. Day-care facilities available.

Graduate School

Enrollment: full-time 210, part-time 457. University faculty: full- and part-time 101. Degrees conferred: M.A., M.A.T., M.E., M.Ed., M.S., M.B.A.

ADMISSION REQUIREMENTS. Transcripts required in support of application. Online application available. TOEFL required for international applicants. Accepts transfer applicants. Apply to Office of Graduate Admissions at least sixty days prior to registration. Application fee $30. Phone: (301)687-7053; fax: (301)687-4597; e-mail: gradservices@frostburg.edu.

ADMISSION STANDARDS. Relatively open. Minimum average: 2.5 (A = 4).

FINANCIAL AID. Scholarships, grants, graduate assistantships, Federal W/S, loans. Apply by April 1 to Director of Financial Aid. Phone: (301)689-4301; fax: (301)687-4937. Use FAFSA.

DEGREE REQUIREMENTS. For M.A., M.Ed., M.A.T.: 33 semester hours minimum. For M.S., M.E.: 36–42 semester hours. For M.B.A.: 45 semester hours.

FIELDS OF STUDY.
Administration and Supervision. M.Ed.
Applied Computer Science. M.S.
Applied Ecology and Conservation Biology. M.S.
Biology. M.Ed.
Business Administration. M.B.A.
Counseling Psychology. M.S.
Curriculum and Instruction. M.Ed.
Educational Technology. M.Ed.
Elementary Administration. M.Ed.
Elementary Education. M.A.T.
Engineering. M.E.
Health and Physical Education. M.Ed.
Human Performance. M.S.
Interdisciplinary. M.Ed.
Modern Humanities. M.A.; Summer only.
Park and Recreation Resource Management. M.S.
Reading. M.Ed.
School Counseling. M.Ed.
Science Education. M.Ed.
Special Education. M.Ed.
Wildlife/Fisheries Management. M.S.

FURMAN UNIVERSITY

Greenville, South Carolina 29613
Web site: www.furman.edu

Founded in 1826. Coed. Private control. Three-term system. Library: 445,900 volumes, 3347 subscriptions. Total University enrollment: 3200.

Tuition: per credit, $315. No on-campus housing available.

Graduate Studies

Enrollment: full-time 44, part-time 165. University faculty teaching graduate students: full-time 15, part-time 39. Degrees conferred: M.A. in Ed.

ADMISSION REQUIREMENTS. Transcripts, bachelor's degree, twelve hours in undergraduate education for Ed. majors required in support of application. Accepts transfer students. Graduates of unaccredited institutions not considered. Apply at least 30 days prior to registration. Application fee $50. Phone: (864)294-2213.

ADMISSION STANDARDS. Usual minimum average: 3.0 (A = 4).

FINANCIAL AID. None available at this time.

DEGREE REQUIREMENTS. For M.A. in Ed.: 30–42 credit program; submit score on Praxis II subject test; master's seminar or comprehensive exam.

FIELDS OF STUDY.
Chemistry,
Early Childhood Education.
Elementary Education.
English as a Second Language.
Middle School Education.
Reading.
School Leadership.
Special Education. Includes learning disabilities, emotional/ behavioral disorders.

GALLAUDET UNIVERSITY
Washington, D.C. 20002-3625
Web site: www.gallaudet.edu

Founded 1864. CGS member. Coed. Private control. Semester system. Special facilities: Center for Auditory and Speech Sciences, Center for Global Education, Center for ASL Literacy, Gallaudet Research Institute, Genetic Counseling Center, Fendall Demonstration School, Model Secondary School for the Deaf, Center for Assessment and Demographic Studies, Center for Studies in Education and Human Development. Library: 220,000 volumes, 372,000 microforms, 1700 current periodicals, 5 PCs.

Tuition: $5790 per semester, per credit $643. On-campus housing for single students only. Average housing cost: $4515 (including board) per semester. Contact Director of Housing for both on- and off-campus housing information. Phone: (202)651-5255.

Graduate School

Enrollment: full-time 258 (men 45, women 213), part-time 114. Graduate faculty: full-time 55, part-time 20. Degrees conferred: M.A., M.S., M.S.W., Au.D., Ph.D.

ADMISSION REQUIREMENTS. Official transcripts, three letters of recommendation, goal statement, GRE or MAT required in support of application. TOEFL required for international applicants. Accepts transfer applicants. Apply by February 15 to Director of Admissions. Application fee $50. Phone: (202)651-5253; fax: (202)651-5744; E-mail: adm_bennetti@gallua.gallaudet.edu.

ADMISSION STANDARDS. Competitive. Usual minimum average: 3.0 (A = 4).

FINANCIAL AID. Scholarships, partial tuition waiver, assistantships, grants-in-aid, Federal W/S, loans. Apply by April 1 to Director of Financial Aid. Use FAFSA and submit FAT. About 60%

of students receive aid other than loans from College and outside sources. Limited aid for part-time students.

DEGREE REQUIREMENTS. For master's: 30–42 hours minimum full-time study; sign language proficiency for some programs; final oral/written exam. For Au.D.: 114–116 credit four-year program; internship; clinical practicum; research project. For Ph.D.: two years minimum beyond the master's, two consecutive semesters in residence; comprehensive exam; sign language proficiency for some programs; internship; dissertation; final written exam.

FIELDS OF STUDY.
Administration. M.S.
American Sign Language/English Bilingual Deaf Education. M.A.T.
Audiology. Au.D., Ph.D.
Change Leadership in Education. Ed.S.
Clinical Psychology. Ph.D.
Deaf Education. M.A., Ed.S., Ph.D.
Deaf Studies. Includes concentrations in sign language teaching, cultural studies, deaf history. M.A.
Hearing, Speech and Language Sciences. M.S.
International Development. M.A.
Interpretation. M.A.
Leisure Services Administration. M.S.
Linguistics. M.A., Ph.D.
Mental Health Counseling. M.A.
School Counseling and Guidance. M.A.
School Psychology. Psy.S.
Social Work. M.S.W.
Special Education Administration. Ph.D.
Speech-Language Pathology. M.S.

GANNON UNIVERSITY
Erie, Pennsylvania 16541-0001
Web site: www.gannon.edu

Founded 1925. Private control. Roman Catholic. Semester system. Library: 300,000 volumes, 2800 subscriptions. Total University enrollment: 3600.

Tuition: per semester credit, Counseling Psychology $825, Nursing and other programs $680; Physical Therapy per semester $11,370. Limited on-campus housing for single graduate students. Contact Director of Student Living. Phone: (814)871-7660.

School of Graduate Studies

Enrollment full-time 300, part-time 716. College faculty teaching graduate students full-time 73, part-time 46. Degrees conferred: M.A., M.S., M.Ed., M.B.A., M.P.A., M.S.N., D.P.T., M.S.N.-M.B.A.

ADMISSION REQUIREMENTS. Transcripts, GRE Subject Tests or GMAT, three letters of recommendation required in support of School's application. Interviews required for some programs. Vita/résumé required for Ph.D. TOEFL required for international applicants. Accepts transfer applicants. Graduates of unaccredited institutions not considered. Apply to Center for Adult Learning well in advance of registration; by March 1 for Ph.D. program. Application fee $25 for most programs; $50 fee for Ph.D. program. Phone: (814)871-5819; fax: (814)871-5827.

ADMISSION STANDARDS. Relatively open. Usual minimum average 2.75 (A = 4); 3.25 for Ph.D. program.

FINANCIAL AID. Scholarship, grants, teaching assistantships, administrative assistantships, Federal W/S, loans. Apply to Director of Financial Aid by March 1 (Fall), November 1 (Spring). Use FAFSA. Phone: (814)871-7337; fax: (814)871-5803.

DEGREE REQUIREMENTS. For M.A., M.S.: 30–48 credit hours; statistics or reading knowledge of one foreign language; thesis/nonthesis option/research project; comprehensive exam. For M.B.A.: 30–48 credit hours minimum, at least 36 in residence; research thesis. For M.P.A.: 36 credit hour program; internship; comprehensive exam. For M.Ed.: 30 credit hours minimum, at least 24 in residence; research essay or project; comprehensive exam. For D.P.T.: 63 credit hours; research thesis; plus clinical practicum. For M.S.N.: 42–48 credit hours; clinical practicum; research thesis. For Ph.D.: 3- to 4-year full-time program; 2000 hours internship; dissertation; final oral exam.

FIELDS OF STUDY.
Business Administration. Includes concentrations in accounting, financial management, human resource management, investments, marketing public administration. M.B.A.
Community Counseling. M.S.
Computer and Information Science. Includes concentrations in computer science, information science, software engineering. M.S.C.I.S.
Counseling Psychology. Ph.D.
Education. Includes concentrations in curriculum and instruction, educational leadership, natural sciences and environmental sciences, reading. M.Ed.
Electrical Engineering. M.S.E.E.
Embedded Software Engineering. M.S.E.S.
Engineering Management. M.S.E.
English. M.A.
Environmental Health and Engineering. M.S.
Mechanical Engineering. M.S.M.E.
Nursing. Includes concentrations in anesthesia, family nurse practitioner, medical-surgical, nursing administration. M.S.N.
Occupational Therapy. M.S.
Organizational Learning and Leadership. Ph.D.
Pastoral Studies. Includes concentrations in pastoral ministry, religious education. M.A.
Physical Therapy. D.P.T.
Physician Assistant. M.P.S.
Public Administration. Includes administrative studies, organizational leadership. M.P.A.

GEORGE MASON UNIVERSITY

Fairfax, Virginia 22030-4444
Web site: www.gmu.edu

Established 1957. CGS member. Coed. Public control. Semester system. Special facilities: Pyramid 90x, CDC CYBER 180/830, DEC/VAX 8500 and 8920, Center for Applied Research and Development in Education, Center for Conflict Analysis and Resolution, Center for Constitutional Rights, Federal Theatre Archives, Institute for Information Technology, Center for Innovative Technology, Center for Market Process, Photographic Archives, Performing Arts Archives, Institute for Computational Sciences and Informatics, Center for Artificial Intelligence, Center for Robotics and Control, Center for Public Choice, Center for Software Engineering. In 2004, the University awarded 149 doctorates which ranked it 100th among all U.S. institutions eligible to award that degree. 3 of the University's faculty members have been elected to National Honor Academies and this ranks it 149th among all U.S. institutions. The Library: approximately 1,500,000 volumes, 22,000 subscriptions. Total University enrollment: 29,700.

Tuition: per credit resident $219, nonresident $651. On-campus housing for both single and married students. Average academic year housing cost: $6480 (including board) for single students, $7500 for married students. Contact Director of Housing for both on- and off-campus housing information. Phone: (703)993-2720. Day-care facilities available.

Graduate School

Graduate study since 1972. Enrollment: full-time 2500, part-time 7043. Faculty: full-time 1000, part-time 800. Degrees M.A., M.A.I.S., M.B.A., M.Ed., M.F.A., M.P.A., M.S., M.S.N., Certificate, D.A.Ed., Ph.D.

ADMISSION REQUIREMENTS. Two official transcripts, three letters of recommendation required in support of School's applications. Online application encouraged. GRE Subject Tests/GMAT/MAT, interview required by some departments. TOEFL (minimum score 575) required of international applicants. Apply to Graduate School's Admissions Office MSN 3A4 by May 1 for most departments. Rolling admissions process. Application fee $30. Phone: (703)993-2407; fax: (703)993-2392.

ADMISSION STANDARDS. Competitive for many departments, selective for others. Usual minimum average: 2.5 (A = 4) for master's, 3.0 for doctoral studies.

FINANCIAL AID. Scholarships and tuition waivers (limited), fellowships, assistantships, career-related internships, Federal W/S, loans. Apply by April 1 to the Dean, Graduate School for fellowships, assistantships, scholarships, and tuition waivers; to Director of Financial Aid for all other programs. Phone: (703) 933-2353. Use FAFSA. Aid available for part-time students.

DEGREE REQUIREMENTS. For master's: 24 semester hours minimum plus thesis; reading knowledge of one foreign language for some programs; final exam/final project for some programs. For D.A.Ed.: 72 credits minimum beyond the bachelor's, at least 32 in residence; written preliminary exam; three comprehensive written exams, dissertation, final oral exam. For Ph.D.: a minimum of 72 semester hours beyond the bachelor's (or 50 beyond the master's); completion of foreign language requirements (if applicable); preliminary exam, dissertation; final written/oral exam.

FIELDS OF STUDY.
Administration of Justice. M.P.A.
Advance Studies in Teaching and Learning. M.Ed.
Anthropology. M.A.
Applied and Engineering Physics. M.S.
Applied Developmental Psychology. M.A., Ph.D.
Art and Visual Technology. M.A., M.A.T., M.F.A.
Art History. M.A.
Arts Management. M.A.
Biodefense. M.S., Ph.D.
Bioinformatics and Computational Biology. M.S., Ph.D.
Biology. M.S.
Biopsychology. Ph.D.
Bioscience Management. M.S.
Biosciences. Ph.D.
Business Administration. M.B.A.
Chemistry. M.S.
Civil and Infrastructure Engineering. M.S.
Civil Engineering. Ph.D.
Climate Dynamics. Ph.D.
Clinical Psychology. Ph.D.
Communication. M.A., Ph.D.
Community College Education. D.A.
Community College Teaching. M.A.I.S.
Computational Science. M.S.
Computational Sciences and Informatics. Ph.D.
Computational Social Science. Ph.D.
Computer Engineering. M.S.
Computer Science. M.S., Ph.D.
Conflict Analysis and Resolution. M.S., Ph.D.

Counseling and Development. M.Ed.
Creative Writing. M.F.A.
Cultural Studies. Ph.D.
Curriculum and Instruction. M.Ed.
Dance. M.F.A.
E-commerce. M.S.
Early Childhood Education. M.Ed.
Earth Systems and Geoinformation Sciences. Ph.D.
Earth Systems Science. M.S.
Economics. M.A., Ph.D.
Education. Ph.D.
Education Leadership. M.Ed.
Educational Psychology. M.Ed.
Electrical Engineering. M.S., Ph.D.
Elementary Education (PK–6). M.Ed.
Emergency Management and Homeland Security. M.P.A.
English. Includes linguistics, literature, professional writing and editing. M.A.
English as a Second Language. M.A.
Environmental Science and Policy. M.S., Ph.D.
Environmental Science and Public Policy. M.P.A.
Epidemiology and Biostatistics. M.S.
Exercise, Fitness and Health Promotion. M.S.
Folklore. M.A.I.S.
Foreign Language (PK–6). M.Ed.
Foreign Languages. Includes French, Spanish. M.A.
Geographic and Cartographic Sciences. M.S.
Gerontology. M.S.
Health Sciences. M.S.
Health Systems Management. Includes assisted living and senior housing, health information systems, health policy, health security and privacy. M.S.
Higher Education. M.A.I.S.
History. Includes applied (M.A.), enrichment (M.A.), teaching (M.A.). Ph.D.
Human Factors, Applied Cognition Psychology. M.A., Ph.D.
Human Resources Management. M.P.A.
Information Policy and Administration. M.P.A.
Information Security and Assurance. M.S.
Information Systems. M.S.
Information Technology. Ph.D.
Instructional Technology. M.Ed.
Interdisciplinary. M.A.I.S.
International Commerce ad Policy. M.A.
International Health. M.S.
International Management. M.P.A.
Justice, Law and Crime Policy. M.A., Ph.D.
Knowledge Management. M.A.
Literacy and Reading. M.Ed.
Mathematics. M.S., Ph.D.
Multilingual/Multicultural Education. M.Ed.
Music. M.A
Neuroscience. Ph.D.
Nonprofit Management. M.P.A.
Nursing. M.S.N., Ph.D.
Operations Research. M.S.
Philosophy. M.A.
Physical Sciences. Ph.D.
Physics. M.S.
Policy Studies. M.P.A.
Political Science. M.A., Ph.D.
Psychology. M.A., Ph.D.
Public Administration. M.P.A.
Public and Nonprofit Management. M.P.A.
Public Management. M.P.A.
Religion, Culture and Values. M.A.I.S.
School Psychology. M.A.
Secondary Education (6–12). M.Ed.
Social Work. M.S.W.
Sociology. M.A.
Software Engineering. M.S.

Special Education. M.Ed.
State and Local Government. M.P.A.
Statistical Science. M.S., Ph.D.
Systems Engineering. M.S., Ph.D.
Teaching of English as a Second Language. M.A.
Technology Management. M.S.
Telecommunications Policy. M.A.
Third-Party Governance. M.P.A.
Transportation Policy, Operations and Logistics. M.A.
Video-Based Production. M.A.I.S.
Women's Studies. M.A.I.S.

School of Law (22201-4426)
Arlington, VA
Web site: www.law.gmu.edu

Affiliated in 1979. ABA approved since 1980. AALS member. Public control. Semester system. Located at the Metro Campus, Arlington. Special facilities: Law and Economics Center, National Center for Technology and Law. Library: 447,746 volumes, 2500 subscriptions; has LEXIS, NEXIS, WESTLAW, LEGALTRAK; has more than 900 network connections.

Annual tuition: resident $15,274, per credit $546; nonresident $26,502, per credit $946. Limited on-campus housing available. Total average annual additional expense: $20,228.

Enrollment: first-year class full-time 110, part-time 104; total 751 (men 62%, women 38%). Faculty: full-time 31, part-time 57. Student to faculty ratio 16.5 to 1. Degrees conferred: J.D., LL.M. (Intellectual Property Law, Law and Economics).

ADMISSION REQUIREMENTS. LSDAS Law School report, bachelor's degree, transcripts, LSAT, writing sample, personal statement, two letters of recommendation required in support of application. TOEFL required of international applicants. Early decision available, apply by December 15, notification by January 15. Preference given to state residents. Graduates of unaccredited colleges not considered. Apply to Admissions Office by April 1. Application fee $35. Phone: (703)993-8010; fax: (703) 993-8260.

ADMISSION STANDARDS. Selective. Accepts 15% of full-time and 17% of part-time applicants. Number of full-time applicants 5199, part-time 751; number of full-time acceptance 787, part-time 127; number enrolled full-time 140, part-time 76; LSAT (75% of full-time students have a score at or above 158, part-time 158); GPA (75% of full-time students have a GPA at or above 3.15, part-time 2.94). *U.S. News & World Report* ranking is tied for 34th of all U.S. law schools.

FINANCIAL AID. Limited to fellowships, Federal W/S, loans. Apply to Admissions Office by March 1. Phone: (703)993-2353. Use FAFSA (School code: 003749) and institutional Financial Aid Application. About 20% of students receive aid from school and outside sources. Aid available for part-time students.

DEGREE REQUIREMENTS. For J.D.: satisfactory completion of three-year program. For LL.M.: Satisfactory completion of 13-course program.

THE GEORGE WASHINGTON UNIVERSITY
Washington, D.C. 20052
Web site: www.gwu.edu

Founded 1821. Located in downtown Washington. CGS member. Coed. Private control. Semester system. Member of consortium of Universities of the Washington Metropolitan Area. Special facilities: Biostatistics Center, The Burdetsky Labor-Management

Institute, Center for the Advanced Study of Human Paleobiology, Center for International Health, Center for International Science and Technology Policy, Center for Nuclear Studies, Center for the Study of Combustion and the Environment, Center for Social and Organizational Learning, Center for Structural Dynamics Research, Center for Washington Area Studies, Center for the Advancement of Small Business, Cyberspace Policy Institute, Educational Resources Information Center, Institute for Artificial Intelligence, Institute on Crime, Justice, and Corrections, Institute for Ethnographic Research, Institute for European, Russian, Eurasian Studies, Institute for History in the Media, Institute for Management Science and Engineering, Institute for Materials Science, Institute for Reliability and Risk Analysis, Institute for the Study of Fatigue Fracture and Structural Reliability, Institute for Urban Development Research, Institute for the Environment, Institute for Medical Imaging and Image Analysis, Institute for Technology and Strategic Research, Institute of Brazilian Business and Public Management Issues, International Water Resource Institute, International Rule of Law Center, Joint Institute for Advancement of Flight Sciences, The Sigur Center for Asian Studies, Space Policy Institute. The University's NIH ranking is 92nd among all U.S. institutions with 64 awards/grants valued at $59,986,074. The University's endowment assets rank it 65th, with a value of $733,000,000. In 2004, the University awarded 255 doctorates which ranked it 57th among all U.S. institutions eligible to award that degree. Three of the University's faculty members have been elected to National Honor Academies and this ranks it 105th among all U.S. institutions. The Library: approximately 1,800,000 volumes, 14,729 subscriptions. Total University enrollment: 20,000.

Tuition: per semester hour $1012. Limited on-campus housing for graduate students based on a first-come, first-served basis. Contact the Office of Residential and Off-Campus Housing for both on- and off-campus housing information. Phone (202)994-6688.

Columbian College of Arts and Sciences

Graduate study since 1886. Enrollment: full-time about 915, part-time 1110. Graduate faculty: full-time 236, part-time 78. Degrees conferred: M.A., M.F.A., M.F.S., M.S.F.S., M.S., Psy.D., Ph.D.

ADMISSION REQUIREMENTS. Transcripts, GRE, statement of purpose, letters of reference required in support of School's application. Online application available. TOEFL (minumum score 550) required for international applicants; TWE recommended, TSE required for international applicants applying for graduate assistantships. GRE subject test, writing samples, portfolio required by some departments. Accepts transfer applicants. Apply to Office of Graduate Admissions by April 1 (Fall), October 1 (Spring), March 1 (Summer). Earlier submission required by some programs. Application fee $55. Phone: (202)994-6211; fax: (202)994-6213; e-mail: asgrad@gwu.edu.

ADMISSION STANDARDS. Very selective for most departments, competitive or selective for the others. Usual minimum average: 3.0 (A = 4).

FINANCIAL AID. Annual award from institutional funds: fellowships, assistantships, Federal W/S, loans. Apply by May 1 to the Office of Student Financial Assistance (January 15 for students in clinical psychology). Phone: (202)994-6620. Use FAFSA. About 20% of students receive aid from School and outside sources. Aid available for part-time students.

DEGREE REQUIREMENTS. For master's: 30–36 semester hours; thesis/nonthesis option; comprehensive exam. For Ph.D.: 72 semester hours beyond the bachelor's; general exam for candidacy; dissertation; final oral exam.

FIELDS OF STUDY.
American Literature.
American Studies.
Anthropology. M.A. only.
Applied Mathematics.
Art. Includes ceramics, design, interior design, printmaking, painting, photography, sculpture, visual communications. M.F.A. only.
Art History.
Art Therapy. M.A. only.
Asian Studies. M.A.
Biochemistry.
Biological Sciences. Includes biology, botany, zoology.
Biostatistics.
Chemical Toxicology. M.S. only.
Chemistry.
Computer Fraud Investigation.
Criminal Justice. M.A. only.
Economics.
English Literature.
Environmental and Resource Policy. M.A. only.
Epidemiology.
Forensic Sciences. M.F.S., M.S.F.S. only.
Genetics.
Geobiology.
Geochemistry. M.S. only.
Geography. M.A. only.
Geology.
Geoscience.
Historic Preservation. M.A. only.
History.
History of Religion.
Hominid Paleobiology.
Human Sciences. Ph.D. only.
Immunology. Ph.D. only.
Industrial and Engineering Statistics. M.S only.
Legislative Affairs. M.A. only.
Materials Science.
Mathematics.
Media and Public Affairs.
Microbiology.
Molecular and Cellular Oncology. Ph.D. only.
Museum Studies. M.A. only.
Neuroscience. Ph.D. only.
Nonprofit Management. M.P.A.
Pharmacology.
Philosophy and Social Policy. M.A. only.
Physics.
Political Management.
Political Science.
Public Policy.
Professional Psychology. Psy.D. only.
Psychology. Includes clinical, cognitive, neuropsychobiology, industrial/organizational/applied social. Ph.D., Psy.D. (Clinical).
Public Policy. Ph.D. only.
Radiological Sciences. Ph.D. only.
Security Management.
Sociology. M.A. only.
Speech-Language Pathology and Audiology. M.A. only.
Statistics.
Telecommunications. M.A. only.
Theater. Includes a concentration in acting, scenic design. M.F.A. only.
Women's Studies. M.A. only.

School of Business and Public Management
710 21st Street, N.W.
Washington, D.C. 20052
Web site: www.sbpm.gwu.edu

Established 1928. School began as Department of Comparative Jurisprudence and Diplomacy in 1898, became a School of Government in 1928, in 1960 name changed to Government, Business and International Affairs, current name adopted in 1990. Private control, Accredited programs: M.B.A. (first M.B.A. awarded in 1954), Accounting; recognized Ph.D. Courses also offered in Loudon County and Alexandria, Virginia. Semester system. Special facilities: Center for Excellence in Municipal Management, Center for Law Practice Strategy and Management, Center for Latin American Issues, Center for Real Estate and Urban Analysis, European Union Research Center, Institute for Global Management and Research, International Institute of Tourism Studies. Special Programs: accelerated MBA program; foreign exchange programs (in Chile, Denmark, France, Germany, Hungary, Portugal, Republic of Korea, Spain, Sweden, Thailand).

Tuition: $1080 per credit. Enrollment: total full-time 834, part-time 1208 (men 60%, women 40%). Faculty: 106 full-time, 44 part-time; 88% with Ph.D./D.B.A. Degrees conferred: M.B.A. (full-time, part-time, day, evening, weekends), M.B.A.I.B. (International Business), E.M.B.A. (weekends only), M.B.A.-M.A. (International Affairs with Elliot School) M.B.A.-J.D., M.Accy., M.P.A., M.P.P. (Public Policy), M.S.A.M. (Acquisition Management), M.S.F., M.S.I.S.T. (Information Systems Technology), M.S.P.M. (Project Management), M.T.A. (Tourism Administration), M.Tax., Ph.D.

ADMISSION REQUIREMENTS. All applicants should have a bachelor's degree from a recognized institution of higher education and a strong mathematics background. Students are required to have their own personal computer. Early applications are encouraged for both admission and financial aid consideration. Submit application for Graduate Study, GMAT (will accept GMAT test results from the last five years, latest acceptable date is March; GRE for M.S.F., M.T.A.), official transcripts from each undergraduate/graduate school attended, three letters of recommendation, statement of purpose, résumé (prefers at least four years of work experience), and an application fee of $60 to the Office of Graduate Enrollment Support Services. An interactive application is also available. In addition, international students (whose native language is other than English) should submit a TOEFL report (minimum score 550), TWE (strongly recommended), certified translations and evaluations of all official transcripts; recommendation should be in English or with certified translations, proof of health/immunization certificate, and proof of sufficient financial resources for two years of academic study. Beginning students are admitted Fall and Winter. Both U.S. citizens and international applicants apply by April 1 (Fall), October 1 (Winter). Accepts transfer applicants. On-campus visits and interviews are encouraged prior to the admissions committee reviewing completed application. Joint degree applicants must apply to and be accepted to both schools; contact the Office of Enrollment Support Services for current information and specific admissions requirements. Rolling admissions process, notification is made within 4–6 weeks of receipt of completed application and supporting documents. Admissions Office phone for M.B.A.: (202)994-6584; fax: (202)994-6382; for E.M.B.A.: (202)729-8282.

ADMISSION REQUIREMENTS FOR DOCTORAL CANDIDATES. Contact the Office of Graduate Enrollment Support Services at (202)994-3900 for application material and information. Beginning students are admitted Fall Only. Both U.S. citizens and international applicants apply by January 15 (Fall). Submit application for Graduate Study, a GMAT/GRE (will accept GMAT/GRE test results from the last five years), two official transcripts from each undergraduate/ graduate schools attended, three applicant evaluation forms, letter of intent, résumé, statement of purpose, and application fee of $60 to the Doctoral Programs Office. In addition, international students (whose native language is other than English) should submit a TOEFL report (minimum score 600), TSE and TWE (strongly recommended), certified (notarized) translations and evaluations of all official, transcripts, recommendation should be in English or with certified translations, proof of health/immunization certificate. Inter-

views strongly recommended with the lead professor from primary field prior to the admissions committee reviewing completed application. Notification is made within four to six weeks of receipt of completed application and all supporting documents. Doctoral Programs Office phone: (202)994-6298; fax (202)994-5225.

ADMISSION STANDARDS. Selective. For M.B.A.: median GMAT: full-time 601, part-time 542; median GPA: full-time 3.32, part-time 3.02 (A = 4) Gourman rating: the M.B.A. program rated in the top 36, the score was 4.50; the Ph.D. program rated in the top 35, the score was 4.49.

FINANCIAL AID. Presidential Merit Fellowships, minority scholarships, graduate fellowships, graduate and teaching assistantships, Federal W/S, loans. Financial aid is available for part-time students. Financial aid may be available for international students. Assistantships/fellowships may be available for joint degree candidates. Financial Aid applications and information are generally available at the on-campus visit/interview or after January 1; apply by April 1. Request scholarship, fellowship, assistantship information from the School of Business. Contact the University's Director of Student Assistance for current need-based financial aid information. Phone: (202)994-6620. Use FAFSA (School code: 001444), also submit Financial Aid Transcript, Federal Income Tax forms. Approximately 20% of students receive some form of financial assistance.

DEGREE REQUIREMENTS. For M.B.A., M.B.A.I.B.: 60-credit program including 15 elective credits, two-year program; degree program must be completed in five years. For M.Accy., M.Tax.; 35–40 credit program. For M.F.S.: 48–69 credit program. For M.S.I.S.T.: 30–33 credit program. For M.S.A.M., M.S.P.M.: 30–36 credit program. For M.T.A.: 36 credit program. For M.B.A.-Master's: 72 credit program, generally a three- to four-year program. For M.B.A.-J.D.: 108-credit program, generally a four- to five-year program. For Ph.D.: three- to five-year program; comprehensive evaluation covering both primary and supporting field; dissertation proposal and oral defense, dissertation; oral defense; degree program must be completed in seven years.

FIELDS OF STUDY.
Accountancy. M.Accy.
Finance. M.S.F.
Information Systems Technology. M.S.I.S.T.
Project Management. M.S.P.M.
Tourism Administration. M.T.A.

M.B.A. AREAS OF CONCENTRATION:
Accountancy.
Environmental Policy and Management.
Finance and Investments.
Health Services Administration
Human Resources Management.
Information Systems, Management.
International Business.
Management Decision Making.
Management of Science, Technology and Innovation.
Marketing.
Non-Profit Organization Management.
Organization Behavior and Development.
Real Estate and Urban Development.
Small Business/Entrepreneurship.
Strategic Management and Public Policy.
Supply Chain Management.
Tourism and Hospitality Management.

P.H.D. AREAS OF CONCENTRATION:
Accountancy.
Decision Sciences.
Finance.

International Business.
Information Systems and Technology Management.
Management.
Marketing.
Strategic Management and Public Policy.

Graduate School of Education and Human Development

Tuition: per hour $1012. Graduate enrollment: full-time 410, part-time 889. School faculty: full-time 65, part-time 56. Degrees conferred: M.A. in Ed., M.Ed., Ed.S., Ed.D.

ADMISSION REQUIREMENTS. Transcripts, GRE/MAT, two letters of recommendation (out-of-area applicants), statement of purpose, résumé, interview required in support of School's application. TOEFL (minimum score 550, 213 on computer-based test) required for international applicants. Accepts transfer applicants. Graduates of unaccredited institutions not considered. Apply to Dean of the School by January 15 (Fall), October 1 (Spring), February 1 (Summer Session); some programs have earlier deadline. Application fee $60. Phone: (202)994-9283; fax: (202)994-7207.

ADMISSION STANDARDS. Selective. Usual minimum average 2.75 (A = 4); 2.3 to 2.74 for provisional admission.

FINANCIAL AID. Fellowships, assistantships are available at Ed.D. level, tuition waivers, Federal W/S, loans. Apply to Office of Student Financial Services by February 15. Phone: (202)994-6620. Use FAFSA. Some employment opportunities are available at the University. Information is available through the Personnel Office. Aid available for part-time students.

DEGREE REQUIREMENTS. For M.A. in Ed., M.Ed.: 24 semester hours minimum in residence; thesis optional for 6 semester hours; comprehensive exam for some programs; additional courses in lieu of comprehensive in some programs. For Ed.S.: 30 semester hours minimum beyond the master's, at least 21 in residence; comprehensive exams; final oral. For Ed.D.: usually about 75 to 90 semester hours beyond the bachelor's, about 60 semester hours in residence and at least one semester in full-time attendance; preliminary exams; dissertation; final oral exam.

FIELDS OF STUDY.
Counseling.
Curriculum and Instruction.
Early Childhood Special Education.
Education Policy Studies.
Educational Administration and Policy Studies.
Educational Leadership and Administration.
Educational Technology Leadership.
Elementary Education.
Higher Education Administration.
Human Resource Development.
Individualized Program.
Infant Special Education.
International Education.
Museum Education.
Rehabilitation Counseling.
School Counseling.
Secondary Education.
Special Education. Includes adolescents with emotional and behavioral disabilities.
Transition to Teaching.

School of Engineering and Applied Science
Web site: www.seas.gwu.edu

Tuition: per credit hour $1012. Graduate enrollment: full-time 416, part-time 1103. Graduate faculty: full-time 70, part-time 97.

Degrees conferred: M.S., M.E.M., professional degrees of Engineer and Applied Scientist; D.Sc.

ADMISSION REQUIREMENTS. Transcripts, statement of purpose, résumé, three letters of recommendation required in support of School's application. GRE Subject Tests recommended; GRE required for Ph.D. applicants and Financial Aid applicants. Interview not required, but desirable for doctoral applicants. TOEFL or IELTS, financial certificate required for international applicants. Accepts transfer applicants. Graduates of unaccredited institutions not considered. Apply to Manager of Engineering Admissions by May 1 (Fall), October 1 (Spring), February 1 (1st Summer Session), April 1 (2nd Summer Session). Application fee $60. Phone: (202)994-6158; fax: (202)994-4522; e-mail: admis@seas.gwu.edu.

ADMISSION STANDARDS. Selective. Usual minimum average: 3.0 (A = 4).

FINANCIAL AID. Annual awards from institutional funds: research/teaching assistantships, fellowships, tuition waivers, Federal W/S, loans. Approved for VA benefits. Apply to the Office of Student Financial Services by March 1 (Summer and Fall), September 1 (Spring). Phone: (202)994-6620; fax: (202)994-7221. Use FAFSA. Aid available for part-time students.

DEGREE REQUIREMENTS: For M.S. (Electrical Engineering and Computer Science): 30 credit hours including thesis; M.S. (Civil, Mechanical, and Environmental and Operations Research): 33 credit hours including thesis; M.S., M.E.M. (Engineering Management): 36 semester hours including thesis. For the Professional Engineering degree: 30 semester hours beyond the master's. For D.Sc.: 30 hours minimum beyond the master's; 54 credit hours beyond the baccalaureate; qualifying exam; dissertation; final oral exam.

FIELDS OF STUDY.
Civil and Environmental Engineering. Includes engineering mechanics, environmental engineering, geotechnical engineering, structural engineering, water resources engineering.
Computer Engineering.
Computer Science. Includes algorithms and theory, artificial intelligence and computer vision, computer and communications security, computer engineering and architecture, graphics and multimedia, industrial engineering, parallel and distributed computing, software engineering and systems.
Electrical and Computer Engineering. Includes biomedical engineering, communications, controls, systems, and signal processing, electrical power and engineering management, electrophysics and fiber optics, energy conversion, power, and transmission, industrial engineering, microelectronics and VLSI systems.
Engineering Management and Systems Engineering. Includes domain-specific engineering management; economics, finance, and cost engineering; engineering management principles, practices, and methods; industrial engineering; information and process engineering; systems engineering; and quantitative analysis.
Mechanical and Aerospace Engineering. Includes aerospace engineering, design of mechanical engineering systems, fluid mechanics, thermal sciences and energy, industrial engineering, solid mechanics and materials science, transportation safety engineering.
Telecommunications and Computers. Includes telecommunications networks, telecommunications network security.

The Elliott School of International Affairs

Established 1898. Name change in 1988. Special facilities: Center for International Science and Technology, Institute for European, Russian, and Eurasian Studies, Sigur Center for Asian Studies, Space Policy Institute.

Tuition: per credit $1018.

Enrollment: full-time 338, part-time 139. School faculty: full-time 50, part-time 21. Degrees conferred: M.A., M.I.S., M.I.P.P., M.A.-M.B.A., M.A.-J.D., M.A.-M.P.H. The Ph.D. is offered through the Graduate School of Arts and Sciences.

ADMISSION REQUIREMENTS. Transcripts, GRE, three letters of recommendation, foreign language proficiency, work experience, personal statement, résumé required in support of School's application. TOEFL (minimum score 600) required for international applicants. TWE is recommended for international applicants. Graduates of unaccredited institutions not considered. Admits Fall only. Apply to Graduate Admissions Office by January 15. International, graduate fellowship, and assistantship applicants apply by January 15. Application fee $60. Phone: (202) 994-7050; fax: (202)994-9537; e-mail: esiagrad@gwu.edu.

ADMISSION STANDARDS. Very selective. Usual minimum average: 3.0 (A = 4).

FINANCIAL AID. Fellowships, assistantships, tuition waivers, off-campus employment, Federal W/S, loans. Apply to the Office of Student Financial Services by January 15. Phone: (202)994-6620; fax: (202)994-0906. Use FAFSA. Aid available for part-time students.

DEGREE REQUIREMENTS. For M.A.: two options (except in Security Policy studies): 30 semester hours minimum in residence including thesis, or 36 semester hours of course work; reading knowledge of one foreign language or specified level of statistics; final comprehensive exam(s). For M.I.S.: 28 credit minimum; proficiency in a modern foreign language; capstone. For M.I.P.P.: 27 hour program; core seminar; skills-based workshops.

FIELDS OF STUDY.
Asian Studies. M.A.
European and Eurasian Studies. M.A.
International Affairs. M.A.
International Development Studies. M.A.
International Policy and Practice. M.I.P.P.
International Studies. Includes conflict and conflict resolution, international security studies, international economic affairs, international affairs and development, international public health, technology and international affairs, international law and organizations, U.S. foreign policy. M.I.S.
International Science and Technology Policy.
International Trade and Investment Policy. M.A.
Latin American and Hemispheric Studies. M.A.
Middle East Studies. M.A.
Security Policy Studies. M.A.

Law School
Web site: www.law.gwu/edu

Established 1865. ABA approved since 1923. AALS member. Private control. Semester system. Special facilities: Creative and Innovative Economy Center (CIEC), Dean Dinwoodey Center for Intellectual Property Studies, Institute for Constitutional Studies, Institute for International Corporate Governance and Accountability, International Rule of Law Center. Summer programs: Augsburg Exchange Program, Munich Intellectual Property Law Program, North American Consortium on Legal Education (NACLE), Oxford-GW Program in International Human Rights Law. Law library: 591,863 volumes, 4304 subscriptions; has LEXIS, NEXIX, WESTLAW, DIALOG, ALADIN.

Annual costs: $38,198, per credit $1343. On- and off-campus housing available. Contact University Housing Office. Total annual average additional expense: $18,490.

Enrollment: first-year class day 413, evening 122; total full-time 1428, part-time 302 (men 52%, women 48%, minorities 18%);

postgraduates 250. Faculty: full-time 96, part-time 200. Student to faculty ration 18.4 to 1. Degrees conferred: J.D., J.D.-M.A., J.D.-M.B.A., J.D.-M.P.H., J.D.-M.P.A. J.D.-M.H.S.A., LL.M. (Environmental Law, Intellectual Property Law, International and Comparative Law, Government Procurement Law, Litigation and Dispute Resolution), LL.M.-M.P.H., S.J.D.

ADMISSION REQUIREMENTS. LSDAS Law School report, bachelor's degree, transcripts, LSAT (no later than December), personal statement, three letters of recommendation required in support of application. Interview not required. Accepts very limited number of transfer applicants. Graduates of unaccredited colleges not considered. Apply to Office of the Dean after October 1, before March 1. Beginning students admitted Fall only. Application fee $80. Phone: (203)739-0648; fax: (203)739-0624; e-mail: jdadmit@law.gwu.edu. For LL.M: apply by June 1 (Fall), November 1 (Spring); nonresidents admitted Fall only. E-mail: grad@law.gwu.

ADMISSION STANDARDS. Selective. Accepts approximately 19% of full-time and 18% of part-time applicants. Number of full-time applicants 9812, part-time 1260; number of full-time acceptance 1888, part-time 225; number full-time enrolled 413, part-time 122; LSAT (75% of full-time students have a score at or above 163, part-time 160); GPA (75% of full-time students have a GPA at or above 3.45, part-time 3.29). *U.S. News & World Report* ranking is in the top 22 of all U.S. law schools.

FINANCIAL AID. Scholarships, teaching fellowships (for LL.M. candidates), assistantships, Federal W/S, loans. Apply to Office of Financial Aid by March 1. Phone: (202)994-7230. Use FAFSA. About 45% of students receive aid other than loans from Law Center.

DEGREE REQUIREMENTS. For J.D.: 84 (32 required) credits with a GPA of at least 2.0 (A = 4), plus completion of upper divisional writing course; three-year program, four-year program. Accelerated J.D. with one summer of course work. For J.D.-Master's: a maximum of 6 credits can be applied to J.D. For LL.M.: 24 credits; a GPA of 2.67 (A = 4) required; thesis; one calendar year full-time, two calendar years part-time. For LL.M. (foreign law school graduates): one full year in residence; a GPA of 2.33 (A = 4) required; thesis/nonthesis option. For S.J.D.: two semesters minimum in residence beyond the master's; dissertation; oral defense.

School of Medicine and Health Sciences (20037)
Web site: www.gwumc.edu

Established 1825. Semester system. Library: 100,000 volumes, 2000 subscriptions. The University's NIH ranking is 92nd among all U.S. institutions with 64 awards/grants worth $59,986,074.

Annual tuition: $44,555. No on-campus housing. Average cost for all other expenses: $19,500.

Enrollment: first-year class 177; total full-time 686 (men 45%, women 55%, minorities 38%, District residents 0%). Faculty: full-time 1648, part-time 626. Degrees conferred: M.D., M.D.-M.P.H. The M.S. and Ph.D. are offered through the Graduate School and School of Engineering.

ADMISSION REQUIREMENTS. AMCAS report and supplemental application, transcripts, MCAT, three letters of recommendation required in support of application. Interview by invitation only. Applicants must have completed at least three years of college study. Has EDP; apply between June 15 and August 1. Accepts transfer applicants. First-year students apply AMCAS after June 15, before December 1. Advanced standing students apply to Admissions Office by December 1. Application fee $80. Phone: (202)994-3506; e-mail: medadmit@gwu.edu.

ADMISSION STANDARDS. Very competitive. Accepts about 4.6% of all applicants. Number of applications 7778 (n/a out-of-

District); number interviewed 1093 (n/a out-of-District); number of acceptance 358 (n/a out-of-District); number enrolled 177 (174 out-of-District). Mean Composite MCAT 9.6; mean UGPA 3.52 (A = 4).

FINANCIAL AID. Scholarships, minority scholarships, grants, NIH stipend, Federal W/S, loans. About 35% of students receive aid other than loans from School. Apply to the Director of Financial Aid after acceptance but by April 15. Phone: (202)994-2960. Use FAFSA (School code: E00197).

DEGREE REQUIREMENTS. For M.D.: satisfactory completion of four-year program; must pass Step 1 of USMLE to advance to third year and pass Step 2 for graduation. For M.S., M.P.H., Ph.D.: see the Graduate listings above.

FIELDS OF GRADUATE STUDY.
Biochemistry.
Cell Biology.
Genetics.
Genomics, Proteomics and Bioinformatics
Immunology.
Microbiology.
Molecular and Cellular Oncology.
Neurosciences.
Pharmacology.

GEORGETOWN COLLEGE
Georgetown, Kentucky 40324-1696
Web site: www.georgetowncollege.edu

Founded 1829. Located 12 miles N of Lexington. Coed. Private control. Baptist. Semester system. Special facility: Center for Leadership and Ethics. Library: 160,000 volumes, 550 subscriptions. Total College enrollment: 1900.
Tuition: per hour $250. No on-campus housing for graduate students.

Graduate Studies

Enrollment: full- and part-time 535. Faculty: full-time 8, part-time 13. Degree conferred: M.A. in Ed.

ADMISSION REQUIREMENTS. Transcripts, letters of recommendation required in support of School's application. GRE is strongly recommended. Interview sometimes required. Accepts transfer applicants. Graduates of unaccredited colleges not considered. Apply to Office of Graduate Study at least 30 days prior to start of semester. Application fee: none. Phone: (502)863-8176; fax: (502)868-7741.

ADMISSION STANDARDS. Relatively open. Minimum average: 2.7 (A = 4).

FINANCIAL AID. Limited to Federal W/S, loans. Approved for VA benefits. Apply to Director of Financial Aid; no specified closing date. Phone: (800)788-9985. Use FAFSA.

DEGREE REQUIREMENTS. For M.A. in Ed.: 30 semester hours minimum, at least 24 in residence; final comprehensive exam.

FIELD OF STUDY.
Education. Includes early elementary, elementary, secondary, middle school.

GEORGETOWN UNIVERSITY
Washington, D.C. 20057
Web site: www.georgetown.edu

Founded 1789. CGS member. Coed. Private control. Roman Catholic, Jesuit affiliated. Semester system. Special facilities: Center for Contemporary Arab Studies, computation center, Joseph and Rose Kennedy Institute of Ethics, Lombardi Cancer Research Center, Center for Child Development, Center for German and European Studies, Center for Latin American Studies, Center for Muslim-Christian Understanding: History and International Affairs, Institute for the Study of Diplomacy. Participates in the Consortium of Universities of the Washington Metropolitan Area, includes the American, Catholic, Gallaudet, George Mason, George Washington, and Howard Universities, the University of the District of Columbia, the University of Maryland College Park, Mt. Vernon and Trinity Colleges. The University's NIH ranking is 82nd among all U.S. institutions with 211 awards/grants valued at $71,798,074. According to The Center at University of Florida, the University is ranked 92nd in receipt of Federal Research funds with $83,745,000. The University's endowment assets rank it 71st, with a value of $680,611,000. Six of the University's faculty members have been elected to National Honor Academies and this ranks it 83rd among all U.S. institutions. The Library: approximately 2,000,000 volumes, 12,800 subscriptions. Total University enrollment: 12,600.
Annual tuition: full-time $33,408; per credit $1392. No on-campus housing available for graduate students. Contact Director of Campus Housing for off-campus housing information. Phone: (202)687-4560.

Graduate School of Arts and Sciences

Graduate study since 1820. Enrollment: full-time 2089, part-time 786. Graduate faculty: full-time 1320, part-time 406. Degrees conferred: M.A., M.S., M.A.T., M.B.A., M.P.P., Ph.D.

ADMISSION REQUIREMENTS. Official transcripts, three letters of reference, statement of purpose required in support of School's application. Online application available. GRE/MAT required by some departments. TOEFL (minimum score 550, some departments require higher scores) required for international applicants. Interview not required. Accepts transfer applicants. Graduates of unaccredited institutions not considered. Apply by February 1 (Fall), November 1 (Spring) to the Graduate School's Admission Office. Application fee $65 for students with an undergraduate degree from a U.S. institution, $70 for students with an undergraduate degree from a non-U.S. institution. Online application fee $55. Phone: (202)687-5568; fax: (202) 687-6802; e-mail: gradmail@georgetown.edu.

ADMISSION STANDARDS. Competitive for most departments. Minimum average: 3.0 (A = 4).

FINANCIAL AID. Annual awards from institutional funds: scholarships, fellowships, assistantships, Federal W/S, loans. Approved for VA benefits. Aid available for international students. Apply by February 1 to the Graduate School Office for scholarships; to Financial Aid Office for all other programs. Phone: (202)687-4547; fax: (202)687-6542. Use FAFSA and graduate student supplement. About 50% of full-time students receive aid other than loans from School and outside sources.

DEGREE REQUIREMENTS. For master's: 24 semester hour minimum, at least 18 in residence; foreign language requirement varies by department; thesis; final written/oral exam; or 30 hour minimum without thesis in some departments. For Ph.D.: 50 hours minimum beyond the bachelor's, at least 45 in residence; preliminary exam; language requirement varies by department; thesis; final written/oral exam.

FIELDS OF STUDY.

American Government. M.A.

Arab Studies. GRE for admission. M.A. only.

Arabic Language, Literature, and Linguistics. M.S., M.S.-Ph.D., Ph.D.

Biochemistry and Molecular Biology. GRE Subject in biology, biochemistry, or chemistry for admission. Ph.D. only.

Biology. GRE Subject for admission. M.S., Ph.D.

Cell Biology. GRE for admission. Ph.D. only.

Chemistry and Biochemistry. GRE for admission. M.S., M.S.-Ph.D., Ph.D.

Communication, Culture and Technology. GRE for admission. M.A. only.

Comparative Government. Ph.D. only.

Demography. GRE for admission. M.A. only.

Economics. GRE for admission. Ph.D. only.

English. GRE for admission. M.A. only.

Eurasian, Russian, and East European Studies. M.A. only.

Foreign Service. GRE for admission. M.S. only.

German. M.S., M.S.-Ph.D., Ph.D.

German and European Studies. GRE for admission. M.A. only.

Government. GRE for admission. M.A., Ph.D.

Health Physics. M.S. only.

History. GRE for admission. Ph.D. only.

Latin American Studies. GRE for admission. M.A. only.

Liberal Studies. M.A. only.

Linguistics. M.A.T., M.S., Ph.D.

Microbiology and Immunology. GRE for admission. Ph.D. only.

Neuroscience. GRE for admission. Ph.D. only.

Pathology. Ph.D. only.

Pharmacology. GRE for admission. Ph.D. only.

Philosophy. GRE for admission. M.A., Ph.D.

Physics. Includes industrial leadership in physics. Ph.D.

Physiology and Biophysics. GRE or MCAT for admission. M.S., Ph.D.

Psychology. GRE Subject for admission. Ph.D. only.

Public Policy. GRE for admission. M.P.P. only.

Russian and East European Studies. M.A. only.

Security Studies. GRE or MAT for admission. M.A. only.

Spanish. M.S., M.S.-Ph.D., Ph.D.

Tumor Biology. M.S., Ph.D.

McDonough School of Business

Web site: www.msb.georgetown.edu

Established 1981. Private control. Accredited programs: M.B.A. Semester system. Special programs: foreign exchange programs (in Australia, Belgium, Czech Republic, Germany, Hong Kong, Japan, Sweden, United Kingdom). Special facilities: Center for International Business, Center for Business-Government Relations, The Connelly Program in Business Ethics, Global Entrepreneurship Program.

Annual tuition: full-time $37,800. Enrollment: total full-time 509. Faculty: full-time 66, part-time 28; 94% with Ph.D./D.B.A. Degrees conferred: M.B.A., G.E.M.B.A., I.E.M.B.A. (International Executive), M.B.A.-J.D., M.B.A.-M.D., M.B.A.-M.P.P. (Public Policy), M.B.A.-M.S.F.S. (Foreign Service).

ADMISSION REQUIREMENTS. All applicants should have a bachelor's degree from a recognized institution of higher education and a strong mathematics background. Beginning students are admitted Fall only. Submit graduate application, GMAT (will accept GMAT test results from the last five years, latest acceptable date is March; GRE may be required for some joint degree programs), official transcripts from each undergraduate/graduate school attended, two letters of recommendation, three essays, résumé (prefers at least four years of work experience), and an application fee of $175 to the office of Graduate Admission. In addition, international students (whose native language is other than English) should submit a TOEFL report (minimum score 600),

certified translations and evaluations of all official transcripts; recommendation should be in English or with certified translations, proof of health/immunization certificate, and proof of sufficient financial resources for two years of academic study. Apply by November 30, for first round consideration; by February 8 for second round consideration; by April 25 for final round; by February 8 for scholarship consideration. Joint degree candidates and international applicants should apply by February 8 (Fall). Transfer applicants are rarely considered. On-campus visits and interviews are required for all applicants prior to the admissions committee reviewing completed application. Joint degree applicants must apply to and be accepted to both schools; contact the admissions offices for current information and specific admissions requirements. Rolling admissions process, notification is made within 6–8 weeks of receipt of completed application and supporting documents. Graduate Business Program office phone: (202) 687-4200.

ADMISSION STANDARDS. Selective. Median GMAT: 662; median GPA: 3.35 (A = 4). *U.S. News & World Report* ranked Georgetown in the top 30 of all U.S. business schools. *Business-Week* listed Georgetown in the top 50 of American business schools.

FINANCIAL AID. Partial and full tuition scholarships, merit scholarships for international students, M.B.A. Scholars Program, minority scholarships, graduate assistantships, Federal W/S, loans. Financial aid is available for international students. Assistantships/fellowships may be available for joint degree candidates. Financial Aid applications and information are generally available at the on-campus visit/interview or after January 1; apply by April 1. Request scholarship, fellowship, assistantship information from the School of Business. Contact the University's Office of Student Financial Services for current need-based financial aid information. Phone: (202)687-4547. Use FAFSA not later than February 15 (School code: 001445), also submit Financial Aid Transcript, Federal Income Tax forms. Approximately 40% of current students receive some form of financial assistance.

DEGREE REQUIREMENTS. For M.B.A.; 60-credit program including 21 elective credits, two-year program; degree program must be completed in three years. For G.E.M.B.A., I.E.M.B.A.: 60-credit program. For M.B.A.-J.D.: 122 credit program, four-and-one-half- to five-year program. For M.B.A.-M.D.: generally a five- to six-year program. For M.B.A.-M.P.P.: 87-credit program. For M.B.A.-M.S.F.S.: 90-credit program.

Law Center (20001)

Web site: www.law.georgetown.edu

Established 1870 and was the first law school established in the United States by a Jesuit institution of higher learning. ABA approved since 1923. AALS member. Private control. Semester system. Special facilities: Center for Law and the Public's Health, Center for the Advancement of the Rule of Law in the Americas, Center for the Study of the Legal Profession, Georgetown Environmental Law and Policy Institute, Human Rights Institute, Institute for the Study of International Migration, Institute of International Economic Law, O'Neill Institute for National and Global Health Law, Supreme Court Institute. Law library: 1,123,199 volumes, 9640 subscriptions; has LEXIS, NEXIS, WESTLAW, DIALOG.

Annual costs: $35,080, per credit $1285. No on-campus housing available. For off-campus housing contact Student Life Office. Total annual average additional expense: $19,875.

Enrollment: first-year class day 454, evening 129; total full-time 1580, part-time 386 (men 57%, women 43%, minorities 24%); postgraduates 320. Faculty: full-time 97, part-time 97. Student to faculty ratio 15.5 to 1. Degrees conferred: J.D., LL.M., M.S.L. (for Journalist), S.J.D.

ADMISSION REQUIREMENTS. LSDAS Law School report, bachelor's degree, transcripts, one reference, LSAT, personal statement, résumé required in support of application. Interview not required. Graduates of unaccredited colleges not considered. Part-time study available. Apply to Law Center Director of Admissions after September 1, before February 1 (Day), March 1 (Evening). First-year students admitted Fall only. Apply by November 1 for early action process. For LL.M. candidates: apply by March 1 (Early Action applicants apply by November 1, international applicants by February 1). For S.J.D.: apply by February 1. Application fee $75. Phone: (202)662-9015; fax: (202)662-9439; e-mail: admis@law.georgetown.edu.

ADMISSION STANDARDS. Selective. Accepts approximately 19% of full-time and 17% of part-time applicants. Number of full-time applicants 10,700, part-time 1002; number of full-time acceptance 2064, part-time 171; number full-time enrolled 454, part-time 129; LSAT (75% of full-time students have a score at or above 167, part-time 160); GPA (75% of full-time students have a GPA at or above 3.42, part-time 3.34). *U.S. News & World Report* ranking is in the top 12 of all U.S. law schools.

FINANCIAL AID. Scholarships including Public Interest Law Scholars Program, Federal W/S, loans. Apply to the Office of Financial Aid by March 1. Phone: (202)662-9210. Use FAFSA (School code: G21075). and institutional FAF. About 28% of students receive aid other than loans from Center. No University aid for part-time students except for students with extreme need.

DEGREE REQUIREMENTS. For J.D.: 83 semester hours required minimum, at least two in residence. For LL.M.: 24 credits beyond the J.D.; one year in residence, two research papers. For M.S.L.: full-time one-year program. For S.J.D.: two years of residence, first year in full-time attendance; publishable thesis.

FIELDS OF GRADUATE STUDY.
Common Law Studies.
International and Comparative Law.
International Legal Studies. For international students only.
Securities and Financial Regulation.
Taxation.
Note: Combined degree programs offered in conjunction with the School of Business, the School of Foreign Service, Department of Government, Department of Philosophy, and the Johns Hopkins School of Hygiene and Public Health.

School of Medicine

Web site: www.som.georgetown.edu

Established 1851. The oldest Catholic and Jesuit-sponsored medical school in U.S. Semester system. Library: 100,000 volumes, 1000 subscriptions. The University's NIH ranking is 82nd among all U.S. institutions with 211 awards/grants worth $71,798,074.

Annual tuition: $42,764. Limited on-campus housing. Average cost for all other expenses: $22,000.

Enrollment: first-year class 190; total full-time 749 (men 48%, women 52%, minorities 23%, District residents 0%). Faculty: full-time 1760, part-time 258. Degrees conferred: M.D., M.D.-M.B.A., M.D.-M.P.H., M.D.-M.S., M.D.-Ph.D. The M.S. and Ph.D. are offered in cooperation the through the Graduate School of Arts and Sciences.

ADMISSION REQUIREMENTS. AMCAS report, transcripts, one-page essay, two references, MCAT required in support of application. Supplemental application required. Interview by invitation only. Accepts transfer applicants. Apply to Office of Admissions after June 1, before November 1 (credentials by February 15). Admits Fall only. Application fee $130. Phone: (202)687-1154; fax: (202)687-3079.

ADMISSION STANDARDS. Very competitive. Accepts about 5.2% of all applicants. Number of applications 7944 (7908 out-of-District); number interviewed 1312 (1298 out-of-District); number of acceptance 413 (407 out-of-District); number enrolled 190 (187 out-of-District). Mean Composite MCAT 10.5; mean UGPA 3.62 (A = 4). *U.S. News & World Report* ranking is in the top 44 of all medical research schools.

FINANCIAL AID. Limited scholarships, Federal and private loans, work-study. Apply, after acceptance, to Office of Student Financial Planning. Phone: (202)687-1693. Apply by April 15. Use FAFSA (School code: E00518). About 88% of students receive aid from School and outside sources.

DEGREE REQUIREMENTS. For M.D.: satisfactory completion of four-year program; must pass Step 1 of USMLE prior to entering third year. For M.S., Ph.D.: see Graduate School listing above.

FIELDS OF GRADUATE STUDY.
Biochemistry and Molecular Biology.
Cell Biology.
Microbiology and Immunology. Includes biohazardous threat agents, emerging infectious diseases.
Neurosciences. Interdisciplinary.
Physiology. M.S., Ph.D.
Tumor Biology. Interdisciplinary.
Note: Special program for fourth-year students to travel in Third World countries to gain practical experience.

GEORGIA COLLEGE AND STATE UNIVERSITY

Milledgeville, Georgia 31061
Web site: www.gcsu.edu

Founded 1889. Located 100 miles SE of Atlanta. State control. Semester system. Library: 170,000 volumes, 1037 subscriptions. Total University enrollment: 5700.

Annual tuition and fees: resident $4954, nonresident $19,814; part-time $207, nonresident $826. Limited on-campus housing available. Average annual housing cost: $4502 (including board); apartment living; $425–$600 per month. Apply to Associate Director of Residence Life. Phone: (478)445-5160.

Graduate School

Graduate study since 1958. Graduate study available at Macon, Warner Robins, and Dublin campuses. Enrollment: full-time 331, part-time 530. Faculty: full-time 130, part-time 80. Degrees conferred: M.A., M.Accy., M.A.T., M.S., M.Ed., M.B.A., M.I.S., M.P.A., M.S.A., M.S.L.S., M.S.N., Ed.S., M.S.N.-M.B.A.

ADMISSION REQUIREMENTS. Transcripts, GRE/GMAT/MAT required in support of School's application. TOEFL required for foreign applicants. T-5 Georgia Certification or equivalent for Specialist. Interview may be requested. Accepts transfer applicants. Graduates of unaccredited institutions not considered. Apply to Office of Enrollment Services at least one month prior to quarter of entrance. Application fee $25. Phone: (478) 445-6289 or (800)342-0471.

ADMISSION STANDARDS. Relatively open. M.B.A. admission formula: GMAT + 200 × UGPA = 1050.

FINANCIAL AID. Annual awards from institutional funds: academic scholarships, assistantships, unlimited internships, Federal W/S, loans. Approved for VA benefits. Apply to Dean of Graduate School; no specified closing date. Use FAFSA and institutional FAF. Phone: (478)445-5149.

DEGREE REQUIREMENTS. For M.A., M.Accy., M.A.T., M.S., M.S.A., M.Ed.: 30–36 semester hours, at least 24 in residence; admission to candidacy; knowledge of one foreign language required by some departments; thesis/nonthesis option. For M.B.A., M.M.I.S., M.P.A.: 30–60 semester hour program. For Ed.S.: minimum of 27 semester hours beyond master's.

FIELDS OF STUDY.

SCHOOL OF ARTS AND SCIENCE:
Biology. M.S.
Creative Writing. M.F.A.
Criminal Justice. M.S.C.J.
English. M.A.
History. Includes archival management, U.S. and Europe. M.A.
Logistics Management. M.S.A.
Psychology. M.S.
Public Administration. M.P.A.
Public Affairs. M.P.A.

SCHOOL OF BUSINESS:
Accountancy. M.Accy.
Business Administration. M.B.A.
Management Information Systems. M.M.I.S.

SCHOOL OF EDUCATION:
Administration and Supervision. M.Ed., Ed.S.
Behavior Disorders. M.Ed.
Education (Grades P–12). Includes art, French, health, Spanish.
Instructional Technology—Distance and Alternative Education. M.Ed.
Instructional Technology—Library Media. M.Ed.
Instructional Technology—Professional Educator. M.Ed.
Instructional Technology—Technology Coordinator. M.Ed.
Secondary Education (Grades 7–12). Includes biology, broad field science, business education, chemistry, English, history, mathematics, physics, political science. M.A.T.
Secondary Education. Includes English, mathematics, natural sciences, social sciences, foreign languages. M.Ed.
Special Education. M.Ed.

SCHOOL OF HEALTH SCIENCES:
Family Health. Includes adult nursing. M.S.N.
Family Nurse Practitioner. M.S.N.
Health and Physical Education. Includes health and physical education, health education, outdoor education and administration. M.Ed., Ed.S.
Kinesiology. M.Ed., Ed.S.
Music Therapy. M.M.T.
Nurse Administration. Includes health informatics, nursing service. M.S.N.

GEORGIA INSTITUTE OF TECHNOLOGY
Atlanta, Georgia 30332-0001
Web site: www.gatech.edu

Founded in 1885. Coed. State control. Semester system. Special facilities: Georgia Tech Research Institute and more than 40 interdisciplinary research centers on campus, including Microelectronics Research Center, Manufacturing Research Center, Bioengineering Research Center, Multimedia Technology Laboratory, video-based master's programs; various mainframe and microcomputing environments; graduate cooperative program; research affiliations Oak Ridge National Labs, Emory University Medical Center, Skidaway Institute of Oceanography. According to The Center at University of Florida, the Institute is ranked 35th

in receipt of Federal Research fund with $203,582,000 and it ranks 29th for total University research expenditures with $364,190,000. The University's endowment assets rank it 42nd, with a value of $1,117,134,000. In 2004, the University awarded 311 doctorates, which ranked it 42nd among all U.S. institutions eligible to award that degree. 30 of the University's faculty members have been elected to National Honor Academies and this ranks it 30th among all U.S. institutions. The Library: approximately 2,100,000 volumes, 23,600 subscriptions.

Tuition: per semester full-time resident $2950, nonresident $10,627; College of Architecture, resident $5262, nonresident $15,101; Prosthetics and Orthotics, resident $5823, nonresident $15,664; M.B.A. resident $3824, nonresident $13,664. On-campus housing for 300 married students. Average academic year housing cost: single students $1625 per semester on-campus, off-campus $1700 per semester; married students from $600 per month for one-bedroom apartments. Apply to Director, Housing Office. Phone: (404)894-2470.

Graduate Studies and Research

Graduate study since 1922. Enrollment: full-time 2730, part-time 833. Graduate faculty: full-time 595, part-time 12. Degrees conferred: M.S., Ph.D.

ADMISSION REQUIREMENTS. Transcripts, GRE, three letters of recommendation required in support of application. GRE Subject Tests or GMAT for most programs. Additional materials required by some departments. TOEFL (minimum score 550) required for international applicants. Interview not required. Accepts transfer applicants. Graduates of unaccredited colleges not considered. Apply directly to individual Schools or Graduate Admissions no later than June 1 (Fall), February 1 recommended for financial aid and international applicants, November 1 (Spring), March 1 (Summer); some programs have later deadlines. Application fee $50. Phone: (404)894-4612.

ADMISSION STANDARDS. Selective. Usual minimum average: 3.0 (A = 4).

FINANCIAL AID. Annual awards from institutional and sponsored funds: fellowships, teaching assistantships, research assistantships, out-of-state tuition waivers, Federal W/S, loans. Apply to appropriate School Directors; no specified closing dates. Phone: (404)894-8160. Use FAFSA for Federal W/S, loans. About 60% of students receive aid other than loans from Institute and outside sources.

DEGREE REQUIREMENTS. For master's: 33 semester hours minimum; candidacy; reading knowledge of one foreign language for some departments; thesis/nonthesis option for some departments. For M.S.M.: two-year, full-time program. For Ph.D.: normally 50 semester hours minimum beyond the bachelor's, at least three semesters in residence; qualifying exam; reading knowledge of one foreign language for some departments; dissertation; final oral/written exams.

FIELDS OF STUDY.

COLLEGE OF ARCHITECTURE:
Architecture. M.S., Ph.D.
Building Construction/Facility Management.
City and Regional Planning.
Industrial Design.
Music Technology.

COLLEGE OF COMPUTING:
Computer Science.
Human-Centered Computing.
Information Security.

COLLEGE OF ENGINEERING:
Aerospace Engineering.
Bioengineering. Interdisciplinary program.
Biomedical Engineering.
Chemical Engineering.
Civil Engineering.
Electrical and Computer Engineering.
Engineering Science and Mechanics.
Environmental Engineering.
Industrial and Systems Engineering.
International Logistics (Executive Master's).
Materials Science and Engineering.
Mechanical Engineering.
Medical Physics.
Nuclear and Radiological Engineering.
Operations Research.
Polymer, Textile & Fiber Engineering.

COLLEGE OF MANAGEMENT:
Global Executive M.B.A.
Management. M.B.A., M.S., Ph.D.
Management of Technology (Executive Master's).

IVAN ALLEN COLLEGE OF LIBERAL ARTS:
Digital Media.
Economics.
History and Sociology of Technology and Science.
International Affairs.
Public Policy. Georgia Tech only.
Public Policy. Joint program with Georgia State University.

COLLEGE OF SCIENCES:
Applied Physiology.
Bioinformatics. Interdisciplinary.
Biology.
Chemistry and Biochemistry.
Earth and Atmospheric Science.
Mathematics.
Physics.
Prosthetics and Orthotics.
Psychology.

MULTIDISCIPLINARY PROGRAMS:
Algorithms, Combinatorics and Optimization.
Bioinformatics.
Computational Science and Engineering.
Human Computer Interaction.
Interdisciplinary Bioengineering Program.
Paper Science and Engineering.
Polymers.
Quantitative and Computational Finance.
Statistics.

MEDICAL COLLEGE OF GEORGIA

Augusta, Georgia 30912-1003
Web site: www.mcg.edu

Chartered 1828. School of Graduate Studies awarded its first degree in 1953. Public control. Semester system. Special facilities: Alzheimer's Disease Center, Center for Biotechnology and Genomic Medicine, Center for Clinical Investigation, Center for Disaster Medicine, Center for Health Care Improvement, Center for Nursing Research, Center for the Study of Occupational Therapy Education, Center for the Study of Physical Therapy Education, Comprehensive Sickle Cell Center, Dental Research Center, Neuroscience Center, Center for Telehealth, Vascular Biology Center, Institute of Molecular Medicine and Genetics, Institute for the Prevention of Human Disease and Accidents,

Institute of Neuroscience. The Medical College's NIH ranking was 127th with 115 awards/grants worth $35,781,988. Library: 176,000 volumes, 1672 subscriptions. Total College enrollment: 2061.

Annual tuition: graduate program, full-time resident $4593, nonresident $18,238. On-campus housing for 108 graduate men, 195 graduate women, 64 married students. Average annual housing cost: $9000–$13,000. Apply to Director of Housing. Phone: (706)721-3471. Day-care facilities available.

School of Graduate Studies

Enrollment: full-time 280, part-time 92 (men 35%, women 65%). Faculty: full-time 176. Degrees conferred: M.S., M.S.N., M.H.E., Ph.D.

ADMISSION REQUIREMENTS. Transcripts, three letters of recommendation, GRE required in support of School's application. Interview required for some departments. TOEFL required of all international applicants. Accepts transfer applicants. Apply to the Dean of School of Graduate Studies: deadlines vary by program. Application fee: none. Phone: (706)721-2725; fax: (706)721-7279.

ADMISSION STANDARDS. Competitive for most departments. Usual minimum average: 3.0 (A = 4).

FINANCIAL AID. Fellowships, scholarships, grants, NIH stipends, assistantships, traineeships, Federal W/S, Federal and private loans. Apply by April 1 to Financial Aid Office. Phone: (706)721-4901. Use FAFSA (College code: 001579). About 85% of students receive aid other than loans from College and outside sources. Aid available for part-time students.

DEGREE REQUIREMENTS. For M.S., M.S.N., M.H.E.; 45 quarter hours minimum, at least 36 in full-time residence; reading knowledge of one foreign language; comprehensive exam; thesis, final oral exam. For M.S. in Medical Illustration: same as above, except graphics project may be submitted in lieu of thesis, and language not required. For Ph.D.: 90 hours and three full years minimum beyond the bachelor's, at least three consecutive quarters or equivalent in full-time residence; preliminary exams; dissertation; final oral exam.

FIELDS OF GRADUATE STUDY.
Adult/Critical Care. M.S.N.
Allied Health Sciences. M.S.
Biomedical Sciences. Ph.D.
Biostatistics. M.S.
Cellular Biology and Anatomy. Ph.D.
Clinical Nurse Leadership. M.S.N.
Family Nurse Practitioner. M.S.N.
Genomic Medicine. Ph.D.
Health Informatics. M.P.H.
Medical Illustration. M.S.
Molecular Medicine. Ph.D.
Neuroscience. Ph.D.
Nursing Anesthesia. M.S.N.
Oral Biology. M.S., Ph.D.
Oral Biology and Maxillofacial Pathology. Ph.D.
Pediatric Nurse Practitioner. M.S.N.
Pharmacology. Ph.D.
Physiology. Ph.D.
Vascular Biology. Ph.D.

School of Dentistry (30912-1020)
Web site: www.mcg.edu/sod

Established 1996. Public control. Semester system.
Annual tuition: resident $14,151. On-campus housing available. Contact Office of Resident Life for both on- and off-campus

housing information. Phone: (706)721-3471. Average academic year living expenses: $11,500. Total cost for all other first-year expenses: $9000.

Enrollment: first-year class 63 (men 42, women 21), total full-time 240 (men 66%, women 34%, minorities 48%, state residents 100%). Faculty: full-time 89, part-time 32. Degrees conferred: D.M.D., D.M.D.-M.S. (Oral Biology), D.M.D.-Ph.D. (Oral Biology).

ADMISSION REQUIREMENTS. Official transcripts, DAT (not later than October), three letters of reference, a pre-dental adviser's recommendation required in support of School's application. Only state residents can apply. Applicants must have completed at least three years of college study. Interviews by invitation only. Apply to Associate Director of Student Affairs after June 1, before October 5. Application fee: $30. Phone: (706) 721-3587; fax: (706)721-6276.

ADMISSION STANDARDS. Competitive. Minimum UGPA: 2.8 (A = 4). Median DAT: Academic 18, PAT 19; median GPA: 3.5 (A = 4). Accepts 75% of total annual applicants. 100% are state residents.

FINANCIAL AID. Scholarships, loans, grants, Federal loans. Apply between January 1 and March 1 to Director of Financial Aid. Phone: (706)721-4901. Use FAFSA (School code: 001579). About 80% of students receive aid other than loans from School.

DEGREE REQUIREMENTS. For D.M.D.: satisfactory completion of 45-month program.

School of Medicine (30912-4760)
Web site: www.mcg.edu/som

Founded 1828. Thirteenth-oldest medical school in the U.S. Semester system. Library: 185,000 volumes, 1300 subscriptions.

Annual tuition: resident $12,996, nonresident $32,360. Total average figure for all other expenses: $14,211.

Enrollment: first-year class 180 (EDP 55); total 734 (men 55%, women 45%, minorities 35%, state residents 95%). Faculty: full-time 466, part-time 118. Degrees conferred: M.D., M.D.-Ph.D.

ADMISSION REQUIREMENTS. AMCAS report, transcripts, references, MCAT, interview, supplemental application required in support of application. Applicants must have completed at least three years of college study. Preference given to Georgia residents. Has EDP, state residents only. Apply between June 15 and August 1. Apply to Associate Dean for Admissions after June 15, before November 1. Application fee none. Phone: (706)721-3186; fax: (706)721-0959.

ADMISSION STANDARDS. Competitive. Accepts about 14.8% of all applicants. Number of applications 1742 (769 out-of-state); number interviewed 447 (10 out-of-state); number of acceptance 258 (3 out-of-state); number enrolled 180 (2 out-of-state). Mean Composite MCAT 10.0; mean UGPA 3.65 (A = 4).

FINANCIAL AID. Scholarships, fellowships, tuition waivers, loans. Apply to Office of Student Financial Aid; no closing date. Phone: (706)721-4901. Use FAFSA (School code: 001579). Approximately 34% of students receive aid other than loans from School.

DEGREE REQUIREMENTS. For M.D.: satisfactory completion of four-year program, at least one year in residence; must take both Step 1 and 2 of USMLE. For Ph.D.: see Graduate School listing above.

FIELDS OF GRADUATE STUDY.
Biomedical Engineering.
Biochemistry and Molecular Biology.
Cellular Biology and Anatomy.
Developmental Biology.
Growth Factor Biology.
Medicinal Chemistry.
Molecular Genetics.
Molecular Immunology.
Molecular Medicine and Genetics.
Molecular Structure.
Neurobiology.

GEORGIA SOUTHERN UNIVERSITY
Statesboro, Georgia 30460-8133
Web site: www.georgiasouthern.edu

Founded 1906. Located 50 miles E of Savannah. CGS member. Coed. State control. Semester system. Library: 568,500 volumes, 3511 subscriptions. Total University enrollment: 16,500.

Annual tuition: resident $2926, nonresident $11,704; per credit, resident $122, nonresident $488. On-campus housing for 1370 men, 1818 women. Average academic year housing cost: $6300. Apply to Director of Housing. Phone: (912)681-5406.

Jack N. Averitt College of Graduate Studies

Enrollment: full- and part-time 1700. University faculty teaching graduate students: full-time 310, part-time 28. Degrees conferred: M.A., M.S., M.B.A., M.F.A., M.H.S.A., M.P.H., M.S.N., M.S.S.M., M.P.A., M.Ed., Ed.S., M.R.A., M.T., Ed.D.

ADMISSION REQUIREMENTS. Two transcripts, GRE (M.A., M.S., M.P.A., M.R.A., M.S.N., M.T., Ed.D.), GMAT (M.B.A.), MAT (M.Ed., Ed.S., M.S.N.) required in support of School's application. Online application available. TOEFL (minimum score 550), certified transcripts and diplomas, financial statement required for international applicants. Interview not required. Accepts transfer applicants. Graduates from unaccredited institutions not considered. Apply to Graduate School by March 1 (Fall), October 1 (Spring), earlier deadlines for international applicants. Application fee: $50. Phone: (912)681-5384; fax: (912) 681-0740; e-mail: gradschool@gasou.edu.

ADMISSION STANDARDS. Selective. Usual minimum average: 2.5 (A = 4).

FINANCIAL AID. Annual awards from institutional funds: scholarships, teaching assistantships, research assistantships, Federal W/S, loans. Apply by April 15 to chair of appropriate division for assistantships; to Financial Aid Office for all other programs. Phone: (912)681-5413. Use FAFSA. About 20% of students receive aid other than loans from College and outside sources. Aid available for both international and part-time students.

DEGREE REQUIREMENT. For M.A., M.S.: 30 semester hours minimum; thesis. For M.Ed., M.R.A.: 45 hours minimum, final comprehensive exam. For Ed.S.: 30 hours minimum; final comprehensive exam. For M.B.A.: 36 hours minimum. For M.P.A.: 45 hours minimum; internship; capstone course; final oral exam. For M.T.: 45 hours minimum; thesis; final oral exam. For M.F.A.: 60 hours; thesis. For M.H.S.A.: 37–39 semester hours; managerial residency or thesis. For M.P.H.: 45 semester hour program; practicum or thesis. For M.S.N.: 45 hours minimum; thesis or project; final exam. Minimum residence requirement for a master's degree is one academic year or three summer sessions. For Ed.D.: 75 hours beyond the master's; comprehensive/qualifying exam; advancement to degree candidacy; dissertation; final oral defense.

FIELDS OF STUDY.

COLLEGE OF BUSINESS ADMINISTRATION:
Accounting. Includes forensic accounting. M.Acc.

Applied Economics. M.S.

Business Administration. Includes concentrations in accounting, health services administration, information systems, international business. M.B.A.

The Georgia WEBMBA.

COLLEGE OF EDUCATION:

Counselor Education. Includes community counseling, student services in higher education, school counseling. M.Ed., Ed.S.

Curriculum Studies. Includes art education, cultural curriculum studies, curriculum theory, instructional improvement, literacy education, mathematics/science/computing, multicultural education. Ed.D.

Educational Administration. Includes higher education, K–12 administration, teacher leadership. Ed.D.

Educational Leadership. M.Ed., Ed.S.

Higher Education Administration. M.Ed.

Instructional Technology (Online). M.Ed.

Reading Education. M.Ed.

School Psychology. M.Ed., Ed.S.

Teaching. Multiple concentrations. M.A.T.

Teaching and Learning. Multiple concentrations. M.Ed., Ed.S.

COLLEGE OF HEALTH AND HUMAN SCIENCES:

Kinesiology. Includes athletic training, coaching (online), exercise science, sports psychology. M.S.

Nursing. Includes nurse practitioner (family, women's health), clinical nurse specialist (community health). M.S.N.

Recreation Administration. M.S.

Sport Management. M.S.

COLLEGE OF LIBERAL ARTS AND SOCIAL SCIENCES:

Art. M.F.A.

Clinical Psychology. M.S., Psy.D.

English. M.A.

Experimental Psychology. Psy.D.

History. M.A.

Music. Includes composition, music education, music technology. M.M.

Public Administration. M.P.A.

Social Sciences. Includes anthropology, political science, psychology, sociology. M.A.

Spanish. M.A.

COLLEGE OF PUBLIC HEALTH:

Biostatistics. M.P.H., Dr.P.H.

Community Health Behavior and Education. Dr.P.H.

Community Health Education. M.P.H.

Environmental Health Sciences. M.P.H.

Epidemiology. M.P.H.

Health Services Administration. M.H.S.A.

Health Services Policy Management. M.P.H.

Public Health Leadership. Dr. P.H..

COLLEGE OF SCIENCE AND TECHNOLOGY:

Biology. M.S.

Mathematics. Includes applied mathematics, computer science, statistics. M.S.

Technology. Includes environmental studies, graphic communications management, informational technology, industrial safety/environmental compliance, industrial management/manufacturing, laser technology. M.T.

GEORGIA STATE UNIVERSITY

Atlanta, Georgia 30302-4038

Web site: www.gsu.edu

Founded 1913. CGS member. Coed. State control. Semester system. Special facilities: Center for Biotechnology and Drug Design, Center for Brain Sciences and Health, Center for Creative Writing, Center for Ethics, Center for Environmental Research, Center for Ethics and Public Affairs, Center for Health Policy, Center for High Angular Resolution Astronomy, Center for Integrative Neurosciences and Health, Center for International Media Research and Training, Center for Latin American Studies, Center for Learning Disorders, Center for Learning and Teaching, Center for Neural Communication and Computation, Center for Professional Communication, Center for Sports Medicine, Gerontology Center, Language Research Center. Library: 2,200,000 volumes, 12,053 subscriptions. Total University enrollment: 25,900.

Tuition: per credit, resident $182, nonresident $728. No on-campus housing. Contact Dean of Students for off-campus housing information. Day-care facilities available.

Division of Graduate Studies— College of Arts and Sciences

Enrollment: full- and part-time 1387. Faculty: full-time 380, part-time 38. Degrees conferred: M A., M.A.Ed., M.H.P., M.S., M.A.T., M.F.A., M.Mu., Certificate, Ph.D.

ADMISSION REQUIREMENTS. Transcripts, GRE required in support of College's application. Some programs require letters of recommendation, portfolio, audition, résumé, interview, writing sample, or list of references. TOEFL required for international applicants. Accepts transfer applicants. Graduates of unaccredited institutions not considered. Apply by August 1 (Fall), December 1 (Spring), June 1 (Summer)—some programs have earlier deadlines—to the Office of Graduate Admissions. Application fee $50. Phone: (404)413-5114; fax: (404)413-5117.

ADMISSION STANDARDS. Competitive. Usual minimum average: 3.0 (A = 4).

FINANCIAL AID. Annual awards from institutional funds: fellowships, scholarships, minority scholarships, graduate assistantships, tuition waivers, Federal W/S, loans. Approved for VA benefits. Apply to head of proposed major department prior to registration; to Office of Financial Aid for all other programs. Phone: (404)413-2400; fax: (404)413-2102. Use FAFSA (School code: 001574).

DEGREE REQUIREMENTS. For M.A., M.S.: 30–33 semester hours minimum, at least 24 hours in residence; thesis/nonthesis option; reading knowledge of one foreign language for some departments; research tool may be substituted in some departments; general exam; thesis. For Certificates: 30 semester hours minimum beyond the master's. For M.A.T.: 36 semester hours minimum; final written/oral exam. For M.F.A.: 60 semester hours minimum; final written/oral exam. For M.M.: 35–36 semester hour program; general written/oral exam. For Ph.D.: four semester in residence, at least two consecutive semsters in full-time attendance; ordinarily, reading knowledge of one or two foreign languages; research skill may be substituted for one or two languages in some departments; general exam; admission to candidacy; dissertation; final exam.

FIELDS OF STUDY.

Anthropology. Includes health policy and planning, urban policy and planning, community development, ethnicity, ethnomedicine, health behavior, urban development, social impact assessment. M.A.

Applied Linguistics. M.A., Ph.D.

Art. Includes ceramics, drawing, interior design, jewelry design and metalsmithing, painting, photography, printmaking, sculpture, textiles. M.A., M.F.A.

Art Education. M.A.E.

Art History. M.A.

Astronomy. Includes astronomy, astrophysics. Ph.D.

Biological Sciences. Ph.D.
Biology. Includes microbiology, molecular genetics, neurobiology and behavior, physiology. M.S.
Chemistry. Includes analytical, biochemical, inorganic, organic, physical chemistry. M.S., Ph.D.
Communication. Includes print journalism, public relations, broadcast journalism, film and video, speech. M.A., Ph.D.
Computer Science. M.S., Ph.D.
Creative Writing. M.F.A.
Earth Science. M.S.
English. Includes American and British literature, creative writing, rhetoric and composition. M.A., Ph.D.
Geography. Includes metropolitan area studies, cartography, physical geography/environmental studies. M.A.
Geology. Includes geochemistry, environmental geology, hydrogeology. M.S.
*Geochemistry.*Ph.D.
German. M.A.
Heritage Preservation. Includes archaeology, planning, architectural history, historical research, urban history. M.H.P.
History. Includes United States, European, Asian, Latin American, African, and Middle-Eastern history. M.A., Ph.D.
Literature. M.A., Ph.D.
Mathematics. Includes statistics. M.A., M.A.T., M.S.
Music. Includes music education, guitar, performance, music theory, choral conducting, instrumental conducting, composition, jazz studies, piano pedagogy, sacred music. M.M.
Philosophy. Includes applied ethics, history of philosophy, Wittgenstein, religious studies. M.A.
Physics. Includes atomic physics, biophysics, molecular physics, nuclear physics, condensed matter physics. M.S., Ph.D.
Political Science. Includes electoral politics, international relations. M.A., Ph.D.
Psychology. Includes clinical psychology, community psychology, neuropsychology and behavioral neurosciences, psychological foundations. M.A., Ph.D.
Sociology. Includes family, life course, social inequality, conflict. M.A.
Spanish. M.A., Ph.D.
Women's Studies. M.A.

J. Mack Robinson College of Business
Web site: www.cba.gsu.edu

Established 1958. Accredited programs: M.B.A., Accounting. Courses offered at University's North Metro Center. Semester system. Special programs: foreign study (in Amsterdam, Frankfurt, London). Special facilities: Center for Business and Industrial Marketing, Center for Digital Commerce, Center for Mature Consumer Studies, Center for Risk Management and Insurance Research, Decision Sciences Institute, Economic Forecasting Center, Institute for Small Business, Institute of Health Administration, Institute of International Business, W. T. Beebe Institute of Personnel and Employment Relations.

Tuition: full-time resident $5298, nonresident $21,182; part-time resident $221 per credit, nonresident $883 per credit. Enrollment: total full-time 648, part-time 1022. Faculty: 151 full-time, 12 part-time; 98% with Ph.D./D.B.A.

Degrees conferred: M.B.A. (full-time, part-time, day, evening), E.M.B.A., F.M.B.A. (Flexible), M.A.S. (Actuarial Science), M.S., M.S.H.A. (Health Administration), M.S.R.E. (Real Estate), M.P.A. (Professional Accounting), M.Tx. (Taxation), M.B.A.-J.D., M.B.A.-M.S.H.A. (Health Administration), Ph.D.

ADMISSION REQUIREMENTS. All applicants should have a bachelor's degree from a recognized institution of higher education and a strong mathematics background. Early applications are encouraged for both admission and financial aid consideration. Submit application, GMAT (will accept GMAT test results from the last five years, latest acceptable date is March), official transcripts from each undergraduate/graduate school attended, three letters of recommendation, résumé (prefers at least four years of work experience), and an application fee of $25 to the Office of Academic Assistance and Master's Admission. In addition, international students (whose native language is other than English) should submit a TOEFL report (minimum score 550), certified translations and evaluations of all official transcripts; recommendation should be in English or with certified translations, proof of health/immunization certificate, and proof of sufficient financial resources to complete entire academic program. Beginning students are admitted into all semesters. Both U.S. citizens and international applicants apply by April 1 (Fall), October 15 (Spring), March 1 (Summer); some programs have earlier dates. On-campus visits are required. Interviews are required for E.M.B.A. applicants prior to the admissions committee reviewing completed application. Joint degree applicants must apply to and be accepted to both colleges; contact the admissions office for current information and specific admissions requirements. Rolling admissions process; notification is made within six to eight weeks of receipt of completed application and supporting documents. Admissions office phone: (404)651-1913; fax: (404)651-0219; E.M.B.A.: (404)651-3760.

ADMISSION REQUIREMENTS FOR DOCTORAL CANDIDATES. Contact the Director of Doctoral Programs, College of Business for application material and information. Beginning students are admitted Fall Only. Both U.S. citizens and international applicants apply by March 1 (Fall). Submit the Doctoral Program Application for Admission, a GMAT (will accept GMAT test results from the last five years), two official transcripts from each undergraduate/graduate schools attended, three letters of recommendation, résumé, statement of purpose, and application fee of $25 to the Doctoral Program Office. In addition, international students (whose native language is other than English) should submit a TOEFL report (minimum score 600); certified translations and evaluations of all official transcripts, recommendation should be in English or with certified translations, proof of health/immunization certificate. Interviews are by invitation and are generally requested prior to the admissions committee reviewing completed application. Notification is made by mid-April.

ADMISSION STANDARDS. For M.B.A.: median GMAT: full-time 580, part-time 570; median GPA: 3.06 (A = 4). U.S. News & World Report ranked College of Business in the top 8 of all U.S. business schools for part-time M.B.A. programs. For Ph.D.: mean GMAT: 660; mean GPA: 3.3 (A = 4).

FINANCIAL AID. Scholarships, merit scholarship, Regent's Opportunity Scholarships, grants, nonresident fee waivers, graduate assistantships, Federal W/S, loans. Financial aid is available for part-time study. Assistantships may be available for joint degree candidates. Financial aid applications and information are generally available at the on-campus visit or after January 1; apply by May 1. Request scholarship and assistantship information from the College of Business; phone: (404)413-2400. For assistantships and scholarships the selection criteria places heavy reliance on GMAT and undergraduate GPA. Contact the University's Financial Aid Office for current need-based financial aid information; phone: (404)413-2400. Use FAFSA (School code: 001574), also submit Financial Aid Transcript, Federal Income Tax forms. Approximately 20% of students receive some form of financial assistance.

DEGREE REQUIREMENTS. For M.B.A.: 39–60 credit, 13–20 course program including four elective courses, two-year program. For E.M.B.A.: 45-credit, eighteen-month program. For M.A.S., M.P.A., M.S.: 30-credit programs. For M.I.B.: 33-credit program; foreign-language proficiency. For M.S.H.A., M.S.R.E.: 36-credit program. M.Tx.: 33-credit program. For M.B.A.-M.S.H.A.: two-and-one-half-year program. For M.B.A.-J.D.: three-and-one-half- to five-year program. For Ph.D.: three- to five-year full-time program; comprehensive exam in major field and related area; dissertation proposal and oral defense, dissertation; oral defense; degree must be completed within seven years.

FIELDS OF STUDY.
Accountancy. Ph.D.
Actuarial Science. M.A.S.
Business Administration. Concentrations in accounting, actuarial science, decision sciences, economics, electronic commerce, entrepreneurship, finance, general business, health administration, hospitality administration, human resource management, information systems, international business, management, marketing, personal financial planning, personnel and employment relations, real estate, risk management and insurance. M.B.A.
Business Economics. M.S.
Computer Information Systems. M.S., Ph.D.
Decision Sciences. M.S.
Finance. M.S., Ph.D.
Health Administration. Includes finance, human resource management, information systems, management, marketing, risk management and insurance. M.S.H.A.
Human Resource Management. M.S.
International Business. M.I.B.
Management. Ph.D.
Marketing. M.S., Ph.D.
Operational Management. M.S., Ph.D.
Organizational Change. M.S.
Personal Financial Planning. M.S.
Professional Accountancy. Includes accounting systems, financial accounting and reporting, management accounting. M.P.A.
Real Estate. M.S.R.E., Ph.D.
Risk Management and Insurance. M.S., Ph.D.
Strategic Management. Ph.D.
Taxation. M.Tx.

College of Education

Special facilities: Center for Sports Medicine, Science, and Technology, Center for the Study of Adult Literacy, Center for Urban Educational Excellence, Instructional Technology Center.

Tuition: per credit resident $182, nonresident $728. Enrollment: full-time 601, part-time 897. College faculty: full-time 97, part-time 61. Degrees conferred: M.Ed., M.L.M., M.S., Ed.S., Ph.D.

ADMISSION REQUIREMENTS. Two official transcripts, two letters of recommendation, goals statement, GRE/MAT/GSTEP (Georgia State Test of English Proficiency) required in support of College's application. TOEFL, GSTEP required for international applicants. Interviews may be required. Accepts transfer applicants. Apply for master's 90 days prior to registration. For Ph.D., application deadlines vary by major; usually accepted once or twice yearly. Rolling admissions process. Application fee $50. Phone: (404)413-8000.

ADMISSION STANDARDS. Usual minimum average master's: 2.5 GPA, GRE 800, MAT 44; Specialist: 3.25 GPA, GRE 900, MAT 48; Ph.D.: varies by degree.

FINANCIAL AID. Fellowships, research assistantships, teaching assistantships, tuition waivers, Federal W/S, loans. Approved for VA benefits. Apply to chairman of appropriate department for fellowships, assistantships; to Director of Financial Aid for all other programs. No specified closing date. Phone: (404)413-2400. Use FAFSA (School code: 001574). About 20% of students receive aid from University and outside sources. Aid available for part-time students.

DEGREE REQUIREMENTS. For M.Ed., M.L.M., M.S.: 36–45 semester hours minimum, at least 27 in residence; comprehensive exam; project, thesis, capstone. For Ed.S.: 30 semester hour program, at least 27 in residence; comprehensive exam; final written/oral exams/projects. For Ph.D.: 54 semester hour pro-

gram, at least 36 in residence; comprehensive exam; candidacy; dissertation; oral defense.

FIELDS OF STUDY.
Art Education. Ed.S.
Behavior/Learning Disabilities. M.Ed.
Communication Disorders. M.Ed.
Counseling. Ph.D.
Counseling Psychology. Ph.D.
Early Childhood Education. M.Ed., Ed.S., Ph.D.
Education of Students with Exceptionalities. Ph.D
Educational Leadership. M.Ed., Ed.S.
Educational Policy Studies. Ph.D.
Educational Psychology. M.S., Ph.D
Educational Research. M.S.
English Education. M.Ed.
Exercise Science. M.S.
Health and Physical Education. M.Ed.
Instructional Technology. M.S., Ph.D.
Library Media Technology. M.L.M.
Mathematics Education. M.Ed.
Middle Childhood Education. M.Ed.
Multiple and Severe Disabilities. M.Ed.
Music Education. Ed.S.
Professional Counseling. M.S., Ed.S.
Reading, Language, and Literacy Education. M.Ed.
Rehabilitation Counseling. M.S., Ed.S.
School Counseling. M.Ed., Ed.S.
School Psychology. M.Ed., Ed.S., Ph.D.
Science Education. M.Ed.
Social Foundations of Education. M.S.
Social Studies Education. M.Ed.
Special Education. Ed.S.
Sports Administration. M.S.
Sport Science. Ph.D.
Teaching and Learning. Ed.S., Ph.D.
Teaching English as a Foreign Language. M.Ed.
Urban Teacher Leadership. M.S.

College of Health and Human Sciences

Tuition: per credit resident $182, nonresident $728. Enrollment: full-time 322, part-time 221. Faculty: full-time 93, part-time 15. Degrees conferred: M.P.H., M.P.T., M.S., M.S.H.S., Ph.D.

ADMISSION REQUIREMENTS. Transcripts, GRE, Certification of Immunization required in support of College's application. Some programs require letters of recommendation, statement of professional goals. TOEFL required for international applicants. Accepts transfer applicants. Graduates of unaccredited institutions not considered. Apply to the Office of Graduate Admissions; application deadlines vary by department. Application fee $50. Phone: (404)413-1000.

ADMISSION STANDARDS. Competitive. Usual minimum average: 3.0 (A = 4).

FINANCIAL AID. Annual awards from institutional funds: scholarships, minority fellowships, fellowships, research assistantships, teaching assistantships, traineeships, Federal W/S, loans. Approved for VA benefits. Apply to head of proposed major department for fellowships, assistantships; to Office of Financial Aid for all other programs. Phone: (404)413-2400. Use FAFSA (School code: 001574).

DEGREE REQUIREMENTS. For M.S., M.S.H.S.: 36–51 semester hours minimum, thesis/nonthesis option; practicum for nursing. For M.P.T.: 107 semester hours minimum; internships. For M.S.W.: 60 semester hours program. For Ph.D.: 51–60 credit program, a minimum of two consecutive semesters in full-time residence; comprehensive exam; candidacy; dissertation; final exam.

FIELDS OF STUDY.

Allied Health Professions. Includes nutrition, physical therapy, respiratory care. M.S.

Criminal Justice. M.S.

Nursing. M.S., Ph.D.

Nutrition. M.S.H.S.

Physical Therapy. M.P.T.

Public Health. M.P.H.

Respiratory Care. M.S.H.S.

Social Work. M.S.W.

College of Law (30302-4049)

Web site: www.law.gsu.edu

Established 1982. ABA approved since 1984. AALS member. Semester system. Special facilities: Capital City Center for State Law and Legislation, Center for Law, Health and Society, Center for the Comparative Study of Metropolitan Growth; Summer programs: Johannes Kepler University of Linz, Austria, University of Warsaw, Poland; and study in Rio de Janeiro. Law library: 342,894 volumes, 2408 subscriptions; has LEXIS, NEXIS, WESTLAW; has more than 800 network connections.

Tuition: full-time resident $7366, nonresident $23,284; part-time resident $6848, nonresident $13,634. No on-campus housing available. Off-campus housing ranges from $475–$600 per month. Total average annual additional expense: $14,974.

Enrollment: first-year class, full-time 151, part-time 68, total full- and part-time 685 (men 51%, women 49%, minorities 34%). Faculty: full-time 33, part-time 20. Student to faculty ratio 16.2 to 1. Degrees conferred: J.D., J.D.-M.A., J.D.-M.B.A., J.D.-M.H.A., J.D.-M.S.H.A.

ADMISSION REQUIREMENTS. LSDAS Law School report, bachelor's degree, transcripts, LSAT, two letters of recommendation, personal statement required in support of application. Accepts transfer applicants. Preference given to state residents. Apply to Admissions Office by March 15. Application fee $50. Phone: (404)651-2048; fax: (404)651-1244.

ADMISSION STANDARDS. Selective. Accepts approximately 21% of full-time and 20% of part-time applicants. Number of full-time applicants 2359, part-time 424; number of full-time acceptance 499, part-time 86; number full-time enrolled 151, part-time 68; LSAT (75% of full-time students have a score at or above 156, part-time 155); GPA (75% of full-time students have a GPA at or above 3.16, part-time 2.95). *U.S. News & World Report* ranking is in the second tier tied at 82nd of all U.S. law schools.

FINANCIAL AID. Scholarships, tuition waiver, research assistantships, grants, Federal W/S, loans. Apply by April 1 to Office of Financial Aid. Phone: (404)651-2227. Use FAFSA. About 25% of students receive some aid from School.

DEGREE REQUIREMENTS. For J.D.: satisfactory completion of 135 quarter hours program. For joint degree programs: see Graduate School listing above.

Andrew Young School of Policy Studies

Established 1996. Semester system. Special facilities: Applied Research Center, Environmental Policy Center, the GSU Economic Forecasting Center, Georgia Health Policy Center.

Tuition: per credit resident $182, nonresident $728. Enrollment: full-time 257, part-time 154. Faculty; full-time 48, part-time 10. Degrees conferred: M.A., M.P.A., M.S.H.R.D., M.S.U.P.S., J.D.-M.P.A., Ph.D.

ADMISSION REQUIREMENTS. Two transcripts, GRE or GMAT, Certification of Immunization required in support of School's application; doctoral application required for Ph.D. applicants. Some programs require letters of recommendation, goal statement, résumé, interview. TOEFL required for international applicants. Accepts transfer applicants. Graduates of unaccredited institutions not considered. Apply to the Office of Academic Assistance; self-managed application process. Master's deadlines: April 1 (Fall), November 1 (Spring), April 12 (Summer); Doctoral deadlines: admits Fall only, Economics March 15, Public Policy February 1. Application fee of $50 for master's and Ph.D. in Economics, for Public Policy $75. Phone: (404)413-0021.

ADMISSION STANDARDS. Competitive. Usual minimum average: 3.0 (A = 4).

FINANCIAL AID. Scholarships, fellowships, research assistantships, teaching assistantships, tuition waivers, Federal W/S, loans. Approved for VA benefits. Apply to head of proposed major department for fellowships, assistantships; to Office of Financial Aid for all other programs. Phone: (404)413-2400. Use FAFSA (School code: 001574). Aid available for part-time students.

DEGREE REQUIREMENTS. For M.A.: 36 credit hour program, at least 30 hours in residence; reading knowledge of one foreign language; research tool may be substituted in some programs; thesis/nonthesis option; written/oral exam. For M.P.A.: 39 semester hours minimum; internship or practicum. For M.S.: 36 credit, two-year full-time program; internship or practicum or thesis. For Ph.D.: 66 credit, full-time program; written qualifying exam; dissertation proposal, defense; dissertation; final oral exam.

FIELDS OF STUDY.

Business Economics. Administered by Robinson College of Business. M.S.

Economics. M.A., Ph.D.

Peace Corps Master's International Program. M.A., M.P.A.

Public Administration. Includes career tracks in criminal justice, management and finance, nonprofit management, planning and economics development, policy analysis and evaluation, public health. M.P.A.

Public Policy. Ph.D.

Urban Policy Studies. Includes career track in nonprofit and civil leadership, planning and economic development, policy analysis, social policy. M.S.U.P.S.

UNIVERSITY OF GEORGIA

Athens, Georgia 30602-7402

Web site: www.uga.edu

Founded 1785. Located 70 miles E of Atlanta. The oldest state university in U.S. CGS member. Coed. State control. Semester system. Sponsoring university of the Oak Ridge Associated Universities. Special facilities: Institute of Behavioral Research, Biomedical and Health Sciences Institute, Center for Tropical and Emerging Diseases, Complex Carbohydrate Research Center, Institute of Ecology, Institute of Higher Education, Marine Institute on Sapelo Island, Poultry Disease Research Center, Institute of Remote Sensing and Mapping, Skidaway Institute of Oceanography, Social Science Research Institute, Organization of Tropical Studies. The University's NIH ranking is 128th among all U.S. institutions with 105 awards/grants valued at $35,243,354. According to The Center at University of Florida, the University is ranked 82nd in receipt of Federal Research funds with $93,884,000. The University's endowment assets rank it 100th, with a value of $474,596,000. In 2004, the University awarded 404 doctorates, which ranked it 71st among all U.S. institutions eligible to award that degree. Ten of the University's faculty members have been elected to National Honor Academies and this ranks it 71st among all U.S. institutions. The Library: approximately 4,000,000 volumes, 51,000 subscriptions. Total University enrollment: 33,660.

Tuition: per credit $211, nonresident $846; Social Work per credit resident $231, nonresident $883; M.B.A. per credit resident $341, nonresident $1127. On-campus housing for 545 married students, unlimited for single students. Average housing costs: $4300–$6500 (including board) for single students. Contact University Housing Office for both on- and off-campus housing information. Phone: (706)542-1421.

Graduate School

Graduate study since 1868. Enrollment: full-time 4290, part-time 1915. Graduate faculty: full-time 1495, part-time none. Degrees conferred: M.A., M.Acc., M.A.E., M.Ag.Ext., M.A.Ed., M.A.M., M.A.M.S., M.A.T., M.B.A., M.C.S.S., M.Ed., M.F.A., M.F.C.S., M.F.R., M.F.T., M.H.P., M.L.A., M.I.T., LL.M., M.M.C., M.M., M.M.Ed., M.P.A., M.P.P.P.M., M.S., M.S.W., Ed.S., D.M.A., D.P.A., Ed.D., Ph.D.

ADMISSION REQUIREMENTS. Two official transcripts, two copies of GRE/GMAT/MAT required in support of School's application (sent directly to Office of Graduate Admission); three letters of recommendation, goal statements, and any other materials are sent to the department or program. TOEFL required for international applicants. Interview not required. Accepts transfer applicants, Graduates of unaccredited institutions not considered. For international applicants apply to Graduate Admissions Office July 15 (Fall), October 15 (Spring), February 15 (Summer); for domestic applicants apply July 1 (Fall), November 15 (Spring), April 1 (Summer); for assistantships apply by January 1; some departments have earlier deadlines, contact department directly. Application fee $50. Phone: (706)542-1787; fax: (706) 542-9480; e-mail: gradadm@uga.edu.

ADMISSION STANDARDS. Selective for most departments. Usual minimum average: 3.0 (A = 4).

FINANCIAL AID. Annual awards from institutional funds: fellowships, scholarships, graduate assistantships, Federal W/S, loans. Approved for VA benefits. Apply by January 1 to Graduate School Office for assistantships; by February 15 to Financial Aid Office for all other programs. Phone: (706)542-6147. Use FAFSA. Aid available for part-time students.

DEGREE REQUIREMENTS. For M.A., M.S., M.Ed.: 28–36 credit hours minimum, at least 24–30 in residence; thesis; reading knowledge of one foreign language for some majors; final oral exam. For M.Acc.: 30 semester hour program. For M.B.A.: 60-credit, full-time program, additional hours may be required depending upon previous preparation. For M.A.Ed.: 30–36 credit hours minimum, at least 24–30 in residence; final written/oral exam. For M.A.E.: 30–36 credit hours minimum depending upon program, at least 24–30 in residence; final written/oral exam. For M.F.A.: 60 semester hours minimum; creative project, depending upon major; final written/oral exam. For M.F.R.: 33-credit program. For M.F.C.S.: 36–55 credit program; internship; project. For M.L.A.: 60 credit hours minimum; thesis; final written/oral exam. For M.M.C.: 30–33 credit program; thesis/nonthesis. For M.S.W.: 60-credit, two-year, full-time program, including instruction and fieldwork; problems course or thesis; practicum. For M.Ag.Ext.: 30 credit hours minimum; written problem. For M.A.M.S.: 33 credit hours minimum; 12 technical reports. For M.A.T.: 33 credit hours minimum in subject area; 15 hours minimum in education; comprehensive exam. For M.A.M.: 30–36 credit program; thesis/research project/practice base paper; oral exam. For M.H.P.: 54–61 credit, two-year program; internship; thesis. For M.I.T.: 32 credit program; technology project. For LL.M.: 27 semester hours; thesis; oral exam. For M.M.: 30–36 credit hours minimum and final project. For M.M.Ed.: 30–36 credit hour minimum. For M.P.P.P.M.: 33 credit hour minimum; two internships; final written and oral exams. For Ed.S.: 33 semester hours beyond master's; student portfolio; final oral exam. For Ph.D.: three years beyond the bachelor's, at least two consecutive semesters in residence; comprehensive written/oral exam; candidacy; research skills requirements; dissertation; final oral exam. For Ed.D., D.M.A., D.P.A.: essentially the same as for the Ph.D.

FIELDS OF STUDY.

COLLEGE OF AGRICULTURAL AND ENVIRONMENTAL SCIENCES:
Agricultural Economics. M.A.E., M.S., Ph.D.
Agricultural Engineering. M.S.
Agricultural Extension. M.A.Ext.
Agronomy. M.S., Ph.D.
Animal and Dairy Science. Ph.D.
Animal Nutrition. Ph.D.
Animal Science. M.S.
Biological and Agricultural Engineering. M.S., Ph.D.
Crop and Soil Science. M.C.S.S.
Dairy Science. M.S.
Entomology. M.S., Ph.D.
Environmental Economics. M.S.
Environmental Health. M.S.
Food Science. M.S., Ph.D.
Food Technology. M.F.T.
Horticulture. M.S., Ph.D.
Plant Pathology. M.S., Ph.D.
Plant Protection and Pest Management.
Poultry Science. M.S., Ph.D.

FRANKLIN COLLEGE OF ARTS AND SCIENCE:
Anthropology. M.A., Ph.D.
Applied Mathematical Sciences. Includes computer science, mathematics, statistics. M.A.M.S.
Art. M.F.A., Ph.D.
Art History. M.A.
Artificial Intelligence. M.S.
Biochemistry and Molecular Biology. M.S., Ph.D.
Cellular Biology. M.S., Ph.D.
Chemistry. M.S., Ph.D.
Classical Languages. M.A.
Comparative Literature. M.A., Ph.D.
Computer Science. M.S., Ph.D.
Drama. M.F.A., Ph.D.
Ecology. M.S., Ph.D.
English. M.A., M.A.T., Ph.D.
French. M.A., M.A.T.
Genetics. M.S., Ph.D.
Geography. M.A., M.S., Ph.D.
Geology. M.S., Ph.D.
German. M.A., M.A.T.
Greek. M.A.
History. M.A., Ph.D.
Latin. M.A.
Linguistics. M.A., Ph.D.
Marine Sciences. M.S., Ph.D.
Mathematics. M.A., Ph.D.
Microbiology. M.S., Ph.D.
Music. M.A., M.M., D.M.A., Ph.D.
Philosophy. M.A., Ph.D.
Physics. M.S., Ph.D.
Plant Biology. M.S., Ph.D.
Political Science. M.A., Ph.D.
Psychology. Ph.D.
Religion. M.A.
Romance Languages. M.A., M.A.T., Ph.D.
Sociology. M.A., Ph.D.
Spanish. M.A., M.A.T.
Speech Communication. M.A., Ph.D.
Statistics. M.S., Ph.D.

TERRY COLLEGE OF BUSINESS:
Accounting. Includes audit and systems track, taxation track. M.Acc.
Business Administration. M.A., M.B.A., Ph.D.
Economics. M.A., Ph.D.
Marketing Research. M.M.R.

COLLEGE OF EDUCATION:
Adult Education. M.A., M.Ed., Ed.S., Ed.D., Ph.D.
Agricultural Education. M.Ed.
Art Education. M.A.Ed., Ed.S., Ed.D.
Business Education. M.Ed.
College Student Affairs Administration. M.A., M.Ed.
Communication Sciences and Disorder. M.A., M.Ed., Ed.S., Ph.D.
Counseling and Pupil Personnel Services. Ph.D.
Counseling Psychology. Ph.D.
Early Childhood Education. M.Ed., Ed.S., Ph.D.
Education of Gifted. Ed.D.,
Educational Psychology. M.A., M.Ed., Ed.S., Ed.D., Ph.D.
Elementary Education. Ph.D.
English Education. M.A., M.Ed., Ed.S.
Exercise Science. M.A., M.Ed., Ed.D., Ph.D.
Family and Consumer Sciences Education. M.Ed.
Guidance and Counseling. M.A., M.Ed., Ed.S.
Health Promotion and Behavior. M.A., M.Ed., Ph.D.
Higher Education. Ed.D., Ph.D.
Instructional Technology. M.Ed., Ed.S., Ed.D., Ph.D.
Kinesiology. M.A., M.Ed., Ed.S., Ed.D.
Language and Literacy Education. Ph.D.
Marketing Education. M.Ed.
Mathematics Education. M.A., M.Ed., Ed.S., Ed.D., Ph.D.
Middle School Education. M.Ed., Ed.S., Ph.D.
Music Education. M.M.Ed., Ed.S., Ed.D., Ph.D.
Occupational Studies. M.Ed., Ed.S., Ed.D., Ph.D.
Physical Education and Sport Studies. M.A., M.Ed., Ed.S., Ed.D., Ph.D.
Reading Education. M.A., M.Ed., Ed.S., Ed.D., Ph.D.
Recreation and Leisure Studies. M.A., M.Ed., Ph.D.
School Psychology. Ed.S.
Science Education. M.A., M.Ed., Ed.S., Ed.D., Ph.D.
Social Foundations of Education. Ph.D.
Social Science Education. M.A., M.Ed., Ed.S., Ed.D., Ph.D.
Special Education. M.A., M.Ed., Ed.S., Ed.D., Ph.D.
Teaching Additional Languages. M.A., M.Ed., Ed.S.
Technological Studies. M.Ed.

COLLEGE OF ENVIRONMENT AND DESIGN:
Conservation Ecology and Sustainable Development. M.S.
Ecology. M.S., Ph.D.
Environmental Design. M.P.H., M.L.A.
Historic Preservation. M.H.P.
Landscape Architecture. M.L.A.

SCHOOL OF FAMILY AND CONSUMER SCIENCES:
Child and Family Development. M.F.C.S., M.S., Ph.D.
Foods and Nutrition. M.F.C.S., M.S., Ph.D.
Housing and Consumer Economics. M.S., Ph.D.
Textile, Merchandising and Interiors. M.S.

DANIEL B. WARNELL SCHOOL OF FORESTRY AND NATURAL RESOURCES:
Forest Resources. MF.R., M.S., Ph.D.
Forestry and Natural Resources. M.S., Ph.D.

GRADY COLLEGE OF JOURNALISM AND MASS COMMUNICATION:
Journalism and Mass Communication. M.A.
Mass Communication. Ph.D.

SCHOOL OF LAW:
Law. LL.M.

COLLEGE OF PHARMACY:
Clinical and Administrative Pharmacy. M.S., Ph.D.
Pharmaceutical and Biomedical Regulatory Affairs. N.D.
Pharmaceutical and Biomedical Sciences. M.S., Ph.D.

SCHOOL OF PUBLIC AND INTERNATIONAL AFFAIRS:
Global Policy Studies. Certificate.
Nonprofit Organizations. M.A.
Nonprofit Organizations: Development and Management. N.D.
Political Science. M.A., Ph.D.
Public Administration. M.P.A., Ph.D.

SCHOOL OF SOCIAL WORK:
Social Work. M.S.W., Ph.D.

COLLEGE OF VETERINARY MEDICINE:
Anatomic and Clinical Pathology. N.D.
Avian Medicine. M.A.M.
Food Animal Medicine. M.F.A.M.
Infectious Diseases. M.S., Ph.D.
Neuroscience. Ph.D.
Pharmacology. Ph.D.
Physiology. Ph.D.
Physiology and Pharmacology. M.S., Ph.D.
Veterinary Pathology. M.S., Ph.D.
Veterinary and Biomedical Sciences. M.S.

School of Law (30602-6012)
Web site: www.lawsch.uga.edu

Established 1859. ABA approved since 1930. AALS member. Semester system. Special facility: The Dean Rusk Center for International and Comparative Law. Law library: 512,418 volumes, 7097 subscriptions; has LEXIS, NEXIS, WESTLAW, INFOTRAC, INNOPAC.

Annual tuition: resident $10,614, nonresident $28,490. On- and off-campus housing available. Total average annual additional cost: $10,400.

Enrollment: first-year class 210; full-time 670 (men 52%, women 48%, minorities 13%). Faculty: full-time 31, part-time 9. Student to faculty ratio 15.3 to 1. Degrees conferred: J.D., LL.M., J.D.-M.B.A., J.D.-M.H.P. (Historic Preservation); J.D.-M.S.W., J.D.-M.P.A., J.D.-M.Spts.Mgt.

ADMISSION REQUIREMENTS. LSDAS Law School report, bachelor's degree, transcripts, LSAT (not later than December), two references, essay required in support of application. Some priority given state residents after January. Interview not required. Four-year undergraduate degree required. Accepts transfer applicants. Apply to the Director of Admissions prior to February 1. First-year students admitted Fall only. Application fee $30. Phone: (706)542-7060; fax: (706)542-5556.

ADMISSION STANDARDS. Selective. Accepts approximately 23% of all students. Number of applicants 2574; number of acceptance 599; number enrolled 210; LSAT (75% of students have a score at or above 158); GPA (75% of students have a GPA at or above 3.28). *U.S. News & World Report* ranking is in the top 36 of all U.S. law schools.

FINANCIAL AID. Scholarships, tuition Equalization scholarships, grants, Federal W/S, loans. Apply by January 31 to Office of Admissions for scholarships, grants; apply to the Office of Financial Aid for all other programs, priority deadline March 1. Phone: (706)542-6147. Use FAFSA (School code: 001598) and School FAF. About 34% of students receive aid from School.

DEGREE REQUIREMENTS. For J.D.: 88 semester hours minimum, at least 30 semester hours in full-time residence. For LL.M.: at least 27 semester hours beyond the J.D.; 2 semesters of graduate study in residence; oral presentation; final thesis.

Note. There are formal exchange agreements with Southhampton University (Great Britain), and the University of Brussels (Belgium).

College of Veterinary Medicine

Web site: www.vet.uga.edu

Professional and graduate study since 1930. College was created in 1946. Semester system. Special facilities: Animal Health Research Center, Poultry Diagnostic and Research Center, Regenerative Biosciences Center.

Annual tuition: resident $12,492, nonresident $34,892. For housing information contact the Division of Housing. Living expenses: $10,000–$13,000.

Enrollment: first-year class 96, total 400, (men 28%, women 72%, minorities 15%, state residents 82%). Faculty: full- and part-time 98. Degrees conferred: D.V.M., M.A.M., M.F.A.M., D.V.M.-M.P.H., D.V.M.-M.S., D.V.M.-Ph.D. (Veterinary Medical Scientist Training Program). The M.A.M., M.F.A.M., M.P.H., M.S. and Ph.D. are offered through the Graduate School.

ADMISSION REQUIREMENTS. Professional program: VMCAS report, transcripts, GRE General/GRE Subject Test in Biology, Analytical Writing test, animal experience, three recommendations (one from an academic adviser), essay required in support of application. At least three years of undergraduate study prior to entrance. Interview by invitation. Admission limited to residents of Georgia, Delaware, South Carolina, West Virginia, and U.S. citizens. Apply to Dean after July 15, before October 1. Admits Fall only. Graduate program: transcripts, GRE, recommendations required in support of application. Apply to individual department at least thirty days prior to beginning of quarter of entry. Application fee $50. Phone: (706)542-3461; fax: (706) 542-8254.

ADMISSION STANDARDS. Competitive. Accepts about 20–25% of all applicants. Number of applications 543 (89 southern state residents, 268 out-of-state); number interviewed n/a (n/a out-of-state); number of acceptance n/a (n/a out-of-state); number enrolled 96 (25 southern state residents, 0 out-of-state). Usual minimum UGPA: 3.0 (A = 4). Mean GRE (V + Q) 1173; mean UGPA 3.53.

FINANCIAL AID. Scholarships, fellowships, assistantships, partial fee waivers, Federal W/S, loans. Apply to Office of Student Aid at least two months prior to entrance; for graduate program, apply to appropriate department; no specified closing date. Use FAFSA. About 60% of students receive aid other than loans from School.

DEGREE REQUIREMENTS. For D.V.M.: Four years in residence. For M.S., Ph.D., see Graduate School listing.

FIELDS OF GRADUATE STUDY.
Anatomic and Clinical Pathology. N.D.
Avian Medicine. M.A.M.
Food Animal Medicine. M.F.A.M.
Infectious Diseases. M.S.
Neuroscience. Ph.D.
Pharmacology. Ph.D.
Physiology. Ph.D.
Physiology and Pharmacology. M.S., Ph.D.
Veterinary and Biomedical Sciences. M.S.
Veterinary Pathology. M.S., Ph.D.

GODDARD COLLEGE

Plainfield, Vermont 05667

Web site: www.goddard.edu

Founded 1938, began offering graduate study leading to the M.A. in 1940. Located 200 miles NW of Boston. Coed. Semester system. Library: 70,000 volumes, 300 active periodicals, on-line databases (DIALOG).

Tuition/fees: per semester $6622 (M.A.), $6878 (Psychology and Counseling), $6878 (M.F.A.). On-campus housing available. Annual academic year housing cost: $5120–$5680 (room and board).

Graduate Program

Enrollment: full- and part-time 220. Combined faculty: full-time 44, part-time 47. Degrees conferred: M.A., M.F.A.

ADMISSION REQUIREMENTS. Self-initiated study plan, transcripts, interview, three letters of recommendation, personal statement, preliminary bibliography required in support of application. Online application available. Accepts transfer applicants. Apply to Director of Admissions; no specified closing date. Rolling admissions process. Application fee $40. Phone: (800)906-8312; e-mail: admissions@goddard.edu.

ADMISSION STANDARDS. Selective. Usual minimum average: 2.75 (A = 4).

FINANCIAL AID. Graduate/teaching assistantships, grants, Federal W/S, loans. Apply to Financial Aid Office; no specified closing date. Use FAFSA (School code: 003686) and CSS Profile. About 50% of students receive aid other than loans from both College and outside sources.

DEGREE REQUIREMENTS. For M.A., M.F.A.: satisfactory completion of individually planned program supervised by a study supervisor and a second reader drawn from the Goddard faculty as a whole.

FIELDS OF STUDY.
Creative Writing.
Education. M.A.Ed.
Health Arts and Science.
Individualized Studies. M.A.
Interdisciplinary Arts. M.F.A.
Psychology and Counseling.
Socially Responsible Business. M.A.

GOLDEN GATE UNIVERSITY

San Francisco, California 94105-2968

Web site: www.ggu.edu

Founded 1853. Coed. Private control. Trimester system. Library: 126,500 volumes, 3335 subscriptions. Total University enrollment: 6360.

Tuition: per 3-unit course $2040, except Taxation $2265. No on-campus housing available. Contact Student Affairs Office for off-campus housing information. Phone: (415)442-7294.

Graduate Programs

Graduate study since 1950. Enrollment: full-time 1297, part-time 2714 (men 50%, women 50%). Graduate faculty: full-time 97, part-time 290. Degrees conferred: M.A., M.Ac., M.B.A., M.P.A., M.S., D.B.A., D.P.A. (C.P.A. exam preparation program also available).

ADMISSION REQUIREMENTS. Transcripts required in support of application. Online application available. GMAT required for M.B.A. applicants. Personal statement optional. TOEFL required for international applicants. Interview not required. Accepts transfer applicants. Graduates of unaccredited institutions not considered. Apply to the Office of Enrollment Services at least one month prior to registration. Rolling admissions process. Application fee $55, doctoral $75, $90 for international applicants. Phone: (415)442-7800; fax: (415)442-7807; e-mail: info@ ggu.edu.

ADMISSION STANDARDS. Selective. Usual minimum average: 2.5 for M.P.A., M.B.A., M.S.; 3.0 for M.Ac. and M.S.T.; 3.0 in graduate work for D.B.A., D.P.A. (A = 4).

FINANCIAL AID. Annual awards from institutional funds: one hundred scholarships, Federal W/S, loans. Approved for VA benefits. Apply to Director of Financial Aid; no specified closing date. Use FAFSA (School code: 001205), Student loan application. Phone: (415)442-7270; fax: (415)442-7807. Aid available for part-time students.

DEGREE REQUIREMENTS. For M.A.: 30 units minimum; thesis; foreign language required by some departments. For M.Ac.: 30-unit program. For M.B.A.: 36 units minimum plus 12 units in general business or undergraduate units if not completed before entrance; thesis optional for 3 units. For M.S.: 30 units minimum, plus 6 general business units if not completed before entrance. For M.P.A.: 39 units minimum plus 9 undergraduate units if act completed before entrance. No language or thesis requirement for master's degrees; limited number of transfer credits considered. For D.B.A., D.P.A.: 56 units in graduate core requirements beyond master's; qualifying exam; dissertation; final oral/written exam.

FIELDS OF STUDY.
Accountancy. M.Ac.
Business Administration. Includes accounting, information technology, finance, human resource management, international business, management, marketing, operations and supply chain management. M.B.A., D.B.A.
Finance. M.S.
Financial Planning. M.S.
Human Resources Management. M.S.
Information Technology. M.S.I.T.M.
Integrated Marketing Communication. Includes public relations. M.S.
Marketing. M.S.
Psychology. Includes marriage, family, and child counseling. M.A.
Public Administration. E.M.P.A.
Taxation. M.S.

School of Law
Web site: www.ggu.edu/law

Established 1901. ABA approved since 1956. AALS member. Private control. Semester system. Summer study abroad in Bangkok, Thailand; Paris, France. Law library: 353,479 volumes, 4259 subscriptions; has LEXIS, WESTLAW, CALI; has more than 500 network connections.

Annual tuition: full-time $31,140, part-time $21,870. On-campus housing available. Total average annual additional expenses: $14,500.

Enrollment: first-year full-time 268, part-time 53; total full- and part-time 759 (men 43%, women 57%, minorities 24%). Faculty: full-time 60, part-time 33. Student to faculty ratio 22.4 to 1. Degrees conferred: J.D., J.D.-M.B.A., J.D.-M.A. (International Relations), J.D.-Ph.D. (Clinical Psychology), LL.M. (Environmental Law, Taxation, Intellectual Property Law, International Legal Studies, U.S. Legal Studies).

ADMISSION REQUIREMENTS. LSDAS Law School report, bachelor's degree, transcripts, LSAT, personal statement, résumé, two letters of recommendation required in support of application. Interview not required. Accepts transfer applicants. Graduates of unaccredited colleges not considered. Apply to Admissions Office by April 1 (Fall), November 15 (Spring). Application fee $60.

Phone: (415)442-6630; fax: (415)442-6631. For LL.M.: submit application and supporting materials by July 1 (Fall), November 1 (Spring).

ADMISSION STANDARDS. Selective. Accepts approximately 36% of full-time and 38% of part-time applicants. Number of full-time applicants 3016, part-time 282; number of full-time acceptance 1077, part-time 107; number full-time enrolled 268, part-time 53; LSAT (75% of full-time students have a score at or above 150, part-time 149); GPA (75% of full-time students have a GPA at or above 3.00, part-time 2.85). *U.S. News & World Report* ranking is in the fourth tier of all U.S. law schools.

FINANCIAL AID. Scholarships, fellowships, assistantships, full and partial tuition waivers, Federal W/S, loans. Apply to Financial Aid Officer by March 1. Phone: (415)442-6635. Use FAFSA. About 37% of students receive scholarships or grants.

DEGREE REQUIREMENTS. For J.D.: 86 semester hours minimum. For LL.M.: at least 24 semester hours beyond the J.D.

Note: School has exchange program with Chulalongkorn University (Thailand).

GONZAGA UNIVERSITY
Spokane, Washington 99258-0001
Web site: www.gonzaga.edu

Founded 1887. Coed. Private control. Jesuit, Roman Catholic. Semester system. Library: 550,000 volumes, 1470 subscriptions. Total University enrollment: 6375.

Tuition: per credit $670, doctoral programs $725. Limited on-campus housing for single graduate students; none for married students. Average annual housing cost: $7270 (double room including board). Contact Residence Life Office for both on- and off-campus housing information. Phone: (509)328-4220, ext. 4103.

Graduate School

Enrollment: full- and part-time 1778. Faculty teaching graduate students: full-time 92, part-time 52. Degrees conferred: M.A., M.Acc, M.B.A., M.B.A.-J.D., M.A.P., M.A.A., M.A.C.E., M.Anthes.Ed., M.Ed., M.E.S., M.P.E., M.T.A., M.I.T., M.A.O.L., M.S.N., M.E.L., Ph.D.

ADMISSION REQUIREMENTS. Two official transcripts, statement of purpose or letter of intent, résumé or vita required in support of School's application. GRE/MAT/GMAT, recommendation/reference letters and interview required by some departments. TOEFL required for international applicants. Accepts transfer applicants. Graduates of unaccredited institutions not considered. Rolling admissions process. Application $45. Phone: (509)328-4220, ext. 3546; fax: (509)324-5399.

ADMISSION STANDARDS. Selective. Usual minimum average: 3.0 G.P.A.; 3.5 G.P.A. for doctoral applicants (A = 4).

FINANCIAL AID. Fellowships, teaching assistantships, tuition waivers, Federal W/S, loans. Approved for VA benefits. Apply by March 1 to appropriate department chair for fellowships, assistantships; to Financial Aid Office for all other programs. Phone: (509)328-4220, ext. 3182. Use FAFSA. Aid sometimes available for part-time students.

DEGREE REQUIREMENTS. For master's: 30–34 semester hours minimum, at least 24 in residence; thesis required for some programs; final oral/written exam; one research skill; reading knowledge of one foreign language for programs in arts. For

Ph.D.: 60 credits minimum beyond the bachelor's, at least 45 in residence; qualifying exam; proficiency in one foreign language; dissertation; final oral exam.

FIELDS OF STUDY.

Accountancy. Includes specializations in professional accounting, taxation. M.Acc.

Anesthesiology Education. M.A.E.

Business Administration. Includes concentrations in accounting, entrepreneurship, ethics, finance, marketing, management of information systems, sport management, supply chain management. M.B.A.

Communication and Leadership. M.A.

Community Counseling. M.A.

Counseling. M.A.

Educational Administration. M.A.

Initial Teaching. Includes elementary, secondary. M.I.T.

Leadership and Administration. M.A.

Leadership Studies. Ph.D.

Literacy. M.Ed.

Nursing. Includes nurse anesthetist, clinical nurse specialist, family nurse practitioner, nursing administration, nurse educator, psychiatric-mental health. M.S.N.

Organizational Leadership. M.A.

Philosophy. Includes history of Western philosophy, social and applied ethics. M.A.

Religious Studies. Includes concentrations in biblical studies, spirituality, theological foundations. M.A.

School Counseling. M.A.

Sport and Athletic Administration. M.A.

Special Education. M.Ed.

Teaching At-Risk Students. M.A.

Teaching English as a Second Language. M.A.

School of Law (Box 3528)

Web site: www.law.gonzaga.edu

Established 1912. ABA approved since 1951. ALS member. Private control. Semester system. Special facility: Center for Law and Justice. Special program: summer program in Florence, Italy. Law library: 283,999 volumes, 2579 subscriptions; has LEXIS, NEXIS, WESTLAW, DIALOG, CARL.

Annual tuition: full-time $27,978, part-time $16,812. No on-campus housing available. Total average annual additional expense: $13,475.

Enrollment: first-year class 192, total 557 (men 56%, women 44%, minorities 10%). Faculty: full-time 22, part-time 45. Student to faculty ratio 18.0 to 1. Degrees conferred: J.D., J.D.-M.B.A., J.D.-M.Acc., J.D.-M.S.W.

ADMISSION REQUIREMENTS. LSDAS Law School report, bachelor's degree, transcripts, LSAT, résumé, personal statement, two letters of recommendation required in support of application. Interview not required. Accepts transfer applicants. Graduates of unaccredited colleges not considered. Apply to Dean by April 1. Admits Fall only. Application fee $50. Phone: (800)793-1710 (Continental U.S.), (509)323-3713; fax (509)323-3697.

ADMISSION STANDARDS. Selective. Accepts approximately 37% of all students. Number of applicants 1485; number of acceptance 546; number enrolled 192; LSAT (75% of students have a score at or above 152); GPA (75% of students have a GPA at or above 3.13). *U.S. News & World Report r*anking is in the third tier of all U.S. law schools.

FINANCIAL AID. Scholarships, full and partial tuition waivers, fellowships, assistantships, Federal W/S, loans. Apply to Law School Financial Aid Office by February 1. Phone: (800)448-2138. Use FAFSA. Approximately 75% of students receive some form of aid from School.

DEGREE REQUIREMENTS. For J.D.: 90 semester hours minimum, at least one year in residence.

GOUCHER COLLEGE

Baltimore, Maryland 21204-2794

Web site: www.goucher.edu

Founded 1885. Private control. Coed. Semester system. Library: 303,000 volumes, 2195 subscriptions. Total College enrollment: 2235.

Tuition: per credit Education $385; M.A., M.F.A. $630; Creative Nonfiction $655. No housing for graduate students.

Graduate Program

Enrollment: full-time 141, part-time 700. Graduate faculty: full-time 6, part-time 90. Degrees conferred: M.A., M.F.A., M.Ed., M.A.T.

ADMISSION REQUIREMENTS. Transcripts, two letters of recommendation, bachelor's required in support of application. TOEFL required for international applicants. Accepts transfer students. Apply to the Office of Graduate and Professional Studies; no specified closing date. Rolling admissions process. Application fee $50. Phone: (410)337-6044; fax: (410)337-6354.

FINANCIAL AID. Limited to grants, loans. Approved for VA benefits. Apply to the Office of Financial Aid. Phone: (410)337-6500. Use FAFSA and institutional FAF.

DEGREE REQUIREMENTS. For M.A., M.Ed.: 35 semester credits; action research project; thesis; internship. For M.A.T.: 36 credits; year-long student teaching internships. For M.F.A.: 36-credit program; three summer residencies; critical paper; internship.

FIELDS OF STUDY.

Arts Administration. M.A.A.A.

Creative Nonfiction. M.F.A.

Education. Includes urban and diverse learners, middle school, the at-risk student, school mediation, school improvement leadership, athletic program leadership/administration. M.Ed.

Historic Preservation. M.A.

Teaching. M.A.T.

GOVERNORS STATE UNIVERSITY

University Park, Illinois 60466

Web site: www.govst.edu

Established 1969. Located 30 miles S of Chicago. Coed. Trimester system. Library: 246,000 volumes, 2700 subscriptions. Total University enrollment: 5400.

Tuition: resident, per hour $157; nonresident, per hour $471. No on-campus housing available. Day-care facilities available.

Graduate Studies

Enrollment: full-time 193, part-time 2580. Faculty: full-time 185, part-time 25. Degrees conferred: M.A., M.S., M.B.A., M.P.A., M.P.T., M.H.S., M.H.A., M.O.T., M.S.N., M.S.W.

ADMISSION REQUIREMENTS. Official transcripts, bachelor's degree required in support of application. TOEFL (minimum score 550) required for international applicants. Accepts transfer applicants. Graduates of unaccredited colleges not considered. Apply by July 15 (Fall), November 1 (Spring) to Office of Admissions. Applications and credentials required approximately two months prior to registration. Rolling admissions process. Application fee: $25. Phone: (708)534-4490; fax: (708) 534-1640.

ADMISSION STANDARDS. Relatively open for some departments, selective for others. Usual minimum average: 2.5 (A = 4).

FINANCIAL AID. Annual awards from institutional funds: scholarships, research assistantships, teaching assistantships, tuition waivers, Federal W/S, loans. Approved for VA benefits. Apply by May 1 to Director of Financial Aid; no specified closing date. Phone: (708)534-5000. Use FAFSA (School code: 009145). About 44% of students receive aid from University and outside sources. Aid available for part-time students.

DEGREE REQUIREMENTS. For master's: at least 32–48 credit hours in graduate-level courses; candidacy; thesis/nonthesis option; at least 2 credit hours are designated as master's final project or practicum/internship.

FIELDS OF STUDY.
Accounting. M.S.
Addiction Studies. M.H.S.
Analytical Chemistry. M.S.
Art. M.A.
Business Administration. M.B.A.
Communication Disorders. M.H.S.
Communication and Training. M.A.
Computer Science. M.S.
Counseling. Includes community, marriage and family, school. M.A.
Early Childhood Education. M.A.
Education. M.A.
Educational Administration. M.A.
English. M.A.
Environmental Biology. M.S.
Health Administration. M.H.A.
Independent Film and Digital Imaging. M.F.A.
Management Information Systems. M.S.
Multicategorical Special Education. M.A.
Nursing. M.S.N.
Occupational Therapy. M.O.T.
Physical Therapy. D.P.T.
Political and Justice Studies. M.A.
Psychology. Includes school. M.A.
Public Administration. M.P.A.
Reading. M.A.
Social Work. M.S.W.

HAMLINE UNIVERSITY
St. Paul, Minnesota 55104-1284
Web site: www.hamline.edu

Founded 1854. Coed. Private control. United Methodist Church. Hamline is the oldest institution of higher learning in the state of Minnesota. Special facility: Center for Excellence in Urban Teaching. Library: 556,450 volumes, 3800 subscriptions. Total University enrollment: 4550.

Tuition: per credit $315. On-campus housing for single students only. Average academic year housing cost: $3936 (room only). Contact Office of Residential Life for both on- and off-campus housing information. Phone: (651)523-2061.

Graduate Studies

Enrollment: full-time 480, part-time 1000. Faculty; full- and part-time 159. Degrees conferred: M.A., M.A.Ed., M.A.T., M.A.P.A., Certificate.

ADMISSION REQUIREMENTS. Official transcripts, three letters of recommendation required in support of School's application. TOEFL (minimum score 550, higher scores required by some departments) required for international applicants. Accepts transfer applicants. Apply by July 1 (Fall), November 1 (Spring) to Graduate Studies Office. Rolling admissions process. Application fee $30. Phone: (651)523-2900; fax: (651)523-2458.

ADMISSION STANDARDS. Selective. Usual minimum average: 2.9 (A = 4).

FINANCIAL AID. Limited to Federal W/S, loans. Approved for VA benefits. Apply by March 1 to the Office of Financial Aid. Phone: (651)523-3000. Use FAFSA (University code: 002354). Aid sometimes available for part-time students.

DEGREE REQUIREMENTS. For M.A.L.A.: 38–40 semester credits; final project/capstone. For M.A.Ed., M.A.T.: 30 credit programs; capstone (thesis). For M.A. in ESL: 41–48 semester credit program; capstone (thesis). For M.A.M., M.A.N.M.: 12 courses; 4 professional development series seminars; internship; capstone project (thesis). For M.A.P.A.: 8 required core courses; independent problem analysis; 4 noncredit one-day public management seminars; final capstone course. For M.F.A.: 10 courses; capstone (thesis). For D.P.A.: 48 semester credits beyond the master's; final comprehensive exam; dissertation; oral defense.

FIELDS OF STUDY.

GRADUATE LIBERAL STUDIES:
Liberal Studies. M.A.L.A.
Writing. M.F.A.

GRADUATE SCHOOL OF EDUCATION:
Education. M.A.Ed.
ESL. M.A. in ESL.
Teaching. M.A.T.

GRADUATE SCHOOL OF MANAGEMENT:
Management. M.A.M.
Nonprofit Management. M.A.N.M.
Public Administration. Includes administering local government, managing state and local government, public dispute resolution, law and government. M.A.P.A.
Public Management. D.P.A.
Public Policy. D.P.A.

School of Law
Web Site: www.hamline.edu/law

Established 1973. ABA approved since 1975. AALS member. Private control. Semester system. Special program: study abroad in London; Bergen, Norway; Hebrew University, Israel; University of Modena, Italy; Central European University, Budapest, Hungary. Library: 268,000, 3865 subscriptions; has LEXIS, NEXIS, WESTLAW, DIALOG; has more than 300 network connections.

Annual tuition: full-time $27,096, part-time $19,528. On-campus housing available. Housing cost: $14,043. Apply to Director of University Housing for off-campus housing.

Enrollment: first-year class 157, part-time 69; total 716 (men 48%, women 52%, minorities 13%). Faculty: full-time 40, part-time 65. Student to faculty ratio 18.5 to 1. Degrees conferred: J.D., J.D.-M.A.P.A., J.D.-M.B.A., J.D.-A.M.B.A. (Accounting, offered with University of St. Thomas), J.D.-M.A.N.M.

ADMISSION REQUIREMENTS. LSDAS Law School report, bachelor's degree, transcripts, LSAT, recommendations, résumé, personal statement required in support of application. Preference given to state residents. Graduates of unaccredited colleges not considered. Apply to Admissions Office by July 1. Phone: (651) 523-2941. Application fee $50.

ADMISSION STANDARDS. Selective. Accepts approximately 40% of full-time and 56% of part-time applicants. Number of full-time applicants 1362, part-time 242; number of full-time acceptance 550, part-time 138; number full-time enrolled 157, part-time 69; LSAT (75% of full-time students have a score at or above 153, part-time 148); GPA (75% of full-time students have a GPA at or above 3.16, part-time 2.88). *U.S. News & World Report* ranking is in the fourth tier of all U.S. law schools.

FINANCIAL AID. Scholarships, Federal W/S, loans. Apply by April 1. Phone: (651)523-3000. Use FAFSA (School code: 002354). About 45% of students receive some aid from School. Public Law forgiveness program available.

DEGREE REQUIREMENTS. For J.D.: satisfactory completion of 88-semester-hour program.

HAMPTON UNIVERSITY
Hampton, Virginia 23668
Web site: www.hamptonu.edu

Founded 1868. Located SE of Richmond. Coed. CGS member. Private control. Semester system. Special facilities: Marine Science Center for Coastal and Environmental Studies, Center for Non-linear Analysis, Nuclear/High Energy Physics Research Center of Excellence, Research Center for Optical Physics, National Center for Minority Special Education Research, Hampton University Museum. Library: 400,000 volumes. Total University enrollment: 5800.

Annual tuition: full-time $12,727; per credit $320. Limited on-campus housing for single students. Average academic year off-campus housing cost: $6750 excluding board. Contact Office of Auxiliary Enterprises for off-campus housing information. Phone: (757)727-5210.

Graduate College

Graduate study since 1928. Enrollment: full- and part-time 415. Graduate faculty: full-time 90, part-time 11. Degrees conferred: M.A., M.S., M.B.A., M.T., D.P.T., Ph.D.

ADMISSION REQUIREMENTS. Transcripts, GRE/GMAT required in support of College's application. TOEFL required for international applicants. Accepts transfer applicants. Apply to Dean of Graduate College at least six weeks prior to registration. Application fee $15. Phone: (757)727-5454 or (757)727-5498; fax: (757)727-5084; e-mail: hugrad@hamptonu.edu.

ADMISSION STANDARDS. Competitive. Usual minimum average: 2.8 (A = 4).

FINANCIAL AID. Fellowships, traineeships, assistantships, Federal W/S, loans. Approved for VA benefits. Apply by May 1 to Dean of Graduate College for fellowships, assistantships; to the Office of Financial Aid for all other programs. Phone: (757)727-5332. Use FAFSA.

DEGREE REQUIREMENTS. For M.A., M.T.: 30–32 hours, at least 24 hours in residence; thesis/special project/comprehensive exam. For M.S.: 32–45 hours; thesis/nonthesis option/comprehensive exam. For M.B.A.: 36–60 semester hours. For Ph.D., D.P.T.: 72 semester hours; qualifying exam; dissertation; final oral exam.

FIELDS OF STUDY.
Applied Mathematics. M.S.
Biology. M.A., M.S.
Business Administration. M.B.A.
Chemistry. M.S.

Communicative Sciences and Disorders. M.A.
Computer Science. M.S.
Counseling. Includes college student development, community agency counseling. M.A.
Early Childhood Education. M.T.
Elementary Education. M.A.
Middle School. M.T.
Nursing. Includes education, administration, practitioner, community health, community mental health/psychiatric, advanced adult nursing. M.S., Ph.D.
Physical Therapy. D.P.T.
Physics. M.S., Ph.D.
Secondary Education. M.T.
Special Education. Includes emotionally disturbed/reeducation specialist, learning disabilities. M.A.

HARDIN-SIMMONS UNIVERSITY
Abilene, Texas 79698-0001
Web site: www.hsutx.edu

Founded 1891. Coed. Private control, Baptist. Semester system. Library: 413,000 volumes, 4000 subscriptions. Total University enrollment: 2450.

Tuition: per credit $465. On-campus housing for 55 married students, 57 graduate men, 67 graduate women. Average academic year housing cost: $4215 (including board). Apply to Director of Housing. Phone: (325)670-1329.

Graduate Studies

Graduate study since 1926. Enrollment: full-time 222, part-time 173. University faculty: full-time 76, part-time 13. Degrees conferred: M.A., M.B.A., M.Ed., M.M., M.Div.

ADMISSION REQUIREMENTS. Transcript, GRE/GMAT, essay or writing sample, résumé, letters of recommendation required in support of School's application. Online application available. TOEFL, English translation of foreign documentation, certificate of financial support required for international applicants. Accepts transfer applicants. Graduates of unaccredited institutions not considered. Apply to Dean of the Graduate School at least two weeks prior to registration. Application fee $25. Phone: (325)670-1298; fax: (325)670-1564; e-mail: gradoff@hsutx.edu.

ADMISSION STANDARDS. Selective for most departments. Usual minimum average: 3.0 (A = 4)

FINANCIAL AID. Annual awards from institutional funds: scholarships, fellowships, graduate assistantships, tuition waivers, Federal W/S, loans. Approved for VA benefits. Apply at least one month prior to registration to Dean of the Graduate School. Phone: (325)670-1331. Use FAFSA (School code: 003571). About 10% of students receive aid other than loans from University and outside sources. Aid sometimes available to part-time students.

DEGREE REQUIREMENTS. For M.A.: 30–36 credit hours minimum, at least 24 in residence; thesis; comprehensive oral exam. For M.Ed.: 36 credit hours minimum, at least 24 in residence; comprehensive oral exam. For M.M.: by advisement. For M.B.A.: 36 credit hours; oral/written exam. For M.Div.: 72 credit hour, full-time program.

FIELDS OF STUDY.
Business Administration. M.B.A.
Counseling and Human Development. M.Ed.
English. M.A.
Environmental Management. M.S.
Family Ministry. M.A. (60 credit hour program).

Family Psychology. M.A. (54 credit hour program).
Gifted and Talented Education. M.Ed.
History. M.A.
Ministry. Includes pastoral ministry, educational ministry, family ministry, spiritual care ministry, missions and cross-cultural ministry. M.Div.
Music. Includes church music, music education, performance, theory and composition. M.M.
Nursing. M.S.
Physical Education. M.Ed.
Physical Therapy. M.P.T.
Reading Specialist Education. M.Ed.
Religion. M.A.
Sports and Recreation Management. M.Ed.

HARDING UNIVERSITY

Searcy, Arkansas 72143-0001
Web site: www.harding.edu

Founded 1924. Located 50 miles N of Little Rock. Coed. Private control. Church of Christ. Semester system. Library: 407,000 volumes, 1350 subscriptions. Total University enrollment: 5700.
Tuition: per credit $435. On-campus housing for 99 married students. Average academic year housing cost: $5312 for single students. Per month $300–$425 for married students. Apply to Director of Housing. Phone: (800)477-4256.

Graduate Program

Enrollment: full-time 71, part-time 362. University faculty: full-time 3, part-time 30. Degrees conferred: M.Ed., M.S.E.

ADMISSION REQUIREMENTS. Two transcripts, letter of recommendation required in support of application. GRE, GMAT, or MAT required for business. TOEFL required for international applicants. Accepts transfer applicants. Apply to Director of Graduate Studies at least two months prior to registration. Application fee $25. Phone: (800)477-4407.

ADMISSION STANDARDS. Selective. Usual minimum average: 2.5 (A = 4).

FINANCIAL AID. Annual awards from institutional funds: academic scholarships, fellowships, Federal W/S, loans. Approved for VA benefits. Apply to Director of Graduate Program; no specified closing date. Phone: (800)477-3243. Use FAFSA. About 25% of students receive aid other than loans from University and outside sources. Aid sometimes available for part-time students.

DEGREE REQUIREMENTS. For M.A.T., M.Ed., M.S.E.: 35 semester hours minimum, at least 29 in residence; final written exam; thesis/nonthesis option (thesis may replace 3–6 hours of course work); comprehensive exam. For M.B.A.: 12–15 month, 36–48 credit hour program. For M.S.N.: 39 credit program.

FIELDS OF STUDY.

COLLEGE OF BIBLE AND RELIGION:
Marriage and Family Therapy.
Mental Health Counseling.
Ministry.

COLLEGE OF BUSINESS ADMINISTRATION:
Business Administration.

COLLEGE OF EDUCATION:
Counseling. M.S., Ed.S.
Early Childhood Education.

Early Childhood Special Education. M.Ed., M.S.Ed.
Educational Leadership. M.Ed., Ed.D.
Educational Technology. M.S.
Elementary Education.
Kinesiology. M.S.Ed.
Literacy. Ed.S.
Reading.
Secondary.
Teaching. M.A.T.

COLLEGE OF SCIENCES:
Physician Assistant Studies. M.S.

UNIVERSITY OF HARTFORD

West Hartford, Connecticut 06117-1599
Web site: www.hartford.edu

Established 1957. CGS member. Private control. Semester system. Library: 522,640 volumes, 3131 subscriptions. Total University enrollment: 7250.
Tuition: Arts and Sciences, per credit $390, Business and Public Administration, per credit hour $595, Engineering per credit hour $510, Education, Nursing, and Health, per credit hour $500, Hartt School of Music, per credit hour $365–$700. On-campus housing for graduate students. Monthly room charge: $525–$700 for single students, $600–$750 for married students. Phone: (860)768-7793.

Graduate Studies

Graduate enrollment: full-time 568, part-time 1100. Faculty: full-time 130, part-time 108. Degrees conferred: M.A., M.A.T., M.Ed., M.Mus., M.M.Ed., M.B.A., M.P.A., M.S.O.B., M.S.T., M.S.I., M.S., M.S.P.A., M.F.A., Certificate, C.A.G.S. Specialist diploma, Sixth-year Certificate.

ADMISSION REQUIREMENTS. Transcripts, GRE/GMAT/ MAT required in support of application. Letters of recommendation, auditions required for some programs. TOEFL required for international applicants. Accepts transfer applicants. Graduates of unaccredited institutions not considered. Apply to Admissions Office by July 1 (Fall), November 15 (Spring). Application fee $40, $55 for international applicants. Phone: (860)768-4371; fax (860)768-5160.

ADMISSION STANDARDS. Selective for most departments. Usual minimum average: 3.0 (A = 4).

FINANCIAL AID. Annual awards from institutional funds: teaching assistantships, research fellowships, internships, Federal W/S, loans. Apply to Dean of appropriate school for assistantships, fellowships by May 1; to the Office of Financial Aid for all other programs: no specified closing date. Phone: (860)768-4296. Use FAFSA and institutional FAF. Very few students receive aid other than loans from University. Aid available for part-time students.

DEGREE REQUIREMENTS. For most master's: 30–45 semester hours minimum, at least two semesters in residence; thesis/ nonthesis option. For M.B.A.: 51 semester hours maximum, at least two semesters in residence. For C.A.G.S., Specialist, Certificate: 30 credit hours minimum beyond the master's; research paper; comprehensive exam.

FIELDS OF STUDY.

BARNEY SCHOOL OF BUSINESS:
Accounting. M.S.A.T.
Business Administration. M.B.A.

Business Administration for Health Care Professionals. E.M.B.A.-H.C.P.

Taxation. M.S.A.T.

COLLEGE OF ARTS AND SCIENCES:
Biology. M.S.
Clinical Psychology. Psy.D.
Clinical Psychology Practices. M.A.
Communication. M.A.
General Experimental Psychology. M.A.
Psychology. M.S.
School Psychology. M.S.

COLLEGE OF EDUCATION, NURSING, AND HEALTH PROFESSIONS:
Counseling. M.Ed., M.S.
Deaf Education. M.Ed.
Early Childhood Education. M.Ed.
Educational Computing and Technology. M.Ed.
Educational Leadership. C.A.G.S., Ed.D.
Educational Technology. M.Ed.
Elementary Education. M.Ed.
Guidance and Counseling. M.Ed., M.S.
Nursing. Includes community and public health nursing, nursing education, nursing management. M.S.N.
Physical Therapy. M.S.P.T.

COLLEGE OF ENGINEERING:
Civil Engineering. M.E.
Electrical and Computer Engineering. M.E.
Environmental Engineering. M.E.
Mechanical Engineering. M.E.

HARTT SCHOOL OF MUSIC:
Choral Conducting.
Composition.
Guitar.
Instrumental Conducting.
Kodaly Training.
Music Education.
Music History.
Music Theory.
Opera.
Performance. Includes voice, instrument, instrument Suzuki pedagogy.
Piano.
Piano Accompanying.
Piano Pedagogy.
Voice.

HARVARD UNIVERSITY
Cambridge, Massachusetts 02138
Web site: www.harvard.edu

Founded 1636. Located adjacent to Boston. Coed. CGS and AAU member. Private control. Semester system. Special facilities: Astronomical and Blue Hill meteorological observatories; Peabody Museum of Archaeology and Ethnology; several art museums; Harvard Forest, geological laboratories; seismograph station; research centers/institutes in International Affairs and Russian, Middle Eastern, East Asian Studies, Jewish Studies, World Religions, Japanese Studies, International Development, Afro-American Studies, Urban Studies, American Political Studies; rare book and manuscript collection; biological, chemical, psychological, and social relations laboratories; biological museums, Herbaria, computer center; engineering and physics laboratories. The University's NIH ranking is 13th among all U.S. Institutions with 682 awards/grants valued at $321,223,983. According to The Center at University of Florida, the University is ranked 13th

in receipt of Federal Research funds with $348,620,000 and it ranks 26th for total University research expenditures with $408,707,000. The University's endowment assets rank it number one, with a value of $22,143,349,000. In 2004, the University awarded 572 doctorates, which ranked it 12th among all U.S. institutions eligible to award that degree. Two hundred sixty-seven of the University's faculty members have been elected to National Honor Academies and this ranks it number one among all U.S. institutions. The Library: approximately 13,400,000 volumes, 97,500 subscriptions. Total University enrollment: 19,400.

On-campus housing for about 350 single graduate students from Graduate School of Arts and Sciences. Approximately 1400 apartment units for which graduate students are eligible. Annual housing cost: $5167–$8115 (room only); apartments $10,920. Contact Harvard Real Estate, Inc., Housing Office, 7 Holyoke Street, for both on- and off-campus housing. Phone: (617)495-5060. Daycare facilities available.

Graduate School of Arts and Sciences
Web site: www.gsas.harvard.edu

Graduate study since 1872. Annual tuition: full-time $31,456. Enrollment: 3000. Faculty teaching graduate students: 1100. Degrees conferred: A.M., S.M., M.F.S., M.E., Ph.D.

ADMISSION REQUIREMENTS. Transcripts, three letters of recommendation, personal statement required in support of College's application. Many departments require GRE. Interview not required. Transfer credit for work done elsewhere considered only for Ph.D. Admits Fall only. Apply by January 2 Natural Sciences, December 14 Social Sciences and Humanities, to the Office of Admissions and Financial Aid. Application fee $75. Phone: (617)495-5315; e-mail: admiss@fas.harvard.edu.

ADMISSION STANDARDS. Very competitive for most departments.

FINANCIAL AID. Annual awards from institutional funds: scholarships, fellowships, research assistantships, teaching assistantships, Federal W/S, loans. File for financial aid with application for admission. Phone: (617)495-5396. FAFSA and institutional FAF. About 85% of students receive aid and/or loans from School and outside sources.

DEGREE REQUIREMENTS. For A.M.: two terms minimum in full-time residence; reading knowledge of one foreign language for most majors; thesis normally not required; final written/oral exam. For S.M., M.E., M.S.F.: two terms minimum in full-time residence; final written/oral exam; no language or thesis requirement. For Ph.D.: minimum of two years in full-time residence and sixteen half courses minimum beyond the bachelor's; general or qualifying exam; reading knowledge of two foreign languages for most majors; thesis; final written/oral exam.

FIELDS OF STUDY.
African American Studies.
African Studies.
Anthropology.
Applied Mathematics.
Applied Physics.
Architecture.
Astronomy.
Biological Sciences in Dental Medicine. Includes molecular, supramolecular, cellular, supracellular processes.
Biological Sciences in Public Health. Includes cellular and molecular biology (nutritional biochemistry, cardiovascular biology, gene regulation, cell/environment interactions, toxicology, cancer, pulmonary inflammation, immunology); infectious diseases (protozoa, helminths, viruses and bacteria); genetic approaches to disease mechanisms.

Biological and Biomedical Sciences. Includes biochemistry, cell biology, genetics, pathology, microbiology, structural biology, pharmacology, virology, developmental biology.
Biophysics.
Biostatistics.
Business Economics.
Celtic Language and Literature.
Chemical Biology.
Chemical Physics.
Chemistry and Chemical Biology.
Classical Archaeology.
Classical Philosophy.
Classics. Includes ancient history, medieval Latin, Byzantine Greek, modern Greek.
Comparative Literature.
Computer Science.
Earth and Planetary Sciences.
East Asian Languages and Civilization.
Economics.
Engineering Science.
English.
Forest Ecology and Biology.
Germanic Literature and Cultural Studies.
Government.
Health Policy.
History.
History and East Asian Languages.
History of American Civilization.
History of Art and Architecture.
Immunology.
Inner Asian and Altaic Studies.
Landscape Architecture.
Linguistics.
Mathematics.
Middle Eastern Studies.
Molecular and Cellular Biology.
Music.
Near Eastern Languages and Civilization. Includes Akkadian and Sumerian Studies, Arabic and Islamic Studies, Archaeology of the Levant, Armenian Studies, Hebrew Bible/Old Testament, Indo-Muslim Culture, Iranian and Persian Studies, Jewish Studies, Semitic Philology, Turkish Studies, Yiddish Language and Literature.
Neuroscience.
Older Germanic Languages, Literature and Cultures. Includes medieval literatures and cultures of Germany, England and Scandinavia.
Organismic and Evolutionary Biology.
Organizational Behavior.
Philosophy.
Physics.
Political Economy and Government.
Psychology.
Public Policy.
Regional Studies—East Asia.
Regional Studies—Russian, Eastern Europe and Central Asia.
Religion.
Romance Languages and Literature. Includes French, Italian, Portuguese, Spanish.
Sanskrit and Indian Studies. Includes Tibetan, Himalayan Studies.
Science, Technology and Management. Joint program with Engineering and Business School.
Slavic Languages and Literature. Includes old church Slavonic, Russian, Ukrainian, Polish, Czech, Serbo-Croatian.
Social Policy.
Sociology.
Statistics.
System Biology.
Urban Planning.
Virology.

Graduate School of Business Administration
Soldiers Field
Web site: www.hbs.edu

Established 1908. Private control. Accredited programs: M.B.A.; recognized D.B.A. (initiated in the 1920s). Term system. Baker Library (largest business library in the world): 2,5000,000 volumes, 6500 subscriptions.

Annual tuition: full-time $41,900. Enrollment: September cohort 560 students, January cohort 330 students; total full-time 1900 (men 75%, women 25%). D.B.A.: full-time 100 students. Faculty: full-time 194; all have Ph.D./D.B.A. Degrees conferred: M.B.A., M.B.A.-J.D., D.B.A. (offered through the Graduate School of Arts and Sciences).

ADMISSION REQUIREMENTS. All applicants should have a bachelor's degree from a recognized institution of higher education and a strong mathematics background. Does not consider transfer applicants. Submit application, GMAT (will accept GMAT test results from the last five years, latest acceptable date is March), official transcripts from each undergraduate/graduate school attended, three letters of recommendation, seven or eight essays, résumé (prefers at least five years of work experience), and an application fee of $235 to the M.B.A. Admission Office. Interview by invitation. In addition, international students (whose native language is other than English) should submit a TOEFL or IELTS, certified translations and evaluations of all official transcripts; recommendation should be in English or with certified translations, proof of health/ immunization certificate, and proof of sufficient financial resources for two years of academic study. Both U.S. citizens and international applicants apply by October 1 (Round 1), January 1 (Round 2), March 12 (Round 3). On-campus visits are encouraged. Interviews are by invitation only. Joint degree applicants must apply to and be accepted to both schools; contact the admissions office for current information and specific admissions requirements. Application materials received by November 10 will have notifications sent by January 15; application materials received by January 6 will have notifications sent by March 30; application materials received by March 1 will have notifications sent by May 15. Admissions Office phone: (617) 495-6128; fax: (617)495-8137; e-mail: admissions@hbs.edu.

ADMISSION REQUIREMENTS FOR DOCTORAL CANDIDATES. Contact either the Graduate School of Arts and Sciences at (617)495-5315 or Graduate School of Business at (617)495-6127 for application material and information. The D.B.A. application materials can be downloaded at: www.hbs.edu/doctoral. Beginning students are admitted to begin study in July only. Both U.S. citizens and international applicants apply by December 30. Submit Graduate School application, GMAT/GRE (will accept GMAT/GRE test results from the last five years), official transcripts from each undergraduate/graduate school attended, three letters of recommendation, four or five essays, résumé, statement of purpose, and application fee of $90 to the Office of Doctoral Programs, Cotting House. In addition, international students (whose native language is other than English) should submit a TOEFL score, both TSE and TWE are encouraged, certified translations and evaluations of all official transcripts; recommendation should be in English or with certified translations, proof of health/immunization certificate. Interviews are encouraged. Notification is made by mid-March. Doctoral Programs phone: (617)495-6101.

ADMISSION STANDARDS. Very selective. Median GMAT: 702; median GPA: 3.5 (A = 4). *U.S. News & World Report* ranked the Business School number one of all U.S. business schools. *BusinessWeek* listed the Business School in the top five of all American business schools.

FINANCIAL AID. Scholarships, merit scholarships, minority scholarships, grants, fellowships, research assistantships, teaching assistantships, international loans, Federal W/S, loans. Financial assistance available for international students. Assistantships/ fellowships may be available for joint degree candidates. Financial Aid applications and information are generally available at the on-campus visit/interview or after January 1; apply by March 1. Request scholarship, fellowship, assistantship and need-based information from the School's Office of Financial Aid Services. Phone: (617)495-6640, fax: (617)496-3955. Use FAFSA (School code: 002155), also submit the School's FAF, a Financial Aid Transcript, Federal Income Tax forms. Approximately 70% of students receive some form of financial assistance. Merit fellowships covering 12 months of study are available for D.B.A. applicants.

DEGREE REQUIREMENTS. For M.B.A.: a four-term full-time program. For M.B.A.-J.D.: four-and-one-half- to five-year program. For D.B.A.: four- to five-year program; teaching experience required; general exam in business; qualifying exam in field of specialization; thesis; oral defense. For Ph.D.: see Graduate School of Arts and Sciences listing above.

FIELDS OF DOCTORAL SPECIALIZATION.
Accounting and Management.
Business Economics.
Health Policy Management.
Marketing.
Organizational Behavior.
Science, Technology and Management.
Strategy.
Technology and Operations Management.

School of Dental Medicine
Web site: www.hsdm.harvard.edu

Established 1867. Located in Boston (02115). Medical-Dental library: 412,000 volumes, 6000 subscriptions.

Annual tuition: $38,600. On-campus housing for single students at Vanderbilt Hall is residence hall for both Medical and Dental students. Married students tend to reside at Harvard@Trilogy, a new apartment facility. Academic year room and board, health insurance and other fees are approximately $21,000.

Enrollment: first-year class 35 (men 60%, women 40%), total 150 (men 60%, women 40%, minorities 6%, state residents 20%). Faculty: full-time 14, part-time 123. Degrees conferred: D.M.D., D.M.D.-M.D., D.M.D.-M.P.H., D.M.D.-M.P.P., D.M.D.-S.M., D.M.D.-ScD., Ph.D.

ADMISSION REQUIREMENTS. AADSAS report, official transcripts, high school and college faculty evaluations, DAT required in support of School's application. Interview by invitation only. Students with three years of undergraduate preparation are considered, but normally four years of college are expected. Does not accept transfer applicants. Graduates of unaccredited colleges not considered. Apply to Assistant Dean after June 1, before December 1. Application fee $70. Phone: (617)432-1443; fax: (617) 432-3881.

ADMISSION STANDARDS. Competitive. Accepts about 5% of all applicants. Number of applications 1500 (n/a out-of-state); number interviewed 130 (n/a out-of-state); number of acceptance n/a (n/a out-of-state); number enrolled 35 (n/a out-of-state). Usual minimum UGPA: 3.0 (A = 4). Mean DAT: academic 22, PAT 22; mean UGPA 3.70.

FINANCIAL AID. Scholarships, fellowships, grants, tuition waivers, DEAL, HEAL, loans. Apply by July 1 to Office of Financial Aid. Phone: (617)432-1527. Use FAFSA (School code: E00508) and CSS profile. About 66% of students receive aid other than loans from School.

DEGREE REQUIREMENTS. For D.M.D.: 53 months minimum, normally at least two years in full-time residence; transfer students occasionally permitted to enter in fourth year. For M.P.H., M.P.P., S.M., Sc.D., Ph.D.: see Graduate Schools listings above.

FIELDS OF GRADUATE STUDY.
Biological Sciences in Dental Medicine. Ph.D.
Oral Biology. M.M.Sc., D.M.Sc.
Public Health. M.P.H., S.M., S.D., D.P.H.
Public Policy. M.P.P.

Specialty Training Programs:
Dental Public Health.
Endodontics.
Oral and Maxillofacial Pathology.
Oral and Maxillofacial Surgery (with Massachusetts General Hospital).
Orthodontics.
Pediatric Dentistry (with Children's Hospital).
Periodontology.
Prostodontics.

Advance Training Programs:
Dental Informatics.
General Practice Residency (with Cambridge Health Alliance, Brigham and Women's Hospital).
Geriatric Dentistry.
Oral Biology.
Oral Epidemiology.
Oral Medicine.
Orofacial and Temporomandibular Disorders.

Graduate School of Design

Annual tuition: full-time $33,438.

Enrollment: full-time 564. Faculty: full-time 32, part-time 66. Degrees conferred: M.Arch., M.L.A., M.Des.S., M.Arch. in Urban Design, M.L.A. in Urban Design, M.U.P., D. Des.

ADMISSION REQUIREMENTS. Transcripts, three letters of recommendation, résumé and essay, portfolio, GRE required in support of School's application. Supplemental forms are required by some programs. TOEFL required for international applicants. Interview not required. Apply to Graduate School of Design by December 1. Fall admission only. Application fee $75. Phone: (617)495-5453; fax: (617)495-8949.

ADMISSION STANDARDS. Very selective.

FINANCIAL AID. Scholarships, grants, Federal W/S, loans (master's candidates); grants, fellowships, teaching/research assistantships (doctoral candidates). Apply by February 15 to the Dean's Office or appropriate department chair. Use FAFSA (School code: E00212) and institutional FAF. No aid for special (nondegree) students.

DEGREE REQUIREMENTS. For M.Arch.: (first professional degree): three and a half years minimum in residence; terminal project. For M.Des.S.: one-year full-time program. For M.U.P.: two years minimum in residence. For M.Arch. (second professional degree): B.Arch. required for admission; one and a half years minimum in residence; terminal project. For M.L.A.: normally three years in residence; terminal project. For D.Des.: a minimum of 32 units of course work; thesis proposal; general exam; thesis. For Ph.D.: see GSAS listing above for degree requirements.

FIELDS OF STUDY.
Architecture. M.Arch. I, M.Arch II., D.Des., Ph.D.
History and Theory. M.Des.S.
Landscape Architecture. M.L.A I, M.L.A.II., D.Des., Ph.D.
Real Estate and Project Management. M.Des.S.
Technology and Design. M.Des.S.
Urban and Housing Studies. M.Des.S.
Urban Planning and Design. M.U.P., M.A.U.D., M.L.AU.D., D.Des., Ph.D.

Divinity School

Theology study since 1636. Annual tuition: full-time M.T.S., M.Div. $21,544, Th.D. $31,456.

Enrollment: full-time 507, part-time 78 (men 45%, women 55%). Faculty: full-time 37, part-time 39. Degrees conferred: M.Div., M.T.S., Th.M., Th.D. The Ph.D. is offered through the Graduate School of Arts and Sciences.

ADMISSION REQUIREMENTS. Official transcripts, 3–5 letters of recommendation, personal statement, résumé, two essays required in support of School's application. GRE optional except for Th.D. applicants. Interview not required. TOEFL required for non-native English speakers. Accepts transfer applicants. Apply by January 1 (Fall), December 1 (Spring), December 31 (Th.D.), March 15 (Th.M.) to Dean of Admissions of School. Rolling admissions process. Application fee $65. Phone: (617) 495-5796; fax: (617)495-0345.

ADMISSION STANDARDS. Selective. Usual minimum average: 3.0 (A = 4).

FINANCIAL AID. Annual awards from institutional funds: scholarships, grants, teaching fellowships (for advanced students only), Federal W/S, loans. Apply to Dean of Admission by January 10 for Th.M., Th.D.; by February 15 for M.Div. Use FAFSA (School code: E00210) and institutional supplementary form. Phone: (617)495-5772. About 81% of students receive aid in the form of grants and/or loans. Aid rarely available for part-time students or Th.M. students.

DEGREE REQUIREMENTS. For M.Div.: 24 half-courses minimum, at least two years in full-time residence; distribution and arts of ministry requirements, senior thesis; reading knowledge of Hebrew, Greek, Latin, German, French, or Spanish. For M.T.S.: 16 half-courses minimum, two years in full-time residence; distribution requirements; reading knowledge of one language of theological scholarship. For Th.M.: 8 half-courses minimum in residence; reading knowledge of two of Hebrew, Greek, Latin, German, French, or Spanish; one major or two smaller research papers; final oral exam. For Th.D.: two years minimum beyond the M.Div. in full-time residence; seven-year limit for degree; knowledge of one classical and two modern languages indicated for M.Div., Th.M.; general exam; dissertation; final oral exam.

Graduate School of Education

Established 1920. Tuition: per semester $15,848. Limited on-campus housing available. Contact Director of Student Affairs for on- and off-campus information. Phone: (617)495-8035. Day care facilities available.

Enrollment: full-time 815, part-time 160. Faculty: full-time 38, part-time 46. Degrees conferred: Ed.M., C.A.S., Ed.D.

ADMISSION REQUIREMENTS. Transcripts, GRE or MAT, three academic/professional references, statement of purpose required in support of School's application. Interview not required. TOEFL (minimum score 600, 250 on computer-based test), TWE (minimum 5) required for international applicants. Graduates of unaccredited institutions and transfer applicants not considered. Doctoral applicants apply to the Office of Admissions by January 2; January 10 for all others. Admits Fall only. Application fee $75. Phone: (617)495-3414; fax: (617)496-3577; e-mail: gseadmissions@harvard.edu.

ADMISSION STANDARDS. Competitive to very selective.

FINANCIAL AID. Scholarships, fellowships, research assistantships, teaching assistantships, grants, Federal W/S, loans. Approved for VA benefits. Apply by January 15 to the Office of Financial Aid. Phone: (617)495-3416; fax: (617)495-0840; Fellowship office phone: (617)496-2805. Use FAFSA (School code: E00213), institutional FAF, CSS profile (doctoral candidates). Students enrolled half-time or more in the Ed.D., Ed.M., and C.A.S. programs are eligible to receive financial aid.

DEGREE REQUIREMENTS. For Ed.M.: One year or equivalent in residence; no transfer of credit permitted; no language, thesis, or comprehensive exam requirement; ordinarily, requirements must be met through full-time study during the academic year. For C.A.S.: one year or equivalent in residence beyond the master's; full-time study during academic year ordinarily required, but exceptions are considered; no language or thesis requirement. For Ed.D.: two years or equivalent beyond the bachelor's, at least two semesters in full-time attendance; written qualifying paper; thesis; final oral exam; no language requirement.

FIELDS OF STUDY.

Administration Planning and Social Policy. Includes communities and schools, elementary and secondary education, higher education, international education, research, urban superintendency. Ed.D., C.A.S., Ed.M.

Arts in Education. Ed.M., C.A.S.

Education Policy and Management. Ed.M., Ed.D.

Higher Education. Ed.M.

Human Development and Psychology. Includes language and literacy. Ed.D., C.A.S.

Individualized Program. Includes self-designed, administration, planning and social policy, human development and psychology, learning and teaching, international education, gender studies, mind, brain and education. Ed.M.

International Education. Ed.M.

Language and Literacy. Ed.M., C.A.S.

Learning and Teaching. Includes learning and knowing, learning in a sociohistorical context. Ed.D., C.A.S., Ed.M.

Risk and Prevention. Ed.M., C.A.S.

School Leadership. Ed.M., C.A.S.

Teacher Certification Programs. Includes teaching and curriculum, midcareer math and science. Ed.M., C.A.S.

Technology Education. Ed.M., C.A.S.

Urban Superintendency. Ed.D.

John Fitzgerald Kennedy School of Government

Web site: www.ksg.harvard.edu

Established 1936 as the Graduate School of Public Administration, changed in 1978 to current name. Special facilities: Belfer Center for Science and International Affairs, Carr Center for Human Rights Policy, Center for Business and Government, Center for International Development at Harvard University, Center for Public Leadership, the Hauser Center for Nonprofit Organizations, the Institute of Politics, Joan Shorenstein Center on the Press, Politics, and Public Policy.

Annual tuition: full-time $34,807.

Enrollment: full-time about 577, no part-time. Faculty: full-time 70. Degrees conferred: M.P.A., M.P.P., M.P.P.-M.U.P., Ph.D.

ADMISSION REQUIREMENTS. Transcripts, three letters of reference, GRE or GMAT, responses to essay questions required in support of School's application. Online application available. Seven years of administrative public-interest work required for Mid-Career M.P.A. TOEFL, TWE, TSE required for foreign applicants. Interview not required. Graduates of unaccredited colleges normally not considered. Apply to Admissions Office by January 4 for M.P.P. and Ph.D.; Mid-Career M.P.A. has rolling admissions from January 15 through May 14. Admits Fall only. Application fee $80. Phone: (617)495-1155; e-mail: ksg-admissions@harvard.edu.

ADMISSION STANDARDS. Competitive.

FINANCIAL AID. Scholarships, grants, assistantships, fellowships, Federal W/S, loans. Apply to Office of Financial Aid by

February 1 for M.P.P. and April 16 for Mid-Career M.P.A. Phone: (617)495-1152. Use FAFSA and CSS profile.

DEGREE REQUIREMENTS. For M.P.P.: two years of full-time study; 18 units of academic credit, 10 in required courses. For the M.P.A.: two years of full-time study; 8 semester-length courses. For Ph.D.: 16 half-course minimum; advancement to candidacy; oral defense of research paper; dissertation; written and oral defense.

FIELDS OF STUDY.

Health Policy.
Political Economy and Government.
Public Administration. Includes international development, mid-career program.
Public Policy.
Social Policy.
Note: Students choose courses from Kennedy School of Government, as well as from other Harvard graduate and professional schools, the Fletcher School of Law and Diplomacy at Tufts University, and MIT.

Law School
Web site: www.law.harvard.edu

Established 1817. The oldest law school in the U.S. Located with most of the other units of the University in Cambridge. ABA approved since 1923. AALS member. Semester system. Full-time, day study only. Law library: 2,192,726 volumes; 15,336 subscriptions; has LEXIS, NEXIS, WESTLAW, DIALOG, OCLC, RLIN, Vu/Text, among others; is a Federal Government Depository. Special facilities: Beckman Center for Internet and Society, Institute for Race and Justice, International Center for Criminal Justice, Center for Law, Economics and Business, Center for Health, Law Policy, Biotechnology and Bioethics, the European Law Research Center. Special programs: The East Asian Legal Studies Program, the Islamic Legal Studies Program, the Human Rights Program, the Program on International Financial Systems, the Program in Law and Economics, the Program on the Legal Profession, the Program on Negotiation.

Annual tuition: $37,100. Total average cost for all other expenses: $22,200.

Enrollment: first-year class 556. Total full-time J.D. students 1719 (men 55%, women 45%, minorities 31%), LL.M. and S.J.D. students 160. Faculty: full-time 76, part-time 17. Student to faculty ratio 11.4 to 1. Degrees conferred: J.D., J.D.-M.B.A., J.D.-M.P.P., J.D.-M.A.L.D., J.D.-M.P.A., J.D.-M.Div., J.D.-Ed.M., J.D.-M.P.H., J.D.-Ph.D., LL.M., J.D.-LL.M (University of Cambridge, England), S.J.D.

ADMISSION REQUIREMENTS. LSDAS Law School report, bachelor's degree, transcripts, two references, LSAT, personal statement required in support of application. International applicants must use LSAC JD Credential Assembly Service. Interview not required. Accepts transfer applicants. Graduates of unaccredited colleges not considered. Apply to Admissions Office of School after September 15, before February 1. Admits Fall only. Application fee $75 (J.D. applicants only). Phone: (617)495-3109.

ADMISSION STANDARDS. Selective. Accepts approximately 12% of all students. Number of applicants 7046; number of acceptance 811; number enrolled 557; LSAT (75% of students have a score at or above 170); GPA (75% of students have a GPA at or above 3.68). *U.S. News & World Report* ranking is in the top 2 of all U.S. law schools.

FINANCIAL AID. Scholarships, fellowships, assistantships, Federal W/S, loans. Apply by March 1 to Financial Aid Office (entering J.D. students), by February 1 to Chair of Division of Graduate Studies (postbaccalaureate students). Phone: (617)495-4606. Use FAFSA. All students receive aid who demonstrate need according to a combination of Federal and institutional guidelines. A Low-Income Protection Plan is available.

DEGREE REQUIREMENTS. For J.D.: three years minimum in residence; advanced standing for study completed in other law schools considered in exceptional cases; final written paper. For LL.M.: at least 24 credits beyond the J.D.; one year in full-time residence; final written essay or thesis. For S.J.D.: one year minimum in full-time residence; dissertation; final oral exam.

Medical School
Web site: www.hms.harvard.edu

Established 1782. Located in Boston (02115-6092). Library: more than 610,000 volumes. NIH ranking is in the top 13 of all U.S. institutions with 682 awards/grants worth $321,223,983.

Annual tuition: $40,279. Total average figure for all other expenses: $11,005. Limited housing available.

Enrollment: first-year class 165, total 771 (men 50%, women 50%, minorities 47%). Faculty: full- and part-time approximately 7500. Degrees conferred: M.D., M.D.-M.B.A., M.D.-M.P.H., M.D.-M.P.P., M.D.-Ph.D. (MSTP in conjunction with both Harvard Graduate School and Massachusetts Institute of Technology).

ADMISSION REQUIREMENTS. AMCAS report, transcripts, MCAT, recommendations, essay, supplemental application required in support of application. Interview by invitation. Applicants must have completed at least two years of college study, but four recommended. Does not have EDP. Apply after June 1, before October 15 to Director of Admissions. Application fee $85. Phone: (617)432-1550; fax: (617)432-3307.

ADMISSION STANDARDS. Competitive. Accepts about 15% of all applicants. Number of applications 1629 (n/a out-of-state); number interviewed 337 (173 out-of-state); number of acceptance n/a (n/a out-of-state); number enrolled 62 (6 out-of-state). Mean Composite MCAT 9.0; mean UGPA 3.62 (A = 4).

FINANCIAL AID. All Financial Aid is based on documented need. Grants, institutional loans, HEAL, alternative loan programs, NIH stipends, Federal Perkins Loans, Stafford Subsidized and Unsubsidized Loans, Service Commitment Scholarship programs are available. Assistantships/fellowships may be available for joint degree candidates. Contact the Financial Aid Office for current information. Phone: (617)432-1575; fax: (617)432-4308; e-mail: financialaid@hms.harvard.edu. For most financial assistance and all Federal programs use FAFSA (School code: E00472), also submit Financial Aid Transcript, Federal Income Tax forms, CSS profile. Approximately 80% of students receive some form of financial assistance.

DEGREE REQUIREMENTS. For M.D.: satisfactory completion of four-year program; pass step 1 and 2 of USMLE for promotion and graduation. For M.B.A., M.P.H., M.P.P., Ph.D.: see Graduate School listing above.

FIELDS OF GRADUATE STUDY.
Biochemistry.
Biomedical Engineering.
Biophysics.
Cell Biology.
Genetics.
Immunology.
Microbiology.
Molecular Biology.
Molecular Pharmacology.
Neurology.
Neurosciences.
Pathology.
Systems Biology.
Urology.

School of Public Health

Founded 1922. Special facilities: Center for Biostatistics in AIDS Research, Center for Health Communication, Center for Quality of Care Research and Education, Center for Risk Analysis, Francois-Xavier Bagnoud Center for Health and Human Rights, Harvard AIDS Institute, Harvard Center for Populations and Development Studies, Harvard Center for Society and Health, Harvard Injury Control Research Center, John B. Little Center for Radiation Sciences and Environmental Health, Kresge Center for Environmental Health.

Annual tuition: full-time $34,085. On-campus housing available. Enrollment: full- and part-time 834. Faculty: full-time 155, part-time 115. Degrees conferred; S.M., M.P.H., M.O.H., S.D., D.P.H.

ADMISSION REQUIREMENTS. Official transcripts, three letters of reference, statement of purpose, résumé, GRE (requests to substitute MCAT/DAT/ GMAT/LSAT are normally approved) required in support of School's application. Online application available. TOEFL (minimum score 560) required for international applicants. Graduates of unaccredited institutions not considered. Apply by December 15 (priority deadline) to SOPHAS (Schools of Public Health Application Service). Admits Fall only. Application fee $75. Phone: (617)432-1031; fax: (617)432-7080.

ADMISSION STANDARDS. Competitive. Usual minimum average: 2.75 (A = 4).

FINANCIAL AID. Fellowships, research/teaching assistantships, tuition grants, Federal W/S, loans. Apply by February 1 to the Office of Student Financial Services. Use FAFSA (School code: E00214). Phone: (617)432-1867. Aid rarely available for part-time or foreign students.

DEGREE REQUIREMENTS. For M.P.H.: 40 credit units minimum, two semesters in residence; applicants ordinarily must be graduates of schools of medicine, dental medicine, veterinary health, law, or hold a doctorate in field related to public health. For S.M.: 42–80 units in residence for students with prior doctoral (and some master's) degree or 80 units minimum in residence for students with relevant bachelor's degrees. For M.O.H.: 40 units minimum in residence; applicants must hold M.D. For S.D.: two years in residence; applicants must hold bachelor's or master's degree depending on department; qualifying exam; thesis; final oral exam. For D.P.H.: essentially the same as the S.D.; applicants must be graduates of schools of medicine, dental medicine, or veterinary medicine, or hold another doctorate in field related to public health; applicants must also hold M.P.H.

FIELDS OF STUDY.
Biostatistics. S.M.
Environmental Health. Ph.D.
Epidemiology. S.M., S.D., D.P.H.
Exposure, Epidemiology and Risk. S.M.
Genetics and Complex Diseases. M.P.H., Ph.D.
Health Care Management. S.M.
Health Communication. S.M., S.D., Ph.D.
Health Policy. Ph.D.
Immunology and Infectious Diseases. M.P.H., S.D., Ph.D.
Industrial Hygiene. S.D.
Maternal and Child Health. S.M., S.D., D.P.H.
Molecular and Integrative Physiological Sciences. S.D., Ph.D.
Nutrition. M.P.H.
Occupational Health. M.O.H., S.M., S.D., D.P.H.
Population and International Health. S.M., S.D., D.P.H.
Public Health. Includes clinical effectiveness, family and community health, health care management, international health, law and public health, occupational and environmental health, quantitative methods. M.P.H.

HAWAII PACIFIC UNIVERSITY
Honolulu, Hawaii 98623-2785
Web site: www.hpu.edu

Coed. Private control. Semester system. Library: 159,000 volumes, 2500 subscriptions. Total University enrollment: 8000.

Annual tuition: full-time $13,440; per credit $560. On-campus housing for single graduate students; none for married students. Average academic year housing cost: $18,500 (including board). Contact Director of Residence Life for both on- and off-campus housing information. Phone: (808)233-3184.

Graduate Studies

Enrollment: full-time 672, part-time 568. University faculty teaching graduate students: full-time 47, part-time 38. Degrees conferred: M.A.G.L., M.A.O.C., M.A.Com., M.A.T.E.S.L., M.A.D.M.S., M.B.A., M.A. in H.R.M., M.S.I S., M.S.N.

ADMISSION REQUIREMENTS. Official transcripts, GMAT/ GRE, two letters of recommendation required in support of application. Online application available. TOEFL required for international applicants. Accepts transfer applicants. Graduates of unaccredited institutions not considered. Apply to the Graduate Admissions Coordinator at least one month prior to registration. Rolling admissions process. Application $50. Phone: (808)544-0279; fax: (808)544-0279; e-mail: gradservctr@hpu.edu.

ADMISSION STANDARDS. Selective. Usual minimum average: 3.0 (A = 4).

FINANCIAL AID. Assistantships, Federal W/S, loans. Approved for VA benefits. Apply after January 1 to Financial Aid Office; no specified closing date. Use FAFSA. Aid sometimes available for part-time students.

DEGREE REQUIREMENTS. For master's: 36–58 semester hours minimum, at least 30 in residence; thesis/nonthesis option.

FIELDS OF STUDY.
Accounting.
Business Administration.
Communication.
Diplomacy and Military Studies.
E-business.
Economics.
Finance.
Global Leadership.
Human Resource Management. M.A. in H.R.M.
Information Systems. M.S.I.S.
International Business.
Management.
Marketing.
Nursing.
Organization Change.
TESL.

UNIVERSITY OF HAWAII AT MANOA
Honolulu, Hawaii 96822
Web site: www.uhm.hawaii.edu

Founded 1907. CGS member. Coed. State control. Semester system. Special facilities: Institute for Astronomy; Computing Center; English Language Institute; Environmental Center; Foreign Languages Laboratories; Hawaii Agricultural Experiment Station; Hawaii Cooperative Fisheries Unit; Hawaii Institute of Geophysics; Hawaii Institute of Marine Biology; Industrial Relations Center; Institute for Astronomy; Instructional Resources Service Center; Laboratory of Sensory Sciences; JKK Look Laboratory of Oceanographic Engineering; Harold L. Lyon Arboretum; Pacific and Asian Linguistics Institute; Pacific Biomedical Research Center; Population Genetics Laboratory; Social Science Research Institute; Social Welfare Development and Research Center; Speech and Hearing Clinic; Survey Research Office; University of Hawaii Press; Waikiki Aquarium; Water Resources Research Center. The University's NIH ranking is 84th among all U.S. institutions with 75 awards/grants valued at $67,517,430. According to The Center at University of Florida, the University is ranked 54th in receipt of Federal Research funds with $143,580,000 and it ranks 78th for total University research expenditures with $179,285,000. In 2004, 6 of the University's faculty members were elected to National Honor Academies and this ranks it 83rd among all U.S. institutions. The Library: approximately 3,100,000 volumes, 26,500 subscriptions. Total University enrollment: 19,000.

Annual tuition: full-time resident $8400, nonresident $11,088; per credit resident $200, nonresident $462. On-campus housing for about 1300 single students, with preference given to Hawaii residents. No on-campus housing facilities for married students. Average academic year housing cost: $6000 (including board) for single students, $9000 (including board) for married students. Contact Student Housing Office for both on- and off-campus housing information. Phone: (808)956-8177.

Graduate Division

Enrollment: full-time 3000, part-time 1500. University faculty: full-time 1320, part-time 192. Degrees conferred: M.Arch., M.A., M.Acc., M.B.A., M.Ed., M.Ed.T., M.F.A., M.L.S., M.M., M.Mus., M.P.A., M.P.H., M.P.S., M.S., M.S.W., M.U.R.P., Ed.D., Dr.P.H., Ph.D.

ADMISSION REQUIREMENTS. Official transcripts; statement of objectives required in support of application. MAT required for some departments; GMAT required by College of Business Administration. GRE required by some fields of study, recommended in others. Two to three letters of recommendation required by some departments. Interview not required. TOEFL (minimum score for most programs 560) required for international applicants. Accepts transfer applicants. Graduates of unaccredited colleges not considered. Apply to Admissions Office, Graduate Division for most programs before January 15 internationals; February 1, U.S. citizens and permanent residents (Fall); August 1 (Spring) internationals; September 1 (Spring) U.S. citizens and permanent residents. Application fee $50. Phone: (808) 956-8544; fax: (808)956-4257.

ADMISSION STANDARDS Selective. Usual minimum average: 3.0 (A = 4); usual minimum GMAT: 500.

FINANCIAL AID. Scholarships; fellowships, assistantships for teaching/research, Federal W/S, loans. Approved for VA benefits. Apply to Dean of Graduate Division for scholarships, fellowships; for East-West Center scholarships, write to East-West Center; to appropriate department chair by February 1 for assistantships; to Financial Aid Office for all other programs. Use FAFSA. About 32% of students receive aid other than loans from University, about 50% from all sources. Aid available for part-time students.

DEGREE REQUIREMENTS. For master's (M.A., M.Ed., M.S.) Plan A: 30 credit hours minimum, at least half of credits in residence; general exam (optional), candidacy; thesis; final written/oral exam. For master's (M.A., M.Ed., M.S.) Plan B: 30 credit minimum, at least 24 credits in residence; general exam (optional); culminating experience; final written/oral or both. For master's (M.A., M.Ed., M.S.) Plan C: preliminary conference to establish plan of study/degree plan; general oral/written exam; fi-

nal written and oral exam. For M.F.A.: 60 credits program minimum depending on field of study offered under Plan A and B; performance/major project/major exhibition. For M.B.A.: 54 credits, thesis/nonthesis option. For M.L.S.: 36 credit hours minimum, thesis/nonthesis program. For M.S.W.: 52 credit hours minimum; final group project or thesis. For M.M.: 28 credit hours minimum plus thesis/composition, or 30 credit hours; performance; final oral exam. For M.P.H.: 30 credit hours minimum; nonthesis program; qualifying exam; final oral exam. For M.Arch., M.U.R.P.: 36 credit hours minimum; thesis. For Ph.D.: 3 semesters minimum in full-time residence beyond the master's; no specific credit requirements; reading knowledge of one foreign language is an optional requirement determined by each field of study; qualifying exam (optional); advancement to candidacy; comprehensive exam; dissertation; final written/oral exam.

FIELDS OF STUDY.
Accounting. GMAT for admission.
American Studies. GRE for admission.
Animal Sciences. GRE/Subject for admission. M.S.
Anthropology. GRE for admission; admits Fall only.
Architecture, ETS Architectural School Test, samples of work, documented evidence of 600 hours of supervised architecture work experience required for admission. M.Arch. only.
Art. M.A. in Asian, Pacific art history; M.F.A. (thesis program only) for creative studio work. M.A., M.F.A. only.
Asian Studies. GRE for admission; interdepartmental program. M.A. only.
Astronomy. GRE/Subject for admission. M.S., Ph.D.
Bioengineering. GRE for admission. M.S., Ph.D.
Biomedical Sciences. M.S., Ph.D.
Botany. GRE for admission; one language for Ph.D.; fields include plant physiology. M.S., Ph.D.
Business Administration. GMAT for admission. M.B.A. only.
Cell and Molecular Biology. GRE for admission. M.S., Ph.D.
Chemistry. GRE/Subject for admission of international applicants, recommended for domestic applicants; one language for Ph.D. M.S., Ph.D.
Chinese. GRE for admission. M.A., Ph.D.
Civil and Environmental Engineering. GRE for admission. M.S., Ph.D.
Classics. M.A.
Communication. M.A.
Communication and Information Sciences. GRE or GMAT for admission. Ph.D.
Computer Science. GRE/Subject for admission. Ph.D.
Counselor and Guidance. GRE for admission. M.Ed.
Curriculum Studies. M.Ed.
Dance. M.A., M.F.A.
Early Childhood Education. M.Ed.
Ecology, Evolution and Conservation Biology. M.S., Ph.D.
Economics. GRE for admission. M.A., Ph.D.
Education. GRE writing assessment for admission. Ph.D.
Educational Administration. Course work or professional experience in education required for admission. Fall admission only. M.Ed.
Educational Foundations. M.Ed.
Educational Psychology. GRE for admission; proficiency in computer language for Ph.D.; Fall admission only. Ph.D.
Educational Technology. GRE for admission. M.Ed.
Electrical Engineering. GRE recommended for admission to M.S., required for Ph.D. program.
English. GRE/Subject for admission. M.A., Ph.D.
English as a Second Language. GRE for all native English speakers. M.A.
Entomology. GRE/Subject for admission. One language for Ph.D. M.S., Ph.D.
Food Science and Technology. GRE for admission. M.S.
French. M.A.
Geography. GRE for admission; one language for Ph.D. M.A., Ph.D.

Geology and Geophysics. GRE for admission; one language for Ph.D. M.S., Ph.D.

German. M.A.

Hawaiian. M.A.

Hawaiian Studies. M.A.

History. GRE for admission; one language for M.A.; two languages for Ph.D.

Human Resource Management. GMAT for admission. M.H.R.M.

Information and Computer Sciences. GRE for admission, Subject recommended, knowledge of programming language required for admission. M.S.

International Management. GMAT for admission. Ph.D.

Japanese. GRE required for admission. M.A., Ph.D.

Kinesiology and Leisure Science. M.S.

Korean. GRE for admission. M.A., Ph.D.

Library and Information Science. GRE for admission. M.L.I.S.

Linguistics. GRE for admission; one language for M.A.; two languages for Ph.D.

Mathematics. GRE/Subject for admission; two languages for Ph.D. M.A., Ph.D.

Mechanical Engineering. GRE for admission. M.S., Ph.D.

Meteorology. GRE recommended for M.S., for Ph.D.; one language for Ph.D. M.S., Ph.D.

Microbiology. GRE for admission; one language for Ph.D. M.S., Ph.D.

Molecular Biosciences and Bioengineering. GRE for admission. M.S., Ph.D.

Music. GRE recommended for M.A., M.M., required for Ph.D.; thesis program only for M.A. in dance ethnology, ethnomusicology, musicology, music education, theory; nonthesis program for M.A. in performance only; M.Mus. in composition and performance; one language for M.A. thesis program; M.A., M.Mus. only.

Natural Resources and Environmental Management. GRE recommended for M.S., required for Ph.D. M.S., Ph.D.

Nursing. Bachelor's degree in nursing, licensure in Hawaii for practice of nursing, GRE for admission; areas of specialization for M.S.: mental health–maternal–child nursing, medical-surgical nursing. M.S.

Nutritional Sciences. GRE recommended for admission; M.S., Ph.D.

Ocean and Resources Engineering. GRE for admission; one language for Ph.D.

Oceanography. GRE for admission; one language, digital computing for Ph.D.

Pacific Islands Studies. GRE for admission; one language for M.A.; M.A.

Philosophy. GRE recommended for native English speakers. Includes Western, Asian, Comparative; two Western languages for Ph.D.

Physics. GRE/Subject for admission. M.S., Ph.D.

Physiology. GRE or MCAT for admission. M.S., Ph.D.

Political Science. GRE for admission.

Psychology. GRE for admission; admits Fall only.

Public Administration. M.P.A. only.

Public Health. GRE for admission; admits Fall only. M.P.H., M.S.

Religion (Asian). M.A.

Russian. M.A.

Second Language Acquisition. GRE for admission. M.A., Ph.D.

Social Welfare. GRE recommended for admission. Ph.D.

Social Work. M.S.W.

Sociology. GRE for admission. M.A., Ph.D.

Spanish. M.A.

Special Education. GRE for admission. M.Ed.

Speech. GRE required for admission.

Speech Pathology and Audiology. GRE required for admission. M.S.

Teaching. M.Ed.T.

Theatre. GRE for admission. Includes history, theory and criticism, fine arts. M.A., M.F.A., Ph.D.

Travel Industry Management. GRE or GMAT for admission. M.S.

Tropical Medicine. GRE/Subject for admission. M.S., Ph.D.

Tropical Plant Pathology. M.S., Ph.D

Tropical Plants and Soil Science. GRE recommended for M.S., required for Ph.D. M.S., Ph.D.

Urban and Regional Planning. GRE for admission. M.U.R.P.

Zoology. GRE/Subject for admission; one language for Ph.D. M.S., Ph.D.

William S. Richardson School of Law (96822)

Web site: www.hawaii.edu/law

Established 1973. ABA approved since 1974. AALS member since 1989. Semester system. Special programs: Environmental/Ocean Law, Pacific-Asian Legal Studies: exchange program with Hiroshima, Japan Law Faculty. Law library: 343,304,4313 subscriptions; has LEXIS, NEXIS, WESTLAW, INNOPAC; more than 250 network connections.

Annual tuition: resident $12,888, nonresident $22,632. On-campus housing available for both single and married students. Estimated living expenses: $13,598.

Enrollment: first-year class 96; total 308 (men 56%, women 44%, minorities 68%). Faculty: full-time 18, part-time 18. Student to faculty ratio 13.6 to 1. Degrees conferred: J.D., J.D.-M.A. (Asian Studies), J.D.-M.B.A., J.D.-M.U.R.P., LL.M. (for foreign legal professionals).

ADMISSION REQUIREMENTS. LSDAS Law School report, bachelor's degree, transcripts, LSAT, two letters of recommendation, residency form required in support of application. Accepts transfer applicants on a space available basis only. TOEFL for applicants from foreign countries. Graduates of unaccredited institutions are not considered. Preference given to state residents; up to 30% of class can be nonresidents. Apply to Office of Admissions by March 1. Application fee $60. Phone: (808)956-3000; fax: (808)956-3813.

ADMISSION STANDARDS. Selective. Accepts approximately 19% of all students. Number of applicants 1091; number of acceptance 203; number enrolled 96; LSAT (75% of students have a score at or above 156); GPA (75% of students have a GPA at or above 3.03). *U.S. News & World Report* ranking is in the second tier tied at 91st of all U.S. law schools.

FINANCIAL AID. Scholarships, Federal W/S, loans. Apply by March 1 to Director of Financial Aid. Phone: (808)956-7251. Use FAFSA. About 35% of students receive some aid from School.

DEGREE REQUIREMENTS. For J.D.: satisfactory completion of 89 credit hours of study. For LL.M.: satisfactory completion of 24-credit two-semester programs.

John A. Burns School of Medicine

Web site: www.jabsom.hawaii.edu

First class entered September 1961, expanded to a four-year program in 1973. Located on Manoa campus. Special facilities: Institute for Biogenesis Research, Sports Medicine and Human Performance, Native Hawaiian Center of Excellence, Center on Aging, Asia-Pacific Institute of Tropical Medicine and Infectious Diseases, Telehealth Research Institute, Clinical Research Center, Pacific Center for Early Human Development, Pacific Center for Emerging Infectious Diseases Research. NIH ranking was 84th with 75 awards/grants worth $67,517,430.

Annual tuition: resident $22,632, nonresident $45,624. No on-campus housing available. Total average figure for all other expenses: $12,000.

Enrollment: first-year class 62 (2 EDP), total 256 (men 45%, women 55%, minorities 79%, state residents 45%); postgraduates 100. Faculty: full-time 225, part-time/volunteers 1297. Degrees conferred: M.D., M.D.-M.S., M.D.-PH.D.

ADMISSION REQUIREMENTS. AMCAS report, MCAT, three years of college, recommendations, and the completion of at least 90 credits are required. Interview by invitation. An evaluation of what the potential student might contribute to the health profession in the Pacific is an integral part of the selection process. Has EDP; apply between June 1 and August 1. Apply through AMCAS after June 1, before November 1. AMCAS application fee $50. Phone: (808)692-1000; fax: (808)956-9547.

ADMISSION STANDARDS. Competitive. Accepts about 15% of all applicants. Number of applications 1629 (n/a out-of-state); number interviewed 337 (173 out-of-state); number of acceptance n/a (n/a out-of-state); number enrolled 62 (6 out-of-state). Mean Composite MCAT 9.0; mean UGPA 3.62 (A = 4).

FINANCIAL AID. Scholarships, NIH stipends, loan fund. Apply after acceptance to University of Hawaii Financial Aids Office. Phone: (808)956-7251. Use FAFSA (School code: 001610). About 80% of students receive some aid from School and outside sources.

DEGREE REQUIREMENTS. For M.D.: satisfactory completion of four-year program and passing USMLE Step 2.

FIELDS OF GRADUATE STUDY.
Cell and Molecular Biology. M.S., Ph.D.
Clinical Research. M.S., Ph.D.
Epidemiology. M.S.
Physiology. M.S., Ph.D.
Tropical Medicine. M.S., Ph.D.

HENDERSON STATE UNIVERSITY
Arkadelphia, Arkansas 71999-0001
Web site: www.hsu.edu

Founded 1890. Located 75 miles SW of Little Rock. Coed. State control. Semester system. Library: 274,639 volumes, 1500 subscriptions. Total University enrollment: 3600.

Tuition: per semester hour, resident $191, nonresident $382. On-campus housing for 600 men, 600 women, 27 married students. Average academic year housing cost: $4100 (room and board) for single students. $400 per month for married students. Apply to Dean, Residence Life. Phone: (870)230-5083.

Graduate Studies

Graduate study since 1954. Enrollment: full-time 105, part-time 265. Faculty teaching graduate students: full-time 55, part-time 9. Degrees conferred: M.A.T., M.L.A., M.S.E., M.S., M B.A.

ADMISSION REQUIREMENTS. Transcripts, GRE/GMAT/MAT required in support of application. TOEFL required for foreign applicants. Accepts transfer applicants. Graduates of unaccredited institutions not considered. Apply to Dean by May 1 (Fall), December 1 (Spring). Application fee none for domestic applicants, $30 for international applicants. Phone: (870)230-5126; fax: (870)230-5479.

ADMISSION STANDARDS. Selective. Usual minimum average: 2.7 (A = 4).

FINANCIAL AID. Annual awards from institutional funds: scholarships, teaching/research assistantships, Federal W/S, loans. Approved for VA benefits. Apply to Dean of Graduate School; no specified closing date. Phone: (870)230-5094; fax: (870)230-5000. Use FAFSA. Aid available for part-time students.

DEGREE REQUIREMENTS. For master's: 30–48 semester hours minimum, at least 24–42 in residence; candidacy; thesis optional for M.S.E.

FIELDS OF STUDY.
Business Administration. M.B.A.
Counseling. Includes community, school. M.S.
Curriculum and Instruction. Includes ESL, middle school, physical education, P–4 education, reading. M.S.E.
Educational Leadership. M.S.E.
English. M.S.E.
Liberal Arts. M.L.A.
Mathematics. M.S.E.
Reading. M.S.E
Recreation. M.S.
School Adminstration. M.S.E.
Social Studies. M.S.E.
Special Education. Includes mild disabilities, early childhood. M.S.E.
Sports Administration. M.S.
Teaching. M.A.T.

HOFSTRA UNIVERSITY
Hempstead, New York 11550-1090
Web site: www.hofstra.edu

Founded 1935. Located 25 miles E of New York City. CGS member. Coed. Private control. Semester system. Library: more than 1,600,000 volumes, 8500 subscriptions. Total University enrollment: 12,900.

Tuition: per credit $670. On-campus housing for both single and married students. Average academic year housing cost: $10,000 (including board). Contact Specialty Housing Coordinator. Phone: (516)463-6936. Day care facilities available.

Graduate Division

Graduate study since 1951. Enrollment: full-time 1200, part-time 1500. Faculty teaching graduate students: full-time 236, part-time 215. Degrees conferred: M.A., M.S., M.B.A., M.P.S., J.D.-M.B.A., C.A.S., Professional Diploma, Ed.D., Psy.D., Ph.D.

ADMISSION REQUIREMENTS. Transcripts, GRE/MAT/GMAT required in support of Divisional application. TOEFL (minimum score 550) required for international applicants. Interview, recommendations required by some departments. Accepts transfer applicants. Graduates of unaccredited institutions not considered. Apply to Admissions Office at least sixty days prior to registration. Application fee $60. Phone: (516)463-4876, fax: (516)463-4664.

ADMISSION STANDARDS. Competitive to very competitive. Usual minimum average: 3.0 (A = 4).

FINANCIAL AID. Scholarships, fellowships, teaching assistantships, tuition waivers, Federal W/S, loans. Approved for VA benefits. Apply to appropriate department chairman for scholarships or assistantships; to the Financial Aid Office of all other programs. Phone: (516)463-6680; fax: (516)463-4936. Use FAFSA. Aid available for part-time students.

DEGREE REQUIREMENTS. For M.A.: 30–36 semester hours minimum, at least 24 in residence; master's essay; one language or knowledge of statistics for many majors; oral/written comprehensive exam; thesis/nonthesis option. For M.S.: 30–37 semester hours minimum, at least 24 in residence; comprehensive exam or alternative; thesis/nonthesis option. For M.B.A.: 36 hours minimum, at least 24 in residence; thesis/nonthesis option; comprehensive exam. For C.A.S., Professional Diploma: 30 hours beyond the master's. For Ed.D.: 90 semester hours minimum; preliminary exam, research project; final oral exam. For Ph.D.: 93 semester hours minimum, at least one year in full-time residence; preliminary exam; reading knowledge of one foreign language; dissertation; final oral exam.

FIELDS OF STUDY.

HOFSTRA COLLEGE OF LIBERAL ARTS AND SCIENCES:
Applied Linguistics. M.A.
Applied Mathematics. M.S.
Audiology. M.A.
Bilingualism. M.A.
Biology. M.A., M.S.
Clinical and School Psychology. Ph.D.
Clinical/School Psychology. Psy.D.
Computer Science. M.A., M.S.
English. M.A.
English and Creative Writing. M.A.
Humanities. M.A.
Industrial/Organizational Psychology. M.A.
Mathematics. M.A.
School-Community Psychology. Psy.D.
Speech-Language Pathology. M.A.

NEW COLLEGE:
Interdisciplinary Studies. M.A.

FRANK G. ZARB SCHOOL OF BUSINESS:
Accounting. M.S.
Accounting and Taxation. M.S.
Accounting Information Systems. M.S.
Business Administration. M.B.A., E.M.B.A.
Computer Information Systems. M.S.
Finance. M.S.
Health Services Management. M.B.A.
Human Resource Management. M.S.
International Business. M.B.A.
Marketing Research. M.S.
Quality Management. M.B.A.
Taxation. M.S.

SCHOOL OF COMMUNICATION:
Journalism. M.A.
Speech Communication and Rhetorical Studies. M.A.

SCHOOL OF EDUCATION AND ALLIED HUMAN SERVICES:
Art Education. M.A., M.S.Ed.
Bilingual Elementary Education. M.S.Ed.
Bilingual Secondary Education. M.S.Ed.
Counseling. M.S., M.S.Ed.
Creative Arts Therapy. M.A.
Early Childhood Education (PreK–6). M.S.
Early Childhood Special Education. M.S.Ed.
Educational Administration. Ed.D.
Educational Administration and Policy Studies. M.S., M.S.Ed.
Elementary Education (PreK–6). M.S.
English Education. M.A., M.S.Ed.
Foreign Language Education. M.A., M.S.Ed.
Gerontology. M.S.
Health Administration. M.A.
Health Education. M.S.Ed.
Literacy Studies. M.S.Ed.
Marriage and Family Therapy. M.A.
Mental Health Counseling. M.A.
Physical Education. M.S.
Program Evaluation. M.S., M.S.Ed.
Reading. M.S.
Reading and Special Education. M.S.Ed.
Reading, Language, and Cognition. Ed.D., Ph.D.
Reading, Language, and Cognition—Bilingual/Bicultural. Ed.D., Ph.D.

Rehabilitation Counseling. M.S., M.S.Ed.
Science Education. M.A., M.S.Ed.
Secondary Education. M.S.
Special Education. M.S., M.S.Ed.
Special Education and Art Therapy. M.S.Ed.
Teaching English as a Second Language. M.S.
Teaching of Writing. M.A.

School of Law
Web site: www.hofstra.edu/law

Established 1970. ABA approved since 1971. AALS member. Private control. Semester system. Special facilities: The Center for Children, Families and the Law, Center for Legal Advocacy, Institute for Health Law and Policy, Institute for the Study of Conflict Transformation, Institute for the Study of Gender, Law and Policy, Institute for the Study of Legal Ethics. Special programs: summer study abroad at the University of Nice, France; Sorrento, Italy; Sydney, Australia. Law library: 550,765 volumes, 5952 subscriptions; has LEXIS, NEXIS, WESTLAW, DIALOG; has more than 150 network connections.

Annual tuition: full-time $35,260, per credit $1235; LL.M. full-time 34,500. part-time $22,000. Law students tend to live off-campus. Off-campus housing and personal expenses: approximately $14,710.

Enrollment: first-year class 269, part-time 117; total full- and part-time 1130 (men 53%, women 47%, minorities 22%). Faculty: full-time 60, part-time 50, minorities 9%. Student to faculty ratio 17.7 to 1. Degrees conferred: J.D., J.D.-M.B.A., LL.M. (American Legal Studies, Family Law, International Law).

ADMISSION REQUIREMENTS. LSDAS report, bachelor's degree, transcript, SAT, one letter of recommendation, personal statement required in support of application. Accepts transfer applicants. Graduates of unaccredited colleges not considered. Apply to Admissions Office after October 1, before April 15. Admits Fall only. For Early Decision program, apply by December 1. Application fee $60. Phone: (516)463-5916; fax: (516)463-6264. For LL.M.: apply by July 1 (Fall), November 1 (Spring).

ADMISSION STANDARDS. Selective. Accepts approximately 38% of full-time and 38% of part-time applicants. Number of full-time applicants 4535, part-time 696; number of full-time acceptance 1724, part-time 267; number full-time enrolled 269, part-time 117; LSAT (75% of full-time students have a score at or above 155, part-time 152); GPA (75% of full-time students have a GPA at or above 3.03, part-time 2.91). *U.S. News & World Report* ranking is in the third tier of all U.S. law schools.

FINANCIAL AID. Scholarships, grants, full and partial tuition waivers, assistantships, Federal W/S, loans. Apply to University Financial Aid Office by April 1. Phone: (516)463-5929. Use FAFSA (School code: 002732). About 56% of students receive aid other than loans from School and outside sources.

DEGREE REQUIREMENTS. For J D.: satisfactory completion of three-year (87 credit hours) program. For J.D.-M.B.A.: 105–108 credit program; thesis/nonthesis option. For LL.M.: 24 credit hour, full-time, two-semester program; a part-time four-semester program is also available.

HOLLINS UNIVERSITY
Roanoke, Virginia 24020-1688
Web site: www.hollins.edu

Established 1842. Located 6 miles N of Roanoke. Coed at graduate level. Private control. Semester system. Library: 220,000 volumes, 6380 subscriptions. Total University enrollment: 1150.

Annual tuition: full-time $23,760, per credit varies by program. No on-campus housing for graduate students.

Graduate Programs

Enrollment: full-time 180, part-time 145. Graduate faculty: full-time 25, part-time 27. Degrees conferred: M.A., M.A.L.S., M.A.T., C.A.S.

ADMISSION REQUIREMENTS. Transcripts, GRE Subject Tests required in support of School's application. Online application avaiable. Interview not required. TOEFL required for international applicants. Transfer applicants, graduates of unaccredited colleges not considered. Apply to Office of Admissions by March 15, one month prior to registration for other sessions. Application fee $40. Phone: (540)362-6575; fax: (540)362-6288.

ADMISSION STANDARDS. Competitive. Usual minimum average: 3.0 (A = 4)

FINANCIAL AID. Scholarships, fellowships, grants, research fellowships, work stipends, Federal W/S, loans. Approved for VA benefits. Apply by April 15 to Chair of Graduate Council for scholarships, grants, fellowships; apply by July 15 to Financial Aid Office for all other programs. Phone: (540)362-6332; fax: (540)362-6093. Use FAFSA and Institutional FAF. All M.A. graduate students receive aid from College. About 50% of students receive aid other than loans from College and outside sources. Aid available for part-time students.

DEGREE REQUIREMENTS. For M.A., M.A.L.S., M.A.T.: 30–40 semester hours minimum; final oral/written exam; thesis/final document. For C.A.S.: 30 semester hours minimum beyond master's; special project.

FIELDS OF STUDY.
Children's Literature. Primarily a summer program. Four to five summer sessions for completion of degree requirements.
Classroom Technology Integration.
Creative Writing.
Dance. M.F.A.
English. One language for M.A.
Humanities. M.A.L.S.
Liberal Studies. Interdisciplinary. M.A.L.S.
Psychology.
Social Science. M.A.L.S.
Screenwriting and Film Studies.
Teaching. At least three years of teaching experience required for admissions. M.A.T.

HOLY NAMES UNIVERSITY
Oakland, California 94619-1699
Web site: www.hnu.edu

Founded 1868. Private control. Roman Catholic. Primarily women. Semester system. Library: 111,062 volumes, 376 subscriptions.
Tuition: per credit $635. On-campus housing for single students only. Average academic year room and board cost: $10,290. Apply to Director of Residents for off-campus housing information. Phone: (510)436-1292.

Graduate Programs

Graduate study since 1956. Enrollment: full-time 125, part-time 219 (men 10%, women 90%). College faculty teaching graduate students: full-time 23, part-time 33. Degrees conferred: M.A., M.S., M.M. in Mus. Ed., M.Ed., M.B.A.

ADMISSION REQUIREMENTS. Two transcripts, two letters of recommendation required in support of Divisional application. TOEFL required for international applicants. Interview and NTE required for Education, Clinical Psychology, Pastoral Counseling. Graduates of unaccredited colleges not considered. Apply to the Office of Adult and Graduate Admission at least six to eight weeks prior to registration. Application fee $65. Phone: (510) 436-1351; fax: (510)436-1325.

ADMISSION STANDARDS. Selective. Minimum average: 2.6 cumulative, 3.0 in major (A = 4).

FINANCIAL AID. Annual awards from institutional funds: Scholarships, Kodaly grants, Federal W/S, loans. Apply to Director of Financial Aid by March 2. Phone: (510)436-1327. Use FAFSA. About 40% of students receive financial aid. Aid available for part-time students.

DEGREE REQUIREMENTS. For master's: 30–36 semester hours; thesis, project or final comprehensive exam, recital.

FIELDS OF STUDY.
Business Administration.
Counseling Psychology.
Culture and Spirituality.
Education.
English.
Music. Includes performance, piano pedagogy, music education with Kodaly emphasis; preliminary qualifying exam.
Nursing.
Pastoral Counseling.

HOOD COLLEGE
Frederick, Maryland 21701-8575
Web site: www.hood.edu

College founded 1895. Located 45 miles from Washington, D.C. CGS member. Private. Semester system. Library: 200,000 volumes, 1200 subscriptions. Total College enrollment: 2100.
Tuition: per credit hour $350. No on-campus housing available.

Graduate School

Enrollment: full-time 59, part-time 875. Faculty: full- and part-time 90. Degrees conferred: M.A., M.B.A., M.S.

ADMISSION REQUIREMENTS. Transcripts, two letters of recommendation, statement of goals required in support of application. GMAT required for Business applicants. TOEFL required for international applicants. Interview recommended. Accepts transfer applicants. Graduates of unaccredited colleges not considered. Apply to Graduate Enrollment Manager. Application fee $35. Phone: (301)696-3600; fax: (301)696-3597; e-mail: hood-grad@hood.edu.

ADMISSION STANDARDS. Selective. Usual minimum average: 2.5 (A = 4).

FINANCIAL AID. Scholarships, internships, tuition waivers, Federal W/S, loans. Phone: (301)696-3411. Use FAFSA (College code: 002076). Aid available for part-time students.

DEGREE REQUIREMENTS. For M.A., M.S.: 30–39 credit hours minimum; thesis required in some programs; comprehensive written exam. For M.B.A.: 36 credit hours minimum.

FIELDS OF STUDY.
Biomedical Sciences. Includes biotechnology/molecular biology, microbiology/immunology/virology, regulatory compliance. M.S.B.S.

Business Administration. Includes accounting, finance, human resource management, information systems, marketing, public management. M.B.A.

Computer and Information Sciences. Includes computer science, information technology. M.S.C.I.S.

Curriculum and Instruction. Includes early childhood education, elementary education, elementary school science and mathematics, reading specialist, secondary education, special education. M.S.C.I.

Educational Leadership. M.S.E.L.

Environmental Biology. M.S.E.B.

Human Science. Includes psychology. M.A.H.S.

Humanities. Includes general/experimental psychology, gerontology, helping relationships. M.A.H.

Management of Information Technology. M.S.M.I.T.

Thanatology. M.A.

UNIVERSITY OF HOUSTON

Houston, Texas 77004
Web site: www.uh.edu

Founded 1934. CGS member. Coed. State control. Semester system. Special facilities: Blaffer Gallery, Center for Critical Cultural Studies, Institute for Molecular Design, Institute for Public History, Center for Public Policy, Southwest Center for International Business, Space Vacuum Epitaxy Center, Center for Study of Issues Management, Texas Center for Superconductivity, Institute for Texas German Studies. Library: 2,100,000 volumes, 15,203 subscriptions; is a depository for U.S. and Texas government documents. Total University enrollment: 35,300.

Tuition: per credit resident $244 (Architecture), $352 (Business), $211 (Liberal Arts, Education), $245 (Engineering), $231 (H&RM), $221 (Natural Sciences, Technology), $365 (Optometry), $233 (Social Work); per credit nonresident $522 (Architecture), $630 (Business), $496 (Liberal Arts), $489 (Education), $523 (Engineering), $509 (H&RM), $499 (Natural Sciences, Technology), $643 (Optometry), $511 (Social Work). On-campus housing for 2600 single students; for 200 married students. Average academic year housing cost: $5475 (including board) for single students; $8856 (including board) for married students. Contact Director of Housing for both on- and off-campus housing information. Phone: (800)247-7184. Day-care facilities available.

Graduate Division

Graduate study since 1939. Enrollment: full-time 3800, part-time 2525. Graduate faculty: full-time 588, part-time 337. Degrees conferred: M.A., M.S., M.S.A., M.B.A., M.Ed., M.M., M.Arch., M.S.Accy., M.S.A., M.S.Ch.E., M.Ch.E., M.S.C.E., M.C.E., M.S.E.E., M.E.E., M.H.M., M.S.I.E., M.I.E., M.S.M.E., M.M.E., M.F.A., M.S.Phar., M.S.O.T., Ed.D., Ph.D., D.M.A., O.D.

ADMISSION REQUIREMENTS. Two official transcripts, GRE/GMAT/MAT required in support of application. Interview required for some departments. Departmental applications in some cases. TOEFL required for international applicants. Accepts transfer applicants. Graduates of unaccredited colleges not considered. Apply to Director of Admissions; deadlines vary by Schools. Rolling admissions process. International applicants should apply to International Student Office by May 1. Application fees vary by Schools. Phone: (713)743-1010; fax: (713)743-9653; e-mail: admissions@uh.edu.

ADMISSION STANDARDS. Very competitive for some departments, selective for others. Usual minimum average: 3.0 for most departments, 2.6 for conditional admission to most departments (A = 4).

FINANCIAL AID. Annual awards from institutional funds: fellowships, assistantships, Federal W/S, loans. Approved for VA benefits. Apply by March 1 to appropriate department chair for assistantships, fellowships; to the Financial Aid Office for all other programs. About 20% of students receive aid from University and outside sources. Aid available for part-time students.

DEGREE REQUIREMENTS. For M.A., M.S.: 30 semester hours minimum, at least 24 in residence; qualifying exam; thesis, final exam; or 36 hours minimum, at least 27 in residence; qualifying exam; final comprehensive exam. For M.B.A.: 48 semester hours minimum, at least 27 in residence. For M.Ed.: 36 semester hours minimum, at least 27 in residence; comprehensive written exam; or 30 semester hours minimum, at least 24 in residence; written comprehensive exam; thesis; final oral exam. For M.M.: 30 semester hours minimum, at least 24 in residence; thesis; final oral exam. For M.S.O.T.: 30–36 semester hours; thesis. For M.F.A.: 60 semester hours; one year in residence; written and oral comprehensive exam. For M.S.W.: 63 semester hours. For Ed.D.: 66 semester hours minimum beyond the master's, at least 30 in residence and 24 consecutive hours in full-time attendance; qualifying exam; dissertation; final written/oral exams. For D.M.A.: 60 semester hours minimum beyond master's; four public performances, written and oral comprehensive exams; research document. For Ph.D.: two to four years beyond the master's, at least one year in full-time residence; reading knowledge of one or two foreign languages; comprehensive exam; dissertation; final oral exams.

FIELDS OF STUDY.

GERALD D. HINES COLLEGE OF ARCHITECTURE:
Architecture.

C. T. BAUER COLLEGE OF BUSINESS:
Accountancy. M.S.
Administration. M.S.
Business Administration. M.B.A.
Decision and Information Sciences. M.B.A., Ph.D.
Finance. M.S., Ph.D.
Management. Ph.D.
Management Information Systems. Ph.D.
Marketing. Ph.D.
Operations Research. Ph.D.
Statistics. Ph.D.
Taxation. Ph.D.

COLLEGE OF EDUCATION:
Allied Health Education and Administration.
Art Education.
Bilingual Education.
Counseling.
Counseling Psychology.
Curriculum and Instruction.
Early Childhood Education.
Educational Administration and Supervision.
Educational Psychology.
Educational Psychology and Individual Differences.
Elementary Education.
Exercise Science.
Gifted and Talented Education.
Health Education.
Higher Education.
Historical, Social and Cultural Education.
Instructional Technology.
Kinesiology.
Mathematics Education.
Physical Education.
Reading and Language Arts.
Science Education.
Second Language Education.

Secondary Education.
Social Studies Education.
Special Education.

CULLEN COLLEGE OF ENGINEERING:
Aerospace Engineering.
Biomedical Engineering.
Chemical Engineering.
Civil and Environmental Engineering.
Computer and Systems Engineering.
Electrical and Computer Engineering.
Environmental Engineering.
Industrial Engineering.
Materials Engineering.
Mechanical Engineering.
Petroleum Engineering.

CONRAD HILTON COLLEGE OF HOTEL AND RESTAURANT
MANAGEMENT:
Hospitality Management.

COLLEGE OF LIBERAL ARTS AND SOCIAL SCIENCES:
Accompanying.
Anthropology.
Applied Music.
Art. Includes interior design, graphic communication, painting, photography, sculpture.
Ceramics.
Clinical Psychology.
Communication.
Communication Disorders.
Composition.
Conducting.
Creative Writing.
Economics.
English.
French.
German.
History.
Literature and Creative Writing.
Mass Communication Studies.
Music Education.
Music Literature.
Music Performance and Pedagogy.
Music Theory.
Organizational and Interpersonal Studies.
Philosophy.
Political Science.
Psychology.
Public History.
Public Relations Studies.
Sociology.
Spanish.
Speech Communication.
Theatre.

COLLEGE OF NATURAL SCIENCE AND MATHEMATICS:
Applied Mathematics.
Biochemical Sciences.
Biochemistry.
Biology. Includes evolutionary.
Chemistry. Includes analytical, biological, inorganic, organic, physical, theoretical.
Computer Science.
Geology.
Geophysics.
Mathematics.
Physics.

COLLEGE OF OPTOMETRY:
Optometry.
Physiological Optics.

COLLEGE OF PHARMACY:
Hospital Pharmacy and Pharmacy Administration.
Pharmaceutics.
Pharmacology.
Pharmacy Administration.

GRADUATE SCHOOL OF SOCIAL WORK:
Social Work.

COLLEGE OF TECHNOLOGY:
Construction Management Technology.
Industrial Technology.
Information and Logistics Technology.
Manufacturing Systems Technology.
Microcomputer Systems Technology.
Occupational Technology. Includes industrial distribution.

Law Center (77204-6390)

Web site: www.law.uh.edu

Established 1974 as a College of Law. Located in metropolitan Houston. ABA approved since 1950. AALS member. Public control. Semester system. Full-time, part-time study. Special facilities: Health Law and Policy Institute, Institute for Higher Education Law and Governance, Institute for Intellectual Property and Information Law, International Law Institute, Trial Advocacy Institute. Special programs: Mexican Legal Studies Program. Law library: 501,862 volumes, 3850 subscriptions; has LEXIS, NEXIS, WESTLAW, DIALOG; is a Federal Government Depository.

Annual tuition: full-time resident $15,922, part-time $8,348. Limited on-campus housing available. Estimated living expense: $15,126.

Enrollment: first-year class 318 (261 day, 57 evening); total full- and part-time 1007 (men 57%, women 43%, minorities 27%); LL.M. total 120. Faculty: full-time 80, part-time 155. Student to faculty ratio 16.6 to 1. Degrees conferred: J.D., J.D.-M.B.A., J.D.-M.P.H. (University of Texas, School of Public Health), J.D.-M.A. (History, Rice University), J.D.-M.S.W., J.D.-Ph.D., J.D.-M.D. (Baylor University), LL.M. (Energy, Environmental, and Natural Resources Law, Health Law, International Economic Law, Intellectual Property Law, Tax), LL.M. (Comparative Law for persons who have completed a basic legal education and received a university degree in law in another country).

ADMISSION REQUIREMENTS. LSDAS report, bachelor's degree, transcripts, LSAT (not later than December), personal statement, résumé, two letters of recommendation required in support of application. Interview not required. Accepts transfer applicants. Graduates of unaccredited colleges not considered. Apply to Law Center after September 1, before February 15. For Early Decision program, applied by November 1. Modified rolling admission process. Part-time students begin studies in summer only. Application fee $50. Phone: (713)743-2280.

ADMISSION STANDARDS. Selective. Accepts approximately 25% of full-time and 19% of part-time applicants. Number of full-time applicants 3242, part-time 430; number of full-time acceptance 813, part-time 83; number full-time enrolled 261, part-time 57; LSAT (75% of full-time students have a score at or above 157, part-time 158); GPA (75% of full-time students have a GPA at or above 3.22, part-time 3.02). U.S. News & World Report ranking is in the second tier tied at 66th of all U.S. law schools.

FINANCIAL AID. Scholarships, teaching assistantships, Federal W/S, loans. Apply after acceptance, by April 1 to Financial Aid Office. Phone (713)743-2269. Use FAFSA. About 40% of students receive aid other than loans from College. Aid available for part-time students.

DEGREE REQUIREMENTS. For J.D.: 88 semester credits minimum, at least 44 in residence. For LL.M.: 24 semester credits, 18 in residence (concentrations in Energy, Environmental, and

Natural Resources Law; Health Law; Intellectual Property Law; International Law; Taxation Law).

UNIVERSITY OF HOUSTON, CLEAR LAKE
Houston, Texas 77058-1098
Web site: www.cl.uh.edu

Founded 1974. Located between Houston and Galveston, adjacent to NASA's Johnson Space Center. CGS member. Coed. State control. Semester system. Library: 405,797 volumes, 2200 subscriptions. Total University enrollment: 7500.

Tuition: per credit resident $218, nonresident $513. No on-campus housing available. Day-care facilities available.

Graduate Studies

Graduate study since 1974. Enrollment: full-time 1075, part-time 2554. Graduate faculty: full- and part-time 234. Degrees conferred: M.A., M.S., M.B.A., M.H.A., M.B.A.-M.H.A.

ADMISSION REQUIREMENTS. Two official transcripts, GRE/GMAT/MAT required in support of application. Interview required for some departments. Departmental applications in some cases. TOEFL (minimum score 550) required for international applicants. Accepts transfer applicants. Graduates of unaccredited colleges not considered. Apply to Office of Enrollment Services by August 1 (Fall), October 1 (Spring), May 1 (Summer); international applicants apply by June 1 (Fall), October 1 (Spring), March 1 (Summer). Some programs have earlier deadlines. Rolling admissions process. Application fees $35, $75 for international applicants. Admissions Office phone: (281)263-2517; fax: (281) 283-2530.

ADMISSION STANDARDS. Selective for most programs. Usual minimum average: 2.75 (A = 4) for most departments.

FINANCIAL AID. Annual awards from institutional funds: scholarships, assistantships, Federal W/S, loans. Approved for VA benefits. Apply by March 1 to appropriate department chair for assistantships; to the Financial Aid Office for all other programs. Phone: (281)283-2480. Use FAFSA (School code: 011711). About 20% of students receive aid from University and outside sources. Aid available for part-time students.

DEGREE REQUIREMENTS. For M.A., M.S.: 30 semester hours minimum, at least 24 in residence; qualifying exam; thesis, final exam; or 36 hours minimum, at least 27 in residence; qualifying exam; final comprehensive exam. For M.B.A., M.H.A.: 36 semester hours minimum, at least 27 in residence.

FIELDS OF STUDY.

SCHOOL OF BUSINESS AND PUBLIC ADMINISTRATION:
Accounting. M.S.
Business Administration. Includes environmental management, international business, human resource management, management information systems, management of technology, studies of the future. M.B.A.
Environmental Management. M.S.
Finance. Includes health care administration. M.S.
Healthcare Administration. M.H.A.
Human Resource Management. M.A.
Management Information Systems. M.S.

SCHOOL OF EDUCATION:
Counseling. M.S.
Curriculum and Instruction. M.S.
Early Childhood Education. M.S.

Education Leadership. Ed.D.
Educational Management. M.S.
Instructional Technology. M.S.
Learning Resources. M.S.
Multicultural Studies in Education. M.S.
Reading. M.S.
School Library and Information Science. M.S.

SCHOOL OF HUMAN SCIENCES AND HUMANITIES:
Behavior Sciences. M.A.
Cross-Cultural Studies. M.A.
Family Therapy. M.A.
Fitness and Human Performance. M.A.
General Clinical Psychology. M.A.
History. M.A.
Humanities. M.A.
Literature. M.A.
Psychology. M.A.
School Psychology. M.A.
Sociology. M.A.
Studies of the Future. M.S.

COLLEGE OF SCIENCE AND COMPUTER ENGINEERING:
Biology. M.S.
Biotechnology. M.S.
Chemistry. M.S.
Computer Engineering. M.S.
Computer Information Systems. M.S.
Computer Science. M.S.
Engineering Management. M.S.
Environmental Science. M.S.
Mathematical Sciences. M.S.
Physics. M.S., Ph.D. (Collaborative program with UH).
Software Engineering. M.S.
Statistics. M.S.
Systems Engineering. M.S.

HOWARD UNIVERSITY
Washington, D.C. 20059-0002
Web site: www.howard.edu

Founded 1867. CGS member. Private control. Howard participates in Joint Graduate Consortium with George Washington, Georgetown, and Catholic universities, the University of the District of Columbia, and three Associate Members (Gallaudet, Mount Vernon, and Trinity colleges). Founders Library for graduate students ranks among top 100 in the United States and Canada. Special facilities: Computer Center, Laser Chemistry Laboratory, Solid-State Electronics Laboratory, Center for Hypertension Control, 5 specialized research institutes, Cancer Research Center, Center for Sickle Cell Disease, modern 500-bed teaching hospital, 5-million-watt public educational television station (WHMM, Channel 32), 24-thousand-watt commercial radio station (WHUF-FM, 96.3 MHz), and the Moorland-Spingarn Research Center, which houses the world's most comprehensive collection of materials on Africa and persons of African descent. The University's NIH ranking is 109th among all U.S. institutions with 42 awards/grants worth $22,619,325. Library: 1,729,875 volumes, 1,453,000 microforms.

Annual tuition: full-time $14,064; part-time, per credit hour, $781. On-campus housing usually unavailable. Off-campus academic year cost: $12,700 (including board). Contact Supervisor of Off-Campus Housing. Phone: (202)806-5749.

Graduate School

Graduate study since 1919. Enrollment: full- and part-time 1200. Graduate faculty: full- and part-time 360. Degrees conferred: M.A., M.S., M.Eng., M.S.C.S., Ph.D.

ADMISSION REQUIREMENTS. Transcripts, GRE, three letters of recommendation, statement of intent, résumé, personal biography required in support of School's application. Online application available. TOEFL required for all international applicants. Interview not required. Transfer applicants accepted. Graduates from unaccredited institutions not considered. Apply to the Office of Student Relations and Enrollment Management by February 15 (Fall), October 1 (Spring), March 15 (Summer). Application fee $45. Phone: (202)806-6800; fax: (202)806-4053; e-mail: hugsadmission@howard.edu.

ADMISSION STANDARDS. Selective. Usual minimum average: 3.0 (A = 4).

FINANCIAL AID. Scholarships, graduate assistantships, fellowships, teaching assistantships, traineeships, Federal W/S, loans. Apply by April 1 (Fall), February 1 (Clinical Psychology), November 1 (Spring), March 15 (Summer) to appropriate department for assistantships; to Financial Aid Office for scholarships and other financial aid programs. Phone: (202)806-2820; fax: (202)806-2818. Use FAFSA (School code: 001448). About 43% of students receive aid other than loans from University and outside sources. No aid for part-time students.

DEGREE REQUIREMENTS. For master's: 30 semester hours minimum, at least two semesters in residence; qualifying exam; admission to candidacy; thesis/nonthesis option; reading knowledge of one foreign language in some departments; demonstrated proficiency in expository writing; final/oral exam. For Ph.D.: 72 semester hours minimum beyond the bachelor's degree, at least four semesters in full-time residence (two of which are consecutive); reading knowledge of two foreign languages in some departments; qualifying exam; admission to candidacy; dissertation; final written/oral (defense) exam.

FIELDS OF STUDY.
African Studies. Includes development studies and public policy. M.A., Ph.D.
Anatomy. Includes cell biology, developmental biology, neuroanatomy & neurophysiology, gross anatomy/paleontology. M.S., Ph.D.
Art. Includes art history. M.A.
Atmospheric Science. Ph.D.
Biochemistry. Includes enzymology, metabolism, molecular biology, biochemical nutrition, clinical biochemistry. M.S., Ph.D.
Biology. Includes cell and molecular biology, ecological, environmental and systematic biology. M.S., Ph.D.
Chemical Engineering. M.S.
Chemistry. Includes analytical, biochemistry, inorganic, laser, organic, physical, theoretical. M.S., Ph.D.
Civil Engineering. Includes environmental and water resources engineering, structural and engineering mechanics, transportation systems engineering, geotechnical engineering. M.S.
Communication and Culture. M.A., Ph.D.
Communication Science and Disorders. Includes speech pathology, audiology (M.S. only). M.S., Ph.D.
Economics. Includes development economics, urban economics, monetary/fiscal economics, human resource economics. M.A., Ph.D.
Education. Includes counseling, school psychology, educational psychology, educational administration and policy, curriculum and instruction, human development. M.A., M.S. Ph.D.
Electrical Engineering. Includes antennas and microwaves, solid state electronics, control engineering and power systems, communications and signal processing (M.Eng.); communications and signal processing, applied microelectronics and solid state electronics, control engineering and power systems (Ph.D.). M.Eng., Ph.D.
English. Includes African American literature, American literature, Caribbean literature, British literature, literary criticism. M.A., Ph.D.

Genetics and Human Genetics. Includes biochemical and molecular genetics, cytogenetics, immogenetics, clinical genetics–genetic counseling. M.S., Ph.D.
Health, Human Performance and Leisure. Includes exercise physiology, recreation and leisure studies, health education. M.S. only.
History. Includes United States history, Africa, African diaspora, Latin American and the Caribbean, modern Europe (M.A. only). M.A., Ph.D.
Mass Communication and Media Studies. M.A., Ph.D.
Material Science and Engineering. Ph.D.
Mathematics. M.S., Ph.D.
Mechanical Engineering. Includes aerospace, applied mechanics, fluid and thermal sciences, CAD/CAM and robotics. M.Eng., Ph.D.
Microbiology. Includes immunology, molecular and cellular microbiology, microbial genetics, microbial physiology, pathogenic bacteriology, medical mycology, medical parasitology, virology. Ph.D.
Modern Languages and Literatures. Includes French, Spanish, Afro-Hispanic. M.A.
Nutritional Sciences. M.S., Ph.D.
Pharmacology. Includes cardiovascular, neurobehavioral, toxicology, biochemical, clinical. M.S., Ph.D.
Philosophy. Includes history of philosophy, philosophy of science, political, African, epistemology metaphysics. M.A.
Physics and Astronomy. Includes astronomy/astrophysics, atomic/molecular physics, biophysics, condensed matter physics, magnetic/optical properties, laser/optical spectroscopy, theoretical physics, M.S., Ph.D.
Physiology and Biophysics. Includes neurophysiology, endocrinology and cellular physiology, cardiovascular physiology, pulmonary physiology, membrane biophysics, renal physiology. Ph.D.
Political Science. Includes American government and politics, public administration and public policy, comparative government, international relations, political theory, black politics and political economy. M.A., Ph.D.
Psychology. Includes clinical, developmental, experimental personality, social. M.S., Ph.D.
Social Work. Ph.D.
Sociology and Anthropology. Includes demography, medical sociology, sociology of aging, social control and deviance, social psychology, urbanization and developmental, race and ethnic relations. M.A., Ph.D.
Systems and Computer Sciences. Includes programming and languages, software engineering, graphics, artificial intelligence, fault-tolerant computing, systems design and analysis. M.C.S.

College of Dentistry
600 W Street, N.W. 20059
Web site: www.dentistry.howard.edu

Organized 1881. Semester system. Library: 85,000 volumes, 850 subscriptions.
Annual tuition: $29,518. No on-campus housing available. Off-campus housing cost: approximately $15,000. Total average cost of all other first year expenses: $7500.
Enrollment: first-year class 83, total 338 (men 45%, women 55%, minorities 78%, state residents 20%). Faculty: full-time 16, part-time 21. Degrees conferred: B.S.-D.D.S. (with Howard University's College of Liberal Arts), D.D.S.

ADMISSION REQUIREMENTS. AADSAS report, transcripts, three letters of recommendation, DAT required in support of College's application. Applicants must have completed at least two years of college study. Apply to Dean after July 1, before February 1. Application fee $45. Phone: (202)806-0400; fax: (202)806-0354.

ADMISSION STANDARDS. Competitive. Accepts about 5–10% of all applicants. Usual minimum UGPA: 2.70 (A = 4). Mean DAT: academic 16, PAT 15; mean UGPA 3.1.

FINANCIAL AID. Limited scholarships, loans. Apply to Financial Aid Committee by July 1. Approximately 83% of students receive some aid from Institution. Phone: (202)806-0375. Use FAFSA (College code: 001448).

DEGREE REQUIREMENTS. For D.D.S.: satisfactory completion of 42-month program.

FIELDS OF POSTGRADUATE STUDY.
Advanced Education Program in General Dentistry.
General Practice Residency.
Oral and Maxillofacial Surgery.
Orthodontics.
Pediatric Dentistry.

College of Medicine

Web site: www.med.howard.edu

Organized 1968. Library: 265,000, 1750 subscriptions. NIH ranking is 169th with 42 awards/grants worth $22,619,328.

Annual tuition: $25,691. Very limited on-campus housing. Contact Dean of Resident Life for both on- and off-campus housing information. Total average figure for all other expenses: $15,600.

Enrollment: first-year class 116, total 458 (men 48%, women 52%, minorities 96%, District residents 4%). Faculty: full-time 240, part-time 168. Degrees conferred: M.D., M.D.-M.S., M.D.-Ph.D. The M.S. and Ph.D. are offered through the Graduate School.

ADMISSION REQUIREMENTS. AMCAS report, transcripts, three letters of recommendation, MCAT, supplemental application required in support of application. Interview by invitation. Applicants must have completed at least three years of college study. Accepts transfer applicants. Does not have EDP. Apply to AMCAS after June 1, before December 15. Application fee $45. Phone: (202)806-6279; fax: (202)806-7934.

ADMISSION STANDARDS. Competitive. Accepts about 5.9% of all applicants. Number of applications 4131 (4031 out-of-District); number interviewed 369 (342 out-of-District); number of acceptance 243 (11 out-of-District); number enrolled 116 (108 out-of-District). Mean Composite MCAT 8.2; mean UGPA 3.34 (A = 4).

FINANCIAL AID. Scholarships, grants, fellowships, assistantships, HEAL, Federal and private loans. Apply to Office of the Dean before May 1. Phone: (202)806-6388. Use FAFSA (College code: 001448). About 92% of students receive some aid.

DEGREE REQUIREMENTS. For M.D.: satisfactory completion of four-year program, at least the final two years in residence; must pass Step 1 of USMLE for promotion to third year, Step 2 of USMLE for graduation. For M.S., Ph.D.: see Graduate School listing above.

FIELDS OF GRADUATE STUDY.
Anatomy.
Biochemistry and Molecular Biology.
Biology.
Chemistry.
Human Genetics.
Microbiology.
Pharmacology.
Physiology and Biophysics.

School of Law (20008)

Web site: www.law.howard.edu

Organized 1868. ABA approved since 1931. AALS member. Private control. Semester system. Special facility: Institute for Intellectual Property and Social Justice. Law library: 620,633 volumes, 2656 subscriptions; has LEXIS, NEXIS, WESTLAW, CALI, OCLC, LEGAL-TRAC; has more than 500 network connections.

Annual tuition: $18,870. Total average annual additional expense: $17,641.

Enrollment: first-year class 140, total 430 (men 39%, women 61%, minorities 84%). Faculty: full-time 33, part-time 33. Student to faculty ratio 13.0 to 1. Degrees conferred: J.D., J.D.-M.B.A., LL.M. (for foreign law graduates).

ADMISSION REQUIREMENTS. LSDAS Law School report, bachelor's degree, LSAT (GMAT for J.D.-M.B.A. program), transcripts, two letters of recommendation, personal statement, résumé required in support of application. International applicants must submit credentials to J.D. Credential Assembly Service. Applicants must have completed at least four years of college study. Accepts transfer applicants. Graduates of unaccredited colleges not considered. Apply to University Office of Admissions after September 1, before March 31. Application fee $60. Phone: (202)806-8009.

ADMISSION STANDARDS. Selective. Accepts approximately 23% of all students. Number of applicants 2373; number of acceptance 551; number enrolled 159; LSAT (75% of students have a score at or above 148); GPA (75% of students have a GPA at or above 2.93). *U.S. News & World Report* ranking is in the 3rd tier of all U.S. law schools.

FINANCIAL AID. Scholarships, grants, Federal W/S, loans. Apply before February 15 to Chairman, Financial Aid Committee. Phone: (202)806-8005. Use FAFSA. About 75% of students receive aid other than loans from School.

DEGREE REQUIREMENTS. For J.D.: satisfactory completion of three-year program, 88 semester hours minimum. For LL.M.: at least 24 credit hours beyond J.D.; thesis.

School of Social Work

Organized 1945. Semester system. Tuition: full-time $14,064. Limited on-campus housing available. Contact Dean of Residence Life. Phone: (202)806-6131.

Enrollment: full- and part-time 358. Faculty: full-time 24, part-time 18. Degrees conferred: M.S.W., Ph.D.

ADMISSION REQUIREMENTS. Transcripts, three letters of recommendation required in support of School's application. Online application available. TOEFL required for international applicants. Accepts transfer applicants. Apply to School by October 1 (Spring), February 1 (Fall). Application fee $45. Phone: (202)806-6450; fax: (202)387-4309.

ADMISSION STANDARDS. Selective. Usual minimum average: 3.0 (A = 4).

FINANCIAL AID. Very limited scholarships, fellowships, and graduate assistantships, federal grants. Apply to Financial Aid Office by March 1 (Fall), November 1 (Spring). Use FAFSA (School code: 005297). Phone: (202)806-2800.

DEGREE REQUIREMENTS. For M.S.W.: satisfactory completion of 60-hour program, at least 30 hours in residence. For Ph.D.: satisfactory completion of 48 semester credit hours beyond the master's; qualifying exam; comprehensive exam; dissertation; oral defense.

FIELDS OF PRACTICE.
Criminal Justice. M.S.W. only.
Displaced Persons.
Family and Child Welfare.
Mental Health.
Social Gerontology.
Social Work in Health Care Settings. M.S.W. only.

HUMBOLDT STATE UNIVERSITY
Arcata, California 95521-8299
Web site: www.humboldt.edu

Founded 1913. Located 300 miles N of San Francisco. CGS member. Coed. State control. Semester system. Special facilities: Arts Center, Marine Biological and Oceanography Station, Natural History Museum, Center for Indian Community Development, Center for the Resolution of Environmental Disputes, Lamphere Dunes, Schatz Tree Farm Experimental Forest, fish hatchery. Library: 900,000 volumes, 3169 subscriptions.

Tuition/fees: resident 0.–6.0 units $1426, 7 or more units $2244, nonresident $399 per semester unit. On-campus housing for graduate students. Average academic year housing cost: $7900 (including board) for single students. Apply to Director of Housing. Phone: (707)826-3451. Day-care facilities available.

Graduate Studies

Enrollment: full- and part-time 501. Faculty teaching graduate students: 276. Degrees conferred: M.A., M.S., M.B.A., M.F.A.

ADMISSION REQUIREMENTS. Transcripts required in support of application. Online application available. GRE Subject Tests for some departments; letters of recommendation for some departments. TOEFL required for international applicants. Interview not required. Accepts transfer applicants. Graduates of unaccredited institutions not considered. Call for application deadlines for individual programs. Application fee $55. Phone: (707)826-3949.

ADMISSION STANDARDS. Selective for most departments. Usual minimum average: 2.5 for last 60 credits (A = 4).

FINANCIAL AID. Annual awards from institutional funds: scholarships, research fellowships, teaching assistantships, research assistantships, Federal W/S, loans. Apply by March 1 to appropriate department or division chair for fellowships and assistantships; to Financial Aid Office for all other programs. Phone: (707)826-4321. Use FAFSA. About 25% of students receive aid other than loans from College and outside sources. Aid available for part-time students.

DEGREE REQUIREMENTS. For M.A., M.S., M.B.A.: 30 semester units minimum, at least 21 in residence; thesis/nonthesis option. For M.F.A.: 60 semester units, at least 42 in residence; creative project.

FIELDS OF STUDY.
Biology. M.A.
Business Administration. M.B.A.
Education. M.A.
English. Includes literature, teaching, or writing. M.A.
Environment and Community. M.A.
Environmental Systems. Includes environmental resource engineering, international development technology, math modeling. M.S.
Kinesiology. M.S.
Natural Resources. Includes fisheries, forestry, planning and interpretation, rangeland resources and wildland soils, wastewater utilization, watershed, wildlife. M.S.

Psychology. Includes academic research, counseling, school psychology. M.A.
Social Science. M.A.
Sociology. M.A.
Theatre Arts. M.F.A., M.A.

HUNTER COLLEGE OF THE CITY UNIVERSITY OF NEW YORK
New York, New York 10021-5085
Web site: www.hunter.cuny.edu

Founded 1870. Coed. Municipal control. Semester system. Special facilities: Brookdale Center on Aging, Center for AIDS, Drugs and Community Health, Center for Biomolecular Structure and Function, Center for Communication Disorders, Center for Occupational and Environmental Health, Center for Puerto Rican Studies, Urban Research Center. University libraries: 789,000 volumes, 4200 subscriptions. Total College enrollment: 20,000.

Annual tuition: resident $6400, per credit $270; nonresident $10,000, per credit $500. No on-campus housing. Contact Graduate Housing Office for off-campus housing information. Phone: (212)481-4310. Day-care facilities available.

Graduate School

Enrollment: full- and part-time 4000. Graduate faculty: full-time 674, part-time 270. Degrees conferred: M.A., M.S., M.U.P., M.S.W., M.F.A., M.S.Ed., M.P.H., Advanced Certificate. The Ph.D. is offered through the University's Graduate Center.

ADMISSION REQUIREMENTS. Official transcripts, three letters of recommendation, GRE (Arts and Sciences areas) required in support of School's application. Interview required for some departments. TOEFL required for international applicants; TWE for some programs. Accepts transfer applicants. Graduates of unaccredited colleges not considered. Apply to Office of Graduate Admissions by February 1 (Fall), November 1 (Spring). Application fee $125. Phone: (212)772-4490; e-mail: admissions @hunter.cuny.edu

ADMISSION STANDARDS. Competitive for most departments, very competitive or selective for others. Usual minimum average: 2.75 (A = 4).

FINANCIAL AID. Scholarships, fellowships, assistantships for teaching/research, tuition waivers, traineeships, grants, Federal W/S, loans. Approved for VA benefits. Apply by April 1 to Office of Graduate Fellowships and Scholarships; to Office of the Dean of Humanities, Sciences, and Mathematics, or Social Sciences for assistantships; to the Office of Financial Aid for all other programs. Phone: (212)772-4820. Closing dates subject to change; consult Financial Aid Office for specific dates. Use FAFSA and CUNY FAF. No aid for part-time students.

DEGREE REQUIREMENTS. For master's: 30–45 semester hours minimum; reading knowledge of one foreign language normally required; thesis/nonthesis option; final comprehensive written exam for most departments.

FIELDS OF STUDY.

SCHOOL OF ARTS AND SCIENCES:
Accounting. M.S.
Anthropology. M.A.
Applied Mathematics. M.A.
Art. M.A., M.F.A.
Biochemistry. M.A.

Biological Sciences. M.A.
Biology 7–12 Teacher. M.A.
Chemistry 7–12 Teacher. M.A.
Creative Writing. M.F.A.
Earth Sciences 7–12 Teacher. M.A.
Economics. M.A.
English. M.A.
English 7–12 Teacher. M.A.
French. M.A.
French 7–12 Teacher. M.A.
Geography. M.A.
History. M.A.
Integrated Media Arts. M.F.A.
Italian 7–12 Teacher. M.A.
Latin 7–12 Teacher. M.A.
Mathematics. M.A.
Mathematics 7–12 Teacher. M.A.
Psychology. M.A.
Social Research. M.S.
Spanish. M.A.
Spanish 7–12 Teacher. M.A.
Statistics and Applied Mathematics. M.A.
Theatre. M.A.
Urban Affairs. M.A.
Urban Planning. M.U.P.

SCHOOL OF EDUCATION:
Behavior Disorders. M.S.Ed.
Biology 7–12. M.A.
Chemistry 7–12. M.A.
Childhood Education. 1–6. M.S.Ed.
Childhood Special Education 1–6. M.S.Ed.
Deaf or Hard of Hearing. M.S.Ed.
Earth Sciences 7–12. M.A.
Early Childhood, Birth–2. M.S.Ed.
English 7–12. M.A.
French 7–12. M.A.
German 7–12. M.A.
Italian 7–12. M.A.
Latin 7–12. M.A.
Learning Disabilities. M.S.Ed.
Literacy: Birth–Grade 6. M.S.Ed.
Mathematics 7–12. M.A.
Physics 7–12. M.A.
Rehabilitation Counseling. M.S.Ed.
School Counselor. M.S.Ed.
Social Studies 7–12. M.A.
Spanish 7–12. M.A.
Special Education. M.S.Ed.
Teaching English to Speakers of Other Languages. M.A.

SCHOOL OF HEALTH SCIENCES:
Communication Sciences. M.S.
Community Health Education. M.P.H.
Environmental and Occupational Health Services. M.P.H.
Physical Therapy. M.P.T.
Public Health Nutrition. M.P.H.
Teachers of Students with Speech and Language Disabilities. M.S.
Urban Public Health. M.P.H., M.S.

SCHOOL OF NURSING:
Adult Health Nursing. M.S.
Adult Nurse Practitioner. M.S.
Community/Public Health Nursing. M.S.
Gerontological Nurse/Adult Nurse Practitioner. M.S.
Psychiatric Nursing. M.S.

SCHOOL OF SOCIAL WORK:
Social Work. M.S.

IDAHO STATE UNIVERSITY
Pocatello, Idaho 83209
Web site: www.isu.edu

Founded 1901. Located 165 miles N of Salt Lake City. CGS member. Coed. State control. Semester system. Library: 406,000 volumes, 1,355,000 microforms, 30 PCs in all libraries.

Annual tuition/fees: full-time, resident $4930, nonresident $13,200; per credit resident $251, nonresident $369. On-campus housing for 150 married and 1200 single students. Average academic year housing cost: $450–$550 per month for married students; $4950–$5800 (including board) for single students. Apply to Housing Office. Phone: (208)282-2120.

Graduate School

Enrollment: full-time 622, part-time 1401 (men 40%, women 60%). Graduate faculty: full-time 219, part-time 0. Degrees conferred: M.A., M.S., M.Ed., M.H.E., M.P.A.S., M.P.E., M.F.A., M.Coun., M.O.T., M.P.T., M.T.D., Ed.S., D.A., M.N.S., Ph.D., Ed.D., D.P.T.

ADMISSION REQUIREMENTS. Two transcripts, GRE/GMAT/MAT required in support of School's application. TOEFL (minimum score 550) required for international applicants. Interview not required. Accepts transfer applicants. Graduates from unaccredited institutions not considered. Apply to Office of Registrar and Admissions by July 1 (Fall), December 1 (Spring), May 1 (Summer). Some programs have earlier deadlines. Application fee $55. Phone: (208)282-5617; International applicants: (208) 282-2270.

ADMISSION STANDARDS. Relatively open for most departments. Usual minimum average: 2.75 (A = 4), 35th percentile on at least one GRE subscore.

FINANCIAL AID. Annual awards from institutional funds: scholarships, teaching and research assistantships, fellowships, Federal W/S, loans. Approved for VA benefits. Apply by March 1 to appropriate department chair for fellowships and assistantships; to Financial Aid Office for all other programs. Use FAFSA. Phone: (208)282-2756, fax: (208)282-4231. About 60% of students receive aid other than loans from University and outside sources. Aid available for part-time students.

DEGREE REQUIREMENTS. For master's: 30–36 semester hours minimum, at least 22 in residence; reading knowledge of a foreign language for some departments; thesis/nonthesis options; final written/oral exam. For M.B.A.: 45-credit program; final oral exam. For M.Ed.: 33-credit program; thesis/field project/case study; final exam. For M.O.T.: 88-credit, 8-semester, full-time program; 4 clinical affiliations; professional project; practicum. For M.P.A.S. 72-credit full-time program; capstone experience. For M.T.D.: 30-credit program; thesis or practicum and research project. For M.Coun.: 48–64-credit program; practicum; internships. For M.P.H.: 47–50-credit program; internships; thesis or project. For Ed.S.: 30 semester hours beyond master's; project. For D.A.: 48 credits minimum beyond master's, at least 30 in residence; comprehensive exam; 2 supervised teaching internships; foreign language proficiency; professional project; final oral exam. For Ed. D.: 64 semester credits, at least 30 in residence; final program of study; comprehensive exam; dissertation; oral defense. For D.P.T.: 98-credit, three-year full-time program; 5 clinical affiliations; practicum; professional project. For Ph.D.: 72 credits minimum beyond bachelor's, at least 30 in residence; reading knowledge of a foreign language for some departments; qualifying exam; admission to candidacy; comprehensive exam; internships for some programs; dissertation; final oral exam.

FIELDS OF STUDY.

COLLEGE OF ARTS AND SCIENCES:
Anthropology. Thesis for M.A., M.S.
Art. One-person show for M.F.A.
Biological Sciences. Includes botany, zoology. M.S., M.N.S., D.A., Ph.D.
Chemistry. Combine B.S.-M.S. with entry at junior level.
Clinical Psychology. M.S., Ph.D.
English. Thesis for M.A., D.A.
General Experimental Psychology. M.S.
Geosciences. Includes environmental. M.S., M.N.S.
History. M.A.
Mathematics. M.S., M.N.S., D.A.
Microbiology. M.S., Ph.D.
Physics. Includes health physics. M.S., M.N.S.
Political Science. M.A., M.P.A., D.A.
Psychology. M.S.
Public Administration. M.P.A.
Sociology. Thesis for M.A.
Speech Communication. Includes organizational communication. M.A.
Theatre. M.A.

COLLEGE OF BUSINESS:
Business Administration. M.B.A.

COLLEGE OF EDUCATION:
Athletic Administration. M.P.E.
Child and Family Studies. M.Ed.
Curriculum Leadership. M.Ed.
Educational Leadership. Ed.D.
Human Exceptionality. Includes special education. M.Ed.
Instructional Technology. M.Ed.
Literacy. M.Ed.
School Psychology. Ed.S.
Special Education. Ed.S.

COLLEGE OF ENGINEERING:
Civil Engineering. M.S.
Engineering and Applied Science. Ph.D.
Engineering Structures and Mechanics. M.S.
Environmental Engineering. M.S.
Measurement and Control Engineering. M.S.
Mechanical Engineering. M.S.
Nuclear Science and Engineering. M.S.

KASISKA COLLEGE OF HEALTH PROFESSIONS:
Audiology. M.S.
Counseling. Ed.S., Ph.D.
Counselor Education. Ph.D.
Deaf Education. M.S.
Health Education. M.H.E.
Health and Nutrition Sciences. M.H.E., M.P.H.
Marriage and Family Counseling. M.Coun.
Mental Health Counseling. M.Coun.
Nursing. M.S.
Occupational Therapy. M.O.T.
Physical Therapy. M.P.T.
Speech-Language Pathology. M.S.
Physician Assistant Studies. M.P.A.S.
Public Health. M.P.A.
School Counseling. M.Coun.
Student Affairs and College Counseling. M.Coun.

COLLEGE OF PHARMACY:
Pharmacy. Includes pharmaceutical chemistry, pharmacology, pharmaceutics, pharmacy administration. M.S.
Pharmaceutical Sciences. Includes biopharmaceutics, biopharmaceutical analysis, pharmacokinetics, pharmacology, pharmacy administration. Ph.D.

COLLEGE OF TECHNOLOGY:
Human Resource Training and Development. Includes technical program management, training management. M.T.D.

INTERDISCIPLINARY PROGRAMS:
Natural Science. M.N.S.
Waste Management and Environmental Science. M.S.

UNIVERSITY OF IDAHO
Moscow, Idaho 83844
Web site: www.uidaho.edu

Founded 1889. Located 85 miles SE of Spokane, Wash. CGS member. Coed. State control. Semester system. Special facilities: Cooperative Fishery Research Unit, Cooperative Park Studies Unit, Cooperative Wildlife Research Unit, Microelectronics Research Center, Institute for Molecular and Agricultural Genetic Engineering, Laboratory of Anthropology, Remote Sensing Research Unit, Graduate Center at Idaho Nuclear Engineering Laboratory, cooperative graduate course program and library usage exchange with Washington State University, Computer Center, Agricultural Experiment Station, Center for Business Development and Research, Bureau of Education Research and Service, Bureau of Mines and Geology, Bureau of Public Affairs Research, Engineering Experiment Station, Forest, Wildlife and Range Experiment Station, Materials Testing Laboratory, U.S. Forest Service, Intermountain Forest Sciences Laboratory, Water Resources Research Institute. Library: 1,400,000 volumes, 14,230 subscriptions. Total University enrollment: 12,500.

Annual tuition fee: full-time, resident $4508, nonresident $8770; part-time per credit, resident $130, nonresident $260. On-campus housing for 276 married students, 1700 men, 1040 women. Housing costs: $8500 per year for married students, $7000 per year (including board) for single students. Apply to Director of Housing. Phone: (208)885-7961. Day care facilities available.

College of Graduate Studies

Graduate study since 1896. Enrollment: full-time 1198, part-time 1319. University faculty: full-time 481, part-time 10. Degrees conferred: M.A., M.S., M.Arch., M.F.A., M.M., M.Ed., M.N.S., M.A.T., M.Acct., M.Engr., M.P.A., Ed.D., Ed.S., Ph.D.

ADMISSION REQUIREMENTS. Transcript required in support of College's application. GRE required by some departments. TOEFL required for international applicants. Interview not required. Accepts transfer applicants. Graduates of unaccredited colleges not considered. Apply to Admissions Officer by August 1 (Fall), December 15 (Spring). International application deadline: June 1 (Fall), December 1 (Spring). Application fee $35, $45 for international applicants. Phone: (208)885-6243; fax: (208)885-6198; e-mail: uigrad@uidaho.edu.

ADMISSION STANDARDS. Selective for most departments. Usual minimum average: 2.8 (A = 4). Some departments require higher GPA.

FINANCIAL AID. Annual awards from institutional funds: scholarships, research fellowships, teaching assistantships, research assistantships, tuition waivers, Federal W/S, loans. Apply by February 15 to appropriate department head for fellowships, assistantships; to Financial Aid Office for all other aid. Phone: (208)885-6312. Use FAFSA and institutional FAF. About 50% of students receive aid other than loans from University and outside sources. Aid available for part-time students.

DEGREE REQUIREMENTS. For M.A., M.S., M.Arch., M.F.A.: 30 credits minimum, at least 18 in residence; thesis; final oral exam. For M.Acct.: 30-credit program; internship; written comprehensive exam or thesis. For M.N.S.: 30 credits minimum, at least 22 in residence; final written exam. For M.M.: 30 credits minimum, at least 22 in residence; thesis, composition, or recital; final written exam. For M.B.A.: 30 credits; calculus and computer proficiency. For M.P.A.: 30 credits minimum, at least 18 in residence; comprehensive exam. For M.Engr.: 30 credits minimum; final document. For Ed.S.: 30 credits beyond the master's. For Ph.D.: 78 credits minimum beyond the bachelor's; at least one year in residence; preliminary exam; reading knowledge of one foreign language required by some departments; dissertation; final written/oral exam. For Ed.D.: essentially the same as for the Ph.D., except no language requirement.

FIELDS OF STUDY.

Accountancy. M.Acct.
Adult Organizational Learning and Leadership. M.S., Ed.S., Ed.D.
Agricultural Economics. M.S.
Agricultural Education. M.S.
Animal Physiology. M.S., Ph.D.
Animal Sciences. M.S.
Anthropology. M.A.
Architecture. M.Arch., M.S.
Art. M.A.T., M.F.A.
Bioinformatics and Computational Biology. M.S., Ph.D.
Biological and Agricultural Engineering. M.S., M.Engr., Ph.D.
Biological Sciences. M.N.S.
Biology. M.S., Ph.D.
Botany. M.S., Ph.D.
Business Education. M.Ed.
Chemical Engineering. M.S., M.Engr., Ph.D.
Chemistry. M.S., M.A.T., Ph.D.
Civil Engineering. M.S., M.Engr., Ph.D.
Computer Engineering. M.S., M.Engr.
Computer Science. M.S., Ph.D.
Counseling and Human Services. M.S., M.Ed., Ed.S.
Creative Writing. M.F.A.
Curriculum and Instruction. M.S., M.Ed.
Earth Science. M.A.T.
Economics. M.S.
Education. Includes elementary, secondary, special education; business, administration, guidance and counseling, distributive. Ed.S., Ed.D., Ph.D.
Educational Leadership. M.S., Ed.S.
Electrical Engineering. M.S., M.Engr., Ph.D.
Elementary Education. M.S., M.Ed.
Engineering Management. M.Engr.
English. M.A., M.A.T.
Entomology. M.S., Ph.D.
Environmental Engineering. M.S., M.Engr.
Environmental Science. M.S.
Family and Consumer Sciences. M.S.
Fishery Resources. M.S.
Food Sciences. M.S., Ph.D.
Forest Products. M.S.
Forest Resources. M.S.
French. M.A.T.
Geography. M.S., M.A.T., Ph.D.
Geological Engineering. M.S.
Geology. M.S., Ph.D.
German. M.A.T.
History. M.A., M.A.T., Ph.D.
Hydrology. M.S.
Industrial Technology Education. M.S., M.Ed.
Interdisciplinary Studies. M.A., M.S.
Landscape Architecture. M.S.
Mathematics. M.S., M.A.T., Ph.D.
Mechanical Engineering. M.S., M.Engr., Ph.D.
Metallurgical Engineering. M.S.
Metallurgy. M.S.
Microbiology, Molecular and Biochemistry. M.S., Ph.D.
Music. Includes performance, history and literature, composition, applied; M.A., M.M.
Natural Resources. M.N.R., Ph.D.
Neuroscience. M.S., Ph.D.
Nuclear Engineering. M.S., M.Engr., Ph.D. (Idaho Falls only).
Philosophy. M.A.
Physical Education. M.S., M.Ed.
Physics. M.S., M.A.T., Ph.D.
Plant Sciences. M.S., Ph.D.
Political Science. M.S., Ph.D.
Psychology. M.S.
Public Administration. M.P.A.
Rangeland Ecology and Management. M.S.
Recreation. M.S.
Resource Recreation and Tourism. M.S.
School Psychology. Ed.S.
Secondary Education. M.S., M.Ed.
Soil and Land Resources. M.S., Ph.D.
Spanish. M.A.T.
Special Education. M.S., M.Ed., Ed.S.
Statistics. M.S.
Systems Engineering. M.Engr.
Teaching English as a Second Language. M.A.
Theater Arts. M.F.A.
Veterinary Science. M.S.
Water Resources. Interdisciplinary. M.S., Ph.D.
Wildlife Resources. M.S.

College of Law (PO Box 442321)

Web site: www.law.uidaho.edu

Establish 1909. ABA approved since 1925. AALS member since 1925. Public control. Semester system. Special facility: Northwest Institute for Dispute Resolution. Library: 235,205, 3996 subscriptions; has LEXIS, NEXIS, WESTLAW, DIALOG; has more than 300 network connections.

Annual tuition: resident no tuition charge, but mandatory fees $9600 per year, nonresident $19,100. On-campus housing available. Estimated living expenses: $12,262.

Enrollment: first-year class 104; total 313 (men 58%, women 42%, minorities 13%). Faculty: full-time 12, part-time 18. Student to faculty ratio 16.7 to 1. Degrees conferred: J.D., M.B.A. (Accounting), J.D.-M.S.(Environmental Science).

ADMISSION REQUIREMENTS. LSDAS Law School report, bachelor's degree, transcripts, LSAT, personal statement, résumé required in support of application. Interview not required. Preference given to state residents. Graduates of unaccredited colleges not considered. Apply to Admissions Officer after September 1, before February 15. Admits to Fall only. Application fee $40. Phone: (208)885-6423; fax: (208)885-5709.

ADMISSION STANDARDS. Selective. Accepts approximately 31% of all students. Number of applicants 828; number of acceptance 260; number enrolled 104; LSAT (75% of students have a score at or above 152); GPA (75% of students have a GPA at or above 3.10). *U.S. News & World Report* ranking is in the third tier of all U.S. law schools.

FINANCIAL AID. Scholarships, assistantships, Federal W/S, loans. Apply by February 15 to Financial Aid Office. Phone: (208)885-6312. Use FAFSA (College code: 001626). About 40% of students receive aid other than loans from institutional funds.

DEGREE REQUIREMENTS. For J.D.: satisfactory completion of three-year program; 88 semester hours.

ILLINOIS INSTITUTE OF TECHNOLOGY
Chicago, Illinois 60616
Web site: www.iit.edu

Formed in 1940 by merger of Armour Institute and Lewis Institute. CGS member. Coed. Private control. Semester system with quarter courses. Special facilities: Center for the Study of Ethics and the Professions, National Center for Food Safety and Technology, Hazardous Waste Management Center, Center for Research on Industrial Strategy and Policy, Centers for Biotechnology, Energy Technology, Fluid Dynamics, Industrial Waste Elimination, Railroad Engineering. Library: 500,000 volumes, 177,000 microforms, 750 current periodicals. Total Institute enrollment: 7400.

Annual tuition: full-time $14,000; per credit $778. On-campus housing for 360 married graduate students, 132 graduate men, 45 graduate women. Average academic year housing cost: $12,000 for married students, $10,000 (including board) for single students. Contact Director of Housing for both on- and off-campus housing information. Phone: (312)567-5076.

Graduate College
Web site: www.grad.iit.edu

Enrollment: full- and part-time 2950. Institute faculty: full-time 202, part-time 114. Degrees conferred: M.S., M.Arch., M.B.A., M.Ch.E., M.C.E., M.C.R.P., M.Met.E., M.M.E., M.P.A., Ph.D.

ADMISSION REQUIREMENTS. Transcripts, GRE, three letters of recommendation, professional statement required in support of application. GRE/Subject Tests required in chemistry, psychology, electrical engineering. TOEFL required for international applicants. Interview not required. Accepts transfer applicants. Graduates of unaccredited institutions not considered. Apply to appropriate department by June 1 (Fall), November 1 (Spring). Deadlines for Architecture and Psychology are earlier. Rolling admissions process. Application fee $40. Phone: (312)567-3020; e-mail: gradstu@iit.edu.

ADMISSION STANDARDS. Very selective for most departments. Usual minimum average: 3.0 (A = 4).

FINANCIAL AID. Annual awards from institutional funds: scholarships, fellowships, teaching assistantships, research assistantships, internships, full or partial tuition waivers, Federal W/S, loans. Approved for VA benefits. Apply by March 1 to appropriate department chair for scholarships, fellowships, assistantships; to Director of Financial Aid for all other programs. Use FAFSA and institutional FAF. Phone: (312)567-7219. About 50% of students receive aid other than loans from Institute and outside sources. No aid for part-time students.

DEGREE REQUIREMENTS. For master's: 32–36 semester hours minimum; comprehensive exam; project; includes 6–8 hours for thesis (when required); final written/oral exam. For Ph.D.: usually 84–96 semester hours beyond the bachelor's, two semesters in full-time residence; foreign language proficiency for some programs; qualifying exam; comprehensive exam; dissertation; final oral exam.

FIELDS OF STUDY.
Analytical Chemistry. M.Chem.
Architectural Engineering. M.S.
Architecture. Includes landscape architecture. Admits Fall only. M.Arch., Ph.D.
Biology. Includes biochemistry, microbiology, physiology. M.S., Ph.D.
Biomedical Engineering. Includes neural engineering, medical imagery, cell and tissue engineering. Ph.D.
Business Administration. GMAT for admission. Includes e-business, entrepreneurship, environmental management, financial management, information management, international business, management science, marketing, operations management, organization and management, quality management, strategic management. M.B.A.
Chemical Engineering. M.S., Ph.D.
Chemistry. One foreign language for Ph.D., M.S., M.C.E., Ph.D.
City and Regional Planning. Admits Fall only. M.C.R.P. only.
Civil Engineering. M.S., Ph.D.
Computer Engineering. M.S.Cp.E
Computer Science. M.S., M.C.S., Ph.D.
Computer Science and Chemical Engineering. M.S., M.C.E.
Construction Engineering and Management. M.S., Ph.D.
Design. Includes photography, product design, visual design. M.S., M.Des., Ph.D.
Electrical and Computer Engineering. M.E.C.E.
Electrical Engineering. M.S.E.E., Ph.D.
Electrical Markets. M.E.M.
Environmental Engineering. M.S., Ph.D.
Environmental Management. M.S.E.M.
Finance. M.S.F.
Financial Markets. M.S.F.M.
Food Processing Engineering. M.S.
Food Safety and Technology. M.F.S.
Gas Engineering. M.G.E.
Geoenvironmental Engineering. M.S., Ph.D.
Geotechnical Engineering. M.S., Ph.D.
Health Physics. M.H.P.
Information Architecture. M.S.
Information Technology and Management. M.I.T.M.
Management Science. Ph.D.
Manufacturing Engineering. M.M.E., M.S.M.E.
Manufacturing Technology and Operations. M.M.T.O.
Marketing Communication. M.S.M.C.
Materials Sciences and Engineering. M.M.E.
Mathematical Finance. M.M.F.
Mathematics Education. M.S., M.S.E.., M.M.E., Ph.D.
Molecular Biochemistry and Biophysics. M.S., Ph.D.
Network Engineering. M.N.E.
Personnel and Human Resource Development. M.S.P.H.R.D.
Physics. M.S., Ph.D.
Power Engineering. M.P.E.
Psychology. Doctoral specializations: clinical, industrial/organizational, rehabilitation. M.S., Ph.D.
Public Administration. Includes specialization in nonprofit management, public works. M.P.A.
Public Works. Includes infrastructure engineering and management. M.S.
Rehabilitation Counseling. M.S.R.C.
Science Education. M.S.S.E., Ph.D.
Structural Engineering. M.S., Ph.D.
Technical Communication and Information Design. M.S.
Telecommunications and Software Engineering. M.T.S.E.
Transportation Engineering. M.S., Ph.D.
VLSI and Microelectronics. M.VLSI.+M.

Chicago-Kent College of Law (60661-3691)
Web site: www.kentlaw.edu

Established 1888. In the late 1800s the Chicago College of Law and Kent College of Law merged to form Chicago-Kent College of Law. In 1969 Chicago-Kent College of Law became an integral part of IIT, in 1992 Chicago-Kent moved to its new quarters in downtown Chicago on Adams Street. ABA approved since 1951. AALS member. Semester system. Full-time, part-time study. Law library: 547,378 volumes, 2313 subscriptions; has LEXIS, NEXIS, WESTLAW, DIALOG, EPIC; is a Federal Government Depository. Special facilities: Global Law and Policy Institute, Institute for Science, Law, and Technology, Institute for Law and the Workplace, Chicago-Kent Institute for the Law and the Humanities, Center for Law and Computers. Special programs: Environmental and Energy Law, Intellectual Property Law, Labor and Employment Law. Special programs: study abroad in London and summer study in Mexico City.

Annual tuition: full-time $31,434, part-time $22,980; LL.M. $22,980. Total average annual additional expenses: $17,765.

Enrollment: first-year class 232, part-time 103; total full- and part-time 1041 (men 53%, women 47%, minorities 21%). Faculty: full-time 65, part-time 85. Student to faculty ratio 12.4 to 1. Degrees conferred: J.D., J.D.-M.B.A., J.D.-M.P.A., J.D.-LL.M. (Financial Services Law, Taxation), J.D.-M.P.H. (with the University of Illinois at Chicago), J.D.-M.S. (Financial Markets and Trading, Environmental Management), LL.M. (Family Law, Financial Services, Taxation), LL.M. (International and Comparative Law for persons who have completed a basic legal education and received a university degree in law in another country).

ADMISSION REQUIREMENTS. LSDAS report, bachelor's degree, transcript, LSAT, two letters of recommendation, personal statement required in support of application. Applicants with foreign transcripts must use J.D. Credential Assembly Service. Minority and disadvantaged applicants encouraged to apply. Transfer applicants accepted from ABA approved law schools only. Apply by March 1. For Early Decision program, apply by December 15. Rolling admission process. Application fee $60. Phone: (312) 906-5020; fax: (312)906-5274.

ADMISSION STANDARDS. Selective. Accepts 26% of full-time and 27% of part-time applicants. Number of full-time applicants 3085, part-time 841; number of full-time acceptance 813, part-time 227; number enrolled full-time 232, part-time 103; LSAT (75% of full-time students have a score at or above 159, part-time 155); GPA (75% of full-time students have a GPA at or above 3.29, part-time 3.03). *U.S. News & World Report* ranking is in the second tier tied at 60th of all U.S. law schools.

FINANCIAL AID. Scholarships, grants, Federal W/S, loans. Apply to Financial Aid Office after acceptance, before April 15. Phone: (312)906-5180. Use FAFSA (College code: 001691) and institutional FAF. About 55% of students receive aid other than loans from the College and outside sources.

DEGREE REQUIREMENTS. For J.D.: 84 credits with a GPA of at least 2.0 (A = 4), plus completion of upper divisional writing course; three-year program, four-year program. Accelerated J.D. with one summer of course work. For J.D.-M.B.A.: up to course reduction: four-year program full-time, five-and-one-half-year program part-time. For J.D.-M.P.A.: up to 7 course reduction; four-year program full-time, five-and-one-half-year program part-time. For J.D.-M.S. (Financial Marketing): up to 7 course reduction; four-year program full-time, five-and-one-half-year program part-time. For J.D.-M.S. (Environmental Management): up to 9 course reduction; four-year program full-time, five-and-one-half-year program part-time. For J.D.-LL.M.: up to 6 credits may be used toward J.D.; one additional semester for LL.M. (full-time study). For LL.M. (Family law, Taxation): 24 credits; a GPA of 2.5 (A = 4) required. For LL.M. (Financial Services): 24 credits; a GPA of 3.0 (A = 4) required; publishable paper. For LL.M. (International and Comparative Law): individually designed degree depending upon previous law degree and legal experience; one full year in residence.

ILLINOIS STATE UNIVERSITY
Normal, Illinois 61790-2000
Web site: www.ilstu.edu

Founded 1857. Located 130 miles S of Chicago. CGS member. Coed. State control. Semester system. Library: 1,900,000 volumes, 8915 subscriptions. Total University enrollment: 20,600.

Annual tuition/fees: full-time, resident $4080 (12 hours each semester), Fall, Spring semester, nonresident $8520; per credit resident $170, nonresident $355. On-campus housing for 292 married students, 125 single men, and 125 single women. Average academic year cost: $5748 for single. Apply to Office of Residential Life. Phone: (309)438-8611 or (800)366-4675. Day care facilities available.

Graduate School

Graduate study since 1943. Enrollment: full-time 1012, part-time 1330. University faculty: full- and part-time 517. Degrees conferred: M.A., M.S., M.S. in Ed., M.M.Ed., M.F.A., M.B.A., M.P.A., M.S.N., S.S.P., Ed.D., Ph.D.

ADMISSION REQUIREMENTS. Two transcripts required in support of School's application. Applicants to degree programs must submit scores of GRE for some departments. Applicants to the Departments of Psychology and Sociology and Anthropology must submit scores on the GRE Subject Test in their field of study. Applicants for Business should submit the GMAT. Doctoral applicants must submit three letters of recommendation. TOEFL required for international applicants. Interview sometimes required. Accepts transfer applicants. Graduates of unaccredited institutions not considered. Apply to Office of Admissions at least three weeks (master's) or two months (doctoral programs) prior to registration. Application fee: $30. Phone: (309)438-2583; fax: (309) 438-9712; e-mail: ugradadm@ilstu.edu.

ADMISSION STANDARDS. Selective. Usual minimum average: 2.6 (A = 4).

FINANCIAL AID. Annual awards from institutional funds: scholarships, grants, fellowships, assistantships, teaching assistantships, internships, traineeships, tuition waivers, Federal W/S, loans. Approved for VA benefits. Apply by April 1 to Graduate Office for fellowships, to head of proposed major department for assistantships; to Financial Aid Office for all other programs. Phone: (309)438-2231; fax: (309)438-3755. Use FAFSA. About 60% of students receive aid other than loans from University and outside sources. No aid for students-at-large or part-time students with less than 5 hours in a degree-seeking program. Departmental tuition waivers are available to part-time students (in-state) on a limited basis.

DEGREE REQUIREMENTS. For master's: 32 semester hours minimum, at least 24 in residence and one semester in full-time attendance for selected majors; optional thesis for 4–6 hours, final oral exam; without thesis, final written exam; reading knowledge of one foreign language (for M.A.). For S.S.P.: 30 semester hours minimum. For Ed.D., Ph.D.: approximately 60 semester hours minimum beyond the master's; research project; final written/oral exam. Knowledge of two foreign languages for Ph.D., or approved substitute; approved alternate research tool for Ed.D. Residency requirements vary.

FIELDS OF STUDY.

COLLEGE OF APPLIED SCIENCE AND TECHNOLOGY:
Agribusiness. M.S.
Applied Computer Science. M.S.
Criminal Justice Sciences. M.A., M.S.
Environmental Health and Safety. M.S.
Family and Consumer Sciences. M.A., M.S.
Health, Physical and Recreation Education. M.S.
Information Technology. M.S.

COLLEGE OF ARTS AND SCIENCES:
Biological Sciences. M.S., Ph.D.
Biology. M.S.
Chemistry. M.S.

Communication. M.A., M.S.
Economics. M.A., M.S.
English. M.A., M.S., Ph.D.
Foreign Languages. M.A.
Genetics. Ph.D.
Geohydrology. M.S.
Historical Archaeology. M.A., M.S.
History. M.A., M.S.,
Mathematics. M.A., M.S.
Mathematics Education. Ph.D.
Political Science. M.A., M.S.
Psychology. M.A., M.S.
School Psychology. S.S.P., Ph.D.
Social Work. M.S.
Sociology. M.A., M.S.
Speech Pathology and Audiology. M.A., M.S.
Writing. M.A., M.S.
Zoology. Ph.D.

COLLEGE OF BUSINESS:
Accounting. M.S., M.P.A.
Business Administration. Includes finance and law; management, quantitative methods, marketing. M.B.A.

COLLEGE OF EDUCATION:
Counselor Education. M.S., M.S. in Ed.
Curriculum and Instruction. M.S. in Ed., Ed.D.
Educational Administration. M.S., M.S. in Ed., Ed.D., Ph.D.
Institutional Technology. M.S. in Ed.
Kinesiology and Recreation. M.S. in Ed.
Reading. M.S. in Ed.
Special Education. M.S. in Ed., Ed.D.

COLLEGE OF FINE ARTS:
Art. M.A., M.S., M.F.A.
Arts Technology. M.S.
Music. M.M., M.M.Ed.
Theater. M.A., M.S., M.F.A.

COLLEGE OF NURSING:
Nursing. M.S.N.

UNIVERSITY OF ILLINOIS AT CHICAGO

Chicago, Illinois 60680
Web site: www.uic.edu

Created in 1992 by combining the resources and facilities of the two University of Illinois campuses in Chicago: the 20-year-old Chicago Circle and the Medical Center in existence for more than 100 years. CGS member. Coed. Public control. Semester system. Special facilities: Anatomy Museum, Institute for Humanities, Pathology Museum, Research and Educational Hospitals, Neuropsychiatric Institute, Molecular Biology Research Facility, Biologic Resource Laboratory, Electron Microscope Facility, Energy Resources Center, Engineering Research Facility, Environmental Stress Facility, Center for Urban Transportation, Center for Women's Studies, Institute for the Study of Developmental Disabilities, Survey Research Laboratory. The University's NIH ranking is 48th among all U.S. institutions with 376 awards/grants valued at $134,411,079. According to The Center at University of Florida, the University is ranked 48th in receipt of Federal Research funds with $168,063,000 and it ranks 41st for total University research expenditures with $291,507,000. In 2004, the University awarded 233 doctorates, which ranked it 66th among all U.S. institutions eligible to award that degree. Six of the University's faculty members have been elected to National Honor Academies and this ranks it 83rd among all U.S. institutions. The

Library: approximately 2,100,000 volumes, 20,800 subscriptions. Total University enrollment: 24,500.

On-campus housing for single students only. Apply to Director of Housing for on-campus information to the Housing Listing Office, 704 CCC, 503 S. Halsted, Chicago, Illinois 60607-7014. Phone: (312)413-5418. Day-care facilities available.

Graduate College

Annual tuition/fees: full-time resident $7790; nonresident $19,788; M.A.S., M.B.A. tuition/fees full-time resident $15,098, nonresident $27,096; nursing tuition/fees full-time resident $14,360, nonresident $26,358.

Enrollment: full-time 2986, part-time 2480. Faculty: full- and part-time 1300. Degrees conferred: M.A., M.Arch., M.A.T., M.B.A., M.Ed., M.F.A., M.P.A., M.S., M.S.T., M.S.W., M.H.P.E., M.A.M.S., D.A., Ph.D.

ADMISSION REQUIREMENTS. Transcripts, three letters of recommendation, GRE/GMAT required in support of College's application. TOEFL required for international applicants. Accepts transfer applicants. Graduates of unaccredited colleges not considered. Apply to Office of Admissions by May 15 (Fall), November 1 (Spring), March 15 (Summer); international applicants March 15 (Fall), July 15 (Spring), December 15 (Summer). Some programs have earlier deadlines. Application fee $50, $60 for international applicants. Phone: (312)413-2550; email: gradcoll@ uic.edu.

ADMISSION STANDARDS. Competitive for most departments, selective for others. Usual minimum average: 2.75 (A = 4).

FINANCIAL AID. Scholarships, research assistantships, teaching assistantships, traineeships, tuition waivers, Federal W/S, loans. Approved for VA benefits. Special support programs exist for minority students. Apply by March 1 to appropriate departments for assistantships, scholarships; to Director of Financial Aid for all other programs. Use FAFSA and institutional FAF. Phone: (312)996-3126; fax: (312)996-3385.

DEGREE REQUIREMENTS. For most master's: 32 semester hours minimum; thesis/nonthesis option; language required for some departments. For M.Ed.: same as most master's programs except no thesis. For M.F.A.: 64 semester hours minimum in residence; written report required for majors in design, painting and printmaking, sculpture, art history; reading knowledge of one foreign language for art history majors. For M.P.A.: 54 semester hours minimum; no thesis. For M.S.W.: 60 semester hours minimum, three semesters in residence; field work experience. For M.H.P.E.: 32 semester hours minimum; thesis; final oral exam. For M.A.M.S.: 45–47 semester hours minimum. For D.A., Ph.D.: 96 semesters hours minimum beyond the bachelor's, at least three consecutive semesters in residence; preliminary exam; dissertation; final oral exam.

FIELDS OF STUDY.
Accounting. M.S.
Anatomy and Cell Biology. M.S., Ph.D.
Anthropology. M.A., Ph.D.
Architecture. M.Arch.
Art History. M.A., Ph.D.
Art Therapy. M.A.
Biochemistry and Molecular Biology. M.S., Ph.D.
Biochemistry and Molecular Genetics. M.S., Ph.D.
Bioengineering. M.S., Ph.D.
Bioinformatics. M.S., Ph.D.
Biological Sciences. Includes cell, developmental, evolutionary, microbiology, molecular, neurobiology, radiation. M.S., D.A., Ph.D.
Biomedical Engineering. Ph.D.
Biomedical Visualization. M.A., M.S.
Business Administration. M.B.A., Ph.D.

Chemical Engineering. M.S., Ph.D.
Chemistry. M.S., Ph.D.
Civil Engineering. M.S., Ph.D.
Communication. M.A.
Computer Science. M.S., Ph.D.
Criminal Justice. M.A., Ph.D.
Curriculum and Instruction. Ph.D.
Disability and Human Development. M.S.
Disability Studies. Ph.D.
Earth and Environmental Sciences. M.S.
Economics. Includes urban, quantitative, information and deci-
   sion science. M.A., Ph.D.
Electrical and Computer Engineering. M.S., Ph.D.
Electronic Visualization. M.F.A.
Energy Engineering. M.E.E.
Engineering. M.Engr.
English. M.A.
Environmental and Urban Geography. M.A.
Film/Animation/Video. M.F.A.
Finance.
French. M.A.
Forensic Science. M.S.
German. M.A., Ph.D.
Graphic Design. M.F.A.
Health Informatics. M.S.
Health Professions Education. M.H.P.E.
Healthcare Administration. M.H.A.
Hispanic Studies. M.A., Ph.D.
History. M.A., M.A.T., Ph.D.
Human Nutrition. M.S., Ph.D.
Industrial Engineering. M.S.
Industrial Design. M.F.A.
Industrial Engineering and Operations Research. Ph.D.
Instructional Leadership. M.Ed.
Learning Sciences. Ph.D.
Linguistics. M.A.
Management Information Systems. M.S., Ph.D.
Marketing. Ph.D.
Materials Engineering. M.S., Ph.D.
Mathematics. Includes applied. M.A., M.S., M.S.T., D.A., Ph.D.
Mathematics and Information Sciences for Industry. M.S.
Mechanical Engineering. M.S., Ph.D.
Medicinal Chemistry. M.S., Ph.D.
Microbiology and Immunology. M.S., Ph.D.
Movement Sciences. M.S., Ph.D.
Nursing. Includes maternity, adult health, administration, medical-
   surgical, pediatric, psychiatric, public health. M.S., Ph.D.
Occupation Therapy. M.S.
Oral Science. M.S.
Pathology. M.S., Ph.D.
Pharmacognosy. M.S., Ph.D.
Pharmacology. M.S., Ph.D.
Pharmacy. M.S., Pharm.D., Ph.D.
Philosophy. M.A., Ph.D.
Photography. M.F.A.
Physical Therapy. M.S.
Physics. M.S., Ph.D.
Physiology and Biophysics. M.S., Ph.D.
Policy Studies in Urban Education. Ph.D.
Political Science. M.A., Ph.D.
Psychology. M.A., Ph.D.
Public Administration. M.P.A., Ph.D.
Public Health. M.P.H., Dr.P.H.
Real Estate. M.A.
Slavic Languages and Literature. Ph.D.
Slavic Studies. M.A.
Social Work. M.S.W., Ph.D.
Sociology. M.A., Ph.D.
Special Education. M.Ed., Ph.D.
Studio Arts. M.F.A.
Surgery. M.D. for admission. M.S.

Urban Education Leadership. Ed.D.
Urban Planning and Policy. M.U.P.P.
Theatre. M.F.A.

College of Dentistry
Web site: www.dentistry.uic.edu

Founded 1898, became part of University of Illinois in 1913. Located at Health Sciences Center. Semester system. Special facility: Center for Molecular Biology of Oral Diseases. Special program: Urban Health Program.

Annual tuition: resident $27,054, nonresident $53,552. On-campus housing for single students only. Average academic year housing cost: $16,500. Total average cost for all other first-year expenses: $8500.

Enrollment: first-year class 65, total 290 (men 41%, women 59%, minorities 17%, state residents 100%). Faculty: full-time 90, part-time 110. Degrees conferred: D.D.S., M.S. (Oral Sciences), Ph.D. (Oral Sciences), D.D.S.-M.S., D.D.S.-Ph.D.

ADMISSION REQUIREMENTS. AADSAS report, transcripts, DAT, recommendations required in support of application. Interview often required. Applicants must have completed at least two years of college study, preferably three years of study. Apply to Office of Admissions and Records after June 1, before December 1. Application fee $40. Phone: (312)996-1020; fax: (312)413-9050.

ADMISSION STANDARDS. Selective. Accepts about 20–25% of all applicants. Usual minimum UGPA: 2.5 (A = 4). Mean DAT: academic 18.7, PAT 18; mean UGPA 3.27.

FINANCIAL AID. Scholarships, research scholarships, grants-in-aid, DEAL, HEAL, loans. Apply to Office of Student Financial and Services of Health Science Center; no specified closing date. Phone: (312)996-5563/4940. Use FAFSA (College code: 001776). About 80% of students receive some aid from College.

DEGREE REQUIREMENTS. For D.D.S.: satisfactory completion of forty-five-month program. The D.D.S.-M.S. program can normally be completed during four-year period.

FIELDS OF GRADUATE STUDY.
Behavior Sciences. M.S.
Biochemistry. M.S.
Biomaterials. M.S.
Biomaterials Science. Ph.D.
Cancer Biology. Ph.D.
Cell Biology. M.S.
Cellular, Molecular and Development Biology. Ph.D.
Clinical Sciences. M.S.
Functional Morphology. M.S.
Histology. M.S.
Immunology. M.S.
Microbiology/Immunology. Ph.D.
Molecular Biology. M.S.
Oral Sciences. M.S., Ph.D.
Pathology. M.S.
Tissue Regeneration. Ph.D.

College of Medicine (60612-7302)
Web site: www.medicine.uic.edu

Founded 1881. The largest medical school in U.S. The College has campuses at Urbana-Champaign, Peoria and Rockford. There are two separate curriculum tracks within the College. Students assigned to the Chicago campus will pursue their full four-year program of medical education under the supervision of the faculty at that site. Students assigned for their first year of instruction to the Urbana-Champaign campus will either remain assigned to that site for the last three years or will transfer to Peoria or Rockford for remaining years of the program. NIH ranking is 48th of all U.S. institutions with 376 awards/grants worth $134,411,079.

Annual tuition: resident $27,676, nonresident $44,730. Total average figure for all other expenses: $13,500.

Enrollment: first-year class 333 (approximately 75–80 students enter UIC), total full-time 1451 (men 51%, women 49%, minorities 52%, state residents 76%). Faculty and volunteers: about 4000 at all four campuses. On-campus housing for 132 single students; none for married students. Average annual housing cost: $6500 for single students. Contact Housing Office, Medical Center. Phone: (312)413-5418. Degrees conferred: M.D., M.D.-M.S., M.D.-Ph.D.

ADMISSION REQUIREMENTS. AMCAS report, transcripts, letters of recommendation, MCAT, interview required in support of application. Transfer applicants considered. Preference given to state students. Applicants must have completed bachelor's or equivalent. Has EDP for state residents only; apply between June 1 and August 1. Apply to Office of Admissions and Records after June 1, before November 15. Application fee $70. Phone: (312) 996-5635; fax: (312)996-6693.

ADMISSION STANDARDS. Competitive. Accepts about 13.2% of all applicants. Number of applications 4856 (3296 out-of-state); number interviewed 828 (256 out-of-state); number of acceptance 640 (185 out-of-state); number enrolled 333 (85 out-of-state). Mean Composite MCAT 10.0; mean UGPA 3.57 (A = 4).

FINANCIAL AID. Scholarships, awards, HEAL, NIH stipends, Federal and private loans. About 52% of students receive aid other than loans from College funds. Apply to Office of Student Affairs by July 1 (priority processing date March 1). Phone: (312)413-0127. Use FAFSA (College code: 001776).

DEGREE REQUIREMENTS. For M.D.: satisfactory completion of four-year program; must pass both Step 1 and 2 of USMLE for graduation. For M.S., Ph.D. requirements refer to Graduate College listing above.

FIELDS OF GRADUATE STUDY.
Anatomy and Cell Biology.
Biochemistry.
Biomedical Engineering.
Biophysics.
Genetics.
Health Professions Education.
Immunology.
Microbiology.
Molecular Biology.
Molecular Genetics.
Pathology.
Pharmacology.
Physiology.

UNIVERSITY OF ILLINOIS AT SPRINGFIELD

Springfield, Illinois 62794-9243
Web site: www.uis.edu

Established 1969 as Sangamon State University, became part of University of Illinois in 1995. Located 100 miles NE of St. Louis. CGS member. Coed. State control. Semester system. Library: 512,000 volumes, 2200 subscriptions. Total University enrollment: 4500.

Tuition: resident per credit $163, nonresident $490. On-campus housing for both single and married students. Average academic year housing cost: $3970 for single students; $5640 for married students. Apply to Housing Office. Day-care facilities available.

Graduate Studies

Enrollment: full-time 467, part time 1152. Faculty: full-time 154, part-time 41. Degrees conferred: M.A., M.S., M.B.A., M.P.A., M.P.H., D.P.A.

ADMISSION REQUIREMENTS. Transcript required in support of College's application. GRE/MAT/GMAT/recommendations/interview/writing exam required by some departments. TOEFL required for international applicants. Accepts transfer applicants. Graduates of unaccredited institutions not considered. Apply to Office of Enrollment Services at least three months in advance of registration, international applicants at least six months in advance of registration. Application fee: $50, $60 for international applicants. Phone: (800)252-8533, (217)206-6626; fax: (217) 206-6720.

ADMISSION STANDARDS. Competitive for most departments. Usual minimum average: 2.5 (A = 4); 3.25 for D.P.A.

FINANCIAL AID. Annual awards from institutional funds: scholarships, fellowships, teaching assistantships, research assistantships, internships, grants, tuition waivers, Federal W/S, loans. Approved for VA benefits. Apply by June 1 to appropriate department head for fellowships, assistantships; for other aid programs apply to Office of Financial Assistance. Use FAFSA. About 20% of students receive aid other than loans from University and outside sources. Aid available for part-time students.

DEGREE REQUIREMENTS. For M.A.: 36-credit program; thesis/project/exam. For M.B.A.: 51–60 credit program depending on previous degree. For M.P.A.: 40–48 credit program; no thesis. For M.P.H.: 48-credit program; internships; comprehensive exam. For M.S.: 36-credit program: thesis/project. For D.P.A.: 66-credit program beyond master's, 20-credit concentration; qualifying exam; admission to candidacy, dissertation; oral defense.

FIELDS OF STUDY
Accountancy.
Biology.
Business Administration.
Communication.
Computer Science.
Educational Leadership.
English.
Environmental Studies.
History.
Human Development Counseling.
Human Services.
Individual Option.
Legal Studies.
Management Information Systems.
Political Studies. Includes practical politics, international affairs.
Public Administration. Includes concentrations in community arts management, criminal justice (M.P.A.); nonprofit management, state government (D.P.A.). M.P.A., D.P.A.
Public Affairs Reporting.
Public Health.
Teacher Leadership. M.A.

UNIVERSITY OF ILLINOIS AT URBANA-CHAMPAIGN

Urbana-Champaign, Illinois 61820
Web site: www.uiuc.edu

Founded 1967. Located 125 miles S of Chicago. CGS and AAU member. Coed. State control. Semester system. Special facilities: Beckman Institution for Advanced Science and Technology, Biotechnology Center, Center for Advanced Construction Technology, Center for African Studies, Center for Latin American and Caribbean Studies, Center for Russian and East European Studies, Center for Complex System Research, Center for Cement Composite Materials, Center for Composite Materials Research, Center for Compound Semiconductor Microelectronics, Center for East Asian and Pacific Studies, Center for South and West Asian Studies, Center for the Study of Reading, National Center for Supercomputing Applications, Illinois Electron Paramagnetic Research Center, Institute for Environmental Studies, Krannert Art Museum, World Heritage Museum. The University's NIH ranking is 94th among all U.S. institutions with 199 awards/grants valued at $58,872,413. According to The Center at University of Florida, the University is ranked 22nd in receipt of Federal Research funds with $266,487,000 and it ranks 14th for total University research expenditures with $493,581,000. The University's endowment assets rank it 66th, with a value of $730,135,000. In 2004, the University awarded 574 doctorates, which ranked it 10th among all U.S. institutions eligible to award that degree. Nineteen of the University's faculty members have been elected to National Honor Academies and this ranks it 52nd among all U.S. institutions. The Library (third-largest university library): approximately 10,200,000 volumes, 90,000 subscriptions. Total University enrollment: 41,000.

Annual tuition fees: full-time, resident $7790, nonresident $19,788. On-campus housing: 750 married student apartments; 1000 graduate dormitory rooms (mixed sex). Average academic year housing cost: $4400–$6000 (plus utilities) for married students, $6800 (including board) for single students. Apply to Division of Housing. Phone: (217)333-5656 (on-campus information), (217)333-1420 (off-campus information).

Graduate College

Graduate study since 1867. Enrollment: full-time 8400, part-time 700. Graduate teaching faculty: full- and part-time 1900. Degrees conferred: A.M., M.S., M.A.S., M.Arch., M.F.A., M.B.A., Ed.M., M.L.A., LL.M., M.C.S., M.M., M.Ext.Ed., M.S.B.A., M.S.W., M.U.P., A.C.Ed., C.A.S., Ed.D., D.M.A., Ph.D.

ADMISSION REQUIREMENTS. Transcript required in support of College's application. GRE/MAT/GMAT/recommendations/interview required by some departments. TOEFL required for international applicants. Accepts transfer applicants. Graduates of unaccredited institutions not considered. Apply to Office of Admissions and Records at least three months in advance of registration, international applicants at least six months in advance of registration. Application fee $50 domestic students, $60 international students. Phone: (217)333-6715.

ADMISSION STANDARDS. Competitive for most departments. Usual minimum average: 3.0 (A = 4).

FINANCIAL AID. Annual awards from institutional funds: academic tuition scholarships, fellowships, administrative assistantships, teaching assistantships, research assistantships, grants, traineeships, tuition waivers, Federal W/S, loans. Approved for VA benefits. Apply by February 15 to appropriate department head for fellowships, assistantships; for other aid programs apply to Office of Financial Aid. Phone: (217)333-0100. Use FAFSA. About 65% of students receive aid other than loans from University and outside sources. Aid available on a limited basis for part-time students.

DEGREE REQUIREMENTS. One unit = 4 semester hours. For most master's: 8 units minimum, at least 4 units in residence; thesis/nonthesis option; language required for some departments. For M.A.S., Ed.M.: same as for most master's, except no thesis requirement. For M.M.: same as for most master's, except reading knowledge of one foreign language for musicology majors. For M.F.A.: 16 units minimum in residence; written report required for majors in design, painting and printmaking, sculpture, art history; no thesis for A.M. in Art Education; reading knowledge of one foreign language for art history majors. For M.B.A.: 18 units minimum; no thesis. For LL.M.: 8 units minimum, at least 2 for research; thesis. For M.S.W.: 16 months in residence and field work. For M.U.P.: normally 2 years in residence; thesis. For A.C.Ed.: 8 units beyond the master's, at least 4 in residence. For Ph.D.: 24 units minimum beyond the bachelor's, at least 16 in residence; departmental qualifying exam; preliminary exam; teaching experience; dissertation; final oral exam. For Ed.D.: essentially the same as for the Ph.D. For D.M.A.: essentially the same as for the Ph.D., except special performance or composition projects in addition to dissertation.

FIELDS OF STUDY.
Accounting.
Advertising. M.S. only.
Aerospace Engineering.
African Studies.
Agricultural and Biological Education. M.S.
Agricultural and Consumer Economics.
American Civilization.
Animal Biology.
Animal Sciences.
Anthropology.
Architecture. Portfolio for admission. M.Arch. only.
Arms Control, Disarment, and International Security.
Art and Design. Includes applied, creative, art education, art history, graphic design; portfolio for admission to creative majors; Ed.D. in art education; Ph.D. in art history.
Astronomy. Includes astrophysics.
Atmospheric Sciences.
Biochemistry.
Bioengeering.
Bioinformatics.
Biology. Interdepartmental.
Biophysics and Computational Biology.
Business Administration.
Cell and Developmental Biology.
Chemical Engineering.
Chemical Physics.
Chemistry. Includes biophysical chemistry.
Civil and Environmental Engineering.
Classics. Includes Latin, Greek, classics; Ph.D. in classical philology only.
Communications. Ph.D.
Community Health.
Comparative Literature. Interdepartmental.
Computer Science and Engineering.
Computer Science.
Crop Sciences.
Dance. Performance; M.F.A. only.
East Asian Languages and Culture.
Economics. GRE for admission; thesis optional for A.M., M.S.
Education. Includes elementary, secondary teaching; administration and supervision, adult curriculum, exceptional children, bilingual education, educational psychology, early childhood teaching, reading research, guidance and counseling, rehabilitation counseling, educational policy studies, history and philosophy, measurement and evaluation, research methods, school psychology; vocational and technical education; all subject fields; thesis for A.M., M.S.
Electrical and Computer Engineering.
English. One language for A.M.; thesis optional.
English as an International Language. A.M. only.
Entomology. Thesis required for M.S.
Finance. Eight units with thesis or ten units without thesis for master's.
Food Science and Human Nutrition.
French.
Genetics. Interdepartmental; Ph.D. only.

Geography.

Geology.

Germanic Languages and Literatures. Thesis, one language in addition to German for A.M.; two additional languages for Ph.D.

Government and Public Affairs.

History. One language for A.M.

Human and Community Development. M.S. or A.M. only; thesis optional.

Human Factors. M.S.

Industrial Engineering. M.S., Ph.D.

Journalism. Thesis or special project for M.S.; M.S. only.

Kinesiology. GRE, MAT for admission; thesis for M.S.

Labor and Industrial Relations. Eight units with thesis, 10 units without thesis for M.S.

Landscape Architecture. Twelve units for M.L.A.; M.L.A. only.

Latin American and Caribbean Studies.

Law. J.D. admission.

Library and Information Science. GRE for admission; 10 units required for M.S.

Linguistics. One language, final essay for A.M.

Materials Science and Engineering.

Mathematics. Includes applied, statistics.

Mechanical and Industrial Engineering.

Microbiology.

Molecular and Integrative Physiology.

Music. Includes performance, musicology, music education, composition; qualifying exam for admission, including performance when appropriate; one language for M.M. in musicology.

Natural Resources and Environmental Science.

Neuroscience.

Nuclear, Plasma, and Radiological Engineering.

Nutritional Science.

Philosophy. GRE for admission; essay for A.M.

Physics.

Plant Biology.

Political Science. Thesis or research paper for A.M.

Psychology. GRE for admission; thesis for A.M.

Recreation, Sports and Tourism. M.S., Ph.D.

Romance Linguistics.

Russian, East European and Eurasian Studies.

Second Language Acquistion and Teacher Education.

Slavic Languages and Literatures.

Social Work.

Sociology. GRE for admission.

Spanish, Italian, and Portuguese. A.M., Ph.D. in all three languages.

Speech and Hearing Science. Includes education of the deaf.

Speech Communication. GRE for admission; thesis for A.M.

Statistics.

Theater.

Urban and Regional Planning. Thesis or master's project required; 12–13½ units for M.U.P.; Ph.D. in regional planning.

Veterinary Medical Science. Includes veterinary biosciences, clinical medicine, pathology, and hygiene; D.V.M. or appropriate B.S. for admission.

Women's Studies.

Writing Studies.

College of Law

Web site: www.law.uiuc.edu

Established 1897. ABA approved since 1923. AALS member. Public control. Semester system. Special programs: Summer study at Oxford University and University of Victoria, B.C. Law library: 709,673 volumes, 8435 subscriptions: has LEXIS, NEXIS, WESTLAW; has more that 800 network connections.

Annual tuition: resident $20,512, nonresident $31,718. Total average annual additional expenses: $14,225.

Enrollment: first-year class 188, total 626 (men 60%, women 40%, minorities 32%); postgraduates 25; no part-time study. Faculty: full-time 48, part-time 48. Student to faculty ratio 12.6 to 1. Degrees conferred: J.D., J.D.-M.D., J.D.-M.Acc., J.D.-M.B.A., J.D.-M.A. (Labor and Industrial Relations, Urban Planning), J.D.-M.Ed., J.D.-Ed.D., J.D.-M.S. (Journalism, Chemistry, Natural Resources, and Environmental Sciences); J.D.-M.U.P., J.D.-D.V.M., J.D.-M.C.S., J.D.-M.S.N.R.E.S. The LL.M., J.S.D. are offered through the Graduate College.

ADMISSION REQUIREMENTS. LSDAS Law School report, bachelor's degree, transcripts, LSAT, résumé, personal statement, two letters of recommendation required in support of application. Interview not required. Accepts transfer applicants. Apply to Admission Office of the College by March 15 (preference given to applications received by January 15). Admits first-year students Fall only. Application fee $50, $60 for non-U.S. citizens. Phone: (217)244-6415.

ADMISSION STANDARDS. Selective. Accepts approximately 15% of all applicants. Number of applicants 2933; number of acceptance 446; number enrolled 188; LSAT (75% of students have a score at or above 162); GPA (75% of students have a GPA at or above 3.04). *U.S. News & World Report* ranking is in the top 25 of all U.S. law schools.

FINANCIAL AID. Scholarships, fellowships, assistantships, full and partial tuition waiver, loans. Apply to Financial Aid Office, preferably by March 15. Phone: (217)244-6415. Use FAFSA. Graduate students apply through Graduate College and use University FAF. About 58% of students receive aid other than loans from College.

DEGREE REQUIREMENTS. For J.D.: 90 hours minimum, at least 6 semesters in full-time residence. Transfer credit from other law schools individually considered. For LL.M.: at least 2 semesters beyond J.D. For J.S.D.: first professional degree required; 16 courses, individually arranged. Refer to Graduate College listings for joint degree requirements.

College of Veterinary Medicine

Web site: www.cvm.uiuc.edu

Established 1944. Semester system. Special facilities: Center for Microscopic Imaging, Center for Zoonoses Research.

Annual tuition and fees: residents $17,012, nonresidents $36,476. Limited on-campus housing available. Contact Tenant Union for both on- and off-campus housing. Phone: (217)333-0112. Total average cost for other expenses: $13,000.

Enrollment: first-year class 100, total 410 (men 25%, women 75%, minorities 8%, state residents 80%); graduate students 100. Faculty: full-time 67, part-time 5. Degrees conferred: D.V.M., D.V.M.-M.P.H., D.V.M.-Ph.D. (Veterinary Medical Scholars Program).

ADMISSION REQUIREMENTS. VMCAS report, transcripts, GRE, essay, animal/veterinary experience, three recommendations (one from an academic adviser) required in support of application. Interview by invitation only. Applicants must have completed at least two years of college study. Preference given to residents and to nonresidents from states that do not have veterinary schools. Apply to Assistant Dean after August 15 but before October 1. Fall admission only. Application fee $60, $75 for international applicants. Phone: (217)333-1192; fax: (217)333-4628; e-mail: admissions@cvm.uiuc.edu.

ADMISSION STANDARDS. Competitive. Accepts about 10–15% of all applicants. Number of applications 500 (n/a out-of-state); number interviewed n/a (n/a out-of-state); number of acceptance n/a (n/a out-of-state); number enrolled 115 (25 out-of-state). Usual minimum UGPA: 3.0 (A = 4), GRE mean score (V + Q) 1150; mean UGPA 3.55 (residents), 3.67 (nonresidents).

FINANCIAL AID. Scholarships, research fellowships, teaching/ research assistantships, full and partial tuition waivers, Federal W/S, Federal and private loans. Apply to University Office of Student Financial Aid by January 15. Use FAFSA.

DEGREE REQUIREMENTS. For D.V.M.: 153 semester hours in full-time residence. For M.S., Ph.D.: see Graduate College listing above.

FIELDS OF GRADUATE STUDY.
Anesthesiology.
Cell/Molecular Biology.
Epidemiology and Preventive Medicine.
Equine Medicine.
Equine Surgery.
Food Animal Medicine.
Food Animal Surgery.
Immunology.
Internal Medicine.
Microbiology.
Morphology.
Ophthalmology.
Parasitology.
Pathology.
Pharmacology.
Physiology.
Radiology.
Small Animal Medicine.
Small Animal Surgery.
Swine Medicine.
Theriogenology. Includes animal reproduction.
Toxicology.

UNIVERSITY OF THE INCARNATE WORD
San Antonio, Texas 78209
Web site: www.uiw.edu

Founded 1881. Coed. Private control—Catholic. Semester system. Library: 257,500 volumes, 3436 subscriptions. Total University enrollment: 5200.

Tuition: per credit $640; $670 Ph.D. On-campus housing for graduate men and women. Annual academic year housing cost: $8300 (including board). Apply to Director of Campus Life. Phone: (210)829-6034.

School of Graduate Studies and Research

Graduate study since 1950. Enrollment: full-time 47, part-time 795. School faculty: full-time 70, part-time 24. Degrees conferred: M.A., M.S., M.B.A., M.S.N., M.Ed., Ph.D.

ADMISSION REQUIREMENTS. Transcripts, GRE/MAT/ GMAT required in support of application. Interview required for some disciplines. TOEFL required for foreign applicants. Accepts transfer applicants. Graduates of unaccredited colleges usually not considered. Apply to Admissions Office at least two months prior to registration. Application fee $20. Phone: (210)829-6005; fax: (210)829-3921.

ADMISSION STANDARDS. Selective. Usual minimum average: 2.5 (3.0 in major) (A = 4).

FINANCIAL AID. Annual awards from institutional funds: fellowships, research assistantships, administrative assistantships, internships, traineeships, Federal W/S, loans. Approved for VA benefits. Apply to the Financial Aid office; no specified closing date. Phone: (210)829-6008. Use FAFSA (School code: 003578). and institutional FAF. Aid available for part-time students.

DEGREE REQUIREMENTS. For M.A., M.Ed., M.S., M.S.N.: 36 credit hours minimum, at least 24 in residence; thesis/nonthesis option. For M.B.A.: 48 credit hours minimum, at least 36 in residence (specific undergraduate prerequisites required). For Ph.D.: minimum of 66 credits beyond the master's; Qualifying Exam; oral and written second language proficiency; dissertation.

FIELDS OF STUDY.
Accounting. M.S.
Administration. Includes concentrations in adult education, applied administration (online only), communication arts, health administration, industrial technology (online only), nutrition, organizational development, sports management. M.A.A.
Biology. M.S.
Business Administration. Includes international business, sports management. M.B.A.
Communication Arts. M.A.
Education. Includes concentrations in adult education, diversity education, early childhood education, instructional technology, kinesiology, organizational leadership, reading, special education. M.A., M.Ed.
International Educational and Entrepreneurship. Ph.D.
Mathematics. M.S.
Mathematics Education. Ph.D.
Mathematics Teaching. M.A.
Multidisciplinary Science. M.A.
Nursing. M.S.N.
Nutrition. M.S.
Organizational Leadership. Ph.D.
Religious Studies. M.A.
Teaching. Includes concentrations in all-level, elementary, secondary. M.A.T.

INDIANA STATE UNIVERSITY
Terre Haute, Indiana 47809-1401
Web site: www.indstate.edu

Founded 1865. Located 170 miles S of Chicago. CGS member. Coed. State control. Semester system. Special facilities: Biotech Center, Center for Governmental Studies, Hearing Disorder Center, Porter School Psychology Center, Special Education Center, Speech Pathology Center, Technology Services Center, Turman Art Gallery, Center for Urban-Regional Studies. Library: 1,500,000 volumes, 5000 subscriptions. Total University enrollment: 10,600.

Tuition: per credit, resident $262, nonresident $521. On-campus housing for 393 married students, limited number of graduate men, women. Average academic year housing cost: $450–$600 per month for married students, $5250 for single students. Apply to Director, University Housing. Phone: (812)237-7697. Day care facilities available.

School of Graduate Studies

Graduate study since 1927. Enrollment: full-time 798; part-time 1210. University faculty teaching graduate students: full-time 343, part-time 72. Degrees conferred: M.A., M.M., M.M.E., M.S., M.B.A., M.P.A., M.F.A., Ed.S., Ph.D., Psy.D.

ADMISSION REQUIREMENTS. Transcript required in support of School's application. Interview required for all Ph.D. applicants. GRE required for some M.A. departments, all Ed.S., doctoral applicants, five letters of recommendation for doctoral applicants. GMAT required for M.B.A. candidates. TOEFL (minimum score 550) required for international applicants. Accepts transfer applicants. Graduates of unaccredited colleges considered. Apply to Dean, School of Graduate Studies one month prior to registration. Application fee $35. Phone: (800)444-4723; (812)237-3111; fax: (812)237-8060; e-mail: gradsch@amber.indstate.edu.

ADMISSION STANDARDS. Selective. Usual minimum average: 2.5 (A = 4).

FINANCIAL AID. Annual awards from institutional funds: scholarships, research fellowships, assistantships, Federal W/S, loans. Apply by March 1 to appropriate department chair for fellowships, assistantships; to Office of Student Financial Aid for all other programs. Phone: (812)237-2215. Use FAFSA. About 50% of full-time students receive aid other than loans from University and outside sources.

DEGREE REQUIREMENTS. For M.A., M.M., M.M.E., M.S., M.B.A., M.P.A., M.F.A.: 32 semester hours minimum; reading knowledge of one foreign language for some departments; GMAT for M.B.A. candidacy; final oral exam with thesis. For Ed.S.: 30 semester hours minimum beyond the master's, at least 20 in residence and one semester in full-time attendance; research project; final oral exam. For Ph.D., Psy.D.: 83–90 semester hours minimum beyond the bachelor's, at least 30 in residence and two consecutive semesters in full-time attendance; preliminary exam; reading knowledge of two foreign languages or one language and statistics or computer science; dissertation final oral exam.

FIELDS OF STUDY.
Art. Includes history, graphic design. M.A., M.F.A.
Athletic Training.
Business Administration.
Clinical Psychology. Admits Fall only.
Communication.
Communication Disorders. Includes speech-language pathology.
Counseling Psychology.
Counselor Education.
Criminology.
Curriculum and Instruction.
Early Childhood Education.
Educational Administration. Includes K–12, higher education.
Electronics and Computer Technology.
Elementary Education.
Elementary School Administration and Supervision.
English.
Family and Consumer Sciences.
Fine Arts.
Geography. Includes economic, physical.
Geology.
Guidance and Psychological Services.
Health and Safety.
History.
Human Resource Development.
Industrial Technology.
Language, Literature, and Linguistics.
Life Sciences. Includes microbiology, systematics, ecology, physiology.
Literacy.
Marriage and Family Therapy
Mathematics.
Mental Health Counseling.
Music.
Nursing.
Physical Education.
Political Science.
Psychology.
Public Administration.
Reading Education.
Recreation and Sports Management.
School Counseling.
Science Education.
Secondary Administration and Supervision.
Social Psychology.
Sociology.
Special Education.
Student Affairs Administration.
Technology Education.
Technology Management.

INDIANA UNIVERSITY
Bloomington, Indiana 47405
Web site: www.iub.edu

Founded 1820. Main campus in Bloomington; Medical Center campus and Law School in Indianapolis. CGS and AAU member. Coed. State control. Semester system. Special facilities: Center for American Studies, Bowen Research Center, CDC CYBER 170/855, Dec VAX-11/780, Geological Field Station in Montana, observatory, biological research station, participant in CIC Traveling Scholar Program with other Big Ten universities, Cyclotron facility, East Asian Languages and Cultures Center, Russian and East European Institute, Fine Arts Museum, Center for Health and Safety Studies, Hilltop and Garden Center, Center for the Study of Law in Action, Indiana Business Research Center, Indiana Museum (anthropology, archaeology, history), Lilly rare book library, Kinsey Sex Institute, Glen Black Archaeological Laboratory, Archives of Traditional Music, Folklore Institute, Nuclear Magnetic Resonance Laboratory, Institute of Psychiatric Research, Institute for Social Research, Semiotics Institute, Transportation Research Center. The University's NIH ranking is 47th among all U.S. institutions with 415 awards/grants valued at $137,418,069. According to The Center at University of Florida, the University is ranked 96th for total University research expenditures with $135,068,000. The University's endowment assets rank it 87th, with a value of $526,608,000. In 2004, the University awarded 391 doctorates, which ranked it 71st among all U.S. institutions eligible to award that degree. Ten of the University's faculty members have been elected to National Honor Academies and this ranks it 71st among all U.S. institutions. The Library: approximately 6,000,000 volumes, 40,000 subscriptions. Total University enrollment: 38,000.

Tuition: per unit, resident $265, nonresident $773. On-campus housing for 1467 married students, 850 graduate men, 850 graduate women. Average academic year housing cost: $3000–$4900, for married students $575–$725 per month. Apply to University Halls of Residence. Phone: (812)855-5601. Day-care facilities available.

Graduate School
Web site: www.indiana.edu/~grdschl/index.html

Graduate study since 1881. Enrollment: full-time 2300, part-time 1760. Graduate faculty: full-time 1080. Degrees conferred: M.A., M.S., M.A.T., M.F.A., M.H.A., D.B.A., Ph.D., LL.M.

ADMISSION REQUIREMENTS. Two transcripts, three reference letters required in support of School's application. GRE or other entrance exams may be required for most programs. Interview not required. Accepts transfer applicants. Graduates of unaccredited institutions not considered. Apply to Office of Graduate School by January 15 (Fall), August 15 (Spring), January 1 (Summer). Application fee $50, $60 for international applicants. Phone: (812)855-0661; fax: (812)855-4266.

ADMISSION STANDARDS. Varies, from relatively open to very competitive. Usual minimum average: 3.0 (A = 4).

FINANCIAL AID. Scholarships; research assistantships, graduate assistantships, faculty assistants, associate instructors, counselors, grants, Federal W/S, loans. Apply by February 1 to proposed major department for fellowships, assistantships; to Financial Aid Office for all other programs. Phone: (812)855-0321. Use FAFSA. About 50% of students receive aid other than loans from University and outside sources. Aid sometimes available for part-time students.

DEGREE REQUIREMENTS. For M.A., M.S.: 30 hours minimum, at least one semester or two summer sessions in full-time attendance; thesis for up to 6 hours' credit; reading knowledge of one foreign language for some programs; final written or oral exam may be required. For M.A.T., M.H.A.: 36 hours minimum, at least 24 in residence and one semester in full-time attendance. For M.F.A.: 60 hours minimum in residence, at least one semester in full-time attendance; final creative project in chosen studio area. For LL.M.: 30 hours minimum in residence; thesis; final oral exam sometimes required. For Ph.D., D.B.A.: 90 hours minimum beyond the bachelor's, at least 60 in residence and two consecutive semesters in full-time attendance; proficiency in depth in one foreign language, reading knowledge in two foreign languages, or reading proficiency in one language and research skill may be required; qualifying exam; dissertation for up to 30 hours' credit; final oral exam.

FIELDS OF STUDY.
African American and African Diaspora Studies. M.A.
American Studies. Ph.D. is combined with related major field.
Anthropology. Thesis or exam required for M.A.
Apparel Merchandising and Interior Design. M.S. only.
Art History. M.A., Ph.D.
Arts Administration. M.A. only.
Astronomy. Thesis ordinarily required for M.A.
Astrophysics. Ph.D. only.
Biochemistry and Molecular Biology. Interdepartmental; programs at Bloomington and Indianapolis campuses; thesis for M.S.; Ph.D.
Biology. M.A.T.; genetics, Ph.D.; microbiology, M.A., Ph.D.; molecular and cellular biology, Ph.D.; plant sciences, M.A., Ph.D.; zoology, M.A., Ph.D.; ecology and evolutionary biology, M.A., Ph.D.
Business. Ph.D. only.
Central Eurasian Studies. M.A., Ph.D.
Chemical Physics. Ph.D. only.
Chemistry. Thesis for M.S., M.A.T., Ph.D.
Classical Studies. Includes Greek, Latin; thesis for M.A., M.A.T.; GRE for admission to Ph.D.
Cognitive Science. Ph.D. is combined with related major field.
Communication and Culture. M.A, M.A.T., Ph.D.
Comparative Literature. Proficiency in one, fluency in one foreign language; thesis for M.A., M.A.T.; fluency in two, proficiency in three foreign languages for Ph.D.
Computer Science. M.S., Ph.D.
Creative Writing. M.F.A.
Criminal Justice. M.A., Ph.D.
Dentistry. Program at Indianapolis campus; apply to Secretary of Dental Graduate Program; thesis for Ph.D.
East Asian Languages and Cultures. Includes Chinese, Japanese, East Asian Studies (M.A. only); one East Asian language for admission; thesis, two languages for M.A.; two languages for Ph.D.
Economics. GRE Subject for admission. M.A., M.A.T., Ph.D.
Education. M.A., Ph.D. through Graduate School; M.S. in Ed., Ed.S., Ed.D. through Graduate School of Education.
English. Includes creative writing major for M.A.; one language for M.A., M.A.T.; two languages for admission to Ph.D. in English language.
Environmental Risk Analysis.
Environmental Science. Ph.D. only.
Fine Arts. Includes studio, art history; one language for M.A. in art history, portfolio for admission to M.F.A., M.A.T.; Ph.D. in art history only.
Folklore. Thesis optional; one language for M.A., Ph.D.

French and Italian. GRE for admission; three languages for Ph.D.; French M.A., M.A.T., Ph.D.; Italian M.A., Ph.D.
General Science. M.A.T. only.
Genetics. Interdepartmental; Ph.D.
Geography. M.A., M.A.T., Ph.D.
Geological Sciences. Includes biogeochemistry, environmental geosciences and hydrogeology, geobiology, geochemistry, geophysics. M.S., Ph.D.
Geology. M.S.
Germanic Studies. M.A., M.A.T., Ph.D.
Health, Physical Education, Recreation. Includes human performance, health behavior, leisure behavior. Ph.D. only; others through School of HPER.
History. GRE, one language for admission. M.A., M.A.T., Ph.D.
History and Philosophy of Science. M.A., Ph.D.
Hungarian Studies. Certificate only.
Informatics. Ph.D.
Information Sciences. Ph.D. only.
Journalism. Thesis or project for M.A., M.A.T., Ph.D.
Latin American and Caribbean Studies. One language for M.A.
Law. LL.M., Ph.D.
Library and Information Science. M.L.S. offered by School of Library and Information Sciences, Ph.D. by Graduate School.
Linguistics. One language; thesis optional for M.A. Includes applied, general. M.A., Ph.D.
Mass Communication. Interdepartmental; GRE for admission. Ph.D. only.
Mathematical Physics. Interdepartmental. Ph.D. only.
Mathematics. M.A., M.A.T., Ph.D.
Medical Sciences (Bloomington). Includes anatomy, M.A., Ph.D.; pathology, M.S., Ph.D.; physiology, M.A., Ph.D.; pharmacology, M.S., Ph.D.; (Indianapolis) anatomy, M.S., Ph.D.; medical biophysics, M.S., Ph.D.; medical genetics, M.S., Ph.D.; medical neurobiology, M.S., Ph.D.; microbiology and immunology, M.S., Ph.D.; pharmacology, M.S., Ph.D.; physiology, M.S., Ph.D.; toxicology, M.S., Ph.D.
Medical Sciences Combined Degree Program (Bloomington and Indianapolis). M.S. or Ph.D., and M.D.
Music. Includes Composition, M.A.; musicology, theory, education, M.A., M.A.T. (music education only), Ph.D. offered by Graduate School; for M.M., M.S.Mus., M.M.Ed., D.Mus.Ed., D.Mus., admission is through School of Music; entrance exams required; thesis for M.A.; several years' experience for admission to M.A.T.
Near Eastern Languages and Cultures. Includes Arabic, Hebrew; for Ph.D.: thesis, one language in addition to Arabic, Hebrew.
Neural Sciences. Ph.D.
Pathology. M.S., Ph.D.
Pharmacology. M.S., Ph.D.
Philosophy. GRE for admission; thesis, one language for M.A., Ph.D.
Physics. M.S., M.A.T., Ph.D.
Physiological Optics. Thesis for M.S., Ph.D.
Physiology. M.A., Ph.D.
Political Science. M.A., M.A.T., Ph.D.
Psychological and Brain Sciences. Ph.D.
Public Affairs. Ph.D.
Public Policy. Ph.D.
Religious Studies. M.A., Ph.D.
Russian and East European. M.A.
Slavic Languages and Literatures. Includes Russian major for M.A., M.A.T., Russian literature or Slavic linguistics for Ph.D., one language in addition to Russian for M.A., two languages in addition to Russian for Ph.D. in Russian literature; comprehensive knowledge of one Slavic language, reading knowledge of French, German, and one other Slavic language for Ph.D. in Slavic linguistics.
Social Studies. M.A.T., M.F.A.
Sociology. Special project for M.A., Ph.D.
Spanish and Portuguese. Includes Spanish major for M.A., M.A.T.; Hispanic literature or Spanish linguistics for Ph.D.;

some knowledge of Latin plus two other languages in addition to Spanish for Ph.D.

Speech and Hearing Sciences. Includes speech pathology and audiology; thesis for M.S.; thesis may be creative in nature; M.A.T., Ph.D.

Studio Arts. M.A.T., M.F.A.

Telecommunication. Thesis for M.A., M.S., Ph.D.

Theater and Drama. M.A., M.A.T., M.F.A., Ph.D.

Vision Sciences. M.S., Ph.D.

Western European Studies. Thesis, comprehensive knowledge of one language, reading knowledge of one other. M.A.

Kelley School of Business

Web site: www.bus.indiana.edu

Established 1936. Public control. Accredited programs: M.B.A., Accounting; recognized Ph.D. Full-time study at Bloomington; part-time study at Indianapolis, Fort Wayne. Semester system. Special facilities: Center for Education and Research in Retailing, Johnson Center for Entrepreneurship and Innovation, Center for International Business Education and Research, Center for Real Estate Studies, Center for Sales Studies and Market Research, Indiana Business Research Center, Indiana Center for Econometric Model Research, Institute for Urban Transportation, Leadership Research Institute, Special Programs: global exchange programs (in Australia, France, Norway, Spain, Switzerland, United Kingdom), international internships (in Germany, Slovenia), summer internships (Germany, France, and People's Republic of China). Library: 160,000 volumes, 1000 subscriptions.

Annual tuition: resident full-time M.B.A. flat fee $16,975, nonresident full-time $33,414; other business programs per credit resident $560, nonresident $1114. On-campus rooms and apartments available for both single and married students.

Enrollment: total full-time 613. Faculty: 109 full-time, 20 part-time; 88% with Ph.D./D.B.A. Degrees conferred: M.B.A., M.B.A.-J.D., M.B.A.-M.A. (East Asian Studies, Russian and East European Studies, West European Studies), M.P.A. (Professional Accountancy), Ph.D. (offered through the Graduate School).

ADMISSION REQUIREMENTS. All applicants should have a bachelor's degree from a recognized institution of higher education. Students are required to have their own personal computer. Beginning M.B.A. and M.P.A. students are admitted Fall only. Submit application, GMAT (will accept GMAT test results from the last five years, latest acceptable date is January), official transcripts from each undergraduate/graduate school attended, two letters of recommendation, three essays, personal statement, résumé (prefers at least four years of work experience), and an application fee of $50 ($60 international applicants) to the Admission Office, School of Business. Accepts MBA Multi-App electronic application in lieu of institutional application. U.S. citizens apply by January 15 (Fall early admission), March 1 (Fall regular admission), international students apply by December 1 (Fall). In addition, international students (whose native language is other than English) should submit a TOEFL report (minimum score 580), certified translations and evaluations of all official transcripts; recommendation should be in English or with certified translations, and proof of sufficient financial resources for two years of academic study. On-campus visits and interviews are strongly urged prior to the admissions committee reviewing completed application. Joint degree applicants must apply to and be accepted to both schools/programs, contact the admissions office for current information and specific admissions requirements. M.B.A. program phone: (812) 855-8006; Accounting graduate program: (812) 855-7200; e-mail: acctgrad@indiana.edu.

ADMISSION REQUIREMENTS FOR DOCTORAL CANDIDATES. Contact Kelley School of Business for application material and information. Beginning students are admitted Fall only. U.S. citizens apply by February 1 (Fall), international students apply by December 15. Submit application, GMAT/GRE (will accept GMAT/GRE test results from the last five years), two official transcripts from each undergraduate/graduate school attended, three letters of recommendation, four or five essays, current résumé, statement of purpose, and application fee of $40 to the Chairperson of the Doctoral Programs, Graduate School of Business. In addition, international students (whose native language is other than English) should submit a TOEFL report (minimum score 600); certified translations and evaluations of all official transcripts; recommendation should be in English or with certified translations, proof of health/immunization certificate. Interviews are strongly encouraged prior to the admissions committee reviewing completed application. Notification is made by mid-April.

ADMISSION STANDARDS. Very competitive for M.B.A., Ph.D. Median GMAT: 630; median GPA: 3.2 (A = 4). *U.S. News & World Report* ranked Kelley in the top 24 of all U.S. business schools. *BusinessWeek* listed Kelley in the top 18 of all American business schools.

FINANCIAL AID. Scholarships, tuition waivers, merit scholarship, fellowships, research and teaching assistantships, Federal W/S, loans. Financial aid may be available for international students. Assistantships/fellowships may be available for joint degree candidates. Financial Aid applications and information generally available at the on-campus visit/interview; apply by March 1. Request all financial aid information from the School of Business. Phone: (812)855-8006. Use FAFSA (School code: 001809), also submit an institutional FAF, a Financial Aid Transcript, Federal Income Tax forms. Approximately 35% of current students receive some form of financial assistance. For Doctoral students there are fee scholarships, teaching appointments, research appointments, and fellowships. For Doctoral Financial Aid information call (812)855-3476.

DEGREE REQUIREMENTS. For M.B.A.: 54 credit program including 18 elective credits, two-year program; degree must be completed within seven years. For M.P.A.: 30 credit program. For M.B.A.-M.A.: 64 credit, generally a two-and-one-half- to seven-year program. For M.B.A.-J.D.: 118 credit, generally four- to seven-year program. For Ph.D.: four- to five-year program; comprehensive exam; candidacy; teaching development component; dissertation proposal and oral defense, dissertation; oral defense.

FIELDS OF STUDY.

Accounting. Includes concentrations in accounting, entrepreneurship, finance, human resource management, individually designed major, information systems, international business, management, marketing, production/operations management. M.B.A., M.S.A.

Finance. M.S.

Global Supply Chain Managment. M.A.

Information Systems. M.S.I.S.

Kelley Direct Online. M.B.A.

Strategic Management. M.S.

FIELDS OF DOCTORAL STUDY.

Accounting.

Business and Public Policy.

Finance.

Management. Includes entrepreneurship, organizational behavior and human performance, strategic management and organization theory.

Marketing.

Operations and Decision Technologies. Includes decision sciences, operations management, information systems.

School of Education—Graduate Studies

Web site: www.education.indiana.edu

Graduate degrees since 1930. Semester system. Special facilities: Center for Adolescent and Family Studies, Center for Human

Growth, Center for Postsecondary Planning and Research, Center for Research on Learning and Technology, Indiana Center for Evaluation, Indiana Education Policy Center, Institute for Child Study, Social Studies Development Center. Tuition: per credit resident $269, nonresident $783. Enrollment: full-time 323, part-time 518. Graduate faculty: full-time 105, part-time 41. Degrees conferred: M.S. in Ed., Ed.S., Ed.D. The M.A. and Ph.D. are awarded by the Graduate School.

ADMISSION REQUIREMENTS. Transcripts, GRE, two letters of recommendation, goal statement required in support of School's application. Online application available. Interview may be required. TOEFL (minimum score 550) required for international applicants. Accepts transfer applicants. Graduates of unaccredited institutions not considered. Apply to Office of Graduate Studies by March 1 (Fall), December 1 (Spring), March 1 (Summer). Earlier deadlines for Counseling, Educational Psychology, School Psychology, Student Affairs Administration. Deadlines for international applicants December 15 (Summer, Fall), September 15 (Spring). Application fee $50, $60 for international applicants. Phone: (812)856-8504; fax: (812)856-8504.

ADMISSION STANDARDS. Selective for most departments. Usual minimum average: 3.0 (A = 4) (master's applicants), average GRE combined score 1225; 3.30 (doctoral applicants), average GRE combined score 1500.

FINANCIAL AID. Annual awards from institutional funds: grants, fellowships, research assistantships, teaching assistantships, internships, other assistantships, Federal W/S, loans. Apply by February 15 to Director of Financial Aid. Phone: (812)855-FAST. Use FAFSA, FAC sheet. About 15% of students receive aid other than loans from both School and outside sources.

DEGREE REQUIREMENTS. For M.S. in Ed.: 36 semester hours minimum without thesis, at least 27 in residence, 15 credits at the campus awarding the degree; some programs require more than 36. For Ed.S.: 65 hours minimum beyond the bachelor's, at least 35 in residence at the Bloomington or Indianapolis campus; 9 credits in full-time attendance in either one semester, or summer. For Ed.D., Ph.D.: 90 hours minimum beyond the bachelor's or 60 credits with a master's degree, at least two consecutive semesters in residence; qualifying written/oral exams; thesis for up to 15 hours; final oral exam.

FIELDS OF STUDY.
Art Education. M.S., Ph.D.
Counseling and Counselor Education. Includes school, agency. 48 credit master's. M.S., Ed.S.
Counseling Psychology. Ph.D.
Curriculum and Instruction. Ed.D., Ph.D.
Educational Leadership. Includes elementary, secondary. M.S., Ed.S., Ed.D.
Educational Psychology. M.S., Ph.D.
Elementary Education. Includes early childhood. M.S., Ed.S., Ph.D.
Higher Education. M.S., Ed.D., Ph.D.
History and Philosophy of Education. M.S., Ph.D.
International and Comparative Education. M.S.
Instructional Systems Technology. M.S., Ed.S., Ed.D., Ph.D.
Language Education. Includes English, foreign language, reading. M.S., Ed.S., Ed.D., Ph.D.
School Psychology. Ed.S., Ph.D.
Secondary Education. Includes mathematics, science. M.S., Ed.S.
Social Studies. M.S., Ed.S.
Special Education. M.S., Ed.S., Ed.D., Ph.D.
Student Affairs Administration. M.S.

School of Health, Physical Education, and Recreation—Graduate Division

In operation since 1946. Tuition: per credit, resident $269, nonresident $783. Enrollment: full- and part-time 270. Faculty teaching graduate students: full-time 50, part-time 12. Degrees conferred: M.S., M.P.H., Director, Ph.D.

ADMISSION REQUIREMENTS. Transcripts, GRE, letters of recommendation required in support of School's application. TOEFL required for international applicants. Interview usually not required. Accepts transfer applicants. Apply by March 1 to Associate Dean for Academic Services for priority consideration. Application fee $50, $60 international applicants. Phone: (812) 855-1561; fax: (812)855-4983.

ADMISSION STANDARDS. Selective. Usual minimum average: for M.S. 2.8; for doctoral degree 3.0 (A = 4).

FINANCIAL AID. Annual awards from institutional funds: fellowships, assistantships, grants, student academic appointments, Federal W/S, loans. Apply to Dean for academic appointments; to Financial Aid Office for all other programs. Use FAFSA. Phone: (812)855-0321.

DEGREE REQUIREMENTS. For M.S.: 35 semester hours minimum, at least 25–30 in residence; 45 credits for exercise physiology. For M.P.H.: 40 credit hours minimum, at least 25–30 in residence. For Director's degree: 65 hours minimum beyond the bachelor's, at least 35 in residence; final project; one year of professional experience; final written exam. For Ph.D. human performance: 90 hours beyond the bachelor's, at least 60 hours in residence; qualifying exams; dissertation; language/statistics option; final oral exam.

FIELDS OF STUDY.
Applied Health Science. Includes public health, human behavior (Ph.D.), human development and family studies, nutrition science, safety management, school and college health education, health promotion. M.P.H., M.S., Ph.D.
Kinesiology. Includes adapted physical education, applied sport science, athletic administration/sport management, biomechanics, ergonomics, exercise physiology, exercise science, clinical exercise physiology, motor control, social science of sport. M.S., Ph.D.
Recreation and Park Administration. Includes leisure behavior (Ph.D.), outdoor recreation, recreation administration, recreational sport administration, therapeutic recreation, tourism management. M.S., Ph.D.

School of Informatics

Web site: www.informatics.indiana.edu

Established 1999. Special facilities: Center for Genomics and Bioinformatics, Informatics Research Institute. Semester system.
Tuition: per credit resident $265, nonresident $773. Enrollment: full- and part-time 81. Faculty: full- and part-time 30. Degree conferred: M.S.

ADMISSION REQUIREMENTS. Transcripts, GRE, three letters of reference, personal statement or sample of creative work required in support of School's application. GRE required for applicants with less than 3.0 GPA. TOEFL (minimum score 600) required for international applicants. Will consider transfer applicants. Graduates of unaccredited colleges not considered. Admits Fall only. Apply to School by January 15 for admissions and financial aid, April 1 admissions only. Application fee $50, $60 international applicants. Phone: (812)856-5754; fax: (812) 856-7464.

ADMISSION STANDARDS. Selective. Usual minimum average: 3.0 (A = 4).

FINANCIAL AID. Annual awards from institutional funds: scholarships, fellowships, assistantships, grants, fee reduction assistance for nonresidents also available, Federal W/S, loans. Approved for VA benefits. Apply by January 15 to School for scholarships, fellowships, assistantships; to Office of Scholarships and Financial Aid for all other programs. Phone: (812)855-0321. Use FAFSA and institutional FAF. About 20% of students receive aid from University and outside sources.

DEGREE REQUIREMENTS. For M.S.: 36 credit interdisciplinary program; 30 credit interdisciplinary program for Media Arts and Science.

FIELDS OF STUDY.
Bioinformatics.
Chemical Informatics.
Health Informatics.
Human–Computer Interaction.
Laboratory Informatics.
Medial Arts and Science.

School of Law
Web site: www.law.indiana.edu

Established 1842. Located on main campus. ABA approved since 1923. AALS member. Public control. Semester system. Full-time, day study only. Special facilities: Center for Constitutional Democracy, Center for the Study of Law and Society. Special programs: study abroad in London, England, Poland, New Zealand, China, Hong Kong; foreign exchange programs with the Universite Pantheon-Assas (Paris II) Law School, Paris, France, and ESADE Law School in Barcelona, Spain. Law library: 739,258 volumes, 9060 subscriptions; has LEXIS, NEXIS, WESTLAW, DIALOG, LEGISLATE.

Annual tuition: resident $15,784, nonresident $30,311, LL.M. $33,154. Total average additional expenses: $14,158.

Enrollment: first-year class 228; total full-time 648 (men 59%, women 41%, minorities 17%). Faculty: full-time 43, part-time 18. Student to faculty ratio 14.1 to 1. Degrees conferred: J.D., J.D.-M.A. (Telecommunication, History, Social Work, Central Eurasian/ Uralic Studies), J.D.-M.B.A., J.D.-M.P.A., J.D.-M.S.E.S. (Environmental Sciences), J.D.-M.L.S., J.D.-Ph.D. (Law and Social Sciences), LL.M., M.C.L. (only for persons who have completed a basic legal education and received a university degree in law in another country), S.J.D.

ADMISSION REQUIREMENTS. LSDAS Law School report, bachelor's degree, transcripts, LSAT, recommendations required in support of application. Graduates of unaccredited colleges not considered. Apply to Admissions Office; no specified closing date. Priority given to applications received before March 1, rolling admissions process. Application fee $35. Phone: (812)855-4765; fax: (812)855-0555; e-mail: lawadmis@indiana.edu. For graduate study contact Graduate Legal Studies Office. Phone: (812)856-0221.

ADMISSION STANDARDS. Selective. Accepts approximately 38% of all students. Number of applicants 2405; number of acceptance 916; number enrolled 228; LSAT (75% of students have a score at or above 158); GPA (75% of students have a GPA at or above 3.03). *U.S. News & World Report* ranking is in the top 36 of all U.S. law schools.

FINANCIAL AID. Scholarships, fellowships, assistantships, Federal W/S, loans. Apply by March 1 to Admissions Office for fellowships, to Office of Scholarships and Financial Aid for loans; no specified closing date. Phone: (812)855-7746. Use FAFSA (School code: 001809). About 74% of students receive some aid from School.

DEGREE REQUIREMENTS. For J.D.: satisfactory completion of an eighty-six-credit-hour program; accelerated twenty-seven-month program is also available. For LL.M., M.C.L.: at least 24 credits minimum beyond J.D.; thesis. For S.J.D.: at least one year of full-time residence; dissertation of publishable quality; oral defense.

School of Library and Information Science
Web site: www.slis.lib.indiana.edu

Organized library and information science study since 1930. Semester system. Special facilities: Center for Applied Semiotics, Center for Social Informatics.

Tuition: per credit, resident $299, nonresident $873. On-campus housing available. Enrollment: full-time 237, part-time 92. Faculty: full-time 12. Degrees conferred: M.L.S., M.I.S., Sp.L.I.S. The Ph.D. is offered by the Graduate School.

ADMISSION REQUIREMENTS. Transcripts, letters of reference, professional goals statement required in support of School's application. Online application available. GRE required for applicants with less than 3.0 GPA. TOEFL required for international applicants. Interview may be required. Accepts transfer applicants. Graduates of unaccredited colleges not considered. Apply to Office of School by May 15 (Fall), November 15 (Spring), March 15 (Summer). Application fee $50, $60 international applicants. Phone: (812)855-2018; fax: (812)855-6166; e-mail: slis@indiana.edu.

ADMISSION STANDARDS. Selective. Usual minimum average: 3.0 (A = 4).

FINANCIAL AID. Annual awards from institutional funds: merit scholarships, fellowships, graduate assistantships, fee reduction assistance for nonresidents also available, Federal W/S, loans. Approved for VA benefits. Apply by January 15 (Fall), October 1 (Spring) to appropriate department for scholarships, fellowships, assistantships; to Office of Scholarships and Financial Aid for all other programs. Phone: (812)855-7787. Use FAFSA and institutional FAF. About 10% of students receive aid from University and outside sources. Aid available for part-time students; part-time work opportunities in the library generally available.

DEGREE REQUIREMENTS. For M.L.S.: 36 hours minimum; computer-based information tool. For M.I.S.: 42 hours minimum; computer-based information tool. For Sp.L.I.S.: 30 hours minimum beyond the master's; computer-based information tool. For Ph.D.: see Graduate School listing above.

FIELDS OF STUDY.
Information Science. Includes information architecture and design, human–computer interaction and communication, strategic information management and leadership, information retrieval systems design. Entire program available in Bloomington and Indiana University–Purdue University Indianapolis. M.I.S., Ph.D.
Library Science. Entire program available in Bloomington, Indiana University–Purdue University Indianapolis, Indiana University South Bend. Courses offered in the Fall, Spring, and during two Summer Sessions. M.L.S.

Jacobs School of Music

Organized music study since 1910. Semester system. Music library: 380,000 volumes. On-campus housing available.

Tuition: per credit, resident $300, nonresident $874. Graduate enrollment: full-time 524, part-time 255. School faculty: full-time 35, part-time 255. Degrees conferred: M.M., M.M.-M.L.S., M.M.Ed., M.S., D.Mus.Ed., D.Mus. The M.A., M.A.T., and Ph.D. are offered through the Graduate School.

ADMISSION REQUIREMENTS. Transcripts, references required in support of application. GRE Music Subject Test strongly recommended for all applicants. GRE required for applicants in Music Education, Music Theory, and Musicology. TOEFL required for international applicants. Audition and/or interview required for most degree and diploma programs. Entrance exams at time of first registration. Accepts transfer applicants. Apply to Director of Admissions by December 1 (Fall), September 1 (Spring), May 1 (Summer). Audition dates: January 11–12, February 1–2, March 1–2. Application fee $100, $110 for international applicants. Phone: (812)855-1738; fax: (812)855-5570; e-mail: musicadm @indiana.edu.

ADMISSION STANDARDS. Selective. Usual minimum average: 3.0 (A = 4).

FINANCIAL AID. Annual awards from institutional funds: research assistantships, teaching assistantships, fellowships, full and partial tuition waivers. Apply to Dean by March 15. Phone: (812)855-3278. Use FAFSA and institutional FAF. About 35% of students receive aid other than loans from School and outside sources.

DEGREE REQUIREMENTS. For master's: 30–35 semester hours minimum, at least 30 in residence and one year or four summer sessions in full-time attendance; reading knowledge of one or more foreign languages for some majors; thesis required for some majors, optional for others; comprehensive exam. For D.M.E., D.M.: 90 semester hours minimum beyond the bachelor's, at least 30 hours and two consecutive semesters in full-time residence; reading knowledge of one to three foreign languages/research techniques, depending upon program; qualifying exam; recitals or other public performance for most majors; dissertation or project (document, essay, lecture/recital, or composition); final oral exam. For M.A., M.A.T., Ph.D.: see Graduate School listing above.

FIELDS OF STUDY.
Arts Administration. M.A.
Ballet. M.S.
Composition. Sample compositions for admission. M.M., D.M.
Computer Music Composition. M.M.
Conducting. Includes choral, instrumental, wind. M.M., D.M.
Early Music. M.M., D.M.
Jazz Studies. M.M.
Music Education. M.A.T., M.M.E., D.M.E., Ph.D.
Music Literature and Pedagogy. D.M.
Music Theatre Scenic Techniques. M.S.
Music Theory. M.A., M.M., Ph.D.
Musicology. M.A., Ph.D.
Organ and Church Music. M.M., D.M.
Performance. Includes most instruments and voice. M.M., D.M.
Stage Direction for Opera. M.S.

INDIANA UNIVERSITY–PURDUE UNIVERSITY INDIANAPOLIS

Indianapolis, Indiana 46202-5143
Web site: www.iupui.edu

Founded 1908. Main campuses in Bloomington and West Lafayette; Medical Center campus and Law School in Indianapolis. Coed. State control. Semester system. According to The Center at University of Florida, the campus is ranked 85th in receipt of Federal Research fund with $92,175,000 and it ranks 68th for total University research expenditures with $202,601,000. The University's endowment assets rank it 97th, with a value of $486,099,000. Seven of the University's faculty members have been elected to National Honor Academies and this ranks it 78th among all U.S. institutions. The Library: approximately 1,500,000 volumes, 29,900 subscriptions. Total University enrollment: 29,900.

Tuition: per credit resident $265, nonresident $773. Limited on-campus housing available. Day-care facilities available.

School of Liberal Arts

Graduate study since 1908. Tuition: per unit, resident $265, nonresident $773. Enrollment: full-time 3200, part-time 800 (men 65%, women 35%). Graduate faculty: full-time 599, part-time 887. Degrees conferred: M.A., M.S., M.A.T., Ph.D.

ADMISSION REQUIREMENTS. Two transcripts, three letters of reference required in support of School's application. GRE or other entrance exams may be required. Interview not required. Accepts transfer applicants. Graduates of unaccredited institutions not considered. Apply to Office of Graduate School by January 15 (Fall), August 15 (Spring), January 1 (Summer). Application fee $50, $60 for international applicants. Phone: (317) 274-1577, fax (317)278-2380.

ADMISSION STANDARDS. Varies, from relatively open to very competitive. Usual minimum average: 3.0 (A = 4).

FINANCIAL AID. Scholarships, research assistantships, graduate assistantships, faculty assistants, associate instructors, counselors. Apply by February 1 to proposed major department for fellowships, assistantships; to Financial Aid Office for all other programs. Use FAFSA. About 50% of students receive aid other than loans from University and outside sources. Aid sometimes available to part-time students.

DEGREE REQUIREMENTS. For M.A., M.S.: 30 hours minimum, at least 1 semester or 2 summer sessions in full-time attendance; thesis for up to 6 hours' credit; reading knowledge of one foreign language for some programs; final written or oral exam may be required. For M.A.T., M.H.A.: 36 hours minimum, at least 24 in residence and 1 semester in full-time attendance. For Ph.D.: 90 hour minimum beyond the bachelor's, at least 60 in residence and 2 consecutive semesters in full-time attendance; proficiency in one foreign language, reading knowledge in two foreign languages, or reading proficiency in one language and research skill may be required; qualifying exam; dissertation for up to 30 hours' credit; final oral exam.

FIELDS OF STUDY.
Applied Communication. M.A.
Economics. M.A.
English. M.A.
Geographic Information Science. M.S.
History. M.A.
Museum Studies. M.A.
Philanthropic Studies. M.A., Ph.D.
Philosophy. M.A.
Political Science. M.A.
Sociology. M.A.
Teaching Spanish. M.A.

Kelley School of Business

Semester systems. Accredited programs: M.B.A., Professional Accounting.
Tuition: M.B.A.: per credit resident $560, nonresident $1114; Accounting: per credit resident $287, nonresident $819.
Enrollment: Total full- and part-time 1130. Faculty: full- and part-time 85. Degrees conferred: M.B.A., M.P.A., M.B.A.-J.D., M.B.A.-M.H.A., M.B.A.-M.D.

ADMISSION REQUIREMENTS. All applicants should have a bachelor's degree from a recognized institution of higher education. Will consider transfer applicants. Submit application, GMAT (will accept GMAT results from the last five years, latest acceptable date is January), official transcripts from each undergraduate/graduate school attended, two recommendations, three essays, personal statement, résumé and an application fee of $50, $65 for international applicants to the Admissions Office, Kelley School of Business. Phone: M.B.A. (317)274-4895; fax: (317)274-2483; Accounting: (317)278-3885. For M.P.A.: there are nine prerequisite courses that need to be completed prior to entrance into the program. For M.B.A.: U.S. citizens apply by April 1 (Fall), November 1 (Spring). For M.P.A.: apply at least two weeks prior to the beginning of semester of preferred entrance. International applicants should apply by February 1 (Fall). In addition, international students (whose native language is other than English) should submit a TOEFL report (minimum score 580), certified translations and evaluations of all official transcripts; recommendation should be in English or with certified translation, and proof of sufficient financial resources for two years of academic study. Dual degree applicants must apply to and be accepted by both schools/programs. Contact the admission office for current information and specific admissions requirements.

ADMISSION STANDARDS. Competitive. For M.B.A.: mean GMAT: 600; mean GPA: 3.0 (A = 4).

FINANCIAL AID. Scholarships, partial tuition waivers, Federal W/S, loans. Request all financial aid information from the School of Business. Phone: (317)278-FAST. Use FAFSA. Also submit an institutional FAF, Financial Aid Transcript, Federal Income Tax forms.

DEGREE REQUIREMENTS. For M.B.A.: 54-credit program including 18 elective credits, at least 45 credits in residence; degree must be complete within 7 years. For M.P.A.: 30-credit program with a bachelor's degree in business or accounting.

FIELDS OF STUDY.
Accounting. Includes specializations in advisory services and consulting, auditing and financial reporting, information systems management, taxation. M.P.A., M.S.
Business Administration. Includes concentration in finance, general administration.

School of Dentistry
Web site: www.iusd.iupui.edu

Established 1879, became part of state system in 1925. Located at the Medical Center in Indianapolis (46202). Semester system. Special facility: Oral Health Research Institute.

Annual tuition: resident $21,148, nonresident $49,200. Medical Center housing available. Average academic year housing cost: $18,500. Total average cost for all other first-year expenses: $11,000.

Enrollment: first-year class 100 (men 65, women 35), total full-time 455, part-time 70 (men 52%, women 48%, minorities 21%, state residents 71%). Faculty: full-time 107, part-time 113. Degrees conferred: D.D.S., M.S., M.S.D., Ph.D. (Oral Sciences), D.D.S.-M.S., D.D.S.-M.S.D., D.D.S.-Ph.D.

ADMISSION REQUIREMENTS. AADSAS report, transcripts, DAT (no later than October), three letters of recommendation required in support of School's application. Applicants must have completed at least three years of college study, prefer four years of study. Interview by invitation only. Preference given to Indiana residents. Accepts transfer applicants from foreign schools at the second-year level on a space available basis. Graduates of unaccredited institutions not considered. Apply to Director of Admissions after June 1, before December 1. Application fee $50, $60 for international applicants. Phone: (317)274-8173; fax: (317)278-9066.

ADMISSION STANDARDS. Competitive. Accepts about 10–15% of all applicants. Number of applications 1844 (1590 out-of-state); number interviewed n/a (n/a out-of-state); number of acceptance n/a (n/a out-of-state); number enrolled 100 (31 out-of-state). Usual minimum UGPA: 2.5 (A = 4) resident, 2.7 nonresident. Mean DAT: academic 18, PAT 18; mean UGPA 3.52.

FINANCIAL AID. Scholarships, fellowships, DEAL, HEAL, loans. Apply to the Loan and Scholarship Committee after acceptance, before March 1. Phone: (317)274-4162. Use FAFSA (School code: 001813). About 88% of students receive aid from School.

DEGREE REQUIREMENTS. For D.D.S.: satisfactory completion of four-year program. For M.S.D.: 30 hours minimum in residence; thesis; final written/oral exam. For M.S., Ph.D.: see Graduate School listing above.

FIELDS OF POSTGRADUATE STUDY.
Dental Diagnostic Sciences. M.S.
Dental Materials. M.S., M.S.D.
Dental Science. Ph.D.
Endodontics. M.S.D.
Operative Dentistry. M.S.D.
Oral and Maxillofacial Surgery. Certificate.
Orthodontics. M.S.D.
Pediatric Dentistry. M.S.D.
Periodontics. M.S.D.
Preventive Dentistry. M.S., M.S.D.
Prosthodontics. M.S.D.

School of Education
Web site: www.education.iupui.edu

Semester systems. Tuition: per credit resident $269, nonresident $783.

Enrollment: Total full- and part-time 810. Faculty: full- and part-time 80. Degrees conferred: M.S. in Education.

ADMISSION REQUIREMENTS. Official transcripts from each undergraduate/graduate school attended, GRE, two letters of recommendation, personal statement required in support of School's application. Online application available. Interview may be requested. TOEFL (minimum score 550) required for international applicants. Accepts transfer applications. Graduates of unaccredited institutions not considered. Apply to School of Education by March 1 (Fall), November 1 (Spring), March 1 (Summer). Application fee $50, $60 for international applicants. Phone: (317) 274-6801; fax: (317)274-6864.

ADMISSION STANDARDS. Selective for most programs. Usual minimum average: 2.75 (A = 4); minimum GRE: combined score: 1300.

FINANCIAL AID. Limited to partial tuition waivers, Federal W/S, loans. Request all financial aid information from the School of Education. No specified closing date. Use FAFSA. Aid available for part-time students.

DEGREE REQUIREMENTS. For M.S.: 36 semester hours minimum without thesis, at least 27 in residence, 15 credits on the campus awarding the degree.

FIELDS OF STUDY.
Educational Leadership. Includes elementary, secondary. M.S.
Educational Psychology. M.S.
Elementary Education. Includes early childhood education, educational technology. M.S.
Higher Education/Student Affairs. A Bloomington program with some classes at IUPUI. M.S.
School Counseling/Counselor Education. M.S.
Secondary Education. Includes education technology. M.S.
Special Education. Includes exceptional needs. M.S.

School of Informatics
Web site: informatics.iupui.edu

Program established 2001. Semester systems. Tuition: per credit resident $269, nonresident $783.

Enrollment: Total full- and part-time 110. Faculty: full- and part-time 10. Degree conferred: M.S.

ADMISSION REQUIREMENTS. Official transcripts from each undergraduate/graduate school attended, three letters of recommendation, statement of purpose, résumé required in support of School's application. Sample of creative work required for News Media. GRE required for applicants with less than 3.0 GPA (A = 4). Online application available. TOEFL (minimum score 600) required for international applicants. Accepts transfer applications. Graduates of unaccredited institutions not considered. Admits Fall only. Apply to School of Informatics by March 1. Application fee $50, $60 for international applicants, Phone (317) 278-4636; e-mail: info@informatics.iupui.edu.

ADMISSION STANDARDS. Selective. Usual minimum average: 3.0 (A = 4).

FINANCIAL AID. Limited to grants, Federal W/S, loans. Apply by March 1 (priority deadline) to the Office of Student Financial Aid Services. Phone: (317)274-4162. Use FAFSA. Aid available for part-time students.

DEGREE REQUIREMENTS. For M.S.: 36-credit interdisciplinary program.

FIELDS OF STUDY.
Bioinformatics.
Chemical Informatics.
Health Informatics.
Human–Computer Interaction.
Media Arts and Sciences. M.S.

School of Law—Indianapolis
Web site: www.indylaw.indiana.edu

Established 1894. Located near downtown. ABA approved since 1936. AALS member. Public control. Semester system. Full- and part-time study. Special facilities: Center for Intellectual Property Law and Innovation, Center for International and Comparative Law, Center for Law and Health. Special programs: summer study abroad in Renmin (People's) University of China, People's Republic of China, and at the Universite of Lille, France. Law library: 590,230 volumes, 3137 subscriptions; has LEXIS, NEXIS, WESTLAW, DIALOG, OCLC; has more than 1100 network connections; is a U.S. Government Depository for the United Nations.

Annual tuition: full-time resident $13,962, nonresident $29,457; part-time resident $9640, nonresident $17,000; graduate tuition $23,285. Limited on-campus housing available. Estimated living expenses: $20,356.

Enrollment: first-year class 196, part-time 81; total full- and part-time 938 (men 52%, women 48%, minorities 11%). Faculty: full-time 36, part-time 32. Student to faculty ratio 26.4 to 1. Degrees conferred: J.D., J.D.-M.B.A., J.D.-M.H.A., J.D.-M.P.A., J.D.-M.P.H., J.D.-M.L.S., J.D.-M.Phil., LL.M.) American Law for Foreign Lawyers, Health Law Policy and Bioethics, Intellectual Property Law, International and Comparative Law International Human Rights Law), S.J.D.

ADMISSION REQUIREMENTS. LSDAS Law School report, bachelor's degree, transcripts, LSAT, personal statement, letters of recommendation required in support of application. Interview not required. Transfer applicants accepted. Apply after September 1, before March 1 to Admission Office. Phone: (317)274-2459. Beginning part-time students admitted May or August only. Application fee $50, $60 for international students. For LL.M.: contact program at (317)278-4783. For S.J.D.: contact programs at (317)274-4900.

ADMISSION STANDARDS. Selective. Accepts approximately 30% of full-time and 33% of part-time applicants. Number of full-time applicants 1537, part-time 401; number of full-time acceptance 464, part-time 134; number full-time enrolled 196, part-time 81; LSAT (75% of full-time students have a score at or above 152, part-time 149); GPA (75% of full-time students have a GPA at or above 3.32, part-time 3.12). *U.S. News & World Report* ranking is in the second tier tied at 85th of all U.S. law schools.

FINANCIAL AID. Scholarships, fellowships, assistantships, partial tuition waivers, Federal W/S, loans. Apply to Office of Student Financial Aid by March 1. Phone: (317)278-2862. Use FAFSA (School code: 001813). About 36% of students receive aid other than loans from School.

DEGREE REQUIREMENTS. For J.D.: 90 semester hours and 6 semesters in full-time residence or 8 semesters in part-time residence. For LL.M.: 24-credit full- or part-time program; thesis. For S.J.D.: satisfactory completion of individually designed program; at least one colloquia; dissertation. For master's degree: see Graduate School listing above.

School of Library and Information Science
Web site: www.slis.iupui.edu

Semester system. Tuition: per credit resident $299, nonresident $873.

Enrollment: total full-time 60, part-time 265. Faculty: full- and part-time 12. Degrees conferred: M.L.S., M.L.S.-M.A. (History), M.L.S. M.P.A., M.L.S.-L.T.M (Library Technology Management).

ADMISSION REQUIREMENTS. Official transcripts from each undergraduate/graduate school attended, three recommendations, personal goals statement required in support of School's application. GRE required for applicants with less than 3.0 GPA (A = 4). All applicants must demonstrate they are computer, network, and information literate. Online application available. TOEFL (minimum score 600) required for international applicants. Accepts transfer applications. Graduates of unaccredited institutions not considered. Dual degree applicants must apply to and be accepted to both Schools/programs, Apply to School of Library and Information Science by July 15. Application fee $50, $60 for international applicants. Phone: (886)758-6254 (toll free); (317)278-2375.

ADMISSION STANDARDS. Selective. Usual minimum average: 3.0 (A = 4).

FINANCIAL AID. Scholarships, tuition waivers, Federal W/S, loans. Apply by March 1 (priority deadline) to the Office of Student Financial Aid Services. Phone: (317)274-4162. Use FAFSA. Aid available for part-time students, part-time work opportunities in the library generally available.

DEGREE REQUIREMENTS, For M.L.S.: 36 credit hours minimum, computer-based, information tool. For M.L.S.-L.T.M: 45 credit hour program, internship. For M.L.S.-M.A.: 50 credit hour program (30 credits taken for M.L.S., 20 credits taken for M.A.). For M.L.S.-M.P.A.: 66 credit hour program (30 credits taken for M.L.S., 36 credits taken for M.P.A.).

FIELDS OF STUDY.
Library Science. Includes library technology management. M.L.S.

School of Medicine (46202-5113)
Web site: www.medicine.iu.edu

Founded 1903. In 1971 School became the hub of statewide medical education. After admission, students select which center they will attend. Centers located at Indianapolis, Bloomington, Gary, South Bend, Fort Wayne, Muncie, Terre Haute, Lafayette, Evansville. Special facilities: Center for Alzheimer Disease and Related Disorders, Automotive Safety Center for Children, Bowen Research Center, Center for Computational Biology and Bioinformatics, Center for Environmental Health, Center of Excellence in Computational Diagnostics, Center for Hispanic Health, Center for Immunobiology, Center for Structural Biology, Center of Excellence in Women's Health, Hartford Center of Excellence in Geriatric Medicine, Herman B. Wells Center for Pediatric Research, Hypertension Research Center, Indiana Alcohol Research Center, Indiana Alzheimer Disease Center, Indiana Area Health Education Centers, Indiana Center for Vascular Biology and Medicine, Indiana Spinal Cord and Head Injury Research Center, Indiana University Breast Care and Research Center, Indiana University Cancer Center, Indiana University Center for Aging Research, Indiana University Center for AIDS Research, Indiana University Center for Bioethics, Indiana University Center for Health Services and Outcomes Research, Indiana University Center for Sports Medicine, Indiana University Diabetes Center, Indiana Children's Health Services Research, Institute of Psychiatric Research, Krannert Institute of Cardiology, Midwest Sexually Transmitted Infections and Topical Microbicide Cooperative Research Center, Multipurpose Arthritis and Musculoskeletal Diseases Center, O'Brien Research Center for Advanced Renal Microscopic Analysis, Riley Child Development Center, Stark Neurosciences Research Institute, Walther Oncology Center, Wells Center for Pediatric Research. Special program for disadvantaged and underrepresented minorities. Library: 202,000 volumes, 1849 subscriptions. NIH ranking is 47th with 415 awards/grants worth $137,418,069.

Annual tuition: resident $24,031, nonresident $43,885. Total average figure for all other expenses $13,000–$16,000. Medical Center housing for 175 married students, 160 men, 130 women.

Enrollment: first-year class 280 (20 EDP), total 1171 (men 56%, women 44%, minorities 22%, state residents 89%). Faculty: full-time 1289, part-time 200. Degrees conferred: M.D., M.D.-M.B.A., M.D.-M.P.H., M.D.-M.S., M.D.-Ph.D. The M.S. and Ph.D. are offered through the Graduate School at either Bloomington or Indianapolis.

ADMISSION REQUIREMENTS. AMCAS report, transcripts, letters of recommendation, MCAT required in support of application. Interview by invitation. Applicants must have completed at least three years of college study. Does have EDP; apply between June 1 and August 1. Preference given to Indiana residents. Accepts transfer applicants. Apply to School Admissions Office after June 1, before December 15. Application fee $50. Phone: (317)274-3772; fax: (317)278-0211.

ADMISSION STANDARDS. Competitive. Accepts about 14.8% of all applicants. Number of applications 2760 (2104 out-of-state); number interviewed 953 (330 out-of-state); number of acceptance 409 (100 out-of-state); number enrolled 280 (38 out-of-state). Mean Composite MCAT 10.1; mean UGPA 3.73. *U.S. News & World Report* ranking is in the top 44 of all medical research schools, 16th in primary care.

FINANCIAL AID. Scholarships, fellowships, assistantships, HEAL, grants, full and partial fee waivers, loans. Apply to Student Financial Services Office. Phone: (317)274-1967. Use FAFSA (School code: 001813). About 32% of students receive aid other than loans from School.

DEGREE REQUIREMENTS. For M.D.: satisfactory completion of four-year program; must pass Step 1 and 2 of USMLE for graduation. For M.S. and Ph.D.: see Graduate School listing above.

FIELDS OF GRADUATE STUDY.
Anatomy and Cell Biology.
Biochemistry and Molecular Biology.
Biomolecular Imaging and Medical Biophysics.

Cellular and Integrative Physiology.
Medical and Molecular Genetics.
Medical Neuroscience.
Microbiology and Immunology.
Pathology and Laboratory Medicine.
Pharmacology.
Toxicology.

PROGRAMS WITH PURDUE UNIVERSITY AT LAFAYETTE:
Engineering.
Medicinal Chemistry.
Molecular Biology.
Neurosciences.

School of Nursing

Established 1945. Located at Indianapolis campus (46202). Tuition: per credit resident $354, nonresident $1072.

Graduate enrollment: full-time 29, part-time 406. Faculty full-time 47, part-time 1. Degrees conferred: M.S.N., M.S.N.-M.P.M., D.N.S., Ph.D.

ADMISSION REQUIREMENTS. Official transcripts, three letters of reference, résumé or vita, interview, current Indiana R.N. license required in support of School's application. GRE required for all applicants without a B.S.N. and for Ph.D. applicants. Online application available. TOEFL (minimum score 550) required for international applicants. Accepts transfer applicants. Graduates of unaccredited institutions not considered. Apply to Graduate Recorder, School of Nursing by April 1 (Fall), October 1 (Spring). Deadline for Ph.D. applicants is February 15. Rolling admissions process. Application fee $50, $60 for international applicants. Phone: (317)274-8094; fax: (317)274-2996.

ADMISSION STANDARDS. Selective. Usual minimum average: 2.8 (A = 4).

FINANCIAL AID. Scholarships, fellowships, research assistantships, teaching assistantships, traineeships, Federal W/S, loans. Apply by May 1 to School of Nursing for fellowships, assistantships, to Traineeships Program for traineeships; to Director of Scholarships and Financial Aid IUPUI for scholarships and all other programs. Use FAFSA. Phone: (317)274-4162. Aid available for part-time students.

DEGREE REQUIREMENTS. For M.S.N.: 36–42 hours minimum, at least 20 in residence; final document. For D.N.S.: Three years minimum beyond the master's, at least one year in full-time residence; qualifying exam; comprehensive exam; dissertation; final oral exam. For Ph.D.: see Graduate School listing above.

FIELDS OF STUDY.
Acute Care Practitioner.
Adult Care Nurse Practitioner.
Adult Nurse Practitioner.
Adult Health Clinical Nurse Specialist.
Adult Psychiatric/Mental Health Clinical Nurse Specialist.
Child/Adolescent Psychiatric Clinical Nurse Specialist.
Community Health Clinical Nurse Specialist.
Family Nurse Practitioner.
Neonatal Nurse Practitioner.
Nursing Administration.
Pediatric Clinical Nurse Specialist.
Pediatric Nurse Practitioner.
Women's Health Nurse Practitioner.

School of Social Work

Main campus for School of Social Work is located in Indianapolis. M.S.W. programs since 1911. Semester system.

Tuition: per credit resident $270, nonresident $720. M.S.W. enrollment: full-time 277, part-time 261. School faculty: full- and part-time 48. Degrees conferred: M.S.W., Ph.D. (offered through the Graduate School).

ADMISSION REQUIREMENT. Official transcript, three letters of recommendation, writing sample required in support of IUPUI and School's application. Online application available. TOEFL and international application required of international application. Call (317)274-7294 for current information. Accepts transfer applicants. Graduates of unaccredited degree programs will not be considered. Submit IUPUI application first and then send the School of Social Work's paper application to the School's Admissions Coordinator by February 1 (Fall priority deadline), June 1 (deadline for part-time evening and part-time Saturday programs). Application fee $50, $60 for international applicants. Phone: (317)274-6727.

ADMISSION STANDARDS. Selective. Usual minimum average: 3.0 (A = 4).

FINANCIAL AID. Fellowships, research assistantships, tuition grants, Federal W/S, loans, Apply by March 1 to the School of Social Work for fellowships, assistantships, tuition grants; to the Office of Students Financial Aid Services for all other assistance. Phone: (317)274-4162. Use FAFSA.

DEGREE REQUIREMENTS. For M.S.W.: 60-credit program, at least 48 credits in residence; field practicum.

FIELDS OF STUDY.
Social Work. Includes concentrations in child welfare, health, families and school, mental health and addictions, social work leadership. M.S.W.

Purdue University School of Engineering and Technology

Semester system. Tuition: per credit resident $286, nonresident $820. Enrollment: full- and part-time 350 (men 50%, women 50%). Faculty: full- and part-time 132. Degrees conferred: M.S., M.S.Bm.E., M.S.E., M.S.E.C.E., M.S.M.E., Ph.D.

ADMISSION REQUIREMENTS. Two official transcripts, GRE, three letters of recommendation, statement of purpose required in support of School's application. Online application available. TOEFL and Financial Information Form with an official letter or statement from bank verifying there are the required funds for at least two years of academic study required for international applicants. Accepts transfer applicants. Graduates of unaccredited institutions not considered. Apply to appropriate major department at least one semester in advance, but not later that May 1 (Fall), October 1 (Spring). Application fee $50, $60 for international applicants. Phone: (317)274-2533; fax: (317)274-4567.

ADMISSION STANDARDS. Selective for most departments, Usual minimum average: 3.0 (A = 4).

FINANCIAL AID. Scholarships, research/teaching assistantships, Federal W/S, loans. Apply by March 15 to department for scholarships, assistantships; to Office of Student Financial Aid Services for all other aid. Phone: (317)274-4162. Use FAFSA. Aid available for part-time students.

DEGREE REQUIREMENTS. For master's: 30 credit hour programs, at least two semesters in residence; thesis/nonthesis option; final written/oral exam. For Ph.D.: 60 credit program beyond bachelor's degree; qualifying exam; preliminary exam; reading knowledge of one foreign language for some programs, dissertation; final oral defense.

FIELD OF STUDY.
Biomedical Engineering. Ph.D. degree program is jointly administered with University in West Lafayette. M.S.Bm.E., Ph.D.
Computer Engineering. M.S., Ph.D.
Electrical Engineering. M.S., M.S.E., M.S.E.C.E.
Interdisciplinary Engineering. M.S., M.S.E.
Mechanical Engineering. M.S., M.S.M.E.
Technology. M.S.

Purdue University School of Science
Web site: www.science.iupui.edu

Semester system. Special facilities: Center for Earth and Environmental Science, Center for Regenerative Biology and Medicine. Tuition: per credit resident $259, nonresident $748. Enrollment: full- and part-time 247 (men 41%, women 59%). Faculty: full- and part-time 132. Degrees conferred: M.S., Ph.D.

ADMISSION REQUIREMENTS. Two official transcripts, GRE, three letters of recommendation, statement of purpose required in support of School's application. Online application available. TOEFL and Financial Information Form with an official letter or statement from bank verifying there are the required funds for at least two years of academic study are required for international applicants. Accepts transfer applicants. Graduates of unaccredited institutions not considered. Apply to appropriate major department at least one semester in advance, but not later that May 1 (Fall), September 1 (Spring). Application fee $45, $55 for international applicants.

ADMISSION STANDARDS. Selective for most departments. Usual minimum average: 3.0 (A = 4).

FINANCIAL AID. Scholarships, research/teaching assistantships, Federal W/S, loans. Apply by March 15 to department for scholarships, assistantships; to Office of Student Financial Aid Services for all other aid. Phone: (317)274-1577. Use FAFSA. Aid available for part-time students.

DEGREE REQUIREMENTS. For M.S.: 30 credit hour programs, at least two semesters in residence, thesis/nonthesis option; final written/oral exam. For Ph.D.: 60-credit program beyond bachelor's degree; qualifying exam; preliminary exam; reading knowledge of one foreign language for some programs; dissertation; final oral defense.

FIELD OF STUDY.
Biology. M.S., Ph.D.
Chemistry. M.S., Ph.D.
Computer and Information Science. M.S., Ph.D.
Geology. M.S.
Information Science and Computer Science. M.S., Ph.D.
Mathematics. Includes applied statistics (M.S.), industrial and applied mathematics (M.S.), pure/applied mathematics. M.S., Ph.D.
Mathematics Secondary School Teaching. M.S.
Physics. M.S., Ph.D.
Psychology. Includes clinical rehabilitation (M.S., Ph.D.), industrial and organizational (M.S.), psychobiology of addictions (Ph.D.). M.S., Ph.D.

INDIANA UNIVERSITY OF PENNSYLVANIA
Indiana, Pennsylvania 15705-1081
Web site: www.iup.edu

Founded 1875. Located 60 miles NE of Pittsburgh. CGS member. Coed. State control. Semester system. Library: 775,000 volumes, 3600 subscriptions; designated Federal Depository. Total University enrollment: 13,400.

Annual tuition: full-time resident $6214, nonresident $9944; per credit, resident $345, nonresident $552. Limited on-campus housing available. Average academic year housing cost: $4020–$6192 (including board). Contact Housing and Residence Life Office for on- and off-campus housing information. Phone: (724) 357-2696. Day-care facilities available.

Graduate School and Research

Graduate study since 1957. Enrollment: full-time 853, part-time 822. University faculty teaching graduate students: full- and part-time 366. Degrees conferred: M.A., M.S., M.B.A., M.Ed., M.F.A. Ed.D., Psy.D., Ph.D.

ADMISSION REQUIREMENTS. Transcripts, two letters of recommendation, GRE/GMAT required in support of application. Interview required by some departments. Praxis II required for Ed.D. in School Psychology. TOEFL required for international applicants. Accepts transfer applicants. Graduates of unaccredited institutions not considered. Apply to the Graduate Office by July 1 (Fall), November 1 (Spring), April 1 (Summer). Some programs have earlier deadlines. Application fee $20. Phone: (724)357-2222; fax (724)357-4862; e-mail: graduate_admissions@grove.iup.edu.

ADMISSION STANDARDS. Selective. Usual minimum average: 2.6 (A = 4).

FINANCIAL AID. Annual awards from institutional funds: scholarships (based on merit and need), research fellowships, teaching assistantships, internships, tuition waivers, Federal W/S, loans. Approved for VA benefits. Apply by March 15 to Assistant Dean of Graduate School for assistantships, fellowships; to Director of Financial Aid for all other programs. Phone: (724)357-2218. Use FAFSA. About 30% of students receive aid other than loans from University. Aid available for part-time students.

DEGREE REQUIREMENTS. For master's: 30–36 credit hours minimum for most, at least 24 in residence; thesis/nonthesis option. For Ed.D., Ph.D., Psy.D.: minimum of 60 credits beyond the bachelor's degree; qualifying exam; dissertation; final oral exam.

FIELDS OF STUDY.
Administration and Leadership Studies.
Adult/Community Education.
Applied Mathematics.
Art.
Art Education.
Biology.
Business Administration.
Business Workplace Development.
Chemistry.
Clinical Psychology.
Community Counseling. Includes certifications in elementary school counselor, secondary school counselor, and supervisor of guidance services.
Criminology.
Curriculum and Instruction.
Early Childhood Education.
Educational Psychology.
Education of Exceptional Persons.
Elementary Education.
Elementary School Mathematics.
Elementary School Counseling.
English. Includes English education, literature and criticism, composition, teaching English to speakers of other languages.
Fine Arts.
Food and Nutrition.
Geography.

Health and Physical Education.
Health Services Administration.
History.
Industrial and Labor Relations.
Leadership Studies. Includes educational, human services.
Literacy.
Mathematics.
Middle School Mathematics.
Music.
Nursing.
Physics.
Political Science.
Professional Growth.
Psychology.
Public Affairs.
Safety Science.
School Psychology.
Science for Disaster Response.
Secondary School Counseling.
Sociology.
Speech-Language Pathology.
Sports Sciences.
Student Affairs in Higher Education.

UNIVERSITY OF INDIANAPOLIS
Indianapolis, Indiana 46227-3697
Web site: www.uindy.edu

Founded 1902. Private control, United Methodist. Semester system. Special facilities: Center for Aging and Community, Center for Business Partnerships, Center of Excellence in Leadership of Learning, Institute for Emerging Careers, Institute for Leadership and Professional Development, Institute for the Study of War and Diplomacy. Library: 173,363 volumes, 1200 subscriptions. Total University enrollment: 4462.

Tuition: $525 per credit. No on-campus housing for graduate students. Estimated annual housing costs $6000–$7000.

Graduate Programs

Graduate enrollment: full-time 440, part-time 587. Faculty teaching graduate students: full-time 81, part-time 42. Degrees conferred: M.A., M.B.A., M.Acc., M.S., M.H.S., M.S.N., D.H.S., D.P.T., O.T.D., Psy.D.

ADMISSION REQUIREMENTS. Transcripts, GRE/GMAT/PRAXIS, statement of purpose, three letters of recommendation, interview required in support of Graduate application. Online application available. TOEFL (minimum score 550) required for international applicants. Accepts transfer applicants. Apply to the individual program offices. Rolling admissions process. Application fee $65. Phone: (800)232-8634; (317)788-6150.

ADMISSION STANDARDS. Relatively open for some programs, selective for others. Usual minimum average: 2.75 (A = 4).

FINANCIAL AID. Fellowships, assistantships, Federal W/S, loans. Approved for VA benefits. Apply to Financial Aid Office; no specified closing date. Phone: (317)788-3217. Use FAFSA (University code: 00184).

DEGREE REQUIREMENTS. For M.A.: 32 semester hours and thesis, or 36 semester hours, without thesis, at least 24 in residence. For M.Acc.: 30 semester hours. For M.S., M.H.S.: 36 semester hours. For M.B.A.: 42 semester hours minimum. For M.S.N.: 40 semester hour program. For D.H.S.: 90 credit programs beyond the bachelor's; critical inquiry; clinical practice. For D.P.T.: 37 credit program beyond the master's. For O.T.D.:

72 credit program beyond bachelor's; plan of study; project; clinical practice; residency. For Psy.D.: 108 semester hour program: final-year internship. All master's degrees must be completed within five years.

FIELDS OF STUDY.
Accounting.
Applied Sociology.
Art.
Art Education.
Business Administration. Includes finance, technology management, organizational leadership.
Clinical Psychology. Psy.D. only.
Curriculum and Instruction.
Elementary Education.
English.
Family Nurse Practitioner. M.S.N. only.
Gerontology.
History and Political Sciences.
Human Biology.
International Relations.
Mental Health Counseling.
Nursing.
Occupational Therapy. Includes administrative, neuroscience, orthopedic tracks at doctoral level. M.S., O.T.D.
Physical Therapy. M.S., M.H.S., D.H.S., D.P.T.
Psychology.
Secondary Education. Includes biology, chemistry, earth science, French, math, physics, Spanish.

INTER AMERICAN UNIVERSITY OF PUERTO RICO
San German, Puerto Rico 00683-5008
Web site: www.sg.inter.edu

College-level study since 1921. Coed. Private control. Semester system. Main campuses at San German and San Juan. Regional colleges at Aguadilla, Arecibo, Barranquitas, Fajardo, Guayama, and Ponce. Library: 162,544 volumes, 1750 subscriptions. Total University enrollment: 5764.

Tuition: per graduate credit hour $170. On-campus housing available only at San German campus for single students. Average academic year housing cost: $3000 (including board). Contact Dean of Students Office for both on- and off-campus housing information. Phone: (787)264-1912, ext. 215.

Graduate Study

Offered at San German campus and San Juan campus. Enrollment: full-time 1000, part-time 563. Graduate faculty: full-time 58, part-time 40. Degrees conferred: M.A., M.A.Ed., M.B.A., M.L.S., M.S., M.S.Ed.

ADMISSION REQUIREMENTS. Official transcripts, two letters of recommendations, PAEG or GRE required in support of application. Accepts transfer applicants. Apply by May 1 (Fall), November 15 (Spring), April 1 (Summer) to the Admissions Director. Rolling admissions process. Application fee $31. Phone: (787)892-4300, ext. 7357; fax: (787)892-6350.

ADMISSION STANDARDS. Selective. Usual minimum average: 3.0 (last 60 credits) or 2.75–2.99 (last 60 credits plus GRE) for full standing (A = 4).

FINANCIAL AID. Limited to assistantships, loans. Apply to appropriate department chair well in advance of registration. Use FAFSA and University's FAF. Phone: (787)264-1912. Aid available for part-time students.

DEGREE REQUIREMENTS. For master's: 36–45 credit hours minimum, at least 30 credits in residence; thesis/nonthesis option; comprehensive exam for some programs.

FIELDS OF STUDY.
Administration of Higher Education.
Art. Includes ceramics, drawing, painting, photography, printmaking.
Business Administration. Includes accounting, finance, human resources, industrial relations, labor relations, marketing.
Curriculum and Instruction.
Educational Administration.
Elementary Education.
English.
Environmental Sciences.
International Business.
Library Science.
Physical Education.
Psychology. Includes counseling, school. 51 credits for M.A.
Science Education.
Special Education.
TESOL.

School of Law (P.O. Box 70351)

Established 1961. ABA approved since 1969. AALS member. Semester system. Located in San Juan (00936). Library: 162,000 volumes, 1658 subscriptions; has LEXIS, NEXIS, DIALOG, DOBIS/LUVEN, MICRO JURIS.

Tuition: resident $10,958, part-time resident $8859. No on-campus housing available. Total average annual additional expense: $8900.

Enrollment: first-year class, full-time 118, part-time 109; total full- and part-time 701 (men 48%, women 52%). Faculty: full-time 23, part-time 28. Student to faculty ratio 21 to 1. Degree conferred: J.D.

ADMISSION REQUIREMENTS. Transcripts, bachelor's degree, LSAT, PAEG, three letters of recommendation, personal interview required in support of application. Interview by invitation. Proficiency in Spanish required, non-Spanish speakers must take PAEG (minimum score 575). Graduates of unaccredited colleges not considered. Apply by March 31. Application fee $63. Phone: (809)751-1912, ext. 2012, 2013.

ADMISSION STANDARDS. Selective. Mean LSAT: full-time 140, part-time 140; mean GPA: full-time 3.17, part-time 3.16 (A = 4). *U.S. News & World Report* ranking is in the fourth tier of all U.S. law schools. Admits approximately 25–30% of total annual applicants.

FINANCIAL AID. Scholarships, grants, Federal W/S, loans, and a deferred payment plan available. Apply to Financial Aid Office by March 31. Use FAFSA (School code: 017202). About 10% of students receive some aid from School.

DEGREE REQUIREMENTS. For J.D.: satisfactory completion of three-year (full-time), four-year (part-time) program, 92 credits hours.

IONA COLLEGE
New Rochelle, New York 10801
Web site: www.iona.edu

Founded 1940. Located 16 miles NE of New York City. Coed. Private control. Roman Catholic. Semester and trimester systems. Library: 270,000 volumes, 1400 subscriptions. Total University enrollment: 4100.

Tuition: per credit $621. No on-campus housing available. Apply to Housing Office for off-campus housing information. Phone: (914)633-2336.

Graduate Study

Graduate enrollment: full- and part-time 1200. Faculty teaching graduate students: full-time 66, part-time 40. Degrees conferred: M.A., M.S., M.S. in Ed., M.S.T., M.B.A.

ADMISSION REQUIREMENTS. Transcripts, three letters of recommendation required in support of application. Online application available. GMAT required in business. GRE and interview required for some programs. TOEFL required for international applicants. Accepts transfer applicants. Apply to Graduate School of Arts and Science for Education and Arts and Sciences, or Hagan School of Business for Business and Management at least one month before intended start date. Admit to Fall, Spring, Summer trimesters. Application fee $50. Phone: (800) 231-IONA, (914)633-2502 (Arts & Science), (914)633-2288 (Business).

ADMISSION STANDARDS. Selective. Usual minimum average: 2.75 (A = 4).

FINANCIAL AID. Scholarships, graduate assistantships, tuition waivers, loans. Approved for VA benefits. Apply to the Office of Financial Aid: no specified closing date. Use FAFSA. Phone: (914)633-2497.

DEGREE REQUIREMENTS. For master's: 30–61 credit hours minimum, at least 24 in residence; written/oral comprehensive exam in some programs.

FIELDS OF STUDY.
Business Administration. Includes financial management, human resources management, information and decision technology management, management, marketing.
Computer Science.
Criminal Justice.
Economics.
Educational Administration.
Educational Technology.
Elementary Education. Includes specialization in science.
English.
Family Counseling.
Health Services Administration.
History.
Journalism. Includes online, print.
Marketing.
Marriage and Family Therapy.
Mass Communication. Includes organizational, public relations.
Multicultural Education.
Pastoral Counseling.
Psychology.
Secondary Education. Includes biology, business education, English, mathematics, Spanish, social studies.
Spanish.
Telecommunications.

IOWA STATE UNIVERSITY OF SCIENCE AND TECHNOLOGY
Ames, Iowa 50011-2010
Web site: www.iastate.edu

Founded 1858. Located 40 miles N of Des Moines. CGS and AAU member. Coed. State control. Semester system. Special facilities: Ames Laboratory, National Soil Tilth Laboratory, Na-

tional Animal Disease Center, Institute for Physical Research and Technology, Iowa Agriculture and Home Economics Experiment Station, Leopold Center for Sustainable Agriculture, Center for Agricultural and Rural Development, Center for Nondestructive Evaluation, Industrial Relations Center, Center for Transportation Research and Education, Veterinary Medical Research Institute, the Institute for Social and Behavioral Research, Utilization Center for Agricultural Products, Plant Sciences Institutes, Center for Immunity Enhancement in Domestic Animals, Computation Center, Center for Designing Foods to Improve Nutrition, Iowa Energy Center. According to The Center at University of Florida, the University is ranked 94th in receipt of Federal Research funds with $82,297,000 and it ranks 70th for total University research expenditures with $199,566,000. In 2004, the University awarded 239 doctorates, which ranked it 63rd among all U.S. institutions eligible to award that degree. Eleven of the University's faculty members have been elected to National Honor Academies and this ranks it 64th among all U.S. institutions. The Library: approximately 2,500,000 volumes, 28,000 subscriptions. Total University enrollment: 25,700.

Annual tuition: resident $6410, nonresident $16,422. Unlimited on-campus housing for married and single students. Housing costs range from $480 per month (double occupancy) to monthly apartment rates of $475–$550. Apply to Director of Residential Life. Phone: (515)294-2900.

Graduate College

Graduate study since 1868, first graduate degree conferred in 1877. Enrollment: full- and part-time 3940. Graduate faculty: full-time 1400. Degrees conferred: M.A., M.S., M.Acc., M.Agr., M.Arch., M.B.A., M.C.R.P., M.Ed., M.Eng., M.F.A., M.F.C.S., M.L.A., M.P.A., M.S.M. specialist, Ph.D.

ADMISSION REQUIREMENTS. Transcripts, letters of reference required in support of College's application. Online application available. GRE required for most departments. Interview not required. Accepts transfer applicants. TOEFL (minimum score 173 on computer-based test) required for international applicants. Graduates of unaccredited colleges not considered. Apply to Graduate College Office at least two months prior to beginning of term (some departments have earlier deadlines); international applicants should apply between nine and twelve months before entering term. Application fee $30, $70 for international applicants. Phone: (800)262-3810; e-mail: grad_admissions@iastate.edu.

ADMISSION STANDARDS. Very competitive for most departments, competitive for some. Usual minimum average: 2.75 (A = 4).

FINANCIAL AID. Scholarships, fellowships, teaching/research assistantships, grants, Federal W/S, loans; deferred payment plan. Approved for VA benefits. Apply to head of proposed major department for scholarships, fellowships, assistantships, preferably by March 15; to Financial Aid Office for all other programs. Use FAFSA and institutional FAF. About 50% of students receive aid other than loans from University and outside sources. Aid available for part-time students.

DEGREE REQUIREMENTS. For master's: 30 credits minimum, at least 22 credits in residence; reading knowledge of one foreign language for some majors; thesis for most majors; final oral exam. For M.Arch.: 30 credits minimum beyond Bachelor's of Architecture degree; 60 credit program beyond B.A., B.S. degree; up to 100 credit program for students with other degrees. For M.Acc.: 32-credit program; creative project. For M.Agr.: 32-credit nonthesis program. For M.B.A.: 48 credits minimum (a combination of integrated core modules and advanced electives). For M.C.R.P.: 48-credit program; thesis/nonthesis option. For M.Ed.: 30–40 credit program; creative project or field-based activity. For M.F.C.S.: 36-credit program; 2 nonthesis options. For M.F.A.: 60–61 credit program; thesis-exhibition or thesis. For

M.L.A.: 36-credit program; thesis or creative project. For M.P.A.: 37-credit program; internship or thesis. For M.S.M.: 36-credit program; creative project. For Ph.D.: 72 credits minimum with 36 credits under supervision of Student's Program of Study Committee; at least 24 credits must be earned during 2 consecutive semesters or a continuous period of 2 semesters in a summer term; preliminary exam; dissertation; final oral exam.

FIELDS OF STUDY.

Accounting. M.Acc. only.
Aerospace Engineering.
Agricultural Economics.
Agricultural Education.
Agricultural Engineering.
Agricultural History and Rural Studies. Ph.D. only.
Agricultural Meteorology.
Agronomy. M.S. only.
Analytical Chemistry.
Animal Breeding and Genetics.
Animal Ecology.
Animal Nutrition.
Animal Physiology.
Animal Science.
Anthropology. M.A. only.
Applied Linguistics and Technology.
Applied Mathematics.
Applied Physics.
Architectural Studies. M.S. only.
Architecture.
Art and Design. M.A. only.
Astrophysics.
Biochemistry.
Bioinformatics and Computational Biology.
Biomedical Sciences.
Biophysics.
Biorenewable Resources and Technology.
Business Administration. M.B.A. only.
Chemical Engineering.
Chemistry.
Civil Engineering.
Community and Regional Planning. M.C.R.P. only.
Computer Engineering.
Computer Science.
Condensed Matter Physics.
Creative Writing and Environment.
Crop Production and Physiology.
Earth Science.
Ecology and Evolutionary Biology.
Economics.
Education. Includes curriculum and instructional, educational leaderships and policy studies.
Electrical Engineering.
Engineering Mechanics.
English. M.A. only.
Entomology.
Environmental Science.
Family and Consumer Sciences. M.F.C.S. only.
Fisheries Biology.
Food Science and Technology.
Forestry.
Genetics.
Geology.
Graphic Design. M.F.A. only.
High Energy Physics.
History. M.A. only.
History of Technology and Science.
Horticulture.
Human Computer Interaction.
Human Development and Family Studies.
Immunobiology.
Industrial and Agricultural Technology.

Industrial Engineering.
Industrial Relations. M.S. only.
Information Assurance. M.S. only.
Inorganic Chemistry.
Integrated Visual Arts. M.F.A. only
Interdisciplinary Graduate Studies. M.A., M.S. only.
Interior Design. M.F.A. only.
Journalism and Mass Communication. M.S. only.
Landscape Architecture. M.L.A. only.
Material Science and Engineering.
Mathematics.
Meat Science.
Mechanical Engineering.
Meteorology.
Microbiology.
Molecular, Cellular, and Developmental Biology.
Neuroscience.
Nuclear Physics.
Nutritional Sciences.
Organic Chemistry.
Physical Chemistry.
Physics.
Plant Breeding.
Plant Pathology.
Plant Physiology.
Political Science. M.A. only.
Professional Agriculture. M.Ag. only.
Psychology.
Public Administration. M.P.A. only.
Rhetoric and Professional Communication. Ph.D. only.
Rural Sociology.
School Mathematics. M.S.M.
Science Education.
Seed Technology and Business.
Sociology.
Soil Science.
Statistics.
Sustainable Agriculture.
Systems Engineering. M.Eng. only.
Teaching English as a Second Lanuage.
Textiles and Clothing.
Toxicology.
Transportation. M.S. only
Veterinary Clinical Sciences.
Veterinary Microbiology.
Veterinary Pathology.
Veterinary Preventive Medicine. M.S. only.
Wildlife Biology.
Note: There are only six approved dual degree programs: M.Arch.-M.B.A., M.Arch.-M.C.R.P., M.C.R.P.-M.B.A., M.L.A.-M.C.R.P., M.P.A.-M.C.R.P., M.S. (Statistics)-M.B.A.

College of Veterinary Medicine (50011)
Web site: www.vetmed.iastate.edu

Formed 1872 as the State Agricultural College and Farm. The College was established in 1879 as the first public veterinary college in the U.S. Semester system. Special facilities: Iowa Center for Advanced Neurotoxicology, Veterinary Medical Research Institute, National Animal Disease Center.

Annual tuition and fees: residents $15,391, nonresidents $36,171. Limited on-campus housing available. Total average cost for other expenses: $9,250.

Enrollment: first-year class 120, total 480 (men 23%, women 77%, minorities 3%, state residents 80%); graduate students 78. Faculty: full-time 106, part-time 17. Degrees conferred: D.V.M., D.V.M.-MS., D.V.M.-Ph.D. The M.S. and Ph.D. are offered through the Graduate College.

ADMISSION REQUIREMENTS. VMCAS report, transcripts, GRE, three letters of recommendation (from an academic adviser veterinarian), personal statement, online supplemental application required in support of application. Applicants must have completed at least three years of college study. Early Decision Option available. Accepts transfer applicants on space available basis only. Preference given to state, Nebraska, New Jersey, North Dakota, and South Dakota residents. Apply to University Director of Admissions and Records before October 1. Fall admission only. Application fee $60, $80 for international applicants. Phone: (515)294-1242, toll-free outside Iowa (800)262-3810.

ADMISSION STANDARDS. Competitive. Accepts about 20–25% of all applicants. Number of applications 510 (contract applicants, 333 out-of-state); number interviewed n/a (n/a out-of-state); number of acceptance n/a (n/a out-of-state); number enrolled 120 (n/a out-of-state). Usual minimum UGPA: 3.0 (resident), 3.2 (nonresident (A = 4). GRE mean score (V + Q) 1150; mean UGPA 3.53.

FINANCIAL AID. Scholarships, fellowships, teaching assistantships, Federal W/S, loans. Apply by March 1 to Student Financial Aid Office (Phone: [515]294-2223), to appropriate department head for fellowships and assistantships. About 50% of students receive aid other than loans from College funds.

DEGREE REQUIREMENTS. For D.V.M.: satisfactory completion of four-year program. For M.S., Ph.D.: see Graduate College listing above.

FIELDS OF GRADUATE STUDY.
Anatomic Pathology.
Cell Biology.
Cellular and Molecular Biology.
Clinical Pathology.
Experimental Anatomy.
Immunobiology.
Molecular, Cellular and Developmental Biology.
Neuroscience.
Pathology.
Parasitology.
Pharmacology.
Physiology.
Theriogenology. M.S. only.
Toxicology. Interdepartmental program.
Veterinary Anatomy.
Veterinary Diagnostic and Production Animal Medicine. M.S. only.
Veterinary Medicine. M.S. only.
Veterinary Preventive Medicine. M.S. only.
Veterinary Microbiology.
Veterinary Surgery. M.S. only.

THE UNIVERSITY OF IOWA
Iowa City, Iowa 52242
Web site: www.uiowa.edu

Founded 1847. Located 250 miles SW of Chicago. CGS and AAU member. Coed. State control. Semester system. Special facilities: Computer-assisted Image Analysis Facility, Electron Microscopy Facility, High Field Nuclear Magnetic Facility, High Resolution Mass Spectrometry Facility, Institute of Hydraulic Research, Laser Science Research Facility, Large Scale Fermentation Facility, Museum of Art, Museum of Natural History, Public Policy Center, Social Science Institute. The University's NIH ranking is 38th among all U.S. institutions with 447 awards/grants valued at $116,119,755. According to The Center at University of Florida, the University is ranked 39th in receipt of Federal Research funds with $197,260,000 and it ranks 40th for total University research expenditures with $292,035,000. The University's endowment assets rank it 64th, with a value of $737,704,000. In 2004, the University awarded 300 doctorates, which ranked it 43rd among all U.S. institutions eligible to award that degree. Twenty of

the University's faculty members have been elected to National Honor Academies and this ranks it 45th among all U.S. institutions. The Library: approximately 4,000,000 volumes, 44,500 subscriptions. Total University enrollment: 28,500.

On-campus housing for 749 married students, 5356 single students. Average academic year housing cost: $6450 for married students, $6700 (including board) for single students. Apply to Family Housing Office. Phone: (319)335-9199 or Housing Assignment Office (319)335-3009; for off-campus housing, the University Housing Clearinghouse (319)335-3055. Day-care facilities available.

Graduate College

Graduate study since 1900. Academic year tuition: resident $6410, nonresident $16,422. Enrollment: full-time 2570, part-time 2144. University faculty teaching graduate students: full-time 1618, part-time 96. Degrees conferred: M.A., M.S., M.Ac., M.F.A., M.A.T., M.H.A., M.P.A., M.P.H., M.P.T., M.S.W., M.S.N., Ed.S., D.M.A., Ph.D.

ADMISSION REQUIREMENTS. Transcripts, three letters of recommendation required in support of College's application. Interview, GRE Subject Tests, GMAT required by some departments. TOEFL required for international applicants. Accepts transfer applicants. Graduates of unaccredited institutions not considered. Apply to University Director of Admissions by July 15 (Fall), December 1 (Spring), April 15 (Summer). Application fee $60, $85 for international applicants. Phone: (319)335-1525; fax: (319)335-1535; e-mail: admissions@uiowa.edu.

ADMISSION STANDARDS. Very selective or competitive for most departments. Usual minimum average: 2.5 (A = 4).

FINANCIAL AID. Annual awards from institutional funds: scholarships, fellowships, teaching assistantships, research assistantships, internships, Federal W/S, loans. Approved for VA benefits. Apply by February 1 to appropriate department for scholarships, fellowships, assistantships: to Director of Financial Aid for all other programs. Use FAFSA and institutional FAF. Phone: (319)335-1450; fax: (319)335-3060. Approximately 50% of students receive aid other than loans from College and outside sources. Aid available for part-time students.

DEGREE REQUIREMENTS. For M.A., M.S., M.Ac.: 30–48 semester hours minimum with or without thesis, at least 24 in residence; comprehensive/final oral exam; candidacy; no language for most majors. For M.F.A.: ordinarily two years of full-time residence, but requirement may be reduced to a minimum of one year at discretion of department head; thesis/creative project. For M.A.T.: 38 hours minimum, at least 24 in residence; final written/oral exam. For M.P.H.: 39–48 semester hour program; practicum; final written report and oral presentation. For M.H.A.: 60 semester hour full-time program; internship. For M.S.W.: 36–60 hours required, at least 24 in residence; final written/oral exam. For M.P.T.: 67 hours minimum, four semesters of full-time residence plus internship; written/oral exam. For M.P.A.: 92 hours minimum, at least 24 in residence; final project/comprehensive exam. For M.S.N.: 40–52 hours required, at least 24 in residence; thesis/nonthesis option; final written/oral exam. For Ed.S.: ordinarily two years, at least one year in residence and 1 semester in full-time attendance; final written/oral exam. For Ph.D.: 72 hours minimum, at least 18 in full-time residence; preliminary written/oral exam; candidacy; dissertation; knowledge of foreign languages or knowledge of special research tools, as determined by department; final oral exam. For D.M.A.: same as for the Ph.D., except qualifying recital and doctoral essay instead of dissertation.

FIELDS OF STUDY.
Accounting. M.Ac.
Acting. M.F.A.
Actuarial Science. M.S.

Afro-American World Studies. M.A.
American Studies. M.A., Ph.D.
Anatomy and Cell Biology. M.S., Ph.D.
Anthropology. M.A.
Applied Mathematical and Computational Sciences. Ph.D.
Art. M.A., M.F.A.
Art Education. M.A., Ph.D.
Art History. M.A., Ph.D.
Asian Civilizations. M.A.
Astronomy. M.S.
Biochemistry. M.S., Ph.D.
Biological Sciences. Includes developmental, ecology, evolutionary, genetics, molecular and cell biology, neurobiology, plant science. M.S., Ph.D.
Biomedical Engineering. M.S., Ph.D.
Biosciences. Ph.D.
Biostatistics. M.S., Ph.D.
Business Administration. Includes accounting, finance, management and organizations, management sciences, marketing. M.A., M.B.A., Ph.D.
Chemical and Biochemical Engineering. M.S., Ph.D.
Chemistry. M.S., Ph.D.
Civil and Environmental Engineering. M.S., Ph.D.
Classics. No thesis for M.A. M.A., Ph.D.
Clinical Investigations. M.S.
Communication Studies. M.A., Ph.D.
Comparative Literature. M.A., Ph.D.
Comparative Literature/Translation. M.F.A.
Computer Science. M.C.S., M.S., Ph.D.
Dance. M.F.A.
Dental Public Health. M.S.
Design. M.F.A.
Developmental Reading. M.A.
Directing. M.F.A.
Dramaturgy. M.F.A.
Economics. M.A., Ph.D.
Education—Counseling, Rehabilitation, and Student Development. Includes counselor education (Ph.D.), rehabilitation counseling (M.A., Ph.D.), school counseling, (M.A.), student development (M.A., Ph.D.), substance abuse counseling (M.A.), student affairs administration and research (Ph.D.).
Education—Educational Policy and Leadership Studies. Includes educational administration (M.A., Ed.S., Ph.D.), higher education (M.A., Ed.S., Ph.D.), social foundations of education (M.A., Ph.D.).
Education—Psychological and Quantitative Foundations. Includes counseling psychology (Ph.D.), educational measurement and statistics (M.A., Ph.D.), educational psychology (M.A., Ph.D.), instructional design and technology (M.A., Ed.S., Ph.D.), school psychology (Ph.D.).
Education—Teaching and Learning. Includes early childhood education (M.A.), elementary education (M.A., M.S., Ph.D.), secondary education (M.A., M.A.T., Ph.D.), special education (M.A., Ph.D.).
Educational Administration. M.A., Ed.S., Ph.D.
Educational Measurement and Statistics. M.A., Ph.D.
Electrical and Computer Engineering. M.S., Ph.D.
English. Includes literary studies (M.A., Ph.D.), nonfiction writing (M.F.A.) creative writing (M.F.A.). M.A., M.F.A., Ph.D.
Environmental Engineering. M.S., Ph.D.
Epidemiology. M.S., Ph.D.
Exercise Science. M.S., Ph.D.
Film and Video Production. M.F.A.
Film Studies. M.A., Ph.D.
Finance. Ph.D.
Free Radical and Radiation Biology. M.S., Ph.D.
French. M.A., Ph.D.
Genetics. Ph.D.
Geography. M.A., Ph.D.
Geoscience. M.S., Ph.D.
German. M.A., Ph.D.

Greek. M.A.
Health and Sport Studies. M.A., Ph.D.
Health Management and Policy. M.H.A., Ph.D.
History. M.A., Ph.D.
Human Toxicology. Ph.D.
Immunology. Ph.D.
Industrial Engineering. M.S., Ph.D.
Journalism. M.A.
Latin. M.A.
Law. LL.M.
Leisure Studies. M.A.
Library and Information Science. M.A.
Linguistics. M.A., Ph.D.
Literacy Studies. M.A., Ph.D.
Management and Organizations. Ph.D.
Management Sciences. Ph.D.
Marketing. Ph.D.
Mass Communication. Ph.D.
Mathematics. M.S., Ph.D.
Mathematics Education. M.A., Ph.D.
Mechanical Engineering. M.S., Ph.D.
Medical Education. M.M.E.
Microbiology. Ph.D.
Molecular and Cellular Biology. Ph.D.
Molecular Physiology and Biophysics. M.S., Ph.D.
Music. M.A., M.F.A., D.M.A., Ph.D.
Music Education. M.A., Ph.D.
Neuroscience. Ph.D.
Nonfiction Writing. M.F.A.
Nursing. Includes clinical nurse leader, nursing practice. M.S., D.N.P., Ph.D.
Occupational and Environmental Health. M.S., Ph.D.
Operative Dentistry. M.S.
Oral and Maxillofacial Surgery. M.S.
Oral Science. M.S., Ph.D.
Orthodontics. M.S.
Pathology. M.S.
Pharmacology. M.S., Ph.D.
Pharmacy. Pharm.D., M.S., Ph.D.
Philosophy. M.A., Ph.D.
Physical Therapy. M.A., M.P.T., Ph.D.
Physician Assistant Studies. M.P.A.
Physics. M.S., Ph.D.
Physiology and Biophysics. M.S., Ph.D.
Playwriting. M.F.A.
Political Science. M.A., Ph.D.
Psychology. M.A., Ph.D.
Public Health. Includes biostatistics (M.S., Ph.D.), epidemiology (M.S., Ph.D.), health management and policy (M.H.A., Ph.D.), occupational and environmental health (M.S., Ph.D.), public health (M.P.H.).
Rehabilitation Counseling. M.A.
Rehabilitation Counselor Education. Ph.D.
Religion. M.A., Ph.D.
School Counseling. M.A.
School Psychology. Ph.D.
Science Education. M.S., Ph.D.
Second Language Acquisition. Ph.D.
Social Studies. M.A.
Social Work. M.S.W., Ph.D.
Sociology. M.A., Ph.D.
Spanish. M.A., Ph.D.
Speech and Hearing Science. Ph.D.
Speech Pathology and Audiology. M.A.
Statistics. Includes actuarial science (M.S.). M.S., Ph.D.
Stomatology. M.S.
Student Affairs Administration and Research. Ph.D.
Theatre Arts. M.F.A.
Translational Biomedicine. M.S., Ph.D.
Urban and Regional Planning. M.A., M.S.
Women's Studies. Ph.D.

College of Dentistry

Web site: www.dentistry.uiowa.edu

Established 1882 as a department of Dentistry, became the College of Dentistry in 1900. Located at the Health Science Center. Semester system. Special facilities: Dows Institute of Dental Research, Center for Clinical Studies, Center for Oral and Maxillofacial Implants, Research Center on Oral Health in Aging, Specialized Caries Research Center. Special programs: summer programs for underrepresented minorities. Health Center library: 373,527 volumes, 14,480 electronic journals, 300 dental subscriptions.

Annual tuition: resident $25,854, nonresident $43,480. Limited on-campus housing available. Most dental students live off-campus. Contact Office of Dental Students Admissions for both on- and off-campus housing information. Phone: (319)335-7157. Average academic year housing cost: $15,000–$18,000. Total average cost for all other first-year expenses: $11,500.

Enrollment: first-year class 75, total full-time 300 (men 72%, women 28%, minorities 19%, state residents 70%). Faculty: full-time 114, part-time 99. Degrees conferred: D.D.S., M.S., Ph.D. (D.S.T.P.-N.I.H. funded program), Certificates.

ADMISSION REQUIREMENTS. AADSAS report, transcripts, DAT (not later than October), three letters of recommendation, interview required in support of application. Preference given to Iowa and Arkansas residents. Applicants must have completed at least three years of college study. Apply to Associate Dean for Academic Affairs after June 1, before November 1. Application fee $60, $85 for international applicants. Phone: (319)335-7157; fax: (319)335-7155.

ADMISSION STANDARDS. Competitive. Accepts about 10–15% of all applicants. Usual minimum UGPA: 3.0 (A = 4). Mean DAT: academic 19, PAT 17; mean UGPA 3.6.

FINANCIAL AID. Scholarships, dental research and teaching awards, federal programs, loans. Apply by November 30 to University Office of Student Aid. Phone: (319)335-1450. Use FAFSA (College code: 001892). About 90% of students receive aid from College.

DEGREE REQUIREMENTS. For D.D.S.: satisfactory completion of forty-five-month program. For M.S.: thirty-hour minimum in residence, final exam. For Ph.D.: see Graduate College listing above.

FIELDS OF POSTGRADUATE STUDY.
Dental Public Health. M.S.
Endodontics. M.S., Certificate.
Operative Dentistry. M.S., Certificate.
Oral and Maxillofacial Pathology. M.S., Certificate.
Oral and Maxillofacial Radiology. M.S., Certificate.
Oral and Maxillofacial Surgery. M.S., Certificate.
Oral Science. M.S.
Orthodontics. M.S., Certificate.
Pediatric Dentistry. Certificate.
Periodontics. M.S., Certificate.
Prosthodontics. M.S., Certificate.

College of Law

Web site: www.law.uiowa.edu

Founded 1865. Oldest law school west of the Mississippi. ABA approved since 1923. AALS member. Semester system. Special facilities: The Institute of Public Affairs, Larned A. Waterman Iowa Nonprofit Resource Center, Law, Health Policy and Disability Center, National Health Law and Policy Recourse Center, UI Center for Human Rights, UI Center for International Finance and Development. Special programs: summer study in London and Iowa Bordeaux program. Law library: 1,154,749 volumes, 10,048 subscriptions; has LEXIS, NEXIS, WESTLAW, ILP; has more that 400 network connections.

Annual tuition: resident $14,542, nonresident $29,986. Total cost for all other expenses: $15,415.

Enrollment: first-year class 225 (Fall), 45 (Summer); total 644 (men 54%, women 46%, minorities 17%). Faculty: full-time 55, part-time 30. Student to faculty ratio 12.2 to 1. Degrees conferred: J.D., J.D.-M.A., LL.M. (International and Comparative Law).

ADMISSION REQUIREMENTS. LSDAS Law School report, bachelor's degree, transcripts, LSAT, at least one letter of recommendation, personal statement required in support of application. Interview not required. Accepts transfer applicants. Preference given to state residents. Graduates of unaccredited colleges not considered. Apply to Director of Admissions after September 1, before March 1. Fall and Summer admission only. Application fee $30, foreign application fee $60, $85 for international applicants. Phone: (800)553-IOWA; phone: (319)335-9095; fax: (319)335-9019; e-mail: law-admissions@uiowa.edu.

ADMISSION STANDARDS. Selective. Accepts approximately 39% of all students. Number of applicants 1339; number of acceptance 519; number enrolled 225; LSAT (75% of students have a score at or above 158); GPA (75% of students have a GPA at or above 3.39). *U.S. News & World Report* ranking is in the top 24 of all U.S. law schools.

FINANCIAL AID. Scholarships, fellowships, assistantships, full and partial tuition waivers, Federal W/S, loans. Apply by January 1 to Associate Director of Admission. Phone: (319)335-9142. Use FAFSA (College code: 001892). About 40% of students receive some aid from College.

DEGREE REQUIREMENTS. For J.D.: 90 credit hours minimum, at least two years in residence. For LL.M.: at least 24 credits minimum beyond the J.D.

Roy J. and Lucille A. Carver College of Medicine (52242-1101)

Web site: www.medicine.uiowa.edu

Establish 1850. Located at Health Science campus. Semester system. Special facilities: Center on Aging, Center for Bioinformatics and Computational Biology, Iowa Cardiovascular Center, The Craniofacial Center, Center for Gene Therapy of Cystic Fibrosis and Other Genetic Diseases, General Clinical Research Center, Holden Comprehensive Cancer Center, Huntington's Disease Center, The Carver Family Center for Macular Degeneration, Wellstone Muscular Dystrophy Cooperative Research Center, Comprehensive Lung Imaging Center, Specialized Center of Research in Osteoarthritis. Library: 260,500 volumes, 2583 subscriptions. NIH ranking is 38th among all U.S. institutions with 447 awards/grants worth $166,119,755.

Annual tuition: resident $21,284, nonresident $41,354. On-campus rooms and apartments available for both single and married students. Annual housing cost: $350–$900 per month. Married students contact Family Housing Office for housing information, phone: (319)335-9199. For off-campus housing in-formation contact the Housing Clearinghouse, phone: (319)335-3055. Off-campus housing and personal expenses: approximately $10,273.

Enrollment: first-year class 142; total 572 (men 51%, women 49%, minorities 20%, state residents 72%). Faculty: full- and part-time 1350. Degrees conferred: M.D., M.D.-M.B.A., M.D.-M.P.H., M.D.-Ph.D. (Medical Scientist Training Program). The M.A., M.S., and Ph.D. are offered through the Graduate College.

ADMISSION REQUIREMENTS. AMCAS report, transcripts, letters of evaluation, MCAT required in support of application. Interviews by invitation. Supplemental application required for admission. Preference given to Iowa residents. Has EDP; apply between June 1 and August 1. Accepts transfer applicants. Applicants must have completed at least three years of college study. Graduates of unaccredited colleges not considered. Apply after

June 1, before November 1. Application fee $60. Phone: (319) 335-8052; fax: (319)335-8049; e-mail: medical-admissions@ uiowa.edu.

ADMISSION STANDARDS. Competitive. Accepts about 11% of all applicants. Number of applications 2513 (2176 out-of-state); number interviewed 640 (377 out-of-state); number of acceptance 300 (170 out-of-state); number enrolled 142 (45 out-of-state). Mean Composite MCAT 10.1; mean UGPA 3.70. *U.S. News & World Report* ranking is in the top 30 of all medical research schools, 18th in primary care.

FINANCIAL AID. Scholarships, summer fellowships, grants, tuition waivers, loans. Apply to Associate Dean by June 1. Phone: (319)335-8059. Use FAFSA (College code: 001892). Approximately 95% of students receive aid from College and outside sources.

DEGREE REQUIREMENTS. For M.D.: satisfactory completion of four-year program. For M.A., M.S., Ph.D., see Graduate College listing above. For M.D.-Ph.D.: generally a seven-year program.

FIELDS OF GRADUATE STUDY.
Anatomy and Cell Biology.
Biochemistry.
Biological Sciences.
Biomedical Engineering.
Biostatistics.
Epidemiology.
Free Radical and Radiation Biology. Interdisciplinary.
Genetics. Interdisciplinary.
Immunology. Interdisciplinary.
Microbiology.
Molecular and Cellular Biology. Interdisciplinary.
Molecular Physiology and Biophysics.
Neuroscience. Interdisciplinary.

ITHACA COLLEGE
Ithaca, New York 14850-7020
Web site: www.ithaca.edu

Founded 1892. Located 50 miles SW of Syracuse. CGS member. Coed. Private control. Semester system. Library: 376,000 volumes, 2500 subscriptions. Total College enrollment: 6400.

Tuition: per credit $790. No on-campus housing for graduate students. Contact Room Assignments Coordinator of Residential Life for off-campus housing information.

Division of Graduate Studies

Enrollment: full-time 290, part-time 14. Faculty: full- and part-time 109. Degrees conferred: M.S., M.M.

ADMISSION REQUIREMENTS. Official transcripts, two letters of recommendation (four letters if applying for an assistantship), GRE scores (for Speech Pathology, Audiology, and Exercise and Sport Science applicants) required in support of application. GMAT required for Business. Auditions required for Music applicants. TOEFL required for international applicants. Accepts transfer applicants. Graduates of unaccredited institutions not considered. Apply to Dean of Graduate Studies by March 1 (Fall), December 1 (Spring). Application fee $40. Phone: (607) 274-3527; fax: (607)274-1263; e-mail: gradstudies @ithaca.edu.

ADMISSION STANDARDS. Selective. Usual minimum average: 3.0. (A = 4).

FINANCIAL AID. Annual awards from institutional funds: teaching assistantships, internships, grants, Federal W/S, loans. Approved for VA benefits. Apply with admission application but not later than March 1 to Dean of Graduate Studies for assistantships; to Financial Aid Office for all other programs. Phone: (607)274-3131; fax: (607)274-1895. Use FAFSA. About 40% of students receive aid other than loans from College. No aid for part-time students.

DEGREE REQUIREMENTS. For M.S.: 30–39 credits minimum; thesis; 36–39 credit hours nonthesis; final oral/written exam. For M.M.: 30 credits minimum; recital; final oral/written exam.

FIELDS OF STUDY.
Adolescence Education.
Business Administration.
Communication.
Exercise and Sports Sciences.
Health Education.
Music. Includes composition, conducting, music education, theory, string, woodwinds, brass.
Occupational Therapy.
Physcial Education.
Professional Accountancy.
Speech-Language, Pathology and Audiology.
Sport Management.
Teaching Students with Speech and Language Disabilities.

JACKSON STATE UNIVERSITY
Jackson, Mississippi 39217-0195
Web site: www.jsums.edu

Founded 1877. CGS member. Coed. State control. Semester system. Library: 400,000 volumes, 2706 subscriptions.

Tuition: per semester hour $247, or $2216 per semester. On-campus housing. Average academic year housing cost: $3334–$5298 for single students. Contact the Director of Residential Life for both on- and off-campus information. Phone: (601)979-2591.

Division of Graduate Studies

Enrollment: full- and part-time about 1349. University faculty teaching graduate students: full-time 200, part-time 0. Degrees conferred: M.A., M.S., M.M.Ed., M.S.Ed., M.S.T., M.A.T., M.B.A., M.Bus.Ed., M.P.A., M.P.P.A., Ed.S., Ed.D., Ph.D.

ADMISSION REQUIREMENTS. Two official transcripts, GRE/ GMAT, three letters of recommendation required in support of application. TOEFL required for international students. Accepts transfer applicants. Apply to Office of Admissions before March 15 (Summer), March 1 (Fall), October 15 (Spring); some programs have earlier deadlines. Application fee $25, $50 for nonresidents. Phone: (601)979-2455; fax: (601)979-4325.

ADMISSION STANDARDS. Relatively open. Usual minimum average: 2.5 (A = 4).

FINANCIAL AID. Scholarships, assistantships, tuition waivers, Federal W/S, loans. Approved for VA benefits. Apply to department of interest before March 1 (Summer), May 1 (Fall), November 1 (Spring) for scholarships, assistantships; to the Office of Aid for all other programs. Phone: (601)979-2227. Use FAFSA.

DEGREE REQUIREMENTS. For master's: 30 semester hours, 36 hours without thesis or project; thesis or project option, written comprehensive exam/final oral exam. For Ed.S.: 30 semester hours beyond the master's. For M.S.W.: 60 semester hours beyond the bachelor's degree. For Ed.D.: 60–66 semester hours. For Ph.D.: 60 semester hours; comprehensive exam; dissertation; final oral exam.

FIELDS OF STUDY.
Accounting. M.P.A.
Biology. M.S.T., M.S.
Business Administration. M.B.A., Ph.D.
Business Education. M.B.Ed.
Chemistry. M.S., Ph.D.
Clinical Psychology. Ph.D.
Communicative Disorders. M.S.
Computer Science. M.S.
Criminal Justice and Sociology. M.A.
Early Childhood. M.S.Ed., Ed.D.
Educational Administration. Ph.D.
Educational Administration and Supervision. M.S.Ed., Ed.S.
Elementary Education. M.S.Ed., Ed.S.
Engineering. M.S.
English. M.A.T., M.A.
Environmental Science. M.S., Ph.D.
Hazardous Materials Management. M.S.
Health, Physical Education, and Recreation. M.S.Ed.
History. M.A.
Mass Communication. M.S.
Mathematics. M.S.T., M.S.
Music Education. M.M.Ed.
Political Science. M.A.
Public Administration. Ph.D.
Public Health. M.P.H.
Public Policy and Administration. M.P.P.A.
Reading. M.S.Ed., Ed.S.
Rehabilitation Services. M.S.
School, Community and Rehabilitation Counseling. M.S., M.S.Ed.
Science Education. M.S.Ed., Ed.S.
Secondary Education. M.S.
Social Work. M.S.W., Ph.D.
Sociology. M.A.
Special Education. M.S.
Technology Education. M.S.Ed.
Urban Higher Education. Executive Ph.D.
Urban and Regional Planning. M.S., Ph.D.

JACKSONVILLE STATE UNIVERSITY
Jacksonville, Alabama 36265-1602
Web site: www.jsu.edu

Founded 1883. Located 76 miles NE of Birmingham. Coed. Public control. Semester system. Library: 685,991 volumes, 4790 subscriptions. Total University enrollment: 9100.

Annual tuition: resident, full-time $4848, nonresident $9696; per credit hour, resident $202, nonresident $404. On-campus housing for all graduate men and women who apply; none for married students. Average academic year housing cost: $2800–$5000 (including board). Apply to Director of University Housing. Phone: (256)782-5122. Day-care facilities available.

College of Graduate Studies

Graduate study since 1957. Enrollment: full-time 424, part-time 1400. Faculty teaching graduate students: full-time 122. Degrees conferred: M.S. in Ed., M.S., M.B.A., M.A., M.M., M.M.Ed., M.P.A.

ADMISSION REQUIREMENTS. Transcripts, GRE Subject Tests/GMAT/MAT required in support of College's application. Interview not required. TOEFL required for international appli-

cants. Accepts transfer applicants. Apply to College of Graduate Studies; no specified closing date. Application fee $20. Phone: (256)782-5329; fax: (256)782-5321; e-mail: graduate@jsu.edu.

ADMISSION STANDARDS. Unconditional admissions; 450 x UGPA + GRE = 2000 or more; or 15 x UGPA + MAT = 60 or more; or 200 x UGPA + GMAT = 950 or more.

FINANCIAL AID. Limited to research assistantships, teaching assistantships, Federal W/S, loans. Approved for VA benefits. Apply by April 1 to Financial Aid Office. Phone: (256)782-5006. Use FAFSA. Aid available for part-time students.

DEGREE REQUIREMENTS. For M.A., M.M.Ed., M.M., M.P.A., M.S., M.S. in Ed.: Plan I, 24–36 semester hours plus thesis. For M.B.A.: Plan II, 30–42 semester hours without thesis. Under both plans, final oral/comprehensive exam.

FIELDS OF STUDY.
Biology.
Business Administration. Includes accounting.
Community Health Nursing.
Computer Systems and Software Design.
Counselor Education.
Criminal Justice.
Early Childhood Education.
Early Childhood Special Education.
Educational Administration.
Elementary Education.
Emergency Managment.
English.
History.
Liberal Studies.
Library Media.
Manufacturing Systems Technology.
Mathematics.
Music.
Music Education.
Nursing.
Physical Education.
Psychology.
Public Administration.
Reading Specialist.
School Counseling.
Secondary Education. Eight subject areas.
Special Education.

JACKSONVILLE UNIVERSITY
Jacksonville, Florida 32211-3394
Web site: www.ju.edu

Founded 1934. Coed. Private control. Semester system. Library: 374,000 volumes, 900 subscriptions; library is an offical depository for both U.S. and Florida government documents. Total University enrollment: 3000.

Tuition: per hour $290; for M.B.A. $495; for Nursing $400. No on-campus housing for married students. Annual housing cost: $6000 (including board). Contact Dean of Students Office for both on- and off-campus housing information. Phone: (904)745-3950.

Graduate Program

Enrollment: full-time 61, part-time 301. Graduate faculty: full-time 60, part-time 20. Degrees conferred: M.A.T., M.B.A., M.S.N.

ADMISSION REQUIREMENTS. Transcripts, GRE/MAT, three letters of recommendation (two for M.B.A.), GMAT (M.B.A.), Florida nursing license (Nursing) required in support of application. Online application available. Interview required for most departments. TOEFL (minimum score 550), TSE, TWE required for international applicants. Accepts transfer applicants. Apply to Director of M.A.T. or M.B.A. program at least 30 days prior to registration. Application fee $30. Phone: Education (904)745-7132; Business (904)745-7466; Nursing (904)745-7280.

ADMISSION STANDARDS. Selective. Usual minimum average: 3.0 (A = 4).

FINANCIAL AID. Scholarships, assistantships, Federal W/S, loans. Approved for VA benefits. Apply by March 15 to the Office of Financial Aid. Phone: (904)745-7060. Use FAFSA.

DEGREE REQUIREMENTS. For M.A.T.: 36 semester hours, at least 30 in residence; six semester hours of internship or three years of teaching; final written exam. For M.B.A.: 30 semester hours, which must be completed within five years of completion of first graduate course. For M.S.N.: 32 semester hours; concentration; practicum.

FIELDS OF STUDY.
Art Education.
Business Administration.
Computing Science.
Educational Leadership.
Educational Technology.
Elementary Education.
English Education.
Entrepreneurship.
Finance.
Foreign Languages.
Integrated Learning with Technology.
Leadership.
Mathematics Education.
Music Education.
Nursing. Includes nursing education, family nurse practitioner, emergency nurse practitioner, nursing administration.
Reading Education.
Social Sciences.

JAMES MADISON UNIVERSITY
Harrisonburg, Virginia 22807
Web site: www.jmu.edu

Established 1908. Located approximately 2½ hours from Washington, D.C. CGS member. Coed. Public control. Semester system. Special facilities: Center for Economics Education, Center for Entrepreneurship, Human Development Center, Speech and Hearing Center. Library: 1,300,000 volumes, 3367 subscriptions. Total University enrollment: 17,000.

Tuition: per credit, resident $246, nonresident $701. Limited on-campus housing for graduate students.

College of Graduate and Outreach Programs

Graduate study since 1954. Enrollment: full-time 682, part-time 385. University faculty: full-time 156, part-time 30. Degrees conferred: M.A., M.S., M.S.Ed., M.B.A., M.A.T., M.Ed., M.M., M.P.A., M.F.A., Ed.S., Psy.D.

ADMISSION REQUIREMENTS. Transcripts, GRE Subject Tests (for some majors), GMAT for M.B.A., MAT required in support of School's application. Online application available. TOEFL required for international applicants. Interview required by some departments. Accepts transfer applicants. Graduates of unaccredited institutions not considered. Apply to Office of Dean by May 1 (Fall), September 1 (Spring). Application fee $55. Phone: (540) 568-6131; fax: (540)568-6266.

ADMISSION STANDARDS. Selective. Usual minimum average: 2.5 (A = 4).

FINANCIAL AID. Annual awards from institutional funds: scholarships, teaching assistantships, research assistantships, internships, service assistantships, Federal W/S, loans. Approved for VA benefits. Apply by March 1 to Dean of Graduate School. Phone: (540)568-7820; fax: (540)568-7994. Use FAFSA and University's FAF. About 30% of students receive aid other than loans from both College and outside sources.

DEGREE REQUIREMENTS. For master's: 30 semester credits minimum; thesis optional for many departments; final written/oral exam. For Ed.S.: 30 semester credits minimum; thesis optional for many departments, final written/oral exam. For Psy.D.: 60 semester credits minimum beyond master's degree; qualifying exam; advancement to candidacy; internship; special project; final written/oral exam.

FIELDS OF STUDY.
Accounting.
Art. Includes art history.
Biology.
Business Administration.
Computer Science.
Communication Sciences and Disorders.
Early Childhood Education (PreK–3).
Elementary Education (PreK–6).
Elementary Education (4–6).
English.
Exceptional Education.
Health Sciences.
History.
Integrated Science and Technology.
Kinesiology.
Learning Technology and Leadership Education.
Mathematics.
Mathematics Education.
Middle School Education.
Music.
Nursing.
Occupational Therapy.
Physician Assistant Studies.
Psychology.
Public Administration.
Reading.
Secondary Education.
Speech-Language Pathology.
Technical and Scientific Communication.

JOHN CARROLL UNIVERSITY
Cleveland, Ohio 44118-4581
Web site: www.jcu.edu

Founded 1886. CGS member. Coed. Private control. Roman Catholic. Semester system. Library: 620,000 volumes, 2198 subscriptions.

Tuition: per credit $645, M.B.A. $793. No separate on-campus housing for graduate students. Apply to Dean of Students Office for off-campus housing. Phone: (216)397-4401.

Graduate School

Enrollment: full-time 187, part-time 606. Graduate faculty: full-time 133, part-time 56. Degrees conferred: M.A., M.S., M.B.A., M.Ed.

ADMISSION REQUIREMENTS. Transcripts required in support of application. GRE Subject Tests/MAT recommended;

M.A.T. required for Community Counseling program. TOEFL required of international students. Accepts transfer applicants. Deadline to Admissions Office, 30 days prior to registration. Application fee $25, $35 for international applicants. Phone: (216)397-4284; fax: (216)397-3009.

ADMISSION STANDARDS. Selective. Usual minimum average: 2.5. Some programs require 3.0 (A = 4).

FINANCIAL AID. Scholarships, teaching and research assistantships, tuition waivers, Federal W/S, loans. Apply by March 1 to Dean, Graduate School. Phone: (216)397-4248. Use FAFSA. About 30% of students receive aid other than loans from School. Aid available for part-time students.

DEGREE REQUIREMENTS. For M.A., M.S., M.Ed.: 30–33 semester hours, at least 24 in residence; reading knowledge of one foreign language for M.A. in some departments; thesis/research essay; oral/written comprehensive exam. For M.A. (Community Counseling): 60-credit full-time program; clinical experience; practicum; internship. For M.B.A.: 60 semester hours.

FIELDS OF STUDY.
Accounting. M.S., M.B.A.
Biology. GRE Subject in Biology for admission.
Business. GMAT for admission.
Communications Management.
Community Counseling.
Education. Includes school counseling, school psychology, administration, professional teacher, instructional technology, reading, educational psychology.
English. GRE for admission to degree programs.
History.
Humanities.
Integrated Science.
Mathematics.
Nonprofit Administration.
Religious Studies. MAT or GRE for admission.
School Counseling.

JOHN JAY COLLEGE OF CRIMINAL JUSTICE
New York, New York 10019-1093
Web site: www.jjay.cuny.edu

Established 1965. A unit of the City University of New York. Coed. Municipal control. Semester system. Special facilities: Center for Crime Prevention and Control, Center for Cybercrime Studies, Center for International Human Rights, Center for Modern Forensic Practice, Center on Race, Crime and Justice, Center on Terrorism, Criminal Justice Center, Criminal Justice Research and Evaluation Center, CUNY Dispute Resolution Consortium, Fire Science Institute, Forensic Psychology Research Institute, Institute for Criminal Justice Ethics, Prisoner Reentry Institute. Library: 310,000 volumes, 1325 subscriptions. Total College enrollment: 14,000.
Tuition: per credit, resident $270, nonresident $500. No on-campus housing. Apply to Dean of Students for off-campus housing information. Phone: (212)237-8737.

Graduate Division

Program intended for students seeking careers in public services, for personnel in various criminal justice agencies. Enrollment: full- and part-time 2000. Faculty: full-time 45, part-time 14. Degrees conferred: M.A., M.S., M.P.A., Ph.D. (program located at CUNY Graduate Center).

ADMISSION REQUIREMENTS. Transcripts, GRE, three letters of recommendation, essay required in support of College's application. Online application available. TOEFL required for all international applicants. Accepts transfer applicants. Apply to Graduate Office of Admissions by June 30 (Fall), December 15 (Spring). Application fee $125. Phone: (212)237-8800; fax: (212) 237-8777. For Ph.D.: apply to CUNY Graduate Center. Phone: (212)817-7470.

ADMISSION STANDARDS. Selective. Usual minimum average: 3.0 in major area of concentration (A = 4).

FINANCIAL AID. Limited to Federal W/S, loans. Approved for VA benefits. Apply to Director of Financial Aid for all programs. Phone: (212)237-8151. Use CUNY's FAFSA (School code: 002693). About 80% of students receive aid other than loans from College and outside sources. Aid available for part-time students.

DEGREE REQUIREMENTS. For master's: credit hours vary from 36–42 credit hours, depending on the selected major. For Ph.D.: three- to four-year, 45–60 credit program; three comprehensive exams; dissertation; final oral defense.

FIELDS OF STUDY.
Criminal Justice. Includes specializations in criminology and deviance, forensic psychology, law and philosophy, public policy and organizational behavior (Ph.D. only). M.A.
Forensic Computing. M.S.
Forensic Psychology. M.A., Ph.D. interdisciplinary.
Forensic Science. M.S.
Protection Management. M.S.
Public Administration. Includes inspector general. M.P.A.

THE JOHN MARSHALL LAW SCHOOL
315 South Plymouth Court
Chicago, Illinois 60604-3968
Web site: www.jmls.edu

Established 1899. Located in the heart of Chicago's legal and financial district. ABA approved since 1951. AALS member. Private control. Semester system. Full- and part-time study. Special facilities: Advocacy and Dispute Resolution Center, Tax Law Center, Employee Benefits Law Center, Fair Housing Legal Support Center, Information Technology and Privacy Law Center, Intellectual Property Law Center, International Business and Trade Law Center, Real Estate Law Center. Special programs: summer abroad in Ireland, Czech Republic, Lithuania, China. Law library: 388,179 volumes, 5514 subscriptions; has LEXIS, NEXIS, WESTLAW, CALI; has more that 75 network connections.
Annual tuition: full-time $28,980, part-time $20,700; per credit $1035. No on-campus housing available. All law students live off campus. Contact Admissions Office for housing information. Off-campus housing and personal expenses: approximately $20,894.
Enrollment: first-year class 419, part-time 122; total full- and part-time 1410 (men 59%, women 41%, minorities 16%); postgraduates 125. Faculty: full-time 33, part-time 96. Student to faculty ratio 21.8 to 1. Degrees conferred: J.D., J.D.-M.A. (Political Science, Roosevelt University), J.D.-M.B.A. (Dominican University), J.D.-M.P.A. (Roosevelt University), J.D.-LL.M. (Intellectual Property Law, Information Technology Law, International Business and Trade, Real Estate Law, Tax Law), LL.M. (Comparative Legal Studies), LL.M. (General, for persons who have completed a basic legal education and received a university degree in law in another country).

ADMISSION REQUIREMENTS. LSDAS Law School report, bachelor's degree, transcripts, LSAT, letters of recommendation required in support of application. Accepts transfer applicants. Apply after October 1, before March 1 (Fall), October 1 (Spring) to Director of Admissions, Application fee $60. Phone: (312)987-1406; outside Chicago (800)537-4280.

ADMISSION STANDARDS. Selective. Accepts approximately 36% of full-time and 38% of part-time applicants. Number of full-time applicants 3141, part-time 562; number of full-time acceptance 1136, part-time 214; number full-time enrolled 419, part-time 122; LSAT (75% of full-time students have a score at or above 152, part-time 151); GPA (75% of full-time students have a GPA at or above 2.80, part-time 2.63). *U.S. News & World Report* ranking is in the fourth tier of all U.S. law schools.

FINANCIAL AID. Scholarships, grants, loans. Apply by June 1 (Fall), November 1 (Spring) to Financial Aid Office. Phone: (800) 537-4280. Use FAFSA (School code: G01698) and JMLS financial aid form.

DEGREE REQUIREMENTS. For J.D.: satisfactory completion of 90 semester hour program. For master's degree: see Dominican University, Roosevelt University listing for requirements. For LL.M.: at least 24 credits minimum beyond J.D.

THE JOHNS HOPKINS UNIVERSITY
Baltimore, Maryland 21218
Web site: www.jhu.edu

Founded 1876. CGS and AAU member. Coed. Private control. Semester system. Special facilities: Center for Astrophysical Sciences, Applied Physics Laboratory, Bologna Center (Italy), Carnegie Institute, Center for Social Organization of Schools, Center for Non-Destructive Testing, Geology Field Station, Homewood Computing Center, McCollum-Pratt Institute, Nanjing Center (PRC), Oceanographic Research Vessels, Space Telescope Science Institute, Villa Spelman (Italy). The University's NIH ranking is number one among all U.S. institutions with 1299 awards/grants valued at $607,222,589. According to The Center at University of Florida, the University is ranked number one in receipt of Federal Research funds with $1,106,671,000 and it ranks number one for total University research expenditures with $1,244,132,000. The University's endowment assets rank it 22nd, with a value of $2,055,542,000. In 2004, the University awarded 367 doctorates, which ranked it 33rd among all U.S. institutions eligible to award that degree. Fifty-five of the University's faculty members have been elected to National Honor Academies and this ranks it 16th among all U.S. institutions. The Library: approximately 3,400,000 volumes, 28,000 subscriptions. Total University enrollment: 5900.

Annual tuition: full-time $35,900. On-campus housing for married students, single men and women. Average academic year housing cost: $8500–$11,500 for married students; $9925 for single students. Apply to Director of Housing. Phone: (410)516-7960.

Zanvyl Krieger School of Arts and Science

Enrollment: full-time 1066, part-time 15. Graduate faculty: full-time 268, part-time 10. Degrees conferred: M.A., Ph.D.

ADMISSION REQUIREMENTS. Two transcripts, two to three letters of recommendation required in support of School's application. Online application available. GRE Subject Tests strongly recommended. Samples of work required by some programs. TOEFL required for international applicants. Accepts transfer applicants. Graduates of unaccredited institutions not considered. Admission requirements vary by department and applicants

should first contact the individual department to obtain pertinent formation. Submit applications as directed, but not later than January 1. Application fee $60. Dean's Phone: (410)516-8174; e-mail: grad_adm@jhu.edu.

ADMISSION STANDARDS. Very competitive.

FINANCIAL AID. Scholarships, fellowships, research assistantships, teaching assistantships, full and partial tuition waivers, Federal W/S, loans. Apply January 15 (for priority consideration) to appropriate department chair for fellowships, assistantships, scholarships; to Office of Student Financial Services for all other programs. Phone: (410)516-8028. Use FAFSA.

DEGREE REQUIREMENTS. For M.A.: One year minimum in full-time residence; reading knowledge of one foreign language optional by department; thesis or comprehensive exam for some departments. For Ph.D.: generally three years minimum beyond the bachelor's; at least one year in full-time residence; reading knowledge of one foreign language optional by department; preliminary oral exam; dissertation; final oral/written exam.

FIELDS OF STUDY.
Anatomy. Ph.D. only.
Anthropology. Ph.D. only.
Art. Includes art history, architecture.
Biochemistry. Ph.D. only. The D.Sc., D.P.H. are offered by School of Hygiene and Public Health.
Biology. Includes chemical biology, developmental biology, genetic biology. Ph.D. only.
Biomedical Engineering. Ph.D. and postdoctoral study only.
Biophysics. Ph.D. only.
Biostatistics. Two years minimum of full-time residence for Ph.D.
Cell Biology.
Chemistry. Generally Ph.D. only.
Classics. Knowledge of Greek and Latin in addition to French, Italian, or German for M.A.; German and French or Italian for admission to Ph.D.
Cognitive Science. Ph.D. only.
Earth and Planetary Sciences. Includes petrology and geochemistry.
Economics. Ph.D. only.
English. Ph.D. only.
Environmental Sciences and Policy. M.S.
German. Oral/written exam for M.A.; qualifying exam for Ph.D.
History. Includes American studies, medieval history.
History of Art.
History of Science, Medicine, and Technology. Offered by School of Medicine; comprehensive written exam, oral qualifying exam for Ph.D. Ph.D. only.
Mathematical Science.
Mathematics.
Medical and Biological Illustration. Offered by School of Medicine; M.A. only.
Microbiology. Offered by School of Medicine.
Near Eastern Studies. Ph.D. only.
Pharmacology and Experimental Therapeutics. Offered by School of Medicine.
Philosophy. Apply to department chair; two years minimum in full-time residence. Ph.D. only.
Physics and Astronomy. Ph.D. only.
Physiological Chemistry. Offered by School of Medicine; Ph.D. only.
Physiology. Offered by School of Medicine; Ph.D. only.
Political Science. Includes public law and jurisprudence, public administration; oral/written exam for M.A.
Psychological and Brain Science.
Public Policy.
Psychology. Comprehensive exam for M.A.
Romance Languages and Literature. Includes French, Italian, Spanish.

Sociology. Includes sociology and public health; Ph.D. only.
Spanish. Ph.D.
Writing. Interdepartmental; M.A. only.

G.W.C. Whiting School of Engineering

Annual tuition: full-time $35,900.

Enrollment: full-time 400, part-time 31. Faculty: full-time 112, part-time 78. Degrees conferred: M.A., M.M.S.E., M.S., M.S.E., Ph.D.

ADMISSION REQUIREMENTS. Official transcripts, GRE, three letters of reference required in support of School's application. TOEFL required for international applicants. Interview not required. Accepts transfer applicants. Graduates of unaccredited institutions not considered. Apply to the Office of Admission by January 15. Application fee $70. Phone: (410)516-8174.

ADMISSION STANDARDS. Selective. Usual minimum average: 3.0 (A = 4).

FINANCIAL AID. Sixty-six fellowships, 207 research assistantships, 90 teaching assistantships, tuition waivers, Federal W/S, loans. Approved for VA benefits. Apply by January 15 (for priority consideration) to Office of Students Financial Services. Phone: (410)516-8028. Use FAFSA.

DEGREE REQUIREMENTS. For master's: One year minimum in full-time residence; thesis or comprehensive exam for some departments. For Ph.D.: generally three years minimum beyond the bachelor's, at least one year in full-time residence; preliminary exam; dissertation; Graduate Board oral exam.

FIELDS OF STUDY.
Applied Mathematics and Statistics. M.A., M.S.E., Ph.D.
Biomedical Engineering. M.S.E., Ph.D. (through the Medical School).
Chemical and Biomolecular Engineering. M.S.E., Ph.D.
Civil Engineering. M.C.E., M.S.E., Ph.D.
Computer Science. M.S.E., Ph.D.
Electrical Engineering. M.S.E., Ph.D.
Geography and Environmental Engineering. M.A., M.S., M.S.E., Ph.D.
Information Security. M.S.
Materials Science and Engineering. M.S.E., Ph.D.
Mechanical Engineering. M.S.E., Ph.D.

ENGINEERING AND APPLIED SCIENCE PROGRAMS FOR PROFESSIONALS:
Applied and Computational Mathematics.
Applied Biomedical Engineering.
Applied Physics.
Bioinformatics.
Chemical and Biomolecular Engineering.
Civil Engineering.
Computer Science.
Electrical and Computer Engineering.
Environmental Engineering, Science and Management.
Information Systems and Technology.
Materials Science and Engineering.
Mechanical Engineering.
Systems Engineering.
Technical Innovation and New Ventures. Certificate only.
Technical Management.

Paul H. Nitze School of Advanced International Studies (22036)

Established 1943. Located in Washington, D.C. Special facilities: Washington Center of Foreign Policy Research, Center for Canadian Studies, Foreign Policy Institute, Center for International Business and Policy, Center for Strategic Education, Center for Transatlantic Relations, Reischauer Center for East Asia Studies. Special programs: European Center in Bologna, Italy; Center in Nanjing, People's Republic of China. Library: 100,000 volumes.

Annual tuition: Washington, D.C. $31,300, Bologna, Italy campus 25,580 Euros; room and board D.C. $13,900, Bologna campus 9820 Euros. Graduate enrollment: full-time 596, part-time 25. School faculty: full-time 43, part-time 102. Degrees conferred: M.A., M.I.P.P., Ph.D.

ADMISSION REQUIREMENTS. Official transcripts, three letters of recommendation required in support of School's application. GRE or GMAT, interview recommended. TOEFL required for international applicants. Graduates of unaccredited colleges not considered. Candidates should have at least nine years of experience. Apply to Director of Admissions by January 15, February 15 (Ph.D.) (Fall), November 1 (Spring). Rolling admissions process. Application fee $90. Phone: (202)663-5700; fax: (202) 663-7788; e-mail: admissions.sais@jhu.edu. Ph.D. phone: (202) 663-5709.

ADMISSION STANDARDS. Competitive. Usual minimum average: 3.5 (A = 4).

FINANCIAL AID. Annual awards from institutional funds: fellowships, research/teaching assistantships, internships, grants, Federal W/S, loans. Apply by February 1 to Office of Admissions. Phone: (202)663-5706. Use FAFSA (School code: E00474). About 50% of students receive aid from School and outside sources. Aid available for part-time students.

DEGREE REQUIREMENTS. For M.A.: two-year, full-time program; two core exams; speaking and reading knowledge of one modern foreign language; final oral exam. For M.I.P.P.: one-year program (midcareer); completion of eight courses within the nine-month period. For Ph.D.: three years minimum beyond the bachelor's; reading knowledge of two foreign languages; comprehensive exam; International Economics competence; dissertation prospectus and defense; dissertation; final oral exam.

FIELDS OF STUDY.
Area Programs. Includes African, American Foreign Policy, Asian (China, Japan, Korea, SE Asia, South Asian), Canadian, European, Latin American, Middle Eastern, Russian and Eurasian Studies. Western Hemisphere.
International Development.
International Economics.
International Public Policy.
International Relations. Includes general international relations, global theory and history, international law, conflict management, strategic studies, energy, environment, science and technology.

PH.D. PROGRAMS ARE OFFERED IN THE FOLLOWING AREAS:
African Studies.
China Studies.
Conflict Management.
Energy, Environmental, Science, and Technology.
European Studies.
Global Theory and History.
International Law and Organizations.
International Relations.
Russian and Eurasian Studies.
SE Asia Studies.
South Asia Studies.
Theory and History.
Western Hemisphere Program.
Note: Joint programs are available. M.A.-M.B.A. with Wharton School at the University of Pennsylvania or from the European Institute of Business Administration (INSEAD), Fontainebleau, France; M.A.-J.D. with Stanford Law School; M.A.-M.H.S. with Bloomberg School of Public Health.

School of Medicine (21205-2196)
Web site: www.hopkinsmedicine.org

Founded 1893. Library: 354,000 volumes 3600 subscriptions. NIH ranking is number one of all U.S. institutions with 1299 awards/grants worth $607,222,589.

Annual tuition: $37,515. On-campus housing available. Total average figure for all other expenses: $13,500.

Enrollment: first-year class 121 (3 EDP), total 482 (men 52%, women 48%, minorities 48%, state residents 22%). Faculty: full-time 2198, part-time 1200. Degrees conferred: M.D., M.D.-M.P.H., M.D.-M.S.E. (Biomedical Engineering), M.D.-Ph.D. (Medical Scientist Training Program).

ADMISSION REQUIREMENTS. AMCAS report, transcripts, MCAT, letters of recommendation, interview required in support of application. Has EDP; apply between June 1 and August 15. Applicants must have completed four years of college study prior to matriculation. Apply to Committee on Admission after June 1, before October 15. Application fee $75. Phone: (410)955-3182.

ADMISSION STANDARDS. Very competitive. Accepts about 6% of all applicants. Number of applications 4289 (3990 out-of-state); number interviewed 643 (591 out-of-state); number of acceptance 255 (232 out-of-state); number enrolled 121 (109 out-of-state). Mean Composite MCAT 11.6; mean UGPA 3.85. *U.S. News & World Report* ranking is in the top 2 of all medical research schools, 28th in primary care.

FINANCIAL AID. Scholarships, summer fellowship, loans. MSTP funded by NIH. Apply to Committee on Admission; no specified closing date. Phone: (410)955-1324. About 78% of students receive some aid from School funds.

DEGREE REQUIREMENTS. For M.D.: satisfactory completion of four-year program for those who enter with bachelor's; satisfactory completion of five- or six-year program for those who enter with less than four years of undergraduate study. For M.P.H., M.S.E., Ph.D.: see Graduate School listing above.

FIELDS OF GRADUATE STUDY.
Biochemistry, Cellular and Molecular Biology.
Biological Chemistry.
Biomedical Engineering.
Cellular and Molecular Medicine.
Cellular and Molecular Physiology.
Functional Anatomy and Evolution.
Health Sciences Informatics.
History of Science, Medicine and Technology.
Human Genetics and Molecular Biology.
Immunology.
Program in Molecular and Computational Biophysics.
Medical and Biological Illustration.
Molecular Biology.
Neuroscience.
Pathobiology.
Pharmacology and Molecular Sciences.

The Peabody Institute of the Johns Hopkins University (21202)
Web site: www.peabody.jhu.edu

Founded 1857. Coed. Private control. Semester system. Music library: 70,000 volumes; audio visual library: 13,510 discs.

Annual tuition: full-time $31,400; diploma programs $25,000. On-campus housing available. Apply to Director of Admissions. Graduate enrollment: full-time 286, part-time 15. Institute faculty: full-time 69, part-time 58. Degrees conferred: M.M., D.M.A., Graduate Performance Diploma, Artist Diploma.

ADMISSION REQUIREMENTS. Official transcripts, entrance audition and entrance exams in music history, theory, and ear training required in support of application. TOEFL required for international applicants. Apply to Director of Admissions by December 15. Application fee $75. Phone: (800)368-2521, (410)659-8110; fax: (410)659-8102.

ADMISSION STANDARDS. Selective.

FINANCIAL AID. Scholarships, assistantships, grants, Federal W/S, loans. Apply by March 1 to Director of Admissions. Phone: (410)659-8100, ext. 3023. Use FAFSA and institutional FAF. Approximately 40% of students receive aid other than loans from Institute; 77% from all sources.

DEGREE REQUIREMENTS. For M.M.: 32 semester hours minimum; recital. For D.M.A.: 90 hours beyond the bachelor's, at least one year in full-time residence; preliminary exam; final written/oral exam; final dissertation or lecture-recital document for all majors; six public recitals; reading knowledge of languages required. For diploma programs: one to two years of full-time study; recital.

FIELD OF STUDY.
Audio Sciences.
Composition.
Computer Music.
Conducting.
Early Music.
Music Performance. Include a pedagogy track.
Music Education.
Music History.
Music Theory Pedagogy.
Vocal Accompanying.
Note: The following Graduate Performance Diplomas (GPD) majors are available: conducting, chamber music, early music, jazz, keyboard instruments, opera, orchestral instruments, voice.

Bloomberg School of Public Health

Established 1916. Semester system. Special facilities: Bill and Melinda Gates Institute for Population and Reproduction, Bioethics Institute, Biostatistics Center, Center for Human Nutrition, Center for a Livable Future, Center for Law and the Public's Health, Education and Research Center in Occupational Safety and Health, Hopkins Population Center, Institute for Vaccine Safety, Johns Hopkins Center in Urban Environmental Health, Johns Hopkins Malaria Research Institute, Mid-Atlantic Health Leadership Institute, Primary Care Policy Center for Underserved Populations.

Annual tuition: full-time $43,680 (M.P.H.), per credit $728. All other programs full-time $34,944, per credit $728. Graduate enrollment: full-time 1139, part-time 400. School faculty: full-time 429, part-time 567. Degrees conferred: M.P.H., Sc.M., M.H.S., Dr.P.H., Sc.D., Ph.D., M.D.-M.P.H., M.S.W.-M.P.H., M.S.N.-M.P.H., J.D.-M.P.H., M.A.-M.P.H.

ADMISSION REQUIREMENTS. Official transcripts, GRE (MCAT, GMAT, LSAT can be substituted for GRE for M.P.H.), three letters of reference, résumé or curriculum vitae, supplemental form (M.P.H. applicants) required in support of School's application. Online appliation available. TOEFL or evidence of proficiency in English required of international students. Interview not required. Accepts transfer applicants. Apply to Admissions Office of School by February 1 for all full-time programs, two terms in advance for part-time programs. Rolling admissions process from October 1 to February 1. Application fee $75, $45 for online applicants. Phone: (410)955-3543; fax: (410)955-0464.

ADMISSION STANDARDS. Selective for most departments. *U.S. News & World Report* ranking is first of all U.S. public health schools. Usual minimum average: 3.0 (A = 4).

FINANCIAL AID. Scholarships, fellowships, research assistantships, teaching assistantships, Federal W/S, loans, and federal
training grants are offered. Approved for VA benefits. Apply to
appropriate departmental chairperson or Master of Public Health
Office for scholarships and traineeships support; the Office of
Student Financial Services for all other aid. Phone: (410)955-
5332; fax: (410)955-0464. Use FAFSA (School code: E00234).
Approximately 70% of students receive either school scholarships, loans, or FWS; 19% receive federal training grants; and
50% receive other aid.

DEGREE REQUIREMENTS. For full-time M.P.H.: Eleven
months, 64–95 credits minimum in residence and satisfactory
completion of approved schedule of studies. For part-time M.P.H.:
64–95 credit units within three years. For Sc.M.: Two years minimum, one in residence; thesis; written exam. For M.H.S.: 64
credit program, one to two academic years in residence; thesis
and field studies vary by department. For Dr.P.H.: Three years
minimum beyond the bachelor's, one year minimum in residence. For Dr.P.H. students who do not already have the M.P.H.,
the first eleven months of study is for M.P.H. degree; preliminary
oral exam; comprehensive written exam; thesis; oral defense of
thesis. For Sc.D.: Two years minimum in residence; preliminary
oral exam; comprehensive written exam; thesis; oral defense of
thesis. For Ph.D.: One year minimum in residence; comprehensive written exam; two to three oral exams; thesis; oral defense of
thesis. For the doctoral degrees, some departments may require
reading knowledge of one foreign language.

FIELDS OF STUDY.
Biochemistry and Molecular Biology.
Biostatistics.
Environmental Health Sciences. Includes toxicological sciences,
   physiology, environmental chemistry and biology, radiation
   health sciences, environmental health engineering, occupational
   health.
Epidemiology.
Graduate Training Program in Clinical Research.
Health Behavior and Society. Includes behavior sciences and
   health education, genetic counseling.
Health Policy and Management. Includes behavioral sciences
   and health education, health finance and management, health
   policy, public health.
International Health. Includes disease control, vaccine sciences,
   human nutrition, health systems.
Internet-Based M.P.H.
Mental Hygiene.
Molecular Microbiology and Immunology.
Population, Family and Reproductive Health.
Public Health.

THE JUILLIARD SCHOOL
New York, New York 10023-6588
Web site: www.juilliard.edu

Founded 1905. Located at Lincoln Center. Coed. Private control. Semester system. Library: 80,793 volumes, 220 subscriptions.
Total School enrollment: 800.
   Annual tuition: full-time $27,150. On-campus housing for 350
students. Annual academic year housing cost: $9500–$13,400.
Apply to Office of Students Affairs for on- and off-campus housing information. Phone: (212)799-5000, ext. 7400 (on-campus),
ext. 200 (off-campus).

Graduate Study

Graduate study since 1924. Enrollment: full-time 298; part-time
29. Faculty: full-time 115, part-time 131. Degrees conferred: M.M.,
D.M.A. Graduate Diploma, Artist's Diploma.

ADMISSION REQUIREMENTS. Transcripts, recommendations, interview, performance audition entrance exam required in
support of School's application. TOEFL (minimum score 570),
TWE required for international applicants. Apply to Admissions
Office by December 1. Fall admission only. Application and entrance exam fees $100. Phone: (212)799-5000, ext. 223; fax:
(212)769-6420.

ADMISSION STANDARDS. Very competitive.

FINANCIAL AID. Scholarships, teaching fellowships, assistant-
ships, Federal W/S, loans. Approved for VA benefits. Apply by
March 1 to Financial Aid Office. Phone: (212)799-5000. Use
FAFSA and institutional FAF.

DEGREE REQUIREMENTS. For M.M.: 54 semester hours minimum, at least two years in full-time residency; graduation performance; final exam. For D.M.A.: 98 semester hours minimum
beyond the bachelor's, at least 60 in full-time residence; preliminary exam; reading knowledge of one foreign language; final pro-
ject/recital/document, depending upon major; final oral exam.

FIELDS OF STUDY.
Collaborative Piano.
Composition.
Conducting (Orchestral).
Guitar. M.M. only.
Harpsichord.
Jazz Studies.
Orchestral Instruments.
Opera Studies.
Organ.
Performance Piano.
String Quartet Studies.
Voice.

KANSAS CITY UNIVERSITY OF MEDICINE AND BIOSCIENCES
1750 Independence Avenue
Kansas City Missouri 64106-1453
Web site: www.kcumb.edu

Founded 1916 as the Kansas City College of Osteopathy and
Surgery. Relocated to current address in 1921. Named changed
in 1980 to University of Health Sciences. Current name changed
in 2005, when the new College of Biosciences was added. Private
control. Semester system. Library: 100,000 volumes, 500 subscriptions; has MEDLINE, ERIC, TOXNET, OSTMED. On-
campus housing available directly across street from University.
Contact the Admission Office for housing information.

College of Osteopathic Medicine

Annual tuition: $36,460. Enrollment: first-year class 250, total
930 (men 60%, women 40%). Faculty: full-time 50, part-time
125. Degrees conferred: D.O., D.O.-M.B.A. (with Rockhurst
University).

ADMISSION REQUIREMENTS. AACOMAS report, bachelor's
degree preferred, transcripts, MCAT, letters of recommendation
from premed advisory committee, evaluation from a physician
(preferably a D.O.) required in support of College's application.
Interview by invitation only. Graduates of unaccredited colleges
not considered. Apply by February 1. Admits first-year students
Fall only. Application fee: $50. Phone: (800)234-4UHS, (816)283-
2339; fax: (816)283-2484.

ADMISSION STANDARDS. Selective. Median MCAT: 8.5; median GPA: 3.37 (A = 4). Accepts approximately 15% of annual applicants. Usual minimum average: 2.75.

FINANCIAL AID. Scholarships, grants, HEAL, loans. Apply after acceptance to Office of Financial Aid. Phone: (816)283-2000. Use FAFSA (University code: G24524).

DEGREE REQUIREMENT. For D.O.: satisfactory completion of four-year program.

KANSAS STATE UNIVERSITY
Manhattan, Kansas 66506-1103
Web site: www.ksu.edu

Founded 1863. Located 55 miles from Topeka. CGS member. Coed. State control. Semester system. Special facilities: nuclear reactor, Flight Research Laboratory, Higuch Biosciences Center, 12 MEV Van de Graaff accelerator, observatory, fish hatchery, botanical garden, Kansas Geological Survey, Konza Prairie Research Area, Natural Science Museum, Wheat Genetics Resource Center, Institute for Environmental Research, Food and Feed Grain Institute, computer center, environmental laboratory, Cereal Technology Laboratory, engineering and agriculture experiment stations. Library: 1,500,000 volumes, 9400 subscriptions. Total University enrollment: 23,100.

Tuition: per credit hour resident $215, nonresident $534. On-campus housing for 625 married students, 400 graduate men, 200 graduate women. Average academic year housing cost: $5100 for married students, $4900 (including board) for single students. Apply to Director of Housing. Phone: (785)532-6453 (on-campus), (785)532-2097 (off-campus). Day-care facilities available.

Graduate School

Graduate study since 1868. Enrollment: full- and part-time 3800. University faculty: full-time 885, part-time 188. Degrees conferred: M.A., M.S., M.Acc., M.B.A., M.F.A., M.M., M.Arch., M.P.A., M.R.P., M.L.A., Ed.D., Ph.D.

ADMISSION REQUIREMENTS. Two transcripts, GRE required in support of School's application. GMAT required for M.B.A., M.Acc. TOEFL (minimum score 550) required for international applicants. Interview sometimes required. Accepts transfer applicants. Graduates of unaccredited institutions not considered. Apply to head of the department concerned at least two months prior to registration; February 1 (Fall), October 1 (Spring) for international applicants. Application fee: $30, $55 for international applicants. Phone: (785)532-7927; fax: (785)532-2983.

ADMISSION STANDARDS. Selective for most departments. Usual minimum average: 2.75 (A = 4).

FINANCIAL AID. Annual awards from institutional funds: scholarships, fellowships, teaching assistantships, internships, grants, research assistantships, Federal W/S, loans. Apply by March 1 to Dean of Graduate School for assistantships; to the Financial Aid Office for all other programs. Phone: (785)532-6420; fax: (785)532-7628. Use FAFSA. About 65% of students receive aid other than loans from University and outside sources. Aid available for part-time students.

DEGREE REQUIREMENTS. For most master's: 30 semester hours minimum including thesis, at least one academic year in full-time residence; transfer credit from other graduate schools individually considered; final oral exam. For M.R.C.P.: 48 hours minimum, at least one academic year in full-time residence. For M.F.A.; 60 hours minimum. For Ph.D.: 90 semester hours mini-

mum beyond the bachelor's, at least one year in full-time residence; preliminary exam; language requirements vary; dissertation; final written/oral exam. For Ed.D.: essentially the same as Ph.D. except no language requirement.

FIELDS OF STUDY.
Accounting. M.Acc.
Agribusiness. M.A.B.
Agricultural Economics. M.S.
Agricultural Technology Management. Ph.D.
Agronomy. M.S., Ph.D.
Anatomy and Physiology. M.S., Ph.D.
Animal Science and Industry. Includes animal breeding and genetics. M.S., Ph.D.
Apparel and Textiles. M.S.
Architectural Engineering. M.S.
Architecture. M.Arch.
Art. M.F.A.
Biochemistry. M.S., Ph.D.
Biological and Agricultural Engineering. M.S.
Biology. M.S., Ph.D.
Business Administration. M.B.A.
Chemical Engineering. M.S., Ph.D.
Chemistry. M.S., Ph.D.
Civil Engineering. M.S., Ph.D.
Clinical Sciences. Includes agricultural practice, anesthesiology, equine medicine and surgery, exotic and wildlife medicine, ophthalmology, radiology, small animal medicine, small animal surgery and theriogenology. M.S.
Computer and Information Science. M.S., Ph.D.
Curriculum and Instruction. M.S., Ed.D., Ph.D.
Economics. M.A., Ph.D.
Education. Includes adult, elementary, secondary, administration, school counseling, student counseling and personnel services, special; three recommendations for admission; GRE for continuance in program.
Educational Leadership. M.S., Ed.D., Ph.D.
Electrical and Computer Engineering. M.S., Ph.D.
Engineering Management. M.E.M.
English. Creative writing major for M.A.; GRE for continuance in program.
Entomology. M.S., Ph.D.
Environmental Design and Planning. Ph.D.
Family Studies and Human Services. M.S.
Food Service, Hospitality Management, and Administrative Dietetics. M.S., Ph.D.
Genetics. M.S., Ph.D.
Geography. M.A., Ph.D.
Geology. M.S., Ph.D.
Grain Science. M.S., Ph.D.
History. Two languages for Ph.D. M.A., Ph.D.
Horticulture. Includes ornamental, floriculture, turfgrass, vegetable crops, fruit crops, horticultural therapy, stress physiology, molecular biology, tissue culture, plant growth regulators. M.S., Ph.D.
Human Ecology. Ph.D.
Human Nutrition. M.S., Ph.D.
Industrial and Manufacturing Systems Engineering. M.S.I.E., M.S.O.R., Ph.D.
Interior Architecture and Product Design. M.I.A.
Journalism and Mass Communication. M.S.
Kinesiology. M.S.
Landscape Architecture. M.L.A.
Mass Communication. M.S.
Mathematics. M.S., Ph.D.
Mechanical Nuclear Engineering. M.S., Ph.D.
Microbiology. M.S., Ph.D.
Modern Languages. Includes French, German, Spanish; one language in addition to major.
Music. Includes applied, music education, music literature; recital for master's. M.M.

Nuclear Engineering. M.S., Ph.D.
Operations Research. M.S.O.R.
Pathobiology. M.S., Ph.D.
Physics. M.S., Ph.D.
Plant Pathology. M.S.
Political Science. M.A.
Psychology. M.S., Ph.D.
Public Administration. M.P.A.
Public Health. M.P.H.
Regional and Community Planning. Interdepartmental. M.R.C.P.
Security Studies. M.A., Ph.D.
Sociology. M.A., Ph.D.
Software Engineering. M.S.E.
Speech. Includes rhetoric/communication, theater. M.A.
Statistics. M.S., Ph.D.
Veterinary Laboratory Medicine. M.S.
Veterinary Pathology. M.S., Ph.D.
Women's Studies. M.A., M.S., Ph.D.

College of Veterinary Medicine

Web site: www.vet.k-state.edu

Founded 1905 as a Department of Veterinary Medicine. In 1963 it was established as a College of the University. Semester system.

Annual tuition and fees: Kansas and North Dakota residents $12,146, nonresidents $31,446. Off-campus housing only. Total average cost for other expenses: $7,500.

Enrollment: first-year class 107, total 472 (men 27%, women 73%, minorities 3%, state residents 60%). Faculty: full-time 62, part-time 17. Degrees conferred: D.V.M. The M.S. and Ph.D. are offered through the Graduate College.

ADMISSION REQUIREMENTS. VMCAS report, transcripts showing completion of seventy hours of preprofessional college work, GRE, animal/veterinary experience, essay, three names and addresses for potential recommendations (one from an academic adviser) required in support of application. Interview by invitation only. Accepts transfer applicants, on a space-available basis. Preference given to state, North Dakota residents, and U.S. residents. Apply to Assistant Dean after September 1, prior to October 1. Rolling admission process. Application fee $50. Phone: (785)532-5660; fax: (785)532-5884.

ADMISSION STANDARDS. Competitive. Accepts about 20–25% of all applicants. Number of applications 970 (16 North Dakota residents, 821 out-of-state); number interviewed 122 (15 North Dakota residents, 262 out-of-state); number of acceptance 47 (9 North Dakota residents, 183 out-of-state); number enrolled 107 (5 North Dakota residents, 55 out-of-state). Usual minimum UGPA: 3.0 (A = 4). GRE mean score (V + Q) 1139 (residents), 1166 (nonresidents); mean UGPA 3.6 .

FINANCIAL AID. Scholarships, assistantships, Federal W/S, loans. Apply by March 1 to Dean after acceptance. Use FAFSA.

DEGREE REQUIREMENTS. For D.V.M.: 164 semester hours and four years in residence. For M.S. and Ph.D.: see Graduate School listing above.

FIELDS OF GRADUATE STUDY.
Anatomy and Physiology.
Biomedical Sciences. M.S., Ph.D.
Clinical Sciences. Includes agricultural practice, anesthesiology, equine medicine and surgery, exotic and wildlife medicine, ophthalmology, radiology, small animal medicine, small animal surgery, theriogenology. M.S.
Veterinary Laboratory Medicine. M.S.
Veterinary Pathology. M.S., Ph.D.

UNIVERSITY OF KANSAS

Lawrence, Kansas 66045
Web site: www.ku.edu

Founded 1866. Main campus is 40 miles W of Kansas City. College of Health Sciences and Hospital located at Kansas City. CGS and AAU member. State control. Semester system. Special facilities: Museum—anthropology, art, invertebrate paleontology, natural history, entomological; Herbarium, computer facilities, Kansas Geological Survey, Higuchi Biosciences Center, Bureau of Child Research, Flight Research Laboratory, Infant Research Laboratory, Retardation Research Center, Gerontology Center, Institute for Social and Environmental Studies, Institute for Economic and Business Research, Transportation Research Group, Space Technology Center, Biological Anthropology Laboratory, Enzyme Laboratory, Chemical Biology Laboratory, Nuclear Reactor Center, field facilities, Water Resources Institute, Paleontological Institute, Tertiary Oil Recovery Project, mineral resources research, animal care units, health and safety research, center for research, children's rehabilitation unit, cancer center program, drug design program. The University's endowment assets rank it 75th, with a value of $662,419,000. In 2004, the University awarded 239 doctorates which ranked it 63rd among all U.S. institutions eligible to award that degree. Six of the University's faculty members have been elected to National Honor Academies and this ranks it 90th among all U.S. institutions. The Library: approximately 4,400,000 volumes, 32,700 subscriptions. Total University enrollment: 29,000.

Annual tuition: full-time, resident $4500, nonresident $11,215; per credit hour, resident $214, nonresident $534. On-campus housing for 300 married students. Average academic year housing cost: $3900–$4900 (including board) for single students, $2950 for married students. Contact Director of Student Housing for both on- and off-campus housing information. Phone: (785)864-7224. Day-care facilities available.

Graduate School

Organized 1894. Enrollment: full-time 3260, part-time 2500. Graduate faculty: full-time 1400, part-time 95. Degrees conferred: M.A., M.S., M.B.A., M.S.Ed., M.F.A., M.M., M.E., M.M.Ed., M.M.E., M.H.D., M.F.A., M.U.P., M.Arch., Ed.S., D.M.A., D.E., Ed.D., Ph.D.

ADMISSION REQUIREMENTS. Two official transcripts required in support of School's application. GRE/MAT, letters of recommendation required by some departments. Interview not required. TOEFL required for international applicants. Accepts transfer applicants. Graduates of unaccredited institutions not considered. Apply to Graduate Advisor of proposed major department by July 1 (Fall), December 1 (Spring), May 1 (Summer); some departments have earlier deadlines. Application fee $50, $60 for international applicants. Phone: (785)864-6161; fax: (785) 864-4555.

ADMISSION STANDARDS. Competitive for most departments, very competitive for others. Usual minimum average: 3.0 (A = 4).

FINANCIAL AID. Annual awards from institutional funds: scholarships, fellowships, teaching assistantships, research assistantships, tuition waivers, internships, grants, Federal W/S, loans. Approved for VA benefits. Apply by February 1 (earlier for some departments) to appropriate department chair for fellowships, assistantships; to Financial Aid Office for all other programs. Phone: (785)864-4700, (785)864-5469. Use FAFSA. About 50% of students receive aid other than loans from University and outside sources. Aid available for part-time students.

DEGREE REQUIREMENTS. For master's: 30 credit hours minimum, at least 24 in residence; research component; thesis/

nonthesis options for some departments; final general exam. For M.Arch.: 60 credit hours; project/thesis; final general exam. For M.B.A.: 60 credit hours; final exam. For M.E., M.M.E.: 36 credit hours; project; internships; final general exam. For M.F.A.: 48–60 credit hours; thesis/exhibition; final general exam. For M.H.D.: 36 credit hours; practicum experience; thesis option; final general exam. For M.M.: 30 credit hours; thesis/recital/project; final general exam. For M.M.Ed.: 30 credit hours; thesis; final general exam. For M.P.A.: 30 credit hours; internship; project; final general exam. For M.U.P.: 50 credit hours; thesis/nonthesis option; final general exam. For Ed.S.: 60 credit hours beyond bachelor's; special project. For Ed.D., D.E., D.M.A.: some variations but all basically the same as for the Ph.D. For Ph.D.: three years beyond the baccalaureate; at least one year in full-time residence; foreign language or other research skills; comprehensive oral exam; candidacy; dissertation; final oral exam.

FIELDS OF STUDY.

SCHOOL OF ARCHITECTURE AND URBAN DESIGN:
Architectural Engineering. M.S.
Architecture. M.Arch.
Urban Planning. M.U.P.

SCHOOL OF BUSINESS:
Accounting. Includes finance concentration.
Business.
Business Administration. M.B.A. only.

COLLEGE OF LIBERAL ARTS AND SCIENCES:
American Studies.
Anthropology.
Applied Behavioral Sciences.
Chemistry.
Child Language.
Classics.
Clinical Child Psychology.
Communication Studies.
Creative Writing.
East Asian Languages and Cultures.
Ecology and Evolutionary Biology.
Economics.
Entomology.
English.
French.
Genetics.
Geography.
Geology.
Germanic Languages and Literature.
Gerontology.
History.
History of Art.
Indigenous Nations Studies.
International Studies.
Latin American Studies.
Linguistics.
Mathematics.
Molecular Biosciences.
Museum Studies.
Philosophy.
Physics.
Political Science.
Psychology.
Public Administration.
Religious Studies.
Russian and East European Studies.
Slavic Languages and Literature.
Sociology.
Spanish.
Theatre and Film.

SCHOOL OF EDUCATION:
Counseling Psychology..
Curriculum and Instruction.
Educational Policy and Leadership.
Educational Psychology and Research.
Foundations of Education.
Health, Sport, and Exercise Sciences.
Higher Education.
Physical Education.
School Administration.
School Psychology.
Special Education.

SCHOOL OF ENGINEERING:
Aerospace Engineering.
Chemical and Petroleum Engineering.
Chemical Engineering. M.S.
Civil Engineering.
Computer Engineering. M.S.
Computer Science.
Construction Engineering. M.S.
Electrical Engineering.
Engineering Management. M.S. only.
Environmental Engineering.
Mechanical Engineering.
Petroleum Engineering.
Water Resources Engineering. M.S.

SCHOOL OF FINE ARTS:
Art. M.F.A. only.
Design. Includes interior, textiles. M.F.A. only.
Music. Includes church, composition, conducting, performance, musicology, opera, theory.
Music Education.
Music Therapy.
Scenography.
Visual Arts Education.

SCHOOL OF JOURNALISM AND MASS COMMUNICATION:
Journalism. M.S.

SCHOOL OF PHARMACY:
Medicinal Chemistry.
Neuroscience. Ph.D.
Pharmacy Practice. M.S.
Pharmaceutical Chemistry.
Pharmacology and Toxicology.

SCHOOL OF SOCIAL WORK:
Social Work. M.S.W., Ph.D.

School of Law
Web site: www.law.ku.edu

Founded 1891. ABA approved since 1923. AALS charter member. Public control. Semester system. Special facility. Tribal Law and Government Center. Special program: study abroad in Istanbul, Turkey, and Limerick, Ireland. Law library: 412,098 volumes, 5891 subscriptions; has LEXIS, NEXIS, WESTLAW, DIALOG.

Annual tuition: full-time resident $10,399, nonresident $19,232. On-campus housing available for both single and married students. Total average cost for all other expenses: $13,642.

Enrollment: first-year class 157, full-time 492 (men 61%, women 39%, minorities 15%); no part-time students. Faculty: full-time 32, part-time 10. Student to faculty ratio is 13.4 to 1. Degrees conferred: J.D., J.D.-M.A. (Economics, Philosophy), J.D.-M.B.A., J.D.-M.H.S.A., J.D.-M.P.A., J.D.-M.S.W., J.D.-M.U.P., LL.M. (Elder Law).

ADMISSION REQUIREMENTS. LSDAS Law School report, bachelor's degree, transcripts, LSAT, personal statement, one letter of recommendation required in support of application. Interview not required. Accepts transfer applicants. Preference given to state residents. Graduates of unaccredited colleges not considered. Apply to Director of Law Admission before March 15 for both Summer and Fall admission. Admits Summer and Fall only. Application fee $50. Phone: (866)220-3654.

ADMISSION STANDARDS. Selective. Accepts approximately 26% of all students. Number of applicants 1145; number of acceptance 303; number enrolled 157; LSAT (75% of students have a score at or above 154); GPA (75% of students have a GPA at or above 3.27). *U.S. News & World Report* ranking is in the second tier tied at 66th of all U.S. law schools.

FINANCIAL AID. Scholarships, assistantships, Federal W/S, loans. Apply to Office of Student Financial Aid by March 1. Phone: (785)864-4700. Use FAFSA. About 76% of students receive aid from School.

DEGREE REQUIREMENTS, For J.D.: 90 hours minimum, at least 30 in full-time residence. For LL.M.: 24-credit program; a two-semester research project; thesis. For master's degree: see Graduate School listings above.

UNIVERSITY OF KANSAS MEDICAL CENTER
Kansas City, Kansas 66103
Web site: www.kumc.edu

Medical study since 1905. Includes Allied Health, Nursing, Medical School, Graduate School (administered by University's Graduate School). Special facilities: Cancer Center, Center for Aging, Radiation Therapy Center, Center on Environmental and Occupational Law. Library: 179,130 volumes, 1500 subscriptions.

Graduate Studies

Tuition: per credit, resident $240.65, nonresident $511.70. Enrollment: full-time 271, part-time 380. Faculty: full-time 235, part-time 40. Degrees conferred: M.A., M.N., M.P.H., M.S., M.S.O.T., M.S.P.T., Ph.D., P.T.-Ph.D.

ADMISSION REQUIREMENTS. Official transcripts, three letters of recommendation, GRE, complete criminal background check required in support of application. TOEFL required for international applicants. Accepts transfer applicants. Graduates of unaccredited institutions not considered. Apply by July 1 (Fall), December 1 (Spring). Rolling admissions process. Application fee: $55. Phone: (913)588-1238; fax: (913)588-5242.

ADMISSION STANDARDS. Competitive. Usual minimum average: 3.0 (A = 4).

FINANCIAL AID. Scholarships, fellowships, assistantships, grants, Federal W/S, Federal and private loans. Approved for VA benefits. Apply by May 1 to appropriate department for assistantships, fellowships; to Financial Aid Office for all other programs. Phone: (913)588-8841. Use FAFSA. Aid available for part-time students.

DEGREE REQUIREMENTS. For M.S., M.A., M.N., M.P.H., M.S.O.T., M.S.P.T., Ph.D.: see University of Kansas Graduate School listing above.

FIELDS OF STUDY.

SCHOOL OF ALLIED HEALTH:
Hearing and Speech. M.A., Ph.D
Dietetics and Nutrition. M.S.
Nurse Anesthesia Education. M.S.
Occupational Therapy Education. M.O.T., M.S., Ph.D.
Physical Therapy and Rehabilitation Sciences. M.S., Ph.D.
Rehabilitation Science. Ph.D.
Speech-Language Pathology. M.A., Ph.D.
Therapeutic Science. Ph.D.

SCHOOL OF GRADUATE STUDIES:
Anatomy and Cell Biology. M.A., Ph.D.
Biochemistry and Molecular Biology. M.S., Ph.D.
Health Policy and Management. M.H.S.A.
Microbiology, Molecular Genetics, and Immunology. M.S., Ph.D.
Molecular and Integrative Physiology. Ph.D.
Pathology. M.A., Ph.D.
Pharmacology, Toxicology, and Therapeutics. M.S., Ph.D.
Public Health. M.P.H.

SCHOOL OF NURSING:
Nursing Specialist. M.S.
Nurse Researcher. Ph.D.

School of Medicine
Web site: www.kumc.edo/som

Founded 1899. Located in Kansas City (66160-7301) at the Medical Center. Special facilities: Center for Biostatistics and Advanced Informatics, Center for Child Health and Development, Center for Environmental and Occupational Health, Center for Healthcare Informatics, Center for Reproductive Sciences, Center for TeleMedicine and TeleHealth, Center on Aging, General Clinical Research Center, Hoglund Brain Imaging Center, The Institute of Maternal-Fetal Biology, Kansas Masonic Cancer Research Institute, Mental Retardation Research Center, The University of Kansas Center for Research. Library: 170,000 volumes, 1200 subscriptions. NIH ranking is 87th with 203 awards/grants worth $64,966,223.

Annual tuition: resident $22,486, nonresident $39,877. No on-campus housing available. Total average figure for all other expenses: $20,000.

Enrollment: first-year class 175 (EDP 35); total 700 (men 55%, women 45%, minorities 21%, state residents 84%). Faculty: full-time 515, part-time 127. Degrees conferred: M.D., M.D.-M.H.A., M.D.-M.P.H., M.D.-M.S., M.D.-Ph.D.

ADMISSION REQUIREMENTS. AMCAS, transcripts, recommendation from premedical adviser, MCAT, supplemental application required in support of application. Interview by invitation. Has EDP; apply between June 1 and August 1. Accepts transfer applicants. Bachelor's degree required for admission. Preference given to Kansas residents. Apply to Office of Student Admissions and Records after June 1, before October 15. Application fee: nonresidents $40. Phone: (913)588-5245; fax: (913)588-5259.

ADMISSION STANDARDS. Competitive. Accepts about 14.7% of all applicants. Number of applications 1553 (1147 out-of-state); number interviewed 443 (136 out-of-state); number of acceptance 229 (60 out-of-state); number enrolled 175 (33 out-of-state). Mean Composite MCAT 9.5; mean UGPA 3.72.

FINANCIAL AID. Scholarships, assistantships, fellowships, loans. Apply by March 30 to Office of Student Financial Aid. Phone: (913)588-5170. About 64% of students receive aid from School.

DEGREE REQUIREMENTS. For M.D.: Satisfactory completion of four-year program; must pass Step 1 of USMLE for advancement to third year and pass Step 2 for graduation. Advanced standing for medical study completed elsewhere considered on individual basis. For Ph.D.: see Graduate School listing above.

FIELDS OF GRADUATE STUDY.
Anatomy and Cell biology. M.A., Ph.D.
Biochemistry and Molecular Biology. M.S., Ph.D.
Biomedical Sciences. Interdisciplinary.
Health Policy and Management. M.H.S.A.
Microbiology, Molecular Genetics and Immunology. M.A., Ph.D.
Molecular and Integrative Physiology. M.S., Ph.D.
Pathology and Laboratory Medicine. M.A., Ph.D.
Pharmacology, Toxicology, and Therapeutics. M.S., Ph.D.
Public Health. M.P.H.

KEAN UNIVERSITY
Union, New Jersey 07083
Web site: www.kean.edu

Founded 1855. Located 15 miles W of New York City. CGS member. Coed. State control. Semester system. Library: 280,000 volumes, 1350 subscriptions. Total University enrollment: 13,000.

Annual tuition: full-time, resident $8280, nonresident $11,512; per hour, resident $391, nonresident $530. No on-campus housing available for graduate students. Day-care facilities available.

Nathan Weiss College of Graduate Studies

Graduate study since 1954. Enrollment: full-time 600, part-time 1650. Faculty: full-time 226, part-time 40. Degrees conferred: M.A., M.P.A., M.S., M.S.N., M.A.L.S., Professional Diploma in School Psychology, Marriage and Family Therapy.

ADMISSION REQUIREMENTS. Official transcripts, recommendations, GRE/MAT/GMAT/PRAXIS required in support of School's application. Interview is usually required. TOEFL required for international applicants. Accepts transfer applicants. Graduates of unaccredited institutions not considered. Apply to Office of Graduate Admissions, T-106 by June 15 (Fall), November 1 (Spring). All documents including test scores must be received by deadline in order for application to be reviewed. Application fee $60, $150 for international applicants. Phone: (908)737-3355.

ADMISSION STANDARDS. Selective for most departments. Usual minimum average: 2.75 (A = 4).

FINANCIAL AID. Annual awards from institutional funds: assistantships; scholarships, tuition waivers, Federal W/S, loans. Approved for VA benefits. Apply to Office of Financial Aid; no specified closing date. Phone: (908)737-3200. About 50% of full-time students receive aid other than loans from both College and outside sources. Aid sometimes available for part-time students.

DEGREE REQUIREMENTS. For master's: 33 credits minimum; comprehensive exam; thesis/nonthesis option. For Professional Diploma: 30 credits minimum beyond master's.

FIELDS OF STUDY.
Accounting. M.S.
Behavioral Sciences. M.A.
Biotechnology. M.S.
Business Administration. M.B.A.
Communication Sciences.
Computing. M.S.
Counselor Education. M.A.
Early Childhood Education. M.A.
Educational Administration. M.A.
Educational Media. M.A.
Educational Psychology. M.A.
Fine Arts. M.A.
Global Management. M.B.A.

Graphic Communication Technology Management. M.S.
Holocaust and Genocide Studies. M.A.
Instruction and Curriculum. M.A.
Liberal Studies. M.A.
Management Information Systems. M.S.
Mathematics. M.S.
Mathematics Education. M.A.
Nursing. M.S.N.
Occupational Therapy. M.S.
Political Science. M.A., M.S.
Public Administration. M.P.A.
Reading. M.A.
School Psychology. Professional Diploma.
Social Work. M.S.W.
Special Education. M.A.
Speech Pathology. M.A.
Statistics. M.S.

KENT STATE UNIVERSITY
Kent, Ohio 44242-0001
Web site: www.kent.edu

Founded 1910. Located 35 miles SE of Cleveland. CGS member. Coed. State control. Semester system. Special facilities: Applied Psychology Center, Center for Aquatic Ecology, Center for Educational Leadership Services, Center for Executive Education and Development, Center for Health Promotion Through Education, Center for International and Comparative Programs, Center for International and Intercultural Education, Center for Literature and Psychoanalysis, Lyman L. Lemnitzer Center for NATO and European Studies, Center for Nuclear Research, Center for Nursing Research, Center for Public Administration and Public Policy, Center for the Study of World Musics, Institute for Applied Linguistics, Institute for Bibliography and Editing, Glen H. Brown Liquid Crystal Institute, Institute for Computational Mathematics, Water Resource Research Institute. Library: 1,800,000 volumes, 14,895 subscriptions.

Annual tuition: resident $8968, nonresident $15,980; per credit, resident $408, nonresident $728. On-campus housing for 250 single students, 259 married students. Average academic year housing cost: $6600–$6900 for married students, $7200–$8000 (including board) for single students. Contact Director of Residence Services for both on- and off-campus housing information. Phone: (330)672-7000.

Division of Research and Graduate Schools

Graduate study since 1935. Enrollment: full-time 1992, part-time 2352. University faculty teaching graduate students: full-time 765. Degrees conferred: M.Arch., M.A., M.A.T., M.B.A., M.Ed., M.F.A., M.L.S., M.M., M.P.A., M.S., M.S.Acct., M.S.N., Ed. Specialist, Ph.D. Graduate work is administered by the Division of Research and Graduate Studies.

ADMISSION REQUIREMENTS. Official transcripts, three letters of recommendation required in support of application. Online application available. GRE/GMAT/MAT required for some programs. TOEFL required for all international applicants. Interview not required. Accepts transfer applicants. Graduates of unaccredited institutions not considered. Apply to appropriate Graduate School at least six weeks prior to registration; some programs have earlier deadlines. Application fee $30. Phone: (330) 672-2661.

ADMISSION STANDARDS. Very selective for most departments, competitive for others. Usual minimum average: 2.75 (A = 4).

FINANCIAL AID. Annual awards from institutional funds: fellowships, research/teaching assistantships, internships, tuition waivers, Federal W/S, loans. Approved for VA benefits. Apply by

March 1 to appropriate department chair for fellowships, assistantships; to the Financial Aid Office for all other programs. Phone: (330)672-2972. Use FAFSA. About 25% of full-time students receive aid other than loans from School and outside sources.

DEGREE REQUIREMENTS. For M.A.: 32 semester hours minimum; thesis in most departments; final exam in some. For M.S.: 32 semester hours; thesis. M.S.Acct.: 33 semester hours beyond the bachelor's in accounting or 64 semester hours beyond other bachelor's; internship. For M.A.T.: 44–45 credit program, at least 39 in residence; internship. For M.Ed.: 32 semester hours minimum; one year teaching experience required in most programs. For M.F.A.: 60 semester hours; studio thesis; qualifying exam. For M.M.: 32 semester hours; recital; essay. For M.L.S.: 36 semester hours; thesis or research paper. For M.S.N.: 36–40 semester hours. For M.P.A.: 45 semester hours; thesis/nonthesis option. For M.Arch.: 32 semester hours minimum. For Ed.S.: 60 semester hours beyond the bachelor's or 30 semester hours beyond the master's; comprehensive exam; final oral exam. For Ph.D.: 60 semester hours beyond the bachelor's minimum, at least two years in residence; qualifying exam; one foreign language for some programs; dissertation; final oral exam.

FIELDS OF STUDY.

COLLEGE OF ARCHITECTURE AND ENVIRONMENTAL DESIGN:
Architecture. M.Arch.
Urban Design. M.U.D.

COLLEGE OF ARTS AND SCIENCE:
Anthropology.
Applied Mathematics.
Biological Sciences. Includes botany, cell, ecology, physiology.
Chemical Physics.
Chemistry.
Clinical Psychology.
Computer Science.
English.
Experimental Psychology.
French.
Geography.
Geology.
German.
Latin.
History.
Justice Studies.
Liberal Studies.
Mathematical Sciences.
Philosophy.
Political Science.
Psychology.
Public Administration.
Sociology.
Spanish.
Translation.

COLLEGE OF ART:
Art.
Art History.
Conducting.
Crafts.
Ethnomusicology.
Fine Arts.
Musicology/Ethnomusicology.
Music Composition.
Music Education.
Music Theory/Composition.
Musicology.
Music Theory.
Performance.
Theatre Studies.

COLLEGE OF COMMUNICATION AND INFORMATION:
Communication Studies.
Information Architecture and Knowledge Management.
Journalism and Mass Communication.
Library and Information Science.
Visual Communication Design.

COLLEGE OF NURSING:
Adult Nurse Practitioner.
Family Nurse Practitioner.
Geriatric Nurse Practitioner.
Nursing and Health Care Management.
Nursing of Adults.
Pediatric Nurse Practitioner.
Psychiatric/Mental Health Nursing.
Women's Health.

GRADUATE SCHOOL OF MANAGEMENT:
Accounting.
Business Administration. Includes finance, human resources management, information systems, international business, marketing.
Economics.
Finance.
Financial Engineering.
Management Systems.
Marketing.

SCHOOL OF BIOMEDICAL SCIENCES:
Biological Anthropology.
Cellular and Molecular Biology.
Neuroscience.
Pharmacology.
Physiology.
Note: Programs offered in cooperation with Northeastern Ohio Universities College of Medicine.

COLLEGE OF EDUCATION, HEALTH AND HUMAN SERVICES:
Audiology.
Career Technical Teacher Education.
Community Counseling.
Counseling.
Counseling and Human Development.
Cultural Foundations.
Curriculum and Instruction.
Early Childhood Education.
Educational Psychology.
Evaluation and Measurement.
Exercise, Leisure and Sport.
Family Studies.
Health Education and Promotion.
Higher Education and Student Personnel.
Instructional Technology.
Intervention Specialist.
Junior High/Middle School.
K–12 Leadership.
Learning and Development.
Math Specialization.
Nutrition.
Physical Education/Exercise Physiology.
Public Health.
Reading Specialist.
Rehabilitation Counseling.
School Counseling.
School Psychology.
Secondary Education.
Special Education.
Speech Pathology and Audiology.

SCHOOL OF TECHNOLOGY:
Technology.

UNIVERSITY OF KENTUCKY
Lexington, Kentucky 40506-0032
Web site: www.uky.edu

Founded 1865. CGS member. Coed. State control. Semester system. Sponsoring university of Oak Ridge Institute of Nuclear Studies in Tennessee. Special facilities: Appalachian Center, Center for the Arts, Center for Business and Economic Research, Maxwell H. Gluck Equine Research Center, Gaines Center for the Humanities, Lucille Parker Mackey Cancer Research Center, Multidisciplinary Center on Gerontology, Institute for Mining/Minerals Research, Sanders-Brown Center for Aging, Survey Research Center, Kentucky Transportation Center, Water Resources Institute. The University's NIH ranking is 69th among all U.S. institutions with 245 awards/grants valued at $83,411,657. According to The Center at University of Florida, the University is ranked 63rd in receipt of Federal Research funds with $120,000,000 and it ranks 47th for total University research expenditures with $272,062,000. The University's endowment assets rank it 94th, with a value of $488,827,000. In 2004, the University awarded 233 doctorates, which ranked it 66th among all U.S. institutions eligible to award that degree. Three of the University's faculty members have been elected to National Honor Academies and this ranks it 105th among all U.S. institutions. The Library: approximately 3,100,000 volumes, 29,580 subscriptions. Total University enrollment: 25,600.

Annual tuition: full-time, resident $7670, nonresident $16,158; per credit, resident $401, nonresident $873; M.B.A. full-time, resident $16,424, nonresident $33,400; per credit, resident $468, nonresident $1046. On-campus housing is available for both single and married students. Room rates: $500–$675 per month. For housing information, call (859)257-1866. Day-care facilities available.

Graduate School

Graduate study since 1870. Enrollment: full-time 2392, part-time 2611. Graduate faculty: full- and part-time 875. Degrees conferred: M.A., M.S., M.S.Acc., M.S.Agr.E., M.S.Ch.E., M.S.C.E., M.S.C.N., M.S.Ed., M.S.E., M.S.E.M., M.S.F.S., M.S.M.E., M.S.R.M.P., M.S.N., M.S.O.R., M.S.R.H., M.S.B.E., M.S.P.H., M.B.A., M.A.T., M.M., M.P.A., M.S.D., M.S.L.S., M.F.A., M.S.W., Ed.S., D.M.A., D.B.A., Ed.D., Ph.D.

ADMISSION REQUIREMENTS. Two official transcripts from each school attended, GRE/GMAT required in support of School's application. TOEFL (minimum score 550) required for international applicants. Interview not required. Accepts transfer applicants. Graduates of unaccredited institutions not considered. Apply to Graduate Admissions Office by July 15 (Fall), November 1 (Spring), April 1 (Summer). Many programs have earlier deadlines; see Fields of Study below. Application fee $40, $55 for international applicants. Phone: (859)257-4613; fax: (859) 323-1928; e-mail: gradapp@uky.edu.

ADMISSION STANDARDS. Relatively open for some departments, selective to very selective for others. Minimum average: 3.0 (A = 4).

FINANCIAL AID. Annual awards from institutional funds: academic scholarships, research/teaching assistantships, fellowships, Federal W/S, loans. Apply by March 1 to Graduate Dean for fellowships, to appropriate department chair for assistantships; to Financial Aid Office for all other programs. Phone: (859)257-3172. Use FAFSA.

DEGREE REQUIREMENTS. For M.A., M.A.T., and all M.S. programs: 30–36 credit hours minimum with or without thesis; final written/oral exam; reading knowledge of one language for some majors. For M.B.A., M.P.A.: same as for M.A. except comprehensive exam instead of thesis. For M.M.: same as M.A., except recital for applied music major, composition for composition major, in lieu of thesis; thesis optional for music education or theory majors. For M.F.A.: 48 credits minimum, at least 40 in residence. For M.S.W.: 60 credits minimum, at least one and a half years in residence; thesis. For Ed.S.: 30 credit hours minimum beyond the master's, research problem and written report included; final written/oral exam. For Ph.D.: three years minimum beyond the bachelor's, at least two semesters in full-time residence; qualifying exam; reading knowledge of one or two foreign languages; dissertation; final written/oral exam. For Ed.D., D.B.A.: same as for Ph.D., except at least 72 credit hours minimum beyond the bachelor's; no foreign language requirement.

FIELDS OF STUDY.

COLLEGE OF AGRICULTURE:
Agricultural Economics.
Animal Sciences.
Biosystems and Agricultural Engineering.
Career, Technology and Leadership Education.
Crop Science.
Entomology.
Family Studies.
Forestry.
Hospitality and Dietetics Administration.
Plant Pathology.
Plant Physiology.
Plant and Soil Science.
Sociology.
Soil Science.
Veterinary Science.

COLLEGE OF ALLIED HEALTH PROFESSIONS:
Clinical Nutrition.
Communication Disorders.
Physical Therapy.
Radiation Sciences.

COLLEGE OF ARTS AND SCIENCES:
Anthropology. Apply by February 15 (Fall).
Applied Mathematics.
Biology.
Chemistry.
Classical Languages. Apply by February 15 (for financial aid consideration).
English. Apply by January 15 (Fall).
French Language and Literature.
Geography.
Geology.
German.
History. Apply by March 1 (Fall for financial aid consideration).
Mathematics.
Philosophy. Apply by April 1 (Fall for financial aid consideration).
Physics and Astronomy.
Political Science.
Psychology—Clinical. Apply by January 15 (Fall).
Psychology—Experimental. Apply by February 1 (Fall).
Sociology. Apply by January 15 (Fall).
Statistics.
Teaching World Languages.

COLLEGE OF BUSINESS AND ECONOMICS:
Accounting.
Business Administration. Apply by March 15 (Fall for financial aid consideration).
Economics.

COLLEGE OF COMMUNICATIONS AND INFORMATION STUDIES:
Communication. Apply by February 1 (Fall), October 1 (Summer)
Library Science. Apply by July 15 (Fall, April 1 for financial aid consideration), November 1 (Spring), March 1 (Summer).

COLLEGE OF DESIGN:
Architecture.
Historic Preservation.
Interior Design, Merchandising and Textiles.

COLLEGE OF EDUCATION:
Administration and Supervision. Apply by July 15 (Fall), December 1 (Spring).
Counseling Psychology.
Curriculum and Instruction.
Early Childhood Education.
Educational and Counseling Psychology. Apply by March 1 (master's degrees), January 15 (doctoral degrees).
Educational Policy Studies and Evaluation. Apply by March 1 (Fall), October 15 (Spring).
Elementary Education.
Exercise Science.
Higher Education.
Kinesiology and Health Promotion.
Middle School Education.
Reading.
Rehabilitation Counseling.
School Psychology.
Secondary Education. Includes English, mathematics, science, social science.
Social and Philosophical Studies in Education.
Special Education.

COLLEGE OF ENGINEERING:
Chemical Engineering.
Civil Engineering.
Computer Science.
Electrical Engineering.
Manufacturing Systems Engineering.
Materials Science and Engineering.
Mechanical Engineering.
Mining and Minerals Engineering.

COLLEGE OF FINE ARTS:
Art Education.
Art History. Apply by June 1 (Fall).
Art Studio.
Composition.
Music. Apply by April 1 (Fall for financial aid consideration).
Music Education.
Music Theory.
Musicology.
Performance.
Theatre Arts.

COLLEGE OF HEALTH SCIENCES:
Athletic Training.
Clinical Sciences.
Communication Disorders.
Physical Therapy.
Physician Assistant Studies.
Radiation Science.
Rehabilitation Sciences. Apply by July 1 (Fall), December 1 (Spring).

COLLEGE OF DENTISTRY:
Dentistry.

COLLEGE OF MEDICINE:
Anatomy and Neurobiology.
Medical Sciences.
Microbiology,
Molecular and Biomedical Pharmacology.
Molecular and Cellular Biochemistry.
Physiology.
Toxicology.

COLLEGE OF NURSING:
Nursing. Doctoral candidates: apply by February 15 (Fall), September 15 (Spring); master's candidates: apply by March 1 (Fall), November 1 (Spring).

COLLEGE OF PHARMACY:
Pharmaceutical Science.

COLLEGE OF PUBLIC HEALTH:
Gerontology.
Public Health.

COLLEGE OF SOCIAL WORK:
Social Work. Apply by February 1 (Fall).

GRADUATE SCHOOL (INTERDISCIPLINARY, INTERDEPARTMENTAL PROGRAMS):
Biomedical Engineering.
Diplomacy and International Commerce. Apply by February 1 (Fall).
Health Administration.
Nutritional Sciences. For assistantships apply by March 1 (Fall), October 1 (Spring).
Public Administration.
Public Policy.

College of Dentistry (40536-0297)
Web site: www.mc.uky.edu/dentistry

First classes 1962. Semester system. Special facility: Center for Oral Health. Medical Center library: 100,000 volumes, 4500 subscriptions.

Annual tuition: resident $21,274, nonresident $41,854. On-campus housing available. Contact Housing Office for both on- and off-campus housing information. Phone: (859)257-3721. Average academic year housing cost: approximately $18,000. Total average cost for all other first-year expenses: $9,000.

Enrollment: first-year class 57 (men 35, women 22), total full-time 221 (men 52%, women 48%, minorities 10%, state residents 71%). Faculty: full- and part-time 77. Degrees conferred: B.S.-D.M.D. (with the University's College of Arts and Sciences), D.M.D. Certificates.

ADMISSION REQUIREMENTS. AADSAS report, transcripts, DAT (not later than October), three letters of recommendation, interview required in support of application. Accepts transfer applicants. Graduates of unaccredited institutions are not considered. Preference given to state residents. Apply to Admissions Office after June 1, before February 1. Rolling admission process. Application fee: $50. Phone: (859)233-6072; fax: (859)257-5550.

ADMISSION STANDARDS. Competitive. Accepts about 10% of all applicants. Number of applications 1461 (n/a out-of-state); number interviewed 174 (80 out-of-state); number of acceptance n/a (n/a out-of-state); number enrolled 57 (16 out-of-state). Usual minimum UGPA: 3.0 (A = 4). Mean DAT: academic 18, PAT 17; mean UGPA 3.5.

FINANCIAL AID. Limited number of scholarships, loans. Apply to Financial Aid Office by April 1. Phone: (859)323-6071. Use FAFSA. About 92% of students receive some aid from College and outside sources.

DEGREE REQUIREMENTS. For D.M.D.: satisfactory completion of forty-month program.

FIELDS OF POSTGRADUATE STUDY.
General Practice Residency. Certificate.
Oral and Maxillofacial Surgery. Certificate.
Orofacial Pain. M.S., Certificate.
Orthodontics. M.S., Certificate.

Pediatric Dentistry. Certificate.
Periodontics. M.S., Certificate.

College of Law (40506-0048)
Web site: www.uky.edu/law

Established 1908. ABA approved since 1925. AALS member since 1912. Semester system. Special facility: The Mineral Law Center. Law library: 425,154 volumes, 3795 subscriptions; has LEXIS, NEXIS, WESTLAW, DIALOG.

Annual tuition: resident $12,842, nonresident $23,272. Limited on-campus housing available. Total average annual additional expense: $14,326.

Enrollment: first-year class 134; total full-time 425 (men 56%, women 44%, minorities 8%); no part-time study. Law faculty: full-time 21, part-time 12. Student to faculty ratio 16.3 to 1. Degrees conferred: J.D., J.D.-M.A., J.D.-M.B.A., J.D.-M.P.A.

ADMISSION REQUIREMENTS. LSDAS Law School report, bachelor's degree, transcripts, LSAT (not later than February), personal statement, résumé, letters of recommendations required in support of application. TOEFL required for applicants whose second language is English. Interview not required. Accepts transfer applicants. Graduates of unaccredited colleges not considered. Approximately 85% of students are state residents. Apply to Associate Dean for Admissions by March 1. Admits Fall only. Application fee $50. Phone: (859)257-6770.

ADMISSION STANDARDS. Selective. Accepts approximately 35% of all students. Number of applicants 1208; number of acceptance 419; number enrolled 172; LSAT (75% of students have a score at or above 157); GPA (75% of students have a GPA at or above 3.30). *U.S. News & World Report* ranking is in the second tier (tied at 60th) of all U.S. law schools.

FINANCIAL AID. Scholarships, full and partial tuition waivers, grants, Federal W/S, loans. Apply to University's Student Financial Aid Office by April 1. Phone: (859)257-3172. Use FAFSA (College code: 001989). About 52% of students receive aid other than loans from both College and outside sources.

DEGREE REQUIREMENTS. For J.D.: 90 semester hours minimum. Note: transfer credit from other ABA-accredited law schools considered.

College of Medicine (40536-0298)
Web site: www.mc.uky.edu/medicine

First class admitted 1960. Medical Center library: 160,000 volumes, 2000 subscriptions. NIH ranking is 69th with 245 awards/grants worth $83,411,657.

Annual tuition: resident $23,752, nonresident 45,155. On-campus housing for both married and single students available. Total average figure for all other expenses: $18,090.

Enrollment: first-year class 103 (EDP 30); total 404 (men 59%, women 41%, minorities 18$, state residents 88%); postgraduates 15. Faculty: full-time 658, part-time 145. Degrees conferred: M.D., M.D.-M.B.A., M.D.-M.P.H., M.D.-M.S., M.D.-Ph.D. The M.S. and Ph.D. are offered through the Graduate School.

ADMISSION REQUIREMENTS. AMCAS report, transcripts, MCAT required in support of application. Interview by invitation only. Accepts transfer applicants. Has EDP; apply between June 1 and August 1. Preference given to state residents. Apply to Office of Admissions after June 1, before November 1. Application fee $30. Phone: (859)323-6161; fax: (859)323-2076.

ADMISSION STANDARDS. Competitive. Accepts about 14% of all applicants. Number of applications 1002 (635 out-of-state); number interviewed 322 (114 out-of-state); number of acceptance 191 (52 out-of-state); number enrolled 103 (17 out-of-state). Mean Composite MCAT 9.8; mean UGPA 3.69.

FINANCIAL AID. Rural Kentucky Medical Scholarship Fund, summer fellowships, assistantships, loans. Apply to Office of Student Financial Aid after acceptance. Phone: (859)323-2461. Use FAFSA. About 95% of students receive aid from College and outside sources.

DEGREE REQUIREMENTS. For M.D.: satisfactory completion of four-year program; must pass Step 1 of USMLE for promotion to third year and pass Step 2 for graduation. For M.S., Ph.D.: see Graduate School listing above.

FIELDS OF GRADUATE STUDY.
Anatomy and Neurobiology.
Integrated Biomedical Sciences.
Medical Science.
Microbiology, Immunology and Molecular Genetics.
Molecular and Biomedical Pharmacology.
Molecular and Cellular Biochemistry.
Physiology.
Toxicology.

KUTZTOWN UNIVERSITY OF PENNSYLVANIA
Kutztown, Pennsylvania 19530-0730
Web site: www.kutztown.edu

Founded 1866. Located 15 miles NE of Reading. CGS member. Coed. State control. Semester system. Library: 500,484 volumes, 1500 subscriptions. Total University enrollment: 9864.

Tuition: per credit, resident $345, nonresident $552. On-campus housing generally not available to graduate students. For information contact Director of Off-Campus Housing: (610) 683-4022. Day-care facilities available.

College of Graduate Studies

Graduate study since 1959. Enrollment: full-time 230, part-time 628. Faculty: full-time 67, part-time 12. Degrees conferred: M.A., M.S., M.Ed., M.L.S., M.P.A., M.B.A.

ADMISSION REQUIREMENTS. One transcript from all postsecondary institutions attended, three letters of recommendation, interview, GRE/GMAT required in support of College's application. TOEFL, TSE required for international applicants. Résumé and statement of goals are needed when applying for M.B.A. Accepts transfer applicants. Graduates of unaccredited institutions not considered. Apply to Graduate Office by February 1 (Fall), July 1 (Spring). Application fee $35. Phone: (610)683-4000; fax: (610)683-1315.

ADMISSION STANDARDS. Selective. Usual minimum average: 2.5 plus test scores (A = 4).

FINANCIAL AID. Assistantships, grants, tuition waivers, Federal W/S, loans. Approved for VA benefits. Apply to Director of Financial Aid. Phone: (610)683-4077. Use FAFSA. Less than 5% of students receive aid other than loans from University.

DEGREE REQUIREMENTS. For master's: 30–57 credit hours minimum, at least 24 in residence (for most programs); thesis/nonthesis option; final written/oral exam.

FIELDS OF STUDY.
Agency Counseling. M.A.
Art Education. M.Ed.
Business Administration. M.B.A.
Computer and Information Science. M.S.
Counseling Psychology. M.A.

Counselor Education. Includes elementary, secondary, student affairs in higher education. M.Ed.

Electronic Media. M.S.

Elementary Education. M.Ed.

English. M.A.

Library Science. M.L.S.

Marital and Family Counseling. M.A.

Mathematics. M.A.

Nursing. M.S.

Public Administration. M.P.A.

Reading. M.Ed.

Secondary Education. Includes biology, curriculum and instruction, English, mathematics, social studies. M.Ed.

Social Work. M.S.W.

THE LAKE ERIE COLLEGE OF OSTEOPATHIC MEDICINE

Erie, Pennsylvania 16509
Web site: www.lecom.edu

Founded in 1992, added a School of Pharmacy in 2001 and in 2004 a School of Osteopathic Medicine at their campus in Bradenton, Florida. Special facility: Cappabianca Research Center. Library: 15,000 volumes, 350 subscriptions.

Annual tuition: resident $25,150, nonresident $26,250. No on-campus housing available. Contact Admissions Office for housing information. Off-campus housing and personal expenses: approximately $14,000–$16,000.

Enrollment: first-year class 389, total full-time 1375 (men 53%, women 47%, minorities 24%, state residents 35%). Faculty: full-time 85, part-time and volunteers 1162. Degree conferred: D.O.

ADMISSION REQUIREMENTS. Preference given to state residents, U.S. citizens, and permanent residents only. Bachelor's degree from an accredited institution required. 100% of applicants have bachelor's degree awarded prior to enrollment. Apply through AACOMAS (file after June 1, before December 1), submit MCAT (will accept test results from last three years), official transcripts for each school attended (should show at least 90 semester credits/135 quarter credits), service processing fee. After review of AACOMAS application and supporting documents decision is made concerning which candidates should receive supplemental materials. The LECOM supplemental application, an application fee of $50, a personal statement, and a premed committee letter and two additional recommendations, one from a D.O. and one general recommendation, should be returned to Office of Admission as soon as possible, but not later than March 1. Interviews are by invitation only and generally for final selection. First-year students admitted Fall only. Rolling admissions process, notification starts in December and is finished when class is filled. Applicant's response to offer and $1500 deposit due within two weeks of receipt of acceptance letter. School does maintain an alternate list. Phone: (814)866-6641; fax: (814)866-8123; e-mail: admissions@lecom.edu.

ADMISSION STANDARDS. Selective. Accepts about 12% of all applicants. Number of applications 4251 (3782 out-of-state); number interviewed 1185 (888 out-of-state); number of acceptance 519 (345 out-of-state); number enrolled 389 (266 out-of-state). Usual minimum UGPA: 3.0 (A = 4). Mean Composite MCAT 8.3, mean UGPA 3.40.

FINANCIAL AID. Scholarships, merit scholarships, minority scholarships, Grants-in-Aid, institutional loans, NOF, HEAL, alternative loan programs, Military and National Health Service program, and Federal loan are available. Financial Aid applications and information are generally available at the on-campus by-invitation interview. Contact the Admissions Office for cur-

rent information. Phone: (814)866-6641. For most programs use FAFSA (School code: G30908), for all Federal programs, also submit Financial Aid Transcript, Federal Income Tax forms. About 90% of students receive some form of financial assistance.

DEGREE REQUIREMENTS. For D.O.: satisfactory completion of 4-year program. All students must pass the National Board of Osteopathic Medical Examination Level I and II prior to the awarding of D.O.

LAMAR UNIVERSITY

Beaumont, Texas 77710
Web site: www.lamar.edu

Founded 1923. CGS member. Coed. State control. Semester system. Special facilities: Dishman Art Gallery, Center for Criminal Justice, Gulf Coast Hazardous Substance Research Center, Center for Public Policy Studies, Space Exploration Center. Library: 698,250 volumes, 2900 subscriptions. Total University enrollment: 10,595.

Tuition: per credit resident $272, nonresident $548, part-time tuition varies according to credit hours. On-campus housing for married, single students. Average annual housing cost: $6700 for married students, $5330 (including board) for single students. Apply to Residence Life Office. Phone: (409)880-2314.

College of Graduate Studies

Graduate study since 1962. Enrollment: full-time 574, part-time 337. Graduate faculty: full-time 175, part-time 20. Degrees conferred: M.A., M.B.A., M.Ed., M.S., M.E.S., M.E., M.E.M., M.Mu., M.Mu.Ed., M.P.A., D.E., Ed.D.

ADMISSION REQUIREMENTS. Transcripts, GRE/GMAT required in support of College's application. Interview not required. TOEFL required for international applicants. Accepts transfer applicants. Graduates of unaccredited colleges not considered. Apply to Dean of College of Graduate Studies at least 4 weeks prior to registration. International students apply 90 days prior to registration. Application fee $25, $50 for international applicants. Phone: (409)880-8356 or (800)443-5638; fax: (409)880-8414; e-mail: gradadmissions@hal.lamar.edu.

ADMISSION STANDARDS. Selective. Usual minimum average: 2.5 (A = 4).

FINANCIAL AID. Annual awards from institutional funds: scholarships, research fellowships, research/teaching fellowships, tuition waivers, grants, Federal W/S, loans. Approved for VA benefits. Apply by April 1 to Dean of College of Graduate Studies for scholarships, fellowships, assistantships; to the Financial Aid Office for all other programs. Phone: (409)880-8450. Use FAFSA. About 15% of students receive aid. Aid available for part-time students.

DEGREE REQUIREMENTS. For M.A., M.E.S., M.Mu.: 30 credit boom minimum, at least 24 in residence; thesis; final oral exam; reading knowledge of one foreign language required for M.A. only. For M.S., M.B.A., M.E., M.E.M., M.P.A., M.Ed.: 30 credit hours minimum, at least 24 in residence; thesis; final oral exam, or 36 credit hours minimum and final written exam in lieu of thesis. For D.E.: 30 credit hours minimum beyond master's; thesis; final oral exam. For Ed.D.: at least 60 credit hours beyond master's; qualifying exam; dissertation; final written/oral exam.

FIELDS OF STUDY.

Applied Criminology. M.S.

Audiology. M.S.

Biology. M.S.

Business Administration. M.B.A.
Chemical Engineering. M.E., M.E.S., D.E.
Chemistry. M.S.
Civil Engineering. M.E., M.E.S., D.E.
Community and Counseling Psychology. M.S.
Computer Science. M.S.
Counseling and Development. M.Ed.
Deaf Studies and Habilitation. M.S.
Education Administration. M.Ed.
Educational Leadership. Ed.D.
Electrical Engineering. M.E., M.E.S., D.E.
Elementary Education. M.Ed.
Engineering Management. M.E.M.
English. M.A.
Environmental Engineering. M.S., M.E.S.
Environmental Studies. M.S.
Family and Consumer Science. M.S.
History. M.A.
Industrial and Organizational Psychology. M.S.
Industrial Engineering. M.E., M.E.S., D.E.
Kinesiology. M.Ed.
Mathematics. M.S.
Mechanical Engineering. M.E., M.E.S., D.E.
Music. M.Mu.
Music Education. M.Mu.Ed.
Nursing Administration. M.S.
Nursing Education. M.S.
Public Administration. M.P.A.
Secondary Education. M.Ed.
Special Education. M.Ed.
Speech-Language Pathology. M.S.
Supervision. M.Ed.
Theater. M.S.
Visual Arts. Includes art history. M.A.

UNIVERSITY OF LA VERNE

La Verne, California 91750-4443
Web site: www.ulv.edu

Founded 1891. Located 30 miles E of Los Angeles. Coed. Independent. Semester system. Library: 250,000 volumes, 4500 subscriptions.

Tuition: per hour $545 (master's), $730 (doctorate). No on-campus housing available.

Graduate Program

Enrollment: full-time 961, part-time 1400. Graduate faculty: full-time 75, part-time 147. Degrees conferred: M.Ed., M.S., M.A., M.H.A., M.P.A., M.B.A., Ed.D., D.P.A.

ADMISSION REQUIREMENTS. Transcripts, three letters of reference required in support of application. Online application available. GRE/GMAT/MAT for some programs. Accepts transfer applicants. TOEFL required for international applicants. Graduates of unaccredited institutions not considered. Apply to Graduate Studies Office; no specified closing date. Application fee $50 (master's), $75 (doctorate). Phone: (909)593-3511, ext. 4244; fax: (909)392-2761.

ADMISSION STANDARDS. Selective. Usual minimum average: 2.5–3.0 for master's programs, 3.0 for doctoral (A = 4).

FINANCIAL AID. Annual awards from institutional funds: departmental scholarships, assistantships, grants, internships, Federal W/S, loans. Apply by May 1 to Financial Aid Office. Phone: (909)543-3511, ext. 4135. Use FAFSA. No aid for part-time students carrying less than half a full-time program.

DEGREE REQUIREMENTS. For master's: 32–50 semester hours minimum (6–12 credits may be transferred into program); thesis or graduate seminar. For Ed.D.: 54 semester hours beyond master's. For D.P.A.: 54 semester hours beyond master's. For Psy.D.: five-year full-time program; clinical practica; internship; dissertation; oral defense.

FIELDS OF STUDY.
Business Administration. M.B.A.
Business Information Technology.
Business Organizational Management. M.S.
Child Development.
Child Life.
Clinical Community Psychology. Psy.D.
College Counseling and Student Services.
Educational Management. M.Ed.
Gerontology.
Health Services Management.
Leadership and Management.
Learning Handicapped.
Marriage and Family Therapy.
Organizational Leadership. Ed.D.
Psychology. Psy.D.
Public Administration. M.P.A., D.P.A.
Reading.
School Counseling.
School Psychology.
Special Education.

LEHIGH UNIVERSITY

Bethlehem, Pennsylvania 18015-3174
Web site: www.lehigh.edu

Founded 1865. Located 60 miles N of Philadelphia. CGS member. Coed. Private control. Semester system. Special facilities: Research centers in Chemical Process Modeling and Control, Design and Manufacture Innovation, Economic Education, Innovation Management Studies, International Studies, Molecular Bioscience and Biotechnology, Polymer Science and Engineering Social Research, Energy Research, Advanced Technology for Large Structural Systems, Environmental Studies, Jewish Studies, Study of Private Enterprise, Materials Research, Business Communications, Solid State Studies, Small Business Development, Technology Studies, Surface Studies; Research institutes in Emulsion Polymers, Fracture and Solid Mechanics, Metal Forming, Study of the High-Rise Habitat, Thermo-Fluid Engineering and Science, 18th-Century Studies, Studies of Commodities, Health Science, Biomedical Engineering and Mathematical Biology. The University's endowment assets rank it 56th, with a value of $796,946,000. In 2004, 11 of the University's faculty members were elected to National Honor Academies and this ranks it 54th among all U.S. institutions. The Library: approximately 1,200,000 volumes, 6271 subscriptions. Total University enrollment: 6500.

Tuition: per credit College of Arts and Sciences $565, College of Business $630, College of Education $510, College of Engineering $565. Limited on-campus housing for both married and single students. Average monthly housing cost: $650–$750 for single graduate students, $10,000 for married students. Apply to Residential Operations Office. Phone: (610)758-3500.

Graduate Studies

Graduate study since 1866. Enrollment: full-time 963, part-time 925. University faculty: full-time 391, part-time 77. Degrees conferred: M.A., M.B.A., M.Ed., M.Eng., M.S., Ed.D., D.A., Ph.D.

ADMISSION REQUIREMENTS. Transcripts, GRE/GMAT/MAT, two letters of recommendation required in support of application. Online application available. International students must submit evidence of competence in English or TOEFL. Interview not required. Accepts transfer applicants. Graduates of unaccredited colleges not considered. Apply to appropriate colleges by July 15 (Fall), December 1 (Spring). Application fee $50. Graduate Studies phone: (610)758-3000; fax: (610)758-4244.

ADMISSION STANDARDS. Competitive for some departments, very selective for others. Minimum average: 2.75 (A = 4).

FINANCIAL AID. Annual awards from institutional funds: scholarships, research assistantships, teaching fellowships, internships, tuition waivers, Federal W/S, loans. Approved for VA benefits. Apply by January 15 to appropriate department chair for scholarships, fellowships, assistantships; to the Financial Aid Office for all other programs. Use either FAFSA. Phone: (610)758-3181. About 75% of students receive aid from University and outside sources.

DEGREE REQUIREMENTS. For master's: 30 credit hours minimum, at least 24 in residence; thesis/research report/comprehensive exam. For Ph.D.: 42–48 credits, three years minimum beyond the bachelor's, at least one year in residence; reading knowledge of foreign languages varies with department; qualifying exam; comprehensive exam; dissertation; final oral exam. For Ed.D.: same as for Ph.D., except no language requirement. For D.A.: same as for Ph.D., except college teaching internship, appropriate project instead of dissertation.

FIELDS OF STUDY.

COLLEGE OF ARTS AND SCIENCES:
American Studies. Interdisciplinary. M.A.
Applied Mathematics. M.S., Ph.D.
Biological Sciences. Includes biochemistry, integrative biology, molecular biology. M.S., Ph.D.
Chemistry. Includes clinical chemistry, pharmaceutical chemistry. M.S., Ph.D., D.A.
Earth and Environmental Sciences. M.S., Ph.D.
English. M.A., Ph.D.
History. M.A., Ph.D.
Human Cognition and Development. M.S., Ph.D.
Mathematics. Includes applied mathematics, statistics. M.S., Ph.D.
Photonics. M.S.
Physics. M.S., Ph.D.
Political Science. M.A.
Polymer Science and Engineering. Interdisciplinary. M.S., Ph.D.
Psychology. M.S., Ph.D.
Sociology and Anthropology. M.A.
Statistics. M.S.

COLLEGE OF BUSINESS AND ECONOMICS:
Accounting. M.S.
Accounting and Information Analysis. M.S.
Business Administration. M.B.A.
Business and Economics. Ph.D.
Economics. M.S.
Finance. M.S.

COLLEGE OF EDUCATION:
Counseling Psychology. Includes counseling and human services. M.Ed., Ph.D.
Education Leadership. M.Ed., Ed.D.
Educational Technology. M.Ed., M.S.
Instructional Technology. M.S.
Learning Sciences and Technology. Ph.D.
School Counseling. M.Ed.
Secondary Education. M.A., M.Ed.
Special Education. M.Ed., Ph.D.

P.C. ROSSIN COLLEGE OF ENGINEERING AND APPLIED SCIENCE:
Chemical Engineering. M.Eng., M.S., Ph.D.
Civil and Environmental Engineering. M.Eng., M.S., Ph.D.
Computational Engineering and Mechanics. M.S., Ph.D.
Computer Engineering. M.S., Ph.D.
Electrical Engineering. M.Eng., M.S., Ph.D.
Engineering and Applied Science. M.Eng., M.S., Ph.D.
Industrial Engineering. M.Eng., M.S., Ph.D.
Information and Systems Engineering. M.Eng., M.S., Ph.D.
Management Science. M.S.
Manufacturing Systems Engineering. M.Eng., M.S., Ph.D.
Material Science and Engineering. M.Eng., Ph.D.
Mechanical Engineering. M.Eng., M.S., Ph.D.
Mechanics. M.Eng., M.S., Ph.D.
Polymer Science and Engineering. M.S.
Quality Engineering. M.S.

HERBERT H. LEHMAN COLLEGE OF THE CITY UNIVERSITY OF NEW YORK
Bronx, New York 10468-1589
Web site: www.lehman.cuny.edu

Founded in 1932 as branch of Hunter College, became independent unit of City University in 1968. Coed. Municipal control. Semester system. Library: 541,944 volumes, 1350 subscriptions. Day-care facilities available.

Tuition: per credit, state resident $230, nonresident $425. No on-campus housing available.

Graduate Division

Enrollment: full-time 83, part-time 1624. Faculty: full-time 110, part-time 36. Degrees conferred: M.A., M.A.T., M.S., M.S.Ed., M.F.A.

ADMISSION REQUIREMENTS. Transcripts, letters of recommendation, GRE/GMAT, TOEFL (for all international applicants) required in support of application. Accepts transfer applicants. Graduates of unaccredited institutions not considered. Apply to Office of Admissions by April 1 (Fall), November 1 (Spring). Application fee $125. Phone: (718)960-8702; fax: (718)960-8172.

ADMISSION STANDARDS. Competitive. Usual minimum average: 3.0 (A = 4).

FINANCIAL AID. Teaching assistantships, tuition waivers, graduate TAP, loans. Apply to Student Financial Aid Office by May 15. Phone: (718)960-8545. Use FAFSA (School code: 007022) and University's FAF. Aid available for part-time students.

DEGREE REQUIREMENTS. For master's: 30 credit hours minimum; thesis and/or comprehensive exams for most majors.

FIELDS OF STUDY.
Accounting. M.S.
Art. M.A., M.F.A.
Art N–12 Teacher. M.A.
Biology. Includes biology 7–12. M.A.
Business Education. Includes secondary and adult education. M.S.Ed.
Computer Science. M.S.
Early Childhood Education. M.S.Ed.
Childhood Education. M.S.Ed.
English. M.A.
English Education. Includes English 7–12. M.S.Ed.
Guidance and Counseling. M.S.Ed.
Health N–12 Teacher. M.S.Ed.
Health Education and Promotion. M.A.

History. M.A.
Liberal Studies. M.A.
Literacy Studies. M.S.Ed.
Mathematics. M.A.
Music. M.A.T.
Nursing. Includes adult health nursing, nursing of older adults, parent-child nursing, pediatric nurse practitioner. M.S.
Nutrition. M.S.
Public Health. M.P.H.
Recreation Education. M.A., M.S.Ed.
School Building Leader. M.S.Ed.
School Counselor. M.A.
School District Leader. M.S.Ed.
Science Education. M.S.Ed.
Social Studies. Includes social science 7–12. M.S.Ed.
Social Work. M.S.W.
Spanish. Includes Spanish 7–12. M.S.Ed.
Speech and Hearing Sciences. M.A.
Speech and Theatre. M.A.
Speech-Language Pathology and Audiology. M.A.
Teacher of Special Education. M.S.Ed.
Teaching English to Speakers of Other Languages. M.S.Ed.

LEWIS AND CLARK COLLEGE
Portland, Oregon 97219-7879
Web site: www.lclark.edu

Founded 1867. Coed. Private control. Presbyterian. Semester system. Library: 270,000 volumes, 1900 subscriptions. Total University enrollment: 3500.

Tuition: $595 per semester hour. No on-campus housing available.

Graduate School of Education

Enrollment: full- and part-time 499. Faculty teaching graduate students: full-time 32, part-time 63. Degrees conferred: M.A., M.S., M.A.T., M.Ed.

ADMISSION REQUIREMENTS. Official transcripts, résumé or vita, personal statement, GRE required in support of School's application. TOEFL required for international applicants. Accepts transfer applicants. Graduates of unaccredited institutions not considered. Apply to the program chairman at least 2 weeks prior to registration for part-time applicants. Applicants in some programs admitted quarterly. Teacher Education applicants apply by January 15. Rolling admissions process. Application fee $50. Phone: (503)768-6200.

ADMISSION STANDARDS. Selective. Usual minimum average: 3.0 (A = 4).

FINANCIAL AID. Limited to Federal W/S, loans. Apply by March 1 to Office of Student Financial Services. Phone: (503) 768-7090. Use FAFSA.

DEGREE REQUIREMENTS. For master's: 10–15 courses minimum, at least 8–12 in residence; thesis/nonthesis option.

FIELDS OF STUDY.
Addictions Treatment. M.A.
Counseling Psychology. Includes addictions. M.A., M.S.
Educational Administration.
Liberal Studies. M.A.
Marriage and Family Therapy. M.A.
School Psychology. M.S.
Special Education. Includes deaf and hard-of-hearing.
Teacher Education. Includes early childhood/elementary, middle level/high school, music. M.A.T.

Northwestern School of Law
Web site: www.law.lclark.edu

Established 1884; affiliated with Lewis and Clark in 1965 and initiated a day division. ABA approved since 1970. AALS member. Private control. Semester system. Special facilities: Pacific Environmental Advocacy Center, Crime Victims Law Institute. Law library: 506,527 volumes, 3975 subscriptions; has LEXIS, NEXIS, WESTLAW, DIALOG, CALI, FIRSTSEARCH, OLSYSTEM.

Annual tuition: $28,970 (day), $21,752 (evening); for LL.M. per credit $1024. No on-campus housing available. Total average annual additional expense: $14,590.

Enrollment: first-year class day 194, evening 39; total day and evening 709 (men 52%, women 48%, minorities 18%). Faculty: full-time 35, part-time 23. Student to faculty ratio 14.1 to 1. Degrees conferred: J.D., LL.M. (Environmental and Natural Resources Law).

ADMISSION REQUIREMENTS. LSDAS Report, bachelor's degree, transcripts, LSAT, personal statement, résumé, two letters of recommendation required in support of application. Accepts transfer applicants, personal visits encouraged. Graduates of unaccredited colleges not considered. Apply to Assistant Dean for Admissions by March 1. Admits Fall only. Application fee $50. Phone: (503)768-6613; fax (503)768-6793. For international applicants, requirements are essentially the same except under certain circumstances the TOEFL may be substituted for LSAT. For LL.M. information contact Director LL.M. program. Phone: (503)768-6649.

ADMISSION STANDARDS. Selective. Accepts approximately 38% of full-time and 39% of part-time applicants. Number of full-time applicants 2190, part-time 205; number of full-time acceptance 828, part-time 79; number full-time enrolled 191, part-time 41; LSAT (75% of full-time students have a score at or above 158, part-time 155); GPA (75% of full-time students have a GPA at or above 3.04, part-time 3.10). *U.S. News & World Report* ranking is in the second tier (tied at 82nd) of all U.S. law schools.

FINANCIAL AID. Scholarships, grants, fellowships, full and partial tuition waivers, Federal W/S, loans. Apply to Financial Aids Office by March 1. Phone: (503)768-7090. Use FAFSA (School code: 003197). Approximately 47% of all students receive some form of financial assistance.

DEGREE REQUIREMENTS. For J.D.: satisfactory completion of three-year (day), four-year (evening) program; 86 credit hours. For LL.M.: one-year full-time program; thesis/nonthesis option.

LINCOLN UNIVERSITY
Jefferson City, Missouri 65102
Web site: www.lincolnu.edu

Founded 1866. Located 125 miles W of St. Louis. Coed. State control. Semester system. Library: 187,956 volumes, 761 subscriptions. Total University enrollment: 3180.

Tuition: per hour, resident $180, nonresident $335. On-campus housing for single students available. Housing cost per semester: $3790 (includes board). Apply to Director of Residential Life. Phone: (573)681-5478.

Graduate Studies

Enrollment: full-time 78, part-time 110. University faculty teaching graduate students: full-time 6, part-time 25. Degrees conferred: M.A., M.Ed., M.B.A.

ADMISSION REQUIREMENTS. Transcripts, three letters of recommendation required in support of application. GRE/MAT required for M.A., M.Ed.; GMAT required for M.B.A. TOEFL required for international applicants. Accepts transfer applicants. Apply to Office of Graduate Studies and Continuing Education by July 1 (Fall), November 30 (Spring). Application fee $17. Phone: (573)681-5247; fax: (573)681-5106; e-mail: gradschool@lincolnu.edu.

FINANCIAL AID. Limited to Federal W/S, loans. Approved for VA benefits. Use FAFSA. Phone: (573)681-6156; fax: (573)681-5566. Aid for part-time students carrying at least six credits.

DEGREE REQUIREMENTS. For M.A.: 33 semester hours minimum; thesis/nonthesis option. For M.Ed.: 36 semester hours minimum. For M.B.A.: 36 semester hours minimum.

FIELDS OF STUDY.
Business Administration. Includes accounting, management. M.B.A.
Educational Leadership. Ed.S.
Elementary Education. M.Ed.
Guidance and Counseling. M.Ed.
History. M.A.
School Administration and Supervision. M.Ed.
Secondary Education. M.Ed.
Social Science. M.A.
Sociology. M.A.
Sociology/Criminal Justice. M.A.
Special Education. M.Ed.

LOMA LINDA UNIVERSITY
Loma Linda, California 92350
Web site: www.llu.edu

Founded in 1905. CGS member. Located in the San Bernardino Redlands area about 5 miles from each city. Coed. Quarter system. Loma Linda University offers programs in graduate professional education through the Graduate School. The programs utilize resources in the Schools of Allied Health Professions, Dentistry, Medicine, Nursing, and Public Health. The University is operated by the Seventh-Day Adventist Church with approximately 40% of its student body belonging to other religious faiths. Library: 322,657 volumes, 1394 subscriptions. Total University enrollment: 3900.

Tuition: per unit $460, graduate dental programs full-time $39,700. On-campus housing for 100 graduate men, 32–64 graduate women, none for married students. Average academic year cost: $8000–$11,730. Apply to Dean of Students. Phone: (909) 558-4510. Day-care facilities available.

Graduate Studies

Opened 1954. Enrollment: full-time 392, part-time 178. University faculty: full-time 36, part-time 58. Degrees conferred: M.A., M.S., M.S.W., M.P.H., Psy.D., Dr.P.H., Ph.D., Ph.D.-M.P.H., Psy.D.-M.P.H., Psy.D.-Dr.P.H.

ADMISSION REQUIREMENTS. Two transcripts, letters of reference, GRE/Subject Tests required in support of School's application. TOEFL required for foreign applicants. Interview not required for most programs. Accepts transfer applicants. Apply to Dean of Graduate School by August 1. Most department prefer Fall entrance. Application fee $50. Phone: (909)558-4528; fax: (909)824-4859.

ADMISSION STANDARDS. Very selective for some departments, selective for others. Usual minimum average: 3.0 (A = 4).

FINANCIAL AID. Annual awards from institutional funds: scholarships, fellowships, stipends, teaching assistantships, grants, full and partial tuition waiver, Federal W/S, loans. Approved for VA benefits. Apply by March 1 to appropriate department chair for scholarships, fellowships, assistantships; to Financial Aid Office for all other programs. Use FAFSA (School code: 001218) and institutional FAF. Phone: (909)558-4509, (800)422-4558. Aid available for part-time students.

DEGREE REQUIREMENTS. For master's: 48 quarter units minimum, at least 12 in residence; advancement to candidacy; thesis/nonthesis option; final written/oral exams. For Ph.D.: 72 quarter units, three years minimum beyond the bachelor's, at least two years in residence and 30 units in full-time attendance; some require reading knowledge of two foreign languages; dissertation; final oral exam. For Psy.D.: essentially the same as Ph.D., except no foreign language; internship; special research project.

FIELDS OF STUDY.
Biology.
Child Life Specialist.
Clinical Social Work.
Counseling.
Counseling and Family Sciences.
Criminal Justice.
Drug and Alcohol Counseling.
Earth and Biological Sciences.
Earth Science.
Family Studies.
Geology.
Gerontology.
Marital and Family Therapy.
Natural Sciences.
Psychology.
Public Administration.
School Counseling.
Social Policy and Research.
Social Work.

School of Allied Health Professions

Established 1966. Quarter system. Tuition: per credit $425. Enrollment: full-time 213, part-time 34. University faculty: full-time 96, part-time 38. Degrees conferred: M.H.I.S., M.O.T., M.P.A., M.P.T., D.P.T.

ADMISSION REQUIREMENTS. Two transcripts, three letters of reference, GRE, statement of professional goals, résumé required in support of School's application. TOEFL (minimum score 550) required for foreign applicants. Preference given to SDA applicants. Accepts transfer applicants. Apply to Director of Admissions by August 1; M.P.A. applicants use CASPA (an online service) by March 1; M.P.A. admits Fall only. Application fee $50. Phone: (909)558-4599; fax (909)558-4291; e-mail: admissions@sahp.llu.edu.

ADMISSION STANDARDS. Selective for most programs. Usual minimum GPA: 3.0 (A = 4); 3.2 for D.P.T.

FINANCIAL AID. Annual awards from institutional funds: scholarships, fellowships, teaching assistantships, grants, internships, tuition waivers, Federal W/S, loans. Approved for VA benefits. Apply by March 1 to appropriate department chair for scholarships, fellowships, assistantships; by March 15 to Financial Aid Office for all other programs. Phone: (909)558-4545 or (800) 422-4558; e-mail: finaid@univ.llu.edu. Use FAFSA (School code: 001218) and institutional FAF. Aid sometimes available for part-time students.

DEGREE REQUIREMENTS. For M.H.I.S.: 54 quarter units, 15-month full-time program; internship. For M.O.T.: 144 quarter unit full-time program; practicum. For M.O.T. (Post-Professional): 45 quarter unit full-time program; practicum. For M.P.T.: two-and-one-half-year full-time program; practicum. For D.P.T.: 189 quarter hour full-time program; clinical experience.

FIELDS OF STUDY.
Occupational Therapy. M.O.T., M.O.T. (Post-Professional).
Physical Therapy. M.P.T., D.P.T.
Physician Assistant. M.P.A.
Rehabilitation Science. Ph.D.
Speech-Language Pathology and Audiology. M.S.

School of Dentistry
Web site: www.llu.edu/llu/dentistry

Founded 1953. Quarter system. Special facility: Center for Oral Health. Special program: Offers an Internationally Trained Dentistry program. Library: 100,000 volumes, 4500 subscriptions.

Annual tuition: $45,279. On-campus housing available. Contact Housing Office for both on- and off-campus housing information. Phone: (859)257-3721. Average academic year housing cost: approximately $18,000. Total average cost for all other first-year expenses: $12,000.

Enrollment: first-year class 95, total full-time 537 (men 69%, women 31%, minorities 39%, state residents 30%). Faculty: full-time 84, part-time 220. Degrees conferred: D.D.S., D.D.S.-M.P.H., D.D.S.-M.S., D.D.S.-Ph.D., Certificates. The M.S. and Ph.D. are offered through the Graduate School.

ADMISSION REQUIREMENTS. AADSAS report, Loma Linda supplemental form, official transcripts, three letters of recommendation, DAT (preference given to October test takers), dexterity test required in support of School's application. Interview by invitation only. Applicants must have completed at least three years of college study, preferably four years of study. Preference given to Seventh-Day Adventist Church members. Graduates of unaccredited institutions not considered. Apply to AADSAS after June 1, before December 1. Rolling admission process. Application fee $75. Phone: (909)558-4621, (800)422-4558; fax: (909) 558-4211.

ADMISSION STANDARDS. Competitive. Accepts about 5–10% of all applicants. Number of applications 1523 (n/a out-of-state); number interviewed n/a (n/a out-of-state); number of acceptance n/a (n/a out-of-state); number enrolled 95 (n/a out-of-state). Usual minimum UGPA: 2.7 (A = 4). Mean DAT: academic 19, PAT 18; mean UGPA 3.5.

FINANCIAL AID. Scholarships, loans. Apply to Financial Aid Office after acceptance, before May 1. Phone: (909)558-4509. Use FAFSA (School code: 001218). About 90% receive aid from School.

DEGREE REQUIREMENTS. For D.D.S.: satisfactory completion of 45-month program. For D.D.S.-M.P.H.: usually requires two additional quarters. For M.S., Ph.D.: see Graduate School listing above.

FIELDS OF POSTGRADUATE STUDY.
Endodontics. M.S., Certificate.
Implant Dentistry. M.S., Certificate.
Oral and Maxillofacial Surgery. M.S., Certificate.
Orthodontics and Dentofacial Orthopedics. M.S., Certificate.
Pediatric Dentistry. M.S., Certificate.
Periodontics. M.S., Certificate.
Prosthodontics. M.S., Certificate.

School of Medicine
Web site: www.llu.edu/llu/medicine

Organized 1909. Quarter system. Special facilities: Center for Perinatal Biology, Center for Health Disparities and Molecular Medicine, Medical Simulation Center. Library: 75,000,800 subscriptions.

Annual tuition: $36,946. Both on- and off-campus housing available. Total average figure for all other expenses: $15,400.

Enrollment: first-year class 166 (EDP 10); total 663 (men 50%, women 50%, minorities 9%, state residents 49%). Faculty: full-time 675, part-time 150. Degrees conferred: M.D., M.D.-M.S., M.D.-Ph.D. The M.S. and Ph.D. are offered through the Graduate School.

ADMISSION REQUIREMENTS. AMCAS report, transcripts, recommendations, MCAT, supplementary form, required in support of application. TOEFL required for international applicants. Interview by invitation. Accepts transfer applicants who have already passed Step 1 of USMLE. Has EDP: apply between June 1 and August 1. Applicants must have completed at least three years of college study. Some preference to members of Seventh-Day Adventist Church. Apply to Dean of Admissions after June 1, before November 1. Application fee $75. Phone: (909)558-4467; fax: (909)558-0359.

ADMISSION STANDARDS. Competitive. Accepts about 10% of all applicants. Number of applications 3024 (n/a out-of-state); number interviewed 338 (n/a out-of-state); number of acceptance n/a (n/a out-of-state); number enrolled 166 (n/a out-of-state). Mean Composite MCAT 10.0; mean UGPA 3.72.

FINANCIAL AID. Scholarships, grants, HEAL, Federal and private loans. Apply to Director of Student Finance; for priority consideration apply by March 2. Phone: (909)558-4509. Use FAFSA (School code: 001218).

DEGREE REQUIREMENTS. For M.D.: satisfactory completion of four-year program; must pass Step 1 of USMLE for promotion to third year and pass Step 2 for graduation. For M.S., Ph.D.: see Graduate School listing above.

FIELDS OF GRADUATE STUDY.
Anatomy.
Biochemistry.
Genetics.
Immunology.
Microbiology and Molecular Genetics.
Molecular Biology.
Neuroscience.
Perinatal Biology.
Pharmacology.
Physiology.

School of Public Health

Established 1967. Quarter system. Special facilities: Center for Health and Development, Center for Health Promotion, Center for Health Research. Annual tuition: $20,150. Enrollment: full-time 266, part-time 101. University faculty: full-time 65, part-time 13. Degrees conferred: M.H.A., M.P.H., Dr.P.H.

ADMISSION REQUIREMENTS. Two transcripts, three letters of reference, GRE (GRE or MCAT for Dr.P.H.), statement of professional goals required in support of School's application. TOEFL (minimum score 550) required for foreign applicants. Interview required for Dr.P.H. Accepts transfer applicants. Apply to Director of Admissions by August 1. Application fee $100. Phone: (909)558-4694; fax (909)558-8087.

ADMISSION STANDARDS. Selective for most programs. Usual minimum GPA: 3.0 (A = 4); 3.2 for Dr.P.H.

FINANCIAL AID. Annual awards from institutional funds: scholarships, fellowships, research assistantships, teaching assistantships, grants, internships, tuition waiver, Federal W/S, loans. Approved for VA benefits. Apply by May 5 to appropriate department chair for scholarships, fellowships, assistantships; to Financial Aid Office for all other programs. Phone: (909)558-4509 or (800)422-4558; e-mail: finaid@univ.llu.edu. Use FAFSA (School code: 001218) and institutional FAF. Aid available for part-time students.

DEGREE REQUIREMENTS. For M.P.H., M.H.A.: 52–54 quarter units minimum; practicum. For Dr.P.H.: 2-year full-time program; comprehensive exam; dissertation; final oral exam.

FIELDS OF STUDY.
Biostatistics. M.P.H., M.S.P.H.
Environmental Epidemiology.
Environmental and Occupational Health. Includes geographic information systems.
Epidemiology. Includes medical epidemiology, research epidemiology.
Global Epidemiology.
Global Health.
Global Health/Maternal and Child Health.
Health Care Administration. M.B.A.
Health Education.
Health Education/Maternal and Child Health.
Health Policy and Leadership.
Health Services Research.
International Health and Development. Dr.P.H.
Maternal and Child Health.
Nutrition. M.S., Dr.P.H.
Nutritional Epidemiology.
Preventive Care. Dr.P.H.
Public Health Nutrition.
Public Health Practice.

LONG ISLAND UNIVERSITY, BROOKLYN CAMPUS

Brooklyn, New York 11201-8423
Web site: www.brooklyn.liu.edu

Founded 1926. Coed. Private control. Semester system. Library: 400,000 volumes, 6500 subscriptions. Total Campus enrollment: 11,100.

Tuition: per credit, $835, Pharmacy $969. Rooms and apartments available for single and married students. Average academic year housing cost: single student $7500 (including board), married $6500 (room only). Apply to Director of Housing. Phone: (718)488-1046.

Enrollment: full-time 694, part-time 1098. Faculty: full-time 143, part-time 148. Degrees conferred: M.A., M.S., M.B.A., M.S.Acc., M.P.A., M.S.Ed., Pharm.D., Ph.D.

Graduate Programs

ADMISSION REQUIREMENTS. Transcripts, GRE/GMAT, two letters of recommendation required in support of application. TOEFL (minimum score 500), affidavit of financial support required for international applicants. Interview not required. Accepts transfer applicants. Graduates of unaccredited institutions not considered. Apply to Graduate Admissions Office at least 1 month prior to beginning of semester. Application fee $30. Phone: (718)403-1011; fax: (718)797-2399.

ADMISSION STANDARDS. Competitive to relatively open. Usual minimum average 2.75 (A = 4).

FINANCIAL AID. Scholarships, teaching fellowships, research assistantships, administrative assistantships, teaching assistantships, Federal W/S, loans. Approved for VA benefits. Apply by

May 1 (Fall), November 1 (Spring), March 1 (Summer) to appropriate department chair for scholarships, fellowships, assistantships; to Graduate Admissions Office for all other programs. Use FAFSA and institutional FAF. Phone: (718)488-1037; fax: (718)488-3343.

DEGREE REQUIREMENTS. For M.A., M.S., M.S.Ed.: 30–36 semester hours minimum, at least 24 in residence; thesis for many departments; final oral/written exam. For M.B.A., M.P.A.: 36 credits beyond core; thesis/nonthesis option; comprehensive exam. For Ph.D.: by advisement.

FIELDS OF STUDY.

SCHOOL OF BUSINESS, PUBLIC ADMINISTRATION AND INFORMATION SCIENCES:
Accounting. M.S.
Business Administration. M.B.A.
Computer Science. M.S.
Health Administration. M.H.A.
Human Resources Management. M.S.
Public Administration. M.P.A.
Taxation. M.S.

SCHOOL OF EDUCATION:
Adolescent Urban Education.
Bilingual Counseling.
Bilingual Education.
Childhood Urban Education
Early Childhood Urban Education.
Education Technology Innovation in Urban Settings.
Literacy.
Mental Health Counseling.
School Counseling.
School Leadership.
School Psychology.
Special Education Childhood and Adolescent.
TESOL.

SCHOOL OF HEALTH PROFESSION:
Advance Athletic Training and Sports Sciences.
Community Health.
Health Sciences.
Occupational Therapy.
Physical Therapy.

RICHARD L. CONOLLY COLLEGE OF LIBERAL ARTS AND SCIENCES:
Biology.
Chemistry.
Communication Sciences and Disorders.
English.
Media Arts.
New Media Art and Performance.
Political Science.
Psychology.
Urban Studies.

SCHOOL OF NURSING:
Adult Nurse Practitioner.
Family Nurse Practitioner.
Geriatric Primary Care Practitioner.
Nursing and Health Care Management.

ARNOLD & MARIE SCHWARTZ COLLEGE OF PHARMACY AND HEALTH SCIENCES:
Cosmetic Science.
Drug Regulatory Affairs.
Pharmaceutics. Ph.D.
Industrial Pharmacy.
Pharmacy Administration.
Pharmacology/Toxicology.

LONG ISLAND UNIVERSITY, C.W. POST CAMPUS

Brookville, New York 11548-1300
Web site: www.cwpost.liu.edu

Established 1954. Coed. Private control. Semester system. Special facilities: Hillwood Art Museum, Center for Aging, Tilles Center for Performing Arts, Accounting and Tax Research Library, Center for Economic Research, Center for Business Research. Library: 1,297,800 volumes, 11,446 subscriptions.

Tuition: per credit $790. Rooms and apartments available for single and married students. Average academic year housing cost: $4500 (room only), $7500 (including board). Contact Director of Housing for both on- and off-campus housing information. Phone: (516)299-2326.

Graduate Division

Graduate study since 1954. Enrollment: full-time 933, part-time 1537. Faculty: full-time 470. Degrees conferred: M.A., M.S., M.B.A., M.S.Ed., M.F.A., M.P.A., A.C., Ph.D., Psy.D.

ADMISSION REQUIREMENTS. Official transcripts, GRE/GMAT, 2 letters of recommendation, personal statement required in support of applications. Department interview may be required. All requirements vary by department. TOEFL or ASPECT program required for international applicants. Accepts transfer applicants. Graduates of unaccredited institutions not considered. Apply to Graduate Admissions Office at least 1 month prior to beginning of semester. Application fee $30. Phone: (516)299-2900; fax: (516)299-2137; e-mail: enroll@cwpost.liu.edu.

ADMISSION STANDARDS. Selective to relatively open. Usual minimum average: 2.5 (A = 4).

FINANCIAL AID. Scholarships, research/teaching assistantships, fellowships, internships, Federal W/S, loans. Approved for VA benefits. Apply by July 1 (Fall), October 1 (Spring), April 1 (Summer) to appropriate department chair for fellowships, assistantships; to Graduate Admissions Office for scholarships; to Financial Aid Office for all other programs. Phone: (516)299-2338. Use FAFSA, TAP for New York State residents. Aid available for part-time students.

DEGREE REQUIREMENTS. For M.A., M.S., 30–36 semester hours minimum, at least 24 in residence; thesis/nonthesis option for many departments; final oral/written exam. For M.B.A., M.P.A.: 48 credits beyond core; thesis/nonthesis option; comprehensive exam. For M.F.A.: 60 credits minimum beyond bachelor's, at least 45 in residence; project.

FIELDS OF STUDY.

COLLEGE OF ARTS AND SCIENCES:
Applied Behavior Analysis.
Applied Mathematics.
Biology.
Clinical Psychology. Psy.D. only.
Earth Science.
English.
Environmental Studies.
History.
Interdisciplinary Studies.
Political Science.
Psychology.
Spanish.

COLLEGE OF INFORMATION AND COMPUTER SCIENCE:
Archives and Records Management. A.C.
Information Studies.
Information Systems.
Information Technology Education.
Library and Information Science.
Management Engineering.
Public Library Director. A.C.
Rare Books and Special Collections.
School Media Specialist. A.C.

COLLEGE OF MANAGEMENT:
Accounting.
Business Administration.
Criminal Justice. Includes security administration.
Finance.
Fraud Examination. Certificate.
Health-Care Administration.
International Business.
Nonprofit Management.
Public Administration.
Strategic Management—Accounting.
Taxation.

SCHOOL OF EDUCATION:
Adolescence Education (Grades 7–12).
Art Education (Birth–Grade 12).
Biology. Includes adolescence, middle childhood.
Childhood Education (Grades 1–6).
Childhood Education/Special Education (Birth–Grade 6).
Childhood Education/Literacy (Birth–Grade 6).
Educational Technology.
Earth Science. Includes adolescence, middle childhood.
Early Childhood Education (Birth–Grade 2).
English. Include adolescence, middle childhood.
Literacy (Birth–Grade 6).
Mathematics. Includes adolescence, middle childhood.
Mental Health Counseling.
Music Education (Birth–Grade 12).
School Building Leader.
School District Leader.
Social Studies. Includes adolescence, middle childhood.
Spanish. Includes adolescence, middle childhood.
Special Education (Grades 1–6).
Speech-Language Pathology.
Teaching English to Speakers of Other Languages.

SCHOOL OF HEALTH PROFESSIONS:
Advanced Practice Nursing.
Biological Science. Includes hematology, immunology, medical chemistry, medical microbiology.
Cardiovascular Perfusion.
Clinical Laboratory Management.
Dietetics.
Family Nurse Practitioner Studies.
Medical Biology.
Nursing Education.
Nutrition.

SCHOOL OF VISUAL AND PERFORMING ARTS:
Art.
Fine Art and Design.
Interactive Media Arts.
Music.
Theater.

LONGWOOD UNIVERSITY

Farmville, Virginia 23909-1800
Web site: www.longwood.edu

Founded 1839. Located 65 miles W of Richmond. CGS member. Coed. State control. Semester system. Library: 325,290 volumes, 5000 subscriptions.

Tuition: per credit, resident $180, nonresident $504. Limited housing for graduate students in Fall and Spring semesters. Contact Director of Housing for on- and off-campus information. Phone: (434)395-2080.

Graduate Studies

Graduate study since 1954. Enrollment: full- and part-time 309. College faculty: full-time 4, part-time 70. Degrees conferred: M.A., M.S.

ADMISSION REQUIREMENTS. Transcripts, 2 letters of recommendation, essay required in support of application. TOEFL required for international applicants. Accepts transfer applicants. Graduates of unaccredited colleges not considered. Apply by May 1 (Fall), October 15 (Spring) to the Director of Graduate Studies. Application fee $40. Phone: (434)395-2012; e-mail: graduate@longwood.lwc.edu.

ADMISSION STANDARDS. Selective. Usual minimum average: 2.5 (A = 4).

FINANCIAL AID. Assistantships, Federal W/S, loans. Apply to the appropriate department for assistantships; to the Office of Financial Aid for loans. Phone: (434)395-2077. No specified closing date. Use FAFSA.

DEGREE REQUIREMENTS. For M.A.: 30 credit hours minimum, at least 24 in residence; thesis; oral defense. For M.S.: 30–36 credit hours minimum, at least 24 in residence; thesis/nonthesis option; comprehensive exam for nonthesis option.

FIELDS OF STUDY.
Business Administration. Includes accounting, general business, retail management. M.B.A.
Communication Sciences and Disorder. M.S.
Education. Includes community and college counseling, curriculum and instruction specialist (K–8 mathematics, LD, E/BD and mild MR, modern languages, music), educational leadership, elementary curriculum and instruction specialist, elementary education, guidance and counseling, literacy and culture, school library media, special education. M.S.
English. Includes creative writing, English education and writing, literature. M.A.
Sociology. Includes criminal justice. M.S.

LORAS COLLEGE
Dubuque, Iowa 52004-0178
Web site: www.loras.edu

Founded 1839. Coed. Private control. Roman Catholic. Semester system. Special facilities: Bioethics Resource Center, Center for Business and Research, Center for Dubuque Area History, Center for Environmental Research. Library: 355,000 volumes, 11,000 subscriptions.

Tuition: per credit hour $400. On-campus housing for graduate students during summer only; none for married students. Average summer housing cost: $650 for six-week summer session. Contact Office of Student Life for housing information. Phone: (563)588-7137.

Graduate Division

Graduate enrollment: full-time 13, part-time 86. Faculty teaching graduate students: full-time 22, part-time 5. Degree conferred: M.A.

ADMISSION REQUIREMENTS. Official transcripts, GRE/MAT, 2 letters of recommendation required in support of application.

Interview required by some departments. TOEFL required for international applicants. Accepts transfer applicants. Apply to Office of Admissions at least 6 weeks prior to registration. Application fee $25. Phone: (563)588-7166, (800)245-6727, ext. 7166.

ADMISSION STANDARDS. Selective. Usual minimum average: 2.75 (A = 4).

FINANCIAL AID. Limited to loans. Phone: (563)588-7339. Use FAFSA.

DEGREE REQUIREMENTS. For M.A.: 30–39 semester hours minimum, at least 24 in residence; admission to candidacy; comprehensive exam (varies by department); reading knowledge of one foreign language; thesis/nonthesis option. For M.M.: 34 semester credits; admission to candidacy; capstone experience; internship.

FIELDS OF STUDY.
Clinical Psychology.
Counseling Psychology.
Educational Leadership.
General Psychology.
Ministry.
Special Education.
Theology.

LOUISIANA STATE UNIVERSITY AND AGRICULTURAL AND MECHANICAL COLLEGE
Baton Rouge, Louisiana 70803
Web site: www.lsu.edu

Established 1860. CGS member. Coed. State control. Semester system. Member institution of Organization for Tropical Studies. Special facilities: Coastal Studies Institute, System Network Computer Center, Center for French and Francophone Studies, Center for Life Course and Population Studies, Southern Regional Climate Center, Louisiana Office of State Climatology, The U.S. Civil War Center, Eric Voegelin Institute for American Renaissance Studies, Public Management Program, Louisiana Real Estate Research Institute, Louisiana Education Policy Research Center, Center for Scientific and Mathematical Literacy, Hazardous Waste Research Center, Louisiana Transportation Research Center, Louisiana Water Resource Research Institute, Institute for Recyclable Materials, Remote Sensing and Image Processing Laboratory, Center for Coastal Energy and Environmental Resources, Basin Research Institute, Center for Energy Studies, Coastal Ecology Institute, Coastal Fisheries Institute, Mining and Mineral Resources Research Institute, Wetland Biogeochemistry Institute, National Ports and Waterways Institute, Office of Sea Grant Development, Louisiana Space Consortium, Museum of Art, Vascular Plant Herbarium, Mycological Herbarium, Rural Life Museum, LSU Agricultural Center, Pennington Biomedical Research Center, Museum of Natural Science, Nuclear Science Center, Center for Advanced Microstructures and Devices, T. Henry Williams Center for Oral History. Founding member of the Council of Sponsoring Institutions of Oak Ridge Associated Universities. According to The Center at University of Florida, the University is ranked 65th for total University research expenditures with $26,677,000. In 2004, the University awarded 240 doctorates, which ranked it 62nd among all U.S. institutions eligible to award that degree. The Library: approximately 1,400,000 volumes, 29,580 subscriptions. Total University enrollment: 31,264.

Annual tuition: full-time resident $2900, nonresident $12,990. On-campus housing for 578 married students, unlimited for graduate men and women. Average academic year housing cost: $3500 for married students, $6330 (including board) for single students. Apply to Director of Housing. Phone: (225)578-8663.

Graduate School

Graduate study since 1868. Enrollment: full-time 3500, part-time 1200. Faculty teaching graduate students: full-time 1200, part-time 27. Degrees conferred: M.A., M.B.A., M.Ed., M.L.A., M.M.Ed., M.M., M.N.S., M.A.H., M.F.A., M.Ap.Stat., M.E., M.P.A., M.S.W., Ed.S., D.M.A., D.V.M., M.M.E., M.L.I.S., C.L.I.S., Ph.D.

ADMISSION REQUIREMENTS. Transcripts, GRE/GMAT required in support of School's application. Online application available. TOEFL (minimum score 550), financial statement required for international applicants. TSE required of international students seeking financial aid. Interview not required. Accepts transfer applicants. Graduates of unaccredited institutions not considered. Apply to the Office of Graduate Admissions by May 15 (Fall), October 15 (Spring), May 15 (Summer). Application fee $25. Phone: (225)578-1641.

ADMISSION STANDARDS. Selective for most departments, very selective for others. Usual minimum average: 3.0 (A = 4).

FINANCIAL AID. Annual awards from institutional funds: scholarships, research assistantships/teaching assistantships, fellowships, internships, grants, Federal W/S, loans. Approved for VA benefits. Apply to appropriate department chair for scholarships, fellowships, assistantships; to Office of Financial Aid for all other programs. No specified closing date; priority date for Fall: January 15. Phone: (225)388-3103; fax: (225)578-6300. Use FAFSA. About 60% of students receive aid other than loans from University and outside sources. Aid sometimes available for part-time students.

DEGREE REQUIREMENTS. For master's: 30 semester hours minimum, at least 24 in residence; thesis; final oral/written exam; or 36 semester hours minimum, at least 30 in residence; final oral/written exam in some departments; reading knowledge of one foreign language for some departments. For Ph.D.: 60 semester hours minimum beyond the master's, at least one year in continuous residence; oral/written qualifying exam in some departments; oral/written general exam; dissertation; final oral exam.

FIELDS OF STUDY.
Accounting.
Agricultural Economics and Agribusiness.
Agronomy.
Animal Science.
Architecture.
Art (School of). Includes art education, art history, photography, studio art.
Biological and Agricultural Engineering.
Biological Sciences. Includes biochemistry, genetics, microbiology, plant biology, zoology.
Business Administration.
Chemical Engineering.
Chemistry.
Civil and Environmental Engineering.
Communication Sciences and Disorders.
Communication Studies.
Comparative Biomedical Science.
Comparative Literature.
Computer Science. Includes systems science.
Construction Management and Industrial Engineering.
Curriculum and Instruction.
Dairy Science.
Economics.
Educational Theory, Policy and Practice.
Electrical and Computer Engineering.
Engineering Sciences.
English.
Entomology.
Environmental Studies.
Experimental Statistics.
Finance.
Food Science.
Foreign Language and Literature.
French Studies.
Genetics.
Geography and Anthropology.
Geology and Geophysics.
History.
Horticulture.
Human Ecology.
Information Systems and Decision Science.
Kinesiology.
Landscape Architecture (School of). •
Liberal Arts.
Library and Information Science (School of).
Linguistics.
Management.
Marketing.
Mass Communication.
Mathematics.
Mechanical Engineering.
Music (School of).
Natural Sciences.
Oceanography and Coastal Sciences.
Pathobiological Sciences.
Petroleum Engineering.
Philosophy and Religious Studies.
Physics and Astronomy.
Plant Pathology and Crop Physiology.
Political Science.
Psychology. Includes clinical, developmental, industrial and organizational, school.
Public Administration.
Renewable Natural Resources.
Social Work (School of).
Sociology.
Theater.
Veterinary Clinical Sciences.

Paul M. Hebert Law Center

Web site: www.law.lsu.edu

Established 1906 as LSU Law School, renamed in 1979. ABA approved since 1926. AALS member. Semester system. Full-time, day study only. Special facility: Center of Civil Law Studies, Louisiana Judicial College, Mineral Law Institute, Pugh Institute for Justice. Special programs: summer study abroad in France at University of Aix-Marseille III Law School. Law library: 836,843 volumes, 10,231 subscriptions; has LEXIS, NEXIS, WESTLAW, DIALOG; is both a State and Federal Government Depository.

Annual tuition: resident $12,124, nonresident $21,220. Off-campus housing and personal expenses: approximately $15,900.

Enrollment: first-year class 233; total full-time 566 (men 51%, women 49%, minorities 10%); no part-time students. Faculty: full-time 35, part-time 18. Student to faculty ratio 16.6 to 1. Degrees conferred: J.D., J.D.-M.B.A., J.D.-M.P.A., LL.M., M.C.L. (only for persons who have completed a basic legal education and received a university degree in law in another country).

ADMISSION REQUIREMENTS. For J.D. program: LSDAS Law School report, bachelor's degree, transcripts, LSAT (not later than December), personal statement, two letters of recommendation required in support of application. Preference given to state residents. Accepts transfer applicants. Graduates from unaccredited institutions not considered. Apply to Admissions Office after November 1, before February 1. Admits Fall only. Application fee $25. For Graduate Program: transcripts required in support of application, TOEFL required for foreign applicants whose native language is not English. Apply to Office of Admissions. Phone: (225)578-8646; fax: (225)578-8647; e-mail: admissions@ law.lsu.edu.

ADMISSION STANDARDS. Selective. Accepts approximately 28% of all students. Number of applicants 1682; number of acceptance 467; number enrolled 218; LSAT (75% of students have a score at or above 154); GPA (75% of students have a GPA at or above 3.23). *U.S. News & World Report* ranking is in the second tier (tied at 91st) of all U.S. law schools.

FINANCIAL AID. Limited scholarships, loans. Apply to LSU Office of Financial Aid by April 1. Phone: (225)578-3103. Use FAFSA (School code: 002010). Approximately 41% of students receive some form of financial assistance.

DEGREE REQUIREMENTS. For J.D.: 97 semester hours minimum, at least 29 in residence. For LL.M., M.C.L.: 24 semester hours minimum, at least two semesters in residence; thesis.

School of Social Work

Graduate study since 1937. Semester system. Annual tuition: resident $2900, nonresident $12,990.

Enrollment: full-time 153, part-time 45. School faculty: full-time 14, part-time 10. Degrees conferred: M.S.W., Ph.D.

ADMISSION REQUIREMENTS. Transcripts, GRE, three letters of recommendation required in support of Graduate School's application as well as the School's application. TOEFL (minimum score 550), financial statement required for international applicants. Interview may be required. Accepts transfer applicants. Graduates of unaccredited institutions not considered. Apply to Office of Student Services of School and Graduate School by February 15. Application fee $25. Phone: (225)578-5875.

ADMISSION STANDARDS. Selective. Usual minimum average: 3.0 (A = 4). GRE combined score (analytic section not included): 1000.

FINANCIAL AID. Child Welfare Stipends, Corrections Stipends, scholarships, teaching assistantships, research assistantships, internships, minority student tuition waivers, Federal W/S, loans. Approved for VA benefits. Apply by March 1 to Office of Admissions. Phone: (225)578-3103; fax: (225)578-6300. Use FAFSA. About 30% of students receive aid from School and outside sources. Aid available for part-time students.

DEGREE REQUIREMENTS. For M.S.W.: 60-hour program, including internship. Advanced standing awarded to qualified B.S.W. degree holders. For Ph.D.: 48 semester hours beyond the master's; at least two semesters in residence; general exam; practicum; dissertation; final defense.

School of Veterinary Medicine
Web site: www.vetmed.lsu.edu

Admitted its first student in 1973–74. Semester system. Library: 40,000 volumes, 1000 subscriptions.

Annual tuition and fees: residents $6734, nonresidents $19,484. Off-campus housing only. Total average cost for other expenses: $7,500.

Enrollment: first-year class 80, total 326 (men 40%, women 60%, minorities 5%, state residents 70%). Faculty: full-time 75, part-time 10. Degrees conferred: D.V.M., D.V.M.-M.S., D.V.M.-Ph.D. The M.S. and Ph.D. are offered through the Graduate School.

ADMISSION REQUIREMENTS. VMCAS report, transcripts showing completion of sixty-six hours of preprofessional college work, GRE, three recommendations, animal/veterinary experience,

essay required in support of application. Interview always required. Accepts transfer applicants. Preference given to state and contract residents. Apply to Assistant Dean after September 1, prior to October 1. Application fee $50. Phone: (225)578-9538; fax: (225)578-9546.

ADMISSION STANDARDS. Selective. Accepts about 30–35% of all applicants. Accepts nine students from Arkansas, fifteen from outside state. Usual minimum UGPA: 2.75 (A = 4). GRE mean score (V + Q) 1121; mean UGPA 3.55.

FINANCIAL AID. Fellowships, assistantships, full tuition waivers, Federal W/S, loans. Apply to Office of Financial Aid after acceptance. Use FAFSA.

DEGREE REQUIREMENTS. For D.V.M.: 152 semester hours and four years in residence. For M.S. and Ph.D.: see Graduate School listing above.

FIELDS OF GRADUATE STUDY.
Comparative Biomedical Sciences. Includes anatomy, cell and molecular biology, cancer cell biology, toxicology (including inhalation toxicology), environmental health science and ecological chemistry, pharmacology, physiology. M.S., Ph.D.
Equine Health Studies. Interdisciplinary and interdepartmental. M.S., Ph.D.
Infectious Disease. Multidisciplinary program. Includes molecular genetics, infectious disease.
Pathobiologicsl Sciences. Includes microbiological sciences. Immunological sciences, zoological sciences, biomolecular sciences. M.S., Ph.D.
Veterinary Clinical Sciences. Includes clinical research, teaching and administration of clinical trials in the private and governmental sectors. M.S. Ph.D.

LOUISIANA STATE UNIVERSITY HEALTH SCIENCES CENTER
New Orleans, Louisiana 70112-2223
Web site: www.lsuhsc.edu

The Health Sciences Center was established as a separate unit in 1965 and includes six professional schools in both New Orleans and Shreveport. CGS member. Public control. Semester system. Special facilities: Pennington Biomedical Research Center, Cardiovascular Center, Center for Arthritis and Rheumatology, Center for Molecular and Human Genetics, Ernest N. Morial Asthma, Allergy, and Respiratory Disease Center, LSU Eye Center, Feist-Weiller Cancer Center, Neuroscience Center, Stanley S. Scott Cancer Center. The University's NIH ranking is 113th among U.S. institutions with 105 awards/grants worth $47,921,427. Library: 389,000 volumes, 3500 subscriptions. Total enrollment at University's Health Sciences Centers: 2965.

Annual tuition: full-time, resident $4626, nonresident $7126. On-campus housing available for both single and married students. Average academic year housing cost: $6800–$9600 (including board); off-campus housing $450 per month. Contact Director of Housing for both on- and off-campus housing information. Phone: (504)568-6260.

School of Graduate Studies

Graduate study since 1967. Enrollment: full-time 83, part-time 21. Faculty teaching graduate students: full-time 138, part-time 29. Degrees conferred: M.S., Ph.D.

ADMISSION REQUIREMENTS. Two official transcripts, two letters of recommendation, GRE required in support of School's application. TOEFL required of international applicants. Interview not required. Accepts transfer applicants. Apply to the Office of Graduate Studies; no specified closing date. Rolling admissions process. Application fee $30. Phone: (504)568-2211; fax: (504)568-5588; e-mail: gradschool@lsuhsc.edu.

ADMISSION STANDARDS. Selective. Usual minimum average: 2.75 (A = 4).

FINANCIAL AID. Fellowships, research assistantships, teaching assistantships, tuition waivers, stipends, Federal W/S, loans. Apply to appropriate department chair for assistantships, fellowships; to Office of Financial Aid for all other programs. Phone: (504)568-4820. Priority deadlines: April 15 (Fall), November 15 (Spring), April 15 (Summer). Use FAFSA and institutional FAF. About 20% of students receive aid other than loans from University and outside sources. Aid sometimes available for part-time students.

DEGREE REQUIREMENTS. For M.S.: 30–36 semester hours minimum, at least 24–36 in residence; thesis/nonthesis option; final written/oral exam for some programs. For Ph.D.: 42 semester hours minimum beyond the master's degree, at least two years in full-time residence; qualifying exam; foreign language proficiency for some programs; dissertation; final oral exam.

FIELDS OF STUDY.
Biochemistry and Molecular Biology.
Biostatistics.
Cell Biology and Anatomy.
Genetics.
Microbiology, Immunology, and Parasitology.
Neuroscience. Ph.D. only.
Oral Biology.
Pathology.
Pharmacology and Experimental Therapeutics. Ph.D. only.
Physiology.

School of Dentistry
Web site: www.lsusd.lsuhsc.edu

Established 1966. Located in New Orleans at Health Science Center. Special facility: Center of Excellence in Oral and Craniofacial Biology. Library: 8000 volumes, 200 subscriptions.

Annual tuition: resident $9,744, nonresident $22,118. No on-campus housing available. Average off-campus living expenses: approximately $12,000. Total average cost for all other expenses: $7,000.

Enrollment: first-year class 60, total 330 (men 56%, women 44%, minorities 9%, state residents 93%). Faculty: full-time 87, part-time 108. Degrees conferred: D.D.S., Certificate.

ADMISSION REQUIREMENTS. Transcripts, DAT, interview, recommendations, at least three years of college required in support of School's application. Preference given to residents of Louisiana and Arkansas. Graduates of unaccredited colleges not considered. Accepts transfer applicants. Apply to Assistant Dean of Admissions after September 1, before February 28. Application fee $50. Phone: (504)619-8579; fax: (504)614-8740.

ADMISSION STANDARDS. Competitive. Accepts about 40–50% of all applicants. Number enrolled 60 (4 Arkansas residents, 5 other out-of-state residents). Usual minimum UGPA: 2.75 (A = 4). Mean DAT: academic 17, PAT 16; mean UGPA 3.5.

FINANCIAL AID. Limited. Scholarships, loans. Apply to Medical Center's Office of Financial Aid after acceptance. Phone: (504)619-8556. About 90% of students receive aid from School and outside sources.

DEGREE REQUIREMENTS. For D.D.S.: satisfactory completion of four-year program.

FIELDS OF POSTGRADUATE STUDY.
Advanced General Dentistry. Certificate.
Endodontics.
Maxillofacial Prosthetics. Certificate.
Oral Biology. M.S.
Oral Medicine. Certificate.
Orthodontics. Certificate.
Pediatric Dentistry. Certificate.
Periodontics. Certificate.
Prosthodontics. Certificate.

School of Medicine
Web site: www.medschool.lsuhsc.edu

Established 1931. Library: 176,000 volumes, 1500 subscriptions. NIH ranking is 113 with 105 awards/grants worth $42,921,427.

Annual tuition: resident $14,086, nonresident $28,233. On-campus housing for 300 married and single students; off-campus housing also available. Total average figure for all other expenses: $15,000-$17,000.

Enrollment: first-year class 171 (EDP 10), total 703 (men 50%, women 50%, minorities 8%, state residents 96%). Faculty: full-time 750, part-time 115. Degrees conferred: M.D., M.D.-Ph.D.

ADMISSION REQUIREMENTS. AMCAS report, transcripts, MCAT required in support of application. Interview by invitation only. Has EDP; apply June 1–August 1. Applicants must have completed at least three years of college study. Accepts state residents only. Accepts transfer applicants. Apply after June 1, before November 15 to Admissions Office. Application fee $50. Phone: (504)568-6262; fax: (504)568-7701.

ADMISSION STANDARDS. Selective. Accepts about 20% of all applicants. Number of applications 897 (n/a out-of-state); number interviewed 407 (n/a out-of-state); number of acceptance n/a (n/a out-of-state); number enrolled 171 (n/a out-of-state). Mean Composite MCAT 10.0; mean UGPA 3.70.

FINANCIAL AID. Scholarships, merit scholarships, minority scholarships, Grants-in-Aid, State and institutional loans, HEAL, alternative loan programs, NIH stipends, Federal Perkins loans, Stafford Subsidized and Unsubsidized Loans, Service Commitment Scholarship programs are available. Stipends/tuition waivers may be available for Combined Degree candidates. Financial Aid applications and information are given out at the on-campus by-invitation interview. For merit scholarships, the selection criteria places heavy reliance on MCAT and undergraduate GPA. Contact the Student Financial Aid Office for current information. Phone: (504) 568-4820. For most financial assistance and all Federal programs submit FAFSA to a Federal processor (School code: 002014), also submit Financial Aid Transcript, Federal Income Tax forms. About 88% of students receive aid from school and outside sources.

DEGREE REQUIREMENTS. For M.D.: satisfactory completion of four-year program; passing Step 2 of the USMLE prior to graduation.

FIELDS OF GRADUATE STUDY.
Biochemistry and Molecular Biology.
Biostatics. M.S. only.
Cell Biology and Anatomy.
Genetics.
Microbiology, Immunology, and Parasitology.
Neurosciences.
Oral Biology. M.S. only.
Pathology.
Pharmacology and Experimental Therapeutics.
Physiology.

School of Medicine in Shreveport

Web site: www.sh.lsuhsc.edu

Established 1966. Located in Shreveport (71130-3932). Semester system. Library: 98,000 volumes, 1300 subscriptions.

Annual tuition: resident $19,452, nonresident $47,850. No on-campus housing available. Total average figure for all other expenses: $13,940.

Enrollment: first-year class 104 (EDP 5), total 387 (men 50%, women 50%, minorities 11%, state residents 98%). Faculty: full-time 125, part-time 22. Degrees conferred: M.D., M.D.-Ph.D.

ADMISSION REQUIREMENTS. AMCAS reports, transcripts, MCAT, recommendations, interview, secondary application required in support of application. Interview by invitation only. Has EDP; apply June 1–August 1. Applicants must have completed at least three years of college. Accepts transfer applicants. Graduates of unaccredited colleges are considered. Accepts state residents only. Apply to Admission Committee after June 1, before November 15. Application fee $50. Phone: (318)675-5190; fax: (318)675-8690.

ADMISSION STANDARDS. Selective. Accepts about 15% of all applicants. Number of applications 967 (n/a out-of-state); number interviewed 226 (n/a out-of-state); number of acceptance n/a (n/a out-of-state); number enrolled 104 (n/a out-of-state). Mean Composite MCAT 9.0; mean UGPA 3.70.

FINANCIAL AID. Scholarships, long-term loans. Apply to Office of Student Affairs after acceptance, before March 31. About 80% of students receive aid from school and outside sources.

DEGREE REQUIREMENTS. For M.D.: satisfactory completion of four-year program.

FIELDS OF GRADUATE STUDY.
Biochemistry and Molecular Biology.
Cellular Biology and Anatomy.
Microbiology and Immunology.
Molecular and Cellular Physiology.
Pharmacology, Toxicology and Neuroscience.

School of Nursing—Graduate Program

Web site: www.nursing.lsuhsc.edu

Graduate study since 1972. Semester system. Annual tuition: resident $3604, nonresident $6104. On-campus housing available. Enrollment: full-time 73, part-time 135. Faculty: full-time 11, part-time 5. Degrees conferred: M.N., D.N.S.

ADMISSION REQUIREMENTS. Transcripts, Louisiana license or current license to practice in any state, GRE/MAT, three letters of recommendation required in support of School's application. TOEFL (minimum score 550) required for foreign applicants. Accepts transfer applicants. Graduates of unaccredited institutions not considered. Apply to Graduate Program by March 15. Application fee $50. Phone: (504)568-4141.

ADMISSION STANDARDS. Selective. Usual minimum average: 3.0 (A = 4); minimum GRE: combined 1500, MAT 50.

FINANCIAL AID. Limited to three graduate assistantships, fifteen grants, Federal W/S, loans. Approved for VA benefits. Apply to the Graduate Program for assistantships, grants; to the Financial Aid Office for all other programs. Phone: (504)568-4820; fax: (504)568-5545. Use FAFSA and institutional FAF.

DEGREE REQUIREMENTS. For M.N.: 38–46 credits minimum, at least three semesters of full-time study; up to 12 credits may be transferred; clinical practice; thesis optional. For D.N.S.:

48 credits minimum, four semesters of full-time study; up to 15 credits may be transferred; candidacy; comprehensive exam; dissertation; oral defense.

FIELDS OF STUDY.
Advanced Public/Community Health Nursing.
Clinical Nurse Specialist.
Nurse Anesthesia.
Nurse Practitioner.
Nursing Administration. M.N., D.N.S.

LOUISIANA STATE UNIVERSITY IN SHREVEPORT

Shreveport, Louisiana 71115
Web site: www.lsus.edu

Founded 1967. Coed. State control. Semester system. Special facilities: Life Science Museum, Pioneer Heritage Center, Social Science Research and Analysis Unit. Library: 279,821 volumes, 1150 subscriptions. Total University enrollment: 4400.

Tuition/fees: per credit, resident $185, nonresident $393. Limited on-campus housing. Contact Director, University Court Apartments for housing information. Phone: (318)797-8588.

Graduate Studies

Graduate study since 1978. Enrollment: full-time 108, part-time 322. Faculty teaching graduate students: full-time 91, part-time 29. Degrees conferred: M.L.S., M.B.A., M.Ed., M.S.T.

ADMISSION REQUIREMENTS. Transcripts, letters of recommendation, GRE/GMAT required in support of application. TOEFL (minimum score 550) and financial affidavit required of international applicants. Interview not required. Accepts transfer applicants. Apply to the Office of Admissions at least 30 days prior to anticipated registration date. Application fee $10, $20 for international applicants. Phone: (318)797-5061; fax: (318)797-5286.

ADMISSION STANDARDS. Selective. Usual minimum average: 3.0 (A = 4).

FINANCIAL AID. Graduate assistantships, Federal W/S, loans. Approved for VA benefits. Apply to appropriate department chair for assistantships; to Office of Financial Aid for all other programs. No specified closing date. Phone: (318)797-5363; fax: (318)797-5180. Use FAFSA and institutional FAF. About 10% of students receive aid other than loans from University and outside sources. Aid sometimes available for part-time students.

DEGREE REQUIREMENTS. For master's: 30–48 semester hours minimum, at least 24–36 in residence; thesis/nonthesis option/final project; final written/oral exam for some programs. For M.B.A.: 54 credit program, at least 30 credits in residence.

FIELDS OF STUDY.
Biochemistry and Molecular Biology. Offered cooperatively with LSU Health Center. M.S.
Business Administration. Includes accounting, finance, health care management, international business, marketing, real estate. M.B.A.
Cellular Biology and Anatomy. Offered cooperatively with LSU Health Center. M.S.
Computer Systems Technology. M.S.
Counseling Psychology. M.S.
Education. Includes elementary, secondary, administration. M.Ed.

English. Offered cooperatively with LSU A&M, Louisiana Tech. M.A.

Environmental Science. Offered cooperatively with LSU A&M. M.S.

Health Administration. M.H.A.

History. Offered cooperatively with Louisiana Tech. M.A.

Human Services Administration. M.S.

Liberal Arts. M.L.A.

Microbiology and Immunology. Offered cooperatively with LSU Health Center. M.S.

Pharmacology and Therapeutics. Offered cooperatively with LSU Health Center. M.S.

Physiology and Biophysics. Offered cooperatively with LSU Health Center. M.S.

School Psychology. S.Sp.

System Technology. Interdisciplinary. M.S.S.T.

LOUISIANA TECH UNIVERSITY

Ruston, Louisiana 71272
Web site: www.latech.edu

Founded 1894. Located 72 miles E of Shreveport. Coed. State control. Quarter system. Special facilities: Center for Applied Physics Studies, Center for Biomedical Engineering and Rehabilitation Science, Center for Entrepreneurship and Information Technology, Center for Numerical Simulation and Modeling, Fitness Institute of Technology, Institute for Micromanufacturing, Trenchless Tech Center, Water Resource Center, Center for Robotics and Automated Manufacturing, Rehabilitation Engineering Research and Development Training Center, Small Business Institute. Library: more than 981,000 volumes, 6700 subscriptions.

Annual tuition: resident $3948, nonresident $9948. On-campus housing for 42 married students, 2052 men, 1860 women. Average academic year housing cost: for 3 quarters $4470–$5970 (including board) for single students. Apply to Director of Housing by July 15. Phone: (318)257-4917.

Graduate School

Authorized 1958. Enrollment: full-time 862, part-time 711. Faculty: full- and part-time 270. Degrees conferred: M.A., M.S., M.B.A., M.P.A., M.F.A., Specialist, D.B.A., Ph.D., D.Engr., Ed.D.

ADMISSION REQUIREMENTS. Transcripts, GRE/GMAT required in support of School's application. Three letters of recommendation, résumé for some programs. TOEFL (minimum score 550), financial affidavit required for foreign applicants. Interview not required. Accepts transfer applicants. Graduates of unaccredited institutions not considered. Apply to Admissions Office at least one month prior to registration. Application fee $30. Phone: (318)257-2924; fax: (318)257-4487.

ADMISSION STANDARDS. Selective. Usual minimum average: 3.0 (A = 4).

FINANCIAL AID. Scholarships, teaching fellowships, research fellowships, Federal W/S, loans. Approved for VA benefits. Apply at least five months prior to registration to department concerned for scholarships, fellowships; to Financial Aid Office for all other programs. Phone: (318)257-2641. Use FAFSA (School code: 002008) and institutional FAF. About 20% of students receive aid other than loans from University and outside sources. Aid sometimes available for part-time students.

DEGREE REQUIREMENTS. For master's: 30 semester hours minimum without thesis or creative project or including thesis or creative project, at least 24 in residence; final written/oral exam; reading knowledge of one foreign language for some majors. For D.B.A., Ph.D.: 60 credits minimum beyond the bachelor's, at least 24 in residence; qualifying exam; language requirement for some majors; dissertation; final oral exam.

FIELDS OF STUDY.

COLLEGE OF APPLIED AND NATURAL SCIENCES:
Biology. Includes cell and molecular biology, environmental biology, organismal biology. M.S.

Family and Consumer Sciences. M.S.

Health Information Management. M.H.I.M.

Molecular Sciences and Nanotechnology. M.S.

Nutrition and Dietetics. Includes clinical dietetics, community dietetics. M.S.

COLLEGE OF BUSINESS:
Accountancy. M.P.A.

Business Administration. M.B.A., D.B.A.

COLLEGE OF EDUCATION:
Adult Education. M.S.

Adapted Physical Education. M.S.

Biology. M.S.

Chemistry. M.S.

Counseling. Includes general, school. M.A.

Early Childhood Education. M.S.

Economics. M.S.

Educational Leadership. M.S.

Educational Psychology. Includes orientation and mobility. M.A.

Exercise Science. M.S.

English. M.S.

History. M.S.

Industrial/Organizational Psychology. M.A.

Library Science. M.S.

Mathematics. M.S.

Physical Education Teacher Preparation. M.S.

Physics. M.S.

Reading. M.S.

Special Education: Early Intervention. M.S.

Special Education: Mild/Moderate. M.S.

Technology. M.S.

COLLEGE OF ENGINEERING AND SCIENCE:
Biomedical Engineering. M.S.E., Ph.D.

Chemical Engineering. M.S.E.

Civil Engineering. M.S.E.

Computational Analysis and Modeling. Ph.D.

Computer Science. M.S.C.S.

Engineering. M.S.E., Ph.D.

Engineering and Technology Management. M.S.E.T.M.

Industrial Engineering. M.S.E.

Mathematics and Statistics. M.S.

Mechanical Engineering. M.S.E.

Microsystems Engineering.

Molecular Sciences and Nanotechnology. M.S.M.S.NT.

Physics. M.S.

COLLEGE OF LIBERAL ARTS:
Architecture. M.Arch.

Art. Includes interior design, communication design, photography, studio. M.F.A.

English. Includes literature, technical writing. M.A.

History. Includes southern history, history of culture and ideas, history of American foreign policy. M.A.

Speech. Includes speech communication, theatre. M.A.

Speech-Language Pathology and Audiology. M.A., D.Aud.

UNIVERSITY OF LOUISIANA AT LAFAYETTE

Lafayette, Louisiana 70504
Web site: www.louisiana.edu

Founded 1900. Located 110 miles W of New Orleans. CGS member. Coed. State control. Semester system. Special facilities: Center for Louisiana Studies, Acadiana Research Laboratory, Center for Crustacean Research, New Iberia Research Center, Center for Advanced Computer Studies, Center for Socioeconomic Education. Library: 986,000 volumes, 5000 subscriptions. Total University enrollment: 17,000.

Annual tuition: full-time, resident $3330, nonresident $9510; per credit, resident $93, nonresident $350. On-campus housing for 150 married students, 1397 men, 1168 women. Average academic year housing costs: single $3478 (including board); married $4500. Contact Director of Housing for both on- and off-campus housing information. Phone: (337)482-6471.

Graduate School

Graduate study since 1956. Enrollment: full-time 826, part-time 460. Faculty: full- and part-time 329. Degrees conferred: M.A., M.S., M.Ed., M.E., M.M., M.B.A., M.M.Ed., Ph.D.

ADMISSION REQUIREMENTS. Two official transcripts, GRE required in support of School's application. TOEFL required for international applicants. Interview not required. Accepts transfer applicants. Graduates of unaccredited institutions not considered. Apply to Dean (P.O. Box 44610) two months prior to registration. Application fee $20 (American), $30 (international). Phone: (337)482-6965; fax: (337)482-1333.

ADMISSION STANDARDS. Selective. Usual minimum average: 2.75 (A = 4).

FINANCIAL AID. Fellowships, research assistantships, teaching assistantships, internships, tuition waivers, Federal W/S, loans. Approved for VA benefits. Apply to Dean of Graduate School by May 1. Use FAFSA. Aid available for part-time students.

DEGREE REQUIREMENTS. For master's: 30 semester hours minimum, at least 24 in residence; final written/oral exam; reading knowledge of one foreign language in some majors; thesis required for most majors. For M.B.A.: 56 semester hours minimum, at least 30 in residence; computer proficiency. For Ph.D.: 50–60 semester hours beyond the master's, one year in full-time residence; proficiency in one language and research tool; general exam; dissertation; final oral exam.

FIELDS OF STUDY.
Applied Language and Speech Sciences. Ph.D.
Architecture.
Biology. Ph.D.
Business Administration. Includes health care administration.
Cognitive Science. Ph.D.
Communication.
Computer Engineering. Ph.D.
Computer Science. Ph.D.
Counselor Education.
Education. Includes administration and supervision, curriculum and instruction, education of the gifted.
Educational Leadership. Ed.D.
Engineering. Includes chemical, civil, mechanical, petroleum.
Engineering Management.
English. Includes American literature, British literature, creative writing, folklore studies, linguistics, rhetoric (Ph.D). M.A., Ph.D.
Francophone Studies. Ph.D.
French.
Geology.

History.
Mathematics. Ph.D.
Music.
Nursing. Includes adult health, adult psychiatric and mental health, nurse educator.
Physics.
Psychology.
Speech Pathology and Audiology.
Telecommunications.

UNIVERSITY OF LOUISIANA AT MONROE

Monroe, Louisiana 71209-0600
Web site: www.ulm.edu

Founded 1931. Located 100 miles E of Shreveport. Coed. State control. Semester system. Special facilities: Cancer Research Center, Louisiana Drug and Poison Information Center, Small Business Development Center, Center for Educational Research and Services, Herbarium, Human Performance Laboratory, Marriage and Family Counseling Center, Institute of Gerontology, Pharmaceutics Research and Technical Service center, Speech and Hearing center, Institute of Toxicology. Library: 645,612 volumes, 2900 current periodicals.

Annual tuition: full-time, resident $3358, nonresident $9316; per credit, resident and nonresident $289. On-campus housing for single students only. Average academic year housing costs: $4800 (including board) for single students. Contact Director of University Housing for both on- and off-campus housing information. Phone: (318)342-5240. Day-care facilities available.

Graduate Studies and Research

Established 1961. Enrollment: full-time 562, part-time 417. Graduate faculty: full-time 222, part-time 36. Degrees conferred: M.A., M.S., M.B.A., M.M., M.M.Ed., Ed.S., Ed.D., Ph.D.

ADMISSION REQUIREMENTS. Official transcripts, GRE or GMAT required in support of application. TOEFL required for international applicants. Interview not required. Accepts transfer applicants. Graduates of unaccredited institutions not considered. Apply to Registrar at least 60 days prior to date of enrollment. Application fee $20, $30 for non-U.S. citizens. Phone: (318)342-1036; fax: (318)342-1042.

ADMISSION STANDARDS. Selective. Usual minimum average: 2.5 (A = 4).

FINANCIAL AID. Annual awards from institutional funds: teaching assistantships, research assistantships, laboratory, nonteaching, Federal W/S, loans. Approved for VA benefits. Apply to Dean of Graduate Studies for assistantships; to Financial Aid for all other programs. No specified closing date. Phone: (318)342-3539. Use FAFSA. About 15% of students receive aid other than loans from University. Aid available for part-time students.

DEGREE REQUIREMENTS. For M.A., M.S., M.M.: 30 semester hours minimum, at least 20 in residence; field study/thesis/nonthesis option or final project (Pharmacy only); comprehensive written/oral exam. For M.B.A.: 33 hours minimum, at least 27 in residence. For M.Ed.: same as for M.A., except thesis is optional. For M.M.Ed.: same as for M.A., except recital for three hours or thesis for six may be elected. For Ed.S.: 60 semester hours minimum beyond the bachelor's, at least two semesters in residence; final written/oral exam. For Ph.D. (Pharmacy only): 60 semester hours minimum beyond the bachelor's, at least two semesters in residence; qualifying exam; reading knowledge of at least one foreign language; dissertation; final oral exam.

FIELDS OF STUDY.
Biology. M.S.
Business Administration. M.B.A.
Communication. M.A.
Communicative Disorders. M.S.
Counseling. M.Ed.
Criminal Justice. M.A.
Curriculum and Instruction. Includes early childhood, elementary education, instructional technology facilitator, middle school education, reading, secondary education, special education (academically gifted, early intervention, educational diagnostics, mild/moderate disabilities). M.Ed., Ed.D.
Educational Leadership. M.Ed., Ed.D.
Educational Technology Leadership. M.Ed.
English. Includes literary studies, creative writing. M.A.
Exercise Science. Includes clinical exercise physiology, applied exercise physiology. M.S.
Gerontology. Includes aging studies, long-term care administration, program administration. M.A.
History. M.A.
Marriage and Family Therapy. M.A., Ph.D.
Music. Includes conducting, music education, performance, theory/composition. M.M.
Pharmaceutical Sciences. Includes hospital pharmacy, medical chemistry, pharmaceutics, pharmacology/toxicology, pharmacy administration, pharmacognosy. M.S., Ph.D., D.Pharm.
Psychology. Includes experimental, psychometrics, school psychology. M.S.
Substance Abuse Counseling. M.A.
Teaching. Includes elementary education (grades 1–5), multiple levels (grades K–12), secondary education (grades 6–12), special education mild/moderate (grades 1–12). M.A.T.

UNIVERSITY OF LOUISVILLE
Louisville, Kentucky 40292-0001
Web site: www.louisville.edu

Founded 1798. Joined state university system in 1970. CGS member. Coed. State control. Semester system. Special facilities: sponsoring university of Oak Ridge Institute of Nuclear Studies in Tennessee, Applied Microcirculation Center, Cancer Center, Center for the Humanities, Institute for the Environment and Sustainable Development, Center for Leadership Studies, Performance Research Laboratory, Water Resources Laboratory, Archaeology Survey, Computer Science Center, Center for Urban and Economic Research, Urban Studies Institute. The University's NIH ranking is 78th among all U.S. institutions with 171 awards/grants valued at $75,587,609. The University's endowment assets rank it 94th, with a value of $488,827,000. The Library: approximately 2,000,000 volumes, 22,580 subscriptions. Total University enrollment: 20,700.

Annual tuition: resident $6006, nonresident $16,554; per credit hour, resident $334, nonresident $940. On-campus housing for 110 married students, 46 graduate women, 82 graduate men. Average academic year housing cost: $2450–$3400 (room only) for single students; $475–$600 per month for married students. Contact Director of Residential Life for both on- and off-campus housing information. Phone: (502)852-6636. Day-care facilities available.

Graduate School

Graduate study since 1907. Enrollment: full-time 2150, part-time 2000. Graduate faculty: full-time 549, part-time 302. Degrees conferred: M.A., M.Ac., M.A.T., M.Ed., M.S., M.Eng., M.M., M.B.A., M.F.A., M.S.N., M.P.A., Ed.S., Ed.D., Ph.D.

ADMISSION REQUIREMENTS. Official transcripts, two letters of recommendation, GRE/MAT required in support of application. GRE Subject required for some departments. GMAT for business. TOEFL required of international applicants. Accepts transfer applicants. Graduates of unaccredited institutions not considered. Apply to Office of Research and Graduate Programs at least two months prior to date of entrance. Application fee: $50. Phone: (502)852-3101; e-mail: graduate@louisville.edu.

ADMISSION STANDARDS. Relatively open for most departments. Usual minimum average: 2.75 (A = 4).

FINANCIAL AID. Annual awards from institutional funds: scholarships, assistantships, research assistantships, fellowships in doctoral programs, tuition remission, Federal W/S, loans. Approved for VA benefits. Apply to appropriate department for assistantships, fellowships; to Office of Financial Aid for all other programs. No specified closing date. Phone: (502)588-5511. Use FAFSA. About 50% of students receive aid other than loans from School and outside sources.

DEGREE REQUIREMENTS. For most master's: 30 semester hours minimum, at least 24 in residence; qualifying exam; thesis for 6 hours required in most departments; final written/oral exam. For M.M.: same as above, except final recital for applied music majors, composition for composition majors in lieu of thesis. For M.F.A. (Theater): 72 hours minimum. For M.S.S.W. (one year advanced-standing program): 42 semesters hours minimum in full-time residence; supervised fieldwork experience. For M.S.S.W. (two-year regular program): 60 semester hours minimum, at least 45 in residence; supervised fieldwork experience. For Ed.S.: 30 hours minimum beyond the master's. For Ph.D., Ed.D.: three years minimum beyond the bachelor's, at least two years in residence and one year in full-time attendance; reading knowledge of two foreign languages or one language and computer science required by some departments; preliminary exam; dissertation; final oral exam.

FIELDS OF STUDY.
Accounting. M.Ac.
Anatomical Sciences and Neurobiology. M.S., Ph.D.
Art Education. M.A.T.
Art History. Ph.D.
Art Therapy. M.A.
Audiology. Ph.D.
Biochemistry and Molecular Biology. M.S., Ph.D.
Biology. M.S., Ph.D.
Biostatistics—Decision Science. Ph.D.
Business and Economics. Includes communications, electronic commerce, entrepreneurship, health care administration, international business. M.B.A.
Chemical Engineering. M.S., Ph.D.
Chemistry. M.S., Ph.D.
Civil Engineering. M.S., Ph.D.
Clinical Investigation Sciences. M.Sc.
Clinical Psychology. Ph.D.
Communicative Disorders. M.S.
Computer Engineering and Computer Science. M.Eng.
Computer Science. M.S.
Computer Science and Engineering. Ph.D.
Counseling and Personnel Services. Includes community counseling, counseling psychology, elementary school, secondary school, college student personnel services. M.Ed., Ph.D.
Curriculum and Instruction. Ph.D.
Early Childhood Education. M.Ed.
Early Elementary Education. M.A.T., M.Ed.
Education. M. Ed., M.A., Ed.S., Ed.D.
Educational Administration. Includes principalship, superintendent, supervision (Ed.S.). M.Ed., Ed.S.
Educational Leadership and Organization Development. Ed.D., Ph.D.
Electrical Engineering. M.Eng., M.S., Ph.D.
Engineering. Includes chemical, civil, electrical, mechanical, computer science, M.S. only; chemical engineering, industrial engineering, computer science and engineering, Ph.D. only.

English. Includes M.A. in creative writing; Ph.D. in Rhetoric and Composition.
Entrepreneurship. Ph.D.
Environmental Biology. Ph.D.
Epidemiology. M.S.
Exercise Physiology. M.S.
Experimental Psychology. Ph.D.
Expressive Therapies. M.A.
Fine Arts. Includes art history, critical and curatorial studies, studio. For creative, art history; one foreign language for M.A. in art history; studio project and paper instead of thesis for M.A. in creative art. M.A., M.A.T.
French. M.A.
Health Education. M.Ed.
Higher Education. Includes sports administration. M.A.
History. M.A.
Humanities. Includes civic leadership, linguistics. M.A., Ph.D.
Human Resource Education. M.Ed.
Industrial Engineering. M.S.
Instructional Technology. M.Ed.
Justice Administration. M.S.
Mathematics. M.A.
Mechanical Engineering. M.S., Ph.D.
Microbiology and Immunology. M.S., Ph.D.
Middle School Education. M.A.T., M.Ed.
Modern Languages. M.A.T. in French, German, Spanish; M.A. in French, German. M.A., M.A.T.
Music (Performance). Includes instrumental conducting, choral conducting, jazz, piano pedagogy. M.M.
Music Education. M.A.T., M.M.E.
Music History and Literature. M.M.
Music Theory and Composition. M.M.
Nursing. M.S.N., Ph.D.
Oral Biology. D.D.S. or equivalent for admission. M.S.
Pan-African Studies. M.A.
Pharmacology and Toxicology. M.S., Ph.D.
Physical Education. M.A.T.
Physics. M.S., Ph.D.
Physiology and Biophysics. M.S., Ph.D.
Political Science. M.A.
Psychology. M.A., Ph.D.
Public Administration. Includes labor–public management relations, public policy and administration, urban development and environment. M.P.A.
Public Health. A.M.P.H.
Public Health Sciences. Ph.D.
Reading Education. M.Ed.
Secondary Education. M.A.T., M.Ed.
Social Work. M.S.S.W.
Sociology. Includes communication, urban geography. M.A., M.A.T.
Spanish. M.A.
Special Education. Includes learning and behavior disorders, learning disabilities, mental retardation, moderate and severe disabilities, severe behavior disorders, visual impairment. M.Ed.
Sport Administration. M.S.
Theatre Arts. Includes African American theatre. M.A., M.F.A.
Urban and Public Affairs. Ph.D. only.
Urban Education. Ed.D.
Urban Planning. Includes land use and environmental planning, administration of planning organizations, spatial analysis for planning. M.U.P.
Visual Sciences. Ph.D.
Women's and Gender Studies. M.A.

School of Dentistry (49292-0001)
Web site: www.dental.louisville.edu

Organized 1886. Located at the Health Sciences Center. Public control. Semester system. Special facilities: Birth Defects Center, the Oral Health and Systemic Disease Group.

Annual tuition: resident $18,850, nonresident $45,094. Medical-dental housing for both single and married students. Average academic year housing cost: $11,000. Total average cost for all other first-year expenses: $5000.

Enrollment; first-year class 80, total 327 (men 57%, women 42%, minorities 13, state residents 55%). Faculty: full-time 61, part-time 77. Degrees conferred: D.M.D., D.M.D.-M.S. (Oral Biology), D.M.D.-Ph.D. Certificates. The M.S. (Oral Biology) and Ph.D. are offered through the Graduate School.

ADMISSION REQUIREMENTS. AADSAS report, official transcripts, recommendations, DAT (October date preferred) required in support of School's application. Interview often required. Applicants must have completed at least three, preferably four, years of college study. Ninety percent of class must be residents. Accepts transfer applicants on a space available basis. Apply to Committee on Admissions between June 1 and February 1. Application fee, none for residents, nonresident $50. Phone: (502)852-5081, (800) 334-8635, ext. 5081; fax: (502)852-1210.

ADMISSION STANDARDS. Competitive. Accepts about 5–10% of all applicants. Number of applications n/a (n/a out-of-state); number interviewed n/a (n/a out-of-state); number of acceptance n/a (n/a out-of-state); number enrolled 80 (36 out-of-state). Usual minimum UGPA: 3.0 (A = 4). Mean DAT: academic 18, PAT 17, mean UGPA 3.62.

FINANCIAL AID. Scholarships, tuition waivers, loans. Apply to Student Affairs Office after acceptance. Phone: (502)852-5075. About 91% of students receive some aid from School.

DEGREE REQUIREMENTS. For D.M.D.: satisfactory completion of forty-five-month program. For M.S., see Graduate School listing above.

FIELDS OF POSTGRADUATE STUDY.
Endodontics.
General Practice.
Oral and Maxillofacial Surgery.
Oral Biology. M.S.
Orthodontics.
Pediatric Dentistry.
Periodontics.

Louis D. Brandeis School of Law (40191)
Web site: www.louisville.edu/brandeislaw

Established 1846. ABA approved since 1931. AALS member. Semester system. Special facilities: Center for Environmental Policy, Center for Women and Families. Special program: Samuel L. Greenbaum Public Service Program. Law library: 415,986 volumes, 5408 subscriptions; has LEXIS, WESTLAW, OCLC.

Annual tuition: full-time resident $11,510, nonresident $23,654; part-time resident $9620, nonresident $15,680. Limited on-campus housing available; moderate cost housing available near campus. Total average annual additional expense: $15,940.

Enrollment: first-year class 81 (day), 40 (evening); total 398 (men 57%, women 47%, minorities 6%). Faculty: full-time 22, part-time 9. Student to faculty ratio 15.0 to 1. Degrees conferred: J.D., J.D.-M.A., J.D.-M.B.A., J.D.-M.Div., (with Louisville Presbyterian Theological Seminary), J.D.-M.S.W.

ADMISSION REQUIREMENTS. LSDAS Law School report, bachelor's degree, transcripts, LSAT (not later than December), personal statement required in support of application. Letters of recommendation and résumé optional. Interview not required. Accepts transfer applicants. Graduates of unaccredited colleges not considered. Preference given to state residents. Apply to Law School Admissions Office after October 1, before March 1. Fall admission only. Application fee $50. Phone: (502)852-6365.

ADMISSION STANDARDS. Selective. Accepts approximately 29% of full-time and 42% of part-time applicants. Number of full-time applicants 1066, part-time 171; number of full-time acceptance 308, part-time 71; number full-time enrolled 99, part-time 38; LSAT (75% of full-time students have a score at or above 155, part-time 150); GPA (75% of full-time students have a GPA at or above 3.43, part-time 3.24). *U.S. News & World Report* ranking is in the second tier (tied at 97th) of all U.S. law schools.

FINANCIAL AID. Scholarships, assistantships, loans. For scholarships, apply to Associate Dean by April 15. Phone: (502)852-6391. Use FAFSA. Students seeking financial aid should contact University's Student Financial Aid Office. Approximately 41% of all students receive financial assistance from the School.

DEGREE REQUIREMENTS. For J.D.: 90 semester hours minimum, at least the last 28 in residence.
Note: School has an exchange program with law schools in England, Finland, France, Germany, Japan, Australia, People's Republic of China, South Africa.

School of Medicine (40292-3866)
Web site: www.louisville.edu/medicine
Founded 1833 as Louisville Medical Institute; affiliated with University in 1984. NIH ranking is 78th among all U.S. institutions with 171 awards/grants worth $75,587,609.
Annual tuition: resident $21,061, nonresident $43,425. On-campus medical-dental housing for married and single students. Off-campus housing near campus also available. Total average figure for all other expenses: $12,000.
Enrollment: first-year class 149 (EDP 10); total 600 (men 59%, women 41%, minorities 15%, state residents 83%). Faculty: full-time 458, part-time 75. Degrees conferred: M.D., M.D.-M.B.A., M.D.-M.S., M.D.-Ph.D. The M.B.A., M.S., Ph.D. are offered through the Graduate School.

ADMISSION REQUIREMENTS. AMCAS report, transcripts, recommendations, MCAT required in support of application. Interview by invitation only. Applicants must have completed at least three years of college study. Preference given to four-year college graduates and state residents. Accepts transfer applicants who are Kentucky residents. Has EDP; apply between June 1 and August 1. Apply to Director of Admissions after June 1, before October 15. Application fee $75. Phone: (502)582-5193.

ADMISSION STANDARDS. Competitive. Accepts about 10% of all applicants. Number of applications 1660 (n/a out-of-state); number interviewed 332 (n/a out-of-state); number of acceptance n/a (n/a out-of-state); number enrolled 149 (n/a out-of-state). Mean Composite MCAT 9.3; mean UGPA 3.52.

FINANCIAL AID. Scholarships, summer research scholarships, HEAL, loans. Apply to Office of Student Affairs by June 1. Phone: (502)852-5187. Use FAFSA (School code: 001999). Approximately 85% of students receive some financial aid.

DEGREE REQUIREMENTS. For M.D.: satisfactory completion of four-year program; must pass Step 1 of USMLE for promotion to third year and take Step 2 of USMLE prior to graduation. For M.S., Ph.D.: see Graduate School listing above.

FIELDS OF GRADUATE STUDY.
Anatomical Sciences and Neurobiology.
Biochemistry and Molecular Biology.
Clinical Research, Epidemiology, and Statistical Training. Multidisciplinary.
Microbiology and Immunology.
Pharmacology and Toxicology.
Physiology and Biophysics.
Structural Biology. Multidisciplinary.

LOYOLA COLLEGE IN MARYLAND
Baltimore, Maryland 21210-2699
Web site: www.loyola.edu

Founded 1852. Coed. Private control. Roman Catholic. Semester system. Library: 380,000 volumes, 2100 subscriptions. Total College enrollment: 6200.
Tuition: per credit $572. No on-campus housing for graduate students. Contact Dean of Students for off-campus housing information.

Graduate Division
Graduate study since 1949. Enrollment: full- and part-time 2631. Graduate faculty: full-time 96, part-time 97. Degrees conferred: M.A., M.Ed., M.S., M.M.S., M.B.A., M.I.B., M.S.F., M.M.S., M.E.S., Psy.D.

ADMISSION REQUIREMENTS. Official transcripts in support of application. GMAT required for M.B.A., M.S.E, and M.P.A. Two letters of recommendation required for M.E.S., three letters for M.A. or M.S. in psychology. Accepts transfer applicants. Graduates of unaccredited institutions not considered. Apply to Graduate Admissions Office by May 15 (Summer), August 15 (Fall), December 15 (Spring). Application fee $50. Phone: (410)617-5020, ext. 2407; fax: (410)617-2002.

ADMISSION STANDARDS. Selective. Usual minimum average: 3.0 (A = 4).

FINANCIAL AID. Internships, graduate assistantships, Federal W/S, loans. Approved for VA benefits. Apply to appropriate department for assistantships; to Financial Aid Office for all other programs. Use FAFSA. Less than 1% of students receive aid other than loans from College and outside sources.

DEGREE REQUIREMENTS. For master's: 30–36 semester hours minimum, at least 24 in residence; thesis for M.A., no language requirement.

FIELDS OF STUDY.
Administration and Supervision.
Business Administration.
Clinical Psychology.
Computer Science.
Counseling Psychology.
Curriculum and Instruction.
Educational Technology.
Finance.
Kodaly Music Education.
Liberal Studies.
Montessori Education.
Pastoral Counseling.
Psychology.
Reading.
School Counseling.
Software Engineering.
Special Education.
Speech-Language Pathology.
Spiritual and Pastoral Care.
Teacher Education with Certification.

LOYOLA MARYMOUNT UNIVERSITY
Los Angeles, California 90045-2659
Web site: www.lmu.edu

Founded 1911. CGS member. Coed. Private control. Roman Catholic. Library: 487,232 volumes, 3100 subscriptions. Total University enrollment: 5000.

Tuition: per unit $770; for Communication Arts and Marriage and Family Therapy per credit $805, for MBA per credit $935. No on-campus housing available for graduate students. Average academic year off-campus housing cost: $500–$1000 per month. Contact Student Housing Office for housing information. Phone: (213)338-2963. Day-care facilities available.

Graduate Division

Graduate Study since 1948. Enrollment: full-time 770, part-time 334. Graduate faculty: full-time 154, part-time 243. Degrees conferred: M.A., M.A.T., M.B.A., M.F.A., M.Ed., M.S., M.S.E.

ADMISSION REQUIREMENTS. Two official transcripts, letters of recommendation, GRE, GMAT (for M.B.A. applicants) required in support of applications. Online application available. Two letters of recommendation required for Counseling Psychology. TOEFL (minimum score 550 for Engineering and Education, 600 for all others) and translation of all foreign credentials required for international applicants. Accepts transfer applicants. Graduates of unaccredited institutions not considered. Apply to Graduate Admissions Office. Application fee $50. Phone: (310)338-2721; fax: (310)338-6086.

ADMISSION STANDARDS. Competitive. Usual minimum average: 3.0 (A = 4).

FINANCIAL AID. Scholarships, grants, internships, assistantships, Federal W/S, loans. Apply by June 1 (Fall), December 1 (Spring) to appropriate department chair for assistantships; to Office of Financial Aid for all other programs. Use FAFSA. Phone: (310)338-2753. About 10% of students receive some aid other than loans from University and outside sources. Aid available for part-time students.

DEGREE REQUIREMENTS. For most master's: 10 courses minimum, at least 8 in residence; thesis/nonthesis option or final written/oral exam. For M.B.A.: 10–18 courses depending on previous degree; project. For M.F.A.: 18 courses, at least 15 in residence; final project.

FIELDS OF STUDY.

COLLEGE OF LIBERAL ARTS:
Bioethics.
English. Includes creative writing, literature.
Pastoral Studies.
Philosophy.
Theology.

COLLEGE OF BUSINESS ADMINISTRATION:
Business Administration. Includes entrepreneurial organization, financial decision systems, human resource management, international business systems, management and organizational behavior, marketing management. M.B.A.

COLLEGE OF SCIENCE AND ENGINEERING:
Civil Engineering.
Computer Science.
Electrical Engineering.
Engineering and Production Management.
Environmental Science.
Mathematics.
Mechanical Engineering.

SCHOOL OF EDUCATION:
Administration.
Bilingual/Bicultural Education.
Catholic School Administration.
Child and Adolescent Literacy.
Counseling.
Educational Leadership.
Educational Psychology.

Elementary Education.
General Education.
Literacy and Language Arts.
School Counseling.
School Psychology.
Secondary Education.
Special Education.
Teaching. Includes biology, English, history, mathematics, social studies.
TESL. Includes multicultural education.

SCHOOL OF FILM AND TELEVISION:
Film Production.
Screenwriting.
Television Production.

DEPARTMENT OF MARITAL AND FAMILY THERAPY:
Clinical Art Therapy.
Marital and Family Therapy.

Loyola Law School (90015-1211)
Web site: www.lls.edu

Establish 1920. ABA approved since 1935. AALS member. Private control. Semester system. Special facilities: Center for Conflict Resolution, Western Law Center for Disability Rights, Disability Mediation Center, Center for Ethical Advocacy, Sports Law Institute. Law library: 576,330 volumes, 7336 subscriptions; has LEXIS, NEXIS, WESTLAW, DIALOG; has more than 1100 network connections.

Annual tuition: full-time $33,793 (day), $22,676 (evening). No on-campus housing available. Estimated housing costs: $18,272.

Enrollment: first-year class day 345, evening 68; total day and evening 1297 (men 53%, women 47%, minorities 39%). Faculty: full-time 64, part-time 50. Student to faculty ratio is 16.1 to 1. Degrees conferred: J.D., J.D.-M.B.A., LL.M. (Tax), International LL.M. at the University of Bologna, Italy.

ADMISSION REQUIREMENTS. LSDAS Law School report, bachelor's degree, transcripts, LSAT (no later than December), letters of recommendation, personal statement required in support of application. TOEFL required for international applicants whose native language is not English. Interview not required. Accepts transfer applicants. Graduates of unaccredited colleges not considered. Apply to Office of Admissions by February 1 (Fall, day), April 17 (Fall, evening). Evaluation fee $65. Phone: (213) 736-1074; fax: (213)736-6523; e-mail: admissions@lls.edu.

ADMISSION STANDARDS. Selective. Accepts approximately 23% of full-time and 19% of part-time applicants. Number of full-time applicants 4213, part-time 622; number of full-time acceptance 984, part-time 121; number full-time enrolled 342, part-time 68; LSAT (75% of full-time students have a score at or above 160, part-time 158); GPA (75% of full-time students have a GPA at or above 3.05, part-time 2.93). *U.S. News & World Report* ranking is in the second tier (tied at 66th) of all U.S. law schools.

FINANCIAL AID. Scholarships, full and partial tuition waivers, assistantships, Federal W/S, loans. Apply to Financial Aid Office after acceptance. Preference given to applications received by March 2. Phone: (213)736-1140. Use FAFSA (School code: 001234). Fellowships available only to advanced students. About 22% of full-time students receive some aid from School. Aid sometimes available for part-time students. Has Public Interest Loan Assistance program.

DEGREE REQUIREMENTS. For J.D.: 87 semester units minimum; completion of three-year program (day), four-year program (evening). For LL.M.: 24-credit program.

Note: Summer programs in San Jose, Costa Rica; Beijing, People's Republic of China; Bologna, Italy.

LOYOLA UNIVERSITY CHICAGO

Chicago, Illinois 60611-2196
Web site: www.luc.edu

Established 1870. CGS member. Coed. Private control, Roman Catholic—Jesuit. Semester system. Special facilities: Center for Catholic Intellectual Heritage, Center for Ethics, Center for Human Rights of Children, Center for Science and Math Education, Center for Urban Environmental Research and Policy, Center for Urban Research and Learning, Gannon Center for Women and Leadership, Parmly Sensory Sciences Institute. The University's NIH ranking is 163rd among all U.S. institutions with 79 awards/grants worth $23,936,661. Library: 1,700,000 volumes, 7800 subscriptions. Total University enrollment: 14,700.

Limited on-campus housing available. Contact Dean, Residence Life for off-campus information. Phone: (773)274-3300. Day-care facilities available.

Graduate School

Graduate study since 1918. Tuition: per credit $750. Enrollment: full-time 1091, part-time 358. Faculty teaching graduate students: full-time 460. Degrees conferred: M.A., M.S., M.B.A., M.Div., M.Ed., M.J., M.P.S., M.R.E., M.S.I.R., M.S.O.D., M.S.N., Ed.D., Ph.D., M.D.-Ph.D., M.D.-M.S., J.D.-M.A.

ADMISSION REQUIREMENTS. Transcripts, statement of purpose, three letters of recommendation required in support of School's application. Online application available. GRE/Subject tests for some departments. Interview required in some departments. TOEFL required for international applicants. Accepts transfer applicants. Graduates of unaccredited institutions not considered. Apply to Dean of Graduate School by February 1 (Fall), December 1 (Spring). Application fee $35. Phone: (773) 508-3396; fax: (773)508-2460.

ADMISSION STANDARDS. Competitive. Usual minimum average: 3.0 (A = 4).

FINANCIAL AID. Annual awards from institutional funds: fellowships, assistantships, internships, Federal W/S, loans. Approved for VA benefits. Apply by March 1 to Dean of School for assistantships, fellowships; to Graduate Financial Assistance for all other programs. Phone: (773)508-3155. Use FAFSA (School code: 001710) and institutional FAF. About 35% of students receive aid other than loans from School and outside sources. Aid available for part-time students.

DEGREE REQUIREMENTS. For master's: generally 30 semester hours minimum; research tool requirement for some departments; final oral/written exam. For Ed.D., Ph.D.: 60 semester hours minimum beyond the bachelor's, at least two semesters in residence; research tool requirement in most departments; preliminary exam; dissertation; final oral exam.

FIELDS OF STUDY.
Applied Statistics.
Biology.
Chemistry.
Child Development.
Computer Science. Includes information technology, scientific and technical computing, software technology.
Criminal Justice.
English.
History.
Mathematical Sciences.
Medical Sciences.
Philosophy.
Political Science.
Psychology. Includes applied social, clinical, development.
Sociology.
Spanish.
Theology.
Women's Studies.

Graduate School of Business

Web site: www.gsb.luc.edu

Graduate School established 1966. Private control. Accredited program: M.B.A. (offered at downtown campus, in Wilmette and Rome, Italy. Quarter, integrated system). Special programs: foreign study programs in Greece, Italy, Republic of Korea, Thailand. Special facilities: Center for Family Business, Center for Financial and Policy Studies, Center for Futures, Center for Values in Business.

Tuition: $3315 per course. Enrollment: total full-time 182, part-time 546. Faculty: full-time 62, part-time 25; 97% with Ph.D./D.B.A. Degrees conferred: M.B.A. (full-time, part-time, evenings and weekends), M.S.A. (Accounting), M.S.I.S.M. (Information Systems Management), M.S.I.M.C. (Integrated Marketing Communication), M.B.A.-J.D., M.B.A.-M.S.N.

ADMISSION REQUIREMENTS. All applicants should have a bachelor's degree from a recognized institution of higher education, a strong mathematics background, a 2.5 (A = 4) GPA, and a GMAT score of 450. Admission is based on a formula, which is 200 × UGPA plus GMAT. Submit application, GMAT results (will accept GMAT test results from the last five years, latest acceptable date is July), official transcripts from each undergraduate/graduate school attended, three letters of recommendation, résumé (prefers at least four years of work experience), and an application fee of $50 to the Committee on Admission, Graduate School of Business. In addition, international students (whose native language is other than English) should submit a TOEFL report (minimum score 550), certified translations and evaluations of all official transcripts, recommendation should be in English or with certified translations, proof of health/immunization certificate, and proof of sufficient financial resources for two years of academic study. U.S. citizens apply by July 31 (Fall), October 1 (Winter), December 31 (Spring), April 1 (Summer), international students apply by June 1 (Fall), August 1 (Winter), November 1 (Spring), February 1 (Summer). Phone: (312)915-8968. On-campus visits are encouraged. Joint degree applicants must apply to and be accepted to both schools; contact the Admissions Office for current information and specific admissions requirements. Rolling admissions process, notification is made within two weeks of receipt of completed application and supporting documents.

ADMISSION STANDARDS. Selective. Usual minimum GPA: 2.5 (A = 4). Median GMAT: 530; median GPA: 3.05 (A = 4).

FINANCIAL AID. Graduate Business Scholars Program (partial tuition reduction), grants, graduate assistantships, internships, Federal W/S, loans. Financial aid is available for part-time study. Assistantships may be available for joint degree candidates. Request scholarship and assistantship information from the Graduate School of Business. Contact the University's Office of Student Financial Assistance for current need-based financial aid information. Phone: (312)915-6636. Apply by April 1 (Fall). Use FAFSA (School code: 001710), also submit Financial Aid Transcript, Federal Income Tax forms. Approximately 30% of students receive some form of financial assistance.

DEGREE REQUIREMENTS. For M.B.A.: 18-course program including 8 elective courses, two-year program; degree program must be completed in five years. For M.S.A., M.S.I.S.M., M.S.I.M.C.: 45 quarter hour programs. For M.B.A.-M.S.N.: 69–81 quarter hour programs. For M.B.A.-J.D.: 128–140 quarter hours, four- to five-year program.

FIELDS OF STUDY.
Accountancy.
Business Administration.
Finance.

Health Care Management.
Human Resources.
Information Systems Management.
Integrated Marketing Communications.
Strategic Financial Services.

School of Education

Semester system. Tuition: per credit $750. Enrollment: full-time 393, part-time 647. Faculty teaching graduate students: full-time 41, part-time 32. Degrees conferred: M.A., M.Ed., Ed.S., Ed.D., Ph.D.

ADMISSION REQUIREMENTS. Transcripts, GRE or MAT, personal statement, three letters of reference required in support of application. Résumé and writing sample required for some programs. Passing scores on State of Illinois Basic Skills and Subject Matter test required for Elementary and Secondary Education programs. Online application available. TOEFL (minimum score 550) required for international applicants. Transfer applicants considered. Apply to the Admission Coordinator by July 1 (Fall), November 1 (Spring), April 1 (Summer); some programs have earlier deadlines, "Self-Managed" application process in effect. Application fee $40. Phone: (312)915-6800; fax: (312)915-6660; e-mail: schleduc@luc.edu.

FINANCIAL AID. Annual awards from institutional funds: fellowships, research assistantships, teaching assistantships, internships, Federal W/S, loans. Apply by April 1 to program directors for fellowships, assistantships; to University's Financial Aid Office for all other programs. Phone: (773)508-3155. About 25% of students receive aid other than loans from School and outside sources. Aid available for part-time students.

DEGREE REQUIREMENTS. For M.Ed.: 10 course, 30 credit program, all in residence; comprehensive exam. For Ed.S.: 22 courses or 66 credits beyond bachelor's (transfer credit accepted); comprehensive exam or culminating portfolio project; internships. For Ed.D.: 60 semester credits beyond bachelor's minimum; comprehensive exams in depth area and two collateral areas; doctoral candidacy; dissertation; oral defense. M.A., Ph.D. are offered through the Graduate School. Consult the Graduate School listing above.

FIELDS OF STUDY.
Administration and Supervision. M.A., M.Ed., Ed.D.
Community Counseling. M.A., M.Ed.
Counseling Psychology. Ph.D.
Cultural and Educational Policy Studies. Includes comparative international education, history of education, philosophy of education, sociology education. M.A., M.Ed., Ph.D.
Curriculum and Instruction. Includes classroom assessment, elementary, school improvement, secondary, technology. M.A., M.Ed., Ed.D.
Educational Policy. Ed.D.
Education Psychology. M.A., M.Ed., Ph.D.
Elementary Education. M.Ed.
Higher Education. M.Ed., Ed.D., Ph.D.
Instructional Leadership. M.Ed.
Reading. M.Ed.
Research Methodology. M.A., M.Ed. Ph.D.
School Counseling. M.A., M.Ed.
School Psychology. Ed.S., Ph.D.
School Technology. M.Ed.
Secondary Education. M.Ed.
Special Education. M.A., M.Ed.

School of Law
Web site: www.luc.edu/law

Established 1908. Located on the Water Tower Campus about 1 mile N of downtown. ABA approved since 1925. AALS member since 1924. Semester system. Private control. Full-time, part-time study. Special facilities: Institute for Consumer Antitrust Studies, Civitas Childlaw Center, Institute for Health Law, Corporate Law Center, Center for Public Service, National Institute for Trial Advocacy. Special program: summer study abroad in Rome at University's campus, Nottingham-Trent University, England, McGill University Center for Medicine, Ethics, and Law, Montreal, Canada. Law library: 408,901 volumes, 4516 subscriptions; has LEXIS, NEXIS, WESTLAW; has more than 300 network connections.

Annual tuition: $34,800 (day), $26,190 (evening), part-time per credit $1160, M.J. per credit $1045, LL.M. per credit $1160. Law students tend to live off-campus. Off-campus housing and personal expenses: approximately $18,040.

Enrollment: first-year class full-time 169, part-time 90; total full-time 607, part-time 252 (men 49%, women 51%, minorities 16%). Faculty: full-time 40, part-time 66. Student to faculty ratio 16.8 to 1. Degrees conferred: J.D., J.D.-M.B.A., J.D.-H.S.H.R., J.D.-M.A. (Political Science), J.D.-M.S.W., LL.M. (Health Law, full- and part-time), M.J. (Child Law, Health Law, evenings), S.J.D. (Health Law and Policy), D.H.L.P. (Health Law and Policy).

ADMISSION REQUIREMENTS. LSDAS Law School report, bachelor's degree, transcripts, LSAT, résumé, personal statement, two letters of recommendation required in support of application. Interview sometimes required. Accepts transfer applicants. Apply to Director of Admission after October 1, before April 1. Fall admission only for beginning students. Application fee $50. Phone: (312)915-7170, (800)545-5744; e-mail: law-admissions@luc.edu. For Graduate Study contact Office of Legal Studies. Phone: (312)915-7161.

ADMISSION STANDARDS. Selective. Accepts approximately 26% of full-time and 33% of part-time applicants. Number of full-time applicants 2180, part-time 407; number of full-time acceptance 558, part-time 134; number full-time enrolled 169, part-time 90; LSAT (75% of full-time students have a score at or above 159, part-time 153); GPA (75% of full-time students have a GPA at or above 3.15, part-time 2.99). *U.S. News & World Report* ranking is in the second tier (tied at 70th) of all U.S. law schools.

FINANCIAL AID. Scholarships, partial tuition waivers, Federal W/S, loans. Apply to Financial Aid Office March 1. Phone: (312)915-7170. Use FAFSA. About 65% of students receive aid other than loans from School.

DEGREE REQUIREMENTS. For J.D.: 86 (46 required) credits with a GPA of at least 2.0 (A = 4), plus completion of upper divisional writing course; a course in philosophical and historical perspective of Law; three-year program, four-year program. Accelerated J.D. with summer course work of up to a maximum of 9 credits. For J.D.-master's: individually designed programs, usually a four-year program (full-time) rather than five years if taken consecutively. For M.J. (Child Law, begins in June): 27 credits; 3 credit thesis; two-year program. For M.J. (Health Law, begins in June): 23 credits of required course work (includes thesis), 7 credits of electives; optional externship. For LL.M. (Child Law): 21 credits; thesis; a GPA of 2.5 (A = 4). For LL.M. (Health Law): 24 credits; a GPA of 2.5 (A = 4); thesis of publishable quality. For D.Law, S.J.D.: two-year full-time programs, thesis in first year, dissertation in second year; presentation of dissertation to Law School Community, Health Law community, where appropriate the Medical community.

Stritch School of Medicine (60153)
Web site: www.meddean.lumc.edu

Established 1870. Located in Maywood, Illinois. Special facilities: Bioethics Institute, Burn and Shock Trauma Institute, Cardiovascular Institute, Neuroscience Institute, Oncology Institute.

Library: 188,400 volumes, 1420 subscriptions. NIH ranking is 163 among all U.S. institutions with 79 awards/grants worth $24,163,537.

Annual tuition: $36,600. Limited on-campus housing available. Apply to Director of Student Personnel Services for both on- and off-campus housing. Total average figure for all other expenses: $18,840.

Enrollment: first-year class 140; total 557 (men 51%, women 49%, minorities 21%, state residents 44%); postgraduates 100. Faculty: full-time 638, part-time 696. Degrees conferred: M.D., M.D.-M.S., M.D.-Ph.D.

ADMISSION REQUIREMENTS. AMCAS report, transcripts, MCAT, essay required in support of application. Interview by invitation only. Applicants must have completed at least 3 years of college study. Does not have EDP. Preference given to residents of Illinois and the Midwest. Accepts transfer applications on a space available basis. Apply to Committee on Admissions of School after June 1, before November 15. Application fee $70. Phone: (708)216-3229.

ADMISSION STANDARDS. Competitive. Accepts about 6.6% of all applicants. Number of applications 4413 (3574 out-of-state); number interviewed 531 (348 out-of-state); number of acceptance 290 (188 out-of-state); number enrolled 140 (75 out-of-state). Mean Composite MCAT 9.9; mean UGPA 3.60.

FINANCIAL AID. Scholarships, grants, loans. Apply to Director of Financial Aid as soon as possible after acceptance. Phone: (708)216-3227. Use FAFSA (School code: G09188). About 94% of students receive aid from School and outside sources.

DEGREE REQUIREMENTS. For M.D.: satisfactory completion of three-year program; take USMLE Step 2 prior to graduation. For M.S., Ph.D.: see Graduate listing above.

FIELDS OF GRADUATE STUDY.
Biomedical Science.
Bioethics and Health Policy.
Cell and Molecular Physiology.
Cell Biology, Neurobiology and Anatomy.
Clinical Research Methods.
Microbiology and Immunology.
Molecular and Cellular Biochemistry.
Molecular Biology.
Neuroscience.
Pharmacology and Experimental Therapeutics.

School of Social Work

Semester system. Tuition: per credit $750. Limited on-campus housing for single students only. Apply to Dean, Residence Life (60626). Phone: (312)508-3300.

Enrollment: full-time 270, part-time 173. Graduate faculty: full-time 18, part-time 23. Degrees conferred: M.S.W., D.S.W.

ADMISSION REQUIREMENTS. Transcripts, letters of recommendation, personal statement required in support of School's application. TOEFL required for international applicants. Accepts transfer applicants. Graduates of unaccredited institutions not considered. Apply to School by July 15. Application fee $50. Phone: (312)915-7005; fax: (312)915-7645; e-mail: socialwork@luc.edu.

ADMISSION STANDARDS. Selective. Usual minimum average: 3.0 (A = 4) plus knowledge of the values of the field and experience in working with people.

FINANCIAL AID. Annual awards from institutional funds: scholarships, research fellowships, internships, tuition waiver, loans. Apply by March 1 to Financial Assistance Office. Phone: (312) 508-3155. Use FAFSA and institutional FAF. About 37% of students receive aid other than loans from School and outside sources. Aid available to part-time students.

DEGREE REQUIREMENTS. For M.S.W.: 55 semester hours minimum; internships. For D.S.W.: 60 semester hours minimum; comprehensive exam; dissertation; final oral exam.
Note: Program emphasis is on the Clinical Practice of Social Work.

LOYOLA UNIVERSITY NEW ORLEANS
New Orleans, Louisiana 70118-6195
Web site: www.loyno.edu

Established 1912. Coed. Private control. Roman Catholic. Semester system. Special facilities: Center for Environmental Communications, Center for the Study of Catholics in the South, Economics Institute, Gillis Long Poverty Law Center, Institute for Politics, Institute for the Study of Catholic Culture and Tradition, International Business Center, Shawn M. Donnelley Center for Nonprofit Communications, Twomey Center for Peace Through Justice, Women's Resource Center. Library: 437,000 volumes, 5111 subscriptions. Total University enrollment: 5500.

Tuition: per credit $379 (Math Teaching, Religious Studies, Loyola Institute for Ministry); $591 (Communication, Counseling, Music); $384 (Nursing); $477 (Criminal Justice). On-campus housing for 24 graduate men, 24 graduate women; none for married students. Average academic year housing costs: $6366 (including board). Apply to Director of Residential Life. Phone: (504)865-3736. Day-care facilities available.

Graduate School

Graduate study since 1912. Enrollment: full-time 658, part-time 946. Faculty: full-time 164, part-time 70. Degrees conferred: M.A., M.B.A., M.M., M.M.E., M.M.T., M.S., M.S.N., M.C.J., M.S.T., M.R.E., M.P.S., J.D.-M.A., J.D.-M.B.A., J.D.-M.C.M.

ADMISSION REQUIREMENTS. Application, transcripts, statement of intent, résumé, letters of recommendation, GMAT (Business), GRE (Criminal Justice, Mass Communications, Nursing), MAT (Education) required in support of School's application. TOEFL required for international applicants. An interview is required for education programs, recommended for other programs. Accepts transfer applicants. Application deadlines: Nursing, April 15 (Fall); Mass Communications, July 1 (Fall), November 1 (Spring); Education, August 1 (Fall), December 1 (Spring), May 1 (Summer); other programs August 1 (Fall), December 1 (Spring), and May 1 (Summer). Application fee $20. Phone: (504)865-3240 or (800)4-LOYOLA; fax: (504)865-3383; e-mail: admit@loyno.edu.

ADMISSION STANDARDS. Selective for most departments. Usual minimum average: 3.0 (A = 4).

FINANCIAL AID. Scholarships, assistantships, tuition waivers, Federal W/S, loans. Apply by May 1 to Financial Aid Office. Phone: (504)865-3231. Use FAFSA. Aid available for part-time students.

DEGREE REQUIREMENTS. For master's: 30–36 semester hours minimum, at least 24 in residence; candidacy; comprehensive exam; thesis/capstone/practicum; final written/oral exam for some departments. For M.S.N.: 45-credit program; comprehensive exam; research project; practicum.

FIELDS OF STUDY.
Counseling.
Criminal Justice.
Mass Communications.

Math Teaching.
Music (Performance).
Music Therapy.
Nursing. Includes family nurse practitioner. M.S.N.
Pastoral Studies. M.P.S.
Religious Education. M.R.E.
Religious Studies. M.A.

Joseph A. Butts, S.J. College of Business Administration
Web site: www.cba.loyno.edu

College founded in 1947, Graduate School established 1961. Private control. Accredited programs: M.B.A. Semester system. Special programs: foreign exchange programs in Belgium, France, and Spain.

Tuition: per credit M.B.A. $761.

Enrollment: total full-time 37, part-time 37. Faculty: full-time 20, part-time 10; all have Ph.D./D.B.A. Degrees conferred: M.B.A. (full-time, part-time, evenings and weekends), M.Q.M. (Quality Management), M.B.A.-J.D.

ADMISSION REQUIREMENTS. All applicants should have a bachelor's degree from a recognized institution of higher education; a strong mathematics background and a 3. 0 (A = 4) GPA. Admission is based on a formula, which is 200 × UGPA plus GMAT. Submit application, GMAT (will accept GMAT test results from the last five years, latest acceptable date is March), official transcripts from each undergraduate/graduate school attended, two letters of recommendation, MBA statement, résumé (prefers at least four years of work experience), and an application fee of $50 to the Office of Graduate Business Programs. Phone: (504)864-7965. Online application available. In addition, international students (whose native language is other than English) should submit a TOEFL (minimum score 580), certified translations and evaluations of all official transcripts, recommendation should be in English or with certified translations, proof of health/ immunization certificate, and proof of sufficient financial resources for two years of academic study. U.S. citizens apply by June 15 (Fall), November 25 (Spring), March 15 (Summer), international students apply by June (Fall). Rolling admissions process. On-campus visits are encouraged. Admissions Committee will consider applicants with some academic course work deficiencies, Joint degree applicants must apply to and be accepted to both schools, contact the admissions office for current information and specific admissions requirements. Notification is made within two weeks of receipt of completed application and supporting documents.

ADMISSION STANDARDS. Selective. Median GMAT: 489; median GPA: 3.0 (A = 4).

FINANCIAL AID. Research assistantships, internships, Federal W/S, loans. Financial aid available for part-time students. Assistantships may be available for joint degree candidates. Apply by May 1. Request assistantship information from the Coordinator, Graduate Business Programs. Contact the University's Financial Aid Office for current need-based financial aid information. Phone: (504)865-3231. Use FAFSA (School code: 002016), also submit Financial Aid Transcript, Federal Income Tax forms. Approximately 24% of students receive some form of financial assistance.

DEGREE REQUIREMENTS. For M.B.A.: 33–56 credit program including 18 elective credits, one- to two-year program; capstone course; degree program must be completed in seven years. For M.Q.M.: 36 credit program. For M.B.A.-J.D.: 105 credit program; four- to five-year program.

FIELDS OF STUDY.
Accounting.
Finance.
International Business.
Management.

School of Law (P.O. Box 901)
Web site: www.law.loyno.edu

Established 1931. ABA approved since 1931. AALS member since 1934. Private control. Semester system. Special facilities: Center for Environmental Law and Land Use, Poverty Law Center, Public Law Center. Law library: 338,150 volumes, 3375 subscriptions; has LEXIS, NEXIS, WESTLAW, DIALOG; has more than 150 network connections.

Annual tuition: $30,566 (day), $20,706 (evening). Limited on-campus housing. Total average annual additional expense: $14,366.

Enrollment: first-year class full-time 220, evening 72; total full- and part-time 796 (men 47%, women 53%, minorities 25%). Faculty: full-time 28, part-time 22. Student to faculty ratio 17.6 to 1. Degrees conferred: J.D., J.D.-M.A. (Communications, Religious Studies). J.D.-M.B.A., J.D.-M.P.A.

ADMISSION REQUIREMENTS. LSDAS Law School report, bachelor's degree, transcripts, LSAT, personal statement, letters of recommendation required in support of application. Interview not required. Graduates of unaccredited colleges not considered. Accepts transfer applicants. Apply to Director of Admissions after September 1, before April 1 for priority consideration. Rolling admissions process. For part-time study, apply by June 1. Admits beginning students Fall only. Application fee $40. Phone: (504)861-5575; fax: (504)801-5772; e-mail: ladmit@ loyno.edu.

ADMISSION STANDARDS. Selective. Accepts approximately 34% of total annual applicants. Number of applicants 1746; number of acceptance 593; number enrolled 215; LSAT (75% of students have a score at or above 151); GPA (75% of students have a GPA at or above 3.16). *U.S. News & World Report* ranking is third tier of all law schools.

FINANCIAL AID. Scholarships, assistantships, full and partial tuition waivers, Federal W/S, loans. Apply to Office of Financial Aid by May 1. Phone: (504)865-3231. Use FAFSA (School code: 002016). About 38% of full-time students receive financial assistance from School. Aid available for part-time study.

DEGREE REQUIREMENTS. For J.D.: 90 credit hours minimum, at least one year in residence. For M.B.A. and M.A.: see Graduate School listing above.
Note: Summer study programs in Brazil, Mexico, Japan, and Eastern Europe available.

LYNCHBURG COLLEGE
Lynchburg, Virginia 24501-3199
Web site: www.lynchburg.edu

Founded 1903. Located 120 miles W of Richmond. Coed. Private control. Semester system. Special facilities: Center for Advanced Engineering, Belle Boone Beard Gerontology Center, Early Childhood Special Education Technical Assistance Center, Center for Economics Education. Library: 287,600 volumes, 636 subscriptions. Total College enrollment: 2400.

Tuition: per credit $335, varies depending on program. On-campus housing for single students only. Average academic year housing cost: $6400 (including board). Contact Office of Residential Living for both on- and off-campus housing. Phone: (434) 544-8320.

Graduate Studies

Graduate study since 1964. Enrollment: full-time 91, part-time 196. Faculty teaching graduate students: full-time 35, part-time 20. Degrees conferred: M.Ad., M.B.A., M.Ed.

ADMISSION REQUIREMENTS. Official transcripts, three letters of recommendation, personal essay, GRE, GMAT (Business) required in support of application. TOEFL required for international applicants. Interview not required. Accepts transfer students. Graduates of unaccredited institutions not considered. Apply to Director of Graduate Studies by May 1 (Summer), July 31 (Fall), November 30 (Spring). Application fee $30. Phone: (434)544-8382 (Education), (434)544-8651 (Business).

ADMISSION STANDARDS. Selective. Usual minimum average: 3.0 (A = 4).

FINANCIAL AID. Scholarships, assistantships, grants, Federal W/S, loans. Apply by March 1 to the Office of Financial Aid. Phone: (434)544-8228. Use FAFSA (College code: 003720).

DEGREE REQUIREMENTS. For M.Ed.: 36–39 semester hours minimum, at least 30 in residence; optional final project/capstone. For M.B.A.: 33 semester hours.

FIELDS OF STUDY.
Business Administration. M.B.A.
Community Counseling. 48 credit program.
Counselor Education. M.Ed.
Educational Leadership. Includes administration/supervision, instructional leadership. M.Ed.
English Education.
School Counseling. 48 credit program.
Special Education. Includes early childhood, mental retardation, learning disabilities, emotional/behavioral disorders. 39 credit program.
Teaching and Learning. M.Ed.

UNIVERSITY OF MAINE
Orono, Maine 04469-5782
Web site: www.umaine.edu

Founded 1865. Located 8 miles N of Bangor. CGS member. Coed. State control. Semester system. School of Law in Portland (04102). Special facilities: Center for Marine Studies, Canadian American Center, Migratory Fish Research Institute, Margaret Chase Smith Center for Public Policy, Institute for Quaternary Studies, College of Forest Resources, computer facilities, Darling Center for Research, Teaching, and Service (marine laboratory at Walpole). Library: 1,000,000 volumes, 17,000 subscriptions. Total University enrollment: 11,400.

Tuition: per credit, resident $325, nonresident $936. Housing for 40 married students, 100 single students. Average housing cost: per semester $6000–$9224 (including board) single students, $4500 married students (room only). Apply to Housing Office, Hilltop Complex. Phone: (207)581-4580.

Graduate School

Graduate study since 1881. Enrollment: total full-time 1115, part-time 689. Graduate faculty: full- and part-time 600. Degrees conferred: M.A., M.S., M.Ed., M.A.T., M.B.A., M.Eng., M.M., M.P.A., M.P.S., M.S.W., M.W.C., C.A.S., Ph.D., Ed.D.

ADMISSION REQUIREMENTS. Transcripts, three letters of reference, GRE required in support of School's application. GRE Subject Test, interview required for some programs. GMAT required for M.B.A. TOEFL required for international applicants. Accepts transfer applicants. Application and all credentials required six weeks prior to registration. Apply to the Graduate School; no specified closing date. Application fee $50. Phone: (207)581-3218; fax: (207)581-3232; e-mail: graduate@maine.edu.

ADMISSION STANDARDS. Selective for some departments, competitive or relatively open for others. Usual minimum average: 2.75 (A = 4).

FINANCIAL AID. Annual awards from institutional funds: scholarships, fellowships, teaching assistantships, research assistantships, traineeships, Federal W/S, loans. Apply by January 15 to department chair for scholarships, assistantships, and fellowships; to Financial Aid Office for all other programs. Use FAFSA. Phone: (207)581-1324; fax: (207)581-3085. About 45% of students receive aid other than loans from School and outside sources. No aid for part-time students.

DEGREE REQUIREMENTS. For M.A., M.S.: 30 semester hours minimum; thesis; final oral exam; nonthesis option in some programs. For M.Ed.: 33 hours minimum. For M.B.A.: 30 hours minimum; additional course work required for those with little or no undergraduate work in business. For M.A.T.: 33 hours minimum. For M.Eng., M.P.S., M.M.: essentially same as M.A., except thesis not required. For M.P.A.: 36 hours minimum. For M.S.W.: 60 hours total; advanced standing for B.S.W. For C.A.S.: 30 hours minimum. For Ed.D., Ph.D.: two consecutive academic years beyond the bachelor's or one year beyond the master's; comprehensive exam; dissertation; final exam. Foreign language requirements in some fields of study. Language requirements vary by department.

FIELDS OF STUDY.
Accounting. M.Acc.
Agricultural and Resource Economics. M.S., M.P.S. only.
Animal Sciences. M.S., M.P.S.
Biochemistry. M.S., M.P.S.
Biochemistry and Molecular Biology. Ph.D.
Biological Engineering. M.E., M.S.
Biological Sciences. Ph.D.
Biomedical Sciences. Ph.D.
Bioresource Engineering. M.S.
Botany and Plant Pathology. M.S. only.
Business Administration. M.B.A. only.
Chemical Engineering. M.E., M.S., Ph.D.
Chemistry. M.S., Ph.D.
Civil Engineering. M.E., M.S., Ph.D.
Clinical Psychology. Ph.D.
Communication. M.A.
Communication Sciences and Disorders. M.A.
Community Development. M.S., M.P.S. only.
Computer Engineering. M.S.
Computer Science. M.S., Ph.D.
Counselor Education. M.A., M.S.
Developmental Psychology. M.A., Ph.D.
Ecology and Environmental Science. Ph.D.
Economics. M.A. only.
Education. M.A., M.S., Ed.D.
Educational Leadership. M.Ed., Ph.D.
Electrical Engineering. M.E., M.S. only.
Elementary Education. M.A., M.A.T., M.S.
Engineering Physics. M.E.
English. M.A. only.
Entomology. M.S. only.
Financial Economics. M.A.
Food and Nutrition Sciences. Ph.D.
Food Science and Human Nutrition. M.S. only.
Forest Resources. Ph.D. only.

Forestry. M.S. only.
French. M.A., M.A.T.
Functional Genomics. Ph.D.
Geological Sciences. M.A., Ph.D.
German. M.A.T.
Higher Education. M.A., Ph.D.
History. M.A., Ph.D.
Horticulture. M.S.
Human Development. M.S.
Individualized Program. Ph.D. only.
Instructional Technology. M.Ed., Ph.D.
Kinesiology and Physical Education. M.A., Ph.D.
Liberal Studies. M.A. only.
Literacy Education. M.A.
Manufacturing Management. M.M.M. only.
Marine Biology. Ph.D.
Marine Bio-Resources. M.S., Ph.D.
Marine Policy. M.A.
Mathematics. M.A. only.
Mechanical Engineering. M.S., M.E.
Microbiology. M.S., Ph.D.
Music. M.M.
Nursing. M.S.
Ocean Engineering. Ph.D.
Oceanography. M.S., Ph.D.
Physics. M.S., Ph.D.
Plant Science. Ph.D.
Plant, Soil, and Environmental Sciences. M.S.
Psychology. M.A., Ph.D.
Public Administration. M.P.A.
Quaternary and Climate Studies. M.S.
Resource Economics and Policy. Ph.D.
Resource Utilization. M.S.
Science Education. M.A.T.
Secondary Education. M.A., M.S.
Social Studies Education. M.A.T.
Social Work. M.S.W.
Spatial Information Sciences and Engineering. M.S., Ph.D.
Special Education. M.A., M.S.
Speech Communication. M.A. only.
Surveying Engineering. M.S. only.
Teaching. M.S.T.
Theater. M.A.
Wildlife Conservation. M.S., M.W.C.
Wildlife Ecology. Ph.D.
Zoology. M.S., Ph.D.

School of Law

Web site: www.mainelaw.maine.edu

Reestablished 1961. Located on the University of Southern Maine Campus in Portland (04102). ABA approved since 1962. AALS member. Public control. Semester system. Special facilities: Maine Law Institute, Technology Law Center, Center for Law and Innovation. Law library: 330,999 volumes, 2974 subscriptions; has LEXIS, NEXIS, WESTLAW.

Annual tuition: full-time resident $16,590, nonresident $26,280.

Enrollment: first-year class 75, total full-time 259 (men 47%, women 53%, minorities 4%); no part-time study. Faculty: full-time 27, part-time 9. Student to faculty ratio 15.5 to 1. Degrees conferred: J.D., J.D.-M.A. (Public Policy and Management), J.D.-M.B.A., J.D.-M.C.P., J.D.-M.H.P.M.

ADMISSION REQUIREMENTS. LSDAS Law School report, bachelor's degree, transcript, LSAT, personal statement, one letter of recommendation required in support of application. TOEFL required for international applicants whose native language is not English. Accepts transfer applicants. Graduates of unaccredited colleges not considered. Apply to Registrar of School after September 1, before March 1. For Early Action program apply by December 1. Transfer applications due June 1. Fall admission only. Application fee $50. Phone: (207)780-4341.

ADMISSION STANDARDS. Selective. Accepts approximately 40% of all students. Number of applicants 694; number of acceptance 280; number enrolled 75; LSAT (75% of students have a score at or above 153); GPA (75% of students have a GPA at or above 3.16). *U.S. News & World Report* ranking is in the third tier of all U.S. law schools.

FINANCIAL AID. Full and partial tuition waivers, Federal W/S, loans. Apply to Financial Aid Office by February 15. Approximately 37% receive aid other than loans from School and outside sources. Phone: (207)780-5250. Use FAFSA (School code: 009762). New England students may qualify for a special rate under the NEBHE Compact. NEBHE is in-state tuition plus 50%.

DEGREE REQUIREMENTS. For J.D.: satisfactory completion of 89 credit hour program; 80 hours of pro bono legal services during the three years of study. For M.A.: see Graduate School listing under the University of Southern Maine.

MANHATTAN COLLEGE

Bronx, New York 10471
Web site: www.manhattan.edu

Founded 1853. Private control. Library: 236,266 volumes, 1590 subscriptions. Total College enrollment: 3425.

Tuition: per semester hour $540 (Education), $675 (Engineering). Limited on-campus housing available for single graduate students. Average academic year housing cost: $7350; $550 per month for off-campus housing. Apply to Director of Residence Life for both on- and off-campus housing information. Phone: (718)862-7200.

Graduate Division

Enrollment: full-time 122, part-time 363. College faculty: full-time 171, part-time 83. Degrees conferred: M.A., M.S.Ed., M.B.A., M.E., M.S.

ADMISSION REQUIREMENTS. Transcripts, GRE/GMAT required in support of application. TOEFL (minimum score 550) required for international applicants. Accepts transfer applicants. Graduates of unaccredited institutions not considered. Apply to Dean of Admissions before May 2 (Fall—Business, Engineering, Biotechnology), August 10 (Fall—all other programs), January 7 (Spring). For full-time Engineering program apply by February 1. Application fee $50. Phone: (718)862-7325; fax: (718)863-8019; e-mail: admit@manhattan.edu.

ADMISSION STANDARDS. Competitive. Usual minimum average; 3.0 (A = 4).

FINANCIAL AID. Scholarships, assistantships, research fellowships, grants, Federal W/S, loans. Apply by February 1 to appropriate departmental chair for scholarships, assistantships, fellowships; to Director of Financial Aid for all other programs; no specified closing date for these programs. Phone: (718)862-7381. Use FAFSA.

DEGREE REQUIREMENTS. For master's: 30–42 credits minimum, at least 24 in residence; thesis/nonthesis option/major research paper/project; internship practicum for some programs. For M.B.A.; 39 credits minimum; master's project.

FIELDS OF STUDY.
Alcohol/Substance Abuse Counseling. M.S.
Biotechnology. Interdisciplinary. M.S.
Chemical Engineering. M.S.
Civil Engineering. M.S.
Computer Engineering. M.S.
Counseling. M.A.
Electrical Engineering. M.S.
Environmental Engineering. M.E.E., M.S.
Mechanical Engineering. M.S.
School Building Leadership. M.S.Ed.
Special Education. Includes adaptive physical education. M.S.Ed.

MANHATTAN SCHOOL OF MUSIC
120 Claremont Avenue
New York, New York 10027-4698
Web site: www.msmnyc.edu

Founded 1918. Coed. Private control. Semester system. Special facilities: 1000-seat auditorium, 3 recital halls, 2 electronic music studios, 1 recording studio. Library: 107,000 volumes, 20,000 recordings. Total School enrollment: 891.

Annual tuition: full-time $26,000. On-campus housing for single students only. Average academic year housing costs: $11,500 (including board). Contact Director of Campus and Residential Life. Phone: (212)749-2802, ext. 462.

Graduate Division

Enrollment: full-time 458, part-time 75. Faculty: full-time 25, part-time 225. Degrees conferred: M.M., D.M.A., Diploma.

ADMISSION REQUIREMENTS. Official transcripts, interview, three letters of recommendation, school entrance exam, audition required in support of application. Online unified application available. TOEFL required for international applicants. Accepts transfer applicants. Apply to Office of Admission at least one month prior to one of the four separately scheduled audition dates, but no later than December 1. Application fee $100. Phone: (212)749-2802, ext. 510; fax (212)749-5471.

ADMISSION STANDARDS. Very competitive for some departments, competitive for others. Talent basis for admission.

FINANCIAL AID. Scholarships, tuition waivers, fellowships, teaching assistantships, Federal W/S, loans. Apply four weeks prior to the scheduled audition date. Phone: (212)749-2802. Use FAFSA. About 50% of students receive aid from School and outside sources.

DEGREE REQUIREMENTS. For M.M.: 56–64 semester credits minimum, at least 54 in residence; recital. For D.M.A.: 54 semester credits minimum, at least 54 in residence; proficiency in one foreign language (French, German, or Italian); thesis; two recitals; oral exam; comprehension exam.

FIELDS OF STUDY.
Accompanying. M.M.
Classical Performance. Includes orchestral instruments, voice, piano, guitar. M.M.
Composition. M.M., D.M.A.
Conducting. M.M.
Guitar. D.M.A.
Jazz/Commercial Music. M.M.
Orchestral Instruments. D.M.A.
Orchestral Performance. M.M.
Organ. D.M.A.
Piano. D.M.A.
Voice. D.M.A.

MANHATTANVILLE COLLEGE
2900 Purchase Street
Purchase, New York 10577-2132
Web site: www.mville.edu

Founded 1841. Located 25 miles NE of midtown New York City and 5 miles from Greenwich, Connecticut. Coed. Private control. Nondenominational. Semester system. Library: 292,000 volumes, 912 subscriptions. Total College enrollment: 2800.

Tuition: per credit $630, $770 (Education). On-campus housing for men, women. Average academic year housing cost: $4850 (including board), $620 for summer. For housing information, phone: (914)694-5217.

Graduate Program

Enrollment: full-time 252, part-time 717. Graduate faculty: full-time 38, part-time 20. Degrees conferred: M.A.T., M.P.S., M.A.L.S., M.S.

ADMISSION REQUIREMENTS. Transcripts, two letters of recommendation required in support of application. Online application available. TOEFL required for international applicants. Accepts transfer applicants. Graduates of unaccredited institutions not considered. For Education, contact School of Education (914)323-5214; Graduate and Professional Studies (914)694-3425; no specified application closing date. Application fee $60.

ADMISSION STANDARDS. Competitive. Usual minimum average: 2.75 (A = 4).

FINANCIAL AID. Fellowships, assistantships, tuition reduction program for recently unemployed, Federal W/S, loans. Apply by April 15 to Committee on Financial Aid. Phone: (914)694-5357. Use FAFSA (School code: 002760). About 20% of students receive aid from College and outside sources.

DEGREE REQUIREMENTS. For master's: 30–39 credit hours minimum; final written/oral exam/project; internships for some programs.

FIELDS OF STUDY.
Elementary and Special Education. M.A.T.
International Management. M.S.
Leadership and Strategic Management. M.S.
Liberal Studies. M.A.L.S.
Management Communication. M.S.
Organizational Management and Human Resource Development. M.S.
Secondary and Special Education. M.A.T.
Writing. M.A.

MANSFIELD UNIVERSITY OF PENNSYLVANIA
Mansfield, Pennsylvania 16933
Web site: www.mansfield.edu

Founded 1857. Located in north-central Pennsylvania. Coed. State control. Semester system. Library: 238,181 volumes, 3110 subscriptions.

Tuition: per credit, resident $345, nonresident $552. On-campus housing for single graduate students; none for married students. Annual academic year housing cost: $6236 including board. Apply to Director of Residence Life for off-campus housing information. Phone: (570)662-4933.

Graduate Division

Graduate study since 1966. Enrollment: full-time 63, part-time 160. Faculty: full-time 1, part-time 35. Degrees conferred: M.Ed., M.A., M.S.

ADMISSION REQUIREMENTS. Transcript required in support of Division's application. GRE/MAT for Psychology only. Audition required for music students. TOEFL required for international applicants. Accepts transfer applicants. Apply to Associate Provost at least 2 weeks prior to registration. Application fee $25. Phone: (570)662-4806; fax: (570)662-4121.

ADMISSION STANDARDS. Selective. Usual minimum average: 3.0 in last 48 semester hours (A = 4).

FINANCIAL AID. Annual awards from institutional funds: internships, assistantships, Federal W/S, loans. Approved for VA benefits. Apply to Associate Provost prior to entrance. Phone: (570) 662-4129; fax: (570)662-4136. Use FAFSA (School code: 003324). About 70% of students receive aid other than loans from University and outside sources. Aid available for part-time students.

DEGREE REQUIREMENTS. For master's: 30–40 credit hour minimum; thesis/nonthesis option; final oral/written exam.

FIELDS OF STUDY.
Art Education. Includes art studio, art history. M.Ed.
Community Psychology. M.A.
Early Childhood Education. M.Ed.
Education. M.S.
Elementary Education. M.Ed.
Music. M.A.
Reading. Specialist Certificate only.
School Library and Information Technologies. M.S.
Secondary Education. M.Ed.
Special Education. M.Ed.

MARQUETTE UNIVERSITY
Milwaukee, Wisconsin 53233
Web site: www.marquette.edu

Founded 1881. CGS member. Coed. Private control. Roman Catholic. Semester system. Special facilities: Center for Biological and Biomedical Research, Bradley Institute for Democracy and Public Values, Center for Applied Economic Analysis, Center for Energy Studies, Center for Ethnic Studies, Center for Highway and Traffic Engineering, Center for Industrial Processes and Productivity, Center for Intelligent Systems, Center for Mass Media Research, Center for Sensor Technology, Hartman Family Literacy Center, Institute of the Catholic Media, Center for Citizenship Public Policy, Institute for Family Studies, Material Science and Technology Center, Parenting Center, Center for Psychological Services, Rapid Prototyping Center, Signal Processing Research Center. Library: 900,000 volumes, 9225 subscriptions.

Tuition: per credit $800, $800 for M.B.A. program, $950 for M.S. Programs in Dentistry, $595 Education. On-campus housing, 260 units for graduate students. Average monthly cost: $450–$900 (apartments and single rooms). Apply to Office of Residence Life. Phone: (414)288-7208. For off-campus housing information: (414)288-7281.

Graduate School

Established 1922. Enrollment: full- and part-time 2348. Faculty: full-time 482, part-time 113. Degrees conferred: M.A., M.S.A.E., M.A.T., M.B.A., M.Ed., M.S., M.S.N., M.S.E.M., M.S.H.R., M.S.A., Ed.D., Ph.D.

ADMISSION REQUIREMENTS. Transcripts required in support of School's application. GRE/MAT/ GMAT, three letters of recommendation, personal statement, résumé required in support of application. Interview required in many programs. Evidence of proficiency in English or TOEFL required of international students. Accepts transfer applicants. Apply to Graduate School at least six weeks prior to registration; some programs have earlier deadlines. Application fee $40. Phone: (414)288-7137; fax: (414) 288-1902; e-mail: mugs@ marquette.edu.

ADMISSION STANDARDS. Competitive for most departments, very competitive or selective for others. Usual minimum average: 3.0 (A = 4).

FINANCIAL AID. Annual awards available from institutional funds: research assistantships, teaching assistantships, fellowships and scholarships, Federal W/S, loans. Approved for VA benefits. Apply by February 15 to Graduate School for fellowships, assistantships, scholarships; to Financial Aid Office for all other programs. Phone: (414)288-7390; fax: (414)288-1718. Use FAFSA. About 35% of graduate students receive some form of financial assistance from School. Aid available for part-time students.

DEGREE REQUIREMENTS. For M.A., M.S., M.A.T.: 30 semester hours minimum, at least 24 in residence; thesis; comprehensive oral/written exam; or 30 semester hours minimum; master's essay; comprehensive oral/written exam; written exam in some departments. For M.B.A.: 33 semester hours minimum. For M.Ed.: 30 semester hours minimum; comprehensive oral/written exam. For Ph.D.: 60 semester hours minimum beyond the bachelor's; two semesters in full-time residence within an eighteen-month period carrying at least nine credits; qualifying exam; dissertation; final oral exam. For Ed.D.: 60 semester hours minimum beyond the bachelor's, at least one year in full-time residence; qualifying exam; dissertation; dissertation defense.

FIELDS OF STUDY.
Accounting.
Bioinformatics.
Biomedical Engineering. GRE for admission.
Broadcast and Electronic Communication.
Business Administration. GMAT for admission. M.B.A. only.
Chemistry. Ph.D.
Civil Engineering. Ph.D.
Clinical Psychology. Ph.D.
Communication Studies.
Computing.
Counseling. Ph.D.
Counseling Psychology. Ph.D.
Dentistry. M.S. only.
Dispute Resolution.
Economics. GRE or GMAT for admission. M.S.A.E. only.
Educational Policy and Leadership. Ed.D.
Educational Psychology. Ph.D.
Electrical and Computer Engineering. Ph.D.
Engineering Management. GRE or GMAT for admission. M.S.E.M. only.
English. GRE for admission. Ph.D.
Foreign Languages and Literature (Spanish).
Healthcare Technologies Management.
History. GRE for admission.
Human Resources. GRE or GMAT for admission. M.S.H.R. only.
Interdisciplinary. Ph.D.
International Affairs. GRE for admission. M.A. only.
Leadership Studies. M.L.S.
Mathematics, Statistics, and Computer Science. Ph.D.
Mechanical and Industrial Engineering. Includes materials science.

Nursing. GRE for admission. M.S.N. only.
Philosophy. GRE for admission. Ph.D.
Physical Therapy. D.P.T.
Physician Assistant. M.P.A.
Political Science. GRE for admission.M.A. only.
Psychology. GRE/Subject, MAT for admission; 36 hours for M.S.
Public Service. GRE for admission. M.A.P.S. only.
Religious Studies. Ph.D.
Speech-Language Pathology. GRE for admission. M.S.
Theology. GRE for admission. Ph.D.
Transfusion Medicine. M.S.T.M.

School of Dentistry

Web site: www.marquette.edu/dentistry

Established 1896. Semester system.

Annual tuition: resident $32,500, nonresident $41,420. No on-campus housing available. For off-campus housing information contact the Office of Student Affairs. Phone: (414)288-7208. Average academic year housing cost: $11,550–$18,460. Total average cost for all other first-year expenses: $10,200.

Enrollment: first-year class 80, total 320 (men 50%, women 50%, minorities 15%, state residents 50%). Faculty: full-time 54, part-time 250. Degrees conferred: D.D.S., M.S., D.D.S.-M.S., D.D.S.-Ph.D. Certificate. The M.S. and Ph.D. are offered through the Graduate School.

ADMISSION REQUIREMENTS. AADSAS report, transcripts, three letters of recommendation, DAT required in support of School's application. Interview by invitation only. Applicants must have completed at least three years of college study. Preference given to Wisconsin, North and South Dakota residents. Accepts transfer applicants. Apply to Director of Admissions after June 1, before January 1. Rolling admission process. Application fee $50. Phone: (414)288-3532 or (800)445-5385; fax: (414) 288-6505.

ADMISSION STANDARDS. Competitive. Accepts about 5–10% of all applicants. Number of applications 2955 (2777 out-of-state); number interviewed n/a (n/a out-of-state); number of acceptance n/a (n/a out-of-state); number enrolled 80 (40 out-of-state). Usual minimum UGPA: 2.75 (A = 4). Mean DAT: academic 18.44, PAT 18.08, mean UGPA 3.50.

FINANCIAL AID. Scholarships, awards, DEAL, HEAL, assistantships, loans. Apply by March 1 to University Office of Financial Aid. Phone: (414)288-7390. Use FAFSA (School code: 003863).

DEGREE REQUIREMENTS. For D.D.S.: satisfactory completion of forty-five-month program. For M.S.: satisfactory completion of one-year program.

FIELDS OF POSTGRADUATE STUDY.
Dental Biomaterials. M.S.
Endodontics. M.S.
General Dentistry. Certificate.
Orthodontics. M.S.
Prosthodontics. M.S.

Law School (P.O. Box 1881)

Web site: www.law.marquette.edu

Established 1892. ABA approved since 1925. AALS member. Private control. Semester system. Special facility: National Sports Law Institute. Law library: 328,048 volumes, 3238 subscriptions; has LEXIS, NEXIS, WESTLAW, DIALOG, LEGALTRAC, CALI, WISCAT, OCLC; has more than 150 network connections.

Annual tuition full-time $27,750, part-time $16,650, No on-campus housing available. Off-campus housing available; contact Office of Residential Life. Phone: (414)288-7208. Total average annual additional expenses: $16,606.

Enrollment: first-year class, full-time 161, part-time 49; total full- and part-time 690 (men 57%, women 43%, minorities 9%). Faculty: full-time 35, part-time 30. Student to faculty ratio 17.3 to 1. Degrees conferred: J.D., J.D.-M.A. (Political Science, International Affairs), J.D.-M.B.A.

ADMISSION REQUIREMENTS. LSDAS Law School report, bachelor's degree, transcripts, LSAT, essay, one letter of recommendation required in support of application. TOEFL required for international applicants whose native language is not English. Interview not required. Accepts transfer applicants. Graduates of unaccredited colleges not considered. Apply to Registrar after October 1, before April 1. Fall admission only. Application fee $50. Phone: (414)288-6767; fax: (414)288-0676.

ADMISSION STANDARDS. Selective. Accepts approximately 40% of full-time and 33% of part-time applicants. Number of full-time applicants 1649, part-time 202; number of full-time acceptance 652, part-time 67; number full-time enrolled 166, part-time 49; LSAT (75% of full-time students have a score at or above 155, part-time 155); GPA (75% of full-time students have a GPA at or above 3.14, part-time 2.96). *U.S. News & World Report* ranking is in the second tier (tied at 97th) of all U.S. law schools.

FINANCIAL AID. Scholarships, Federal W/S, loans. Apply to the Office of Financial Aid by March 1. Phone: (414)288-7390. Use FAFSA. About 39% (full-time), 49% (part-time) of students receive aid other than loans from School.

DEGREE REQUIREMENTS. For J.D.: satisfactory completion of 90 semester-hour program. For master's degree: see Graduate School listing above.

MARSHALL UNIVERSITY

Huntington, West Virginia 25755-2100
Web site: www.marshall.edu

Founded 1837. CGS member. Coed. State control. Semester system. Special facilities: WMUL-FM, WPBY-TV, Robert C. Byrd Institute for Advanced Flexible Manufacturing Systems, Research and Economic Development Center. Library: 1,400,000 volumes, 13,405 subscriptions. Library is repository for General Chuck Yeager memorabilia and Blake Collection of antebellum American literary materials. Total University enrollment: 14,000.

Annual tuition and fees; full-time area resident $8292, state resident $4606, nonresident $12,548; per credit area resident $460, state resident $255, nonresident $697. On-campus housing for 84 married students, 1050 graduate men, 1050 graduate women. Average academic year housing cost: approximately $4800–$6818 for married students, $5200 for single students (including board). Apply to Director of Student Housing. Phone: (304)696-3171; (304)696-2564 (off-campus housing information). Day-care facilities available.

Graduate College

Graduate study since 1938. Graduate College established 1948. Enrollment: full-time 1400, part-time 2013. Graduate faculty: full-time 200, part-time 20. Degrees conferred: M.A., M.B.A., M.S., M.A.J., M.A.T., M.S.N., Ph.D.

ADMISSION REQUIREMENTS. Transcript, GRE, MAT, GMAT (for M.B.A.) required in support of School's application. Online application available. TOEFL required of international students. Interview required by some departments. Accepts transfer applicants. Graduates of unaccredited institutions not considered. Apply to Admissions Office at least one month prior to registration. Some departments have earlier deadlines. Application fee residents $40, nonresidents $100. Phone: (800)642-3499 or (304) 746-2500, ext. 1900; fax: (304)746-1902.

ADMISSION STANDARDS. Vary by department. Usual minimum average: 2.75 (A = 4).

FINANCIAL AID. Scholarships, fellowships, grants, academic tuition waivers, research assistantships, teaching assistantships, administrative assistantships, internships, tuition waivers, Federal W/S, loans. Approved for VA benefits. Apply to Director of Financial Aid; no specified closing date. Phone: (304)696-3162; fax: (304)696-3242. Use FAFSA and institutional FAF. Aid available for part-time students.

DEGREE REQUIREMENTS. For master's: 32 credit hours minimum including thesis or 36 credit hours minimum without thesis; final written/oral exam. For Ph.D.: at least 60 credits beyond the master's; reading knowledge of one foreign language for some departments; qualifying exam; dissertation; final oral exam.

FIELDS OF STUDY.

COLLEGE OF BUSINESS:
Business Administration. Includes accounting, finance management, marketing economics. M.B.A.
Human Resource Management. M.S.
Industrial Relations. M.S.

COLLEGE OF EDUCATION:
Adult and Technical Education. Includes business, career, cooperative, marketing, vocational-technical. M.A., M.S.
Counseling. Includes elementary, secondary school, higher education, agency counseling. M.A.
Educational Administration. Includes elementary and secondary principal studies, higher education, supervision, school superintendent studies. M.A., Ed.D.
Family and Consumer Science. Includes food and nutrition, home management, consumer economics, teacher education. M.A.
Health and Physical Education. Includes athletic training, adult physical fitness, cardiac rehabilitation. M.S.
School Psychology. Ed.S.
Teacher Education. Includes early childhood, elementary, middle childhood, secondary, reading, special (behavioral disorders, gifted, learning disabilities, mentally impaired, physical handicapped). M.A.
Teaching. M.A.T.

COLLEGE OF FINE ARTS:
Art. Includes art education, art history, ceramics, drawing, graphics, painting, sculpture. M.A.
Music. Includes instrumental, vocal, church, performance, history, literature, theory, composition, music supervisor, teacher education. M.A.

COLLEGE OF LIBERAL ARTS:
Communication Studies. Includes speech communication. M.A.
Criminal Justice. Includes correction, law enforcement. M.S.
English. Includes American and English literature and language. M.A.
Geography. Includes cultural geography, conservation cartography. M.A., M.S.
History. Includes American, European, Asian. M.A.
Humanities. M.A.
Political Science. Includes American national and state government, comparative government, international government, public administration, theory. M.A.
Psychology. Includes general-theoretical, clinical, school. M.S.
Sociology and Anthropology. Includes general, community development, industrial relations, sociology of the Appalachian region, medical anthropology. M.A.

COLLEGE OF SCIENCE:
Biological Sciences. Includes aquatic ecology, biological science education, evolutionary biology and systematics, plant cell chemistry, plant and animal toxonomy, environmental biology. M.A., M.S.
Chemistry. Includes organic, physical, analytical chemistry. M.S.
Mathematics. Includes algebra, topology, analysis, teacher education. M.A.
Physical Science and Physics. Includes interdisciplinary program in physical science, teacher education. M.S.

COLLEGE OF INFORMATION TECHNOLOGY AND ENGINEERING:
Engineering. Includes chemical, engineering management, environmental engineering. M.S.
Environmental Science. M.S.
Information Systems. M.S.
Safety Technology. Includes ergonomics, industrial hygiene, occupational safety and health, safety management, mine safety. M.S.
Technology Management. M.S.

SCHOOL OF MEDICINE:
Biological Sciences. Includes anatomy, biochemistry, microbiology, pharmacology, physiology. M.S., Ph.D.
Forensic Science. M.S.

COLLEGE OF NURSING AND HEALTH PROFESSIONALS:
Communication Disorders. Includes speech pathology and audiology. M.A.
Dietetics. M.S.
Nursing. Includes family nurse practitioner studies. M.S.N.

COLLEGE OF JOURNALISM AND MASS COMMUNICATION.
Journalism. Includes news-editorial writing, public relations, broadcast-TV journalism, advertising, teacher education.

Joan C. Edwards School of Medicine (25701)
Web site: www.musom.marshall.edu

Established 1978. Special Facilities: Edwards Comprehensive Cancer Center, Robert C. Byrd Biotechnology Science Center, Clinical Education and Outreach Center, Center for Rural Health Research. Library: 8000 volumes, 300 subscriptions.

Annual tuition: resident $16,100, nonresident $40,930. On-campus housing available. Total average figure for all other expenses: $16,000.

Enrollment: first-year class 60; total 277 (men 57%, women 43%, minorities 21%, state residents 84%). Faculty: full-time 155, part-time 25. Degrees conferred: M.D., M.D.-M.S.

ADMISSION REQUIREMENTS. AMCAS report, transcripts, MCAT, recommendations, supplemental application required in support of application. Interview by invitation only. Preference given to state residents and residents from states contiguous to West Virginia. Apply to Admissions Office after June 1, before December 1. Application fee resident $50, nonresident $100. Phone: (304)691-1738; (800)544-8514; fax: (304)691-1744.

ADMISSION STANDARDS. Competitive. Accepts about 15–20% of all applicants. Number of applications 785 (n/a out-of-state); number interviewed 157 (n/a out-of-state); number of acceptance n/a (n/a out-of-state); number enrolled 60 (n/a out-of-state). Mean Composite MCAT 8.7; mean UGPA 3.60.

FINANCIAL AID. Scholarships, tuition waiver, HEAL, loans. Apply after acceptance to University's Office of Financial Assistance. Phone: (304)696-3162. Use FAFSA (School code: G06869). Approximately 94% of students receive some financial assistance.

DEGREE REQUIREMENTS. For M.D.: satisfactory completion of four-year program; must pass Step 1 of USMLE for promotion to third year and must pass Step 2 of USMLE prior to awarding M.D.

FIELDS OF GRADUATE STUDY.
Cancer Biology.
Cardiovascular Disease, Obesity and Diabetes.
Molecular Mechanisms of Pathogenesis.
Neuroscience and Developmental Biology.
Toxicology and Environmental Health Sciences.

MARYGROVE COLLEGE
Detroit, Michigan 48221-2599
Web site: www.marygrove.edu

Founded 1910. Moved to Detroit in 1927. Coed. Private control. Roman Catholic. Semester system. Library: 187,000 volumes, 16,000 microforms.

Tuition: per credit $552, M.A.T. $340–$424. On-campus housing available for single students only. Annual academic year housing cost: $5600–$6800. Apply to Residence Director.

Graduate Division

Enrollment: full- and part-time 250. College faculty: full-time 9, part-time 18. Degrees conferred: M.A., M.Ed., M.A.T.

ADMISSION REQUIREMENTS. Transcripts, career plan, interview (for some programs) required in support of application. Teacher certification required for some programs. TOEFL (minimum score 500) required for international applicants. Accepts transfer applicants. Apply to Graduate Admissions Office; no specified closing dates. Application fee $25. Phone: (313)927-1509.

ADMISSION STANDARDS. Selective. Usual minimum average: 3.0 (A = 4).

FINANCIAL AID. Scholarships, tuition grants, Federal W/S, loans. Approved for VA benefits. Apply by March 1 to Financial Aid Office. Phone: (313)927-1692. Use FAFSA.

DEGREE REQUIREMENTS. For M.Ed., M.A.T.: 30 semester hours minimum, at least 24 in residence; no language or thesis requirement. For M.A. (Pastoral Ministry): 36 semester hours minimum, internship; final project. For M.A. (Administration): 36 semester hours minimum.

FIELDS OF STUDY.
Adult Learning. M.Ed.
Educational Leadership. M.A.
Educational Technology. M.Ed.
English. M.A.
Human Resources Management. M.A.
Reading Education. M.Ed.
Social Justice. M.A
Teaching. M.A.T.

MARYLAND INSTITUTE COLLEGE OF ART
Baltimore, Maryland 21217
Web site: www.mica.edu

Founded 1826. Coed. Private control. Semester system. Library: 80,000 volumes, 366 subscriptions. Total College enrollment: 1700.

Annual tuition: full-time $26,140, per credit $1090. Limited on-campus housing. Annual academic year housing cost: $7200. Apply to Housing and Residence Life Office for on- and off-campus housing information. Phone: (410)225-2398.

Graduate Studies

Enrollment: full-time 149, part-time 71. Faculty: full-time 9, part-time 7. Degree conferred: M.F.A.

ADMISSION REQUIREMENTS. Transcripts, three letters of recommendation, portfolio required in support of application. TOEFL required for international applicants. Apply by March 1 (Fall), October 1 (Spring) for painting, ceramics, sculpture, printmaking, and photography. Fall admission for all majors except art education. Application $50. Phone: (410)225-2255; fax: (410)225-2408; e-mail: graduate@mica.edu.

ADMISSION STANDARDS. Competitive for most departments, relatively open for others. Usual minimum average: 2.75 (A = 4).

FINANCIAL AID. Scholarships, grants, teaching assistantships, internships, loans. Apply to Dean, Graduate Studies, before March 1. Phone: (410)225-2285; fax: (410)669-9206. Use FAFSA. About 65% of students receive aid other than loans from College. No aid for part-time students.

DEGREE REQUIREMENTS. For M.F.A.: 60 semester hours minimum, at least 54 in full-time residence; thesis/creative project; no language requirement.

FIELDS OF STUDY.
Art Education. Portfolio required for admission to all programs.
Community Arts.
Digital Arts.
Graphic Design.
M.F.A. for Art Educators. Four summers in residence.
Mixed Media.
Painting. Private studios for full-time students.
Photography and Digital Imaging. Private studios for full-time students.
Sculpture. Private studios for full-time students; large shop and foundry.
Studio Art.

UNIVERSITY OF MARYLAND
College Park, Maryland 20742-5121
Web site: www.umd.edu

Established 1856. CGS and AAU member. College Park campus located 10 miles N of Washington, D.C.; Schools of Medicine, Dentistry, Nursing, Pharmacy, Social Work, and Law are located in Baltimore. Coed. State control. Semester system. Special facilities: Center for Aging, Automation Research Center, Institute for Criminal Justice and Criminology, Center for Estuarine and Environmental Sciences, Center for Language, Institute for Philosophy and Public Policy, Institute for Physical Science and Technology, Center for Renaissance and Baroque Studies, Survey Research Center, electron microscope, linear accelerator, wind tunnel, marine laboratory, research farms, laboratory-equipped vessels for water research, Transportation Studies Center. The University's NIH ranking is 164th among all U.S. institutions with 97 awards/grants worth $23,483,942. Library: more than 3,000,000 volumes, 32,290 subscriptions. Total University enrollment: 35,300.

Tuition: per hour, resident $409, nonresident $731. On-campus housing for 476 married students, limited number of single graduate students. Average academic year housing cost: $550–$750 per month. Contact Office of Residential Life. Phone: (301)314-2100, (301)314-5274 (off-campus housing information). Day-care facilities available.

Graduate School

Established 1919. Enrollment: full-time 4919, part-time 3585 (men 50%, women 50%). Graduate faculty: full-time more than 2690, part-time 914. Degrees conferred: M.A., M.S., M.Ed., M.F.A., M.L.S., M.M., M.B.A., M.C.P., M.A.A., M.Arch., M.Eng., A.G.S., Ed.D., D.M.A., Ph.D.

ADMISSION REQUIREMENTS. Transcripts, GRE/MAT/GMAT, three letters of recommendation required in support of School's application. Online application available. GRE Subject Test for many programs. TOEFL, TWE required for international applicants. Interview usually not required. Accepts transfer applicants. Graduates of unaccredited institutions not considered. Apply to Director of Graduate Admission and Records by March 1 (Fall), October 1 (Spring), May 1 (Summer); international February 1 (Fall), June 1 (Spring). Application fee $60. Phone: (301)405-4198; fax: (301)314-9305; e-mail: grschool@deans.umd.edu.

ADMISSION STANDARDS. Selective for most departments. Usual minimum average: 3.0 (A = 4).

FINANCIAL AID. Annual awards from institutional funds: grants, scholarships, teaching/research/administrative assistantships, research fellowships, internships, tuition waivers, Federal W/S, loans. Approved for VA benefits. Apply by February 1 to appropriate department for scholarships, assistantships, fellowships; to Financial Aid Office for all other programs. Phone: (301)314-8313; fax: (301)314-9587. Use FAFSA and FATS. About 31% of students receive aid other than loans from School and outside sources. Aid available for part-time students.

DEGREE REQUIREMENTS. For most master's: 30–39 semester hours minimum, at least 24 in residence: thesis/nonthesis option; final oral exam. For M.L.S.: 36 hours minimum. For A.G.S.: 30 semester hours beyond the master's. For Ph.D.: three years minimum beyond the bachelor's, at least one in residence; qualifying exam; oral comprehensive exam; dissertation; final oral exam. For D.M.A.: essentially the same as for the Ph.D., except reading knowledge of one language required; composition/final recital.

FIELDS OF STUDY.
Aerospace Engineering. M.S., M.E., Ph.D.
Agricultural and Resource Economics. M.S., Ph.D.
Agronomy. M.S., Ph.D.
American Studies. M.A., Ph.D.
Animal Sciences. M.S., Ph.D.
Anthropology. M.A.A.
Applied Mathematics and Scientific Computation. M.S., Ph.D.
Architecture. M.Arch.
Art. Includes studio. M.F.A.
Art History and Archaeology. M.A., Ph.D.
Astronomy. M.S., Ph.D.
Behavior, Ecology, Evolution, and Systematics. M.S., Ph.D.
Biochemistry. M.S., Ph.D.
Bioengineering. M.S., Ph.D.
Biological Resource Engineering. M.S., Ph.D.
Biology. M.S., Ph.D.
Business and Management. GMAT for admission. M.S., M.B.A., M.S., Ph.D.
Cell Biology and Molecular Genetics. M.S., Ph.D.
Chemical Engineering. M.S., M.E., Ph.D.
Chemical Physics. Interdepartmental. M.S., Ph.D.
Chemistry. M.S., Ph.D.
Civil and Environmental Engineering. M.E., Ph.D.
Classics. M.A.
Clinical Audiology. Au.D., Ph.D.
Communication. M.A., Ph.D.
Comparative Literature. M.A., Ph.D.
Computer Science. M.S., Ph.D.
Counseling and Personnel Services. M.Ed., M.A., Ph.D., A.G.S.

Creative Writing. M.F.A.
Criminal Justice and Criminology. M.A., Ph.D.
Curriculum and Instruction. Includes elementary and secondary. M.Ed., M.A., Ed.D., Ph.D., A.G.S.
Dance. M.F.A.
Economics. M.A., Ph.D.
Education Policy and Leadership. M.A., M.Ed., Ed.D., Ph.D., A.G.S.
Electrical and Computer Engineering. M.S., M.E., Ph.D.
English Language and Literature. M.A., Ph.D.
Entomology. M.S., Ph.D.
Epidemiology. M.P.H., Ph.D.
Family Studies. M.S., Ph.D.
Fire Protection Engineering. M.S., M.E.
Food Science. M.S., Ph.D.
French Language and Literature. M.A., Ph.D.
Geography. M.A., Ph.D.
Geography/Library and Information Systems. M.A., M.L.S.
Geology. M.S., Ph.D.
Germanic Language and Literature. M.A., Ph.D.
Government and Politics. M.A., Ph.D.
Health Services. Ph.D.
Hearing and Speech Science. M.A., Ph.D.
Historical Preservation. M.H.P.
History. M.A., Ph.D.
History/Library and Information. M.A., M.L.S.
Human Development. M.Ed., M.A., Ed.D., Ph.D., A.G.S.
Information Management. M.I.M.
Journalism. M.A., Ph.D.
Kinesiology. M.A., Ph.D.
Leadership, Higher Education and International Education. M.A., Ed.D., Ph.D.
Library and Information Services. M.L.S., Ph.D.
Life Sciences. M.L.S.
Linguistics. M.A., Ph.D.
Marine-Estuarine-Environmental Sciences. M.S., Ph.D.
Material Sciences and Engineering. M.S., M.E., Ph.D.
Mathematical Statistics. M.A., Ph.D.
Mathematics. M.A., Ph.D.
Measurement, Statistics, and Evaluation. M.A., Ph.D.
Mechanical Engineering. M.S., M.E., Ph.D.
Meteorology. M.S., Ph.D.
Modern French Studies. Ph.D.
Molecular and Cell Biology. Ph.D.
Music. M.M., M.A., M.Ed., D.M.A., Ph.D., Ed.D.
Natural Resources Sciences. M.S., Ph.D.
Neuroscience and Cognitive Science. M.S., Ph.D.
Nuclear Engineering. M.S., M.E., Ph.D.
Nutrition. M.S., Ph.D.
Philosophy. M.A., Ph.D.
Physics. M.S., Ph.D.
Policy Studies. M.A., M.Ed., Ph.D.
Psychology. M.A., M.S., Ph.D.
Public Affairs. Includes policy studies, public management. M.P.M., M.P.P.
Public and Community Health. M.P.H., Ph.D.
Public Policy. M.P.P.
Real Estate Development. M.R.E.D.
Reliability Engineering. M.S., M.E., Ph.D.
Russian Language and Linguistics. M.A.
Second Language Acquistion and Application. M.A., Ph.D.
Sociology. M.A., Ph.D.
Spanish Language and Literature. M.A., Ph.D.
Special Education. M.Ed., M.A., Ed.D., Ph.D.
Speech-Language Pathology. M.A.
Survey Methodology. M.S., Ph.D.
Sustainable Development and Conservation Biology. M.S.
Systems Engineering. M.S., M.E.
Telecommunications. M.S.
Theatre. M.A., M.F.A., Ph.D.
Urban and Regional Planning and Design. Ph.D.

Urban Studies and Planning. M.C.P.
Veterinary Medical Science. M.S., Ph.D., D.V.M.
Women's Studies. M.A., Ph.D.

UNIVERSITYF OF MARYLAND AT BALTIMORE
Baltimore, Maryland 21201-1627
Web site: www.umaryland.edu

Founded 1807. CGS member. Coed. Semester system. Special facilities: Aquatic Pathology Center, Cancer Center, Clinical Stroke Research Center, Biotechnology Research Center, Center for Health Policy Research, Center for Human Virology, Center for Drugs and Public Policy, Center for Vaccine Development. Library: 650,740 volumes, 7072 subscriptions. Total University enrollment: 5800.

Tuition: per credit, resident $409, nonresident $731. On-campus housing available for graduate men and women. Annual academic year average cost: $4000 (room only). Apply to Office of Residential Life. Phone: (410)706-7766.

Graduate School
Web site: www.graduate.umaryland.edu

Enrollment: full-time 682, part-time 496. Faculty: full-time 146, part-time 4. Degrees conferred: M.S., Ph.D.

ADMISSION REQUIREMENTS. Transcripts, GRE, three letters of recommendation required in support of School's application. Online application available. TOEFL required of international applicants. Accepts transfer applicants. Graduates of unaccredited colleges not considered. Apply to Graduate Admission and Records Office; no specified closing date. Application fee $50. Phone: (410)706-7131; fax: (410)706-3473; e-mail: gradinfo@graduate.umaryland.edu.

ADMISSION STANDARDS. Selective in some departments, competitive in others. Usual minimum average: 3.0 (A = 4).

FINANCIAL AID. Annual awards from institutional funds: fellowships, teaching assistantships, research assistantships, internships, grants, traineeships, tuition waivers, Federal W/S, loans. Approved for VA benefits. Use FAFSA. Phone: (410)455-7347; fax: (410)706-0824. About 30% of students receive aid other than loans from both University and outside sources. Aid available for part-time students.

DEGREE REQUIREMENTS. For M.S.: 30 semester hours minimum; thesis/nonthesis option; final exam. For Ph.D.: three years of full-time study, at least one year in residence; preliminary exam; dissertation; final exam.

FIELDS OF STUDY.
Anatomy and Neurobiology.
Applied and Professional Ethics.
Biochemistry.
Dental Hygiene.
Epidemiology.
Gerontology. Ph.D. only.
Human Genetics.
Marine-Environmental-Estuarine Studies.
Medical and Research Technology.
Medical Pathology.
Microbiology and Immunology.
Molecular and Cell Biology.
Neuroscience and Cognitive Science.
Nursing.
Oral and Craniofacial Biological Science. Includes cellular and molecular biology, infectious disease, neuroscience.
Oral Biology.
Oral Pathology.
Pathology. Includes forensic toxicology, medical pathology.
Pharmaceutical Health Service Research.
Pharmaceutical Sciences.
Pharmacology and Experimental Therapeutics.
Physical and Rehabilitative Science.
Physiology.
Preventive Medicine.
Social Work. Ph.D. only.
Toxicology.

Baltimore College of Dental Surgery
Web site: www.dental.umaryland.edu

Established 1840, the first dental school in U.S. Located in Baltimore (21201). Semester system. Special facilities: Organized Research Center on Persistent Pain, Center for Clinical Studies, Brotman Facial Pain Clinic.

Annual tuition: resident $24,340, nonresident $42,794. Both on- and off-campus housing available. For housing information contact the Residence Life Office. Phone: (410)706-7766 Average academic year housing cost: $11,550–$15,000. Total average cost for all other first-year expenses: $5,200.

Enrollment: first-year class 114, total 440 (men 56%, women 44%, minorities 11%, state residents 55%). Faculty: full-time 117, part-time 98. Degrees conferred: B.S.-D.D.S., D.D.S., D.D.S.-M.S., D.D.S.-Ph.D. Certificate. The M.S. and Ph.D. are offered through the Graduate School.

ADMISSION REQUIREMENTS. AADSAS report, transcripts, DAT (not later than October), three letters of recommendation required in support of application. Interviews by invitation only. Applicants must have completed at least three but preferably four years of study in an accredited college of arts and sciences. Transfer applicants accepted. Preference given to state residents. Accepts transfer applicants. Apply after June 1, before January 1 to the Office of Admissions of the Dental School. Application fee $60. Phone: (410)706-7472.

ADMISSION STANDARDS. Competitive. Accepts about 10–15% of all applicants. Usual minimum UGPA: resident 3.0 (A = 4), nonresident 3.2. Mean DAT: academic 19.5, PAT 17, mean UGPA 3.40.

FINANCIAL AID. Scholarships, work-study; Federal, state, and private loans. Apply to Office of Student Financial Aid, University of Maryland at Baltimore; priority consideration given applications received by February 15. Phone: (410)706-7347. Use FAFSA (School code: 002104). About 70% of students receive some aid from the School.

DEGREE REQUIREMENTS. For B.S.-D.D.S.: satisfactory completion of seven-year program. For D.D.S.: satisfactory completion of forty-five-month program. For Ph.D.: see Graduate School listing above.

FIELDS OF POSTGRADUATE STUDY.
Advanced Education in General Dentistry. M.S., Certificate.
Biomedical Science. Includes molecular and cell biology, infectious diseases and immunology, neuroscience.
Endodontics. M.S., Certificate.
Experimental Pathology.
Neuroscience. NIH Training Program.
Oral and Craniofacial Biological Sciences.
Oral and Maxillofacial Pathology. Includes research in connective tissue, bone, stress proteins, retroviruses, and epidemiology of oral disease. M.S., Ph.D.
Oral Biology. NIH Training Program.
Orthodontics. M.S., Certificate.
Pediatric Dentistry. M.S., Certificate.
Periodontics. M.S., Certificate.
Prosthodontics. M.S., Certificate.

School of Law (21201-1786)

Web site: www.law.umaryland.edu

Founded 1816. Located in downtown Baltimore in the business and legal district. ABA approve since 1930. AALS member. Public control. Semester system. Special facilities: Center for Dispute Resolution at the University of Maryland, Center for Health and Homeland Security, Legal Resource Center for Tobacco Regulation, Litigation and Advocacy, Maryland Intellectual Property Legal Resource Center. Law library: 468,320 volumes, 3885 subscriptions; has LEXIS, WESTLAW, DIALOG, CARL, UNCOVER, OCLC; has more than 1200 network connections.

Annual tuition: full-time resident $19,105, nonresident $30,384; part-time resident $14,460, nonresident $14,460, No on-campus housing available. Estimated living expenses: $23,848.

Enrollment: first-year class, full-time 230, part-time 28; total full- and part-time 826 (men 42%, women 58%, minorities 32%). Faculty: full-time 60, part-time 42. Student to faculty ratio 11.9 to 1. Degrees conferred: J.D., J.D.-Master's. (Business Administration, Community Planning, Criminal Justice, Marine and Environmental Sciences, Nursing, Policy Sciences, Public Health, Public Management, Social Work).

ADMISSION REQUIREMENTS. LSDAS Law School report, bachelor's degree, transcript, LSAT (no later than February), personal statement, two letters of recommendation required in support of application. Interview not required. TOEFL required for international applicants whose native language is not English. Accepts transfer applicants. Graduates of unaccredited colleges not considered. Apply to Director of Admissions after September 1, before March 1 (priority deadline). Fall admission only for beginning students. Application fee $65. Phone: (410)706-3492; fax: (410)706-4045.

ADMISSION STANDARDS. Selective. Accepts approximately 16% of full-time and 11% of part-time applicants. Number of full-time applicants 3587, part-time 527; number of full-time acceptance 578, part-time 60; number full-time enrolled 230, part-time 28; LSAT (75% of full-time students have a score at or above 158, part-time 157); GPA (75% of full-time students have a GPA at or above 3.35, part-time 3.30). *U.S. News & World Report* ranking is in the top 36 of all U.S. law schools.

FINANCIAL AID. Scholarships, grants, loans. Apply by March 15 to Financial Aid Office. Phone: (410)706-0873. Use FAFSA (School code: 002104). About 54% of full-time and 28% of part-time of students receive aid other than loans from School. Aid available for part-time students.

DEGREE REQUIREMENTS. For J.D.: satisfactory completion of three-year program, at least one year in residence; 85 semester-hours program. For J.D.-Masters: see Graduate School listing above.

School of Medicine

Web site: www.medschool.umaryland.edu

Chartered 1808. The fifth-oldest medical school in U.S. Located in Baltimore (21201). Special facilities: R. Adams Cowley Shock Trauma Center, the Institute of Human Virology, the University of Maryland Center for Vaccine Development, the Baltimore VA Medical Center. Library: 240,000 volumes, 3100 subscriptions. NIH ranking is 32nd among all U.S. institutions with 425 awards/grants worth $181,548,023.

Annual tuition: resident $20,919, nonresident $37,262. On- and off-campus housing available. Total average figure for all other expenses: $18,490.

Enrollment: first-year class 150 (EDP 10), total 621 (men 40%, women 60%, minorities 37%, state residents 82%). Faculty: full- and part-time 1300. Degrees conferred: M.D., M.D.-M.S., M.D.-M.P.H., M.D.-Ph.D.

ADMISSION REQUIREMENTS. AMCAS report, transcripts, MCAT, letters of recommendation required in support of application. A second-stage application is required. Interview by invitation only. Applicants must have completed at least three years of college study. Preference given to Maryland residents. Accepts transfer applicants in second and third years on a space available basis. Graduates of unaccredited colleges not considered. Has EDP for Maryland residents only; apply between June 1 and August 1. Apply to Director of Admissions after June 1, before November 1. Application fee $70. Phone: (410)706-7478.

ADMISSION STANDARDS. Competitive. Accepts about 8% of all applicants. Number of applications 3713 (2965 out-of-state); number interviewed 572 (247 out-of-state); number of acceptance 311 (120 out-of-state); number enrolled 150 (27 out-of-state). Mean Composite MCAT 10.2; mean UGPA 3.66. *U.S. News & World Report* ranking is in the top 41 of all medical research schools, 30th in primary care.

FINANCIAL AID. Scholarships, Summer fellowships, HEAL, NIH stipends, loans. Apply by June 1 to Office of Financial Aid. Phone: (410)706-7347. Use FAFSA (School code: 002104). About 88% of students receive some aid from School.

DEGREE REQUIREMENTS. For M.D.: satisfactory completion of four-year program, at least one year in residence; must pass Step 1 of USMLE for promotion to third year. For M.S., Ph.D.: see Graduate School listing above.

FIELDS OF GRADUATE STUDY.
Anatomy.
Biochemistry and Molecular Biology.
Epidemiology and Preventive Medicine.
Gerontology.
Human Genetics.
Microbiology and Immunology.
Molecular and Cell Biology.
Molecular Medicine.
Molecular Microbiology and Immunology.
Neuroscience.
Pathology.
Pharmacology and Experimental Therapeutics.
Physical Rehabilitation Science.
Physiology.
Toxicology.

UNIVERSITY OF MARYLAND, BALTIMORE COUNTY

Baltimore, Maryland 21250
Web site: www.umbc.edu

Founded 1807. CGS member. Coed. Semester system. Special facilities: Bioimaging Center, Center for Educational Research and Development, Bradley Center for Employment and Training, Center for Fluorescience Spectrocopy, Molecular Graphic Center, Institute for Policy Analysis and Research, Sargent and Eunice Shriver Center, Structural Biochemistry Center. Library: 766,000 volumes, 4700 subscriptions. Total Campus enrollment: 11,650.

Tuition: per credit, resident $395, nonresident $652. On-campus housing for single students only. Average academic year housing cost: $7000 (including board). Contact Office of Residential Life for both on- and off-campus housing information.

Graduate School

Web site: www.umbc.edu/umgsb

Enrollment: full-time 881, part-time 1363. Faculty: full-time 333, part-time 17. Degrees conferred: M.A., M.F.A., M.P.S., M.S., Ph.D.

ADMISSION REQUIREMENTS. Transcripts, GRE, three letters of recommendation required in support of School's application. TOEFL required of international applicants. Accepts transfer applicants. Graduates of unaccredited colleges not considered. Apply to Director, Graduate Admissions and Records Office; no specified closing date. Application fee $45. Phone: (410)455-2944; fax: (410)455-1130.

ADMISSION STANDARDS. Selective in some departments, competitive in others. Usual minimum average: 3.0 (A = 4).

FINANCIAL AID. Annual awards from institutional funds: fellowships, teaching assistantships, research assistantships, internships, grants, traineeships, Federal W/S, loans. Approved for VA benefits. Apply by April 1 to the Dean's Office for fellowships, assistantships; to the Financial Aid Office for all other programs. Use FAFSA. About 30% of students receive aid other than loans from both University and outside sources. Aid available for part-time students.

DEGREE REQUIREMENTS. For master's: 30–39 semester hours minimum; thesis/nonthesis option; final exam. For M.F.A.: 60 semester hours minimum, all in full-time residence or equivalent; special final project. For Ph.D.: three years of full-time study, at least one year in residence; preliminary exam; dissertation; final exam.

FIELDS OF STUDY.
Applied and Professional Ethics.
Applied Developmental Psychology.
Applied Mathematics.
Applied Molecular Biology.
Applied Physics.
Atmospheric Physics.
Biochemistry.
Biological Sciences.
Biotechnology.
Chemical and Biochemical Engineering.
Chemistry.
Civil and Environmental Engineering.
Computer Science.
Economic Policy Analysis.
Education.
Electrical Engineering.
Emergency Health Services.
Engineering Management.
Geography and Environmental Systems.
Gerontology.
Historical Studies.
Human-Centered Computing.
Human Services Psychology.
Imaging and Digital Arts.
Information Systems.
Instructional Systems Development.
Intercultural Communication.
Language, Literacy, and Culture. Includes French, German, Spanish.
Management of Aging.
Marine-Estuarine-Environmental Sciences.
Mechanical Engineering.
Molecular and Cell Biology.
Neuroscience and Cognitive Sciences.
Operations Analysis.
Physics.
Policy Sciences.
Psychology. Includes human services psychology.
Sociology. Includes applied.
Statistics.
Systems Engineering.
Teaching.

MARYVILLE UNIVERSITY OF SAINT LOUIS
St. Louis, Missouri 63141-7299
Web site: www.maryville.edu

Founded 1872. Coed. Semester system. Library: 149,483 volumes, 3700 subscriptions.

Annual tuition: $18,600; per credit $580, Ed.D. $650. On-campus housing semi-private and private accommodations. Annual academic year housing cost: $4750 (includes board). Apply to Director of Residential Life. Phone: (314)529-9505.

Graduate Studies

Graduate study for Education since 1982, for Business since 1990. Enrollment: full-time 90, part-time 392 (men 25%, women 75%). Faculty: full-time 56, part-time 36. Degrees conferred: M.A., M.B.A., M.M.T., M.O.T., M.P.T., M.H.A., M.S.N.

ADMISSION REQUIREMENTS. Transcripts required in support of application. For Business: GMAT, personal letter explaining qualifications for graduate study. For Education: three letters of recommendation, essay. For Music Therapy: letter of intent, letters of recommendation, audition. TOEFL required for international applicants. Accepts transfer applicants. Graduates of unaccredited institutions not considered. Apply to Admission Office of appropriate school; no specified closing date. Application fee $35. School of Education phone: (314)529-9542; fax: (314)519-9921; e-mail: teachered@maryville.edu; School of Business phone: (314)529-9382; fax: (314)529-9975; e-mail: business@maryville.edu; School of Health Professions phone: (314)529-9625; fax: (314)529-9139; e-mail: hlthprofessions@ maryville.edu.

FINANCIAL AID. Professional educator scholarships, corporate reimbursement, Federal W/S, loans. Approved for VA benefits. Apply to Financial Aid Office; no specified closing date. Use FAFSA (School code: 002482). Phone: (314)576-9360; fax: (314) 542-9085; e-mail: fin_aid@maryville.edu.

DEGREE REQUIREMENTS. For master's: 30 credits minimum; thesis/nonthesis option. M.B.A.: 36 credits.

FIELDS OF STUDY.
Actuarial Science. M.S.
Business Administration. M.B.A.
Early Childhood. M.A.Ed.
Early Childhood and Leadership. M.A.Ed.
Educational Leadership. M.A.
Elementary Education. M.A.Ed.
Environmental Education. M.A.Ed.
Gifted Education. M.A.
Health Administration. M.H.A.
Middle School Education. M.A.Ed.
Music Therapy. M.M.T.
Nursing. Includes adult nurse practitioner, gerontological clinical nurse specialist. M.S.N.
Occupational Therapy. M.O.T.
Physical Therapy. M.P.T.
Reading. M.A.
Rehabilitation Counseling. M.A.
Secondary Education. M.A.Ed.

MARYWOOD UNIVERSITY
Scranton, Pennsylvania 18509-1598
Web site: www.marywood.edu

Founded 1915. Located approximately 100 miles W of New York City and 100 miles N of Philadelphia. Coed. Private control. Roman Catholic. Semester system. Library: 202,000 volumes, 221,000 microforms, 1100 subscriptions. Total University enrollment: 3000.

Tuition: per credit $695; $695 for M.F.A; doctoral programs $750. On-campus housing for single students only. Average academic year housing cost: $3948–$9100 (including board). Contact Office of Student Affairs for on- and off-campus housing information. Phone: (570)348-6236. Day-care facilities available.

Graduate School of Arts and Sciences

Graduate study since 1922. Enrollment: full-time 181, part-time 466. Graduate faculty: full-time 80, part-time 63. Degrees conferred: M.A., M.S., M.P.A., M.B.A., M.F.A., M.P.A.-M.S.W., C.A.G.S., Ph.D.

ADMISSION REQUIREMENTS. Transcripts, two letters of recommendation, GRE or MAT, GMAT (Business) required in support of School's application. Online application available. TOEFL required for international applicants. Accepts transfer applicants. Graduates of unaccredited institutions not considered. Apply to Graduate Admission Office by July 1 (Fall), December 1 (Spring), April 15 (Summer). Application fee $30. Phone: (570)340-6002; fax: (570)961-4759; e-mail: gsas_adm@ac.marywood.edu.

ADMISSION STANDARDS. Selective. Usual minimum average: 3.0 (A = 4).

FINANCIAL AID. Annual awards from institutional funds: scholarships, assistantships, internships, tuition waivers, loans. Apply by February 15 to Dean of Graduate School of Arts and Sciences for scholarships, assistantships; to Financial Aid Office for loans. Phone: (570)348-6225. Use FAFSA. About 55% of students receive aid other than loans from College and outside sources. Aid available for part-time students.

DEGREE REQUIREMENTS. For master's: 30–60 credits; thesis/professional contribution; comprehensive exams. For C.A.G.S.: 30 credits beyond the master's; special project. For Ph.D.: 60 credits beyond the master's minimum, at least one year in full-time residence; qualifying exam; dissertation; final oral exam.

FIELDS OF STUDY.
Art. Includes two-dimensional, three-dimensional. M.F.A.
Art Education. M.A.
Art Therapy. M.A.
Biotechnology. M.S.
Business Administration. M.B.A.
Business and Managerial Science. M.S.
Church Music. M.A.
Communication Arts. M.A.
Communication Sciences and Disorders. M.S.
Counseling. Includes addictions, agency, pastoral. M.A.
Counseling. Includes elementary, secondary. M.S.
Criminal Justice. M.P.A.
Dietetics. M.S.
Early Childhood Intervention. M.S.
Education. Includes school leadership, early childhood, elementary, instructional technology, reading. M.S.
Elementary Education. M.A.T.
Finance and Investments. M.B.A.
Fine Arts. M.F.A.
Foods and Nutrition. Includes nutrition, sports nutrition, critical care/nutritional support, food systems management, gerontology. M.S.
Gerontology. M.P.A.
Health Services Administration. M.B.A., M.P.A.
Higher Education Administration. M.S.
Human Development. Interdisciplinary. M.A., Ph.D.

Industrial Management. M.B.A.
Information Sciences. M.S.
Instructional Leadership. M.A.
Instructional Technology. M.S.
Management Information Systems. M.S.
Management of Nonprofit Organizations. M.P.A.
Music. M.A.
Music Education. M.A.
Music Therapy. M.M.T.
Nursing. M.S.
Nutrition. M.S.
Psychology. Includes clinical services, general/theoretical, school/child. M.A.
Public Administration. M.P.A.
Reading. M.S.
School Leadership. M.S.
Secondary Education. M.A.T.
Social Work. M.S.W.
Special Education. M.S.
Speech-Language Pathology. M.S.
Sport Nutrition and Exercise Science. M.S.
Studio Art. M.A.
Teaching. M.A.
Theological Studies. M.A.
Visual Arts. M.F.A.

MASSACHUSETTS COLLEGE OF ART
Boston, Massachusetts 02115-5882
Web site: massart.edu

Founded 1873. Coed. State control. Semester system. Library: 231,586 volumes, 757 subscriptions. Total College enrollment: 2150.

Tuition: per credit $483. No on-campus housing available for graduate students. Contact Housing Office for off-campus housing information. Phone: (617)879-7750.

Graduate Program

Enrollment: full-time 73, part-time 28. Faculty: full-time 13, part-time 13. Degrees conferred: M.S., M.S.A.E., M.F.A.

ADMISSION REQUIREMENTS. Transcripts, bachelor's degree, three letters of recommendation, statement of purpose, portfolio required in support of application. TOEFL required for international applicants. Accepts transfer applicants. Apply to Admissions Office by February 1. Application fee $50. Phone: (617)879-7163; fax: (617)879-7171.

ADMISSION STANDARDS. Competitive. Portfolio/talent-based selection process.

FINANCIAL AID. Annual awards from institutional funds: administrative assistantships, teaching assistantships, technical assistantships, internships, Federal W/S, loans. Apply by May 1 to the Financial Aid Office. Phone: (617)879-7850. Use FAFSA (College code: 002180). Aid available for part-time students.

DEGREE REQUIREMENTS. For M.S., M.S.A.E.: 36 semester hours. For M.F.A.: 60 semester hours.

FIELDS OF STUDY.
Art Education. M.S.A.E.
Fine Arts. Includes ceramics, painting, printmaking, sculpture, design, fibers, glass, metalsmithing, photography, film/video, studio for interrelated media. M.F.A.

MASSACHUSETTS COLLEGE OF PHARMACY AND ALLIED HEALTH SCIENCES

Boston, Massachusetts 02115-5896
Web site: www.mcphs.edu

Founded 1823. Coed. Private control. Has campuses in Worcester and Manchester, NH. Special facilities: Samuel M. Best Research Laboratory, Pfeiffer Pharmaceutics Laboratory. Library: 75,000 volumes, 790 subscriptions.

Tuition: per hour $810. Housing on nearby campus. Annual academic year housing cost: approximately $6500–$9240.

Graduate Study

Enrollment: full-time 33, part-time 61. Graduate faculty: full-time 18, part-time 3. Degrees conferred: M.S., Ph.D.

ADMISSION REQUIREMENTS. Transcripts, GRE, two letters of recommendation, 500-word essay, résumé required in support of application. TOEFL, TSE required for international applicants. Interview not required. Accepts transfer applicants. Graduates of unaccredited colleges not considered. Apply by February 1 for September admission. Some programs have later deadlines. Admits normally to Fall only. Application fee $70. Phone: (617) 732-2850; fax: (617)732-2118; e-mail: admission@mcphs.edu.

ADMISSION STANDARDS. Selective. Usual minimum average: 3.0 (A = 4).

FINANCIAL AID. Annual awards from institutional funds: teaching fellowships, research assistantships, tuition waivers, Federal W/S, loans. Approved for VA benefits. Apply to Associate Dean for Graduate Studies by March 15 for assistantships, fellowships; to Financial Aid Office for all other programs. Phone: (617)732-2861; fax: (617)732-2801. Use FAFSA. About 25% of students receive aid other than loans from the College, 30% from other sources. No aid for part-time students.

DEGREE REQUIREMENTS. For M.S.: 30 semester hours minimum, normally in full-time residence; thesis; final oral exam. For Ph.D.: 50 semester hours minimum beyond bachelor's, normally in full-time residence; one language or research skill; preliminary exam; dissertation; final written/oral exam.

FIELDS OF STUDY.
Applied Natural Products. M.A.N.P.
Chemistry/Medicinal Chemistry. M.S., Ph.D.
Chemistry/Pharmaceutical Chemistry. B.S./M.S.
Drug Discovery and Development. M.S.
Pharmaceutics. M.S., Ph.D.
Pharmacology. M.S., Ph.D.
Physician Assistant Studies. M.P.A.S.
Radiologist Assistant Studies. M.R.A.S.
Regulatory Affairs and Health Policy. M.S.

MASSACHUSETTS INSTITUTE OF TECHNOLOGY

Cambridge, Massachusetts 02139
Web site: www.mit.edu

Founded 1861. Located adjacent to Boston. CGS and AAU member. Coed. Private control. 4-1-4 system. Special facilities: Biotechnology Process Engineering Center, Center for Cognitive Science, Center for Environmental Health Sciences, Center for Global Change Science, Center for Information Systems Research, Center for International Studies, Center for Materials Science and Engineering, Materials Processing Center, Center for Space Research, Center for Transportation, Computation Center, Joint Center for Urban Studies with Harvard University, Laboratory for Nuclear Science, Haystack Observatory, Lincoln Laboratory for Research and Development in Advanced Electronics, media laboratory, Leaders for Manufacturing, National Magnet Laboratory, Operations Research Center, Research Laboratory of Electronics, nuclear reactor, Whitehead Institute for Biomedical Research, MIT-Japan Science and Technology, spectroscopy laboratory. The Institute's NIH ranking is 35th among all U.S. institutions with 280 awards/grants valued at $172,184,305. According to The Center at University of Florida, the Institute is ranked 12th in receipt of Federal Research funds with $356,206,000 and it ranks 15th for total Institute research expenditures with $485,764,000. The Institute's endowment assets rank it 5th, with a value of $5,865,212,000. In 2004, the Institute awarded 467 doctorates, which ranked it 119th among all U.S. institutions eligible to award that degree. Two hundred thirty-eight of the Institute's faculty members have been elected to National Honor Academies and this ranks it 3rd among all U.S. institutions. The Library: approximately 2,700,000 volumes, 22,000 subscriptions. Total Institute enrollment: 10,500.

Annual tuition: full-time $32,100. On-campus housing for 40 married students, 800 graduate men and women. Average monthly room and board cost: $2200–$2500 for married students, $1425 for single students. Apply to Manager of Ashdown House (single students) or to Campus Housing Office (married students). Phone: (617)253-5148; apply to Off-Campus Housing Service for off-campus housing information. Phone: (617)253-4449.

Graduate School

Graduate study since 1886. Enrollment: full-time 5831. Faculty: full-time 933, part-time 14. Degrees conferred: M.Arch., M.B.A., S.M., M.Eng., Engineer, Sc.D., M.Arch.A.S., M.C.P., Ph.D.

ADMISSION REQUIREMENTS. Transcripts, three references, statement of purpose required in support of School's application. Online application available. GRE required by some departments, recommended for the others. Interview not required. TOEFL required of international students. Accepts transfer applicants. Graduates of unaccredited institutions not considered. Contact individual Departments for most current information. Apply to your Department of choice by December 15 (Fall or Summer), September 15 (Spring). Later applications are considered if vacancies still exist. Application fee $70. Phone: (617)253-2917; fax: (617)253-8304; e-mail: mitgrad@mit.edu.

ADMISSION STANDARDS. Competitive. Usual minimum average: 3.5 (A = 4).

FINANCIAL AID. Annual awards from institutional funds: scholarships, fellowships, teaching assistantships, research assistantships, traineeships, Federal W/S, loans. Apply by January 15 to Director of Admissions for scholarships or traineeships, loans; to appropriate department chair for assistantships. Phone: (617) 253-4971; fax: (617)258-8301. Use FAFSA and institutional FAF. About 80% of students receive aid other than loans from School and outside sources. No aid for part-time students. Aid may be available for international students after the first year of full-time study.

DEGREE REQUIREMENTS. For S.M.: 66 subject units minimum, at least one term in residence; thesis. For M.Eng.: 90 subject units minimum, at least one term in residence; thesis. For M.C.P.: 126 subject units; at least two terms in residence; thesis. For M.Arch.: 164 subject units minimum, at least 96 in residence; thesis. For Engineering: 162 units minimum beyond the bachelor's, at least one year in residence; thesis. For Sc.D., Ph.D.: three years minimum beyond the bachelor's, at least four terms full-time in residence; general written exam in two fields; language requirements vary with department; dissertation; final oral exam.

FIELDS OF STUDY.

SCHOOL OF ARCHITECTURE AND PLANNING:
Architecture. M.Arch.
Architecture Studies. M.S.
Building Technology. M.S., Ph.D.
City Planning. M.C.P.
Design and Computation. Ph.D.
History and Theory of Art and Architecture. Ph.D.
Media Arts and Sciences. M.S., Ph.D.
Media Technology. M.S.
Real Estate Development. M.S.
Urban Studies and Planning. M.S., Ph.D.
Visual Studies. M.S.

SCHOOL OF ENGINEERING:
Aeronautics and Astronautics.
Biological Engineering.
Chemical Engineering.
Civil and Environmental Engineering.
Electrical Engineering and Computer Science.
Materials Science and Engineering.
Mechanical Engineering.
Nuclear Science and Engineering.
Ocean Engineering.

SCHOOL OF HUMANITIES AND SOCIAL SCIENCE:
Anthropology.
Comparative Media Studies.
Foreign Languages and Literatures. Includes Chinese, French, German, Italian, Japanese, Spanish.
History.
Linguistics.
Literature.
Music and Theater Arts.
Philosophy.
Political Science.
Science Technology and Science.

SCHOOL OF SCIENCE:
Biology.
Brain and Cognitive Sciences.
Chemistry.
Earth, Atmospheric, and Planetary Sciences.
Mathematics.
Physics.

WHITAKER COLLEGE OF HEALTH SCIENCES AND TECHNOLOGY:
Biomedical Engineering.
Biomedical Enterprise.
Biomedical Informatics.
Medical Engineering and Medical Physics.
Radiological Sciences.
Speech and Hearing Bioscience and Technology.

INTERDEPARTMENTAL PROGRAMS:
Biomedical Engineering.
Computation for Design and Optimization.
Computational and System Biology.
Economics and Urban Studies.
Health Sciences and Technology.
Leaders for Manufacturing.
Logistics.
Medical Engineering and Medical Physics.
Microbiology.
Oceanography.
Operations Research.
Polymer Science and Technology.
Real Estate Development.
Systems Design and Management.
Technology and Policy.

Technology, Management and Policy.
Transportation.

Sloan School of Management
Web site: mitsloan.mit.edu

Established 1925. Private control. Accredited programs: M.B.A. Semester system. Special programs: foreign exchange programs in Spain, United Kingdom. Special facilities: Center for Computational Research in Economics and Management Science, Center for Coordination Science, Center for Energy and Environmental Policy Research, Center for Information Systems Research, Center for Innovation in Product Development, Finance Research Center, International Center for Research on the Management of Technology, the MIT Entrepreneurship Center, Operations Research Center.

Annual tuition: full-time $44,556. Estimated annual budget for tuition, room and board, and personal expenses: $72,282; Ph.D. $33,400. Enrollment: total full-time 714 (men 70%, women 30%). Faculty: 91 full-time, 5 part-time; all have Ph.D./D.B.A. Degrees conferred: M.B.A. (full-time only) (concentrations in Entrepreneurship, Finance, Management, Management Information Systems, Management Science, Marketing, Operations Management, Strategic Management), M.S. (majors in Management, Management Information Systems, Management Science, Operations Management, Strategic Management), Ph.D.

ADMISSION REQUIREMENTS. All applicants should have a bachelor's degree from a recognized institution of higher education, a strong mathematics background, a 3.0 (A = 4) GPA, and a GMAT score of 600. Students are required to have their own personal computer. Early applications are encouraged for both admission and financial aid consideration. Submit application, GMAT results (will accept GMAT test results from the last five years, latest acceptable date is January), official transcripts from each undergraduate/graduate school attended, cover letter of at least 500 words, two letters of recommendation, two essays, résumé (prefers at least four years of work experience), and an application fee of $230 to the Director of Master's Admission. Interview by invitation. Beginning students are admitted Fall only. Both U.S. citizens and international applicants apply by October 30 (Round 1), January 15 (Round 2). In addition, international students (whose native language is other than English) should submit a TOEFL report (minimum score 600), certified translations and evaluations of all official transcripts, recommendation should be in English or with certified translations, proof of health/immunization certificate, and proof of sufficient financial resources for two years of academic study. Admissions Office phone: (617)253-3730; fax: (617) 253-6405.

ADMISSION REQUIREMENTS FOR DOCTORAL CANDIDATES. Contact Sloan Doctoral Programs at (617)253-7188 for application material and information. Beginning students are admitted Fall only. Both U.S. citizens and international applicants apply by January 7 (Fall). Submit application, GMAT/GRE (General only; will accept GMAT/GRE test results from the last five years), official transcripts from each undergraduate/graduate schools attended, three letters of recommendation, written description of background, interests, and career expectations, résumé, statement of purpose, and application fee of $75 to Sloan Doctoral Programs Office. Online applications available. In addition, international students (whose native language is other than English) should submit a TOEFL report (minimum score 575), certified translations and evaluations of all official transcripts, recommendation should be in English or with certified translations, proof of health/immunization certificate. International students' contact: (617)253-3795. Interviews by invitation. Notification is made by mid-March.

ADMISSION STANDARDS. For M.B.A.: median GMAT: 650; median GPA: 3.5 (A = 4). For Ph.D.: number of applications

400–500; number enrolled 15–20. Gourman rating: the M.B.A. was rated in the top five the score was 4.91; the Ph.D. was rated in the top five, the score was 4.91. *U.S. News & World Report* ranked Sloan School in the top four of all U.S. business schools. *Business-Week* listed Sloan School in the top ten of all U.S. business schools.

FINANCIAL AID. Fellowships, research and teaching assistant-ships, Federal W/S, loans. Financial aid may be available for in-ternational students. Financial Aid applications and information are generally available at the on-campus interview or included in application materials; apply by January 15. Request fellowship and assistantship information from the Sloan School. Contact the University's Financial Aid Office for current need-based finan-cial aid information; phone: (617)258-5775. Use FAFSA (School code: 002103), also submit Financial Aid Transcript, Federal In-come Tax forms. Approximately 60% of students receive some form of financial assistance.

DEGREE REQUIREMENTS. For M.B.A., M.S.: 18–24 month programs. For M.Acc., M.P.A., M.S.T.: 32-credit program. For M.B.A.-master's: generally a three-and-one-half- to five-year pro-gram. For M.B.A.-J.D.: four-and-one-half- to five-year program. For Ph.D.: three- to five-year program; general exam in major and minor field; dissertation proposal and oral defense, dissertation; oral defense.

AREAS OF DOCTORAL STUDY.
Management Science. Includes information technologies, mar-keting, operations management, system dynamics.
Behavioral and Policy Studies. Includes economic sociology, global economics and management, organization studies, work and employment research, technological innovation and entre-preneurship, strategy and international management.
Economics, Finance and Accounting. Includes financial econom-ics, accounting and control.

UNIVERSITY OF MASSACHUSETTS AMHERST

Amherst, Massachusetts 01003-0001
Web site: www.umass.edu

Founded 1863. Located 90 miles W of Boston. Amherst campus is primary graduate school location. CGS member. State control. Semester system. Special facilities: University Computing Center, Donahue Institute for Government Services, Institute for Advanced Studies in the Humanities, Polymer Research Institute, Labor Relations and Research Center, Environmental Institute, Water Resources Center, Hampshire Inter-Library Center, Marine Sta-tion, Suburban Experiment Station, University of Massachusetts Abroad, Center for Instructional Resources and Improvement, Office of Research Services, University Press, Center for Busi-ness and Economic Research, Polymer Research Institute. Five-College (Amherst, Hampshire, Mount Holyoke, Smith, University of Massachusetts) cooperative undergraduate and graduate pro-grams. The University's NIH ranking is 58th among all U.S. institutions with 315 awards/grants valued at $114,697,778. Ac-cording to The Center at University of Florida, the University is ranked 66th in receipt of Federal Research funds with $109,082,000 and it ranks 92nd for total University research ex-penditures with $148,823,000. In 2004, the University awarded 274 doctorates, which ranked it 51st among all U.S. institutions eligible to award that degree. Seven of the University's faculty members have been elected to National Honor Academies and this ranks it 78th among all U.S. institutions. The Library: ap-proximately 4,700,000 volumes, 15,300 subscriptions. Total In-stitute enrollment: 25,000.

Tuition: per hour, resident $120, nonresident $420, New En-gland region $192. Mandatory fees: full-time resident $3727, nonresident $4620. On-campus housing for 300 graduate single students; 345 married students. Average academic year housing cost: $6310 (including board) for single students; $7200–$10,000 for married students. Apply to Housing Office. Phone: (413)545-2100. Day-care facilities available.

Graduate School
Web site: www.umass.edu/gradschool

Graduate study since 1876. Enrollment: full-time 2013, part-time 2319. University faculty: full-and part-time 1161. Degrees conferred: M.A., M.S., M.S.E.C.E., M.R.P., M.A.T., Ch.E., M.S.C.E., M.S.Envr.E., M.S.I.E.O.R., M.S.M.E., M.P.A., M.P.H., M.Ed., M.B.A., M.F.A., M.L.A., M.M., C.A.G.S., Ed.D., Ph.D., Five-College Ph.D.

ADMISSION REQUIREMENTS. Transcripts, two recommen-dations, GRE or GMAT, proof of residency form required in sup-port of School's application. Interview not required. TOEFL required for international applicants. Graduates of unaccredited institutions not considered. Apply to Graduate Admissions Of-fice by March 1 (Fall and Summer), October 1 (Spring). Some programs may have earlier deadline. Application fee $40, $65 for international applicants. Phone: (413)545-0721; fax: (413)577-0010; e-mail: gradinfo@ resgs.umass.edu.

ADMISSION STANDARDS. Very selective for most depart-ments. Usual minimum average: 3.0 (A = 4).

FINANCIAL AID. Annual awards from institutional funds: fel-lowships, internships, teaching assistantships, research assistant-ships, grants, tuition waivers, NSF and NIH traineeships, Federal W/S, loans. Apply to Financial Aid Office; no specified closing date. Phone: (413)545-0801. Use FAFSA. About 50% of students receive aid other than loans from University and outside sources.

DEGREE REQUIREMENTS. For most master's: 30 credits; the-sis; final general exam. For M.A.T.: 39–45 credits. For M.Ed.: 33 credits. For M.B.A.: 55 credits. For M.F.A.: 60 credits; final M.F.A. creative project (English, Art, Theater). For M.R.P., M.L.A.: 46 credits; internships; research project; thesis optional. For M.M.: 33 credits; one original composition in lieu of thesis for composition majors. For C.A.G.S.: 30 credits beyond mas-ter's. For Ph.D., Ed.D.: course work as specified by program, at least two consecutive semesters in full-time residence; compre-hensive exam; foreign language requirement varies by program; dissertation; final oral exam. The Statute of Limitations (maxi-mum time allowed in which to earn the degree) is six years for the doctorate, four years for the M.F.A., and three years for all other master's degree programs; a part-time student may apply for an additional year in which to complete a program.

FIELDS OF STUDY.
Accounting.
Afro-American Studies.
Animal Science.
Anthropology.
Applied Mathematics.
Architecture and Design.
Art.
Art History.
Astronomy.
Audiology.
Chemical Engineering.
Chemistry.
Chinese.
Civil Engineering.
Communication.
Communication Disorders.
Comparative Literature.
Computer Science.
Economics.

Education.
Electrical and Computer Engineering.
Engineering Management.
English.
Entomology.
Environmental Engineering.
Food Science.
Forest Resources.
French and Francophone Studies.
Geography.
Geology.
Geosciences.
Germanic and Scandinavian Studies.
Hispanic Literature and Linguistics.
History.
Hotel and Tourism Management.
Industrial Engineering and Operations Research.
Italian Studies.
Japanese.
Kinesiology.
Labor Studies.
Landscape Architecture.
Latin and Classical Humanities.
Linguistics.
Management.
Mathematics.
Mechanical Engineering.
Microbiology.
Molecular and Cellular Biology.
Music.
Neuroscience and Behavior.
Nursing.
Nutrition.
Organismic and Evolutionary Biology.
Philosophy.
Physics.
Plant and Soil Sciences.
Plant Biology.
Political Science.
Polymer Science and Engineering.
Psychology.
Public Administration.
Public Health.
Regional Planning.
Resource Economics.
School Psychology.
Sociology.
Sport Management.
Theater.
Wildlife and Fisheries Conservation.

Medical School

Web site: www.umassmed.edu

Established 1962. Located in Worcester (01655-0115). Special facilities: Brudnick Neuropsychiatric Research Institute, Cancer Center, Cardiovascular Thrombosis Research Center, Center for Adoption Research, Center for AIDS Research, Center for Comparative Neuroimaging, Center for Health Policy and Research, Center for Infectious Diseases and Vaccine Research, Center for Mental Health Services Research, Center for Platelet Function Studies, Center for Outcomes Research, Meyers Primary Care Institute, Shriver Center. Library: 100,000 volumes, 1200 subscriptions. NIH ranking is 58th among all U.S. institutions with 315 awards/grants worth $114,692,778.

Annual tuition: resident $14,062, nonresident not applicable. No on-campus housing available. Total average figure for all other expenses: $15,300.

Enrollment: first-year class 102 (EDP 10); total 423 (men 45%, women 55%, minorities 21%, state residents 99%). Faculty: full- and part-time 1000. Degrees conferred: M.D., M.D.-Ph.D.

ADMISSION REQUIREMENTS. AMCAS report, transcripts, MCAT, recommendations, interview required in support of application. Non-Massachusetts residents, graduates of unaccredited colleges not considered. Accepts transfer applicants on a space available basis. Has EDP; apply between June 1 and August 1. Apply after June 1, before November 1. Application fee $75. Phone: (508)856-2323; fax: (508)856-3629.

ADMISSION STANDARDS. Competitive. Accepts about 21% of all applicants. Number of applications 795 (122 out-of-state); number interviewed 440 (16 out-of-state); number of acceptance 181 (5 out-of-state); number enrolled 102 (2 out-of-state). Mean Composite MCAT 10.4; mean UGPA 3.58. *U.S. News & World Report* ranking is in the top 49 of all medical research schools, 10th in primary care.

FINANCIAL AID. Scholarships, minority scholarships, grants, institutional loans, HEAL, alternative loan programs, learning contracts, tuition waivers, loans, Service Commitment Scholarships to the Commonwealth in primary care are available. Tuition waivers/stipends may be available for M.D.-Ph.D. degree candidates. Financial Aid applications and information are given out at the on-campus by-invitation interview or sent with the letter of acceptance. Contact the Financial Aid Office for current information. Phone: (508)856-2265. Use FAFSA (School code: G09756), also submit Financial Aid Transcript, Federal Income Tax forms; use CSS profile for all campus-based funds. Approximately 89% of students receive some form of financial assistance.

DEGREE REQUIREMENTS. For M.D.: satisfactory completion of four-year program; all students required to take both Step 1 and Step 2 of USMLE. For M.D.-Ph.D.: generally a six- to seven-year program.

FIELDS OF GRADUATE STUDY.
Biomedical Engineering and Medical Physics. A joint program with Worcester Polytechnic Institute.
Biochemistry and Molecular Pharmacology.
Cancer Biology.
Cell Biology.
Cellular and Molecular Physiology.
Clinical and Population Health Research.
Immunology and Virology.
Molecular Genetics.
Microbiology.
Neuroscience.

UNIVERSITY OF MASSACHUSETTS BOSTON

Boston, Massachusetts 02125-3393
Web site: www.umb.edu

Founded 1964. CGS member. Coed. State control. Semester system. Special facilities: Center for the Advancement of Teaching in the Sciences, Asian-American Institute, Gerontology Institute, Gaston Institute for Latino Affairs, Institute for Learning and Teaching, McCormack Institute of Public Affairs, Center for Survey Research, Joiner Center for the Study of War and Social Consequences, Trotter Institute for the Study of Black Culture, Urban Harbors Institute. Library: 572,000 volumes, 3120 subscriptions. Total University enrollment: 13,500.

Tuition: per credit, resident $110, nonresident $414. No on- or off-campus housing available (commuter institution). Day-care facilities available.

Graduate Studies and Research

Enrollment: full-time 770, part-time 1950. University faculty: full-time 488, part-time 71. Degrees conferred: M.A., M.S., M.Ed., M.B.A., C.A.G.S., Ph.D., Ed.D., Graduate Certificate.

ADMISSION REQUIREMENTS. Transcripts, GRE/MAT/GMAT, three letters of recommendation, statement of intent required in support of application. TOEFL required for international applicants. Accepts transfer applicants. Graduates of unaccredited institutions not considered. Apply to Office of Graduate Admissions and Records. Application deadlines vary by program; priority deadlines March 1 (Fall), November 1 (Spring); for international applicants apply by May 1 (Fall), October 1 (Spring). Some programs have earlier deadlines. Application fee $40 (residents), $60 (nonresidents). Phone: (617)287-6400; fax: (617)287-7173.

ADMISSION STANDARDS. Selective. Usual minimum average: 2.75 (A = 4).

FINANCIAL AID. Academic scholarships, grants, research assistantships, administrative assistantships, teaching assistantships, internships, tuition waivers, Federal W/S, loans. Approved for VA benefits. Apply by March 1 to Director of Financial Aid. Phone: (617)287-6300; fax: (617)287-6323. Use FAFSA and institutional FAF. Aid available for part-time students.

DEGREE REQUIREMENTS. For master's: 30 credits minimum; thesis and general exam for some departments. For Ph.D.: 60 credits beyond the master's minimum; two semesters in full-time residence; qualifying exam; one foreign language required for some departments; dissertation; final oral exam. For Ed.D.: essentially the same as Ph.D. except no foreign language requirement.

FIELDS OF STUDY.
Accounting. M.S.
Adapting the Curriculum. M.Ed.
American Studies. M.A.
Applied Linguistics. M.S.
Applied Physics. M.S.
Applied Sociology. M.A.
Bilingual Education. M.A.
Biology. M.S.
Biomedical Engineering and Biotechnology. M.S.
Biotechnology and Biomedical Science. M.S.
Business Administration. M.B.A.
Chemistry. M.S.
Clinical Psychology. Ph.D.
Computer Science. M.S., Ph.D.
Counseling. M.Ed., C.A.G.S.
Critical and Creative Thinking. M.A., Graduate Certificate.
Database Technology. M.S.
Dispute Resolution. M.A., Graduate Certificate.
Education/Higher Educational Administration. Ed.D.
Education/Leadership in Urban Schools. Ed.D.
Educational Administration. M.Ed., C.A.G.S.
English. M.A.
Environmental Sciences. M.S., Ph.D.
Environmental Sciences—Environmental Biology. M.S., Ph.D.
Environmental Sciences—Environmental, Coastal, and Ocean Sciences. M.S., Ph.D.
Environmental Sciences—Green Chemistry. M.S., Ph.D.
Environmental Sciences—Molecular, Cellular and Organismal Biology. M.S., Ph.D.
Forensic Services. M.S.
Gerontology. Ph.D.
History. M.A.
History/Archival Methods. M.A.
History/Historical Archaeology. M.A.
Human Services. M.S.
Instructional Design. M.Ed.
Instructional Technology Design. M.Ed.
International Relations. M.A.
Marine Sciences and Technology. M.S.
Nursing. M.S., Ph.D.
Nursing/Business Administration. M.S.
Public Affairs. M.S.
Public Policy. Ph.D.
School Psychology. M.Ed., C.A.G.S.
Special Education. M.Ed.
Teacher Education. M.Ed.
Teachers of Visually Impaired. M.Ed.
Teaching of Spanish. Certificate.
Women in Politics and Public Policy. M.A.

UNIVERSITY OF MASSACHUSETTS DARTMOUTH

North Dartmouth, Massachusetts 02747-2300
Web site: www.umassd.edu

Founded 1895. Located 50 miles S of Boston. Coed. State control. Semester system. Special facilities: Center for Marine Science and Technology (CMAST), Northeast Regional Aquaculture Center; research affiliations with Brookhaven National Lab (physics), Marine Biological Lab (marine sciences), and Woods Hole Oceanographic Institute (marine sciences); 2 Digital VAX 6610 mainframe computers; 150 IBM and Macintosh personal computers in cluster labs. Library: 947,000 volumes, 4500 subscriptions. Total Campus enrollment: 8550.

Annual tuition/fees: full-time (9 credits each semester) resident $6740, nonresident $18,426. Limited on-campus housing for graduate students. Average academic year housing cost: $7537. Contact Office of Residential Life for both on- and off-campus housing information. Phone: (508)999-8140. Day-care facilities available.

Graduate School

Enrollment: full-time 331, part-time 445, Graduate faculty: full-time 279, part-time 138. Degrees conferred: M.A., M.S., M.F.A., M.B.A., M.A.E.

ADMISSION REQUIREMENTS. Official transcripts, three letters of recommendation required in support of School's application. GRE Subject Test/GMAT/MAT required by some programs. Interview not required. TOEFL required for international applicants. Accepts transfer applicants. Graduates of unaccredited institutions not considered. Apply to Graduate Admissions Office by April 20 (September), November 20 (January); international applicants apply by February 20 (September), September 15 (January). Application fee resident $50, nonresident $60. Phone: (508)999-8604; fax: (508)999-8183; e-mail: graduate@umass.edu.

ADMISSION STANDARDS. Selective. Usual minimum average: 2.75 (A = 4).

FINANCIAL AID. Research fellowships, teaching assistantships, internships, tuition waivers, Federal W/S, loans. Approved for VA benefits. Apply by March 1 to Dean, Graduate School for fellowships, assistantships; to Financial Aid Office for all other programs. Phone: (508)999-9632. Use FAFSA and University's FAF. About 20% of students receive aid other than loans from University. Aid available for part-time study.

DEGREE REQUIREMENTS. For master's: 30 credits minimum, at least 24 in residence; comprehensive exam; thesis/nonthesis option.

FIELDS OF STUDY.
Art Education.
Artisanry. Includes ceramics, jewelry/metals, textile/fiber arts, wood and furniture design.
Biomedical Engineering/Biotechnology. Joint Ph.D. program with University of Massachusetts, Lowell.

Biology/Marine Biology.

Business Administration.

Chemistry. Joint Ph.D. program with University of Massachusetts, Lowell.

Civil and Environmental Engineering.

Computer Engineering.

Computer Science.

Design. Portfolio for admission.

Electrical Engineering.

Elementary Education.

Fine Arts. Includes studios in drawing, painting, printmaking, sculpture.

Graphic Design.

Luso-Afro-Brazilian Studies and Theory.

Marine Sciences and Technology. University-of-Massachusetts-wide joint Ph.D.

Mechanical Engineering.

Middle Education.

Nursing.

Physics.

Policy Studies.

Portuguese Studies.

Professional Writing.

Psychology.

Secondary Education. Includes business, English, foreign literature and languages (French, Portuguese, Spanish), history, mathematics, social studies.

Teaching.

Textile Chemistry.

Textile Technology.

Visual Design. Includes studios in graphic design, electronic imaging, illustration, multimedia, photography, typography.

UNIVERSITY OF MASSACHUSETTS LOWELL

Lowell, Massachusetts 01854-2881

Web site: www.uml.edu

Founded 1897. Located 25 miles N of Boston. CGS member. State control. Semester system. Special facilities: Center for the Arts, Center for Criminal Justice, Center for Family and Community Studies, Center for Field Service, Center for Health Promotion, Center for Lowell History, Pinaski Energy Center, Institute for Plastics Innovation, Center for Productivity Enhancement, Toxic Use Reduction Center, Tsongas Industrial History Center. Library: 549,000 volumes, 7855 subscriptions. Total University enrollment: 10,600.

Tuition/fees: per credit resident $472, New England region $528, nonresident $929. On-campus housing available. Average academic year housing cost: $6500 (including board). Contact Housing Officer for on- and off-campus housing information. Phone: (978)934-2107.

The Graduate School

Founded 1935. Enrollment: full-time 613, part-time 1840 (men 55%, women 45%). Faculty: full-time 450, part-time 50. Degrees conferred: M.S., M.Ed., M.B.A., M.M.S., M.S.Eng., M.A., C.A.G.S., M.M., Ph.D., D.Sc., D.Eng., D.Ed., Certificate.

ADMISSION REQUIREMENTS. Transcripts, three references, GRE/GMAT/MAT required in support of School's application. Online application available. TOEFL required for international applicants. Interview not required. Accepts transfer applicants. Graduates of unaccredited institutions not considered. Apply to Graduate School Office by May 1 (Fall), October 1 (Spring). Application fee $35, $55 for international applicants. Phone:

(800)656-GRAD or (978)934-2380; fax: (978)934-3010; e-mail: graduate_school@uml.edu.

ADMISSION STANDARDS. Selective. Usual minimum average: 2.75 (A = 4).

FINANCIAL AID. Annual awards from institutional funds: scholarships, research assistantships, teaching assistantships, fellowships, Federal W/S, loans. Approved for VA benefits. Apply by April 1 to appropriate department chair for assistantships; to Financial Aid Office for all other programs. Use FAFSA. Phone: (978)934-4220. About 10% of students receive aid other than loans from University and outside sources. Aid available for part-time students.

DEGREE REQUIREMENTS. For master's: 30 credit hours minimum including thesis, at least one year in residence; final written/oral exam. For C.A.G.S.: 30 credits beyond the master's; project for some programs. For Certificates: twelve credits minimum; all credits applicable to master's degree. For Ph.D.: two to three years minimum in residence beyond the master's, depending upon previous preparation; preliminary exam; qualifying exam; dissertation; final oral exam. For D.Sc., D.Eng.: requirements are essentially the same as for Ph.D.

FIELDS OF STUDY.

Biological Sciences. Includes biotechnology.

Biomedical Engineering and Biotechnology.

Business Administration.

Chemical Engineering.

Chemistry. Includes biochemistry, environmental studies.

Civil Engineering. Includes geotechnical, structural, transportation, environmental, and geoenvironmental.

Clinical Laboratory Sciences.

Community and Social Psychology.

Computer Engineering.

Computer Science. Includes computational mathematics, mathematical science.

Criminal Justice.

Curriculum and Instruction. Includes ESL.

Economic and Social Development of Regions.

Educational Administration.

Electrical Engineering. Includes opto-electronics.

Energy Engineering. Includes solar, nuclear.

Environmental Studies. Includes atmospheric sciences.

Health Management Policy.

Language Arts and Literacy.

Leadership in Schooling.

Marine Sciences and Technology.

Mathematics. Includes applied, mathematics for teachers, scientific computing, statistic and operators research.

Mathematics and Science Education.

Mechanical Engineering.

Music Education.

Music Performance.

Nursing. Includes gerontological, family health, adult psychiatric/mental health, health promotion.

Physical Therapy.

Physics. Includes applied mechanics, energy engineering, optical sciences.

Plastics Engineering. Includes coatings and adhesives, fiber/composites.

Polymer Science. Includes polymer science/plastics engineering.

Radiological Sciences and Protection.

Reading and Language.

Sound Recording Technology.

Work Environment. Includes industrial hygiene, occupational ergonomics, epidemiology, work environment policy, cleaner production and pollution prevention.

MAYO CLINIC AND MAYO FOUNDATION

Rochester, Minnesota 55905
Web site: www.mayo.edu

Founded 1863. There are three sites: Rochester, Minnesota; Jacksonville Florida; Scottsdale, Arizona. Private control. One of the world's largest group practices. Special facilities: Cancer Center, Mass Spectrometry Resource Laboratory, Analytical Nuclear Magnetic Resonance Resource Laboratory, Electron Microscopy Resource Laboratory, Molecular Biology Resource Laboratory, Biomedical Imaging Resource Laboratory. The Mayo Clinic's NIH ranking is 39th among all U.S. institutions with 362 awards/ grants worth $162,922,675. The Mayo Medical Center is a member of Council of Teaching Hospitals. *U.S. News & World Report* Hospital/Medical Center national rankings for all hospitals placed the Mayo Clinic in the top 20 of all U.S. hospitals. Library: 353,000 volumes, 4300 subscriptions.

Mayo Medical School

Web site: www.mayo.edu/mms

Established 1972. Graduate programs affiliated with the University of Minnesota since 1914. In 1983, Mayo Clinic became an independent institution.

Annual tuition: $24,250. Mayo scholarships and Minnesota state funds reduces this cost for residents of Arizona, Florida and Minnesota to $6125 and for nonresidents to $12,250. Only off-campus housing available. Contact Admissions Office for off-campus housing information. Off-campus housing and personal expenses: approximately $12,250.

Enrollment: first-year class 43, total 165 (men 48%, women 52%, minorities 36%, state residents 22%). Faculty: full- and part-time/volunteers 2254. Degrees conferred: M.D., M.D.-M.P.H., M.D.-Ph.D.

ADMISSION REQUIREMENTS. AMCAS report, transcripts, MCAT, bachelor's degree, interview, recommendations required in support of application. Interview by invitation only. Preference given to residents of Arizona, Florida, and Minnesota. Graduates of unaccredited colleges not considered. Does not have EDP. Apply to Director of Admissions after June 1, before November 1. Application fee $85. Phone: (507)284-3671; fax: (507)284-2634.

ADMISSION STANDARDS. Very competitive. Accepts about 2% of all applicants. Number of applications 2883 (2573 out-of-state); number interviewed 295 (250 out-of-state); number of acceptance 65 (51 out-of-state); number enrolled 43 (32 out-of-state). Mean Composite MCAT 10.9; mean UGPA 3.82. *U.S. News & World Report* ranking is in the top 23 of all U.S. medical research schools, 45th in primary care.

FINANCIAL AID. Full-tutition scholarships, merit scholarships, NIH stipends, loans. Apply to Office of Student Affairs after appointment but not later than May 1. Phone: (507)284-4839. There are special merit scholarships for residents of Arizona, Florida, and Minnesota. Use FAFSA.

DEGREE REQUIREMENTS. For M.D.: satisfactory completion of four-year program; all students required to take Step 1 and 2 of USMLE. For M.S.: one year beyond M.D.; knowledge of one foreign language; thesis/nonthesis option. For Ph.D.: at least two years beyond M.D.; knowledge of two foreign languages; one language/research tool; preliminary oral/written exam thesis; final oral exam.

FIELDS OF GRADUATE STUDY.
Biochemistry and Molecular Biology.
Biomedical Engineering.
Immunology.
Molecular Neurosciences.
Molecular Pharmacology and Experimental Therapeutics.
Virology and Gene Therapy.

MCDANIEL COLLEGE

Westminster, Maryland 21157-4390
Web site: www.mcdaniel.edu

Founded 1867. Located 32 miles NW of Baltimore. Coed. Private control. Semester system. Library: 200,000 volumes, 750 subscriptions.

Tuition: per credit $300. Limited on-campus housing available during academic year and Summer session for single students only. Average academic year housing costs: $5465. Contact Housing Office for both on- and off-campus housing information. Phone: (410)857-2240.

Graduate Studies

Enrollment: full-time 76; part-time 1102 (men 30%, women 70%). Graduate faculty: full-time 25, part-time 60. Degrees conferred: M.S., M.L.A.

ADMISSION REQUIREMENTS. Official transcripts, three letters of reference, interview; GRE or MAT required in support of application. TOEFL required for international applicants. Accepts transfer applicants. Apply to Dean of Graduate Admissions. Application fee $50. Phone: (410)857-2500; fax: (410)857-2515.

ADMISSION STANDARDS. Selective. Usual minimum average: 2.75 (A = 4).

FINANCIAL AID. Graduate assistantships available in housing, education department, physical education department, grants, loans. Approved for VA benefits. Apply to the Office of Graduate and Professional Studies; no specified closing date. Phone: (410) 857-2235; fax: (410)386-4608. Use FAFSA. About 5% of students receive aid other than loans from both College and outside sources.

DEGREE REQUIREMENTS. For master's: 30-33 hours; thesis/ nonthesis option; comprehensive exam.

FIELDS OF STUDY.
Counselor Education.
Curriculum and Instruction.
Deaf Education. Includes the teaching of sign language, the teaching of interpreting.
Educational Administration.
Elementary Education.
Exercise Science and Physical Education.
Gerontology.
Human Resource Development.
Human Services Management.
Liberal Arts.
Reading.
School Library Media.
Secondary Education.
Special Education.

MCNEESE STATE UNIVERSITY

Lake Charles, Louisiana 70609-2495
Web site: www.mcneese.edu

Founded 1938. Located 130 miles W of Baton Rouge. Coed. State control. Semester system. Library: 351,700 volumes, 1700 subscriptions. Total University enrollment: 8800.

Annual tuition, depending upon credit load: $3154 resident, nonresident $9220; 0–3 credits, resident $505, nonresident $925. On-campus housing for 116 married students, 1177 men, 425 women. Average annual housing cost: $5500 married students, $4000 (including board) for single students. Apply to Office of Student Housing for housing information. Phone: (337)475-5606.

School of Graduate Studies

Enrollment: full-time 382, part-time 502. Graduate faculty: full-time 97, part-time 20. Degrees conferred: M.A., M.S., M.F.A., M.Eng., M.B.A., M.Ed., M.M., Ed.S.

ADMISSION REQUIREMENTS. Transcripts, GRE/GMAT required in support of School's application. TOEFL (minimum score 550) and affidavit of support required for international applicants. Interview not required. Accepts transfer applicants. Graduates of unaccredited colleges not considered. Apply to Office of Graduate Admissions by May 1 (Fall), October 1 (Spring). Application fee $20, international students $40. Phone: (337)475-5356.

ADMISSION STANDARDS. Selective. Usual minimum score of 1100 (150 × UGPA + GRE) required for consideration.

FINANCIAL AID. Scholarships, research assistantships, teaching assistantships, Federal W/S, loans. Apply by May 1 to appropriate department head for scholarships, assistantships; to Office of Financial Aid for all other programs. Use FAFSA (University code: 002017) and University's FAF. Phone: (337)475-5065. About 3% of students receive aid other than loans from University and outside sources. Aid available for part-time students.

DEGREE REQUIREMENTS. For master's: 30 semester hours minimum, at least 24 in residence; thesis required (for 6 hours) for M.A., M.S., optional for other master's; reading knowledge of one foreign language for some majors; final oral exam for all majors; final written exam for some majors. For Ed.S.: 30 semester hours minimum beyond the master's in residence; three years' teaching experience.

FIELDS OF STUDY.

COLLEGE OF BUSINESS:
Business Administration.

BURTON COLLEGE OF EDUCATION:
Administration and Supervision. Includes principalship, supervision of instruction.
Early Childhood Education.
Educational Leadership.
Educational Technology. Includes computer, instructional technology.
Elementary Education.
Health and Human Performance. Includes exercise science, health education. health promotion.
Psychology. Includes counseling, general-experimental, school psychology.
School Counseling.
Secondary Education. Includes business, English, mathematics, science, social studies, speech.
Special Education. Includes curriculum/materials, early childhood, educational diagnostician.

COLLEGE OF ENGINEERING AND TECHNOLOGY:
Chemical Engineering.
Civil Engineering.
Electrical Engineering.
Engineering Management.
Mechanical Engineering.

COLLEGE OF LIBERAL ARTS:
Creative Writing.
English.
Music Education.

COLLEGE OF NURSING:
Nursing. Includes clinical nurse specialist, nurse practitioner.
Nursing Administration.
Nursing Education.

COLLEGE OF SCIENCE:
Computer Science.
Environment and Chemical Sciences. Includes environmental science.
Environmental and Chemical Sciences. Includes chemistry, chemistry education, environmental science education.
Mathematical Sciences. Includes computer science, mathematics, statistics.

UNIVERSITY OF MEDICINE AND DENTISTRY OF NEW JERSEY
Newark, New Jersey 07103-2400
Web site: www.umdnj.edu

Established 1970, became a free-standing University in 1981. CGS member. Coed. State control. Quarter system. Special facilities: Center for Advanced Biotechnology and Medicine, Environmental and Occupational Health Science Center, New Jersey Cancer Institute, New Jersey Eye Institute. The University's NIH ranking is 55th among all U.S. institutions with 287 awards/grants valued at $120,750,579. According to The Center at University of Florida, the University is ranked 73rd in receipt of Federal Research funds with $105,495,000 and it ranks 74th for total University research expenditures with $190,763,000. In 2004, the University awarded 185 doctorates, which ranked it 80th among all U.S. institutions eligible to award that degree. The Library: approximately 258,300 volumes, 6450 subscriptions. Total Institute enrollment: 3500.

Graduate School of Biomedical Science

Established in 1956 as part of the former Seton Hall College of Medicine and Dentistry and became a separate School of the State's Health Sciences University in 1969. Branch campuses located in Newark, Piscataway, and Stratford.

Annual tuition: resident full-time $5556, nonresident $8049; resident per credit $456–$512, nonresident $570–$642. Enrollment: full-time 729, part-time 29. Degrees conferred: M.S., Ph.D.

ADMISSIONS REQUIREMENTS. Official transcripts, GRE or MAT, statement of purpose, three letters of recommendation required in support of application. TOEFL required for all international applicants. Apply to the specific campus and program by February 1 (Fall), October 1 (Spring). Some programs have earlier deadlines. Phone: (973)972-4511 (Newark); (732)235-5016 (Piscataway); (856)566-6282 (Stratford). Application fee $40.

ADMISSIONS STANDARDS. Selective. Usual minimum GPA 3.0 (A = 4).

FINANCIAL AID. Fellowships, research assistantships, teaching assistantships, traineeships, tuition waivers, Federal W/S, loans. Apply by May 1 to appropriate campus Financial Aid Office. Use FAFSA (School code: 013645).

DEGREE REQUIREMENTS. For M.S.: two-year full-time programs; thesis/nonthesis option. For Ph.D.: two- to three-year full-time program; qualifying exam; dissertation; final oral defense.

FIELDS OF STUDY.

NEWARK CAMPUS:
Biochemistry and Molecular Biology.
Biomedical Engineering. Joint program with N.J.I.T.
Biomedical Sciences.
Cell Biology and Molecular Medicine.
Experimental Pathology.
Microbiology, Molecular Genetics and Immunology.
Neurosciences.
Pharmacology and Physiology.

PISCATAWAY CAMPUS:
Biochemistry and Molecular Biology.
Cell and Development Biology.
Cellular and Molecular Pharmacology.
Environmental Science/Exposure Assessment.
Molecular Genetics, Microbiology and Immunology.
Physiology and Neurobiology.
Toxicology.

STRATFORD CAMPUS:
Biomedical Sciences. M.B.S.
Cell and Molecular Biology. Ph.D. only.
Molecular Biology. M.S.

New Jersey Dental School

Web site: www.dentalschool.umdnj.edu

Established 1956. Located in Newark. Semester system.

Annual tuition: resident $24,340, nonresident $42,794. Both on- and off-campus housing available. For housing information contact the Admissions Office. Phone: (973)972-5362. Average academic year housing cost: $11,550–$15,000. Total average cost for all other first-year expenses: $12,000.

Enrollment: first-year class 84, total 390 (men 45%, women 55%, minorities 4%, state residents 98%), postgraduates 35. Faculty: full-time 91, part-time 15. Degrees conferred: D.M.D., D.M.D.-Ph.D., Certificate.

ADMISSION REQUIREMENTS. AADSAS report, transcripts, 3 letters of recommendation, DAT required in support of application. Interview by invitation only. Preference given to state residents. Applicants must have completed at least 3 but preferably 4 years of college study; most applicants have bachelor's degree. Accepts transfer applicants on a space available basis. Apply to AADSAS after June 1, before February 1. Application fee $75. Phone: (973)972-5362; fax: (973)972-0309.

ADMISSION STANDARDS. Competitive. Accepts about 10–15% of all applicants. Usual minimum UGPA: 3.0 (A = 4). Mean DAT: academic 19, PAT 17, mean UGPA 3.40.

FINANCIAL AID. Scholarships, fellowships, loans. Apply after acceptance to Office of Financial Aid. Priority deadline May 1. Phone: (973)972-4376. Use FAFSA. About 91% of students receive aid from School.

DEGREE REQUIREMENTS. For D.M.D.: satisfactory completion of four-year program.

FIELDS OF POSTGRADUATE STUDY.
Advanced Education in General Dentistry. Certificate.
Dental Science. M.D.S.
Dentistry. M.S.D.
Endodontics. Certificate.
Oral and Maxillofacial Pathology. Certificate.
Oral Biology. Ph.D.
Orthodontics. Certificate.
Pediatric Dentistry. Certificate.
Periodontics. Certificate.
Prosthodontics. Certificate.

New Jersey Medical School

Web site: www.njms.umdnj.edu

Founded 1954. Located in Newark (07101) since 1977. Library: 70,000 volumes, 2000 subscriptions. NIH ranking is 55th among all U.S. institutions with 287 awards/grants worth $120,750,579.

Annual tuition: resident $25,198, nonresident $37,763. Both on- and off-campus housing available. Total average figure for all other expenses: $18,000–$20,000.

Enrollment: first-year class 170 (EDP 10); total 705 (men 48%, women 52%, minorities 59%, state residents 80%); postgraduates 250. Faculty: full-time 737, part-time 93. Degrees conferred: B.A./B.S.-M.D., M.D., M.D.-J.D., M.D-M.B.A., M.D.-M.P.H., M.D.-Ph.D.

ADMISSION REQUIREMENTS. AMCAS report, transcripts, MCAT, supplemental application required in support of application. Applicants must have completed at least three years of college study. Preference given to New Jersey residents. Interviews by invitation only. Has EDP; apply between June 1 and September 1. Apply to Director of Admissions after June 1, before December 1. Application fee $75. Phone: (973)972-4631; fax: (973) 972-7986; e-mail: njmsadmiss@ umdnj.edu.

ADMISSION STANDARDS. Competitive. Accepts about 10% of all applicants. Number of applications 4057 (3054 out-of-state); number interviewed 751 (n/a out-of-state); number of acceptance 415 (100 out-of-state); number enrolled 170 (29 out-of-state). Mean Composite MCAT 10.0; mean UGPA 3.57.

FINANCIAL AID. Academic Excellence Scholarships, minority scholarships, Grants-in-Aid, institutional loans, HEAL, alternative loan programs, NIH stipends, loans. Service Commitment Scholarship programs are available. The UMDNJ Financial Aid applications and information are available at the on-campus, by-invitation interview. All students are considered for all aid they are eligible for. Assistantships/fellowships may be available for Dual Degree candidates. Contact the Financial Aid Office for current information. Phone: (973)972-7030. Use FAFSA (School code: 013465), also submit Financial Aid Transcript, Federal Income Tax forms. Approximately 85% of students receive some form of financial assistance.

DEGREE REQUIREMENTS. For M.D.: satisfactory completion of four-year program. All students must pass USMLE Step 1 prior to entering third year; all students must pass USMLE Step 2 prior to awarding of M.D.

FIELDS OF GRADUATE STUDY.
Biochemistry.
Bioinformatics.
Cell Biology.
Immunology.
Molecular Biology.
Molecular Genetics.
Microbial Pathogenesis.
Neurosciences.
Pathology.
Pharmacology.
Physiology.

Robert Wood Johnson Medical School

Web site: www.rwjms.umdnj.edu

Established 1961, formerly know as Rutgers Medical School; became part of University in 1970. Located in Piscataway (08854-5635) and has a division in Camden. Special facilities: The Cancer Institute of New Jersey, Center for Advanced Biotechnology and Medicine, Environmental and Occupational Health Sciences Institute, Stem Cell Institute of New Jersey, Center for Agricultural Molecular Biology, The New Jersey Center for Biomaterials, Child Health Institute of New Jersey, Waksman Institute.

Annual tuition: resident $25,313, nonresident $37,878. No on-campus housing available. Total average figure for all other expenses: $12,295.

Enrollment: first-year class 157 (EDP 5); total 659 (men 43%, women 57%, minorities 53%, state residents 95%). Faculty: full- and part-time 973. Degrees conferred: M.D., M.D.-M.P.H., M.D.-Ph.D., M.D.-J.D. (Rutgers Law School), M.D.-M.S. (Seton Hall Law School), M.D.-M.D.-M.S. (Medical Informatics with N.J. Institute of Technology), M.D.-M.B.A. (Rutgers School of Management).

ADMISSION REQUIREMENTS. AMCAS report, transcripts, MCAT required in support of application. Interview by invitation only. Applicants should have completed four years of college study. Preference given to state residents. Has EDP; apply between June 1 and August 1. Accepts transfer applicants. Apply to Committee on Admissions of School after June 1, before December 1 (Fall). Application fee $75. Phone: (732)235-4576; fax: (732) 235-5078.

ADMISSION STANDARDS. Competitive. Accepts about 12.3% of all applicants. Number of applications 2815 (1795 out-of-state); number interviewed 580 (106 out-of-state); number of acceptance 345 (45 out-of-state); number enrolled 157 (2 out-of-state). Mean Composite MCAT 10.2; mean UGPA 3.57.

FINANCIAL AID. Scholarships, minority scholarships, Grants-in-Aid, institutional loans, HEAL, alternative loan programs, Federal Perkins Loans, Stafford Subsidized and Unsubsidized Loans. Service Commitment Scholarship programs are available. Assistantships/fellowships may be available for Dual Degree candidates. UMDNJ Financial Aid applications and information are given out at the on-campus by-invitation interview. Most aid is based on demonstrated need. Contact the University's Financial Aid Office for current information. Phone: (732)235-4689. Use FAFSA (School code: 013645), also submit Financial Aid Transcript, Federal Income Tax forms, statement of educational purpose and default/refund statement. Approximately 82% of students receive some form of financial assistance.

DEGREE REQUIREMENTS. For M.D.: satisfactory completion of four-year program. All students must pass USMLE Step 1 prior to entering third year; all students must pass USMLE Step 2 prior to awarding of M.D.

FIELDS OF GRADUATE STUDY.
Biochemistry and Molecular Biology.
Biomedical Engineering.
Cell and Developmental Biology.
Cellular and Molecular Pharmacology.
Environmental Science/Exposure Assessment.
Molecular Genetics, Microbiology and Immunology.
Neuroscience.
Physiology and Integrative Biology.

School of Osteopathic Medicine
Web site: www.som.umdnj.edu

Founded 1976. Located in Stratford (08084-1501). Special facilities: New Jersey Institute for Successful Aging, University Headache Center, University Pain Care Center. No on-campus housing available. Contact the Office of Student affairs for housing information. Phone: (856)566-6482. Total housing and personal expenses: approximately $12,000.

Annual tuition: resident $24,833, nonresident $36,059.

Enrollment: first-year class 100, total 397 (men 41%, women 59%, minorities 52%, state residents 99%). Faculty: full-time 165, part-time 34. Degrees conferred: D.O., D.O.-J.D., D.O.-M.P.A., D.O.-M.P.H., D.O.-Ph.D.

ADMISSION REQUIREMENTS. Bachelor's degree from an accredited institution required. Apply through AACOMAS (file after June 1, before February 1), submit MCAT (will accept test results from last three years), official transcripts for each school attended (should show at least 90 semester credits/135 quarter credits), service processing fee. Preference given to state residents. After a review of the AACOMAS application and supporting documents a decision is made concerning which candidates should receive supplemental materials. The supplemental application, an application fee of $75, a personal statement, and three recommendations (one from a D.O.) should be returned to Office of Admission by February 1. Joint Degree applicants must apply to and be accepted to both Schools, contact the admissions office for current information and specific admissions requirements. Interviews are by invitation only and generally for final selection. In addition, international applicants must submit foreign transcripts to the World Education Service for translation and evaluation. TOEFL may be required of those applicants whose native language is other than English. First-year students admitted Fall only. Rolling admissions process, notification starts in January and is finished when class is filled. Applicants response to offer due within two weeks of receipt of acceptance letter. Phone: (856)566-7050; fax: (856)566-6895.

ADMISSION STANDARDS. Competitive. Accepts about 6% of all applicants. Number of applications 2401 (2028 out-of-state); number interviewed 285 (170 out-of-state); number of acceptance 190 (112 out-of-state); number enrolled 100 (0 out-of-state). Usual minimum UGPA: 3.0 (A = 4). Mean Composite MCAT 8.8, mean UGPA 3.50.

FINANCIAL AID. Scholarships, merit scholarship, MLK scholarships, grants, institutional loans, NOF, HEAL, alternative loan programs, NIH stipends, Federal Perkins Loans, Stafford Subsidized and Unsubsidized Loans. Service Obligation Scholarship programs, Military and National Health Service programs are available. Financial Aid applications and information are generally available at the by-invitation interview; however, all accepted students are sent applications and information. All accepted applicants are considered for merit scholarships. Contact the Financial Aid Office for current information. Phone: (856)566-6008. Use FAFSA (School code: 013465), also submit Financial Aid Transcript, Federal Income Tax forms. Approximately 90% of students receive some form of financial assistance.

DEGREE REQUIREMENTS. For D.O.: satisfactory completion of four-year program. All students must pass the National Board of Osteopathic Medical Examination Level I and II prior to the awarding of D.O.

MEHARRY MEDICAL COLLEGE
Nashville, Tennessee 37208-9989
Web site: www.mmc.edu

Founded 1876. CGS member. Coed. Private control. Semester system. The College's NIH ranking is 141st among all U.S. institutions with 35 awards/grants worth $30,508,564. Library: 98,000 volumes, 1100 subscriptions. Total College enrollment: 900.

On-campus housing for single students only. Average academic year housing cost: $7200 (including board).

School of Graduate Studies

Established 1938. Annual tuition: $11,845; M.S.P.H. $ 11,845. Enrollment: full-time 151, part-time 11. Faculty: full-time 9. Degrees conferred: M.S.P.H., Ph.D.

ADMISSION REQUIREMENTS. Official transcripts, GRE, two letters of recommendation, statement summarizing research interests and career plans required in support of School's application. TOEFL required for international applicants. Accepts transfer applicants. Graduates of unaccredited institutions not considered. Apply to Director of Admissions and Records by June 1. Application fee $45. Phone: (615)327-6533; fax: (615)321-2933.

ADMISSION STANDARDS. Competitive. Usual minimum average: 3.0 (A = 4).

FINANCIAL AID. Annual awards from institutional funds: fellowships, scholarships, assistantships, internships, Federal W/S, loans. Apply to Financial Aid Office by April 1. Phone: (615) 327-6826. Use FAFSA.

DEGREE REQUIREMENTS. For M.S.P.H.: 60 credits minimum; thesis and extensive fieldwork. For Ph.D.: 40 credits minimum beyond the bachelor's, at least 30 in residence; qualifying exam; dissertation; final oral exam.

FIELDS OF STUDY.
Biochemistry.
Biomedical Sciences.
Cancer Biology.
Clinical Investigation.
Microbiology and Immunology.
Molecular Biology.
Neurosciences.
Pharmacology.
Physiology.
Public Health.

School of Dentistry
Web site: www.mmc.edu/education/dentistry

Organized 1886. Semester system. Special facilities: Center of Excellence, Regional Research Center for Minority Oral Health.

Annual tuition: $28,800. No on-campus housing available. For housing information contact the Student Service Office. Phone: (615)327-6387. Average academic year housing cost: $11,550–$15,000. Total average cost for all other first-year expenses: $10,000.

Enrollment: first-year class 55, total 212 (men 45%, women 55%, minorities 98%, state residents 15%), postgraduates 10. Faculty: full-time 62, part-time 39. Degrees conferred: D.D.S., Certificate.

ADMISSION REQUIREMENTS. AADSAS report, transcripts, three letters of recommendation, DAT, supplemental application required in support of School's application. Applicants must have completed at least three years of college study. Interview not required. Preference given to SREB member states. Accepts transfer applicants from U.S. and Canadian dental schools. Apply to Office of Admissions and Records after June 1 and before March 1. Application fee $60. Phone: (615)327-6223; fax: (615)327-6228.

ADMISSION STANDARDS. Competitive. Accepts about 15–20% of all applicants. Usual minimum UGPA: 2.70 (A = 4). Mean DAT: academic 15.8, PAT 16, mean UGPA 3.00.

FINANCIAL AID. Scholarships, grants, loans. Apply to Director of Financial Aid after acceptance. Phone: (615)327-8626. Use FAFSA. About 95% of students receive some aid from School funds.

DEGREE REQUIREMENTS. For D.D.S.: satisfactory completion of forty-four-month program.

FIELDS OF POSTGRADUATE STUDY.
General Practice Residency. Certificate.
Oral and Maxillofacial Pathology. Certificate.

School of Medicine
Web site: www.mmc.edu

Founded 1876 as Medical Department of Central Tennessee College; became independent in 1915. Special facilities: Asthma Disparities Center, Center for AIDS Health Disparities Research, Center for Molecular and Behavioral Neurosciences, Center for Optimal Health, Center for Research in Reproduction, Center for Women's Health Research, Center for Molecular and Behavioral Neuroscience, Center on Aging, Meharry Community Wellness Center, Sickle Cell Center. Library: 50,000 volumes, 1000 subscriptions.

Annual tuition: $29,596. On-campus housing available. Total average cost for all other expenses: $12,000.

Enrollment: first-year class 80 (EDP 0); total 322 (men 49%, women 51%, minorities 74%; state residents 17%). Degrees conferred: M.D., M.D.-M.S., M.D.-Ph.D.

ADMISSION REQUIREMENTS. AMCAS, transcripts, MCAT, interview required in support of application. Applicants must have completed at least three years of college study. Accepts transfer applicants. Has EDP; apply between June 1 and August 1. Apply to Director of Admissions after June 1, before December 15. Application fee $60. Phone: (615)327-6223; fax: (615)327-6228.

ADMISSION STANDARDS. Competitive. Accepts about 10% of all applicants. Number of applications 3069 (n/a out-of-state); number interviewed 499 (n/a out-of-state); number of acceptance n/a (n/a out-of-state); number enrolled 80 (n/a out-of-state). Mean Composite MCAT 8.0, mean UGPA 3.30.

FINANCIAL AID. Scholarships, Grants-in-Aid, institutional loans, HEAL, alternative loan programs, Federal Perkins Loans, Stafford Subsidized and Unsubsidized Loans. Service Commitment Scholarship programs are available. Assistantships/fellowships may be available for Combined Degree candidates. Financial Aid applications and information are given out at the on-campus by-invitation interview. Contact the Financial Aid Office for current information. Phone: (615)327-6826. Use FAFSA (School code: G03506), also submit Financial Aid Transcript, Federal Income Tax forms. Approximately 85% of students receive some form of financial assistance.

DEGREE REQUIREMENTS. For M.D.: satisfactory completion of four- or five-year program. All students must pass USMLE Step 1 prior to entering third year; all students must pass USMLE Step 2 prior to awarding of M.D. For M.D.-M.S.: generally a four-and-one-half- to five-and-one-half-year program. For M.D.-Ph.D.: generally a seven-year program.

FIELDS OF GRADUATE STUDY.
Cancer Biology.
Microbiology and Immunology.
Neuroscience.
Pharmacology.

THE UNIVERSITY OF MEMPHIS
Memphis, Tennessee 38152
Web site: www.memphis.edu

Established in 1912, name changed from Memphis State University in 1994. CGS member. Coed. State control. Semester system. Special facilities: Center for Applied Psychological Research, Center for Earthquake Research and Information, Center for Research Initiatives and Strategies for the Communicatively Impaired, Center for Research in Educational Policy, the Institute of Egyptian Art and Archaeology, Institute for Intelligent Systems. Library: more than 1,100,000 volumes, 12,000 subscriptions. Total University enrollment: 20,000.

Annual tuition: resident $6990, nonresident $16,226; per credit resident $377, nonresident $830. On-campus housing for single students and families. Apply to Director of Residence Life. Phone: (901)678-2295. Day-care facilities available.

Graduate School

Graduate study since 1951. Enrollment: full-time 1718, part-time 2575. Faculty: full-time 524, part-time 63. Degrees conferred: M.A., M.A.T., M.B.A., M.H.A., M.S., M.F.A., M.P.A., M.C.R.P., D.M.A., M.Mu., Ed.S., Ed.D., Ph.D.

ADMISSION REQUIREMENTS: Transcripts, GRE/GMAT/MAT required in support of School's application. Online application available. For additional requirements contact individual program chair. TOEFL required of international students. Accepts transfer applicants. Graduates of unaccredited colleges not considered. Graduate School application deadlines: August 1 (Fall), December 1 (Spring), May 1 (Summer). Some programs may have earlier deadlines. Apply to both Graduate Admissions and to the appropriate Department. Application fee $35, $60 for international applicants. Phone: (901)678-2531; fax: (901)678-3003; e-mail: gradsch@memphis.edu.

ADMISSION STANDARDS. Selective for most departments, very selective for some departments. Usual minimum average: 2.75 (A = 4).

FINANCIAL AID. Fellowships, research assistantships, administrative assistantships, teaching assistantships, grants, internships, Federal W/S, loans. Apply to individual chairs for assistantships; to Financial Aid Office for all other programs. Phone: (901)678-4825; fax: (901)678-3590. Use FAFSA (University code: 003509). Aid available for part-time students.

DEGREE REQUIREMENTS. For master's: 30 semester hours minimum; thesis; final oral/written exam; or 36 semester hours minimum; no thesis; final oral/written exam for most departments. For M.F.A.: 60 semester hour program; comprehensive exam; thesis/exhibition. For Doctorates: 72 credits, three years, at least one year in full-time residence; reading knowledge of one foreign language or statistics/research tool or both; comprehensive exam; admission to candidacy; dissertation; final oral exam. Contact program chair for additional degree requirements.

FIELDS OF STUDY.
Accounting. Includes accounting systems, taxation. M.S.
Anthropology. Includes medical, public archaeology, urban. M.A.
Applied Computer Science. M.S.
Art. Includes ceramics, graphic design, interior design, painting, printmaking/photography, sculpture. M.F.A.
Art History. Includes Egyptian art and archeology. M.A.
Audiology. Au.D.
Bioinformatics. M.S.
Biology. Includes microbiology, molecular cell sciences. M.S., Ph.D.
Biomedical Engineering. Ph.D.
Business Administration. Includes accounting, economics, finance, insurance and real estate, international business, law, management, management information systems, management science and operations, marketing. I.M.B.A., M.B.A., M.S., Ph.D.
Chemistry. Includes analytical, computational, inorganic, physical. M.S., Ph.D.
City and Regional Planning. M.C.R.P.
Civil Engineering. Includes environmental, foundation, structural, transportation, water resources. M.S.
Clinical Nutrition. M.S.
Communication. Includes film and video production. M.A.
Communication Arts. Ph.D.

Computer Science. M.S., Ph.D.
Counseling and Personnel Services. Includes community agency, rehabilitation, school, student personnel services. M.S., Ed.D.
Counseling Psychology. Ph.D.
Creative Writing. M.F.A.
Criminal Justice. M.A.
Earth Sciences. M.A., M.S., Ph.D.
Economics. M.A.
Education. Ed.S.
Educational Psychology and Research. M.S., Ph.D.
Electrical Engineering. Includes automatic control systems, communication and propagation systems, electro-optical systems, engineering computer systems. M.S.
Electronic Commerce. M.S.
Engineering. Includes civil, electrical, mechanical. Ph.D.
Engineering Technology. Includes architectural, electronics, manufacturing. M.S.
English. Includes applied linguistics, ESL, language and linguistics, literature, writing (creative and professional). M.A.
Geography. M.A., M.S.
Geological Sciences. Includes geology, geophysics. M.S.
Health Administration. M.H.A. only.
Higher and Adult Education. Ed.D.
History. Includes ancient Egyptian. M.A., Ph.D.
Human Movement Science. Includes exercise and sport sciences, health promotion, sport and leisure commerce. M.S.
Instruction and Curriculum Leadership. Includes early childhood, elementary, secondary, special. M.A.T., M.S., Ed.D.
Journalism. Includes journal administration. M.A.
Leadership and Policy Studies. Includes leadership, school administration and supervision (M.S.), community education, educational leadership, policy studies (Ed.D.). M.S., Ed.D.
Liberal Studies. M.A.L.S.
Mathematics. Includes applied, applied statistics, bioinformatics, computer science, statistics. M.S., Ph.D.
Mechanical Engineering. Includes design and mechanical systems, energy systems, mechanical systems, power systems. M.S.
Merchandise and Consumer Science. M.S.
Music. Includes composition, jazz and studio, music education, music history, pedagogy, performance, Orff-Schulwerk, sacred (M.Mu.), composition, music education, performance, sacred (D.M.A.), musicology (Ph.D.). M.Mu., D.M.A., Ph.D.
Nursing. M.S.N.
Philosophy. M.A., Ph.D.
Physics. M.S.
Political Science. M.A.
Psychology. Includes general (M.S.), clinical, experimental, school (Ph.D). M.S., Ph.D.
Public Administration. Includes general, health services administration, human resources administration, nonprofit administration, urban management and planning. M.P.A.
Public Health. M.P.A.
Romance Languages. Includes French, Spanish. M.A.
School Psychology. M.A.
Sociology. M.A.
Theatre. M.F.A.
Women's Studies. M.A.

Cecil C. Humphreys School of Law (38152)
Web site: www.law.memphis.edu

Founded 1962. ABA approved since 1965. AALS member. Public control. Semester system. Law library: 279,886 volumes, 2327 subscriptions; has LEXIS, NEXIS, WESTLAW, DIALOG.

Annual tuition: full-time resident $10,116, nonresident $28,446; part-time resident $8704, nonresident $23,768. On-campus housing available. Apply to Director of Residence Life. Estimated living expenses: $12,982.

Enrollment: first-year class, full-time 129, part-time 16; total full- and part-time 398 (men 56%, women 44%, minorities 18%).

Faculty: full-time 19, part-time 18. Student to faculty ratio 18.4 to 1. Degrees conferred: J.D., J.D.-M.B.A.

ADMISSION REQUIREMENTS. LSDAS Law School report, bachelor's degree, transcripts, LSAT, personal statement required in support of application. Interview not required. Accepts transfer applicants. Graduates of unaccredited colleges not considered. Apply by March 1. Fall admission only. Application fee $25. Phone: (901)678-5403; fax: (901)678-5210.

ADMISSION STANDARDS. Selective. Accepts approximately 23% of full-time and 48% of part-time applicants. Number of full-time applicants 1166, part-time 42; number of full-time acceptance 266, part-time 20; number full-time enrolled 129, part-time 16; LSAT (75% of full-time students have a score at or above 154, part-time 144); GPA (75% of full-time students have a GPA at or above 3.07, part-time 3.06). *U.S. News & World Report* ranking is in the third tier of all U.S. law schools.

FINANCIAL AID. Scholarships, assistantships, Federal W/S, loans. Apply to Financial Aid Office by April 1. Phone: (901) 678-3737. Use FAFSA (School code: 003509). About 24% of students receive aid other than loans from School.

DEGREE REQUIREMENTS. For J.D.: satisfactory completion of three-year program; 90 credit-hour program.

MERCER UNIVERSITY
Macon, Georgia 31207-0003
Web site: www.mercer.edu

Founded 1833. Located 92 miles S of Atlanta. Private control. Baptist. Semester system. Library: 692,200 volumes, 12,000 subscriptions. Total University enrollment: 7100.

Tuition: per credit hour Education $370, Business $550, Engineering $670. On-campus housing for 70 married students, 650 men, 510 women. Average academic year housing cost: $5000–$7000 for married students, $6500 (includes full board) for single students. Phone: (478)301-2687.

Graduate Studies

Enrollment: full-time 952, part-time 500. University faculty teaching graduate students: full-time 101, part-time 16. Degrees conferred: M.Ed., M.B.A., M.S.E., M.S., M.S.M., M.F.S., S.Ed.

ADMISSION REQUIREMENTS. Transcripts, letters of reference, GRE/NTE/MAT/GMAT tests required in support of application. Online application available. TOEFL (minimum score 550) required for international applicants. Interview not required. Accepts transfer applicants. Graduates of unaccredited institutions sometimes considered. Apply to Director of Graduate Programs; no specified closing dates. Application fee: $50, $100 for international applicants. Phone: (478)301-2700; fax: (478)301-2828; e-mail: admissions@mercer.edu.

ADMISSION STANDARDS. Selective for most departments. Usual minimum average: 3.0 (A = 4); GRE score: 35th percentile.

FINANCIAL AID. Supervising teacher scholarships, internships, Federal W/S, loans (academic year). Approved for VA benefits. Apply to the Financial Aid Office; no specified closing date. Phone: (478)301-2670. Use FAFSA (School code: 001580). Aid available for part-time students.

DEGREE REQUIREMENTS. For M.Ed., M.B.A.: 36 semester hours minimum. For M.S.E., M.S.: 33 semester hours minimum; thesis. For M.S.M., M.F.S.: 45 semester hours minimum. For S.Ed.: 30 semester hours minimum; special project.

FIELDS OF STUDY.

MACON CAMPUS

SCHOOL OF EDUCATION:
Collaborative Educator.
Educational Leadership.
Middle Grades Education (4–8).

SCHOOL OF ENGINEERING:
Biomedical Engineering.
Computer Engineering.
Electrical Engineering.
Engineering Management.
Mechanical Engineering.
Software Engineering.
Software Systems.
Technical Communication Management.
Technical Management.

STETSON SCHOOL OF BUSINESS AND ECONOMICS:
Business Administration. M.B.A.

CECIL B. DAY CAMPUS (ATLANTA)

SCHOOL OF EDUCATION:
Early Childhood Education (P–5).
Educational Leadership.
Middle Grades Education (4–8).
Reading (P–12).
Secondary Education.
Teacher Leadership.

SCHOOL OF ENGINEERING:
Electrical Engineering.
Engineering Management.
Mechanical Engineering.
Software Engineering.
Software Systems.
Technical Communication Management.
Technical Management.

STETSON SCHOOL OF BUSINESS AND ECONOMICS:
Business Administration.
Executive Business Administration.
Health Care Management.

Walter F. George School of Law
Web site: www.law.mercer.edu

Established 1873. Oldest private law school in U.S. ABA approved since 1925. AALS member since 1923. Private control. Semester system. Special facility: Center for Legal Ethics and Professionalism. Law library: 333,658 volumes, 3300 subscriptions; has LEXIS, NEXIS, WESTLAW, DIALOG.

Annual tuition: full-time $30,146. No on-campus housing available. Total average annual additional expenses: $14,200.

Enrollment: first-year class 155; total 451 (men 57%, women 43%, minorities 16%). Faculty: full-time 25, part-time 30. Student to faculty ratio 13.5 to 1. Degrees conferred: J.D., J.D.-M.B.A.

ADMISSION REQUIREMENTS. LSDAS Law School report, bachelor's degree, transcripts, LSAT, personal statement, two letters of recommendation required in support of application. Interviews are encouraged. Accepts transfer applicants. Graduate of unaccredited colleges not considered. Apply to Director of Admissions after September 1, before March 15. Beginning students admitted Fall only. Application fee $50. Phone: (478)301-2605; fax: (478)301-2989.

ADMISSION STANDARDS. Selective. Accepts approximately 30% of all students. Number of applicants 1489; number of acceptance 450; number enrolled 155; LSAT (75% of students have a score at or above 153); GPA (75% of students have a GPA at or above 3.02). *U.S. News & World Report* ranking is in the second tier (tied at 100) of all U.S. law schools.

FINANCIAL AID. Scholarships, Federal W/S, loans. Apply by January 15 (Scholarships), May 1 (flexible) to Director of Admissions. Phone: (478)301-2064. Use FAFSA (School code: E00561). About 32% of students receive aid other than loans from School.

DEGREE REQUIREMENTS. For J.D.: satisfactory completion of three-year program; 90 credit-hour program. For M.B.A.: see Graduate School listing above.

School of Medicine

Web site: www.medicine.mercer.edu

Established 1982. Library: 60,000 volumes, 500 subscriptions. Annual tuition: $30,220. Both on- and off-campus housing available. Total average figure for all other expenses: $13,500.

Enrollment: first-year class 60; total 245 (men 52%, women 48%, minorities 14%, state residents 100%). Faculty: full-time 186, part-time 81. Degree conferred: M.D.

ADMISSION REQUIREMENTS. AMCAS report, transcripts, MCAT, two letters of recommendation or one premedical committee evaluation, personal history, Certificate of Georgia residency required in support of application. Interview by invitation only. Accepts only state residents. Has EDP; apply between June 1 and August 1. Graduates of unaccredited colleges not considered. Apply to Office of Admissions and Student Affairs after June 1, before November 1. Application fee $50. Phone: (478)301-2542.

ADMISSION STANDARDS. Competitive. Accepts about 12.9% of all applicants. Number of applicants 689 (0 out-of-state); number interviewed 237 (0 out-of-state); number of acceptance 89 (0 out-of-state); number enrolled 60 (0 out-of-state). Mean Composite MCAT 8.9, mean UGPA 3.52.

FINANCIAL AID. Scholarships, loans. Apply after acceptance to Office of Admissions and Student Affairs. Phone: (478)301-2853. Use FAFSA (School code: E00560). About 94% of students receive some aid from School.

DEGREE REQUIREMENTS. For M.D.: satisfactory completion of four-year program. All students must pass USMLE Step 1 prior to entering third year; all students must pass USMLE Step 2 prior to awarding of M.D.

MIAMI UNIVERSITY
Oxford, Ohio 45056
Web site: www.muohio.edu

Founded 1809. Located 35 miles NW of Cincinnati. CGS member. Coed. State control. Semester system. Special facilities: academic centers located in Hamilton, Middletown; Bachelor Wildlife Reserve, Willard Sherman Turrell Herbarium, Ecology Research Center, Institute of Environmental Sciences, Scripps Gerontology Center. Library: 1,800,000 volumes, 12,200 subscriptions. Total University enrollment: 16,000.

Annual fees: full-time, resident $11,765, nonresident $24,624. Limited on-campus housing available. Annual academic year housing cost: $6500. Apply to Office of Student Housing for housing information. Phone: (513)529-5000. Day-care facilities available.

Graduate School

Graduate study since 1826, became Graduate School 1947. Enrollment: full-time 996, part-time 231. Faculty teaching graduate students: full- and part-time 623. Degrees conferred: M.A., M.A.T., M.B.A., M.Ed., M.F.A., M.M., M.S., M.Arch., M.Env.Sci., M.G.S., M.S. in Stats., M.Acc., Specialist, Ph.D.

ADMISSION REQUIREMENTS. Two transcripts, GRE/MAT/GMAT required in support of School's application. Online application available. Proof of proficiency in English or TOEFL required of international applicants. Accepts transfer applicants. Graduates of unaccredited institutions not considered. Apply to School at least one month prior to registration. Financial Aid applicants apply by March 1 (Fall), December 1 (Spring). Application fee $35. Phone: (513)529-3734; fax: (513)529-4127.

ADMISSION STANDARDS. Selective for all departments. Minimum average: 2.75 (A = 4).

FINANCIAL AID. Annual awards from institutional funds: scholarships, grants, tuition waivers, research assistantships, administrative assistantships, teaching assistantships, fellowships, internships, Federal W/S, loans. Apply by March 1 to Office of Student Financial Assistance. Phone: (513)529-8734. Use FAFSA. About 75% of full-time students receive aid other than loans from both School and outside sources. Aid available for part-time students.

DEGREE REQUIREMENTS. For M.A.: 30 credit hours minimum, at least 15 in residence; preliminary oral/written exam; thesis; final oral/written exam. For M.A.T.: 30 credit hours minimum, at least 15 in residence; thesis; preliminary oral/written exam; final oral/written exam. For M.B.A.: 76 credit hours minimum, all in residence; oral/written comprehensive exam. For M.Env.Set.: 36 credit hours minimum; written comprehensive exam; thesis. For M.Ed.: 30 credit hours minimum; field study; preliminary oral/written exam; comprehensive oral/written exam. For M.F.A., M.Arch.: 60 credit hours minimum; preliminary oral/written exam; thesis; final project; final oral/written exam. For M.M.: 33 credit hours generally required. For M.S., M.S. in Stats.: 30 hours minimum, at least 15 in residence; preliminary oral/written exam; final oral/written exam. For M.T.S.C.: 32 credit hours minimum, at least 16 in residence; thesis or internship; qualifying exam; final oral/written exam. For M.Acc.: 33 credit hours minimum, at least 17 in residence; oral/written comprehensive exam. For M.G.S., Specialist: 30 credits beyond the master's, at least 24 in residence. For Ph.D.: 60 credit hours beyond the master's, at least 48 in residence; language requirement determined by department; oral/written comprehensive exam; dissertation; final exam.

FIELDS OF STUDY.
Accountancy. GMAT for admission. Master's only.
Adolescent Education. M.A.T., M.Ed.
Architecture. Master's only.
Art. Master's only.
Art Education. Master's only.
Biological Sciences. Master's only.
Botany. M.A., M.S., M.A.T., Ph.D.
Business Administration. GMAT for admission. Master's only.
Chemistry. M.S., Ph.D.
College Student Personnel.
Comparitive Religion. M.A.
Computer Sciences. M.C.S.
Ecology. M.S., Ph.D.
Education. Includes adolescent, educational administration, student personnel services, curriculum and leadership, elementary, secondary, reading, sport studies, exercise and health studies, educational psychology. Ph.D./Ed.D. in administration and curriculum only.

English. Includes composition, creative writing, literature. M.A., M.A.T., Ph.D.
Environmental Sciences. MAT for admission. Master's only.
Exercise and Health Studies.
Family and Child Studies.
Finance. GMAT for admission. Master's only.
French. Master's only.
Geography. Master's only.
Geology. M.A., M.S., Ph.D.
Gerontological Studies. Master's only.
History. Master's only.
Instructional Design and Technology. M.A., M.Ed.
Kinesiology and Health. M.S.
Management. GMAT for admission. Master's only.
Management Information Systems. Master's only.
Marketing. GMAT for admission. Master's only.
Mass Communication. Master's only.
Mathematics. Master's only.
Microbiology. M.A., M.S., Ph.D.
Molecular Biology.
Music. Includes music education, performance. Master's only.
Paper Science and Engineering. Master's only.
Philosophy. Master's only.
Physics. Master's only.
Political Science. M.A., M.A.T., Ph.D.
Psychology. GRE for admission. Ph.D. only.
School Psychology. Nine-month internship for M.S. M.S., Ed.S.
Software Development.
Spanish. Master's only.
Speech Communication. Master's only.
Speech Pathology and Audiology. Master's only.
Sport Studies. M.S.
Statistics. Master's only.
System Analysis. Master's only.
Theater. Master's only.
Women's Studies.
Zoology. M.A., M.S., M.A.T., Ph.D.

UNIVERSITY OF MIAMI
Coral Gables, Florida 33124
Web site: www.miami.edu

Founded 1925. Located 12 miles SW of Miami. CGS member. Coed. Private control. Semester system. Special facilities: Lowe Art Museum, Bascome Palmer Eye Institute, Comprehensive Cancer Center for Florida, Rosenstiel School of Marine and Atmospheric Sciences, Graduate School International Studies, Mailman Center for Child Development, the Ungar Computing Center; Organization for Tropical Studies, Inc., sponsoring university of the Oak Ridge Associated Universities in Oak Ridge, Tennessee, special environmental-ecology field stations, Long Pine Key, Fairchild Tropical Gardens. The Institute's NIH ranking is 63rd among all U.S. institutions with 246 awards/grants valued at $92,011,838. According to The Center at University of Florida, the University is ranked 52nd in receipt of Federal Research funds with $130,863,000 and it ranks 79th for total University research expenditures with $177,709,000. In 2004, the University awarded 159 doctorates, which ranked it 93rd among all U.S. institutions eligible to award that degree. 2 of the University's faculty members have been elected to National Honor Academies and this ranks it 117th among all U.S. institutions. The Library: approximately 2,030,000 volumes, 17,100 subscriptions. Total Institute enrollment: 15,700.

Tuition: per credit $1350. On-campus housing for married and single students. Average academic year housing cost: $6935. Apply to Director, Residence Halls. Phone: (305)284-4505.

Graduate School

Organized 1941. Enrollment: full-time 2577, part-time 669. Graduate faculty: full- and part-time 750. Degrees conferred: M.A., M.S., M.B.A., M.S.Ed., M.Arch., M.M., M.F.A., M.P.Acc., M.S.Tax., M.P.H., M.S.P.H., M.P.A., M.P.T., M.S.P.T., M.S.N., M.S.B.E., M.S.I.E., M.S.C.E., M.S.M.E., M.S.E.C.F., M.S.O.E., Spec.M., Ed.S., Ed.D., Ph.D., D.M.A., D.A.

ADMISSION REQUIREMENTS. Transcripts, letters of recommendation, GRE Subject Tests required in support of School's application. Online applications available. GMAT for M.B.A. TOEFL required for international applicants. Interview required for some programs. Graduates of unaccredited institutions not considered. Apply to individual program directors. Admissions by March 1 (Fall). Application fee $50. Phone: (305)284-4154; fax: (305)284-5441; e-mail: graduateschool@miami.edu.

ADMISSION STANDARDS. Selective for most departments, very competitive for others. Usual minimum average: 3.0 (A = 4).

FINANCIAL AID. Annual awards from institutional funds: scholarships, fellowships, research assistantships, teaching assistantships, internships, Federal W/S, loans. Approved for VA benefits. Apply by March 1 to individual program directors for scholarships, assistantships, fellowships; to Financial Aid Office for all other programs. Phone: (305)284-5212; fax: (305)284-4082. Use FAFSA. About 50% of students receive aid other than loans from University and outside sources. Aid available for part-time students.

DEGREE REQUIREMENTS. For M.A., M.S.: 30 semester credits minimum, at least 24 in residence; reading knowledge of one foreign language for many departments; thesis/comprehensive exam; up to 6 credits for thesis if required. For M.B.A.: 39 credits minimum, at least 30 in residence; additional study may be required, depending upon previous preparation. For M.S.Ed.: 30–60 credits, depending on department, at least 30 in residence. For M.M.: 30 credits minimum, at least 24 in residence; thesis for up to 6 credits for majors in music education or theory-composition; recital for three credits for applied music major; final oral exam in defense of thesis for music education majors. For M.F.A.: 36–60 credits, depending on department. For D.M.A.: 90 credits beyond the bachelor's, essentially the same as for the Ph.D., except a creative effort/performance and doctoral essay instead of dissertation. For D.A.: essentially the same as for the Ph.D., except a college teaching internship and scholarly investigation replace the dissertation. For Ph.D.: 60 credits minimum beyond the bachelor's, at least 24 in residence and two consecutive semesters in full-time attendance; qualifying exam; dissertation for at least 12 credits; final oral exam; final written exam sometimes required. For Ed.D.: 85 credits minimum beyond the bachelor's, at least 30 in residence and two consecutive semesters in full-time attendance; preliminary exam; written comprehensive exam; proficiency in four research tools, which may include language, statistics, or similar methods; research project; final oral exam.

FIELDS OF STUDY.

COLLEGE OF ARTS AND SCIENCES:
Art. Includes art history (M.A.), painting, sculpture, weaving, graphic design, printmaking, art studio. M.F.A.
Biology.
Chemistry.
Computer Science.
English and Creative Writing.
Foreign Languages. Includes French, German, Portuguese, Russian, Spanish; three languages for M.A.
Geography and Regional Studies.
History.
International Studies.

Latin American Studies.
Liberal Studies.
Mathematics.
Philosophy.
Physics.
Psychology.
Sociology.

SCHOOL OF BUSINESS ADMINISTRATION:
Accounting.
Business Administration.
Computer Information System.
Economics and Business. Ph.D.
Finance.
International Business.
Management.
Marketing.
Public Administration.

SCHOOL OF EDUCATION:
Counseling Psychology.
Elementary Education. Includes ESOL.
Exceptional Student Education. Includes prekindergarten disabilities, ESOL, reading.
Exercise Physiology.
Higher Education Administration. Includes enrollment management, student life and development.
Mathematics and Science Education.
Mental Health Counseling.
Reading. Includes ESOL.
Research, Measurement and Evaluation.
Sport Administration.
Sport Medicine.
Teaching and Learning. Includes reading, ESOL.

COLLEGE OF ENGINEERING:
Architectural Engineering.
Biomedical Engineering.
Civil Engineering. Includes environmental emphasis.
Computer Engineering.
Electrical and Computer Engineering.
Electrical Engineering.
Environmental Health and Safety.
Industrial Engineering.
Management of Technology.
Mechanical Engineering. Includes management option.

SCHOOL OF ARCHITECTURE:
Architecture.

SCHOOL OF COMMUNICATION:
Communication. Ph.D. only.
Communications Studies.
Film Studies.
Motion Picture Production.
Periodismo.
Print Journalism.
Public Relations.
Screenwriting.
TV Broadcast Journalism.

ROSENSTILL SCHOOL OF MARINE AND ATMOSPHERIC SCIENCES:
Applied Marine Physics.
Marine Affairs and Policy.
Marine and Atmospheric Chemistry.
Marine Biology and Fisheries.
Marine Geology and Geophysics.
Meteorology and Physical Oceanography.
Joint Degree. Programs with Engineering and Law Schools available.

SCHOOL OF MEDICINE—LIFE SCIENCES:
Biochemistry and Molecular Biology.
Cellular and Molecular Biology.
Epidemiology and Public Health.
Microbiology and Immunology.
Molecular and Cellular Pharmacology.
Molecular Cell and Development Biology.
Neuroscience.
Pharmacology.
Physiology and Biophysics.
Physical Therapy.
Radiological Science.

FROST SCHOOL OF MUSIC:
Accompanying and Chamber Music.
Choral Conducting.
Composition.
Electronic Music.
Instrumental Conducting.
Instrumental Music.
Instrumental Performance.
Jazz Composition.
Jazz Pedagogy.
Jazz Performance. Includes instrumental, vocal.
Keyboard Performance and Pedagogy.
Media Writing and Production.
Multiple Woodwinds Performance.
Music Business and Entertainment Industries.
Music Education.
Music Engineering Technology.
Music Therapy.
Piano Performance.
Studio Jazz Writing.
Vocal Pedagogy.
Vocal Performance.

SCHOOL OF NURSING:
Acute Care Practitioner.
Adult Health Practitioner.
Family Health Practitioner.
Nurse Anesthesia.
Nurse Midwifery.
Nursing Science. Includes health disparities and minority health, HIV/AIDS and infectious diseases, family and maternal/neonatal health, patient safety. Ph.D. only.
Psychiatric Mental Health Practitioner.
Women's Health Practitioner.

School of Law (P.O. Box 248087)

Web site: www.law.miami.edu

Established 1926. ABA approved since 1941. AALS member. Semester system. Full-time (day), part-time (evening) study. Special facilities: Center for the Study of Human Rights, Center for Ethics and Public Service. Special program: summer study abroad at University College, London, England. Law library: 596,242 volumes, 6923 subscriptions; has LEXIS, NEXIS, WESTLAW, DIALOG, CCH; has more than 250 network connections.

Annual tuition: full-time $32,820, part-time $24,316. On-campus housing available for both single and married students. Contact Department of Residence Halls. Phone: (305)284-4505. Law students tend to live off-campus. Contact office of Student Recruitment for off-campus information. Off-campus housing and personal expenses: approximately $16,820.

Enrollment: first-year class full-time 414, part-time 51; total full- and part-time 1208 (men 56%, women 44%, minorities 23%). Faculty: full-time 60, part-time 99. Student to faculty ratio 19.6 to 1. Degrees conferred: J.D., J.D.-M.B.A., J.D.-M.P.H., J.D.-M.Marine Affairs. LL.M. (Taxation, Estate Planning, Real Property Development), LL.M. (Inter-American Law, International Law,

Ocean and Coastal Law), LL.M. (Comparative Law; for persons who have completed a basic legal education and received a university degree in law in another country).

ADMISSION REQUIREMENTS. LSDAS Law School report, bachelor's degree, transcripts, LSAT, two letters of recommendation, personal statement required in support of application. Interview not required. Accepts transfer applicants. Graduates of unaccredited colleges not considered. Admits Fall only. Apply to Director of Law Admissions after September 1, before July 1. Application fee $60. Phone: (305)284-2795; fax: (305) 284-3084.

ADMISSION STANDARDS. Selective. Accepts approximately 37% of full-time and 10% of part-time applicants. Number of full-time applicants 4946, part-time 114; number of full-time acceptance 1838, part-time 11; number full-time enrolled 414, part-time 1; LSAT (75% of full-time students have a score at or above 156, part-time N/A; GPA (75% of full-time students have a GPA at or above 3.22, part-time N/A). *U.S. News & World Report* ranking is in the second tier (tied at 70th) of all U.S. law schools.

FINANCIAL AID. Scholarships, Federal W/S, loans. Apply to Financial Aid Office by March 1 (Fall), July 1 (Spring). Phone: (305)284-3115. Use FAFSA (School code: E00532). About 34% of students receive aid other than loans from School funds.

DEGREE REQUIREMENTS. For J.D.: 88 credits minimum, at least the last 28 credits and 36 weeks in residence. For LL.M.: at least 24 credits minimum beyond the J.D. and 36 weeks in resident; thesis.

Miller School of Medicine (33136)
Web site: www.med.miami.edu

Established 1952. Located next to Jackson Memorial Hospital in the Civic Center area of Miami and in Boca Raton at Florida Atlantic University. Starting in 2007 students admitted to the Boca Raton program will complete all four years there in residence. Special facilities: Applebaum Magnetic Resonance Imaging Center, Bascombe Palmer Eye Institute, Anne Bates Leach Eye Hospital, Sylvester Comprehensive Cancer Center, Ryder Trauma Center, Diabetes Research Institute, Mailman Center for Child Development. Special programs: Summer program for underrepresented minorities. Library: 180,000 volumes, 2100 subscriptions. NIH ranking is 63rd among all U.S. institutions with 246 awards/grants worth $92,011,838.

Annual tuition: Florida resident $30,048, nonresident $38,854. No on-campus housing available. Contact Admissions Officer for off-campus housing availability. Off-campus housing and personal expenses: $22,700.

Enrollment: first-year class 182 (32 at Boca Raton); total 651 (men 52%, women 48%, minorities 43%, residents 79%). Faculty: full-time 1146, part-time 9. Degrees conferred: B.S.-M.D., M.D., M.D.-M.P.H., M.D.-M.S., M.D.-Ph.D. The M.S. and Ph.D. are offered through the Graduate School.

ADMISSION REQUIREMENTS. AMCAS, transcripts, undergraduate faculty evaluation, two personal references, MCAT (preferably in Spring), supplemental application required in support of application. Interview by invitation only. Applicants must have completed at least three years of college study. Preference given to Florida residents. Has EDP; apply after June 1, before August 1. Apply to Office of Admissions after June 1, before December 1. Application fee $65. Phone: (305)243-6791; fax: (305)243-6548. For M.D.-Ph.D. program GRE required. Application fee $65.

ADMISSION STANDARDS. Competitive. Accepts about 8.6% of all applicants. Number of applications 3739 (2492 out-of-state); number interviewed 473 (161 out-of-state); number of acceptance

323 (86 out-of-state); number enrolled 182 (32 out-of-state). Mean Composite MCAT 10.3, mean UGPA 3.7.

FINANCIAL AID. Scholarships, diversity scholarship, grants, Federal and private loans. Apply to Office of Financial Aid after acceptance, before April 1. Phone: (305)243-6211. Use FAFSA. About 88% of students receive aid from School and outside sources.

DEGREE REQUIREMENTS. For B.S.-M.D.: satisfactory completion of seven-year program. For M.D.: satisfactory completion of four-year program. For Ph.D. to M.D.: satisfactory completion of two-year M.D. program. For M.P.H., M.S., Ph.D.: see Graduate School listing above.

FIELDS OF GRADUATE STUDY.
Biochemistry and Molecular Biology.
Cancer Biology.
Epidemiology.
Microbiology and Immunology.
Molecular, Cell and Developmental Biology.
Molecular and Cellular Pharmacology.
Neuroscience.

MICHIGAN STATE UNIVERSITY
East Lansing, Michigan 48824-1020
Web site: www.msu.edu

Founded 1855. Located 80 miles NW of Detroit. CGS and AAU member. Coed. State control. Semester system. Special facilities: Abrams Planetarium, African Studies Center, Agricultural Experiment Station, Alumni Memorial Chapel, Animal Health Diagnostic Laboratory, Asian Studies Center, Bioelectromagnetics Laboratory, Biological Research Center, Breslin Student Events Center, Carcinogenesis Laboratory, Career Information Center, Center for Advanced Study of International Development, Center for Electron Optics, Center for Environmental Toxicology, Center for International Programs, Center for International Transportation Exchange, Center for Remote Sensing, Center for Urban Affairs, Clinical Center (outpatient facility), Cooperative Extension Service, Counseling Center, English Language Center, Fairchild Theater, Forest Akers Golf Courses, Genetics Clinic, Hematology Oncology Clinic, Hidden Lake Gardens, Institute for Research on Teaching, Institute for Water Research, Institute of Agricultural Technology, Institute of International Agriculture, Institute of Nutrition, Institute of Public Utilities, IPTV (3 TV stations, TV teaching auditorium, closed-circuit TV), Jenison Gymnasium and Fieldhouse, Journalism/Law Institute, Kellogg Center (hotel/restaurant), Kellogg Center for Continuing Education, Kresge Art Center and Museum, Laboratory Animal Care Service, Language Laboratory, Latin American Studies Center, Learning Resources Center, Livestock Pavilion, Living-Learning (dorm-classroom) Centers, MSU/DOE Plant Research Laboratory, MSU Laboratory Preschool, MSU Union, Munn Ice Arena, National Superconducting Cyclotron, Olin Health Center, Pesticide Research Center, Psychological Clinic, Service-Learning Center (volunteers), Social Science Research Bureau, Spartan Nursery School, Spartan Stadium, Speech and Hearing Clinic, University Auditorium, University Center for International Rehabilitation, University Museum, university radio stations (AM/FM), Veterinary Clinical Center, Wharton Center for Performing Arts (Festival Stage and Great Hall), W. J. Beal Botanical Garden and Campus Plant Collection, and W. K. Kellogg Biological Station. Graduate study available through many of seven off-campus extensions centers. The University's NIH ranking is 114th among all U.S. institutions with 142 awards/grants valued at $42,106,03. According to The Center at University of Florida, the University is ranked 56th in receipt of Federal Research funds with $132,820,000 and it ranks 34th for total University research expenditures with $321,410,000. The University's endowment assets rank it 62nd, with a value of $749,365,000. In 2004, the University awarded 430 doctorates, which ranked it 22nd among all U.S. institutions eligible to award that degree. Six of the University's faculty members have been elected to National Honor Academies and this ranks it 73rd among all U.S. institutions. The Library: approximately 4,400,000 volumes, 29,000 subscriptions. Total University enrollment: 45,100.

Tuition: per credit, resident $376–$582, nonresident $762–$930. On-campus housing: Owen Graduate Center (476 graduate men and 396 graduate women at $4400 per academic year with minimum board included) and 2175 apartments available to undergraduate and graduate single and married students (1160 one-bedroom apartments, each available to 1-2 students at average monthly cost of $400 per apartment, and 1025 one- and two-bedroom family apartments at average monthly cost of $425 per apartment). Apply to University Housing Office or University Apartments for on-campus housing or to Off-Campus Housing Office. Phone: (517)355-7457. Day-care facilities available.

Graduate School

Graduate study since 1863. Enrollment: full-time 4383, part-time 3274. University faculty teaching students: full- and part-time 1977. Degrees conferred: M.A., M.A.T., M.B.A., M.F.A., M.L.R.H.R., M.Mus., M.P.A., M.S., M.S.N., M.S.W., M.U.R.P., Ed.S., D.M.A., Ed.D., Ph.D.

ADMISSION REQUIREMENTS. Transcripts, three letters of recommendation required in support of School's application. Online application available. TOEFL (minimum score 580; some programs have higher minimums) required for international applicants. GRE/GMAT/MAT required by some departments. Interview usually not required. Accepts transfer applicants. Graduates of unaccredited institutions not considered. Apply to Office of Admissions and Scholarships at least forty-five days prior to registration. Application fee $50, $60 for international applicants. Phone: (517)355-8332; fax: (517)353-1674; e-mail: admis@msu.edu.

ADMISSION STANDARDS. Selective or very selective for most departments, competitive for others. Usual minimum average: 3.0 (A = 4).

FINANCIAL AID. Annual awards from institutional funds: grants/scholarships, fellowships, teaching assistantships, research assistantships, internships, tuition waivers, Federal W/S, loans. Approved for VA benefits. Apply by February 1 to appropriate department chair for assistantships, fellowships; to Financial Aid Office for all other programs. Phone: (517)353-5940; fax: (517)432-1155. Use FAFSA. About 57% of students receive aid other than loans from School and outside sources. Aid available for part-time students.

DEGREE REQUIREMENTS. For M.A., M.F.A., M.L.R.H.R., M.Mus., M.P.A., M.S.: 30–33 credits minimum, at least 6 in residence; thesis/nonthesis options; oral exam required with thesis option; final written and/or oral certifying exam may be required with nonthesis option; no language requirements for most majors. For M.S.N.: 37 credits minimum, at least 6 in residence; thesis/nonthesis option; final written and/or oral certifying exam (oral exam when thesis is offered). For M.B.A.: 37 credits minimum, at least 27 in residence. For M.U.P.: 48 credits minimum, at least 24 in residence. For M.S.W.: 57 credits minimum, at least 29 in residence (Social Work Plan I), and 61 credits minimum, at least 6 in residence (Social Work Plan II). For M.A.T.: 30 credits minimum, at least 9 in residence; completion of requirements for the secondary provisional certificate; thesis usually not required. For Ed.S.: normally two years beyond bachelor's; 30 credits minimum beyond the master's, at least 22 in residence; competence

in statistics or a reading knowledge of a foreign language may be required. For Ph.D.: normally at least three years beyond the bachelor's, at least 12 credits or one year in residence; qualifying exam for some departments; written and/or oral comprehensive exams; language requirements vary by department; thesis; final oral exam. For D.M.A., Ed.D.: essentially the same as for the Ph.D. For D.O.: completion of eleven-term professional program, including 6 semesters of clerkships; endorsement of the Committee on Student Evaluation; an affirmative vote from College faculty. For D.V.M.: completion of 12 semesters professional program (minimum of 163 credits), including three terms (minimum of 60 credits) of clerkships. For M.D.: completion of three-phase professional program (normally extending from 10 to 13 semesters), including clinical clerkships in community hospitals; preclinical comprehensive exams (NBME Exams, Parts I and II).

FIELDS OF STUDY.

COLLEGE OF AGRICULTURE AND NATURAL RESOURCES:
Agribusiness Strategy and Management. M.S., Ph.D.
Agricultural and Extension Education. GRE or MAT for admission. M.S., Ph.D.
Agricultural Markets and Price Analysis. Thesis required for M.S., Ph.D.
Agricultural Technology and Systems Management. Thesis required for M.S. M.S., Ph.D.
Animal Science. M.S., Ph.D.
Biosystems Engineering. M.S., Ph.D.
Building Construction Management. Thesis required for M.S. M.S. only.
Crop and Soil Sciences. M.S., Ph.D.
Ecology and Evolutionary Biology. Includes crop and soil sciences, fisheries and wildlife, forestry, horticulture. M.S., Ph.D.
Entomology. M.S., Ph.D.
Environmental and Resource Economics. M.S., Ph.D.
Environmental Toxicology. Includes animal science, crop and soil sciences, fisheries and wildlife, food science, resource development. M.S., Ph.D.
Evolutionary Biology and Behavior. Ph.D.
Finance and Production Economics. M.S., Ph.D.
Fisheries and Wildlife. GRE Subject (biology) for admission. M.S., Ph.D.
Food Science. Includes food science and foods, human nutrition and institution administration; GRE for admission. M.S., Ph.D.
Forestry. M.S., Ph.D.
Horticulture. M.S., Ph.D.
Human Nutrition. M.S., Ph.D.
Packaging. GRE for admission. M.S., Ph.D.
Park, Recreation, and Tourism Resources. GRE for admission. M.S., Ph.D.
Plant Breeding and Genetics. Includes crop and soil sciences, forestry, horticulture or botany, plant pathology. Thesis required for M.S., Ph.D.
Plant Pathology. M.S., Ph.D.
Resource Development. GRE for admission. M.S., Ph.D.
Resource Economics. Includes agricultural economics, fisheries and wildlife, forestry, park, recreation, and tourism resources, resource development. M.S., Ph.D.
Urban Studies. Includes forestry, park, recreation, and tourism resources, resource development. M.S., Ph.D.
Note: Oral final exam required for all M.S. degrees.

COLLEGE OF ARTS AND LETTERS:
African American and African Studies. M.A.
American Studies. M.A., Ph.D.
Comparative Literature. GRE for admission; qualifying exam for M.A.; M.A. only.
Critical Studies in Literacy and Pedagogy. M.A.
Digital Rhetoric and Professional Writing. M.A.
English. GRE Subject (English literature or a cognate area) for admission; GPA of 3.5 in English courses for admission to M.A.

program; two years of college-level foreign language for admission; predissertation exam required for Ph.D.; M.A., Ph.D.

English: Teaching of English to Speakers of Other Languages. GRE Subject (English literature or a cognate area) and overall GPA of 3.25 for admission. M.A., Ph.D.

French. GRE Subject (French) and department proficiency exam in French for admission. M.A.

French Language and Literature. GRE Subject (French) and qualifying exam for admission; reading proficiency in two languages other than major language required. Ph.D. only.

German Studies. Oral and written exams, nonthesis option for M.A. M.A., Ph.D.

Hispanic Cultural Studies. Ph.D.

Hispanic Literature. M.A.

History. Includes urban studies. GPA of 3.5 in history courses, GRE Subject (history) and term paper for admission; oral exam and competence in one foreign language required for M.A.; competence in two foreign languages and written and oral comprehensive required for Ph.D. M.A., Ph.D.

History of Art. GRE for admission. Two years college-level French, German, Italian, and minimum of 18 credits in History of Art upper-level courses or the equivalent for admission. M.A. only.

History—Urban Studies. M.A.

Linguistics. Two years of a college-level foreign language for admission; major linguistic research paper and qualifying exam required for admission to Ph.D. program; written exam required for M.A.; nonthesis option; demonstrated ability in two foreign languages required for Ph.D. M.A., Ph.D.

Literature in English. Includes literary studies, creative writing.

Philosophy. Sample of philosophic writing for admission; GRE optional. Public demonstration of philosophic competence required for M.A. with nonthesis option; reading knowledge of one foreign language, written comprehensive exam for Ph.D. M.A., Ph.D.

Russian. Oral and written exams and reading knowledge of another foreign language required. M.A. only.

Second Language Studies. Ph.D.

Spanish. GRE Subject (Spanish) and department proficiency exam in Spanish for admission. M.A. only.

Spanish Language and Literature. GRE Subject (Spanish) and qualifying exam for admission; reading proficiency in two languages other than major language required. Ph.D. only.

Theater. Audition required for admission to M.F.A., program; written and oral exams required for M.A. nonthesis option. M.A., M.F.A. (production design, acting).

Note: GRE and personal statement required for admission for most programs.

ELI BROAD GRADUATE SCHOOL OF MANAGEMENT:

Accounting. M.S., Ph.D.

Accounting and Business Process. M.S.

Business Administration. M.B.A., Ph.D.

Business Information Systems. M.B.A.

Business Management in Manufacturing. M.S.

Corporate Accounting. M.B.A.

Finance. M.B.A., Ph.D.

Financial Administration. M.B.A. only.

Foodservice Management. M.S.

Hospitality Business. M.B.A.

Human Resource Management. M.B.A.

Integrative Management. M.B.A.

International Business. M.B.A.

Logistics. M.S.

Management Policy and Strategy. Ph.D. only.

Management Science. M.B.A.

Manufacturing and Engineering Management. M.S.

Manufacturing and Innovation. M.S.

Marketing. M.S., Ph.D.

Materials and Logistics Management—Operations Management. M.B.A. only.

Materials and Logistics Management—Purchasing Management. M.B.A. only.

Materials and Logistics Management—Transportation/Physical Distribution Management. M.B.A. only.

Operations and Sourcing Management. Ph.D.

Operations Research Management. Comprehensive oral exam on course work required. M.S. only.

Organizational Behavior: Human Resource Management. Ph.D. only.

Personnel—Human Relations. M.B.A. only.

Professional Accounting. Minimum overall GPA of 3.25 and personal statement for admission. M.S.

Strategic Management. Ph.D.

Supply Chain Management. M.S.

Transportation Distribution. M.B.A. and Ph.D. only.

Note: GMAT required for admission to M.B.A. program; oral and written comprehensive exams required for D.B.A. and Ph.D. programs.

COLLEGE OF COMMUNICATION ARTS AND SCIENCES:

Advertising. Minimum third- or fourth-year undergraduate GPA of 3.25 for admission. M.A. only.

Communication. M.A., Ph.D.

Communication—Urban Studies. Interdepartmental. 33 credit master's. M.A. only.

Communicative Sciences and Disorders. M.A., Ph.D.

Health Communication. 33 credit master's. M.A.

Journalism. GRE, autobiography, and personal statement for admission. M.A. only.

Mass Media. Ph.D.

Public Relations. Minimum third- or fourth-year undergraduate GPA of 3.25 for admission. M.A. only.

Retailing. M.A., Ph.D.

Telecommunication. Minimum third- or fourth-year undergraduate GPA of 3.25 for admission. 40 credit master's. Includes information and telecommunication management, digital media arts and technology, information policy and society. M.A. only.

Telecommunication—Urban Studies. Interdepartmental. Includes multichannel/broadcast management (37 credit master's), information technologies and services management (40 credit master's), social effects of media (34 credit master's), media arts (31 credit master's). M.A.

Note: Written and oral exams required for nonthesis option.

COLLEGE OF EDUCATION:

Counseling. Interview and one-year counseling experience for admission to Ed.S. program; internship (21 credits) required for M.A. in rehabilitation counseling; one major and two minor field exams, prepracticum, three terms of practicum, and one-year internship required for Ed.D. and Ph.D.

Counseling Psychology. Ph.D.

Curriculum and Teaching. M.A. only.

Curriculum, Teaching and Educational Policy. Ed.S., Ph.D.

Education. M.A.

Educational Policy. Ph.D.

Educational Technology. M.A.

Higher, Adult and Lifelong Education. M.A., Ph.D.

K–12 Educational Administration. Personal statement for admission; interview and short, written essay exam for admission to Ed.S., Ed.D., and Ph.D. programs.

Kinesiology. M.S., Ph.D.

Kinesiology—Urban Studies. Interdepartmental. M.S.

Learning Technology and Culture. Ph.D.

Literary Instruction. M.A.

Measurement and Quantitative Methods. M.A., Ph.D.

Rehabilitation Counseling. M.A.

Rehabilitation Counselor Education. Ph.D.

School Psychology. Ed.S., Ph.D.

Special Education. Elementary or secondary teaching credential, eligibility for additional endorsement as a teacher of severely or mildly impaired learner, and one full year of successful teaching experience for admission to M.A. program; interview and samples of both scholarly and spontaneous writing required for admission to Ed.D. and Ph.D. programs; internship (1 term) required for Ed.S.

Student Affairs Administration. M.A.

Note: GRE required for Ed.S., Ed.D., and Ph.D. admission; M.A., M.A.T. (joint with College of Natural Science); Ed.S., Ed.D., and Ph.D.

COLLEGE OF ENGINEERING:

Chemical Engineering.
Civil Engineering.
Civil Engineering: Urban Studies. M.S. only.
Computer Science.
Electrical Engineering.
Engineering Mechanics.
Environmental Engineering.
Environmental Engineering—Environmental Toxicology. Ph.D.
Materials Science and Engineering.
Mechanical Engineering.

Note: GRE required for all international applicants, GRE strongly recommended for domestic applicants; certifying exam or thesis defense for M.S. degrees; qualifying exams for all Ph.D. degrees.

COLLEGE OF HUMAN MEDICINE:

Biochemistry. GRE Subject or MCAT (M.D.-Ph.D.) for admission.
Bioethics, Humanities and Society. M.S.
Cell and Molecular Biology. GRE Subject for admission.
Epidemiology. M.S., Ph.D.
Integrative Pharmacology.
Microbiology and Molecular Genetics. Ph.D.
Molecular Biology. M.S., Ph.D.
Neuroscience. GRE Subject for admission.
Pharmacology and Toxicology. GRE for admission to Ph.D. program.
Physiology. M.S., Ph.D.

Note: Thesis/oral exam required for master's degrees; see separate listings below.

COLLEGE OF MUSIC:

Music Composition.
Music Conducting.
Music Education.
Music Performance.
Musicology.
Piano Pedagogy.
Music Theory.
Music Therapy.

COLLEGE OF NATURAL SCIENCE:

Applied Mathematics.
Astrophysics and Astronomy.
Biochemistry and Molecular Biology. GRE Subject for admission.
Biological Science. Interdepartmental. Teacher's certificate, or candidacy for, required for admission to M.A.T. program; reading knowledge of one foreign language and one term's residency at a recognized biological station required for M.S. M.S., M.A.T. only.
Biomedical Laboratory Operations. M.S.
Biotechnology. Interdepartmental.
Cell and Molecular Biology. Interdepartmental. GRE for admission.
Chemical Physics. GRE for admission.
Chemistry. Orientation exam required for admission; teacher's certificate, or candidacy for certificate, required for admission to M.A.T. program; qualifying exam required for M.S. and M.A.T. degrees and for admission to Ph.D. program; reading knowledge of German, Russian, or French and preoral exam required for Ph.D. M.S., M.A.T., and Ph.D.
Clinical Laboratory Science.
Computational Chemistry. Ph.D.
Computational Mathematics.

Earth Science. Interdepartmental. Teacher's certificate, or candidacy for certificate, required for admission. M.A.T. only.
Ecology and Evolutionary Biology. Interdepartmental.
Environmental Geoscience.
Environmental Toxicology. Interdepartmental.
General Science. Interdepartmental. Teacher's certificate, or candidacy for certificate, required for admission; M.A.T. only.
Genetics. Ph.D. only.
Geological Sciences. GRE for admission. M.S., M.A.T., Ph.D.
Human Nutrition. M.S.
Industrial Mathematics. M.S.
Industrial Microbiology. M.S.
Inorganic Chemistry.
Mathematics. Reading knowledge of two foreign languages required for Ph.D. M.A., M.S., M.A.T., Ph.D.
Mathematics Education.
Microbiology. GRE Subject (biology) and personal statement for admission; final oral exam required. M.S. only.
Neuroscience. Ph.D.
Nuclear Chemistry. M.S., Ph.D.
Operations Research Statistics. M.S. only.
Pathology. Ph.D. only.
Physical Science. Interdepartmental. Certifying exam required for M.S. M.S., M.A.T. only.
Physics. Qualifying exam required for M.S. and Ph.D.; one term of half-time teaching required for Ph.D. M.S., M.A.T., Ph.D.
Physiology. GRE for admission; thesis/oral exam required for M.S.; qualifying exam required for Ph.D.
Plant Biology. M.S., Ph.D.
Statistics. Qualifying exam and reading ability in French, German, or Russian required for Ph.D. M.A., M.S., Ph.D.
Zoology. GRE for admission. M.S., M.A.T., Ph.D.

Note: Requirements for secondary provisional certificate must be met for M.A.T.

COLLEGE OF NURSING:

Nursing. Includes adult, family and gerontological nursing. GRE (within the last five years), personal interview, statistics course, B.S.N. from accredited nursing program with GPA of 3.0 for years three and four; one-year work experience as R.N. during previous five years or the equivalent, current licensure to practice nursing in the U.S., and eligibility for Michigan licensure required for admission; 42 credit program. M.S.N. only.

COLLEGE OF OSTEOPATHIC MEDICINE:

Biochemistry and Molecular Biology. GRE/Subject for admission.
Microbiology. GRE/Subject (Biology) and personal statement for M.S., plus lab teaching, predissertation oral exam, publishable manuscript for Ph.D. M.S. Ph.D.
Microbiology and Molecular Genetics. Ph.D.
Pharmacology. GRE for admission to Ph.D.
Physiology. GRE for admission; thesis/oral exam required for M.S.; qualifying exam required for Ph.D.

Note: Final oral exam required for M.S. Also see separate listing below.

COLLEGE OF SOCIAL SCIENCE:

Anthropology. Thesis/oral exam required for M.A. (can substitute qualifying exam or doctoral comprehensive exam if directly admitted to doctoral program without M.A.). Includes professional applications in anthropology. M.A., Ph.D.
Chicano/Latin Studies. Ph.D.
Criminal Justice. GRE or MAT (social science professional scale) and minimum overall undergraduate GPA of 3.2 for admission; policy paper and oral exam required for nonthesis option. M.S., Ph.D.
Economics. Includes history of economic thought, advanced economic theory, econometrics, labor economics, industrial organization, advanced macro and monetary economics, public

economics, international economics, economic development. M.A., Ph.D.

Environmental Design. M.A.

Forensic Sciences. M.S.

Geographic Information Science. M.A., M.S., Ph.D.

Geography. GRE and a minimum GPA of 3.4 in all geography courses and all junior-senior courses for admissions to M.A. or M.S. programs; minimum GPA of 3.6 for admission to Ph.D. M.A., M.S., Ph.D.

Geography—Urban Studies. GRE and a minimum GPA of 3.4. Interdepartmental. M.A. only.

History. M.A.

Human Resources and Labor Relations. M.A.

Industrial Relations and Human Resources. Ph.D.

Infant Studies. Interdepartmental. M.A.

Labor Relations and Human Resources. Includes collective bargaining and employment relations, and employment and training programs options; GRE for admission. M.L.R.H.R. only.

Labor Relations and Human Resources—Urban Studies. Interdepartmental.

Political Science. GRE and 3.2 GPA for admission. M.A., Ph.D.

Political Science—Urban Studies. GRE and 3.2 GPA for admission. Interdepartmental. M.A., Ph.D.

Psychology. GRE/Subject (Psychology) for admission to M.A., Ph.D.; thesis/oral exam required for M.A. M.A., Ph.D.

Psychology—Urban Studies. GRE/Subject (Psychology) for admission. M.A., Ph.D.

Public Policy. M.P.P.

Social Work. Includes administration and program evaluation and interpersonal intervention; MSWI (two-year) and MSWII (one-year) program options; bachelor's in social work from CSEW-accredited program and full-time student status required for admission to MSWII program. M.S.W., Ph.D.

Sociology. GRE for admission; master's thesis or original research paper for admission to Ph.D. program.

Sociology—Urban Studies. GRE for admission; master's thesis or original research paper for admission to Ph.D. program; thesis/oral exam required for M.A.

Urban and Regional Planning. M.U.R.P. only.

Urban and Regional Planning—Urban Studies. Interdepartmental. M.U.R.P.

COLLEGE OF VETERINARY MEDICINE:

Anatomy. GRE for admission; thesis/oral exam or publishable manuscript required for M.S.; publishable manuscript required for Ph.D.

Comparative Medicine and Integrative Biology. Ph.D.

Environmental Toxicology. Multidepartmental program, granting a Ph.D. only, anatomy (GRE for admission), microbiology (GRE/Subject (Biology) for admission), pathology, pharmacology (GRE for admission), physiology (GRE/Subject for admission).

Food Safety. Inter-College program. M.S., Ph.D.

Large Animal Clinical Sciences. M.S., Ph.D.

Microbiology. GRE/Subject (Biology) and personal statement for admission; final oral exam required. M.S., Ph.D.

Pathology. Thesis/oral exam and publishable manuscript required for M.S.; publishable manuscript required for Ph.D.

Pharmacology and Toxicology. GRE for admission to Ph.D. program.

Physiology. GRE/Subject for admission; thesis/oral exam required for M.S.; qualifying exam required for Ph.D.

Small Animal Clinical Sciences. M.S. only.

Note: Also see separate listing below.

College of Human Medicine (48824-1317)

Web site: www.humanmedicine.msu.edu

First class entered 1964. Students spend their first year or two years on the main MSU campus, located in East Lansing, Michigan. The remainder of their CHM education is spent at one of six community campuses located throughout the state: Grand Rapids for years two through four or Flint, Kalamazoo, Lansing, Saginaw, or the Upper Peninsula for years three and four. NIH ranking is 114th among U.S. institutions with 142 awards/grants worth $42,106,033.

Annual tuition: resident $25,544, nonresident $55,544. On-campus housing available. Total average figure for all other expenses: $18,500.

Enrollment: first-year 106, total 454 (men 44%, women 56%, minorities 34%, state residents 78%). Faculty: full-time 400, part-time 200. Degrees conferred: M.D., M.D.-M. A., M.D.-M.S., M.D.-Ph.D. The M.A., M.S., and Ph.D. are available through the Graduate School.

ADMISSION REQUIREMENTS. AMCAS report, transcripts, letters of recommendation, MCAT, autobiographical statement required in support of application. Interview by invitation only. Has EDP; apply between June 1 and August 1. Applicants must have completed at least three years of college study. Preference given to state residents. Accepts transfer applicants on a space available basis. Apply to Office of Admissions after June 1, before November 15. Application fee $60. Phone: (517)353-9620; fax: (517)432-0021; e-mail: MDadmissions@msu.edu.

ADMISSION STANDARDS. Competitive. Accepts about 6.6% of all applicants. Number of applications 3165 (2123 out-of-state); number interviewed 369 (106 out-of-state); number of acceptance 210 (59 out-of-state); number enrolled 106 (23 out-of-state). Mean Composite MCAT 9.4; mean UGPA 3.51. *U.S. News & World Report* ranking is 18th of all U.S. medical schools for primary care.

FINANCIAL AID. Scholarships, minority scholarships, Grants-in-Aid, institutional loans, HEAL, alternative loan programs, NIH stipends, Federal Perkins Loans, Stafford Subsidized and Unsubsidized Loans, Service Commitment Scholarship programs are available. All Financial Aid is based on proven need. Assistantships/fellowships may be available for M.D.-Advanced Graduate Degree candidates. Financial Aid applications and information are available at the on-campus, by-invitation interview. For scholarships, the selection criteria places heavy reliance on MCAT and undergraduate GPA. Contact the MSU Health Professions Financial Aid Office for current information. Phone: (517)353-5940. Apply for aid as soon as possible. For most financial assistance and all Federal programs submit FAFSA to a Federal processor (School code: 002290), also submit Financial Aid Transcript, Federal Income Tax forms. Approximately 75% of students receive some form of financial assistance.

DEGREE REQUIREMENTS. For B.A./B.S.-M.D.: an eight-year program. For M.D.: satisfactory completion of four-year program. All students must pass USMLE Step 1 prior to entering third year; all students must pass USMLE Step 2 prior to awarding of M.D. For M.D.-M.A., M.D.-M.S.: generally a four-and-one-half- to five-and-one-half-year program. For M.D.-Ph.D.: generally a seven-year program.

FIELDS OF GRADUATE STUDY.
Biochemistry and Molecular Biology.
Bioethics, Humanities and Society.
Epidemiology.
Microbiology and Molecular Genetics.
Pharmacology and Toxicology.
Physiology.

College of Osteopathic Medicine

Web site: www.com.msu.edu

College opened in 1971. Located on main campus. Semester system.

Annual tuition: resident $25,544, nonresident $55,544. On-campus rooms and apartments available for both single and married students. Contact Housing Office for both on- and off-campus housing information. Phone: (571)353-7457. Off-campus housing and personal expenses: approximately $19,170.

Enrollment: first-year class 205, total 708 (men 46%, women 54%, minorities 19%, state residents 91%). Faculty: Full-time 180, part-time 25. Degrees conferred: D.O., H.O.-M.H.H. (Health and Humanities), D.O.-M.P.H., D.O.-M.S., D.O.-Ph.D., M.S.T.P.

ADMISSION REQUIREMENTS FOR FIRST-YEAR APPLICANTS. Preference given to state residents, U.S. citizens, and permanent residents only. Has EDP for state residents only. EDP applicants must apply through AMCAS (official transcripts sent by mid-May) between June 1 and August 1. Early applications are encouraged. Submit secondary/supplemental application, a personal statement, two recommendations to Office of Admission within two weeks of receipt of application. Interviews are by invitation only and generally for final selection. Notification normally begins October 1. All other applicants apply through AACOMAS (file after June 1, before December 1), submit MCAT (will accept test results from last three years), official transcripts for each school attended (should show at least 90 semester credits/135 quarter credits) and service processing fee. After a review of the AACOMAS application and supporting documents a decision is made concerning which candidates should receive supplemental materials. The supplemental application (return by February 15), an application fee of $60, a personal statement, and three recommendations (one from a D.O.) should be returned to Office of Admission as soon as possible. Phone: (517)353-7740. International applicants are subject to Michigan State University's requirements for international students. Contact the Office of International Students and Scholars, 103 Center for International Programs, MSU, East Lansing, Michigan 48824 for current information and specific requirements. Interviews are by invitation only and generally for final selection. Applicants to joint degree programs and M.S.T.P. must be accepted by both the College and the Graduate School. Request applications from both schools and mark M.S.T.P. clearly on both forms. First-year students admitted Fall only. Priority deadline December 1. Rolling admissions process; notification starts in October and is finished when class is filled.

ADMISSION STANDARDS. Selective. Accepts about 18% of all applicants. Number of applicants 1943 (1394 out-of-state); number interviewed 375 (87 out-of-state); number of acceptance 335 (79 out-of-state); number enrolled 205 (20 out-of-state). Usual minimum UGPA: 3.0 (A = 4). Mean Composite MCAT 8.4, mean UGPA 3.51.

FINANCIAL AID. Scholarships, minority scholarships, grants, institutional loans, NOF, HEAL, alternative loan programs, NIH stipends; Service Obligation Scholarship programs, Military and National Health Service programs are available; private loans. All aid is based on documented need. Assistantships/fellowships may be available for joint degree and M.S.T.P. applicants. Financial Aid applications and information are sent out periodically during the year. Contact the MSU Health Professions Financial Aid Office for current information. Phone: (517)353-5188. Use FAFSA for all Federal programs (School code: 002290), also submit Financial Aid Transcript, Federal Income Tax forms. Approximately 90% of students receive some form of financial assistance.

DEGREE REQUIREMENTS. For D.O.: satisfactory completion of Units I, II, and III. For D.O.-M.H.H., D.O.-M.P.H.: generally a five- to six-year program. For M.D.-Ph.D.: generally a seven-year program.

FIELDS OF GRADUATE STUDY.
Biochemistry and Molecular Biology.
Bioethics, Humanities and Society. M.A.

Cell and Molecular Biology.
Environmental Toxicology. Interdepartmental program.
Genetics.
Microbiology and Molecular Biology.
Neuroscience.
Pharmacology and Toxicology.
Physiology.
Public Health. M.P.H.

College of Veterinary Medicine (48824-1316)
Web site: www.cvm.msu.edu

Semester system. Library: 40,000 volumes, 1000 subscriptions. Special facilities: Center for emerging Infectious Diseases, Center for Feline Health and Well-being, Center for Integrative toxicology, Diagnostic Center for Population and Animal Health, Equine Performance Center, Training Center for Dairy Professionals, National Food Safety and Toxicology Center, Center for Comparative Epidemiology.

Annual tuition and fees: residents $17,230, nonresidents $36,030. Both on- and off campus housing available. Total average cost for other expenses: $15,394.

Enrollment: first-year class 107, total 435 (men 20%, women 80%, minorities 5%, state residents 80%). Faculty: full-time 82, part-time 10. Degrees conferred: D.V.M., D.V.M.-M.P.H. The M.S. and Ph.D. are offered through the Graduate School.

ADMISSION REQUIREMENTS. VMCAS report, completion of required preveterinary courses, transcripts, MCAT or GRE, interview, autobiography, three recommendations required in support of application. TOEFL required if English is not the applicant's primary language. Has EDP; apply after August 1, before October 15. Preference given to Michigan residents. Graduates of unaccredited colleges not considered. All application materials must be received by the Office of Admissions and Scholarships by October 1. Application fee $65. Phone: (517)353-9793; fax: (517) 353-3041.

ADMISSION STANDARDS. Selective. Accepts about 10–15% of all applicants. Number of applicants 883 (672 out-of-state); number interviewed 226 (108 out-of-state); number of acceptance 115 (42 out-of-state); number enrolled 107 (22 out-of-state). Usual minimum UGPA: 3.0 (A = 4). GRE mean score (V + Q) 1131; mean UGPA 3.62 .

FINANCIAL AID. Fellowships, research assistantships, tuition reimbursement, Federal W/S, loans. Apply to Office of Admissions and Scholarships. Use FAFSA.

DEGREE REQUIREMENTS. For D.V.M.: satisfactory completion of three-year, year-round, professional curriculum. For M.S., Ph.D.: see Graduate School listing above.

FIELDS OF GRADUATE STUDY.
Comparative Medicine & Integrative Biology. M.S., Ph.D.
Comparative Orthopaedics. M.S.
Food Safety. Professional M.S.
Large Animal Clinical Sciences. M.S., Ph.D.
Microbiology and Molecular Genetics.
Molecular Genetic Research. M.S.
Pharmacology and Toxicology. Ph.D.
Physiology.
Pathobiology and Diagnostic Investigation. Ph.D.

MSW COLLEGE OF LAW
368 Law College Building
East Lansing, Michigan 48824-1300
Website: www.law.mus.edu

Established in 1891. Located at Michigan State University. Name changed from Detroit College of Law to MSU College of Law in 2004. ABA approved since 1941. AALS member. Private control. Semester system. Full- and part-time study. Special facilities: Center for Canadian–U.S. Law, Grand Rapids Law Centers, Fieger Trial Practice Institute. Special programs; Summer study abroad at University of Ottawa, Canada, and Panamericana University, Zapopan, Jalisco, Mexico. Law library: 271,426 volumes, 3960 subscriptions; has LEXIS, NEXIS, WESTLAW, INFOTRAC, MERIT; has more than 1200 network connections.

Annual tuition: full-time $28,182, part-time $21,434. On-campus housing available for both single and married students at Michigan State University. Contact University's Housing Office for both on- and off-campus housing information. Phone: (800) 678-4679, (517)355-7460. Off-campus housing and personal expenses: approximately $11,118.

Enrollment: first-year class 197, part-time 83; total full- and part-time 948 (men 55%, women 45%, minorities 13%). Faculty: full-time 43, part-time 40. Faculty to faculty ratio 20.8 to 1. Degrees conferred: J.D., J.D.-M.A.(Bioethics, Humanities & Society, English, Interdisciplinary Programs in Health and Humanities, Labor Relations and Human Resources), J.D.-M.B.A., J.D.-M.S. (Community, Agricultural, Recreation, and Resources Studies, Fisheries & Wildlife, Forestry), J.D.-M.U.R.P., LL.M. (American Legal System), LL.M. (Intellectual Property & Communications Law), M.J.

ADMISSION REQUIREMENTS. LSDAS Law School report, LSAT (not later that December test date; if more than one LSAT, highest is used), bachelor's degree from an accredited institution, résumé, personal statement, interview, transcripts (must show all schools attended and at least three years of study) required in support of application. Letters of recommendation are optional. Applicants must have received bachelor's degree prior to enrollment. Interview not required but may be requested by School. In addition, international applicants for whom English is not their native language must submit TOEFL (not older than two years). Apply to Director of Admission after September 30, before March 1. First-year students admitted Fall only. Rolling admissions process, notification starts in November and is finished by late May. Application fee $50. Phone: (517)432-6800; fax: (517)432-0098; e-mail: law@msu.edu.

ADMISSION STANDARDS. Selective. Accepts approximately 35% of full-time and 50% of part-time applicants. Number of full-time applicants 2473, part-time 368; number of full-time acceptance 876, part-time 134; number full-time enrolled 197, part-time 83; LSAT (75% of full-time students have a score at or above 155, part-time 150; GPA (75% of full-time student have a GPA at or above 3.04, part-time 3.07). *U.S. News & World Report* ranking is in the third tier of all U.S. law schools.

FINANCIAL AID. Scholarships, minority scholarships, Grants-in-Aid, institutional loans; Federal loans and Federal W/S offered through University's Financial Aid Office. Assistantships may be available for upper divisional Joint Degree candidates. Apply to Office of Financial Aid after January 1 and before April 15. Phone: (517)432-6810. For all other programs use FAFSA (College code: G02254). Approximately 38% full-time, 14% part-time of first-year class receive scholarships/Grants-in-Aid. Approximately 43% of students receive some form of financial assistance.

DEGREE REQUIREMENTS. For J.D.: 85 (60 required) credits with a GPA of at least a 2.0 (A = 4), plus completion of upper divisional writing course; three-year program, four-year program. Accelerated J.D. with one summer of course work. For J.D.-M.B.A.: up to 6 M.B.A. credits can be used for the J.D., up to 9 J.D. credits can be used for the M.B.A. For LL.M.M.J.: full-time 24 credit individualized program.

MICHIGAN TECHNOLOGICAL UNIVERSITY
Houghton, Michigan 49931-1295
Web site: www.mtu.edu

Founded 1885. Located 400 miles N of Chicago. CGS member. Coed. State control. Semester system. Special facilities: A.E. Seaman Mineralogical Museum, National Center for Clean Industrial and Treatment Technologies, Center for Advanced Manufacturing and Material Processing, Environmental Engineering Center, Keweenaw Research Center, Center for Clean Manufacturing and Research, Ford Forestry Center, Remote Sensing Institute, Institute of Wood Research, Institute of Materials Processing, Regional Groundwater Education in Michigan Center. Library: 992,197 volumes, 10,500 subscriptions. Total University enrollment: 6500.

Annual tuition: full-time, resident $11,232, nonresident $16,500. On-campus housing for 352 married units, 110 single units. Average academic year housing cost: $6375 (including board) for single students; $4377 for married students. Contact Director of Housing for both on- and off-campus housing information. Phone: (906)487-2682.

Graduate School

Enrollment: full-time 674, part-time 203. University faculty: full-time 303, part-time 76. Degrees conferred: M.S., Ph.D.

ADMISSION REQUIREMENTS. Official transcripts, GRE, GMAT required in support of School's application. TOEFL required for international applicants. Interview not required. Accepts transfer applicants. Graduates of unaccredited institutions not considered. Apply to Graduate School Office at least six weeks prior to the desired semester of registration. Application fee $40, $45 for international applicants. Phone: (906)487-2327; fax: (906)487-2463; e-mail: gradadm@mtu.edu.

ADMISSION STANDARDS. Selective. Usual minimum average: 2.7 (A = 4).

FINANCIAL AID. Fellowships, research assistantships, teaching assistantships, internships, grants, Federal W/S, loans. Approved for VA benefits. Apply February 1 to Dean, Graduate School for fellowships, assistantships; to Financial Aid Office for all other programs. Phone: (906)487-2622. Use FAFSA. About 71% of students receive aid other than loans from University and outside sources. Aid available for part-time students.

DEGREE REQUIREMENTS. For M.S.: 30 credits minimum, at least 24 in residence; 6 credits may be assigned to thesis; final oral exam. For Ph.D.: total number of credits variable, at least four semesters in residence; preliminary written/oral exam; foreign language proficiency recommended by some departments; dissertation; final oral exam.

FIELDS OF STUDY.
Applied Ecology. M.S.
Applied Natural Resource Economics. M.S.
Atmospheric Sciences. Ph.D.
Biomedical Engineering. Ph.D.
Biotechnology. M.S., Ph.D.
Business. M.S.
Business Administration. M.B.A.
Chemical Engineering. M.S., Ph.D.
Civil Engineering. M.Eng., M.S., Ph.D.
Composites. M.S., Ph.D.
Computational Science and Engineering. Ph.D.
Computer Science. M.S., Ph.D.
Computational Science and Engineering. Ph.D.
Electrical Engineering. M.S., Ph.D.

Engineering Mechanics. M.S.
Engineering Physics. Ph.D.
Environmental Engineering. M.Eng., M.S., Ph.D.
Environmental Policy. M.S.
Forest Ecology and Management. M.S.
Forest Molecular Genetics and Biotechnology. M.S., Ph.D.
Forest Science. Ph.D.
Forestry. M.F., M.S., Ph.D.
Geological Engineering. M.Eng., M.S., Ph.D.
Industrial Archaeology. M.S.
Industrial Heritage and Archaeology. Ph.D.
Information Technology. M.S., Ph.D.
International Civil and Environmental Engineering. Peace Corps
 program. M.S.
Materials Science and Engineering. M.S., Ph.D.
Mechanical Engineering. M.Eng., Ph.D.
Mining Engineering. M.S., Ph.D.
Nanotechnology. M.S., Ph.D.
Remote Sensing. M.S., Ph.D.
Rhetoric and Technical Communication. M.S., Ph.D.
Transportation. M.S., Ph.D.

THE UNIVERSITY OF MICHIGAN
Ann Arbor, Michigan 48109
Web site: www.umich.edu

Founded 1817. Located 40 miles W of Detroit. CGS and AAU member. Coed. State control. Trimester system. Special facilities: computer center; four astronomical laboratories; experimental school; nuclear reactor; statistical research laboratory; installations for handling radioisotopes and high-intensity radiation sources; centers for ancient and modern studies, Afro-American and African studies, Chinese studies, Near Eastern and North African studies, Russian and East European studies, South and Southeast Asian studies, Western European studies, research on economic development, human growth and development, research on learning and teaching; institutes for environmental quality, labor and industrial relations, mental health research, public policy, science and technology, social research. The University's NIH ranking is 7th among all U.S. institutions with 975 awards/grants valued at $386,627,410. According to The Center at University of Florida, the University is ranked 3rd in receipt of Federal Research funding with $516,818,000, and it ranks 3rd for total University research expenditures with $780,054,000. The University's endowment assets rank it 8th, with a value of $4,163,382,000. In 2004, the University awarded 660 doctorates, which ranked it 6th among all U.S. institutions eligible to award that degree. Seventy-seven of the University's faculty members have been elected to National Honor Academies and this ranks it 13th among all U.S. institutions. The Library: approximately 7,000,000 volumes, 62,000 subscriptions. Total University enrollment: 40,000.

Annual tuition: full-time (9 or more credits), resident $14,000 (some programs may have additional charges), nonresident $28,500. On-campus housing for 2100 married students, 750 graduate men, 750 graduate women. Average academic year housing cost: $8200–$9000 for married students, $4888–$6000 for 8 months (including board) for single students. Apply to Housing Office. Phone: (734)763-2084.

Horace H. Rackham School of Graduate Studies

Graduate study since 1849. Enrollment: 6850. Graduate faculty: full-time 4100. Degrees conferred: A.M., M.S., M.F.A., M.I.L.S., M.L.Arch., M.L.S., M.P.A., M.P.P., M.S.Pharm., M.U.P., M.S.E., Engineer, Ed.S., Ed.D., A.Mus.D., Ph.D.

ADMISSION REQUIREMENTS. Transcripts, letters of reference required in support of School's application. GRE either required or strongly recommended for most departments. TOEFL or MELAB required of international students. Interview not required. Accepts transfer applicants. Graduates of unaccredited institutions not considered. Apply by January 15. Application fee $60, $75 for international applicants. Phone: (734)764-8129.

ADMISSION STANDARDS. Selective to competitive for most departments. Usual minimum average: 3.0 (A = 4).

FINANCIAL AID. Annual awards from institutional funds: fellowships, assistantships, internships, traineeships, tuition waivers, Federal W/S, loans. Approved for VA benefits. Apply by February 1 to Fellowships, Assistantships Office; to Financial Aid Office for all other programs. Use FAFSA and University's FAF. 1040 IRS form must be submitted. Phone: (734)763-6600; fax: (734)647-3081. About 75% of students receive aid other than loans from University and outside sources. Aid available for part-time students.

DEGREE REQUIREMENTS. For master's: 30–36 hours minimum, at least 18 in residence; thesis, final written/oral exam for most majors; reading knowledge of one foreign language for some majors. For M.S.E.: 30 hours minimum, at least 24 in residence. For Engineering: 30 hours minimum beyond the bachelor's, at least 24 in residence. For Ed.S.: 54 hours minimum beyond the bachelor's, at least 48 in residence; final research report. For Ph.D.: six terms of study/research minimum beyond the bachelor's, at least two terms of not less than eight hours each in residence; no specific hour requirement except 60 hours minimum for education; language requirements vary by major; qualifying exam; preliminary exam; candidacy; dissertation; final oral exam. For Ed.D.: 72 hours minimum beyond the bachelor's, at least two terms in residence; preliminary exam; dissertation; final oral exam. For A.Mus.D.: essentially the same as for the Ph.D.

FIELDS OF STUDY.
Aerospace Engineering. GRE for admission. M.S., Ph.D.
American Culture. GRE for admission; interdepartmental. A.M., Ph.D.
Anthropology. GRE for admission. Ph.D.
Anthropology and History. GRE for admission; interdepartmental. Ph.D.
Applied Physics. GRE for admissions. Ph.D.
Architecture. M.S., Ph.D.
Archives and Records Management. M.S.I.
Art and Design. Includes photography, art education; portfolio for admission. M.A., M.F.A.
Asian Languages and Culture. GRE for admission; includes Chinese language and literature, Japanese language and literature, Buddhist studies; one language for M.A. candidacy, plus two years study in Far Eastern language.
Asian Studies. GRE for admission; interdepartmental; includes China, Japan, South and Southeast Asia. A.M.
Astronomy and Astrophysics. GRE/Subject for admission. Ph.D.
Atmospheric, Oceanic and Space Sciences. GRE recommended. M.S., Ph.D.
Bioinformatics. M.S., Ph.D.
Biological Chemistry. GRE for admission. Ph.D.
Biology. GRE for admission. M.S., Ph.D.
Biomedical Engineering. GRE for admission; interdepartmental.
Biophysics. Interdepartmental. Ph.D.
Biostatistics. GRE for admission. M.S., Ph.D.
Business Administration. M.B.A., M.A.S., M.H.A. granted by School of Business Administration. Ph.D.
Cell and Development Biology. Ph.D.
Cellular and Molecular Biology. GRE for admission; interdepartmental. Ph.D.
Cellular Biotechnology. Indepartmental. Ph.D.
Chemical Biology. Ph.D.
Chemical Engineering. GRE for admission. M.S.E., Ph.D.
Chemistry. GRE for admission. Ph.D.

Civil and Environmental Engineering. Includes civil, construction engineering and management, environmental engineering. GRE for admission. M.S.E., Ph.D.

Classical Art and Archaeology. GRE for admission; interdepartmental. Ph.D.

Classical Studies. GRE for admission. A.M. in Greek and Latin; Ph.D. in Classical Studies.

Clinical Research Design and Statistical Analysis. M.S.

Communication Studies. GRE for admission. Includes radio, TV, film, journalism.

Comparative Literature. Interdepartmental; one language for admission; substantial knowledge of two languages, some facility in another for Ph.D.

Computer Science and Engineering. M.S., M.S.E., Ph.D.

Dentistry. D.D.S. for admission, except in biomaterials (M.S., Ph.D.), dental hygiene (M.S.), endodontics (M.S.), oral health sciences (Ph.D.), Orthodontics (M.S.), pediatrics dentistry (M.S.), periodontics (M.S.), Prosthodontics (M.S.), restorative dentistry (M.S.).

Design Science. Ph.D.

Ecology and Evolutionary Biology. M.S., Ph.D.

Economics. Includes applied (A.M.). GRE/Subject for admission. Ph.D.

Education. GRE for admission. Includes educational studies, higher and postsecondary education. A.M., M.S., Ph.D.

Education and Psychology. GRE for admission; interdepartmental. Ph.D.

Electrical and Computer Engineering. GRE for admission. M.S., M.S.E., Ph.D.

English and Education. GRE for admission; interdepartmental. Ph.D.

English and Women's Studies. Ph.D.

English Language and Literature. GRE, writing sample for admission. Ph.D.

Environmental Health Science. M.S., Ph.D.

Epidemiologic Science. GRE for admission. Normally admits to Ph.D. only.

Financial Engineering. M.S.E.

Geological Sciences. GRE for admission. M.S., Ph.D.

Geoscience and Remote Sensing. Ph.D.

Germanic Languages and Literatures. GRE for admission. A.M., Ph.D.

Greek and Roman History. Ph.D.

Health Behavior and Health Education. GRE for admission. Ph.D.

Health Services Organization and Policy. Ph.D.

History. GRE for admission. Ph.D.

History and Women's Studies. Ph.D.

History of Art. GRE for admission. One language for A.M. Ph.D.

Human Genetics. GRE for admission. M.S., Ph.D.

Immunology. Ph.D.

Industrial and Operations Engineering. GRE for admission. M.S., M.S.E., Ph.D.

Industrial Health. M.S., Ph.D.

Information and Library Studies. M.I.L.S., Ph.D.

Journalism. A.M.

Judaic Studies. A.M.

Kinesiology. A.M., M.S., Ph.D.

Landscape Architecture. M.L.Arch., Ph.D.

Library and Information Services. M.S.I.

Linguistics. GRE for admission. Ph.D.

Linguistics and Germanic Language and Literatures. Ph.D.

Linguistics and Romance Languages and Literatures. Ph.D.

Macromolecular Science and Engineering. GRE for admission. Interdepartmental. M.S., Ph.D.

Materials Science and Engineering. GRE for admission. M.S.E., Ph.D.

Mathematics. GRE for admission. Includes applied and interdisciplinary. A.M., M.S., Ph.D.

Mechanical Engineering. M.S.E., Ph.D.

Medical Scientist Training Program. M.D.-Ph.D. program.

Medicinal Chemistry. GRE for admission. Interdepartmental. Ph.D.

Microbiology and Immunology. GRE for admission. Ph.D.

Mineralogy. M.S., Ph.D.

Modern Middle Eastern and North African Studies. GRE for admission; interdepartmental. A.M.

Molecular, Cellular, and Developmental Biology. M.S., Ph.D.

Music. Includes composition (A.Mus.D., A.M.), composition and music theory (Ph.D.), conducting (band, choral, orchestral, A.Mus.D.), dance (M.F.A.), music education (Ph.D.), music theory (A.M., Ph.D.), musicology—ethnomusicology (A.M., Ph.D.); musicology—history (A.M., Ph.D.), performance (all instruments and voice, A.Mus.D.), piano accompanying and chamber music (A.Mus.D.), piano pedagogy and performance (A.Mus.D.).

Natural Resources and Environment. GRE for admission. M.S., Ph.D.

Naval Architecture and Marine Engineering. GRE for admission. M.S., M.S.E., Ph.D.

Near Eastern Studies. GRE for admission. A.M., Ph.D.

Neuroscience. GRE for admission; interdepartmental. Ph.D.

Nuclear Engineer. M.S., M.S.E.

Nuclear Engineering. Ph.D.

Nuclear Engineering and Radiological Sciences. Ph.D.

Nuclear Science. M.S., Ph.D.

Nursing. GRE for admission. Includes community health nursing (M.S.), gerontological nursing (M.S.), medical-surgical nursing (M.S.), nursing (Ph.D.), nurse health services administration (M.S.), nursing business and health systems (M.S.), parent–child nursing (M.S.), psychiatric–mental health nursing (M.S.). M.S., Ph.D.

Nutritional Science. M.S.

Oceanography—Marine Geology and Geochemistry. M.S., Ph.D.

Oceanography—Physical. M.S., Ph.D.

Pathology. Ph.D.

Pharmaceutical Chemistry. GRE for admission. Ph.D.

Pharmaceutical Sciences. GRE for admission. Ph.D.

Pharmacology. GRE for admission. Ph.D.

Philosophy. GRE, writing sample for admission. A.M., Ph.D.

Physics. GRE for admission. M.S., Ph.D.

Physiology. GRE for admission. Ph.D.

Political Science. GRE for admission. Ph.D.

Psychology. GRE for admission; admits to Ph.D. only, additional departmental application required for admission. Ph.D.

Psychology and Women's Studies. Ph.D.

Public Administration. GRE for admission. M.P.A.

Public Policy Studies. GRE for admission; interdepartmental. Includes public policy (M.P.P.), public policy and economics (Ph.D.), public policy and political science (Ph.D.), public policy and sociology (Ph.D). M.P.P., Ph.D.

Romance Languages and Literature. Includes French, Italian, Spanish. GRE for admission. A.M., Ph.D.

Russian and East European Studies. GRE for admission; interdepartmental. A.M.

Scientific Computing. Ph.D.

Screen Arts and Cultures. Ph.D.

Slavic Languages and Literatures. GRE for admission. A.M., Ph.D.

Social Work and Social Science. Includes social work and anthropology, social work and economics, social work and political science, social work and psychology, social work and sociology. Ph.D. only.

Sociology. GRE/Subject for admission. Ph.D.

Space and Planetary Physics. Ph.D.

Statistics. GRE for admission. Includes applied statistics (A.M. only). A.M., Ph.D.

Survey Methodology. M.S., Ph.D.

Teaching Arabic as a Foreign Language. A.M.

Theatre. Includes theatre practice (Ph.D.), design (M.F.A.). M.F.A., Ph.D.

Toxicology. M.S., Ph.D.

Urban Planning. GRE for admission. M.U.P. only.

Urban, Technological, and Environmental Planning. GRE for admission. Ph.D.

Ross School of Business
Web site: www.bus.umich.edu

Established 1924. Public control. Accredited programs: M.B.A., Accounting; recognized Ph.D. Courses offered in Dearborn. Semester (both seven- and fourteen-week courses) system. Special programs: foreign exchange programs in Australia, Austria, Costa Rica, Denmark, Finland, France, Germany, Italy, the Netherlands, Republic of Singapore, Spain, Sweden, United Kingdom; there are domestic (Washington Campus Program) and international internships, overseas business residencies. Special facilities: Center for International Business Education, Frederick A. and Barbara M. Erb Environmental Management Institute, Mitsui Life Financial Research Center, National Quality Research Center, Paton Center for Research in Accounting, Tauber Manufacturing Institute, William Davidson Institute. Library: 144,000 volumes, 3,100 subscriptions.

Annual tuition: resident full-time $38,289, M.S.C.M. $39,581; nonresident full-time $43,289, M.S.C.M. $44,581.

Enrollment: total full-time 1100, part-time 825. Faculty: full-time 121, part-time 57; 98% with Ph.D./D.B.A. Degrees conferred: M.B.A. (full-time, part-time, day, evening), M.B.A.-M.Arch., M.B.A.-M.A. (Chinese Studies, Japanese Studies, Middle Eastern and North African Studies, Russian and East European Studies, South and Southeast Asian Studies), M.B.A.-M.H.S.A. (Health Service Administration), M.B.A.-J.D., M.B.A.-M.P.P. (Public Policy), M.B.A.-M.M. (Music), M.B.A.-M.M.E. (Manufacturing Engineering), M.B.A.-M.S. (Construction Engineering, Engineering, Industrial and Operations Engineering, Natural Resources and Environment, Nursing Administration), M.B.A.-M.S.W. (Social Work), Ph.D.

ADMISSION REQUIREMENTS. All applicants must have a bachelor's degree from a recognized institution of higher education. Students are required to have their own personal computer. Application can be downloaded from Web site, Adobe Acrobat Reader required. Accepts MBA Multi-App application in lieu of institutional application. Early applications are encouraged for both admission and financial aid consideration. Beginning full-time students are admitted Fall only, part-time admitted both Fall and Spring. For full-time Decision I applicants apply by November 1; Decision II deadline January 1; Decision III deadline March 1; international applicants are encouraged to apply for either Decision I or II. Part-time applicants apply by May 1 (Fall), October 1 (Spring). Submit an MBA/Graduate School application, a GMAT results (will accept GMAT test results from the last five years, latest acceptable date is January (full-time), March (part-time), official transcripts from each undergraduate/graduate school attended, two letters of recommendation, four essays, résumé (prefers at least four years of work experience), and an application fee of $125 to the Office of Admission. In addition, international students (whose native language is other than English) should submit a TOEFL report (minimum score 600), TSE, TWE (recommended), certified translations and evaluations of all official transcripts, recommendation should be in English or with certified translations and proof of sufficient financial resources for two years of academic study. Interviews are strongly recommended prior to the admissions committee reviewing completed application. Joint degree applicants must apply to and be accepted to both schools/programs, contact the Admissions Office for current information and specific admissions requirements. Notification for Decision I applicants is made on February 1; Decision II applicants are notified March 15; Decision III applicants are notified May 1. Part-time Fall applicants are notified on July 1 and Spring applicants are notified December 1. Admissions Office phone: (734) 763-7233; e-mail: umbusmba@umich.edu, ummbaeve@umich.edu (part-time applicants).

ADMISSION REQUIREMENTS FOR DOCTORAL CANDIDATES. Contact Ph.D. Office at (734)764-2343 for application material and information. Beginning students are admitted Fall Only. Both U.S. citizens and international applicants apply by January 15. U.S. citizens and permanent residents mail the following items to Rackham Graduate School: application form—Rackham copy, application fee of $55. Mail the following items to the Business School Doctoral Studies Office: application form—Department copy, official GRE or GMAT test scores from ETS, official transcripts from each college or university in sealed envelopes, three letters of recommendation, and statement of purpose. International applicants mail the following items to Rackham Graduate School: application form—Rackham copy, application fee of $60, $75 for international applicants, one set of official transcripts from each college or university in sealed envelopes. Mail the following items to the Business School Doctoral Studies Office: application form—department copy, Official TOEFL and GRE or GMAT test scores from ETS, one set of official transcripts from each college or university in sealed envelopes, three letters of recommendation, and statement of purpose. Interviews strongly encouraged. Notification is made by mid-March. E-mail: umbusphd@umich.edu.

ADMISSION STANDARDS. Very selective. Mean GMAT: 645; mean GPA: 3.3 (A = 4). *U.S. News & World Report* ranked the Business School in the top 11 of all U.S. business schools and rated the part-time MBA program in the top 7. *BusinessWeek* listed Business School in the top 5 of all American business schools.

FINANCIAL AID. Business School scholarships, fellowships, Dean's Fellowships, graduate assistantships, Federal Perkins Loans, Stafford Subsidized and Unsubsidized Loans, Federal W/S available; Loan Repayment Assistance Program for students entering the nonprofit or public sectors. Aid is available for part-time study. Aid for international students is limited to scholarships only. Assistantships/fellowships may be available for joint degree candidates. Financial Aid applications and information are generally available at the on-campus interview or included with admissions application; apply by March 1 (Fall), by September 30 (Spring). Request scholarship, fellowship, assistantship, and need-based information from the Business School. Phone: (734) 764-5139. For most financial assistance and all Federal programs submit FAFSA (School code: 002325), also submit Financial Aid Transcript, Federal Income Tax forms. Approximately 50% of students receive some form of financial assistance.

DEGREE REQUIREMENTS. For M.B.A.: 60-credit program including 29 elective credits (of which 10 credits may be taken at any graduate school at University of Michigan), two-year program; degree program must be completed in six years. For M.B.A.-M.Arch.: 90-credit program. For M.B.A.-M.A., M.M., M.S.: 65–81 credits, two-and-one-half- to four-year programs. For M.B.A.-M.H.S.A.: 90-credit program. For M.B.A.-M.P.P.: 90-credit program. For M.B.A.-M.S.W.: 84-credit program. For M.B.A.-J.D.: four-and-one-half- to five-year program. For Ph.D.: at least three years in full-time residency; preliminary written exam; dissertation proposal and oral defense; dissertation; oral defense; offered through the Rackham Graduate School.

FIELDS OF STUDY.
Accounting. M.Acc.
Business Administrations. M.B.A.
Global. M.B.A.
Supply Chain Management. M.S.C.M.

PH.D. CONCENTRATIONS:
Accounting.
Business Information Technology.
Finance.
International Business and Business Economics.
Management and Organizations.
Marketing.
Operations and Management Science.
Strategy.

School of Dentistry (48109-1078)
Web site: www.dent.umich.edu

Organized 1875. Semester system. Special facility: Sindecuse Museum of Dentistry. Special program: offers an Internationally Trained Dentist Program for graduates of foreign dental schools.

Annual tuition: resident $22,750, nonresident $40,855. Both on- and off-campus housing available. For housing information contact the Housing Office. Phone: (734)763-3164. Average academic year housing cost: $11,550–$15,000. Total average cost for all other first-year expenses: $8,500.

Enrollment: first-year class 110, total 450 (men 45%, women 55%, minorities 42%, state residents 55%). Faculty: full-time 115, part-time and volunteers 145. Degrees conferred: D.D.S., M.S., D.D.S.-M.P.H., D.D.S.-Ph.D. Certificate. The M.S., M.P.H., and Ph.D. are offered through the School of Graduate Studies.

ADMISSION REQUIREMENTS. AADSAS, transcripts, three letters of recommendation, DAT (not later than October) required in support of School's application. Interview often required. Applicants must have completed at least two but preferably three years of college study. Preference given to state residents. Accepts transfer applicants from U.S. and Canadian dental schools. Apply to AADSAS after June 1, before December 1. Application fee $50. Phone: (734)763-3316; fax: (734)647-6805.

ADMISSION STANDARDS. Competitive. Accepts about 5–10% of all applicants. Usual minimum UGPA: 3.0 (A = 4). Mean DAT: academic 19.5, PAT 18.2, mean UGPA 3.46.

FINANCIAL AID. Scholarships, minority scholarships, research stipends, grants, institutional loans, State Loan Programs, DEAL, HEAL, alternative loan programs; Federal Perkins Loans, Stafford Subsidized and Unsubsidized Loans, Military Service Commitment Scholarship programs are available. Assistantships/fellowships may be available for Combined Degree candidates. Institutional Financial Aid applications and information are generally available at the on-campus by-invitation interview and applications are sent to all accepted applicants. Contact the Office of Student Affairs and Financial Aid for current information. Phone: (734)763-3313. All awards are made through the University's Office of Financial Aid. For most financial assistance and all need-based programs use FAFSA (School code: 002325), also submit Financial Aid Transcript, Federal Income Tax forms, and use of Federal Funds Certification. Approximately 75% of students receive some form of financial assistance.

DEGREE REQUIREMENTS. For D.D.S.: satisfactory completion of four-year program. For D.D.S.-M.P.H.: generally a five-year program. For D.D.S.-M.S.: generally a four-and-one-half- to five-and-one-half-year program, thesis/nonthesis option; research project. For D.D.S.-Ph.D.: generally a six- to seven-year program; candidacy; dissertation; oral defense; final exam.

FIELDS OF STUDY FOR POSTDOCTORAL
SCHOLAR PROGRAM.
Biomaterials.
Dental Hygiene.
Dental Public Health.
Endodontics.
Oral and Maxillofacial Surgery.
Orthodontics.
Pediatric Dentistry.
Periodontics.
Prosthodontics.
Restorative Dentistry. Includes programs in Occlusion and Operative Dentistry.

RESIDENCY PROGRAMS:
Advance Education in General Dentistry Residency.
General Practice Residency.
Geriatric Dentistry.

School of Law (48109-1215)
Web site: www.law.umich.edu

Opened 1869 and is one of the oldest in the U.S. ABA approved since 1923. AALS member. Semester system. Full-time day only. Special facilities: Center for International and Comparative Law, Olin Center for Law and Economics, Institute for Continuing Legal Education. Special programs: Summer "Start Program"; formal arrangements with University of Leiden (the Netherlands), University of Paris II, University College London, Katholieke University (Belgium), Bucerius Law School (Germany), Tel Aviv Law School and European Institute (Florence); traineeships at International Court of Justice; clerkships at European Court of Justice; externships. Law library: 965,069 volumes, 9514 subscriptions; has LEXIS, NEXIS, WESTLAW, LEXCALIBUR; has more that 400 network connections; is a Federal Government Depository.

Annual tuition: resident $35,502, nonresident $38,502. On-campus housing available for both single and married students. Contact Housing Office at (734)763-1316 or Lawyers Club at (734)764-1116 for both on- and off-campus housing information. Law students tend to live off-campus. For family housing contact Officer of University Housing. Phone: (734)763-3164. Off-campus housing and personal expenses: approximately $14,480.

Enrollment: first-year class 367; total full-time 1130 (men 55%, women 45%, minorities 28%). Faculty: full-time 70, part-time 27. Student to faculty ratio 16.9 to 1. Degrees conferred: J.D., J.D.-M.B.A., J.D.-M.H.S.A., J.D.-M.A. (Modern Middle Eastern and North African Studies, Russian and East European Studies, Law and Philosophy, History), J.D.-M.S. (Natural Resources), J.D.-M.P.H., J.D.-M.P.P. (Public Policy), J.D.-M.U.R., J.D.-Ph.D. (Economics), LL.M. (General, International Tax), M.C.L. (only for persons who have completed a basic legal education and received a university degree in law in another country), LL.M.-S.J.D.

ADMISSION REQUIREMENTS. LSDAS Law School report, bachelor's degree, transcripts, LSAT, personal statement, letters of recommendation required in support of application. TOEFL required of international students. Interview not required. Accepts transfer applicants. Graduates of unaccredited colleges not considered. Apply to Director of Admissions after September 1, before February 15. For Early Decision Plan apply by November 1. Application fee $60. Phone: (734)764-0537.

ADMISSION REQUIREMENTS. For LL.M., M.C.L., LL.M.-S.J.D. Applicants must have an accredited B.S., B.S. degree or its equivalent and LL.B. or J.D. from accredited Law School; achieved High Honors (Order of the Coif or equivalent academic distinction); letters of recommendation from Law School faculty, official transcripts should include an explanation of grading and rank-in-class, résumé, personal statement, a statement of purpose including academic interest and ability to benefit from graduate study are required in support of International and Graduate Application. In addition, international applicants from non-English-speaking countries are required to take TOEFL (usual minimum 600) or MELAB before December 1 (one calendar year before year for which admission is sought). Admits Fall only. Apply by January 1 to Office of International and Graduate Programs. Phone: (734)764-0537; fax: (734)936-1973; e-mail: law.grad.Admissions@umich.edu. Notification of decision is generally made in March. The LL.M., M.C.L. class is 35–45, the LL.M.-S.J.D. class is no more than 10.

ADMISSION STANDARDS. Selective. Accepts approximately 19% of all students. Number of applicants 5771; number of acceptance 1125; number enrolled 366; LSAT (75% of students have a score at or above 166); GPA (75% of student have a GPA at or above 3.45). *U.S. News & World Report* ranking is in the top eight of all U.S. law schools.

FINANCIAL AID. Scholarships, grants, fellowships (overseas travel fellowships for legal studies abroad), assistantships, Federal

W/S, loans. Apply for financial aid by February 1. Phone: (734) 764-5289. Use FAFSA (School code: E00506). Apply to Director of Advanced Studies for fellowships for advanced degrees. About 61% of students receive aid from School. Most state residents with need are aided. Has a Debt Management Program.

DEGREE REQUIREMENTS. For J.D.: 83 (31 required) credits with a GPA of at least a 2.0 (A = 4), plus completion of upper divisional writing course; four-year program. For J.D.-master's: individually designed programs, generally completed in three and a half to four years rather than four and a half to five years if each degree were taken consecutively. For LL.M.: 24 credits at least two semester in full-time residence; a 3.0 (A = 4) GPA required. For M.C.L. (International): 20 credits; at least two semesters in full-time residence; one course in U.S. Constitutional Law; research paper; GPA of 2.3 (A = 4) required. For LL.M.-S.J.D.: completion of a LL.M. of 24 credits taken in two semesters; research paper, thesis project; a GPA of 3.0 (A = 4); admission to candidacy; thesis; oral exam; completion of program within five years.

Medical School (48109-0611)

Web site: www.med.umich.edu/medschool

Established 1850. Located at Medical Center. Special facilities: Comprehensive Cancer Center, Geriatrics Center, Historical Center for the Health Sciences, Howard Hughes Medical Institute at University of Michigan, Kresge Hearing Research Institute, Mental Health Research Institute, Michigan Human Genome Center, Michigan Transplant Center, Multipurpose Arthritis and Musculoskeletal Disease Center, Center for Organogensis. Special programs: summer programs for underrepresented minorities. For information contact Director. Phone: (734)763-1296. Library: 200,000 volumes, 2900 subscriptions. NIH ranking is 7th among all U.S. institutions with 975 awards/grants worth $386,027,410.

Annual tuition: resident $24,755, nonresident $39,117. Limited on-campus housing available. Contact Office of University for both on- and off-campus housing information. Phone: (734)763-3164. Medical students tend to live off-campus. Off-campus housing and personal expenses: approximately $19,530.

Enrollment: first-year class 177 (M.D.-Ph.D. approximately 8 each year), total 682 (men 53%, women 47%, minorities 44%, state residents 45%), Faculty: full-time 1905, over 500 part-time and volunteer. Degrees conferred: B.A., B.S.-M.D. (Interflex Program), M.D., M.D.-M.B.A., M.D.-M.P.H., M.D.-M.S., M.D.-Ph.D. (MSTP). The M.S. and Ph.D. are offered through the School of Graduate Studies.

ADMISSION REQUIREMENTS. AMCAS report, transcripts, references, MCAT, interview required in support of application. Secondary application required. Interview by invitation only. Applicants must have completed at least 90 semester hours of university work. Does not have EDP. Apply after June 1, before November 15. Application fee $70, after initial screening procedure. Phone: (734)764-6317; fax: (734)763-0453.

ADMISSION STANDARDS. Very competitive. Accepts about 7.8% of all applicants. Number of applications 4938 (4048 out-of-state); number interviewed 807 (567 out-of-state); number of acceptance 387 (297 out-of-state); number enrolled 177 (98 out-of-state). Mean Composite MCAT 11.4; mean UGPA 3.73. *U.S. News & World Report* ranking is in the top 10 of all U.S. medical research schools, 45th in primary care.

FINANCIAL AID. Scholarships, minority scholarships, Grants-in-Aid, institutional loans, HEAL, alternative loan programs, NIH stipends; Federal Perkins Loans, Stafford Subsidized and Unsubsidized Loans, Service Commitment Scholarship programs are available. Students selected for M.S.T.P. receive full tuition, health insurance, and $15,000 stipend. Assistantships/fellowships may be available for Joint Degree candidates. Financial Aid applications and information are given out at the on-campus by-invitation interview. Contact the Financial Aid office for current information. Phone: (734)763-4147; e-mail: medfi-

naid@ umich.edu. For most financial assistance and all Federal programs use FAFSA (School code: E00398), also submit Financial Aid Transcript, Federal Income Tax forms. Approximately 85% of students receive some form of financial assistance.

DEGREE REQUIREMENTS. For B.A./B.S.-M.D.: an eight-year program. For M.D.: satisfactory completion of four-year program. All students must pass USMLE Step 1 prior to entering third year; all students must pass USMLE Step 2 prior to awarding of M.D. For M.D.-M.B.A., M.D.-M.P.H.: generally a five-year program. For M.D.-M.S.: generally a four-and-one-half- to five-and-one-half-year program. For M.D.-Ph.D.: generally a seven- to eight-year program.

FIELDS OF GRADUATE STUDY.
Bioinformatics.
Biological Chemistry.
Biomedical Engineering.
Biophysics.
Cell and Developmental Biology.
Chemical Biology.
Human Genetics.
Medicinal Chemistry.
Microbiology and Immunology.
Molecular, Cellular and Pathology.
Molecular and Integrative Physiology.
Pharmacology.
Public Health.

School of Music

Web site: www.music.umich.edu

Organized 1880.

Annual tuition: resident $15,892, nonresident $31,802; per credit, resident $894, nonresident $1675.

Enrollment: full-time 280, part-time 25. Faculty: full-time 84, part-time 34. Degrees conferred: M.M., M.M.-M.B.A., Specialist in Music. The A.M., A.Mus.D., D.M.A., Ph.D. are offered through the School of Graduate Studies

ADMISSION REQUIREMENTS. Varies by department, but generally one official transcript, audition, or tape (for M.M., D.M.A.), GRE (for some majors) required in support of School's application. MELAB required for international applicants. Accepts transfer applicants. Apply to Associate Dean by December 15 (Fall). Some programs have earlier deadlines. Application fee $75. Phone: (734)764-0593; fax: (734)763-5097; e-mail: music.admissions@umich.edu.

ADMISSION STANDARDS. Selective for most programs, very selective for others. Usual minimum average: 3.0 (A = 4).

FINANCIAL AID. Annual awards from institutional funds: scholarships, teaching assistantships, internships, Federal W/S, loans. Approved for VA benefits. Apply February 1 to Associate Dean for scholarships, assistantships; to Financial Aid Office for all other programs. Phone: (734)763-6600; fax: (734)747-3081. Use FAFSA (School code: 002325). About 40% of students receive aid other than loans from School and outside sources. No aid available for part-time students.

DEGREE REQUIREMENTS. For M.M.: 30–36 semester hours minimum; placement exam in theory; thesis, composition, final exam, or public recital, depending upon major. For Specialist in Music: 30-credit programs; 16-hour concentration. For other degree requirements, consult the Associate Dean, or see the School of Graduate Studies listing above.

FIELDS OF STUDY.
Arts Administration. Joint M.M.-M.B.A. program.
Chamber Music. Includes bassoon, cello, clarinet, double bass,

euphonium, flute, horn, oboe, saxophone, trombone, trumpet, tuba, viola, violin. M.M.
Church Music. M.M., Spec.M.
Collaborative Piano. M.M., Spec.M.
Composition. M.M.
Conducting. Includes band/wind ensemble, choral, orchestral. M.M.
Early Keyboard Instruments. M.M.
Ethnomusicology. Spec.M.
Improvisation. M.M.
Keyboard Instruments. M.M.
Music Education. M.M., Spec.M.
Performance. All instruments and voice. M.M., Spec.M.
Piano Pedagogy and Performance. M.M.
Wind Instruments. M.M.

RACKHAM PROGRAMS (Administered jointly by School and Graduate Studies):
Collaborative Piano. A.Mus.D.
Composition. MA., A.Mus.D.
Composition and Music Theory. Ph.D.
Conducting. Includes band/wind ensemble, choral, orchestral. A.Mus.D.
Dance. M.F.A.
Liturgical Church and Synagogue Music. A.Mus.D.
Music Education. A.Mus.D.
Musicology: Historical Musicology or Ethnomusicology. M.A., Ph.D.
Performance. A.Mus.D.
Performance Arts Technology. M.A.
Piano Pedagogy and Performance. A.Mus.D.
Theatre. Ph.D.

School of Public Health
Web site: www.sph.umich.edu

Established 1941.
Annual tuition: resident $19,124, nonresident $32,712.
Enrollment: full- and part-time 838. Faculty; full-time 109. Degrees conferred: M.P.H., M.H.S.A., Dr.P.H., M.H.S.A.-M.B.A., M.H.S.A.-M.N.A., M.H.S.A.-M.P.P., M.P.H.-M.P.P., M.H.S.A.-M.S.I.O.E., M.H.S.A.-J.D., M.P.H.-J.D., M.P.H.-M.D., M.P.H.-D.O. The M.S. and Ph.D. are offered through the School of Graduate Studies.

ADMISSION REQUIREMENTS. Transcript, three letters of recommendation, GRE required in support of School's application. Interview required for M.P.H. only. TOEFL required for international applicants. Joint degree applicants must apply to and be accepted by both degree programs/departments/schools. Apply to Office of Student Affairs. School-wide application deadline is February 1. Application fee $60, $75 for international applicants. Phone: (734)764-5425; fax: (734)763-5425.

ADMISSION STANDARDS. Very selective for most programs, selective for others. Usual minimum average: 3.0 (A = 4).

FINANCIAL AID. Fellowships, teaching assistantships, internships, grants, Federal W/S, loans. Approved for VA benefits. Apply by March 1 to the Office of Student Affairs and to the University of Michigan Office of Financial Aid. Phone: (734)763-0931. Use FAFSA.

DEGREE REQUIREMENTS. For M.P.H.: 60 credit hours; field experience. For M.H.S.A.: 60 credit hours; field experience. For Dr.P.H.: two years minimum beyond master's; preliminary exam; dissertation; final oral exam. Joint degree programs generally reduce the time needed to complete both degrees by half a year or more if the degrees had been taken separately. For M.S., Ph.D. see Horace H. Rackham School of Graduate Studies listing above.

FIELDS OF STUDY.
Biostatistics.
Dental Public Health.
Environmental Health Sciences.
General Epidemiology.
Health Behavior and Health Education.
Health Management and Policy.
Health Services Organization and Policy.
Hospital and Molecular Epidemiology.
Human Nutrition.
Industrial Hygiene.
International Health.
Occupational and Environmental Epidemiology.
Occupational and Environmental Medicine.
Public Health.
Toxicology.

School of Social Work (48109-1285)
Web site: www.ssw.umich.edu

Established 1921. Semester system. Annual tuition: resident $18,430, nonresident $30,288.
Enrollment: full-time 570, part-time 23. School faculty: full-time 50, part-time 35. Degrees conferred: M.S.W., M.S.W.-Ph.D. (Anthropology, Economics, Political Science, Psychology, Sociology). The Ph.D. is offered through the Horace H. Rackham School of Graduate Studies.

ADMISSION REQUIREMENTS. Transcripts, letters of reference, supplementary statement dealing with applicant's career objectives and personal qualifications, interviews required in support of School's application. TOEFL or MELAB TSE (recommended) required for international applicants. Apply to M.S.W. program director by March 1 (Fall), Ph.D. application January 2 (Fall). Application fee $60, $75 for international applicants. Phone: (734)764-3309.

ADMISSION STANDARDS. Selective. Usual minimum average: 3.0 (A = 4).

FINANCIAL AID. Grants, scholarships, fellowships, traineeships, Federal W/S, loans. Apply at the same time as admission to University's Office of Financial Aid. Phone: (734)763-6600. Use FAFSA (School code: 002325).

DEGREE REQUIREMENTS. For M.S.W.: 60 credit hours; full-time program; research papers. For Ph.D.: see Horace H. Rackham School of Graduate Studies listing above.

SPECIALIZATIONS AND CERTIFICATIONS.
Jewish Communal Service and Judaic Studies. Certificate.
Social Work in Public School.
Social Work in the Workplace.
Specialization in Aging. Certificate.

MIDDLEBURY COLLEGE
Middlebury, Vermont 05753-6002
Web site: www.middlebury.edu

Founded 1800. Located 35 miles S of Burlington. Coed. Private control. 4-1-4 system. Special facilities: Music Library, Performing Arts Center, Museum of Art. Library: 853,000 volumes, 2900 subscriptions. Total College enrollment: 2450.
Tuition: summer study (includes room and board) on campus $4855–$8406, academic year abroad at Language Schools (Florence, Italy; Madrid, Spain; Mainz, Germany; Paris, France) $16,600–$24,960.

Graduate Study

Graduate study since 1915. Enrollment: full- and part-time 959. Faculty: full-time 109. Degrees conferred: M.A., D.M.L. The M.A. and D.M.L. may be earned either during a series of summers in Vermont, or by combining summer study in Vermont with an academic year at one of College's five schools abroad.

ADMISSION REQUIREMENTS. For M.A.: transcripts, proficiency in the language equivalent to an undergraduate major required in support of College's application. For D.M.L.: transcripts, equivalent of an M.A. in the primary language. Apply to Language School Office of the primary language of interest. Rolling admissions process. Application fee $50. Phone: (802)443-5158.

FINANCIAL AID. Awards from institutional funds: scholarships, grants, Federal W/S, loans. Approved for VA benefits. Apply to Office of Financial Aid as soon as possible after January 1. Use FAFSA. Phone: (802)443-5158.

DEGREE REQUIREMENTS. For M.A. in foreign languages: 12 course units. Transfer credits limited to 3 approved course units. For M.S.: 9 courses, at least 6 in residence; laboratory teaching. For D.M.L.: 12 units beyond the M.A.; teaching experience; residence in country of primary language; proficiency in one other language in addition to primary language; dissertation; final written/oral exams.

FIELDS OF STUDY.

ACADEMIC YEAR LANGUAGE PROGRAMS:
Chinese.
French.
German.
Italian.
Russian.
Spanish.

LANGUAGE SCHOOLS SUMMER PROGRAMS:
Arabic.
Chinese.
French.
German.
Hebrew.
Italian.
Japanese.
Portuguese.
Russian.
Spanish.

MIDDLE TENNESSEE STATE UNIVERSITY

Murfreesboro, Tennessee 37132
Web site: www.mtsu.edu

Founded 1911. Located 30 miles SE of Nashville. CGS member. Coed. State control. Semester system. Library: 1,000,000 volumes, 3600 subscriptions.

Annual tuition: full-time, resident $6666, nonresident $16,942; per hour, resident $340, nonresident $786. Annual academic year housing cost for single students: $2900–$6520 (excluding board). Contact Housing Office for both on- and off-campus housing information. Phone: (615)898-2971. Day-care facilities available.

College of Graduate Studies

Enrollment: full-time 227, part-time 1477. Faculty teaching graduate students: full-time 350, part-time 38. Degrees conferred:

M.A., M.A.T., M.B.A., M.B.E., M.C.J., M.Ed., M.S., M.S.T., M.V.T.E., Ed.S., D.A.

ADMISSION REQUIREMENTS. Transcripts, three letters of reference, MAT/GRE/GMAT in support of School's application. Online application available. TOEFL required for international applicants. Accepts transfer applicants. Graduates of unaccredited institutions not considered. Apply to Dean of Graduate School, by June 1 (Fall), October 1 (Spring). Application fee $25. Phone: (615)898-2840; fax: (615)904-8020.

ADMISSION STANDARDS. Selective. Usual minimum average: 3.0 (A = 4).

FINANCIAL AID. Fellowships, research assistantships, administrative assistantships, teaching assistantships, internships, tuition waivers, Federal W/S, loans. Approved for VA benefits. Contact the Office of Financial Aid; no specified closing date. Phone: (615)898-2830. Use FAFSA and University's FAF. Aid available for part-time students.

DEGREE REQUIREMENTS. For M.A., M.S.: 30 semester hours minimum; admission to candidacy; reading knowledge of one foreign language or approved research tool; thesis (three semester hours minimum). For M.A.T., M.S.T., M.V.T.E.: 30 semester hours minimum; teaching certification; admission to candidacy; comprehensive exam. For M.Ed.: 33 semester hours; admission to candidacy; comprehensive exam. For M.B.A.: 36 semester hours; admission to candidacy; comprehensive exam. For M.B.E.: 32 semester hours; admission to candidacy; comprehensive exam. For M.C.J.: 36 semester hours; admission to candidacy; comprehensive exam. For Ed.S.: 30 semester hours; admission to candidacy; comprehensive exam. For D.A.: 48 semester hours beyond master's; qualifying exam; admission to candidacy; 3 hours externship, 3 hours internship; dissertation (6 semester hours minimum); defense of dissertation.

FIELDS OF STUDY.
Accounting/Information Systems. M.S.
Administration and Supervision. Includes K–12 public school, higher education. M.Ed., Ed.S.
Aerospace Education. M.Ed.
Aviation Administration. Includes airline/airport management, aviation assist management. M.S.
Biology. M.S., M.S.T.
Business Administration. M.B.A.
Business Education. Includes marketing education, office management. M.B.E.
Chemistry. M.S., D.A.
Computer Science. M.S.
Criminal Justice Administration. M.C.J.
Curriculum and Instruction. Includes ESL, early childhood, elementary. M.Ed., Ed.S.
Economics. Includes industrial relations, financial economics. M.A., D.A.
Engineering Technology and Industrial Studies. M.S.
English. M.A., D.A.
Exercise Science and Health Promotion. M.S.
Foreign Language. Includes French, German, Spanish. M.A.T.
Health, Physical Education, Recreation, and Safety. Includes health, physical education (M.S., Ph.D.), recreation, sport management. M.S., Ph.D.
History. Includes public history, historic preservation. M.A., D.A.
Human Performance. Ph.D.
Human Sciences. Includes nutrition and food science, child development and family studies. M.S.
Industrial Studies. Includes engineering technology, occupational health and safety. M.S.
Literacy Studies. Ph.D.
Mass Communications. M.S.

Mathematics. Includes general mathematics, industrial mathematics, research preparation (M.S.); middle grades mathematics, secondary mathematics (M.S.T.). M.S., M.S.T.
Music. M.A.
Professional Counseling. M.Ed.
Professional Science. Includes biostatistics, biotechnology. M.S.
Psychology. Includes clinical, experimental, industrial/organizational, quantitative, school psychology. M.A.
Reading. M.Ed.
Recording Arts and Technology. M.F.A.
Sociology. M.A.
Special Education. Includes mildly/moderately disabled, preschool disabled, severe/profoundly disabled, vision disabilities. M.Ed.

MIDWESTERN STATE UNIVERSITY
Wichita Falls, Texas 76308-2096
Web site: www.mwsu.edu

Founded 1922. Coed. State control. Semester system. Library: 366,350 volumes, 1100 subscriptions.

Annual tuition: full-time, resident $5374, nonresident $6274; per credit, resident $179, nonresident $210. On-campus housing for single students. Average academic year housing cost: $5230 (including board). Apply to Director of Housing. Phone: (940) 397-4217.

Graduate School

Graduate study since 1952. Enrollment: full-time 132, part-time 526 (men 45%, women 55%). Graduate faculty: full-time 58, part-time 12. Degrees conferred: M.A., M.S., M.Ed., M.S.K., M.B.A.

ADMISSION REQUIREMENTS. One official transcript from each institution attended, GRE or GMAT required in support of School's application. Online application available. TOEFL required for international applicants. Accepts transfer applicants. Graduates of unaccredited institution. Admission deadlines: August 7 (Fall), December 15 (Spring), May 15 (Summer I), June 15 (Summer II). International applications must be received 5 months prior to registration. Application fee $35, $50 for international applicants. Phone: (940)397-4334; fax: (940)397-4672; e-mail: admissions@mwsu.edu.

ADMISSION STANDARDS. Varies with program. Usual minimum average: 3.0 (A = 4). Must meet index GRE/GMAT + (200 times the GPA on last 60 hours of undergraduate work.)

FINANCIAL AID. Annual awards from institutional funds: scholarships, research assistantships, teaching assistantships, internships, Federal W/S, loans. Approved for VA benefits. Apply by March 1 to Division Director of major field. Phone: (940)397-4214. Use FAFSA. Aid sometimes available for part-time students.

DEGREE REQUIREMENTS. For M.A.: 30 semester hours minimum, at least 24 in residence; reading knowledge of one foreign language; thesis; final comprehensive exam. For M.Ed., M.B.A., M.S., M.S.K.: 36 hours minimum, at least 30 in residence; final comprehensive exam; substantial research paper.

FIELDS OF STUDY.
Biology.
Business Administration.
Computer Science.
Counseling.
Curriculum and Instruction.
Educational Leadership.
Educational Technology.
Elementary Education.
English.
Family Nurse Practitioner.
Health Services Administration.
History.
Human Rescource Development.
Kinesiology.
Liberal Arts.
Nurse Educator.
Nurse Practitioner.
Political Science.
Psychology.
Public Administration.
Radiologic Administration.
Radiologic Education.
Radiologic Sciences.
Reading.
School Counseling.
Special Education.
Training and Development.

MIDWESTERN UNIVERSITY
Downers Grove, Illinois 60515-1235
Web site: www.midwestern.edu

Founded 1900. Located 25 miles W of Chicago. Private control. Graduate study only. Quarter system. Library: 85,000 volumes, 1500 subscriptions. Total University enrollment 3200.

On-campus apartments and residence halls available. Contact Housing Director for both on- and off-campus housing information. Phone: (630)971-6400. Medical students tend to live off-campus. Off-campus housing and personal expenses: approximately $15,000.

The University's Graduate Colleges at Downers Grove campus include the Chicago College of Osteopathic Medicine, College of Pharmacy, College of Health Sciences; at Glendale campus, the Arizona College of Osteopathic Medicine, College of Pharmacy, College of Health Sciences.

Downers Grove Campus
Chicago College of Osteopathic Medicine
Web site: www.midwestern.edu/downersgrove

Established 1900 as the College of Osteopathic Medicine and Surgery, merged and created Littlejohn College and Hospital, name changed to Chicago College in 1970.

Annual tuition: resident $38,211, nonresident $42,517.

Enrollment: first-year class 174, total 700 (men 47%, women 53%, minorities 24%, state residents 46%). Faculty: full-time 141, part-time 244. Degrees conferred: D.O., D.O.-Ph.D.

ADMISSION REQUIREMENTS. Preference given to state residents, U.S. citizens and permanent residents only. Bachelor's degree from an accredited institution required. Apply through AACOMAS (file after June 1, before December 1), submit MCAT (will accept test results from last three years), official transcripts for each school attended (should show at least 90 semester credits/135 quarter credits), service processing fee. After a review of the AACOMAS application and supporting documents a decision is made concerning which candidates should receive supplemental materials. Supplemental applications are sent to all students with a 2.75 (A = 4) science GPA. The supplemental application, an application fee of $50, a personal statement, and three recommendations (one from a D.O.) should be returned to Office of Admission by January 1. Interviews are by invitation only and generally for final selection. Accepts transfer applicants. First-year students admitted Fall only. Rolling admissions process, notification starts in October and is finished when class is filled. Phone: (630)515-6171; e-mail: admiss@midwestern.edu.

ADMISSION STANDARDS. Selective. Accepts about 23% of all applicants. Number of applications 1645 (1406 out-of-state); number interviewed 519 (365 out-of-state); number of acceptance 382 (267 out-of-state); number enrolled 174 (103 out-of-state). Usual minimum UGPA: 2.7 (A = 4). Mean Composite MCAT 8.7, mean UGPA 3.5.

FINANCIAL AID. Scholarships, institutional loans, NOF, HEAL, alternative loan programs, Federal Perkins Loans, Stafford Subsidized and Unsubsidized Loans, Service Obligation Scholarship programs, Military and National Health Service programs are available. Financial Aid applications and information are available at the on-campus, by-invitation interview. Contact the Financial Aid Office for current information. Phone: (630)515-6101. Use FAFSA (School code: 001657), also submit Financial Aid Transcript, Federal Income Tax forms. Approximately 87% of students receive some form of financial assistance.

DEGREE REQUIREMENTS. For D.O.: satisfactory completion of 4-year (45-month) program. All students must pass the National Board of Osteopathic Medical Examination Level I to advance to the third year. All students must take the National Board of Osteopathic Medical Examination Level II prior to the awarding of D.O.

College of Health Sciences

Founded 1992. Quarter system. Annual tuition: resident $21,176–$26,997 (depending on program), nonresident $21,176–$28,941 (depending on program). Enrollment: total full- and part-time 258. Faculty: full-time 22, part-time 61. Degrees conferred: M.B.S., M.M.S., M.O.T., M.P.T., Psy.D.

ADMISSION REQUIREMENTS. Official transcripts, GRE or MCAT or PCAT, two letters of recommendation required in support of application. Online application available. Apply to the Office of Admissions by May 15. Application fee $50. First-year students admitted Fall only. Rolling admissions process. Phone: (800)458-6253; fax: (630)971-6086; e-mail: admissil@midwestern.edu.

ADMISSION STANDARDS. Selective. Usual minimum average: 2.75 (A = 4).

FINANCIAL AID. Scholarships, grants, assistantships, Federal W/S, loans. Contact the Office of Financial Services for current information. Apply by April 1. Phone: (630)515-6101. Use FAFSA (School code: 001657). Approximately 90% of students receive some type of financial assistance.

DEGREE REQUIREMENTS. For M.B.S.: 72 quarter hour, full-time program; research project; thesis. For M.M.S.: 27-month full-time program. For M.O.T.: 27-month, full-time program; field placement. For M.P.T.: 30-month, full-time program. For Psy.D.: four-year program; internship; clinical dissertation.

FIELDS OF STUDY.
Biological Sciences. M.B.S.
Clinical Psychology. Psy.D.
Occupational Therapy. M.O.T.
Physical Therapy. M.P.T.
Physician Assistant Studies. M.M.S.

Glendale Campus
Arizona College of Osteopathic Medicine
19555 North 59th Avenue
Glendale, Arizona 85308
Web site: www.midwestern.edu/azcom

Established 1995. Located 15 miles NW of Phoenix, one of the newest schools of osteopathic medicine. Also on-campus are the College of Pharmacy, the College of Health Sciences. Quarter system.

Annual tuition: $14,242. On-campus apartments available for both single and married students. Contact Manger of Residence Life for both on- and off-campus housing information. Phone: (602)572-3848. Housing and personal expenses: approximately $14,000.

Enrollment: first-year class 152, total 580 (men 65%, women 35%, minorities 16%, state residents 33%). Faculty: full- and part-time 195. Degrees conferred: D.O.

ADMISSION REQUIREMENTS. Bachelor's degree from an accredited institution required. 100% of applicants have bachelor's degree awarded prior to enrollment. Apply through AACO-MAS (file after June 1, before January 1), submit MCAT (will accept test results from last three years), official transcripts for each school attended (should show at least 90 semester credits/135 quarter credits), service processing fee. After a review of the AACOMAS application and supporting documents a decision is made concerning which candidates should receive supplemental materials. The supplemental application, an application fee of $50, a personal statement, and two recommendations (one from a D.O.) should be returned to Office of Admission by January 1. In addition, international applicants must submit foreign transcripts to the World Education Service for translation and evaluation. TOEFL may be required of those applicants whose native language is other than English. Interviews are by invitation only and generally for final selection. Accepts transfer applicants. First-year students admitted Fall only. Rolling admissions process, notification starts in October and is finished when class is filled. School does maintain an alternate list. Phone: (888)247-9277; (623)572-3215; e-mail: admissaz@arizona.midwestern.edu.

ADMISSION REQUIREMENTS FOR TRANSFER APPLICANTS. Accepts transfers from other accredited U.S. osteopathic medical schools. Admission limited to space available. Contact the Office of Admissions for current information and specific requirements.

ADMISSION STANDARDS. Selective. Accepts about 12% of all applicants. Number of applications n/a (n/a out-of-state); number interviewed n/a (n/a out-of-state); number of acceptance n/a (n/a out-of-state); number enrolled 140 (n/a out-of-state). Usual minimum UGPA: 2.75 (A = 4). Mean Composite MCAT 9.0, mean UGPA 3.45.

FINANCIAL AID. Scholarships, institutional loans, NOF, HEAL, alternative loan programs, Federal Perkins Loans, Stafford Subsidized and Unsubsidized Loans, Service Obligation Scholarship programs, Military and National Health Service programs are available. Financial Aid applications and information are available from either the Arizona campus or from Downers Grove. Contact the Financial Aid Office for current information. Phone Glendale: (623)572-3321, Downers Grove: (630)515-6101. Use FAFSA (School code: 001657), also submit Financial Aid Transcript, Federal Income Tax forms. Approximately 87% of students receive some form of financial assistance.

DEGREE REQUIREMENTS. For D.O.: satisfactory completion of four-year (45-month) program. All students must pass the National Board of Osteopathic Medical Examination Level I and all must take level II prior to the awarding of D.O.

MILLERSVILLE UNIVERSITY OF PENNSYLVANIA
Millersville, Pennsylvania 17551-0302
Web site: www.millersville.edu

Founded 1855. Located 3 miles SW of Lancaster. CGS member. Coed. Semester system. State control. Library: 503,100 volumes, 5000 subscriptions. Total University enrollment: 8000.

Tuition: per credit, resident $327, nonresident $523. On-campus housing for single graduate students. Housing cost: $5500 (including board). Apply to Office of Resident Life. Phone: (717)872-3162.

Graduate School

Graduate study since 1959. Enrollment: full-time 116, part-time 409. Faculty: full-time 205, part-time 67. Degrees conferred: M.Ed., M.S., M.A.

ADMISSION REQUIREMENTS. Transcripts, statement of academic and professional goals, three recommendations, GRE/GMAT or MAT required in support of application. TOEFL required for international applicants. Accepts transfer applicants. Graduates of unaccredited institutions not considered. Apply to Graduate Office by March 1 (Summer, Fall), October 1 (Spring). Rolling admissions process. Application fee: $35. Phone: (717) 872-3099; fax: (717)871-2022; e-mail: gradstu@millersville.edu.

ADMISSION STANDARDS. Selective for most departments, Usual minimum average: 2.75 (A = 4).

FINANCIAL AID. Annual awards from institutional funds: assistantships, internships, Federal W/S, loans. Approved for VA benefits. Apply by March 15 to Dean, Graduate School for assistantships; to Financial Aid Office for all other aid. Use FAFSA. Phone: (717)872-3026. About 20% of students receive aid other than loans from College and outside sources. Loans available for part-time students.

DEGREE REQUIREMENTS. For M.Ed.: 30 credit hours minimum, 36 credit hours without research papers; qualifying exam; research paper. For M.A., M.S.: 30 credit hours minimum; qualifying exam; thesis/nonthesis option by program.

FIELDS OF STUDY.
Art.
Biology.
Business Administration.
Early Childhood Education.
Educational Leadership.
Elementary Education.
Emergency Management.
English.
Foreign Language. Includes French, German, Spanish.
Gifted Education.
History.
Language and Literacy Education.
Mathematics.
Psychology.
Reading and Language Arts.
Reading Supervision. Post-master's program only.
School Psychology.
Special Education.
Sports Management.
Technology Education.

MILLS COLLEGE
Oakland, California 94613-1000
Web site: www.mills.edu

Founded 1852. Located 12 miles E of San Francisco. Coed on graduate level. Private control. Semester system. Library: 254,500 volumes, 4000 subscriptions. Total College enrollment: 1375.

Annual tuition: full-time $20,350; Art $25,350. On-campus housing for single graduate students. Average academic year cost: $10,290 (including board). Contact Director of Residence Life. Phone: (510)430-2130. Day-care facilities available.

Graduate Programs

Graduate study since 1920. Enrollment: full-time 400, part-time 55. College faculty teaching graduate students: full-time 67, part-time 72. Degrees conferred: M.A., M.A.L.A., M.F.A.

ADMISSION REQUIREMENTS. Two transcripts, GRE, three letters of recommendations required in support of application. Samples of creative work required for art, music, and writing majors. Interview required for some programs. TOEFL required for international applicants. Apply to Director of Graduate Study by February 1 (Fall), November 1 (Spring). Some programs have earlier deadlines. Application fee $50. Phone: (510)430-3309; fax: (510)430-2159; e-mail: grad-studies@ mills.edu.

ADMISSION STANDARDS. Very selective. Usual minimum average: 3.2 (A = 4).

FINANCIAL AID. Limited annual awards from institutional funds: academic scholarships, teaching assistantships, special scholarships, music lesson scholarships, internships, grants, Federal W/S, loans. Apply to Director of Graduate Study by February 1 for scholarships, assistantships; to Financial Aid Office for all other programs. Use FAFSA and FAF of CSS. Phone: (510) 430-2134. About 46% of students receive some form of financial aid, including loans. Aid available for part-time students.

DEGREE REQUIREMENTS. For M.F.A., M.A., M.A.L.A.: 10–12 semester course credits minimum, two years in residence; petition for candidacy; thesis or final project; final written/oral exam. Thesis is credited as a two-semester course.

FIELDS OF STUDY.
Art. Includes ceramics, intermedia, electronic, painting, sculpture, photography. M.F.A. only, admits Fall term only.
Business. M.B.A.
Computational Science. Interdisciplinary.
Creative Writing. Includes fiction, nonfiction, poetry. M.F.A. only.
Dance. Includes choreography, performance. M.A., M.F.A.
Education. Includes child development, early childhood, elementary, secondary, child life in hospitals. M.A., teaching credentials.
Educational Leadership.
English. Includes American literature. M.A.
Interdisciplinary Computer Science. M.A.
Liberal Studies. M.A. (part-time evening program).
Management. B.A.-M.B.A.
Music. Composition (M.A.), performance and literature (M.F.A.), electronic music and recording media (M.F.A.). M.A., M.F.A.

MILWAUKEE SCHOOL OF ENGINEERING
Milwaukee, Wisconsin 53201-3109
Web site: www.msoe.edu

Founded 1903. Coed. Private control. Quarter system. Graduate study available on part-time evening basis only. Special facilities: Applied Industrial Research Institute, Applied Technology Center, Biomedical Research Center, Center for Biomolecular Modeling, Fluid Power Institute, Photonics and Applied Optics Center, High Impact Materials and Structures Center. Library: 60,000 volumes, 750 subscriptions. Total enrollment: 2300.

Tuition: per credit $505. Limited on-campus housing as most students are part-time evening. Contact Housing Office for information. Phone: (414)277-7400.

Graduate School

Enrollment: part-time only, about 225. Faculty teaching graduate students: 30. Degrees conferred: M.S.E., M.S.E.E., M.S.E.M., M.S.Ev., M.S.M.I., M.S.S.T., M.S.P.

ADMISSION REQUIREMENTS. Transcripts, GRE/GMAT, two letters of recommendation, interview required in support of School's application. Online application available. TOEFL (minimum score 550) required for international applicants. Accepts transfer applicants. Apply to Graduate School by July 1. Application fee $30. Phone: (414)277-6763 or (800)332-6763; fax: (414)277-7475.

ADMISSION STANDARDS. Selective. Usual minimum average: 2.8 (A = 4).

FINANCIAL AID. Limited to three research assistantships, loans. Use FAFSA.

DEGREE REQUIREMENTS. For master's: 50–54 quarter hours minimum, at least 41–45 quarter hours in residence; thesis/oral presentation/special projects.

FIELDS OF STUDY.
Cardiovascular Studies.
Engineering.
Engineering Management.
Environmental Engineering.
Marketing and Export Management.
Medical Informatics.
New Product Management.
Nursing—Clinical Nurse Leadership.
Perfusion.
Structural Engineering.

MINNESOTA STATE UNIVERSITY, MANKATO

Mankato, Minnesota 56002-8400
Web site: www.mnsu.edu

Founded 1867. Located 80 miles SW of Minneapolis–St. Paul. CGS member. Coed. State control. Semester system. Special facilities: Biotechnology Research Center, Andreas and Standeford Astronomy Observatories, Performing Arts Center, Trafton Science Center, Water Resource Center, Urban Studies Institute, Conkling Art Gallery. Library: 1,100,000 volumes, 3400 subscriptions. Total University enrollment: 14,350.

Tuition: per credit hour, resident $243, nonresident $400 (out-of-state students from Wisconsin, North Dakota, South Dakota, Manitoba may be eligible for reciprocity or an out-of-state tuition scholarship). On-campus housing available for single students only. Average academic year housing cost: $4595 (including board). Contact the Office of Residential Life for both on- and off-campus housing information. Phone: (507)389-1011. Daycare facilities available.

College of Graduate Studies

Graduate degrees authorized in 1953. Enrollment: full-time 677, part-time 1002. Graduate faculty: full- and part-time 405. Degrees conferred: M.A., M.B.A., M.S., M.A.T., M.F.A., M.M., Specialist.

ADMISSION REQUIREMENTS. Two official transcripts required in support of application. GRE/Subject/MAT/ GMAT required for some majors. TOEFL (minimum score 500) and Financial Statement Form required for international applicants. Accepts transfer applicants. Graduates of unaccredited institutions not considered. Apply to Graduate Studies Office by August 15 (Fall), December 1 (Spring); for international applicants May 22 (Fall), October 9 (Spring). Applicants for Graduate assistantships apply by February 3 for the Fall. Application fee $40. Phone: (800)772-0544 or (507)389-2321; fax: (507)389-5974; e-mail: grad@mnsu.edu.

ADMISSION STANDARDS. Selective for most departments, relatively open for others. Usual minimum average: 2.75 (A = 4).

FINANCIAL AID. Annual awards from institutional funds: fellowships, assistantships, tuition waivers, internships, Federal W/S, loans. Approved for VA benefits. Apply by March 15 to the Dean for assistantships; to Financial Aid Office for all other programs. Use FAFSA. Phone: (507)389-1185. About 50% of full-time students receive aid other than loans from College and outside sources. Aid available for part-time students.

DEGREE REQUIREMENTS. For M.A.: 30 credit hours with thesis, or 34 credit hours plus research paper; final written/oral exams. For M.S.: same as for M.A., no language requirement. For M.B.A.: 30-credit program hours; research paper. For M.A.T.: similar to M.A., but includes teaching internships. For Specialist: 30-credit program beyond master's. For M.F.A.: 60 credit hour program; special project.

FIELDS OF STUDY.

COLLEGE OF ALLIED HEALTH AND NURSING:
Communication Disorders. M.S.
Health Science. M.S.
Human Performance. M.A., M.S.
Nursing. M.S.N.
Rehabilitation Counseling. M.S.

COLLEGE OF ARTS AND HUMANITIES:
Art. Includes studio (M.A.). M.A., M.S.
English. Includes literature (M.A.), TESL (M.A.), technical communication (M.A.), creative writing (M.F.A.). M.A., M.F.A.
French. M.A.
Music. M.M.
Spanish. M.S.
Speech Communication. M.A., M.S.
Theatre. M.A., M.F.A.

COLLEGE OF BUSINESS:
Business Administration. M.B.A.

COLLEGE OF EDUCATION:
Counseling and Student Personnel. M.S.
Curriculum and Instruction.
Educational Leadership.
Educational Technology. M.S.
Elementary Education. M.S.
Experiential Education. M.S.
Library Media Education. M.S.
Special Education. M.S.
Teaching. Includes secondary education in art, earth science, English, English/TESL, family consumer science, French, general science, life science, mathematics, music, physical education, school health, social studies, Spanish, speech, speech/theatre, theatre arts. M.A.T.
Teaching and Learning. Includes middle and secondary education, curriculum and instruction, environmental education. M.S.

COLLEGE OF SCIENCE, ENGINEERING, AND TECHNOLOGY:
Biology. M.S.
Computer Science. M.S.
Electrical Engineering. M.S.
Environmental Science. M.S.
Manufacturing Engineering Technology. M.S.
Mathematics. M.A.
Mechanical Engineering. M.A.
Physics. M.S.
Science Education. M.S.

COLLEGE OF SOCIAL AND BEHAVIORAL SCIENCES:
Anthropology. M.S.
Ethnic and Multicultural Studies. M.A.

Geography. M.S.
Gerontology. M.S.
History. M.A., M.S.
Political Science. M.A.
Psychology. Includes clinical, industrial/organizational. M.A.
Public Administration. M.A.P.A.
Social Work. M.S.W.
Sociology. Includes corrections (M.S.), human services planning and administration (M.S.). M.A., M.S.
Urban and Regional Studies. Includes urban planning. M.A.
Women's Studies. M.S.

MINNESOTA STATE UNIVERSITY, MOORHEAD

Moorhead, Minnesota 56563
Web site: www.mnstate.edu

Founded 1887. Located 260 miles NW of Minneapolis. Coed. State control. Semester system. Library: 367,000 volumes, 1539 subscriptions.

Tuition: per credit hour, resident $169, nonresident $169. No on-campus housing available. Contact Housing Office for off-campus housing information. Phone: (218)236-2118.

Graduate Studies

Graduate study since 1952. Enrollment: full-time 90 (men 39%, women 61%); part-time 284. Graduate faculty: full-time 55, part-time 28. Degrees conferred: M.A., M.S., M.B.A., M.F.A., M.L.A., Specialist.

ADMISSION REQUIREMENTS. Transcripts required in support of application. Online application available. GRE/GMAT/MAT may be required by some programs. Immunization record required for all applicants. TOEFL required for international applicants. Interview required for some programs. Accepts transfer applicants. Apply to Graduate Admissions Office by April 15 (Fall semester), November 1 (Spring semester). International students apply by February 1 (Fall), October 15 (Spring). Some programs have earlier deadlines. Application fee $20, $35 for international applicants. Phone: (218)236-2344; fax: (218)236-2168.

ADMISSION STANDARDS. Selective. Usual minimum average: 2.75 or 3.25 (A = 4) in last 30 semester hours of graded course work.

FINANCIAL AID. Annual awards from institutional funds: graduate assistantships, internships, Federal W/S, loans. Approved for VA benefits. Apply by July 15 to Dean of Academic Services for assistantships; to Financial Aid Office for all other programs. Use FAFSA and institutional FAF. About 20% of students receive aid from all sources. Aid available for part-time students.

DEGREE REQUIREMENTS. For master's Plan A: 30-credit minimum; written comprehensive exam; thesis; final oral exam. For master's Plan B: 32-credit minimum; written comprehensive exam; project paper; oral exam. For M.F.A.: 42-credit minimum; thesis; oral discourse. For M.L.A.: 32-credit minimum; thesis; oral exam. For M.S.N.: Plan A & B; written comprehensive exam; thesis or classroom-based research project; oral exam. For Specialist: 30 semester hours minimum beyond master's.

FIELDS OF STUDY.
Counseling and Student Affairs. Includes community counseling, student affairs, school counseling. Plan B: 48-credit, full-time program. M.S.

Creative Writing. M.F.A.
Curriculum and Instruction. Plan B: 32 credit program. M.S.
Educational Leadership. Plan A: 33–47 credit program.
Liberal Studies. M.L.A.
Music. Plan A and B. M.A.
Music Education. Plan A and B. M.S.
Nursing. Includes clinical nurse specialist in adult health, family nurse practitioner, nurse educator, parish nurse specialist, transcultural nurse specialist. M.S.N.
Public Human Service and Health Administration. Plan B: 35 credit program. M.S.
Reading. Plan A and B: 33 credit program. M.S.
School Psychology. Plan A. M.S.
Special Education. Includes developmental disabilities, early childhood special education, emotional/behavioral disorders, learning disabilities, physical and health disabilities. Plan A and B. M.S.
Speech/Language Pathology. Plan A and B: 48 credit program; clinical practica. M.S.

UNIVERSITY OF MINNESOTA, TWIN CITIES

Minneapolis, Minnesota 55455-0213
Web site: www.umn.edu

Established 1851. Coed. State control. CGS and AAU member. Semester system. Member of Committee on Institutional Cooperation with other Big Ten universities and the University of Chicago. Graduate study also offered at the Duluth campus. Special facilities: Bell Museum of Natural History, Dairy Foods Research Center, Rural Health Research Center, MIS Research Center, Avian Research Center, Limnological Research Center, Center for Advanced Research in Language Acquisition, Water Resource Center, Center for Infectious Disease Research and Policy, Center for Insurance Research, Agricultural Research Center, Immigration Health Research Center, Center for Violence Prevention and Control. The University's NIH ranking is 24th among all U.S. institutions with 575 awards/grants valued at $227,338,684. According to The Center at University of Florida, the University is ranked number 19th in receipt of Federal Research funds with $293,266,000 and it ranks number 11th for total University research expenditures with $508,557,000. The University's endowment assets rank it 25th, with a value of $1,730,063,000. In 2004, the University awarded 592 doctorates, which ranked it 9th among all U.S. institutions eligible to award that degree. Twenty-six of the University's faculty members have been elected to National Honor Academies and this ranks it 37th among all U.S. institutions. The Library: approximately 6,000,000 volumes, 45,000 subscriptions. Total University enrollment: 51,200.

Annual tuition: full-time resident $8748, nonresident $15,848; per credit resident $729, nonresident $1321; some programs have higher tuition costs, contact University for current charges. On-campus housing for married students, single men and women. Average academic year housing costs: $380–$450 per month for married students; $3100 per semester (including board) for single students. Apply to the Housing office. Phone: (612)624-2994. Day-care facilities available.

Graduate School

Graduate study since 1879. Enrollment: full- and part-time 11,000. Faculty: full- and part-time 2700. Degrees conferred: M.A., M.Ed., M.S., M.Arch., M.B.A., M.F.A., M.E., M.F., M.P.P., M.P.A., M.U.R.P., M.S.W., Ed.D., Ph.D., and many other designated degrees.

ADMISSION REQUIREMENTS. Transcripts required in support of School's application. GRE Subject Tests, MAT, GMAT required for some departments. TOEFL required for international applicants. Accepts transfer applicants. Graduates of unaccredited institutions not considered. Apply to Graduate School by June 15 (Fall), October 15 (Spring), March 15 (Summer). Application fee $55, $75 for international applicants. Phone: (612) 625-3014.

ADMISSION STANDARDS. Acceptance ratios vary among degree programs; admission based on competition generated by spaces available and applications received.

FINANCIAL AID. Individual departments award and administer graduate assistantships. Limited number of fellowships; program nomination is required for consideration. Apply to individual department. Use FAFSA.

DEGREE REQUIREMENTS. For M.A., M.S. Plan A: 30-credit program; thesis; final written/oral exam. For M.A., M.S. Plan B: 32-credit program; three lengthy papers; final written exam. For M.F.A.: three-year program; thesis. For M.P.P., M.U.R.P.: 45–48 credit programs. For M.S.: 40-credit, two-year program; capstone project. For Ph.D.: 60-credit, full-time program; minor field of study; reading knowledge of two foreign languages or one language/research tool/collateral field in some departments; comprehensive oral and written exam; thesis; final oral. For Ed.D.: 84-credit, full-time program beyond bachelor's; a minor field of study; supervised internship/clinical experience/fieldwork; preliminary written/oral exam; thesis/project; final oral exam.

FIELDS OF STUDY.
Accountancy.
Aerospace Engineering.
Agricultural and Applied Economics.
Agricultural Engineering.
American Studies.
Animal Sciences.
Anthropology.
Applied Plant Sciences.
Arabic.
Architecture.
Art.
Art Education.
Art History.
Astrophysics.
Biochemistry, Molecular Biology, and Biophysics.
Biological Science.
Biomedical Engineering.
Biophysical Sciences and Medical Physics.
Biostatistics.
Biosystems and Agricultural Engineering.
Business Administration.
Business Taxation.
Cellular and Integrative Physiology.
Chemical Engineering.
Chemical Physics.
Chemistry.
Child Psychology.
Chinese.
Civil Engineering.
Classical and Near Eastern Studies.
Clinical Laboratory Science.
Clinical Research.
Communication Disorders.
Communication Studies.
Comparative Literature.
Comparative Studies in Discourse and Society.
Computer Sciences.
Conservation Biology.
Control Science and Dynamical Systems.
Creative Writing.
Culture and Teaching.
Dentistry.

Design, Housing, and Apparel.
East Asian Studies.
Ecology, Evolution, and Behavior.
Economics.
Education. Includes curriculum and instruction, educational policy and administration, recreation, park and leisure studies, work, community and family education.
Educational Policy and Administration.
Educational Psychology. Includes counseling and student personnel psychology, psychological foundations of education, school psychology, special education.
Electrical Engineering.
English.
English as a Second Language.
Entomology.
Environmental Health.
Epidemiology.
Experimental Surgery.
Family Social Science.
Feminist Studies.
Finance.
Fisheries and Aquatic Biology.
Food Science.
French.
Geographic Information Science.
Geography.
Geological Engineering.
Geology.
Geophysics.
German and Scandinavian Studies.
Health Informatics.
Health Journalism.
Health Services Research, Policy, and Administration.
Hispanic and Luso-Brazilian Literatures and Linguistics.
Hispanic Linguistics.
Hispanic Literature.
History.
History of Medicine and Biological Sciences.
History of Science and Technology.
Human Resources and Industrial Relations.
Industrial Engineering.
Information and Decision Sciences.
Infrastructure Systems Engineering.
Japanese.
Journalism.
Kinesiology.
Landscape Architecture.
Latin.
Liberal Studies.
Linguistics.
Luso-Brazilian Literature.
Management of Technology.
Manufacturing Systems Engineering.
Marketing and Logistics Management.
Mass Communication.
Materials Science and Engineering.
Mathematics.
Mechanical Engineering.
Mechanics.
Medicinal Chemistry.
Microbial Engineering.
Microbiology, Immunology, and Cancer Biology.
Molecular, Cellular, Developmental Biology and Genetics.
Molecular Veterinary Biosciences.
Music.
Music Education.
Musicology.
Natural Resources Science and Management.
Neuroscience.
Nursing.
Nutrition.

Occupational Therapy.
Operations and Management Science.
Oral Biology.
Otolaryngology.
Pharmaceutics.
Pharmacology.
Philosophy.
Physical Therapy.
Physics.
Planning.
Plant Biological Sciences.
Plant Breeding/Plant Molecular Genetics.
Plant Pathology.
Political Science.
Psychology.
Public Affairs.
Public Policy.
Recreation, Parks and Leisure Studies
Rehabilitation Science.
Rhetoric and Scientific and Technical Communication.
Russian Area Studies.
Science, Environmental, and Technology Policy.
Scientific and Technical Communication.
Scientific Computation.
Social, Administrative, and Clinical Pharmacy.
Social Work.
Sociology.
Software Engineering.
Soil Science.
South Asian Languages.
Spanish.
Special Education.
Speech-Language-Hearing Sciences.
Statistics.
Studio Arts.
Surgery.
Theatre Arts. Includes directing, design.
Toxicology.
Urban and Regional Planning.
Veterinary Medicine.
Water Resources Science.
Work and Human Resource Education.

School of Dentistry
Web site: dentistry.umn.edu

Founded 1888, became School of Dentistry in 1932. Located at the University's Health Sciences Center. Quarter system. Special facilities: Dental Research Institute, Minnesota Dental Research Center for Biomaterials and Biomechanics, Minnesota Oral Health Clinical Research Center. Special Programs: externships; Summer Research Fellowships; foreign exchange in Denmark, Norway, Germany, and Peru.

Annual tuition: resident $27,904, nonresident $39,934. On-campus housing available. Average academic year housing cost: $14,000. Contact Housing Office at (612)624-2994. Total average cost for all other first-year expenses: $7500.

Enrollment: first-year class 97, total 390 (men 49%, women 51%, minorities 11%, state residents 65%); postgraduates: about 800. Degrees conferred: D.D.S., B.A.-D.D.S., D.D.S.-M.S., D.D.S.-Ph.D. The M.S. and Ph.D. are offered through the Graduate School.

ADMISSION REQUIREMENTS. AADSAS report, transcripts, three letters of recommendations, DAT (not later than October) required in support of School's application. TOEFL, TWE required for nonnative speakers of English. Applicants must have completed at least three years of college study. Has early admission program. Interview by invitation only. Accepts transfer applicants from U.S. and Canadian dental schools. Preference given to residents of Minnesota, nearby states, and Manitoba.

Apply to the Office of Enrollment Management after June 1, before January 1. Application fee $60. Phone: (612)625-7477; fax: (612)624-2120.

ADMISSION STANDARDS. Competitive. Accepts about 5–10% of all applicants. Usual minimum UGPA: 3.0 (A = 4). Mean DAT: academic 19, PAT 18, mean UGPA 3.60.

FINANCIAL AID. Scholarships, summer research fellowships, loans. Apply to University Student Financial Aid Office after acceptance; no specified closing date. Phone: (612)626-1665. Use FAFSA. Approximately 90% of students demonstrating need receive financial assistance.

DEGREE REQUIREMENTS. For B.D.: satisfactory completion of three-year undergraduate program and one year at School. For D.D.S.: satisfactory completion of forty-five-month program. For M.S., Ph.D.: requirements vary with department; see Graduate School listing above.

FIELDS OF POSTGRADUATE STUDY.
Endodontics. M.S.
Geriatrics. Certificate.
Oral and Maxillofacial Surgery. Certificate.
Oral Biology. M.S., Ph.D.
Orthodontics. M.S., Certificate.
Pediatric Dentistry. M.S., Certificate.
Pedodontics. M.S., Certificate.
Periodontics. Advanced training program.
Prosthodontics. M.S.
Research. Multi-disciplinary. M.S.
TMD, Orofacial Pain and Oral Medicine. M.S., Certificate.

Law School
Web site: www.law.umn.edu

Established 1888. ABA approved since 1923. AALS member. Public control. Semester system. Special facilities: Center for Computer-Assisted Legal Instruction; Consortium on Law and Values in Health, Environment & the Life Sciences; Human Rights Center; Institute for Law & Economics; Institute for Law & Politics; Institute for Law & Rationality; Institute on Race & Poverty; Kommerstad Center for Business Law and Entrepreneurship; Minnesota Center for Legal Studies. Law library: 1,020,040 volumes, 10,574 subscriptions; has LEXIS, NEXIS, WESTLAW, LUMINA.

Annual tuition: full-time. Resident $21,984, nonresident $31,484. Limited on-campus housing available. Total average annual additional expenses: $13,392.

Enrollment: first-year class 241; total 800 (men 57%, women 43%, minorities 16%); no part-time students. Faculty: full-time 55, part-time 70. Student to faculty ratio 12.5 to 1. Degree conferred: J.D., J.D.-M.A., J.D.-M.B.A., J.D.-M.B.S., J.D.-M.B.T., J.D.-M.P., J.D.-M.P.A., J.D.-M.P.H., J.D.-M.P.P., J.D.-M.S., LL.M. (only for persons who have completed a basic legal education and received a University degree in law in another country).

ADMISSION REQUIREMENTS. LSDAS Law School report, bachelor's degree, transcripts, LSAT, personal statement, résumé, two letters of recommendation required in support of application. Interview not required. Occasionally accepts transfer applicants. Graduates of unaccredited colleges not considered. Apply to the Director of Admission after October 1, before March 1. For Early Decision Program apply by November 15. Application fee $70. Phone: (612)625-3487; fax: (612)626-1874. For LL.M. go to www.law.umn.edu/LL.M.

ADMISSION STANDARDS. Selective. Accepts 28% of total annual applicants. Number of applicants 3068; number of acceptance 866; number enrolled 273; LSAT (75% of class have a score at or above 162); GPA (75% of class have a GPA at or above 3.30). *U.S. News & World Report* ranking is in the top 20 of all U.S. law schools.

FINANCIAL AID. Scholarships, full and partial tuition waivers, Federal W/S, loans. Apply to the University's Office of Financial Aid by March 1. Phone: (612)625-3487. Use FAFSA (School code: 003969). About 53% of students receive some aid from School.

DEGREE REQUIREMENTS. For J.D.: satisfactory completion of three-year program; 88 credit hours. For LL.M.: at least 24 credit hours beyond the J.D.; one year in full-time residence.

Note: Summer study available at Université Jean Moulin, Lyon (France), and Uppsala University Law School (Sweden). Joint degree programs exist with Hubert H. Humphrey Institute of Public Affairs and Curtis L. Carlson School of Management.

Medical School (55455-0310)
Web site: www.med.umn.edu

Founded 1888. NIH ranking is 24th among all U.S. institutions with 575 awards/grants worth $227,338,684.

Annual tuition: resident $31,941, nonresident $39,038. Limited on-campus housing available. Contact the Admissions Office for both on- and off-campus housing information. Total average figure for all other expenses: $17,500.

Enrollment: first-year class 165 (EDP 9), total 929 (men 51%, women 49%, minorities 9%, state residents 78%). Faculty: full-time 919, part-time 1500. Degrees conferred: M.D., M.D.-M.B.A., M.D.-M.P.H., M.D.-M.H.I., M.D.-M.S., M.D.-Ph.D., Medical Scientist Training Program. The M.S. and Ph.D. are offered through the Graduate School.

ADMISSION REQUIREMENTS. AMCAS report, transcripts, letters of evaluation, MCAT, supplementary applications required in support of application. Applicants must have completed bachelor's degree. Preference given to residents of Minnesota. Interview by invitation only. Accepts transfer students from University of Minnesota-Duluth. Has EDP; apply between June 1 and August 1. Apply to AMCAS after June 1, before November 15. Application fee $75. Phone: (612)624-7977; fax: (612)624-4200; e-mail: meded@umn.edu.

ADMISSION STANDARDS. Competitive. Accepts about 9% of all applicants. Number of applications 2528 (1874 out-of-state); number interviewed 525 (n/a out-of-state); number of acceptance n/a (n/a out-of-state); number enrolled 165 (34 out-of-state). Mean Composite MCAT 10.1; mean UGPA 3.64. *U.S. News & World Report* ranking is in the top 39 of all medical research schools, 13th in Primary Care.

FINANCIAL AID. Scholarships, merit scholarship, minority scholarships, graduate assistantship, Grants-in-Aid, institutional loans, HEAL, alternative loan programs, NIH stipends; Federal W/S, Federal Perkins Loans, Stafford Subsidized and Unsubsidized Loans, Service Commitment Scholarship programs are available. All M.D.-Ph.D. students are accepted into fully funded positions which include stipends, tuition waivers, fees, and health insurance. Financial Aid applications and information are generally available at the on-campus, by-invitation interview. Contact the Financial Aid Office for current information. Priority deadline March 1. Phone: (612)625-4998. Use FAFSA (School code: E00477), also submit Financial Aid Transcript, Federal Income Tax forms, ACT-FFS needs analysis form. Approximately 90% of students receive some form of financial assistance.

DEGREE REQUIREMENTS. For M.D.: satisfactory completion of four-year program. All students must pass USMLE Step 1 prior to entering third year; all students must pass USMLE Step 2 prior to awarding of M.D. For M.D.-Ph.D.: generally a seven-year program.

FIELDS OF GRADUATE STUDY.
Biochemistry.
Biomedical Engineering. M.S.

Biophysics.
Cancer Biology.
Cell Biology.
Chemistry.
Genetics.
Health Informatics.
Immunology.
Medicinal Chemistry.
Microbiology.
Molecular Biology.
Molecular, Cellular and Development Biology.
Neuroscience.
Pharmacology.
Public Health.

College of Veterinary Medicine
Web site: www.cvm.umn.edu

Established 1947. Located in St. Paul (55108) at the Veterinary Medical Center. Semester system. Special facilities: Veterinary Dental Education Center, Clinical Investigation Center, Equine Center.

Annual tuition: Minnesota and North Dakota contract residents $20,699, nonresidents $39,357. Off-campus housing only. Total annual housing expenses: $12,000–$15,000. Total average cost for other expenses: $5,500.

Enrollment: first-year class 90, total 400 (men 24%, women 76%, minorities 5%, state residents 60%). Faculty: full-time 153, part-time 17. Degrees conferred: D.V.M., M.S., Ph.D., D.V.M.-M.P.H., D.V.M.-Ph.D. The M.S. and Ph.D. are offered through the Graduate School.

ADMISSION REQUIREMENTS. VMCAS report, transcripts, GRE General, animal/veterinary knowledge, three references required in support of application. Online application available. Interview by invitation only. Preference given to state residents, then to residents of North Dakota, South Dakota, Manitoba. Applicants must have completed at least three years of college study (by Spring prior to entrance) with a specific area distribution. Accepts a limited number of transfer applicants. Apply to the Office of Student Affairs and Admissions after August 1, before October 1. Admits Fall only. Preference given to state and contract residents. Application fee $50. Phone: (612)624-4747.

ADMISSION STANDARDS. Competitive. Accepts about 15–20% of all applicants. Number of applications 1010 (813 out-of-state); number interviewed n/a (n/a out-of-state); number of acceptance n/a (n/a out-of-state); number enrolled 90 (36 out-of-state). Usual minimum UGPA: 2.90 (A = 4). GRE mean score (V + Q) 1170; mean UGPA 3.52.

FINANCIAL AID. Awards, scholarships, fellowships, assistantships, internships, Federal W/S, loans. Apply to University Office of Student Financial Aid by March 1. Use FAFSA. Most students receive loans or have part-time employment.

DEGREE REQUIREMENTS. For D.V.M.: satisfactory completion of four-year program. For M.S., Ph.D.: see Graduate School listing above.

FIELDS OF GRADUATE STUDY.
Comparative and Molecular Biosciences. Multidisciplinary program. Includes Molecular Mechanism of Pathogenesis in Animals, comparative animal biomedical sciences. M.S., Ph.D.
Public Health. Includes biostatistics, community health education, environmental health, epidemiology, public health administration and policy, public health nutrition, public health medicine, veterinary public health.
Veterinary Medicine. Includes infectious disease, comparative medicine and Pathology, population medicine, surgery/radiology/anesthesiology, theriogenology. M.S., Ph.D

UNIVERSITY OF MINNESOTA, DULUTH

Duluth, Minnesota 55812-2596
Web site: www.d.umn.edu

Founded in 1895. State control. Semester system. Special facilities: Alworth Institute for International Studies, Large Lakes Observatory, Marshall Performing Arts Center, Natural Resource Research Institute, Small Business Development Center, Tweed Museum of Art. Library: 707,000 volumes, 4500 subscriptions. Total campus enrollment: 10,500.

Annual tuition: resident $9740, nonresident $16,838; per credit, resident $811, nonresident $1403. On-campus housing for single graduate men and women; none for married students. Average academic year housing cost: $6500 (including board) for single students. Phone: (218)726-9119.

Graduate School

Graduate study since 1957. Enrollment: full-time 292, part-time 128. Faculty teaching graduate students: full- and part-time 283. Degrees conferred: M.A., M.S., M.B.A., M.L.S., M.M., M.S.W.

ADMISSION REQUIREMENTS. Two transcripts required in support of School's application. GRE/GMAT/MAT required for some departments. TOEFL required for international applicants. Accepts transfer students. Apply to Associate Dean of Graduate School at least eight weeks prior to registration. Application fee $50, $75 for international applicants. Phone: (218)726-7523; fax: (218)726-6970; e-mail: grad@umn.edu.

ADMISSION STANDARDS. Selective. Usual minimum average: 3.0 (A = 4).

FINANCIAL AID. Annual awards from institutional funds: fellowships, teaching assistantships, research assistantships, tuition remission for TA, RA, and fellowship recipients, internships, grants, Federal W/S, loans. Approved for VA benefits. Apply to director of each program for fellowships, assistantships; to director of Financial Aid for loans. No specified closing date. Use FAFSA. About 60% of students receive aid other than loans from University and outside sources.

DEGREE REQUIREMENTS. For master's Plan A: 44 credit minimum, thesis, final written/oral exam. Plan B: 30 credit minimum without thesis; reading knowledge of one foreign language; two major projects; comprehensive final written and oral exam.

FIELDS OF STUDY.
Advocacy and Political Leadership.
Applied and Computational Mathematics. M.S. (Plans A and B).
Art. Includes graphic design, M.F.A. (Plan B).
Biochemistry, Molecular Biology and Biophysics. M.S.
Business Administration. M.B.A. (Plan B).
Chemistry. Includes analytical, inorganic, physical, organic. M.S. (Plans A and B).
Communication Sciences and Disorders. M.A. (Plan B).
Computer Science. M.S. (Plans A and B).
Criminology. M.A.
Educational Psychology. M.A. (Plan B).
Electrical and Computer Engineering. M.S.E.C.E.
Engineering Management. M.S.E.M. (Plan B).
English. Includes teaching of English. M.A. (Plan B).
Geological Sciences. M.S. (Plan A and B).
Integrated Bioscience. M.S.
Liberal Studies. M.L.S. (Plan B).
Music. Includes music education, performance. M.M. (Plan B).
Physics. M.S. (Plan A and B).
Social Work. M.S.W. (Plan B).

Toxicology. M.S. (Plans A and B); Ph. D. (offered jointly with Twin Cities Campus).
Water Resources Science. M.S. (Plan A and B); Ph.D. (offered jointly with Twin Cities Campus).

Medical School—Duluth Campus

Web site: www.med.umn.edu/duluth

Founded 1972. Special facility: Center of American Indian and Minority Health.

Annual tuition: resident $31,941, nonresident $39,038. No on-campus housing available. Contact the Admissions Office for both on- and off-campus housing information. Total average figure for all other expenses: $11,500.

Enrollment: first-year class 55 (EDP 9), total 111 (men 47%, women 53%, minorities 9%, state residents 93%). Faculty: full-time 45, part-time and volunteers 250. Degree conferred: none, two-year transfer program.

ADMISSION REQUIREMENTS. AMCAS report, transcripts, MCAT, recommendations, screening questionnaire required in support of application. Interview by invitation only. Preference given to state residents and residents of North Dakota, South Dakota, Iowa, and northern Wisconsin. Has EDP; apply between June 1 and August 1. Graduates of unaccredited colleges not considered. Apply to Associate Dean after June 1, before November 15 (firm). Application fee $75. Phone: (218)726-8511; fax: (218)726-7057; e-mail: medadmis@d.umn.edu.

ADMISSION STANDARDS. Competitive. Accepts about 10–15% of all applicants. Number of applications 954 (1874 out-of-state); number interviewed 162 (n/a out-of-state); number of acceptance n/a (n/a out-of-state); number enrolled 55 (n/a out-of-state). Mean Composite MCAT 9.3; mean UGPA 3.60.

FINANCIAL AID. Scholarships, loans. Apply to University Financial Aid Program following admission. Phone: (218)726-8786. Use FAFSA (School code: E00477). About 93% of students eligible for aid receive assistance.

DEGREE REQUIREMENTS. Satisfactory completion of two-year program; must pass Step 1 of USMLE to transfer to University of Minnesota, Minneapolis. All students transfer to University of Minnesota Medical School in Minneapolis to complete studies for M.D.

MINOT STATE UNIVERSITY

Minot, North Dakota 58702-0002
Web site: www.minotstateu.edu

Founded 1913. Coed. State control. Semester system. Library: 420,971 volumes, 1400 subscriptions. Total University enrollment: 3800.

Annual tuition: resident $5264, nonresident $14,844. Limited on-campus housing available. Average academic year housing cost: $3914–$4224 (including board). Contact Housing Office for both on- and off-campus housing information. Phone: (701) 858-3360.

Graduate School

Enrollment: full- and part-time 267. University faculty teaching graduate students: full- and part-time 100. Degrees conferred: M.S., M.M.E., M.A.T.

ADMISSION REQUIREMENTS. Official transcripts from all colleges/universities attended, GRE/GMAT, three letters of recommendation, autobiography required in support of School's application. Online application available. TOEFL required for international applicants. Apply to the Dean of the Graduate School at least four weeks prior to registration. Application fee $25. Phone: (701)858-3250; fax: (701)858-4286.

ADMISSION STANDARDS. Selective. Usual minimum average: 3.00 (A = 4).

FINANCIAL AID. Annual awards from institutional funds: scholarships, Federal W/S, loans. Approved for VA benefits. Apply to Financial Aid Office by April 15, February 15 for scholarship consideration. Phone: (701)858-3375; fax: (701)858-4310. Use FAFSA (School code: 002994).

DEGREE REQUIREMENTS. For master's: 30–36 semester hours minimum; thesis option/written comprehensive exam; oral exam.

FIELDS OF STUDY.
Communication Disorders.
Criminal Justice.
Education.
Information Systems.
Management. M.S.
Music Education. M.M.E.
School Psychology.
Science. M.A.T.
Special Education.
Teaching Mathematics. M.A.T.

MISSISSIPPI COLLEGE
Clinton, Mississippi 39058
Web site: www.mc.edu

Founded 1826. Located 5 miles W of Jackson. Coed. Private control. Semester system. Library: 276,245 volumes, 5300 subscriptions. Total College enrollment: 3000.

Tuition: per hour $405. On-campus housing for single students only. Average academic year housing cost: $5500–$6100 (including board); off-campus housing cost: $550–$750 per month. Contact the Dean of Students Office for both on- and off-campus housing information. Phone: (601)925-3248.

Graduate School

Graduate study since 1950. Enrollment: full-time 87, part-time 417. College faculty: full-time 67, part-time 12. Degrees conferred: M.A., M.Ed., M.B.A., M.F.A., M.M., M.C.C., M.C.P., M.C.S., M.H.S., M.S., M.S.S., Ed.Sp.

ADMISSION REQUIREMENTS. Two transcripts, two photographs, GRE/NTE/GMAT, two letters of recommendation required in support of application. GRE Subject for some programs. Interview required for most departments. TOEFL required for foreign applicants. Accepts transfer applicants. Graduates of unaccredited colleges not considered. Apply to Graduate Office by August 20 (Fall), May 15 (Summer). Rolling admissions process. Application fee $25, $75 for international applicants. Phone: (601) 925-3260; fax: (601)925-3889; e-mail: graduate@mc.edu.

ADMISSION STANDARDS. Relatively open. Usual minimum average: 2.75 (A = 4).

FINANCIAL AID. Annual awards from institutional funds: teaching assistantships, internships, tuition waivers, loans. Apply by April 1 to appropriate department chair; to Financial Aid Office for all other programs. Use FAFSA (School code: 002415). About 20% of students receive aid other than loans from College and outside sources. Aid sometimes available for part-time students.

DEGREE REQUIREMENTS. For master's: 30–36 semester hours minimum, at least 24–36 in residence; thesis or final project; reading knowledge of one foreign language for M.A.; internship for M.Ed.; final oral/written comprehensive exam. For M.F.A.: 60 credit program; project.

FIELDS OF STUDY.
Accounting. M.B.A.
Administration of Justice. M.S.S.
Applied Communication. M.S.C.
Art. M.A.
Art Education. M.Ed.
Athletic Administration. M.S.
Biology Medical Sciences. M.S..
Biological Sciences. M.S.C.
Biology Education. M.Ed.
Business Administration. M.B.A.
Business Education. M.Ed.
Chemistry. M.C.S., M.S.
Combined Sciences. M.C.S.
Community Psychology. M.Ed.
Computer Science. M.S.
Computer Science Education. M.Ed.
Counseling. Ed.Sp.
Dyslexia Therapy. M.Ed.
Educational Leadership. M.Ed., Ed.Sp., Ed.D.
Elementary Education. M.Ed., Ed.Sp.
English. M.A.
Health Services Administration. M.H.S.A.
Higher Education Administration. M.S.
History. M.A., M.Ed., M.S.S.
Liberal Studies. M.L.S.
Marriage and Family Therapy. M.S.
Mass Communication. M.S.
Mathematics. M.C.S., M.S.
Mathematics Education. M.Ed.
Mental Health Counseling. M.S.C.
Music. Includes applied, education, performance, accompanying. M.M.
Political Science. M.S.S.
Public Relations and Corporate Communication. M.S.C.
School Administration. M.Ed.
School Counseling. M.Ed.
Science Education. M.Ed.
Secondary Education. Includes art, biological sciences, business education, computer science, English, mathematics, social sciences (history), teaching arts (elementary/secondary). M.Ed.
Social Sciences. M.S.S.
Sociology. Includes general. M.S.S.
TESOL. M.A.
Visual Arts. M.F.A.

School of Law (39201-1391)
Web site: www.law.mc.edu

Established 1975. Approved 1980. AALS member. Located in downtown Jackson. Private control. Semester system. Law library: 330,590 volumes, 3491 subscriptions.

Annual tuition: full-time $20,140. No on-campus housing available. Total average annual additional expenses: $17,200.

Enrollment: first-year class, full-time 199, total 528 (men 60%, women 40%, minorities 8%). Faculty: full-time 14, part-time 22. Student to faculty ratio is 21.4 to 1. Degrees Conferred: J.D., J.D.-M.B.A.

ADMISSION REQUIREMENTS. LSDAS Law School report, bachelor's degree, transcripts, LSAT (not later than March), personal statement, recommendations required in support of application. Graduates of unaccredited colleges not considered. Apply to Office of Admissions by June 1. Rolling admissions process. Application fee $50. Phone: (601)925-7151; fax: (601)925-7185.

ADMISSION STANDARDS. Selective. Accepts 39% of total annual applicants. Number of applicants 1274; number of acceptance 491; number enrolled 199; LSAT (75% of class have a score at or above 149); GPA (75% of class have a GPA at or above 2.99). *U.S. News & World Report* ranking is fourth tier of all U.S. law schools.

FINANCIAL AID. Full and partial scholarships, Federal W/S, loans. Apply to Office of Financial Aid by May 1. Phone: (601) 925-7110. Use FAFSA (School code: E00479). About 22% of students receive some aid from School.

DEGREE REQUIREMENTS. For J.D.: satisfactory completion of three-year (full-time), four-year (extended division) program; 88 credit hours. For J.D.-M.B.A.: J.D. (84 credits), M.B.A. (21 credits), combined 105 credit program.

MISSISSIPPI STATE UNIVERSITY
Mississippi State, Mississippi 39762
Web site: www.msstate.edu

Founded 1878. Located 130 miles NE of Jackson. CGS member. Coed. State control. Semester system. Special facilities: Institute for Humanities, Cobb Institute for Archaeology, Center for Robotics, Automation, and Artificial Intelligence, electron microscope, Mississippi Energy Research Center, Mississippi State Chemical Laboratory, Radiological Safety Office, Water Resource Research Institute, Center for International Security and Strategic Studies, Mississippi Alcohol Safety Education Program, John C. Stennis Institute of Government, Social Science Research Center, Gulf Coast Research Laboratory at Ocean Springs. According to The Center at University of Florida, the University is ranked 98th in receipt of Federal Research funds with $79,837,000 and it ranks number 82nd for total University research expenditures with $165,922,000. The Library: approximately 1,600,000 volumes, 15,500 subscriptions. Total University enrollment: 16,100.

Annual tuition: full-time, resident $4312, nonresident $9772; per credit, resident $240, nonresident $543. On-campus housing for 268 married students. Average academic year housing cost: $4188 for married students, $3000 (room only) for single students. Contact Housing Director. Phone: (662)325-3557. Day-care facilities available.

Graduate Studies

Graduate study since 1893. Enrollment: full-time 1748, part-time 1506 (men 55%, women 45%). University faculty: full-time 934, part-time 122. Degrees conferred: M.A., M.S., M.Ag., M.A.B.M., M.B.A., M.F.A., M.P.P.A., M.Prof.Acc., M.Tax., Ed.S., Ed.D., Ph.D.

ADMISSION REQUIREMENTS. Official transcripts, GRE, GMAT, three letters of recommendation required in support of School's application. Interview not required. TOEFL required of international students. Accepts transfer applicants. Apply to Office of Admissions at least twenty days prior to registration. Application fee $30. Phone: (662)325-4104; fax: (662)325-8872; e-mail: admit@admission.msstate.edu.

ADMISSION STANDARDS. Selective for some departments, relatively open for others. Usual minimum average: 2.5 for master's, 3.0–3.5 for Ed.S., Ed.D., Ph.D. (A = 4).

FINANCIAL AID. Annual awards from institutional funds: scholarships, grants, teaching assistantships, research assistantships, Federal W/S, loans. Approved for VA benefits. Apply by March 1 to Dean of the Graduate School for assistantships; to Financial Aid Office for all other programs. Use FAFSA and institutional FAF. Phone: (662)325-2450; fax: (662)325-0702. About 40% of students receive aid other than loans from University and outside sources. Aid sometimes available for part-time students.

DEGREE REQUIREMENTS. For M.A., M.S.: 30 semester hours minimum, at least 24 in residence; reading knowledge of one foreign language for majors in English, physical and biological sciences; final oral exam. For M.Ag.: same as for M.A., except thesis is optional; no language requirement; final written/oral exam. For M.B.A., M.Prof.Acc.: 30 semester hours minimum, at least 24 in residence; no thesis or language requirement; final written/oral exam. For Ed.S.: 30 semester hours beyond the master's, at least 24 in residence; special problem or thesis included; final written/oral exam. For Ph.D.: three years beyond the bachelor's, at least one year in full-time residence, preliminary exam; foreign language proficiency for some programs; qualifying exam; dissertation; final oral exam. For Ed.D.: essentially the same as for the Ph.D., except no language requirement.

FIELDS OF STUDY.
Accounting.
Aerospace Engineering.
Agribusiness Management. M.Agri.Bus.Mgt. only.
Agricultural and Biological Engineering.
Agricultural and Extension Education.
Agricultural Economics.
Agronomy.
Animal Physiology. Interdepartmental. Ph.D. only.
Applied Anthropology.
Applied Economics. Ph.D. only.
Architecture.
Art.
Biochemistry and Molecular Biology..
Biological Engineering.
Biological Sciences.
Biomedical Engineering.
Botany.
Business Administration.
Business Information Systems.
Business Technology.
Chemical Engineering. M.S. only.
Chemistry. Includes analytical, inorganic, organic, physical. Placement exam; one language for M.S.
Civil Engineering.
Cognitive Science. Ph.D. only.
Communication.
Community College Leadership. Ph.D. only.
Computational Engineering.
Computer Engineering.
Computer Science and Engineering.
Counselor Education.
Curriculum and Instruction.
Dairy Science.
Economics.
Education.
Educational Leadership.
Electrical Engineering.
Electronic Visualization. M.F.A. only.
Elementary Education.
Engineering.
Engineering Mechanics.
Engineering Physics.
English. One language for M.A.; M.A. only.
Entomology and Plant Pathology.
Environmental Toxicology. Ph.D. only.
Finance and Economics.
Fisheries.
Food Science and Technology.
Foreign Languages. French, German, Spanish; M.A. only.
Forest Products.

Forest Resources. Includes forest products, forestry, and wildlife and fisheries science. Ph.D. only.

Forestry. M.F., M.S. only.

General Engineering.

Genetics. Interdisciplinary; one language for M.S.

Geosciences.

Gerontology.

History.

Horticulture.

Human Sciences. Interdisciplinary.

Industrial Engineering. M.S. only.

Industrial Technology.

Instructional System, Leadership and Workforce Development.

Landscape Architecture. M.L.A. only.

Management and Information Systems.

Mathematics. Includes applied mathematics, statistics. One language for M.S.

Mechanical Engineering.

Molecular Biology.

Nutrition.

Physics and Astronomy. One language for M.S.

Plant and Soil Sciences.

Political Science. Master's only.

Poultry Science.

Project Management.

Psychology. Master's only.

Public Policy and Administration. M.P.P.A. only.

School Psychology. Ed.SP.

Secondary Education.

Sociology.

Special Education. Master's, Ed.S. only.

Statistics.

Taxation. Master's only.

Technology and Education.

Veterinary Medical Science.

Weed Science.

Wildlife and Fisheries.

Women's Studies.

Zoology.

College of Veterinary Medicine (PO Box 6100)

Web site: www.cvm.msstate.edu

Established 1977. Located on campus. Semester system. Special facility: Animal Health Center, Center for Environmental Health Sciences.

Annual tuition: residents $12,202, nonresidents $30,944. On-campus housing available. Total average expenses for both on- and off-campus housing: $6,000–$10,000. Total average cost for other expenses: $5,500.

Enrollment: first-year class 72, total 300 (men 30%, women 70%, minorities 3%, state residents 50%), postgraduate 65. Faculty: full-time 62, part-time 11. Degrees conferred: D.V.M., M.S., M.V.S., Ph.D., D.V.M.-M.S. The M.S. and Ph.D. are offered through the Office of Graduate Studies.

ADMISSION REQUIREMENTS. VMCAS report, transcripts showing completion of sixty-five hours of preprofessional college work, VCAT or GRE, recommendations, animal/veterinary experience, essay required in support of application. Supplemental application required. Interview by invitation only. Accepts transfer applicants on a space-available basis. Preference given to state residents. Apply to Assistant Dean after August 1, prior to October 1. Application fee $30. Phone: (662)325-1129.

ADMISSION STANDARDS. Selective. Accepts about 35–40% of all applicants. Number of applications n/a (n/a out-of-state); number interviewed n/a (n/a out-of-state); number of acceptance n/a (n/a out-of-state); number enrolled 72 (36 out-of-state include 5 South Carolina contract students). Usual minimum

UGPA: 2.80 (A = 4). GRE mean score (V + Q) 1100; mean UGPA 3.59.

FINANCIAL AID. Fellowships, research assistantships, Federal W/S, loans. Apply by April 1 to Dean. Use FAFSA.

DEGREE REQUIREMENTS. For D.V.M.: 152 semester hours and four years in residence. For M.S., M.V.S., and Ph.D.: see Graduate Studies listing above.

FIELDS OF GRADUATE STUDY.

Aquatic Medicine.

Avian Medicine.

Infectious Diseases.

Pathology.

Production Animal Medicine.

Toxicology.

MISSISSIPPI UNIVERSITY FOR WOMEN

Columbus, Mississippi 39701-9998

Web site: www.muw.edu

Founded 1884. State control. Semester system. Library: 426,500 volumes, 1629 subscriptions. Total University enrollment: 2300.

Annual tuition: resident $4209, nonresident $10,723. On-campus housing for 250 graduate students. Average academic year housing cost: $2780–$5160 (including meals). Apply to Graduate Housing Office for both on- and off-campus housing. Phone: (662)329-7215. Day-care facilities available.

Graduate Studies

Enrollment: full-time 21, part-time 110. College faculty teaching graduate students: full-time 5, part-time 3. Degrees conferred: M.Ed., M.S., M.S.N.

ADMISSION REQUIREMENTS. Official transcripts, letters of recommendation, GRE required in support of School's application. TOEFL and Graduate English Proficiency required of international applicants. Accepts transfer applicants. Apply to the Dean of the Graduate School by April 1. Application fee: none. Phone: (662)329-7110; fax: (662)329-8515.

ADMISSION STANDARDS. Selective. Usual minimum average: 2.75; 3.0 in area of study (A = 4).

FINANCIAL AID. Annual awards from institutional funds: fellowships, federal traineeships (when available), in-state scholarships, Federal W/S, loans. Apply by April 1 to Dean of the Graduate School. Phone: (662)329-7142. About 80% of students receive aid other than loans from College and outside sources.

DEGREE REQUIREMENTS. For master's: 30–36 semester hour minimum, at least 30 in residence; written/oral final exam; thesis/nonthesis option; language optional with department/student.

FIELDS OF STUDY.

Differentiated Instruction. M.Ed.

Gifted Studies. M.Ed.

Health Education. M.S.

Nursing. Includes family, gerontological practitioner.

Reading/Literacy. M.S.

Speech/Language Pathology. M.S.

Teaching. M.A.

THE UNIVERSITY OF MISSISSIPPI

University, Mississippi 38677
Web site: www.olemiss.edu

Founded 1848. Located 76 miles SE of Memphis, Tenn. CGS member. Coed. State control. Semester system. New Science Center complex. Special facilities: Center for Computational Hydroscience and Engineering, Center for the Study of Southern Culture, Mary Buie Museum, National Center for Physical Acoustics, Research Institute for Pharmaceutical Sciences. The University's NIH ranking is 193rd among all U.S. institutions with 48 awards/grants worth $18,307,189. Library: 951,259 volumes, 8495 subscriptions. Total University enrollment: 14,900.

Annual tuition: full-time, resident $4320, nonresident $9744; per credit, resident $240, nonresident $301. On-campus housing for both single and married students. Average academic year housing cost: $2952 (room only) for single students; $4000 for married students. Contact Director of Housing for both on- and off-campus housing. Phone: (662)915-7328.

Graduate School

Graduate study since 1870. Enrollment: full-time 1255, part-time 682. Graduate faculty: full- and part-time 578. Degrees conferred: M.A., M.S., M.B.A., M.Ed., M.F.A., M.M., M.Acc., M.S.S., M.Tax., D.A., Ed.Sp., Ed.D., Ph.D.

ADMISSION REQUIREMENTS. Official transcripts, three letters of recommendation, GRE, GMAT (Business), NTE (Education) required in support of School's application. Interview usually not required. TOEFL required for international applicants. Accepts transfer applicants. Graduates of unaccredited institutions not considered. Apply by April 1 (Fall), October 1 (Spring) to the Registrar's Office. Rolling admissions process. Application fee: none, $25 for international applicants. Phone: (662)915-7474; fax: (662) 915-7577.

ADMISSION STANDARDS. Selective. Usual minimum average: 3.0, 2.75 for last 60 credits (A = 4).

FINANCIAL AID. Scholarships, fellowships, special minority fellowships, teaching/research assistantships, internships, Federal W/S, loans. Approved for VA benefits. Apply by March 1 to Graduate School for Honors Fellowships and Minority Fellowships; to appropriate department for assistantships; to Office of Financial Aid for all other programs. Phone: (662)915-7175. Use FAFSA. About 55% of students receive aid other than loans from University and outside sources. Aid available to part-time students.

DEGREE REQUIREMENTS. For M.A., M.S., M.S.S., M.Acc., M.Tax.: 30 semester hours minimum, at least 24 in residence; thesis included for six hours; reading knowledge of one foreign language for some majors; final oral exam. For M.B.A.: one year minimum in residence; specific number of hours depends upon previous preparation. For M.Ed.: 30 hours minimum, at least 24 in residence; final oral exam. For M.F.A.: 60 hours minimum, at least two years in residence; creative project included for six hours; final exhibition and final oral exam may be required. For M.M.: 30 hours minimum, at least 24 in residence; recital, composition, or thesis; final oral exam. For Ed.Sp.: 30 hours beyond the master's; special project; final oral exam. For D.A., Ed.D.: 60 hours of course work beyond the master's degree; one year of continuous full-time attendance; internship; doctoral essay; comprehensive exam. For Ph.D.: three years minimum beyond the bachelor's, at least two years in residence, and one year of continuous full-time attendance; preliminary exam; written, oral comprehensive exam; dissertation; final oral exam.

FIELDS OF STUDY.
Accountancy. GMAT for admission. M.Acc., Ph.D.
Anthropology. M.A.

Art. Includes art education, ceramics, painting, printmaking, sculpture. M.A., M.F.A. only.
Art History. M.A.
Biological Sciences. M.S., Ph.D.
Business Administration. GMAT required for admission. M.B.A., Ph.D. (Concentrations in finance, management, marketing.)
Chemistry. M.S., Ph.D., D.A.
Classics. Greek, Latin, classical archaeology; one language in addition to major. M.A. only.
Communicative Disorders. Includes audiology, speech pathology. M.S., Sp.Ed.
Computational Engineering Science. M.S., Ph.D.
Counselor Education. M.Ed., Ed.Sp., Ph.D.
Creative Writing. M.F.A.
Criminal Justice. M.C.J.
Curriculum and Instruction. M.A., M.Ed., Ed.Sp.
Economics. M.A., Ph.D.
Education. Includes curriculum and instruction, educational leadership (K–12), educational psychology. M.A., M.Ed., Ed.Sp., Ph.D.
Elementary Education. Ed.D.
Engineering. Includes aeroacoustics, civil, environmental engineering, computer science, geology and geological engineering, hydrology, mechanical engineering, chemical engineering, electrical engineering, telecommunication. M.S., Ph.D.
English. M.A., Ph.D.
Exercise Science. M.S., Ph.D.
Fine Arts. Includes art, creative writing, theatre. M.F.A.
Geology. M.S.
Health Promotion. M.S.
Higher Education and Student Personnel. M.A.
History. One language for M.A., Ph.D.
Journalism. M.A. only.
Leisure Management. M.A. only.
Mathematics. M.A., M.S., Ph.D.
Modern Languages. Includes French, German, Spanish, TESL.
Music. Includes conducting, performance, music education. M.M., D.A.
Parks and Recreation Management. M.A.
Pharmaceutical Sciences. Includes environmental toxicology, pharmacology, medicinal chemistry, pharmaceutics, pharmacognosy, pharmacy administration. M.S., Ph.D.
Philosophy. M.A. only.
Physics. One language for M.A., M.S., Ph.D.
Political Science. M.A., Ph.D.
Psychology. M.A., Ph.D.
Social Science. M.S.
Social Work. M.S.W.
Sociology. One language or research tool for M.A. M.A., M.S.S. only.
Southern Studies. M.A. only.
Taxation. M.T.
Theater Arts. M.A., M.F.A. only.

School of Law (P.O. Box 1848)

Web site: www.olemiss.edu/depts/law_school

Established 1854 as a Department of Law: fourth-oldest state-supported law school in U.S. Public control. Semester system. Special facilities: Croft Institute for International Studies, Mississippi Judicial College, Mississippi Law Research Institute, National Center for Justice and the Rule of Law, National Center for Remote Sensing, Air and Space Law. Special program: Cambridge Study Abroad Program. Law library: 328,134 volumes, 2144 subscriptions; has LEXIS, NEXIS, WESTLAW, DIALOG; has more than 700 network connections.

Annual tuition: resident $8715; nonresident $16,595. On-campus housing available, but most law students live off-campus in local apartments. Total average annual expense: $14,858.

Enrollment: full-time, J.D. program, first year class 187, total full-time 505 (men 55%, women 45%, minorities 12%); graduate program 25. School faculty: full-time 22, part-time 14. Student to faculty ratio 16.9 to 1. Degrees conferred: J.D., J.D.-M.B.A.

ADMISSION REQUIREMENTS. For J.D.: LSDAS Law School report, bachelor's degree, transcripts, LSAT, personal statement, one letter of recommendation required in support of application. Accepts a limited number of transfer applicants. Apply to Law School Director of Admissions by March 1 (nonresidents for Summer, Fall), April 1 (residents for Summer). Fall or Summer admission only. Preference given to state residents. Application fee $40. Phone: (662)915-6910; fax: (662)915-1289. For graduate degrees: transcripts required in support of application. Applicants should have graduated in upper half of law school class. Apply to Chair of the Graduate Program at least twenty days prior to registration.

ADMISSION STANDARDS. Selective. Accepts 27% of total annual applicants. Number of applicants 1678; number of acceptance 456; number enrolled 187; LSAT (75% of class have a score at or above 151); GPA (75% of class have a GPA at or above 3.26). *U.S. News & World Report* ranking is in the third tier of all U.S. law schools.

FINANCIAL AID. Scholarships, fellowships, assistantships, Federal W/S, loans. Apply to University Financial Aid Officer for loans, to Scholarship Coordinator for all others by March 1; to Chair of Graduate Programs by March 1. Phone: (800)891-4596. Use FAFSA (School code: 002440). About 32% of students receive aid other than loans from School.

DEGREE REQUIREMENTS. For J.D.: satisfactory completion of ninety credit-hour program. For M.B.A.: see Graduate School listing above.

UNIVERSITY OF MISSISSIPPI MEDICAL CENTER
Jackson, Mississippi 39216-4505
Web site: www.umc.edu

Medical Center opened in 1955. Includes the Schools of Dentistry, Medicine, Health-Related Professions, Nursing and the University Hospital. Library: 237,765 volumes, 2202 subscriptions. Limited on-campus housing. Contact Housing Office for both on- and off-campus housing information. Phone: (601)984-1491. Total Medical Center enrollment: 1800. Total full- and part-time faculty: 776.

School of Dentistry
Web site: dentistry.umc.edu

Established 1973. Public control. Quarter system. Special facility: J. Perry McGinnis, Jr. Clinical Dental Research Center.

Annual tuition: residents $9,030. No on-campus housing available. For housing information contact the Student Service Office. Phone: (615)327-6387. Average academic year housing cost: $9,500. Total average cost for all other first-year expenses: $7500.

Enrollment: first-year class 30, total 125 (men 59%, women 41%, minorities 6%, state residents 100%), postgraduates 15. Faculty: full-time 27, part-time 120. Degrees conferred: D.M.D., Certificate.

ADMISSION REQUIREMENTS. Transcripts, DAT, three letters of recommendation required in support of School's application. Interview by invitation only. Applicants must have completed at least three years of college study. Strong preference given to state residents. Accepts transfer applicants. Apply to Office of Student

Services and Records after July 1, before December 1. Rolling admission process. Application fee: resident $50, nonresident $75. Phone: (601)984-6009; fax: (601)984-6014.

ADMISSION STANDARDS. Competitive. Accepts about 30% of all applicants. Usual minimum UGPA: 2.70 (A = 4). Mean DAT: academic 17.2, PAT 17, mean UGPA 3.60.

FINANCIAL AID. Scholarships, grants, tuition waivers, loans. Apply to Financial Aid Office; no specified closing date. Preference given to applications received before April 30. Phone: (601) 984-1117. Use FAFSA (School code: 004688). About 85% of students receive aid from School and outside sources.

DEGREE REQUIREMENTS. For D.M.D.: satisfactory completion of forty-five-month program; advanced standing for work completed at other dental schools considered.

FIELDS OF POSTGRADUATE STUDY.
Advanced Education in General Dentistry Residency.
Craniofacial and Dental Research. M.S., Ph.D.
General Practice Residency. Certificate.
Residency Training in Pediatric Dentistry.

School of Medicine
Web site: som.umc.edu

Founded 1903, became four-year school in 1955. Located in Jackson, Mississippi. Quarter system. Library: 300,000 items, 2368 subscriptions. NIH ranking is 193rd among all U.S. institutions with 48 awards/grants worth $18,307,891.

Annual tuition: resident $10,649, nonresident $16,327. No on-campus housing available. Contact the Admissions Office for both on- and off-campus housing information. Total average figure for all other expenses: $11,500.

Enrollment: first-year class 105 (EDP 10), total 386 (men 70%, women 30%, minorities 11%, state residents 100%). Faculty: full-time 375, part-time and volunteers 1069. Degrees conferred: M.D., M.D.-M.S., M.D.-Ph.D.

ADMISSION REQUIREMENTS. For M.D. program: AMCAS report, transcripts, MCAT, recommendations, secondary application required in support of application. Interview by invitation only. Applicants must have completed at least three years of college study. Preference given to state residents only. Has EDP; apply between June 1 and August 1. For graduate program: transcripts, five references, GRE/Subject Tests required in support of application. Interview required for most departments. Accepts transfer applicants for M.D. and graduate program. Graduates of unaccredited colleges not considered. Apply to Registrar after June 1, before October 15 (M.D.). Application fee: residents $50, nonresidents $100. Phone: (601)984-5010; fax: (601)984-5008.

ADMISSION STANDARDS. Selective. Accepts about 65% of all applicants. Number of applications 210 (n/a out-of-state); number interviewed 156 (0 out-of-state); number of acceptance n/a (n/a out-of-state); number enrolled 105 (0 out-of-state). Mean Composite MCAT 9.1; mean UGPA 3.64.

FINANCIAL AID. Scholarships and loans available to medical students; research fellowships and teaching/research assistantships for graduate programs. Apply to Division of Student Services and Records for scholarships and loans, to appropriate department chair for fellowships and assistantships; no specified closing date, April 15 suggested. Use FAFSA (School code: 004688). Approximately 90% of all students receive some form of aid from either school or outside sources.

DEGREE REQUIREMENTS. For M.D.: satisfactory completion of four-year program; advanced standing for work completed at other medical schools considered; all students must record a score on both Step 1 and 2 of USMLE. For M.S., Ph.D.: see graduate degree program at the University of Mississippi.

FIELDS OF GRADUATE STUDY.
Anatomy.
Biochemistry.
Microbiology.
Pathology.
Pharmacology and Toxicology.
Physiology and Biophysics.
Preventive Medicine.

School of Nursing

Graduate program began in 1970. Tuition: full-time resident $4616, nonresident $10,753; per credit, resident $262, nonresident $593. On-campus housing available for single and married students. Average academic year cost: $5500–$6500 (room only). Contact Housing Office for married student information. Phone: (601)984-1490.

Enrollment: full-time 59, part-time 81. Faculty with graduate appointment: full-time 23, part-time 5. Degree conferred: M.S.N.

ADMISSION REQUIREMENTS. Transcript, B.S.N., GRE, license (R.N.), at least one year of nursing experience, one page biography, plan of study, three letters of recommendation required in support of School's application. Online application available. Accepts transfer applicants. Applicants accepted for admission each semester. Apply to Registrar by March 30. Application fee $25. Phone: (601)984-6211; fax: (601)984-5957.

ADMISSION STANDARDS. Selective. Usual minimum average: 2.75 cumulative; 3.0 for nursing courses (A = 4). Combined GRE: 900.

FINANCIAL AID. Grants, Federal Nurse Traineeships, loans. Approved for VA benefits. Apply to Director of Student Financial Aid; no specified closing date. Preferred date April 1. Phone: (601) 984-1117; fax: (601)984-1099. Use FAFSA (School code: 004688). Aid available for part-time students.

DEGREE REQUIREMENTS. For M.S.N.: 46–50 credits minimum; accepts up to 9 hours in transfer; thesis or non-thesis option.

FIELDS OF STUDY.
Adult Acute Care.
Family Nurse Practitioner.
Nurse Anesthesia.
Nurse Educator.
Nurse Researcher.
Nursing and Health Care Administrator.
Psych/Mental Health Practitioner.
Note: A R.N.-B.S.N.-M.S.N program is available for qualified students.

MISSOURI UNIVERSITY OF SCIENCE AND TECHNOLOGY

Rolla, Missouri 65409-1060
Web site: www.mst.edu

Founded 1871. Formerly the University of Missouri–Rolla. Name changed 2004. Located 100 miles SW of St. Louis. Coed. State control. Special facilities: nuclear reactor, Graduate Center for Materials Research, Graduate Center for Cloud Physics Research, Rock Mechanics and Explosives Research Center, Institute for River Studies, fully equipped mine for research and study. Library: 440,000 volumes, 1495 subscriptions.

Annual tuition and fees: full-time, resident $7058, midwest student exchange $9641, nonresident $15,229; per credit, resident $263, nonresident $680. On-campus housing for 50 married students, 1340 single students. Average academic year housing cost: $6115 (including board) for single students; $7500 per for married students. Off-campus housing cost: $430–$600 per month. Contact Housing office for on- and off-campus housing information. Phone: (573)341-4218.

Graduate School

Enrollment: full-time 621, part-time 232. University faculty: full-time 238, part-time 52. Degrees conferred: M.S., M.S.T., Ph.D., D.E.

ADMISSION REQUIREMENTS. Official transcripts, GRE/GMAT, three letters of recommendation required in support of School's application. Electronic application available. Interview not required. TOEFL required of international students. Accepts transfer applicants. Graduates of unaccredited institutions not considered. Apply to the Admission Office by July 15 (Fall), December 1 (Spring), May 1 (Summer). Rolling admissions process. Application fee $50. Phone: (573) 341-4165; fax: (573) 341-4082.

ADMISSION STANDARDS. Competitive for most departments. Usual minimum average: 2.75 (A = 4).

FINANCIAL AID. Academic scholarships, fellowships, teaching and research assistantships, internships, tuition waivers, Federal W/S, loans. Approved for VA benefits. Apply by March 1 to chair of proposed major department for fellowships, assistantships; to Financial Aid Office for all other programs. Phone: (573)341-4282. Use FAFSA. About 35% of students receive aid. Aid available for part-time students.

DEGREE REQUIREMENTS. For M.S.: 30 semester hours with thesis, 33 without thesis; final oral exam. For M.S.T.: 36 semester hours minimum, at least 24 in residence; final written exam; no thesis. For Ph.D., D.E.: about 90 semester hours beyond the bachelor's, at least two semesters in full-time residence; proficiency in foreign language for Ph.D.; dissertation; final oral exam.

FIELDS OF STUDY.
Aerospace Engineering.
Applied and Environmental Biology.
Applied Mathematics. M.S. only.
Biomaterials.
Business Administration.
Ceramic Engineering.
Chemical Engineering.
Chemistry.
Civil Engineering.
Computer Engineering.
Computer Science.
Earth Sciences.
Economics.
Electrical Engineering.
Engineering Management.
Engineering Mechanics.
English.
Environmental Engineering. M.S. only.
Geological Engineering.
Geology and Geophysics.
Geotechnics.
History.
Information Systems and Technology. M.S. only.
Manufacturing Engineering. M.S. only.
Materials Science and Engineering.
Mathematics.
Mechanical Engineering.
Metallurgical Engineering.

Mining Engineering.
Nuclear Engineering.
Petroleum Engineering.
Physics.
Systems Engineering. M.S. only.
Technical Communication.

UNIVERSITY OF MISSOURI— COLUMBIA

Columbia, Missouri 65211
Web site: www.missouri.edu

Founded 1839. Located 120 miles W of St. Louis. CGS and AAU member. Coed. State control. Semester system. Special facilities: Center for Aging, Agricultural Experiment Station Research Farms, Business and Public Administration Research Center, Capsule Pipeline Research Center, Dalton Center for Cardiovascular Research, Financial Research Institute, Freedom of Information Center, Geographic Resource Center, Nuclear Magnetic Resonance Center, Power Electronics Research Center, Research Reactor Center, Center for Research in Social Behavior, Space Sciences Center, Water Resources Research Center; Museums of Anthropology Art and Archaeology, Entomology, Geological Sciences; herbarium; extensive acreage for research in soils, field crops, horticulture; art collections. The University's NIH ranking is 110th among all U.S. institutions with 140 awards/grants valued at $44,559,595. According to The Center at University of Florida, the University is ranked 91st in receipt of Federal Research funds with $84,211,000 and it ranks 67th for total University research expenditures with $205,212,000. The University's endowment assets rank it 82nd, with a value of $570,866,000. In 2004, the University awarded 251 doctorates, which ranked it 59th among all U.S. institutions eligible to award that degree. Five of the University's faculty members have been elected to National Honor Academies and this ranks it 90th among all U.S. institutions. The Library: approximately 3,200,000 volumes, 20,500 subscriptions. Total University enrollment: 27,900.

Tuition: per credit resident $287, nonresident $454. On-campus housing for 352 married students, 2100 single men, 2880 single women. Average academic year housing cost: $4200 (double room, including board). Apartments per month $335–$400 (one-bedroom), $410–$450 (two-bedroom); meal plans $2000–$2800. Apply to Residential Life Office. Phone: (573)882-7275.

Graduate School

Graduate study since 1846. Enrollment: full-time 1813, part-time 1651. Faculty: full-time 1179, part-time 35. Degrees conferred: M.A., M.S., M.Acc., M.P.A., M.H.A., M.H.S., M.A.P.E., M.S.W., M.S.P.H., M.B.A., M.S.T., M.F.A., M.Ed., M.M., Ed.Sp., Ed.D., Ph.D.

ADMISSION REQUIREMENTS. Transcripts required in support of School's application. GRE/GMAT/MAT, recommendations required by some departments. Interview not required. TOEFL required for international applicants. Accepts transfer students. Graduates of unaccredited institutions not considered. Apply to Director of Admissions by July 1 (Fall), December 1 (Winter), May 1 (Summer). Two-part application process; 1 application for Graduate School, second part for departments. Some departmental application deadlines may be earlier. Application fee $45, $60 for international applicants. Phone: (573)882-3292.

ADMISSION STANDARDS. Very selective for most departments, selective to very competitive for others. Usual minimum average: 3.0 (A = 4).

FINANCIAL AID. Annual awards from institutional funds: academic scholarships/fellowships, teaching assistantships, research assistantships, internships, traineeships, tuition waivers, Federal W/S, loans. Approved for VA benefits. Apply by January 1 to appropriate department chair for assistantships; to Financial Aid Office for all other programs. Phone: (573)882-7506. Use FAFSA (School code: 002516). Aid available for part-time study.

DEGREE REQUIREMENTS. For master's: 30 hours minimum; thesis required for many majors; final written/oral exam. For Ed.Sp.: 30 hours minimum beyond the master's; final written/oral exam. For Ph.D.: 72 credits beyond the bachelor's (all in residence), at least 18 semester hours within an 18-month period; language requirements vary by department; comprehensive exam; dissertation; final oral exam. For Ed.D.: 82 hours minimum beyond the bachelor's (all in residence), at least 18 semester hours within an 18-month period; knowledge of statistics; matriculation exam; no language requirement; dissertation; final oral exam.

FIELDS OF STUDY.

COLLEGE OF AGRICULTURE, FOOD, AND NATURAL RESOURCES:
Agricultural Economics.
Agricultural Education.
Agronomy.
Animal Sciences.
Biochemistry.
Biological Engineering.
Crop, Soil, and Pest Management.
Entomology.
Fisheries and Wildlife Sciences.
Food Science.
Forestry.
Horticulture.
Park, Recreation, and Tourism. M.S. only.
Plant Biology and Genetics.
Plant Microbiology and Plant Sciences.
Rural Sociology.
Soil and Atmospheric Sciences.

COLLEGE OF ARTS AND SCIENCE:
Anthropology.
Applied Mathematics. M.S. only.
Art.
Art History and Archaeology.
Biological Sciences.
Chemistry.
Classical Studies.
Economics.
English.
French.
Geography. M.A. only.
Geological Sciences.
German. M.A. only.
History. M.A. only.
Mathematics.
Music.
Philosophy.
Physics.
Political Science.
Psychological Sciences. Includes clinical psychology, cognition and neurosience psychology, development psychology, quantitative psychology, social psychology.
Religious Studies. M.A. only.
Russian. M.A. only.
Sociology.
Spanish.
Statistics.
Theatre.

ROBERT J. TRULASKE, SR. COLLEGE OF BUSINESS:
Accountancy. M.Acc., Ph.D.
Business. Ph.D. only.
Business Administration. M.B.A.
Finance. Ph.D.
Management. Includes organizational sciences. Ph.D.
Marketing. Ph.D.

COLLEGE OF EDUCATION:
Art Education.
Autism.
Behavioral Disorders.
Business and Marketing Education. M.Ed. only.
Counseling Psychology.
Cross Categorical Disabilities.
Curriculum Development, Learners with Disabilities. Ed.S. only.
Early Childhood Education.
Early Childhood Special Education.
Educational Administration. Ph.D. only.
Educational Leadership.
Educational Psychology.
Educational Technology.
Elementary Education.
English Education.
Gifted Education.
Health Education and Promotion.
Higher and Continuing Education.
Information Science and Learning Technologies. Ph.D. only.
Learning Disabilities.
Library Science. M.A. only.
Mathematics Education.
Music Education.
Principal Preparation.
Reading and Literacy Education.
School Psychology.
Science Education.
Social Studies Education.
Superintendent Preparation. Ed.S. only.

COLLEGE OF ENGINEERING:
Biological Engineering.
Chemical Engineering.
Civil and Environmental Engineering.
Computer Engineering. M.S. only.
Computer Science. M.S. only.
Electrical and Computer Engineering. Ph.D.
Electrical Engineering.
Industrial Engineering.
Mechanical and Aerospace Engineering.
Nuclear Engineering.

GRADUATE SCHOOL (INTERDIVISIONAL):
Dispute Resolution.
Genetics Program. Ph.D. only
Neuroscience.
Research Resource.

HARRY S. TRUMAN SCHOOL OF PUBLIC AFFAIRS:
Public Administration.

COLLEGE OF HUMAN ENVIRONMENTAL SCIENCES:
Apparel Marketing and Merchandising.
Apparel Product Development and Management.
Architectural Studies.
Child Development and Education.
Child Life Specialist.
Dietetics.
E-Consumer Studies.
Family Studies.
Human Development.

Human Environmental Sciences. Ph.D. only.
Interior Design.
International Apparel Marketing and Merchandising.
International Apparel Product Development and Management.
Nutrition and Fitness.
Nutritional Sciences.
Personal Financial Planning. Also available online.
Personal Financial Management.
Social Work. M.S.W., Ph.D.

SCHOOL OF JOURNALISM:
Journalism. Includes advertising, broadcast news, design, editing, environmental reporting, international, magazine, media management, new media, news media and society, photo journalism, public policy, reporting/writing.
Journalism-Law Program.

SCHOOL OF LAW:
Dispute Resolution. LL.M.

SCHOOL OF MEDICINE:
Biochemistry.
Health Administration. M.H.A. only.
Health Informatics. M.S. only.
Microbiology—Medicine.
Pathology. M.S. only.
Pharmacology.
Physiology.
Public Health. M.S. only.

SINCLAIR SCHOOL OF NURSING:
Nursing. Also available online. M.S.N.
Nursing. Ph.D.

SCHOOL OF HEALTH PROFESSIONS:
Communication Science and Disorders. M.H.S.
Diagnostic Medical Ultrasound.
Health Psychology.
Occupational Therapy and Occupational Science. M.O.T.
Physical Therapy. M.P.T., D.P.T.
Speech Language Pathology.

COLLEGE OF VETERINARY MEDICINE:
Biomedical Sciences. M.S. only.
Laboratory Animal Medicine.
Pathobiology Area Program. Ph.D. only.
Physiology Area Program. Ph.D. only.
Veterinary Biomedical Sciences.
Veterinary Clinical Sciences.
Veterinary Pathobiology.

School of Law
Web site: www.law.missouri.edu

Established 1872. ABA approved since 1923. AALS charter member. Semester system. Special facility: Center for the Study of Dispute Resolution. Law library: 363,074 volumes, 3138 subscriptions; has LEXIS, WESTLAW, INFOTRAC, LUMIN/OCLC.

Annual tuition: resident $14,752; nonresident $28,175. On-campus housing available, but most law students live off-campus in local apartments. Total average annual additional expense: $14,592.

Enrollment: first year class 150, total full-time 446 (men 63%, women 37%, minorities 12%). Faculty: full-time 36, part-time 8. Student to faculty ratio 13.2 to 1. Degrees conferred: J.D., J.D.-M.A. (Consumer and Family Economics, Educational Leadership and Policy, Human Development and Family Studies, Journalism, Library and Information Science), J.D.-M.B.A., J.D.-M.P.A., LL.M. (Dispute Resolution).

ADMISSION REQUIREMENTS. LSDAS Law School report, bachelor's degree, transcripts, LSAT, personal statement, résumé, two letters of recommendation required in support of application. Interview not required. Accepts transfer applicants. Graduates of unaccredited colleges not considered. Apply to Admissions Office, preferably by March 1. Students accepted for Fall only. Application fee $50. Phone: (573)882-6042; fax: (573)882-9625. For LL.M.: phone: (573)882-2020.

ADMISSION STANDARDS. Selective. Accepts 32% of total annual applicants. Number of applicants 977; number of acceptance 314; number enrolled 150; LSAT (75% of class have a score at or above 156); GPA (75% of class have a GPA at or above 3.31). *U.S. News & World Report* ranking is in the second tier (tied at 66th) of all U.S. law schools.

FINANCIAL AID. Scholarships, assistantships, Federal W/S, loans. Apply to School of Law Scholarship Committee by March 1. Phone: (573)882-6643. Use FAFSA (School code: 002516). About 38% of students receive aid other than loans from School.

DEGREE REQUIREMENTS. For J.D.: 89 hours minimum, at least two years in residence. For LL.M.: successful completion of 24-credit program.
Note: On\e-semester study abroad program in London, England; Bucerius University, Hamburg, Germany, available for second- and third-year students.

School of Medicine
Web site: www.muhealth.org/~medicine

Founded 1872 as a two-year school, expanded to four-year school in 1956. Library: 190,000 volumes, 2000 subscriptions. NIH ranking is 110th among all U.S. institutions with 140 awards/grants worth $44,559,595.

Annual tuition: resident $22,987, nonresident $44,749. On-campus housing available. Apply to Housing Office. Total average figure for all other expenses: $16,000.

Enrollment: first-year class 96 (EDP 3), total 370 (men 51%, women 49%, minorities 19%, state residents 98%), postgraduates 317. Faculty: full-time 451, part-time 91. Degrees conferred: M.D., M.D.-M.S., M.D.-Ph.D. The M.S. and Ph.D. are offered through the Graduate School.

ADMISSION REQUIREMENTS. AMCAS report, transcripts, letters of recommendation, MCAT required in support of application. Applicants must have completed at least three years of college study. Interview by invitation only. Has EDP; apply between June 1 and August 1. Preference given to Missouri residents. Accepts transfer applicants into third year and applicants must have a passing score on Step 1 of USMLE. Apply to Assistant Dean after June 1, before November 1. Application fee $75. Phone: (573) 882-9219; fax: (573)884-2988.

ADMISSION STANDARDS. Competitive. Accepts about 17% of all applicants. Number of applications 959 (557 out-of-state); number interviewed 301 (76 out-of-state); number of acceptance 155 (30 out-of-state); number enrolled 96 (10 out-of-state). Mean Composite MCAT 10.0; mean UGPA 3.77.

FINANCIAL AID. Scholarships, Federal and private loans. Apply to Financial Aid Office after acceptance. Phone: (573)882-2923. Use FAFSA (School code: 002516). About 85% of students receive some aid from School.

DEGREE REQUIREMENTS. For M.D.: satisfactory completion of four-year program and passing Step 2 of USMLE for graduation. For M.S., Ph.D.: see Graduate School listing above.

FIELDS OF GRADUATE STUDY.
Biochemistry.
Immunology.
Microbiology.
Pharmacology.
Physiology.
Psychology.

College of Veterinary Medicine
Web site: vetmed.missouri.edu

Established 1949. Semester system.
Annual tuition: resident $15,754, nonresident $30,126. On-campus housing available. Total average expenses for both on- and off-campus housing: $8720. Total average cost for other expenses: $7,200.

Enrollment: first-year class 75, total 450 (men 22%, women 78%, minorities 6%, state residents 78%), postgraduate 65. Faculty: full-time 111, part-time 2. Degrees conferred: D.V.M., M.S., M.V.S., Ph.D., D.V.M.-M.S. The M.S. and Ph.D. are offered through the Graduate School.

ADMISSION REQUIREMENTS. UMCAS report, transcripts, MCAT or GRE (must be received by February 1), two recommendations, animal/veterinary experience, essay, interview required in support of application. For combined programs, a bachelor's degree is required. Accepts transfer applicants on a space-available basis. Will consider American students with two years in foreign college of veterinary medicine. Graduates of unaccredited colleges not considered. Applicants must have completed at least two years of preprofessional college study. Preference given to state residents; Utah and Arkansas residents. Apply to Dean, School of Veterinary Medicine after September 1, before November 1. Fall admission only. Application fee $50. Phone: (573)882-3554.

ADMISSION STANDARDS. Selective. Accepts about 25–30% of all applicants. Number of applications 585 (462 out-of-state); number interviewed n/a (n/a out-of-state); number of acceptance n/a (n/a out-of-state); number enrolled 75 (17 out-of-state). Usual minimum UGPA: 3.0 (A = 4). GRE mean score (V + Q) 1130; mean UGPA 3.68.

FINANCIAL AID. Scholarships, fellowships, assistantships, internships, tuition waivers, Federal W/S, loans, grants. Apply to Director of Student Aids; no specified closing date. Phone: (573) 882-1600. Use FAFSA.

DEGREE REQUIREMENTS. For D.V.M.: satisfactory completion of four-year program. For M.S., Ph.D.: see Graduate School listing above.

FIELDS OF GRADUATE STUDY.
Biomedical Sciences. Multidisciplinary. Includes molecular, cellular organ, integrative biology. Ph.D. only.
Comparative Medicine. Includes infectious disease, pathology, molecular biology, mouse biology, cardiovascular physiology. M.S., Ph.D.
Veterinary Medicine and Surgery. Includes comparative orthopaedics and oncology; food animal, equine, and small animal medicine and surgery; physiology; pharmacology; cell and molecular biology; imaging; neurology; nuclear medicine; ophthalmology; tissue engineering. M.S. , Ph.D.
Veterinary Pathobiology. Includes Veterinary pathobiology (M.S.), laboratory animal medicine (M.S.), pathology, laboratory animal medicine. M.S., Ph.D.

UNIVERSITY OF MISSOURI—KANSAS CITY
Kansas City, Missouri 64110-2499
Web site: www.umkc.edu

Founded 1929. Coed. State control. CGS member. Semester system. Special facilities: Institute for Study in American Music,

Electronic Music Laboratory, Center for Underground Space Studies, Drug Information Center, Biopharmacokinetics Laboratory, Hormone Research Laboratory, Family Study Center, Center for the Study of Metropolitan Problems in Education, Center for Labor Studies, Institute for Human Development. Library: 942,000 volumes, 1,773,000 microforms, 7200 subscriptions. Total University enrollment: 14,300.

Tuition and fees: per credit hour, resident $263, nonresident $679 plus prorated tuition 7–10 hours. On-campus housing for single students only. Average academic year housing cost: $6670 (including board). Contact University Housing Office for both on- and off-campus housing information. Phone: (816)235-2800.

Graduate Studies

Graduate study since 1939. Enrollment: full- and part-time 4606. University faculty teaching graduate students: full-time 489, part-time 233. Degrees conferred: M.A., M.S., M.A. in Ed., M.Ed., M.B.A., M.P.A., LL.M., M.M., M.M.Ed., Ed.S., D.M.A., Ph.D.

ADMISSION REQUIREMENTS. Two official transcripts, GRE/GMAT required in support of application. Interview not required. TOEFL required of international applicants whose first language is not English. Accepts transfer applicants. Graduates of unaccredited institutions not considered. Apply to the Admissions Office by February 1 (Summer and Fall), September 1 (Winter). Application fee: $35, $50 for international applicants. Phone: (816)235-1111; fax: (816)235-5544.

ADMISSION STANDARDS. Selective for some departments, competitive for most departments. Usual minimum average: 3.0; probationary status: 2.75 (A = 4).

FINANCIAL AID. Chancellor nonresident awards, scholarships, teaching assistantships, internships, full and partial fee waiver, Federal W/S, loans. Apply by March 1 to appropriate department chair for assistantships, scholarships; to the Financial Aid Office for all other programs. Use FAFSA. About 10% of students receive aid other than loans from University. No aid for part-time students.

DEGREE REQUIREMENTS. For M.A., M.S.: 30 semester hours minimum, at least 24 in residence; reading knowledge of one foreign language for some departments; qualifying exam for many departments; thesis/nonthesis option; final master's competency written/oral exam. For M.A. in Ed., M.Ed.: 30 semester hours minimum, at least 24 in residence; thesis not required. For M.B.A.: 36 hours minimum or 43 hours minimum, depending upon previous education, at least 30 or 37 hours in residence; thesis sometimes required for 6 hours. For M.P.A.: 36 hours minimum, at least 30 in residence; thesis optional for 6 hours. For LL.M.: 24 hours minimum beyond the J.D.; thesis for 8 hours. For M.M.: 30 semester hours minimum, at least 24 in residence, qualifying exam sometimes required; thesis/recital/research project; final oral/written exam. For M.M.Ed.: 30 semester hours minimum, at least 24 in residence; thesis for 4–6 hours; final written/oral exam. For Ed.S.: 60 hours minimum beyond the bachelor's, at least 20 in residence and one semester in full-time attendance; field project; final oral exam; offered in counseling and guidance, educational administration, and reading. For Ph.D.: usually 90 hours minimum beyond the bachelor's, at least 45 hours in residence and two consecutive semesters, one summer session in full-time attendance; qualifying exam; reading knowledge of two foreign languages or one language and one other acceptable research tool; comprehensive exam; dissertation; final oral exam. For D.M.A., Ed.D.: essentially the same as for the Ph.D., except composition/recitals may replace thesis in appropriate fields.

FIELDS OF STUDY.
Accounting. M.S. only.
Anesthetics. M.S. only.

Art. Includes art history, graphic design, photography. Portfolio and interview required. M.A. only.
Biology. M.A., M.S. only.
Business Administration. GMAT for admission. M.B.A. only.
Cellular and Molecular Biology.
Chemistry. Includes analytical, inorganic, organic, physical. M.S., Ph.D.
Computer Science. M.S.
Counseling and Guidance. M.A.
Counseling Psychology.
Criminal Justice and Criminology. M.S.
Curriculum and Instruction.
Dental Hygiene Education. B.S. in dental hygiene for admission. M.S. only.
Dentistry. Includes anatomy, biochemistry, microbiology, oral histology and embryology, oral medicine and diagnosis, oral radiology, periodontics, restorative dentistry, oral surgery, orthodontics, pedodontics, prosthodontics, oral pathology; D.D.S. for admission. M.S. only.
Economics. GRE for admission. M.A., Ph.D.
Education. Includes elementary and secondary curriculum and instruction, administration and community leadership, adult foundations and philosophy of education. M.A., Ed.S.; Ph.D. in curriculum and instruction, administration and community leadership, counseling, and guidance.
Engineering. Includes civil, electrical, industrial, mechanical; degrees awarded by University of Missouri—Columbia. M.S., Ph.D.
English Language and Literature. One language for M.A. M.A., Ph.D.
Environmental and Urban Geosciences.
Health Psychology.
History. M.A., Ph.D.
Liberal Studies.
Mathematics and Statistics. M.S., Ph.D.
Microbiology. Interdivisional. M.S. only.
Molecular Biology and Biochemistry. Ph.D.
Music. Includes applied music, history & literature, theory, composition, conducting, performance, sacred music, music education; GRE Subject, audition for admission. M.M., Ph.D.
Nursing. Includes child-care nursing.
Oral Biology. M.S., Ph.D.
Pharmaceutical Sciences. M.S., Ph.D.
Physics. M.S., Ph.D.
Political Science. GRE for admission. M.A., Ph.D.
Psychology. M.A.
Public Administration. GRE for admission. M.P.A. only.
Reading. M.Ed.
Romance Languages and Literature. M.A. only.
Social Sciences.
Social Work.
Sociology. M.A.
Special Education. M.Ed.
Studio Art.
Theater. Includes acting, directing, design and technology. Production thesis or new play may replace thesis. M.A. only.

School of Dentistry
Web site: www.umkc.edu/dentistry

Founded 1881. In 1963 Dental School joined University of Missouri. Semester system.

Annual tuition: resident $25,094, nonresident $45,766. No on-campus housing available. Average academic year off-campus housing costs: $12,000–$15,000. Contact Office of Student Support Services for housing information. Phone: (816)235-1428. Total average cost for all other first-year expenses: $8500.

Enrollment: first-year class 86; total 396 (men 60%, women 40%, minorities 11%, state residents 85%). Faculty: full-time 99, part-time 67. Degree conferred: D.D.S., Certificates. The M.S. and Ph.D. are offered through the School of Graduate Studies.

ADMISSION REQUIREMENTS. AADSAS report, official transcripts, DAT (no later than October), three letters of recommendation required in support of School's application. Interviews of students under serious consideration are required. Applicants must have completed at least two years of college study. Accepts transfer applicants on a space available basis only. Preference given to residents of Missouri, Arkansas, Kansas, New Mexico. Apply to Office of Student Affairs after June 1, before January 1. Application fee $35, $50 for international applicants. Phone: (816)235-2080 (local), (800)776-8652; fax: (816)235-2157.

ADMISSION STANDARDS. Selective. Accepts about 15–20% of all applicants. Usual minimum UGPA: 2.70 (A = 4). Mean DAT: academic 18, PAT 17; mean UGPA 3.60.

FINANCIAL AID. Limited scholarships, grants, loans. Apply to Student Financial Aid Office. Phone: (816)235-1154. Use FAFSA (School code: G24821). About 90% of students receive some form of financial assistance.

DEGREE REQUIREMENTS. For D.D.S.: satisfactory completion of forty-month program. For M.S.: see School of Graduate Studies listing above.

FIELDS OF POSTGRADUATE STUDY.
Advanced Education in General Dentistry. Certificate.
Endodontics. Certificate.
Oral and Maxillofacial Radiology. Certificate.
Oral and Maxillofacial Surgery. Certificate.
Oral Biology. M.S., Interdisciplinary Ph.D.
Orthodontics and Dentofacial Orthopedics.
Pediatric Dentistry. Certificate.
Periodontics. Certificate.

School of Law
Web site: www.law.umkc.edu

Founded 1895. ABA approved since 1923. AALS member. Semester system. Law library: 325,344 volumes, 1812 subscriptions; has LEXIS, NEXIS, WESTLAW, DIALOG.

Annual tuition: full-time, resident $13,183; nonresident $25,234; part-time, resident $9486, nonresident $16,800 . No on-campus housing available. Total average annual additional expense: $19,600.

Enrollment: first year class full-time 172, part-time 6, total full- and part-time 489 (men 58%, women 42%, minorities 9%). Faculty: full-time 30, part-time 27. Student-to-faculty ratio is 20.4 to 1. Degrees conferred: J.D., J.D.-M.B.A., J.D.-M.P.A., LL.M. (Taxation, Urban Affairs).

ADMISSION REQUIREMENTS. LSDAS Law School report, bachelor's degree, transcripts, LSAT, personal statement, two letters of recommendation required in support of application. Interview not required. Accepts transfer applicants. Preference given to state residents. Graduates of unaccredited institutions not considered. Apply to Office of the Associate Dean by March 1. Rolling admission process. Fall admission only for beginning law students. Application fee $50. Phone: (816)235-1644; fax (816) 235-5276.

ADMISSION STANDARDS. Selective. Accepts approximately 38% of full-time and 30% of part-time students. Number of full-time applicants 1207, part-time 47; number of acceptance full-time 461, part-time 14; number enrolled full-time 172, part-time 6; LSAT (75% of full-time students have a score at or above 152, part-time 152); GPA (75% of full-time student have a GPA at or above 3.14, part-time 2.76). *U.S. News & World Report* ranking is in the third tier of all U.S. law schools.

FINANCIAL AID. Scholarships, loans. Apply by March 1 to Office of the Dean for scholarships, to University's Financial Aid

Office for loans. Phone: (816)235-1154. Use FAFSA (School code: 002518) and UMKC FAF. About 38% of students receive some form of financial assistance from the school.

DEGREE REQUIREMENTS. For J.D.: 90 credit hours minimum, at least the last year in residence. For LL.M.: at least 24 credit hours beyond the J.D., at least one year in residence. For M.B.A.: see Graduate School listing above.
Note: A one semester study abroad program in China and Ireland available.

School of Medicine
Web site: www.med.umkc.edu

Established 1969. Six-year baccalaureate medical program and a M.D.-only program, which started in 2003.

Annual tuition: resident $28,102, nonresident $53,398. Limited on-campus housing available for married and single students. Total average figure for all other expenses: $15,000.

Enrollment: first-year class 117, total 392 (men 40%, women 60%, minorities 0%, state residents 74%). Faculty: full-time 543, part-time 824. Degrees conferred: B.A.-M.D., M.D.

ADMISSION REQUIREMENTS. Transcripts, ACT, three letters of recommendation, screening interview, supplemental application required in support of application. Preference given to state residents. Accepts a limited number of upper division applicants between the program's second and third years. MCAT required for transfer applicants. Graduates of unaccredited colleges not considered. Apply to Director of Admissions and Registrar after August 1, before November 15. Application fee: resident $35, nonresident $50. Phone: (816)235-1870; fax: (816)235-5277.

ADMISSION STANDARDS. Selective. Accepts about 20–30% of all applicants. Number of applications 536 (n/a out-of-state); number interviewed 245 (n/a out-of-state); number of acceptance n/a (n/a out-of-state); number enrolled 117 (31 out-of-state). Mean Composite MCAT n/a; mean UGPA n/a.

FINANCIAL AID. Scholarships, Federal W/S, Federal and private loans. Apply to University's Financial Aid Office by March 15. Phone: (816)235-1242. Use FAFSA (School code: 002518). About 80% of students receive some form of financial assistance.

DEGREE REQUIREMENTS. For M.D.: satisfactory completion of six-year program; all students must pass USMLE Step 2 prior to awarding of M.D.

UNIVERSITY OF MISSOURI— ST. LOUIS
St. Louis, Missouri 63121-4499
Web site: www.umsl.edu/

Founded 1963. CGS member. Coed. State control. Semester system. Special facilities: Art Gallery 210, Center for Business and Industrial Studies, Center for Humanities, Center for International Studies, Center for Molecular Electronics, Center for Neurodynamics, International Center for Tropical Ecology, Joint Center for East Asian Studies (in cooperation with Washington University), Public Policy Research Center, Center for Trauma Recovery, Center for Transportation Studies, Center for Science and Technology, St. Louis Historical Research Center. Library: 1,100,000 volumes, 3807 subscriptions. Total University enrollment: 15,500.

Tuition: per credit hour, resident $263, nonresident $680. On-campus housing available for single graduate students only. Apartments located approximately three blocks from campus. Average academic year housing cost: $6000 (including board). Day-care facilities available.

Graduate School

Graduate study since 1968. Enrollment: full-time 443, part-time 1910 (men 35%, women 65%). Faculty: full-time 401. Degrees conferred: M.A., M.S., M.B.A., M.M.E., M.Ed., M.P.P.A., M.Acc., Ed.D., Ph.D.

ADMISSION REQUIREMENTS. Transcripts, GRE/GMAT required in support of School's application. Online application available. TOEFL required of all foreign students. Accepts transfer applicants. Graduates of unaccredited colleges not considered. Apply to Director of Admissions by July 1 (Fall), December 1 (Spring), May 1 (Summer); Clinical Psychology, doctoral programs, M.F.A. programs have earlier deadlines. Application fee $35, $40 for international applicants. Phone: (314)516-5458; fax: (314)516-5310; e-mail: gradadm@umsl.edu.

ADMISSION STANDARDS. Selective. Usual minimum average: 2.75 (A = 4).

FINANCIAL AID. Annual awards from institutional funds: scholarships, teaching assistantships, research assistantships, graduate-school-funded dissertation fellowships, summer research fellowships, internships, Federal W/S, loans. Approved for VA benefits. Apply by July 1 to department chair for fellowships, assistantships; to Financial Aid Office for all other programs. Phone: (314)516-5526; fax: (314)516-5310. Use FAFSA. Aid available for part-time students.

DEGREE REQUIREMENTS. For master's: 30 credits minimum, at least 21 credits in residence; thesis required by some departments; final written/oral exam. For Ph.D.: at least three academic years of full-time study or equivalent, at least two years in residence; two consecutive semesters full-time; qualifying exam; reading knowledge of two foreign languages or one language and one research skill; dissertation; final exam.

FIELDS OF STUDY.
Accounting.
Applied Mathematics. Ph.D.
Biochemistry and Biotechnology. M.S. only.
Biology. M.S., Ph.D.
Business Administration. GMAT for admission; 39–60 credits. M.B.A., M.S., M.Acc.
Chemistry. M.S., Ph.D.
Communications.
Computer Science.
Counseling.
Creative Writing.
Criminology and Criminal Justice. M.A., Ph.D.
Economics. M.A. only.
Education. Includes counseling, educational administration, elementary education, secondary education, special education, learning-instructional processes, and behavioral developmental processes. M.Ed., Ed.D., Ph.D.
English. M.A. only.
Gerontology. M.A. only.
History. M.A. only.
Information Systems.
Logistics and Supply Chain Management. Ph.D.
Mathematics. M.A.
Museum Studies.
Music Education. M.M.E. only.
Nursing. M.S., Ph.D.
Philosophy.
Physics. M.S., Ph.D.
Physiological Optics. M.S., Ph.D.
Political Science. Includes urban and regional politics, American politics, political process and behavior, international public administration, M.A.; politics, comparative politics, Ph.D.

Psychology. Includes behavior, clinical, industrial/organizational. M.A., Ph.D.
Public Policy Administration. Includes policy analysis, public administration, management, accounting and economics.
School Psychology. Ed.S..
Social Work.
Sociology. M.A. only.
Special Education.

MONMOUTH UNIVERSITY
West Long Branch, New Jersey 07764-1898
Web site: www.monmouth.edu

Founded in 1933. Located 50 miles S of New York City, 75 miles NE of Philadelphia. Private control. Semester system. Library: 248,000 volumes, 1300 subscriptions. Total University enrollment: 6000.

Tuition: per credit hour $673. Limited on-campus housing for graduate students but available for international students. Annual academic year housing cost: $4500–$5500. For off-campus housing contact Office of Student Services. Phone: (732)571-3465.

Graduate School

Graduate study since 1967. Enrollment: full- and part-time 1800. Degrees conferred: M.B.A., M.A., M.A.L.A., M.S., M.A.T., M.S.Ed.

ADMISSION REQUIREMENTS. Transcripts, two letters of recommendation, GRE, GMAT Test (for M.B.A.) required in support of application. TOEFL required for foreign applicants. Accepts transfer applicants. Graduates of unaccredited institutions not considered. Apply to Director of Graduate Admissions by August 15 (Fall), November 15 (Spring). Rolling admissions process. Application fee $35. Phone: (732)571-3452; (800)320-7754; fax: (732)263-5123; e-mail: gradadm@ monmouth.edu.

ADMISSION STANDARDS. Selective. Usual minimum average: 2.5 overall, 3.0 in major. For M.B.A. program only: GPA x 200 + GMAT = 1000.

FINANCIAL AID. Research assistantships, internships, tuition waivers, Federal W/S, loans. Apply by March 1 to Financial Aid Office. Phone: (732)571-3463; fax: (732)571-3629. Use FAFSA. Aid available for part-time students.

DEGREE REQUIREMENTS. For M.B.A.: 30–60 semester hours depending upon previous preparation. For M.S. Computer Science: 33 semester hours. For M.S. Software Engineering: 36 semester hours depending upon previous preparation. For M.S. Electronic Engineering: 30 semester hours. For M.A.L.A., M.A. (History): 36 semester hours. For M.A.T. with certification, M.A.T. Advanced, M.S.Ed. Student Personnel Services: 36 semester hours. For M.S.N.: 40 semester hours. For the M.A. Psychological Counseling: 30 semester hours. For the M.A. Criminal Justice: 36 semester hours.

FIELDS OF STUDY.
Business Administration. Includes health care management. M.B.A.
Computer Science. M.S.
Corporate and Public Communications.
Criminal Justice. M.A.
Education. Includes elementary, secondary, supervision, principal, school administrator, school business administrator, special education, student personnel services, reading. M.S.Ed.
Educational Counseling. M.S.Ed.
Electronic Engineering. M.S.

History. M.A.
Liberal Arts. M.A.L.A.
Nursing. M.S.N.
Professional Counseling. M.A.
Psychological Counseling. M.A.
Public Policy. M.A.
Reading Specialist Studies.
Social Work. M.S.W.
Software Engineering. M.S.
Special Education.

Public Administration. M.P.A.
Public Relation. M.S.P.R.

COLLEGE OF EDUCATION AND HUMAN SERVICES:
Curriculum and Instruction (K–8). M.Ed.
Early Childhood. M.Ed.
Educational Technology. M.Ed.
Interdisciplinary Studies. M.Ed.
Reading. M.Ed.
School Counseling (K–12). M.Ed.
Special Education. M.S.S.E.
Sport Management. M.S.S.M.

MONTANA STATE UNIVERSITY
Billings, Montana 59101-0298
Web site: www.msubillings.edu

Founded 1927. Coed. State control. Semester system. Special facilities: Montana Center for Disabilities, Native American Cultural Institute, Red Mountain Biological Field Station. Library: 488,000 volumes, 2000 subscriptions. Total University enrollment: 4900.

Annual tuition: resident $4626, nonresident $10,800. On-campus housing for graduate men, women; none for married students. Average academic year housing cost: $3000–$6000. Apply to Director of Resident Life for both on-campus housing and off-campus information. Phone: (408)657-2333.

Graduate Studies

Established 1954. Enrollment: full-time 200, part-time 325. University faculty teaching graduate students: full-time 72. Degrees conferred: M.Ed., M.S.Psyc., M.S.P.R., M.S.R.M.H.C., M.S.S.E., M.S.R.C., M.S.I.P.C., M.S.S.M.

ADMISSION REQUIREMENTS. Transcripts, GRE/MAT required in support of application. Online application available. TOEFL and certified statement of support required for international applicants. Accepts transfer applicants. Graduates of unaccredited institutions not considered. Apply to Office of Graduate Studies at least six weeks prior to registration. Application fee $40. Phone: (406)657-2053; fax: (406)657-2299.

ADMISSION STANDARDS. Selective for most departments. Usual minimum average: 3.0 (A = 4).

FINANCIAL AID. Annual awards from institutional funds: scholarships, grants, graduate assistantships, Federal W/S, loans. Approximately thirty resident fee waivers and five nonresident fee waivers available. Approved for VA benefits. Apply to Director of Graduate Studies for scholarships, assistantships; to Office of Financial Aid for all other programs. Phone: (406)657-2188; fax: (406)657-2302. Use FAFSA. About 30% of students receive aid other than loans from both University funds and outside sources.

DEGREE REQUIREMENTS. For M.Ed., M.S.: 36–45 semester hours minimum, at least 30 in residence; thesis/nonthesis options. For M.S.R.C.: 60 semester hours.

FIELDS OF STUDY.

COLLEGE OF ALLIED HEALTH PROFESSIONS:
Athletic Training. M.S.A.T.
Health Administration. M.H.A.
Rehabilitation and Mental Health Counseling. M.S.R.M.H.C.
Sport, Recreation, and Fitness Management. M.S.S.R.F.M.

COLLEGE OF ARTS AND SCIENCE:
Psychology. M.S. Psyc.

MONTANA STATE UNIVERSITY
Bozeman, Montana 59717
Web site: www.montana.edu

Founded 1893. Located 90 miles N of Yellowstone Park. CGS member. Coed. State control. Semester system. Special facilities: Animal Research Center, Engineering Research Center, Local Government Center, Marsh Laboratory, Water Center. Library: 569,000 volumes, 5000 subscriptions. Total University enrollment: 12,100.

Annual tuition: full-time, resident $4132, nonresident $11,332. On-campus housing for 704 married students, 50 single students. Average academic year housing cost: $5500 (including board) for single students; $6000 for married students. Apply to Housing Office. Phone: (406)994-2661.

College of Graduate Studies

Graduate study since 1898. Enrollment: full-time 535; part-time 741. Graduate faculty: 425, part-time 20. Degrees conferred: M.A., M.Ed., M.N., M.S., Ed.D., Ph.D.

ADMISSION REQUIREMENTS. Transcripts, GRE, three letters of recommendation required in support of College's application. Online application available. Interview may be required by some departments. TOEFL and GRE required for international applicants. Apply to appropriate department by July 15 (Fall), December 1 (Spring), April 1 (Summer). Some departments have earlier deadlines. Late applicants considered as nondegree students. Rolling admissions process. Application fee $30. Phone: (406)994-4145; fax: (406)994-4733; e-mail: gradstudy@montana.edu.

ADMISSION STANDARDS. Selective. Usual minimum average: 3.0 (A = 4).

FINANCIAL AID. Annual awards from institutional funds: scholarships, fellowships, teaching assistantships, research assistantships, internships, grants, Federal W/S, loans. Approved for VA benefits. Apply by March 1 to appropriate department chair for fellowships, assistantships; to Financial Aid Office for all other programs. Phone: (406)994-2845; fax: (406)994-6962. Use FAFSA. About 70% of students receive aid from College and outside sources. Aid available for part-time students.

DEGREE REQUIREMENTS. For master's Plan A: 30-credit program; one foreign language for some programs; thesis. For master's Plan B: 30-credit program; professional paper or project. For Ed.D.: 44 credits beyond the master's, at least 30 credits in residence; qualifying exam may be required; reading knowledge of one foreign language required by some departments; written/oral comprehensive exam; thesis; final written/oral exam. For Ph.D.: normally three years minimum beyond the bachelor's, at least 48 credits in residence; qualifying exam may be required; language requirements vary by department; oral/

written comprehensive exam; dissertation; final written/oral exam.

FIELDS OF STUDY.

COLLEGE OF AGRICULTURE:
Agricultural Education.
Animal and Range Sciences.
Entomology.
Land Resources and Environmental Sciences.
Land Rehabilitation.
Plant Pathology.
Plant Science. Includes plant genetics.
Veterinary Molecular Biology.

COLLEGE OF ARTS AND ARCHITECTURE:
Architecture.
Art.
Science and Natural History Filmmaking.

COLLEGE OF BUSINESS:
Professional Accountancy.

COLLEGE OF EDUCATION, HEALTH AND HUMAN DEVELOPMENT:
Adult and Higher Education.
Counseling.
Curriculum and Instruction.
Education Administration.
Exercise and Nutrition Science.
Family and Consumer Sciences.
Health Promotion and Education.
School Counseling.

COLLEGE OF ENGINEERING:
Chemical Engineering.
Civil Engineering.
Computer Science.
Construction Engineering Management.
Electrical Engineering.
Engineering.
Environmental Engineering.
Industrial and Management Engineering.
Mechanical Engineering.

COLLEGE OF LETTERS AND SCIENCE:
Applied Economics.
Applied Psychology.
Biochemistry.
Biological Sciences.
Chemistry.
Earth Sciences.
Ecological and Environmental Statistics.
English.
Fish and Wildlife Management.
History.
Mathematics.
Microbiology.
Native American Studies.
Neuroscience.
Physics.
Public Administration.
Statistics.

COLLEGE OF NURSING:
Nursing. Includes clinical nurse specialist, family health practitioner.

INTERCOLLEGE:
Land Rehabilitation.
Science Education.

MONTANA TECH OF THE UNIVERSITY OF MONTANA
Butte, Montana 59701-8997
Web site: www.mtech.edu

Founded in 1900. Located 300 miles E of Spokane, Washington, and 400 miles N of Salt Lake City. Coed. State control. Semester system. Special facilities: Mineral Research Center for Advanced Mining Processing, Montana Bureau of Mines and Geology. Library: 165,700 volumes, 1200 subscriptions. Total Campus enrollment: 2230.

Annual tuition: full-time, resident $5133, nonresident $15,746. On-campus housing limited. Housing for married students both on- and off-campus. Average academic year housing cost: $4738 double (includes board) for single students; $3800 for married students (60 apartments on campus). Apply to Director, Resident Life. Phone: (406)496-4425. Day-care facilities available.

Graduate School

Graduate study since 1929. Enrollment: full-time 62, part-time 35. Faculty teaching graduate students: full-time 36, part-time 6. Degree conferred: M.S.

ADMISSION REQUIREMENTS. Transcripts, GRE Subject Tests, three references required in support of application. Interview not required. TOEFL required for international applicants. Accepts transfer applicants. Apply to Administrator of Graduate School before March 31. Application fee $30 (for U.S./Canada), $90 for international applicants. Phone: (406)496-4304; fax: (406)496-4710.

ADMISSION STANDARDS. Very competitive. Usual minimum average: 3.0 (A = 4).

FINANCIAL AID. Annual awards from institutional funds: fellowships, teaching assistantships, research assistantships, fee waivers, Federal W/S, loans. Approved for VA benefits. Apply by April 1 to Administrator, Graduate School. Phone: (406)496-4212; fax: (406)496-4133. Use FAFSA and institutional FAF. Aid available for part-time students.

DEGREE REQUIREMENTS. For M.S. (thesis required): 30 semester hours. For M.S. (nonthesis): 36 semester hours.

FIELDS OF STUDY.
Environmental Engineering.
Geochemistry.
Geological Engineering.
Geology.
Geophysical Engineering.
Hydrogeological Engineering.
Industrial Hygiene.
Metallurgical/Mineral Processing Engineering.
Mining Engineering.
Petroleum Engineering.
Project Engineering and Management. Joint program with Montana State University.
Technical Communications. In affiliation with University of Montana.

UNIVERSITY OF MONTANA
Missoula, Montana 59812
Web site: www.umt.edu

Established 1893. CGS member. Coed. State control. Semester system. Special facilities: University Biological Station, Wood

Chemistry Laboratories, Animal Behavior Laboratory, Bureau of Business and Economic Research, Computer Center, Lubrecht Forestry Camp, Montana Forest and Conservation Experiment Station, Performing Arts and Radio/TV Center, Institute for Social Science Research, Bureau of Government Research, Wildlife Research Unit, Division of Educational Research and Services, Bureau of Press and Broadcasting, Stella Duncan Memorial Institute for Respiratory Disease Research Center, Mansfield Center of Ethics and Asian Affairs. Library: 700,000 volumes, 6248 subscriptions. Total University enrollment: 13,602.

Tuition: per credit resident $267, nonresident $665. On-campus housing for 394 married students, limited number for single graduate students. Average per month housing cost: $400–$650 for married students; academic year housing cost for single students: $2500–$4000. Apply to Family Housing Office. Phone: (406) 549-0134 (married students); to Off-Campus Housing Clearinghouse. Phone: (406)243-4636 (off-campus housing information).

Graduate School

Enrollment: full-time 678, part-time 549 (men 50%, women 50%). Faculty: full-time 380, part-time 109. Degrees conferred: M.A., M.Acc., M.A.S., M.A.T., M.B.A., M.Ed., M.F., M.S.T., M.M.Ed., M.I.S., M.F.A., M.M., M.P.A., M.S., Ed.S., Ed.D., Ph.D.

ADMISSION REQUIREMENTS. One official transcript, GRE, three letters of recommendation required in support of School's application. Online application available. GMAT required for business. Interview not required. TOEFL required for international applicants. Accepts transfer applicants. Graduates of unaccredited institutions not considered. Apply to department concerned at least two months prior to registration. Some departments have earlier deadlines. Application fee $45. Phone: (406)243-2572; fax: (406)243-4593.

ADMISSION STANDARDS. Very competitive for some departments, competitive or selective for others. Usual minimum average: 3.0 (A = 4).

FINANCIAL AID. Annual awards from institutional funds: scholarships, research assistantships, teaching assistantships, internship, grants, Federal W/S, loans. Approved for VA benefits. Apply by March 1 to department for assistantships; to Financial Aid Office for all other programs. Phone: (406)243-5373. Use FAFSA. About 40% of students receive aid other than loans from School and outside sources. Aid sometimes available for part-time students.

DEGREE REQUIREMENTS. For master's: 30 semester credits minimum, at least 12 in residence; final oral/written exam; thesis/final project; reading knowledge of one foreign language required by some departments. For Ed.D.: 90 semester credits minimum, at least 30 in residence; comprehensive exam; dissertation; final oral exam. For Ph.D.: three years minimum beyond the bachelor's, at least three semesters in residence; language requirement varies with department; comprehensive exam; dissertation; final oral exam.

FIELDS OF STUDY.
Accounting. M.Acc.
Anthropology. Includes cultural heritage, forensic linguistics. M.A.
Art. Includes art (M.A.), integrated arts and education (M.A.), art history (M.F.A.), ceramics (M.F.A.), painting and drawing (M.F.A.), photography (M.F.A.), printmaking (M.F.A.), sculpture (M.F.A.). Portfolio for admission to M.F.A. program. M.A., M.F.A.
Biochemistry. M.S.
Biochemistry-Microbiology. Includes microbial ecology. Ph.D. only.
Biological Sciences. M.S.T.
Biomedical Sciences. Ph.D..

Business Administration. M.B.A.
Chemistry. Includes analytical/environmental, inorganic, organic, physical, teaching. M.S., M.S.T.C., Ph.D.
Communication Studies. M.A.
Computer Science. M.S.
Counselor Education. Includes mental health counseling, school counseling (M.A.). M.A., M.Ed., Ed.S.
Creative Writing. Includes fiction, nonfiction, poetry. M.F.A.
Curriculum and Instruction. Includes curriculum studies, elementary education, library media services, literacy education, secondary education. M.Ed., Ed.D.
Drama. Includes acting, design technology, directing, drama (M.A.). M.A., M.F.A.
Economics. M.A.
Ecosystem Management. M.E.M.
Educational Leadership. M.Ed., Ed.S., Ed.D.
English. Includes literature. M.A.
Environmental Studies. M.S.
Fish and Wildlife Biology. Ph.D.
Foreign Languages. Includes French, German, Spanish. M.A.
Forestry. M.S., Ph.D.
Geography. Includes cartography and GIS, community and environmental planning. M.A.
Geology. M.S., Ph.D.
Health and Human Performance. Includes exercise science, health promotion. M.S.
History. M.A.
Integrative Microbiology and Biochemistry. Ph.D.
Interdisciplinary Studies. Includes individualized interdisciplinary studies (Ph.D.). M.I.S., Ph.D.
Journalism. Includes photojournalism, print, radio and TV. M.A.
Linguistics. Includes applied, general. M.A.
Mathematics. Includes mathematics education, college teaching and general practitioner (Ph.D.), traditional (Ph.D.). M.A., Ph.D.
Media Arts. M.F.A.
Microbiology. Includes microbial ecology. M.S.
Modern Language and Literature. Includes French, German, Spanish. M.A.
Music. Includes music history and literature (M.A.), composition/technology, music education, performance. M.A., M.M.
Organismal Biology and Ecology. M.S., Ph.D.
Pharmacology/Pharmaceutical Sciences. Ph.D.
Pharmacy. M.S.
Philosophy. Includes teaching ethics. M.A.
Physical Therapy. M.S.
Political Science. M.A.
Psychology. Includes animal behavior, clinical, developmental, school. M.A., Ph.D.
Public Administration. M.P.A.
Recreation Management. M.S.
Resource Conservation. Includes international resource management. M.S.
School Psychology. M.A., Ed.S.
Social Work. M.S.W.
Sociology. Includes criminology, rural environmental change. M.A.
Technical Communications. M.S.
Toxicology. Ph.D.
Wildlife Biology. M.S.

School of Law
Web site: www.umt.edu/law

Established 1911. ABA approved since 1923. AALS member since 1914. Semester system. Law library: 125,000 volumes, 1946 subscriptions; has LEXIS, WESTLAW; has more than 100 network connections.

Annual tuition: full-time, resident $9978, nonresident $20,414. On-campus housing available. Total average annual additional expense: $11,764.

Enrollment: first-year class 83; total full-time 251 (men 54%, women 46%, minorities 10%). Faculty: full-time 11, part-time

15. Student to faculty ratio 18.2 to 1. Degrees conferred: J.D., J.D.-M.B.A., J.D.-M.S. (Environmental Studies), J.D.-M.P.A.

ADMISSION REQUIREMENTS. LSDAS Law School report, bachelor's degree, transcripts, LSAT (not later than February), two personal statements, three letters of recommendation required in support of application. Interview not required. Preference given to state residents. Graduates of unaccredited colleges not considered. Apply to Dean of the Law School after September 1, before March 15, applications received after this date will be considered on a space available basis. Fall admission only. Application fee $60. Phone: (406)243-4311.

ADMISSION STANDARDS. Selective. Accepts 38% of total annual applicants. Number of applicants 458; number of acceptance 172; number enrolled 85; LSAT (75% of class have a score at or above 151); GPA (75% of class have a GPA at or above 3.17). *U.S. News & World Report* ranking is in the third tier of all U.S. law schools.

FINANCIAL AID. Limited to loans; research assistantships for third-year students only. Apply by March 1 to Financial Aid Office. Phone: (406)243-5524. Use FAFSA (School code: 00256) and Montana FAF. About 40% of students receive aid other than loans from School.

DEGREE REQUIREMENTS. For J.D.: satisfactory completion of three-year program; 90 credit-hour program.

MONTCLAIR STATE UNIVERSITY
Upper Montclair, New Jersey 07043-1624
Web site: www.montclair.edu

Founded 1908. Located 15 miles W of New York City. CGS member. Coed. State control. Semester system. Special facilities: Center for Adult Learning, Center for Archaeological Studies, Center for Child Advocacy, Center for Community-Based Learning, Center for Pedagogy, Center for Economic Research on Africa, DuMont TV Center, International Trade Counseling Center, Preparatory Center for the Arts, Institute for the Advancement of Philosophy for Children, Institute for the Humanities, Institute for Community Studies. Library: 455,185 volumes, 2900 subscriptions. Total University enrollment: 16,000.

Tuition: per credit: resident $535, nonresident $767. Limited on-campus housing for graduate students. Contact Office of Residence Life for both on- and off-campus housing information. Phone: (973)655-5188. Day-care facilities available.

Graduate School

Graduate study since 1932. Enrollment: full-time 828, part-time 2300. Faculty: full- and part-time 465. Degrees conferred: M.A., M.B.A., M.A.T., M.Ed., M.S., Ed.D.

ADMISSION REQUIREMENTS. Official transcripts, GRE/GMAT/MAT/NTE, two letters of recommendation, statement of objective required in support of application. Online application available. Portfolios, auditions required for some programs. TOEFL required for international applicants. Accepts transfer applicants. Graduates of unaccredited institutions not considered. To be considered for matriculation, applications and credentials need to be received by the Graduate Office before April 1 (Summer and Fall), November 1 (Spring). Some programs have earlier deadlines. Application fee $60. Phone: (800)331-9207, (973) 655-5147; e-mail: gradstudies@montclair.edu.

ADMISSION STANDARDS. Admission decisions based on combination of GPA and standardized test score. Usual minimum average: 2.75 (A = 4).

FINANCIAL AID. Annual awards from institutional funds: scholarships, graduate assistantships, Federal W/S, loans. Apply by March 1 to the Office of Graduate Studies for assistantships; to Office of Financial Aid for all other programs. Phone: (973)655-4461. Use FAFSA. Aid available for part-time students.

DEGREE REQUIREMENTS. For M.A., M.S.: 32 semester hours minimum, at least 30 in residence; additional hours may be required depending on undergraduate major; thesis/special project/comprehensive exam. For M.A.T.: 45 semester hours minimum, at least 30 in residence. For M.B.A.: 45–60 semester hours depending on undergraduate major, at least 30 in residence. For Ed.D.: 60 credit program; dissertation seminar; dissertation; final defense.

FIELDS OF STUDY.
Accounting. M.B.A.
Addictions Counseling. M.S.
Applied Linguistics. M.A.
Aquatic and Coastal Sciences. M.S.
Art Teaching. M.A.T.
Arts Management. M.A.
Audiology. D.S.C.D.
Biochemistry. M.S.
Biological Science Teaching. M.A.T.
Biology. M.S.
Biology Science Education. M.S.
Business Administration. M.B.A.
Chemical Business. M.S.
Child/Adolescent Clinical Psychology. M.A.
Child Advocacy. M.A.
Clinical Psychology for Spanish-English Bilinguals. M.A.
Coaching and Sport Administration. M.A.
Communication Sciences and Disorders. M.A.
Communication Studies. M.A.
Community Counseling. M.S.
Computer Science. M.S.
Counseling. M.S.
Dispute Resolution. M.A.
Early Childhood and Elementary Education. M.E.D., M.A.T.
Earth Science Teaching. M.A.T.
Ecology and Evolution. M.S.
Educational Leadership. M.A.
Educational Psychology. M.A.
Elementary Education. M.A.T.
English. M.A.
Environmental Education. M.A.
Environmental Management. M.A., D.Env.M.
Exercise Science and Physical Education. M.A.
Finance. M.B.A.
Fine Arts. M.A.
French. Includes literature, studies. M.A., M.A.T.
Geoscience. M.S.
Governance, Compliance and Regulation. M.A.
Health and Physical Education. M.A., M.A.T.
History. M.A.
Industrial and Organizational Psychology. M.A.
Informatics. M.S.
Intellectual Property. M.A.
International Business. M.B.A.
Learning Disabilities. M.Ed.
Legal Management, Information and Technology. M.A.
Legal Studies. M.A.
Management. M.B.A.
Management Information Systems. M.B.A.
Marketing. M.B.A.
Mathematics. Includes pure and applied. M.A.T., M .S., Ed.D.
Molecular Biology. M.S.
Museum Management. M.A.
Music. Includes education, pedagogy, performance, theory/composition. M.A., M.A.T.
Music Therapy. M.A.

Nutrition and Food Science. M.S.
Organizational Communication. M.A.
Physical Education. M.A.T.
Physical Science. M.A.T.
Physiology. M.S.
Production/Stage Management. M.A.
Psychology. M.A.
Public Child Welfare. M.A.
Public Relations. M.A.
Reading. M.A.
School Counseling. M.A.
Social Studies. M.A.T.
Spanish. M.A.T.
Special Education. M.Ed.
Speech Communication. M.A.
Statistics. M.S
Student Affairs/Counseling in Higher Education. M.A.
Studio Art. M.F.A.
Teacher Leadership. M.Ed.
TESL. M.A.T.
Theatre. M.A.

MONTEREY INSTITUTE OF INTERNATIONAL STUDIES

Monterey, California 93940-2691
Web site: www.miis.edu

Founded 1955. Located 124 miles S of San Francisco. An affiliate of Middlebury College. Coed. Private control. Semester system. Library: 92,000 volumes, 575 subscriptions. Total Institute enrollment: 750.

Annual tuition: full-time $25,500. No on-campus housing available for graduate students. Average academic year housing and food expense: $9000.

Graduate Programs

Enrollment: full-time 626, part-time 91. Institute's faculty: full-time 59, part-time 25. Degrees conferred: M.A., M.A.C.D., M.A.C.I., M.A.I.E.P., M.A.I.P.S., M.A.T., M.A.TESOL, M.A.T.F.L., M.A.T.I., M.B.A., M.P.A.

ADMISSION REQUIREMENTS. Transcripts, two letters of recommendation, statement of purpose, résumé required in support of application. All students must be able to work at the third-year university level in the proposed language of study. GRE for native English speakers for M.A. Translation and Interpretation applicants. GMAT required for M.B.A. applicants. TOEFL (minimum score 550) required for international applicants. Campus visits/interviews recommended. Apply to the Admission Office by June 1. M.B.A. admitted in August, January, and June. Application fee $50. Phone: (831)647-4123; fax (831)647-6405; e-mail: admit@miis.edu.

ADMISSION STANDARDS. Selective. Usual minimum average: 3.0 (A = 4).

FINANCIAL AID. Annual awards from institutional funds: scholarships, grants, assistantships, internships, Federal W/S, loans. Approved for VA benefits. Apply by March 15 to Financial Aid Office. Phone: (831) 647-4119; fax: (831)647-4199. Use FAFSA. About 65% of full-time students receive aid other than loans from Institute and outside sources.

DEGREE REQUIREMENTS. For M.A.I.P.S., M.A.I.E.P., M.P.A., M.A.C.D.: 60 credit, two-year, full-time programs; capstone project/master's project. For M.A.TESOL, M.A.T.F.L.: 48 credit programs. For M.A.T., M.A.T.I., M.A.C.I.: 60 credit, four-

semester, full-time programs; comprehensive professional exam; research project/translation thesis. For M.B.A.: two-year full-time program (also have 12-month program for advanced entry candidates, a summer language program and master's international in cooperation with the Peace Corps).

FIELDS OF STUDY.

FISCHER GRADUATE SCHOOL OF INTERNATIONAL BUSINESS:
Business Administration. Specializations in entrepreneurial management, international trade management, international marketing, international finance and economics, international human resources management, regional business environments, global business management, international environmental management, nonprofit and public management. M.B.A.

GRADUATE SCHOOL OF INTERNATIONAL POLICY STUDIES:
International Environmental Policy. M.A.I.E.P.
International Management. M.P.A.
International Policy Studies. M.A.I.P.S.
International Trade Policy. M.A.I.T.P.

GRADUATE SCHOOL OF LANGUAGE AND EDUCATIONAL LINGUISTICS:
Teaching English to Speakers of Other Languages. M.A.TESOL.
Teaching Foreign Language. M.A.T.F.L.

GRADUATE SCHOOL OF TRANSLATION AND INTERPRETATION:
Conference Interpretation. M.A.C.I.
Translation. M.A.T.
Translation and Interpretation. M.A.T.I.
Translation/Localization Management. M.A.T.L.M.
Note: Study available in the following languages: Arabic, Chinese, English, French, German, Japanese, Russian, Spanish.

UNIVERSITY OF MONTEVALLO

Montevallo, Alabama 35115
Web site: www.montevallo.edu

Founded 1896. Located 32 miles from Birmingham. Coed. State control. Semester system. Library: 248,000 volumes, 868 subscriptions.

Tuition: per credit hour resident $208, nonresident $416. On-campus housing in Summer for 200 men, 200 women; none for married students. Annual academic year housing cost: $2700–$4622; board cost $800–$1500. Single students apply to Director of Housing and Residence Life. Phone: (205)665-6235. Married students make own arrangements for off-campus housing.

Graduate Studies

Graduate study since 1955. Enrollment: full-time 124, part-time 295. University faculty teaching graduate students: full- and part-time 97. Degrees conferred: M.A., M.S., M.Ed., M.M.

ADMISSION REQUIREMENTS. Transcripts, GRE/MAT required in support of application. Interview not required. TOEFL (minimum score 550) required for international applicants. Accepts transfer applicants. Graduates of unaccredited colleges not considered. Apply to Office of Graduate Studies two to three months prior to registration. Application fee $25. Phone: (205)665-6350; fax: (205)665-6353.

ADMISSION STANDARDS. Relatively open. Usual minimum average: 2.5, 2.75 last 60 credits (A = 4).

FINANCIAL AID. Limited to Federal W/S, loans. Approved for VA benefits. Apply to Office of Financial Aid; no specified closing date. Phone: (205)665-6050. Use FAFSA.

Morehouse School of Medicine *399*

DEGREE REQUIREMENTS. For master's: 30 semester hours minimum; comprehensive exam; thesis/nonthesis option. For Ed.S.: 30 semester hours beyond master's; comprehensive exam.

FIELDS OF STUDY.
Counseling. M.Ed.
Early Childhood Education. M.Ed.
Educational Administration. M.Ed.
Educational Leadership. Ed.S.
Elementary Education. M.Ed.
English. M.A.
Music.
Preschool to 12th Grade Education (P–12). M.Ed.
Secondary Education (6–12). M.Ed.
Speech Pathology and Audiology. M.S.
Teacher Leader. Ed.S.

MOREHEAD STATE UNIVERSITY
Morehead, Kentucky 40351
Web site: www.moreheadstate.edu

Founded 1922. Located 65 miles E of Lexington. CGS member. Semester system. Library: 400,000 volumes, 2600 subscriptions. Total University enrollment: 9100.

Annual tuition: full-time, resident $5730, nonresident $14,550; per credit resident $320, nonresident $810. On-campus housing for married and single students. Average academic year housing cost: $2800–$5100 for single students; $4800 for married students. Contact Director of Housing for both on- and off-campus housing information. Phone: (606)783-2060.

Graduate Programs

Enrollment: full- and part-time 1060. Faculty: full-time 139, part-time 38. Degrees conferred: M.A., M.B.A., M.S., M.M., M.A.Ed., M.S.W., Ed.S., Ed.D. (cooperative program with University of Kentucky), Ph.D. (cooperative program with University of Kentucky).

ADMISSION REQUIREMENTS. Official transcripts, GRE required in support of application. Online application available. TOEFL required for international applicants. Accepts transfer applicants. Graduates of unaccredited colleges not considered. Apply to Graduate Admissions Office at least two months prior to registration. Rolling admissions process. Application fee: $0, $55 for international applicants. Phone: (606)783-2039; fax: (606)783-5061.

ADMISSION STANDARDS. Selective. Usual minimum average: 2.5 (A = 4).

FINANCIAL AID. Annual awards from institutional funds: research/teaching assistantships, internships, Federal W/S, loans. Approved for VA benefits. Apply by April 1 to Dean of Graduate and Extended Campus Programs for assistantships; to Financial Aid Office for all other programs. Phone: (606)783-2039. Use FAFSA and University's FAF. About 15% of students receive aid from University. No aid available for part-time students.

DEGREE REQUIREMENTS. For master's: 33–45 semester hours minimum, at least 27–36 in residence; thesis/nonthesis optional; final written/oral exams. For Ed.S.: 30 semester hours beyond the master's. For Ph.D.: 60 credits minimum, at least one year in full-time residence; qualifying exam; proficiency in one foreign language for some programs; dissertation; final oral exam.

FIELDS OF STUDY.
Adult and Higher Education. M.A., Ed.S.
Art. Includes art education, graphic design, studio art. M.A.

Biology. M.S.
Business Administration. M.B.A.
Career and Technical Education. Includes agriculture, human sciences, industrial education. M.S.
Communications. Includes advertising/public relations, electronic media, journalism, speech, theatre. M.A.
Counseling. M.A.
Curriculum and Instruction. Ed.S.
Education. Includes elementary (P–5), elementary (5–9), educational technology, reading/writing, secondary (8–12), secondary guidance, special education. M.A.Ed.
Educational Policy Studies and Evaluation. Cooperative doctoral program with University of Kentucky.
Educational Psychology.
English. M.A.
Guidance and Counseling. Ed.S.
Health, Physical Education, and Recreation. Includes health and physical education, sports administration. M.A.
Industrial Technology. M.S.
Instructional Leadership. Ed.S.
Instruction and Administration. Cooperative doctoral program with University of Kentucky.
Kinesiology and Health Promotion. Cooperative doctoral program with University of Kentucky.
Music. Includes music education, performance.
Psychology. Includes general-experimental, clinical, counseling.
Public Administration. M.P.A.
School Administration. M.A.
Social Work. M.S.W. Cooperative program with University of Kentucky.
Sociology. Includes chemical dependency, criminology, general, social gerontology. M.A.
Special Education and Rehabilitation Counseling. Cooperative doctoral program with the University of Kentucky.
Teaching. Includes business and marketing education, French, health, middle grades (English language, math, science, social studies), secondary (biology, chemistry, earth science, English, math, physics, social studies), physical education, Spanish, special education (MSD, LBD). M.A.T.

MOREHOUSE SCHOOL OF MEDICINE
Atlanta, Georgia 30310-1495
Web site: www.msm.edu

Established 1978. Primary mission is to provide physicians for medically underserved rural and inner-city area. Special facilities: Cardiovascular Research Institute, Center of Excellence on Health Disparities, Center of Laboratory Animal Resources, Clinical Research Center, Cooperative Reproductive Science Research Center, Cork Institute, NASA Space Medicine Life Sciences Research Center, National Center for Primary Care, Research Centers in Minority Institutions, Prevention Research Center, Center of Excellence for Sexual Health. Library: 95,000 volumes, 800 subscriptions. NIH ranking is 145th among all U.S. institutions with 40 awards/grants worth $28,505,979.

Annual tuition and fees: $26,000, student fees $6252. No on-campus housing available. Total average figure for all other expenses: $20,000.

Enrollment: first-year 52 (EDP 2), total 196 (men 36%, women 64%, minorities 86%, state residents 51%). Faculty: full-time 216, part-time and volunteers 100. Degrees conferred: M.D., M.D.-M.P.H. (with Clark Atlanta University), M.D.-Ph.D.(Biomedical Sciences).

ADMISSION REQUIREMENTS. AMCAS report, transcripts, MCAT, three letters of recommendation, biographical questionnaire, personal statement, supplemental application required in support of application. Has EDP; apply between June 1 and August 1. Interview by invitation. Preference given to state residents. Accepts transfer applicants into second year only and on a space available basis. Apply to Office of Admissions and Student Affairs after June 1, before December 1. Application fee $50. Phone: (404)752-1650; fax: (404)752-1512.

ADMISSION STANDARDS. Selective. Accepts about 10–15% of all applicants. Number of applications 2003 (n/a out-of-state); number interviewed 267 (n/a out-of-state); number of acceptance n/a (n/a out-of-state); number enrolled 52 (31 out-of-state). Mean Composite MCAT 8.5; mean UGPA 3.29.

FINANCIAL AID. Scholarships, limited merit scholarships, minority scholarships, Grants-in-Aid, institutional loans, HEAL, alternative loan programs, Federal Perkins Loans, Stafford Subsidized and Unsubsidized Loans, Service Commitment Scholarship programs are available. All Financial Aid is based on documented need. For merit scholarships, the selection criteria places heavy reliance on MCAT and undergraduate GPA. Contact the Office of Student Fiscal Affairs for current information. Phone: (404)752-1656. For most financial assistance and all Federal programs use FAFSA (School code: G24821), also submit Financial Aid Transcript, Federal Income Tax forms. Approximately 95% of students receive some form of financial assistance.

DEGREE REQUIREMENTS. For M.D.: satisfactory completion of four-year program. All students must pass USMLE Step 1 prior to entering third year; all students must pass USMLE Step 2 prior to awarding of M.D.

MORGAN STATE UNIVERSITY
Baltimore, Maryland 21239
Web site: www.morgan.edu

Founded 1867. CGS member. Coed. State control. Semester system. Library: 652,000 volumes, 2526 subscriptions.

Tuition: per credit, resident $272, nonresident $478. No on-campus housing for graduate students during academic year, some housing during Summer session. Annual academic year housing cost: $3950 (including board). Apply to Director, Residence Life. Phone: (443)885-3217. Day care facilities available.

School of Graduate Studies

Graduate study since 1964. Enrollment: full-time 390, part-time 359. Graduate faculty: full-time 70, part-time 10. Degrees conferred: M.A., M.S., M.B.A., M.Arch., M.L.A., M.C.R.P., M.E., M.P.H., D.E., Ed.D., Ph.D.

ADMISSION REQUIREMENTS. Transcripts, GRE/GMAT/MAT required in support of School's application. Interview not required. TOEFL required for international applicants. Accepts transfer applicants. Apply to Graduate School by February 1 (Fall), October 1 (Spring), June 1 (Summer). Application fee, none. Phone: (443)885-3185; fax: (443)885-8226.

ADMISSION STANDARDS. Selective. Usual minimum average: 3.0 (unconditional), 2.5 (conditional) (A = 4).

FINANCIAL AID. Annual awards from institutional funds: scholarships, fellowships, teaching assistantships, minority fellowships, internships, grants, Federal W/S, loans. Approved for VA benefits. Phone: (443)885-3170; fax: (443)885-3852. Use FAFSA and University's FAF. Aid available for part-time students.

DEGREE REQUIREMENTS. For M.A., M.S.: 30–42 semester hours, depending upon major, at least 25–36 hours in residence; thesis/final written/oral exam. For M.B.A.: 30–51 hours depend-

ing upon academic background. For M.C.R.P.: 51 semester hours. For M.Arch.: 30–90 semester hours, depending on academic background. For M.L.A.: 90 semester hours, depending on academic background. For D.E., Ed.D.: 60 semester hours minimum beyond the master's. For Ph.D.: 60 semester hours minimum beyond the master's, qualifying exam; one foreign language and research tool for some programs, dissertation; final oral exam.

FIELDS OF STUDY.
African American Studies. M.A.
Architecture. M.Arch.
Bio-Environmental Sciences. Ph.D. only.
Bioinformatics. M.A.
Business Administration. Includes accounting, finance, international, management, marketing. M.B.A., Ph.D.
City and Regional Planning. M.C.R.P.
Community College Leadership. Ed.D.
Economics. M.A.
Educational Administration and Supervision. M.S.
Elementary and Middle School Education. M.S.
Engineering. M.E., D.E.
English. M.A., Ph.D.
Higher Education Administration. Ph.D. only.
History. M.A., Ph.D.
International Studies. M.A.
Landscape Architecture. M.L.A.
Mathematics. M.A.
Mathematics Education. M.S., Ed.D.
Music. Includes choral and instrumental conducting, musicology, theory, performance. M.A.
Nursing. M.S.N.
Physics. M.S.
Psychometrics. M.S., Ph.D.
Public Health. M.P.H., Dr.P.H.
Science. M.S.
Science Education. Ed.D.
Social Work. M.S.W., Ph.D.
Sociology. M.S.
Teaching. M.A.T.
Telecommunication and Management. M.S.
Transportation Studies. M.S.
Urban Education Leadership. Ed.D. only.

MORNINGSIDE COLLEGE
Sioux City, Iowa 51106-1751
Web site: www.morningside.edu

Founded 1894. Coed. Private control. Methodist affiliation. Semester system. Library: 168,000 volumes, 650 subscriptions.

Tuition: per credit $150. On-campus housing for graduate men, women; some for married students. Average academic year expenses: $6000. Contact Director of Housing for on- and off-campus information. Phone: (712)274-5104.

Graduate Program

Summer study with evening program during academic year. Enrollment: part-time only, 300. College faculty teaching graduate students: full-time 18, part-time 3. Degree conferred: M.A.T.

ADMISSION REQUIREMENTS. Transcripts, writing sample, MAT required in support of application. Online application available. TOEFL required for international applicants. Accepts transfer applicants. Apply to Director of Graduate Study at least one month prior to registration. Application fee: $25. Phone: (712)274-5375.

ADMISSION STANDARDS. Relatively open. Minimum average: 3.0 (A = 4).

FINANCIAL AID. Rebates for qualified students, Federal W/S, loans. Apply to Director of Graduate Studies; no specified closing date. Phone: (712)274-5159. Use FAFSA (School code: 001879). More than 90% of students receive financial assistance.

DEGREE REQUIREMENTS. For M.A.T.: 31–32 semester hours minimum; final written comprehensive exam; three final research papers.

FIELDS OF STUDY.
Special Education—Instructional Strategist 1: K–6. M.A.T.
Special Education—Instructional Strategist 1: 7–12. M.A.T.
Special Education—Instructional Strategist 2: K–12. BD/LD. M.A.T.
Special Education—Instructional Strategist 2: K–12. M.D. M.A.T.
Professional Educator. M.A.T.

MOUNT ST. MARY'S COLLEGE

Los Angeles, California 90049-1599
Web site: www.msmc.la.edu

Founded 1925. Coed. Private control. Roman Catholic. Semester system. Special facility: Center for Cultural Fluency. Library: 140,000 volumes, 800 subscriptions. Total College enrollment: 2480.

Tuition: per credit $662. No on-campus housing.

Graduate School

Graduate study since 1931. Enrollment: full- and part-time 500. Graduate faculty: full-time 16, part-time 23. Degrees conferred: M.A., M.S.

ADMISSION REQUIREMENTS. Transcripts, MAT, letters of recommendation required in support of application. TOEFL required of foreign students. Accepts transfer applicants. Apply to Director of Admissions at least six weeks prior to registration (earlier deadline for Physical Therapy program). Application fee $40. Phone: (213)477-2800; fax: (213)477-2519.

ADMISSION STANDARDS. Relatively open. Usual minimum average: 2.5 (A = 4).

FINANCIAL AID. Limited to loans. Tuition discount available for employees of the Archdiocese of Los Angeles and Orange Counties. Approved for VA benefits. Apply to Financial Aid Office; no specified closing date. Phone: (213)477-2800. Use FAFSA.

DEGREE REQUIREMENTS. For master's: 30 units minimum, at least 24 in residence; final written/oral exams; final project or thesis. For master's (no project/thesis): 39 unit program; oral integration interview.

FIELDS OF STUDY.
Business Administration.
Counseling Psychology. Includes human services and marriage, family, and child counseling.
Elementary Education.
Humanities.
Instructional Leadership.
Nursing Education.
Physical Therapy.
Religious Studies. Includes certificate programs in advanced religious studies, Hispanic pastoral ministry, pastoral care/counseling, youth and young adult ministry.
Secondary Education.
Special Education. Includes mild/moderate disabilities.

MOUNT SINAI SCHOOL OF MEDICINE

New York, New York 10029-6572

Mount Sinai Medical Center

One Gustave L. Levy Place
New York, New York 10029

Established 1852. Public Control. Mount Sinai Hospital is a member of Council of Teaching Hospitals. Special facilities: Division of Environment and Occupational Medicine, Clinical Genetics Center, Gerald A. Ruttenberg Cancer Center, General Clinical Research Center, Global Health Center, Institute for Gene Therapy and Molecular Medicine, Center for Jewish Genetic Diseases, Institute for Medicare Practice, Fishberg Research Center for Neurobiology of Aging, Recanati/Miller Transplantation Institute, Wiener Cardiovascular Institute, Lucy Moses Cardiothoracic Center. The School's NIH ranking is number 34 among all U.S. institutions with 400 awards/grants valued at $174,415,661. According to The Center at University of Florida, the School is ranked 52nd in receipt of Federal Research funds with $152,719,000 and it ranks 61st for total research expenditures with $214,514,000. Twelve of the School's faculty members have been elected to National Honor Academies and this ranks it 62nd among all U.S. institutions. The Library: approximately 154,000 volumes, 2,500 subscriptions.

Graduate School of Biological Sciences
(P.O. Box 1022)

Web site: www.mssm.edu/gradschool

Graduate study since 1965. Annual tuition: $23,175. Enrollment: full- and part-time 218. Faculty: full- and part-time 200. Degrees conferred: M.S., M.P.H., Ph.D.

ADMISSION REQUIREMENTS. Official transcripts, GRE or MCAT, three letters of recommendation required in support of School's application. Interviews by invitation. TOEFL or evidence of proficiency in English required for international students. Accepts transfer applicants. Graduates of unaccredited institutions not considered. Admits Fall only. Apply by February 15 (Fall), January 15 (for priority consideration) to Graduate School (P.O. Box 1022). Rolling admissions process. Application fee $75. Phone: (212)241-3267; fax (212)241-0651; e-mail: grads@mssm.edu.

ADMISSION STANDARDS. Competitive for most departments, selective for all others. Usual minimum average: 3.0 (A = 4).

FINANCIAL AID. Traineeships, fellowships, assistantships, loans. Apply by February 1 to Dean for assistantships, fellowships; to Financial Aid Office for all other programs. Phone: (212)241-5245. Use FAFSA.

DEGREE REQUIREMENTS. For M.P.H., M.S.: two-year part-time program; field practicum: thesis/project. For Ph.D.: three-year full-time program; qualifying exam; selection of preceptor's laboratory; thesis proposal; dissertation: dissertation defense.

FIELDS OF STUDY.
Biomedical Sciences. M.S.
Biomedical Sciences and Neuroscience. Ph.D.
Clinical Research. M.S.
Dermatology. M.S.
Genetic Counseling. M.S.
Public Health. M.P.H.

Mount Sinai School of Medicine (10029-6574)

Web site: www.mssm.edu

Established 1968. In July 1999, Mount Sinai School of Medicine changed its academic affiliation to New York University and, hence, its diplomas read Mount Sinai School of Medicine of New York University. Special programs: an Early Acceptance program with Amherst College, Brandeis University, Princeton University, Wesleyan University, Williams College, Cooper Union; a seven-year Biomedical Education program with City College of City University of New York; prematriculation summer sessions.

Annual tuition: $37,450. On-campus rooms for single students and off-campus school-owned apartments available for married students. Contact Office of Student Affairs for both on- and off-campus information. Annual on-campus housing cost: $15,000. Medical students tend to live off-campus. Off-campus housing and personal expenses: approximately $16,500

Enrollment: first-year class 120 (EDP 5); total 587 (men 46%, women 54%, minorities 42%, state residents 43%). Faculty: full-time 1000, part-time 250. Degrees conferred: M.D., M.D.-M.B.A., M.D.-M.P.H., M.D.-M.S., M.D.-Ph.D., M.S.T.P.

ADMISSION REQUIREMENTS. AMCAS report, transcripts, MCAT, references, interview required in support of application. Online application available. Interview by invitation only. Has EDP; apply between June 1 and August 1. Accepts transfer applicants. Applicants must have completed at least three years of college study. Apply to Office for Admissions after June 1, before November 1. Application fee $105. Phone: (212)241-6696; fax: (212)369-6013.

ADMISSION STANDARDS. Very competitive. Accepts about 5% of all applicants. Number of applications 6591 (5059 out-of-state); number interviewed 737 (484 out-of-state); number of acceptance 329 (217 out-of-state); number enrolled 120 (73 out-of-state). Mean Composite MCAT 11.1; mean UGPA 3.65. *U.S. News & World Report* ranking is in the top 27 of all medical schools.

FINANCIAL AID. Scholarships, fellowships, Federal and private loans. Apply to Financial Aid Officer after acceptance. Phone: (212)241-5245. MSTP funded by NIH. Use FAFSA (School code: G07026). About 45% of students receive aid other than loans from School; over 90% receive some form of financial assistance.

DEGREE REQUIREMENTS. For M.D.: satisfactory completion of four-year program.

FIELDS OF GRADUATE STUDY.
Biomedical Sciences. M.S.
Biophysics, Structural Biology, and Biomathematics.
Clinical Research. M.S.
Molecular, Cellular, Biochemical, and Developmental Sciences.
Genetics and Genomic Sciences.
Genetic Counseling. M.S.
Mechanisms of Disease and Therapy.
Microbiology.
Neurosciences.

MURRAY STATE UNIVERSITY
Murray, Kentucky 42071-0009
Web site: www.murraystate.edu

Founded 1922. Located 110 miles W of Nashville, Tennessee. CGS member. Coed. State control. Semester system. Library: 831,000 volumes, 3000 subscriptions.

Annual tuition: full-time, resident $6156, nonresident $17,316; per credit, resident $342, nonresident $962. On-campus housing for 144 married students, 1383 men, 1449 women. Average annual housing cost: $4870 for married students, $3000–$4000 for single students. Contact Housing Office for on- and off-campus information. Phone: (270)809-2310.

Graduate Studies

Graduate study since 1936. Enrollment: full-time 439, part-time 1225. University faculty: full- and part-time 319. Degrees conferred: M.A., M.S., M.B.A., M.A.Ed., M.S.N., M.M.E., M.A.T., M.P.A., Ed.S.

ADMISSION REQUIREMENTS. Transcripts, GRE Subject Tests/GMAT required in support of School's application. TOEFL (minimum score 500) required for international applicants. Interview required by some departments. Accepts transfer applicants. Graduates of unaccredited colleges not considered. Apply to Graduate Office at least one month prior to registration. Application fee $30. Phone: (270)809-3895; fax: (270)809-3780.

ADMISSION STANDARDS. Relatively open. Usual minimum average: 2.75 (A = 4).

FINANCIAL AID. Annual awards from institutional funds: scholarships, teaching fellowships, research assistantships, internships, Federal W/S, loans. Apply by April 1 to chair of proposed major department for fellowships and assistantships; to Financial Aid Office for all other programs. Phone: (270)809-2546. Use FAFSA. About 10% of students receive aid other than loans from University and outside sources. Aid available for part-time students.

DEGREE REQUIREMENTS. For master's: 30–45 semester hours, at least 18–33 in residence; final written/oral exams; reading knowledge of one foreign language for some degrees, majors; thesis usually required for M.A., M.S. For Ed.S.: 30 semester hours minimum beyond master's.

FIELDS OF STUDY.
Agriculture.
Biology.
Business Administration. GMAT for admission. Includes accounting and e-business options.
Career and Technical Education.
Chemistry.
Creative Writing.
Director of Special Education.
Economics. Includes a finance emphasis.
Elementary Education.
English.
Geosciences.
Guidance and Counseling.
History.
Human Development and Leadership.
Information Systems.
Interdisciplinary Early Childhood Education.
Management of Technology.
Mass Communications.
Mathematics.
Middle School Education.
Music Education.
Nursing.
Nutrition Services.
Occupational Safety and Health.
Organizational Communication.
Professional Accountancy.
Psychology. Includes clinical, general.
Public Administration.
Reading and Writing.
School Administration.
Secondary Education. Includes specializations in biology, business and marketing, chemistry, earth science, economics, English, French, German, Spanish, geography, health, history, industrial education, mathematics, physical education, psychology, school safety, teaching area in studio art, special edu-

cation (mild learning and behavior disorders (P–12), moderate to severe disabilities (P–12), advanced studies in learning behavior disorders).
Speech-Language Pathology.
Teacher Education and Professional Development.
Teaching English to Speakers of Other Languages.
Telecommunications Systems Management.
Water Science.

NATIONAL-LOUIS UNIVERSITY
Evanston, Illinois 60201-1796
Web site: www.nl.edu

Founded 1866 as National College of Education. Name changed in 1992. Regional campuses located in Atlanta, Chicago area, McLean/Washington, Milwaukee/Beloit, Orlando, Tampa, Heidleberg, Nowy Sacz. Coed. Private control. Semester system. Library: 180,000 volumes, 1200 subscriptions. Total University enrollment: 7345.

Tuition: per credit, Education $630, Management and Business $618. On-campus housing for limited number of men, women; none for married students. Average annual housing expense $2200–$3300. Apply to Director of Housing. Phone: (847)475-1100.

Graduate Programs

Graduate study since 1951. Enrollment: full-time 1360, part-time 3825. Graduate faculty: full-time 125, part-time 456. Degrees conferred: M.Ed., M.A.T., M.S.Ed., Ed.S., Ed.D.

ADMISSION REQUIREMENTS. Transcripts, three letters of recommendation, MAT required in support of School's application. GRE for Ed.S. and doctoral program. TOEFL, financial affidavits required for international applicants. Accepts transfer applicants. Graduates of unaccredited institutions not considered. Apply to Director of Admission by April 15 (Fall), October 15 (Spring). Rolling admissions process. Application fee $40. Phone: (847)465-0575, ext. 5571.

ADMISSION STANDARDS. Selective. Usual minimum average: 3.0 (A = 4).

FINANCIAL AID. Annual awards from institutional funds: scholarships, fellowships, Federal W/S, loans. Apply to Office of Financial Assistance; no specified closing date. Use FAFSA. Phone: (800)443-5522, ext. 5350. Aid sometimes available for part-time students.

DEGREE REQUIREMENTS. For master's: 32–38 credits minimum; internship option; thesis/nonthesis option. No language requirement. For Ed.S.: at least 30 credits beyond master's. For Ed.D.: 63 credits minimum; qualifying exam; dissertation; final oral exam.

FIELDS OF STUDY.

COLLEGE OF ARTS AND SCIENCES:
Health Services Administration.
Psychology.
Public Policy.
Written Communication.

COLLEGE OF MANAGEMENT AND BUSINESS:
Business Administration.
Human Resources Management.
Management.

NATIONAL COLLEGE OF EDUCATION:
Administration and Supervision.
Adult Education.
Adult Education Leadership.
Adult Literacy/Developmental Studies.
Community College Leadership.
Curriculum and Instruction. Includes ESL/bilingual education, health education, mathematics education, school nurse, science education, social studies education teaching for conceptual integration.
Disability and Equity in Education.
Early Childhood Administration.
Early Childhood Education.
Educational Leadership.
Educational Psychology/Human Learning and Development.
Educational Psychology/School Psychology.
Elementary Education.
Interdisciplinary Studies in Curriculum and Instruction.
Language and Literacy.
Leadership in Curriculum and Instruction.
Middle Level Education.
Reading.
Reading and Language.
School Library Information Specialist in Language and Literacy.
Secondary Education.
Special Education.
Technology in Education.

NATIONAL UNIVERSITY
La Jolla, California 92037-1011
Web site: www.nu.edu

Chartered 1971. Fourteen branch campuses—San Diego, Vista, La Jolla, Costa Mesa, San Bernadino, Bakersfield, Redding, Orange, Twenty-Nine Palms, Irvine, Riverside, Los Angeles, Sacramento, San Jose, Fresno, Stockton. CGS member. Coed. Private control. One-course-per-month format, quarter system. Library: 226,000 volumes, 3700 subscriptions. Total University enrollment: 26,000.

Tuition: $1188 per 4.5 quarter-hour course. No on-campus housing available.

Graduate Studies

Graduate study since 1975. Enrollment: full-time 6554, part-time 12,322. Graduate faculty: full-time 100, part-time 2645. Degrees conferred: M.A., M.B.A., M.F.A., M.F.S., M.P.A., M.S.

ADMISSION REQUIREMENTS. Official transcripts, three letters of recommendation required in support of application. TOEFL required for international applicants. Accepts transfer applicants. Graduates of unaccredited institutions not considered. Apply to Admission Office: no specified closing date. Rolling admissions process. Application fee $60, $100 for international applicants. Phone: (800) NAT-UNIV, (858)642-8180; fax: (858)642-8709; e-mail: advisor@nu.edu.

ADMISSION STANDARDS. Relatively open. Usual minimum average: 2.5 (A = 4).

FINANCIAL AID. Annual awards from institutional funds: scholarships, grants, Federal W/S, loans. Approved for VA benefits. Apply to Office of Financial Assistance; no specified closing date. Phone: (858)642-8500. Use FAFSA. Aid available for part-time students.

DEGREE REQUIREMENTS. For master's: 45–60 credits minimum, at least 35 in residence; thesis/nonthesis option; no foreign language requirement.

FIELDS OF STUDY.

SCHOOL OF ARTS AND SCIENCES:
Counseling Psychology. M.A.
Creative Writing. M.F.A.
Film Arts Studies. M.F.A.
English. M.A.
Human Behavior. M.A.
Industrial Organizational Psychology. M.S.
Instructional Technology. M.S.
Nursing. M.S.

SCHOOL OF BUSINESS AND TECHNOLOGY:
Business Administration. Includes accountancy, e-commerce, environmental management, financial management, health care management, human resource management, international management, marketing, public administration, technology management. M.B.A.
Electronic Commerce. M.S.
Finance. M.S.
Forensic Sciences. M.F.S.
Health Care Administration. M.H.C.A.
Human Resource Management. M.A.
Management. M.A.
Organization Leadership. M.S.
Public Administration. M.P.A.
Software Engineering. M.S.
Taxation. M.S.
Technology Management. M.S.
Telecommunication Systems Management. M.S.

SCHOOL OF EDUCATION AND HUMAN SERVICES:
Cross-Cultural Teaching. M.Ed.
Educational Administration. M.S.
Educational Counseling. M.A.
Educational Technology. M.S.
School Psychology. M.S.
Special Education. M.S.

NAVAL POSTGRADUATE SCHOOL
Monterey, California 93943-5100
Web site: www.nps.edu

Organized 1909. Located 125 miles S of San Francisco. Enrollment limited to military officers and sponsored civilian federal employees and selected international officers. CGS member. Federal control. Quarter system. Library: 500,000 volumes, 1200 subscriptions.

Annual tuition: fully funded. On-campus housing for single and married students. Average academic year housing cost: $10,000. Day care facilities available.

Enrollment: full-time 1439, 253 international. Faculty: full-time 348; part-time 34. Degrees conferred: M.A., M.S., Engr., D.Eng., Ph.D.

ADMISSION REQUIREMENTS. Official transcripts, recommendations required in support of application. Interview not required. TOEFL, TWE required for international applicants. Officers on active duty with all branches of the armed services eligible for enrollment. Apply to branch personnel division; no specified closing dates. Phone: (831)656-3093; fax: (831)656-2891.

ADMISSION STANDARDS. Competitive. Usual minimum average: 2.5 (A = 4).

DEGREE REQUIREMENTS. For M.A., M.S.: 45 quarter hours minimum in full-time residence; thesis; no language requirement. For M.B.A.: 44 credit hour program. For Engineering: 45 quarter hours beyond the master's; special project. For Ph.D.: 72 credits; three years minimum beyond the bachelor's, at least two years in full-time residence; qualifying exam; reading knowledge of one foreign language; advancement to candidacy; dissertation; final oral exam. D.Eng.: essentially the same as Ph.D., except no foreign language requirement.

FIELDS OF STUDY.

GRADUATE SCHOOL OF BUSINESS AND PUBLIC POLICY:
Applied Mathematics.
Applied Physics.
Applied Science.
Astronautical Engineering.
Astronautical Engineer.
Combat Systems Technology.
Electrical Engineering.
Electrical Engineer.
Electrical and Computer Engineering.
Engineering Acoustics.
Engineering Science.
Mechanical Engineering.
Meteorology.
Meteorology and Physical Oceanography.
Physical Oceanography.
Physics.
Systems Engineering.
Systems Engineering and Analysis.

GRADUATE SCHOOL OF ENGINEERING AND APPLIED SCIENCE:
Applied Mathematics.
Applied Physics.
Applied Science.
Astronautical Engineering.
Astronautical Engineer.
Combat Systems Technology.
Electrical Engineering.
Electrical Engineer.
Electrical and Computer Engineering.
Engineering Acoustics.
Engineering Science.
Mechanical Engineering.
Meteorology.
Meteorology and Physical Oceanography.
Physical Oceanography.
Physics.
Systems Engineering.
Systems Engineering and Analysis.

SCHOOL OF INTERNATIONAL GRADUATE STUDIES:
Civil-Military Relations.
Combating Terrorism—Planning and Strategy.
Defense Decision-Making and Planning.
Homeland Security and Defense.
Regional Security Studies. Includes Europe and Eurasia.
Regional Security Studies. Includes Far East, Southeast Asia, and the Pacific.
Regional Security Studies. Includes Middle East, South Asia, and sub-Saharan Africa.
Regional Security Studies. Includes Western Hemisphere.
Security Studies. Ph.D. only.
Stabilization and Reconstruction.

GRADUATE SCHOOL OF OPERATIONS AND INFORMATION SCIENCES:
Computer Science.
Computing Technology.
Defense Analysis.
Human Systems Integration.

Information Operations.
Information Science.
Information Systems and Operations.
Information Technology Management.
Information Warfare Systems Engineering.
Modeling, Virtual Environments, and Simulation.
Operations Research.
System Analysis.
Software Engineering.
Systems Technology.

UNIVERSITY OF NEBRASKA AT KEARNEY

Kearney, Nebraska 68849-0001
Web site: www.unk.edu

Founded 1903. Located 125 miles W of Lincoln. CGS member. Coed. State control. Semester system. Special facilities: Center for Economic Education, Center for Rural Research, Museum of Nebraska Art, Nebraska Business Development Center, Nebraska State Arboretum, Safety Center. Library: 320,915 volumes, 1650 subscriptions.

Tuition: per credit hour, resident $170, nonresident $351. Limited on-campus housing available for single graduate students, about 100 apartments for married students. Housing cost: $1350 per semester for single students; $1800 per semester for married students. Contact Director of Residence Life for on- and off-campus housing information. Phone: (308)865-8519.

College of Graduate Study

Graduate study since 1956. Enrollment: full-time 140, part-time 445. Graduate faculty: full-time 90, part-time 50. Degrees conferred: M.S. in Ed., M.A. in Ed., M.B.A., Specialist.

ADMISSION REQUIREMENTS. Transcripts, GRE/GMAT required in support of College's application. TOEFL required for foreign applicants. Interview not required. Accepts transfer applicants. Graduates of unaccredited institutions not considered. Apply to Dean of Graduate School prior to registration. Application fee $45. Phone: (800)717-7881; (308)865-8838; fax: (308) 865-8837.

ADMISSION STANDARDS. Selective. Usual minimum average: 2.75 (A = 4); GRE: minimum 750–950.

FINANCIAL AID. Annual awards from institutional funds: academic scholarships, nonresident tuition scholarships, grants, teaching/research assistantships, internships, Federal W/S, loans. Approved for VA benefits. Apply to Dean of Graduate Studies for scholarships, assistantships; to Financial Aid Office for all other programs. Apply by March 1. Phone: (308)865-8520; fax: (308) 865-8096. Use FAFSA (School code: 002551). About 5% of students receive aid from College and outside sources. Aid sometimes available for part-time students.

DEGREE REQUIREMENTS. For M.A. and M.S. in Ed.: 36 credit hours minimum, at least 27 in residence; optional thesis included; comprehensive written exam. For M.B.A.: 36 credit hours; final exam. For Specialist: 30 credits beyond the master's.

FIELDS OF STUDY.
Art Education.
Biology.
Business Administration.
Community Counseling.
Counseling and School Psychology.
Curriculum and Instruction.

Educational Administration.
Elementary/Early Childhood Education.
Elementary School Counseling.
English.
Exercise Science.
History.
Instructional Technology.
Modern Languages. Includes French, German, Spanish.
Music Education.
Physical Education. Includes sports administration, recreation and leisure.
Reading K–12.
School Counseling.
School Principalship.
School Psychology. Specialist only.
Science Teaching.
Speech/Language Pathology.
Student Affairs.
Teaching the Secondary School. Usual subject fields.

UNIVERSITY OF NEBRASKA AT LINCOLN

P.O. Box 880434
Lincoln, Nebraska 68588-0434
Web site: www.unl.edu

Founded 1869. CGS and AAU member. Coed. State control. Semester system. Special facilities: Barkley Memorial Center, G.W. Beadle Center for Genetics and Biomaterial Research, Bureau of Sociological Research, Government Research Institute, Lied Center for Performing Arts, Midwestern Center for Mass Spectrometry, Nebraska State Museum of Natural History, Sheldon Art Gallery. Library: 2,200,000 volumes, 20,000 subscriptions. Total University enrollment: 24,300.

Tuition: per credit hour, resident $224, nonresident $604. On-campus housing for single graduate students. Apartment housing for 70 married students. Average monthly housing cost: $350–$475 for married students. Average academic year housing cost for single students: $4600. Contact Office of University Housing for both on- and off-campus housing information. Phone: (402) 472-3561.

Graduate College

Web site: www.unl.edu/gradstud

Graduate study since 1886. Graduate enrollment: full-time 1775, part-time 1292. Graduate faculty: full-time 860, part-time 43. Degrees conferred: M.A., M.S., M.Arch., M.Ed., M.A.T., M.Sc.T., M.F.A., M.B.A., M.L.S., M.P.A., M.M., M.P.E., M.C.R.P., M.S.T., Ed.S., Ed.D., D.M.A., Ph.D.

ADMISSION REQUIREMENTS. Two transcripts, three letters of recommendation required in support of College's application. online application available. GRE/Subject Tests/MAT required by some programs. GMAT required for business programs. TOEFL required for international applicants. Interview not required. Accepts transfer applicants. Graduates of unaccredited institutions not considered. Apply to Graduate Office by March 1 (Fall), September 1 (Spring), February 1 (Summer). Admission fee $45. Phone: (800)742-8800, (402)472-2878; fax: (402)472-0589; e-mail: grad_admissions@unl.edu.

ADMISSION STANDARDS. Competitive for most departments, very competitive or selective for others. Usual minimum average: 2.5 for master's, 3.0 for doctoral candidates (A = 4).

FINANCIAL AID. Fellowships, teaching and research assistantships, internships, Federal W/S, loans. Approved for VA benefits.

Apply by February 15 to Office of Graduate Studies for information regarding fellowships, to appropriate department chair for assistantships; to Office of Financial Aid for all other programs. Phone: (402)472-8670. Use FAFSA. About 33% of students receive aid other than loans from College. Aid available for part-time students.

DEGREE REQUIREMENTS. For M.A., M.S., M.S.T., M.Sc.T.: 30 semester credits minimum, at least 12 in residence; thesis; final oral/written exams; or 36 credits minimum, at least 18 in residence; final oral/written exam in some departments. For M.Ed., M.A.T., M.P.E.: 30 semester hours minimum, at least 12 in residence; qualifying exam; thesis; final oral/written comprehensive exam; or nonthesis option, 36 semester hours minimum, at least 18 in residence. For M.F.A., M.Arch., M.C.R.P.: 60 semester hours minimum; final project; final exam. For M.B.A., M.P.A.: 48 hours minimum, at least 18 in residence. For Ed.S.: 64 hours beyond bachelor's. For Ed.D., Ph.D., D.M.A.: three full years minimum; 90 semester hours; reading knowledge of one foreign language, plus reading knowledge of second language or comprehensive knowledge of one foreign language or proficiency in research techniques or evidence of knowledge of a collateral field; residency, 27 hours graduate work within a consecutive 18-month period or less; comprehensive exam; dissertation; final oral exam.

FIELDS OF STUDY.

COLLEGE OF AGRICULTURAL SCIENCES AND NATURAL RESOURCES:
Agricultural and Biological Systems Engineering.
Agricultural Economics.
Agriculture. M.Ag. only.
Agronomy.
Animal Science.
Biochemistry.
Entomology.
Food Science and Technology.
Horticulture. Includes horticulture and forestry.
Integrative Biomedical Sciences.
Leadership Education. M.S. only.
Mechanized Systems Management. M.S. only.
Natural Resource Sciences. M.S. only.
Nutrition.
Statistics.
Veterinary and Biomedical Science.

COLLEGE OF ARCHITECTURE:
Architecture. M.Arch., M.S.
Community and Regional Planning. M.C.R.P.

COLLEGE OF ARTS AND SCIENCES:
Anthropology. M.A. only
Biochemistry.
Biological Sciences.
Chemistry.
Communication Studies.
Computer Science.
English.
Geography.
Geosciences.
History.
Mathematics. M.A., M.S., M.A.T.
Modern Languages and Literatures.
Philosophy.
Physics and Astronomy.
Political Science.
Psychology.
Sociology.
Statistics.
Survey Research and Methodology.

COLLEGE OF BUSINESS ADMINISTRATION:
Accountancy. M.P.A.
Actuarial Science. M.S.
Business. Includes agribusiness (M.B.A.), finance (M.A.), management (M.A.), marketing (M.A.). M.A., M.B.A., Ph.D.
Economics.
Finance.
Management.
Marketing.

COLLEGE OF ENGINEERING AND TECHNOLOGY:
Agricultural and Biological System Engineering. M.S.
Architectural Engineering. M.A.E.
Biomedical Engineering.
Chemical Engineering. M.S.
Chemical and Material Engineering.
Civil Engineering. M.S.
Computer Engineering.
Construction Engineering.
Electrical Engineering. M.S.
Engineering.
Engineering. Unified doctoral program. Ph.D.
Engineering Mechanics. M.S.
Environmental Engineering. M.S.
Environmental Studies. M.S.
Industrial and Management Systems Engineering. M.S.
Manufacturing Systems. M.S.
Mechanical Engineering. M.S.
Telecommunications Engineering. M.S.

COLLEGE OF EDUCATION AND HUMAN SCIENCES:
Architecture Education. Ed.D., Ph.D.
Child, Youth, and Family Studies. M.S., Ph.D.
Cognition, Learning, and Development. Ph.D.
Communication Disorders. Ph.D.
Counseling Psychology. Ph.D.
Educational Administration. M.A., M.Ed., joint Ph.D. program with UNO.
Educational Leadership and Higher Administration. Ed.D., Ph.D.
Educational Psychology. M.A., Ed.S.
Educational Studies. Ed.D., Ph.D.
Gerontology. Ph.D.
Human Sciences. Ed.D., Ph.D.
Instructional Technology. Ed.D., Ph.D.
Internet-based Education. Ed.D., Ph.D.
Leadership Studies. Ed.D., Ph.D.
Nutrition. M.S., Ph.D.
Nutrition and Health Sciences. M.S., Ph.D.
Psychological Studies in Education. Ed.D., Ph.D.
Quantitative, Qualitative, and Psychometric Methods. Ph.D.
School Psychology. Ph.D.
Special Education. M.A., M.Ed., Ed.D., Ph.D.
Special Education and Communication Disorders. Ed.S.
Speech-Language Pathology and Audiology. M.S.
Teaching, Curriculum and Learning. Ed.D., Ph.D.
Teaching, Learning and Teacher Education. M.A., M.Ed., Ed.S.
Textiles Clothing and Design. M.A., M.S., Ph.D.

COLLEGE OF JOURNALISM AND COMMUNICATION:
Journalism. M.A.

COLLEGE OF LAW:
Legal Studies. M.L.S.

HIXON-LIED COLLEGE OF FINE AND PERFORMING ARTS:
Art. M.F.A.
Music. M.M., D.M.A.
Music Education. Ed.D., Ph.D.
Theater Arts. M.F.A.

College of Dentistry (68583-0740)
Web site: unmc.edu/dentistry

Founded 1899 as Lincoln Dental College. Affiliated with University in 1917, became part of the University's Medical Center in 1976, but is located in Lincoln. Semester system. Special facilities: Cruzan Center for Applied Clinical Research, Nebraska Center for Cellular Signaling, Biomaterials Group, Bioregulation Group.

Annual tuition: resident $32,700, nonresident $62,500. On-campus housing available. Average academic year off-campus housing costs: $12,000–$15,000. Contact Division of University Housing (P.O. Box 880622) for both on- and off-campus housing information. Phone: (402)472-3561. Total average cost for all other first-year expenses: $5500.

Enrollment: first-year class 45; total 176 (men 52%, women 48%, minorities 8%, state residents 76%), postgraduates 50. Faculty: full-time 52, part-time 31. Degree conferred: D.D.S., Certificates. The M.S. and Ph.D. are offered through the Graduate College (Medical Sciences Interdepartmental Area) with specializations in the Biomedical disciplines.

ADMISSION REQUIREMENTS. AADSAS report, transcripts, DAT (no later than October) required in support of application. TOEFL (minimum score 575) and Certification of Financial Support required of international students whose first language is not English. Interview by invitation only. At least three years of college preferred. Preference given to Nebraska residents and residents of North Dakota and Wyoming. Apply to Admissions Committee after July 1, before December 15. Phone: (402)472-1363; fax: (402)472-5290. Application fee $50.

ADMISSION STANDARDS. Selective. Accepts about 5–10% of all applicants. Usual minimum UGPA: 3.0 (A = 4). Mean DAT: academic 18.5, PAT 17.2; mean UGPA 3.8.

FINANCIAL AID. Scholarships, merit scholarships, minority scholarships, Grants-in-Aid, institutional loans, State Loan Programs, DEAL, HEAL, alternative loan programs, Federal Perkins Loans, Stafford Subsidized and Unsubsidized Loans, Military Service Commitment Scholarship programs are available. Institutional Financial Aid applications and information are generally available at the on-campus by-invitation interview. Contact the Financial Aid Office at Medical Center for current information. Priority deadine March 15. Phone: (402)559-4199. For most financial assistance and all need-based programs use FAFSA (School code: 006895); also submit Financial Aid Transcript, Federal Income Tax forms, and Use of Federal Funds Certification. Approximately 95% of students receive some form of financial assistance. Average award: resident $20,312, nonresident $32,667.

DEGREE REQUIREMENTS. For D.D.S.: satisfactory completion of forty-four-month program.; three summer sessions required. For graduate degrees, see Graduate College listing above.

FIELDS OF POSTGRADUATE STUDY.
Endodontics. Certificate.
General Practice. Certificate.
Oral Biology. M.S., Ph.D.
Orthodontics. Certificate.
Pediatric Dentistry. Certificate.
Periodontics. Certificate.

College of Law (P.O. Box 830902)
Web site: www.law.unl.edu

Established 1891. ABA approved since 1923. AALS charter member. Public control. Semester system. Full-time, day only. Special programs: summer programs at Cambridge University, England and University of Limerick, Ireland. Law library: 401,745 volumes, 2571 subscriptions; has LEXIS, NEXIS, WESTLAW, DAILOG.

Annual tuition: resident $9213, nonresident $21,580. On-campus housing available for both single and married students. Contact Housing Office for both on- and off-campus housing information. Phone: (402)472-3561. Law students tend to live off-campus. Off-campus housing and personal expenses: approximately $11,430.

Enrollment: first-year class 121; total full-time 396 (men 52%, women 48%, minorities 13%); no part-time students. Faculty: full-time 24, part-time 15. Student to faculty ratio 13.3 to 1. Degrees conferred: J.D., J.D.-M.A. (Economics, International Affairs, Political Sciences, Psychology), J.D.-M.B.A., J.D.-M.P.Acc., J.D.-Ph.D. (Psychology, Educational Administration), M.L.S.

ADMISSION REQUIREMENTS. LSDAS Law School report, bachelor's degree, transcripts, LSAT, personal statement, two letters of recommendation required in support of application. Interview not required. Transfer applicants and graduates of unaccredited colleges not considered. Apply to Dean of College after September 1, before March 1 for preferred consideration. First-year students admitted September only. Application fee $25. Phone: (402)472-2161; fax: (402)472-5185; e-mail: lawadm@unl.edu.

ADMISSION STANDARDS. Selective. Accepts approximately 41% of all students. Number of applicants 865; number of acceptance 352; number enrolled 136; LSAT (75% of students have a score at or above 153); GPA (75% of student have a GPA at or above 3.30). *U.S. News & World Report* ranking is in the second tier (tied at 77th) of all U.S. law schools.

FINANCIAL AID. Scholarships, fellowships, assistantships, Federal W/S, loans. Apply to the University Financial Aid Office by May 1. Phone: (402)472-2161. Use FAFSA (College code: 002565) and College's need-based grant application. Approximately 44% of first-year class receives some form of financial assistance.

DEGREE REQUIREMENTS. For J.D.: satisfactory completion of three-year program, last two semesters required in residence; 96 credit-hour program. For M.L.S., 33 credit programs; oral final exam. For J.D.-master's and doctoral programs: see Graduate school listing above.

UNIVERSITY OF NEBRASKA AT OMAHA
Omaha, Nebraska 68101
Web site: www.unomaha.edu

Founded 1908. CGS member. Coed. State control. Semester system. Special facilities: Center for Afghanistan Studies, Aviation Institute, Center for Faculty Development, Center for International Telecommunications Management, Center for Urban Education, Small Business Development Center. Library: 750,000 volumes, 3200 subscriptions. Total University enrollment: 14,000.

Tuition: per credit hour, resident $192, nonresident $507. No on-campus housing. For off-campus housing, contact Office of Student Housing. Day-care facilities available.

Graduate College

Graduate study since 1931. Enrollment: full-time 578, part-time 1716. Faculty teaching graduate students: full-time 376, part-time 15. Degrees conferred: M.A., M.S., M.B.A., M.M., M.P.A., M.S.W., Ed.S., Ph.D.

ADMISSION REQUIREMENTS. Transcripts, GRE/MAT/GMAT required in support of College's application. Online application available. Evidence of English proficiency or TOEFL required of international students. Accepts transfer applicants. Graduates of unaccredited institutions not considered. Apply to Director of Admissions by March 1 (Fall), October 1 (Spring), May 1 (Summer). Application fee $45. Phone: (402)554-2341; fax: (402)554-3143; e-mail: graduate@unomaha.edu.

ADMISSION STANDARDS. Selective for most departments. Usual minimum average: 3.0 (A = 4).

FINANCIAL AID. Annual awards from institutional funds: fellowships, graduate assistantships, internships, tuition waivers, Federal W/S, loans. Approved for VA benefits. Apply by March 1 to appropriate department chair for assistantships; to Financial Aid Office for all other programs. Phone: (402)554-2327. Use FAFSA. Aid sometimes available to part-time students.

DEGREE REQUIREMENTS. For M.A.: 30 semester hours minimum, at least 24 in residence; thesis included; final written/oral exam. For M.B.A., M.S., M.M., M.P.A., M.S.W.: 36 semester hours minimum, at least 30 in residence; final written/oral exam. For Ed.S.: one year minimum beyond the master's, at least one semester and one summer in full-time residence; field project; final oral exam. For Ph.D.: three years minimum, 90 semester hours, 27 hours graduate work within a consecutive 18-month period or less; reading knowledge of one foreign language, plus reading knowledge of one foreign language or proficiency in research techniques or evidence of knowledge of a collateral field; comprehensive exam; dissertation; final oral exam.

FIELDS OF STUDY.
Accounting.
Biology.
Business Administration.
Communication.
Computer Science.
Counseling.
Criminal Justice.
Economics.
Educational Administration and Supervision.
English.
Geography.
Gerontology.
Health, Physical Education, and Recreation.
History.
Information Technology.
Language Teaching.
Management Information Systems.
Mathematics.
Music.
Political Science.
Psychology. Includes educational, school industrial, organizational.
Public Administration.
Public Health.
Social Work.
Special Education and Communication Disorders.
Teacher Education.
Theatre.
Urban Studies.
Writing.

UNIVERSITY OF NEBRASKA MEDICAL CENTER
600 South 42nd Street
Omaha, Nebraska 68198-6585
Web site: www.unmc.edu

Established 1902. Public Control. Nebraska Health System is a member of Council of Teaching Hospitals. Schools located at

Medical Center are the College of Dentistry, College of Medicine, College of Nursing, College of Pharmacy, Graduate College, School of Allied Health. Special facilities; Geriatric Center, Eppley Cancer Research Institute, C. Louis Meyer Children's Rehabilitation Center. The Medical Center's NIH ranking was 115th with 110 awards/grants worth $41,728,648. Library: 247,434 volumes, 1741 subscriptions.

Graduate College
Web site: www.unmc.edu/grad.html

Tuition: per semester-hour credit, resident $211, Nursing $229; nonresident $569, Nursing $640. On- and off-campus housing is available. Phone: (402)559-5201.

Enrollment: full- and part-time 500. Graduate faculty: 350. Degrees conferred: M.P.H., M.S., Ph.D.

ADMISSION REQUIREMENTS. Transcripts, GRE, three letters of recommendation required in support of College's application. TOEFL (minimum score 550) required for foreign applicants. Accepts transfer applicants. Graduates of unaccredited colleges not considered. Deadlines for applications vary by program. Application fee $45. Phone: (402)559-6448; fax: (402)559-9671.

ADMISSION STANDARDS. Selective. Usual minimum average: 3.0 for M.S. and Ph.D. (A = 4).

FINANCIAL AID. Scholarships, fellowships, assistantships for teaching and research, internships, traineeships, tuition waivers, loans. Approved for VA benefits. Phone: (402)559-4199; fax: (402)559-9671. Use FAFSA. About 50% of students receive aid other than loans from all sources. Aid available for part-time students.

DEGREE REQUIREMENTS. For master's: six didactic courses; seminars; admission to candidacy; thesis/final document; final oral/written exam. For Ph.D.: three years minimum; reading knowledge of foreign language(s)/research tool may be required; admission to candidacy; dissertation; final oral/written exam.

FIELDS OF GRADUATE STUDY.
Biochemistry and Molecular Biology. M.S., Ph.D.
Cancer Research. M.S., Ph.D.
Cellular and Integrative Physiology. M.S., Ph.D.
Genetics, Cell Biology, and Anatomy. M.S., Ph.D.
Medical Sciences Interdepartmental Area. M.S., Ph.D.
Nursing. M.S.N., Ph.D.
Pathology and Microbiology. M.S., Ph.D.
Pharmaceutical Sciences. M.S., Ph.D.
Pharmacology and Experimental Neuroscience. M.S., Ph.D.
Public Health. M.P.H.
Toxicology. M.S., Ph.D.

College of Medicine
Web site: www.unmc.edu/dept/com

Established 1880 as Omaha Medical College. Joined University in 1902. Located in Omaha since 1913. Library: 284,000 volumes, 2200 subscriptions.

Annual tuition: resident $23,088, nonresident $50,988. Off-campus housing only. Contact Student Services for housing information. Total average figure for all other expenses: $14,400.

Enrollment: first-year class 122 (20 EDP), total 476 (men 57%, women 43%, minorities 9%, residents 88%). Faculty: full-time 579, part-time and volunteers 1100. Degrees conferred: M.D., M.D.-M.S., M.D.-Ph.D.

ADMISSION REQUIREMENTS. AMCAS report, transcripts, MCAT, screening interview required in support of application. Applicants must have completed at least three years of college study but degree recommended. Has EDP. Apply between June 1 and August 1. Preference given to state residents. Accepts transfer applicants. Apply to Office of Dean of College after June 1, before November 1. Application fee $45. Phone: (402)559-2259; fax: (402)559-6804.

ADMISSION STANDARDS. Competitive. Accepts about 13% of all applicants. Number of applications 1101 (807 out-of-state); number interviewed 382 (112 out-of-state); number of acceptance 169 (35 out-of-state); number enrolled 122 (17 out-of-state). Mean Composite MCAT 9.5; mean UGPA 3.71. *U.S. News & World Report* ranking for primary care medical school is 10th among all U.S. medical schools.

FINANCIAL AID. Scholarships, some merit scholarships, Grants-in-Aid, institutional loans, HEAL, alternative loan programs, Primary Care Loan Program, Federal Perkins Loans, Stafford Subsidized and Unsubsidized Loans, Service Commitment Scholarship programs are available. Assistantships/fellowships may be available for Combined Degree candidates. Financial Aid applications and information are sent out with the letter of acceptance and are due back within 30 days of date of acceptance. Contact the Financial Aid Office for current information. Phone: (404) 559-4199. Use FAFSA (School code: 006895); also submit Financial Aid Transcript, Federal Income Tax forms. Approximately 100% of students receive some form of financial assistance.

DEGREE REQUIREMENTS. For M.D.: satisfactory completion of four-year program. All students must pass USMLE Step 1 prior to entering third year; taking USMLE Step 2 is required. For M.D.-M.S.: generally a four-and-one-half- to five-and-one-half-year program. For M.D.-Ph.D.: generally a seven-year program.

FIELDS OF GRADUATE STUDY.
Biochemistry and Molecular Biology.
Cancer Research.
Cellular and Integrative Physiology.
Genetics, Cell Biology, and Anatomy.
Medical Sciences Interdepartmental Area.
Pathology and Microbiology.
Pharmaceutical Sciences.
Pharmacology and Experimental Neuroscience.
Public Health.
Toxicology.

UNIVERSITY OF NEVADA, LAS VEGAS
Las Vegas, Nevada 89154-9900
Web site: www.unlu.edu

Founded 1957. CGS member. Coed. State control. Semester system. Special facilities: Desert Biology Research Center, Education Equity Resource Center, Center for Energy Research, Harry Reid Center, Information Science Research Center, Center for In-Service Training and Educational Research, International Gaming Institute, Limnological Research Center, Nevada Small Business Development Center, Arnold Shaw Popular Music Research Center, Center for Public Data Research, Supercomputing Center for Energy and the Environment, Center for the Study of Public Policy, Sports Injury Research Center, Transportation Research Center, Center for Volcanic and Tectronic Studies. Library: 1,200,000 volumes, 9500 subscriptions. Total University enrollment: 27,300.

Tuition: per credit, resident $150, nonresident $315. Limited on-campus housing. Room and board: $3900–$4500 per semester. Contact the Office of Student Personnel Services for both on- and off-campus information. Phone: (702)895-3489.

Graduate College

Enrollment: full-time 1600, part-time 2000. Faculty: full-time 600, part-time 200. Degrees conferred: M.A., M.S., M.Ed., M.Arch., M.B.A., Ed.S., M.M., M.F.A., M.P.A., Ed.D., Ph.D.

ADMISSION REQUIREMENTS. Transcripts, two letters of recommendation; appropriate undergraduate background required in support of College's application. Individual departments may impose special requirements such as GRE, GMAT, MAT. Interview not normally required. TOEFL (minimum score 550) required for international applicants. Transfer applicants considered. Graduates of unaccredited institutions not considered. Apply to Dean, Graduate College; deadlines vary by department for U.S. applicants; May 1 (Fall), October 1 (Spring) for international applicants. Application fee $60, $75 for international applicants. Phone: (702)895-3320; fax: (702)895-4180.

ADMISSION STANDARDS. Selective. Usual minimum average: 2.75; 3.0 for last two years (A = 4).

FINANCIAL AID. Fellowships, partial scholarships, assistantships, internships, tuition waivers, Federal W/S, loans. Approved for VA benefits. Apply to Graduate Dean by March 1 for fellowships, scholarships, assistantships; to Financial Aid Office for all other programs. Phone: (702)895-3424. Use FAFSA and institutional FAF. Aid available for part-time students.

DEGREE REQUIREMENTS. Minimum of 30 hours. Varies with department and degree. Final examination required in all programs except M.B.A. Thesis required in most programs. For Ph.D., Ed.D.: 72 semester credits (Ph.D.), 90 credits (Ed.D.) beyond the bachelor's degree; seven-year time limit; at least two successive semesters in full-time residence; qualifying exam; comprehensive exam; dissertation; final oral exam.

FIELDS OF STUDY.

COLLEGE OF BUSINESS:
Accountancy. M.S.
Business Administration. M.B.A., E.M.B.A.
Economics. M.A.
Management Information Systems. M.S.

COLLEGE OF EDUCATION:
Curriculum and Instruction. Includes educational computing and technology, elementary education, English language arts education, library science, mathematics education, middle level education, multicultural education (K–12), postsecondary teaching English as a second language, reading and language arts, secondary education, TESOL. M.Ed., M.S.
Early Childhood Education. M.Ed.
Educational Leadership. Includes higher education administration, educational leadership (K–12), executive educational leadership (K–12, Ed.D.), higher education administration (Ph.D.). M.Ed., M.S., Ed.S., Ed.D., Ph.D.
Educational Psychology. Includes school counseling. M.Ed., M.S.
Executive Educational Leadership. Ed.D., Ph.D
Learning and Technology. Ph.D. only.
Physical Education. M.Ed. only.
Special Education. Includes generalist–mild disabilities, severe mental retardation, severe emotional disturbance, early childhood special education, gifted and talented, special education administration, school psychology, general special education in higher education (Ph.D). M.Ed., M.S., Ed.S., Ed.D., Ph.D.
Sports Educational Leadership. Ph.D.
Teacher Education. Ph.D. only.

COLLEGE OF ENGINEERING:
Biomedical Engineering. M.S.
Civil and Environmental Engineering. M.S.E., Ph.D.

Computer Science. M.S., Ph.D.
Construction Management. M.S.C.M.
Electrical Engineering. M.S., Ph.D.
Materials and Nuclear Engineering.
Mechanical Engineering. M.S., Ph.D.
Transportation. M.S.T.

COLLEGE OF FINE ARTS:
Architecture. M.Arch.
Art. Includes ceramics, drawing, painting, photography, print-making, sculpture. M.F.A.
Film/Screenwriting. M.F.A.
Music. Includes applied music, composition, music education. M.M., D.M.A.
Screenwriting. M.F.A.
Theatre Arts. Includes design technology, music theatre performance, playwriting. M.A., M.F.A.

COLLEGE OF HEALTH SCIENCES:
Health Physics. M.S. only.
Health Promotion. M.Ed.
*Kinesioiogy.*M.S.
Nursing. Includes family nurse practitioner, pediatric nurse practitioner, geriatric nurse practitioner. M.S.N.
Physical Therapy. M.S.
Public Health. M.P.H.

WILLIAM F. HARRAH COLLEGE OF HOTEL ADMINISTRATION:
Hospitality Administration. Includes executive hotel administration. M.H.A., Ph.D.
Hotel Administration. Includes food service administration, hotel management, tourism and convention administration. M.S.
Sport and Leisure Service Management. M.S.

COLLEGE OF LIBERAL ARTS:
Anthropology.
Creative Writing. M.F.A. only.
English.
Ethics and Policy Studies. M.A. only.
Foreign Languages. Includes French, Spanish. M.A. only.
History.
Political Science. M.S. only.
Psychology. Includes clinical, experimental.
Sociology.

COLLEGE OF SCIENCES:
Biochemistry. M.S. only.
Biological Sciences.
Chemistry. Includes analytical, biological, organic. M.S. only.
Geoscience. Includes economic geology, environmental geology, geochemistry, geochronology, geographic information systems, geomorphology, hydrogeology, igneous and metamorphic petrology, invertebrate paleontology, palynology, quaternary geology, sedimentology, soil studies, stratigraphy, structural geology, surficial process, tectonics, volcanology.
Mathematical Sciences. Includes applied mathematics, applied statistics, pure mathematics. M.S. only.
Physics. Includes astronomy.
Science. M.A.S. only.
Water Resources Management. M.S. only.

GREENSPUN COLLEGE OF URBAN AFFAIRS:
Communication Studies. M.A. only.
Counseling. Includes community, marriage and family. M.S. only.
Criminal Justice. M.A. only.
Crisis and Emergency Management. M.S.
Environmental Studies. Includes environmental policy, environmental chemistry.
Public Administration. M.P.A. only.
Public Affairs. Ph.D.
Social Work. M.S.W. only.

William S. Boyd School of Law (P.O. Box 451003)

Web site: www.law.unlv.edu

Established 1998. ABA approved since 2000. Public control. Semester system. Special facilities: Saltman Center for Conflict Resolution. Law library: 284,593 volumes, 4013 subscriptions; has LEXIS, NEXIS, WESTLAW, DIALOG, OCLC, CALE; has more than 1000 network connections.

Annual tuition: resident full-time $9568, nonresident $18,468; part-time per credit, resident $350, nonresident $700. Limited on-campus housing available. Contact Admission Office for both on- and off-campus information. Off-campus housing and personal expenses: approximately $13,350.

Enrollment: first-year class, full-time 106, part-time 45; total full- and part-time 471 (men 52%, women 48%, minorities 27%). Faculty: full-time 25, part-time 15. Student-to-faculty ratio is 15 to 1. Degrees conferred: J.D., J.D.-M.B.A., M.D.-M.S.W.

ADMISSION REQUIREMENTS. LSDAS Law School report, LSAT (not later than February test date; if more than one LSAT, repeated scores are used if higher), bachelor's degree from an accredited institution, personal statement, one recommendation, transcripts (must show all schools attended and at least three years of study) required in support of application. Applicants must have received bachelor's degree prior to enrollment. Interview not required but may be requested by School. In addition, international applicants whose native language is not English must submit TOEFL (not older than two years), International Student Financial Certificate form, degree must be certified as equivalent to an American baccalaureate, certified transcripts must be sent directly to School. Apply to Office of Admission after September 15, before March 15 (priority deadline). First-year students admitted Fall only. Rolling admissions process, notification starts in November and is finished by late April. Application fee $50. Phone: (702) 895-2440; e-mail: request@ law.unlv.edu.

ADMISSION STANDARDS. Selective. Accepts approximately 12% of full-time and 22% of part-time students. Number of full-time applicants 2134, part-time 274; number of full-time acceptances 258, part-time 59; number of full-time enrolled 106, part-time 45; LSAT (75% of full-time students have a score at or above 155, part-time 152); GPA (75% of full-time students have a GPA at or above 3.55, part-time 3.01). *U.S. News & World Report* ranking is in the second tier (tied at 100) of all U.S. law schools.

FINANCIAL AID. Scholarships, merit scholarships, Grants-in-Aid, private and institutional loans, Federal loans, Federal W/S available. For all other programs apply after January 1, before February 1 to Financial Aid Office. Phone: (702)895-0630. Use FAFSA, also submit Financial Aid Transcript, Federal Income Tax forms. Approximately 54% of students receive some form of financial assistance. Average scholarships grant: $7000 (full-time), $2500 (part-time).

DEGREE REQUIREMENTS. For J.D.: three-year full-time program; four-year part-time program. For joint degree programs see graduate programs above.

UNIVERSITY OF NEVADA, RENO

Reno, Nevada 89557-0035
Web site: www.unr.edu

Founded 1864. CGS member. Coed. State control. Semester system. Special facilities: Center for Advanced Study, Agricultural Experiment Station; Biological Science Center, Bureaus of Business, Economics, and Government Research; Desert Research Institute; Engineering Research and Development Center, Energy and Environmental Engineering Center, Fleischmann Atmospherium-Planetarium; nuclear reactor; Nevada Mining Analytical Laboratory; Mackay Mineral Resource Research Institute;

Nevada Bureau of Mines; Reno Metallurgy Research Center, Water Resource Center. The University's NIH ranking is 185th among all U.S. institutions with 41 awards/grants valued at $19,946,198. Two of the University's faculty members have been elected to National Honor Academies and this ranks it 117th among all U.S. institutions. The Library: approximately 1,100,000 volumes, 15,000 subscriptions. Total University enrollment: 16,300.

Tuition: per credit, resident $150, nonresident $315. On-campus housing for both single and married students. Average academic year housing cost: $7440–$10,125. Contact Housing Services Office for both on- and off-campus housing information. Phone: (775)784-6107.

Graduate School

Semester enrollment: full-time 1020, part-time 1312. University faculty teaching graduate students: full-time 600, part-time 32. Degrees conferred: M.A., M.Acc., M.S., M.Ed., M.B.A., M.J.S., M.M., M.S.W., Ph.D., Ed.D.

ADMISSION REQUIREMENTS. Two official transcripts from each college or institution attended, GRE/Subject Tests, GMAT (for M.B.A.) required in support of School's application. Online application available. Written statement of purpose, biography, writing sample, letters of recommendation required by some programs. TOEFL, financial statement, and medical history and exam for international applicants. Accepts transfer applicants. Graduates of unaccredited institutions not considered. Apply to Office of Admissions and Records three weeks prior to registration. Many departments have earlier deadlines. Application fee $40. Phone: (775)784-6869; fax: (775)784-6064; e-mail: gradadmissions@unr.edu.

ADMISSION STANDARDS. Selective, for most departments. Usual minimum average: 2.75 for master's; 3.0 for doctoral programs (A = 4).

FINANCIAL AID. Annual awards from institutional funds: 20 scholarships, 214 teaching assistantships, 517 research assistantships, 30 internships, Federal W/S, loans. Apply by March 1 to Chair of Scholarships, Committee for Scholarships; to Dean of College for internships and fellowships; to department concerned for assistantships; to Financial Aid Office for all other programs. Use FAFSA. Phone: (775)784-4666. About 50% of full-time students receive aid other than loans from School and outside sources.

DEGREE REQUIREMENTS. For M.A., M.S., M.Acc., M.B.A., M.M.: 30–33 semester credits minimum, at least 21 in residence; thesis/nonthesis option; reading knowledge of one foreign language required by some departments; final oral/written exam. For M.Ed., M.S.W.: 32 credits minimum, at least 24 in residence; two years' educational experience; final paper or comprehensive exam; final oral/written exam; six-year time limit. For Ph.D., 72 semester credits; comprehensive exam; dissertation; final oral defense. For Ed.D.: 90 semester credits minimum beyond the bachelor's; eight-year time limit; at least two successive semesters in full-time residence; qualifying exam; comprehensive exam; dissertation; final oral exam.

FIELDS OF STUDY.
Accountancy. M.Acc. only.
Animal Science. M.S. only.
Anthropology.
Atmospheric Sciences.
Basque Studies. Ph.D. only.
Behavior Analysis.
Biochemistry.
Biology. M.S. only.
Biomedical Engineering.
Business Administration. M.B.A. only.
Cell and Molecular Biology. Ph.D.

Cellular and Molecular Pharmacology and Physiology. Ph.D. only.
Chemical Engineering.
Chemical Physics. Ph.D. only.
Chemistry.
Civil and Environmental Engineering.
Computer Engineering.
Computer Science. M.S. only.
Counseling and Educational Psychology.
Criminal Justice.
Curriculum and Instruction. Ed.D., Ph.D.
Ecology, Evolution, and Conservation Biology. Ph.D. only.
Economics. M.A., M.S. only.
Educational Leadership.
Electrical Engineering.
Elementary Education. M.A., Ed.D., M.S. only.
English.
Environmental Science. M.S. only.
Finance.
Fine Arts.
Foreign Languages and Literatures. Includes French, German, Spanish. M.A. only.
Geochemistry.
Geo-Engineering. Ph.D. only.
Geography. M.S. only.
Geological Engineering. M.S. only.
Geology and Related Earth Sciences.
Geophysics. Ph.D. only.
Health Ecology. M.S. only.
History.
Human Development and Family Studies. M.S. only.
Hydrogeologic Sciences.
Information Systems.
Journalism. M.A. only.
Judicial Studies. For sitting judges only. M.J.S.
Justice Management.
Land Use Planning. M.S. only.
Literacy Studies.
Mathematics and Statistics. M.S. only.
Mechanical Engineering.
Metallurgical Engineering.
Mining Engineering. M.S. only.
Music. M.A., M.M. only.
Natural Resources and Environmental Science.
Nursing. M.S. only.
Nutrition. M.S. only.
Philosophy. M.A. only.
Physics.
Political Science.
Psychology. Includes behavior analysis, clinical, experimental.
Public Administration and Policy. M.P.A. only.
Public Health. M.P.H.
Resource Economics. M.S. only.
Secondary Education. M.A., M.Ed., M.S. only.
Social Psychology. Ph.D. only.
Social Work. M.S.W. only.
Sociology. M.A. only.
Special Education. M.A., M.Ed., M.S. only.
Speech Communication. M.A. only.
Speech Pathology. Ph.D. only.
Speech Pathology and Audiology. M.S. only.
Teaching of English as a Second Language. M.A. only.
Teaching of Mathematics. M.A.T.M. only.

School of Medicine
Web site: www.unr.edu/med

Established 1969. NIH ranking is 185th among all U.S. institutions with 41 awards/grants worth $19,946,198.

Annual tuition: resident $13,638, nonresident $31,848. No on-campus housing available. Total average figure for all other expenses: $18,000.

Enrollment: first-year class 52 (first-year class will be expanded to 62 by 2008) (EDP 2), total 200 (men 49%, women 51%, minorities 6%, state residents 93%). Faculty: full-time 120, part-time 50. Degrees conferred: M.D., M.D.-Ph.D.

ADMISSION REQUIREMENTS. AMCAS report, transcripts, MCAT, three letters of evaluation required in support of application. Interview by invitation only. Graduates of unaccredited colleges not considered. Preference given to residents of Nevada and residents of Alaska, Idaho, Montana, and Wyoming. Will consider transfer applicants. Has EDP; apply between June 1 and October 1. Apply to Admissions Office after June 1, before November 1. Application fee $45. Phone: (775)784-6063; fax: (775)784-6096.

ADMISSION STANDARDS. Selective. Accepts about 10–15% of all applicants. Number of applications 794 (n/a out-of-state); number interviewed 190 (n/a out-of-state); number of acceptance n/a (n/a out-of-state); number enrolled 52 (n/a out-of-state). Mean Composite MCAT 9.5; mean UGPA 3.70.

FINANCIAL AID. Scholarships, loans. Apply to Director of Student Affairs; no specified closing date. Phone: (775)784-4666. Use FAFSA (School code: 002568). About 77% of students receive some aid from School and outside sources.

DEGREE REQUIREMENTS. For M.D: satisfactory completion of four-year program; all students must take both Step 1 and Step 2 of USMLE prior to awarding of M.D. Third and fourth years are spent in Reno, Las Vegas, and rural Nevada. For Ph.D.: see Graduate School listing above.

FIELDS OF GRADUATE STUDY.
Biochemistry.
Biomedical Engineering.
Cellular and Molecular Pharmacology and Physiology.
Cell and Molecular Biology.
Microbiology.
Speech-Language Pathology.

NEW ENGLAND CONSERVATORY OF MUSIC

Boston, Massachusetts 02115-5000
Web site: www.newenglandconservatory.edu

Founded 1867. Coed. Private control. Semester system. Library: 78,000 volumes, 275 subscriptions. Total enrollment: 800.

Annual tuition: full-time $27,500. On-campus housing available for single students. Average academic year housing cost: $10,950 (including board).

Graduate Program

Enrollment: full-time 370, part-time 19. Faculty: full-time 81, part-time 123. Degrees conferred: M.M., Graduate Diploma, Artist Diploma, D.M.A.

ADMISSION REQUIREMENTS. Transcripts, bachelor's, three letters of recommendation, audition required in support of application. Interview required by some departments. TOEFL required for international applicants. Apply by January 15 (Fall), November 1 (Spring) to the Dean of Admissions and Financial Aid. Application fee $100. Phone: (617)585-1101; fax: (617)585-1115.

ADMISSION STANDARDS. Selective. Usual minimum average: 3.0 (A = 4).

FINANCIAL AID. Scholarships, teaching fellowships, teaching assistantships, tuition waivers, Federal W/S, loans. Apply to the Financial Aid Office; no specified closing date. Phone: (617)585-1110. Use FAFSA (School code: 002194) and institutional FAF. Approximately 60% of students receive aid other than loans from School. Aid sometimes available for part-time students.

DEGREE REQUIREMENTS. For master's: 32 credits. For diplomas: at least 30 credits beyond the master's; music history exam, music theory exam, language exam (for vocal pedagogy and vocal performance); public performance; special project for some programs. For D.M.A.: 60 semester hours beyond the master's degree, at least 30 credits in full-time residence; reading knowledge of one foreign language/research technique, depending on program; qualifying exam; three recitals or other public performance for most programs; dissertation or final document; final oral exam.

FIELDS OF STUDY.
Brass and Percussion. Includes horn, trumpet, trombone, tuba, percussion.
Composition.
Conducting. Includes choral, orchestral, wind ensemble.
Contemporary Improvisation.
Historical Performance.
Jazz Studies.
Keyboard Instruments. Includes piano, collaborative piano.
Music History and Musicology.
Professional Piano Trio Training Program.
Professional String Quartet Training Program.
Theoretical Studies.
Strings. Includes violin, viola, violoncello, double bass, guitar, harp.
Voice. Includes performance, pedagogy, opera.
Woodwinds. Includes flute, oboe, clarinet, bassoon, saxophone.

NEW ENGLAND SCHOOL OF LAW

154 Stuart Street
Boston, Massachusetts 02116
Web site: www.nesl.edu

Established 1908 as Portia Law School; it was the first law school in the nation exclusively for women. Name changed 1969. ABA approved since 1969. AALS member. Private control. Semester system. Full-time (day), part-time (evening), part-time (flexible to accommodate child-care responsibilities). Special facilities: Center for International Law and Policy, Center for Law and Social Responsibility, Center for Business Law. Special program: foreign study in London, Galway, Malta, the Czech Republic, the Netherlands. Law library: 309,423 volumes, 3104 subscriptions; has LEXIS, NEXIS, WESTLAW, DIALOG, OCLC, CALI.

Annual tuition: full-time $25,865, part-time $19,415. No on-campus housing available. Law students live off-campus. Contact Admissions Office for off-campus information. Off-campus housing and personal expenses: approximately $15,530.

Enrollment: first-year class 239, part-time 105; total full- and part-time 1200 (men 47%, women 53%, minorities 12%). Faculty: full-time 45, part-time 70. Student to faculty ratio 25.2 to 1. Degree conferred: J.D.

ADMISSION REQUIREMENTS. LSDAS Law School report, bachelor's degree, transcripts, LSAT, personal statement, two letters of recommendation required in support of application. Accepts transfer applicants. Graduates of unaccredited colleges not considered. Apply to Director of Admissions by March 15. Application fee $65. Phone: (617)422-7210; fax: (617)422-7200.

ADMISSION STANDARDS. Selective. Accepts approximately 37% of full-time and 45% of part-time students. Number of full-time applicants 2803, part-time 580; number of full-time acceptance 1044, part-time 261; number of full-time enrolled 253, part-time 129; LSAT (75% of full-time students have a score at or above 150, part-time 148); GPA (75% of full-time students have a GPA at or above 3.12, part-time 2.92). *U.S. News & World Report* ranking is in the fourth tier of all U.S. law schools.

FINANCIAL AID. Minority and disadvantaged scholarships, grants, Federal W/S, loans. Apply to Office of Financial Aid by April 15. Phone: (617)422-7298. Use FAFSA (School code: G08916) and NESL financial aid application. Approximately 42% of students receive some form of financial assistance.

DEGREE REQUIREMENTS. For J.D.: satisfactory completion of 84 credit-hour program.

UNIVERSITY OF NEW ENGLAND
11 Hills Beach Road
Biddeford, Maine 04005-9526
Web site: www.une.edu

The University's charter dates back to 1831; however, the University was formed in 1978. A 20-minute drive from Portland. University has a suburban campus in Portland. Private control. Semester system. Special facilities: Harold Alfond Center for Health Sciences, Center for Human Services. Library: 86,000 volumes, 1280 subscriptions. Total University enrollment: 2500.

The University's graduate programs include College of Osteopathic Medicine, the College of Professional and Continuing Studies.

College of Osteopathic Medicine

College established 1970 as St. Francis College of Osteopathic Medicine, merged with University in 1978. Affiliated with 20 community hospitals and medical centers.

Annual tuition: $39,330. No on-campus housing available. Contact Graduate Housing office for off-campus housing information. Phone: (297)283-0171, ext 2272.

Enrollment: first-year class 121, total 496 (men 46%, women 54%, minorities 10%, state residents 19%). Faculty: full-time 101, part-time 431. Degrees conferred: D.O., D.O.-M.P.H.

ADMISSION REQUIREMENTS. Preference given to students who will practice in New England; U.S. citizens and permanent residents only. For serious consideration an applicant should have a 2.75 (A = 4) GPA or above. Bachelor's degree from an accredited institution required. Apply through AACOMAS (file after June 1, before February 1), submit MCAT (will accept test results from last two years; MCAT should be taken no later than September of the year prior to the year of anticipated enrollment), official transcripts from each school attended (should show at least 90 semester credits/135 quarter credit), service processing fee. After a review of the AACOMAS application and supporting documents a decision is made concerning which candidates should receive supplemental materials. The supplemental application, an application fee of $55, a personal statement, and three recommendations (at least two from science faculty; one from a D.O. is highly recommended) should be returned to Office of Admission as soon as possible. In addition, international applicants must submit foreign transcripts to the World Education Service for translation and evaluation. TOEFL may be required of those applicants whose native language is other than English. Interviews are by invitation only and generally for final selection. First-year students admitted Fall only. Rolling admissions process, notification starts in October and is finished when class is filled. Phone: (800)477-4UNE, (207)283-0171 ext. 218; fax: (207)283-3249.

ADMISSION STANDARDS. Competitive. Accepts about 8% of all applicants. Number of applications 2448 (2396 out-of-state); number interviewed 306 (269 out-of-state); number of acceptance 221 (188 out-of-state); number enrolled 121 (93 out-of-state). Usual minimum UGPA: 2.75 (A = 4). Mean Composite MCAT 8.8, mean UGPA 3.40.

FINANCIAL AID. Scholarships, minority scholarships, grants, institutional loans, Maine Osteopathic Loan Fund, NOF, HEAL, alternative loan programs, Federal Perkins Loans, Stafford Subsidized and Unsubsidized Loans, Service Obligation Scholarship programs, Military and National Health Service programs are available. Financial Aid applications and information are generally available at the on-campus, by-invitation interview. Apply by April 15. Contact the Office of Financial Aid for current information. Phone: (207)283-0171. Use FAFSA (School code: 002050); also submit Financial Aid Transcript, Federal Income Tax forms. Approximately 80% of students receive some form of financial assistance.

DEGREE REQUIREMENTS. For D.O.: satisfactory completion of four-year program.

UNIVERSITY OF NEW HAMPSHIRE
Durham, New Hampshire 03824-3547
Web site: www.unh.edu

Founded in 1866. Located 60 miles N of Boston. CGS member. Coed. State control. Semester system. Special facilities: Agricultural Experiment Station, Center for Business and Economics Research, Family Research Center, Center for Humanities, Institute on Disabilities, Environmental Research Group, Manchester Manufacturing Management Center, New Hampshire Small Business Development Center, Institute for Policy and Social Science Research, Institute for the Study of Earth, Oceans and Space, Center for Venture Research, Water Resources Research Center. Library: more than 1,800,000 volumes, 6500 subscriptions. Total University enrollment: 14,500.

Annual tuition: full-time resident $8010, nonresident $19,730; part-time, resident $445 per credit, nonresident $810. On-campus housing available for married students (154 units) and single students (180 rooms). Average academic year housing cost: $8400. For on-campus housing, apply to Residential Life, Pettee House. Phone: (603)862-2120; for off-campus housing, contact Commuter Transfer Center. Phone: (603)862-3612.

Graduate School

Graduate study since 1928. Enrollment: full-time 1237, part-time 1244. Graduate faculty: 602. Degrees conferred: M.A., M.A.L.A., M.S., M.A.T., M.S.W., M.S.T., M.A.O.E., M.B.A., M.Ed., M.H.A., M.P.A., C.A.G.S., Ph.D.

ADMISSION REQUIREMENTS. Transcripts, three letters of recommendation required in support of School's application. Online application available. GRE required by some departments; GMAT required for M.B.A. applicants. TOEFL required for international applicants. International applicants admitted Fall only. Apply to Dean of the Graduate School by April 1 (Fall), December 1 (Spring), April 1 (Summer), by February 15 to ensure financial aid consideration (earlier applications encouraged). Application fee $60. Phone: (603)862-3000; fax: (603)862-0275; e-mail: grad.school@unh.edu.

ADMISSION STANDARDS. Selective to competitive. Usual minimum average: 2.75 (A = 4).

FINANCIAL AID. Annual awards from institutional funds: academic scholarships, tuition scholarships, teaching assistantships, internships, tuition waivers, Federal W/S, loans. Approved for VA benefits. Apply by February 15 to Graduate School for scholarships, assistantships; to Financial Aid Office for all other programs. Phone: (603)862-3600. Use FAFSA. Financial aid available for part-time students.

DEGREE REQUIREMENTS. For master's: 30 credits minimum; thesis/nonthesis option in some departments. For C.A.G.S.: 32–40 credits beyond master's. For Ph.D.: three years beyond bachelor's, at least one year in residence; written exam; language required in some programs.

FIELDS OF STUDY.
Accounting. M.S.
Adult and Occupational Education. M.A.O.E.
Animal and Nutritional Sciences. M.S., Ph.D.
Animal Science. M.S.
Biochemistry. M.S., Ph.D.
Biology. M.S.
Business Administration. M.B.A.
Chemical Engineering. M.S.
Chemistry. M.S., M.S.T., Ph.D.
Civil Engineering. M.S.
Communication Science and Disorders. M.S.
Computer Science. M.S., Ph.D.
Counseling. M.A., M.Ed.
Earth and Environmental Sciences. Includes geology, oceanography. M.S., Ph.D.
Economics. M.A., Ph.D.
Education. Includes administration/supervision, elementary, secondary, early childhood, reading, reading/writing instruction, special, teacher leadership. M.A., M.A.T., C.A.G.S., M.Ed., Ph.D.
Electrical and Computer Engineering. M.S.
Engineering. Ph.D.
English. Includes literature, language and linguistics, and writing. M.A., M.S.T., Ph.D.
Environmental Education. M.A.
Family Studies. Includes marriage and family therapy. M.S.
Genetics. M.S., Ph.D.
History. Includes museum studies. M.A., Ph.D.
Hydrology. M.S.
Justice Studies. M.S.
Kinesiology. M.S.
Liberal Studies. M.A.L.S.
Literacy and Schooling. Ph.D.
Materials Science. M.S.
Mathematics. Includes applied mathematics, statistics. M.S., M.S.T. (Summer only), Ph.D.
Mechanical Engineering. M.S.
Microbiology. M.S., Ph.D.
Music. M.A., M.S.
Natural Resource. Includes environmental conservation, forestry, soil science, water resources, wildlife. M.S., Ph.D.
Nursing. M.S., Ph.D.
Nutritional Science. M.S.
Ocean Engineering. M.S.
Ocean Mapping. M.S.
Ocean Systems Design. Ph.D.
Occupational Therapy. M.S.
Painting. M.F.A.
Physical Education. M.S.
Physics. M.S., Ph.D.
Plant Biology. M.S., Ph.D.
Political Science. M.A.
Psychology. Ph.D.
Public Administration. M.P.A.
Public Health. M.P.H.
Recreation Management. M.S.
Resource Administration and Management. M.S.
Resource Economics. M.S.
Sociology. M.A., Ph.D.
Social Work. M.S.W.
Spanish. M.A.
Zoology. M.S., Ph.D.

UNIVERSITY OF NEW HAVEN
West Haven, Connecticut 06516-1916
Web site: www.newhaven.edu

Established 1920. CGS member. Coed. Trimester system. Private control. Library: 300,000 volumes; 1400 subscriptions.
Tuition: per credit $545. Limited on-campus housing available. Contact the Residential Services office for on- and off-campus housing information. Phone: (203)932-7176.

Graduate School

Graduate study since 1969. Enrollment: full- and part-time 1600. Faculty: full-time 250, part-time 150. Degrees conferred: M.A., M.S., M.B.A., M.P.A., M.S.I.E., Sc.D., M.B.A.-M.S.I.E., M.B.A.-M.P.A.

ADMISSION REQUIREMENTS. Transcripts, two letters of recommendation required in support of School's application. GRE required for M.S.-Forensic Science, GMAT for business. TOEFL and certified financial support form required of all international applicants. Accepts transfer applicants. Graduates of unaccredited colleges not considered. Apply to Graduate School by June 15 (Fall), October 1 (Winter), January 15 (Spring). Application fee $50. Phone: (800)DIAL-UNH, ext. 7133, (203)932-7133; fax: (203)932-7137.

ADMISSION STANDARDS. Competitive. Usual minimum average: 2.75 (A = 4).

FINANCIAL AID. Annual awards from institutional funds: thirty-five fellowships, twenty-seven administrative assistantships, eighteen research assistantships, nineteen teaching assistantships, Federal W/S, loans. Approved for VA benefits. Apply by April 15 to Dean for fellowships, assistantships; to Director of Financial Aid for all other programs. Phone: (203)932-7315. Use FAFSA. About 12% of students receive aid other than loans from University and outside sources. Aid sometimes available for part-time students.

DEGREE REQUIREMENTS. For M.A., M.S.: 36–48 credit hours minimum, depending on program; 30 credits in residence; thesis/nonthesis option. For M.P.A.: 42 credit hours minimum, 30 credits in residence; internship; special project. For M.B.A.: 57 credit hours minimum, at least 30 in residence; thesis/nonthesis option. For Sc.D.: 30 credits beyond the master's minimum; dissertation; final oral exam.

FIELDS OF STUDY.
Accounting.
Aviation Science.
Business Administration. Includes options in accounting, finance, global marketing, technology management, marketing, health care administration, human resources, public relations, sports management.
Cellular and Molecular Biology.
Community Psychology.
Computer and Informational Science.
Criminal Justice.
Education.
Electrical Engineering.
Environmental Engineering.
Environmental Science.
Executive Engineering Management.
Executive M.B.A.

Finance and Financial Services.
Fire Science.
Forensic Science.
Health Care Administration.
Hospitality and Tourism.
Human Nutrition.
Industrial Engineering.
Industrial Hygiene.
Industrial/Organizational Psychology.
Labor Relations.
Management Systems. Sc.D. only.
Mechanical Engineering.
National Security.
Occupational Safety and Health Management.
Operations Research.
Public Administration.
Taxation.

Educational Technology.
Elementary Education.
English.
ESL.
Health Education.
Marriage and Family Therapy. Ed.S. only.
Music. Includes applied, composition, conducting, education.
Nursing.
Physical Education.
Reading.
Secondary Education.
Special Education. Includes teaching developmentally handicapped, learning disabilities; Ed.S. only.
Speech. Includes speech correction, pathology.
Speech Pathology.
Teaching English as a Second Language.

COLLEGE OF NEW JERSEY

P.O. Box 7718
Ewing, New Jersey 08628
Web site: www.tcnj.edu

Established 1855. CGS member. Coed. State control. Semester system. Library: 560,000 volumes, 1400 subscriptions. Total enrollment: 6700.

Tuition: per credit, resident $569, nonresident $763. No on-campus housing available. Contact Off-campus Housing Office for off-campus information. Phone: (609)771-2466. Day-care facilities available.

Graduate Division

Graduate study since 1947. Enrollment: full-time 130, part-time 743. Graduate faculty: full-time 41, part-time 12. Degrees conferred: M.A., M.S., M.Ed., M.A.T., M.S.N., Ed.S.

ADMISSION REQUIREMENTS. Transcripts, GRE or MAT, letters of recommendation required in support of application. TOEFL required for international applicants. Accepts transfer applicants. Graduates of unaccredited institutions are not considered. Apply to the Office of Graduate Admission by April 15 (Fall), October 15 (Spring). Some programs have earlier deadlines. Application fee $50. Phone: (609)771-2300; fax: (609)637-5105; e-mail: graduate@tcnj.edu.

ADMISSION STANDARDS. Selective. Usual minimum average: 2.75 (A = 4).

FINANCIAL AID. Graduate assistantships, internships, Federal W/S, loans. Apply by May 1 to Dean of Graduate Study for assistantships, Financial Aid Office for all other programs. Phone: (609)771-2211. Use FAFSA. About 2-5% of students receive aid other than loans from College and outside sources. Aid available for part-time students.

DEGREE REQUIREMENTS. For master's: 30 credits minimum; final written exam. For M.A.T.: 40–56 credits; final written exam. For M.S.N.: 36 credits; final written exam.

FIELDS OF STUDY.
Applied Spanish Studies.
Audiology.
Counselor Education.
Developmental Reading.
Early Childhood Education.
Education.
Educational Leadership.

NEW JERSEY CITY UNIVERSITY

Jersey City, New Jersey 07305-1957
Web site: www.njcu.edu

Founded 1927. Name changed 1998. Coed. Public control. Semester system. Special facilities: ADA Technology Center, Center for the Advancement of Teaching and Learning, Peter W. Rodino Jr. Institute of Criminal Justice. Library: 250,000 volumes, 1550 current periodicals. Total University enrollment: 8500.

Tuition: per credit, resident $414, nonresident $764. No on-campus housing for graduate students. Contact Director of Student Services for off-campus housing information. Phone: (201)200-2338. Day-care facilities available.

Graduate Studies

Graduate study since 1960. Enrollment: full-time 41, part-time 974. Graduate faculty: full-time 87, part-time 22. Degrees conferred: M.A., M.F.A., M.S., Professional Diploma.

ADMISSION REQUIREMENTS. Official transcripts, two letters of recommendation, interview, GRE/MAT required in support of application. TOEFL required for all international applicants. Accepts transfer applicants. Graduates of unaccredited institutions not considered. Apply to Director of Graduate Studies by August 1 (Fall), December 1 (Spring), May 1 (Summer). Application fee: none. Phone: (877)NJCUGRAD, (201)200-3409.

ADMISSION STANDARDS. Selective. Usual minimum average: 2.75 (A = 4).

FINANCIAL AID. Assistantships, Federal W/S, loans. Approved for VA benefits. Apply by June 1 to Office of Graduate Studies. Use FAFSA and institutional FAF. About 4% of students receive aid from all sources. Aid sometimes available to part-time students.

DEGREE REQUIREMENTS. For M.A., M.S.: 32 credit hours minimum, at least 24 in residence; thesis or final document; practicum or comprehensive exam. For M.F.A.: 60 credit hours minimum, at least 45 in residence; special project. For M.S. in Health, Criminal Justice, Nursing: 36–42 credit programs; residency; thesis/project. For Professional Diploma: 33 credits minimum beyond the master's.

FIELDS OF STUDY.

GRADUATE COLLEGE OF ARTS AND SCIENCE:
Art.
Art Education.
Counseling.
Educational Psychology.

Mathematics Education.
Music Education.
Performance.
School Psychology.

GRADUATE COLLEGE OF EDUCATION:
Early Childhood Education.
Educational Leadership.
Educational Technology.
Literacy Education.
Multicultural Education.
Special Education.
Urban Education.

GRADUATE COLLEGE OF PROFESSIONAL STUDIES:
Accounting.
Criminal Justice. Includes law enforcement and criminal justice.
Finance. Includes professional financial planning, financial analysis, financial management.
Health Sciences. Includes community health education, health administration, school health education.
Nursing. Includes urban health, holistic nursing.

NEW JERSEY INSTITUTE OF TECHNOLOGY

Newark, New Jersey 07102-1982
Web site: www.njit.edu

Founded 1881. CGS member. Coed. State control. Semester system. Special facilities: Biomedical Engineering Center for Manufacturing Systems, Hazardous Substance Management Research Center, Center for Transportation Studies and Research. Library: 204,471 volumes, 1100 subscriptions. Total Institute enrollment: 8000.

Annual tuition: full-time resident $9620, nonresident $13,542. Limited on-campus housing available. Average academic year housing cost: $5500–$7800. Contact the Office of Residence Life for both on- and off-campus housing information. Phone: (973) 596-3041. Day-care facilities available.

Graduate Studies

Enrollment: full-time 1261, part-time 1797. Faculty: full-time 416, part-time 223. Degrees conferred: M.Arch., M.F.S., M.S., Ph.D.

ADMISSION REQUIREMENTS. Two official transcripts, GRE, three letters of recommendation required in support of application. Online application available. TOEFL required for international applicants. Interview not required. Accepts transfer applicants. Graduates of unaccredited institutions not considered. Apply to Office of University Admissions by June 1 (Fall), October 15 (Spring); Architecture applicants apply by April 1 (fall), October 15 (Spring). Application fee $60. Phone: (973)596-3300; fax: (973)596-3461; e-mail: admissions@njit.edu.

ADMISSION STANDARDS. Selective for most departments. Usual minimum average: master's, GPA of at least 2.5; doctoral, GPA of at least 3.5.

FINANCIAL AID. More than 400 annual awards from institutional funds: teaching/research assistantships, tuition remission, Federal W/S, loans. Approved for VA benefits. Apply by March 15 to appropriate department chair for assistantships; to Financial Aid Office for all other programs. Phone: (973)-596-3479. Use FAFSA. About 50% of full-time students receive aid other than loans from College and outside sources.

DEGREE REQUIREMENTS. For master's: 30 credit hours minimum; thesis/project. For Ph.D.: 60 credit hours minimum beyond the master's degree, at least one year in residence; qualifying exam; thesis/research design; final oral exam.

FIELDS OF STUDY.
Applied Mathematics. M.S.
Applied Physics. M.S., Ph.D.
Applied Statistics. M.S.
Architecture. M.Arch.
Architectural Studies. M.S.
Bioinformatics. M.S.
Biology. M.S., Ph.D.
Biomedical Engineering. M.S., Ph.D.
Biomedical Informatics. M.S., Ph.D.
Business Administration in Management of Technology. M.S.
Chemical Engineering. M.S., Ph.D.
Chemistry. Ph.D.
Civil Engineering. M.S., Ph.D.
Computational Biology. M.S.
Computer Engineering. M.S., Ph.D.
Computer Science. M.S., Ph.D.
Electrical Engineering. M.S., Ph.D.
Emergency Management and Business Continuity. M.S.
Engineering Management. M.S.
Engineering Science. M.S.
Environmental Engineering. M.S., Ph.D.
Environmental Policy Studies. M.S.
Environmental Science. M.S., Ph.D.
History. M.S.
Industrial Engineering. M.S., Ph.D.
Information Systems. M.S., Ph.D.
Infrastructure Planning. M.S.
Internet Engineering. M.S.
Management. M.S., Ph.D. (cooperatively with Rutgers—Newark).
Manufacturing Systems Engineering. M.S.
Materials Science and Engineering. M.S., Ph.D.
Mathematical Sciences. M.S., Ph.D.
Mechanical Engineering. M.S., Ph.D.
Occupational Safety and Health Engineering. M.S.
Occupational Safety and Industrial Hygiene. M.S.
Pharmaceutical Engineering. M.S.
Physics. M.S.
Professional and Technical Communication. M.S., Ph.D.
Public Health. M.S.
Telecommunication. M.S.
Transportation. M.S., Ph.D.
Urban Systems. M.S., Ph.D.

NEW MEXICO HIGHLANDS UNIVERSITY

Las Vegas, NM 87701
Web site: www.nmhu.edu

Founded 1893. CGS member. Located 60 miles E of Santa Fe. Coed. State control. Semester system. Library: 551,276 volumes, 4700 subscriptions. Total University enrollment: 3750.

Annual tuition: full-time resident $2280, nonresident $3420; per credit, resident $101, nonresident $151. On-campus housing for 64 married and 154 single graduate students. Average academic year housing cost: $3900 for married students; $4800 for single students. Apply to Coordinator of Housing. Phone: (505) 454-3197. Day-care facilities available.

Graduate Studies

Enrollment: full-time 480; part-time 314. University faculty teaching graduate students: full-time 81, part-time 32. Degrees conferred: M.A., M.S., M.B.A., M.S.W.

ADMISSION REQUIREMENTS: Transcripts required in support of Divisional application. TOEFL required for international applicants. Interview required for some programs. Accepts transfer applicants. Graduates of unaccredited institutions not considered. Apply to Graduate Division, Office of the Vice President for Academic Affairs at least 30 days prior to registration. Application fees: $15. Phone: (505)454-3220 (Social Work); (505)454-3266; fax: (505)454-3558; e-mail: portega@merlin.nmhu.edu.

ADMISSION STANDARDS: Selective for some disciplines, relatively open for others. Usual minimum average: 3.0 in major field (A = 4).

FINANCIAL AID: Awards from institutional funds: academic scholarships, fellowships, assistantships, stipends, internships, tuition waivers, Federal W/S, loans. Approved for VA benefits. Apply by March 1 to Office of Vice President for assistantships; to Financial Aid Office for all other programs. Use FAFSA. Phone: (505)454-3318; fax: (505)454-3398. About 45% of students receive aid from University and outside sources. Aid sometimes available for part-time students.

DEGREE REQUIREMENTS: For master's: 34 credits minimum; thesis/nonthesis option; case/field study; comprehensive exam.

FIELDS OF STUDY.

COLLEGE OF ARTS AND SCIENCES:
Anthropology. M.A.
Applied Chemistry. M.S.
Applied Sociology. M.A.
Cognitive Science. M.A., M.S.
English. Includes literature, language, rhetoric and composition, creative writing. M.A.
Life Science. Includes biology, environmental science and management. M.S. only.
Media Arts and Computer Science. Includes cognitive science, computer graphics, design studies, digital audio and video production, multimedia systems, networking technology. M.A., M.S.
Public Affairs. Includes administration, applied sociology, historical and cross-cultural perspective, political and governmental process. M.A.
Southwest Studies. Includes Hispanic language and literature, history/political science. M.A.
Psychology. Includes general, clinical. M.S.

SCHOOL OF BUSINESS:
Business Administration. Includes electronic commerce, general management, government and not-for-profit management, international business, management information systems. M.B.A.

SCHOOL OF EDUCATION:
Counseling and Guidance. Includes school counseling, professional counseling, rehabilitation counseling. M.A.
Curriculum and Instruction. Includes English, math, history, bilingual education. M.A.
Educational Administration. M.A.
Educational Leadership. M.A.
Human Performance and Sport. Includes exercise and sport science, sport administration, teacher education. M.A.
Special Education. M.A.

SCHOOL OF SOCIAL WORK:
Social Work. Includes clinical social work practice, community and administration practice, direct practice. M.S.W.

NEW MEXICO INSTITUTE OF MINING AND TECHNOLOGY
Saceur, New Mexico 87801
Web site: www.nmt.edu

Founded 1889. Located 75 miles S of Albuquerque. State control. Special facilities: Center for Explosive Technology Research, Geophysical Research Center, Joint Observatory for Cometary Research, Waldo Experimental Mine, Petroleum Recovery Research Center, New Mexico Bureau of Mines and Mineral Resources, Langmuir Laboratory for Atmospheric Physics, Sullivan Center of In-Situ Mining Research, Very Large Array radio telescope, Very Large Baseline Array. Cooperative research opportunities with Sandia National Laboratories. Library: 137,000 volumes, 766 subscriptions. Total Institute enrollment: 2000.

Tuition: per credit, resident $206, nonresident $661. On-campus housing for 36 married students, 10 graduate dorms for men, 10 graduate dorms for women. Average academic year housing cost: $5500 for married students, $10,000 (including board) for single students. Apply to Office of Auxiliary Services. Phone: (505) 835-5900. Day-care facilities available.

Graduate Studies

Graduate study since 1946. Enrollment; full-time 400, part-time 75. Institute faculty: full-time 29, part-time 7. Degrees conferred: M.E.M., M.S., Ph.D.

ADMISSION REQUIREMENTS. Transcripts, GRE/Subject Test, three letters of reference required in support of application. TOEFL required for international applicants. Interview not required. Accepts transfer applicants. Graduates of unaccredited institutions not considered. Apply to Dean of Graduate Studies by March 15 (Fall). Application fee $16. Phone: (505)835-5513 or (800)428-8324; fax: (505)835-5476; e-mail: graduate@nmt.edu.

ADMISSION STANDARDS. Selective for most departments. Usual minimum average: 3.0 (A = 4).

FINANCIAL AID. Annual awards from institutional funds: teaching fellowships, research fellowships, HEW fellowships, Federal W/S, loans. Approved for VA benefits. Apply by March 15 to Dean of Graduate Studies for fellowships, assistantships; to Financial Aid Office for all other programs. Use FAFSA. Phone: (505)835-5300. About 70% of students receive aid from Institute and outside sources.

DEGREE REQUIREMENTS. For M.E.M., M.S.: 30 credit hours minimum, at least 24 in residence; thesis/nonthesis option; final oral exam; faculty review. For Ph.D.: three years minimum beyond the bachelor's, at least two in residence; reading knowledge of one foreign language; dissertation; preliminary exam/faculty review; oral defense.

FIELDS OF STUDY.
Biology. M.S., Ph.D.
Chemistry. M.S., Ph.D.
Computer Science. M.S., Ph.D.
Electrical Engineering. M.S.
Engineering Management. M.E.M.
Engineering Mechanics. M.S.
Environmental Engineering. M.S.
Geological Engineer. M.S.
Geochemistry. M.S., Ph.D.
Geology. M.S., Ph.D.
Geophysics. M.S., Ph.D.
Hydrology. M.S., Ph.D.
Materials Engineering. M.S., Ph.D.

Mathematics. M.S.
Mineral Engineering. M.S.
Petroleum Engineering. M.S., Ph.D.
Physics. M.S., Ph.D.
Teaching. Includes mathematics, science. M.S.

NEW MEXICO STATE UNIVERSITY
Las Cruces, New Mexico 88003-8001
Web site: www.nmsu.edu

Established 1899. Located 40 miles N of El Paso, Texas. CGS member. Coed. State control. Semester system. Special facilities: Agricultural Experiment Station, Arts and Sciences Research Center, Astrophysical Research Consortium, Border Research Institute, Center for Business Research and Services, Center for Educational Development, Center for Latin American Studies, Computer Center, Computing Research Laboratory, Consortium for International Development, Cooperative Extension Service, Educational Research Center, Engineering Research Center, Branson Hall Library and New Library, New Mexico Department of Agriculture, New Mexico Regional Primate Research Laboratory, New Mexico Water Resources Research Institute, Physical Science Laboratory, Plant Genetic Engineering Laboratory, Southwest Technology Development Institute, United States Department of Agriculture (Cotton Genetics, Ars-Jornada Experimental Range, Southwest Cotton Ginning Research Laboratory, Economics Research), University Statistics Center, cooperative program with White Sand Missile Range. Library: 1,600,000 volumes, 11,700 suscriptions. Total University enrollment: 16,700.

Annual tuition: full-time, resident $3156, nonresident $12,510; per credit, resident $175; nonresident $565. On-campus housing for married students, single men and women. Average academic year housing cost: $5300 for single students (including board), $450 per month for married students. Contact the Director of Housing for on- and off-campus housing information. Phone: (505)646-3203. Day-care facilities available.

Graduate School
Web site: www.nmsu.edu/~gradcolg

Graduate study since 1895. Enrollment: full-time 1670, part-time 1450. University faculty teaching graduate students: full- and part-time 566. Degrees conferred: M.A., M.B.A., M.Acc., M.Ag., M.A.G., M.C.J., M.F.A., M.A.T., M.S., M.M., M.S.N., M.P.H., M.P.A., M.S.W., Ed.S., Ed.D., Ph.D.

ADMISSION REQUIREMENTS. Two transcripts, letters of recommendation, letter of intent required in support of School's application. Online application available. Interview, GRE/Subject Tests/GMAT/MAT required by some departments. TOEFL required for international applicants. Accepts transfer applicants. Graduates of unaccredited colleges not considered. Apply to Dean of Graduate School by July 1 (Fall), November 1 (Spring), April 1 (Summer). Application fee $30, $50 for international applicants. Phone: (505)646-2736; fax: (505)646-7721.

ADMISSION STANDARDS. Selective for most departments. Usual minimum average: 3.0 (A = 4).

FINANCIAL AID. Annual awards from institutional funds: minority assistantships, minority/women fellowships, teaching/research assistantships, internships, traineeships, grants, Federal W/S, loans. Approved for VA benefits. Apply by March 15 to appropriate department chairman for assistantships, fellowships; to Financial Aid Office for all other programs. Phone: (505)646-4205; fax: (505) 646-7381. Use FAFSA. Aid available for part-time students.

DEGREE REQUIREMENTS. For master's: 30–36 semester hours minimum, at least 24 in residence; reading knowledge of one foreign language for some departments; thesis/nonthesis option; final oral/written exam. For Doctorate: three years minimum beyond the bachelor's, at least one year in residence: language requirements and psychometric tools vary by department; preliminary exam; dissertation; final oral/written exam.

FIELDS OF STUDY.
Accounting.
Agricultural Biology.
Agricultural Economics.
Agricultural Engineering.
Agricultural Extension Education.
Agronomy and Horticulture.
Animal and Range Science.
Anthropology.
Art. Includes art history.
Astronomy.
Biochemistry.
Biology.
Business Administration. Includes agribusiness, finance, information systems, international business.
Chemical Engineering.
Chemistry.
Civil Engineering.
Communication Studies.
Computer Science.
Counseling and Guidance.
Counseling Psychology.
Creative Writing.
Criminal Justice.
Curriculum and Instruction.
Economics.
Educational Administration.
Electrical Engineering.
Engineering.
English.
Entomology.
Environmental Engineering.
Experimental Statistics.
Family and Consumer Science.
Fine Arts. Includes ceramics, drawing, graphic design, jewelry and metalsmithing, painting, photography, printmaking, sculpture.
Geography.
Geology.
Government.
Health Science.
History. Includes public history.
Horticulture.
Industrial Engineering.
Mathematical Sciences.
Mechanical Engineering.
Molecular Biology.
Music.
Nursing.
Physics.
Psychology.
Public Administration.
Public Health.
Range Science.
School Psychology.
Social Work.
Sociology.
Spanish.
Special Education/Communication Disorders.
Wildlife Science.

THE UNIVERSITY OF NEW MEXICO
Albuquerque, New Mexico 87131-2039
Web site: www.unm.edu

Founded 1889. CGS member. State control. Semester system. Coed. Special facilities: Bureau of Engineering Research, Bureau of Business and Economic Research, Center for Southwest Research, Office of Contract Archeology, Maxwell Museum of Anthropology, Museum of Southwestern Biology, New Mexico Engineering Research Center, Technology Application Center; Centers for Advanced Studies, Alcohol and Substance Abuse, Design and Assistance, Economic Development, Communications, Health Sciences, High Performance Computing and Education and Research, High Technology Materials Integrative Studies, Microelectronics Research, MicroEngineering Ceramics, Radioactive Waste Management; Institutes for Applied Research Services, Astrophysics, Environmental Education, Latin American Institute, Meteoritics, Modern Optics, New Mexico Engineering Research Institute, Organizational Communication, Plastics, Public Policy, Social Research, Space and Nuclear Power Studies, Southwest Hispanic Research, Manufacturing Engineering and Development; UNM Business Link, Latin American Institute, Tamarind Institute. The University's NIH ranking is 85th among all U.S. institutions with 139 awards/grants valued at $67,474,792. According to The Center at University of Florida, the University is ranked 70th in receipt of Federal Research funds with $106,541,000 and it ranks 84th for total University research expenditures with $158,239,000. In 2004, the University awarded 195 doctorates, which ranked it 74th among all U.S. institutions eligible to award that degree. Three of the University's faculty members have been elected to National Honor Academies and this ranks it 105th among all U.S. institutions. The Library: approximately 2,700,000 volumes, 17,000 subscriptions. Total University enrollment: 26,100. Off-Campus Graduate Center: Los Alamos, Santa Fe, and Taos.

Tuition and fees: per credit hour, resident $209, $264 for business; nonresident $640, $695 for business. Housing available for single and married graduate students; 200 apartments for married students. Annual academic year housing cost: $6500 (including board). Contact Housing Reservations for both on- and off-campus housing information. Phone: (505)277-2606. Day care facilities available.

Graduate Studies

Graduate study since 1916. Enrollment: full-time 2643, part-time 1868. Faculty: full- and part-time 857. Degrees conferred: M.A., M.S., M.B.A., M.F.A., M.P.A., M.P.H., M.Mu., M.Arch., M.C.R.P., M.E.M.E., M.W.R.A., E.M.B.A., Ed.D., Ph.D.

ADMISSION REQUIREMENTS. Transcripts required in support of application. Online application available; Self-Managed Application Process. GRE/Subject Tests/GMAT recommended or required by some departments. TOEFL required for international students. Interview generally not required. Accepts transfer applicants. Graduates of unaccredited institutions not considered. U.S. applicants apply to Graduate Studies by published departmental deadline dates. Application fee $40. Phone: (505)277-2711; fax: (505)277-7405. International applicants apply to International Admissions, Student Services Center. Phone: (505)277-3136.

ADMISSION STANDARDS. Selective for most departments. Usual minimum average: 3.0 (A = 4).

FINANCIAL AID. Annual awards from institutional funds: scholarships, research fellowships, research assistantships, teaching assistantships, internships, grants, tuition waivers, Federal W/S, loans. Apply by March 1 to the appropriate departmental chair for fellowships, assistantships; to Student Financial Aid Office for all other programs. Application dates vary by department. Use FAFSA. Phone: (505)277-2041. About 33% of students receive aid through loans from School and outside sources. Aid available for part-time students.

DEGREE REQUIREMENTS: For master's: thesis/nonthesis options offered by many departments, others designate one of the two plans. PLAN I: minimum of 24 semester hours of course work, thesis; final oral/written exam. PLAN II: minimum of 32 semester hours of course work, no thesis; final oral/written exam. Some programs require demonstration of competence in one or more foreign languages. For Ph.D., Ed.D., M.F.A.: minimum of 48 semester hours of course work beyond the bachelor's degree; at least 18 semester hours exclusive of dissertation credit must be earned in courses numbered 500 or above at UNM (some programs require more course work). Ph.D. requires at least three years of intensive study and research beyond the bachelor's degree.

FIELDS OF STUDY.
American Studies.
Anthropology.
Architecture.
Art Education.
Art History.
Art Studio.
Biology.
Biomedical Sciences.
Business Administration.
Chemical Engineering.
Chemistry and Chemical Biology.
Civil Engineering.
Clinical Laboratory Science.
Communication.
Community and Regional Planning.
Comparative Literature and Cultural Studies.
Computational Science and Engineering.
Computer Engineering.
Computer Science.
Construction Management.
Counseling.
Counselor Education.
Creative Writing.
Curriculum and Instruction.
Dance.
Dental Hygiene.
Dramatic Writing.
Earth and Planetary Sciences.
Economics.
Educational Leadership.
Educational Linguistics.
Educational Psychology.
Electrical Engineering.
Elementary Education.
English.
Family Studies.
French. M.A.
French Studies. Ph.D.
Geography.
German Studies.
Hazardous Waste Engineering.
Health Education.
Historic Preservation and Regionalism.
History.
Intensive Social, Language, and Behavioral Needs.
Landscape Architecture.
Language, Literacy, and Sociocultural Studies.
Latin American Studies.
Linguistics.
Manufacturing Engineering.
Mathematics.
Mechanical Engineering.

Multicultural Teacher and Childhood Education.
Music.
Nanoscience and Microsystems.
Nuclear Engineering.
Nursing, M.S.N., NurCP., Ph.D.
Nutrition.
Occupational Therapy.
Optical Science and Engineering.
Organizational Learning and Instructional Technology.
Pharmaceutical Science.
Philosophy.
Physical Education. M.S.
Physical Education, Sports and Exercise Science. Ph.D.
Physical Therapy.
Physics.
Political Science.
Portuguese. M.A.
Psychology.
Public Administration.
Public Health.
Secondary Education .
Sociology.
Spanish. M.A.
Spanish and Portuguese. Ph.D.
Special Education.
Speech-Language Pathology.
Statistics.
Systems Engineering.
Theatre and Dance.
Town Design.
Water Resources.
Women Studies

School of Law

Web site: lawschool.unm.edu

Founded 1947. ABA approved since 1948. AALS member. Public control. Semester system. Special facilities: American Indian Law Center, Institute of Public Law, Natural Resource Center, Transboundary Resource Center, Center for Environmental Law, Center for Wildlife. Law library: 425,093 volumes, 3290 subscriptions; has LEXIS, NEXIS, WESTLAW, DIALOG, Q/L; has more than 300 network connections.

Annual tuition: resident $10,561, nonresident $24,467. Total average annual additional expense: $13,188.

Enrollment: first-year class 119; total 343 (men 50%, women 50%, minorities 45%). Faculty: full-time 32, part-time 20. Student-to-faculty ratio is 11.4 to 1. Degrees conferred: J.D., J.D.-M.A. (Latin American Studies), J.D.-M.B.A., J.D.-M.P.A.

ADMISSION REQUIREMENTS. LSDAS Law School report, bachelor's degree, two transcripts, LSAT (no later than December), personal statement, résumé, one letter of recommendation required in support of application. Interview not required. Accepts transfer applicants. Graduates of unaccredited institutions not considered. Preference given to state residents. Apply to School of Law after September 1, before February 15. Admits beginning students Fall only. Application fee $50. Phone: (505)277-0572.

ADMISSION STANDARDS. Selective. Accepts approximately 21% of all students. Number of applicants 1161; number of acceptance 242; number enrolled 119; LSAT (75% of students have a score at or above 150); GPA (75% of student have a GPA at or above 3.07). *U.S. News & World Report* ranking is in the second tier (tied at 70th) of all U.S. law schools.

FINANCIAL AID. Scholarships; grants for Native Americans; loans. Apply to Financial Aid Office, School of Law, by March 1. Phone: (505)277-0572. Use FAFSA (School code: 002663) and UNM supplemental application. About 20% of students receive aid other than loans from School.

DEGREE REQUIREMENTS. For J.D.: 86 semester hours program, at least two years in full-time residence. For master's program see graduate school listing above.

School of Medicine

Web site: hsc.unm.edu/som

Medical study since 1964. Special facilities: Biomedical Research and Integrative Neuroimaging (BRAIN Imaging) Center, Cancer Research and Treatment Center, Center for Community Partnerships, Center for Development and Disability, Center for Disaster Medicine, Center for Environmental Health Sciences, Center for Health Promotion and Disease Prevention, Center for Infectious Disease and Immunity, Center for Telehealth, Center on Aging, Geriatric Education Center, HSC Ethics Institute, Institute for Public Health. Library: 100,000 volumes, 1200 subscriptions. NIH ranking is 85th among all U.S. institutions with 139 awards/grants worth $67,474,792.

Annual tuition: resident $16,081, nonresident $40,994. No on-campus housing available. Total average figure for all other expenses: $15,500.

Enrollment: first-year class 75 (EDP 25), total 329 (men 47%, women 53%, minorities 38%, state residents 98%). Faculty: full-time 636, part-time 137. Degrees conferred: M.D., M.D.-M.P.H., M.D.-Ph.D.

ADMISSION REQUIREMENTS. AMCAS report, transcripts, MCAT required in support of application. Interview by invitation only. Applicants must have completed at least three years of college study. Preference given to New Mexico and WICHE residents. Accepts transfer applicants on a space available basis. Has EDP; apply between June 1 and August 1. Graduates of unaccredited colleges not considered. Apply to Director of Admissions after June 1, before November 15. Application fee $50. Phone: (505)272-4766; fax: (505)272-8239.

ADMISSION STANDARDS. Competitive. Accepts about 9.3% of all applicants. Number of applications 994 (760 out-of-state); number interviewed 197 (7 out-of-state); number of acceptances 92 (4 out-of-state); number enrolled 75 (4 out-of-state). Mean Composite MCAT 9.4; mean UGPA 3.61. *U.S. News & World Report* ranking is 38th among all U.S. medical schools in primary care programs.

FINANCIAL AID. Scholarships, loans (short-term, and no-interest). Apply after acceptance to Office of Student Affairs Graduate Committee. Phone: (505)272-8008. Use FAFSA (School code: G24593). About 90% of students receive some form of financial aid from School and outside sources.

DEGREE REQUIREMENTS. For M.D.: satisfactory completion of four-year program; all students must pass Step 1 and Step 2 of USMLE prior to awarding of M.D.

FIELDS OF GRADUATE STUDY.
Anatomy.
Biochemistry.
Biomedical Engineering.
Biophysics.
Cell Biology.
Genetics.
Immunology.
Microbiology.
Molecular Biology.
Neurosciences.
Pathology.
Pharmacology.
Physiology.
Public Health.

UNIVERSITY OF NEW ORLEANS

New Orleans, Louisiana 70148

Web site: www.uno.edu

Opened 1958. Formerly Louisiana State University at New Orleans. CGS member. Coed. State control. Semester system. Special facilities: Center for Energy Resource Management, Energy and Environmental Materials Research Institute, Environmental Social Science Research Institute, Gulf Coast Region Maritime Technology Center, Center for the Industrial Application of Electric Power and Instrumentation, Small Business Development Center, Urban Waste Management and Research Center, Computer Research Center. Library: 864,400 volumes, 4900 subscriptions. Total University enrollment: 12,000.

Annual tuition: resident $3292, nonresident $10,336. On-campus housing for 360 graduate men, 252 graduate women; 120 apartments for married students. Annual cost: single student $4200–$5210; married $420–$520 per month. Contact Director, Auxiliary Enterprises for both on- and off-campus housing information. Phone: (504)286-6590.

Graduate School

Enrollment: full-time 1673, part-time 2452. University faculty teaching graduate students: full- and part-time 600. Degrees conferred: M.A., M.A.E.T., M.A.S.T., M.S., M.B.A., M.F.A., M.Ed., M.E.D., M.U.R.P., Ph.D., Ed.D.

ADMISSION REQUIREMENTS. Official transcripts required in support of application. GRE Subject Tests required by many departments; GMAT for M.B.A., M.S. in accounting majors. Interview for some departments. TOEFL (TSE recommended) required for international applicants. Accepts transfer applicants. Graduates of unaccredited institutions not considered. Apply to Dean of Graduate School by July 1 (Fall), November 15 (Spring), May 1 (Summer). Application fee $20. Phone: (504)280-6836; fax: (504)280-6298.

ADMISSION STANDARDS. Very selective for some departments. Usual minimum average: 2.5 (A = 4).

FINANCIAL AID. Annual awards from institutional funds: fellowships, teaching assistantships, research assistantships, internships, grants, Federal W/S, loans. Approved for VA benefits. Apply by April 15 to the appropriate department chairman for assistantships; to Financial Aid Office for all other programs. Phone: (504)286-6689. Use FAFSA (University code: 002015). About 30% of students receive aid other than loans from University and outside sources. Aid sometimes available for part-time students.

DEGREE REQUIREMENTS. For master's: 30–48 credits, at least 24 in residence; thesis for most majors; reading knowledge of one foreign language in some programs; final written/oral exam. For Ph.D., Ed.D.: 60 credits minimum beyond the bachelor's, normally at least one year in residence; reading knowledge of one or two foreign languages; qualifying exam; general exam; dissertation; final oral exam.

FIELDS OF STUDY.
Accounting. Tax option available. M.S. only.
Art. Includes fine arts, graphic design, photography. M.A., M.F.A.
Arts Administration. M.A.
Biological Sciences. M.S. only.
Business Administration. Additional study may be required for students lacking previous preparation in the field. M.B.A. only.
Chemistry.
Civil Engineering.
Computer Science.
Communication.
Conservation Biology.
Counselor Education.
Creative Writing.
Curriculum and Instruction.
Drama and Communications. M.A., M.F.A.
Earth and Environmental Sciences.
Economics. M.A., Ph.D.
Educational Administration.
Electrical Engineering.
Engineering and Applied Science.
Engineering Management.
English. M.A. only.
English Teaching. M.A.E.T. only
Film, Theatre, and Communication Arts.
Financial Economics.
Fine Arts.
Geology and Geophysics.
Geography. M.A. only.
Gerontology.
Health Care Management.
History. M.A. only.
History Teaching.
Hospitality and Tourism Management.
Mathematics. M.S. only.
Mechanical Engineering.
Music. M.M. only.
Naval Architecture and Marine Engineering.
Physics. Includes applied. M.S. only.
Political Science. M.A., Ph.D.
Psychology. M.S., Ph.D.
Public Administration. M.P.A. only.
Romance Languages. Options in French and Spanish; M.A. only.
Science Teaching. M.A.S.T only.
Sociology. M.A. only.
Special Education.
Taxation.
Urban and Regional Planning. M.U.R.P.
Urban Studies. M.S. only.

COLLEGE OF NEW ROCHELLE

New Rochelle, New York 10805-2339

Web site: www.cnr.edu

Founded 1904. Composed of 4 schools. Located 16 miles NE of New York City. CGS member. Coed. Private control. Semester system. Library: 220,000 volumes, 1440 subscriptions. Total enrollment: 2300.

Tuition: per credit $650. On-campus housing available for single students only. Average academic year housing cost: $3800–$6000. Contact Director Residence for both on- and off-campus housing information. Phone: (914) 654-5365.

Graduate School

Established 1969. Enrollment: full-time 211, part-time 1000. Faculty: full-time 25, part-time 66. Degrees conferred: M.A., M.S.

ADMISSION REQUIREMENTS. Transcripts, three references, personal interview required in support of School's application. TOEFL required for international applicants. Accepts transfer applicants. Graduates of unaccredited colleges not considered. Apply by August 2 (Fall), December 1 (Spring) to the Office of the Dean. Rolling admissions process. Application fee $35. Phone: (914)654-5334; fax: (914)654-5593.

ADMISSION STANDARDS. Selective. Usual minimum average: 2.7, 3.0 in major field (A = 4).

FINANCIAL AID. Scholarships, research assistantships, staff assistantships, internships, tuition waivers, grants, Federal W/S, loans. Apply to the Office of the Dean for assistantships; to the Financial Aid Office for all other programs. No specified closing date. Phone: (914)654-5434. Use FAFSA and College's FAF.

DEGREE REQUIREMENTS. For master's: 33–45 credits minimum (depending on program), at least 28–35 in residence.

FIELDS OF STUDY.
Art Education. M.A.
Art Therapy. M.S.
Art Therapy/Counseling. M.S.
Career Development. M.S.
Childhood Education. M.S.Ed.
Childhood Special Education. M.S.Ed.
Communication Studies. M.S.
Creative Teaching and Learning. M.S.Ed.
Early Childhood Education. M.S.Ed.
Early Childhood Special Education. M.S.Ed.
Gerontology. M.S.
Guidance and Counseling. M.S.
Literacy Education. M.S.Ed.
Mental Health Counseling. M.S.
Multilingual/Multicultural Education. M.S.Ed.
School Building Leadership. M.S.
School District Leadership. M.S.
School Psychology. M.S.
Studio Art. M.S.

THE NEW SCHOOL: A UNIVERSITY

New York, New York 10011-8603
Web site: www.newschool.edu

Founded 1919. Coed. Private control. Semester system. Special facilities: Center for Economic Policy Analysis, Center for Studies of Social Change, Community Development Research Center, Center for the Study of Politics, Theory, and Policy, Environmental Simulation Center, European Union Center of New York, International Center for Migration, Ethnicity, and Citizenship, Transregional Center for Democratic Studies. Library: 4,100,000 volumes, 15,000 subscriptions. Total University enrollment: 9300.

Tuition: full-time per credit $1090. Off-campus housing for graduate students. Average academic year housing costs: $17,000 (including board). Contact Director of Housing for both on- and off-campus housing information. Phone: (212)229-5459.

The New School for Social Research

Founded 1933.
Tuition: per credit: $1430. Enrollment: full-time 797, part-time 226. Graduate faculty: full-time 74, part-time 55. Degrees conferred: M.A., M.Phil., M.S.Sc. Ph.D., D.S.Sc.

ADMISSION REQUIREMENTS. Transcripts, letters of reference, GRE required in support of application. TOEFL required for international applicants. Interview not required. Accepts transfer applicants. Graduates of unaccredited institutions not considered. Apply to Director of Admissions by August 1 (Fall), December 1 (Spring), May 1 (Summer). Rolling admissions process. Application fee $30. Phone: (800)523-5411; fax: (212)229-5665; e-mail: gfadmit@newschool.edu.

ADMISSION STANDARDS. Selective for most departments. Usual minimum average: 3.0 (A = 4).

FINANCIAL AID. One hundred fifty scholarships, 55 teaching/research assistantships, Federal W/S, loans. Approved for VA benefits. Apply by January 15 to the department chair for scholarships and assistantships; to the Office of Financial Aid for all other aid. Phone: (212)741-5714. Use FAFSA. About 30% of students receive aid other than loans from School, 50% from all sources. Loans available for part-time study.

DEGREE REQUIREMENTS. For M.A., M.Phil.: 30-36 credits, thesis/ nonthesis option; other requirements vary by department. For Ph.D.: 60 credits minimum beyond the bachelor's, at least 30 credits in full-time residence; written qualifying exam; oral comprehensive exam; reading knowledge of one foreign language, computer/statistics substitute possible; dissertation; final oral defense. For D.S.Sc.: 92 credits minimum beyond the bachelor's; other requirements essentially the same as for Ph.D.

FIELDS OF STUDY.
Anthropology.
Economics.
Global Political Economy and Finance.
Historical Studies. Interdisciplinary. M.A.
Liberal Studies. Interdisciplinary. M.A.
Philosophy.
Political Science.
Psychoanalytic Studies. Interdisciplinary. M.A.
Psychology.
Sociology.

Robert J. Milano The New School of Management and Urban Policy

Graduate study since 1975. Semester system. Tuition: per credit $1090. Enrollment: full-time 154, part-time 451. Graduate faculty: full-time 24, part-time 79. Degrees conferred: M.S., Adv.C.

ADMISSION REQUIREMENTS. Transcripts, letters of reference required in support of School's application. GMAT considered if available. TOEFL required for international applicants. Accepts transfer students. Graduates of unaccredited institutions not considered. Apply to Admission Office by August 1 (Fall), December 1 (Spring), May 1 (Summer). Application fee $30. Phone: (212)229-5462; fax: (212)229-8935.

ADMISSION STANDARDS. Selective for most departments. Usual minimum average: 3.0 (A = 4).

FINANCIAL AID. Academic scholarships, grants, fellowships, research assistantships, administrative assistantships, teaching assistantships, tuition waivers, Federal W/S, loans. Approved for VA benefits. Apply by March 1 to department chair for scholarships, fellowships, assistantships; to the Office of Financial Aid for all other programs. Phone: (212)229-5462; fax: (212)229-8935. Use FAFSA and CSS/FA Profile. Aid available for part-time students.

DEGREE REQUIREMENTS. For M.S.: 42 credits minimum; internship (strongly encouraged); thesis/nonthesis option. For Adv.C.: 18 credits minimum beyond master's. For Ph.D.: 60 credit minimum beyond bachelor's, at least 30 credits in residence; qualifying exam; comprehensive exam; dissertation; oral defense.

FIELDS OF STUDY.
Health Services Management and Policy.
Human Resources Management.
Nonprofit Management.
Organization Change Management.
Public and Urban Policy. Ph.D. only.
Urban Policy Analysis and Management.

The New School for General Studies

The University's founding division. Semester system. Tuition: per credit $1020; Creative Writing $1158, International Affairs $1066, TESOL $1000. Enrollment: full-time 307, part-time 221.

Graduate faculty: full-time 15, part-time 60. Degrees conferred: M.A., M.S., M.F.A.

ADMISSION REQUIREMENTS. Transcripts, letters of reference required in support of School's application. GMAT considered if available. TOEFL required for international applicants. Accepts transfer students. Graduates of unaccredited institutions not considered. Apply to Admission Office by August 1 (Fall), December 1 (Spring), May 1 (Summer). Application fee $30. Phone: (212)229-5613.

ADMISSION STANDARDS. Selective for most departments. Usual minimum average: 3. 0 (A = 4).

FINANCIAL AID. Scholarships, fellowships, research assistantships, teaching assistantships, internships, grants, Federal W/S, loans. Approved for VA benefits. Apply by March 1 to department chair for scholarships, fellowships, assistantships; to the Office of Financial Aid for all other programs. Use FAFSA. Aid available for part-time students.

DEGREE REQUIREMENTS. For master's: 42 credits minimum; internship (strongly encouraged); thesis/nonthesis option.

FIELDS OF STUDY.
Creative Writing. M.F.A.
International Affairs. M.A., M.S.
Media Studies. M.A.
Teacher Education. M.S.T.
Teaching English to Speakers of Other Language. M.A.

Parsons The New School for Design

Web site: www.parsons.edu

Annual tuition: $32,760; per credits $1158. Enrollment: full-time 285; part-time 96. Faculty: full-time 15, part-time 30. Degrees conferred: M.A., M.Arch., M.F.A.

ADMISSION REQUIREMENTS. Transcripts, three letters of recommendation, résumé, statement of intent, portfolio of 15–20 pieces of work required in support of School's application. Interview sometimes required. TOEFL required for international applicants. Apply to Admissions Committee by March 1. Application fee $40. Phone: (800)252-0852 or (212)229-8910; fax: (212)229-8975.

ADMISSION STANDARDS. Selective. Admission based on portfolio review.

FINANCIAL AID. Annual awards from institutional funds: scholarships, fellowships, assistantships, internships, tuition waivers, Federal W/S, loans. Apply by April 1 to Financial Aid Office; no specified closing date. Phone: (212)229-8930; fax: (212)229-8975. Use FAFSA, institutional FAF, and CSS profile. About 20% of students receive aid other than loans from School and outside sources.

DEGREE REQUIREMENTS. For M.A.: 32 credits minimum, at least 24 in residence; thesis option. For M.Arch.: 30–36 credits minimum, at least 24 in residence; master's project. For M.F.A.: 48 credits minimum, at least 40 in residence; departmental requirements determined by portfolio review; final essay; applied project, gallery exhibition.

FIELDS OF STUDY.
Architecture.
Design and Technology.
Fine Arts.
History of Decorative Arts.
Lighting Design.
Painting.
Photography.
Sculpture.

THE CITY UNIVERSITY OF NEW YORK
The Graduate School and University Center
365 Fifth Avenue
New York, New York 10016-4039
Web site: www.gc.cuny.edu

Established 1961. CGS member. Public control. Semester system. Special facilities: Center for Advanced Study in Education, Center for Jewish Studies, Center for Research in Cognition and Affect, Center for Research in Speech and Hearing Sciences, Center for Social Research, Center for Urban and Policy Studies, Center for the Study of Women and Sex Roles. Library: 272,000 volumes, 1680 subscriptions.

Tuition: per credit Doctoral students residents $325, nonresidents $560; Master's students residents $270, nonresidents $500. On-campus housing available. Contact the Office of Residence Life for current information. Phone: (212)817-7480.

Graduate Studies

Enrollment: full-time 3648, part-time 368. Faculty: full- and part-time 1500. Degrees conferred: M.A., D.M.A., D.S.W., Ph.D.

ADMISSION REQUIREMENTS. Official transcripts, GRE, GMAT (Business Ph.D. program only), two faculty recommendations required in support of application. TOEFL required for international applicants. Accepts transfer applicants. Apply to Admissions Office by March 1 for most programs (Fall), November 15 (Spring). Application fee $125. Phone: (212)817-7470.

ADMISSION STANDARDS. Selective. Usual minimum average: 3.0 (A = 4).

FINANCIAL AID. Fellowships (service and nonservice), grants, assistantships, traineeships, Federal W/S, loans. Apply to the Office of Financial Aid by February 1. Phone: (212)642-2811. Use CUNY Student Aid form.

DEGREE REQUIREMENTS. For M.A.: 30 credits minimum, at least 24 in residence; final comprehensive exam; thesis. For D.S.W.: 30 credits minimum beyond the master's, at least two terms in residence; preliminary exam; dissertation; final oral/written exam. For D.M.A., Ph.D.: 60 credits minimum, at least 30 in residence and two consecutive semesters in full-time residence; preliminary exam; candidacy exam; dissertation; final defense of dissertation.

FIELDS OF STUDY.
Anthropology. Admits Fall only. Apply by January 8.
Art History.
Audiology. Au.D.
Biochemistry.
Biology. Apply by February 1.
Business. Admits Fall only.
Chemistry.
Classics.
Comparative Literature.
Computer Science. Admits Fall only.
Criminal Justice. Admits Fall only. Apply by January 15.
Earth and Environmental Sciences.
Economics.
Educational Psychology. Admits Fall only. Apply by February 15.
Engineering.
English. Admits Fall only. Apply by January 15.
French. Apply by February 1.
Hispanic and Luso-Brazilian Literature. Apply by January 15.
History.
Journalism.
Liberal Studies.
Linguistics. Admits Fall only. Apply by January 15.

Mathematics.
Music. Admits Fall only. Apply by January 1.
Philosophy.
Physical Therapy.
Physics.
Political Science.
Psychology. Admits Fall only. Apply by March 1, January 1 for clinical and neuropsychology, February 1 for social-personality, March 15 for learning processes.
Public Health.
Social Welfare. Admits Fall only. D.S.W. only.
Sociology. Admits Fall only.
Speech and Hearing Sciences.
Theater. Admits Fall only.
Urban Education. Admits Fall only. Apply by February 15.

NEW YORK INSTITUTE OF TECHNOLOGY

Old Westbury, New York 11568-8000
Web site: www.nyit.edu

Main campus located 35 miles E of New York City; other branches are located in NYC and Islip, Long Island, New York. CGS member. Coed. Private control. Semester system. Special facilities: Center for Labor and Industrial Relations, Management Information Systems Center, Science and Technology Research Center, Video Center. Library: 213,600 volumes, 3500 subscriptions. Total enrollment: 11,100.

Tuition: per credit $705. On-campus housing available. Average academic year housing cost: $7000 (including board) for single students; $5700 for married students. Off-campus housing cost: $700–$1000 per month. Contact Office of Residential Life for both on- and off-campus housing information. Phone: (516)348-3340.

Graduate Division

Enrollment: full-time 1012, part-time 2175. University faculty teaching graduate students: full-time 256, part-time 145. Degrees conferred: M.A., M.B.A., M.P.S., M.S.

ADMISSION REQUIREMENTS. Transcripts, GMAT (Business) required in support of application. Online application available. GRE required by some programs. TOEFL required for international applicants. Interview not required. Accepts transfer applicants. Graduates of unaccredited institutions not considered. Apply to Graduate Admissions Office by July 1 (Fall), December 1 (Spring). Rolling admissions process. Application fee $50. Phone: (516)686-7925; fax: (516)686-7613.

ADMISSION STANDARDS. Selective. Usual minimum average: 2.85 (A = 4).

FINANCIAL AID. Scholarships, fellowships, assistantships, grants, tuition waivers, Federal W/S, loans. Apply to appropriate dean for assistantships; to Financial Aid Office for all other programs. No specified closing date. Use FAFSA. Aid available for part-time students.

DEGREE REQUIREMENTS. For master's: 33–45 credit hours minimum; at least 30 credit hours in residence; thesis/nonthesis option; final oral exam for some programs.

FIELDS OF STUDY.

SCHOOL OF ALLIED HEALTH AND LIFE SCIENCES:
Clinical Nutrition. M.S.
Human Relations. M.P.S.
Occupational Therapy. M.S.

Physical Therapy. M.S.
Physician Assistant. M.S.

SCHOOL OF ARCHITECTURE AND DESIGN:
Urban and Regional Design. M.Arch.

SCHOOL OF ARTS, SCIENCES, AND COMMUNICATION:
Communication Arts. Includes advertising, corporate communication, design graphics, electronic cinematography, intercultural communication, mass communication, media management, writing for media, journalism, painting, public relations, studio art. M.A.

SCHOOL OF EDUCATION:
Counseling. Includes mental health. M.S.
Elementary Education. M.S.
Instructional Technology. M.S.
School Leadership and Technology. M.S.

SCHOOL OF ENGINEERING AND TECHNOLOGY:
Computer Science. M.S.
Electrical Engineering and Computer Engineering. M.S.
Energy Management. M.S.
Engineering and Technology. M.S.
Environmental Technology. Includes pollution prevention, regulatory compliance, waste management. M.S.

SCHOOL OF MANAGEMENT:
Business Administration. Includes accounting, finance, general management, international business, management of information systems, marketing, personnel and industrial relations. M.B.A.
Human Resources Management and Labor Relations. M.S.
Management. M.B.A., M.S.

New York College of Osteopathic Medicine

Web site: www.nyit.edu/nycom

Founded 1977. Private control. Located on main campus. Semester system. Library: 60,000 volumes, 1500 subscriptions.

Annual tuition: $36,503. Off-campus housing only. Off-campus housing and personal expenses: approximately $21,000.

Enrollment: first-year class 310, total 1220 (men 45%, women 55%, minorities 44%, state residents 63%). Faculty: Full-time 38, part-time and volunteers 1000. Degrees conferred: D.O., D.O.-M.B.A., D.O.-M.S. (Clinical Nutrition).

ADMISSION REQUIREMENTS. AACOMAS report, bachelor's degree, official transcripts, MCAT (no later than September), three letters of recommendation, one from premed advisory committee, evaluation from a physician (preferably a D.O.), supplemental form required in support of application. Interview by invitation only. Graduates of unaccredited colleges not considered. Apply by February 1 to the Director of Admissions. Admits first-year students Fall only. Application fee: $60. Phone: (516)686-3747; fax: (516)686-3831.

ADMISSION STANDARDS. Selective. Accepts about 15% of all applicants. Number of applications 3297 (2637 out-of-state); number interviewed 720 (353 out-of-state); number of acceptance 540 (254 out-of-state); number enrolled 310 (112 out-of-state). Usual minimum UGPA: 2.75 (A = 4). Mean Composite MCAT 8.5, mean UGPA 3.5.

FINANCIAL AID. Scholarships, fellowships, grants, tuition waivers, loans. Apply by April 1 to the Financial Aid Office. Phone: (516)686-7960. Use FAFSA (College code: 002782). About 90% of students receive some form of financial assistance.

DEGREE REQUIREMENT. For D.O.: satisfactory completion of four-year program.

NEW YORK LAW SCHOOL

57 Worth Street
New York, New York 10013-2960
Web site: www.nyls.edu

Established 1891. Located in lower Manhattan in TriBeCa. ABA approved since 1954. AALS member. Private control. Semester system. Special facilities: Communication Media Center, Justice Action Center, Center for Real Estate Studies, Center for New York City Law, Center for International Law. Special programs: Law School exchange with Vermont Law; externships and judicial internships. Law library: 513,597 volumes, 5504 subscriptions; has LEXIS, NEXIS, WESTLAW, LEGALTRAC, OCLC, RLIN; has more than 350 network connections.

Annual tuition: Full-time $24,478, part-time $31,124. Total full-time 1150, total part-time 361. No on-campus housing available. Students live off-campus. Contact New York Law School Housing Office for off-campus information. Phone: (212)431-2166. Off-campus housing and personal expenses: $19,950.

Enrollment: first-year class, full-time 400, part-time 135; total full-time 1150, total part-time 361. Faculty: full-time 60, part-time 75. Student-to-faculty ratio is 20.3 to 1. Degrees conferred: J.D., J.D.-M.B.A., J.D.-M.P.A. (with Baruch College of CUNY), LL.M. (Taxation).

ADMISSION REQUIREMENTS. LSDAS Law School report, bachelor's degree, transcripts, LSAT, personal statement, one letter of recommendation required in support of application. Applicants must have completed four years of college. Accepts transfer applicants. Graduates of unaccredited institutions not considered. Apply to Admissions Office after September 1, before April 1. Admits full-time students in Fall and Spring. Application fee $60. Phone: (212)431-2888.

ADMISSION STANDARDS. Selective. Accepts approximately 39% of full-time and 33% of part-time students. Number of full-time applicants 4606, part-time 1008; number of full-time acceptance 1782, part-time 331; number of full-time enrolled 403, part-time 135; LSAT (75% of full-time students have a score at or above 153, part-time 151); GPA (75% of full-time students have a GPA at or above 3.12, part-time 2.91). *U.S. News & World Report* ranking is in the third tier of all U.S. law schools.

FINANCIAL AID. Scholarships, grants, Federal W/S, loans. Apply to Office of Financial Aid, preferably by April 15. Phone: (212)431-2828. Use FAFSA (School code: G02783) and NEED ACCESS application. About 31% of students receive aid other than loans from School.

DEGREE REQUIREMENTS. For J.D.: satisfactory completion of three-year day program or four-year evening program; 86 credit hour program. For M.B.A., M.P.A.: see appropriate Graduate School listing in Baruch College, CUNY.

NEW YORK MEDICAL COLLEGE

Valhalla, New York 10595
Web site: www.nymc.edu

Established 1960. Located about 25 miles N of New York City. CGS member. Special facilities: Brander Cancer Research Institute, Cardiovascular Research Institute, Center for Lyme Disease, Center for Pediatric Hypotension, Center for Primary Care Education and Research, Institute for Genetic Analysis of Common Diseases, Institute for Bioethics at New York Medical College, Institute for International Health, Institute for Trauma Emergency Care, Westchester Institute for Human Development. The College's NIH ranking is 168th among all U.S. institutions

with 56 awards/grants worth $22,621,817. Library: 148,000 volumes, 1200 subscriptions.

Annual tuition: graduate program, per credit $645. Very limited on-campus housing available. Average academic year housing cost: $15,000 for married students, $13,000 for single students; off-campus cost: $700–$1200 per month. Contact Housing Office for both on- and off-campus housing information. Phone: (914) 993-4532.

Graduate School of Basic Medical Sciences

Established 1963. Tuition: per credit $645. Enrollment: full-time 200, part-time 54. Faculty: full- and part-time 83. Degrees conferred: M.S., Ph.D.

ADMISSION REQUIREMENTS. Official transcripts, GRE, personal statement, two letters of recommendation required in support of School's application. GRE Subject test may be required for some programs. TOEFL, or evidence of proficiency in English required of international applicants. Accepts transfer applicants. Apply to Dean of the School by July 1 (Fall), December 1 (Spring); February 1 (Fall, Ph.D.), October 1 (Spring, Ph.D.). Application $35, $60 for international applicants. Phone: (914)594-4110; fax: (914)594-4944.

ADMISSION STANDARDS. Competitive. Usual minimum average: 3.3 (A = 4).

FINANCIAL AID. Scholarships, fellowships, assistantships, internships, grants, loans. Apply to Dean of the School; no specified closing date. Phone: (914)594-4491. Use FAFSA. Aid available for part-time students.

DEGREE REQUIREMENTS. For M.S.: 30–36 credits minimum, at least 24–30 credits in residence; qualifying exam; thesis. For Ph.D.: 60 credits minimum beyond the bachelor's; at least two years in full-time residence; reading knowledge of one foreign language or research tool; qualifying exam; dissertation; final oral exam.

FIELDS OF STUDY.
Basic Medical Sciences. Interdisciplinary.
Biochemistry and Molecular Biology.
Cell Biology.
Experimental Pathology.
Experimental Pathology: Applied Environmental Science.
Experimental Pathology: Environmental Pathology.
Experimental Pathology: Toxicological Pathology.
Microbiology and Immunology.
Pharmacology,
Physiology.

Medical College

Web site: www.nymc.edu

Established 1860. Located in Valhalla (10595). Library: 203,000 volumes, 1500 subscriptions. NIH ranking is 168th among all U.S. institutions with 54 awards/grants worth $22,621,817.

Annual tuition: $41,836. On-campus housing available. Most students live on campus for the first two years. Total figures for all other expenses: $17,968.

Enrollment: first-year class 186 (EDP 2), total 774 (men 49%, women 51%, minorities 41%, state residents 33%). Faculty: full-time 1246, part-time and volunteers 1000. Degrees conferred: M.D., M.D.-M.P.H., M.D.-Ph.D.

ADMISSION REQUIREMENTS. AMCAS report, transcripts, MCAT, recommendations required in support of application. Supplemental online application may be requested. Interview by invitation only. Applicants must possess bachelor's degree. Has EDP; apply between June 1 and August 1. Apply to Admissions Office after June 1, before December 15. Application fee $100. Phone: (914)594-4507; fax: (914)594-4976.

ADMISSION STANDARDS. Selective. Accepts about 10% of all applicants. Number of applications 7073 (5628 out-of-state); number interviewed 1394 (1016 out-of-state); number of acceptance 743 (508 out-of-state); number enrolled 186 (129 out-of-state). Mean Composite MCAT 10.0; mean UGPA 3.50.

FINANCIAL AID. Scholarships, loans. Apply to Director of Financial Aid; no specified closing date. Phone: (914)594-4491. Use FAFSA. About 85% of students receive some aid from College.

DEGREE REQUIREMENTS. For M.D.: satisfactory completion of four-year program; must pass Step 1 of USMLE for promotion to fourth year, pass Step 2 CK for graduation and take Step 2 CS.

FIELDS OF GRADUATE STUDY.
Basic Medical Sciences. Interdisciplinary.
Biochemistry and Molecular Biology.
Cell Biology.
Experimental Pathology.
Experimental Pathology: Applied Environmental Science.
Experimental Pathology: Environmental Pathology.
Experimental Pathology: Toxicological Pathology.
Microbiology and Immunology.
Pharmacology.
Physiology.
Public Health.

School of Public Health

Founded 1981. Courses offered in Suffern, New York, and Danbury, Connecticut. Special facility: Center for Disaster Medicine. Tuition: per credit $680. Enrollment: full- and part-time 500. Faculty: full-time 10, part-time 50. Degrees conferred: M.S., M.P.H.

ADMISSION REQUIREMENTS. Official transcripts, GRE, personal statement, two letters of recommendation required in support of School's application. Separate applications for Physical Therapy and Speech-Language Pathology. TOEFL (minimum score 600) or evidence of proficiency in English required for international students. Accepts transfer applicants. Graduates of unaccredited institutions not considered. Apply by August 1 (Fall), December 1 (Spring) to Office of Admissions. Rolling admissions process. Application fee $50, $100 for international applicants. Phone: (914)594-4510.

ADMISSION STANDARDS. Competitive for some departments, selective for all others. Usual minimum average: 3.0 (A = 4).

FINANCIAL AID. Traineeships, assistantships, loans. Apply by June 15 to Dean for assistantships, to Office of Student Financial Planning for all other programs. Phone: (914)594-4491. Use FAFSA.

DEGREE REQUIREMENTS. For M.S., M.P.H.: 36–45 credit program, one and a half years minimum, at least 24–30 credits in residence; thesis and defense/research report/qualifying exam.

FIELDS OF STUDY.
Behavioral Sciences and Health Promotion.
Biostatistics.
Disability and Human Development.
Environmental Health Science.
Epidemiology.
Health Policy and Management.
Health Informatics.
International/Global Health.
Physical Therapy.
Public Health.
Speech-Language Pathology.

STATE UNIVERSITY OF NEW YORK AT BINGHAMTON
Binghamton, New York 13902-6000
Web site: www.binghamton.edu

Founded 1950. CGS member. Coed. State control. Special facilities: Center for Cognitive and Psycholinguistic Sciences, Center for Developmental Psychobiology, Center for Global Cultural Studies, Integrated Electronic Engineering Center, Center for Leadership Studies, Center for Medieval and Early Renaissance Studies, Center for Research in Translation, Center for Women's Studies, Institute for Research on Multicultural and International Labor. Library: 1,700,000 volumes, 9100 subscriptions.

Annual tuition: residents $6336 (Business $6512), nonresident $10,010 (Business $10,406); per credit resident $288 (Business $296), nonresidents $455 (Business $473). On-campus housing available in a new graduate apartment complex consisting of three- and four-person apartments each with living room, dining area, kitchen, and bathroom. Annual academic year housing cost: $3180 for a single, $4630 for family apartment. Apply to Coordinator, Graduate Community. Phone: (607)777-2904. Day-care facilities available.

Graduate School

Graduate study since 1961. Enrollment: full-time 1335, part-time 1380. University faculty teaching graduate students: full-time 467, part-time 196. Degrees conferred: M.A., M.S., M.A.T., M.Eng., M.M., M.S.Ed., M.S.T., M.B.A., M.P.A., Certificate, Ed.D., Ph.D.

ADMISSION REQUIREMENTS. Transcripts, GRE, personal statement, two letters of recommendation required in support of School's application. Online application available. GMAT and résumé required for School of Management. GRE Subject required by some departments. Interview is not required. TOEFL required for international applicants. Accepts transfer applicants. Graduates of unaccredited institutions not considered. Apply to Graduate School Admissions Office by April 15 (Fall), November 15 (Spring). Some programs have earlier deadlines, consult department for both Fall and Spring deadlines. Application fee $60 (online), $75 (paper application). Phone: (607)777-2151.

ADMISSION STANDARDS. Competitive. Usual minimum average: 3.0 (A = 4).

FINANCIAL AID. Annual awards from institutional funds: tuition scholarships, teaching assistantships, research assistantships, fellowships, internships, tuition waivers, Federal W/S, loans. Approved for VA benefits. Apply by February 15 to appropriate Academic Program Directors for assistantships, fellowships, internships; to Director of Student Financial Aid for all other programs. Phone: (607)777-2702. Use FAFSA (School code: 002836). About 64% of students receive aid other than loans from University and outside sources. Aid available for part-time students.

DEGREE REQUIREMENTS. For master's: 30 credit hours minimum, at least 24 in residence; thesis and nonthesis options; final oral/written exam; most departments require reading knowledge of one foreign language. For Ph.D.: 60 credit hours, at least 24 in full-time residence; knowledge of at least one foreign language; dissertation; final written/oral exam.

FIELDS OF STUDY.
Accounting. M.S.
Anthropology. M.A., M.S., Ph.D.
Art History. M.A., Ph.D.
Biological Sciences. M.A., M.A.T., M.S.T., M.S.Ed., Ph.D.
Business Administration. M.B.A., Ph.D.
Chemistry. M.A., M.S., Ph.D.
Comparative Literature. M.A., Ph.D.

Computer Science. M.S., M.Eng., Ph.D.
Economics. M.A., Ph.D.
Education. Includes early childhood elementary, reading, secondary, special. M.S.Ed.
Electrical Engineering. M.S., M.Eng., Ph.D.
English. M.A., M.A.T., M.S.T., M.S.Ed., Ph.D.
Geography. M.A.
Geological Sciences. Includes earth science. M.A., M.A.T., M.S.T., M.S.Ed., Ph.D.
History. M.A., Ph.D.
Industrial Engineering. M.S., M.Eng.
Materials Engineering. M.S., Ph.D.
Materials Science. M.S., Ph.D.
Mathematical Sciences. M.A., Ph.D.
Mechanical Engineering. M.S., M.Eng., Ph.D.
Music. M.A., M.M.
Nursing. M.S. Includes family nurse practitioner, Certificate; gerontological nurse practitioner, Certificate; community health/primary care nurse practitioner, Certificate.
Philosophy. M.A., Ph.D.
Physics. Includes applied physics and astronomy. M.A., M.A.T., M.S., M.S.T., M.S.Ed.
Political Science. M.A., Ph.D.
Psychology. Includes general experimental psychology, clinical psychology, and psychobiology. M.A., Ph.D.
Public Administration. M.A.
Romance Languages and Literatures. Includes French (M.A., M.A.T., M.S.T.), Italian (M.A.), Spanish (M.A., M.A.T., M.S.T.).
Social Sciences. M.A., M.A.T., M.S.T., M.S.Ed.
Social Work. M.S.W.
Sociology. M.A., Ph.D.
Systems Science. Includes manufacturing systems. M.S., Ph.D.
Theater. M.A., M.F.A.
Translation Research and Instruction Program. Ph.D.

OTHER PROGRAMS:
M.B.A. Management with M.A. History. M.B.A.-M.A.
M.B.A. with Specialization in Arts Administration. M.B.A.

STATE UNIVERSITY OF NEW YORK COLLEGE AT BROCKPORT
Brockport, New York 14420-2997
Web site: www.brockport.edu

Founded 1841. Located 18 miles W of Rochester. CGS member. Coed. State control. Semester system. Special facilities: Center for Applied Aquatic Science and Aquaculture, Center for Philosophic Exchange, Child and Adolescent Stress Management Institute, Congress on Research in Dance, Monroe County Historian's office. Library: more than 584,600 volumes, 1800 subscriptions. Total College enrollment: 8500.

Annual tuition: full-time, resident $6900, nonresident $10,920; per credit, resident $288, nonresident $455. On-campus housing for single graduate students. Average academic year housing cost: $8000. Contact Director of Residential Life for on- and off-campus housing information. Phone: (585)395-2122.

Graduate Studies

Graduate study since 1948. Enrollment: full-time 345, part-time 940. Faculty teaching graduate students: full- and part-time 208. Degrees conferred: M.A., M.F.A., M.S., M.S.Ed., M.P.A., M.S.S.W. (in collaboration with Nazareth College of Rochester), C.A.S.

ADMISSION REQUIREMENTS. Transcripts, three letters of recommendation required in support of application. GRE required for some programs. Portfolio in lieu of GRE for M.F.A. TOEFL required for international applicants. Accepts transfer applicants. Apply to the Office of Graduate Admission; closing date varies

by program. Application fee $50. Phone: (585)395-5465; fax: (585)395-2515; e-mail: gradadmit@brockport.edu.

ADMISSION STANDARDS. Selective. Usual minimum average: 3.0 (A = 4).

FINANCIAL AID. Annual awards from institutional funds: full and partial scholarships, fellowships, research assistantships, teaching assistantships, minority fellowships, Federal W/S, loans. Approved for VA benefits. Apply by April 15 to academic department for fellowships, assistantships; to Financial Aid Office for all other programs. Phone: (800)295-9150, (585)395-2501; fax: (585) 395-5445. Use FAFSA.

DEGREE REQUIREMENTS. For master's: 30 credits minimum. For C.A.S., M.F.A.: 60 credits minimum beyond the bachelor's.

FIELDS OF STUDY.
Biological Sciences. Includes botany, zoology. M.S.
Communication. M.A.
Computational Science. M.S.
Counselor Education. M.S.Ed., C.A.S.
Dance. M.F.A.
Educational Administration. Includes school administration, school business administration. M.S.Ed., C.A.S.
Educational and Human Development. Includes adolescence education, bilingual, elementary, reading teacher, secondary (English, mathematics, science, social studies).
English.
Family Nurse Practitoner and Studies. M.S.
Health Education. M.S.Ed.
History.
Liberal Studies.
Mathematics.
Physical Education.
Psychology.
Public Administration. M.P.A.
Recreation and Leisure Studies. M.S.
Social Work. M.S.S.W.
Special Physical Education.
Visual Studies. Includes book arts, computer imaging, photography, video. M.F.A.

STATE UNIVERSITY OF NEW YORK COLLEGE AT BUFFALO
Buffalo, New York 14222-1095
Web site: www.buffalostate.edu

Established 1871. CGS member. Coed. State control. Semester system. Special facilities: Burchfield Center, Center for Development of Human Services, Great Lakes Center for Environmental Research and Education, Prevention Resources Center, Center for Study in Creativity. Library: 359,433 volumes, 3000 subscriptions.

Annual tuition: full-time, resident $6900, nonresident $10,920; per semester hour, resident $288, nonresident $455. On-campus housing for men and women; none for married students. Average annual housing cost: $5000–$8000 (including board). Apply to Director of Residential Life. Phone: (716)878-3000. Day-care facilities available.

Graduate Studies and Research

Established 1945. Enrollment: full-time 382, part-time 1631. College faculty teaching graduate students: full-time 185, part-time 31. Degrees conferred: M.A., M.S., M.S.Ed., M.P.S., C.A.S.

ADMISSION REQUIREMENTS. Transcripts, GRE/MAT required in support of application. Supplemental materials required by most departments. TOEFL required for international applicants. Accepts transfer applicants. Apply to Office of Graduate Studies by May 1 (Fall), October 1 (Spring), March 1 (Summer). Application fee $50. Phone: (716)878-5601; e-mail: gradoffc@ buffalostate.edu.

ADMISSION STANDARDS. Relatively open. Usual minimum average: 2.75 for M.A.; 2.5 for M.S., M.S.Ed. for last two years (A = 4).

FINANCIAL AID. Research assistantships, fellowships, minority fellowships, internships, tuition waivers, Federal W/S, loans. Approved for VA benefits. Apply by March 1 to individual graduate departments for fellowships, assistantships; to Office of Financial Aid for all other programs. Phone: (716)878-4901. Use FAFSA (School code: 002842). About 50% of students receive aid other than loans from outside agencies. Aid available for part-time students.

DEGREE REQUIREMENTS. For master's: 30 semester hours minimum, at least 24 in residence; comprehensive exam/thesis for M.A. For C.A.S.: 30 semester hours beyond master's, at least 27 in residence.

FIELDS OF STUDY.
Adult Education.
Applied Economics.
Art Conservation.
Art Education (K–12).
Biology.
Biology Education (7–12).
Business and Marketing Education.
Career and Technical Education.
Chemistry Education (7–12).
Childhood and Early Childhood Curriculum and Instruction.
Childhood Education (Grades 1–6).
Creative Studies.
Criminal Justice.
Early Childhood Education (Birth–Grade 2).
Earth Science Education (7–12).
Educational Computing.
Educational Leadership.
Elementary Education (Pre-K–6).
English.
English Education (7–12).
History. Includes museum studies.
Industrial Technology.
Literary Specialist (5–12).
Mathematical Education (7–12).
Multidisciplinary Studies. Includes environmental research and education, human services administration, public relations management.
Physics Education (7–12).
Social Studies Education (7–12).
Spanish Education (7–12).
Special Education. Includes adolescence, childhood, early childhood.
Speech-Language Pathology.
Student Personnel Administration.
Teaching Bilingual Exceptional Individuals.
Technology Education.

STATE UNIVERSITY OF NEW YORK COLLEGE AT CORTLAND

Cortland, New York 13045
Web site: www.cortland.edu

Founded 1868. Located 35 miles S of Syracuse. Coed. State control. Semester system. Library: 396,200 volumes, 2744 sub-

scriptions. Annual tuition: resident, full-time $6900, nonresident $10,920, per credit $288; nonresident $455. No on-campus housing for graduate students. Apply to Office of Campus Activities for off-campus housing information. Phone: (607)753-2321. Daycare facilities available.

Graduate Studies

Graduate study since 1947. Enrollment: full- and part-time 1350. Faculty: full- and part-time 62. Degrees conferred: M.A., M.S., M.S.E., M.A.T., M.S.T., C.A.B., C.A.S.

ADMISSION REQUIREMENTS. Transcripts required in support of application. GRE/MAT, letters of recommendation required by some departments. TOEFL required for international applicants. Interview not required. Accepts transfer applicants. Graduates of unaccredited institutions not considered. Apply to Office of Graduate Admissions by July 1 (Fall), December 1 (Spring), April 1 (Summer). Application fee $50. Phone: (607)753-4800; fax: (607) 753- 5988.

ADMISSION STANDARDS. Selective. Usual minimum average: 3.0 (A = 4).

FINANCIAL AID. Annual awards from institutional funds: teaching fellowships, internships, tuition waivers, Federal W/S, loans. Approved for VA benefits. Apply to Director of Financial Aid by March 15. Phone: (607)753-4717; fax: (607)753-5999. Use FAFSA and TAP application.

DEGREE REQUIREMENTS. For master's: 30 semester hours minimum, at least 24 in residence; admission to candidacy; written comprehensive exam/thesis/special project. For C.A.S., C.A.B.: 30 semester hours beyond the master's.

FIELDS OF STUDY.
Adolescence Education (7–12). Includes biology, chemistry, earth science, English, mathematics, physics, physics and mathematics, social studies. M.A.T.
Childhood Education (1–6). Includes math and science, social studies, technology. M.S. Ed., M.S.T.
Elementary and Early Secondary English. M.S.Ed.
Elementary and Early Secondary Science. M.S.Ed.
Elementary and Early Secondary Social Studies. M.S.Ed.
Elementary Education. Includes curriculum and instruction, foundations of education, mathematics, reading teacher, science. M.S.Ed.
English. M.A.
Exercise Science. M.S.
Health Education (K–12). M.S.Ed., M.S.T.
History. M.A.
Literacy Education (Birth–12). M.S.Ed.
Physical Education (K–12). M.S.Ed.
Reading Teacher (K–12). M.S.Ed.
Recreation. Includes environmental and outdoor education, management of leisure services, therapeutic recreation. M.S.
Recreation Education. Includes environmental and outdoor education, management of leisure services, therapeutic recreation. M.S.Ed.
Second Language Education. Includes English as second language, French, Spanish. M.S.Ed.
Secondary Education (7–12). Includes biology, chemistry, earth science, English, French, mathematics, physics, physics and mathematics, social studies. M.A.T., M.S.Ed.
Sport Management. M.S.
Teaching Students with Disabilities. Includes severe and multiple disabilities. M.S.Ed.
Teaching (1–6). M.S.T.

STATE UNIVERSITY OF NEW YORK COLLEGE AT FREDONIA

Fredonia, New York 14063
Web site: www.fredonia.edu

Established 1948. Located 45 miles from Buffalo. Coed. State control. Semester system. Library: 396,000 volumes, 2270 subscriptions. Total College enrollment: 5400.

Annual tuition: full-time, resident $6900, nonresident $10,920; per credit, resident $288, nonresident $455. On-campus housing for single students only. Annual academic year housing cost: $4350; $7330 (including board). Contact Director of Housing for off-campus housing information. Phone: (716)673-3341.

Graduate Studies

Graduate study since 1956. Enrollment: full-time 155, part-time 263. Graduate faculty: full-time 45, part-time 12. Degrees conferred: M.A., M.S., M.S. in Ed., M.M., C.A.S.

ADMISSION REQUIREMENTS. Transcripts, two letters of recommendation required in support of application. Online application available. TOEFL required for international applicants. Interview sometimes required. Accepts transfer applicants. Apply to Graduate Admissions, Fenner House, by August 5 (Fall), December 1 (Spring), April 20 (Summer). Application fee $50. Phone: (716)673-3808; fax: (716)673-3338.

ADMISSION STANDARDS. Relatively open for most departments. Usual minimum average: 2.5 (A = 4).

FINANCIAL AID. Annual awards from institutional funds: graduate assistantships, various research assistantships, tuition waivers; free tuition for disadvantaged students, internships, tuition waivers, Federal W/S, loans. Approved for VA benefits. Apply by March 15 to appropriate department chair for fellowships and assistantships; to Financial Aid Office for all other programs. Phone: (716)673-3253. Use FAFSA. About 12% of students receive aid other than loans from College and outside sources. Aid available for part-time students.

DEGREE REQUIREMENTS. For master's: 30 credits minimum, at least 15 in residence; thesis/final oral/written exam for some departments. For C.A.S.: 30 hours beyond the master's; internship; research paper.

FIELDS OF STUDY.
Biology.
Chemistry.
Education. Includes elementary, secondary teaching; most subject fields; speech pathology and audiology; reading, TESL.
Educational Administration.
English.
Interdisciplinary Studies.
Literacy Education.
Mathematics.
Music. Includes music education, performance, theory/composition.
Speech Pathology and Audiology.

STATE UNIVERSITY OF NEW YORK COLLEGE AT GENESEO

Geneseo, New York 14454-1401
Web site: www.geneseo.edu

Founded 1871. Located 30 miles S of Rochester. Coed. State control. Semester system. Library: 576,700 volumes, 2200 subscriptions. Total College enrollment: 5500.

Annual tuition: full-time resident $6900, nonresident $10,920; per credit, resident $288, nonresident $455. No on-campus housing available. Day care facilities available.

Graduate Studies

Graduate study since 1952. Enrollment: full-time 63, part-time 108. Graduate faculty: full-time 25, part-time 7. Degrees conferred: M.A., M.S.A., M.S.Ed.

ADMISSION REQUIREMENTS. Transcripts, two letters of recommendation, interview, GRE required in support of application. TOEFL required for international applicants. Accepts transfer applicants. Apply to Graduate Studies by June 1 (Fall), October 1 (Spring), May 1 (Summer). Application fee $50. Phone: (585)245-5546; fax: (585)245-5005; e-mail: tag@geneseo.edu.

ADMISSION STANDARDS. Selective. Usual minimum average: 2.75 (A = 4).

FINANCIAL AID. Annual awards from institutional funds: fellowships, teaching assistantships, internships, Federal W/S, loans. Apply by April 1 to appropriate department chair for assistantships; to Financial Aid Office for all other programs. Phone: (585)245-5731. Use FAFSA and TAP application. About 65% of students receive aid from College and outside sources. Aid available for part-time students.

DEGREE REQUIREMENTS. For master's: 33–42 credit hours minimum; final written/oral exam or thesis.

FIELDS OF STUDY.
Accounting.
Adolescence Education (Grade 7–12). Includes English, French, mathematics, social studies, Spanish.
Communicative Disorders and Sciences. Includes speech-language pathology.
Early Childhood Education (Birth–Grade 2).
Reading and Literacy (Birth–Grade 6).
Reading and Literacy (Grade 5–12).
Teaching in Mulicultural Education (Grade 1–6).

STATE UNIVERSITY OF NEW YORK AT NEW PALTZ

New Paltz, New York 12561-2449
Web site: www.newpaltz.edu

Founded 1885. Located 80 miles N of New York City. Coed. State control. Semester system. Library: 524,000 volumes, 4900 subscriptions.

Tuition: full-time, resident $6900, nonresident $10,920; per credit, resident $288, nonresident $455. On-campus housing for single students; none for married students. Average annual housing cost: $4350, $7330 (including board). Apply to Director of Residence Life. Phone: (845)257-4444. Day-care facilities available.

Graduate Division

Graduate study since 1947. Enrollment: full-time 385, part-time 789. Faculty teaching graduate students: full-time 116, part-time 90. Degrees conferred: M.S., M.S.Ed., M.S.T., M.A.T., M.A., M.F.A., M.P.S., C.A.S.

ADMISSION REQUIREMENTS. Transcripts, GRE/MAT/ GMAT required in support of application. Provisional or permanent teaching certificate for M.S. in Ed. TOEFL required for international applicants. Interview not required. Accepts transfer applicants. Graduates of unaccredited colleges not considered. Apply to Director of Graduate Admissions at least two month prior to registration. Application fee $50. Phone: (845)257-3285.

ADMISSION STANDARDS. Selective. Usual minimum average: 3.0 (A = 4).

FINANCIAL AID. Annual awards from institutional funds: minority student scholarships, teaching assistantships, internships, tuition waivers, Federal W/S, loans. Approved for VA benefits. Apply one month prior to registration to Division chair for scholarships, assistantships; to Director of Financial Aid for all other programs. Phone: (845)257-3250. Use FAFSA. About 4% of students receive aid other than loans from School. No aid for part-time students.

DEGREE REQUIREMENTS. For master's: 30–36 semester hours minimum, at least 24 in residence; final comprehensive exam. For C.A.S.: 30 hours minimum beyond the master's.

FIELDS OF STUDY.
Accounting.
Adolescence Education. Includes biology, chemistry, earth science, English, French, mathematics, social studies, Spanish.
Art Studio. Includes ceramics, metal, painting, printmaking, sculpture.
Business Administration.
Childhood Education. Includes early childhood, environmental, humanistic, math, science and tech., reading/literacy, special education.
Computer Science.
Communication Disorders.
Early Childhood Education (Birth–Grade2).
Electrical Engineering.
Humanistic/Multicultural Education.
Literacy Education. Includes literacy and adolescent special education, literacy and childhood special education.
Mental Health Counseling.
Music Therapy.
Nursing.
Public Accountancy.
School Leadership.
Secondary Language Education.
Special Education. Includes adolescence education, childhood education, early childhood education.
Speech-Language Pathology.
Speech and Language Disabilities.
Teaching. Includes biology, chemistry, earth science, English, French, geology, mathematics, psychology, social studies, Spanish.
Visual Arts Education. Interdisciplinary Summer program. Includes art studio–art education.

STATE UNIVERSITY OF NEW YORK COLLEGE AT ONEONTA
Oneonta, New York 13820
Web site: www.oneonta.edu

Founded 1889. Located 200 miles NW of New York City. CGS member. Coed. State control. Semester system. Library: 546,700 volumes, 2200 subscriptions. Total College enrollment: 5900.

Annual tuition: full-time, resident $6900, nonresident $10,920. Limited dormitory housing for single students. No housing for married students. Average academic year housing cost: $3850. Contact Housing Office for both on- and off-campus housing information. Phone: (607)436-3725. Day-care facilities available.

Graduate Studies

Established 1948. Enrollment: full-time 36, part-time 163. College faculty teaching graduate students: full- and part-time 144. Degrees conferred: M.A., M.S., M.S.Ed., C.A.S.

ADMISSION REQUIREMENTS. Transcripts, GRE required in support of application. TOEFL required for international applicants. Accepts transfer applicants. Graduates of unaccredited institutions not considered. Apply to Graduate Office by March 15 (Summer and Fall), October 1 (Spring). Application fee $50. Phone: (800)786-9123; (607)436-2523; fax: (607)436-3084.

ADMISSION STANDARDS. Selective. Usual minimum average: 2.8 (A = 4).

FINANCIAL AID. Annual awards from institutional funds: fellowships, teaching assistantships, Federal W/S, loans. Apply to Financial Aid Office by April 15. Use FAFSA and TAP application. Financial aid largely in form of federal and state loan programs.

DEGREE REQUIREMENTS. For M.A., M.S.: 30–48 semester hours minimum, at least 24 in residence; reading knowledge of one foreign language sometimes required for M.A.; thesis sometimes required; written/oral comprehensive exam. For C.A.S.: 27 semester hours beyond master's; thesis required for some programs.

FIELDS OF STUDY.
Adolescence Education (Grades 7–12).
Biology.
Childhood Education (Grades 1–6).
Earth Science.
Family and Consumer Science Education (Grades K–12).
History Museum Studies.
Literacy Education.
School Counselor (Grade K–12).

STATE UNIVERSITY OF NEW YORK AT OSWEGO
Oswego, New York 13126
Web site: www.oswego.edu

Founded 1861. Located 35 miles NW of Syracuse. CGS member. Coed. State control. Semester system. Library: 477,900 volumes, 1802 subscriptions. Total enrollment: 8300.

Annual tuition: full-time, resident $6900, nonresident $10,920; per credit, resident $288, nonresident $455. On-campus dormitory housing available. Average academic year housing cost: $4000, $8340 (including board). Contact Director of Housing for both on- and off-campus housing information. Phone: (315)341-2246. Day care facilities available.

Division of Graduate Studies and Research

Graduate study since 1948. Enrollment: full-time 377, part-time 513. Faculty: full-time 75, part-time 31. Degrees conferred: M.A., M.S., M.S. Ed., C.A.S., M.S.-C.A.S.

ADMISSION REQUIREMENTS. Transcripts, letters of recommendation, GRE Subject Test, GMAT required in support of application. Interview required by some departments. TOEFL required for international applicants. Accepts transfer applicants. Graduates of unaccredited colleges not considered. Apply to Office of Graduate Studies by February 1 (Fall), October 1 (Spring). Application fee $50. Phone: (315)341-3152; fax: (315)341-3577.

ADMISSION STANDARDS. Selective. Usual minimum average: 3.0 (A = 4).

FINANCIAL AID. Annual awards from institutional funds: scholarships, teaching assistantships, research fellowships, internships, tuition waivers, Federal W/S, loans. Approved for VA benefits. Apply by November 15 (Spring), April 1 (Fall) to Graduate Office for scholarships, fellowships, assistantships; to Financial Aid Office for all other programs. Phone: (315)341-2248. Use FAFSA and TAP application. About 20% of students receive aid other than loans from College and outside sources.

DEGREE REQUIREMENTS. For master's: 30–36 credit hours minimum; thesis required for some programs. For C.A.S.: 60 credit hours minimum; thesis required for some programs.

FIELDS OF STUDY.

COLLEGE OF ARTS AND SCIENCES:
Art.
Chemistry.
English.
History.
Human-Computer.

SCHOOL OF BUSINESS:
Accounting, Finance, and Law.
Business Administration. Includes concentrations in accounting, management.
International Business.
Management and Marketing.

SCHOOL OF EDUCATION:
Counseling and Psychological Services.
Curriculum and Instruction.
Educational Administration.
Technology.
Vocational Teacher Preparation.

STATE UNIVERSITY OF NEW YORK AT PLATTSBURGH
Plattsburgh, New York 12901
Web site: www.plattsburgh.edu

Organized 1889. Located 60 miles S of Montreal, Canada, 160 miles N of Albany, New York. Coed. State control. Semester system. Library: 378,000 volumes, 1400 subscriptions. Total enrollment: 6000.

Annual tuition: full-time, resident $6900, nonresident $10,920; per credit, resident $288, nonresident $455. On-campus housing for single students only. Annual academic year housing cost: $2900–$3600. Contact the Office of Campus Life/Housing for housing information. Phone: (518)564-3824.

Graduate Studies

Graduate study since 1950. Enrollment: full-time 259, part-time 269. Faculty: full-time 32, part-time 7. Degrees conferred: M.A., M.S., C.A.S.

ADMISSION REQUIREMENTS. Transcripts, statement of purpose, three letters of reference, GRE/MAT/GMAT required in support of application. Interview required for some departments. TOEFL (minimum score 550) required for international applicants. Accepts transfer applicants. Apply to Admissions Office by March 1 (Fall) School Psychology, Counselor Education, Speech-Language Pathology; May 15 (Fall) Education, Liberal Studies; October 15 (Spring) Liberal Studies, Education, Counselor Education; February 15 (Summer) Counselor Education, Speech-Language Pathology. Application fee $50. Phone: (518)564-4723; fax: (518)564-4722; e-mail: graduate@plattsburgh.edu.

ADMISSION STANDARDS. Selective. Usual minimum average: 2.5 (A = 4).

FINANCIAL AID. Annual awards from institutional funds: assistantships. Federal W/S, loans. Approved for VA benefits. Apply to Office of Financial Aid; no specified closing date. Phone: (518)564-2072; fax: (518)564-4079. Use FAFSA and TAP application. About 1% of students receive aid other than loans from College, 27% from all sources.

DEGREE REQUIREMENTS. For M.A., M.S.: 30 credits minimum, at least 18 in residence. For C.A.S.: 60 credits.

FIELDS OF STUDY.
Adolescence Education (Grades 7–12). Includes biology, chemistry, earth science, English, French, mathematics, physics, social studies, Spanish.
Childhood Education.
College and Agency Counseling. Includes student affairs professional practice.
Curriculum and Instruction.
Educational Leadership.
Liberal Studies. Includes leadership, natural science.
Literacy (Birth–Grades 6).
Literacy (Grades 5–12).
Mental Health Counseling.
School Counselor.
School Psychology.
Special Education. Includes birth–grade 2, grade 1–6, grade 7–12.
Speech-Language Pathology.

STATE UNIVERSITY OF NEW YORK COLLEGE AT POTSDAM
Potsdam, New York 13676
Web site: www.potsdam.edu

Founded 1816. Located 120 miles NW of Albany. Coed. State control. Semester system. Library: 408,000 volumes, 1300 subscriptions. Total College enrollment: 4300.

Annual tuition: full-time, resident $6900, nonresident $10,920; per credit, resident $288, nonresident $455. On-campus housing available for graduate students. Annual housing cost: $4350, $7330 (including board). Apply to Director of Residence Life. Phone: (315)267-2350. On-campus day-care facilities available.

Graduate Studies

Enrollment: full-time 287, part-time 282. College faculty teaching graduate students: full-time 48. Degrees conferred: M.A, M.S.Ed., M.M., M.S.T.

ADMISSION REQUIREMENTS. Transcripts, NYSTCE required in support of application. TOEFL required for international applicants. Accepts transfer applicants. Graduates of unaccredited institutions not considered. Apply to Admissions Office by April 1 (Summer and Fall), October 15 (Spring) for M.S. Ed., M.S.T.; no specified closing date for M.A., M.M. Application fee $50. Phone: (315)267-2515; fax: (315)267-4802.

ADMISSION STANDARDS. Usual minimum average: 2.75 (A = 4) final 60 semester credits of undergraduate studies.

FINANCIAL AID. Scholarships, graduate assistantships, minority graduate fellowships, Federal W/S, loans. Approved for VA benefits. Apply to the Financial Aid Office; no specified closing date. Phone: (315)267-2162. Use FAFSA. Aid available for part-time students.

DEGREE REQUIREMENTS. For master's: 30–33 credits minimum, 24 in residence. For M.S.T.: 42 credits minimum.

FIELDS OF STUDY.

SCHOOL OF ARTS AND SCIENCES:
English. M.A.
Mathematics. M.A.

SCHOOL OF EDUCATION:
Elementary Education. M.S.Ed., M.S.T.
General Professional Education. M.S.Ed.
Instruction Technology. M.S.Ed.
Reading. M.S.Ed.
Secondary Education. Includes biology, chemistry, English, earth science, mathematics, physics, social studies. M.S.Ed., M.S.T.
Special Education. M.S.Ed.

CRANE SCHOOL OF MUSIC:
Composition. M.M.
Music Education. M.M.
Music History and Literature. M.M.
Music Theory. M.M.
Performance. M.M.

STATE UNIVERSITY OF NEW YORK COLLEGE OF ENVIRONMENTAL SCIENCE AND FORESTRY AT SYRACUSE

Syracuse, New York 13210-2779
Web site: www.esf.edu

Coed. State control. Semester system. Special facilities: Archer and Anna Huntington Wildlife Forest, Adirondack Ecological Center, Cranberry Lake Biological Station, Empire State Paper Research Institute, Heiberg Memorial Forest, Wanakena Campus, Institute of Environmental Program Affairs, State University Polymer Research Center, U.S. Forest Service Cooperative Research Unit. Library: 137,300 volumes, 2000 subscriptions. Total enrollment: 1900.

Annual tuition (9 months): resident $6900, nonresident $10,920; per credit, resident $288, nonresident $455. On-campus housing available for married and single students. Housing cost: married students $500–$640 per month, single $6820, $8310 (including board). Phone: (315)443-2567. Day-care facilities available.

Graduate Studies

Graduate study since 1913. Enrollment: full-time 272, part-time 170. College faculty: full- and part-time 121. Degrees conferred: M.L.A., M.P.S., M.S., Ph.D.

ADMISSION REQUIREMENTS. Transcripts, GRE, bachelor's degree, three letters of reference, statement of educational objectives required in support of application. GRE Subject test for some programs. Interview desirable. TOEFL required of international students. Accepts transfer applicants. Apply to Office of Instruction and Graduate Studies by April 15 (Fall), November 15 (Spring). Application fee $50. Phone: (315)470-6599; fax: (315)470-6978; E-mail: esfgrad@esfedu.

ADMISSION STANDARDS. Very selective for most departments. Usual minimum average: 3.0 (A = 4).

FINANCIAL AID. Annual awards from institutional funds: teaching assistantships, research assistantships, fellowships, intern-

ships, Federal W/S, loans. Apply to Financial Aid Office; no specific closing date. Phone: (315)470-6670. Use FAFSA. About 70% of students receive aid other than loans from outside sources.

DEGREE REQUIREMENTS. For M.S. and M.L.A.: 30–37 semester hours minimum; thesis; project; oral exam. For M.P.S.: 30–39 semester hours minimum; internship or course work and comprehensive exam or terminal experience depending on area of study. For Ph.D.: 60 credit, three-year program beyond the bachelor's; written/oral candidacy exam; advancement to dissertation; oral exam. Additional requirements upon decision of student's program director.

FIELDS OF STUDY.

DEPARTMENT OF ENVIRONMENTAL AND FOREST BIOLOGY:
Applied Ecology. M.P.S.
Chemical Ecology. M.P.S., M.S., Ph.D.
Conservation Biology. M.P.S., M.S., Ph.D.
Ecology. M.P.S., M.S., Ph.D.
Entomology. M.P.S., M.S., Ph.D.
Environmental Interpretation. M.P.S., M.S., Ph.D.
Environmental Physiology. M.S., Ph.D.
Fish and Wildlife Biology and Management. M.P.S., M.S., Ph.D.
Forest Pathology and Mycology. M.P.S., M.S., Ph.D.
Plant Biotechnology. M.P.S.
Plant Science and Biotechnology. M.P.S., M.S., Ph.D.

DEPARTMENT OF ENVIRONMENT AND FOREST CHEMISTRY:
Biochemistry. M.S., Ph.D.
Environmental Chemistry. M.S., Ph.D.
Organic Chemistry of Natural Products. M.S., Ph.D.
Polymer Chemistry. M.S., Ph.D.

DEPARTMENT OF ENVIRONMENTAL AND RESOURCE ENGINEERING:
Chemistry of Pulping and Bleaching. M.S., Ph.D.
Colloid Chemistry and Fiber Flocculation. M.S., Ph.D.
Construction and Construction Management. M.P.S., M.S., Ph.D.
Ecological Engineering. M.S., Ph.D.
Engineering Wood Products and Structures: Timber Structure Design. M.S., Ph.D.
Environmental Management. M.P.S.
Fiber and Paper Mechanics. M.S., Ph.D.
Forest Engineering. M.S., Ph.D.
Geo-spatial Information Science and Engineering. M.S., Ph.D.
Mapping Sciences. M.P.S.
Process and Environmental System Engineering. M.P.S., M.S., Ph.D.
Pulp and Paper Technology. M.P.S., M.S., Ph.D.
Renewable Energy and Engineering. M.S., Ph.D.
Tropical Timbers. M.S., Ph.D.
Water Resources Engineering. M.S., Ph.D.
Wood Anatomy and Ultrastructure. M.S., Ph.D.
Wood Science and Technology. M.S.P., M.S., Ph.D.
Wood Treatments. M.S., Ph.D.

DEPARTMENT OF ENVIRONMENTAL SCIENCE:
Environmental and Community Land Planning. M.P.S., M.S., Ph.D.
Environmental and Natural Resource Study. Ph.D.
Environmental Communication and Participatory Processes. M.P.S., M.S., Ph.D.
Environmental Policy and Democratic Processes. M.P.S., M.S., Ph.D.
Environmental Systems and Risk Management. M.P.S., M.S., Ph.D.
Water and Wetland Resource Studies. M.P.S., M.S., Ph.D.

DEPARTMENT OF FOREST RESOURCES MANAGEMENT:
Environmental and Natural Resources Policy. M.P.S., M.S., Ph.D.
Forest Ecosystem Science and Application. M.P.S., M.S., Ph.D.
Forest Management and Operation. M.F.

Natural Resources Management. M.P.S., M.S., Ph.D.
Quantitative Methods in Forest Science and Management. M.P.S., M.S., Ph.D.
Recreation and Resource Management. M.P.S., M.S., Ph.D.
Watershed Management and Forest Hydrology. M.P.S., M.S., Ph.D.

DEPARTMENT OF LANDSCAPE ARCHITECTURE:
Community Design and Planning. M.L.A., M.S.
Cultural Landscape Studies and Conservation. M.L.A., M.S.
Landscape and Urban Ecology. M.L.A., M.S.

STATE UNIVERSITY OF NEW YORK DOWNSTATE MEDICAL CENTER AT BROOKLYN

Brooklyn, New York 11203-2098
Web site: www.downstate.edu

Founded 1860; merged with State University of New York in 1950. Name changed 1986. Coed. State control. Semester system. The Center's NIH ranking is 175th among all U.S. institutions with 40 awards/grants worth $21,045,766. Medical library: 357,200 volumes, 2104 subscriptions. Total Center enrollment: 1567.

School of Graduate Studies

Founded 1966.
Annual tuition: resident $6900, nonresident $10,920. Enrollment: full-time 71, part-time 1. Faculty: full-time 115, part-time none. Degrees conferred: M.S., Ph.D.

ADMISSIONS REQUIREMENTS. Transcripts, three letters of recommendation, GRE required in support of application. TOEFL, TSE required for international applicants. Interview may be arranged. Accepts transfer applicants. Apply to Office Graduate Studies by February 1. Application fee $35. Phone: (718)270-2738; fax: (718)270-3378.

ADMISSION STANDARDS. Competitive. Usual minimum average: 3.0 (A = 4).

FINANCIAL AID. Fellowships, research assistantships, teaching assistantships, internships, full and partial tuition waivers, Federal W/S, loans. Apply to Office of Financial Aid, no specified closing date. Use FAFSA.

DEGREE REQUIREMENTS. For M.S.: 30 credit hours; no residency required; thesis defense. For Ph.D.: 90 credit hours beyond bachelor's, 24 credit hours in full-time residency; qualifying exam; dissertation defense.

FIELDS OF STUDY.
Biomedical Engineering. Joint program with Polytechnic University.
Molecular and Cellular Biology.
Neural and Behavioral Science.

College of Medicine

Web site: www.downstate.edu

Founded 1860. Library: 357,000 volumes, 2100 subscriptions.
Annual tuition: resident $21,413, nonresident $36,113. On-campus housing for both single and married students. For both on- and off-campus housing information contact the Office of Residential Life and Services. Phone: (718)270-1466. Total average figure for all other expenses: $16,500.
Enrollment: first-year class 185, total 769 (men 49%, women 51%, minorities 10%, state residents 87%). Faculty: full- and

part-time and volunteers approximately 2500. Degrees conferred: B.A.-M.D. (with Brooklyn College), M.D., M.D.-Ph.D.

ADMISSION REQUIREMENTS. AMCAS report, transcripts, letters of recommendation, MCAT required in support of application. Has EDP; apply between June 1 and August 1. Interviews by invitation only. Applicants must have completed at least three years of college study. Accepts transfer applicants. Preference given to state residents. Apply to Office of Admissions after June 1, before December 15. Application fee $80. Phone: (718)270-2446; fax: (718)270-7592.

ADMISSION STANDARDS. Competitive. Accepts about 10% of all applicants. Number of applications n/a (n/a out-of-state); number interviewed n/a (n/a out-of-state); number of acceptance n/a (n/a out-of-state); number enrolled 185 (18 out-of-state). Mean Composite MCAT 10.6; mean UGPA 3.67.

FINANCIAL AID. Scholarships, fellowships, grants, loans, work-study. Financial aid application materials are sent to all selected applicants. Use FAFSA (School code: 002839) and institutional application. About 85% of students receive some aid from College.

DEGREE REQUIREMENTS. For M.D.: satisfactory completion of four-year program. All students must pass USMLE Step 1 prior to entering third year.

FIELDS OF GRADUATE STUDY.
Biomedical Engineering.
Molecular and Cellular Biology.
Neural and Behavioral Science.

STATE UNIVERSITY OF NEW YORK INSTITUTE OF TECHNOLOGY AT UTICA/ROME

Utica, New York 13504-3050
Web site: www.sunyit.edu

Founded 1966. Coed. State control. Upper Division institution. Semester system. Library: 193,600 volumes, 1090 subscriptions. Total Institute enrollment: 2660.
Annual tuition: full-time resident $6900, nonresident $10,920; per credit resident $288, nonresident $455. On-campus housing available for graduate students. Annual housing cost: $4380, $7330 (including board). Apply to Director of Residence Life.

Graduate Studies (P.O. Box 3050)

Enrollment: full-time 86, part-time 384. College faculty teaching graduate students: full-time 54, part-time 7. Degrees conferred: M.B.A., M.S., M.S.A.T.

ADMISSION REQUIREMENTS. Transcripts, GRE/MAT, statement of educational objective required in support of application. Letters of recommendation, interviews required by some programs. TOEFL (minimum score 550) required for international applicants. Accepts transfer applicants. Graduates of unaccredited institutions not considered. Apply to Director of Admission by June 15 (Fall), November 15 (Spring). Application fee $50. Phone: (866)2-SUNYIT, (315)792-7500, fax (315)792-7837; e-mail: admission@sunyit.edu.

ADMISSION STANDARDS. Usual minimum average: 3.0 (A = 4) final 60 semester credits of undergraduate studies.

FINANCIAL AID. Assistantships, graduate minority fellowships, tuition waivers, Federal W/S, loans. Approved for VA benefits.

Apply to the Financial Aid Office; no specified closing date. Phone: (315)792-7210. Use FAFSA. Aid available for part-time students.

DEGREE REQUIREMENTS. For master's: 30–36 credits minimum, 24 in residence; professional project.

FIELDS OF STUDY.
Accountancy.
Advanced Technology.
Adult Nurse Practitioner.
Applied Sociology.
Computer and Information Science.
Family Nurse Practitioner.
Gerontological Nurse Practitioner.
Health Services Administration.
Health Services Management. M.B.A.
Information Design and Technology.
Nursing Administration.
Nursing Education.
Technology Management. M.B.A.
Telecommunication.

STATE UNIVERSITY OF NEW YORK UPSTATE MEDICAL UNIVERSITY AT SYRACUSE
Syracuse, New York 13210-2334

Founded 1834; merged with State University of New York in 1950. Name changed in 1986. Name changed to Upstate Medical University in 1999. CGS member. Coed. State control. Semester system. The University's NIH ranking is 195th among all U.S. institutions with 63 awards/grants worth $18,213,522. Library: 132,500 volumes, 1800 subscriptions. Total University enrollment: 950.

On-campus housing available for both single and married students. Annual academic year housing cost: $4800 for single students, $5400 for married students.

College of Graduate Studies

Annual tuition: resident $6900, nonresident $10,920. Enrollment: full-time 123, part time 5. Center faculty: 62. Degrees conferred: M.S., Ph.D., M.D.-Ph.D.

ADMISSION REQUIREMENTS. Transcripts, three letters of recommendation, GRE required in support of College's application. TOEFL, TSE required for international applicants. Interviews may be arranged. Accepts transfer applicants. Graduates of unaccredited institutions not considered. Apply to Office of Graduate Studies by February 1. Application fee $25, $50 for international applicants. Phone: (315)464-4538; fax: (315)464-4544; e-mail: gradstud@mail.upstate.edu.

ADMISSION STANDARDS. Competitive. Usual minimum average: 3.0 (A = 4).

FINANCIAL AID. Predoctoral fellowships, graduate/research assistantships, tuition waivers, Federal W/S, loans. Approved for VA benefits. Contact Office of the Dean for information. Use FAFSA.

DEGREE REQUIREMENTS. For M.S.: 30 credit hours; no residency required; thesis defense. For Ph.D.: 90 credit hours, 24 credit hours in full-time residency; qualifying exam; dissertation defense. For M.D. requirements refer to College of Medicine listing below.

FIELDS OF STUDY.
Anatomy and Cell Biology.
Biochemistry and Molecular Biology.
Cell and Developmental Biology.
Cell and Molecular Biology.
Microbiology and Immunology.
Neuroscience.
Pharmacology.
Physiology.

College of Medicine
Web site: www.upstate.edu

Established 1834 as General Medical School. Joined Syracuse University in 1871. Moved to SUNY system in 1950. Library: 130,000 volumes, 2200 subscriptions.

Annual tuition: resident $19,840, nonresident $34,540. On-campus housing for 235 married students, 180 for single students. For on-campus housing information contact the Director of Housing. Phone: (315)464-6498. Total average figure for all other expenses: $11,500.

Enrollment: first-year class 153, total 613 (men 46%, women 54%, minorities 9%, state residents 90%). Faculty: full-time 366, part-time 182. Degrees conferred: M.D., M.D.-Ph.D. (Medical Scientist training Program).

ADMISSION REQUIREMENTS. AMCAS report, transcripts, MCAT, recommendations required in support of application. Interview by invitation only. Applicants must have completed at least three years of college study. Preference given to state residents. Has EDP; apply between June 1 and August 1. Apply to Admissions Committee after June 1, before November 1 (firm). Application fee $100. Phone: (315)464-4570; fax: (315)464-8867.

ADMISSION STANDARDS. Competitive. Accepts about 12% of all applicants. Number of applications 3227 (1352 out-of-state); number interviewed 908 (248 out-of-state); number of acceptance 396 (92 out-of-state); number enrolled 153 (31 out-of-state). Mean Composite MCAT 9.6, mean UGPA 3.60

FINANCIAL AID. Scholarships, grants, tuition waivers, loans. Apply to Office of Admissions and Student Affairs by May 1. Phone: (315)464-4329. Use FAFSA (College code: 002840) and ACT needs analysis. About 44% of students receive aid other than loans from College.

DEGREE REQUIREMENTS. For M.D.: satisfactory completion of four-year program. All students must take USMLE Step 1 and Step 2.

FIELDS OF GRADUATE STUDY.
Biochemistry and Molecular Biology.
Cell and Developmental Biology
Microbiology and Immunology.
Neuroscience.
Pharmacology.
Physiology.

NEW YORK UNIVERSITY
New York, New York 10276-0907
Web site: www.nyu.edu

Founded 1831. CGS and AAU member. Coed. Private control. Semester system. Special facilities: Center for Latin American and Caribbean Studies, Institute for Developmental Studies, Maison Française, Courant Institute of Mathematical Sciences, National Academy of Television Arts and Sciences Archives, Institute of French Studies, Institute of Physical Medicine and Rehabilitation, Grey Art Gallery, Institute of Fine Arts, Murray and

Leonie Guggenheim Foundation, Institute for Dental Research, C. J. Devine Institute of Finance, C.V. Starr Center for Applied Economics, Hargop Kevorkian Center for Near Eastern Studies, Institute of Retail Management, Institute of Planning and Housing, Institute of Labor Relations, Institute of Environmental Medicine, Henry W. and Albert A. Berg Institute for Experimental Physiology, Surgery, and Pathology, Institute of Judicial Administration, Institute of International Law, Copyright Publications Center, Onassis Center for Hellenic Studies. The University's NIH ranking is 45th among all U.S. institutions with 401 awards/grants valued at $152,238,328. According to The Center at University of Florida, the University is ranked 49th in receipt of Federal Research funds with $166,033,000 and it ranks 53rd for total University research expenditures with $241,593,000. The University's endowment assets rank it 28th, with a value of $1,449,500,000. In 2004, the University awarded 407 doctorates, which ranked it 25th among all U.S. institutions eligible to award that degree. Thirty-three of the University's faculty members have been elected to National Honor Academies and this ranks it 28th among all U.S. institutions. The Library: approximately 4,500,000 volumes, 32,700 subscriptions. Total University enrollment: 50,000.

Limited on-campus housing for married students, 602 graduate men and women. Housing cost: $700–$900 per month for married students, $11,000–$16,000 per academic year for single students. Apply to Office of Director of Housing. Phone: (212) 998-4600.

Graduate School of Arts and Sciences

Graduate study since 1886. Tuition: per credit $1024. Enrollment: full-time 2888, part-time 1394. School faculty: full-time 597, part-time 393. Degrees conferred: M.A., M.Phil., M.S., Ph.D.

ADMISSION REQUIREMENTS. Transcripts, three letters of recommendation required in support of School's application. Interview, GRE, TSE required for some departments. TOEFL required for international applicants. Accepts transfer applicants. Graduates of unaccredited institutions not considered. Apply to Office of Graduate Enrollment Services by January 4 (priority deadline). International applicants apply to International Student Center by November 1. Application fee $80 (online), $90 (paper application). Phone: (212)998-8050; fax: (212)995-4557; e-mail: gsas.admission@nyu.edu.

ADMISSION STANDARDS. Selective to very competitive. Usual minimum average: 3.3 (A = 4).

FINANCIAL AID. Annual awards from institutional funds: scholarships, grants, fellowships, teaching/research/administrative assistantships, tuition waivers, Federal W/S, loans. Multiyear fellowships available for Ph.D. students. Approved for VA benefits. Apply by January 4 to Fellowship Office for scholarships, internships, and fellowships; to appropriate department head for assistantships; to Financial Aid Office for Federal W/S, loans. Phone: (212)998-4486. Use FAFSA. About 30% of students receive aid other than loans from School.

DEGREE REQUIREMENTS. For M.A., M.S., M.Phil.: 32 credits minimum, at least 24 in residence; reading knowledge of one foreign language; thesis for most departments; final written exam for some departments. For Ph.D.: 72 credits minimum beyond the bachelor's, at least 32 in residence; reading knowledge of two foreign languages for most departments; qualifying exam; dissertation; final oral exam.

FIELDS OF STUDY.
Africana Studies.
American Studies.
Ancient Near Eastern and Egyptian Studies.
Anthropology. Research papers, oral exam for M.A.

Atmospheric Ocean Science.
Basic Medical Sciences. Includes anatomy, biochemistry, biophysics, microbiology, pathology, pharmacology, physiology; combined M.D.-Ph.D. programs available.
Bioethics.
Biology. Includes training program in basic cancer research, cell and molecular, developmental, environmental, evolutionary, physiology, neurobiology, population biology; preliminary oral exam for Ph.D.
Biomaterials Science.
Biomedical Science.
Chemistry.
Cinema Studies.
Classics. Includes Greek, Latin, Byzantine, and Hellenic studies.
Comparative Literature. Three languages for Ph.D.
Computer Science.
Creative Writing.
East Asian Studies.
Economics.
English. Essay required for M.A. in lieu of thesis.
English and American Literature.
Environmental Health Sciences.
Ergonomics and Biomechanics.
European and Mediterranean Studies. M.A. only.
Fine Arts. Includes history of art, archaeology, conservation, anatorial studies; creative art major offered by School of Education; French and German for M.A.; for Ph.D. in Far Eastern art and archaeology, competence in Chinese/Japanese for Ph.D. in Near Eastern art and archaeology, reading knowledge of Arabic and Persian, or Akkadian/Sumerian; written comprehensive exam for M.A.; final oral/written exam for Ph.D.
French Studies. Includes French literature.
Germanic Languages and Literatures.
Hebrew and Judaic Studies.
History.
Humanities and Social Thought.
Irish Studies. M.A.
Italian Studies. Includes Italian literature.
Journalism. M.A. only.
Latin American and Caribbean Studies. M.A. only.
Law and Society.
Library and Information Science.
Linguistics.
Mathematics. Thesis/nonthesis options for M.S.
Middle Eastern Studies.
Museum Studies. Certificate program only.
Music. Includes musicology, theory, composition.
Near Eastern Studies. M.A. only.
Neural Science. Ph.D. only.
Performance Studies.
Philosophy. M.A. only.
Physics.
Poetics and Theory.
Politics. Includes international relations, American government and politics, comparative politics; regional study programs are available.
Psychology. Includes developmental, individual and organizational, social.
Religious Studies. M.A. only.
Russian and Slavic Studies. Includes Russian; written comprehensive exam for M.A. in Russian; qualifying exam for Ph.D. in Slavic philology and linguistics.
Sociology.
Spanish and Portuguese Languages and Literatures.
Trauma and Violence.
Transdisciplinary Studies. M.A.

Tisch School of the Arts—Graduate Division
721 Broadway, 7th Floor, 10003-6807

Graduate study since 1968. Semester system.

Annual tuition: full-time $36,708. On-campus housing available. Average academic year housing cost: $15,000.

Enrollment: full-time 811, part-time 105. School faculty teaching graduate students: full-time 101. Degrees conferred: M.F.A., M.P.S. The M.A., Ph.D. awarded through the Graduate School of Arts and Sciences.

ADMISSION REQUIREMENTS. Transcripts, two or three letters of recommendation, interview/audition or portfolio required in support of School's application. Deadlines vary. Please consult Office of Graduate Admissions at (212)998-1918. Application fee $50. Admits Fall only. Apply by February 1 to Director of Graduate Admission, 721 Broadway, 7th Floor, New York, NY 10003-6807. Some programs have earlier deadlines. Phone: (212)998-1918; fax: (212)995-4060; e-mail: tisch.gradadmissions@nyu.edu.

ADMISSION STANDARDS. Competitive. Evidence of professional promise.

FINANCIAL AID. Annual awards from institutional funds: fellowships, graduate teaching assistantships, funded awards, internships, grants, tuition waivers, Federal W/S, loans. Apply by February 15 to Financial Aid Office. Phone: (212)998-1900; fax: (212)995-4060. Use FAFSA (School code: 002785) and Tisch FAF.

DEGREE REQUIREMENTS. For M.F.A.: Design, 108 credits; Dance, 72 credits; Acting, 108 credits; Dramatic Writing, 70 credits; Film, 108 credits; Musical Theater, 72 credits. For M.P.S.: Interactive Telecommunications, 60 credits. For M.A., Ph.D., see Graduate School of Arts and Sciences listing above.

FIELDS OF STUDY.
Arts Politics. M.A.
Cinema Studies. M.A., Ph.D.
Dramatic Writing. Includes writing for film, theater, television.
Film and Television. Includes film production-direction, cinematography, animation degree program by advisement.
Interactive Telecommunications. Focus on application of new media and telecommunications technologies.
Performance Studies. M.A., Ph.D.
Theater. Includes acting, dance, design, musical, theatre writing.

Leonard N. Stern School of Business Administration, Graduate Division

Web site: www.stern.nyu.edu

Graduate study since 1916. Semester system. Located at 44 West 4th Street, New York, NY 10012-1126. Annual tuition: $39,800. Enrollment: full-time 882, part-time 1937. Faculty: full-time 202, part-time 122. Degrees conferred: M.S. (Accounting), M.B.A., Ph.D.

ADMISSION REQUIREMENTS. Transcripts, letters of recommendation, GMAT, personal essay, résumé required in support of application. Interview by invitation only. TOEFL (minimum score 600) required for international applicants. Graduates of unaccredited colleges not considered. Apply to Admissions Office of the School by February 1 (Ph.D. only), March 15 (Fall), May 15 (part-time only Fall), September 15 domestic (part-time only Spring). Application fee $175, international students $125. Phone: (212)998-0900; fax: (212)995-4212.

ADMISSION STANDARDS. Very selective. Mean undergraduate average: 3.32 (A = 4); mean GMAT: 646. *U.S. News & World Report* ranking is in the top 15 of all U.S. business schools. *Business Week* ranked Stern in the top 14 of all U.S. business schools; *Financial Times* ranked Ph.D. program second in 2002, 2003, 2004.

FINANCIAL AID. Annual awards from institutional funds; scholarships, research fellowships, graduate assistantships, internships,

tuition waivers, Federal W/S, loans. Approved for VA benefits. Apply by January 15 to the Office of Financial Aid. Use FAFSA (School code: 002785). About 40% of students receive aid other than loans from School and outside sources. Loans available for part-time students.

DEGREE REQUIREMENTS. For M.B.A.: 60 credits (20 courses) plus comprehensive business project; calculus, computer economics and business writing proficiencies. For M.S. in Accounting: 60 credits. For Ph.D.: 72 credits.

FIELDS OF DOCTORAL STUDY.
Accounting.
Economics.
Entertainment, Media, and Technology.
Finance.
Information Systems.
International Business. Multidisciplinary program.
Management.
Marketing.
Operations Management.
Statistics and Operations Research.
Strategy.

College of Dentistry—David B. Kriser Dental Center

Web site: www.nyu.edu/dental

Founded 1865. Located 345 East 24th Street, New York 10010. Special facilities: NYU/Forsyth Center for Minority Oral Health, Research for Adolescent and Adult Health Promotion Center. Waldman Memorial Library: 38,000 volumes, 550 subscriptions.

Annual tuition: $49,347. On-campus housing for both married students and single students. Average academic year housing cost: $18,400. Apply to Office of the Manager, Hall of Residence, New York University Medical Center. Total average cost for all other first-year expenses: $13,500.

Enrollment: first-year class 230, total 920 (men 58%, women 42%, minorities 52%, residents 41%). Faculty: full-time 135, part-time 455. Degrees conferred: A.B.-D.D.S., D.D.S., D.D.S.-M.S. (Management), D.D.S.-M.B.A., D.D.S.-M.P.H., D.D.S.-Ph.D., Certificates (Advanced Education Programs).

ADMISSION REQUIREMENTS. For D.D.S. program: AADSAS, transcripts, three letters of recommendation, DAT required in support of College's application. Interviews by invitation only. Applicants must have completed at least three years of college study. TOEFL required for international applicants. Accepts transfer applicants from U.S. and Canadian dental Schools. International transfer applicants accepted into a three-year program for foreign-trained dentists. Apply to Director of Admissions after July 15, before June 1. Fall admission only. Application fee $75. Phone: (212)998-9818; fax: (212)995-4240. For Certificate programs: official transcripts, two letters of recommendation, D.D.S. or D.M.D., interview required in support of College's application. Apply to Director of Advanced Education of School by March 31. Fall admission only.

ADMISSION STANDARDS. Competitive. Accepts about 10% of all applicants. Number of applications 3907 (3493 out-of-state); number interviewed 697 (582 out-of-state); number of acceptances 460 (394 out-of-state); number enrolled 232 (173 out-of-state). Usual minimum UGPA: 3.0 (A = 4). Mean DAT: academic 19, PAT 18; mean UGPA 3.28.

FINANCIAL AID. Scholarships, grants, loans. Apply by March 1 to Dental Center Financial Aid Office after acceptance. Phone: (212)998-9825. Use FAFSA (College code: 002785). About 100% of students receive some aid from College and outside sources.

DEGREE REQUIREMENTS. For A.B.-D.D.S.: satisfactory completion of seven-year program. For D.D.S.: satisfactory completion of forty-five-month program. For Advanced Education Programs: varies by program.

FIELDS OF POSTGRADUATE STUDY.

Biology/Oral Biology. M.S.
Biomaterials. M.S.
Clinical Research. M.S.
Endodontics. Certificate.
Global Public Health. Interuniversity program with five concentration: oral public health, epidemiology, heath policy and management, health promotion, disease prevention and human migration. M.P.H.
Oral and Maxillofacial Surgery. Certificate.
Oral Epidemiology. Concurrent enrollment at either Columbia University, Yale University, Johns Hopkins University. Ph.D.
Orthodontics and Dentofacial Orthopedics. Certificate.
Pediatric Dentistry. Certificate.
Periodontics. Certificate.
Prosthodontics. Certificate.

The Steinhardt School of Culture, Education, and Human Development

Web site: www.education.nyu.edu

Graduate study since 1980. Semester system. Special facilities: Center for Research and Community Service, Center for Nursing Research, Center for the Study of American Culture and Education, Center for Urban Community College Leadership, Metropolitan Center for Urban Education, New York University Institute for Education and Social Policy, Reading Recovery Teacher Leader Training Center.

Tuition: per credit $1097. Enrollment: full-time 1980, part-time 1591. School faculty: full-time 224, part-time 536. Degrees conferred: M.A., M.S., M.P.H., Sixth-Year Certificate, D.A., Ed.D., Psy.D., Ph.D.

ADMISSION REQUIREMENTS. Transcripts required in support of application. GRE required for all doctoral applicants. TOEFL (minimum score 550) required for all non-native speakers of English. Interview required for some graduate applicants. Apply to School of Education, Graduate Admissions, by March 1 for master's and February 1 for doctoral programs (Fall), and December 1 for master's only (Spring). Application fee $40, international students $60. Phone: (212)998-5030; fax: (212) 995-4328.

ADMISSION STANDARDS. Selective to very selective (varies by program).

FINANCIAL AID. Annual awards from institutional funds: fellowships, teaching and research assistantships, graduate assistantships, internships, tuition waivers, Federal W/S, loans. Approved for VA benefits. Apply by February 1 for Fall term and by November 1 for Spring term to Office of Graduate Admissions. Phone: (212) 998-4444. Use FAFSA (School code: 002785), and New York State residents use TAP application. About 44% of full-time students receive aid other than loans from University and outside sources. Aid available for part-time students.

DEGREE REQUIREMENTS. For M.A.: 34 credits minimum without thesis, at least 24 in residence; or 30 credits minimum plus thesis, at least 24 in residence. For Sixth-Year Certificate: 30 credits minimum beyond a 34-credit master's degree, at least 24 credits in residence. For Ph.D., Ed.D., Psy.D., D.A.: 30 credit basic core, plus department requirements, at least 54 credits in residence beyond bachelor's, at least 30 credits in residence beyond master's; departmental candidacy exam; final oral exam; tool requirement for research; research proposal; dissertation; one or two semesters in full-time residence for some departments.

FIELDS OF STUDY.

Art Education.
Art Therapy.
Arts and Humanities Education.
Bilingual Education.
Business Education.
Childhood Education.
Childhood Special Education.
Community Health.
Counseling and Guidance.
Counseling Psychology.
Dance Education.
Deafness Rehabilitation.
Drama Therapy.
Early Childhood Education.
Education and Jewish Studies.
Education Policy.
Educational Leadership.
Educational Communication and Technology.
Educational Psychology.
Educational Leadership.
Educational Theatre.
English Education.
Environmental Conservation Education.
Food Studies and Food Management.
Foreign Language Education.
Graphic Communications Management and Technology.
Health Education.
Higher Education Administration.
History of Education.
International Education.
Literacy Education.
Mathematics Education.
Media Ecology—Studies in Communication.
Music Business.
Music Education.
Music Performance. Includes jazz instruments, piano, voice.
Music Technology.
Music Therapy.
Nutrition and Dietetics.
Occupational Therapy.
Performing Arts Administration.
Philosophy of Education.
Physical Therapy.
Psychology and Social Interventions.
Psychology Development.
Public Health.
Rehabilitation Counseling.
School Psychology.
Science Education.
Social Studies Education.
Sociology of Education.
Special Education.
Speech-Language Pathology.
Speech-Language Pathology and Audiology.
Studio Art.
Teaching and Learning.
TESOL
Visual Arts Administration.
Visual Culture.

School of Law

Web site: www.law.nyu.edu

Established 1835. Located at the Washington Square campus. ABA approved since 1930. AALS member. Private control. Semester system. Full-time day only. Special facilities: Institute for International Law and Justice; Center for Human Rights and Global Justice; Jean Monnet Center for International and Regional Economic Law and Justice; Labor and Employment Law; Center for Labor and Employment Law; Center for Law, Economics; and Organization; Pollack Center for Law and Business; Institute for Law and Society; Center for the Study of Central Banks; Center on Environmental and Land Use Law; Engelberg Center on Innovation Law and Policy; Furman Center for Real Estate and Urban Policy; Institute for Law and Society; Brennan Center for Justice; Center for Community Problem Solving; Center for Human Rights and Global Justice; Migration Policy Institute; Public Interest Law Center; National Center on Philanthropy and the Law. Special programs: Study abroad programs are currently established with the Universities of Amsterdam (The Netherlands), Kyushu (Japan), Copenhagen (Denmark), Leuven (Belgium), Palermo (Argentina), Paris II and Paris X (France), Sydney (Australia), the European University Institute (Italy), Bucerius Law School (Germany), and the National University of Singapore. Law Library: 1,080,282 volumes, 7025 subscription; has LEXIS, NEXIS, WESTLAW, DIALOG; has more than 1800 network connections; is a Federal Government Depository.

Annual tuition: $38,980; LL.M. and J.S.D $22,225, per credit $1950. On-campus housing available for both single and married students. Law School has more than 400 on-campus accommodations. Annual on-campus housing cost: $22,760. Contact Law School Residence Hall for both on- and off-campus housing information. Many law students live in off-campus housing. Off-campus housing and personal expenses: approximately $18,555.

Enrollment: first-year class 448, total full-time 1442, (men 54%, women 46%, minorities 24%). Faculty: full-time 130, part-time 65. Student-to-faculty ratio 11.1 to 1. Degrees conferred: J.D., J.D.-M.A.(Economics, French, History, Philosophy, Politics, Sociology), J.D.-M.B.A., J.D.-M.P.A (Princeton University or N.Y.U.), J.D.-M.P.A.K.S., J.D.-M.U.P., J.D.-M.S.W., J.D.-LL.M., LL.M. (Corporate Law, International Legal Studies, International Tax Program for Foreign Students, Taxation, Trade Regulations), LL.M.C.J. (only for persons who have completed a basic legal education and received a university degree in law in another country), J.S.D.

ADMISSION REQUIREMENTS. For J.D.: LSDAS Law School report, bachelor's degree, transcripts, LSAT, three letters of recommendation required in support of application. Interview not required or encouraged. Evidence of proficiency in English required for international applicants. Accepts transfer applicants. Apply to Committee on Admissions of the School by February 1 (Fall), October 15 (Spring). Accepts full-time students only. Application fee $65. Phone: (212)998-6060; fax: (212)995-4527. For graduate program: transcripts, personal statement, résumé, one letter of recommendation in support of application. English language proficiency evaluation by American Language Institute at NYU for international applicants. Apply to Graduate Office of School by August 10 (Fall), December 10 (Spring), May 10 (Summer). Phone: (212)998-6060. Application fee $75.

ADMISSION STANDARDS. Selective. Accepts approximately 21% of all students. Number of applicants 7872; number of acceptances 1655; number enrolled 448; LSAT (75% of students have a score at or above 168); GPA (75% of student have a GPA at or above 3.60). *U.S. News & World Report* ranking is in the top four of all U.S. law schools.

FINANCIAL AID. For J.D.: scholarships, Federal W/S, loans. Apply to Committee on Admissions by April 15. About 50% of students receive aid other than loans from School. For graduate program: fellowships, assistantships; apply to Financial Aid Office of the School by May 1. Phone: (212)998-6050. Use FAFSA (School code: 002785). About 31% of students receive aid other than loans from School. Public service loan forgiveness plan available.

DEGREE REQUIREMENTS. For J.D.: 82 semester hours minimum, six semesters in full-time residence. For LL.M.: at least 24 credit hours beyond the J.D. minimum, at least 16 in residence. For LL.M.C.J.: at least one year in full-time residence; essay; for foreign lawyers other than those trained in Common Law countries. For J.S.D.: an NYU LL.M. required; 36 credit hours minimum, at least one year in full-time residence; advancement to candidacy; oral exam; dissertation. Refer to other Graduate School listings for joint degree requirements.

FIELDS OF GRADUATE STUDY.
Comparative Jurisprudence. Open only to lawyers whose training is in civil law.
Corporation Law
General Studies.
International Legal Studies.
International Taxation.
Labor and Employment Law.
Public Service Law.
Taxation.
Trade Regulation.
Note: Joint degree program in public affairs with Woodrow Wilson School, Princeton University, also available.

School of Medicine (P.O. Box 1924)
Web site: www.med.nyu

Organized 1841. Located 550 First Avenue, New York 10016. Special facility: Institute of Environmental Medicine at Sterling Forrest. The NIH ranking is 45th among U.S. institutions with 401 awards/grants worth $152,238,328. Library: 100,000 volumes, 1600 subscriptions.

Annual tuition: $40,750. On-campus housing for married students and single students. Apply to Housing Department, New York University Medical Center. Total average figure for all other expenses: $18,000.

Enrollment: first-year class 160, total 711 (men 50%, women 50%, minorities 36%, state residents 46%). Faculty: full-time 1531, part-time 2000. Degrees conferred: M.D., M.D.-M.P.H., M.D.-Ph.D. (Medical Scientist Training Program).

ADMISSION REQUIREMENTS. AMCAS report, transcripts, two letters of recommendation, MCAT, screening interview, secondary application required in support of application. Interview for serious candidates only. Applicants must have completed at least three years of college study. TOEFL required for foreign applicants. Does not have EDP. Accepts transfer applicants. Graduates of unaccredited colleges not considered. Apply to Office of Admissions of School after August 15, before October 15. Foreign students apply to International Student Center. Fall admission only. Application fee $100. Phone: (212)263-5290; fax: (212) 725-0720.

ADMISSION STANDARDS. Very competitive. Accepts about 5.8% of all applicants. Number of applications 8028 (6561 out-of-state); number interviewed 940 (705 out-of-state); number of acceptances 468 (330 out-of-state); number enrolled 160 (93 out-of-state). Mean Composite MCAT 10.6; mean UGPA 3.77. *U.S. News & World Report* ranking is in the top 34 of all medical schools.

FINANCIAL AID. Scholarships, research fellowships, assistantships, Federal W/S, loans, MSTP funded by NIH. Apply to Office of the Associate Dean; no specified closing date. Phone: (212)263-5286. Use FAFSA (School code: G24543). About 60% of students receive aid other than loans from School.

DEGREE REQUIREMENTS. For M.D.: satisfactory completion of four-year program, at least two years in residence; taking Step 1 and Step 2 of USMLE is optional. For M.D.-Ph.D.: consult Director, Institute of Graduate Biomedical Sciences.

FIELDS OF GRADUATE STUDY.
Bioethics.
Cellular and Molecular Biology.
Clinical Investigation.

Computational Biology.
Developmental Genetics.
Environmental Health Sciences.
Medical and Molecular Parasitology.
Medical Education.
Medical Informatics.
Microbiology.
Molecular Oncology and Immunology.
Molecular Pharmacology.
Neuroscience.
Physiology.
Public Health.
Structural Biology.

College of Nursing
246 Greene Street
Web site: www.nyu.edu/nursing

Department of Nursing founded in 1947 as part of the School of Education, Became a division of the School and in 2001 the College of Nursing was established and is now located at the College of Dentistry. Semester system. Special facilities: Center for Continuing Education in Nursing, International Programs and W.H.O. Collaborating Center, Hartford Institute for Geriatric Nursing, Martha E. Rogers Center, Leadership Institute for Black Nurses.

Tuition: per credit $1124.

Enrollment: full- and part-time 1100. Faculty: full-time 50, part-time 87. Degrees conferred: M.S., Ph.D.

ADMISSION REQUIREMENTS. Transcripts, two letters of recommendation, personal statement, résumé required in support of College's application. TOEFL required for international applicants. Accepts limited number of transfer applicants. Graduates of unaccredited colleges not considered. Apply by July 1 (Fall), December 1 (Spring) to Office of Student Affairs and Admissions. Phone: (212)998-5317. Rolling admission process. Application fee $65.

ADMISSION STANDARDS. Competitive. Usual minimum average: 3.0 (A = 4).

FINANCIAL AID. Scholarships, assistantship, internships, grants, Federal loans. Apply by March 1 to Office of Financial Aid. Use FAFSA (School code 002785) and New York State residents use TAP application.

DEGREE REQUIREMENTS. For M.S.: 30–36 credit program at least 24 credits in residence; thesis, nonthesis option. For Ph.D.: 54 credit program beyond master's; dissertation; oral exam.

FIELDS OF STUDY.
Adult Acute Care.
Adult Primary Care.
Adult Primary Care/Geriatrics.
Adult Primary Care/Holistic Nursing.
Adult Primary Care/Palliative Care Nursing.
Geriatrics.
Mental Health Nursing.
Midwifery.
Nursing Administration.
Nursing Education.
Nursing Informatics.
Pediatrics.

Robert F. Wagner Graduate School of Public Service
Web site: www.wagner.nyu.edu

Established 1938. Semester system. Tuition: per credit $831. Enrollment: full-time 440, part-time 429. Faculty: full-time 27, part-time 58. Degrees conferred: M.S., M.P.A., M.U.P., Ph.D., Advanced Professional Certificates.

ADMISSION REQUIREMENTS. Transcripts required in support of application. GRE required for doctoral students. Interview not required. TOEFL, TWE required for international applicants. Accepts transfer applicants. Graduates of unaccredited institutions not considered. Apply to Office of Admissions of School by June 1 (Fall), November 1 (Spring). Application fee $70. Phone: (212) 998-7414; fax: (212)995-4164.

ADMISSION STANDARDS. Selective. Usual minimum average: 3.0 (A = 4); 3.3–3.5 for doctoral applicants.

FINANCIAL AID. Annual awards from institutional funds: scholarships, fellowships, research assistantships, internships, tuition waivers, Federal W/S, loans. Approved for VA benefits. Apply by January 15 to Office of Admissions. Phone: (212)998-4486. Use FAFSA. About 40% of students receive aid other than loans from School and outside sources. Aid available for part-time students.

DEGREE REQUIREMENTS. For M.P.A., M.U.P.: 60 credits minimum, at least 32 in residence; capstone project. For Ph.D.: 72 credits minimum beyond the bachelor's, at least 32 in residence; written preliminary exam; three comprehensive written exams; foreign language or advanced statistics; dissertation; final oral exam. For Adv. Prof. Cert.: 20 credits minimum beyond the master's, at least 15 in residence.

FIELDS OF STUDY.
Health Finance.
Health Policy Analysis
Health Policy and Management.
Infrastructure Management.
Management.
Management/International.
Public and Nonprofit Management and Policy.
Public Service.
Urban Planning.

Shirley M. Ehrenkranz School of Social Work

Established in 1960. Semester system. Tuition: per credit $831 (M.S.W.), $794 (Ph.D.). Enrollment: full-time 661, part-time 394. Faculty: full-time 36, part-time 128. Degrees conferred: M.S.W,. Ph.D.

ADMISSION REQUIREMENTS. Transcripts, personal essay, letters of recommendation required in support of School's application. Interview may be required. TOEFL required for international applicants. Accepts limited number of transfer applicants. Graduates of unaccredited colleges not considered. Apply to Director of Admissions of School by March 1 (Fall), November 1 (Spring). Fall admission for full-time program. Rolling admissions process. Application fee $50. Phone: (212)998-5910; fax: (212)995-4171.

ADMISSION STANDARDS. Competitive. Usual minimum average: 3.0 (A = 4).

FINANCIAL AID. Assistantships, internships, tuition remission program, grants, tuition waivers, Federal W/S, loans. Apply by March 1 to the Director of Admissions. Use FAFSA, and New York State residents use TAP application. About 85% of students receive aid other than loans from School and outside sources. Only loans available for part-time students.

DEGREE REQUIREMENTS. For M.S.W.: 65 credits minimum, at least one year in full-time residence. For Ph.D.: 60 credits beyond the master's.

FIELD OF STUDY.
Clinical Social Work.

NIAGARA UNIVERSITY

Niagara University, New York 14109
Web site: www.niagara.edu

Founded 1856, located 25 miles NW of Buffalo. Coed. Private control. Roman Catholic. Semester system. Library: exceeds 313,895 volumes, 4500 subscriptions. Total University enrollment: 4000.

Tuition: per credit Elementary and Secondary Education $535, other Education programs $510, M.B.A. $655, Criminal Justice $545. Limited on-campus housing. Annual academic year housing cost: $6660. Apply to Director of University Housing. Phone: (716)285-8568.

Graduate Studies

Enrollment: full-time 573, part-time 298. University faculty: full-time 35, part-time 24. Degrees conferred: M.S., M.B.A., M.S.Ed.; Professional Diploma in Educational Administration, School Counseling.

ADMISSION REQUIREMENTS. Transcripts, two letters of recommendation, GRE/GMAT scores, personal statement, interview required in support of application. TOEFL required for international applicants. Accepts transfer applicants. Graduates of unaccredited institutions not considered. Apply to Director of Graduate Recruitment at least one month prior to registration. Phone: (716)286-8769; fax: (716)286-8710. Application fee $30.

ADMISSION STANDARDS. Selective. Usual minimum average: 3.0 (A = 4).

FINANCIAL AID. Scholarships, fellowships, research assistantship, Federal W/S, loans. Apply by March 1 to Financial Aid Office; no specified closing date. Phone: (716)286-8686. Use FAFSA. About 40% of students receive aid other than loans from University and outside sources. Aid available for part-time students.

DEGREE REQUIREMENTS. For M.S.: 33–36 semester hours minimum; thesis/oral exam; comprehensive exam. For M.S. Ed.: 36 semester hours; comprehensive exam. For M.B.A.: 48 semester hours. For Professional Diplomas: 30 hours beyond the master's.

FIELDS OF STUDY.

GRADUATE DIVISION OF ARTS AND SCIENCES:
Criminal Justice. M.S.
Criminal Justice Administration. M.S.

GRADUATE DIVISION OF BUSINESS:
Business Administration. Includes accounting, human resource management, international business, strategic management. M.B.A. only.

GRADUATE DIVISION OF EDUCATION:
Educational Administration and Supervision.
Elementary Education.
Foundations of Teaching.
Literacy Instruction.
Mental Health Counseling.
School Counseling.
School Psychology.
Secondary Education.
Teacher Education.

UNIVERSITY OF NORTH ALABAMA

Florence, Alabama 35632-0001
Web site: www.una.edu

Founded 1830. Located 120 miles N of Birmingham. Coed. State control. Semester system. Library: 350,000 volumes, 3100 subscriptions. Total University enrollment: 6400.

Tuition: per credit, resident $180, nonresident $360. On-campus housing for 50 married students, unlimited for single graduate men and women. Average annual housing cost: $4034–$4310 (including board) for single students; $5000 for married students. Contact Office of Student Affairs for both on- and off-campus housing information. Phone: (256)765-4280. Day-care facilities available.

Graduate Division

Enrollment: full-time 194, part-time 650. University faculty teaching graduate students: full- and part-time 68. Degrees conferred: M.A., M.A.Ed., M.B.A., M.S.

ADMISSION REQUIREMENTS. Transcripts, GRE Subject Tests or MAT/GMAT required in support of application. Online application available. TOEFL required for international applicants. Interview not required. Accepts transfer applicants. Apply to Director of Admissions at least two months prior to registration. Application fee $25. Phone: (256)765-4608; fax: (256)765-4960.

ADMISSION STANDARDS. Selective. Usual minimum average: 2.75 unconditional, 2.0 conditional (A = 4).

FINANCIAL AID. Limited to Federal W/S, loans. Apply to Financial Aid Office; no specified closing date. Phone: (256)765-4278. Use FAFSA.

DEGREE REQUIREMENTS. For master's: 33 credit hours minimum; at least 24 credit hours in residence; thesis/nonthesis option; final oral exam.

FIELDS OF STUDY.

COLLEGE OF ARTS AND SCIENCE:
Criminal Justice. M.S.
English. M.A.

COLLEGE OF BUSINESS:
Business Administration. M.B.A.

COLLEGE OF EDUCATION:
Counseling (P–12). M.A.Ed.
Educational Administration. Ed. S.
Elementary Education (K–6). M.A.Ed.
Health Education (P–12). M.A.Ed.
Health, Physical Education, and Recreation. M.A.
Learning Disabilities. M.A.Ed.
Non-School Counseling. M.A.
Non-School Based Teaching. M.A.
Physical Education (P–12). M.A.Ed.
Secondary Education (6–12). Includes biology, business and office education, chemistry, English/language arts, general science, geography, history, mathematics, mathematics/computer science, physics, political science, social science. M.A.Ed.
Special Education Collaborative. Includes K–6 grades, 6–12 grades, K–12 grades. M.A.Ed.
Supervision of Instruction. M.A.Ed.

NORTH CAROLINA AGRICULTURAL AND TECHNICAL STATE UNIVERSITY

Greensboro, North Carolina 27411
Web site: www.ncat.edu

Founded 1891. CGS member. Coed. State control. Semester system. Special facilities: Center for Advanced Materials and Smart Structures, Center of Aerospace Research, Center for Autonomous Control Engineering, Center for Composite Materials

Research, Center for Electronics Manufacturing, Center for Energy Research and Technology, Center for Environmental Remediation and Pollution Prevention, Institute for Human–Machine Studies, International Trade Center, Transportation Institute, Waste Management Institute. Library 483,700 volumes, 4500 subscriptions.

Annual tuition: full-time resident $3186, nonresident $12,771 On-campus housing for single students only. Average academic year cost: $5000–$6500 (including board). Contact Dean of Students for both on- and off-campus housing information, Phone: (336)334-7920. Day-care facilities available.

School of Graduate Studies

Graduate study since 1939. Enrollment: full- and part-time 1310. Faculty: full-time 360, part-time 102. Degrees conferred: M.A., M.S., M.S.E., M.S.A.E., M.S.M.E., M.S.I.T., Ph.D.

ADMISSION REQUIREMENTS. Two official transcripts, GRE, letter of intent required in support of School's application. TOEFL required for international applicants. Interview not required. Accepts transfer applicants. Graduates of unaccredited institutions not considered. Apply to Graduate Office by July 1 (Fall), November 1 (Spring). Rolling admissions process. Application fee $35. Phone: (336)334-7920; fax: (336)334-7282.

ADMISSION STANDARDS. Selective. Usual minimum average: 2.5 (A = 4).

FINANCIAL AID. Fellowships, research assistantships, teaching assistantships, internships, Federal W/S, loans. Approved for VA benefits. Apply to Dean of Graduate School for fellowships, assistantships; to Financial Aid Office for all other programs. No specified closing date. Use FAFSA. About 10% of students receive aid other than loans from School. Aid available for part-time students.

DEGREE REQUIREMENTS. For master's: 30–36 semester hours minimum, at least 22 in residence; a reading knowledge of one foreign language required by some programs; qualifying exam; thesis/nonthesis option; comprehensive oral/written exam. For Ph.D.: minimum of 36 semester hours beyond the master's; qualifying exam; reading knowledge of one foreign language required by some programs; preliminary oral exam; admission to candidacy; dissertation; final oral exam.

FIELDS OF STUDY
Adult Education. M.S.
Agricultural and Biosystems Engineering. M.S.
Agricultural Economics. M.S.
Agricultural Education. M.S.
Animal Health Science. M.S.
Applied Mathematics. M.S.
Applied Physics. M.S.
Architectural Engineering. M.S.
Biology. M.S.
Chemical Education. M.A.
Chemical Engineering. M.S.Ch.E.
Chemistry. M.S.
Civil and Environmental Engineering. M.S.
Computational and Science Engineering. M.S.
Computer Science. M.S.
Counselor Education. M.S.
Elementary Education. M.A.Ed
Electrical and Computer Engineering. M.S., Ph.D.
Energy and Environmental Studies. Ph.D.
English and African American Literature. M.A.
English Education. M.S.
Food and Nutrition. M.S.
Health and Physical Education. M.S.

History Education. M.S.
Human Environmental and Family Sciences. M.S.
Human Resource. Includes business and industry, community/agency. M.S.
Industrial Engineering. M.S., Ph.D.
Industrial Technology. Includes manufacturing systems, electronic and computer technology, graphic communication systems, construction management, occupational safety and health. M.S.I.T.
Instructional Technology. M.S.
Leadership Studies. Ph.D.
Management Information Systems. M.S.
Mathematics Secondary Education. M.S.
Mechanical Engineering. M.S.M.E., Ph.D.
Natural Resources and Environmental Design. M.S.
Physics. M.S.
Plant and Soil Science. M.S.
Professional Physics. M.S.
Social Work. Joint programs with University of North Carolina, Greensboro. M.S.W.
Technology Education. M.S.
Technology Management. Ph.D.
Transportation and Logistics. M.S.M.

NORTH CAROLINA CENTRAL UNIVERSITY
Durham, North Carolina 27707-3129
Web site: www.nccu.edu

Founded 1910. CGS member. Coed. State control. Semester system. Library: 614,000 volumes, 860,000 microforms, 4500 current periodicals, 30 PCs.

Annual tuition: full-time, resident $2690, nonresident $12,270. On-campus housing for single students only. Average academic year housing cost: $6800 (including board). Contact Director of Residence Operations for both on- and off-campus for housing information. Phone: (919)530-6517. Day-care facilities available.

Graduate Studies

Enrollment: full-time 253, part-time 560. Faculty: full-time 194, part-time 77. Degrees conferred: M.A., M.S., M.Ed., M.B.A., M.I.S., M.L.S., M.P.A.

ADMISSION REQUIREMENTS. Official transcripts, GRE/GMAT, two letters of reference required in support of application. TOEFL (minimum score 500) required for international applicants. Interview not required. Accepts transfer applicants. Graduates of unaccredited institutions not considered. Apply to the Admissions Office at least one month (45 days for Business) prior to registration. Application fee $40. Phone: (919)530-7396.

ADMISSION STANDARDS. Selective. Usual minimum average: 2.5, 3.0 in undergraduate major (A = 4).

FINANCIAL AID. Assistantships, teaching/research fellowships, internships, grants, Federal W/S, loans. Approved for VA benefits. Apply by May 1 to the Vice Chancellor's Office for assistantships, fellowships; to the Financial Aid Office for all other programs. Phone: (919)530-6202. Use FAFSA and University's FAF. About 25% of students receive aid other than loans from College and outside sources. Aid available for part-time students.

DEGREE REQUIREMENTS. For master's: 30–48 semester hours minimum with at least three summers in full-time attendance; thesis/nonthesis option or research project; reading knowledge of one foreign language or other research tool for some programs; final oral/written exam.

FIELDS OF STUDY.

COLLEGE OF ARTS AND SCIENCES:
Biology. M.S.
Chemistry M.S.
Criminal Justice. M.S.
Earth Science. M.S.
English. M.A.
History. M.A.
Human Sciences. M.S.
Mathematics. M.S.
Physical Education and Recreation. M.S.
Psychology M.A.
Public Administration. M.S.
Recreation Administration.
Sociology.

SCHOOL OF BUSINESS:
Business Administration. M.B.A.

SCHOOL OF EDUCATION:
Behavioral-Emotional Disabilities.
Career Counseling
Communication Disorders.
Community Agency Counseling.
Curriculum and Instruction.
Early Education and Language Development.
Educational Technology.
Instructional Technology.
Learning Disabilities.
Orientation and Mobility.
Rehabilitation Counseling.
School Administration.
School Counseling.
Special Education.
Visual Impairment.

SCHOOL OF LIBRARY AND INFORMATION SCIENCE:
Information Science. Includes project management, information network management, information counseling, database management, institutional research. M.I.S.
Library Science.

School of Law

Web site: www.nccu.edu/law

Established 1939. ABA approved since 1950. AALS member. Public control. Semester system. Special facilities: Biotechnology and Pharmaceutical Law Institute, Dispute Resolution Institute. Law library: 340,040 volumes, 4250 subscriptions; has LEXIS, NEXIS, WESTLAW, DIALOG.

Annual tuition: resident $4711, nonresident $16,571; per credit $1941. On-campus housing available for single students only. Apply to Housing Office. Phone: (919)560-6627. Total average annual additional expense: $19,061.

Enrollment: first-year class, 89 (day), 26 (evening); full-time 426, part-time 111 (men 43%, women 57%, minorities 52%). Faculty: full-time 11, part-time 12. Student to faculty ratio 23.1 to 1. Degrees conferred: J.D., J.D.-M.B.A., J.D.-M.L.S. (Law Librarianship).

ADMISSION REQUIREMENTS. LSDAS Law School report, bachelor's degree, transcript, personal statement, two letters of recommendation, LSAT required in support of application. Interview not required. Accepts transfer applicants. Graduates of unaccredited colleges not considered. Apply to Office of Admissions after September 1, before April 1. Application fee $40. Phone: (919)530-5243.

ADMISSION STANDARDS. Selective. Accepts approximately 20% of full-time and 19% of part-time students. Number of full-

time applicants 1747, part-time 693; number of full-time acceptance 350, part-time 131; number of full-time enrolled 171, part-time 30; LSAT (75% of full-time students have a score at or above 143, part-time 149); GPA (75% of full-time students have a GPA at or above 2.80, part-time 2.90). *U.S. News & World Report* ranking is in the fourth tier of all U.S. law schools.

FINANCIAL AID. Scholarships, assistantships, Federal W/S, loans. Apply to Director of Student Financial Aid by February 1. Phone: (919)530-6409. Use FAFSA (School code: 002950). About 20% of students receive aid other than loans from School. Aid sometimes available for part-time students.

DEGREE REQUIREMENTS. For J.D.: satisfactory completion of three-year program; 88 semester hour program.

NORTH CAROLINA STATE UNIVERSITY AT RALEIGH
Raleigh, North Carolina 27695
Web site: www.ncsu.edu

Established 1987. CGS member. Coed. State control. Semester system. Special facilities: Center for Electric Power Research, Center for Sound and Vibration, Electron Microscope Facilities, Highlands Biological Station, Reproductive Physiology Research Laboratory, Phytotron, Triangle Universities Nuclear Laboratory, Mars Mission Research Center, Nuclear Reactor Program Facilities, Pesticide Residue Research Laboratory, Precision Engineering Center, Southeastern Plant Environment Laboratories, Sea Grant College Program, Triangle Universities Computation Center, Institute of Statistics, member Institution Research Program at Oak Ridge, Water Resources Research Institute. Library: 2,398,000 volumes, 18,500 subscriptions.

Annual tuition/fees: full-time, resident $4268, $10,892 (M.B.A.), $9580 (M.A.C.), nonresident $16,316, $22,816 (M.B.A.), $21,566 (M.A.C.); part-time, graduated scale depending upon number of credits. On-campus housing for 300 married students, 4000 men, 1500 women. Average academic year housing cost: $450–$575 per month for married student housing; $3800 for single students. Off-campus housing cost: $690 per month. Contact Director of Student Housing for both on- and off-campus housing information. Phone: (919)515-2440.

Graduate School

Graduate study since 1993. Enrollment: full-time 3336, part-time 1756. University faculty: full-time 1800. Degrees conferred: M.S., M.A., M.A.C., M.B.A., Master of a Designated Field, Ed.D., Ph.D.

ADMISSION REQUIREMENTS. Official transcripts, GRE/MAT/GMAT required in support of School's application. GRE Subject Test recommended for some programs. Online application available. TOEFL (minimum score 550) required for international applicants. Interview not required. Accepts transfer applicants. Graduates of unaccredited institutions not considered. Apply to Graduate Admissions Office by June 15 (Fall), November 15 (Spring). Some programs have earlier deadlines. Application fee $65, $75 international applicants. Phone: (919) 737-2871.

ADMISSION STANDARDS. Selective. Usual minimum average: 3.0 (A = 4).

FINANCIAL AID. Annual awards from institutional funds: scholarships, fellowships, research assistantships, teaching assistantships, traineeships, Federal W/S, loans. Approved for VA benefits. Apply by March 1 to appropriate department chair for fellowships, assistantships; to Financial Aid Office for all other programs.

Phone: (919)737-2421. Use FAFSA (School code: 002972) and University's FAF. About 50% of students receive aid other than loans from School and outside sources.

DEGREE REQUIREMENTS. For master's: 33–48 credits minimum, at least one academic year in residence; thesis/nonthesis option; final oral/written exam. For professional degrees: 30–36 credits, at least one academic year in residence; project paper required by some departments; final oral exam. For Ph.D.: 6 semesters beyond the bachelor's, at least two semesters in full-time residence; reading knowledge of at least one foreign language required by some departments; dissertation; oral/written qualifying exam; final oral exam. For Ed.D.: essentially the same as Ph.D., except no language requirement.

FIELDS OF STUDY.
Accounting.
Adult and Community College Education.
Aerospace Engineering.
Agency Counseling.
Agricultural and Resource Economics.
Agricultural Education.
Analytics.
Animal Science.
Anthropology.
Applied Mathematics.
Architecture.
Art and Design.
Biochemistry.
Bioinformatics.
Biological and Agricultural Engineering.
Botany.
Business Administration.
Chemical Engineering.
Chemistry.
Civil Engineering.
Communication.
Comparative Biomedical Sciences.
Computer Engineering.
Computer Networking.
Computer Science.
Counselor Education.
Creative Writing.
Crop Science.
Curriculum and Instruction. Includes elementary, English, reading, social studies.
Design.
Economics.
Educational Administration and Supervision.
Educational Research and Policy Analysis.
Electrical Engineering.
English.
Entomology.
Extension Education.
Fiber and Polymer Science.
Financial Mathematics.
Fisheries and Wildlife Sciences.
Food Science.
Forestry.
French Language and Literature.
Functional Genomics.
Genetics.
Graphic Design.
Higher Education Administration.
History.
Horticultural Science.
Human Development and Family Studies.
Immunology.
Industrial Design.
Industrial Engineering.
Instructional Technology—Computers.

Integrated Manufacturing Systems Engineering.
International Affairs.
Landscape Architecture.
Liberal Studies.
Marine, Earth, and Atmospheric Sciences.
Materials Science and Engineering.
Mathematics.
Mathematics Education.
Mechanical Engineering.
Microbial Biotechnology.
Microbiology.
Middle School Education.
Natural Resources.
Nuclear Engineering.
Nutrition.
Operations Research.
Parks, Recreation, and Tourism Management.
Physics.
Physiology.
Plant Biology.
Plant Pathology.
Poultry Science.
Psychology.
Public Administration.
Public History.
School Administration.
Science Education.
Social Work.
Sociology.
Soil Science.
Spanish Language and Literature.
Special Education. Includes behavior disorders, learning disabilities, mental retardation.
Specialized Veterinary Medicine.
Statistics.
Technical Communication.
Technical Education.
Textile and Apparel Technology Management.
Textile Chemistry.
Textile Technology Management.
Toxicology.
Training Development.
Veterinary Public Health.
Wood and Paper Science.
Zoology.

College of Veterinary Medicine (P.O. Box 8401)
Web site: www.cvm.unsu.edu

Established 1981. Semester system. Special facilities: Center for Comparative Medicine and Translational Research, Center for Chemical Toxicology Research and Pharmacokinetics.

Annual tuition: residents $10,580, nonresidents $33,343. On-campus housing available. Total average expenses for both on- and off-campus housing: $10,750. Total average cost for other expenses: $6400.

Enrollment: first-year class 80, total 340 (men 22%, women 78%, minorities 6%, state residents 78%), postgraduate 100. Faculty: full-time 140, part-time 2. Degrees conferred: D.V.M., M.V.P.H., M.S., Ph.D., D.V.M.-M.B.A., D.V.M.-M.S. The M.B.A., M.S., and Ph.D. are offered through the Graduate School.

ADMISSION REQUIREMENTS. VMCAS report, transcripts, GRE, recommendations, personal essay, animal/veterinary experience required in support of application. Supplemental application required. Preference given to state residents. Graduates of unaccredited colleges not considered. Considers transfer applicants on a space-available basis. Apply to the College after July 31. Application packets must be completed and returned by October 1. Application fee $45. Phone: (919)513-6448; fax: (919) 513-6197.

ADMISSION STANDARDS. Selective. Accepts about 25–30% of all applicants. Number of applications 493 (293 out-of-state); number interviewed n/a (n/a out-of-state); number of acceptances n/a (n/a out-of-state); number enrolled 80 (18 out-of-state). Usual minimum UGPA: 3.0 (residents), 3.2 (nonresidents) (A = 4). GRE mean score (V + Q) 1199; mean UGPA 3.66.

FINANCIAL AID. Scholarships, fellowships, assistantships, Federal W/S, loans available. Apply to the Financial Aid Office after acceptance. No specified closing date. Use FAFSA.

DEGREE REQUIREMENTS. For D.V.M., satisfactory completion of four-year program. For M.B.A., M.S., Ph.D., see Graduate School listing above.

FIELDS OF GRADUATE STUDY.
Comparative Biomedical Sciences.
Immunology.
Physiology.
Specialized Veterinary Medicine.
Veterinary Public Health.

THE UNIVERSITY OF NORTH CAROLINA AT CHAPEL HILL
Chapel Hill, North Carolina 27599
Web site: www.unc.edu

Chartered 1789; first state university in U.S. Located 28 miles NW of Raleigh. CGS and AAU member. Coed. State control. Semester system. Special facilities: Biological Sciences Research Center, Cancer Research Center, Center for Urban and Regional Studies, Center for Alcohol, Institute for Research in Social Science, Institute for Environmental Studies, Child Development Institute, Institute of Statistics, Institute of Marine Science, Institute of Government, Institute of Latin American Studies, Research Laboratories of Anthropology, Member of the Research Triangle Institute of North Carolina. The University's NIH ranking is 16th among all U.S. institutions with 782 awards/grants valued at $296,566,365. According to The Center at University of Florida, the University is ranked 20th in receipt of Federal Research funds with $280,678,000 and it ranks 27th for total University research expenditures with $390,542,000. The University's endowment assets rank it 32nd, with a value of $1,317,211,000. In 2004, the University awarded 439 doctorates, which ranked it 21st among all U.S. institutions eligible to award that degree. Thirty-six of the University's faculty members have been elected to National Honor Academies and this ranks it 27th among all U.S. institutions. The Library: approximately 4,900,000 volumes, 44,000 subscriptions. Total University enrollment: 25,000.

Annual tuition: full-time, resident $5680, nonresident $19,678. On-campus housing for 306 married students, 325 men, 325 women. Average academic year housing cost: $750–$850 per month (housing only) for married students, $1980–$2650 per semester for single students. Contact the Director of Housing for both on- and off-campus housing information. Phone: (919)966-5661. Day-care facilities available.

Graduate School
Web site: www.gradschool.unc.edu

Graduate study since 1853. Enrollment: full- and part-time 8000. Graduate faculty: 1200. Degrees conferred: M.A., M.B.A., M.M., M.Ed., M.P.H., M.R.P., M.S., M.S.L.S., M.S.S.E., M.S.P.H., M.S.W., M.P.A., M.F.A., M.A.T., Ed.D., D.P.H., Ph.D.

ADMISSION REQUIREMENTS. Two transcripts, three letters of reference, GRE/Subject Tests/GMAT, statement of purpose re-

quired in support of School's application. Interview required by some departments. TOEFL required for international applicants. Accepts transfer applicants. Graduates of unaccredited institutions not considered. Apply to Office of the Dean by January 1 (Fall), October 15 (Spring). Some programs have earlier deadlines. Application fee $73. Phone: (919)962-6309, -6307, -6322.

ADMISSION STANDARDS. Selective to competitive. Usual minimum average: 3.0 (A = 4).

FINANCIAL AID. Annual awards from institutional funds: scholarships, fellowships, traineeships, teaching/research assistantships, tuition waivers, Federal W/S, loans. Approved for VA benefits. Apply by January 31 to the Graduate School. Phone: (919)962-8396; fax: (919)962-2716. Use FAFSA. About 57% of students receive aid other than loans from University and outside sources. Aid sometimes available for part-time students.

DEGREE REQUIREMENTS. For M.A., M.S.: 30 semester hours minimum, at least two semesters in residence; reading knowledge of one foreign language or approved options in some departments; thesis or acceptable option; written/oral comprehensive exam. For M.B.A.: two years minimum. For M.Ed.: 30 semester hours minimum; written comprehensive exam. For M.A.T., M.P.H., M.S.P.H., M.S.S.E.: 30 semester hours minimum, at least two semesters in residence; final written/oral exam. For M.F.A.: 40 semester hours minimum, at least two semesters in residence; oral exam. For M.S.L.S.: 48 semester hours minimum, at least two semesters in residence; final written exam. For M.P.A.: 45 semester hours minimum, at least two semesters in residence; oral exam. For M.S.W.: 53 semester hours minimum, at least two semesters in residence; final written/oral exam. For Ph.D.: four semesters minimum in residence, at least two semesters in continuous attendance; reading knowledge of two foreign languages or approved options in some departments; doctoral oral exam; written exam; dissertation; final oral exam. For D.P.H., Ed.D.: requirements essentially the same as for the Ph.D., except no language requirement.

FIELDS OF STUDY.
Anthropology.
Art. Includes studio art, art history; Ph.D. in art history only.
Audiology. Au.D.
Biochemistry and Biophysics.
Bioinformatics and Computational Biology.
Biology.
Biomedical Engineering.
Biostatistics.
Business Administration. GMAT for admission to M.B.A.
Cell and Development Biology.
Cell and Molecular Physiology.
Chemistry.
City and Regional Planning. Two years for M.R.P.
Classics.
Communication Studies.
Comparative Literature. Latin for Ph.D.
Computer Science.
Dramatic Art. M.F.A.
Ecology.
Economics.
Education. M.A.T., M.A. in college teaching; internship, comprehensive written exam for M.A.; includes administration and supervision, adult education, curriculum and instruction, educational media, elementary, higher education, educational psychology, educational leadership, counseling, school psychology, reading and language arts, physical education, social foundations of education, special education.
English. Latin for Ph.D.
Environmental Sciences and Engineering.
Epidemiology.
Folklore. M.A. only.

Genetics and Molecular Biology. Interdepartmental.
Geography.
Geological Sciences.
German Languages. French for M.A., Ph.D.
Health Behavior and Health Education.
Health Policy and Administration.
History.
Human Movement Science.
Information and Library Science. Thirty-six hours for M.S.L.S., Ph.D.
Journalism and Mass Communication. M.A. only; interdepartmental program, mass communications research for Ph.D.
Linguistics.
Marine Sciences.
Materials Sciences.
Maternal and Child Health.
Mathematics. Written qualifying exam for M.S.; apply by February 11 (Fall).
Microbiology and Immunology.
Music. Original composition for M.S.; other requirements as for M.A.
Neurobiology. Ph.D. only.
Nursing.
Nutrition.
Occupational Sciences. M.S. only.
Oral Biology.
Pathology.
Pharmaceutical Sciences.
Pharmacology.
Philosophy.
Physics and Astronomy.
Political Science. Includes public administration; M.P.A. only; 40 hours, internship, comprehensive written exam, final oral exam.
Psychology. GRE, MAT for admission.
Public Administration.
Public Health. Includes environmental sciences and engineering, biostatistics, epidemiology, maternal and child health, health behavior and health education, public health nursing, nutrition, health policy and administration.
Public Health Leadership.
Public Policy Analysis. Ph.D. only.
Radio, Television, and Motion Pictures. M.A.
Recreation and Leisure Studies.
Rehabilitation Counseling and Psychology. M.S. only.
Religious Studies.
Romance Languages. Includes Spanish; Latin, German for Ph.D.
Russian/East European Studies.
Slavic Languages and Literature.
Social Work. GRE, MAT for admission; four semesters, one Summer term in residence for M.S.W.; M.S.W., Ph.D.
Sociology.
Speech Communications. M.A. only.
Speech and Hearing Science. M.S. only.
Statistics and Operations Research.
Toxicology.

School of Dentistry (27540-7450)
Web site: www.dent.unc.edul

Founded 1950. Semester system. Special facilities: Center for Neurosensory Disorders, Center for Oral and Systemic Diseases, Comprehensive, General Clinical Research Center, UNC Craniofacial Center.

Annual tuition: resident $12,635, nonresident $28,117. On-campus housing available. Average academic year housing cost: $12,400. Total average cost for all other first-year expenses: $7,500.

Enrollment: first-year class 81, total 330 (men 50%, women 50%, minorities 32%, residents 84%). Faculty: full-time 80, part-time 35. Degrees conferred: D.D.S., M.S., Ph.D., D.D.S.-M.S., D.D.S.-M.P.H., D.D.S.-Ph.D., Certificates.

ADMISSION REQUIREMENTS. For D.D.S.: AADSAS report, official transcripts, DAT (April test in Junior year preferred) required in support of School's application. UNC Supplementary Application also required. Applicants must have completed at least three years of college study, prefer four years of study. TOEFL required for international applicants. Preference given to state residents. Interview by invitation only. Accepts transfer students on a space available basis. Apply to Office of Admission, School of Dentistry after June 1, before November 1. Application fee $65. Phone: (919)966-4451. For graduate study: official transcripts, GRE required in support of School's application. Graduates of unaccredited colleges not considered.

ADMISSION STANDARDS. Competitive. Accepts about 10% of all applicants. Usual minimum UGPA: 3.0 (A = 4). Mean DAT: academic 19.7, PAT 18.1; mean UGPA 3.53.

FINANCIAL AID. Board of Governors Scholarships (for minority and disadvantaged students), Dental Scholars Program, merit scholarships, North Carolina School of Dentistry Minority Grants, institutional loans, North Carolina Loan Programs, DEAL, HEAL, alternative loan programs; Federal Perkins Loans, Stafford Subsidized and Unsubsidized Loans, Military Service Commitment Scholarships programs are available. All Financial Aid is based on documented need. Fellowships may be available for Joint Degree candidates. Institutional Financial Aid applications and information are available after January 1. Apply for Financial Aid by March 1 (priority deadline). Contact the University's Office of Scholarships and Student Aid for current information. Phone: (919)962-8936. Use FAFSA (School code: 002974), also submit Financial Aid Transcript, Federal Income Tax forms, and Use of Federal Funds Certification. Approximately 72% of students receive some form of financial assistance. Graduate study: fellowships, assistantships, loans. Apply after acceptance to Office of Admissions, School of Dentistry. About 76% of graduate students receive aid from School and outside sources.

DEGREE REQUIREMENTS. For D.D.S.: satisfactory completion of four-year program. For M.S.: 45–60 credits; thesis; final oral exam. Refer to other Graduate School listings above for joint degree requirements.

FIELDS OF POSTGRADUATE STUDY.
Advanced Education in General Dentistry. Certificate.
Endodontics. M.S.
General Practice Residency. Certificate.
Operative Dentistry. M.S.
Oral and Maxillofacial Pathology. M.S.
Oral and Maxillofacial Radiology. M.S.
Oral and Maxillofacial Surgery. Certificate.
Oral Biology. Ph.D.
Oral Epidemiology. Ph.D.
Orthodontics. M.S.
Pediatric Dentistry. M.S.
Periodontology. M.S.
Prosthodontics. M.S.

School of Law (CB No. 3380)
Web site: www.law.unc.edu

Opened 1845. ABA approved since 1923. AALS member since 1920. Public control. Semester system. Special facilities: Center for Banking and Finance, Center for Civil Rights. Special programs: Summer programs in Sydney, Australia; Universität Augsburg Summer Law Program; Germany; Nice Summer Law Program, France-Hofstra University; semester long exchange programs with Université Jean Moulin LYON 3, France; Radboud Universiteit Nijmegen, The Netherlands; Universidad Iberoamericana, Mexico; University of Manchester, England; University of Glasgow, Scotland. Law library: 519,776 volumes, 6725 subscriptions; has LEXIS, NEXIS, WESTLAW; has more than 550 network connections.

Annual tuition: resident $12,947, nonresident $25,365. Total average annual additional expenses: $16,848.

Enrollment: first-year class 324; total 712 (men 52%, women 48%, minorities, 21%). Faculty: full-time 38, part-time 40. Student-to-faculty ratio is 16.9 to 1. Degrees conferred: J.D., J.D.-M.B.A., J.D.-M.P.A., J.D.-M.P.H., J.D.-M.P.P. (with Duke University), J.D.-M.R.P., J.D.-M.S.W.

ADMISSION REQUIREMENTS. LSDAS Law School report, bachelor's degree, transcripts, LSAT (no later than December), personal statement, résumé, two letters of recommendation, North Carolina Residency form required in support of application. TOEFL required for international applicants whose native language is not English. Accepts transfer applicants. Graduates of unaccredited institutions not considered. Preference given to state residents. Apply to Admissions Office after September 1, before February 1. Application fee $70. Phone: (919)962-5109.

ADMISSION STANDARDS. Selective. Accepts approximately 15% of all students. Number of applicants 3648; number of acceptance 557; number enrolled 231; LSAT (75% of students have a score at or above 158); GPA (75% of student have a GPA at or above 3.47). *U.S. News & World Report* ranking is 36th among all U.S. law schools.

FINANCIAL AID. Chancellor's scholarships, merit scholarships, minority presence scholarships, Grants-in-Aid, institutional loans; Federal loans and Federal W/S offered through University's Financial Aid Office. Assistantships may be available for upper-divisional Joint Degree candidates. All accepted students are automatically considered for both merit- and need-based scholarships (selection criteria places heavy reliance on LSAT and Undergraduate GPA). For all other programs apply after January 1, before March 1 to University's Office of Scholarship and Student Aid. Phone: (919)962-8396. Use FAFSA (School code: 002974). Also submit Financial Aid Transcript, Federal Income Tax forms. Approximately 20% of first-year class received scholarships/Grants-in-Aid. Approximately 78% of students receive some form of financial assistance.

DEGREE REQUIREMENTS. For J. D.: satisfactory completion of three-year program; 86 credit hour program. For master's degrees, see Graduate School listing above.

School of Medicine (27599-7000)

Web site: www.med.unc.edu

Established 1879. Library: 263,000 volumes, 4000 subscriptions. NIH ranking is 16 among U.S. institutions with 782 awards/grants worth $296,566,365.

Annual tuition: resident $11,373, nonresident $35,039. On-campus housing available. Total average figure for all other expenses: $21,000.

Enrollment: first-year class 160 (EDP 7), total 656 (men 51%, women 49%, minorities 29%, state residents 86%). Faculty: full-time 1238, part-time 127. Degrees conferred: M.D., M.D.-M.P.H., M.D.-Ph.D.

ADMISSION REQUIREMENTS. AMCAS report, transcripts, two letters of recommendation, MCAT, supplementary application, interview required in support of application. Do not send recommendations until or unless an interview is requested. Applicants must have completed at least three years of college study. Preference given to state residents. Has EDP; apply between June 1 and August 1. Accepts transfer applicants on a space available basis. Graduates of unaccredited colleges not considered. Apply to Office of the Dean after June 1, before November 15. Application fee $68. Phone: (919)962-8331; fax: (919)966-9930.

ADMISSION STANDARDS. Very competitive. Accepts about 6% of all applicants. Number of applications 3154 (2322 out-of-state); number interviewed 565 (85 out-of-state); number of acceptances 224 (38 out-of-state); number enrolled 160 (18 out-of-state). Mean Composite MCAT 10.7; mean UGPA 3.71. *U.S. News & World Report* ranking is in the top 20 of all U.S. medical schools.

FINANCIAL AID. Scholarships, loans. Apply after acceptance to Chair, Student Aid Committee. Priority deadline March 1. Phone: (919)962-6118. Use FAFSA (School code: 002974). About 84% of students receive aid other than loans from School.

DEGREE REQUIREMENTS. For M.D.: satisfactory completion of four-year program. Passing USMLE Step 1 is required to enter third year, and passing USMLE Step 2 is required for graduation. Refer to other Graduate School listings above for joint degree requirements.

FIELDS OF GRADUATE STUDY.
Anatomy.
Biochemistry.
Biomedical Engineering.
Biophysics.
Biostatistics.
Cell and Molecular Physiology.
Cell Biology.
Environmental Sciences.
Epidemiology.
Genetics and Molecular Biology.
Health Policy and Administration.
Health Care and Prevention.
Immunology.
Maternal and Child Health.
Molecular Biology.
Neurobiology.
Pathology.
Pharmacology.
Physiology.
Public Health.
Toxicology.

THE UNIVERSITY OF NORTH CAROLINA AT CHARLOTTE

Charlotte, North Carolina 28223
Web site: www.uncc.edu

Established 1965. CGS member. Coed. State control. Semester system. Special facilities: Cameron Applied Research Center, Small Business and Technology Development Center, Urban Institute. Library: 916,218 volumes, 5000 subscriptions. Total University enrollment: 20,700.

Annual tuition: full-time, resident $2504, nonresident $12,711; per credit, graduated scale for resident, nonresident students. Limited on-campus housing for graduate men and women, none for married students. Average academic year housing cost: $6573 (including board). Contact the Director of Residence Life for both on- and off-campus housing information. Phone: (704) 687-2585.

Graduate School

Enrollment: full-time 1077, part-time 1996. University faculty: full-time 511, part-time 148. Degrees conferred: M.A., M.A.L.S., M.B.A., M.Ed., M.S.A., M.S.E., M.S.C.E., M.S.E.E., M.S.M.E., M.L.S., M.S.N., M.P.A., C.A.S., Ph.D.

ADMISSION REQUIREMENTS. Two transcripts, GRE, three letters of recommendation, statement of purpose required in support of School's application. MAT/GMAT required by some departments. Interview/auditions/portfolio required by some departments. Online application available. TOEFL required for international applicants. Accepts transfer applicants. Apply to the Assistant Dean for Graduate Admissions by May 1 (Fall), October 1 (Spring); many programs have early deadlines. Application fee $55. Phone: (704)687-3372; fax: (704) 687-3279.

ADMISSION STANDARDS. Competitive. Usual minimum average: 2.75 (A = 4).

FINANCIAL AID. Annual awards from institutional funds: fellowships, teaching assistantships, research assistantships, internships, traineeships, Federal W/S, loans. Approved for VA benefits. Apply by April 1 to appropriate department chair for fellowships, assistantships; to Office of Financial Aid for all other programs. Use FAFSA. About 40% of students receive aid from School and outside sources. Aid available for part-time students.

DEGREE REQUIREMENTS. For master's: 30–32 semester hours minimum; thesis; written/oral candidacy exam; reading knowledge of one foreign language for many departments. For M.Arch.: 42 credit, full-time program; thesis. For M.Ed.: 32 semester hours minimum; final written exam. For M.L.S.: 36 semester hours minimum; written/oral exam. For M.B.A., M.P.A.: 42 semester hours minimum; written exam. For M.S.N.: 49–55 semester hours minimum; internship, practicum; thesis; written/oral exam. For C.A.S.: 30 semester hours beyond the master's. For Ph.D.: six full semesters minimum beyond the bachelor's, at least two consecutive semesters or equivalent in full-time residence; reading knowledge of one or more foreign languages or equivalent in some departments; preliminary exam; dissertation; final oral exam.

FIELDS OF STUDY.

COLLEGE OF ARCHITECTURE:
Architecture.

COLLEGE OF ARTS AND SCIENCES:
Biology.
Chemistry.
Communication Studies. Includes international public relations.
Criminal Justice.
Earth Science. Includes climatology and hydrology, environmental systems analysis, solid earth sciences.
English. Includes applied linguistics, children's literature, English for specific purposes, literature, rhetoric and writing, technical/professional writing.
English Education.
Ethics and Applied Philosophy.
Geography. Includes community planning, location analysis, international studies.
Geography and Urban Regional Analysis.
Gerontology.
Health Psychology. Includes community health psychology, general health psychology.
History.
Latin American Studies.
Liberal Studies.
Mathematics. Includes applied, general, statistics.
Mathematics Education.
Nanoscale Science. Interdisciplinary Ph.D.
Optical Science and Engineering. Interdisciplinary Ph.D.
Organizational Science. Interdisciplinary Ph.D.
Physics. Includes applied.
Psychology. Includes clinical/community, industrial/organizational.

Public Administration. Includes arts administration, emergency management, non-profit management, urban management and policy.
Public Policy.
Religious studies.
Sociology.
Spanish. Includes language, literature and culture, translating and translation studies.

COLLEGE OF BUSINESS:
Accountancy
Business Administration. Includes economics, finance, financial institutions/commercial banking, global business and strategy in Monterrey, Mexico, information and technology, international business, management, marketing, real estate finance and development, supply chain management.
Economics.
Mathematical Finance.
Sports Marketing and Management.

COLLEGE OF EDUCATION:
Art Education.
Child and Family Studies.
Counseling.
Curriculum and Instruction. Includes urban literacy, urban math.
Curriculum and Supervision.
Dance Education.
Educational Leadership. Includes community, school.
Elementary Education.
Foreign Language Education.
Instructional Systems Technology.
Middle Grades. Includes English/language arts, mathematics, science, social studies.
Music Education.
Reading Education.
School Administration.
Secondary Education. Includes biology, chemistry, comprehensive science, earth science, English, history/social studies, mathematics, physics, social studies.
Special Education. Includes academically gifted, adapted.
Teaching English as a Second Language.
Theatre Education.

COLLEGE OF ENGINEERING:
Civil Engineering.
Electrical and Computer Engineering. Includes communication and signal, computer engineering, control systems, analog, mixed-signal and RF electronic design, microelectronics and optoelectronics, power system.
Engineering Management.
Infrastructure and Environmental Systems. Interdisciplinary. Includes science, management. Ph.D. only.
Mechanical Engineering. Includes precision engineering and manufacturing, Computational modeling, bioengineering.

COLLEGE OF HEALTH AND HUMAN SERVICES:
Clinical Exercise Physiology.
Health Administration.
Health Services Research. Interdisciplinary Ph.D.
Nursing. Includes nurse anesthesia, adult nurse practitioner, family nurse practitioner, systems/population (concentrations in community public health nursing, nurse educator, nurse administration, nursing and health administration).
Public Health.
Social Work.

COLLEGE OF COMPUTING AND INFORMATICS:
Computer Science.
Information Technology. Includes bioinformatics, business infor-

mation systems and operations management, computer science, software and information systems.
Professional Science.

THE UNIVERSITY OF NORTH CAROLINA AT GREENSBORO

Greensboro, North Carolina 27412-5001
Web site: www.uncg.edu

Established 1891. CGS member. Coed. State control. Semester system. Special facilities: Three College Observatory, Center for Applied Research, Center for Critical Inquiry into the Liberal Arts, Center for Educational Research and Evaluation, Center for Social Research, Center for Social Welfare, Center for Applied Research, Weatherspoon Art Gallery. Library: 914,000 volumes, 5300 subscriptions. Total University enrollment: 16,000.

Annual tuition: full-time, resident $2426, nonresident $10,714; per credit, graduated scale for resident, nonresident students. Limited on-campus housing for graduate men and women, none for married students. Average academic year housing cost: $6573 (including board, medical services fee). Contact the Director of Residence Life for both on- and off-campus housing information. Phone: (336)334-5636.

Graduate School

First graduate degree conferred in 1922. Enrollment: full-time 1257, part-time 2512. University faculty: full-time 487, part-time 38. Degrees conferred: M.A., M.B.A., M.Ed., M.F.A., M.M., M.S., M.A.L.S., M.I.L.S., M.S.A., M.S.N., M.P.A., Ed.S., Ph.D., Ed.D., D.M.A.

ADMISSION REQUIREMENTS. Transcripts, GRE required in support of School's application. MAT/NTE/GMAT required by some departments. Interview/auditions/portfolio required by some departments. TOEFL required for international applicants. Accepts transfer applicants. Apply to Graduate School (P.O. Box 26176) at least sixty days prior to date of desired registration; many programs have early deadlines. Application fee $45. Phone: (336)334-4884; (336)334-4424.

ADMISSION STANDARDS. Competitive. Usual minimum average: 2.75 (A = 4).

FINANCIAL AID. Annual awards from institutional funds: fellowships, academic scholarships, Minority Presence Grants, teaching assistantships, research assistantships, administrative assistantships, internships, Federal W/S, loans. Approved for VA benefits. Apply by March 1 to appropriate department chair for assistantships; to Office of Financial Aid for all other programs. Phone: (336)334-5702; fax: (336)334-3010. Use FAFSA. About 90% of students receive aid other than loans from School and outside sources. Aid not available to part-time students.

DEGREE REQUIREMENTS. For M.A., M.S.: 30 semester hours minimum; thesis; written/oral exam; reading knowledge of one foreign language for many departments. For M.Ed.: 32 semester hours minimum; final written exam. For M.F.A.: 60 semester hours minimum (except for creative writing, 36 semester hours); final written/oral exam; thesis/final project. For M.M.: 30 semester hours minimum; recital. For M.A.L.S., M.I.L.S.: 36 semester hours minimum; written/oral exam. For M.P.A.: 36 semester hours minimum; written exam. For M.S.N.: 36 semester hours minimum; thesis; written/oral exam. For Ed.S.: 30 semester hours beyond the master's. For Ph.D., Ed.D.: six full semesters minimum beyond the bachelor's, at least two consecutive semesters or equivalent in full-time residence; reading knowledge of one or

more foreign languages or equivalent in some departments; preliminary exam; dissertation; final oral exam. For D.M.A.: requirements essentially the same as for Ph.D. except a final project/recital/performance required.

FIELDS OF STUDY.
Accounting.
Applied Economics.
Art. Includes fine arts, interior design, studio, art education.
Biochemistry.
Biology.
Business Administration.
Business Education.
Chemistry.
Community Counseling.
Communication Studies.
Computer Science.
Conflict Resolution.
Counseling and Development.
Counselor Education.
Creative Writing.
Curriculum and Teaching.
Dance.
Drama. Includes film/video, acting, directing, design, theater for youth.
Economics.
Educational Leadership.
Educational Research, Measurement, and Evaluation.
Educational Supervision.
Elementary Education.
English.
Exercise and Sport Science.
French.
Genetic Counseling.
Geography.
Gereontology.
Health Management.
Higher Education.
History.
Housing and Interior Design.
Human Development and Family Studies.
Information Systems and Operations Management.
Interior Architecture.
Latin.
Liberal Studies.
Library and Information Studies.
Mathematics.
Music. Includes accompanying, composition, conducting, education, performance, theory.
Nursing. Includes nurse anesthesia, administration, gerontological.
Nutrition and Food Service Systems.
Parks and Recreation Management. Includes therapeutic recreation.
Physics.
Political Science.
Psychology. Includes clinical.
Public Affairs.
Public Health.
Public History.
Romance Languages.
School Administration.
School Counseling.
Secondary Education. Includes the usual majors.
Social Work.
Sociology.
Spanish.
Special Education.
Speech Pathology and Audiology.
Studio Art.
Textile Products Design and Marketing.
Theatre Education.
Women's and Gender Studies.

THE UNIVERSITY OF NORTH CAROLINA AT WILMINGTON
Wilmington, North Carolina 28403-5955
Web site: www.uncw.edu

Established 1975. CGS member. Coed. State control. Semester system. Special facility: Center for Marine Science Research. Library: 852,000 volumes, 4300 subscriptions. Total University enrollment: 11,650.

Annual tuition: full-time, resident $4698, nonresident $14,564; M.B.A. full-time resident $5202, nonresident $15,062; per credit, graduated scale for resident, nonresident students. Limited on-campus housing for graduate men and women, none for married students. Average academic year housing cost: $5500 (including board). Contact the Housing Office for both on- and off-campus housing information. Phone: (910)962-3241.

Graduate School

Enrollment: full-time 374, part-time 578. University faculty: full-time 295, part-time 12. Degrees conferred: M.A., M.A.T., M.B.A., M.Ed., M.F.A.

ADMISSION REQUIREMENTS. Transcripts, GRE, three letters of recommendation, a statement of purpose required in support of School's application. MAT/NTE/GMAT required by some departments. Interview required by some departments. TOEFL required for international applicants. Accepts transfer applicants. Apply to the Assistant Dean for Graduate Admissions at least 60 days prior to date of desired registration; some programs have early deadlines. Rolling admissions process. Application fee $45. Phone: (910)962-7303.

ADMISSION STANDARDS. Competitive. Usual minimum average: 2.75 (A = 4).

FINANCIAL AID. Annual awards from institutional funds: scholarships, fellowships, teaching assistantships, research assistantships, administrative assistantships, internships, Federal W/S, loans. Approved for VA benefits. Apply by March 15 to appropriate department chair for fellowships, assistantships; to Office of Financial Aid for all other programs. Phone: (910)962-3177. Use FAFSA. About 20% of students receive aid from School and outside sources. Aid available for part-time students.

DEGREE REQUIREMENTS. For M.A: 30 semester hours minimum; thesis; written/oral exam; reading knowledge of one foreign language for some departments. For M.Ed.: 32 semester hours minimum; final written exam. For M.B.A.: 36 semester hours minimum; written exam. For M.F.A.: 48 credit program; thesis; M.F.A. exam.

FIELDS OF STUDY.

COLLEGE OF ARTS AND SCIENCES:
Biology.
Chemistry.
Computer Science and Information Systems.
Creative Writing.
English.
Geology.
History.
Liberal Studies.
Marine Biology.
Marine Science.
Mathematics.
Psychology.
Public Administration.
Social Work.

CAMERON SCHOOL OF BUSINESS:
Accountancy.
Business Administration.

WATSON SCHOOL OF EDUCATION:
Curriculum Instruction/Supervision.
Elementary Education.
Instructional Technology.
Language and Literacy.
Middle Grades Education.
Reading Education.
School Administration.
Secondary Education.
Special Education.
Teaching.

SCHOOL OF NURSING:
Nursing.

NORTH DAKOTA STATE UNIVERSITY
Fargo, North Dakota 58105-5790
Web site: www.ndsu.edu

Founded 1890. CGS member. Coed. State control. Semester system. Special facilities Agricultural Experiment Station, the Center for Main Group Chemistry, the Center for Cooperatives, Computer Systems Institute, Natural Resources and Economic Development Institute, North Dakota Census Data Center, North Dakota Institute for Regional Studies, Center for Agriculture Policy and Trade Studies, Upper Great Plains Transportation Institute, Radiation Research Laboratory, Water Resources Institute. Library: 518,921 volumes, 5095 subscriptions. Total University enrollment: 12,100.

Tuition: per credit resident $194, $242 for Minnesota residents, $292 for residents of Saskatchewan, Manitoba, South Dakota, and Montana, $520 for all other nonresidents. On-campus housing for 305 married students, limited for single students. Average academic year housing cost: for single students $5130 with seven day meals, $5520–$8075 for married students. Contact the Director of Housing for both on- and off-campus housing information. Phone: (701)231-7557. Day-care facilities available.

Graduate School

Graduate study since 1895. Enrollment: full- and part-time 1477. Faculty: full-time 400, part-time 26. Degrees conferred: M.A., M.S., M.Ed., M.B.A., Ed.S., Ph.D.

ADMISSION REQUIREMENTS. Official transcript, three letters of reference, personal statement required in support of School's application. GRE or MAT or GMAT required by some departments. TOEFL required for foreign applicants. Interview not required. Accepts transfer applicants. Graduates of unaccredited institutions not considered. Apply to Graduate School Admission Office at least two months prior to registration; some departments have earlier deadlines. Application fee $45, $60 for international applicants. Phone: (701)231-8909; fax: (701)231-6524.

ADMISSION STANDARDS. Very selective for most departments. Usual minimum average: 3.0 (A = 4).

FINANCIAL AID. Annual awards from institutional funds: scholarships, teaching assistantships, research assistantships, tuition waivers, Federal W/S, loans. Approved for VA benefits. Apply by March 15 to Graduate Dean for scholarships, to appropriate department chair for assistantships; to Financial Aid Office for all other programs. Phone: (701)231-7533. Use FAFSA. About 35% of students receive aid other than loans from University and outside sources. Aid available for part-time students.

DEGREE REQUIREMENTS. For all master's: 30 semester hours minimum, at least 20 in residence; thesis/nonthesis option; final oral exam. For M.Ed.: two seminar papers. For M.B.A.: 30 semester hours minimum. For Ed.S.: 30 semester hours beyond the master's, at least 24 in residence. For Ph.D.: normally three years beyond the bachelor's; comprehensive exam; dissertation; final written/oral exam.

FIELDS OF STUDY.
Agribusiness and Applied Economics. M.S. only.
Agricultural and Biosystems Engineering.
Agricultural Education. M.S. only.
Animal and Range Sciences.
Biochemistry and Molecular Biology.
Biology.
Botany.
Business Administration.
Cereal Science.
Chemistry.
Child Development and Family Science.
Civil Engineering.
Computer Science.
Communication.
Conservation and Environmental Sciences.
Counselor Education.
Criminal Justice.
Education.
Educational Administration.
Electrical Engineering.
Emergency Management.
Engineering.
English.
Entomology.
Environmental Engineering.
Family and Consumer Sciences Education.
Food Safety.
Genomics and Bioinformatics.
Health, Nutrition, and Exercise Sciences.
History.
Horticulture.
Human Development.
Industrial Engineering and Management.
International Agribusiness.
Manufacturing Engineering.
Mass Communication.
Mathematics.
Mechanical Engineering.
Microbiology.
Molecular Pathogenesis.
Music.
Musical Arts.
Natural Resources and Management.
Nursing.
Nutrition and Exercise Science.
Pharmaceutical Sciences.
Physics.
Plant Pathology.
Plant Sciences.
Polymers and Coatings Science.
Psychology.
Secondary Education.
Social Science.
Software Engineering.
Soil Science.
Speech Communication.
Statistics.
Transportation and Logistics.
Zoology.

UNIVERSITY OF NORTH DAKOTA
Grand Forks, North Dakota 58201
Web site: www.und.edu

Established 1883. CGS member. Located 300 miles NW of Minneapolis. Coed. State control. Semester system. Special facilities: Center for Aerospace Studies, Ireland Cancer Research Laboratory, Energy and Environmental Research Center, biological field stations. Library: 925,367 volumes, 10,400 subscriptions. Total University enrollment: 12,900.

Tuition: per credit resident $164, nonresident $359. On-campus housing for 892 married students, 3100 single students. Average academic year housing cost: single students $6148 (including board); married students $4500. Contact the Director of Housing for both on- and off-campus housing information. Phone: (701)777-4251. Day-care facilities available.

Graduate School

Graduate study since 1883. Enrollment: full-time 446, part-time 1549. University faculty: full-time 492, part-time 18. Degrees conferred: M.A., M.S., M.Ed., M.B.A., M.P.A., M.F.A., M.Engr., Specialist, Ed.D., D.A., Ph.D.

ADMISSION REQUIREMENTS. Transcripts, GRE/MAT/GMAT/NTE, letters of recommendation required in support of School's application. Interview not required. TOEFL required for international applicants. Accepts transfer applicants. Graduates of unaccredited institutions not considered. Apply to Graduate School by March 1 (Fall), October 15 (Spring); some programs have earlier deadlines. Application fee $35. Phone: (701)777-2945; fax: (701)777-3619.

ADMISSION STANDARDS. Selective for most departments. Usual minimum average: 3.0 (A = 4).

FINANCIAL AID. Annual awards from institutional funds: scholarships, fellowships, teaching assistantships, research assistantships, internships, tuition waivers, Federal W/S, loans. Approved for VA benefits. Apply by March 15 to Dean of Graduate School for fellowships, assistantships; to Financial Aid Office for all other programs. Phone: (701)777-3121. Use FAFSA. Aid available for part-time students.

DEGREE REQUIREMENTS. For master's: 30–32 credits minimum; thesis and nonthesis programs; comprehensive exam; final oral/written exam. For M.F.A.: 60 credit program with at least two semesters in residence; advancement to candiacy; comprehensive evaluation; professional exhibition; final evaluation. For Ed.D.: 96 credits minimum beyond the bachelor's, at least two consecutive semesters in full-time residence; preliminary exam; dissertation for 10 credits; final oral exam. For D.A.: 90 semester hours, two years in residence; comprehensive exam; research project/oral exam. For Ph.D.: 90 credits minimum beyond the bachelor's, at least two consecutive semesters in full-time residence; competence in scholarly tools as specified by department; preliminary exam; advancement to candidacy; dissertation; final oral exam.

FIELDS OF STUDY.
Accountancy.
Anatomy and Cell Biology.
Art.
Atmospheric Sciences.
Aviation.
Biochemistry and Molecular Biology.
Biology.
Business Administration.
Career and Technical Education.
Chemical Engineering.

Chemistry.
Civil Engineering.
Clinical Laboratory Science.
Communication.
Communication and Public Discourse.
Communication Sciences and Disorders.
Computer Science.
Counseling.
Counseling Psychology.
Criminal Justice.
Early Childhood Education.
Earth System Science and Policy.
Educational Leadership.
Education—General Studies.
Electrical Engineering.
Elementary Education.
Engineering.
English.
Environmental Engineering.
Geography.
Geological Engineering.
Geology.
History.
Industrial Technology.
Instructional Design and Technology.
Kinesiology.
Linguistics.
Mathematics.
Mechanical Engineering.
Microbiology and Immunology.
Music.
Music Education.
Nursing.
Occupational Therapy.
Pharmacology, Physiology, and Therapeutics.
Physical Therapy.
Physician Assistant.
Physics.
Psychology.
Public Administration.
Reading Education.
Social Work.
Sociology.
Space Studies.
Special Education.
Speech-Language Pathology.
Teaching and Learning.
Technology Education.
Theatre Arts.
Visual Arts.

School of Law (P.O. Box 9003)

Web site: www.law.und.nodak.edu

Established 1899. ABA approved since 1923. AALS member since 1910. Public control. Semester system. Special facilities: Agricultural Law Center, Center for American Indian Legal Program and Resources. Law library: 317,000 volumes, 2001 subscriptions; has LEXIS, NEXIS; has more than 150 network connections.

Annual tuition: resident $8,386, nonresident $18,038. Total average annual additional expenses: $13,500.

Enrollment: first-year class 90; total 236 (men 54%, women 46%, minorities, 10%). Faculty: full-time 10, part-time 13. Student-to-faculty ratio is 19.0 to 1. Degrees conferred: J.D., J.D.-M.P.A.

ADMISSION REQUIREMENTS. LSDAS Law School report, bachelor's degree, transcripts, LSAT, two letters of recommendation required in support of application. Interview not encouraged. Accepts transfer applicants. Preference given to state residents.

Graduates of unaccredited colleges not considered. Admits beginning students in Fall only. Apply to Office of the Dean after August 15, before May 1. Application fee $35, $45 after April 1. Phone: (701)777-2260; fax: (701)777-2217.

ADMISSION STANDARDS. Selective. Accepts approximately 45% of all students. Number of applicants 430; number of acceptances 194; number enrolled 90; LSAT (75% of students have a score at or above 147); GPA (75% of student have a GPA at or above 3.25). *U.S. News & World Report* ranking is in the fourth tier of all U.S. law schools.

FINANCIAL AID. Scholarships, full and partial tuition waivers, Federal W/S, loans. Apply to Dean of the School for scholarships by April 1; for loans apply to the University's Financial Aid Office. Phone: (701)777-6265. Use FAFSA (School code: 003005). About 42% of students receive aid other than loans from School. No aid available for part-time students.

DEGREE REQUIREMENTS. For J.D.: 90 credits minimum, at least one year in residence. Up to 30 transfer credits of advance standing may be accepted from another accredited school.
Note: An exchange program at the University of Oslo in Norway is available.

School of Medicine and Health Sciences

Web site: www.med.und.nodak.edu

Established 1905. Four year programs since 1973. Special facilities: Basic Science Imaging Center, Center for Biomedical Research, Center for Health Promotion and Translation Research, Center for Rural Health, Center of Excellence in Neurosciences, National Center of Excellence in Women's Health, National Resource Center on Native American Aging, North Dakota AIDS Education and Training Center, Rural Assistance Center, The Mass Spectrometry Center. Library: 100,000 volumes, 1800 subscriptions.

Annual tuition: resident $21,753, nonresident $39,131. On- and off-campus housing available. Total average figure for all other expenses: $11,000.

Enrollment: first-year class 61, total 242 (men 50%, women 50%, minorities 13%, state residents 86%). Faculty: full-time 163, part-time and volunteers 1218. Degrees conferred: M.D., M.D.-M.P.H., M.D.-M.S., M.D.-Ph.D.

ADMISSION REQUIREMENTS. Transcripts, letters of recommendation, personal statement, MCAT, interview required in support of application. Has special program for Native Americans wishing to enter medicine (INMED). Special consideration for residents of Minnesota and WICHE states. Does not have EDP. Apply to Secretary of Admissions of School after July 1, before November 1. Application fee $50. Phone: (701)777-4221; fax: (701)777-4942.

ADMISSION STANDARDS. Selective. Accepts about 32% of all applicants. Number of applications 250 (122 out-of-state); number interviewed 153 (59 out-of-state); number of acceptances 84 (28 out-of-state); number enrolled 61 (17 out-of-state). Mean Composite MCAT 9.2; mean UGPA 3.62.

FINANCIAL AID. Scholarships, merit scholarships, minority scholarships, Grants-in-Aid, institutional loans, HEAL, alternative loan programs, Federal Perkins Loans, Stafford Subsidized and Unsubsidized Loans, Service Commitment Scholarship programs are available. Assistantships/fellowships may be available for Dual Degree candidates. Immediately after acceptance, Financial Aid applications and information are sent to students. All Financial Aid is based on demonstrated need. Contact the Financial Aid Office for current information. Phone: (701)777-2849; fax: (701)777-4942. Use FAFSA (School code: 003005); also submit Financial Aid Transcript, Federal Income Tax forms. Approximately 98% of students receive some form of financial assistance.

DEGREE REQUIREMENTS. For M.D.: successful completion of four-year program. For Ph.D.: see Graduate School listing above.

FIELDS OF GRADUATE STUDY.
Anatomy and Cell Biology. M.S., Ph.D.
Biochemistry and Molecular Biology. M.S., Ph.D.
Clinical Laboratory Science. M.S.
Microbiology and Immunology. M.S., Ph.D.
Occupational Therapy. M.S.O.T.
Pharmacology, Physiology, and Therapeutics. M.S., Ph.D.
Physical Therapy. M.P.T.

UNIVERSITY OF NORTH FLORIDA
Jacksonville, Florida 32224-2645
Web site: www.unf.edu

Authorized by Florida Legislature in 1965 and opened in 1972. Coed. Public control. Semester system. Special facilities: Center for Membrane Physics, Florida Institute of Education, Center for Local Government, Small Business Development Center. Library: more than 746,600 volumes, 3000 subscriptions. Total University enrollment: 15,200.

Tuition: per semester hour, resident $244, nonresident $835. On-campus housing for 100 married students and unlimited housing for single students. Annual academic year housing costs: $3800–$6640. Contact the Director of Residential Life for both on- and off-campus housing information. Phone: (904)620-2636. On-campus day-care facilities available.

Graduate Studies

Enrollment: full-time 591, part-time 1034. University faculty: full-time 288, part-time 20. Degrees conferred: M.A., M.P.A., M.S., M.B.A., M.Ed., M.H.A., M.H.R.M., M.Acc.

ADMISSION REQUIREMENTS. Transcripts, bachelor's degree, GRE/GMAT required in support of application. Online application available. TOEFL (minimum score 550) required for international applicants. Accepts transfer applicants. Graduates of unaccredited institutions not considered. Apply by July 1 (Fall), November 1 (Spring). Application fee $30. Phone: (904)620-1360; fax: (904)620-1362.

ADMISSION STANDARDS. Selective. Usual minimum average: 3.0 (A = 4), a composite score of 1000 or more on GRE (College of Education and Human Services), a score of 500 or more on GMAT (College of Business Administration).

FINANCIAL AID. Annual awards from institutional funds: scholarships, research/teaching assistantships, tuition waivers, Federal W/S, loans. Approved for VA benefits. Apply by April 1 to Financial Aid Office. Phone: (904)620-2604; fax: (904)620-2703. Use FAFSA and University's FAF. Aid available for part-time students.

DEGREE REQUIREMENTS. For M.A.: 30–39 credit program; thesis/nonthesis option. For M.S.: 36 credit program; thesis or comprehensive exam. For M.A. in Mathematical Sciences: 30 semester hours. For M.P.A.: 36 credit hours for those with significant government experience or 39 credit hours for those who do not have background. For M.S. Criminal Justice: 37 credit hours. For M.A. in Counseling: 40 semester hours. For M.B.A.: Part I—a foundation for regular graduate study; Part II—36 semester hours. For M.Acc.: 36 semester hours. For M.H.R.M.: 36 credit

hours. For M.Ed.: 36–39 hours selected from component cores. For M.S. in Allied Health Services: 36 semester hours.

FIELDS OF STUDY.

COLLEGE OF ARTS AND SCIENCES:
Applied Sociology.
Biology.
Counseling Psychology.
Criminal Justice.
English.
General Psychology.
History.
Mathematics and Statistics.
Public Administration.

COGGIN COLLEGE OF BUSINESS ADMINISTRATION:
Accountancy.
Business Administration.
Human Resource Management.

COLLEGE OF COMPUTING SCIENCES AND ENGINEERING:
Computer and Information Sciences.

COLLEGE OF EDUCATION AND HUMAN SERVICES:
Counselor Education. Includes mental health counseling, school guidance.
Deaf Education.
Educational Leadership. Includes instructional leadership, school principal.
Elementary Education. Includes reading (K–6).
Secondary Education. Includes adult learning, English education (6–12), reading education (6–12).
Special Education. Includes disability services, emotionally handicapped, learning disabilities, mentally handicapped, hearing impaired, varying exceptionalities.

COLLEGE OF HEALTH:
Community Health.
Geriatric Management.
Health Administration.
Health Promotion/Health Education.
Nursing.
Nutrition.
Physical Therapy.
Rehabilitation Counseling.

UNIVERSITY OF NORTH TEXAS
Denton, Texas 76203-5449
Web site: www.unt.edu

Founded 1890. Located 35 miles NW of Dallas. CGS member. Coed. State control. Semester system. Special facilities: Institute for Studies in Addiction, Institute for Applied Sciences, Institute of Criminal Justice, Center for Economic Education, Center for Environmental Economic Studies and Research, Center for Inter-American Studies and Research, Center for Network Neuroscience, Center for Organometallic Research and Education, Center for Public Service, Center for Remote Sensing and Land-Use Analysis, University Center for Texas Studies. Library: 2,100,000 volumes, 12,243 subscriptions. Total University enrollment: 32,000.

Tuition: per credit, resident $181, nonresident $451. On-campus housing for 50 married students, unlimited for single students. Average academic year housing costs: $5365 (including board) for single students; $3700 for married students. Contact Director of Housing for both on- and off-campus housing information. Phone: (940)565-2605.

Robert B. Toulouse School of Graduate Studies
(Box 305459)

Graduate study since 1935. Enrollment: full-time 2411, part-time 4328. Graduate faculty: full-time 623, part-time 200. Degrees conferred: M.A., M.S., M.B.A., M.F.A., M.J., M.P.A., M.Ed., M.L.S., M.M., M.M.Ed., Ed.D., D.M.A., Ph.D., D.F.A.

ADMISSION REQUIREMENTS. Official transcripts, GRE/MAT/GMAT (for business) required in support of School's application. TOEFL required for international applicants. Interview not required. Accepts transfer applicants. Graduates of unaccredited institutions not considered. Apply to Dean of Graduate School at least six weeks prior to registration, some departments have earlier deadlines. Application fee: $50, $75 for international students. Phone: (940)565-2383; fax: (940)565-2141.

ADMISSION STANDARDS. Selective. Usual minimum average: 2.80, 3.0 on last 60 hours of undergraduate study (A = 4).

FINANCIAL AID. Annual awards from institutional funds: scholarships, teaching fellowships, research assistantships, Federal W/S, loans. Approved for VA benefits. Apply by March 1 to appropriate department chair for fellowships and assistantships; to Financial Aid Office for all other programs. Phone: (940)565-2016. Use FAFSA. About 25–30% of students receive aid other than loans from University and outside sources. Aid generally not available for part-time students.

DEGREE REQUIREMENTS. For M.A., M.S.: 30–36 credit hours minimum, depending upon program and degree; comprehensive oral/written exam; reading knowledge of one foreign language for some departments; for 30-hour M.A. program, thesis or research problem. For M.B.A.: 36 credit hours minimum; final oral/written exam. For M.Ed., M.L.S., M.P.A.: 36 credit hours minimum; final oral/written exam. For M.M.: 32 credit hours; thesis; reading knowledge of one foreign language; final oral/written exam. For M.F.A.: 60 credit hours minimum; final oral/written exam. For M.M.Ed.: 36 credit hours minimum; final written/oral exam. For D.M.A., Ph.D., D.F.A.: normally 60 credit hours or three years in residence beyond the bachelor's and at least two consecutive semesters in full-time attendance; reading knowledge of one or two foreign languages or completion of tool subject; qualifying exam; dissertation; final written/oral exam. For Ed.D.: 60 credit hours beyond the master's, at least two consecutive semesters in full-time residence; qualifying exam; dissertation; final oral exam.

FIELDS OF STUDY.

COLLEGE OF ARTS AND SCIENCES:
Applied Geography.
Audiology.
Biochemistry.
Biology.
Chemistry.
Clinical Psychology.
Communication Studies.
Counseling Psychology.
Creative Writing.
Economic Research.
Economics.
Engineering Technology.
English.
English as a Second Language.
Environmental Science.
Experimental Psychology.
Foreign Languages and Literature.
French.
Health Psychology and Behavioral Medicine.
History.

Industrial-Organizational Psychology.
Journalism.
Labor and Industrial Relations.
Linguistics.
Mathematics.
Molecular Biology.
Philosophy.
Physics.
Political Science.
Radio, Television, and Film.
Psychology.
Spanish.
Speech and Hearing Sciences.
Technical Writing.

COLLEGE OF BUSINESS ADMINISTRATION:
Accounting.
Business Administration.
Business Computer Information Systems.
Decision Technologies.
Finance.
Health Services Management.
Information Technologies.
Logistics and Supply Chain Management.
Management.
Management Science.
Marketing.
Operations and Supply Chain Management.
Organizational Behavior and Human Resource Management.
Real Estate.
Strategic Management.
Taxation.

COLLEGE OF EDUCATION AND HUMAN SERVICES:
Applied Technology and Development.
Computer Education and Cognitive Systems.
Counseling.
Curriculum and Instruction.
Development and Family Studies.
Early Childhood Education.
Educational Administration.
Educational Computing.
Higher Education.
Kinesiology.
Reading Education.
Recreation and Leisure Studies.
Secondary Education.
Special Education.

COLLEGE OF MUSIC:
Composition.
Jazz Studies.
Music.
Music Education.
Music Theory.
Musicology.
Performance.

COLLEGE OF PUBLIC AFFAIRS AND COMMUNITY SERVICE:
Administration of Long-Term Care, Senior Housing, and Aging Services.
Applied Anthropology.
Applied Economics.
Applied Gerontology.
Behavior Analysis.
Criminal Justice.
General Studies in Aging.
Public Administration.
Rehabilitation Services.
Sociology.

SCHOOL OF LIBRARY AND INFORMATION SCIENCE:
Information Science.
Library and Information Science.

SCHOOL OF MERCHANDISING AND HOSPITALITY MANAGEMENT:
Hotel Management.
Merchandising.

SCHOOL OF VISUAL ARTS:
Art Education.
Art History.
Ceramics.
Communication Design.
Drawing and Painting.
Fashion Design.
Fibers.
Interior Design.
Metalsmithing and Jewelry.
Photography.
Printmaking.
Sculpture.
Studio Art.

Texas College of Osteopathic Medicine

Web site: www.hsc.unt.edu

Founded 1970. State control. Affiliated with University of North Texas in 1975. Library: 38,000 volumes, 520 subscriptions.

Annual tuition: resident $13,964, nonresident $29,714. No on-campus housing available. Contact the Office of Student affairs for housing information. Total housing and personal expenses: approximately $15,000.

Enrollment: first-year class 135, total 555 (men 48%, women 52%, minorities 48%, state residents 95%). Faculty: full-time 293, part-time 200. Degrees conferred: D.O., D.O.-M.P.H., D.O.-Ph.D.

ADMISSION REQUIREMENTS. Bachelor's degree preferred, official transcripts, MCAT (no later than the Spring of junior year), three recommendations (one from premed advisory committee, one evaluation from a physician, preferably a D.O.), supplemental form required in support of application. Has EDP (apply September 1). Interview by invitation only. Graduates of unaccredited colleges not considered. Preference given to state residents. Apply by October 1 to Texas Medical and Dental Schools Application Service (TMDSAS). Supplemental application deadline October 15. Admits first year students Fall only. Application fee $55. Phone: (800)735-TCOM, (817)735-2204; fax: (817) 735-2225.

ADMISSION STANDARDS. Selective. Accepts about 10% of all applicants. Number of applications 1701 (197 out-of-state); number interviewed 569 (47 out-of-state); number of acceptances 177 (29 out-of-state); number enrolled 135 (13 out-of-state). Usual minimum UGPA: 3.0 (A = 4). Mean Composite MCAT 8.9, mean UGPA 3.50.

FINANCIAL AID. Scholarships, fellowships, assistantships, grants, loans. Apply by May 1 to the Financial Aid Office. Phone: (800)346-8266. Use FAFSA (College code: 003954) and institutional FAF. Approximately 80% of students receive some form of financial assistance.

DEGREE REQUIREMENTS. For D.O.: satisfactory completion of four-year program. For M.P.H., Ph.D: see Graduate Studies listing above.

FIELDS OF GRADUATE STUDY.
Cell Biology and Genetics.
Biochemistry and Molecular Biology.
Integrative Biomedical Science.
Integrative Physiology.
Microbiology and Immunology.
Pharmacology and Neuroscience.

NORTHEASTERN ILLINOIS UNIVERSITY

Chicago, Illinois 60625-4699
Web site: www.neiu.edu

Founded 1896, this campus 1961. CGS member. Coed. State control. Trimester system. Special facilities: Mazon Creek Paleontological Collection, Center for Exercise Science and Cardiovascular Research, Center for Inner Cities Studies. Library: 498,000 volumes, 3451 subscriptions.

Tuition: per credit, resident $160, nonresident $320. No on-campus housing. Day-care facilities available.

Graduate College

Graduate study since 1961. Enrollment: full-time 238, part-time 1354. Graduate faculty: full-time 257, part-time 164. Degrees conferred: M.A., M.B.A., M.Ed., M.S.

ADMISSION REQUIREMENTS. Official transcripts, statement of goals/objectives, two letters of recommendation, GRE/GMAT required in support of College's application. TOEFL (minimum score 500) required for international applicants. Interview not required. Accepts transfer applicants. Graduates of unaccredited institutions not considered. Apply to Graduate Office by February 15 (Fall), August 15 (Spring). Application fee, $25. Phone: (773)442-6008; fax: (773)442-6020.

ADMISSION STANDARDS. Competitive. Usual minimum average: 2.75 (A = 4).

FINANCIAL AID. Annual awards from institutional funds: research assistantships, teaching assistantships, internships, tuition waivers, Federal W/S, loans. Apply to appropriate department chair for assistantships; to Financial Aid Office for all other programs. Phone: (773)442-6002. No specified closing date. Use FAFSA. About 5–10% of students receive aid other than loans from College and outside sources. Aid available for part-time students.

DEGREE REQUIREMENTS. For master's: 30–48 hours minimum, at least 24–42 in residence; thesis or final paper for most majors; final written/oral exam.

FIELDS OF STUDY.

COLLEGE OF ARTS AND SCIENCES:
Biology.
Chemistry.
Communication, Media, and Theatre.
Computer Science.
Earth Science.
English. Includes literature, composition/writing.
Geography and Environmental Studies.
Gerontology.
History.
Latin American Literature and Culture.
Linguistics.
Mathematics. Includes applied mathematics, secondary education.
Mathematics for Elementary School Teachers.
Music.
Political Science.

COLLEGE OF BUSINESS AND MANAGEMENT:
Accounting.
Business Administration. Includes accounting, finance, marketing, management, international management, interdisciplinary.

COLLEGE OF EDUCATION:
Bilingual/Bicultural Education.
Counseling. Includes community counseling, school counseling.

Educational Leadership. Includes higher education leadership, chief school business official, school leadership.
Exercise Science.
Family Counseling.
Gifted Education.
Human Resource Development.
Inner City Studies.
Language Arts. Includes elementary, secondary.
Reading.
Special Education. Includes educating children with behavior disorders, educating individuals with mental retardation, early childhood special education, teaching children with learning disabilities.

NORTHEASTERN OHIO UNIVERSITIES
Rootstown, Ohio 44272-0095
Web site: www.neoucom.edu

College of Medicine (P.O. Box 95)

Established 1973 as a medical school consortium. Public control. Library: 110,000 volumes, 1050 subscriptions.

Annual tuition: resident $27,900, nonresident $52,296. On-campus housing available for 1st and 2nd year medical students. Total average figure for all other expenses: $16,000.

Enrollment: first-year class, B.S.-M.D. 85, M.D. 35, total 455 (men 48%, women 52%, minorities 41%, state residents 97%). Faculty: full- and part-time 1900. Degrees conferred: B.S.-M.D., M.D.

ADMISSION REQUIREMENTS. AMCAS report, transcripts, MCAT, recommendations, supplemental application required in support of application. Interview by invitation only. Preference given to state residents. For B.S.-M.D.: preference given to applicants from Kent State, University of Akron, Youngstown State University. Has EDP; apply between June 1 and September 1. Graduates of unaccredited colleges not considered. For M.D.: apply to Office of Student Affairs after June 1, before November 1. Application fee $30. Phone: (800)686-2511 (in Ohio); (330)325-6270 (outside Ohio); e-mail: admissions@neoucom.edu.

ADMISSION STANDARDS. Selective. Accepts about 14.9% of all applicants. Number of applications 1623 (574 out-of-state); number interviewed 368 (35 out-of-state); number of acceptance 242 (16 out-of-state); number enrolled 120 (5 out-of-state). Mean Composite MCAT 9.1; mean UGPA 3.69.

FINANCIAL AID. Scholarships, loans. Apply after acceptance to Fellowships and Awards Committee. Phone: (330)325-6481. Use FAFSA (College code: G24544). About 82% of students receive some aid from School.

DEGREE REQUIREMENTS. For B.S.-M.D.: satisfactory completion of six-year program. For M.D.: satisfactory completion of four-year program. All students required to pass Step 1 and Step 2 of the USMLE.

NORTHEASTERN STATE UNIVERSITY
Tahlequah, Oklahoma 74464-7099
Web site: www.nsuok.edu

Founded 1846. Located 75 miles SE of Tulsa. Coed. State control. Semester system. Library: 424,800 volumes, 3983 subscriptions.

Tuition: per credit, resident $101, nonresident $288 plus fees. On-campus housing for 140 married students, 800 men, 800 women. Cost varies with type of accommodation; approximate costs: $2960–$4328 per year. Contact Director of Housing for both on- and off-campus housing information. Phone: (918)456-5511, ext. 4700.

Graduate College

Graduate study since 1954. Enrollment: full- and part-time 1050. College faculty teaching graduate students: full-time 121, part-time 42. Degrees conferred: M.A., M.B.A., M.Ed., M.S.

ADMISSION REQUIREMENTS. Official transcripts, three letters of reference, GRE/MAT/GMAT required in support of College's application. TOEFL required for international applicants. Interview not required. Accepts transfer applicants. Graduates of unaccredited institutions not considered. Apply to Office of Graduate Dean by June 1 (Fall), December 1 (Spring), May 1 (Summer). Application fee: none for domestic, $25 for international applicants. Phone: (918)456-5511; fax: (918)458-2061.

ADMISSION STANDARDS. Relatively open. Usual minimum average: 2.5 overall (A = 4), 2.75 (for last 60 hours).

FINANCIAL AID. Annual awards from institutional funds: scholarships, research assistantships, teaching assistantships, internships, grants, Federal W/S, loans. Approved for VA benefits. Apply by March 1 to Dean of Graduate College for assistantships; to Financial Aid Office for all other programs. Phone: (918)456-5511. Use FAFSA.

DEGREE REQUIREMENTS. For master's: 32–36 semester hours minimum, at least 24 hours including the last 8 in residence.

FIELDS OF STUDY.
Collegiate Scholarships and Services. M.S.
Communication. M.A.
Counseling. M.S.
English. M.A.
Health and Kinesiology. M.S.
Industrial Management. M.S.
Library Media and Information Technology. M.S.
Mathematics Education. M.Ed.
School Administration. M.Ed.
School Counseling. M.Ed.
Science Education. M.Ed.
Speech-Language Pathology. M.S.
Teaching. M.Ed.

NORTHEASTERN UNIVERSITY
Boston, Massachusetts 02115-5096
Web site: www.neu.edu

Founded 1898. CGS member. Coed. Private control. Semester system. Special facilities: Center for Advanced Microgravity, Center for Applied Social Research, Barnett Institute of Chemical Analysis and Materials Science, Burdnick Center for the Study of Conflict and Violence, Center for Biotechnology Engineering, Center for Comparative Democracy, Center for Criminal Justice Policy Research, Cultural and Arts Policy Research Institute, Center for Digital Signal Processing, Domestic Violence Institute, Center for Electromagnetic Research, Electron Microscopy Center, Center for European Economic Studies, Center for Labor Market Studies, Marine Science Center, Center for the Study of Sports in Society, Center for Innovation in Urban Education, Institute on Writing and Teaching, World History Center. Library: 965,800 volumes, 8590 subscriptions. Total University enrollment: 19,500.

Tuition varies with program; see school listing below. On-campus housing for single students only. Housing costs per quarter: $1715–$1925. Apply to Director of Residential Life for both on- and off-campus housing information. Phone: (617)373-4872.

Graduate School of Arts and Sciences

Tuition: per quarter hour $980. Enrollment: full-time 571, part-time 207. School faculty: full-time 234, part-time 25. Degrees conferred: M.A., M.A.T., M.S., M.P.A., M.S.H.S., M.S.E.P.P., M.J.N.M.M., M.T.P.W., C.A.G.S., Ph.D.

ADMISSION REQUIREMENTS. Official transcripts, two or three letters of recommendation required in support of School's application. GRE, GRE Subject Tests required for many departments. Online application available. TOEFL and certification of finances required from international applicants. Accepts transfer applicants. Graduates of unaccredited institutions not considered. Apply by March 15 (in many cases) to the Graduate School of Arts and Sciences. Application fee $50. Phone: (617)373-3982; fax: (617)373-2942; e-mail: a&sgradinfo@casdn.neu.edu.

ADMISSION STANDARDS. Selective for most departments. Usual minimum average: 2.75 (A = 4).

FINANCIAL AID. Annual awards from institutional funds: research fellowships, teaching assistantships, Northeastern tuition assistantships, minority fellowships and MLK scholarships, tuition waivers, Federal W/S, loans. Approved for VA benefits. Apply by March 1 to Graduate School for assistantships, fellowships; to the Financial Aid Office for all other programs. Phone: (617) 373-5899. Use FAFSA (School code: 002199). Aid available for part-time students.

DEGREE REQUIREMENTS. For master's: 30–33 hours minimum, at least 24 in residence; thesis/final comprehensive exam/language required for most departments. For Ph.D.: normally 30 hours beyond the master's, at least one year in residence; qualifying exam; final written/oral exams; reading knowledge of one or two foreign languages; dissertation; final oral exam. For C.A.G.S.: 30 hours beyond the master's degree; comprehensive exam.

FIELDS OF STUDY.
Architecture.
American Government and Politics.
Bioinformatics.
Biology. GRE Subject, three references for admission; M.S. in biology, research, or literature, thesis required; M.S. in health science, thesis optional; M.S. full- or part-time; two languages for Ph.D. or research tool.
Biotechnology. M.S.
Chemistry. Includes analytical, clinical, organic, inorganic, physical; two references for admission, M.S. full- and part-time; one language for Ph.D.
Comparative and International Policy and Politics. Ph.D.
Economics. Includes economic policy and planning; two references for admission, comprehensive exam for M.A., M.S.E.P.P.; thesis optional for M.A., M.S.E.P.P.
English. Includes linguistics, literature, writing. Three references for admission; one language for M.A., thesis optional, Master of Technical and Professional Writing, C.A.G.S. in humanistic literary study also offered.
History. GRE Subject, two references for admission; one language and comprehensive exam for M.A., thesis optional; includes historical agencies and administration, public history, world history.
Journalism. Includes news media management, technical and professional writing, technical writing, writing; GRE, two references for admission. M.A., M.J.N.M.M.; comprehensive exam for both degrees.

Law, Policy, and Society. M.S., Ph.D.; interdisciplinary programs; one language for Ph.D.
Mathematics. Includes applied and pure mathematics; three references for admission, one language for Ph.D.
Operations Research. Offered jointly with the School of Engineering. M.S.O.R.
Physics. GRE recommended, two references for admission. M.S. full- and part-time.
Political Science. Includes comparative government, international relations, political theory. Three references for admission; comprehensive exam for M.A., thesis optional. M.P.A. full- and part-time study.
Psychology. GRE Subject, MAT for Ph.D.; three references for admission; includes applied behavior analysis, experimental; thesis required for M.A.
Public Administration. Includes development, public policy, personnel administration, policy and planning, public financing, health administration.
Sociology-Anthropology. GRE, three references for admission; thesis optional for M.A.; comprehensive, dissertation, research tool for Ph.D.; full- and part-time study.
Technical and Professional Writing.

Graduate School of Professional Accounting

Graduate study since 1965. Semester system. Fifteen-month cooperative program includes three-month internship where student is able to earn $8000–$10,000.

Total tuition: $27,960. On-campus housing available. Contact University's Housing Office. Phone: (617)373-5877.

Enrollment: full-time 48, part-time 13. School faculty: full-time 15, part-time 1. Degree conferred: M.S., M.S.T.

ADMISSION REQUIREMENTS. Transcripts, three letters of reference, interview, GMAT or LSAT required in support of School's application. Online application available. TOEFL required for international applicants. Applicants cannot be undergraduate accounting majors. Apply to Director of School, preferably before April 1. Classes start in June. Application fee $100. Phone: (617) 373-5072; fax: (617)373-8890; E-mail: GSPA@neu.edu.

ADMISSION STANDARDS. Very selective. Usual minimum average: 3.2 (A = 4).

FINANCIAL AID. Annual awards from institutional funds: scholarships, research assistantships, teaching assistantships, internships, Federal W/S, loans. Approved for VA benefits. Apply by March 1 to Director of School. Use FAFSA and institutional FAF. About 75% of students receive aid other than loans from School and outside sources. Aid available for part-time students.

DEGREE REQUIREMENTS. For M.S., M.S.T.: 30 credit hours; 6 required, seven electives; successful completion of internship.

FIELDS OF STUDY.
Accounting.
Taxation.

Graduate School of Business Administration

Special facilities: DEC VAX 8650 computer, 300 IBM PCs. Tuition: per credit $1110.

Enrollment: full-time 219, part-time 547. Faculty: full-time 102, part-time 46. On-campus housing available. Degrees conferred: M.B.A., E.M.B.A., M.S., M.S.F.

ADMISSION REQUIREMENTS. Official transcripts, GMAT, references required in support of School's application. Online application available. TOEFL required for international applicants. Accepts transfer applicants. Graduates of unaccredited institutions not considered. Apply by May 1 to the Director of Admission. Rolling admissions process. Application fee $50. Phone: (617)373-5992; fax: (617)373-8564.

ADMISSION STANDARDS. Selective. Usual minimum average: 3.2 (A = 4); average GMAT 540.

FINANCIAL AID. Annual awards from institutional funds: fellowships, teaching assistantships, research assistantships, internships, Federal W/S, loans. Approved for VA benefits. Apply by March 1 to appropriate department chair for fellowships, assistantships; to the Director of Financial Aid for all other programs. Phone: (617)373-3190. Use FAFSA. About 25% of students receive aid other than loans from School and outside sources. Aid available for part-time students.

DEGREE REQUIREMENTS. For master's: 45–60 credits minimum, at least 45 in residence.

FIELD OF STUDY.
Accounting. M.S.
Business Administration. Includes finance, marketing, production, human relations, quantitative methods, economics, management, management systems, international business.
Finance. M.S.F.
Taxation. M.S.

Graduate School of Computer Science
Web site: www.ccs.neu.edu

Graduate study since 1988. Tuition: per credit $1050. On-campus housing available. Contact University's Housing Office for both on- and off-campus housing information. Phone: (617) 373-5877.

Enrollment: full-time 169, part-time 25. Faculty: full-time 27, part-time 3. Degrees conferred: M.S., Ph.D.

ADMISSION REQUIREMENTS. Transcripts, three letters of recommendation, GRE required in support of School's application. TOEFL required for international applicants. Accepts transfer applicants. Graduates of unaccredited institutions not considered. Apply to Graduate School Office by August 15 (Winter), November 1 (Spring). Application fee $50. Phone: (617)373-2462; fax: (617)373-5121.

ADMISSION STANDARDS. Selective. Usual minimum average: 3.0 (A = 4).

FINANCIAL AID. Annual awards from institutional funds: fellowship, research assistantships, teaching assistantships, internships, Federal W/S, loans. Approved for VA benefits. Apply by January 15 to Graduate School Office for fellowships, assistantships; to Financial Aid Office for all other programs. Phone: (617) 373-3190; fax: (617)373-8735. Use FAFSA.

DEGREE REQUIREMENTS. For M.S.: 30–32 hours minimum, including required courses and concentration area. For Ph.D.: normally 45 hours beyond master's, at least one year in residence; qualifying exam, reading knowledge of one foreign language; dissertation; final oral exam.

FIELD OF STUDY.
Computer Science. Includes artificial intelligence, communications and networks, databases, distributed systems, programming languages, operating systems, theory.
Health Informatics.
Information Assurance.

Graduate School of Criminal Justice

Graduate study since 1974. Semester system. Tuition: $980 per credit.

Enrollment: full-time 64, part-time 20. Faculty: full-time 16, part-time 5. Degree conferred: M.S.

ADMISSION REQUIREMENTS. Official transcripts, three letters of recommendation from academic and professional sources, GRE or LSAT, essay expressing academic and personal objectives required in support of School's application. Online application available. TOEFL required for international applicants. Accepts transfer applicants. Apply by March 1, full-time (admits Fall only); June 1, part-time (Fall), November 1 (Winter), February 1 (Spring). Application fee $50. Phone: (617)373-2813; fax: (617) 373-8723.

ADMISSION STANDARDS. Selective. Usual minimum average: 3.0 (A = 4), but lower considered for provisional admission.

FINANCIAL AID. Annual awards from institutional funds: research assistantships, teaching assistantships, Federal W/S, loans. Approved for VA benefits. Apply by March 31 to the Graduate School for assistantships; to Financial Aid Office for all other programs. Phone: (617)372-3190; fax: (617)373-8735. Use FAFSA and institutional FAF. Aid available for part-time students.

DEGREE REQUIREMENTS. For master's: 30–32 hours minimum; comprehensive exam; thesis optional. Full-time students may complete program in one year.

FIELD OF STUDY.
Criminal Justice.
Criminology and Justice Policy. Ph.D.

Graduate School of Engineering
Web site: www.neu.edu/gradschool/engineering.html

Tuition: per credit $1050. Enrollment: full-time 483, part-time 298. Faculty: full-time 104, part-time 21. Degrees conferred: M.S., M.S.C.E., M.S.C.S.E., M.S.E.E., M.S.E.M., M.S.I.E., M.S.I.S., M.S.M.E., M.S.O.R., Ph.D., E.Engr., I.Engr., M.Engr.

ADMISSION REQUIREMENTS. Transcripts, GRE, two letters of recommendation required in support of School's application. For Ph.D.: statement of purposes required. TOEFL required for international applicants. Accepts transfer applicants. Graduates of unaccredited colleges not considered. Apply to Graduate School Admissions Office by April 15. Rolling admissions process. Application fee $50. Phone: (617)373-2711; fax: (617)373-2501; e-mail: grad-eng@coe.neu.edu.

ADMISSION STANDARDS. Selective. Usual minimum average: 2.8 (A = 4).

FINANCIAL AID. Annual awards from institutional funds: fellowships, teaching assistantships, research assistantships, internships, tuition waivers, Federal W/S, loans. Approved for VA benefits. Apply by February 15 to appropriate department chair for fellowships, assistantships; to Financial Aid Office for all other programs. Phone: (617)373-3190. Use FAFSA. About 35% of students receive aid other than loans from School and outside sources. Aid available for part-time students.

DEGREE REQUIREMENTS. For master's: 30–36 credit hours minimum, at least 28 in residence; thesis in most programs, or project, written report, and final exam. For Ph.D.: full-time program credit, requirements vary; reading knowledge of one foreign language for some programs; qualifying exam; final written/oral exam; thesis; final oral exam.

FIELDS OF STUDY.
Chemical Engineering. Apply by April 15 for Ph.D.; one language for Ph.D. M.S., M.S.C.E., Ph.D.

Civil Engineering. Includes construction, environmental, geotechnical/geoenvironmental, public works engineering management, transportation; thesis option for M.S.; apply by April 15 for Ph.D. M.S., M.S.C.E., Ph.D.

Computer Engineering. Ph.D.

Computer Systems Engineering. Includes CAD/CAM, engineering software design, robotics. M.S.C.S.E.

Electrical Engineering. Includes communications and signal processing, computer, control systems and signal processing, electromagnetics, plasma and optics, electronic circuits and semiconductor devices, power systems; thesis option for M.S.; apply by April 15 for Ph.D.; one language for Ph.D. M.S., M.S.E.E., Ph.D., E.Engr.

Engineering Management. Includes computer and information systems, manufacturing, operations research, quality control and reliability analysis; thesis for M.S.E.M.; M.S.E.M.

Industrial Engineering. Includes computer and information systems, manufacturing, operations research, quality control and reliability analysis; thesis for M.S., M.S.I.E.; apply by April 15 for Ph.D. M.S., M.S.I.E., Ph.D., I.Engr.

Information Systems. Thesis for M.S.I.S.; M.S.I.S.

Interdisciplinary Engineering. M.S., Ph.D.

Mechanical Engineering. Includes materials science and engineering, mechanics and design, thermofluids; thesis normally required for M.S.; apply by April 15 for Ph.D.; one language for Ph.D. M.S., M.S.M.E., Ph.D., M.Engr.

Operations Management. M.S.O.R. only.

Telecommuncation Systems Management. M.S.

Bouve College of Health Sciences

Web site: www.neu.edu/gradschool/bouve.html

Tuition: per credit $980. Enrollment: full-time 767, part-time 239. Faculty: full-time 128, part-time 65. Degrees conferred: M.S., C.A.G.S., M.H.P., Ph.D., Pharm.D.

ADMISSION REQUIREMENTS. Official transcripts, references, essay, test (vary by program and degree), required in support of School's application. TOEFL (miminum score 600) required of those applicants whose native language is not English. Accepts transfer applicants. The application deadline for the Pharm.D. program is February 1; Ph.D. program deadline is April 15. All application materials for master's program must be submitted to the Director of Graduate Admissions at least one month prior to registration. Application fee $50. Phone: (617) 373-2708; fax: (617)373-4701.

ADMISSION STANDARDS. Selective for most departments. Usual minimum average: 3.0 (A = 4).

FINANCIAL AID. Scholarships, fellowships, assistantships, a limited number of minority fellowships and Martin Luther King, Jr. Scholarships, internships, tuition waivers, Federal W/S, loans. Approved for VA benefits. Need-based financial aid is available only to American citizens or permanent residents of the United States. Apply by March 1 to appropriate department for assistantships, fellowships; to Office of Financial Aid for all other programs. Phone: (617)373-5899. Use FAFSA. Aid available for part-time students.

DEGREE REQUIREMENTS. For M.S.: 30–45 credit hours minimum; comprehensive exam. For C.A.G.S.: one year beyond the master's; qualifying exam; comprehensive exam. For Pharm.D.: 60 credit hours beyond the master's; qualifying exam; comprehensive exam; dissertation; final oral exam. For Ph.D.: normally 45 credit hours beyond master's, at least one year in residence; qualifying exam; dissertation; final oral exam.

FIELDS OF STUDY.

Applied Behavior Analysis. M.S.

Audiology. Au.D.

Biotechnology. M.S.

Clinical Exercise Physiology. M.S.

College Student Development and Counseling. M.S.

Counseling Psychology. M.S., Ph.D.

Critical Care. Includes acute care nurse practitioner, neonatal nurse practitioner. M.S.

Health Informatics. M.S.

Nursing. Ph.D.

Nursing Administration. M.S.

Pharmaceutical Science. M.S., Ph.D.

Physician Assistant Studies. M.S.

Primary Care Nursing. M.S.

Psychiatric/Mental Health Nursing. M.S.

School Counseling. M.S.

School/Counseling Psychology. Ph.D.

School Psychology. M.S.

Speech-Language Pathology. M.S.

School of Law

Web site: www.slaw.neu.edu

Established 1968. ABA approved since 1969. AALS member. Private control. Quarter system. Based on cooperative plan of legal education. Special facilities: Center for Artificial Intelligence and Law, Domestic Violence Institute, Public Health Advocacy Institute, Urban Law and Public Policy Institute. Law library: 275,908 volumes, 3057 subscriptions; has LEXIS, NEXIS, WESTLAW, DIALOG.

Annual tuition: $36,455. No on-campus housing available. Total average annual additional expense: $17,500.

Enrollment: first-year class 193; total 606 (men 41%, women 59%, minorities 27%). Faculty: full-time 29, part-time 20. Student-to-faculty ratio is 17.0 to 1. Degrees conferred: J.D., J.D.-M.B.A., J.D.-M.P.H., J.D.-M.S. (Accounting).

ADMISSION REQUIREMENTS. LSDAS Law School report, bachelor's degree, transcripts, LSAT, personal statement, essay, two letters of recommendation required in support of application. Interviews are recommended. Accepts transfer applicants. Graduates of unaccredited colleges not considered. Apply to Director of Admissions by March 1. Admits first-year students Fall only. Begin study in August. Application fee $75. Phone: (617)373-2395; fax: (617)373-8793.

ADMISSION STANDARDS. Selective. Accepts approximately 27% of all students. Number of applicants 3708; number of acceptances 986; number enrolled 212; LSAT (75% of students have a score at or above 159); GPA (75% of students have a GPA at or above 3.10). *U.S. News & World Report* ranking is in the second tier (tied at 85th) of all U.S. law schools.

FINANCIAL AID. Full and partial tuition waivers, fellowships, assistantships, Federal W/S, loans. Apply to Director of Financial Aid by March 1. Phone: (617)373-4620. Use FAFSA (School code: 002199). About 70% of students receive aid other than loans from School and outside sources.

DEGREE REQUIREMENTS. For J.D.: satisfactory completion of two-year, nine-month (103 quarter hours) continuous co-op program; public interest requirement. Cooperative legal education program integral part of J.D. For M.B.A.: see Graduate School listing above.

NORTHERN ARIZONA UNIVERSITY

P.O. Box 4125
Flagstaff, Arizona 86011-4125
Web site: www.nau.edu

Founded 1899. CGS member. Coed. State control. Semester system. Special facilities: Arizona Center for Research in Vocational Education, Arizona Earthquake Center, Bilby Research Center, Center for Colorado Plateau Studies, Center for Excellence in Education, Institute for Human Development, Center for Ecological Research, Center for Quaternary Studies. Library: 523,800 volumes, 6253 subscriptions. Total University enrollment: 18,000.

Annual tuition: full-time resident $2481, nonresident $14,644; per credit, $260, nonresident $610. On-campus housing with attractive options available for single students. Annual academic year housing costs: $4800 (including board), $3900 for married students. On-campus family housing limited (one-year waiting list). Phone: (928)523-3978.

Graduate School

Enrollment: full-time 1500, part-time 3800. University faculty: full-time 533, part-time 337. Degrees conferred: M.A., M.A.T., M.Ed., M.B.A., M.M., M.P.A., M.P.T., M.V.E., M.S., M.S.N., Ph.D., Ed.D.

ADMISSION REQUIREMENTS: Transcripts, GRE/GMAT/ MAT required in support of application. Online application available. TOEFL required for international applicants. Accepts transfer applicants. Graduates of unaccredited institutions not considered. Apply to Director of Admissions by March 1. Application fee $50. Phone: (928)523-4348; fax: (928)523-8950.

ADMISSION STANDARDS. Selective. Usual minimum average: 2.9 (A = 4).

FINANCIAL AID. Annual awards from institutional funds: academic scholarships, fellowships, research assistantships, teaching assistantships, internships, tuition waivers, Federal W/S, loans. Approved for VA benefits. Apply by March 1 to department chair for assistantships; to Financial Aid Office for all other programs. Phone: (928)523-4951. Use FAFSA. Loans and part-time work available.

DEGREE REQUIREMENTS. For master's: Thesis Plan—32 hours including thesis or practicum; Comprehensive Examination Plan—33 hours plus written comprehensive exam; Extended Coursework Plan—36–45 hours, 8–10 hours of transfer credit may be accepted. For Ed.D.: 90 semester hours beyond bachelor's; residence requirement; dissertation; final oral exam. For Ph.D.: 75 semester hours, two semesters in full-time study; foreign language; dissertation; final oral exam.

FIELDS OF STUDY.
Administration. M.Adm.
Anthropology. M.A.
Applied Communication. M.A.
Applied Geographic Information Sciences. M.S.
Applied Physics. M.S.
Applied Sociology. M.A.
Bilingual/Multicultural Education. M.Ed.
Biology. M.S., Ph.D.
Business Administration. M.B.A.
Career and Technical Education. M.Ed.
Chemistry. M.S.
Clinical Speech Pathology. M.S.
Counseling. Includes human relations, school counseling, student affairs (M.Ed.only). M.A., M.Ed.
Criminal Justice. M.S.
Curriculum and Instruction. M.Ed.
Early Childhood Education. M.Ed.
Earth Science. M.S.
Educational Leadership. M.Ed., Ed.D.
Educational Psychology. Includes counseling psychology, school psychology, learning and instruction. Ph.D.
Educational Technology. M.Ed.
Elementary Education. M.Ed.

Engineering. M.E.
English. Includes TESL, applied linguistics. M.A., Ph.D.
Environmental Science and Policy. M.S.
Forestry. M.F., M.S.
Forest Science. Ph.D. only.
Geology. M.S.
Liberal Arts. M.L.S.
Mathematics. M.A.T., M.S.
Music. M.M.
Nursing. M.S.N.
Physical Therapy. D.P.T.
Political Science. M.A., Ph.D.
Public Administration. M.P.A.
Psychology. M.A.
Quaternary Science. M.S.
Rural Geography. M.S.
School Psychology. M.A.
Science Teaching. M.A.
Secondary Education. M.Ed.
Spanish. M.A.T.
Special Education. M.Ed.
Statistics. M.S.

UNIVERSITY OF NORTHERN COLORADO
Greeley, Colorado 80639
Web site: www.unco.edu

Founded 1889. Located 50 miles N of Denver. CGS member. Coed. State control. Semester system. Special facilities: Center for Educational Technology, Mathematics and Science Teaching Center, Laboratory School (K-12). Library: 1,000,000 volumes, 3219 subscriptions. Total University enrollment: 13,100.

Annual tuition: full-time resident $4968, nonresident $14,688. On-campus housing for 94 married students, 20 graduate men, 20 graduate women. Average academic year housing costs: $3150–$3600 (room only) for single students; $550 per month for married students; off-campus housing $550–$800 per month. Contact Director of Residence Life for both on- and off-campus housing information. Phone: (970)351-2721.

Graduate School

Graduate study since 1913. Enrollment: full-time 1127, part-time 458. Graduate faculty: full-time 229, part-time 27. Degrees conferred: M.A., M.S., M.P.H., Ed.S., D.A., Ed.D., Psy.D., Ph.D.

ADMISSION REQUIREMENTS. Two transcripts, GRE, three letters of reference (Ed.S., D.A., Psy.D. applicants) required in support of School's application. TOEFL required for international applicants. Accepts transfer applicants. Graduates of unaccredited institutions not considered. Apply to Dean of Graduate School, preferably at least sixty days prior to registration. Application fee $50, $60 for international applicants. Phone: (800)776-GRAD, or (970)351-1807; fax: (970)351-2371.

ADMISSION STANDARDS. Selective. Usual minimum average 2.7, 3.0 for doctoral applicants (A = 4).

FINANCIAL AID. Annual awards from institutional funds: fellowships, teaching/graduate assistantships with stipend and partial/full tuition waiver, internships, Federal W/S, loans. Approved for VA benefits. Apply by March 1 to appropriate department chair for fellowships, assistantships; to Financial Aid Office for all other programs. Phone: (970)351-2502. Use FAFSA. About 30% of students receive aid other than loans from University and outside sources. Aid available for part-time students.

DEGREE REQUIREMENTS. For M.A., M.S.: 30 semester hours minimum; thesis or creative project/internship; comprehensive exams or capstone project. For Ed.S.: 30 semester hours beyond the master's; practicum report; final written exam. For Ph.D., Ed.D., D.A., Psy.D.: 64 semester hours minimum beyond the master's, at least 18 hours residence and two semesters in full-time attendance; dissertation; final written/oral exam. Ph.D. students must also demonstrate competency in using two research tools (foreign language, applied statistics, mathematical statistics, or computer languages/application).

FIELDS OF STUDY.
Applied Statistics and Research Methods. M.S., Ph.D.
Art and Design. M.A.
Audiology. Au.D.
Biological Education. Ph.D.
Biological Sciences. M.S.
Chemical Education. Ph.D.
Chemistry. Includes education, research. M.S.
Clinical Counseling. Includes couples, family therapy. M.A.
Communication. Includes human communication.
Counseling Psychology. Psy.D.
Counselor Education and Supervision. Ph.D.
Earth Sciences. M.A.
Educational Leadership. M.A., Ed.S., Ed.D.
Educational Mathematics. Ph.D.
Educational Technology. M.A., Ph.D.
Educational Studies. Includes elementary education, curriculum studies. M.A.T., Ed.D.
English. M.A.
Foreign Language. Includes Spanish teaching. M.A.
Gerontology. M.A.
Higher Education and Student Affairs Leadership. Ph.D.
History. M.A.
Human Rehabilitation. Ph.D.
Mathematics. M.A.
Music. Includes collaborative keyboard, conducting, instrumental performance, jazz studies, music education, music history and literature, theory and composition, vocal performance. M.M., D.A.
Nursing. Includes education, clinical nurse specialist in chronic illness, family nurse practitioner. M.S.
Nursing Education. Ph.D.
Public Health. Includes community health education. M.P.H.
Reading. M.A.
Rehabilitation Counseling. M.A.
School Counseling. M.A.
School Library Education. M.A.
School Psychology. Ed.S., Ph.D.
Social Science. M.A.
Special Education. Includes early childhood, deaf/hard of hearing, generalist, gifted and talented, visual impairment. M.A., Psy.D.
Speech Language Pathology. M.A.
Sports and Exercise Science. Includes exercise science, sports administration, sport pedagogy. M.S., Ph.D.

NORTHERN ILLINOIS UNIVERSITY
De Kalb, Illinois 60115-2864
Web site: www.niu.edu

Founded 1895. Located 65 miles W of Chicago. CGS member. Coed. State control. Semester system. Special facilities: Center for Black Studies, Center for Biochemical and Biophysics Studies, Center for Governmental Studies, Plant Molecular Biology Center, Regional History Center, Social Science Research Center, Center for Southeast Asian Studies, Center for Burma Studies. Library: 2,100,000 volumes, 21,000 subscriptions. Total University enrollment: 25,200.

Tuition: per credit, resident $191, nonresident $382. On-campus housing for 80 married students, 3400 single men, 3200 single women. Average academic year housing costs: $5484–$8618 (including board) for single students; $4500 for married students. Contact the Office of Housing Services for information on both on- and off-campus housing. Phone: (815)753-1525. Day-care facilities available.

Graduate School
Web site: www.niu.edu/grad

Graduate study since 1951. Enrollment: full-time 2200, part-time 3293. Graduate faculty: full-time 693, part-time 66. Degrees conferred: M.A., M.S., M.B.A., M.A.S., M.M., M.S.Ed., M.F.A., M.P.A., M.P.H., Ed.S., Performer's Certificate, Ed.D., Ph.D.

ADMISSION REQUIREMENTS. Transcripts, two letters of recommendation for master's (three for doctorate) required in support of School's application. GRE/GMAT/MAT may be required for some programs. TOEFL required for applicants whose native language is not English; TSE for international applicants applying for teaching assistantships and M.A. program in Communication Studies. GRE Subject Test required by Department of Biological Sciences. Interview typically not required. Accepts transfer applicants. Graduates of unaccredited institutions not considered. Apply to Graduate School by June 1 (Fall), November 1 (Spring), April 1 (Summer); international applicant deadlines May 1 (Fall), October 1 (Spring). Application fee: $30. Phone: (815)753-0395; fax: (815)753-6366; e-mail: gradsch@niu.edu.

ADMISSION STANDARDS. Selective. Usual minimum average: 2.75 (A = 4).

FINANCIAL AID. Annual awards from institutional funds: academic scholarships, fellowships, assistantships, internships, tuition waivers, Federal W/S, loans. Approved for VA benefits. Apply to specific department for fellowships, assistantships; to Office of Financial Aid for all other programs. No specified closing date. Phone: (815)753-1395; fax: (815)753-9475. Use FAFSA and institutional FAF. Aid available for part-time students.

DEGREE REQUIREMENTS. For most M.A.s, M.M., M.P.A., M.P.H., M.M., M.S., M.S.Ed.: 30 semester hours minimum; final comprehensive exam in most programs; some departments require thesis; some require a reading knowledge of one foreign language. For M.B.A., M.A.S.: 30 semester hours plus 0–18 hours of deficiencies; no thesis required. For M.F.A.: 60 semester hours beyond the bachelor's degree; qualifying exam; final written/oral exam; final individual show or project. For Ed.S.: 30 semester hours minimum beyond the master's; final written/oral exam. For Performer's Certificate: 24 semester hours; two public recitals. For Ed.D., Ph.D.: about 90 semester hours beyond the bachelor's degree; qualifying exam in some programs; candidacy exam; final oral exams; proficiency in foreign language/research tool for Ph.D.; dissertation.

FIELDS OF STUDY.
Accountancy. GMAT for admission. M.A.S.
Adult and Higher Education. Thesis optional for M.S.Ed. M.S.Ed., Ed.D.
Anthropology. Thesis optional. M.A.
Applied Family and Child Studies. Includes marriage and family therapy.
Applied Probability and Statistics. Thesis optional. M.S.
Art. Includes studio, art history, art education, art therapy; studio art M.A., M.F.A; one language, thesis for art history M.A., M.F.A.
Audiology, Au.D.
Biochemistry and Biophysics. Interdepartmental.

Biological Sciences. Includes human anatomical sciences; GRE Subject Test in Biology for admission; thesis optional for M.S. M.S. Ph.D.

Business Administration. GMAT for admission; M.B.A.; joint M.B.A.-J.D.

Chemistry. Thesis required for M.S. M.S., Ph.D.

Communication Studies. Thesis optional. M.A.

Communicative Disorders. Includes speech language pathology, audiology, deafness rehabilitation counseling; thesis optional. M.A.

Computer Science. No thesis. M.S. only.

Counseling. Thesis optional for M.S.Ed. M.S.Ed., Ed.S., Ed.D.

Curriculum and Instruction. Includes outdoor teacher education, secondary education. Thesis optional for M.S.Ed. M.S.Ed., Ed.S., Ed.D.

Curriculum and Supervision. Thesis optional for M.S.Ed. M.S.Ed., Ed.S., Ed.D.

Early Childhood Education. Thesis optional. M.S.Ed.

Economics. Thesis optional for M.A. M.A., Ph.D.

Educational Administration. Thesis optional for M.S.Ed. M.S.Ed., Ed.S., Ed.D.

Educational Research and Evaluation. M.S.Ed.

Educational Psychology. Thesis optional for M.S.Ed. M.S.Ed., Ed.D.

Electrical Engineering. Thesis required; M.S.

Elementary Education. Thesis optional; M.S. Ed.

English. Thesis optional for M.A. M.A., Ph.D.

Family and Child Studies. See Human and Family Resources.

Finance. GMAT for admission; thesis optional. M.S.

Foreign Languages and Literatures. Includes French, Spanish; thesis optional. M.A.

Foundation of Education. Thesis optional. M.S. Ed.

Geography. Thesis optional. M.S.

Geology. Thesis optional for M.S. M.S., Ph.D.

Gerontology. Interdepartmental program.

Higher Education. Interdepartmental.

History. Thesis optional for M.A. M.A., Ph.D.

Human and Family Resources. Includes applied family and child studies; home economics, resources, and services; marriage and family therapy; nutrition and dietetics; thesis optional. M.S.

Industrial Engineering. Thesis required. M.S.

Industrial Management. Thesis optional. M.S.

Instructional Technology. Thesis optional for M.S.Ed. M.S.Ed., Ed.D.

Law. Joint M.B.A.-J.D.

Literacy Education. M.S.Ed.

Management. See Business Administration.

Management Information Systems. M.S.

Marketing. See Business Administration.

Marriage and Family Therapy. See Human and Family Resources.

Mathematical Sciences. Includes applied, computational, pure mathematics, mathematics education; thesis optional for M.S. M.S., Ph.D.

Mechanical Engineering. Thesis required. M.S.

Music. Includes music education, theory and composition, history and literature, performance and pedagogy; individualized major, thesis or recital required. M.M., Performer's Certificate.

Nursing. Thesis optional. M.S.

Nutrition and Dietetics. M.S.

Philosophy. Thesis optional. M.A.

Physical Education. Includes adapted, exercise physiology/ fitness leadership; thesis optional. M.S.Ed.

Physical Therapy. M.S.

Physics. Thesis optional. M.S.

Political Science. Includes public administration (M.P.A.); no thesis for M.P.A.; thesis optional for M.A. M.A., M.P.A., Ph.D.

Psychology. Thesis optional for M.A. M.A., Ph.D.

Public Administration. Includes comparative and development, fiscal, human services administration, urban management; no thesis. M.P.A. only.

Public Health. Thesis optional. M.P.H. only.

Reading. Thesis optional for M.S.Ed. M.S.Ed., Ed.D.

School Business Management. Thesis optional. M.S.Ed.

Secondary Education. Thesis optional. M.S.Ed., Ed.S., Ed.D.

Sociology. Includes criminology; thesis optional. M.A.

Southeast Asian Studies. Interdepartmental.

Special Education. Thesis optional. M.S.Ed. only.

Speech Communication. For M.A. see Communication Studies.

Sports Management.

Statistics. Thesis optional. M.S. only.

Taxation.

Theater Arts. Includes acting, design, technology; thesis optional. M.A., M.F.A.

Women's Studies. Interdepartmental.

College of Law (60115-2890)

Web site: www.law.niu.edu

Established 1975. Located in downtown DeKalb. ABA approved since 1978. AALS member. Public control. Semester system. Law library: 242,270 volumes, 3264 subscriptions; has LEXIS, WESTLAW, LIS.

Annual tuition: full-time resident $11,938, nonresident $21,490; part-time per credit $498. No on-campus housing available. Total average annual additional expenses: $12,966.

Enrollment: first-year class, full-time 128, part-time 4; total full- and part-time 297 (men 50%, women 50%, minorities 21%). Faculty: full-time 16, part-time 10. Student-to-faculty ratio is 18.4 to 1. Degrees conferred: J.D., J.D.-M.B.A., J.S.-M.P.A.

ADMISSION REQUIREMENTS. LSDAS Law School report, bachelor's degree, transcripts, LSAT, personal goal statement, two letters of recommendation required in support of application. Preference given to state residents. Graduates of unaccredited institutions not considered. Apply by May 15. Rolling admissions process. Application fee $50. Phone: (815) 753-9485; fax: (815) 753-4501.

ADMISSION STANDARDS. Selective. Accepts approximately 35% of full-time and 29% of part-time students. Number of full-time applicants 1452, part-time 28; number of full-time acceptances 506, part-time 8; number of full-time enrolled 128, part-time 4; LSAT (75% of full-time students have a score at or above 154, part-time 156); GPA (75% of full-time students have a GPA at or above 3.05, part-time 2.59). *U.S. News & World Report* ranking is in the fourth tier of all U.S. law schools.

FINANCIAL AID. Scholarships, grants, assistantships, loans. Apply by March 1 to Financial Aid Office. Phone: (815)753-9485. Use FAFSA (School code: 001737). About 23% of students receive some aid from School.

DEGREE REQUIREMENTS. For J.D.: satisfactory completion of three-year program. For M.B.A.: see Graduate School listing above.

Note: Summer study abroad at University of Bordeaux-Montesquieu, Agen, France.

UNIVERSITY OF NORTHERN IOWA

Cedar Falls, Iowa 50614

Web site: www.uni.edu

Founded 1876. Located 96 miles NE of Des Moines. CGS member. Coed. State control. Semester system. Special facilities: Iowa Teachers Conservation Camp, Iowa Lakeside Laboratory, Institute for Environmental Education. Library: 1,200,000 volumes, 6781 subscriptions. Total University enrollment: 12,600.

Annual tuition: full-time resident $5708, nonresident $13,532; per hour resident $317, nonresident $966. On-campus housing for

365 married graduate students, limited for single graduate students. Average academic year housing costs: $4700 (including board) for single students; $4000 for married student apartments. Apply to Director of Housing for both on- and off-campus housing information. Phone: (319)273-2333. Day-care facilities available.

The Graduate College

Graduate study since 1951. Enrollment: full-time 635, part-time 630. Graduate faculty: full- and part-time 536. Degrees conferred: M.A., M.Acc., M.A.Ed., M.M., M.B.A., M.P.P., M.S., Ed.S., D.I.T., Ed.D., P.S.M. (Professional Science Master's).

ADMISSION REQUIREMENTS. Official transcripts required in support of College's application. GRE/GMAT required for some programs. Interview not required. TOEFL required for international applicants. Accepts transfer applicants. Apply to Registrar by August 10 (Fall), January 15 (Spring). Rolling admissions process. Application fee $30, $50 for international applicants. Phone: (319)273-2623; fax: (319)273-6792.

FINANCIAL AID. Annual awards from institutional funds: scholarships, fellowships, assistantships, internships, tuition waivers, Federal W/S, loans. Approved for VA benefits. Apply by February 1 to major department for fellowships, assistantships; to Financial Aid Office for all other aid. Phone: (319)273-2700. Use FAFSA. About 40% of students receive aid other than loans from College and outside sources. Aid available for part-time students.

DEGREE REQUIREMENTS. For P.S.M., master's: 30 or 32 semester hours minimum; qualifying exam; thesis/nonthesis option; final written exam for nonthesis plan. For Ed.S.: 30 hours minimum beyond the master's, at least 20 in residence and one semester or two Summer sessions in full-time attendance; final written exam often required; final oral exam. For Ed.D.: 60 semester hours minimum beyond the master's, at least 45 in residence; GRE required prior to starting dissertation; dissertation; final oral exam. For D.I.T.: 64 semester hours minimum beyond the master's, at least 52 in residence; GRE required prior to starting dissertation; dissertation; final oral exam.

FIELDS OF STUDY.
Accounting. M.Acc.
Applied Chemistry and Biochemistry. P.S.M.
Applied Physics. P.S.M.
Art. Includes studio, education; final creative project optional. M.A.
Athletic Training. M.S.
Biology. M.A., M.S.
Biotechnology. P.S.M.
Business Administration. M.B.A.
Chemistry. M.A., M.S.
Communication Studies. M.A.
Computer Science. M.S.
Computer Science Education. M.A.
Criminology. M.A.
Curriculum and Instruction. Includes education of the gifted, education technology, elementary education, literacy education, middle level education. M.A.Ed., Ed.D.
Ecosystems Management. P.S.M.
Educational Leadership. Ed.D.
Educational Psychology. Includes professional development for teachers. M.A.Ed.
English. M.A.
Environmental Science/Technology and Health. M.S.
French. M.A.
Geography. M.A.
German. M.A.
Health Education. M.A.
History. M.A.
Industrial Mathematics. M.A.

Industrial Technology. D.I.T.
Leisure, Youth, and Human Services. M.A., Ed.D.
Mathematics. M.A.
Mathematics for Middle Grades (4–8). M.A.
Mental Health Counseling. M.A.
Music. M.A., M.M.
Performance and Training Technology. M.A.
Philanthropy and Nonprofit Development. M.A.
Physical Education. M.A.
Physics Education. M.A.
Postsecondary Education. Includes student affairs. M.A.Ed.
Principalship. M.A.Ed.
Psychology. M.A.
Public Policy. M.P.P.
School Counseling. M.A.Ed.
School Library Media Studies. M.A.
School Psychology. Ed.S.
Science Education. M.A.
Science Education for Elementary Schools (K–6). M.A.
Social Work. M.S.W.
Sociology. M.A.
Spanish. M.A.
Special Education. Includes career/vocational programming and transition, consultant, M.A.Ed.
Speech-Language Pathology. M.A.
TESOL. M.A.
Two Languages. Includes French/German, Spanish/French, German/Spanish. M.A.
Women's Studies. M.A.

SALMON P. CHASE COLLEGE OF LAW OF NORTHERN KENTUCKY UNIVERSITY
Highland Heights, Kentucky 41099
Web site: www.nku.edu/~chase

Established 1893. ABA approved since 1954. AALS member. State control. Semester system. Special facilities: Local Government Law Center, Children's Law Center, Ohio Valley Environmental and Natural Resources Law Institute. Law library: 317,855 volumes, 2290 subscriptions; has LEXIS, NEXIS, WESTLAW, DIALOG.

Annual tuition: full-time resident $11,112, nonresident $24,240; part-time per credit, resident $463, nonresident $1010. On-campus housing available. Total average annual additional expenses: $15,299.

Enrollment: first-year class 110, part-time 78; total full- and part-time 516 (men 45%, women 55%, minorities, 8%). Faculty: full-time 20, part-time 12. Student-to-faculty ratio is 17.4 to 1. Degrees conferred: J.D., J.D.-M.B.A.

ADMISSION REQUIREMENTS. LSDAS Law School report, bachelor's degree, transcripts, LSAT, two letters of recommendation required in support of application. Transfer applicants accepted. Preference given to state residents. Graduates of unaccredited colleges not considered. Apply to the Office of Admissions, after October 1, before April 1. Rolling admissions process. Application fee $40. Phone: (859)572-5841.

ADMISSION STANDARDS. Selective. Accepts approximately 25% of full-time and 53% of part-time students. Number of full-time applicants 858, part-time 187; number of full-time acceptances 213, part-time 100; number of full-time enrolled 110, part-time 78; LSAT (75% of full-time students have a score at or above 152, part-time 150); GPA (75% of full-time student have a GPA at or above 3.01, part-time 3.03). *U.S. News & World Report* ranking is in the fourth tier of all U.S. law schools.

FINANCIAL AID. Scholarships, tuition waivers, Federal W/S, loans. Apply to Financial Aid Office of University by March 1. Phone: (859)572-6437. Use FAFSA (College code: 009275). Approximately 30% of all students receive some form of financial assistance.

DEGREE REQUIREMENTS. For J.D.: satisfactory completion of three-year (full-time) or four-year (part-time) program; 90 credit hour program.

NORTHERN MICHIGAN UNIVERSITY

Marquette, Michigan 49855-5301

Web site: www.nmu.edu

Founded 1899. Located 300 miles N of Milwaukee. Coed. State control. Semester system. Library: 511,000 volumes, 2200 subscriptions.

Tuition: per semester hour resident $340, nonresident $487. On-campus housing for 3200 students, 200 apartments for married students. Average academic year housing costs: $7220 (room and board) for single students; $3900 for married students. Contact Director of Housing for both on- and off-campus housing information. Phone: (906)227-2622.

College of Graduate Studies

Graduate study since 1960. Enrollment: full-time 120, part-time 254. University faculty: full-time 98, part-time 7. Degrees conferred: M.A., M.A.Ed., M.M.E., M.P.A., M.S.

ADMISSION REQUIREMENTS. Official transcripts required in support of School's application. Online application available. GRE/GMAT/MAT required for some programs. TOEFL required for international applicants. Suggest international students allow one year to complete all application procedures. Accepts transfer applicants. Apply to Dean of Graduate Studies by July 1 (Fall), November 15 (Spring), March 15 (Summer). Rolling admissions process. Application fee: $50. Phone: (906)227-2300; e-mail: gdcoll@nmu.edu.

ADMISSION STANDARDS. Selective. Usual minimum average: 3.0 (A = 4). May be higher for some departments.

FINANCIAL AID. Scholarships, graduate assistantships, grants, tuition waivers, Federal W/S, loans. Approved for VA benefits. Apply by March 1 to Director of Financial Aid. Phone: (906)227-2327. Use FAFSA.

DEGREE REQUIREMENTS. For master's: 32 semester hours minimum, at least 28 in residence and one semester or one Summer session in full-time residence; thesis/nonthesis option/ special project.

FIELDS OF STUDY.
Administrative Service. Includes community planning, general administration, public administration.
Biology.
Communication Disorders.
Creative Writing.
Criminal Justice.
Educational Administration.
Elementary Education.
English. Includes writing, pedagogy.
Enhanced Mathematics/Science Education.
Exercise Science.
Individualized Studies. M.I.S.
Instructional Leadership.

Mathematics Education.
Nursing. Includes advanced practice nursing, nursing administration.
Public Administration. Includes general administration, health care administration, personnel and labor relations, state and local administration, community planning, financial administration, criminal justice.
Reading Specialist K–12.
School Guidance and Counseling.
Science Education.
Secondary Education. Includes nine major disciplines.
Special Education.
Training and Development.

NORTHERN STATE UNIVERSITY

Aberdeen, South Dakota 57401-7198

Web site: www.northern.edu

Founded 1801. Located 288 miles W of Minneapolis. Coed. State control. Semester system. Library: 192,000 volumes, 1000 subscriptions. Total University enrollment: 2600.

Annual tuition: per hour resident $116, nonresident $341. On-campus housing for 411 graduate men and 582 graduate women; none for married students. Annual academic year housing costs: $3000–$3890. Apply to Director of Student Housing. Phone: (605) 626-3007. Day-care facilities available.

Graduate Study

Graduate study since 1956. Enrollment: full-time 22, part-time 123; Summer, full-time 200. College faculty teaching graduate students: full- and part-time 80. Degree conferred: M.S. in Ed.

ADMISSION REQUIREMENTS. Transcripts required in support of application. GRE required for some programs. TOEFL required for international applicants. Accepts transfer applicants. Apply to Director of Graduate Studies at least one month prior to registration. Application fee $35. Phone: (605)626-2558; fax: (605)626-2542.

ADMISSION STANDARDS. Selective. Usual minimum average: 2.75 (A = 4).

FINANCIAL AID. Annual awards from institutional funds: graduate assistantships, internships, Federal W/S, loans. Approved for VA benefits. Apply by March 1 to Director of Graduate Studies for assistantships; to Financial Aid Office for all other programs. Phone: (605)622-2640; fax: (605)626-3022. Use FAFSA. Aid available for part-time students.

DEGREE REQUIREMENTS. For master's: 24 semester hours minimum plus 6-hour thesis, or 27 semester hours and a 3-hour project paper, or 32 semester hours; admission to candidacy; final oral exam. Guidance and Counseling: 48-hour program.

FIELDS OF STUDY.
E-Learning.
E-Learning Design and Instruction.
E-Learning Technology and Administration.
Guidance and Counseling. Includes agency, school.
Leadership and Administration. Includes elementary principalship, secondary principalship.
Teaching and Learning. Includes education studies, elementary classroom teaching, guidance and counseling, health, physical education and coaching, language and literacy, secondary classroom teaching, special education.

NORTHWEST MISSOURI STATE UNIVERSITY
Maryville, Missouri 64468-6001
Web site: www.nwmissouri.edu

Founded 1905. Located 95 miles N of Kansas City. Coed. State control. Trimester system. Special facilities: Alternative Crop Center, Biomass Applied Research Center, Institute for Quality Productivity, Poultry Compost Research Center. Library: 335,000 volumes, 1469 subscriptions. Total University enrollment: 6250.

Tuition: per credit hour resident $231, nonresident $406. On-campus housing available for graduate students. Annual academic year housing costs; $3643 (excluding board). Apply to Housing Office. Phone: (660)562-1363.

Graduate School

Enrollment: full-time 247; part-time 384. Faculty teaching graduate students: full- and part-time 165. Degrees conferred: M.A., M.S., M.S. in Ed., M.B.A., Ed.S.

ADMISSION REQUIREMENTS. Transcripts, GRE required in support of School's application. GMAT for M.B.A. applicants. Online application available. TOEFL required for international applicants. Accepts transfer applicants. Graduates of unaccredited institutions not considered. Apply to Dean of Graduate School by July 1 (Fall), November 15 (Spring), March 1 (Summer). Application fee: none, $50 for international students. Phone: (660)562-1145; fax: (660)562-1096.

ADMISSION STANDARDS. Relatively open. Usual minimum average: 2.5 (A = 4).

FINANCIAL AID. Annual awards from institutional funds: assistantships, teaching assistantships, Federal W/S, loans. Approved for VA benefits. Apply by March 1 to Dean of the Graduate School for assistantships; to Director of Financial Aid for all other programs. Phone: (660)562-1363. Use FAFSA. About 10% of students receive aid other than loans from University and outside sources.

DEGREE REQUIREMENTS. For master's: 32 semester hours minimum, at least 24 in residence; admission to candidacy; thesis optional; final comprehensive exam; no language requirement. For Ed.S.: 32 credits beyond the master's, at least 24 in residence.

FIELDS OF STUDY.
Agriculture. M.S.
Biology. M.S.
Business Administration. Includes accounting, agriculture economics, management information systems. M.B.A.
Counseling Psychology. M.S.
Educational Leadership. Includes elementary, secondary. M.S.Ed.
English. Includes speech. M.A., M.S.Ed.
Elementary Principalship. Ed.S.
Guidance and Counseling. M.S.Ed.
Health and Physical Education. M.S.Ed.
History. M.A.
Learning Disabilities. Includes elementary, elementary/secondary, secondary. M.S.Ed.
Mentally Handicapped. Includes elementary, elementary/secondary, secondary. M.S.Ed.
Reading. M.S.Ed.
School Computer Studies. M.S.
Secondary Principalship. Ed.S.
Science Education. M.S. Ed.
Superintendency. Ed.S.

Teaching. Includes agriculture, early childhood, elementary, English, history, instructional technology, mathematics, middle school, music, secondary science. M.S.Ed.
Teacher Leadership. M.S.Ed.

NORTHWESTERN OKLAHOMA STATE UNIVERSITY
Alva, Oklahoma 73717-2799
Web site: www.nwosu.edu

Founded 1897. Located 150 miles NW of Oklahoma City. Coed. State control. Library: 225,000 volumes, 1411 subscriptions. Total University enrollment: 2100.

Tuition: per credit, resident $133, nonresident $365. On-campus housing available for graduate students. Average academic year housing costs: $3700 (including board). Apply to Housing Director. Phone: (580)327-8418.

Graduate School

Graduate study since 1954. Enrollment: full-time 48, part-time 122. College faculty: full-time 25, part-time 12. Degrees conferred: M.Ed., M.C.P.

ADMISSION REQUIREMENTS. Transcripts, GRE or MAT required in support of School's application. Interview not required. Accepts transfer applicants. Apply to Dean of Graduate School; no specified closing dates. Application fee $15. Phone: (580) 327-8589.

ADMISSION STANDARDS. Selective. Usual minimum average: 2.75 overall or 3.0 in last 60 hours (A = 4).

FINANCIAL AID. Limited to Oklahoma tuition grants, fellowships, Federal W/S, loans. Apply by May 1 to Director of Financial Aid. Phone: (580)327-8542. Use FAFSA. Aid available for part-time students.

DEGREE REQUIREMENTS. For M.Ed.: 32–34 credit hours minimum, optional paper; final written/oral exam. For M.C.P.: 48 credit program; practicum.

FIELDS OF STUDY.
Adult Education Management and Administration.
Counseling Psychology.
Curriculum and Instruction.
Educational Leadership.
Elementary Education
Guidance Counseling PF–12.
Reading Specialist.
School Counselor.
Secondary Education.
Special Education.

NORTHWESTERN STATE UNIVERSITY OF LOUISIANA
Natchitoches, Louisiana 71497
Web site: www.nsula.edu

Founded 1884. Located 75 miles SW of Shreveport. CGS member. Coed. State control. Semester system. Special facilities: Northwest Louisiana Lignite Institute, Southern Studies Institute, Williamson Museum. Library: 330,145 volumes, 2500 subscriptions. Total University enrollment: 9800.

Annual tuition: full-time resident $2992, nonresident $11,779. On-campus housing for 40 married students, 1000 men, 1240 women. Average academic year housing costs: $350–$450 per month for married students, $4300 (including board) for single students. Apply to Director of Housing. Phone: (318)357-6703. On-campus day-care facilities available.

Graduate Studies and Research

Graduate work since 1954. Enrollment: full-time 240, part-time 608. Graduate faculty: full-time 55, part-time 12. Degrees conferred: M.A., M.Ed., M.S., M.M., M.M.Ed., M.S.N., Ed.S.

ADMISSION REQUIREMENTS. Transcripts, GRE required in support of application. GMAT required for Business. Interview not required. TOEFL required of international students. Accepts transfer applicants. Apply to Dean of Graduate School by March 15 (Fall), October 15 (Spring). Application fee $20, foreign students $30. Phone: (318)357-5851; fax: (318)357-5019.

ADMISSION STANDARDS. Selective. Usual minimum average: 2.5 (A = 4).

FINANCIAL AID. Annual awards from institutional funds: fellowships, teaching assistantships, service assistantships, research assistantships, internships, Federal W/S, loans. Approved for VA benefits. Apply by June 15 to appropriate department head for assistantships; to Financial Aid Office for all other programs. Phone: (318)357-5961. Use FAFSA (School code: 002021). About 75% of full-time and 30% of all students receive aid other than loans from School and outside sources. Aid available for part-time students.

DEGREE REQUIREMENTS. For master's: 30 semester hours minimum including thesis, at least 24 in residence; admission to candidacy; comprehensive final written exam. For M.A. in Ed., M.S. in Ed., M.M.Ed., M.Ed.: same as above, except student may elect 33 semester hour program and special research report instead of thesis. For Ed.S.: 60 hours minimum beyond the bachelor's degree; one semester or two consecutive summers of full-time residence; thesis.

FIELDS OF STUDY.
Adult and Continuing Education. M.A.
Art. M.A.
Clinical Psychology. M.S.
Curriculum and Instruction. Includes educational technology, elementary school, English education, mathematics, reading, science education. M.Ed.
Early Childhood Education Grades PK–3. M.A.T., M.Ed.
Educational Leadership. M.Ed.
Educational Technology Leadership. M.Ed.
Elementary Education Grades 1–5. M.A.T.
English. Includes literature, folklife/southern culture, writing and linguistics. M.A.
Health and Human Performance. Includes health promotion, physical education, sport administration. M.S.
Heritage Resources. M.A.
Middle School Education Grades 4–8. M.A.T.
Music. M.M.
Nursing. Includes acute care nurse practitioner, adult nursing, critical care nursing of the adult, family nurse practitioner, maternal child and family nursing, mental health/psychiatric, neonatal nurse practitioner, pediatric nurse practitioner, women's health nurse practitioner. M.S.N.
Secondary Education Grades 6–12. M.A.T.
Special Education. Includes gifted, general, mild/moderate. M.Ed.
Student Personnel Services. M.A.

NORTHWESTERN UNIVERSITY
Evanston, Illinois 60208
Web site: www.northwestern.edu

Founded 1851. Located 12 miles N of Chicago. CGS and AAU member. Coed. Private control. Quarter system. Special facilities: Basic Industry Research Laboratory, Biomedical Engineering laboratory, Center for Experimental Animal Resources, Materials Science Research Center, Center for Mathematical Studies in Economics and Management, Center for Urban Affairs and Policy, Vogelback Computing Center, Van de Graaff accelerator, cooperative arrangement with Argonne National Laboratory, Gas Dynamics Laboratory, Transportation Center. On the Chicago campus are the Medical School, School of Law, Dental School, Kellogg Graduate School of Management. The University's NIH ranking is 37th among all U.S. institutions with 469 awards/grants valued at $168,376,712. According to The Center at University of Florida, the University is ranked 37th in receipt of Federal Research funds with $200,316,000 and it ranks 35th for total University research expenditures with $319,722,000. The University's endowment assets rank it 12th, with a value of $3,668,405,000. In 2004, the University awarded 367 doctorates, which ranked it 25th among all U.S. institutions eligible to award that degree. Thirty-eight of the University's faculty members have been elected to National Honor Academies and this ranks it 25th among all U.S. institutions. The Library: approximately 4,400,000 volumes, 39,000 subscriptions. Total University enrollment: 17,000.

Annual tuition: full-time $35,064, per course $4160. On-campus housing for limited number of graduate students. Average academic year housing costs: $8200 for married students, $6000 for single students. Apply to Director of Graduate Housing. Phone: (847)491-5127.

Graduate School

Graduate study since 1893. Enrollment: full-time 6500, part-time 100. Faculty: full- and part-time 2155. Degrees conferred: M.A., M.E.M., M.S., M.F.A., Ph.D.

ADMISSION REQUIREMENTS. Transcripts, two letters of recommendation required in support of School's application. TOEFL required for international applicants. GRE required for financial aid applicants, recommended for admission; GRE or GMAT required for management. Interview required for some departments. Accepts transfer applicants, but no advanced standing toward master's degree. Apply to Admissions Office of the Graduate School by December 31, by January 15 for financial aid consideration. Application fee $65, international students $75. Phone: (847)491-8532; fax: (847) 491-5070.

ADMISSION STANDARDS. Selective for most departments, very competitive for some.

FINANCIAL AID. Traineeships, research assistantships, teaching assistantships, fellowships, internships, Federal W/S, loans. Apply by January 15 to Office of the Graduate School for scholarships, to appropriate chairperson for assistantships; to Financial Aid Office for all other programs. Phone: (847)491-7264. Use FAFSA. About 60% of students receive aid other than loans from University and outside sources. No aid available for part-time students.

DEGREE REQUIREMENTS. For master's: equivalent of three quarters of full-time study; thesis required by many departments; no language requirement; final written/oral exam. For Ph.D.: equivalent of nine quarters of full-time study with at least three consecutive quarters in full-time study with at least three consecutive quarters in full-time attendance; admission to candidacy; qualifying exam; dissertation; final oral exam.

FIELDS OF STUDY.

WEINBERG COLLEGE OF ARTS AND SCIENCES:
Arican-American Studies.
Anthropology.
Art History.
Art Theory and Practice.
Biological Sciences Program. Interdepartmental.
Chemistry.
Comparative Literature.
Earth and Planetary Sciences.
Economics.
English.
French and Italian.
German Literature and Critical Thought.
History.
Linguistics.
Mathematics.
Neurobiology and Physiology.
Philosophy.
Physics and Astronomy.
Political Science.
Psychology.
Religion.
Slavic Language and Literature.
Sociology.
Statistics.

SCHOOL OF COMMUNICATION:
Communication Sciences and Disorders. Includes audiology and hearing sciences, learning disabilities, speech and language pathology.
Communication Studies.
Media, Technology, and Society.
Performance Studies.
Radio/Television/Film.
Theatre.
Writing for the Screen and Stage.

SCHOOL OF EDUCATION:
Human Development and Social Policy.
Learning Sciences.

MCCORMICK SCHOOL OF ENGINEERING AND APPLIED SCIENCE:
Applied Mathematics.
Biomedical Engineering.
Biotechnology.
Chemical and Biological Engineering.
Civil and Environmental Engineering.
Computer Information Systems.
Computer Science.
Electrical Engineering and Computer Science.
Engineering Design and Innovation.
Engineering Management.
Industrial Engineering and Management Sciences.
Information Technology.
Management and Manufacturing.
Materials Science and Engineering.
Mechanical Engineering.
Production Development.
Project Management.
Theoretical and Applied Mechanics.

KELLOGG SCHOOL OF MANAGEMENT:
Accounting Information and Management.
Finance.
Management and Organizations.
Managerial Economics and Strategy.
Marketing.

FEINBERG SCHOOL OF MEDICINE:
Clinical Investigation.
Clinical Psychology.
Genetic Counseling.
Integrated Graduate Program in the Life Science.
Public Health. Includes Ph.D. concentrations in medical anthropology, life sciences and public health.

SCHOOL OF MUSIC:
Music Cognition.
Music Education.
Musicology.
Music Technology.
Music Theory.

INTERDISCIPLINARY DEGREE PROGRAMS:
Counseling Psychology.
Liberal Studies.
Literature.
Management and Organization and Sociology.
Mathematical Methods/Social Sciences.
Medical Scientist Training Program.
Public Health.

Medill School of Journalism

Evanston campus. Annual tuition: $30,834 (M.S.J.), $35,064 (I.M.C.). Graduate enrollment: full-time 260 (men 45%, women 55%). School faculty: full-time 45, part-time 29. Degrees conferred: I.M.C., M.S.J.

ADMISSION REQUIREMENTS. Transcripts, GRE/GMAT/ LSAT, three letters of recommendation, résumé, 500-word autobiography, 500-word report on a news event or marketing campaign, news writing test clip of any published material (editorial candidates) required in support of School's application. TOEFL (minimum score 650) required for international applicants. Interview required for domestic M.S.M.C. applicants. Graduates of unaccredited colleges not considered. Apply to Office of Graduate Admissions by January 15 (Fall). Rolling admission process. Application fee $75. Phone: (847)491-5228; fax: (847)491-2052.

ADMISSION STANDARDS. Competitive. Usual minimum average: 3.0 (A = 4).

FINANCIAL AID. Scholarships, fellowships, grants, Federal W/S, loans. Approved for VA benefits. Apply by February 1 to Office of Graduate Admissions. Phone: (847)491-5224; fax: (847)467-2451. Use FAFSA (School code: E00513) and Medill's FAF. About 80% of students receive aid other than loans from School and outside sources.

DEGREE REQUIREMENTS. For M.S.J.: a twelve-unit, twelve-month program; capstone. For I.M.C.: fifteen-month, full-time program, includes a summer residency.

FIELDS OF STUDY.
Integrated Marketing Communication. I.M.C.
Journalism. Has concentrations in business and economics, government, policy and politics, health and science. Includes specialization basic reporting and writing, videography/broadcast, magazine writing, editing and publishing, interactive storytelling. M.S.J.

School of Law (P.O. Box 11064)

Founded 1859. Located in downtown Chicago. The national headquarters for ABA and AALS are located in the Northwestern University Law School complex. ABA approved since 1923. AALS member. Semester system. Full-time, day study only. Special facilities: Center for International Human Rights, Children and Family Justice Center, Center on Wrongful Convictions, Center for Urban Affairs and Research, Pritzker Legal Research Center. Law library: 733,026 volumes, 5452 subscriptions; has LEXIS, NEXIS, WESTLAW, DIALOG, CCH Access; has more than 200 network connections.

Annual tuition: $42,672; for LL.M. $43,792. On-campus housing available for both single and married students. Law students tend to live off-campus. Contact Admissions Office for both on- and off-campus housing information. Total on-campus living expenses: $19,706.

Enrollment: first-year class 243; total 768 (men 54%, women 46%, minorities, 35%). Faculty: full-time 52, part-time 36. Student-to-faculty ratio is 11.9 to 1. Degrees conferred: J.D., J.D.-M.B.A., J.D.-Ph.D., two-year J.D. (for persons who have completed a basic legal education and received a university degree in law in another country). LL.M. (Executive, taxation, International).

ADMISSION REQUIREMENTS. LSDAS Law School report, bachelor's degree, transcripts, LSAT (not later than December), one recommendation, personal statement, résumé required in support of application. Graduates of unaccredited colleges not considered. Apply after October 1, before February 15. For Early Decision program apply by December 15. Candidates for LL.M. must submit two additional recommendations, but not the LSAT. Apply to Law School Office of Admissions preferably no later than February 1. Admits first-year students Fall only. Application fee $80 ($90 after February 1). Phone: (312)503-8465; fax: (312)503-0178.

ADMISSION STANDARDS. Selective. Accepts approximately 17% of all students. Number of applicants 4678; number of acceptances 781; number enrolled 243; LSAT (75% of students have a score at or above 167); GPA (75% of students have a GPA at or above 3.46). *U.S. News & World Report* ranking is in the top twelve of all U.S. law schools.

FINANCIAL AID. Need-based scholarships, minority scholarships, Grants-in-Aid, private and institutional loans, Federal loans, Federal W/S. Assistantships may be available for upper-divisional joint degree candidates. All accepted students who show need are automatically considered for scholarships (selection criteria places heavy reliance on LSAT and undergraduate GPA). Apply by February 15. For all other programs, apply to the Office of Financial Aid. Phone: (312)503-8465. Use FAFSA (School code: E00293) and the University Aid application; also submit Financial Aid Transcript, Federal Income Tax forms, and use Access Disk. Approximately 33% of first-year students receive scholarships/Grants-in-Aid. Approximately 70% of students receive some form of financial assistance. For LL.M.: fellowships in the form of grants, Graduate-Professional Alternative Loans (GPAL) available. Apply on LL.M. Admissions application form and complete LL.M. Financial Aid Form. Apply by March 15. If eligible for Federal programs, submit FAFSA. No employment opportunities are available.

DEGREE REQUIREMENTS. For J.D.: satisfactory completion of 86 semester hour program. For LL.M.: at least 24 credits beyond the J.D.; one year in full-time residence; thesis; final written/oral exam. Refer to Graduate School listings above for joint degree requirements.

J. L. Kellogg Graduate School of Management
Web site: www.kellogg.northwestern.edu

Established in 1908 as the School of Commerce.

Quarter system. Annual tuition: $43,935. Full-time program located on Evanston campus, part-time (evening) program on Chicago campus. On-campus housing for single, married students. Contact Assistant Director of Student Affairs for housing information. Phone: (708)491-3300.

Enrollment: full-time 1201, part-time 1300. Faculty: full- and part-time 183. Degrees conferred: M.B.A., M.M. Manufacturing (combined program with School of Engineering). The Ph.D. is offered through the Graduate School.

ADMISSION REQUIREMENTS. Transcripts, GMAT (GRE required for doctoral applicants), data form, essays, résumé, 2 career progress surveys required in support of School's application. TOEFL (minimum score 600) required of international applicants. Transfer applicants not accepted. For M.B.A. apply to Office of Admissions by October 1 (round 1), December 15 (round 2), February 15 (round 3); round 1 notification by January 7, round 2 by March 3, round 3 by May 12; for Ph.D. apply by February 1. Admits Fall only. Application fee $225 (M.B.A.), $75 (Ph.D.). Phone: (847)491-3308; fax: (847)491-4960. Phone: (847)491-3308; fax: (847)491-4960.

ADMISSION STANDARDS. Very selective. No minimum G.P.A. or GMAT required. Mean LSAT: 702; mean GPA: 3.45. *U.S. News & World Report* ranking is in the top five of all business schools.

FINANCIAL AID. Annual awards are from government, institutional, and corporate funds, including minority fellowships, grants, scholarships, internships, loans. Apply by February 1 to Office of Admission. Phone: (847)491-3308. Use FAFSA (School code: E00302). Ph.D. students should apply by January 15; there are approximately 40 research assistantships. About 60% of students receive aid. Aid available for part-time students.

DEGREE REQUIREMENTS. For M.B.A., M.M.M.: six quarters in residence, beginning in September, for candidates other than graduates of accredited business schools. For Ph.D.: see Graduate School listing above.

FIELDS OF DOCTORAL STUDY.
Accounting Information and Management.
Finance.
Management and Organizations.
Managerial Economics and Strategy.
Marketing.
Operations Management.

The Feinberg Medical School
Web site: www.feinberg.northwestern.edu

Founded 1859. Chicago campus (60611). Quarter system. Medical library: 250,000 volumes, 1865 subscriptions. NIH ranking is 37th among all U.S. institutions with 469 awards/grants worth $168,376,712.

Annual tuition: $44,500. On-campus housing for single students, limited for married students with children. Total average figure for all other expenses: $12,078.

Enrollment: first-year class 170, total 695 (men 54%, women 43%, minorities 49%, state residents 29%). Faculty: full- and part-time 1900. Degrees conferred: M.D., M.D.-M.A., M.D.-M.B.A., M.D.-M.P.H., M.D.-Ph.D. (Medical Scientist Training Program). The M.B.A. is offered through Kellogg Graduate School of Management, M.A., Ph.D. offered through the Graduate School.

ADMISSION REQUIREMENTS. AMCAS report, transcripts, two letters of recommendation, MCAT, supplemental application required in support of application. At least three years of pre-medical work required for admission. Does not have EDP. Interview required for all applicants under serious consideration. Accepts transfer applicants. Apply to Office of Admissions after June 15, before October 15. Application fee (after screening) $70. Phone: (312) 503-8206.

ADMISSION STANDARDS. Very competitive. Accepts about 6% of all applicants. Number of applications 6897 (6033 out-of-state); number interviewed 713 (600 out-of-state); number of acceptances 399 (350 out-of-state); number enrolled 170 (124 out-of-state). Mean Composite MCAT 11.2; mean UGPA 3.70. *U.S. News & World Report* ranking is in the top 21 of all U.S. medical research schools, 44th in primary care.

FINANCIAL AID. Scholarships, fellowships, loans. Apply to Financial Aid Committee after acceptance, but before March 15. Phone: (312)503-8722. Use FAFSA (School code: E00295). MSTP funded by NIH. About 76% of students receive some aid from School.

DEGREE REQUIREMENTS. For B.A., B.S.-M.D.: satisfactory completion of seven-year program. For M.D.: satisfactory completion of four-year program. For M.B.A.: see J. L. Kellogg Graduate School of Management listing above. For M.P.H.: one year beyond M.D., in certain cases it can be accomplished during four-year M.D. program; see Graduate School listing above. For M.A., Ph.D.: see the Graduate School listing above.

FIELDS OF GRADUATE STUDY.
Anatomy.
Biochemistry.
Biology.
Bioethics. M.A.
Biomedical Engineering.
Biophysics.
Cell Biology.
Chemical and Biological Engineering.
Chemistry.
Genetics.
Immunology.
Life Science.
Management. M.B.A.
Medical Humanities. M.A.
Microbiology.
Molecular Biology.
Neuroscience.
Pathology.
Pharmacology.
Physiology.
Public Health. M.P.H.

School of Music

Established 1895. Annual tuition: full-time $35,064. On-campus housing is available for graduate students. Enrollment: full-time 236, part-time 6. School of Music faculty: 60 full-time, 53 part-time. Degrees conferred: M.M., D.M. The Ph.D. is offered through the Graduate School.

ADMISSION REQUIREMENTS. Transcripts, personal statement, performance résumé or vitae, two recommendations required in support of School's application. Online application available. GRE required for Ph.D. applicants only. TOEFL required for international applicants. Accepts transfer applicants. For M.M.: audition or recording for performance majors, scores for composition majors, research papers for theory majors, music history and literature majors, essays for music education majors. For D.M.: theory and music history exams; interview and audition for performance majors; scores and tape recording of compositions for composition majors. Transfer credits for M.M. not accepted. Limited transfer credit for D.M. from an accredited college accepted. Apply to Office of Music Admission and Financial Aid. Apply by January 1 (Fall), April 15 (Summer, M.M. Music Education). Early filing is given preference. Application fee $50. Phone: (847)491-3141; fax: (847)467-7440.

ADMISSION STANDARDS. Highly selective. Minimum usual average 3.0 (A = 4).

FINANCIAL AID. Annual awards from institutional funds: grants, fellowships, graduate assistantships, internships, tuition waivers, stipends, Federal W/S, loans. Approved for VA benefits. Financial Aid application sent out after admissions application is received. Apply by January 15 for D.M., February 15 for M.M. to Office of Admissions and Financial Aid. Phone: (847)491-3141. Use FAFSA and institutional FAF. About 80% of students receive aid other than loans from School of Music and outside sources. No aid is offered part-time students.

DEGREE REQUIREMENTS. For M.M.: 12 units minimum in residence; recital for performance and conducting majors; large composition for composition majors; comprehensive exams for music theory, music history, and music education majors; optional thesis or project for music education majors. For D.M.: 18 units minimum in residence, at least 9 units in full-time attendance; recitals-projects, lecture-recitals, or document, depending on major; reading knowledge of one or two foreign languages, depending on major; qualifying exam; final oral exam.

FIELDS OF STUDY:
Conducting. M.M., D.M.
Music Cognition. Ph.D.
Music Composition. D.M.
Music Education. M.M., Ph.D.
Music Education and Piano Pedagogy. M.M.
Music Education and String Pedagogy. M.M.
Music Technology. M.M., D.M.
Music Theory. M.M
Musicology. M.M., Ph.D.
Musicology and Library Science. M.M.
Piano Performance. Includes performance and collaborative arts, performance and pedagogy. M.M., D.M.
String Performance. Includes performance and pedagogy, chamber and orchestral literature. M.M.
Vocal and Opera Performance. D.M.
Voice Performance and Literature. M.M.
Wind and Percussion Performance. Includes performance and literature. M.M, D.M.

NOTRE DAME DE NAMUR UNIVERSITY
Belmont, California 94002-1997
Web site: www.ndnu.edu

Established 1851. Located 25 miles S of San Francisco. CGS member. Coed. Private control. Roman Catholic affiliation. 4-4-4 system. Library: 115,000 volumes, 726 subscriptions. Total University enrollment: 1588.

Tuition: per credit $655. On-campus housing available. Annual cost: $8000–$12,000. Contact Director of Housing for both on- and off-campus housing information. Phone: (650)508-3513.

Graduate Studies

Graduate study since 1972. Enrollment: full-time 195, part-time 503. College faculty: full-time 24, part-time 103. Degrees conferred: M.A., M.M., M.Ed., M.B.A., M.P.A., M.A.-A.T., M.A.-C.P., M.S.S.M., M.A.-Geron.

ADMISSION REQUIREMENTS. Official transcripts, GMAT (business), two letters of recommendation required in support of application. Online application available. GRE required for some programs. Interview required for some programs. TOEFL (minimum score 550) and a statement of financial and family support required for international applicants. Accepts transfer applicants. Graduates of unaccredited colleges not considered. Apply to Graduate Office at least one month prior to date of registration. Rolling admissions process. Application fee $50. Phone: (800)263-0545; (800)263-3600; fax: (650)508-3426.

ADMISSION STANDARDS. Selective. Usual minimum average: 2.5 (A = 4).

FINANCIAL AID. Scholarships, teaching assistantships, Federal W/S, loans. Apply to Director of Financial Aid. Scholarship deadlines: July 15 (Fall), December 1 (Spring). Phone: (650) 508-3509. Use FAFSA.

DEGREE REQUIREMENTS. For master's: 30–39 credits minimum, at least 24–33 in residence; advancement to candidacy; thesis/nonthesis option.

FIELDS OF STUDY.

SCHOOL OF ARTS AND HUMANITIES:
English. M.A.
Music. M.M.

SCHOOL OF BUSINESS AND MANAGEMENT:
Business Administration. M.B.A.
Management. M.S.M.
Public Administration. M.P.A.

SCHOOL OF EDUCATION AND LEADERSHIP:
Curriculum and Instruction. Includes literacy.
Educational Technology. M.Ed.
Educational Technology Administration. M.S.
Reading. M.A.
Special Education. M.A.
Teaching. M.A.

SCHOOL OF SCIENCE:
Art Therapy Psychology. M.A.
Clinical Psychology. M.A.
Clinical Gerontology. M.A.
Marital and Family Therapy. M.A.

UNIVERSITY OF NOTRE DAME
Notre Dame, Indiana 46556-5602
Web site: www.nd.edu

Founded 1842. Located 80 miles SE of Chicago. CGS member. Coed on graduate level. Private control. Roman Catholic affiliation. Semester system. Special facilities: Center for Applied Mathematics, Center for Bioengineering and Pollution Control, Computing Center with IBM 3033 system with peripheral equipment, Center for Catalysis and Reaction Engineering, Center for Environmental Science and Technology, Center for Molecularly Engineering Materials, Center for Nano Science and Technology, Center for the Philosophy of Religion, Center for Tropical Disease and Training, Center for Zebrafish Research, Cushwa Center for the Study of American Catholicism, Center for the Study of Contemporary Society, Hessert Center for Aerospace Research, Institute for Latino Studies, Institute for Pastoral Liturgy, Joan B. Kroc Institute of International Peace Studies, Helen Kellogg Institute for International Studies, Keough Institute for Irish Studies, LOBUND Laboratory (germfree life equipment), Radiation Laboratory, The Library of the Medieval Institute, Center for the Study of Man in Contemporary Society, Nanovic Institute for European Studies, Reilly Center for Sciences, Technology and Values, Walther Cancer Research Center. Library 2,800,000 volumes, 18,416 subscriptions. Total University enrollment: 10,563.

Annual tuition: full-time $34,580, per credit $1922. On-campus housing for 132 married students and 253 single students. Aver-

age academic year housing cost: $470–$605 (per month) for married students, $7700 (including board) for single students. Apply to Director of Student Residences. Phone: (574)631-5878. Daycare facilities available.

Graduate School

Organized 1918. Enrollment: full-time 1404, part-time 53. University faculty: full- and part-time 615. Degrees conferred: M.A., M.B.A., M.S., M.Div., M.F.A., M.M., M.Arch., M.M.S., Ph.D.

ADMISSION REQUIREMENTS. Transcripts, three letters of recommendation, vitae/résumé, GRE/Subject Tests required in support of School's application. Online application available. TOEFL required for international applicants. Interview not required. Accepts transfer applicants. Graduates of unaccredited institutions not considered. Apply to Director of Graduate Admissions, preferably by February 1 (Fall), November 1 (Spring). Some programs have earlier deadlines. New students normally begin Fall only. Application fee $50. Phone: (574)631-7706; fax: (574) 631-4183; e-mail: gradad@nd.edu.

ADMISSION STANDARDS. Selective for most departments. Usual minimum average: 3.0 in area of concentration (A = 4).

FINANCIAL AID. Annual awards from institutional funds: scholarships, teaching assistantships, research assistantships, fellowships, internships, grants, Federal W/S, loans. Apply to Director of Graduate Admissions by February 1. Phone: (574) 631-6436. Use FAFSA. About 90% of students receive aid other than loans from University and outside sources. Aid available for part-time students.

DEGREE REQUIREMENTS. Degree programs are all determined by departmental advisement. The following are illustrative degree programs. For M.A., M.S.: Plan I—30 semester hours minimum; thesis (6 semester boom), admission to candidacy; final written/oral exam. Plan II—30 semester hours minimum; admission to candidacy; no thesis or language requirement; normally a terminal degree. For M.A. (Art): 32 semester hours minimum; final portfolio and essay. For M.B.A.: 60 semester hours minimum in residence. For M.F.A.: 60 semester boom minimum; final portfolio; studio thesis. For M.M.: 36 semester hours minimum; final music project. For M.M.S.: 38 semester hours minimum and knowledge of Latin required for entrance. For M.Div.: 72 semester hours. For Ph.D.: 72 semester hours, at least four consecutive semesters in full-time residence; foreign language requirements determined by department; candidacy exam; dissertation; defense of dissertation.

FIELDS OF STUDY.
Aerospace—Mechanical Engineering.
American Studies. Interdepartmental; master's only.
Applied Mathematics.
Architecture. M.Arch. only.
Art. Includes art history (M.A.), studio, design. M.F.A.
Biochemistry. Interdisciplinary.
Bioengineering.
Biological Sciences.
Chemical and Biomolecular Engineering.
Chemical Physics. Interdisciplinary.
Chemistry.
Civil Engineering and Geological Sciences.
Computer Science and Engineering.
Creative Writing.
Early Christian Studies.
Economics.
Education.
Educational Administration.
Electrical Engineering.

English.
Government and International Studies.
History.
History and Philosophy of Science.
Literature. Interdisciplinary.
Mathematics.
Medieval Studies.
Peace Studies. Master's only.
Philosophy.
Physics.
Political Sciences.
Psychology
Romance Languages and Literature. Master's only.
Sacred Music.
Sociology.
Theology.

Mendoza College of Business
P.O. Box 399
Web site: www.nd.edu/~cba

Graduate Business School established 1967. Private control. Accredited programs: M.B.A. Institution draws from a national and international population. Located on main campus; suburban environment. Semester system. Special facilities: Center for Accounting Research and Education, Center for Ethics and Religious Values, Center for U.S.–Japanese Studies, Fanning Center for Business Communication, Gigot Center for Entrepreneurial Studies, Institute for Ethical Business Worldwide. Special programs: accelerated M.B.A. program for students with an undergraduate degree in business; foreign exchange programs in London, England, Santiago, Chile, Monterrey, Mexico; international internships.

Annual tuition: $35,490. On-campus rooms and apartments available for both single and married students. Enrollment: full-time 629, part-time 45. Faculty: full-time 107, part-time 12. Degrees conferred: M.B.A., E.M.B.A. (weekends only), M.S.A. (Administration), M.S.Acct., M.B.A.-J.D.

ADMISSION REQUIREMENTS. All applicants should have a bachelor's degree from a recognized institution of higher education and a strong mathematics background. Contact College of Business for application material and information; phone: M.B.A. (574)631-8671; E.M.B.A. (800)631-3622; Accountancy (574)631-9732. Early applications are encouraged for both admission and financial aid consideration. Beginning students are admitted Fall and Summer. Both U.S. citizens and international applicants should apply by April 15 (Fall, two-year program), March 1 (Summer, one-year program). Submit an application, GMAT (will accept GMAT test results from the last five years; latest acceptable date is June), official transcripts, two letters of recommendation, four essays, résumé (prefers at least four years of work experience), and an application fee of $75 to the Office of Admission. In addition, international students (whose native language is other than English) should submit a TOEFL report (minimum score 600), certified translations and evaluations of all official transcripts, recommendation should be in English or with certified translations, proof of health/immunization certificate, and proof of sufficient financial resources for two years of academic study. Interviews are strongly encouraged prior to the admissions committee reviewing completed applications. Joint degree applicants must apply to and be accepted to both schools; contact the Admissions Office for current information and specific admissions requirements. Rolling admissions process.

ADMISSION STANDARDS. Selective. Median GMAT: 611, median GPA: 3.16 (A = 4). *U.S. News & World Report* ranked the College of Business in the top 39 of all U.S. business schools. *BusinessWeek* listed the College of Business in the top 26 of all American business schools.

FINANCIAL AID. Scholarships, merit fellowships, minority stipend program, grants, M.B.A. fellowship, graduate assistantships, Federal Perkins Loans, Stafford Subsidized and Unsubsidized Loans, Federal W/S available. Financial aid is available for part-time study and may be available for international students. Assistantships/fellowships may be available for joint degree candidates. Financial aid applications and information are generally available at the on-campus visit/interview and is included with the admissions application; apply by February 15. Request scholarship, fellowship, assistantship, and all need-based information from the College of Business. Phone: (574)631-8488. For assistantships, fellowships, scholarships the selection criteria places heavy reliance on GMAT and undergraduate GPA. Use FAFSA (School code: 001840); also submit Financial Aid Transcript, Federal Income Tax forms. Approximately 70% of students receive some form of financial assistance.

DEGREE REQUIREMENTS. For M.B.A.: 44–63 credit program including 24 elective credits, one- or two-year program; degree program must be completed in five years. For E.M.B.A.: 48-credit program. For M.S.A.: 42-credit intensive Summer program; some electives can be completed through a distance learning option. For M.S.Acct.: 30–36 credit program. For M.B.A.-J.D.: 123-credit, four-and-one-half- to five-and-one-half-year program.

FIELDS OF STUDY.
Accountancy. M.S.Acct.
Nonprofit Administration. M.N.A.

Law School (46556-0780)
Web site: www.law.nd.edu

Established 1869. ABA approved since 1925. AALS member. Semester system. Special facilities: Center for Civil and Human Rights, Thomas J. White Center on Law and Government. Law library: 634,905 volumes, 7203 subscriptions; has LEXIS, NEXIS, VU/TEXT, WESTLAW, DIALOG; has more than 100 network connections.

Annual tuition: $34,120. On-campus housing available. Total average additional expenses: $14,100.

Enrollment: first-year class 175; total 570 (men 63%, women 37%, minorities, 22%). Faculty: full-time 40, part-time 31. Student-to-faculty ratio is 14.3 to 1. Degrees conferred: J.D., J.D.-M.B.A., LL.M. (Comparative and International Law), J.S.D.

ADMISSION REQUIREMENTS. LSDAS Law School report, bachelor's degree transcript, LSAT, personal statement, two letters of recommendation required in support of application. TOEFL required for international applicants. Interview usually not required. Accepts transfer applicants. Apply to the Director of Admission for the School after September 1, before February 15. Application fee $55, after February 15, $70. Phone: (574)631-6626; fax: (574)631-3980. For LL.M., J.S.D.: apply by February 1; use LL.M. Credential Assembly Service of LSAC.

ADMISSION STANDARDS. Selective. Accepts approximately 18% of all students. Number of applicants 3507; number of acceptance 637; number enrolled 1753; LSAT (75% of students have a score at or above 163); GPA (75% of student have a GPA at or above 3.28). *U.S. News & World Report* ranking is 28th of all U.S. law schools.

FINANCIAL AID. Scholarships, fellowships, resident assistantships, Federal W/S, loans. Apply to the Financial Aid Office by February 15. Phone: (574)631-6626. Use FAFSA (School code: 001840). About 60% of students receive aid other than loans from School.

DEGREE REQUIREMENTS. For J.D.: satisfactory completion of three-year program. For LL.M., J.S.D.: at least 24 credit hours beyond the J.D.; thesis; for J.S.D. one year in full-time study and a final written/oral exam. For M.B.A., see Graduate School listing above.

Note: Academic year and summer program in London for J.D. candidates.

NOVA SOUTHEASTERN UNIVERSITY

Fort Lauderdale, Florida 33314-7721

Web site: www.nova.edu

Chartered 1964. Merged with Southeastern University of Health Sciences in 1994. Offers degree programs throughout United States and four foreign countries. CGS member. Coed. Private control. Special facilities: Family Center for Child Development, Institute for Marine and Coastal Studies, Institute for Social Services to Families, Center for Youth Policy. Library: 668,700 volumes, 8821 subscriptions. Total University enrollment: 26,300.

Tuition: per credit $500–$726, varies by program. On-campus housing for married and single graduate students. Average academic year housing costs: $7800 (including board), $7344–$14,676 for married students. Contact Director of Residential Life for both on- and off-campus housing information. Phone: (954) 262-7052.

Graduate Programs

Enrollment: full-time 2854, part-time 5610. Faculty: full-time 290, part-time 569. Degrees conferred: M.S., M.B.A., M.P.A., M.Acc., M.A., M.I.B.A., M.O.T., M.P.T., M.P.H., D.I.B.A., Sc.D., Psy.D., D.S., D.A., D.P.A., D.O.T., Ed.S., Ed.D., Ph.D., D.B.A., D.I.B.A.

ADMISSION REQUIREMENTS. Official transcripts, letters of recommendation required in support of application. Online application available. GRE Subject Tests, GMAT required for some programs. Accepts transfer applicants. Graduates of unaccredited institutions not considered. Apply to Office of Admissions for the program of interest, or the Registrar's Office. Closing date varies with the program; rolling admissions for most programs. Application fee $50. Phone: (800)541-6682.

ADMISSION STANDARDS. Selective. Usual minimum average: 3.0 (A = 4).

FINANCIAL AID. Scholarships, research fellowships, research assistantships, Federal W/S, loans. Approved for VA benefits. Apply to appropriate department for fellowships/assistantships; to Financial Aid Office for all other programs. Phone: (800)806-3680. Use FAFSA (University code: 001509). About 20% of students receive aid other than loans from both University and outside sources.

DEGREE REQUIREMENTS. For master's: generally 36–45 hours minimum, varies with program; thesis/nonthesis option. For Ed.S.: 36 hours beyond the master's. For doctorate: satisfactory completion of core instructional sequence, areas of specialization and research experiences; dissertation; final exam. Residence requirements: varies with program; Ph.D. and other doctoral programs typically require three to four years and 90 credits beyond baccalaureate.

FIELDS OF STUDY.

COLLEGE OF ALLIED HEALTH AND NURSING:
Health Science. M.H.S., D.H.S.
Nursing. M.S.N.
Occupational Therapy. M.O.T., Ph.D.
Physical Therapy. Ph.D.
Physician Assistant. M.M.S.

COLLEGE OF BIOMEDICAL SCIENCES:
Biomedical Sciences. M.B.S.

CRIMINAL JUSTICE INSTITUTE:
Child Protection. M.H.S.
Criminal Justice. M.S.

GRADUATE SCHOOL OF COMPUTER AND INFORMATION SCIENCES:
Computer Information Systems. M.S., Ph.D.
Computer Science. M.S., Ph.D.
Computing Technology in Education. M.S., Ed.D., Ph.D.
Information Security. M.S.
Management Information Systems. M.S.

H. WAYNE HUIZENGA GRADUATE SCHOOL OF BUSINESS
AND ENTREPRENEURSHIP:
Accounting. M.Acc., D.B.A.
Business Administration. M.B.A.
Entrepreneurship. M.B.A.
Finance. D.B.A.
Human Resource Management. M.S., D.B.A.
International Business. M.I.B.A., D.B.A.
Leadership. M.S.
Management. D.B.A.
Marketing. D.B.A.
Operations Management. D.B.A.
Public Administration. M.P.A., D.P.A.
Real Estate Development. M.B.A.
Taxation. M.T.

FISCHLER SCHOOL OF EDUCATION AND HUMAN SERVICES:
Bilingual Education. M.S.Ed.
Charter School Education/Leadership. M.S.Ed.
Child and Youth Care Administration. M.S.H.S.
Child, Youth, and Human Services. Includes curriculum development, early childhood, early literacy and reading, family systems and services, human services administration, special education/special education administration. Ed.D.
Cognitive and Behavioral Disabilities. M.S.Ed.
Computer Science Education. M.S.Ed., Ed.S.
Curriculum and Instruction. M.A.T.L., Ed.S.
Curriculum, Instruction, and Technology. M.S.Ed.
Early Childhood Education Administration. M.S.H.S.
Early Literacy Education. M.S.Ed., Ed.S.
Educational Leadership. M.S.Ed., Ed.S., Ed.D.
Educational Media. M.S.Ed., Ed.S.
Educational Technology. M.S.Ed.
Elementary Education. M.S.Ed., Ed.S.
Elementary Mathematics. M.A.T.L.
Elementary Reading. M.A.T.L.
English Education. M.S.Ed.
Environmental Education. M.S.Ed.
Exceptional Student Education. M.S.Ed.
Family Support Studies. M.S.H.S.
Gifted Child Education. M.S.Ed., Ed.S.
Health Care Education. Ed.D.
Higher Education Leadership. Includes adult education, health care education, higher educational leadership, organizational leadership. Ed.D.
Human Services Administration. Ed.D.
Instructional Technology and Distance Education. M.S., Ed.D.
Interdisciplinary Arts. M.S.Ed.
Jewish Education. M.S.Ed.
K–12 Technology Integration. M.A.T.L.
Leadership. M.S.
Literacy Education. M.S.Ed.
Management and Administration of Educational Programs. M.S.Ed.
Mathematics Education. M.S.Ed., Ed.S.
Organizational Leadership. Includes adult education leadership, community college leadership, conflict resolution, educational

leadership, health care education leadership, higher education leadership, international education, instructional technology, human resource development, nonprofit sector, service leadership, student affairs leadership in higher education. Ed.D.

Prekindergarten and Primary Education. M.S.Ed.
Reading Education. M.S.Ed.
Science Education. M.S.Ed.
Social Studies Education. M.S.Ed.
Spanish Language Education. M.S.Ed.
Special Education. Ed.D.
Speech-Language and Communication Disorders. S.L.P.D.
Speech-Language Pathology. M.S.
Substance Abuse Counseling and Education. M.S.

GRADUATE SCHOOL OF HUMANITIES AND SOCIAL SCIENCES:
College Student Affairs. M.S.
Conflict Analysis and Resolution. M.S., Ph.D.
Cross Disciplinary Studies. M.A.
Family Therapy. M.A., Ph.D., D.M.F.T.

OCEANOGRAPHIC CENTER:
Coastal Zone Management. M.S.
Marine Biology. M.S., Ph.D.
Marine Environmental Sciences. M.S.
Oceanography. Ph.D.

CENTER FOR PSYCHOLOGICAL STUDIES:
Clinical Psychology. Ph.D., Psy.D.
Mental Health Counseling. M.S.
Psychopharmacology. M.S.
School Guidance and Counseling. M.S.
School Psychology. Psy.S.

College of Dental Medicine

Established 1996. Located on main campus. Basic science courses are taught by both the College's and Medical Sciences' faculty. Postgraduate specialties: Endodontics, Orthodontics, Pediatric Dentistry, Periodontics.

Annual tuition: resident $37,585, nonresident $39,585. No on-campus housing available at this time. Contact Office of Residential Life for both on- and off-campus housing information. Phone: (954)262-7052. Off-campus housing, food, transportation, and personal expenses: approximately $21,000. Estimated additional first-year expense: $18,000. Enrollment: first-year class 95; total full-time 425. Faculty: full-time 76, part-time/volunteers 25. Degree conferred: D.M.D.

ADMISSION REQUIREMENTS. Preference given to state residents, U.S. citizens, and permanent residents only. The Junior College transfer credit is limited to 60 credits. For serious consideration, applicants should have at least a 2.5 GPA (A = 4). Will consider applicants with only three years of undergraduate preparation; prefer applicants who will have a bachelor's degree prior to enrollment. Apply through AADSAS (file after June 1, before March 1), send official transcripts (should show at least 90 semester credits/135 quarter credits), service processing fee; at the same time submit official DAT scores directly to the Office of Admission. TOEFL may be required of applicants whose native language is other than English. Submit the following materials only after being contacted by an Admissions Officer: an application fee of $50, a secondary/supplemental application, official transcripts, predental committee evaluation or two recommendations from science professors and one from a humanities professor to Office of Admission within two weeks of receipt of supplemental materials. Interviews are by invitation only and generally for final selection. First-year students admitted Fall only. Rolling admissions process; notification starts in December and is finished when class is filled, but generally no later than June 1. School does maintain an alternate/waiting list. Phone: (954)262-1108, (800)356-0026; fax: (954)916-2282.

ADMISSION STANDARDS. The College's first year was 1997; median DAT: Academic 18, PAT 18; median GPA: 3.31 (A = 4).

FINANCIAL AID. Limited number of scholarships, grants, institutional loans, State Loan Programs, DEAL, HEAL, alternative loan programs, loans, Military Service Commitment Scholarship programs. Institutional Financial Aid applications and information are generally available at the on-campus, by-invitation interview. Contact the Financial Aid Office for current information. Phone: (954)262-1114. Use FAFSA (School code: 001509); also submit Financial Aid Transcript, Federal Income Tax forms, and Federal Funds Certification.

DEGREE REQUIREMENTS. For D.M.D.: satisfactory completion of four-year program.

Shepard Broad Law Center (33314-7721)

Web site: www.nsulaw.nova.edu

Established 1974. ABA approved since 1975. AALS member. Private control. Semester system. Special facilities: Disability Law Institute, Center for the Study of Youth Policy. Library: 359,673 volumes, 5467 subscriptions; has LEXIS, NEXIS, WESTLAW, DIALOG, CALI.

Annual tuition: full-time $27,550, part-time $20,788. On-campus housing available. Total average annual additional expense: $17,346.

Enrollment: first-year class full-time 270, part-time 66; total full- and part-time 927 (men 55%, women 45%, minorities 41%). Faculty: full-time 46, part-time 62. Student to faculty ratio 16.2 to 1. Degrees conferred: J.D., J.D.-M.B.A., J.D.-M.S. (Computer Science, Dispute Resolution, Psychology), J.D.-M.U.R.P.

ADMISSION REQUIREMENTS. LSDAS Law School report, bachelor's degree, transcripts, LSAT, personal statement, résumé, required in support of application. Accepts transfer students. Apply to Office of Admissions by March 1. Rolling admissions process. Application fee $50. Phone: (954)262-6117; fax: (954) 262-3844.

ADMISSION STANDARDS. Selective. Accepts approximately 28% of full-time and 26% of part-time students. Number of full-time applicants 2442, part-time 371; number of full-time acceptances 680, part-time 95; number of full-time enrolled 270, part-time 66; LSAT (75% of full-time students have a score at or above 148, part-time 148); GPA (75% of full-time students have a GPA at or above 2.93, part-time 2.68). *U.S. News & World Report* ranking is in the fourth tier of all U.S. law schools.

FINANCIAL AID. Scholarships, grants, partial tuition waivers, assistantships, Federal W/S, loans. Apply to the Financial Aid Office by April 1. Phone: (954)262-7412. Use FAFSA (School code: 001509). About 19% of full-time students and 20% of part-time students receive some aid from School.

DEGREE REQUIREMENTS. For J.D.: satisfactory completion of 87 credit hour program. For master's degrees: see Graduate School listing above.

College of Osteopathic Medicine

Web site: medicine.nova.edu

Founded 1979. Private control. Located on main campus. Semester system. Library: 45,000 volumes, 600 subscriptions.

Annual tuition: resident $27,585, nonresident $33,995. No on-campus housing available. Off-campus housing is within two blocks of campus. Off-campus housing and personal expenses: approximately $10,500.

Enrollment: first-year class 236, total 883 (men 48%, women 52%, minorities 34%, state residents 50%). Faculty: full-time 94, part-time and volunteers 835. Degrees conferred: D.O., D.O.-M.B.A., D.O.-M.P.H.

ADMISSION REQUIREMENTS. AACOMAS report, bachelor's degree, official transcripts, MCAT (no later than the Spring of junior year), three recommendations (one from premed advisory committee, one evaluation from a physician, preferably a D.O.), supplemental form required in support of application. Interview by invitation only. Graduates of unaccredited colleges not considered. Preference given to state residents. Apply by March 1 to AACOMAS, April 1 (for supplemental materials) to the Director of Admissions. Rolling admissions process. Admits first year students Fall only. Application fee $50. Phone: (800)356-0026, ext. 1101, or (954)262-1101.

ADMISSION STANDARDS. Selective. Accepts about 24% of all applicants. Number of applications 2541 (2070 out-of-state); number interviewed 423 (165 out-of-state); number of acceptances 366 (131 out-of-state); number enrolled 236 (112 out-of-state). Usual minimum UGPA: 2.75 (A = 4). Mean Composite MCAT 8.5, mean UGPA 3.43.

FINANCIAL AID. Scholarships, fellowships, Federal W/S, loans. Apply by April 1 to the Financial Aid Office. Phone: (954)262-3380. Use FAFSA (College code: 001509) and institutional FAF. Approximately 90% of students receive some form of financial assistance.

DEGREE REQUIREMENT. For D.O.: satisfactory completion of four-year program. All students must take and pass the National Board of Osteopathic Medical Examination Parts I and II prior to the awarding of D.O.

OAKLAND UNIVERSITY
Rochester, Michigan 48309-4401
Web site: www.oakland.edu

Founded 1957. Located 25 miles N of Detroit. CGS member. Coed. State control. Trimester system. Special facilities: Eye Research Institute, Biochemistry and Biotechnology Institute, Center for Robotics and Advanced Automation, Cumulative Trauma Research Institute, Institute for Action Research, Michigan Center for Automotive Research, Public Affairs Research Laboratory, Meadow Brook Health Enhancement Institute. Library: 688,000 volumes, 2600 subscriptions. Total University enrollment: 17,300.

Tuition: per credit resident $383, nonresident $666. On-campus housing for graduate men and women, 48 units for married students. Average academic year housing costs: $6080 (including board) for single students; $6400 for married students. Contact Director, Residence Halls for both on- and off-campus housing information. Phone: (248)370-3570.

Graduate Studies

Enrollment: full-time 1209, part-time 2451. University faculty: full- and part-time 397. Degrees conferred: M.A., M.Ed., M.S., M.A.T., M.M., M.P.A., M.P.T., M.B.A., M.S.N., Ed.S., Ph.D.

ADMISSION REQUIREMENTS. Official transcripts, two recommendations required in support of application. GRE/GMAT required for some programs. Interview not required. Online application available. TOEFL and GRE required for international applicants. Accepts transfer applicants. Apply to Office of Admission by July 15 (Fall), November 20 (Winter), March 15 (Spring), May 15 (Summer). Application fee $30. Phone: (248)370-3167; fax: (248)370-4114; e-mail: gradmail@oakland.edu.

ADMISSION STANDARDS. Selective for some departments, competitive for others. Usual minimum average: 3.0 (A = 4).

FINANCIAL AID. Annual awards from institutional funds: fellowships, teaching assistantships, research assistantships, internships, full tuition waivers, Federal W/S, loans. Apply to appropriate department chairman by March 15. Use FAFSA and University's FAF. Phone: (248)370-3370. About 10% of students receive aid other than loans from University and outside sources. Aid available for part-time students.

DEGREE REQUIREMENTS. For master's: 36–45 semester hours minimum, at least 30 in residence; candidacy; thesis/non-thesis option. For Ed.S.: 30 semester hours beyond master's. For Ph.D.: 60 credits beyond the bachelor's minimum, at least one year in full-time residence; proficiency in at least one foreign language for some programs; qualifying exam; dissertation; final oral exam.

FIELDS OF STUDY.
Accounting. M.S.
Applied Mathematical Sciences. Ph.D.
Applied Statitics. M.S.
Biological Sciences. M.S., Ph.D.
Biology. M.S.
Biomedical Sciences. Includes health and environmental chemistry, medical physics. Ph.D.
Business Administration. M.B.A.
Cellular Biology. M.S., Ph.D.
Chemistry. M.S., Ph.D.
Computer Education. M.Ed.
Computer Science and Engineering. M.S.
Counseling. M.A.
Curriculum and Instruction. M.Ed.
Early Childhood Education. M.Ed.
Educational Leadership. M.Ed., Ed.S.
Electrical and Computer Engineering. M.S.
Engineering Management. M.S.
English. M.A.
Exercise Science. M.S.
History. M.A.
Industrial Applied Mathematics. M.S.
Information Systems Engineering. M.S.
Information Technology. M.S.
Liberal Studies. M.A.
Linguistics. M.A.
Management. M.S.
Mathematics. M.S., M.A.
Mechanical Engineering. M.S.
Music. M.M.
Nursing. M.S.N.
Physical Therapy. M.P.T.
Physics. M.S., Ph.D.
Public Administration. M.P.A.
Reading. Ph.D.
Reading and Language Arts. M.A.T.
School Administration. Ed.S.
Software Engineering. M.S.
Special Education. M.Ed.
Systems Engineering. M.S., Ph.D.
Training and Development. M.S.

OHIO NORTHERN UNIVERSITY
Ada, Ohio 45810-1599
Web site: www.onu.edu

Founded 1885. Located 85 miles SE of Toledo. Private control. Methodist affiliation. Semester system. Special facilities: Pharmacy Law Institute. Total University enrollment: 2900.

Claude W. Pettit College of Law

Established 1885. ABA approved since 1948. AALS member. Law Library: 378,086 volumes, 2296 subscriptions; has LEXIS, NEXIS, WESTLAW; has more than 200 network connections.

Annual tuition: $35,050. On-campus housing available. Total average annual additional expenses: $12,495.

Enrollment: first-year class 116; total 311 (men 53%, women 47%, minorities 10%); no part-time students. College faculty: full-time 15, part-time 10. Student-to-faculty ratio is 14.8 to 1. Degrees conferred: J.D., LL.M.(Democratic Governance).

ADMISSION REQUIREMENTS. LSDAS Law School report, bachelor's degree, transcripts, four character references, LSAT, personal statement, résumé required in support of application. TOEFL required for international applicants. Interview not required. Accepts transfer applicants. Graduates of unaccredited colleges not considered. Apply to Director of Admissions, preference given to applications received by March 15. Rolling admissions process. Admits first-year students in Fall only. Application fee $40. Phone: (877)452-9668; fax: (419)772-3402.

ADMISSION STANDARDS. Selective. Accepts approximately 27% of all students. Number of applicants 1553; number of acceptance 421; number enrolled 116; LSAT (75% of students have a score at or above 150); GPA (75% of students have a GPA at or above 3.15). *U.S. News & World Report* ranking is in the fourth tier of all U.S. law schools.

FINANCIAL AID. Scholarships, need-based grants, assistantships, Federal W/S, loans. Apply to Financial Aid Office by June 1. Phone: (419)772-2272. Use FAFSA (College code: 003089). About 40% of students receive aid other than loans from College.

DEGREE REQUIREMENTS. For J.D.: satisfactory completion of required 87 semester hour program. For LL.M.: 24 credit full-time program.
Note: Exchange program with the University of Iceland.

THE OHIO STATE UNIVERSITY
Columbus, Ohio 43210-1270
Web site: www.osu.edu

Established 1870. CGS and AAU member. Coed. State control. Quarter system. Special facilities: Advanced Computing Center for the Arts and Design, Center for Advanced Study in Telecommunication, Atmospheric Sciences Program, Ohio State Biochemistry Program, Laboratory for Artificial Intelligence Research, Biomedical Engineering Center, Biostatistics Program, Byrd Polar Research Center, Campus Chemical Instrument Center, Chemical Physics Program, Center for Cognitive Science, Criminal Justice Research Center, Electroscience Laboratory, Engineering Research Center for Net Shape Manufacturing, Environmental Biology Program, Center for Human Resource Research, International Area Studies, Center for Lake Erie Area Research, Center for Mapping, Center for Materials Research, Center for Medieval and Renaissance Studies, Mershon Center for Research and Education in National Security and Public Policy, Molecular, Cellular, and Developmental Biology Program, National Regulatory Research Institute, OSU Comprehensive Cancer Center, OSU Nisonger Center for Mental Retardation and Developmental Disabilities, Ohio Supercomputer Center, Physiological Optics Program, Slavic and East European Studies Program, Comprehensive Program in Vocational Education, Water Resources Center. The University's NIH ranking is 54th among all U.S. institutions with 374 awards/grants valued at $121,398,233. According to The Center at University of Florida, the University is ranked 38th in receipt of Federal Research funds with $198,488,000 and it ranks 13th for total University research expenditures with $496,438,000.

The University's endowment assets rank it 27th, with a value of $1,541,175,000. In 2004, the University awarded 561 doctorates, which ranked it 13th among all U.S. institutions eligible to award that degree. Forty-nine of the University's faculty members have been elected to National Honor Academies and this ranks it 18th among all U.S. institutions. The Library: approximately 5,400,000 volumes, 42,700 subscriptions. Total University enrollment: 58,300.

Annual tuition: full-time resident $9972, nonresident $24,126. On-campus housing for 396 married students, 890 single students. Average annual housing cost: $12,100 (including board) for single students. Apply to the Office of Contracts and Assignments. Phone: (614)292-8266.

Graduate School

Graduate study since 1878. Enrollment; full-time 7200, part-time 2500. Graduate faculty: 2877. Degrees conferred: M.Appl.Stat., M.Arch., M.A., M.B.A., M.C.R.P., M.Ed., M.F.A., M.H.A., M.L.H.R., M.Land.Arch., M.Mus., M.O.T., M.P.A., M.P.H., M.S., M.S.W., D.M.A., Ph.D., Cert.Sp'l., Edu'l.Adm., Cert.Sp'l. (Latin American Studies), Cert.Sp'l. (Russian Area Studies), Cert.Sp'l. (Medieval and Renaissance Studies).

ADMISSION REQUIREMENTS. Transcripts, three letters of recommendation, statement of intent, vitae/résumé required in support of School's application. Additional items may be required by individual departments. GRE Subject Tests for most departments. GMAT required for some departments. Interview required by some departments. Evidence of proficiency in English required of international applicants TOEFL (minimum score 550). Accepts transfer applicants. Graduates of unaccredited institutions not considered. Apply online by August 15 (Autumn), December 1 (Winter), March 1 (Spring), May 15 (Summer); prior to January 15 if a fellowship applicant. Earlier dates established by individual departments. Application fee $40; international applicants $50. Phone: (614)292-9444; fax: (614)292-3895; e-mail: admissions@osu.edu.

ADMISSION STANDARDS. Very competitive for some departments, competitive for the others. Minimum average required (unless otherwise specified by individual graduate program): 3.0 (A = 4).

FINANCIAL AID. Annual awards from institutional funds: fellowships, research associateships, administrative associateships, teaching associateships, internships, Federal W/S, loans. Apply before January 15 (prior to the intended academic year of enrollment) to Admissions Office for fellowships; by April 1 to appropriate department chair for associateships; to Office of Financial Aid for all other programs. Phone: (800)678-6440 (outside 614 area code); (614)292-0300; fax: (614) 292-9264. Use FAFSA. About 47% of students receive aid other than loans from institution and outside sources. Aid available to part-time students.

DEGREE REQUIREMENTS. For master's: 45 quarter hours minimum, at least 36 in residence; either a thesis and an oral and/or written exam or a four-hour written comprehensive exam which may include an oral portion. For Ph.D.: 135 quarter hours minimum beyond the bachelor's degree, a minimum of 90 credits in residence; a minimum of three out of four consecutive quarters in full-time study; foreign language requirement for some departments; general comprehensive exam; candidacy exam; dissertation; final oral exam. For D.M.A.: essentially the same as for Ph.D., except a D.M.A. document and performance for some areas.

FIELDS OF STUDY.
Accounting. M.Acc.
Accounting and Management Information Systems. GMAT and additional requirements for admission; contact department for additional materials. Ph.D.

Aeronautical and Astronautical Engineering. GRE required for admission, additional department materials required; contact department. Admits primarily for Autumn quarter, apply by January 15. M.S., Ph.D.

African American and African Studies.

Agricultural and Extension Education. M.Ed., M.S., Ph.D.

Agricultural, Environmental, and Developmental Economics. GRE or GMAT required for admission, GRE required for fellowship applicants.

Agricultural Engineering. GRE Subject Test strongly recommended. Fifty-hour M.S., if nonthesis.

Allied Medical Professions. GRE required for all applicants whose GPA is below 3.5. Health professions certification, registration, or licensure required. M.S. only.

Anatomy. GRE Subject Test in Biology required for admission. M.S., Ph.D.

Animal Science. GRE required for admission. Thesis for M.S. M.S., Ph.D.

Anthropology. GRE required for admission. Prefer Autumn quarter applicants.

Architecture. Admits Autumn quarter only. Applicants for three-year plus (90 hour) program admitted Summer quarter. GRE, portfolio required for admission. Thesis (45 hour program)/nonthesis (50 hours).

Art. Admits Autumn quarter only. Application completed by January 20. For additional admission requirements contact department. 90-hour program; public exhibition of studio work, thesis.

Art Education. Apply by April 5 (Autumn), January 5 (Summer). GRE for fellowship applicants and Art Administration. For additional admissions requirements contact department. 60- or 70-hour master's; thesis.

Arts Policy and Administration.

Astronomy. Admits Summer and Autumn quarters only; apply by January 15. GRE Subject Test in Physics for admission. Thesis required. M.S., Pd.D.

Atmospheric Sciences. Autumn quarter preferred. Apply by February 1 for associateships. GRE required for admission; thesis required for M.S. M.S., Ph.D.

Audiology. Au.D.

Biochemistry Program (OSBP). Autumn quarter applications strongly recommended; apply by February 1. GRE required for admission. Thesis for M.S. M.S., Ph.D.

Biomedical Engineering. GRE required for admission; thesis required for M.S. Statement of purpose, title and abstract of master's thesis for Ph.D.; M.S., Ph.D.

Biophysics. GRE recommended for all applicants, required if GPA is below 3.0. M.S., Ph.D.

Biostatistics. GRE required for admission; Summer quarter applications strongly recommended; January 15 deadline for fellowship consideration. Ph.D. only.

Business Administration. Admits Autumn quarter only. GMAT for admission, except for organizational behavior, GRE may be substituted; 104-hour full-time M.B.A. program. M.B.A. applicants apply by March 1, February 1 for Financial Aid; Ph.D. applicants apply by February 1. M.B.A., Ph.D.

Business Logistic Engineering. GRE or GMAT for admission. M.B.L.E.

Chemical Engineering. GRE recommended for all applicants and required of graduates of foreign universities, holders of non-engineering degrees and applicants whose GPA is below 3.0; thesis required for M.S. M.S., Ph.D.

Chemical Physics. Summer and Fall quarters preferred. GRE Subject Test in Physics or Chemistry required of graduates of foreign universities and highly recommended for all other applicants, particularly if GPA is below 3.0. M.S., Ph.D.

Chemistry. Admits Summer (international applicants preferred) and Autumn (domestic applicants preferred). Apply by February 1. GRE Subject Test in Chemistry required. M.S., Ph.D.

City and Regional Planning. GRE for master's applicants with GPA below 3.0 and all Ph.D.s and fellowship applicants. 90 hours for M.C.R.P. M.C.R.P., Ph.D.

Civil Engineering. No Summer quarter admission. GRE required of all applicants with undergraduate GPA below 2.7 and of applicants with graduate GPA below 3.0, of nonengineering majors, of fellowship applicants and of engineering graduates from non-ABET-accredited or non-CAB-accredited institutions. GPA of 3.6 of fellowships. M.S., Ph.D.

Communication. Admits Autumn quarter only. Apply by May 15, by March 1 for associateships consideration. GRE required for admission. Contact department for additional requirements. 50 hours for M.A. M.A., Ph.D.

Comparative Studies. Apply by April 1 (Summer and Autumn quarter), January 1 (for financial aid consideration), November 1 (Winter), January 15 (Spring). GRE required for admission. 50 hours for M.A. M.A. only.

Computer and Information Science. Admits Autumn quarter only. GRE Subject Test required for admission. M.S., Ph.D.

Dance. Admits Autumn quarter only. Qualifying audition required for admission. 90 hours for M.F.A.; M.A., M.F.A.

Dance Studies. GRE for admission. Ph.D.

Dentistry. Admits Summer quarter only. Apply by October 1. GRE; D.D.S. or D.M.D. required for admission, except those wanting dental materials or oral biology. Thesis required. M.S. only.

East Asian Languages and Literature. No Summer quarter admission; prefer Autumn quarter. Apply by February 15, prefer earlier submission. GRE for financial aid consideration and if GPA is less than 3.0. 65 hours for M.A. M.A., Ph.D.

Economics. Admits Autumn quarter only. Apply by February 15 for priority financial aid consideration. GRE required for admission; Subject Test in Economics recommended. M.A., Ph.D.

Education. No Summer quarter admission. GRE/MAT required for most programs. Includes educational policy and leadership, educational services and research, educational studies, teaching and learning. Contact the School of Education for specific program listing for requirements and contact information. M.Ed., M.A., Ph.D., Certificate of Specialist in Education Administration.

Electrical and Computer Engineering. GRE required of M.S. applicants and if GPA is less than 3.0, and of all graduates of foreign universities. Ph.D. applicants should submit thesis or thesis abstract (in English) and letter of recommendation from thesis adviser. 50 hours required for nonthesis M.S. M.S. Ph.D.

English. Admits Autumn quarter only. Apply by January 15. GRE, sample of critical writing required of M.A., Ph.D. applicants; subject test recommended. 50 hours for M.A. 65 hours for M.F.A. M.A., M.F.A., Ph.D.

Entomology. GRE Subject Test in Biology, curriculum vitae required for admission. M.S., Ph.D.

Environmental Science. Admits Autumn quarter only. Apply by May 1 (preferably by March 1), February 15 for financial aid consideration. GRE required for admission. Contact department for additional application materials. M.S., Ph.D.

Evaluation, Ecology, and Organismal Biology.

Family Resource Management. GRE required for admission. M.S., Ph.D.

Food, Agricultural, and Biological Engineering.

Food Science and Nutrition. GRE required for admission. 50 hours required for nonthesis M.S. M.S., Ph.D.

French and Italian. Admits Autumn quarter only. Apply by February 15 for associateships consideration. GRE required for all applicants with degrees from American universities. Scholarly paper required for Ph.D. applicants. M.A., Ph.D.

Geodetic Science and Surveying. Autumn quarter preferred; Summer quarter if prerequisites required. Mathematics through differential and integral calculus required for admission; one course in linear algebra and knowledge of computer programs recommended. M.S., Ph.D.

Geography. Autumn quarter admission preferred. GRE required for admission. Statement of purpose for Ph.D. applicants; contact department for details. M.A., Ph.D.

Geological Sciences. GRE Subject Test in Geology or allied science in undergraduate area of study required for admission; thesis required for M.S. M.S., Ph.D.

German Languages and Literature. Autumn quarter strongly recommended. Apply by January 15 for priority consideration. GRE required for admission. M.A., Ph.D.

Greek and Latin. GRE for admission. M.A., Ph.D.

Health Services Management and Policy. Admits Autumn quarter only. Apply by March 15 for priority consideration. GRE/GMAT required for admission. Contact department for additional admission materials. 84 hours for M.H.A. M.H.A. only.

History. Admits Summer and Autumn quarter only. Apply by January 10. GRE required for all U.S. citizens. Sample of written work required. M.A., Ph.D.

History of Art. Admits Summer and Autumn quarters only. Apply by January 15 for associateship or fellowship consideration. GRE, writing sample required for admission. 50-hour nonthesis option for M.A. M.A., Ph.D.

Horticulture and Crop Science. GRE required for admission. M.S., Ph.D.

Hospitality Management. GRE or GMAT for admission. M.S., Ph.D.

Human and Community Resource Development. Includes family relations and human development, family resource management, home economics education, human nutrition and food management, and textiles and clothing. Contact School of Human Ecology for specific admission requirements. M.S., Ph.D.

Human Nutrition and Food Management. GRE required for admission. M.S., Ph.D.

Industrial and System Engineering. Admits Autumn quarter only. Apply by March 1; February 1 for financial aid consideration. GRE required for admission. M.S., Ph.D.

Industrial, Interior, and Visual Communication Design. Admits Autumn only. Apply by April 15. Portfolio of recent academic or professional visual work required. Contact department for additional admission requirements. 60-hour nonthesis option for M.A. M.A. only.

Labor and Human Resources. Admits Ph.D. applicants to Autumn quarter only; apply by February 1. Apply for M.L.H.R. by July 1 (Autumn), October 1 (Winter), February 1 (Spring), April 1 (Summer). GRE/GMAT required for admission. 50 hour nonthesis option for M.L.H.R. M.L.H.R., Ph.D.

Landscape Architecture. Prefer applicants for Autumn quarter. Apply by March 31. Applicants with landscape architecture or allied field may apply for Winter or Spring quarter. GRE, portfolio, statement of intent required for admission. Contact department for additional admission requirements. M.Land, Arch. only.

Linguistics. Admits Autumn quarter only. Apply by December 15. GRE required for admission. M.A., Ph.D.

Materials Science and Engineering. GRE required for graduates of foreign universities and of holders of nonengineering degrees. M.S., Ph.D.

Mathematics. Prefer applicants for Summer quarter. GRE Subject Test in mathematics required for admission. Contact department for additional admission requirements. 51 hours for M.A.; writing project. 50-hour nonthesis M.S. M.A., M.S., Ph.D.

Mechanical Engineering. Apply by July 1 (Autumn), November 1 (Winter), February 1 (Spring), May 1 (Summer); January 1 for associateship consideration. GRE required for M.S. applicants with below 3.3 GPA. M.S. applicants who hold nonengineering baccalaureate or degrees from a foreign university; all doctoral applicants with GPA below 3.7, applicants with a master's degree from a foreign university, and fellowships applicants. M.S., Ph.D.

Medical Science. M.D. or D.O. for admission. M.S. only.

Microbiology. Autumn quarter application strongly recommended. Apply by February 1. GRE required for admission. Subject Test in Biology or Biochemistry recommended. 60-hour nonthesis M.S. option. M.S., Ph.D.

Molecular, Cellular, and Developmental Biology. Prefer Autumn quarter applicants. GRE/Subject Test (Biology, Chemistry, or Biochemistry, Cell and Molecular Biology preferred) required for admission. Thesis required for M.S. M.S., Ph.D.

Molecular Genetics. Includes genetics. GRE Subject Test (Biology or Biochemistry, Cell and Molecular Biology) required for admission. Thesis required for M.S. M.S., Ph.D.

Music. GRE required for M.A., Ph.D. applicants in music education, music history and music theory; and for M.Mus. D.M.A. in music composition. Contact department for additional requirements. 50-hour nonthesis M.A. option. 45 hours for M.Mus., plus tape-recorded recital. M.A., M.Mus., D.M.A., Ph.D.

Natural Resources. Apply by February 15. GRE required for admission. 55-hour nonthesis M.S. option. M.S. only.

Near Eastern Languages and Literature. GRE recommended. M.A. only.

Neuroscience. GRE/Subject Test (Biology, Psychology, Biochemistry, Cell and Molecular Biology) required for admission. Contact department for statement of purpose guidelines. Ph.D. only.

Nuclear Engineering. GRE required for admission. 50-hour nonthesis M.S. option, plus written task report. M.S., Ph.D.

Nursing. Admits M.S. May 1 (Autumn), November 1 (Winter), February 1 (Spring). Admits Ph.D. January 15 (Autumn only). GRE required for admission. Applicants must hold or be eligible for licensure as an RN in Ohio. Contact department for additional admission requirements. 52-hour nonthesis M.S. option. M.S., Ph.D.

Occupational Therapy. Admits Summer only. GRE for admission. M.O.T.

Oral Biology. Admits Autumn quarter only. GRE required for admission. Ph.D. only

Pathology. GRE Subject (Biology, Cell, and Molecular Biology required for admission. Contact department for additional admission requirements. Thesis required M.S. M.S., Ph.D.

Pharmacology. Admits Autumn quarter only. GRE Subject (Biology or Chemistry, Cell and Molecular) required for admission. MCAT scores in lieu of GRE for M.D.-Ph.D. applicants. M.S., Ph.D.

Pharmacy. Includes pharmaceutical administration (admits Autumn quarter only, GRE or GMAT for applicants with GPA below 3.0), pharmacology (GRE for admission), pharmaceutical chemistry (GRE for admission), medicinal chemistry and Pharmacognosy (GRE for admission). M.S., Ph.D.

Philosophy. Autumn quarter strongly recommended. Apply by February 1 for priority consideration. GRE, sample of work required for admission. M.A., Ph.D.

Physical Therapy. Admits Summer only. GRE for admission. D.P.T.

Physics. Admits Summer and Autumn quarters; Summer preferred. GRE Subject Test in Physics required for admission. 50 hour nonthesis M.S. option. M.S., Ph.D.

Plant, Cellular and Molecular Biology. Apply by March 15 for associateship consideration. GRE Subject Test in Biology required for admission. TOEFL, TSE required for applicants whose native language is not English. 55-hour nonthesis M.S. option. M.S., Ph.D.

Plant Pathology. GRE required for admission. M.S., Ph.D.

Political Science. Admits Autumn quarter only. Apply by March 1; January 1 for fellowships consideration. GRE required for admission. M.A., Ph.D.

Psychology. Admits Autumn quarter only. Apply by February 1; January 1 for fellowship consideration. GRE Subject Test in Psychology required for admission. Contact department for additional admission requirements. Thesis required for M.A. M.A., Ph.D.

Public Health. GRE, GMAT, or MCAT for admission; admits Fall only. M.P.H., M.S., Ph.D.

Public Policy and Management. Autumn quarter applicants preferred. GRE/GMAT (all M.P.A. applicants), GRE/GMAT (M.A. applicants with GPA below 2.7), GRE (for all Ph.D. applicants) required for admission. 50 hours for M.A., 74 hours for M.P.A. M.A., M.P.A., Ph.D.

Rural Sociology. GRE or GMAT for admission. M.S., Ph.D.

Slavic and East European Languages and Literature. Autumn quarter applicants preferred. GRE required for admission. M.A., Ph.D.

Slavic and East European Studies. GRE recommend for admission. 50 hour M.A. M.A. only.

Social Work. Admits M.S.W. Autumn and Summer quarters; Ph.D. Autumn quarter only (apply by April 1). Contact programs for additional admission requirements. 90 hours for M.S.W.; 60 hours for M.S.W. for applicants with advance standing available. M.S.W., Ph.D.

Sociology. Admits Autumn quarter only. Apply by March 1 for associateship consideration. GRE required for admission. Contact department for additional admissions requirements. Thesis required for M.A. M.A., Ph.D.

Soil Science.

Spanish and Portuguese. Autumn Quarter application strongly recommended. Apply by March 1 for associateship consideration. GRE (for all graduates from U.S. and Canadian Universities), TSE (for all applicants required to take TOEFL/MELAB; minimum score 230 for teaching associateships), tape recordings (for all nonnative Spanish speakers); telephone interview, scholarly paper required for Ph.D. applicants. M.A., Ph.D.

Speech and Hearing Science. Admits M.A. Autumn quarter only; Ph.D. all quarters. Apply by January 15 for financial aid consideration. GRE required for admission. 57-hour nonthesis M.A. option. M.A., Ph.D.

Speech-Language Pathology. Admits Fall only. GRE for admission. M.A.

Statistics. Summer quarter strongly recommended. Apply by January 15 for fellowship consideration. GRE required for admission. 50 hours for M.Appl.Stat. M.Appl.Stat., M.S., Ph.D.

Textiles and Clothing. Admits Autumn quarter only. Apply by February 1. GRE required for admission. Contact program for statement of purpose guidelines. 50-hour nonthesis M.S. option. M.S., Ph.D.

Theater. Admits mainly Autumn and Winter quarters for M.A., Ph.D. programs. Apply by January 1 (fellowship consideration), February 15 (associateships); April 15 (M.F.A. acting and design associateships). Acting program accepting for Autumn 1996, 1997. GRE required for M.A., Ph.D. applicants; audition for M.F.A.(acting), portfolio (design). Thesis required for M.A.; M.F.A. in design. 99 hours for M.F.A. M.A., M.F.A., Ph.D.

Veterinary Biosciences. D.V.M. or equivalent required. GRE required for applicants with GPA below 3.0 (unless they have a completed master's degree at time of evaluation) and of all graduates of foreign universities. Thesis required for M.S. M.S., Ph.D.

Veterinary Clinical Sciences. D.V.M. or equivalent required. Most applicants admitted through AAVC's Residency MATCH Program. Contact program for admission procedures. GRE required of all graduates of foreign universities and to theriogenology and equine exercise physiology. Thesis required for M.S. M.S., Ph.D.

Veterinary Preventive Medicine. D.V.M. or equivalent required. GRE required of all graduates of non-AVMA-accredited veterinary colleges. Thesis required for M.S. M.S., Ph.D.

Vision Science. GRE for admission. M.S., Ph.D.

Welding Engineering. GRE Subject Test in Engineering required for applicants with GPA below 2.7. M.S., Ph.D.

Women's Studies. Admits Autumn quarter only. Apply by January 15. GPA of 3.0 and at least four women's studies courses required for admission. Duplicate copies of all application materials must be sent to program. M.A. only.

College of Dentistry

Web site: www.dent.ohio-state.edul

Organized 1890. Joined Ohio State University in 1914. Quarter system.

Annual tuition: resident $24,663, nonresident $53,724. On-campus housing available for both married and single students.

For off-campus housing contact the Office of Off-campus Student Services. Average academic year housing cost: $14,184. Total average cost for all other first-year expenses. $6400.

Enrollment: first-year class 104, total 420 (men 70%, women 30%, minorities 15%, state residents 75%). Faculty: full- and part-time 400. Degrees conferred: B.A., B.S.-D.D.S. (Ohio State University undergraduates only), D.D.S., D.D.S.-M.S., D.D.S.-Ph.D. The M.S. and Ph.D. are offered through the Graduate School.

ADMISSION REQUIREMENTS. AADSAS, transcripts, DAT (not later than October) required in support of application. Interview by invitation only. Accepts transfer applicants. Applicants must have completed at least two years of college study. Preference given to state residents. Apply to Director of Admissions after June 1, before September 15. Application fee $60, $70 for international applicants. Phone: (614)292-3361; fax: (614)292-0813.

ADMISSION STANDARDS. Competitive. Accepts about 21% of all applicants. Number of applications 1110 (875 out-of-state); number interviewed n/a (n/a out-of-state); number of acceptances n/a (n/a out-of-state); number enrolled 102 (26 out-of-state). Usual minimum UGPA: 3.0 (A = 4). Mean DAT: academic 19, PAT 18.98; mean UGPA 3.52.

FINANCIAL AID. Scholarships, grants, loans. Apply to University's Financial Aid Office after acceptance, before July 1. Phone: (614)292-7768. Use FAFSA (School code: 003090). About 91% of students receive some aid from College-controlled and outside sources.

DEGREE REQUIREMENTS. For D.D.S.-B.A./B.S.: satisfactory completion of seven-year program. For D.D.S.: satisfactory completion of forty-five-month program. For M.S., see Graduate School listing above.

FIELDS OF POSTGRADUATE STUDY.
Anesthesiology. M.S., Certificate.
Dental Materials. M.S., Certificate.
Endodontics. M.S., Certificate.
General Practice Residency. M.S., Certificate.
Oral Pathology. M.S., Certificate.
Oral and Maxillofacial Surgery. M.S., Certificate.
Oral Biology. Includes research in biomaterials, cellular and molecular biology, hard tissue, immunology and inflammation, and neuroscience. Ph.D.
Orthodontics. M.S., Certificate.
Pediatric Dentistry. M.S., Certificate.
Periodontics. M.S., Certificate.
Prosthodontics. M.S., Certificate.

Michael E. Moritz College of Law

Web site: www.moritzlaw.osu.edu

Established 1891. ABA approved since 1923. AALS member. Public control. Semester system. Special facilities: Comprehensive National Resource Center, Kirwan Institute, Center for Interdisciplinary Law and Policy Studies. Law Library: 789,615 volumes, 7876 subscriptions; has LEXIS, NEXIS, WESTLAW, DIALOG.

Annual tuition: full-time resident $17,551, nonresident $31,969. On-campus housing available for married and single students. Total average annual additional expenses: $16,694.

Enrollment: first-year class 217; total 688 (men 57%, women 43%, minorities 23%); no part-time students. College faculty: full-time 51, part-time 27. Student-to-faculty ratio is 14.1 to 1. Degrees conferred: J.D., J.D.-M.A., J.D.-M.B.A., J.D.-M.H.A., J.D.-M.P.A., J.D. –M.P.H., LL.M. (for foreign educated lawyers only).

ADMISSION REQUIREMENTS. LSDAS Law School report, bachelor's degree, transcripts, writing sample, two letters of recommendation, résumé, LSAT (not later than February) required in support of application. Interview required for final selection. Accepts transfer applicants. Graduates of unaccredited institutions not considered. Apply to Director of Admissions after October, before March 1. Admits first-year students Fall only. Application fee $60. Phone: (614)292-8810; fax: (614)292-1492; e-mail: lawadmit@osu.edu.

ADMISSION STANDARDS. Selective. Accepts approximately 28% of all students. Number of applicants 2282; number of acceptances 629; number enrolled 217; LSAT (75% of students have a score at or above 158); GPA (75% of students have a GPA at or above 3.33). *U.S. News & World Report* ranking is 33rd of all U.S. law schools.

FINANCIAL AID. Scholarships, grants, Federal W/S, loans. Apply to the Financial Aid Office by March 1. Phone: (614)292-8807. Use FAFSA (College code: 003090). About 75% of students receive aid other than loans from College.

DEGREE REQUIREMENTS. For J.D.: 88 semester hours minimum, three years in residence. For LL.M.: 24-credit full-time, one-year program.
Note: Has summer programs with Oxford University (Great Britain).

College of Medicine (43210-1238)
Web site: medicine.osu.edu

Established 1914. Started as Starling–Ohio Medical College. Library: 200,000 volumes, 2899 subscriptions. NIH ranking is 54th among all U.S. institutions with 374 awards/grants worth $121,398,233.

Annual tuition: resident $27,225, nonresident $41,643. Limited on-campus housing available. Off-campus housing available within walking distance of campus. Total average figure for all other expenses: $15,760.

Enrollment: first-year class 210, total 832 (men 61%, women 39%, minorities 30%, state residents 87%). Degrees conferred: M.D., M.D.-M.B.A., M.D.-M.H.A., M.D.-M.P.H., M.D.-Ph.D.

ADMISSION REQUIREMENTS. For M.D. program: AMCAS report, transcripts, letters of recommendation, bachelor's degree, MCAT, interview required in support of application. Has EDP; apply between June 1 and August 1. Accepts transfer applicants. Preference given to Ohio residents. Apply to AMCAS after June 1, before December 1. Application fee $60. Phone: (614)292-7137; fax: (614)247-7959.

ADMISSION STANDARDS. Competitive. Accepts about 9% of all applicants. Number of applications 4180 (3159 out-of-state); number interviewed 665 (407 out-of-state); number of acceptances 400 (217 out-of-state); number enrolled 210 (91 out-of-state). Mean Composite MCAT 10.8; mean UGPA 3.72. *U.S. News & World Report* ranking is in the top 31 of all U.S. medical research schools, 38th in primary care.

FINANCIAL AID. Scholarships, assistantships, grants, Federal and private loans. About 87% of students receive aid other than loans from College. Apply to the Office of Financial Aid. Phone: (614)688-4955. Use FAFSA.

DEGREE REQUIREMENTS. For M.D.: satisfactory completion of four-year program. All students must pass USMLE Step 1 prior to entering third year; all students must pass USMLE Step 2 prior to awarding of M.D.

FIELDS OF GRADUATE STUDY.
Anatomy.
Biochemistry.
Biomedical Engineering.

Biostatistics.
Environmental Health Science.
Epidemiology.
Health Behavior and Health Promotion.
Health Services Management and Policy.
Integrated Biomedical Science.
Molecular, Cellular, and Development Biology.
Neuroscience.

College of Veterinary Medicine
Web site: www.vet.ohio-state.edu

Established 1885. Third oldest veterinary college. Quarter system. Special facilities: Center for Retrovirus Research, Comprehensive Cancer Center, Galbreath Equine Trauma, Intensive Care and Research Center.

Annual tuition: residents $17,585, nonresidents $53,583. On-campus housing available. Total average expenses for both on- and off-campus housing: $17,500. Total average cost for other expenses: $5000.

Enrollment: first-year class 140, total 670 (men 22%, women 78%, minorities 6%, state residents 78%), postgraduate 100. Faculty: full-time 105, part-time 2. Degrees conferred: D.V.M., D.V.M.-M.P.H., D.V.M.-M.S., D.V.M.-Ph.D. The M.S. and Ph.D. are offered through the Graduate School.

ADMISSION REQUIREMENTS. VMCAS report, transcripts, MCAT or GRE, two recommendations, animal/veterinary experience, required in support of application. Interview by invitation only. Preference given to state and contract state residents. Applicants must have completed at least 101 quarter hours of college study. Accepts transfer applicants on a space-available basis. Apply to Chairperson, Admissions Committee, by October 1. Application fee $40, $50 for international applicants. Phone: (614) 292-1171; fax: (614)262-6989.

ADMISSION STANDARDS. Selective. Accepts about 15–20% of all applicants. Number of applications n/a (n/a out-of-state); number interviewed n/a (n/a out-of-state); number of acceptance n/a (n/a out-of-state); number enrolled 140 (35 out-of-state, 5 West Virginia contract residents). Usual minimum UGPA: 3.0 (residents), 3.4 (nonresidents) (A = 4). GRE mean score (V + Q) 1150; mean UGPA 3.66.

FINANCIAL AID. Scholarships, grants, fellowships, assistantships, Federal W/S, loans. Apply to Financial Aid Officer of the College after acceptance, before March 15. About 50% of students receive aid other than loans from College. Aid available to part-time students.

DEGREE REQUIREMENTS. For D.V.M.: satisfactory completion of four-year program. For M.S., Ph.D.: successful completion of first year of veterinary curriculum required for consideration; see Graduate School listing above.

FIELDS OF GRADUATE STUDY.
Anesthesiology.
Cellular and Molecular Biology.
Clinical Pharmacology.
Equine Medicine and Surgery.
Food Animal Medicine and Surgery.
Integrated Biomedical Sciences. Interdisciplinary.
Microbiology and Immunology.
Molecular, Cellular, and Developmental Biology. Interdisciplinary.
Neuroscience. Interdisciplinary.
Nutrition.
Oncology.
Pathophysiology and Pharmacology.
Radiology.
Small Animal Medicine.
Small Animal Surgery.

Theriogenology.
Veterinary Medicine.
Veterinary Public Health. M.P.H.

OHIO UNIVERSITY

Athens, Ohio 45701
Web site: www.ohiou.edu

Chartered 1804. Located 76 miles SE of Columbus. CGS member. Coed. State control. Quarter system. Library: 2,800,000 volumes, 20,800 subscriptions. Total University enrollment: 20,400.

Annual tuition: full-time, resident $7605, nonresident $15,597; per credit resident, $314, nonresident, $645. Limited on-campus housing for married and single graduate students. Average annual housing cost: $8200 (12 months, room only) for married students; $8900 (12 months) for single students. Phone: (740)593-4090. Day-care facilities available.

Graduate College

Graduate study since 1950. Enrollment: full-time 2250, part-time 723. University faculty: full-time 718, part-time 99. Degrees conferred: M.A., M.S., M.S.S., M.M., M.B.A., M.Ed., M.F.A., M.H.S.A., M.P.A., M.P.T., M.S.A., Ph.D.

ADMISSION REQUIREMENTS. Transcripts required in support of School's application. GRE Subject Tests, MAT, GMAT, interview required for some departments. Online application available. TOEFL required for international applicants; TSE required by some departments. Accepts transfer applicants. Graduates of unaccredited institutions not considered. Apply to Office of Graduate Student Services at least six weeks prior to registration; international application at least six months prior to registration. Application fee $45. Phone: (740)593-2800; fax: (740)593-4625.

ADMISSION STANDARDS. Relatively open for many departments, competitive or very competitive for the others. Usual minimum GPA: 2.75 (A = 4).

FINANCIAL AID. Scholarships, research assistantships, teaching assistantships, internships, grants, tuition waivers, Federal W/S, loans. Approved for VA benefits. Apply to the individual departmental Graduate Committee chairman for scholarships, assistantships; to the Financial Aid Office for all other programs. Phone: (740)593-4141; fax: (740)593-4140. Use FAFSA. About 50% of students receive aid other than loans from College and outside sources.

DEGREE REQUIREMENTS. For master's: 45–60 quarter hours minimum; thesis; final oral exam; nonthesis option in some departments. For M.B.A.: 90 quarter hours minimum. For Ph.D.: 9 quarters minimum beyond the bachelor's, at least 3 quarters in full-time residence; comprehensive exam; scholarly disciplines are determined by department; dissertation; final oral exam.

FIELDS OF STUDY.

COLLEGE OF ARTS AND SCIENCES:
Biological Sciences. Includes biology, microbiology, neurobiology.
Chemistry. Includes analytical, biological, inorganic, organic, physical.
Economics. M.A. only.
English Language and Literature.
Environmental Plant Biology. Includes biochemistry, cell biology, ecology, ethnobotany, evolution, molecular biology, plant morphology, mycology, paleobotany, plant physiology, plant systematics.
Environmental Studies. M.S. only.

Geography. M.S. only.
Geological Sciences. Includes geology, hydrogeology, environmental geography, environmental geochemistry, geophysics. M.S. only.
History.
Linguistics. Includes general linguistics, teaching English as a second or foreign language. M.A.
Mathematics. Includes applied, computer science, mathematics for secondary school teachers, pure (M.S.); algebra, analysis, topology, applied (Ph.D.).
Modern Languages. Includes French, Spanish. M.A. only.
Philosophy. M.A. only.
Physics and Astronomy.
Political Science. Includes public administration.
Psychology. Includes clinical, experimental, industrial/organizational psychology.
Social Work. M.S.W. only.
Social Sciences. M.S.S. only.
Sociology. M.A. only.

COLLEGE OF BUSINESS:
Business. M.B.A.

SCRIPPS COLLEGE OF COMMUNICATION:
Communication and Development Studies. M.A.
Communication Technology and Policy. M.C.T.P.
Health Communication. Ph.D.
Journalism. M.S.
Mass Communication. Ph.D.
Mass Communication/Telecommunication. Ph.D.
Public Broadcasting. M.A.
Relating and Organizing. Ph.D.
Rhetoric and Public Culture. Ph.D.
Telecommunication. M.S.
Visual Communication. M.A.

COLLEGE OF EDUCATION:
Adolescent-to-Young Adult Education. Includes science, education, life science, earth/space science, French, German, Spanish, integrated languages, arts, mathematics, social studies, integrated science. M.Ed.
College Student Personnel. M.Ed.
Community/Agency Counseling. M.Ed.
Community/Rehabilitation. M.Ed.
Community/Rehabilitation/School Counseling. M.Ed.
Computer Education and Technology. M.Ed.
Counselor Education. M.Ed., Ph.D.
Cultural Studies. M.Ed., Ph.D.
Curriculum and Instruction. M.E., Ph.D.
Educational Administration. M.E., Ed.D.
Educational Research and Evaluation. M.Ed., Ph.D.
Higher Education. M.E., Ph.D.
Instructional Technology. Ph.D.
Intervention Specialist. Includes mild to moderate needs, moderate to intensive needs. M.Ed.
Mathematics Education. M.Ed., Ph.D.
Middle Childhood Education. M.Ed., Ph.D.
Reading Education. M.Ed.
Reading/Language Arts Education. Ph.D.
Rehabilitation Counseling. M.Ed.
School Counseling. M.Ed.
School/Community Counseling. M.Ed.
School/Rehabilitation Counseling. M.Ed.
Science Education. M.Ed., Ph.D.
Social Studies Education. Ph.D.
Special Education. M.E., Ph.D.

RUSS COLLEGE OF ENGINEERING AND TECHNOLOGY:
Biomedical Engineering. M.S.
Chemical Engineering. M.S., Ph.D.
Civil Engineering. M.S.

Computer Science. M.S.
Electrical Engineering. M.S., Ph.D.
Industrial Engineering. M.S.
Integrated Engineering. Ph.D.
Mechanical Engineering. M.S.

COLLEGE OF FINE ARTS:
Art. Includes art history (M.A.), ceramics, graphic design, painting, photography, printmaking, sculpture, studio/art history. M.A., M.F.A.
Film. Includes film production (M.F.A.), film studies (M.A.).
Music. Includes composition, education, history and literature, performance (accompanying, conducting, vocal, instrumental, pedagogy), theory, therapy. M.M.
Theater. Includes playwriting (M.F.A.), production design and technology (M.F.A.), theater (M.A.), theater history and criticism (M.A.), M.A., M.F.A.

COLLEGE OF HEALTH AND HUMAN SERVICES:
Athletic Administration. M.S.
Athletic Training. M.S.
Clinical Audiology. Au.D., Ph.D.
Coaching Education. M.S.
Early Childhood Education. M.S.
Family Nurse Practitioner. M.S.
Family Studies. M.S.
Food and Nutrition. M.S.
Health Administration. M.H.A.
Hearing Science. Ph.D.
Language Science. Ph.D.
Nurse Administrator. M.S.
Nurse Educator. M.S.
Physical Therapy. D.P.T.
Physiology of Exercise. Includes clinical, research. M.S.
Public Health. M.P.H.
Recreation Studies. M.S.
Speech and Language Pathology. M.A.
Speech Science. Ph.D.
Sport Administration. M.S.A.

CENTER FOR INTERNATIONAL STUDIES:
International Affairs. Includes African studies, communication and development studies, Latin American studies, Southeast Asian studies. M.A. only.

College of Osteopathic Medicine

Web site: www.oucom.ohiou.edu

Founded 1975. Public control. Located on main campus. Semester system. Special facilities: Center of Excellence for Multicultural Medicine, Center for Osteopathic Research and Education. Library: 70,000 volumes, 900 subscriptions.

Annual tuition: resident $24,288, nonresident $34,287. No on-campus housing available. Contact the Office of Student Affairs for online internet housing information. Off-campus housing and personal expenses: approximately $10,071.

Enrollment: first-year class 108, total 435 (men 48%, women 52%, minorities 24%, state residents 83%). Faculty: full-time 80, part-time and volunteers 506. Degrees conferred: D.O., D.O.-M.A., D.O.-M.B.A., D.O.-M.H.A., D.O.-M.P.H., D.O.-M.S., D.O.-Ph.D.

ADMISSION REQUIREMENTS. AACOMAS report, bachelor's degree preferred, official transcripts, MCAT (no later than September), three letters of recommendation, one from premed advisory committee, evaluation from a physician (preferably a D.O.), supplemental form required (before March 1) in support of application. Interview by invitation only. Graduates of unaccredited colleges not considered. Preference given to state residents. Apply by February 1 to the Director of Admissions. Admits first year students Fall only. Application fee: $30. Phone: (800)345-1560, or (740)593-4313; fax: (740)593-0761.

ADMISSION STANDARDS. Selective. Accepts about 6% of all applicants. Number of applications 2338 (1971 out-of-state); number interviewed 210 (41 out-of-state); number of acceptances 157 (26 out-of-state); number enrolled 108 (14 out-of-state). Usual minimum UGPA: 3.0 (A = 4). Mean Composite MCAT 8.1, mean UGPA 3.55.

FINANCIAL AID. Scholarships, fellowships, Federal W/S, loans. Apply by March 1 (priority deadline) to the Financial Aid Office. Phone (740)593-2152. Use FAFSA (College code: E00306) and institutional FAF. About 90% of students receive aid from College and outside sources.

DEGREE REQUIREMENT. For D.O.: satisfactory completion of four-year program; all students must pass the National Board of Osteopathic Medical Examination Part I and Part II. For Ph.D., see Graduate College listing above.

OKLAHOMA CITY UNIVERSITY
Oklahoma City, Oklahoma 73106-1402
Web site: www.okcu.edu

Founded 1904. Coed. Private control. Methodist affiliation. Semester system. Library: 280,400 volumes, 5600 subscriptions. Total University enrollment: 3700.

On-campus housing for married and single graduate students. Average academic year housing costs: $8200 for married students, $8200–$10,500 (including board) for single students. Contact Dean of Students Office for both on- and off-campus housing information. Phone: (405)208-9164.

Petree College of Arts and Science

Tuition: per credit $780. Enrollment: full-time 288, part-time 266. Faculty: full-time 40, part-time 34. Degrees conferred: M.A., M.A.R., M.Ed., M.L.A., M.C.J., M.S.N.

ADMISSION REQUIREMENTS. Official transcripts, two letters of recommendation required in support of College's application. Interview sometimes required. TOEFL required for international applicants. Accepts transfer applicants. Graduates of unaccredited institutions not considered. Apply by August 25 (Fall), January 15 (Spring) to Office of Graduate Admissions. Rolling admissions process. Application fee $35, $70 for international applicants. Phone: (405)208-5351 or (800)633-7242, ext. 4; fax: (405)208-5356; e-mail: gadmissions@okcu.edu.

ADMISSION STANDARDS. Selective for some programs, very selective for others. Usual minimum average: 3.0 (A = 4).

FINANCIAL AID. Fellowships, internships, full and partial tuition waivers, Federal W/S, loans. Approved for VA benefits. Apply by August 1 to the Dean's Office for fellowships; to Financial Aid Office for all other programs. Use FAFSA. Phone: (800)633-7242, ext. 5211. About 35% of students receive aid from University and outside sources. Aid available to part-time students.

DEGREE REQUIREMENTS. For master's: 36–45 semester hours minimum, at least 27 in residence; thesis/nonthesis option.

FIELDS OF STUDY.
Applied Behavioral Studies and Counseling. M.Ed.
Computer Science. Includes database systems, general. M.S.
Criminal Justice. M.C.J.
Dance. M.F.A.
Liberal Arts. Includes general studies, graphic design, leadership/management, literature, mass communication, philosophy, photography, studio arts, writing. M.L.A.

Music. Includes composition, conducting, music theatre, performance (instrumental, vocal, opera, piano, keyboard). M.M.
Nursing. Includes nursing administration, nursing education. M.S.N.
Performing Arts. M.A.
Religion. M.A.R.
Technical Theatre. Includes costume design, scene design. M.A.
TESOL. M.A.
Theatre. M.A.
Theatre for Young Audiences. M.A.

Meinders School of Business
Web site: www.okcu.edu/business

Graduate study since 1904. Semester system. Tuition: per credit $780. Enrollment: full-time 325, part-time 335. Graduate faculty: full-time 25, part-time 24. Degrees conferred: M.B.A., M.S.A.

ADMISSION REQUIREMENTS. Transcripts, GMAT required in support of School's application. TOEFL required for international applicants. Interview not required. Accepts transfer applicants. Apply to Director of M.B.A. Program by August 25 (Fall), January 15 (Spring). Application fee $35, $70 for international applicants. Phone: (800)683-7242, ext. 4; fax: (405)208-5356.

ADMISSION STANDARDS. Relatively open. Usual minimum average: 2.75 (A = 4).

FINANCIAL AID. Scholarships, fellowships, tuition waivers, Federal W/S, loans. Approved for VA benefits. Apply by August 1 to Financial Aid Office. Phone: (405)208-5211; fax: (405)208-5466. Use FAFSA (School code: 003166). Aid available for part-time students.

DEGREE REQUIREMENTS. For M.S. Accounting: 30 semester hours, 24 in residence. For M.B.A.: 36 semester hours minimum, at least 24 in residence; comprehensive written exam.

FIELDS OF STUDY.
Accounting. M.S.A. only.
Business Administration (Generalist).
Finance.
Health Administration.
Information Technology.
Integrated Marketing Communications.
International Business. Includes international finance, international information technology.
Marketing.
Note: M.B.A.-J.D. available.

School of Law (73106-1493)
Web site: www.okcu.edu/law

Established 1952. ABA approved since 1969. AALS member. Private control. Semester system. Special facilities: Center on Alternative Dispute Resolution, Center for the Study of State Constitutional Law and Government, Native American Legal Resource Center. Law Library: 311,643 volumes, 4354 subscriptions; has LEXIS, NEXIS, WESTLAW, OCLC; has more than 150 network connections.

Annual tuition: full-time $27,200, part-time $18,420. Limited on-campus housing available for married and single students. Total average annual additional expenses: $14,260

Enrollment: first-year class 184 (day), 33 (evening); total day and evening 605 (men 59%, women 41%, minorities 18%). Faculty: full-time 28, part-time 20. Student-to-faculty ratio is 18.6 to 1. Degrees conferred: J.D., J.D.-M.A., J.D.-M.B.A., J.D.-M.Div.

ADMISSION REQUIREMENTS. LSDAS Law School report, bachelor's degree, transcripts, LSAT, two letters of recommendation, personal statement, and résumé required in support of application. Accepts limited transfer applicants. Graduates of unaccredited colleges not considered. Apply by August 1 to the School. Beginning students Fall admission only. Application fee $50. Phone: (866)529-6281.

ADMISSION STANDARDS. Selective. Accepts approximately 41% of full-time and 46% of part-time students. Number of full-time applicants 1241, part-time 136; number of full-time acceptances 505, part-time 62; number of full-time enrolled 184, part-time 33; LSAT (75% of full-time students have a score at or above 148, part-time 146); GPA (75% of full-time students have a GPA at or above 2.78, part-time 2.54). *U.S. News & World Report* ranking is in the fourth tier of all U.S. law schools.

FINANCIAL AID. Scholarships, tuition remission, fellowships, assistantships, Federal W/S, loans. Apply to the Director of Financial Aid by March 1. Phone: (800)633-7242. Use FAFSA (School code: 003166). About 27% of students receive aid other than loans from School.

DEGREE REQUIREMENTS. For J.D.: day students may complete the J.D. degree in 24 months by year-round attendance, evening students in 33 months by year-round attendance; 90 hour semester program.

OKLAHOMA STATE UNIVERSITY
Stillwater, Oklahoma 74078-1019
Web site: www.okstate.edu

Founded 1890. Located in north-central Oklahoma approximately one hour from Tulsa and Oklahoma City. CGS member. Special facilities: Twenty-First Century Center for Agriculture and Renewable Natural Resources, University Center for Water Research, Center for Applications of Remote Sensing, Center for Global Studies, Center for Laser and Photonics Research, Center for Local Government and Technology, Center for Poets and Writers, Center for Science Literacy, Center for Sensors and Sensor Technologies, Educational Technology Center, Ethics Center, Multicultural Development and Assessment Center, Institute for Energy Analysis, Center for International Trade and Development, Oklahoma Center for the Advancement of Science and Technology, Oklahoma Food and Agricultural Products Research and Technology Center, Oklahoma Industrial Assessment Center, Virgin Prairie and Woodland Study and Research Site, Wes Watkins Center for International Trade Development. Library: 2,500,000 volumes, 35,600 subscriptions. Total University enrollment: 23,400.

Tuition: per credit hour resident $139, nonresident $485. On-campus housing available for graduate students. Average academic year housing costs: $5800 (including board) for single students; $7000 for married student housing. Contact the Graduate Student Housing Office for both on- and off-campus housing information. Phone: (405)744-9164.

Graduate College

Graduate study since 1905. Enrollment: full-time 1791, part-time 2212. Faculty: full-and part-time 941. Degrees conferred: M.A., M.Ag., M.M.S.E., M.S., M.Arch., M.Arch.Eng., M. Eng., M.B.A., Ed.S., Ed.D., Ph.D.

ADMISSION REQUIREMENTS. Two official transcripts required in support of College's application. GRE/MAT/GMAT required for some programs. Online application available. TOEFL required of international applicants. Accepts transfer applicants. Graduates of unaccredited institutions not considered. Apply to Graduate College at least thirty days prior to the semester of expected enrollment; international students five months prior to enrollment. Application fee $40, $75 for international applicants. Phone: (405)744-6368; fax: (405)744-0355.

ADMISSIONS STANDARDS. Competitive for most departments, selective for the others. Usual minimum average: 2.75 (A = 4).

FINANCIAL AID. Scholarships, research assistantships, teaching assistantships, internships, tuition waivers, social justice waiver, Federal W/S, loans. Approved for VA benefits. Apply directly to the academic department or unit in which the student desires the appointment for assistantships. Contact individual department for date. Apply by March 1 to the Office of Financial Aid for all other programs. Phone: (405)744-6604. Use FAFSA. Approximately 35% of students receive aid from both College and outside agencies. Aid available for part-time students.

DEGREE REQUIREMENTS. For master's: Plan I—30 credit hours including 6 hours for thesis, 21 hours in residence; thesis. Plan II—32 credit hours including 2 credit hours for special report, 23 credit hours in residence; special report. Plan III—32 credit hours, 23 credit hours in residence; creative component/project. For Ed.S.: 60 credit hours beyond the bachelor's degree; one year or equivalent in residency; qualifying exam; thesis with final exam. For Ed.D.: 90 hours beyond the bachelor's degree; 75% of course work at 5000 and 6000 level; 10-hour thesis; maintain B average; qualifying exams; thesis defense. For Ph.D.: 60 hours minimum beyond the bachelor's degree or 30 hours minimum beyond the master's degree; one year in residence; one or two foreign languages for some departments; qualifying exam; dissertation (minimum 15 credit hours); final oral exam.

FIELDS OF STUDY.

COLLEGE OF AGRICULTURAL SCIENCE AND NATURAL RESOURCES:
Agricultural Communication.
Agricultural Economics.
Agricultural Education.
Animal Breeding and Reproduction. Ph.D. only
Animal Nutrition. Ph.D. only.
Animal Sciences.
Biochemistry and Molecular Biology.
Biosystems and Agricultural Engineering.
Crop Science.
Entomology.
Food Science.
Forest Resources.
Horticulture.
Natural Resource Ecology and Management.
Plant Pathology. Ph.D. only.
Plant Sciences.
Soil Science. Ph.D. only.

COLLEGE OF ARTS AND SCIENCES:
Botany. M.S. only.
Chemistry.
Communication Sciences and Disorders. M.S. only.
Computer Science.
Environmental Sciences.
Fire and Emergency Management. M.S. only.
Geography. M.S. only.
Geology. M.S. only.
History.
Mass Communications. M.S. only.
Mathematics.
Microbiology, Cell, and Molecular Biology.
Music.
Philosophy. M.A. only.
Physics.
Plant Science. Ph.D. only.
Political Science. M.A. only.
Psychology.
Sociology.
Statistics.
Theater. M.A. only.
Zoology.

SPEARS SCHOOL OF BUSINESS:
Accounting.
Business Administration.
Business Geographics.
Economics.
Finance. Ph.D.
Management. Ph.D.
Management Information Systems. M.S.
Management Science and Information Systems. Ph.D.
Marketing. Ph.D.
Quantitative Financial Economics.
Telecommunication.

COLLEGE OF EDUCATION:
Applied Educational Studies.
Counseling. Includes community counseling, school counseling.
Educational Leadership Studies. Includes college student development, school administration, higher education.
Educational Psychology. Includes educational research and evaluation.
Educational Technology. Includes school library media.
Health and Human Performance. Includes applied-exercise science, health promotion, physical education.
Higher Education.
Leadership and Policy Studies.
Leisure Studies.
Natural and Applied Sciences. Includes aviation and space science.
School Administration.
Teaching, Learning, and Leadership. Includes curriculum and leadership studies, elementary, middle secondary and K–12 education, occupational education studies. reading and literacy, special education.

COLLEGE OF ENGINEERING, ARCHITECTURE, AND TECHNOLOGY:
Biosystems and Agricultural Engineering.
Chemical Engineering.
Civil Engineering.
Electrical Engineering.
Engineering and Technology Management. M.S. only.
Environmental Engineering.
Industrial Engineering and Management.
Mechanical Engineering.

COLLEGE OF HUMAN ENVIRONMENTAL SCIENCES:
Design, Housing, and Merchandising.
Hospitality Administration.
Human Development and Family Sciences.
Nutritional Sciences.

College of Veterinary Medicine
Web site: www.cvm.okstate.edu

Located at Center for Veterinary Health Sciences. Semester system. Special facilities: Equine Breeding facilities, Cohn Family Animal Shelter, Biosensor and Molecular Diagnostics Oklahoma Technology and Research Park.

Annual tuition: residents $13,129, nonresidents $30,404. On-campus housing available. Total average expenses for both on- and off-campus housing: $17,500. Total average cost for other expenses: $5000.

Enrollment: first-year class 82, total 312 (men 28%, women 72%, minorities 6%, state residents 75%), postgraduate 55. Faculty: full-time 118, part-time n/a. Degrees conferred: D.V.M., D.V.M.-M.S., D.V.M.-Ph.D. The M.S. and Ph.D. are offered through the Graduate College.

ADMISSION REQUIREMENTS. VMCAS, transcripts, GRE/Subject Biology, recommendations, personal essay, animal/veterinary experience required in support of application. Interview by invitation only. Preference given to state residents. Accepts transfer applicants on a space-available basis only. Graduates of unaccredited colleges not considered. Apply to the College after July 1, before October 1. Rolling admission process. Application fee $15. Phone: (405)744-6653; fax: (405)744-0356.

ADMISSION STANDARDS. Selective. Accepts about 15–20% of all applicants. Number of applications 481 (399 out-of-state); number interviewed n/a (n/a out-of-state); number of acceptances n/a (n/a out-of-state); number enrolled 82 (24 out-of-state). Usual minimum UGPA: 2.80 (A = 4). GRE mean score (V + Q) 1123; mean UGPA 3.49.

FINANCIAL AID. Scholarships, fellowships, assistantships, partial tuition waivers, Federal W/S, loans available. Apply to Office of Financial Aid by March 1. Use FAFSA.

DEGREE REQUIREMENTS. For D.V.M.: satisfactory completion of four-year program. For M.S., Ph.D., see Graduate College listing above.

FIELDS OF GRADUATE STUDY.
Anesthesia and Pain Management.
Infectious Diseases. Includes pathogenesis of infectious respiratory disease, arthropod-borne diseases and zoonoses, chemical and biological warfare agent detection, animal models of human disease, vaccine development, bacterial and mycobacterial biology.
Physiological Sciences
Reproductive Sciences.
Surgical and Non-Surgical Therapeutic Uses of Lasers.
Toxicology. Include organophosphate toxicology, lung epithelial cell differentiation and oxidative stress, active site studies of human sulfotransferases.

OKLAHOMA STATE UNIVERSITY CENTER FOR HEALTH SCIENCES
Tulsa, Oklahoma 74107-1898
Web site: healthsciences.okstate.edu

College of Osteopathic Medicine

Founded 1972 as the Oklahoma College of Osteopathic Medicine and Surgery. Joined OSU in 1988. Public control. Semester system. Library: 57,979 volumes, 1200 subscriptions.

Annual tuition: resident $16,938, nonresident $32,158. No on-campus housing available. Contact the Office of Student Affairs for housing information. Off-campus housing and personal expenses: approximately $8,500.

Enrollment: first-year class 88, total 343 (men 53%, women 47%, minorities 21%, state residents 89%). Faculty: full-time 71, part-time and volunteers 406. Degrees conferred: D.O., D.O.-M.B.A., D.O.-Ph.D.

ADMISSION REQUIREMENTS. AACOMAS report, bachelor's degree preferred, official transcripts, MCAT (no later than Spring of year prior to application) from premed advisory committee, evaluation from a physician (preferably a D.O.), supplemental form required in support of application. Interview by invitation only. Graduates of unaccredited college not considered. Preference given to state residents. Apply by February 1 to the Assistant Dean of Students. Admits first year students Fall only. Rolling admissions process. Application fee $25. Phone: (800)677-1972 or (918)528-8421; fax: (918)561-8412.

ADMISSION STANDARDS. Selective. Accepts about 27% of all applicants. Number of applications 422 (224 out-of-state); number interviewed 216 (41 out-of-state); number of acceptances 116 (23 out-of-state); number enrolled 88 (12 out-of-state). Usual minimum UGPA: 3.0 (A = 4). Mean Composite MCAT 8.3, mean UGPA 3.62.

FINANCIAL AID. Scholarships, grants, partial tuition waivers, Federal W/S, loans. Apply by June 1 to the Financial Aid Office. Phone: (918)561-1228. Use FAFSA and institutional FAF. About 90% of all students receive some form of financial assistance.

DEGREE REQUIREMENT. For D.O.: satisfactory completion of four-year program. For D.O.-Ph.D.: 7-year full-time program, must be completed within 9 years; research proposal; a written and oral qualifying exam; dissertation.

FIELDS OF GRADUATE STUDY.
Anatomy.
Biochemistry.
Cell Biology.
Microbiology.
Pathology.
Pharmacology.
Physiology.

UNIVERSITY OF OKLAHOMA
Norman, Oklahoma 73019-4076
Web site: www.ou.edu

Founded 1890. Located 18 miles S of Oklahoma City. CGS member. Coed. State control. Special facilities: Center for the Investigation of Mesoscale Meteorological Systems; permanent biological station on Lake Texoma; earth sciences observatory at Leonard; geological field camp at Canon City, Colo.; aquatic biology and fisheries research center in Noble; virgin prairie and woodland plots for study and research; Sarkey's Energy Center; Surfactant Institute; Rock Mechanics Institute; Ground Water Institute; cooperative program with Oak Ridge Institute of Nuclear Studies. The University's NIH ranking is 108th among all U.S. institutions with 107 awards/grants valued at $47,411,188. In 2004, 2 of the University's faculty members were elected to National Honor Academies and this ranks it 117th among all U.S. institutions. The Library: approximately 4,300,000 volumes, 22,000 subscriptions; features Western History Collection, Degolyer Collection in the History of Science and Technology and the Bass Business Collection. Total University enrollment: 27,000.

Tuition: per credit resident $126, nonresident $450. On-campus housing for 922 married students, 100 men, list women. Average annual housing cost: $5200–$7500 for married students, $7900 (including board) for single students. Apply to Director of the Office of Housing. Phone: (405)325-2511. Day-care facilities available.

Graduate College

Graduate study since 1899. Enrollment: full-time 2748, part-time 3232. Graduate faculty: full-time 956. Degrees conferred: M.Ac., M.A., M.Arch., M.A. in Art, M.A. in L.Sci., M.P.A., M.B.A., M.Ed., M.Ed. in HPER., M.Env.Sci., M.F.A. in Art, M.F.A. in Dance, M.F.A. in Design, M.F.A. in Drama, M.H.R., M.L.S., M.Land.Arch., M.L.Sc., M.Mus., M.Mus.Ed., M.Nat.Sci., M.P.H., M.R.C.P., M.S., M.S. in Const.Set., M.S. in Metr., M.Soc.Sci., M.Soc.Work, D.Mus.Arts, Ed.D., Ph.D., Dr.P.H., D.P.A.

ADMISSION REQUIREMENTS. Transcripts required in support of College's application. GRE/GMAT/MAT/interview for some departments. TOEFL required for international applicants. Accepts transfer applicants. Graduates of unaccredited institutions not considered. Apply to Office of Admissions and Records by June 1 (Fall), November 1 (Spring), April 1 (Summer); international applicants April 1 (Fall), September 1 (Spring), February 1 (Summer). Application fee $25, $50 for international applicants. Phone: (405)325-3811; fax: (405)325-5346; e-mail: cs@ou.edu.

ADMISSION STANDARDS. Selective for most departments, very selective for others. Usual minimum average: 3.0 (A = 4).

FINANCIAL AID. Annual awards from institutional funds: fee waiver scholarships, fellowships, teaching assistantships, research assistantships, internships, tuition waivers, Federal W/S, loans. Approved for VA benefits. Apply by March 31 to Graduate College and appropriate department chair for scholarships, assistantships; to Financial Aid Office for all other programs. Phone: (405)325-4521; fax: (405)325-7608. Use FAFSA. About 30% of students receive aid other than loans from College and outside sources. Aid sometimes available for part-time students.

DEGREE REQUIREMENTS. For most master's: 30 semester hours minimum, at least 22 in residence; thesis; comprehensive oral/written exam sometimes required; 32 semester hours minimum, at least 24 in residence; comprehensive oral/written exam for some departments. For M.Ac.: 33 hours minimum; comprehensive oral/written exam. For M.B.A.: 36 hours minimum; comprehensive written exam. For M.R.C.P.: 54 hours minimum, final project. For M.S.W.: 60 hours minimum; fieldwork; thesis/final project. For M.L.A.: 62 hours minimum; research project. For M.F.A.: 60 hours minimum; final project/exhibition. For Ph.D.: 3 years minimum and at least 90 semester hours beyond the bachelor's degree, at least 2 semesters in residence; general oral/written exam, dissertation; final oral exam. For Ed.D.: evidence of proficiency in statistics/methods of research or reading knowledge of one foreign language; other requirements essentially the same as the Ph.D. For D.P.A., D.Mus.Arts, essentially the same as for the Ph.D.

FIELDS OF STUDY.

NORMAN CAMPUS:

COLLEGE OF ARCHITECTURE:
Architecture. M.Arch.
Construction Science. M.S.
Landscape Architecture. M.L.A.
Regional and City Planning. M.R.C.P.

COLLEGE OF ARTS AND SCIENCES:
Anthropology. M.A., Ph.D.
Botany and Microbiology. M.S., M.N.S., Ph.D.
Cellular and Behavioral Neurobiology. Ph.D.
Chemistry and Biochemistry. M.S., Ph.D.
Communication. M.A., Ph.D.
Ecology and Evolutionary Biology. Ph.D.
Economics. M.A., Ph.D.
English. M.A., Ph.D.
Health and Exercise Science. M.S., Ph.D.
History. M.A., Ph.D.
History of Science. M.A., Ph.D.
Human Relations. M.H.R.
Library and Information Studies. M.L.I.S.
Mathematics. M.A., M.S., Ph.D.
Modern Languages. Includes Arabic, Mandarin Chinese, French, German, Italian, Japanese, Modern Hebrew, Portuguese, Russian, Spanish. M.A., Ph.D.
Natural Science. M.N.S.
Philosophy. M.A., Ph.D.
Physics. M.S., M.N.S., Ph.D.
Political Science. M.A., M.P.A., Ph.D.

Psychology. M.S., Ph.D.
Social Work. M.S.W.
Sociology. M.A., Ph.D.
Zoology. M.S., Ph.D.

COLLEGE OF ATMOSPHERIC AND GEOGRAPHIC SCIENCES:
Geography. M.A., Ph.D.
Meteorology. M.S. Metr., Ph.D.

MICHAEL F. PRICE COLLEGE OF BUSINESS:
Accounting. M.Acc., Ph.D.
Business Administration. M.B.A.
Business Administration. Includes accounting, finance, management, information systems, marketing. Ph.D.
Management Information Systems. M.S. M.I.S.

COLLEGE OF EARTH AND ENERGY:
Managerial Energy Economics. M.A.
Geology and Geophysics. M.S., Ph.D.
Petroleum and Geological Engineering. M.S., Ph.D.

COLLEGE OF EDUCATION:
Adult and Higher Education. M.Ed., Ph.D.
Education Administration–Curriculum/Supervision. M.Ed., Ed.D., Ph.D.
Educational Studies. M.Ed., Ph.D.
Educational Instructional Psychology and Technology. M.Ed., Ph.D.
Instructional Leadership and Academic Curriculum. M.Ed., Ph.D.
School Counseling. M.Ed.
Special Education. M.Ed., Ph.D.

COLLEGE OF ENGINEERING:
Aerospace and Mechanical Engineering. M.S., Ph.D.
Bioengineering. Ph.D.
Chemical, Biological, and Materials Engineering. M.S., Ph.D.
Civil Engineering and Environmental Science. M.S., Ph.D.
Computer Science. M.S., Ph.D.
Electrical and Computer Engineering. M.S., Ph.D.
Engineering. M.S., Ph.D.
Engineering Physics. M.S., Ph.D.
Industrial Engineering. M.S., Ph.D.
Natural Gas Engineering and Management. M.S.
Petroleum and Geological Engineering. M.S., Ph.D.

COLLEGE OF FINE ARTS:
Art. Includes art (M.F.A.), art history (M.A.), Art of the American West (Ph.D.), native American arts (Ph.D.).
Dance. M.F.A.
Drama. M.A., M.F.A.
Music. M.M., M.M.Ed., D.M.A., Ph.D.

GAYLORD COLLEGE OF JOURNALISM AND MASS COMMUNICATION:
Journalism and Mass Communication. M.A.
Mass Communication. Ph.D.
Professional Writing. M.P.W.

COLLEGE OF LIBERAL STUDIES:
Liberal Studies. M.L.S.

SCHOOL OF INTERNATIONAL AND AREAS STUDIES:
International and Area Studies. M.S.I.A.

HEALTH SCIENCES CENTER:
Allied Health Sciences. Ph.D.
Biochemistry and Molecular Biology. Ph.D.
Biological Psychology. M.S., Ph.D.
Biostatistics and Epidemiology. M.S., Ph.D,
Cell Biology. M.S., Ph.D.
Communication Sciences and Disorders. M.S., Ph.D.
Health Administration and Policy. M.S., Ph.D.

Health Promotion Sciences. M.S., Ph.D.
Microbiology and Immunology. M.S., Ph.D.
Neuroscience. M.S., Ph.D.
Nursing. M.S.
Nutritional Sciences. M.S.
Occupational and Environmental Health. M.S., Ph.D.
Orthodontics. M.S.
Pathology. Ph.D.
Periodontics. M.S.
Pharmaceutical Sciences. M.S., Ph.D.
Physiology. M.S., Ph.D.
Radiological Sciences. M.S., Ph.D.
Rehabilitation Sciences. M.S.

College of Law (73019-5081)

Web site: www.law.ou.edu

Organized 1909. Semester system. Special facility: American Indian Law and Policy Center. Library: 345,394 volumes, 4914 subscriptions; has LEXIS, WESTLAW, OLIN; has more than 100 network connections.

Annual tuition: full-time resident $13,564, nonresident $23,493. On-campus housing available. Total average annual additional expense: $15,185.

Enrollment: first-year class 174; total 500 (men 56%, women 44%, minorities 24%). Faculty: full-time 29, part-time 20. Student-to-faculty ratio 15.3 to 1. Degrees conferred: J.D., J.D.-M.B.A., J.D.-M.P.A., J.D.-M.S. (Health Administration, Environmental Management, Occupational Health).

ADMISSION REQUIREMENTS. LSDAS Law School report, bachelor's degree, transcripts, LSAT, personal statement, two letters of recommendation required in support of application. Accepts transfer applicants. Graduates of unaccredited colleges not considered. Apply to the Admissions Office by March 15. Application fee $50 (nonresident only). Phone: (405)325-4728.

ADMISSION STANDARDS. Selective. Accepts approximately 26% of all students. Number of applicants 1278; number of acceptances 336; number enrolled 174; LSAT (75% of students have a score at or above 154); GPA (75% of students have a GPA at or above 3.32). *U.S. News & World Report* ranking is in the second tier (tied at 70th) of all U.S. law schools.

FINANCIAL AID. Scholarships, full and partial tuition waivers, fellowships, assistantships, Federal W/S, loans. Apply to the Office of Financial Aid, preferably by March 1. Phone: (405)325-4521. Use FAFSA (College code: 003184). About 65% of students receive aid other than loans from College.

DEGREE REQUIREMENTS. For J.D.: 90 credit minimum, at least final year in residence. For master's degrees, see Graduate College listing above.
Note: Summer study abroad at Oxford University (Great Britain) available.

UNIVERSITY OF OKLAHOMA HEALTH SCIENCES CENTER

Oklahoma City, Oklahoma 73190
Web site: www.ouhsc.edu

CGS member. Coed. State control. Semester system. Special facilities: Alcohol Research Center, Child Study Center, John W. Keys Speech and Hearing Center, Oklahoma Center for Neurosciences, Toxicology Center. Library: 268,000 volumes, 2600 subscriptions; has MEDLINE, HEALTHLINE. No on-campus housing available.

Graduate College

Awarded first degree in 1921.
Tuition: per credit, resident $143, nonresident $374. Enrollment: full- and part-time 558. Faculty: full-time 320, part-time 141. Degrees conferred: M.P.H., M.S., Dr.P.H., Ph.D., M.D.-Ph.D. (Biomedical Sciences), M.P.H.-M.B.A. (with Oklahoma State University).

ADMISSION REQUIREMENTS. Official transcripts, three letters of recommendation, résumé/vitae, statement of career goals required in support of College's application. GRE required by some programs. TOEFL (minimum score 550), TWE required for international applicants. Interviews may be arranged. Accepts transfer applicants. Graduates of unaccredited institutions not considered. Apply to Office of Graduate Admissions (P.O. Box 26901) by April 1. Rolling admissions process. Application fee $45. Phone: (405)271-2359; fax: (405)271-2480; e-mail: admissions@ouhsc.edu.

ADMISSION STANDARDS. Competitive. Usual minimum average: 3.0 (A = 4).

FINANCIAL AID. Fellowships, research assistantships, teaching assistantships, tuition waivers, Federal W/S, loans. Approved for VA benefits. Apply by March 1 to the Office of the Dean for fellowships, assistantships; to the Financial Aid Office for all other programs. Phone: (405)271-2118. Use FAFSA (School code: 005889). Aid available for part-time students.

DEGREE REQUIREMENTS. For M.S.: 30 credit hours; no residency required; thesis defense. For M.P.H.: 36 credit hours minimum, at least 30 in residence; thesis. Dr.P.H.: at least one and up to three years in full-time residence, depending upon previous preparation and experience; qualifying exam; dissertation; final oral exam. For Ph.D.: 60 credit hours minimum beyond the bachelor's, 30 credit hours in full-time residency; qualifying exam; dissertation defense. For M.D. requirements refer to College of Medicine listing below.

FIELDS OF STUDY.
Allied Health Sciences. M.S., Ph.D.
Biochemistry and Molecular Biology. Ph.D.
Biological Psychology. M.S., Ph.D.
Biostatistics and Epidemiology. M.P.H., M.S., Ph.D., Dr. P.H.
Cell Biology. Ph.D.
Communication Sciences and Disorders. M.S., Ph.D.
Genetic Counseling. M.S.
Health Administration and Policy. M.P.H., M.H.A.
Health Promotion Sciences. M.S., M.P.H., Dr.P.H.
Microbiology and Immunology. Ph.D.
Neuroscience. Ph.D.
Nursing. M.S.
Nutritional Sciences. M.S.
Occupational and Environmental Health. M.P.H., M.S., Dr.P.H., Ph.D.
Orthodontics. M.S.
Pathology. Ph.D.
Periodontics. M.S.
Pharmaceutical Sciences. M.S., Ph.D.
Physiology. M.S., Ph.D.
Radiological Sciences. M.S., Ph.D.
Rehabilitation Sciences. M.S.

School of Dentistry (P.O. Box 26901)

Web site: www.dentistry.ouhsc.edu

Established 1972. Located in Oklahoma City (73190). Special facility: Native American Center of Excellence.
Annual tuition: resident $20,157, nonresident $39,612. No on-campus housing available, but off-campus housing is just

two blocks away. For housing contact the Office of Student Affairs. Phone: (405)325-2511. Average academic year housing cost: $17,416. Total average cost for all other first-year expenses: $6800.

Enrollment: first-year class 54, total 205 (men 68%, women 32%, minorities 35%, state residents 95%). Faculty: full-time 62, part-time 103. Degrees conferred: D.D.S., M.S., D.D.S.-M.S., Certificate.

ADMISSION REQUIREMENTS. AADSAS, official transcripts, three letters of recommendation, DAT (no later than October) required in support of School's application. Applicants must have completed at least two years of college study. Interviews by invitation only. Preference given to state residents and Arkansas residents. Apply to Office of Admissions after July 1, before September 1 (nonresident), before December 1 (resident). Rolling admission process. Application fee $50, $75 for international applicants. Phone: (405)271-3530; fax: (405)271-3423.

ADMISSION STANDARDS. Competitive. Accepts about 10–15% of all applicants. Usual minimum UGPA: 2.70 (A = 4). Mean DAT: academic 19, PAT 17; mean UGPA 3.50.

FINANCIAL AID. Limited to scholarships, tuition waivers, grants, loans. Apply to Director, University Office of Financial Aid after acceptance and before March 1. Phone: (405)271-2118. Use FAFSA (College code: 005889). About 81% of students receive some aid from School and outside sources.

DEGREE REQUIREMENTS. For D.D.S.: satisfactory completion of forty-five-month program. For M.S.: satisfactory completion of one-year program.

FIELDS OF POSTGRADUATE STUDY.
Advanced Education in General Dentistry.
Oral and Maxillofacial Surgery. M.S.
Orthodontics. M.S.
Periodontics. M.S.

College of Medicine (P.O. Box 26901)

Web site: www.medicine.ouhsc.edu

Established 1900. Located in Oklahoma City (73190). Library: 156,000 volumes, 850 subscriptions. NIH ranking is 108th of all U.S. institutions with 107 awards/grants worth $47,411,188.

Annual tuition: resident $19,246, nonresident $46,776. Limited on-campus housing available. Total average figure for all other expenses: $17,416.

Enrollment: first-year class 152 (EDP 10), total 601 (men 51%, women 49%, minorities 23%, state residents 94%). Faculty: full-time 734, part-time 162. Degrees conferred: M.D., M.D.-M.P.H., M.D.-M.S., M.D.-Ph.D. The M.S. and Ph.D. are offered through the Graduate College.

ADMISSION REQUIREMENTS. AMCAS report, transcripts, letters of recommendation, MCAT required in support of application. Interview by invitation only. Applicants must have completed at least three years of college study. Preference given to state residents. Does have EDP; apply after June 1, before August 1. Apply to Assistant Dean for Admissions after June 1, before October 15. Application fee $65. Phone: (405)271-2331; fax: (405) 271-3032.

ADMISSION STANDARDS. Selective. Accepts about 19.6% of all applicants. Number of applications 1012 (633 out-of-state); number interviewed 241 (38 out-of-state); number of acceptances 198 (31 out-of-state); number enrolled 152 (15 out-of-state). Mean Composite MCAT 9.5; mean UGPA 3.66.

FINANCIAL AID. Scholarships, fee waivers, loans. Apply to Director of Financial Aids; no specified closing dates. Phone: (405)

271-2118. Use FAFSA (School code: 005889). About 90% of students receive some financial assistance.

DEGREE REQUIREMENTS. For M.D.: satisfactory completion of four-year program; all students must take USMLE Step 1 and Step 2 prior to graduation. For M.S., Ph.D.: see Graduate College listing above.

FIELDS OF GRADUATE STUDY.
Anatomical Sciences.
Biochemistry.
Biophysics.
Biostatistics.
Cell Biology.
Epidemiology.
Health Administration and Policy.
Health Promotion Sciences.
Immunology.
Microbiology.
Neuroscience.
Occupational and Environmental Health.

OLD DOMINION UNIVERSITY

Norfolk, Virginia 23529
Web site: www.odu.edu

Established 1930. CGS member. Coed. State control. Semester system. Special facilities: Applied Research Center, Center for Advance Ship Repair and Maintenance, Center for Coastal Physical Oceanography, Center for Global Business and Executive Education, Center for Real Estate and Economic Development, Frank Reidy Research Center for Bioelectrics, International Maritime, Ports and Logistics Management Institute, Laser and Plasma Engineering Institute, NASA Langley Research Center, Social Science Research Center, Virginia Center for Innovative Technology, Virginia Spaceflight Center. Library: 985,800 volumes, 7985 subscriptions. Total University enrollment: 21,200.

Tuition: per credit, resident $263, nonresident $661. On-campus housing for 750 graduate men, 750 graduate women; none for married students. More housing available on competitive basis with undergraduate students. Average annual housing cost; $5600 (including board). Apply to Housing Office. Phone: (757)683-3843.

School of Graduate Studies

Enrollment: full-time 1147, part-time 2596. Faculty teaching graduate students: full-time 579, part-time 72. Degrees conferred: M.A., M.S., M.B.A., M.E., M.S.Ed., M.S.N., M.U.S., M.P.A., M.P.H., M.P.T., M.E.M., M.F.A., M.Tx., C.A.S., Psy.D., Ph.D., D.B.A.

ADMISSION REQUIREMENTS. Transcripts, three references (depending on program) required in support of School's application. GRE/GMAT required for certain programs. TOEFL required for international applicants. Accepts transfer applicants. Graduates of unaccredited institutions not considered. Apply to appropriate graduate program director at least two months prior to registration. Application fee $40. Phone: (757)683-3685; fax: (757)683-3255; e-mail: admit@odu.edu.

ADMISSION STANDARDS. Selective. Usual minimum average: regular status 2.5, 3.0 for major (A = 4).

FINANCIAL AID. Scholarships, assistantships, grants-in-aid, internships, tuition waivers, Federal W/S, loans. Approved for VA benefits. Apply by February 15 to appropriate graduate program director for fellowships, assistantships; to Financial Aid Office for all other programs. Use FAFSA and institutional FAF. Phone: (757)683-3638; fax: (757)683-5920.

DEGREE REQUIREMENTS. For master's: 30–33 semester hours minimum, at least 24 in residence; thesis/nonthesis option; final oral/written exam. For C.A.S.: 30 semester hours beyond the master's. For Ph.D.: up to 48 semester hours beyond the master's; preliminary exam; language requirement; research tool; dissertation; final oral defense.

FIELDS OF STUDY.

COLLEGE OF ARTS AND LETTERS:
Applied Linguistics. M.A.
Applied Sociology. M.A.
Creative Writing. M.F.A.
Criminology. Ph.D.
English. M.A., Ph.D.
History. M.A.
Humanities. M.A.
International Studies. M.A., Ph.D.
Music Education. M.M.E.
Visual Studies. M.A., M.F.A.

COLLEGE OF BUSINESS AND PUBLIC ADMINISTRATION:
Accounting. M.S.
Business Administration. M.B.A., Ph.D.
Economics. M.A.
Finance. Ph.D.
Management. Ph.D.
Marketing. Ph.D.
Public Administration. M.P.A., Ph.D.
Taxation. M.Tx.
Urban Services. Includes urban management. Multidisciplinary. Ph.D.
Urban Studies. M.U.S.

DARDEN COLLEGE OF EDUCATION:
Counseling. M.S.Ed., Ed.S., Ph.D.
Community College Leadership. Ph.D.
Curriculum and Instruction. Ph.D.
Early Childhood Education. M.S.Ed., Ph.D.
Educational Leadership. M.S.Ed., Ed.S., Ph.D.
Higher Education. M.S.Ed., Ed.S., Ph.D.
Instructional Design and Technology. Includes elementary/middle school, secondary. M.S.Ed., Ed.S., Ph.D.
Library Science. M.S.Ed.
Occupational and Technical Studies. M.S., Ph.D.
Physical Education. Includes athletic training (M.S.Ed.), exercise science and wellness (M.S.Ed.), human movement science (Ph.D.), recreation and tourism studies (M.S.Ed.), sport management (M.S.Ed.).
Reading Education. Includes literacy leadership (Ph.D.). M.S., Ph.D.
Secondary Education. M.S.Ed.
Special Education. M.S.Ed.
Speech–Language Pathology and Audiology. M.S.Ed.

COLLEGE OF ENGINEERING AND TECHNOLOGY:
Aerospace Engineering. M.E., M.S., Ph.D.
Civil Engineering. M.E., M.S., Ph.D.
Computer Engineering. M.E., M.S.
Electrical and Computer Engineering. Ph.D.
Electrical Engineering. M.E., M.S.
Engineering Management. M.S., M.E.M., Ph.D.
Environmental Engineering. M.E., M.S., Ph.D.
Mechanical Engineering. M.E., M.S., Ph.D.
Modeling and Simulation. M.E., M.S., Ph.D.
Systems Engineering. M.E.

COLLEGE OF HEALTH SCIENCES:
Community Health. M.S.
Dental Hygiene. M.S.
Health Services Research. Ph.D.

Nursing. M.S.N.
Physical Therapy. M.P.T.
Public Health. M.P.H.
Urban Services. Includes health services. Multidisciplinary. Ph.D.

COLLEGE OF SCIENCES:
Biochemistry.
Biology. M.S.
Biomedical Sciences. Ph.D.
Chemistry. M.S.
Clinical Psychology. Psy.D.
Computer Science. M.S., Ph.D.
Computational and Applied Mathematics. M.S., Ph.D.
Ecology Sciences. Ph.D.
Geology. M.S.
Industrial/Organizational Psychology. Ph.D.
Oceanography. M.S., Ph.D.
Physics. M.S., Ph.D.
Psychology. M.S.

OLIVET NAZARENE UNIVERSITY
Bourbonnais, Illinois 60914
Web site: www.olivet.edu

Founded 1907. Located 50 miles S of Chicago. Coed. Semester system. Private control. Church of the Nazarene affiliation. Library: 155,000 volumes, 1500 subscriptions. Total University enrollment: 4600.

Annual tuition: full-time $6700, per credit $230. Limited on-campus housing for graduate students. Contact the Admissions Office for housing information. Phone: (815)939-5203.

School of Graduate and Continuing Studies

Graduate study since 1961. Enrollment: full- and part-time 1000. Graduate faculty: full-time 48, part-time 119. Degrees conferred: M.A., M.A.E., M.A.T., M.B.A., M.C.M., M.A.P.C., M.P.C.

ADMISSION REQUIREMENTS. Official transcripts, three references, interview, photograph required in support of application. GRE required for some programs. TOEFL required for international applicants. Accepts transfer applicants. Apply by July 1 (Fall), December 1 (Spring), May 1 (Summer). Phone: (815)939-5291; fax: (815)935-4991; e-mail: gradadmissions@olivet.edu.

ADMISSION STANDARDS. Selective. Usual minimum average: 3.0 (A = 4).

FINANCIAL AID. Thirty-seven grants, three teaching assistantships, Federal W/S, loans. Approved for VA benefits. Apply by March 1 to Office of Financial Aid. Phone: (815)939-5249; fax: (815)935-4990. Use FAFSA (School code: 001741) and institutional FAF.

DEGREE REQUIREMENTS. For M.A., M.A.E., M.C.M., M.P.C.: 30–39 semester hours minimum; thesis or scholarly option of 2–4 credits. For M.B.A., M.A.T.: 36 semester hours minimum; project.

FIELDS OF STUDY.
Business Administration.
Curriculum and Instruction.
English.
Ethical Leadership. Ed.D.
Library Information Specialist.
Ministry.
Nursing.
Organizational Leadership.
Practical Ministries (for Salvation Army Officers).

Professional Counseling.
Reading Specialist.
Religion.
School Leadership.
Youth Ministry.

ORAL ROBERTS UNIVERSITY

Tulsa, Oklahoma 74171-0001

Web site: www.oru.edu

Founded 1965. Coed. Private control. Semester system. Library: 210,625 volumes, 5613 subscriptions.

Limited on-campus housing available. Rooms/apartments for both single and married students. Average academic year on- and off-campus housing costs: $5200–$7300. Apply to Director, Residential Life. Phone: (918)495-7700.

Graduate School of Business

Graduate study since 1978. Tuition: per credit $460. Enrollment: full-time 27, part-time 40. Faculty: full-time 6, part-time 3. Degrees conferred: M.B.A., M.M.

ADMISSION REQUIREMENTS. Transcripts, personal sketch, letters of recommendation, GMAT (minimum score 500) required in support of School's application. TOEFL required (minimum score 600) for international applicants. Accepts transfer students. Apply by July 1 (Fall), December 1 (Spring). Application fee $35. Phone: (800)643-7926, ext. 21; (918)495-6117; fax: (918) 495-7965.

ADMISSION STANDARDS. Selective. Usual minimum average: 3.0 (A = 4).

FINANCIAL AID. Scholarships, grants, assistantships, fellowships, career-related internships, Federal W/S, loans. Approved for VA benefits. Apply by March 15 to Director of University Financial Aid. Use FAFSA (School code: 003985). Phone: (918)495-6602; fax: (918)395-7965. About 30% of students receive aid other than loans from University and outside sources.

DEGREE REQUIREMENTS. For M.B.A.: 36–42 credits minimum; final exam. For M.M.: 35 credit hour program.

FIELDS OF STUDY.
Accounting. M.B.A.
Business Administration. M.B.A.
Finance. M.B.A.
Human Resource Management. M.M.
International Business. M.B.A.
Management. M.B.A.
Marketing. M.B.A.
Non-Profit Management. M.M.

Graduate School of Education

Graduate study since 1965. Tuition: per credit $425. Enrollment: full-time 39, part-time 272. Faculty: full-time 7, part-time 7. Degree conferred: M.A.Ed.

ADMISSION REQUIREMENTS. Transcripts, letters of recommendation, GRE/MAT, personal biographical summary required in support of School's application. TOEFL (minimum score 500) required for international applicants. Accepts transfer students. Apply by July 1 (Fall), December 1 (Spring). Application fee $35. Phone: (800)643-7976, ext. 14; (918)495-6553; fax: (918) 495-6959.

ADMISSION STANDARDS. Selective. Usual minimum average: 3.0 (A = 4).

FINANCIAL AID. Scholarships, grants, assistantships, internships, Federal W/S, loans. Approved for VA benefits. Apply by June 15 to Director of University Financial Aid. Phone: (918) 495-6510; fax: (918)395-6803. Use FAFSA (School code: 003985). About 30% of students receive aid other than loans from University and outside sources. Aid available for part-time students.

DEGREE REQUIREMENTS. For M.A.Ed.: 30–36 credit hours depending upon program; thesis optional. For Ed.D.: 60–65 credit program; dissertation.

FIELDS OF STUDY.
Christian School Administration (PK–12). M.A., Ed.D.
College and Higher Education Administration. M.A., Ed.D.
Curriculum Development. M.A.
Public School Administration. M.A., Ed.D.
Teaching. M.A.
Teaching English as a Second Language (TESL). M.A.

Graduate School of Theology and Missions

Graduate study since 1965. Tuition: per credit $400. Enrollment: full-time 264, part-time 156. Faculty: full-time 16, part-time 15. Degrees conferred: M.A., M.Div., D.Min.

ADMISSION REQUIREMENTS. Transcripts, letters of recommendation, photograph, GRE/MAT/GMAT required in support of School's application. TOEFL (minimum score 550) required for international applicants. Accepts transfer students. Apply by July 1 (Fall), December 1 (Spring). Application fee $35. Phone: (800)643-7976, ext. 13, (918)495-6618; fax: (918)495-7965.

ADMISSION STANDARDS. Selective. Usual minimum average: 2.5 (A = 4).

FINANCIAL AID. Scholarships, assistantships, grants, Federal W/S, loans. Approved for VA benefits. Apply by June 1 to Director of University Financial Aid. Phone: (918)495-6510; fax: (918) 395-6803. Use FAFSA (School code: 003985). About 30% of students receive aid other than loans from University and outside sources.

DEGREE REQUIREMENTS. For M.A.: 51–57 credit hours depending upon program; thesis/nonthesis option. For M.Div.: 88 credits minimum in full-time residence; final comprehensive exam or research paper. For D.Min.: 36 credits minimum beyond M.Div., at least two semesters in full-time residence; thesis.

FIELDS OF STUDY.
Biblical Literature. Includes advanced languages concentration, Judaic-Christian concentration. M.A., M.Div.
Christian Counseling. M.A.C.C.
Christian Counseling, Marital, and Family Therapy. M.A.C.C/ M.F.T.
Christian Education. M.A.C.E.
Church Ministries and Leadership. D.Div.
Missions. M.A.M.
Pastoral Care and Counseling. D.Div.
Practical Theology. M.A.P.T.
Practices of Ministry. M.Div.
Theological/Historical Studies. M.A., M.Div.

OREGON HEALTH AND SCIENCES UNIVERSITY

Portland, Oregon 97239-3098

Web site: www.ohsu.edu

Founded in 1867. Located on top of Marquam Hill, a short distance from downtown. In 1974 the University of Oregon's Schools of Dentistry, Medicine, and Nursing were unified at the

University of Oregon Health Sciences Center in Portland; in 1981 it was renamed the Oregon Health Sciences University and it became an Independent Non-Profit Public Corporation. It is an upper-level/graduate institution. In 2001 it merged with Oregon Graduate Institute of Science and Technology and the name was changed to Oregon Health and Sciences University. Special facilities: Center for Human Computer Communication, Center for Ethics in Health Care, Center for Information Technology, General Clinical Research Center, Heart Research Center, Cancer Institute, Oregon Hearing Research Center, Oregon Health Policy Institute, Oregon Institute on Disability and Development, Vaccine and Gene Therapy Institute, Vollum Institute for Advanced Biomedical Research, Oregon Regional Primate Research Center, Center for Research on Occupational and Environmental Toxicology, Biomedical Information Communication Center, Center for the Application of Advanced Materials Science and Engineering Concepts, Center for Coastal and Land-Margin Research, Center for Groundwater Research, Center for Molecular Cardiology, Center for Semiconductor Research, Center for Spoken Language Understanding, Data-Intensive Systems Center, Change Research Center, Pacific Software Research Center. University Hospital is a member of the Council of Teaching Hospitals. The University's NIH ranking is 33rd among all U.S. institutions with 505 awards/grants valued at $175,443,012. According to The Center at University of Florida, the University is ranked 50th in receipt of Federal Research funds with $164,221,000 and it ranks 71st for total University research expenditures with $197,178,000. In 2004, four of the University's faculty members were elected to National Honor Academies and this ranks it 97th among all U.S. institutions. The Library: approximately 250,000 volumes, 2800 subscriptions. Total University enrollment: 1900.

On-campus housing available. Contact Student Housing Office for current information. Phone (503)494-7878. Annual housing cost: $19,278.

OGI School of Science and Technology

Located in Beaverton, Oregon, 97006-8921. Graduate study only. Coed. Quarter system.

Tuition: per credit $625. Enrollment: full-time 319, part-time 261. Faculty: full-time 63, part-time 40. Degrees conferred: M.S., Ph.D.

ADMISSION REQUIREMENTS. Transcripts, GRE, three letters of recommendation, statement of purpose required in support of Institute's application. TOEFL (minimum score 550) required for international applicants. Accepts transfer applicants. Graduates of unaccredited institutions not considered. Apply to the Department of Graduate Education at least two months prior to the date of registration. Rolling admissions process. Application fee $65. Phone: (800)685-2423, (503)748-1137.

ADMISSION STANDARDS. Selective for most departments, competitive for the others. Usual minimum average: 3.0 (A = 4).

FINANCIAL AID. Fellowships, scholarships, assistantships, Federal W/S, loans. Apply to the appropriate department chair for fellowships, assistantships; to Financial Aid Office for all other programs. Phone: (503)494-7800. Use FAFSA (School code: 004883). About 65% of students receive aid from Institute and outside sources.

DEGREE REQUIREMENTS. For M.S.: 45 credit hours minimum, at least 30 credits in residence; thesis/nonthesis option; final written/oral exam. For Ph.D.: three years minimum beyond the bachelor's degree; residency requirement; qualifying exam; candidacy; dissertation; final exam.

FIELDS OF STUDY.
Biochemistry and Molecular Biology.
Biomedical Engineering.
Computational Bioscience.
Computer Engineering and Design.
Computer Science and Engineering.
Electrical Engineering.
Engineering Management. M.S.
Environmental Science and Engineering. Includes environmental information technology.
Machine Learning and Adaptive Systems.
Management in Science and Technology. M.S.
Speech, Language and Interactive System.

School of Dentistry (97239-3098)
Web site: www.ohsu.edu/sod

Founded 1900. Joined state system in 1945. Quarter system.

Annual tuition: resident $18,582, nonresident $32,562. No on-campus housing available. For housing contact the Office of Student Affairs. Average academic year housing cost: $17,880. Total average cost for all other first-year expenses. $12,750.

Enrollment: first-year class 75, total 310 (men 67%, women 33%, minorities 16%, state and WICHE residents 92%). Faculty: full-time 72, part-time 91. Degrees conferred: D.M.D., M.S., D.M.D.-M.S., Certificate.

ADMISSION REQUIREMENTS. Priority given to state residents and WICHE residents, U.S. citizens and permanent residents only. The Junior College transfer credit limit is 60/90 credits. Applicants must have completed at least one year at a four-year institution prior to enrollment. Will consider applicants with only three years of undergraduate preparation, prefer applicants who will have a bachelor's degree prior to enrollment. Around 68 out of 70 enrolled students have bachelor's degree awarded prior to enrollment. Apply through AADSAS (file after July 1, before November 1), submit official transcripts for each school attended (should show at least 90 semester credits/135 quarter credits), service processing fee; at the same time as you send in AADSAS materials submit Official DAT scores (taken no later than October of the year prior to the year of anticipated enrollment) directly to the Office of Admission and Student Affairs. Preference given to state residents and residents of certified WICHE program. TOEFL may be required of an applicant whose native language is other than English. Submit the following materials only after being contacted by an Admissions Officer: an application fee of $75, a supplemental application, official transcripts, predental committee evaluation or three recommendations from science professors to the Office of Admission and Student Affairs. Interviews are by invitation only and generally for final selection. Joint Degree applicants must apply to and be accepted to both Schools, contact the Office of Admissions and Student Affairs for current information and specific requirements. First-year students admitted Fall only. Rolling admissions process, notification starts December 1 and is finished when class is filled. School does maintain an alternate list. Phone: (503)494-5274; fax: (503)494-6244; e-mail: cromleyn@ohsu.edu.

ADMISSION STANDARDS. Competitive. Accepts about 10–15% of all applicants. Usual minimum UGPA: 3.0 (A = 4). Mean DAT: academic 19.55, PAT 18.87; mean UGPA 3.58.

FINANCIAL AID. Grants, scholarships, loans. Apply to Financial Aid Office by March 1; Financial Aid interview required. Phone: (503)494-7800; fax: (503)494-4629. Use FAFSA (School code: 003223). About 97% of students receive some aid from School and outside sources.

DEGREE REQUIREMENTS. For D.M.D.: satisfactory completion of forty-five-month program. Students take Part I of the National Board Exam after their sophomore year and Part II in December of their senior year. For M.S.: 45 quarter hours minimum, at least three quarters in residence; thesis; final oral exam.

FIELDS OF POSTGRADUATE STUDY.
Endodontology. M.S., Certificate.
Oral and Maxillofacial Surgery. M.S., Certificate.
Orthodontics. M.S., Certificate.
Pediatric Dentistry. M.S., Certificate.
Periodontics. M.S., Certificate.

School of Medicine

Web site: www.ohsu.edu/som

Established 1887. Academic year has three terms. Library: 150,000 volumes, 2500 subscriptions. NIH ranking is 33rd among all U.S. institutions with 505 awards/grants worth $175,443,012.

Annual tuition: resident $30,277, nonresident $40,675. On-campus housing available. Phone (503)494-7747. Total average figure for all other expenses: $15,000.

Enrollment: first-year class 112, total 483 (men 45%, women 55%, minorities 18%, state residents 59%), graduate programs 100. Faculty: full-time 1466, part-time 292. Degrees conferred: M.D., M.D.-M.P.H., M.D.-M.S., M.D.-Ph.D.

ADMISSION REQUIREMENTS. For M.D. program: AMCAS report, transcripts, letters of recommendation, MCAT, interview required in support of application. Applicants must have completed at least three years of college study. Preference given to Oregon residents, ethnic minorities, and residents of WICHE states without medical schools. Does not have EDP. Apply to Office of Admissions after June 1, before October 15. Application fee $75. Phone: (503)494-2998; fax: (503)494-3400. For graduate study: transcripts, letters of recommendation, GRE Subject Tests required in support of application. Interview sometimes required. Accepts transfer applicants. Graduates of unaccredited colleges not considered. Apply to Director of Admissions at least three months prior to date of expected entrance.

ADMISSION STANDARDS. Competitive. Accepts about 5% of all applicants. Number of applications 3601 (3242 out-of-state); number interviewed 521(353 out-of-state); number of acceptances 223 (138 out-of-state); number enrolled 112 (44 out-of-state). Mean Composite MCAT 10.3; mean UGPA 3.63. *U.S. News & World Report* ranking is in the top 32 of all U.S. medical research schools, 4th in primary care.

FINANCIAL AID. For M.D. program: scholarships, loans. Apply to Financial Aid Office; no specified closing date. For graduate study: research fellowships, assistantships. Apply to appropriate department chair; no specified closing date. Phone: (503)494-7800. About 95% of students receive some aid from School.

DEGREE REQUIREMENTS. For M.D.: satisfactory completion of four-year program; must pass Step 1 and Step 2 of USMLE for graduation. For M.S.: 45 credit hours minimum, at least three terms in residence; thesis; final oral exam. For Ph.D.: 135 credit hours minimum, at least six terms in residence; reading knowledge of one foreign language; written qualifying exam; thesis; final oral exam.

FIELDS OF GRADUATE STUDY.
Behavioral Neuroscience.
Biomedical Informatics. M.S. Ph.D.
Biostatistics. M.P.H.
Clinical Nutrition.
Clinical Research
Epidemiology. M.P.H.
Neuroscience.
Molecular and Cellular Biosciences. Includes Biochemistry and Molecular Biology, Cell and Developmental Biology, Molecular and Medical Genetics, Molecular Microbiology and Immunology, Physiology and Pharmacology.

OREGON STATE UNIVERSITY

Corvallis, Oregon 97331
Web site: www.orst.edu

Founded 1868. Located 85 miles S of Portland. CGS member. Coed. State control. Quarter system. Special facilities: Agricultural Experiment Station, Center for Advanced Materials Research, Center for Gene Research and Biotechnology, Center for Analysis of Environmental Change, Computer Center, Cooperative Center for Marine Resources Studies, Engineering Experiment Station, Environmental Health Sciences Center, Environmental Remote Sensing Laboratory, Forest Research Laboratory, Center for Humanities, Integrated Plant Protection Center, Mark O. Hatfield Marine Science Center, Nuclear Science and Engineering Institute, Nutrition Research Institute, Radiation Center, Sea Grant College Program, Survey Research Center, Transportation Research Institute, Water Resources Research Institute, the Western Rural Development Center. According to The Center at University of Florida, the University is ranked 76th in receipt of Federal Research funds with $100,499,000 and it ranks 81st for total University research expenditures with $167,631,000. In 2004, the University awarded 173 doctorates, which ranked it 84th among all U.S. institutions eligible to award that degree. Five of the University's faculty members have been elected to National Honor Academies and this ranks it 90th among all U.S. institutions. The Library: approximately 1,225,000 volumes, 12,254 subscriptions. Total University enrollment: 19,200.

Annual tuition: full-time resident $8139, nonresident $14,376; per credit resident $301, nonresident $532. On-campus housing includes dormitories, cooperative living groups, apartments for married students, and miscellaneous rental properties owned by the University. Average annual (12 month) housing costs: $6930 (including board). Apply to Director of Housing and Dining Services. Phone: (541)737-4771. Day-care facilities available.

Graduate School

Web site: www.oregonstate.edu/dept/grad_school

Graduate study since 1876. Enrollment: full-time 1996, part-time 499. Graduate faculty: full- and part-time 840. Degrees conferred: M.A., M.Agr., M.A.I.S., M.A.T., M.B.A., Ed.M., M.Eng., M.F., M.Oc.E., M.P.H., M.P.P., M.S., Ed.D., Ph.D.

ADMISSION REQUIREMENTS. Transcripts, letters of recommendation, statement indicating special fields of interest required in support of School's application. GRE/GMAT/NTE required by some departments. TOEFL and certification of financial support required for international applicants. Accepts transfer applicants. Graduates of unaccredited institutions not considered. Apply by March 15 to Office of Admission and Orientation. Some departments may establish earlier deadlines. Application fee $50. Phone: (541)737-4411; fax: (541)737-2482.

ADMISSION STANDARDS. Selective. Usual minimum average: 3.0 (A = 4) on the last 90 graded quarter hours of undergraduate work.

FINANCIAL AID. Annual awards from institutional funds: teaching assistantships, research assistantships, internships, Federal W/S, loans. Approved for VA benefits. Apply to appropriate department chair for assistantships; to Financial Aid Office for all other programs. Phone: (541)737-2241; fax: (541)737-2400. Use FAFSA. Aid available for part-time students.

DEGREE REQUIREMENTS. For master's: 45 credit hours minimum, at least 30 in residence; thesis/nonthesis option; final exam for some programs. For Ph.D.: three years minimum beyond the bachelor's; residency requirement; preliminary exam; thesis; final exam. For Ed.D.: two years teaching experience; other requirements essentially the same as for the Ph.D.

FIELDS OF STUDY.
Adult Education. Ed.M.
Agricultural and Resource Economics. M.S., Ph.D.
Agricultural Education. M.S.
Agriculture. M.Agr.
Animal Science. M.S., Ph.D.
Applied Anthropology. M.A.
Applied Physics. M.S.
Atmospheric Sciences. M.A., M.S., Ph.D.
Biochemistry and Biophysics. M.A., M.S., Ph.D.
Biological and Ecological Engineering. M.Eng., M.S., Ph.D.
Botany and Plant Pathology. M.A., M.S., Ph.D.
Business Administration. M.B.A.
Chemical Engineering. M.S., Ph.D.
Chemistry. M.A., M.S., Ph.D.
Civil Engineering. M.S., Ph.D.
College Student Services Administration. Ed.M., M.S.
Comparative Veterinary Medicine. Ph.D.
Computer Science. M.A., M.S., Ph.D.
Construction Engineering Management. M.B.E.
Counseling. M.S., Ph.D.
Creative Writing. M.F.A.
Crop Science. M.S., Ph.D.
Design and Human Environment. M.A., M.S., Ph.D.
Economics. M.A., M.S., Ph.D.
Education. Ed.M., M.S., Ed.D., Ph.D.
Electrical and Computer Engineering. M.S., Ph.D.
English. M.A.
Entomology. M.A., M.S., Ph.D.
Environmental Health and Occupational Safety Management. M.S.
Environmental Science. M.A., M.S., Ph.D.
Exercise and Sport Science. M.S., Ph.D.
Fisheries Sciences. M.S., Ph.D.
Food Science and Technology. M.S., Ph.D.
Forest Engineering. M.F., M.S., Ph.D.
Forest Products. M.F.
Forest Resources. M.F., M.S., Ph.D.
Forest Science. M.F., M.S., Ph.D.
Genetics. M.A., M.S., Ph.D.
Geography. M.A., M.S., Ph.D.
Geology. M.A., M.S., Ph.D.
Geophysics. M.A., M.S., Ph.D.
Health Promotion and Health Behavior. M.S.
Health and Safety Administration. M.S.
History of Science. M.A., M.S., Ph.D.
Horticulture. M.S., Ph.D.
Human Development and Family Studies. M.S., Ph.D.
Industrial Engineering. M.S., Ph.D.
Interdisciplinary Studies. M.A.I.S.
Marine Resource Management. M.A., M.S.
Materials Science. M.S.
Mathematics. M.A., M.S., Ph.D.
Mathematics Education. M.A., M.S., Ph.D.
Mechanical Engineering. M.S., Ph.D.
Microbiology. M.A., M.S., Ph.D.
Molecular and Cellular Biology. Ph.D.
Movement Studies in Disability. M.S.
Nuclear Engineering. M.S., Ph.D.
Nutrition and Food Management. M.S., Ph.D.
Ocean Engineering. M.Oc.E.
Oceanography. M.A., M.S., Ph.D.
Operations Research. M.A., M.S.
Pharmacy. M.S., Ph.D.
Physics. M.A., M.S., Ph.D.
Plant Physiology. M.S., Ph.D.
Poultry Science. M.S., Ph.D.
Public Health. M.P.H., M.S., Ph.D.
Public Policy. M.P.P.
Radiation Health Physics. M.A., M.S., Ph.D.
Rangeland Ecology and Management. M.S., Ph.D.
Science Education. M.A., M.S., Ph.D.

Soil Science. M.S., Ph.D.
Statistics. M.A., M.S., Ph.D.
Teaching. M.A.T.
Toxicology. M.S., Ph.D.
Veterinary Science. M.S.
Water Resources Engineering. M.S., Ph.D.
Water Resources Policy and Management. M.S.
Water Resurces Science. M.S., Ph.D.
Wildlife Science. M.S., Ph.D.
Wood Science. M.S., Ph.D.
Zoology. M.A., M.S., Ph.D.

College of Veterinary Medicine (97331-4801)
Web site: oregonstate.edu/vetmed

Established 1949. Quarter system.

Annual tuition: resident and WICHE contract nonresidents $15,585, nonresidents $29,733. On-campus housing available. Estimated living expenses: $7344. Total all other expenses: $4500.

Enrollment: first year class 48, total 196 (men 19%, women 81%, minorities 15%, state residents 85%). Faculty: full-time 37, part-time 6. Degree conferred: D.V.M. The M.S. and Ph.D. are offered through the Graduate School.

ADMISSION REQUIREMENTS. VMCAS report, transcripts, GRE, three recommendations, animal/veterinary experience, essay required in support of application. Interview by invitation only. Accepts transfer applicants on a space-available basis only. Graduates of unaccredited colleges not considered. Applicants must have completed at least two years of preprofessional college study. Preference given to state and Western Regional Compact state residents. Apply to Dean, College of Veterinary Medicine after July 1, before October 1. Fall admission only. Application fee $50. Phone: (541)737-2098; fax: (541)737-4245.

ADMISSION STANDARDS. Selective. Accepts about 10–15% of all applicants. Number of enrolled students 48 (8 out-of-state). Usual minimum UGPA: 3.0 (A = 4). GRE mean score (V + Q) 1150; mean UGPA 3.60.

FINANCIAL AID. Scholarships, fellowships, assistantships, Federal W/S, loans, grants. Apply by February 1 to Director of Student Aids. Use FAFSA.

DEGREE REQUIREMENTS. For D.V.M.: satisfactory completion of four-year program. For Compact state residents: first year at OSU, second and third years at Washington State University, fourth year back at OSU. For M.S., Ph.D.: see Graduate School listing above.

FIELDS OF GRADUATE STUDY.
Veterinary Sciences. Includes anatomy, clinical sciences, immunology, microbiology, pathology, physiology, toxicology. M.S.
Comparative Veterinary Medicine. Includes in basic sciences—anatomy, biochemistry, histology, immunology, molecular biology; in biological fields—microbiology, nutrition. pathology, toxicology. Ph.D.

UNIVERSITY OF OREGON
Eugene, Oregon 97403-1217
Web site: www.uoregon.edu

Established 1871. CGS and AAU member. Coed. State control. Quarter system. Special facilities: Institute for Chemical Physics, Humanities Center, Institute for Molecular Biology, Institute for Neuroscience, Institute of Theoretical Science, Computing Center, Advanced Science and Technology Institute, Bureau of Government Research, Institute on Violence and Destructive Behavior, Center for the Study of Women in Society, Oregon Institute of

Marine Biology, Solar Energy Center. Library: 2,600,000 volumes, 18,500 subscriptions. Total University enrollment: 20,300.

Tuition: full-time, per term resident $3345, nonresident $4933. On-campus housing for married students and single students. Average academic year housing costs: $500–$900 (per month) for married students off-campus; $6800 (including board) for single students on-campus. Contact Housing Office for both on- and off-campus housing information. Phone: (541)346-4277. Day-care facilities available.

Graduate School

Organized 1900. Enrollment: full- and part-time 3933. Faculty: full-time 615, part-time 55. Degrees conferred: M.A., M.Arch., M.B.A., M.Ed., M.F.A., M.Mus., M.S., M.U.P., Ed.D., D.M.A., Ph.D.

ADMISSION REQUIREMENTS. Two different sets of materials must be submitted to the University. Official transcripts, $50 application fee, and the graduate application should be sent to the Office of Admissions. Official transcripts, letters of recommendation, GRE/MAT (if required), and the graduate application should be sent directly to the major department. Online application available. TOEFL (minimum score 500), TSE (required for assistantship applicants), and the International Students Financial Statement are required for international applicants. Accepts transfer applicants. Graduates of unaccredited institutions not considered. Apply to appropriate department or school at least one month prior to registration. Most departments admit Fall only. Rolling admissions process. Application fee $50. Phone: (541) 346-5129.

ADMISSION STANDARDS. Selective. Usual minimum average: 3.0 (A = 4).

FINANCIAL AID. Annual awards from institutional funds: research/teaching assistantships, full tuition waiver, Federal W/S, loans. Approved for VA benefits. Apply by February 1 to appropriate department for fellowships, assistantships; to the Office of Student Financial Aid for all other programs. Phone: (541)346-3221. Use FAFSA. About 30% of students receive aid other than loans from School. Aid available for part-time students.

DEGREE REQUIREMENTS. For most master's: 45 quarter hours minimum, at least 39 in residence; reading knowledge of one foreign language for M.A.; qualifying exam/final exam/thesis required for some departments. For M.F.A.: two years minimum, at least one year in full-time residence; final project; oral/written final exam. For M.Arch., M.L.A., M.U.P.: 45 quarter hours minimum, at least 39 in residence; thesis/final project. For Ph.D.: three years minimum beyond the bachelor's, at least one year in residence; qualifying exam; advancement to candidacy; oral/written comprehensive exam; thesis; oral/written final exam. For Ed.D.: essentially the same as for the Ph.D., except no specified language requirement.

FIELDS OF STUDY.

SCHOOL OF ARCHITECTURE AND ALLIED ARTS:
Architecture. M.Arch. only.
Art. M.F.A. only.
Art History.
Arts Management.
Ceramics. M.F.A.
Community and Regional Planning. M.C.R.P. only.
Digital Arts. M.F.A.
Fibers. M.F.A.
Historic Preservation. M.S. only.
Interior Architecture. M.I.Arch.
Landscape Architecture. Includes planning, public policy, and management. M.L.A. only.

Metalsmithing and Jewelry. M.F.A.
Painting. M.F.A.
Photography. M.F.A.
Printmaking. M.F.A.
Public Policy and Management. M.A., M.S.
Sculpture. M.F.A.
Visual Design. M.F.A.

COLLEGE OF ARTS AND SCIENCES:
Anthropology. Includes archaeology, cultural, linguistics, physical.
Applied Physics. M.S. only.
Asian Studies. Interdisciplinary. Includes China, Japan, Southeast Asia. M.A., M.S.
Biology. Includes cell, developmental, ecology, genetics, marine, microbiology, molecular, neuroscience.
Chemistry. Includes biochemistry, cell biology, chemical physics, materials science, organic, physical, theoretical.
Classics. Includes classics, Greek, Latin. M.A. only.
Comparative Literature. Interdisciplinary.
Computer Science and Information Science.
Creative Writing. M.A. only.
East Asian Languages and Literatures.
Economics. Includes advanced macroeconomics, applied econometrics, economic growth and development, industrial organization, international, labor, public finance, urban-regional.
English. Includes American literature, creative writing, English literature.
Environmental Sciences, Studies, and Policy. Ph.D. only.
Environmental Studies. M.A., M.S.
Exercise and Movement Science. Includes biomechanics, human physiology, motor control, physiology of exercise, social psychology of sport, sport medicine.
French. M.A. only.
Geography. Includes biogeography, cultural, physical, quaternary geography.
Geological Sciences. Includes mineral deposits, mineralogy-petrology-geochemistry, stratigraphy-sedimentary petrology, paleontology, structural geology-geophysics, volcanology.
Germanic Languages and Literature.
History. Includes ancient, Britain and its empire, East Asia and Southeast Asia, German-speaking world, Latin American, medieval, early modern and modern Europe, Soviet Union, United States.
Human Physiology. M.S., Ph.D.
International Studies. Interdisciplinary. M.A. only.
Italian. M.A. only.
Linguistics. Includes applied, general. M.S., Ph.D.
Mathematics. Includes algebra, analysis, combinatorics, differential and algebraic geometry, geometry, mathematical physics, numerical analysis, probability, statistics, topology.
Philosophy.
Physics. Includes astronomy, astrophysics, cosmology; atomic and molecular; optical; biophysics; condensed-matter; elementary-particle; fluid and superfluid mechanics; nuclear.
Political Science. Includes American government, classical and contemporary political theory, comparative politics, international relations, public policy, research methodology.
Psychology. Includes clinical, cognitive, developmental, physiological-neuroscience, social and personality.
Romance Languages. Includes French, Italian, Spanish language and literature.
Russian and East European Studies. M.A.
Sociology. Includes sex and gender; labor, organization, and political; environment; social psychology; language and culture; theory.
Spanish. M.A.
Theater Arts.

CHARLES H. LUNDQUIST COLLEGE OF BUSINESS:
Accounting.
Decision Sciences. Includes business statistics, production, and operations management.

Finance.

Management. Includes corporate strategy and policy (Ph.D.), general business (M.B.A.), human resources management (Ph.D.), organizational studies (Ph.D.).

Marketing.

COLLEGE OF EDUCATION:

Communication Disorders and Sciences.

Counseling, Family, and Human Services. Includes community and other agency settings, early intervention, employment and vocational, individual and family.

Counseling Psychology. Ph.D. only.

Educational Leadership.

School Psychology.

Special Education. Includes developmental disabilities, handicapped learner, rehabilitation (Ph.D.).

Teaching and Learning. M.Ed.

GRADUATE SCHOOL:

Applied Information Management. M.S.

Folklore. M.A.

Individualized Program. M.A.

SCHOOL OF JOURNALISM AND COMMUNICATION:

Communication and Society. Ph.D. only.

Journalism. Includes advertising, magazine, news-editorial. M.A., M.S. only.

SCHOOL OF MUSIC:

Composition. M.Mus.

Conducting. M.Mus.

Dance. M.A.

Intermedia Music Technology. M.Mus.

Jazz Studies. M.Mus.

Music Education.

Music History.

Music Performance.

Music Theory.

Piano Pedagogy.

School of Law (97403-1221)

Web site: www.law.uoregon.edu

Established 1884. Located in Eugene. ABA approved since 1923. AALS member. Public control. Semester system. Special facilities: Environment and Natural Resources Law Center, Center for Law and Entrepreneurship, Ocean and Coastal Law Center, the Wayne Morse Center for Law and Politics. Summer study available. Law library: 358,470 volumes, 2814 subscriptions; has LEXIS, NEXIS, WESTLAW; has more than 1000 network connections.

Annual tuition: resident $18,690, nonresident $223,262, LL.M. $35,358. On campus housing available. Total average annual additional expenses: $12,265.

Enrollment: first-year class 179; total full-time 536 (men 57%, women 43%, minorities 18%). Faculty: full-time 30, part-time 20. Student to faculty ratio 19.7 to 1. Degrees conferred: J.D., J.D.-M.A. (International Studies), J.D.-M.B.A., J.D.-M.S. (Environmental Studies), LL.M. (Conflict and Dispute Resolution, Environmental and Natural Resource Law).

ADMISSION REQUIREMENTS. LSDAS law school report, bachelor's degree, transcripts, LSAT, personal statement, résumé, two letters of recommendation required in support of application. Accepts transfer applicants. Graduates of unaccredited institutions not considered. Apply to Admissions Office after September 1, before March 1. Fall admission only. Application fee $50. Phone: (541)346-3846, (541)346-0532. For LL.M. information phone: (541)346-0532.

ADMISSION STANDARDS. Selective. Accepts approximately 37% of all students. Number of applicants 1944; number of acceptances 726; number enrolled 179; LSAT (75% of students have a score at or above 156); GPA (75% of students have a GPA at or above 3.17). *U.S. News & World Report* ranking is in the second tier (tied at 82nd) of all U.S. law schools.

FINANCIAL AID. Scholarships, partial tuition waivers, Federal W/S, loans, grants for second- and third-year students. Apply to Office of Financial Aid by March 1. Phone: (800)760-6953. Use FAFSA (School code: 003223). About 49% of students receive aid other than loans from School.

DEGREE REQUIREMENTS. For J.D.: satisfactory completion of three-year program. For M.B.A., M.S.: see Graduate School listing above. For LL.M.: 20 credit full-time programs; LL.M. seminar; written comprehensive paper or project.

OUR LADY OF THE LAKE UNIVERSITY
San Antonio, Texas 78207-4666
Web site: www.ollusa.edu

Founded 1985. Coed. Independent. Roman Catholic. Semester system, except Weekend College's M.B.A. is on trimester system. Library: 166,000 volumes, 3000 subscriptions. Total University enrollment: 2900.

Tuition: per credit hour $628 (Master's), $728 (Doctoral). On-campus housing available for single and married students. Average academic year housing costs: $6193. Apply to Office of Campus Activities and Services. Phone: (210)434-6711.

College of Art and Sciences

Graduate study since 1911. Enrollment: full-time 5 and part-time 30. Graduate faculty: full-time 5, part-time 3. Degrees conferred: M.A., Psy.D.

ADMISSION REQUIREMENTS. Transcripts, GRE required in support of application. Online application available. TOEFL required for foreign applicants. Accepts transfer applicants. Apply to Director of Admissions by August 15 (Fall), December 15 (Spring), May 5 (Summer). Application fee $25, $50 for international applicants. Phone: (210)434-6711, ext. 314; fax: (210)434-4036; e-mail: gradadm@lake.ollusa.edu.

ADMISSION STANDARDS. Selective. Usual minimum average: 2.5, or 3.0 (A = 4) in last 60 undergraduate credits.

FINANCIAL AID. Scholarships, assistantships, internships, tuition waivers, Federal W/S, loans. Approved for VA benefits. Apply by April 15 to the Office of Financial Aid. Phone: (210)434-6711.Use FAFSA.

DEGREE REQUIREMENTS. For M.A.: 30–36 credits minimum; thesis/nonthesis. For Psy.D.: 54 credits in residence beyond master's degree, at least 30 credits in residence; candidacy; clinical case study; final oral exam.

FIELDS OF STUDY.

English Communication Arts.

English Education.

English Language and Literature.

Note: Cooperative programs with University of the Incarnate Word and St. Mary's University.

School of Business and Public Administration

Graduate study since 1978. Coed. Trimester system. A weekend instructional format.

Tuition: per credit $586. Enrollment: full-time 22, part-time 304. Graduate faculty: full-time 12, part-time 9. Degree conferred: M.B.A.

ADMISSION REQUIREMENTS. Transcripts, GRE/MAT/ GMAT, two letters of recommendation, detailed résumé required in support of School's application. TOEFL required for international applicants. Accepts transfer applicants. Graduates of unaccredited institutions not considered. Apply to Director of Admission by at least one week prior to Weekend College orientation for the trimester of registration. Application fee $25, $50 for international applicants. Phone: (210)434-6711; fax: (210)434-0821.

ADMISSION STANDARDS. Selective. Usual minimum average: 2.5, or 3.0 (A = 4) in last 60 undergraduate credits.

FINANCIAL AID. Grants, loans. Approved for VA benefits. Apply by April 15 to the Office of Financial Aid. Phone: (210)434-6711. Use FAFSA.

DEGREE REQUIREMENTS. For M.B.A.: 36 credits minimum; advancement to candidacy; thesis/professional project option in lieu of six semester hours of electives.

FIELDS OF STUDY.
Business Administration. Includes finance, international business, management.
Electronic Commerce Management.
Health Care Management.

School of Education and Clinical Studies

Graduate study since 1950. Tuition: per credit $628; doctoral tuition per credit $728.
Enrollment: full-time 148, part-time 458. Graduate faculty: full-time 29, part-time 21. Degrees conferred: M.A., M.Ed., M.S., Psy.D.

ADMISSION REQUIREMENTS. Transcripts, GRE/MAT, two letters of recommendation required in support of School's application. Online application available. TOEFL required for foreign applicants. Accepts transfer applicants. Apply to School of Education by August 6 (Fall), January 4 (Spring), May 5 (Summer); some programs have earlier deadlines. Application fee $25, $50 for international applicants. Phone: (210)434-6711; fax: (210) 434-2314.

ADMISSION STANDARDS. Selective. Usual minimum average: 2.5, or 3.0 (A = 4) in last 60 undergraduate credits.

FINANCIAL AID. Fellowships, assistantships for teaching/ research, internships, grants, Federal W/S, loans. Approved for VA benefits. Apply by April 15 to the Office of Financial Aid. Phone: (210)434-6711, ext. 314. Use FAFSA.

DEGREE REQUIREMENTS. For M.A.: 36 credits minimum, at least 24 in residence; final oral/written exam. For M.Ed.: 36 credits minimum, at least 30 in residence; final written exam. For M.S. (Psychology): 60 credits minimum; comprehensive exam. For Psy.D.: 119 credits beyond the bachelor's degree, two consecutive 9-hour semesters in residence; dissertation; written/oral exam.

FIELDS OF STUDY.
Curriculum and Instruction. Includes bilingual, early childhood, English as a second language, integrated math teaching, integrated science teaching, master reading teacher, master technology teacher—online, reading specialist. M.Ed.
Early Elementary Education. Includes bilingual, early childhood, generic special education, professional studies. M.Ed.

Intermediate Education. Includes math/science education, professional studies. M.Ed.
Learning Resources Specialist. M.Ed.
Principal. M.Ed.
School Counseling. M.Ed.
Secondary Education. Includes math/science education, professional studies. M.Ed.
Special Education. Includes early childhood, generic special education, educational diagnostician, severely emotionally disturbed autistic, severe to profound handicapped. M.A.

Worden School of Social Services

Graduate study since 1942. Coed. Semester system.
Enrollment: full-time 59, part-time 22. Graduate faculty: full-time 7, part-time 3. Degree conferred: M.S.W.

ADMISSION REQUIREMENTS. Transcripts, GRE/MAT, three letters of recommendation required in support of School's application. TOEFL required for international applicants. Interview may be required. Accepts transfer applicants. Graduates of unaccredited institutions not considered. Apply to Director of Admission by April 2 (Fall), November 1 (Spring). Application fee $25, $50 for international applicants. Phone: (210)434-7111, ext. 231; fax: (210)434-2314.

ADMISSION STANDARDS. Selective. Usual minimum average: 2.5, or 3.0 (A = 4) in last 60 undergraduate credits.

FINANCIAL AID. Assistantships, internships, tuition waivers, Federal W/S, loans. Approved for VA benefits. Apply by April 15 to the Office of Financial Aid. Phone: (210)434-6711, ext. 319. Use FAFSA.

DEGREE REQUIREMENTS. For M.S.W.: 58 credits minimum, at least one year in residence; field practicum; final oral/written exam.
Note: A 36 credit hour program is available for eligible undergraduates with a B.S.W. from a CSWE accredited program.

FIELDS OF STUDY.
Social Work. Includes concentrations in services to children and families, program planning and administration. M.S.W.

PACE UNIVERSITY
New York, New York 10038
Web site: www.pace.edu

Founded 1906. Westchester campuses at Pleasantville/Briarcliff and White Plains. CGS member. Not all programs available at all campuses. Private control. Semester system. Special facilities: Center for Applied Research, Center for International Business, Center for Nursing Research and Clinical Practice. Library: 825,000 volumes, 2637 subscriptions. Total University enrollment: 14,100.
Tuition: per credit $856. On-campus housing for single students at all campuses. Average academic year housing costs: $10,320.

Lubin School of Business Graduate Programs

Graduate study since 1906. Tuition: per credit $856. Enrollment: full-time 175, part-time 846. Graduate faculty: full-time 128, part-time 42. Degrees conferred: M.S., M.B.A.

ADMISSION REQUIREMENTS. Transcript, GMAT, personal statement, résumé required in support of School's application. TOEFL required for international applicants. Interview may be required. Accepts transfer applicants. Graduates of unaccredited colleges not considered. Apply to Graduate Admissions Office by July 31 (Fall), November 30 (Spring); for D.P.S.: July 31 (Fall), November 30 (Spring). Application fee $65. Phone: (212)346-1585; fax: (212)346-1963; e-mail: gradnyc@pace.edu.

ADMISSION STANDARDS. Selective. Usual minimum average: 3.0 (A = 4).

FINANCIAL AID. Scholarships, research/administrative assistantships, internships, tuition waivers, Federal W/S, loans. Approved for VA benefits. Apply to Graduate Admissions Office by May 15 (Summer and Fall), December 15 (Spring). Phone: (212)346-1300. Use FAFSA. About 65% of students receive aid from University and outside sources. Aid available to part-time students.

DEGREE REQUIREMENTS. For M.B.A.: 36 credits minimum, at least 33 in residence. For M.S.: 36 credit hours minimum, at least 30 in residence.

FIELDS OF STUDY.
Accounting. M.B.A., M.S.
Banking and Finance. M.B.A.
Business Economics. M.B.A., M.S.
Economics. M.S.
Financial Management. M.B.A., M.S.
Human Resource Management. M.S.
Information Systems. M.B.A.
International Business. M.B.A.
International Economics. M.B.A.
Investment Management. M.S.
Management. M.B.A., M.S.
Management Science. M.B.A.
Managerial Accounting. M.B.A.
Marketing. M.B.A.
Operations Planning and Analysis. M.B.A., M.S.
Taxation. M.B.A., M.S.
Note: Special degree programs include J.D./M.B.A., International Exchange Programs; M.S. Accounting/Internship Program; Dual concentration M.B.A.

Dyson College of Arts and Science

Graduate study since 1906. Tuition: per credit $856. Enrollment: full-time 188, part-time 114. Graduate faculty: full-time 26, part-time 56. Degrees conferred: M.S., M.S.Ed., M.P.A., Psy.D.

ADMISSION REQUIREMENTS. Transcript, GRE/MAT required in support of College's application. TOEFL required for international applicants. Interview may be required. Accepts transfer applicants. Graduates of unaccredited colleges not considered. Apply to Graduate Admissions Office by August 15 (Fall), December 15 (Spring), March 15 (May term), May 1 (Summer). Rolling admissions process. Application fee $65. Phone: (212)346-1531; fax: (212)346-4283; e-mail: gradnyc@pace.edu.

ADMISSION STANDARDS. Selective. Usual minimum average: 3.0 (A = 4).

FINANCIAL AID. Scholarships, research assistantships, teaching assistantships, internships, tuition waivers, Federal W/S, loans. Approved for VA benefits. Apply to Financial Aid Office at 1 Pace Plaza by May 15 (Summer and Fall), December 15 (Spring). Phone: (212)346-1300. Use FAFSA. About 25% of students receive aid from University and outside sources. Aid available for part-time students.

DEGREE REQUIREMENTS. For M.P.A.: 36 credits minimum, at least 33 in residence. For M.S.: 36 credit hours minimum, at least 30 in residence. For Psy.D.: 57 credits beyond the master's;

qualifying exam; internship; written/oral exam; special research project.

FIELDS OF STUDY.
Bilingual School Psychology. M.S.Ed.
Counseling. Includes substance abuse. M.S.
Environmental Science. M.S.
Forensic Science. M.S.
Government Management. M.P.A.
Health Care Administration. M.P.A.
Psychology. M.A.
Public Administration. Includes management of government, health care, nonprofit organization. M.P.A.
Publishing. M.S.
School-Clinical Child Psychology. Psy.D.
School Psychology. M.S.Ed.

Seidenberg School of Computer Science and Information Systems

Established 1983. Classes take place in New York City, Pleasantville, White Plains campuses. Special facilities. Center for Advanced Media, Center for the Advancement of Formal Method Education.

Tuition: per credit $856. Enrollment: full- and part-time 461. Graduate faculty: full-time 23, part-time 29. Degrees conferred: M.S., D.P.S.

ADMISSION REQUIREMENTS. Transcript, GRE, personal statement, two letters of recommendation, interview, supplemental information required in support of College's application. Online application available. TOEFL required for international applicants. Interview may be required. Accepts transfer applicants. Graduate of unaccredited colleges not considered. Apply to Graduate Admissions Office by June 1 (Fall), December 15 (Spring); for D.P.S. applicants July 31 (Fall), November 30 (Spring). Rolling admissions process. Application fee $65. Phone: (212)346-1531; fax: (212)346-4283.

ADMISSION STANDARDS. Selective. Usual minimum average: 3.0 (A = 4).

FINANCIAL AID. Research assistantships, tuition waivers, Federal W/S, loans. Approved for VA benefits. Apply to Graduate Admissions Office by March 15 (Summer and Fall), December 15 (Spring). Phone: (212)346-1300. Use FAFSA (School code: 002727). About 25% of students receive aid from University and outside sources. Aid available for part-time students.

DEGREE REQUIREMENTS. For M.S.: 36 credits minimum, at least 33 in residence; thesis. For D.P.S.: three- to four-year, 48 credit program; qualifying exam; written/oral exam; dissertation; final oral defense.

FIELDS OF STUDY.
Computer Science. M.S.
Computing. D.P.S.
Information Systems. M.S.
Internet Technology. M.S.
Software Development and Engineering. M.S.
Telecommunication. M.S.

School of Education

Special facilities: Center for Urban Education, Center for Literacy, Center for Economic Education, Center for Care Studies.
Tuition: per credit $734. Enrollment: full-time 66, part-time 1700. Graduate faculty: full-time 20, part-time 35. Degrees conferred: M.S.Ed., M.S.T.

ADMISSION REQUIREMENTS. Transcript, personal statement, two letters of recommendation required in support of College's application. Online application available. TOEFL required for international applicants. Interview may be required. Accepts transfer applicants. Graduates of unaccredited colleges not considered. Apply to Graduate Admissions Office by August 1 (Fall), December 15 (Spring). Rolling admissions process. Application fee $65. Phone: (212)346-1652.

ADMISSION STANDARDS. Selective. Usual minimum average: 3.0 (A = 4).

FINANCIAL AID. Research assistantships, internships, tuition waivers, Federal W/S, loans. Approved for VA benefits. Apply to Graduate Admissions Office by March 15 (Summer and Fall), December 15 (Spring). Phone: (914)422-4050. Use FAFSA (School code: 002791). About 25% of students receive aid from University and outside sources. Aid available for part-time students.

DEGREE REQUIREMENTS. For M.S.: 36 credit program, at least 30 in residence.

FIELDS OF STUDY.
Adolescent Education. M.S.T.
Childhood Education. M.S.T.
Educational Leadership. NYC campus only. M.S.Ed.
Educational Technology. M.S.Ed.
Literacy. M.S.Ed.
Special Education. M.S.Ed.

School of Law

Web site: www.law.pace.edu

Established 1976. Located in White Plains (10603), Westchester County's seat. ABA approved since 1978. AALS member. Semester system. Full-time, part-time study. Special facilities: Land Use Law Center, Real Estate Law Institute, Social Justice Center Pace Institute for International Law, Women's Justice Center. Law Library: 382,538 volumes, 4014 subscriptions; has LEXIS, NEXIS, WESTLAW, DIALOG, OCLC, EPIC, RLIN; has more than 250 network connections; is a Federal Government Depository.

Annual tuition: $35,900, part-time $26,758. On-campus housing available for single students. Contact Law School's Residence Halls for on-campus information; the Admissions Office for off-campus information. Law students tend to live off-campus. Annual on-campus housing costs: single room $6500, double room $5400. Off-campus housing and personal expenses approximately $20,182.

Enrollment: first-year class full-time 172, part-time 88; total full- and part-time 755 (men 43%, women 57%, minorities 17%). Faculty: full-time 30, part-time 30. Student to faculty ratio is 17.5 to 1. Degrees conferred: J.D., J.D.-M.B.A., J.D.-M.P.A., J.D.-M.E.M., J.D.-M.S., LL.M. (Environmental Law, Comparative Legal Studies), S.J.D.(Environmental Law).

ADMISSION REQUIREMENTS. For J.D.: LSDAS Law School report, LSAT (not later that February test date; if more than one LSAT, highest is used), bachelor's degree from an accredited institution, personal statement, two appraisals (recommendations), official transcripts (must show all schools attended and at least three years of study) required in support of application. Applicants must have received bachelor's degree prior to enrollment. Interview not required but may be requested by School. In addition, international applicants whose native language is not English must submit a TOEFL report (minimum score 600). Accepts transfer applicants. Graduates of unaccredited institutions not considered. Apply to Office of Admission after September 30, before March 1; February 1 for scholarships consideration. First-year students admitted Fall only. Rolling admissions process. Notification starts in January and is finished by late April. Application fee $65. Phone: (914)422-4210; fax: (914)422-4010; e-mail: admissions@law.pace.edu. For LL.M., S.J.D.: Applicants must

hold a final degree in law (J.D., LL.B) approved by the section of Legal Education of ABA. Submit all official transcripts, at least two professional recommendations, résumé, personal statement to the Office of Admission before March 1. Phone: (914)422-4338. Admits Fall only. Application fee $65. S.J.D. applicants must apply to and be accepted for LL.M.; completion of LL.M. program required before advancement to candidacy.

ADMISSION STANDARDS. Selective. Accepts approximately 33% of full-time and 32% of part-time students. Number of full-time applicants 2708, part-time 509; number of full-time acceptances 889, part-time 161; number of full-time enrolled 172, part-time 88; LSAT (75% of full-time students have a score at or above 153, part-time 151); GPA (75% of full-time students have a GPA at or above 3.09, part-time 2.91). *U.S. News & World Report* ranking is in the third tier of all U.S. law schools.

FINANCIAL AID. Scholarships, merit scholarships, minority scholarships, Grants-in-Aid, institutional loans; Federal loans and Federal W/S offered through University's Financial Aid Office. Assistantships may be available for upper-divisional Joint Degree candidates. Apply to Admissions Office by February 1. For all other programs apply before April 30. Phone: (914)422-4048. Use FAFSA (School code: 002727)), TAP application (New York State residents only), also submit Financial Aid Transcript, Federal Income Tax forms. Approximately 56% of students receive some form of financial assistance.

DEGREE REQUIREMENTS. For J.D.: 90 (40 required) credits with a GPA of at least 2.0. (A = 4), plus completion of upper divisional writing course; three-year program, four-year part-time program. Accelerated J.D. with summer course work. For J.D.-master's: a four-year program rather than a five-year program if both degrees are taken consecutively. For LL.M. (Environmental Law): 24 credits; one year full-time, two years part-time; major research paper. For S.J.D.: completion of LL.M., advancement to candidacy; one year in full-time residence; thesis of publishable quality; oral defense.
Note: School has summer program in conjunction with the University of London (Great Britain).

Lienhard School of Nursing

Tuition: per credit $734. Enrollment: full-time 16, part-time 63. Graduate faculty: full-time 5, part-time 17. Degrees conferred: MA., M.S.N.

ADMISSION REQUIREMENTS. Transcript, GRE, personal statement, two letters of recommendation required in support of School's application. Online application available. TOEFL required for international applicants. Interview may be required. Accepts transfer applicants. Graduates of unaccredited colleges not considered. Apply to Graduate Admissions Office by July 31 (Fall), November 30 (Spring). Rolling admissions process. Application fee $65. Phone: (212)346-1585.

ADMISSION STANDARDS. Selective. Usual minimum average: 3.0 (A = 4).

FINANCIAL AID. Research assistantships, internships, tuition waivers, Federal W/S, loans. Approved for VA benefits. Apply to Graduate Admissions Office by March 15 (Summer and Fall), December 15 (Spring). Phone: (914)422-4050. Use FAFSA (School code: 002791). About 25% of students receive aid from University and outside sources. Aid available to part-time students. For M.A.: 32 credit program; practicum.

DEGREE REQUIREMENTS. For M.S.N.: 42 credit program.

FIELDS OF CONCENTRATION.
Family Nurse Practitioner. M.S.N.
Nursing Education. M.A.

PACIFIC LUTHERAN UNIVERSITY
Tacoma, Washington 98447
Web site: www.plu.edu

Founded 1890. Coed. Private control. Lutheran affiliation. 4-1-4 calendar system. Library: 365,021 volumes, 2186 subscriptions. Total University enrollment: 3680.

Tuition: $731 per credit hour. On-campus housing for 27 married students; single students accommodated in dormitories. Average academic year housing cost: $6765 (including board) for single students. Contact Assistant Director for Residential Life for both on- and off-campus housing information. Phone: (253) 535-7200.

Division of Graduate Studies

Enrollment: full-time 204, part-time 98. Faculty: full-time 23, part-time 14. Degrees conferred: M.A., M.A. in Ed., M.A. in Social Sci., M.B.A., M.S. in Nursing.

ADMISSION REQUIREMENTS. Transcripts, two references, statement of goals, MAT or GRE (Education) required in support of application. GMAT for admission to M.B.A. program. TOEFL required for international applicants. Interview required for M.A.S.S. (Marriage and Family Therapy) and M.A.E. Accepts transfer applicants. Apply to Office of Admissions at least one month prior to registration. Rolling admissions process. Application fee $35. Phone: (800)274-6758, (253)535-7151; fax: (253) 536-5136; E-mail: admission@plu.edu.

ADMISSION STANDARDS. Selective for most departments. Usual minimum average: 2.75 (A = 4).

FINANCIAL AID. Annual awards from institutional funds: summer scholarships, fellowships, research assistantships, internships, Federal W/S, loans. Approved for VA benefits. Apply to Dean of Graduate Studies by March 1. Use FAFSA. Phone: (253) 535-7161. Aid available for part-time students.

DEGREE REQUIREMENTS. For master's: 32 semester hours minimum, at least 24 in residence; thesis or research paper; final oral/written exam.

FIELDS OF STUDY.
Business Administration. Includes technology, innovative management. M.B.A.
Creative Writing. M.A.
Education. Includes concentrations in educational administration, classroom teaching, literacy education, special education; teaching experience required. M.A.
Nursing. Includes care and outcomes manager, nurse practitioner studies. M.S.N.
Social Sciences. Includes concentrations in marriage and family therapy.

PACIFIC UNIVERSITY
Forest Grove, Oregon 97116-1797
Web site: www.pacificu.edu

Founded 1842. Located 23 miles W of Portland. Coed. Private control. United Church of Christ. Semester system. Special facilities: Malheur Field Station, Blodget Arboretum. Library: 225,000 volumes, 1908 subscriptions. Total University enrollment: 2563.

Tuition: per credit $499–$1100. On-campus housing for graduate men and women; none for married students. Average academic year housing costs: $6356 (including board) for single students. Contact Dean of Students Office for both on- and off-campus housing information. Phone: (503)357-6151, ext. 2200.

Graduate Division

Enrollment: full-time 847; part-time 145. University faculty teaching graduate students: full-time 92, part-time 65. Degrees conferred: M.F.A., M.S., M.A. in Ed., M.A.T., M.S.P.T., M.S.T.

ADMISSION REQUIREMENTS. Official transcripts, three letters of recommendation, brief essay required in support of application. TOEFL required for international applicants. Accepts transfer applicants. Apply by March 15 (Fall), October 15 (Spring) to Director of Admissions for Professions programs, School of Education (rolling admissions process), February 15 (Fall) for School of Physical Therapy, December 15 (Fall) for School of Professional Psychology. Application fee $40. Phone: (800)677-6712, (503)359-2900; fax: (503)359-2975.

ADMISSION STANDARDS. Selective or relatively open. Usual minimum average: 2.75 (A = 4).

FINANCIAL AID. Annual awards from institutional funds: research/teaching assistantships, internships, grants, Federal W/S, loans. Approved for VA benefits. Apply by May 1 to Director of the Professional Programs for assistantships; to Financial Aid Office for all other programs. Phone: (503)352-2222. Use FAFSA (School code: 003212). About 35% of students receive aid other than loans from University and outside sources. Aid available for part-time students.

DEGREE REQUIREMENTS. For master's: 30 semester hours minimum, at least 21 in residence; GRE for candidacy; thesis/final project. For Psy.D.: 45 semester hours beyond the master's, at least two years in residence or equivalent; qualifying exam; internship; research paper; final exam.

FIELDS OF STUDY.
Dental Health.
Education. Includes early childhood, elementary, middle school, high school.
Occupational Therapy.
Optometry.
Pharmacy.
Physical Therapy.
Physician Assistant.
Professional Psychology.
Writing.

UNIVERSITY OF THE PACIFIC
Stockton, California 95211-0197
Web site: www.uop.edu

Founded 1851. Located 90 miles E of San Francisco. CGS member. Coed. Private control. Semester system. Library: 689,733 volumes, 3747 subscriptions. Total University enrollment: 6196.

Annual tuition: full-time $25,658. On-campus housing available. Average academic year housing costs: $8292–$10,350 (including board). Apply to Director of Housing. Phone: (209)946-2331.

Graduate School

Enrollment: full-time 834, part-time 249. University faculty: full-time 144, part-time 3. Degrees conferred: M.A., M.S., M.Ed., M.A.T., Mus.M., Ed.D., D.P.T., Ph.D.

ADMISSION REQUIREMENTS. Transcripts, references, GRE Subject Tests required in support of School's application. TOEFL score of 550 required for international applicants. Accepts transfer applicants. Apply to Dean of Graduate School by March 1

(Summer, Fall), October 15 (Spring). Rolling admission process. Application fee $75. Phone: (209)946-2261; fax: (209)946-2858; e-mail: gradschool@uop.edu.

ADMISSION STANDARDS. Selective. Usual minimum average: 3.0 (A = 4).

FINANCIAL AID. Annual awards from institutional funds: scholarships, fellowships, grants, teaching assistantships, Federal W/S, loans. Approved for VA benefits. Apply by March 1 to the Dean for assistantships; to Financial Aid Office for all other programs. Use FAFSA. Phone: (209)946-2421. About 20% of students receive aid other than loans from University and outside sources. Aid available for part-time students.

DEGREE REQUIREMENTS. For master's: 28–32 units minimum, at least 24 in residence; thesis/nonthesis option; final oral exam. For Ph.D.: 45 units beyond master's; preliminary written/oral exam, reading knowledge of 2 foreign languages; dissertation; final oral exam. For Ed.D.: 65 units minimum beyond the bachelor's, at least 36 in residence and 2 semesters in full-time attendance; preliminary written/oral exam; foreign language usually not required; dissertation; final oral exam. For D.P.T.: 92 credit program; internship.

FIELDS OF STUDY.
Biological Sciences. Includes microbiology, botany, zoology; M.S. only.
Business Administration. M.B.A.
Communication. M.A.
Education. Includes curriculum and instruction, educational administration, educational/school psychology.
Intercultural Relations. M.A.
Music (Pacific Conservatory of Music). Includes applied music, theory and composition, music education. M.A., Mus.M. only.
Music Therapy. M.A.
Pharmaceutical and Medical Chemistry. Includes chemistry, pharmacy practice, physiology and pharmacology.
Physical Therapy. D.P.T.
Psychology. M.A. only.
Speech-Lanquage, Pathology. M.S.
Sports Sciences. M.A.

Arthur A. Dugoni School of Dentistry
Web site: dental.uop.edu

Established 1896 as the College of Physicians and Surgeons. Located in San Francisco, 2155 Webster Street (94115). Quarter system. Special facility: The Institute of Dental History and Craniofacial Study. Special programs: Advanced Education in General Dentistry program, International Dental Studies program for foreign dental graduates.

Annual tuition: $48,888. Off-campus University-owned housing available. Average academic year housing costs: $14,000–$17,325. Contact Pacific Housing Committee for University-owned housing information or Office of Student Services for off-campus housing information. Phone (415)929-6491. Total average cost for all other first-year expenses: $17,500.

Enrollment: first-year class 139, total 500 (men 62%, women 38%, minorities 2%, state residents 90%). Faculty: full-time 50, part-time 75. Degrees conferred: B.A.-D.D.S., D.D.S., M.S. (Orthodontics).

ADMISSION REQUIREMENTS. AADSAS report, official transcripts, DAT (no later than November), three letters of recommendation required in support of School's application. TOEFL, TSE, TWE required for international applicants whose native language is not English. Interview by invitation only. Applicants must have completed at least three years of college study. Preference given to Asia Pacific Islanders and state residents. Apply to Office Admission after June 1, before January 1. Application fee $75. Phone: (415)929-6491; fax: (415)929-6654.

ADMISSION STANDARDS. Competitive. Accepts about 10–15% of all applicants. Usual minimum UGPA: 3.0 (A = 4). Mean DAT: academic 21, PAT 20; mean UGPA 3.37.

FINANCIAL AID. Scholarships, grants, loans. Apply to Office of Financial Aid after acceptance. Phone: (415)929-6452. Use FAFSA (School code: O13292). About 85% of students receive aid from School and outside sources.

DEGREE REQUIREMENTS. For D.D.S.: satisfactory completion of thirty-six-month, twelve-quarter program.

McGeorge School of Law
Web site: www.mcgeorge.edu

Founded 1924, amalgamated with the University in 1966. Located in Sacramento (95817). ABA approved since 1969. AALS member. Semester system. Special facility: Center for Global Business and Development. Law library: 481,402 volumes, 4546 subscriptions; has LEXIS, NEXIS, WESTLAW, DIALOG. Day and evening programs.

Annual tuition: $34,474 (day), $22,920 (evening), $23,800 (LL.M.). On-campus housing available. Apply to Housing Office. Early applications advised. Total average figure for all other expenses: $19,371.

Enrollment: first-year class 243 (day), 97 (evening); total full-time 605 (men 55%, women 45%, minorities 23%), part-time 396. Faculty: full-time 100, part-time 48. Student to faculty ratio 13.4 to 1. Degrees conferred: J.D., M.D.-M.B.A., J.D.-M.P.P.A., LL.M. (Government Law and Policy, International Law, International Water Resource Law).

ADMISSION REQUIREMENTS. LSDAS Law School report, bachelor's degree, transcripts, LAST, personal statement required in support of application. TOEFL required for all international applicants whose native language is other than English. Applicants must have completed at least three years of college study. Interview not required. Accepts transfer applicants. Apply by May 1 (by March 15th for priority consideration) to Admission Committee. Application fee: $50. Phone: (916)739-7105.

ADMISSION STANDARDS. Selective. Accepts approximately 31% (day), 41% (evening) of all students. Number of applicants 3027 (day), 374 (evening); number of acceptances 939 (day), 155 (evening); number enrolled 243 (day), 97 (evening); LSAT (75% of students have a score at or above 156 (day), 152 (evening)); GPA (75% of students have a GPA at or above 3.00 (day), 2.89 (evening). *U.S. News & World Report* ranking is in the top 100 of all U.S. law schools.

FINANCIAL AID. Scholarships, Federal W/S, loans. Apply to Financial Aid Office by April 1. Phone: (916)739-7158. Use FAFSA (School code: G03592) and institutional financial aid form. About 53% of students receive aid other than loans from School and outside sources.

DEGREE REQUIREMENTS. For J.D.: 88 credit hour program, at least 84 in residence. For LL.M.: at least 24 credit hours beyond the J.D.; one year in residence; thesis.

PENNSYLVANIA COLLEGE OF OPTOMETRY
Elkins Park, Pennsylvania 19027-1598
Web site: www.pco.edu

Founded 1919. Coed. Private control. Quarter systems. Special facilities: Feinbloom Vision Rehabilitation Center, Lynch Pediatric Center, the Eye Institute. Library: 21,000 volumes, 280 subscriptions.

Annual tuition: $28,500 (D.O.); per credit $535 (Graduate). On-campus housing available. For off-campus housing information contact the Office of Student Affairs. Phone: (800) 824-6262.

Enrollment: O.D.: first-year class 158, total 593. M.S./M.Ed. part-time 33. College faculty: full-time 49, part-time 21. Degrees conferred: O.D., M.S., M.Ed.

ADMISSION REQUIREMENTS. O.D. program: transcripts, OAT, essay, letters of recommendation required in support of College's application. Graduates of unaccredited institutions not considered. Apply to the Office of Admissions by March 31 for priority consideration. Rolling admissions process. For M.S./ M.Ed.: O.D. required for admission. Apply by May 20 for priority consideration. Application fee $50. Phone: (800)824-6242, (215)780-1280; fax: (215)276-6081.

ADMISSION STANDARDS. Competitive.

FINANCIAL AID. Scholarships, Federal W/S, loans. Some surrounding states have contractual arrangements with College. Contact Admissions Office for pertinent information. For other aid apply by May 1 to Office of Admissions. Phone: (215)780-1330. Use FAFSA. About 55% of students receive aid other than loans from College and outside sources.

DEGREE REQUIREMENTS. For O.D.: four years beyond minimum three years of pre-optometry college study; final written exam; passage of National Board of Examiners in Optometry part 1 and part 2. For M.S., M.Ed.: 51 quarter hour program; field practice; internship.

FIELDS OF GRADUATE STUDY.
Audiology.
Education of Children and Youth with Visual and Multiple Impairments. M.S.
Low Vision Rehabilitation. M.S.
Orientation and Mobility. M.S.
Optometry.
Physician Assistant Studies. M.M.S.
Vision Rehabilitation Therapy. M.S.

PENNSYLVANIA STATE UNIVERSITY
University Park, Pennsylvania 16802
Web site: www.psu.edu

Founded 1855. Located 90 miles NW of Harrisburg. CGS and AAU member. Coed. State control. Semester system. Special facilities: Agricultural Experiment Station, Agricultural and Home Economics Extension Services, Computation Center, Nuclear Reactor, Psychology Clinic, Reading Center, Institute of Public Administration, Ionosphere Research Laboratory, Materials Research Laboratory, Earth and Mineral Sciences Experiment Station, Applied Research Laboratory, Petroleum Refining Laboratory. Graduate work is offered in the Milton S. Hershey Medical Center in Hershey, Penn State Great Valley Center in Malvern near Philadelphia, Penn State Harrisburg, and the Penn State Erie; cooperative program with the Jefferson Medical College of Philadelphia. The University's NIH ranking is 66th among all U.S. institutions with 281 awards/grants valued at $86,737,404. According to The Center at University of Florida, the University is ranked 21st in receipt of Federal Research funds with $280,678,000 and it ranks 17th for total University research expenditures with $480,084,000. In 2004, the University awarded 539 doctorates, which ranked it 14th among all U.S. institutions eligible to award that degree. Thirty-seven of the University's faculty members have been elected to National Honor Academies and this ranks it 27th among all U.S. institutions. The Library:

approximately 4,300,000 volumes, 39,879 subscriptions. Total University enrollment: 45,000.

Annual tuition: full-time resident $12,518, nonresident $23,000; per credit resident $522, nonresident $959. On-campus housing available for graduate students. Annual academic year housing costs: $5500–$8550 (including board) for single students, $4914 for one- and two-bedroom apartments. Apply to Assignment Office for Campus Residences, 101 Shields Building. Phone: (814) 865-7501. Day-care facilities available.

Graduate School
Web site: www.gradsch.psu.edu

Graduate study since 1862. Enrollment: full-time 4249, part-time 1914. Graduate faculty: 2600. Degrees conferred: M.A., M.S., M.Agr., M.B.A., M.C.P., M.Ed., M.Eng., M.E.P.C., M.F.A., M.F.R., M.H.A., M.J., M.H.R.I.M., M.L.A., M.P.A., M.Mgt., M.Mus., D.Ed., Ph.D.

ADMISSION REQUIREMENTS. Two transcripts, GRE/GMAT/ MAT (varies by department) required in support of School's application. TOEFL required for international applicants. Accepts transfer applicants. Apply to Office of Graduate Admissions; completed forms must be received at least one month prior to registration. Application fee $45. Phone: (814)865-1795; fax: (814)863-4627; e-mail: gadm@psu.edu.

ADMISSION STANDARDS. Usual minimum average: 3.0 (A = 4).

FINANCIAL AID. Annual awards from institutional funds: fellowships, research/teaching assistantships, tuition waivers, traineeships, Federal W/S, loans. Approved for VA benefits. Apply to departments for assistantships, fellowships; to the Office of Student Aid for all other aid. Phone: (814)865-6301. Use FAFSA. About 65% of students receive aid other than loans from School and outside sources.

DEGREE REQUIREMENTS. For M.A., M.S.: 30 credits minimum, at least 20 in residence; thesis for most M.S. and M.A. candidates. For M.Agr.: 30 credits minimum, at least 20 in residence; final paper/report of internship training. For M.B.A.: 48 credits minimum; project paper. For M.C.P.: 36 credits minimum, at least 20 in residence. For M.Ed.: 30 credits minimum, at least 20 in residence. For M.Eng.: 30 credits minimum; final document. For M.E.P.C.: 30 credits minimum, at least 20 in residence; thesis/paper. For M.F.A.: 48 credits minimum; professional project plus monograph. For M.H.A.: 51 credits minimum; professional paper. For M.H.R.I.M.: 36 credits minimum; professional paper. For M.J.: 30 credits minimum. For M.L.A.: 44 credits minimum, at least 34 in residence; individual project. For M.Mgt.: 33 credits minimum. For M.P.A.: 45 credits minimum; professional paper. For M.Mus.: 36 credits minimum, at least 30 in residence; paper. For M.F.R.: 30 credits minimum. For Ph.D.: two consecutive semesters minimum in residence; candidacy exam; language requirement varies by department; comprehensive oral/written exam; final oral exam; thesis. For D.Ed.: minimum six semesters full-time or equivalent; 30 credits in residence; comprehensive exam; final oral exam; thesis.

FIELDS OF STUDY.
Acoustics.
Adult Education.
Aerospace Engineering.
Agricultural and Biological Engineering.
Agricultural and Extension Education.
Agronomy.
Animal Science.
Anthropology.
Applied Linguistics.
Applied Statistics.

Architectural Engineering.
Architecture.
Art.
Art Education.
Art History.
Astronomy and Astrophysics.
Biobehavioral Health.
Biochemistry, Microbiology, and Molecular Biology.
Bioengineering.
Biology.
Biotechnology.
Business Administration.
Cell and Developmental Biology.
Chemical Engineering.
Chemistry.
Civil Engineering.
Communication Arts and Sciences.
Communication Sciences and Disorders.
Community Psychology and Social Change.
Community and Economic Development.
Comparative and International Education.
Comparative Literature.
Composition/Theory.
Computer Science and Engineering.
Conducting.
Counseling Psychology.
Counselor Education.
Crime, Law, and Justice.
Curriculum and Instruction.
Demography.
Earth Sciences.
Ecology.
Economics.
Educational Leadership.
Educational Psychology.
Educational Theory and Policy.
Electrical Engineering.
Energy and Geo-Environmental Engineering.
Engineering Mechanics.
Engineering Science.
Engineering Science and Mechanics.
English.
Entomology.
Environmental Engineering.
Environmental Pollution Control.
Finance.
Food Science.
Forensic Science.
Forest Resources.
French.
Fuel Science.
Genetics.
Geoenvironmental Engineering.
Geography.
Geosciences.
German.
Health Policy and Administration.
Higher Education.
History.
Horticulture.
Hotel, Restaurant, and Institutional Management.
Human Development and Family Studies.
Human Nutrition.
Immunology and Infectious Diseases.
Industrial Engineering.
Industrial Relations and Human Resources.
Information Science.
Information Sciences and Technology.
Information Systems.
Instructional Systems.

Integrative Biosciences.
Kinesiology.
Landscape Architecture.
Leadership Development.
Leisure Studies.
Manufacturing Engineering.
Manufacturing Systems Engineering.
Mass Communications.
Materials.
Materials Science and Engineering.
Mathematics.
Mechanical Engineering.
Media Studies.
Meteorology.
Molecular Medicine.
Molecular Toxicology.
Music and Music Education.
Music Theory and History.
Musicology.
Neuroscience.
Nuclear Engineering.
Nursing.
Nutrition.
Operations Research.
Pathobiology.
Performance.
Petroleum and Mineral Engineering.
Philosophy.
Physics.
Physiology.
Piano Pedagogy and Performance.
Plant Physiology.
Political Science.
Psychology.
Quality and Manufacturing Management.
Recreation, Parks, and Tourism Management.
Rural Sociology.
Russian and Comparative Literature.
School Psychology.
Sociology.
Soil Science.
Spanish.
Special Education.
Statistics.
Supply Chain Management.
Teaching and Curriculum.
Teaching English as a Second Language.
Telecommunications Studies.
Theater Arts.
Voice Performance and Pedagogy.
Wildlife and Fisheries Science.
Women's Studies.
Workforce Education and Development.
Youth and Family Education.

Dickinson School of Law

Carlisle, Pennsylvania 17013-2899
Web site: www.dsl.psu.edu

Established 1834. Effective July 1, 1997, Dickinson affiliated with Pennsylvania State University and will be known as Dickinson School of Law of the Pennsylvania State University. ABA approved since 1931. AALS member. Semester system. Special facilities: Agricultural Law Research and Education Center, Institute of Arbitration Law and Practice, Institute for Sport Law, Policy and Research. Special programs: ABA-approved summer study abroad at the University of Florence, Italy, and in the Cities of Brussels, Strasbourg, Vienna; externship. Law library: 506,566 volumes, 6730 subscriptions; has LEXIS, NEXIS, WESTLAW; is a depository for U.S. government documents.

Annual tuition: $28,054. On-campus housing available for single students only. Law students tend to live off campus. Contact Administrative Service Office for both on- and off-campus housing information. Phone: (717)240-5000. Annual on-campus housing costs: $7000–$8000. Off-campus housing and personal expenses: approximately $16,284.

Enrollment: first-year class 205; total 540 (men 54%, women 46%, minorities 23%); no part-time students. Faculty: full-time 40, part-time 45. Student-to-faculty ratio is 13.8 to 1. Degrees conferred: J.D., J.D.-M.B.A., J.D.-M.P.A. (Penn State at Harrisburg), J.D.-M.S.I.S. J.D.-M.Eng. (Environmental Pollution Control), J.D.-M.E.P.C. (Environmental Pollution Control), J.D.-M.S.E.P.C. (Environmental Pollution Control), LL.M. (only for persons who have completed a basic legal education and received a university degree in law in another country).

ADMISSION REQUIREMENTS. LSDAS Law School report, bachelor's degree, transcripts, résumé, two examples of written expression, two letters of recommendation. LSAT required in support of application. Interview not required. Accepts transfer applicationts. Graduates of unaccredited colleges not considered. Apply to Office of Admissions preferably after September 1, before March 1, before June 15 (transfers). Fall admission only. Application fee $60 (online), $70 with paper application. Phone (800)840-1122; fax: (717)241-3503. For LL.M. use LL.M. Credential Assembly Service of LSAC.

ADMISSION STANDARDS. Selective. Accepts approximately 29% of all students. Number of applicants 2491; number of acceptances 732; number enrolled 205; LSAT (75% of students have a score at or above 154); GPA (75% of students have a GPA at or above 3.11). *U.S. News & World Report* ranking is in the second tier (tied at 91st) of all U.S. law schools.

FINANCIAL AID. Scholarships, grants Federal W/S, loans. Apply to Chair, Scholarship Committee by February 15. Phone: (800) 840-1122. Use FAFSA (School code: G03254). About 40% of students receive aid other than loans from School.

DEGREE REQUIREMENTS. For J.D.: satisfactory completion of 88 semester hours minimum, summer session abroad available. For LL.M.: at least 24 credits beyond J.D.; thesis.

PENNSYLVANIA STATE UNIVERSITY AT HARRISBURG—THE CAPITAL COLLEGE

Middletown, Pennsylvania 17057-4898
Web site: www.hbg.psu.edu

Established 1966. Public. Coed. Semester system. Library: 285,100 volumes, 2600 subscriptions. Total University enrollment: 3500.

Annual tuition: resident $12,518, nonresident $17,592; per credit resident $522, nonresident $733. On-campus housing for single and 20 married students. Annual academic year housing costs: $3300–$5500 single students, $4700 for married students.

Enrollment: full- and part-time 1670. Faculty: full-time 83, part-time 20. Degrees conferred: M.A., M.B.A., M.E.P.C., M.Ed., M.E.E., M.Eng., M.H.A., M.P.A., M.S., M.S.I.S., Ph.D., Ed.D., M.Com.Psy.

Graduate Center

ADMISSION REQUIREMENTS. Transcripts, recommendations required in support of College's application. GRE/GMAT/MAT required for some programs. TOEFL (minimum score 550) required for international applicants. Accepts transfer applicants. Apply to Office of Enrollment Services. Rolling admission process. Application fee $45. Phone: (717)948-6250; fax: (717)948-6325.

ADMISSION STANDARDS. Selective. Usual minimum average: 2.5 (A = 4).

FINANCIAL AID. Scholarships, fellowships, research assistantships, grants, Federal W/S, loans. Approved for VA benefits. Apply to Financial Aid Office; no specified closing date. Use FAFSA. Phone: (717)654-7728. About 1% of students receive aid other than loans from both College and outside sources.

DEGREE REQUIREMENTS. For master's: 30 credits minimum; research paper. For Doctorate: 90 credits minimum; qualifying exam; dissertation; final oral exam.

FIELDS OF STUDY.
Adult Education.
American Studies.
Applied Behavioral Analysis.
Applied Clinical Psychology.
Applied Psychological Research.
Business Administration.
Community Psychology and Social Change.
Computer Science.
Criminal Justice.
Electrical Engineering.
Engineering Science.
Environmental Pollution Control.
Health Administration.
Health Education.
Humanities.
Information Systems.
Public Administration.
Teaching and Curriculum.
Training and Development.

PENNSYLVANIA STATE UNIVERSITY MILTON S. HERSHEY MEDICAL CENTER

500 University Drive
Hershey, Pennsylvania 17033
Web site: www.hmc.psu.edu

Founded 1967. Located about 8 miles from Harrisburg. Public control. The Medical Center is a member of the Council of Teaching Hospitals. Special facilities: Animal Research Farm, Biomedical Research Building, Penn State Center for Sports Medicine, University Hospital. Library: 100,000 volumes, 2000 subscriptions. NIH ranking is 66th among all U.S. institutions with 255 awards/grants worth $85,011,365.

College of Medicine

P.O. Box 850
Hershey, Pennsylvania 17033-0650
Web site: www.hmc.psu.edu/med

Established 1967. Located at the Medical Center. Special Program: overseas study program for selected fourth-year students.

Annual tuition: resident $32,590, nonresident $44,452. On-campus rooms and apartments available for both single and married students. Annual on-campus housing cost: single students $5000 (room only), married students $8000. Contact Office of Admissions for both on- and off-campus housing information.

Some medical students live off-campus. Off-campus housing and personal expenses: approximately $15,000.

Enrollment: first-year class 125; total full-time 480 (men 50%, women 50%, minorities 13%, state residents 45%) . Faculty: full-time 485, part-time 40. Degrees conferred: M.D., M.D.-Ph.D.

ADMISSION REQUIREMENTS. Preference given to State residents, U.S. citizens, and permanent residents only. Bachelor's degree from an accredited institution required. All applicants must have bachelor's degree awarded prior to enrollment. Accepts transfer applicants. Has EDP; applicants must apply through AMCAS (official transcripts sent by mid-May) between June 1 and August 1. Early applications are encouraged. Submit secondary/supplemental application, personal statement, four recommendations to Office of Admissions within two weeks of receipt of application. Notification normally begins October 1. Apply through AMCAS (file after June 1, before November 15), submit MCAT (will accept MCAT test results from 1995), official transcripts for each school attended (should show at least 90 semester credits/135 quarter credits; submit transcripts by mid-May to AMCAS), service processing fee. Submit an application fee of $65, a supplemental application, a personal statement, pre-professional committee evaluation, and two recommendations from science faculty to Office of Admissions within two to three weeks of the receipt of supplemental materials, but no later than January 15. Interviews are by invitation only and generally for final selection. M.D.-Ph.D. degree applicants must apply to and be accepted to both Schools; contact Office of Admissions for current information and specific admissions requirements. First-year students admitted Fall only. Rolling admissions process; notification starts October 15 and is finished when class is filled. School does maintain an alternate list. Phone: (717)531-8755; e-mail: studentadmissions@ hmc.psu.edu.

ADMISSION STANDARDS. Selective. Accepts about 10–12% of all applicants. Number of applications 5611 (n/a out-of-state); number interviewed 918 (n/a out-of-state); number of acceptances n/a (n/a out-of-state); number enrolled 125 (64 out-of-state). Mean Composite MCAT 10.0; mean UGPA 3.70.

FINANCIAL AID. Scholarships, merit scholarships, minority scholarships, Grants-in-Aid, institutional loans, HEAL, alternative loan programs, NIH stipends; Federal Perkins Loans, Stafford Subsidized and Unsubsidized Loans, Service Commitment Scholarship programs are available. Assistantships/fellowships may be available for dual degree candidates. Financial Aid applications and information are generally available at the on-campus by invitation interview. For scholarships assistance, the selection criteria places heavy reliance on MCAT and undergraduate GPA; suggested deadline February 15. Contact the Office of Student Affairs for current information. Phone: (717)531-4103. Use FAFSA (School code: G06813); also submit Financial Aid Transcript, Federal Income Tax forms. Approximately 85% of students receive some form of financial assistance; 60% receive funds from College sources.

DEGREE REQUIREMENTS. For M.D.: satisfactory completion of four-year program; research project. All students must pass USMLE Step 1 prior to entering third year; all students must record a score on USMLE Step 2 prior to awarding of M.D. For M.D.-Ph.D.: generally a seven-year program.

FIELDS OF GRADUATE STUDY.
Anatomy.
Biochemistry and Molecular Biology.
Bioengineering.
Cell and Molecular Biology.
Genetics.
Health Evaluation Sciences. M.S.
Immunology and Infectious Diseases.
Integrative Biosciences.

Laboratory Animal Sciences. M.S.
Microbiology and Immunology.
Molecular Medicine.
Molecular Toxicology.
Neuroscience.
Pharmacology.
Physiology.

UNIVERSITY OF PENNSYLVANIA
Philadelphia, Pennsylvania 19104
Web site: www.upenn.edu

Founded 1740 by Benjamin Franklin. CGS and AAU member. Coed. Private control. Semester system. Special facilities: University Museum, Institute for Environmental Studies, Ackoff Center for Advancement of Systems Approaches, Center for Bioinformatics, Center for Health, Achievement, Neighborhood, Growth and Ethnic Studies (CHANGE), Center for Human Modeling and Simulation, Center for Science and Engineering of Nanoscale Systems, Institute for Medicine and Engineering, Institute for Research in Cognitive Science, International Literacy Institute, National Center on Fathers and Families, National Institute on Adult Literacy, Institute of Neurological Sciences, Lauder Institute, Population Studies Center, Leonard Doves Institute of Health Economics, Center for the Study of Aging, Early American Studies Center, Center for Urban Ethnography, Wistar Institute of Anatomy and Biology. The University's NIH ranking is 2nd among all U.S. institutions with 1153 awards/grants valued at $471,350,481. According to The Center at University of Florida, the University is ranked 6th in receipt of Federal Research funds with $415,631,000 and it ranks 9th for total University research expenditures with $564,716,000. The University's endowment assets rank it 10th, with a value of $4,018,660,000. In 2004, the University awarded 414 doctorates, which ranked it 23rd among all U.S. institutions eligible to award that degree. Eighty-five of the University's faculty members have been elected to National Honor Academies and this ranks it 11th among all U.S. institutions. The Library: approximately 4,400,000 volumes, 33,000 subscriptions. Total University enrollment: 22,760.

Average academic year housing costs: $19,700 for single students. Apply to Director of Residential Living for on-campus housing, to office of Off-Campus Living for off-campus housing. Phone: on-campus information, (215)989-3676, off-campus information (215)898-8500.

School of Arts and Sciences—Graduate Division

Annual tuition: $33,630, per course $4258.
Enrollment: full-time 1688, part-time 366. Faculty: 1022. Degrees conferred: A.M., M.S., Ph.D., postdoctoral study in most departments.

ADMISSION REQUIREMENTS. Transcripts, letters of recommendation, GRE required in support of School's application. GRE Subject Tests for fellowships. Online application available. Evidence of proficiency in English, TOEFL/TSE required for international applicants. Accepts transfer applicants. Graduates of unaccredited institutions not considered. Apply by January 1 (for fellowships), July 15 (Fall), December 1 (Spring), May 1 (First Summer Session), June 1 (Second Summer Session). Application fee $65. Phone: (215)898-5720; fax: (215)898-0821.

ADMISSION STANDARDS. Very selective. Usual minimum average: 3.0 (A = 4).

FINANCIAL AID. Annual awards from institutional funds: grants, fellowships, assistantships for teaching/research, traineeships, tuition waivers, loans. Approved for VA benefits. Apply by January 15 for fellowships. GRE required of all financial aid applicants. Use FAFSA. Phone: (215)898-1988; fax: (215)898-5428. About 60% of students receive aid other than loans from School. Aid available for part-time students.

DEGREE REQUIREMENTS. For A.M., M.S.: 8 units minimum in residence; thesis/final project; oral/written exam. For Ph.D.: 20 units minimum, at least 12 in residence; reading knowledge of two foreign languages for most departments; preliminary exam; dissertation; final oral/written exam.

FIELDS OF STUDY.
Ancient History. Ph.D. only.
Anthropology.
Applied Mathematics and Computational Science. Ph.D.
Art and Archaeology of the Mediterranean World. Ph.D. only.
Bioethics. M.B.E.
Biology. Ph.D. only.
Chemistry. Ph.D. only.
Classical Studies.
Comparative Literature and Literary Theory.
Criminology.
Demography.
Earth and Environment Science.
East Asian Language and Civilization.
Economics. Ph.D. only.
English.
Environmental Studies. M.E.S.
Folklore and Folklife.
Germanic Languages and Literatures.
Government. M.G.A.
History.
History and Sociology of Science.
History of Art.
International Studies. A.M., M.B.A.
Liberal Arts. M.L.A. only.
Linguistics.
Mathematics.
Medical Physics.
Music. Ph.D. only.
Near Eastern Language and Civilizations.
Organizational Dynamics. M.S., M.Phil.
Philosophy. Ph.D. only.
Physics and Astronomy.
Plant and Microbial Biology. Ph.D. only.
Political Science.
Psychology. Ph.D. only.
Religious Studies. Ph.D. only.
Romance Languages. Ph.D.
Sociology. Ph.D. only.
South Asia Regional Studies.

Annenberg School for Communication

Founded 1959. Annual tuition: full-time $33,630. Enrollment: full-time 70, part-time 5. Faculty: full- and part-time 27. Degrees conferred: Ph.D.

ADMISSION REQUIREMENTS. Transcripts, three letters of recommendation, personal statement, GRE required in support of application. Online application available. TOEFL required for international applicants. Transfer applicants not accepted. Apply to School by December 15 (Fall). Application fee $65. Phone: (215)898-7041; fax: (215)898-2024.

ADMISSION STANDARDS. Competitive. Usual minimum average: 3.0 (A = 4).

FINANCIAL AID. Scholarships, fellowships, assistantships, Federal W/S, loans. Approved for VA benefits. Apply at date of application for admission, but before January 1. Phone: (215) 898-2046. Use FAFSA. About 80% of students receive aid other than loans from School and outside sources.

DEGREE REQUIREMENTS. For Ph.D.: 20 courses minimum; qualification evaluation; comprehensive exam, proposal defense; dissertation.

FIELD OF STUDY.
Communication. Includes these areas of faculty interest: children and media, culture, society and communication, global communication, health communication, media institutions, mew media and information technologies, political communication, visual communication.

School of Dental Medicine (19104-6003)
Web site: www.dental.upenn.edu

Established 1878 as the Dental Department of the University and in 1915 it was housed in the Thomas W. Evans Museum and Dental Institute. Name changed in 1964. Semester system. Special facility: Center for Oral Health Research. Special programs: foreign exchange programs at 17 different international locations, Programs for Advannced Standing Students (PASS) for foreign trained dental graduates.

Annual tuition: $51,420. On-campus rooms and apartments available for both single and married students. Average academic year housing costs: $13,300. Contact Graduate Housing Office for both on- and off-campus housing information. Phone: (215) 898-8271. Total average cost for all other first-year expenses: $11,500.

Enrollment: first-year class 117, total 410 (men 45%, women 55%, minorities 50%, state residents 18%). Faculty: full- and part-time/volunteers 260. Degrees conferred: B.S.-D.M.D. (with the College of Arts and Sciences of the University, Hampton University, Leigh University, Muhlenberg College, Villanova University, Xavier University), D.M.D., D.M.D.-M.B.A., M.S. D.M.D.-Ph.D. (no formal program, but is available with special arrangements).

ADMISSION REQUIREMENTS. AADSAS, official transcript indicating completion of at least six semesters or their equivalent of college work, three letters of recommendation, DAT (April test of junior year preferred) required in support of School's application. Interviews by invitation only. Accepts transfer applicants from U.S. schools only. Graduates of unaccredited institutions not considered. Apply to Director of Admissions after June 1, before January 15. Application fee $50. Phone: (215)898-8943; fax: (215)898-5243.

ADMISSION STANDARDS. Competitive. Accepts about 5–10% of all applicants. Number of applications 2206 (n/a out-of-state); number interviewed n/a (n/a out-of-state); number of acceptances n/a (n/a out-of-state); number enrolled 117 (n/a out-of-state). Usual minimum UGPA: 3.0 (A = 4). Mean DAT: academic 21, PAT 19; mean UGPA 3.68.

FINANCIAL AID. Scholarships, research fellowships, grants, loans. Apply after acceptance to Director of Student Affairs. Phone: (215)898-4550. Use FAFSA (School code: 009737). About 82% of students receive some aid from School and outside sources.

DEGREE REQUIREMENTS. For D.M.D.: satisfactory completion of four-year program. For M.S., Ph.D.: see Graduate School of Arts and Sciences listing above.

FIELDS OF POSTGRADUATE STUDY.
Endodontics.
Oral Medicine.
Oral and Maxillofacial Surgery.
Oral Biology. M.S.
Orthodontics.
Pediatric Dentistry.

Periodontics.
Periodontics/Orthodontics.
Periodontal/Prosthesis.

Graduate School of Education

Graduate study since 1930. Annual tuition: $33,630, per course unit $4258.

Enrollment: full-time 551, part-time 299. Faculty: full- and part-time 84. Degrees conferred: M.S.Ed., Ed.D., Ph.D.

ADMISSION REQUIREMENTS. All undergraduate and graduate transcripts, three letters of recommendation, GRE Subject Test/MAT required in support of School's application. Online application available. Evidence of proficiency in English required of international applicants. Interview not required. Accepts transfer applicants. Graduates of unaccredited institutions not considered. Apply to Graduate School of Education by July 15 (Fall), December 1 (Spring), May 1 (Summer). Some programs have earlier deadlines. Application fee $45. Phone: (215)898-6415; fax: (215)746-6884; e-mail: admissions@ gse.upenn.edu.

ADMISSION STANDARDS. Competitive. Usual minimum average: 3.0 (A = 4).

FINANCIAL AID. Scholarships, fellowships, research assistants, teaching assistantships, tuition waivers, Federal W/S, loans. Approved for VA benefits. Apply by February 1 to the appropriate department for fellowships, assistantships; to Financial Aid Office for all other programs. Use FAFSA (School code: 003378) and institutional FAF. Phone: (215)898-1501; fax: (215)573-2166. About 80% of students receive aid other than loans from School and outside sources. Aid available for part-time students.

DEGREE REQUIREMENTS. For M.S.: 10 units minimum; specialization exam; comprehensive exam. For Ph.D.: 20 units minimum, at least 12 in residence; qualifying exam; written major exam; written comprehensive exam; thesis; final oral exam. For Ed.D.: essentially the same as for the Ph.D.

FIELDS OF STUDY.
Education, Culture, and Society. M.S.Ed., Ph.D.
Educational Leadership. M.S.Ed., Ed.D.
Educational Linguistics. Ph.D.
Educational Policy. M.S.Ed., Ph.D.
Higher Education. M.S.Ed., Ed.D., Ph.D.
Intercultural Communication. M.S.Ed.
Interdisciplinary Studies in Human Development. M.S.Ed., Ph.D.
International Educational Development. M.S.Ed.
Language and Literacy. M.S.Ed.
Policy Research, Evaluation, and Measurement. M.Phil., Ph.D.
Psychological Services. Includes school counseling. M.S.Ed.
Reading, Writing, and Literacy. M.S.Ed., Ed.D., Ph.D.
Statistics, Measurement, and Research Technology. M.S.
Teacher Education. M.S.Ed.
Teaching, Learning, and Curriculum. M.S.Ed., Ed.D., Ph.D.
TESOL. M.S.Ed.

School of Engineering and Applied Science— Graduate

Web site: www.seas.upenn.edu

Established 1852. Annual tuition: full-time $33,630.

Enrollment: full- and part-time 833. Graduate faculty: full- and part-time 190. Degrees conferred: M.S.E., Ph.D.

ADMISSION REQUIREMENTS. Transcripts, GRE, two letters of recommendation required in support of School's application. Online application available. TOEFL score of 600 required for international applicants. Accepts transfer applicants. Graduates of unaccredited institutions not considered. Apply to Graduate Admissions Office for doctoral programs (admits Fall only) by January 1 (some programs have earlier deadlines), Master's programs June 1 (Fall), November 1 (Spring). Application fee $65. Phone: (215)898-8241; fax: (215)573-5577.

ADMISSION STANDARDS. Competitive. Usual minimum average: 3.0 (A = 4).

FINANCIAL AID. Fellowships, teaching assistantships, research assistantships, Federal W/S, loans. Approved for VA benefits. Apply by February 1 to Office of Student Financial Services. Phone: (215)898-1988. Use FAFSA (School code: 003378) and institutional FAF.

DEGREE REQUIREMENTS. For M.S.E.: 10 course units; thesis optional for some departments. For Ph.D.: 20 course units; dissertation; preliminary exam; final oral/written exam.

FIELDS OF STUDY.
Bioengineering.
Biotechnology. Interdisciplinary. M.B. only.
Chemical and Biomolecular Engineering.
Computer and Information Science.
Computer and Information Technology. M.C.I.T. only.
Electrical Engineering.
Engineering. M.S.E.
Materials Science and Engineering.
Mechanical Engineering and Applied Mechanics.
Robotics. M.S.E.
Systems Engineering.
Technology Management. E.M.T.M. only.
Telecommunications.
Telecommunications and Networking. Interdisciplinary. T.C.O.M. only.

School of Design

Name changed in 2003. Annual tuition: full-time $33,630.

Enrollment: full-time 512, part-time 26. School faculty: full- and part-time 126. Degrees conferred: M.Arch., M.C.P., M.L.A., M.F.A., M.C.P., M.S., Ph.D.

ADMISSION REQUIREMENTS. Official transcripts, personal statement, three letters of recommendation, personal statement, GRE, portfolio required in support of application. Writing samples required for some programs. Online application available. TOEFL required for international applicants. Interview not required. Transfer applicants considered. Graduates of unaccredited institutions not considered. Apply to appropriate department chair by February 1 (January 15 for Architecture). Fall admission only. Application fee $75. Admissions Coordinator's phone: (215) 898-6520; fax: (215)573-3927.

ADMISSION STANDARDS. Competitive for most departments. Usual minimum average: 3.0 (A = 4).

FINANCIAL AID. Fellowships, research assistantships, teaching assistantships, full and partial tuition waivers, grants, internships, Federal W/S, loans. Approved for VA benefits. Apply by January 1 to Graduate School of Fine Arts for fellowships, assistantships; for Financial Aid Office for all other programs. Use FAFSA (School code: 003378). About 75% of students receive aid other than loans from School and outside sources.

DEGREE REQUIREMENTS. For M.S.: one year in full-time residence; thesis/nonthesis option; final exam. For M.Arch.: two to four years, depending upon previous education; thesis. For M.C.P.: four terms minimum of full-time study; one summer of office practice; thesis. For M.L.A.: generally two-year program, including one summer semester; thesis. For M.F.A.: two to three years, depending upon previous education. For Ph.D.: three to

University of Pennsylvania *505*

four years, depending upon previous education; at least two years in residence; reading knowledge of two foreign languages or one language and research tool; preliminary exam; dissertation; final oral/written exam.

FIELDS OF STUDY.
Architecture. M.Arch., M.S., Ph.D.
City and Regional Planning. A.M., M.C.P., Ph.D.
Fine Arts. Includes painting and sculpture. M.F.A.
Historic Preservation. M.S.
Landscape Architecture. M.L.A.

Law School
Web site: www.law.upenn.edu

Established 1852. ABA approved since 1923. AALS member. Private control. Semester system. Special facilities: Institute for Law and Economics, Institute for Law and Philosophy. Law library: 826,096 volumes, 7558 subscriptions: has LEXIS, NEXIS, WESTLAW, DIALOG, BRS, VU/TEXT; has more than 200 network connections; is a Federal depository for governmental documents.

Annual tuition/fees: $39,330. On-campus housing for 166 single students. Apply to Office of Graduate Housing. Total average annual additional expenses: $17,050.

Enrollment: first-year class 251; total 765 (men 53%, women 47%); postgraduates 25; no part-time students. Faculty: full-time 44, part-time 45. Student to faculty ratio 12.8 to 1. Degrees conferred: J.D., J.D.-M.A. (Economics, Islamic Studies, Public Policy Analysis), J.D.-M.B.A., J.D.-M.B.E., J.D.-M.C.P., J.D.-M.E.S., J.D.-M.G.A., J.D.-M.P.H., J.D.-M.S.W., J.D.-Ph.D., LL.M., LL.C.M., S.J.D.

ADMISSION REQUIREMENTS. For J.D. program: LSDAS Law School report, bachelor's degree, transcripts, personal statement, two letters of recommendation, LSAT required in support of application. TOEFL required of international students. Interview not required. Accepts transfer applicants. Graduates of unaccredited institutions not considered. Apply to Assistant Dean for Admissions and Student Aid after August 30, before March 1. For Early Decision apply by November 1. Fall admission only. Application fee $75. Phone: (215)898-7400; fax: (215)572-9606.

ADMISSION REQUIREMENTS. For LL.M., LL.C.M., S.J.D.: all applicants must have J.D. or LL.B (or the equivalent) from a U.S. ABA/AALS-approved Law School. If applicants are from outside the U.S., the Law School/Faculty must be approved by organization/government agency of comparable standing. Official transcripts, two recommendations, résumé, personal statement, writing sample required in support of Graduate Application. Admits Fall only (new class enrollment is normally 40–50 each Fall). Apply by February 15 to Graduate Admissions Office. Application fee $70. Phone: (215)898-0407; fax: (215)573-2025. For S.J.D.: this degree is normally open only to those candidates who have spent at least one academic year in residence at the Law School, have earned an LL.M., and have a fully developed scholarly project before admission. Normally admits 6–7 candidates each year.

ADMISSION STANDARDS. Selective. Accepts approximately 13% of all students. Number of applicants 6396; number of acceptances 801; number enrolled 243; LSAT (75% of students have a score at or above 166); GPA (75% of students have a GPA at or above 3.43). *U.S. News & World Report* ranking is in the top six of all U.S. law schools.

FINANCIAL AID. For J.D. program: scholarships, Federal W/S, loans. Apply to Dean of Admissions and Student Aid by March 1. Phone: (215)898-7400. Use FAFSA (School code: 003378) and institutional financial aid application. There is a Public Interest Loan Repayment Assistance program. For graduate program: apply to the Assistant Dean, Graduate Studies and Research before February 1. About 75% of J.D. students receive some aid from School. A loan forgiveness program for those who work in the public sector is available.

DEGREE REQUIREMENTS. For J.D.: satisfactory completion of three-year program. For LL.M., LL.C.M.: at least 24 credits minimum beyond the J.D.; one year in full-time residence. For S.J.D.: one year minimum in full-time residence; dissertation of publishable quality; oral defense. For M.A., M.B.A., M.C.P., Ph.D.: see Graduate School listing above.

School of Medicine (19104-6055)
Web site: www.med.upenn.edu

Established 1765; the first medical school in U.S. Special facilities: Abramson Cancer Center; Cardiovascular Institute; Center for AIDS Research; Center for Bioethics; Center for Clinical Epidemiology and Biostatistics; Center for Research on Reproduction and Women's Health; Center for Sleep and Respiratory Neurobiology; Institute for Diabetes, Obesity, and Metabolism; Institute for Environmental Medicine; Institute for Medicine and Engineering; Institute for Translational Medicine and Therapeutics; Institute on Aging; Leonard Davis Institute; Mahoney Institute of Neurological Sciences; Penn Comprehensive Neuroscience Center; Penn Medicine Transplant Institute; Pennsylvania Muscle Institute. Library: 100,000 volumes, 2000 subscriptions. NIH ranking is 2nd among all U.S. institutions with 1153 awards/grants worth $471,350,481.

Annual tuition: $41,173. Limited on-campus housing available. Apply to Residence Office for both on- and off-campus housing information. Total annual average figure for all other expenses: $18,050.

Enrollment: first-year class 147, total 606 (men 50%, women 50%, minorities 33%, state residents 38%). Faculty: full-time 2047, part-time 1000. Degrees conferred: M.D., M.D.-M.B.A., M.D.-M.B.E., M.D.-M.P.H., M.D.-M.S., M.D.-M.S. C.E., M.D.-Ph.D. (Medical Scientist Training Program).

ADMISSION REQUIREMENTS. AMCAS report, transcripts, two letters of recommendation (one from premed advisor), MCAT required in support of application. Bachelor's required for matriculation. Has EDP; apply after June 1, before August 1. Interview by invitation only. Accepts transfer applicants. Apply to Director of Admissions of School after June 1, before October 15 (Fall). Application fee $80. Phone: (215)898-8001; fax: (215) 573-6645.

ADMISSION STANDARDS. Very competitive. Accepts about 4% of all applicants. Number of applications 4671 (4138 out-of-state); number interviewed 833 (685 out-of-state); number of acceptances 223 (176 out-of-state); number enrolled 147 (110 out-of-state). Mean Composite MCAT 11.4; mean UGPA 3.80. *U.S. News & World Report* ranking is in the top 3 of all medical research schools, 16th in primary care.

FINANCIAL AID. Scholarships, Federal and private loans. Apply to Director of Admissions after admission. Phone: (215) 573-3423. MSTP-funded by NIH. Use FAFSA. About 84% of students receive some aid from School.

DEGREE REQUIREMENTS. For M.D.: satisfactory completion of four-year programs; must pass step 1 and step 2 of USMLE for graduation. For M.B.A., M.B.E., M.P.H., M.S., M.S.C.E., Ph.D.: see graduate schools listing above.

FIELDS OF GRADUATE STUDY.
Biochemistry and Molecular Biophysics.
Bioengineering.
Bioethics. M.B.E.
Cell and Molecular Biology.

Clinical Epidemiology. M.S.C.E.
Epidemiology and Biostatistics. M.P.H.
Genomics and Computational Biology.
Health Policy Research. M.S.
Immunology.
Neuroscience.
Pharmacological Sciences.
Public Health. M.P.H.
Translational Medicine. M.S.

School of Nursing—Graduate Division
Web site: www.nursing.upenn.edu

Graduate study since 1961. Annual tuition: full-time $45,146 (12 month program). Enrollment: full-time 165; part-time 204. Faculty: full- and part-time 189. Degrees conferred: M.S.N., M.S.N.-M.B.A., Ph.D., Ph.D.-M.B. (Bioethics), Ph.D.-M.B.A.

ADMISSION REQUIREMENTS. Transcripts, three letters of reference, essay, CV or résumé, current RN license, interview, GRE required in support of School's application. GMAT required for M.S.N.-M.B.A. applicants. Online application available. TOEFL required for international applicants. Accepts transfer applicants. Graduates of unaccredited institutions not considered. For master's: apply by February 15. Apply to the Office of Enrollment Management. Rolling admission process. Application fee $70. Phone: (866)867-6877, (215)898-4271; fax: (215)898-8439.

ADMISSION STANDARDS. Usual minimum average for M.S.N. applicants: 3.0 (A = 4). Usual minimum average for doctoral applicants: 3.2 (A = 4) at the master's level.

FINANCIAL AID. Fellowships, teaching/research assistantships, Federal W/S, loans. Approved for VA benefits. Apply by January 1 to School for fellowships, assistantships; to the Office of Student Financial Services for all other programs. Phone: (215)898-8191. Use FAFSA (School code: 003378) and institutional FAF. Aid available for part-time students.

DEGREE REQUIREMENTS. For M.S.N.: 12 course units minimum; 16 course units for Nurse-Midwifery, Nursing Administration, Family Nurse Practitioner, and Occupational Health Nursing programs. For Ph.D.: 13 required courses; maximum seven calendar years allowed beyond master's, one year or more of full-time study recommended; qualifying exam; preliminary exam; dissertation; related field final oral exam.

FIELDS OF STUDY.
Adult Acute Care Nurse Practitioner.
Adult Health Nurse Practitioner.
Adult Home Care.
Adult Oncology Nurse Practitioner.
Clinical Nurse Specialist.
Family Health Nurse Practitioner.
Gerontological Nurse Practitioner.
Health Leadership.
Neonatal Nurse Practitioner.
Nurse Anesthesia.
Nurse—Midwifery.
Nursing and Health Care Administration. In cooperation with the Wharton School. M.S.N.-M.B.A., Ph.D.-M.B.A.
Occupational and Environmental Health.
Pediatric Acute/Chronic Care Nurse Practitioner.
Pediatric Critical Care Nurse Practitioner.
Pediatric Nurse Practitioner.
Pediatric Oncology Nurse Practitioner.
Psychiatric Mental Health Nursing.
Women's Health Care Nurse Practitioner.

School of Social Policy and Practice

Established 1909. Annual tuition: $30,832. Enrollment: full-time 210, part-time 87. Faculty: full-time 19, part-time 42. Degrees conferred: M.S., M.S.W., Ph.D., M.S.W.-M.B.A., M.S.W.-M.S.Ed., M.S.W.-M.C.P., M.S.W.-J.D.

ADMISSION REQUIREMENTS. Official transcript, three references required in support of School's application. TOEFL required for international applicants. Online application available. Interview may be required. Accepts transfer applicants. Graduates of unaccredited institutions not considered. Apply to Office of Admissions before March 31. Rolling admission process. Application fee $70. Phone: (215)898-5550; fax: (215)573-2099.

ADMISSION STANDARDS. Selective. Usual minimum average: 3.0 (A = 4).

FINANCIAL AID. Fellowships, research assistantships, teaching assistantships, grants, internships, Federal W/S, loans. Apply by March 1 to the Dean's Office for fellowships, assistantships; to the Financial Aid Office for all other programs. Use FAFSA (School code: 003378). Fifty percent of students receive aid from University and outside sources. Aid available for part-time students.

DEGREE REQUIREMENTS. For M.S., M.S.W.: 65 credits minimum, at least one year in full-time residence; thesis. For Ph.D.: one year minimum beyond M.S.W.; qualifying exam; field practice; dissertation; final oral exam.

FIELDS OF STUDY.
Nonprofit/NGO Leadership. M.S.
Social Policy. M.S.S.P.
Social Welfare. Ph.D.
Social Work. M.S.W.

School of Veterinary Medicine (19104-6008)
Web site: www.vet.upenn.edu

Established 1884. Semester system. Special facilities: Center for Animal Health and Productivity, Center for Animal Transgenesis and Germ Cell Research, Center for Aquatic Animal Medicine and Pathology, Allam Center for Equine Sports Medicine and Imaging, Center for Infectious Disease Research and Food Safety, Center for Interaction of Animals and Society, Goodman Center for Comparative Medical Genetics, Lowe Center for Comparative Oncology Research, Rosenthal Imaging and Treatment Center,
Annual tuition: residents $31,725, nonresidents $37,775. On-campus housing available. Estimated living expenses: $16,400. Total all other expenses: $8500.
Enrollment: first-year class 110, total 450 (men 19%, women 81%, minorities 15%, state residents 51%). Faculty: full- and part-time 250. Degrees conferred: V.M.D., V.M.D.-M.B.A., V.M.D.-Ph.D. (Veterinary Medical Scientist Training Program).

ADMISSION REQUIREMENTS. VMCAS report, transcript, completion of 90 credits or three years of college study with prescribed courses, animal/veterinary experience, three recommendations, GRE General required in support of application. Interview by invitation only. Graduates of unaccredited colleges not considered. Transfer applicants not considered. Apply to Admissions Office after July 1, before October 1. Application fee $65. Phone: (215)898-5434, (215)898-5435.

ADMISSION STANDARDS. Competitive. Accepts about 5–10% of all applicants. Number of applications 1300 (1050 out-of-state); number interviewed n/a (n/a out-of-state); number of acceptances n/a (n/a out-of-state); number enrolled 110 (54 out-of-state). Usual minimum UGPA: 3.0 (A = 4). GRE mean score (V + Q) 1258; mean UGPA 3.58.

FINANCIAL AID. Scholarships, fellowships, internships, Federal W/S, loans available. VMSTP funded by NIH. Apply after acceptance to Associate Dean for Student Affairs. Use FAFSA. About 50% of students receive aid other than loans from all sources.

DEGREE REQUIREMENTS. For V.M.D.: satisfactory completion of four-year program. For M.B.A., Ph.D.: see Graduate School listings above.

FIELDS OF GRADUATE STUDY.
Biomedical Research.
Human and Animal Health.
Pharmaceutical Research.
Public Health.

The Wharton School
Web site: www.wharton.upenn.edu

Established 1881. Accredited programs: M.B.A., Accounting; recognized Ph.D. Semester and quarter system: first year is quarter system; second year is semester system. Special programs: four week pre-term program; foreign exchange programs in Australia, Brazil, France, Italy, Japan, the Netherlands, the Philippines, Spain, Sweden, United Kingdom, Wharton Global Immersion Program, Wharton/Johns Hopkins School of Advanced International Studies. Special facility: Joseph H. Lauder Institute of Management and International Studies. Library: 200,000 volumes, 3500 subscriptions.

Annual tuition: full-time $47,236 (M.B.A.), $36,142 (Doctoral programs). Enrollment: total full-time 1871 (men 63%, women 37%, minorities 28%). Faculty: full-time 215, part-time 41; all have Ph.D./D.B.A. Degrees conferred: M.B.A., W.E.M.B.A., M.S. (Accounting, for Wharton undergraduates only), M.B.A.-J.D., M.B.A.-M.A. (International Relations, Communications), M.B.A.-M.D., M.B.A.-D.M.D., M.B.A.-D.V.M., M.B.A.-M.S.E. (Engineering), M.B.A.-M.S.N., M.B.A.-M.S.W., M.B.A.-Ph.D. (Nursing, Medical Sciences at Wharton), Ph.D.

ADMISSION REQUIREMENTS. All applicants should have a bachelor's degree from a recognized institution of higher education and a strong mathematics background. Students are required to have their own personal computer. Contact Wharton for application material and information; phone: M.B.A. (215)898-6183, W.E.M.B.A. (215)898-1776. Early applications are encouraged for both admission and financial aid consideration. Beginning students are admitted Fall only. Both U.S. citizens and international applicants apply by October 11 (Round 1, Decision released December 20), January 3 (Round 2, Decision released March 27), February 28 (Round 3, Decision released May 15). Submit application, GMAT results (will accept GMAT test results from the last five years, latest acceptable date is March), official transcripts from each undergraduate/graduate school attended, three letters of recommendation, four essays, résumé (prefers at least four years of work experience), and an application fee of $225 to the Director of MBA Admission. Interviews by invitation only. Online application available. In addition, international students (whose native language is other than English) should submit a TOEFL score, certified translations and evaluations of all official transcripts; recommendation should be in English or with certified translations and proof of sufficient financial resources for two years of academic study. On-campus interviews are strongly encouraged prior to the admissions committee reviewing completed application. Dual Degree applicants must apply to and be accepted to both schools/programs. Contact the Admissions Office for current information and specific admissions requirements. Phone: (215) 898-6183; fax: (215)898-0120. Rolling admissions process; notification is made within 8–10 weeks of receipt of completed application and supporting documents.

ADMISSION REQUIREMENTS. Contact Doctoral Programs at (215)898-4877 for application material and information. Beginning students are admitted Fall Only. Both U.S. citizens and international applicants apply by December 15 (Fall). Submit two-part application form, GMAT (will accept GMAT test results from the last five years), official transcripts from each undergraduate/graduate school attended, three letters of recommendation, résumé, statement of purpose, and application fee of $65 to the University of Pennsylvania Office of Graduate Admission. In addition, international students (whose native language is other than English) should submit TOEFL, TSE, and TWE scores; certified translations and evaluations of all official transcripts; recommendation should be in English or with certified translations. International students' contact: (215)898-4877. All accepted students are invited for interviews. Notification is made on or near April 1.

ADMISSION STANDARDS. Very selective. Usual minimum average: M.B.A. 3.0, Ph.D. 3.3 (A = 4). Mean M.B.A. GMAT: 712; median M.B.A. GPA: 3.54 (A = 4). *U.S. News & World Report* ranked Wharton's M.B.A. program in the top three of all U.S. business schools. *BusinessWeek* listed Wharton as number one among all U.S. business schools. For Ph.D.: approximately 600–800 applications; 30–40 will enroll.

FINANCIAL AID. Scholarships, international scholarships, minority scholarships, grants, fellowships, graduate assistantships, Federal Perkins Loans, Stafford Subsidized and Unsubsidized Loans, Federal W/S available. Some financial assistance is available for international students. Assistantships/fellowships may be available for joint degree candidates. Financial Aid applications and information are included with admission materials; apply by March 1. Request scholarship, fellowship, assistantship, and need-based information from Wharton. Use FAFSA (School code: 003378); also submit an institutional FAF, a Financial Aid Transcript, Federal Income Tax forms. Approximately 65% of students receive some form of financial assistance.

DEGREE REQUIREMENTS. For M.B.A.: 19 course, two-year program; degree program must be completed in two years. For W.E.M.B.A.: two-year program. For M.B.A.-Masters: generally a three-and-one-half- to five-year program. For M.B.A.-J.D.: four-and-one-half- to five-year program. For M.B.A.-D.M.D., M.D., D.V.D.: generally a five- to six-year program. For Ph.D.: three- to five-year program, 20 course units; teacher development program; preliminary exam; candidacy; dissertation proposal; dissertation; oral defense.

DOCTORAL PROGRAMS.
Accounting.
Applied Economics. Includes business and public policy, insurance and risk management, real estate.
Ethics and Legal Studies.
Finance.
Health Care Management and Economics.
Management.
Marketing.
Operations and Information Management.
Statistics.

PEPPERDINE UNIVERSITY
Los Angeles, California 90045
Web site: www.pepperdine.edu

Founded 1937. Coed. Private control. Church of Christ. Trimester system. Library: 110,000 volumes, 875 subscriptions.

Tuition: per unit, varies from $890 (Master's), $1115 (Doctoral programs). No on-campus housing available.

Graduate Programs

Enrollment: full- and part-time 3375. Faculty: full-time 136, part-time 135. Degrees conferred: M.A., M.P.P., M.S., M.S.O.D., M.S.T.M., M.B.A., M.I.B., Ed.D., Psy.D.

ADMISSION REQUIREMENTS. Official transcripts, GRE/GMAT/MAT, recommendations required in support of application. TOEFL and evidence of financial support required for international applicants. Interview may be required. Accepts transfer applicants. Graduates of unaccredited institutions not considered. Apply by May 1 (Fall), February 28 (April trimester) to the Director of Admission for appropriate School. Some programs have earlier deadlines. Application fee $55. Phone: (310)568-5555.

ADMISSION STANDARDS. Selective. Usual minimum average: 2.5 (A = 4).

FINANCIAL AID. Scholarships, research assistantships, teaching assistantships, internships, Federal W/S, loans. Approved for VA benefits. Apply by July 1 to appropriate department chair for assistantships; to Financial Aid Office for all other programs. Phone: (310)568-5530. Use FAFSA (University code: 001264). Aid available for part-time students.

DEGREE REQUIREMENTS. For master's: 30 semester units minimum, at least 24 in residence; thesis/nonthesis option. For M.B.A.: 48 units, at least 40 in residence. For M.P.P.: 64 credit program. For Ed.D., Psy.D.: GRE Subject Tests for candidacy; thesis or research project; final written/oral exam.

FIELDS OF STUDY.

GRADUATE SCHOOL OF EDUCATION AND PSYCHOLOGY:
Administration.
Clinical Psychology.
Education.
Educational Leadership, Administration and Policy.
Educational Technology.
General Psychology.
Organizational Change.
Organizational Leadership.
Psychology.
School Counseling.

GRADUATE SCHOOL OF BUSINESS AND MANAGEMENT:
Applied Finance.
Business Administration.
Executive Business Administration.
Global Business.
International Business.
Management and Leadership.
Organizational Development.
Technology Management.

PEPPERDINE UNIVERSITY
Pacific Coast Highway, Malibu, California 90263-0001
Web site: www.pepperdine.edu

Founded 1937. CGS member. Coed. Private control—Church of Christ. Trimester system. Has centers in West Los Angeles, Encino, Irvine, Long Beach, Pasadena, Santa Clara, and Westlake Village. Special facilities: Ira Sherman Center for Ethical Awareness, Center for Educational Leadership, National School Safety Center, Institute for the Study of Asian Culture. Library: 800,000 volumes, 3880 subscriptions.

Tuition: per unit, varies from $890 (Master's), $1115 (Doctoral programs). On-campus housing available for single students only. Average academic year housing costs: $16,000. Contact the Office of Residential Life for both on- and off-campus housing information. Phone: (310)456-4104.

Graduate Programs

Enrollment: full-time 11, part-time 109. Faculty: full-time 34, part-time 5. Degrees conferred: M.A., M.S., M.Div.

ADMISSION REQUIREMENTS. Transcripts, GRE, three recommendations required in support of College's application. TOEFL required for international applicants. Interview may be required. Accepts transfer applicants. Graduates of unaccredited institutions not considered. Apply by May 1 (Fall), September 1 (Spring) to Admissions Office. Rolling admissions process. Application fee $55. Phone: (310)506-4000.

ADMISSION STANDARDS. Selective. Minimum average: 2.5 (A = 4).

FINANCIAL AID. Scholarships, fellowships, research assistantships, teaching assistantships, grants, Federal W/S, loans. Approved for VA benefits. Apply by February 15 to Dean's Office for assistantships; to Financial Aid Office for all other programs. Phone: (310)568-5530. Use FAFSA (School code: 001264). Aid available for part-time students.

DEGREE REQUIREMENTS. For master's: 30 semester units minimum and at least 24 in residence; thesis/nonthesis option; comprehensive exam.

FIELDS OF STUDY.

SEAVER COLLEGE:
American Studies.
Communications.
History.
Psychology.
Public Policy.
Religion.

GRADUATE SCHOOL OF EDUCATION:
Administration.
Clinical Psychology.
Education.
Educational Leadership, Administration and Policy.
Educational Technology. Ed.D. only.
General Psychology.
Organizational Change.
Organizational Leadership.
Psychology.
School Counseling.

GRAZIADO SCHOOL OF BUSINESS AND MANAGEMENT:
Applied Finance.
Business Administration.
Executive Business Administration.
Global Business.
International Business.
Management and Leadership.
Organizational Development.
Technology Management.

SCHOOL OF PUBLIC POLICY:
Public Policy and Economics.
Public Policy and American Politics.
Public Policy and International Relations.
State and Local Policy.

School of Law
Web site: law.pepperdine.edu

Formerly Orange University College of Law. Affiliated 1969. Located in Malibu (90263). ABA approved since 1972. AALS member. Private control. Semester system. Special facilities: Center for Entrepreneurship and the Law; Institute for Dispute Resolution; Institute on Law, Religion, and Ethics. Special programs; exchange programs with University of Copenhagen, University of Augsburg. Law library: 375,160 volumes, 3600 subscriptions: has LEXIS, NEXIS, WESTLAW, DIALOG.

Annual tuition/fees: $35,460. University housing available near campus. Total average annual additional expenses: $20,000.

Enrollment: first-year class 243, total 637 (men 49%, women 51%, minorities 18%). Student to faculty ratio is 19.8 to 1. Faculty: full-time 27, part-time 34. Degrees conferred: J.D., J.D.-M.B.A., J.D.-M.Div., M.D.R., (Dispute Resolution), J.D.-M.D.R., J.D. –M.P.P.

ADMISSION REQUIREMENTS. LSDAS Law School report, bachelor's degree, transcripts, LSAT, personal statement, résumé, two letters of reference, response to University's mission statement required in support of application. Accepts transfer applicants. Graduates of unaccredited colleges not considered. Apply to Admissions Office by February 1. Application fee $50. Phone: (310)506-4631; fax: (310)506-7668.

ADMISSION STANDARDS. Selective. Accepts approximately 25% of all students. Number of applicants 3314; number of acceptances 839; number enrolled 243; LSAT (75% of students have a score at or above 157); GPA (75% of students have a GPA at or above 3.38). *U.S. News & World Report* ranking is in the second tier (tied at 66th) of all U.S. law schools.

FINANCIAL AID. Scholarships, assistantships, Federal W/S, loans. Apply to Director of Financial Aid by April 1. Phone: (310) 506-4633. Use FAFSA. About 85% of students receive some aid from School.

DEGREE REQUIREMENTS. For J. D.: satisfactory completion of three-year program; 88 credit hour program. For M.D.R.: 32 units; thesis/project or externship.
Note: Study abroad program in London (Great Britain) available each Fall term for second- and third-year students.

PHILADELPHIA COLLEGE OF OSTEOPATHIC MEDICINE
4170 City Avenue
Philadelphia, Pennsylvania 19131
Web site: www.pcom.edu

Founded 1899. In 2002 a branch campus was established in Suwanee, Georgia. Private control. Semester system. Special facilities: Rural Health Care Center in Sullivan County, Pennsylvania, the Center of Medical Informatics, Education Outreach, Center for the Study of Chronic Diseases of Aging. Library: 71,000 volumes, 900 subscriptions.

Annual tuition: $35,298. No on-campus housing available. Contact the Office of Student Affairs for housing information. Off-campus housing and personal expenses: approximately $15,500.

Enrollment: first-year class 266, total 1047 (men 44%, women 56%, minorities 9%, state residents 59%). Faculty: full-time 55, part-time and volunteers 800. Degrees conferred: D.O., M.S., D.O.-M.B.A. (with St. Joseph's University), D.O.-M.P.H. (with Temple University), D.O.-Ph.D.

ADMISSION REQUIREMENTS. AACOMAS report (deadline February 1), bachelor's degree, official transcripts, MCAT, three recommendations (one from premed advisory committee, one evaluation from a physician, preferably a D.O.), supplemental form required in support of application. Interview by invitation only. Graduates of unaccredited colleges not considered. Preference given to state residents. Apply by February 1 (supplemental deadline March 1) to the Assistant Dean for Admissions and Enrollment. Admits first year students Fall only. Rolling admissions process. Application fee: $50 for nonresidents. Phone: (800)999-6998; (215)871-6100; e-mail: admissions@pcom.edu.

ADMISSION STANDARDS. Competitive. Accepts about 11% of all applicants. Number of applications 3825 (3272 out-of-state); number interviewed 568 (259 out-of-state); number of acceptances 414 (177 out-of-state); number enrolled 266 (105 out-of-state). Usual minimum UGPA: 2.75 (A = 4). Mean Composite MCAT 8.0, mean UGPA 3.30.

FINANCIAL AID. Scholarships, minority scholarships, fellowships, assistantships, grants, Federal W/S, loans. Apply by April 1 to the Financial Aid Office. Phone: (215)871-6170. Use FAFSA (College code: 015979) and institutional FAF. About 90% of students receive some form of financial assistance.

DEGREE REQUIREMENT. For D.O.: satisfactory completion of four-year program; all students must pass the National Board of Osteopathic Medical Exam Part I and take Part II. For M.S.: 36 credit program; comprehensive exam; thesis for some programs.

FIELDS OF GRADUATE STUDY.
Biomedical Sciences. M.S.
Clinical Psychology. Psy.D.
Counseling and Clinical Health Psychology. M.S.
Forensic Medicine. M.S.
Health Policy. Ph.D.
Health Sciences—Physician Assistant. M.S.
Organizational Development and Leadership. M.S.
Public Health. M.P.H.
School Psychology. M.S., Ed.S., Psy.D.

UNIVERSITY OF PHOENIX
Phoenix, Arizona 85072-2069
Web site: www.phoenix.edu

Chartered 1976. Classes offered at more than 125 campuses and Learning centers in 37 states, two Provinces in Canada and Puerto Rico. University offers programs in Alabama, Arkansas, Arizona, California, Connecticut, District of Columbia, Florida, Georgia, Hawaii, Iowa, Idaho, Illinois, Indiana, Kansas, Kentucky, Louisiana, Massachusetts, Maryland, Michigan, Minnesota, Missouri, North Carolina, Nebraska, New Jersey, New Mexico, Nevada, Ohio, Oklahoma, Oregon, Pennsylvania, South Carolina, Tennessee, Texas, Utah, Virginia, Washington, Wyoming, Alberta, British Columbia, and Puerto Rico. Not all programs are offered at all locations. Coed. Private proprietary (Apollo Group) control. One-course-per-month format, six weeks in duration. Special facilities: Center for Distance Learning, Center for Higher Education and Economic Development. Library: 27,000,000 volumes, 1,366,000 microforms, 2500 current subscriptions, several thousand PCs at all campuses and Learning Centers. Total University enrollment: 125,364; 80,000 on campuses, 48,000 using online instruction or distance learning.

Tuition: varies by campus. No on-campus housing available.

Graduate Programs

Graduate study since 1975. Enrollment: full- and part-time approximately 25,000. Graduate faculty: full-time 30, part-time 1100. Degrees conferred: M.A.Ed., M.A.O.M., M.B.A., M.H.A., M.I.S., M.S, M.S.N., M.S.C.I.S.

ADMISSION REQUIREMENT. Official transcripts, proof of at least three years of significant full-time work experience required in support of application. Some programs have additional admission requirements. TOEFL, TOEIC, or IELTS required for international applicants. Accepts transfer applicants. Graduates of unaccredited institutions not considered. Apply to appropriate Admissions Office at least one month prior to date of registration. Some programs have earlier deadlines. Rolling admission process. Phone (800)MY-SUCCESS. Application fee $110. Contact Web site for appropriate Admissions Office number.

ADMISSION STANDARDS. Relatively open. Usual minimum average: 2.5 (A = 4).

FINANCIAL AID. Annual awards from institutional funds: Federal W/S, loans. Most sites are approved for VA benefits. Apply to Office of Financial Assistance at each site; no specified closing date. Use FAFSA. Aid available for part-time students.

DEGREE REQUIREMENTS. For master's: 36–51 credits minimum, at least 30–45 in residence; thesis/nonthesis option; no foreign language requirement; final exams/internships in some programs.

FIELDS OF STUDY.
Accountancy. M.S.
Administration of Justice and Security. M.S.
Business Administration. Includes accounting, global management, health care management, human resource management, marketing, public administration, technology management, Spanish. M.B.A.
Counseling. Includes community counseling, marriage and family counseling, marriage, family and child therapy, mental health counseling, school counseling. M.S.
Education. Includes administration and supervision, adult education & training, cross categorical special education, curriculum and instruction (computer education, English and language arts education, mathematics education), early childhood education, elementary education, elementary teacher education, secondary education, secondary teacher education. M.A.Ed.
Health Administration. Includes gerontology, health care education, health care informatics. M.H.A.
Information Systems. M.I.S.
Information Systems/Management. M.I.S.M.
Management. Includes international, human resource management, public administration. M.M.
Nursing. Includes nurse practitioner, family nurse practitioner. M.S.N.
Psychology. M.S.
Note: The above fields of study were obtained by visiting the main University of Phoenix Web site. Consult the campus closest to you to obtain current and complete information.

PIKEVILE COLLEGE SCHOOL OF OSTEOPATHIC MEDICINE

147 Sycamore Street
Pikeville, Kentucky 41501
Web site: pcom.pc.edu

Founded 1997. Private control. Semester system. Library: 30,000 volumes, 350 subscriptions.

Annual tuition: $29,250. No on-campus housing available. Contact the Office of Student Affairs for housing information. Off-campus housing and personal expenses: approximately $12,000.

Enrollment: first-year class 80, total 301 (men 54%, women 44%, minorities 12%, state residents 46%). Faculty: full-time 26, part-time 249. Degree conferred: D.O.

ADMISSION REQUIREMENTS. AACOMAS report (deadline February 1), bachelor's degree, official transcripts, MCAT, three recommendations (one from science faculty member, a premedical source, one evaluation from a physician, preferably a D.O.), supplemental from required in support of application. Accepts transfer applicants. Interview by invitation only. Graduates of unaccredited colleges not considered. Apply by February 1 (supple-

mental deadline March 1) to the admission office. Admits first year student Fall only. Rolling admission process. Application fee $75. Phone: (606)218-5400; fax: (606)218-5405

ADMISSION STANDARDS. Selective. Accepts about 27% of all applicants. Number of applications 521 (464 out-of-state); number interviewed 167 (113 out-of-state); number of acceptances 140 (90 out-of-state); number enrolled 80 (44 out-of-state). Usual minimum UGPA: 2.75 (A = 4). Mean Composite MCAT 7.3, mean UGPA 3.30.

FINANCIAL AID. Scholarships, grants, federal w/s, Federal or private loans. Apply by April 1 to Financial Aid Office. Use FAFSA. About 90% of students receive some form of financial assistance.

DEGREE REQUIREMENTS. For D.O.: satisfactory completion of four-year program; all students must take the National Board of Osteopathic Medical Exam Level I and Level II.

PITTSBURG STATE UNIVERSITY

Pittsburg, Kansas 66762-5880
Web site: www.pittstate.edu

Founded 1903. Located 125 miles S of Kansas City. CGS member. Coed. State control. Semester system. Library: 639,100 volumes, 5000 subscriptions. Total University enrollment: 6825.

Annual tuition: resident $4590, nonresident $11,254; per credit, resident $194, nonresident $472. On-campus housing for 47 married students, 630 men, 700 women. Average academic year housing costs: $5000 (including board). Apply to Director of Residence Life. Phone: (620)235-4245.

Graduate School

Graduate study since 1929. Enrollment: full-time 331, part-time 865. College faculty teaching graduate students: 268. Degrees conferred: M.A., M.S., M.B.A., M.M., M.S.N., Ed.S.

ADMISSION REQUIREMENTS. Official transcripts, recommendations required in support of application. GRE/GMAT required by several departments. TOEFL (minimum score 520–550 depending on department) required for international applicants. Accepts transfer applicants. Apply by July 15 (Fall), December 5 (Spring), April 30 (Summer) to the Office of Graduate Studies and Research. Rolling admissions process. Application fee: $30, international applicants $50. Phone: (620)235-4220; fax: (620)235-4219.

ADMISSION STANDARDS. Selective. Usual minimum average: 2.5 (A = 4).

FINANCIAL AID. Annual awards from institutional funds: teaching assistantships, research assistantships, internships, fee waivers, Federal W/S, loans. Approved for VA benefits. Apply to Graduate Office for assistantships; to Financial Aid Office for all other programs. Phone: (620)235-7000. Use FAFSA. About 60% of students receive aid other than loans from College and outside sources.

DEGREE REQUIREMENTS. For master's: 30–36 semester hours minimum; admission to candidacy; comprehensive exam; research problem, seminar; or thesis/nonthesis option. For Ed.S.: 30 semester hours minimum beyond the master's; thesis problem; comprehensive exam; admission to candidacy.

FIELDS OF STUDY.

COLLEGE OF ARTS AND SCIENCES:
Art. Includes art studio, art education.
Biology.

Chemistry.
Communication.
English. Includes creative writing, literature, professional writing and rhetoric, teaching English in community college.
History.
Mathematics.
Music. Includes conducting. education, pedagogy, performance.
Nursing. Includes family health administration, family health education, family health gerontology, family nurse practitioner.
Physics.

COLLEGE OF BUSINESS:
Accounting.
General Administration.
International Business.

COLLEGE OF EDUCATION:
Counseling. Includes community counseling, school counseling.
Educational Leadership.
Educational Technology. Includes technology facilitator, library media.
Health, Human Performance, and Recreation. Includes human performance and wellness, sport and leisure service management.
Psychology. Includes clinical psychology.
Reading. Includes classroom reading teacher.
Special Education Teaching Specialist. Includes community college, higher education.
Specialist in Education. Includes general school administration.
Teaching. Includes elementary, secondary, ESOL.

COLLEGE OF TECHNOLOGY:
College Teaching.
Engineering Technology.
Human Resource Development. Includes management and consulting.
Technology. Includes printing management.
Technical Teacher Education.
Workforce Development and Education.
Note: Cooperative Ph.D. and Ed.D. programs available from University of Kansas, Kansas State University, University of Arkansas.

UNIVERSITY OF PITTSBURGH
Pittsburgh, Pennsylvania 15261
Web site: www.pitt.edu

Chartered 1787. CGS and AAU member. Coed. State related. Trimester system. Regional campuses in Titusville, Bradford, Greensburg, Johnstown. Special facilities: Allegheny Observatory, Applied Research Center, Center for Biotechnology and Bioengineering, Cancer Institute, Cleft-Palate-Craniofacial Center, Frick Fine Arts Building, Center for International Studies, Learning Research and Development Center, Mid-Atlantic Technology Application Center, Center for Neuroscience, Center for Philosophy of Science, Pittsburgh Cancer Institute, Center for Social and Urban Research, Surface Science Center. The University's NIH ranking is 9th among all U.S. institutions with 969 awards/grants valued at $395,680,084. According to The Center at University of Florida, the University is ranked 14th in receipt of Federal Research funds with $345,625,000 and it ranks 25th for total University research expenditures with $4,019,684,000. The University's endowment assets rank it 31st, with a value of $1,364,882,000. In 2004, the University awarded 382 doctorates, which ranked it 29th among all U.S. institutions eligible to award that degree. Twenty-two of the University's faculty members have been elected to National Honor Academies and this ranks it 44th among all U.S. institutions. The Library: approximately 3,600,000 volumes, 32,000 subscriptions. Total University enrollment: 26,500.

Annual tuition: varies by school. No on-campus housing. For off-campus housing, contact Graduate Housing Office. Phone: (412)624-7115.

School of Arts and Sciences—Graduate Studies

Former Divisions of Humanities, Natural Sciences, and Social Sciences combined into the School of Arts and Sciences. Annual tuition: full-time resident $14,880, nonresident $26,920; per credit resident $604, nonresident $1103. Graduate enrollment: full-time 1648, part-time 122. Faculty teaching graduate students: full-time 720, part-time 146. Degrees conferred: M.A., M.F.A., M.S., Ph.D.

ADMISSION REQUIREMENTS. Transcripts, three letters of recommendation, personal statement, GRE required in support of application. Online application available. TOEFL required for international applicants. Accepts transfer applicants. Graduates of unaccredited institutions not considered. Apply to chair of proposed graduate department by August 1 (Fall), December 1 (Winter), April 1 (Spring), June 1 (Summer). Earlier deadlines may be applicable for some programs. Rolling admission process. Application fee $40, $50 for international applicants. Phone: (412) 624-6094; fax: (412)624-6855.

ADMISSION STANDARDS. Selective for most departments, competitive for others. Usual minimum average: 3.0 (A = 4).

FINANCIAL AID. Annual awards from institutional funds: scholarships, fellowships, research assistantships, teaching assistantships, internships, Mellon fellowships, full and partial tuition waivers, Federal W/S, loans. Approved for VA benefits. Apply by April 1 to departmental chairperson for fellowships, assistantships; to the Financial Aid Office for all other programs. Use FAFSA (School code: 008815) and institutional FAF. About 60% of full-time students receive aid other than loans from University and outside sources.

DEGREE REQUIREMENTS. For master's: 9 courses minimum; comprehensive exam; thesis/nonthesis. For Ph.D.: 72 credit minimum or 24 courses minimum beyond the bachelor's; preliminary, comprehensive exams; dissertation; final oral exam; additional requirements may be determined by each department.

FIELDS OF STUDY.
Anthropology.
Applied Mathematic.
Art History.
Astronomy.
Bioethics. M.A. only.
Biological Sciences. Includes molecular, cellular and developmental biology, molecular biophysics, ecology and evolution.
Chemistry.
Classics. Includes Greek history and literature, Latin literature.
Communication.
Computer Engineering.
Computer Science. Includes information science.
East Asian Studies. M.A. only.
Ecology and Evolution.
Economics.
English. Includes composition, cultural and critical studies, writing.
French and Italian Language and Literature.
Geology and Planetary Sciences. Includes environmental science, GIS/remote sensing, paleontology.
Germanic Languages and Literatures.
Hispanic Languages and Literatures. Includes Portuguese, Spanish.
History.
History and Philosophy of Science.
History of Art and Architecture. Includes fine arts.
Integrative Molecular Biology.
Intelligent Systems Studies.

Linguistics.
Mathematics.
Music.
Neuroscience.
Philosophy.
Physics.
Political Science.
Psychology. Includes clinical, cognitive, developmental, health, social, individualized.
Religion. Ph.D. only.
Religious Studies. M.A. only.
Slavic Languages and Literatures.
Sociology.
Statistics.
Theatre Arts. Includes dramatic arts, speech, theatre and performance studies.

The Joseph M. Katz Graduate School of Business
Web site: www.katz.pitt.edu

Established 1960. Special facilities: Center for Economic Development, Small Business Development Center, Center for International Business, Strategic Management Institute, Program in Corporate Culture, Business, Society, and Government Research Institute, and Center for Research on Contracts and the Structure of Enterprise.

Annual tuition: resident $29,676, nonresident $44,418.

Enrollment: full-time 183, part-time 462. Faculty: full-time 70, part-time 23. Degrees conferred: M.B.A., E.M.B.A., M.S. in MOIS, M.H.A., M.B.A.-J.D., Ph.D., M.I.B., M.B.A.-M.S.N., M.B.A.-M.P.I.A.

ADMISSION REQUIREMENTS. Baccalaureate or higher degree; introductory calculus; GMAT required in support of School's application. Online application available. TOEFL (minimum score 600) required for international applicants. Accepts transfer applicants. Graduates of unaccredited institutions not considered. Apply prior to March 1 (Fall), November 1 (Spring) to the Admission Office. Full-time M.B.A. applicants admitted Fall only. Part-time applicants admitted Fall, Spring, Summer terms. Rolling admission process. Application fee $50. Phone: (412)648-1700; fax: (412)648-1659.

ADMISSION STANDARDS. Very selective. Mean GMAT: 621; mean GPA: 3.20 (A = 4). Usual minimum average: 3.1 (A = 4), usual GMAT range 550–650.

FINANCIAL AID. Annual awards from institutional funds: scholarships, tuition fellowships, research assistantships, teaching assistantships, grants, Federal W/S, loans. Approved for VA benefits. Apply to Dean's Office for fellowships, assistantships; to Financial Aid Office for all other programs. Submit FAFSA (School code: 008815) and completed institutional application with GMAT scores by March 15. Phone: (412)624-PITT. No scholarship aid is available for part-time students or international students in M.B.A. program. Approximately 70% of M.B.A. students and 90% of doctoral students receive some form of financial assistance.

DEGREE REQUIREMENTS. For master's: 39–51 credit hours depending on previous degree and experience; thesis/nonthesis option; final comprehensive exam for some programs. For Ph.D.: 72 credit hours; comprehensive exam in major and minor fields; dissertation; final oral exam.

FIELDS OF STUDY.
Accounting. Ph.D.
Business Administration. Includes concentrations in accounting, information systems, marketing, operations, organizational behavior and human resource management, strategy, environment and organizations. M.B.A.
Finance. Ph.D.

Information Systems. Ph.D.
Marketing. Ph.D.
Operations, Decision Sciences, and Artificial Intelligence. Includes data mining and business analytics, project management, revenue management, simulation methodology, stochastic modeling and applied statistical methods, supply chain management. Ph.D.
Organizational Behavior and Human Resource Management. Ph.D.
Strategic Management. Ph.D.

School of Dental Medicine (15261-1945)
Web site: www.dental.pitt.edu

Established 1878. Semester system. Special program: Program for International/Advanced Standing Program for foreign-trained dental graduates.

Annual tuition: resident $32,460, nonresident $39,788. Limited on-campus housing available. Average academic year housing costs: $17,000. Contact Graduate Housing Office for both on- and off-campus housing information. Phone: (215)898-8271. Total average cost for all other first-year expenses: $14,500.

Enrollment: first-year class 90, total 387 (men 55%, women 45%, minorities 5%, state residents 30%). Faculty: full-time 86, part-time 81. Degrees conferred: D.M.D., M.D.S., M.S., Ph.D., Certificates.

ADMISSIONS REQUIREMENTS. For D.M.D. program: AADSAS report, official high school and college transcripts, three letters of recommendation, essay, DAT (April test in junior year preferred) required in support of School's application. Interview by invitation only. Applicants must have completed at least three years of college study. Transfer applicants considered on a space available basis only. Preference given to state residents. Apply to Office of Admissions after August 1, before December 1. Application fee $35. Phone: (412)648-8437; fax: (412)648-9571. For graduate program: official transcripts, three letters of recommendation required in support of School's application. Apply to Director, Graduate Education by December 1. Phone: (412)648-8500.

ADMISSION STANDARDS. Competitive. Accepts about 10–15% of all applicants. Usual minimum UGPA: 3.0 (A = 4). Mean DAT: academic 18.85, PAT 18; mean UGPA 3.57.

FINANCIAL AID. D.M.D. programs: scholarships, grants, loans. Apply to University Office of Financial Aid after acceptance. Approximately 89% of all D.M.D. students receive some form of financial assistance. For Graduate students: fellowships, assistantships, loans. Apply April 1 to Financial Aid Office. Phone: (412)648-8422. Use FAFSA (School code: 024824).

DEGREE REQUIREMENTS. For D.M.D.: satisfactory completion of four-year program. For M.D.S.: two to three year, full-time program, thesis. For M.S., Ph.D.: see Graduate School listing above.

FIELDS OF POSTGRADUATE STUDY.
Advanced Education in General Dentistry.
Dental Anesthesiology.
Dental Informatics. A concentration in the Biomedical Informatics Training Program. M.S., Ph.D.
Endodontics. Certificate.
Oral and Maxillofacial Surgery.
Orthodontics and Dentofacial Orthopedics. M.D.S., Certificate.
Pediatric Dentistry. Certificate.
Periodontics. M.D.S., Certificate
Prothodontics.

School of Education
Web site: www.pitt.edu/education.html

Graduate study since 1910. Semester system.

Annual tuition: full-time resident $14,880, nonresident $26,920, per credit resident $604, nonresident $1103.

Enrollment: full-time 560, part-time 653. Faculty: full-time 102, part-time 28. Degrees conferred: M.A., M.Ed., M.A.T., M.S., Ed.D., Ph.D.

ADMISSION REQUIREMENTS. Official transcripts, GRE required in support of School's application. Interview/MAT required by some departments. TOEFL required for international applicants. Accepts transfer applicants. Graduates of unaccredited institutions not considered. Apply to the Office of Student Personnel Services, School of Education, by February 1 (Fall), November 15 (Spring). Rolling admission process. Application fee $50, international applicants $60. Phone (412)648-2230; fax: (412)648-1899.

ADMISSION STANDARDS. Selective for master's, usual minimum average 3.0; 3.3 (A = 4) for doctorate.

FINANCIAL AID. Five scholarships, teaching assistantships, research assistantships, internships, traineeships, tuition waivers, Federal W/S, loans. Approved for VA benefits. Apply by April 15 to department chair for fellowships, assistantships; to Office of Financial Aid for all other programs. Phone: (412)624-PITT. Use FAFSA and institutional FAF. Aid available for part-time students.

DEGREE REQUIREMENTS: For master's: 36 credit hours minimum; comprehensive exam. For Ed.D., Ph.D.: 90 credit hour minimum beyond bachelor's degree, at least 60 credits in residence; comprehensive written exam; dissertation; final oral exam.

FIELDS OF STUDY
Administrative and Policy Studies. Includes higher education management, school leadership, social and comparative analysis in education.
Health and Physical Activity. Includes adapted physical education, development movement, exercise physiology, youth health and fitness.
Instruction and Learning. Includes early childhood education, early intervention special education, education of deaf and hard of hearing, education of mentally and physically disabled, elementary education, elementary education and foreign language education, English and communication education, foreign language education, mathematics education, reading education, science education, severe disabilities special education, social studies education, special education, visual studies special education.
Psychology. Includes research methodology, applied developmental psychology.

School of Engineering

Annual tuition: resident $17,060, nonresident $30,908; per credit resident $839, nonresident $1465.

Enrollment; full-time 388, part-time 141. Faculty: full-time 94, part-time 40. Degrees conferred: M.S., M.S.B.Eng., M.S.C.E., M.S.Ch.E., M.S.E.E., M.S.E.R., M.S.I.E., M.S.M.E., M.S.Met.E., M.S.Mf.S.E., M.S.M.S.E., M.S.P.E., Ph.D.

ADMISSION REQUIREMENTS. Official transcript, GRE required in support of School's application. GRE Subject Test required for some programs. Interview not required. Online application available. TOEFL required for international applicants. Accepts transfer applicants. Graduates of unaccredited institutions not considered. Apply to appropriate department chair by April 1 (Fall), August 1 (Spring), April 1 (Summer). Rolling admissions process. Application fee $40, international applicants $50. Phone: (412)624-9800; fax: (412)624-9808.

ADMISSION STANDARDS. Selective. Usual minimum average: 3.0 (A = 4) from ABET-accredited undergraduate institu-

tion. Applicants with lower averages considered on limited and exceptional basis.

FINANCIAL AID. Fellowships, teaching assistantships, research assistantships, grants, Federal W/S, loans. Approved for VA benefits. Apply by February 1 to appropriate department chair for assistantships, fellowships; to Financial Aid Office for all other programs. Phone: (412) 624-7488. Use FAFSA (School code: 008815).

DEGREE REQUIREMENTS. For master's: 30 credit hours minimum; comprehensive exam; thesis/nonthesis option; final exam. For Ph.D.: 72 credit hours minimum, at least two consecutive terms in residence; qualifying exam; comprehensive exam; dissertation; final oral exam.

FIELDS OF STUDY.
Bioengineering. M.S.B.Eng., Ph.D.
Chemical Engineering. M.S.Ch.E., Ph.D.
Civil Engineering. M.S.C.E., Ph.D.
Electrical Engineering. M.S.E.E., Ph.D.
Industrial Engineering. M.S.I.E., Ph.D.
Materials Science and Engineering. M.S.M.E., Ph.D.
Mechanical Engineering. M.S.M.E., Ph.D.
Metallurgical Engineering. M.S.Met.E., Ph.D.
Petroleum Engineering. M.S.P.E.

School of Health and Rehabilitation Sciences
4019 Forbes Tower (15260)

Annual tuition: full-time resident $17,448, nonresident $31,590; per credit, resident $714, nonresident $1298.

Enrollment: full-time 387, part-time 90. Faculty: full- and part-time 63. Degrees conferred: M.S., M.P.T., Ph.D.

ADMISSION REQUIREMENTS. Official transcripts, three recommendations required in support of School's application. GRE required for M.P.T., Ph.D. applicants. TOEFL required for international applicants. Accepts transfer applicants. Application deadlines: M.S. June 1 (Fall), November 15 (Spring); M.P.T. January 31; Ph.D. April 1 (Fall), September 1 (Spring). Application fee $30, international applicants $40, M.P.T. application fee $50. Phone: (412)383-6558; fax: (412)383-6535.

FINANCIAL AID. Scholarships, teaching fellowships, teaching assistantships, internships, grants, Federal W/S, loans. Approved for VA benefits. Apply to departmental chair for fellowships, assistantships; to Financial Aid Office for all other programs. Use FAFSA and institutional FAF. Phone: (412) 624-7488; fax (412) 648-8815. Financial assistance also available for selected minority students. About 50% of students receive aid other than loans from School and outside sources.

DEGREE REQUIREMENTS. For M.S., M.P.T.: 8-course minimum; comprehensive exam; thesis/nonthesis option. For Ph.D.: 90 credit hours minimum beyond the bachelor's degree, at least 60 credits in residence; qualifying exam; candidacy; dissertation; final oral exam.

FIELDS OF STUDY.
Communication Science and Disorders. Includes Audiology, speech language pathology.
Dietetics.
Health Information Management. Includes healthcare supervision and management, health information systems.
Health and Rehabilitation Sciences. Includes clinical dietetics and nutrition, occupational therapy, physical therapy, sports medicine, wellness and human performances.
Occupational Therapy. M.O.T.
Physical Therapy. D.P.T.

Rehabilitation Science and Technology. Includes rehabilitation counseling, rehabilitation science and technology.
Rehabilitation Science. Interdisciplinary. Ph.D.

School of Information Science

Web site: www.lis.pitt.edu

Established 1962.

Annual tuition: full-time resident $15,646, nonresident $28,308; per credit resident $640, nonresident $1168.

Enrollment: full-time 287, part-time 319. Faculty: full-time 32, part-time 12. Degrees conferred: M.L.S., M.S.I.S., M.S.T., C.A.S., Ph.D.

ADMISSION REQUIREMENTS. Official transcripts, GRE, letters of recommendation required in support of School's application. TOEFL required for international applicants. Accepts transfer applicants. Graduates of unaccredited institutions not considered. Apply to School by June 1 (Fall), April 1 (Fall, international), October 1 (Spring). Application fee $50, international applicants $60. Phone: (412)624-5230; fax: (412)624-5231.

FINANCIAL AID. Annual awards from institutional funds: Twenty-five fellowships, three assistantships, Federal W/S, loans. Approved for VA benefits. Apply to the School for fellowships, assistantships; to the Office of Financial Aid for all other programs. Phone: (412) 624-7488; fax: (412)648-8815. Use FAFSA and institutional FAF. Financial assistance also available for selected minority students.

DEGREE REQUIREMENTS. M.L.S., M.S.I.S.,: 36 credit hours minimum, at least 30 in residence. For M.S.T.: 48 credit hours minimum, at least 36 in residence. For Ph.D. in L.S.: 54 credit hours minimum beyond the Master's; preliminary exam; comprehensive exam; proficiency in language determined by Committee on Doctoral Studies; dissertation. For Ph.D. in I.S.: 60 credit hours minimum beyond the Master's; 6 credits in linguistics; preliminary exam; comprehensive exam; 18 dissertation credits. For Certificate: 24 credit hours minimum beyond the master's.

FIELDS OF STUDY.
Information Science.
Library and Information Science.
Telecommunications.

School of Law (15260)

Web site: www.law.pitt.edu

Founded 1895. ABA approved since 1923. AALS charter member. Public control. Semester system. Special facility: Center for International Legal Education. Law library: 440,116 volumes, 2672 subscriptions: has LEXIS, NEXIS, WESTLAW; has more than 300 network connections.

Annual tuition: resident $20,758, nonresident $29,056. On-campus housing available. Total average annual additional expenses: $16,860.

Enrollment: first-year class 243, total 731 (men 58%, women 42%, minorities 13%). Faculty: full-time 52, part-time 48. Student to faculty ratio is 14.4 to 1. Degrees conferred: J.D., J.D.-M.A., J.D.-M.B.A., J.D.-M.P.A., J.D.-M.P.I.A., J.D.-M.P.H., J.D.-M.S. (Carnegie Mellon's Schools of Industrial Management and Urban and Public Affairs), J.D.-M.S.I.A., J.D.-M.U.R.P., LL.M. (for persons who have completed a basic legal education and received a university degree in law in another country), J.S.D.

ADMISSION REQUIREMENTS. LSDAS Law School report, bachelor's degree, transcripts, LSAT, personal statement, two letters of recommendation required in support of application. Accepts transfer applicants. Graduates of unaccredited institutions not considered. Apply to Director of Admissions after September 1, before March 1. Dual degree applicants must apply to and be

accepted to both Schools/programs. Application fee $55. Phone: (412)648-1415.

ADMISSION STANDARDS. Selective. Accepts approximately 29% of all students. Number of applicants 2349; number of acceptances 671; number enrolled 243; LSAT (75% of students have a score at or above 157); GPA (75% of student have a GPA at or above 3.12). *U.S. News & World Report* ranking is in the second tier (tied at 57th) of all U.S. law schools.

FINANCIAL AID. Scholarships, fellowships, assistantships, Federal W/S, loans. Apply to the Financial Aid Office by March 1. Phone: (412)648-1415. Use FAFSA (School code: 008815) and institutional financial aid form. Approximately 50% of all students receive some form of financial assistance.

DEGREE REQUIREMENTS. For J.D.: three years minimum, at least the final year in full-time residence; 88 credit hour program. For LL.M.: at least 24 credit hours minimum beyond J.D.; final project. For J.S.D.: 2–4 year program beyond LL.M.; dissertation. *Note:* School has a faculty exchange program with the University of Augsburg (Germany).

School of Medicine (15261)

Web site: www.medschool.pitt.edu

Established 1886 as Western Pennsylvania Medical College. In 1892 it affiliated with Western University of Pennsylvania, which became University of Pittsburgh. Library: 175,000 volumes, 2000 subscriptions. NIH ranking is 9th among U.S. institutions with 969 worth $395,680,084.

Annual tuition: resident $33,834, nonresident $38,714. No on-campus housing available. Total average figure for all other expenses: $15,000.

Enrollment: first-year class 148, total 589 (men 53%, women 49%, minorities 40%, state residents 29%). Faculty: full- and part-time about 1800. Degrees conferred: M.D., M.D.-M.A., M.D.-M.S., M.D.-M.P.H., M.D.-Ph.D. (Medical Scientist Training program with both the University of Pittsburgh and Carnegie-Mellon University).

ADMISSION REQUIREMENTS. AMCAS report, transcripts, three letters of recommendation, preprofessional committee evaluation, MCAT, interview required in support of application. Accepts transfer applicants on a space available basis only. Has EDP; apply between June 1 and August 1. Apply to Office of the Associate Dean of the School after June 1, before December 1 (firm). Dual degree applicants must apply to and be accepted to both Schools/programs. Application fee $75. Phone: (412)648-9891; fax: (412)648-8768. M.D.-Ph.D.: (412)648-2324.

ADMISSION STANDARDS. Competitive. Accepts about 9% of all applicants. Number of applications 5300 (4506 out-of-state); number interviewed 1188 (1024 out-of-state); number of acceptances 462 (397 out-of-state); number enrolled 148 (125 out-of-state). Mean Composite MCAT 13.3; mean UGPA 3.68. *U.S. News & World Report* ranking is in the top 15 of all medical research schools, 18th in primary care.

FINANCIAL AID. Scholarships, Federal and private loans, research fellowships. MSTP funded by NIH. Apply after acceptance to Financial Aid Committee. Phone: (412)648-9891. Use FAFSA (School code: E00516). About 86% of students receive some form of financial assistance.

DEGREE REQUIREMENTS. For M.D.: satisfactory completion of four-year program; all students must pass USMLE Step 1 prior to entering third year; all students must pass USMLE Step 2 prior to awarding of M.D. For M.S.: 32 credit hours minimum; final project/thesis.

FIELDS OF GRADUATE STUDY.

Biomedical Engineering. With both University of Pittsburgh and Carnegie Mellon University.
Biological Sciences. With Carnegie Mellon University.
Biochemistry and Molecular Genetics.
Bioinformatics and Biomedical Informatics.
Cell Biology and Molecular Physiology.
Cellular and Molecular Pathology.
Chemical and Petroleum Engineering.
Chemistry.
Computational Biology.
Epidemiology.
Ethics. M.A.
Human Genetics.
Immunology.
Integrative Molecular Biology.
Medical Humanities. It draws upon the fields of anthropology, cultural studies, ethics, history, law, literature, philosophy, religion, writing, and women's studies.
Molecular Biophysics/Structural Biology.
Molecular Pharmacology.
Molecular Toxicology.
Molecular Virology and Microbiology.
Neuroscience.
Robotics. With Carnegie Mellon University.

School of Nursing—Graduate Division

Annual tuition: full-time resident $17,448, nonresident $22,236; per credit resident $714, nonresident $911.
Enrollment: full-time 167, part-time 175. Faculty: full-time 68, part-time 24. Degrees conferred: M.S.N., Ph.D.

ADMISSION REQUIREMENTS. Transcripts, GRE, three references, résumé, current nursing license required in support of School's application. Interview may be required. TOEFL required for international applicants. Accepts transfer applicants. Graduates of unaccredited colleges not considered. Apply to the School by February 1 (Fall), September 15 (Spring). Rolling admission process. Application fee $50, international applicants $60. Phone: (412)624-9670; fax: (412)624-2409.

ADMISSION STANDARDS. Competitive. Usual minimum average: 3.0 (A = 4).

FINANCIAL AID. Scholarships, fellowships, research assistantships, teaching assistantships, internships, Federal W/S, loans. Approved for VA benefits. Apply by March 1 to Assistant Dean of the School for assistantships; to Financial Aid Office for all other programs. Phone: (412)624-6302. Use FAFSA and School's FAF. About 45% of students receive aid other than loans. Aid available for part-time students.

DEGREE REQUIREMENTS. For M.S.N.: 42 credits minimum. For Ph.D.: 42 credits minimum beyond the master's; comprehensive exam; dissertation; final oral defense.

FIELDS OF STUDY.
Clinical Nurse Specialist. Includes adult/medical/surgery nursing, psychiatric/mental health nursing.
Nurse Anesthesia.
Nurse Practitioner. Includes acute care, adult, family, neonatal, pediatric, psychiatric, primary care.
Nursing. Includes adolescent health, chronic disorders, critical care, genetics, technology, women's health. Ph.D.
Nursing Administration.
Nursing Education.
Nursing Informatics.
Nursing Research.

School of Pharmacy—Graduate Studies (15261)

Founded 1878. Coed. Semester system.
Tuition: per credit resident $1443, nonresident $1814; Pharm.D. per credit resident $715, nonresident $985.
Enrollment: full-time 417, part-time 2. Faculty full-time 80, part-time 35. Degrees conferred: Pharm.D., M.S., Ph.D.

ADMISSION REQUIREMENTS. Transcripts, GRE, personal statement outlining goals, letters of reference required in support of School's application. TOEFL, TSE, TWE required for international applicants. Interview not required, but may be requested. Accepts transfer applicants. Apply to Director of Graduate Programs by March 1 (Fall). Admits Fall only. Application fee $50, international students $60. Phone: (412)383-9000; fax: (412)383-9995.

ADMISSION STANDARDS. Very selective. Usual minimum average: 3.0 (A = 4).

FINANCIAL AID. Scholarships, teaching assistantships, internships, Federal W/S, loans. Apply by March 1 to Director of Graduate Programs for scholarships, assistantships; to the Financial Aid Office for all other programs. Phone: (412)648-7488. Use FAFSA and institutional FAF. Nearly 100% of students receive aid from School or outside sources.

DEGREE REQUIREMENTS. For M.S.: at least 24 credits, but usually 30 credits of approved graduate study; comprehensive written exam; thesis; final oral exam. For Pharm.D: six-year "lock step" program with two years of preprofessional study; experiential learning sequence. For Ph.D.: at least 72 credits; thesis; preliminary exam; dissertation; final oral exam.

FIELDS OF STUDY.
Pharmaceutical Sciences.
Pharmacy.

Graduate School of Public and International Affairs
Web site: www.pitt.edu/~gspia

Graduate study since 1957. Semester system.
Annual Tuition: full-time resident $14,880, nonresident $26,920, per credit resident $604, nonresident $1103.
Enrollment: full-time 335, part-time 87. Faculty: full-time 35, part-time 17. Degrees conferred: M.I.D., M.P.A., M.P.I.A., M.P.P.M., Ph.D.

ADMISSION REQUIREMENTS. Transcripts, essay, letters of reference required in support of School's application. GRE and a major paper required of doctoral applicants, recommended for master's applicants. Online application available. Evidence of proficiency in English required of international students. Interview not required. Accepts transfer applicants. Graduates of unaccredited institutions not considered. Apply to Office of Admissions by February 1 (Fall), October 1 (Spring). Rolling admissions process. Application fee $50, international applicants $60. Phone: (412) 648-7643; fax (412)648-7641.

ADMISSION STANDARDS. Selective. Usual minimum average: 3.0 (A = 4).

FINANCIAL AID. Scholarships, minority scholarships, fellowships, research fellowships, teaching assistantships, internships, Federal W/S, loans. Apply by February 1 to Admissions Office of School for scholarships, fellowships, assistantships; to the Financial Aid Office for all other programs. Phone: (412)648-7647; fax: (412)648-2605. Use FAFSA and institutional FAF. About 41% of students receive aid other than loans from School.

DEGREE REQUIREMENTS. For master's: 48 hours minimum in residence; policy seminar, and internship. For Ph.D.: 78 credit hours minimum, at least four terms in residence; proficiency in advanced research and quantitative analysis; preliminary exam; comprehensive exam; dissertation; final oral exam.

FIELDS OF STUDY.
Development Planning and Environmental Sustainability. M.I.D.
Global Political Economy. M.P.I.A.
Nongovernmental Organizations and Civil Society. M.I.D.
Policy Research and Analysis. M.P.A.
Public and International Affairs. Ph.D.
Public and Nonprofit Affairs. M.P.A.
Public Policy and Management. M.P.P.M.
Security and Intelligence Studies. M.P.I.A.
Urban and Regional Affairs. M.P.A.

Graduate School of Public Health

Established 1948.

Annual tuition: resident $17,448, nonresident $31,590; per credit resident $714 nonresident $1298. No on-campus housing available.

Enrollment: full-time 314, part-time 166. Faculty: full-time 110, part-time 20. Degrees conferred: M.P.H., M.H.A., M.S., M.H.P.E., D.P.H., Ph.D.

ADMISSION REQUIREMENTS. Transcripts, two letters of recommendation, GRE, GMAT (Health Administration) required in support of application. TOEFL, statement of financial responsibility required of all international applicants. Interview not required for most programs. Accepts transfer applicants. Graduates of unaccredited colleges not considered. Apply to Admissions Office of the School; deadlines vary by program. Fall and Winter admission for most programs. Application fee $50; international fee $60. Phone (412)624-5200; fax (412)624-3755.

ADMISSION STANDARDS. Competitive. Usual minimum average: 3.0 (A = 4).

FINANCIAL AID. Annual awards from institutional funds vary from year to year; scholarships, research assistantships, teaching assistantships, internships, postdoctoral positions, Federal W/S, loans. Approved for VA benefits. Apply to appropriate department chairman for scholarships, assistantships, internships, postdoctoral positions; to the Financial Aid Office for all other programs. Phone: (412)624-3002. Use FAFSA and institutional FAF. About 50% of Students receive aid other than loans from School and outside sources. Limited aid for part-time students.

DEGREE REQUIREMENTS. For master's program by advisement: thesis/final document; final oral/written exam. For doctoral programs by advisement: knowledge of one computer language; preliminary exam; comprehensive exam; dissertation; final oral exam.

FIELDS OF STUDY.
Behavioral and Community Health Sciences.
Biostatistics.
Environmental and Occupational Health.
Epidemiology.
Genetic Counseling.
Health Policy and Management.
Human Genetics.
Infectious Diseases and Microbiology.
Multidisciplinary Public Health.
Occupational Medicine.
Public Health Genetics.
Note: Joint programs with the School of Arts and Science, School of Law, School of Medicine, Pittsburgh Theological Seminary, School of Public and International Affairs, School of Social Work.

School of Social Work—Graduate Division

Graduate study since 1942. Semester system.

Annual tuition: full-time resident $14,880, nonresident $26,920; per credit resident $604, nonresident $1103.

Enrollment: full-time 350, part-time 281. Faculty: full-time 22, part-time 45. Degrees conferred: M.S.W., Ph.D.

ADMISSION REQUIREMENTS. Transcripts required in support of School's application. Interview may be required. TOEFL required for international applicants. Accepts transfer applicants. Graduates of unaccredited colleges not considered. Apply to the School by March 31. Fall admission only. Rolling admission process. Application fee $50, $60 for international applicants. Phone: (412)624-6302; fax: (412)624-6323.

ADMISSION STANDARDS. Competitive. Usual minimum average: 3.0 (A = 4).

FINANCIAL AID. Scholarships, traineeships, research assistantships, teaching assistantships, internships, tuition waivers, Federal W/S, loans. Approved for VA benefits. Apply by March 31 to Assistant Dean of Admissions of the School for assistantships; to Financial Aid Office for all other programs. Phone: (412)624-6302. Use FAFSA and School's FAF. About 45% of students receive aid other than loans. No aid for part-time students.

DEGREE REQUIREMENTS. For M.S.W.: 58 credits minimum, including 18 credits field practicum. For Ph.D.: 42 credits minimum beyond the Master's; comprehensive exam; dissertation; final oral defense.

FIELDS OF STUDY.
Social Work. Includes concentrations in direct practice with individuals, families and groups, community organization and social administration; specializations in children, youth and families, health, mental health. M.S.W., Ph.D.
Note: Joint programs with the Hebrew Union College (New York State), Pittsburgh Theological Seminary, Graduate School of Public and International Affairs, Graduate School of Public Health.

PLYMOUTH STATE UNIVERSITY
Plymouth, New Hampshire 03264
Web site: www.plymouth.edu

Founded 1871. Located 125 miles N of Boston. Coed. State control. Semester system. Library: 315,000 volumes, 1065 subscriptions. Total University enrollment: 5260.

Tuition: per credit resident $415, nonresident $452. On-campus housing available for married and single students. Average annual housing cost: $5400 (room and board). Apply to Office of Residential Life. Phone: (603)535-2260.

College of Graduate Studies

Graduate study since 1948. Enrollment: full-time 28, part-time 1100. College faculty teaching graduate students: full-time 73, part-time 25. Degrees conferred: M.A.T., M.B.A., M.Ed., M.S.

ADMISSION REQUIREMENTS. Transcripts, GRE/MAT/GMAT, recommendations required in support of application Online application available. TOEFL required for international applicants. Accepts transfer applicants. Apply to Director of Graduate Studies at least 60 days prior to the semester of preferred registration. Application fee $40, international applicants $75. Phone: (603)535-2737; fax: (603)535-2572.

ADMISSION STANDARDS. Minimum average: 2.75 (A = 4).

FINANCIAL AID, Scholarships, assistantships, internships, Federal W/S, loans. Apply by April 1 to the Office of Graduate Studies. Use FAFSA. Aid available for part-time students.

DEGREE REQUIREMENTS. For M.B.A.: 36 credit program, research project option. For M.A.T., M.Ed., M.S.: 33–42 credit programs; thesis/nonthesis option.

FIELDS OF STUDY.
Applied Meteorology. M.S.
Art Education. M.A.T., M.Ed.
Athletic Training. Includes entry level, advanced Master's in sport medicine, advanced Master's in higher education. M.Ed., M.S.
Biology. M.S.
Biology Education. M.Ed.
Counselor Education. M.Ed.
Criminal Justice. M.S.
Educational Leadership. M.Ed.
Elementary Education. M.Ed.
Emotional Handicaps K–12. M.Ed.
English Education. M.Ed.
Environmental Science and Policy. M.S.
General Management. M.B.A.
Health Education. M.Ed.
Heritage Studies. M.Ed.
Integrated Arts. M.Ed.
Learning Disabilities. M.Ed.
Library Media Specialist. M.Ed.
Mathematics Education. M.Ed.
Music Education. M.Ed.
Neurodevelopmental Approach to Teaching. M.Ed.
Physical Science Education. M.Ed.
Reading and Writing Specialist. M.Ed.
School Psychology. M.Ed.
Science Education. M.A.T., M.S.
Self-Designed Programs. Includes adult learning and development, adventure learning, curriculum and instruction, eating disorders, middle level education, online teaching and learning. M.Ed.
Social Studies Education. M.Ed.
Spanish Education. M.Ed.
Special Education. M.Ed.
Teaching English to Speakers of Other Languages. M.Ed.
Note: Doctoral partnerships with Argosy University and Franklin Pierce College.

POINT LOMA NAZARENE UNIVERSITY
San Diego, California 92106-2899
Web site: www.pointloma.edu

Founded 1902 in Los Angeles, California; located in Pasadena, California, 1910–1973. Formerly Pasadena College. Branch campuses in Arcadia, Bakersfield, Mission Valley. Coed. Private control. Church of the Nazarene. Semester system. Library: 160,000 volumes, 637 subscriptions.

Tuition: per unit $445–$465 Education, $600 M.B.A., $580 M.S., $525 Biology, $255 Religion and Ministry. On-campus housing for a limited number of single graduate students. Average annual housing cost: $7280–$8170 (including board) for single students. Apply to Associate Dean for Residential Life. Phone: (619)221-2482.

Graduate Studies

Enrollment: full-time 280, part-time 149. College faculty teaching graduate students: full-time 10, part-time 40. Degrees conferred: M.A., M.Min., Ed.S.

ADMISSION REQUIREMENTS. Transcripts, personal essay, two recommendations, MAT or GRE General/Subject Tests/GMAT required in support of application. Online application available. TOEFL (minimum score 550) required of international applicants. Accepts transfer applicants. Apply to Director of Admissions by May 15 (priority Fall consideration), November 1 (Spring). Rolling admissions process. Application fee $35. Phone: (619)849-2639; fax: (619)849-7018; e-mail: gradinfo@ptloma.edu.

ADMISSION STANDARDS. Selective. Usual minimum average: 3.0 in upper division courses (A = 4).

FINANCIAL AID. Limited to Federal W/S, loans. Apply to the Office of Financial Aid; no specified closing date. Phone: (619)221-2296. Use FAFSA.

DEGREE REQUIREMENTS. For M.A., M.Min.: 36-credit program without thesis, or 32 including thesis; reading knowledge of Greek for M.A. in Religion. For Ed.S.: 32 credit hour program beyond the master's; internship; written comprehensive exam.

FIELDS OF STUDY.
Biology. M.A., M.S.
Business Administration. M.B.A.
Education. Includes counseling and guidance, educational leadership, special education, teaching and learning. M.A., Ed.S.
Ministry. M.M.
Nursing. M.S.
Religion. Includes biblical studies, theology. M.A.

POLYTECHNIC UNIVERSITY
6 Metrotech Center
Brooklyn, New York 11201-2990
Web site: www.poly.edu

Founded 1854 as Polytechnic Institute of Brooklyn, became Polytechnic University in 1973. Polytechnic is the second oldest private institution of science and engineering in the United States. CGS member. Coed. Private control. Semester system. Three campuses: Brooklyn, Long Island, Westchester. The Brooklyn Center is the focus of an exciting new environment with the arrival of Metrotech, a joint University-industry development. Four major industrial companies now share a common campus with Polytechnic University, with the university as its core. Specialized facilities: Center for Advanced Technology in Telecommunications, Aerospace Research Laboratories, Center for Applied Large-Scale Computing, Center for Digital Systems, Center for Transportation Research, Dibner Library/Center for Advanced Technology in Communications, Microwave Research Institute, Philosophy and Technology Center, Polymer Research Institute, Institute for Imaging Sciences, and the Weber Research Institute. Library: 200,000 volumes, 1621 subscriptions. Total University enrollment: 2800.

Tuition: per unit $1027. On-campus housing for 150 students. Average academic year housing costs: $5250 (including board). Apply to Dean of Student Life. Phone: (718)260-3600.

Graduate Studies

Graduate study since 1902. Enrollment: full- and part-time 927 (men 85%, women 15%). Faculty: full-time 66, part-time 66. Degrees conferred: M.S., Engineer, Ph.D.

ADMISSION REQUIREMENTS. Transcripts, two letters of recommendation required in support of application. TOEFL required for international applicants. Accepts transfer applicants. Graduates of unaccredited colleges not considered. Apply to Office of Admissions by July 1 (Fall), November 1 (Spring), May 1 (Summer). Rolling admission process. Application fee $55. Phone: (800) POLYTECH, (718)260-3200; fax: (718)260-3446.

ADMISSION STANDARDS. Competitive. Usual minimum average: 2.75 (A = 4).

FINANCIAL AID. Annual awards from institutional funds: teaching assistantships, teaching fellowships, research fellowships, stipends, Federal W/S, loans. Apply by March 1 to Office of Financial Aid or major department. Phone: (718)260-3300. Use FAFSA. Aid available for part-time students.

DEGREE REQUIREMENTS. For M.S.: 36 semester units minimum, at least 27 in residence; thesis/project optional. For Engineer: 36 semester units beyond the M.S., at least 27 in residence; thesis/project, required; final oral exam. For Ph.D.: three years minimum, at least one year in residence; reading knowledge of one foreign language, two foreign languages required by some departments; qualifying oral/written exam; dissertation; final oral defense.

FIELDS OF STUDY.
Bioinformatics. M.S.
Biomedical Engineering. M.S.
Biotechnology. M.S.
Biotechnology and Entrepreneurship. M.S.
Chemical Engineering. Includes polymer science. M.S., Ph.D.
Chemistry. M.S.
Civil Engineering. M.S., Ph.D.
Computer Engineering. M.S.
Computer Science. M.S., Ph.D.
Construction Management. M.S.
Electrical Engineering. M.E., Ph.D.
Electrophysics. M.S., Ph.D.
Environment-Behavior Studies. M.S.
Environment and Engineering Science. M.S., Ph.D.
Environmental Science. M.S.
Financial Engineering. M.S.
History of Science. M.S.
Informatics in Chemistry and Biology. M.S.
Information Systems Engineering. M.S.
Integrative Digital Media. M.S.
Management. M.S., Ph.D.
Management of Technology. M.S.
Manufacturing and Industrial Engineering. M.S.
Materials Chemistry. Ph.D.
Materials Science. M.S.
Mathematics. M.S., Ph.D.
Mechanical and Aerospace Engineering. M.S., Ph.D.
Organizational Behavior. M.S.
System Engineering. M.S.
Systems Integration. M.S.
Technical Writing and Journalism. M.S.
Telecommunication Networks. M.S.
Transportation Management. M.S.
Transportation Planning and Engineering. M.S., Ph.D.
Urban Systems Engineering and Management. M.S., Ph.D.
Wireless Innovation. M.S.

PONCE SCHOOL OF MEDICINE
P.O. Box 7004
Ponce, Puerto Rico 00732-7004
Web site: www.psm.edu

Formerly Catholic University of Puerto Rico School of Medicine, reorganized in 1980. Graduate program in Biomedical Sciences was initiated in 1988. Library: 37,316 volumes, 6200 subscriptions.

Annual tuition: resident $17,835, nonresident $26,597, student fees $3625. No on-campus housing available.

Enrollment: first-year class 66, total 260 (men 52%, women 48%, minorities 95%, residents 90%). Faculty: full-time 257, part-time 115. Degrees conferred: M.D., M.D.-Ph.D.

ADMISSION REQUIREMENTS. AMCAS report, transcripts, MCAT, three letters of recommendations required in support of application. Interview by invitation. Has EDP (for Puerto Rican students only); apply between June 1 and August 1. Fluency in Spanish required. Preference given to residents of Puerto Rico. Apply to Admissions Office after June 1, before December 15. Rolling admission process. Application fee $100. Phone: (787) 840-2575; fax: (787)842-0461.

ADMISSION STANDARDS. Selective. Accepts about 15% of all applicants. Number of applications 968 (n/a out-of-state); number interviewed n/a (n/a out-of-state); number of acceptances n/a (n/a out-of-state); number enrolled 66 (n/a out-of-state).

FINANCIAL AID. Scholarships, graduate assistantship, fellowships, grants, Federal and private loans. Apply after acceptance to Student Financial Aid Office. Phone: (787)840-2511. Use FAFSA (School code: 024824). About 90% of students receive some aid from School.

DEGREE REQUIREMENTS. For M.D.: satisfactory completion of four-year progam. All students must pass step 1 of USMLE for promotion to the third year and pass step 2 prior to graduation. For Ph.D.: 70 credit programs; qualifying exam; research proposal; dissertation; dissertation defense.

FIELDS OF GRADUATE STUDY.
Anatomy.
Biochemistry.
Microbiology.
Pharmacology.
Physiology.

PONTIFICAL CATHOLIC UNIVERSITY OF PUERTO RICO
Ponce, Puerto Rico 00731-6382
Web site: www.pucpr.edu

Founded 1949. Located 140 miles S of San Juan. Coed. Private control. Semester system. Library: 286,800 volumes, 3700 subscriptions.

The University's other Graduate Colleges/Schools: College of Arts and Humanities, College of Business Administration, College of Education, College of Sciences. Total University enrollment at main campus: 11,800.

School of Law
Las Americas Avenue, Suite 543
Ponce, Puerto Rico 00731-6382

Established 1961. Located on main campus. ABA approved since 1967. AALS member. Semester system. Full-time, part-time study. Law library: 193,714 volumes, 2400 subscriptions; has LEXIS, NEXIS, WESTLAW, DIALOG; is a Federal Government and United Nations Depository.

Annual tuition: full-time $10,159, part-time $7247. On-campus housing available for single students only. Annual on-campus housing cost: single students $6327 (including board). Housing deadline July 15. Contact Housing Office for both on- and off-campus housing information. Phone: (787)841-2000, ext. 232. Law students generally prefer to live off-campus. Off-campus housing and personal expenses: approximately $9900.

Enrollment: first-year class full-time 116, part-time 63; total full- and part-time 524 (men 48%, women 52%). Faculty: full-time 22, part-time 18. Student to faculty ratio 17.5 to 1. Degrees conferred: J.D., J.D.-M.B.A.

ADMISSION REQUIREMENTS. LSDAS Law School report, LSAT (not later than February test date; if more than one LSAT, highest is used), PAEG, bachelor's degree from an accredited institution, personal statement, personal interview, two recommendations; transcripts (must show all schools attended and at least three years of study) required in support of application. Applicants must have received bachelor's degree prior to enrollment. Joint Degree applicants must apply to and be accepted to both Schools. Apply to Office of Admission after November 1, before April 15. First-year students admitted Fall only. Rolling admissions process. Application fee $75. Phone: (787)841-2200, ext. 1839 or 1837.

ADMISSION STANDARDS. Selective. Mean LSAT: full-time 136, part-time 134; mean GPA: full-time 3.28, part-time 3.11 (A = 4). Gourman rating: 2.28. *U.S. News & World Report* ranking is in the fourth tier of all law schools. Accepts 68% of total annual applicants. Most enrolled students are from Puerto Rico.

FINANCIAL AID. Scholarships, merit scholarships, Grants-in-Aid, private and institutional loans; Federal W/S, loans offered through University's Financial Aid Office. For scholarships apply to Admissions Office after January 1, before April 1. For all other programs apply to University's Office of Financial Aid. Use FAFSA (School code: 003936), also submit Financial Aid Transcript, Federal Income Tax forms. Approximately 50% of students receive some form of financial assistance. Aid available for part-time students.

DEGREE REQUIREMENTS. For J.D.: 94 (82 required) credits with a GPA of at least 2.0 (A = 4), plus completion of upper-divisional writing course; three-year program, four-year part-time program. For J.D.-M.B.A.: a four-year program rather than a five-year program if both degrees are taken consecutively.

PORTLAND STATE UNIVERSITY
Portland, Oregon 97270-0751
Web site: www.pdx.edu

Established 1946. CGS member. Coed. State control. Quarter system. Library: more than 1,800,000 volumes, 10,230 subscriptions. Total University enrollment: 24,100.

Annual tuition: resident $6648, nonresident $11,319. Limited on- and off-campus housing for married and graduate students. Annual academic year housing costs: $6300 single students, $6900 for married students. Apply through College Housing Northwest, 1802 SW 10th Ave. (97201). Phone: (800)547-8887, ext. 4333, (503)725-4333.

Graduate Studies

Enrollment: full-time 2000, part-time 2100. University faculty: full-time 590; part-time 200. Degrees conferred: M.A., M.E., M.I.M., M.S., M.Ed., M.P.A., M.P.H., M.T., M.U.S., M.U.R.P., M.A.T., M.S.T., M.B.A., M.F.A., M.S.W., Ed.D., Ph.D.

ADMISSION REQUIREMENTS. Two official transcripts required in support of application. GRE required for most programs, GMAT required for M.B.A., M.I.M., M.T. TOEFL required for international applicants. Accepts transfer applicants. Apply to Office of Graduate Admissions by April 1, March 1 for international applicants. Application fee $50. Phone: (503)725-3511; fax: (503)725-4882.

ADMISSION STANDARDS. Relatively open or selective. Usual minimum average: 2.75, or 3.0 for last two years (A = 4).

FINANCIAL AID. Annual awards from institutional funds: academic scholarships, fellowships, research assistantships, teaching assistantships, internships, Federal W/S, loans. Approved for VA benefits. Apply to Graduate Office; no specified closing dates. Phone: (503)725-3461; fax: (503)725-5965. Use FAFSA and institutional FAF. About 18% of students receive aid other than loans from University and outside sources. Aid available for part-time students.

DEGREE REQUIREMENTS. For master's: 45–90 quarter hours depending on degree program, at least 30 in residence; thesis/final exam varies by department. Reading knowledge of one foreign language for M.A., M.A.T. For Ed.D., Ph.D.: three years beyond the bachelor's, at least three consecutive terms in full-time residence; competency in at least one foreign language (Ph.D. only); comprehensive written/oral exam; dissertation; final oral exam.

FIELDS OF STUDY.

COLLEGE OF LIBERAL ARTS AND SCIENCES:
Anthropology. M.A.
Applied Linguistics. M.A.
Biology. M.A., M.S., Ph.D.
Chemistry. M.A., M.S., Ph.D.
Communication Studies. M.A., M.S.
Conflict Resolution. M.A., M.S.
Economics. M.A., M.S.
English. M.A., M.A.T.
Foreign Language. M.A., M.A.T.
Geography. M.A., M.S.
Geology. M.A., M.S.
History. M.A.
Mathematics. M.A., M.S., M.A.T., M.S.T.
Physics. M.A., M.S.
Psychology. Includes applied. M.A., M.S., Ph.D.
Science. M.A.T., M.S.T.
Sociology. M.A., M.S.
Speech and Hearing Sciences. M.A., M.S.
Speech Communication. M.A., M.S.
Statistics. M.A., M.S.
TESOL. M.A.
Writing. M.A., M.S.

MASEEH COLLEGE OF ENGINEERING AND COMPUTER SCIENCE:
Civil and Environmental Engineering.
Computer Science.
Electrical and Computer Engineering.
Engineering Management. Includes project management, technology management.
Manufacturing Engineering.
Materials Science and Engineering.
Mechanical Engineering.
Software Engineering.
Systems Engineering.

COLLEGE OF URBAN AND PUBLIC AFFAIRS:
Criminology and Criminal Justice. M.S.
Health Administration. M.P.A.
Health Education. Includes health studies, health promotion. M.A., M.P.H., M.S.
Health Management and Policy. M.P.H.
Political Science. M.A., M.S.
Public Administration. M.P.A.
Public Administration and Policy. Ph.D.
Urban and Regional Planning. M.U.R.P.
Urban Studies. M.U.S., Ph.D.

GRADUATE SCHOOL OF EDUCATION:
Counseling. M.A., M.S.
Curriculum and Instruction. M.A., M.S.
Education. Includes elementary, secondary. M.Ed.
Educational Leadership. Includes administration, postsecondary education, curriculum and instruction, special and counselor education. Ed.D.
Media and Librarianship. M.A., M.S.
Policy, Foundations, and Administrative Studies. M.A., M.S.
Special Education. M.A., M.S.

GRADUATE SCHOOL OF SOCIAL WORK:
Social Work. M.S.W.
Social Work and Social Research. Ph.D.

SCHOOL OF FINE AND PERFORMING ARTS:
Art. Includes painting, sculpture. M.F.A.
Music. Includes conducting, educator, jazz studies, performance. M.A.T., M.M., M.S.T.
Theater Arts. M.A., M.S.

SCHOOL OF BUSINESS ADMINISTRATION
Business Administration. Includes management of innovation and technology, finance international. M.B.A.
Financial Analysis. M.S.
International Management. M.I.M.

UNIVERSITY OF PORTLAND
Portland, Oregon 97203-5798
Web site: www.up.edu

Founded 1901. Coed. Private control. Semester system. Library: 310,000 volumes, 1446 subscriptions. Total University enrollment: 3400.

Tuition: per credit $650. Limited on-campus housing for graduate students during academic year. Average academic year housing costs: $8900 (including board). Apply to Dean of Students for both on- and off-campus information. Phone: (503)943-7205.

Graduate School

Graduate study since 1936. Enrollment: full-time 144, part-time 297. Graduate faculty: full-time 84, part-time 11. Degrees conferred: M.A., M.Ed., M.F.A., M.M., M.M.Ed., M.B.A., M.A.T., M.S.M.E., M.S.E.E., M.S.C.E., M.S.N.

ADMISSION REQUIREMENTS. Transcripts, three letters of recommendation, GRE/GMAT/MAT/NTE required in support of School's application. Online application available. TOEFL required for international applicants. Accepts transfer applicants. Apply to Dean of Graduate School by July 15 (Fall), December 15 (Spring). Application fee $50. Phone: (503)943-7107; fax: (503)943-7178; e-mail: gradschl@up.edu.

ADMISSION STANDARDS. Competitive for some departments, selective for others. Usual minimum average: 3.0 (A = 4).

FINANCIAL AID. Internships, Federal W/S, loans. Approved for VA benefits. Apply by March 15 to the Office of Financial Aid. Phone: (503)283-7311. Use FAFSA.

DEGREE REQUIREMENTS. For master's: 30 semester hours minimum, at least 21 in residence; comprehensive exam; thesis or final research project required for M.A.; final oral/written exam.

FIELDS OF STUDY.
Business Administration. Includes health care programs. M.B.A.
Communication Studies. M.A.
Directing. M.F.A.

Education. 36 hours minimum for M.Ed., M.A.T., M.A.
Engineering. Includes civil, electrical, mechanical. M.S.M.E., M.S.E.E., M.S.C.E.
History and Government. M.A.
Management Communication. M.S.
Music. Includes theory, performance, education. M.A.
Nursing. M.S.N.
Theology. M.A.

PRAIRIE VIEW A&M UNIVERSITY
Prairie View, Texas 77446-0188
Web site: www.pvamu.edu

Founded 1876. Located 45 miles NW of Houston. Coed. State control. Semester system. A unit of the Texas A&M University system. Special facilities: Cooperative Agricultural Research Center, Particle Detector Research Center, Center for Social and Economic Research. Library: 347,477 volumes, 1300 subscriptions. Total University enrollment: 7900.

Tuition: per credit, resident $80, nonresident $358. On-campus housing for single students only. Average academic year housing costs: $6200 (including board). Average off-campus housing costs: $375–$550 per month. Contact the Housing Office for both on- and off-campus housing information.

Graduate School

Founded 1938. Enrollment: full-time 737, part-time 950. Faculty: full-time 75, part-time 40. Degrees conferred: M.A., M.C.D., M.Ed., M.S., M.S.Ag., M.S.Eng., M.S.N., M.B.A.

ADMISSION REQUIREMENTS. Official transcripts, three letters of recommendation, GRE/GMAT (Business) required in support of application. TOEFL required for international applicants. Accepts transfer applicants. Graduates of unaccredited institutions not considered. Apply by July 1 (Fall), November 1 (Spring) to Dean of Graduate School. Rolling admissions process. Application fee $50, $75 for international applicants. Phone: (936)857-2315; fax: (936)857-4521.

ADMISSION STANDARDS. Relatively open. Usual minimum average: 2.75 (A = 4).

FINANCIAL AID. Fellowships, teaching assistantships, research assistantships, tuition waivers, Federal W/S, loans. Apply by April 1 to the Dean of the Graduate School for assistantships; to Financial Aid Office for all other programs. Use FAFSA. About 65% receive aid from School and outside sources. Aid available for part-time students.

DEGREE REQUIREMENTS. For master's: 30–36 semester hours minimum (depending upon program), at least 20 hours in residence; thesis usually required for M.A., M.S.

FIELDS OF STUDY.

COLLEGE OF AGRICULTURE AND HUMAN SCIENCES:
Agriculture. Includes agricultural economics, animal science, soil science. M.S.Ag.
Human Sciences. Includes marriage and family studies, family and consumer studies, interdisciplinary studies in human sciences. M.S.

COLLEGE OF ARTS AND SCIENCES:
Chemistry. M.S.
English. M.A.
Mathematics. M.S.
Sociology. M.A.

COLLEGE OF BUSINESS:
Accounting. M.S.A.
Business Administration. M.B.A.

COLLEGE OF EDUCATION:
Counseling. Includes counselor education. M.A., M.S.Ed.
Curricula and Instruction. Includes agriculture education, educational media and technology, elementary education (early childhood), home economics education, industrial education, mathematics education, reading education, science education (biology, chemistry). M.A. Ed., M.Ed., M.S.Ed.
Educational Administration. M.Ed., M.S.Ed.
Educational Leadership. Ph.D.
Health and Physical Education. M.Ed., M.S.Ed.
School Administration. M.Ed., M.S.Ed.
Special Education. M.Ed., M.S.Ed.

COLLEGE OF ENGINEERING:
Computer Information Systems. M.S.C.I.S.
Computer Science. M.S.C.S.
Engineering. Includes chemical, civil, environmental, mechanical. M.S. Engr.
Electrical Engineering. M.S.E.E., Ph.D.

COLLEGE OF JUVENILE JUSTICE AND PSYCHOLOGY:
Clinical Adolescent Psychology. Ph.D.
Juvenile Justice. M.S., Ph.D.
Juvenile Forensic Psychology. M.S.

COLLEGE OF NURSING:
Family Nurse Practitioner. M.S.N.

SCHOOL OF ARCHITECTURE:
Architecture. M.Arch.
Community Development. M.C.D.

PRATT INSTITUTE
Brooklyn, New York 11205-3899
Web site: www.pratt.edu

Founded 1887. Coed. Private control. Semester system. Special facilities: Center for Community and Environmental Development, Printmaking/Fine Arts Center, Schaffler Art Gallery. Library: 220,000 volumes, 540 subscriptions. 100,000 pictures and prints. Total enrollment: 4600.

Annual tuition: full-time $24,240; per credit $1010. On-campus housing for married and single students. Average academic year housing costs: $10,580 for married students, $13,780 (including board) for single students. Contact Residential Life Office for both on- and off-campus housing information. Phone: (718)636-3669.

Graduate Programs

Graduate study since 1950. Enrollment: full-time 950, part-time 323. Faculty: full- and part-time 134. Degrees conferred: M.Arch., M.Arch.I, M.S., M.S.C.R.P., M.I.D., M.S.U.E.S.M., M.S.U.D., M.F.A., M.L.S.

ADMISSION REQUIREMENTS. Official transcripts, three letters of reference required in support of application. Interview often required. GRE Subject Tests recommended. Portfolio required for Art, Design, and Architecture Departments. TOEFL recommended for international applicants. Accepts transfer applicants. Graduates of unaccredited institutions not considered. Apply to Graduate Admissions Office by March 1 (Fall), October 1 (Spring). Rolling admissions process. Application fee $40, $90 for international applicants. Phone: (718)636-3683; fax: (718) 636-4242.

ADMISSION STANDARDS. Very competitive for some departments, very selective for most. Usual minimum average: 2.5 (A = 4).

FINANCIAL AID. Scholarships, fellowships, assistantships, internships, Federal W/S, loans. Approved for VA benefits. Apply by February 1 to Director of Graduate Program of the appropriate program for fellowships, assistantships; to Financial Aid Office for all other programs. Use FAFSA. About 20–25% of students receive aid from Institute and outside sources. Aid available for part-time students.

DEGREE REQUIREMENTS. For M.Arch.: 36 credits minimum, at least 22 in residence. For M.S.: 36–50 credits minimum, at least 24 in residence. For M.I.D.: 34 credits minimum, at least 26 in residence. For M.L.S.: 36 credits minimum, at least 30 in residence. For M.F.A.: 48 credits minimum, at least 40 in residence. For M.S.C.R.P., M.S.U.E.S.M., M.S.U.D.; 62 credits minimum, at least 45 in full-time residence; special project.

FIELDS OF STUDY.

SCHOOL OF ARCHITECTURE:
Architecture. M.Arch., M.Arch. I
City and Regional Planning. M.S.
Facilities Management. M.S.
Historic Preservation. M.S.
Planning and Law. M.S.
Urban Environmental Systems Management. M.S.

SCHOOL OF ART AND DESIGN:
Art and Design Education. M.S.
Art Therapy. M.P.S.
Art Therapy and Creativity Development. M.P.S.
Arts and Cultural Management. M.P.S.
Communications Design. M.S.
Dance/Movement Therapy. M.S.
Design Management. M.P.S.
Digital Arts. M.F.A.
Drawing. M.F.A.
Fine Arts. M.F.A.
History of Art and Design. M.S.
Industrial Design. Includes products, furniture, transportation, exhibition, and tabletop. M.I.D.
Interior Design. M.S.
Packaging Design. M.S.
Painting. M.F.A.
Photography. M.F.A.
Printmaking. M.F.A.
Sculpture. M.F.A.

SCHOOL OF INFORMATION AND LIBRARY SCIENCE:
Library and Information Science. M.S.

PRINCETON UNIVERSITY
Princeton, New Jersey 08544-1019
Web site: www.princeton.edu

Founded 1746. Located 50 miles SW of New York City. CGS and AAU member. Private control. Semester system. Special facilities: cooperative with the Institute for Advanced Study, Center for Human Values, Geophysical Fluid Dynamics Lab of NOAA, Plasma Physics Fusion Research Laboratory; affiliation with Princeton Theological Seminary, Office for Survey Research and Statistical Studies, Princeton Materials Institute, Textile Research Institute, Center for Studies in Twentieth-Century American State craft and Public Policy, Center of International Studies. According to The Center at University of Florida, the University is ranked 74th in receipt of Federal Research funds with $104,011,000 and it ranks 77th for total University research expenditures with $179,951,000. The University's endowment assets rank it 3rd, with a value of $9,928,200,000. In 2004, the University awarded 276 doctorates, which ranked it 50th among all U.S. institutions eligible to award that degree. Ninety of the University's faculty members have been elected to National Honor Academies and this ranks it 10th among all U.S. institutions. The Library: approximately 4,000,000 volumes, 39,000 subscriptions.

Annual tuition: full-time $34,000. On-campus housing for more than 400 married students, 570 single students. Average academic year housing costs: $664–$1231 per month plus $525 for each child for married students, $1236 per month plus partial board for single students. Apply to Assistant Director for Graduate Housing no later than April 15. Phone: (609)258-3720.

Graduate School

Established 1869. Enrollment: full-time 1769 (men 63%, women 37%); no part-time students. Faculty: full-time 693, part-time 69. Degrees conferred: M.A., M.Eng., M.F.A., M.P.A., M.P.P., M.S., M.Arch., M.S.E., Ph.D.

ADMISSION REQUIREMENTS. Transcripts, three letters of recommendation, personal statement, statement of financial resources, GRE Test required in support of School's application. GRE Subject Test strongly recommended or required according to department. Online application available. TOEFL required of international applicants. Apply by the first Wednesday in January (domestic applicants), December 1 (international applicants). Some programs have earlier deadines. Admits full-time students only. Fall admission only. Application fee $65, $105 for international students. Phone: (609)258-3034; fax: (609)258-6180.

ADMISSION STANDARDS. Very competitive for some departments, competitive for the others.

FINANCIAL AID. Annual awards from institutional funds: fellowships, teaching/research assistantships, Federal W/S, loans. Apply by first Wednesday in January to Graduate School Office for fellowships, assistantships; to Financial Aid Office for all other programs. Phone: (609)258-3028; fax: (609)258-6180. Use FAFSA and University's FAF. About 95% of students receive aid other than loans from School and outside sources.

DEGREE REQUIREMENTS. For master's: one year minimum in full-time residence; general exam (one year minimum full-time before sitting for general exam); thesis for M.S. and for M.A. in Near Eastern Studies; M.A. generally regarded as incidental degree. For Ph.D.: one year minimum in full-time residence; oral/written general exam; dissertation; final public oral exam.

FIELDS OF STUDY.
African Studies. Interdepartmental.
Afro-American Studies. Interdepartmental program in combination with an established discipline.
Anthropology. Ph.D. in cultural anthropology; competence in one foreign language, usually French.
Applied and Computational Mathematics. Interdepartmental in combination with science and engineering departments.
Architecture. One- and two-year M.Arch. program; design project and oral exam for M.Arch.
Art and Archaeology. Includes joint program in classical archaeology; two languages for Ph.D.
Astrophysical Sciences. Includes astronomy, astrophysics, plasma physics.
Atmospheric and Oceanic Sciences. Ph.D.
Chemical Engineering. M.Eng., M.S.E., Ph.D.
Chemistry. Includes cooperative program in physics and chemical physics; Ph.D. applicants given preference for admission; one language appropriate to study of chemistry for Ph.D.; M.S. available for local and regional firms (part-time).
Chinese Art and Archaeology. Interdepartmental; proficiency in classical and modern Chinese; also French or German for Ph.D.
Civil and Environmental Engineering. M.Eng., M.S.E., Ph.D.
Classical Philosophy. Interdepartmental; proficiency in Greek, Latin, French, and German for Ph.D.
Classics. Competence in Greek and Latin plus French and German for Ph.D.
Comparative Literature. Competence in two foreign languages plus Greek or Latin for Ph.D.
Computer Science. M.Eng., Ph.D.
Demography. Admission to Ph.D. program granted to students in economics, sociology, statistics; language requirement of that department must be fulfilled.
East Asian Studies. High degree of competence in Chinese or Japanese plus one European language for Ph.D.
Ecology and Evolutionary Biology.
Economics. Strong mathematical/statistical background recommended.
Economics and Demography.
Electrical Engineering. M.Eng., Ph.D.
English. Reading knowledge of Latin or Greek and reading knowledge of German and French.
French and Italian.
Geosciences.
Germanic Languages and Literatures. Two languages in addition to German for Ph.D.
History. Reading knowledge of at least one language; more may be required depending on area of study.
History of Science. French and German required for students of history of science; French or German for students of philosophy of science; Latin/Greek for medieval or ancient periods.
History and Theory of Architecture.
History and Theory of Engineering and Building Technology.
History and Theory of Landscape.
History and Theory of Urbanism.
Mathematical Physics.
Mathematics. Reading knowledge of mathematical texts in German or Russian for Ph.D.
Mechanical and Aerospace Engineering. M.Eng., M.S.E., Ph.D.
Molecular Biology. Ph.D.
Music. Includes music history, theory, composition; reading knowledge of at least one of the following—German, French, or Italian for Ph.D.
Near Eastern Studies. M.A.
Operations Research and Financial Engineering. M.Eng., M.S.E., Ph.D.
Philosophy. Reading knowledge of French or German for Ph.D.
Physics. Includes mathematical, chemical, plasma.
Plasma Science and Technology.
Political Economy. Ph.D.
Political Philosophy. Interdepartmental.
Politics.
Psychology.
Psychology and Neuroscience.
Public Affairs. Two-year M.P.A.
Public Affairs and Demography.
Public Policy. M.P.P.
Quantitative and Computational Biology. Ph.D.
Religion. Two languages in addition to competence in biblical, classical, Oriental languages as required in field of specialization.
Slavic and Theoretical Linguistics. Ph.D.
Slavic Languages and Literature.
Social Policy. Joint Ph.D. program.
Sociology. One language and knowledge of general sociological theory, statistical theory and procedure, competence in research methodology including computer application for Ph.D.
Spanish and Portuguese Language and Culture.
Transportation. Interdepartmental.

Woodrow Wilson School of Public and International Affairs (08544-1013)

Web site: www.wws.princeton.edu

Established 1930. Special facilities: Bendheim-Thoman Center for Research on Child Wellbeing, Center for Arts and Cultural Policy Studies, Center for Health and Wellbeing, Center for the Study of Democratic Politics, Liechtenstein Institute on Self-Determination, Niehaus Center for Globalization and Governance, Policy Research Institute for the Region.

Graduate enrollment: full-time, M.P.A., 130, Ph.D. 25. Faculty: full-time 55, adjunct 20. Degrees conferred: M.P.A., M.P.P., M.P.A.-J.D. (with Columbia University, NYU, Stanford University), M.P.A.-U.R.P., Ph.D.

ADMISSION REQUIREMENTS. Transcripts, three letters of reference, public policy essay, personal statement, GRE required in support of School's application. TOEFL required for international applicants. Accepts transfer applicants. Graduates of unaccredited institutions not considered. Apply to Office of Graduate Admissions by January 8. Fall admission only. Application fee $65, $105 if mailed outside the United States, Canada, and Mexico. Phone: (609)258-4836; fax: (609)258-2095; e-mail: wwsadmit@princeton.edu.

ADMISSION STANDARDS. Very competitive. Usual minimum average: 3.6 (A = 4).

FINANCIAL AID. Academic scholarships, research fellowships, teaching fellowships, research assistantships, internships, Federal W/S, loans. Approved for VA benefits. Apply in early January to Graduate School for scholarships, fellowships, assistantships; to Financial Aid Office for all other programs. Phone: (609)258-3037. Use FAFSA and University's FAF. About 92% of M.P.A.s and 100% of Ph.D.s receive aid from School and outside sources.

DEGREE REQUIREMENTS. For M.P.A., M.P.P.: two-year program, one year in residence; two qualifying examinations. For M.P.A.-J.D.: three semesters in residence. For M.P.A.-U.R.P.: four semesters in residence. For Ph.D.: at least ten courses; reading knowledge of one foreign language; general exam; dissertation; final oral exam.

FIELDS OF STUDY.
Politics and Public Policy. Ph.D.
Political Economy. Ph.D.
Population and Public Policy. Ph.D.
Public Affairs. M.P.A., Ph.D.
Public Policy. One year program for qualified physician, Ph.D. Scientist, lawyers. M.P.P.
Science, Technology, and Environmental Policy. Ph.D.

PROVIDENCE COLLEGE

Providence, Rhode Island 02918
Web site: www.providence.edu

Founded 1917. Private control. Roman Catholic affiliation. Semester system. Library: 536,200 volumes, 8000 subscriptions. Total College enrollment: 4830.

Tuition: per credit $969, $1140 (M.B.A.). Limited on-campus housing available. Usual housing cost: $4300–$6250; board cost: $1950–$3800. Contact Director of Life for both on- and off-campus housing information. Phone: (401)865-2392.

Graduate Studies

Graduate study since 1965. Enrollment: full-time 112, part-time 380. Faculty teaching graduate students: full-time 33, part-time 43. Degrees conferred: M.A., M.A.T. (Math), M.B.A., M.Ed.

ADMISSION REQUIREMENTS. Transcripts, two letters of recommendation, GMAT/MAT required in support of School's application. Interview required for some programs. TOEFL required for foreign applicants. Accepts transfer applicants. Apply to Office of Admissions; no specified closing date. Application fee $55. Phone: (401)865-2247; fax: (401)865-1147.

ADMISSION STANDARDS. Selective. Usual minimum average: 3.0 (A = 4).

FINANCIAL AID. Annual awards from institutional funds: scholarships, grants, assistantships, Federal W/S, loans. Approved for VA benefits. Apply by March 15 to appropriate department chair for assistantships; to Financial Aid Office for all other programs. Phone: (401)865-2286. Use FAFSA. About 10% of students receive aid other than loans from School and outside sources.

DEGREE REQUIREMENTS. For M.A. (History), M.S.: 30 credit hours minimum; reading knowledge of one foreign language; comprehensive exam; thesis/final document. For M.B.A., M.Ed.: 36 credit hours; comprehensive exam.

FIELDS OF STUDY.
Biblical Studies. M.A.
Business Administration.
Education.
History.
Literacy.
Mathematics. M.A.T. only.
Theology.

UNIVERSITY OF PUERTO RICO, MAYAGUEZ

Mayaguez, Puerto Rico 00681-9020
Web site: www.uprm.edu

Established in 1911. CGS member. Public control. Coed. Semester system. Formerly the College of Agriculture and Mechanic Arts. Special facilities: Center for Applied Social Research, Center for Computing Research and Development, Center for Energy and Environmental Research, Civil Infrastructure Research Center, Engineering Research Center, Mechatronics Center, Puerto Rico Commercial Aquaculture Research and Development Center, Puerto Rico and U.S. Virgin Island Climatology Center, Agricultural Experimental Station, Tropical Center for Earth and Space Studies, Water Resource Research Institute. Library: 921,300 volumes, 12,000 subscriptions.

Tuition: U.S. citizens, residents of Puerto Rico, $100 per credit; U.S. nonresidents of Puerto Rico $294. Foreign students: $3800 per year. There are also applicable regular or special fees. Limited on-campus housing available. Average off-campus housing costs: $650–$900 per month. Contact Office of Residential Life for on- and off-campus housing information. Phone: (787)834-0589.

Graduate Studies

Graduate study since 1957. Graduate enrollment: full-time 390, part-time 400. Graduate faculty: 400. Degrees conferred: M.A., M.B.A., M.S., M.E., Ph.D.

ADMISSION REQUIREMENTS. Bachelor's degree, transcript, three letters of recommendation, working knowledge of Spanish and English required in support of application. GRE/GMAT required for some programs. Interview required for some departments. Apply to the Director, Office of Graduate Studies by

February 15 (Fall), September 15 (Winter). Rolling admission process. Application fee $20. Phone: (787)265-3811; fax: (787)834-5265.

ADMISSION STANDARDS. Selective. Usual minimum average: 2.5 (A = 4).

FINANCIAL AID. Annual awards from institutional funds: scholarships, research assistantships, teaching assistantships, grants, Federal W/S, loans. Approved for VA benefits. Apply to Director of Financial Aid; no specified closing date. Phone: (787)832-4040; fax: (787)265-1920. Use FAFSA and institutional FAF. Approximately 72% of all students receive some form of financial aid.

DEGREE REQUIREMENTS. Master's: 36 credits minimum, at least 24 in residence; candidacy; thesis; final oral exam. For Ph.D.: 72 credits beyond the bachelor's minimum; at least 30 credits in residence; comprehensive exam; candidacy; dissertation; final exam.

FIELDS OF STUDY.

COLLEGE OF AGRICULTURAL SCIENCES:
Agricultural Economics.
Agricultural Education.
Agronomy and Soils.
Crop Protection.
Food Science and Technology.
Horticulture.
Soils.

COLLEGE OF ARTS AND SCIENCES:
Applied Mathematics.
Biology.
Chemistry.
Computational Sciences.
English.
Geology.
Hispanic Studies.
Marine Sciences. Includes biological oceanography, chemical oceanography, geological oceanography, physical oceanography.
Mathematics.
Physics.
Pure Mathematics.
Statistics.

COLLEGE OF BUSINESS ADMINISTRATION:
Business Administration.
Finance.
Human Resources.
Industrial Management.
Marketing.

COLLEGE OF ENGINEERING:
Chemical Engineering.
Civil Engineering.
Electrical and Computer Engineering.
Industrial Engineering.
Mechanical Engineering.

INTERDISCIPLINARY PROGRAMS:
Computer and Information Sciences and Engineering. Ph.D.
Food Science and Technology. Ph.D.

UNIVERSITY OF PUERTO RICO

Rio Piedras, Puerto Rico 00931-3315
Web site: www.uprrp.edu

Founded 1903. Located 8 miles S of San Juan. CGS member. Coed. Public control. Semester system. Special facilities: Center for Studies of American Arts, Center for Archaeological Research, Caribbean Studies Institute, Institute of Cooperativism, Economic Research Center, Center for Historical Research, Natural Science Academic Computer Center, Resource Center for Scientific Engineering, Social Science Research Center. Library: 4,091,000 volumes, 5599 subscriptions. Total University enrollment: 21,000.

Tuition: per credit resident $100, nonresident $294. Limited on-campus housing for single graduate students. Average academic year housing costs: $2200 (room only). Contact Dean of Students Office for both on- and off-campus housing information. Phone: (787)764-0000, ext. 5651. Day-care facilities available.

Graduate Division

Graduate study since 1927. Enrollment: full-time 1400, part-time 1600. Graduate faculty: full-time 195, part-time 146. Degrees conferred: M.A., M.S., M.B.A., M.L.S., M.Ed., M.P., M.P.A., M.S.W., M.Arch., M.C.R., Ed.D., Ph.D.

ADMISSION REQUIREMENTS. Two official transcripts required in support of application. GRE, interview required for some departments. Accepts transfer applicants. Apply February 15 to Office of Admissions of appropriate College/School. Earlier application deadline for some departments. Application fee $17. Phone: Education (787)764-0000, ext. 2607; Humanities (787)764-0000, ext. 3525; Social Sciences (787)767-2040; Natural Science (787)763-5101; Business (787)764-0000, ext. 4142; Librarianship, (787)764-0000, ext. 5827; Planning (787)764-0000, ext. 3182; Architecture (787)764-0000, ext. 3449; Communication (787)764-0000, ext. 5043; Rehabilitation Counseling (787)764-0000, ext. 2177.

ADMISSION STANDARDS. Competitive. Usual minimum average: 3.0 (A = 4).

FINANCIAL AID. Scholarships, fellowships, assistantships, partial tuition waivers, Federal W/S, loans. Apply by May 31 to appropriate department chair for fellowships, assistantships; to Financial Aid Office for all other programs. Phone: (787)764-0000, ext. 3148. Use FAFSA and University's FAF. About 60% of students receive aid from University and outside sources.

DEGREE REQUIREMENTS. For master's: one year minimum in residence; thesis/nonthesis; final oral exam; final written exam. For Ph.D.: 30 semester hours minimum beyond the master's, at least two semesters in full-time attendance; reading knowledge of two foreign languages for most programs; qualifying written exam; dissertation; final oral exam. For Ed.D.: essentially the same as Ph.D., except no language requirement.

FIELDS OF STUDY.

COLLEGE OF EDUCATION:
Biology Education. M.Ed.
Chemistry Education. M.Ed.
Child Education. M.Ed.
Curriculum and Teaching. Ed.D.
Educational Research and Evaluation. M.Ed.
English Education. M.Ed.
Guidance and Counseling. M.Ed., Ed.D.
History Education. M.Ed.
Mathematics Education. M.Ed.
Physics Education. M.Ed.
School Administration and Supervision. M.Ed., Ed.D.
Secondary Education. M.Ed.
Spanish Education. M.Ed.
Special Education. M.Ed.
TESL. M.Ed.

COLLEGE OF HUMANITIES:
Comparative Literature. M.A.
English. M.A.

Hispanic Studies. M.A., Ph.D.
History. M.A., Ph.D.
Humanities. M.A., Ph.D.
Linguistics. M.A.
Philosophy. M.A. only.
Translation. M.A.

COLLEGE OF SOCIAL SCIENCES:
Economics. M.A. only.
Psychology. M.A., Ph.D.
Public Administration. M.P.A.
Rehabilitation Counseling. M.C.R.
Social Sciences. M.A., Ph.D.
Social Work. M.S.W.
Sociology. M.A.

FACULTY OF NATURAL SCIENCES:
Biology. M.S., Ph.D.
Chemical Physics. Ph.D.
Chemistry. M.S., Ph.D.
Mathematics. M.A. only.
Natural Sciences. M.S., Ph.D.
Physics. M.S. only.

GRADUATE SCHOOL OF BUSINESS ADMINISTRATION:
Business Administration. M.B.A.

GRADUATE SCHOOL OF INFORMATION SCIENCES AND TECHNOLOGY:
Librarianship and Information Services. M.L.S.

GRADUATE SCHOOL OF PLANNING:
Planning. M.P.

SCHOOL OF ARCHITECTURE:
Architecture. M.Arch.

SCHOOL OF COMMUNICATION:
Public Communication. M.A.

School of Dentistry

Established 1956. Located in San Juan (00936-5067). Annual tuition: resident $5340, nonresident varies. Limited on-campus housing available for single students only. Average academic year housing costs: $6500. Contact Dean of Students Office for both on- and off-campus housing information. Total average cost for all other first-year expenses: $8500.

Enrollment: D.M.D. programs, first-year class 40; total 202 (men 35%, women 65%, minorities 80%, residents 95%); graduate program, full-time 16 (men 15, women 1). Faculty: full-time 91, part-time 53. Degrees conferred: D.M.D., M.S.

ADMISSION REQUIREMENTS. For D.M.D. program: AAD-SAS, official transcripts, three letters of recommendation, DAT (no later than October), proficiency in Spanish required in support of application. Preference given to Puerto Rican students. Interview by invitation only. Applicants must have completed at least three years of college study. Accepts transfer applicants. Apply to Director of Admissions after June 30, before December 15. Application fee $15. Phone: (787)758-2525, ext. 1113; fax: (787) 751-0990. For graduate programs: official transcripts, two letters of recommendation, interview required in support of School's application. Accepts transfer applicants. Enrollment limited to residents. Apply to Chair of Graduate Committee by December 1. Application fee $20.

ADMISSION STANDARDS. For D.M.D. program: Mean DAT: Academic 16, PAT 16; mean GPA: 3.55. Accepts 65% of total annual applicants; 100% are residents of Puerto Rico. For graduate program: competitive. Usual minimum GPA: 3.0 (A = 4).

FINANCIAL AID. For D.M.D. program: scholarships, grants, loans for Puerto Rican resident students only; apply by May 15 to the University's Dean of Students Office. About 75% of students receive aid from School and outside sources. For graduate program: fellowships for hospital residency. All graduate students receive aid during residency.

DEGREE REQUIREMENTS. For D.M.D.: satisfactory completion of 46-month program. For M.S. (oral surgery): 36 months minimum, at least 2 semesters in hospital residency; thesis; final written exam. For M.S.: 24 months minimum, hospital residency; thesis; final written exam.

FIELDS OF GRADUATE STUDY.
General Dentistry.
Oral and Maxillofacial Surgery.
Orthodontics.
Pediatric Dentistry.
Prosthodontics.

School of Law (P.O. Box 23349)
San Juan, Puerto Rico 00931-3349

Established 1913. Located in metropolitan San Juan. ABA approved since 1945. AALS member. Semester system. Full-time, part-time study. Exchange program with the University of Arizona, the University of Connecticut; summer study abroad at University of Barcelona. Law library: 290,300 volumes, 4250 subscriptions; has LEXIS, NEXIS, WESTLAW, DIALOG, COMPU-CLERK, CUMPULEQ, LEGALTRAC, INFOTRAC; is a selective depository for U.S. Government Documents and European Document Center.

Annual tuition: full-time $2395, residents and American citizens; nonresident, non-American citizens $3595. Annual on-campus living expenses: single $9975. Housing deadline June 15. Contact Housing Office for both on- and off-campus housing information. Phone: (787)764-0000, ext. 5651. Law students tend to live off-campus. Off-campus housing and personal expenses: approximately $10,040.

Enrollment: first-year class full-time 111, part-time 41; total 669 (men 47%, women 53%, minorities 100%, residents 100%). Faculty: full-time 23, part-time 21. Student to faculty ratio 16.4 to 1. Degrees conferred: J.D., J.D.-M.B.A., J.D.-M.P.P. (University of Minnesota), LL.M. (For Latin American Lawyers), J.D.-Lic. en Derecho (University of Barcelona).

ADMISSION REQUIREMENTS. LSDAS Law School report, bachelor's degree, two transcripts, LSAT, PAEG required in support of application. Interview not required. Accepts transfer applicants. Graduates of unaccredited colleges not considered. Apply to Office of Admission after September 1, before February 1. Fall admission only. Application fee $17. Phone: (787)764-2675; fax: (787)764-2675.

ADMISSION STANDARDS. Selective. Mean LSAT: full-time 149, part-time 146; mean GPA: full-time 3.56, part-time 3.55 (A = 4). Gourman rating: 2.32. *U.S. News & World Report* ranking is in the fourth tier of all U.S. law schools. Accepts 20–25% of total annual applicants.

FINANCIAL AID. Scholarships, grants, tuition waivers, assistantships, Federal W/S, Federal and private loans. Apply to the University's Office of Financial Aid in San Juan after acceptance, before May 31. Use FAFSA (School code: 007108). About 10% of students receive aid other than loans from outside sources.

DEGREE REQUIREMENTS. For J.D.: 92 credits minimum, at least 60 in residence, three-year (day) or four-year (evening) program; 92 credit hour program. For LL.M.: 24 credit program.

Medical Sciences Campus— Graduate Studies

Web site: www.rcm.upr.edu

Established 1960. Located in San Juan (00936-5067). Public control. Special facilities: Caribbean Primate Research Center, Center for Environmental and Toxicological Studies, Center for Informatics and Technology, Center for Sports, Health, and Exercise Sciences, Puerto Rican Cancer Center, Puerto Rican Geriatric Education Center, Center for the Study of Sexually Transmitted Disease, Center for Energy and Environmental Research, Clinical Research Center. The University's NIH ranking is 100th among all U.S. institutions with 53 awards/grants worth $50,047,578. Library: 50,000 volumes, 1250 subscriptions.

Tuition: per credit $100. No on-campus housing available. Off-campus housing costs: $300–$600 per month. Enrollment: full-time 509 (men 70%, women 30%). Faculty: full-time 41, part-time 3. Degrees conferred: M.S., M.S.N., M.P.H., Ph.D.

ADMISSION REQUIREMENTS. Transcripts, GRE and Subject Tests, interview, two recommendations, proficiency in English and Spanish required in support of application. Online application available. Accepts transfer applicants. Apply by February 15 (Fall), by October 15 (Spring) to Director of Graduate Studies. Application fee $20. Phone: (787)758-2525, ext. 1814.

ADMISSION STANDARDS. Selective for most departments. Usual minimum average: 2.75 (A = 4).

FINANCIAL AID. Annual awards from institutional funds: scholarships, assistantships, fellowships, loans. Apply to appropriate department chairman for fellowships, assistantships. Use FAFSA. About 30% of students receive aid other than loans from university and outside sources.

DEGREE REQUIREMENTS. For M.S., M.P.H.: 30–36 credit hours minimum, at least 24 in residence; reading knowledge of one foreign language; thesis/nonthesis; final oral exam. For M.S.N.: 48 credit program; research project. For Ph.D.: 60 credit hours minimum beyond the bachelor's, at least 40 in residence; qualifying exam; reading knowledge of two foreign languages; comprehensive exam; advancement to candidacy; dissertation; final oral exam.

FIELDS OF STUDY.
Anatomy.
Biochemistry.
Biology.
Clinical Nurse Specialist.
Environmental Health.
Epidemiology.
Health Services Administration.
Microbiology and Medical Zoology.
Nursing Anesthesia.
Nursing Services Administration.
Occupational Health.
Pharmacy.
Pharmacology and Toxicology.
Physiology.
Public Health.
Speech Pathology.
Teaching of Nursing in Higher Education.

School of Medicine

P.O. Box 365067

Established 1949. Located in San Juan (00936-5067). Library: 100,000 volumes. Annual tuition: $6965. Tuition varies for nonresident students according to program; approximately $12,000. Total average figure for all other annual expenses: $11,500.

Enrollment: first-year class 115, total 419 (men 39%, women 61%); Faculty: about 400, full- and part-time. Degrees conferred: M.D., M.D.-M.S., M.D.-Ph.D.

ADMISSION REQUIREMENTS. For M.D. program: AMCAS report, two transcripts, letters of recommendation, fluency in English and Spanish, MCAT required in support of application. Does not have EDP. Interview by invitation only. Applicants must have completed at least three years of college study. Accepts limited number of nonresidents. Apply to Office of Dean after June 1, before December 1. Application fee $20. Phone: (787)758-2525, ext. 5231; fax: (787)282-7117.

ADMISSION STANDARDS. Selective. Mean MCAT: 7.0; mean GPA: 3.69 (A = 4). Gourman rating: 4.03. Accepts 25–30% of total annual applicants. Approximately 100% are residents.

FINANCIAL AID. Scholarships for resident students only. Apply by April 30 to Financial Aid Office. Use FAFSA (School code: 003945). About 50% of students receive some aid from School.

DEGREE REQUIREMENTS. For M.D.: satisfactory completion of four-year program. For M.S., Ph.D.: see Graduate Division listing above.

FIELDS OF GRADUATE STUDY.
Anatomy and Neurobiology.
Biochemistry.
Biology.
Microbiology and Medical Zoology.
Pharmacology and Toxicology.
Physicology.

UNIVERSITY OF PUGET SOUND

Tacoma, Washington 98416-0005
Web site: www.ups.edu

Founded 1888. Coed. Private control. Methodist affiliation. Semester system. Library: 363,000 volumes, 4510 subscriptions. Total University enrollment: 2900.

Tuition: per unit $3910 (M.A.T.), $2600 (M.Ed.), $4000 (M.O.T., M.S.O.T., D.P.T.). No on-campus housing for graduate students.

Graduate Studies

Enrollment: full-time 184, part-time 79. University faculty: full-time 21, part-time 22. Degrees conferred: M.A.T., M.Ed., M.O.T., M.S.O.T., D.P.T

ADMISSION REQUIREMENTS. Official transcripts, three letters of recommendation, GRE/MAT required in support of application. Interview required for Education. Online application available. Proficiency in English or TOEFL required of international students. Accepts transfer applicants. Graduates of unaccredited institutions not considered. Apply to Office of Admissions one month prior to registration. Application deadline for M.O.T. and D.P.T. is February 1. Rolling admissions process. Application fee $65. Phone: (253)879-3211; e-mail: admission@ups.edu.

ADMISSION STANDARDS. Selective for all departments. Usual minimum average: 3.0 (A = 4). 50th percentile or higher on tests.

FINANCIAL AID. Scholarships, fellowships, research assistantships, teaching assistantships, Federal W/S, loans. Approved for VA benefits. Apply by March 1 to appropriate school for assistantships; to Financial Aid Office for all other programs. Phone:

(253)879-3214. Use FAFSA (University code: 003797). About 25% of students receive aid from both University and outside sources. Aid available for part-time students.

DEGREE REQUIREMENTS. For master's: 8 units (32 semester hours) minimum, at least 6 units in residence; oral/written comprehensive exam; thesis/nonthesis option for some degrees. For D.P.T.: a minimum of 80 credits; comprehensive written exam; 31 weeks full-time clinical internship.

FIELDS OF STUDY.
Counseling. Includes agency, pastoral. M.Ed.
Education Administration. M.Ed.
Occupational Therapy. M.O.T., M.S.O.T.
Physical Therapy. D.P.T.
Teaching. M.A.T.

PURDUE UNIVERSITY
West Lafayette, Indiana 47907-1968
Web site: www.purdue.edu

Founded 1869. Located 65 miles NW of Indianapolis. CGS and AAU member. Coed. State control. Semester system. Special facilities: Agricultural Experiment Station, Animal Science Research Center, Center for Applied Ethology and Human/Animal Interaction, Center for Applied Mathematics, Center for Artistic Endeavors, Center for Asian Studies, Hellenbrand Biomedical Engineering Center, Center for Classical Studies, Center for Comparative Literature, Engineering Research Center for Intelligent Manufacturing Systems, Engineering Experiment Station, Center for Film Studies, Gifted Education Resource Center, Center for Humanistic Studies, Jet Propulsion Center, Center for Leadership Studies, Center for Medieval Studies, Center for AIDS Research, Center for Intelligent Manufacturing Systems, Marriage and Family Center, Center for Paralysis Research, Center for Plant Environmental Stress Physiology, Policy Center for Life Long Learning, Retail Institute, Center for Research on the Aging, Center for Rural Development, Social Research Center, Center for Technology Transfer and Pollution Prevention, University Research Park. The University's NIH ranking is 118th among all U.S. institutions with 127 awards/grants valued at $40,695,266. According to The Center at University of Florida, the University is ranked 59th in receipt of Federal Research funds with $129,199,000 and it ranks 37th for total University research expenditures with $309,476,000. The University's endowment assets rank it 38th, with a value of $1,207,131,000. In 2004, the University awarded 446 doctorates, which ranked it 20th among all U.S. institutions eligible to award that degree. Fifty-seven of the University's faculty members have been elected to National Honor Academies and this ranks it 14th among all U.S. institutions. The Library: approximately 2,400,000 volumes, 19,500 subscriptions. Total University enrollment: 38,700.

Annual tuition: full-time resident $7316, nonresident $15,474, $16,090 (Business); per hour resident $261, nonresident $493. On-campus housing for 1300 married students, 800 graduate men and women. Average annual housing cost: $6200 for married students, $5800–$10,500 for single students. Apply to Director's Office, Young Graduate House, Purdue University, for graduate housing; Director, Married Student Housing, Nimitz Drive, Purdue University, for married student housing; for off-campus housing, apply to Off-Campus Housing Services, Hovde Hall, Office of the Dean of Students. Phone: (765)494-7045.

Graduate School

Enrollment: full-time 4800, part-time 1839. Graduate faculty: full- and part-time 1800. Degrees conferred: M.A., M.Agr., M.F.A., M.A.T., M.S., full- and part-time M.S.A.A.E., M.S.Ag.E., M.S.C.E., M.S.Ch.E., M.S.Ed., M.S.E.E., M.S.F., M.S.I.A., M.S.I.E., M.S.Met.E., M.S.N.E., Ed.S., Ph.D.

ADMISSION REQUIREMENTS. Official transcripts, three letters of reference required in support of School's application. Online applications available. GRE/MAT/GMAT required by many departments. TOEFL required for international applicants. Accepts transfer applicants. Graduates of unaccredited institutions not considered. Apply to department of major interest one semester in advance and not later than May 1 (Fall), September 1 (Spring), March 1 (Summer). Rolling admission process. Application fee $55. Phone for general information: (765)494-2600; fax: (765)494-0136; e-mail: gradinfo@purdue.edu.

ADMISSION STANDARDS. Selective for most departments, very selective for the others. Usual minimum average: 3.0 (A = 4).

FINANCIAL AID. Annual awards from institutional funds: scholarships, fellowships (including minority fellowships), teaching assistantships, research fellowships, administrative assistantships, full and partial tuition waivers, grants, Federal W/S, loans. Approved for VA benefits. Apply by February 1 to appropriate department for fellowships, assistantships; to Financial Aid Office for all other programs. Use FAFSA. About 60% of full-time students receive aid from University and outside sources. Aid available for part-time students.

DEGREE REQUIREMENTS. For master's: usually about 33 hours, at least two semesters in residence; thesis/nonthesis option: final written/oral exams for most majors; reading knowledge of one foreign language for some majors. For Ph.D.: usually 50–60 hours minimum beyond the bachelor's, at least one year in residence; qualifying exam for most majors; preliminary exam; reading knowledge of one foreign language for most majors; thesis; final written/oral exam.

FIELDS OF STUDY.
Accounting. M.S., Ph.D.
Aeronautics and Astronautics. M.S., M.S.A.A.E., M.S.E., Ph.D.
Agricultural and Biological Engineering. M.S., M.S.Ag.E., M.S.E., Ph.D.
Agricultural Economics. M.S., Ph.D.
Agronomy. M.S., Ph.D.
American Studies. M.A., Ph.D.
Animal Sciences. M.S., Ph.D.
Anthropology. M.S., Ph.D.
Art and Design. M.A.
Audiology and Speech Sciences. M.S., Ph.D.
Basic Medical Sciences. M.S., Ph.D.
Biochemistry. Interdisciplinary program. M.S., Ph.D.
Biochemistry and Molecular Biology. M.S., Ph.D.
Biomedical Engineering and Bioengineering. Interdisciplinary.
Botany and Plant Pathology. M.S., Ph.D.
Chemical Engineering. M.S., M.S.Ch.E., M.S.E., Ph.D.
Chemistry. Includes analytical, geochemistry, inorganic, organic, physical.
Child Development and Family Studies. M.S.Ed., M.S., Ph.D.
Civil Engineering. M.S., M.S.C.E., M.S.E., Ph.D.
Communication. M.A., M.S., Ph.D.
Comparative Literature. Interdisciplinary. M.A., Ph.D.
Comparative Pathobiology. Ph.D.
Computational Life Sciences. Interdisciplinary. M.S., Ph.D.
Computational Science and Engineering. Interdisciplinary. M.S., Ph.D.
Computer Sciences. M.S., Ph.D.
Consumer Sciences and Retailing. M.S., Ph.D.
Counseling and Development. M.S., M.S.Ed., Ph.D., Ed.S.
Curriculum and Instruction. M.S.Ed., Ph.D.
Earth and Atmospheric Sciences. M.S., Ph.D.

Ecology, Evolutionary, and Population Biology. M.S., Ph.D.
Economics. Ph.D.
Educational Studies. M.S.Ed., Ph.D.
Electrical and Computer Engineering. M.S., M.S.E., M.S.E.E., Ph.D.
English.
Entomology. M.S., Ph.D.
Food Science. M.S., Ph.D.
Foods and Nutrition. M.S.
Foreign Language and Literature. M.A., Ph.D.
Forestry and Natural Resources. M.S., M.S.F., Ph.D.
Geographic Information System and Remote Sensing. Interdisciplinary.
Gerontology. M.S., Ph.D.
Health and Kinesiology. M.S.
Health Sciences. M.S., Ph.D.
History. M.A., Ph.D.
Horticulture. M.Agr., M.A., Ph.D.
Hospitality and Tourism Management. M.S.
Human Resource Management. M.S.
Industrial Engineering. M.S.I.E., Ph.D.
Industrial and Physical Pharmacy. Ph.D.
Information Security. M.S., Ph.D.
Linguistics. M.A., Ph.D.
Management Information Systems. M.S., Ph.D.
Management. M.S., Ph.D.
Materials Engineering. M.S., M.S.E., Ph.D.
Mathematics. M.S., Ph.D.
Mechanical Engineering. M.S., M.S.M.E., Ph.D.
Medicinal Chemistry and Molecular Pharmacology. M.S., Ph.D.
Nuclear Engineering. M.S., M.S.N.E., Ph.D.
Nursing. Ph.D.
Organizational Behavior and Human Resource Management. M.S., Ph.D.
Pharmacy Practice. M.S.
Philosophy. M.A., Ph.D.
Physics. M.S., Ph.D.
PILSe (Purdue University Interdisciplinary Life Science Ph.D. Program). Includes biomolecular structure and biophysics, chemical biology, chromatin and regulation of gene expression, integrative neuroscience, membrane biology, microbes and the environment, microbial pathogenesis, molecular evolutionary genetics, molecular signaling and cancer biology, molecular virology, plant biology,. Ph.D.
Political Science. M.A., Ph.D.
Psychological Sciences. M.S., Ph.D.
Sociology. M.S., Ph.D.
Speech and Hearing Science. M.S., Ph.D.
Speech and Language Pathology. Ph.D.
Statistics. M.S.
Technology. M.S.
Theater. M.A., M.F.A.
Veterinary Clinical Sciences. M.S., Ph.D.
Visual and Performing Arts. Includes art, design, theater. M.A., M.F.A.
Youth Development and Agriculture Education. M.S., Ph.D.

Graduate Study at Other Campuses

Purdue University maintains a system-wide graduate school under which some courses and/or programs are offered at the regional campuses located at Hammond and Westville, as well as at the Indiana University–Purdue University campuses at Fort Wayne and Indianapolis.

School of Veterinary Medicine (47907-2026)

Web site: www.vet.purdue.edu

Established 1957. Semester system. Special facilities: Purdue Comparative Oncology Program, Equine Sports Medicine Center,

Center for Human/Animal Bond, Center for Paralysis Research. Library: 72,000 volumes, 458 subscriptions.

Annual tuition: residents $14,790, nonresidents $35,656. On-campus housing available. Estimated living expenses: $7500. Total all other expenses: $4500.

Enrollment: first-year class 70, total 268 (men 17%, women 83%, minorities 5%, state residents 63%), graduate/residency students 105 Faculty: full- and part-time 108. Degrees conferred: D.V.M., D.V.M.-M.S., D.V.M.-Ph.D.

ADMISSION REQUIREMENTS. VMCAS report, two transcripts, GRE, animal/veterinary experience, essay required in support of application. Interview by invitation only. Applicants must have completed at least two years of college study. Accepts transfer applicants on a space-available basis only. Preference given first to Indiana residents, second to residents of states without veterinary schools. Apply to Student Services Office after July 1 and before October 1. Fall admission only. Application fee: none. Phone: (765)494-7893; e-mail: admissions@vet.purdue.edu.

ADMISSION STANDARDS. Competitive. Accepts about 5–10% of all applicants. Number of applications 711 (590 out-of-state); number interviewed 222 (159 out-of-state); number of acceptances 109 (64 out-of-state); number enrolled 70 (26 out-of-state). Usual minimum UGPA: nonresidents 3.0 (A = 4). GRE mean score (V + Q) residents 1098, nonresidents 1170; mean UGPA residents 3.65, nonresidents 3.79.

FINANCIAL AID. Scholarships, assistantships, fellowships, full and partial tuition waivers, Federal W/S, grants. Apply to Office of Financial Aid by March 1. Use FAFSA.

DEGREE REQUIREMENTS. For D.V.M.: satisfactory completion of four-year program, at least three years in residence. For Ph.D., see Graduate School listing above.

FIELDS OF GRADUATE STUDY.
Anesthesiology.
Animal Behavior.
Animal Biosecurity.
Biomedical Engineering Research.
Cancer Research.
Cardiovascular.
Clinical Epidemiology.
Comparative Oncology.
Dermatology.
Diagnostic Imaging.
Endocrine and Reproductive Biology.
Equine Sports Medicine.
Infectious Disease Research.
Human-Animal Bond.
Immunology and Vaccine Development.
Metabolism.
Molecular Virology and Gene Therapy.
Neuroscience/Neurotrauma Intervention Research.
Orthopedics.
Pharmacology and Toxicology.
Production Medicine.
Tissue Engineering.
Urogenital.

PURDUE UNIVERSITY CALUMET
Hammond, Indiana 46323-2094
Web site: www.calumet.purdue.edu

Established 1948. Coed. State control. Semester system. Library: 205,000 volumes, 1300 subscriptions. Total Campus enrollment: 9600.

Tuition: per credit hour, resident $261, nonresident $493. No on-campus housing for graduate students. Day-care facilities available.

Graduate School

Enrollment: full-time 96, part-time 907. Faculty: full-time 140, part-time 16. Degrees conferred: M.A., M S., M.S.E.

ADMISSION REQUIREMENTS. Two transcripts, three letters of recommendation, statement of purpose required in support of application. GRE/GMAT/MAT required by some departments. Online application available. TOEFL required for international applicants. Accepts transfer applicants. Apply to the Office of Graduate Study; no specified closing date. Application fee $55. Phone: (219)989-2257; e-mail: grad@calumet.purdue.edu.

ADMISSION STANDARDS. Selective. Usual minimum average: 3.0 (A = 4).

FINANCIAL AID. Research fellowships, teaching assistantships, Federal W/S, loans. Apply to appropriate departments for fellowships, assistantships; to Financial Aid Office for all other programs. Phone: (219)989-2660. Use FAFSA.

DEGREE REQUIREMENTS. For master's: 33–48 semester hours; knowledge of one foreign language required by some departments; candidacy; final oral/written exam.

FIELDS OF STUDY.
Accountancy. M.Acc.
Addictions Counseling. M.S.
Behavior Sciences. Includes marriage and family therapy. M.S.
Biological Sciences. Includes biology, biotechnology, teaching. M.S.
Business Administration. M.B.A.
Communication. M.A.
Computer Engineering. M.S.E.
Educational Administration. M.S.
Electrical Engineering. M.S.E.
Elementary Education. M.S.
English. M.A.
Family and Marriage Therapy. M.S.
History. M.A.
Human Services. M.S.
Instructional Technology. Includes school personnel, business/industry folk. M.S.
Mathematics. M.S.
Mechanical Engineering. M.S.E.
Nursing. Includes clinical nurse specialist, family nurse practitioner, nursing administration. M.S.N.
School Mental Health. M.S.
Secondary Education. M.S.
Special Education. M.S.
Technology. M.S.

QUEENS COLLEGE OF THE CITY UNIVERSITY OF NEW YORK

Flushing, New York 11367-1597
Web site: www.qc.edu

Established 1937. CGS member. Coed. New York State control. Semester system. Library: 985,550 volumes, 3800 subscriptions. Total Campus enrollment: 17,600.

Tuition: full-time, state resident per credit $270; nonresident per credit $360. No housing available. Day-care facilities available.

Division of Graduate Studies

Graduate study since 1950. Enrollment: full- and part-time 4100. Faculty: full-time 456, part-time 189. Degrees conferred: M.A., M.A.S.S., M.L.S., M.F.A., M.S.Ed., M.A.L.S., Professional Diploma.

ADMISSION REQUIREMENTS. Transcripts required in support of application. GRE and GRE Subject Test, interview required for some departments. TOEFL required for international applicants. Accepts transfer applicants. Graduates of unaccredited institutions not considered. Apply to Office of Graduate Admissions by April 1 (Fall; some programs have earlier deadline), November 1 (Spring; not all programs admit in Spring). Application fee $125. Phone: (718)997-5200; fax: (718)997-5193.

ADMISSION STANDARDS. Selective or very selective. Usual minimum average: 2.75, 3.0 for major (A = 4).

FINANCIAL AID. Fellowships, assistantships, tuition waivers, Federal W/S, loans. Approved for VA benefits. Apply by April 1 to appropriate department chair for fellowships, assistantships; to Financial Aid Office for all other programs. Use FAFSA and University's FAF. Phone: (718)977-5100. Aid available for part-time students.

DEGREE REQUIREMENTS. For master's: generally 30 semester hours; thesis and comprehensive exam required for some degrees. For Post-Baccalaureate Certificate (teacher certification): 30 credits beyond the bachelor's degree. For Advanced Certificate: 30 semester hours beyond the master's.

FIELDS OF STUDY.
Accounting. M.S.Ed.
Applied Linguistics. M.A.
Art History. M.A., M.F.A.
Bilingual Elementary Education. M.S.Ed.
Biology. M.A.
Biochemistry. M.A.
Chemistry. M.A.
Computer Science. M.A.
Counselor Education. M.S.Ed.
Elementary Education. M.S.Ed.
English. M.A.
Family and Consumer Sciences. M.S.Ed.
French. M.A.
Fine Arts. M.F.A.
Geology. M.A.
History. M.A.
Italian. M.A.
Liberal Studies. M.A.L.S.
Library Science. Includes specializations in school or public, academic and special; M.L.S.; Advanced Certificate in Librarianship.
Literacy Education. M.S.Ed.
Mathematics. M.A.
Media Studies. M.A.
Music. M.A.
Music Performance. M.A.
Nutrition and Exercise Sciences. M.A.
Physics. M.A.
Psychology. M.A.
Reading. M.S.Ed.
School Psychology. M.S.Ed.
Secondary Education. Includes art, English, French, general science (biology, chemistry, earth science, physics), home economics, Italian, mathematics, music, physical education, social studies, Spanish. M.S.Ed.
Social Sciences. M.A.S.S.
Sociology. M.A.
Spanish. M.A.
Special Education. M.S.Ed.

Speech Pathology. M.A.
Studio Arts. M.F.A.
TESOL. M.S.Ed.
Urban Affairs. M.A.

City University of New York School of Law at Queens College
Flushing, New York 11367-1358
Web site: www.law.cuny.edu

Established 1983. Located on the Queens College campus in Flushing. ABA approved since 1985. AALS member. Semester system. Public control. Full-time, day study only. Law library: 278,498 volumes, 3094 subscriptions; has LEXIS, NEXIS, WESTLAW, DIALOG.

Annual tuition: resident $10,562, nonresident $16,462. No on-campus housing available. Law students tend to live off-campus. Contact Admissions Office for off-campus information. Off-campus housing and personal expenses: approximately $10,588. Enrollment: first-year class 166; total full-time 419 (men 34%, women 66%, minorities 31%); no part-time students. Faculty: full-time 26, part-time 17. Student to faculty ratio 12.2 to 1. Degree conferred: J.D.

ADMISSION REQUIREMENTS. LSDAS Law School report, LSAT (not later than February test date; if more than one LSAT, highest is used), bachelor's degree from an accredited institution, personal statement, two recommendations, transcripts (must show all schools attended and at least three years of study) required in support of application. Applicants must have received bachelor's degree prior to enrollment. Accepts transfer applicants. Interview not required but may be requested by School. In addition, international applicants whose native language is not English must submit TOEFL (not older than two years). Apply to Office of Admission after October 1, before March 15. First-year students admitted Fall only. Rolling admissions process. Application fee $50. Phone: (718)340-4210.

ADMISSION STANDARDS. Selective. Accepts 21% of total annual applicants. Number of applicants 2415; number of acceptances 497; number enrolled 166; LSAT (75% of class have a score at or above 149); GPA (75% of class have a GPA at or above 3.03). *U.S. News & World Report* ranking is in the fourth tier of all law schools.

FINANCIAL AID. Scholarships, Grants-in-Aid, private and institutional loans, Federal W/S, loans. For scholarships apply to Admissions Office after January 1, before May 1; use CUNY's Financial Aid Form, also submit Financial Aid Transcript, Federal Income Tax forms. Phone: (718)340-4284. Approximately 30% of first-year class received scholarships/Grants-in-Aid. Approximately 80% of students receive some form of financial aid.

DEGREE REQUIREMENTS. For J.D.: 92 (70 required) credits with a GPA of at least 2.0 (A = 4), plus completion of upper-divisional writing course; three-year program.

QUINNIPIAC UNIVERSITY
Hamden, Connecticut 96518-1940
Web site: www.quinnipiac.edu

Founded 1929. Located 20 miles S of Hartford. Coed. Semester system. Special facilities: Albert Schweitzer Institute, Bioanthroplogy Research Institute, Center for Excellence in Teaching and Service to Students. Center for Health Law and Policy, Center on Dispute Resolution, Equity Compensation Institute, National Institute for Community Health Education, Quinnipiac University Polling Institute, Professional Athlete Transition Cen-

ter. Library: 285,000 volumes, 4400 subscriptions. Total University enrollment: 7290.

Tuition: per credit $675. On-campus housing available for single students only. Average academic year housing costs: $6800 (including board); off-campus housing costs: $550–$750 per month. Contact Housing Office for both on- and off-campus housing information. Phone: (203)582-8666.

Graduate Programs

Graduate study since 1965. Enrollment: full-time 450, part-time 450. Graduate faculty: full-time 89, part-time 34. Degrees conferred: M.A.T., M.B.A., M.H.A., M.H.S., M.S.P.T.

ADMISSION REQUIREMENTS. Official transcripts required in support of application. Interviews required for some programs. TOEFL required for international applicants. Accepts transfer applicants. Graduates of unaccredited institutions not considered.

Apply to Director of Graduate Admissions at least one month prior to date of registration; for Physician Assistant program apply by December 1, Pathologist program apply by January 15. Rolling admissions process. Application fee $45. Phone: (203) 582-8672, (203)582-5238; e-mail: graduate@quinnipiac.edu.

ADMISSION STANDARDS. Selective. Usual minimum average: 2.75 (A = 4).

FINANCIAL AID. Annual awards from institutional funds: assistantships, Federal W/S, loans. Approved for VA benefits. Apply to Office of Financial Assistance; no specified closing date. Phone: (800)462-1944. Use FAFSA. Aid available for part-time students.

DEGREE REQUIREMENTS. For master's: 32–60 credits minimum, at least 26–54 in residence; thesis/nonthesis option; no foreign language requirement; final exams/internships in some programs.

FIELDS OF STUDY.
Accounting.
Biomedical Sciences.
Business Administration.
Computer Information Systems.
Elementary Education.
E-Media.
Forensic Nursing.
Health Management.
Journalism.
Medical Laboratory Sciences.
Middle School Education.
Molecular and Cell Biology.
Nurse Practitioner Studies.
Pathologist Assistant Studies.
Physical Therapy.
Physician Assistant Studies.
Secondary Education.
Teaching.

School of Law
Web site: www.law.quinnipiac.edu

Founded 1979 as part of the University of Bridgeport, name changed in 1995 and School moved to Hamden, Connecticut. ABA approved since 1992. AALS member. Private control. Semester system. Special facilities: Center for Dispute Resolution, Center for Health Law and Policy. Special programs: Summer program at Trinity College, Ireland; externships, Pre-Admission Summer Program. Law library: 401,505 volumes, 2601 subscriptions; has LEXIS, WESTLAW, DIALOG; has more than 400 network connections.

Annual tuition: full-time $33,840, part-time $23,840. On-campus housing available. Total average annual additional expenses: $17,206.

Enrollment: first-year class full-time 82, part-time 50; total full- and part-time 464 (men 52%, women 48%, minorities 11%). Faculty: full-time 33, part-time 28. Student to faculty ratio is 14.5 to 1. Degrees conferred: J.D., J.D.-M.B.A., J.D.-M.H.A., LL.M. (Health Law, Taxation, Taxation and Business).

ADMISSION REQUIREMENTS. LSDAS Law School report, LSAT, transcripts, personal statement, two letters of recommendation, required in support of application. Graduates of unaccredited colleges not considered. Apply by March 1 to the Office of Admissions. Admissions on a rolling basis, early applicants given special consideration. Application fee $40. Phone: (203)582-3400; fax: (203)582-3339.

ADMISSION STANDARDS. Selective. Accepts approximately 23% of full-time and 29% of part-time students. Number of full-time applicants 2225, part-time 355; number of full-time acceptances 515, part-time 103; number of full-time enrolled 82, part-time 50; LSAT (75% of full-time students have a score at or above 155, part-time 152); GPA (75% of full-time students have a GPA at or above 3.08, part-time 2.95). *U.S. News & World Report* ranking is in the third tier of all U.S. law schools.

FINANCIAL AID. Scholarships, Federal W/S, loans. Apply to Financial Aid Office by May 1. Phone: (203)582-3405. Use FAFSA (School code: E00545) and Quinnipiac Financial Aid Application. About 60% of students receive some aid from school.

DEGREE REQUIREMENTS. For J.D.: 86 semester hour program, minimum of two years in residence. For LL.M.: at least 24 credits beyond J.D.

RADFORD UNIVERSITY
Radford, Virginia 24142
Web site: www.radford.edu

Founded 1913. Located 40 miles SW of Roanoke. CGS member. Coed. State control. Semester system. Special facilities: Center for Brain Research and Informational Sciences, Curriculum Materials Center, Economics Research Center, Geography Research Center, Institute for Engineering Geosciences. Library: 527,789 volumes, 3200 subscriptions. Total University enrollment: 9500.

Annual tuition: resident $4284, nonresident $7884; per credit hour resident $238, nonresident $438. On-campus housing for single students only. Annual academic year housing costs: $6120 for single students, $7300 for married students living off-campus. Contact Director of Residential Life for off-campus housing information. Phone: (540)831-5375. Day-care facilities available.

Graduate College

Enrollment: full-time 444, part-time 663. Graduate faculty: full-time 210, part-time 24. Degrees conferred: M.A., M.B.A., M.F.A., M.S., M.S.W., Ed.S.

ADMISSION REQUIREMENTS. Transcripts, two letters of recommendation, GRE/GMAT/MAT/NTE required in support of College's application. Online application available. TOEFL required for international applicants. Accepts transfer applicants. Graduates of unaccredited institutions not considered. Apply to Graduate Studies Admissions (Box 6905) by March 1 (Fall), October 1 (Spring), April 1 (Summer). Application fee $40. Phone: (540)831-5431; fax: (540)831-6061.

ADMISSION STANDARDS. Relatively open. Usual minimum average: 2.75, for candidacy 3.0 (A = 4).

FINANCIAL AID. Fellowships, research assistantships, teaching assistantships, internships, grants, Federal W/S, loans. Approved for VA benefits. Apply by February 1 to Graduate Office for assistantships; to Financial Aid Office for all other programs. Phone: (540)831-5408. Use FAFSA. About 50% of full-time Graduate students receive aid other than loans from University and outside sources.

DEGREE REQUIREMENTS. For master's: 30–49 semester hours minimum; thesis/nonthesis; NTE, GRE, or MAT required for admission to candidacy; GMAT required for admission to candidacy for business majors in the nonteaching option. For M.F.A.: 60-credit program. For M.S.W.: 61-credit program. For Ed.S.: 30 semester hours beyond master's.

FIELDS OF STUDY.
Arts. M.F.A.
Business Administration. M.B.A.
Communication Sciences and Disorders. Includes speech and language pathology. M.A., M.S.
Corporate and Professional Communication. M.S.
Counseling and Human Development. Includes community counseling, school counseling, student affairs (administration, counseling). M.S.
Counseling Psychology. Psy.D.
Criminal Justice. M.A., M.S.
Education. Includes curriculum and instruction, early childhood education, educational technology, information technology, library science, literacy, music education. M.S.
Educational Leadership. M.S.
English. M.A., M.S.
Music. Includes music therapy. M.A., M.S.
Nursing. Includes adult clinical nurse specialist, family nurse practitioner, gerontology clinical nurse specialist, nurse midwifery. M.S.N.
Psychology. Includes clinical experimental, industrial/organization. M.A., M.S.
Reading. M.S.
School Psychology. M.S.
Social Work. M.S.W.
Special Education. Includes deaf and hard of hearing, early childhood special education. high incidence disabilities, severe disabilities. M.S.

UNIVERSITY OF REDLANDS
Redlands, California 92373-0999
Web site: www.redlands.edu

Founded 1907. Located 60 miles east of Los Angeles. Coed. Private control. Modified semester system. Library: 262,893 volumes, 2200 subscriptions. Total University enrollment: 2454.

Tuition: per credit $551. Limited on-campus housing for graduate students. Contact Director of Housing for both on- and off-campus housing information. Phone: (909)793-2121.

Graduate Studies

Enrollment: full-time 40, part-time 200. Faculty: full-time 20, part-time 100. Degrees conferred: M.A., M.M., M.S., M.B.A.

ADMISSION REQUIREMENTS. Official transcripts, three letters of recommendation, statement of intent, résumé usually required in support of application, GRE/GMAT required for some programs. Online application available. TOEFL (minimum score 550) required for international applicants. Accepts transfer applicants.

Apply to appropriate department, preferably by March 31. Some programs have earlier deadlines. Rolling admission process. Application fee $40. Phone: (909)793-2121, ext. 2200.

ADMISSION STANDARDS. Selective. Usual minimum average: 2.5 or 3.0, depending on program (A = 4).

FINANCIAL AID. Assistantships, internships, Federal W/S, loans. Approved for VA benefits. Apply to Director of Financial Aid. Phone: (909)-793-2121. Use FAFSA.

DEGREE REQUIREMENTS. For master's: 36–48 units minimum; thesis/nonthesis option; final oral/written exam.

FIELDS OF STUDY.

COLLEGE OF ARTS AND SCIENCES:
Communication Disorder. M.S.
Geographic Information Systems. M.S.
Music. M.M.

SCHOOL OF BUSINESS:
Business Administration. M.B.A.
Information Technology. M.S.
Management. M.A.

SCHOOL OF EDUCATION:
Education. Includes counseling, curriculum and instruction, educational administration, higher education. M.A.
Educational Leadership. Ed.D.

REGENT UNIVERSITY
Virginia Beach, VA 23464-9800
Web site: www.regent.edu

Founded 1977. Has branch campus located in Northern Virginia. Coed. Private control. Christian Broadcasting Network affiliation. Primarily graduate studies. Offers both campus-based classroom programs and online courses via Regent Worldwide Campus; some degree programs are offered only online and some are offered in a combination of both. Special facilities: Center for Applied Domestic and International Studies, Center for Career Advancement and Training, Center for Grassroots Politics, Center for Latin American Leadership, Institute for Christ-Centered Counseling. Library: 600,000 volumes, 2000 subscriptions. Total University enrollment: 3900.

Tuition: varies by school, see listings below. No on-campus housing available. Off-campus housing within a mile of campus. Annual average housing costs: $350–$400 per month single students; $600–$725 per month married students. Contact Regent Village, phone: (757)226-4890; fax: (757)226-4896.

Graduate School of Business

Tuition: per credit $700 (M.A., M.B.A.), $880 (E.M.B.A.). Enrollment: full-time 431, part-time 173. Faculty: full-time 9, part-time 21. Degrees conferred: M.B.A., E.M.B.A., P.M.B.A., M.A. in Management.

ADMISSION REQUIREMENTS, Transcripts, GMAT, Community Life Form, personal goals statement, two letters of recommendation required in support of application. Online application available. TOEFL (minimum score 577), TWE, and official translations of transcript required for international applicants. Apply by April 1 (Fall priority date), October 15 (Spring priority date) to the Central Enrollment Management Office. Phone: (800)373-5504; fax: (757)226-4033: e-mail: admissions@regent.edu. Application fee $40.

ADMISSION STANDARDS. Selective. Usual minimum academic average: 2.75 (A = 4).

FINANCIAL AID. Scholarships, research assistantships, internships, grants, loans. Apply to the Central Financial Aid Office by April 1. Phone: (757)226-4125; fax: (757)266-4118. Use FAFSA.

DEGREE REQUIREMENTS. For M. A. in Management: 16- to 20-month, 33 credit program; culminating experience. For M.B.A.: 16- to 20-month, 48–54 full-time credit program. For P.M.B.A.: 24- to 48-month, 48 credit program (combines classroom attendance and distance education). For E.M.B.A.: 36 credit program.

FIELDS OF STUDY.
Business Administration. Includes specialization in e-business, entrepreneurship, finance and accounting, human resource management, international business, leadership, marketing, not-for-profit management, organizational change and development. M.B.A., P.M.B.A., E.M.B.A.
Management. Includes specialization in e-business, entrepreneurship, finance and accounting, human resource management, international business, marketing, not-for-profit management, organizational change and development. M.A. in Management.

School of Communication and the Arts

Tuition: per credit $800 (M.A.), $850 (Ph.D.). Enrollment: full-time 160, part-time 187. Faculty: full-time 18, part-time 27, Degrees conferred: M.A., M.F.A., Ph.D

ADMISSION REQUIREMENTS. For master's candidates: transcripts, GRE or MAT, Community Life Form, personal goals statement, two letters of recommendation required in support of application. For Ph.D. candidates: master's in communication preferred, transcripts, GRE, Community Life Form, three letters of recommendation, writing sample, interview required in support of application. For distance candidates: submit résumé/vitae, computer literacy survey. Online application available. TOEFL (minimum score 550) and official translations of transcript required for international applicant. Apply by February 15 (doctoral candidates), March 1 (Fall), October 15 (Spring) to the Central Enrollment Management Office. Application fee $40. Phone: (800) 477-5504; fax: (757)226-4033: e-mail admissions@regent.edu.

ADMISSION STANDARDS. Selective. Usual minimum academic average: 2.75 (A = 4).

FINANCIAL AID, Scholarships, research assistantships, internships, grants, loans. Apply to the Central Financial Aid office by March 15 (priority deadline), April 1 (for scholarships). Phone: (757)226-4125; fax: (757)226-4118. Use FAFSA.

DEGREE REQUIREMENTS. For M.A., M.F.A.: 38 credit program; thesis/portfolio. For M.A., M.F.A.: 39 credit program; internship; comprehensive written/oral exam. For Ph.D.: at least two years in full-time residency; qualifying exam; dissertation proposal defense; dissertation; oral defense.

FIELDS OF STUDY.
Communication. Includes communication studies, cinema/T.V., design and technical theater, performance studies. M.A., Ph.D.
Digital Animation. M.A.
Journalism. Includes news journalism, professional writing/magazine, journalism, public relation. M.A.
Script and Screenwriting. M.F.A.
Theatre Arts. M.A.

School of Education

Tuition: per credit $560 (master's), $720 (Ed.S., Ed.D.). Enrollment: full-time 208, part-time 313, Faculty: full-time 25, part-time 34. Degrees conferred: M.Ed., Ed.D.

ADMISSION REQUIREMENTS. Transcripts, GRE, Community Life Form, writing sample, two letters of recommendation, interview required in support of application. Online application available. TOEFL (minimum score 550) and official translations of transcript required for international applicant. Apply by February 15 (doctoral candidates), April 1 (Fall), October 15 (Spring) to the Central Enrollment Management Office. Application fee $50. Phone: (800)477-5504; fax: (757)226-4033: e-mail: admissions @regent.edu.

ADMISSION STANDARDS. Selective. Usual minimum academic average: 2.75 (A = 4).

FINANCIAL AID. Scholarships, tuition remission, internships, grants, loans. Apply to the Central Financial Aid Office by March 15 (priority deadline), April 1 (for scholarships). Use FAFSA.

DEGREE REQUIREMENTS. For M.Ed.: 33–45 credit programs; internship; professional project. For Ed.D.: 60 credit, 3- to 4-year full-time program; one cognate area of specialization; candidacy; comprehensive exam; culminating experience.

FIELDS OF STUDY.
Christian School. M.Ed.
Cross-Categorical Special Education. M.Ed.
Education. Includes K–12 school leadership, higher education administration, staff development/adult education, educational psychology, special education, distance education. Ed.D.
Educational Leadership. M.Ed.
Individualized Degree Plan. M.Ed.
Master Teacher Program. M.Ed.
TESOL. M.Ed.

Robertson School of Government

Tuition: per credit $655. Enrollment: full-time 60, part-time 51. Faculty: full-time 8, part-time 6. Degrees conferred: M.P.A., M.P.M., M.P.P.

ADMISSION REQUIREMENTS, Transcripts, Community Life Form, three letters of recommendation, public policy writing sample, personal essay, résumé, interview required in support of application. Online application available. TOEFL (minimum score 550) and official translations of transcript required for international applicant. Apply by May 1 (Fall), November 15 (Spring) to the Central Enrollment Management Office. Application fee $40. Phone: (800)477-5504; fax: (757)226-4033; e-mail: admissions@ regent.edu.

ADMISSION STANDARDS. Selective. Usual minimum academic average: 2.75 (A = 4).

FINANCIAL AID. Scholarships, research assistantships, internships, grants, loans, Apply to the Central Financial Aid office by March 15 (priority deadline), April 1 (for scholarships). Phone: (757)226-4125; fax: (757)226-4118. Use FAFSA.

DEGREE REQUIREMENTS. For M.P.A.: 39-credit, two-year full-time program; internship; administrative project. For M.P.M.: 39-credit, two-year full-time program. For M.P.P.: 36-credit, two-year full-time program; culminating experience.

FIELDS OF STUDY.
Government. M.A.
Political Management. Includes campaign management. M.P.M.
Public Administration. Includes leadership studies. M.P.A.
Public Policy. Includes domestic policy analysis, economic policy analysis, political philosophy, strategic leadership. M.P.P.

School of Law
Web site: www.regent.edu/law

Established 1986 as successor to O.W. Coburn School of Law at Oral Roberts University. Located on main campus. ABA approved since 1989. AALS member. Private control. Semester system. Special facility: Institute for Christian Legal Studies. Law library: 387,451 volumes, 2242 subscriptions; has NEXIS, LEXIS, WESTLAW, DIALOG, INFORTRAC, LEGALTRAC; has more than 250 networks connections.

Annual tuition: full-time $25,616, part-time $19,056. Law students live in off-campus housing. Contact Admissions Office for off-campus information. Off-campus housing and personal expenses: approximately $14,993.

Enrollment: first-year class full-time 156, part-time 5; total full- and part-time 492 (men 49%, women 51%, minorities 12%). Faculty: full-time 25, part-time 13. Student to faculty ratio is 19.3 to 1. Degrees conferred: J.D., J.D.-M.A. (Communications, Counseling, Government, Journalism, Management, Public Policy), J.D.-M.B.A., LL.M. (only offered online), M.I.T. (Only offered online).

ADMISSION REQUIREMENTS. LSDAS Law School report, LSAT (not later that February test date; if more than one LSAT, average is used), bachelor's degree from an accredited institution, personal statement, résumé, three recommendations, transcripts (must show all schools attended and at least three years of study), a clergy/spiritual life letter of recommendation required in support of application. Applicants must have received bachelor's degree prior to enrollment. Interview not required but may be requested by School. In addition, international applicants whose native language is not English must submit TOEFL (not older that two years). Joint degree applications must apply to and be accepted to both Schools. Apply to Office of Admission after September 30, before June 1. First-year students admitted Fall only. Rolling admissions process. Application fee $50. Phone: (757)226-4584; fax: (757)226-4139; e-Mail: lawschool@regent.edu.

ADMISSION REQUIREMENTS FOR TRANSFER APPLICANTS. Accepts transfers from other ABA-accredited schools. Admission limited to space available. At least one year of enrollment, Dean's letter indicating the applicant is in good standing, prefer applicants in the upper half of first-year class, LSAT, LSDAS, personal statement regarding reason for transfer, current law school transcript required in support of School's application. Apply to Admission Office by June 15. Admission decision made by mid-July. Application fee $40. Will consider visiting students.

ADMISSION STANDARDS. Selective. Accepts approximately 45% of full-time and 44% of part-time students. Number of full-time applicants 720, part-time 25; number of full-time acceptances 322, part-time 11; number of full-time enrolled 156, part-time 5; LSAT (75% of full-time students have a score at or above 150, part-time 149); GPA (75% of full-time students have a GPA at or above 3.08, part-time 3.30). *U.S. News & World Report* ranking is in the fourth tier of all U.S. law schools.

FINANCIAL AID. Scholarships, merit scholarships, minority scholarships, private and institutional loans; Federal loans and Federal W/S offered through University's Financial Aid Office. Phone: (757)226-4559. Apply to University's Central Financial Aid Office after January 1, before April 15. Use FAFSA (School code: 030913), also submit Financial Aid Transcript, Federal Income Tax forms. Approximately 70% of students receive some form of financial assistance.

DEGREE REQUIREMENTS. For J.D.: 90 (66 required) credits with a GPA of at least 2.0 (A = 4), plus completion of upper-divisional writing course; 3-year program. For LL.M., M.I.T.: 24 credit online programs. For J.D.-Master's: three-and-one-half- or four-year program rather than a four- or five-year program if both degrees are taken consecutively.

FIELDS OF GRADUATE STUDY.
International Taxation. LL.M., M.I.T.

School of Leadership Studies

Tuition: per credit $575 (master's), $800 (doctoral). Enrollment: full-time 55, part-time 336, Faculty: full-time 11, part-time 15. Degrees conferred: M.O.L., D.S.L., Ph.D.

ADMISSION REQUIREMENTS. Transcripts, GRE/MAT/GMAT, Community Life Form, two letters of recommendation, personal goals statement, résumé or curriculum vitae required in support of application. Three years of relevant professional experience, a master's degree, and a writing sample required for doctoral applicants. Online application available. TOEFL (minimum score 575) and official translations of transcript required for international applicants. Apply by February 1 (doctoral applicants), May 1 (Fall), October 15 (Spring) to the Central Enrollment Management Office. Application fee $100. Phone: (800)477-5504; fax: (757)226-4033; e-mail admissions@regent.edu.

ADMISSION STANDARDS. Selective. Usual minimum academic average: 2.75 (A = 4).

FINANCIAL AID. Scholarships, research assistantships, internships, grants, loans. Apply to the Central Financial Aid office by March 15 (priority deadline), April 1 (for scholarships). Phone: (757)226-4125; fax: (757)226-4118. Use FAFSA.

DEGREE REQUIREMENTS. For M.O.L.: 33-credit program; culminating experience. For D.S.L.:. 60 credits (beyond the master's) four-year full-time program; candidacy; three residencies; culminating integrative paper; D.S.L. project. For Ph.D.: 60-credit (beyond the master's) three-year minimum full-time program; comprehensive exam; admission to candidacy; dissertation, oral defense.

FIELDS OF STUDY.
Organizational Leadership. Includes church and ministry leadership, computer-mediated communication, corporate communication leadership, leadership in business, interdisciplinary studies, leadership in education, leadership in government. M.O.L., Ph.D.
Strategic Leadership. D.S.L.

School of Psychology and Counseling

Tuition: per credit $575 (Counseling M.A.), $695 (Psy.D., Counseling Ph.D.). Enrollment: full-time 237, part-time 164. Faculty: full-time 25, part-time 11. Degrees conferred: M.A., Psy.D., Ph.D.

ADMISSION REQUIREMENTS. For master's candidates: transcripts, GRE or MAT, Community Life Form, two letters of recommendation required in support of application. For doctoral candidates: transcripts, GRE, writing sample, Community Life Form, three letters of recommendation, interview required in support of application. A video, 10-page writing sample, personal goals statement required for Ph.D. applicants. Online application available. TOEFL (minimum score 550) and official translations of transcript required for international applicants. Apply by February 15 (doctoral candidates), April 1 (Fall), November 1 (Spring) to the Central Enrollment Management Office. Application fee $40, $50 for doctoral applicant. Phone: (800)477-5504; fax: (757) 226-4033; e-mail: admissions@regent.edu.

ADMISSION STANDARDS. Selective. Usual minimum academic average: 2.75 for M.A., 3.0 UGPA, 3.2 (A = 4) in graduate studies for doctoral candidates.

FINANCIAL AID. Scholarships, tuition remission, internships, grants, loans. Apply to the Central Financial Aid Office by March 15 (priority deadline), April 1 (for scholarships). Use FAFSA.

DEGREE REQUIREMENTS. For M.A.: 51 credit full-time program; practicum; internship. For Psy.D.: 123 credit, four- to five-year full-time program; clinical internships; dissertation, oral defense. For Ph.D.: 60 credit three- to four-year full-time program, yearlong internship; dissertation proposal defense; dissertation; oral defense.

FIELDS OF STUDY.
Clinical Psychology. Psy.D.
Counseling. Includes community, school guidance. M.A.
Counselor Education and Supervision. Ph.D.
Human Services Counseling. M.A.

RENSSELAER POLYTECHNIC INSTITUTE
Troy, New York 12180-3590
Web site: www.rpi.edu

Founded 1824. Located 10 miles N of Albany. CGS member. Coed. Private control. Special facilities: Rensselaer Design Research Center, Center for Composite Materials and Structure, Lighting Research Institute, Center for Infrastructure and Transportation Studies, Clean Room, Materials Research Center, Fresh Water Institute, G. M. Low Center for Industrial Innovation, Geo technical Centrifuge Research Center, Center for Manufacturing Productivity, Center for Integrated Electronics, Scientific Computation Center, Center for Science and Technology Policy. University-affiliated Technology Park. Library: 420,0000 volumes, 10,200 subscriptions. Total University enrollment: 7250.

Tuition: per credit $1320. On-campus housing for 265 married students, unlimited housing for graduate men and women. Average academic year housing costs: $8200 for single students, per month $550–$730 for married students. Apply to Residence Life and Student Dining. Phone: (518)276-6284. Day-care facilities available.

Graduate School

Graduate study since 1826. Enrollment: full-time 1144, part-time 1146. Graduate faculty: full- and part-time 400. Degrees conferred: M.Eng., M.S., M.B.A., M.F.A., M.Arch., M.Arch.I, D.Eng., Ph.D.

ADMISSION REQUIREMENTS. Two transcripts, two letters of reference in support of School's application. GRE Subject Test required for some programs, recommended for others; GMAT required for M.B.A. TOEFL required for international applicants. Interview not required. Accepts transfer applicants. Graduates of unaccredited institutions not considered. Apply by January 15 (Fall), August 1 (Spring) to Dean of Enrollment Management. Application fee $75. Phone: (518)276-6216; fax: (518)276-4072; e-mail: admissions@rpi.edu.

ADMISSION STANDARDS. Competitive to very selective. Usual minimum average: 3.0 (A = 4).

FINANCIAL AID. Scholarships, fellowships, teaching assistantships, tuition waivers, Federal W/S, loans. Approved for VA benefits. Apply by February 1 to Department Chair for scholarship, fellowships, assistantships; to Office of Financial Aid for all other programs. Use FAFSA. About 65% of students receive aid other than loans from Institute and outside sources. Aid available for part-time students.

DEGREE REQUIREMENTS. For master's: 30 credit hours minimum, except M.Arch., which is three-and-one-half years of study beyond master's, and M.B.A. in School of Management, which requires 60 credits; M.S. in Lighting requires 48; M.S. in Environmental Management and Policy requires 45 credits, at least 24 in residence; thesis required by some departments. For Ph.D., D.Eng.: 90 credit hours minimum beyond the bachelor's, at least 45 in residence; candidacy exam; thesis; final oral exam.

FIELDS OF STUDY.

SCHOOL OF ARCHITECTURE:
Architecture. M.Arch., M.Arch.I, M.S.
Architecture Sciences. M.S., Ph.D.
Building Conservation. M.S.
Informatics and Architecture. M.S.
Lighting. M.S.

SCHOOL OF ENGINEERING:
Aeronautical Engineering.
Biomedical Engineering.
Chemical Engineering.
Civil Engineering.
Computer and Systems Engineering.
Decision Sciences and Engineering Systems.
Electrical Engineering.
Electric Power Engineering.
Engineering Physics.
Environmental Engineering.
Industrial and Management Engineering.
Manufacturing Systems.
Materials Engineering.
Mechanical Engineering.
Mechanics.
Nuclear Engineering.
Operations Research and Statistics.
Transportation Engineering.

SCHOOL OF HUMANITIES AND SOCIAL SCIENCES:
Cognitive Science.
Communication and Rhetoric.
Ecological Economics.
Ecological Economics, Values, and Policy.
Economics.
Electronic Arts.
Human Computer Interaction.
Science and Technology Studies.
Technical Communication.

LALLY SCHOOL OF MANAGEMENT AND TECHNOLOGY:
Environment Management and Policy.
Management.

SCHOOL OF SCIENCE:
Applied Mathematics.
Applied Science.
Astronomy.
Biology.
Biochemistry and Biophysics.
Chemistry.
Computer Science.
Engineering Principles in Technology Education.
Geology.
Hydrogeology.
Mathematics.
Multidisciplinary Science. Includes applied science, biochemistry and biophysics, bioformatics and molecular biology, ecological economics, values and policy, environmental studies, environmental science, information technology, interdisciplinary science, mind and machine, product design and innovation.
Natural Science.
Physics.

Rensselaer at Hartford
Hartford, Connecticut 06120-2991
Web site: www.hgc.edu/hartford

Established 1955. Located in Hartford, Connecticut. Coed. Library: 30,000 volumes, 535 subscriptions.

Tuition: per credit $1167. No on-campus housing. Enrollment: part-time 1800 (men 68%, women 32%). Faculty: full-time 37, part-time 53. Degrees conferred: M.S., M.B.A. Certificate Programs.

ADMISSION REQUIREMENTS. Transcripts, GMAT/GRE, two letters of recommendation, résumé required in support of Center's application. TOEFL required for international applicants. Accepts transfer applicants. Graduates of unaccredited institutions not considered. Apply to Director of Admissions at least 30 days prior to the start of term. Application fee $75. Phone: (860) 548-2420; fax: (860)548-7823.

ADMISSION STANDARDS. Selective. Usual minimum average: 3.0 (A = 4).

FINANCIAL AID. Grants, scholarships, research assistantships, tuition waivers, loans. Approved for VA benefits. Apply to Office of Student Affairs; no specified closing date. Phone: (800)433-4723, ext. 2406. Use FAFSA (School code: E01127). Aid available for part-time students.

DEGREE REQUIREMENTS. For M.S.: 30–39 credit hours minimum, at least 24 in residence; thesis/nonthesis option. For M.B.A.: 46 credit hours minimum. For certificates: minimum of four courses.

FIELDS OF STUDY.
Business Administration. M.B.A.
Computer and Systems Engineering. M.S.
Computer Science. Includes graduate certificates in bioinformatics, computer network communication, database systems, graphical user interface, information systems, software engineering. M.S.
Electrical Engineering. M.S.
Engineering. Includes graduate certificates in high-temperature materials for propulsion and power generation, pollution and waste prevention in manufacturing, quality and reliability engineering, systems modeling and analysis. M.S.
Engineering Science. M.S.
Information Technology. M.S.
Management. M.S.
Mechanical Engineering. M.S.

RHODE ISLAND COLLEGE
Providence, Rhode Island 02908-1924
Web site: www.ric.edu

Founded 1854. CGS member. Coed. State control. Semester system. Library: 639,400 volumes, 2000 subscriptions. Total College enrollment: 9000.

Tuition: per credit, resident $260, nonresident $546. Limited on-campus housing for graduate students. Average academic year housing costs: $6500–$8400 (including board). Contact the Director of Housing for both on- and off-campus housing information. Phone: (401) 456-8240. Day-care facilities available.

Graduate Studies

Graduate study since 1924. Enrollment: full-time 285, part-time 1091. College faculty teaching graduate students: full-time 80, part-time 28. Degrees conferred: M.A., M.Ed., M.F.A., M.A.T., M.M.Ed., M.P.A., M.S.W., C.A.G.S., M.S.

ADMISSION REQUIREMENTS. Transcripts, three letters of recommendation required in support of School's application. GRE/MAT required by some programs. TOEFL required for foreign applicants. Accepts transfer applicants. Graduates of unaccredited institutions not considered. Apply to Graduate Office by April 1 (Fall), November 1 (Spring), February 1 (M.S.W. deadline). Application fee $50. Phone: (401)456-8700; fax: (401)456-8117.

ADMISSION STANDARDS. Selective for most departments. Usual minimum average: 3.0 (A = 4).

FINANCIAL AID. Fellowships, research and teaching assistantships, internships, tuition waivers, Federal W/S, loans. Approved for VA benefits. Apply by March 15 to Dean of Graduate Studies for assistantships; to Office of Financial Aid for all other programs. Phone: (401)456-8700. Use FAFSA. About 30% of students receive aid other than loans from College and outside sources. Aid available for part-time students.

DEGREE REQUIREMENTS. For master's: 30 credit hours minimum; final written comprehensive exam. For M.A. (Agency Counseling): 45 credit program. For M.A.T.: 35–45 credit programs. For M.Ed.: 36 credit program. For M.S.W.: 61 credits minimum, at least 30 in residence; individual or group thesis. For C.A.G.S.: 30 credit hours minimum beyond the master's.

FIELDS OF STUDY.
Accounting. M.P.A.
Art.
Art Education.
Bilingual/Bicultural Education.
Biology.
Counseling. Includes agency, alcohol and substance abuse, school counseling.
Counselor Education.
Educational Administration. Includes elementary, secondary.
Educational Psychology.
Elementary Education. Includes early childhood education.
English.
French.
General Science.
Health Education.
History.
Mathematics.
Media Studies.
Music.
Personal Financial Planning.
Physical Science.
Physics.
Psychology.
Reading.
Secondary Education.
Secondary School Administration.
Social Work. Includes clinical practice, organizing policy and administration.
Spanish.
Special Education. Includes behavior disorders, learning disabilities, preschool disabilities, secondary special needs, severe and profound disabilities.
Teaching English as a Second Language (TESL).
Technology Education.
Theatre.

RHODE ISLAND SCHOOL OF DESIGN
Providence, Rhode Island 02903-2784
Web site: www.risd.edu

Founded 1877. Coed. Private control. Semester system, Special facility: Museum of Art. Library: 115,000 volumes, 423 subscriptions. Total School enrollment: 2337.

Annual tuition and fees: full-time $32,858. On-campus housing available for single graduate students. Average academic year housing costs: $9900 (including board). Off-campus housing per month: $450–$600. Contact Housing and Residence Life for on- and off-campus housing information. Phone: (401)454-6650.

Graduate Studies

Enrollment: full-time 330 (men 45%, women 55%). Faculty: full-time 51, part-time 10. Degrees conferred: M.A.Art.Ed., M.Arch., M.A.T., M.F.A., M.I.A., M.I.D., M.L.A.

ADMISSION REQUIREMENTS. Transcripts, full portfolio, three letters of recommendation required in support of application. TOEFL required for international applicants. Interview not required, but recommended. Accepts transfer applicants. Apply to Division of Graduate Studies by January 15. Online application available. Fall admission only. Application fee $60. Phone: (401)454-6300; fax: (401)454-6309; e-mail: admissions@risd.edu.

ADMISSION STANDARDS. Competitive. Admission based on talent.

FINANCIAL AID. Grants, scholarships, assistantships, fellowships, internships, grants, Federal W/S, loans. Approved for VA benefits. Apply by February 15 to Graduate Studies Committee. Phone: (401)454-6661; fax: (401)454-6412. Use FAFSA (School code: 003409) and CSS Profile. About 30% of students receive aid from School and outside sources.

DEGREE REQUIREMENTS. For M.I.A., M.I.D., M.F.A., M.L.A.: 66 semester credits minimum, two years in residence; thesis. For M.A.T.: 34–37 semester credits minimum; thesis. For M.A.Art.Ed.: 33–39 semester credits minimum; thesis. M.Arch.: 111 credits, three years in residence.

FIELDS OF STUDY.
Architecture.
Art and Design Education.
Art History.
Ceramics.
Digital Media.
Furniture Design.
Glass.
Graphic Design.
Industrial Design.
Interior Architecture.
Jewelry/Metalsmithing.
Landscape Architecture.
Painting.
Photography.
Printmaking.
Sculpture.
Textile.

UNIVERSITY OF RHODE ISLAND
Kingston, Rhode Island 02681
Web site: www.uri.edu

Founded 1888. Located 30 miles S of Providence. CGS member. Coed. State control. Semester system. Special facilities: Biotechnology Center, Research Center in Business, Child Development Center, Center for Energy Studies, Institute of Human Sciences and Services, Labor Research Center, International Center for Marine Resource Development, Marriage and Family Center, Center for Ocean Management, Robotics Research Center. Library: 1,200,000 volumes, 7966 subscriptions. Total University enrollment: 15,000

Annual tuition: full-time, resident $13,872, regional $20,808, nonresident $38,088. On-campus housing for single and married students. Average academic year housing costs: $8114 (including board) for single students; $8500 for married students. Contact Residential Life Office for both on- and off-campus housing information. Phone: (401)874-2935. Day-care facilities available.

Graduate School

Enrollment: full-time 1296, part-time 2642. Faculty: full-time 659, part-time 10. Degrees conferred: M.A., M.E.S.M., M.S., M.O., M.P.A., M.C.P., E.M.B.A., M.B.A., M.L.I.S., M.M.A., M.M., Ph.D.

ADMISSION REQUIREMENTS. Two official transcripts, three letters of recommendation required in support of School's application. GRE or MAT required for most departments, GRE Subject Test for some departments, GMAT for business programs. Interview required in some programs. TOEFL required of international students. Accepts transfer applicants. Graduates of unaccredited colleges not considered. Apply to Dean of Graduate School by April 15 (Fall), November 15 (Spring). Earlier dates in some programs. Application fee $35. Phone: (401)874-9500; fax: (401)874-5491.

ADMISSION STANDARDS. Very competitive to selective. Usual minimum average: 2.75 (A = 4).

FINANCIAL AID. Scholarships, fellowships, diversity fellowships, teaching/research assistantships, tuition waivers, Federal W/S, loans. Approved for VA benefits. Apply by February 15 to Dean for scholarships and fellowships; to appropriate departments for assistantships; to Financial Aid Office for all other programs. Phone: (401)874-9500. Use FAFSA. Aid available for part-time students.

DEGREE REQUIREMENTS. For master's: 30 credits minimum, at least 24 in residence; thesis with oral defense (6 credits) for most departments, or nonthesis with major paper; comprehensive exam. For Ph.D.: 72 credits minimum beyond the bachelor's, at least 24 in full-time residence or two consecutive semesters in full-time attendance; preliminary exam; proficiency in research tool/foreign language required in some programs; dissertation; final oral exam.

FIELDS OF STUDY.
Accounting. M.S.
Adult Education. M.A.
Applied Mathematics. Ph.D.
Applied Pharmaceutical Sciences. M.S., Ph.D.
Applied Probability. Ph.D.
Audiology. Au.D.
Biochemistry. M.S.
Biological Sciences. M.S., Ph.D.
Biomedical Engineering. M.S.
Biotechnology. M.S.
Business Administration. M.B.A., Ph.D.
Chemical Engineering. M.S., Ph.D.
Chemistry. M.S., Ph.D.
Civil and Environmental Engineering. M.S., Ph.D.
Clinical Laboratory Science. M.S.
Clinical Psychology. Ph.D.
College Student Personnel. M.S.
Communication Studies. M.A.
Community Planning. M.C.P.
Computer Engineering. M.S.
Computer Science. M.S., Ph.D.
Cytotechnology. M.S.
Earth and Hydrologic Science. M.E.S.M.
Economics. M.A.
Education. Ph.D.

Electrical Engineering. M.S., Ph.D.
Elementary Education. M.A., M.S.
English. M.A., Ph.D.
Entomology. M.S., Ph.D.
Environmental and Natural Resources Economics. M.S., Ph.D.
Environmental Policy and Management. M.E.S.W.
Experimental Psychology. Ph.D.
Finance. M.B.A.
Fisheries, Animal, and Veterinary Science. M.S., Ph.D.
Food Science and Nutrition. Ph.D.
French. M.A.
Geosciences. M.S., Ph.D.
History. M.A.
Human Development and Family Studies. M.S.
Industrial and Manufacturing Engineering. Ph.D.
International Business. M.B.A.
International Sports Management. M.B.A.
Kinesiology. M.S.
Labor and Industrial Relations. M.S.
Library and Information Studies. M.L.I.S. only.
Management. M.B.A.
Manufacturing Engineering. M.S.
Marine Affairs. M.A., M.M.A., Ph.D.
Marketing. M.B.A.
Marriage and Family Therapy. M.S.
Mathematics. M.S., Ph.D.
Mechanical Engineering and Applied Mechanics. M.S., Ph.D.
Medicinal Chemistry and Pharmacognosy. M.S., Ph.D.
Microbiology. M.S., Ph.D.
Music. M.M.
Natural Resources Science. M.S., Ph.D.
Nursing. Includes nursing service administration, teaching of nursing. M.S., Ph.D.
Nutrition and Food Sciences. M.S.
Ocean Engineering. M.S., Ph.D.
Oceanography. M.O., M.S., Ph.D.
Operations Research. Ph.D.
Pharmaceutics and Pharmacokinetics. M.S.
Pharmacoepidemiology and Pharmacoenomics. M.S.
Pharmacology and Toxicology. M.S., Ph.D.
Pharmacy Administration. M.S.
Physical Education. M.S.
Physical Therapy. M.S.
Physics. M.S., Ph.D.
Plant Sciences. M.S.
Political Science. M.A.
Public Administration. M.P.A.
Reading Education. M.A.
Remote Sensing and Spatial Analysis. M.E.S.M.
School Psychology. M.S., Ph.D.
Secondary Education. M.A.
Spanish. M.A.
Speech-Language Pathology. M.S.
Statistics. M.S., Ph.D.
Sustainable Systems. M.E.S.M.
Textiles, Fashion Merchandising, and Design. M.S.
Wetland, Watershed, and Ecosystem Science. M.E.S.M.

RICE UNIVERSITY

Houston, Texas 77005-1892
Web site: www.rice.edu

Founded 1891. CGS and AAU member. Coed. Private control. Semester system. Special facilities: James A. Baker III Institute for Public Policy, Center for Applied Psychological Systems, Center for Biological and Environmental Nanotechnology, Center for Chemical Processing Technology, Center for Computational Geophysics, Center for High Performance Software

Research, Center for the History of Leadership Institutions, Center for Medical Ethics and Health Policy, Center for Multimedia Communication, Center for Nanoscale Science and Technology, Center for the Study of Cultures, Center for the Study of Environment and Society, Center for the Study of Institutions and Values, Center for the Study of Languages, Center for Sustainability in the Built Environment, Center for Technology in Teaching and Learning, Center for Urbanism, Center on the Management of Information Technology, Computer and Information Technology Institute, Environmental and Energy Systems Institute, Goethe Center for Central European Studies, Hazardous Substances Research Center/South and Southwest, Institute of Biosciences and Bioengineering, National Center for Ground Water Research, W. M. Keck Center for Computational Biology, Rice Center for Organizational Effectiveness Studies, Rice Quantum Institute, Texas Center for Crystallography. Library: 2,000,000 volumes, 14,000 subscriptions. Total University enrollment: 4500.

Annual tuition: full-time $29,960, part-time per credit $1560. On-campus housing available for graduate students. Average housing costs: $475–$735 for single students, $545–$735 (room only) for married students. Contact the Housing Office for both on- and off-campus information. Phone: (713)348-4723.

Graduate Division

Enrollment: full-time, 1587; part-time 56. University faculty: full-time 434, part-time 150. Degrees conferred: M.A., M.B.A., M.M., M.Arch., M.S., M.Stat., D.Arch., D.M.A., Ph.D.

ADMISSION REQUIREMENTS. Transcripts, three letters of recommendation, GRE or GMAT required in support of application. Online application available. TOEFL (minimum score 600) required for foreign applicants. Interview not required. Accepts transfer applicants. Graduates of unaccredited institutions not considered. Apply to Dean by February 1. Some departments have earlier deadlines and additional requirements. Most students enter Fall semester. Application fee $40. Phone: (713) 348-4002.

ADMISSION STANDARDS. Competitive. Usual minimum average: 3.0 (A = 4).

FINANCIAL AID. Scholarships, fellowships, research assistantships, teaching assistantships, internships, tuition waivers, Federal W/S, loans. Approved for VA benefits. Apply by February 1 to appropriate department chair for fellowships, assistantships; to Financial Aid Office for all other programs. Phone: (713)348-4958. Use FAFSA. About 90% of all thesis students receive aid other than loans from University and outside sources. No aid for part-time students.

DEGREE REQUIREMENTS. For master's: 30 semester hours minimum, at least 24 in residence; qualifying exam; final oral exam; thesis/nonthesis option. For M.M.: 43–57 semester hours, at least 36 in residence. For M.B.A.: a minimum of two years in residence. For Ph.D., D.Arch.: 90 credit program, normally three or more years beyond the bachelor's degree, at least two years in full-time residence; qualifying exam; candidacy; final oral exam; thesis.

FIELDS OF STUDY.

SCHOOL OF ARCHITECTURE:
Architecture. M.Arch., D. Arch.
Urban Design. M.Arch.

GEORGE R. BROWN SCHOOL OF ENGINEERING:
Bioengineering. M.S., Ph.D.
Chemical Engineering. M.ChE., M.S., Ph.D.
Civil and Environmental Engineering. M.C.E., M.E.E., M.E.S., M.S., Ph.D.

Computational and Applied Mathematics. M.C.A.M., M.C.S.E., M.A., Ph.D.
Computer Science. M.C.S., M.S., Ph.D.
Electrical and Computer Engineering. M.E.E., M.S. Ph.D.
Mechanical Engineering and Materials Sciences. M.M.E., M.M.S., M.S., Ph.D.
Statistics. M.Stat., M.A., Ph.D.

SCHOOL OF HUMANITIES:
English. M.A., Ph.D.
French Studies. M.A., Ph.D.
Hispanic Studies. M.A.
History. M.A., Ph.D.
Linguistics. Ph.D.
Philosophy. M.A., Ph.D.
Religious Studies. M.A., Ph.D.

JESSE H. JONES GRADUATE SCHOOL OF MANAGEMENT:
Business Administration. Includes informal concentrations in accounting, entrepreneurship, finance, general management, international business, information technology, marketing, operations management, organizational behavior and human resource management, health-care management, strategic management and planning. M.B.A., M.B.A. for Executives.

SHEPHERD SCHOOL OF MUSIC:
Composition. M.Mus.
Choral and Instrumental Conducting. M.Mus.
Historical Musicology. M.Mus.
Music Theory. M.Mus.
Performance. M.Mus.

WIESS SCHOOL OF NATURAL SCIENCES:
Biochemistry and Cell Biology. M.A., Ph.D.
Chemistry. M.A., Ph.D.
Ecology and Evolutionary Biology. M.A., Ph.D.
Earth Science. M.A., Ph.D.
Mathematics. M.A., Ph.D.
Physics and Astronomy. M.A., M.S., Ph.D.

SCHOOL OF SOCIAL SCIENCES:
Anthropology. M.A., Ph.D.
Economics. M.A., Ph.D.
Political Science. M.A., Ph.D.
Psychology. M.A., Ph.D.

INTERDEPARTMENTAL PROGRAMS:
Applied Physics. Master's, Ph.D.
Computational Science and Engineering. Master's, Ph.D.
Environmental Analysis and decision Making. Master's.
Material Science and Engineering. Master's, Ph.D.
Nanoscale Physics. Master's.
Subsurface Geoscience. M.S.

COOPERATIVE PROGRAMS:
Biomedical Ethics. With University of Texas Health Science Center at Houston. M.A. Ph.D.
Computational Biology. With Baylor College of Medicine and University of Houston. Ph.D.

UNIVERSITY OF RICHMOND
Richmond, Virginia 23173
Web site: www.richmond.edu

Founded 1830. Private control. Baptist affiliation. Semester system. Library: 1,100,000 volumes, 3579 subscriptions. Total University enrollment: 3700.

Annual tuition: full-time $26,300, per credit $1320. No on-campus housing available.

Arts and Sciences Graduate School

Graduate study since 1921. Enrollment: full-time 17, part-time 40. Faculty: full-time 105, part-time 8. Degrees conferred: M.A., M.L.A., M.S.

ADMISSION REQUIREMENTS. Transcripts, three letters of recommendation, statement of purpose, GRE/GMAT required in support of School's application. TOEFL (minimum score 550) required of international students. Interview not required. Transfer applicants considered. Graduates of unaccredited institutions not considered. Apply to Graduate School by March 15 (Fall). Application fee $30. Phone: (804)289-8417; fax: (804) 289-8818.

ADMISSION STANDARDS. Selective for most departments. Usual minimum average: 3.0 (A = 4).

FINANCIAL AID. Tuition remission program for full-time students; special tuition rates for part-time students. Fellowships, academic scholarships, teaching and research assistantships, Federal W/S, loans. Approved for VA benefits. Apply by March 15 to Dean of Graduate School for assistantships, scholarships; to the Office of Financial Aid for all other programs. Phone: (804)289-8438. Use FAFSA. About 60% of full-time students receive aid other than loans from University and outside sources.

DEGREE REQUIREMENTS. For M.A., M.S.: 27–36 semester hours; thesis/nonthesis; comprehensive exam. For M.L.A.: 30 hours minimum; thesis/nonthesis option.

FIELDS OF STUDY.
Biology.
English.
History.
Liberal Arts. Cross-disciplinary.
Psychology.

The E. Claiborne Robins School of Business— Graduate Division

Annual tuition: $26,300. Enrollment: full-time 10, part-time 262. Faculty: full-time 39, part-time 10. Degree conferred: M.Acc., M.B.A.

ADMISSION REQUIREMENTS. Transcripts, three letters of recommendation, statement of purpose, GMAT required in support of School's application. TOEFL required of international students. Interview not required. Transfer applicants considered. Graduates of unaccredited institutions not considered. Apply to Graduate Division by May 1 (Fall), November 1 (Spring). Rolling admissions process. Application fee $50. Phone: (804)289-8553; fax: (804)287-1228.

ADMISSION STANDARDS. Selective. Mean GMAT: 617; mean GPA: 3.0 (A = 4). Usual minimum average: 2.75 (A = 4).

FINANCIAL AID. Assistantships, loans. Approved for VA benefits. Apply to Financial Aid Office; no specified closing date. Use FAFSA (School code: 003744). Phone: (804)289-8438. About 60% of full-time students receive aid other than loans from University and outside sources. Aid available for part-time students.

DEGREE REQUIREMENTS. For M.Acc., M.B.A.: 30–51 semester hours minimum; degree program must be completed in 5 years.

FIELDS OF STUDY.
Accounting. M.Acc.
Business Administration, M.B.A.

T. C. Williams School of Law
Web site: law.richmond.edu

Established 1870. ABA approved since 1928. AALS member. Private control. Semester system. Special facilities: Children's Law Center, Institute for Actual Innocence, Intellectual Property Institute, Mid-Atlantic Juvenile Defender Center, National Center for Family Law, Robert R. Merhige Jr. Center for Environmental Studies. Law library: 382,741 volumes, 4573 subscriptions; has LEXIS, NEXIS, WESTLAW, DIALOG, VU/TEXT; has more than 700 network connections.

Annual tuition: $28,390. Limited on-campus housing for single students. Total average annual additional expenses: $14,040.

Enrollment: first-year class 171; total 500 (men 54%, women 46%, minorities 10%). Faculty: full-time 70, part-time 35. Student to faculty ratio is 14.3 to 1. Degrees conferred: J.D., J.D.-M.B.A., J.D.-M.H.A., J.D.-M.P.A., J.D.-M.S.W., J.D.-M.U.P.

ADMISSION REQUIREMENTS. LSDAS Law School report, bachelor's degree, transcripts, LSAT, narrative statement, two letters of recommendation required in support of application. Personal interviews optional. Accepts transfer applicants. Graduates of unaccredited institutions not considered. Apply to School after September 1, before April 1. Admits beginning students Fall only. Application fee $35. Phone: (804) 289-8189.

ADMISSION STANDARDS. Selective. Accepts approximately 26% of all students. Number of applicants 2203; number of acceptances 581; number enrolled 171; LSAT (75% of students have a score at or above 160); GPA (75% of students have a GPA at or above 3.10). *U.S. News & World Report* ranking is in the second tier (tied at 77th) of all U.S. law schools.

FINANCIAL AID. Scholarships, assistantships, Federal W/S, loans. Apply to Financial Aid Office by February 25. Phone: (804)289-8438. Use FAFSA (School code: 030913). About 50% of students receive aid other than loans from School.

DEGREE REQUIREMENTS. For J.D.: satisfactory completion of three-year program; 86 semester hours minimum. For master's degrees, see Graduate School listing above.
Note: Summer program in Cambridge (Great Britain).

RIDER UNIVERSITY
Trenton, New Jersey 08648-3001
Web site: www.rider.edu

Founded 1865. Coed. Private control. Semester system. Library: 404,353 volumes, 2763 subscriptions. Total university enrollment: 5600.

Tuition: per credit, $735 (Business), $540 (Education), $930 (Westminster). On-campus housing for single students available. Average housing costs: $2800–$3800, $6800–$7800 (including board). Contact Graduate Housing Office for both on- and off-campus housing information. Phone: (609)996-5102.

Graduate Studies

Enrollment: full-time 235, part-time 688. Faculty: full-time 75, part-time 35. Degrees conferred: M.A., M.Acc., M.B.A., M.M.

ADMISSION REQUIREMENTS. Official Transcript, two professional recommendations required in support of application. GMAT and Audition required for some programs. Online application available. TOEFL required for international applicants. Accepts transfer applicants. Graduates of unaccredited institutions not considered. Apply to Director of Graduate Services at least one month prior to registration. Rolling admissions process. Application fee $35. Phone: (609)896-5036; fax: (609)895-6645; Westminster Choir College: (800)962-4647.

ADMISSION STANDARDS. Selective. Usual minimum average: 2.5 (A = 4).

FINANCIAL AID. Fellowships, research assistantships, teaching assistantships, internships, Federal W/S, loans. Approved for VA benefits. Apply by April 1 to the Director of Financial Aid. Phone: (609)896-5360. Use FAFSA.

DEGREE REQUIREMENTS. For M.A., M.Acc.: 30–36 credit hours minimum, depending on program; thesis/nonthesis option. For M.B.A.: 30–57 credit hours, depending on previous degree and number of foundation courses waived. For M.M.: 30–36 credit hours minimum; thesis/nonthesis option/recital. For Ed.S.: 30-credit program; special project.

FIELDS OF STUDY.

COLLEGE OF BUSINESS ADMINISTRATION:
Accountancy. M.Acc.
Business Administration. M.B.A.

SCHOOL OF GRADUATE EDUCATION AND HUMAN SERVICES:
Counseling Services. M.A., Ed.S.
Curriculum, Instruction, and Supervision. M.A.
Education Administration. M.A.
Organizational Leadership. M.A.
Reading Language Arts. M.A.
School Psychology. Ed.S.
Special Education. M.A.
Teaching. M.A.

WESTMINSTER CHOIR COLLEGE OF RIDER UNIVERSITY:
Choral Conducting. M.M.
Composition. M.M.
Music Education. M.M., M.M.Ed.
Organ Performance. M.M.
Piano Accompanying and Coaching. M.M.
Piano Pedagogy and Performance. M.M.
Piano Performance. M.M.
Sacred Music. M.M.
Voice Pedagogy and Performance. M.M., M.A.T., M.V.P.

RIVIER COLLEGE
Nashua, New Hampshire 03060-5086
Web site: www.rivier.edu

Founded 1933. Located NW of Boston. Coed. Private control—Roman Catholic. Semester system. Library: 150,000 volumes, 1800 subscriptions. Total College enrollment: 2100.

Tuition: per credit $425; Nursing $727. No on-campus housing for graduate students.

School of Graduate Studies

Enrollment: full-time 73, part-time 674. Graduate faculty: full-time 35, part-time 43. Degrees conferred: M.A., M.B.A., M.A.T., M.Ed., M.S., C.A.G.S.

ADMISSION REQUIREMENTS. Transcripts, three letters of recommendation, personal statement required in support of School's application. Online application available. MAT required for education applicants. TOEFL required for international applicants. Accepts transfer applicants. Apply to Office of Graduate Admission by August 1 (Fall), November 30 (Spring). Rolling admission process. Application fee $25. Phone: (603)897-8219; fax: (603)897-8810; e-mail: gadmissions@rivier.edu

ADMISSION STANDARDS. Selective. Usual minimum average: 2.75 (A = 4).

FINANCIAL AID. Limited to assistantships, Federal W/S, loans. Approve for VA benefits. Phone: (603)897-8510. Use FAFSA. Aid available for part-time students.

DEGREE REQUIREMENTS. For M.A., M.S., M. Ed.: 30 semester hours minimum including thesis, or 33 hours without thesis; final written exam. For M.B.A.: 36–45 semester hours. For C.A.G.S.: 30 credit program beyond master's.

FIELDS OF STUDY.
Business Administration. Includes accounting, marketing, organizational management. M.B.A.
Clinical Mental Health Counseling. M.A.
Computer Information System. M.S.
Computer Science. M.S.
Curriculum and Instruction. M.Ed.
Early Childhood Education. M.Ed.
Educational Administration. M.Ed.
Educational Studies. M.Ed.
Elementary Education. M.Ed.
Elementary Education and General Special Education. M.Ed.
Elementary Education and Learning Disabilities. M.Ed.
Emotional and Behavior Disabilities. M.Ed.
English. M.A.T.
Learning Disabilities. M.Ed.
Learning Disabilities and Reading. M.Ed.
Mathematics Education. M.A.T.
Nursing. Includes family nursing, nurse education, psychiatric mental health nursing. M.S.
Reading. M.Ed.
School Counseling. M.Ed.
Secondary Education. M.Ed.
Social Studies. M.A.T.
Spanish. M.A.T.
Writing and Literature. M.A., M.A.T.

ROBERT MORRIS UNIVERSITY
Moon Township, Pennsylvania 15108-1189
Web site: www.rmu.edu

Founded 1921. A second campus is located in downtown Pittsburgh. Coed. Private control. Semester system. Library: 212,000 volumes, 853 subscriptions. Total College enrollment: 5100.

Tuition: per credit $640 (M.B.A., Taxation), $625 (Business M.S.), $595 (Education), $660 (Engineering Management), $650 (Nursing), $550 (Organizational Studies), $615 (Information Systems); per semester $12,652 (D.Sc.). Limited on-campus housing available. Annual average housing cost: $4650, $7670 (including board). Contact Housing Office for both on- and off-campus housing information. Phone: (412)262-8408.

Graduate Studies

Enrollment: 1124 part-time. Faculty: full-time 52, part-time 28. Degrees conferred: M.B.A., M.S., D.Sc., Ph.D.

ADMISSION REQUIREMENTS. Official transcript, two professional recommendations required in support of application. TOEFL required for international applicants. Online application available. GRE/GMAT/MAT strongly recommended. Interview required for M.S. in Communication and Information Systems and D.Sc. Accepts transfer applicants. Apply to Office of Graduate Enrollment at least two months prior to registration. Some programs have earlier deadlines. Rolling admission process. Application fee $35. Phone: (800)762-0097; fax (412)299-2425.

ADMISSION STANDARDS. Selective. Usual minimum average: 2.5 (A = 4)

FINANCIAL AID. Limited to assistantships, loans. Apply to the Financial Aid Office; no specified closing date. Use FAFSA (School code: 003359). Aid available for part-time students.

DEGREE REQUIREMENTS. For M.S.; 33–36 credit hours minimum, depending on program. For M.B.A.: 30–57 credit hours, depending on previous degree and number of foundation courses waived. For D.Sc.: 60 credit program; doctoral candidacy; field project.

FIELDS OF STUDY.
Business Administration. M.B.A.
Business Education. M.S.
Communications and Information Systems. M.S.
Competitive Intelligence Systems. M.S.
Engineering Management. M.S.
Human Resource Management. M.S.
Information Security and Assurance. M.S.
Information Systems Management. M.S.
Information Technology Project Management. M.S.
Instructional Leadership. Includes corporate training, elementary education, English, leadership, mathematics education, sport management. M.S.
Internet Information Systems. M.S.
Nonprofit Management. M.S.
Nursing. Includes leadership and management, nursing education. M.S.
Organizational Studies. Includes employee relations, leadership. M.S.
Taxation. M.S.

ROCHESTER INSTITUTE OF TECHNOLOGY
Rochester, New York 14623-5604
Web site: www.rit.edu

Founded 1829. CGS member. Coed. Private control. Quarter system. Special facilities: Chester F. Carlson Center for Imaging Science, Center for Excellence in Mathematics, Science, and Technology, Center for Integrated Manufacturing Studies. Library: 408,000 volumes, 4300 subscriptions. Total Institute enrollment: 15,000.

Annual tuition: full-time $26,900; part-time $755 per quarter hour. On-campus housing for married students on space-available basis. Annual housing costs: $8451 (including board). Apply to Center for Residence Life for on- and off-campus housing information. Phone: (585)475-8815 (on-campus), (585)475-2575 (off-campus). Day-care facilities available.

Graduate Studies

Graduate study since 1959. Enrollment: full-time 1158, part-time 937. Institute faculty: full-time 500, part-time varies by quarter. Degrees conferred: M.B.A., M.E., M.F.A., M.S., M.S.T., Ph.D.

ADMISSION REQUIREMENTS. Transcripts, personal statement, two letters of recommendation required in support of application. Online application available. GMAT required for M.B.A.; GRE, MAT for some programs. Slide portfolio for some programs. Evidence of proficiency in English (TOEFL or Michigan Test of English administered at RIT) required of international students. Interview required for some departments. Accepts transfer applicants. Apply to Office of Graduate Enrollment Services by March 1; some programs have earlier deadlines. Application fee $50. Phone: (585)475-7284; fax: (585)475-7164; e-mail: gradinfo @rit.edu.

ADMISSION STANDARDS. Selective. Usual minimum average varies by department.

FINANCIAL AID. Annual awards from institutional funds: scholarships, research and teaching assistantships, tuition waivers, Federal W/S, loans. Approved for VA benefits. For scholarships, apply at time of admission to appropriate department head and to Dean of Graduate Studies (but not later that March 15); to Financial Aid Office for all other programs. Phone: (585)475-2186. Use FAFSA. Loans are also available under New York State's Supplemental Higher Education Loan Financing Program. Aid available for part-time students.

DEGREE REQUIREMENTS. For M.S.: 45–72 quarter hours minimum. For M.F.A.: 85–90 quarter hours minimum. For M.S.T.: 48 quarter hours minimum. For M.B.A.: 76 quarter hours minimum. For M.E.: 48 quarter hours minimum. Thesis required for some programs. Ph.D.: as determined by committee review.

FIELDS OF STUDY.

COLLEGE OF APPLIED SCIENCE AND TECHNOLOGY:
Cross-Disciplinary Professional Studies. Individualized study program. M.S.
Environmental, Health, and Safety Management. M.S.
Facility Management. M.S.
Health Systems Administration. M.S.
Hospitality—Tourism Management. M.S.
Human Resource Development. M.S.
Manufacturing and Mechanical Systems Integration. M.S.
Packaging Science. M.S.
Service Management. M.S.
Telecommunication Engineering Technology. M.S.
Training and Instructional Design. M.S.

COLLEGE OF BUSINESS:
Accounting. M.B.A.
Business Administration. M.B.A.
Finance. M.S.
Innovation Management. M.S.
Management. M.S.

COLLEGE OF COMPUTING AND INFORMATION SCIENCES:
Computer Science. M.S.
Computer Security and Information Assurance. M.S.
Computing and Information Sciences. Ph.D.
Game Design and Development. M.S.
Information Technology. M.S.
Learning and Knowledge Management Systems. M.S.
Networking and Systems Administration. M.S.
Software Engineering. M.S.

COLLEGE OF ENGINEERING:
Applied Statistics. M.S.
Computer Engineering. M.S.
Electrical Engineering. M.S.
Engineering Management. M.E.
Industrial Engineering. M.E., M.S.
Manufacturing Engineering. M.E.
Manufacturing Leadership. M.S.
Materials Science and Engineering. M.S.
Mechanical Engineering. M.S.
Microelectronic Engineering. M.S.
Microelectronic Manufacturing Engineering. M.E.
Microsystems Engineering. Ph.D.
Product Development. M.S.
Systems Engineering. M.E.

COLLEGE OF IMAGING ARTS AND SCIENCES:
Art Education. M.S.T.
Ceramics. M.F.A.

Computer Graphics Design. M.F.A.
Fine Arts Studio. M.F.A.
Glass. M.F.A.
Graphic Design. M.F.A.
Imaging Arts/Film. M.F.A.
Imaging Arts/Photography. M.F.A.
Industrial design. M.F.A.
Medical Illustration. M.F.A.
Metals. M.F.A.
Print Media. M.S.
Wood. M.S.

COLLEGE OF LIBERAL ARTS:
Applied Experimental Engineering Psychology. M.S.
Communication and Media Technologies. M.S.
School Psychology. M.S.
Science, Technology, and Public Policy. M.S.

COLLEGE OF SCIENCE:
Applied Mathematics. M.S.
Bioinformatics. M.S.
Chemistry. M.S.
Clinical Chemistry. M.S.
Color Science. M.S., Ph.D.
Environmental Science. M.S.
Imaging Science. M.S., Ph.D.

NATIONAL TECHNICAL INSTITUTE FOR THE DEAF:
Secondary Education of Students Who Are Deaf and Hard of Hearing. M.S.

UNIVERSITY OF ROCHESTER
Rochester, New York 14627-0250
Web site: www.rochester.edu

The University of Rochester, established in 1850, is independent and coeducational, and operates on a semester system. CGS and AAU member. Three of the University's 6 schools and colleges are on the River Campus. The School of Medicine and Dentistry and the School of Nursing are within a 5-minute walk, and the Eastman School of Music is 2 miles away. Special facilities include a large biology-chemistry-mathematics complex, a nuclear structure research laboratory with a 24-MeV tandem Van Degraaff accelerator, the Mees Observatory (at the highest location in the eastern United States), an atomic energy ERDA project (radiation biology and biophysics), a well-staffed computing center, campus-wide access to the Internet, and several hundred microcomputers linked to the campus network, the Managerial Economics Research Center, Center for Environmental Health Sciences, the New York State Center for Optical Technology, Center for Photoinduced Charge Transfer, Center for Superconductive Circuits, the Center for Visual Science, the Laboratory for Laser Energetics, Center for Research in Government Policy and Business. The University's NIH ranking is 40th among all U.S. institutions with 414 awards/grants valued at $162,312,479. According to The Center at University of Florida, the University is ranked 32nd in receipt of Federal Research funds with $208,148,000 and it ranks 43rd for total University research expenditures with $285,768,000. The University's endowment assets rank it 35th, with a value of $1,261,526,000. In 2004, the University awarded 210 doctorates, which ranked it 70th among all U.S. institutions eligible to award that degree. Twenty-four of the University's faculty members have been elected to National Honor Academies and this ranks it 39th among all U.S. institutions. The Library: approximately 3,000,000 volumes, 11,254 subscriptions. Total University enrollment: 10,000.

Tuition: per credit $795, Simon School $1010; Eastman School of Music $820. On-campus housing available; contact Housing Coordinator. Phone: (716)275-5521.

Graduate Studies

Graduate study since 1851. Enrollment: full-time 2300, part-time 700. Graduate faculty: full-time 1000, part-time 200. Degrees conferred: M.A., M.S., M.B.A., M.H.P., M.M., M.A.T., Ed.D., D.M.A., Ph.D.

ADMISSION REQUIREMENTS. Transcripts, three letters of recommendation required in support of application. GRE Subject Tests, GMAT recommended. TOEFL required for international applicants. Accepts transfer applicants. Graduates of unaccredited institutions not considered. Apply by February 1 to department offering specific degree program. Application fee $25 (Simon School $75). Phone: (716)275-2121 (general information number).

ADMISSION STANDARDS. Competitive. Usual minimum average: 3.0 (A = 4).

FINANCIAL AID. Most Ph.D. candidates receive grants, assistantships, or fellowships. For M.A., M.S., M.M., D.M.A., M.B.A. candidates: scholarships, fellowships, tuition waivers, Federal W/S, loans. Approved for VA benefits. To be eligible for aid, new students must apply by February 1. Phone: (585)275-3226. Use FAFSA. Phone appropriate department for information regarding assistantships, fellowships.

DEGREE REQUIREMENTS. For M.A., M.A.T.: 30 semester hours minimum, at least 20 in residence; thesis; final oral exam; for nonthesis option, master's essay for some departments; comprehensive exam. For M.B.A.: 64–67 semester hours minimum, at least 48 semester hours in residence; comprehensive exam; thesis not required. For M.S.: 36–39 credit programs. For Ed.D.: 90 semester hours minimum beyond the bachelor's, comprehensive exam; dissertation; final oral exam. For Ph.D.: 90 semester hours beyond the bachelor's degree or 60 semester hours minimum beyond the master's, at least two consecutive semesters in full-time residence; competence in foreign languages required by some departments; written/oral qualifying exam; dissertation; final oral exam. For D.M.A.: 60 semester hours minimum beyond the master's, at least one year in full-time residence; demonstrated proficiency in performance; oral/written exam; qualifying exam; dissertation; final oral exam. For joint M.D.-Ph.D.: same requirements for both programs individually, although course work and research may overlap.

FIELDS OF STUDY.

COLLEGE OF ARTS AND SCIENCES:
Applied Mathematics. M.S.
Biochemistry. M.S., Ph.D.
Biology. M.S., Ph.D.
Brain and Cognitive Sciences. M.A., Ph.D.
Chemistry. M.S., Ph.D.
Clinical Psychology. Ph.D.
Computer Science. M.S., Ph.D.
Developmental Psychology. Ph.D. (Through the Department of Clinical and Social Psychology.)
Developmental Psychology. Ph.D. (Through the Department of Brain and Cognitive Sciences.)
Economics. M.A., Ph.D.
English. M.A., Ph.D.
Genetics. M.S., Ph.D.
Geological Sciences. M.S., Ph.D.
History. M.A., Ph.D.
Mathematics. M.A., Ph.D.
Mathematics—Statistics. M.A.
Microbiology. M.S.
Microbiology and Immunology. Ph.D.
Neuroscience. M.S., Ph.D.
Philosophy. M.A., Ph.D.
Physics. M.A., M.S., Ph.D.

Physics and Astronomy. Ph.D.
Political Science. M.A., Ph.D.
Psychology. M.A.
Social-Personality Psychology. Ph.D.
Statistics. M.A., Ph.D.
Visual and Cultural Studies. M.A., Ph.D.

SCHOOL OF ENGINEERING AND APPLIED SCIENCES:
Biomedical Engineering. M.S., Ph.D.
Chemical Engineering. M.S., Ph.D.
Electrical Engineering. M.S., Ph.D.
Materials Science. M.S., Ph.D.
Mechanical Engineering. M.S., Ph.D.
Optics. M.S., Ph.D.

EASTMAN SCHOOL OF MUSIC:
Conducting. D.M.A.
Conducting (Choral). M.M.
Jazz Studies and Contemporary Media. M.M.
Music Composition. M.A,, M.M., D.M.A., Ph.D.
Music Education. M.A., M.M., D.M.A., Ph.D.
Music Theory. M.A., Ph.D.
Musicology. M.A., Ph.D.
Pedagogy of Music Theory. M.A.
Performance and Literature. M.M., D.M.A.
Piano Accompanying and Chamber Music. M.M., D.M.A.

MARGARET WARNER GRADUATE SCHOOL OF EDUCATION
AND HUMAN DEVELOPMENT:
Counseling.
Educational Leadership.
Human Development.
Teaching and Curriculum. Includes urban teaching and leadership.

SCHOOL OF MEDICINE AND DENTISTRY:
Biochemistry. M.S., Ph.D.
Biomedical Genetics. M.S., Ph.D.
Biophysics. M.S., Ph.D.
Dental Sciences. M.S.
Epidemiology. Ph.D.
Genetics. M.S., Ph.D.
Health Services Research and Policy. Ph.D.
Marriage and Family Therapy. M.S.
Medical Statistics. M.S.
Microbiology. M.S.
Neurobiology and Anatomy. M.S., Ph.D.
Pathology. M.S., Ph.D.
Pharmacology. M.S., Ph.D.
Physiology. M.S., Ph.D.
Public Health. M.P.H.
Statistics. M.A., Ph.D.
Toxicology. M.S., Ph.D.

SCHOOL OF NURSING:
Health Practice Research. Ph.D.
Leadership Programs. Includes clinical nurse leader for RNs, disaster response and emergency preparedness, health promotion, education and technology. M.S.
Nurse Practitioner Programs. Includes acute care nurse, adult nurse, family nurse, care of children and families/pediatric nurse, psychiatric mental health nurse (adult/family, child adolescent). M.S.
Nursing Practice. D.N.P.

WILLIAM E. SIMON GRADUATE SCHOOL
OF BUSINESS ADMINISTRATION:
Accountancy. M.S.
Business Administration. Includes specializations in accounting and information systems, business and public policy, competitive and organizational strategy, computers and information systems, corporate accounting, electronic commerce, entrepreneurship, finance, health sciences management, international management, marketing, operations management—manufacturing, operations management—service, public accounting. M.B.A., Ph.D.
Finance. M.S.
Information Management. M.S.
Manufacturing Management. M.S.
Medical Management. M.S.
Science and Technology Commercialization. M.S.
Technology Transfer and Commercialization. M.S.

DOCTORAL PROGRAMS:
Accountancy.
Applied Economics.
Applied Statistics.
Computed Information Systems.
Competitive and Organizational Strategy.
Finance.
Macroeconomics.
Management Science.
Marketing.
Operational Management.

School of Medicine and Dentistry (14642)

Web site: www.urmc.rochester.edu

Founded 1920. Library: 200,000 volumes, 3000 subscriptions. NIH ranking is 40th among all U.S. institutions with 414 awards/grants worth $162,312,479.

Annual tuition: $40,384. On-campus housing available for married, single students. Apply to the Housing Coordinator, Medical Center. Total average figure for all other expenses: $15,500.

Enrollment: first-year class 100, total 402 (men 46%, women 54%, minorities 33%, state residents 40%); postgraduates 350. Faculty: full-time 1302, part-time 800. Degrees conferred: M.D., M.D.-M.B.A., M.D.-M.P.H., M.D.-M.S., M.D.-Ph.D. (Medical Scientist Training Program), Graduate study only in Dentistry, no D.D.S.

ADMISSION REQUIREMENTS. For M.D.: AMCAS report, transcripts, letters of recommendation, personal statement, MCAT, supplemental application required in support of application. Applicants must have completed at least three years of college study. Interview by invitation only. Does not have EDP. Does not accept transfer or foreign applicants. Apply to Director of Admission (Medical Center Box 601A) after June 1, before November 15. Application fee $75. Phone: (585)275-4542; fax: (585)756-5479.

ADMISSION STANDARDS. Competitive. Accepts about 7.5% of all applicants. Number of applications 3449 (2517 out-of-state); number interviewed 636 (420 out-of-state); number of acceptances 260 (170 out-of-state); number enrolled 100 (63 out-of-state). Mean Composite MCAT 10.6; mean UGPA 3.66. *U.S. News & World Report* ranking is in the top 34 of all U.S. medical research schools, 13th in primary care.

FINANCIAL AID. For M.D.: scholarships, Federal and private loans. Apply to Financial Aid Office. Phone: (585)275-4523. MSTP funded by NIH. Use FAFSA (School code: G24601). About 92% of students receive some aid from School.

DEGREE REQUIREMENTS. For M.D.: satisfactory completion of four-year program. For M.S., Ph.D., see Graduate Studies above.

FIELDS OF GRADUATE STUDY.
Biochemistry, Molecular, and Cell Biology. Ph.D.
Biological Engineering. Ph.D.
Biophysics. Ph.D.
Biostatistics. Ph.D.
Clinical Investigation. M.S.
Dental Sciences. M.S.

Epidemiology. M.P.H., Ph.D.
Genetics, Genomics, and Development. Ph.D.
Health Care Management. M.B.A.
Health Services Research and Policy. Ph.D.
Marriage and Family Therapy. M.S.
Medical Neurobiology. M.S.
Medical Statistics. M.S.
Microbiology. M.S.
Microbiology and Immunology. Ph.D.
Neuroscience. Ph.D.
Pathology. Ph.D.
Pharmacology. Ph.D.
Physiology. Ph.D.
Public Health. M.P.H.
Statistics. M.A., Ph.D.
Toxicology. Ph.D.

THE ROCKEFELLER UNIVERSITY
New York, New York 10065
Web site: www.rockefeller.edu

Founded 1901. CGS member. Coed. Private control. Graduate study only. Special facilities: Center for Biochemistry, Structural Biology, and Chemistry, Bio-Imaging Resource Center, Chemical Biology Spectroscopy Resource Center, DNA Sequencing Resource Center, Flow Cytometry Resource Center, Gene Array Resource Center, High-Throughput Screening Resource Center, Center for Human Genetics, Laboratory Animal Research Center, Media and Glassware Resource Center, Media Resource Center, Protein Resource Center, Research Center for Ecology and Ethology, Center for Research on Alzheimer's Disease, Center for Studies in Physics and Biology. According to The Center at University of Florida, the University is ranked 72nd for total University research expenditures with $192,143,000. The University's endowment assets rank it 30th, with a value of $1,394,736,000. In 2004, 45 of the University's faculty members were elected to National Honor Academies and this ranks it 22nd among all U.S. institutions. The Library: approximately 200,000 volumes, 900 subscriptions.

No tuition charge. On-campus housing for married and single students. Average academic year housing costs: $7000–$10,000. Contact the Office of the Dean for all housing information.

Graduate Programs

Established 1954. Enrollment: full-time 225, part-time 179. Faculty: full-time 265. Degree conferred: Ph.D., M.D.-Ph.D. (M.D. through Weill Medical College of Cornell.)

ADMISSION REQUIREMENTS. Transcripts, at least three letters of recommendation, letter from applicant, personal statement, interview required in support of application. Online application available. GRE and GRE Subject Test strongly recommended. TOEFL recommended for international applicants. Applications should be completed by December 1, October 16 for M.D.-Ph.D. applicants. Address inquiries to Office of Graduate Studies. Application fee $80. Phone: (212)327-8086; fax: (212)327-8505; e-mail: phd@mail.rockefeller.edu.

ADMISSION STANDARDS. Very competitive.

FINANCIAL AID. All students receive a stipend and tuition remission.

DEGREE REQUIREMENTS. For Ph.D.: Five years of research and study generally required; dissertation; final oral exam.

FIELDS OF STUDY.
Biochemistry, Structural Biology, Chemistry.
Immunology, Virology, and Microbiology.
Molecular, Cell, and Developmental Biology.
Medical Sciences and Human Genetics.
Neuroscience.
Physics and Mathematical Biology.

ROCKFORD COLLEGE
Rockford, Illinois 61108-2393
Web site: www.rockford.edu

Founded 1847. Located on new campus 90 miles NW of Chicago. Coed. Private control. Semester system. Library: 165,000 volumes, 7400 microforms.

Tuition: per credit $610. On-campus housing for graduate students; no married student housing. Average academic year housing costs: $6500. Contact the Dean, Student Services for housing information. Phone: (815)226-4045.

Graduate Study

Graduate study since 1950. Enrollment: full-time 51, part-time 300. Faculty: full-time 15, part-time 27. Courses offered evenings and Summer. College does not seek full-time or nonlocal students, although such applicants are considered. Degrees conferred: M.A.T., M.B.A.

ADMISSION REQUIREMENTS. Transcripts, GRE/GMAT for M.B.A., three letters of recommendation required in support of application. TOEFL required for international applicants. Interview sometimes required. Accepts transfer applicants. Apply to Office of Graduate Studies prior to registration. Application fee $50. Phone: (815)226-4040; fax: (815)226-4119.

ADMISSION STANDARDS. Selective. Usual minimum average: 3.0 (A = 4).

FINANCIAL AID. Grants, loans. Approved for VA benefits. Apply to Office of Graduate Studies; no specified closing date. Phone: (815)226-3383; fax: (815)226-4119. Use FAFSA.

DEGREE REQUIREMENTS. For M.A.T.: 32–36 semester hours minimum, at least 24 in residence; candidacy; no language requirement; thesis required for some programs. For M.B.A.: 36 semester hours minimum; prerequisite courses or competency test, in economics, accounting, finance, statistics, mathematics; ten required courses and two electives required.

FIELDS OF STUDY.
Business Administration.
Elementary Education.
Instructional Strategies.
Reading
Secondary Education. Includes modern languages (Spanish, French, German), physical education, theatre arts, visual arts.
Special Education.

ROGER WILLIAMS UNIVERSITY
Bristol, Rhode Island 02809
Web site: www.rwu.edu

Founded 1967. Located on a peninsula 20 miles from Providence. Coed. Private control. Semester system. Library: 168,460 volumes, 1225 subscriptions. Total University enrollment: 1500.

Ralph R. Papitto School of Law

Web site: law.rwu.edu/

Established 1992. Located on main campus. ABA approved since 1995. Semester system. Full-time, part-time study. Special facilities: Marine Affair Institute, Feinstein Institute. Law library: 287,384 volumes, 3657 subscriptions; has LEXIS, NEXIS, WESTLAW, DIALOG; has more than 200 network connections.

Tuition: per credit $990. On-campus housing available for both single and married students. Contact the University's Housing Office for both on- and off-campus housing information. Law students tend to live off-campus. Off-campus housing and personal expenses: approximately $16,200.

Enrollment: first-year class full-time 198; total 511 (men 50%, women 50%). Faculty: full-time 18, part-time 16. Student to faculty ratio 19.9 to 1. Degrees conferred: J.D. joint degree programs with the University of Rhode Island: J.D.-M.S.C.P., J.D.-M.M.A., J.D.-M.L.R.H.R. (Labor Relations and Human Resources).

ADMISSION REQUIREMENTS. LSDAS Law School report, LSAT (not later that February test date; if more than one LSAT, highest is used), bachelor's degree from an accredited institution, personal statement, résumé, one letter of recommendation, transcripts (must show all schools attended and at least three years of study) required in support of application. International applicants use J.D. Credential Assembly Service (LSAC) and submit TOEFL. Applicants must have received bachelor's degree prior to enrollment. Interview and recommendations not required. Accepts transfer candidates. Apply to Office of Admission after September 30, before April 15 (priority deadline). First-year students admitted Fall only. Rolling admissions process; notification starts in January and is finished when class is filled. Application fee $60. Phone: (800)633-2727, (401)254-4555; fax: (401)254-4516.

ADMISSION STANDARDS. Selective. Accepts approximately 41% of all students. Number of applicants 1743; number of acceptances 716; number enrolled 198; LSAT (75% of students have a score at or above 151); GPA (75% of students have a GPA at or above 2.94). *U.S. News & World Report* ranking is in the fourth tier of all U.S. law schools.

FINANCIAL AID. Scholarships, merit scholarships, minority scholarships, Grants-in-Aid, institutional loans; Federal loans and Federal W/S offered through University's Financial Aid Office. For scholarships apply to Admissions Office after January 1 before May 15; use School's Financial Aid Form. For all other programs apply to the University's Office of Financial Aid. Phone: (401)254-4641. Use FAFSA (School code: 003410), also submit Financial Aid Transcript, Federal Income Tax forms. Approximately 5% (full-time), 2–6% (part-time) of 1st year class received scholarships/Grants-in-Aid. Approximately 41% of students receive some form of financial assistance. Average scholarships grant $3000 for both full- and part-time.

DEGREE REQUIREMENTS. For J.D.: 90 (54 required) credits with a GPA of at least 2.0 (A = 4), plus completion of upper-divisional writing course; three-year program, four-year part-time program. For J.D.-M.C.P., J.D.-M.M.A., J.D.-M.S.: four-year programs rather than five-year programs if both degrees are taken consecutively.

ROLLINS COLLEGE

Winter Park, Florida 32789-4499
Web site: www.rollins.edu

Established 1885. Located adjacent to Orlando. Coed. Private control. Semester system. Special facilities: Leadership Center, Entrepreneurship Center, Philanthropy and Nonprofit Leadership

Center. Library: 288,323 volumes, 1500 subscriptions. Total College enrollment: 2500.

No on-campus housing available for graduate students. Annual average housing cost: $12,000. Contact the Office of Residential Life for off-campus housing information. Phone: (407)646-2405.

Roy E. Crummer Graduate School of Business

Web site: www.crummer.rollins.edu

Graduate study since 1957. Total tuition cost for degree: E.A.M.B.A. $56,600; part-time C.M.B.A. $59,000; P.M.B.A. $46,400; S.M.B.A. $55,491. Enrollment: full-time 224, part-time 212. Faculty: full-time 23, part-time 4. Degree conferred: M.B.A.

ADMISSION REQUIREMENTS. Transcripts, GMAT, essays, two letters of recommendation, personal interview required in support of School's application. TOEFL (minimum score 550) required for international applicants. Apply by April 1 (Fall), December 1 (Spring). Rolling admissions process. Late applications considered on a space available basis. Application fee $50. Phone: (407)691-1195; fax: (407)628-6336.

ADMISSION STANDARDS. Selective. Mean LSAT: full-time 569, part-time 537; full- and part-time mean GPA: 3.23 (A = 4). Usual minimum average: 3.2 (A = 4).

FINANCIAL AID. Scholarships, fellowships, administrative assistantships, grants, Federal W/S, loans. Apply by March 1 to the Office of Student Financial Planning. Phone: (407)646-2395. Use FAFSA (School code: 001515) and institutional FAF. About 50% of students receive aid other than loans from College and outside sources.

DEGREE REQUIREMENTS. For E.A.M.B.A. (Early Advantage): 21 month full-time program. For C.M.B.A. (Corporate): 19 month part-time program for executives. For P.M.B.A. (Professional): 32 month part-time evening program. For S.M.B.A. (Saturday): 19 month part-time Saturday program.

FIELD OF STUDY.
Business Administration.

Hamilton Holt School—Graduate Division

Tuition: per credit Counseling $422, Human Resources $430, Teaching $364, Liberal Studies $310. Enrollment: full-time 186, part-time 129. Faculty: full-time 31, part-time 11. Degrees conferred: M.A., M.A.T., M.H.R., M.L.S.

ADMISSION REQUIREMENTS. Transcripts, GRE required in support of School's application. TOEFL required for international applicants. Accepts transfer applicants. Graduates of unaccredited institutions not considered. Apply to Coordinator of Records and Registration; no specified closing date. Rolling admissions process. Late applications considered on a space available basis. Application fee $50. Phone: (407)646-2232; fax: (407)646-1551.

ADMISSION STANDARDS. Selective. Usual minimum average: 2.75 (A = 4).

FINANCIAL AID. Scholarships, fellowships, assistantships, loans. Approved for VA benefits. Apply by March 15 to the Dean for scholarships, fellowships, assistantships; to Financial Aid Office for loans. Phone: (407)646-2395. Use FAFSA (College code: 001515) and institutional FAF. About 35% of students receive aid other than loans from College and outside sources. Aid available for part-time students.

DEGREE REQUIREMENTS. For master's: 30–36 credit hour program; thesis/nonthesis option.

FIELDS OF STUDY.
Elementary Education. M.A.T., M.Ed.
Human Resources. M.H.R.
Liberal Studies. M.L.S.
Mental Health Counseling. M.A.

ROOSEVELT UNIVERSITY

Chicago, Illinois 60605-1394
Web site: www.roosevelt.edu

Founded 1945. Coed. Private control. Semester system. Branch campus at Schaumburg, IL (60173). Library: 225,000 volumes, 1200 subscriptions. Total University enrollment: 7300.

Tuition: per hour $688. Limit on-campus housing for single students only. Annual housing costs: $7160–$9356. Apply to Office of Residence Life for housing information. Phone: (312)341-2004.

Graduate Division

Enrollment: full-time 887, part-time 2400. Faculty: full-time 212, part-time 76. Degrees conferred: M.A., M.B.A., M.M., M.P.A., M.S., M.S.J., M.G.S.

ADMISSION REQUIREMENTS. Transcripts required in support of application. GMAT required for Business. Accepts transfer applicants. Apply to Coordinator of Graduate Admissions by June 1 (Fall), December 1 (Spring); international students apply three months prior to the intended semester. Application fee $25, $35 for international applicants. Phone: (877)277-5978; fax: (312) 341-3523. Schaumberg Admission Office phone: (877)277-5978; fax: (847)619-8636.

ADMISSION STANDARDS. Selective. Usual minimum average: 2.7–3.0 (A = 4) depending on program.

FINANCIAL AID. Scholarships, teaching assistantships, grants, tuition waivers, Federal W/S, loans. Approved for VA benefits. Apply by February 15 to Graduate Admissions for scholarships; to appropriate department chair for assistantships; to Financial Aid Office for all other programs. Phone: (312)341-3565. Use FAFSA. Limited merit awards available for part-time students.

DEGREE REQUIREMENTS. For master's: 30–60 semester hours of graduate work; thesis/nonthesis option; final written/oral exam; research paper.

FIELDS OF STUDY.
Accounting. M.S.
Acting. M.F.A.
Biotechnology and Chemical Sciences. M.S.
Business Administration. Includes E.M.B.A. in international leadership. M.B.A.
Clinical Profession Psychology. M.A.
Clinical Psychology. M.A., Ph.D.
Composition. M.M.
Computer Science. M.S.
Counseling and Human Services. M.A.
Creative Writing. M.F.A.
Directing. M.A.
Directing/Dramaturgy. M.F.A.
Early Childhood Education. M.A.
Early Childhood Professions. M.S.
Economics. M.A.
Educational Leadership. M.A., Ed.D.
Elementary Education. M.A.
English. M.A.
History. M.A.
Hospitality and Tourism Management. M.S.
Human Resource Management. M.S.
Industrial/Organization. M.S.

Information Systems. M.S.
Integrated Marketing Communication. M.S.
International Business. M.S.
Jazz Studies. M.M.
Journalism. M.S.
Legal Studies. M.A., M.P.A.
Mathematics. M.S.
Music Theory. M.M.
Musicology. M.M.
Orchestral Studies. M.M.
Performance. M.M.
Piano Performance. M.M.
Public Administration. M.P.A.
Reading. M.A.
Real Estate. M.S.
Secondary Education. M.A.
Sociology. M.A.
Spanish. M.A.
Special Education. M.A.
Teacher Leadership. M.A.
Telecommunications. M.S.
Theatre Arts. M.A.
Training and Development. M.A.
Women's and Gender Studies. M.A.

ROSALIND FRANKLIN UNIVERSITY OF MEDICINE AND SCIENCES

3333 Green Bay Road
North Chicago, Illinois 60064-3095
Web site: www.rosalindfranklin.edu

Founded in 1912. University established in 1968, with Chicago Medical School as core component of three allied units. Named change in 2004. CGS member. Private control. Quarter system. Special facilities: Electron Microscopy Center, Protein Sequence Laboratory, Special Pathogen-Free Swine Facility. Library: 100,000 volumes, 1200 subscriptions. Total University enrollment: 1500.

On- and off-campus housing available. Contact Office of Student Housing. Phone (847)578-8350. Average living expenses: $1600 per month.

School of Graduate and Postdoctoral Studies

Graduate study since 1968. Annual tuition: $20,496.

Enrollment: full- and part-time 313. Faculty: full- and part-time 92. Degrees conferred: M.S., Ph.D.

ADMISSION REQUIREMENTS. Completed application, transcripts, three letters of recommendation, GRE required in support of School's application. Interview recommended. TOEFL, TWE, financial statement required for international applicants. Graduates of unaccredited institutions not considered. Early application advised for applicants seeking fellowships. All applications must be completed by November 1; December 1 for Clinical Psychology. Apply to the Office of Graduate Admissions. Application fee $50. Phone: (847)578-3209.

ADMISSION STANDARDS. Competitive for most departments. Usual minimum average: 3.0 (A = 4).

FINANCIAL AID. Fellowships, research assistantships, research grants, tuition waivers, Federal and private loans. Approved for VA benefits. Apply to chairman of department for fellowships and assistantships; to the Office of Financial Aid for loans. Phone: (847)578-3217. Use FAFSA (School code: 001659). Almost all students in basic medical science doctoral programs who are in good standing receive some sort of financial aid through University fellowships, research grants, and/or other sources.

DEGREE REQUIREMENTS. For M.S. (research master's): minimum of 30 units of course work and 15 units of research; minimum of one year of full-time residence; thesis; final oral exam. For Ph.D.: minimum of 60 units of course work and 75 units of research credit; minimum of two years of full-time residence; preliminary exam; thesis; final oral exam.

FIELDS OF STUDY.
Cancer/Cell/Developmental Biology.
Clinical Psychology.
Neurosciences.
Structural Biology.

Chicago Medical School

Founded 1912. Has NIH grants worth $26,700,000.

Annual tuition: $36,900. No on-campus housing available. Total average cost for all other expenses: $16,000.

Enrollment: first-year class 185 (EDP 5); total full-time 750 (men 57%, women 43%, minorities 46%, state residents 24%). School faculty: full-time 683, part-time 430. Degrees conferred: M.D., M.D.-Ph.D.

ADMISSION REQUIREMENTS. AMCAS report, transcripts, references, MCAT, interview, supplemental school specific application required in support of application. Online application available. Applicants must have completed at least four years of college study. Transfer applicants considered. Has EDP; apply between June 1 and August 1. Apply to Office of Admissions after June 15, before November 1 (firm). Application fee $95. Phone: (847)578-3204; fax: (847)578-3284.

ADMISSION STANDARDS. Selective. Accepts about 7.5% of all applicants. Number of applications 6442 (5202 out-of-state); number interviewed 589 (485 out-of-state); number of acceptance 485 (383 out-of-state); number enrolled 185 (148 out-of-state). Mean Composite MCAT 9.7; mean UGPA 3.45.

FINANCIAL AID. Scholarships, loans. Apply to Associate Dean (Student Affairs); no specified closing date. Phone: (847)578-3217. Use FAFSA. About 40% of students receive aid other than loans from School funds.

DEGREE REQUIREMENTS. For M.D.: satisfactory completion of three-, four-, or five-year program; must pass Step 1 and Step 2 of the USMLE before graduation. For M.D.-M.S.: satisfactory completion of five-year program. For M.D.-Ph.D.: satisfactory completion of program.

FIELDS OF GRADUATE STUDY.
Biochemistry and Molecular Biology.
Biomedical Sciences. Interdisciplinary.
Cell Biology and Anatomy.
Cellular and Molecular Pharmacology.
Clinical Psychology.
Microbiology and Immunology.
Molecular Cell Sciences.
Neuroscience.
Pathology.
Physiology and Biophysics.

ROSE-HULMAN INSTITUTE OF TECHNOLOGY
Terre Haute, Indiana 47803-3920
Web site: www.rose-hulman.edu

Founded 1874. Coed. Private control. Quarter system. Special facilities: digital computers, high-flux neutron generator, observatory, Center of Applied Optics, Center of Technology Assessment. Library: more than 150,000 volumes, 589 subscriptions. Total enrollment: 2000.

Annual tuition: full-time $28,530, per credit $840. On-campus housing for 700 students; none for graduate students. Average academic year housing costs: $4236, $7419 (including board). Apply to Dean of Students. Phone: (812)877-8257.

Graduate Studies

Graduate study since 1894. Enrollment: full-time 38, part-time 86. Institute faculty: full-time 77, part-time 2. Degree conferred: M.S.

ADMISSION REQUIREMENTS. Transcripts, GRE, three references required in support of application. Interview desirable. TOEFL (minimum score 580) and GRE required for international applicants. Accepts transfer applicants. Apply to Dean for Research and Graduate Studies; no specified closing dates, though preference is given to those applying by February 1. Application fee: none. Phone: (800)248-7448; fax: (812)877-8061.

ADMISSION STANDARDS. Selective. Usual minimum average: 3.0 (A = 4).

FINANCIAL AID. Annual awards from institutional funds: international fellowships, graduate assistantships, research assistantships, grants, tuition waivers, Federal W/S, loans. Apply by April 1 to Dean of Research and Graduate Studies for fellowships, assistantships; to Financial Aid Office for all other programs. Phone: (812)877-8403. Use FAFSA. About 60–80% of students receive aid other than loans from Institute and outside sources.

DEGREE REQUIREMENTS. For M.S.: 51 quarter hours minimum; thesis; final oral exam; no language requirement.

FIELDS OF STUDY.
Biomedical Engineering.
Chemical Engineering.
Civil Engineering.
Electrical and Computer Engineering.
Engineering Management.
Environmental Engineering.
Mechanical Engineering.
Optical Engineering.

ROWAN UNIVERSITY
Glassboro, New Jersey 08028-1701
Web site: www.rowan.edu

Founded 1923. Name changed in 1992, granted university status in 1997. Located 35 miles SE of Philadelphia. CGS member. Coed. State Control. Semester system. Library: 350,000 volumes, 2000 subscriptions; is a U.S. government depository. Total University enrollment: 10,000.

Annual tuition: full-time resident $9886, nonresident $14,662; per credit resident $594, nonresident $880. No on- or off-campus housing available. Day-care facilities available.

Graduate School

Graduate study since 1950. Enrollment: full-time 177, part-time 570. Graduate faculty: full-time 110, part-time 20. Degrees conferred: M.A., M.B.A., M.S. in Teaching.

ADMISSION REQUIREMENTS. Transcripts, letters of recommendation, GRE/GMAT/MAT/NTE required in support of application. Personal interview required for some programs. TOEFL required for international applicants. Interview required by some departments. Accepts transfer applicants. Apply to Graduate Admissions Office prior to registration. Application fee $50. Phone: (856)256-4050; fax (856)256-4436.

ADMISSION STANDARDS. Selective. Usual minimum average: 2.8 for last 60 credits (A = 4).

FINANCIAL AID. Annual awards from institutional funds: graduate and residence assistantships (non-teaching), internships, tuition waivers, Federal W/S, loans. Apply to Graduate Office. Phone: (856)256-4250. Use FAFSA. About 10% of students receive aid from University. Aid available for part-time students.

DEGREE REQUIREMENTS. For master's: 32–48 credit hours minimum; thesis or final project; written comprehensive exam.

FIELDS OF STUDY.

COLLEGE OF BUSINESS:
Business Administration. Includes specializations in accounting, entrepreneurship, finance. M.B.A.

COLLEGE OF COMMUNICATION:
Public Relations. M.A.
Writing. M.A.

COLLEGE OF EDUCATION:
Counseling in Educational Settings. M.A.
Educational Leadership. Ed.D.
Educational Services. Includes school psychologist specialist. Ed.S.
Higher Education. M.A.
Learning Disabilities. M.A.
Reading. M.A.
School Administration. M.A.
School and Public Librarianship. M.A.
School Psychology. M.A.
Special Education. M.A.
Standards-Based Practice. M.Ed.
Supervision and Curriculum Development. M.A.
Teaching. Includes elementary/secondary. Collaborative teaching, theatre education. M.S T.

COLLEGE OF ENGINEERING:
Chemical Engineering.
Civil and Environmental Engineering.
Electrical and Computer Engineering.
Mechanical Engineering.

COLLEGE OF FINE AND PERFORMING ARTS:
Music. M.M.
Theatre. M.A.

COLLEGE OF LIBERAL ARTS AND SCIENCES:
Criminal Justice. M.A.
Mathematics. M.A.
Mental Health Counseling and Applied Psychology. M.A.

RUSH UNIVERSITY
Chicago, Illinois 60612-3832
Web site: www.rushu.rush.edu

Private control. Special facilities: Computer Research Institute, Comparative Research Center, Electron Microscope. The University's NIH ranking is 111th among all U.S. institutions with 80 awards/grants worth $44,559,595. Library: 596,600 volumes, 2050 subscriptions. Total University enrollment at main campus: 1350.

On-campus rooms and apartments available for both single and married students. Annual on-campus housing cost: single students $5200 (room only), married students $8960. Contact Admissions Office for both on- and off-campus housing information. Medical students tend to live off-campus. Off-campus housing and personal expenses: approximately $17,500.

Rush Medical College

Established 1837, closed in 1942. Reopened in 1971 and merged with Presbyterian-St. Luke's Medical Center. Located on the University's campus. Quarter system. Affiliated hospitals: Holy Family Medical Center, Illinois Masonic Medical, Lake Forest Hospital, Oak Park Hospital, Riverside Medical Center, Rush-Copley Medical, Rush North Shore Medical Center, Westlake Community Hospital, Johnston R. Bowman Health Center for the Elderly. Special programs: Primary Care Preceptorships. Library: 97,000 volumes, 2050 subscriptions.
Annual tuition: $43,680.
Enrollment: first-year class 128, total 527 (men 42%, women 52%, minorities 40%, state residents 80%). Faculty: full-time 462, part-time 179. Degrees conferred: M.D., M.D.-M.S., M.D.-Ph.D.

ADMISSION REQUIREMENTS. AMCAS report, transcripts, MCAT, two recommendations (one from premedical committee), supplemental application required in support of application. Interview by invitation only. Preference given to state residents. Will consider transfer applicants on a space-available basis. Has EDP; apply between June 1 and August 1. Apply through AMCAS after June 1, before November 1. Application fee $65. Phone: (312)942-6913; fax: (312)942-2333; e-mail: rmc_admissions@rush.edu.

ADMISSION STANDARDS. Competitive. Accepts about 6% of all applicants. Number of applications 4247 (2925 out-of-state); number interviewed 458 (95 out-of-state); number of acceptances 263 (69 out-of-state), number enrolled 128 (22 out-of-state). Mean Composite MCAT 10.1; mean UGPA 3.63.

FINANCIAL AID. Scholarships, assistantships, loans, grants. Apply to Financial Aid Office after acceptance; before May 1. Phone: (312)942-6256. Use FAFSA (College code: 009800). About 87% of students receive some aid from College.

DEGREE REQUIREMENTS. For M.D.: satisfactory completion of four-year curricular plan; all students must pass USMLE Step 1 prior to entering third year and must take USMLE Step 2 and record a score prior to awarding of M.D. For M.D.-Ph.D.: generally a seven-year program.

FIELDS OF GRADUATE STUDY.
Anatomy and Cell Biology.
Biochemistry.
Immunology.
Medical Physics.
Microbiology.
Molecular Biophysics and Physiology.
Neurosciences.
Pharmacology.
Physiology.

RUTGERS, THE STATE UNIVERSITY OF NEW JERSEY, CAMDEN
Camden, New Jersey 08102-1401
Web site: camden-www.rutgers.edu

Established 1950. Coed. State control. Semester system. Library: 300,000 volumes, 1300 subscriptions. Campus enrollment: 5000.

Annual tuition: full-time resident $12,380, nonresident $18,404; per credit resident $515, nonresident $766. On-campus housing available. Average academic year housing costs: $5000 for single students, $9200 for married students. Contact the Housing Office for both on- and off-campus housing information. Phone: (856) 225-6471.

Graduate School

Established 1981. Enrollment: total full-time 45, part-time 250. Faculty: full-time 82, part-time 18. Degrees conferred: M.A., M.S., M.P.A., M.P.T.

ADMISSION REQUIREMENTS. Transcripts, GRE/GMAT required in support of School's application. Online application available. TOEFL required for international applicants. Accepts transfer applicants. Graduates of unaccredited institutions not considered. Apply to Director of Graduate Admissions by July 1 (Fall), December 1 (Spring); for P.T. program, December 15 (Fall admission only). Application fee $50. Phone: (856)225-6104; fax: (856)225-6498.

ADMISSION STANDARDS. Competitive. Usual minimum average: 2.5 (A = 4).

FINANCIAL AID. Annual awards from institutional funds: fellowships, teaching assistantships, research assistantships, internships, grants, Federal W/S, loans. Approved for VA benefits. Apply by March 15 to Dean for assistantships; to Director of Financial Aid for all other programs. Phone: (609)225-6039. Use FAFSA.

DEGREE REQUIREMENTS. Essentially the same as those for main campus.

FIELDS OF STUDY.
Biology.
Chemistry.
Childhood Studies.
Computer Science.
Criminal Justice.
English.
History. Includes American, public.
Liberal Studies.
Mathematical Sciences.
Physical Therapy.
Psychology.
Public Policy and Administration.
Social Work.

School of Business

Web site: camden-www.rutgers.edu

Established 1988. Public control. Accredited programs: M.B.A. Courses offered in Atlantic City. Semester system.

Annual tuition: full-time resident $17,162, nonresident $25,944; part-time per credit resident $710, nonresident $1076. Enrollment: total full-time 13, part-time 169 (men 75%, women 25%). Faculty: full-time 32, part-time 4; all have Ph.D./D.B.A. Degrees conferred: M.B.A., M.B.A.-J.D.

ADMISSION REQUIREMENTS. All applicants should have a bachelor's degree from a recognized institution of higher education; a strong mathematics background; a 2.5 GPA (A = 4); and a GMAT score of 500. Admission is based on the formula 200 × UGPA + GMAT. Beginning students are admitted Fall and Spring. U.S. citizens apply by August 1 (Fall), December 1 (Spring), April 1 (Summer); international students apply by December 12 (Fall only). Submit an application, GMAT results (will accept GMAT test results from the last five years, latest acceptable date is June), official transcripts from each undergraduate/graduate school attended, three letters of recommendation, personal statement, résumé (prefers at least four years of work experience), and an application fee of $50 to the Office of Graduate and Undergraduate Admission. Phone: (732)932-4636. Accepts transfer candidates. In addition, international students (whose native language is other than English) should submit a TOEFL report (minimum score 550), certified translations and evaluations of all official transcripts, recommendation should be in English or with certified translations, proof of health/immunization certificate, and proof of sufficient financial resources for one year of academic study. On-campus visits are encouraged. Joint degree applicants must apply to and be accepted to both schools, contact the admissions office for current information and specific admissions requirements. Rolling admissions process; notification is made within two weeks of receipt of completed application and supporting documents.

ADMISSION STANDARDS. Selective. Mean GMAT: 566; mean GPA: 3.2 (A = 4).

FINANCIAL AID. Graduate and Professional Scholar awards, New Jersey State Grants, research assistantships, Federal Perkins Loans, Federal W/S, loans. Assistantships may be available for joint degree candidates. Financial Aid applications and information are generally included with the admissions materials; apply by April 1. Request assistantship information from the School of Business. Contact the University's Financial Aid Office for current need-based financial aid information. Phone: (609)225-2074. Use FAFSA (School code: 004741), also submit Financial Aid Transcript, Federal Income Tax forms. Approximately 5% of students receive some form of financial assistance. Aid available for part-time students.

DEGREE REQUIREMENTS. For M.B.A.: 36–60 credit program including 24 elective credits, one- to two-year program; degree program must be completed in six years. For M.B.A.-J.D.: 108–120 credit, four- to five-year program.

M.B.A. FIELDS OF CONCENTRATION.
Accounting.
E-commerce and Information Technology.
Finance.
Health Care Management.
International Business.
Management.
Marketing.
Operations Management.

School of Law (08102-1203)

Web site: camlaw.rutgers.edu

Established 1926. ABA approved since 1951. AALS member. Public control. Semester system. Law library: 439,801 volumes, 4457 subscriptions; has LEXIS, NEXIS, WESTLAW; has more than 175 network connections.

Annual tuition: resident $19,867, nonresident $28,220; part-time resident $15,851, nonresident $18,500. No on-campus housing available. Total average annual additional expenses: $13,684.

Enrollment: first-year class 175 (day), 50 (evening); total day and evening 766 (men 60%, women 40%, minorities 21%). Faculty: full-time 42, part-time 50. Student to faculty ratio is 15.7 to 1. Degrees conferred: J.D., J.D.-M.A. (Political Science), J.D.-M.B.A., J.D.-M.C.R.P., J.D.-M.P.A., J.D.-M.S.W.

ADMISSION REQUIREMENTS. LSDAS Law School report, bachelor's degree, transcripts, letters of recommendation, LSAT, personal statement required in support of application. Online application available. Interview sometimes required. Accepts transfer applicants. Graduates of unaccredited colleges not considered. Apply to Admissions Office by April 1. Application fee $60. Admits Fall only. Phone: (800)466-7561; fax: (856)225-6537.

ADMISSION STANDARDS. Selective. Accepts approximately 14% of full-time and 9% of part-time students. Number of full-time applicants 2481, part-time 2481; number of full-time acceptances 344, part-time 140; number of full-time enrolled 121, part-time 31; LSAT (75% of full-time students have a score at or above 159, part-time 154); GPA (75% of full-time students have a GPA at or above 3.10, part-time 3.10). *U.S. News & World Report* ranking is in the second tier (tied at 70th) of all U.S. law schools.

FINANCIAL AID. Scholarships, fellowships, Federal W/S, loans, legal employment. Apply to Director of Financial Aid by March 15. Phone: (856)225-6039. Use FAFSA (School code: 004741) and Institutional financial aid application. About 40% of full-time and 8% of part-time students receive some aid from School.

DEGREE REQUIREMENTS. For J.D.: 84 credits minimum, at least final two terms in residence. Evening program: nine semesters plus one summer session. For master's degrees: see Graduate School listing, main campus, below.

RUTGERS UNIVERSITY
New Brunswick, New Jersey 08901
Web site: www.rutgers.edu

Established 1766. Located 33 miles SW of New York City. CGS and AAU member. Coed. State control. Semester system. Special facilities: Center for Advanced Biotechnology and Medicine, Center for Advanced Food Technology, Center for Agriculture, Center for Alcohol Studies, American Affordable Housing Institute, Center for American Women in Politics, Art Museum, Institute for Biostatistics, Center for Ceramic Research, Center of Cognitive Sciences, Center for Computer Aids for Industrial Productivity, Center for Discrete Mathematics and Theoretical Computer Science, Controlled Drug-Delivery Research Center, Institute for Criminological Research, Center for the Critical Analysis of Contemporary Culture, Eagleton Institute of Politics, Environmental and Occupational Health Sciences Institute, Fiber Optics Materials Research, Institute for Health, Health Care Policy and Aging Research, Center for Historical Analysis, Center for International Conflict Resolution and Peace Studies, Institute of Marine and Coastal Sciences, Center for Materials Synthesis, Center for Operations Research, Laboratory for Surface Modification, Center for Urban Policy Research, Waksman Institute of Microbiology, Wireless Information Network Laboratory, Institute for Research on Women. According to The Center at University of Florida, the University is ranked 81st in receipt of Federal Research funds with $94,393,000 and it ranks 52nd for total University research expenditures with $244,373,000. In 2004, the University awarded 382 doctorates, which ranked it 29th among all U.S. institutions eligible to award that degree. Thirty of the University's faculty members have been elected to National Honor Academies and this ranks it 30th among all U.S. institutions. The Library: approximately 5,267,000 volumes, 28,000 subscriptions. Total University enrollment: 34,500.

Annual tuition: full-time residents $12,380, nonresidents $18,400; per credit residents $515, nonresidents $766. On-campus housing for 380 married students, 703 single students. Average academic year housing costs: $8000–$10,000 for single students; per month $575–$800 for family housing. Contact Graduate and Family Housing Office for both on- and off-campus information. Phone: (732)445-2215. Day-care facilities available.

The Graduate School

Graduate study since 1876. Enrollment: full-time 1621, part-time 1975. Graduate faculty: full- and part-time 1842. Degrees conferred: M.A., M.A.T., M.C.R.P., M.S., M.S.T., M.Phil., Dr.P.H., Ph.D.

ADMISSION REQUIREMENTS. Transcripts, GRE, two or three letters of recommendation required in support of School's application. GRE Subject Test required for many programs. TOEFL required for international applicants. Interview not required. Accepts transfer applicants. Graduates of unaccredited colleges not considered. Apply to Admissions Office by July 1 (Fall), December 1 (Spring), March 1 (Summer). Applicants seeking financial support should apply by February 1 for the Fall term. Application fee $50. Phone: (732)932-7711; fax: (732)932-7407.

ADMISSION STANDARDS. Very competitive or selective.

FINANCIAL AID. Academic scholarships, fellowships, teaching assistantships, graduate assistantships, internships, grants, tuition waivers, Federal W/S, loans. Approved for VA benefits. Apply by February 1 to appropriate department Chair for assistantships, fellowships; to Admissions Office for all other programs. Phone: (732)932-7755; fax: (732)932-7385. Use FAFSA and institutional FAF. About 80% of students receive aid other than loans from School and outside sources. Aid available for part-time students.

DEGREE REQUIREMENTS. For master's: 30 credit hours minimum; thesis required by some departments; final oral/written comprehensive exam. For Ph.D.: 3 years minimum beyond the bachelor's, at least one year in full-time residence required by some programs; reading knowledge of one or two foreign languages required by some programs; qualifying exam; thesis; final oral exam.

FIELDS OF STUDY.
Anthropology. M.A., Ph.D.
Art History. M.A., Ph.D.
Atmospheric Science. M.S., Ph.D.
Biochemistry. M.S., Ph.D.
Biomedical Engineering. M.S., Ph.D.
Cell and Developmental Biology. M.S., Ph.D.
Chemical and Biochemical Engineering. M.S., Ph.D.
Chemistry and Chemical Biology. M.S., M.S.T., Ph.D.
Civil and Environmental Engineering. M.S., Ph.D.
Classics. M.A., M.A.T., Ph.D.
Communication, Information and Library Studies. Ph.D.
Comparative Literature. Ph.D.
Computational Biology and Molecular Biophysics. Ph.D.
Computer Science. M.S., Ph.D.
Ecology and Evolution. M.S., Ph.D.
Economics. M.A., Ph.D.
Education. Ph.D.
Electrical and Computer Engineering. M.S., Ph.D.
Endocrinology and Animal Bioscience. M.S., Ph.D.
English. Ph.D.
Entomology. M.S., Ph.D.
Environmental Sciences. M.S., Ph.D.
Food and Business Economics. M.S.
Food Science. M.S., Ph.D.
French. M.A., M.A.T., Ph.D.
Geography. M.A., M.S., Ph.D.
Geological Sciences. M.S., Ph.D.
German. M.A., Ph.D.
History. Ph.D.
Industrial and System Engineering. M.S., Ph.D.
Industrial Relations and Human Resources. Ph.D.
Italian. M.A., M.A.T., Ph.D.
Linguistics. Ph.D.
Materials Science and Engineering. M.S., Ph.D.
Mathematics. M.S., Ph.D.
Mechanical and Aerospace Engineering. M.S., Ph.D.
Mechanics. M.S., Ph.D.
Medicinal Chemistry. M.S., Ph.D.
Microbiology and Molecular Genetics. M.S., Ph.D.
Music. M.A., Ph.D.
Nutritional Sciences. M.S., Ph.D.
Oceanography. M.S., Ph.D.
Operations Research. Ph.D.
Pharmaceutical Science. M.S., Ph.D.
Pharmacology, Cellular and Molecular. Ph.D.
Philosophy. Ph.D.
Physics and Astronomy. M.S., M.S.T., Ph.D.
Physiology and Integrative Biology. Ph.D.
Planning and Public Policy. Ph.D.
Plant Biology. M.S., Ph.D.

Political Science. Ph.D.
Psychology. Ph.D.
Public Health. Ph.D., (Offered jointly with and administered by UMDNJ-SPH.)
Social Work. Ph.D.
Sociology. M.A., Ph.D.
Spanish. M.A., M.A.T., Ph.D.
Statistics and Biostatistics. M.S., Ph.D.
Toxicology. M.S., Ph.D.
Urban Planning and Policy Development. Ph.D.
Women's and Gender Studies. M.A., Ph.D.

Mason Gross School of the Arts

Web site: www.masongross.rutgers.edu

Graduate study since 1998. Semester system.

Enrollment: full-time 250, part-time 75. Faculty: full-time 67, part-time 69. Degrees conferred: M.F.A., M.M., D.M.A., A.D.

ADMISSION REQUIREMENTS. Transcripts, three letters of recommendation, graduate audition questionnaire form (Music Program), personal statement required in support of School's application. TOEFL (minimum score 550) required for international applicants. Accepts transfer applicants. Graduates of unaccredited institutions not considered. Apply to Graduate Admissions Office by March 1 (Fall). Application fee $50. Phone: (732)932-7711; fax (732)932-8231.

ADMISSION STANDARDS. Selective. Usual minimum average: 2.75 (A = 4.).

FINANCIAL AID. Scholarships, fellowships, assistantships, teaching assistantships, internships, Federal W/S, loans. Approved for VA benefits. Apply to program chair for scholarships, fellowships, assistantships; to Office of Financial Aid; no specified closing date. Phone: (732)932-7755; fax: (732)932-7385. Use FAFSA and institutional FAF. About 20% of students receive aid from School and outside sources. Aid available for part-time students.

DEGREE REQUIREMENTS. For M.F.A.: 75 credit, three-year full-time program; internship (playwriting); special showcase/thesis production/thesis play. For M.M.: 36 credit, two-year full-time program; one solo recital; comprehensive exam. For D.M.A.: three-year full-time residency; reading knowledge of either German, French, or Italian; comprehensive exam; two solo recitals; two lecture recitals; one chamber music program; final written/oral comprehensive exam.

FIELDS OF STUDY.
Acting.
Design and Costume Technology.
Directing.
Music.
Playwriting.
State Management.
Visual Arts.

Rutgers Business School

Web site: www.business.rutgers.edu

Established 1965. Private control. Accredited programs: M.B.A. and Accounting. Located on Newark and New Brunswick campuses, courses offered at Princeton and Morristown. Trimester system. Special Programs: Foreign Exchange programs in France, Italy, the Netherlands, United Kingdom, Republic of Singapore; E.M.B.A., offered entirely in Singapore; foreign study (joint E.M.B.A. with Dalian University of Technology in People's Republic of China). Special facilities: Center for Entrepreneurial Management, Center for Information Management, Integration and Connectivity, Center for International Business Education and Research, Center for Research in Regulated Industries, New Jersey Center for Research in Financial Services, New Jersey Small Business Development Center, Rutgers Accounting Research Center, Technology Management Research Center.

Annual tuition: full-time resident $17,162, nonresident $25,944; part-time per credit resident $710, nonresident $1076. On-campus rooms and apartments available for single students only.

Enrollment: total full-time 394, part-time 1132 (men 65%, women 35%) Faculty: full-time 136, part-time 60; 98% with Ph.D./D.B.A. Degrees conferred: M.B.A., M.B.A. in Professional Accounting, E.M.B.A., M.Accy., M.B.A.-J.D., M.B.A.-M.D., M.B.A.-M.P.H., M.B.A.-M.S. (Biomedical Sciences), M.Q.F., Ph.D. in Management (in cooperation with New Jersey Institute of Technology), Ph.D.

ADMISSION REQUIREMENTS. Transcripts, two letters of recommendation, two essays, GMAT required in support of School's application. TOEFL required for international applicants. Accepts transfer applicants. Graduates of unaccredited institutions not considered. For M.B.A.: apply to Admissions Office, 190 New Street, Newark, NJ 07102. Most full-time programs admit Fall and Spring, except M.B.A. in Management (admits Fall only) M.B.A. in Professional Accounting (admits Spring only). Most part-time programs admit Spring and Fall, except M.S.-M.B.A. (admits Fall only). Apply by May 1 (Summer), June 1 (Fall), November 1 (Spring). For Ph.D., apply to Admissions Office, Graduate School-Newark, 249 University Avenue, Newark, NJ 07102. Application fee $50. M.B.A. phone: (973)353-1234; Ph.D. phone: (973)353-5371.

ADMISSION STANDARDS. Competitive. Usual minimum average: 3.0, mean GPA: 3.27 (A = 4); mean GMAT: 580; work experience: full-time students three years, part-time students five years.

FINANCIAL AID. Annual awards from institutional funds: scholarships, fellowships, teaching assistantships (Ph.D. only), internships, tuition waivers, Federal W/S, loans. Apply by March 1 to Dean for scholarships, fellowships, assistantships; to Admissions Office for all other programs. Phone: (973)353-1234. Use FAFSA (School code: 002631). About 25% of students receive aid other than loans from School. No aid for part-time students.

DEGREE REQUIREMENTS. For M.B.A.: 60–61 credits, at least 49 in residence. For M.B.A. in Professional Accounting: 63 credits. For M.Accy.: 30 credits. For Ph.D.: 72 credits, at least 65 in residence; qualifying exam; dissertation; final oral exam.

FIELDS OF STUDY.
Accounting. Ph.D.
Accounting Information Systems. Ph.D.
Accountancy in Financial Accounting. M.Accy.
Business Administration. M.B.A.
Finance. Ph.D.
Governmental Accounting. M.Accy.
Information Technology. Ph.D.
International Business. Ph.D.
Management Science. Ph.D.
Mathematical Finance. M.S.
Organization Management. Ph.D.
Pharmaceutical Management. M.B.A.
Professional Accounting. M.B.A.
Quantitative Finance. M.Q.F.
Supply Chain Management. Ph.D.
Taxation. M.Accy.

School of Communication, Information and Library Studies

Graduate study since 1953. Semester system.

Enrollment: full-time 179, part-time 208. Faculty: full-time 39, part-time 14. Degrees conferred: M.L.I.S., M.C.I.S., Ph.D.

ADMISSION REQUIREMENTS. Transcripts, GRE, three letters of reference, personal statement required in support of School's application. Online application available. TOEFL required of international students. Interview not required. Accepts transfer applicants. Graduates of unaccredited institutions not considered. Apply to Director of Admissions by March 1 (Fall), October 1 (Spring). Rolling admission process. Application fee $50. Phone: (732)932-7711; fax: (732)932-8231.

ADMISSION STANDARDS. Selective. Usual minimum average: 3.0 (A = 4).

FINANCIAL AID. Scholarships, fellowships, teaching assistantships, internships, tuition waivers, Federal W/S, loans. Approved for VA benefits. Apply as part of admission application. Phone: (732)932-7755; fax: (732)932-7385. Use FAFSA and institutional FAF. About 5% of students receive aid other than loans from School and outside sources. Aid available for part-time students.

DEGREE REQUIREMENTS. For M.L.I.S.: 36 credit hours. For M.C.I.S.: 36 credit hours, at least 30 in residence.

FIELDS OF STUDY.
Communications. Ph.D. is offered through the Graduate School.
Communication and Information Studies. M.C.I.S.
Library and Information Science. M.L.I.S.

Graduate School of Education

Graduate study since 1924. Semester system.
Enrollment: full-time 323, part-time 499. Faculty: full-time 53, part-time 30. Degrees conferred: Ed.M., Ed.S., Ed.D.

ADMISSION REQUIREMENTS. Transcripts, GRE, three letters of recommendation, personal statement, essay required in support of School's application. Online application available. TOEFL required for international applicants. Accepts transfer applicants. Graduates of unaccredited institutions not considered. Apply to Graduate Admissions Office by February 1 (Fall), November 1 (Spring); Counseling Psychology by January 15. Application fee $50. Phone: (732)932-7711; fax: (732)932-8206.

ADMISSION STANDARDS. Selective. Usual minimum average: master's 3.0 (A = 4) and GRE 1000, doctorate 3.5 and GRE 1100.

FINANCIAL AID. Academic scholarships, grants, fellowships, research assistantships, teaching assistantships, internships, Federal W/S, loans. Approved for VA benefits. Apply by March 1 to appropriate department chair for scholarships, fellowships, assistantships; to Office of Financial Aid for all others. Phone: (732) 932-7755; fax: (732)932-7385. Use FAFSA and institutional FAF. About 20% of students receive aid from School and outside sources. Aid available for part-time students.

DEGREE REQUIREMENTS. For Ed.M.: 30 credit hours minimum; comprehensive written exam/thesis for some departments. For Ed.S.: 64 credit hours minimum beyond the bachelor's, at least 24 in residence; qualifying exam. For Ed.D.: 72 credit hours minimum beyond the bachelor's, at least 42 at Rutgers; qualifying exam; dissertation; final oral exam.

FIELDS OF STUDY.
Adult and Continuing Education. Ed.M.
Counseling Psychology. Ed.M.
Early Childhood/Elementary Education. Ed.M., Ed.D.
Educational Administration and Supervision. Ed.D.
Educational Policy. Ph.D.
Educational Psychology. Ph.D.
Educational Statistics, Measurement and Evaluation. Ed.M.
Language Education. Ed.M., Ed.D.
Language and Literacy Education. Ph.D.
Learning, Cognition and Development. Ed.M.

Literacy Education. Ed.M., Ed.D.
Math Education. Ed.M., Ed.D., Ph.D.
Principal. Ed.M.
Principal and Supervisor. Ed.M
Science Education. Ed.M., Ed.D.
Social and Philosophical Foundations of Education. Ed.M., Ed.D.
Social Studies Education. Ed.M., Ed.D.
Special Education. Ed.M., Ed.D.

Edward J. Bloustein School of Planning and Public Policy

Graduate study since 1965. Semester system. Special facilities: Bloustein Center for Survey Research, Center for Energy, Economics and Environmental Policy, Center for Government Services, Center for Negotiation and Conflict Resolution, Center for Urban Policy Research, Community Development Institute, Institute for Meadowlands Studies, New Jersey Public Policy Research Institute, New Jersey Sustainable State Institute, National Transit Institute, Voorhees Transportation Center.
Enrollment: full- and part-time 436. Faculty: full-time 45, part-time 35. Degrees conferred: M.C.R.P., M.C.R.S., M.P.A.P., M.P.P., M.P.A.P.-J.D., M.P.A.P.-M.B.A., M.C.R.P.-J.D., M.C.R.P.-M.S. (Agricultural Economics), M.C.R.S.-M.B.A.

ADMISSION REQUIREMENTS. Transcripts, GRE, three letters of recommendation, personal statement or essay required in support of School's application. TOEFL required for international applicants. Accepts transfer applicants. Graduates of unaccredited institutions not considered. Apply to the Office of Graduate and Professional Admissions by January 15 (Fall); for Urban Planning June 1 (Fall), November 1 (Spring); Public Policy admits Fall only, apply by February 15. International applicants apply by April 1 (Fall), November 1 (Spring). Application fee $50. Phone: (732)932-7711; fax: (732)932-8231.

ADMISSION STANDARDS. Selective. Usual minimum average: master's 3.0 (A = 4).

FINANCIAL AID. Diversity scholarships, graduate awards, fellowships, graduate assistantships, teaching assistantships, traineeships, Federal W/S, loans. Approved for VA benefits. Apply to program chair for scholarships, fellowships, awards, assistantships; to Office of Financial Aid for all other programs. Financial Aid applications due for Urban Planning by February 1 Fall), November 1 (Spring); for Public Policy by February 15 (Fall). Phone: (732)932-7057; fax: (732)932-7385. Use FAFSA and institutional FAF. Aid available for part-time students.

DEGREE REQUIREMENTS. For M.C.R.P., M.C.R.S.: 30 credit hours minimum; comprehensive written exam. For M.C.R.S.: 48 credit full-time program. For M.P.A.P., M.P.P.: two-year full-time program.

FIELDS OF STUDY.
City and Regional Planning. M.C.R.P.
City and Regional Studies. Includes international development planning. M.C.R.S.
Planning and Public Policy. Ph.D. awarded through the Graduate School.
Public Affairs and Politics. M.P.A.P.
Public Policy. M.P.P.
Urban Planning and Policy Development. Ph.D. awarded through the Graduate School.
Note: Programs in Public Health are offered jointly with the Graduate School, New Brunswick, and the University of Medicine and Dentistry of New Jersey.

School of Social Work

Graduate study since 1955. Located at Camden, Newark, and New Brunswick.

Enrollment: full-time 361, part-time 343. Faculty: full-time 29, part-time 31. Degrees conferred: M.S.W., Ph.D.: (offered through Graduate School).

ADMISSION REQUIREMENTS. Transcripts, personal statement, three letters of recommendation required in support of School's application. Online application available. GRE required for doctoral applicants. TOEFL required for international applicants. Accepts transfer applicants. Graduates of unaccredited institutions not considered. Apply to Office of Graduate Admissions by May 1 (Fall); March 1 (advanced standing accelerated program), November 1 (Spring). Application fee $35. Phone: (732)932-7711; fax: (732)932-8231.

ADMISSION STANDARDS. Selective. Usual minimum average: 3.0 (A = 4).

FINANCIAL AID. Fellowships, research assistantships, field placement, stipends, Federal W/S, loans. Approved for VA benefits. Apply to University Financial Aid Office by March 1. Phone: (732)932-7057; fax: (732)932-7385. Use FAFSA and institutional FAF. About 46% of students receive aid other than loans from School and outside sources.

DEGREE REQUIREMENTS. For M.S.W.: 60 credit hours minimum, at least 36 in residence; research project.

FIELDS OF STUDY.
Administration, Policy, and Planning.
Children and Families.
Direct Practice.
Health, Mental Health, and Aging.
Social Work. Ph.D. awarded through the Graduate School.

School of Law—Newark Campus (07102-3094)
Web site: law.newark.rutgers.edu

Established 1908. ABA approved since 1941. AALS member. Public control. Semester system. Special facility: Institute on Education Law and Policy. Law library: 522,600 volumes, 3100 subscriptions; has LEXIS, NEXIS, WESTLAW, DIALOG; has more than 500 network connections.
Annual tuition: resident $19,623, nonresident $27,976; part-time resident $12,691, nonresident $14,500. No on-campus housing available. Total average annual additional expense: $18,000.
Enrollment: first-year class 181 (day), 68 (evening); total day and evening 815 (men 58%, women 42%, minorities 17%). Faculty: full-time 42, part-time 30. Student to faculty ratio is 15.4 to 1. Degrees conferred: J.D., J.D.-M.A. (Criminal Justice, Political Science), J.D.-M.B.A., J.D.-M.C.R.P., J.D.-M.S.W., J.D.-Ph.D.

ADMISSION REQUIREMENTS. LSDAS Law School report, bachelor's degree, transcripts, LSAT, one letter of recommendation required in support of application. Interview not required. Accepts transfer applicants. Graduates of unaccredited institutions not considered. Minority Student Program available. Apply to Director of Admissions of School by March 15. Application fee $60. Fall admission only. Phone: (973)353-5554; fax: (973)353-3459.

ADMISSION STANDARDS. Selective. Accepts approximately 24% of full-time and 20% of part-time students. Number of full-time applicants 2886, part-time 606; number of full-time acceptances 690, part-time 121; number of full-time enrolled 181, part-time 68; LSAT (75% of full-time students have a score at or above 154, part-time 153); GPA (75% of full-time students have a GPA at or above 3.06, part-time 3.02). *U.S. News & World Report* ranking is in the second tier (tied at 77th) of all U.S. law schools.

FINANCIAL AID. Scholarships, fellowships, Federal W/S, loans. Apply to the University's Financial Aid Office by March 1. Phone: (973)353-1702. Use FAFSA (School code: 002631) and institu-

tional FAF. About 45% of full-time and 22% of part-time students receive aid other than loans from School. Has loan repayment assistance program (Public Interest/Public Service).

DEGREE REQUIREMENTS. For J.D.: satisfactory completion of three-year program; 84 credits hours minimum.
Note: Semester study abroad program with the University of Leiden, Netherlands.

THE SAGE COLLEGES
Troy, New York 12180-4115
Web site: www.sage.edu

Founded 1916. Located 10 miles E of Albany; has two campuses, one in Troy and one in Albany. Coed on graduate level. Private control. Semester system. Library: 379,736 volumes, 1070 subscriptions. Library fully automated.
Tuition: per credit: $515. Limited on-campus housing. Average annual costs: $8520 (including board). Contact the Director of Residence Life for both on- and off-campus housing information. Phone: (518)270-2008.

Sage Graduate School

Graduate study since 1949. Enrollment: full- and part-time 926. Faculty: full-time 44, part-time 32. Degrees conferred: M.A., M.S., M.B.A., M.S.Ed.

ADMISSION REQUIREMENTS. Transcripts, two recommendations, résumé, career essay required in support of School's application. GRE/GMAT required for some programs. TOEFL required for international applicants. Accepts transfer applicants. Graduates of unaccredited institutions not considered. Apply to Dean, Sage Graduate School; no specified closing date. Rolling admissions process. Application fee $40. Phone: (518)244-2443; fax: (518)244-6880; e-mail: sgsadm@sage.edu.

ADMISSION STANDARDS. Selective. Usual minimum average: 2.75 (A = 4).

FINANCIAL AID. Grants, teaching assistantships, federal traineeships, Federal W/S, loans. Approved for VA benefits. Apply by March 1 to Sage Graduate School for assistantships; to Financial Aid Office for all other programs. Phone: (518)270-2341.Use FAFSA.

DEGREE REQUIREMENTS. For master's: 31–54 credits; thesis/nonthesis option; seminar/comprehensive exam.

FIELDS OF STUDY.
Business Administration. Includes finance, management, human resources. M.B.A.
Child Care and Children's Services.
Chemical Dependence.
Chemical Dependence Administration.
Childhood Education.
Community Counseling.
Community Health Education.
Community Psychology.
Counseling.
Elementary Education. Includes reading, special education. M.S.Ed.
Forensic Psychology.
General Psychology.
Guidance Counseling.
Health Education. Includes community health education, school health education. M.S.
Health Services Administration. Includes administration, health education. M.S.

Literacy Education.
Nursing. Includes adult health, community health nursing, gerontological, nurse practitioner studies, medical-surgical nursing, nurse practitioner studies, psychiatric-mental health nursing. M.S., M.S.-M.B.A.
Nutrition. M.S.
Occupational Therapy. M.S.
Organizational Management.
Physical Therapy.
Public Administration. Includes communications, human services administration, public management. M.S.
Reading/Special Education. M.S.Ed.
School Health Education. M.S.
Secondary Education. Includes usual academic subjects. M.S.Ed.
Special Education. Includes childhood special education.

SAGINAW VALLEY STATE UNIVERSITY
University Center, Michigan 48710
Web site: www.svsu.edu

Founded 1963. Located 8 miles from Saginaw. State control. Coed. Early semester system. Library: 358,000 volumes, 2000 subscriptions. Total University enrollment: 9600.

Tuition: per credit hour, resident $285, nonresident $549. Limited on-campus housing available for single students only. Average housing costs: $6150 (including board). Contact Director of Housing for both on- and off-campus housing information. Phone: (989)964-4255. Day-care facilities available.

Graduate Program

Enrollment: full-time 166, part-time 1488. Faculty: full- and part-time 101. Degrees conferred: M.A., M.A.T., M.B.A., M.Ed.

ADMISSION REQUIREMENTS. Transcripts, GRE/GMAT, letters of recommendation, interview required in support of application. Michigan Teaching Certificate required for M.A.T., M.Ed. TOEFL required for international applicants. Accepts transfer applicants. Graduates of unaccredited institutions not considered. Apply to Director of Admissions; no specified closing date. Rolling admissions process. Application fee $25. Phone: (989)964-2184; fax: (989)790-2173; e-mail: gradadm@svsu.edu.

ADMISSION STANDARDS. Selective. Usual minimum average: 3.0 (A = 4).

FINANCIAL AID. Fellowships, assistantships, Federal W/S, loans. Approved for VA benefits. Apply by April 1 to the Office of Financial Aid. Phone: (989)964-4103; fax: (989)964-0180. Use FAFSA. Aid available for part-time students.

DEGREE REQUIREMENTS. For M.A., M.A.T., M.Ed.: 33–39 hours; thesis/nonthesis option/project. For M.B.A.: 36–48 credit hours minimum depending upon previous preparation, 24 in residence.

FIELDS OF STUDY.
Administrative Science. M.A.S.
Business Administration. M.B.A.
Chief Business Official. M.Ed.
Communication and Digital Media Design. M.A.
Educational Leadership. M.Ed.
E-learning. M.A.
Health Leadership. M.S.
Instructional Technology. M.A.
Nursing. Includes advanced clinical practice, health system nurse specialist. M.S.N.
Occupational Therapy. M.S.O.T.

Principalship. M.Ed.
Superintendency. M.Ed.
Teaching. Includes adapted physical activity, early childhood, elementary classroom, middle level classroom, natural science, reading, secondary classroom, special. M.A.T.

ST. BONAVENTURE UNIVERSITY
Bonaventure, New York 14778-2284
Web site: www.sbu.edu

Established 1859. Located 70 miles SE of Buffalo. CGS member. Coed. Private control. Roman Catholic. Semester system. Library: 372,090 volumes, 1621 subscriptions.

Tuition: per credit $650. On-campus housing for single students only. Average academic year housing costs: $3670 (including board). Contact Coordinator of Residence Living for both on- and off-campus housing information. Phone: (716)375-2512.

School of Graduate Studies

Graduate study since 1920. Enrollment: full- and part-time 475. Faculty: full-time 65, part-time 28. Degrees conferred: M.A., M.A.T., M.S., M.S.Ed., M.B.A.

ADMISSION REQUIREMENTS. Official transcripts, two letters of recommendation, GRE/GMAT/MAT required in support of School's application. Online application available. GRE Subject Test, interview required by some departments. TOEFL required for international applicants. Accepts transfer applicants. Graduates of unaccredited institutions not considered. Apply to Graduate School at least thirty days prior to registration. Rolling admission process. Application fee $30. Phone: (716)375-2021; fax: (716) 375-7834; e-mail: gradsch@sbu.edu.

ADMISSION STANDARDS. Selective for many departments. Usual minimum average: 2.5 (A = 4).

FINANCIAL AID. Research assistantships, teaching assistantships, internships, tuition waivers, Federal W/S, loans. Approved for VA benefits. Apply by April 1 to School of Graduate Studies for assistantships; to Financial Aid Office for all other programs. Use FAFSA (School code: 002817). Phone: (716)375-2528. About 10% of students receive aid from School and outside sources. Aid available for part-time students.

DEGREE REQUIREMENTS. For master's: 30 semester hours minimum, at least 24 in residence; thesis/nonthesis option; final oral exam for some departments; reading knowledge of one foreign language for some departments; written/oral comprehensive exam.

FIELDS OF STUDY.

SCHOOL OF ARTS AND SCIENCES:
English. M.A.

SCHOOL OF BUSINESS:
Business Administration. Includes accounting/finance, general business, international business, management/marketing. M.B.A.
Professional Leadership. M.S.

SCHOOL OF EDUCATION:
Adolescence Education. M.S.Ed.
Advanced Inclusive Process. M.S.Ed.
Counselor Education. M.S.Ed., M.S.
Educational Leadership. M.S.Ed.
Literacy (Reading B–6th grade). M.S.Ed.
Literacy (Reading 5–12 grade). M.S.Ed.

SCHOOL OF FRANCISCAN STUDIES:
Franciscan Studies. M.A.

SCHOOL OF JOURNALISM AND MASS COMMUNICATION:
Integrated Marketing Communication. M.A.

ST. CLOUD STATE UNIVERSITY

St. Cloud, Minnesota 56301-4498
Web site: www.stcloudstate.edu

Founded 1869. Located 62 miles NW of Minneapolis on Interstate 94. CGS member. Coed. State control. Semester system. Library: 897,973 volumes, 8300 subscriptions. Total University enrollment: 15,900.

Tuition: per credit resident $277, nonresident $379. On-campus housing for single students only. Average academic year housing costs: $4600 (including board). Apply to Director of Housing. Phone: (320)308-2166. Day-care facilities available.

School of Graduate Studies

Graduate study since 1953. Enrollment: full-time 530, part-time 984. Graduate faculty: full-time 338, part-time 67. Degrees conferred: M.A., M.M., M.S., M.B.A., Specialist program.

ADMISSION REQUIREMENTS. Two transcripts, GRE required in support of application. GMAT required for Business applicants. TOEFL required of international applicants. Interview required for Applied Psychology. Apply to Graduate Studies Office; no specified closing dates. Rolling admission process. Application fee $35. Phone: (320)308-2113; fax: (320)308-5371.

ADMISSION STANDARDS. Selective for most departments. Usual minimum average: 2.75 (A = 4).

FINANCIAL AID. Scholarships, full/part-time assistantships, Federal W/S, loans. Apply by March 1 to appropriate department Chair for scholarships, assistantships; to Financial Aid Office for all other programs. Phone: (320)308-2047; fax: (320)308-5424. Use FAFSA and University's FAF. Aid sometimes available for part-time students.

DEGREE REQUIREMENTS. For master's: Plan A—36–39 credits, at least 30 in residence; thesis or creative work; final written/oral exam. Plan B—32–36 credits minimum, at least 30 in residence; final comprehensive exam; no thesis; starred paper required by some departments. For Specialist program: 30 credits beyond master's; field study.

FIELDS OF STUDY.
Applied Behavioral Analysis.
Applied Economics.
Art.
Biological Sciences. Includes cell and molecular, ecology and natural resources.
Business Administration. GMAT for admission.
Child and Family Studies. Includes early childhood special education, early education, family studies.
College Counseling and Student Development.
Communication Disorders.
Community Education.
Computer Science.
Counseling. Includes college student development, community, rehabilitation, school.
Criminal Justice.
Cultural Resources Management.
Curriculum and Instruction. Includes elementary, middle school/junior high, senior high, reading.
Educational Administration. M.S., Specialist.

Educational Media.
Electrical Engineering.
English. Includes TESL. M.A., M.S.
Exercise Science.
Geography. Includes geographic information science, tourism planning and development.
Gerontology.
Higher Education Administration.
History. Includes public history.
Human Resource Development/Training.
Industrial/Organizational Psychology.
Information Media.
Information Technologies.
Mass Communications.
Mathematics.
Mechanical Engineering.
Music Conducting. M.M.
Music Education. M.M.
Music—Piano Pedagogy. M.M.
Physical Education.
Public and Nonprofit Institutions.
Public Safety Executive Leadership.
Social Responsibility.
Social Work.
Special Education.
Sports Management.

ST. EDWARD'S UNIVERSITY

Austin, Texas 78704-6489
Web site: www.stedwards.edu

Founded in 1885. Coed. Independent. Trimester system. Evening sessions. Library: 186,100 volumes, 2100 subscriptions. Total University enrollment: 5000.

Tuition: per credit $598. On-campus housing available for 40–60 single students. Annual academic year costs: $9062 (including board). Phone: (512)448-8400.

Graduate Program

Graduate study since 1970. Enrollment: full-time 164, part-time 782. Faculty: full-time 18, part-time 38. Degrees conferred: M.B.A., M.A.C., M.A.H.S., M.L.A., M.S.C.I.S., M.S.O.L.E.

ADMISSION REQUIREMENTS. Transcripts, GRE/GMAT required in support of application. Online application available. TOEFL required for international applicants. Accepts transfer applicants. Graduates of unaccredited institutions not considered. Apply by August 1 (Fall), December 1 (Spring) to Graduate admissions office. Application fee $30, international applicants $50. Phone: (512)428-1061; fax: (512)428-1032.

ADMISSION STANDARDS. Selective. Usual minimum average: 2.75 (A = 4).

FINANCIAL AID. Scholarships, loans. Approved for VA benefits. Apply by March 1 to Financial Aid Office. Phone: (512)448-8520. Use FAFSA. Aid available for part-time students.

DEGREE REQUIREMENTS. For M.B.A.: 36–60 semester hours. For M.A.H.S.: 36 semester hours. For M.L.A.: 33-credit program. For M.A.C.: 54-credit program; practicum; comprehensive exam. For M.S.C.I.S.: 36-credit program. For M.S.O.L.E.: 36-credit program; leadership capstone.

FIELDS OF STUDY.
Business Administration. Includes concentrations in accounting, business management, corporate finance, entrepreneurship, glo-

bal business, human resources management, management information systems, marketing, operations management. M.B.A.
College Student Development. M.A.
Computer Information Systems. M.S.C.I.S.
Counseling. M.A.C.
Digital Media Management. M.B.A. in D.M.M.
Human Services. M.A.H.S.
Liberal Arts. M.L.A.
Organizational Leadership and Ethics. M.S.O.L.E.
Project Management. M.S.P.M.
Teaching. M.A.T.

UNIVERSITY OF ST. FRANCIS
2701 Spring Street
Fort Wayne, Indiana 46808-3994
Web site: www.sf.edu

Founded 1890. Coed. Private Control. Roman Catholic. Semester system. Library: 88,000 volumes, 580 subscriptions. Total University enrollment: 2000.

Tuition: per hour $620. On-campus housing for 46 men, 170 women; none for married students. Average academic year housing costs: $5000–$6200 (including board). Contact Director of Residence Life for both on- and off-campus housing information. Phone: (260)434-7411.

Graduate School

Graduate study since 1961. Enrollment: full-time 88, part-time 153. Graduate faculty: full-time 20, part-time 17. Degrees conferred: M.A.F.A., M.B.A., M.S., M.S.Ed., M.S.N.

ADMISSION REQUIREMENTS. Transcripts, interview required in support of School's application. GMAT required for business; MAT required for Nursing and Education. Accepts transfer applicants. Apply to Dean of Graduate Studies two months prior to registration. Rolling admission process. Application fee $20. Phone: (260) 434-3279; fax: (260)434-7601.

ADMISSION STANDARDS. Relatively open. Usual minimum average: 2.5 (A = 4).

FINANCIAL AID. Scholarships, assistantships, internships, Federal W/S, loans. Approved for VA benefits. Apply to Dean of Graduate Studies for assistantships; to Director of Financial Aid for all other programs. No specified closing date. Phone: (260) 434-3283; fax: (260)434-3183. Use FAFSA. Aid available for part-time students.

DEGREE REQUIREMENTS. Varies according to program.

FIELDS OF STUDY.
Business Administration. M.B.A.
Environmental Science. M.S.
Exceptional Needs. M.S.Ed.
Healthcare Administration. M.S.
Leadership Studies. M.A.
Mental Health Counseling. M.S.
Nursing. Includes community and health education, family nurse practitioner. M.S.N.
Pastoral Counseling. M.S.
Physician Assistant Studies. M.S.
Psychology. M.S.
School Counseling. M.S.Ed.
Studio Art. M.A.
Theology. M.A.

ST. FRANCIS UNIVERSITY
Loretto, Pennsylvania 15940-0600
Web site: www.sfcpa.edu

Founded 1847. Located 90 miles E of Pittsburgh. Private control. Roman Catholic. Semester system. Special facilities: Center for International Education and Outreach, DiSepio Institute, Institute for Ethnics, Renewable Energy Center, Science Outreach Center, Center for the Study of Government and Law. Library: 188,800 volumes, 975 subscriptions.

Tuition: per credit $701. Limited on-campus housing for single students. Average academic year housing cost: $6800 (including board). Contact the Office of Residence Life for on- and off-campus housing information. Phone: (814)472-3029.

Graduate Program

Graduate study since 1961. Enrollment: full-time 175, part-time 402. Graduate faculty: full-time 31, part-time 35. Degrees conferred: M.A., M.B.A., M.H.R.M., M.M.S., M.O.T., M.P.T., M.P.A.S.

ADMISSION REQUIREMENTS. Transcripts, GRE/GMAT/MAT, essay, letters of reference required in support of School's application. TOEFL required for international applicants. Accepts transfer applicants. Graduates of unaccredited institutions not considered. Apply to Director of Graduate School by August 1 (Fall), one month prior to registration for other sessions. Rolling admissions process. Application fee $30. Phone: (814)472-3004; fax: (814)472-3365.

ADMISSION STANDARDS. Selective. Usual minimum average: 2.5 (A = 4).

FINANCIAL AID. Annual awards from institutional funds: scholarships, fellowship, research assistantship, loans. Approved for VA benefits. Apply by March 31 to individual programs for scholarships, fellowships, assistantships; to Financial Aid Office for loans. Phone: (814)472-3010; fax: (814)472-3335. Use FAFSA. About 3–5% of students receive aid other than loans from School and outside sources. Aid available for part-time students.

DEGREE REQUIREMENTS. For master's: 30 credit hours minimum, research project or comprehensive exam. For M.B.A.: 48 credit programs.

FIELDS OF STUDY.
Business Administration. Includes accounting, finance, health care administration, human resource management, labor relations, marketing. M.B.A.
Education. M.Ed.
Educational Leadership. M.Ed.
Health Science. M.H.S.
Human Resources Management. M.A., M.H.R.M.
Industrial Relations. M.A.
Medical Science. M.M.S.
Occupational Therapy. M.O.T.
Physical Therapy. M.P.T.
Physician Assistant. M.P.A.
Reading. M.Ed.R.

ST. JOHN'S SCHOOL
Collegeville, Minnesota 56321
Web site: www.csbsju.edu

Founded 1857. Located 80 miles NW of Minneapolis. Coed on the graduate level. Private control. Roman Catholic. Semester system. Library: 600,000 volumes, 4200 subscriptions.

Tuition: per credit $635. On-campus housing for graduate students. Average academic year housing cost: $2800. Apply to Director of Admissions. Phone: (320)363-2102.

Graduate School of Theology

Open to clerical, religious, and lay students. Enrollment: summer full-time 65, part-time 152; academic year, full-time 76, part-time 64. Graduate faculty: full-time 6, part-time 16. Degrees conferred: M.A., M.Div.

ADMISSION REQUIREMENTS. Transcripts, GRE/MAT, letters of recommendation required in support of application. Online application available. TOEFL required for international applicant. MAT or GRE required during first semester. Interview not required. Accepts transfer applicants. Apply to Director of Admissions; no specified closing date. Application fee $25. Phone: (320)363-2102; fax: (320)363-3145.

ADMISSION STANDARDS. Selective. Usual minimum average: 3.0 (A = 4.0).

FINANCIAL AID. Scholarships, fellowships, assistantships, grants, Federal W/S, loans. Apply to Director of Admissions; no specified closing date. Phone: (320)363-2102. Use FAFSA. About of 90% of full-time students receive aid other than loans from University and outside sources. Some aid for part-time students.

DEGREE REQUIREMENTS. For M.A. (Theology; Liturgical Studies): 30 credit minimum; reading knowledge of one foreign language; final comprehensive exam. For M.A. (Liturgical Music; Pastoral Ministry), M.Div.: 30 credits minimum; final comprehensive exam.

FIELDS OF STUDY.
Divinity. M.Div.
Liturgical Music. M.A.
Liturgical Studies. M.A.
Pastoral Ministry. M.A.
Theology. Includes Scripture, systematic, church history, liturgy, monastic studies, spirituality. M.A.

ST. JOHN'S UNIVERSITY
Queens Campus
Jamaica, New York 11439
Staten Island Campus
Staten Island, New York 10301
Web site: www.stjohns.edu

Founded 1870. CGS member. Coed. Private control. Roman Catholic. Semester system. Library: 3,400,000 volumes, 7000 subscriptions. Total University enrollment: 20,350.

Tuition: per credit varies between $820 and $990 depending upon program. No on-campus housing for graduate or married students. Contact Dean of Students for off-campus housing information. Phone: (718)990-6161, ext. 6573.

College of Liberal Arts and Sciences

Queens campus only. Enrollment: full-time 335, part-time 705. Faculty: full-time 161, part-time 111. Degrees conferred: M.A., M.L.S., M.S., M.Div., M.A.-M.L.S., M.L.S.-M.S., D.A., Ph.D.

ADMISSION REQUIREMENTS. Transcripts, two letters of recommendation required in support of School's application. GRE required for Ph.D. programs, GRE/interview for some departments. TOEFL required for international applicants. Graduates of unaccredited institutions not considered. Accepts transfer ap-

plicants. Apply to Office of Dean of Admissions by May 1 (Fall), November 1 (Spring). Application fee $40. Phone: (718)990-2000; fax: (718) 990-2096; e-mail: admissions@stjohns.edu.

ADMISSION STANDARDS. Selective. Usual minimum average: 3.0 for master's, 3.5 (in major) for doctorates (A = 4).

FINANCIAL AID. Annual awards from institutional funds: scholarships, doctoral fellowships, graduate assistantships, research assistantships, Federal W/S, loans. Apply by March 1 to the Office of the Dean for fellowships, assistantships; to the Financial Aid Office for all other programs. Phone: (718)990-6161. Use FAFSA. About 19% of students receive aid other than loans from School. Aid available for part-time students.

DEGREE REQUIREMENTS. For master's programs: varies between 30 and 60 semester hours, at least one year in residence; research tool for some departments; written/oral comprehensive exam; thesis/nonthesis option. For M.Div.: 99 semester hours required. For program: 45 semester hours minimum beyond the master's; two-year minimum residence; foreign language/research tool required; written comprehensive exam; research essay. For Ph.D.(Biology): minimum of 60 credits beyond the B.S. degree, or 32 hours beyond the master's, at least two years in residence; foreign language/research tool required; written comprehensive exam; dissertation; oral exam. For Ph.D. (Clinical Psychology): 90 semester hours beyond the bachelor's; full-time residency; one-year internship; written/oral comprehensive exam; dissertation; oral exam.

FIELDS OF STUDY.
Audiology. Au.D.
Biological and Pharmaceutical Biotechnology. M.S.
Biology. M.S., Ph.D.
Chemistry. M.S.
Chinese Studies. M.A.
Clinical Psychology. Ph.D.
Criminology and Justice. M.A.
East Asian Studies. M.A.
English. M.A., D.A.
General Experimental Psychology. M.A.
Government and Politics. M.A.
Government and Politics/International Relations. M.A.
History. Includes world history (D.A.). M.A., D.A.
International Relations. M.A.
Liberal Studies. Includes global development and social justice, women's and genders studies. M.A.
Library and Information Sciences. M.L.S.
Mathematics. M.A.
Ministerial Studies. M.Div.
School Psychology. M.S., Psy.D.
Sociology. M.A.
Spanish. M.A.
Speech Language Pathology. M.A.
Theology. M.A.
Theology—Catechetical Ministry. M.A.

The Peter J. Tobin College of Business

Graduate division established 1959. The School of Risk Management, Insurance, and Actuarial Science evolved in 2001 with the merger of College of Insurance and the College of Business. Special facilities: Center for Professional Education, Financial Services Institute, Global Institute for Taxation.

Tuition: per credit $835. Enrollment: full-time 225, part-time 440. Graduate faculty: full-time 90, part-time 63. Degrees conferred: M.B.A., M.S., Advanced Professional Certificate.

ADMISSION REQUIREMENTS. Official transcripts, GMAT, two letters of recommendation, written statement of objectives required in support of School's application. TOEFL required for international applicants. Interview not required. Accepts transfer applicants. Graduates of unaccredited institutions not considered. Apply to Office of Dean of Admission and Registrar at least three months prior to registration. Application fee $40. Phone: (718) 990-2599; fax: (718)990-5242.

ADMISSION STANDARDS. Selective. Usual minimum average: 3.0 (A = 4).

FINANCIAL AID. Scholarships, research assistantships, tuition awards, stipends, Federal W/S, loans. Approved for VA benefits. Apply by March 1 to the Financial Aid Office. Phone: (718)990-6403; fax: (718)969-4773. Use FAFSA, TAP. Aid available for part-time students.

DEGREE REQUIREMENTS. For M.B.A.: 36 credits minimum; thesis optional. For M.S.: 33 credit program. For A.P.C.: 18 credits beyond the M.B.A.

FIELDS OF STUDY.
Accounting. M.B.A., M.S., A.P.C.
Business Administration. Includes specializations in accounting, taxation, decision science, executive management, finance, insurance financial management, international business, marketing management, risk management, computer information systems for managers, controllership. M.B.A.
Computer Information Systems for Managers. M.B.A., A.P.C.
Decision. Sciences. M.B.A., A.P.C.
Executive Management. M.B.A., A.P.C.
Finance. M.B.A., A.P.C.
Financial Services. M.B.A., A.P.C.
Insurance Financial Management. M.B.A.
International Business. M.B.A., A.P.C.
International Finance. A.P.C.
Marketing Management. M.B.A., A.P.C.
Management of Risk. M.B.A.
Taxation. M.B.A., M.S., A.P.C.
Note: The School's center for study in Rome, Italy, has concentrations in finance, international business, marketing management.

School of Education and Human Services

Tuition: $820. Enrollment: full-time 146, part-time 1630. Faculty: full-time 41, part-time 70. Degrees conferred: M.S. Professional Diploma, Ed.D., Ph.D.

ADMISSION REQUIREMENTS. Transcripts, GRE required in support of School's application. TOEFL required for international applicants. Accepts transfer applicants. Apply to Office of Dean, at least three months prior to registration. Rolling admissions process. Application fee $40. Phone: (718)990-2303; fax: (718)990-6096.

ADMISSION STANDARDS. Very competitive for some departments, selective in others. Usual minimum average: 3.0 (A = 4).

FINANCIAL AID. Annual awards from institutional funds: scholarships, fellowships, assistantships, internships, Federal W/S, loans. Approved for VA benefits. Apply by March 1 to department chair for scholarships, fellowships, assistantships; to Financial Aid Office for all other programs. Phone: (718)990-6403; fax: (718)990-4773. Use FAFSA. Aid available for part-time students.

DEGREE REQUIREMENTS. For M.S.: 33 semester hours minimum, at least 27 in residence; comprehensive written exam. For Professional Diploma: 60 semester hours minimum beyond the bachelor's. For Ph.D.: 90 semester hours minimum beyond the bachelor's; reading knowledge of one foreign language or statistics; written comprehensive exam; dissertation; final oral exam. For Ed.D.: 90 semester hours minimum beyond the bachelor's; written comprehensive exam; dissertation; final oral exam.

FIELDS OF STUDY.
Adolescent Education. M.S.
Childhood Education. M.S.
Early Childhood Education. M.S.
Educational Administration and Supervision. Ed.D.
Instructional Leadership. P.D., Ed.D.
School Building Leadership. M.S.
School Counselor. Includes bilingual extension. M.S., P.D.
School District Leadership. P.D.
Teaching Children with Disabilities in Childhood Education. M.S.
TESOL. M.S.
Teaching Literacy (B–6). M.S.
Teaching Literacy (5–12). M.S.
Teaching Literacy (B–12). M.S.

School of Law
Web site: www.law.stjohns.edu

Established 1925. Located at Jamaica (Queens) campus (11439). ABA approved since 1937. AALS member. Private control. Semester system. Special facilities: Trial Advocacy Institute, Center for Civil Rights and Economic Development. Law library: 487,264 volumes, 4805 subscriptions; has LEXIS, NEXIS, WESTLAW, DIALOG; has more than 150 network connections.

Annual tuition: $35,000 (day), $26,925 (evening), $39,000 (LL.M.). No on-campus housing available. Total average annual additional expenses: $18,110.

Enrollment: 236 (day), 89 (evening); total day and evening 724 (men 52%, women 48%, minorities 24%). Faculty: full-time 67, part-time 50. Student to faculty ratio is 17 to 1. Degrees conferred: J.D., J.D.-M.A. (Government and politics), J.D.-M.B.A., LL.M. (Bankruptcy), JD.-LL.M.

ADMISSION REQUIREMENTS. LSDAS Law School report, bachelor's degree, transcripts, LSAT, personal statement, two letters of recommendation required in support of application. Accepts transfer applicants. Graduates of unaccredited institutions not considered. Apply to Director of Admissions by April 1 (Fall), October 1 (Spring). Application fee $60. Phone: (718)990-6474.

ADMISSION STANDARDS. Selective. Accepts approximately 31% of full-time, 33% of part-time students. Number of full-time applicants 3314, part-time 756; number of full-time acceptances 1035, part-time 249; number of full-time enrolled 236, part-time 89; LSAT (75% of full-time students have a score at or above 158, part-time 152); GPA (75% of full-time students have a GPA at or above 3.18, part-time 3.07). *U.S. News & World Report* ranking is in the second tier (tied at 70th) of all U.S. law schools.

FINANCIAL AID. Scholarships, assistantships, Federal W/S, loans. Apply to University's Financial Aid Office by March 1. Phone: (718)990-1485. Use FAFSA (School code: 002823) and institutional financial aid form. Aid available for part-time students. About 49% of full-time and 23% of part-time students received aid other than loans from school.

DEGREE REQUIREMENTS. For J.D.: 86 semester hours minimum, at least 30 in residence. For LL.M.: 30-credit program.

College of Pharmacy and Allied Health Professions

Graduate study since 1929.
Tuition: per credit $955. No on-campus housing available. Contact Student Life Office for off-campus housing information. Phone: (718)990-6783.

Enrollment: full-time 300, part-time 140. Faculty: full-time 52, part-time 17. Degrees conferred: M.S., Ph.D., Pharm.D., M.S.-M.L.S.

ADMISSION REQUIREMENTS. Transcripts, GRE, two letters of recommendation required in support of application. TOEFL required for foreign applicants. Interview required for Pharm.D. only. Accepts transfer applicants. Graduates of unaccredited institutions not considered. Apply to Office of Graduate Admissions by May 1 (Fall), November 1 (Spring). Rolling admission process. Application fee $40. Phone: (718)990-2000; fax: (718) 990-2096.

ADMISSION STANDARDS. Selective. Usual minimum average: 3.0 (A = 4).

FINANCIAL AID. Annual awards from institutional funds: doctoral fellowships, graduate assistantships, internships, Federal W/S, loans. Approved for VA benefits. Apply by March 1 to Dean of Graduate Division of College for fellowships, assistantships; to Financial Aid Office for all other programs. Phone: (718)990-6403; fax: (718)969-4773. Use FAFSA. About 30% of students receive aid other than loans from College and outside sources. Aid available for part-time students.

DEGREE REQUIREMENTS. For Pharm.D.: 66 semester hours minimum; comprehensive oral/written exam; thesis. For M.S.: 30–33 semester hours minimum; comprehensive oral/written exam; thesis. For Ph.D.: 36 semester hours beyond the master's, exclusive of dissertation research; dissertation; comprehensive written/oral exam.

FIELDS OF STUDY.
Biological and Pharmaceutical Biotechnology. M.S.
Pharmaceutical Sciences. M.S., Ph.D.
Pharmacy Administration. M.S.
Toxicology. M.S.

ST. JOSEPH COLLEGE

West Hartford, Connecticut 06117-2700
Web site: www.sjc.edu

Founded 1932. Located 3 miles W of Hartford. Coed on graduate level. Private control. Roman Catholic affiliation. Semester system. Special facilities: Athletic Center, Gengras Center for Exceptional Children, Marriage and Family Center, School for Young Children. Library: 164,283 volumes, 600 subscriptions. Total College enrollment: 1900.

Annual tuition: per credit $540. On-campus housing for graduate students available. Annual cost: $8200–$11,000 (including board). Apply to Director, Residential Life. Phone: (860)232-4571, ext. 214.

Graduate School

Graduate study since 1959. Enrollment: full-time 89, part-time 342. College faculty: full-time 36, part-time 28. Degrees conferred: M.A., M.S., M.A.M.F.T., six year certificate.

ADMISSION REQUIREMENTS. Transcripts, two references, interview, GRE or MAT required in support of application. TOEFL required for international applicants. Accepts transfer applicants. Apply to Graduate Office; no specified closing date. Rolling admission process. Application fee $50. Phone: (860)231-5381; fax: (860)231-6754.

ADMISSION STANDARDS. Selective. Usual minimum average: 3.0 (A = 4).

FINANCIAL AID. Scholarships, assistantships, internships, tuition waivers, loans. Approved for VA benefits. Apply by July 15 to Director of Financial Aid. Phone: (860)231-5223. Use FAFSA (College code: 001409) and institutional FAF. Aid available for part-time students.

DEGREE REQUIREMENTS. For M.A.: 30 semester hours minimum; thesis optional, may supply 6 credits; final comprehensive evaluation. For S.Y.C.: 32 credits minimum beyond the master's.

FIELDS OF STUDY.
Biology. M.S.
Chemistry. Includes biochemistry online. M.S.
Community Counseling. Includes specializations in child welfare, pastoral counseling. M.A.
Education. Includes specialization in curriculum and instruction, reading and language (elementary, secondary), special education (urban education). M.A.
Early Childhood/Special Education. M.A.
Human Development/Gerontology. M.A.
Management. M.S.
Marriage and Family Therapy. M.A.
Nutrition. M.S.
Nursing. Includes family health nursing, psychiatric/mental health nursing. M.S.
School Counseling. M.A.

ST. JOSEPH'S UNIVERSITY

Philadelphia, Pennsylvania 19131-1395
Web site: www.sju.edu

Founded 1851. Coed. Private control. Roman Catholic (Jesuit). Semester system. Library: 350,000 volumes, 2600 subscriptions. Total University enrollment: 7700.

Tuition: per credit $765 (M.B.A., Financial Services, Human Resources), $738 (Computer Science, Education, Psychology), $781 (Ed.D. in Educational Leadership), $687 all other programs. No on-campus housing for graduate and married students. Average annual housing cost: $6500. Apply to Residence Life Office for off-campus housing. Phone: (610)660-1063.

Graduate Program

Enrollment: full-time 406, part-time 1736. Graduate faculty: full- and part-time 111. Degrees conferred: M.S., M.B.A.

ADMISSION REQUIREMENTS. Transcripts, three letters of recommendation, résumé required in support of application. Online application available. GRE required for some programs. GMAT for M.B.A. programs. TOEFL required for international applicants. Accepts transfer applicants. Graduates of unaccredited colleges not considered. Apply to appropriate School at least two months prior to registration. Application fee $35. Phone: (610)660-1101; fax: (610) 660-1224.

ADMISSION STANDARDS. Selective. Usual minimum average: 3.0 (A = 4).

FINANCIAL AID. Annual awards from institutional funds: scholarships, assistantships, tuition waivers, Federal W/S, loans. Apply by February 15 to Chairman, Chemistry Department, for teaching assistantships; to Director, Computer Science Graduate Program, for teaching assistantships: to Chairman, Criminal Justice, for research assistantships; to Chairman, Education Department, for assistantships; to Director of M.B.A. Program, for assistantships. Phone: (610)660-1760. Use FAFSA. About 5–10% of students receive aid other than loans from University. Aid available for part-time students.

DEGREE REQUIREMENTS. For M.S. Biology: 36 credits minimum. For M.S. Chemistry: 31 credits minimum. For M.S. Computer Sciences: 31 credits. For M.S. Criminal Justice: 30 credits. For M.S. Education or Health Education: 36 credits. For M.S. Health Administration: 36 credits. For M.S. Gerontological Services: 36 credits. For M.S. Public Safety: 33 credits minimum. For M.S. Training and Development: 36 credits. For M.B.A.: 33 credits minimum.

FIELDS OF STUDY.

SCHOOL OF ARTS AND SCIENCES:
Biology.
Chemistry.
Chemistry Education.
Computer Science.
Criminal Justice.
Education.
Educational Leadership. Ed.D.
Environmental Protection.
Gerontological Services.
Health Administration.
Nurse Anesthesia.
Psychology.
Public Safety.
Training and Organizational Development.
Writing Studies.

SCHOOL OF BUSINESS:
Business Administration. Includes concentrations in accounting, decision and system sciences, finance, general business, health and medical services, human resource management, information systems, international business, international marketing, management and marketing, nonprofit management. M.B.A.
Business Intelligence. M.S.
Financial Services. M.S.
Food Marketing. Executive M.S.
Human Resource Management. M.S.
International Marketing. M.S.
Pharmaceutical Marketing. Executive M.B.A.

SAINT LOUIS UNIVERSITY
St. Louis, Missouri 63103-2097
Web site: www.slu.edu

Founded 1818. CGS member. Coed. Private control. Roman Catholic affiliation. Semester system. Special facilities: Center for Applied Behavior Science, Center for Irish Law, Institute for Molecular Virology, Seismographic Stations Network, Center for Public Policy, Center for Jewish Law, Center for Medieval and Renaissance Studies, Yalem Computing Center, Reis Biological Station, Doisy Hall of Medical Research, Vatican Film Library. The University's NIH ranking is 120th among all U.S. institutions with 97 awards/grants valued at $39,910,752. The University's endowment assets rank it 67th, with a value of $702,064,000. In 2004, the University awarded 150 doctorates, which ranked it 97th among all U.S. institutions eligible to award that degree. The Library: approximately 1,900,000 volumes, 14,700. Total University enrollment: 11,800.

Tuition: per credit $760. On-campus housing for 400 single students. Average academic year housing costs: $9680 (including board) for single students. Contact the Director of Residence Life for both on- and off-campus housing information. Phone: (314)977-2797.

Graduate School

Graduate study since 1832. Enrollment: full-time 1106, part-time 984. Graduate faculty: full-time 512, part-time 98. Degrees conferred: M.A., M.A.U.A., M.S., M.S. in Dent., M.S. in Diet., M.S.S. in N.R., M.H.A., M.P.A., M.A.P.A., M.P.H., M.S.D., M.S.N., M.Pr.Gph., M.Pr.Met., M.U.P.R.ED., Ed.S., Ed.D., Ph.D., Certificates.

ADMISSION REQUIREMENTS. Transcripts, GRE, three references, autobiographical sketch, goals statement required in support of School's application. GMAT required for Business. TOEFL required for international applicants. Accepts transfer applicants. Apply to Dean of Graduate School at least two months prior to registration. Application fee $50. Phone: (800)SLU-FORU; (314)977-2240; fax: (314)977-3943.

ADMISSION STANDARDS. Relatively open to very competitive. Usual minimum average 3.0 in last 60 credits for master's (A = 4).

FINANCIAL AID. Annual awards from institutional funds: fellowships, teaching assistantships, research assistantships, specialized assistantships, traineeships, tuition waivers, Federal W/S, loans. Approved for VA benefits. Apply preferably by February 1 to Dean of the Graduate School for fellowships, assistantships; to Office of Student Financial Services by April 1 for all other programs. Phone: (314)977-2350. Use FAFSA (School code 002506). About 65% of all students receive aid other than loans from University and outside sources.

DEGREE REQUIREMENTS. For master's: 30 semester hours minimum including 6 hours of thesis for research degree; research tool (foreign language, computer literacy, statistics); final oral exam. For Ed.S.: 30 semester hours minimum beyond master's. For Ed.D.: about 75 hours beyond bachelor's degree; research-methods sequences; preliminary exam; culminatory project. For Ph.D.: about 48–60 hours, plus 12 hours research, beyond the bachelor's degree, minimum one year in full-time residence, preliminary written and oral exams; research tool; dissertation.

FIELDS OF STUDY.
Accounting. M.Acc.
American Studies.
Anatomy.
Biochemistry. Ph.D. only.
Biology.
Biomedical Engineering.
Biosecurity and Disaster Preparedness.
Business Administration. GMAT for admission. Includes accounting, economics, international business, management and decision sciences, marketing, personnel and industrial relations.
Chemistry. M.S. only.
Clinical Psychology.
Communication. M.A. only.
Communication Sciences and Disorders. M.A. only.
Community Health. M.P.H. only.
Counseling and Family Therapy. M.A., Ph.D.
Dietetics. M.S. only.
Economics.
Educational Leadership. M.A., Ed.S., Ed.D., Ph.D.
Educational Studies. M.A., M.A.T., Ph.D.
Endodontics. M.S. only.
English.
Experimental Psychology.
Finance.
French. M.A. only.
Geology. M.S. only.
Geophysics.
Health Administration. M.H.A.
Health-Care Ethics. Ph.D.
Historical Theology.
History.
Industrial/Organizational Psychology.
International Business.
Mathematics.
Meteorology.
Microbiology. Ph.D. only.
Neurobiology. Ph.D. only.
Nursing.
Nutrition and Dietetics. M.S. only.
Orthodontics. M.S. only.

Pathology. Ph.D.
Periodontics. M.S.
Pharmacological and Physiological Sciences. Ph.D.
Philosophy.
Physical Therapy.
Physician Assistant.
Psychology.
Public Administration. M.A.P.A.
Public Health.
Public Policy Analysis. Ph.D.
Social Work.
Spanish. M.A. only.
Theology. M.A. only.
Urban Affairs. M.A.U.A. only.
Urban Planning and Real Estate Development. M.U.P.R.E.D.

John Cook School of Business

Established 1910. Private control. Accredited programs: M.B.A.; recognized Ph.D. Semester system. Special programs: foreign exchange programs in Hong Kong, Spain, Sweden. Special facilities: Emerson Electric Center for Business Ethics, Institute for International Business, Jefferson Smurfit Center for Entrepreneurial Studies, Small Business Development Center.

Annual tuition: full-time $47,785, part-time $840 per credit.

Enrollment: total full-time 74, part-time 275. Faculty: full-time 61, part-time 23; 97% with Ph.D./D.B.A. Degrees conferred: M.B.A. (full-time, part-time, day, evening, weekends), E.M.I.B. (Executive Masters in International Business), M.P.A. (Professional Accounting), M.S.F. (Finance), M.B.A.-M.H.A. (Health Administration).

ADMISSION REQUIREMENTS. All applicants should have a bachelor's degree from a recognized institution of higher education and a strong mathematics background (competency in calculus). Admission is based on the formula: 200 × UGPA + GMAT. Early applications are encouraged for both admission and financial aid consideration. Beginning students are admitted Fall, Spring, and Summer. U.S. citizens apply by July 1 (Fall), December 1 (Spring), April 15 (Summer), international students apply by January 15 (Fall), June 1 (Spring), November 15 (Summer). Submit an application, GMAT (will accept GMAT test results from the last five years, latest acceptable date is June), official transcripts from each undergraduate/graduate school attended, two letters of recommendation, statement of intent, résumé (prefers at least four years of work experience), and an application fee of $40 to the Office of Admission. Online application available. In addition, international students (whose native language is other than English) should submit a TOEFL (minimum score 550) or the Michigan Language Test (minimum score 4.5); certified translations and evaluations of all official transcripts; recommendations should be in English or with certified translations; proof of health/immunization certificate; and proof of sufficient financial resources for two years of academic study. On-campus visits are encouraged. Joint degree applicants must apply to and be accepted to both schools/programs. Contact the admissions office for current information and specific admissions requirements. Rolling admissions process; notification is made within four weeks of receipt of completed application and supporting documents.

ADMISSION REQUIREMENTS FOR DOCTORAL CANDIDATES. Contact either the Graduate School at (314)977-2240 or the Director of Graduate and Professional Programs, School of Business, at (314)977-3801 for application material and information. A preliminary application may be required for Ph.D. in Business. Beginning students are admitted Fall only. Both U.S. citizens and international applicants apply by February 15 (Fall). Submit a Graduate School application, GMAT/GRE (will accept GMAT/GRE test results from the last five years), official transcripts from each undergraduate/graduate school attended, three

letters of recommendation, biographical sketch, résumé, statement of purpose, and application fee of $40 to the Dean, Graduate School. In addition, international students (whose native language is other than English) should submit TOEFL (minimum score 600); certified translations and evaluations of all official transcripts; recommendations should be in English or with certified translations; proof of health/immunization certificate. International students' contact: (314)977-2318. Interviews are strongly encouraged prior to admissions committee reviewing completed application. Notification is generally made by mid-April.

ADMISSION STANDARDS. Selective. Mean GMAT: full-time 577, part-time 554; mean GPA: 3.19 (A = 4).

FINANCIAL AID. Fellowships, research and teaching assistantships, Federal Perkins Loans, Stafford Subsidized and Unsubsidized Loans, Federal W/S available. Financial aid is available for part-time study. Assistantships/fellowships may be available for Joint Degree candidates. Financial Aid applications and information are included in admissions materials; apply by June 1. Request fellowship and assistantship information from the School of Business. Contact the University's Financial Aid Office for need-based financial aid information. Phone: (314)977-2350. Use FAFSA (School code: 002506), also submit Financial Aid Transcript, Federal Income Tax forms. Approximately 40% of students receive some form of financial aid.

DEGREE REQUIREMENTS. For M.B.A.: 39–57 credit program including 12 elective credits, one- to two-year program; degree program must be completed in five years. For E.M.I.B.: 36 credit program. For M.M.S., M.S.F.: 30–48 credit programs. For M.P.A.: 30–63 credit program. For M.B.A.-J.D.: 130 credit, four-and-one-half- to five-year program. For M.B.A.-M.H.A.: 91 credit program. For Ph.D.: 54 credits beyond master's, three- to five-year program, at least three years in full-time residence; comprehensive exam in area of study; dissertation proposal and oral defense; dissertation; oral defense.

FIELDS OF STUDY.
Accounting. M.Acc.
Business Administration. Includes areas of emphasis in accounting, economics, entrepreneurship, finance, international business. Management, management information systems, marketing, operations and supply chain management (M.B.A.); international business, marketing (Ph.D. offered through the Graduate School). M.B.A./Ph.D.
Finance. M.S.F.
International Business. E.M.I.B.

School of Law
Web site: www.law.slu.edu

Established 1842. ABA approved since 1924. AALS member. Private control. Semester system. Full-time, part-time study. Special facilities: Center for Health Law Studies, Center for International and Comparative Law, Wefel Center for Employment Law. Special programs: Summer Institute at University's Madrid, Spain, campus; has faculty exchange programs with Sichuan University in the People's Republic of China, Ruhr University in Bochum, Germany; University of Warsaw, Poland. Law library: 639,517 volumes, 36537 subscriptions; has LEXIS, NEXIS, WESTLAW, DIALOG; has more than 700 network connections; is a Federal Government Depository.

Annual tuition: full-time $30,040, part-time $21,920. On-campus housing available for both single and married students. Contact Office of Housing for both on- and off-campus housing information. Phone: (314)977-2797. Law students generally live off-campus. Off-campus housing sand personal expenses: approximately $18,792.

Enrollment: first-year class full-time 225, part-time 75; total full-time 712, part-time 233 (men 51%, women 49%, minorities

11%). Faculty: full-time 35, part-time 21. Student to faculty ratio 17.6 to one.

Degrees conferred: J.D., J.D.-M.B.A., J.D.-M.H.A., J.D.-M.A. (Public Affairs, Urban Affairs), J.D.-M.P.A., J.D.-M.P.H., J.D.-M.S.W., LL.M. (Health Law, Employment Law), LL.M. (American Law for Foreign Lawyers who have completed a basic legal education and received a university degree in law in another country).

ADMISSION REQUIREMENTS. LSDAS Law School report, transcripts, LSAT (not later than December), personal statement, résumé, two letters of recommendation required in support of application. Interview not required. Accepts transfer applicants. Graduates of unaccredited colleges not considered. Apply to Director of Admissions by March 1. Rolling admission process. Admits first-year students. Fall only. Application fee $55. Phone: (314) 977-2800; fax: (314)977-1464; e-mail: admissions@law.slu.edu.

ADMISSION REQUIREMENTS. For LL.M. (Health Law, Employment Law): Applicants must have a J.D. from an ABA/AALS-accredited/approved Law School. Official transcripts from undergraduate, graduate, and law schools, résumé/curriculum vitae, two letters of recommendation, personal statement including interest and career goals required in support of application. Approximately five students accepted each year. For LL.M. (Foreign Lawyers): Applicants must have a degree in law from a foreign university. Certified translations and evaluations of all foreign academic credentials, TOEFL (for those whose native language is not English, minimum score 575), two letters of recommendation, personal statement including your interests and career goals, résumé/curriculum vitae required in support of application. All LL.M. programs admit Fall only. Apply by May 1 to School of Law—Graduate Programs. Phone: (314)977-3067.

ADMISSION STANDARDS. Selective. Accepts approximately 40% of full-time, 28% of part-time students. Number of full-time applicants 1845, part-time 487; number of full-time acceptances 734, part-time 249; number of full-time enrolled 236, part-time 135; LSAT (75% of full-time students have a score at or above 154, part-time 151); GPA (75% of full-time students have a GPA at or above 3.35, part-time 3.12). *U.S. News & World Report* ranking is in the second tier (tied at 85th) of all U.S. law schools.

FINANCIAL AID. Scholarships, full and partial tuition waivers, fellowships, Federal W/S, loans. Apply to the Financial Aid Office by March 1. Phone: (314)977-3369. Use FAFSA (School code: 002506). About 48% of full-time and 20% of part-time students receive aid other than loans from School.

DEGREE REQUIREMENTS. For J.D.: 88 (36 required) credits with a GPA of at least 2.0 (A = 4), plus completion of upper-divisional writing course; three-year program, four-year part-time program. Accelerated J.D. with summer course work. For J.D.-master's: four-year programs rather than five-year programs if both degrees are taken consecutively. For LL.M. (Health Law, Employment Law): 24 credits completed over two years, full- and part-time study; thesis of publishable quality; oral defense. For LL.M. (Foreign Lawyers): 24 credits; at least two semesters in residence; thesis of publishable quality; oral defense.

School of Medicine
Web site: medschool.slu.edu

Established 1836. Present school acquired in 1903. Semester system. Special facilities: SLU Anheuser-Busch Eye Institute, Institute of Molecular Virology. Special program: summer programs for underrepresented minorities. Library: 113,000 volumes, 1421 subscriptions. NIH ranking is 120 among all U.S. institutions with 97 awards/grants worth $39,910,752.

Annual tuition: $41,158. Limited housing available. Contact Director of Housing for current information. Total average figure for all other expenses: $15,500.

Enrollment: first-year class 164, total 668 (men 57%, women 43%, minorities 27%, state residents 46%). Faculty: full-time 584, part-time 1160. Degrees conferred: M.D., M.D.-M.B.A., M.D.-M.P.H., M.D.-Ph.D.

ADMISSION REQUIREMENTS. AMCAS report, transcripts, recommendations, MCAT, interview required in support of application. Interview by invitation only. Has EDP; apply between June 1 and August 1. Apply to Committee on Admissions after June 1, before December 15. Accepts transfer applicants. Admits Fall only. Applicants planning to begin medical studies after only three years of college work considered. Application fee $100. Phone: (314)577-9870; fax: (314)577-9825.

ADMISSION STANDARDS. Competitive. Accepts about 11% of all applicants. Number of applications 5687 (5254 out-of-state); number interviewed n/a (n/a out-of-state); number of acceptances 493 (389 out-of-state); number enrolled 164 (104 out-of-state). Mean Composite MCAT 10.4; mean UGPA 3.68.

FINANCIAL AID. Scholarships, loans. Apply by May 1 to Office of Student Financial Planning. Phone: (314)977-9840. Use FAFSA (School code: 002506). About 87% of students receive aid other than loans from School.

DEGREE REQUIREMENTS. For M.D.: satisfactory completion of four-year program. All students must pass USMLE Step 1 prior to entering third year and Step 2 prior to awarding of M.D.

FIELDS OF GRADUATE STUDY.
Biochemistry and Molecular Biology.
Cell and Molecular Biology.
Health Care Ethics.
Molecular Micobiology and Immunology.
Neurobiology.
Pathology.
Pharmacological Sciences.
Physiological Sciences.

SAINT MARY'S UNIVERSITY OF MINNESOTA
Winona, Minnesota 55987-1399
Web site: www.smumn.edu

Founded 1912. Private control. Roman Catholic affiliation. Courses offered in Twin Cities and Nairobi. Semester system. Special facilities: De La Salle Language Institute, Hendrickson Institute for Ethical Leadership, Institute in Pastoral Ministries, Maryknoll Institute of African Studies, St. Teresa Leadership and Services Institute for Women. Library: 168,900 volumes, 2600 subscriptions. Total University enrollment: 5800.

Tuition: per credit $450 (Geographic Information Science), $350 (Human Development), $365 (Instruction), $395 (M.B.A.), $420 (Organizational Leadership), $310 (all other Master's), $475 (Ed.D.). No on-campus housing available.

Graduate Programs

Enrollment: full-time 675, part-time 2800. Faculty: full-time 43, part-time 312. Degrees conferred: M.A., M.A.I., M.S.

ADMISSION REQUIREMENTS. Official transcripts, personal statement, three letters of recommendation, résumé required in support of application. Additional requirements vary by program. TOEFL (minimum score 550) required for international applicants. Accepts transfer applicants. Graduates of unaccredited institutions not considered. Apply to the Graduate Office at least one month prior to registration. Rolling admissions process. Application fee $25. Phone: (612)728-5207; fax: (612)728-5121.

ADMISSION STANDARDS. Selective for most programs. Usual minimum average: 2.75 (A = 4).

FINANCIAL AID. Limited to scholarships, assistantships, loans. Apply to the Financial Aid Office; no specified closing date. Phone: (800)635-5987. Use FAFSA (School code: 002380).

DEGREE REQUIREMENTS. For master's: 41–48 semester hours depending on program; thesis/nonthesis option; final oral colloquia presentation for most programs. For M.S.: 3–4 semester individually designed programs.

FIELDS OF STUDY.
Business Administration. M.B.A.
Geographic Information Science. M.S.
Instruction. M.A.
International Business. M.A.
Leadership. Ed.D.
Literacy Education. M.A.
Organizational Leadership. M.A.
Pastoral Administration. M.A.
Pastoral Ministries. M.A.
Philanthropy and Development. M.A.
Teaching and Learning. M.Ed.

ST. MARY'S UNIVERSITY
San Antonio, Texas 78228-8572
Web site: www.stmarytx.edu

Founded 1852. Coed. Private control. Semester system. Library: 525,000 volumes, 1500 subscriptions. Total University enrollment: 3950.

Tuition: per credit $585. On-campus housing available for single students only. Average academic year housing costs: $3916–$4200 (room only). Contact Housing office for both on- and off-campus housing information. Phone: (210)436-3534.

Graduate School

Graduate study since 1936. Enrollment: full- and part-time 750. Graduate faculty: full-time 44, part-time 25. Degrees conferred: M.A., M.B.A., M.J.A., M.P.A., M.S., Ph.D.

ADMISSION REQUIREMENTS. Transcripts, two letters of recommendation, GRE/GMAT required in support of School's application. Online application available. TOEFL required for international applicants. Interview not required. Accepts transfer applicants. Apply to Graduate School by August 1 (Fall), two weeks prior to registration for other semesters. Rolling admission process. Application fee $35. Phone: (210)436-3101; fax: (210)431-2220.

ADMISSION STANDARDS. Selective. Usual minimum average: 3.0 (A = 4).

FINANCIAL AID. Assistantships, Federal W/S, loans. Approved for VA benefits. Apply by March 31 to Dean of the Graduate School for assistantships; to Financial Aid Office for all other programs. Use FAFSA. About 5–10% of students receive aid other than loans from university.

DEGREE REQUIREMENTS. For master's: 30–36 semester hours minimum, at least 24 in residence, thesis; 30–36 hours, nonthesis option for all departments; reading knowledge of 1 foreign language for some departments; final oral/written exam. For Ph.D.: 78 semester hours beyond master's; reading knowledge of one foreign language; comprehensive exam; dissertation; final oral exam.

FIELDS OF STUDY.
Business Administration. GMAT for admission.
Catholic School Leadership.
Communication.
Community Counseling.
Computer Information Systems.
Computer Science.
Counselor Education and Supervision. Ph.D. only.
Education.
Educational Leadership.
Electrical Engineering.
Engineering Systems Management.
English Literature and Language.
History.
Industrial Engineering.
Industrial/Organizational Psychology.
International Relations.
Marriage and Family Therapy. 48 credit master's program.
Mathematics.
Mental Health Counseling.
Pastoral Ministry.
Political Science.
Psychology. 42 credit program.
Public Administration.
Reading.
Software Engineering.
Theology.

School of Law (78228-8601)
Web site: law.stmarytx.edu

Established 1927. ABA approved since 1948. AALS member. Semester system. Full-time study; an evening part-time program started in 2007. Special facilities: Center for Legal and Social Justice, Center for Conciliation and Arbitration, Center for International Legal Studies, Institute for World Legal Problems in Innsbruck, Austria, Institute for International Human Rights in Guatemala. Special programs: Judicial Internships. Law library: 411,734 volumes, 4397 subscriptions; has LEXIS, NEXIS, WESTLAW, DIALOG; has more than 600 network connections.

Annual tuition: $22,258. On-campus housing available for single students only. Contact Housing Office for both on- and off-campus housing information. Telephone: (210)436-3534. Law students tend to live off-campus. Off-campus housing and personal expenses: approximately $14,000.

Enrollment: first-year class 267; total full-time 742 (men 58%, women 42%, minorities 30%). Faculty: full-time 33, part-time 43. Student to faculty ratio 23.5 to 1. Degrees conferred: J.D., J.D.-M.B.A., J.D.-M.P.A., J.D.-E.C., J.D.-I.R., J.D.-M.Theo., J.D.-M.C.I.S., LL.M. (International and Comparative Law for U.S.-trained attorneys), LL.M. (American Legal Studies for persons who have completed a basic legal education and received a university degree in law in another country).

ADMISSION REQUIREMENTS. LSDAS Law School report, bachelor's degree, transcripts, LSAT, personal statement, two letters of recommendation required in support of application. Graduates of unaccredited colleges not considered. Apply to Chairperson, Faculty Admissions Committee by March 1. Application fee $55. Phone: (210)436-3523; fax: (210)431-4202.

ADMISSION STANDARDS. Selective. Accepts approximately 37% of full-time students. Number of full-time applicants 2069; number of full-time acceptances 769; number of full-time enrolled 267; LSAT (75% of full-time students have a score at or above 151); GPA (75% of full-time students have a GPA at or above 2.81). *U.S. News & World Report* ranking is in the fourth tier of all U.S. law schools.

FINANCIAL AID. Scholarships, assistantships, Federal W/S, loans. Apply to Director of Financial Aid by April 1. Phone: (210)

431-6743. Use FAFSA (School code: 003623). About 46% of students receive some aid from School.

DEGREE REQUIREMENTS. For J.D.: 90 (46 required) credits with a GPA of at least 2.0 (A = 4), plus completion of upper-divisional writing course; three-year program. Accelerated J.D. with summer course work. For J.D.-Master's: four-year programs rather than five-year programs if both degrees are taken consecutively. For LL.M. (International and Comparative Law): 24 credits, at least two semesters in full-time residence; thesis of publishable quality. For LL.M. (American Legal Studies): 24 credits; at least two semesters in residence in full-time residence; three required courses in U.S. legal system; thesis of publishable quality.

ST. MICHAEL'S COLLEGE
Colchester, Vermont 05439
Web site: www.smcvt.edu

Founded 1904. Located near Burlington. Private control. Roman Catholic affiliation. Semester system. Library: 210,800 volumes, 1200 subscriptions. Total College enrollment: 2474.

Tuition: per credit $435. Limited on-campus housing available for single students only. Average academic year housing costs: $4510 (room only). Contact assistant Dean of Students for both on- and off-campus housing information. Phone: (802)654-2566. Day-care facilities available.

Graduate Programs

Graduate study since 1926. Enrollment: full-time 78, part-time 235. Faculty: full-time 9, part-time 84. Degrees conferred: M.A., M.Ed., M.S.A.

ADMISSION REQUIREMENTS. Transcripts, two letters of recommendation, personal essay, GRE required in support of School's application. Online application available. TOEFL (minimum score 550) required for international applicants. Interview recommended for some programs. Accepts transfer applicants. Apply to Dean at least one month prior to registration. Application fee $35. Phone: (802)654-2251; fax: (802)654-2906; e-mail: gradprograms@smcvt.edu.

ADMISSION STANDARDS. Selective. Usual minimum average: 2.8 (A = 4).

FINANCIAL AID. Three assistantships, grants, Vermont loans and scholarships, Federal W/S, loans. Apply by March 15 to Director of Financial Aid. Phone: (802)654-3243; fax: (802)654-2591. Use FAFSA (College code: 003694) and institutional FAF.

DEGREE REQUIREMENTS. For master's: 36–42 semester hours.

FIELDS OF STUDY.
Administration and Management. M.S.A. only.
Clinical Psychology. Sixty semester hours. M.A.
Education.
Teaching English as a Second/Foreign Language.
Theology and Pastoral Ministry.

THE COLLEGE OF SAINT ROSE
Albany, New York 12203-1419
Web site: www.strose.edu

Founded 1920. CGS member. Coed. Private control. Semester system. Library: 200,987 volumes, 975 subscriptions. Total College enrollment: 5149.

Tuition: per credit $527. Limited housing for graduate students. Average monthly housing costs: $400–$575. Contact the Direc-

---

tor of Residence Life for off-campus housing information. Phone: (518)454-5295.

Graduate School

Graduate study since 1949. Enrollment: full-time 560; part-time 1109. Graduate faculty: full-time 68, part-time 101. Degrees conferred: M.A., M.S., M.S.Ed., M.B.A., M.B.A.-J.D. (with Albany Law School).

ADMISSION REQUIREMENTS. Transcripts, two letters of recommendation, statement of purpose required in support of application. GMAT required for Business Administration and Accounting. TOEFL required for international applicants. Accepts transfer applicants. Apply to Dean of Graduate, Adult, and Continuing Education Admissions at least three months prior to registration. Rolling admissions process. Application fee $35. Phone: (518)454-5143; fax: (518)458-5479.

ADMISSION STANDARDS. Selective. Usual minimum average: 2.75 (A = 4).

FINANCIAL AID. Scholarships, assistantships, internships, grants, Federal W/S, loans. Approved for VA benefits. Apply by March 1 to appropriate Department for internships, scholarships, assistantships; to Financial Aid Office for all other programs. Phone: (518)454-5168. Use FAFSA and institutional FAF. Some aid for part-time students.

DEGREE REQUIREMENTS. For master's: 30 semester hours minimum, at least 24 in residence; thesis/nonthesis option; written comprehensive exam for some departments.

FIELDS OF STUDY.

SCHOOL OF ARTS AND HUMANITIES:
Art Education. M.S.Ed.
Communications. M.A.
English. M.A.
History/Political Science. M.A.
Music Education. M.S.Ed.
Music Technology. M.A.

SCHOOL OF BUSINESS:
Accounting. M.A.
Business Administration. M.B.A.

SCHOOL OF EDUCATION:
Adolescence Education. M.S.Ed.
Applied Technology Education. M.S.Ed.
Childhood Education. M.S.Ed.
Counseling. M.S.Ed.
Early Childhood Education. M.S.Ed.
Educational Leadership and Administration. M.S.Ed.
Educational Psychology. M.S.Ed.
Literacy. M.S.Ed.
Professional Teacher Education. M.S.Ed.
School Psychology. M.S.
Special Education. M.S.Ed.

SCHOOL OF MATHEMATICS AND SCIENCES:
Computer Information Systems. Includes bioinformatics, computer game design, internet programming, embedded real-time systems. M.S.

COLLEGE OF ST. SCHOLASTICA
Duluth, Minnesota 55811-4199
Web site: www.css.edu

Founded 1912. Coed. Private. Church related. Semester system. Library: 137,000 volumes, 828 subscriptions. Total College enrollment: 3250.

Tuition: per credit $583. On-campus housing available for single students. Average academic year housing costs: $7000. Contact the Housing Office for both on- and off-campus housing information. Phone: (218)723-6483. Day-care facilities available.

Graduate Studies

Graduate study since 1972. Enrollment: full-time 365, part-time 242. Faculty: full-time 38, part-time 31. Degrees conferred: M.A., M.Ed.

ADMISSION REQUIREMENTS. Transcripts, GRE (Nursing, Exercise Physiology program only), two letters of recommendations required in support of application. TOEFL required for international applicants. Accepts transfer applicants. Apply to Graduate Office by March 1 for Physical Therapy, January 31 for Occupational Therapy; apply to all other programs at least one month prior to each quarter. Application fee $50. Phone: (800) 447-5444, (218) 723-6285; fax: (218)723-2275.

ADMISSION STANDARDS. Selective. Usual minimum average: 3.0 for last two years (A = 4). TOEFL minimum score 575.

FINANCIAL AID. Scholarships, traineeships, Federal W/S, loans. Approved for VA benefits. Apply to Director of Financial Aid; no specified closing date. Phone: (218)723-6047; fax: (218) 723-6290. Use FAFSA. Aid available for part-time students.

DEGREE REQUIREMENTS. For M.Ed.: 34 credit program. For M.A. Nursing: 38–47 credit program. For M.A. Management: 39 credit program. For M.A. Physical Therapy: 85 credit program; internship. For M.A. Occupational Therapy: 76 credit program; fieldwork experience. For M.A. Exercise Physiology: 32 credit program; thesis/internship.

FIELDS OF STUDY.
Curriculum and Instruction.
Educational Media and Technology.
Exercise Physiology.
Health Information Management.
Information Technology Leadership.
Management.
Nursing.
Occupational Therapy.
Physical Therapy.
Teaching.

ST. THOMAS UNIVERSITY

Miami, Florida 33054-6459
Web site: www.stu.edu

Founded 1966. Located about 5 miles NW of Miami. Coed. Private control (Roman Catholic affiliation). Semester system. Library: 190,000 volumes, 990 subscriptions. Total University enrollment at main campus: 2500.

School of Law

Web site: www.stu.edu/lawschool

Established 1984. Located on main campus. ABA approved since 1988. AALS member. Semester system. Full-time, day study only. Special program: full year or summer study at the University of Madrid, Spain. Law library: 324,202 volumes, 3071 subscriptions; has LEXIS, NEXIS, WESTLAW, DIALOG, TOMCAT.

Annual tuition: $26,580. On-campus housing available for single students only. Law students tend to live off-campus. Contact University's Housing Office for both on- and off-campus housing information. Phone: (305)628-6692. Housing deadline July 1. Annual on-campus housing cost: single students $17,578 (room and board). Off-campus housing and personal expenses: approximately $18,000.

Enrollment: first-year class 328; total 665 (men 55%, women 45%, minorities 41%). Faculty: full-time 30, part-time 34. Student to faculty ratio is 19.1 to 1. Degrees conferred: J.D., J.D.-M.B.A. (Accounting, International Business, Sport Administration), J.D.-M.S. (Marriage and Family), LL.M. (Intercultural Human Rights), JD.-LL.M.-M.A. (International Human Rights).

ADMISSION REQUIREMENTS. LSDAS Law School report, LSAT (not later that February test date; if more than one LSAT, average is used), bachelor's degree from an accredited institution, personal statement, two recommendations, transcripts (must show all schools attended and at least three years of study) required in support of application. TOEFL required for international applicants. Applicants must have received bachelor's degree prior to enrollment. Interview not required but may be requested by School. Accepts transfer applicants from other ABA-accredited schools on a space-available basis. Apply to Office of Admission after September 30, before May 1. First-year students admitted Fall only. Rolling admissions process. Application fee $60. Phone: (800)254-4569, (305)623-2311; fax: (305)623-2357.

ADMISSION STANDARDS. Selective. Accepts approximately 39% of all students. Number of full-time applicants 2379; number of full-time acceptances 925; number of full-time enrolled 328; LSAT (75% of full-time students have a score at or above 147); GPA (75% of full-time students have a GPA at or above 2.58). *U.S. News & World Report* ranking is in the fourth tier of all U.S. law schools.

FINANCIAL AID. Scholarships, minority scholarships, Grants-in-Aid, private and institutional loans; Federal loans and Federal W/S offered through Financial Aid Office. For scholarships/grants (selection criteria places heavy reliance on LSAT and Undergraduate GPA) apply to before May 1 (priority deadline). For all other programs apply to Financial Aid Officer. Phone: (305)628-6725. Use FAFSA (School code: 001468), also submit Financial Aid Transcript, Federal Income Tax forms. Approximately 34% of first-year class received scholarships/Grants-in-Aid. Approximately 80% of students receive some form of financial aid. Average scholarships grant $7,826.

DEGREE REQUIREMENTS. For J.D.: 90 (49 required) credits with a GPA of at least a 2.0 (A = 4), plus completion of upper-divisional writing course; three-year program. For LL.M.: 24 credit program.

UNIVERSITY OF ST. THOMAS

Houston, Texas 77006-4694
Web site: www.stthom.edu

Founded 1885. CGS member. Coed. Private control. Roman Catholic affiliation. Semester system. Library: 226,500 volumes, 2400 subscriptions. Total University enrollment: 3800.

Tuition: per credit $630. On-campus housing for single students only. Average academic year housing costs: $6700 (including board). Contact Director of Residence Life for both on- and off-campus housing information. Phone: (713)525-3836.

Graduate Study

Enrollment: full-time 268, part-time 909. Graduate faculty: full-time 48, part-time 38. Degrees conferred: M.A., M.B.A., M.Ed., M.I.B., M.L.A., M.S.Acc., M.S.I.S., M.Div., M.A.Th., Ph.D.

ADMISSION REQUIREMENTS. Official transcripts, three letters of recommendation, GMAT (for Business), essay required in support of application. TOEFL required for international applicants. Accepts transfer applicants. Graduates of unaccredited colleges not considered. Apply to Director of Admissions at least two months prior to entrance. Rolling admissions process. Application $25. Phone: (713)525-3500; fax: (713)525-3532; e-mail: admissions@stthom.edu.

ADMISSION STANDARDS. Selective. Usual minimum average: 2.75 (A = 4).

FINANCIAL AID. Fellowships, assistantships, tuition waivers, Federal W/S, loans. Apply to the appropriate School for fellowships, assistantships; to the Office of Financial Aid for all other programs. No specified closing dates. Use FAFSA.

DEGREE REQUIREMENTS. For most master's: 32–36 credits minimum final written/oral exam; no thesis or language requirement. For M.B.A.: 36–42 semester credits. For M.Div.: at least two years in residence; thesis; reading knowledge of either Hebrew, Latin, Greek. For Ph.D.: 60 credits minimum beyond the bachelor's degree; qualifying exam; reading knowledge of two foreign languages; dissertation; final oral exam.

FIELDS OF STUDY.

CAMERON SCHOOL OF BUSINESS:
Accounting. M.S. Acc.
Business Administration. M.B.A.

CENTER FOR THOMISTIC STUDIES:
Philosophy. M.A., Ph.D.

SCHOOL OF EDUCATION:
Education. M.Ed.

SCHOOL OF THEOLOGY AT ST. MARY'S SEMINARY:
Divinity. M.Div.
Pastoral Studies. M.A.P.S.
Theological Studies. M.A.T.S.

LIBERAL ARTS:
Liberal Arts. M.L.A.

UNIVERSITY OF ST. THOMAS
St. Paul, Minnesota 55105-1089
Web site: www.stthomas.edu

Founded 1885. Coed on the graduate level. Private control. Roman Catholic affiliation. Semester system. Library: 460,000 volumes, 2530 subscriptions. Total University enrollment: 11,000.
Tuition: per credit $572–$852. No on-campus housing available. Contact Director of Residence Life for both on- and off-campus housing information. Phone: (651)962-6150.

Graduate Study

Graduate study since 1950. Enrollment: full-time 655, part-time 4509. Graduate faculty: full-time 367, part-time 159. Degrees conferred: M.A., M.A.T., M.B.A., M.I.M., M.M., M.B.C., M.S.M.S.E., M.S.D.D., M.S.S., M.S.W., Ed.S.

ADMISSION REQUIREMENTS. Official transcripts, three letters of recommendation, GRE/MAT, GMAT (for Business), personal statement required in support of application. Online application available. TOEFL required for international applicants. Accepts transfer applicants. Graduates of unaccredited colleges not considered. Apply to Director of Admissions by June 1 (Fall), November 1 (Spring). Rolling admissions process. Application $50. Phone: (651)962-4550; fax: (651)962-6410.

ADMISSION STANDARDS. Selective. Usual minimum average: 2.75 (M.A.), 3.0 (M.B.A.), 3.25 (Ed.S.)

FINANCIAL AID. Fellowships, research assistantships, teaching assistantships, grants, Federal W/S, loans. Apply to the Office of Financial Aid; no specified closing dates. Phone: (651)647-5232. Use FAFSA. Aid available for part-time students.

DEGREE REQUIREMENTS. For most master's: 32–36 credits minimum final written/oral exam; no thesis or language requirement. For M.B.A., M.I.M.: 36–42 semester credits. For Ed.S.: 33 credits beyond the master's; final written/oral exams; final project.

FIELDS OF STUDY.

OPUS COLLEGE OF BUSINESS:
Accounting. M.B.A.
Business Administration. M.B.A., E.M.B.A.
Business Communication. M.B.C.
Health Care. M.B.A.
Real Estate. M.S.

GRADUATE SCHOOL OF ARTS AND SCIENCES:
Art History. M.A.
Catholic Studies. M.A.
English. M.A.
Music Education. M.A.

SCHOOL OF EDUCATION:
Athletics and Activities Administration. M.A.
Community Education Administration. M.A.
Curriculum and Instruction. M.A.
Educational Leadership and Administrative. M.A.
Gifted, Creative, and Talented Education. M.A.
Human Resource and Change Leadership. M.A.
Leadership. Ed.D.
Leadership in Student Affairs. M.A.
Learning Technology. M.A.
Organizational Development. Ed.D.
Police Leadership. M.A.
Public Policy and Leadership.
Reading. Includes reading K–12.
Special Education. Includes developmental disabilities, early childhood, emotional behavioral disorders, learning disabilities.
Special Education—Autism Spectrum Disorder. M.A.
Teaching. M.A.

SCHOOL OF ENGINEERING:
Manufacturing Systems. M.A.
Manufacturing Systems Engineering. M.M.S.E.
System Engineering. M.S.
Technology Management. M.S.

GRADUATE SCHOOL OF PROFESSIONAL PSYCHOLOGY:
Counseling. M.A.
Psychology. Psy.D.

SCHOOL OF SOCIAL WORK:
Social Work. M.S.W. offered jointly with the College of St. Catherine.

SAINT PAUL SEMINARY SCHOOL OF DIVINITY:
Divinity. Seminary program. M.Div.
Religious Education. M.A.
Theology. M.A.

GRADUATE PROGRAMS IN SOFTWARE:
Software Engineering. M.S.S.E.
Software Management. M.S.S.M.
Software Systems. M.S.S.

ST. XAVIER UNIVERSITY

Chicago, Illinois 60655-3105
Web site: www.sxu.edu

Founded 1847. Coed. Roman Catholic. Semester system. Library: 173,700 volumes, 2150 subscriptions. Total University enrollment: 5700.

Tuition: per credit $625 (Applied Computer Science), $650 (Business, Nursing, Speech-Language Pathology), $550 (Business Cohort), $600 (Education), $500 (Education Cohort). On-campus housing for 285 graduate students. Average academic year housing costs: $6350. Contact the Director of Campus Life for both on- and off-campus housing information. Phone: (773) 298-3499.

Graduate Studies

Enrollment: full- and part-time 2200. College faculty teaching graduate students: full-time 92, part-time 46. Degrees conferred: M.A., M.A.C.S., M.S., M.B.A., M.P.H.

ADMISSION REQUIREMENTS. Transcripts, three letters of recommendation, GRE/GMAT/MAT in support of application. Online application available. TOEFL required for international applicants. Accepts transfer applicants. Apply to Director of Admissions at least one month prior to registration. Rolling admission process. Application fee $35. Phone: (773)298-3053; fax: (773)298-3076; e-mail: admission @sxu.edu.

ADMISSION STANDARDS. Selective. Usual minimum average: 3.0 (A = 4).

FINANCIAL AID. Scholarships, research assistantships, internships, Federal W/S, loans. Approved for VA benefits. Apply by July 15 to Director of Financial Aid. Phone: (773)298-7071; fax: (773)298-3076. Use FAFSA. Aid available for part-time students.

DEGREE REQUIREMENTS. For master's: 30 semester hours minimum; research project.

FIELDS OF STUDY.

GRAHAM SCHOOL OF MANAGEMENT:
Business Administration. Includes concentrations in finance, financial analysis and investment, financial fraud examination, financial planning, health administration, management, marketing, project management, public and nonprofit, service management, training and workplace learning management. M.B.A.
Finance. M.S.
Management. M.S.
Public and Non-profit Management. M.S.
Service Management. M.S.

SCHOOL OF ARTS AND SCIENCE:
Applied Computer Science. M.A.C.S.
Speech-Language Pathology. M.S.

SCHOOL OF EDUCATION:
Counseling. Includes community, agency, school. M.A.
Educational Administration and Supervision. M.A.
Curriculum and Instruction. M.A.
Multicategorical Special Education. M.A.
Reading. M.A.
Teaching and Leadership.

SCHOOL OF NURSING:
Clinical Nurse Specialist in Adult. M.S.
Family Nurse Practitioner. M.S.
Leadership in Nursing and Community Health. M.S.
Mental Health Nursing. M.S.

SALEM STATE COLLEGE

Salem, Massachusetts 01970–5353
Web site: www.salemstate.edu

Founded 1854. CGS member. Located 20 miles NE of Boston. Coed. State control. Semester system. Library: 230,500 volumes, 1400 subscriptions.

Tuition/fees: per credit resident $250, nonresident $340. No on-campus housing available.

Graduate School

Enrollment: full-time 225, part-time 1054. Graduate faculty: full-time 38, part-time 77. Degrees conferred: M.A., M.A.T., M.B.A., M.Ed., M.S., M.S.N., M.S.W., M.S.N.-M.B.A.

ADMISSION REQUIREMENTS. Transcripts, three letters of reference, statement of purpose, GRE/GMAT/MAT required in support of School's application. TOEFL required for international applicants. Interview not required. Accepts transfer applicants. Graduates of unaccredited institutions not considered. Apply to Dean of Graduate School by November 1 (Spring), July 1 (Fall) for M.B.A.; by January 1 for M.S.W.; all others on rolling admissions. Application fee $35. Phone: (978)542-6323.

ADMISSION STANDARDS. Selective. Usual minimum average: 2.5 (A = 4) and 2.7 in major field of study.

FINANCIAL AID. Scholarships, graduate assistantships, Federal W/S, loans. Approved for VA benefits. Apply by May 1 to the Dean of Graduate School for assistantships; to Financial Aid Office for all other programs. Phone: (978)542-6112. Use FAFSA.

DEGREE REQUIREMENTS. For M.Ed., M.A.T.: 36–39 semester hours minimum, at least 27 in residence; final written/oral exam. For M.A.: 33 semester hours; one foreign language or computer statistics; final written exam. For M.S. in Geo Information, Science: 40 semester hours. For M.S. in Math: 30 semester hours. For M.S.N.: 39 semester hours. For M.B.A.: 54 semester hours; computer proficiency. For M.S.W.: 60 semester hours.

FIELDS OF STUDY.
Art. M.A.T.
Bilingual Education. M.Ed.
Biology. M.A.T.
Business Administration. M.B.A.
Chemistry. M.A.T.
Counseling and Psychological Services. M.S.
Criminal Justice. M.S.
Early Childhood. M.Ed.
Educational Leadership. M.Ed.
Elementary Education. M.Ed.
English. MA., M.A.T.
ESL. M.A.T.
Geo-Information Science. M.S.
Higher Education in Student Affairs. M.Ed.
History. M.A., M.A.T.
Industrial/Organizational Psychology. M.S.
Library Media Studies. M.Ed.
Mathematics. M.A.T.
Middle School General Science. M.A.T.
Middle School Mathematics. M.A.T.
Middle School Education. M.Ed.
Nursing. Includes direct entry. M.S.
Physical Education. M.Ed.
Reading. M.Ed.
School Business Officer. M.Ed.
School Counseling. M.Ed.
Secondary Education. M.Ed.
Spanish. M.S.
Special Education. M.Ed.
Technology in Education. M.Ed.

SALISBURY STATE UNIVERSITY

Salisbury, Maryland 21801-6837
Web site: www.salisbury.edu

Founded 1925. Located 125 miles SE of Baltimore. Coed. State control. Semester system. Special facilities: Center for Technology in Education, Research Center for Delmarva History and Culture, Small Business Development Center. Library: 249,700 volumes, 1762 subscriptions. Total University enrollment: 7000.

Tuition: per credit resident $249, nonresident $535. No on- or off-campus housing for graduate students.

Graduate Program

Graduate study since 1962. Enrollment: full-time 184, part-time 428. Graduate faculty: full- and part-time 89. Degrees conferred: M.Ed., M.A., M.B.A., M.S., M.S.W.

ADMISSION REQUIREMENTS. Official transcripts, GRE/GMAT/MAT/NTE required in support of application. TOEFL required for international applicants. Accepts transfer applicants. Graduates of unaccredited institutions not considered. Apply by August 1 (Fall), January 1 (Spring) to the Graduate Admissions Office. Rolling admission process. Application fee $45. Phone: (410)546-6161; fax: (410)546-6016; e-mail: admissions@ssu.edu.

ADMISSION STANDARDS. Varies by department.

FINANCIAL AID. Fellowships, graduate assistantships, internships, grants, loans. Approved for VA benefits. Apply to appropriate department chair for assistantships; to the Financial Aid Office for all other programs. Phone: (410)546-6165; fax: (410)546-6168. Use FAFSA. Aid available for part-time students.

DEGREE REQUIREMENTS. For M.Ed.: 33 semester hours. For M.S.-Nursing: 39 semester hours. For M.A.-English: 33 credits minimum. For M.B.A.: 30 semester hours. For M.S.W.: 60 credit program.

FIELDS OF STUDY.
Applied Health Physiology. M.S.
Business Administration. M.B.A.
Conflict Analysis and Dispute Resolution. M.A.
Education. Includes English, history, mathematics, music, science. M.Ed.
Elementary Education. M.Ed.
English. M.A.
Geographic Information Systems and Public Administration. M.S.
History. M.A.
Nursing. Includes family nurse practitioner. M.S.
Psychology. M.A.
Public School Administration. M.Ed.
Reading. M.Ed.
School Administration. M.Ed.
Social Work. M.S.W.
Teaching. M.A.T.

SAMFORD UNIVERSITY

Birmingham, Alabama 35229-0002
Web site: www.samford.edu

Founded 1941. Coed. Private control. Baptist affiliation. Semester system. Library: 508,000 volumes, 3700 subscriptions. Total University enrollment: 4500.

Tuition: per credit $480. No on-campus housing available. Monthly housing costs: $450–$625. Contact Director, Residence Life for both on- and off-campus housing information. Phone: (205)870-2932.

Graduate Studies

Graduate study since 1965. Enrollment: full-time 825, part-time 243. Faculty: full-time 101, part-time 15. Degrees conferred: M.S. in Ed., M.S. in Environ. Mgt., M.S.N., M.B.A., M.S., M.Mus., M.Mus.Ed., Ed.S., M.Div., D. Min., M.Mus., Pharm.D.

ADMISSION REQUIREMENTS. Transcripts, photograph required in support of School's application. GRE/NTE required for Education, Liberal Arts majors; GMAT for Business majors; MAT for Music. TOEFL required for international applicants. Interview desirable. Accepts transfer applicants. Graduates of unaccredited institutions not considered. Apply to Graduate Dean at least one month prior to entrance. Application fee $25. Phone: (205)726-2871; fax: (205)726-2171.

ADMISSION STANDARDS. Selective. Usual minimum average: 2.5 (A = 4).

FINANCIAL AID. Annual awards from institutional funds: scholarships, assistantships, tuition waivers, Federal W/S, loans. Approved for VA benefits. Apply by March 1 to the Financial Aid Office. Phone: (205)870-2905; fax: (205)870-2171. Use FAFSA and institutional FAF. About 10% of students receive aid other than loans from University and outside sources.

DEGREE REQUIREMENTS. For M.A.: 33 semester hours minimum including thesis, at least 24 in residence; reading knowledge of one foreign language; comprehensive exam. For M.S. in Ed., M.Mus.: 32–33 hours minimum, at least 24 in residence; no thesis or language requirement; comprehensive exam. For M.B.A.: 36–45 hours, depending upon previous preparation, at least 24 in residence. For M.Mus.Ed.: essentially the same as for M.S. in Ed., except 37 semester hours required. Final written/oral exams for all master's. For Ed.S.: 30 semester hours beyond the master's. For Pharm.D.: 65 credits, plus 139 professional credits.

FIELDS OF STUDY.
Accounting. M.Acc.
Business Administration. M.B.A.
Church Music. M.M.
Comparative Law. M.C.L.
Divinity. M.Div.
Early Childhood Education. M.S.F.
Educational Leadership. Ed.D.
Elementary Education. M.S.E.
Environmental Management. M.S.E.M.
Ministry. D.Min.
Music. M.M.
Music Education. M.M.E.
Nursing. M.S.N., D.N.P.
Pharmacy. Pharm.D.
Theological Studies. M.T.S.

Cumberland School of Law

Web site: cumberland.samford.edu

Established 1847. School acquired by Samford University in 1961. ABA approved since 1949. AALS member since 1952. Semester system. Special facilities: Center for Law and Civic Education, Center for Biotechnology, Center for the Study of Law and the Church. Special programs: Summer programs in Cambridge, England, Victoria, British Columbia, Fortaleza, Brazil. Law library: 290,954 volumes, 2029 subscriptions; has LEGALTRAC, LEXIS, NEXIS, WESTLAW, OCLC; has more than 200 network connections.

Annual tuition: full-time $26,190, part-time $15,426. Limited on-campus housing available. Average annual living expenses: $19,310.

Enrollment: first-year class 173; total 498 (men 56%, women 44%, minorities 12%). Faculty: full-time 23, part-time 21. Student to faculty ratio is 18 to 1. Degrees conferred: J.D., J.D.-M.Acc., J.D.-M.B.A., J.D.-M.P.A., J.D.-M.P.H., J.D.-M.Div., J.D.-M.S. (Environmental Management), M.C.L. (for International Law School graduates).

ADMISSION REQUIREMENTS. LSDAS Law School report, bachelor's degree, transcripts, personal statement, two references, LSAT degree required in support of application. Interview recommended. Accepts transfer applicants. Graduates of unaccredited colleges usually not considered. Apply to Admission Office after October 1, before May 1 (priority deadline February 28.). Admits Fall only. Application fee $50. Phone: (205)726-2702, (800)888-7213; fax: (205)726-2057.

ADMISSION STANDARDS. Selective. Accepts approximately 32% of all students. Number of full-time applicants 1420; number of full-time acceptance 450; number of full-time enrolled 173; LSAT (75% of full-time students have a score at or above 154); GPA (75% of full-time students have a GPA at or above 2.98). *U.S. News & World Report* ranking is in the third tier of all U.S. law schools.

FINANCIAL AID. Scholarships, Federal W/S, loans. Apply to University's Director of Financial Aid by March 1. Phone: (205) 726-2905. Use FAFSA (School code: 001036). Approximately 30% of students receive financial assistance from school.

DEGREE REQUIREMENTS. For J.D.: 90 semester hours program. For master's degrees, see Graduate School listing above.

SAM HOUSTON STATE UNIVERSITY
Huntsville, Texas 77341-2448
Web site: www.shsu.edu

Founded 1879. Located 70 miles N of Houston. Coed. State control. Semester system. Special facilities: Sam Houston Memorial Museum, Texas Regional Institute for Environmental Studies. Library: 1,800,000 volumes, 3297 subscriptions. Total University enrollment: 15,000.

Tuition: per credit resident $184, nonresident $462. On-campus housing for 102 married students, unlimited for single students. Average academic year housing costs: $5600 (including board) for single students; $4456 for married students. Contact Director of Housing for both on- and off-campus housing information. Phone: (936)294-1812.

Graduate Studies

Graduate study since 1938. Enrollment: full-time 446, part-time 1100. College faculty teaching graduate students: full- and part-time 220. Degrees conferred: M.A., M.B.A., M.Ed., M.M., M.M.Ed., M.S., M.F.A., M.L.S., Ed.D. Ph.D.

ADMISSION REQUIREMENTS. Two official transcripts, GRE/GMAT/MAT required in support of application. Recommendations, résumés, departmental application, writing samples required by some departments. TOEFL required for international applicants. Accepts transfer applicants. Graduates of unaccredited institutions not considered. Apply to Graduate Studies Office at least two months prior to registration. Rolling admissions process. Application fee $20. Phone: (936)294-1971; fax: (936)294-1271.

ADMISSION STANDARDS. Selective. Usual minimum average: 2.5 (A = 4).

FINANCIAL AID. Annual awards from institutional funds: scholarships, teaching fellowships, research assistantships, internships,

Federal W/S, loans. Approved for VA benefits. Apply well in advance of registration to the Graduate Office for assistantships, fellowships; to the Financial Aid Office for all other programs. Phone: (936)294-2328. Use FAFSA (School code: 003606). About 10% of students receive aid from College and outside sources. Aid available for part-time students.

DEGREE REQUIREMENTS. For M.A., M.L.S.: 30 semester hours minimum including thesis, at least 24 in residence; candidacy; comprehensive exam. For M.Ed., M.S., M.B.A.: 36 semester hours minimum, at least 30 in residence; candidacy; thesis optional for six credits; comprehensive oral/written exam. For Ph.D.: 90 semester hours beyond the bachelor's, at least 30 in residence; two semesters for supervised teaching; written/oral exam; dissertation.

FIELDS OF STUDY.

COLLEGE OF ARTS AND SCIENCES:
Agriculture. M.S.
Biology. M.A., M.S.
Chemistry. M.S.
Computing and Information Science. M.S.
Dance. M.F.A.
Digital Forensics. M.S.
Industrial Technology. M.A.
Information Assurance and Security. M.S.
Mathematics. M.A., M.S.
Music. Includes conducting, Kodaly pedagogy, performance, musicology, theory/composition. M.M.
Music Education. Includes elementary instrumental, Kodaly pedagogy, vocal. M.Ed.
Statistics. M.S.

COLLEGE OF BUSINESS ADMINISTRATION:
Accounting. M.S.
Business Administration. M.B.A.
Finance. M.S.

COLLEGE OF CRIMINAL JUSTICE:
Criminal Justice. Ph.D.
Criminal Justice and Criminology. M.A.
Criminal Justice Leadership and Management. M.S.
Forensic Science. M.S.
Security Studies. M.S.
Victim Services Management. M.S.

COLLEGE OF EDUCATION AND APPLIED SCIENCE:
Administration. M.A., M.Ed.
Counseling. M.A., M.Ed.
Counselor Education. Ph.D.
Educational Leadership. Ed.D.
Health. M.A., M.Ed.
Instructional Technology. M.Ed.
Kinesiology. M.A., M.Ed.
Library Science. M.L.S.
Reading. M.Ed., Ed.D.
Special Education. M.A., M.Ed.

COLLEGE OF HUMANITIES AND SOCIAL SCIENCES:
Dietetics. M.S.
English. M.A.
Family and Consumer Sciences. M.S.
History. M.A., Ph.D.
Political Science. M.A
Psychology. Includes clinical (Ph.D.), school. M.A., Ph.D.
Public Administration. M.P.A.
Sociology. M.A.
Speech Communication. M.A.

SAN DIEGO STATE UNIVERSITY

San Diego, California 92182-7416
Web site: www.sdsu.edu

Founded 1897. CGS member. Coed. State control. Semester system. Special facilities: Center on Aging, Lupinski Institute for Judaic Studies, Production Center for Documentary and Drama, Institute for International Security and Conflict Resolution, Mt. Laguna Observatory, Center for Energy Studies, Molecular Biology Institute, Institute for Public Health. Library: 1,300,000 volumes, 12,000 subscriptions. Total University enrollment: 33,000.

Annual tuition/fees: full-time, resident $4070, nonresident $4070 plus $339 per unit. On-campus housing for 2077 single students; none for married students. Average academic year housing costs: $10,904 (including board). Contact the Director of Housing and Residential Life for both on- and off-campus housing information. Phone: (619)594-5742. Day-care facilities available.

Graduate and Research Affairs

Enrollment: full-time 3073, part-time 2950. Faculty: full- and part-time over 750. Degrees conferred: M.A., M.S., M.B.A., M.C.P., M.F.A., M.M., M.P.A., M.P.H., M.S.W., Ph.D.

ADMISSION REQUIREMENTS. Two transcripts, GRE required in support of application. TOEFL (minimum score 550) required for international applicants. GRE Subject Test, GMAT, interview required by some departments. Accepts transfer applicants. Graduates of unaccredited colleges not considered. Apply to Admissions Office of the University by July 1 (Fall), December 1 (Spring). Applicants for doctoral programs must be admitted as a regular student at the appropriate campus as well as to San Diego State University. Rolling admissions process. Application fee $55. Phone: (619)594-6336.

ADMISSION STANDARDS. Selective. Usual minimum average: 2.75 (A = 4).

FINANCIAL AID. Teaching associates, fellowships, scholarships, graduate/research/student assistantships, Federal W/S, loans. Apply by February 15 to appropriate department chairman for assistantships; to Financial Aid Office for all other programs. Phone: (619)594-6323. Use FAFSA (School code: 001151). About 20% of students receive aid other than loans from University and other sources. Aid available for part-time students.

DEGREE REQUIREMENTS. For M.A., M.S., M.M.: 30 units minimum, at least 21 in residence; thesis/comprehensive exam; reading knowledge of one foreign language for some majors. For M.S. (Counseling): 60 units minimum, at least 30 in residence; comprehensive exam. For M.C.P.: 57 units minimum, at least 30 in residence. For M.B.A.: 30–60 units, at least 21 in residence. For M.F.A.: 60 units, at least 30 in residence. For M.P.A.: 36 units, at least 21 in residence. For M.S.W.: 56 units, at least 28 in residence. For M.P.H.: 48–55 units, depending on concentration, at least 39 in residence. For Ph.D. (Biology, Chemistry, Clinical Psychology, Engineering Sciences/Applied Mechanics, Language and Communicative Disorders, Mathematics and Science Education, Public Health): at least two years in full-time residence, one year on the campus of the University of California at San Diego and one year at San Diego State University; preliminary written exam; dissertation; final oral exam. For Ph.D. (Ecology): at least two years in full-time residence, one year at University of California at Davis and one year at San Diego State University; qualifying exam; dissertation; final oral exam. For Ph.D. (Education): 48 semester units of residency, 24 at Claremont Graduate School and 24 at San Diego State University; qualifying exam; dissertation; final oral exam. For Ph.D. (Geography): at least two years in full-time residence, one year at University of California Santa Barbara and one year at San Diego State University; qualifying exam; dissertation; final oral exam.

FIELDS OF STUDY.
Accountancy. M.S.
Aerospace Engineering. M.S.
Anthropology. Thesis, one language, final oral exam for M.A.
Applied Mathematics. Includes mathematical theory of communication systems. M.S.
Art. Includes art history, studio arts; thesis or creative project for M.A., M.F.A.
Asian Studies. Interdepartmental. M.A.
Astronomy. M.S.
Audiology. Au.D.
Biology. GRE Subject for admission. Includes ecology, evolutionary biology, molecular biology, physiology. Thesis, final oral exam for M.A., M.S.; one foreign language for M.A. M.A., M.S.; joint doctoral (Ph.D.) program with University of California at San Diego.
Business Administration. GMAT for admission. Includes entrepreneurship, finance, financial and tax planning, human resource management, information systems, international business, management, marketing, operations management, real estate, taxation, total quality management (M.S.). Thesis or comprehensive exam for M.S., M.B.A.
Chemistry. Thesis, final oral exam for M.A., M.S. M.A., M.S; joint doctoral (Ph.D.) program with University of California at San Diego.
Child Development. M.S.
City Planning. M.C.P.
Civil Engineering. Includes environmental engineering. M.S.
Clinical Psychology. Joint doctoral (Ph.D.) program with University of California at San Diego.
Communication. M.A.
Computational Science. M.S.
Computer Science. M.S.
Counseling. M.A. Full-time, Fall admission only. Includes marriage, family, and child counseling, school counseling, school psychology.
Creative Writing. M.F.A.
Criminal Justice and Criminology. M.S.
Drama. Thesis for M.A., M.F.A.
Ecology. Joint doctoral (Ph.D.) program with University of California at Davis.
Economics. M.A.
Education. Includes counseling, educational leadership, educational research, educational technology, elementary curriculum and instruction, policy studies in language and cross-cultural education, reading, secondary curriculum and instruction, special education. M.A.; joint doctoral (Ed.D.) program with Claremont Graduate University.
Electrical Engineering. M.S.
Engineering Sciences/Applied Mechanics. Joint doctoral (Ph.D.) program with University of California at San Diego.
English. One foreign language for M.A. M.A.
Exercise Physiology. M.S.
Executive. M.B.A.
French. M.A.
Geography. Includes natural resources and environmental policy, transportation. M.A.; joint doctoral (Ph.D.) program with University of California at Santa Barbara.
Geological Sciences. M.S.
Gerontology. M.S.
History. One foreign language for M.A.
Homeland Security. M.S.
Interdisciplinary Studies. M.S.
Journalism and Media Studies. M.A.
Language and Communicative Disorders. Joint doctoral (Ph.D.) program with University of California at San Diego.
Latin American Studies. Interdepartmental. M.A.
Liberal Arts. Interdepartmental. M.A.
Linguistics. M.A.
Mathematics. M.A.
Mathematics and Science Education. Joint doctoral (Ph.D.) program with University of California at San Diego.

Mechanical Engineering. M.S.
Microbiology. M.S.
Music. Public recital or thesis for M.A., M.M.
Nursing. Includes advanced practice nursing of adults and the elderly, community health nursing, nursing systems administration. M.S.
Nutritional Sciences. M.S.
Philosophy. M.A.
Physical Education. M.A.
Physics. One foreign language for M.A. M.A., M.S.
Political Science. M.A.
Psychology. GRE Subject for admission. Includes applied. Thesis, final exam for M.A., M.S. M.A., M.S.; joint doctoral (Ph.D.) program in clinical psychology with University of California at San Diego.
Public Administration. Includes city planning, criminal justice administration. M.P.A.
Public Health. Includes biometry, environmental health, epidemiology, health promotion, health services administration (M.P.H.); environmental health science, industrial hygiene, toxicology (M.S.). M.S., M.P.H.; joint doctoral (Ph.D.) program with University of California at San Diego.
Radiological Health Physics. Thesis. M.S.
Regulatory Affairs. M.S.
Rehabilitation Counseling. Fall admission only. M.S.
Social Work. Admits Fall only; apply to Director of School of Social Work between November 1 and April 15; interview required for admission. M.S.W.
Sociology. M.A.
Spanish. M.A.
Speech, Language and Hearing Sciences. M.A.
Sport Business Management. M.B.A.
Statistics. Includes biostatistics. M.S.
Television, Film, and New Media Production. M.A.
Theatre Arts. Includes acting, design and technical theatre, musical theatre. M.A., M.F.A.
Women's Studies. M.A.

UNIVERSITY OF SAN DIEGO
San Diego, California 92110-2492
Web site: www.sandiego.edu

Founded 1949. CGS member. Private control. Roman Catholic. Semester system. Special facilities: Children's Advocacy Institute, Patient Advocacy Clinic, Public Interest Law Center. Library: 825,000 volumes, 10,450 subscriptions. Total University enrollment: 7550.

Tuition: per credit master's programs $1010 (School of Leadership & Education Sciences), $1020 (Business), $1025 (Nursing, Arts & Science); per credit doctoral $1025 (Education), $1040 (Nursing). On-campus for both single and married graduate students. Average academic year housing costs: $7100 (including board) for single students; $7500 for married students. Contact Director of Graduate Housing for both on- and off-campus housing information. Phone: (619)260-4777.

Graduate Programs

Enrollment: full-time 553, part-time 745. Graduate faculty: full-time 121, part-time 25. Degrees conferred: M.A., M.F.A., M.S. (Tax), M.A.T., M.Ed., M.B.A., M.I.B., M.S.N., D.N.Sci., Ed.D.

ADMISSION REQUIREMENTS. Two official transcripts, GRE/MAT/GMAT, three letters of recommendation required in support of School's application. Online application available. TOEFL (minimum score 600) and financial information form required for international applicants. Accepts transfer applicants. Graduates of unaccredited colleges not considered. Apply to the Office of Graduate Admissions; for most master's programs May 1 (Fall),

November 15 (Spring), March 15 (Summer), other degree programs have specific deadlines consult Graduate Application for those deadlines. Rolling admissions process. Application fee $45 (master's), $50 (doctoral). Phone: (800)248-4873, (619)260-4524; fax: (619)260-4158; e-mail: grads@acusd.edu.

ADMISSION STANDARDS. Selective. Usual minimum average: 3.0 recommended (A = 4); GMAT score minimum of 525; GRE Verbal, Quantitative, and Analytical score minimum of 500.

FINANCIAL AID. Annual awards from institutional funds: assistantships, traineeships, fellowships, Federal W/S, loans. Approved for VA benefits. Apply by May 1 to the Office of Financial Services. Phone: (800)248-4873, (619)260-4514. Use FAFSA. About 37% of students receive aid other than loans from University and outside sources. Aid available to part-time students.

DEGREE REQUIREMENTS. For M.A.: 30 units minimum, at least 24 in residence; reading knowledge of one foreign language; thesis included; final written exam. For M.A.T., M.Ed., M.S.N.: same as for M.A., except no language requirement. For M.B.A., M.I.B.: 60 units minimum; computer proficiency. For M.S.(Tax): 36-unit program. For D.N.Sc.: 54 units minimum, at least 1 semester in full-time study; written exam; dissertation; oral defense. For Ed.D.: 60 units minimum beyond master's degree, at least two semesters in residence; qualifying exam; candidacy; dissertation; final oral exam.

FIELDS OF STUDY.

COLLEGE OF ARTS AND SCIENCES:
Dramatic Arts. In conjunction with The Old Globe Theatre. M.F.A.
History. M.A.
International Relations. M.A
Marine Science. Includes biological, chemical, geological oceanography. M.S.
Pastoral Care and Counseling. M.A.
Peace and Justice Studies. M.A.
Practical Theology. M.A.

SCHOOL OF BUSINESS:
Accounting. M.S.
Business Administration. Includes emphasis in electronic commerce, finance, management, marketing, project management, supply management, venture management. M.B.A.
Electronic Commerce. M.S.
Executive Leadership. M.S.
Global Leadership. M.S.
International Business. I.M.B.A.
Real Estate. M.S.R.E.
Supply Chain Management. M.S.

SCHOOL OF LEADERSHIP AND EDUCATION:
Counseling. M.A.
Educational Leadership/Administration. M.Ed.
Educational Technology. Joint doctoral (Ed.D.) Program with San Diego State University.
Leadership Studies. M.A., Ed.D.
Learning and Teaching. M.Ed.
Marital and Family Therapy. M.A.
Special Education. M.A.
Teaching and Learning (Literacy). Joint doctoral (Ed.D.) program with San Diego State University.

HAHN SCHOOL OF NURSING AND HEALTH SCIENCE:
Adult Nurse Practitioner. M.S.N.
Case Management of Vulnerable Populations. Includes acute, long-term community, home health. M.S.N.
Family Nurse Practitioner. M.S.N.
Health Care Systems Administration. M.S.N.
Nursing. Ph.D.
Pediatric Nurse Practitioner. M.S.N.

School of Law
Web site: www.sandiego.edu

Established 1954. Located on main campus. ABA approved since 1961. AALS member since 1952. Private control. Semester system. Full-time, part-time study. Special facilities: Center for Public Interest Law, Center for the Study of Constitutional Originalism, Institute on International and Comparative Law, Pardee Legal Research Center, Children's Advocacy Institute, Institute for Law and Philosophy. Law library: 523,054 volumes, 2034 subscriptions; has LEGALTRAC, LEXIS, NEXIS, WESTLAW, CALI; has more than 200 network connections.

Annual tuition: full-time $35,896, part-time $26,516. No on-campus housing available. Average annual living expenses: $14,310.

Enrollment: first-year class full-time 266, part-time 99; total full- and part-time 1035 (men 55%, women 45%, minorities 29%). Faculty: full-time 50, part-time 39. Student to faculty ratio is 14.1 to 1. Degrees conferred: J.D., J.D.-M.A. (International Relations), J.D.-M.B.A., J.D.-I.M.B.A., J.D.-LL.M., LL.M. (General, Tax), LL.M. (International Law, for persons who have completed a basic legal education and received a university degree in law in another country).

ADMISSION REQUIREMENTS. LSDAS Law School report, bachelor's degree, transcripts, LSAT, personal statement, résumé required in support of application. Photograph required after admittance. Interview not required. Accepts transfer applicants. Graduates of unaccredited colleges not considered. Apply to Admissions Office after September 1, before March 1 (priority deadline February 1); evening students May 1. Admits first-year students Fall and Summer only. Application fee $35. Phone: (619) 260-4528, (800)248-4873; e-mail: jdinfo@acusd.edu.

ADMISSION REQUIREMENTS FOR LL.M. APPLICANTS. Must possess a J.D. or an equivalent foreign law degree. Official transcripts with rank-in-class, résumé, personal statement with rationale for graduate study required in support of application. In addition, international applicants whose native language is not English must submit a TOEFL report. Admits Fall, Spring, Summer. Apply by May 1 (Fall), November 1 (Spring), April 1 (Summer) to the Office of Graduate Programs. Rolling admission process. Notification of admission decision normally begins within six weeks of receipt of completed application. Application fee $50. Phone: (619)260-4596.

ADMISSION STANDARDS. Selective. Accepts approximately 25% of full-time, 44% of part-time students. Number of full-time applicants 4580, part-time 583; number of full-time acceptance 1139, part-time 235; number of full-time enrolled 266, part-time 235; LSAT (75% of full-time students have a score at or above 160, part-time 156); GPA (75% of full-time students have a GPA at or above 3.11, part-time 3.08). *U.S. News & World Report* ranking is in the second tier (tied at 85th) of all U.S. law schools.

FINANCIAL AID. Scholarships, fellowships, assistantships, Federal W/S, loans. Apply to Office of Financial Aid by March 1. Phone: (619)260-4570. Use FAFSA (School code: G06976). About 38% of full-time and 23% of part-time students receive aid other than loans from School.

DEGREE REQUIREMENTS. For J.D.: 85 credits minimum, three-year (day), four-year (evening) program, at least 55 in residence. For LL.M.: at least 24 credits minimum beyond the J.D.; one-year of full-time study and research.
Note: Summer study abroad programs in England, France, Ireland, Italy, Mexico, Russia, and Spain.

SAN FRANCISCO ART INSTITUTE
San Francisco, California 94133-2299
Web site: www.sfai.edu

Founded 1871. Coed. Private control. Library: 35,000 volumes, 210 subscriptions. Total enrollment: 600.

Annual tuition: full-time $27,150, per unit $1175. No on-campus housing available. Studio space for graduate students. Contact the Student Services Department for off-campus housing information. Phone: (415)749-4525.

Graduate Program

Enrollment: full-time 171, part-time 42. Faculty: full- and part-time 38. Degree conferred: M.F.A.

ADMISSION REQUIREMENTS. Transcripts, portfolio of original artwork, statement of purpose required in support of application. TOEFL, TSE required for international applicants. Accepts transfer applicants, but no credits are transferred. Apply to Graduate Program Committee by January 15 (Fall), November 1 (Spring). Application fee $75, $85 for international applicants. Phone: (800)345-7324; fax: (415)749-4592; e-mail: admissions@sfai.edu.

ADMISSION STANDARDS. Very competitive. Admission based primarily on portfolio and statement of purpose. TOEFL score minimum 500.

FINANCIAL AID. Academic scholarships, fellowships, grants, Federal W/S, loans. Approved for VA benefits. Apply to Director of Financial Aid; recommended deadline July 15. Phone: (415) 749-4500, (415)749-4590. Use FAFSA. About 67% of students receive aid other than loans from Institute.

DEGREE REQUIREMENTS. For M.F.A.: 60 semester units; final examination of work and an exhibition. No language or thesis requirements.

FIELDS OF STUDY.
Design and Technology.
Filmmaking.
New Genres.
Painting.
Performance/Video.
Photography.
Printmaking.
Sculpture.

SAN FRANCISCO CONSERVATORY OF MUSIC
San Francisco, California 94102-6011
Web site: www.sfcm.edu

Founded 1917. Coed. Private control. Semester system. Library: 36,800 volumes, 80 subscriptions, 6000 individual recordings and tapes. Total enrollment: 375.

Annual tuition: $19,300; per credit $860. No on-campus housing. Contact Admission Office for off-campus housing information.

Graduate Division

Graduate study since 1960. Enrollment: full-time 124, part-time 3. Faculty: full-time 20, part-time 25, plus private instructors. Degree conferred: M.M.

ADMISSION REQUIREMENTS. Transcripts, two letters of recommendation, audition required in support of application. TOEFL required for international applicants. Accepts transfer applicants. Graduates of unaccredited institutions not considered. Apply to Unified Application for Conservatory Admission by December 1 (Fall), October 1 (Spring) for most majors. Admits Fall and Spring. Application fee $150. Phone: (415)503-6231; fax: (415) 503-6299.

ADMISSION STANDARDS. Musical proficiency more important than undergraduate GPA.

FINANCIAL AID. Scholarships, fellowships, assistantships, Federal W/S, loans. Apply to Director of Student Services by March 1; preference given to early applicants. Phone: (415)503-6214. Use FAFSA (School code: 001278) and institutional FAF. About 65% of students receive aid other than loans from School and outside sources. Aid available for part-time students.

DEGREE REQUIREMENTS. For M.M.: 30 semester hours minimum, all in residence; two public recitals.

FIELDS OF STUDY.
Chamber Music.
Classical Guitar.
Composition.
Conducting.
Keyboard Instruments.
Orchestral Instruments.
Piano Accompanying.
Voice.

SAN FRANCISCO STATE UNIVERSITY
San Francisco, California 94132-1722
Web site: www.sfsu.edu

Founded 1899. CGS member. Coed. State control. Semester system. Library: 900,000 volumes, 3800 subscriptions, 200 PCs in all libraries.

Annual fees/tuition: full-time, resident $3414, nonresident and foreign students $3414 plus $339 per unit. Limited on-campus housing for graduate students. Average academic year housing cost: $5800–$11,500 for single students. Contact Housing Office for both on- and off-campus housing information. Phone: (415)338-1067.

Graduate Division

Enrollment: full-time 2015, part-time 2408. Faculty: full-time 475, part-time 236. Degrees conferred: M.A., M.S., M.B.A., M.F.A., M.M., M.P.A., M.P.H., M.P.T., M.S.W., Ed.D., Ph.D.

ADMISSION REQUIREMENTS. Two official transcripts required in support of application. Interview, GRE/GMAT/MAT/NTE, letter of intent required for some departments. TOEFL required for international applicants. Accepts transfer applicants. Graduates of unaccredited institutions not considered. Apply to Office of Graduate Admissions at least two months prior to registration. Application fee $55. Phone: (415)338-2233; fax: (415)338-2514.

ADMISSION STANDARDS. Very selective for several departments, competitive for the others. Usual minimum average: 3.0 (A = 4). TOEFL score required 550.

FINANCIAL AID. Annual awards from institutional funds: Graduate Equity Fellowships, assistantships, Federal W/S, loans. Approved for VA benefits. Apply by March 1 to appropriate department chair for fellowships, assistantships; to Financial Aid Office for all other programs. Phone: (415)338-7000; e-mail: finaid@sfsu.edu. Use FAFSA (School code: 001154). About 60% of students receive aid other than loans from University funds. No aid for part-time or foreign students.

DEGREE REQUIREMENTS. For M.A., M.S., M.M.: 30 units minimum, at least 24 in residence; advancement to candidacy; thesis, creative project/final written/oral exam; usually no language requirement. For M.B.A.: 30–54 units minimum, at least 24 in residence; advancement to candidacy; thesis/research project; no language requirement. For M.P.A.: 37–41 units minimum, at least 24 in residence. For M.P.H.: 53-credit program; practicum; internship. For M.P.T.: offered jointly with University of California, San Francisco; 64 units in residence. For M.S.W.: 60 units minimum, at least 30 in residence; advancement to candidacy; fieldwork/thesis; no language requirement. For M.F.A.: 60 units, at least 30 in residence. For Ed.D., Ph.D.: offered jointly in Special Education with University of California, Berkeley; requirements vary with degree program. For D.P.T.S.: offered jointly with University of California, San Francisco; requirements vary based on past experience.

FIELDS OF STUDY.
Accounting.
Anthropology. M.A.
Applied Geosciences. M.S.
Art. M.A., M.F.A.
Asian American Studies. M.A.
Biology. Includes cell and molecular, conservation, ecology and systematic, marine, microbiology, physiology and behavioral biology. M.A.
Biomedical Laboratory Science. M.S.
Business Administration. M.B.A., M.S.
Chemistry. Includes biochemistry. M.S.
Chinese. M.A.
Cinema. M.F.A.
Cinema Studies. M.A.
Classics. M.A.
Clinical Science. M.S.
Communicative Disorders. M.S.
Communication Studies. M.A.
Comparative Literature. M.A.
Computer Science. M.S.
Counseling. Includes marriage, family, and child counseling. M.S.
Creative Arts. M.F.A.
Drama. M.A.
Economics. M.A.
Education. Includes adult education, early childhood education, educational administration, elementary, equity and social justice in education, instructional technologies, language and literacy education, mathematics education, secondary, special-interest program. M.A.
Engineering. M.S.
English. Includes composition, creative writing, linguistics, literature, teaching English as a foreign language. M.A.
Ethnic Studies. M.A.
French. M.A.
Geography. Includes resource management and environmental planning. M.A.
Geoscience.
German. M.A.
Gerontology. M.A.
Health Science.
History. M.A.
Home Economics.
Human Sexuality Studies. M.A.
Humanities. M.A.
Industrial Arts. M.A.
International Relations. M.A.
Italian. M.A.
Japanese. M.A.
Kinesiology. Includes exercise physiology, movement science, sports science. M.A.
Marine Science. M.S.
Mathematics. M.A.
Museum Studies. M.A.
Music. M.A., M.M.
Nursing. Includes family nurse practitioner. M.S.
Philosophy. M.A.
Physical Therapy. M.S.
Physical Therapy Science. Joint doctoral (D.P.T.S.) program with University of California, San Francisco.
Physics. M.S.

Political Science. M.A.

Psychology. Includes developmental, psychological research, social psychology (M.A.); clinical, industrial/organizational, school (M.S.).

Public Administration. M.P.A.

Public Health. M.P.H.

Radio and Television. M.A.

Recreation. M.S.

Rehabilitation Counseling. M.S.

Science. Interdisciplinary.

Social Science. Includes interdisciplinary studies. M.A.

Social Work. M.S.W.

Spanish. M.A.

Special Education. M.A.; joint doctoral (Ed.D., Ph.D.) program with University of California, Berkeley.

Special Major. M.A., M.S.

Speech Communication. M.A.

Taxation.

Theatre Arts. Includes design/technical production. M.F.A.

Women Studies. M.A.

UNIVERSITY OF SAN FRANCISCO

San Francisco, California 94117-1080

Web site: www.usfca.edu

Founded 1855. Coed. Private control. Roman Catholic, Jesuit affiliation. Semester system. Special facilities: Center for Child and Family Development, Center for Latin American Business, Center for Latino Studies in the Americas, Center for the Pacific Rim, Family Business Resource Center, Fromm Institute, Institute for Catholic Educational Leadership, Institute for Nonprofit Organization Management, International Institute of Criminal Justice Leadership, Ricci Institute. Library: 1,100,000 volumes, 2418 subscriptions. Total University enrollment: 8500.

Tuition: per unit $1005 (Arts & Sciences), $965 (Arts & Science–Chemistry, biology, theology), $1080 (M.B.A.), $815 (Professional Studies), $920 (Nursing), $890 (Education–master's), $995 (Education–doctoral programs). On-campus housing for 1050 men, 580 women, limited number of married students. Average academic year housing costs: $8500–$11,000 (including board) for single students. Apply to Director of Residence Life. Phone: (415) 422-6824.

Graduate Programs

Graduate study since 1867. Enrollment: full- and part-time 2450. Faculty: full-time 72, part-time 105. Degrees conferred: M.A., M.S., M.B.A., M.F.A., M.H.R.O.D., M.N.O., M.R.E., M.P.A., M.S.N., M.S.I.S., Ed.D.

ADMISSION REQUIREMENTS. Two transcripts, two letters of recommendation required in support of application. GRE for M.A. programs; GMAT for M.B.A. TOEFL required for international applicants. Interview not required. Accepts transfer applicants. Graduates of unaccredited institutions not considered. Admissions deadlines vary by program, contact Office of Graduate Admission at least three months prior to desired registration period for specific deadlines. Application fee $40, foreign applicants $55, $65 for international applicants. Phone: (800)CALL-USF (outside California), or (415)422-6563; fax: (415)422-2217; e-mail: graduate@usfca.edu.

ADMISSION STANDARDS. Competitive. Usual minimum average: 3.0 (A = 4).

FINANCIAL AID. Merit scholarships, research assistantships, teaching assistantships, tuition grants, Federal W/S, loans. Approved for VA benefits. Apply by March 1 to appropriate departmental chair for fellowships, assistantships; to Financial Aid Office for all other programs. Phone: (415)422-6303. Use FAFSA. About 60% of students receive aid other than loans from University. Loans available for part-time students.

DEGREE REQUIREMENTS. For M.A., M.S., M.S.N, M.S.I.S.: 24–36 units minimum including thesis, at least 20 in residence; reading knowledge of one foreign language for some majors; final written/oral exam. For M.F.A.: 33 credit, two-year program. For M.B.A.: 30–48 units minimum including thesis, at least 25 in residence; additional study may be required depending upon previous preparation; final oral exam; no language requirements. For M.F.A.: 33 credit, two-year program. For M.H.R.O.D., M.N.O., M.P.A.: 48 credits minimum, at least 30 in residence; final exam. For Ed.D.: 60 semester hours of course work beyond master's degree, at least 48 in residence; qualifying exam; dissertation; final oral exam.

FIELDS OF STUDY.

COLLEGE OF ARTS AND SCIENCES:

Asian-Pacific Studies. M.A.

Biology. M.S.

Chemistry. M.S.

Computer Science. M.S.

Economics.

Environmental Management. M.S.

Financial Economics. M.S.

Sport and Fitness Management. Joint degree with the McLaren School of Business.

Theology.

Writing. M.A., M.F.A.

COLLEGE OF PROFESSIONAL STUDIES:

Human Resources and Organizational Development. M.H.R.O.D.

Information Systems. Includes emphasis in health service administration, human resources, information systems, nonprofit administration, organization development. M.S.I.S.

Nonprofit Organization. M.N.O.

Organizational Development. M.S.

Public Administration. Includes health services administration. M.P.A.

SCHOOL OF BUSINESS MANAGEMENT:

Business Administration. Includes emphasis entrepreneurship, finance, international business, management, marketing. M.B.A.

SCHOOL OF EDUCATION:

Catholic School Leadership. Ed.D.

Counseling Psychology. Includes adult development, marriage and family therapy, educational counseling. M.A.

Education. Includes elementary, secondary, Catholic school leadership, educational technology. M.A.

International and Multicultural Education. M.A., Ed.D.

Learning and Instruction. M.A., Ed.D.

Organizational Leadership. M.A., Ed.D.

Private School Administration. Ed.D.

Special Education. M.A.

Teaching English as a Second Language. M.A.

SCHOOL OF NURSING:

Adult Health/Advanced Practice Nurse. M.S.N.

Clinical Nurse Specialist. M.S.N.

Family Nurse Practitioner. M.S.N.

Nursing Administration. M.S.N.

School of Law

Web site: www.law.usfca.edu

Established 1912. Located on main campus. ABA approved since 1935. AALS member. Semester system. Full-time, part-time study. Special facilities: Center for Applied Legal Ethics, Center for Law and Global Justice, Institute for Intellectual Property and Technology Law. Special programs: Asian Pacific Legal

Studies Program; summer study abroad at Trinity College, Ireland, Charles University, Czech Republic, Nayana University, Bali. Faculty exchange programs with schools in Ireland, Czech Republic, Indonesia, PRC, Vietnam. Law library: 354,849 volumes, 3293 subscriptions; has LEXIS, NEXIS, WESTLAW, DIALOG, INNOPAC; has more than 1000 network connections.

Annual tuition: $32,190, part-time $1150 per credit. Law students tend to live off-campus. Off-campus housing and personal expenses: approximately $18,000.

Enrollment: first-year class full-time 208, part-time 51; total full- and part-time 702 (men 49%, women 51%, minorities 36%). Student to faculty ratio 16.7 1o 1. Degrees conferred: J.D., J.D.-M.B.A., LL.M. (International Transactions and Comparative Law, for foreign lawyers who have completed a basic legal education and received a university degree in law in another country; full- and part-time study).

ADMISSION REQUIREMENTS. LSDAS Law School report, bachelor's degree, transcripts, LSAT, personal statement, two recommendations required in support of application. Accepts transfer applicants. Graduates of unaccredited institutions not considered. Apply to Director of Admissions by February 1, June 1 (evening). Admits first-year students September only. Application fee $60. Phone: (415)422-6586; fax: (415)422-6433.

ADMISSION REQUIREMENTS FOR LL.M. APPLICANTS. Must have a first law degree from a foreign university authorized by the government of the country to confer such a degree and must be fluent in English. Official transcripts with certified translations and evaluations, personal statement, two letters of recommendation (if not in English they should be accompanied by an English translation), personal statement (no more than two double-spaced typewritten pages), résumé, evidence of financial support required in support of LL.M. application. In addition, TOEFL (minimum score 600) is required for those whose native language is not English. Admits Fall only. Apply by April 1. Application fee $60. Phone: (415) 422-6946; fax: (415)422-6433, attn: LL.M. Director; Web site: www.usfca.edu/law/llm. About 25 students admitted each year.

ADMISSION STANDARDS. Selective. Accepts approximately 32% of full-time, 21% of part-time students. Number of full-time applicants 3674, part-time 480; number of full-time acceptance 1165, part-time 100; number of full-time enrolled 208, part-time 51; LSAT (75% of full-time students have a score at or above 157, part-time 154); GPA (75% of full-time students have a GPA at or above 3.13, part-time 2.94). *U.S. News & World Report* ranking is in the second tier (tied at 100) of all U.S. law schools.

FINANCIAL AID. Scholarships, Federal W/S, loans. Apply by February 1 to Financial Aid Office. Phone: (415)422-6210. Use FAFSA. About 30% of full-time, 20% of part-time students receive aid other than loans from School. Aid available for part-time students.

DEGREE REQUIREMENTS. For J.D.: satisfactory completion of three-year (day), four-year (evening) program; 86 semester hours program. For LL.M.: 25 course unit program, at least two semesters in full-time residence, four semesters in part-time residence.

SAN JOSE STATE UNIVERSITY

San Jose, California 95192-0025
Web site: www.sjsu.edu

Founded 1857. Located 50 miles S of San Francisco. CGS member. Coed. State control. Semester system. Library: 1,100,000 volumes, 2504 subscriptions. Total University enrollment: 30,000.

Annual fees/tuition: full-time resident $2840, nonresident $2840 plus $339 per unit. On-campus housing for married and single students. Average academic year housing costs: $7600 (including board). Contact Housing Office for both on- and off- campus housing information. Phone: (408)924-6160. Day-care facilities available.

Graduate Studies and Research

Graduate study since 1946. Enrollment: full-time 3100, part-time 4100. Faculty: 300 full-time, 124 part-time. Degrees conferred: M.A., M.S., M.B.A., M.S.W., M.P.A., M.U.R., M.P.H., M.F.A.

ADMISSION REQUIREMENTS. Transcripts required in support of application. Online application available. GRE Subject Tests/GMAT/MAT required or recommended for some programs. TOEFL required for international applicants. Interview not required. Accepts transfer applicants. Graduates of unaccredited institutions not considered. Apply to Graduate Studies Office by June 30 (Fall), November 30 (Spring). Applications considered after above dates on a space-available basis. Application fee $55. Phone: (408)924-2480; fax: (408)924-2477.

ADMISSION STANDARDS. Selective for most majors. Usual minimum average: 2.5 for last 60 credits (A = 4).

FINANCIAL AID. Fellowships, scholarships, research/teaching assistantships, internships, tuition waivers, Federal W/S, loans. Approved for VA benefits. Apply to Financial Aid Office; no closing date specified. Phone: (408)924-6100. Use FAFSA. Aid available for part-time students.

DEGREE REQUIREMENTS. For master's: 30 semester units minimum, at least 24 in residence; final written/oral exam; thesis/nonthesis option; creative project; reading knowledge of one foreign language for some departments.

FIELDS OF STUDY.

COLLEGE OF APPLIED SCIENCE AND ARTS:
Justice Studies. M.S.
Kinesiology. M.A.
Mass Communications. M.S.
Nursing. M.S.
Nutritional Science. M.S.
Occupational Therapy. M.S.
Public Health. M.P.H.
Recreation. M.S.

COLLEGE OF BUSINESS:
Accounting. M.S.
Business Administration. M.B.A.
Taxation. M.S.
Transportation Management. M.S.

COLLEGE OF EDUCATION:
Administration and Supervision. M.A.
Child and Adolescent Development. M.A.
Communication Disorder and Sciences. M.A.
Counselor Education. M.A.
Curriculum and Instruction. M.A.
Higher Education. M.A.
Instructional Technology. M.A.
Special Education. M.A.

COLLEGE OF ENGINEERING:
Aerospace Engineering. M.S.
Chemical Engineering. M.S.
Civil Engineering. M.S.
Computer Engineering. M.S.
Electrical Engineering. M.S.
Engineering. M.S.
Human Factors/Ergonomics. M.S.
Industrial and Systems Engineering. M.S.
Materials Engineering. M.S.

Mechanical Engineering. M.S.
Quality Assurance. M.S.
Software Engineering. M.S.

COLLEGE OF HUMANITIES AND THE ARTS:
Art. Includes creative, art history, graphic design. M.A., M.F.A.
Creative Writing. M.F.A.
English. GRE Subject for candidacy. Includes creative writing; one foreign language for M.A. M.A.
French. GRE for candidacy; working knowledge of second language for M.A. M.A.
Linguistics. M.A.
Music. Includes performance, literature, theory and composition, education; GRE, Music Subject Tests for candidacy; thesis project, recital or composition for M.A. M.A.
Philosophy. M.A.
Spanish. GRE for candidacy; working knowledge of second language for M.A. M.A.
TESOL. M.A.
Theatre Arts. M.A.

COLLEGE OF SCIENCE:
Biology. M.A., M.S.
Biotechnology. M.B.T.
Chemistry. Includes analytical, inorganic, organic, physical. M.A., M.S.
Computer Science. M.S.
Geology. M.S.
Marine Science. M.S.
Mathematics. M.S.
Meteorology. M.S.
Molecular Biology and Microbiology. M.S.
Physics. M.S.
Physiology. M.S.

COLLEGE OF SOCIAL SCIENCES:
Communication. M.A.
Criminology. M.A.
Economics. M.A.
Environmental Studies. M.S.
Geography. M.A.
History. M.A.
Psychology. Includes clinical/counseling, industrial/organizational; project or thesis for M.S.
Public Administration. M.P.A.
Sociology. GRE Subject for candidacy; thesis, one foreign language for M.A. M.A.
Speech Communication. GRE/Subject for candidacy; thesis or project for M.A.
Urban and Regional Planning. M.U.P.

COLLEGE OF SOCIAL WORK:
Mexican American Studies. M.A.
Social Work. M.S.W
Urban Planning. Thesis or project for M.U.P.

GRADUATE STUDIES AND RESEARCH:
Human Factors/Ergonomics. M.S.
Interdisciplinary Studies. M.A.
Library and Information Science. M.L.I.S.

SANTA CLARA UNIVERSITY
Santa Clara, California 95053-0001
Web site: www.scu.edu

Founded 1851. Located 45 miles S of San Francisco. CGS member. Coed. Private control, Roman Catholic affiliation. Quarter system. Special facilities: Bannan Center for Jesuit Education, Center for Advanced Study and Practice of Information Assurance, Cen-

ter for Innovation and Entrepreneurship, Center for Multicultural Learning, Center for Professional Development, Center for Science, Technology, and Society, Civil Society Institute, East San Jose Community Law Center, Environmental Studies Institute, Food and Agribusiness Institute, High Tech Law Institute, Howard Hughes Medical Institute, Institute for Information Storage Technology, Institute of Globalization, Markkula Center for Applied Ethics, Retail Management Institute. Library: 1,200,000 volumes, 8919 subscriptions. Total University enrollment 8,100.

Tuition: per unit $739 (Business), $669 (Engineering), $425 (Education, Counseling, Pastoral Ministries). On-campus housing for graduate students on a space-available basis. Contact Director of Housing for off-campus housing information. Phone: (408)554-4900. Day-care facilities available.

Graduate Programs

Graduate study since 1951. Enrollment: full-time 556, part-time 1752. Graduate faculty: full-time 135, part-time 108. Degrees conferred: M.A., M.B.A., M.S. (Engineering), Engineer.

ADMISSION REQUIREMENTS. Two transcripts, three letters of recommendation required in support of application. Online applications available. GRE/GMAT required for some programs. TOEFL required for international applicants. Interview usually not required. Accepts transfer applicants. Graduates of unaccredited institutions not considered. Apply to Dean's Office, School of Engineering June 1 (Fall), January 1 (Spring); Graduate Admissions, School of Business, June 1 (Fall), December 1 (Spring); Graduate Admissions, School of Education, April 1 (Fall), February 1 (Spring). Application fee $45–$75 (fee varies from division to division), international application fee $100. Phone: School of Business (408)554-4593, Engineering (480)554-4313, Education (408)554-4656.

ADMISSION STANDARDS. Competitive. Usual minimum average: 2.75 (Engineering), 3.0 (all other departments) (A = 4).

FINANCIAL AID. Scholarships, fellowships, assistantships, Federal W/S, loans. Approved for VA benefits. Apply by February 1 to appropriate Dean's Office for fellowships, assistantships; to Financial Aid Office for all other programs. Phone: (408)554-4505. Use FAFSA.

DEGREE REQUIREMENTS. For M.A.: 45 quarter units minimum; final written/oral exam may also be required. For M.B.A.: minimum of 18 courses beyond basic courses, at least 16 in residence. For Engineer: minimum of 45 units beyond the master's; thesis. For Ph.D. (Engineering, electrical only): 135 units minimum of graduate credit, at least 11 months in full-time residence; 45 units research credit for the master's and doctor's theses; language requirement to be determined; thesis; final oral exam.

FIELDS OF STUDY.

LEAVEY SCHOOL OF BUSINESS:
Business Administration. M.B.A.
Information Systems. M.S.I.S.

SCHOOL OF EDUCATION, COUNSELING PSYCHOLOGY AND
PASTORAL MINISTRIES:
Catholic Education.
Counseling.
Counseling Psychology. Includes marriage and family therapy.
Curriculum and Instruction.
Early Childhood Special Education.
Educational Administration.
Environmental Literacy and Ethics.
Higher Education Administration.
Literacy and Language Development.
Pastoral Ministries. Includes catechetics, liturgical music, pastoral liturgy, spirituality.

Reading.
Special Education. Includes mild/moderate disabilities.
Teaching and Learning. Includes teaching and learning with technology.

SCHOOL OF ENGINEERING:
Applied Mathematics.
Computer Engineering.
Electrical Engineering.
Engineering Management.
Mechanical Engineering.

School of Law
Web site: www.scu.edu/law

Established 1912. ABA approved since 1937. AALS member. Private control. Semester system. Special facilities: Institute of International and Comparative Law, Center for Global Law, Center for Trial and Appellate Advocacy, Center for Social Justice and Public Service, High Tech Law Institute, Institute for Redress and Recovery. Law library: 351,098 volumes, 4183 subscriptions; has LEXIS, NEXIS, WESTLAW, OSCAR; has more than 800 network connections.

Annual tuition: full-time $35,250, part-time $24,676; LL.M. per credit: $1310. No on-campus housing available. Average annual living expenses: $18,400.

Enrollment: first-year class full-time 239, part-time 67; total full- and part-time 743 (men 50%, women 50%, minorities 41%). Faculty: full-time 50, part-time 38. Student to faculty ratio is 17.8 to 1. Degrees conferred: J.D., J.D.-M.B.A., J.D.-M.S.T., LL.M. (International Law, Intellectual Property Law).

ADMISSION REQUIREMENTS. LSDAS Law School report, bachelor's degree, transcripts, LSAT, personal statement required in support of application. Accepts transfer applicants. Graduates of unaccredited colleges not considered. Apply to Office of Admissions after September 1, before February 1. Rolling admissions process. Admits beginning students Fall only. Application fee $75. Phone: (408)554-4800; fax: (408)554-7897.

ADMISSION STANDARDS. Selective. Accepts approximately 37% of full-time, 34% of part-time students. Number of full-time applicants 4112, part-time 375; number of full-time acceptance 1539, part-time 126; number of full-time enrolled 247, part-time 63; LSAT (75% of full-time students have a score at or above 157, part-time 156); GPA (75% of full-time students have a GPA at or above 3.21, part-time 2.94). *U.S. News & World Report* ranking is in the second tier (tied at 91st) of all U.S. law schools.

FINANCIAL AID. Scholarships, fellowships, assistantships, Federal W/S, loans. Apply to Office of the Dean for Scholarships by February 1; Director of Financial Aid for loans by March 1 for all other aid. Phone: (408)544-4447. Use FAFSA (School code: 001326). About 30% of full-time and 20% of part-time students receive aid other than loans from School.

DEGREE REQUIREMENTS. For J.D.: 86 credit hours minimum, at least three years in residence for day students, at least four years in residence for part-time students. For LL.M.: 24-credit program, either full-time or part-time.
Note: Summer programs in Australia, France, Germany, Hungary, Malaysia, Switzerland, England, Hong Kong, Singapore, Korea, Vietnam, Thailand, Japan, and People's Republic of China.

SARAH LAWRENCE COLLEGE
Bronxville, New York 10708
Web site: www.sarahlawrence.edu

Founded 1928. Located 15 miles N of New York City. CGS member. Coed on graduate level. Private control. Semester sys-

tem. Library: 288,000 volumes, 1135 subscriptions. Total College enrollment: 1700.

Tuition: per credit $884–$1034, depending on program. No on-campus housing for graduate students. Average on-campus costs: $15,390. Contact Student Affairs Office for off-campus housing information. Phone: (914)395-2373.

Graduate Studies

Graduate study since 1950. Enrollment: full-time 238, part-time 88. Faculty: full-time 25, part-time 20. Degrees conferred: M.A., M.F.A., M.S., M.P.S., M.S.Ed., M.A.-M.S.W. (with NYU School of Social Work).

ADMISSION REQUIREMENTS. Transcripts, two letters of recommendation required in support of application. Interview sometimes requested. TOEFL required for international applicants. Accepts transfer applicants. Graduates of unaccredited colleges not considered. Apply to Committee on Graduate Studies by February 1. Fall admission. Application fee $45. Phone: (914)395-2371; fax: (914)395-2664.

ADMISSION STANDARDS. Very selective for most departments, competitive for all others. Usual minimum average: 3.0 (A = 4).

FINANCIAL AID. Annual awards from institutional funds: grants, assistantships, loans. Apply by March 1 to Committee on Graduate Studies. Phone: (914)395-2570. Use FAFSA. About 25% of students receive aid other than loans from College and outside sources. Aid sometimes available for part-time students.

DEGREE REQUIREMENTS. For M.F.A. and most M.A.: 36 credits, at least two years in residence; thesis or project. For some M.A.'s: 40 credits, at least two years in residence; fieldwork. For M.S., M.P.S.: 40 credits, at least two years in residence; fieldwork. For M.S.: 38 credits; fieldwork.

FIELDS OF STUDY.
Art of Teaching. M.S.Ed.
Child Development. M.A.
Dance. M.F.A.
Education. Includes early childhood, elementary.
Health Advocacy. M.A., M.P.S.
Human Genetics. Includes genetic counseling. M.P.S., M.S.
Theater. M.A., M.F.A.
Women's History. M.A.
Writing. Includes creative, nonfiction, poetry. M.F.A.

UNIVERSITY OF SCRANTON
Scranton, Pennsylvania 18510-4631
Web site: www.scranton.edu

Founded 1888. CGS member. Coed. Private control. Catholic affiliation. Semester system. Library: 465,800 volumes, 7550 subscriptions. Total University enrollment: 5200.

Tuition: per credit $647 (tuition guarantee program). No on-campus housing available. Average off-campus housing cost per month: $450–$600. Contact Director, Residence Life for off-campus housing information. Phone: (570)941-6226.

Graduate School

Graduate study since 1951. Enrollment: full-time 306, part-time 719. Graduate faculty: full-time 70, part-time 34. Degrees conferred: M.A., M.B.A., M.H.A., M.S.N., M.S.

ADMISSION REQUIREMENTS. Transcripts, letters of recommendation required in support of School's application. GMAT required for business applicants. Software Engineering applicants may submit either the GMAT or GRE. TOEFL required for international applicants. Interview required for some programs. Accepts transfer applicants. Graduates of unaccredited institutions not considered. Apply to School at least thirty days prior to registration date. Foreign applicants should apply at least three months prior to registration date. Rolling admissions process. Application fee $50. Phone: (800)366-4723, (570)941-6304; fax: (570)941-5995.

ADMISSION STANDARDS. Selective for most departments. Usual minimum average: 2.75 (A = 4).

FINANCIAL AID. Annual awards from institutional funds: fellowships, graduate assistantships, internships, Federal W/S, loans. Approved for VA benefits. Apply by March 1 to Graduate Dean. Phone: (570)941-7700. Use FAFSA and University's FAF. Aid available for part-time students.

DEGREE REQUIREMENTS. For master's: 30–48 semester credits; thesis/nonthesis option; final written/oral exam.

FIELDS OF STUDY.
Administration (Principal K–12).
Biochemistry.
Business. GMAT for admission. Includes specializations in accounting, enterprise management technology, finance, international business, management information systems, marketing, operations management. M.B.A. only.
Chemistry.
Clinical Chemistry.
Community Counseling.
Curriculum and Instruction.
Early Childhood Education.
Elementary Education.
English.
Health Administration.
History.
Human Resources Administration.
Nursing. Includes specializations in adult health, family nurse practitioner, nurse anesthesia.
Occupational Therapy. Program is for applicants with an undergraduate degree in occupational therapy. 24-credit master's.
Organizational Leadership. M.S.
Physical Therapy.
Reading Education.
Rehabilitation Counseling.
School Counseling.
Secondary Education.
Software Engineering.
Special Education.
Theology.

UNIVERSITY OF THE SCIENCES IN PHILADELPHIA
Philadelphia, Pennsylvania 19104-4495
Web site: www.usip.edu

Founded 1821. Name changed in 1998. Coed. Private control. Semester system. Special facilities: McNeil Research Center, Institute for Pharmaceutical Economics, Pharmacology/Toxicology Research Center. Library: 87,125 volumes, 809 subscriptions. Total University enrollment: 2800.

Tuition: per credit $999. No on-campus housing available for graduate students. Contact Dean of Student Affairs for off-campus housing information. Phone: (215)596-8844.

College of Graduate Studies

Graduate study since 1921. Enrollment: full-time 85, part-time 190. Graduate faculty: full-time 69, part-time 19. Degrees conferred: M.S., Ph.D.

ADMISSION REQUIREMENTS. Official transcripts, GRE, written statement of professional goals, three letters of recommendation required in support of School's application. Online application available. TOEFL, TWE, and certification of finances required for international applicants. GMAT required for Biomedical Writing, Pharmacy Administration. Interview, GRE Subject Tests recommended. Accepts transfer applicants. Graduates of unaccredited institutions not considered. Apply to Dean of Graduate School. Admits to Fall and Spring. Application fee $50. Phone: (215)596-8937; e-mail: graduate@usip.edu.

ADMISSION STANDARDS. Very selective. Usual minimum average: 3.0 (A = 4).

FINANCIAL AID. Annual awards from institutional funds: fellowships, teaching assistantships, tuition scholarships, tuition waivers, Federal W/S, loans. Apply to appropriate department chair for fellowships, assistantships; to Financial Aid Office for all other programs. No specified closing date. Use FAFSA and PHEAA. Phone: (215)596-8894; fax: (215)895-1100. About 80% of students receive aid other than loans from College and outside sources.

DEGREE REQUIREMENTS. For M.S. (nonthesis): 30 semester hours of didactic credit. For M.S. (thesis): 20 semester hours of didactic credit; 24 semester hours of credit in research; thesis; proficiency exam may be required. For Ph.D.: 20 semester hours of didactic credit; 48 semester hours of credit in research; at least eight months in full-time residence; proficiency exam may be required; dissertation; final oral/written exam.

FIELDS OF STUDY.
Biochemistry.
Bioinformation.
Biomedical Writing.
Cell Biology and Biotechnology.
Chemistry.
Clinical Health Psychology.
Health Policy.
Medicinal Chemistry.
Pharmaceutical Business.
Pharmaceutics.
Pharmacognosy.
Pharmacology and Toxicology.
Pharmacy Administration.
Toxicology.

SEATTLE PACIFIC UNIVERSITY
Seattle, Washington 98119-1997
Web site: www.spu.edu

Founded 1891. Coed. Private control. Free Methodist. Quarter system. Library: 200,000 volumes, 1192 subscriptions. Total University enrollment: 3900.

Limited on-campus housing for single and married graduate students. Average academic year housing costs: $6000 (including board) for single students, $7600 for married students. Contact Coordinator of Housing for both on- and off-campus housing information. Phone: (206)281-2779.

Graduate Studies

Tuition: per credit $390–$440 (Arts & Sciences), $625 (Business), $440 (Educational Counseling), $522 (Leadership), $566 (Ed.D.), $504 (Nursing), $511 (MFT, Organizational Psychology), $569 (Ph.D.). Enrollment: full-time 199, part-time 554. Enrollment: full-time 157, part-time 500. Graduate faculty: full-time 51, part-time 54. Degrees conferred: M.Ed., M.A., M.S., M.S.N., M.B.A., Ed.D., Ph.D.

ADMISSION REQUIREMENTS. Transcripts, two letters of reference, GRE or MAT required in support of application. GMAT for M.B.A. program. Interview required for some departments. TOEFL required for foreign applicants. Accepts transfer applicants. Apply to Graduate School at least four weeks prior to registration. Application fee $50. Phone: (206)281-2125; fax: (206) 281-2115.

ADMISSION STANDARDS. Competitive. Usual minimum average: 3.0. (A = 4), 3.0 in last 45 credits. TOEFL minimum score 550; for M.B.A., I.S.M. 575; TESOL 600.

FINANCIAL AID. Teaching/research assistantships, traineeships, Federal W/S, loans. Approved for VA benefits. Apply by April 1 to appropriate School for assistantships, fellowships; to Financial Aid Office for all other programs. Phone: (206)281-2046. Use FAFSA.

DEGREE REQUIREMENTS. For master's: 45 quarter hours minimum, last 15 in residence; three credit course in Christian thought; candidacy; comprehensive exam; thesis/nonthesis option/project. For Ed.D., Ph.D.: 90–96 quarter hours beyond master's degree; qualifying exam; comprehensive exam; dissertation; clinical internship for psychology; final oral exam.

FIELDS OF STUDY.

COLLEGE OF ARTS AND SCIENCES:
Creative writing. M.F.A.
Fine Arts. M.F.A.
TESOL. M.A.

SCHOOL OF BUSINESS AND ECONOMICS:
Business Administration. M.B.A.
Information Systems Management. M.S.

SCHOOL OF EDUCATION:
Curriculum and Instruction. M.Ed.
Education. M.Ed., Ed.D.
Educational Leadership. M.Ed.
School Counseling. M.Ed.
Teaching. M.A.T.

SCHOOL OF HEALTH SCIENCES:
Nursing. M.S.N.

SCHOOL OF PSYCHOLOGY, FAMILY AND COMMUNITY:
Clinical Psychology. Ph.D.
Marriage and Family Therapy. M.F.T.
Organizational Psychology. M.A., Ph.D.

SEATTLE UNIVERSITY
Seattle, Washington 98122-1090
Web site: www.seattleu.edu

Founded 1891. Coed. Private control. Jesuit affiliation. Quarter system. Library: 216,000 volumes, 2500 subscriptions. Total University enrollment: 5800.

Tuition: per credit $645 (Business, Software Engineering), $540 (Criminal Justice, Nonprofit Leadership, Psychology, Sport Administration), $497 (Ed.S., Teaching), $502 (Nursing, Theology & Ministry), $527 (Organizational Design). Limited on-campus housing for graduate single students. Average academic year hous-

ing costs: $6768–$7422 (including board). Contact Residential Life Office for both on- and off-campus housing information. Phone: (206)296-6274. Day-care facilities available.

Graduate School

Graduate study since 1901. Enrollment: full-time 353, part-time 1261. Faculty: full-time 119, part-time 58. Degrees conferred: M.A., M.A.P.S., M.A.T.S., M.S., M.Ed., M.B.A., M.I.B., M.A. in Ed., Ed.D., M.C., M.S.E., M.Div., M.M., M.N.P.L., M.I.T., M.S.N., M.P.A., M.S.F., M.A.E., Ed.S.

ADMISSION REQUIREMENTS. Transcripts required in support of School's application. Online application available. GRE/GMAT/MAT, interview required for some programs. TOEFL required for non-English-speaking international applicants. Accepts transfer applicants. Graduates of unaccredited institutions not considered. Apply to Graduate Admissions Office at least four weeks prior to registration. Application fee $55. Phone: (206) 296-2000; fax: (206)298-5656; e-mail: grad_admissions@seattleu.edu.

ADMISSION STANDARDS. Selective. Usual minimum average: 2.75 (A = 4).

FINANCIAL AID. Scholarships, assistantships, internships, grants, Federal W/S, loans. Approved for VA benefits. Apply to Financial Aid Office; no specified closing date. Phone: (206)296-5840; fax: (206)296-5656. Use FAFSA. Aid available for part-time students.

DEGREE REQUIREMENTS. For master's: 45–60 quarter hours minimum, at least 25 in residence; thesis; final oral/written exam depending upon program. For Ed.D.: 90 quarter hours minimum; preliminary exam; dissertation; final exam.

FIELDS OF STUDY.

ALBERS SCHOOL OF BUSINESS AND ECONOMICS:
Accounting. M.P.A.C.
Business Administration. M.B.A.
Finance. M.S.F.
International Business. M.I.B.
Leadership Executive. M.B.A.
Professional Accounting. M.P.A.C.

COLLEGE OF ARTS AND SCIENCES:
Arts Leadership. M.F.A.
Criminal Justice. M.A.C.J.
Executive Nonprofit Leadership. M.N.P.L
Organizational Systems Renewal. M.A.O.D.R.
Psychology. M.A.P.
Public Administration. M.P.A.
Sport Administration and Leadership. M.S.A.L.

SCHOOL OF EDUCATION:
Adult Education and Training. M.A., M.Ed.
Counseling. M.A.
Curriculum and Instruction. M.A., M.Ed.
Educational Administration. M.A., M.Ed., Ed.S.
Educational Leadership. Ed.D.
Literacy for Special Needs. M.A.
School Psychology. Ed.S.
Special Education. M.Ed., Ed.S.
Student Development Administration. M.A., M.Ed.
Teaching English to Speakers of Other Languages. M.A., M.Ed.
Teaching. M.I.T.

SCHOOL OF NURSING:
Advanced Practice Nurse Practitioner. M.S.N.
Nursing. M.S.N.

SCHOOL OF SCIENCE AND ENGINEERING:
Software Engineering. M.S.E.

SCHOOL OF THEOLOGY AND MINISTRY:
Divinity. M.Div.
Pastoral Counseling. M.A.P.C.
Pastoral Studies. M.A.
Transforming Spirituality. M.A.

School of Law (P.O. Box 222000)

Web site: www.law.seattleu.edu

Established 1972. Formerly Puget Sound School of Law. Acquired by Seattle University in 1994. ABA approved since 1994. AALS member. Private control. Semester system. Special facilities: Access to Justice Institute, Center on Corporations, Law and Society. Law library: 356,028 volumes, 3143 subscriptions; has LEXIS, NEXIS, WESTLAW, DIALOG, BRS, VUTEXT, WILSONLINE, DATATIMES; has more than 100 network connections.

Annual tuition: full-time $27,826, part-time $18,552. No on-campus housing available. Total average annual additional expenses: $15,797.

Enrollment: first-year class full-time 297, part-time 60; total full- and part-time 990 (men 45%, women 55%, minorities 24%). Faculty: full-time 54, part-time 35. Student to faculty ratio is 15.6 to 1. Degrees conferred: J.D., J.D.-M.B.A., J.D.-M.S.F., J.D.-M.I.B., LL.M. (for foreign trained lawyers only).

ADMISSION REQUIREMENTS. LSDAS Law School report, bachelor's degree, transcripts, LSAT, personal statement, résumé, two letters of recommendation required in support of application. Interviews by invitation only. Accepts transfer applicants. Graduates of unaccredited colleges not considered. Apply to the Office of Admissions by April 1. Admits Fall only. Application fee $50. Phone: (206)398-4200; fax: (206)398-4058.

ADMISSION STANDARDS. Selective. Accepts approximately 26% of full-time, 38% of part-time students. Number of full-time applicants 2857, part-time 267; number of full-time acceptance 743, part-time 102; number of full-time enrolled 297, part-time 68; LSAT (75% of full-time students have a score at or above 152, part-time 153); GPA (75% of full-time students have a GPA at or above 3.17, part-time 2.90). *U.S. News & World Report* ranking is in the second tier (tied at 85th) of all U.S. law schools.

FINANCIAL AID. Scholarships, tuition waivers, assistantships, Federal W/S, loans. Apply to Student Aid Office by April 1. Phone: (206)398-4250. Use FAFSA (School code: E00615). About 48% of full-time and 38% of part-time students receive aid other than loans from School.

DEGREE REQUIREMENTS. For J.D.: satisfactory completion of 90 semester hour program. For LL.M.: 24 credit full-time program.

SETON HALL UNIVERSITY

South Orange, New Jersey 07079-2697
Web site: www.shu.edu

Founded 1856. Located 20 miles SW of New York City. CGS member. Coed. Private control. Roman Catholic. Semester system. Special facilities: Alberto Italian Studies Institute, Center for Applied Catalysis, Center for Catholic Studies, Center for Community Research and Engagement, Center for Leadership Studies, Center for Public Service, Center for Sport Management, Center for Women's Studies, Institute on Work, Joseph A. Unanue Latino Institute, Nonprofit Sector Resource Institute, Teaching, Learning & Technology Center. Walsh Library: 484,500 volumes, 2400 subscriptions. Total University enrollment: 10,500.

Tuition: per credit nonbusiness $826, business $889. Limited on-campus housing for graduate students. Average academic year housing costs: $9300 (including board), Contact Director of Housing for on- and off-campus housing information. Phone: (973)761-9172.

Graduate Division

Graduate study since 1943. Enrollment: full-time 724, part-time 2027. Faculty: full-time 335, part-time 307. Degrees conferred: M.A., M.A.S.C.L., M.B.A., M.H.A., M.S., M.P.A., Ed.S., Ed.D., Ph.D. (Chemistry and Education).

ADMISSION REQUIREMENTS. Two transcripts, three letters of recommendation, statement of purpose or résumé required in support of application. Interview, MAT/GRE/GMAT required by some departments. TOEFL required for international applicants. Accepts transfer applicants. Graduates of unaccredited institutions not considered. Apply to Graduate Office by July 1 (Fall), November 1 (Spring), May 1 (Summer). Some programs have earlier deadlines. Rolling admission process. Application fee $30. Phone: (973)761-9343.

ADMISSION STANDARDS. Selective for most departments. Usual minimum average: 3.0 (A = 4).

FINANCIAL AID. Annual awards from university funds: academic scholarships, fellowships, administrative assistantships, teaching assistantships, internships, Federal W/S, loans. Approved for VA benefits. Apply by February 1 to appropriate departmental chair for assistantships, fellowships; to Financial Aid Office for all other programs. Phone: (973)761-9350; fax: (973)761-7954. Use FAFSA. About 30% of students receive aid other than loans from University and outside sources.

DEGREE REQUIREMENTS. For master's: 30 credits minimum; qualifying exam/thesis required in some departments; competency in one foreign language required in some programs in the College of Arts and Sciences; comprehensive exam. For Ed.D., Ph.D.: 70 credits minimum beyond the bachelor's degree; matriculation exam; dissertation; final oral exam.

FIELDS OF STUDY.

COLLEGE OF ARTS AND SCIENCES:
Asian Studies. M.A.
Biology. Includes neuroscience. M.S.
Chemistry. M.S., Ph.D.
English. M.A.
Healthcare Administration. M.H.A.
History. M.A.
Jewish-Christian Studies. M.A.
Microbiology. M.S.
Molecular Bioscience. Ph.D.
Museum Professions. M.A.
Psychology. M.S.
Public Administration. M.P.A.
Strategic Communication. M.A.

COLLEGE OF EDUCATION AND HUMAN SERVICES:
Bilingual Fellowship Program. Ed.D.
Catholic School Leadership. M.A.
College Students Personnel Administration. M.A.
Counseling. M.A.
Counseling Psychology. Ph.D.
Educational Leadership, Management and Policy. M.A.
Educational Administration. Ed.D.
Educational Administration K–12. Ed.D.
Educational Media Specialist. M.A., Ed.S.
Family Psychology. Ph.D.
Higher Education Administration. Ed.D.

Higher Education Policy and Research. Ph.D.
Higher Education—College Teaching. Ed.D.
Human Resource Training and Development. M.A.
Instructional Design and Technology. M.A.
Marriage and Family Therapy. M.S., Ed.S.
State Police Graduate Studies Program. M.A.
Professional Development in Education. M.A.
Psychological Studies. M.A.
School and Community Psychology. Ed.S.
School Counseling. M.A.

W. PAUL STILLMAN SCHOOL OF BUSINESS:
Accounting. M.B.A., M.S.
Business. M.B.A.
Economics.
Finance. M.B.A.
Financial Marketing, Institution and Instruments. M.B.A.
Information Systems. M.B.A.
International Business. M.S.
Management. M.B.A.
Marketing. M.B.A.
Pharmaceutical Operations. M.B.A.
Professional Accounting. M.S.
Sports Management. M.B.A.
Taxation. M.S.
Note: Evening program requires GMAT for admission; M.B.A.,
   M.S. Taxation. Joint M.B.A.-J.D., M.B.A.-M.P.A., M.B.A.-
   M.S. (Nursing), M.S. (International Business)-M.A. (Diplo-
   macy and International Relations).

COLLEGE OF NURSING:
Acute Care Nurse Practitioner. M.S.N.
Adult Nurse Practitioner. M.S.N.
Advanced Practice Nurse. M.S.N.
Case Management/Health Administration. M.S.N.
Gerontological Nurse Practitioner. M.S.N.
Health Systems Administration. M.S.N.
Pediatric Nurse Practitioner. M.S.N.
School Nursing. M.S.

SCHOOL OF DIPLOMACY AND INTERNATIONAL RELATIONS:
Diplomacy and International Relations. M.A.

SCHOOL OF GRADUATE MEDICAL EDUCATION:
Athletic Training. M.S.
Audiology. Sc.D.
Health Sciences. Includes movement science. M.S., Ph.D.
Occupational Therapy. M.S.
Physical Therapy. D.P.T.
Physician Assistant. M.S.
Speech Pathology. M.S.

SCHOOL OF THEOLOGY:
Pastoral Ministry. Includes church management, catechetical
   health care, liturgical, spirituality, youth.
Theology. Include biblical studies, ecclesia history, Judaeo-
   Christian studies, moral theology, systematic.

School of Law
Web site: www.law.shu.edu

Established 1951. Located 20 minutes from New York City in
Newark (07102-5210). ABA approved since 1951. AALS mem-
ber. Semester system. Full-time, part-time study. Special facili-
ties: Center for Social Justice, Legal Education Opportunities
Institute, Institute of Law, Science, and Technology. Special pro-
grams: summer study abroad at University of Parma in Parma
(Milan, Florence, Genoa), Italy, American University of Cairo,
Egypt. Law library: 446,916 volumes, 10,000 subscriptions; has
LEXIS, NEXIS, WESTLAW, DIALOG; has more than 200 net-
work connections.

Annual tuition: full-time $35,400, part-time $26,054. No on-
campus housing available. Contact Admission Officer for off-
campus information. Off-campus and personal expenses: $17,354.

Enrollment: first-year class full-time 205, part-time 162; total
full- and part-time 1193 (men 56%, women 44%, minorities 17%).
Faculty: full-time 39, part-time 110. Student to faculty ratio is
21.5 to 1. Degrees conferred: J.D., J.D.-M.B.A., J.D.-M.A. (Diplomacy and International Relations), J.D.-M.D. (Robert Wood Johnson Medical School of the UMDNJ), LL.M. (Health Law, full- or
part-time program), M.S.J. (Health Law for Health Care Professionals, full- or part-time).

ADMISSION REQUIREMENTS. LSDAS Law School report,
LSAT (not later that February test date; if more than one LSAT,
average is used), bachelor's degree from an accredited institution, personal statement, résumé, two recommendations, transcripts
(must show all schools attended and at least three years of study)
required in support of application. Applicants must have received
bachelor's degree prior to enrollment. Interview not required but
may be requested by School. In addition, international applicants
whose precollege language was not English and they score 150
or less on the LSAT must submit TOEFL (not older that two
years), certified copies of all transcripts and evaluations of all
foreign credentials. Joint degree applicants must apply to and be
accepted by both Schools; GMAT for M.B.A. Apply to Office of
Admission after September 30, before April 1. First-year students
admitted Fall only. Rolling admissions process, notification starts
in January and is finished by early May. Application fee $65.
Phone: (888)415-7271, (973)642-8747.

ADMISSION STANDARDS. Selective. Accepts approximately
25% of full-time, 61% of part-time students. Number of full-time
applicants 2498, part-time 582; number of full-time acceptance
627, part-time 357; number of full-time enrolled 205, part-time
162; LSAT (75% of full-time students have a score at or above
158, part-time 152); GPA (75% of full-time students have a GPA
at or above 3.00, part-time 3.00). *U.S. News & World Report*
ranking is in the second tier (tied at 70th) of all U.S. law schools.

FINANCIAL AID. Centennial Scholarships, need-based merit
scholarships, minority scholarships, Grants-in-Aid, private and
institutional loans; Federal loans and Federal W/S offered through
University's Financial Aid Office. Assistantships may be available
for upper-divisional joint degree candidates. All accepted students
are automatically considered for scholarships (selection criteria
places heavy reliance on LSAT and Undergraduate GPA). For all
other programs apply after January 1, before April 15 to Office of
Financial Resource Management. Phone: (973)642-8850. Use
FAFSA (School code: G09986), also submit Financial Aid Transcript, Federal Income Tax forms. Approximately 66% of first-
year class received scholarships/Grants-in-Aid. Approximately
52% of full-time and 12% of part-time students receive some
form of financial assistance.

DEGREE REQUIREMENTS. For J.D.: 85 (46 required) credits
with a GPA of at least 2.0 (A = 4), plus completion of upper divisional writing course; three-year program, four-year part-time
program. Accelerated J.D. with one summer of course work. For
J.D.-M.B.A.: total 118 credits (J.D. 73 credits, M.B.A. 45 credits); four-year full-time program only. For LL.M., M.S.J.: 24
credit program.

SHIPPENSBURG UNIVERSITY OF PENNSYLVANIA
Shippensburg, Pennsylvania 17257-2299
Web site: www.ship.edu

Founded 1871. Located 40 miles SW of Harrisburg. CGS member. Coed. State control. Semester credit hour system. Special

facilities: Center for Applied Research and Policy Analysis. Center for Education and Human Services, Center for Interdisciplinary Science, The Frehn-Center for Professional Organizational Development, Center for Juvenile Justice Training and Research, Center for Local and State Government. Library: 445,600 volumes, 1453 subscriptions. Total University enrollment: 7500.

Tuition: per credit resident $327, nonresident $523. On-campus housing for graduate men and women. Average annual housing costs: $5000–$6700. Contact Dean of Students Office for both on- and off-campus housing information. Phone: (717)532-1164. Day-care facilities available.

School of Graduate Studies

Graduate studies since 1959. Enrollment: full-time 250, part-time 634. College faculty teaching graduate students: full-time 148, part-time 22. Degrees conferred: M.A., M.Ed., M.S., M.P.A.

ADMISSION REQUIREMENTS. Transcripts, GRE/MAT required in support of School's application. Online application available. Some departments require interview, goal statement, or letters of recommendation. TOEFL required for international applicants. Accepts transfer applicants. Apply to Dean of Graduate Studies at least eight weeks prior to registration. Rolling admissions process. Application fee $30. Phone: (717)477-1213; fax: (717)477-4016; e-mail: admiss@ship.edu.

ADMISSION STANDARDS. Selective for most departments. Usual minimum average: 2.75 (A = 4).

FINANCIAL AID. Annual awards from institutional funds: assistantships, internships, Federal W/S, loans. Apply by March 1 to Dean of the Graduate Studies for assistantships; to the Financial Aid Office for all other programs. Phone: (717)477-1131. Use FAFSA and University's FAF. Aid available for part-time students.

DEGREE REQUIREMENTS. For master's: 30–48 semester hours minimum, 24 in residence; thesis/nonthesis option.

FIELDS OF STUDY.
Administration of Justice.
Applied History.
Biology.
Business Administration.
Communication Study.
Computer Science. GRE required.
Counseling.
Curriculum and Instruction.
Geoenvironmental Studies.
Information Systems.
Organizational Development and Leadership.
Psychology.
Public Administration.
Reading.
School Administration.
Social Work.
Special Education.

SIENA HEIGHTS UNIVERSITY
Adrian, Michigan 49221-1796
Web site: www.sienaheights.edu

Founded 1919. Located 65 miles SW of Detroit. Coed. Private control. Roman Catholic. Semester system. Library: 125,000 volumes, 650 subscriptions. Total University enrollment: 2000.

Tuition: per credit $399. No on-campus housing for graduate students. Contact Director, Residence Life for off-campus housing information. Phone: (517)264-7170.

Graduate Division

Graduate study since 1953. Enrollment: full-time 36, part-time 167. Graduate faculty: full- and part-time 28. Degree conferred: M.A.

ADMISSION REQUIREMENTS. Transcripts, three letters of recommendation required in support of application. Online application available. TOEFL required for international applicants. Interview recommended. Accepts transfer applicants. Apply to Graduate Office by April 1 (Summer), August 1 (Fall). Application fee $25. Phone: (517)264-7185.

ADMISSION STANDARDS. Selective for most departments. Usual minimum average: 3.0 (A = 4).

FINANCIAL AID. Limited Federal W/S, loans. Approved for VA benefits. Apply by March 1 to Financial Aid Office. Phone: (800) 521-0009, ext. 7130. Use FAFSA (School code: 007316).

DEGREE REQUIREMENTS. For M.A.: 36–48 semester hours; thesis/research project.

FIELDS OF STUDY.
Community Counseling.
Early Childhood Education. Includes Montessori.
Educational Leadership.
Elementary Education. Includes reading K–12.
Emergency Management.
Health Care Leadership.
Homeland Security.
Mathematics Education. Includes technology.
Middle Level Education.
Not for Profit Leadership.
Nuclear Power Administration.
Organizational Leadership.
Public Service Leadership.
School Counseling.
Secondary Education. Includes reading K–12.

SIMMONS COLLEGE
Boston, Massachusetts 02115-5898
Web site: www.simmons.edu

Founded 1899. Coed on graduate level. Private control. Semester system. Library: 285,700 volumes, 1861 subscriptions.

Tuition: per credit $850 (A&S), $725 (Education), $879 (Health), $868 (Library), $975 (Management), $811 (Social Work). On-campus housing for graduate students. Average academic year housing costs: on-campus $12,448 (including board), off-campus $16,500. Contact the Office of Student Housing for both on- and off-campus housing information. Phone: (617)521-1102.

Graduate Division

Enrollment: full-time 650, part-time 1462. College faculty: full-time 119, part-time 99. Degrees conferred: M.A., M.S., M.S.Ed., M.B.A., M.A.T., M.Phil., M.S.W., Ph.D., D.A.

ADMISSION REQUIREMENTS. Transcripts, references required in support of application. Online application available. TOEFL required for international applicants. Interview, GRE/GMAT/MAT sometimes necessary. Apply to Director of appropriate program. Call for information regarding deadlines and application fees; they vary by graduate program. Rolling admissions process. Phone: (617)521-2915 (A & S); (617)521-3137 (Health); (617)521-3840 (Management); (617)521-3939 (Social Work).

ADMISSION STANDARDS: Selective. Usual minimum average: 2.75 (A = 4).

FINANCIAL AID. Grants, scholarships, assistantships, internships, tuition waivers, Federal W/S, loans. Type and amount of aid varies according to program of study. Apply by March 1 to Director of Financial Aid. Phone: (617)521-2910. Use FAFSA. Aid available for part-time students.

DEGREE REQUIREMENTS. For master's: 32–56 semester hours, dependent upon the program; thesis required in some programs. For Ph.D.: 70 credits minimum beyond bachelor's, at least 32 in residence; competency in 2 foreign languages, or computer tool may be substituted for 1 language; dissertation; final oral exam. For D.D.T.: Three-year, full-time, 99-credit program; clinical placement.

FIELDS OF STUDY.

COLLEGE OF ARTS AND SCIENCES:
Applied Behavior Analysis. Ph.D.
Children's Literature. M.A.
Educational Leadership. M.S.Ed.
English. M.A.
Gender/Cultural Studies. M.A.
Health Professions Education. Ph.D.
Spanish. M.A.
Special Education. Includes administrator, assistive technology, behavior education, language & literacy, moderate/severe. M.S.Ed.
Teaching English as a Second Language. M.A.T.E.S.L.
Urban Education. M.S.Ed.
Writing for Children. M.F.A.

SCHOOL OF HEALTH STUDIES:
Health Administration. M.H.A.
Nutrition and Health Promotion. M.S.
Physical Therapy. D.P.T.
Primary Health Care Nursing. M.S.

GRADUATE SCHOOL OF LIBRARY AND INFORMATION SCIENCE:
Archives Management. M.S.
Library and Information Science. Ph.D.
Managerial Leadership in the Information Professions. D.A., Ph.D.
Preservation Management. M.S.
School Library Teacher. M.S.

SCHOOL OF MANAGEMENT:
Business Administration. M.B.A.

SCHOOL OF SOCIAL WORK:
Social Work. M.S.W., Ph.D.
Urban Leadership. M.S.W.

SLIPPERY ROCK UNIVERSITY OF PENNSYLVANIA
Slippery Rock, Pennsylvania 16057
Web site: www.sru.edu

Established 1889. Located 50 miles N of Pittsburgh. Coed. State control. Library: 774,723 volumes, 4100 subscriptions. Total University enrollment: 8100.

Annual tuition: full-time resident $7637, nonresident $11,764; per credit resident $327, nonresident $523. On-campus housing for single students only. Average academic year housing cost: $5300 (including board). Contact Office of Director of Residence Life for both on- and off-campus housing. Phone: (724) 738-2082. Day-care facilities available.

Graduate School

Enrollment: full-time 390, part-time 301. Faculty: full- and part-time 65. Degrees conferred: M.Ed., M.A., M.S., M.S.N., M.P.A., D.P.T.

ADMISSION REQUIREMENTS. Transcripts, GRE, interview (Physical Therapy) required in support of application. TOEFL required for international applicants. Interview not required. Accepts transfer applicants. Graduates of unaccredited institutions not considered. Apply to Graduate School Office at least two months prior to registration. Application fee $25, $35 for D.P.T., Nursing. Phone: (724)738-2051; fax: (724)738-2146.

ADMISSION STANDARDS. Selective. Usual minimum average: 2.75, some programs required 3.0 (A = 4).

FINANCIAL AID. Annual awards from institutional funds: scholarships, assistantships, internships, grants, tuition waivers, Federal W/S, loans. Apply by May 1 to appropriate department chair for assistantships; to Office of Financial Aid for all other programs. Phone: (724)738-2044; fax: (724)738-2922. Use FAFSA. About 35% of students receive aid other than loans from College and outside sources. Aid available for part-time students.

DEGREE REQUIREMENTS. For master's: 30 credit hours minimum, at least 18 in residence; thesis or final document; final written/oral exam. For D.P.T.: 60 credits beyond the master's degree, at least two years in full-time residence; qualifying exam; dissertation; internship; final oral exam.

FIELDS OF STUDY.
Community Counseling. Includes addiction, adult, child & adolescent. M.A.
English. Includes traditional, professional writing. M.A.
Environmental Education. M.Ed.
History. M.A.
Nursing. M.S.
Park and Resource Management. M.S.
Physical Education. M.Ed.
Physical Therapy. Ph.D.
Reading. Includes elementary, early childhood. M.Ed.
School Counseling. M.Ed.
Secondary Education. Includes teaching English, mathematics & science, social studies/history. M.Ed.
Special Education. M.Ed.
Special Education School Supervision. M.Ed.
Sport Management. M.S.
Student Affairs in Higher Education. M.A.
Sustainable Systems. M.S.

SMITH COLLEGE
Northampton, Massachusetts 01063
Web site: www.smith.edu

Founded 1871. Located 100 miles W of Boston. Coed on graduate level. Private control. Semester system. Special facilities: Fine Arts Center, Center for the Performing Arts, Clarke Science Center. Cooperative M.E.D. program with the Clarke School for the Deaf; cooperative Ph.D. program with Amherst, Hampshire, Mount Holyoke, University of Massachusetts. Library: 1,200,000 volumes, 5119 subscriptions. Total enrollment: 3100.

Annual tuition: $33,940, per credit $1060. On-campus housing for 25 graduate students; none for married students. Average annual housing cost: $8400 (including board). Phone: (413)585-3050.

Graduate Study

Graduate study since 1879. Enrollment: full-time 48, part-time 23. College faculty: full-time 98, part-time 38. Degrees conferred: M.A., M.A.T., M.Ed., M.E.D., (Teaching of the Deaf), M.F.A. (Dance), M.S. in Exercise and Sport Studies.

ADMISSION REQUIREMENTS. Transcripts, GRE/MAT, three letters of recommendation required in support of application. TOEFL required for international applicants. Interview not required. Apply to Director of Graduate Study by January 15 M.E.D. (April 15 without financial aid); April 1 M.F.A.; March 1 all other programs. Application fee $60. Phone: (413)585-3051; fax: (413) 585-3054; e-mail: gradstdy@smith.edu.

ADMISSION STANDARDS. Competitive for most departments. Usual minimum average: 3.0 (A = 4).

FINANCIAL AID. Scholarships, grants, fellowships, assistantships, Federal W/S, loans. Apply by January 15 to Director of Graduate Study for scholarships, fellowships; to Financial Aid Office for all other programs. Phone: (413)585-3050; fax: (413)858-2075. Use FAFSA and CSS Profile. About 80% of students receive aid from College and outside sources. Aid available for part-time students.

DEGREE REQUIREMENTS. For M.A., Ed.M., M.E.D., M.F.A.: 8 semester courses minimum in residence; thesis or final project. For M.A.T.: 8 semester courses minimum in residence, usually one academic year plus one summer internship. For M.S. in Exercise and Sport Studies: usually two years in full-time residence.

FIELDS OF STUDY.
Biological Sciences. M.S.
Dance. M.F.A.
Education of the Deaf. M.Ed.
Elementary Education. M.Ed.
Exercise and Sport Studies. M.S.
Middle School Education. M.Ed.
Playwriting. M.F.A.
Secondary Education. Includes biological sciences, chemistry, English, French, geology, history, mathematics, physics, Spanish. M.A.T.

School for Social Work

Since 1918. Quarter system. Annual tuition: full-time $13,328. On-campus housing available. Summer session room and board: $2306.
Enrollment: full-time 373. School faculty: full-time 10, part-time 92. Degrees conferred: M.S.W., Ph.D.

ADMISSION REQUIREMENTS. Official transcripts, MAT required in support of School's application. TOEFL required for international applicants. Accepts transfer applicants. Graduates of unaccredited institutions not considered. Apply by February 15 to the Office of Admissions. Application fee $60. Phone: (413) 585-7960; fax: (413)585-7994.

ADMISSION STANDARDS. Competitive. Usual minimum average: 3.0 (A = 4).

FINANCIAL AID. Scholarships, tuition waivers, internships, grants, loans. Apply by April 1 to the Financial Aid Office. Use FAFSA. About 50% of students receive aid from the School and outside sources.

DEGREE REQUIREMENTS. For M.S.W: three quarters (56 quarter hours) in full-time studies; field work experience; final research project. For Ph.D.: two and one-half summers and two intervening eight-month clinical practice internships; written & oral Clinical Qualifying Exam; comprehensive exam; dissertation proposal; dissertation; dissertation defense.

SONOMA STATE UNIVERSITY
Rohnert Park, California 94928-3609
Web site: www.sonoma.edu

Founded 1960. Located 45 miles N of San Francisco. Coed. State control. Semester system. Library: 636,613 volumes, 2400 subscriptions. Total University enrollment: 7749.
Annual fee: full-time resident $4588, nonresident $4588 plus $339 per unit. On-campus housing for single students only. Average academic year housing costs: $5200 (including board). Contact Housing Office for both on- and off-campus housing information. Phone: (707)664-4033. Day-care facilities available.

Graduate Programs

Enrollment: full-time 481, part-time 140. College faculty teaching graduate students: full-time 75, part-time 61. Degrees conferred: M.A., M.S., M.B.A., M.P.A.

ADMISSION REQUIREMENTS. Transcripts, GRE/GMAT/MAT required in support of application. Online application available. TOEFL required for international applicants. Accepts transfer applicants. Graduates of unaccredited institutions not considered. Apply to Office of Admissions and Records by January 31 (Fall), October 31 (Spring). Application fee $55. Phone: (707)664-2778; fax: (707)664-2060.

ADMISSION STANDARDS. Varies by department. Usual minimum average: 3.0 (A = 4).

FINANCIAL AID. Fellowships, internships, assistantships, Federal W/S, loans. Apply by April 1 to Financial Aid Office. Phone: (707)664-2389. Use FAFSA. Aid available for part-time students.

DEGREE REQUIREMENTS. For master's: 30–60 units minimum, at least 21 in residence; thesis/nonthesis option; final oral exam/projects.

FIELDS OF STUDY.
Biology. Includes environmental. M.A.
Business Administration. M.B.A.
Computer and Engineering. M.S.
Counseling. Concentrations in marriage, family, and child counseling (M.F.C.C.), school counseling (P.P.S.). M.A.
Cultural Resource Management. Includes anthropology. M.A.
Education. Concentrations in curriculum and instruction, early childhood education, educational administration, reading and language, special education. M.A.
English. M.A.
History. M.A.
Interdisciplinary Studies. M.A., M.S.
Kinesiology. M.A.
Nursing. Concentrations in family nurse practitioner, leadership and management. M.S.
Psychology. Includes art therapy, organizational development, special-interest areas. M.A.
Public Administration. M.P.A.

UNIVERSITY OF THE SOUTH
Sewanee, Tennessee 37383-1000
Web site: www.sewanee.edu

Founded 1857. Located 50 miles W of Chattanooga. Coed. Private control. Semester system. Library: 457,526 volumes, 6495 subscriptions.
Tuition: per credit $660. On-campus housing for 50 graduate students in apartments only. Average academic year housing costs

for single or married seminary students: $385–$1100 per month. Day-care facilities available.

School of Theology

Founded 1872. Enrollment: full-time 97, part-time 17 (M.Dir., and M.A.). Faculty: full-time 9, part-time 6. Degrees conferred: M.Div. (S.T.M. and D.Min. are only in Summer), S.T.M., D.Min., M.A.

ADMISSION REQUIREMENTS. Transcripts, letter of recommendation, GRE, interview required in support of application. TOEFL required for international applicants. Accepts transfer applicants. Apply to Admissions Office before April 1 (Fall), November 15 (Spring). Application fee $25. Phone: (931)598-1283; fax: (931)598-1852.

ADMISSION STANDARDS. Competitive. Usual minimum average: 3.0 (A = 4).

FINANCIAL AID. 75 grants which are need-based, institutional work program for M.Div., M.A. students only. Contact Financial Aid Office for application deadlines. Phone: (615)598-1312; fax: (615)598-1667.

DEGREE REQUIREMENTS. For M.Div.: 91 credits minimum, at least 30 in residence and two semesters in full-time study. For M.A.: 48 hours including thesis. For S.T.M.: 30 credits minimum beyond the M.Div., four summers in residence; thesis. For D.Min.: 30 credits minimum beyond the M.Div., normally takes four summers in residence.

FIELD OF STUDY.
Theology.

UNIVERSITY OF SOUTH ALABAMA
Mobile, Alabama 36688-0002
Web site: www.usouthal.edu

Founded 1964. Semester system. CGS member. Coed. Special facilities: Electron Microscopy Center, Mass Spectroscopy Center, Flow Cytometry Center, DBNA-Protein Sequencing and Synthesis Center, Sickle-Cell Center, Cancer Center. Library: 1,000,000 volumes, 2800 subscriptions. Total University enrollment: 13,000.

Tuition/fees: basic fee of $176 per semester; per credit, resident $176, nonresident $352. On-campus housing available for 502 married students, 1690 single students. Average academic year housing costs: $3600–$4400 (including board). Contact Director of Housing for both on- and off-campus housing information. Phone: (251)460-6195.

Graduate School

Created 1968. Enrollment: full-time 1838, part-time 835. Graduate faculty: full-time 287. Degrees conferred: M.A., M.Acct., M.B.A., M.Ed., M.P.A., M.S., M.S.Ch.E., M.S.E.E., M.S.M.E., M.S.N., Ed.S., Ed.D., Ph.D.

ADMISSION REQUIREMENTS. Transcripts required in support of School's application. Standardized test, recommendation required by some programs. TOEFL required for international applicants. Accepts transfer applicants. Graduates of unaccredited institutions considered. Apply to Director of Admissions by July 15 (Fall), December 15 (Spring), May 1 (Summer). Deadlines for all admissions documents for International students is at least three months prior to date of registration. Rolling admissions process. Application fee $25. Phone: (800)872-5247, (251)460-6141.

ADMISSION STANDARDS. Selective. Usual minimum average: 3.0 (provisional 2.5) (A = 4).

FINANCIAL AID. Research assistantships, teaching assistantships, fellowships, stipends, internships, traineeships, Federal W/S, loans. Approved for VA benefits. Apply by April 1 to appropriate department for fellowships, assistantships; to the Office of Financial Aid for all other programs. Use FAFSA and University's FAF. Approximately 30% of graduate students receive aid other than loans from the University or outside sources. Aid available for part-time students.

DEGREE REQUIREMENTS. For master's: 48 quarter hours minimum, at least 3 quarter hours in residence; foreign language may be required by some programs; comprehensive exam; thesis/nonthesis option. For Ed.S.: 45 quarter hours beyond the master's. For doctoral programs: 90 quarter hours minimum, at least 6 quarters in residence; preliminary exam; dissertation; reading knowledge of one language, a research tool or computer technique; final oral exam.

FIELDS OF STUDY.

COLLEGE OF ALLIED HEALTH PROFESSIONS:
Communication Sciences and Disorders. Ph.D.
Occupational Therapy. M.S.
Physical Therapy. M.P.T.
Physician Assistant Studies. M.H.S.
Speech and Hearing Science. M.S.

COLLEGE OF ARTS AND SCIENCES:
Basic Medical Sciences. Specialization in biochemistry, microbiology/immunology, pharmacology, physiology, structural and cellular biology. Ph.D.
Biological Sciences. M.S.
Communication. M.A.
English. M.A.
History. M.A.
Marine Sciences. M.S., Ph.D.
Mathematics. M.S.
Psychology. M.S.
Public Administration. M.P.A.
Sociology. M.A.

MITCHELL COLLEGE OF BUSINESS:
Accounting. M.Acc.
Business Administration. M.B.A.

SCHOOL OF COMPUTER AND INFORMATION SCIENCES:
Computer and Information Sciences. M.S.

COLLEGE OF EDUCATION:
Alternative Education. M.Ed.
Alternative Secondary Education. M.Ed.
Community Counseling. M.S.
Counselor Education. Ed.S.
Early Childhood Education. M.Ed., Ed.S.
Educational Leadership. M.Ed., Ed.S.
Educational Media. M.Ed., Ed.S.
Elementary Education. M.Ed., Ed.S.
Exercise Technology. M.S.
Health Education. M.Ed., Ed.S.
Instructional Design and Development. M.S., Ph.D.
Physical Education. M.Ed., Ed.S.
Recreation Administration. M.S.
Rehabilitation Counseling. M.S.
School Counseling. M.Ed.
School Psychometry. M.Ed.
Science Education. M.Ed.
Secondary Education. M.Ed., Ed.S.
Special Education. Ed.S.
Therapeutic Recreation. M.S.

COLLEGE OF ENGINEERING:
Chemical Engineering. M.S.
Civil Engineering. M.S.
Electrical and Computer Engineering. M.S.
Mechanical Engineering. M.S.

COLLEGE OF NURSING:
Nursing. M.S.N.
Nursing Practice. D.N.P.

College of Medicine (36688-0002)

Web site: www.southmed.usouthal.edu

Established 1967. Library: 65,000 volumes, 2500 subscriptions.
Annual tuition: resident $14,654, nonresidents $26,908. Both on- and off-campus housing available. Total average figure for all other expenses: $12,000.

Enrollment: first-year class 64, total 302 (men 49%, women 51%, minorities 22%, state residents 89%). Faculty: full-time 206, part-time 18. Degrees conferred: M.D., M.D.-Ph.D.

ADMISSION REQUIREMENTS. AMCAS report, transcripts, MCAT, recommendations required in support of final application. Interview by invitation. Applicants must have completed at least three years of college study. Has EDP (Alabama residents only); apply between June 1 and August 1. Preference given to state residents. Graduates of unaccredited colleges not considered. Apply after June 1, before November 1. Application fee $50, submitted with supplemental application. Phone: (251)460-7176; fax: (251)460-6278.

ADMISSION STANDARDS. Competitive. Accepts about 10–15% of all applicants. Number of applications 809 (n/a out-of-state); number interviewed 162 (n/a out-of-state); number of acceptance n/a (n/a out-of-state); number enrolled 70 (n/a out-of-state). Mean Composite MCAT 10.0; mean UGPA 3.65 (A = 4.).

FINANCIAL AID. Limited scholarships, medical student summer research program, loans. Apply after acceptance to Office of Financial Aid. Phone: (251)460-7918. Use FAFSA (College code: 001057). About 5% of students receive some aid from School.

DEGREE REQUIREMENTS. For M.D.: satisfactory completion of four-year program; all students must pass USMLE Step 1 prior to entering the third year and pass USMLE Step 2 prior to awarding of M.D. For Ph.D., see Graduate listing above.

FIELDS OF GRADUATE STUDY.
Biochemistry & Molecular Biology.
Cancer Biology.
Cell Biology & Neuroscience.
Lung Biology.
Microbiology & Immunology.
Molecular & Cellular Pharmacology.
Physiology.

MEDICAL UNIVERSITY OF SOUTH CAROLINA

Charleston, South Carolina 29425-0002
Web site: www.musc.edu

Founded 1824. CGS member. Coed. State control. Semester system. Special facilities: Alcohol Research Center, Bone and Joint Center, Center for Appearance, Center for Drug and Alcohol Programs, Center for Health Care Research, Center for Advanced Imaging Research, Center on Aging, Cholesterol Center, Cystic Fibrosis Center, Digestive Disease Center, Gazes Cardiac Research

Institute, General Clinical Research Center, Hollings Cancer Center, Institute of Human Values in Health Care, Institute of Psychiatry, Magil Laser Center, National Crime Victims Research and Treatment Center, Pre-Conception Care Resource Center, Resource Centers of Minority Aging Research, Sarcoidosis Center. The University's NIH ranking is number 67th among all U.S. Institutions with 255 awards/grants valued at $85,011,365. According to The Center at University of Florida, the University is ranked number 84th in receipt of Federal Research fund with $92,893,000 and it ranks number 89th for total University research expenditures with $150,551,000. In 2004, 2 of the University's faculty members had been elected to National Honor Academies and this ranks it 117th among all U.S. institutions. The Library: approximately 255,000 volumes, 2180 subscriptions. Total University enrollment: 2500.
No on-campus housing available.

College of Graduate Studies

Annual tuition: full-time resident $9926 (M.S. degree), $9340 (Ph.D.), nonresident $13,260 (M.S. degrees), $11,842 (Ph.D.). Enrollment: full-time 227, part-time 35. Degrees conferred: M.S., Ph.D.

ADMISSION REQUIREMENTS. Transcripts, three letters of recommendation, GRE Subject Tests, interview required in support of application. Online application available. Accepts transfer applicants. Apply by January 15 to Director of Student Programs. Phone: (800)792-3391; fax: (843)792-6590. Application fee: none, $75 for international applicants. Approximately 90% are state residents.

ADMISSION STANDARDS. Selective. Usual minimum average: 3.0 (A = 4) residents.

FINANCIAL AID. Teaching research/fellowships, teaching assistantships, full and partial tuition waivers, Federal W/S, loans. Apply by April 1 to appropriate department chair for fellowships; to Office of Financial Aid for all other aid. Use FAFSA (College code: 003438). Aid available for part-time students.

DEGREE REQUIREMENTS. For M.S.: 30 semester hours minimum, at least 18 in residence; reading knowledge of one foreign language; thesis; final oral exam. For Ph.D.: 60 credits minimum beyond the bachelor's, at least one year in continuous residence; reading knowledge of two foreign languages; written/oral qualifying exam; dissertation; final oral exam.

FIELDS OF STUDY.
Biochemistry and Molecular Biology. M.S.
Biomedical Sciences. Ph.D.
Biostatistics, Bioinformatics and Epidemiology. M.S.
Cell and Molecular Pharmacology and Experimental Therapeutics. M.S., Ph.D.
Cell Biology and Anatomy. Ph.D.
Clinical Research. M.S.
Marine Biomedicine and Environmental Sciences. Ph.D.
Molecular, Cellular Biology, and Pathobiology. Ph.D.
Microbiology and Immunology. M.S.
Neurosciences. M.S.
Nursing. Ph.D.
Pathology and Laboratory Medicine. M.S., Ph.D.
Pharmaceutical Sciences. Ph.D.
Physiology/Neuroscience. M.S., Ph.D.

College of Dental Medicine

Web site: www.musc.edu/dentistry

First class admitted fall 1967. Semester system. Special facility: Center for Oral Health Research.

Annual tuition: resident $19,204, nonresident $53,686. Limited on-campus housing. Average academic year housing costs:

$12,300. Total average cost for all other first-year expenses: $11,500.

Enrollment: first-year class 54, total 220 (men 58%, women 42%, minorities 14%, state residents 94%). Faculty: full-time 47, part-time 25. Degrees conferred: D.M.D., D.M.D.-Ph.D.(Dental Medicine Scientist Training Program).

ADMISSION REQUIREMENTS. AADSAS report, transcripts, DAT required in support of College's application. Interview by invitation only. Preference given to state residents. Applicants must have completed at least three years of college study. Apply to Office of Enrollment Services after June 1, before December 1. Application fee $75. Phone: (843)792-7345; fax: (843)792-1521.

ADMISSION STANDARDS. Selective. Accepts about 10–15% of all applicants. Usual minimum UGPA: 2.7 (A = 4). Mean DAT: academic 19, PAT 18; mean UGPA 3.50.

FINANCIAL AID. Scholarships, grants, loans. Apply to Director of Financial Aid after acceptance; priority deadline March 15. Phone: (843)792-2536. Use FAFSA (College code: 003438). About 90% of students receive some aid from School and outside sources.

DEGREE REQUIREMENTS. For D.M.D.: satisfactory completion of four-year program. For Ph.D.: see College of Graduate Studies listing above.

FIELDS OF POSTGRADUATE STUDY.
Oral and Maxillofacial Surgery.
Orthodontics.
Pediatric Dentistry.
Periodontics.

Medical School (P.O. Box 250203)
Web site: www.musc.edu

Established 1834 and is the South's oldest medical school. Library: 230,000 volumes, 1700 subscriptions. NIH ranking is 67th among all U.S. institutions with 255 awards/grants worth $85,011,365.

Annual tuition: resident $23,152, nonresidents $62,808. No on-campus housing available. For off-campus housing information contact Off-campus Housing Office. Phone (843)792-0394. Total average figure for all other expenses: $12,000-$18,000.

Enrollment: first-year class 138, total 609 (men 54%, women 46%, minorities 24%, state residents 90%). Faculty: full- and part-time 1075. Degrees conferred: M.D., M.D.-M.H.A., M.D.-M.P.H., M.D.-Ph.D.

ADMISSION REQUIREMENTS. AMCAS report, transcripts, MCAT, recommendations, interview required in support of application. Supplemental application required. Interview by invitation only. Has EDP (South Carolina residents only); apply between June 1 and August 1. Applicants must have completed at least three years of college study. Preference given to state residents. Accepts transfer applicants. Apply to Registrar after June 1, before December 1 (Fall). Application fee $25. Phone: (843)792-2055; fax: (843)792-3764.

ADMISSION STANDARDS. Competitive. Accepts about 17% of all applicants. Number of applications 1064 (658 out-of-state); number interviewed 357 (48 out-of-state); number of acceptance 188 (20 out-of-state); number enrolled 138 (4 out-of-state). Mean Composite MCAT 9.6; mean UGPA 3.61 (A = 4.).

FINANCIAL AID. Scholarships, internships, loans. Apply to Office of the Dean by April 24. Phone: (843)792-2536. Use FAFSA (School code: 003438). About 82% of students receive aid other than loans from School.

DEGREE REQUIREMENTS. For M.D.: successful completion of four-year program; all students must pass USMLE Step 1 prior to beginning third year; Step 2 required for graduation. For Ph.D.: see Graduate School listing above.

FIELDS OF GRADUATE STUDY.
Anatomy and Cell Biology.
Bioinformatics.
Biochemistry and Molecular Biology.
Epidemiology.
Cell and Molecular Pharmacology and Experimental Therapeutics.
Gene Medicine.
Microbiology and Immunology.
Molecular and Cellular Biology.
Neuroscience and Proteomics.
Pathobiology.
Pathology.
Structural Biology.
Toxicology.

SOUTH CAROLINA STATE UNIVERSITY
Orangeburg, South Carolina 29117
Web site: www.scsu.edu

Founded 1896. Located 50 miles S of Columbia. CGS member. Coed. State control. Semester system. Special facilities: Biology Center of Excellence, Savannah River Field Station, National Summer Transportation Institute, University Transportation Center. Library: 273,000 volumes, 1650 subscriptions. Total University enrollment: 4500.

Tuition: per credit resident $257, nonresident $431; student fees resident $3162, nonresident $6510.

Limited on-campus housing. Average academic year housing costs: $2660–$5200. Contact Director of Housing for both on- and off-campus housing information. Phone: (803)536-8560.

School of Graduate Studies

Established 1946. Enrollment: full-time 250, part-time 475. Faculty: full- and part-time 76. Degrees conferred: M.A., M.A.T., M.Ed., M.S., Ed.S., Ed.D.

ADMISSION REQUIREMENTS. Transcripts, GRE or MAT, NTE (for M.Ed.), enrollment objectives, résumé, two recommendations required in support of School's application. Online application available. Interview not required. Accepts transfer applicants. Apply to Dean of Graduate Studies by June 15 (Fall), November 1 (Spring). Rolling admissions process. Application fee $25. Phone: (803)536-8809; fax: (803)536-8812.

ADMISSION STANDARDS. Relatively open for master's, selective for all other degrees. Usual minimum for all master's: 2.5 (A = 4), for Ed.S.: 3.25 GPA, GRE total 850, for Ed.D.: 3.25 GPA, GRE total 1000.

FINANCIAL AID. Fellowships, research assistantships, Federal W/S, loans. Approved for VA benefits. Apply to Director of Financial Aid by June 1. Phone: (803)536-7067; fax: (803)536-8420. Use FAFSA (School code: 003446).

DEGREE REQUIREMENTS. For master's: 36 semester hours minimum, at least 30 in residence; GRE, English Subject Test, NTE for candidacy (M.Ed.); comprehensive exams; thesis/nonthesis option.

FIELDS OF STUDY.
Agribusiness.
Business Administration. M.B.A.
Counselor Education.

Education. M.Ed., Ed.S., Ed.D.
Entrepreneurship.
Individual and Family Development.
Nutritional Sciences.
Rehabilitation Counseling.
Speech Pathology and Audiology.
Teaching. M.A.T.
Transportation.

UNIVERSITY OF SOUTH CAROLINA
Columbia, South Carolina 29208
Web site: www.sc.edu

Founded 1801. CGS member. State control. Coed. Semester system. Special facilities: Ira and Nancy Koger Center for the Arts, Belle W. Baruch Institute for Marine Biology and Coastal Research, Counseling and Human Development Center, Center for Developmental Disabilities, Earth Sciences and Resources Institute, Center for Economic Education, Center for Fracture Mechanics and Nondestructive Evaluation, Center for Industrial Research, Center for Industry Policy and Strategy, International Center for Public Health Research, Center for Machine Intelligence, Center for Science Education, Southeast Manufacturing Technology Center, Institute for Southern Studies, Center for the Study of Suicide and Life Threatening Behavior, McKissick Museum. The University's NIH ranking is 147th among all U.S. institutions with 73 awards/grants valued at $27,532,968. In 2004, the University awarded 241 doctorates which ranked it 60th among all U.S. institutions eligible to award that degree. The Library: approximately 2,675,000 volumes, 20,400 subscriptions.

Annual tuition: full-time resident $8288, nonresident $17,916; per credit resident $411, nonresident $874. On-campus housing for married students, graduate men, graduate women. Average academic year housing costs: $3500–$4500 for married students, $5500–$6500 (including board) for single students. Contact Director of Family, Conference & Summer Housing for on- and off-campus housing information. Phone: (803)777-4571. Day-care facilities available.

Graduate School

Established 1906. Enrollment: full-time 3500, part-time 3769. Faculty: full- and part-time 1300. Degrees conferred: M.A., M.Acc., M.A.T., M.B.A., M.C.J., M.E., M.Ed., M.E.R.M., M.F.A., M.H.A., M.I.B.S., M.L.I.S., MM., M.M.A., M.M.Ed., M.N., M.P.A., M.P.E.R., M.S., M.S.W., M.Tax., D.M.A., M.N., Ed.D., Dr.Ph., Ph.D.

ADMISSION REQUIREMENTS. Transcripts, two letters of recommendation, GRE Subject Tests/MAT, GMAT (business majors) required in support of School's application. Online application available. TOEFL required for international applicants. Interview not required. Accepts transfer applicants. Graduates of unaccredited institutions not considered. Apply to Graduate School with complete credentials by July 1 (Fall), November 15 (Spring), May 1 (Summer). Rolling admissions process. Application fee $35. Phone: (803)777-4243; fax: (803)777-2972.

ADMISSION STANDARDS. Selective for most departments. Usual minimum average: 3.0 (A = 4).

FINANCIAL AID. Annual awards from institutional funds: scholarships, fellowships, teaching assistantships, research assistantships, internships, grants, tuition waivers, Federal W/S, loans. Approved for VA benefits. Apply to Dean of Graduate School for scholarships; to appropriate department chairman for assistantships, fellowships; to Financial Aid Office for all other programs; no specified closing date. Use FAFSA. About 55% of students receive aid other than loans from University and outside sources. Aid available to part-time students.

DEGREE REQUIREMENTS. For M.A., M.S.: 30 semester hours minimum, at least 24 in residence; one language for some programs; thesis/nonthesis option; comprehensive exam. For other master's: usually, language requirement is eliminated and course work is allowed in lieu of thesis. For doctoral programs: 72 hours minimum beyond the bachelor's degree, at least two years in residence; reading knowledge of one foreign language varies by department, research tool, or computer technique; qualifying exam; candidacy; dissertation; final oral exam.

FIELDS OF STUDY.
Accounting. M.Acc.
Anthropology.
Applied Art History. M.A.
Art. M.F.A.
Art Education. M.A., M.A.T.
Art History. M.A.
Art Studio. M.A., M.F.A.
Biological Sciences. M.S., Ph.D.
Biomedical Science. M.B.S., Ph.D.
Biomedical Engineering. M.S., Ph.D.
Biostatistics. M.P.H., Dr.P.D.
Business Administration. Ph.D.
Business Education. M.A., M.A.T.
Chemical Engineering. M.E., M.S., Ph.D.
Chemistry and Biochemistry. M.S., Ph.D.
Civil and Environmental Engineering. M.E., M.S., Ph.D.
Clinical Community Psychology. Ph.D.
Clinical Nursing. M.S.N.
Communication Sciences and Disorders. M.C.D., M.S.P., Ph.D.
Community Mental Health and Psychiatric Nursing. M.S.N.
Comparative Literature. M.A., Ph.D.
Computer Science and Engineering. M.E., M.S., Ph.D.
Counselor Education. Ed.S., Ph.D.
Creative Writing. M.F.A.
Criminology and Criminal Justice. M.A.
Curriculum and Instruction. Ed.D.
Early Childhood Education. M.A.T., M.Ed., Ph.D.
Earth and Environmental Resource Management. M.E.R.M.
Economics. M.A., Ph.D.
Educational Administration. M.Ed., Ed.S., Ph.D.
Educational Research. M.Ed.
Elementary Education. M.A.T., Ph.D.
Electrical Engineering. M.E., M.S., Ph.D.
English. M.A., M.A.T., Ph.D.
Environmental Health Sciences. M.P.H., M.S., M.S.P.H.
Epidemiology. M.P.H., M.S.P.H., Dr.P.H., Ph.D.
Exercise Science. M.S., Ph.D.
Experimental Psychology. M.A., Ph.D.
Foreign Languages. M.A.T.
Foundations of Education. Ph.D.
French. M.A.
Genetic Counseling. M.S.
Geography. M.A., M.S., Ph.D.
Geology. M.S., Ph.D.
German. M.A.
Health Care Administration. M.H.A.
Health Education. M.A.T., M.S.
Health Nursing. M.S.N.
Health Promotion, Education and Behavior. M.P.H., M.S.P.H., Dr.P.H., Ph.D.
Higher Education and Student Affairs. M.Ed.
History. M.A., Ph.D.
Human Resources. M.H.R.
Industrial Statistics. M.I.S.
International Business. Includes a concentration in Europe. I.M.B.A.
International Hospitality and Tourism Management. M.I.H.R.T.M.
International Studies. M.A.
Jazz Studies. M.M.
Journalism and Mass Communications. M.A., M.M.C.

Language and Literacy. M.Ed., Ph.D.
Library and Information Science. M.L.I.S., Ph.D.
Linguistics. M.A., Ph.D.
Marine Science. M.S., Ph.D.
Mass Communication. Ph.D.
Media Arts. M.M.A.
Mechanical Engineering. M.E., M.S., Ph.D.
Music Composition. M.M., D.M.A.
Music Conducting. M.M., D.M.A.
Music Education. M.M.E., Ph.D.
Music History. M.M.
Music Performance. M.M., D.M.A.
Music Theory. M.M.
Nuclear Engineering. M.E., M.S., Ph.D.
Nursing. N.D.
Nursing Administration. M.S.N.
Nursing Anesthesia. M.N.A.
Nursing Science. Ph.D.
Opera Theater. M.M.
Pharmaceutical Science. M.S., Ph.D.
Philosophy. M.A., Ph.D.
Physical Activity and Public Health. M.P.H.
Physical Education. M.A., M.A.T., M.S., Ph.D.
Physical Therapy. D.P.T.
Physics. M.S., Ph.D.
Piano Pedagogy. M.M., D.M.A.
Political Science. M.A., Ph.D.
Public Administration. M.P.A.
Public Health Administration. M.P.H., Dr.P.H., Ph.D.
Public Health. M.P.H.
Public History. M.A.
Rehabilitation Counseling. M.R.C.
Religious Studies. M.A.
Retailing. M.R.
School Psychology. Ph.D.
Sciences. M.A., M.A.T.
Secondary Education. M.T., Ph.D.
Social Studies. M.A.T.
Social Work. M.S., Ph.D.
Sociology. M.A., Ph.D.
Spanish. M.A.
Special Education. M.A.T., M.Ed., Ph.D.
Speech Language Pathology and Audiology. Ph.D.
Speech Pathology. M.C.D., M.S.P.
Sport and Entertainment Management. M.S.E.M.
Statistics. M.S., Ph.D.
Teaching. M.Ed., Ed.S.
Theater. M.A., M.A.T., M.F.A.

School of Law
Web site: www.law.sc.edu

Established 1867. ABA approved since 1925. AALS member since 1924. Semester system. Special facility: National Judicial Advocacy Center. Law library: 521,597 volumes, 3347 subscriptions; has LEXIS, NEXIS, WESTLAW, DIALOG, RLIN, OCLC.

Annual tuition: full-time resident $16,156, nonresident $32,048. On-campus housing available. Total average annual additional expense: $15,092.

Enrollment: first-year class 225; total 706 (men 56%, women 44%, minorities 11%); no part-time students. Faculty: full-time 48, part-time 30. Student to faculty ratio 17.8 to 1. Degrees conferred: J.D., J.D.-M.A. (Economics, Criminology, Human Resources), J.D.-M.B.A., J.D.-M.I.B.S., J.D.-M.Acc., J.D.-M.P.A, J.D.-M.S. (Health Administration, Earth and Environmental Resources Management).

ADMISSION REQUIREMENTS. LSDAS Law School report, bachelor's degree, transcripts, LSAT, personal statement, two letters of recommendation required in support of application. Interview not required. Accepts transfer applicants. Preference given to state residents. Graduates of unaccredited colleges not considered. Apply to Director of Admissions after September 1, before April 1; transfer application deadline May 15. Admits beginning students Fall only. Application fee: residents $60, nonresidents $70. Phone: (803)777-6605/6606.

ADMISSION STANDARDS. Selective. Accepts approximately 34% of all students. Number of applicants 1503; number of acceptance 516; number enrolled 225; LSAT (75% of students have a score at or above 154); GPA (75% of students have a GPA at or above 3.19). *U.S. News & World Report* ranking is in the second tier (tied at 91st) of all U.S. law schools.

FINANCIAL AID. Scholarships, fellowships, Federal W/S, loans. Apply to University's Financial Aid Office after acceptance, before April 15 (priority date February 1). Phone: (803)777-6605. Use FAFSA (School code: 003448). Approximately 17% of all students receive aid from School funds.

DEGREE REQUIREMENTS. For J.D.: 6 semesters minimum, at least two years in residence; 90 semester credit programs. For master's degree, see Graduate School listing above.

School of Medicine
Web site: www.med.sc.edu

Established 1974. Library: 80,000 volumes, 1200 subscriptions. NIH ranking is 147th among all U.S. institutions with 73 awards/grants worth $27,532,968.

Annual tuition: resident $22,544, nonresidents $59,860. On-campus housing available for married students only. Total average figure for all other expenses: $11,600.

Enrollment: first-year class 80, total 310 (men 54%, women 46%, minorities 15%, state residents 97%). Faculty: full- and part-time 400. Degrees conferred: M.D., M.D.-M.P.H., M.D.-Ph.D.

ADMISSION REQUIREMENTS. AMCAS report, transcripts, MCAT, recommendations required in support of final application. Interview by invitation only. Personal essay may be requested. Has EDP; apply between June 1 and August 1. Preference given to state residents. Accepts transfer applicants on a space-available basis. Graduates of unaccredited colleges not considered. Apply to Associate Dean for Admissions after June 1, before December 1. Application fee $75. Phone: (803)733-3325; fax: (803)733-3328.

ADMISSION STANDARDS. Competitive. Accepts about 10% of all applicants. Number of applications 1383 (1015 out-of-state); number interviewed 265 (60 out-of-state); number of acceptance 138 (23 out-of-state); number enrolled 80 (10 out-of-state). Mean Composite MCAT 9.3; mean UGPA 3.59 (A = 4.).

FINANCIAL AID. Scholarships, loans. Apply after acceptance to Office of Student Affairs. Phone: (803)733-3135. Use FAFSA (School code: 003448). About 91% of students receive aid from School.

DEGREE REQUIREMENTS. For M.D.: satisfactory completion of four-year program; all students must pass USMLE Step 1 prior to entering the third year and must pass USMLE Step 2 prior to awarding of M.D. For Ph.D.: see Graduate School listing above.

FIELDS OF GRADUATE STUDY.
Anatomy.
Cell Biology.
Immunology.
Microbiology.
Molecular Biology.
Neurosciences.
Pathology.
Pharmacology.
Physiology.
Public Health.

SOUTH DAKOTA SCHOOL OF MINES AND TECHNOLOGY

Rapid City, South Dakota 57701-3995
Web site: www.sdsmt.edu

Founded 1885. CGS member. Coed. State control. Semester system. Special facilities: Institute for the Study of Mineral Deposits, Mining and Mineral Resources Institute, Engineering and Mining Experiment Station, Institute of Atmospheric Sciences, Museum of Geology. Library: 273,000 volumes, 2000 subscriptions. Total School enrollment: 2650.

Tuition: per credit, resident $116, nonresident $391. On-campus housing for single students only. Average academic year housing cost: $3000–$4500 (including board). Contact Housing Director for both on- and off-campus housing information. Phone: (605) 394-2348.

Graduate Division

Graduate study since 1900. Enrollment: full-time 144, part-time 112. School faculty: full-time 98, part-time 30. Degrees conferred: M.S., Ph.D.

ADMISSION REQUIREMENTS. Transcripts, three letters of recommendation required in support of application. GRE/GMAT required by some departments. Online application available. TOEFL (minimum score 520) required for foreign applicants. Interview not required. Accepts transfer applicants. Graduates of unaccredited institutions not considered. Apply to Dean of Graduate Division at least two months prior to registration, at least three months for international applicants. Application fee domestic students $35, foreign students $100. Phone: (605)394-2342; fax: (605)394-5360; e-mail: admissions@sdsmt.edu.

ADMISSION STANDARDS. Selective for most departments. Usual minimum average: 2.75 (A = 4). TOEFL score 560 for admission without tutoring.

FINANCIAL AID. Annual awards from institutional funds: teaching assistantships, research assistantships, fellowships, Federal W/S, loans. Approved for VA benefits. Apply to Dean, Graduate Division at least three months prior to registration. Use FAFSA. About 50% of students receive aid other than loans from School and outside sources. Aid sometimes available for part-time students.

DEGREE REQUIREMENTS. For M.S.: 30 credit hours minimum, at least 18 in residence; thesis; final oral exam; or 32 hours without thesis, at least 18 in residence; final oral exam. For Ph.D.: four years beyond the bachelor's degree, at least 80 credits (includes M.S. allowance); research requirement; foreign language requirement; qualifying exam; comprehensive exams; thesis; final oral exam.

FIELDS OF STUDY.
Atmospheric, Environmental, and Water Resources. GRE for admission. Ph.D. only.
Atmospheric Sciences. M.S. only.
Chemical Engineering. M.S. only.
Civil Engineering. M.S. only.
Computer Science. GRE for admission. M.S. only.
Electrical Engineering. GRE for admission. M.S. only.
Geology/Geological Engineering. GRE Subject for admission.
Materials Engineering and Science. GRE for admission.
Mechanical Engineering. M.S. only.
Metallurgical Engineering. M.S. only.
Meteorology. GRE Subject for international applicants.
Mining Engineering. M.S. only.
Nanoscience and Nanoengineering. Ph.D.
Paleontology. GRE Subject for admission. One language for M.S. M.S. only.
Technology Management. GMAT or GRE for admission. M.S. only.

SOUTH DAKOTA STATE UNIVERSITY

Brookings, South Dakota 57007
Web site: www.sdstate.edu

Founded 1881. Coed. State control. Semester system. Library: 525,000 volumes, 3000 subscriptions.

Tuition: per credit resident $125, nonresident $369. On-campus housing for 88 married students, 1688 men, 1644 women. Average academic year housing costs: on-campus for single students, $2200 (double room), $4600 (including board). Varies for married students because of off-campus costs. Contact Director of Student Housing for both on- and off-campus housing information. Phone: (605)688-5148. Day-care facilities available.

Graduate School

Graduate study since 1891. Enrollment: full-time 280, part-time 796. Graduate faculty: full-time 286, part-time none. Degrees conferred: M.A., M.S., M.Ed., Ph.D.

ADMISSION REQUIREMENTS. Transcripts, two letters of recommendation required in support of School's application. GRE required for some departments. Online application available. TOEFL required of international students. Interview not required. Accepts transfer applicants. Graduates of unaccredited colleges not considered. Apply to Graduate Office at least one month prior to registration. Application fee $35. Phone: (605)688-4181; fax: (605)688-6167; E-mail: davisd@adm.sdstate.edu.

ADMISSION STANDARDS. Selective for most departments. Usual minimum average: 2.5 (with condition), 3.0 (unconditional) (A = 4).

FINANCIAL AID. Scholarships, fellowships, teaching assistantships, research assistantships, Federal W/S, loans. Approved for VA benefits. Apply to appropriate department chair for assistantships, scholarships; to Financial Aid Office for all other programs. Phone: (605)688-4695; fax: (605)688-5882. Use FAFSA (School code: 003471).

DEGREE REQUIREMENTS. For M.A.: 30 credit hours minimum, at least 22 in residence; thesis; final oral exam. For M.Ed.: 32 credit hours minimum, at least 22 in resident; final research/design report; final oral exam; or 35 hours minimum, at least 22 in residence; comprehensive written exam; final oral exam. For M.S.: 30 credit hours minimum, 5–7 credits thesis or 32 credits with research/design paper; 48 credits required for M.S. in Counseling and Human Resource Development. For Ph.D.: 90 credit program (may be reduced to 60 with prior master's degree), at least 50 in residence; preliminary exam; dissertation; final oral exam.

FIELDS OF STUDY.
Agricultural and Biosystems Engineering.
Agronomy.
Animal and Range Sciences.
Biological Sciences.
Chemistry and Biochemistry.
Civil and Environmental Engineering.
Communication Studies and Journalism.
Computer Science.
Counseling and Human Resource Development.
Dairy Science.
Economics.
Education.
Electrical Engineering.
English.
Geography.
Geospatial Science and Engineering.
Health, Physical Education and Recreation.
Human Development, Consumer and Family Sciences.
Human Nutrition and Food Science.

Industrial Management.
Mathematics and Statistics.
Mechanical Engineering.
Merchandising.
Nursing.
Pharmaceutical Science.
Physics.
Plant Science.
Sociology.
Veterinary Science.
Wildlife and Fisheries Sciences.

UNIVERSITY OF SOUTH DAKOTA
Vermillion, South Dakota 57069-2390
Web site: www.usd.edu

Founded 1882. Located 60 miles S of Sioux Falls. Coed. State control. Semester system. Special facilities: Business Research Center, Government Research Bureau, Historical Preservation Center, Institute of American Indian, Missouri River Institute, Oral History Center, South Dakota Geological Society, W. H. Over Museum. Library: 1,200,000 volumes, 2810 subscriptions. Total University enrollment: 8600.

Tuition: per credit resident $125, $251 Minnesota residents, nonresident $369. On-campus housing for 80 married students. Average annual housing cost: $2800 for married students, $4000 (including board) for single students. Contact Resident Services for both on- and off-campus housing information. Phone: (605) 677-5663.

Graduate School

Graduate study since 1889. Enrollment: full- and part-time 2200. University faculty: full- and part-time 249. Degrees conferred: M.A., M.B.A., M.F.A., M.M., M.N.S., M.P.A., M.S., Ed.S., Ed.D., Ph.D., M.D.-Ph.D

ADMISSION REQUIREMENTS. Two official transcripts, GRE Subject Tests/GMAT, three letters of recommendation required in support of School's application. Special applications for Physical Therapy, Physician Assistants, School of Education. Interview not required. TOEFL, financial statement required for international applicants. Accepts transfer applicants. Graduates of unaccredited institutions not considered. Apply to Dean of Graduate School by July 15. Application fee $35. Phone: (605) 677-6287.

ADMISSION STANDARDS. Selective for most departments. Usual minimum average: 3.0 (A = 4).

FINANCIAL AID. Scholarships, research assistantships, teaching assistantships, internships, Federal W/S, loans. Approved for VA benefits. Apply by March 15 to appropriate department for assistantships; to Financial Aid Office for all other programs. Phone: (605)677-5446. Use FAFSA. About 25% of students receive aid other than loans from School, 40% from all sources. Aid available for part-time students.

DEGREE REQUIREMENTS. For M.A., M.M.: 30–32 semester hours minimum, at least 20 in residence; thesis/nonthesis option; final oral/written exam. For M.N.S.: 30 hours minimum, at least 20 in residence; thesis; final oral/written exam. For M.B.A., M.P.A.: one calendar year in residence; otherwise same as for M.A. For Ed.S.: 64 semester hours minimum; preliminary exam; research project; comprehensive exam; final oral exam. For Ed.D.: 90 hours minimum beyond the bachelor's degree, at least 30 in residence; preliminary written exam; comprehensive exam; dissertation; final oral exam. For Ph.D.: 84 hours minimum beyond the bachelor's degree, at least two years in residence; preliminary exam; dissertation; final oral exam.

FIELDS OF STUDY.

COLLEGE OF ARTS AND SCIENCES:
Audiology. Au.D.
Biological Sciences. M.A., M.N.S., M.S., Ph.D.
Chemistry. M.A., M.N.S.
Communication Disorders. Includes speech-language pathology. M.A.
Communication Studies. Includes organizational communication, political communication. M.A.
Computational Science and Statistics. Ph.D.
Computer Science. M.S.
English. Includes literature, creative writing, TESOL. M.A., Ph.D.
History. M.A.
Literary Studies. Includes critical, creative. Ph.D.
Mathematics. M.A., M.S.
Political Science. Includes American politics & public policy, international relations, public law. M.A., Ph.D.
Psychology. Includes clinical, clinical/disaster, human factors. Ph.D. M.A. available if pursuing Ph.D.
Public Administration. Includes criminal justice, health services administration, information systems, leadership studies, nonprofit administration. state & local government administration, M.P.A.

SCHOOL OF BUSINESS:
Business Administration. Includes general, health services administration. M.B.A.
Professional Accountancy. M.P.A.

SCHOOL OF EDUCATION:
Counseling and Psychology in Education. Includes school counseling community agency, college counseling, substance counseling (M.A.); mental health counseling, marriage and family counseling (Ed.S.); counselor education and supervision, counseling practice (Ph.D.).
Educational Administration. Includes elementary School principal, secondary school principal, school district superintendent, director of curriculum, adult and higher education (M.A., Ed.S., Ed.D.); director of special education (Ed.S., Ed.D.).
Curriculum and Instruction. Ed.S., Ed.D.
Elementary Education. Includes curriculum director, early childhood, reading recovery. M.A.
Health, Physical Education and Recreation. Includes athletic administration, curriculum, exercise science, general and therapeutic recreation, school and community health. M.A.
Secondary Education. Includes curriculum, curriculum director. M.A.
Special Education. Includes behavior disorders, early childhood special education, multi-categorical mild/moderate, learning disabilities, mental disabilities, gifted education. M.A.
Technology for Education and Training. Includes K–12 education, training and development. M.S.

COLLEGE OF FINE ARTS:
Art. Includes painting, printmaking, sculpture, studio art. M.F.A.
Music. Includes history of musical instrument, music education, music history, music performance. M.M.
Theatre. Includes design/production, directing. M.A., M.F.A.

GRADUATE SCHOOL:
Administrative Studies. Includes health services administration, human resources, interdisciplinary, organizational leadership, criminal justice (Rapid City, SD only), long term care administration (online only). M.S.
Biomedical Engineering. M.S., Ph.D.
Interdisciplinary. M.A.
Natural Sciences. Includes biology, chemistry, physics. M.N.S.

School of Law (57069-2390)

Web site: www.usd.edu/law

Established 1901. Located on main campus. ABA approved since 1923. AALS member. Semester system. Full-time, day study only. Law library: 205,506 volumes, 1874 subscriptions; has LEXIS, NEXIS, WESTLAW, DIALOG, SDLN; has more than 200 network connections.

Annual tuition: resident $8326, nonresident $16,609. On-campus housing available for single students in the Graduate and Professional Dormitory and for married students in University-owned apartments. Annual on-campus living expense: $14,000. Contact Office of Residential Life for both on- and off-campus housing information. Phone: (605)677-5663. Law students tend to live off-campus. Off-campus housing and personal expenses: approximately $12,000.

Enrollment: first-year class 90; total full-time 231 (men 58%, women 42%, minorities 4%). Faculty: full-time 11, part-time 1. Student to faculty ratio 12.7 to 1. Degrees conferred: J.D., J.D.-M.Acc., J.D.-M.B.A., J.D.-M.Econ., J.D.-M.P.A., J.D.-M.A. (Educational Administration, English, History, Political Science, Psychology).

ADMISSION REQUIREMENTS. LSDAS Law School report, bachelor's degree, transcripts, personal statement, two letters of recommendation, LSAT, two photos, personal statement required in support of application. Accepts transfer applicants. Preference given to state residents. Graduates of unaccredited institutions not considered. Apply by March 1 to the Admissions Office. Application fee $35. Phone: (605)677-5443.

ADMISSION STANDARDS. Selective. Accepts approximately 35% of all students. Number of applicants 516; number of acceptance 180; number enrolled 90; LSAT (75% of students have a score at or above 150); GPA (75% of students have a GPA at or above 2.95). *U.S. News & World Report* ranking is in the fourth tier of all U.S. law schools.

FINANCIAL AID. Scholarships, assistantships, Federal W/S, loans. Apply to Financial Aid Office by May 1. Phone: (605)677-5446. Use FAFSA (School code: 003474). About 29% of students receive aid other than loans from school.

DEGREE REQUIREMENTS. For J.D.: 90 semester hour program, at least two years residence.

Sanford School of Medicine (57069-2390)

Web site: www.usd.edu/med/md

Established in 1907 as a 2-year basic sciences institution. Expanded to a degree-granting medical school was approved by legislature in 1974. Special facilities: Cardiovascular Research Institute, Center for Disabilities, Center for Ethics and Caring, Cystic Fibrosis Center.

Annual tuition: resident $17,528, nonresident $36,733. On-campus housing available. Total average figure for all other expenses: $19,430.

Enrollment: first-year class 50, total 210 (men 54%, women 46%, minorities 4%, state residents 95%). Faculty: full-time 246, part-time 696. Degrees conferred: M.D., M.D.-Ph.D.

ADMISSION REQUIREMENTS. AMCAS report, transcripts, letters of recommendation, MCAT, supplemental application, interview required in support of application. Applicants must have completed at least three years of college study. Does not have EDP. Preference given to South Dakota residents. Accepts transfer applicants on a space-available basis. Apply after June 1, before November 15. Application fee $35, fee after screening $15. Phone: (605)677-6886; fax: (605)677-5109.

ADMISSION STANDARDS. Competitive. Accepts about 10% of all applicants. Number of applications 717 (573 out-of-state); number interviewed 158 (26 out-of-state); number of acceptance 66 (4 out-of-state); number enrolled 50 (2 out-of-state). Mean Composite MCAT 9.5; mean UGPA 3.65 (A = 4).

FINANCIAL AID. Tuition waivers, scholarships, fellowships. Apply after Fall classes begin to Office of Student Affairs. Phone: (605)677-5112. Use FAFSA (School code: 003474). About 96% of students receive some aid from School.

DEGREE REQUIREMENTS. For M.D.: satisfactory completion of four-year program and the passing of Step 1 and Step 2 of the USMLE prior to graduation. For Ph.D. see Graduate School listing above.

FIELDS OF GRADUATE STUDY.
Anatomy and Structural Biology.
Biochemistry.
Cellular Biology.
Immunology.
Microbiology.
Molecular Biology.
Neuroscience.
Pharmacology.
Physiology.

UNIVERSITY OF SOUTH FLORIDA

Tampa, Florida 33620-9951
Web site: www.usf.edu

Founded 1956. CGS member. Coed. State control. Semester system. Special facilities: H. Lee Moffitt Cancer Center and Research Institute, Florida Mental Health Institute, Florida Institute of Oceanography, Gerontology Center, Center for Nearshore Marine Science, Center for Urban Transportation Research, Center of Microelectronics Research, Center for Engineering Development and Research, Institute Biomolecular Science, Institute on Black Life. The University's NIH ranking is 109th among all U.S. institutions with 83 awards/grants valued at $46,591,809. According to The Center at University of Florida, the University is ranked 71st in receipt of Federal Research funds with $106,102,000 and it ranks 64th for total University research expenditures with $213,249,000. In 2004, the University awarded 179 doctorates which ranked it 81st among all U.S. institutions eligible to award that degree. The Library: approximately 2,000,000 volumes, 8500 subscriptions. Total University enrollment: 42,600.

Tuition: per semester hour resident $278, nonresident $922. On-campus housing available for single students only. Average academic year housing costs: $8500–$10,500. Contact Director of University Housing for both on- and off-campus housing information. Phone: (813)974-2764.

Graduate Studies

Enrollment: full-time 3312, part-time 4113. Faculty: full- and part-time 1400. Degrees conferred: M.A., M.Acc., M.Arch., M.B.A., M.Ed., Ed.S., Ed.D., M.C.E., M.E., M.F.A., M.M., M.P.A., M.P.H., M.S.P.H., M.S.C.E., M.S.C.S., M.S.E., M.S.E.E., M.S.E.M., M.S.E.S., M.S.I.E., M.S.M.E., M.S.W., M.S., Ph.D.

ADMISSION REQUIREMENTS. Transcripts, GRE Subject Tests (GMAT for business only). Online application available. TOEFL (minimum score 550) and TSE required for international applicants. Interview required by some departments. Three letters of recommendation required by Natural Science Division. Accepts transfer applicants. Graduates of unaccredited institutions not considered. Apply by February 1. Some programs have earlier deadlines. Rolling admission process. Application fee $35. Phone: (813) 974-8800; e-mail: admissions@grad.usf.edu.

ADMISSION STANDARDS. Selective for most departments. Usual minimum average: 2.75 (A = 4).

FINANCIAL AID. Fellowships, assistantships for teaching/research, Federal W/S, loans. Approved for VA benefits. Apply by February 1 to department chair for fellowships, assistantships; to Director of Financial Aid for all other programs. Phone: (813)974-4700. Use FAFSA.

DEGREE REQUIREMENTS. For master's: 30–36 semester hours minimum, at least 18 credits in residence; reading knowledge of one foreign language for some majors; thesis/nonthesis option; final oral/written exam. For Ed.S.: 30 semester hours beyond the master's. For Ed.D.: essentially the same as for the Ph.D., except no foreign language requirement. For Ph.D.: minimum of 90 credits beyond bachelor's degree; preliminary exam; reading knowledge of two foreign languages or equivalent; dissertation; final oral/written exam.

FIELDS OF STUDY.

SCHOOL OF ARCHITECTURE AND COMMUNITY DESIGN:
Architecture. Joint program with Florida Agricultural and Mechanical University. M.Arch.

COLLEGE OF ARTS AND SCIENCES:
Africana Studies.
Aging Studies.
American History.
American Studies.
Analytical Chemistry.
Ancient History.
Applied Anthropology.
Aqueous Geochemistry.
Atmospheric Physics.
Atomic and Molecular Physics.
Audiology.
Aural Rehabilitation.
Bio-Cultural Medical Anthropology.
Biochemistry.
Biogeochemistry.
Biology.
Cell and Molecular Biology.
Chemistry.
Classic: Latin/Greek.
Clinical Psychology.
Coastal Geology.
Coastal Marine Ecology Biology.
Cognitive and Neural Sciences.
Communication.
Communication Sciences and Disorders.
Computational Chemistry.
Conservation Biology.
Creative Writing.
Criminal Justice Administration.
Criminology.
Cultural Resource Management.
Economic, Social and Planning Issues in the Urban Environment.
English.
Environmental Chemistry.
Environmental Geophysics.
Environmental Science and Policy.
European History.
Florida Studies.
Geographic Information Systems and Spatial Analysis.
Geography.
Geography and Environmental Science and Policy.
Geology.
Geomorphology.
Gerontology.

Hearing Sciences and Audiology.
History.
Humanities.
Hydrogeology.
Industrial-Organizational Psychology.
Inorganic Chemistry.
Journalism Studies.
Laser Physics.
Latin American History.
Liberal Studies.
Library and Information Science.
Linguistics. Includes ESL.
Literature.
Marriage and Family Therapy.
Mass Communication.
Materials Physics.
Mathematics. Includes pure & applied.
Media Studies.
Medical Physics.
Medieval History.
Microbiology.
Multimedia Journalism.
Natural/Technological Hazards and Environmental Justice.
Neurocommunicative Sciences.
Optical Physics.
Organic Chemistry.
Paleoclimatology.
Petrology.
Philosophy.
Physical Chemistry.
Physics. Includes applied.
Political Science.
Polymer Chemistry.
Psychology.
Public Administration.
Rehabilitation and Mental Health Counseling.
Religious Studies.
Rhetoric and Composition.
Semiconductor Physics.
Social and Political Thought.
Social Work.
Sociology.
Solid State Physics.
Spanish.
Speech-Language Pathology.
Statistics.
Strategic Communication Management.
Tectonophysics.
Urban and Regional Planning.
Women's Studies.

COLLEGE OF BUSINESS:
Accountancy. M.Acc.
Business Administration. Includes Saturday M.B.A.
Business Economics.
Executive M.B.A.
Executive M.B.A. for Physicians.
Finance.
Leadership and Organizational Effectiveness. M.S.
Management.
Management Information Systems.
Marketing. M.S.M.

COLLEGE OF EDUCATION:
Administration of Special Education.
Adult Education.
Business and Office Education.
Career and Technical Education.
Career and Workforce Education.
College Leadership.

College Student Affairs.
Counselor Education.
Curriculum and Instruction.
Distributive and Marketing Education.
Early Childhood Education.
Educational Leadership.
Educational Program Development.
Elementary Education.
English Education.
Exercise Science.
Foreign Language Education.
Guidance and Counselor Education.
Higher Education Administration.
Higher Education College Teaching.
Higher Education Community College Teaching.
Human Resource Development.
Industrial Arts—Technology Education.
Instructional Technology.
Interdisciplinary Education.
Language Arts.
Mathematics Education.
Measurement and Evaluation.
Middle Grades Education. Includes English, mathematics, science, social studies.
Music Education.
Physical Education.
Reading and Language Arts Education.
Reading Education.
School Psychology.
Science and Mathematics.
Science Education. Includes biology, chemistry, physics.
Secondary Education.
Social Science Education.
Special Education. Includes behavior disorders, gifted, learning disabilities, mental retardation, motor disabilities, varying exceptionalities.
Student Affairs Administration.
Teaching and Learning in Content Areas.
Theatre Education.
Vocational Education.

COLLEGE OF ENGINEERING:
Biomedical and Biotechnology.
Biomedical Engineering.
Chemical Engineering.
Circuits, Controls and Systems.
Civil Engineering.
Communications and Signal Processing.
Computer Engineering.
Computer Science.
Computer Science and Engineering.
Digital Architecture and Design.
Electric Power Systems.
Electrical Engineering.
Engineering.
Engineering Management.
Engineering Science.
Environmental Engineering.
Geotechnical Engineering.
Industrial Engineering.
Manufacturing Engineering.
Materials
Mechanical Engineering.
Microelectronics.
Physics.
Quantitative Analysis.
Structures.
Transportation.
Water Resources.
Wireless Circuits and Systems.

COLLEGE OF MARINE SCIENCE:
Biological Oceanography.
Chemical Oceanography.
Geological Oceanography.
Interdisciplinary.
Marine Science.
Physical Oceanography.

COLLEGE OF NURSING:
Nursing. Includes adult health, child health, critical care, family health, gerontological, health systems informatics, nurse anesthesia, nursing education, occupational health, oncology, psychiatric-mental health.

COLLEGE OF PUBLIC HEALTH:
Behavior Health.
Bioinformatics.
Biostatistics.
Community and Family Health.
Environmental and Occupational Health.
Environmental Health.
Epidemiology.
Global Communicable Diseases.
Health Administration.
Health-Care Organizations and Management.
Health Policies and Programs.
Health Policy and Management.
Industrial Hygiene.
International Health Management.
Maternal and Child Health/Clinical Social Work.
Occupational Health.
Public Health.
Public Health Administration.
Public Health Education.
Safety Management.
Social and Behavioral Science.
Toxicology and Risk Assessment.
Tropical/Communicable Diseases.

COLLEGE OF VISUAL AND PERFORMING ARTS:
Art.
Art History.
Chamber Music.
Composition.
Conducting.
Dramatic Writing.
Electro-Acoustic Music.
Jazz Composition.
Jazz Performance.
Music.
Music Education.
Performance.
Piano Pedagogy.
Theory.

Sanford School of Medicine (57069-2390)
Web site: www.usf.edu/med/md

Established 1965, first class enter 1971. Special facilities: Archie A. & Mary-Louise Silver Child Development Center; Cardiac Hormone Center; Center for Aging & Brain Repair; Center for Hospice, Palliative Care & End of Life Studies; Diabetes Center; Florida Infectious Disease Center; Joy McCann Culverhouse Center for Swallowing Disorders; Pediatrics Epidemiology Center; Suncoast Alzheimer's & Gerontology Center; USF Parkinson's Disease and Movement Disorders Center; NPF Center of Excellence. NIH ranking is 109 among all U.S. institutions with 83 awards/grants worth $46,591,809.

Annual tuition: resident $18,431, nonresident $50,515. On-campus housing available. Total average figure for all other expenses: $15,430.

Enrollment: first-year class 120, total 483 (men 47%, women 53%, minorities 38%, state residents 99%). Faculty: full-time 504, part-time 93. Degrees conferred: M.D., M.D.-M.B.A., M.D.-M.P.H., M.D.-Ph.D.

ADMISSION REQUIREMENTS. For M.D.: transcripts, MCAT, recommendations required in support of application. Has EDP (Florida residents only); apply between June 1 and August 1. Preference given to Florida residents. Graduates of unaccredited colleges not considered. Apply to Assistant Dean for Admissions after October 1, before December 1. For Graduate Program: transcripts, GRE required in support of application. TOEFL required of foreign students. Accepts transfer applicants. Apply before August 15 to Graduate Office. Application fee $20. Phone: (813) 974-2229; fax: (813)974-4990.

ADMISSION STANDARDS. Competitive. Accepts about 10% of all applicants. Number of applications 1822 (531 out-of-state); number interviewed 336 (12 out-of-state); number of acceptance 202 (6 out-of-state); number enrolled 120 (5 out-of-state). Mean Composite MCAT 9.9; mean UGPA 3.70 (A = 4.).

FINANCIAL AID. For M.D.: limited scholarships, loans. Apply to Office of Financial Aid after acceptance. Use FAFSA (College code: E00568). For Graduate Program: fellowships, assistantships. Apply to Financial Aid Office by March 1. Phone: (813) 974-2068. Approximately 80% of students receive some form of assistance.

DEGREE REQUIREMENTS. For M.D.: satisfactory completion of three to four-year program. For Ph.D., M.P.H.: see Graduate School listings above.

FIELDS OF GRADUATE STUDY.
Allergy, Immunology and Infectious Diseases.
Biomedical Engineering.
Cancer Biology.
Molecular Medicine.
Molecular Pharmacology and Physiology.
Nanomedicine.
Neuromusculoskeletal Disorders.
Neuroscience.
Pathology and Cell Biology.
Pharmacogenomics.
Regenerative Medicine.
Sports Medicine.
Women's Health.

SOUTH TEXAS COLLEGE OF LAW

1303 San Jacinto
Houston, Texas 77002-7000
Web site: www.stcl.edu

Established 1923. ABA approved since 1959. AALS member. Private control. Semester system. Full-time, part-time study. Special facilities: Center for Conflict Resolution, Corporate Compliance Center, Center for Legal Responsibility, Legal Institute for Medical Studies. Special programs: exchange programs in the Netherlands or Denmark: summer study in Malta, Turkey, Ireland, England, Czech Republic and Mexico. Law Library: 504,656 volumes, 4325 subscriptions; has LEXIS, NEXIS, WESTLAW, DIALOG, EPIC; has more than 1000 network connections.

Annual tuition: full-time $22,440, part-time $15,160. No on-campus housing available. Contact Admission Officer for off-campus information. Off-campus and personal expenses: $15,422.

Enrollment: first-year class full-time 344, part-time 109; total full- and part-time 1237 (men 56%, women 44%, minorities 23%).

Faculty: full-time 52, part-time 39. Student to faculty ratio is 19.7 to 1. Degrees conferred: J.D.

ADMISSION REQUIREMENTS. LSDAS Law School report, bachelor's degree, transcripts, LSAT, personal statement, résumé, two letters of recommendation required in support of application. Graduates of unaccredited colleges not considered. Accepts transfer applicants. Transfers admitted Fall and Spring. Apply to Director of Admission by February 15 (Fall), October 1 (Spring), January 15 (Summer). Application fee $50. Phone: (713)646-1810.

ADMISSION STANDARDS. Selective. Accepts approximately 37% of full-time, 36% of part-time students. Number of full-time applicants 2524, part-time 428; number of full-time acceptance 932, part-time 154; number of full-time enrolled 344, part-time 109; LSAT (75% of full-time students have a score at or above 151, part-time 150); GPA (75% of full-time students have a GPA at or above 2.98, part-time 2.84). *U.S. News & World Report* ranking is in the third tier of all U.S. law schools.

FINANCIAL AID. Scholarships, tuition equalization, grants, Federal W/S, loans. Apply to Financial Aid Office before May 1 (Fall), October 1 (Spring). Phone: (713)646-1820. Use FAFSA (College code: G04977). About 40% of full-time and 29% of part-time students receive aid other than loans from College and outside sources.

DEGREE REQUIREMENTS. For J.D.: 90 semester hours, at least 24 semester hours and last 3 semesters in residence.

SOUTHEAST MISSOURI STATE UNIVERSITY

Cape Girardeau, Missouri 63701-4799
Web site: www.semo.edu

Founded 1873. Located 125 miles S of St. Louis. CGS member. Coed. State control. Semester system. Library: 429,000 volumes, 6200 subscriptions.

Fees: per semester, resident $3063, nonresident $5626; per credit part-time resident $204, nonresident $375. On-campus housing for married and single students. Average academic year housing costs: single students $6335 (including board); married students $5000. Contact Residence Life Office for on- and off-campus housing information. Phone: (573)651-2274.

School of Graduate Studies and Research

Graduate study since 1965. Enrollment: full-time 205, part-time 1119. Faculty: full-time 217. Degrees conferred: M.A., M.B.A., M.M.E., M.N.S., M.S.A., M.S.C.J., M.S.I.S., M.S.N., Ed.S.

ADMISSION REQUIREMENTS. Transcripts required in support of application. GRE required for some programs. TOEFL required for international applicants. Accepts transfer applicants. Graduates of unaccredited institutions not considered. Apply to Dean of Graduate Study by August 1 (Fall), November 15 (Spring), February 1 (Summer). Rolling admissions process. Application fee $20, $100 for international applicants. Phone: (573)651-2192; fax: (573)651-2001.

ADMISSION STANDARDS. Selective. Usual minimum average: 2.5 (A = 4), 3.0 GPA for some programs.

FINANCIAL AID. Graduate scholarships, teaching assistantships, research assistantships, internships, Federal W/S, loans. Approved for VA benefits. Apply with admission application to appropriate department head for assistantships; to Financial Aid Office for all other programs. Phone: (573)651-2253. Use FAFSA (School code: 002501). About 15% of students receive aid other than loans from University and outside sources. No aid other than loans for part-time students.

DEGREE REQUIREMENTS. For master's: 32 semester hours minimum, at least 24 in residence; thesis or final document. For Ed.S.: one year beyond the master's.

FIELDS OF STUDY.
Accounting. M.B.A.
Athletic Administration. M.S.A.
Biology. M.N.S.
Chemistry. M.N.S.
Communication Disorders. M.A.
Community Counseling. M.A.
Community Wellness and Leisure Services. M.P.A.
Counseling Education. Ed.S.
Criminal Justice. M.S.C.J.
Educational Administration. Ed.S.
Elementary Education. M.A.
English. M.A.
Environmental Management. M.B.A.
Exceptional Child Education. M.A.
Financial Management. M.B.A.
General Management. M.B.A.
Geosciences. M.N.S.
Health Fitness Administration. M.S.A.
Higher Education Administration. M.A.
History. Includes historic preservation, research, teaching. M.A.
Human Environmental Studies Education. M.A.
Industrial Management. M.B.A.
International Business. M.B.A.
Mathematics. M.N.S.
Music Education. M.M.Ed.
Nursing. M.S.N.
Nutrition and Exercise Science. M.S.N.E.S.
Public Administration. M.P.A.
School Administration. M.A.
School Counseling. Includes elementary school counseling, secondary school counseling. M.A.
Science Education. M.N.S.
Secondary Education. Includes art, business, educational studies, educational technology, middle studies, social studies. M.A.
Teaching English to Speakers of Other Languages. M.A.

SOUTHEASTERN LOUISIANA UNIVERSITY

Hammond, Louisiana 70402-0752
Web site: www.selu.edu

Founded 1925. Located 60 miles N of New Orleans. Coed. State control. Semester system. Special facilities: Center for Regional Studies, Biological Turtle Cove Research Station, Agricultural and Educational Research Station, JFK Assassination Resources Center, Institute for Human Development. Library: 554,000 volumes, 2100 subscriptions. Total University enrollment: 15,500.

Annual tuition: full-time resident $3131, nonresident $7127; per semester, part-time resident $174, nonresident $396, plus nonresident fee. On-campus housing for 60 married students, unlimited for single students. Average academic year housing costs: $5180 (including board) for single students; $3500–$4800 for married students. Contact Director of Housing for both on- and off-campus housing information. Phone: (985)549-2118.

Graduate School

Graduate study since 1960. Enrollment: full-time 395, part-time 817. Graduate faculty: full-time 201, part-time 5. Degrees conferred: M.A., M.M., M.Ed., M.S.N., M.B.A., Ed.S.

ADMISSION REQUIREMENTS. Official transcripts, GRE required in support of application. Copy of teaching certificate required for Education majors. GMAT required for M.B.A. applicants. GRE Subject required by some programs. TOEFL required for international applicants. Interview not required. Accepts transfer applicants. Graduates of unaccredited institutions not considered. Apply to Office of Graduate Admissions at least 30 days prior to registration. Rolling admissions process. Application fee $20, $30 for international applicants. Phone: (985)549-2066; fax: (985)549-5632.

ADMISSION STANDARDS. Relatively open. Usual minimum average: 2.5, 3.0 for candidacy (A = 4).

FINANCIAL AID. Fellowships, research assistantships, teaching assistantships, internships, Federal W/S, loans. Apply by May 1 to appropriate department head for fellowships, assistantships; to Financial Aid Office for all other programs. Phone: (985)549-2244. Use FAFSA. About 30% of students receive aid from University and outside sources.

DEGREE REQUIREMENTS. For M.Ed.: 30 semester hours minimum, except Secondary Guidance and Counseling 33 hours, at least 21 in residence; final written/oral exams. For Ed.S.: 30 semester hours minimum, at least 21 in residence; thesis or research project. For M.S.: 30 semester hours minimum; thesis. For M.B.A.: one-year program for students with degree in business, two-year for non-degree holders.

FIELDS OF STUDY.

COLLEGE OF ARTS, HUMANITIES AND SOCIAL SCIENCES:
Applied Sociology. M.A.
Biology. M.S.
English. M.A.
History. M.A.
Integrated Science and Technology. M.S.
Music. M.M.
Organizational Communication. M.A.
Psychology. M.A.

COLLEGE OF BUSINESS AND TECHNOLOGY:
Business Administration. M.B.A.
Integrated Science and Technology. M.S.

COLLEGE OF EDUCATION AND HUMAN DEVELOPMENT:
Counselor Education. M.Ed.
Curriculum and Instruction. M.Ed.
Educational Leadership. M.Ed., Ph.D.
Special Education. M.Ed.
Teaching in Elementary Education. M.A.

COLLEGE OF NURSING AND HEALTH SCIENCES:
Communication Sciences and Disorders. M.S.
Health and Kinesiology. M.A.
Nursing. M.S.N.

COLLEGE OF SCIENCE AND TECHNOLOGY:
Biology. M.S.
Integrated Science and Technology. M.S.

SOUTHEASTERN OKLAHOMA STATE UNIVERSITY

Durant, Oklahoma 74701-0609
Web site: www.sosu.edu

Established 1909. Located 90 miles N of Dallas, Texas. Coed. State control. Semester system. Library: 192,000 volumes, 1300 subscriptions. Total University enrollment: 4100.

Tuition: per credit resident $138, nonresident $301. On-campus housing for 36 married students, 125 single men, 100 single women. Average academic year housing costs: single students $5400 (including board), married students $7700. Contact Housing Director for both on- and off-campus housing information. Phone: (580)745-2948.

Graduate School

Graduate study since 1954. Enrollment: full-time 121, part-time 228. Faculty teaching graduate students: full-time 97, part-time 4. Degrees conferred: M.A.S., M.B.S., M.Ed., M.T.

ADMISSION REQUIREMENTS. Transcripts, GRE/GMAT, interview required in support of School's application. TOEFL required for international applicants. Accepts transfer applicants. Graduates of unaccredited colleges not considered. Apply to Dean of Graduate School at least two months prior to date of registration. Application fee: $20, $65 for international applicants. Phone: (580)745-2200; fax: (580)745-7474.

ADMISSION STANDARDS. Selective. Usual minimum average: 2.75 (A = 4).

FINANCIAL AID. Scholarships, teaching assistantships, tuition waivers, Federal W/S, loans. Apply by June 15 to the Director of Financial Aid. Phone: (580)745-2186; fax: (580)745-7469. Use FAFSA and institutional FAF. Aid available for part-time students.

DEGREE REQUIREMENTS. For master's: 33 semester hours minimum, at least 24 in semester hours in residence; thesis/nonthesis option.

FIELDS OF STUDY.
Behavioral Studies. Includes counseling.
Business Administration.
Education. Includes secondary education, elementary education, school counseling, educational administration, educational technology.
Occupational Safety and Health.
Technology. Includes electronics, design, manufacturing processes, computer science, safety, sciences.

SOUTHERN CALIFORNIA COLLEGE OF OPTOMETRY

Fullerton, California 92631-1615
Web site: www.scco.edu

Founded 1904. Coed. Private control. Quarter system. Library: 17,100 volumes, 300 subscriptions.

Annual tuition: full-time $29,625. No on-campus housing available.

Graduate Study

Enrollment: full-time 379. Faculty: full-time 43, part-time 37. Degree conferred: O.D.

ADMISSION REQUIREMENTS. Transcripts, bachelor's degree, OAT, three letters of recommendation, interview required in support of application. Accepts transfer applicants. Apply to Admissions Office by March 15. Admits Fall only. Rolling admissions process. Application fee $50. Phone: (714)449-7445; fax: (714)992-7878.

ADMISSION STANDARDS. Selective. Usual minimum average: 2.75 (A = 4).

FINANCIAL AID. Scholarships, internships, Federal W/S, loans. Approved for VA benefits. Apply by June 1 to Financial Aid Office. Phone: (714)449-7447. Use FAFSA. About 89% of students receive aid other than loans from College.

DEGREE REQUIREMENTS. For O.D.: 4 years and 241 quarter units.

UNIVERSITY OF SOUTHERN CALIFORNIA

Los Angeles, California 90089-0913
Web site: www.usc.edu

Founded 1880. CGS and AAU member. Coed. Private control. Semester system. Special facilities: Annenberg Center for Communication, U.S.C.-Atelier Art Gallery, Arnold Schoenberg Institute, East Asian Studies Center, Center for Feminist Research, Fisher Gallery, Signal and Image Processing Institute, Information Science Institute, Hydrocarbon Research Institute, Center for International Business Education and Research, Center for Laser Studies, Alzheimer's Disease Research Center, Gerontology Research Institute, Center for the Management of Engineering Research and Technology, Center for Multiethnic and Transnational Studies, Information Sciences Institute, Pacific Center for Health Policy and Ethics, Social Science Research Institute, Robotics and Intelligent Systems Institute, Center for Future Research, Center for Software Engineering, Center for Urban Affairs, Von Kleinsmid Center for International and Public Affairs, Wrigley Institute for Environmental Studies. The University's NIH ranking is 31st among all U.S. institutions with 334 awards/grants valued at $181,838,243. According to The Center at University of Florida, the University is ranked 17th in receipt of Federal Research funds with $310,195,000 and it ranks 24th for total University research expenditures with $410,099,000. The University's endowment assets rank it 20th, with a value of $2,399,960,000. In 2004, the University awarded 573 doctorates which ranked it 11th among all U.S. institutions eligible to award that degree. Forty of the University's faculty members have been elected to National Honor Academies and this ranks it 24th among all U.S. institutions. The Library: approximately 3,000,000 volumes, 20,000 subscriptions. Total University enrollment: 33,000.

Tuition: per unit $1059. On-campus housing available. Average monthly housing costs: $450–$535 for a one-bedroom/two-person unit, $350–$500 for a two-bedroom/four-person unit, $680–$900 per month for family units. Contact Housing Office for detailed information. Phone: (800)872-4632. Day-care facilities available.

Graduate School

Graduate study since 1910. Enrollment: full-time 7088, part-time 3455. Graduate faculty: 1614. Degrees conferred: M.A., M.A.E.D.P., M.F.A., M.P.T., M.P.P., M.P.A.S., M.S., M.S.N., M.S.S., M.S.S.M., M.U.D., Ph.D.

ADMISSION REQUIREMENTS. Official transcripts, an earned bachelor's degree, GRE required in support of School's application. Online application available. GRE Subject Test required by some departments. TOEFL encouraged for international applicants. Accepts transfer applicants. Graduates of unaccredited institutions not considered. Apply to University Office of Admissions, preferably early in the preceding semester. Application fee $65, $75 for international applicants. Phone: (213)740-1111; fax: (213) 740-8826.

ADMISSION STANDARDS. Competitive for most departments, selective or very competitive for the others. Usual minimum average: 3.0 (A = 4).

FINANCIAL AID. Fellowships, research assistantships, teaching assistantships, Federal W/S, loans. Approved for VA benefits. Apply by February 1 to Dean of Graduate School for scholarships and fellowships, to appropriate department chair for assistantships; to Financial Aid Office for all other programs. Phone: (213)740-1111. Use FAFSA. Most full-time students receive some financial support. About 50% of all students receive aid other than loans from University and outside sources. Aid sometimes available for part-time students.

DEGREE REQUIREMENTS. For master's: 24 units minimum, at least 20 in residence; thesis/nonthesis; final written/oral exam; some departments require language, some permit comprehensive exam in lieu of thesis. For Ph.D.: 60 units minimum beyond the bachelor's, at least three years in residence; preliminary exam; reading knowledge of one foreign language for most programs; dissertation; final oral exam.

FIELDS OF STUDY.
American Studies and Ethnicity.
Anthropology.
Applied Mathematics.
Art History.
Biology.
Chemical Chemistry.
Chemistry.
Classics.
Comparative Literature.
Computational Biology and Bioinformatics.
Computational Molecular Biology.
East Asian Studies.
East Asian Languages and Cultures.
East Asian Linguistics.
Economics Development Programming.
Economics.
English.
Environmental Studies.
Environmental Risk Analysis.
French.
Geographic Information Science and Technology.
Geological Sciences.
German.
Hispanic Linguistics.
History.
Integrative and Evolutional Biology.
International Relations.
Kinesiology.
Liberal Studies.
Linguistics.
Literature and Creative Writing.
Marine and Environmental Biology.
Mathematical Finance.
Mathematics.
Molecular and Computational Biology.
Molecular Biology.
Neurosciences.
Ocean Sciences.
Philosophy.
Physics.
Physics for Business Applications.

Political Economy and Public Policy.
Politic and International Relations.
Professional Writing.
Psychology.
Public Diplomacy.
Religion and Social Ethics.
Slavic Language and Literature.
Slavic Linguistics.
Sociology.
Spanish.
Statistics.

School of Architecture

Established 1919. School's library: 60,000 volumes, 200,000 slides.

Tuition: per credit $1185. Enrollment: full-time 41. School faculty: full-time 12, part-time 1. Degrees conferred: M.Arch., M.B.S., M.L.A.

ADMISSION REQUIREMENTS. Transcripts, GRE, design portfolio, three letters of reference, statement of intent, résumé required in support of application. TOEFL required for foreign applicants. Graduates of unaccredited colleges not considered. Applicants with nonarchitecture degrees not considered for M.Arch. program. Apply to University Office of Admissions by January 15. Application fee $85. Phone: (213)740-1879.

ADMISSION STANDARDS. Competitive. Usual minimum average: 3.0 (A = 4).

FINANCIAL AID. Scholarships, fellowships, teaching assistantships, Federal W/S, loans. Apply by May 1 to Financial Aid Office. Phone: (213)740-1111. Use FAFSA (School code: 001328) and University's FAF.

DEGREE REQUIREMENTS. For master's: one to three years minimum, at least one to two in residence; thesis.

FIELDS OF STUDY.
Architecture.
Building Science.
Historic Preservation.
Landscape Architecture.

Marshall School of Business
Web site: www.marshall.usc.edu

Established 1951, name changed in 1997. Accredited programs: M.B.A., Accounting; recognized Ph.D. Semester (11-week terms) system. Special facilities: Center for Accounting Research, Center for Effective Organization, SEC and Financial Reporting Institute, Center for Service Excellence, Center for Telecommunications Management, Center for International Business Education and Research, Leadership Institute. Special programs: foreign exchange programs in Argentina, Australia, Austria, Brazil, Chile, China (PRC), Costa Rica, Denmark, France, Germany, Hong Kong, Indonesia, Japan, Korea, Mexico, Philippines, Singapore, Spain, Switzerland, Taiwan. Library: 100,000 volumes, 1000 subscriptions.

Tuition: per credit M.B.A. $1217, M.Acc., M.B.T. $1173, M.M.M. full-time $39,750. Enrollment: total full-time 1284, part-time 506; full-time Ph.D. 60-70. Faculty: 173 full-time, 43 part-time: 90% with Ph.D./D.B.A. Degrees conferred: M.Acc., M.B.A. (full-time, part-time; concentrations in accounting [financial reporting & analysis, designing and re-engineering enterprise systems], business of creative industries, business of entertainment, business of education, entrepreneurship [entrepreneurship & venture management, technology commercialization], entrepreneurship & operations, finance and business economics [corporate finance, investments & financial markets, real estate finance], health care advisory services, information systems, management & organization [strategic management & consulting, leadership & organization], marketing [product innovation & brand management, integrative marketing communication management, strategic marketing management and analysis], operations management), E.M.B.A. (weekends only), IBEAR M.B.A. (International Business Education and Research; one-year program International Business, day and evening sessions), M.B.A.P.M. (for Professionals and Managers; concentrations in Business Economics and Public Policy, Business of Entertainment, Business Entrepreneurship, Consulting Services, Finance, General Management, Health Care Advisory Services, Human Resource Management, Information Systems, International Finance and Economics, Marketing, Operations Management, Real Estate, Statistics, Technology Management, Venture Management), M.B.T. (Business Taxation), M.M.M. (Medical Management), M.S.B.A., M.S.I.O.M. (Information and Operations Management), M.B.A.-D.D.S., M.B.A.-J.D., M.B.A.-M.A. (East Asian Studies), M.B.A.-M.PL. (Planning), M.B.A.-Pharm.D., M.B.A.-M.R.E.D. (Real Estate Development), M.B.A., M.S. (Industrial and Systems Engineering), M.B.A.-M.S.G. (Gerontology), M.B.A.-M.S.N. (Nursing), Ph.D.

ADMISSION REQUIREMENTS. Transcript, GMAT or GRE, introduction to calculus prior to enrollment, letters of recommendation required in support of School's application. Two years of professional work experience preferred. TOEFL required for international applicants. Graduates of unaccredited institutions not considered. Apply online only, full-time applicants by April 15, part-time applicants by June 1, April 1 (Fall) October 1 (Spring). Application fee $90 domestic, $125 for international applicants. Phone: (213)740-8846; fax: (213)749-8520.

ADMISSION STANDARDS. Selective. Usual minimum average: 3.2 (A = 4), GMAT 626.

FINANCIAL AID. Annual awards from institutional funds: each year qualified full-time M.B.A. students are offered merit-based fellowships ranging from partial to full-tuition, loans. Approved for VA benefits. Apply by February 15 (Fall). Phone: (213)743-1111. Use FAFSA (School code: 001328). About 33% receive aid other than loans from School, outside sources, and interested individuals.

DEGREE REQUIREMENTS. For M.B.A., M.S.I.O.M., M.S.B.A.: contact (213)740-8846; for Accounting contact (213)740-4867; for Ph.D.: contact (213)740-0674.

FIELDS OF STUDY.
Accounting. M.Acc.
Business Administration. M.B.A., M.S., Ph.D.
Business Taxation. M.B.T.
Digital Supply Chain Management. M.D.S.C.M.
Medical Management. M.M.M.

FIELDS OF DOCTORAL STUDY.
Accounting.
Finance and Business Economics.
Information and Operations Management.
Management and Organization.
Marketing.

School of Cinematic Arts

Graduate study since 1914. Semester system. Special facility: Institute for Multimedia Literacy.
Annual tuition: $24,238 (8–14 units for two semesters), $35,750 (15–18 units for two semesters).
Graduate enrollment: full- and part-time 657. Faculty: total full-time 89, part-time 230. Degrees conferred: M.A., M.F.A., Ph.D.

ADMISSION REQUIREMENTS. Two transcripts, GRE, reference, personal statement, supplementary application required in

support of USC Application. Portfolios and writing samples required for some programs. Online application available. Accepts transfer applicants. Application deadlines vary by program, contact School for application information. Phone: (213)740-8358; e-mail: admissions@cinema.usc.edu. Application fee $85.

ADMISSION STANDARDS. Competitive. Usual minimum average: 3.0 (A = 4).

FINANCIAL AID. Annual awards from institutional funds: scholarships, assistantship, grants, Federal W/S, loans. Approved for VA benefits. Apply by February 15 to University Financial Aid Office. Phone (213)740-1111. Use FAFSA (School code 001328) and University's FAF.

DEGREE REQUIREMENTS. For M.A.: 36-credit program; comprehensive exam. For M.F.A: (Interactive Media) 56-unit, three-year program; advanced interactive project. (Film & TV) 52-unit program; thesis. (Peter Stark Producing Program) 44-unit program; internship. (Writing) 44–48 unit, two-year program; practicum. For Ph.D.: See Graduate School listing above.

FIELDS OF STUDY.
Animation and Digital Arts.
Business of Entertainment.
Critical Studies.
Film and Television Production.
Interactive Media. Includes game design & innovation, interactive entertainment.
Producing.
Writing for Screen and Television.

Annenberg School for Communication

Graduate study since 1971. Semester system. Special facilities: Center for Communication Law and Policy, Center for Communication Leadership, Center for Digital Future, Center for Public Diplomacy, Center for the Study of Journalism and Democracy, Norman Lear Center, Strategic Public Relations Center, Institute for Justice and Journalism.
Tuition: per credit $1185.
Graduate enrollment: full-time 250, part-time 85, Ph.D. full-time 18. Faculty: full-time 75. Degrees conferred: M.A., M.C.M., M.G.C., M.P.D., Ph.D.

ADMISSION REQUIREMENTS. Two transcripts, GRE, reference, personal statement, Annenberg supplementary application required in support of USC Application. Accepts transfer applicants. Apply to the USC Graduate Admission Office by February 1 (for Ph.D. apply by December 1). Some master's programs have earlier deadlines. Phone: (213)740-1111. For Global Communication, apply directly to London School of Economics and Political Science (LSE). Application fee $85.

ADMISSION STANDARDS. Competitive. Usual minimum average: 3.0 (A = 4).

FINANCIAL AID. Annual awards from institutional funds: scholarships, assistantship, grants, Federal W/S, loans. Approved for VA benefits. Apply by February 15 to University Financial Aid Office. Phone (213)740-1111. Use FAFSA and University's FAF.

DEGREE REQUIREMENTS. For M.A.: 40-credit program; comprehensive exam option/thesis option. For M.C.M.: 32-credit program; Capstone Communication Professional Practicum. For M.D.P.: 52-credit program; internship. For M.G.C.: two-year program, first year spent at London School of Economics, second year at USC; research course; final research project. For Ph.D.: see Graduate School listing above.

FIELDS OF STUDY.
Communication. Includes information and society, interpersonal and health communication, media, culture and communication, organizational communication, rhetoric and political communication. Ph.D.
Communication Management. Includes online communities. M.C.M.
Global Communication. M.G.C.
Journalism. Includes print, broadcast, online journalism. M.A.
Public Diplomacy. Includes communication and International Relations. M.P.D.
Specialized Journalism. M.A.
Strategic Public Relations. M.A.

School of Dentistry (90089-0641)
Web site: www.usc.edu/dental

Founded 1897. Trimester system. Special facility: Center for Craniofacial Molecular Biology. Special program: Advanced Standing Program for International Dentists.

Annual tuition: $55,347. Limited on-campus housing available. Average academic year housing costs: $14,500. Contact Housing Office in Student Union Building for both on- and off-campus housing information. Total average cost for all other first year expenses: $9,645.

Enrollment: first year class 144, total 622 (men 64%, women 36%, minorities 33%, state residents 62%), postgraduates 111, graduate students 42. Faculty: full- and part-time 230. Degrees conferred: D.D.S, D.D.S.-M.B.A., D.D.S.-M.S. (Gerontology). The M.S. and PhD. in Craniofacial Biology are offered through the Graduate School.

ADMISSION REQUIREMENTS. AADSAS, official transcripts, three letters of reference, DAT (no later than October) required in support of School's application. Applicants must have at least two years of college study. Interview by invitation only. Accepts transfer applicants from U.S. and Canadian dental schools on a space available basis. Graduates of unaccredited colleges not considered. Apply to Office of Admissions and Student Affairs after June 1, before March 1. Deadline for transfer applicants March 1. Application fee $65, $145 for international applicants. Phone: (213)740-2811; fax: (213)740-8109.

ADMISSION STANDARDS. Selective. Accepts about 10–15% of all applicants. Usual minimum UGPA: 3.0 (A = 4). Mean DAT: academic 19, PAT 18; mean UGPA 3.44.

FINANCIAL AID. Scholarships, grants, loans. Apply to Office of Admissions and Student Affairs; no specified closing date. Phone: (213)740-2841. Use FAFSA (School code: 001328). About 75% of students receive some form of financial assistance.

DEGREE REQUIREMENTS. For D.D.S.: satisfactory completion of 11 consecutive 15 week trimesters. For M.S., Ph.D.: see Graduate School listing above.

FIELDS OF POSTGRADUATE STUDY.
Craniofacial Biology. M.S., Ph.D.
Endodontics.
General Dentistry Residency (AEGD).
General Practice Residency.
Integrated M.D. Degree/ Oral and Maxillofacial Surgery Certificate Program.
Oral & Maxillofacial Surgery.
Orthodontics.
Orofacial Pain and Oral Medicine.
Pediatric Dentistry.
Periodontology.
Prosthodontics.

Rossier School of Education
Doctoral degrees in education awarded since 1927.

Tuition: $1185 per unit. Graduate enrollment: full-time 488, part-time 455. Faculty: full-time 48, part-time 100. Degrees conferred: M.Ed., M.S., M.F.C.C., Ed.D. The Ph.D.: is administered by the Graduate School.

ADMISSION REQUIREMENTS. Official transcripts, GRE required in support of Schools application. Interview not required. TOEFL required for international applicants. International students whose first language is English are exempted. Accepts transfer applicants. Graduates of unaccredited institutions not considered. Apply to University Office of Admissions one month prior to registration. Application fee $85. Phone: (213)743-1111; School of Education Student Services phone: (213)740-2606.

ADMISSION STANDARDS. Competitive for most departments. Usual minimum average: 3.0 (master's), 3.0 (doctorate) (A = 4).

FINANCIAL AID. Scholarships, fellowships, research assistantships, teaching assistantships, training grants, Federal W/S, loans. Approved for VA benefits. Apply by February 15 to Dean of School of Education for fellowships, assistantships; to Financial Aid for all other programs. Use FAFSA (School code: 001328). Phone: (213)740-1111. About 50% of students receive aid other than loans from University and outside sources. Aid available for part-time students.

DEGREE REQUIREMENTS. For M.Ed.: 41 unit program; thesis. For M.S.: 28 units minimum, at least 24 in residence; thesis/nonthesis option or master's seminar. For M.F.C.C.: 51 units, at least four semesters in residence; practicum. For Ed.D.: 96 units minimum beyond the bachelor's, at least 66 in residence; preliminary review; qualifying exam; candidacy; dissertation; final oral exam. For Ph.D., see Graduate School listing above.

FIELDS OF STUDY.
Education. Includes multiple subjects, single subject, music education, public school music. M.A.T.
Education. Includes educational psychology, instructional technology, reading & writing, M .Ed.
Educational Psychology. Ed.D., Ph.D.
Higher Education/Community College Leadership. Ed.D., Ph.D.
K–12 Leadership in Urban Education Settings. Ed.D., Ph.D.
Marriage and Family Therapy. M.M.F.T.
Post Secondary Administration and Student Affairs. M.Ed.
School Counseling. M.Ed.
Teacher Education in Multicultural Societies. Ed.D., Ph.D.
Teaching English to Speakers of Other Languages. M.S.
Teaching English as a Foreign Language. M.Ed.

Viterbi School of Engineering
Web site: www.usc.edu

Graduate study since 1931. Semester system.

Tuition: per credit $1293. Graduate enrollment: full-time 1297, part-time 1209. Graduate teaching faculty: full-time 140, part-time 38. Degrees conferred: M.S., Engineer. The Ph.D. is administered by the Graduate School.

ADMISSION REQUIREMENTS. Two transcripts, GRE required in support of School's application. Some majors also require GRE Subject Test. Interview not required. Accepts transfer applicants. Graduates of unaccredited institutions not considered. Apply to University Office of Admissions by June 15 (Fall), October 1 (Spring), February 1 (Summer). Application fee $85. Phone: (213) 740-1111; fax: (213)740-8493.

ADMISSION STANDARDS. Selective for most departments. Usual minimum average: 3.0 (A = 4) for M.S., 3.5 for Ph.D.

FINANCIAL AID. Annual awards from institutional funds: fellowships, scholarships, teaching/research assistantships, Federal W/S, loans. Approved for VA benefits. Apply by February 15 to chair of major department for assistantships; to Financial Aid Office for all other programs. Use FAFSA (School code: 001328) and University's FAF. Phone: (213)740-1111; fax: (213)740-0680. About 35% of full-time students receive aid other than loans from both School and outside sources. Loans available for part-time students.

DEGREE REQUIREMENTS. For M.S.: 27 units minimum, at least 23 in residence; thesis/nonthesis option. For Engineer: 30 units beyond the master's degree, at least 26 units in residence; Engineer's exam. For Ph.D.: see Graduate School listing above.

FIELDS OF STUDY.
Aerospace and Mechanical Engineering. Includes computational fluid and solid mechanics, dynamics and control.
Aerospace Engineering.
Applied Mechanics.
Astronautical Engineering.
Biomedical Engineering. Includes medical imaging and imaging informatics.
Chemical Engineering.
Civil Engineering. Includes construction, environmental, geotechnical, structural, transportation.
Computer-aided Engineering.
Computer Engineering.
Computer Science. Includes computer networks, computer security, game development, high performance computing and simulations, intelligent robotics, multimedia and creative technologies, software engineering.
Construction Management.
Electrical Engineering. Includes computer networks, multimedia and creative technologies, VLSI design.
Engineering Management.
Environmental Quality Management.
Industrial and Systems Engineering.
Manufacturing Engineering.
Materials Engineering.
Materials Science.
Mechanical Engineering.
Medical Device and Diagnostic Engineering.
Operations Research Engineering.
Petroleum Engineering. Includes smart oilfield technologies.
Production Development Engineering.
Systems Architecting and Engineering.
System Safety and Security.
Structural Design.

Roski School of Fine Arts (90089-0292)

Tuition: per credit $1185.
Graduate enrollment: full-time 27, part-time 3. School faculty: full-time 12, part-time 14. Degrees conferred: M.A., M.F.A.

ADMISSION REQUIREMENTS. Two transcripts, three letters of reference (GRE required for Public Art Studies), twenty-slide portfolio for studio M.F.A., supplemental application and materials for M.A. TOEFL required for international applicants. Apply to both School of Fine Arts and Graduate School by February 1. Application fee $85. Phone: (213)740-2787 Art Office, (213) 743-1111 University Office of Admissions.

ADMISSION STANDARDS. Competitive. Usual minimum average: 3.0 (A = 4).

FINANCIAL AID. Teaching assistantships, internships, grants, Federal W/S, loans. Approved for VA benefits. Apply by February 1 to School's Financial Aid Office. Phone: (213)740-1111; fax: (213)740-0680. Use FAFSA (School code: 001328) and University's FAF.

DEGREE REQUIREMENTS. For M.A.: 40 units; internships. For M.F.A.: 48 credits; thesis/exhibition.

FIELDS OF STUDY.
Fine Arts. M.F.A.
Public Art Studies. M.P.A.S.

Gould School of Law (90089-0071)
Web site: www.usc.law.edu

Established 1896. Located on main campus in Law Center. ABA approved since 1924. AALS member since 1907. Semester system. Full-time, day study only. Special facilities: Center for Communication Law and Policy, Center in Law, Economics and Organization, Center for Law, History and Culture, Center for Law and Philosophy, Center for the Study of Law and Politics, Initiative & Referendum Institute, Pacific Center for Health Policy and Ethics. Special programs: faculty exchange programs with Hebrew University, Tel Aviv University, Israel; Oxford University, England; China University of Political Science, People's Republic of China; judicial externships; internships. Law library: 413,501 volumes, 4818 subscriptions; has LEXIS, NEXIS, WESTLAW, DIALOG; is a Federal Government Depository.
Annual tuition: full-time $40,262. On-campus housing available. Total average annual additional expenses: $17,354.
Enrollment: first-year class 205, total 605 (men 52%, women 48%, minorities 39%). Faculty: full-time 40, part-time 45. Student to faculty ratio is 15.4 to 1. Degrees conferred: J.D., J.D.-M.A. (Communications Management, Economics, International Relations, Politics, Religion), J.D.-M.B.A., J.D.-M.B.T., J.D.-M.P.A., J.D.-M.P.P., J.D.-M.R.E.D., J.D.-M.S.W., J.D. Ph.D. (Social Sciences with California Institute of Technology), LL.M., M.C.L.

ADMISSION REQUIREMENTS. LSDAS Law School report, bachelor's degree, transcripts, LSAT (not later than December), personal statement, two letters of recommendation required in support of application. Interview not required. Accepts transfer applicants. Graduates of unaccredited colleges not considered. Apply to Admissions Office after September 1, before February 1. Fall admission only. Application fee $70. Phone: (213)740-2523. For Graduate degree information: Phone: (213)821-5916. Apply by March 1.

ADMISSION STANDARDS. Selective. Accepts approximately 20% of all students. Number of applicants 7075; number of acceptance 1438; number enrolled 205; LSAT (75% of students have a score at or above 164); GPA (75% of student have a GPA at or above 3.51). *U.S. News & World Report* ranking is in the top 16 of all U.S. law schools.

FINANCIAL AID. Scholarships, merit scholarships, minority scholarships, Grants-in-Aid, institutional loans; Federal loans and Federal W/S (for second- and third-year students only) available. Assistantships may be available for upper-divisional joint degree candidates. All accepted students are automatically considered for all scholarships. Apply by February 15 to Director of Financial Aid for all programs. Phone: (213)740-2523; use Law Center's Financial Aid Form. Use FAFSA (School code: 001328), also submit Financial Aid Transcript, Federal Income Tax forms. Approximately 58% of first-year class received scholarships/Grants-in-Aid. Approximately 55% of students receive some form of financial assistance. USC Loan Repayment Assistance Program for public-interest employment available.

DEGREE REQUIREMENTS. For J. D.: 88 (33 required) credits with a GPA of at least 70 (scale: 0–100), plus completion of upper-divisional writing course; three-year program. Accelerated J.D. with summer course work. For J.D.-M.B.A.: 105–121 total credits. For J.D.-M.P.A.: 93 total credits. For J.D.-M.B.T.: 94–110 total credits. For J.D.-M.A.: Communications, 88 total credits; Economic, 89 total credits; International Relations, 94 total credits;

Religion, 88 total credits. For J.D.-M.R.E.D.: 108 total credits. For J.D.-M.S.W.: 118 total credits. For LL.M., M.C.L.: at least 24 credits beyond the J.D.; thesis.

Keck School of Medicine (90033)
Web site: www.usc.edu/keck

Organized 1885. Library: 300,000 volumes, 2500 subscriptions. NIH ranking is 31 among all U.S. institutions with 334 awards/grants worth $181,838,243.

Annual tuition: $42,164. On-campus housing available. Total average figure for all other expenses: $16,900.

Enrollment: first-year class 171, total 672 (men 50%, women 50%, minorities 42%, state residents 75%). Faculty: full-time 1222, part-time 150. Degrees conferred: M.D., M.D.-M.B.A., M.D.-M.H.A., M.D.-M.P.H., M.D.-M.S., M.D.-Ph.D.

ADMISSION REQUIREMENTS. AMCAS report, letters of recommendation, MCAT supplement application required for admission. Interview by invitation only. Applicants must have completed at least three years of college study. Has EDP; apply between June 1 and August 1. Accepts transfer applicants. Graduates of unaccredited colleges not considered. Apply after June 1, before November 1. Application fee $90. Phone: (323)442-2552.

ADMISSION STANDARDS. Very competitive. Accepts about 6% of all applicants. Number of applications 5461 (2249 out-of-state); number interviewed 625 (209 out-of-state); number of acceptance 384 (118 out-of-state); number enrolled 171 (46 out-of-state). Mean Composite MCAT 10.8; mean UGPA 3.60 (A = 4.). *U.S. News & World Report* ranking is in the top 38 of all U.S. medical schools.

FINANCIAL AID. Scholarships, loans. Apply to University Financial Aid Office. Phone: (323)442-1016. Use FAFSA (School code: 001328). About 90% of students receive some aid from School.

DEGREE REQUIREMENTS. For M.D.: satisfactory completion of four-year program; transfer students from other medical schools may be admitted to advanced standing in second- or third-year class; all students must pass USMLE Step 1 prior to entering third year, and must pass USMLE Step 2 prior to awarding of M.D. For M.S., Ph.D., see Graduate School listing above.

FIELDS OF GRADUATE STUDY.
Biochemistry and Molecular Biology. M.S., Ph.D.
Biostatistics and Epidemiology. M.S., Ph.D.
Cell and Neurobiology. M.S., Ph.D.
Epidemiology. M.S., Ph.D
Health Behavior Research. M.S.
Medical Education. M.S.
Molecular Epidemiology. M.S., Ph.D.
Molecular Microbiology and Immunology. M.S., Ph.D.
Pathology. M.S., Ph.D.
Physiology and Biophysics. M.S., Ph.D.
Preventive Medicine. M.S.

Thornton School of Music

Observed its centennial in 1984. Semester system.
Tuition: per credit $1185.
Graduate enrollment: full-time 234, part-time 189. Faculty: full-time 54, part-time 75. Degrees conferred: M.M., M.M.Ed., D.M.A. The M.A. and Ph.D. are offered through the Graduate School.

ADMISSION REQUIREMENTS. Transcripts, supplementary application required in support of regular University application. Personal or taped performance audition required for all performance majors; original scores for composition majors; research paper or thesis for M.A. or Ph.D. Accepts transfer applicants. Apply to both USC Admissions Office and Office of Admission, School of Music by December 1 (Fall), October 1 (Spring). Application fee $85. Phone: (213)740-1111; fax: (213)740-8995.

ADMISSION STANDARDS. Selective. Talent weighted more heavily than GPA in most programs.

FINANCIAL AID. Tuition awards, scholarships, teaching assistantships, Federal W/S, loans. Apply by February 15 to School's Office of Financial Aid; no specified closing date. Phone: (213) 740-1111; fax: (213)740-0680. Use FAFSA (School code: 001328). Application details accompany application for admission.

DEGREE REQUIREMENTS. For M.M.: 30 units minimum, at least 26 in residence. For M.M.Ed.: 30 units minimum, at least 26 in residence; Music Graduate Entrance Exam; one or two recitals for performance majors; thesis for music education majors, thesis and recital for composition majors. For D.M.A.: 65 units minimum beyond the bachelor's, at least 35 units in residence and two consecutive semesters in full-time attendance; reading knowledge of one foreign language; qualifying exam; dissertation for composition, music education, and church music majors; two solo recitals and two other appropriate appearances for performance majors; final oral exam. For M.A., Ph.D., see Graduate School listing above.

FIELDS OF STUDY.
Choral Music.
Composition.
Conducting.
Early Music Performance.
Jazz Studies.
Jazz Voice.
Music Education.
Music History.
Musicology. M.A., Ph.D.
Performance. Includes keyboard collaborative arts, classical guitar, studio guitar, early music, jazz studies, orchestral instruments, keyboard (piano, organ, harpsichord), voice, opera.
Sacred Music.

School of Pharmacy

Founded in 1905. Semester system.
Annual tuition: full-time $36,172; per credit $1206.
Enrollment: full-time 754, part-time 67. Faculty: full-time 25, part-time and courtesy clinical 300. Degrees conferred: Pharm.D.; M.S. and Ph.D. administered by the Graduate School.

ADMISSION REQUIREMENTS. Pharm.D.: two transcripts documenting completion of required preprofessional courses, written essay; two letters of recommendation, personal interview required in support of School's application. Accepts transfer applicants. Graduates of unaccredited institutions not considered. Apply through the Pharmacy College Application Service by November 1 (Fall). Graduate program: two official transcripts, three letters of recommendation, GRE required in support of application. Transfer applicants accepted. Apply to Director of Admissions by March 1 (Fall), December 15 (Spring). Application fee $85. Phone: (323) 442-1369.

ADMISSION STANDARDS. Selective. Accepts 23% of applicants in professional and graduate programs. Usual minimum average: 2.75 (A = 4).

FINANCIAL AID. Professional program: loans and scholarships based upon financial eligibility and merit. Institutional FAF included with application package. Graduate programs: fellowships, teaching assistantships, Federal W/S, loans. Apply by February 15 to Coordinator, Graduate Programs Committee. Phone: (323) 442-1369. Use FAFSA (School code: 001328).

DEGREE REQUIREMENTS. Professional program: four-year curriculum following two years of preprofessional undergraduate college study. For M.S. and Ph.D.: see the Graduate School listing above.

FIELDS OF STUDY.
Molecular Pharmacology and Toxicology. M.S. Ph.D.
Pharmaceutical Economics and Policy. M.S., Ph.D.
Pharmaceutical Sciences. M.S., Ph.D.
Pharmacy. Pharm.D.
Regulatory Science. M.S.

School of Policy, Planning, and Development

Established 1929. Semester system. Campuses located in Sacramento, California, Washington, D.C., and its home campus in Los Angeles.

Tuition: per credit $1185. Enrollment: full-time 445, part-time 213. Faculty: full-time 28, part-time 70. Degrees conferred: M.P.A., M.H.A., M.H.M., M.Pl., M.P.D.S., D.P.P., D.P.A., Ph.D., M.Pl.-M.Arch., M.Pl.-M.B.A., M.Pl.-M.A. (Economics, International Relations), M.Pl.-M.R.E.D., M.Pl.-M.S.G., M.Pl.-M.L.A., M.Pl.-M.P.A., M.Pl.-M.P.A.S., M.Pl.-M.S.W., M.R.E.D.-J.D., M.P.A.-M.S.G., M.H.A.-M.S.G., M.P.A.-M.A.I.R., M.P.A.-J.D., M.P.P.-J.D., M.P.A.-M.S.W., M.P.A.-M.A. (Jewish Communal Service).

ADMISSION REQUIREMENTS. U.S.C. Graduate Admission Application, School Supplemental Application, two official transcripts, three letters of recommendation, résumé, GRE or GMAT or LSAT test scores required in support of School's application. TOEFL required for international applicants. Interview not required. Accepts transfer applicants (up to 8 units can be transferred). Apply to School by July 1 (most master's programs), December 1 (Doctoral programs). Application fee $85. Phone: (213)740-1111. The School's Student Affairs Officer: (213)740-6842.

ADMISSION STANDARDS. Selective. Usual minimum GPA of 3.0 (A = 4) in last 60 semester units or 90 quarter units. GRE (or equivalent GMAT or LSAT) score of 1000 on verbal and quantitative sections.

FINANCIAL AID. Awards from institutional funds: partial tuition scholarships, doctoral fellowships, assistantships, graduate internships, tuition waivers, Federal W/S, loans. Approved for VA benefits. Apply to School by February 15 for Fall awards, November 1 for Spring awards. Financial aid application for Federal programs are due March 10. Use FAFSA (School code: 001328) and University's FAF.

DEGREE REQUIREMENTS. For M.P.D.S.: 28 unit program. For M.H.M., M.Pl., M.P.A.: 40–41 units of study. For M.P.P., M.H.A.: 48 units, at least 36 in residence; internship, comprehensive exam. For Ph.D., D.P.A., D.P.D.S.: completion of 60 units beyond the bachelor's degree, at least 30 in residence; qualifying exam; dissertation; systems requirement for D.P.A., a foreign language requirement for Ph.D.

FIELDS OF STUDY.
Construction Management. Jointly offered with Department of Civil Engineering. M.C.M.
Health Administration. M.H.A.
International Public Policy and Management. M.I.P.P.A.M.
Planning. M.Pl., Ph.D.
Planning and Development Studies. M.P.D.S., D.Pl.D.S.
Policy, Planning and Development. Ph.D.
Public Administration. M.P.A., Ph.D., D.P.A.
Public Policy. M.P.P.
Public Policy and Management. M.P.P.M.
Real Estate Development. M.R.E.D.

School of Social Work

Graduate study since 1920. Semester system.
Tuition: per credit $1185.
Graduate enrollment: full-time 371, part-time 144. Faculty: full-time 13, part-time 47. Degrees conferred: M.S.W., Ph.D.

ADMISSION REQUIREMENTS. Two transcripts, references, personal statement, résumé, required in support of School's application. TOEFL, TSE required for international applicants. Accepts transfer applicants. Apply online only by April 1. Fall admission only. Application fee $85. Phone: (213)740-2013.

ADMISSION STANDARDS. Competitive. Usual minimum average: 3.0 (A = 4).

FINANCIAL AID. Annual awards from institutional funds: scholarships, fellowships, research/teaching assistantships, internships, Federal W/S, loans. Approved for VA benefits. Apply by February 15 to the University Financial Aid Office. Phone: (213)740-1111. Use FAFSA (School code: 001328) and University's FAF. About 45% of students receive aid other than loans from School and outside sources. No aid for part-time students.

DEGREE REQUIREMENTS. For M.S.W.: 56 units minimum in residence. For Ph.D.: see Graduate School listing above.

M.S.W. FIELDS OF CONCENTRATION.
Community Organization, Planning and Administration.
Families and Children.
Health.
Mental Health.
Work and Life.

School of Theatre

Graduate study since 1985. Semester system.
Tuition: per credit $1185.
Graduate enrollment: full-time 185, part-time 5. Faculty: full-time 22, part-time 56. Degrees conferred: M.F.A.

ADMISSION REQUIREMENT. Two transcripts, GRE, reference, personal statement, audition, theatre supplementary application required in support of USC Application. Interviews required for Design applicants. Accepts transfer applicants. For information contact the Office of Admission and Recruitment, School of Theatre. Phone: (213)740-1286. Application fee $85.

ADMISSION STANDARDS. Competitive. Usual minimum average: 3.0 (A = 4).

FINANCIAL AID. Annual awards from institutional funds: scholarships, assistantships, grants, Federal W/S, loans. Approved for VA benefits. Apply by February 15 to University Financial Aid Office. Phone (213)740-1111. Use FAFSA (School code: 001328) and University's FAF.

DEGREE REQUIREMENT. For M.F.A.: 48-credit program (directing and theatrical design); 64-credit program (dramatic writing), 72-credit program (acting); thesis; final project and oral defense (design).

FIELDS OF STUDY.
Acting.
Directing.
Dramatic Writing.
Theatrical Design.

SOUTHERN COLLEGE OF OPTOMETRY

Memphis, Tennessee 38104
Web site: www.sco.edu

Founded 1932. Coed. Accredited by Southern Association of Colleges and Schools and by Council on Optometric Education. Private control. Semester system. Library: 20,500 volumes, 531 microforms, 25 PCs.

Annual tuition: regional $15,448, nonregional $20,448. No on-campus housing available. Contact the Records and Admissions Office for off-campus housing information. Phone: (800) 238-0180.

Enrollment: full-time 480. College faculty: full-time 39, part-time 4. Degree conferred: O.D.

ADMISSION REQUIREMENTS. Transcripts showing satisfactory completion of 90 semester hours of prescribed preoptometry courses (bachelor's degree preferred), two letters of recommendation, interview, OAT, essays required in support of College's application. Online application available. Apply to Admissions Office by March 1 (priority date). Rolling admissions process. Application fee $50. Phone: (901)722-3224, (800)238-0180.

ADMISSION STANDARDS. Competitive. Usual minimum average: 2.5 (A = 4).

FINANCIAL AID. Scholarships, awards, Federal W/S, loans. Approved for VA benefits. Apply by April 1 to Financial Aid Office. Phone: (901)722-3207. Use FAFSA (School code: 003517).

DEGREE REQUIREMENTS. For O.D.: 188 credit hours minimum; externship.

SOUTHERN CONNECTICUT STATE UNIVERSITY

New Haven, Connecticut 06515-1355
Web site: www.southernct.edu

Founded 1893. CGS member. Coed. State control. Semester system. Special facilities: Business and Economic Development Center, Child Abuse Center, Center for Communication Disorders, Center for Computing and Society, Center for Environment, Reading Center, Research in Behavioral Science Center, Urban Studies Center. Library: 510,000 volumes, 2800 subscriptions.

Annual tuition: full-time resident $4376, nonresident $12,196; per credit $449. Some on-campus housing in summer for single graduate students. Average academic year housing costs: $6800 (including board). Contact Housing Office for both on- and off-campus housing information. Phone: (203)392-5869.

School of Graduate Studies

Graduate study since 1947. Enrollment: full- and part-time 3800. Graduate faculty: full-time 154, part-time 70. Degrees conferred: M.A., M.M.F.T., M.B.A., M.L.S., M.P.H., M.S., M.S.Ed., M.S.N., M.S.W., Sixth Year Professional Diploma.

ADMISSION REQUIREMENTS. Transcripts, GRE (nursing, library science), GRE Subject Test (biology, foreign language departments), GMAT (business economics), letters of recommendation or departmental form, interview required in support of School's application. TOEFL required for international applicants. Accepts transfer applicants. Graduates of unaccredited institutions not considered. Apply to Dean of Graduate Studies by July 15 (Fall), November 15 (Spring), May 15 (Summer). Rolling admission process. Application fee $50. Phone: (203)392-5656.

ADMISSION STANDARDS. Usual minimum average: 2.75 (A = 4) and/or 3.3 in graduate major area.

FINANCIAL AID. Fellowships, assistantships for teaching/research, Federal W/S, loans. Approved for VA benefits. Apply to appropriate department chair for fellowships, assistantships; to Financial Aid Office for all other programs. Phone: (203)392-4232. Use FAFSA. About 10% of students receive aid other than loans from College and outside sources. Aid available for part-time students.

DEGREE REQUIREMENTS. For master's: 30 semester hours minimum, at least 21 credits in residence; comprehensive exam; thesis/nonthesis option. For Professional Diploma: 30 semester hours beyond the master's, all in residence; final comprehensive exam.

FIELDS OF STUDY.
Art Education.
Bilingual/Bicultural Education.
Biology.
Business Administration.
Chemistry.
Communications Disorders.
Counseling.
Educational Foundations.
Educational Leadership.
Elementary Education.
English.
Environmental Education.
Exercise Science.
History.
Library Science.
Marriage and Family Therapy.
Mathematics.
Nursing.
Political Science.
Psychology.
Public Health.
Reading.
Recreation and Leisure.
Research, Measurement, and Evaluation.
Romance Languages. Includes French, Italian, Spanish.
School Health Education.
School Psychology.
Science Education.
Social Work.
Sociology.
Special Education.
Urban Studies.
Women's Studies.

SOUTHERN ILLINOIS UNIVERSITY

Carbondale, Illinois 62901-6806
Web site: www.siuc.edu

Founded 1869. Located 100 miles SE of St. Louis, Missouri. CGS member. Coed. State control. Semester system. Special facilities: Center for Archaeological Investigation, Coal Extraction and Utilization Center, Center for Dewey Studies, Materials Technology Center. Library: 4,200,000 volumes, 15,000 subscriptions. Total University enrollment: 22,000.

Annual tuition: full-time resident $8350, nonresident $20,625; per credit resident $275, nonresident $687.50. On-campus housing for married, single graduate students. Average housing costs: $375–$525 per month. Contact University Housing Office for both on- and off-campus housing information. Phone: (618)453-2301. Day-care facilities available.

Graduate School

Graduate study since 1944. Enrollment: full- and part-time 3263. Graduate faculty: full-time 780, part-time 14. Degrees conferred: M.A., M.S., M.F.A., M.B.A., M.Acc., M.S. in Ed., M.M., M.P.A., Ph.D., Rh.D., D.B.A.

ADMISSION REQUIREMENTS. Official transcripts required in support of School's application. GRE/GMAT/MAT, letters of recommendation required by some departments. TOEFL (minimum score 550) required for international applicants. Accepts transfer applicants. Graduates of unaccredited institutions not considered. Contact departments directly for admission material and requirements. Rolling admissions process. Application fee $20. Phone: (618)536-7791; fax: (618)453-4562; e-mail: gradschl@siu.edu.

ADMISSION STANDARDS. Selective for most departments, very selective or competitive for others. Usual minimum average: 2.7 (A = 4).

FINANCIAL AID. Annual awards from institutional funds: scholarships, fellowships, teaching assistantships, research assistantships, other grants, Federal W/S, loans. Approved for VA benefits. Apply by February 1 to appropriate department chair for fellowships, assistantships; to Financial Aid Office for all other programs. Phone: (618)453-4334; fax: (618)453-7305. Use FAFSA. Over 70% of full-time students are given some type of financial assistance.

DEGREE REQUIREMENTS. For M.A., M.S.: 30–45 semester hours minimum, at least half in residence; foreign language optional with some departments; thesis for many majors; final written/oral exam. For M.F.A.: 40–60 hours minimum, at least half in residence; thesis; final exhibit of creative work; final exam. For M.B.A., M.P.A., M.Acc.: 30–36 hours minimum, at least half in residence; final written/oral exam. For M.S. in Ed.: same as for M.A., M.S. For M.M.: same as for M.S. in Ed., except recital required in some fields. For Ph.D., Rh.D., D.B.A.: no set hourly requirements (some departments set hourly minimum); at least two semesters in full-time residence; departments establish research tools; dissertation for 24 hours; final written/oral exam.

FIELDS OF STUDY.
Accountancy. M.Acc.
Administration of Justice. M.A.
Agribusiness Economics. M.S.
Animal Science. M.S.
Anthropology. M.A., Ph.D.
Applied Linguistics. M.A.
Architecture. M.Arch.
Art. M.F.A.
Behavior Analysis and Therapy. M.S.
Biological Sciences. M.S.
Business Administration. M.B.A., Ph.D.
Chemistry. M.S., Ph.D.
Cinema and Photography. M.F.A.
Civil Engineering. M.S.
Communication Disorders and Sciences. M.S.
Computer Science. M.S., Ph.D.
Creative Writing. M.F.A.
Curriculum and Instruction. M.S. in Ed., Ph.D.
Economics. M.A., M.S., Ph.D.
Education. Ph.D. in 8 concentrations.
Educational Administration. M.S. in Ed., Ph.D.
Educational Psychology. M.S. in Ed., Ph.D.
Electrical and Computer Engineering. M.S.
Engineering Science. Ph.D.
English. M.A., Ph.D.
Environmental Resources and Policy. Ph.D.

Food and Nutrition. M.S.
Foreign Languages and Literatures. Includes French, German, Spanish. M.A.
Forestry. M.S.
Geography and Environmental Resources. M.S., Ph.D.
Geology. M.S., Ph.D.
Health Education. M.S. in Ed., Ph.D.
Higher Education. M.S. in Ed.
Historical Studies. Ph.D.
History. M.A.
Kinesiology. M.S.Ed.
Legal Studies. M.L.S.
Manufacturing System. M.S.
Mass Communication and Media Arts. M.A., M.F.A., Ph.D.
Mathematics. M.A., M.S., Ph.D.
Mechanical Engineering. M.S.
Media Theory and Research. M.A.
Mining Engineering. M.S.
Molecular Biology, Microbiology, and Biochemistry. M.S.
Molecular, Cellular, and Systemic Physiology. M.S., Ph.D.
Music. M.M.
Pharmacology. M.S., Ph.D.
Philosophy. M.A., Ph.D.
Physician Assistant. M.S.P.A.
Physics. M.S.
Physiology.
Plant Biology. M.A., M.S., Ph.D.
Plant and Soil Science. M.S.
Political Science. M.A., Ph.D.
Psychology. M.A., Ph.D.
Public Administration. M.P.A.
Recreation. M.S. in Ed.
Rehabilitation Administration and Services. M.S., Ph.D.
Rehabilitation Counseling. M.S.
Social Work. M.S.W.
Sociology. M.A., Ph.D.
Special Education. M.S., Ed.D., Ph.D.
Speech Communication. M.A., M.S., Ph.D.
TESOL. M.A.
Theater. M.F.A.
Workforce Education and Development. M.S. in Ed., Ph.D.
Zoology. M.S., Ph.D.

School of Dental Medicine (62002)

Web site: www.siue.edu/dentalmedicine

Founded 1969. Located in Alton Illinois, near St. Louis Missouri. Semester system.

Annual tuition: resident $20,343, nonresident $61,938. No on-campus housing available. Average academic year housing costs: $13,600. Total average cost for all other first year expenses: $12,200.

Enrollment: first year class 48, total 205 (men 49%, women 51%, minorities 13%, state residents 93%). Faculty: full-time 43, part-time 44. Degrees conferred: D.M.D.

ADMISSION REQUIREMENTS. AADSAS, official transcripts, DAT (October test preferred), three letters of recommendation required in support of School's application. Applicants must have completed at least two years of college study, prefer three years of study. Interview by invitation only. Preference is given to state residents. Accepts transfer applicants on a space available basis only. Graduates of unaccredited colleges not considered. Apply after June 1, before February 1. Application fee $20. Phone: (618) 474-7120; fax: (618)474-7249.

ADMISSION STANDARDS. Selective. Accepts about 15–20% of all applicants. Usual minimum UGPA: there is no minimum UGPA or DAT score. Mean DAT: academic 18.4, PAT 17.6; mean UGPA 3.50.

FINANCIAL AID. Limited scholarships, grants, loans. Apply after acceptance to Office of Student Affairs. Phone: (618)474-7175. Use FAFSA (School code: E00606). About 94% of students receive aid from School and outside sources.

DEGREE REQUIREMENTS. For D.M.D.: satisfactory completion of forty-six-month program.

School of Law

Web site: www.law.siu.edu

Established 1973. ABA approved since 1974. AALS member. Private control. Semester system. Special facility: Center for Health Law and Policy. Law library: 393,131 volumes, 3960 subscriptions; has LEXIS, NEXIS, WESTLAW, LEGALTRAC.

Annual tuition: resident $10,861, nonresident $28,621. On-campus housing available. Apply to Housing Office. Phone: (618) 453-2301. Total average annual additional expenses: $11,674.

Enrollment: first-year class full-time 122; total 353 (men 59%, women 41%, minorities 8%). Faculty: full-time 25, part-time 10. Student to faculty ratio is 13 to 1. Degrees conferred: J.D., J.D.-M.Acc., J.D.-M.B.A., J.D.-M.Ed., J.D.-M.P.A., J.D.-M.S.W., J.D.-M.D., LL.M. (General, Health Law and Policy), M.L.S.

ADMISSION REQUIREMENTS. LSDAS Law School report, bachelor's degree, transcripts, LSAT, résumé, two letters of recommendation required in support of application. Graduates of unaccredited institutions not considered. Apply by March 1 to Admissions Office. Rolling admissions process. Application fee $50. Phone: (800)739-9187, (618)453-8858.

ADMISSION STANDARDS. Selective. Accepts approximately 37% of all students. Number of applicants 713; number of acceptance 262; number enrolled 122; LSAT (75% of students have a score at or above 152); GPA (75% of students have a GPA at or above 3.13). *U.S. News & World Report* ranking is in the third tier of all U.S. law schools.

FINANCIAL AID. Scholarships, grants, full and partial tuition waivers, fellowships, assistantships, loans. Apply to Office of Student Work and Financial Assistance by April 1. Phone: (618) 453-4334. Use FAFSA (School code: 001758). Approximately 46% of all students receive some form of financial assistance.

DEGREE REQUIREMENTS. For J.D.: satisfactory completion of 90 semester hour program. For LL.M.: 24-credit program; substantial research paper of publishable quality. For M.L.S.: 30-credit program. For combined degree programs: normally requires one additional year; see Graduate School listing above.

School of Medicine (P.O. Box 19620)

Web site: www.siumed.edu

Established 1969. Located at Springfield (62794-9624); the first year of medical school is spent on Carbondale campus. Library: 113,000 volumes, 1600 subscriptions.

Annual tuition/fees: resident $23,284, $62,572. Only off-campus housing in Springfield. Total average figure for all other expenses: $16,500.

Enrollment: first-year class 72, total 289 (men 47%, women 53%, minorities 23%, state residents 100%). Faculty: full-time 301, part-time 9300. Degrees conferred: M.D., M.D. J.D.

ADMISSION REQUIREMENTS. AMCAS report, transcripts, MCAT, recommendations, screening interview required in support of application. Must be Illinois resident. Accepts transfer applicants. Does not have EDP. Graduates of unaccredited colleges not considered. Apply after June 1, before November 15. Application fee $50. Phone: (217)545-6013; fax: (217)545-5538.

ADMISSION STANDARDS. Selective. Accepts about 15% of all applicants. Number of applications 1013 (40 out-of-state);

number interviewed 284 (3 out-of-state); number of acceptance 192 (2 out-of-state); number enrolled 72 (0 out-of-state). Mean Composite MCAT 9.0; mean UGPA 3.53 (A = 4.).

FINANCIAL AID. Scholarships, merit scholarships, minority scholarships, Grants-in-Aid, institutional loans, HEAL, alternative loan programs, Federal Perkins Loans, Stafford Subsidized and Unsubsidized Loans, Illinois Health Improvement Associate Loans are available. Financial aid applications and information are generally available at the on-campus by invitation interview. Scholarships and grants limited to students with demonstrated exceptional need. Contact the Financial Aid Office for current information. Phone: (217)545-2224. For most financial assistance and all Federal programs use FAFSA (School code: E00569), also submit Financial Aid Transcript, Federal Income Tax forms. Approximately 93% of students receive some form of financial assistance.

DEGREE REQUIREMENTS. For M.D.: satisfactory completion of four-year program; first year is spent in Carbondale. All students must pass USMLE Step 1 prior to graduation. For M.D.-J.D.: generally a six-year program.

SOUTHERN ILLINOIS UNIVERSITY AT EDWARDSVILLE

Edwardsville, Illinois 62026-1046
Web site: www.siue.edu

Located 20 miles from St. Louis, Missouri. CGS member. Coed. State control. Semester system. Library: 788,000 volumes, 7500 subscriptions. Total University enrollment: 13,500.

Annual tuition: full-time resident $5670, nonresident $14,174; special part-time tuition reduction program for Missouri residents. On-campus housing available for 248 married students, 1000 single students. Annual academic year housing costs: $3200–$3360 single students (room only); $7200 married students. Contact Housing Office for on- and off-campus housing information. Phone: (618)892-3931. Day-care facilities available.

Graduate Studies and Research

Enrollment: full-time 750, part-time 1378. Faculty: full-time 350, part-time 115. Degrees conferred: M.A., M.B.A., M.F.A., M.M., M.M.R., M.P.A., M.S.A., M.S.C.E., M.S., M.S.Ed., M.S.E., M.S.E.E., Specialist, Ed.D.

ADMISSION REQUIREMENTS. Transcripts required in support of School's application. GRE/MAT/GMAT, letters of recommendation required in some programs. Online application available. TOEFL required for international applicants. Graduates of unaccredited institutions considered. Apply to Graduate Admissions Office (Box 1047) at least three months prior to registration. Application fee $30. Phone: (618)692-3010; fax: (618) 650-3523.

ADMISSION STANDARDS. Selective. Usual minimum average: 2.5 (A = 4).

FINANCIAL AID. Annual awards from institutional funds: academic scholarships, fellowships, assistantships, stipends, tuition remission program, internships, grants, Federal W/S, loans. Approved for VA benefits. Apply by March 1 to appropriate department Chair for assistantships; to Office of Financial Aid for all other programs date. Use FAFSA. Aid available for part-time students.

DEGREE REQUIREMENTS. For master's: minimum 32 credit program, at least 27 in residence; thesis/nonthesis option/

research project; internships/practicum; exhibitions/recitals; final exam. For Specialist: 30 credits beyond the master's degree. For Ed.D.: 72 credits, at least two years in residence; qualifying exam; dissertation; final oral exam.

FIELDS OF STUDY.

COLLEGE OF ARTS AND SCIENCES:
Art Studio. M.F.A.
Art Therapy Counseling. M.A.
Biological Sciences. M.A., M.S.
Chemistry. M.S.
English. M.A.
Environmental Sciences. M.S.
Geographical Studies. M.S.
History. M.A.
Mass Communications. M.S.
Mathematics. M.S.
Music. M.M.
Physics. M.S.
Public Administration. M.P.A.
Social Work. M.S.W.
Sociology. M.A.
Speech Communication. M.A.

SCHOOL OF BUSINESS:
Accountancy. M.S.A.
Business Administration. M.B.A.
Computer Management and Information Systems. M.S.
Economics and Finance. M.A., M.S.
Marketing Research. M.M.R.

SCHOOL OF EDUCATION:
Educational Administration. M.S., S.D.
Elementary Education. M.S.Ed.
Instructional Design and Learning Technologies. M.S.Ed.
Kinesiology. M.S.Ed.
Learning, Culture and Society. M.S.Ed.
Literacy Education (K–12). M.S.Ed.
Psychology. M.A., M.S., S.D.
Secondary Education. M.S.Ed.
Special Education. M.S.Ed.
Speech Pathology. M.S.
Teaching. M.A.T.

SCHOOL OF ENGINEERING:
Civil Engineering. M.S.
Computer Science. M.S.
Electrical and Computer Engineering. M.S.
Mechanical Engineering. M.S.

SCHOOL OF NURSING:
Nursing. M.S.

UNIVERSITY OF SOUTHERN MAINE
Portland, Maine 04103-9300
Web site: www.usm.maine.edu

Founded in 1878 as Gorham State College and in 1970 merged with the University of Maine at Portland to form the University of Southern Maine. Library: 620,000 volumes, 7600 subscriptions.

Tuition: per hour resident $297, nonresident $844. Limited on-campus housing during academic year. On-campus housing available in summer. Contact Resident Life Office for both on- and off-campus housing information. Phone: (207)780-5158. Day-care facilities available.

Graduate Studies and Research

Graduate study authorized in 1964. Enrollment: full-time 700, part-time 1100. Graduate programs are evenings, Saturdays and Summer sessions. Graduate faculty: full- and part-time 140. Degrees conferred: M.A., M.B.A., M.O.T., M.S., M.S.A., M.S.Ad.Ed., M.S.Ed.

ADMISSION REQUIREMENTS. Two transcripts, three references, GRE/GMAT/MAT, essay required in support of application. Additional materials may be required. Interview recommended. TOEFL required for international applicants. Accepts transfer applicants. Apply to Office of Graduate Affairs by March 1 for priority consideration. Departmental deadlines may vary. Rolling admissions process. Application fee $50. Phone: (207)780-4386; fax: (207)780-4959.

ADMISSION STANDARDS. Competitive. Usual minimum average: 2.75 (A = 4).

FINANCIAL AID. Graduate assistantships, internships, tuition waivers, Federal W/S, loans. Approved for VA benefits. Apply to Office of Graduate Affairs by February 15. Phone: (207)780-5250. Use FAFSA (School code: 009762).

DEGREE REQUIREMENTS. Variable by program; most master's degree require 32–36 credits; thesis/nonthesis option. Nearly all degree programs are offered at the Portland or Gorham campuses, Occupational Therapy offered at Lewiston-Auburn campus.

FIELDS OF STUDY.

COLLEGE OF ARTS AND SCIENCES:
American and New England Studies. M.A.
Biology. M.S.
Creative Writing. M.F.A.
Music. M.M.
Social Work. M.S.W.
Statistics. M.S.

COLLEGE OF EDUCATION AND HUMAN DEVELOPMENT:
Adult Education. M.S.A.Ed.
Counselor Education. Includes school, clinical counseling, rehabilitation counseling, psychosocial rehabilitation counseling. M.S.Ed.
Educational Leadership. Includes teacher leadership administration, special education administration. M.S.Ed.
Literacy Education. Includes ESL. M.S.Ed.
School Psychology. M.S.Ed., Psy.D.
Special Education. Includes elementary education, gifted child education, secondary education. M.S.Ed.
Teaching and Learning. M.S.Ed.

COLLEGE OF NURSING AND HEALTH PROFESSIONS:
Nursing.

SCHOOL OF APPLIED SCIENCE, ENGINEERING AND TECHNOLOGY:
Applied Medical Sciences.
Computer Science.

SCHOOL OF BUSINESS:
Accounting.
Business Administration.

EDMUND S. MUSKIE SCHOOL OF PUBLIC SERVICE:
Community Planning and Development.
Health Policy and Management.
Public Policy.
Public Policy and Management.

SOUTHERN METHODIST UNIVERSITY
Dallas, Texas 75275
Web site: www.smu.edu

Founded 1911. CGS member. Located 5 miles N of downtown. Coed. Private control. Methodist affiliation. Semester system. Special facilities: university herbarium, Dallas Seismological Observatory, Statistical Research Laboratory, Shuler Museum of Paleontology, Institute for the Study of Earth and Man, Electron Microscopy Laboratory, Fort Burgwin Research Center, The Meadows Collection of Art, Computing Laboratory, Environmental Engineering Science Center. Library: 3,100,000 volumes, 11,200 subscriptions. Total University enrollment: 11,100.

Tuition: per credit $771. On-campus housing for married and single graduate students. Approximate average academic year housing costs: $5000 for married students, $3400–$4500 (room only) for single students. Contact Office of Housing for both on- and off-campus housing information. Phone: (214)768-2407. Day-care facilities available.

Dedman College

Tuition: per credit $1145.
Enrollment: full-time 160, part-time 275. Faculty: full- and part-time 175. Degrees conferred: M.A., M.B.E., M.S., Ph.D.

ADMISSION REQUIREMENTS. Two transcripts, GRE, two to four letters of recommendation required in support of College's application. GRE Subject Test required for some departments. TOEFL required for international applicants. Interview not required. Accepts transfer applicants. Graduates of unaccredited institutions not considered. Apply to Office of Research and Graduate Studies; no specified closing date. Application fee $60. Phone: (214)768-4202.

ADMISSION STANDARDS. Selective. Minimum average: 3.0 or GRE V + Q score of 1100. TOEFL minimum score 550.

FINANCIAL AID. Annual awards from institutional funds: scholarships, teaching fellowships, research fellowships, full and partial tuition waivers, internships, Federal W/S, loans. Apply by May 1 to appropriate department for fellowships, assistantships; to Financial Aid Office for all other aid. Phone: (214)768-3314. Use FAFSA. About 60% of students receive aid other than loans from College and outside sources. Aid available for part-time students.

DEGREE REQUIREMENTS. For M.A., M.S.: 30 semester hours minimum, at least one year or its equivalent in residence for most programs; thesis/nonthesis option; comprehensive written/oral exam. For Ph.D.: generally three years beyond the bachelor's degree, at least one year in residence; qualifying exam; reading knowledge of one foreign language for most programs; dissertation; final oral exam.

FIELDS OF STUDY.
Anthropology. Includes medical anthropology. M.A., Ph.D.
Applied Geophysics. M.S.
Biology. GRE Subject Test in biology required for admission. M.A., M.S., Ph.D.
Chemistry. GRE Subject Test in chemistry required for admission. M.S.
Computational and Applied Mathematics. M.A., Ph.D.
Economics. Includes applied, GRE if GPA is below 3.0. M.A., Ph.D.
English. GRE Subject Test in literature required for admission. M.A., Ph.D.
Geology. M.S., Ph.D.
Geophysics. M.S., Ph.D.
History. M.A., Ph.D.
Latin American Studies. M.A. only.

Liberal Arts.
Mathematical Sciences. Includes applied (M.S.), mathematics (M.A.).
Medieval Studies. M.A.
Physics. M.S., Ph.D.
Psychology. Includes general/experimental (M.A., Ph.D.), clinical and counseling (Ph.D. only); MMPI release form required for clinical and counseling.
Religious Studies. M.A., Ph.D.
Statistical Sciences. M.S., Ph.D.

Meadows School of the Arts

Tuition: per credit $1145.
Enrollment: full-time 91, part-time 83. Graduate faculty: full-time 88, part-time 25. Degrees conferred: M.A., M.F.A., M.M., M.M.T., M.S.M.

ADMISSION REQUIREMENTS. Transcripts, three letters of recommendation, résumé, qualifying audition required in support of School's application. GRE sometimes required. TOEFL required for international applicants. Apply to Director of Admissions and Records by February 1. Application fee $50. Phone: (214)768-3765; fax: (214)768-3272.

ADMISSION STANDARDS. Selective for most departments, competitive for the others. For most programs talent given greater weight than GPA.

FINANCIAL AID. Scholarships, fellowships, assistantships for teaching/research, internships, Federal W/S, loans. Apply to Financial Aid Office by March 15. Phone: (214)768-3314. Use FAFSA. About 60% of students receive aid from School and outside sources. Aid sometimes available for part-time students.

DEGREE REQUIREMENTS. For M.A.: 36-48 semester hours; reading knowledge of foreign language for some departments; thesis/internship. For M.F.A.: 60–66 semester hours; project. For M.M., M.M.T., M.S.M.: 30 semester hours minimum; recital/final project.

FIELDS OF STUDY.
Art. Includes ceramics, drawing, painting, photography, printmaking, sculpture. M.F.A.
Art History. M.A.
Choral Conducting. M.M.
Dance. M.F.A.
Instrumental Conducting. M.M.
Music Composition. M.M.
Music Education. M.M.
Music History and Literature. M.M.
Music Performance. M.M.
Music Theory. M.M.
Music Therapy. M.P.T.
Piano Performance and Pedagogy. M.M.
Theatre. Includes acting, design. M.F.A.
TV/Radio. Includes mass communication. M.F.A., M.A.

Edwin L. Cox School of Business—
Graduate Division

Graduate study since 1950. Semester system. Special facilities: Maguire Energy Institute, Caruth Institute of Owner-Managed Business, J.C. Penny Center for Retail Exellence.

Annual tuition: full-time M.B.A. $35,530, per credit $1676; $1245 (master's degree); E.M.B.A. $32,534. Enrollment: full-time 268, part-time 656. Graduate faculty: full- and part-time 71. Degrees conferred: M.B.A., E.M.B.A., M.S.A.

ADMISSION REQUIREMENTS. Official transcripts, recommendation, GMAT, interview required in support of School's application. TOEFL required of international applicants. Accepts transfer applicants. Graduates of unaccredited institutions not considered. Apply by April 30 (Fall), December 30 (Spring) to Graduate Admissions Office. Rolling admissions process. Application fee $75. Phone: (214)768-3012; fax: (214)768-3713.

ADMISSION STANDARDS. Competitive. Usual minimum average: 3.0 (A = 4).

FINANCIAL AID. Merit-based scholarships, fellowships, research assistantships, internships, tuition waivers, Federal W/S, loans. Approved for VA benefits. Apply by March 1 to the Office of the Dean for assistantships; to Office of Financial Aid for all other programs. Phone: (214)768-3417. Use FAFSA (School code: 003613). Aid available for part-time students.

DEGREE REQUIREMENTS. For M.B.A.: 45–60 semester hours, depending upon previous degree program. For M.S.A.: 30-credit program.

FIELDS OF STUDY.
Accounting. M.S.
Business Administration. M.B.A.
Entrepreneurship. M.S.
Management. M.S.

School of Engineering and Applied Science—Graduate Division
Web site: www.seas.smu.edu

Graduate study since 1949. Semester system.
Tuition: per credit $870. Enrollment: full-time 205, part-time 904. Graduate faculty: full-time 51, part-time 15. Degrees conferred: M.S., D.Eng., Ph.D.

ADMISSION REQUIREMENTS. Official transcripts, GRE required in support of School's application. TOEFL required for international applicants. Interview not required. Accepts transfer applicants with up to 6 hours of transfer credits. Graduates of unaccredited institutions not considered. Apply to Director of Graduate Division, School of Engineering and Applied Science by application deadline on back of form. Application fee $30. Phone: (214)768-1456; fax: (214)768-3845.

ADMISSION STANDARDS. Selective. Usual minimum average: 3.0 (A = 4).

FINANCIAL AID. Annual awards from institutional funds: research/teaching fellowships, research/teaching assistantships, internships, tuition waivers, Federal W/S, loans. Approved for VA benefits. Apply by May 1 to Director of Graduate Division for assistantships, fellowship; to Financial Aid Office for all other programs. Phone: (214)768-3417; fax: (214)768-3878. Use FAFSA. About 90% of students receive aid other than loans from School and outside sources.

DEGREE REQUIREMENTS. For M.S.: 30 semester hours minimum, 24 in residence; thesis/nonthesis option. For Ph.D.: 78 semester hours minimum, at least 30 in residence; qualifying exam; dissertation; final exam. For D.Eng.: 78 hours required; essentially the same as for Ph.D., praxis required.

FIELDS OF STUDY.
Applied Science. M.S., Ph.D.
Civil Engineering. M.S., Ph.D.
Computer Engineering. M.S., Ph.D.
Computer Science. M.S., Ph.D.
Electrical Engineering. M.S., Ph.D.
Engineering Management. M.S., D.Eng.
Environmental Systems Management. M.S.
Facilities Management. M.S.F.M.

Hazardous and Waste Materials Management. M.S.
Information Engineering and Management. M.S.I.E.
Manufacturing Systems Management. M.S.
Mechanical Engineering. M.S., Ph.D.
Operations Research. M.S., Ph.D.
Packaging of Electronic and Optical Devices. M.S.
Security Engineering. M.S.
Software Engineering. M.S.
Systems Engineering. M.S.
Telecommunication. M.S.

School of Law (75275-0110)
Web site: www.law.smu.edu

Established 1925. Graduate program since 1950. ABA approved since 1927. AALS member. Semester system. Full- and part-time study; LL.M. both full- and part-time study. Special facilities: Center for Pacific Rim Legal Studies, Center for NAFTA and Latin American Legal Studies. Special programs: Summer study abroad at University College, Oxford University, England. Law library: 601,946 volumes, 5260 subscriptions; has LEXIS, WESTLAW; is a Federal Government Depository.

Annual tuition: full-time $32,844, part-time $24,633, LL.M. $32,844. On-campus housing available for both single and married students. Annual on-campus housing cost: $18,000 single students, married students $20,200. Contact Office of Housing for both on- and off-campus housing information. Phone: (214)768-2407. Law students can live off-campus. Off-campus housing and personal expenses: approximately $13,000.

Enrollment: first-year class full-time 181, part-time 109; total full-time 554, part-time 328 (men 54%, women 46%, minorities 23%); very few part-time students. Faculty: full-time 40, part-time 25. Student to faculty ratio 15.4 to 1. Degrees conferred: J.D., J.D.-M.B.A., J.D.-M.A. (Economics), LL.M. (General, Taxation), LL.M. (Comparative and International Law; for persons who have completed a basic legal education and received a university degree in law in another country), S.J.D.

ADMISSION REQUIREMENTS. For J.D. program: LSDAS Law School report, bachelor's degree, transcripts, personal statement, résumé, two letters of recommendation, LSAT required in support of application. Accepts transfer applicants. Apply to School of Law by February 15; beginning students admitted Fall only. For graduate program: transcripts, letters of recommendation required in support of application. Interview not required. Graduates of unaccredited colleges not considered. Apply to Secretary, Committee on Graduate Studies, School of Law, by February 15. Application fee $60. Phone: (214)768-2550; fax: (214)768-4390.

ADMISSION REQUIREMENTS FOR LL.M. APPLICANTS (General, Taxation). Must have a J.D. from an ABA-accredited law school; must have graduated in the top half of class. Official transcripts including rank-in-class, two letters of recommendation, a statement of interest in graduate study required in support of application. Admits Fall and Spring, for full- and part-time study. Apply by April 1 (Fall), December 1 (Spring). Application fee $60. Phone: (214)768-2550.

ADMISSION REQUIREMENTS FOR LL.M. APPLICANTS. (Comparative and International Law). Must be graduates of a recognized foreign law school. Official U.S. Law School transcripts or certified translation and evaluation of all foreign credentials; TOEFL for all applicants whose native language is not English, short curriculum vitae, two letters of recommendation, evidence of financial ability to pay degree expenses required in support of application. Admits full-time and Fall only. Application fee $60. Phone: (214)768-2550.

ADMISSION STANDARDS. Selective. Accepts approximately 23% of full-time, 29% of part-time students. Number of full-time applicants 2399, part-time 578; number of full-time acceptance

545, part-time 169; number of full-time enrolled 181, part-time 109; LSAT (75% of full-time students have a score at or above 155, part-time 153); GPA (75% of full-time students have a GPA at or above 3.31, part-time 2.98). *U.S. News & World Report* ranking is in the top 46 of all U.S. law schools.

FINANCIAL AID. For J.D. program: scholarships, Federal W/S, loans. Apply to Director of Financial Aid by February 15. Phone: (214)768-1588. Use FAFSA. For graduate program: scholarships, fellowships; apply to Chair of Committee on Graduate Studies by May 1. About 75% of full-time and 17% of part-time students receive aid other than loans from School.

DEGREE REQUIREMENTS. For J.D.: 90 semester hours minimum, at least last 6 semesters in residence. For LL.M.: at least 24 semester hours minimum, one year in full-time residence. For S.J.D.: one year minimum in residence; thesis; oral exam.

UNIVERSITY OF SOUTHERN MISSISSIPPI
Hattiesburg, Mississippi 39406-0066
Web site: www.usm.edu

Founded 1910. Located 90 miles SE of Jackson. CGS member. Coed. State control. Semester system. Special facilities: Automation and Robotics Application Center, Bureau of Educational Research, Gulf Coast Research Laboratory, Health Related Sciences Institute, Institute of Environmental Science, the Mississippi Polymer Institute, Physical Fitness Institute. Library: 872,000 volumes, 4500 subscriptions.

Annual tuition: full-time resident $6778, nonresident $12,784. On-campus housing for 296 married and 4700 single students. Average academic year housing cost: $4500 for married students, $3200 for single students. Contact Resident Life Office for both on- and off-campus housing information. Phone: (601)266-4783. Day-care facilities available.

Graduate School

Established 1947. Enrollment: full-time 1242, part-time 1124. Faculty: full-time 654, part-time 73. Degrees conferred: M.A., M.S., M.Ed., M.B.A., M.F.A., M.L.S., M.M., M.M.E., M.P.A., M.S.N., M.S.W., Ed.S., Ed.D., Ph.D.

ADMISSION REQUIREMENTS. Two transcripts, GRE/GMAT/MAT/NTE Test, two recommendations required in support of School's application. Interview may be required. TOEFL required for international applicants. Accepts transfer applicants. Apply by July 15 (Fall), November 15 (Spring) to Director of Graduate Admissions. Some programs have earlier deadlines. Rolling admissions process. Application fee $0, $25 for international applicants. Phone: (601)266-5137; fax: (601)266-5138.

ADMISSION STANDARDS. Selective for most departments. Usual minimum average: 2.75 (A = 4).

FINANCIAL AID. Annual awards from institutional funds: scholarships, teaching assistantships, fellowships, internships, tuition waivers, Federal W/S, loans. Apply by March 15 to Dean for assistantships, fellowships; to Financial Aid Office for all other programs. Phone: (601)266-4774. Use FAFSA. About 60% of students receive aid from School and outside sources. Aid available for part-time students.

DEGREE REQUIREMENTS. For master's: 30 semester hours minimum, at least 15 in residence; reading knowledge of one foreign language; thesis required for many majors; final written/oral exam. For M.Ed., M.S. in Teaching: same as above, except no thesis requirement. For Ed.S.: 30 hours minimum beyond the master's, at least one quarter in full-time residence; final written exam. For Ph.D.: 78 hours minimum beyond the bachelor's, at least two consecutive semesters in full-time residence; reading knowledge of two foreign languages or one language and statistics; preliminary exam; dissertation; final written/oral exam. For Ed.D.: essentially same as for Ph.D., except MAT for candidacy, no language requirement; knowledge of statistics required.

FIELDS OF STUDY.
Accounting. M.P.A.
Administration of Justice. Includes corrections, forensics juvenile. M.A., M.S., Ph.D.
Adult Education. M.Ed.
Anthropology. M.A.
Art Education. M.A.Ed.
Biological Sciences. Includes environmental biology, marine biology, microbiology, molecular biology. Ph.D.
Business Administration. M.B.A.
Chemistry. Includes biochemistry. M.S., Ph.D.
Child and Family Studies. M.S.
Coastal Sciences. M.S., Ph.D.
Communication. Includes mass, speech. M.A., M.S., Ph.D.
Computational Sciences. Includes computer science, mathematics, physics. Ph.D.
Computer Science. Includes computational science. M.S.
Counseling and Personnel Services. Includes college student personnel, school counseling. M.S.
Early Intervention. M.S.
Economic Development. M.S.
Education. Includes adult, elementary, educational administration, secondary, special. Ed.D., Ph.D.
Educational Administration/Supervision. M.Ed.
Educational Curriculum and Instruction. Includes early childhood, elementary, reading, secondary. M.Ed., M.S.
Engineering Technology. Includes architecture and construction visualization, construction management and technology, logistics management and technology. M.S.
English. Includes creative writing, literature. M.A., Ph.D.
Geography. M.S., Ph.D.
Geology. M.S.
Higher Educational Administration. Ed.D., Ph.D.
History. Includes European, international studies, Latin American, war & society, United States. M.A., M.S., Ph.D.
Human Capital Development. Ph.D.
Human Performance. Includes exercise, physical education. M.S., Ph.D.
Hydrographic Science. M.S.
International Development. Ph.D.
Interscholastic Athlete Administration. M.S.
Instructional Technology. M.S.
Library Information Science. M.L.I.S.
Marine Science. Includes biological, chemical, geological, physical. M.S., Ph.D.
Marriage Family Therapy. M.S.
Mathematics. Includes computational science. M.S.
Medical Technology. M.S.
Music. Includes conducting, history and literature, performance-piano accompany, performance, theory and composition, woodwind performance and pedagogy. M.M.
Music Education. M.M.E., Ph.D.
Nursing. Includes adult health nursing, community health nursing, family nurse practitioner, nursing service administration, psychiatric nursing, psychiatric nurse practitioner (M.S.N.), ethics, leadership, policy analysis (Ph.D.).
Nutrition and Food Systems. M.S., Ph.D.
Philosophy. M.A.
Physics. Includes computational science, polymer physics. M.S.
Political Science. M.A., M.S.
Polymer Science. M.S.
Polymer Science and Engineering. Ph.D.

Psychology. Includes counseling, experimental (M.S.), clinical, counseling, experimental school (Ph.D.).

Public Health. Includes epidemiology, health education, health policy and administration, health services administration, occupational and environmental, public health nutrition. M.P.H.

Public Relations. M.S.

Recreation and Leisure Administration. M.S.

Science Education. Includes biology, chemistry, coastal, earth science, mathematics, physics. M.S., Ph.D.

Social Work. M.S.W.

Special Education. Includes behavioral disorders, gifted, learning disabilities, mental retardation, severe mental retardation. M.Ed.

Speech/Hearing Science. Includes education of deaf, speech-language pathology. M.A., M.S.

Sport Coaching Education. M.S.

Sport and High School Performance Material. M.S., Ph.D.

Teaching of Languages. Includes French, Spanish, TESOL. M.A.T.L.

Technology Education. Includes business technology, technology and occupational education. M.S.

Theatre. Includes design and technical theatre, performance. M.F.A.

SOUTHERN NAZARENE UNIVERSITY
Bethany, Oklahoma 73008-2694
Web site: www.snu.edu

From 1920–1955 was known as Bethany-Peniel College; name changed in 1986. Coed. Semester system. Affiliated with Church of the Nazarene. Library: 105,000 volumes, 325 subscriptions, 10 PCs.

Tuition: per semester hour $385. On-campus housing available for 60 married students, limited for single graduate students. Average academic year housing costs: single students $3800–$5500 (including board); married students per month $350–$500. Contact Dean of Student Services for both on- and off-campus housing information. Phone: (405)491-6316.

Graduate Studies

Graduate program began in 1963. Enrollment: full-time 168, part-time 102 (men 132, women 139). Faculty: full-time 25. Degrees conferred: M.A., M.A.M.F.T., M.S.Mgt., M.Min., M.S.C.P.

ADMISSION REQUIREMENTS. Transcripts, MAT/GMAT, three letters of recommendation required in support of College's application. Interview strongly recommended. TOEFL (minimum score 550) required for international applicants. Accepts transfer applicants. Graduates of unaccredited institutions considered on a conditional basis. Apply to Director of Graduate Studies by August 1 (Fall), December 1 (Spring). Application fee $25. International application fee $35. Phone: (405)491-6316, (405)491-6302. Tulsa campus phone: (918)644-4100.

ADMISSION STANDARDS. Selective. Usual minimum average: 2.5 (A = 4) on last 60 hours.

FINANCIAL AID. Limited teaching fellowships, loans. Approved for VA benefits. Apply to the Financial Aid Office by March 1. Phone: (405)491-6685; fax: (405)491-6381. Use FAFSA.

DEGREE REQUIREMENTS. For master's: 32 semester hours minimum; thesis optional; comprehensive exam.

FIELDS OF STUDY.
Business Administration.
Church Leadership.
Counseling Psychology.
Curriculum and Instruction.
Educational Leadership.
Executive M.B.A. in Ethical Leadership.

Management.
Marriage and Family Therapy.
Nursing.
Theology.

SOUTHERN OREGON UNIVERSITY
Ashland, Oregon 97520
Web site: www.sou.edu

Founded 1926. Located 300 miles S of Portland. Coed. State control. Quarter system. Library: 275,000 volumes, 760,000 microforms, 2137 current periodicals.

Annual tuition: full-time resident $10,620, nonresident $17,541. On-campus housing: 60 units for married students, 2000 single students. Average academic year housing costs: $4800 for married students, $7941 for single students (includes board). Apply to Director of Student Services for off-campus housing information. Phone: (541)552-6371 (single students), (541)488-4401 (married students).

Graduate Division

Graduate study since 1952. Enrollment: full-time 163, part-time 162. College faculty: full-time 170, part-time 10. Degrees conferred: M.A., M.S., M.M., M.A.P.

ADMISSION REQUIREMENTS. Transcripts, GRE/GMAT/NTE, three letters of recommendation, goal statement or letter of intent required in support of application. Online application available. TOEFL (minimum score 540) required for applicants whose native language is not English. Interview may be required for some programs. Accepts transfer applicants. Apply to Admission Office by April 15 (Fall), October 15 (Winter), January 15 (Spring and Summer). Application fee $50. Phone: (541)552-6411.

ADMISSION STANDARDS. Selective. Usual minimum average: 3.0 (A = 4).

FINANCIAL AID. Graduate assistantships, loans. Approved for VA benefits. Apply to Director of Financial Aid by February 15. Phone: (541) 482-6181. Use FAFSA (School code: 003219).

DEGREE REQUIREMENTS. For master's: 45 quarter hours minimum, at least 30 in residence; thesis or project option; final oral/written comprehensive exam.

FIELDS OF STUDY.
Applied Psychology. M.A.P.
Arts and Letters (Foreign Languages). M.A.L.
Arts and Letters (Theatre Arts). M.A., M.A.
Business Administration. M.B.A.
Conducting. In association with American Band College. M.M.
Elementary Education. M.A., M.S.
Environmental Education. M.S.
Management. M.M.
Mathematical and Computer Sciences. M.A., M.S.
Secondary Education. M.A., M.S.
Teaching. M.A.T.

SOUTHERN UNIVERSITY AND AGRICULTURAL AND MECHANICAL COLLEGE
P.O. Box 9860
Baton Rouge, Louisiana 70813
Web site: www.subr.edu

Founded 1880. CGS member. Coed. State control. Semester system. Special facilities: Health Research Center, Environmental and Energy Institute, Center for Sickle Cell Disease Research, National Plant Data Center, Small Farm Family Resource Development Center, Research Institute of Pure and Applied Sciences, Center for Social Research. Library: 808,300 volumes, 4000 subscriptions. Total University enrollment: 10,000.

Annual tuition: full-time resident $3724, nonresident $5166; part-time varies according to course load. On-campus housing available for single students only. Average academic year housing costs: $7700–$8800 (including board). Contact Housing Office for both on- and off-campus housing. Phone: (225)771-3590.

Graduate School

Established 1956. Enrollment: full-time 656, part-time 679. Faculty: full- and part-time 146. Degrees conferred: M.A., M.Ed., M.P.A., M.S., Ph.D.

ADMISSION REQUIREMENTS. Transcripts required in support of School's application. GRE/GMAT recommended. Interview not required. TOEFL required for international applicants. Accepts transfer applicants. Graduates of unaccredited institutions not considered. Apply to Graduate Office by April 15 (Fall), November 1 (Spring), May 1 (Summer). Rolling admissions process. Application fee $25. Phone: (225)771-5390; fax: (225)771-5723.

ADMISSION STANDARDS. Selective for most departments. Usual minimum average: 2.5 (A = 4).

FINANCIAL AID. Annual awards from institutional funds: teaching assistantships, research assistantships, Federal W/S, loans. Approved for VA benefits. Apply at least thirty days prior to registration to Dean of the Graduate School for assistantships; to the Office of Financial Aid for all other programs. Phone: (225)771-2790. Use FAFSA. About 10% of students receive aid other than loans from School. Aid available for part-time students.

DEGREE REQUIREMENTS. For master's: 30–36 semester hours minimum, at least 24 in residence and 18 weeks in full-time attendance; thesis required for M.A., optional for other degrees; final written/oral exam. For Ph.D.: 60 credit minimum beyond bachelor's; foreign language requirement; qualifying exam; candidacy; dissertation; oral defense.

FIELDS OF STUDY.
Accountancy. M.P.A.
Administration and Supervision. M.Ed.
Biochemistry. M.S.
Biology. M.S.
Chemistry. Includes analytical, environmental, inorganic, organic, physical. M.S.
Computer Science. Includes operating/information systems, educational computing. M.S.
Counselor Education. M.A.
Criminal Justice. M.C.J.
Elementary Education. M.Ed.
Engineering. M.E.
Environmental Sciences. M.S.
Environmental Toxicology. Ph.D.
Information Systems. M.S.
Mass Communication. M.A.
Mathematics. M.S.
Media. M.Ed.
Mental Health Counseling. M.A.
Micro/Minicomputer Architecture. M.S.
Nursing. M.S.N., Ph.D.
Physics. M.S.
Public Policy and Urban Affairs. Ph.D.
Public Administration. M.P.A.
Rehabilitation Counseling. M.S.
Secondary Education. Includes agriculture, biology, business education, chemistry, English, health and physical education, home economics, industrial arts, mathematics, music, social studies. M.Ed.
Science/Mathematics Education. Ph.D.
Social Sciences. Interdisciplinary. Includes history, political science, sociology. M.A.
Special Education. M.Ed., Ph.D.
Speech-Language Pathology. M.S.
Therapeutic Recreation. M.S.
Urban Forestry. M.S., Ph.D.

Law Center

P.O. Box 9294

Founded 1947. ABA approved since 1953. AALS member. Semester system. Law library: 426,386 volumes, 4402 subscriptions; has LEXIS, NEXIS, WESTLAW, DIALOG.

Annual tuition: resident $6611, nonresident $11,211. On-campus housing available. Total average annual additional expense: $12,300.

Enrollment: first-year class 112; total full-time 394 (men 46%, women 54%, minorities 58%). Faculty: full-time 24, part-time 7. Student to faculty ratio 11.9 to 1. Degree conferred: J.D.

ADMISSION REQUIREMENTS. LSDAS Law School report, bachelor's degree, transcripts, LSAT (prior to March test date), two letters of recommendation, narrative on why one selects the field of law required in support of application. Interview may be requested. Accepts transfer applicants. Graduates of unaccredited colleges not considered. Apply to Office of Admissions by March 30. Beginning students admitted Fall only. Application fee $25. Phone: (504)771-5340, (800)537-1135.

ADMISSION STANDARDS. Selective. Mean LSAT: 146; mean GPA: 2.68 (A = 4). *U.S. News & World Report* ranking is in the fourth tier of all U.S. law schools. Accepts 35% of total annual applicants.

FINANCIAL AID. Scholarships, assistantships, Federal W/S, loans. Apply Financial Aid Committee by April 15. Use FAFSA (Law Center code: 002025). About 26% of students receive aid other than loans from School.

DEGREE REQUIREMENTS. For J.D.: 96 semester hours, 6 semesters in residence.

SOUTHWEST MISSOURI STATE UNIVERSITY
Springfield, Missouri 65897
Web site: www.missouristate.edu

Founded 1905. CGS member. Semester system. State control. Special facilities: Center for Archaeological Research, Center for Business and Research, Center for Cultural Programs and Development, Center for Economic Research, Center for Gerontological Studies, Center for Ozarks Studies, Center for Human Resources and Service, Center for Resource Planning and Management. Library: 771,300 volumes, 9000 subscriptions. Total University enrollment: 17,000.

Tuition: per credit, resident $206, nonresident $349. On-campus housing available. Average academic year housing costs: $5000–$6000 room/suite style (includes 20 meals per week); $375–$500 per month apartment style. Contact Residence Life for both on- and off-campus housing information. Phone: (417) 836-5536. Day-care facilities available.

Graduate College

Enrollment: full-time 854, part-time 2150. Faculty: full-time 396, part-time 19. Degrees conferred: M.A., M.B.A., M.P.A., M.M., M.S., M.S.Ed., M.S.N., M.S.W., Ed.S.

ADMISSION REQUIREMENTS. Official transcripts, letters of recommendation, résumé required in support of application. On-line application available. TOEFL required for foreign applicants. GRE/GMAT/MAT required for some programs. Accepts transfer applicants. Graduates of unaccredited institutions not considered. Apply to Graduate College at least six weeks prior to registration. Rolling admissions process. Application fee $35, $50 for international applicants. Phone(417)836-5335; fax: (417)836-6888.

ADMISSION STANDARDS. Selective. Usual minimum average: 2.75 (A = 4) or satisfactory GRE or GMAT scores.

FINANCIAL AID. Assistantships, internships, grants, Federal W/S, loans. Apply by April 1 to department head for assistantships; to Financial Aid Office for all other programs. Phone: (417)836-5262; fax: (417)836-8392. Use FAFSA (School code: 002503).

DEGREE REQUIREMENTS. For master's: 32-47 semester hours minimum; research project; comprehensive exam. For Ed.S.: 70 semester hours minimum; research project; comprehensive exam.

FIELDS OF STUDY.
Accounting.
Administrative Studies.
Applied Anthropology.
Audiology.
Biology.
Business Administration.
Cell and Molecular Biology.
Chemistry.
Communication.
Communication Sciences and Disorders.
Computer Information Systems.
Counseling.
Criminology.
Defense and Strategic Studies.
Early Childhood and Development.
Educational Administration.
Elementary Education.
English.
Geospatial Sciences in Geography and Geology.
Health Administration.
Health Promotion and Wellness Management.
History.
Instructional Media Technology.
International Affairs and Administration.
Materials Science.
Mathematics.
Music.
Natural and Applied Science.
Nurse Anesthesia.
Nursing.
Physical Therapy.
Physician Assistant Studies.
Plant Science.
Project Management.
Psychology.
Public Administration.
Public Health.
Reading.
Religious Studies.
Resource Planning.
Secondary Education.
Social Work.
Special Education.
Student Affairs.
Teaching.
Theater.
Writing.

SOUTHWESTERN OKLAHOMA STATE UNIVERSITY
100 Campus Drive
Weatherford, Oklahoma 73096-3098
Web site: www.swosu.edu

Founded in 1903. Located 70 miles west of Oklahoma City. Coed. State control. Semester system. Library: 250,000 bound volumes, 1300 subscriptions.

Tuition: per credit hour, resident 3000–4000 level—$125; 5000 level—$150, nonresident 3000–4000 level—$285; 5000 level—$350. On-campus housing for 64 married students, 1547 single students. Average academic year housing costs: $4140 (including board) for single students; $3890 for married students. Contact the Director of Student Housing for both on- and off-campus housing information. Phone: (580)774-3024.

Graduate School

Graduate study since 1953. Enrollment: full-time 454, part-time 242. Faculty: full- and part-time 131. Degrees conferred: M.Ed., M.S.A.P., M.B.A., M.M.

ADMISSION REQUIREMENTS. Official transcripts, GRE/GMAT required in support of School's application. Letters of reference for some programs. TOEFL (minimum score 550) required for international applicants. Interview not required. Accepts transfer applicants (maximum transfer credits: 9 hours). Graduates of unaccredited institutions not considered. Apply to Dean of the Graduate School; no specified closing date. Application fee $15. Phone: (580)774-3790; fax: (580)774-7043.

ADMISSION STANDARDS. Usual minimum average: 2.5 (A = 4). Applicants must meet minimum formula of undergraduate GPA plus GRE or GMAT score.

FINANCIAL AID. Fellowships, research assistantships, teaching assistantships, internships, tuition waivers, Federal W/S, loans. Approved for VA benefits. Apply to Director of Financial Aid by March 1. Phone: (580)774-3786; fax: (580)774-3795. Use FAFSA and institutional FAF. Aid available for part-time students.

DEGREE REQUIREMENTS. For M.Ed.: 32 semester hours. For M.B.A.: 33 semester hours. For M.S.A.P.: 36 semester hours. For M.M.: 32 semester hours; final comprehensive exam.

FIELDS OF STUDY.
Art.
Business Administration.
Community Counseling.
Early Childhood.
Educational Administration.
Elementary Education.
English.
Health and Physical Education.
Mathematics.
Music Education. Includes choral, conducting, church music, instrumental, performance. M.M. only.
Natural Sciences.
Reading Specialist.
School Counseling.
School Psychology.
School Psychometry.
Secondary Education. Includes English, mathematics, natural sciences, social sciences, technology.
Social Sciences.
Special Education.
Technology.

SOUTHWESTERN UNIVERSITY SCHOOL OF LAW

675 South Westmoreland Avenue
Los Angeles, California 90010-1106
Web site: www.swlaw.edu

Established 1911. Located in downtown Los Angeles. ABA approved since 1970. AALS member. Private control. Semester system. Full-time, part-time study. Special facility: National Institute of Entertainment and Media Law. Special programs: Southwestern Conceptual Approach to Legal Education (SCALE, a two-year J.D. program), Part-Time Legal Education Alternative at Southwestern (PLEAS, a program designed for students with child care responsibilities); summer study in Entertainment Law; study abroad in Buenos Aires, Argentina; London, England; Vancouver, British Columbia; University of Guanajuato, Mexico; externships. Law library: 467,579 volumes, 4500 subscriptions; has LEXIS, NEXIS, WESTLAW, RLIN, LEGALTRAC, WILSONLINE; has more than 750 network connections.

Annual tuition: full-time $31,700, part-time $19,100. No on-campus housing available. Contact the Admission Office for off-campus housing information. Off-campus housing and personal expenses: approximately $15,650.

Enrollment: first-year class full-time 248, part-time 86; total full- and part-time 964 (men 48%, women 52%, minorities 36%). Faculty: full-time 50, part-time 24. Student to faculty ratio is 15.7 to 1. Degrees conferred: J.D., LL.M. (Entertainment and Media Law).

ADMISSION REQUIREMENTS. LSDAS Law School report, bachelor's degree, transcripts, LSAT, personal statement, up to three letters of recommendation required in support of application. Interviews required for SCALE. Letters of recommendation and supplementary essay recommended. Accepts transfer applicants from ABA approved law schools. Apply to Office of Admissions by April 1. Application fee $60. Phone: (213)738-6717; fax: (213)383-1688. For LL.M.: apply by June 30 (Fall), November 15 (Spring), April 15 (Summer). Phone: (213)738-6602.

ADMISSION STANDARDS. Selective. Accepts approximately 26% of full-time, 25% of part-time students. Number of full-time applicants 3332, part-time 583; number of full-time acceptance 857, part-time 146; number of full-time enrolled 248, part-time 86; LSAT (75% of full-time students have a score at or above 154, part-time 151); GPA (75% of full-time students have a GPA at or above 3.11, part-time 3.10). *U.S. News & World Report* ranking is in the third tier of all U.S. law schools.

FINANCIAL AID. Scholarships, public interest fellowship, tuition waiver, assistantships, Federal W/S, loans. Apply to Financial Aid Office by June 1. Phone: (213)738-6719. Use FAFSA (School code: G01295). About 33% of full-time and 14% of part-time students receive aid other than loans from School or outside sources. Public-Interest Loan Forgiveness Program available.

DEGREE REQUIREMENTS. For J.D.: 87 semester credits in full- or part-time program; completion of two calendar years in SCALE program. For LL.M.: 24-credit program; thesis.

SPALDING UNIVERSITY

Louisville, Kentucky 40203-2188
Web site: www.spalding.edu

Founded 1814. CGS member. Coed. Private control. Roman Catholic. Semester system. Library: 200,000 volumes, 800 subscriptions.

Tuition: per credit hour $595 (most master's), $665 (Ed.D.), $665 (master's in Psychology), $665 (Psy.D.). On-campus housing 20 single graduate students. Average academic year housing costs: $3180. Contact Director of Housing for both on- and off-campus housing information. Phone: (502)858-7139.

Graduate Study

Enrollment: full- and part-time 650. College faculty teaching graduate students: full-time 27, part-time 8. Degrees conferred: M.A., M.A.T., M.F.A., M.S.N., Specialist, Psy.D., Ed.D.

ADMISSION REQUIREMENTS. Official transcripts, GRE required in support of application. TOEFL required for international applicants. Accepts transfer applicants. Graduates of unaccredited institutions not considered. Apply to Graduate Admissions Office at least four weeks prior to registration. Psychology, Social Work, Ed.D. programs admit Fall only; Occupational Therapy admits Spring only. Application fee $30. Phone: (502)585-7111; fax: (502)902-2418.

ADMISSION STANDARDS. Selective. Usual minimum average: 3.0 (proposed major) (A = 4).

FINANCIAL AID. Scholarships, administrative/research assistantships, Federal W/S, loans. Approved for VA benefits. Apply to the Director of Student Financial Aid. Phone: (502)585-9911, ext. 200. Use FAFSA and institutional FAF.

DEGREE REQUIREMENTS. For M.A.: 30 semester hours minimum, at least 24 in residence; written comprehensive exam; research papers. For M.A.T., M.A.L.S.: 36 semester hours minimum. For M.S.N.: 39 semester hours minimum, written comprehensive exam; thesis. For M.F.A.: 60 semester hour program; special project. For Specialist: 30 semester hours beyond the master's. For Psy.D.: M.A. plus 69 semester hours; internship and dissertation; final oral exam. For Ed.D.: M.A. plus 60 semester hours; dissertation; final oral exam. Limit of eight years to complete doctorate.

FIELDS OF STUDY.
Business Communication.
Clinical Psychology. Includes health psychology.
Creative Writing.
Early Elementary Education.
Education.
Elementary Education.
High School Education.
Instructional Computer Technology.
Leadership Education.
Learning Behavior Disorders.
Middle School Education.
Montessori Education.
Nursing. Includes adult nurse practitioner studies, family nurse practitioner, leadership in nursing and health care, pediatric nurse practitioner.
Occupational Therapy.
Pastoral Ministries. M.A.
Reading and Writing.
Religious Studies.
School Guidance.
School Principalship.
Social Work.
TESOL.
Writing. Includes creative writing, fiction, poetry, writing for children. M.F.A.

SPRINGFIELD COLLEGE

Springfield, Massachusetts 01109-3797
Web site: www.spfldcol.edu

Founded 1885. Located 85 miles W of Boston. Coed. Private control. Semester system. Library: 150,000 volumes, 850 subscriptions. Total enrollment: 3150.

Tuition: per credit hour $646. On-campus housing for limited number of married, single students. Average academic year housing costs (room only): $6200 for single students, $8670 for married students. Contact Housing Director for both on- and off-campus housing information. Phone: (413)748-3102. Day-care facilities available.

School of Graduate Studies

Graduate study since 1899. Enrollment: full-time 1048, part-time 375. College faculty: full-time 156, part-time 15. Degrees conferred: M.S., MED., M.P.E., M.S.W., C.A.S., D.P.E.

ADMISSION REQUIREMENTS. Transcripts, letter of recommendation required in support of application. GRE required for M.P.T. and doctoral applicants. TOEFL required for international applicants. Interview sometimes required. Apply to Office of Graduate Admissions, preferably by January 1 (Fall), November 1 (Spring); Occupational Therapy, Physical Therapy January 1 (Fall only), Social Work (March 15). Rolling admission process. Application fee $50. Phone: (413)748-3225; fax: (413)748-3694.

ADMISSION STANDARDS. Selective for most majors. Usual minimum average: 2.5 (A = 4).

FINANCIAL AID. Scholarships, teaching/research assistantships, fellowships, rehabilitation traineeships, residence hall directorships, internships, tuition waivers, Federal W/S, loans. Approved for VA benefits. Apply by March 1 to director of appropriate graduate program for fellowships, assistantships; to Financial Aid Office for all other programs. Phone: (413)748-3108. Use FAFSA, Financial Aid transcript. About 60% of full-time students receive aid other than loans from College and outside sources. No aid for part-time students.

DEGREE REQUIREMENTS. For master's: 32 semester hours minimum, at least 26 in residence; may include thesis with final oral/written exam. For C.A.S.: 32 semester hours minimum beyond the master's, at least 26 in residence. For D.P.E.: 90 semester hours minimum, at least 45 in residence and 30 in full-time attendance; preliminary exam; dissertation; final oral exam.

FIELDS OF STUDY.
Art Therapy. Includes clinical art therapy, studio art therapy.
Education. Includes educational administration, educational studies, early childhood education (Pre-K–2), elementary education (1–6), secondary education, special education.
Exercise Science and Sports Studies. Includes athletic training, exercise physiology, health promotion & disease prevention, sport & exercise psychology, strength & conditioning.
Health Care Management. Includes Health Care Management in Long-term Facilities.
Occupational Therapy.
Physical Education. Includes adapted physical education, advanced-Level Coaching, athletic administration, sport performance.
Physical Therapy.
Physician Assistant.
Psychology and Counseling. Includes athletic counseling, clinical mental health counseling, industrial/organizational psychology, marriage and family therapy, school guidance counseling, student personnel administration in higher education.
Rehabilitation Counseling and Services. Includes alcohol and substance abuse counseling, management and administration, pediatric and development disabilities, psychiatric rehabilitation & mental health counseling, rehabilitation counseling, rehabilitation counseling for the deaf, rehabilitation services.
Social Work.
Sport Management and Recreation. Includes sport management, recreation management, therapeutic recreation management.

STANFORD UNIVERSITY
Stanford, California 94305-9991
Web site: www.stanford.edu

Founded 1891. Graduate study since 1891. Located near Palo Alto, 30 miles SE of San Francisco. CGS and AAU member. Coed. Private control. Quarter system. Special facilities: Center for Chicano Studies, Hopkins Marine Station at Pacific Grove, California, Hoover Institution of War, Revolution, and Peace, Humanities Center, Institute for Energy Studies, Center for International Studies, Institute for Research on Women and Gender, Stanford Medical Center, Computation Center, Center for Materials Research, Stanford Linear Accelerator Center; special laboratories for study in high voltage, electronics, nuclear engineering, physics, biophysics, and microwaves. The University's NIH ranking is 15th among all U.S. institutions with 763 awards/grants valued at $395,561,055. According to The Center at University of Florida, the University is ranked 4th in receipt of Federal Research funds with $483,540,000 and it ranks 8th for total University research expenditures with $603,227,000. The University's endowment assets rank it 4th, with a value of $9,922,000,000. In 2004, the University awarded 625 doctorates which ranked it 2nd among all U.S. institutions eligible to award that degree. Two-hundred fifty-three of the University's faculty members have been elected to National Honor Academies and this ranks it 2nd among all U.S. institutions. The Library: approximately 7,000,000 volumes, 44,000 subscriptions. Total University enrollment: 14,000.

Annual tuition: full-time $34,800, Engineering $37,110. On-campus housing for graduate students: 3000 men and women. Average academic year housing costs: $16,212 single students, $20,000 married students. Contact the Housing Assignment Services for on-campus housing. Phone: (650)725-2810 and Community Housing Service for off-campus housing. Phone: (650)723-3906.

Graduate Study

Graduate study since 1891. Enrollment: full-time 6500. Faculty: full-time 1740. Degrees conferred: A.M., M.S., M.A.T., Engineer, M.F.A., Ed.S., D.M.A., Ed.D., Ph.D.

ADMISSION REQUIREMENTS. Two official copies of all transcripts, GRE, three letters of recommendation in duplicate, statement of purpose required in support of application. GRE Subject Test required for some programs. Online application available. Interview not required. TOEFL/TSE required for international applicants. Accepts transfer applicants. Graduates of unaccredited institutions not considered. Apply to Office of Graduate Admissions by January 1 (Fall). Some programs have earlier deadlines. Most programs admit Fall only. Application fee $105 (online), $125 (paper). Phone: (650)723-4291; fax: (650)725-8371.

ADMISSION STANDARDS. Very competitive for most departments, competitive for the others.

FINANCIAL AID. Annual awards from institutional funds: scholarships, teaching fellowships, research fellowships, Federal W/S, loans. Most scholarships and fellowships have no teaching or research requirements. Apply to Financial Aid Office by December 15 for art, history, biological sciences, and biophysics. Apply by January 1 for schools of Education, Earth Science, Humanities and Science, Medicine (non-M.D.); and chemical, civil, and electrical engineering, and computer science. Apply by February 15 for all other engineering departments, for scholarships and fellowships; to appropriate department for assistantships. Phone: (650)723-3058 or (888)FAO-3773. Use FAFSA. Contact Financial Aid Office for loans. About 72% of students receive aid other than loans from University and outside sources.

DEGREE REQUIREMENTS. For M.A., M.S.: three quarters (36–45 units) minimum in residence, some departments require more; thesis/nonthesis option; written/oral exams in some departments; reading knowledge of one foreign language for some departments. For M.A.T.: three quarters (45 units) minimum in full-time residence; teaching credential. For Engineer: six quarters (71–90 units) minimum, at least three quarters in residence; thesis. For Ed.D.: nine quarters (108–135 units) minimum beyond the bachelor's degree, at least six quarters in residence and two quarters in consecutive full-time attendance; candidacy; dissertation, final oral exam. For D.M.A.: same as for Ed.D., except final project usually replaces dissertation. For Ph.D.: nine quarters (109–135 units) minimum beyond the bachelor's degree, at least six quarters in residence, full-time attendance requirement for most departments; preliminary/final written exams in most departments; candidacy; dissertation; final oral exams.

FIELDS OF STUDY.

SCHOOL OF EARTH SCIENCES:
Earth Energy and Environmental Sciences. M.S., Ph.D.
Energy Resource Engineering. Includes petroleum Engineering. Engr., M.S., Ph.D.
Environment and Resources. Interdisciplinary. M.S., Ph.D.
Geological and Environmental Sciences. M.S., Ph.D.
Geophysics. M.S.

SCHOOL OF EDUCATION:
Administration and Policy Analysis. Ph.D., Ed.D.
Anthropology of Education. Ph.D.
Child and Adolescent Development. Ph.D.
Economics of Education. Ph.D.
Educational Linguistics. Ph.D.
Educational Psychology. Ph.D.
English Education/Literacy Studies. Ph.D.
Evaluation. M.A.
General Curriculum Studies. Ph.D.
Higher Education. Ph.D.
History of Education. Ph.D.
History/Social Sciences Education. Ph.D.
International Comparative Education. M.A., Ph.D.
Interdisciplinary Studies. Ph.D.
Learning, Design, and Technology. M.A., Ph.D.
Mathematics Education. Ph.D.
Science Education. Ph.D.
Social Studies Education. Ph.D.
Sociology of Education. Ph.D.
Stanford Teacher Education Program (STEP). M.A.
Symbolic Systems in Education. Ph.D.
Teacher Education. Ph.D.

SCHOOL OF ENGINEERING:
Aeronautics and Astronautics. M.S., Ph.D., Engr.
Chemical Engineering. M.S., Ph.D., Engr.
Civil and Environmental Engineering. M.S., Ph.D., Engr.
Computational and Mathematical Engineering. M.S., Ph.D.
Computer Science. M.S., Ph.D.
Electrical Engineering. M.S., Ph.D., Engr.
Management Science and Engineering. M.S., Ph.D.
Materials Science and Engineering. M.S., Ph.D., Engr.
Mechanical Engineering. M.S., Ph.D., Engr.

SCHOOL OF HUMANITIES AND SCIENCES:
African Studies. M.A.
Anthropological Sciences. M.A., M.S., Ph.D.
Applied Physics. M.S., Ph.D.
Art History. Ph.D.
Art Studio. M.F.A.
Asian Languages. M.A., Ph.D.
Biological Sciences. M.S.
Biophysics. Ph.D.
Chemistry. Ph.D.
Classics. M.A., Ph.D.
Communication. M.A., Ph.D.

Comparative Literature. Ph.D.
Drama. Ph.D.
East Asian Studies. M.A.
Economics. Ph.D.
English. M.A., Ph.D.
Financial Mathematics. M.S.
French. M.A., Ph.D.
German Studies. M.A., Ph.D.
History. M.A., Ph.D.
Humanities. M.A.
International Policy Studies. M.A.
Italian. M.A., Ph.D.
Latin American Studies. M.A.
Linguistics. M.A., Ph.D.
Mathematics. Ph.D.
Modern Thought and Literature. Ph.D.
Music. M.A., D.M.-A., Ph.D.
Philosophy. M.A., Ph.D.
Physics. Ph.D.
Political Science. Ph.D.
Psychology. Ph.D.
Religious Studies. M.A., Ph.D.
Russian and East European Studies. M.A.
Slavic Languages and Literature. M.A., Ph.D.
Sociology. Ph.D.
Spanish and Portuguese. M.A., Ph.D.
Statistics. Ph.D.
Symbolic Systems. M.S.

Graduate School of Business
Web site: www.gsb.stanford.edu

Established 1925. Private control. Accredited programs: M.B.A.; recognized Ph.D. Special facilities: Center for Entrepreneurial Studies, Center for Social Innovation, Global Organization of Business Enterprise, Global Supply Chain Management Forum, Process of Change Laboratory, Stanford Project on Emerging Companies, Rosenberg Corporation Research Center. Special programs: Stanford Integrated Manufacturing Association, foreign exchange programs in Singapore and Hong Kong, Global Management Immersion Experience.

Annual tuition: full-time $45,921. On-campus rooms and apartments available for both single and married students. Enrollment: M.B.A. full-time 730, part-time 15 (men 70%, women 30%); Ph.D. full-time 105 (men 60%, women 40%). Faculty: 120 full- and part-time; all have Ph.D./D.B.A. Degrees conferred: M.B.A., M.S.M. (Stanford Sloan Program—nine-month program for midcareer managers with at least eight years experience), M.B.A.-J.D., M.B.A.-M.S.E. (Engineering), Ph.D.

ADMISSION REQUIREMENTS. All applicants should have a bachelor's degree from a recognized institution of higher education and a strong mathematics background. Students are required to have their own personal computer. Early applications are encouraged for both admission and financial aid consideration. Beginning students are admitted Fall only. U.S. citizens and international applicants apply by October 15, for first decision period, by January 8 for second round, and by March 19 for final round. Submit an application, online only, GMAT results, (will accept GMAT test results from the last five years; latest acceptable date is March), official transcripts from each undergraduate/graduate school attended, three letters of reference/evaluations, two essays, résumé (prefers at least four years of work experience), and an application fee of $250 to the Director of Admission. In addition, international students (whose native language is other than English) should submit a TOEFL score (TWE recommended), certified translations and evaluations of all official transcripts, recommendation should be in English or with certified translations, proof of health/immunization certificate, and proof of sufficient financial resources for two years of academic study. On-campus visits are encouraged. Joint degree applicants must apply to and be accepted to both schools. Contact the admissions office for current information and specific admissions requirements. Phone: (650)723-2766. Rolling admissions process; notification is made within six weeks of receipt of completed application and supporting documents.

ADMISSION REQUIREMENTS FOR DOCTORAL CANDIDATES. Contact Doctoral Programs, Graduate School of Business, at (650)723-2149 for application material and information. Applications and instructions available at www.gsb.stanford.edu/phd. Beginning students are admitted Fall Only. U.S. citizens and international applicants apply by January 1 (for most years) Submit an application (online only), GMAT, GRE for Organizational Behavior (will accept GMAT/GRE test results from the last five years), official transcripts from each undergraduate/graduate school attended, three letters of recommendation, résumé, statement of purpose, a confidential Financial Statement, and application fee of $105 to the Office of Graduate Admission. In addition, international students (whose native language is other than English) should submit certified translations and evaluations of all official transcripts (transcripts should show at least 16 years of full-time academic work commencing with elementary school), recommendation should be in English or with certified translations, proof of health/immunization certificate; TOEFL is not required. International students contact: (650)723-2831. Interviews are not required or encouraged. Notification is made on or about April 1.

ADMISSION STANDARDS. Very competitive. Mean GMAT: 720; mean GPA: 3.61 (A = 4). *U.S. News & World Report* ranking is in the top 2 of all U.S. business schools. *BusinessWeek* listed GSB in the top 10 American business schools. Accepts approximately 10% of total annual applicants.

FINANCIAL AID. Scholarships, Partnership for Diversity Fellowship Program, State Grants, fellowships, graduate assistantships, Federal Perkins Loans, Stafford Subsidized and Unsubsidized Loans, Federal W/S available; the Graduate School of Business has a Loan Forgiveness Program. Financial aid is available for international students in the form of fellowships. Assistantships/fellowships may be available for joint degree candidates. Financial aid applications and information are generally included with the application materials; apply by March 1. Request both fellowship and current need-based financial aid information from the Graduate School of Business. Phone: (650)723-3282. Use FAFSA (School code: G22249), also submit Financial Aid Transcript, Federal Income Tax forms. Approximately 65% of students receive some form of financial assistance. For Ph.D.: fellowships typically cover full tuition and 85% of students' living expenses.

DEGREE REQUIREMENTS. For M.B.A.: 102 quarter hour program including 62 elective credits, two-year program; Capstone experience. For M.S.M.: 52 quarter hour program. For Ph.D.: four- to five-year program; annual faculty evaluations; research assistantship; field exam; University oral exam; advancement to candidacy; dissertation; oral defense.

FIELDS OF DOCTORAL STUDY.
Accounting.
Economic Analysis and Policy.
Finance.
Marketing.
Operations, Information, and Technology Management.
Organizational Behavior.
Political Economics.

Law School (94605-8610)
Web site: www.law.stanford.edu

Established 1893. located on main campus. ABA approved since 1923. AALS member. Semester system. Full-time, day study only.

Special facilities: John and Terry Levin Center for Public Service and Public Interest Law, Martin Daniel Gould Center for Conflict Resolution, Stanford Center on International Conflict and Negotiation, Stanford Criminal Justice Center, Stanford Constitutional Law Center, Arthur and Toni Rembe Rock Center for Corporate Governance, John M. Olin Program in Law and Economics, Center for E-Commerce, Center for Internet and Society, Center for Law and the Biosciences, Stanford Center for Computers and Law. Special programs: Stanford Program in International Legal Studies (SPILS); externships. Law library: 539,300 volumes, 6792 subscriptions: has LEXIS, WESTLAW; has more than 250 network connections; is a Federal Government Depository.

Annual tuition: $37,836, graduate education $39,500. On-campus housing available for both single and married students. Law students tend to live off-campus. Off-campus housing and personal expenses: approximately $19,872.

Enrollment: first-year class 173; total 534 (men 57%, women 43%, minorities 31%). Faculty: full-time 48, part-time 38. Student to faculty ratio is 9.2 to 1.

Degrees conferred: J.D., J.D.-M.B.A., J.D.,-M.A. (Economics, History, Political Science), J.D.-M.I.P.S., J.D.-M.P.A. (Woodrow Wilson School of Public and International Affairs, Princeton University), J.D.-M.A. (Johns Hopkins School of Advanced International Studies), LL.M. (for persons who have received a university degree in law in another country or have an advanced degree in law from outside the U.S. and will be returning overseas upon completion of degree; specializations in either Corporate Governance and Practice, Law, Science and Technology), M.L.S. (a nonprofessional degree for those who do not have a law degree but are pursuing a doctoral degree, have earned another advanced degree, or possess exceptional relevant experience), J.S.D.

ADMISSION REQUIREMENTS. LSDAS Law School report, bachelor's degree, transcripts, personal statement, two recommendations, LSAT required in support of application. Interview not required. Accepts transfer applicants. Graduates of unaccredited colleges not considered. Apply to Director of Admissions and Financial Aid by February 1. Earlier filing strongly advised. Admits Fall only. Application fee $75. Phone: (650)723-4985.

ADMISSIONS REQUIREMENTS FOR J.S.D. APPLICANTS. A J.D. from an approved ABA/AALS Law School or equivalent degree required for consideration. Official transcripts, two or three letters of recommendation, résumé or other evidence of significant professional accomplishment, personal statement, proposed dissertation research project required in support of Graduate application. Admits Fall only. Apply by April 1 to the Office of Graduate programs. Phone: (650)723-4985.

ADMISSION REQUIREMENTS FOR LL.M., M.L.S. APPLICANTS. Certified translations and evaluation of all foreign credentials, résumé, personal statement, at least two recommendations, copies of research or published works are required in support of Graduate application. Admits Fall only. Apply by April 1 to Stanford Program in International Legal Studies. Phone: (650)723-4985; fax: (650)725-0253. Selection of SPILS fellows announced by June 1.

ADMISSION STANDARDS. Selective. Accepts approximately 8% of all students. Number of applicants 4863; number of acceptance 379; number enrolled 173; LSAT (75% of students have a score at or above 167); GPA (75% of students have a GPA at or above 3.80). *U.S. News & World Report* ranking is in the top 2 of all U.S. law schools.

FINANCIAL AID. Scholarships, public service fellowships, Federal W/S, loans. Apply by March 15 (scholarships, no closing date for loans) to Director of Admissions and Financial Aid. Phone: (650)723-9247. Use FAFSA. About 38% of students receive aid from School. Miles and Nancy Rubin Loan Forgiveness Program (for graduates who take low-paying public-interest jobs).

DEGREE REQUIREMENTS. For J.D.: 86 (27 required) credits with a GPA of at least 2.0 (A = 4), plus completion of upper-divisional writing course, one course in legal ethics, one inter-disciplinary course examining the American Legal System or examining a foreign or international legal system; three-year program. Accelerated J.D. with summer course work. For J.D.-M.B.A.: four-year program rather than five-year program if both degrees are taken consecutively. For J.D.-Master's: individually designed program, four- to four-and-one-half-year program rather than a five- to five-and-one-half-year program if both degrees are taken consecutively. For LL.M.: one core seminar, three to five advanced courses or seminars, a multidisciplinary research workshop; written research project. For M.L.S.: 30 credits, must be completed within two consecutive academic years; one writing seminar or directed research project resulting in a written paper. For J.S.D.: at least one year in full-time residence; dissertation of publishable quality, oral defense.

School of Medicine (94305-5404)

Web site: www.med.stanford.edu

Incorporated 1908. Special facilities: Stanford Comprehensive Cancer Center, Stanford Institute for Stem Cell Biology and Regenerative Medicine, Stanford Cardiovascular Institute, The Neuroscience Institute at Stanford, Stanford Institute for Immunity, Transplantation and Infection. NIH ranking is 15th among all U.S. institutions with 763 awards/grants worth $395,561,055. Library: 280,000 volumes, 3000 subscriptions.

Annual tuition: $39,981. On-campus apartments available for both single and married students. Total average figure for all other expenses: $19,872.

Enrollment: first-year class 86, total 456 (men 52%, women 48%, minorities 53%, state residents 41%). Faculty: full-time 736, part-time and volunteer 800. Degrees conferred: M.D., M.D.-M.P.H., M.D.-M.S., M.D.-Ph.D.

ADMISSION REQUIREMENTS. AMCAS report, transcripts, recommendations, MCAT, interview required in support of application. Supplemental application required. Applicants must have completed at least three years of college. Has EDP; apply between June 1 and August 1. Will consider transfer applicants under special circumstances. Apply to Director of Admission after June 1, before October 15. Graduate program: transcripts, GRE required in support of a supplementary application. Apply by February 1 to chair of appropriate department. Application fee $75. Phone: (650)723-6861; fax: (650)723-7855.

ADMISSION STANDARDS. Very competitive. Accepts about 3% of all applicants. Number of applications 5648 (3593 out-of-state); number interviewed 362 (227 out-of-state); number of acceptance 163 (113 out-of-state); number enrolled 86 (54 out-of-state). Mean Composite MCAT 11.4; mean UGPA 3.71. *U.S. News & World Report* ranking is in the top 7 of all U.S. medical research schools.

FINANCIAL AID. Scholarships, research fellowships, teaching/research assistantships, Federal and private loans. MSTP funded by NIH. Apply to Office of Student Financial Services after admission, as soon as possible after January 1. Phone: (650)723-6958. Use FAFSA (School code: G24552). About 65% of students receive some aid from the School.

DEGREE REQUIREMENTS. For M.D.: satisfactory completion of thirteen quarters of academic work and passing USMLE Step 2. For Ph.D.: nine quarters minimum beyond the bachelor's, some departments require reading knowledge of one or more languages; preliminary written exam; dissertation; final oral exam.

FIELDS OF GRADUATE STUDY.
Bioengineering. Ph.D.
Biomedical Informatics. M.S., Ph.D.
Biosciences. Ph.D.

Biochemistry. Ph.D.
Biological Sciences. Ph.D.
Biophysics. Ph.D.
Cancer Biology. Ph.D.
Developmental Biology. Ph.D.
Epidemiology. M.S., Ph.D.
Genetics. Ph.D.
Health Services Research. M.S.
Immunology. Ph.D.
Medicine. M.M.
Microbiology and Immunology. Ph.D.
Molecular and Cellular Physiology. Ph.D.
Molecular Pharmacology/Chemical and Systems Biology. Ph.D.
Neurosciences. Ph.D.
Structural Biology. Ph.D.

THE COLLEGE OF STATEN ISLAND OF THE CITY UNIVERSITY OF NEW YORK

Staten Island, New York 10301
Web site: www.csi.cuny.edu

Founded 1976. Coed. Municipal control. Semester system. Special facilities: Center for Developmental Neurosciences and Developmental Disabilities, Center for Environmental Science, Center for Immigrant and Population Studies. Library: 220,000 volumes, 3000 subscriptions. Total Campus enrollment: 12,000.

Tuition: per credit, city resident $270, nonresident $500. No on-campus housing. Day-care facilities available.

Division of Graduate Studies

Enrollment: full-time 95, part-time 960. Faculty: full-time 56, part-time 10. Degrees conferred: M.A., M.S., M.S. in Ed., Advanced Certificate.

ADMISSION REQUIREMENTS. Transcripts, GRE (except teacher education), letters of recommendation required in support of divisional application. TOEFL required for international applicants. Accepts transfer applicants. Graduates of unaccredited institutions not considered. Apply to Office of Admissions well in advance of registration. Application fee $40. Phone: (718)982-2010; fax: (718)982-2500.

ADMISSION STANDARDS. Selective. Usual minimum average: 3.0 (A = 4).

FINANCIAL AID. Fellowships, research assistantships, teaching assistantships, internships, traineeships, tuition waivers, Federal W/S, loans. Approved for VA benefits. Apply to Director of Financial Aid; no specified closing date. Phone: (718)982-2030. Use University's FAF. Aid available for part-time students.

DEGREE REQUIREMENTS. For master's: 30 semester hours minimum, at least 24 in residence; thesis/final written exam.

FIELDS OF STUDY.
Adult Health Nursing.
Biology.
Business Management.
Cinema and Media Studies.
Computer Science.
Educational Leadership. Includes adolescence, childhood education.
Elementary Education.
English.
Environmental Sciences.
History.
Liberal Studies.

Mental Retardation and Development Disabilities.
Neuroscience.
Physical Therapy.
Secondary Education. Includes biology, English, mathematics, social studies.
Special Education.

STEPHEN F. AUSTIN STATE UNIVERSITY
Nacogdoches, Texas 75962
Web site: www.sfasu.edu

Founded 1921. Located 140 miles NE of Houston. Coed. State control. Semester system. Library: 850,000 volumes, 4000 subscriptions. Total University enrollment: 11,500.

Annual tuition: per credit resident $146, nonresident $422. On-campus housing for 416 married students, 1661 men, 2343 women. Average annual housing cost: $4800 (including board). Contact Director of Housing. For both on- and off-campus housing information. Phone: (936)468-2601.

Graduate School

Graduate study since 1937. Enrollment: full-time 616, part-time 955. Graduate faculty: full-time 289, part-time 75. Degrees conferred: M.A., M.B.A., M.Ed., M.F., M.F.A., D.F. (Forestry), M.I.S., M.M., M.P.A., M.S., M.S.F., M.S.W., Ph.D. in Forestry (cooperative with Texas A&M University).

ADMISSION REQUIREMENTS. Transcripts, GRE, GMAT (for M.B.A.) required in support of School's application. Online application available. TOEFL, TWE required for international applicants. Interview not required. Accepts transfer applicants. Graduates of unaccredited institutions not considered. Apply to Graduate School by July 1 (Fall), November 1 (Spring). Application fee $25, $50 for international students. Phone: (936)468-2807; fax: (936)468-1251; e-mail: gschool@titan.sfasu.edu.

ADMISSION STANDARDS. Selective. Usual minimum average: 2.8 (A = 4).

FINANCIAL AID. Annual awards from institutional funds: scholarships, teaching assistantships, research assistantships, internships, Federal W/S, loans. Approved for VA benefits. Apply by March 1 to Director of Scholarships and Loans for scholarships, to head of major department for assistantships, to Financial Aid Office for all other programs. Phone: (936)468-2403. Use FAFSA. About 50% of students receive aid other than loans from College and outside sources. Aid available for part-time students.

DEGREE REQUIREMENTS. For master's: 30 semester hours minimum including thesis, or 36 semester hours minimum without thesis, at least 24 in residence; final oral/written comprehensive exams. For M.F.: 38 semester hour program; final oral, written or both comprehensive exam. For M.F.A.: 60 semester hour program beyond baccalaureate; written and oral comprehensive; thesis. For M.S.W.: 63 semester hour, two-year full-time or four-year part-time program. For Ph.D.: 66 semester hour program beyond the master's, at least two consecutive semesters in residence; foreign language competency; candidacy, qualifying exam; dissertation; final exam.

FIELDS OF STUDY.
Accounting.
Agriculture.
Art. Includes applied, design, fine arts.
Athletic Training.
Biology.

Biotechnology.
Business. GMAT required for admission. Includes general business, management. M.B.A. only.
Chemistry.
Communication. Includes speech communication, journalism, organizational, radio-television-film.
Computer Science.
Counseling.
Early Childhood Education.
Educational Leadership.
Elementary Education.
English.
Environmental Science.
Forestry. Includes forest management, forest economics, forest ecology, forest entomology, recreation management, wildlife management, range management, silviculture, urban forestry, wood science. M.F., M.S.F., D.F.
Geology.
History.
Human Sciences.
Interdisciplinary Studies.
Kinesiology.
Management.
Mathematics. Includes teaching.
Music. Includes music education.
Natural Science.
Physical Education.
Physics. Thesis usually required.
Psychology. Thesis usually required for M.A.
Public Administration.
Reading Specialist.
School Psychology.
Secondary Education.
Social Work.
Spatial Science.
Special Education.
Speech Pathology and Audiology.
Statistics.

STETSON UNIVERSITY
De Land, Florida 32720
Web site: www.stetson.edu

Founded 1883. Located 40 miles N of Orlando. Coed. Private control. Semester system. Library: 491,000 volumes, 1400 current periodicals. Total University enrollment: 3650.

Tuition: per semester hour $575. Limited on-campus housing. Average academic year off-campus housing costs: $700–$800 per month. Contact Dean of Students Office for both on- and off-campus housing information. Phone: (386)822-7201.

College of Arts and Sciences Graduate Programs

Graduate study since 1902. Enrollment: full-time 25, part-time 87. Faculty: full-time 10, part-time 5. Degrees conferred: M.A., M.S., M.A.T., M.Ed., Ed.S.

ADMISSION REQUIREMENTS. Official transcripts, three letters of references, GRE/MAT required in support of application. Online application available. Interview required for some departments. Accepts transfer applicants. Apply to Office of Graduate Studies by March 1 (Fall), November 1 (Spring). Application fee $25. Phone: (386)822-7075.

ADMISSION STANDARDS. Selective. Usual minimum average: 3.0 (A = 4).

FINANCIAL AID. Scholarships, internships, tuition waivers, Federal W/S, loans. Apply to the Financial Aid Office; no specified closing date. Phone: (386)822-7501. Use FAFSA.

DEGREE REQUIREMENTS. For master's: 30 semester hours minimum, at least 24 in residence; reading knowledge of one foreign language for some majors; thesis or final oral exam. For Ed.S.: 30 semester hours beyond master's.

FIELDS OF STUDY.
Counselor Education.
Educational Leadership.
English.
Marital, Couples and Family Counseling/Therapy.
Mental Health Counseling.
Reading.
School Counseling.

School of Business Administration
Graduate Programs

Established 1885. Accredited programs: M.B.A., Accounting. Located on main campus, courses offered in St. Petersburg at College of Law. Semester system.

Tuition: $575 per credit, $675 at Celebration Campus. Enrollment: total full-time 77, part-time 121. Faculty: 36 full- and part-time; 95% with Ph.D./D.B.A. Degrees conferred: M.B.A. (Concentrations in Finance), M.B.A.-J.D., M.Acc.

ADMISSION REQUIREMENTS. All applicants should have a bachelor's degree from a recognized institution of higher education, a strong mathematics background, and GPA of at least 2.5 (A = 4). Contact Director of Graduate Business at (386)822-7410 for application material and information. Online application available. Early applications are encouraged for both admission and financial aid consideration. Beginning students are admitted Fall, Spring, and Summer. U.S. citizens apply by July 15 (Fall), December 15 (Spring), April 15 (Summer), International students apply by July 1 (Fall), November 15 (Spring), March 15 (Summer). Submit an application, GMAT results (will accept GMAT test results from the last five years, latest acceptable date is March), two official transcripts from each undergraduate/graduate school attended, two letters of recommendation, personal statement, résumé (prefers at least two years of work experience), and an application fee of $25 to the Office of Admission. In addition, international students (whose native language is other than English) should submit a TOEFL (minimum score 550), certified translations and evaluations of all official transcripts, recommendation should be in English or with certified translations, proof of health/immunization certificate, and proof of sufficient financial resources for two years of academic study. On-campus visits and interviews are strongly recommended. Admissions Committee may consider applicants with some academic course work deficiencies. Joint degree applicants must apply to and be accepted to both schools; contact the admissions office for current information and specific admissions requirements.

ADMISSION STANDARDS. Selective. Usual minimum average 2.5 (A = 4). Mean GMAT: 540; mean GPA: 3.1 (A = 4).

FINANCIAL AID. Graduate assistantships, Federal Perkins Loans, Stafford Subsidized and Unsubsidized Loans, Federal W/S available. Financial aid is available for part-time study. Assistantships may be available for joint degree candidates. Financial Aid applications and information are generally available at the on-campus visit/interview; apply by March 15. Request assistantship information from the Director of Graduate Business Programs. Contact the University's Student Financial Planning Office for current need-based financial aid information. Phone: (386)822-7120. Use FAFSA (School code: 001531), also submit Financial Aid Transcript, Federal Income Tax forms. Approximately 20% of students receive some form of financial assistance.

DEGREE REQUIREMENTS. For M.B.A.: 30–59 credit program including 10 elective credits, one- to two-year program;

degree program must be completed in eight years. For M.Acc.: 30–60 credit program. For M.B.A.-J.D.: four- to five-year program (both programs will accept 12 credits from the other degree program).

College of Law
Web site: www.law.stetson.edu

Established 1900. Located in St. Petersburg (33707). ABA approved since 1930. AALS member since 1931. Private control. Semester system. Special programs: summer programs in Granada, Spain. Law library: 403,644 volumes, 3854 subscriptions: has LEXIS, WESTLAW; has more than 500 network connections.

Annual tuition: full-time $27,860, part-time $19,300. On-campus housing available. Apply to Director, Stetson Inn. Phone: (727) 562-7886. Total average annual additional expense: $15,800.

Enrollment: first-year class full-time 276, part-time 69; total full- and part-time 1033 (men 47%, women 53%, minorities 19%). Faculty: full-time 40, part-time 44. Student to faculty ratio is 17.3 to 1. Degrees conferred: J.D., J.D.-M.B.A., LL.M. (International Law and Business).

ADMISSION REQUIREMENTS. LSDAS Law School report, bachelor's degree, transcripts, personal statement, LSAT required in support of application. Résumé and letter of recommendation are optional. Accepts transfer applicants. Graduates of unaccredited colleges not considered. Apply to Director of Admissions by March 15. Admits new students to Fall, Spring, Summer. Application fee $55. Phone: (727)562-7802.

ADMISSION STANDARDS. Selective. Accepts approximately 23% of full-time, 30% of part-time students. Number of full-time applicants 2968, part-time 489; number of full-time acceptance 696, part-time 145; number of full-time enrolled 276, part-time 69; LSAT (75% of full-time students have a score at or above 152, part-time 149); GPA (75% of full-time students have a GPA at or above 3.28, part-time 2.75). *U.S. News & World Report* ranking is in the second tier (tied at 100) of all U.S. law schools.

FINANCIAL AID. Scholarships, grants, research/teaching assistantships, Federal W/S, loans. Apply to Financial Aid Office by February 15. Phone: (727)562-7813. Use FAFSA (College code: E00342). About 24% of full-time and 10% of part-time students receive aid other than loans from College.

DEGREE REQUIREMENTS. For J.D.: 88 semester hours minimum; advanced standing for work completed at other accredited law schools considered. For LL.M.: 24 credit program. For M.B.A.: see Graduate School of Business listing above.

STEVENS INSTITUTE OF TECHNOLOGY
Hoboken, New Jersey 07030
Web site: www.stevens.edu/sit

Founded 1870. Coed. Private control. Semester system. Special facilities: Automotive Research Laboratory, Davidson Laboratory for Fluids Research, Plastics Institute of America Laboratory, Laboratory of Psychological Studies, Computer Center, Energy Center, Polymer Processing Institute, Center for Surface Engineered Materials, Schacht Management Laboratory, Specialized Department Laboratories. Library: 135,000 volumes, 200 subscriptions. Total Institute enrollment: 4700.

Tuition: per credit $965; School of Technology $825. Average academic year housing costs: $9900 for married students; $4475–$8875 for single students. Contact Director of Residence Halls for both on- and off-campus housing information. Phone: (210) 216-5128.

Graduate School

Enrollment: full-time 661, part-time 1978. Faculty: full-time 102, part-time 80. Degrees conferred: M.E., M.Eng., M.S., Engineer (chemical, civil, computer, electrical, mechanical), Ph.D.

ADMISSION REQUIREMENTS. Two official transcripts, two letters of recommendation required in support of School's application. Online application available. GRE/GMAT for management. TOEFL required for international applicants. Interview not required. Transfer applicants accepted. Graduates of unaccredited institutions not considered. Apply to Graduate School at least one month prior to beginning of semester, for international applicants at least four months prior to beginning of semester. Rolling admissions process. Application fee $55. Phone: (800) 496-4935; fax: (201)216-8044.

ADMISSION STANDARDS. Selective. Usual minimum average: 2.5 (A = 4).

FINANCIAL AID. Annual awards from institutional funds: fellowships, teaching assistantships, research assistantships, graduate assistantships, internships, tuition waivers, Federal W/S, loans. Approved for VA benefits. Apply to individual department heads for assistantships, fellowships; to Financial Aid Office of all other programs. Use FAFSA. Phone: (201)216-5291. About 30% of full-time students receive aid from Institute.

DEGREE REQUIREMENTS. For master's: 30 credit hours minimum; thesis/nonthesis option. For Ph.D.: equivalent of three years of course work, at least one year in residence; reading knowledge of one foreign language for some departments; preliminary and/or comprehensive exam; dissertation; final oral exam.

FIELDS OF STUDY.

CHARLES V. SCHAEFER, JR. SCHOOL OF ENGINEERING AND SCIENCE:
Applied Mathematics. M.S.
Biomedical Engineering. M.Eng., Ph.D.
Chemical Biology. Includes analytical chemistry, organic, physical, polymer. M.S., Ph.D.
Chemical Engineering. Includes polymer engineering. M.Eng., Ch.E., Ph.D.
Chemistry. Includes analytical, chemical biology, organic, physical, polymer. M.S., Ph.D.
Civil Engineering. Includes geotechnical/geoenvironmental engineering, hydrologic modeling, stormwater management, structural engineering, water resources engineering. M.Eng., C.E., Ph.D.
Computer Engineering. Includes computer systems, data communications and networks, digital systems design, image processing and multimedia, information systems, information systems security, intelligent systems, real-time and embedded systems. M.Eng., C.E., Ph.D.
Computer Science. Includes databases and service-oriented architecture, databases, security and privacy, health informatics, mobile and embedded systems, network and systems administration, software and security engineering, software engineering and databases, web application development. M.S., Ph.D.
Construction Management. M.S.
Electrical Engineering. Includes autonomous robots, computer architecture and digital systems, embedded systems, microelectronic devices and systems, microelectronics and photonics science and technology (interdisciplinary), signal processing for communications, telecommunications systems engineering, wireless communication. M.Eng., E.E., Ph.D.
Engineering Physics. Includes applied optics, solid state physics, microelectronics and photonics science and technology. Interdisciplinary. M.Eng.
Enterprise Computing. Includes data management and service-oriented architecture, management, security and privacy, software engineering, systems administration. M.S.

Environmental Engineering. Includes environmental control process, groundwater and soil pollution control in land and coastal environmental hydrodynamics. M.Eng., Ph.D.
Integrated Products Development. Includes armament engineering, electrical and computer engineering, manufacture technologies, systems reliability and design. Interdisciplinary. M.Eng.
Maritime Systems. Includes environmental engineering, structural engineering, management, marine transportation. M.S.
Materials Engineering. Includes microelectronics and photonics science and technology (interdisciplinary). M.Eng., Ph.D.
Mathematics. M.S., Ph.D.
Mechanical Engineering. Includes manufacturing systems, product design, pharmaceutical manufacturing, thermal engineering. M.Eng, M.E., Ph.D.
Multimedia Experience and Management. Includes multimedia experience, multimedia management. M.S.
Network Information Systems. Includes data communication networks, information networks, multimedia information systems, multimedia technologies, networked information systems (business practices), network systems technologies, secure network systems design. M. Eng.
Ocean Engineering. Includes coastal engineering, hydrodynamics, maritime systems, naval architecture oceanography. M.Eng., Ph.D.
Pharmaceutical Manufacturing. M.Eng., M.Sc.
Physics. Includes nanoscale science and technology. Interdisciplinary. M.S., Ph.D.
Product-Architecture and Engineering. Interdisciplinary. M.Eng.
Quantitative Software Engineering. M.S.
Security and Privacy. Includes cybersecurity, enterprise computing. M.S.
Service-Oriented Computing. Includes health informatics, internet software engineering, software engineering. M.S.
Stochastic Systems. M.S.

SCHOOL OF SYSTEMS AND ENTERPRISES:
Business Administration in Technology Management. Includes engineering management, financial engineering. M.B.A.
Engineering Management. M.Eng., Ph.D.
Enterprise Systems. M.S., Ph.D.
Financial Engineering. M.S.
Systems Engineering. M.Eng., Ph.D.

WESLEY J. HOWE SCHOOL OF TECHNOLOGY MANAGEMENT:
Management. Includes global innovation management, information management (Ph.D. available), project management, technological management (Ph.D. available), pharmaceutical management, technology commercialization. M.S.
Information Systems. Includes business process management and service innovation, computer science (interdisciplinary), e-commerce, enterprise systems, entrepreneurial IT, global innovation management, human resource management, information management (Ph.D. available), information security (interdisciplinary), integrated information architecture (interdisciplinary), IT in financial services, IT in pharmaceutical industry, IT outsourcing management, knowledge management/data mining, legal issues in IT, management consulting, project management, quantitative software engineering (interdisciplinary), service-oriented architecture, supply chain management, systems engineering (interdisciplinary), telecommunications management (Ph.D. available). M.S.
Technology Management for Experienced Professionals. Includes engineering management, financial engineering, global technology management, information management, IT in financial services industry, IT in pharmaceutical industry, project management, telecommunications management, pharmaceutical management, IT outsourcing. E.M.B.A. M.B.A., E.M.T.M., M.S.
Telecommunication Management. Includes business management, global innovation management, management of wireless networks, online technology, business & security, project man-

agement, security management & forensics, technical management. M.S.

STONY BROOK UNIVERSITY, STATE UNIVERSITY OF NEW YORK

Stony Brook, New York 11794-4433
Web site: www.sunysb.edu

Founded 1957. Located 60 miles E of New York City on Long Island's north shore. CGS and AAU member. Coed. State control. Semester system. Special facilities: Humanities Institute, Institute for American Studies, Institute for Decision Sciences, Institute for Mathematical Science, Institute for Theoretical Physics, Nuclear Structure Laboratory, Marine Sciences Research Center, Institute for Pattern Recognition, Health Sciences Center. The University's NIH ranking is 88th among all U.S. institutions with 203 awards/grants valued at $64,966,223. According to The Center at University of Florida, the University is ranked 65th in receipt of Federal Research funds with $112,452,000 and it ranks 69th for total University research expenditures with $200,330,000. In 2004, the University awarded 285 doctorates which ranked it 48th among all U.S. institutions eligible to award that degree. Fourteen of the University's faculty members have been elected to National Honor Academies and this ranks it 57th among all U.S. institutions. The Library: approximately 2,200,000 volumes, 19,000 subscriptions. Total University enrollment: 22,000.

The Graduate School

Web site: www.grad.sunysb.edu

Annual tuition: full-time, resident $6900, nonresident $10,920; per credit, resident $288, nonresident $455. On-campus housing available for married and single graduate students. Housing application mailed with acceptance to degree program. Monthly housing cost: $350–$1300 per month, including most utilities.

Enrollment: full-time 2617, part-time 390. Graduate faculty: full-time approximately 714, part-time approximately 59. Degrees conferred: M.A., M.M., M.F.A., M.P.S., M.S., D.M.A., D.A., Ph.D.

ADMISSION REQUIREMENTS. Two transcripts from all undergraduate and graduate programs (Certified English translations of all international transcripts), GRE, three letters of recommendation required in support of School's application. GRE Subject Test required for some programs. TOEFL or TSE required for international applicants. Apply by January 15 (Fall), October 1 (Spring). Use online application only. Application $60. Information available by e-mail at Graduate_School_Admissions@ notes.cc.sunyabsb.edu.

ADMISSION STANDARDS. Competitive. Minimum GPA of 2.75 (A = 4), a GPA of 3.0 in the major or related courses. Very competitive programs require higher GPA. For international applicants: minimum TOEFL score 550 or TSE of 240.

FINANCIAL AID. Current awards from institutional funds: tuition scholarships, teaching and graduate assistantships, graduate research assistantships, state-supported fellowships, internships, tuition waivers, Federal W/S, loans. Approved for VA benefits. Apply by January 15 to the Graduate Office for scholarships, fellowships, assistantships; to Financial Aid Office for all other programs. Use FAFSA and CSS Profile. About 134 students supported on stipends from outside sources. No aid for part-time students.

DEGREE REQUIREMENTS. For master's: 30 credits minimum with a 3.0 GPA, time limit of three years; reading knowledge of one foreign language for some programs; practicum in teaching; thesis/comprehensive exam/written exam varies by program. For doctoral degrees: at least three years in residence, a minimum of two semesters in full-time study, time limit of seven years after completion of the first 24 credits; GPA of 3.0; preliminary exam; reading knowledge of two foreign languages for some programs; advancement to candidacy; dissertation, dissertation defense; practicum in teaching; final oral/written examination varies by program.

FIELDS OF STUDY.
Anatomical Sciences. Ph.D.
Anthropology. Includes anthropological sciences. M.A.
Applied Mathematics and Statistics. M.S., Ph.D.
Art History and Criticism. M.A., Ph.D.
Art, Studio. M.F.A.
Atmospheric Science. M.S., Ph.D.
Biochemistry and Structural Biology. Ph.D.
Biological Science. M.A.
Biomedical Engineering. M.S., Ph.D.
Business Administration. M.B.A.
Cellular and Developmental Biology. Ph.D.
Chemistry. M.S., Ph.D.
Clinical Psychology. Ph.D.
Coastal Oceanography. Ph.D.
Comparative Literacy and Cultural Studies. M.A., Ph.D.
Computer Science. M.S., Ph.D.
Dramaturgy. M.F.A.
Earth and Space Science. Includes geosciences. M.S., Ph.D.
Ecology and Evolution. Ph.D.
Economics. M.A., Ph.D.
Electrical and Computer Engineering. M.S., Ph.D.
English. Includes comparative literature. M.A., Ph.D.
Environmental and Waste Management. M.S.
Experimental Psychology. Ph.D.
Foreign Language Instruction. Includes French, Italian. M.A.
Genetics. Ph.D.
Geoscience. M.S., Ph.D.
Germanic Languages and Literature. M.A.
Global Operations Management. M.S.
Health Care Polilcy and Management. M.S.
Hispanic Languages and Literature. M.A., Ph.D.
History. M.A., Ph.D.
Human Resources Management. M.P.S.
Linguistics. M.A., Ph.D.
Management and Policy. M.S.
Marine Science. M.S., Ph.D
Materials Science and Engineering. M.S., Ph.D.
Mathematics. M.A., Ph.D.
Mechanical Engineering. M.S., Ph.D.
Molecular and Cellular Biology. Ph.D.
Molecular and Cellular Pharmacology. Ph.D.
Molecular Genetics and Microbiology. Ph.D.
Music. M.A., Ph.D.
Music Performance. M.M., D.M.A.
Neuroscience. Ph.D.
Oral Biology and Pathology. Ph.D.
Philosophy. M.A., Ph.D.
Physics. Includes instrumentation, modern research. M.A., M.S., Ph.D.
Physiology and Biophysics. Ph.D.
Political Science. M.A., Ph.D.
Professional Studies. M.P.S.
Psychology. M.A.
Public Affairs. M.P.S.
Romance Languages and Literature. Includes French, Italian. M.A.
Slavic Languages and Literature. M.A.
Social/Health Psychology. Ph.D.
Social Welfare. Ph.D.
Sociology. M.A., Ph.D.
Teaching of English to Speakers of Other Languages (TESOL). M.A.
Technological Systems Management. M.S.
Theater. M.A., Ph.D.
Writing and Literature. M.F.A.

College of Business

Graduate study since 1974. Annual tuition: resident $5100, nonresident $8416.

Enrollment: full-time 39, part-time 91. Faculty: full-time 45, part-time 2. Degrees conferred: M.B.A., Ph.D. (through Graduate School).

ADMISSION REQUIREMENTS. Transcripts, GRE or other relevant admission exam, three letters of reference, essay, registration, certification or licensure; at least one year of full-time practice in the professional field required in support of School's application. TOEFL required for international applicants. Accept transfer applicants. Apply to the Office of Student Services of the Graduate School by March 1. Application fee $60. Phone: (631) 444-3240; fax: (631)444-7621.

ADMISSIONS STANDARDS. Selective. Usual minimum average: 3.0 (A = 4).

FINANCIAL AID. Internships, Federal W/S, loans. Apply by March 15 to the Financial Aid Office with admissions application. Use FAFSA.

DEGREE REQUIREMENTS. For M.B.A.: 48–60 credits minimum.

AREAS OF CONCENTRATION:
Finance.
Management Information Systems.
General Management.
Human Resources.
Health Care Management.
Marketing.

School of Dental Medicine
Web site: www.hsc.stonybrook.edu

Graduate study since 1973. Semester system. Special facility: Dental Care Center.

Annual tuition: resident $16,200, nonresident $32,500. On-campus housing available. Contact the Division of Campus Residences for on-campus housing information. Average academic year housing costs: $12,100. Total average cost for all other first year expenses: $9,070.

Enrollment: first year class 40, total 158 (men 44%, women 56%, minorities 28%, state residents 90%). Faculty: full-time 31, part-time 61. Degrees conferred: D.D.S. (with specialties in Children's Dentistry, General Dentistry, Dental Medicine, Oral Biology and Pathology, Oral & Maxillofacial Surgery, Periodontics). M.S., Ph.D. The M.S. and Ph.D. are offered through the Graduate School.

ADMISSION REQUIREMENTS. AADSAS, transcripts, DAT (no later than October), three letters of recommendation from science faculty, personal interviews required in support of application. Applicants must have completed at least three years of college work. Preference given to state residents. Accepts transfer applicants from U.S. and Canadian dental schools. Graduates of unaccredited institutions not considered. Apply through AADSAS after July 1, before January 15. Application fee $75. Phone: (631)632-8871; fax: (631)632-9105.

ADMISSION STANDARDS. Competitive. Accepts about 5–10% of all applicants. Usual minimum UGPA: 3.0 (A = 4). Mean DAT: academic 21 PAT 17; mean UGPA 3.60.

FINANCIAL AID. Full and partial scholarships, Federal W/S, loans. Apply to Financial Aid Office after acceptance. Phone: (631)632-3027. Use FAFSA. About 92% of students receive aid from School and outside sources.

DEGREE REQUIREMENTS. For D.D.S.: satisfactory completion of forty-three-month program. For M.S., Ph.D.: see Graduate School listing.

FIELDS OF POSTGRADUATE STUDY.
Dental Care for the Developmentally Disabled.
Endodontics.
General Practice Residency.
Oral Biology & Pathology. M.S., Ph.D.
Orthodontics.
Pediatric Dentistry Residency.
Periodontics.

School of Medicine (11794-8434)
Health Science Center
Web site: www.hsc.sunysb.edu/som

Established 1971. Located at Health Science Center. Semester system. Library: 238,000 volumes, 4400 subscriptions. Affiliated hospitals: University Hospital, Nassau County Medical Center, Northport VA Hospital, Winthrop University Hospital. Special programs: M.S.T.P. combines research training at the School of Medicine with research at Cold Spring Harbor Laboratory and Brookhaven National Laboratory.

Annual tuition: resident $19,740, nonresident $34,440. On-campus rooms and apartments available for both single and married students. Total average cost for all other expenses: $19,500. Contact Student Affairs Office for both on- and off-campus housing information. Phone: (631)632-6750. Medical students tend to live off-campus. Off-campus living expenses: approximately $15,900.

Enrollment: first-year class 100, total 438 (men 49%, women 51%, minorities 51%, state residents 98%). Faculty: full-time 500, part-time and volunteer 800. Degrees conferred: M.D., M.D.-M.P.H., M.D.-Ph.D. (M.S.T.P.).

ADMISSION REQUIREMENTS. AMCAS report, transcript, MCAT, letter of evaluation, recommendations, supplemental application required in support of application. Accepts transfer applicants. Interview by invitation only. Has EDP; apply between June 1 and August 1. Apply to Committee on Admissions after June 1, before December 15. Application fee $75. Phone: (631) 444-2113; fax: (631)444-6032.

ADMISSION STANDARDS. Competitive. Accepts about 10.5% of all applicants. Number of applications 2755 (816 out-of-state); number interviewed 573 (53 out-of-state); number of acceptance 288 (25 out-of-state); number enrolled 101 (7 out-of-state). Mean Composite MCAT 10.7; mean UGPA 3.60.

FINANCIAL AID. Scholarships, fellowships, assistantships, internships, grants, Federal W/S, Federal and private loans. Apply after acceptance to Office of Student Affairs. Phone: (631)444-2341. Use FAFSA (School code: 002838). About 87% of students receive some aid from school.

DEGREE REQUIREMENTS. For M.D.: satisfactory completion of four-year program; must pass Step 1 of USMLE for advancement to third year and pass Step 2 for graduation. For M.D.-Ph.D.: satisfactory completion of six- to eight-year program. For Ph.D.: see Graduate School listing above.

FIELDS OF GRADUATE STUDY.
Anatomy.
Biochemistry.
Biophysics.
Cancer Biology.
Cell and Developmental Biology.
Cell Structure.
Cellular Immunology.
Cellular Pharmacology.
Epidemiology.

Genetics.
Membrane Biology and Biophysics.
Molecular Biology and Molecular Genetics.
Molecular Microbiology.
Neurobiology.
Neuropharmacology.
Pharmacology.
Physiology.
Tumorigenesis.
Structure and Physical Biochemistry.
Vertebrate Morphology.
Virology.

School of Nursing

Graduate study since 1970. Annual tuition: resident $6900, nonresident $10,920; per credit $288 resident, nonresident $455.

Enrollment: full-time and part-time 471. Faculty: full-time 27, part-time 22. Degrees conferred: M.P.S., M.S., B.S./M.S., Post Master's Advance Certificate.

ADMISSION REQUIREMENTS. Transcripts, three letters of reference, personal statement, registered professional nurse licensure within one year of admission, CPR certification, B.S. with major in nursing required in support of School's application. Midwives' M.S. completion program applicants must be ACC certified. Neonatal M.S. applicants must have at least two years of full-time nursing experience in the neonatal intensive care setting. Non-nursing bachelor's degree applicants must pass Regents College Examination in Health Restoration I and II, and Health Support I and II within one year of admission. Accepts transfer applicants. Graduates of unaccredited institutions not considered. Apply to Admissions Office by March 1. Application fee $50. Phone: (631)444-3262; fax: (631)444-3136.

ADMISSIONS STANDARDS. Selective. Usual minimum average: 3.0 (A = 4).

FINANCIAL AID. Partial tuition scholarships for full-time study, fellowships, assistantships, internships, Federal W/S, loans. Apply at time of Admissions. Use FAFSA.

DEGREE REQUIREMENTS. For master's: 45 credits in required core courses in clinical specialty; minimum 3.0 GPA. Certificates of Advanced Standing: 18–24 credits in required courses and clinicals; minimum 3.0 GPA.

FIELDS OF STUDY.
Adult Health Nursing.
Child Health Nursing.
Family Nurse Practitioner.
Gerontological Nursing.
Mental Health Nursing.
Neonatal Nurse Practitioner.
Nurse Midwifery.
Pediatric Nurse Practitioner.
Perinatal/Women's Health.
Psychiatric/Mental Health Nurse Practitioner.

The School of Professional Development and Continuing Studies

Annual tuition: full-time resident $6900, nonresident $10,920; per credit resident $288, nonresident $455.

Enrollment: full-time 346, part-time 1380. Faculty: full-time 25, part-time 101. Degrees conferred: M.A., M.A.T., M.P.S., Advance Certificate.

ADMISSION REQUIREMENTS. Transcripts, essay, three letters of recommendation required in support of School's application. Online application available. GRE and undergraduate major

in related field is required for the MAT candidates. TOEFL required for international applicants. Accepts transfer applicants. Apply to Director of Admissions and Advisement by July 15 (Fall), December 15 (Spring). Rolling admission process. Application fee $50. Phone: (631)632-7050; fax: (631)632-9046.

ADMISSION STANDARDS. Selective. Usual minimum average: 2.75 (A = 4). TOEFL score of 550 for international applicants.

FINANCIAL AID. Assistantshps, internships, Federal W/S, loans. Apply to the Financial Aid Office with admissions application. Use FAFSA. Aid available for part-time students.

DEGREE REQUIREMENTS. For master's: 30–36 credits minimum with a 3.0 GPA; time limit five years. For certificates: 18–24 credits with a 3.0 GPA; time limit five years.

FIELDS OF STUDY.
English Language and Literature. M.A.T.
Foreign Languages. Includes programs in French, German, Italian, Spanish. M.A.T.
Liberal Studies. Includes areas of interest in education, educating the non-traditional K–12 students, environmental studies, studies in the arts, youth & society. M.A.L.S.
Mathematics. M.A.T.
Professional Studies. Includes concentrations in human resource management, waste management. M.P.S.
Science. Includes programs in biology, chemistry, earth science, physics. M.A.T.
Social Studies. M.A.T.

School of Social Welfare

Graduate study since 1971. Semester system. Annual tuition: resident $6900, nonresident $10,920; per credit resident $288, nonresident $455.

Enrollment: full-time 346, part-time 15. Faculty: full-time 20, part-time 18. Degree conferred: M.S.W.

ADMISSION REQUIREMENTS. Transcript, three letters of reference, essays, evidence of commitment to profession and social concern required in support of School's application. Accepts transfer students. Apply to Office of Admissions by March 1. Phone: (631)444-3174; fax: (631)444-7565. Application fee $50.

ADMISSION STANDARDS. Selective. Usual minimum average: 2.5 (A = 4).

FINANCIAL AID. Fellowships, assistantships, internships, Federal W/S, loans. Apply by March 15 to the Office of Financial Aid. Use FAFSA.

DEGREE REQUIREMENTS. For M.S.W.: 64 credits minimum, 16 in field instruction; master's project; 3.0 GPA.

SUFFOLK UNIVERSITY
Boston, Massachusetts 02108-2770
Web site: www.suffolk.edu

Founded 1906. Located in historic Beacon Hill. Coed, Private control, Semester system. Special facilities: Center for Global Business Law and Ethics, Center for Innovation and Change Leadership, Center for Public Management, Center for Entrepreneurship Studies, Center for Advanced Legal Studies, Juvenile Justice Center, Institute on Public Policy and Political Leadership, Center for Restorative Justice, Center for Women's Health and Human Rights, Center for Crime and Justice Policy Research, Suffolk University Political Research Center. Library: 292,000 volumes, 6500 subscriptions. Total University enrollment: 8500.

Annual tuition: full-time $14,745 (M.B.A., M.S.A., M.S.T.), $12,240 (M.H.A., M.P.A.), $9106 (M.Ed.), $10,055 (M.A.C., M.S.P.S.), $10,374 (M.S.I.E.), $9895 (M.S.C.J., M.A.W.H., M.A.I.D., M.A.G.D.), $13,200 (Ph.D.). No on-campus housing for graduate students. Average academic year off-campus housing costs: $600 per month. Contact Dean of Students for off-campus housing information. Phone: (617)573-8647.

College of Arts and Sciences—Graduate Programs

Enrollment: full-time 182, part-time 391. University faculty: full-time 111, part-time 27. Degrees conferred: M.S., M.A., M.A.W.H., M.Ed., M.B.A., M.H.A., M.P.A., M.S.A., M.S.F., M.S.I.E., M.S.C.S., M.S.C.J., M.S.P.S., M.S.T., C.A.G.S., C.A.P.S., Ph.D., J.D.-M.B.A., J.D.-M.S.I.E., J.D.-M.P.A.

ADMISSION REQUIREMENTS. Official transcripts required in support of application. MAT or GRE, two letters of reference for M.A., M.S., M.S. in Ed., M.Ed., M.S.P.S., Ph.D. applicants. GMAT for M.B.A., M.S.F., M.S.A., M.S.T. applicants. GMAT or GRE for M.S.I.E. applicants. Online application available. TOEFL required for international applicants. Accepts transfer applicants. Apply to Director of Graduate Admissions by June 15 (Fall), November 15 (Spring). Application fee $35. Phone: (617)573-8302; fax: (617)573-0116.

ADMISSION STANDARDS. Very selective. Usual minimum average: 2.7 (A = 4).

FINANCIAL AID. Annual awards from institutional funds: scholarships, fellowships, internships, assistantships, Federal W/S, loans. Approved for VA benefits. Apply by March 15 to Director of Financial Aid. Phone: (617)573-8470. Use FAFSA and University's FAF. About 10% of students receive aid other than loans from University and outside sources. Aid available for part-time study.

DEGREE REQUIREMENTS. For M.A., M.S.Ed., M.S.I.E., M.S.P.S., M.S.C.S., M.S.C.J.: 30–36 hours minimum, at least 24 in residence. For M.B.A.: 30–36 hours, except students without previous training may be required to complete up to 59 hours. For M.P.A.: 36 hours minimum, at least 30 in residence; For M.S.A., M.S.F., M.S.T.: 30 hours beyond M.B.A., 57–60 without master's. For Ph.D.: 60 hours minimum beyond master's degree, at least 45 hours in residence; reading knowledge of two foreign languages for some departments or one language and a research tool; qualifying exam; candidacy; dissertation; final oral exam.

FIELDS OF STUDY.
Administration of Higher Education. M.Ed.
Clinical Psychology. Ph.D.
Communication. M.A.C.
Computer Science. M.S.C.S.
Criminal Justice. M.S.C.J.
Economics. Ph.D.
Economic Policy. M.S.E.P.
Ethics and Public Policy. M.S.
Foundation of Education. M.Ed.
Graphic Design. M.A.G.D.
Human Resource. M.S.
Interior Design. M.A.I.D.
International Economics. M.S.I.E.
Mental Health Counseling. M.S.M.H.C.
Middle School Teacher. M.Ed.
Organizational Learning and Development. M.S.O.L.D.
Political Science. M.S.P.S.
Professional Development for Secondary and Middle School Teaching. M.Ed.
Women's Health. M.A.W.H.
School Counseling. M.Ed.

Frank Sawyer School of Management
Web site: www.sawyer.suffolk.edu

Established 1937, expanded to include graduate study in 1948. Accredited programs: M.B.A., Accounting. Located on main campus; courses offered at Cape Cod Community College. Semester system. Special Programs: accelerated MBA program; foreign exchange programs (in Czech Republic, France, Ireland, Italy, Spain, United Kingdom); internships.

Tuition: per semester M.B.A., M.S.A., M.S.T. $14,745; M.S.F. per credit $1073; M.H.A., M.P.A. $12,240. E.M.B.A. tuition: per credit $1337. On-campus rooms and apartments available for both single and married students. Contact Graduate Housing Office for both on- and off-campus housing information. Phone: (617)573-8239.

Enrollment: total full-time 231, part-time 789. Faculty: 39 full-time, 45 part-time; 95% with Ph.D./D.B.A. Degrees conferred: M.B.A. (full-time, part-time, day, late afternoons, evenings, and weekends); accelerated programs; M.B.A. for Attorneys, M.B.A. for CPAs, M.B.A. for Berklee College of Music Management majors; E.M.B.A. (weekends only), eM.B.A. (Online M.B.A.), M.H.A. (Health Administration), M.P.A. (Public Administration), M.S.A. (Accounting), M.S.F. (Finance), M.S.F.S.B. (Financial Services and Banking), M.S.T. (Taxation), M.B.A.-J.D., M.B.A.-M.S.A., M.B.A.-M.S.T., M.B.A.-M.S.F., M.B.A.-M.P.A., M.P.A.-M.S. (Criminal Justice, Mental Health Counseling, Political Science), M.P.A.-J.D.

ADMISSION REQUIREMENTS. All applicants should have a bachelor's degree from a recognized institution of higher education, a strong mathematics background, and GPA 2.6 (A = 4). Contact either the Director of Graduate Admissions at (617) 573-8302, fax: (617)573-0116, or Director MBA Programs at (617)573-8306 for application material and information. Online application available. Early applications are encouraged for both admission and financial aid consideration. Beginning students are admitted Fall, Spring, and Summer except for M.S.F. and E.M.B.A. (Fall and Spring only). Both U.S. citizens and international applicants apply by June 1 (Fall), November 1 (Spring), April 1 (Summer). Submit an application, GMAT results (will accept GMAT test results from the last five years, latest acceptable date is June), official transcripts from each undergraduate/graduate school attended, two letters of recommendation, a statement of personal goals, résumé (prefers at least four years of work experience), and an application fee of $50 to the Office of Graduate Admission. In addition, international students (whose native language is other than English) should submit a TOEFL (550 minimum score) report, certified translations and evaluations of all official transcripts, recommendation should be in English or with certified translations, proof of health/immunization certificate, and proof of sufficient financial resources for two years of academic study. On-campus visits are encouraged prior to the admissions reviewing completed application. Admissions Committee may consider applicants with some academic course work deficiencies. Joint degree applicants must apply to and be accepted to both schools; contact the admissions office for current information and specific admissions requirements. Rolling admissions process.

ADMISSION STANDARDS. Selective. Mean GMAT: 520, mean GPA: 2.9 (A = 4). Accepts approximately 65% of total annual applicants.

FINANCIAL AID. Scholarships, grants, fellowships, Federal Perkins Loans, Stafford Subsidized and Unsubsidized Loans, Federal W/S available. Financial aid is available for part-time study in the form of Graduate Management part-time Scholarship Grants. Merit-based financial aid available for international applicants. Fellowships may be available for joint degree candidates. Financial aid applications and information are generally included with the admissions materials. Apply by April 1 (Fall). Request merit-based aid, fellowship information from the School of Management. Phone: (617)573-8088. Contact the University's Financial Aid Office for current need-based financial aid information. Phone: (617)573-8470. Use FAFSA (School code: 00218), also submit institutional FAF, a Financial Aid Transcript, Federal Income Tax forms. Approximately 30% of students receive some form of financial assistance.

DEGREE REQUIREMENTS. For M.B.A.: 30–54 credit (19 courses) program including 24 elective credits, two-year program; degree program must be completed in five years. For E.M.B.A.: 54-credit program. For M.S.A., M.S.T.: 30–60 credit programs. For M.S.E.S.: 48-credit program. For M.S.F., M.S.F.S.B.: 30–48 credit programs. For M.B.A.-J.D.: 117-credit programs, four- to five-year program.

FIELDS OF STUDY.
Accounting. M.S.A.
Banking and Financial Services. M.S.
Business Administration. Includes concentrations in accounting, corporate finance, entrepreneurship, finance, health management, human resource management, international business, management, marketing, nonprofit management, organizational behavior, taxation.
Finance. Includes financial services and banking (M.S.F.S.B.). M.S.F.
Health Administration. M.H.A.
Management. M.B.A.
Public Administration. Includes disability studies, finance and human resources, health administration, nonprofit management, state and local government, philanthropy and media.
Taxation. M.S.T.

Law School

Web site: www.law.suffolk.edu

Established 1906. ABA approved since 1953. AALS member. Private control. Semester system. Special facility: Juvenile Justice Center. Special program: summer program at University of Lund, Sweden. Law library: 360,624 volumes, 6620 subscriptions: has LEXIS, NEXIS, WESTLAW, DIALOG; has more than 1000 network connections.

Annual tuition: $35,948 (day), $26,960 (evening); per credit $1497 (LL.M.). No on-campus housing available. Total average annual additional expense: $16,319.

Enrollment: first-year class 359 (day), 195 (evening); total day and evening 1644 (men 50%, women 50%, minorities 13%). Faculty: full-time 78, part-time 80. Student to faculty ratio is 17.1 to 1. Degrees conferred: J.D., J.D.-M.B.A., J.D.-M.P.A., J.D.-M.S.F., J.D.-M.S.I.E., J.D.-M.S.C.J., LL.M.(Global Law and Technology).

ADMISSION REQUIREMENTS. LSDAS Law School report, bachelor's degree, transcript, LSAT (no later than February), personal statement, one letter of recommendation required in support of application. Interview not required. Accepts limited number of transfer applicants. Graduates of unaccredited institutions not considered. Apply to Director of Admissions by March 1. Application fee $60. Phone: (617)573-8144; fax: (617)523-1367.

ADMISSION STANDARDS. Selective. Accepts approximately 42% of full-time, 52% of part-time students. Number of full-time applicants 2623, part-time 578; number of full-time acceptance 1112, part-time 299; number of full-time enrolled 359, part-time 195; LSAT (75% of full-time students have a score at or above 154, part-time 151); GPA (75% of full-time students have a GPA at or above 3.10, part-time 3.00). *U.S. News & World Report* ranking is in the third tier of all U.S. law schools.

FINANCIAL AID. Scholarships, grants, fellowships, assistantships, Federal W/S, loans. Apply to Financial Aid Office by

March 1. Phone: (617)573-8147. Use FAFSA (School code: E00517) and institutional FAF. About 54% of full-time and 22% of part-time students receive University aid other than loans. Has a loan repayment assistance program.

DEGREE REQUIREMENTS. For J.D.: 90 semester hours minimum, at least the last year in residence. For LL.M.: 24 credit program; substantial piece of written work. For master's degrees: see Graduate School listing above.
Note: Summer program abroad in Lund, Sweden.

SUL ROSS STATE UNIVERSITY
Alpine, Texas 79832
Web site: www.sulross.edu

Founded 1920. Located 300 miles W of San Antonio. Coed. State control. Semester system. Library: 275,000 volumes, 1800 subscriptions. Total University enrollment: 2400.

Tuition: per credit resident $112, nonresident $390. On-campus housing for 155 married students, 320 men, 480 women. Average academic year housing costs: $325–$375 per month for married students, $2000–$2500 (room and board) or $950–$1450 (room only) for single students. Contact Housing Officer for both on- and off-campus housing information. Phone: (432)837-8190.

Graduate Division

Graduate study since 1930. Enrollment: full-time 229, part-time 751 (men 55%, women 45%). Graduate faculty: full-time 60, part-time 20. Degrees conferred: M.A., M.B.A., M.Ed., M.S.

ADMISSION REQUIREMENTS. Two official transcripts, GRE, GMAT required in support of application. Online application available. TOEFL (minimum score 520), interview required for international applicants. Interview not required for domestic applicants. Accepts transfer applicants. Graduates of unaccredited institutions not considered. Apply to Office of Admissions and Record by July 15 (Fall), December 1 (Spring), May 1 (First Summer Session), June 25 (Second Summer Session). Accepts Texas Common Application. Application fee: none for domestic applicants, $50 for international applicants. Phone: (432)837-8052; fax: (432)837-8431.

ADMISSION STANDARDS. Relatively open. Usual minimum average: 2.5 (A = 4); minimum GRE: 850; minimum GMAT: 400.

FINANCIAL AID. Annual awards from institutional funds: twelve scholarships, ten research assistantships, twenty-four administrative assistantships, four internships, Federal W/S, loans. Approved for VA benefits. Apply by June 1 to Dean, Graduate Division. Phone: (432)837-8055. Use FAFSA (School code: 003625). About 68% of students receive aid other than loans from University. Aid sometimes available for part-time students.

DEGREE REQUIREMENTS. For M.A., M.S.: 30 semester hours minimum, at least 18 in residence; thesis; comprehensive exam. For M.Ed.: 36 semester hours minimum, at least 24 in residence; thesis/nonthesis option; comprehensive exam. For M.B.A.: 56 semester hours minimum, at least 30 hours in residence; computer proficiency; thesis/nonthesis option; comprehensive exam.

FIELDS OF STUDY.
Animal Science.
Art. Includes applied, design, education, history.
Biology.
Business Administration. Includes business, international trade, management.

Counseling.
Criminal Justice.
Educational Diagnostician.
Elementary Education.
English.
Geology.
History.
Industrial Arts Education.
Liberal Arts.
Physical Education.
Political Science.
Psychology.
Public Administration.
Range and Wildlife Management.
Reading.
School Administration.
Secondary Education.

SYRACUSE UNIVERSITY

Syracuse, New York 13244-0003
Web site: www.syracuse.edu

Founded 1871. CGS and AAU member. Coed. Private control. Semester system. Special facilities: Center for Advanced Technology in Computer Application and Software Engineering, Science and Technology Center, Northeast Parallel Architectures Center, Center for Membrane Engineering and Science, Center for the Study of Citizenship, Institute for Energy Research, Institute for Sensory Research, Interdisciplinary Institute for Literacy, Advance Graphics Research Laboratory, Natural Sciences Computing Center, Centro de Estudios Hispanicos, Gerontology Center, Robert H. Brethen Operations Management Institute, Better Audio Laboratory and Archive, George Arents Research Library. Library: 3,100,000 volumes, 12,000 subscriptions. Total University enrollment: 17,300.

Tuition: per credit $1068. On-campus housing for both married and single graduate students. Average academic year housing costs: $6670 (room only) for single students, $11,270 (including board) for married students. Apply to Office of South Campus Housing for both on- and off-campus housing information. Phone: (315)443-2567.

Graduate School

Graduate study since 1876. Enrollment: full-time 3132, part-time 1447. Graduate faculty: full-time 830, part-time 565. Degrees conferred: M.Arch.I., M.Arch.II, M.A., M.S., Ph.D., D.A., Ed.D., C.A.S., E.E., C.E., M.L.S., M.B.A., M.P.A., M.S.C., M.P.S., M.S.W., M.F.A., M.I.D., M.Mus. Combined degree programs: J.D.-M.L.S., J.D.-M.B.A., J.D.-M.S., J.D.-Ph.D., J.D.-M.P.A.

ADMISSION REQUIREMENTS. Two official transcripts, three letters of recommendation, interview for some programs, GRE for most programs, GMAT for Management required in support of School's application. Online application available. TOEFL required for international applicants. Accepts transfer applicants. Graduates of unaccredited institutions not considered. Apply to Graduate School by January 15 (Fall), November 1 (Spring). Rolling admission process. Application fee $65. Phone: (315)443-4492; e-mail: grad@syr.edu.

ADMISSION STANDARDS. Very competitive for some departments, competitive or selective for the others. Usual minimum average: 3.0 (A = 4).

FINANCIAL AID. Scholarships, fellowships, teaching/research assistantships, internships, tuition waivers, Federal W/S, loans. Approved for VA benefits. Apply by January 10 for fellowships, March 1 for assistantships and scholarships to appropriate department; to Financial Aid Office for all other programs. Phone: (315)443-1513. Submit FAFSA by February 28. About 65% of students receive aid other than loans from University. Aid available for part-time students.

DEGREE REQUIREMENTS. For most master's: 30 semester hours minimum, at least 24 in residence; thesis/nonthesis option for some departments; comprehensive oral/written exam. For Ph.D., Ed.D.; D.A.: 48–90 credit hours, 50% of program in residence; one foreign language and other research tool requirement; qualifying exam; dissertation; final oral exam; recital for D.A.

FIELDS OF STUDY.

SCHOOL OF ARCHITECTURE:
Architecture.

COLLEGE OF ARTS AND SCIENCES:
Applied Statistics.
Art History.
Audiology.
Biology.
Chemistry.
Clinical Psychology.
College Science Teaching.
Composition and Cultural Rhetoric.
Creative Writing.
English.
Experimental Psychology.
French Language, Literature, and Culture.
General Science.
Geology.
Linguistic Studies.
Mathematics.
Pan African Studies.
Philosophy.
Physics.
Religion.
School Psychology.
Social Psychology.
Spanish Language, Literature, and Culture.
Speech-Language Psychology.
Structural Biology, Biophysics, and Biochemistry.

SCHOOL OF EDUCATION:
Art Education.
Childhood Education.
Community Counseling.
Counselor Education.
Cultural Foundations of Education.
Early Childhood Special Education.
Educational Leadership.
Elementary Education N–6.
English Education.
Exercise Science.
Higher Education.
Instructional Design, Development, and Evaluation.
Literacy Education.
Mathematics Education.
Music Education.
Reading.
Rehabilitation Counseling.
School Counseling.
Science Education. Includes biology, chemistry, earth science, physics.
Social Studies Education.
Special Education. Includes educating infants and young children with special needs, learning disabilities, mental retardation.
Speech Education.
Teaching and Curriculum.

L. C. SMITH COLLEGE OF ENGINEERING AND COMPUTER SCIENCE:
Aerospace Engineering.
Bioengineering.
Chemical Engineering.
Civil Engineering.
Computer Information Science and Engineering.
Computer Engineering.
Computer Science.
Electrical and Computer Engineering.
Engineering Management.
Environmental Engineering.
Environmental Engineering Sciences.
Mechanical and Aerospace Engineering.
Neuroscience.
Systems Assurance.
System and Information Science.

COLLEGE OF HUMAN SERVICES AND HEALTH PROFESSIONS:
Child and Family Studies.
Marriage and Family Therapy.
Nutrition Science.
Social Work.

SCHOOL OF INFORMATION STUDIES:
Information Management. E.M.S., M.S.
Information Management (In Washington D.C.). M.S.
Information Science and Technology. Ph.D.
Library and Information Science. Includes school media. M.S.
Telecommunication and Network Management. M.S.

WHITMAN SCHOOL OF MANAGEMENT:
Accounting. M.S.
Business Administration. M.B.A., Ph.D.
Finance. M.S.
Media Management. M.S.

DOCTORAL FIELDS OF STUDY:
Accounting.
Entrepreneurship.
Finance/Managerial Statistics.
Management.
Management Information Systems.
Marketing.
Supply Chain.

THE MAXWELL SCHOOL:
Anthropology.
Economics.
Geography.
History.
International Relations.
Political Science.
Public Administration.
Social Science.
Sociology.

S. I. NEWHOUSE SCHOOL OF PUBLIC COMMUNICATION:
Advertising.
Broadcast Journalism.
Communications Management.
Documentary Film and History.
Magazine, Newspaper, and Online Journalism.
Mass Communication. Includes media ethics & diversity, media sociology, new media, political communication, popular television, public relations, social effects. Ph.D.
Media Management.
Media Studies.
New Media.
Newspaper.
Photography.
Public Diplomacy.
Public Relations.
Television-Radio-Film.

COLLEGE OF VISUAL AND PERFORMING ARTS:
Advertising Design.
Art Education.
Art Photography.
Art Video.
Ceramics.
Communication and Rhetorical Studies.
Computer Arts.
Environmental Arts.
Fiber Arts/Material Studies.
Film.
Illustration.
Jewelry and Metalsmithing.
Museum Studies.
Music Composition.
Music Conducting.
Music Education.
Music Theory.
Organ.
Painting.
Percussion.
Piano.
Printmaking.
Sculpture.
Strings.
Voice.
Wind Instruments.

College of Law (13244-1030)
Web site: www.law.syr.edu

Established 1895. Located on main campus. ABA approved since 1923. AALS charter member. Semester system. Full-time, day study, limited part-time program. Special facilities: Business Law Center, Family Law and Social Policy Center, Center for Global Law and Practice, Center for Law and Business Enterprise, Center for Law, Technology and Management, New Technology Law Center, Center on Human Policy, Law and Disability Studies. Special program: Law and Economics Program. Law library: 453,680 volumes, 3364 subscriptions: has LEXIS, NEXIS, WESTLAW, DIALOG.

Annual tuition: $35,790. On-campus housing available for both single and married students. Contact Office of South Campus Housing. Phone: (345)443-2567. Total average annual additional expense: $16,020. Law students tend to live off-campus. Off-campus housing and personal expense: approximately $14,500.

Enrollment: first-year class 264, total 683 (men 56%, women 44%, minorities 20%). Faculty: full-time 39, part-time 22. Student to faculty ratio is 15.7 to 1. Degrees conferred: J.D., J.D.-M.A. (Communications, Economics, History, International Relations, Media, Political Science), J.D.-M.B.A., J.D.-M.P.A., J.D.-M.S. (Accounting, Bioengineering, Environmental Science, Engineering), J.D.-Ph.D.

ADMISSION REQUIREMENTS. LSDAS Law School report, bachelor's degree, transcripts, LSAT (no later than April 1), up to three letters of recommendation required in support of application. Interview not required. Accepts transfer applicants. Graduates of unaccredited institutions not considered. Apply to Director of Admissions after September 15, before April 1. Rolling admission process. Fall admission only. Application fee $70. Phone: (315)443-1962; fax: (315)443-9568.

ADMISSION STANDARDS. Selective. Accepts approximately 34% of full-time, 13% of part-time students. Number of full-time applicants 2719, part-time 46; number of full-time acceptance 920, part-time 6; number of full-time enrolled 264, part-time 2; LSAT (75% of full-time students have a score at or above 153, part-time

N/A); GPA (75% of full-time students have a GPA at or above 3.12, part-time N/A). *U.S. News & World Report* ranking is in the third tier of all U.S. law schools.

FINANCIAL AID. Scholarships, grants, partial tuition waivers, fellowships, assistantships, Federal W/S, loans. Apply to Office of Admissions and Financial Aid by March 1. Phone: (315)443-1963. Use FAFSA (College code: 002882). Approximately 80% of students receive some aid from School.

DEGREE REQUIREMENTS. For J.D.: 87 (40 required) credits with a GPA of at least 2.0 (A = 4), plus completion of upper-divisional writing course; three-year program, four-year part-time program. Accelerated J.D. with summer course work. For J.D.-M.B.A., J.D.-M.S. Accounting: four-year program rather than five-year program if both degrees are taken consecutively. For J.D.-M.P.A.: three-year program rather than four-year program if both degrees are taken consecutively. For J.D.-M.A.: three-and-one-half-year program rather than four-and-one-half-year program if both degrees are taken consecutively. For J.D.-M.S.: three-year program rather than four-year program if both degrees are taken consecutively. J.D.-Ph. D.: six-year program rather than seven-year program if both degrees are taken consecutively.

TARLETON STATE UNIVERSITY
Stephenville, Texas 76402
Web site: www.tarleton.edu

Founded 1899. Located 65 miles SW of Fort Worth. Tarleton is a member of the Texas A&M University system. Coed. State control. Semester system. Library: 664,500 volumes, 2800 subscriptions. Total University enrollment: 9150.

Tuition: per credit hour, resident $140, nonresident $406. On-campus housing available. Average academic year housing costs: $4480 (including board) single students; $2500 (room only) married students. Contact Dean of Students for both on- and off-campus housing information. Phone: (254)968-9680. Day-care facilities available.

College of Graduate Studies

Graduate study since 1971. Enrollment: full-time 357, part-time 1200. Faculty: full-time 104, part-time 80. Degrees conferred: M.A., M.S., M.Ed., M.B.A., M.C.J.

ADMISSION REQUIREMENTS. Official transcripts, GRE/GMAT required in support of School's application. Online application available. TOEFL required for international applicants. Accepts transfer applicants. Graduates of unaccredited colleges not considered. Apply to Dean by August 1 (Fall), December 1 (Spring). Rolling admission process. Application fee $30, $75 for international applicants. Phone: (254)968-9104; fax: (254)968-9670.

ADMISSION STANDARDS. Relatively open. Usual minimum average: 2.5 (A = 4).

FINANCIAL AID. Annual awards from institutional funds: scholarship, teaching assistantships, internships, tuition waivers, Federal W/S, loans. Approved for VA benefits. Apply by May 1 to Graduate Dean. Phone: (254)968-9070; fax: (254)968-9670. Use FAFSA (School code: 003631) and institutional FAF. Aid available for part-time students.

DEGREE REQUIREMENTS. For master's: 36-48 hours minimum; comprehensive exam; thesis/nonthesis; project for some programs.

FIELDS OF STUDY.
Agriculture. M.S.
Agriculture Education. M.S.
Animal Science. M.S.
Biology. M.S.
Business Administration. M.B.A.
Counseling. M.Ed.
Counseling Psychology. M.S.
Criminal Justice. M.C.J.
Curriculum and Instruction. M.Ed.
Educational Administration. M.Ed.
Educational Leadership. Ed.D.
Educational Psychology. M.S.
Elementary Administration. M.Ed.
Elementary Education. M.Ed.
English. M.A.
Environmental Science. M.S.
Government. M.A.
History. M.A.
Human Resource Management. M.S.
Information Systems. M.S.
Liberal Studies. M.S.
Management and Leadership. M.S.
Manufacturing Quality and Leadership. M.S.
Mathematics. M.S.
Physical Education. M.Ed.
Political Science. M.A.
Psychology. M.S.
Reading. M.Ed.
Secondary Education. M.Ed.
Special Education. M.Ed.

TEMPLE UNIVERSITY
Philadelphia, Pennsylvania 19122-6096
Web site: www.temple.edu

Founded 1894. CGS member. Coed. State related. Semester system. Special facilities: Center for African American History and Culture, Center for Frontier Sciences, Center for Neurovirology and Cancer Biology, Center for Professional Development in Career and Technical, Center for Public Policy, Center for Social Policy and Community Development, Center for Student Professional Development, Center for Substance Abuse Research, Center for the Study of Federalism, Center for the Study of Force and Diplomacy, Institute on Aging, Institute on Disabilities, Institute for the Study of Literature, Literacy, and Culture, Institute for Survey Research. The University's NIH ranking is 119th among all U.S. institutions with 116 awards/grants worth $39,917,683. Libraries: 3,300,000 volumes, 16,700 subscriptions. Total University enrollment: 33,600.

Tuition: per credit resident $541, $559 (Tyler, Art), $574 (Business, Tourism & Hospitality), $563 (Health Profession); nonresident $790, $823 (Tyler, Art), $851 (Business, Tourism & Hospitality), $18,400 (Pharmacy resident), $27,256 (Pharmacy nonresident); per semester resident/nonresident $16,756 (International Business), E.M.B.A. $36,582. On-campus housing available. Average academic year housing cost: $5200 for single students; $10,300 for married students. Contact Office of Student Residences for both on- and off-campus housing information. Phone: (215)204-7184.

Graduate School

Enrollment: full-time 1988, part-time 3863. Faculty: full-time 1177, part-time 200. Degrees conferred: M.A., M.B.A., Ed.M. M.F.A., M.J., M.L.A., M.M., M.M.T., M.P.T., M.S., M.S.D., M.S.Ed., M.S.E., M.S.N., M.S.W., D.M.A., Ed.D., Ph.D.

ADMISSION REQUIREMENTS. Transcripts, letters of recommendation, statement of educational objectives required in support of School's application. GRE/Subject Tests/MAT/ GMAT, auditions, performances, portfolio, and/or interview required by some departments. TOEFL required of all international applicants. Accepts transfer applicants. Apply directly to Academic Department; closing dates vary by department, consult Bulletin or Web site. Application fee $40. Phone: (215)204-6575; fax: (215) 204-8781.

ADMISSION STANDARDS. Competitive or selective for most departments. Usual minimum average: 3.0 (A = 4).

FINANCIAL AID. Fellowships, research assistantships, teaching assistantships, administrative assistantships, graduate assistant, internships, tuition waivers, Federal W/S, loans. Approved of VA benefits. Apply by March 1 to appropriate department for scholarships, fellowships, teaching/research assistantships; to Director of Financial Aid for all other programs. Use FAFSA and institutional FAF. Phone: (215)204-1405; fax: (215)204-5897. Aid available for part-time students.

DEGREE REQUIREMENTS. For M.A., M.S.: 24 semester hours minimum; thesis for some departments; final oral/written exam usually required. For M.B.A.: 45–60 semester hours minimum, research paper; final oral/written exam. For M.S.E., M.Ed.: 30 semester hours minimum; final written exam; or 24 semester hours minimum; thesis. For M.F.A.: 48–52 semester hours minimum; thesis; final oral exam. For M.L.A.: 30 semester hours minimum; qualifying essay. For M.M.: 30 semester hours minimum, at least 24 in residence; comprehensive exam. For M.J.: 40 semester hours minimum; written exam; written project; oral exam. For M.S.W.: four semesters in full-time residence; field work experience; final project. For D.M.A.: 38 hours minimum beyond the master's; written/oral qualifying exam; final oral exam; dissertation/final project. For Ed.D.: 68 semester hours minimum beyond the bachelor's degree; preliminary written exam; dissertation; final oral/written exam. For Ph.D.: three years minimum beyond the bachelor's; dissertation; final oral exam.

FIELDS OF STUDY.
Accounting. M.B.A.
Accounting and Financial Management. M.S.
Actuarial Science. M.S.
Adult and Organizational Development. Ed.M.
African American Studies. M.A., Ph.D.
Anatomy. Ph.D.
Anthropology. Ph.D.
Art Education. Ed.M.
Art History. M.A., Ph.D.
Bassoon. M.M., D.M.A.
Biochemistry. M.S., Ph.D.
Bioengineering. M.S.
Biology. M.S., Ph.D.
Biomedical Neuroscience. M.S., Ph.D.
Broadcasting Telecommunication Mass Media. M.A.
Business Administration. Includes accounting (M.B.A., Ph.D.), business management (M.B.A.), finance (Ph.D.), financial management-corporate financial management (M.B.A.), financial management-investment management (M.B.A.), healthcare management (M.B.A.), human resource management (M.B.A., Ph.D.), information technology management (M.B.A.), international business management (M.B.A., Ph.D.), management information systems (Ph.D.), marketing management (M.B.A.), risk, insurance and healthcare (Ph.D.), risk management (M.B.A.), strategic management (M.B.A., Ph.D.), tourism (Ph.D.).
Career and Technical Education. M.S. Ed.
Cell Biology. M.S.
Cello. M.M., D.M.A.
Ceramics and Glass. M.F.A.
Chemistry. M.A., Ph.D.

Choral Conducting. M.M.
Civil Engineering. M.S.E.
Clarinet. M.M., D.M.A.
Communication Management. Includes media management, government and social policy, strategic and corporate communication management. M.S.
Communication Sciences. Ph.D.
Community and Regional Planning. M.S.
Community Health Education. M.P.H.
Computer and Information Science. Includes artificial intelligence and applications, information systems, software systems. Ph.D.
Counseling Psychology. Ed.M., Ph.D.
Criminal Justice. M.A., Ph.D.
Curriculum, Instruction and Technology in Education. Includes applied behavior analysis, career and technical education, early childhood education, English education, mathematics education, reading, science education, second and foreign language education, special education, TESOL. M.S.Ed.
Curriculum, Instruction and Technology in Education/Language Arts Education. Ed.D.
Curriculum Instruction and Technology in Education/Math and Science Education. Ed.D.
Dance. Includes cultural studies (Ed.M.), dance education (Ed.M.). M.Ed., M.F.A., Ph.D.
Economics. M.A., Ph.D.
Educational Administration. Ed.M., Ed.D.
Educational Psychology. Ed.M., Ph.D.
Electrical Engineering. M.S.E.
Engineering. Ph.D.
English. Includes creative writing. Ph.D.
Environmental Health. M.S.
Epidemiology. M.S.
Fiber and Fabric Design. M.F.A.
Film ad Media Arts. M.F.A.
Finance. M.S.
Geography. M.A.
Geology. M.S.
Graphic and Interactive Arts. M.F.A.
Health Studies. Ph.D.
Healthcare Financial Management. M.S.
History. M.A., Ph.D.
Human Resource Administration. M.B.A., M.S., Ph.D.
Journalism. M.J.
Kinesiology. Ed.M., Ph.D.
Liberal Arts. M.L.A.
Lighting Design. M.F.A.
Linguistics. M.A.
Management Information Systems. M.S.
Marketing. Includes marketing communication, management, research. M.S.
Mass Media and Communication. Ph.D.
Mathematics. M.A., Ph.D.
Mechanical Engineering. M.S.E.
Microbiology and Immunology. M.S., Ph.D.
Molecular Biology and Genetics. Ph.D.
Music Composition. M.M., D.M.A.
Music Education. M.M., Ph.D.
Music History. M.M.
Music Performance. Includes bassoon, cello, clarinet, classical guitar, double bass, flute, French horn, harp, harpsichord, oboe, percussion, piano, saxophone, trombone, trumpet, tuba, viola, violin, voice. M.M., D.M.A.
Music Theory. M.M., M.M.T.
Music Therapy. Ph.D.
Nursing. Includes adult nurse practitioner, family nurse practitioner, nurse educator, pediatric nurse practitioner. M.S.N.
Oboe. M.M., D.M.A.
Occupational Therapy. M.S., M.O.T.
Opera. M.M.
Oral Biology. M.S.
Painting. M.F.A.

Pathology. Ph.D.
Pharmaceutical Sciences/Medicinal Chemistry. M.S., Ph.D.
Pharmaceutical Sciences/Pharmaceutics. M.S., Ph.D.
Pharmaceutical Sciences/Pharmacodynamics. M.S., Ph.D.
Pharmacology/Medicine. Ph.D.
Philosophy. M.A., Ph.D.
Photography. M.F.A.
Physical Education. Ed.M., Ph.D.
Physical Therapy. D.P.T., Ph.D.
Physics. M.S., Ph.D.
Physiology. M.S., Ph.D.
Piano. M.M., D.M.A.
Piano Accompanying. Includes chamber music, opera coaching. M.M.
Piano Pedagogy. M.M.
Political Science. M.A., Ph.D.
Printmaking. M.F.A.
Psychology. Ph.D.
Public Health. Includes community health education (M.P.H.), school health education (Ed.M.), environmental health (M.S.).
Quality Assurance and Regulatory Affairs. M.S.
Religion. M.A., Ph.D.
School Health Education. Includes counseling, curriculum and learning. Ed.M.
School Psychology. Ed.M., Ph.D.
Sculpture. M.F.A.
Social Work. M.S.W.
Sociology. M.A., Ph.D.
Spanish. M.A., Ph.D.
Speech Language and Hearing Science. M.A.
Sport and Recreation Administration. Ed.M.
Statistics. M.S., Ph.D.
String Pedagogy. M.M.
Theater. Includes acting, design (costume construction, costume design, lighting design, scene design), directing, playwriting. M.F.A.
Therapeutic Recreation. Ed.M.
Tourism and Hospitality Management. M.T.H.M.
Urban Education. Ed.M, Ph.D.
Urban Planning. M.S.
Urban Studies. M.A.

Kornberg School of Dentistry (19140)

Web site: www.temple.edu/dentistry

Organized 1863 as Philadelphia Dental College. Joined Temple University in 1907. Located at the Health Sciences Campus. Semester system. Special facility: Rosenthal Clinic Center.

Annual tuition: resident $32,220, nonresident $45,620. On-campus housing available. Average academic year off-campus housing costs: $13,500. Contact the Office of University Housing. Phone: (215)704-7184. Total average cost for all other first-year expenses: $7500.

Enrollment: first year class 125, total 500 (men 62%, women 38%, minorities 8%, state residents 42%), graduate program 60. Faculty: full-time 79, part-time 79. Degrees conferred: D.D.S., D.D.S.-M.B.A., M.S., Ph.D., Certificates.

ADMISSION REQUIREMENTS. For D.D.S. program: AADSAS, official transcripts, DAT required in support of School's application. Evidence of proficiency in English required of international students. Applicants must have completed at least three years of college study, four years of study preferred. Preference given to state residents. Accepts transfer applicants. Graduates of unaccredited colleges not considered. Apply to Assistant Dean after August 1, before March 1. Application fee $30. Phone: (215) 707-7667; fax: (215)707-2917. For graduate program: official transcripts, D.D.S. or D.M.D. degree, interview required in support of School's application. Transfer applicants, graduates of unaccredited institutions not considered. Apply to School by March 1 (Fall). Application fee $30.

ADMISSION STANDARDS. Selective. Accepts about 5–10% of all D.D.S. applicants. Usual minimum UGPA: 2.75 (A = 4). Mean DAT: academic 19 PAT 17; mean UGPA 3.30. For graduate programs: usual minimum average 3.0 (A = 4).

FINANCIAL AID. For D.D.S. program: Scholarships, Federal loans, private loans. Contact the Student Affairs Office after acceptance for Financial Assistance. Phone: (215)707-7663. Use FAFSA (School code: E00353). About 90% of students receive aid other than loans from the School and outside sources. For graduate programs: fellowships, teaching/research assistantships, loans. Apply by July 1 to Dean of School. Use FAFSA.

DEGREE REQUIREMENTS. For D.D.S.: satisfactory completion of forty-five-month program. For Postgraduate Certificate Programs: four semesters minimum (two years) in full-time residence. For M.S.: two semesters minimum (one year) in full-time residence; thesis; final exam. For Ph.D.: see Graduate School listing above.

FIELDS OF GRADUATE STUDY.
Endodontology.
General Dentistry.
Informatics.
Oral Biology. M.S.
Oral Surgery.
Orthodontics.
Periodontology.

James E. Beasley School of Law

Web site: www.law.temple.edu

Established 1895. Located on main campus. ABA approved since 1933. AALS member. Semester system. Full-time, part-time study. Special facilities: Institute for International Law and Public Policy, Center for Community Non-Profit Organizations, Cyperspace Law Institute. Special programs: semester abroad in Tokyo, Japan; summer abroad in Rome, Italy, Tel Aviv, Israel, Beijing, People's Republic of China, Cork, Ireland. Law library: 573,568 volumes, 3048 subscriptions, has LEXIS, NEXIS, WESTLAW, DIALOG, RLN, INNOPAC, CALI; has more than 400 network connections; is a Federal Government Depository.

Tuition: per semester, full-time resident $15,200, nonresident $26,498; full-time evening resident $12,176, nonresident $21,200; part-time per credit resident $589, nonresident $1083; LL.M. (international) full-time per semester $21,020, part-time $980; LL.M. (Trial Advocacy) per semester resident and nonresident $20,056; LL.M. (Tax) per credit resident $639, nonresident $877. On-campus housing available for single and married LL.M. students (about half of entering LL.M. class live on-campus). Annual on-campus housing cost: $13,000–$15,000. Housing deadline June 1. Contact Office of University Housing for both on- and off-campus housing. Phone: (218)207-7223. J.D. students tend to live off-campus. Off-campus housing and personal expenses: approximately $19,254.

Enrollment: first-year class full-time 250, part-time 73; total full- and part-time 1126 (men 52%, women 48%, minorities 12%). Faculty: full-time 65, part-time 86. Student to faculty ratio 15.9 to 1. Degrees conferred: J.D., J.D.-M.B.A., J.D.-LL.M. (Tax, Trial Advocacy), LL.M. (Tax full- and part-time program; Trial Advocacy, evening and weekend program), LL.M. (international graduates who have completed a basic legal education and received a university degree in law in another country), S.J.D.

ADMISSION REQUIREMENTS. LSDAS Law School report, bachelor's degree, transcripts, LSAT (not later than February), personal statement, up to three letters of recommendation required in support of application. Accepts transfer applicants. Graduates of unaccredited colleges not considered. Apply to School Admissions Office, preferably by March 1. Application fee $60. Phone: (800)560-1428; fax: (215)204-1185.

ADMISSION STANDARDS. Selective. Accepts approximately 29% of full-time, 34% of part-time students. Number of full-time applicants 4846 part-time 397; number of full-time acceptance 1409, part-time 135; number of full-time enrolled 250, part-time 73; LSAT (75% of full-time students have a score at or above 160, part-time 156); GPA (75% of full-time students have a GPA at or above 3.09, part-time 2.92). *U.S. News & World Report* ranking is in the second tier (tied at 60th) of all U.S. law schools.

FINANCIAL AID. Scholarships, Federal W/S, loans. Apply to the Office of Financial Aid by March 1. Phone: (800)560-1428. Use FAFSA (School code: E00354). About 45% of full-time and 16% of part-time students receive aid other than loans from School. There is a Public Interest Loan Repayment program.

DEGREE REQUIREMENTS. For J.D.: satisfactory completion of three-year day or four-year evening program: 83 unit program. For LL.M.: at least 24 credits beyond the J.D.; one year minimum; final research project. For S.J.D.: at least one full year in residence; a dissertation of publishable quality.

School of Medicine (19140)

Web site: www.medschool.temple.edu

Established 1901. Special facilities: Center for Biomedical Physics, Center for Cardiovascular Research, Center for Neurovirology, Center for Obesity Research and Education, Center for Substance Abuse Research, Fels Institute for Cancer Research & Molecular Biology, Sol Sherry Thrombosis Research Center. NIH ranking is 119th among all U.S. institutions with 116 awards/grants worth $39,917,683.

Annual tuition: resident $38,378, nonresident $46,880. No on-campus housing available. Total averaged figure for all other expenses: $13,821.

Enrollment: first-year class 176, total 713 (men 54%, women 46%, minorities 40%, state residents 56%). Faculty: full-time 450, part-time 69. Degrees conferred: M.D., M.D.-M.B.A., M.D.-M.P.H., M.D.-Ph.D.

ADMISSION REQUIREMENTS. For M.D. program: AMCAS report, transcripts, letters of recommendation, MCAT, final screening interview, supplemental application required in support of application. Preference given to state residents. Interview by invitation only. Has EDP; apply between June 1 and August 1. Accepts transfer applicants. Apply to Director of Admissions after June 1, before December 15. Application fee $70. Phone: (215) 707-3656; fax: (215)707-6932. For graduate program: transcripts, two letters of recommendation, GRE Subject Tests, interview required in support of application. Accepts transfer applicants. Graduates of unaccredited colleges not considered. Apply to Associate Dean of Health Sciences Center prior to registration. Application fee $10.

ADMISSION STANDARDS. Competitive. Accepts about 7% of all applicants. Number of applications 7504 (6556 out-of-state); number interviewed 978 (725 out-of-state); number of acceptance 589 (366 out-of-state); number enrolled 176 (83 out-of-state). Mean Composite MCAT 10.0; mean UGPA 3.61 (A = 4.).

FINANCIAL AID. For M.D. program: scholarships, loans; apply to Director, Health Sciences Center Financial Aid Office, by April 1. Phone: (215)707-2667. Use FAFSA and GAPSFAS (School code: E00352). About 89% of students receive some type of aid. For graduate program: scholarships, fellowships, assistantships for teaching/research. Apply to Associate Dean of Graduate School for scholarships, fellowships, to appropriate department chair for assistantships; no specified closing date. About 20% of graduate students receive aid other than loans from School.

DEGREE REQUIREMENTS. For M.D.: satisfactory completion of four-year program; all students must pass USMLE Step 1

prior to entering third year, and pass Step 2 prior to awarding of M.D. For M.B.A., M.S., Ph.D.: see Graduate School listing above.

FIELDS OF GRADUATE STUDY.
Anatomy and Cell Biology. M.S., Ph.D.
Biochemistry. M.S., Ph.D.
Microbiology and Immunology. Ph.D.
Molecular Biology and Genetics. Ph.D.
Neuroscience. M.S., Ph.D.
Pathology. Ph.D.
Pharmacology. Ph.D.
Physiology. M.S., Ph.D.

TENNESSEE STATE UNIVERSITY

Nashville, Tennessee 37209-1561
Web site: www.tnstate.edu

Founded 1912. CGS member. Coed. State control. Semester system. Special facilities: Center of Excellence in Information Systems and Engineering Management, Center of Excellence in Research and Policy on Basic Skills, Small Business Development Center. Library: 580,650 volumes, 2500 subscriptions. Total University enrollment: 8900.

Annual tuition: full-time resident $5446, nonresident $15,722; per credit resident $288, nonresident $754. On-campus housing for single students. Apply to Dean of Women or Dean of Men. Average annual housing expenses $3400, $5200 (including board). Day-care facilities available.

Graduate School

Graduate study since 1941. Enrollment: full- and part-time 1750. Faculty: full-time 129, part-time 34. Degrees conferred: M.A., M.A.Ed., M.E., M.Ed., M.B.A., M.P.A., M.S., M.S.N., M.C.J., Ed.D.

ADMISSION REQUIREMENTS. Transcripts, GRE required in support of School's application. Online application available. TOEFL required for international foreign applicants. Accepts transfer applicants. Apply to Dean, Graduate School, at least six weeks prior to registration. Rolling admission process. Application fee $25. Phone: (615)963-5901; fax: (615)963-5963.

ADMISSIONS STANDARDS. Relatively open to selective. Usual minimum average: 2.5 (A = 4).

FINANCIAL AID. Fellowships, assistantships, internships, Federal W/S, loans. Approved for VA benefits. Apply to Director of Financial Aid; no specified closing date. Use FAFSA. Aid available for part-time students.

DEGREE REQUIREMENTS. For master's: 30–33 semester hours minimum, at least 27 in residence; thesis in some departments. For Ed.D.: 69 hours maximum beyond the master's; comprehensive exam; advancement to candidacy; dissertation or special project; final oral exam.

FIELDS OF STUDY.

AGRICULTURE AND CONSUMER SCIENCES:
Agricultural Science. Includes agricultural education, agribusiness, animal science, plant science.
Family and Consumer Sciences.

COLLEGE OF ARTS AND SCIENCES:
Biological Sciences.
Biology.
Chemistry.

Criminal Justice.
Language, Literature and Philosophy.
Mathematical Sciences.
Music.

COLLEGE OF BUSINESS:
Business Administration. Includes concentrations in accounting, healthcare economics and management, management information systems, supply chain management.

COLLEGE OF EDUCATION:
Advanced Studies in Teaching and Learning.
Curriculum and Instruction. Includes concentrations in adult education, educational technology, history, teaching of non-English language children, reading, secondary school instruction (M.Ed.); curriculum planning, secondary education, reading, special education (Ed.D.).
Educational Administration and Supervision. Includes concentrations in K–12 administration, higher education administration.
Elementary Education.
Guidance and Counseling. Includes concentration in pre-K–12 school counseling.
Health, Physical Education and Recreation.
Human Performance and Sports Sciences. Includes concentrations in exercise science, sports administration.
Psychology. Includes concentrations in counseling psychology, school psychology.
Special Education.

COLLEGE OF ENGINEERING, TECHNOLOGY, AND COMPUTER SCIENCE:
Computer and Information Systems Engineering. Includes computer communication and networks, control systems and signal processing, manufacturing, robotics and computer integration.
Engineering. Includes biomedical, civil, electrical, environmental, manufacturing, mechanical.

COLLEGE OF HEALTH SCIENCES:
Occupational Therapy.
Physical Therapy.
Speech and Hearing Science.

INSTITUTE OF GOVERNMENT:
Professional Studies.
Public Administration.

SCHOOL OF NURSING:
Nursing. Includes concentrations in holistic nursing, family nurse practitioner, nursing administration, nursing education, nursing informatics.

TENNESSEE TECHNOLOGICAL UNIVERSITY
Cookeville, Tennessee 38505
Web site: www.tntech.edu

Established 1915. Located 80 miles E of Nashville. CGS member. Coed. State control. Semester system. Special facilities: Center for Electric Power, Center for Manufacturing Research, Water Resources Center. Library: 640,500 volumes, 4800 subscriptions. Total University enrollment: 9300.

Annual tuition: full-time resident $8421, nonresident $22,389. On-campus housing for 300 married students (2000 men, 1800 women). Average academic year housing costs: $4000 for married students, $8700 (include board) for single students. Contact Director of Housing for both on- and off-campus housing. Phone: (931)372-3414. Day-care facilities available.

Graduate School

Graduate study since 1958. Enrollment: full-time 581, part-time 856. Faculty: full-time 315, part-time 40. Degrees conferred: M.A., M.S., M.B.A., Ed.S., Ph.D. (Engineering only).

ADMISSION REQUIREMENTS. Transcripts, letters of recommendation required in support of School's application. MAT required for education majors. GRE required for science and engineering majors. GMAT required for M.B.A. applicants. TOEFL required for international applicants. Accepts transfer applicants. Apply to Dean of Graduate School by March 1 (Fall), August 1 (Spring); international students apply at least six months in advance. Application fee $25, $30 for international applicants. Phone: (931)372-3233; fax: (931)372-3497.

ADMISSION STANDARDS. Selective. Usual minimum average: 2.75 (A = 4).

FINANCIAL AID. Annual awards from institutional funds: scholarships, teaching assistantships, research assistantships, internships, Federal W/S, loans. Approved for VA benefits. Apply by April 1 to appropriate department chair for assistantships, scholarships; to Financial Aid Office for all other programs. Phone: (931)372-3073; fax: (931)372-6335. Use FAFSA and University's FAF. About 50% of students receive aid from University. Aid available for part-time students.

DEGREE REQUIREMENTS. For master's: 30 semester credits minimum, at least 24 in residence; thesis; final oral exam. For M.B.A.: 36 hours. For Ed.S.: 30 credits minimum beyond the master's. For Ph.D.: 60 hours minimum; one year in residence; qualifying exam; advancement to candidacy; dissertation; final oral exam.

FIELDS OF STUDY.

COLLEGE OF ARTS AND SCIENCE:
Biology. Includes fisheries management, general biology.
Chemistry.
Computer Science.
English.
Environmental Sciences.
Mathematics. Includes applied mathematics, statistics.

COLLEGE OF BUSINESS ADMINISTRATION:
Business Management.
Distance MBA Program.

COLLEGE OF EDUCATION:
Advanced Studies in Teaching and Learning.
Curriculum and Instruction. Includes curriculum, early childhood, elementary, library science, reading, secondary, special.
Educational Psychology and Counselor Education. Includes agency counselor, education psychology, school counselor, school psychology.
Exceptional Learning. Includes applied behavior and learning, literacy, young children and families.
Health and Physical Education. Includes adapted physical education, elementary and middle school physical education, lifetime wellness.
Instructional Leadership. Includes developmental and administrative studies, elementary education, health and physical education/wellness, materials supervision, music performance and music education, reading, secondary education special education technology.

COLLEGE OF ENGINEERING:
Chemical Engineering.
Civil Engineering. Includes environmental, structural, transportation.

Electrical Engineering. Includes electromagnetic fields and physical electronics, communications theory and electronics, networks and control systems, power systems and energy conversion, computers and digital systems, nuclear systems.
Engineering.
Mechanical Engineering. Includes acoustics, control systems, design/mechanical systems, materials, thermal science/systems.

SCHOOL OF NURSING:
Nursing.

UNIVERSITY OF TENNESSEE AT CHATTANOOGA

Chattanooga, Tennessee 37403-2504
Web site: www.utc.edu

Founded 1886 as University of Chattanooga, merged July 1969 with the University of Tennessee. CGS member. Coed. State control. Semester system. Special facilities: Center for Economic Education, Cadek Conservatory of Music, Center for Environmental/Energy Education, Institute of Archaeology, Odor Research Center. Library: 491,179 volumes, 2768 subscriptions. Total University enrollment: 8650.

Tuition: per credit resident $327, nonresident $829. On-campus housing for limited number of single graduate students; none for married students (except during Summer). Average academic year housing costs: $3300 (excluding board). Contact Dean of Student Affairs Office for both on- and off-campus housing information. Phone: (423)425-4246. Day-care facilities available.

Graduate Division

Enrollment: full-time 536, part-time 782. University faculty teaching graduate students: full-time 149, part-time 38. Degrees conferred: M.A., M.B.A., M.Ed., M.M., M.P.A., M.S., M.S.C.J., M.S.N.

ADMISSION REQUIREMENTS. Transcripts, GRE, MAT for M.Ed., M.S.C.J., M.A., M.M., and M.S. in Psychology; GMAT for M.B.A., three letters of reference, required in support of application. Interview sometimes required. TOEFL required for international applicants. Accepts transfer applicants. Apply to Graduate Office by August 1 (Fall), well in advance of registration for other semesters. Application fee $25. Phone: (423)425-4666; fax: (423)425-5223.

ADMISSION STANDARDS. Relatively open. Usual minimum average: 2.5 (A = 4).

FINANCIAL AID. Fellowships, assistantships, internships, Federal W/S, loans. Approved for VA benefits. Apply to the Financial Aid Office; no specified closing date. Phone: (423)425-4677. Use FAFSA and University's FAF. Aid available for part-time students.

DEGREE REQUIREMENTS. For M.A., M.S., M.S.N.: 33 semester hours minimum, at least 27 in residence; thesis/nonthesis option. For M.B.A., M.P.A.: 31–36 semester hours minimum, at least 30 in residence. For M.Ed.: 33 semester hours minimum, at least 24 in residence; final comprehensive exam. For M.S.C.J.: 36 semester hours minimum, at least 30 in residence; qualifying exam; thesis optional; internship. For M.M.: 33 semester hours minimum, at least 30 in residence. Additional requirements depend upon major.

FIELDS OF STUDY.
Accountancy.
Business Administration.
Computational Engineering.
Computer Science.
Counseling.
Criminal Justice.
Educational Technology.
Elementary Education.
Engineering.
Engineering Management.
English.
Environmental Science.
Health and Human Performance.
Learning and Leadership.
Music.
Nursing.
Occupational Therapy.
Physical Therapy.
Psychology.
Public Administration.
School Leadership.
School Psychology.
Secondary Education.
Special Education.

UNIVERSITY OF TENNESSEE

Knoxville, Tennessee 37996
Web site: www.utk.edu

Founded 1794. CGS member. Coed. State control. Semester system. Special facilities: Institute of Agriculture, Center for Business and Economic Research, Energy, Environment and Resources Center, Forensic Anthropology Center, Management Development Center, McClung Museum, Measurement and Control Engineering Center, Social Science Research Institute, Space Institute, Stokey Institute of Liberal Arts, Transportation Center, cooperating University in Oak Ridge Associate Universities Program. The University's NIH ranking is 105th among all U.S. institutions with 137 awards/grants valued at $48,552,748. According to The Center at University of Florida, the University is ranked 77th in receipt of Federal Research funds with 100,486,000 and it ranks 60th for total University research expenditures with $217,389,000. The University's endowment assets rank it 92nd, with a value of $506,225,000. In 2004, the University awarded 280 doctorates which ranked it 49th among all U.S. institutions eligible to award that degree. Two of the University's faculty members have been elected to National Honor Academies and this ranks it 117th among all U.S. institutions. The Library: approximately 2,400,000 volumes, 17,628 subscriptions. Total University enrollment: 25,500.

Tuition: resident $5932, nonresident $18,174. On-campus housing for 800 married students, 7500 men, 7500 women. Average annual housing cost: $5800 for single students, $7150 for married students. Apply to Office of Residence Halls or Rental Properties. Phone: (865)974-3411. Day-care facilities available.

Graduate School

Graduate study since 1928. Enrollment: full-time 3518, part-time 1771. University faculty: full-time 1238, part-time 62. Degrees conferred: M.A., M.S., M.Arch., M.B.A., M.F.A., M.P.H., M.P.A., M.Acc., M.Math., M.Music., M.S.N., M.S.P., M.S.S.W., Ed.S., Ed.D., Ph.D.

ADMISSION REQUIREMENTS. Official transcripts, letters of recommendation required in support of School's application. Online application available. GRE Subject/GMAT required for many departments. TOEFL required for international applicants. Interview not required. Additional application materials may be required by some schools; please contact individual schools for current information. Accepts transfer applicants. Graduates of unaccredited institution. Apply to Office of Graduate Admissions and Records by February 1 (Fall). Foreign students apply at least six months prior to registration. Application fee $15. Phone: (865) 974-3251; fax: (865)974-6541; e-mail: gsinfo@utk.edu.

ADMISSION STANDARDS. Very selective for most departments, competitive or selective for the others. Usual minimum average: 2.7 (A = 4).

FINANCIAL AID. Scholarships, fellowships, research assistantships, teaching assistantships, administrative assistantships, internships, Federal W/S, loans. Approved for VA benefits. Apply by March 1 to the Graduate School for fellowships, to appropriate department chairman for assistantships; to Financial Aid Office for all other programs. Phone: (865)974-3131. Use FAFSA. About 65% of students receive aid other than loans from School and outside sources. Aid available for part-time students.

DEGREE REQUIREMENTS. For master's: 30 semester hours minimum; thesis/final project; final oral/written exam. For Ed.S.: 60 semester hours minimum; one to two semesters in full-time attendance; qualifying exam may be required; thesis/nonthesis option; final oral/written exam. For Doctorates: 24 hours minimum beyond the master's, at least one year in full-time residence; comprehensive written exam; reading knowledge of one foreign language or proficiency in research techniques; dissertation; final oral exam.

FIELDS OF STUDY.

INTERCOLLEGIATE PROGRAMS:
Aviation Systems. Offered at UT Space Institute. M.S.
Comparative and Experimental Medicine. GRE for admission.

COLLEGE OF AGRICULTURAL SCIENCES AND NATURAL RESOURCES:
Agricultural and Extension Education.
Agricultural Economics. GRE for admission. Includes agribusiness.
Animal Science. GRE for admission. Includes animal genetics, animal health and well-being, animal management, animal nutrition, animal physiology.
Biosystems Engineering. GRE required for international applicants.
Biosystems Engineering Technology. GRE required for international applicants.
Entomology and Plant Pathology. M.S.
Food Science and Technology. GRE for admission.
Forestry. GRE for admission. M.S.
Natural Resources. GRE for admission. Ph.D.
Ornamental Horticulture and Landscape Design. Includes landscape design horticulture, turfgrass, wood ornamentals. M.S.
Plant and Soil Sciences. GRE for admission. Ph.D.
Plant Sciences. M.S.
Wildlife and Fisheries Science. GRE for admission. M.S.

COLLEGE OF ARCHITECTURE AND DESIGN:
Architecture. GRE for admission. M.Arch.
Landscape Architecture. M.L.A.

COLLEGE OF ARTS AND SCIENCES:
Anthropology. GRE for admission.
Art. Portfolio for admission. M.F.A. only. Includes ceramics, drawing, graphic design, media arts, painting, printmaking, sculpture, watercolor.
Audiology. GRE for admission. Includes aural habilitation. M.A. only.
Biochemistry, Cellular, and Molecular Biology. GRE for admission.
Chemistry. GRE for admission.
Computer Science.
Ecology and Evolutionary Biology. GRE for admission.
English. GRE General/Subject for admission. Includes writing.

French. M.A.
Geography. GRE for admission.
Geology. GRE for admission.
German. M.A.
History. GRE for admission.
Life Sciences. GRE for admission. Includes genome science and technology, plant physiology and genetics.
Mathematics. Includes applied mathematics, mathematical ecology. M.M.
Microbiology. GRE for admission.
Modern Foreign Languages. Ph.D.
Music. Audition required for admission. M.M.
Philosophy. GRE for admission. Includes medical ethics, religious studies.
Physics.
Planning. GRE for admission. M.S.P.
Political Science. GRE for admission.
Psychology. GRE/Subject for admission.
Public Administration. GRE for admission. M.P.A.
Sociology. GRE for admission.
Spanish. M.A.
Speech and Hearing Science. GRE for admission. Ph.D.
Speech Pathology. GRE for admission. M.A.
Theatre. Audition for admission. M.F.A.

COLLEGE OF BUSINESS ADMINISTRATION:
Accounting. GMAT for admission. M.Acc.
Business Administration. GMAT for admission. Includes accounting, finance, logistics and transportation, management, marketing, operations management.
Economics. GRE or GMAT for admission.
Human Resource Development. M.S.
Industrial and Organizational Psychology. GRE for admission.
Management Science. GRE or GMAT for admission. M.S., Ph.D.
Statistics. GRE or GMAT for admission. M.S.

COLLEGE OF COMMUNICATIONS:
Communication and Information. GRE for admission. M.S., Ph.D.
Information Sciences. M.S.

COLLEGE OF EDUCATION, HEALTH AND HUMAN SCIENCES:
Child and Family Studies. M.S.
College Student Personnel. GRE for admission. M.S.
Consumer Services Management. M.S.
Counseling. Includes mental health counseling, rehabilitation counseling, school counseling. M.S.
Education. Includes Counselor education, cultural studies of educational foundations, educational psychology and research, exercise science, higher education administration, instructional technology, leadership studies in education, literacy studies, school psychology, special education, sport studies, teacher education. Ph.D.
Educational Administration. M.S., Ed.S.
Educational Psychology. M.S.
Exercise Science. M.S.
Health and Human Sciences. Includes child and family studies; community health; hospitality and tourism management, nutrition science, retail and consumer sciences. Ph.D.
Instruction Technology and Educational Studies. M.S., Ed.S.
Nutrition. M.S.
Public Health. Includes community health education, health planning/administration, veterinary public health. M.P.H.
Recreation and Leisure Studies. M.S.
Safety. M.S.
School Counseling. Ed.S.
School Psychology. Ed.S.
Sports Studies. M.S.
Teacher Education. Includes elementary teaching, middle grades teaching, modified and early childhood special education, secondary teaching (M.S.); elementary education, English education, foreign language/ESL education, mathematics education,

reading education, science education, social science education, special education (Ed.S.).

COLLEGE OF ENGINEERING:
Aerospace Engineering. GRE for international applicants.
Biomedical Engineering. GRE for admission.
Chemical Engineering. GRE for admission.
Civil Engineering. GRE for international applicants.
Computer Engineering. GRE for admission.
Electrical Engineering. GRE for Ph.D. candidates.
Engineering Science. GRE for international applicants.
Environmental Engineering. GRE for international applicants. M.S.
Industrial Engineering. GRE for admission. M.S.
Materials Science and Engineering. GRE for international applicants.
Mechanical Engineering. GRE for international applicants.
Nuclear Engineering. GRE for admission.
Polymer Engineering. GRE for international applicants.
Reliability and Maintainability. GRE for admission.

COLLEGE OF NURSING:
Nursing. GRE for admission. Includes adult health nursing, family nurse practitioner, mental health nursing, nurse anesthesia, nursing administration, nursing of women and children.

COLLEGE OF SOCIAL WORK:
Social Work. GRE for admission. Includes clinical social work practice, social welfare management, community practice.

College of Law

Web site: www.law.utk.edu

Established 1890. Located in Knoxville (37996-1810). ABA approved since 1925. AALS charter member. Semester system. Special facilities: Center for Entrepreneurial Law, Center for Advocacy and Dispute Resolution. Special Programs: summer program in Cambridge, England. Law library: 558,262 volumes, 6650 subscriptions; has LEXIS, WESTLAW, INFORTRAC; has more than 150 network connections.

Annual tuition: resident $9934, nonresident $25,290. On-campus housing available. Total average annual additional expense: $12,800.

Enrollment: first-year class 158, total 449 (men 50%, women 50%, minorities 16%). Faculty: full-time 29, part-time 27. Student to faculty ratio is 13.7 to 1. Degrees conferred: J.D., J.D.-M.B.A., J.D.-M.P.A.

ADMISSION REQUIREMENTS. LSDAS Law School report, bachelor's degree, transcripts, LSAT (not later than December), two letters of recommendation, personal statement, essay required in support of application. Interview not required. Preference given to state residents (70–80% state residents). Accepts transfer applicants. Graduates of unaccredited colleges not considered. Apply to Admissions Office after October 1, before March 1. Application fee $15. Phone: (865)974-4131; fax: (865)974-1572.

ADMISSION STANDARDS. Selective. Accepts approximately 20% of all students. Number of applicants 1622; number of acceptance 322; number enrolled 158; LSAT (75% of students have a score at or above 155); GPA (75% of students have a GPA at or above 3.36). *U.S. News & World Report* ranking is in the second tier (tied at 60th) of all U.S. law schools.

FINANCIAL AID. Scholarships, fellowships, Federal W/S, loans. Apply to Financial Aid Office by March 1. Phone: (865)974-4131. Use FAFSA (College code: 006725). About 45% of students receive aid other than loans from College.

DEGREE REQUIREMENTS. For J.D.: satisfactory completion of three-year program; 89 credit hour program.

College of Veterinary Medicine (37996-4550)
Web site: www.vet.utk.edu

Established 1974. Semester system. Special facilities: Hyperbaric Oxygen Therapy Chamber for Horses, Center for Disease Control and Prevention, Center for Management of Animal Pain. Library: 120,000 volumes, 1200 subscriptions.

Annual tuition: residents $14,590, nonresidents $38,658. On-campus housing available. Estimated living expenses: $7500. Total all other expenses: $4500.

Enrollment: first-year class 70, total 268 (men 21%, women 79%, minorities 5%, state residents 63%). Faculty: full- and part-time 108. Degrees conferred: D.V.M., D.V.M.-M.P.H.

ADMISSION REQUIREMENTS. VMCAS report, transcripts, VCAT, recommendations/evaluations, personal essay, animal/veterinary experience required in support of application. Interview by invitation only. Preference given to state residents. Graduates of unaccredited colleges not considered. Apply to the College (P.O. Box 1071) after July 1, before October 1. Application fee $25. Phone: (865)974-7354.

ADMISSION STANDARDS. Competitive. Accepts about 5–10% of all applicants. Number of applications 760 (628 out-of-state); number interviewed 244 (157 out-of-state); number of acceptance n/a (n/a out-of-state); number enrolled 70 (16 out-of-state). Usual minimum UGPA: nonresidents 3.2 (A = 4). GRE mean score (V + Q) 1142; mean UGPA residents 3.54, nonresidents 3.74.

FINANCIAL AID. Scholarships, fellowships, assistantships, internships, loans available. Apply after acceptance to Office of Financial Aid. Use FAFSA.

DEGREE REQUIREMENTS. For D.V.M.: satisfactory completion of four-year, nine-semester program.

FIELD OF GRADUATE STUDY.
Comparative and Experimental Medicine. M.S., Ph.D.

UNIVERSITY OF TENNESSEE AT MARTIN
Martin, Tennessee 38238-1000
Web site: www.utm.edu

Traces its origin to Hall-Moody Institute founded in 1900. State controlled since 1927. Located 125 miles NE of Memphis. CGS member. Semester system. Special facilities: Reelfoot Lake Research and Teaching Center, Center for Excellence in Science and Mathematics Education, Center for Environmental and Conservation Education. Library: 621,000 volumes, 2654 subscriptions. Selected by the Humanities Research Corporation as one of the exemplary institutions of higher education with regard to the use of the computer for learning and teaching. Total University enrollment: 6500.

Annual tuition: full-time resident $5200, nonresident $9000; per credit resident $291, nonresident $794. On-campus housing for 226 married students, 1155 men, 1427 women. Average annual housing cost: $3800–$4500 for married students, $4500 (including board) for single students. Contact Director of Housing for both on- and off-campus housing information. Phone: (731) 587-7730. Day-care facilities available.

Graduate Studies

Enrollment: full- and part-time 483. Graduate faculty: full-time 134, part-time 12. Degrees conferred: M.S., M.Acc., M.B.A.

ADMISSION REQUIREMENTS. Two official transcripts, GMAT (business) required in support of School's application. Online application available. GRE/MAT/NTE required before the completion of 6 semester hours. TOEFL required for international applicants. Interview not required. Accepts transfer applicants. Apply to Graduate Studies Office by August 1 (Fall), January 1 (Spring). Application fee $25, $50 for international applicants. Phone: (731)881-7012; fax: (731)881-7019.

ADMISSION STANDARDS. Relatively open. Usual minimum average: 2.5 cumulative, or 3.0 in upper divisional work (A = 4).

FINANCIAL AID. Annual awards from institutional funds: fellowships, scholarships, assistantships, residence hall assistantships, internships, tuition waivers, loans. Approved for VA benefits. Apply by March 1 to Dean of the School for assistantships; to Financial Aid Director for all other programs. Phone: (731)881-7040. Use FAFSA. About 30% of students receive aid other than loans from University and outside sources. Aid available for part-time students.

DEGREE REQUIREMENTS. For master's: 30–48 semester hours minimum, the equivalent of two semesters in residence unless transferring within the University of Tennessee system; thesis optional in Human Environmental Science, education; final written/oral exam.

FIELDS OF STUDY.

COLLEGE OF AGRICULTURE AND APPLIED SCIENCES:
Agricultural Education and Leadership.
Family and Consumer Sciences. Includes dietetics.
Natural Recourses Systems Management.

COLLEGE OF BUSINESS AND PUBLIC AFFAIRS:
Business Administration.

COLLEGE OF EDUCATION AND BEHAVIORAL SCIENCES:
Educational Administration and Supervision.
Counseling. Includes community, school.
Teaching. Includes advanced elementary, secondary, subject area.

UNIVERSITY OF TENNESSEE HEALTH SCIENCE CENTER
Memphis, Tennessee 38163-0002
Web site: www.utmem.edu

Founded 1911. CGS member. Coed. State control. Semester system. Special facilities: DEC PDP-11/70, 11/34, IBM 370/3031; Stout Neuroscience Mass Spectrometry Laboratory, Memorial Research Center, Clinical Research Center, Molecular Resource Center, Center for Neurosciences, Materials Science Toxicology Laboratory. The University's NIH ranking is 105th among all U.S. institutions with 137 awards/grants worth $48,552,748. Library: 263,000 volumes, 1784 subscriptions. Total University enrollment: 2000.

On-campus housing available for 147 single men, 205 single women. Average academic year housing costs: $7800. Contact the Director of Housing for both on- and off-campus housing information. Phone: (901)448-5609.

College of Allied Health Sciences

Founded 1972. Annual tuition: full-time resident $10,055 (Cytopathology, Clinical Laboratory Science), $8249 (Health Information Management), $10,245 (Occupational Therapy), $10,455 (Physical Therapy); nonresident $21,654 (Cytopathology, Clinical Laboratory Science), $19,391 (Health Information Management), $21,349 (Occupational Therapy), $21,549 (Physical Therapy).

Enrollment: full-time 253, part-time 7. Faculty: full-time 10, part-time 12. Degrees conferred: M.P.T. (degree completion program for undergraduates: students transfer 90 approved credits, spend an additional three years in full-time study to receive M.P.T.), M.C.P., M.H.I.M., M.S.P.T., M.S.C.L.S.

ADMISSION REQUIREMENTS. Official transcripts, two recommendations, GRE, interview required in support of College's application. Online application available. Interview encouraged. TOEFL (minimum score 550) required for international applicants. Graduates of unaccredited colleges not considered. Preference given to Tennessee residents. Apply to the Director of Admissions by January 15 (Fall priority date, M.P.T., M.S.), September 1 (Winter priority date, M.S.), March 1 (Spring priority date, M.S.). Rolling admission process. Application fee: $50. Phone: (901)448-5560.

ADMISSION STANDARDS. Selective. Usual minimum average: 3.0 (A = 4).

FINANCIAL AID. Scholarships, assistantships, internships, tuition waivers, Federal W/S, loans. Apply by March 1 to the Financial Aid Office. Phone: (901)448-5568. Use FAFSA (School code: 006725).

DEGREE REQUIREMENTS. For M.P.T.: three-year full-time program. For Master's: 36 credit program; admission to candidacy; practicum.

FIELDS OF STUDY.
Clinical Laboratory Sciences. M.S.C.L.S.
Cytopathology. M.C.P.
Health Information Management. M.H.I.M.
Occupational Therapy.
Physical Therapy.

College of Graduate Health Sciences

Annual tuition: full-time resident $8267, nonresident $20,747. Enrollment: full-time 259, part-time 29. Faculty: full-time 170, part-time 12. Degrees conferred: M.S., Ph.D.

ADMISSION REQUIREMENTS. Official transcripts, three recommendations, GRE Test required in support of College's applications. Online application available. Interview encouraged. Four-year bachelor's degree or equivalent required. TOEFL (minimum score 550) required for international applicants. Graduates of unaccredited colleges not considered. Apply to University Office of Admissions, before May 15 (Fall). Application fee: $50. Phone: (901)448-5560; fax: (901)448-7772.

ADMISSION STANDARDS. Selective. Usual minimum average: 3.0 (A = 4).

FINANCIAL AID. Scholarships, teaching assistantships, research assistantships, fellowships, tuition waivers, Federal W/S, loans. Apply by February 15 to the Financial Aid Office. Phone: (901)448-5569. Use FAFSA (School code: 006725). Most full-time students receive aid from School; aid sometimes available for part-time students.

DEGREE REQUIREMENTS. For M.S.: 30 semester hours minimum, at least 18 in residence; thesis; comprehensive oral/written exam for some departments. For Ph.D.: at least one year in residence; oral/written candidacy exam; dissertation; final oral exam.

FIELDS OF STUDY.
Biomedical Engineering and Imaging.
Dental Sciences. Includes orthodontics, pediatric dentistry, Periodontics, Prosthodontics.
Epidemiology.
Health Outcomes and Policy Research. Includes pharmacoeconomics, health policy, health systems pharmacy management.

Integrated Program in Biomedical Sciences. Combines the following programs: anatomy and neurobiology, interdisciplinary, molecular sciences, pathology, pharmacology, physiology.
Nursing.
Pharmaceutical Sciences. Includes medicinal chemistry, pharmaceutics.

College of Dentistry

Web site: www.utmem.edu/dentistry

Founded 1878. Located at the Health Sciences Center in Memphis. Semester system.

Annual tuition: resident $15,670, nonresident $36,640. On-campus housing available. Average academic year off-campus housing costs: $10,000–$12,000. Contact the Housing Office for both on- and off-campus housing information. Phone: (901)448-5609. Total average cost for all other first-year expenses: $13,100.

Enrollment: first-year class 80, total 313 (men 49%, women 51%, minorities 15%, Arkansas and state residents 87%). Faculty: full-time 68, part-time 56. Degrees conferred: D.D.S., M.D.S., Certificates.

ADMISSION REQUIREMENTS. For D.D.S. program: official transcripts, DAT, three letters of recommendation required in support of College's application. Interview by invitation only. Applicants must have completed at least three years of college study, four years of study preferred. Preference given to Tennessee and Arkansas residents. Accepts transfer applicants. Apply to Assistant Dean after June 1, before December 31. Application fee $50. Phone: (901)448-6201; (800)788-0040; fax: (901)448-1625. For graduate program: official transcripts, D.D.S. or equivalent degree. Interview by invitation. Transfer applicants, graduates of unaccredited institutions not considered. Apply to College by December 1. Phone: (901)448-6201.

ADMISSION STANDARDS. Selective. Accepts about 20–25% of all D.D.S. applicants. Usual minimum UGPA: 3.0 (A = 4). Mean DAT: academic 18, PAT 17; mean UGPA 3.50. For graduate programs: usual minimum average 3.0 (A = 4).

FINANCIAL AID. Scholarships, minority scholarship, grants, loans, Federal W/S; fellowships for periodontics program only. Apply to Financial Aid Office within thirty days of acceptance. Phone: (901)488-5568. Use FAFSA (College code: 006725). About 89% of students receive aid from College and outside sources.

DEGREE REQUIREMENTS. For D.D.S.: Satisfactory completion of forth five month program. For D.M.S.: two-year full-time program; comprehensive general exam; admission to candidacy; thesis.

FIELDS OF POSTGRADUATE STUDY.
Advanced Education in General Dentistry. Certificate.
Oral & Maxillofacial Surgery. Certificate.
Orthodontics. M.D.S., Certificate.
Periodontics. M.D.S., Certificate.
Pediatric Dentistry. M.D.S., Certificate.
Prosthodontics. M.D.S., Certificate.

College of Medicine (38163-2166)

Web site: www.utmed.edu/medicine

Founded 1851, moved to Memphis in 1911. Library: 172,000 volumes, 1200 subscriptions. NIH ranking is 105th among all U.S. institutions with 137 awards/grants worth $48,552,748.

Annual tuition: resident $20,222, nonresident $37,612. On-campus housing available. Total averaged figure for all other expenses: $12,000.

Enrollment: first-year class 150, total 601 (men 54%, women 46%, minorities 24%, state residents 97%). Faculty: full-time 721, part-time 141. Degrees conferred: M.D., M.D.-Ph.D.

ADMISSION REQUIREMENTS. AMCAS report, transcripts, letters of recommendation, MCAT, interview required in support of application. Interview by invitation only. Preference given to Tennessee and the eight contiguous states' residents. Accepts transfer applicants who are state residents. Does not have EDP. Apply to Director of Admissions after June 1, before November 15. Application fee $50. Phone: (901)448-5559; fax: (901)448-1740.

ADMISSION STANDARDS. Selective. Accepts about 19% of all applicants. Number of applications 1051 (486 out-of-state); number interviewed 375 (51 out-of-state); number of acceptance 248 (27 out-of-state); number enrolled 150 (9 out-of-state). Mean Composite MCAT 9.3; mean UGPA 3.64 (A = 4).

FINANCIAL AID. Scholarships, Federal and private loans. Apply to Director of Admissions after acceptance. Phone: (901)448-5568. Use FAFSA (College code: 006725). About 90% of students receive aid from College.

DEGREE REQUIREMENTS. For M.D.: satisfactory completion of four-year, 45-month program; pass Step 1 and Step 2 of USMLE for graduation.

FIELDS OF GRADUATE STUDY.
Biomedical Engineering and Imaging.
Biomedical Sciences. Includes Anatomy and Neurobiology, Molecular Sciences, Pathology, Pharmacology, and Physiology. Interdisciplinary.

College of Nursing

Graduate study since 1976. Annual tuition: full-time, resident $9914, nonresident $20,694.

Enrollment: full-time 181, part-time 5. Faculty: full-time 20, part-time 8. Degrees conferred: M.S.N., D.N.P., Ph.D.

ADMISSIONS REQUIREMENTS. Official transcripts, bachelor's degree, Graduate Program Data Form, three Graduate Rating Forms required in support of College's application. Online application available. TOEFL, TSE required for international applicants. Accepts transfer applicants. Graduates of unaccredited colleges not considered. Preference given to Tennessee residents. Apply by February 1 (Fall), September 1 (Winter). Application fee $50. Phone: (901)448-5560; fax: (901)448-7272.

ADMISSIONS STANDARDS. Selective. Usual minimum average: 3.0 (A = 4).

FINANCIAL AID. Fellowships, assistantships, traineeships, Federal W/S, loans. Approved for VA benefits. Apply to Financial Aid Office by February 15. Phone: (901)448-5568. Use FAFSA and institutional FAF.

DEGREE REQUIREMENTS. For M.S.: 36 semester hours; thesis. For Ph.D., D.N.P.: 42 semester hours beyond master's; qualifying exam; dissertation; final oral exam.

FIELDS OF STUDY.
Acute Critical Care Nurse Practitioner.
Clinical Nurse Specialist.
Family Nurse Practitioner.
Neonatal Nurse Practitioner.
Nurse Anesthesia.

DOCTORAL TRACKS:
Acute Care. Ph.D.
Acute Critical Care. D.N.P.
Chronic Care. Ph.D.
Forensics Nursing. D.N.P.
Gerontology. D.N.P.
Health Promotion. Ph.D.

Psychiatric/Family Nurse Practitioner. D.N.P.
Primary Care. D.N.P.
Public Health Nursing. D.N.P.

College of Pharmacy

Established 1928. Located in Memphis (38163).

Annual tuition: resident $14,962, nonresident $27,795. On-campus housing at Medical Units campus in Memphis for 195 men, 233 women; none for married students. (Note: There is no separation of graduate from undergraduate students.) Apply to Office of Student Housing for both on- and off-campus housing. Phone: (901)448-5609.

Enrollment: full-time 541. College faculty teaching graduate students: full-time 43, part-time 37. Degrees conferred: M.S., Ph.D., Pharm.D.-Ph.D.

ADMISSION REQUIREMENTS. Transcripts, GRE required in support of application. TOEFL required, TSE recommended for international applicants. Accepts transfer applicants. Apply by February 1 to Office of Dean. Rolling admission process. Application fee $50. Phone: (901)448-5560; fax: (901)448-7772.

ADMISSION STANDARDS. Very selective for most departments. Usual minimum average: 3.0 (A = 4), GRE combined score 1500.

FINANCIAL AID. Annual awards from institutional funds: fellowships, teaching assistantships, research assistantships, internships, tuition waivers, Federal W/S, loans. Approved for VA benefits. Apply by February 15 to Office of Dean for assistantship, to Financial Aid Office for all other programs. Phone: (901)448-5568. Usa FAFSA. All full-time students receive aid other than loans from College and outside sources.

DEGREE REQUIREMENTS. For M.S.: 30 semester hours minimum; thesis/research project; final written/oral exam. For Ph.D.: minimum of six semesters beyond the B.S.; at least one year in full-time residence; proficiency in designated research tools; dissertation; final written/oral exam.

FIELDS OF STUDY.
Bioanalytical Technologies.
Health Science Administration.
Medicinal Chemistry.
Pharmaceutics.

UNIVERSITY OF TENNESSEE SPACE INSTITUTE

Tullahoma, Tennessee 37388-8897
Web site: www.utsi.edu

Located 100 miles SE of Nashville. Coed. State control. Graduate study only. Semester system. Special facilities: Arnold Engineering Development Center, Aviation Systems Flight Research, Gas Dynamic Facilities, Center for Laser Application, Wind Tunnel, Water Tunnel, E-Beam and Energy Conversion Facilities. Library: 24,700 volumes, 172 subscriptions.

Annual tuition: full-time resident $5908, nonresident $17,850. On-campus housing for single students only. Average academic year on-campus housing costs: $2200; off-campus housing costs: $375–$500 per month. Contact Director of Housing for both on- and off-campus housing information. Phone: (931)393-7218.

Graduate Programs

Enrollment: full- and part-time 310. Graduate faculty: full-time 26, part-time 8. Degrees conferred: M.S., Ph.D.

ADMISSION REQUIREMENTS. Two official transcripts, GRE, three letters of recommendation required in support of application. Online application available. TOEFL required for international applicants. Interview not required. Accepts transfer applicants. Apply to Assistant Dean for Admissions and Student Affairs at least 2 months prior to registration. Rolling admissions process. Application fee $35. Phone: (931)393-7432; fax: (931)393-7346.

ADMISSION STANDARDS. Very selective. Usual minimum average: 3.0 (A = 4).

FINANCIAL AID. Annual awards from institutional funds: fellowships, research assistantships, internships, full and partial tuition waivers, Federal W/S, loans. Approved for VA benefits. Apply to appropriate department for fellowships, assistantships; to Assistant Dean for Admissions and Student Affairs for all other programs. Phone: (931)393-7432. No specified closing date. Use FAFSA. Aid available for part-time students.

DEGREE REQUIREMENTS. For master's: 30–36 semester hours minimum, the equivalent of two semesters in residence unless transferring within the University of Tennessee system; thesis/nonthesis option; written/oral exam. For Ph.D.: 24 credit hours minimum beyond the master's, at one year in full-time residence; comprehensive written exam; reading knowledge of one foreign language or proficiency in research technique; dissertation; final oral exam.

FIELDS OF STUDY.
Aerospace Engineering.
Aviation Systems.
Biomedical Engineering.
Computer Engineering.
Electrical Engineering.
Engineering Science.
Industrial Engineering. Includes engineering management.
Materials Science and Engineering.
Mathematics.
Mechanical Engineering.
Physics.

TEXAS A&M UNIVERSITY

College Station, Texas 77843-1244
Web site: www.tamu.edu

Founded 1876. Located 100 miles N of Houston. CGS and AAU member. Coed. Semester system. State control. Special facilities: Center for Advanced Invertebrate Molecular Sciences, Center for Alcohol and Drug Education Studies, Center for Asphalt and Materials Chemistry, Center for Bioacoustics, Center for Chemical Characterization and Analysis, Center for Comparative Animal Genetics, Center for Demographic and Socioeconomic Research and Education, Center for Electronic Materials, Devices and Systems, Center for Food Processing, Center for Fuzzy Logic, Robotics, and Intelligent Systems, Center for Health Systems and Design, Center for Human Resource Management, Center for Marine Geotechnical Engineering, Center for Nanostructure Materials and Quantum Device Fabrication, Center for Natural Resource Information Technology, Center for North American Studies, Center for Space Power, Center for Structural Biology, Center for Telecommunications Technology Management, Institute for Biosciences and Technology, Center for Biotechnology, Policy, and Ethics, Center for International Business Studies, Aerospace Vehicle Systems Institute, Global Petroleum Research Institute, Institute for Equine Science and Technology, Institute for Manufacturing Systems, Institute for Marine Life Sciences, Institute for Oil Spill Technology, Institute for Plant Genomics and Biotechnology, Institute for Scientific

Computation, Institute for Nautical Archaeology, Nuclear Science Center, Offshore Technology Research Center, Polymer Technology Center, Wildlife and Exotic Animal Center, Public Policy Research Institute, Race and Ethnic Studies Center, Texas Agricultural Experiment Station, Texas Engineering Station, Texas Institute of Oceanography, Texas Transportation Institute, Texas Water Resources Institute, Runyon Art Collection, Sustainable Enterprise Institute, Space Research Center, Cyclotron Institute. According to The Center at University of Florida, the University is ranked 46th in receipt of Federal Research funds with $117,119,000 and it ranks 20th for total University research expenditures with $456,235,000. The University's endowment assets rank it 9th, with a value of $4,023,641,000. In 2004, the University awarded 515 doctorates which ranked it 15th among all U.S. institutions eligible to award that degree. Forty-five of the University's faculty members have been elected to National Honor Academies and this ranks it 20th among all U.S. institutions. The Library: approximately 3,000,000 volumes, 25,000 subscriptions. Total University enrollment: 44,900.

Tuition: per credit, resident $187, nonresident $463. Limited on-campus housing available. Average academic year housing costs: $2986–$6350. Contact Director of Campus Housing for both on- and off-campus housing information. Phone: (979)862-3158.

Office of Graduate Studies

Graduate study since 1923. Enrollment: full-time 6500, part-time 2000. Graduate faculty: full-time 1525, part-time 120. Degrees conferred: M.A., M.S., M.Agr., M.Arch., M.B.A., M.C.S., M.Ed., M.Eng., M.L.A., M.P.A., M.U.P., D.E.D., Ph.D., Ed.D., D.Eng.

ADMISSION REQUIREMENTS. Official transcripts, statement of purpose, three letters of recommendation, GRE/GMAT required in support of application. Online application available. TOEFL (minimum score 550) required non-native English speakers. Interview, portfolio may be required by some departments or schools/ colleges. Accepts transfer applicants. Graduates of unaccredited colleges not considered. Apply to Office of Admissions at least six weeks prior to registration; international applicants at least six months prior to registration. Application fee $50, $75 for international applicants. Phone: (979)845-1044; fax: (979)845-0727.

ADMISSION STANDARDS. Competitive for some departments, very competitive for the others. Usual minimum average: 3.0 (A = 4).

FINANCIAL AID. Annual awards from institutional funds: scholarships, teaching assistantships, nonteaching assistantships, research assistantships, Federal W/S, loans. Approved for VA benefits. Apply to appropriate department for assistantships; to Financial Aid Office for all other programs. No specified closing date. Phone: (979)845-3236. Use FAFSA. About 65% of students receive aid other than loans from College and outside sources. Aid sometimes available for part-time students.

DEGREE REQUIREMENTS. For M.A.: 30 semester hours minimum, 9 credit hours during one semester or two consecutive six-week summer terms in residents; knowledge of one foreign language; thesis; final oral/written exam. For M.S.: 32 semester hours minimum, 9 credit hours during one semester or two consecutive six-week summer terms in residence; thesis; final oral/ written exam. For M.Agr.: 36 semester hours minimum, at least 12 hours on Main Campus; balance on-campus to satisfy residence; final project; final oral/written exam. For M.Arch.: 52 hours for nonthesis program, 12 hours on Main Campus; balance on-campus to satisfy residence. For M.B.A.: 36 hours minimum, at least 12 hours on Main Campus; balance on-campus to satisfy residence; final oral/written exam. For M.C.S.: 36 hours minimum, at least 12 hours on Main Campus; balance on-campus to satisfy residence; final comprehensive exam. For M.Ed.: 36 hours minimum, at least 12 hours on Main Campus; balance on-campus

to satisfy residence; final oral/written exam. For M.Eng.: 36 hours minimum, at least 16 in residence; written reports; final oral/written exam. For M.L.A.: 40 hours minimum, 12 hours on Main Campus to satisfy residence. For M.P.A.: 36 hours minimum; 12 hours on Main Campus to satisfy residence. For M.U.P.: 48 hours minimum, at least 12 hours on Main Campus; balance on-campus to satisfy residence; comprehensive oral exam. For doctorate (D.ED., Ed.D., D.Eng.): 6 semesters full-time study or its equivalent, at least 9 credit hours during two consecutive semesters or during one semester and one adjacent twelve-week summer session to satisfy residence; reading knowledge of one or two foreign languages depending on department and degree; qualifying exam; dissertation; final oral exam.

FIELDS OF STUDY.

COLLEGE OF AGRICULTURE AND LIFE SCIENCES:
Agricultural Chemistry.
Agricultural Development.
Agricultural Economics.
Agricultural Education.
Agricultural Systems Management.
Agronomy.
Animal Breeding.
Animal Science.
Biochemistry.
Biological and Agricultural Engineering.
Biophysics.
Dairy Science.
Economic Entomology.
Entomology.
Fisheries Science.
Floriculture.
Food Science and Technology.
Forestry.
Horticulture.
Natural Resources Development.
Physiology of Reproduction.
Plant Breeding.
Plant Pathology.
Plant Protection.
Plant Sciences.
Poultry Science.
Rangeland Ecology and Management.
Recreation and Resources Development.
Recreation, Park, and Tourism Sciences.
Rural Sociology.
Soil Science.
Wildlife and Fisheries Sciences.
Wildlife Science.

COLLEGE OF ARCHITECTURE:
Architecture.
Construction Management.
Land Development.
Landscape Architecture.
Urban and Regional Planning.
Urban and Regional Science.
Visualization Sciences.

LOWRY MAYS GRADUATE SCHOOL OF BUSINESS:
Accounting.
Business Administration.
Finance.
Information and Operations Management.
Land Economics and Real Estate.
Management.
Management Information Systems.
Marketing.

Operations Management.
Real Estate.

COLLEGE OF EDUCATION:
Agricultural Education.
Counseling Psychology.
Curriculum and Instruction.
Educational Administration.
Education Human Resource Development.
Educational Psychology.
Educational Technology.
Health Education.
Kinesiology.
Physical Education.
School Psychology.

DWIGHT LOOK COLLEGE OF ENGINEERING:
Aerospace Engineering.
Agricultural Engineering.
Biomedical Engineering.
Chemical Engineering.
Civil Engineering.
Computer Engineering.
Computer Science.
Electrical Engineering.
Engineering.
Health Physics.
Industrial Distribution.
Industrial Engineering.
Industrial Hygiene.
Interdisciplinary Engineering.
Mechanical Engineering.
Nuclear Engineering.
Ocean Engineering.
Petroleum Engineering.
Safety Engineering.

COLLEGE OF GEOSCIENCES:
Atmospheric Sciences.
Geosciences.
Geography.
Geology.
Geophysics.
Oceanography.

COLLEGE OF LIBERAL ARTS:
Anthropology.
Comparative Literature and Cultures.
Economics.
English.
Hispanic Studies.
History.
Modern Languages.
Philosophy.
Political Science.
Psychology.
Sociology.
Spanish.
Speech Communication.

COLLEGE OF SCIENCE:
Applied Physics.
Biology.
Botany.
Chemistry.
Mathematics.
Microbiology.
Physics.
Statistics.
Zoology.

COLLEGE OF VETERINARY MEDICINE:
Biomedical Sciences.
Epidemiology.
Laboratory Animal Medicine.
Veterinary Public Health.

GEORGE BUSH SCHOOL OF GOVERNMENT AND PUBLIC SERVICE:
International Affairs.
Public Service and Administration.

INTERDISCIPLINARY PROGRAMS:
Agribusiness.
Biotechnology.
Engineering Systems Management.
Food Science and Technology.
Genetics.
Materials Science and Technology.
Molecular and Environmental Plant Sciences.
Nutrition.
Toxicology.
Water Management and Hydrological Science.

College of Veterinary Medicine and Biomedical Sciences (77843-4461)

Web site: www.cvm.tamu.edu

Established 1916. Semester system. Special facilities: Michael E. DeBakey Institute, Center for Environmental and Rural Health, Stevenson Companion Animal Life-care Center, National Center for Foreign Animal and Zoonotic Disease Defense, Schubot Center.

Annual tuition: residents $12,969, nonresidents $23,769. No on-campus housing available. Estimated off-campus living expenses: $9651. Total all other expenses: $5000.

Enrollment: first-year class 132, total 602 (men 22%, women 78%, minorities 5%, state residents 100%). Faculty: full- and part-time 95. Degrees conferred: D.V.M., D.V.M.-M.B.A., M.S., Ph.D.

ADMISSION REQUIREMENTS. Transcripts, GRE, three evaluations, personal essay, animal/veterinary experience required in support of application. Supplemental application required. Interview by invitation only. Preference given to state residents. Accepts transfer applicants on a state available basis. Apply after July 1, before October 1 through Texas Medical and Dental Schools Application Service (TMDSAS). Application fee $50. Contact Dean's office for information. Phone: (979)845-1169.

ADMISSION STANDARDS. Competitive. Accepts about 5–10% of all applicants. Number of applications 338 (86 out-of-state); number interviewed 251 (24 out-of-state); number of acceptance 151 (16 out-of-state); number enrolled 132 (8 out-of-state). Usual minimum UGPA: 2.9 (A = 4). GRE mean score (V + Q) 1172; mean UGPA 3.67.

FINANCIAL AID. Fellowships, assistantships, partial tuition waivers, Federal W/S, loans available. Apply to Director of Student Financial Aid. Phone: (979)845-5054. Use FAFSA.

DEGREE REQUIREMENTS. For D.V.M.: satisfactory completion of three-year program. For M.S.: 36 semester hour program; thesis. For Ph.D.: 96 semester hour program; dissertation. For M.B.A.: see Mays Business School listing above.

FIELDS OF GRADUATE STUDY.
Biomedical Sciences. M.S., Ph.D.
Epidemiology. M.S.
Laboratory Animal Medicine. M.S.
Veterinary Microbiology. M.S., Ph.D.
Veterinary Pathology. M.S., Ph.D.
Veterinary Public Health. M.S.

TEXAS A&M UNIVERSITY—COMMERCE

Commerce, Texas 75429
Web site: www.tamu-commerce.edu

Founded 1889. In 1996 East Texas State University entered the Texas A&M University System. Located 65 miles NE of Dallas. CGS member. Coed. State control. Semester system. Library: 1,500,219 volumes, 7900 subscriptions. Total Campus enrollment: 8800.

Tuition: per credit, resident $246, nonresident $500. On-campus housing for 250 married students, 1558 single students. Average academic year housing cost: $2850 for married students, $4500 (including board) for single students. Apply to Director of Housing. Phone: (903)886-5797. Day-care facilities available.

Graduate School

Graduate study since 1936, Enrollment: full-time 816, part-time 2300. Faculty: full-time 160, part-time 85. Degrees conferred: M.A., M.S., M.M., M.F.A., M.Ed., M.B.A., M.S.L.S., Ph.D., Ed.D.

ADMISSION REQUIREMENTS. Transcript, GRE GMAT, four recommendations (Ph.D.) required in support of School's application. TOEFL required for foreign applicants. Interview not required. Accepts transfer applicants. Graduates of unaccredited institutions not considered. Apply to the Graduate School at least one month (90 days for international applicants) prior to registration. Phone: (903)886-5167; fax: (903)886-5165.

ADMISSION STANDARDS. Selective. Usual minimum average 2.75 (A = 4).

FINANCIAL AID. Assistantships for teaching/research, Federal W/S, loans. Approved for VA benefits. Apply to Financial Aid Office at least four months before aid is needed. Phone: (903) 886-5096. Use FAFSA (School code: 003565) and institutional FAF.

DEGREE REQUIREMENTS. For M.A.: 30 semester hours minimum, at least 24 credits in residence; reading knowledge of one foreign language; admission to candidacy; thesis; final comprehensive exam. For M.S., M.M., M.B.A., M.S.L.S.: ten graduate courses minimum, at least eight in residence; thesis and final oral exam; or twelve graduate courses without thesis. For M.Ed.: 36 semester hour program; final comprehensive exam. For M.F.A.: 62 semester hour program; thesis/creative exhibit. For Ph.D.: 90 semester hours minimum beyond the bachelor's, at least one year in residence; reading knowledge of two foreign languages; qualifying exam; dissertation; final oral exam. For Ed.D.: generally the same as for the Ph.D., except proficiency in computer science, statistics or foreign language.

FIELDS OF STUDY.

COLLEGE OF ARTS AND SCIENCES:
Agricultural Education.
Agricultural Sciences.
Art.
Biological Sciences,
Broadfield Science.
Chemistry.
College Teaching of English. Ph.D. only.
Computer Science.
Earth Science.
History.
English.
Interdisciplinary Studies.
Mathematics.
Music
Music Education.
Music Performance.
Music Theory.
Physics.
Social Sciences.
Social Work.
Sociology.
Spanish.
Theatre.

COLLEGE OF BUSINESS AND TECHNOLOGY:
Business Administration.
Economics.
Electronic Commerce.
Finance.
Industrial Technology.
Management.
Marketing.

COLLEGE OF EDUCATION AND HUMAN SERVICES:
Counseling.
Curriculum and Instruction.
Early Childhood Education.
Educational Administration.
Educational Psychology. Ph.D. only.
Elementary Education.
Health, Kinesiology, and Sport Studies.
Higher Education Administration.
Higher Education Teaching.
Instructional Training and Design.
Learning Technology and Information Systems. Includes educational computing, library and information science, media and technology.
Psychology.
Reading.
Secondary Education.
Special Education.
Supervision, Curriculum, and Instruction—Elementary Education. Ed.D. only.
Supervision, Curriculum, and Instruction—Higher Education. Ed.D. only.
Training and Development.
Vocational/Technical Education.

TEXAS A&M UNIVERSITY—CORPUS CHRISTI

Corpus Christi, Texas 78412-5503
Web site: www.tamucc.edu

Established 1947. Name changed 1989. Coed. Semester system. State control. Special facilities: Center for Coastal Studies, Environmental Research Consortium, Haite Research Institute for Gulf of Mexico Studies, Conrad Bluche Institute for Surveying and Science, Center for Water Supply Studies, Center for Educational Development, Evaluation, and Research, Center for Business and Economic Research, Natural Resource Center, Social Science Research Center, Wells Gallery. Library: 500,000, 2204 subscriptions. Total University enrollment: 8600.

Tuition: per credit resident $215, nonresident $493. Limited on-campus housing available for single students, none for married students. Average academic year housing costs: $8648 (including board); off-campus housing costs: $500–$575 per month. Contact Director of Housing for both on- and off-campus housing information. Phone: (361)825-2612.

Graduate Studies and Research

Enrollment: full-time 262, part-time 977. Graduate faculty: full-time 109, part-time 49. Degrees conferred: M.A., M.Acc., M.B.A., M.P.A., M.S., M.S.N., Ed.D.

ADMISSION REQUIREMENTS. Official transcripts, GRE/GMAT, statement of purpose required in support of application. Letters of recommendation, writing samples, portfolio may be required by some degree programs. TOEFL (minimum score 550) required non-native English speakers. Interview not required. Accepts transfer applicants. Graduates of unaccredited colleges not considered. Apply to Office of Graduate Studies and Research by July 15 (Fall), November 15 (Spring). Some programs have earlier deadlines. Application fee $40, $70 for international applicants. Phone: (361)825-2177.

ADMISSION STANDARDS. Selective. Usual minimum average: 2.75 (A = 4).

FINANCIAL AID. Annual awards from institutional funds: scholarships, assistantships, Federal W/S, loans. Approved for VA benefits. Apply by February 1 to Financial Aid Office. Phone: (361)825-2338. Use FAFSA. About 25% of students receive aid other than loans from College and outside sources. Aid available to part-time students.

DEGREE REQUIREMENTS. For M.A., M.S., M.S.N.: 30–36 semester hours minimum, thesis/nonthesis option; final oral/written exam. For M.B.A., M.Acc.: 36 hours minimum, final oral/written exam. For M.P.A.: 36 hours minimum; comprehensive oral exam. For Ed.D.: six semesters full-time study or its equivalent, at least 9 credit hours during two consecutive semesters or during one semester and one adjacent twelve-week summer session to satisfy residence; qualifying exam; dissertation; final oral exam.

FIELDS OF STUDY.
Accountancy.
Art. Includes fine art, studio art.
Biology.
Business Administration.
Coastal Marine System Science.
Computer Science.
Counseling.
Curriculum and Instruction.
Early Childhood Education.
Educational Administration.
Educational Leadership.
Educational Technology.
Elementary Education.
English.
Environmental Sciences.
Geospatial Surveying Engineering.
History.
Kinesiology.
Mariculture.
Mathematics.
Nursing.
Occupational Training and Development.
Psychology.
Public Administration.
Reading.
School Counseling.
Secondary Education.
Special Education.
Studio Arts.

TEXAS A&M UNIVERSITY— KINGSVILLE
Kingsville, Texas 78363
Web site: www.tamuk.edu

Founded 1925. Became part of Texas A&M system 1989. Located 40 miles SW of Corpus Christi. Coed. State control. Semester system. Special facilities: Caesar Kleberg Wildlife Research Institute, Citrus Center, Monoclonal Antibody Facility. Library 500,000 volumes, 2300 subscriptions. Total University enrollment: 6000.

Annual tuition: full-time resident $2994, nonresident $7962. On-campus housing for married students. Average academic year housing cost: $450–$625 per month. Contact Campus Housing Office for both on- and off-campus housing information. Phone: (361)593-3419. Day-care facilities available.

College of Graduate Studies

Enrollment: full-time 360, part-time 763. Faculty: full-time 120, part-time 26. Degrees conferred: M.A., M.S., M.M., M.P.A., M.B.A., M.Engineering, M.Ed., Ed.D. (BiLing.Ed., Ed. Admin.), Ph.D. (Wildlife Sciences).

ADMISSION REQUIREMENTS. Transcripts, GRE/GMAT required in support of College's application. TOEFL (minimum score 500) required for international applicants. Accepts transfer applicants. Apply by July 1 (Fall), November 15 (Spring) to Director of Admissions. Application fee $35, $50 for international applicants. Phone: (361)593-2808.

ADMISSION STANDARDS. Selective. Usual minimum average: 3.0 (A = 4).

FINANCIAL AID. Scholarships, fellowships, assistantships, internships, tuition waivers, Federal W/S, loans. Apply by May 15 to Director of Financial Aid. Phone: (361)593-3911. Use FAFSA.

DEGREE REQUIREMENTS. For master's: 30 semester hours minimum, thesis often required; final written/oral exam. For Ed.D.: 60 semester hours minimum beyond master's degree, at least 48 in residence; qualifying exam; candidacy; dissertation; final oral exam.

FIELDS OF STUDY.

COLLEGE OF AGRICULTURE, NATURAL RESOURCES AND HUMAN SCIENCES:
Agribusiness.
Agriculture Science.
Animal Science.
Human Science. M.S.H.S. only.
Plant and Soil Science.
Range and Wildlife Management.
Wildlife Science. Joint Ph.D. program with Texas A&M University, College Station.

COLLEGE OF ARTS AND SCIENCES:
Art.
Biology.
Chemistry.
Communication Science and Disorders.
English.
Hispanic Studies.
History and Politics.
Mathematics.
Music Education.
Psychology.
Sociology.
Spanish.

COLLEGE OF BUSINESS ADMINISTRATION:
Accounting.
Business Administration.

COLLEGE OF EDUCATION:
Adult Education.
Bilingual Education.
Counseling and Guidance.

Early Childhood Education.
Educational Administration.
Educational Leadership.
English as a Second Language.
Instructional Technology.
Kinesiology.
Reading.
Special Education.
Supervision.

COLLEGE OF ENGINEERING:
Chemical Engineering.
Civil Engineering.
Computer Science.
Electrical Engineering.
Environmental Engineering.
Industrial Engineering.
Mechanical Engineering.
Natural Gas Engineering.

TEXAS A&M UNIVERSITY SYSTEM HEALTH SCIENCE CENTER
College Station, Texas 77840-7896
Web site: www.tamushsc.edu

Coed. State control. Semester system. Has locations in Dallas, Temple, and Houston. Library: 200,000 volumes, 2000 subscriptions. The Health Science Center's NIH ranking is 167th among all U.S. institutions with 79 awards/grants worth $23,076,106.

The Graduate School of Biomedical Sciences includes the following units: Baylor College of Dentistry (Dallas), College of Medicine (College Station, Temple), Institute of Biosciences and Technology (Houston), School of Rural Public Health (College Station; M.S. and Ph.D. are under development.). On-campus housing available at all locations.

Baylor College of Dentistry
P.O. Box 660677
Dallas, Texas 75266-0677
Web site: www.bcd.tamhsc.edu

Founded 1905. Affiliated with Baylor University from 1918–1971. Became independent corporation in 1971. Joined the Texas A&M System in 1996 and became the founding school at Health Science Center. Semester system. Special facility: Center for Craniofacial Research & Diagnosis. Library: 32,000 volumes, 6000 subscriptions.

Annual tuition: resident $9648, nonresident $20,448. On-campus housing available. Average academic year off-campus housing costs: $14,000. Contact the Housing Office for both on- and off-campus housing information. Phone: (214)828-8210. Total average cost for all other first-year expenses: $8,500.

Enrollment: first-year class 90, total 375 (men 58%, women 42%, minorities 33%, state residents 90%). Graduate students 75. Faculty: full-time 110, part-time 130. Degrees conferred: D.D.S., D.D.S.-M.D., D.D.S.-M.S., D.D.S.-Ph.D., M.S., Ph.D., Certificate.

ADMISSION REQUIREMENTS. For D.D.S. program: official transcripts, three letters of recommendation, DAT, personal interview required in support of College's application. Out-of-state applicants use AADSAS. Accepts transfer applicants. Applicants must have completed at least three years of college study. Apply through the Texas Medical and Dental Schools Application Service after June 1, before October 1 (flexible). Application fee $35. Phone: (214)828-8230; fax: (214)874-4567.

For graduate study: official transcripts, three letters of recommendation, GRE, interview required in support of College's application. Accepts transfer applicants. Graduates of unaccredited colleges not considered. Apply to Registrar of the College after May 1, before November 1. Application fee $35.

ADMISSION STANDARDS. Selective. Accepts about 20–25% of all applicants. Usual minimum UGPA: 3.0 (A = 4). Mean DAT: academic 19.7, PAT 17; mean UGPA 3.50.

FINANCIAL AID. For D.D.S. program: scholarships, grants, tuition waivers, loans. Apply to Office Financial Aid; no specified closing date. Use FAFSA. Phone: (214)828-8236. For graduate study: fellowships, assistantships for teaching/research. Apply as soon as possible to Head of Department. Use FAFSA (College code: 004448). About 88% of students receive aid other than loans from University and outside sources.

DEGREE REQUIREMENTS. For D.D.S.: Satisfactory completion of forty-five-month program. For M.S.: 32-credit full-time program; comprehensive oral exam; thesis. For Ph.D.: a minimum of 60-credit program beyond master's; preliminary exam; reading knowledge of two foreign languages; final written exam; dissertation; final oral exam.

FIELDS OF POSTGRADUATE STUDY.
Biomedical Science. Offered through Graduate School of Biomedical Sciences. M.S., Ph.D.
Dental Hygiene. M.S.
Endodonitcs. Certificate.
General Dentistry. Certificate.
Health Professional Education. M.S.
Oral Biology. M.S.
Oral and Maxillofacial Pathology. Certificate.
Oral and Maxillofacial Radiology. Certificate.
Oral and Maxillofacial Surgery. Certificate.
Oral Surgery. M.D.-D.D.S.
Pediatric Dentistry. Certificate.
Periodontics. Certificate.
Prosthodontics. Certificate.
Public Health. Certificate.

College of Medicine (77843-1114)
Web site: www.medicine.tamhsc.edu

Established 1973. Joined the Texas A & M University System Health Science Center 1999. Library: 104,000 volumes, 1600 subscriptions. NIH ranking is 167th among all U.S. institutions with 79 awards/grants worth $23,076,106.

Annual tuition: resident $9012, nonresident $38,650. On-campus housing available. Total average figure for all other expenses: $14,500.

Enrollment: first-year class 100, total 350 (men 48%, women 52%, minorities 40%, state residents 90%). Faculty: full-time 719, part-time 81. Degrees conferred: M.D., M.D.-M.B.A., M.D.-Ph.D.

ADMISSION REQUIREMENTS. Transcripts, MCAT, three letters of recommendation required in support of a College specific application. Interview by invitation. Preference given to state residents. Does not have EDP. Apply through the Texas Medical and Dental Schools Application Service after May 1 before November 1. Applicants to the M.D.-Ph.D. program must complete the AMCAS application as the primary application and pay the required application fee to AMCAS. Application fee $55. Phone: (979)845-7743; fax: (979)845-5533.

ADMISSION STANDARDS. Selective. Accepts about 12% of all applicants. Number of applications 2108 (225 out-of-state); number interviewed 694 (38 out-of-state); number of acceptance 245 (16 out-of-state); number enrolled 100 (9 out-of-state). Mean Composite MCAT 9.3; mean UGPA 3.74 (A = 4).

FINANCIAL AID. Scholarships, loans. Apply after acceptance to Student Affairs Office. Phone: (979)845-8854. Use FAFSA (School code: 003632). About 86% of students receive some aid from School.

DEGREE REQUIREMENTS. For M.D.: satisfactory completion of four-year program. For M.B.A., M.P.H., Ph.D.: see Graduate College listing above.

FIELDS OF GRADUATE STUDY.
Biochemistry and Structural Biology.
Cardiovascular and Integrative Biology.
Cell and Molecular Biology.
Microbial and Molecular Pathogenesis.
Neurosciences.
Pharmaceutical Sciences and Therapeutics.

TEXAS CHRISTIAN UNIVERSITY
Fort Worth, Texas 76129-0002
Web site: www.tcu.edu

Founded 1873. CGS member. Coed. Private control. Semester system. Special facilities: Center for Remote Sensing, Center for Texas Studies, Experimental Mesocosm Facility, Lake Worth Fish Hatchery, Institute of Behavioral Research, cooperative association with Oak Ridge Institute of Nuclear Studies. Library: 1,300,000 volumes, 4700 subscriptions. Total University enrollment: 8750.

Tuition: per credit $740, M.B.A. $935. Campus housing for married students at Brite Divinity School campus housing; none for graduate single students. Contact the Housing Office for both on- and off-campus housing information. Phone: (817)257-7865.

Graduate Studies

Enrollment: full-time 618, part-time 960. Faculty: full-time 230. Degrees conferred: M.A., M.Acc., M.B.A., M.Ed., M.F.A., M.L.A., M.M., M.M.Ed., M.S., M.S.E., Certificate program, D.M., Ph.D.

ADMISSION REQUIREMENTS. Official transcripts, GRE/GMAT required in support of graduate application. Online application available. TOEFL and International Student and Scholar Form required for international applicants. Interview not required. Accepts transfer applicants. Graduates of unaccredited institutions not considered. Apply directly to School or progam at least six weeks prior to registration. Application fee $50. Phone: (817) 257-7515, (800)828-3764; fax: (817)257-7134. For M.B.A.: phone: (817)257-7531; fax: (817)257-6431.

ADMISSION STANDARDS. Very selective for most departments. Usual minimum average: 3.0 (A = 4).

FINANCIAL AID. Annual awards from institutional funds: fellowships, teaching assistantships, research assistantships, internships, traineeships, Federal W/S, loans. Approved for VA benefits. Apply by March 1 to Graduate School for fellowship, assistantships, internships; to Financial Aid Office for all other programs. Use FAFSA and institution FAF. Phone: (817)257-7872; fax: (817)257-7333. About 77% of students receive aid other than loans from School and outside sources. Limited aid for part-time students.

DEGREE REQUIREMENTS. For master's: 30 semester hours minimum, at least 24 in residence; thesis; final oral exam. For Administrator's Certificate: 60 semester hours beyond the bachelor's degree; special project. For D.M., Ph.D.: three years mini-

mum beyond the bachelor's degree, the second year or its equivalent in full-time residence; reading knowledge of one or two foreign languages, depending upon department; qualifying exam; dissertation; final oral exam.

FIELDS OF STUDY.
Accounting. M.Acc.
Art History. Comprehensive exam for candidacy. M.F.A. only.
Ballet. Final artistic project for degree. M.F.A. only.
Biology.
Business. GMAT for admission. Includes management statistics. M.B.A. only.
Chemistry. German proficiency, cumulative exam required for Ph.D.
Communication in Human Relations. M.S.
Communication Sciences and Disorders.
Computer Science.
Counseling.
Economics. M.A. only.
Educational Foundations.
Educational Leadership.
Educational Studies.
Elementary Education.
English. Candidacy exam for M.A.; one modern language, qualifying exam for Ph.D.
Environmental Sciences.
Geology. Preliminary exam for M.S.
History. One modern language, qualifying exam for Ph.D.
Journalism. Includes news, editorial, advertising, public relations.
Kinesiology.
Liberal Arts. M.L.A. only.
Mathematics.
Media Arts. Final written exam for M.S. M.S. only.
Modern Dance.
Music. Includes performance, musicology, theory. M.M., M.M.Ed. only.
Nurse Anesthesia.
Nursing.
Nursing Practice.
Physics and Astronomy. One language, qualifying exam for Ph.D.
Psychology. One language, other exams for Ph.D.
Science Education.
Secondary Education.
Special Education.
Studio Arts.

TEXAS SOUTHERN UNIVERSITY
Houston, Texas 77004-4584
Web site: www.tsu.edu

Founded 1947. CGS member. State control. Semester system. Special facilities: Cancer Prevention Awareness Center, Center for Excellence in Education, Economic Development Center, Center for Excellence in Urban Education, Center for Transportation Training and Research, Mickey Leland Center on World Hunger and Peace, Center on the Family, Research Center for Minority Institutions, Environmental Science Institute, Center for Toxicological Studies, Minority Biomedical Research Support Program, Environmental Research and Technology Transfer Center, Center for Aging for Horizon Intergenerational Wellness, Center for Cardiovascular Research. Library: 473,500 volumes, 1715 subscriptions. Total University enrollment: 8000.

Annual tuition/fees: full-time resident $7258, nonresident $14,668. On-campus housing for married and single students. Average academic year housing costs: $5000–$7500 for married students, $6526 (including board) for single students. Off-campus housing costs: $480–$600 per month. Contact Director of Housing for both on- and off-campus housing information. Phone: (713)527-7205.

Graduate School

Established 1947. Enrollment: full- and part-time 900. Faculty: full-time 118, part-time 38. Degrees conferred: M.A., M.S., M.Ed., M.B.A., M.Mus.Ed., M.C.R., M.P.A., Ed.D., Ph.D., D.Pharm.

ADMISSION REQUIREMENTS. Official transcripts, GRE/ GMAT required in support of School's application. TOEFL (minimum score 550) required of international applicants. Accepts transfer applicants. Graduates of unaccredited institutions not considered. Apply to the School by July 15 (Fall), November 15 (Spring), May 1 (Summer). Application fee $75. Phone: (713) 313-7232; fax: (713)313-1876.

ADMISSION STANDARDS. Selective. Usual minimum average: 2.5, or 3.0 last 60 credits (A = 4); for M.B.A., 2.75 minimum average (undergraduate GPA plus 200) plus GMAT score = 950; for Ed.D., average GPA for the last 60 semester hours times 100 plus the verbal and quantitative must = at least 1000, minimum average must be at least 2.5.; for Ph.D., 2.75 GPA, GRE score at least 950.

FINANCIAL AID. Fellowships, assistantships, internships, grants, Federal W/S, loans. Approved for VA benefits. Apply by April 15 to Graduate School for assistantships; to Financial Aid Office for all other programs. Phone: (713)313-7207. Use FAFSA (School code: 003642) and University's FAF. About 25% of students receive aid other than loans from University and outside sources.

DEGREE REQUIREMENTS. For master's: 36 semester hours minimum, at least 30 in residence; thesis/nonthesis option. For M.B.A.: 36 semester hours minimum; 27 in residence. For M.P.A. (Accounting): 36 semester hours minimum, 30 in residence. For M.C.P., M.P.A. (Public Administration), M.A. (Psychology): 48 semester hours minimum; 42 in residence; thesis/no thesis option. For Ed.D.: 72 semester hours minimum, 57 in residence; qualifying exam; dissertation; final oral exam. For Ph.D.: 75 semester hours minimum, at least 66 in residence; candidacy; reading knowledge of one or two foreign languages; dissertation; final oral exam.

FIELDS OF STUDY.

TAVIS SMILEY SCHOOL OF COMMUNICATION:
Communication. M.A.

COLLEGE OF LIBERAL ARTS AND BEHAVIORAL SCIENCES:
English. M.A.
History. M.A.
Human Services and Consumer Sciences. M.S.
Music. Includes performing arts. M.A.F.A.
Psychology. M.A.
Sociology. M.A.

COLLEGE OF EDUCATION:
Counseling. M.Ed.
Counselor Education. Ed.D.
Curriculum and Instruction. M.Ed., Ed.D.
Educational Administration. M.Ed., Ed.D.
Health. M.S.
Human Performance. M.S.
Secondary Education. M.Ed.

JESSE H. JONES SCHOOL OF BUSINESS:
Business Administration.
Management Information Systems. M.S.

COLLEGE OF PHARMACY AND HEALTH SCIENCES:
Health Care Administration. M.S.
Pharmaceutical Science. Ph.D.

BARBARA JORDAN–MICKEY LELAND SCHOOL OF PUBLIC AFFAIRS:
Administration of Justice. M.S., Ph.D.
Public Administration. M.P.A.
Urban Planning and Environmental Policy. M.S., Ph.D.

COLLEGE OF SCIENCE AND TECHNOLOGY:
Biology. M.S.
Chemistry. M.S.
Environmental Toxicology. M.S., Ph.D.
Industrial Technology. M.S.
Mathematics. M.S.
Teaching Mathematics. M.Ed.
Transportation Planning and Management. M.S.

Thurgood Marshall School of Law (77004)
Web site: www.tsu.edu/academics/law

Established 1947. ABA approved since 1949. AALS member. Public control. Semester system. Special facilities: Center for Legal Pedagogy, Earl Carl Institute, Institute for International & Immigration, Center for Government Law. Law library: 623,753 volumes, 2734 subscriptions; has LEXIS, WESTLAW, DIALOG; has more than 900 network connections.

Annual tuition: resident $11,228, nonresident $14,978. No on-campus housing available. Total average annual additional expenses: $12,000.

Enrollment: first-year class 236, total 658 (men 48%, women 52%, minorities 83%). Faculty: full-time 29, part-time 27. Student to faculty ratio is 16.3 to 1. Degrees conferred: J.D., J.D.-M.A. (History), J.D.-M.B.A., J.D. -M.P.A.

ADMISSION REQUIREMENTS. LSDAS Law School report, bachelor's degree, two transcripts, LSAT, personal statement, résumé, two letters of recommendation required in support of application. Accepts transfer applicants. Interview not required. Graduates of unaccredited colleges not considered. Preference given to state residents. Admits to Fall semester only. Apply to the Office of Admissions by April 1. Application fee $55. Phone: (713)313-7114.

ADMISSION STANDARDS. Selective. Accepts approximately 22% of all students. Number of applicants 2102; number of acceptance 459; number enrolled 236; LSAT (75% of students have a score at or above 144); GPA (75% of students have a GPA at or above 2.58). *U.S. News & World Report* ranking is in the third tier of all U.S. law schools.

FINANCIAL AID. Scholarships, partial tuition waivers, Federal W/S, loans. Apply to Director of Financial Aid by April 1. Phone: (713)313-7243. Use FAFSA (School code: 003642). About 40% of students receive some of aid.

DEGREE REQUIREMENTS. For J.D.: 90 semester hours minimum, at least 45 in residence. For master's degrees: see Graduate School listing above.

TEXAS STATE UNIVERSITY— SAN MARCOS
San Marcos, Texas 78666-4605
Web site: www.txstate.edu

Founded 1899. Name change in 2003. Located 28 miles SW of Austin. CGS member. Coed. State control. Semester system. Library: 1,200,000 volumes, 6200 subscriptions. Total University enrollment: 28,100.

Tuition: per credit resident $275, nonresident $553. On-campus housing for 100 married students, 2000 men, 2250 women. Average annual housing cost: $8500 for married students, $6800 (including board) for single students. Contact Director of Residential Life for both on- and off-campus housing information. Phone: (512)245-2382.

Graduate School

Graduate study since 1935. Enrollment: full-time 1100, part-time 2000. Graduate faculty: full-time 256, part-time 38. Degrees conferred: M.A., M.Accy., M.A.Geo., M.A.I.S., M.A.T., M.B.A., M.Ed., M.F.A., M.H.A., M.M., M.P.A., M.S., M.S.C.D., M.S.C.J., M.S.H.P., M.S.T., M.P.A., M.S.I.S., M.S.P.T., M.S.W., Ph.D.

ADMISSION REQUIREMENTS. Transcripts, GRE/GMAT required in support of School's application. Online application available. Interview not required for most programs. TOEFL, TSE (for M.B.A., M.P.A., History) required for international applicants. Accepts transfer applicants. Graduates of unaccredited institutions not considered. Apply to Dean of Graduate School by October 15 (Spring), April 15 (Summer), June 15 (Fall). International applicants must submit application at least one month prior to deadlines above. In addition, if applicant is submitting foreign credentials, a $50 evaluation fee accompany application and $40 application fee. Application fee $40. Phone: (512)245-2581; fax: (512)245-8365; e-mail: gradcollege@txstate.edu.

ADMISSION STANDARDS. Selective. Usual minimum average (some programs are higher): 2.75 (A = 4) on last 60 hours of bachelor's degree. Minimum GMAT score 400, minimum TOEFL score 550, minimum TSE score 45.

FINANCIAL AID. Annual awards from institutional funds: minority scholarships, fellowships, teaching assistantships, internships, Federal W/S, loans. Approved for VA benefits. Apply by April 1 to Office of Financial Assistance for fellowships, loans; to appropriate department chair for assistantships. Phone: (512) 245-2315. Use FAFSA. About 10% of students receive aid other than loans from University and outside sources. Aid available for part-time students.

DEGREE REQUIREMENTS. For M.A.: 30 semester hours minimum including thesis, at least 24 in residence; final oral/written exams. For M.A.T., M.Ed., M.M.: 36 semester hours minimum, at least 30 in residence; no thesis required. For M.Acc., M.B.A.: 30 semester hours minimum, but usually 36. For M.S.C.J., M.P.A.: 39 semester hours minimum. For M.A.G, M.S.H.P., M.S.I.S., M.S.T.: 39 semester hours minimum; up to 9 hours may be granted for work/life experience in M.S.I.S. program. For Ph.D.: 46 credit program beyond master's; qualifying exam; dissertation; oral defense.

FIELDS OF STUDY.

COLLEGE OF APPLIED ARTS:
Agricultural Education.
Criminal Justice.
Family and Child Studies.
Human Nutrition.
Management of Technical Studies.
Occupational Education.

MCCOY COLLEGE OF BUSINESS:
Accounting.
Accounting and Information Technology.
Business Administration.

COLLEGE OF EDUCATION:
Adult, Professional and Community Education.
Athletic Training.
Counseling & Guidance.

Developmental & Adult Education.
Educational Administration.
Educational Technology.
Elementary Education.
Elementary Education—Bilingual/Bicultural.
Elementary Education—Early Childhood Education.
Health Education.
Interdisciplinary Studies—Health, P.E., and Recreation.
Physical Education.
Professional Counseling.
Reading Education.
Recreation & Leisure Services.
School Improvement.
School Psychology.
Secondary Education.
Special Education.

COLLEGE OF FNE ARTS AND COMMUNICATION:
Communication Design.
Communication Studies.
Mass Communication.
Music.
Music Education.
Theatre.

COLLEGE OF HEALTH PROFESSIONS:
Communication Disorders.
Healthcare Administration.
Health Services Research.
Healthcare Human Resources.
Physical Therapy.
Social Work.

COLLEGE OF LIBERAL ARTS:
Anthropology.
Applied Sociology. Interdisciplinary.
Creative Writing.
Environmental Geography.
Geographic Education.
Geographic Information Science.
Geography.
Health Psychology.
History.
International Studies.
Legal Studies.
Literature.
Modern Languages. Interdisciplinary.
Political Science. Interdisciplinary.
Psychology. Interdisciplinary.
Rhetoric and Composition.
Sociology.
Spanish.
Technical Communication.

COLLEGE OF SCIENCE:
Aquatic Resources.
Biochemistry.
Biology. Interdisciplinary.
Chemistry.
Computer Science.
Industrial Mathematics.
Industrial Technology.
Interdisciplinary Studies—General Elementary Mathematics/ Science/Technology.
Materials Physics.
Mathematics.
Middle School Mathematics Teaching.
Physics.
Population & Conservation Biology.
Software Engineering.
Wildlife Ecology.

TEXAS TECH UNIVERSITY
Lubbock, Texas 79409
Web site: www.ttu.edu

Founded 1923. CGS member. Coed. State control. Semester system. Special facilities: Center for Agricultural Technology, Center for Applied Research in Industrial/Automation and Robotics, Institute for Banking and Financial Studies, Institute for Communications Research, Community Design Center, Institute for Disaster Research, Institute for Ergonomics Research, Center for Feed and Industry Research and Education, Center for Forensic Studies, Center for Historic Preservation and Technology, Child Development Center, Center for Petroleum Mathematics, International Textile Research Center, International Center for Arid and Semi-Arid Land Studies, Center for the Study of Addiction, Center for Professional Development, Institute of Environmental and Human Health, Plant Stress and Water Conservation Institute, Center for Public Service, Ranching Heritage Center, Center for the Study of the Vietnam Conflict, Texas Wine Marketing Research Center, Turkish Oral Archives, Wildlife and Fisheries Management Institute. Library: 2,400,000 volumes, 27,000 subscriptions. Total University enrollment: 28,000.

Annual tuition: full-time resident $4296; nonresident $10,920; per credit resident $179, nonresident $455. On-campus housing for single students, none for married students. Annual housing costs: $6875 (including board). Apply to Director of Housing Reservation: Phone: (806)742-2261; to Student Association off-campus housing information: Phone: (806)742-3631. Day-care facilities available.

Graduate School

Graduate study since 1927. Enrollment: full-time 2797, part-time 1497. Faculty: full-time 740, part-time 44. Degrees conferred: M.A., M.B.A., M.Ed., M.F.A., M.Eng., M.Ag., M.A.Ed., M.P.A., M.M.E., M.S.Ch.E., M.S.C.E., M.S.E.E., M.S.I.E., M.S.M.E., M.S.P.E., M.S.H.E., M.S., Ed.D., Ph.D.

ADMISSION REQUIREMENTS. Official transcripts, GRE/GMAT required in support of School's application. Online application available. Letters of recommendation required for some departments. TOEFL required for international applicants. Interview not required. Accepts transfer applicants. Graduates of unaccredited institutions not considered. Apply to Office of the Dean of Graduate Admissions by March 1 (Fall), October 1 (Spring). Application fee $50, $60 for international applicants. Phone: (806)742-2781; fax: (806)742-4038; e-mail: gradschool@ttu.edu.

ADMISSION STANDARDS. Selective for most departments. Usual minimum average: 3.0 (A = 4) or 1000 GRE.

FINANCIAL AID. Annual awards from institutional funds: scholarships, fellowships, teaching assistantships, research assistantships, out-of-state tuition waivers, Federal W/S, loans. Approved for VA benefits. Apply by April 15 to appropriate department chairman for assistantships; to Financial Aid Office for all other programs. Phone: (806)742-3681; fax: (806)742-0880. Use FAFSA and University's FAF. About 20% of students receive aid other than loans from College and outside sources. Aid available for part-time students.

DEGREE REQUIREMENTS. For master's: 30–36 semester hours minimum, at least 24 in residence; thesis/nonthesis option; final comprehensive exam; foreign language requirements vary by department. For doctorates: 72 semester hours minimum, at least two consecutive semesters in residence; oral/written preliminary exam; oral/written qualifying exam for candidacy; foreign language requirements vary by department and program; dissertation; final oral exam.

FIELDS OF STUDY.

GRADUATE SCHOOL:
Interdisciplinary Studies. Includes biotechnology, heritage management, multidisciplinary science, museum science, public administration.

COLLEGE OF AGRICULTURAL SCIENCES AND NATURAL RESOURCES:
Agricultural and Applied Economics.
Agricultural Education.
Agronomy.
Animal Science.
Crop Science.
Entomology.
Fisheries Science.
Food Technology.
Horticulture.
Landscape Architecture. M.L.A. only.
Range Science.
Soil Science.
Wildlife Science.

COLLEGE OF ARCHITECTURE:
Architecture. Master's only.
Land Use Planning, Management, and Design.

COLLEGE OF ARTS AND SCIENCES:
Anthropology.
Applied Linguistics.
Applied Physics.
Atmospheric Science.
Biological Informatics.
Biology.
Chemistry.
Classics.
Communication Studies.
Economics.
English.
Environmental Toxicology.
Exercise and Sport Sciences.
French.
Geosciences.
German.
History.
Mass Communication.
Mathematics.
Microbiology.
Philosophy.
Physics.
Political Science.
Psychology. Includes clinical, counseling, experimental.
Public Administration.
Sociology.
Spanish.
Sports Health.
Statistics.
Technical Communication and Rhetoric.
Zoology.

COLLEGE OF BUSINESS ADMINISTRATION:
Accounting. Includes auditing/financial reporting, information systems assurance, accounting information systems design, controllership, taxation.
Business Administration. Includes accounting, business statistics, finance, management, management information systems, marketing, production and operations management, taxation, telecom technology management.
General Business. Includes health organization management.

COLLEGE OF EDUCATION:
Bilingual Education.
Counselor Education.
Curriculum and Instruction.
Educational Leadership.
Educational Psychology.
Elementary Education.
Higher Education.
Instructional Technology.
Literacy.
Secondary Education.
Special Education.

COLLEGE OF ENGINEERING:
Chemical Engineering.
Civil Engineering.
Computer Science.
Electrical Engineering.
Environmental Engineering.
Environmental Technology Management. Master's only.
Industrial Engineering.
Manufacturing Systems and Engineering.
Mechanical Engineering.
Petroleum Engineering.
Software Engineering.
Systems and Engineering Management.

COLLEGE OF HUMAN SCIENCES:
Environmental Design.
Environmental Design and Consumer Economics.
Family and Consumer Sciences Education.
Food and Nutrition.
Hospitality Administration.
Human Development and Family Studies.
Human Sciences.
Marriage and Family Therapy.
Personal Financial Planning.
Restaurant, Hotel, and Institutional Management.

COLLEGE OF VISUAL AND PERFORMING ARTS:
Art.
Art Education.
Fine Arts (Interdisciplinary). Includes arts, music, theatre.
Music. Includes instrument, voice.
Music Composition.
Music Conducting.
Music Education.
Music History and Literature.
Music Performance.
Music Piano Pedagogy.
Music Theory.
Theatre Arts.

School of Law
Web site: www.law.ttu.edu

Established 1967. ABA approved since 1969. AALS member since 1969. Semester system. Special facilities: Center for Biodefense, Law and Public Policy, Center of Military Law & Policy, Center for Water Law & Policy. Law library: 297,238 volumes, 2931 subscriptions; has LEXIS, NEXIS, WESTLAW; has more than 800 network connections.

Annual tuition: resident $14,253, nonresident $21,693. On- and off-campus housing available. Apply to Housing Office. Total average annual additional expense: $12,282.

Enrollment: first-year class 269, total 702 (men 56%, women 44%, minorities 20%). Faculty: full-time 32, part-time 14. Student to faculty ratio is 16.6 to 1. Degrees conferred: J.D., J.D.-M.A. (History), J.D.-M.B.A., J.D.-M.E.T. (Environmental Toxicology), J.D.-M.P.A., J.D.-M.S. (Accounting, Agricultural Economics, Biotech).

ADMISSION REQUIREMENTS. LSDAS Law School report, bachelor's degree, transcripts, LSAT, personal statement, résumé, two letters of recommendation required in support of application. Accepts transfer applicants. Graduates of unaccredited colleges not considered. Apply to Dean by February 1. Rolling admissions process. Admits Fall only. Application fee $50. Phone: (806)742-3791; fax: (806)742-1629.

ADMISSION STANDARDS. Selective. Accepts approximately 35% of all students. Number of applicants 1805; number of acceptance 636; number enrolled 270; LSAT (75% of students have a score at or above 151); GPA (75% of students have a GPA at or above 3.28). *U.S. News & World Report* ranking is in the third tier of all U.S. law schools.

FINANCIAL AID. Scholarships, assistantships, Federal W/S, loans. Apply to Office of the Director of Financial Aid by June 1. Phone: (806)742-3681. Use FAFSA (School code: 003644). Approximately 50% of students receive some form of financial assistance.

DEGREE REQUIREMENTS. For J.D.: satisfactory completion of 90 credit hour program. For master's degree: see Graduate School listing above.

TEXAS TECH UNIVERSITY HEALTH SCIENCES CENTER
Lubbock, Texas 79430
Web site: www.ttuhsc.edu

Founded 1979. Located adjacent to main campus. Schools located at Health Sciences Center are Graduate School of Biomedical Sciences, School of Allied Health, School of Medicine, School of Nursing, School of Pharmacy. Library: 259,300 volumes, 2600 subscriptions.

School of Allied Health Sciences (79430)
Founded 1981. Tuition: per credit, resident $88, nonresident $306. Enrollment: full- and part-time 500. Faculty: full-time 162, part-time 22. Degrees conferred: M.A.T., M.S.O.T., M.S.R.S., M.S.P.A., M.S.M.P., M.V.R., Au.D., Sc.D., Ph.D.

ADMISSION REQUIREMENTS. Official transcripts, two recommendations, GRE, interview required in support of School's application. Online application available. Interview encouraged, TOEFL required for international applicants. Graduates of unaccredited colleges not considered. Preference given to Texas residents. Apply to the Office of Registrar before February 15. Application fee: $40. Phone: (806)743-3220; fax: (806)473-2656.

ADMISSION STANDARDS. Selective. Usual minimum average: 2.7–3.0 (A = 4).

FINANCIAL AID. Scholarships, assistantships, fellowships, internships, tuition waiver, Federal W/S, loans. Apply by April 1 to the Financial Aid Office. Phone: (806)743-3025. Use FAFSA (School code: 016024).

DEGREE REQUIREMENTS. For M.A.T.: 47 credit program; thesis/nonthesis option. For M.S.O.T.: 102 credit full-time, three-year program; fieldwork experience; thesis/nonthesis. For M.S.M.P.: 42 credit full-time; clinical preceptorship. For M.S.P.A.: 31-month full-time program. For M.S.R.S.: 48 credit program, internships; clinical practice. For M.C.P.M.: 48 credit program; clinical internship; practicum. For Au.D.: 125 credit four-year program; clinical internship; clinical practicum; dissertation; oral defense. For Sc.D.: 38 credit program with master's (70 credit program with bachelor's); clinical internship; clinical project. For Ph.D.: 72 credit minimum, at least two consecutive semesters in residence; oral/written preliminary exam; oral written qualifying exam for candidacy; foreign language requirements vary by program; dissertation; final oral exam.

FIELDS OF STUDY.
Athletic Training. M.A.T.
Audiology. Au.D.
Clinical Practice Management. M.C.P.M.
Communication Sciences and Disorders. Ph.D.
Molecular Pathology. M.S.M.P.
Occupational Therapy. M.S.O.T.
Physical Therapy. M.S.P.T., Sc.D.
Physician Assistant Program. M.S.P.A.
Rehabilitation Counseling. M.S.
Rehabilitation Science. Includes management track, gerontology track. M.S.R.S.
Speech-Language Pathology. M.S.

School of Medicine

Web site: www.ttuhsc.edu/som

Established 1969 and is part of the University Health Science Center, Lubbock (79430). Library: 100,000 volumes, 1500 subscriptions. NIH ranking is 167th among all U.S. institutions with 79 awards/grants worth $23,076,106.

Annual tuition: resident $11,314, nonresident $24,414. No on-campus housing available. Total average figure for all other expenses: $13,500.

Enrollment: first-year class 140, total 550 (men 56%, women 44%, minorities 40%, state residents 96%). Faculty: full-time 482, part-time 82. Degrees conferred: M.D., M.D.-M.B.A., M.D.-Ph.D.

ADMISSION REQUIREMENTS. Applicants from Texas, Southwestern Oklahoma, Eastern New Mexico given preference, U.S. citizens and permanent residents only. Bachelor's degree from an accredited institution required. Has EDP; applicants must apply directly to Office of Admission between June 1 and August 1. Early applications are encouraged. All other applicants request publication forms and procedural information from the Texas Medical and Dental Schools Application Service and submit application and application fee (resident $55, nonresident $100), MCAT, official transcripts, a personal statement, two recommendations to the Application Service Center. A secondary application and application fee of $50 is required by the TTUHSC School of Medicine. Interviews are by invitation only and generally for final selection. Notification for EDP normally begins October 15. For regular admission apply after June 1, before November 1. Submit MCAT (will accept MCAT test results from the last three years), official transcripts for each school attended (should show at least 90 semester credits/135 quarter credits; submit transcripts by mid-May to AMCAS), an application and application fee of $50, a personal statement, preprofessional committee evaluation and three recommendations from science faculty to Office of Admission. Interviews by invitation only and generally for final selection. Dual degree applicants must apply to and be accepted to both Schools; contact the Office of Admission for current information and specific admissions requirements. First-year students admitted Fall only. Rolling admissions process; notification starts October 15 and is finished when class is filled. School does maintain an alternate list. Phone: (806)743-2297; fax: (806)743-2725.

ADMISSION STANDARDS. Competitive. Accepts about 6% of all applicants. Number of applications 2656 (298 out-of-state); number interviewed 776 (28 out-of-state); number of acceptance 173 (13 out-of-state); number enrolled 140 (8 out-of-state). Mean Composite MCAT 9.6; mean UGPA 3.64 (A = 4).

FINANCIAL AID. Scholarships, merit scholarships, minority scholarships, Grants-in-Aid, HEAL, loans. Apply to Office of Student Financial Aid after acceptance. Phone: (806)743-3025. Use FAFSA (School code: 016024). About 78% of students receive financial assistance.

DEGREE REQUIREMENTS. For M.D.: satisfactory completion of four-year program; all students spend the first two years in Lubbock then the third and fourth years in Lubbock, Amarillo, or El Paso; must pass Step 1 of USMLE for promotion to fourth year. For M.B.A., Ph.D.: see Texas Tech University listing above.

FIELDS OF GRADUATE STUDY.
Biochemistry & Molecular Genetics. Ph.D.
Biotechnology. M.S., Ph.D.
Cell & Molecular Biology. Ph.D.
Health Services Research. M.S.
Medical Microbiology. Ph.D.
Pharmaceutical Sciences. Ph.D.
Pharmacology & Neuroscience. Ph.D.
Physiology. Ph.D.

TEXAS WESLEYAN UNIVERSITY
Fort Worth, Texas 76102-1536
Web site: www.law.txwes.edu

Founded 1990. Coed. Private control, Methodist affiliation. Semester system. Library: 192,044 volumes, 632 subscriptions.

The University's graduate programs include Business Administration, Education, and Health Sciences. Total University enrollment at main campus: 2800.

School of Law (76102)

Established 1989, became part of the University in 1992. School of Law moved to current site in 1997. ABA approved since 1994. AALS member. Private control. Semester system. Full-time, part-time study. Special program: externship. Law library: 240,437 volumes, 4836 subscriptions; has LEXIS, NEXIS, WESTLAW.

Annual tuition: full-time $21,660, part-time $15,630. University housing available for both single and married students. Annual on-campus housing cost: $13,886. Contact Director of Housing for University owned housing information. Phone: (817)531-4432. Law students tend to live off-campus. Contact Admissions Office for off-campus housing information. Off-campus housing and personal expenses: approximately $10,500.

Enrollment: first-year class full-time 141, part-time 112; total full- and part-time 670 (men 50%, women 50%, minorities 19%). Faculty: full-time 35, part-time 30. Student to faculty ratio is 17.9 to 1. Degree conferred: J.D.

ADMISSION REQUIREMENTS. LSDAS Law School report, bachelor's degree, transcripts, LSAT, personal statement, two letters of recommendation required in support of application. Accepts transfer applicants from ABA approved schools. Apply to Office of Admissions by March 31. Application fee $55. Phone: (800)733-9529, (817)212-4040; fax: (817) 212-4002.

ADMISSION STANDARDS. Selective. Accepts approximately 29% of all students. Number of applicants 1671; number of acceptance 484; number enrolled 141; LSAT (75% of students have a score at or above 153); GPA (75% of students have a GPA at or above 2.89). *U.S. News & World Report* ranking is in the fourth tier of all U.S. law schools.

FINANCIAL AID. Scholarships, Federal W/S, loans. Apply to Financial Aid Office by March 1. Phone: (817)212-4090. Use FAFSA. About 36% of full-time and 17% of part-time students receive aid other than loans from School or outside sources.

DEGREE REQUIREMENTS. For J.D.: 88 semester cretits in full- or part-time program.

TEXAS WOMAN'S UNIVERSITY
Denton, Texas 76204-0479
Web site: www.twu.edu

Established 1901. Located 35 miles NW of Dallas. CGS member. Coed on graduate level. State control. Special facilities: Animal Care Facility, CompuPASS Learning Laboratory, Food Testing Laboratory, Speech and Hearing Clinic, Textile Research Laboratory, Institute for Clinical Services and Applied Research, Institute for Women's Health, The Stroke Center. Library: 788,000 volumes, 6000 subscriptions. Total University enrollment: 11,300.

Tuition: per semester hour, resident $163, nonresident $443. On-campus housing for 2880 graduate women, 70 graduate men, 53 married students. Average academic year housing costs: $4800 (including board) for single students; $5700 for married students. Apply to the Office of University Housing. Phone: (940)898-3676.

Graduate School

Graduate study since 1930. Enrollment: full-time 1505, part-time 3022. Faculty: full-time 292, part-time 100. Degrees conferred: M.A., M.B.A., M.F.A., M.S., M.Ed., M.O.T., M.L.S., M.Ed., Ed.D., Ph.D.

ADMISSION REQUIREMENTS. Official transcript, GRE/GMAT required in support of School's application. Online application available. Some programs require interview, letters of recommendation. TOEFL required for international applicants. Accepts transfer applicants. Graduates of unaccredited schools not considered. Apply to Office of Student Processing by June 30 (Fall), December 1 (Spring). Application fee $30, $50 for international applicants. Phone: (940)898-3188; fax: (940)898-3081; e-mail: gradschool@twu.edu.

ADMISSION STANDARDS. Selective for most departments. Usual minimum average: 3.0 (A = 4).

FINANCIAL AID. Scholarships, research assistantships, teaching assistantships, internships, grants, tuition waivers, Federal W/S, loans. Approved for VA benefits. Apply to appropriate departmental chair for assistantships; to Director of Financial Aid for all other programs. No specified closing date. Phone: (940)898-3050. Use FAFSA. Aid available for part-time students.

DEGREE REQUIREMENTS. For master's: 30 semester hours with thesis or 36 semester hours with professional paper or project; additional requirements vary from program to program. For Ph.D.: at least 90 hours beyond the bachelor's; proficiency in two research tools; qualifying exam; dissertation, final oral/written exam. For Ed.D.: essentially the same as Ph.D., but requires a proficiency in statistics as a research tool. Some doctorates require a residency of two consecutive semesters.

FIELDS OF STUDY.

THE COLLEGE OF ARTS AND SCIENCES (M.A., M.B.A., M.F.A., M.S., PH.D.):
Art.
Art Education.
Art History.
Biology.
Biology Teaching.
Business Administration.
Chemistry.
Chemistry Teaching.
Counseling Psychology.
Dance.
Design. Includes advertising, fashion illustrating, medical illustration.
Drama.
English.
Fashion Merchandising.
Fashion and Textiles.
Government.
History.
Mathematics.
Mathematics Teaching.
Molecular Biology.
Music.
Music Education.
Music Therapy.
Psychology.
Rhetoric.
School Psychology.
Science Teaching.
Sociology.
Studio Art. Includes ceramics, fabric and printed textile, jewelry and metalsmithing, painting, photography, sculpture.
Women's Studies.

COLLEGE OF PROFESSIONAL EDUCATION (M.A.T., M.S., M.ED., M.L.S., ED.D., PH.D.):
Administration.
Child Development.
Consumer Sciences.
Counseling and Development.
Early Childhood Education.
Elementary Education.
Family Studies.
Family Therapy.
Home and Family Life.
Library Science.
Marriage and Family Counseling.
Reading Education.
Special Education. Includes educational diagnostician, mental retardation, physically handicapped.
Teaching.

COLLEGE OF HEALTH SCIENCES (M.A., M.S., ED.D., PH.D.):
Education of the Deaf.
Exercise and Sport Nutrition.
Food Science.
Food Systems Administration.
Health Care Administration.
Health Education.
Health Studies.
Institutional Administration.
Kinesiology.
Nutrition,
Speech-Language Pathology.

COLLEGE OF NURSING (M.S., PH.D.):
Clinical Nurse Specialist.
Nurse Practitioner.
Nursing Education.
Nursing Practice.
Nursing Science.
Nursing Systems Management.

SCHOOL OF OCCUPATIONAL THERAPY (M.A., M.O.T.):
Occupational Therapy.
Rehabilitation Technology.

SCHOOL OF PHYSICAL THERAPY (M.S., PH.D.):
Physical Therapy (Clinical Level).
Physical Therapy (Entry Level).

THE UNIVERSITY OF TEXAS AT ARLINGTON

Arlington, Texas 76019
Web site: www.uta.edu

Founded 1895. Located in the Center of Dallas–Fort Worth. CGS member. Coed. Public control. Semester system. Special facilities: Automation and Robotics Research Institute, Community Services Research Center, Center for Research in Contemporary Art, Energy Systems Research Center, Center for Rhetorical and Critical Theory, Center for Positron Studies, Center for Social Research, Center for Greater Southwestern Studies and History of Cartography. Library: 1,500,000 volumes, 8500 subscriptions. Total University enrollment: 25,500.

Tuition: per credit, resident $56, nonresidents $278. On-campus housing for 330 married students, 800 single students. Annual housing cost: $5345 (including board) single students; $5800 for married students. Contact Director of Housing for both on- and off-campus housing information. Phone: (817)272-2791.

Graduate School

Graduate study since 1952. Enrollment: full-time 2555, part-time 3205. Faculty: full-time 411, part-time 42. Degrees conferred: M.A., M.Arch., M.B.A., M.Engr., M.C.R.P., M.S.N., M.C.S., M.E.T., M.P.A., M.S., M.S.S.W., D.Sc., Ph.D.

ADMISSION REQUIREMENTS. Official transcripts, GRE/GMAT (M.B.A., M.P.A.) required in support of School's application. Portfolio required for M.Arch. TOEFL required of international applicants. Accepts transfer applicants. Graduates of unaccredited colleges not considered. Apply to Director of Admissions 60 days prior to beginning of semester; international applicants should apply at least 120 days prior to beginning of semester. Application fee $35, $50 for international applicants. Phone: (817)272-3186; e-mail: graduate.school@uta.edu.

ADMISSION STANDARDS. Very selective or selective. Usual minimum average: 3.0 (A = 4).

FINANCIAL AID. Annual awards from institutional funds: fellowships, teaching assistantships, research assistantships (TSE required of those whose primary language is not English), internships, tuition waivers, Federal W/S, loans. Apply by June 1 to Dean for scholarships, to appropriate departmental chair for fellowships/assistantships; to Financial Aid Office for all other programs. Phone: (817)272-3561. Use FAFSA.

DEGREE REQUIREMENTS. For master's: Plan I—30 semester hours minimum; thesis; final oral exam. Plan II—33 semester hours minimum; internship/project; comprehensive exam. Plan III—36 semester hours minimum; comprehensive exam. For Ph.D., D.Sc.: four years beyond the bachelor's degree minimum, at least one year in residence; qualifying exam; dissertation; final oral exam.

FIELDS OF STUDY.

GRADUATE SCHOOL:
Interdisciplinary Studies. M.A., M.S.
Management of Technology. M.S.

COLLEGE OF BUSINESS ADMINISTRATION:
Accounting. Includes flexible M.B.A., business administration (Ph.D.). M.P.A., M.S., Ph.D.
Economics. Includes flexible M.B.A., business administration (Ph.D.). M.A., Ph.D.
Finance and Real Estate. Includes flexible M.B.A., quantitative finance (M.S.), real estate (M.S.), business administration (Ph.D.). M.S., Ph.D.
Information Systems and Management Science. Includes flexible M.B.A., business statistics (Ph.D.), information systems (M.S.),

business administration (Ph.D.), mathematical sciences (Ph.D.), operations management (M.B.A.). M.S., Ph.D.
Management. Includes flexible M.B.A., human resource management (M.S.), business administration (Ph.D.). M.S., Ph.D.
Marketing. Includes flexible M.B.A., marketing research (M.S.), business administration (Ph.D.).
Professional Accounting. M.P.A.
Taxation. M.S.

COLLEGE OF EDUCATION:
Curriculum and Instruction. M.Ed.
Educational Leadership and Policy Studies. M.Ed., Ph.D.
Physiology in Exercise (Kinesiology). M.S.
Teaching. M.Ed.T.

COLLEGE OF ENGINEERING:
Aerospace Engineering. M.S., M.Engr., Ph.D.
Biomedical Engineering. M.S., Ph.D.
Civil Engineering. M.S., M.Engr., Ph.D.
Computer Science and Engineering. Includes online computer science (M.S.), online computer science and engineering (M.S.), software engineering (M.SW.Engr.). M.S., M.C.S., M.SW.Engr., Ph.D.
Computer Sciences. M.S., Ph.D.
Electrical Engineering. Includes online electrical engineering (M.S.). M.S., M.Engr., Ph.D.
Engineering Management. M.S.
Industrial and Manufacturing Engineering. Includes logistics (M.S.), management of technology (M.S.). M.S., M.Engr., Ph.D.
Materials Science and Engineering. M.S., M.Engr., Ph.D.
Mechanical Engineering. M.S., M.Engr., Ph.D.

COLLEGE OF LIBERAL ARTS:
Anthropology. M.A.
Art. M.F.A.
Communication. M.A.
Criminology and Criminal Justice. M.A.
English. M.A., Ph.D.
History. M.A.
Humanities. M.A.
Linguistics. M.A., Ph.D.
Modern Languages. Includes French, Spanish. M.A.
Music Education. M.M.
Philosophy. Ph.D.
Political Science. M.A.
Sociology. M.A.
TESOL. M.A.

COLLEGE OF SCIENCE:
Biology. Includes mathematical sciences (Ph.D.), quantitative biology (Ph.D.). M.S., Ph.D.
Chemistry. M.S., Ph.D.
Environmental and Earth Sciences. M.S., Ph.D.
Interdisciplinary Science. M.A.
Mathematics. Includes mathematics, general statistics. M.A., M.S., Ph.D.
Physics. Includes physics and applied physics (Ph.D.). M.S., Ph.D.
Psychology. Includes experimental (M.S., Ph.D.), industrial organizational (M.S.). M.S., Ph.D.

SCHOOL OF ARCHITECTURE:
Architecture. M.Arch.
Landscape Architecture. M.L.A.

SCHOOL OF EDUCATION:
Curriculum and Instruction. M.Ed.
Educational Leadership. M.Ed.
Teaching. M.Ed.T.

SCHOOL OF NURSING:
Nurse Practitioner Programs. Includes acute care nursing, adult nursing, emergency nursing, family nursing, gerontological nursing, pediatric nursing, psychiatric-mental health nursing.

Nursing Administration. M.S.N.
Nursing. Ph.D.

SCHOOL OF SOCIAL WORK.
Social Work. M.S.S.W., Ph.D.

SCHOOL OF URBAN AND PUBLIC AFFAIRS:
City and Regional Planning. M.C.R.P.
Public Administration. M.P.A.
Public and Urban Administration. Ph.D.
Urban Affairs. M.A.
Urban Planning and Public Policy. Ph.D.

THE UNIVERSITY OF TEXAS AT AUSTIN
Austin, Texas 78712-7666
Web site: www.utexas.edu

Founded 1883. CGS and AAU member. Coed. State control. Semester system. Special facilities: Americo Paredes Center for Cultural Studies, Biochemical Institute, Center for African and African American Studies, Center for Asian Studies, Center for Asian American Studies, Center for Mexican American Studies, Center for Middle Eastern Studies, Center for Russian, East European and Eurasian Studies, Computation Center, Drug Dynamics Institute, Bureau of Economic Geology, Bureau of Engineering Research, Harry Huntt Ransom Humanities Research Center, Lyndon B. Johnson Library and Museum, Bureau of Business Research, Institute of Marine Science, Jack S. Blanton Museum of Art, McDonald Observatory, Population Research Center, Speech and Hearing Center, Teresa Lozano Long Institute of Latin American Studies, Texas Memorial Museum. The University's NIH ranking is 104th among all U.S. institutions with 190 awards/grants valued at $48,995,231. According to The Center at University of Florida, the University is ranked 26th in receipt of Federal Research funds with $231,996,000 and it ranks 31st for total University research expenditures with $343,854,000. The University's endowment assets rank it 23rd, with a value of $2,038,938,000. In 2004, the University awarded 702 doctorates which ranked it 3rd among all U.S. institutions eligible to award that degree. Fifty-three of the University's faculty members have been elected to National Honor Academies and this ranks it 18th among all U.S. institutions. The Library: approximately 6,680,000 volumes, 50,000 subscriptions. Total University enrollment: 54,000.

Tuition: per credit, resident $437–$457, nonresident $797–$817; M.B.A., M.P.A. nonresidents $1561. Average academic year housing costs: extremely wide range. Contact Housing and Food Service Division for both on- and off-campus housing information. Phone: (512)471-3136. Day-care facilities available.

Graduate School

Graduate study since 1909. Enrollment: full-time 10,576 (men 50%, women 50%). Faculty: full-time 1774. Degrees conferred: M.A., M.Arch., M.B.A., M.Ed., M.F.A., M.L.I.S., M.M., M.P.A., M.P.Aff., M.S.Appl.Phy., M.S.Arch.St., M.S.C.R.P., M.S.C.A.M., M.S.C.S., M.S.Econom., M.S.E., M.S.Geo.Sci., M.S.Info.Stds., M.S.Marine.Sci., M.S.N., M.S.Phr., M.S.S.T.C., M.S.S.W., M.S.Stat., Ed.D., D.M.A., Ph.D.

ADMISSION REQUIREMENTS. Official transcripts, GRE/GMAT required in support of School's application. Interview required by some departments. Online application available. TOEFL required for international applicants. Graduates of unaccredited colleges not considered. Apply to Graduate and International Admission Center. Departmental deadlines vary, contact appropriate department for this information, or visit the Web site.

Application fee $50; $75 for international applicants. Phone: (512)475-7390.

ADMISSION STANDARDS. Selective for most departments. Usual minimum average: 3.0 (A = 4).

FINANCIAL AID. Annual awards from institutional funds: scholarships, fellowships, assistantships, internships, grants, tuition waivers, Federal W/S, loans. Approved for VA benefits. Apply by March 31 to appropriate Graduate Adviser for scholarships, assistantships; to Financial Services Office for all other aid. No specified closing date. Phone: (512)475-6282. Use FAFSA. "Substantial numbers" of students receive aid other than loans from School and outside sources. Aid available for part-time students.

DEGREE REQUIREMENTS. For most master's: 30 semester hours minimum, at least one year in residence; thesis; comprehensive oral/written exam for some departments. For M.B.A., M.P.A., M.Arch., M.L.I.S., M.S.S.W., M.S.Pharm., M.S.CRP., M.S.C.S.: 30–60 hours depending on previous background, at least 30 hours in residence; thesis/final report. For M.Ed.: 36 hours minimum, at least 30 in residence; final competency exam. For Ph.D.: at least one year in residence; foreign language requirement set by department; oral/written candidacy exam; dissertation; final oral exam. For Ed.D.: comprehensive oral/written exam; other requirements essentially the same as for Ph.D. For D.M.A.: requirements essentially the same as for Ph.D., except original composition/dissertation/performance.

FIELDS OF STUDY.

SCHOOL OF ARCHITECTURE:
Architectural History. M.A.
Architectural Studies. M.S.Arch.St.
Architecture—First Professional. M.Arch.
Architecture—Post Professional. M.Arch.
Architecture. Ph.D.
Community and Regional Planning. M.S.C.R.P., Ph.D.
Historical Preservation. M.S.
Sustainable Design. M.S.S.D.
Urban Design. M.S.U.D.

RED MCCOMBS GRADUATE SCHOOL OF BUSINESS:
Accounting. Ph.D.
Business Administration. Includes executive M.B.A. in Mexico City, evening option. M.B.A.
Finance. Ph.D.
Management Science and Information Systems. Ph.D.
Management. Ph.D.
Marketing. Ph.D.
Professional Accounting. M.P.A.
Risk Analysis and Decision Making. Ph.D.
Supply Chain and Operations Management. Ph.D.

COLLEGE OF COMMUNICATION:
Advertising. M.A., Ph.D.
Communication Sciences and Disorders. M.A., Ph.D.
Communication Studies. M.A., Ph.D.
Journalism. M.A., Ph.D.
Radio-Television-Film. M.A., M.F.A., Ph.D.

COLLEGE OF EDUCATION:
Curriculum and Instruction. M.A., M.Ed., Ed.D., Ph.D.
Educational Administration. M.Ed., Ed.D., Ph.D.
Educational Psychology. Includes counseling (Ph.D.), school (Ph.D.). M.A., M.Ed., Ph.D.
Foreign Language Education. M.A., Ph.D.
Health Education. M.A., M.Ed., Ed.D., Ph.D.
Kinesiology. M.A., M.Ed., Ed.D., Ph.D.
Mathematics Education. M.A. M.Ed., Ph.D.
Science Education. M.A., M.Ed., Ph.D.
Special Education. M.A., M.Ed., Ed.D., Ph.D.

COLLEGE OF ENGINEERING:
Advanced Manufacturing. M.S.E.
Aerospace Engineering. M.S.E., Ph.D.
Architectural Engineering. M.S.E.
Biomedical Engineering. M.S.E., Ph.D.
Chemical Engineering. M.S.E., Ph.D.
Circuit Design. M.S.E.
Civil Engineering. M.S.E., Ph.D.
Electrical and Computer Engineering. Includes biomedical engineering, communications, networks and systems, computer engineering, electromagnetics and acoustics, energy systems, executive software engineering, plasma, quantum electronics and optics, solid-state electronics. M.S.E., Ph.D.
Energy and Mineral Resources. M.A.
Engineering Management. M.S.E.
Engineering Mechanics. M.S.E., Ph.D.
Environmental and Water Resources. M.S.E.
Executive Engineering Management. M.S.E.
Materials Science and Engineering. M.S.E., Ph.D.
Mechanical Engineering. M.S.E., Ph.D.
Operations Research and Industrial Engineering. M.S., Ph.D.
Petroleum and Geosystems Engineering. M.S.E., Ph.D.

COLLEGE OF FINE ARTS:
Art Education. M.A.
Art History. M.A., Ph.D.
Dance. M.F.A.
Design. M.F.A.
Music Composition. M.M., D.M.A.
Music Education. M.M., D.M.A., Ph.D.
Music Performance. M.M., D.M.A.
Music Theory. M.M., Ph.D.
Musicology/Ethnomusicology. M.M., Ph.D.
Studio Art. M.F.A.
Theatre. Includes acting, directing, drama & theatre for youth, playwriting, theatre technology, theatrical design. M.F.A.

COLLEGE OF LIBERAL ARTS:
American Studies. M.A., Ph.D.
Anthropology. Includes folklore and public culture. M.A., Ph.D.
Arabic Studies. M.A., Ph.D.
Asian Culture and Languages. M.A., Ph.D.
Asian Studies. M.A.
Classics. M.A., Ph.D.
Comparative Literature. M.A., Ph.D.
Economics. M.A., M.S.Econ., Ph.D.
English. Includes creative writing (M.A.). M.A., Ph.D.
French. M.A., Ph.D.
Geography. M.A., Ph.D.
Germanic Studies. M.A., Ph.D.
Government. M.A., Ph.D.
History. M.A., Ph.D.
Latin American Studies. M.A., Ph.D.
Linguistics. M.A., Ph.D.
Mexican American Studies. M.A.
Middle Eastern Studies. M.A.
Philosophy. M.A., Ph.D.
Psychology. Includes clinical. Ph.D.
Russian, East European, and Eurasian Studies. M.A.
Slavic Languages. M.A., Ph.D.
Sociology. M.A., Ph.D.
Spanish, Portuguese. M.A., Ph.D.
Women's and Gender Studies. M.A.

SCHOOL OF INFORMATION:
Information Science. M.L.I.S., Ph.D.

COLLEGE OF NATURAL SCIENCES:
Astronomy. M.A., Ph.D.
Biochemistry. M.A., Ph.D.
Cell and Molecular Biology. M.A., Ph.D.

Chemistry. M.A., Ph.D.
Computer Sciences. M.A., M.S.C.S., Ph.D.
Ecology, Evolution, and Behavior. M.A., Ph.D.
Geological Sciences. M.A., Ph.D.
Human Development and Family Sciences. M.A., Ph.D.
Marine Science. M.A., Ph.D.
Mathematics. M.A., Ph.D.
Microbiology. M.A., Ph.D.
Nutritional Sciences. Ph.D.
Physics. M.A., Ph.D.
Statistics. M.S.Stat.
Textile and Apparel Technology. M.S.

JACKSON SCHOOL OF GEOSCIENCES:
Energy and Earth Sciences Resources. Interdisciplinary.
Geological Sciences. M.S., Ph.D.
Hydrogeology. M.A.
Petroleum Geology. M.A.

SCHOOL OF NURSING:
Nursing. M.S.N., Ph.D.

COLLEGE OF PHARMACY:
Pharmacy. M.S.Phr., Ph.D.

L.B.J. SCHOOL OF PUBLIC AFFAIRS:
Public Affairs. M.P.Aff.
Public Policy. Ph.D.

SCHOOL OF SOCIAL WORK:
Social Work. M.S.S.W., Ph.D.

INTERCOLLEGIAL PROGRAMS:
Computational and Applied Mathematics. M.S.C.A.M., Ph.D.
Medieval Studies. Ph.D.
Neuroscience. M.A., Ph.D.
Science and Technology Commercialization. M.S.S.T.C.
Writing. M.F.A.

JOINT DEGREE PROGRAMS:
Advertising/Business Administration. M.A.-M.B.A.
Asian Studies/Business Administration. M.A.-M.B.A.
Asian Studies/Public Affairs. M.A.-M.P.Aff.
Communication/Business Administration. M.A.-M.B.A.
Community and Regional Planning/Geography. M.S.C.R.P.-Ph.D.
Journalism/Business Administration. M.A.-M.B.A.
Latin American Studies/Business Administration. M.A.-M.B.A.
Latin American Studies/Communication. M.A.-M.A.
Latin American Studies/Community and Regional Planning. M.A.-M.S.C.R.P.
Latin American Studies/Law. M.A.-J.D.
Latin American Studies/Public Affairs. M.A.-M.P.Aff.
Law/Business Administration. J.D.-M.B.A.
Law/Public Affairs. J.D.-M.P.Aff.
Law/Russian, East European, and Eurasian Studies. J.D.-M.A.
Mechanical Engineering/Business Administration. M.S.E.-M.B.A.
Middle Eastern Studies/Business Administration. M.A.-M.B.A.
Middle Eastern Studies/Communication. M.A.-M.A.
Middle Eastern Studies/Law. M.A.-J.D.
Middle Eastern Studies/Library and Information Science. M.A.-M.L.I.S.
Middle Eastern Studies/Public Affairs. M.A.-M.P.Aff.
Nursing/Business Administration. M.S.N.-M.B.A.
Public Affairs/Business Administration. M.P.Aff.-M.B.A.
Public Affairs/Communication. M.P.Aff.-M.A.
Public Affairs/Engineering. M.P.Aff.-M.S.E.
Russian, East European, and Eurasian Studies/Business Administration. M.A.-M.B.A.
Russian, East European, and Eurasian Studies/Communication. M.A.-M.A.

Russian, East European, and Eurasian Studies/Public Affairs. M.A.-M.P.Aff.

School of Law (78705-3299)

Web site: www.utexas.edu/law

Established 1883. Located on main campus. ABA approved since 1923. AALS member since 1907. Semester system. Full-time, day study only. Special facilities: Center for Human Rights and Justice, Center for Law, Business and Economics, The Center on Lawyers, Civil Justice and Media, the William Wayne Center for Public Interest Law, Center for Public Policy and Dispute Resolution, Institute for Transnational Law. Special programs: study abroad at the University of Nottingham, England; University of Edinburgh, Scotland; University of Pais Vasco, Spain; University of Paris X (Nanterre), France; Bucerius Law School, Germany; University of Siena, Italy; Australian National University, Australia; University of Leiden, Netherlands; Universidad Torcuato de Tella, Argentina; Universidade Federal do Rio Grande do Sul, Brazil. Law library: 1,026,598 volumes, 8322 subscriptions; has LEXIS, NEXIS, WESTLAW, DIALOG, CALI; has more than 300 network connections; is a State and Federal Depository.

Annual tuition: resident $20,632, nonresident $35,130. Limited on-campus housing available. Law students generally prefer to live off-campus. Contact University of Texas Housing Division for off-campus information. Phone: (512)471-3136. Off-campus housing and personal expenses: approximately $13,116.

Enrollment: first-year class 477; total full-time 1313 (men 60%, women 40%, minorities 32%); no part-time students. Faculty: full-time 64, part-time 51. Student to faculty ratio 17.6 to 1. Degrees conferred: J.D., J.D.-M.B.A., J.D.-M.P.A., J.D.-M.A. (Latin American Studies, Russian, East European, and Eurasian Studies, Middle Eastern Studies), J.D.-M.S.C.R.P., J.D.-Ph.D. (History, Philosophy), LL.M. (for foreign law school graduates who have completed a basic legal education and received a university degree in law in another country), LL.M. (Latin American and International Law), M.C.J.

ADMISSION REQUIREMENTS. Bachelor's degree, transcripts, LSAT, personal statement, résumé required in support of application. Letters of recommendation are optional, but encouraged. Interview not required. Accepts transfer applicants. Graduates of unaccredited institutions not considered. Apply to University Director of Admissions by February 1 (Fall). Application fee $70, $75 for international applicants. Phone: (512)232-1200.

ADMISSION STANDARDS. Selective. Accepts approximately 19% of all students. Number of applicants 5442; number of acceptance 1017; number enrolled 442; LSAT (75% of students have a score at or above 161); GPA (75% of students have a GPA at or above 3.41). *U.S. News & World Report* ranking is in the top 18 of all U.S. law schools.

FINANCIAL AID. Law School scholarships, Townes-Rice Scholarships, minority scholarships, Texas Grants, Law School and private loans; Federal loans and Federal W/S offered through University's Financial Aid Office. Assistantships may be available for upper-divisional joint degree candidates and second- and third-year law students. For scholarships, apply to Loans and Scholarships office after January 1, before March 31. For all other programs, apply to University's Office of Student Financial Services, Wooldridge Hall, 600 W. 24th Street. Phone: (512)232-1130. Use FAFSA (School code: 003658), also submit Financial Aid Transcript, Federal Income Tax forms. Approximately 80% of first-year class received scholarships/Grants-in-Aid. No aid available for LL.M. students.

DEGREE REQUIREMENTS. For J.D.: 86 (39 required) credits with a GPA of at least 2.0 (A = 4.), plus completion of upper-divisional writing seminar, one course in Professional Responsibility; three-year program. Accelerated J.D. with two summers of course work. For J.D.-Master's: four-year programs rather than five-year programs if both degrees are taken consecutively. For LL.M. (foreign law graduates): 24 credits; at least two semesters in residence; satisfactory completion of "Introduction to U.S. Law and Legal Research"; completion of a substantial paper. For M.C.J.: degree program is currently inactive.

THE UNIVERSITY OF TEXAS AT BROWNSVILLE AND TEXAS SOUTHMOST COLLEGE

Brownsville, Texas 78520-4991
Web site: www.utb.edu

CGS member, Coed. State control. Semester system. Library: 174,660 volumes, 4400 subscriptions. Total University enrollment: 13,300.

Tuition: per credit, resident $120, nonresident $265. No on-campus housing available. Day-care facilities available.

Graduate Studies

Graduate Enrollment: full-time 77, part-time 772. Graduate faculty: full- and part-time 175. Degrees Conferred: M.A., M.A.I.S., M.B.A., M.Ed., M.S.P.H.N, M.S.I.S.

ADMISSION REQUIREMENTS. Two official transcripts, GRE/GMAT, essay, statement of goals, two letters of recommendation required in support of application. TOEFL (minimum score 550) required for international applicants. Accepts transfer students. Graduates of unaccredited institutions not considered. Apply to the Director of Admissions and Records by July 1 (Fall), December 1 (Spring) for priority consideration. Rolling admissions process. Application fee: $30. Phone: (800)860-0287, (956)548-6552; fax: (956)882-7279.

ADMISSION STANDARDS. Selective. Usual minimum average: 3.0 (A = 4).

FINANCIAL AID, Scholarships, assistantships, internships, tuition waivers, Federal W/S, loans. Approved for VA benefits. Apply by April 1 to the appropriate department for scholarships and assistantships; to Director of Financial Aid for all other programs. Use FAFSA. Aid available for part-time students.

DEGREE REQUIREMENTS. For M.A., M.S.: 30 semester credits minimum, at least 24 credits in residence; thesis/nonthesis option; comprehensive written/oral exam. For M.Ed.: 36 semester credits minimum, at least 30 credits in residence. For M.B.A.: 36–45 semester credits minimum, at least 30–39 credits in residence; computer proficiency. For M.S.P.H.N.: 36 semester credits minimum, at least 30 credits in residence; practicum; comprehensive exam.

FIELDS OF STUDY.
Bilingual Education. M.Ed., M.S.
Biology. M.S., M.S.I.S.
Business Administration. M.B.A.
Computer Science. M.S.I.S.
Counseling and Guidance. M.Ed.
Curriculum and Instruction. M.Ed., Ed.D.
Early Childhood Education. M.Ed.
Educational Leadership. M.Ed.
Education Technology. M.Ed.
Elementary Education. M.Ed.
English as a Second Language. M.Ed.
English. M.A., M.A.I.S.
Government. M.A.I.S.
History. M.A.I.S.
Mathematics. M.S.

Music Education. M.M.
Nursing. M.S.N.
Public Health Nursing. M.S.P.H.N.
Public Policy and Management. M.P.P.M.
Reading Specialist. M.Ed.
Sociology. M.A.I.S.
Spanish. M.A., M.A.I.S.
Special Education. Includes educational diagnostician option. M.Ed.
Technology. M.S.

THE UNIVERSITY OF TEXAS AT DALLAS

Richardson, Texas 75083-0688
Web site: www.utdallas.edu

Created 1969. CGS member. Coed. State control. Semester system. Special facilities: Callier Center for Communications Disorders, Center for Applied Optics, Center for Lithospheric Studies, Center for Quantum Electronics, Center for Space Sciences, Center for Genetic Technology, Institute for Environmental Sciences, Communications and Learning Center, Center for China and U.S. Management Studies, Center for Research and Teaching, Bruton Center for Development Studies, Morris Hite Center for Product Development and Marketing Science, Center for International Accounting Development, Translation Center. Library: 797,719 volumes, 5100 subscriptions. Total University enrollment: 14,500.

Tuition: per credit, resident $303, nonresident $703. On-campus housing available for single and married students. Average academic year housing costs: $5799 (including board); off-campus costs: $375–$700 per month. Day-care facilities available.

Graduate School

Graduate study since 1969. Graduate enrollment: full-time 2072, part-time 2259. Graduate faculty: full-time 312, part-time 57. Degrees conferred: M.A., M.A.T., M.B.A., M.S., M.S.E.E., M.S.E.S., M.P.A., Ph.D., D.Chem.

ADMISSION REQUIREMENTS. Official transcripts, bachelor's degree, GRE, GMAT (School of Management) required in support of School's application. Online application available. TOEFL required for international applicants. Accepts transfer students. Graduates of unaccredited institutions not considered. Apply to Director of Admissions by July 15 (Fall), November 15 (Spring). Rolling admissions process. Application fee: $25, international students $75. Phone: (214)883-2294; information line: (214)883-2341; fax: (214)883-2599.

ADMISSION STANDARDS. Selective. Usual minimum average: 3.0 (A = 4).

FINANCIAL AID. Scholarships, assistantships, internships, partial tuition waivers, grants, Federal W/S, loans. Approved for VA benefits. Apply by April 30 to the appropriate department for scholarships and assistantships; to Financial Aid Office for all other aid. Phone: (214)883-2941; fax: (214)883-2947. Use FAFSA and Institutional FAF. About 65% of students receive aid from University and outside sources. Aid available for part-time students.

DEGREE REQUIREMENTS. For master's: 36–45 semester credits minimum; at least 30–39 credits in residence; thesis/nonthesis option; comprehensive written/oral exam. For Ph.D., D.Chem.: 60 credits minimum beyond bachelor's, at least one year in full-time study; proficiency in one foreign language for some programs; qualifying exam; advancement to candidacy; dissertation; final oral exam.

FIELDS OF STUDY.

SCHOOL OF ARTS AND HUMANITIES:
Arts and Technology. M.A., M.F.A.
History. M.A.
Humanities. Includes aesthetic studies, history of ideas, studies in literature. M.A., M.A.T., Ph.D.

SCHOOL OF BEHAVIORAL AND BRAIN SCIENCES:
Applied Cognition and Neuroscience. M.S.
Audiology. Au.D.
Cognition and Neuroscience. Ph.D.
Communication Disorders. M.S.
Communication Sciences and Disorders. Ph.D.
Human Development and Early Childhood Disorders. M.S.
Psychological Sciences. M.S., Ph.D.

SCHOOL OF ECONOMIC, POLITICAL AND POLICY STUDIES:
Applied Sociology. M.S.
Criminology. M.S., Ph.D.
Economics. M.S., Ph.D.
Geospatial Information Sciences. M.S., Ph.D.
International Political Economy. M.S.
Political Science. Ph.D.
Public Affairs. M.P.A.
Public Policy. M.P.P., Ph.D.
Public Policy and Political Economy. Ph.D.

ERIK JOHNSON SCHOOL OF ENGINEERING AND COMPUTER SCIENCE:
Computer Engineering. M.S., Ph.D.
Computer Science. Includes software engineering (M.S.). M.S., Ph.D.
Electrical Engineering. Includes microelectronics, (M.S.), telecommunications (M.S.). M.S., Ph.D.
Materials Science and Engineering. M.S., Ph.D.
Software Engineering. Ph.D.
Telecommunications Engineering. M.S., Ph.D.

SCHOOL OF MANAGEMENT:
Accounting and Information Management. M.S.
Business Administration. Includes global leadership executive, global (Online), project management. M.B.A.
Healthcare Management. M.S.
Information Technology Management. M.S.
International Management Studies. M.A., Ph.D.
Management and Administration Sciences. M.S.
Management Sciences. Ph.D.

SCHOOL OF NATURAL SCIENCES AND MATHEMATICS:
Applied Physics. M.S.
Bioinformatics and Computational Biology. M.S.
Biotechnology. M.S.
Chemistry. M.S., Ph.D.
Geosciences. M.S., Ph.D.
Mathematical Sciences. Includes applied mathematics (M.S., Ph.D.), engineering mathematics (M.S.), Statistics (M.S., Ph.D.). M.S., Ph.D.
Mathematics Education. M.A.T.
Molecular and Cell Biology. M.S., Ph.D.
Physics. M.S., Ph.D.
Science Education. M.A.T.

THE UNIVERSITY OF TEXAS AT EL PASO

El Paso, Texas 79968-0001
Web site: www.utep.edu

Established 1913. CGS member. Coed. State control. Semester system. Special facilities: NSF Material Science Center, El Paso

Centennial Museum, Center for Environmental Resource Management, Center for Entrepreneurial Development, Advancement Research and Support, El Paso Solar Pond Research Station, Institute for Manufacturing and Materials Management, Center for Environmental Resource Management, the Hemispheric Trade Center, the Inter-American and Border Studies Center, NSF Materials Science Center, Oral History Institute, Center for Public Policy, Bureau of Business and Economics Research. Library: 850,000 volumes, 2499 subscriptions. Total University enrollment: 19,500.

Tuition: per credit, resident $171, nonresident $449, resident Business, Nursing $181, nonresident $459 (Business, Nursing). On-campus housing for 60 married students, 328 men, 122 women. Average academic year housing costs: $400–$450 per month for married students, $300–$450 for single students. Contact Housing Office for both on- and off-campus housing information. Phone: (915)747-5352.

Graduate School

Graduate study since 1940. Enrollment: full-time 222, part-time 2047. University faculty teaching graduate students: full-time 341, part-time 330. Degrees conferred: M.A., M.Ed., M.B.A., M.M., M.P.A., M.Acy., M.S., M.S.I.S., M.A.T., M.A.I.S., M.S.N., Ph.D.

ADMISSION REQUIREMENTS. Two official transcripts, GRE/GMAT, statement of purpose, letters of recommendation required in support of School's application. Online application available. MAT may be required for nursing students. Interview not required. TOEFL required for international applicants. Accepts transfer applicants. Graduates of unaccredited institutions not considered. Apply by August 31 (Fall), December 31 (Spring) to Graduate Student Services Office. Application fee $30, $65 for international applicants. Phone: (915)747-5491; fax: (915)747-5788.

ADMISSION STANDARDS. Selective. Usual minimum average: 2.75 (A = 4).

FINANCIAL AID. Scholarships, fellowships, research/teaching assistantships, internships, partial tuition waivers, Federal W/S, loans. Approved for VA benefits. Apply to the appropriate department for fellowships, assistantships; to the Office of Student Financial Aid for all other programs. No specified closing date, although applicants are advised to submit their applications before March 1 for the upcoming academic year. Office of Student Financial Aid. Phone: (915)747-5204. Use FAFSA and institutional FAF. Aid available for part-time students.

DEGREE REQUIREMENTS. For M.A., M.S.: 30 semester hours minimum, at least 24 in residence; thesis; comprehensive oral/written exam. For M.Ed.: 36 semester hours minimum, at least 30 in residence. For M.B.A., M.Acc.: 36 semester hours minimum, at least 30 in residence; computer proficiency. For M.P.A.: 36 semester hours minimum, at least 30 in residence; internship; comprehensive exam. For M.S.N.: 36 semester hours minimum, at least 30 in residence; practicum; comprehensive exam. For M.S.I.S.: 36 semester hours minimum, at least 30 in residence; report. For M.A.T.: 36 semester hours minimum, at least 30 in residence; comprehensive exam. For M.A.I.S.: 36 semester hours minimum, at least 30 in residence; final project; oral examination. For Ph.D.: 30 semester hours minimum beyond the master's; qualifying exam; proficiency in one foreign language for some programs; dissertation; final oral exam.

FIELDS OF STUDY.

COLLEGE OF BUSINESS ADMINISTRATION:
Accounting. M.Acc.
Business Administration. M.B.A.
Economics. M.S.E.
Information Technology. M.I.T.
International Business. Ph.D.

COLLEGE OF EDUCATION:
Counseling. M.Ed.
Education Administration. M.Ed.
Education Diagnostician. M.Ed.
Educational Leadership and Administration. M.Ed.
Instructional Specialist. M.Ed.
Reading Education. M.Ed.
Special Education. M.Ed.

COLLEGE OF ENGINEERING:
Civil Engineering. M.S., Ph.D.
Computer Engineering. M.S., Ph.D.
Computer Science. M.S., Ph.D.
Electrical Engineering. M.S.
Environmental Engineering. M.S.En.E., M.E.En.E.
Environmental Sciences and Engineering. Ph.D.
Industrial Engineering. M.S.
Information Technology. M.I.T.
Manufacturing Engineering. M.S.
Materials Science and Engineering. Ph.D.
Mechanical Engineering. M.S.
Metallurgical and Materials Engineering. M.S.

COLLEGE OF HEALTH SCIENCES:
Health Promotion. M.S.
Interdisciplinary Health Sciences. Ph.D.
Kinesiology. M.S.
Occupational Therapy. M.O.T.
Physical Therapy. M.P.T.
Speech Language Pathology. M.S.

COLLEGE OF LIBERAL ARTS:
Art Education. M.A.
Art Studio. M.A.
Communication. M.A.
Creative Writing. M.A.
English and American Literature. M.A.
English Teaching. M.A.T.
English Rhetoric and Writing Studies. M.A.
History. M.A., Ph.D.
Interdisciplinary Studies in Liberal Arts. M.A.I.S.
Latin American and Border Studies. M.A.
Linguistics. M.A.
Music Performance. M.M.
Political Science. M.A.
Psychology. Ph.D.
Rhetoric and Composition. Ph.D.
Sociology. M.A.
Spanish. M.A.
Theater Arts. M.A.

SCHOOL OF NURSING:
Family Nurse Practitioner. M.S.N.
Interdisciplinary Health Sciences. Ph.D.
Nurse Clinician Educator. M.S.N.
Nursing Administration. M.S.N.
Women's Health Care Nurse Practitioner. M.S.N.

COLLEGE OF SCIENCE:
Biology. M.S., Ph.D.
Bioinformatics. M.S.
Chemistry. M.S., Ph.D.
Environmental Science. M.S.
Geological Sciences. Ph.D.
Geology. M.S.
Geophysics. M.S.
Interdisciplinary Studies in Science. M.S.I.S.
Mathematics. M.S.
Physics. M.S.
Statistics. M.S.
Teaching Mathematics. M.A.T.

THE UNIVERSITY OF TEXAS AT SAN ANTONIO

San Antonio, Texas 78249
Web site: www.utsa.edu

Founded in 1969. CGS member. Coed. State control. Semester system. Special facilities: Institute for Studies in Business, Economics and Human Resources; Center for Archaeological Research; Center for Applied Research and Technology. Library: 521,000 volumes, 2665 subscriptions. Total University enrollment: 22,000.

Annual tuition: full-time resident $3618, nonresident $13,626; per credit, resident $201, nonresident $757. On-campus housing for both single and married students. Average academic year housing costs: $6500 (including board) for single students; $4800 for married students. Contact Director of Chisholm Hall, Phone: (210)458-6700; or Director of University Oaks Apartments. Phone: (210)458-8699.

Graduate School

Graduate study since 1973. Graduate enrollment: full-time 668, part-time 2043. Graduate faculty: full-time 376, part-time 60. Degrees conferred: M.A., M.Acy., M.B.A., M.P.Acct., M.F.A., M.M., M.S., M.P.A., Ph.D.

ADMISSION REQUIREMENTS. Official transcripts, GRE/GMAT, statement of purpose, résumé, letters of recommendation required in support of School's application. Auditions/portfolio review required for music/art applicants. TOEFL required for international applicants. Accepts transfer students. Graduates of unaccredited institutions not considered. Applications processed on a rolling basis. Apply to the Director of Admissions and Registrar April 1 (Summer), July 1 (Fall), November 1 (Spring) for priority consideration. Some programs have earlier deadlines. Application fee $25. Phone: (210)458-4335.

ADMISSION STANDARDS. Selective. Usual minimum average for last 60 credits for unconditional admission: 3.0 (A = 4).

FINANCIAL AID. Scholarships, assistantships, internships, Federal W/S, loans. Approved for VA benefits. Apply by February 15 to the appropriate department for scholarships and assistantships; apply by March 31 to Director of Financial Aid for all other forms of aid. Phone: (210)458-8000. Use FAFSA. Aid sometimes available for part-time study.

DEGREE REQUIREMENTS. For M.A., M.S.: 30 semester credits minimum, at least 24 credits in residence; thesis/nonthesis option; comprehensive written/oral exam. For M.B.A., M.Acy., M.P.Acct.: 36–45 semester credits, at least 30–39 credits in residence; computer proficiency. For M.P.A.: 36 semester credits minimum, at least 30 credits in residence; comprehensive exam. For M.M.: 30 semester credits minimum, at least 24 in residence; recital; written/oral exam. For M.F.A.: 60 semester credits minimum, at least 48 credits in residence; gallery level exhibition/special project; written/oral exam. For Ph.D.: 60 credits minimum beyond the master's degree, at least 48 in residence; foreign language proficiency set by department; qualifying exam; candidacy; dissertation; final oral exam.

FIELDS OF STUDY.
Accounting. M.Acy.
Anthropology. M.A., Ph.D.
Applied Demography. Ph.D.
Applied Mathematics. Includes industrial mathematics. M.S.
Applied Statistics. Ph.D.
Architecture. M.Arch., M.S.
Art. Includes ceramics, drawing, painting, photography, printmaking, sculpture. M.F.A.

Art History. M.A.
Bicultural–Bilingual Studies. M.A.
Biology. M.S.
Biomedical Engineering. M.S.
Biotechnology. M.S.
Business Administration. Includes business economics, finance, health care management, information assurance, information systems, international business, management accounting, management of technology, management science, marketing management, project management, real estate finance, tourism (destination development). M.B.A.
Business Administration. Includes accounting, finance, information technology, marketing, organization and management studies. Ph.D.
Cellular and Molecular. Ph.D.
Chemistry. M.S., Ph.D.
Civil Engineering. M.S.
Communication. M.A.
Computer Engineering. M.S.
Computer Science. M.S., Ph.D.
Counseling. M.A.
Counselor Education and Supervision. Ph.D.
Culture, Literacy and Language. Ph.D.
Economics. M.A.
Education. Includes curriculum & instruction, early childhood & elementary education, instructional technology, kinesiology & health promotion, reading & literacy, special education. M.A.
Educational Leadership. Includes higher education. Ed.D.
Electrical Engineering. M.S., Ph.D.
English. M.A., Ph.D.
Environmental Science. M.S., Ph.D.
Finance. Includes real estate. M.S.
Geology. M.S.
History. M.A.
Information Technology. Includes infrastructure assurance. M.S.
Justice Policy. M.S.
Management of Technology. Includes distance learning. M.S., M.O.T.
Mathematics. M.S.
Mathematics Education. M.S.
Mechanical Engineering. M.S.
Music. Includes conducting, education, piano pedagogy & performance. M.M.
Neurobiology. Ph.D.
Physics. M.S., Ph.D.
Political Science. Includes American government, international politics, political economy, political theory & public law. M.A.
Psychology. M.S.
Public Administration. M.P.A.
Social Work. M.S.W.
Sociology. M.S.
Spanish. Includes Hispanic culture, Hispanic literature. M.A.
Statistics. M.S.
Teaching English as a Second Language. M.A.

THE UNIVERSITY OF TEXAS AT TYLER

Tyler, Texas 75799-0001
Web site: www.uttyler.edu

Coed. State control. Semester system. Special facilities: Zuckerman Electron Microscope Laboratory, University of Texas High Speed Computational Center, Center for Policy Studies, Child and Family Abuse Clearinghouse. Library: 216,000 volumes, 1534 subscriptions. Total University enrollment: 5800.

Annual tuition: full-time, residents $5272, nonresident $13,522; per credit, resident $530, nonresident $805. No on-campus housing available.

Graduate Studies

Graduate Enrollment: full-time 106, part-time 561. Graduate faculty: full-time 115, part-time 73. Degrees Conferred: M.A., M.B.A., M.Ed., M.P.A., M.S.N., M.S.

ADMISSION REQUIREMENTS. Two official transcripts, letters of recommendation, GRE/GMAT required in support of application. Online application available. TOEFL required for international applicants. Accepts transfer students. Graduates of unaccredited institutions not considered. Apply through "Apply Texas" (applytexas.org) by April 1 (Summer), July 1 (Fall), November 1 (Spring) for priority consideration. Rolling admissions process. Application fee none, $50 for international applicants. Phone: (903)566-5642; fax: (903)566-7068.

ADMISSION STANDARDS. Selective. Usual minimum average: 2.75 (A = 4).

FINANCIAL AID. Scholarships, fellowships, assistantships, internships, full and partial tuition waivers, Federal W/S, loans. Approved for VA benefits. Apply to the appropriate department for scholarships and assistantships; to Director of Financial Aid for all other programs. No specified closing date. Phone: (903)566-7221. Use FAFSA and Institutional FAF. Aid available for part-time students.

DEGREE REQUIREMENTS. For M.A., M.S.: 30 semester credits minimum, at least 24 credits in residence; thesis/nonthesis option; comprehensive written/oral exam. For M.Ed.: 36 semester credits minimum, at least 30 in residence. For M.B.A., M.P.A.: 36–45 semester minimum, at least 30–39 credits in residence; computer proficiency. For M.S.N.: 36 semester credits minimum, at least 30 credits in residence; practicum; comprehensive exam.

FIELDS OF STUDY.
Accounting.
Art. Includes art history.
Biology.
Business Administration.
Chemistry.
Civil Engineering.
Clinical Exercise Physiology.
Clinical Psychology.
Communication.
Computer Information Systems.
Computer Sciences.
Counseling Psychology.
Criminal Justice.
Curriculum and Instruction.
Early Childhood Education.
Educational Administration.
Economics.
Electrical Engineering.
Engineering.
English.
Finance.
General Business.
General Studies.
Health and Kinesiology.
Health Professions.
History.
Human Resource Development.
Industrial Management.
Industrial Safety.
Interdisciplinary Studies.
Journalism.
Kinesiology.
Liberal Studies. Interdisciplinary.
Management.
Marketing.
Mathematics.
Mechanical Engineering.
Music.
Nursing.
Political Science.
Public Administration.
Reading.
School Counseling.
Sociology.
Special Education.
Teaching.
Technology.

THE UNIVERSITY OF TEXAS HEALTH SCIENCE CENTER AT HOUSTON
Houston, Texas 77225-0036
Web site: www.uthouston.edu

Established 1972. Located 2 miles SW of downtown. Public control. Semester system. The Health Science Center includes the Medical School, the Dental Branch (formerly Texas Dental College), the Graduate School of Biomedical Sciences, the School of Public Health, the School of Allied Health Sciences and the School of Nursing. Special facilities: AIDS Education and Training Center for Texas and Oklahoma, Center on Aging, Center for Health Policy Studies, Center for Health Promotion Research, Center for Infections Diseases, Center for the Prevention of Injury and Violence, Epidemiology Research Center, Health Policy Institute, Houston Center for Bone Research Human Genetics Center, Human Nutrition Center, Neuroscience Research Center, Positron Diagnostic and Research Center, Southwest Center for Occupational and Environmental Health, Southwest Center for Prevention Research, Speech and Hearing Institute, UT Mental Science Institute. The University's NIH ranking is 71st among all U.S. institutions with 193 awards/grants valued at $81,548,352. According to The Center at University of Florida, the University is ranked 69th in receipt of Federal Research funds with $107,481,000 and it ranks 90th for total University research expenditures with $149,294,000. In 2004, 6 of the University's faculty members have been elected to National Honor Academies and this ranks it 90th among all U.S. institutions. The Library: approximately 368,000 volumes, 2800 subscriptions. Total University enrollment: 3,400.

On-campus housing available for both single and married students. Phone: (713)500-8444.

Graduate School of Biomedical Sciences
Web site: www.gsbs.gs.uth.tmc.edu

Established 1963. Coed. Tuition: per credit resident $116–$161, nonresident $394–$439. Enrollment: full-time 545. Faculty: full-time 479, part-time 11. Degrees conferred: M.S., Ph.D., M.D.-Ph.D.

ADMISSION REQUIREMENTS. Transcripts, GRE, three letters of recommendation, personal statement background, research interests, and professional goals required in support of School's application. Online application available. GRE Subject Test recommended. TOEFL and TWE required of international students. Interview optional. Apply to Office of the Registrar, UT Health Science Center, P.O. Box 20036, Houston, Texas 77225, eight weeks prior to registration. Priority deadline for Fall admission is January 15 (Fall), November 1 (Spring). Application fee $10. Phone: (800)UTH-GSBS, (713)500-9860; fax: (713)500-9877.

ADMISSION STANDARDS. Competitive. Usual minimum average: 3.0 (A = 4).

FINANCIAL AID. Scholarships, fellowships, research assistant-ships, teaching assistantships, training grants, loans. Nearly all admitted students are awarded financial aid. Apply by January 15 to the Office of Student Financial Aid. Phone: (713)500-3860. Use FAFSA for all nonmerit aid. About 95% of students receive aid from School and outside sources.

DEGREE REQUIREMENTS. For M.S.: 24 hours of course work, two semesters of registration for thesis. For Ph.D.: three tutorial laboratory rotations; four area courses, one ethics course; qualifying exam; dissertation; final oral exam.

FIELDS OF STUDY.
Biochemistry and Molecular Biology.
Biomathematics and Biostatistics.
Biomedical Sciences. Includes medical physics. M.S. only.
Biophysics.
Cancer Biology.
Cell and Regulatory Biology.
Environmental and Molecular Carcinogenesis.
Genes and Development.
Genetics Counseling. M.S. only.
Human and Molecular Genetics.
Immunology.
Medical Physics.
Microbiology and Molecular Genetics.
Molecular Biology.
Molecular Pathology.
Neurosciences.
Oral Biomaterials. M.S. only.
Toxicology.
Virology and Gene Therapy.

Dental Branch at Houston

Web site: www.db.uth.tmc.edu

Established 1905 as Texas Dental College. Joined University of Texas system in 1972. Semester system. Library: 25,000 volumes, 1500 subscriptions.

Annual tuition: resident $10,216, nonresident $21,016. Limited on-campus housing available. Average academic year off-campus housing costs: $14,000. Contact the Office of Student Affairs for both on- and off-campus housing information. Phone: (713)500-4151. Total average cost for all other first-year expenses: $8,500.

Enrollment: first-year class 80, total 320 (men 59%, women 41%, minorities 22%, state residents 100%). Faculty: full-time 88, part-time 72. Degrees conferred: D.D.S., M.S., Certificate.

ADMISSION REQUIREMENTS. AADSAS (nonresidents), offi-cial transcripts, three letters of recommendation, DAT required in support of School's application. Applicants must have completed at least three years of college study, four years of study preferred. Interview by invitation only. Preference given to state residents. Accepts transfer students. Apply to UT System, Medical and Den-tal Application Center, Austin, Texas 78701, after May 1, before November 1. Application fee $55 resident, $190 nonresident. Den-tal School Admissions Office Phone: (713)500-4151; fax: (713) 500-4425.

ADMISSION STANDARDS. Selective. Accepts about 15–20% of all applicants. Usual minimum UGPA: 3.0 (A = 4). Mean DAT: academic 19, PAT 18; mean UGPA 3.50.

FINANCIAL AID. Scholarships, grants, loans. Apply to the Health Science Center's Financial Aid Office; no specified closing date. Phone: (713)500-3860. Use FAFSA (School code: 013956). About 90% of students receive some aid from University and outside sources.

DEGREE REQUIREMENTS. For D.D.S.: satisfactory comple-tion of forty-six-month program.

FIELDS OF POSTGRADUATE STUDY.
Advanced in General Dentistry. Certificate.
Endodontics. M.S., Certificate.
General Practice Residency.
Oral & Maxillofacial Surgery. Certificate.
Oral Biomaterials. Offered through the Graduate School of Bio-
    medical Sciences. M.S.
Pediatric Dentistry. Certifcate.
Periodontics. M.S., Certificate.
Prosthodontics. M.S., Certificate.

Medical School at Houston

Web site: www.med.uth.tmc.edu

Established 1969. Special facilities: Brown Foundation Institute of Molecular Medicine for the Prevention of Human Diseases, Clinical Genetics Research Center, Gulf States Hemophilia & Thrombophilia Center/Pediatric AIDS Center, John P. McGovern, MD, Center for Health, Humanities and the Human Spirit, Keck Center for the Neurobiology of Learning and Memory, Mental Sciences Institute, Neuroscience Research Center, Structural Biology Center, Texas Kidney Institute, Texas Renal-Pancreas Center, The Texas Gulf Coast Digestive Diseases Center, Trauma Research Center, University Clinical Research Center. Library: 362,000 volumes, 3200 subscriptions. NIH ranking is 71st among all U.S. institutions with 193 awards/grants worth $81,548,352.

Annual tuition: resident $14,439, nonresident $26,538. No on-campus housing available, a University of Texas housing com-plex one block away. Total average figure for all other expenses: $18,730.

Enrollment: first-year class 210, total 868 (men 54%, women 46%, minorities 27%, state residents 97%). Faculty: full-time 795, part-time 105. Degrees conferred: M.D., M.D.-M.P.H., M.D.-Ph.D.

ADMISSION REQUIREMENTS. Transcripts, MCAT, recommen-dations required in support of application. Interview by invitation. Preference given to state residents. Graduates of unaccredited colleges not considered. 90% of class must be state residents. Apply to University of Texas, Medical and Dental Schools Ap-plication Service, Austin, Texas 78701, after May 1. before Octo-ber 15. Application fee $55 (resident) plus $5 for each additional school, $100 (nonresident) plus $5 for each additional school. Phone: (713)500-5116; fax: (713)500-0604.

ADMISSION STANDARDS. Competitive. Accepts about 8% of all applicants. Number of applications 3245 (496 out-of-state); number interviewed 1212 (26 out-of-state); number of accep-tance 256 (10 out-of-state); number enrolled 210 (8 out-of-state). Mean Composite MCAT 9.4; mean UGPA 3.67 (A = 4).

FINANCIAL AID. A limited number of scholarships from memo-rial funds and foundations, institutional loans, HEAL, alternative loan programs, NIH stipends, Federal Perkins Loans, Stafford Sub-sidized and Unsubsidized Loans, Service Commitment Scholarship programs are available. Assistantships/fellowships may be avail-able for combined degree candidates. Most aid is awarded based on demonstrated need. Financial aid applications and information are available by contacting the Office of the Registrar. Phone: (713) 500-3860. Use FAFSA (School code: 013956), also submit Finan-cial Aid Transcript, Federal Income Tax forms. Approximately 98% of students receive some form of financial assistance.

DEGREE REQUIREMENTS. For M.D.: satisfactory completion of four-year program. All students must pass USMLE Step 1 prior to entering fourth year; must take Step 2 during fourth year. For M.D.-M.P.H.: generally from four-and-one-half- to five-and-one-half-year program. For M.D.-Ph.D.: generally a six- to seven-year program.

FIELDS OF GRADUATE STUDY.
Behavioral Sciences.
Biochemistry.
Bioinformatics.
Biostatistics.
Cancer Biology.
Cell Biology.
Developmental Biology.
Genetic Counseling.
Genetics.
Immunology.
Medical Physics.
Microbiology.
Molecular Biology.
Pathology.
Neuroscience.
Oral Biomaterials.
Pharmacology.
Physiology.
Reproductive Biology.
Structural Biology.
Toxicology.
Virology.

School of Public Health

Founded 1967. Coed. Semester system. Special facilities: Center for Health Policy Studies, Center for Health Promotion and Prevention Research, Center for Health Services Research, Center for Infectious Diseases, Center for Society and Population Health, Coordinating Center for Clinical Trials, Human Genetics Center, Human Nutrition Center, Southwest Center for Occupational and Environmental Health.

Tuition: per credit, resident $161, nonresident $439. Enrollment: full-time 327, part-time 521. Faculty: full-time 142, part-time 10. Degrees conferred: M.P.H., M.S., D.P.H., Ph.D.

ADMISSION REQUIREMENTS, Transcripts, two letters of recommendation, written statement of goals, GRE required in support of application. TOEFL (minimum score 565) required for international applicants. Accepts transfer applicants. Graduates of unaccredited institutions considered. Apply to Office of Registration by February 1 (Fall), August 1 (Spring). Application fee $10. Phone: (713)792-4425.

ADMISSION STANDARDS. Very selective. Usual minimum average: 3.0 (A = 4); GRE: 1000 (combined), 1200 (for doctoral programs).

FINANCIAL AID. Scholarships, fellowships, traineeships, grants and contracts, internships, loans. Approved for VA benefits. Apply to the Financial Aid Office by May 1. Phone: (713)500-3860; fax: (713)500-3863. Use FAFSA. About 33% of students receive aid other than loans from School and outside sources.

DEGREE REQUIREMENTS. For master's: satisfactory completion of 36 credit, 18- to 24-month program; thesis. For D.P.H.: at least one academic year in preparation for qualifying exam; research project. For Ph.D.: satisfactory completion of prescribed course of study, at least to semesters in residence; qualifying exam; dissertation; final oral exam.

THE UNIVERSITY OF TEXAS HEALTH SCIENCE CENTER AT SAN ANTONIO

San Antonio, Texas 78284
Web site: www.uthscsa.edu

Formed in 1959. Coed. State control. Semester system. Special facilities: DEC system -20, DEC/VAX 8650, 8700, 11-/785;

Center for Research in Reproductive Biology; Scanning Electron Microscope facility. The University's NIH ranking is 72nd among all U.S. institutions with 231 awards/grants valued at $81,440,359. According to The Center at University of Florida, the University is ranked 88th in receipt of Federal Research funds with $86,683,000 and it ranks 97th for total University research expenditures with $133,304,000. The Library: approximately 250,000 volumes, 2500 subscriptions. Total University enrollment: 3,000.

Graduate School of Biomedical Sciences

Graduate study since 1972. Tuition: per credit resident $116–$161, nonresident $394–$439. Enrollment: full- and part-time 272 (men 55%, women 45%). Faculty: full-time 225, part-time 36. Degrees conferred: M.S., M.S.N., Ph.D.

ADMISSION REQUIREMENTS. Transcripts, GRE, three letters of recommendation, research interests, and professional goals statement required in support of School's application. Online application available. GRE Subject Test recommended. TOEFL and TWE required of international applicants. Interview optional. Graduates of unaccredited institutions not considered. Apply to Office of the Registrar, eight weeks prior to registration. Priority deadline for Fall admission is January 15. Application fee $10. Phone: (210) 567-3709; fax (210) 567-3719.

ADMISSIONS STANDARDS. Selective. Usual minimum average: 3.0 (A = 4).

FINANCIAL AID. Scholarship, assistantships, fellowships for teaching/research, loans. Apply to appropriate department by March 31; for Federal programs apply to Student Services. Phone: (210)567-2635. Use FAFSA (School code: 003659) for all nonmerit aid. About 35% of students receive aid from School and outside sources.

DEGREE REQUIREMENTS. For M.S.: 30 semester hours minimum, at least 24 in residence; thesis; comprehensive oral/written exam for some departments. For Ph.D.: at least one year in residence; foreign language requirement set by department; oral written exam for candidacy; dissertation; final oral exam.

FIELDS OF STUDY.
Allied Health. M.S.
Biochemistry. M.S.
Biomedical Engineering. M.S., Ph.D.
Cellular and Structural Biology. M.S.
Clinical Investigation. M.S.
Dental Sciences. M.S.
Integrated Multidisciplinary Graduate Programs. Includes biology of aging, cancer biology, cell & molecular biology, genetics, genomics & development, membrane biology & cell signaling, metabolism & metabolic disorders, microbiology & immunology, molecular biophysics & biochemistry, molecular, cellular & integrative physiology, neuroscience, pharmacology. Ph.D.
Microbiology and Immunology. M.S.
Molecular Biology. M.S.
Molecular Medicine. Ph.D.
Nursing. M.S., Ph.D.
Pharmacology. M.S.
Physiology. M.S.
Radiological Sciences. M.S., Ph.D.

Dental School (78229-3900)

Web site: www.dental.uthscsa.edu

Established 1969. Located at Health Science Center. Semester system. Special program: International Dentist Education Program for graduates of foreign dental programs.

Annual tuition: resident $11,125, nonresident $21,925. No on-campus housing available. Average academic year off-campus housing costs: $14,000. Contact the Office of Student Affairs for off-campus housing information. Phone: (210)567-3180. Total average cost for all other first-year expenses: $8,500.

Enrollment: first year class 90, total 360 (men 57%, women 43%, minorities 5%, state residents 95%), graduate students 80. Faculty: full-time 88, part-time 72. Degrees conferred: D.D.S., M.S., D.D.S.-Ph.D. Certificate. The M.S. and Ph.D. are offered through the Graduate School of Biomedical Sciences.

ADMISSION REQUIREMENTS. AADSAS (nonresidents), official transcripts, DAT (not later than October), three letters of recommendation required in support of School's application. Preference given to state residents and veterans. Interview by invitation only. Accepts transfer applicants. Graduates of unaccredited institutions not considered. Apply to UT System, Medical and Dental Application Center, Austin, Texas 78701, after May 1, before October 15. Application fee: resident $55, nonresident $100; School's fee $40. Dental School's Admissions Office. Phone: (210)567-3752; fax: (210)567-4776.

ADMISSION STANDARDS. Selective. Accepts about 5–10% of all applicants. Usual minimum UGPA: 3.0 (A = 4). Mean DAT: academic 18, PAT 17; mean UGPA 3.60.

FINANCIAL AID. Limited state, federal scholarships, loans. Apply to Student Financial Aid office after acceptance. Phone: (210)567-2365. Use FAFSA (School code: 010115). About 90% of students receive aid from School and outside sources.

DEGREE REQUIREMENTS. For D.D.S.: satisfactory completion of thirty-nine-month program.

FIELDS OF POSTGRADUATE STUDY.
Advanced Education in General Dentistry. Certificate.
Biomedical Sciences. D.D.S.-Ph.D.
Dental Diagnostic Science. M.S., Certificate.
Dental Public Health Residency.
Endodontics. M.S., Certificate.
General Practice Residency.
Oral & Maxillofacial Surgery Residency.
Orthodontics. Certificate.
Pediatric Dentistry. Ph.D., Certificate.
Periodontics. M.S., Certificate.
Prosthodontics. M.S., Certificate

Medical School (78229-7702)

Web site: www.uthscsa.edu

Established 1969. Special facilities: Greehey Children's Cancer Research Institute, The Center for Medical Humanities and Ethics, South Texas Health Research Center, Transplant Center, Pharmacotherapy Education and Research Center, Institute for Health Promotion Research. Library: 362,000 volumes, 3200 subscriptions. NIH ranking is 72nd among all U.S. institutions with 231 awards/grants worth $81,440,359.

Annual tuition: resident $14,439, nonresident $26,538. On-campus housing available for women; none for married and men. Total average figure for all other expenses: $17,583.

Enrollment: first-year class 200, total 849 (men 42%, women 48%, minorities 23%, state residents 96%). Faculty: full-time 823, part-time 111. Degrees conferred: M.D., M.D.-Ph.D.

ADMISSION REQUIREMENTS. Transcripts, letter of recommendation from Premedical Committee, two additional letters of recommendation, MCAT required in support of application. Interview by invitation only. Applicants must have completed at least three years of college study. 90% of class must be state residents. Apply to University of Texas Medical and Dental Schools Application Service at Austin (78701) after May 1, before October 15. Application center fee: residents $55 plus $5 for each additional school, nonresidents $100 plus $10 for each ad-

ditional school. Medical School phone: (210)567-6080; fax: (210) 567-6962.

ADMISSION STANDARDS. Competitive. Accepts about 8% of all applicants. Number of applications 2701 (n/a out-of-state); number interviewed 1027 (n/a out-of-state); number of acceptance n/a (n/a out-of-state); number enrolled 200 (n/a out-of-state). Mean Composite MCAT 9.6; mean UGPA 3.76 (A = 4).

FINANCIAL AID. Limited scholarships, loans. Apply after acceptance, before July 1 to Office of Student Services. Phone: (210)567-2635. Use FAFSA (School code: 010115). About 45% of students receive some aid from School.

DEGREE REQUIREMENTS. For M.D.: satisfactory completion of four-year program.

FIELDS OF GRADUATE STUDY.
Biochemistry.
Biomedical Engineering.
Cellular and Structural Biology.
Microbiology and Immunology.
Molecular Medicine.
Pathology.
Pharmacology.
Physiology.

UNIVERSITY OF TEXAS MEDICAL BRANCH AT GALVESTON

Galveston, Texas 77555
Web site: www.utmb.edu

Established 1891. CGS member. Coed. State control. Semester system. Special facilities: DEC/VAX11/750, IBM 3081, Biomedical Engineering Center, Marine Biomedical Institute, Molecular Science Institute, Institute for Medical Humanities, Shriner's Burn Institute. The University's NIH ranking is 57th among all U.S. institutions with 253 awards/grants valued at $114,922,154. According to The Center at University of Florida, the University is ranked 83rd in receipt of Federal Research funds with $93,639,000 and it ranks 86th for total University research expenditures with $153,122,000. In 2004, 2 of the University's faculty members have been elected to National Honor Academies and this ranks it 119th among all U.S. institutions. The Library: approximately 270,000 volumes, 1986 subscriptions. Total University enrollment: 2200.

Limited graduate housing available for single students, none for married students. Average academic year housing costs: $280–$350 per month (room only). Phone: (409)772-1898.

Graduate School of Biomedical Science

Web site: www.utmb.edu/gsbs/programs/html

Graduate study since 1969. Annual tuition: full-time resident $3598, nonresident $11,024; per credit resident $180, nonresident $550.

Enrollment: full-time 330, part-time 40. Faculty: full-time 323, part-time 15. Degrees conferred: M.A., M.M.S., M.S., M.S.N., Ph.D.

ADMISSION REQUIREMENTS. Official transcripts, three recommendations, GRE required in support of School's application. Online application available. Four-year bachelor's degree or equivalent required. Interview encouraged. TOEFL (minimum score 550) required for all international applicants. Accepts transfer applicants. Graduates of unaccredited institutions given consideration. Apply to Office of the Registrar by March 1 (Fall), October 1 (Spring), February 1 (Summer). Application fee $30,

$70 for international applicants. Phone: (409)772-2665; fax: (409) 747-0772.

ADMISSION STANDARDS. Selective. Usual minimum average: 3.0 (A = 4).

FINANCIAL AID. Scholarships, fellowships, research assistantships, internships, Federal W/S, loans. Approved for VA benefits. Apply to Financial Aid Office; no specified closing date. Phone: (409)722-4955; fax: (409)722-4466. Use FAFSA. About 35% of students receive aid other than loans from School. Aid available for part-time students.

DEGREE REQUIREMENTS. For master's: 36 semester hours minimum, at least 24 in residence; thesis; comprehensive oral/written exam for some departments. For Ph.D.: at least one year in residence; foreign language requirement set by department; oral/written candidacy exam; dissertation, final oral exam.

FIELDS OF STUDY.
Biochemistry and Molecular Biology. Ph.D.
Cell Biology. Ph.D.
Cellular Physiology & Molecular Biophysics. Ph.D.
Experimental Pathology. Ph.D.
Medical Humanities. M.A., Ph.D.
Medical Sciences. M.M.S. only.
Microbiology and Immunology. Ph.D.
Neuroscience. Ph.D.
Nursing. Ph.D.
Pharmacology and Toxicology. Ph.D.
Preventive Medicine and Community Health. M.S., Ph.D.
Public Health. M.P.H.

School of Medicine (77555-0133)
Web site: www.utmb.edu

Established 1969. Library: 250,000 volumes, 2800 subscriptions. NIH ranking is 57th among all U.S. institutions with 253 awards/grants worth $114,922,154.

Annual tuition: resident $14,439, nonresident $26,538. On-campus housing available for women; none for married and men. Total average figure for all other expenses: $16,944. Apply to Manager, Dormitories and Apartments. Phone: (409)772-1898.

Enrollment: first-year class 210, total 861 (men 50%, women 50%, minorities 43%, state residents 94%). Faculty: full-time 1074, part-time 111. Degrees conferred: M.D., M.D.-M.A. (Medical Humanities), M.S.-M.S., M.D.-Ph.D.

ADMISSION REQUIREMENTS. Transcripts, letter of recommendation from Premedical Committee, two additional letters of recommendation, MCAT required in support of application. Interview by invitation only. Applicants must have completed at least three years of college study. Does not have EDP. Accepts transfer applicants. 90% of class must be state residents. Apply to University of Texas Medical and Dental Schools Application Service at Austin (78701) after May 1, before November 1. Application center fee: residents $55 plus $5 for each additional school, nonresidents $100 plus $10 for each additional school. School's application fee: none. Phone: (409)772-3517.

ADMISSION STANDARDS. Competitive. Accepts about 8% of all applicants. Number of applications 3154 (435 out-of-state); number interviewed 974 (84 out-of-state); number of acceptance 265 (25 out-of-state); number enrolled 210 (12 out-of-state). Mean Composite MCAT 9.6; mean UGPA 3.76 (A = 4).

FINANCIAL AID. Limited scholarships, loans. Apply after acceptance, before July 1 to Office of Student Affairs. Phone: (409) 772-4955. Use FAFSA (School code: 013976). About 84% of students receive some aid from School.

DEGREE REQUIREMENTS. For M.D.: satisfactory completion of four-year program.

FIELDS OF GRADUATE STUDY.
Biochemistry and Molecular Biology. Ph.D.
Cancer Cell Biology. Ph.D.
Cellular Physiology and Molecular Biophysics. Ph.D.
Clinical Investigation. M.S., Ph.D.
Experimental Pathology. Ph.D.
Health Services Research. M.S., Ph.D.
Medical Humanities. M.A., Ph.D.
Medical Science. M.M.S.
Microbiology and Immunology. Ph.D.
Neuroscience and Cell Biology. Ph.D.
Pharmacology and Toxicology. Ph.D.
Preventive Medicine and Community Health. M.S. and Ph.D.
Public Health. M.P.H.

THE UNIVERSITY OF TEXAS OF THE PERMIAN BASIN
Odessa, Texas 79762-0001
Web site: www.utpb.edu

Coed. State control. Semester system. Special facilities: Center for Energy and Economic Diversification, Center for Behavioral Analysis. Library: 270,000 volumes, 1,074,000 microforms, 723 current periodicals.

Tuition: per credit, resident $198, nonresident $462. On-campus housing for single and married students. Average academic year housing costs: single students $2500, married students $4000. Contact Director of Graduate Housing for both on- and off-campus housing information. Phone: (432)552-2743.

Graduate Studies and Research

Enrollment: full-time 61, part-time 256. Faculty: full-time 48, part-time 7. Degrees conferred: M.A., M.B.A., M.S.

ADMISSION REQUIREMENTS. Two transcripts, GRE/GMAT required in support of application. Online application available. TOEFL (minimum score 550) required for international applicants. Accepts transfer students. Graduates of unaccredited institutions not considered. Applications processed on a rolling basis. Apply to the Registrar at least 60 days prior to the date of registration. Application fee: none. Phone: (432)552-2530; fax: (432) 552-2109.

ADMISSION STANDARDS. Selective. Usual minimum average: 3.0 last 60 credits (A = 4).

FINANCIAL AID. Limited to Federal W/S, loans. Approved for VA benefits. Apply to Director of Financial Aid; no specified closing date. Phone: (432)552-2620. Use FAFSA (School code: 00930) and Institutional FAF. Aid available for part-time students.

DEGREE REQUIREMENTS. For M.A., M.S.: 30 semester credits minimum, at least 24 credits in residence; thesis/nonthesis option; comprehensive written/oral exam. For M.B.A.: 36–45 semester credits, at least 30–39 credits in residence; computer proficiency.

FIELDS OF STUDY.

COLLEGE OF ARTS AND SCIENCES:
Biology.
Computer Science.
Criminal Justice Administration.

English.
Geology.
History.
Kinesiology.
Psychology.
Public Administration.

SCHOOL OF BUSINESS:
Professional Accountancy.
Business Administration.
M.B.A. Online.

SCHOOL OF EDUCATION:
Counseling.
Early Childhood Education.
Educational Leadership.
Professional Education.
Reading.
Special Education.

THE UNIVERSITY OF TEXAS— PAN AMERICAN

Edinburg, Texas 78539-2999
Web site: www.utpa.edu

Founded 1927. CGS member. Coed. State control. Semester system. Special facilities: Speech and Hearing Clinic, Coastal Marine Biology Laboratory, Rio Grande Valley Archives. Library: 572,100 volumes, 5600 subscriptions. Total University enrollment: 17,000.

Tuition/fees: per semester, resident $1420, nonresident $6290. On-campus housing for single students only. Annual housing cost: $4700 (including board). Contact Director of Student Services for both on- and off-campus housing information. Phone: (956)381-3439.

Office of Graduate Studies

Enrollment: full-time 537, part-time 1568. Graduate faculty: full-time 200, part-time 34. Degrees conferred: M.A., M.B.A., M.Ed., M.S., M.S.I.S.

ADMISSION REQUIREMENTS. Two transcripts, GRE/GMAT required in support of application. TOEFL required for international students. Accepts transfer students. Graduates of unaccredited institutions not considered. Applications processed on a rolling basis. Apply to the Director of Admissions and Records by April 1 (Summer), July 1 (Fall), November 1 (Spring) for priority consideration. Application fee none. Phone: (956)381-3661.

ADMISSION STANDARDS. Selective. Usual minimum average: 2.75 (A = 4).

FINANCIAL AID. Scholarships, assistantships, partial tuition waivers, grants, Federal W/S, loans. Approved for VA benefits. Apply by April 15 to the appropriate department for scholarships and assistantships; to Office of Financial Services for all other programs. Phone: (956)381-2501. Use FAFSA (School code: 003599). Aid available for part-time students.

DEGREE REQUIREMENTS. For M.A., M.S., M.S.I.S.: 30 semester credits minimum, at least 24 credits in residence; thesis/nonthesis option; comprehensive written/oral exam. For M.Ed.: 36 semester credits minimum, at least 30 in residence. For M.B.A.: 36–45 semester credits, at least 30–39 credits in residence; computer proficiency.

FIELDS OF STUDY.

COLLEGS OF ARTS AND HUMANITIES:
Art. M.F.A.
Communication. M.A.
Creative Writing. M.A.
English. M.A.
English as a Second Language. M.A.
History. M.A.
Interdisciplinary. Includes concentration in English, history, music, Spanish. M.A.
Music. M.A.
Spanish. M.A.
Theatre. M.A.

COLLEGE OF BUSINESS ADMINISTRATION:
Accountancy. M.Accy., M.S.
Business Administration. Includes international business (Ph.D.). M.B.A., Ph.D.

COLLEGE OF EDUCATION:
Bilingual Education.
Early Childhood Education.
Education Leadership.
Educational Administration.
Educational Diagnostician.
Elementary Education.
Gifted Education.
Guidance and Counseling.
Kinesiology.
Reading.
School Psychology.
Secondary Education.
Special Education.
Supervision.

COLLEGE OF HEALTH SCIENCES AND HUMAN SERVICES:
Communication Sciences and Disorders. M.S.
Nursing. Includes concentrations in adult health nursing, family nurse practitioner, pediatric nurse practitioner. M.S.N.
Occupational Therapy. M.S.
Rehabilitation Counseling. M.S.
Social Work. M.S.S.W.

COLLEGE OF SCIENCE AND ENGINEERING:
Biology. M.S.
Chemistry. M.S.
Computer Science. M.S.
Electrical Engineering. M.S.E.
Engineering Management. M.S.E.
Information Technology. M.S.
Interdisciplinary Science. Includes concentration in Physics. M.S.
Manufacturing Engineering. M.S.E.
Mathematical Sciences. M.S.
Mathematics Teaching. M.S.
Mechanical Engineering. M.S.E.

COLLEGE OF SOCIAL AND BEHAVIORAL SCIENCES:
Clinical Psychology. M.A.
Criminal Justice. M.S.
Experimental Psychology. M.A.
Interdisciplinary Studies. Includes concentration in anthropology. M.A.
Public Administration. M.P.A.
Sociology. M.S.

THE UNIVERSITY OF TEXAS SOUTHWESTERN MEDICAL CENTER AT DALLAS

Dallas, Texas 75235-9096
Web site: www.swmed.edu

Established 1943. Coed. State control. Semester system. Special facilities: Howard Hughes Medical Institute; Zale Lipshy Hospital; Cain Center for Biomedical Research; James M. Collins Center for Biomedical Research; Cecil H. and Ida Green Center for Reproductive Biology Sciences; Robert T. Hayes Center for Mineral Metabolism Research; Erik Jonson Center for Research on Molecular Genetics and Human Disease; Kimberly-Clark Center for Breast Cancer Research; Eugene McDermott Center for Human Growth and Development; Eugene McDermott Center for Pain Management; Mobility Foundation Center for Rehabilitation Research; W. A. "Tex" and Deborah Moncrieg, Jr., Center for Cancer Genetics; Harry S. Ross Heart Center; Frank M. Ryburn, Jr., Cardiac Center; Harold C. Simmons Arthritis Research Center; Harold C. Simmons Comprehensive Cancer Center; Kent Waldrep Foundation Center for Basic Neuroscience Research; Cancer Immunobiology Center; Center for Basic Research in Transplantation Immunology; the Nuclear Medicine Center. The Medical Center's NIH ranking is 36th among all U.S. institutions with 423 awards/grants valued at $170,541,372. According to The Center at University of Florida, the Center is ranked 45th in receipt of Federal Research funds with $177,196,000 and it ranks 45th for total research expenditures with $276,692,000. The Center's endowment assets rank it 55th, with a value of $804,305,000. In 2004, 29 of the Center's faculty members have been elected to National Honor Academies and this ranks it 32nd among all U.S. institutions. The Library: approximately 257,780 volumes, 2865 subscriptions. Total campus enrollment: 2400.

Southwestern Graduate School of Biomedical Sciences

Tuition: per credit, resident $50, nonresident $328; Biomedical Engineering resident $100, nonresident $378.

Enrollment: full-time 522, part-time 568. Faculty: full-time 345, part-time 65. Degrees conferred: M.A., M.S., Ph.D.

ADMISSION REQUIREMENTS. Official transcripts, three recommendations, GRE required in support of School's application. Online application available. Four-year bachelor's degree or equivalent required. Interviews encouraged. TOEFL required for international applicants. Accepts transfer applicants. Graduates of unaccredited colleges not considered. Apply to Registrar, University of Texas Southwestern Medical Center, deadlines vary by program. Application fee none. Phone: (214)648-5617, fax: (214) 648-3289.

ADMISSION STANDARDS. Selective. Usual minimum average: 3.45 (A = 4). GRE average score 1250.

FINANCIAL AID. Scholarships, fellowships, teaching/research assistantships, internships, grants, tuition waivers, Federal W/S, loans. Approved for VA benefits. Apply by March 1 to Financial Aid Office; no specified closing date. Phone: (214)648-3611; fax: (214)648-3289. Use FAFSA. Most Ph.D. students receive stipends.

DEGREE REQUIREMENTS. For master's: 30 semester hours minimum, at least 24 in residence; thesis; comprehensive oral/written exam for some departments. For Ph.D.: at least one year in residence; foreign language requirement set by department; oral/written candidacy exam; dissertation; final oral exam.

FIELDS OF STUDY.
Bioinstrumentation and Human Performance. M.S., Ph.D.
Biological Chemistry. Includes biochemistry, chemistry. Ph.D.
Biomaterials and Tissue Engineering. M.S., Ph.D.
Biomechanics. M.S., Ph.D.
Cell Regulation. Includes cell biology, cell signaling, pharmacological sciences. Ph.D.
Clinical Psychology. Ph.D.
Clinical Sciences. M.S.
Genetics and Development. Includes cancer biology. Ph.D.
Immunology. Ph.D.
Integrative Biology. Includes mechanism of disease. Ph.D.
Medical Imaging. M.S., Ph.D.
Molecular and Computational Biomedical Engineering. Ph.D.
Molecular Biophysics. Includes computational biology. Ph.D.
Molecular Microbiology. Ph.D.
Neuroscience. Ph.D.
Orthopedics. M.S., Ph.D.
Radiological Sciences. M.S., Ph.D.
Rehabilitation Counseling Psychology. M.S.

Southwestern Medical School (75390-9162)

Web site: www.utsouthwestern.edu

Established 1943. Special facilities: Advanced Imaging Research Center, Alzheimer's Center, Cancer Immunobiology Center, Center for Basic Neuroscience, Center for Developmental Biology, Center for Diabetes Research, Center for Human Nutrition, Center for Immunology, Green Center for Reproductive Biology Sciences, Hamon Center for Therapeutic Oncology Research, McDermott Center for Human Growth Development, McDermott Center for Pain Management, Simmons Comprehensive Cancer Center. Library: 270,000 volumes, 2400 subscriptions. NIH ranking is 36th among all U.S. institutions with 423 awards/grants worth $170,541,372.

Annual tuition: resident $11,632, nonresident $24,732. On-campus housing available. Total average figure for all other expenses: $15,736.

Enrollment: first-year class 229, total 925 (men 55%, women 45%, minorities 47%, state residents 87%). Faculty: full-time 1458, part-time 209. Degrees conferred: M.D., M.D.-M.B.A., M.D.-M.P.H., M.D.-M.S., M.D.-Ph.D. (Medical Scientist Training Program).

ADMISSION REQUIREMENTS. Transcripts, letter of recommendation from Premedical Committee, two additional letters of recommendation, MCAT required in support of application. Interview by invitation only. Applicants must have completed at least three years of college study. Does not have EDP. Accepts transfer applicants. 90% of class must be state residents. Apply to University of Texas Medical and Dental Schools Application Service at Austin (78701) after May 1, before October 1. Application center fee: residents $55 plus $5 for each additional school, nonresidents $100 plus $10 for each additional school. School's application fee $65. Phone: (214)648-5617; fax: (214)648-3289. Applications to M.D.-Ph.D. program are made through AMCAS.

ADMISSION STANDARDS. Competitive. Accepts about 13% of all applicants. Number of applications 3268 (678 out-of-state); number interviewed 723 (101 out-of-state); number of acceptance 434 (61 out-of-state); number enrolled 229 (36 out-of-state). Mean Composite MCAT 10.7; mean UGPA 3.83. *U.S. News & World Report* ranking is in the top 19 of all medical research schools, 18th in primary care.

FINANCIAL AID. A limited number of scholarships from memorial funds and foundations, institutional loans, HEAL, alternative loan programs, NIH stipends, Federal Perkins Loans, Stafford Subsidized and Unsubsidized Loans, Service Commitment Scholarship programs are available. Assistantships/fellowships may be available for combined degree candidates. Most aid is awarded based on demonstrated need. Financial aid applications and information are available by contacting the Office of the Registrar. Phone: (214)648-3611. Use FAFSA (School code: 010019), also submit Financial Aid Transcript, Federal Income Tax forms. Approximately 92% of students receive some form of financial assistance.

DEGREE REQUIREMENTS. For M.D.: satisfactory completion of 4-year program. All students must pass USMLE Step 1 prior to entering fourth year and Step 2 for graduation. For M.D.-M.A., M.D.-M.S.: generally from four-and-one-half- to five-and-one-half-year programs. For M.D.-Ph.D.: generally a six- to seven-year program.

FIELDS OF GRADUATE STUDY.
Biological Chemistry. Includes Biochemistry, Chemistry.
Biomedical Communications.
Biomedical Engineering. Includes Bioinstrumentation & Human Performance, Biomaterials & Tissue Engineering, Biomechanics, Medical Imaging, Molecular & Computational Biomedical Engineering, Orthopedics.
Cell Regulation. Includes Cell Biology, Cell Signaling, Pharmacological Sciences.
Genetics and Development. Includes Cancer Biology.
Immunology.
Integrative Biology.
Molecular Biophysics. Includes Computational Biology.
Molecular Microbiology.
Neuroscience.

THOMAS M. COOLEY LAW SCHOOL
P.O. Box 13038
Lansing, Michigan 48901-3038
Web site: www.cooley.edu

Established 1972. Campuses in Lansing, Rochester at Oakland University, Grand Rapids. ABA approved since 1975, AALS member. Private control. Morning, afternoon, evening divisions. Special facilities: Center for Ethics and Responsibility, Indian Law Center, Forensics Science Institute. Law library, 541,986 volumes, 6281 subscriptions; has LEXIS, NEXIS, WESTLAW; has more than 50 network connections.

Annual tuition: full-time $24,260, part-time $17,340; LL.M. $527 per credit. No on-campus housing available. Total average annual additional expense: $11,160.

Enrollment: first-year class full-time 385, part-time 1129; total full- and part-time 3106 (men 53%, women 47%, minorities 22%). Faculty: full-time 46, part-time 125. Student to faculty ratio is 23.0 to 1. Degree conferred: J.D., J.D.-M.P.A., LL.M. (Intellectual Property, Taxation).

ADMISSION REQUIREMENTS. LSDAS Law School report, bachelor's degree, transcripts, LSAT required in support of application. Accepts transfer applicants. Apply to Admissions Office at least one month prior to beginning of trimester. Rolling admissions process. Admits September (morning classes), January (afternoon classes), and May (evening classes). Application fee, none. Phone: (517)371-5140, ext. 2244; fax: (517)334-5718. For LL.M.: contact Graduate Program Office. Phone: (800)874-3511.

ADMISSION STANDARDS. Selective. Accepts approximately 69% of full-time, 51% of part-time students. Number of full-time applicants 4226, part-time 588; number of full-time acceptance 2895, part-time 297; number of full-time enrolled 385, part-time 129; LSAT (75% of full-time students have a score at or above 146, part-time 144); GPA (75% of full-time students have a GPA at or above 2.72, part-time 2.71). *U.S. News & World Report* ranking is in the fourth tier of all U.S. law schools.

FINANCIAL AID. Honor scholarships, Federal W/S, loans. Apply to the Financial Aid Office; no specified closing date. Phone: (517)371-5140. Use FAFSA (School code: G12627). About 55% of full-time and 44% of part-time students receive some aid from School.

DEGREE REQUIREMENTS. For J.D.: satisfactory completion of 90 credit hour program. For LL.M.: 24 credit program; full-time one year; part-time program must be completed in less than five years.

THOMAS JEFFERSON SCHOOL OF LAW
2121 San Diego Avenue
San Diego, California 92110
Web site: www.tjsl.edu

Established 1969. Located in historic "Old Town" section of San Diego. ABA approved since 1996. AALS member. Private control. Semester system. Full-time (day), part-time (day or evening) study. Special facilities: Center for Law, Technology, and Communication, Center for Global Legal Studies, Center for Law and Social Justice. Special programs: externships. Law library: 250,613 volumes, 3393 subscriptions; has LEXIS, NEXIS, WESTLAW.

Annual tuition: full-time $30,250, part-time $19,050. No on-campus housing available. Contact Admissions Office for off-campus information. Off-campus housing and personal expenses: approximately $23,898.

Enrollment: first-year class full-time 232, part-time 44; total full- and part-time 770 (men 56%, women 44%, minorities 21%). Faculty: full-time 26, part-time 19. Student to faculty ratio is 21.9 to 1. Degree conferred: J.D.

ADMISSION REQUIREMENTS. LSDAS Law School report, LSAT (not later that June (Fall), December 1 (Spring) test date; if more than one LSAT, highest is used), bachelor's degree from an accredited institution, résumé, personal statement, two recommendations, transcripts (must show all schools attended and at least three years of study) required in support of application. Applicants must have received bachelor's degree prior to enrollment. Interview not required but telephone and personal interviews are available. Accepts transfer applicants. In addition, international applicants whose native language is not English must submit TOEFL (not older than two years). First-year students admitted Fall, Spring. Apply by April 30 (Fall), October 1 (Spring). Rolling admissions process. Application fee $35. Phone: (800)936-7529, (619)297-9700, ext. 1600; fax: (619)294-4713; e-mail: info@tjsl.edu.

ADMISSION REQUIREMENTS FOR TRANSFER APPLICANTS. Accepts transfers from other ABA-accredited schools. Admission limited to space available. At least one year of enrollment, Dean's letter indicating the applicant is in good standing, LSAT, LSDAS, personal statement regarding reason for transfer, undergraduate transcript, current law school transcript required in support of School application. Rolling admissions process. Application fee $35. Will consider visiting students.

ADMISSION STANDARDS. Selective. Accepts approximately 24% of full-time, 24% of part-time students. Number of full-time applicants 4170, part-time 406; number of full-time acceptance 1003, part-time 98; number of full-time enrolled 232, part-time 44; LSAT (75% of full-time students have a score at or above 151, part-time 150); GPA (75% of full-time students have a GPA at or above 2.74, part-time 2.65). *U.S. News & World Report* ranking is in the fourth tier of all U.S. law schools.

FINANCIAL AID. Scholarships, merit scholarships, minority scholarships, private loans, State grants, Federal loans and Federal W/S available. All accepted students are considered for scholarships (a student with a LSAT score of 150 or higher automatically receives either a partial or full scholarship). Apply as soon as possible after January 1. Phone: (619)279-9700, ext. 1350. Use FAFSA (School code: 013780), also submit Financial Aid Transcript, Federal Income Tax forms. Approximately 64% (full-time), 49% (part-time) of first year class received scholarships/Grants-in-Aid. Approximately 60% of students receive some form of financial assistance.

DEGREE REQUIREMENTS. For J.D.: 88 (33 required) credits with a GPA of at least a 2.0 (A = 4), plus completion of upper-divisional writing course; three-year program, four-year part-time program. Accelerated J.D. with summer course work.

THOMAS JEFFERSON UNIVERSITY
Philadelphia, Pennsylvania 19107-5083
Web site: www.tju.edu

Founded 1824. CGS member. Private control. Semester system. The University's NIH ranking is 81st among all U.S. institutions with 211 awards/grants worth $71,798,074. Medical library: 192,000 volumes, 2100 subscriptions.

Annual Graduate School tuition: $20,340; per credit $818 (M.P.H., M.S.). On-campus housing available. Average academic year housing costs: apartments $800–$1760/month, dormitory $340–$485/month. Contact the Director of University Housing Office for both on- and off-campus housing information. Phone: (215)955-8913. On-campus day-care facilities available.

College of Graduate Studies

Enrollment: full-time 264, part-time 252 (men 35%, women 65%). Faculty: full-time 200, part-time 11. Degrees conferred: M.S., Ph.D.

ADMISSION REQUIREMENTS. Official transcripts, three letters of recommendation, GRE required in support of College's application. TOEFL required for international applicants. Accepts transfer applicants. Graduates of unaccredited institutions not considered. Apply to Director of admission; no specified closing date. Application fee $40. Phone: (215)503-0155; fax: (215)503-3433.

ADMISSION STANDARDS. Competitive. Usual minimum average: 3.0 (A = 4).

FINANCIAL AID. Fellowships, research assistantships, traineeships, grants, Federal W/S, loans. Approved for VA benefits. Apply by May 1 to the Dean for fellowships, assistantships; to Financial Aid Office for all other programs. Phone: (215)955-2867; fax: (215)955-5186. Use FAFSA and institutional FAF. Aid available for part-time students.

DEGREE REQUIREMENTS. For M.S.: minimum 30 credits, maximum 44; final project or thesis. For Ph.D.: minimum of 45 credits beyond the master's, at least one year in full-time residence; qualifying exam; dissertation; final written/oral exam.

FIELDS OF GRADUATE STUDY.
Biomedical Sciences. M.S.
Biochemistry and Molecular Biology.
Cell and Development Biology. M.S.
Genetics.
Immunology and Microbial Pathogenesis.
Microbiology. M.S.

Molecular Pharmacology and Structural Biology.
Neuroscience.
Pharmacology. M.S.
Tissue Engineering and Regenerative Medicine.

Jefferson Medical College
Web site: www.tju.edu

Established 1824, one of the oldest medical colleges in the nation. Semester system; the first two years are spent in studying the basic sciences. Affiliated hospitals: Thomas Jefferson University Hospital, Stein Research Center, Wills Eye Hospital, Veterans Administration Hospital. Special facility: Bodine Center for Radiation Therapy. Special programs: prematriculation summer sessions; a decelerated program available during first two years.

Annual tuition: $39,625; student fees, none. On-campus apartments available for both single and married students. Contact Housing Office for both on- and off-campus housing information. Phone: (215)955-8913. Medical students tend to live off-campus. Off-campus housing and personal expenses: approximately $15,609.

Enrollment: first-year class 255 (EDP 30); total full-time 966 (men 49%, women 51%, minorities 26%, state residents 46%). Faculty: full-time 2000, part-time/volunteers 1500. Degrees conferred: M.D., B.S.-M.D. (with Penn State University), M.D.-M.B.A. (with Widener University), M.D.-M.H.A. (Widener University), M.D.-M.P.H. (in cooperation with Johns Hopkins School of Public Health), M.D.-Ph.D.

ADMISSION REQUIREMENTS. Preference given to U.S. citizens and permanent residents and children of alumni and faculty. Bachelor's degree from an accredited institution required. Has EDP; applicants must apply through AMCAS (official transcripts sent by mid-May) between June 1 and August 1. Early applications are encouraged. Submit secondary/supplemental application, a personal statement, two recommendations to Office of Admission within two weeks of receipt of application. Interviews are by invitation only and generally for final selection. Notification normally begins October 1. Accepts transfer and international (students must have four-year degree from U.S. institution) applicants. All other candidates apply through AMCAS (file after June 1, before November 15), submit MCAT (will accept MCAT test results from the last three years), official transcripts for each school attended (should show at least 90 semester credits/135 quarter credit; submit transcripts by mid-May to AMCAS), service processing fee. Submit an application fee of $80, a supplemental application, a personal statement, pre-professional committee evaluation, and three recommendations from science faculty to Office of Admission within two to three weeks of the receipt of supplemental materials, but no later than January 15. Interviews are by invitation only and generally for final selection. Phone: (215)503-8877. M.D.-Ph.D. applicants must apply to and be accepted to both Schools, contact the Director of Admission and Recruitment of the College of Graduate Studies for current information and specific admissions requirements. Phone: (215)955-0155. First-year students admitted Fall only. Rolling admissions process; notification starts October 15 and is finished when class is filled. Phone: (215)955-6983; fax: (215)955-5151.

ADMISSION STANDARDS. Very competitive. Accepts about 6.7% of all applicants. Number of applications 7702 (6739 out-of-state); number interviewed 771 (506 out-of-state); number of acceptance 517 (334 out-of-state); number enrolled 255 (147 out-of-state). Mean Composite MCAT 10.4; mean UGPA 3.51.

FINANCIAL AID. Scholarships, merit scholarships, minority scholarships, Grants-in-Aid, institutional loans, HEAL, alternative loan programs, Federal Perkins Loans, Stafford Subsidized and Unsubsidized Loans, Primary Care Service Commitment Scholarship programs are available. Fellowships, tuition waivers, and stipends may be available for M.D.-Ph.D. candidates. All aid is based on demonstrated need. Financial Aid applications and the Financial Aid Handbook are available after December 18; applications must be completed and returned no later than April 1. For scholarships, the selection criteria places heavy reliance on MCAT and undergraduate GPA. Contact the Office of Student Financial Aid for current information. Phone: (215)955-2867. Use FAFSA (School code: 010021), also submit Financial Aid Transcript, Federal Income Tax forms. Approximately 48% of students receive some form of financial assistance.

DEGREE REQUIREMENTS. For M.D.: satisfactory completion of four-year program; all students must pass USMLE Step 1 prior to entering third year and all students must pass USMLE Step 2 prior to awarding of M.D. For M.D.-M.B.A.: generally a five-year program. For M.D.-M.P.H.: generally a five-year program. For M.D.-Ph.D.: generally a seven-year program.

FIELDS OF GRADUATE STUDY.
Biomedical Sciences. M.S.
Biochemistry and Molecular Biology.
Cell and Development Biology. M.S.
Genetics.
Immunology and Microbial Pathogenesis.
Microbiology. M.S.
Molecular Pharmacology and Structural Biology.
Neuroscience.
Pharmacology. M.S.
Tissue Engineering and Regenerative Medicine.

THUNDERBIRD, SCHOOL OF GLOBAL MANAGEMENT
Glendale, Arizona 85306-6000
Web site: www.t-bird.edu

Founded 1946. Located in a suburban area near Phoenix with campuses in Japan and France. Coed. Private control. Trimester system. Special facilities: International Studies Research Center, Dom Pedro II Research Center on Iberia, Ibero-American and Lusohispanphone Africa Center, International Business Information Center. Library: 72,900 volumes, 1612 subscriptions, 60 PCs.

Total tuition per program: $41,000 (Global–Latin American Managers, $59,850 (Global On-Demand), $73,300 (M.B.A.-GM), $39,500 (E.M.B.A.-Europe), $67,000 (E.M.B.A.-Arizona); per trimester $17,050 (M.B.A.-Global Management). On-campus housing available for single students only. Average academic year housing costs: $3900 (including board). Contact the Housing Office for off-campus housing information. Phone: (602) 978-7132.

Graduate Programs

Enrollment: full-time 1102, part-time 0. Graduate faculty: full-time 50, part-time 39. Degrees conferred: M.B.A.I.M., M.I.M.L.A., M.I.M.-M.B.A.

ADMISSION REQUIREMENTS. Official transcripts, GMAT, required in support of School's application. Online application available. TOEFL required for international applicants. Accepts transfer applicants. Graduates of unaccredited institutions not considered. Apply by January 15 (Fall), July 31 (Spring) to Dean of Admissions. Rolling admissions process. Application fee $100. Phone: (602)978-7210; fax: (602)439-5432.

ADMISSION STANDARDS. Selective. Usual minimum average: 2.75 (A = 4). Ranked number one in International Management by *U.S. News & World Report.*

FINANCIAL AID. Scholarships, fellowships, assistantships, partial tuition waivers, Federal W/S, loans. Approved for VA benefits. Apply by February 15 to appropriate program chair for fellowships, assistantships; to Financial Aid Office for all other programs. Use FAFSA (School code: G01070). About 65% of students receive aid from School and outside sources.

DEGREE REQUIREMENTS. For M.B.A.I.M.: 48–60 credit program; language/nonlanguage option. For M.I.M.: 30–42 credits minimum, all in full-time residence, one- to two-year program; language proficiency for some programs; final oral/written exam. For M.I.M.L.A.: 50-credit program.

FIELDS OF STUDY.
Executive M.B.A. Offered in Arizona or Europe.
Global Affairs and Management. M.A.
Global M.B.A. On-Demand.
Global M.B.A. for Latin American Managers.
Global Management. M.B.A., M.S.

UNIVERSITY OF TOLEDO
Toledo, Ohio 43606-3390
Web site: www.utoledo.edu

Founded 1872, became a state university in 1967. CGS member. Coed. State control. Semester system. Special facilities: VAX-11/785, Humanities Institute, Polymer Institute, Center for International Studies, Center for Institutional Research and Services, Eitel Institute for Silicate Research, Ritter Astrophysical Research, Polymer Institute, Opinion Research Institute, Urban Affairs Center. Library: 1,600,000 volumes, 4500 subscriptions. Total University enrollment: 20,000.

Annual tuition: full-time resident $9828, nonresident $18,638. Off-campus housing only. Average monthly housing costs: $300–$450. Contact Coordinator of Commuter and Off-Campus Housing Services. Phone: (419)530-2941. On-campus day-care facilities available.

Graduate School

Graduate study since 1912. Enrollment: full- and part-time 2500. Graduate faculty: full-time 408, part-time 50. Degrees conferred: M.A., M.B.A., M.Ed., M.M., M.S., Ed.S., Ed.D., Ph.D.

ADMISSION REQUIREMENTS. Three official transcripts, three letters of recommendation, GMAT/GRE and Subject Tests required in support of School's application. Online application available. TOEFL required for international applicants. Accepts transfer applicants. Graduates of unaccredited institutions not considered. Apply to Director of Admissions at least one month prior to registration. All requirements must be completed at least 2 weeks prior to registration. Rolling admissions process. Application fee $30. Phone: (800)914-7764; fax: (419)530-4724; e-mail: grdsch@utnet.utoledo.edu.

ADMISSION STANDARDS. Selective. Usual minimum average: 2.7–3.0 (A = 4).

FINANCIAL AID. Annual awards from institutional funds: scholarships, fellowships, stipends, tuition waivers, internships, teaching assistantships, research assistantships, Federal W/S, loans. Approved for VA benefits. Apply by March 1 to Graduate School for assistantships; to Financial Aid for all other programs. Phone: (419)530-8700. Use FAFSA. About 25% of students receive aid other than loans from School and outside sources. Aid available for part-time students.

DEGREE REQUIREMENTS. For master's: 30–33 credit hours minimum, at least 24 in residence; thesis/comprehensive exam/

one language for some departments. For Ed.D.: 90 credit hours minimum beyond the bachelor's, at least three consecutive Summers in full-time residence; written comprehensive exam; knowledge of statistics; dissertation; final oral exam. For Ph.D.: 90 credit hours minimum beyond the bachelor's, at least two semesters in full-time residence; reading knowledge of one foreign language for some departments; comprehensive exam; dissertation; final exam.

FIELDS OF STUDY.
Accounting.
Administrative Pharmacy.
Art Education.
Athletic Training.
Bioengineering.
Biology. Includes cell and molecular biology, ecology.
Biomedical Engineering.
Biomedical Sciences. Includes bioinformatics and proteomics/genomics, cancer biology, cardiovascular and metabolic disease, infection, immunity and transplantation, neurosciences and neurological disorders, oral biology, orthopedic sciences, urological sciences.
Business Administration. Includes administration, finance, human resource management, information systems, international business, management, marketing, operations management.
Career and Technical Education.
Chemical Engineering.
Chemistry.
Civil Engineering.
Communication Disorders.
Communication Studies.
Community Counseling.
Computer Science.
Counselor Education.
Criminal Justice.
Curriculum and Instruction.
Early Childhood Education.
Economics.
Education. Interdisciplinary programs with Arts and Science include anthropology, biology, chemistry, classics, economics, English, ESL, French, geology, German, history, mathematics, physics, political science, sociology, Spanish.
Educational Administration and Supervision.
Educational Psychology.
Educational Research and Measurement.
Educational Sociology.
Educational Technology and Media.
Educational Theory and Social Foundations.
ESL.
English Literature.
Environmental Sciences.
Exercise Science.
Foreign Languages. Includes French, German, Spanish.
Geographic Information Systems.
Geography.
Gifted Education.
Health Education.
Higher Education.
History.
History of Education.
Industrial Engineering.
Industrial Pharmacy.
Kinesiology. Includes applied and clinical physiology, biomechanics, clinical kinesiotherapy, exercise physiology.
Liberal Arts.
Manufacturing Management.
Mathematics.
Mechanical Engineering.
Medical Physics.
Medical Sciences.
Medicinal Chemistry.

Middle Childhood Education.
Music Education.
Music Performance.
Nursing. Includes adult nurse practitioner, clinical nurse leader, family nurse practitioner, nurse educator, pediatric nurse practitioner, psychiatric–mental health.
Occupational Health.
Occupational Therapy.
Pharmacology Toxicology.
Philosophy.
Philosophy of Education.
Physical Education.
Physical Therapy.
Physician Assistant.
Physics.
Political Science.
Psychology. Includes clinical, experimental.
Public Administration.
Public Health. Includes administration, environmental and occupational health and safety sciences, epidemiology, health promotion and education, nutrition, occupational health/industrial hygiene.
Public Health and Emergency Response.
Radiation Oncology.
Radiological Sciences.
Radiology. Includes diagnostics.
Recreation Administration.
Research and Measurement.
School Counseling.
School Psychology.
Secondary Education.
Social Work.
Sociology.
Special Education.
Speech Language Pathology.
Teaching of Writing.

College of Law (43606-3390)
Web site: www.utlaw.edu

Organized 1906. ABA approved since 1939. AALS member. Public control. Semester system. Special facilities: Legal Institute of the Great Lakes, Cybersecurities Law Institute. Law library: 344,863 volumes, 3351 subscriptions; has LEXIS, NEXIS, WESTLAW.

Annual tuition: full-time resident $14,839, nonresident $25,082; per credit resident $617, nonresident $1044. No on-campus housing available. For off-campus housing contact either the Student Bar Association or the University's Off-Campus Living Officer. Total average annual additional expense: $13,860.

Enrollment: first-year class 85 (day), 89 (evening); total full- and part-time 524 (men 60%, women 40%, minorities 7%). Faculty: full-time 32, part-time 20. Student to faculty ratio is 13.4 to 1. Degrees conferred: J.D., J.D.-M.B.A., J.D.-M.P.A., J.D.-M.P.H., J.D.-M.S.E.

ADMISSION REQUIREMENTS. LSDAS Law School report, bachelor's degree, transcripts, LSAT, two letters of recommendation required in support of application. Personal statement optional. Campus visit encouraged. Evidence of proficiency in English required of foreign students. Interview not required. Accepts transfer applicants. Graduates of unaccredited colleges not considered. Apply to Office of Admissions by July 1. Fall admission only. Rolling admission process. Application fee $40. Phone: (419) 530-4131; fax: (419)530-4345.

ADMISSION STANDARDS. Selective. Accepts approximately 19% of full-time, 42% of part-time students. Number of full-time applicants 1231, part-time 266; number of full-time acceptance 231, part-time 111; number of full-time enrolled 85, part-time 89; LSAT (75% of full-time students have a score at or above

155, part-time 152); GPA (75% of full-time students have a GPA at or above 2.98, part-time 3.00). *U.S. News & World Report* ranking is in the second tier (tied at 85th) of all U.S. law schools.

FINANCIAL AID. Scholarships, grants, assistantships, Federal W/S, loans. Apply to Office of Financial Aid by August 1. Phone: (419)530-7929. Use FAFSA (College code: 003131). About 48% of full-time and 6% of part-time students receive aid other than loans from College.

DEGREE REQUIREMENTS. For J.D.: successful completion of three-year program (day), four-year program (evening); 87 credit hour program.

College of Medicine
Web site: hsc.utoledo.edu

Established 1968. Formerly Medical College of Ohio, merged with University of Toledo in 2006. Located at the Health Science Campus. Library: 100,000 volumes, 850 subscriptions.

Annual tuition: resident $23,494, nonresident $53,590. No on-campus housing available. Total average figure for all other expenses: $12,270.

Enrollment: first-year class 155, total 601 (men 53%, women 47%, minorities 22%, state residents 70%). Faculty: full-time 250, part-time/volunteers 1100. Degrees conferred: M.D., M.D.-M.P.H., M.D.-M.S., M.D.-Ph.D.

ADMISSION REQUIREMENTS. AMCAS report, transcripts, MCAT, recommendations required in support of application. Interviews by invitation only. Preference given to state residents. Accepts transfer applicants from Ohio only. Has EDP; apply between June 1 and November 1. Graduates of unaccredited colleges not considered. Apply to Director of Admissions after June 1, before November 1. Application fee $80. Phone: (419)383-4229; fax: (419)383-4005.

ADMISSION STANDARDS. Selective. Accepts about 11% of all applicants. Number of applications 2787 (1903 out-of-state); number interviewed 477 (n/a out-of-state); number of acceptance n/a (n/a out-of-state); number enrolled 155 (50 out-of-state). Mean Composite MCAT 10.0; mean UGPA 3.60.

FINANCIAL AID. Need-based scholarships, merit scholarships, minority scholarships, Grants-in-Aid, institutional loans, HEAL, alternative loan programs, NIH stipends, Federal Perkins Loans, Stafford Subsidized and Unsubsidized Loans, Service Commitment Scholarship programs are available. Assistantships/fellowships may be available for Dual Degree candidates. All accepted students receive Financial Aid applications in early February. Contact the Financial Aid Office for current information. Phone: (419)383-4232. Use FAFSA to a Federal processor (Title IV School code: G07737); also submit Financial Aid Transcript, Federal Income Tax forms. Approximately 90% of students receive some form of financial assistance.

DEGREE REQUIREMENTS. For M.D.: satisfactory completion of four-year program. Students required to pass Step 1 of USMLE and Step 2 for graduation. For M.S.: 32 semester hours minimum; thesis or comprehensive exam. For Ph.D.: at least 90 credits beyond bachelor's. Foreign language required by some departments; comprehensive exam; dissertation; final oral exam.

FIELDS OF GRADUATE STUDY.
Bioinformatics/Proteomics/Genomics. M.S.
Cancer Biology. M.S., Ph.D.
Cardiovascular and Metabolic Diseases. M.S., Ph.D.
Diagnostic Radiology. M.S.
Infection, Immunity, and Transplantation. M.S., Ph.D.
Medical Physics. M.S.

Medical Sciences. M.S.
Neurosciences and Neurological Disorders. M.S., Ph.D.
Oral Biology. M.S.
Orthopaedic Sciences. M.S.
Public Health. M.P.H.
Radiation Oncology. M.S.
Urological Sciences. M.S.

TOURO COLLEGE
300 Nassau Road
Huntington, New York 11743

Jacob D. Fuchsberg Law Center
Web site: www.tourolaw.edu

Established 1980. Located on Long Island's north shore approximately 30 miles E of New York City. Private control. Semester system. ABA approved since 1983. AALS member. Semester system, Full-time, part-time study. Special facilities: Institute of Local and Suburban Law, Institute of Jewish Law. Special programs: summer study abroad at Moscow State University, Russia, Shimla, India; international summer internships in London, Cork, Paris, Brussels, Lisbon, Tel Aviv, Jerusalem. Law library: 423,805 volumes, 4584 subscriptions; has LEXIS, NEXIS, WESTLAW, DIALOG, OCLC, DOWJONES, AUTO-LITE.

Annual tuition: full-time $32,900, part-time $24,300. On-campus apartments available for both single and married students. Total average annual additional expenses: $22,271. Law students tend to live off-campus. Contact Admissions Office for both on- and off-campus information.

Enrollment: first-year class full-time 227, part-time 71; total 732 (men 55%, women 45%, minorities 23%). Faculty: full-time 26, part-time 20. Student to faculty ratio 16.5 to 1. Degrees conferred: J.D., J.D.-M.B.A. (with Dowling College or C.W. Post College), J.D.-M.P.A. (Long Island University, C.W. Post College), J.D.-M.S. (Tax), LL.M. (full- or part-time, for foreign lawyers who have completed a basic legal education and received a university degree in law in another country), LL.M. (General).

ADMISSION REQUIREMENTS. LSDAS Law School report, LSAT (not later that December test date; if more than one LSAT, highest is used), LSAT writing sample, bachelor's degree from an accredited institution, personal statement, two letters of recommendation, transcripts (must show all schools attended and at least three years of study) required in support of application. Applicants must have received bachelor's degree prior to enrollment. Campus visits are encouraged. In addition, international applicants whose native language is not English must submit TOEFL (not older that five years), certified translations and evaluations of all foreign credentials. Accepts transfer applicants. Joint degree applicants must apply to and be accepted to both schools. Apply to Office of Admission after September 30, before July 15 (priority deadline). First-year students admitted Fall only. Rolling admissions process; notification starts within four to six weeks from the time application is complete and continues until class is filled. Application fee $60. Phone: (631) 421-2244, ext. 312; fax: (631)421-2675; e-mail: admissions@tourolaw.edu.

ADMISSION REQUIREMENTS FOR LL.M. (Foreign Lawyers). All applicants must have the foreign equivalent of an American J.D. Official transcript with certified translation and evaluations, two letters of recommendation, personal statement required in support of LL.M. application. TOEFL required for those applicants whose native language is not English. Admits Fall only. Full-time day, part-time day, part-time evening study available. Apply to Admissions Office at least three months prior to preferred date of entrance. Application fee $50.

ADMISSION STANDARDS. Selective. Accepts approximately 35% of full-time, 32% of part-time students. Number of full-time applicants 1976, part-time 496; number of full-time acceptance 683, part-time 158; number of full-time enrolled 227, part-time 71; LSAT (75% of full-time students have a score at or above 150, part-time 147); GPA (75% of full-time students have a GPA at or above 2.87, part-time 2.69). *U.S. News & World Report* ranking is in the fourth tier of all U.S. law schools.

FINANCIAL AID. Scholarships, Dean's Fellowships, Merit Scholarships and Incentive Awards, grants, private and institutional loans, Summer Public Interest Fellowships, State grants (TAP), Federal loans and Federal W/S available. All accepted students are automatically considered for scholarships. Apply to Admissions Office as soon as possible after January 1 but not later than May 1. Phone: (631)421-2244, ext. 322. Use FAFSA, also submit Financial Aid Transcript, Federal Income Tax forms. Approximately 44% (full-time), 55% (part-time) of first-year class received scholarships/Grants-in-Aid. Approximately 55% of students receive some form of financial assistance. Public Interest Loan Repayment Program available.

DEGREE REQUIREMENTS. For J.D.: 87 (44–46 required) credits program with a GPA of at least 2.0 (A = 4), plus completion of upper-divisional writing course; three-year full-time program, four-year part-time program. Accelerated J.D. with two summers of course work. For J.D.-Master's: four-year programs rather than five-year programs if both degrees are taken consecutively. For LL.M. (Foreign Lawyers): 27 credits, at least two semesters in residence; successful completion of "Introduction to the U.S. Legal System." For LL.M. (General): 24 credit program.

TOURO UNIVERSITY

1310 Johnson Lane
Vallejo, California 94592
Web site: www.tu.edu

Founded 1997. The University is a division of Touro College, a Jewish sponsored non-for-profit educational system located on Long Island, New York. Graduate programs only. Branch campus in Henderson, Nevada.

College of Osteopathic Medicine,
Mare Island Campus

Web site: www.tu.edu

Founded 1997. Semester system. Library: 35,000 volumes, 900 subscriptions.

Annual tuition: $35,715. On- and off-campus housing available, but best housing is on campus. Contact the Office of Student Affairs for housing information. On-campus housing and personal expenses: approximately $17,500.

Enrollment: first-year class 125, total 526 (men 49%, women 51%, minorities 9%, state residents 51%). Faculty: full-time 48, part-time 0. Degree conferred: D.O.

ADMISSION REQUIREMENTS. AACOMAS report (deadline February 1), bachelor's degree, official transcripts, MCAT, three recommendations (one from science faculty member, a premedical source, one evaluation from a physician, preferably a D.O.) required in support of application. Supplemental applications are sent to applicants after initial review. Accepts transfer applicants. Interviews by invitation only. Graduates of unaccredited colleges not considered. Apply to the Office of Admissions by April 1. Admits first year student Fall only. Rolling admission process. Application fee $75. Phone: (888)880-7336; (707)638-5270; fax: (707)638-5252.

ADMISSION STANDARDS. Selective. Accepts about 13% of all applicants. Number of applications 2084 (n/a out-of-state); number interviewed 425 (n/a out-of-state); number of acceptance 278 (n/a out-of-state); number enrolled 125 (n/a out-of-state). Usual minimum UGPA: 3.0 (A = 4). Mean Composite MCAT 8.7, mean UGPA 3.35.

FINANCIAL AID. Scholarships, grants, Federal W/S, Federal or private loans. Apply by April 1 to Financial Aid Office. Phone: (707)638-5280. Use FAFSA. About 90%of students receive some form of financial assistance.

DEGREE REQUIREMENTS. For D.O.: satisfactory completion of four-year program.

TOWSON UNIVERSITY

Baltimore, Maryland 21204
Web site: www.towson.edu

Founded 1866. CGS member. Coed. State control. Semester system. Special facilities: Center for Mathematics and Sciences Education, Center for Applied Informatoin Technology, Center for Suburban and Regional Studies, Center for the Teaching and Research on Women, Center for the Teaching and Study of Writing. Library: 574,100 volumes, 2400 subscriptions. Total University enrollment: 18,000.

Tuition: per credit, $267 resident, nonresident $560. Limited on-campus housing. Average academic year on-campus housing costs: $7000; off-campus costs: $730–$850 per month. Contact the Director, Residence for both on- and off-campus housing information. Phone: (410)830-2516.

Graduate School

Graduate study since 1957. Enrollment: full-time 819, part-time 2697. Graduate faculty: full-time 260, part-time 19. Degrees conferred: M.A., M.S., M.Ed., M.F.A., M.M., M.A.T.

ADMISSION REQUIREMENTS. Transcripts required in support of application. GRE, interview required for some programs. TOEFL required for international applicants. Apply to the Graduate School; no specified closing date, some programs have deadlines. Rolling admissions process. Application fee $40. Phone: (410)704-2501; fax: (410)704-4675.

ADMISSION STANDARDS. Selective. Usual minimum average: 2.75 (A = 4).

FINANCIAL AID. Annual awards from institutional funds: fellowships, research assistantships, teaching assistantships, internships, Federal W/S, loans. Approved for VA benefits. Apply by April 1 to Dean of Graduate School for assistantships; to Financial Aid Office for all other programs. Phone: (410)704-2098. Use FAFSA and University's FAF. Aid available for part-time students.

DEGREE REQUIREMENTS. For master's: 30–60 semester hours; thesis/nonthesis option; final written/oral exam.

FIELDS OF STUDY.
Applied and Industrial Mathematics.
Applied Gerontology.
Applied Information Technology.
Art Education.
Audiology.
Biology.
Communication Management.
Computer Science.
Early Childhood Education.

Elementary Education.
Environmental Sciences.
Geography and Environmental Planning.
Health Science.
Hunan Resource Development.
Instructional Technology.
Liberal and Professional Studies.
Mass Communication.
Mathematics Education.
Music Composition.
Music Education.
Music Performance.
Nursing.
Occupational Science.
Occupational Therapy.
Physician's Assistant Studies.
Professional Writing.
Psychology. Includes clinical, counseling, experimental, school.
Reading.
Science Education.
Secondary Education.
Special Education.
Speech-Language Pathology.
Studio Arts.
Teaching.
Theater.
Women's Studies.

TRINITY COLLEGE
Hartford, Connecticut 06106
Web site: www.trincoll.edu

Founded 1823. Coed. Private control. Semester system. Library: 962,700 volumes, 3400 subscriptions. Total College enrollment: 2550.

Tuition: per credit $500. No on-campus housing available. Day-care facilities available.

Graduate Program

Graduate study since 1988. Offered in evenings during academic year, and during Summer term. Graduate enrollment: part-time 123. Faculty: full-time 11, part-time 9. Degrees conferred: M.A.

ADMISSION REQUIREMENTS. Transcripts, writing sample, letters of academic recommendation required in support of application. Online application available. Accepts transfer applicants. Graduates of unaccredited institutions not considered. Apply to Office of Graduate Studies by April 15 (Fall), November 15 (Spring). Application fee $50. Phone: (860)297-2151; fax: (860) 297-5362.

ADMISSION STANDARDS. Relatively open when provisional acceptees are included. Usual minimum average: 3.0 (A = 4).

FINANCIAL AID. Fellowships, grants, loans. Apply by April 1 to Office of Graduate Studies. Use FAFSA and College's FAF. Aid available for part-time students.

DEGREE REQUIREMENTS. For M.A.: ten courses, includes thesis or comprehensive exam.

FIELDS OF STUDY.
American Studies.
Economics.
English.
History.
Public Policy Studies.

TRINITY UNIVERSITY
San Antonio, Texas 78212-7200
Web site: www.trinity.edu

Founded 1869. CGS member. Coed. Private control. Presbyterian affiliation. Semester system. Special facilities: working agreements with Southwest Research Institute, Southwest Foundation for Research and Education, United States Air Force School for Aerospace Medicine, University of Texas Health Science Center. Library: 917,700 volumes, 3450 subscriptions. Total University enrollment: 2750.

Tuition: per credit $964. No housing for graduate students.

Graduate School

Graduate study since 1950. Enrollment: full-time 134, part-time 96. University faculty: full-time 15, part-time 23. Degrees conferred: M.A., M.A.T., M.Ed., M.S.

ADMISSION REQUIREMENTS. Transcripts, letters of recommendation, GRE/GMAT required in support of School's application. TOEFL (minimum score 600) required of international applicants. Accepts transfer applicants. Apply to Graduate Admissions Office at least one month prior to registration. Application fee $40. Phone: (210)999-8424; fax: (210)999-8108.

ADMISSION STANDARDS. Selective. Usual minimum average: 3.0 (A = 4).

FINANCIAL AID. Annual awards from institutional funds: thirty-six departmental assistantships, Federal W/S, loans. Approved for VA benefits. Apply to department of choice for assistantships, to Financial Aid Office for all other programs. No specified closing date. Phone: (210)999-7207. Use FAFSA. About 20% of students receive aid other than loans from School and outside sources.

DEGREE REQUIREMENTS. For master's: 30–36 semester hours minimum, at least 80% in residence; thesis for some departments; nonthesis option includes research project/comprehensive exam/internship.

FIELDS OF STUDY.
Accounting.
Health Care Administration. Two-year program includes one-year residency; external degree (three-year program).
School Administration. Two-year program; includes two-semester internship.
School Psychology.
Teaching.

TROY UNIVERSITY
Troy, Alabama 36082
Web site: www.troyst.edu

Founded 1887. Located 55 miles SE of Montgomery. Coed. State control. Semester system. Library: 443,415 volumes, 1800 subscriptions. Total University enrollment: 26,800.

Tuition: per hour resident $182, nonresident per hour $364. On-campus housing for 48 married students, 1500 single students. Average academic year housing costs: $4812 (including board). Contact Director, University Housing for both on- and off-campus housing information. Phone: (334)670-3346. Day-care facilities available.

Graduate School

Graduate study since 1958. Enrollment: full-time 3100, part-time 4930. Graduate faculty: full-time 232, part-time 147. Degrees conferred: M.S., M.B.A., Ed.S.

ADMISSION REQUIREMENTS. Transcripts, GRE Subject Tests, GMAT/MAT/NTE required in support of School's application. Online application available. TOEFL required for international applicants. Accepts transfer applicants. Graduates of unaccredited institutions not considered. Apply to Dean of Graduate School at least one month prior to registration. Rolling admissions process. Application fee $50. Phone: (334)670-3178; fax: (334)670-3733.

ADMISSION STANDARDS. Selective. Usual minimum average: 2.5, 3.0 for last two years (A = 4).

FINANCIAL AID. Scholarships, fellowships, internships, Federal W/S, loans. Approved for VA benefits. Apply by May 1 to the Financial Aid Office. Phone: (334)670-3186; fax: (334)670-3702. Use FAFSA. Aid available for part-time students.

DEGREE REQUIREMENTS. For M.S.: 39–48 credit minimum, at least 36 in residence; thesis/nonthesis option; final written exam. For M.B.A.: 33 credits. For Ed.S.: 36 credit minimum beyond the master's.

FIELDS OF STUDY.

COLLEGE OF ARTS AND SCIENCES:
Computer Science. M.S.
Criminal Justice. M.S.
Environmental and Biological Sciences. M.S.
International Relations. M.S.
Public Administration. M.P.A.

SORREL COLLEGE OF BUSINESS:
Business Administration. M.B.A., E.M.B.A.
Human Resource Management. M.S.
Management. M.S.

COLLEGE OF EDUCATION:
Counseling and Psychology. Includes clinical mental health, community counseling, corrections counseling, rehabilitation, counseling, school counseling, school psychometry, social services counseling, student affairs counseling, substance abuse counseling. M.S.
Education. Includes collaborative teacher, early childhood education, elementary education, gifted education, reading specialist, secondary education. M.S.Ed.

COLLEGE OF HEALTH AND HUMAN SERVICES:
Nursing. Includes clinical nurse specialist (adult health, maternal infant health, educator, administrator), nursing informatics, family nurse practitioner. M.S.N.
Sport and Fitness Management. Includes athletic administration, fitness, sport & club management. M.S.

TROY UNIVERSITY AT DOTHAN
Dothan, Alabama 36304-0368
Web site: dothan.troy.edu

Established 1961. Coed. State control. Semester system. Library: 100,000 volumes, 600 subscriptions.
Tuition: per credit, resident $267; nonresident $560. No on-campus housing available.

Graduate School

Enrollment: full- and part-time 394. Graduate faculty: full- and part-time 62. Degrees conferred: M.S., M.B.A., M.S.Ed., Ed.S.

ADMISSION REQUIREMENTS. Transcripts, GRE/GMAT/MAT/NTE required in support of School's application. Online

application available. Class B Alabama certification or equivalent required for some programs. Accepts transfer applicants. Graduates of unaccredited colleges not considered. Apply to Director of Admissions and Records at least one month prior to registration. Rolling admissions process. Application fee $20. Phone: (334) 983-6556, ext. 1230; fax: (334)983-6322.

ADMISSION STANDARDS. Selective. Usual minimum average: 2.5, 3.0 for last two years (A = 4).

FINANCIAL AID. Scholarships, grants, Federal W/S, loans. Approved for VA benefits. Apply by May 1 to the Financial Aid Office. Use FAFSA. Aid available for part-time students.

DEGREE REQUIREMENTS. For M.S., M.S.Ed.: 30 credits minimum, at least 24 in residence; thesis/nonthesis option; final comprehensive written/oral exam. For M.B.A.: 33 credits, at least 30 in residence; final exam. For Ed.S.: 45 credits minimum beyond the master's.

FIELDS OF STUDY.

COLLEGE OF ARTS AND SCIENCES:
International Studies. M.S.

SORREL COLLEGE OF BUSINESS:
Business Administration. Includes accounting, general business. M.B.A.
Human Resource Management. M.S.

COLLEGE OF EDUCATION:
Counseling and Psychology. Includes advanced community counseling, community counseling corrections counseling, abuse counseling. M.S.
Education. Includes early childhood education, elementary education, gifted education, instructional support programs (educational leadership, school counseling, school psychometry), secondary education (biology, English, history, mathematics, comprehensive general science, social science, language arts), special education. M.S.Ed.

TROY UNIVERSITY IN MONTGOMERY
Montgomery, Alabama 36103-4419
Web site: montgomery.troy.edu

Established 1990. Coed. State control. Semester system. Library: 34,800 volumes, 476 subscriptions.
Tuition: per hour, resident $267, nonresident $560. No on-campus housing available.

Graduate School

Enrollment: full-time 131, part-time 316. Graduate faculty: full-time 22, part-time 18. Degrees conferred: M.A., M.S., M.S.M., M.S.P.A., M.B.A., Ed.S.

ADMISSION REQUIREMENTS. Transcripts, GRE/GMAT/MAT required in support of School's application. Online application available. Class B Alabama certification or equivalent required for some programs. Accepts transfer applicants. Graduates of unaccredited colleges not considered. Apply to Dean of Graduate Studies at least one month prior to registration. Rolling admissions process. Application fee $30. Phone: (334)241-9581; fax: (334) 241-9586.

ADMISSION STANDARDS. Selective. Usual minimum average: 2.5, 3.0 for last two years (A = 4).

FINANCIAL AID. Scholarships, grants, Federal W/S, loans. Approved for VA benefits. Apply by May 1 to the Financial Aid Office. Use FAFSA. Aid available for part-time students.

DEGREE REQUIREMENTS. For M.A., M.S., M.S.M., M.S.P.A.: 30 credit hours minimum, at least 24 in residence; candidacy; thesis/nonthesis option; final written exam. For M.B.A.: 33 credit hours; candidacy; research paper; written/oral comprehensive exam. For Ed.S.: 30 credit hours minimum beyond the master's.

FIELDS OF STUDY.
Adult Education. M.S.
Business Administration. M.B.A.
Computer Science. M.S.
Counseling and Psychology. Includes community counseling, rehabilitation counseling, school counseling, social services, school psychometry, substance abuse. M.S.
Elementary Education. M.S.
Human Resource Management. M.S.
Management. Includes applied, public. M.S.
Post Secondary Education. Includes English, history, mathematics, political science, psychology. M.S.

TRUMAN STATE UNIVERSITY
Kirksville, Missouri 63501-4221
Web site: www.truman.edu

Founded 1897. Formerly Northeast Missouri State University, name changed in 1996. CGS member. Located 200 miles NW of St. Louis. Coed. State control. Semester system. Library: 492,900 volumes, 3700 subscriptions. Total University enrollment: 5800.

Annual tuition: full-time, resident $4572, nonresident $7812; per credit, resident $254, nonresident $434. On-campus housing for 30 married students, 48 men, 48 women. Average academic year housing costs: $4850 (including board); off-campus housing $375–$480 per month. Contact Housing Office for both on- and off-campus housing information. Phone: (660)785-4227.

Graduate School

Enrollment: full-time 181, part-time 47. Faculty: full- and part-time 120. Degrees conferred: M.A., M.S., M.Ac., M.A.E.

ADMISSION REQUIREMENTS. Transcripts, GRE/GMAT required in support of application. Online application available. TOEFL required for international applicants. Accepts transfer applicants. Graduates of unaccredited institutions not considered. Apply by June 15 to Dean for Graduate Studies. Application fee, none. Phone: (660)785-4109; fax: (660)785-7460; e-mail: gradinfo @truman.edu.

ADMISSION STANDARDS. Selective. Usual minimum average: 2.75 (A = 4).

FINANCIAL AID. Annual awards from institutional funds: fellowships, scholarships, research assistantships, teaching assistantships, Federal W/S, loans. Approved for VA benefits. Apply to the Dean for Graduate Studies; no specified closing date. Phone: (660)785-4130. Use FAFSA. About 13% of students receive aid other than loans from University and outside sources. Aid available for part-time students.

DEGREE REQUIREMENTS. For master's: 30–48 credits minimum; thesis or capstone project; final oral/written comprehensive exam.

FIELDS OF STUDY.
Accountancy. GMAT for admission.
Biology. GRE for admission.
Communication Disorders. GRE for admission.

Counseling. GRE for admission.
Education. GRE for admission.
English. GRE for admission.
Music.

TUFTS UNIVERSITY
Medford, Massachusetts 02155
Web site: www.tufts.edu

Founded 1852. Located 5 miles NW of Boston. CGS member. Coed. Private control. Semester system. Special facilities: Center for Applied Child Development, Electro-Optics Technology Center, Center for Environmental Management, Lincoln Filene Center for Science and Math Teaching, Science and Technology Center. The University's NIH ranking is 73rd among all U.S. Institutions with 206 awards/grants valued at $80,857,027. According to The Center at University of Florida, the University is ranked 99th in receipt of Federal Research funds with $78,942,000. The University's endowment assets rank it 66th, with a value of $752,426,000. In 2004, 5 of the University's faculty members have been elected to National Honor Academies and this ranks it 90th among all U.S. institutions. The Library: approximately 1,600,000 volumes, 8,000 subscriptions. Total University enrollment: 9800.

Limited on-campus housing for single students; none for married students. Average academic year housing costs: $900 per month. Contact Campus Housing Office for both on- and off-campus housing information. Phone: (617)627-3248. Day-care facilities available.

Graduate School of Arts and Science
Web site: www.tufts.edu/as/gsas/gsashome.hmtl

Graduate study since 1875. Annual tuition: Master's programs: $35,052, $30,704 (M.F.A. Studio Arts), $26,288 (Occupational Therapy), $30,670 (School Psychology), $26,288 (Urban and Environmental Policy and Planning); Doctoral programs: $35,052, $26,888 (Occupational Therapy).

Enrollment: full- and part-time 1289. University faculty teaching graduate courses: full-time 304, part-time 216. Degrees conferred: M.A., M.A.T., M.F.A., M.S., Ph.D.

ADMISSION REQUIREMENTS. Official transcripts, three letters of recommendation, GRE Subject Tests, personal statement required in support of School's application. Online application available. TOEFL (minimum score 550) required for international applicants. Interview sometimes required. Apply to Director of Admission of Graduate School by February 15 (Fall); some departments have other deadlines. Application fee $65. Phone: (617) 627-3395; fax: (617)627-3016.

ADMISSION STANDARDS. Very selective for most departments. Usual minimum average: 3.0 (A = 4).

FINANCIAL AID. Annual awards from institutional funds: scholarships, teaching assistantships, research assistantships, fellowships, internships, Federal W/S, loans. Approved for VA benefits. Apply to the Dean by February 15. Phone: (617)627-3528. Use FAFSA. About 65% of students receive aid other than loans from School and outside sources. Aid available for part-time students.

DEGREE REQUIREMENTS. For master's: 8 courses minimum, at least two terms in residence; thesis/nonthesis option; reading knowledge of one foreign language for some majors; final oral exam. For Ph.D.: 30 courses minimum, at least 10 in residence; qualifying exam; reading knowledge of one or more foreign languages, depending upon department; qualifying exam; dissertation; final written/oral exam.

FIELDS OF STUDY.
Art. M.A.T.
Art History. M.A.
Art History and Museum Studies. M.A.
Biology. M.S., Ph.D.
Chemistry. M.S., Ph.D.
Chemistry/Biotechnology. M.S., Ph.D.
Child Development. M.A., M.A.T., Ph.D.
Classical Archaeology. M.A.
Classics. Includes Latin, Greek. M.A. only.
Drama. Theater arts majors must have practical knowledge of stagecraft; Ph.D. is academic, does not include performance or technical practice. M.A., Ph.D.
Economics. M.A.
Education. Includes elementary, secondary, early childhood. M.A.T., Ph.D.
Engineering Management. M.S.
English. M.A., Ph.D.
Fine Arts. M.F.A.: thesis is creative project with written discussion. M.A., M.F.A.
French. M.A., Ph.D.
German. M.A. study offered at Medford and in Germany. M.A. only.
History. M.A., Ph.D.
History and Museum Studies. M.A.
Interdisciplinary Doctorate. Ph.D.
Mathematics. M.A., M.S., Ph.D.
Mechanical Engineering. M.S., Ph.D.
Museum Education. M.A.
Music. Includes musicology, theory and composition. M.A. only.
Occupational Therapy. M.S., M.A., D.O.T.
Philosophy. M.A. only.
Physics. M.S., Ph.D.
Psychology. M.S., Ph.D.
Public Policy. M.P.P.
School Psychology. M.A., M.S., Ph.D.
Urban and Environmental Policy and Planning. M.A.

School of Dental Medicine
Web site: tufts.edu/dental

Established 1868 as Boston Dental College, incorporated into Tufts University in 1899. Located at Health Science Center in Boston. Semester system. Special program: Dental International Students Program for foreign trained dentist.

Annual tuition: $52,969. On-campus housing available for single students only. Average academic year off-campus housing costs: $14,000. Contact the Student Housing Coordinator for both on- and off-campus housing information. Phone: (617)636-6639. Total average cost for all other first-year expenses: $8,500.

Enrollment: first-year class 150, total 545 (men 53%, women 47%, minorities 41%, state residents 14%). Faculty: full-time 88, part-time 72. Degrees conferred: B.S.-D.M.D. (with Adelphi University), D.M.D., M.S., Certificate.

ADMISSION REQUIREMENTS. AADSAS report, transcripts, three letters of recommendations (one from a biology instructor, one from a chemistry instructor), DAT, interview required in support of School's application. Accepts transfer applicants from foreign dental schools. Apply to Admissions Office after July 1, before March 1. Application fee $60. Phone: (617)636-6639; fax: (617)636-0309.

ADMISSION STANDARDS. Selective. Accepts about 5–10% of all applicants. Usual minimum UGPA: 3.0 (A = 4). Mean DAT: academic 19, PAT 19; mean UGPA 3.41.

FINANCIAL AID. Scholarships, loans. Apply by May 1 to Admissions, Financial Aid and Housing Office after acceptance. Use FAFSA (School code: E00519). About 82% of students receive some aid from School.

DEGREE REQUIREMENTS. For D.M.D.; satisfactory completion of forty-four month program. For M.S.: 40 credit full-time program; thesis.

FIELDS OF POSTGRADUATE STUDY.
Advanced Education in Esthetic Dentistry. Certificate.
Craniomandibular Disorders and Orofacial Pain. Certificate.
Dental Research. M.S.
Endodontics. Certificate.
General Practice Residency.
Implant Dentistry. Certificate.
Oral & Maxillofacial Surgery.
Orthodontics. M.S., Certificate.
Pediatric Dentistry. Certificate.
Periodontology. Certificate.
Prosthodontics and Operative Dentistry. Certificate.

The Fletcher School of Law and Diplomacy
Web site: www.tufts.edu/fletcher

Established 1933. Semester system. Special facilities: William L. Clayton Center for International Economic Affairs, Global Development and Environmental Institute, Edward R. Murrow Center, Hitachi Center for Technology and International Affairs, Center for Human Rights and Conflict Resolution, Institute for Human Security. Programs in International Development, International Environment and Resource Policy, International Information and Communication, International Negotiation and Conflict, Southwest Asia and Islamic Civilization.

Annual tuition: $33,852 (M.A.L.D., M.A., Ph.D.), $38,852 (LL.M.), $39,600 (M.I.D.). Enrollment: full-time 478, part-time 11. Faculty: full-time 35, part-time 31. Degrees conferred: M.A., M.A.L.D., M.I.D., LL.M., Ph.D.; J.D.-M.A.L.D. in conjunction with Harvard Law School and U.C. Berkeley-Boalt Hall Law School; M.B.A.-M.A.L.D. in conjunction with Amos Tuck School of Business Administration, Dartmouth College; M.S.J.-M.A.L.D. in conjunction with Medill School of Journalism, Northwestern University.

ADMISSION REQUIREMENTS. Official transcripts, three letters of reference, GRE or GMAT required in support of School's application. Online application available. Interview recommended. TOEFL required for international applicants. Apply to Director of Admissions of School after September 1, before January 15. Normally admits Fall only. Application fee $65. Phone: (617) 627-2410; fax: (617)627-3712.

ADMISSION STANDARDS. Highly competitive. Usual minimum average: 3.0 (A = 4).

FINANCIAL AID. Scholarships, fellowships, teaching assistantships, internships, grants, Federal W/S, loans. Approved for VA benefits. Apply by January 15 to Director of Admissions of School. Phone: (617)627-3528. Use FAFSA and Fletcher's FAF. About 65% of students receive aid other than loans from School and outside sources.

DEGREE REQUIREMENTS. For M.A.: one year in residence including 8 semester courses; reading and oral competency in one foreign language; final oral exam and application limited to midcareer professionals only. For M.A.L.D., M.I.D.: two years in residence; 16 semester courses, thesis; oral competency in one language; final oral exam. For Ph.D.: two and a half years in residence including 20 semester courses; written and oral comprehensive exam; reading and oral competency in one language; dissertation; final oral exam.

FIELDS OF STUDY.
International Affairs. Includes development economics, human security, international business and economic law, international environment and resource policy, international information and

communication, international monetary theory and policy, international negotiation and conflict resolution, international organizations, international political economy, international security studies, international trade and commercial policies, law and development, pacific Asia, political systems and theories, public international law, southwest Asia and Islamic civilization, United States. M.I.B.

International Business. Includes international finance & banking, international marketing, international public and NGO management, strategic management, & international consultancy. Interdisciplinary. M.I.B.

International Relations. Ph.D.

International Studies. G.M.A.P.

Law and Diplomacy. Includes development economics, human security, international business and economic law, international business relations, international environment and resource policy, international information and communication, international monetary theory and policy, international negotiation and conflict resolution, international organizations, international political economy, international security studies, international trade and commercial policies, law and development, pacific Asia, political systems and theories, public international law, self-designed, southwest Asia and Islamic civilization, United States. M.A.L.D.

School of Medicine
Web site: www.tufts.edu/med

Established 1943. Library: 110,000 volumes, 1400 subscriptions. NIH ranking is 73rd among all U.S. institutions with 206 awards/grants worth $80,857,027.

Annual tuition: $48,034. Off-campus housing available within one block of campus. Total average figure for all other expenses: $15,500.

Enrollment: first-year class 168, total 698 (men 54%, women 46%, minorities 37%, state residents 39%). Faculty: full-time 1346, part-time 1500. Degrees conferred: M.D., M.D.-M.B.A., M.D.-M.P.H., M.D.-Ph.D. (Medical Scientist Training Program).

ADMISSION REQUIREMENTS. AMCAS report, transcripts, recommendations, MCAT, required in suport of application. Interviews by invitation only. Supplemental application required. Applicants must have completed at least three years of college study. Accepts transfer applicants. Has EDP; apply between June 1 and August 1. Apply to Director of Admissions after June 1, before November 1 (firm). Application fee $95. Phone: (617)636-6571.

ADMISSION STANDARDS. Competitive. Accepts about 7% of all applicants. Number of applications 6794 (6204 out-of-state); number interviewed 893 (624 out-of-state); number of acceptance 473 (324 out-of-state); number enrolled 168 (107 out-of-state). Mean Composite MCAT 10.5; mean UGPA 3.61. *U.S. News & World Report* ranking is 47th among all U.S. medical research schools.

FINANCIAL AID. Limited number of scholarships, loans. Apply to the Committee on Financial Aid after acceptance, before May 1. Phone: (617)636-6574. Use FAFSA (School code: E00520). About 33% of students receive some aid from School.

DEGREE REQUIREMENTS. For M.D.: satisfactory completion of four-year program; all students must pass USMLE Step 1 prior to entering the third year and pass USMLE Step 2 prior to the awarding of the M.D.

FIELDS OF GRADUATE STUDY.
Biochemistry.
Cell, Molecular and Developmental Biology.
Cellular and Molecular Physiology.
Genetics.

Health Communication.
Health Management.
Immunology.
Molecular Microbiology.
Neurosciences.
Pain Research, Education and Policy.
Pharmacology and Experimental Therapeutics.
Public Health.

Cummings School of Veterinary Medicine
Web site: www.tufts.edu/vet

Founded 1978. Located in North Grafton (01536). Semester system. Special facilities: Center for Animal and Public Policy, National Center for Botulinum Therapies Research and Development, Tufts Center for Conservation Medicine. Special program; member institution of the Food and Waterborne Diseases Integrated Research network.

Annual tuition: $36,190, Maine and New Hampshire contract residents $24,190. No on-campus housing available. Estimated off-campus living expenses: $11,000- $13,000. Total all other expenses: $7000.

Enrollment: first-year class 80, total 300 (men 11%, women 89%, minorities 5%, state residents 52%). Faculty: full- and part-time 95. Degree conferred: D.V.M., D.V.M.-M.A., D.V.M.-M.P.H., D.V.M.-M.S., D.V.M.-Ph.D.

ADMISSION REQUIREMENTS. Transcripts, GRE, recommendations, personal essay, animal/veterinary experience required in support of application. Interviews by invitation only. Preference given to state residents. School has contractual agreements with Maine (1), New Hampshire (1–2), New Jersey (6). Accepts transfer applicants (apply by June 1 for following September). Graduates of unaccredited colleges not considered. Apply to the School after July 1, before December 1. Application fee $80. Phone: (508)839-7920; fax: (508)839-2953.

ADMISSION STANDARDS. Competitive. Accepts about 5–10% of all applicants. Number of applications 696 (n/a out-of-state); number interviewed n/a (n/a out-of-state); number of acceptance n/a (n/a out-of-state); number enrolled 80 (42 out-of-state). Usual minimum UGPA: 3.0 (A = 4). GRE mean score (V + Q) 1300; mean UGPA 3.58.

FINANCIAL AID. Scholarships, assistantships, Federal W/S, loans available. Apply to Office of Financial Aid by March 15. Phone: (508)839-8733. Use FAFSA.

DEGREE REQUIREMENTS. For D.V.M.: satisfactory completion of four-year program. For M.P.H., M.S., Ph.D.: see Graduate College listing above.

FIELDS OF GRADUATE STUDY.
Animals and Public Policy. D.V.M.-M.S. (with Tufts Center for Animals and Public Policy).
Applied Biotechnology. D.V.M.-M.S. (with Worcester Polytechnic Institute).
Basic Medical Sciences. D.V.M.-Ph.D. (with University of Massachusetts Medical Center). Includes concentrations biochemistry, cell biology, immunology and virology, molecular genetics and microbiology, pharmacology, physiology.
Biomedical Sciences. D.V.M.-Ph.D. (with Tufts University Sackler School of Graduate Biomedical Sciences.
Comparative Biomedical Sciences. A training program in Infectious Diseases with specialties in Cryptosporidiosis, Microsporidiosis, *E. Coli* Disease, Molecular Helminthology, Tick borne diseases and Tularemia, enteric Viruses, Staphylococcal Infectious and Enterotoxins. D.V.M.-M.S., Ph.D.
International Policy-Making. D.V.M.-M.A. (with Fletcher School of Law and Diplomacy).
Laboratory Animal Medicine. D.V.M.-M.S.

Public Health. D.V.M.-M.P.H. (with Tufts University School of Medicine).

TULANE UNIVERSITY
New Orleans, Louisiana 70118-5669
Web site: www.tulane.edu

Founded 1834. CGS and AAU member, Coed. Private control. Semester system. Special facilities: Amistad Research Center, Center for Archaeology, Newcomb College Center for Research on Women, Center for Bioenvironmental Research, Roger Thayer Stone Center for Latin American Studies, Southeastern Architectural Archives, William Ranson Hogan Jazz Archives, Delta Regional Primate Research Center, Lindy Boggs Center for Energy and Biotechnology, Murphy Institute of Political Economy, Middle American Research Institute, Southern Center of the National Institute for Global Environmental Change, Tulane Research and Teaching Center, U.S.-Japan Cooperative Biomedical Research Laboratories. The University's NIH ranking is 79th among all U.S. institutions with 123 awards/grants valued at $73,392,850. According to The Center at University of Florida, the University is ranked 95th in receipt of Federal Research funds with $82,118,000. The University's endowment assets rank it 70th, with a value of $692,665,000. In 2004, three of the University's faculty members have been elected to National Honor Academies and this ranks it 105th among all U.S. institutions. The Library: approximately 2,300,000 volumes, 15,000 subscriptions. Total University enrollment: 9700.

Annual tuition: full-time $33,500, per credit $1861. Limited on-campus housing available. Average academic year housing costs: $10,600 for married students, $8500 (including board) for single students. Apply to Housing Office. Phone: (504)865-5724.

School of Liberal Arts

Graduate study since 1883. Enrollment: full-time 875, part-time 51. Graduate faculty: full-time 350. Degrees conferred: M.A., M.F.A., M.L.A., Ph.D.

ADMISSION REQUIREMENTS. Official transcripts of all undergraduate and graduate work, three recommendation forms, statement of career objective, GRE required in support of application. GRE Subject for some departments. TSE (minimum score 220) required for international applicants, if not available in applicant's area submit TOEFL (minimum score 600). Application deadlines: July 1 (Fall), December 1 (Spring) May 1 (Summer). Application fee $45. Phone: (504)865-5100; fax: (504)865-5274.

ADMISSION STANDARDS: Competitive for most departments and selective for all others. Usual minimum average: 2.75 to 3.0 (A = 4).

FINANCIAL AID. Fellowships, teaching/research assistantships, scholarships, internships, tuition waivers, Federal W/S, loans. Approved for VA benefits. Apply by February 1 (Fall semester) to Office of Financial Aid. Phone: (504)865-5723. Use FAFSA (School code: 002029).

DEGREE REQUIREMENTS. For M.A.: 24 semester hours plus thesis, 30 hours without thesis; reading knowledge of one foreign language for some programs; final written/oral exam. For M.F.A.: 30 hours minimum; creative project or recital; final essay. For Ph.D.: 48 hours minimum; reading knowledge of two foreign languages; preliminary or general exam; dissertation; final oral exam.

FIELDS OF STUDY.
Anthropology. M.A., Ph.D.
Art History. M.A.
Art Studio. M.F.A.

Classical Studies. M.A.
Economics. Include policy economics. M.A.
English. M.A.
French and Italian. M.A.
History. M.A., Ph.D.
Interdisciplinary. Ph.D.
Latin American Studies. M.A., Ph.D.
Latin American Studies and Art History. Ph.D.
Music. Includes musicology, composition, performance (Ph.D.). M.A., Ph.D.
Philosophy. M.A., Ph.D.
Political Science.
Sociology. Includes applied sociology. M.A.
Spanish and Portuguese. M.A., Ph.D.
Theatre. Includes design, technical production. M.F.A.

A. B. Freeman School of Business
Web site: www.freeman.tulane.edu

Established 1914. Private control. Accredited programs: M.B.A., Accounting; recognized Ph.D. Graduate study since 1940. E.M.B.A. offered in Taiwan, Mexico, and Chile. Semester system. Special facilities: Burkenroad Institute, Goldring Institute, Levy-Rosenblum Institute for Entrepreneurship, Management Communication Center. Special programs: foreign exchange programs (in Argentina, Austria, Brazil, Chile, Columbia, Czech Republic, Ecuador, Finland, France, Germany, Hong Kong, Hungary, Mexico, People's Republic of China, Spain, Taiwan, United Kingdom), internships. Library: 35,000 volumes, 28,744 microforms, 910 current periodicals/subscriptions.

Annual tuition: full-time $37,470; per credit $1175. Enrollment: total full-time 151, part-time 164 (men 60%, women 40%). Faculty: 60 full-time, 16 part-time; 98% with Ph.D./D.B.A. Degrees conferred: M.B.A. (full-time, part-time, day and evening), E.M.B.A. (alternate weekends), Prof. M.B.A., M.Acc., M.Fin., M.B.A.-J.D., M.B.A.-M.A. (Latin American Studies), M.B.A.-M.P.H., Ph.D.

ADMISSION REQUIREMENTS. Official transcripts, two recommendations, GMAT, personal essay, résumé of professional experience required in support of School's application. Online application available. TOEFL required for international applicants. Evaluative interviews required for all applicants living in the U.S. or Canada. Must have baccalaureate degree from an accredited institution. Apply for Fall admission to the Director of Admissions; applications calendar: first submissions date November 2, second submissions date January 2, third submission date March 3, fourth submission date May 2. Application fee $40 (domestic), $50 (international). Phone: (504)865-5410 or (800)223-5402; fax: (504)865-6770; e-mail: freeman.admissions@tulane.edu. Doctoral programs: (504)865-5495.

ADMISSION STANDARDS. Competitive. Usual minimum average 3.2 (A = 4); average GMAT 610. *U.S. News & World Report* ranking is in the top 45 of all U.S. business schools.

FINANCIAL AID. Fellowships, research assistantships, administrative assistantships, teaching assistantships, internships, tuition waivers, Federal W/S, loans. Approved for VA benefits. Apply by April 15 to Office of Financial Aid. Phone: (504)865-5273; fax: (504)862-8750. FAFSA (School code: 002029) required for Federal W/S, loans. Phone fellowships are merit based and are awarded to approximately half of the entering class. Research/administrative/teaching assistantships are arranged through faculty and staff. Aid available for part-time students.

DEGREE REQUIREMENTS. For M.B.A.: 63-credit (including 30 elective credits), two-year program; degree program must be completed in seven years. For E.M.B.A.: 49-credit, 19-month program. Professional M.B.A.: 55-credit, three- to seven-year program. For M.Acc.: 30-credit program. For M.Fin: 37-credit, 12-month full-time program. For M.B.A.-M.A.: 75-credit program. For

M.B.A.-M.P.H.: 93-credit program. For M.B.A.-J.D.: 130-credit program.

FIELDS OF STUDY.
Accounting. M.Acc.
Business Administration. Includes concentrations in accounting, finance, international management, management, management information systems, marketing, operations management, organizational behavior, strategic planning (MBA); accounting, finance, organizational behavior (Ph.D.). M.B.A., E.M.B.A., Ph.D.
Finance. M.Fin.
Global M.B.A. Offered in conjunction with three Latin American universities.

School of Science and Engineering— Graduate Division

Founded 1894. Special facilities: Center for Bioenvironmental Research, National Institute for Global Environmental Change, U.S.-China Energy and Environmental Technology Center, Livingston Digital Millennium Center for Computational Science, Center for Ballistic Missile Defense, Tulane Institute for Macromolecular Science and Engineering.

Annual tuition: $35,100. Enrollment: full-time 144, part-time 16. Faculty: full-time 50, part-time 7. Degrees conferred: M.Eng., M.S.E., Ph.D., Sc.D.

ADMISSION REQUIREMENTS. Official transcripts, GRE, three letters of recommendation required in support of School's application. Online application available. Interview sometimes required. TOEFL required for international applicants. Accepts transfer applicants. Graduates of unaccredited institutions not considered. Apply by August 15 (Fall), January 1 (Spring) to Graduate Division, School of Engineering. Application fee $25. Phone: (504) 865-5764; fax (504)862-8747; e-mail: gradengr@tulane.edu.

ADMISSION STANDARDS. Competitive. Usual minimum average: 3.0 (A = 4).

FINANCIAL AID. Scholarships, fellowships, research assistantships, teaching assistantship, Federal W/S, loans. Apply by February 1 to Graduate Division. Use FAFSA (School code: 002029).

DEGREE REQUIREMENTS. For M.Eng.: 30-credit program; no thesis. For M.S.E.: 24-credit program plus thesis. For Ph.D., Sc.D.: 48-credit programs, at least one year in full-time residence; qualifying exam; admission to candidacy; dissertation; written/oral exams.

FIELDS OF STUDY.
Biomedical Engineering.
Biology. Includes cell and molecular biology, ecology and evolutionary biology.
Chemical and Biomolecular Engineering.
Chemistry.
Earth and Environmental Sciences.
Interdisciplinary. Ph.D.
Mathematics.
Neuroscience.
Physics.
Psychology.
Statistics. M.S. only.

Law School (70118-6231)

Web site: www.law.tulane.edu

Established 1847. Twelfth oldest U.S. law school. ABA approved since 1925. AALS member. Semester system. Full-time, day study only. Special facilities: Maritime Law Center, Eason Weinmann Center for Comparative Law, Institute for Environmental Law. Special programs: summer study abroad at McGill University, Canada; Trinity College Cambridge, England; Tulane Institute of European Legal Studies, Paris, France; Hebrew University, Israel; University of Siena, Italy; Tulane Center for European Union Law, Amsterdam, the Netherlands. Law library: 512,117 volumes, 4932 subscriptions; has LEXIS, NEXIS, WESTLAW, DIALOG, EELS, ORBIT, QUICKLAW, VU/TEXT; is a Federal Government Depository.

Annual tuition: $34,696. On-campus housing available for both single and married students. Total annual on-campus housing cost: $17,300.

Enrollment: first-year class 300; total full-time 768 (men 56%, women 44%. minorities 16%). Faculty: full-time 46, part-time 30. Student to faculty ratio 17.2 to 1. Degrees conferred: J.D., J.D.-M.B.A., J.D.-M.H.A., J.D.-M.P.H., J.D.-M.S.P.H., LL.M. (General, Admiralty, American Business Law, Energy and Environmental Law, International and Comparative Law; for persons who have completed a basic legal education and received a university degree in law in another country), LL.M.-M.A. (Latin American Studies, International Affairs), S.J.D.

ADMISSION REQUIREMENTS. LSDAS Law School report, bachelor's degree, transcripts, LSAT, personal statement required in support of application. Letters of recommendation are optional. Interview not required. Accepts transfer applicants. Graduates of unaccredited colleges not considered. Apply to Admissions Office after October 1, before March 15 (February 1 strongly recommended). Rolling admissions process. Application fee $60. Phone: (504)865-5930.

ADMISSION STANDARDS. Selective. Accepts approximately 26% of all students. Number of applicants 4126; number of acceptance 1055; number enrolled 300; LSAT (75% of students have a score at or above 158); GPA (75% of students have a GPA at or above 3.28). *U.S. News & World Report* ranking is in the top 47 of all U.S. law schools.

FINANCIAL AID. Scholarships, fellowships, Federal W/S, loans. Apply to Director of Financial Aid by February 15; preliminary Financial Aid form due with admissions application. Phone: (504) 865-5931. Use FAFSA (School code: 002029). About 70% of students receive aid other than loans from School.

DEGREE REQUIREMENTS. For J.D.: 6 semesters minimum, at least 2 in full-time residence; 88 semester credits; 30-hour pro bono community service obligation. For LL.M.: 24 hours minimum beyond the J.D.; one year in full-time residence; thesis; final written exam. For S.J.D.: usually at least two years in full-time resident beyond the J.D.; dissertation; final written exam.

School of Medicine (70112-2699)

Web site: www.som.tulane.edu

Founded 1834 as the Medical College of Louisiana, became Medical Department of the University of Louisiana in 1945. Name changed to Tulane in 1884. Special facilities: Center for Gene Therapy, Center for Infectious Diseases, General Clinical Research Center, Hayward Genetics Center, Hypertension and Renal Center, Tulane Center for Clinical Effectiveness and Prevention, Center for Bioenvironmental Research at Tulane and Xavier Universities. Library: 150,000 volumes, 1200 subscriptions. NIH ranking is 79th among all U.S. institutions with 123 awards/grants worth $73,392,850.

Annual tuition: $42,666. On-campus housing available for both single and married students. Total average figure for all other expenses: $13,500.

Enrollment: first-year class 155, total 623 (men 56%, women 44%, minorities 13%, state residents 44%). Faculty: full-time 800, part-time 200. Degrees conferred: M.D., M.D.-M.P.H., M.D.-M.S., M.D.-Ph.D. (Medical Scientist Training Program).

ADMISSION REQUIREMENTS. AMCAS report, transcripts, recommendations, MCAT required in suport of application. Interview by invitation only. Secondary application required. Applicants must have completed at least three years of college study. Accepts transfer applicants. Has EDP; apply between June 1 and August 1. Apply to Chair of the Committee on Admissions after June 1, before December 1. Application fee $95. Phone: (504) 588-5331.

ADMISSION STANDARDS. Competitive. Accepts about 5% of all applicants. Number of applications 6602 (n/a out-of-state); number interviewed 808 (n/a out-of-state); number of acceptance n/a (n/a out-of-state); number enrolled 155 (n/a out-of-state). Mean Composite MCAT 10.3; mean UGPA 3.47.

FINANCIAL AID. Scholarships, Federal and private loans. Apply to the Chair, Financial Aid Committee, by April 1. Phone: (504) 988-6135. Use FAFSA (School code: 002029). About 90% of students receive some aid from School.

DEGREE REQUIREMENTS. For M.D.: satisfacotry completion of four-year program; must take Step 1 of USMLE and record a score. For M.S., M.P.H., Ph.D.: see Graduate Schools listings above.

FIELDS OF GRADUATE STUDY.
Biochemistry.
Human Genetics.
Microbiology and Immunology.
Molecular and Cellular Biology.
Neuroscience.
Pharmacology.
Physiology.
Structural and Cellular Biology.

School of Public Health and Tropical Medicine (70112-2824)

Founded 1912. Special facilities: Center for Applied Environmental Public Health, Center for Bioenvironmental Research, Center for Infectious Diseases, Environmental Diseases Prevention Research Center, International Communication Enhancement Center, South Center for Public Health Preparedness, South Center Public Health Leadership Institute, South Center Public Health Training Center, Tulane/Xavier Center of Excellence in Women's Health.

Tuition: per credit hour $832. Enrollment: full-time 630, part-time 370 (men 45%, women 55%). Faculty: full-and part-time 101. Degrees conferred: M.P.H., M.S.P.H., M.H.A., M.S.W.-M.P.H., M.A.-M.P.H., M.P.H. & T.M., Dr.P.H., Sc.D., M.D.-M.P.H., M.D.-M.P.H. & T.M., M.D.-M.S.P.H., J.D.-M.P.H. The Ph.D. is offered through the Graduate School.

ADMISSION REQUIREMENTS. Transcripts, three recommendations, GRE/MCAT required in support of School's application. Online application available. TOEFL required for international applicants. Interview may be required. Accepts transfer applicants. Apply to the Office of Admissions and Students Affairs by April 15 (Fall), October 15 (Spring), March 15 (Summer). Admits both semesters. Application fee $40. Phone: (800)676-5389, (504)988-5388.

ADMISSION STANDARDS. Very selective. Usual minimum average: 3.0 (A = 4).

FINANCIAL AID. Annual awards from institutional funds: scholarships, research fellowships, research assistantships, Federal W/S. loans. Traineeships available to U.S. citizens. Approved for VA benefits. Apply, preferably by February 1, to Director of the School for scholarships, fellowships, assistantships; to Admission Office for all other programs. Phone: (504)588-5387. Use FAFSA (School code: 002029). About 75% of students receive aid other than loans from School and outside sources.

DEGREE REQUIREMENTS. For M.P.H., M.S.P.H., M.H.A.; 36–45 credit hours minimum, at least one year in residence; capstone experience. For M.P.H. & T.M.: essentially same as for M.P.H., except candidates must hold the M.D. or equivalent. For Dr.P.H., Sc.D.: at least one and up to three years in full-time residence (minimum of 72 credits), depending upon previous preparation and accomplishment; comprehensive exam; dissertation; final oral exam.

FIELDS OF STUDY.
Applied Development.
Biostatistics.
Community Health Sciences.
Environmental Health Education.
Environmental Health Sciences. Includes industrial hygiene, environmental health for developing countries, environmental policy, general technical track (midcareer), industrial hygiene (midcareer), natural resource management, sustainable/toxic and waste management, toxicology and risk assessment, water and sustainable resource management, water quality management.
Epidemiology.
Health Administration.
Health Education and Communication.
Health Systems Management.
International Health and Development.
International Health Systems Management.
Maternal and Child Health.
Medical Management.
Nutrition.
Parasitology.
Public Health. Includes environmental health (midcareer), occupational health, occupational health and safety management (midcareer).
Tropical Medicine.

School of Social Work

Founded 1927. Graduate study only. Special facilities: Center for Lifelong Learning, Porter-Cason Institute for the Advancement of Family Practice, Tulane Center on Aging Research, Education, and Services, Elizabeth Wisner Social Welfare Center for Families and Children.

Tuition: per credit $832. Enrollment: full-time 158, part-time 50. Faculty: full-time 19, part-time 37; clinical instructors 100. Degrees conferred: M.S.W., Ph.D., M.S.W.-M.P.H.

ADMISSION REQUIREMENTS. Official transcripts, two academic references and one current or most recent work reference, autobiographical statement or personal essay required in support of School's application. GRE required for Ph.D program. Online application available. Interview sometimes required. TOEFL required for international applicants. Accepts transfer applicants. Graduates of unaccredited institutions not considered. Apply by March 31 (Fall full-time program), November 15 (Spring part-time program) to Assistant Dean for Admissions and Student Affairs. Application fee $40. Phone: (504)865-5314; fax (504)862-8727.

ADMISSION STANDARDS. Competitive. Usual minimum average: 3.0 (A = 4).

FINANCIAL AID. Merit and need-based scholarships, fellowships, grants, teaching assistantships, Federal W/S, loans. Apply by March 31 to office of Student Affairs of the School. Phone: (504)865-5723. Use FAFSA (School code: (002029).

DEGREE REQUIREMENTS. For M.S.W.: 60 semester hours minimum, at least 30 in full-time residence (accelerated program available); no language or thesis requirement. For Ph.D.: a minimum of 16 courses (49 credits); qualifying exam; at least one year in full-time residence; dissertation; written/oral exams. For M.S.W.-M.P.H.: M.S.W. awarded after four semesters, M.P.H. after fifth semester.

THE UNIVERSITY OF TULSA
Tulsa, Oklahoma 74104-3126
Web site: www.utulsa.edu

Founded 1894. CGS member. Coed. Private control. Special facilities: Enterprise Development Center, Venture Capital Exchange, anthropological research sites. Library: approximately 940,105 volumes, 8000 subscriptions; special authors collection, U.S. Civil War collection, and American Indian Law Collection. Total University enrollment: 4000.

Annual tuition: full-time $12,132, per credit hour $674. On-campus housing for 632 women, 632 men, 200 married students. Average academic year housing cost: $6868 (including board). Contact Director of University Housing for both on- and off-campus housing information. Phone: (918)631-5249. Day-care facilities available.

Graduate School

Established 1933. Enrollment: full-time 450, part-time 220. Faculty: full-time 178, part-time 51. Degrees conferred: M.A., M.S., M.B.A., M.Acc., M.Tax., M.Eng., M.Engineering and Technology Management, M.S.M.S.E., M.S.Eng., M.M.E., M.M., M.T.A., M.F.A., M.N.A., Ph.D., M.N.A.-M.B.A., J.D.-M.S. (Biological Sciences, Geosciences), J.D.-M.A. (Anthropology, Clinical Psychology, English Language and Literature, History, Industrial/Organizational Psychology), J.D.-M.B.A.

ADMISSION REQUIREMENTS. Official transcripts, three letters of recommendation, GRE/GMAT required in support of School's application. Online application available. Evidence of English proficiency and TOEFL required for international students. Interview not required. Transfer students accepted. Graduates of unaccredited institutions not considered. Apply to Graduate School at least one month prior to enrollment. Application fee $30. Phone: (800)882-4723 or (918)631-2336; fax: (918)631-2156; e-mail: grad@utulsa.edu.

ADMISSIONS STANDARDS. Selective. Usual minimum average: 3.0 (A = 4).

FINANCIAL AID. Scholarships, fellowships, teaching assistantships, research assistantships, internships, tuition waivers, Federal W/S, loans. Approved for VA benefits. Apply by February 1 for Fall term. Phone: (918)631-2526; fax: (918)631-2073. Use FAFSA. About 63% of graduate students receive aid other than loans from both the University and outside sources. Aid available for part-time students.

DEGREE REQUIREMENTS. For master's: 30 semester hours minimum, at least 24 in residence; thesis/nonthesis option; final oral exam in some departments. For Ph.D.: 60 semester hours minimum beyond the master's; one foreign language and/or computer language may be required; candidacy exam; qualifying exam; dissertation; comprehensive written/oral exam.

FIELDS OF STUDY.
Accounting. M.Acc.
Acounting and Information Systems. M.A.I.S.
Anthropology. M.A.
Art. M.F.A., M.T.A.
Biological Science. Includes environmental science, genetics, organismic biology. M.S., Ph.D.
Business Administration. GMAT for admission. M.B.A.
Chemical Engineering. M.S. in Engineering, M. of Engineering, Ph.D.
Chemistry. M.S.
Clinical Psychology. M.A., Ph.D.
Computer Science. M.S., Ph.D.
Education. Includes elementary, secondary, school counseling. M.A., M.S.M.S.E., M.T.A.

Electrical Engineering. M.S. in Engineering, M. of Engineering.
Engineering and Technology Management. In cooperation with College of Business Administration. M. of Engineering and Technology Management.
English Language and Literature. Includes rhetoric and writing, writing in the professions, and research in and analysis of literature. M.A., Ph.D.
Finance. M.S.
Fine Arts. M.F.A.
Geosciences. Includes geochemistry, geology, geophysics. M.S., Ph.D.
History. M.A.
Industrial/Organizational Psychology. M.A., Ph.D.
Information Systems. M.S.
Mathematics. M.S.
Math/Science Education. M.S.
Mechanical Engineering. M.S. in Engineering, M.Eng., Ph.D.
Music. Includes composition, applied music. M.M., M.M.E.
Nursing. M.N.A.
Petroleum Engineering. M.Eng., M.S. in Engineering, Ph.D.
Speech/Language Pathology. M.S.
Taxation. M.S.Tax.

College of Law
Web site: www.law.utulsa.edu

Established 1923. ABA approved since 1950. AALS member. Semester system. Full-time, part-time study. Special facilities: National Energy-Environment Law and Policy Institute, Native American Law Center, International and Comparative Law Center. Special programs: study abroad in Dublin, Ireland; London, England; Geneva, Switzerland; Buenos Aires, Argentina. Law library: 285,167 volumes, 3293 subscriptions; has LEXIS, NEXIS, WESTLAW, DIALOG, LEGALTRAC; has more that 400 network connections.

Annual tuition: full-time $25,264, part-time $17,688. On-campus housing available for both single and married students. Total average annual additional expense: $12,606. Law students tend to live off-campus. Contact Director of Housing for both on- and off-campus housing information. Phone: (918)631-2378.

Enrollment: first-year class full-time 188, part-time 20; total full- and part-time 540 (men 66%, women 34%, minorities 11%). Faculty: full-time 31, part-time 28. Student to faculty ratio is 16.3 to 1. Degree conferred: J.D., J.D.-M.Acc., JU.D.-M.A. (Anthropology, Clinical Psychology, English, History, Industrial and Organizational Psychology), J.D.-M.B.A., J.D.-M.S. (Biological Science, Geosciences), J.D.-M.S.Tax., LL.M. (American Law for foreign graduates; American Indian and Indigenous Law).

ADMISSION REQUIREMENTS. LSDAS Law School report, Bachelor's degree, LSAT required in support of application. Interview not required. Accepts transfer applicants in good standing from accredited law schools. Graduates of unaccredited colleges not considered. Apply to Admissions Office after September 1, before May 15 (flexible). Application fee $30. Phone: (918)631-2709; fax: (918)631-3630.

ADMISSION STANDARDS. Selective. Accepts approximately 34% of full-time, 29% of part-time students. Number of full-time applicants 1486, part-time 110; number of full-time acceptance 509, part-time 32; number of full-time enrolled 188, part-time 20; LSAT (75% of full-time students have a score at or above 150, part-time 150); GPA (75% of full-time students have a GPA at or above 2.80, part-time 3.10). *U.S. News & World Report* ranking is in the fourth tier of all U.S. law schools.

FINANCIAL AID. Scholarships mainly for advanced students, Federal W/S, loans. Apply to Office of Dean by February 1 (flexible). Phone: (918)631-2526. Use FAFSA (School code: 003185). About 34% of full-time and 33% of part-time students receive aid other than loans from College and outside sources.

DEGREE REQUIREMENTS. For J.D.: 88 credit hours minimum, at least the last 30 in residence. For LL.M.: 24 credit full-time program. For master's degree: see Graduate School listing above.

TUSKEGEE UNIVERSITY
Tuskegee, Alabama 36088
Web site: www.tuskegee.edu

Founded 1881. Located 38 miles E of Montgomery. Coed. Private and state-related control. Semester system. Special facilities: George Washington Carver Research Foundation. Library: 623,000 volumes, 3157 subscriptions. Total University enrollment: 2900.

Annual tuition: full-time resident $12,400. On-campus housing for 48 married students, 150 men, 150 women. Average academic year housing costs: $5200–$6400 for married students, $3280–$7887 (including board) for single students. Apply to Manager of Auxiliary Enterprises by May 1. Phone: (334)727-8915. Day-care facilities available.

Graduate Programs

Graduate study since 1944. Enrollment: full-time 95, part-time 39. University faculty teaching graduate students: full-time 20, part-time 5. Degrees conferred: M.Ed., M.S., M.S.E.E., M.S.M.E., M.S.N.E., Ph.D.

ADMISSION REQUIREMENTS. Official transcripts, GRE required in support of application. TOEFL required for international applicants. Interview not required. Accepts transfer applicants. Apply to Admissions Office by July 15 (Fall), November 15 (Spring), April 15 (Summer). Application fee $25, $35 for international applicants. Phone: (334)727-8580; fax: (334)727-5750.

ADMISSION STANDARDS. Selective. Usual minimum average: 2.7 (A = 4).

FINANCIAL AID. Annual awards from institutional funds: research assistantships, teaching assistantships, graduate assistantships, internships, Federal W/S, loans. Approved for VA benefits. Apply by April 15 to appropriate department chair for assistantships; to Financial Aid Office for all other programs. Use FAFSA. About 35% of students receive aid other than loans from University and outside sources. Aid available for part-time students.

DEGREE REQUIREMENTS. For master's: 30–36 semester hours; thesis/nonthesis option; final oral/written exam. For Ph.D.: three-year, full-time program; qualifying exam; research proposal; dissertation; oral exam.

FIELDS OF STUDY.
Agricultural and Resource Economics.
Animal and Poultry Science.
Biology.
Chemistry.
Counseling and Student Development.
Electrical Engineering.
Environmental Sciences.
Food and Nutritional Science. Includes food science, nutritional science.
Forest Resources. Three plus two program.
General Science Education.
Integrative Biosciences. Ph.D. only.
Materials Science and Engineering. Ph.D. only.
Mechanical Engineering.
Plant and Soil Science.

College of Veterinary Medicine, Nursing and Allied Health
Web site: www.tuskegee.edu/cvmnah

Established 1945. Semester system. Special facilities: Center for Computational Epidemiology, Bioinformatics & Risk Analysis, Center for Excellence in Veterinary Education, Center for Integrated Study of Food Animal & Plant Systems, International Center for Tropical Animal Health, Center for the Study of Human-Animal Interdependent Relationships. Veterinary library: 31,098 volumes, 400 subscriptions.

Annual tuition: $13,520. Both on- and off-campus housing available. Estimated living expenses: $6000–$9000. Total all other expenses: $5000.

Enrollment: first-year class 60, total 244 (men 35%, women 65%, minorities 100%, state residents 25%). Faculty: full- and part-time 60. Degree conferred: D.V.M., D.V.M.-M.S., D.V.M.-Ph.D.

ADMISSION REQUIREMENTS. Transcripts, VCAT/MCAT/GRE, recommendations, animal/veterinary experience required in support of application. Interview by invitation only. Applicants must have completed at least two years of college study. Preference given to state and contract state residents (Kentucky; New Jersey, South Carolina, West Virginia). Apply to Dean of School by first Monday in December. Graduate study: Bachelor's degree, transcripts required in support of application. Apply to Dean of School after July 1, before first Monday in December. Rolling admission process. Application fee $25, $35 for international applicants. Phone: (334)727-8174; fax: (334)727-8177.

ADMISSION STANDARDS. Selective. Accepts about 20–25% of all applicants. Usual minimum UGPA: 2.70 (A = 4). GRE mean score (V + Q) 1500; mean UGPA 3.42.

FINANCIAL AID. For information and forms write to the University's Director of Financial Aid. Apply by April 15. Use FAFSA.

DEGREE REQUIREMENTS. For D.V.M.: satisfactory completion of four-year program. Students in combined programs take graduate course during summer only. For M.S., Ph.D. requirements: see Graduate School listing above.

FIELDS OF GRADUATE STUDY.
Integrative Biosciences. Ph.D. only.
Tropical Animal Health. M.S.
Veterinary Science. M.S.

UNIFORMED SERVICES UNIVERSITY OF THE HEALTH SCIENCES
4301 Jones Bridge Road
Bethesda, Maryland 20814-4799
Web site: www.usuhs.mil

Founded 1972. Located on the grounds of the Naval Medical Center, Bethesda. Federal control. Semester system. Special affiliations: Armed Forces Institute of Pathology, National Library of Medicine, National Institutes of Health, U.S. Armed Forces Radiobiology Research Institute, Walter Reed Army Institute of Research.

The University's Schools include the Graduate School of Nursing, School of Medicine, and Graduate programs in Biomedical Sciences and Public Health. Total University enrollment at main campus: 757.

F. Edward Hebert School of Medicine
Room A-10411

Admitted charter class 1976. The academic year is 48 weeks. Special programs: 20% of clinical experience may be taken in other areas of the world. Library: 75,000 volumes, 1500 current periodical/subscriptions.

Annual tuition: none. No on-campus housing available. Annual living expenses are expected to be covered by the student's annual salary.

Enrollment: first-year class 169; total full-time 673 (men 70%, women 30%, minorities 22%, state residents 6%). Faculty: full-time 269, part-time 1837. Degree conferred: M.D.

ADMISSION REQUIREMENTS. Preference given to both military and civilian U.S. citizens between the ages of 18 and 30. All military applicant must submit a "Letter of Approval" to apply. Bachelor's degree from an accredited institution required. All applicants have bachelor's degree awarded prior to enrollment. Does not have EDP. Does not accept transfer applicants. Apply through AMCAS (file after June 1, before November 1), submit MCAT (will accept MCAT test results from the last three years); official transcripts for each school attended (should show at least 90 semester credits/135 quarter credit; submit transcripts by mid-May to AMCAS). Service processing fee: none, nor a supplementary application fee. Submit a supplemental application, a photograph, a personal statement, preprofessional committee evaluation and three recommendations from science faculty to Office of Admission within two to three weeks of receipt of supplemental materials. Phone: (800)772-1743, (301)295-3101; fax: (301)295-3545; e-mail: admissions@usuhs.mil. Interviews are by invitation only and generally for final selection. First-year students admitted Fall only. Rolling admissions process; notification starts November 1 and is finished when class is filled. Applicant's response to offer due within two weeks of receipt of acceptance letter. Prior to enrollment a student can expect to have a background check performed and will have to pass a medical examination.

ADMISSION STANDARDS. Selective. Accepts about 16% of all applicants. Number of applications 1725 (n/a out-of-state); number interviewed 498 (n/a out-of-state); number of acceptance 263 (n/a out-of-state); number enrolled 169 (n/a out-of-state). Mean Composite MCAT 9.8; mean UGPA 3.54.

FINANCIAL AID. Upon matriculation the student becomes an active reserve officer in one of the military service branches and receives a full salary, free health benefits for the student and his or her family, a housing allowance, commissary privileges, and 30 days' paid leave.

DEGREE REQUIREMENTS. For M.D.: satisfactory completion of four-year program. All students must pass USMLE Step 1 prior to entering third year and must pass USMLE Step 2 prior to awarding of M.D. Upon graduation there is a military commitment of not less than seven years on active duty and six years of inactive ready reserve. For M.D.-Ph.D.: generally a seven to eight year program.

FIELDS OF GRADUATE STUDY.
Applied Human Biology (Undersea Medicine). Ph.D.
Clinical Psychology. Ph.D.
Emerging Infectious Diseases. Interdisciplinary. Ph.D.
Environmental Health Sciences. Ph.D.
Medical Psychology. Ph.D.
Medical Zoology. Ph.D.
Molecular and Cellular Biology. Interdisciplinary. Ph.D.
Neuroscience. Interdisciplinary. Ph.D.
Pathology. Ph.D.

UNION COLLEGE
Barbourville, Kentucky 40906-1499
Web site: www.unionky.edu

Founded 1879. Located 100 miles S of Lexington. Coed. Private control. Methodist affiliation. Semester system. Library: 120,000 volumes, 2450 subscriptions.

Tuition: per hour $285. Limited on-campus housing for 30 married students, 50 men, 50 women. Average academic year housing costs: $3300 (including board) for single students. Contact Dean of Students. Phone: (606)546-1230.

Graduate School

Enrollment: full-time 5, part-time 250. Graduate faculty: full-time 6, part-time 18. Degree conferred: M.A. in Ed.

ADMISSION REQUIREMENTS. Two official transcripts, GRE/PRAXIS II, two letters of recommendation, teaching certificates required in support of School's application. Online application available. TOEFL required for international applicants. Interview desirable. Accepts transfer applicants. Graduates of unaccredited institutions not considered. Apply to Dean of the Graduate School by August 15 (Fall), December 15 (Spring). Application fee $25. Phone: (606)546-1210; fax: (606)546-1792.

ADMISSION STANDARDS. Selective. Usual minimum average: 2.5 (A = 4).

FINANCIAL AID. Limited to loans. Approved for VA benefits. Apply to Financial Aid Office. Phone: (606)546-1224; fax: (606)546-1217. Use FAFSA.

DEGREE REQUIREMENTS. For M.A. in Ed.: 30 semester hours minimum, at least 24 in residence and one semester or Summer session in full-time attendance; thesis optional for 6 hours; final written exam.

FIELDS OF STUDY.
Elementary Education. Includes language arts, science, social studies.
Middle School Education. Includes language arts, science, social studies.
P–12 Education. Includes health/physical education, educational leadership/principalships, reading and writing, special education.
Psychology.
Secondary Education. Includes language arts, science, social studies.

UNION GRADUATE COLLEGE
Schenectady, New York 12308-3107
Web site: www.union.edu

Union Graduate College chartered in 2003, affiliated with Union College. Named changed in 2006. Graduate only institution. Coed. Private control. Semester system. Library: 496,000 volumes, 6500 subscriptions.

Tuition: per course, $1850 (Education), $2500 (Engineering/Computer Science), $2300 (Management), $2485 (Bioethics). No on-campus housing available. Contact Housing Office for off-campus housing information. Phone: (518)388-6061. Day-care facilities available near campus.

Graduate School

Graduate study since 1904. Enrollment: full-time 280, part-time 175. Faculty: full-time 14, part-time 19. Degrees conferred: M.A., M.A.T., M.S., M.B.A., M.S.T., Ph.D.

ADMISSION REQUIREMENTS. Official transcripts, three letters of recommendation required in support of application. Interview not required except for M.A.T./M.S.T. program. Accepts transfers with one or two courses (depending on program). GMAT scores required for admission to Graduate Management Institute. Apply to Graduate Studies Office by May 1, April 1 for M.A.T.; part-time applicants may apply throughout year. Part-time students may complete between one and three courses (depending on program) at Union before applying for degree status. Application fee $60. Phone: (518)388-6238; fax: (518)388-6686.

ADMISSION STANDARDS. Selective. Usual minimum average: 3.0 (A = 4).

FINANCIAL AID. Scholarships, fellowships and assistantships available for full-time students in the Graduate Management Institute, occasional assistantship available in engineering departments internships, tuition waivers, loans. Phone: (518)388-6642; fax: (518)388-6686. Use FAFSA and College's FAF. No institutional aid for part-time students.

DEGREE REQUIREMENTS. For M.A., M.A.T., M.S., M.S.T.: 10 full courses (33 credits) required in most departments; thesis for some departments. For M.S. from Graduate Management Institute: 15 full courses; for M.B.A.: 18 full courses; thesis/final oral/written exam. For Ph.D.: 15 courses minimum, one year of residency; dissertation; final oral/written exam.

FIELDS OF STUDY.
Bioethics.
Business Administration. Includes areas of focus in economics, finance, marketing & operations, management & human resources.
Clinical Leadership.
Computer Science.
Electrical Engineering.
Engineering and Management Systems.
Healthcare Management.
Mechanical Engineering.
Teachers of Mathematics and Science.
Teaching.

THE UNION INSTITUTE AND UNIVERSITY

Cincinnati, Ohio 45206-1925
Web site: www.tui.edu

Founded 1964. Coed. Private control. Semester system. External, nonresidential, self-paced, interdisciplinary, independent study program. Master's programs are offered at Vermont College, Montpelier, Vermont, and Dade County, Florida. Library: 50,000 volumes, it also houses Institute's doctoral dissertation: approximately 3500. Total University enrollment: 2400.

Annual tuition: $18,096. No on-campus housing available.

Graduate College

Graduate study since 1969. Enrollment: full-time 1432, part-time 0. Graduate faculty: full- and part-time 86. Degrees conferred: M.A., M.Ed., M.F.A., Ph.D.

ADMISSION REQUIREMENTS. Master's degree, two official transcripts, three letters of recommendation, three detailed narrative essays (autobiography, statement of interests, proposed program overview) required in support of School's application. Interview not required. Apply to the Dean at least two months prior to preferred date of enrollment. Application fee $50. Rolling admissions process. Phone: (800)486-3116 or (513)861-6400; fax (513)861-0779; e-mail: admission@tui.edu.

ADMISSION STANDARDS. Selective. No minimum GPA or test score required. Individualized admission process based on evidence of ability to self-direct, conceptualize, define, and carry out a doctoral-level research program.

FINANCIAL AID. Limited to Federal W/S, loans. Apply by May 1 to the Financial Aid Office. Phone: (800)486-3116. Use FAFSA and institutional FAF.

DEGREE REQUIREMENTS. For M.A.: 12-month individually designed program. For M.Ed.: entry colloquium; four required residencies; three seminars. For M.F.A. 60 credits individually designed program. For Ph.D.: at least six semesters (24 months) in continuous full-time enrollment; attendance at a ten-day entry colloquium and three five-day seminars; internship; dissertation.

FIELDS OF STUDY.
Business Management.
Clinical Psychology.
Communication.
Creative and Performing Arts.
Educational Leadership.
Health and Health Care.
Higher Education.
Interdisciplinary Arts and Science.
Literature.
Multicultural Studies.
Peace Studies.
Philanthropy and Leadership.
Philosophy/Religion.
Psychology. Includes general, marital and family therapy, social.
Public Policy.
Racial and Ethnic Studies.
Science/Mathematics.
Social sciences.
Sociology and Social Work.
Women's Studies.
Note: All fields of study are interdisciplinary, and programs are individually designed.

FIELDS OF STUDY—VERMONT COLLEGE.
Adult and Higher Education. M.Ed.
Art History. M.A.
Curriculum and Instruction. M.Ed.
Education. M.A.
Educational Leadership. M.Ed.
Environmental Education. M.A.
Issues in Education. M.Ed.
Literature and Writing. M.A.
Visual Arts. Interdisciplinary. Includes craft as fine art, drawing, electronic media, painting, performance, photography, printmaking, sculpture, video/film. M.F.A.
Writing. M.F.A.
Writing for Children and Young Adults. M.F.A.
Women's Studies. M.A.

FIELDS OF STUDY—DADE COUNTY.
Curriculum and Instruction. M.Ed.
Educational Leadership. M.Ed.
Elementary Education. M.Ed.
Gifted Education. M.Ed.
Guidance and Counseling. M.Ed.
Issues in Education. M.Ed.
Mathematics Education. M.Ed.
Mentally Handicapped. M.Ed.
PreK–Primary Education. M.Ed.
Reading. M.Ed.
School Psychology. M.Ed.
TESOL. M.Ed.

THE UNIVERSITY OF THE ARTS
Philadelphia, Pennsylvania 19102-9762
Web site: www.uarts.edu

Founded 1876. Coed. Private control. Semester system. Special facilities: electronic media laboratory, video editing studios, Oxberry Animation Stand, analog and digital electronic music studios, music calligraphy laboratory, Borowsky Center for Publication Arts, laser scanner laboratory, industrial design computer-aided product design center. Merriam, Drake, and Black Box Theaters. Library: 118,500 volumes, 5321 subscriptions.

Annual tuition: full-time $27,220; per credit hour $1328. No on-campus housing available. Contact the Director of Residential Life for off-campus housing information. Phone: (215)717-6046.

Graduate Program

Enrollment: full-time 81, part-time 63. University faculty teaching graduate students: full-time 26, part-time 12. Degrees conferred: M.A., M.F.A., M.A.T., M.I.D., M.M.

ADMISSION REQUIREMENTS. Official transcripts, audition, portfolio, interview, statement of purpose required in support of application. TOEFL (550 minimum) required for international applicants. Accepts transfer applicants in Music and Art Education. Apply to the Director of Admission by January 15 (Fall & Summer), November 1 (Spring). Application fee $60, $75 for international applicants. Phone: (800)616-ARTS, (215)717-6049; fax: (215)717-6045.

ADMISSION STANDARDS. Selective. Usual minimum average: 3.0 (A = 4). Talent is usual basis for most admissions decisions.

FINANCIAL AID. Scholarships, assistantships, internships, Grants-in-Aid, Federal W/S, loans. Approved for VA benefits. Apply with application for admission to Director of Admissions by March 1 (priority consideration). Phone: (215) 875-4858. Use FAFSA (School code: 003350). About 24–36% of students receive aid other than loans from University and outside sources.

DEGREE REQUIREMENTS. For M.A., M.M.: 36 semester hours minimum, at least 24 in residence; thesis; creative project. For M.F.A.: 60 semester hours, all in residence; thesis; four years for completion required. For part-time M.F.A.: 60 semester hours over four six-week summer residencies; eight independent study projects; thesis/exhibition during fifth summer.

FIELDS OF STUDY.
Art Education. Includes concentration in educational media.
Book Arts/Printmaking.
Ceramics.
Industrial Design.
Jazz Studies.
Museum Communication.
Museum Education.
Museum Exhibition, Planning, and Design.
Music Education.
Painting.
Sculpture.
Teaching Visual Arts.

UTAH STATE UNIVERSITY
Logan, Utah 84322-0900
Web site: www.usu.edu

Founded 1888. Located 80 miles N of Salt Lake City. CGS member. Coed. State control. Semester system. According to The Center at University of Florida, the University is ranked number

80th in receipt of Federal Research fund with $95,494,000 and it ranks number 95th for total University research expenditures with $138,862,000. The Library: approximately 1,500,000 volumes, 14,000 subscriptions. Total University enrollment: 14,500.

Tuition: per credit resident $574.40, nonresident $1509.54. On-campus housing for 670 married students, 1058 men, 1002 women. Average academic year housing costs: $4100 (including board), $6300 for married students. Contact Director, Housing and Residential Life, for both on- and off-campus housing information. Phone: (435)797-3113. Day-care facilities available.

School of Graduate Studies

Graduate study since 1914. Enrollment: full-time 2000, part-time 576. Faculty: full-time 574, part-time 163. Degrees conferred: M.A., M.Ac., M.A.I., M.B.A., M.C.E.D., M.E., M.Ed., M.E.S., M.F., M.F.A., M.L.A., M.M.T., M.S., M.S.S., Ed.S., C.E., E.E., Ed.D., Ph.D.

ADMISSION REQUIREMENTS. Two official transcripts from each postsecondary institution attended, three letters of recommendation, GRE/GMAT (Business) required in support of School's application. Online application available. TOEFL (minimum score 550) required for international applicants. Accepts transfer applicants. Graduates of unaccredited colleges not considered. Apply to Graduate Office by June 15 (Fall), October 15 (Spring), March 15 (Summer). Application fee $50, $60 for international applicants. Phone: (435)797-1190; fax: (435)797-1192.

ADMISSION STANDARDS. Selective. Usual minimum average GPA: 3.0 (A = 4); admission test score in the 40th percentile of above.

FINANCIAL AID. Fellowships, scholarships, teaching assistantships, tuition waivers and nonresident tuition waivers, internships, Federal W/S, loans. Approved for VA benefits. Apply by February 15 to appropriate department head for fellowships, assistantships; to Financial Aid Office for all other programs. Phone: (435)797-0173; fax: (435)797-0654. Use FAFSA. Aid available for part-time students.

DEGREE REQUIREMENTS. For master's: 30–36 credit hours minimum, at least 24 in residence; reading knowledge of one foreign language for M.A.; thesis/final report in some departments; final exam. For M.F.A.: generally two-year program. For M.B.A.: one to two-year program, depending on background of candidate. For M.F. (for holders of Bachelor's in field other than forestry): 60 credit hours minimum. For Ed.S., C.E., E.E.: 30 credit hours beyond the master's; project. For Ed.D.: 60 credits minimum beyond the master's, at least four semesters in residence; dissertation; comprehensive written exam; final oral exam. For Ph.D.: 60 credits minimum beyond the master's, at least four semesters in residence; dissertation; preliminary exam; comprehensive written exam; final oral exam.

FIELDS OF STUDY.

COLLEGE OF AGRICULTURE:
Agricultural Systems Technology. M.S.
Animal Science. M.S., Ph.D.
Applied Economics. M.S.
Biometeorology. M.S., Ph.D.
Bioveterinary Science. M.S., Ph.D.
Dairy Science. M.S.
Dietetics Administration. M.D.A.
Ecology. M.S., Ph.D.
Economics. M.S., Ph.D.
Food and Agribusiness. M.B.A.
Food Microbiology and Safety. M.F.M.S.
Nutrition and Food Science. M.S., Ph.D.
Plant Science. M.S., Ph.D.

Professional Studies in Horticulture. M.P.S.H.
Soil Science. M.S., Ph.D.

COLLEGE OF BUSINESS:
Accounting. M.Acc.
Applied Economics. M.S.
Business Administration. M.B.A.
Business Information Systems. M.S., Ph.D.
Economics. M.S., Ph.D.
Food and Agribusiness. M.B.A., M.S.
Human Resource. M.B.A.

COLLEGE OF EDUCATION:
Audiology. Au.D.
Communicative Disorders and Deaf Education. M.A., M.Ed.,
    M.S. Ed.S.
Disability Discipline. Ph.D.
Education. Includes business, information systems and educa-
    tion, communicative disorders, elementary education, research
    and evaluation, educational audiology; Ed.D., Ph.D.
Elementary Education. M.A., M.Ed., M.S.
Family and Human Development. M.F.H.D., M.S.
Health, Physical Education, and Recreation. M.S., M.Ed.
Instructional Technology. M.S., M.Ed., Ed.S.
Psychology. M.S., Ph.D.
Rehabilitation Counseling. M.R.C.
Secondary Education. M.A., M.Ed., M.S.
Special Education. M.S., M.Ed., Ed.S.

COLLEGE OF ENGINEERING:
Biological Engineering. M.S., Ph.D.
Civil and Environmental Engineering. M.S., C.E., M.E., Ph.D.
Electrical Engineering. E.E., M.S., M. E., Ph.D.
Engineering and Technology Education. M.S., Ph.D.
Irrigation Engineering. M.S., Ph.D.
Mechanical Engineering. M.S., M.E., Ph.D.

COLLEGE OF HUMANITIES, ARTS, AND SOCIAL SCIENCES:
American Studies. M.A., M.S.
Art. M.A., M.F.A.
Bioregional Planning. M.S.
Communication. M.A., M.S.
English. M.A., M.S.
History. M.A., M.S.
Landscape Architecture. M.S., M.L.A.
Management and Human Resources. M.S.
Political Science. M.A., M.S.
Second Language Teaching. M.S.L.T.
Social Sciences.
Social Work. M.S.W.
Sociology. M.A., M.S., Ph.D.
Theater Arts. M.A., M.F.A.

COLLEGE OF NATURAL RESOURCES:
Ecology. M.S., Ph.D.
Fisheries Biology. M.S., Ph.D.
Forestry. M.S., Ph.D.
Geography. M.A., M.S.
Human Dimensions of Ecosystems Science and Management.
    M.S., Ph.D.
Natural Resources. M.N.R.
Range Science. M.S., Ph.D.
Recreation Resource Management. M.S., Ph.D.
Watershed Science. M.S., Ph.D.
Wildlife Biology. M.S., Ph.D.

COLLEGE OF SCIENCE:
Biochemistry. M.S., Ph.D.
Biology. M.S., Ph.D.
Biology Ecology. M.S., Ph.D.
Chemistry. M.S., Ph.D.

Computer Science. M.S., M.C.S., Ph.D.
Geology. M.S., Ph.D.
Industrial Mathematics. M.S.
Mathematical Sciences. Ph.D.
Mathematics. M.S., M.Math.
Physics. M.S., Ph.D.
Statistics. M.S.
Toxicology. M.S., Ph.D.

UNIVERSITY OF UTAH
Salt Lake City, Utah 84112
Web site: www.utah.edu

Founded 1850. CGS member. State control. Semester system.
Special facilities: Advanced Combustion Engineering Research
Center, American West Center, Archaeological Center, Center of
Architectural Studies, Center for Atmospheric and Remote Sound-
ing Studies, Institute for Biomedical Engineering, Center for Con-
trolled Chemical Delivery, Cosmic Ray Observatory, Center for
Excellence in Nuclear Technology, Engineering, and Research,
Center for Health Care, Hinckley Institute of Politics, Intermoun-
tain Burn Center, Obert C. and Grace A. Tanner Humanities Cen-
ter, Center for Human Toxicology, Garn Institute for Finance,
Gerontology Center, Huntsman Cancer Institute, Jon A. Dixon
Laser Institute, Middle East Center, Social Research Center,
Utah Museum of Fine Arts, Utah Museum of Natural History.
The University's NIH ranking is 49th among all U.S. institutions
with 364 awards/grants valued at $127,067,754. According to
The Center at University of Florida, the University is ranked
53rd in receipt of Federal Research funds with $152,112,000
and it ranks 58th for total University research expenditures with
$223,739,000. In 2004, the University awarded 216 doctorates
which ranked it 88th among all U.S. institutions eligible to award
that degree. Twenty of the University's faculty members have
been elected to National Honor Academies and this ranks it
45th among all U.S. institutions. The Library: approximately
3,300,000 volumes, 21,000 subscriptions. Total University enrollment: 29,000.

Tuition: full-time resident $2932, nonresident $10,350; part-
time per credit, resident $369, nonresident $1302. On-campus
housing for 1092 married students, 102 men, 52 women. Average
academic year housing costs: $4000 for single students; $5000
for married students. Contact Director of Residential Living for
both on- and off-campus housing information. Phone: (801)581-
6667. Day-care facilities available.

Graduate School

Enrollment: full-time 3372, part-time 1418. Faculty: full- and
part-time 1134. Degrees conferred: M.A., M.Arch., M.A.T.,
M.B.A., M.E., M.E.A., M.Ed., M.F.A., M.H.R.M., M.Mus.,
M.Pr.A., M.P.A., M.S., M.S.P.H., M.S.W., M.Phil., M.Stat.,
Ed.S., Ph.D., Ed.D., Pharm.D., D.S.W., E.E.

ADMISSION REQUIREMENTS. Official transcripts GRE/
GMAT/MAT required in support of School's application. Online
application available. GRE Subject required for some programs.
TOEFL required for international applicants. Interview may be
required. Accepts transfer applicants. Graduates of unaccredited
institutions not considered. Apply to the Director of Admissions
by April 1 (Fall), November 1 (Spring); some departments may
have earlier deadlines. Application fee $45, $65 for international
applicants. Phone: (801)581-7283; fax: (801)585-7864.

ADMISSION STANDARDS. Selective to very competitive.
Usual minimum average: 3.0 (A = 4).

FINANCIAL AID. Annual awards from institutional funds:
teaching/research assistantships, teaching/research fellowships,

internships, traineeships, tuition waivers, Federal W/S, loans. Approved for VA benefits. In addition, all departments have established teaching positions for graduate students with stipends. Apply by March 1 to Graduate Fellowship Office for fellowships; to appropriate department chair for assistantships; to Financial Aid Office for all other programs. Phone: (801)581-6211. Use FAFSA. About 20% of students receive aid other than loans from School and outside sources. Aid available for part-time students.

DEGREE REQUIREMENTS. For master's: 30–48 credit hours minimum, at least 24 in residence; foreign language qualifying exam for M.A.; admission to candidacy; thesis; final oral/written exam. For E.E., Ed.S.: 30 credit hours beyond master's. For Ph.D.: 60 credits minimum, at least one year in full-time residence; foreign language requirements vary by department; qualifying exam; thesis; final oral exam. For Ed.D.: language requirements vary from department to department, some have none at all; other requirements essentially the same as for the Ph.D.

FIELDS OF STUDY.

DAVID ECCLES SCHOOL OF BUSINESS:
Accounting. GMAT for admission; includes professional accounting. M.B.A., M.Pr.A., Ph.D.
Business Administration. GMAT for admission. M.B.A., Ph.D.
Finance. GMAT for admission. M.B.A., M.S., Ph.D.
Human Resource Management. GRE for admission. M.B.A., M.H.R.M., Ph.D.
Management. M.S.
Marketing. GMAT for admission. M.B.A., Ph.D.

GRADUATE SCHOOL OF EDUCATION:
Counseling Psychology. M.Ed., Ph.D.
Early Childhood Special Education (B–5). M.Ed., M.S.
Education, Culture and Society. M.A., M.Ed., M.Phil, M.S., Ph.D.
Educational Leadership and Policy (PreK–12). M.Ed., Ph.D.
Hearing Impairments (B–5, or K–12). M.Ed., M.S.
Instructional Design and Educational Technology. M.Ed., M.S.
Learning and Cognition. M.Phil., M.S., Ph.D.
Mild-Moderate Disabilities (K–12). M.Ed., M.S.
Professional Practice in Special Education. M.Ed., M.S.
Research in Special Education. M.S.
Research Methods. M.Stat.
School Psychology. M.S., Ph.D.
Severe Disabilities (K–12). M.Ed., M.S.
Special Education. Ph.D.
Teaching and Learning. M.Ed., M.S., Ph.D.
Visual Impairment (B–5 or K–12). M.Ed., M.S.

COLLEGE OF ENGINEERING:
Biomedical Engineering. M.E., M.S., Ph.D.
Chemical Engineering. M.E., M.Phil., M.S., Ph.D.
Civil Engineering. M.E., M.S., Ph.D.
Computer Science. M.E., M.Phil., M.S., Ph.D.
Electrical Engineering. M.E., M.S., Ph.D.
Engineering Administration. M.E.A.
Environmental Engineering. M.E., M.S., Ph.D.
Fuels Engineering. M.E., M.S., Ph.D.
Materials Science and Engineering. Interdepartmental. M.E., M.S., Ph.D.
Mechanical Engineering. M.E., M.Phil., M.S., Ph.D.
Nuclear Engineering. M.E., M.S., Ph.D.

COLLEGE OF FINE ARTS:
Art. Includes art teaching, ceramics, drawing and painting, graphic design, illustration, intermedia, sculpture, photography/digital imaging, printmaking. M.A., M.F.A.
Art History. Includes Asian art, Western European art, American art, 20th-century art. M.A.
Ballet. Includes character dance, performance, teaching. M.A., M.F.A.

Film Studies. Includes critical studies, film and video production, screenwriting. M.F.A.
Modern Dance. Includes performance, choreography, education, history, kinesiology. M.F.A., M.A.
Music. Includes conducting, history, instrumental and vocal performance, jazz studies, music composition, music education, musicology, theory. M.A., M.Mus., Ph.D.
Theatre. Includes acting and directing, design, history, literature, playwriting, production and stage management, theatre education. M.F.A., Ph.D.

SCHOOL OF HEALTH:
ATOD/Violence Prevention and Education. M.S.
Audiology. Au.D.
Community Health. M.S.
Exercise Physiology. M.S., Ph.D.
Integrative Health. M.S.
Natural Resource Management. M.S.
Nutrition Sciences. M.S.
Physical Acivity and Weight Management. M.S.
Psychosocial Aspects of Sport. M.S., Ph.D.
Special Physical Education. M.S., Ph.D.
Sport Pedagogy. M.S.
Therapeutic Recreation Assessment. M.S.
Therapeutic Recreation Counseling and Clinical Interventions. M.S.
Therapeutic Recreation Leisure Education. M.S.
Tourism Marketing and Finance. M.S.
Tourism Planning and Development. M.S.

COLLEGE OF HUMANITIES:
Communication. Includes mass communication, journalism, speech communication; interdisciplinary programs in environmental and science communication, conflict resolution, peace and conflict studies, new media technologies, critical-cultural studies. M.A., M.Phil., Ph.D.
English. Includes literature and creative writing (Ph.D.), fiction and poetry (M.F.A.), British and American literature (M.A., Ph.D.), American studies (M.A., Ph.D.), rhetoric & composition (Ph.D.). M.A., Ph.D.
History. Includes United States, Middle East, modern Europe, medieval Europe. M.A., M.S., Ph.D.
Language and Literature. Includes comparative literacy and cultural studies, French, German, Spanish (M.A.), CLCS, French, German, Spanish (M.A.L.P.), CLCS, German, French (Ph.D.). M.A., M.A.L.P., Ph.D.
Linguistics. Includes applied (M.A.), theoretical (M.A.). M.A., Ph.D.
Philosophy. Includes applied ethics, philosophy of biology, philosophy of mind & cognitive science, ancient Greek philosophy, Chinese philosophy, practical reason, philosophy of law, early modern philosophy. M.A., M.S., Ph.D.

COLLEGE OF MINES AND EARTH SCIENCES:
Environmental Earth Science.
Geological Engineering. M.E., M.S., Ph.D.
Geology. M.S., Ph.D.
Geophysics. M.S., Ph.D.
Metallurgical Engineering. M.E., M.S., Ph.D.
Meterology. M.S., Ph.D.
Mines and Earth Sciences. M.E., M.S., Ph.D.
Mining Engineering. M.E., M.S., Ph.D.

COLLEGE OF NURSING:
Clinical Nurse Leader.
Gerontology. Interdisciplinary. M.S.
Nursing Informatics.
Nurse Midwifery.
Nursing. Ph.D.
Psychiatric/Mental Health.

Teaching Nursing.
Women's Health.

COLLEGE OF PHARMACY:
Medical Chemistry. M.S., Ph.D.
Pharmaceutics and Pharmaceutical Chemistry. M.S., Ph.D.
Pharmacology and Toxicology. M.S., Ph.D.
Pharmacy. Pharm.D.
Pharmacy Practice. M.S.

COLLEGE OF SCIENCE:
Biological Chemistry. Ph.D.
Biology. M.S.
Cell Biology. Ph.D.
Chemical Physics. Ph.D.
Chemistry. Ph.D.
Computational Engineering and Science. Interdisciplinary. M.S.
Ecology and Evolutionary Biology. M.S., Ph.D.
Genetics. M.S., Ph.D.
Mathematics. M.A., M.Phil., M.S., Ph.D.
Medical Physics. Ph.D.
Molecular Biology. Ph.D.
Physics. M.A., M.Phil., M.S., Ph.D.
Secondary School Teachers of Science and Mathematics. M.S.

COLLEGE OF SOCIAL AND BEHAVIORAL SCIENCE:
Anthropology. M.A., Ph.D.
Economics. M.A., M.Phil., M.S., M.Stat., Ph.D.
Family Ecology. M.S.
Geography. M.A., M.S., Ph.D.
Political Science. M.A., M.S., Ph.D.
Psychogy. GRE/MAT for admission; M.A., M.S., M.Stat., Ph.D.
Public Administration. M.P.A.
Public Policy. M.P.P.
Sociology. M.A., M.S., Ph.D.

GRADUATE SCHOOL OF ARCHITECTURE:
Architecture. M.Arch., M.S.

GRADUATE SCHOOL OF SOCIAL WORK:
Social Work. M.S.W., D.S.W.

S.J. Quinney College of Law
Web site: www.law.utah.edu

Established 1914. ABA approved since 1927. AALS member. Public control. Semester system. Special facilities: Wallace Stegner Center for Land, Resources and the Environment, Disabilities Law Center, Rocky Mountain Innocence Center. Law library: 334,119 volumes, 4804 subscriptions; has LEXIS, WESTLAW; has about 600 network connections.

Annual tuition: resident $4758, nonresident $25,116. On-campus housing available for both single and married students. Annual on-campus housing cost: $7800. Phone: (801)581-6611. Law students tend to live off-campus. Off-campus housing and personal expense: approximately $15,000.

Enrollment: first-year class day 129; total 391 (men 62%, women 38%, minorities 10%). Faculty: full-time 27, part-time 20. Student to faculty ratio is 11.5 to 1. Degrees conferred: J.D., J.D.-M.B.A., J.D.-M.P.A., LL.M. (Environmental and Natural Resource Law).

ADMISSION REQUIREMENTS. LSDAS Law School report, Bachelor's degree, transcripts, LSAT, personal statement required in support of application. Accepts transfer applicants. Apply to Office of Dean of College by February 1 (for priority consideration). Rolling admissions process. Admits Fall only. Application fee $60. Phone: (801)581-7479; fax: (801)581-6897.

ADMISSION STANDARDS. Selective. Accepts approximately 31% of all students. Number of applicants 1176; number of acceptance 359; number enrolled 129; LSAT (75% of students have

a score at or above 158); GPA (75% of students have a GPA at or above 3.46). *U.S. News & World Report* ranking is tied at 57th of all U.S. law schools.

FINANCIAL AID. Scholarships, tuition waivers, fellowships, assistantships, Federal W/S, loans. Apply to Financial Aid Office of University by March 15 for priority consideration. Phone: (801)581-6211. Use FAFSA (College code: 003675). About 43% of students receive aid other than loans from College.

DEGREE REQUIREMENTS. For J.D.: 88 semester hours minimum. For LL.M.: at least 24 credit hours beyond the J.D.; one year in full-time residence.
Note: Study-abroad program in London available.

College of Medicine (84132-2101)
Web site: www.uuhsc.utah.edu/som

Founded 1905, expanded to a four-year program in 1942. Library: 100,000 volumes, 1750 subscriptions. NIH ranking is 49th among U.S. institutions with 364 awards/grants worth $127,067,754.

Annual tuition: state resident $19,272, Idaho resident $20,287, nonresident $35,864. On-campus housing available for both single and married students. Total average figure for all other expenses: $8964.

Enrollment: first-year class 102, total 404 (men 63%, women 37%, minorities 14%, state residents 86%). Faculty: full-time 951, part-time 265. Degrees conferred: M.D., M.D.-M.P.H., M.D.-Ph.D. The Ph.D. is offered through the Graduate School.

ADMISSION REQUIREMENTS. AMCAS, transcripts, letters of recommendation, MCAT required in support of application. Interviews by invitation only. Applicants must have completed at least three years of college study. Preference given to state residents and residents of Idaho. Nonresidents must apply under EDP; apply between June 1 and August 1. Apply to Admissions Office after June 15, before November 1. Application fee: $100. Phone: (801)581-7498; fax: (801)585-3300.

ADMISSION STANDARDS. Selective. Accepts about 11% of all applicants. Number of applications 1074 (650 out-of-state); number interviewed 442 (161 out-of-state); number of acceptance 138 (45 out-of-state); number enrolled 102 (27 out-of-state). Mean Composite MCAT 9.8; mean UGPA 3.65.

FINANCIAL AID. Scholarships, Grants-in-Aid, institutional loans, HEAL, alternative loan programs, NIH stipends, Federal Perkins Loans, Stafford Subsidized and Unsubsidized Loans, Service Commitment Scholarship programs are available. Assistantships/fellowships may be available for dual degree candidates. Financial aid applications and information are generally available at the on-campus by-invitation interview. Apply by March 15. Contact the Financial Aid Office for current information. Phone: (801) 581-6474. Use FAFSA (School code: 003675), also submit Financial Aid Transcript, Federal Income Tax forms. Approximately 91% of students receive some form of financial assistance.

DEGREE REQUIREMENTS. For M.D.: satisfactory completion of four-year program. All students must take USMLE Step 1 and Step 2 and record scores. For M.D.-M.S.P.H, M.D.-M.P.H.: generally a four-and-one-half- to five-and-one-half-year programs. For M.D.-Ph.D.: generally a seven- to eight-year program.

FIELDS OF GRADUATE STUDY.
Biomedical Informatics.
Biochemistry.
Human Genetics.
Neurobiology and Anatomy.
Oncological Sciences.
Neuroscience.

Pathology.
Physiology.

VALDOSTA STATE COLLEGE
Valdosta, Georgia 31698
Web site: www.valdosta.edu

Founded 1906. Located 75 miles NE of Tallahassee, Florida. CGS member. Coed. State control. Semester system. Library: 467,560 volumes, 3262 subscriptions. Total College enrollment: 10,503.

Annual tuition: resident $3516, nonresident $14,060; per credit resident $147, nonresident $586. On-campus housing for 601 graduate men, 1082 graduate women; 12 units for married students. Average academic year housing costs: $4200 for single students; $5800 for married students. Contact Director, Housing and Residence Life for both on- and off-campus housing information. Phone: (229)333-5920.

Graduate School

Graduate study since 1968. Enrollment: full-time 776, part-time 334. College faculty teaching graduate students: full-time 193, part-time 10. Degrees conferred: M.A., M.M.E., M.S., M.B.A., M.Ed., M.P.A., Ed.S., Ed.D.

ADMISSION REQUIREMENTS. Two official transcripts, GRE (for education applicants; M.A., M.S. applicants), GRE or GMAT (for M.P.A. applicants), GMAT (for business) required in support of application. Online application available. TOEFL required for international applicants. Accepts transfer applicants. Graduates of unaccredited institutions not considered. Apply to Director of Graduate Admissions at least sixty days prior to the beginning of the semester of registration. Rolling admission process. Application fee $20. Phone: (229)333-5694; fax: (229)245-3853.

ADMISSION STANDARDS. Relatively open. Usual minimum average: 2.5 (A = 4).

FINANCIAL AID. Scholarships, research assistantships, teaching assistantships, internships, traineeships, tuition waivers, Federal W/S, grants, loans. Approved for VA benefits. Apply by May 1 to Director of Student Aid. Phone: (229)333-5935; fax: (229) 333-5430. Use FAFSA and institutional FAF. About 20% of students receive aid other than loans from College and outside sources. Aid available for part-time students.

DEGREE REQUIREMENTS. For M.A.: 30 credit hours minimum plus thesis, at least 24 in residence; or 33 credit hours minimum without thesis, at least 25 in residence; reading knowledge of one foreign language; comprehensive/oral exam. For M.Ed., M.M.E.: 30 credit hours minimum plus thesis, at least 25 in residence; or 36 credit hours minimum without thesis, at least 30 in residence; comprehensive written/oral exam. For M.S.: 30 credit hours minimum plus thesis, at least 24 in residence; or 30 hours minimum without thesis, at least 30 in residence; comprehensive written/oral exam. For M.B.A., M.P.A.: 45 credit hours minimum, at least 30 in residence; comprehensive written/oral exam. For Ed.S.: 30 credit hours beyond the master's; thesis/nonthesis option. For. Ed.D.: at least 60 credit hours beyond the master's; qualifying exam; candidacy; dissertation; final oral exam.

FIELDS OF STUDY.

GRADUATE SCHOOL:
Library and Information Science. M.L.I.S.

COLLEGE OF ARTS:
Music Education. M.M.E.

COLLEGE OF ARTS AND SCIENCES:
Criminal Justice. M.S.
English. M.A.
History. M.A.
Marriage and Family Therapy. M.S.
Public Administration. M.P.A.
Sociology. M.S.

LANGDALE COLLEGE OF BUSINESS ADMINISTRATION:
Business Administration. M.B.A.

COLLEGE OF EDUCATION:
Adult and Career Education. Includes business education, technical, trade and industrial, training and development. M.Ed., Ed.D.
Business Education. M.Ed.
Career Education. Includes business education, general career education. Ed.S.
Curriculum and Instruction. Ed.D.
Early Childhood Education. M.Ed., Ed.S.
Educational Leadership. Includes public school leadership, higher education leadership. M.Ed., Ed.S., Ed.D.
Instructional Technology. Includes library media technology, technology applications. M.Ed., Ed.S.
Middle Grades. M.Ed., Ed.S.
Physical Education. M.Ed.
Psychology. Includes clinical/counseling, industrial/organizational. M.S.
Reading. M.Ed.
School Counseling. Ed.S.
School Psychology. Ed.S.
Secondary Education. M.Ed., Ed.S.
Special Education. Includes communication disorders, early childhood special education, general, mild disabilities, mental retardation, interrelated. M.Ed., Ed.S.

COLLEGE OF NURSING:
Nursing. M.S.N.

COLLEGE OF SOCIAL WORK:
Social Work. M.S.W.

VALPARAISO UNIVERSITY
Valparaiso, Indiana 46383-6493
Web site: www.valpo.edu

Founded 1959. Coed. Private control. Lutheran affiliation. Semester system. Library: 1,100,000 volumes, 18,000 subscriptions. Total University enrollment: 3900.

Tuition: per credit hour $420; Nursing $500; M.B.A. $510; M.E.M. $570. No on-campus housing available. For off-campus information contact Director of Housing. Phone: (219)464-5413.

Graduate Division

Graduate study since 1963. Classes offered in evening and Summer session. Enrollment: full-time 193, part-time 138, Faculty: full-time 20, part-time 21. Degrees conferred: M.A., M.A.L.S., M.Ed., M.M., M.S.N., M.S., Ed.S.

ADMISSION REQUIREMENTS. Official transcripts, interview required in support of application. GRE recommended; required for M.A., M.E., M.S., Ed.S. Online application available. TOEFL required for international applicants. Accepts transfer applicants. Graduates of unaccredited institutions not considered. Apply to Director of Graduate Studies one month prior to registration for Spring, Summer, and Fall. Application fee $30, $50 for international applicants. Phone: (800)349-2611, (219)464-5313; fax: (219)464-5381.

ADMISSION STANDARDS. Selective. Usual minimum average: 3.0 (A = 4).

FINANCIAL AID. Limited to internships, assistantships, Federal W/S, loans. Approved for VA benefits. Apply to the Office of Financial Aid: no specified closing date. Phone: (800) 348-2611. Use FAFSA.

DEGREE REQUIREMENTS. For M.A.: 30 credit program; practicum; internships. For M.Ed., M.M., M.S.: 30–36 semester hours minimum, at least 24 in residence; no thesis or language requirement. For M.A.L.S.: 42 semester hours minimum, at least 30 in residence; research project. For Ed.S.: 30 credit program beyond master's; special project.

FIELDS OF STUDY.
Business Administration. M.B.A.
Chinese Studies. M.A.
Clinical Mental Health Counseling. M.A.
Community Counseling. M.A.
Deaconess. M.A.L.S.
Educational Specialist in School Psychology. M.Ed.
Engineering Management. M.E.M.
English. M.A.L.S.
English Studies and Communication. M.A.
Ethics and Values. M.A.L.S.
Gerontology. M.A.L.S.
History. M.A.L.S.
Human Behavior and Society. M.A.L.S.
Individualized. M.A.L.S.
Information Technology. M.S.
International Commerce and Policy. M.S.
Nursing. M.S.
Sports Administration. M.S.
Teaching and Learning. M.Ed.
Theology and Ministry. M.A.L.S.

School of Law
Web site: www.valpo.edu/law

Founded 1879. ABA approved since 1929. AALS member. Private control. Semester system. Law library: 319,604 volumes, 2348 subscriptions; has NEXIS, LEXIS, WESTLAW, DIALOG, VU/TEXT.

Annual tuition: full-time $28,940, part-time $1131 per credit. On-campus housing available. Law students tend to live off-campus. Off-campus housing and personal expenses: approximately $10,650.

Enrollment: first-year class full-time 172, part-time 22; total full- and part-time 485 (men 54%, women 46%, minorities 12%). Faculty: full-time 19, part-time 30. Student to faculty ratio is 15.5 to 1. Degrees conferred: J.D., J.S.-M.A. (Psychology), J.D.-M.B.A., J.D.-M.A.L.S., J.D.-M.S. (Sports), LL.M. (for international lawyers).

ADMISSION REQUIREMENTS. LSDAS Law School report, Bachelor's degree, transcripts, LSAT required in support of application. Recommendations strongly suggested. Interview sometimes required. Accepts transfer applicants. Graduates of unaccredited institutions not considered. Apply to Dean by April 1 for priority consideration. Application fee $50. Phone: outside Indiana (888) 825-7652, (219)548-7703; fax: (219)465-7872.

ADMISSION STANDARDS. Selective. Accepts approximately 21% of full-time, 31% of part-time students. Number of full-time applicants 2918, part-time 175; number of full-time acceptance 627, part-time 55; number of full-time enrolled 172, part-time 27; LSAT (75% of full-time students have a score at or above 150, part-time 144); GPA (75% of full-time students have a GPA at or above 2.97, part-time 2.78). *U.S. News & World Report* ranking is in the fourth tier of all U.S. law schools.

FINANCIAL AID. Scholarships, grants, full and partial tuition waivers, Federal W/S, loans. Apply to the Financial Aid Office, preferably before March 1. Phone: (219)465-7818. Use FAFSA (School code: 001842). About 32% of students receive aid other than loans from School. Loan Repayment Assistance Program for Public Service employment.

DEGREE REQUIREMENTS. For J.D. 90 hours, at least 30 in residence; final written exam; 20 hours of pro bono work. For LL.M.: 24 credit hour program.
Note: Summer study abroad in Cambridge (England).

VANDERBILT UNIVERSITY
Nashville, Tennessee 37240-1001
Web site: www.vanderbilt.edu

Founded 1873. CGS member. Coed. Private control. Semester system. Special facilities: Arthritis and Joint Replacement Center, Bill Wilkerson Center for Otolaryngology and Communication Sciences, Center for Baudelaire Studies, Center for Child and Family Policy, Center for Crime and Justice Policy, Center for Entrepreneurship Education, Center for Evaluation Research and Methodology, Center for Environmental Management Studies, Center for Health Policy, Center for Health Services, Center for Innovation in Engineering Education, Center for Intelligent Systems, Center for Latin American and Iberian Studies, Center for Mental Health Policy, Center for Molecular Neuroscience, Center for Molecular Toxicology, Center for Psychotherapy Research and Policy, Center for Space Physiology and Medicine, Center for State and Local Policy, Center for Support of Professional Practice in Education, Center for Teaching, Fine Arts Gallery, Robert Penn Warren Center for the Humanities, Free Electron Laser Center, Informatics Center, Institute for Public Policy Studies, Institute for Software Integrated Systems, John F. Kennedy Center for Research on Education and Human Development, Stevenson Center for Natural Sciences, Arthur J. Dyer Observatory, Vanderbilt Institute for Public Policy Studies. The University's NIH ranking is 19th among all U.S. institutions with 668 awards/grants valued at $266,236,625. According to The Center at University of Florida, the University is ranked 28th in receipt of Federal Research funds with $221,979,000 and it ranks 46th for total University research expenditures with $276,074,000. The University's endowment assets rank it 21st, with a value of $2,296,262,000. In 2004, the University awarded 193 doctorates which ranked it 78th among all U.S. institutions eligible to award that degree. Seventeen of the University's faculty members have been elected to National Honor Academies and this ranks it 51st among all U.S. institutions. Joint libraries (with George Peabody and Scarritt Colleges): approximately 2,000,000 volumes, 21,608 subscriptions. Total University enrollment: 11,500.

Tuition: per credit $1283. On-campus housing for 140 married students, 110 men, 105 women. Annual housing costs: $5500 single students, $6800 married students. Contact Office of Residential Affairs for both on- and off-campus housing information. Phone: (615)322-2591. Day-care facilities available.

Graduate School

Graduate study since 1875. Enrollment: full-time 1948, part-time 112. University faculty: full-time 710. Degrees conferred: M.A., M.S., M.A.T., M.L.A.S., Ph.D.

ADMISSION REQUIREMENTS. Two official transcripts, three letters of recommendation, GRE, statement of purpose required in support of School's application. Interview not required. Online application available. TOEFL (minimum score 550) required for international applicants. TSE recommended for international applicants wanting to be considered for teaching assistantships. Accepts transfer applicants. Graduates of unaccredited institutions not considered. Apply to Dean of Graduate School by January 15 (Fall), November 1 (Spring), May 1 (Summer). Application fee $40. Phone: (615)343-2727; fax: (615)322-9936.

ADMISSION STANDARDS. Competitive for some departments, selective for others. Usual minimum average: 3.0 (A = 4).

FINANCIAL AID. Fellowships, scholarships, assistantships, research fellowships, assistantships, traineeships, tuition waivers, Federal W/S, loans. Approved for VA benefits. Apply by January 15 to Graduate School for fellowships, assistantships; to Financial Aid Office for all other programs. Use FAFSA. About 70% of students receive aid other than loans from University, 75% from all sources. Aid available for part-time students.

DEGREE REQUIREMENTS. For M.A., M.S.: 24 semester hours minimum; reading knowledge of one foreign language in some programs; thesis/nonthesis option for some departments. For M.A.T: 30–36 semester hours minimum. For Ph.D.: 72 semester hours minimum beyond the Bachelor's degree, at least one year in residence; reading knowledge of one foreign language in some programs; qualifying exam; dissertation; final exam.

FIELDS OF STUDY.
Anthropology.
Art History. Master's only.
Biochemistry. Ph.D. only.
Biological Sciences. Ph.D. only.
Biomedical Engineering.
Biomedical Informatics.
Cancer Biology.
Cell and Development Biology.
Chemical and Physical Biology.
Chemical Engineering.
Chemistry.
Classical Studies.
Community Research and Action.
Comparative Literature.
Computer Science.
Creative Writing.
Earth and Environmental Sciences.
Economic Development.
Economics.
Electrical Engineering.
English.
Environmental and Water Resources Engineering.
Environmental Engineering.
French.
German.
Hearing and Speech Sciences.
History.
Human Genetics.
Interdisciplinary Materials Science.
Latin American and Iberian Studies.
Leadership and Policy Studies. Ph.D. only.
Liberal Arts and Science. Master's only.
Management. Ph.D. only.
Management of Technology.
Materials Science and Engineering.
Mathematics.
Mechanical Engineering.
Microbiology and Immunology.
Molecular Physiology and Biophysics. Ph.D. only.
Neurosciences.
Nursing Science. Ph.D. only.
Pathology.
Pharmacology. Ph.D. only.
Philosophy.
Physics and Astronomy. Includes astronomy (M.S. only).
Political Science.
Psychology. Includes clinical.
Psychology and Human Development.
Religion.
Sociology.
Spanish-Portuguese. Ph.D. only.
Special Education.

Divinity School

Graduate study since 1875. Coed. Semester system.
Tuition: per credit $800. On-campus housing available.
Enrollment: full- and part-time 154. School faculty teaching professions students: full-time 30, part-time 19. Degrees conferred: M.Div., M.T.S.

ADMISSION REQUIREMENTS. Official transcripts, three letters of recommendation, essay required in support of School's application. TOEFL (minimum score 600) required for international applicants. Interview recommended. Accepts transfer applicants. Apply to Director of Admissions by May 1 (Fall), November 1 (Spring). Rolling admission process. Application fee $50. Phone: (615)343-3963; fax: (615)343-9957.

ADMISSION STANDARDS. Selective. Minimum acceptable GPA: 2.9 (A = 4).

FINANCIAL AID. Scholarships, tuition grants, internships, tuition waivers, Federal W/S, loans. Approved for VA benefits. Apply by May 1 to Director of Admissions. Use FAFSA plus CSS Profile.

DEGREE REQUIREMENTS. For M.Div.: 84 credits. For M.T.S.: 51 credits. The M.A. and Ph.D. are offered through the Graduate School.

FIELDS OF STUDY.
Divinity. M.Div.
Theological Studies. M.T.S.

Peabody College of Education and Human Development

Merged with Vanderbilt in 1979. Coed. Semester system. Tuition: per credit $1020. Enrollment: full-time 332, part-time 155. College faculty: full-time 97, part-time 45. Degrees conferred: M.S., M.P.P., M.Ed., Ed.S., Ed.D., Ph.D.

ADMISSION REQUIREMENTS. Official transcripts, GRE/MAT required in support of College's application. Online application available. TOEFL required for international applicants. Interviews required for doctoral programs. Apply to Director of Admissions by February 15 (Fall), November 1 (Spring). Rolling admission process. Application fee $40. Phone: (615)322-8410; fax: (615) 322-8401.

ADMISSION STANDARDS. Very selective for most departments. Usual minimum average: 3.0 for last two years (A = 4).

FINANCIAL AID. Annual awards from institutional funds: scholarships, fellowships, research assistantships, teaching assistantships, internships, grants, traineeships, Federal W/S, loans. Approved for VA benefits. Apply by February 1 to department chair for fellowships, assistantships; to Director of Financial Aid for all other programs. Phone: (615)322-3591. Use FAFSA and CSS Profile. About 60% of students receive aid from College and outside sources. Aid available for part-time students.

DEGREE REQUIREMENTS. For master's: 30 credit hours minimum, at least 24 in residence; final oral/written exam. For Ed.S.;

30 credit hours minimum beyond the master's, at least one semester in residence; final project. For Ph.D.: 72 credit hours minimum beyond the bachelor's, at least two semesters in full-time residence; qualifying exam; dissertation; proficiency in appropriate research methods; final oral exam. For Ed.D.: essentially the same as Ph.D. except 84 credit hours minimum.

FIELDS OF STUDY.
Child Studies.
Community Development Action.
Curriculum and Instructional Leadership.
Early Childhood Education.
Education Policy.
Elementary Education.
English Education.
English Language Learners.
Higher Education Administration.
Human Development Counseling.
Human Resource Development.
International Education Policy and Management.
Mathematics Education.
Organizational Leadership.
Reading Education.
Science Education.
Secondary Education.
Special Education.

School of Engineering

Graduate study since 1875. Coed. Semester system.
Tuition: per credit $1100.
Enrollment: full-time 380, part-time 35. School faculty teaching graduate students: full-time 150, part-time 12. Degrees conferred: M.S., M.Eng., Ph.D.

ADMISSION REQUIREMENTS. Official transcripts, letters of recommendation, GRE required in support of application. Online application available. TOEFL required for international applicants. Interview not required. Accepts transfer applicants. Graduates of unaccredited colleges not considered. Apply to Dean of Graduate School by January 15 (Fall), October 15 (Spring). Application fee $40. Phone: (615)343-3773; fax: (615)343-8006.

ADMISSION STANDARDS. Selective. Usual minimum average: 3.0 (A = 4).

FINANCIAL AID. Fellowships, research assistantships, teaching assistantships, internships, traineeships, tuition waivers, Federal W/S, loans. Approved for VA benefits. Apply by January 15 to Dean of the School for fellowships, assistantships; to Financial Aid Office for all other programs. Phone: (615)322-3591; fax: (615)343-8512. Use FAFSA and CSS Profile. Aid available for part-time students.

DEGREE REQUIREMENTS. For M.S., M.E.: 30 semester hours minimum, at least 12 in residence; thesis/research project; final oral exam. For Ph.D.: 72 semester hours, at least 24 credits of course work beyond the master's, at least two semesters in residence; comprehensive exam; dissertation; final oral exam.

FIELDS OF STUDY.
Biomedical Engineering.
Chemical Engineering.
Civil Engineering.
Computer Science.
Electrical and Computer Engineering.
Environmental Engineering.
Materials Science and Engineering.
Mechanical Engineering.

Owen Graduate School of Management

Web site: mba.vanderbilt.edu

Established 1969. Accredited programs: M.B.A.; recognized Ph.D. Located on main campus, some courses offered in Miami, Florida. Half-semester module system. Special programs: foreign exchange programs with Manchester Business School (England), Ecole Superieure de Sciences Economiques et Commerciales (France), Monterrey Institute of Technology (Mexico), Karlsruhe University (Germany), Norwegian School of Economics and Business (Norway), University of Sao Paulo School of Economics, Management, and Accounting (Brazil), INCAE (Costa Rica), IESA (Venezuela), the Universidad Pontificia Catolica (Chile), and the Copenhagen Business School (Denmark). Library: 44,000 volumes, 1100 subscriptions.

Annual tuition: full-time $37,834, EMBA $43,234, Ph.D. $19,000. Enrollment: total full-time 490. Faculty: 37 full-time, 30 part-time; all have Ph.D./D.B.A. Degrees conferred: M.B.A. (full-time only), E.M.B.A. (weekends only, alternating Fridays, Saturdays), I.E.M.B.A. (International Executive, in conjunction with University of Florida), M.B.A.-J.D., M.B.A.-M.A. (Latin American Studies), M.B.A.-M.S.N., M.B.A.-M.T., (Technology, with School of Engineering), Ph.D.

ADMISSION REQUIREMENTS. All applicants should have a bachelor's degree from a recognized institution of higher education and a strong mathematics background. Students are required to have their own personal computer. Contact Owen School of Management for application material and information; phone: MBA (615)322-6469; EMBA (615)322-2513; IEMBA (615)343-4087; Ph.D. (615)343-1989). Early applications are encouraged for both admission and financial aid consideration. Beginning students are admitted Fall only. Both U.S. citizens and international applicants apply by November 30 (first round), January 31 (second round), March 15 (third round), April 15 (fourth round). Online application available. Submit an application, GMAT (will accept GMAT test results from the last five years, latest acceptable date is March), official transcripts from each undergraduate/graduate school attended, two letters of recommendation, two essays, résumé (prefers at least four years of work experience), and an application fee of $100 to Owen School of Management. In addition, international students (whose native language is other than English) should submit a TOEFL report (minimum score 600), certified translations and evaluations of all official transcripts, recommendation should be in English or with certified translations, proof of health/immunization certificate, and proof of sufficient financial resources for two years of academic study. Interviews required prior to the Admissions Committee reviewing completed application. Joint degree applicants must apply to and be accepted to both schools/programs, contact the admissions office for current information and specific admissions requirements. Rolling admissions process; notification is made within four weeks of receipt of completed application and supporting documents.

ADMISSION REQUIREMENTS FOR DOCTORAL CANDIDATES. Contact Ph.D. Program Administrator, Owen School (phone: (615)343-1989) for application material and information. Applications may be downloaded from Graduate School Web site. Beginning students are admitted Fall Only. Both U.S. citizens and international applicants apply by January 15 (Fall). Submit a Graduate School application, a GMAT/GRE (will accept GMAT/GRE test results from the last five years), two official transcripts from each undergraduate/graduate school attended, three letters of recommendation, résumé, statement of purpose, and application fee of $50 to the Graduate School. In addition, international students (whose native language is other than English) should submit a TOEFL report (minimum score 600), certified translations and evaluations of all official transcripts, recommendation should be in English or with certified translations, proof of health/immunization certificate. Interviews are by invitation for final candidates only. Notification is generally made by mid-April.

ADMISSION STANDARDS. Selective. Mean GMAT: 642; mean GPA: 3.21 (A = 4). *U.S. News & World Report* ranked Owen in the top 35 of all U.S. business schools. *BusinessWeek* listed Owen in the top 25 of all U.S. business schools. Accepts about 40% of total annual applicants.

FINANCIAL AID. Scholarships, scholar awards, fellowships, graduate assistantships, internships, grants, Federal W/S, loans available. Financial aid may be available for international students in the form of merit-based scholarships. Assistantships/fellowships may be available for joint degree candidates. Financial aid applications and information are generally available at the on-campus visit/interview and are also included with the admission materials, apply by May 1. Contact Owen School's Associate Director for Student Services and Admissions for current need-based financial aid information. Phone: (615)322-6469. Use FAFSA (School code: E00528), also submit CSS Profile, a Financial Aid Transcript, Federal Income Tax forms. Approximately 50% of students receive some form of financial assistance.

DEGREE REQUIREMENTS. For M.B.A.: 60 credit program including 36 elective credits, two-year program; degree program must be completed in six years. For E.M.B.A.: 50 credit, 21-month program. For I.E.M.B.A.: 50 credit, 18-month program. For M.B.A.-M.A., M.B.A.-M.T.: 72 credit programs. For M.B.A.-M.S.N.: 69 credit program. For M.B.A.-J.D.: 151 credit, four-and-one-half- to five-and-one-half-year program. For Ph.D.: three- to five-year program, preliminary exam in a basic discipline or minor area; qualifying exam in major area; research paper; teaching assistantship; dissertation proposal and oral defense; dissertation; oral defense.

FIELDS OF STUDY.
Accountancy. M.Accy.
Business Administration. Second year concentrations in accounting, finance, human and organizational performance, information technology, marketing, operations, strategy. M.B.A.
Finance. Ph.D.
Marketing. Ph.D.
Operations Management. Ph.D.
Organization Studies. Ph.D.

School of Law
Web site: www.vanderbilt.edu/law

Established 1874. Located on main campus. ABA approved since 1925. AALS member. Semester system. Full-time, day study only. Special facilities: Vanderbilt Institute for Public Policy Studies, Freedom Forum First Amendment Center. Special programs: Transnational Legal Studies Program; clerkships, internships. Law library: 588,413 volumes, 6959 subscriptions; has LEXIS, NEXIS, WESTLAW, INFOTRAC; has more than 400 network connections; is a Federal Government Depository.

Annual tuition: $36,622. On-campus housing available. Apply to Office of Residential and Judicial Affairs. Total average annual additional expenses: $20,350.

Enrollment: first-year class 200; total 630 (men 54%, women 46%, minorities 18%). Faculty: full-time 37, part-time 25. Student to faculty ratio is 16.4 to 1. Degrees conferred: J.D., J.D.-M.B.A., J.D.-M.P.P., J.D.-M.T.S., J.D.-M.Div., LL.M. (for persons who have completed a basic legal education and received a university degree in law in another country). A concurrent M.A. and Ph.D. available through the Graduate School.

ADMISSION REQUIREMENTS. LSDAS Law School report, bachelor's degree, transcripts, two letters of recommendation, personal statement, J.D. Financial Aid statement require in support of application. Foreign applicants whose native language is

not English must submit TOEFL and use LSAC J.D. Credential Assembly Service. Accepts transfer application. Graduates of unaccredited institutions not considered. Apply to Director of Admissions by March 15 (flexible). Application fee $50. Phone: (615)322-6452; fax: (615)322-1531.

ADMISSION REQUIREMENTS FOR LL.M. APPLICANTS. All applicants must have obtained a J.D. (or equivalent) from a U.S. law school or the first (basic) law degree from a foreign law school. Official transcripts (a certified translation and evaluation in addition to original international credentials for international applicants), two letters of recommendation, personal statement required in support of Graduate Programs in Law application. In addition, international candidates whose native language is not English and have attended a law school in a non-English-speaking countries must submit TOEFL. The TSE is strongly encouraged although not required. Admits Fall only. Apply by March 1. Application Fee $50. Phone: (615)322-6452.

ADMISSION STANDARDS. Selective. Accepts approximately 23% of all students. Number of applicants 3437; number of acceptance 791; number enrolled 200; LSAT (75% of students have a score at or above 163); GPA (75% of students have a GPA at or above 3.52). *U.S. News & World Report* ranking is in the top 16 of all U.S. law schools.

FINANCIAL AID. Scholarships, loans. Apply to the Office of Financial Aid by February 15 for priority consideration. Phone: (615)322-6452. Use FAFSA (School code: E00529). About 63% of students receive aid other than loans from School.

DEGREE REQUIREMENTS. For J.D.: satisfactory completion of three-year program; 88 semester hour program. For LL.M.: 24 credit full-time program. For master's degree: see Graduate School listing above.

School of Medicine (37232-2104)
Web site: www.mc.vanderbilt.edu

Founded 1873. Special facilities: Center for Biomedical Ethics and Society, Center for Bone Biology, Center for Child Development, Center for Clinical Toxicology, Center for Evaluation and Program Improvement, Center for Human Genetics Research, Center for Matrix Biology, Center for Molecular Neuroscience, Center for Molecular Toxicology, Center for Pharmacology and Drug Toxicology, Center for Pain Research and Neuromagnetics, Center for Space Physiology and Medicine, Center for Structural Biology, Clinical Nutrition Research Unit, Digestive Disease Research Center, General Clinical Research Center, Informatics Center, Institute for Global Health, Mass Spectrometry Research Center, Mouse Metabolic Phenotyping Center, Vanderbilt Center for Evidence-based Medicine, Vanderbilt Center for Stem Cell Biology, Vanderbilt Addiction Research Center, Vanderbilt Bill Wilkerson Center, Vanderbilt Brain Institute, Vanderbilt Diabetes Center, Vanderbilt-Ingram Cancer Center, Vanderbilt Institute of Chemical Biology, Vanderbilt Kennedy Center for Research on Human Development, Vanderbilt University Institute of Imaging Science, Women's Reproductive Health Research Center. Library: 201,000 volumes, 1850 subscriptions; has MEDLINE. NIH ranking is 19th among all U.S. institutions with 668 awards/grants worth $266,236,625.

Annual tuition: $38,050. On-campus housing available. Total average figure for all other expenses: $12,500.

Enrollment: first-year class 105, total 428 (men 54%, women 46%, minorities 27%, state residents 16%). Faculty: full-time 1630, part-time 800. Degrees conferred: M.D., M.D.-M.B.A., M.D.-M.P.H., M.D.-M.S., M.D.-Ph.D. (Medical Scientist Training Program).

ADMISSION REQUIREMENTS. AMCAS report, transcripts, recommendations, MCAT, bachelor's degree required in support of application. Interview and final application by invitation only. Has EDP; apply between June 1 and August 1. Apply to AMCAS after June 1, before November 15. Application fee $50. Phone: (615)322-2145; fax: (615)343-8397.

ADMISSION STANDARDS. Very competitive. Accepts about 7% of all applicants. Number of applications 4369 (4052 out-of-state); number interviewed 993 (948 out-of-state); number of acceptance 291 (270 out-of-state); number enrolled 105 (88 out-of-state). Mean Composite MCAT 11.3; mean UGPA 3.76. *U.S. News & World Report* ranking is in the top 18 of all medical research schools, 30th in primary care.

FINANCIAL AID. Scholarships, fellowships, Federal and private loans. MSTP funded by NIH. Apply to Assistant Dean, Student Services by March 1 (priority date). Phone: (615)343-6310. Use FAFSA. About 30% of students receive aid other than loans from School.

DEGREE REQUIREMENTS. For M.D.: satisfactory completion of four-year program. For Ph.D.: see Graduate School listing above.

FIELDS OF GRADUATE STUDY.
Biochemistry.
Biomedical Engineering.
Biomedical Informatics.
Cell and Development Biology.
Microbiology and Immunology.
Molecular Biology.
Molecular Physiology and Biophysics.
Neurosciences.
Pathology.
Pharmacology.

VERMONT LAW SCHOOL
Chelsea Street
South Royalton, Vermont 05506-0096
Web site: www.vermontlaw.edu

Established 1972. Located in a national historic district along the White River. ABA approved since 1975. AALS member. Private control. Coed. Semester system. Full-time, day study only. Special facility: Environmental Law Center. Special program: Law School Exchange Program. Law library: 239,606 volumes, 1856 subscriptions; has LEXIS, NEXIS, WESTLAW, DIALOG; has more than 100 network connections; is a Federal Government Selective Depository.

Annual tuition: $31,514. On-campus housing available for single students only. Contact Business Office for both on- and off-campus housing information. Off-campus housing and personal expenses: approximately $17,695.

Enrollment: first-year class 196; total 552 (men 48%, women 52%, minorities 14%); 25 new M.S.E.L. students. Faculty: full-time 37, part-time 20. Student to faculty ratio is 13.3 to 1. Degrees conferred: J.D., M.S.E.L. (Environmental Law), LL.M. (Environmental Law), J.D.-M.S.E.L.

ADMISSION REQUIREMENTS. LSDAS Law School report, bachelor's degree or equivalent, transcripts, LSAT, recommendations, personal statement required in support of application. Graduates of unaccredited colleges not considered. Apply to Admissions Office by March 1 for priority consideration. Application fee $60. Phone: in Vermont (802)763-8303, ext. 2239; (888) 277-5985.

ADMISSION STANDARDS. Selective. Accepts approximately 51% of all students. Number of applicants 1116; number of acceptance 565; number enrolled 196; LSAT (75% of students have

a score at or above 151); GPA (75% of students have a GPA at or above 2.89). *U.S. News & World Report* ranking is in the third tier of all U.S. law schools.

FINANCIAL AID. Scholarships, tuition grants, Federal W/S, Federal and private loans. Apply to Admissions Office by March 1. Phone: (888)277-5985. Use FAFSA. About 60% of students receive some aid from School.

DEGREE REQUIREMENTS. For J.D.: satisfactory completion of 84 semester hour program. For M.S.E.L., LL.M.: at least 24 credits beyond the J.D.: one year of full-time study.

UNIVERSITY OF VERMONT
Burlington, Vermont 05405-0160
Web site: www.uvm.edu

Founded 1791. Located 95 miles S of Montreal, Canada. CGS member. Coed. State control. Semester system. Library: 2,400,000 volumes, 20,200 subscriptions. The University's NIH ranking is 89th among all U.S. institutions with 164 awards/grants worth $64,906,596. Total University enrollment: 11,600.

Tuition: per credit, resident $410, nonresident $1034. University on-campus housing for married students and for single students. Average academic year housing costs: $11,000 for single students; $16,000 for married students. Contact Director, Than Allen Housing for both on- and off-campus housing information. Phone: (802)655-0661.

Graduate College

Graduate study since 1807. Enrollment: full- and part-time 1300. Faculty: full-and part-time 361, Degrees conferred: M.A., M.S., M.Ed., M.A.T., M.S.T., M.B.A., M.Ext.Ed., M.P.A., M.S.W., Ed.D., Ph.D.

ADMISSION REQUIREMENTS. Official transcripts, GRE/MAT/GMAT (Business), letters of recommendation required in support of College's application. Online application available. GRE Subject for some programs. Interview required for some departments. Accepts transfer applicants. Graduates of unaccredited institutions not considered. Apply to Graduate College Admissions Office by April 1, except for Anatomy and Neurobiology, Botany, Field Naturalist Studies, Civil and Environmental Engineering, Communication Services, Counseling, Higher Education and Student Affairs, Microbiology and Molecular Genetics, Public Administration, Social Work, February 1; Cell and Molecular Biology, Pharmacology, Physical Therapy, Psychology, January 1; Curriculum and Instruction, Educational Leadership, Educational Studies, French, Interdisciplinary, Reading and Language Arts, Special Education, August 1; Educational Leadership and Policy Study, May 1; Forestry, Geography, Historic Preservation, Natural Resource Planning, Water Resources, Wildlife and Fisheries Biology, March 1; March 1 if applying for scholarships and fellowships. Rolling admission process. Application fee $40. Phone: (802) 656-3160; fax: (802)656-0519.

ADMISSION STANDARDS. Very competitive for most departments. Usual minimum average: 3.0 (A = 4).

FINANCIAL AID. Annual awards from institutional funds: fellowships, research assistantships, teaching assistantships, internships, tuition waivers, traineeships, Federal W/S, loans. Approved for VA benefits. Apply by March 1 to the appropriate Chair for fellowships, assistantships; to Office of Financial Aid for all other programs. Phone: (802)656-3156; fax: (802)656-4076. Use FAFSA. Aid available for part-time students.

DEGREE REQUIREMENTS. For M.A., M.S., M.S.T., M.Ed., M.Ext.Ed.: 30 semester hours minimum, at least 22 in residence; thesis/nonthesis option; final oral/written exam. For M.A.T.: same as above, except no thesis. For M.B.A.: 48 semester hours; may be reduced depending upon previous preparation; final written/oral exam. For Ph.D.: 75 semester hours minimum beyond the bachelor's, at least 51 in residence; reading knowledge of one foreign language for some programs; comprehensive exam; dissertation; final oral defense.

FIELDS OF STUDY.
Animal Sciences.
Animal Nutrition and Food Sciences.
Biochemistry.
Biology.
Biomedical Engineering. M.S. only.
Biostatistics. M.S. only.
Botany.
Business Administration. M.B.A. only.
Cell and Molecular Biology.
Chemistry. One language for M.S.
Civil and Environmental Engineering.
Communication Sciences. M.S. only.
Community Development and Applied Economics.
Computer Science. M.S. only.
Counseling. M.S. only.
Curriculum and Instruction.
Dietetics.
Ecological Economics.
Educational Leadership. Ed.D.
Educational Studies.
Electrical Engineering.
English. One language for M.A.; M.A., M.A.T. only.
Field Naturalist Studies. M.S. only.
French. M.A., M.A.T. only.
Geology. M.S., M.A.T., M.S.T. only.
German. M.A., M.A.T. only.
Greek and Latin. M.A., M.A.T. only.
Higher Education and Student Affairs. M.Ed. only.
Historic Preservation. M.S. only.
History. Sample research paper for admission to M.A. M.A., M.A.T. only.
Materials Science.
Mathematical Sciences. Ph.D. only.
Mathematics. M.S. only.
Mechanical Engineering.
Microbiology and Molecular Genetics.
Molecular Physiology and Biophysics.
Natural Resources. Ph.D. only.
Neuroscience.
Nursing. M.S. only.
Nutrition and Food Sciences. M.S. only.
Pathology. M.S. only.
Pharmacology.
Physical Therapy.
Physics. M.S. only.
Plant and Soil Science.
Psychology.
Public Administration. M.P.A. only.
Reading and Language Arts.
Social Work. M.S.W. only.
Special Education.
Statistics. M.S. only.

College of Medicine (37232-2104)
Web site: www.med.uvm.edu

Established in 1822, seventh oldest medical school. Special facilities: Cardiovascular Research Institute, General Clinical Research Center, Health Behavior Research Center, McClure Musculoskeletal Research Center, Microscopy Imaging Center (Cell Imaging Facility), Treatment Research Center, UVM Substance Abuse Treatment Center, Vermont Cancer Center, Vermont Lung Center. Library: 100,000 volumes, 1450 subscriptions. NIH ranking is 89th among all U.S. institutions with 164 awards/grants worth $64,906,596.

Annual tuition: residents $26,055, nonresidents $44,425. No on-campus housing available: off-campus housing within working or biking distance of campus. Total average figure for all other expenses: $13,500.

Enrollment: first-year class 102, total 425 (men 40%, women 60%, minorities 16%, state residents 32%). Faculty: full-time 512, part-time 600. Degrees conferred: M.D., M.D.-Ph.D.

ADMISSION REQUIREMENTS. AMCAS report, transcripts, MCAT, letters of evaluation required in support of application. Supplemental application required. Interview by invitation only. Has EDP; apply between June 1 and August 1. Preference given to residents of Vermont, Maine. Apply to Associate Dean for Admission after June 1, before November 1. Application fee $85. Phone: (802)656-2154; fax: (802) 656-8577.

ADMISSION STANDARDS. Competitive. Accepts about 6% of all applicants. Number of applications 3482 (3390 out-of-state); number interviewed 497 (431 out-of-state); number of acceptance 205 (154 out-of-state); number enrolled 102 (59 out-of-state). Mean Composite MCAT 9.9; mean UGPA 3.60. *U.S. News & World Report* ranking is in the top 6 of all primary care medical schools.

FINANCIAL AID. Scholarships, merit scholarships, minority scholarships, Grants-in-Aid, UVM 21st-Century Loan Program, HEAL, alternative loan programs, Federal Perkins Loans, Stafford Subsidized and Unsubsidized Loans, Service Commitment Scholarship programs are available. Assistantships/fellowships may be available for M.D.-Ph.D. candidates. Financial aid applications and information are generally available at the on-campus by invitation interview. For scholarships assistance, the selection criteria places heavy reliance on MCAT and undergraduate GPA. Contact the Financial Aid Office for current information. Phone: (802)656-5700. Use FAFSA prior to March 1 (School code: 03696), also submit Financial Aid Transcript, Federal Income Tax forms. Approximately 90% of students receive some form of financial assistance.

DEGREE REQUIREMENTS. For M.D.: satisfactory completion of 45-month program. Taking USMLE Step 1 and Step 2 are required for graduation. For M.D.-Ph.D.: generally a six- to seven-year program.

FIELDS OF GRADUATE STUDY.
Biochemistry.
Cell and Molecular Biology.
Genetics.
Molecular Biology.
Microbiology and Molecular Genetics.
Molecular Physiology and Biophysics.
Neurosciences.
Pathology.
Pharmacology.

VILLANOVA UNIVERSITY
Villanova, Pennsylvania 19085-1688
Web site: www.villanova.edu

Founded 1843. Located 10 miles W of Philadelphia. CGS member. Coed. Private control. Roman Catholic. Semester system. Library: 1,000,000 volumes, 8000 subscriptions. Total University enrollment: 10,450.

No on-campus housing available. For off-campus housing information, contact housing office. Phone: (610)519-4154.

Graduate School of Liberal Arts and Sciences

Graduate study since 1931. Tuition: per credit $585 (Arts), $650 (Sciences). Enrollment: full-time 420, part-time 588. Degrees conferred: M.A., MS., Ph.D.

ADMISSION REQUIREMENTS. Two official transcripts required in support of School's application. Online application available. Recommendations, GRE, interview required for program. TOEFL required for international applicants. Deadlines vary by program. Contact Dean's office for deadlines. Rolling admissions process. Application fee $50. Phone: (610)519-7090; fax: (610)519-7096.

ADMISSION STANDARDS. Competitive for some departments, selective for others. Usual minimum average: 3.0 (A = 4).

FINANCIAL AID. From the University, graduate assistantships, scholarships, fellowships, research assistantships, internships, Federal W/S, loans. Deadline for applications for University aid vary by program. Contact Graduate Dean for specific dates with reference to assistantships, fellowships. Contact Financial Aid Office for all other programs. Phone: (610)519-4010. Use FAFSA and Graduate School FAF. Aid available for part-time students.

DEGREE REQUIREMENTS. For master's: 30–48 semester hours; comprehensive exam; reading knowledge of one foreign language for some majors; thesis/nonthesis option; final oral/written exam. For Ph.D.: 60 semester hours beyond the master's, at least two semesters in residence; qualifying exam, candidacy; dissertation; final oral exam.

FIELDS OF STUDY.
Applied Statistics.
Biology.
Chemistry.
Classical Studies.
Computer Science.
Counseling and Human Relations. Includes community, elementary, secondary.
Criminal Justice Administration.
Elementary Education.
English.
Hispanic Studies.
History.
Human Resource Development.
Liberal Studies.
Mathematics.
Philosophy.
Political Science.
Psychology.
Public Administration.
Theater.
Theology.

School of Business

Established 1922, graduate studies since 1982. Accredited programs: M.B.A. Semester system.

Tuition: $815 per credit.

Enrollment: total full-time 97, part-time 715 (men 60%, women 40%). Faculty: 69 full-time, 44 part-time; 94% with Ph.D./D.B.A. Degrees conferred: M.B.A. (full-time, part-time, evening only), M.T. (Taxation), M.B.A.-J.D.

ADMISSION REQUIREMENTS. All applicants should have a bachelor's degree from a recognized institution of higher education. Admission is based on the formula 200 × UGPA + GMAT. Contact College of Commerce at (610)519-4336 for application material and information. Beginning students are admitted Fall, Spring, and Summer. Both U.S. citizens and international applicants apply by June 30 (Fall), November 15 (Spring), April 15 (Summer). Submit an application, GMAT (will accept GMAT test results from the last five years, latest acceptable date is June), official transcripts from each undergraduate/graduate school attended, three letters of recommendation, two essays, personal statement, résumé (prefers at least four years of work experience), and an application fee of $50 to the Office of Graduate Admission. In addition, international students (whose native language is other than English) should submit a TOEFL report (minimum score 600), certified translations and evaluations of all official transcripts, recommendation should be in English or with certified translations, proof of health/immunization certificate, and proof of sufficient financial resources for two years of academic study. On-campus visits are encouraged. Admissions Committee may consider applicants with some academic course work deficiencies. Joint degree applicants must apply to and be accepted to both schools, contact the admissions office for current information and specific admissions requirements. Rolling admissions process; notification is made within four-weeks of receipt of completed application and supporting documents.

ADMISSION STANDARDS. Selective. Usual minimum average: 3.0 (A = 4). Mean GMAT: 560; mean GPA: 3.1 (A = 4).

FINANCIAL AID. Graduate assistantships, Federal Perkins Loans, Stafford Subsidized and Unsubsidized Loans, Federal W/S available. Aid is available for part-time study. Financial aid may be available for international students in the form of graduate assistantships. Assistantships/fellowships may be available for joint degree candidates. Financial aid applications and information are generally included with admissions materials; apply by July 1. Request assistantship information from the College of Commerce. Contact the University's Financial Aid Office for current need-based financial aid information. Phone: (610)519-4010. Use FAFSA (School code: 003368) and PHEAA, also submit Financial Aid Transcript, Federal Income Tax forms. Approximately 10% of students receive some form of financial assistance.

DEGREE REQUIREMENTS. For M.B.A.: 33–48 credit program including 12 elective credits, one- to two-year program; degree program must be completed in ten years. For M.T.: 24-credit program. For M.B.A.-Masters: generally a three-and-one-half- to five-year program. For M.B.A.-J.D.: four-and-one-half- to six-year program.

FIELDS OF STUDY.
Accounting. M.Ac.
Business Administration. M.B.A., E.M.B.A.
Church Management. M.S.
Finance. M.S.F.
Taxation. M.T.
Technology Management. M.T.M.

College of Engineering

Tuition: per credit $845.

Enrollment: full-time 72, part-time 371. Faculty: full-time 58, part-time 35. Degrees conferred: M.C.E., M.Ch.E., M.S.C.E., M.S.E.E., M.M.E., M.S.T.E.

ADMISSION REQUIREMENTS. Two official transcripts, GRE required in support of College's application. Online application available. TOEFL required for international applicants. Accepts transfer applicants. Graduates of unaccredited institutions not considered. Apply to Director of Admissions; no specified closing date. Rolling admissions process. Application fee $50. Phone: (610) 519-4940; fax: (610)519-4941.

ADMISSION STANDARDS. Selective. Usual minimum average: 3.0 (A = 4).

FINANCIAL AID. Scholarships, research assistantships, teaching assistantships, Federal W/S, loans. Approved for VA benefits.

Apply to Dean for assistantships, to Financial Aid Office for all other programs. Phone: (610)519-4010. Use FAFSA and institutional FAF.

DEGREE REQUIREMENTS. For master's: 30–36 hours; thesis/nonthesis option; comprehensive exam.

FIELDS OF STUDY.
Chemical Engineering.
Civil Engineering.
Computer Engineering.
Electrical Engineering.
Mechanical Engineering.
Transportation Engineering.
Water Resources and Environmental Engineering.

School of Law
Web site: www.law.villanova.edu

Founded 1953. ABA approved since 1954. AALS member. Private control. Semester system. No part-time summer or evening study. Special facility: Center for Information Law and Policy. Law library: 516,273 volumes, 3554 subscriptions; has LEXIS, NEXIS, WESTLAW, DIALOG; has more than 300 network connections.

Annual tuition: $29,340. No on-campus housing available. Contact Student Bar Association in June for off-campus housing information. Off-campus housing and personal expenses: approximately $18,688.

Enrollment: first-year class 245; total 725 (men 52%, women 48%, minorities 17%). Faculty: full-time 40, part-time 33. Student to faculty ratio is 17.7 to 1. Degrees conferred: J.D., J.D.-M.B.A., J.D.-Ph.D. (Law and Psychology), LL.M. (Taxation), J.D.-LL.M.

ADMISSION REQUIREMENTS. LSDAS Law School report, bachelor's degree, transcripts, LSAT required in support of application. Interview not required. Transfer applicants considered for admission into second-year class; one full year of superior work at another accredited/approved law school is required. Graduates of unaccredited colleges not considered. Apply to Admissions Office after September 1, before March 1. Application fee $75. Phone: (610)519-7010; fax: (610)519-6291.

ADMISSION STANDARDS. Selective. Accepts approximately 32% of all students. Number of applicants 2994; number of acceptance 945; number enrolled 245; LSAT (75% of students have a score at or above 161); GPA (75% of students have a GPA at or above 3.30). *U.S. News & World Report* ranking is in the second tier (tied at 60th) of all U.S. law schools.

FINANCIAL AID. Scholarships, special minority scholarships, partial tuition waivers, resident assistantships, counselorships, Federal W/S, loans. For resident assistantships, apply to Dean of Residence Life. Apply to Financial Aid Office by March 1 for all other programs. Phone: (610)519-7015. Use FAFSA (School code: E00428). About 20% of students receive aid from Law School sources.

DEGREE REQUIREMENTS. For J.D.: satisfactory completion of three-year program; 87 semester hour program. For LL.M.: at least 24 credits beyond the J.D.: one year in full-time residence.

College of Nursing

Tuition: per credit $650.
Enrollment: full-time 41, part-time 141. Faculty: full-time 15, part-time 4. Degree conferred: M.S.N.

ADMISSION REQUIREMENTS. Two official transcripts, GRE required in support of College's application. TOEFL required for international applicants. Accepts transfer applicants. Graduates of unaccredited institutions not considered. Apply to Director of

Admissions by July 1 (Fall), December 1 (Spring). Rolling admissions process. Application fee $50. Phone: (610)519-4934; fax: (610)519-7650.

ADMISSION STANDARDS. Selective. Usual minimum average: 3.0 (A = 4).

FINANCIAL AID. Assistantships, scholarships, traineeships, Federal W/S, loans. Approved for VA benefits. Apply by March 1 to Dean for assistantships; to Financial Aid Office for all other programs. Phone: (610)519-4010. Use FAFSA and institutional FAF. Aid available for part-time students.

DEGREE REQUIREMENTS. For master's: 30–36 semester hours; thesis; comprehensive exam.

FIELDS OF STUDY.
Adult Nurse Practitioner.
Clinical Case Management.
Community Nurse Service Administration.
Geriatric Nurse Practitioner.
Nursing Administration.
Staff Administration.
Teaching of Nursing.

VIRGINIA COMMONWEALTH UNIVERSITY
Richmond, Virginia 23284-3051
Web site: www.vcu.edu

Founded 1838. University formed with merger of Richmond Professional Institute and Medical College of Virginia in 1968. CGS member. Coed. State control. Semester system. Special facilities: Anderson Art Gallery, Burn Trauma Clinic, Institute of Biotechnology, Business Management Center, Massey Cancer Center, Sickle Cell Anemia Center, Institute of Statistics, Virginia Center on Aging, Virginia Center for Public/Private Initiative, Virginia Institute for Developmental Disabilities. The University's NIH ranking is 80th among all U.S. institutions with 231 awards/grants valued at $73,030,895. According to The Center at University of Florida, the University is ranked 97th in receipt of Federal Research funds with $81,201,000 and it ranks 100th for total University research expenditures with $126,451,000. In 2004, the University awarded 153 doctorates, which ranked it 97th among all U.S. institutions eligible to award that degree. Two of the University's faculty members have been elected to National Honor Academies and this ranks it 117th among all U.S. institutions. The Library: approximately 1,500,000 volumes, 10,000 subscriptions. Total University enrollment: 29,300.

Annual tuition: resident $6268, nonresident $15,904; per credit resident $405, nonresident $940. Limited on-campus housing for graduate students. Average academic year housing costs: $4200–$5800. Contact Director of residence Life for both on- and off-campus hosing information. Phone: (804)828-7666.

School of Graduate Studies

Enrollment: full-time 4299, part-time 4585. Faculty: full-time 875. Degrees conferred: M.A., M.Acc., M.A.E., M.B.A., M.Ed., M.F.A., M.H.A., M.I.S., M.M., M.P.A., M.P.H., M.S., M.S.H.A., M.S.N.A., M.S.O.T., M.S.W., M.Tax., M.T., M.U.R.P., Ph.D., J.D.-M.H.A., J.D.-M.U.R.P., J.D.-M.S.W., M.S.-D.D.S., M.S.-M.D., Pharm.D., Ph.D., Ph.D.-D.D.S., Ph.D.-M.D., Ph.D.-Pharm.D., C.Acc., C.A.S., C.A.S.R., C.C.S., C.C.J.A., C.I.S., C.P.I., C.P.C., C.P.M., C.T.

ADMISSION REQUIREMENTS. Transcripts, GRE/GMAT/MAT required in support of School's application. TOEFL required for international applicants. Accepts transfer applicants. Graduates of unaccredited institutions not considered. Apply to Director of Admissions. Application deadlines vary by program. Application fee $50. Phone: (804)828-6916; fax: (804)828-6949; e-mail: vcu-grad@vcu.edu.

ADMISSION STANDARDS. Selective. Minimum acceptable GPA: 2.7 (A = 4).

FINANCIAL AID. Annual awards from institutional funds: teaching/research assistantships, full and partial tuition waivers, Federal W/S, loans. Approved for VA benefits. Apply to appropriate department chair for assistantships, fellowships; to Financial Aid Office for all other aid; no specified closing dates. Phone: (804)828-6669; fax: (804)828-6187. Use FAFSA. About 15% of students receive aid other than loans from University and outside sources. Aid available for part-time students.

DEGREE REQUIREMENTS. Vary by program.

FIELDS OF STUDY.
Accountancy. Includes finance and auditing, information systems. M.Acc.
Accounting. Ph.D.
Adult Learning. Includes adult literacy, adults with disabilities, human resource development. M.Ed.
Anatomy and Neurobiology. Includes anatomical sciences (M.S., Ph.D.), molecular biology and genetics (M.S., Ph.D.), neurobiology (M.S., Ph.D.), neuroscience (Ph.D.), physical therapy (Ph.D.). M.S., Ph.D.
Art Education. M.A.E.
Arts History. Includes architectural history, historical studies, museum studies. M.A., Ph.D.
Athletic Training. M.S.A.T.
Biochemistry. Includes molecular biology & genetics, neuroscience. M.S., Ph.D.
Bioinformatics. Includes biological/genomic, computational, quantitative/statistical. M.Bin, M.S.
Biology. M.S.
Biomedical Engineering. M.S., Ph.D.
Biostatistics. M.S., Ph.D.
Business. Includes accounting (Ph.D.), decision sciences (M.S.), finance (M.S.), global marketing management (M.S.), human resource management and industrial relations (M.S.), information systems Ph.D.), management (Ph.D.), real estate valuation (M.S.). M.S., Ph.D.
Business Administration. M.B.A.
Chemistry. M.S., Ph.D.
Clinical Laboratory Sciences. M.S.
Clinical Psychology. Ph.D.
Computer Science. M.S.
Counseling Psychology. Ph.D.
Counselor Education. M.Ed.
Creative Writing. M.F.A.
Criminal Justice. M.S.
Dentistry. Includes endodontics, orthodontics, pediatric dentistry, periodontics. M.S.D.
Design. Includes interior environments, visual communications. M.F.A.
Economics. Includes financial economics. M.A.
Education. Includes educational leadership, instructional leadership, research and evaluation, special education and disability policy leadership, urban services leadership. Ph.D.
Educational Leadership. Includes administration and supervision, leadership studies. M.Ed.
Engineering. Includes chemical and life science engineering (M.S., Ph.D.), computer science (Ph.D.), electrical and computer engineering (M.S., Ph.D.), engineering (Ph.D.), mechanical engineering (M.S., Ph.D.), nuclear engineering (M.S.). M.S., Ph.D.
English. Includes literature, writing and rhetoric. M.A.
Environmental Studies. M.Env., M.S.
Epidemiology. Ph.D.

Fine Arts. Includes ceramics, fibers, furniture design, glassworking, jewelry/metalworking, kinetic imaging, painting, photography and film, printmaking, sculpture. M.F.A.
Forensic Science. M.S.
Genetic Counseling. M.S.
Gerontology. Includes education, health care planning and organization, psychogeriatrics, public administration, research, social services. M.S.
Health Administration. M.H.A., M.S.H.A.
Health and Movement Sciences. Includes exercise science, teacher education. M.S.
Health Related Sciences. Includes clinical laboratory sciences, gerontology, health administration, nurse anesthesia, occupational therapy, physical therapy, radiation sciences, rehabilitation leadership. Ph.D.
Health Services Organization and Research. Ph.D.
History. M.A.
Homeland Security and Emergency Preparedness. M.A.
Human Genetics. Includes molecular biology and genetics (M.S., Ph.D.), genetic epidemiology (Ph.D.). M.S., Ph.D.
Information Systems. M.S.
Integrative Life Sciences. Ph.D.
Interdisciplinary Studies. M.I.S.
Mass Communication. Includes advertising (art direction, communication strategy, copywriting, creative brand management), multimedia journalism, scholastic journalism, strategic public relations. M.S.
Mathematical Sciences. Includes applied, operations research statistics. M.S.
Media, Art and Text. Ph.D.
Medical Physics. M.S., Ph.D.
Microbiology and Immunology. Includes molecular geology & genetics. M.S., Ph.D.
Music. Includes composition, education, performance. M.M.
Nurse Anesthesia. M.S.N.A., D.N.A.P.
Nursing. Includes adult health (acute care, primary care), child health, family health, integrative psychiatric mental health, nursing administration and leadership, women's health (M.S.); behavioral clinical, biology of health and human illness, healing, health systems, human health and illness, immunocompetence, nursing systems, risk and resilience (Ph.D.). M.S., Ph.D.
Occupational Therapy. M.S., M.S.O.T.
Pathology. Ph.D.
Patient Counseling. M.S.
Pharmaceutical Sciences. Includes medicinal chemistry, pharmaceutics, pharmacotherapy, pharmacy administration. M.P.S., M.S., Ph.D.
Pharmacology and Toxicology. Includes molecular biology and genetics (M.S., Ph.D.), neuroscience (Ph.D.). M.S., Ph.D.
Physics. Includes applied physics. M.S.
Physiology. M.S., Ph.D.
Psychology. Includes clinical, counseling. Ph.D.
Public Administration. M.P.A.
Public Health. Includes addiction studies, environmental health, epidemiology. M.P.H.
Public Policy and Administration. Ph.D.
Reading. M.Ed.
Recreation, Parks and Sport Leadership. M.S.
Rehabilitation and Movement Science. Includes exercise physiology, neuromusculoskeletal dynamics. Ph.D.
Rehabilitation Counseling. M.S.
Social Work. M.S.W., Ph.D.
Sociology. M.S., Ph.D.
Special Education. Includes early childhood, emotional disturbance, learning disabilities, mental retardation, severe disabilities. M.Ed.
Taxation. M.Tax.
Teaching. Includes early childhood, elementary education, middle education, secondary (biology, chemistry, English, French, German, history-social studies, interdisciplinary science, mathematic physics, Spanish), special Education. M.T.

Theatre. Includes acting, costume design, directing, pedagogy (acting, directing, literature), stage design/technical theatre. M.F.A.

Urban and Regional Planning. Includes community revitalization, environmental planning, international development planning, metropolitan planning, planning management. M.U.R.P.

School of Dentistry (23298-0566)

Web site: www.dentistry.vcu.edu

Established 1893 as the Dental department in the College of Medicine. Located at Health Science Complex. Semester system. Special facilities: Philips Institute, Clinical Research Center for Periodontal Disease.

Annual tuition: resident $15,798, nonresident $31,060. On-campus housing available for both single and married students. Average academic year off-campus housing costs: $9,000–$13,500. Contact the Office of Residential Life & Housing for both on- and off-campus housing information. Phone: (804)828-7666. Total average cost for all other first-year expenses: $8,500.

Enrollment: first year class 83, total 374 (men 62%, women 38%, minorities 7%, state residents 60%). Faculty: full-time 46, part-time 92. Degrees conferred: D.D.S., D.D.S. –M.S., D.D.S.-Ph.D.

ADMISSION REQUIREMENTS. AADSAS report, transcripts, DAT (no later than October), recommendations, interview required in support of School's application. Applicants must have completed at least 90 semester hours of college study, School prefers 120 semester hour applicants. Interview by invitation only. Accepts transfer applicants. Preference given to state residents. Apply to Director of Admissions after June 1, before November 1. Application fee $70. Phone: (804)828-9196; fax: (804)828-5288.

ADMISSION STANDARDS. Selective. Accepts about 10–15% of all applicants. Usual minimum UGPA: 3.0 (A = 4). Mean DAT: academic 19, PAT 19; mean UGPA 3.45.

FINANCIAL AID. Limited. Apply to Financial Aid officer of School; no specified closing date. Phone: (804)828-9196. Use FAFSA (School code: 003735). Approximately 85% of class receives some form of financial assistance.

DEGREE REQUIREMENTS. For D.D.S.: satisfactory completion of four-year program, least two years in residence. For D.D.S.-M.S.: satisfactory completion of four to five year program. For D.D.S.-Ph.D.: satisfactory completion of six- to seven-year program. Offered jointly with School of Graduate Studies.

FIELDS OF POSTGRADUATE STUDY.
Endodontics. M.S.
General Dentistry.
General Practice Residency.
Oral & Maxillofacial Surgery.
Orthodontics. M.S.
Pediatric Dentistry. M.S.
Periodontics. M.S.

School of Medicine (23298-0565)

Web site: www.medschool.uvc.edu

Established in 1838, as a medical department at Hampden-Sidney College, became Medical College of Virginia in 1954, a totally independent institution. Located near the financial and governmental areas of downtown. Special facility: Medical College of Virginia Clinical Research Center. Library: 100,000 volumes, 1450 subscriptions. NIH ranking is 80th among all U.S. institutions with 231 awards/grants worth $73,030,895.

Annual tuition: residents $26,952, nonresidents $39,436. On-campus housing available. Total average figure for all other expenses: $13,300.

Enrollment: first-year class 184, total 727 (men 51%, women 49%, minorities 41%, state residents 58%). Faculty: full-time 749, part-time 40. Degrees conferred: M.D., M.D.-M.H.A., M.D.-M.P.H., M.D.-Ph.D.

ADMISSION REQUIREMENTS. AMCAS report, transcripts, MCAT, recommendations, interview required in support of application. Applicants must have completed at least 90 hours of college study. Interview by invitation only. Preference given to state residents. Accepts transfer applicants. Has EDP; apply between June 1 and August 1. Apply to AMCAS after June 1, before October 15. Application fee $80. Phone: (804)828-9629; fax: (804)828-1246.

ADMISSION STANDARDS. Competitive. Accepts about 8% of all applicants. Number of applications 4877 (4068 out-of-state); number interviewed 685 (368 out-of-state); number of acceptance 368 (180 out-of-state); number enrolled 184 (80 out-of-state). Mean Composite MCAT 9.8; mean UGPA 3.50.

FINANCIAL AID. Scholarships, fellowships, loans, Federal W/S. Apply to Financial Aid Office (phone: (804)828-4006) of the School for scholarships, to Dean of the School for fellowships by September 1. Use FAFSA (School code: 003735). About 38% of students receive aid other than loans from school.

DEGREE REQUIREMENTS. For M.D.: satisfactory completion of four-year program, at least final two years in residence; all students must take USMLE Step 1 and Step 2 and record a score. See Graduate Division entry for Ph.D. requirements.

FIELDS OF GRADUATE STUDY (M.D.-PH.D.).
Addiction and Drugs of Abuse.
Brain Response to Trauma.
Cancer Biology.
Cancer Immunology.
Genetics of Health.
Infectious Disease and Vaccinology.
Immunology and Allergy.
Integrated Cell and Molecular Signaling.
Mixtures Toxicology and Statistics.
Molecular Pathogenesis.
Pharmacology of Abused Drugs.
Psychiatric and Statistical Genetics.
Structural Biology.

Graduate Education

Graduate study since 1934 and is now under the School of Medicine's administrative authority. Annual tuition/fees: full-time resident $6784, nonresident $15,904.

Enrollment: full-time 248, part-time 99. Graduate faculty: full-time 190, part-time 0. Degrees conferred: M.P.H., M.S., Ph.D., M.D.-Ph.D., Specialized Master's, Certificates.

ADMISSION REQUIREMENTS. Transcripts, three letters of recommendation, interview (for most departments), GRE Subject Tests required in support of application. Online application available. TOEFL required of all international applicants. Accepts transfer applicants. Graduates of unaccredited institutions not considered. Apply to the Office of Graduate Education by January 1 (Fall). Some programs have earlier deadlines. Admits Fall only. Application fee $50. Phone: (804)828-1023; fax: (804)828-1473.

ADMISSION STANDARDS. Competitive for most departments. Usual minimum average: 2.75 (A = 4).

FINANCIAL AID. Scholarships, NIH traineeships, fellowships, research assistantships, teaching assistantships, internships, Federal W/S, loans. Approved for VA benefits. Apply to Office of Dean for assistantships, fellowships, to Financial Aid Office for all other programs. No specified closing date. Phone: (804)828-

0523; fax: (804)828-2703. Use FAFSA. About 75% of students receive aid other than loans from School and outside sources.

DEGREE REQUIREMENTS. For master's: one year minimum in residence; thesis; final exam. For Ph.D.: two years in residence beyond the master's; comprehensive written; advancement to candidacy; dissertation; final oral exam.

FIELDS OF STUDY.
Anatomy.
Biochemistry.
Biostatistics.
Epidemiology. M.P.H.
Genetic Counseling. M.S.G.C.
Human Genetics.
Immunology.
Microbiology and Immunology.
Molecular Biology and Genetics. Ph.D. only.
Neuroscience.
Pathology.
Pharmacology and Toxicology.
Physiology.
Public Health. M.P.H.
Structural Biology.

School of Nursing

Master's study since 1968; doctoral study since 1986. Located at the Health Sciences complex.

Annual tuition/fees: full-time resident $6784, nonresident $15,904. Enrollment: full-time 129, part-time 115. Graduate faculty: full-time 21, part-time 4; volunteers 65. Degrees conferred: M.S., Ph.D.

ADMISSION REQUIREMENTS. Official transcripts, personal statement, GRE, nursing license, B.S. in nursing from a NLN accredited school, three references required in support of School's application. TOEFL (minimum score 550) required of international applicants. Graduates of foreign nursing schools who are licensed outside the United States are required to pass the Qualifying Exam of the Commission on Graduates of Foreign Nursing Schools prior to application and include the exam report with their application materials. Accepts transfer applicants. Graduates of unaccredited institutions not considered. Apply by February 1 to School of Graduate Studies. Application fee $50. Phone: (804)282-5171; fax (804)282-7743.

ADMISSION STANDARDS. Competitive. Usual minimum average: 3.0 (A = 4).

FINANCIAL AID. Annual awards from institutional funds. Scholarships, fellowships, grants, teaching assistantships, internships, Federal W/S, loans. Apply by May 1 to the Office of Enrollment Services. Phone: (804)828-5171. Use FAFSA and institutional FAF. About 68% of students receive aid other than loans from both School and outside sources.

DEGREE REQUIREMENTS. For M.S.: 36–48 semester credits minimum (up to 12 approved credits may be transferred), qualifying exam; clinical experience; thesis option. For Ph.D.: 60 credits minimum (up to 15 approved credits may be transferred); qualifying exam; dissertation; oral exam.

FIELDS OF STUDY.
Adult Health. Includes acute care, primary care. Post-master's certificate.
Adult Health Nursing. Includes acute care nursing, primary care nursing. M.S.
Child Health. Post-master's certificate.
Child Health Nursing. M.S.
Clinical Nurse Manager. Post-master's certificate.

Family Health. Certificate.
Family Health Nursing. M.S.
Healing. Ph.D.
Immunocompetence. Ph.D.
Nurse Executive. Post-master's certificate.
Nursing Systems—Clinical Nurse Manager. M.S.
Nursing Systems—Nurse Executive. M.S.
Psychiatric Mental Health Nursing. M.S. Post-master's certificate.
Risk and Resilience. Ph.D.
Women's Health. Post-master's certificate.
Women's Health Nursing. M.S.

VIRGINIA POLYTECHNIC INSTITUTE AND STATE UNIVERSITY
Blacksburg, Virginia 24061-0325
Web site: www.vt.edu

Founded 1872. Located 40 miles W of Roanoke. CGS member. Coed. State control. Semester systems. Special facilities: Center for Geospatial Information Technology, Center for Gerontology, Center for Human-Computer Interaction, Center for Survey Research, Fralin Biotechnology Center, Institute for Particle Physics and Astrophysics, Metropolitan Institute, Virginia Bioinformatics Institute, Virginia Center for Coal and Energy Research, Virginia Center for Housing Research, Virginia Tech Transportation Institute, Virginia Water Resources Research Center. The University's NIH ranking is 184th among all U.S. institutions with 41 awards/grants valued at $19,996,106. According to The Center at University of Florida, the University is ranked 78th in receipt of Federal Research funds with $98,143,000 and it ranks 50th for total University research expenditures with $247,807,000. In 2004, the University awarded 290 doctorates which ranked it 46th among all U.S. institutions eligible to award that degree. Twelve of the University's faculty members have been elected to National Honor Academies and this ranks it 62nd among all U.S. institutions. The Library: approximately 2,200,000 volumes, 22,000 subscriptions. Total University enrollment: 28,000.

Annual tuition: full-time resident $6558, nonresident $11,296; part-time, per credit resident $364, nonresident $628. Limited on-campus housing. Average academic year housing costs: $2100 (room only) single students. Contact Manager, Campus Housing, for both on- and off-campus housing information. Phone: (540) 231-6204.

Graduate School
Web site: www.grad.vt.edu

Enrollment: full-time 4090, part-time 2272. Faculty: full-time 1500. Degrees conferred: M.A., M.Acc., M.B.A., M.F., M.F.A., M.A.Ed., M.S.Ed., M.Arch., M.A.I.S., M.S., M.S.L.F.S., M.Engr., M.P.A., M.I.S., M.L.A., M.U.A., M.U.R.P., C.A.G.S., Ed.D., Ph.D.

ADMISSION REQUIREMENTS. Official transcripts, three letters of recommendation required in support of application. Online application available. GRE/GMAT, interview required for some departments. GRE/Subject Tests strongly recommended. TOEFL (minimum score 550) and GRE required for international applicants. Accepts transfer applicants. Graduates of unaccredited colleges not considered. Apply to School by January 15 (for Financial Aid consideration), or at least two months prior to registration; May 15 (Fall), October 15 (Spring) for international applicants. Application fee $45. Phone: (540)231-3092; fax: (540) 231-3750.

ADMISSION STANDARDS. Very selective for many departments. Usual minimum average: 3.0, 2.7 for provisional (A = 4).

FINANCIAL AID. Annual awards from institutional funds: scholarships, fellowships, teaching/research assistantships, internships, tuition waivers, Federal W/S, loans. Approved for VA benefits. Apply to appropriate department chairman for scholarships, fellowships, assistantships; to Financial Aid Office for all other programs. Phone: (540)231-5179. Use FAFSA. About 60% of students receive aid other than loans from School and outside sources. Aid available for part-time students.

DEGREE REQUIREMENTS. For master's: 30 semester hours minimum, at least 24 in residence; thesis/nonthesis option; final oral/written exam. For C.A.G.S.: 30 semester hours beyond the master's; final written exam. For Ph.D.: 90 semester hours minimum beyond the bachelor's, at least 30 in full-time attendance; reading knowledge of one foreign language in some departments; preliminary exam; dissertation; final oral/written exam. For Ed.D.: essentially the same as for the Ph.D., except no language requirement.

FIELDS OF STUDY.

COLLEGE OF AGRICULTURE AND LIFE SCIENCES:
Agricultural and Extension Education. M.S., Ph.D.
Agriculture and Applied Economics. M.S.
Animal and Dairy Science. Ph.D.
Animal and Poultry Sciences. M.S., Ph.D.
Biochemistry. M.S.L.F.S., Ph.D.
Crop and Soil Environmental Sciences. M.S., Ph.D.
Dairy Science. M.S.
Economics in Agricultural and Life Sciences. Ph.D.
Entomology. M.S.L.F.S., Ph.D.
Food Science and Technology. M.S.L.F.S., Ph.D.
Horticulture. M.S., Ph.D.
Human Nutrition, Foods and Exercise. M.S., Ph.D.
Plant Pathology, Physiology, and Weed Science. M.S.L.F.S., Ph.D.

COLLEGE OF ARCHITECTURE AND URBAN STUDIES:
Architecture. M.Arch., M.S.
Architecture and Design Research.. Ph.D.
Building Construction. M.S.
Environmental Design and Planning. Ph.D.
Landscape Architecture. M.L.A.
Public Administration and Public Affairs. M.P.A., Ph.D.
Public and International Affairs. M.P.I.A.
Urban and Regional Planning. M.U.R.P., Ph.D.

COLLEGE OF LIBERAL ARTS AND HUMAN SCIENCES:
Apparel, Housing and Resource Management. M.S., Ph.D.
Communication. M.S.
Creative Writing. M.F.A.
Career and Technical Education. M.S.Ed., Ed.S., Ed.D., Ph.D.
Counselor Education. M.A.Ed., Ed.S., Ed.D., Ph.D.
Curriculum and Instruction. M.A.Ed., Ed.S., Ed.D., Ph.D.
Educational Research, Evaluation. Ph.D.
English. M.A.
Foreign Languages, Cultures and Literatures. M.A.
Health and Physical Education. M.S.Ed.
History. M.A.
Human Development. M.S., Ph.D.
Leadership and Policy. M.A.Ed., Ed.S., Ed.D., Ph.D.
Philosophy. M.A.
Political Science. M.A.
Rhetoric and Writing. Ph.D.
Science and Technology Studies. M.S., Ph.D.
Sociology. M.S., Ph.D.
Special Education Administration. Ed.S., Ed.D., Ph.D.
Theatre Arts. M.F.A.

PAMPLIN COLLEGE OF BUSINESS:
Accounting and Information Systems. M.A.I.S., Ph.D.
Business Administration. M.B.A.
Business Information Technology. M.S., Ph.D.
Finance. M.S., Ph.D.
Hospitality and Tourism Management. M.S., Ph.D.

Management. M.S., Ph.D.
Marketing. M.S., Ph.D.

COLLEGE OF ENGINEERING:
Aerospace Engineering. M.S., M.Eng., Ph.D.
Biological Systems Engineering. M.S., M.Eng., Ph.D.
Chemical Engineering. M.S., M.Eng., Ph.D.
Civil Engineering. M.S., M.Eng., Ph.D.
Computer Engineering. M.S., Ph.D.
Computer Science and Applications. M.S., Ph.D.
Electrical Engineering. M.S., Ph.D.
Engineering Mechanics. M.S., M.Eng., Ph.D.
Environmental Engineering. M.S., M.Eng.
Environmental Sciences and Engineering. M.S.
Industrial and Systems Engineering. M.S., M.Eng., Ph.D.
Information Systems. M.I.S.
Materials Science and Engineering. M.S., M.Eng., Ph.D.
Mechanical Engineering. M.S., M.Eng., Ph.D.
Mining Engineering. M.S., M.Eng., Ph.D.
Ocean Engineering. M.S., M.Eng.
Systems Engineering. M.S., M.Eng.

COLLEGE OF NATURAL RESOURCES:
Fisheries and Wildlife Sciences. M.S., Ph.D.
Forestry. M.S., M.F., Ph.D.
Forest Products. M.S., M.F., Ph.D.
Geography. M.S., Ph.D.
Natural Resources. M.N.R.

VIRGINIA—MARYLAND REGIONAL COLLEGE OF VETERINARY MEDICINE:
Veterinary Medical Sciences. M.S., Ph.D.

INTERDISCIPLINARY DEGREES:
Biomedical Engineering. M.S., Ph.D.
Genetics, Bioinformatics, and Computational Biology. Ph.D.
Information Technology. M.I.T., M.S., Ph.D.
Macromolecular Science and Engineering. M.S., Ph.D.

Virginia–Maryland Regional College of Veterinary Medicine (24061-0442)
Web site: www.vetmed.vt.edu

Founded 1978. The College has three campuses: at Virginia Tech, at Avrum Gudelsky Veterinary Center at College Park, at the Marion DuPont Scott Equine Medical Center in Leesburg. Admission office located in Blackburg. Semester system. Special facilities: Center for Molecular Medicine & Infectious Diseases, Center for Comparative Oncology, Center for Public and Corporate Veterinary Medicine, Center for Reproductive Excellence Using Advanced Technology and Endocrinology.

Annual tuition: Virginia and Maryland residents $15,590, nonresidents $35,896. Both on- and off-campus housing available. Estimated living expenses: $11,000–$15,000. Total all other expenses: $5000.

Enrollment: first-year class 90, total 385 (men 28%, women 72%, minorities 5%, Virginia and Maryland residents 90%). Faculty: full- and part-time 60. Degree conferred: D.V.M., D.V.M.-M.S., D.V.M.-Ph.D.

ADMISSION REQUIREMENTS. VMCAS report (nonresidents), transcripts, GRE, Advanced Biology, three recommendations, animal/veterinary experience required in support of application. Interview by invitation only. Applicants must have completed at least two years of college study. Preference given to state (50 positions), Maryland (30 positions), and Delaware (3 positions) residents; remaining 7–10 for nonresidents. Apply to the Office of Student Services after September 1, before November 15. Application fee $45. Phone: (540)231-4699; fax: (540)231-9290.

ADMISSION STANDARDS. Competitive. Accepts about 5–10% of all applicants. Number of applications 914 (180 Virginia, 109

Maryland, 625 out-of-state); number interviewed 200 (91 Virginia, 59 Maryland, 50 out-of-state); number of acceptance n/a (n/a out-of-state); number enrolled 90 (50 Virginia, 30 Maryland, 10 out-of-state). Usual minimum UGPA: 2.80 (A = 4). GRE mean score (V + Q + A) 1837; mean UGPA 3.66.

FINANCIAL AID. Scholarships, fellowships, assistantships, tuition reimbursement, Federal W/S, loans. Apply to Financial Aid Office before February 1. Use FAFSA.

DEGREE REQUIREMENTS. For D.V.M.: satisfactory completion of four-year program. For M.S. and Ph.D.: see Graduate School listing above.

FIELDS OF GRADUATE STUDY.
Aquatic Medicine.
Immunology.
Infectious Diseases.
Informatics.
Neuroscience.
Nutrition.
Toxicology.

VIRGINIA STATE UNIVERSITY
Petersburg, Virginia 23806-0001
Web site: www.vsu.edu

Founded 1882. Located 25 miles S of Richmond. Coed. State Control. Semester system. Library: 282,500 volumes, 1150 subscriptions.

Annual tuition/fees: full-time resident $6490, nonresident $13,898; per credit resident $190, nonresident $630. On-campus housing available for single students only. Average academic year housing costs: $7350 (including board) for single students. Contact Dean of Students Office for both on- and off-campus housing information. Phone: (804)524-5862.

School of Graduate Studies

Enrollment: full-time 52, part-time 828. College faculty teaching graduate students: full-time 44, part-time 5. Degrees conferred: M.A., M.S., M.Ed., M.I.S., C.A.G.S.

ADMISSION REQUIREMENTS: Two official transcripts, GRE required in support of application. Online application available. TOEFL required for international applicants. Accepts transfer applications. Apply to Graduate School by May 1 (Fall), November 1 (Spring). Application Fee $25. Phone: (804)524-5984; fax: (804)524-5104.

ADMISSION STANDARDS. Selective. Usual minimum average: 2.6 (A = 4) for unconditional admission.

FINANCIAL AID. Annual awards from institutional funds. Fellowships, asistantships, Federal W/S, loans. Approved for VA benefits. Apply by March 31 to Financial Aid Office. Phone: (804)524-5990; fax: (804)524-6818. Use FAFSA (School code: 003764). About 10% of students receive aid other than from University and outside sources.

DEGREE REQUIREMENTS. For M.A., M.S.: 24–27 semester hours minimum; thesis for 3–6 hours, 21 semester hours in residence. For M.Ed.: 33 hours including project or 36 hours including statistics and research; comprehensive examination. For C.A.C.S.: 30 semester hours beyond the master's.

FIELDS OF STUDY.
Administration and Supervision. Ed.D. only.
Biology.
Career and Technical Studies.

Counselor Education.
Criminal Justice.
Economics.
Education. Includes elementary education, educational technology, special education.
Educational Administration and Supervision.
English.
History.
Interdisciplinary Studies.
Mathematics.
Physics.
Psychology.
Sports Management.

UNIVERSITY OF VIRGINIA
Charlottesville, Virginia 22906-3196
Web site: www.virginia.edu

Established 1819. Located 66 miles W of Richmond, 120 miles S of Washington. CGS and AAU member. Coed. State control. Semester system. Special facilities: Olsson Center for Applied Ethics, Center for Biological Timing, Center for Electrochemical Sciences and Engineering, Institute for Environmental Negotiation, Center for High Temperature Composites, Taylor Murphy International Business Studies Center, Institute for Nuclear and Particle Physics, Center for Russian and East European Studies, Center for South Asian Studies, University Transportation Center. The University's NIH ranking is 44th among all U.S. institutions with 438 awards/grants valued at $152,679,824. According to The Center at University of Florida, the University is ranked 47th in receipt of Federal Research funds with $173,442,000 and it ranks 66th for total University research expenditures with $206,199,000. The University's endowment assets rank it 17th, with a value of $2,793,225,000. In 2004, the University awarded 358 doctorates which ranked it 34th among all U.S. institutions eligible to award that degree. Twenty-five of the University's faculty members have been elected to National Honor Academies and this ranks it 38th among all U.S. institutions. The Library: approximately 4,900,000 volumes, 51,000 subscriptions. Total University enrollment: 23,800.

Annual tuition: full-time resident $7731, nonresident $18,672; part-time per semester minimum, resident $1475, nonresident $4100. Average academic year housing costs: $5200 (including board) for single students; $5000 for married students. Contact Office of Housing, Station 1, Page House, University of Virginia 22904, for both on- and off-campus housing information. Phone: (434)924-6873. Day-care facilities available.

Graduate School of Arts and Sciences

Graduate study since 1904. Enrollment: full-time 1577, part-time 92. University faculty teaching graduate students: full-time 613, part-time 78. Degrees conferred: M.A., M.A.T., M.A.P.A., M.F.A, M.S., Ph.D.

ADMISSION REQUIREMENTS. Transcripts, GRE, two letters of recommendation required in support of School's application. Online application available. TOEFL (minimum score 600) required for international applicants. Accepts transfer applicants. Graduates of unaccredited institutions not considered. Apply to Office of the Graduate School by July 15 (Fall), December 1 (Spring); international applicants apply by April 1. Application fee $60. Phone: (434)924-7184; fax: (434)924-6737.

ADMISSION STANDARDS. Very selective for most departments, competitive for others. Usual minimum average: 3.0 (A = 4).

FINANCIAL AID. Annual awards from institutional funds: teaching assistantships, research assistantships, fellowships, traineeships, partial tuition waivers, Federal W/S, loans. Approved for VA benefits. Apply by February 1 (December 1 for international applicants) to individual departments for fellowships, assistantships; to the Office of Financial Aid for all other programs. Phone: (434) 924-3725. Use FAFSA. About 60% of students receive aid other than loans from School and outside sources.

DEGREE REQUIREMENTS. For master's: 24 semester hours minimum plus thesis, 30–36 credit without thesis; reading knowledge of one foreign language (by completion of two years of college credit or equivalent) for some programs; final oral/written exam. For Ph.D.: a minimum of 72 semester hours (or 50 beyond the master's); proficiency in one or two foreign languages (if applicable); preliminary/qualifying exam; dissertation; final/oral exam.

FIELDS OF STUDY.
Anthropology. M.A., Ph.D.
Astronomy. M.A., Ph.D.
Biology. M.A., M.S., Ph.D.
Biomedical Ethics. M.A.
Chemistry. M.S., Ph.D.
Classics. M.A., Ph.D.
Creative Writing. M.F.A.
Drama. M.F.A.
East Asian Studies. M.A.
Economics. M.A., Ph.D.
English. M.A., Ph.D.
Environmental Sciences. M.A., M.S., Ph.D.
French. M.A., Ph.D.
German. M.A., Ph.D.
Government. M.A., Ph.D.
History. M.A., Ph.D.
History of Art and Architecture. M.A., Ph.D.
Italian. M.A.
Linguistics. M.A.
Mathematics. M.A., M.S., Ph.D.
Music. M.A., Ph.D.
Nursing. Ph.D.
Philosophy. M.A., Ph.D.
Physics. M.A., M.A.P.E., M.S., Ph.D.
Politics. M.A., Ph.D.
Psychology. M.A., Ph.D.
Public Health Sciences. M.S., M.P.H.
Religious Studies. M.A., Ph.D.
Slavic Languages and Literature. M.A., Ph.D.
Sociology. M.A., Ph.D.
Spanish. M.A., Ph.D.
Statistics. M.S., Ph.D.

School of Architecture

School founded in 1919.
Enrollment: full-time 153, no part-time students. Faculty: full-time 36, part-time 19. Degrees conferred: M.Arch., M.Arch.H., M.L.A., M.U.E.P., Ph.D.

ADMISSION REQUIREMENTS. Transcripts, GRE required in support of application. Online application available. TOEFL required for international applicants. Accepts transfer applicants. Graduates of unaccredited institutions not considered. Apply to Dean of School by January 15 for Architecture, Architecture History, Landscape Architecture; February 1 for, M.U.E.P. Application fee $60. Phone: (434)924-6442; fax: (434)982-2678.

ADMISSION STANDARDS. Very selective. Usual minimum average: 3.0 (A = 4).

FINANCIAL AID. Grants and fellowships. Architecture School Financial Aid form should be filed with application. Loans, Federal W/S available through University's Office of Financial Aid,

Michie North, Emmet Street, Charlottesville, Virginia 22903. Phone: (434)982-6000. Apply by March 31 for Fall semester. Use FAFSA and School's FAF.

DEGREE REQUIREMENTS. For M.Arch.: Summer session plus 92 semester hours (less for B.S. in Arch. recipients), at least two years in residence. For M.L.A.: Summer session plus 94 semester hours, at least two years in residence. For M.Arch.H.: 36 semester hours, 24 hours in residence; comprehensive exam; one foreign language; thesis; final oral exam. For M.U.E.P.: 50 semester hours, summer internship. For Ph.D.: 48 semester hours plus 18 semester hours of nontopical research; written and oral exam; additional foreign language; dissertation; oral defense.

FIELDS OF STUDY.
Architectural History. M.Arch.H., Ph.D.
Architecture. Includes American urbanism, preservation; M.Arch.
Landscape Architecture. M.L.A.
Urban and Environmental Planning. Includes urban, environmental land use, policy. M.U.E.P.
Note: Study abroad available in Venice.

Colgate Darden Graduate School of Business Administration
PO Box 6550
Web site: www.darden.edu

Established 1954. Public control. Accredited programs: M.B.A.; recognized Ph.D. First year semester system, second year quarter system. Special facilities: Ballen Center for Entrepreneurial Leadership, Olsson Center for Applied Ethics, Taylor Murphy International Business Studies Center. Special programs: foreign exchange programs in Belgium, Hong Kong, Japan. Library: 80,000 volumes, 1110 subscriptions.

Annual MBA tuition: full-time resident $43,000, nonresident $48,000; Ph.D. full-time resident $7731, nonresident $18,672. Limited on-campus rooms and apartments available for single students.

Enrollment: total full-time 632. Faculty: 56 full-time, 35 part-time; 96% with Ph.D./D.B.A. Degrees conferred: M.B.A. (full-time only), M.B.A.-J.D., M.B.A.-M.A. (Asian Studies, Government, Foreign Affairs), M.B.A.-M.E., M.B.A.-M.S.N., M.B.A.-Ph.D., Ph.D.

ADMISSION REQUIREMENTS. All applicants should have a bachelor's degree from a recognized institution of higher education. Students are required to have their own personal computer. Contact Darden School of Business (phone: (800)UVA-MBA1; (434)924-7281) for application material and information. Early applications are encouraged for both admission and financial aid consideration. Does not accept transfer applicants. Beginning students are admitted Fall only. There are three application periods. The first ends December 1, the second ends February 1, and the last ends on March 15. Both U.S. citizens and international applicants should apply no later than March 15 (Fall). Online application available. Submit an application, GMAT results (will accept GMAT test results from the last five years, latest acceptable date is January), two official transcripts from each undergraduate/graduate school attended, two letters of recommendation, four essays, résumé (prefers at least four years of work experience), and an application fee of $140 ($165 for international applicants) to the office of Admission. Phone: (434)924-4809. Online application available. In addition, international students (whose native language is other than English) should submit a TOEFL report (minimum score 600), TSE score, certified translations and evaluations of all official transcripts, recommendation should be in English or with certified translations, proof of health/immunization certificate, and proof of sufficient financial resources for one year of academic study. Interviews are strongly recommended prior to the Admissions Committee reviewing completed application. All interview requests from applicants are scheduled from August 1 through February; after February 1 interviews are scheduled at the request of Admissions Committee. Joint degree applicants must apply to and be accepted to both schools, contact the admissions office for current information and specific admissions requirements. Rolling admissions process; notification is made within six to eight weeks of receipt of completed application and supporting documents.

ADMISSION REQUIREMENTS FOR DOCTORAL CANDIDATES. Contact Director of Doctoral Program, Darden School of Business at (434)924-7247 (e-mail: dardendoctoral@darden. gbus.virginia.edu) for application material and information. MBA is generally required for all doctoral applicants. Beginning students are admitted Fall Only. Both U.S. citizens and international applicants apply by February 15. Online application available. Submit a doctoral application, a GMAT score (will accept GMAT test results from the last five years), official transcripts from each undergraduate/graduate school attended, three letters of recommendation, essays, résumé, statement of purpose, and application fee of $60 to the Director of Doctoral Program. In addition, international students (whose native language is other than English) should submit a TOEFL report (minimum score 600), TSE scores, certified translations and evaluations of all official transcripts, recommendation should be in English or with certified translations, proof of health/immunization certificate. Interviews strongly encouraged. Notification is generally made by mid-April.

ADMISSION STANDARDS. Very selective. Mean GMAT: 677; median GPA: 3.27 (A = 4). *U.S. News & World Report* ranked Darden in the top 12 of all U.S. business schools. *BusinessWeek* listed Darden in the top 5 of all American business schools. Accepts approximately 15–20% of total annual applicants.

FINANCIAL AID. International scholarships, scholarships (some scholarship programs may require a essay), special minority stipend program, fellowships, graduate assistantships, Federal W/S, loans available. Financial aid is available for international students. Assistantships/fellowships may be available for joint degree candidates. Financial aid applications and information are generally included with the admission materials; apply by March 15 (for Darden Scholarships apply by February 15). Request Darden scholarship and fellowship information from Darden. Phone: (434)924-7559. Contact the University's Financial Aid Office for need-based financial aid information. Phone: (434) 243-5033. Use FAFSA (School code: 003745), also submit the University's FAF, the Darden Statement of Financial Aid, a Financial Aid Transcript, Federal Income Tax forms. Approximately 65% of students receive some form of financial assistance.

All doctoral candidates are considered for all merit- or need-based awards, stipends, assistantships, and tuition waivers. Some Darden Loans may be canceled if recipient receives the Ph.D. and serves as a full-time faculty member at an accredited school of business for three years.

DEGREE REQUIREMENTS. For M.B.A.: 78-credit program including 21 elective credits, two-year program; degree program must be completed in two years. For M.B.A.-Masters: generally a three- to four-year programs. For M.B.A.-J.D.: four-and-one-half-year program. For M.B.A.-Ph.D.: four year full-time program. For Ph.D.: three- to four-year program, at least two consecutive academic semester in full-time residence; major field exam; major field research paper; dissertation proposal exam; dissertation; oral defense.

FIELDS OF STUDY.
Business Administration. M.B.A.
Finance. Ph.D.
Management. Includes business ethics, entrepreneurship, general management, strategic management. Ph.D.

Marketing. Ph.D.
Operations Management. Ph.D.

The Curry School of Graduate Education

Graduate study since 1905. Semester system.
Annual tuition: full-time resident $7731, nonresident $18,672. Enrollment: full-time 728, part-time 168. Faculty: full-time 100, part-time 5. Degrees conferred: M.Ed., M.T., Ed.S., Ed.D., Ph.D.

ADMISSION REQUIREMENTS. Official transcripts, GRE Subject Tests, three letters of recommendation required in support of School's application. Online application available. TOEFL required for international applicants. Accepts transfer applicants. Graduates of unaccredited institutions not considered. Apply to Office of School, preferably by March 1 (Fall), November 15 (Spring). Application fee $60. Rolling admission process. Phone: (434)924-0741.

ADMISSION STANDARDS. Selective. Usual minimum average: 3.0 (A = 4).

FINANCIAL AID. Scholarships, fellowships, grants, teaching assistantships, internships, Federal W/S, loans. Approved for VA benefits. Apply to Office of the School by April 1. Phone: (434) 924-6000. Use FAFSA.

DEGREE REQUIREMENTS. For M.Ed., M.T.: 30–48 semester hours minimum, at least 24 in residence; comprehensive exam. For Ed.S.: 30 semester hours beyond the master's; comprehensive exam. For Ed. D.: at least one semester in full-time residence; preliminary exam; comprehensive exam; final dissertation; final oral exam. For Ph.D.: same as for Ed.D., except research project; proficiency in research methodology and statistics, and two years residency.

FIELDS OF STUDY.
Administration and Supervision.
Clinical and School Psychology.
Communication Disorders.
Counselor Education.
Curriculum and Instruction.
Educational Psychology. Includes gifted education, learning and development.
Educational Research, Statistics and Evaluation.
Elementary Education.
English Education.
Foreign Language Education.
Higher Education. Includes student affairs practice in higher education.
Instructional Technology.
Kinesiology. Includes adapted physical education, athletic training & sports medicine, exercise physiology, health & physical education/pedagogy.
Mathematics Education.
Reading Education.
Risk and Prevention in Education Sciences.
Science Education.
Social Foundations.
Social Studies Education.
Special Education. Includes early childhood & developmental risk, higher incident disabilities, severe disabilities.
Teacher Education.

School of Engineering and Applied Science— Graduate Division

Graduate study since 1946. Semester system.
Annual tuition: full-time resident $7731, nonresident $18,672.
Enrollment: full-time 629, part-time 16. Faculty teaching graduate students: full-time 170. Degrees conferred: M.S., M.E., Ph.D.

ADMISSION REQUIREMENTS. Official transcripts, three letters of recommendation, GRE required in support of School's application. Online application available. TOEFL, financial statement certifying $22,000 available for first year of study required for international applicants. Accepts transfer applicants. Interview not required. Apply to Dean of School by August 1 (Fall), December 1 (Spring); international applicants apply by April 1 (Spring); September 1 (Fall). Application fee $60. Rolling admission process. Phone: (434)924-3897; fax: (434)982-2214.

ADMISSION STANDARDS. Selective. Usual minimum average: 3.0 (A = 4). TOEFL Score: 600.

FINANCIAL AID. Fellowships, teaching assistantships, research assistantships, traineeships, internships, Federal W/S, loans. Approved for VA benefits. Apply by February 1 to Dean for fellowships, assistantship; to Financial Aid Office for all other programs. Phone: (434)924-3897. Use FAFSA. About 85% of students receive aid other than loans from School and outside sources. Aid rarely available to part-time students.

DEGREE REQUIREMENTS. For M.E., M.S.: 24–30 semester hours minimum, at least one semester in residence for M.S.; thesis/research project; final oral thesis exam. For Ph.D.: 48 semester hours, at least 24 credits of research beyond the master's, at least two semesters in residence; comprehensive exam; dissertation; final oral exam.

FIELDS OF STUDY.
Biomedical Engineering.
Chemical Engineering.
Civil and Environmental Engineering.
Computer Engineering.
Computer Science.
Electrical and Computer Engineering.
Engineering Physics.
Materials Science and Engineering.
Mechanical and Aerospace Engineering.
System and Information Engineering.

School of Law (22903-1738)
Web site: www.law.virginia.edu

Founded 1825. ABA approved since 1923. AALS member. Public control. Semester system. Full-time day study only. Special program: foreign study in Hamburg, Germany, Melbourne, Australia, Nottingham, England; Clerkships. Law library: 882,770 volumes, 11,275 subscriptions; has LEXIS, NEXIS, WESTLAW; is a Federal Government Depository.

Annual tuition: resident $33,500, nonresident $38,500, LL.M. $38,600. On-campus housing available. Total average annual additional expense: $15,600

Enrollment: first-year class 336; total 1146 (men 56%, women 44%, minorities 17%). Faculty: full-time 80, part-time 100. Student to faculty ratio is 13.0 to 1. Degrees conferred: J.D., J.D.-M.S. (Accounting at the Graduate School of Arts and Science of the University of Virginia), J.D.-M.P.A. (Public Affairs in the Woodrow Wilson School of Public and International Affairs at Princeton University), J.D.-M.A. (International Relations and International Economics at Johns Hopkins University School of Advanced International Studies), J.D.-M.A.L.D. (Law and Diplomacy in the Fletcher School of Law and diplomacy at Tufts University), LL.M. (three-quarters of accepted students are foreign lawyers), S.J.D.

ADMISSION REQUIREMENTS. For J.D. program: transcripts, LSAT, personal statement, two recommendations required in support of application. Applicants must have completed four years of college study. Interview not required. TOEFL required for international applicants whose native language is not English. Accepts transfer applicants. Graduates of unaccredited colleges not considered. Apply to Admissions Office of School, preferably by January 15 (Fall), Application fee $70. Phone: (434)924-7351. For graduate program: transcripts, GRE required in support of application. Interview may be required. Graduates of unaccredited colleges not considered. Apply to Admissions Office of the School; closing date varies by school.

ADMISSION REQUIREMENTS FOR LL.M. All applicants must have received the J.D. or equivalent first professional degree in law from an accredited U.S. law school or comparable foreign law school. Official transcripts with rank-in-class, two letters of recommendation required in support of LL.M. application. In addition, international applicants whose native language is not English must submit TOEFL and certified translations and evaluations of all foreign credentials. Personal interviews may be arranged with the Director of LL.M. Program. Admit Fall only. Apply by April 1 to Graduate Studies Office. Application fee $40. Phone: (434)924-3154; e-mail: gradadmit@law.virginia.edu.

ADMISSION REQUIREMENTS FOR S.J.D. Applicants must submit all materials required for LL.M. In addition, a personal statement expressing the rationale for pursuing the S.J.D. and its relevance to the applicant's planned career; submit dissertation proposal and candidate research plan with an endorsement of the proposal by a resident faculty member who has agreed to supervise the research and writing of dissertation; most candidates have completed the Law School's LL.M.

ADMISSION STANDARDS. Selective. Accepts approximately 20% of all students. Number of applicants 5495; number of acceptance 1111; number enrolled 374; LSAT (75% of students have a score at or above 167); GPA (75% of students have a GPA at or above 3.53). *U.S. News & World Report* ranking is in the top ten of all U.S. law schools.

FINANCIAL AID. Scholarships, fellowships, assistantships, Federal W/S, federal and law school loans. Apply to Federal Students Aid Center by February 15 for scholarships and Federal programs. Phone: (434)924-7805. Use FAFSA (School code: 003745). Apply to Chair of Graduate Commission for fellowships, assistantships. About 59% of students receive some aid from all sources.

DEGREE REQUIREMENTS. For J.D.: 86 (27 required) credits with a GPA of at least 2.0 (A = 4), plus completion of upper-divisional writing course; six semesters in residence program. For J.D.-M.S. (Accounting): 98 total credits (J.D. up to 12 credits, M.S. up to 6 credits). For J.D.-M.A.L.D., J.D.-M.A., J.D.-M.P.A.: individualized programs at each university; up to 14 credits may be applied to the J.D. and one semester of residence. For LL.M.: 24 credits, at least two semesters in full-time residence; substantial written work, either within a seminar or as supervised research; specialization in Oceans Law and Policy requires 30 credits. For S.J.D.: completion of a LL.M.; at least one year in full-time study; dissertation must make an original contribution to legal literature and be of publishable quality; oral defense.

School of Medicine (22908-0793)
Web site: www.med.virginia.edu

Established in 1825. Special facilities: Asthma and Allergic Diseases Center, Beirne B. Carter Center for Immunology Research, Cancer Center, Center for Biomedical Ethics and Humanities, Center for Cell Signaling, Center for Global Health, Center on Health Disparities, Center for Research in Contraceptive and Reproductive Health, Center for Research in Reproduction, Center for Structural Biology, Center for the Study of Neurodegenerative Disease, Diabetes Center, Diabetes and Hormone Center of Excellence, Digestive Health Center of Excellence, General Clinical Research Center, International Health Care Worker Safety Center, Keck Center for Cellular Imaging, Medical Automation Research Center, Morphogenesis & Regenerative Medicine Institute, Myles H. Thaler Center for AIDS & Human Retrovirus Research, O'Brien Urologic Research Center, Paul Mellon Prostate Cancer Research Institute, Robert M. Berne Cardiovascular Research Center. Library: 140,000 volumes, 3000 subscriptions; has MEDLINE. NIH ranking is 44th among all U.S. institutions with 438 awards/grants worth $152,679,824.

Annual tuition: residents $31,305, nonresidents $41,305. On-campus housing available for single students, limited for married students. Total average figure for all other expenses: $17,000.

Enrollment: first-year class 141, total 554 (men 54%, women 46%, minorities 26%, state residents 65%). Faculty: full-time 882, part-time 104. Degrees conferred: M.D., M.D.-M.P.H., M.D.-M.S., M.D.-Ph.D. (Medical Scientist Training Program).

ADMISSION REQUIREMENTS. AMCAS report, transcripts, letters of recommendation, MCAT, final screening interview required in support of application. Interview by invitation only. Applicants must have completed at least three years of college study. Accepts transfer applicants who are Virginia residents on a space available basis only. Does not have EDP. Preference given to Virginia residents. Apply to Director of Admissions (P.O. Box 800725) after June 1, before November 1. Application fee $75. Phone: (434)924-5571; fax: (434)982-2586.

ADMISSION STANDARDS. Competitive. Accepts about 9% of all applicants. Number of applications 3604 (2892 out-of-state); number interviewed 505 (324 out-of-state); number of acceptance 314 (182 out-of-state); number enrolled 141 (48 out-of-state). Mean Composite MCAT 11.0; mean UGPA 3.73. *U.S. News & World Report* ranking is in the top 23 of all medical research schools, 38th in primary care.

FINANCIAL AID. Scholarships, loans. MSTP funded by NIH. Apply to Financial Aid Director by January 1. Phone: (434)924-0033. Use FAFSA (School code: 003745). About 87% of students receive some type of aid.

DEGREE REQUIREMENTS. For M.D.: satisfactory completion of four-year program. Ph.D. is granted through the Graduate School of Arts and Sciences.

FIELDS OF GRADUATE STUDY.
Biochemistry. Ph.D.
Bioethics. M.A.
Biomedical Engineering. Ph.D.
Cancer Biology. Ph.D.
Cell Biology. Ph.D.
Clinical Research. M.S.
Microbiology and Immunology. Ph.D.
Molecular Genetics. Ph.D.
Molecular Physiology and Biological Physics.
Neurobiology and Behavior. Ph.D.
Neuroscience. Ph.D.
Pathology. Ph.D.
Pharmacology. Ph.D.

School of Nursing

Graduate study since 1928, first Ph.D. awarded in 1982. Semester system. Special facilities: Center for Nursing Research, Southeastern Rural Mental Health Research Center, Center for Nursing Historical Inquiry, Center for the Study of Complementary & Alternative Therapies, Rural Health Care Research Center, Health Care Product Evaluation Center.

Annual tuition/fees: full-time resident $10,565, nonresident $20,565. Enrollment. Full- and part-time 257. Faculty: full-time 52, part-time 42. Degrees conferred: M.S.N., M.S.N.-M.B.A., D.N.P., Ph.D.

ADMISSION REQUIREMENTS. Official transcripts, three letters of recommendation, GRE required in support of School's application. Online application available. TOEFL, financial statement

certifying at least $25,000 available for first year of study required for international applicants. Accepts transfer applications. Interview not required. Apply to Admissions & Student Services by April 1 (Fall), November 1 (Spring). Phone: (434)924-0141. Rolling admission process. Application fee $60.

ADMISSION STANDARDS. Selective. Usual minimum average: 3.0 (A = 4).

FINANCIAL AID. Scholarships, graduate assistantship, traineeship, Federal W/S, loans. Approved for VA benefits. Apply by February 1 to Dean for fellowships, assistantships; to Financial Aid Office for all other programs. Phone: (434)924-0068. Use FAFSA. Abut 60% of doctoral students receive aid other than loans from School and outside sources.

DEGREE REQUIREMENTS: For M.S.N.: full-time, 20–24 month program; clinical experience. For D.N.P., Ph.D.: 38–46 credit program beyond M.S.N.; research practicum; cognate requirement; dissertation; defense.

FIELDS OF STUDY.
Acute and Specialty Care Clinical Nurse Specialist.
Acute Care Nurse Practitioner.
Clinical Nurse Leader.
Community/Public Health Leadership.
Family Care Nurse Practitioner.
Geriatric Care Nurse Practitioner.
Health Systems Management.
Pediatric Care Nurse Practitioner.
Psychiatric—Mental Health.

WAGNER COLLEGE
Staten Island, New York 10301
Web site: www.wagner.edu

Founded 1883. Coed. Private control. Receives some support from the Lutheran Church of America. Semester system. Library: 310,000 volumes, 1000 subscriptions. Total College enrollment: 2900.

Tuition: per credit $820. On-campus housing for single students only. Average academic year housing cost: $7300 (including board). Contact Director of Residence Life for both on- and off-campus housing information. Phone: (718)390-3412. Day-care facilities available.

Division of Graduate Studies

Graduate study since 1952. Enrollment: full-time 163, part-time 162. College faculty: full-time 21, part-time 28. Degrees conferred: M.B.A., M.S., M.S.Ed., M.S.N.

ADMISSION REQUIREMENTS. Official transcripts, MAT/NTE/GMAT required in support of application. Interview not required. TOEFL required for international applicants. Accepts transfer applicants. Graduates of unaccredited institutions not considered. Apply to Director of Graduate Admissions at least six weeks prior to registration. Rolling admissions process. Application fee $50; $85 for international applicants. Phone: (718)390-3411.

ADMISSION STANDARDS. Selective for most departments. Usual minimum average: 2.75 (A = 4).

FINANCIAL AID. Fellowships, teaching assistantships, tuition waivers, internships, Federal W/S, loans. Approved for VA benefits. Apply by May 1 to Director of Graduate Studies for fellowships, assistantships; to Office of Financial Aid for all other programs. Phone: (718)390-3183. Use FAFSA. About 20% of students receive aid from College. Aid available for part-time students.

DEGREE REQUIREMENTS. For M.S., M.S.N.: 30–42 credits depending upon department; thesis/nonthesis option. For M.B.A.: 45–51 credits, at least 39 in residence; thesis/nonthesis option. For M.S. in Ed.: 34 credit hours minimum; 36 credit hours minimum in special education; thesis/nonthesis option.

FIELDS OF STUDY.
Accounting. M.S.
Adolescent Education/Special Education (7–9). M.S.Ed.
Advanced Physician Assistant Studies. M.S.
Business Administration. M.B.A.
Childhood Education/Special Education (1–6). M.S.Ed.
Early Childhood Education/Special Education (B–2). M.S.Ed.
Microbiology. M.S.
Middle Level Education/Special Education (5–9). M.S.Ed.
Nursing. M.S.N.
Teaching Literacy (B–6). M.S.Ed.

WAKE FOREST UNIVERSITY
Winston-Salem, North Carolina 27106
Web site: www.wfu.ed.

Founded 1834. CGS member. Coed. Private control. Baptist affiliation. Semester system. The University's NIH ranking is number 51st among all U.S. Institutions with 271 awards/grants valued at $125,545,373. According to The Center at University of Florida, the University is ranked number 67th in receipt of Federal Research fund with $108,467,000 and it ranks number 98th for total University research expenditures with $130,405,000. The University's endowment assets rank it 54th, with a value of $812,192,000. The Library: approximately 1,600,000 volumes, 7,500 subscriptions. Total University enrollment: 6716.

Annual tuition: full-time $28,340; per credit $1010. Limited on-campus housing for graduate students. Contact the Director of Residence Life and Housing for both on- and off-campus housing information. Phone: (336)758-5185.

Graduate School

Graduate study since 1866. Enrollment: full-time 275, part-time 136 (men 184, women 227). Faculty: full-time 404. Degrees conferred: M.A.Ed., M.A.L.S., M.S.A., M.S., Ph.D.

ADMISSION REQUIREMENTS. For Arts and Sciences: official transcripts, three letters of evaluation, statement of interest, interview for most departments, GRE/GMAT (accountancy) required in support of School's application. Online application available. TOEFL required for international applicants. Accepts transfer applicants. Apply to Dean of Graduate School by February 15. Application fee $25. Phone: (800)257-3166; fax: (336)759-6074. For Bowman Gray School of Medicine-Graduate Program: official transcripts, three letters of evaluation, GRE Subject Tests required in support of School's application. TOEFL required for international students. Accepts transfer applicants. Graduates of unaccredited institutions not considered. Apply to Dean of the Graduate School by January 15. Application fee $45, $55 for international applicants. Phone: (336)758-5301 or (800)257-3166; fax: (336)758-4230.

ADMISSION STANDARDS. Very selective for most departments, selective for the others. Usual minimum average: 3.0 (A = 4).

FINANCIAL AID. For Arts and Sciences: annual awards from institutional funds: scholarships, fellowships, assistantships (varies on availability), Federal W/S, loans. Apply at the time of application to Dean of Graduate School. Phone: (336)758-4743; fax: (336)758-4924. Use FAFSA (School code: E00429). About 85% of students receive aid other than loans from School and outside sources. For Bowman Gray School of Medicine-Graduate Program: scholarships, teaching/ research fellowships, research assistantships. Apply at time of application for admission to Dean of Graduate School. About 34% of students receive aid other than loans from School, 90% for all sources. No aid for part-time students.

DEGREE REQUIREMENTS. For master's: 30 semester hours minimum, at least 24 in residence; reading knowledge of one foreign language for some departments, substitution allowed in others; thesis/nonthesis option; final oral/written exam. For Ph.D.: three years minimum beyond the bachelor's, at least one year in residence; reading knowledge of two foreign languages in some departments, with substitutions allowed in others for one or both; preliminary oral/written exam; dissertation; final exam.

FIELDS OF STUDY.
Accountancy. M.S.A.
Biochemistry and Molecular Biology. Ph.D.
Biology. Includes cell and molecular, ecology/evolution/systematics, physiology and behavior, plant biology, M.S., Ph.D.
Biomedical Engineering. M.S., Ph.D.
Cancer Biology. Ph.D.
Chemistry. M.S., Ph.D.
Clinical and Population Translational Sciences. M.S.
Communication. M.A.
Comparative Medicine, M.S.
Computer Science. M.S.
Counseling. M.A.
Education. M.A.Ed.
English. M.A.
Health and Exercise Science. M.S.
Liberal Studies. M.A.L.S.
Mathematics. M.A.
Microbiology and Immunology. Ph.D.
Molecular and Cellular Pathobiology. Ph.D.
Molecular Genetics and Genomics. Ph.D.
Molecular Medicine. M.S., Ph.D.
Neurobiology and Anatomy. Ph.D.
Neuroscience. Ph.D.
Physics. M.S., Ph.D.
Physiology and Pharmacology. Ph.D.
Psychology. M.A.
Religion. M.A.

School of Law (PO Box 7206)
Web site: www.law.wfu.edu

Founded 1884. ABA approved since 1935. AALS member. Private control. Semester system. Full-time day study only. Special program: Sister School programs in Pecs, Hungary; summer study abroad in London, England, Vienna, Austria, Venice, Italy. Law library: 432,306 volumes, 5442 subscriptions; has LEXIS, NEXIS, WESTLAW, DIALOG, EPIC, ACES; has more than 100 network connections.

Annual tuition: $29,500, LL.M. $29,500. No on-campus housing available. Contact the Admissions Office for off-campus housing information. Total average annual additional expenses: $16,050.

Enrollment: first-year class 154; total 454 (men 58%, women 42%, minorities 14%). Faculty: full-time 35, part-time 15. Student to faculty ratio is 10.2 to 1. Degrees conferred: J.D., J.D.-M.B.A., LL.M. (American Law for foreign lawyers who have completed a basic legal education and received a university degree in law in another country).

ADMISSION REQUIREMENTS. LSDAS Law School report, Bachelor's degree, transcripts, LSAT, one academic recommendation, Dean's Certification required in support of application. Interviews are recommended only. Accepts transfer applicants on a space available basis. Graduates of unaccredited institutions not considered. Apply to Admissions Office after September 1, before March 1. Rolling admissions process. Application fee $60. Phone: (336)758-5437; fax (336)758-4632.

ADMISSION REQUIREMENTS FOR LL.M. APPLICANTS. All applicants must have a law degree from an approved degree-granting institution in the applicant's home country. Official transcripts in the language of the institution and certified English translation), two recommendations (one from a current or former faculty member), documentation of financial resources from bank or sponsor required in support of LL.M. application. In addition, TOEFL (minimum score 600) is required for those whose native language is not English. Admits Fall only. Apply by March 15 to Director LL.M. Program. Phone: (336)758-4496; e-mail: llm-admission@law.wfu.edu. Application fee $60.

ADMISSION STANDARDS. Selective. Accepts approximately 24% of all students. Number of applicants 2424; number of acceptance 571; number enrolled 154; LSAT (75% of students have a score at or above 162); GPA (75% of students have a GPA at or above 3.17). *U.S. News & World Report* ranking is in the top 36 of all U.S. law schools.

FINANCIAL AID. Need-based scholarships, merit scholarships, minority scholarships, assistantships, private and institutional loans, Federal loans; Federal W/S available for second- and third-year students only. Assistantships may be available for upper-divisional joint degree candidates. All accepted students are automatically considered for scholarships. For all other programs apply to Admissions and Financial Aid Office after January 1, before May 1. Phone: (336)758-5431. Use FAFSA (School code: E00514), also submit Financial Aid Transcript, Federal Income Tax forms. Approximately 25%, of first-year class receive scholarships/Grants-in-Aid. Approximately 46% of students receive some form of financial assistance.

DEGREE REQUIREMENTS. For J.D.: 89 credits with a GPA of at least 73 (scale: 0–100), plus completion of upper-divisional writing course; three-year program, four-year program. Accelerated J.D. with summer course work. For J.D.-M.B.A.: a four-year program rather than a five-year program if both degrees are taken consecutively. For LL.M. (foreign lawyers): 24 credits, at least two semesters in residence; "Introduction to American Law" course; thesis/seminar paper; a GPA of 73 (scale 0–100) required.

Babcock Graduate School of Management
7659 Reynolda Station
Web site: www.mba.wfu.edu

Established 1969. Private control. Accredited program: M.B.A. Located on main campus, courses offered at Charlotte, North Carolina, and Munich, Germany; suburban environment. Semester system. Special facilities: Angell Center for Entrepreneurship, Center for Economic Studies, Center for Management Communications, Flow Institute of International Studies, Worrell Professional Center for Law and Management. Special Programs: foreign exchange programs; in East Asia, Germany, United Kingdom; International Internships Program. Library: 22,000 volumes, 350 subscriptions.

Annual tuition: full-time $29,500–$33,400; evening M.B.A. $59,000 (total cost for degree program); fast-track E.M.B.A. $65,000 (total cost for program). No on-campus housing available. Estimated annual off-campus budget for M.B.A. tuition, room and board, and personal expenses: approximately $39,385.

Enrollment: total full-time 565, part-time 216. Faculty: full-time 42, part-time 15; 93% with Ph.D./D.B.A. Degrees conferred: M.A., M.B.A. (full-time, part-time, day and evening), E.M.B.A. (weekends only, alternating Fridays, Saturdays), M.B.A.-J.D., M.B.A.-M.D., M.B.A.-M.S.A., M.B.A.-Ph.D.

ADMISSION REQUIREMENTS. All applicants should have a bachelor's degree from a recognized institution of higher education and a strong mathematics background. Students are required to have their own personal computer. Contact Babcock Graduate School of Management for application material and information; phone: full-time M.B.A. (336) 758-5422, E.M.B.A. and evening M.B.A. (336)758-4584, E.M.B.A. and evening M.B.A. at Charlotte (704)365-1717. Early applications are encouraged for both admission and financial aid consideration. Does not accept transfer students. Beginning students are admitted Fall only. Both U.S. citizens and international apply by April 1 (Fall), December 1 (for Early Decision applicants). Online application available. Submit an application, GMAT (will accept GMAT test results from the last five years, latest acceptable date is June), two official transcripts from each undergraduate/graduate school attended, two letters of recommendation, three essays, résumé (work experience is not required), and an application fee of $75 to the Office of Admission and Financial Aid. In addition, international students (whose native language is other than English) should submit a TOEFL report (minimum score 580), certified translations and evaluations of all official transcripts, recommendation should be in English or with certified translations, proof of health/immunization certificate, and proof of sufficient financial resources for two years of academic study. Interviews are required for applicants lacking postgraduate work experience, for all other applicants an interview is strongly recommend. Joint degree applicants must apply to and be accepted to both schools; contact the Admissions Office for current information and specific admissions requirements. Rolling admissions process; notification is made within four weeks of receipt of completed application and supporting documents.

ADMISSION STANDARDS. Selective. Mean GMAT: 647; mean GPA: 3.2 (A = 4). *U.S. News & World Report* ranking is in the top 49 of all U.S. business schools. *BusinessWeek* listed Babcock in the top 50 of all U.S. business schools. Accepts about 40–50% of total annual applicants.

FINANCIAL AID. Scholarships, minority scholarships, fellowships, graduate assistantships, Federal W/S, loans. Financial aid is available for part-time study. Assistantships/fellowships may be available for joint degree candidates. Financial Aid applications and information are generally available at the on-campus visit/interview and are included with the admission materials; apply by February 15 for the Babcock Scholars (full-tuition scholarships); by March 1 for merit-based scholarships; final deadline April 1. Contact the Assistant Director, Admissions and Financial Aid for current need-based financial aid information. Phone: (336)758-4424. Use FAFSA (School code: E00515), also submit Financial Aid Transcript, Federal Income Tax forms. Approximately 20% of students receive some form of financial assistance.

DEGREE REQUIREMENTS. For M.A.: one year full-time program; thesis/nonthesis option. For M.B.A.: 66-credit program including 22 elective credits, two-year program; degree program must be completed in five years. For part-time evening M.B.A.: 54-credit program. For E.M.B.A.: 51-credit, 22-month program. For M.B.A.-J.D.: 125-credit, four-and-one-half- to five-year program. For M.B.A.-M.D.: 192-credit, five-and-one-half- to six-year program.

FIELDS OF STUDY.
Business Administration. Includes career concentrations in consulting/general management, entrepreneurship, finance (corporate finance/treasury, financial analysis, investment banking, security analysis/asset management), marketing, operations management. M.B.A.
Management. M.A.

Bowman Gray School of Medicine (27157-1090)
Web site: www.wfubmc.edu

Established 1902. Renamed in 1941. Library: 150,000 volumes, 2300 subscriptions. NIH ranking is 51 among all U.S. institutions with 271 awards/grants worth $125,545,373.

Annual tuition: $35,706. no on-campus housing available, off-campus housing within easy walking distance. Total average figure for all other expenses: $19,000.

Enrollment: first-year class 108, total 446 (men 57%, women 43%, minorities 44%, state residents 37%). Faculty: full-time 869, part-time 491. Degrees conferred: M.D., M.D.-M.A. (International Studies), M.D.-M.B.A., M.D.-M.S. (Clinical Epidemiology and Health Services Research), M.D.-Ph.D. (Medical Scientist training Program). The M.S. and Ph.D. are offered through the Graduate School.

ADMISSION REQUIREMENTS. AMCAS report, transcripts, MCAT, recommendations, including premedical advisory committee, required in support of application. Accepts transfer applicants on a space available basis only. Has EDP; apply between June 1 and August 1. Interviews and supplemental application by invitation only. Preference given to state residents. Apply after June 1, before November 1 to Associate Dean for Admissions. Application fee $55. Phone: (336)716-4264, fax: (336)716-9593.

ADMISSION STANDARDS. Very competitive. Accepts about 4% of all applicants. Number of applications 5983 (5356 out-of-state); number interviewed 518 (378 out-of-state); number of acceptance 280 (78 out-of-state); number enrolled 108 (67 out-of-state). Mean Composite MCAT 10.2; mean UGPA 3.59. *U.S. News & World Report* ranking is in the top 44 of all U.S. research medical schools; 18th in Primary Care.

FINANCIAL AID. Scholarships, loan funds. Apply by April 1 to Financial Aid Director. Phone: (336)716-2889. About 85% of students receive some financial aid.

DEGREE REQUIREMENTS. For M.D.: satisfactory completion of four-year program; must pass Step 1 of USMLE for promotion to 3rd year and pass Step 2 for graduation. For M.B.H., M.S., Ph.D.: see Graduate School listing above.

FIELDS OF GRADUATE STUDY.
Biochemistry and Molecular Biology.
Biology.
Biomedical Engineering.
Cancer Biology.
Cell Biology.
Clinical Epidemiology and Health Services.
Microbiology and Immunology.
Molecular and Cellular Pathobiology.
Molecular Genetics.
Molecular Medicine.
Molecular Physiology and Biological Physics.
Neurobiology and Behavior.
Neuroscience.
Physics.
Physiology and Pharmacology.

WALLA WALLA UNIVERSITY
College Place, Washington 99324-1198
Web site: www.wallawalla.edu

Founded 1892. Located 160 miles SW of Spokane. Coed. Private control. Seventh-Day Adventist. Quarter system. Library: 235,000 volumes, 1105 subscriptions. Total University enrollment: 2000.

Tuition: per credit $489. On-campus housing for 1480 single students, 110 units for married students. Average academic year housing costs: $3100 (room only) for a single student; $4000 for married students. Contact Village Life for on- and off-campus housing information. Phone: (509)527-2109.

Graduate School

Graduate study since 1900. Enrollment: full-time 232, part-time 42. Graduate faculty: full-time 34, part-time 13. Degrees conferred: M.A., M.Ed., M.S., M.S.W.

ADMISSION REQUIREMENTS. Official transcripts required in support of School's application. Online application available. Interview not required. GRE and Subject Test for M.S. Biology. TOEFL required for international applicants. Accepts transfer applicants. Apply to Dean of Graduate Studies at least three months prior to registration. Application fee $40. Phone: (509) 527-2421; fax: (509)527-2253.

ADMISSION STANDARDS. Selective. Usual minimum average: 2.75 (A = 4).

FINANCIAL AID. Scholarships, teaching assistantships, internships, tuition waivers, Federal W/S, loans. Approved for VA benefits. Apply by April 1 to the Financial Aid Office for scholarships, to department chair for assistantships. Use FAFSA and institutional FAF. Phone: (509)527-2815; fax: (509)527-2253. About 30% of students receive aid other than loans from College, 35% from all sources. Aid available to part-time students.

DEGREE REQUIREMENTS. For master's: 45 credits minimum, at least 30 in residence; thesis required for M.S., M.A.; final oral/written exams. For M.S.W.: two-year full-time program.

FIELDS OF STUDY.
Biology. M.S.
Counseling Psychology. M.A.
Education. Includes curriculum and instruction, education leadership, literacy instruction, special education, students-at-risk. M.A., M.Ed.
Social Work. Master's program has clinical focus.
Teaching. Includes curriculum & instruction, educational leadership, professional practice, special education. M.A.T.

WASHBURN UNIVERSITY OF TOPEKA
Topeka, Kansas 66621
Web site: www.washburn.edu

Founded 1865. Located 65 miles W of Kansas City. Coed. Municipal control. Semester system. Special facilities: Center for Diversity Studies, Center for Kansas Studies, Center on Violence and Victim Studies, Washburn Leadership Institute. Library: 500,000 volumes, 7000 subscriptions. Total University enrollment: 7300.

Tuition: per hour, resident $225, nonresident $458. On-campus housing for graduate students available. Average academic year housing costs: $4700. Contact Director of Housing for both on- and off-campus housing information. Phone: (785)231-1065. Day-care facilities available.

Graduate Program

Enrollment: full-time 591, part-time 246. Graduate faculty: full-time 32, part-time 9. Degrees conferred: M.A., M.B.A., M.Ed., M.S.W.

ADMISSION REQUIREMENTS. Official transcripts, references, GMAT, interview required in support of application. Online application available. TOEFL required for international applicants. Accepts transfer applicants. Apply to Director of Graduate Programs at least one month prior to registration. Application fee: none. Phone: (785)231-1561.

ADMISSION STANDARDS. Selective. Usual minimum average: 3.0 (A = 4).

FINANCIAL AID. Scholarships, research fellowships, research assistantships, teaching assistantships, internships, Federal W/S, loans. Approved for VA benefits. Apply by February 15 to Dean's office for fellowships, assistantships: to Financial Aid Office all other programs. Phone: (785)231-1151. Use FAFSA. Aid available for part-time students.

DEGREE REQUIREMENTS. For M.A., M.Ed., M.S.W.: 32 semester hours minimum, at least 24 in residence; final document. For M.B.A.: 30 semester hours minimum; computer proficiency.

FIELDS OF STUDY.

COLLEGE OF ARTS AND SCIENCES:
Clinical Psychology. M.A.
Education. M.Ed.
Educational Leadership. M.Ed.
Liberal Studies. M.L.S.
Psychology. M.A.
Reading. M.Ed.
Special Education. M.Ed.

SCHOOL OF APPLIED STUDIES:
Criminal Justice. M.C.J.
Social Work. M.S.A.

SCHOOL OF BUSINESS:
Accounting. M.B.A.
Business Administration. M.B.A.

School of Law
Web site: www.washburnlaw.edu

Organized 1903. ABA approved since 1923. AALS member since 1905. Semester system. Special facilities: Business and Transactional Law Center, Children and Family Law Center, Center for Excellence in Advocacy. Special programs: summer program at University of Utrecht, the Netherlands. Law library: 379,814 volumes, 4064 subscriptions; has LEXIS, NEXIS, WESTLAW, DIALOG; has more than 75 network connections.

Annual tuition: residents $14,400, nonresidents $22,500. On-campus housing available. Annual housing cost: $13,805.

Enrollment: first-year class 152; total 449 (men 59%, women 41%, minorities 14%). Faculty: full-time 25, part-time 20. Student to faculty ratio is 14.4 to 1. Degree conferred: J.D.

ADMISSION REQUIREMENTS. LSDAS Law School report, bachelor's degree, transcripts, LSAT, at least one letter of recommendation required in support of application. Interview not required. Accepts transfer applicants. Preference given to state residents. Graduates of unaccredited institutions not considered. Admits to both Fall and Spring semesters. Apply to Admissions Office by April 1 (Fall), September 15 (Spring). Later applications considered on space-available basis only. Application fee $40. Phone: (800)927-4529; fax: (785)232-8087.

ADMISSION STANDARDS. Selective. Accepts approximately 36% of all students. Number of applicants 397; number of acceptance 152; number enrolled 154; LSAT (75% of students have a score at or above 151); GPA (75% of students have a GPA at or above 3.04). *U.S. News & World Report* ranking is in the third tier of all U.S. law schools.

FINANCIAL AID. Scholarships, Federal W/S, loans. Apply to Financial Aid Office by March 15 (Fall), September 15 (Spring). for priority consideration. Phone: (785)231-1151. Use FAFSA (School code: 001949). About 43% of students receive aid other than loans from School.

DEGREE REQUIREMENTS. For J.D.: 90 credit hours minimum, at least 24 hours and the last year in residence.
Note: Six-week program of international study at Brunel University of West London (Great Britain) available.

WASHINGTON AND LEE UNIVERSITY
Lexington, Virginia 24450-0303
Web site: www.wlu.edu

Founded 1849. Located 50 miles NE of Roanoke. Private control. Special facilities: Lewis Law Center, Center for Law and History, Transnational Law Institute. Special program: exchange programs with Bucerius Law School , Hamburg, Germany, Trinity College, Dublin, University of Western Ontario. Law library: 427,978 volumes, 4086 subscriptions: has LEXIS, NEXIS, WEST LAW; has more than 300 network connections.

On-campus housing available. Average annual housing cost: $4500 for single students. Apply to Director of University Services.

School of Law
Web site: www.law.wlu.edu

Established 1849. ABA approved since 1923. AALS member. Semester system.

Annual tuition: full-time $31,300. Total average annual additional expenses: $15,695.

Enrollment: first-year class 136, total 390 (men 59%, women 41%, minorities 16%). Faculty: full-time 35, part-time 3. Student to faculty ratio 10.6 to 1. Degree conferred: J.D.

ADMISSION REQUIREMENTS. LSDAS Law School report, bachelor's degree, transcripts, two letters of recommendation, LSAT required in support of application. Interview not required. Accepts transfer applicants. Graduates of unaccredited colleges not considered. Apply to office of Dean of School after July 1, before February 1 for priority consideration. Application fee $40. Admits beginning students to Fall only. Phone: (540)458-8504; fax: (540)458-8546.

ADMISSION STANDARDS. Selective. Accepts approximately 21% of all students. Number of applicants 4007; number of acceptance 847; number enrolled 136; LSAT (75% of students have a score at or above 163); GPA (75% of students have a GPA at or above 3.25). *U.S. News & World Report* ranking is in the top 25 of all U.S. law schools.

FINANCIAL AID. Scholarships, grants, fellowships, Federal W/S, loans. Apply to Dean of School by February 15. Phone: (540) 458-8729. Use FAFSA (School code: 003768). About 65% of students receive financial assistance.

DEGREE REQUIREMENTS. For J.D.: 85 semester hours minimum, at least final four semesters in residence.

WASHINGTON STATE UNIVERSITY
Pullman, Washington 99164-1068
Web site: www.wsu.edu

Founded 1890. Located 80 miles S of Spokane. Campuses located in Spokane, Tri-cities and Vancouver. CGS member. Coed.

State control. Semester system. Special facilities: Humanities Research Center, Small Business Research Center, Social and Economic Sciences Research Center, Computing Center, Nuclear Reactor Center, Electron Microscope Laboratory, Agricultural Research Centers, College of Engineering Research Division, State of Washington Water Research Center, Bioanalytical Research Center, Laboratory Animal Facility, Molecular Biophysics Laboratory. Library: 2,000,000 volumes, 28,120 subscriptions. Total University enrollment: 23,500.

Annual tuition: full-time resident $6295, nonresident $15,949; per credit, resident $336, nonresident $819. On-campus housing for 648 married students, unlimited for single students. Average academic year housing costs: $410–$550 per month for married students; $8500 (including board) for single students. Contact Program Coordinator Residence Halls (509)335-9574 for on-campus housing information: Program Coordinator Housing Commission (509)355-4577 for off-campus housing information. Day-care facilities available.

Graduate School

Graduate study since 1902. Enrollment: full-time 2200, part-time 469. Graduate faculty: full-time 721, part-time 49. Degrees conferred: M.A., M.S., M.F.A., M.A.T., Ed.M., M.B.A., M.Nurs., M.R.P., Ed.D., Ph.D.

ADMISSION REQUIREMENTS. Two official transcripts, GRE/GMAT/MAT required in support of School's application. Online application available. TOEFL required for international applicants. Accepts transfer applicants. Foreign students apply at least six months prior to registration. Apply to the Director of Admissions at least three months prior to registration. Application fee $35. Phone: (509)335-6424; fax: (509)335-1949.

ADMISSION STANDARDS. Very selective for most departments, relatively open to very competitive for others. Usual minimum average: 3.1 (last two years) (A = 4).

FINANCIAL AID. Annual awards from institutional funds: fellowships, teaching assistantships, research assistantships, internships, traineeships, tuition waivers, Federal W/S, loans. Approved for VA benefits. Apply by February 1 to the Dean of Graduate School for assistantships, fellowships; to Financial Aid Office for all other programs. Phone: (509)335-9711. Use FAFSA (School code: 003800). About 70% of students receive aid other than loans from University and outside sources. Aid available for part-time students.

DEGREE REQUIREMENTS. For M.A., M.S.: 30 credits minimum, at least one year in residence; language requirements vary by department; thesis/nonthesis option; final exam in all departments. For M.A.T.: 30 credits minimum, at least 24 in residence; final oral exam. For Ed.M.: qualifying exam; other requirement, same as for M.A.T. For M.B.A., M.R.P.: 30 credits minimum, no thesis; final oral exam. For M.N.: 45 credits, thesis; final oral exam. For Ed.D., Ph.D.: six semesters minimum beyond the bachelor's, at least four semester, in residences language requirements vary by department; oral/written preliminary exam; thesis; final oral exam.

FIELDS OF STUDY
Accounting. M.Acct., Ph.D.
Agribusiness. M.A.
Agriculture. M.S.
Agricultural Economics. M.A., Ph.D.
American Studies. M.A., Ph.D.
Animal Sciences. M.S., Ph.D.
Anthropology. M.A., Ph.D.
Apparel Merchandising and Textile. M.A.
Applied Economics. M.A.
Architecture. M.S., M.Arch.

Biochemistry. M.S., Ph.D.
Biological and Agricultural Engineering. M.S., Ph.D.
Biology. M.S., Ph.D.
Biotechnology. M.S.
Botany. M.S., Ph.D.
Business Administration. M.B.A., Ph.D.
Chemical Engineering. M.S., Ph.D.
Chemistry. Includes analytical, inorganic, organic, physical. M.S., Ph.D.
Civil Engineering. M.S., Ph.D.
Communication. M.A., Ph.D.
Computer Science. M.S., Ph.D.
Criminal Justice. M.A., Ph.D.
Crop Science. M.S., Ph.D.
Design. D.Des.
Economics. M.A., Ph.D.
Education. Includes educational leadership, counseling psychology, educational psychology, higher education, sport management, teaching and learning. M.A., Ed.M., Ed.D., Ph.D.
Electrical and Computer Engineering. Ph.D.
Electrical Engineering. M.S.
Engineering. M.S.
Engineering Management. M.Eng.Mgt. only.
Engineering Science. Ph.D.
English. M.A., Ph.D.
Entomology. M.S., Ph.D.
Environmental and Natural Resource Sciences. Ph.D.
Environmental Engineering. M.S.
Environmental Research. Interdisciplinary. M.S.
Environmental Science. M.S.
Finance. Ph.D.
Fine Arts. M.F.A.
Food Science. M.S., Ph.D.
Foreign Languages and Literatures. M.A.
Genetics and Cell Biology. M.S., Ph.D.
Geology. M.S., Ph.D.
Health Policy and Administration. M.H.P.A.
History. M.A., Ph.D.
Horticulture. M.S., Ph.D.
Human Development. M.A.
Human Nutrition. M.S.
Individual Ph.D. Interdisciplinary. Ph.D.
Interior Design. M.A.
Landscape Architecture. M.S.
Management and Operations. Ph.D.
Management Information Systems. Ph.D.
Marketing. Ph.D.
Materials Science. Ph.D.
Materials Science and Engineering. M.S.
Mathematics. M.S., Ph.D.
Mechanical Engineering. M.S., Ph.D.
Microbiology. M.S., Ph.D.
Molecular Plant Science. M.S.
Music. M.A.
Natural Resource Sciences. M.S.
Natural Resources. M.S.
Neurosciences. M.S., Ph.D.
Nursing. M.Nurs., Ph.D.
Nutrition. Ph.D.
Pharmacology and Toxicology. M.S., Ph.D.
Philosophy. M.A.
Physics. M.S., Ph.D.
Plant Pathology. M.S., Ph.D.
Political Science. M.A., Ph.D.
Psychology. Includes clinical, experimental. Ph.D.
Public Affairs. M.P.A.
Regional Planning. M.R.P.
Sociology. M.A., Ph.D.
Soil Science. M.S., Ph.D.
Speech and Hearing Science. M.A.
Statistics. M.S.

Technology Management. M.T.M.
Veterinary Science. M.S., Ph.D.
Zoology. M.S., Ph.D.

College of Veterinary Medicine (99164-7012)
Web site: www.vetmed.wsu.edu

Founded 1899. The fifth oldest College of Veterinary Medicine in U.S. Semester system. Special facility: Monoclonal Antibody Center.

Annual tuition: Washington, Idaho, WICHE residents $16,044, nonresidents $39,636. Both on- and off-campus housing available. Estimated living expenses: $15,000. Total all other expenses: $6200.

Enrollment: first-year class 103, total 420 (men 28%, women 72%, minorities 5%, Washington residents 50%). Faculty: full- and part-time 60. Degrees conferred: D.V.M., D.V.M.-M.S., D.V.M.-Ph.D.

ADMISSION REQUIREMENTS. VMCAS report, transcripts, GRE, three recommendations, animal/veterinary experience required in support of application. Interview by invitation only. Applicants must have completed at least two years of college study. Preference given to state, Idaho, Oregon, and WICHE residents; accepts about 5 students who are nonresidents and not from WICHE. Accepts transfer applicants under special circumstances only. Apply to the Office of Student Services after August 1, before October 1. Rolling admission process. Application fee $40. Phone: (509)335-5107; fax: (509)335-0160.

ADMISSION STANDARDS. Competitive. Accepts about 15–20% of all applicants. Number of applications 949 (150 Washington and Idaho, 200 WICHE, 599 out-of-state); number interviewed n/a (n/a out-of-state); number of acceptance 178 (66 Washington and Idaho, 62 WICHE, 51 out-of-state); number enrolled 103 (65 Washington and Idaho, 15 WICHE, 15 out-of-state). Usual minimum UGPA: 2.80 (A = 4). GRE mean score (V + Q) 1150; mean UGPA 3.71.

FINANCIAL AID. Scholarships, assistantship, fellowships, Federal W/S, loans. Use FAFSA before March 1.

DEGREE REQUIREMENTS. For D.V.M.: satisfactory completion of four-year program. For M.S., Ph.D.: see Graduate School listing above.

FIELDS OF GRADUATE STUDY.
Anesthesiology. M.S., Ph.D.
Clinical Neurology and Neurosurgery. M.S.
Equine Surgery. M.S.
Field Disease Investigation. M.S., Ph.D.
Infectious Diseases. M.S., Ph.D.
Immunology. M.S., Ph.D.
Neuroscience. M.S., Ph.D.
Pathology. M.S., Ph.D.
Radiology. M.S., Ph.D.
Small Animal Medicine. M.S.
Small Animal Surgery. M.S.
Theriogenology. M.S., Ph.D.
Veterinary Clinical Pathology. M.S., Ph.D.
Veterinary Science. M.S., Ph.D.

WASHINGTON UNIVERSITY
St. Louis, Missouri 63130-4899
Web site: www.wustl.edu

Founded 1853. CGS and AAU member and charter member of Association of Graduate Schools. Coed. Private control. Semester system. Special facilities: Center for Air Pollution and Trend Analysis, Center for the Study of American Business, Center for American Indian Studies, Institute for Biomedical Computing, Business, Law and Economics Center, McDonnell Center for Cellular and Molecular Neurobiology, Center for Computational Mechanics, Computer and Communications Research Center, Construction Management Center, Center for the Study of Data Processing, Carolyne Roehm Electronic Media Center, Center for Engineering Computing, Center for Genetics in Medicine, McDonnell Center for Studies of Higher Brain Function, Center for the History of Freedom, Center for Intelligent Computer Systems, International Writers Center, Center for the Study of Islamic Societies and Civilizations, Management Center, Markey Center for Research in Molecular Biology of Human Disease, Center for Optimization and Semantic Control, Center for Plant Science and Biotechnology, Center for Political Economy, Center for the Study of Public Affairs, Center for Robotics and Automation, Social Work Research Development Center, McDonnell Center for Space Sciences, Center for Technology Assessment and Policy, Center for the Application of Information Technology, Urban Research and Design Center, Central Institute for the Deaf. The University's NIH ranking is 5th among all U.S. institutions with 855 awards/grants valued at $394,788,334. According to The Center at University of Florida, the University is ranked 11th in receipt of Federal Research funds with $357,364,000 and it ranks 18th for total University research expenditures with $474,328,000. The University's endowment assets rank it 11th, with a value of $4,000,823,000. In 2004, the University awarded 241 doctorates which ranked it 60th among all U.S. institutions eligible to award that degree. Forty-four of the University's faculty members have been elected to National Honor Academies and this ranks it 23rd among all U.S. institutions. The Library: approximately 3,000,000 volumes, 18,000 subscriptions. Total University enrollment: 12,100.

Annual tuition: full-time $27,590. No on-campus housing available. Average academic year housing costs: $450–$950 per month.

Graduate School of Arts and Sciences

Formal graduate study since 1898. Enrollment: full-time 1365, part-time 25. School faculty: full-time 500, part-time 80. Degrees conferred; A.M., M.S., M.L.A., M.A.Ed., M.A.T., M.M., M.F.A.W., M.S.S.H., A.G.C., Ph.D.

ADMISSION REQUIREMENTS. Official transcripts, GRE Subject Test required in support of application. Official TOEFL or TSE required for international applicants. Interview required in some programs. Accepts transfer applicants. Graduates of unaccredited institutions not considered. Apply to Office of the Dean (Campus Box 1187), preferably by January 15 (January 1 for the Division of Biology and Biomedical Sciences, April 1 for Speech and Hearing). Rolling admissions process. Application $35. Phone: (314)935-6880; fax: (314)935-4887.

ADMISSION STANDARDS. Competitive for most departments. Usual minimum average: 3.0 (A = 4).

FINANCIAL AID. Annual awards from institutional funds: 700 scholarships, 120 fellowships, 300 research assistantships, 250 teaching assistantships, 20 internships, grants, Federal W/S, loans. Approved for VA benefits. Apply by January 15 to Dean for scholarships, to appropriate department head for fellowships, internships, assistantships; to the Financial Aid Office for all other programs. Phone: (314)935-6880. Use FAFSA and University's FAF. About 65% of students receive aid other than loans from School and outside sources.

DEGREE REQUIREMENTS. For A.M., M.L.A., M.S.: 24 semester hours plus thesis, or 30 hours plus essay, at least one year in residence; 6 hours maximum in transfer; final written exam. For

M.A.Ed., M.A.T., M.S.S.H: 30 hours minimum, at least 27 in residence; final written exam. For M.M.: 33–37 hours minimum, at least 27 in residence; includes graduate recital; reading knowledge of two modern languages. For M.F.A.W.: 39 hours minimum, at least 33 in residence, up to 15 hours in workshops or tutorials of directed writing. For A.G.C. (Education): normally 30 hours minimum beyond the master's, at least 24 in residence; qualifying written exam; final written project; final oral exam. For Ph.D.: 72 hours minimum beyond the bachelor's, at least 48 in residence; reading knowledge of one or two languages may be specified by major department; qualifying exam; candidacy; dissertation; final oral defense.

FIELDS OF STUDY.
American Culture Studies. A.M.
Anthropology. A.M., Ph.D.
Art History and Archaeology. One language for A.M., two for Ph.D.
Asian and Near Eastern Languages and Literature. A.M.
Biochemistry. Ph.D.
Biology. A.M.
Bioorganic Chemistry. Ph.D.
Business Administration. Ph.D.; M.B.A., E.M.B.A. offered through Graduate School of Business Administration.
Chemistry. Includes organic, bioorganic, polymer, physical, biophysical, inorganic, organometallic, bioinorganic, nuclear, radiochemistry. A.M., Ph.D.
Chinese and Comparative Literature. Ph.D.
Chinese Language and Literature. A.M.
Classics. A.M.
Comparative Literature. Includes literary theory, European and American literature, Chinese and Japanese literature. A.M., Ph.D.
Computational Biology. Ph.D.
Developmental Biology. Ph.D.
Earth and Planetary Sciences. Includes sedimentary geology, planetary exploration. A.M., Ph.D.
East Asian Studies. Includes economic development, law, political, economic, and intellectual history, literature and culture, art history and archaeology. A.M.
Economics. Includes economic history, economic theory, econometrics, industrial organization, monetary economics, political economy, public economics, public finance. A.M., Ph.D.
Education. Includes teacher education (preservice and inservice), educational research. M.A.Ed., M.A.T., Ph.D.
Engineering. Includes aerospace, biomedical, computer, electrical, energy, environmental and chemical, mechanical, structural, systems science and mathematics. Ph.D
English and American Literature. A.M., Ph.D.
English and Comparative Literature. Ph.D.
Evolution, Ecology and Population Biology. Ph.D.
French. A.M.
French and Comparative Literature. Ph.D.
French Language and Literature. Ph.D.
German and Comparative Literature. Ph.D.
Germanic Languages and Literatures. GRE for admission; one language in addition to German for A.M., two for Ph.D.
Hispanic Language and Literature. Ph.D.
History. A.M., Ph.D.
Human and Statistical Genetics. Ph.D.
Human Resources Management. A.M.
Immunology. Ph.D.
International Affairs. A.M.
Islamic and Near Eastern Studies. A.M.
Japanese and Comparative Literature. Ph.D.
Japanese Language and Literature. A.M.
Jewish Studies. A.M.
Liberal Arts. M.L.A.
Mathematics. Includes analysis, geometry, algebra. M.S., Ph.D.
Molecular Biophysics. Ph.D.
Molecular Cell Biology. Ph.D.
Molecular Genetics and Genomics. Ph.D.
Molecular Microbiology and Microbial Pathogenesis. Ph.D.

Movement Science. Ph.D.
Music. Includes musicology, theory, composition; entrance exam for Ph.D.; qualifying exam for master's; two languages for Ph.D. M.M., A.M., Ph.D.
Neurosciences. Ph.D.
Nonprofit Management. A.M.
Performing Arts. Includes dramatic literature, criticism, theory, modern drama, Renaissance Drama, theater. A.M.
Philosophy. A.M., Ph.D.
Physics. A.M., Ph.D.
Physics and Electrical Engineering. Ph.D.
Plant Biology. Ph.D.
Political Economy and Public Policy. Includes public choice, international political economy public policy. A.M.
Political Science. A.M., Ph.D.
Psychology. Includes experimental, development and aging, social. Ph.D.
Social Work. Ph.D. only. M.S.W. offered through School of Social Work.
Spanish. A.M.
Spanish and Comparative Literature. Ph.D.
Speech and Hearing Sciences. Ph.D.
Writing Program. Includes fiction, poetry, nonfiction, playwriting. Writing samples must be included with application materials. M.F.A.

School of Art

Annual tuition: $27,590. Enrollment: full-time 45. School faculty: full-time 17, part-time 5. Degree conferred: M.F.A.

ADMISSION REQUIREMENTS. Transcripts, BFA or equivalent, twenty slide portfolio, three recommendations, statement of purpose, résumé required in support of application. Online application available. TOEFL required for international students. Graduates of unaccredited colleges not considered. Apply to Graduate Office by January 15. Application fee $75. Phone: (314)935-6500; fax: (314)935-6462; e-mail: cbaldwin@art.wustl.edu.

ADMISSION STANDARDS. Competitive. Usual minimum average: 3.0 (A = 4).

FINANCIAL AID. Scholarships, fellowships, teaching assistantships, technical assistantships, internships, Federal W/S, loans. Approved for VA benefits. Apply to Graduate Office; various deadlines in January and February. Phone: (314)935-4761, fax: (315)935-4862. Use FAFSA and University's FAF. Approximately 100% of students receive aid other than loans from both School and outside sources.

DEGREE REQUIREMENTS. For M.F.A.: 60 credit, full-time program; candidacy; thesis; exhibition.

FIELDS OF STUDY.
Ceramics. Includes glass.
Digital Imaging.
Electronic Media.
Painting.
Photography.
Printmaking/Drawing.
Sculpture.

John M. Olin School of Business (Campus Box 1133)
Web site: www.olin.wustl.edu

Established 1917, added M.B.A. in 1950, E.M.B.A. in 1983, P.M.B.A. in Health Science, and E.M. in Manufacturing Management in 1997. Accredited program: M.B.A.; recognized Ph.D. Semester system. Special facilities: Business Law and Economics Center, Center for Technology Information and Manufacturing, Center for the Study of American Business. Special Programs:

foreign exchange programs (in France, Germany, Hong Kong, United Kingdom, Venezuela), internships. Library: 28,700 volumes, 400 subscriptions.

Annual tuition: full-time $40,500; E.M.B.A. $83,900. No on-campus housing available.

Enrollment: total full-time 507, part-time 349. Faculty: full-time 61, part-time 15; all have Ph.D./D.B.A. Degrees conferred: M.B.A. (full-time, part-time, day and evening), P.M.B.A. (part-time, evening), E.M.B.A. (weekends only, alternating Fridays, Saturdays), E.M.B.A. in Health Services, E.M.M.M., M.B.A.-J.D., M.B.A.-M.A. (East Asian Studies), M.B.A.-M.Arch., M.B.A.-M.S.W., Ph.D.

ADMISSION REQUIREMENTS. All applicants should have a bachelor's degree from a recognized institution of higher education and a strong mathematics background. Contact Director of M.B.A. Admissions for application material and information; phone: (314)935-7301; e-mail: mba@olin.sustl.edu.; E.M.B.A. (314)935-4572. Online application available. Early applications are encouraged for both admission and financial aid consideration. Beginning students who are full-time students admitted Fall only, part-time admitted Fall and Spring. Both U.S. citizens and international applicants apply by November 1 (Round #1, notification by January 31), January 15 (Round #2, notification by March 31), March 1 (Round #3, notification May 31), May 1 (Round #4, notification by June 30), Rolling admissions (Round #5); part-time applicants apply by February 25 (Round #1), April 7 (Round #2), May 5 (Round #3), June 16 (Round #4). Submit M.B.A. application, GMAT (will accept GMAT test results from the last five years, latest acceptable date is March), official transcripts from each undergraduate/graduate school attended, two letters of recommendation, four essays, Work History Form (prefers at least three years of work experience), and an application fee of $100 to the Director of M.B.A. Admissions. In addition, international students (whose native language is other than English) should submit a TOEFL report (minimum score 550), certified translations and evaluations of all official transcripts, recommendation should be in English or with certified translations, proof of health/immunization certificate, and proof of sufficient financial resources for two years of academic study. Interviews are encouraged. Joint degree applicants must apply to and be accepted to both schools/programs, contact the admissions office for current information and specific admissions requirements.

ADMISSION REQUIREMENTS FOR DOCTORAL CANDIDATES. Contact Director for Business Ph.D. Admissions at (314)935-6340 for application material and information. Beginning students are admitted Fall Only. Both U.S. citizens and international applicants apply by January 15. Submit an application, GMAT (will accept GMAT test results from the last five years), official transcripts from each undergraduate/graduate school attended, three letters of recommendation, résumé, statement of objectives and application fee of $75 to the Director of Business Ph.D. Admissions. Online application available. In addition, international students (whose native language is other than English) should submit a TOEFL report (minimum score 600), certified translations and evaluations of all official transcripts, recommendation should be in English or with certified translations, proof of health/immunization certificate. Interviews are encouraged. Notification is generally made mid-April.

ADMISSION STANDARDS. Selective. Mean GMAT: 647; mean GPA: 3.2 (A = 4). Gourman rating: the M.B.A. was rated in the top 31, the score was 4.60; the Ph.D. was rated in the top 35, the score was 4.54. *U.S. News & World Report* ranked Olin in the top 30 of all U.S. business schools; the E.M.B.A. in the top 15. *BusinessWeek* listed Olin in the top 16 of all U.S. business schools.

FINANCIAL AID. Scholarships, special minority stipends, Consortium Fellowships, fellowships, graduate assistantships, Federal W/S, loans. Financial aid is available for part-time study. Financial aid for international students may be available in the form of merit awards. Assistantships/fellowships may be available for joint degree candidates. Financial aid applications and information are generally available at the on-campus visit/interview and are included with admissions materials obtained directly from Olin School of Business; apply by March 31. Request both need- and merit-based information from the School of Business. Phone: (314)935-6610. Use FAFSA (School code: 002520); also submit the School's FAF, a Financial Aid Transcript, Federal Income Tax forms. Approximately 65% of students receive some form of financial assistance. Ph.D. applicants for an Olin Fellowship for Women or a Chancellor's Graduate Fellowship apply in early January.

DEGREE REQUIREMENTS. For M.B.A.: 60-credit program including 24 elective credits, two-year program; degree program must be completed in seven years. For P.M.B.A.: 54-credit, part-time evening program. For E.M.B.A.: 21-month program. For E.M.B.A. in Health Services: 60 credit program. For E.M.M.M.: 60 credit program. For M.B.A.-Master's: generally a three- to five-year program. For M.B.A.-J.D.: four-and-one-half- to five-year program. For Ph.D.: four- to five-year program in full-time residence (and M.S.B.A. may be earned while pursuing the Ph.D.); oral presentation of a research paper; completion of a minor field requirement; comprehensive exam in major; dissertation proposal and oral defense; dissertation; oral defense.

FIELDS OF STUDY.

Accounting. M.Acc., Ph.D.

Business Administration. Includes concentrations in accounting analysis, entrepreneurship, finance, international management, manufacturing and operations, marketing, Organizational leadership, strategy consulting. M.B.A.

Business Economics. Ph.D.

Finance. M.S., Ph.D.

Marketing. Ph.D.

Operations and Manufacturing Management. Ph.D.

Organizational Behavior and Strategy. Ph.D.

Sever School of Engineering and Applied Science

Founded 1948. Tuition: per unit $1450. Graduate enrollment: full-time 330, part-time 460. Institute faculty: full-time 80, part-time 20. Degrees conferred: M.S., M.C.E., M.S.C.E., M.E.M., M.I.M., M.T.M., D.Sc.

ADMISSION REQUIREMENTS. Official transcripts, letters of recommendation required in support of School's application. Online application available. Interview desirable. GRE required for all financial aid applicants. TOEFL (minimum score 550) required for international applicants. Accepts transfer applicants. Graduates of unaccredited institutions not considered. Apply to Chairman of the Department; no specified closing dates. Application fee: paper $40, Online $20. Phone: (314)935-6166.

ADMISSION STANDARDS. Selective. Usual minimum average: 2.75 (last 2 years) (A = 4).

FINANCIAL AID. Annual awards from institutional funds: scholarships, research assistantships, traineeships, Federal W/S, loans. Apply by February 15 to appropriate department for scholarships, assistantships; to Financial Aid Office for all other programs. Use FAFSA. Phone: (314)935-4761. About 48% of students receive aid other than loans from Institute and outside sources.

DEGREE REQUIREMENTS. For master's: 30 units minimum, at least 24 in residence; thesis/nonthesis option; final written/oral exam. For D.Sc.: 72 units minimum beyond the bachelor's, at least 48 in full-time residence; qualifying exam; dissertation; final written/oral exams.

FIELDS OF STUDY.
Biomedical Engineering.
Chemical Engineering.
Civil Engineering. Includes material science, international project management, structural (advanced design, earthquake, applied mechanics, structures, transportation).
Computer Engineering. M.S.CoE.
Computer Science.
Construction Engineering. M.C.E. only.
Electrical Engineering.
Electrical Engineering/Physics. Ph.D. only.
Engineering Management. M.E.M. only.
Environmental Engineering. Multidisciplinary.
Information Management. M.I.M. only.
Mechanical and Aerospace Engineering.
Silicon Technology. M.S. only.
Systems Science and Mathematics.
Telecommunications Management. M.T.M. only.
Transportation Engineering. D.Sc.

School of Law (Box 1120)
Web site: www.law.wustl.edu

Established 1867. Oldest private law school west of Mississippi. Moved to new facilities in 1997. Located on main campus. ABA approved since 1923. AALS member. Semester system. Full-time, day study only. Special facilities: Center for Interdisciplinary Studies, Institute for Global Legal Studies, Center for Research on Innovation and Entrepreneurship. Special programs: foreign exchange programs with Utrecht University, Utrecht, the Netherlands; Inns of Court School of Law, London, England; The Gerd Bucerius Law School, Hamburg, Germany; Monash University Faculty of Law, Melbourne, Australia; National Law School of India, Bangalore, India; Indian Law Society Law College, Pune, India; National University of Singapore; Tribhuvan University, Kathmandu, Nepal; Kobe University Graduate School of Law, Japan. Law library: 675,776 volumes, 6109 subscriptions; has LEXIS, NEXIS, WESTLAW, LEGI-SLATE, Congressional Information Systems; has more than 700 network connections.

Annual tuition: $36,380. No on-campus housing available. Law students live off-campus. Contact University Housing Office for off-campus information, phone: (800)874-4330 or (314)935-5092; for University Apartment Referral Service, phone: (314)935-5092. Off-campus housing and personal expenses: approximately $19,600.

Enrollment: first-year class 222; total full-time 788 (men 58%, women 42%, minorities 16%) Faculty: full-time 55, part-time 39. Student to faculty ratio 13.2 to 1. Degrees conferred: J.D., J.D.-M.B.A., J.D.-M.H.A., J.D.-M.A. (East Asian Studies, European Studies, Environmental Policy, Islamic Studies, Political Science), J.D.-M.S.W., J. D.-M.S. (Engineering and Policy), M.J.S. (limited to five students per year), LL.M. (Tax, Intellectual Property), LL.M. (for international persons who have completed a basic legal education and received a university degree in law in another country), LL.M.-J.S.D.

ADMISSION REQUIREMENTS. LSDAS Law School report, bachelor's degree, transcripts, LSAT, personal statement required in support of application. Résumé and letters of recommendation optional. Interview not required. Accepts transfer applicants. Graduates of unaccredited colleges not considered. Apply to Office of Admissions by March 1 for priority consideration. Admits Fall only. Application fee $70. Phone: (314)935-4525; fax: (314) 935-8778.

ADMISSION REQUIREMENTS FOR LL.M. APPLICANTS. For LL.M.: all applicants must have received the LL.B. or J.D. from a law school approved by AALS. Official undergraduate transcripts, official law school transcripts with rank-in-class, verification of LSAT, personal statement, résumé required in support of graduate application. Apply to LL.M. program. Application fee $50. Phone: (314)935-4525. For LL.M. (international applicants): all applicants must have the basic law degree recognized in their own country. Official transcripts with certified translations and evaluations, TOEFL (minimum score 600) for those who native language is not English, letter of credit indicating sufficient financial support required in support of graduate application. Personal interviews may be requested. Admits Fall only. Apply to LL.M. program for International Students. Application fee $60. Phone: (314)935-6404.

ADMISSION REQUIREMENTS FOR LL.M.-J.S.D. (RESEARCH DEGREE) APPLICANTS. All applicants must have received the LL.B. or J.D. from a law school approved by AALS. Official undergraduate transcripts, official law school transcripts with rank-in-class, verification of LSAT, personal statement, résumé required in support of graduate application. Admits Fall only. Apply to Graduate program by March 15. Application fee $50. Phone: (314)935-4525.

ADMISSION STANDARDS. Selective. Accepts approximately 25% of all students. Number of applicants 3767; number of acceptance 954; number enrolled 222; LSAT (75% of students have a score at or above 161); GPA (75% of students have a GPA at or above 3.20). *U.S. News & World Report* ranking is in the top 19 of all U.S. law schools.

FINANCIAL AID. Olin Scholarship, scholarships, grants, Federal W/S, loans. Apply to Office of Financial Aid by March 1. Phone: (314)935-4605.Use FAFSA. About 55% of students receive scholarships from School.

DEGREE REQUIREMENTS. For J.D.: 85 hours minimum, at least two semesters in full-time residence. For M.J.S.: 30 credits, all in residence; thesis of publishable quality; all course work completed in four years; thesis must be completed within one year of completion of course work. For LL.M.: at least 24 credits beyond the J.D.; one year in full-time residence; Capstone. For J.S.D.: individualized program; thesis.

School of Medicine (63110)
Web site: www.medschool.wustl.edu

Formed 1891. Library: 290,000 volumes, 5400 subscriptions; has MEDLINE. NIH ranking is 5 among all U.S. institutions with 855 awards/grants worth $394,788,334.

Annual tuition: $41,910. On-campus housing available. Total average figure for all other expenses: $14,000–$16,000.

Enrollment: first-year class 123, total 589 (men 53%, women 47%, minorities 36%, state residents 9%). Faculty: full-time 1500, part-time 600. Degrees conferred: M.D., M.D.-M.A., M.D.-Ph.D. (Medical Scientist training Program).

ADMISSION REQUIREMENTS. AMCAS report, transcripts, recommendations, MCAT required in support of application. Interview by invitation only. Applicants must have completed at least three years of college study. Accepts transfer applicants on a space available basis and compelling personal reason. Does not have EDP. Apply through AMCAS after June 1, before December 15. Application fee $50. Phone: (314)362-6858; fax: (314) 362-4658.

ADMISSION STANDARDS. Very competitive. Accepts about 4% of all applicants. Number of applications 3298 (3141 out-of-state); number interviewed 1195 (1142 out-of-state); number of acceptance 326 (315 out-of-state); number enrolled 123 (117 out-of-state). Mean Composite MCAT 12.2; mean UGPA 3.84. *U.S. News & World Report* ranking is in the top 4 of all U.S. research medical schools; 38th in Primary Care.

FINANCIAL AID. Scholarships, fellowship, Federal and private loans. MSTP funded by NIH. About 63% of students receive aid other than loans from School. Apply to Financial Aid Officer following acceptance. For scholarships apply by February 1. Phone: (314)362-6862. Use FAFSA (School code: G24620). About 90% of students receive some form of financial assistance.

DEGREE REQUIREMENTS. For M.D.: satisfactory completion of four-year program; taking the USMLE Step 1 and Step 2 is recommended. For M.A.-M.D.: satisfactory completion of five-year program. For Ph.D.: see Graduate School listing above.

FIELDS OF GRADUATE STUDY.
Biochemistry.
Computational Biology.
Developmental Biology.
Evolution, Ecology and Population Biology.
Human and Statistical Genetics.
Immunology.
Molecular Biophysics.
Molecular Cell Biology.
Molecular Genetics and Genomics.
Molecular Microbiology and Microbial Pathogenesis.
Neuroscience.
Plant Biology.

George Warren Brown School of Social Work

Established 1925. Semester system. Special facilities: Buder Center for American Indian Studies, Center for Mental Health Services Research, Center for Social Development, Comorbidity and Addictions Center.

Annual tuition $28,890. Off-campus housing only. Contact Graduate Housing Office for off-campus housing information. Phone: (314)935-5092.

Enrollment: full-time 351, part-time 29. School faculty: full-time 31, part-time 47. Degrees conferred: M.S.W., M.S.W.-J.D., M.S.W.-M.B.A., Ph.D. (awarded by the Graduate school of Arts and Sciences).

ADMISSION REQUIREMENTS. Transcripts, references required in support of application. Interview may be required. MAT/GRE required for Ph.D. applicants. Online application available. TOEFL (minimum 575) required for international applicants. Accepts transfer applicants. Graduates of unaccredited institutions not considered. Apply to Director of Admissions and Student Resources by March 1 (Fall), October 15 (Spring). Earlier application encouraged. Rolling admissions process. Application fee $60, $40 for online applicants. Phone: (314)935-6676; fax (314)935-4859.

ADMISSION STANDARDS. Very selective. Usual minimum average: 3.0 (A = 4).

FINANCIAL AID. Fellowships, teaching assistantships, scholarships, tuition remission grants, internships, tuition waivers, Federal W/S, loans. Approved for VA benefits. Apply by March 1 to Dean's Office for fellowships, assistantships; to Director of Financial Aid for all other programs, Phone: (314) 935-6655. Use FAFSA (School code: 002520) and Institutional FAF. Approximately 80% of students receive some form of financial assistance. Aid available for part-time students.

DEGREE REQUIREMENTS. For M.S.W.: 45–60 credits minimum, depending on previous academic preparation; 10 of 60 credits are in field practicum, normally in two different social work settings. For Ph.D.: 51 credits beyond the M.S.W. or 72 beyond the baccalaureate; at least one year in full-time residence; qualifying exams; dissertation; final oral exam.

FIELDS OF STUDY.
Social Work (Clinical). Includes children, youth and family, gerontology, mental health, social and economic development. M.S.W.
Social Work. Interdisciplinary. Ph.D.

UNIVERSITY OF WASHINGTON
Seattle, Washington 98195
Web site: www.washington.edu

Founded 1861. CGS and AAU member. Coed. State control. Quarter System. Special facilities: arboretum, Bureau of Governmental Research Services, Botanical and Drug Plant Gardens, Burke Memorial Washington State Museum, Center for Advanced Research Technology in the Arts and Humanities, Center for Advanced Study and Research on Intellectual Property, Center for AIDS and Sexually Transmitted Diseases, Center for American Politics and Public Policy, Center for Child Environmental Health Risks Research, Center for Conservation Biology, Center for Cost and Outcomes Research, Center for Disability Policy and Research, Center for Ecogenetics and Environmental Health, Center for Experimental Nuclear Physics and Astrophysics, Center for Expression Arrays, Center for Health Education and Research, Center for Human Development and Disability, Center for Instructional Development and Research, Center for International Business and Research, Center for International Trade in Forest Products, Center for Internet, Center for Labor Studies, Center for Law, Commerce and Technology, Center for Mind, Brain, and Learning, Center for Multicultural Education, Center for Nanotechnology, Center for Process Analytical Chemistry, Center for Research on Family, Center for Social Science Computation and Research, Center for Spanish Studies, Center for Statistics and Social Sciences, Center for Studies in Demography and Ecology, Center for Technology Entrepreneurship, Center for Urban Horticulture, Center for Urban Water Resources Management, Center for Videoendoscopic Surgery, Center for West European Studies, Center for Women and Democracy, Center for Women's Health Research, Child Health Institute, Fisheries Research Institute, Friday Harbor Laboratories, Henry Art Gallery, Human Services Policy Center, Institute on Aging, Institute for Ethnic Studies in the United States, Institute for International Policy, Institute for Nuclear Theory, Institute for Public Health Genetics, Institute for Risk Analysis and Risk Communication, Institute for the Study of Educational Policy, Institute for Transnational Studies, Laboratory of Radiation Biology, Northwest Center for Research on Women, Regional Primate Research Center, Washington Mining and Mineral Resources Research Institute, oceanographic research vessels. The University's NIH ranking is 3rd among all U.S. institutions with 997 awards/grants valued at $462,021,658. According to The Center at University of Florida, the University is ranked 2nd in receipt of Federal Research funds with $565,602,000 and it ranks 5th for total University research expenditures with $684,814,000. The University's endowment assets rank it 33rd, with a value of $1,315,894,000. In 2004, the University awarded 503 doctorates which ranked it 16th among all U.S. institutions eligible to award that degree. Seventy-eight of the University's faculty members have been elected to National Honor Academies and this ranks it 12th among all U.S. institutions. The Library: approximately 5,800,000 volumes, 50,000 subscriptions. Total University enrollment: 35,600.

Annual tuition: full-time resident $9874, nonresident $20,921; $29,000 (Business), $24,077 (Nursing), $25,555 (Pharmacy). On-campus housing for 672 married students, 4400 units for men and women. Average academic year housing cost: $6500 for married students; $4200 for single students. Contact Student Services Office: (206)543-4059 for on-campus housing information; (206)

543-8997 for off-campus housing information. Day-care facilities available.

Graduate School

Established 1911. Enrollment: full-time 6698 (men 50%, women 50%), part-time 2129. Graduate faculty: full- and part-time 2500. Degrees conferred: M.A., M.Arch., M.A.I.S., M.A.T., M.B.A., M.Comm., M.Ed., M.F.A., M.I.S., M.L.A., M.Lib., M.O.T., M.P.T., M.S.W., M.S.P.A., M.H.A., M.S., M.S.Aero. & Astro., M.S.B.C.M., M.S.Cer.Eng., M.S.Chem.Eng., M.S.Civ.Eng., M.S.D., M.S.E.E., M.For.Res., M.S.Mech.Eng., M.S.Met.Eng., M.M., M.S.Nuc.Eng., M.N., M.P.A., M.P.H., M.S.P.E., M.S.P.H., M.S.Rad.Sci., M.U.P., Ph.D., Ed.D., D.M.A., D.A.

ADMISSION REQUIREMENTS. Two official transcripts, letters of recommendation, GRE Test required in support of School's application. Online application available. Satisfactory score on TOEFL required for international students. Accepts transfer applicants. Graduates of unaccredited institutions not considered. Apply to Office of Graduate Admissions by May 15 (Summer), July 1 (Fall), November 1 (Winter), February 1 (Spring). Application fee $50. Phone: (206)543-5929 (request school/program); fax: (206)543-8798; e-mail: uwgrad@u.washington.edu.

ADMISSION STANDARDS. Very competitive for some departments, competitive and selective for the others. Minimum average: 3.0 for last two years (A = 4).

FINANCIAL AID. Scholarships, teaching/research assistantships, internships, grants, tuition waivers, Federal W/S, loans. Approved for VA benefits. Apply by February 28 to appropriate department chair/graduate program coordinator. Phone: (206)543-6101. Use FAFSA. About 35% of students receive aid other than loans from School. Aid available for part-time students.

DEGREE REQUIREMENTS. For master's: 36 credits minimum, at least three quarters (27 credits) in residence; foreign language and thesis for some departments; final oral/written exam. For doctorates: three years minimum, at least one year in full-time residence; reading knowledge of two foreign languages in some programs for Ph.D.; candidacy exam; dissertation; final exam.

FIELDS OF STUDY.
Accounting. M.Prof.Acc.
Aeronautics and Astronautics. M.S.A.A., Ph.D.
Anthropology. M.A., Ph.D.
Applied Mathematics. M.S., Ph.D.
Aquatic and Fishery Sciences. M.S., Ph.D.
Architecture. M.Arch., M.S.Arch.
Art. M.F.A.
Art History. M.A., Ph.D.
Art Studio. M.F.A.
Asian Languages and Literature. M.A., Ph.D.
Astronomy. M.S., Ph.D.
Atmospheric Sciences. M.S., Ph.D.
Biochemistry. Ph.D.
Bioengineering. M.S.Bio., Ph.D.
Biological Structure. M.S., Ph.D.
Biology Teaching. M.S.
Biomedical and Health Informatics. M.S., Ph.D.
Biomedical Regulatory Affairs. M.S.
Biostatistics. M.P.H., M.S., Ph.D.
Botany. M.S., Ph.D.
Business Administration. M.B.A., Ph.D.
Chemical Engineering. M.S.Ch.E., M.S.E., Ph.D.
Chemistry. Ph.D.
Civil and Environmental Engineering. M.S., M.S.Civ.E., M.S.E., Ph.D.
Classics. M.A., Ph.D.
Communication. M.A., M.C., Ph.D.

Communications—Digital Media. M.C.
Comparative Literature. M.A., Ph.D.
Comparative Medicine. M.S.
Computer Science and Engineering. M.S., Ph.D.
Construction Management. M.S.C.M.
Dance. M.F.A.
Dentistry. Includes endodontics, oral medicine, orthodonotics, periodontics, pediatric dentistry, prosthodontics. M.S.D.
Drama. Includes acting, costume design, directing, history, lighting design, playwriting, scenic design, theater criticism, theater history. M.F.A., Ph.D.
Earth and Space Sciences. M.S., Ph.D.
Economics. M.A., Ph.D.
Education. Includes curriculum (educational communication and technology, instructional leadership, language, literacy and culture, mathematics education, multicultural education, science education, social studies education, teaching and curriculum), educational leadership (higher education, intercollegiate athletic leadership, leadership in learning, organization and policy, social and cultural foundations), educational psychology (human development and cognition, learning sciences, measurement, statistics and research design, school psychology), special education (applied behavior analysis, early childhood special education, emotional behavior disorder, learning disabilities, severe disabilities), teacher education (elementary, secondary). M.Ed., M.I.T., Ed.D., Ph.D.
Electrical Engineering. M.S.E.E., Ph.D.
Engineering. Interengineering graduate studies. M.S.E., M.Engr., M.S.
English. Includes creative writing (M.F.A.). M.A., M.A.T., Ph.D.
English Language and Literature. M.A., Ph.D.
Environmental and Occupational Health. M.P.H., M.S., Ph.D.
Epidemiology. Includes global health, maternal and child health. M.P.H., M.S., Ph.D.
Forest Resources. M.F.R., M.S., Ph.D.
French Studies. M.A., Ph.D.
Genetic Epidemiology. M.S.
Genome Sciences. Ph.D.
Geography. M.A., Ph.D.
Germanics. M.A., Ph.D,
Health Services Administration. M.H.A.
Health Services. M.P.H., M.S., Ph.D.
Hispanic Studies. M.A.
History. Includes international studies (M.A. only), comparative religion, East Asian studies, Middle Eastern studies, Russian and East European studies, South Asian studies. M.A., Ph.D.
Immunology. Ph.D.
Individual Ph.D.
Industrial Engineering. M.S., Ph.D.
Information Management. M.S., Ph.D.
Information Science. Ph.D.
International Studies. Includes China studies, comparative religion, Japan studies, Korea studies, Middle Eastern studies, Russian/East European/Central Asian studies, South Asian studies. M.I.S. only.
Italian Studies. M.A.
Laboratory Medicine. M.S.
Landscape Architecture. M.L.A.
Law. LL.M., Ph.D.
Linguistics. Includes romances linguistics. M.A., Ph.D.
Manufacturing Engineering. M.S.
Marine Affairs. M.M.A.
Materials Science and Engineering. M.S.M.S.&E., Ph.D.
Mathematics. M.A., M.S., Ph. D.
Mechanical Engineering. M.S.M.E., M.S.E., Ph.D.
Medical Engineering. M.M.E.
Medical History and Ethics. M.A.
Medicinal Chemistry. Ph.D.
Microbiology. Ph.D.
Museology. Interdisciplinary. M.A.
Music. M.A., M.M., D.M.A., Ph.D.

Near and Middle Eastern Studies. Interdisciplinary. Ph.D.
Near East Language and Civilization. M.A.
Neurobiology and Behavior. Ph.D.
Nursing. M.N., M.S., Ph.D.
Nutritional Sciences. M.P.H., M.S., Ph.D.
Oceanography. Includes biological, chemical, physical. M.S., Ph.D.
Oral Biology. M.S., Ph.D.
Pathobiology. M.S., Ph.D.
Pathology. Ph.D.
Pharmaceutics. Ph.D.
Pharmacology. M.S., Ph.D.
Philosophy. M.A., Ph.D.
Physics. M.S., Ph.D.
Physiology and Biophysics. Ph.D.
Political Science. Ph.D.
Psychology. Includes clinical, school. Ph.D.
Public Affairs. M.P.A.
Public Health Genetics. M.P.H., Ph.D.
Quantitative Ecology and Resource Management. M.S., Ph.D.
Rehabilitation Medicine. M.R.M., M.S., M.O.T., M.P.T.
Scandinavian Studies. M.A., Ph.D.
Slavic Languages and Literature. M.A., Ph.D.
Social Work. M.S.W.
Social Welfare. Ph.D.
Sociology. Ph.D.
Speech and Hearing Sciences. M.S., Au.D., Ph.D.
Statistics. M.S., Ph.D.
Strategic Planning for Critical Infrastructure. M.S.P.C.I.
Technical Communication. M.S., Ph.D.
Urban Design and Planning. M.U.P., Ph.D.
Women's Studies. Ph.D.
Zoology. Ph.D.

School of Dentistry (98195-6365)
Web site: www.dental.washington.edu

Established 1945. Located at Health Sciences Center. Semester system. Special facilities: Northwest/Alaska Center to Reduce Oral Health Disparities, Regional Clinical Dental Research Center, Center for Leadership Training in Pediatric Dentistry.

Annual tuition: resident $15,872, nonresident $37,694. On-campus housing available for both single and married students. Average academic year off-campus housing costs: $11,500. Contact the Housing Office for both on- and off-campus housing information. Total average cost for all other first-year expenses: $7,500.

Enrollment: first-year class 55, total 216 (men 62%, women 38%, minorities 7%, state residents 60%), postgraduate students 100. Faculty: full-time 59, part-time 35, volunteers 504. Degrees conferred: D.D.S., D.D.S.-M.S., D.D.S.-Ph.D.

ADMISSION REQUIREMENTS. AADSAS report, transcripts, DAT, recommendations required in support of application. Applicants must have completed at least three years of college study. Interview by invitation only. Preference given to state and WICHE residents. Apply through AADSAS after June 1, before November 1. Application fee $35. Phone: (206)543-5840; fax: (206)616-2612; e-mail: askuwsod@u.washington.edu.

ADMISSION STANDARDS. Selective. Accepts about 5% of all applicants. Usual minimum UGPA: 3.0 (A = 4). Mean DAT: academic 21, PAT 19; mean UGPA 3.6.

FINANCIAL AID. Scholarships, grants, loans. About 20% of students receive aid other than loans from School. Apply to Financial Aid Office by March 1. Phone: (206)543-1511. Use FAFSA. About 80% of students receive some form of financial assistance.

DEGREE REQUIREMENTS. For D.D.S.: satisfactory completion of 12 quarters of study, including summer quarters after year two, and year three. For M.S.D.: satisfactory completion of one-year program. For M.S., Ph.D.: see Graduate School listing above.

FIELDS OF POSTGRADUATE STUDY.
Endodontics. M.S.D.
General Dentistry.
General Practice Residency.
Oral & Maxillofacial Surgery. Certificate.
Oral Biology. Includes oral pathology. M.S.D. M.S., Ph.D.
Oral Medicine. M.D.S.
Orthodontics. M.D.S.
Pediatric Dentistry. M.D.S., Certificate.
Periodontics. M.D.S.
Prosthodontics. M.D.S.

School of Law (98195-3020)
Web site: www.law.washington.edu

Established 1899. Located on main campus. ABA approved since 1924. AALS member. Quarter system. Full-time, day study only. Special facilities: Asian Law Center, Center for Advanced Study and Research on Intellectual Property, Center for Law, Science and Global Health, Native American Law Center, Shidler Center for Law, Commerce & Technology. Law library: 591,741 volumes, 5550 subscriptions; has LEXIS, NEXIS, WESTLAW, DIALOG.

Annual tuition: resident $16,255, nonresident $23,878. On-campus housing available for both single and married students. Contact Housing Office for both on- and off-campus housing information. Phone: (206)543-4059. Law students tend to live off-campus. Off-campus housing and personal expenses: approximately $14,913.

Enrollment: first-year class 180; total full-time 544 (men 43%, women 57%, minorities 20%). Faculty: full-time 37, part-time 40. Student to faculty ratio 11.7 to 1. Degrees conferred: J.D., J.D.-M.B.A., J.D.-M.A. (International Studies), LL.M. (Asian Law, Law and Marine Affairs, International Environmental Law, Law of Sustainable International Development, Taxation).

ADMISSION REQUIREMENTS. LSDAS Law School report, Bachelor's degree, transcripts, LSAT (not later than December) required in support of application. Letters of recommendation are optional. TOEFL required for foreign students. Interview not required. Graduate of unaccredited colleges not considered. Priority given to state residents (70% of entering class). Apply to Admission Office after September 15, before January 15. Admits Fall only. Application fee $50. Phone: (206)543-4078; fax: (206)543-5671. For graduate study, apply to Director, Graduate Program, School of Law.

ADMISSION REQUIREMENTS FOR TRANSFER APPLICANTS. Accepts transfers from other AALS-approved schools. Admission limited to space available. At least one year of enrollment, Dean's letter indicating the applicant is in good standing, prefer applicants in the top quarter of first-year class, LSAT, LSDAS, personal statement regarding reason for transfer, undergraduate transcript, current law school transcript required in support of School's application. Apply to Admission Office by July 10 (Fall only). Admission decision made by mid-August. Application fee $50. Will consider visiting students.

ADMISSION REQUIREMENT FOR LL.M. APPLICANTS. All applicants must hold a J.D. or equivalent degree from a law school that is a member of AALS and is approved by ABA. International applicants must have a first law degree or equivalent and must receive permission from Director of Graduate Admission. Original application, one official transcript, and application fee of $45 should be sent to the Office of Graduate Admission (Box 351280). A second official transcript including ranking-in-class, one or two letters of recommendation, a statement of purpose, a résumé and the goldenrod copy of the application should be sent to the Law School Graduate Admission Office. Admits to all quarters. Deadlines: July 1 (Fall, full- and part-time), November 1 (Winter, part-time only), February 1 (Spring, part-time only),

May 15 (Summer, part-time only). Phone: (206)616-5964; fax: (206)685-4469.

ADMISSION STANDARDS. Selective. Accepts approximately 21% of all students. Number of applicants 2465; number of acceptance 529; number enrolled 180; LSAT (75% of students have a score at or above 159); GPA (75% of students have a GPA at or above 3.51). *U.S. News & World Report* ranking is in the top 28 of all U.S. law schools.

FINANCIAL AID. Scholarships, partial tuition waivers, fellowships, assistantships, Federal W/S, loans. About 42% of students receive aid other than loans from School. Apply to Assistant Dean of School by March 1. Phone: (206)543-4552. Use FAFSA (School code: 003798).

DEGREE REQUIREMENTS. For J.D.: 135 quarter credits with a GPA of at least 2.0 (A = 4), plus completion of upper-divisional writing course; 60 hours of public service; three-year program. Accelerated J.D. with summer course work. For LL.M. (Asian Law): 36 quarter credits; proficiency in either Japanese, Chinese, or Korean; one comparative law seminar, one graduate research course; research project. For LL.M. (International Environmental Law): 40 quarter credits, at least 15 credits earned in law school; seminar on Problems in International Environmental Law; research paper. For LL.M. (Sustainable International Development): 40 quarter credits, at least 15 credits earned in law school; seminar in Legal Problems of Economic Development; research paper. For LL.M. (Law and Marine Affairs): 40 quarter credits, at least 15 credits earned in law school; one course in Marine Affairs (course must be at the 500 level); Ocean Policy and Resource Seminar. For LL.M. (Tax): 36 quarter credits.

School of Medicine
Web site: www.uwmedicine.edu

Founded in 1945. Library: 120,000 volumes, 2300 subscriptions. NIH ranking is 3 among all U.S. institutions with 997 awards/grants worth $462,021,658.

Annual tuition: residents $16,272, nonresident $38,094. No on-campus housing available. Total average figure for all other expenses: $14,000-$16,000.

Enrollment: first-year class 180, total 806 (men 49%, women 51%, minorities 23%, state residents 88%). Faculty: full-and part-time and volunteers 1977. Degrees conferred: M.D., M.D.-M.H.A., M.D.-M.P.H., M.D.-Ph.D. (Medical Scientist Training Program). The Ph.D. is offered through the Graduate School.

ADMISSION REQUIREMENTS. AMCAS report, transcripts, three letters of recommendation, MCAT, autiobiography, final screening interview required in suport of application. Does not have EDP. Interview and supplemental materials by invitation only. Accepts transfer applicants. Graduates of unaccredited colleges not considered. Preference given to WAMI residents. Apply to Assistant Dean for Admissions after June 1, before November 1. Application fee $50. Phone: (206)543-7212; fax: (206)616-3341.

ADMISSION STANDARDS. Very competitive. Accepts about 6% of all applicants. Number of applications 3224 (2234 out-of-state); number interviewed 803 (100 out-of-state); number of acceptance 232 (33 out-of-state); number enrolled 180 (16 out-of-state). Mean Composite MCAT 10.4; mean UGPA 3.64. *U.S. News & World Report* ranking is in the top 6 of all U.S. research medical schools; number one in Primary Care.

FINANCIAL AID. Scholarships, research fellowships, loans. MSTP funded by NIH. Apply to School's Financial Aid Office after acceptance, but before February 28. Phone: (206)685-9229. Use FAFSA (School code: 003798). About 92% of students receive some aid from School.

DEGREE REQUIREMENTS. For M.D.: satisfactory completion of four-year program; all students must pass USMLE Step 1 prior to entering third year, and pass Step 2 prior to awarding of M.D. For M.H.A., M.P.H., Ph.D.: see graduate school listings above.

FIELDS OF GRADUATE STUDY.
Biochemistry.
Bioengineering.
Biostatistics.
Biomedical and Health Informatics.
Biological Structure.
Epidemiology.
Environmental Health.
Genome Sciences.
Immunology.
Microbiology.
Molecular and Cellular Biology.
Neurobiology and Behavior.
Pathology.
Pharmacology.
Physiology and Biophysics.
Zoology.

WAYNE STATE COLLEGE
Wayne, Nebraska 68787
Web site: www.wsc.edu

Founded 1891. Located 100 miles NW of Omaha. CGS member. Coed. State control. Semester system. Library: 350,000 volumes, 1200 subscriptions. Total College enrollment 3450.

Tuition: per credit, resident $139.50, nonresident $279. On-campus housing available. Average academic year housing costs: $4780 (including board) for single students; $5500 for married students. Contact Housing Office for both on- and off-campus housing information. Phone: (402)375-7318.

Graduate Studies

Enrollment: full-time 31, part-time 247. Faculty teaching graduate students: full-time 0, part-time 73. Degrees conferred: M.S.E., M.B.A., Ed.S.

ADMISSION REQUIREMENTS. Official transcripts, GRE/GMAT, health form required in support of College's application. Online application available. TOEFL and Financial Resources Certification form required for international applicants. Accepts transfer applicants. Apply to Office of Admissions at least one month prior to date of registration. Rolling admissions process. Application fee $30; $50 for international applicants. Phone: (800) 228-9972, (402)375-7234.

ADMISSION STANDARDS. Relatively open. Usual minimum average 2.5 (A = 4).

FINANCIAL AID. Annual awards from institutional funds: scholarships, teaching assistantships, loans. Apply by April 1 to Director of Graduate Studies Office for assistantships; to Financial Aid Office for all other programs. Phone: (402)375-7204. Use FAFSA (College code: 002566). About 10% of students receive aid other than loans from College and outside sources. No aid for part-time students.

DEGREE REQUIREMENTS. For M.S.E.: 30 semester hours minimum; thesis optional; final oral/written exam. For M.B.A.: 36 credit program. For Specialist: 33 semester hours beyond the master's degree; special project.

FIELDS OF STUDY.
Alternative Education.
Business Administration.
Business Education.
Communication Arts Education
Curriculum and Instruction.
Early Childhood Education.
Elementary Education.
English Education.
English as a Second Language.
Exercise Science.
Family and Consumer Science.
Industrial Technical Education/Vocational Education.
Instructional Manager.
Learning Community.
Mathematics Education.
Music Education.
Organizational Management. M.S.O.M.
Physical Education.
School Administration (K–6, 7–12, P–12).
School Counseling (K–6, 7–12, K–12).
Science Education.
Social Sciences.
Special Educator.

WAYNE STATE UNIVERSITY
Detroit, Michigan 48202
Web site: www.wayne.edu

Founded 1868. CGS member. Coed. State control. Semester system. Special facilities: Addiction Research Center, Bioengineering Center, Center for Automotive Research, Center for Chicano Boricua Studies, Center for Health Research, Center for Healthcare Effectiveness Research, Center for International Business Studies, Center for Legal Studies, Center for Molecular Medicine and Genetics, Center for Peace and Conflict Studies, Center for the Study of Arts and Public Policy, Center for Urban Studies, Institute of Environmental Health Sciences, Institute for Information Technology and Culture, Institute for Learning and Performance Improvement, Institute for Manufacturing Research, Institute for Organizational and Industrial Competitiveness, Institute for Scientific Computing, Ligon Research Center for Vision, Manufacturing Information Systems Center, Merrill-Palmer Institute, Research Institute for Engineering Sciences, Institute of Gerontology, Barbara Ann Karmanos Cancer Institute, Cohn-Haddow Center for Judaic Studies, C.S. Mott Center for Human Growth and Development, Developmental Disabilities Institute, Douglas A. Fraser Center for Workplace Issues, Hilberry Classic Repertory Theatre, Humanities Center, Labor Studies Center, Morris J. Hood, Jr. Comprehensive Diabetes Center, National Teachers Corps Center, Charles Grosberg Religious Center, Mass Communications Center (equipped for closed-circuit TV and portable videotaping operation), Skillman Center for Children, State Policy Center. The University's NIH ranking is 77th among all U.S. institutions with 234 awards/grants valued at $76,915,164. According to The Center at University of Florida, the University is ranked 75th in receipt of Federal Research funds with $102,963,000 and it ranks 63rd for total University research expenditures with $213,717,000. In 2004, the University awarded 194 doctorates which ranked it 76th among all U.S. institutions eligible to award that degree. Four of the University's faculty members have been elected to National Honor Academies and this ranks it 97th among all U.S. institutions. The Library: approximately 2,800,000 volumes, 24,000 subscriptions. Total University enrollment: 33,100.

Tuition: per credit, resident $402, nonresident $889. On-campus housing for 800 single students. Average annual housing cost: $1000 per semester in dormitory; $475–$600 per month in apartments. Apply to Housing Authority. Phone: (313)577-2116.

Graduate School

Graduate study since 1930. Enrollment: full- and part-time 10,640. Graduate faculty: full- and part-time 939. Degrees conferred: M.A., M.S., M.Ed., M.A.I.R., M.A.T., M.S.L.S., M.B.A., M.F.A., M.L.I.S., M.M., M.P.A., M.U.P., M.S.W., Ed.S., Ed.D., Ph.D.

ADMISSION REQUIREMENTS. Official transcripts required in support of School's application. Online application available. GRE, MAT, GMAT/other entrance exams, letters of recommendation, interviews required by many departments. TOEFL required for international applicants. Accepts transfer applicants. Graduates of unaccredited institutions not considered. Apply to Office of University Admissions by July 1 (Fall), November 1 (Winter), March 1 (Spring), June 1 (Summer). Application fee $30; $50 for international applicants. Rolling admission process. Phone: (313) 577-9753; fax: (313)577-7536; e-mail: admissions@wayne.edu.

ADMISSION STANDARDS. Selective for most departments. Usual minimum average: 2.6 (A = 4).

FINANCIAL AID. Annual awards from institutional funds: scholarships, graduate fellowships, minority fellowships, graduate assistantships, internships, Federal W/S, loans. Approved for VA benefits. Apply in early Winter to Graduate Dean for scholarships and fellowships, to department chair for assistantships; to Financial Aid Office for all other programs. Phone: (313)577-2172 (scholarships and fellowships), (313)577-3378 (loans). Use FAFSA and University's FAF. About 30% of students receive aid other than loans from University and outside sources. Aid available for part-time students.

DEGREE REQUIREMENTS. For most master's: Plan A—24 semester hours minimum plus thesis; Plan B—28 semester hours minimum plus essay; Plan C—30 semester hours minimum without thesis or essay, at least 24 in residence; final written/oral exam; no language for most majors. For Ed.S.: 30 hours minimum beyond the master's, at least 24 in residence; terminal project or field study. For Ed.D.: 100 hours minimum beyond the bachelor's, at least 30 in residence; preliminary, qualifying, final written/oral exam; dissertation. For Ph.D.: 90 hours minimum beyond the bachelor's, including dissertation, at least 30 in residence; preliminary exam for some majors; written/oral qualifying exams; final oral exam; reading knowledge of one or more foreign languages required in some fields.

FIELDS OF STUDY.

SCHOOL OF BUSINESS ADMINISTRATION:
Accounting. M.S.
Business Administration. M.B.A.
Taxation. M.S.

COLLEGE OF EDUCATION:
Administration and Supervision. Ed.D.
Art Education. M.Ed.
Bilingual/Bicultural Education. M.Ed.
Career and Technical Education. M.Ed., Ed.D., Ph.D.
Counseling. M.A., M.Ed., Ed.D., Ph.D.
Curriculum and Instruction. Ed.D., Ph.D.
Early Childhood Education. M.Ed.
Education Evaluation and Research. M.Ed., Ed.D., Ph.D.
Educational Leadership. M.Ed.
Educational Leadership and Policy Studies. Ed.D., Ph.D.
Educational Psychology. M.Ed., Ph.D.
Elementary Education. M.A., M.A.T., M.Ed.
English Education (Secondary). M.Ed.
Foreign Language Education. M.Ed.
Health Education. Includes clinical/community health education. M.Ed.
Instructional Technology. M.Ed., Ed.D., Ph.D.

Kinesiology. M.Ed.
Mathematics Education. M.Ed.
Reading. M.Ed., Ed.D.
Reading, Language, and Literature. Ed.D.
Rehabilitation Counseling and Community Inclusion. M.A.
School and Community Psychology. M.A.
Science Education. M.Ed.
Secondary Education. M.A.T.
Social Studies Education (Secondary). M.Ed.
Special Education. M.Ed., Ed.D., Ph.D.
Sports Administration. Includes interscholastic/intercollegiate, professional. M.A.

COLLEGE OF ENGINEERING:
Alternative Energy Technology. M.S.
Biomedical Engineering. M.S., Ph.D.
Chemical Engineering. M.S., Ph.D.
Civil Engineering. M.S., Ph.D.
Computer Engineering. M.S., Ph.D.
Electrical Engineering. M.S., Ph.D.
Electronic and Computer Control Systems. M.S.
Engineering Management. M.S.
Engineering Technology. M.S.
Environmental Auditing.
Hazardous Materials Management on Public Lands.
Hazardous Waste Management. M.S.
Industrial Engineering. M.S., Ph.D.
Manufacturing Engineering. M.S.
Materials Science and Engineering. M.S., Ph.D.
Mechanical Engineering. M.S., Ph.D.
Polymer Engineering.

COLLEGE OF FINE, PERFORMING, AND COMMUNICATION ARTS:
Art. M.A., M.F.A.
Art History. Includes museum practice. M.A.
Communication. Includes communication studies, public relations and organizational communication, radio-TV-film, speech communication. M.A., Ph.D.
Design and Merchandising. M.A.
Dispute Resolution. M.A.
Music. Includes composition, choral conducting, music education, performance, theory. M.A., M.M.
Theatre. M.A., M.F.A., Ph.D.

GRADUATE SCHOOL:
Alcohol and Drug Abuse Studies.
Archival Administration.
Gerontology.
Infant Mental Health.
Library and Information Science. M.L.I.S.
Molecular and Cellular Toxicology. M.S., Ph.D.
Molecular Biology and Genetics. M.S., Ph.D.

COLLEGE OF LIBERAL ARTS AND SCIENCES:
Anthropology. M.A., Ph.D.
Audiology. Au.D.
Biological Science. M.A., M.S., Ph.D.
Chemistry. M.A., M.S., Ph.D.
Classics. M.A.
Communication Sciences and Disorders. Ph.D.
Comparative Literature. M.A.
Computer Science. M.A., M.S., Ph.D.
Criminal Justice. M.S.
Economics. M.A., Ph.D.
English. M.A., Ph.D.
Geology. M.S.
German. M.A.
History. M.A., Ph.D.
Human Development. M.A.
Industrial Relations. M.A.
Interdisciplinary Studies. M.I.S.

Language Learning. M.A.
Linguistics. M.A.
Mathematical Statistics. M.A.
Mathematics. Includes applied. M.A., Ph.D.
Modern Languages. Ph.D.
Molecular Biotechnology. M.S.
Multidisciplinary Science. M.A.
Near Eastern Languages. M.A.
Nutrition and Food Science. M.A., M.S., Ph.D.
Philosophy. M.A., Ph.D.
Physics. M.A., M.S., Ph.D.
Political Science. M.A., Ph.D.
Psychology. Includes industrial/organizational. M.A., Ph.D.
Public Administration. M.P.A.
Romance Languages. M.A.
Sociology. M.A., Ph.D.
Speech Language Pathology. M.A.
Urban Planning. M.U.P.

COLLEGE OF LIFELONG LEARNING:
Interdisciplinary Studies. M.I.S.

COLLEGE OF NURSING:
Adult Acute Care Nursing. M.S.
Adult Primary Care Nursing. M.S.
Community Health Nursing. M.S.N.
Neonatal Nurse Practitioner.
Nursing. Ph.D.
Nursing Education.
Psychiatric Mental Health Nurse Practitioner. M.S.N.
Transcultural Nursing. M.S.

EUGENE APPLEBAUM COLLEGE OF PHARMACY AND ALLIED HEALTH PROFESSIONS:
Anesthesia. M.S.
Clinical Laboratory Science. M.S.
Health Systems Pharmacy Management. M.S.
Occupational and Environmental Health Sciences. M.S.
Occupational Therapy. M.O.T., M.S.O.T
Pharmaceutical Sciences. M.S., Ph.D.
Physical Therapy. D.P.T.
Physician Assistant Studies. M.S.

SCHOOL OF SOCIAL WORK:
Social Work. Includes administration and community, family, children and youth services, health care services, mental health services. M.S.W., Ph.D.

Law School
Web site: www.wayne.edu

Established 1927. Located on main campus. ABA approved since 1927. AALS member. Semester system. Full-time, day, part-time (day or evening) study. Special facilities: Intellectual Property Law Institute, Center for Legal Studies. Special programs: summer study abroad at the Academy of International Law, the Hague, the Netherlands; the London Law Programme; exchange program with the School of Law, University of Warwick, England. Law library: 620,018 volumes, 4863 subscriptions; has LEXIS, NEXIS, WESTLAW, CALI; has more than 150 network connections.

Annual tuition: full-time resident $18,526, nonresident $34,462; part-time $584 per credit. University owned apartments available for both single and married students. Contact University's Housing Office for both on- and off-campus housing information. Law students tend to live off-campus. Off-campus housing and personal expenses: approximately $21,536.

Enrollment: first-year class full-time 207; total 670 (men 52%, women 48%, minorities 19%). Faculty: full-time 40, part-time 26. Student to faculty ratio is 19.6 to 1. Degrees conferred: J.D., J.D.-M.A. (History, Political Science), J.D.-M.B.A., J.D.-M.A. D.R. (Dispute Resolution), LL.M.

ADMISSION REQUIREMENTS. LSDAS Law School report, LSAT (not later than February test date; if more than one LSAT, highest is used), bachelor's degree from an accredited institution, personal statement, one recommendation, transcripts (must show all schools attended and at least three years of study) required in support of application. Applicants must have received bachelor's degree prior to enrollment. Interview not required. In addition, international applicants whose native language is not English must submit TOEFL scores (not older than two years), certified translations and evaluations of all foreign documents use J.D.-CAS. Apply to Office of Admission after October 1, before March 15. First-year students admitted Fall only. Accepts transfer applicants. Rolling admissions process. Application fee $50. Phone: (313) 577-3937; e-mail: inquire@novell.law.wayne.edu.

ADMISSION REQUIREMENTS FOR TRANSFER APPLICANTS. Accepts transfers from other ABA accredited schools. Admission limited to space available. At least one year of enrollment, Dean's letter indicating the applicant is in good standing, prefer applicants in the top quarter of first year class, LSAT, LSDAS, personal statement regarding reason for transfer, undergraduate transcript, current law school transcript required in support of School's application. Apply to Admission Office by July 1 (Fall). Admission decision made within one month of the receipt of a completed application. Application fee $50. Will consider visiting students.

ADMISSION REQUIREMENTS FOR LL.M. APPLICANTS. All applicants must have an equivalent J.D. (LL.B.) degree from a Common Law–based country or have completed a distinguished academic record in legal studies from a non–Common Law country, approved by the Director of Graduate Studies. Official transcripts, a personal statement, résumé, recommendations (optional) required in support of the Graduate application. In addition, international students must submit TOEFL scores (if English is not their native language), a special Graduate International Application, and a statement of financial support. Admits Fall, Winter, Spring/Summer. Apply by July 1 (Fall), November 1 (Winter), March 15 (Spring/Summer) to the Office of University Admissions. Application fee $50. Contact the Director of Graduate Studies for LL.M. for program information. Phone (313)577-3947; fax: (313)577-1060. International applicants should contact the Office of University Admissions for specific admissions information. Phone: (313)577-3577.

ADMISSION STANDARDS. Selective. Accepts approximately 40% of full-time, 27% of part-time students. Number of full-time applicants 1206, part-time 156; number of full-time acceptance 447, part-time 42; number of full-time enrolled 207, part-time 31; LSAT (75% of full-time students have a score at or above 153, part-time 151); GPA (75% of full-time students have a GPA at or above 3.33, part-time 3.28). *U.S. News & World Report* ranking is in the fourth tier of all U.S. law schools.

FINANCIAL AID. Need-based scholarships, minority (Kenneth Cockrel, Wade McCree) scholarships, law alumni fellowships, Board of Governor's Grants; private and institutional loans, Federal loans and Federal W/S offered through University's Financial Aid Office. Assistantships may be available for upper-divisional joint degree candidates. All accepted student are automatically considered for scholarships. For scholarship information, contact the Law School at (313)577-5142. Apply for Financial Aid after January 1, before April 30. Phone: (313)577-2172. Use FAFSA (School code: E00435), also submit Financial Aid Transcript, Federal Income Tax forms. Approximately 54% of first-year class received scholarships/Grants-in-Aid. Approximately 85% of students receive some form of financial assistance. Aid available for part-time students.

DEGREE REQUIREMENTS. For J.D.: 86 (36 required) credits with a GPA of at least a 2.0 (A = 4), plus completion of upper-divisional writing course; three-year program, four- to six-year part-time program. Accelerated J.D. with summer course work. For J.D.-Master's: three-and-one-half- to four-year programs rather than four- to five-year programs if both degrees are taken consecutively. For LL.M. (Tax): primarily a part-time evening program; 26 credits, at least 16 credits taken at the Law School; 3.0 (A = 4) GPA required; master's essay.

FIELDS OF GRADUATE STUDY.
Corporate and Finance Law. LL.M.
Labor Law. LL.M.
Tax Law. LL.M.

School of Medicine (48201)
Web site: www.med.wayne.edu

Founded 1868. Located at Detroit Medical Center. Special facilities: Addiction Research Institute, Barbara Ann Karmanos Cancer Institute, Center for Healthcare Effectiveness Research, Center for Molecular Medicine and Genetics, EHS Center in Molecular and Cellular Toxicology with Human Applications, Institute of Environmental Health Sciences, Ligon Research Center of Vision, Morris J. Hood, Jr. Comprehensive Diabetes Center, NanoBioScience Institute. Library: 150,000 volumes, 2500 subscriptions. NIH ranking is 77th among all U.S. institutions with 234 awards/grants worth $76,915,164.

Annual tuition: resident $25,891, nonresident $53,878. Off-campus housing only. Total average for all other expenses: $16,000–$18,000.

Enrollment: first-year class 288, total 1150 (men 51%, women 49%, minorities 29%, state residents 88%). Faculty: full-time 384, part-time 1000, Degrees conferred: M.D., M.D.-M.S., M.D.-Ph.D. The M.S., Ph.D. are offered through the Graduate School.

ADMISSION REQUIREMENTS. AMCAS report, transcripts, recommendations, MCAT (prefer Spring results) required in support of application. Interview required of those candidates under serious consideration. Applicants must have completed at least three years of college study. Has EDP; apply between June 1 and August 1. Accepts transfer applicants. Preference given to state residents. Apply to Office of Admissions after June 1, before November 1. Application fee $50. Phone: (313)577-1466; fax: (313) 577-9420.

ADMISSION STANDARDS. Competitive. Accepts about 15% of all applicants. Number of applications 3385 (2220 out-of-state); number interviewed 668 (213 out-of-state); number of acceptance n/a (n/a out-of-state); number enrolled 288 (59 out-of-state). Mean Composite MCAT 9.77 mean UGPA 3.54.

FINANCIAL AID. Scholarships, loans, college work-study. Summer fellowships. Apply to Committee on Financial Aid and Scholarships after acceptance. Phone: (313)577-1039. Use FAFSA (School code: E00570). About 41% of students receive aid other than loans from School.

DEGREE REQUIREMENTS. For M.D.: satisfactory completion of four-year program; Step 1 of USMLE must be passed prior to entering third year; all students must pass USMLE Step 2 for graduation. For Ph.D.: see Graduate Division listing above. Combined M.D.-Ph.D. program is available. Apply during first year in medical school.

FIELDS OF GRADUATE STUDY.
Anatomy and Cell Biology.
Biochemistry and Molecular Biology.
Cancer Biology.
Cellular and Clinical Neurobiology.
Community Medicine.
Genetic Counseling.
Immunology and Microbiology.

Medical Physics.
Molecular and Cellular Toxicology.
Molecular Biology and Genetics.
Pathology.
Pharmacology.
Physiology.
Psychiatry and Behavioral Neurosciences.
Radiological Physics.

WEBSTER UNIVERSITY
Webster Groves, Missouri 63119-3194
Web site: www.webster.edu

Founded 1915. Located in St. Louis and 40 locations worldwide. Coed. Private control. Semester system. Special facility (St. Louis): Center for International Education. Library: 250,000 volumes, 1400 subscriptions. Total University enrollment: 17,725.

Tuition (St. Louis): per credit hour $520, M.A.T. $435, online M.B.A. and online M.A. $485. No on-campus housing available.

Graduate Program

Graduate study since 1963. Enrollment: full-time 3626, part-time 8679. Faculty: full-time 76, part-time 1115. Degrees conferred: M.A., M.B.A., M.F.A., M.A.T., M.M., M.S., M.S.N., D.Mgt.

ADMISSION REQUIREMENTS. Official transcripts, bachelor's degree required in support of application. Online application available. TOEFL required for international applicants. Accepts transfer applicants. Graduates of unaccredited institutions not considered. Application fee $20. Phone: (314)968-7100 or (800)75-ENROL; fax: (314)968-7116.

ADMISSION STANDARDS. Relatively open. Usual minimum average: 2.5 (A = 4).

FINANCIAL AID. Internships, Federal W/S, loans. Approved for VA benefits. Apply by April 1 to the Financial Aid Office. Phone: (314)968-6992; fax: (314)968-7125. Aid available for part-time students.

DEGREE REQUIREMENTS. For M.A., M.S.: 36 credit program; thesis/nonthesis option. For M.B.A.: 36 credit program. For M.A.T.: 33 credit program. For M.M.: 32–34 credit program. For D.Mgt.: 42 credit program.

FIELDS OF STUDY.
Art. M.A.
Arts Management and Leadership. M.F.A.
Advertising and Marketing Communication. M.A.
Business Administration. M.B.A.
Business and Organizational Security Management. M.A.
Communication Arts. M.A.T.
Communications Management. M.A.
Computer Science/Distributed Systems. M.S.
Counseling. M.A.
Early Childhood Education. M.A.T.
Educational Technology. M.A.T.
Environmental Management. M.S.
Finance. M.S.
Gerontology. M.A.
Global. M.B.A.
Health Administration. M.H.A.
Health Care Management. M.A.
Human Resource Development. M.A.
Human Resource Management. M.A.
Information Technology Management. M.A.
International Business. M.A.

International Nongovernmental Organization. M.A.
International Relations. M.A.
Legal Analysis. M.A.
Legal Studies. M.A.
Management. D.Mgt.
Management and Leadership. M.A.
Marketing. M.A.
Mathematics. M.A.T.
Media Communications. M.A.
Media Literacy. M.A.
Multidisciplinary Studies. M.A.T.
Music. M.A., M.M.
Nurse Anesthesia. M.S.
Nursing. M.S.N.
Patent Agency. M.A.
Procurement and Acquisitions Management. M.A.
Professional Science Management and Leadership. M.A.
Public Administration. M.P.A.
Public Relations. M.A.
Reading. M.A.T.
Social Science. M.A.T.
Space Systems Operations Management. M.S.
Special Education. M.A.T.

WESLEYAN UNIVERSITY
Middletown, Connecticut 06459-0260
Web site: www.wesleyan.edu

Founded 1831. Located 16 miles S of Hartford. CGS member. Coed. Private control. Semester system. Special facilities: Center for the Arts, Davison Art Center, Freeman Athletic Center, Science Center, Van Vleck Observatory. Library: 2,000,000 volumes, 2719 subscriptions. Total University enrollment: 3200.

Annual tuition: full-time $24,732, per course $4122. On-campus housing for married students, 93 graduate men, 65 graduate women. Average academic year housing cost: $702–$910 per month for married students, $626–$702 (room only) for single students. Apply to Graduate Admissions Office in Middletown for both on- and off-campus housing information. Phone: (860) 685-3550. Day-care facilities available.

Graduate Program

Graduate study since 1965. Enrollment: full-time 193, part-time 259. University faculty: full-time 97. Degrees conferred: M.A., M.A.L.S., C.A.S., Ph.D.

ADMISSION REQUIREMENTS. Transcripts, three letters of recommendation, GRE required in support of application. Online application available. GRE Subject Test recommended. TOEFL required for international applicants. Interview often useful. Accepts transfer applicants. Apply to Graduate Admissions Office by April 1 for most programs, by January 15 for music. Application fee $40. Phone: (860)685-1390; fax: (860)685-2001.

ADMISSION STANDARDS. Very competitive for some departments, competitive for others. Usual minimum average: 3.0 (A = 4).

FINANCIAL AID. Annual awards from institutional funds: scholarships, grants, teaching assistantships, Federal W/S, loans. Approved for VA benefits. Apply, normally by March 15, to appropriate department chair for assistantships; to Financial Aid Office for all other programs. Phone: (860)685-2800. Use FAFSA and institutional FAF. About 98% of students receive aid from University and outside sources. Aid available for part-time students.

DEGREE REQUIREMENTS. For M.A.: one year in full-time study or the equivalent, but no more than four years for completion and at least two-thirds of total program in residence; reading knowledge of one foreign language for most majors, more for some programs; thesis or creative project; final written/oral exam. For M.A.L.S.: 30 semester hours, at least 24 in residence; designed for those who want an interdisciplinary education; credit may be earned solely in Summer sessions or in one calendar year of full-time study. For C.A.S. (for those who hold the master's degree): requirements essentially the same as for M.A.L.S. (transfer credits not accepted). For Ph.D.: normally at least 16 semester courses beyond the bachelor's, usually at least three years in residence; reading knowledge of two foreign languages; preliminary/qualifying exams; dissertation; final written/oral exam.

FIELDS OF STUDY.
Astronomy. Qualifying exam, apprenticeships for M.A. M.A. only.
Biochemistry. Ph.D.
Biology. Ph.D.
Chemistry. Ph.D.
Computer Science.
Earth and Environmental Science. M.A. only.
Ethnomusicology. Ph.D.
Mathematics. Apply by March 15.
Molecular Biology.
Molecular Biophysics. Interdepartmental. Ph.D.
Music. Includes choral conducting and composition in Western music.
Physics. Two years for M.A.
Psychology. Apply by March 15. M.A. only.
Note: Special programs leading to the M.A.L.S. and C.A.S. utilize the course offerings of several University departments, with specializations in arts, humanities, mathematics, general studies, science, social science.

UNIVERSITY OF WEST ALABAMA
Livingston, Alabama 35470
Web site: www.uwa.edu

Founded 1835. Name changed from Livingston University in 1995. Located 120 miles SW of Birmingham. Coed. State control. Semester system. Library: 141,700 volumes, 2000 subscriptions.
Tuition: per credit, resident $140, nonresident $290. On-campus housing for both single and married students. Average academic year housing costs: $3200 (including board) for single students; $4000 for married students (including board). Contact Director of Housing for both on- and off-campus housing information. Phone: (205)652-3400.

School of Graduate Studies

Graduate study since 1958. Enrollment: full- and part-time 329. Graduate faculty: full-time 50, part-time 2. Degrees conferred: M.Ed., M.S.C.Ed., M.A.T.

ADMISSION REQUIREMENTS. Transcripts, GRE/MAT/NTE, Alabama Class B certificate, or equivalent required in support of School's application. (Certificate not required for master's in Continuing Education or M.A.T.) TOEFL required for international applicants. Interview not required. Accepts transfer applicants. Apply to Director of Admissions; no specified closing dates. Rolling admissions process. Application fee $20, $50 for international applicants. Phone: (205)652-3647.

ADMISSION STANDARDS. Selective. Usual minimum average: 2.5 (A = 4).

FINANCIAL AID. Scholarships, assistantships, internships, Federal W/S, loans. Apply to Office of Financial Aid by April 1.

Phone: (205)652-3576. Use FAFSA and University's FAF. About 10% of students receive aid other than loans from University, 26% from all sources. Aid available for part-time students.

DEGREE REQUIREMENTS. For M.Ed.: 33-credit program, must take 9–12 credit in full-time residence; no thesis; admission to candidacy; final written exam. For M.S.C.Ed.; 33-credit program, must take 9–12 credits in full-time residence; admission to candidacy; final written exam. For M.A.T. 36-credit program, must take 9–12 credits in full-time residence; admission to candidacy; final written exam. No language requirement for any degrees.

FIELDS OF STUDY.
Continuing Education.
Counseling/Psychology.
Early Childhood Education.
Educational Leadership.
Elementary Education.
Guidance and Counseling.
Library Media.
Nursery—Grade 12 Education.
Physical Education.
School Counseling.
Secondary Education.
Social Science Education.
Special Education. Includes K–6, 6–12.

WEST CHESTER UNIVERSITY OF PENNSYLVANIA
West Chester, Pennsylvania 19383
Web site: www.wcupa.edu

Founded 1871. Located 25 miles W of Philadelphia and 17 miles north of Wilmington. CGS member. Coed. State control. Semester system. Library: 744,900 volumes, 4500 subscriptions. Total University enrollment: 12,988.
Tuition: per credit, resident $327, nonresident $523. Limited on-campus housing for graduate students. Average academic year housing costs: $3300–$4100 (including board). Apply to Director, Residence Life, for on-campus housing information; to the Office of Off-Campus Life for all off-campus housing information. Phone: (610)436-3307.

Graduate Studies

Graduate study since 1959. Enrollment: full-time 571, part-time 1579. Faculty: full- and part-time 232. Degrees conferred: M.Ed., M.A., M.S., M.M., M.B.A., M.S.A.

ADMISSION REQUIREMENTS. Two official transcripts, letters of recommendation required in support of application. Some programs require GRE and Subject Test, MAT, or GMAT scores, interviews. TOEFL required for international applicants. Apply to Office of Graduate Studies by April 15 (Fall), October 15 (Spring). Application fee $35. Phone: (610)436-2943; fax: (610) 436-2763; e-mail: gradstudy@wcupa.edu.

ADMISSION STANDARDS. Vary with program. Usual minimum average: 2.75, 3.00 for full degree status (A = 4).

FINANCIAL AID. Scholarships, awards, graduate assistantships, loans. Apply by February 15 to Dean of Graduate Studies and department chair for assistantships, scholarships, awards; to Financial Aid for all other programs. Phone: (610)436-2943. Use FAFSA.

DEGREE REQUIREMENTS. For master's: 30 credits minimum plus thesis, or 36 credits minimum without thesis; final written/oral exam in most programs.

FIELDS OF STUDY.
Administration. M.S. only.
Applied Statistics. M.S.
Biology. M.A. only.
Business Administration. Includes economics/finance, general business, management, technology and electronic commerce. M.B.A.
Chemistry. Includes clinical, general. M.S. only.
Communication Studies. M.A. only.
Communicative Disorders. M.A. only.
Computer Science. M.S. only.
Counselor Education. M.Ed., M.S.
Criminal Justice. M.S. only.
Early Childhood Education. M.Ed.
Educational Research. M.S. only.
Elementary Education. M.Ed. only.
Elementary School Counseling. M.Ed.
English. M.A. only.
Environmental Health. M.S. only.
French. M.A., M.Ed.
Geography. M.A. only.
German. M.Ed. only.
Health Services. M.S.A. only.
Higher Education Counseling. M.S. only.
History. M.A., M.Ed.
Holocaust and Genocide Studies. M.A. only.
Human Resources Management. M.S.A. only.
Instructional Media. M.Ed., M.S.
Latin. M.Ed. only.
Leadership for Women. M.S.A. only.
Long-Term Care. M.S.A.
Mathematics. M.A. only.
Music Composition. M.M.
Music Education. M.M. only.
Music History. M.A. only.
Music Performance. M.M.
Music Theory. M.M. only.
Nursing. M.S. only.
Philosophy. M.A. only.
Physical Education. M.S. only.
Physical Science. Includes earth science. M.A. only.
Psychology. Includes clinical, industrial/organizational. M.A. only.
Public Administration. M.S.A. only.
Public Health. M.P.H.
Reading. M.Ed. only.
School Health. M.Ed. only.
Secondary Education. M.Ed. only.
Secondary School Counseling. M.Ed. only.
Social Work. M.S.W.
Spanish. M.A., M.Ed.
Special Education. M.Ed. only.
Sport and Athletic Administration. M.S.A. only.
TESL. M.A.
Training and Development. M.S.A. only.
Urban and Regional Planning. M.S.A. only.

UNIVERSITY OF WEST GEORGIA

Carrollton, Georgia 30118
Web site: www.westga.edu

Became a junior college in 1933. Located 48 miles W of Atlanta. CGS member. Coed. State control. Semester system. Library: 391,330 volumes, 2095 subscriptions. Total University enrollment: 10,200.

Annual tuition: full-time resident $2196, nonresident $8784; per semester credit, resident $122; nonresident $488. No on-campus housing for married students. Average academic year housing costs: $5828 (including board). Contact Director of Residential Life for off-campus housing information. Phone: (678)836-6426. Day-care facilities available.

Graduate School

Graduate study since 1967. Enrollment: full-time 422, part-time 1386. College faculty teaching graduate students: full-time 199, part-time 43. Degrees conferred: M.A., M.S., M.M., M.Ed., M.B.A., M.P.A., M.P.Acc., Ed.S., Ed.D., Ph.D.

ADMISSION REQUIREMENTS. Official transcripts, NTE, GRE/GMAT, MAT, recommendations required in support of School's application. Interview for psychology majors. TOEFL (minimum score 550) required for international applicants. Accepts transfer applicants. Graduates of unaccredited institutions not considered. Apply to Dean of the Graduate School by August 1 (Fall), December 15 (Winter), March 10 (Spring), June 6 (Summer). All doctoral applicants must apply by February 28 for summer start. Application fee $20. Phone: (678)836-6419; fax: (678)830-2301.

ADMISSION STANDARDS. Selective. Usual minimum average: 2.5 (A = 4).

FINANCIAL AID. Annual awards from institutional funds: graduate assistantships, research assistantships, internships, tuition waivers, Federal W/S, loans; varying number of dormitory hosts and hostesses. Approved for VA benefits. Apply to Dean of the Graduate School; no specified closing date. Phone: (678)836-6421. Use FAFSA. About 20% of students receive aid other than loans from University and outside sources.

DEGREE REQUIREMENTS. For M.A., M.S.: Plan A—30 semester hours, reading knowledge of one foreign language; thesis; oral defense. Plan B—36 semester hours without thesis; reading knowledge of one foreign language; final comprehensive. For M.M.: 36 semester hours; thesis/nonthesis option; admission to candidacy; recital. For M.P.A.: 36 semester hours, professional seminar; research paper; oral defense. For M.Ed.: 36 semester hours (except 48 for Guidance and Counseling); final written/oral exam. For M.B.A.: 30–57 semester hours (depending on previous academic work), at least 30 credits in residence. For M.P.Acc.: 30 semester hours minimum beyond foundation and basic accounting courses; comprehensive exam. For M.S.N.: 36 semester hour program. For Ed.S.: at least 27 semester hours beyond the master's; admission to candidacy; research project. For Ed.D., Ph.D.: 60 semester hour program; school improvement project; admission to candidacy; dissertation; oral defense.

FIELDS OF STUDY.
Administration and Supervision. M.Ed., Ed.S.
Applied Computer Science. M.S.
Art Education. M.Ed.
Biology. M.S.
Business Education. M.Ed., Ed.S.
Business Administration. M.B.A.
Early Childhood Education. M.Ed., Ed.S.
Educational Leadership. M.Ed.
English. M.A.
French. M.A.T., M.Ed.
German. M.A.T.
Gerontology. Includes direct service, administration and supervision, policy and planning. M.A.
Guidance and Counseling. M.Ed., Ed.S.
History. Includes public history. M.A.
Individual, Organizational and Community Transformation. Ph.D.
Mathematics.
Media. M.Ed., Ed.S.
Middle Grades Education. M.Ed., Ed.S.
Music. Includes music education, performance.
Nursing. Includes nurse education track, health system leadership track. M.S.N.
Physical Education. M.Ed., Ed.S.
Professional Accounting. M.P.Acc.
Professional Counseling. M.Ed.

Psychology. Includes organizational development. M.A.
Public Administration. M.P.A.
Reading Education. M.Ed.
School Improvement. Ed.D.
Secondary Education. Includes English, mathematics, science, social science. M.Ed., Ed.S.
Sociology. Includes criminology, resources and methods, women's studies. M.A.
Spanish. M.A.T., M.Ed.
Special Education. Includes adapted curriculum. M.Ed., Ed.S.
Speech-Language Pathology. M.Ed.
Rural and Small Town Planning. M.S.

WEST TEXAS A&M UNIVERSITY

Canyon, Texas 79016-0001
Web site: www.wtamu.edu

Established 1909. Located 15 miles S of Amarillo. Coed. State control. Semester system. Special facilities: Drylands Agriculture Institute, Equine Center, Killgore Research Center, Pan Handle Plains Historical Museum, Texas Engineering Experiment Station Regional Division. Library: 349,224 volumes, 5900 subscriptions. Total University enrollment: 6650.

Tuition: per credit resident $184, border state residents $214, nonresident $462. On-campus housing costs: $3000–$4500 (includes board). Apply to Director of Housing. Phone: (806) 651-3300.

Graduate School

Graduate study since 1932. Enrollment: full- and part-time 1250. Graduate faculty: full-time 180, part-time 45. Degrees conferred: M.A., M.B.A., M.Ed., M.S., M.Ag., M.M., M.P.A., M.S.N., M.F.A.

ADMISSION REQUIREMENTS. Official transcripts, MAT/GRE, GMAT (Business) required in support of School's application. Interview required by some departments. TOEFL required for international applicants. Accepts transfer applicants. Graduates of unaccredited institutions not considered. Apply to Director of Admissions. Rolling admissions process. Application fee for international applications $25. Phone: (806)651-2730; fax: (806)651-2733.

ADMISSION STANDARDS. Relatively open. Usual minimum average: 2.60, 2.85 for last two years (A = 4).

FINANCIAL AID. Annual awards from institutional funds: teaching assistantships, research assistantships, internships, grants, Federal W/S, loans. Approved for VA benefits. Apply to appropriate department chair for assistantships; to Financial Aid Office for all other programs. Phone: (806)651-2055; fax: (806)651-2924. Use FAFSA (School code: 003665). About 10% of students receive financial assistance. Aid available to part-time students.

DEGREE REQUIREMENTS. For master's: 30 credit hours with thesis or 36 credit hours with nonthesis option (available in most departments); at least 18 hours in residence comprehensive final exam.

FIELDS OF STUDY.
Accounting. M.P.A.
Agriculture. M.S., Ph.D.
Agricultural Business and Economics. M.S.
Animal Science. M.S.
Art. M.A.
Biology. M.S.
Business Administration. Includes agriculture, management, marketing. M.B.A.

Chemistry. M.S.
Communication. M.A.
Communication Disorders. M.S.
Computer Information Systems. M.B.A.
Counseling. M.A., M.Ed.
Criminal Justice Studies. M.A.
Curriculum and Instruction. M.Ed.
Educational Administration. M.Ed.
Educational Diagnostician. M.Ed.
Engineering Technology. M.S.
English. M.A.
Environmental Science. M.S.
Finance and Economics. M.S.
History. M.A.
Instructional Technology and Design. M.Ed.
Interdisciplinary Studies. M.A., M.S.
Mathematics. M.S.
Music. Includes performance. M.A., M.M.
Nursing. Includes administration, education, practitioners.
Plant, Soil and Environmental Science. M.S.
Political Science. M.A.
Psychology. M.A.
Reading Education. M.Ed.
Special Education. M.Ed.
Sport and Exercise Sciences. M.S.
Studio Art. M.F.A.

UNIVERSITY-WIDE PROGRAMS:
Interdisciplinary Studies. M.A., M.S.

WEST VIRGINIA SCHOOL OF OSTEOPATHIC MEDICINE

400 North Lee Street
Lewisburg, West Virginia 24901-1128
Web site: www.wvsom.edu

Founded 1974 as Greenbrier College of Osteopathic Medicine, became part of West Virginia State System of Higher Education in 1976. Located in rural Appalachia. Public control. Three-phase system. Library: 18,660 volumes, 468 subscription.

Annual tuition: resident $19,086, nonresident $46,936. No on-campus housing available. Contact Admissions Office for off-campus housing information. Off-campus housing and personal expenses: approximately $16,500.

Enrollment: first-year class 104; total full-time 503 (men 52%, women 48%, minorities 15%, state residents 44%). Faculty: full-time 38, part-time 98. Degree conferred: D.O.

ADMISSION REQUIREMENTS. Preference given to state residents, then to SREB contract states, and then to residents of the Southern Appalachian states; U.S. citizens and permanent residents only. Bachelor's degree from an accredited institution required. All applicants have bachelor's degree awarded prior to enrollment. Apply through AACOMAS (file after June 1, before January 2), submit MCAT (will accept test results from last three years), official transcripts for each school attended (should show at least 90 semester credits/135 quarter credit), service processing fee. After a review of the AACOMAS application and supporting documents a decision is made concerning which candidates should receive supplemental materials. Online application available. The supplemental application, an application fee of $40 ($80 for nonresidents), a personal statement, and three recommendations (one from a D.O.) should be returned to the Office of Admissions as soon as possible, no later than February 15. Interviews are by invitation only and generally for final selection. First-year students admitted Fall only. Rolling admissions process; notification starts in November and is finished when class is filled. School does maintain an alternate/waiting list. CPR Certification is required prior to enrollment. Phone: (800)356-7836, (304)645-6270, ext. 373; fax: (304)645-4859; e-mail: admission@wvsom.edu.

ADMISSION REQUIREMENTS FOR TRANSFER APPLICANTS. Accepts transfers from other accredited U.S. osteopathic medical schools. Admission limited to space available. Contact the Office of Admissions for current information and specific requirements.

ADMISSION STANDARDS. Selective. Accepts about 26% of all applicants. Number of applications 1635 (1512 out-of-state); number interviewed 420 (343 out-of-state); number of acceptance 310 (250 out-of-state); number enrolled 104 (61 out-of-state). Usual minimum UGPA: 2.75 (A = 4). Mean Composite MCAT 7.6, mean UGPA 3.4. The *U.S. News & World Report* ranking is in the top 50 of all U.S. Medical Schools for Primary Care.

FINANCIAL AID. Tuition fee waivers, scholarships, grants, institutional loans, NOF, HEAL, alternative loan programs, West Virginia Board of Trustees Medical Student Loan Program, Federal W/S, loans. Service Obligation Scholarship programs, Armed Forces and National Health Service programs are available. Financial Aid applications and information are given out at the on-campus, by-invitation interview. Contact the Financial Aid Office for current information. Phone: (304) 645-6270. Apply by April 1 to the Financial Aid Office. Use FAFSA (School code: 011245), also submit Financial Aid Transcript, Federal Income Tax forms. Approximately 90% of students receive some form of financial assistance.

DEGREE REQUIREMENTS. For D.O.: satisfactory completion of four-year program; must pass part I of the National Osteopathic Board Exam for promotion to clinical years; pass part II for graduation.

WEST VIRGINIA UNIVERSITY
Morgantown, West Virginia 26506-6009
Web site: www.wvu.edu

Established 1867. Located 70 miles S of Pittsburgh, Pennsylvania. CGS member. Coed. State control. Semester system. Special facilities: Agricultural Experiment Station, Center for Black Culture and Research, Bureau of Business Research, Bureau of Government Resource, Energy Research Center, Concurrent Engineering Research Center, Fluidization Center, Engineering Experiment Station, Gerontology Center, Institute for the History of Technology and Industrial Archeology, Institute for Labor Relations, NASA facility, National Research Center for Coal and Energy, Regional Research Institute, Water Research Institute, Westvaco Natural Resource Center. Women Studies Center. Library: 1,877,000 volumes, 7900 subscriptions. Total University enrollment: 26,000.

Annual tuition: full-time resident $4582, nonresident $13,820; per credit resident $258, nonresident $741. Limited on-campus housing for single and married students. Annual housing costs: $6342 (including board) for single student; $5800 for married students. Off-campus housing costs: $375–$550 per month. Contact Housing and Residence Life for both on- and off-campus housing information. Phone: (304)293-3621.

Graduate Studies

Enrollment: full-time 4185, part-time 1990. Faculty: full-time 737, part-time 488. Degrees conferred: M.A., M.S., M.Agr., M.M., M.B.A., M.F.A., M.P.A. (Professional Accountancy), M.P.A., M.S.F., M.S.E., M.S.E.E., M.S.A.E., M.S.C.E., M.S.Ch.E., M.S.E.E., M.S.E.M., M.S.F., M.S.I.E., M.S.M.E., M.S.N., M.S.PNGE., M.S.W., M.S.J., M.A.L.S., C.A.S., Ed.D., D.M.A., Ph.D.

ADMISSION REQUIREMENTS. Official transcripts required in support of application. Online application available. GRE Subject Tests/GMAT, letters of recommendation, interviews required for some departments. TOEFL required for foreign applicants. Accepts transfer applicants. Graduates of unaccredited colleges not considered. Apply to Director of Admissions and Records by June 30 (Fall), November 15 (Spring). Rolling admissions process. Application fee $50. Phone: (800)344-WVU1; fax: (304) 293-3080.

ADMISSION STANDARDS. Selective for most departments, very selective or competitive for the others. Usual minimum average: 2.75 (A = 4).

FINANCIAL AID. Annual awards from institutional funds: scholarships/fellowships, teaching assistantships, research assistantships, tuition waivers, internships, Federal W/S, loans. Approved for VA benefits. Apply by February 1 to appropriate department chairman for fellowships, assistantships; to the Office of Financial Assistance for all other programs. Phone: (304) 293-5242. Use FAFSA. Aid available for part-time students.

DEGREE REQUIREMENTS. For master's: 30 semester hours minimum, at least 24 in full-time residence; thesis/nonthesis option; final report for many departments; final oral/written exam in many programs. For C.A.S.: 30 hours minimum beyond the master's, at least 24 in residence including one semester or Summer session in full-time study; research report; final oral exam. For Ed.D.: 72 semester hours minimum beyond the bachelor's, at least two consecutive semesters in full-time residence; advancement to candidacy exams; dissertation; final oral exam. For D.M.A.: three years full-time study, at least one year in full-time residence; written research project; reading knowledge of one foreign language. For D.M.A., Performance: same as above except major solo recital. For D.M.A., Composition: major composition project; final oral exam. For Ph.D.: three years minimum beyond the bachelor's, at least two semesters in full-time residence; foreign language competency required by most departments; dissertation; final oral exam.

FIELDS OF STUDY.

DAVIS COLLEGE OF AGRICULTURE, FORESTRY, AND CONSUMER SCIENCES:
Agricultural and Extension Education. M.S., Ph.D.
Agricultural and Resource Economics. M.S.
Agriculture, Forestry and Consumer Sciences. M.S.
Agronomy. M.S.
Animal and Food Sciences. Ph.D.
Animal and Nutritional Sciences. M.S.
Entomology. M.S.
Environmental Microbiology. M.S.
Family and Consumer Sciences. M.S.
Forest Resources Science. Ph.D.
Forestry. M.S.
Genetics and Developmental Biology. M.S., Ph.D.
Horticulture. M.S.
Human and Community Development. Ph.D.
Natural Resource Economics. Ph.D.
Plant and Soil Sciences. Ph.D.
Plant Pathology. M.S.
Recreation, Park and Tourism Resources. M.S.
Reproductive Physiology. M.S., Ph.D.
Resource Management. Ph.D.
Wildlife and Fisheries Resources. M.S.

EBERLY COLLEGE OF ARTS AND SCIENCES:
Biology. M.S., Ph.D.
Chemistry. M.S., Ph.D.
Communication Studies. M.A., Ph.D.
Creative Writing. M.A.

English. M.A., Ph.D.
Foreign Languages. M.A.
Geography. M.A., Ph.D.
Geology. M.S., Ph.D.
History. M.A., Ph.D.
Legal Studies. M.L.S.
Liberal Studies. M.A.L.S.
Mathematics. M.S., Ph.D.
Physics. M.S., Ph.D.
Political Science. M.S., Ph.D.
Professional Writing and Editing. M.A.
Psychology. M.A., Ph.D.
Public Administration. M.P.A.
Social Work. M.S.W.
Statistics. M.S.

COLLEGE OF BUSINESS AND ECONOMICS:
Accounting. M.Acc.
Business Administration. M.B.A.
Economics. M.A., Ph.D.
Industrial Relations. M.S.
Professional Accountancy. M.P.A.

COLLEGE OF CREATIVE ARTS:
Art. M.A.
Art Education. M.A.
Art History. M.A.
Music. M.M., D.M.A.
Theatre. M.F.A.
Visual Arts. M.F.A.

COLLEGE OF ENGINEERING AND MINERAL RESOURCES:
Aerospace Engineering. M.S.A.E., Ph.D.
Chemical Engineering. M.S.Ch.E., Ph.D.
Civil Engineering. M.S.C.E., Ph.D.
Computer Engineering. Ph.D.
Computer Science. M.S.C.S., Ph.D.
Electrical Engineering. M.S.E.E., Ph.D.
Engineering. M.S.E.
Industrial Engineering. M.S.I.E., Ph.D.
Industrial Hygiene. M.S.
Mechanical Engineering. M.S.M.E., Ph.D.
Mining Engineering. M.S.E.M., Ph.D.
Occupational Safety and Health. Ph.D.
Petroleum and Natural Gas Engineering. M.S.PNGE., Ph.D.
Safety Management. M.S.
Software Engineering. M.S.

COLLEGE OF HUMAN RESOURCES AND EDUCATION:
Audiology. Au.D.
Child Development and Family Studies. M.A.
Counseling. M.A.
Counseling Psychology. Ph.D.
Curriculum and Instruction. Ed.D.
Education Leadership. M.A., Ed.D.
Educational Psychology. M.A., Ed.D.
Elementary Education. Includes multidisciplinary studies. M.A.
Instruction Design and Technology. M.A., Ed.D.
Reading. M.A.
Rehabilitation Counseling. M.S.
Secondary Education. Includes English, foreign languages, mathematics, science, social studies. M.A.
Special Education. M.A., Ed.D.
Speech Pathology. M.S.

PERLEY ISAAC REED SCHOOL OF JOURNALISM:
Integrated Marketing Communications. M.A.
Journalism. M.S.J.

SCHOOL OF MEDICINE:
Anatomy. M.S.
Biochemistry. M.S.
Biochemistry and Molecular Biology.
Biomedical Sciences. Interdisciplinary. Ph.D.
Cancer Cell Biology. Ph.D.
Cellular and Integrative Physiology. Ph.D.
Community Health Education. M.S.
Exercise Physiology. M.S., Ph.D.
Immunopathology and Microbial Pathogenesis. Ph.D.
Microbiology and Immunology. M.S.
Neuroscience. Ph.D.
Occupational Therapy. M.O.T.
Pathologist's Assistant. M.S.
Pharmaceutical and Pharmacological Sciences. Ph.D.
Physical Therapy. D.P.T.
Physiology. M.S.
Public Health. M.P.H., Ph.D.
Public Health Sciences. Ph.D.
School Health Education. M.S.

SCHOOL OF NURSING:
Nursing. M.S.N., D.S.N.

SCHOOL OF PHARMACY:
Pharmaceutical Sciences. M.S., Ph.D.
Pharmacy. Pharm.D.

SCHOOL OF PHYSICAL EDUCATION:
Athletic Coaching Education. M.S.
Athletic Training. M.S.
Kinesiology. Ed.D.
Physical Education/Teacher Education. M.S., Ed.D.
Sport and Exercise Psychology. M.S., Ed.D.
Sport Management. M.S.

School of Dentistry (P.O. Box 9400)
Web site: www.hsc.wvu.edu/sod

Established 1957. Located at Health Sciences Center. Semester system.

Annual tuition: resident $12,000, nonresident $29,960. On-campus housing available. Average academic year off-campus housing costs: $11,500. Contact the Director of Housing for both on- and off-campus housing information. Phone: (304)293-4491. Total average cost for all other first-year expenses: $7,500.

Enrollment: first-year class 50, total 216 (men 46%, women 54%, minorities 12%, state residents 78%), postgraduates 15. Faculty: full-time 42, part-time 21. Degrees conferred: D.D.S., D.D.S.-M.S., D.D.S.-Ph.D.

ADMISSION REQUIREMENTS. AADSAS report, transcripts, DAT (not later than November 1) required in support of application. Interview by invitation only. Applicants must have completed at least three years of college study for admission. West Virginia residents given preference. Graduates of unaccredited institutions not considered. Apply to Dean of Admissions after June 1, before January 31. Rolling admission process. Application fee $50. Phone: (304)293-6646; fax: (304)293-8561.

ADMISSION STANDARDS. Selective. Accepts about 5% of all applicants. Usual minimum UGPA: 2.75 (A = 4). Mean DAT: academic 17, PAT 16; mean UGPA 3.52.

FINANCIAL AID. Scholarships, loans. Apply by March 1 to Financial Aid Officer for scholarships and loans. Phone: (304) 293-3706. Use FAFSA (School code: 003827). Approximately 82% of all students receive some form of financial assistance.

DEGREE REQUIREMENTS. For D.D.S.: satisfactory completion of three- to four-year program. For M.S.: satisfactory completion of one-year program. For Ph.D.: see Graduate School listing above.

FIELDS OF POSTGRADUATE STUDY.
Advanced Education in General Dentistry.
Dental Hygiene. M.S.
Endodontics. M.S.
General Practice Residency.
Oral and Maxillofacial Surgery. Certificate.
Orthodontics. M.S.
Prosthodontics.

College of Law (P.O. Box 6130)
Web site: www.wvu.edu/~law

Established 1878. Located on main campus. ABA approved since 1923. AALS member since 1914. Semester system. Full-time, day and limited part-time study. Special programs: Appalachian Center for Law and Public Service. Law library: 347,393 volumes, 3222 subscriptions; has LEXIS, WESTLAW, CALI; is a Federal Government Depository.

Annual tuition: resident $9342, nonresident $21,710. On-campus housing available for both single and married students. Contact University's On-campus Housing Office for information. Phone: (304)293-3621. Law students tend to live off-campus. Contact University's Off-campus Housing Office for off-campus information. Phone: (304)293-5613. Off-campus housing and personal expenses: approximately $12,481.

Enrollment: first-year class 151; total full-time 474 (men 56%, women 44%, minorities 10%); limited part-time study. Faculty: full-time 22, part-time 20. Student to faculty ratio 23.2 to 1. Degrees conferred: J.D., J.D.-M.B.A., J.D.-M.P.A.

ADMISSION REQUIREMENTS. LSDAS Law School report, bachelor's degree, transcripts, LSAT, three letters of recommendation required in support of application. West Virginia residents given preference. Accepts a limited number of transfer applicants. Graduates of unaccredited colleges not considered. Apply to Office of Admission, after September 1, before February 1. Admits beginning students Fall only. Application fee $50. Phone: (304) 293-5304; fax: (304)293-6891.

ADMISSION STANDARDS. Selective. Accepts approximately 39% of all students. Number of applicants 850; number of acceptance 324; number enrolled 151; LSAT (75% of students have a score at or above 148); GPA (75% of students have a GPA at or above 3.19). *U.S. News & World Report* ranking is in the third tier of all U.S. law schools.

FINANCIAL AID. Scholarships, Federal W/S, loans. Apply to the Financial Aid Counselor by March 1. Phone: (304)293-5302. Use FAFSA (College code: 003827) and institutional application (due by April 1). About 33% of students receive aid other than loans from College. No aid for part-time students.

DEGREE REQUIREMENTS. For J.D.: 90-credit-hour program, at least 55 in residence.

School of Medicine (P.O. Box 9111)
Web site: www.hsc.wvu.edu/som

Medical training since 1902. Located at Medical Center. Special facilities: Cancer Cell Biology Research Center, Cardiovascular Sciences Research Center, Diabetes, Obesity and Metabolic Disorders Research Center, Immunopathology & Microbial Pathogenesis Research Center, Respiratory Biology & Lung Disease Research Center, Neuroscience Research Center, Center for Advanced Imaging, Center of Excellence in Women's Health, Center for Rural Emergency Medicine, Health Research Center, Injury Control Research Center, Mary Babb Randolph Cancer Center, Prevention Research Center. Library: 264,000 volumes, 2227 subscriptions.

Annual tuition: resident $19,204, nonresident $41,900. On-campus housing available. Total average for all other expenses: $12,000–$14,000.

Enrollment: first-year class 98, total 424 (men 53%, women 47%, minorities 23%, state residents 46%); postgraduates 204. Faculty: full-time 584, part-time 113. Degrees conferred: M.D., M.D.-Ph.D. The Ph.D. is offered through the Graduate School.

ADMISSION REQUIREMENTS. AMCAS Report, transcripts, recommendations, MCAT, final screening interview required in support of application. Has EDP (state residents only); apply between June 1 and August 1. Interview by invitation only. Applicants must have completed at least three years of college study for admission. West Virginia residents given preference. Accepts transfer applicants. Graduates of unaccredited colleges not considered. Apply to Chair, Committee on Admissions, after June 1, before November 15. Admits beginning students Fall only. Application fee $50. Phone: (304)293-2408; fax: (301) 293-7814.

ADMISSION STANDARDS. Competitive. Accepts about 13% of all applicants. Number of applications 1307 (1121 out-of-state); number interviewed 258 (140 out-of-state); number of acceptance 170 (85 out-of-state); number enrolled 98 (43 out-of-state). Mean Composite MCAT 9.8 mean UGPA 3.72.

FINANCIAL AID. Scholarships, loans; fellowships, assistantships for teaching/research. Apply to Financial Aid Officer for scholarships, loans; to appropriate department chair for fellowships, assistantships; no specified closing date. Phone: (304)293-3706. Use FAFSA (School code: 003827). Approximately 88% of students receive some form of financial assistance.

DEGREE REQUIREMENTS. For M.D.: satisfactory completion of four-year program; all students must pass USMLE Step 1 prior to entering third year, and must pass USMLE Step 2 prior to awarding of M.D. For M.P.H., Ph.D.: see Graduate School listing above.

FIELDS OF GRADUATE STUDY.
Biochemistry and Molecular Biology.
Cancer Cell Biology.
Cellular and Integrative Physiology.
Exercise Physiology.
Immunology and Microbial Pathogenesis.
Neuroscience.
Pharmaceutical and Pharmacological Sciences.
Public Health Sciences.

WESTERN CAROLINA UNIVERSITY
Cullowhee, North Carolina 28723-9022
Web site: www.wcu.edu

Founded 1889; college work began 1907. Located 52 miles W of Asheville. CGS member. Coed. State control. Semester system. Special facility: Computer Center with two DEC VAX 4000/700A, Mountain Aquaculture Center, Mountain Heritage Center, Center for Improving Mountain Living. Library: 527,866 volumes, 2900 subscriptions. Total University enrollment: 6500.

Annual tuition full-time resident $2314, nonresident $11,893. On-campus housing for 1570 graduate men, 1733 graduate women; 45 units for married students. Average academic year housing costs: single students $5000 (including board), married students $500–$600 per month. Contact Director of Housing for both on- and off-campus housing information. Phone: (828)227-7303.

Graduate School

Graduate study since 1951. Enrollment: full-time 367, part-time 634. Graduate faculty: full-time 273, part-time 20. Degrees conferred: M.A., M.A.Ed., M.H.S., M.I.E., M.B.A., M.M.E., M.P.A., M.P.M., M.S., Ed.S., C.A.S.

ADMISSION REQUIREMENTS. Official transcripts, letters of reference in most programs (GRE for M.A., M.A.Ed., M.H.S., M.I.E., M.M.E., M.P.A., M.S., Ed.S., C.A.S.; GMAT for M.B.A., M.P.M.) required in support of School's application. TOEFL required for international applicants. Accepts transfer applicants. Graduates from unaccredited institutions not considered. Apply to and have all credentials at Graduate School by February 1, international applicants by April 1. Application fee $35. Phone: (800) 364-9854, (828)227-7398; fax: (828)227-7480.

ADMISSION STANDARDS. Selective. Usual minimum average: 3.0 (A = 4).

FINANCIAL AID. Annual awards from institutional funds: Chancellors' fellowships, teaching/service assistantships, tuition waivers, study grants, Federal W/S, loans. Approved for VA benefits. Apply by March 31 to Dean of Graduate School or department chair for assistantships, fellowships; to the Financial Aid for all other programs. Phone: (828)227-7290. Use FAFSA (School code: 002981). About 25% of students receive aid other than loans from University and outside sources. Aid sometimes available for part-time students.

DEGREE REQUIREMENTS. For master's: 30-36 semester hours, at least 24 in residence; comprehensive exam; thesis for M.A., M.H.S., M.S.; some M.A., M.S. programs require one foreign language. For Ed.S.: 30 semester hours beyond the master's; special project.

FIELDS OF STUDY.
Accountancy. M.Acc.
Art. M.F.A.
Art Education. M.A.Ed., M.A.T.
Biology. M.S., M.A.Ed., M.A.T.
Birth–Kindergarten Education. M.A.Ed., M.A.T.
Business Administration. M.B.A.
Chemistry. M.S., M.A.Ed., M.A.T.
College Student Personnel. M.Ed.
Communication Sciences and Disorders. M.S.
Community College Administration. M.A.Ed.
Community College Teaching. M.A.Ed.
Construction Management. M.C.M.
Counseling, Community. M.S.
Counseling, School. M.A.Ed.
Educational Leadership. Ed.S., Ed.D.
Educational Supervision. M.A.Ed.
Elementary Education. M.A.Ed.
English. M.A., M.A.Ed., M.A.T.
Entrepreneurship. M.E.
Health Sciences. M.H.S.
History. M.A.
Human Resources. M.S.
Mathematics. M.S., M.A.Ed., M.A.T.
Middle Grades Education. M.A.Ed., M.A.T.
Music. M.A.Ed., M.A.T., M.M.
Nursing. M.S.
Physical Education. M.A.Ed., M.A.T.
Physical Therapy. M.P.T.
Project Management. M.P.M.
Psychology. M.A.
Public Affairs. M.P.A.
School Administration. M.S.A.
Science and Entrepreneurship. M.S.
Social Sciences Education. M.A.Ed., M.A.T.
Social Work. M.S.W.
Special Education. M.A.Ed., M.A.T.
Sport Management. M.S.
Technology. M.S.
TESOL. M.A., M.A.T., M.A.Ed.

WESTERN CONNECTICUT STATE UNIVERSITY
Danbury, Connecticut 06810-6885
Web site: www.wcsu.edu

Established 1903. Located 60 miles N of New York City. Coed. State control. Semester system. Library: 261,328 volumes, 2500 subscriptions.

Tuition: per semester hour $363 (master's), $575 (doctoral). On-campus housing available. Average academic year housing costs: $4200-$5200. Contact Office of Housing for both on- and off-campus housing information. Phone: (203)837-8531.

Graduate Studies

Graduate study since 1955. Enrollment: full-time 22, part-time 611 (men 30%, women 70%). College faculty: full-time 46, part-time 6. Degrees conferred: M.A., M.B.A., M.S., M.H.A., M.S.N.

ADMISSION REQUIREMENTS. Official transcripts, interview required in support of application. GRE/MAT/GMAT required for some programs. TOEFL required for international applicants. Accepts transfer applicants. Graduates of unaccredited colleges not considered. Apply to Dean, Office of Graduate Studies at least 30 days in advance of the beginning of semester of choice. Application fee $50. Phone: (203)837-8244; fax: (203)837-8338.

ADMISSION STANDARDS. Selective for some departments, relatively open for others. Usual minimum average: 2.7 (A = 4).

FINANCIAL AID. Fellowships, assistantships, internships, Federal W/S, loans. Approved for VA benefits. Apply by May 1 to Director of Financial Aid. Phone: (203)837-8581; fax: (203)837-8320. Use FAFSA and University's FAF. About 5% of students receive aid other than loans from outside sources. Aid available for part-time students.

DEGREE REQUIREMENTS. For M.A., M.S.: 30 semester hours minimum, at least 21 in residence; thesis/nonthesis option. For M.S.N.: 40 semester hours. For M.B.A.: 57 semester hours.

FIELDS OF STUDY.
Biological and Environmental Sciences. M.A.
Business Administration. M.B.A.
Early Childhood Education. M.S.
Education. Includes curriculum, instructional technology, reading, special education. M.S.Ed.
Counselor Education. Includes community counseling, school counseling. M.S.
Earth and Planetary Sciences. M.A.
English. Includes literature, TESOL, writing. M.A., M.S.
Health Administration. M.H.A.
History. M.A.
Instructional Leadership. Ed.D.
Justice Administration. M.S.J.A.
Mathematics. M.A., M.S.
Music Education. M.S.M.Ed.
Nursing. Includes adult nurse practitioner, clinical nurse specialist. M.S.N.
Professional Writing. M.F.A.
Visual Arts. M.F.A.

WESTERN ILLINOIS UNIVERSITY
Macomb, Illinois 61455-1390
Web site: www.wiu.edu

Founded 1895. Located 250 miles SW of Chicago. CGS member. Coed. State control. Semester system. Library: 1,000,000 volumes, 3200 subscriptions. Total University enrollment: 13,400.

Tuition/fees: per credit, resident $200, nonresident $400. On-campus housing for 336 married students, 3148 men, 2972 women. Average annual housing cost: $5625 for married students, $4500–$6000 (including board) for single students. Contact Graduate and Family Housing Office for on-campus (309)298-3331, off-campus (309)298-3285.

School of Graduate Studies

Graduate study since 1945. Enrollment: full-time 726, part-time 1046. Graduate faculty: full-time 392, part-time 16. Degrees conferred: M.A., M.S., M.S. in Ed., M.B.A., M.Acc., M.F.A., Ed.S., S.S.P.

ADMISSION REQUIREMENTS. Two official transcripts, GRE Subject Test (Psychology, Political Science only), GMAT (M.B.A. and Accounting only) required in support of School's application. Online application available. Interview required for some departments. TOEFL (minimum score 550) required for international applicants. Accepts transfer applicants. Graduates of unaccredited institutions not considered. Apply to Graduate Admissions at least three weeks prior to registration. Application fee $30. Phone: (309)298-1806; fax: (309)298-2345; e-mail: grad_office@ wiu.edu.

ADMISSION STANDARDS. Relatively open. Usual minimum average: 2.5 (A = 4).

FINANCIAL AID. Annual awards from institutional funds: grants, research assistantships, teaching assistantships, internships, Federal W/S, loans. Approved for VA benefits. Apply by March 1 to appropriate chair for assistantships; to Financial Aid Office for all other programs. Phone: (309)298-2446; fax: (309)298-2353. Use FAFSA. About 50% of students receive aid other than loans from University and outside sources.

DEGREE REQUIREMENTS. For master's: 30-36 semester hours minimum, at least 24 in residence; thesis/nonthesis option; final written/oral exam. For Ed.S. (Educational Administration only): 32 hours minimum beyond the master's; 12 credits within a period of three consecutive semesters. For M.F.A. (Theater): 60 hours minimum, two academic years, and one Summer in residence.

FIELDS OF STUDY.
Accountancy.
Biology.
Business Administration.
Chemistry.
College Student Personnel. Interview required for admission.
Communication.
Communication Sciences and Disorders.
Computer Science.
Counseling.
Economics.
Educational and Interdisciplinary Studies.
Educational Leadership.
Educational Specialist.
Elementary Education.
English.
Geography.
Gerontology.
Health Education.
History.
Instructional Design and Technology.
Kinesiology.
Law Enforcement and Justice Administration.
Manufacturing Engineering Systems.
Mathematics.
Music.
Physics.
Political Science.

Psychology.
Reading.
Recreation, Park, and Tourism Administration.
Secondary Education.
Sociology.
Special Education.
Specialist in School Psychology.
Sport Management.
Theater. Interview required for admission.

WESTERN KENTUCKY UNIVERSITY
Bowling Green, Kentucky 42101-3576
Web site: www.wku.edu

Founded 1906. Located 120 miles S of Louisville, 65 miles N of Nashville. CGS member. Coed. State control. Semester system. Library: 875,000 volumes, 5260 subscriptions, 50 PCs in all libraries. Total University enrollment: 18,600.

Annual tuition: full-time resident $5816, nonresident $6356; per credit resident $219, nonresident $326. On-campus housing available for single students only. Average academic year housing costs: $2800. Off-campus housing costs: $450–$600 per month. Contact Director of Housing for both on- and off-campus housing information. Phone: (270)745-2100.

Graduate Studies and Research

Graduate study since 1931. Enrollment: full-time 443, part-time 1156. Graduate faculty: full-time 211, part-time 37. Degrees conferred: M.A., M.S., M.A.E., M.B.A., M.H.A., M.P.A., M.P.Acc., Ed.S.

ADMISSION REQUIREMENTS. Transcripts, GRE/GMAT (business) required in support of application. TOEFL required for international applicants. Accepts transfer applicants. Graduates of unaccredited institutions not considered. Apply to Office of Graduate Studies by July 1 (Fall), November 1 (Spring). Rolling admission process. Application fee $35. Phone: (800)896-6960, (270) 745-2446; fax: (270)745-6950.

ADMISSION STANDARDS. Selective. Usual minimum average: 2.75 (3.0 for some departments) (A = 4).

FINANCIAL AID. Annual awards from institutional funds: teaching assistantships, research assistantships, internships, tuition waivers, Federal W/S, loans. Approved for VA benefits. Apply by April 1 to Office of Graduate Studies for assistantships; to the Office of Financial Aid for all other programs. Phone: (270)745-2755; fax: (270)745-6586. Use FAFSA. Aid available for part-time students.

DEGREE REQUIREMENTS. For master's: 30 credit hours minimum; thesis/nonthesis option. For Specialist (Ed.S.), S.S.P.: 30 credit hours beyond the master's degree.

FIELDS OF STUDY.
Administrative Dynamics. M.A.
Adult Education. M.A.E.
Agriculture. M.S.
Biology. M.S.
Business Administration. M.B.A.
Chemistry. M.S.
Communication. M.A.
Communication Disorders. M.S.
Computer Science. M.S.
Education and Behavioral Science Studies. M.A.E.
Educational Administration (School Principal). M.A.E.
Elementary Education (P–5). M.A.E., Ed.S.

English. M.A.
Exceptional Education. M.A.E.
Folk Studies. M.A.
Geoscience. M.S.
Health Administration. M.H.A.
History. M.A.
Interdisciplinary Early Childhood Education. M.A.E.
Library Science. M.S.
Mathematics. M.S.
Mental Health Counseling. M.A.E.
Middle Grades Education (5–9). M.A.E.
Music Education. M.A.E.
Nursing. M.S.N.
Physical Education. M.S.
Psychology. Includes applied experimental, clinical, industrial.
  M.A.
Public Administration. M.P.A.
Public Health. Includes education, environmental. M.P.H.
Recreation. M.S.
School Administration. Ed.S.
School Counseling. M.A.E., Ed.S.
School Psychology. Ed.S.
Secondary Education. Includes agriculture, art, biology, chemistry, English & allied languages arts, geography, health, history, mathematics. M.A.E., Ed.S.
Social Work. M.S.W.
Sociology. M.A.
Student Affairs in Higher Education. M.A.E.
Technology Management. M.S.

WESTERN MICHIGAN UNIVERSITY
Kalamazoo, Michigan 49008-5242
Web site: www.wmich.edu

Founded 1903. Located 150 miles W of Detroit. CGS member. Coed. State control. Semester system. Special facilities: Applied Mechanics Institute, Behavior Research and Development Center, Business Research and Service Institute, Center for Communications Research, Concurrent Computation Research Center, Design Center, Center for Electron Microscopy, Enabling Technology Center, Center for Research on Educational Accountability and Teacher Evaluation, Geographic Information System Research Center, Medieval Institute, Printing and Research Center, Kercher Center for Social Research, Institute for Water Sciences, Women's Center. Library: 1,649,000 volumes, 600,000 microforms, 540 current periodicals, 288 PCs in all libraries. Total University enrollment: 26,200.

Tuition: per semester credit hour, resident $305.67, nonresident $688.85. On-campus housing available for both married and single students. Average academic year housing cost: $6821 (including board) for single students; $547–$767 per month for married students. Contact Housing Director for both on- and off-campus housing information. Phone: (800)882-9819.

The Graduate College

Enrollment: full- and part-time 4800. University faculty teaching graduate students: full-time 725, part-time 401. Degrees conferred: M.S., M.A., M.F.A., M.B.A., M.D.A., M.M., M.P.A., M.S., M.S.A., M.S.E., M.S.W, Ed.S., Ed.D., D.P.A., Ph.D.

ADMISSION REQUIREMENTS. Transcripts, GRE Subject (doctoral programs only) required in support of application. Online application available. Interview required for admission to specialist and doctoral programs. TOEFL or MTELP required for international applicants. Accepts transfer applicants. Graduates of unaccredited institutions not considered. Apply by July 1 (Fall), November 1 (Winter), March 1 (Spring) to Office of Graduate Admissions and Orientation. Rolling admissions process. Application fee $40. Phone: (616)387-8212; fax: (616)387-8232.

ADMISSION STANDARDS. Selective to relatively open. Usual minimum average: 2.75 (A = 4).

FINANCIAL AID. Annual awards from institutional funds: fellowships, teaching assistantships, research assistantships, tuition grants, Federal W/S, loans. Approved for VA benefits. Apply by February 15 to Graduate College for scholarships, fellowships; to department head for assistantships; to Financial Aid Office for all other programs. Phone: (616)387-6000. Use FAFSA. About 35% of full-time students receive aid from University and outside sources. Aid available for part-time students.

DEGREE REQUIREMENTS. For master's: 30 hours minimum, at least 24 in residence; thesis, one language required for some majors; final written/oral exams; final review. For Ed.S: 30 hours minimum beyond the master's, at least 30 in residence in most cases; final project. For Ph.D.: 90 hours minimum beyond the bachelor's, at least one year in full-time residence, knowledge of two research tools, one of which will normally be a language; qualifying exam; dissertation, for which 15 hours is given; final written/oral exams. For Ed.D., D.P.A.: same as for Ph.D., except only one research tool, which may be a language.

FIELDS OF STUDY.
Accounting. M.S.A.
Anthropology. M.A.
Applied Economics. M.A., Ph.D.
Applied Mathematics. M.S.
Art. M.A., M.F.A.
Audiology. Au.D.
Biological Sciences. M.S., Ph.D.
Biostatistics. M.S.
Business Administration. M.B.A.
Career and Technical Education. M.A.
Chemistry. Includes environmental. M.A., Ph.D.
Communication. M.A.
Comparative Religion. M.A., Ph.D.
Computational Mathematics. M.S.
Computer Engineering. M.S.E.
Computer Science. M.S., Ph.D.
Construction Management. M.S.
Counseling Psychology. M.A., Ed.D.
Counselor Education. M.A., Ed.D.
Creative Writing. M.F.A.
Development Administration. M.D.A.
Earth Science. M.S.
Economics. M.A.
Education and Professional Development. M.A.
Educational Leadership. M.A., Ed.S., Ed.D., Ph.D.
Educational Technology. M.A.
Electrical and Computer Engineering. M.S.E., Ph.D.
Engineering Management. M.S.
English. M.A., M.F.A., Ph.D.
Family and Consumer Sciences. M.A.
Fine Arts. 60 credits for M.F.A.
Geography. M.A.
Geology. M.S., Ph.D.
Health Care Administration. M.P.A.
History. M.A., Ph.D.
Home Economics.
Industrial Engineering. M.S.E., Ph.D.
Manufacturing Engineering. M.S.E.
Marriage and Family Therapy. M.A.
Materials Science and Engineering. M.S.E.
Mathematics. M.A., Ph.D.
Mathematics Education. M.A. Ph.D.
Medicine. M.S.
Mechanical Engineering. M.S.E., Ph.D.

Medieval Studies. M.A.
Molecular Biotechnology. M.S.
Music. M.M.
Occupational Therapy. M.S.
Operations Research. M.S.
Paper and Imaging Science and Engineering. M.S., Ph.D.
Philosophy. M.A.
Physical Education. M.A.
Physician Assistant Studies. M.S.
Physics. M.A., Ph.D.
Political Science. M.A., Ph.D.
Psychology. M.A., Ph.D.
Public Administration. M.P.A., D.P.A.
Rehabilitation Teaching. M.A.
School Psychology. Ed.S., Ph.D.
Science Education. M.A., Ph.D.
Social Work. M.S.W.
Sociology. M.A., Ph.D.
Spanish. M.A., Ph.D.
Special Education. M.A., Ph.D.
Speech Pathology and Audiology. M.A.
Statistics. M.S., Ph.D.
Teaching in the Elementary School. M.A.
Teaching of Geography. M.A.
Teaching in the Middle School. M.A.
Teaching of Music. M.M.

WESTERN NEW ENGLAND COLLEGE
Springfield, Massachusetts 01119-2654
Web site: www.wnec.edu

Founded in 1919. Coed. Semester system. Library: 289,000 volumes, 2900 subscriptions. Total College enrollment: 3700.

Tuition: per credit hour $599 (Business), $260 (Education), $800 (Engineering). No on-campus housing available for graduate students. For off-campus housing, contact Office of Student Housing.

Graduate Programs

Graduate study since 1978. Enrollment: part-time 900. Faculty: full-time 50, part-time 19. Degrees conferred: M.A.E.T., M.A.M.T., M.B.A., M.B.A. Sport, M.E.E.E, M.S.E., M.S.E.M., M.B.A.-J.D.

ADMISSION REQUIREMENTS. Official transcripts required in support of application. GRE recommended; two letters of recommendation for Engineering applicants, GMAT for Business. Apply to Division of Continuing Education at least one month prior to date of enrollment. Application fee $30. Phone: (413) 782-1249; fax: (413)782-1779.

ADMISSION STANDARDS. Selective. Usual minimum average: 2.5 (2.75 Engineering Programs) (A = 4).

FINANCIAL AID. Limited to four assistantships, Federal W/S, loans. Approved for VA benefits. Apply Director of Financial Aid. No specified closing date. Phone: (413)782-1258. Use FAFSA.

DEGREE REQUIREMENTS. For Master's: 30 semester hours required. For M.B.A.: 30-48 semester hours depending upon undergraduate courses.

FIELDS OF STUDY.

SCHOOL OF ARTS AND SCIENCES:
Elementary Education. M.E.E.E.
English for Teachers. M.A.E.T.
Mathematics for Teachers. M.A.M.T.

SCHOOL OF BUSINESS:
Accounting. Includes forensic accounting & fraud, investigation, taxation. M.S.A.
Business Administration. M.B.A.
Business Administration Sport Program. M.B.A. Sport.

SCHOOL OF ENGINEERING:
Engineering. M.S.E.
Engineering Management. M.S.E.M.

School of Law (01119-2684)
Web site: www.law.wnec.edu

Founded in 1919 as part of the Springfield Division of Northeastern University and incorporated as part of Western New England College in 1951. ABA approved since 1974. AALS member. Semester system. Special facilities: Legislative and Governmental Affairs Institute, Law and Business Center for Advancing Entrepreneurship. Law library: 384,167 volumes, 5171 subscriptions: has LEXIS, NEXIS, WESTLAW, DIALOG, MEDIS, OCLC; has more than 40 network connections.

Annual tuition: full-time $30,522, part-time $22,566, LL.M. $1294 per credit. Limited on-campus housing available. Total average annual additional expenses: $18,485.

Enrollment: first-year class full-time 139, part-time 53; total full-time 384, part-time 169 (men 55%, women 45%, minorities 9%). Student to faculty ratio 16.5 to 1. Degrees conferred: J.D., J.D.-M.B.A., J.D.-M.S.W. (with Springfield College, J.D.-M.R.P. (with University of Massachusetts-Amherst), LL.M. (Estate Planning and Elder Law).

ADMISSION REQUIREMENTS. LSDAS Law School report, bachelor's degree, transcripts, LSAT, two letters of recommendation, personal statement required in support of application. Apply to Admissions Office by March 15 (full-time program), May 1 (part-time program). Rolling admissions process. Application fee $45. Phone: (800)782-6665; (413)782-1406; fax: (413)796-2067.

ADMISSION STANDARDS. Selective. Accepts approximately 43% of full-time, 44% of part-time students. Number of full-time applicants 1600, part-time 249; number of full-time acceptance 688, part-time 109; number of full-time enrolled 139, part-time 53; LSAT (75% of full-time students have a score at or above 151, part-time 149); GPA (75% of full-time student have a GPA at or above 2.70, part-time 2.78). *U.S. News & World Report* ranking is in the fourth tier of all U.S. law schools.

FINANCIAL AID. Scholarships, grants, Federal W/S, loans. Apply to Financial Aid Office by April 1. Phone: (413)796-2080. Use FAFSA (School code: 002226). About 65% of students receive some aid from School.

DEGREE REQUIREMENTS. For J.D.: satisfactory completion of three-year (full-time), four-year (part-time) program; 88 credit hour program. For LL.M.: 28 credit program; final project.

WESTERN NEW MEXICO UNIVERSITY
Silver City, New Mexico 88061-0680
Web site: www.wnmu.edu

Founded 1893, Located 200 miles SW of Albuquerque. Coed. State control. Semester system. Library: 245,000 volumes, 236 subscriptions.

Annual tuition/fees: resident $3390, nonresident $12,078. On-campus housing for 65 married students, 250 graduate men, 150 graduate women. Average annual housing cost: $3800 (including board) for single students, $3300 for married students. Apply to Director of Residence Life. Phone: (575)538-6629.

Graduate Division

Graduate study since 1950. Enrollment: full- and part-time 368. Graduate faculty: full-time 42, part-time 7. Degrees conferred: M.A., M.A.T., M.B.A.

ADMISSION REQUIREMENTS. Transcripts, GMAT (MBA applicants) required in support of application. Online application available. GRE required for applicants with a GPA between 2.75 and 3.19. Admission formula for M.B.A. applicants is UGPA × 200 + GMAT score must equal 950 or higher. TOEFL (minimum score 550) required for international applicants. Interview not required. Accepts transfer applicants. Graduates of unaccredited institutions not considered. Apply to Office of Admissions by June 1 (Fall), October 1 (Spring). Application fee $10. Phone: (575)538-6106; fax: (575)538-6127.

ADMISSION STANDARDS. Selective. Usual minimum average: 3.0 (A = 4).

FINANCIAL AID. Annual awards from institutional funds: graduate assistantships, teaching assistantships, internships, tuition waivers, Federal W/S, loans. Approved for VA benefits. Apply to Director of Graduate Division by April 1. Phone: (575)538-6173. Use FAFSA. About 10% of students receive aid other than loans from University and outside sources.

DEGREE REQUIREMENTS. For M.A., M.A.T.: 30–36 semester hours minimum with thesis, at least 30 in residence; or 36 semester hours without thesis, at least 30 in residence. For M.B.A.: 36 semester hours minimum.

FIELDS OF STUDY.
Business Administration.
Counseling. 48 credit M.A. program.
Educational Leadership.
Elementary Education.
Reading Education.
Secondary Education. Includes art, English, history, mathematics, movement sciences, music.
Special Education (K–12). 39-credit M.A.T.

WESTERN OREGON UNIVERSITY
Monmouth, Oregon 97361-1394
Web site: www.wou.edu

Organized 1882. Located 64 miles SW of Portland. Coed. State control. Semester system. Special facilities: Regional Resource Center on Deafness, Educational Evaluation Center, Teaching Research Center. Library: 257,000 volumes, 1700 subscriptions. Total University enrollment: 4500.

Annual tuition: full-time resident $8307, nonresident $14,049; part-time, resident $246 per credit, nonresident $438. On-campus housing for both single and married students available. Average academic year housing costs: $6700 (including board) for single students; $4700 for married students; off-campus housing costs: $425–$600 per month. Contact Student Affairs Office for both on- and off-campus housing information. Phone: (503)838-8311. Day-care facilities available.

Graduate Programs

Enrollment: full-time 155, part-time 175. Faculty: full-time 111, part-time 25. Degrees conferred: M.A., M.A.T., M.S.Ed.

ADMISSION REQUIREMENTS. Transcripts, GRE/MAT required in support of application. Interview required for some programs. TOEFL required for international applicants. Accepts transfer applicants. Graduates of unaccredited institutions not

considered. Apply by May 15 (Fall), January 15 (Spring) to Director of Admission. Rolling admissions process. Application fee $50. Phone: (503)838-8492; fax: (503)838-8067.

ADMISSION STANDARDS. Competitive. Usual minimum average: 2.75 (A = 4).

FINANCIAL AID. Research assistantships, teaching assistantships, full and partial tuition waivers, internshpis, Federal W/S, loans. Approved for VA benefits. Apply by March 1 to Provost for assistantships; to Financial Aid Office for all other programs. Phone: (503)838-8475. Use FAFSA (University code: 003209) and College's FAF. About 5% of students receive aid from College and outside sources. Aid available for part-time students.

DEGREE REQUIREMENTS. For master's: 30–36 semester hours minimum, at least 24–30 in residence; thesis/nonthesis option; final oral/written exam.

FIELDS OF STUDY.
Contemporary Music. M.M.
Criminal Justice. M.S.
Information Technology. M.S.Ed.
Mathematics. M.A.T.
Rehabilitation Counseling. M.S.Ed.
Secondary Education. Includes humanities, science, social science, socially and educational different. M.A.T., M.S.Ed.
Science. M.A.T.
Social Science. M.A.T.
Special Educator. M.S.Ed.
Teacher Preparation: Deaf Education. M.S.Ed.

WESTERN UNIVERSITY OF HEALTH SCIENCES
Pomona, California 91766-1889
Web site: www.westernu.edu

Founded 1977 as the College of Osteopathic Medicine of the Pacific, name changed in 1996 and is a graduate university of medical sciences. Located 35 miles E of Los Angeles. Private control. Semester system. Special facilities: a partner with San Bernardino County's Arrowhead Medical Center in an Academic Center for Excellence in the Health Sciences at San Bernardino County's Arrowhead Medical Center, Center for Disability Issues and the Health Professional. Library: 30,000 volumes, 3300 subscriptions.
Total University enrollment at main campus: 1885.

College of Osteopathic Medicine of the Pacific

Established 1977. Curriculum based on a three phase system. Special program: Summer Anatomy program for underrepresented minorities.

Annual tuition: $37,230. No on-campus housing available. Contact Admissions Office for off-campus housing information. Off-campus housing and personal expenses: approximately $15,500.

Enrollment: first-year class 212, total 762 (men 49%, women 51%, minorities 49%, state residents 63%). Faculty: full-time 100, part-time and volunteers 500. Degrees conferred: D.O.

ADMISSION REQUIREMENTS. Preference given to state residents, U.S. citizens, and permanent residents only. Bachelor's degree from an accredited institution required. All applicants have bachelor's degree awarded prior to enrollment. Does not have EDP. Early applications are encouraged. Submit supplemental application, a personal statement, three recommendations to Office of Admission within two weeks of receipt of application, but not later than August 1. For serious consideration an applicant should have at least a 3.30 (A = 4) in both Sciences and overall GPA and a minimum average MCAT of 9.0. Interviews are by invitation only and generally for final selection. Notification normally begins in October. Apply through AACOMAS (file after June 1, before January 1), submit MCAT (will accept test results from last three years), official transcripts for each school attended (should show at least 90 semester credits/135 quarter credit), service processing fee. After a review of the AACOMAS application and supporting documents, a decision is made concerning which candidates should receive supplemental materials. The supplemental application, an application fee of $65, a personal statement, and three recommendations (one from a D.O.) should be returned to Office of Admission as soon as possible, but not later than April 15. Interviews are by invitation only and generally for final selection. Accepts transfer applicants on a space-available basis. First-year students admitted Fall only. Rolling admissions process; notification starts in October and is finished when class is filled. School does maintain an alternate list. Phone: (909)469-5335; fax: (909)469-5570.

ADMISSION STANDARDS. Selective. Accepts about 23% of all applicants. Number of applications 2342 (1606 out-of-state); number interviewed 601 (312 out-of-state); number of acceptance 542 (281 out-of-state); number enrolled 212 (80 out-of-state). Usual minimum UGPA: 3.0 (A = 4). Mean Composite MCAT 9.0, mean UGPA 3.49.

FINANCIAL AID. Scholarships, grants, California State Graduate Fellowships, institutional loans, NOF, HEAL, alternative loan programs, Federal Perkins Loans, Stafford Subsidized and Unsubsidized Loans, Service Obligation Scholarship programs, Armed Forces and National Health Service programs are available. Financial aid applications and the Financial Aid Handbook are generally available at the on-campus, by-invitation interview. All financial aid is based on demonstrated need. Contact the Financial Aid Office for current information. Phone: (800)346-1610; (909)469-5350. Use FAFSA (School code: 024827), also submit Financial Aid Transcript, Federal Income Tax forms. Approximately 75% of students receive some form of financial assistance.

DEGREE REQUIREMENTS. For D.O.: satisfactory completion of four-year program. All students must take the National Board of Osteopathic Medical Examination Level 1 and Level 2.

WESTERN WASHINGTON UNIVERSITY
Bellingham, Washington 98225-5996
Web site: www.wwu.edu

Established 1893. Located 85 miles N of Seattle. CGS member. Coed. State control. Quarter system. Library: 1,300,000 volumes, 4800 subscriptions. Total University enrollment: 14,200.

Annual tuition: full-time, resident $5628, nonresident $16,176; per credit resident $188, nonresident $539. On-campus housing for 1460 women, 1164 men; 13 coed units, 1 woman only; 3 apartment buildings, 268 apartment units for single and married students. Average academic year housing costs: $6242 (including board) for single students. Contact Director, University Residences for both on- and off-campus housing information. Phone: (360)650-2950.

Graduate School

Graduate study since 1947. Enrollment: full-time 773, part-time 227. Faculty teaching graduate students: full-time 300, part-time 25. Degrees conferred: M.A., M.S., M.Ed., M.B.A., M.Mus.

ADMISSION REQUIREMENTS. Transcripts, letters of recommendation, GRE, GMAT, current résumé required in support of School's application. Interview required for some programs. TOEFL required for non-native English-speaking applicants. Accepts transfer applicants. Graduates of unaccredited colleges not considered. Apply to Dean of Graduate School by June 1 (Fall), October 1 (Winter), February 1 (Spring), May 1 (Summer). Many programs admit Fall Quarter only; some programs have earlier deadlines. Application fee $50. Phone: (360)650-3170; fax: (360) 650-6811; e-mail: gradschl@wwu.edu.

ADMISSION STANDARDS. Selective. Required average: 3.0 (A = 4) last 90 quarter credits (60 semester hours).

FINANCIAL AID. Scholarships, fellowships, teaching assistantships, research assistantships, tuition waivers, Federal W/S, loans. Approved for VA benefits. Early application is encouraged. Apply by February 15 to Graduate School for scholarships, fellowships, assistantships, fee waivers; the Student Financial Services Office for all other programs. Phone: (360)650-3470; fax: (360)650-7291. Use FAFSA. About 25% of students receive aid other than loans from College and outside sources. Aid available for part-time students.

DEGREE REQUIREMENTS. For master's: 45 quarter hours minimum with thesis, or 48 quarter hours minimum without thesis and written comprehensive exam; reading knowledge of foreign language required for some departments.

FIELDS OF STUDY.
Anthropology. M.A.
Archives and Records Management. M.A.
Biology. M.S.
Business Administration. M.B.A.
Chemistry. M.S.
Computer Science. M.S.
Continuing and College Education. M.Ed.
Creative Writing. M.A.
Educational Administration. Includes instructional technology. M.Ed.
Environmental Education. M.Ed.
Environmental Science. M.S.
English Studies. M.A.
Exercise Science. M.S.
Experimental Psychology. M.S.
Geography. M.S.
Geology. M.S.
History. M.A.
Mathematics. M.S.
Mental Health Counseling. M.S.
Music. M.M.
Political Science. Includes environmental Studies. M.A.
Professional Accounting. M.P.A.
Rehabilitation Counseling. M.A.
School Counselor. M.Ed.
Science Education. M.Ed.
Special Education. M.Ed.
Speech Language Pathology. M.A.
Sport Psychology. M.S.
Student Affairs Administration in Higher Education. M.Ed.
Teaching. M.T.

WESTFIELD STATE COLLEGE
Westfield, Massachusetts 01086
Web site: www.wsc.ma.edu

Founded 1838. Located 12 miles W of Springfield. Coed. State control. Semester system. Library: 166,721 volumes, 1100 subscriptions. Total College enrollment: 5350.

Tuition: per semester hour, resident $175, nonresident $185. No on-campus housing available for graduate students. Contact Director, Residential Life, for off-campus housing information. Phone: (413)572-5402.

Division of Graduate and Continuing Education

Graduate study since 1963. Enrollment: full-time 37, part-time 239. Faculty teaching graduate students: 21 full-time, 29 part-time. Degrees conferred: M.A., M.S., M.Ed., C.A.G.S.

ADMISSION REQUIREMENTS. Transcripts required in support of application. TOEFL required for international applicants. GRE, MAT recommended. Interview may be requested. Accepts transfer applicants. Graduates of unaccredited colleges not considered. Apply to Dean, Graduate Studies and Continuing Education prior to registration. Rolling admission process. Application fee $30. Phone: (413)572-8022; fax: (413)572-5227.

ADMISSION STANDARDS. Selective. Usual minimum average: 2.6 (A = 4).

FINANCIAL AID. Graduate assistantships, grants, New England Regional Student Program, Federal W/S, loans. Apply by April 1 to Dean, Graduate Studies and Continuing Education for assistantships; to Financial Aid Office for all other programs. Phone: (413)572-5407. Use FAFSA. Aid available for part-time students.

DEGREE REQUIREMENTS. For master's: 33 semester hours minimum; comprehensive exam; thesis/nonthesis option in some programs. For C.A.G.S.: 30 semester hours minimum beyond the master's; comprehensive exam.

FIELDS OF STUDY.
Accountancy. M.S.
Applied Behavior Analysis. M.A.
Criminal Justice. M.S.
Early Childhood (Pre-K–12). M.Ed.
Elementary (1–6). M.Ed.
English. Includes teacher of English (5–8, 8–12). M.A.
History. M.Ed.
Mental Health. M.A.
Music. M.Ed.
Physical Education. M.Ed.
Psychology. M.A.
School Guidance. M.A.
School Principal. Includes elementary, middle, secondary. M.Ed.
Secondary Education. Includes biology, chemistry, general science, history, mathematics. M.Ed.
Teacher of Students with Moderate Disabilities. Includes Pre-K–8, 5–12. M.Ed.

WESTMINSTER COLLEGE

New Wilmington, Pennsylvania 16142-0001
Web site: www.westminster.edu

Founded 1852. Located 60 miles NE of Pittsburgh. Coed. Private control. Presbyterian affiliation. Semester system. Library: 283,000 volumes, 933 subscriptions.
Tuition: $1680. No on-campus housing available.

Graduate Program

Graduate study since 1944. Enrollment: part-time 147. Graduate faculty: full-time 5. Degree conferred: M.Ed.

ADMISSION REQUIREMENTS. Transcripts required in support of application. MAT occasionally required. Graduates of unaccredited colleges not considered. Accepts transfer applicants. Apply to Director of Admissions by August 30 (Fall), January 15 (Spring). Rolling admissions process. Application fee $20. Phone: (724)946-7180; fax: (724)946-7171.

ADMISSION STANDARDS. Selective. Usual minimum average: 2.75 (A = 4).

FINANCIAL AID. Internships, loans, grants. Apply to Financial Aid Office; no specified closing date. Phone: (724)946-7100. Use FAFSA.

DEGREE REQUIREMENTS. For M.Ed.: 10 courses minimum, at least 8 in residence; final written exam.

FIELDS OF STUDY.
Education.
Elementary Counselor.
English
History.
Principal (K–12).
Reading Specialist.
Secondary Counselor.
Superintendent.

WHEELOCK COLLEGE

Boston, Massachusetts 02215-4176
Web site: www.wheelock.edu

Founded 1888. Private control. Semester system. Library: 96,000 volumes, 546 subscriptions. Total College enrollment: 1000.
Tuition: per credit $755. On-campus housing available. Apply to Director of Graduate Admissions.

Graduate Division

Graduate study since 1953. Enrollment; full-time 200, part-time 175. Graduate faculty: full-time 36, part-time 32. Degree conferred: M.S.

ADMISSION REQUIREMENTS. Transcripts, three references, essay, interview in support of application. Online application available. TOEFL required for international applicants. Accepts transfer applicants. Graduates of un accredited institutions not considered. Apply to Director of Graduate Admissions by July 1 (Fall), October 1 (Spring). Application fee $40, international applicants $45. Rolling admissions process. Phone: (617)879-2206; fax: (617)879-2449.

ADMISSION STANDARDS. Selective. Usual minimum average: 3.0 (A = 4).

FINANCIAL AID. Scholarships, grants, assistantships, Federal W/S, loans. Apply by April 1 to Director of Financial Aid, Graduate School. Phone: (617)879-2178. Use FAFSA and institutional graduate FAF. About 50% of students receive aid other than loans from College. Aid available for part-time students.

DEGREE REQUIREMENTS. For M.S.: 32-40 semester hours minimum.

FIELDS OF STUDY.
Care and Education in Early Childhood Settings.
Child Life and Family Centered Care.
Early Childhood Education.
Educational Studies: Elementary Education.
Educational Studies: Special Education.
Elementary Education (1–6).
Language and Literacy Studies.
Social Work
Special Education (Pre-K–8).
Teacher of Reading.

WHITTIER COLLEGE
Whittier, California 90608-0634
Web site: www.whittier.edu

Chartered 1901. Located adjacent to Los Angeles. Coed. Private control. Quaker affiliation. Library: 225,300 volumes, 1357 subscriptions. Total College enrollment: 1325.

Tuition: per credit $400. No on-campus housing available. Day care facilities available.

Graduate Program

Enrollment: full- and part-time 75. College faculty teaching graduate students: full-time 4, part-time 9. Degree conferred: M.A.

ADMISSION REQUIREMENTS. Transcripts, CBEST, personal statement, two letters of recommendation, interview required in support of application. Online application available. TOEFL required for international applicants. Accepts transfer applicants. Apply to the Graduate Program by September 1 (Fall), February 1 (Spring). Rolling admissions process. Application fee $60. Phone: (562)907-4200, ext. 4204.

ADMISSION STANDARDS. Selective. Usual minimum average: 2.8 (A = 4).

FINANCIAL AID. Fellowships, assistantships, internships, tuition waivers, loans. Apply to the Office of Financial Aid; no specified closing date. Use FAFSA (School code: 001342).

DEGREE REQUIREMENTS. For M.A.: 30–36 credits minimum, at least 18 in residence; thesis.

FIELD OF STUDY.
Educational Designs. All M.A. programs are an individually designed course of study.

Whittier Law School
3333 Harbor Boulevard
Costa Mesa, California 92626-1501
Web site: www.law.whitter.edu

Founded in 1966 as Beverly Law School, merged with Whittier College in 1975. Now located in Costa Mesa, Orange County, two blocks north of the San Diego Freeway. ABA approved since 1978. AALS member since 1987. Private control. Semester system. Full-time, part-time study. Special facilities: Center for Children's Rights, Center for Intellectual Property, Center for International and Comparative Laws. Special programs: Summer study abroad at Nanjing University, China, Universite de Toulouse, France, Bar-Ilan University, Israel, Universidade de Cantabria, Spain, Universiteil Van Amsterdam, the Netherlands. Law library: 421,678 volumes, 3791 subscriptions; has LEXIS, NEXIS, WESTLAW, DIALOG; has more than 200 network connections; is a State and Federal Document Repository.

Annual tuition: full-time $30,750, part-time $20,500. No on-campus housing available. Contact Office of the Assistant Dean for off-campus housing information. Off-campus housing and personal expenses: approximately $17,056.

Enrollment: first-year class full-time 162, part-time 111; total full- and part-time 673 (men 50%, women 50%, minorities 32%). Faculty: full-time 25, part-time 38. Student to faculty ratio is 16.6 to 1. Degrees conferred: J.D., LL.M. (U.S. Legal Studies—for foreign lawyers who have completed a basic legal education and received a university degree in law in another country).

ADMISSION REQUIREMENTS. LSDAS law school report, LSAT (not later than February (Fall), June (Spring) test date; if more than one LSAT, highest is used), bachelor's degree from an accredited institution, personal statement (not to exceed three pages), two recommendations, transcripts (must show all schools attended and at least three years of study) required in support of application. International applicants whose native language is not English must submit a TOEFL report (minimum score 550 and not older than two years), certified translations and evaluations of all foreign credentials; use the Credential Evaluation Service, 5353 West Third Street, Los Angeles, California 90020. Phone: (310)390-6276. Apply to Office of Admission by March 15 (Fall), October 15 (Spring). First-year students admitted Fall and Spring. Rolling admissions process. Application fee $50. Phone for both J.D. and LL.M. applicants: (800)808-8188, (714)444-4141; fax: (714)444-0250; e-mail: info@law.whittier.edu.

ADMISSION REQUIREMENTS FOR TRANSFER APPLICANTS. Accepts transfers from other ABA-accredited schools. Admission limited to space available. At least one year of enrollment, Dean's letter indicating the applicant is in good standing, LSAT, LSDAS, personal statement regarding reason for transfer, two letters of recommendation, undergraduate transcript, current law school transcript required in support of School's application. Apply to Admission Office by June 1. Admission decision made by late July. Application fee $50. Will consider visiting students.

ADMISSION STANDARDS. Selective. Accepts approximately 30% of full-time, 38% of part-time students. Number of full-time applicants 2526, part-time 618; number of full-time acceptance 747, part-time 235; number of full-time enrolled 162, part-time 111; LSAT (75% of full-time students have a score at or above 152, part-time 150); GPA (75% of full-time students have a GPA at or above 2.86, part-time 2.69). *U.S. News & World Report* ranking is in the fourth tier of all U.S. law schools.

FINANCIAL AID. Need-based scholarships, merit scholarships, diversity scholarships, private and institutional loans, state grants, Federal W/S, loans. All accepted students who have signed and returned the preliminary financial aid applications with the admissions application are automatically considered for scholarships. For all other programs apply by April 1 (Fall), November 1 (Spring). Phone: (714)444-4141. Use FAFSA (School code: E00480), also submit Financial Aid Transcript, Federal Income Tax forms. Approximately 26% (full-time), 26% (part-time) of first-year class received scholarships/Grants-in-Aid. Approximately 78% of current students receive some form of financial assistance.

DEGREE REQUIREMENTS. For J.D.: 87 (40 required) credits with a GPA of at least 77 or higher (C = 77–84), plus completion of upper-divisional writing course; three-year program, four-year plus two summer session part-time program. Accelerated J.D. with summer course work. For LL.M. (U.S. Legal Studies): 24 credit, full-time, twelve-month program.

WHITWORTH COLLEGE
Spokane, Washington 99251-0001
Web site: www.whitworth.edu

Founded 1890. Coed. Private control. Presbyterian affiliation. 4-1-4 system. Library: 135,300 volumes, 725 subscriptions. Total College enrollment: 2450.

Tuition: per credit $385. No on-campus housing available for graduate students. Contact Housing Office for both on- and off-campus housing information. Phone: (509)466-3287.

Graduate Study

Enrollment: full- and part-time 205. College faculty teaching graduate students: full-time 16, part-time 35. Degrees conferred: M.A.T., M.Ed., M.I.M., M.I.T.

ADMISSION REQUIREMENTS. Official transcripts, GRE required in support of application. Online application available. Interview sometimes requested. TOEFL required for international applicants. Accepts transfer applicants. Apply by April 1 (Fall), November 1 (Spring) to Office of Admissions. Rolling admissions process. Application fee $35. Phone: (800)929-6892.

ADMISSION STANDARDS. Selective. Usual minimum average: 2.75 (A = 4).

FINANCIAL AID. Fellowships, internships, grants, Federal W/S, loans. Apply by March 1 to Office of Financial Aid. Use FAFSA. Aid available for part-time students.

DEGREE REQUIREMENTS. For master's: 30-38 semester credits minimum, thesis/nonthesis option, research paper or internship; comprehensive exam.

FIELDS OF STUDY.
Administrative Leadership. M.Ed.
Business Administration. M.B.A.
Community–Agency Counseling. M.A., M.Ed.
Educational Administration. M.Ed.
Elementary Education. M.Ed.
Gifted Education. M.A.T.
International Management. M.I.M.
School Counseling. M.A.
Secondary Education. M.Ed.
Special Education. M.A.T.
Teaching. M.I.T.
Theology. M.A.

WICHITA STATE UNIVERSITY
Wichita, Kansas 67260-0004
Web site: www.wichita.edu

Founded 1895. CGS member. Coed. State control. Semester system. Special facilities: Administrative Assessment Center, National Institute for Aviation Research, Digital Computing Center, Center for Economics Development and Business Research, Center for Energy Studies, Center for Entrepreneurship, Center for Forensic Science, Center for Urban Studies, Rehabilitation Engineering Center, Gerontology Center, Reading Assessment Center, two low-speed and two supersonic-speed wind tunnels, Water Tunnel. Library: 1,100,000 volumes, 12,000 subscriptions. Total University enrollment: 15,000.

Tuition: per credit resident $182.90, nonresident $532.80 On-campus housing available. Average academic year housing costs: $5340–$6780 (including board) for single students; $8000–$11,000 for married students. Contact Office of Student Housing for both on- and off-campus housing information. Phone: (316) 689-3693.

Graduate School
Web site: www.wichita.edu/gradsch

Graduate study since 1928. Enrollment: full-time 1000, part-time 1750. University faculty: full-time 440, part-time 39. Degrees conferred: M.A., M.S., M.A.J., M.B.A., M.Ed., M.S.E., M.F.A., M.M., M.M.Ed., M.C.S., M.S.N., M.P.A., M.P.F., M.P.T., Ed.S., Ed.D., Ph.D.

ADMISSION REQUIREMENTS. Two official transcripts required in support of School's application. Online application available. GRE/GMAT may be required by some programs. Portfolio required for M.F.A. applicants. TOEFL required for international applicants; TSE required for assistantship consideration. Interview not required. Accepts transfer applicants. Apply to Graduate Office at least three months prior to registration. Some programs have earlier deadlines. Application fee: $35, $50 for international applicants. Phone: (316)689-3095; fax: (316)689-3253.

ADMISSION STANDARDS. Selective. Usual minimum average: 2.75 for last two years (A = 4).

FINANCIAL AID. Fellowships, assistantships for teaching/research, traineeships, internships, tuition waivers, Federal W/S, loans. Apply by April 1 to appropriate department chair for assistantships and fellowships; to Financial Aid Office for all other programs. Phone: (316)689-3430. Use FAFSA and University's FAF. About 20% of students receive aid other than loans from University and outside sources. Aid available for part-time students.

DEGREE REQUIREMENTS. For M.A., M.S.: 30 credit hours minimum; final written/oral exam; reading knowledge of one language for many departments. For M.A.J., M.P.T.: 33 hours minimum including thesis, internships, or practicum. For M.B.A.: 33-54 hours, depending upon previous academic background. For M.Ed., M.S.N.: 30 hours plus thesis or 36 hours without thesis; final written exam. For M.S.E.: 36 hours without thesis, final oral/written exam. For M.F.A.: 60 hours minimum in art, 48 minimum in creative writing, including final creative project or thesis; final written/oral exam. For M.M.: 30 hours minimum, including thesis or recital; final oral exam. For M.M.Ed.: 30 hours including thesis or recital; or 32 hours, including research seminar, final oral exam. For M.P.A.: 39 hours minimum, including urban affairs core and internships or practicum. For Ed.S.: normally 30 hours beyond the master's; final written/oral exam. For Ph.D., Ed.D.: 90 hours beyond the bachelor's; preliminary written exam; foreign languages or research tools; dissertation; final oral exam.

FIELDS OF STUDY.
Accounting. GMAT for admission. M.P.A., M.B.A. only.
Aerospace Engineering. GRE for admission. M.S., Ph.D.
Anthropology. M.A.
Art Education. Portfolio for admission. M.A.
Audiology. Au.D.
Biology. GRE Subject Test, three letters of recommendation for admission. M.S. only.
Business Administration. GMAT for admission. M.B.A. only.
Chemistry. GRE Subject Test, two letters of reference, statement for goals and research interest. Apply by second Monday in November (Spring), second Monday in April (Fall). M.S., Ph.D.
Communication. Includes communications, theater/drama. GRE for admissions. M.A.
Communicative Disorders and Sciences. GRE, three letters of recommendation for admission. Apply by March 1 (Summer and Fall), October 1 (Spring). M.A., Ph.D.
Computer Science. GRE taken during first year. M.S. only.
Counseling. Statement of Goals, three letters of recommendation for admission. M.Ed.
Creative Writing. Includes fiction, poetry. M.F.A.
Criminal Justice. M.A.
Curriculum and Instruction. GRE/MAT, three recommendations for admission. M.Ed.
Economics. GRE taken during first year. M.A.
Educational Leadership. GRE, three letters of recommendation. M.Ed., Ed.D.
Educational Psychology. M.Ed.
Electrical Engineering. GRE for admission. M.S., Ph.D.
Engineering Management. M.E.M.
English. M.A.
Exercise Science. M.Ed.
Gerontology. Names of three references for admission. M.S.
History. One language for M.A. M.A. only.
Industrial Engineering. GRE for admission. M.S., Ph.D.
Liberal Studies. Essay, personal interview for admission. M.A. only.
Mathematics. M.S., Ph.D.
Mathematics—Applied. GRE Subject Test for admission. Ph.D.
Mechanical Engineering. GRE for admission. M.S., Ph.D.

Music. Includes history/literature, instrumental conducting, opera performance, performance piano/organ, piano pedagogy, theory/composition. M.M.

Music Education. Includes choral, elementary, instrumental, music in special education, vocal music. M.M.Ed.

Nursing. Includes administration, education. M.S.N.

Physical Therapy. Departmental application, three references for admission. M.P.T.

Physician Assistant. M.P.A.

Physics. M.S.

Psychology. Includes community/clinical, human factors. GRE General/Subject required for admission; one language or research tool for M.A. M.A., Ph.D.

Public Administration. GRE desirable. M.P.A.

School Psychology. GRE, three reference, Statement of Goals and research interest. Ed.S. only.

Social Work. M.S.W.

Sociology. One language depending upon thesis topic. M.A.

Spanish. One language in addition to Spanish. M.A.

Special Education. GRE, one-year teaching experience for admission. M.Ed.

Sport Administration. Three references, personal interview for admission. M.Ed.

Studio Art. Includes ceramics, painting, printmaking, sculpture. M.F.A.

WIDENER UNIVERSITY
Chester, Pennsylvania 19013-5792
Web site: www.widener.edu

Founded 1821. Located 15 miles S of Philadelphia. CGS member. Coed. Independent. Semester system. Special facilities: CDC CYBER 930, Digital VAX-11/750, Prime 9955, Prime 2555, Child Development Center, Engineering Research Center, University Art Museum. Prime-Medusa Computer Aided Design Laboratory, Center for Computer Assisted Instruction, Business Research Center. Library: 300,000 volumes, 2256 subscriptions. Total University enrollment: 7500.

Tuition: Master's per credit $720 (Business), $570 (Education), $790 (Engineering), $600 (Hospitality Management), $495 (Liberal Arts), $545 (Public Administration/Criminal Justice). $680 (Nursing), $615 (Social Work); Doctoral part-time $725 (Education), $700 (Nursing), $715 (Social Work), $770 (Psy.D.), $830 (P.T.); Doctoral full-time $23,350 (P.T.), $21,105 (Psychology). No on-campus housing available. Off-campus housing available within walking distance of the campus. Average academic year housing costs $8000 (including board). Contact Director of Housing by May 30 for housing information. Phone: (610)499-4393.

Graduate Studies

Enrollment: full- and part-time 3550. Faculty: full-time 156, part-time 216. Degrees conferred: M.A., M.B.A., M.Ed., M.S., M.S.N., M.E., M.H.P., M.P.A., M.S.W., Psy.D., D.N.Sc., Ed.D., M.E.-M.B.A., J.D.-M.B.A., J.D.-Psy.D., Psy.D.-M.H.A., Psy.D.-M.S. (Human Resource Management), Psy.D.-M.A. (Criminal Justice), Psy.D.-M.P.A.

ADMISSION REQUIREMENTS. Transcripts required in support of application. GRE/GMAT required for some departments. TOEFL required of international applicants. Accepts transfer applicants. Graduates of unaccredited institutions not considered. Apply to Assistant Provost at least one month prior to preferred entrance date. Application fee $25-$40. Phone: (610)499-4372.

ADMISSION STANDARDS. Usual minimum average: 2.5 (A = 4) master's level, 3.0 for doctoral programs.

FINANCIAL AID. Limited to assistantships, loans. Approved for VA benefits. Apply by April 15 to Director of Financial Aid for all programs. Phone: (610)499-4152. Use FAFSA and institutional FAF.

DEGREE REQUIREMENTS. For master's: 30-45 semester hours minimum with or without thesis, at least 24 in residence, final written/oral exam in some programs. For D.N.Sc., 60-63 credits; computer literacy, preliminary exam; dissertation; final written/oral exam. For Ed.D., Psy.D.: 60-65 credits beyond master's; preliminary exam; dissertation/project; final written/oral exam.

FIELDS OF STUDY.

COLLEGE OF ARTS AND SCIENCES:
Criminal Justice. M.A.
Liberal Studies. M.L.S.
Public Administration. M.P.A.

SCHOOL OF BUSINESS ADMINISTRATION:
Business Administration. M.B.A.
Health Care Management. M.B.A.
Human Resource and Organizational Leadership. M.S.
Information Systems. Includes accounting information systems, management information systems. M.S.
Taxation and Financial Planning. M.S.

SCHOOL OF ENGINEERING:
Chemical Engineering. M.E.
Civil Engineering. M.E.
Computer and Software Engineering. M.E.
Electrical and Telecommunication Engineering. M.E.
Engineering Management. M.E.
Mechanical Engineering. M.E.

SCHOOL OF HOSPITALITY MANAGEMENT:
Hospitality Management. M.S.

SCHOOL OF HUMAN SERVICE PROFESSION:
Adult Education.
Clinical Psychology. Includes concentrations in brief psychotherapies, cognitive-behavioral therapy, cross-cultural & diversity, psychology, family therapy, forensic psychology, group psychotherapy, health psychology, neuropsychology, organizational psychology, psychoanalytic psychology, school psychology. Psy.D.
Counselor Education.
Early Childhood Education.
Educational Foundations.
Educational Leadership/Principalship.
Educational Psychology.
Elementary Education.
English and Language Arts Education.
Home and School Visitor.
Human Sexuality Education.
Instructional Technology.
Mathematics Education.
Middle School Education.
Physical Therapy. D.P.T.
Reading.
Science and Technology Education.
Secondary Education.
Social Studies Education.
Social Work. M.S.W., Ph.D.
Special Education.
Student Personnel Services and Counseling in Higher Education.
Supervisor.

SCHOOL OF NURSING:
Clinical Nurse Specialist in Adult Health. M.S.N.
Community-Based Nursing. M.S.N.
Emergency/Critical Care. M.S.N.

Family Nurse Practitioner. M.S.N.
Nurse Educator. M.S.N.
Nursing. D.N.Sc.
Psychiatric/Mental Health Nursing. M.S.N.

School of Law—Delaware (P.O. Box 7474)
4601 Concord Pike
Wilmington, Delaware 19803-0474
Web site: www.law.widener.edu

Founded 1971, affiliated with Widener in 1975. ABA approved since 1975. AALS member. Semester system. Full-time, part-time day study. Special facilities: Health Law Institute, Trial Advocacy Institute. Special programs: summer study abroad at the International Law Institute, University of Geneva, Switzerland; the International Law Institute, University of Nairobi, Kenya; the International Law Institute, Macquarie University, Sidney Australia. Law library: 416,717 volumes, 5196 subscriptions; has LEXIS, NEXIS, WEST-LAW, DIALOG, LEGALTRAC, INFOTRAC.

Annual tuition: full-time $30,800, part-time $23,060, LL.M. $915 per credit. On-campus housing available. Contact Admissions Office for both on- and off-campus information. Off-campus housing and personal expenses: approximately $13,494.

Enrollment: first-year class full-time 375, part-time 175; total full- and part-time 1424 (men 56%, women 44%, minorities 13%). Faculty: full-time 75, part-time 50. Student to faculty ratio 17.5 to 1. Degrees conferred: J.D., J.D.-M.B.A., J.D.-Psy.D., J.D.-M.M.P. (with University of Delaware), J.D.-M.S.L.S. (with Clarion University), LL.M. (Corporate Law and Finance, Health Law).

ADMISSION REQUIREMENTS. LSDAS Law School report, bachelor's degree, transcripts, LSAT required in support of application. Letters of recommendations are suggested, but not required. Accept transfer applicants. Graduates of unaccredited colleges not considered. Apply to Admissions Office by May 15. Rolling admissions process. Application fee $60, none, if you apply Online. Phone: (302)477-2162; fax: (302)477-2224.

ADMISSION STANDARDS. Selective. Accepts approximately 36% of full-time, 42% of part-time students. Number of full-time applicants 2932, part-time 717; number of full-time acceptance 1067, part-time 303; number of full-time enrolled 375, part-time 175; LSAT (75% of full-time students have a score at or above 150, part-time 149); GPA (75% of full-time students have a GPA at or above 2.81, part-time 2.75). *U.S. News & World Report* ranking is in the fourth tier of all U.S. law schools.

FINANCIAL AID. Scholarships, Federal W/S, loans. Apply to Office of Financial Aid by April 15. Phone: (302)477-2272. Use FAFSA (School code: 003313). About 30% of full-time and 15% of part-time students receive some aid from School. A Loan Repayment Assistance Program is available.

DEGREE REQUIREMENTS. For J.D.: satisfactory completion of three-year (day) or four-year (evening) program; 87-credit-hour program. For LL.M.: at least 24 credits beyond the J.D.; two semesters in full-time residence.

School of Law (P.O. Box 69381)
Harrisburg, Pennsylvania 17106-9381
Web site: www.law.widener.edu

Established 1989. Located 7 miles from Pennsylvania's State Capital. Students have same access to facilities and programs as those students at Wilmington campus. ABA approved since 1989. Semester system. Full-time, part-time study. Special facilities: Law and Government Institute, Trial Advocacy Institute. Special programs: summer programs offered in Nairobi, Kenya; Geneva, Switzerland; Sydney, Australia; Venice, Italy. Law library: 188,600 volumes/microforms, 4207 subscriptions, 52 computer worksta-

tions; has LEXIS, NEXIS, WESTLAW, DIALOG, LEGALTRAC, INFOTRAC.

Annual tuition: full-time $30,800, part-time $23,060. No on-campus housing available. Law students live Off-campus. Contact Admissions Office for off-campus information. Off-campus housing and personal expenses: approximately $11,970.

Enrollment: first-year class full-time 97, part-time 54; total 397 (men 54%, women 46%). Faculty: full-time 16, part-time 15. Student to faculty ratio 17.9 to 1. Degrees conferred: J.D., J.D.-M.S.L.S. (with Clarion University).

ADMISSION REQUIREMENTS. LSDAS Law School report, LSAT (not later than February test date; if more than one LSAT, highest is used), bachelor's degree from an accredited institution, transcripts (must show all schools attended and at least three years of study) required in support of application. Letters of recommendation are suggested, but not required. Applicants must have received bachelor's degree prior to enrollment. Interview not required. Campus visits encouraged. Apply to Office of Admission by May 15 (Fall), March 31 is preferred date, December 1 (Spring). Rolling admissions process. Application fee $60, none, if you apply online. Phone: (717)541-3903.

ADMISSION REQUIREMENTS FOR TRANSFER APPLICANTS. Accepts transfers from other ABA-accredited schools. Admission limited to space available. At least one year of enrollment, Dean's letter indicating the applicant is in good standing, LSAT, LSDAS, personal statement regarding reason for transfer, personal interview, current law school transcript required in support of School's application. Apply to Admission Office by July 1. Admission decision made within one month of the receipt of completed application. Application fee $60. Will consider visiting students.

ADMISSION STANDARDS. Selective. Accepts approximately 36% of full-time, 42% of part-time students. Number of full-time applicants 2932, part-time 717; number of full-time acceptance 1067, part-time 303; number of full-time enrolled 375, part-time 175; LSAT (75% of full-time students have a score at or above 150, part-time 149); GPA (75% of full-time students have a GPA at or above 2.81, part-time 2.75). *U.S. News & World Report* ranking is in the fourth tier of all U.S. law schools.

FINANCIAL AID. Full and half scholarships, State scholarship, Grants-in-Aid, private and institutional loans, Federal loans and Federal W/S available. All accepted students are automatically considered for scholarships; use School's Institutional Data Form. For all other programs apply as soon as possible after January 1, but not later than April 5. Use FAFSA (School code: E00651), also submit Financial Aid Transcript, Federal Income Tax forms. Approximately 30% of full-time and 15% of part-time students receive aid other than loans from School. Loan Repayment Assistance Program available.

DEGREE REQUIREMENTS. For J.D.: 87 (44 required) credits with a GPA of at least a 2.3 (A = 4), plus completion of upper-divisional writing course; three-year full-time program, four-year part-time program. Accelerated J.D. with summer course work.

WILKES UNIVERSITY
Wilkes-Barre, Pennsylvania 18766-0002
Web site: www.wilkes.edu

Founded 1933. Located 100 miles NW of Philadelphia. Coed. Private control. Semester system. Library: 236,900 volumes, 4800 subscriptions. Total University enrollment: 4500.

Tuition: per semester hour $685, Education $345. Limited on-campus housing for graduate students.

Graduate Studies

Graduate study since 1959. Enrollment: full-time 429, part-time 1860. Faculty: full- and part-time 113. Degrees conferred: M.A., M.S., M.B.A., M.H.A.

ADMISSION REQUIREMENTS. Transcripts, GRE/MAT/ GMAT letters of recommendation required in support of School's application. Online application available. Interview may be required. Accepts transfer applicants. Apply to Dean of Admissions; no specified closing date. Rolling admission process. Application fee $35. Phone: (570)408-4235; fax: (570)408-7846.

ADMISSION STANDARDS. Selective. Usual minimum average: 2.75 (A = 4).

FINANCIAL AID. Graduate assistantships, counselorships, Federal W/S, loans. Apply to Director of Graduate Studies by March 1; no specified closing date. Phone: (570)408-4345. Use FAFSA and University's form (PHEAA).

DEGREE REQUIREMENTS. For master's: 30-39 credit hours minimum, at least 24 in residence. For Ph.D.: at least 60 credits beyond the bachelor's degree, two years in residence; foreign language requirement varies by department; preliminary exam; candidacy; dissertation; final oral exam.

FIELDS OF STUDY.
Business Administration. M.B.A.
Creative Writing. M.A., M.F.A.
Education. Includes elementary, secondary, educator, teacher leader. M.Ed., M.S.
Electrical Engineering. M.S.
Engineering Operations and Strategy. M.S.
Mathematics. M.S.
Nursing. Includes clinical nurse specialist (gerontological, psychiatric mental health nursing), nursing education, nursing management. M.S.

WILLAMETTE UNIVERSITY

Salem, Oregon 97301-3931
Web site: www.willamette.edu

Founded 1842. Located 42 miles S of Portland. The University consists of a College of Liberal Arts, College of Law, and the Atkinson Graduate School of Management. Library: 408,000 volumes, 3100 subscriptions.

Limited on-campus housing available for graduate students. Average academic year housing costs: $8000–$12,000 (including board). Contact Dean of Residence Life for both on- and off-campus housing information. Phone: (503)370-6212.

George H. Atkinson Graduate School of Management

Web site: www.willamette.edu/agsm

Graduate study since 1974. Coed. Semester system. Special facilities: Atkinson School Technology Center (includes 23 PCs), Public Policy Research Center.

Annual tuition: full-time $22,680; per course $3830.

Enrollment: full-time 151, part-time 21. Faculty: full-time 14, part-time 12. Degrees conferred: M.B.A., M.B.A.-J.D.

ADMISSION REQUIREMENTS. Transcripts, GMAT, letters of reference, résumé, application form and essay required in support of School's application. Online application available. TOEFL required for applicants. Graduates of unaccredited institutions not considered. Apply by April 1 (May entrance), August 1 (Septem-

ber entrance), December 1 (January entrance). Rolling admissions process after that on a space-available basis only. Application fee $50. Phone: (503)808-9902; e-mail: pmba@willamette.edu.

ADMISSION STANDARDS. Selective. Usual minimum average: 3.0 (A = 4).

FINANCIAL AID. Scholarships, research assistantships, internships, Federal W/S, loans. Approved for VA benefits. Apply by July 1. Phone: (503)370-6273. Use FAFSA.

DEGREE REQUIREMENTS. For M.B.A.: 63 semester hours. Joint Law and Management degree requires four years of full-time study.

FIELD OF STUDY.
Business, Government, and Not-for-Profit Management.

College of Law (97301-3922)
Web site: www.willamette.edu/wucl

Established 1883. ABA approved since 1938. AALS member. Semester system. Full-time, day study only. Special facility: Center for Dispute Resolution, Truman Wesley Collins Legal Center. Special programs: summer study abroad in Germany, People's Republic of China, and Ecuador. Law library: 288,204 volumes, 3110 subscriptions; has LEXIS, NEXIS, WESTLAW, DIALOG, CALI; has more than 100 network connections.

Annual tuition: $27,000. On-campus housing available for single students only. Contact Office of Residential Life for both on- and off-campus housing information. Phone: (503)370-6212. Law students tend to live off-campus. Off-campus housing and personal expenses: approximately $15,480.

Enrollment: first-year class 145; total 422 (men 58%, women 42%, minorities 8%). Faculty: full-time 35, part-time 20. Student to faculty ratio 15.6 to 1. Degrees conferred: J.D., J.D.-M.B.A., LL.M. (Transnational Law).

ADMISSION REQUIREMENTS. LSDAS Law School report, bachelor's degree, transcripts, references, LSAT, personal statement, résumé required in support of application. TOEFL required for all applicants whose native language is not English. Accepts transfer applicants. Graduates of unaccredited colleges not considered. Apply to Dean after September 1, before April 1 for priority consideration. Applications will be accepted as long as space is available. Rolling admissions process. Admits beginning student Fall only. Application fee $50; none, if applying online. Phone for both J.D. and LL.M. applicants: (503)370-6282.

ADMISSION STANDARDS. Selective. Accepts approximately 35% of all students. Number of applicants 1554; number of acceptance 546; number enrolled 145; LSAT (75% of students have a score at or above 153); GPA (75% of students have a GPA at or above 3.12). *U.S. News & World Report* ranking is in the fourth tier of all U.S. law schools.

FINANCIAL AID. Scholarships, partial tuition waivers, Federal W/S, Federal and private loans. Apply to the Office of Financial Aid by February 1. Phone: (503)370-6273. Use FAFSA. About 59% of students receive aid other than loans from School and outside sources.

DEGREE REQUIREMENTS. For J.D.: 88 semester hours minimum; writing requirements; final exam. For LL.M.: 25-credit program; required paper.
Note: Study-abroad program in Shanghai (China) available.

THE COLLEGE OF WILLIAM AND MARY

Williamsburg, Virginia 23187-8795
Web site: www.wm.edu

Founded 1693. Located 50 miles SE of Richmond. CGS member. Coed. State control. Semester system. Special facilities: Applied Research Center, Archaeological Conservation Center, Center for Archaeological Research, Center for Conservation Biology, Center for Gifted Education, Center for Public Policy, Institute for the Bill of Rights, Omohundro Institute of Early American History and Culture, National Institute of American History and Democracy, National Planned Giving Institute, Reves Center for International Studies, Roy R. Charles Center, Virginia Institute of Marine Science (VINIS), Writing Resources Center, Millington Life Sciences Hall, Muscarelle Museum, William Small Physical Laboratory; research opportunities at Colonial Williamsburg Foundation, Continuous Electron Beam Accelerator Facility (CEBAF), the Eastern State Hospital, the National Center for State Courts, and the Langley Research Center (LaRC) of the National Aeronautics and Space Administration. Graduate students work at the national laboratories and accelerator installations throughout the world. Libraries of the College are the central Earl Gregg Swem; the chemistry, physics, geology, biology, and music libraries; the Marshall-Wythe Law Library; the School of Marine Science; the Professional Resource Center (School of Business Administration); Learning Resource Center/curriculum Library (School of Education); 2,000,000 volumes, 9500 subscriptions. Total College enrollment: 7500.

Annual tuition: full-time resident $9414, nonresident $19,882 (Arts & Science, Education, Marine Science), resident $10,368, nonresident $27,972 (Clinical Psychology); resident $13,956, nonresident $25,478 (M.B.A.); resident $12,271, nonresident $22,631 (M.A.C.). On-campus housing for 122 graduate men and women, and 10 married students' apartments. Average academic year housing costs: $12,350 (including board) single students; $9000 for married students. Contact Office of Residence Life for on-campus information, phone: (757)221-4314; Office of Off-Campus Housing for off-campus information, phone: (757)221-3302. Daycare facilities available.

Graduate Studies

Enrollment: full- and part-time 1400. Graduate faculty: full- and part-time 675. Degrees conferred: M.A., M.A.Ed., M.S., M.Ed., M.B.A., M.L.&T., M.P.P., Ed.D., Psy.D., Ph.D., M.B.A.-J.D., M.B.A.-M.P.P.

ADMISSION REQUIREMENTS. Official transcripts, letters of reference required in support of application. Online application available. GRE/GMAT, interview required for some departments. TOEFL required for international applicants. Accepts transfer applicants. Apply to appropriate department chair or dean of professional school by May 1 for priority consideration. Application fees and deadlines vary by school. Phone: (757)221-2467 (Arts and Sciences), (757)221-2900 (M.B.A., M.A.C.), (804)684-7106 (Marine Science), (757)221-2317 (Education), (757)368-1820 (Clinical Psychology).

ADMISSION STANDARDS. Competitive for some departments, selective for all others. Minimum average: 2.5 (A = 4).

FINANCIAL AID. Awards from institutional funds: fellowships, scholarships, research fellowships, teaching assistantships, internships, Federal W/S, loans. Approved for VA benefits. Apply to appropriate department chair for fellowships, assistantships; to Financial Aid Office for all other programs. Phone: (757)221-1220; fax: (757)221-2515. Use FAFSA. About 50% of students receive aid other than loans from College and outside sources.

DEGREE REQUIREMENTS. For M.A.: 24 semester credits, at least one year in residence; reading knowledge of one foreign language for some departments; thesis; final exam. For M.S.: 32 semester credits minimum; thesis not required. Other requirements same as for M.A. For M.P.P.: 48 semester credits over two years; ten-week internship in summer between first and second years. For M.Ed., M.A. in Ed. 30 semester credits minimum, at least 18 in residence; thesis/final project (except for Secondary School Teaching); comprehensive exam. For M.B.A.: 60 semester credits minimum; thesis optional. For M.L.&T: one year minimum beyond the J.D. or equivalent. For Ed.D.: 90 semester credits minimum, at least 60 in residence; preliminary exam; dissertation; final oral exam. For Psy.D.: three years minimum, three terms per year, at least two years in residence; one year internship, comprehensive exam; final written or oral exam. For Ph.D.: three years minimum, at least one year in residence; reading knowledge of one or two foreign languages in some departments; comprehensive exam; dissertation; final oral exam.

FIELDS OF STUDY.

ARTS AND SCIENCES:
American Studies. M.A., Ph.D.
Anthropology. Includes historical archaeology. M.A. only.
Applied Sciences. Includes applied mathematics and computer science, chemical physics, atmospheric and plasma science, materials science; thesis optional. M.S., Ph.D.
Biology. M.S.
Chemistry. M.A., M.S.
Computer Science. Includes computational operations research. M.S., Ph.D.
History. Includes M.A. apprenticeship and Ph.D. internship programs in historical archaeology, historical editing, historical libraries. M.A., Ph.D.
Physics. Includes computational science. M.S., Ph.D.
Psychology. M.A. in general psychology, Psy.D. in clinical.
Public Policy. M.P.P.

MASON SCHOOL OF BUSINESS:
Accounting. M.Acc.
Business Administration. M.B.A., E.M.B.A.

SCHOOL OF EDUCATION:
Administration and Supervision Pre-K–12. M.Ed., Ed.D, Ph.D.
Curriculum and Educational Technology. Ed.D., Ph.D.
Curriculum Leadership. Ed.D., Ph.D.
Elementary Education. M.A.Ed.
Gifted Education. M.A.Ed.
Gifted Education Administration. M.Ed., Ed.D., Ph.D.
Higher Education Administration. M.Ed., Ed.D., Ph.D.
Reading, Language & Literacy. M.A.Ed.
School Psychology. M.Ed., Ed.S.
School Counseling. Includes community, community & addictions, family (M.Ed.); counselor education (Ed.D., Ph.D.).
Secondary Education. Includes English, mathematics, modern language, science, social studies. M.A.Ed.
Special Education. M.A.Ed.
Special Education Administration. Ed.D., Ph.D.

SCHOOL OF MARINE SCIENCES:
Marine Science. Includes research in Biological Sciences, environmental and aquatic animal health, fisheries science, physical science, marine & environmental policy. M.S., Ph.D.

THOMAS JEFFERSON PROGRAM IN PUBLIC POLICY:
Environmental Policy. M.P.P.
Globalization and Development. M.P.P.
Health Policy. M.P.P.
Social Policy. M.P.P.

JOINT DEGREE PROGRAMS:
Business and Public Policy.
Law and Public Policy.
Marine Science and Public Policy.
Computational Operations Research and Public Policy.

Marshall-Wythe Law School (P.O. Box 8795)

Web site: www.wm.edu/law

Established 1779. Located on main campus. ABA approved since 1932. AALS member. Semester system. Full-time, day study only. Special facility: Institute of Bill of Rights Law. Special programs: summer study abroad at University of Exeter, Devonshire, England; University of Madrid, Spain; University of Adelaide, Australia. Law library: 386,618 volumes, 4387 subscriptions; has LEXIS, NEXIS, WESTLAW, DIALOG; is a Federal Government Depository.

Annual tuition: resident $16,600, nonresident $26,800; LL.M. resident $18,336, nonresident $28,536. On-campus housing available for both single and married students. Contact Resident Life Office for both on- and off-campus housing information. Phone: (757)221-4314. Law students tend to live off-campus. Off-campus housing and personal expenses: approximately $13,500.

Enrollment: first-year class 205; total full-time 607 (men 53%, women 47%, minorities 16%); no part-time students. Faculty: full-time 26, part-time 27. Student to faculty ratio 16.7 to 1. Degrees conferred: J.D., J.D.-M.B.A., J.D.-M.P.P., J.D.-M.A., LL.M. (American Legal System—for foreign attorneys who have completed a basic legal education and received a university degree in law in another country).

ADMISSION REQUIREMENTS. LSDAS Law School report, bachelor's degree, transcripts, LSAT, two letters of recommendation required in support of application. TOEFL required for international applicants. Accepts transfer applicants. Graduates of unaccredited colleges not considered. Apply to Admissions Office after September 1, before March 1 for priority consideration. Application fee $50. Phone: (757)221-3785; fax: (757)221-3261.

ADMISSION REQUIREMENTS FOR TRANSFER APPLICANTS. Accepts transfers from other ABA-accredited schools. Admission limited to space available. At least one year of enrollment, Dean's letter indicating the applicant is in good standing (prefer applicants in the top quarter of first-year class), LSAT, LSDAS, personal statement regarding reason for transfer, two letters of recommendation, current law school transcript with rank in class required in support of School's application. Apply to Admission Office by April 1. Admission decision made by early August. Application fee $50. Will consider visiting students.

ADMISSION REQUIREMENTS FOR LL.M. APPLICANTS. All applicants must have a basic law degree from a country other than the U.S.; the institution must be fully accredited and recognized by the relevant educational authority of that country; and applicant can not be a permanent resident of U.S. citizen. Original or certified copies of all original official transcripts/academic record, certified English translations of all non-English credentials, two letters of recommendation, personal statement required in support of LL.M. application. TOEFL required for all international applicants. Admits Fall only. Apply by February 1 to the School of Law's Admissions Office. Application fee $50.

ADMISSION STANDARDS. Selective. Accepts approximately 22% of all students. Number of applicants 4116; number of acceptance 924; number enrolled 205; LSAT (75% of students have a score at or above 160); GPA (75% of students have a GPA at or above 3.31). *U.S. News & World Report* ranking is 31st of all U.S. law schools.

FINANCIAL AID. Scholarships, fellowships, assistantships, Federal W/S, loans. Apply to the Office of Financial Aid by February 1.

Phone: (757)221-2420. Use FAFSA (School code: 003705). About 40% of students receive aid other than loans from School.

DEGREE REQUIREMENTS. For J.D.: 90 semester credit program, at least final year in residence. For LL.M.: at least 24 credits beyond J.D.; one year in full-time residence.

WILLIAM CAREY COLLEGE

Hattiesburg, Mississippi 39401-5499
Web site: www.wmcarey.edu

Founded 1906. Located 125 miles from New Orleans, Louisiana. Additional campuses in Gulfport, New Orleans. Coed. Semester system. Library: 107,000 volumes, 30,000 microforms, 628 subscriptions.

Tuition: per credit hour $275 (M.Ed., M.B.A.), $260 (Psychology). Limited on-campus housing available.

Graduate Division

Founded in 1969. Enrollment: full- and part-time 185 (men 13, women 10). Faculty: full-time 21, part-time 11. Degrees conferred: M.Ed., M.B.A.

ADMISSION REQUIREMENTS. Transcripts, letters of recommendation, teaching certificate (for Education) required in support of application. TOEFL required for international applicants. Accepts transfer applicants. Apply to the Chair Graduate Division; no specified closing date. Rolling admissions process. Application fee $10. Phone: (601)318-6774; fax: (601)318-6765.

ADMISSION STANDARDS. Selective. Usual minimum average: 2.5 (A = 4).

FINANCIAL AID. Scholarships, Scholar Grants, Federal W/S, loans. Phone: (601)318-6153. Use FAFSA (College code: 002447) and College's FAF. About 10% of students receive aid from College and outside sources. Aid available for part-time students.

DEGREE REQUIREMENTS. For M.B.A., M.Ed.: 30-36 semester hours minimum; evaluation tests; comprehensive exam.

FIELDS OF STUDY.
Business Administration. M.B.A.
Counseling Psychology.
Education. Includes art education, art of teaching, elementary education, English, gifted education, mild/moderate disabilities, secondary education. M.Ed.
Nursing. M.S.N.
Psychology. M.S.
Specialist in Education. Includes elementary education. Ed.S.

WILLIAM MITCHELL COLLEGE OF LAW

875 Summit Avenue
St. Paul, Minnesota 55105-3076
Web site: www.wmitchell.edu

Established 1900. Located in downtown St. Paul. ABA approved since 1938. AALS member. Private control. Semester system. Special program: belongs to the Consortium for Innovative Legal Education, or CILE, a partnership with California Western School of Law in San Diego, New England School of Law in Boston, and South Texas College of Law in Houston; summer study in Galway, Ireland, Malta; semester abroad programs in Aarhus,

Denmark, Leiden, the Netherlands. Law library: 334,632 volumes, 3988 subscriptions; has LEXIS, WESTLAW; has more than 200 networks connections.

Annual tuition: full-time (three-year program) $29,020, part-time (four-year program) $21,000. No on-campus housing available. Contact Student Services for off-campus housing information. Off-campus housing and personal expenses: approximately $14,300.

Enrollment: first-year class full-time 271, part-time 121; total full- and part-time 1103 (men 46%, women 54%, minorities 11%). Faculty: full-time 35, part-time 20. Student to faculty ratio 23.6 to 1. Degrees conferred: J.D.

ADMISSION REQUIREMENTS. Bachelor's degree, transcripts, LSAT, writing sample, two letters of recommendation, personal statement, résumé required in support of application. Accepts transfer applicants. Graduates of unaccredited colleges not considered. Apply to Admissions Office by May 1 for priority consideration. Rolling admissions process. Admits beginning student Fall only. Application fee $50. Phone: (651)290-6476.

ADMISSION STANDARDS. Selective. Accepts approximately 48% of all students. Number of applicants 1591; number of acceptance 763; number enrolled 270; LSAT (75% of students have a score at or above 151); GPA (75% of students have a GPA at or above 3.24). *U.S. News & World Report* ranking is in the third tier of all U.S. law schools.

FINANCIAL AID. Scholarships, minority scholarships, Federal W/S, loans. Approved for VA benefits. Apply to Financial Aid Office before March 15. Phone: (651)290-6403. Use FAFSA (College code: G02391). About 50% of students receive aid other than loans from College. Aid available for part-time, third-, and fourth-year students.

DEGREE REQUIREMENTS. For J.D.: 86-semester-hour program; advanced standing considered. For LL.M.: at least 24 credits beyond J.D.

WILLIAM PATERSON UNIVERSITY OF NEW JERSEY
Wayne, New Jersey 07470-2103
Web site: www.wpunj.edu

Founded 1855, Located 20 miles W of New York City. CGS member. Coed. State control. Semester system. Special facility: New Sarah Byrd Askew library. Library: 305,100 volumes, 1950 subscriptions. Total University enrollment: 11,000.

Tuition: per credit resident $476, nonresident $717. On-campus housing available for single graduate students only. Average academic year housing costs: $3750 (including board). Contact Director of Residence Life for both on- and off-campus housing information. Phone: (973)720-2714.

Graduate Programs

Graduate study since 1966. Enrollment: full-time 355, part-time 1500. Faculty: full-time 238, part-time 3. Degrees conferred: M.A., M.A.T., M.B.A., M.Ed., M.S., M.S.N.

ADMISSION REQUIREMENTS. Official transcripts, interview, GRE or MAT, GMAT (Business) required in support of application. Online application available. TOEFL, W.E.S. required for international applicants. Accepts transfer applicants. Apply to Office of Graduate Studies and Research by August 1 (Fall), November 1 (Spring) for most departments. Application fee $50. Phone: (973)720-2237; fax: (973)720-2035.

ADMISSION STANDARDS. Selective. Usual minimum average: 3.0 (A = 4).

FINANCIAL AID. Graduate assistantship, internships, loans. Approved for VA benefits. Apply to the Office of Graduate Studies and Research for assistantships, internships; to the Financial Aid Office for all other programs. Phone: (973)720-2022. Use FAFSA.

DEGREE REQUIREMENTS. For master's: 30-42 credit hours minimum, at least 24 in residence; research thesis; project; comprehensive exam. For M.B.A.: 60 credit hours minimum.

FIELDS OF STUDY.
Applied Clinical Psychology. M.A.
Biological Sciences. M.A., M. S.
Biology. M. S.
Biotechnology and Communication Disorders. Includes speech-language pathology. M.S.
Communication Arts. Includes interpersonal communication, television. M.A. only.
Community-Based Nursing. Includes tracks in educational, administrative, advanced practice. M.S.N.
Counseling Services. Includes agency, school; M. Ed.
Education. Includes bilingual/English as a second language, early childhood, educational leadership, educational media, language arts, learning technologies, teaching children mathematics. M.Ed. only.
Educational Leadership. M.Ed.
Elementary Education. M.A.T.
English. Includes literature, writing. M.A. only.
Finance. M.B.A.
General Business. M.B.A.
History. M.A.
Jazz Studies. M.M.
Management. M.B.A.
Marketing. M.B.A.
Media Studies. M.A.
Music Education. M.M.
Music Management. M.M.
Public Policy and International Affairs. M.A.
Reading. M.Ed.
Sociology. Includes diversity studies, crime and justice. M.A.
Special Education. Includes development disability, learning disability. M.Ed. only.
Visual Arts. Includes painting, sculpture, ceramics, furniture design, metals, photography, printmaking, textiles. M.F.A. only.
Note: Certification Programs in Education available.

WINONA STATE UNIVERSITY
Winona, Minnesota 55987-5838
Web site: www.winona.msus.edu

Founded 1858. Located 110 miles SE of Minneapolis. Coed. State control. Quarter system. Library: 244,000 volumes, 1950 subscriptions. Total University enrollment: 8236.

Tuition: per credit, resident $251, nonresident $378. Average academic year housing cost: $3850 (including board). Limited on-campus housing for graduate students. Contact Director of Student Housing for both on- and off-campus housing information. Phone: (507)457-5305. Day-care facilities available.

Graduate Studies

Graduate study since 1953. Enrollment: full-time 101, part-time 295. College faculty teaching graduate students: full-time 57, part-time none. Degrees conferred: M.S., M.A., M.B.A., Specialist Degree in Educational Administration.

ADMISSION REQUIREMENTS. Transcripts GRE/GMAT required in support of application. Online application available. Interview not required. TOEFL required for international applicants. Accepts transfer applicants. Graduates of unaccredited institutions not considered. Apply to Office of Graduate Studies at least one month prior to registration. Application fee $20. Phone: (507)457-5346; fax: (507)457-5578.

ADMISSION STANDARDS. Selective. Usual minimum average: 2.5 (A = 4).

FINANCIAL AID. Annual awards from institutional funds: assistantships, traineeships, internships, Federal W/S, loans. Approved for VA benefits. Apply at least six months prior to registration to appropriate department chair for assistantships; to Financial Aid Office for all other programs. Phone: (507)457-5090. Use FAFSA. Aid available for part-time students.

DEGREE REQUIREMENTS. Thesis plan: 45 quarter hours minimum; final written/oral exam. Nonthesis plan: 48-72 quarter hours; final written exam. Specialist: 45 quarter hours beyond the master's; special project.

FIELDS OF STUDY.
Counselor Education. Includes community counseling (chemical dependency counseling), professional development, school counseling. M.S.
Education. Includes learning community, graduate induction program. M.S.
Educational Leadership. Includes K–12, teacher leadership, outdoor education/adventure-based leadership, sports management (M.S.); Pre-K–12, superintendent (Ed.S.). M.S., Ed.S.
English. Includes literature & language, TESOL (M.A.), studies in literature, language & education (M.S.). M.A., M.S.
Nursing. Includes adult nurse practitioner, family nurse practitioner, nurse administrator, clinical nurse specialist, nurse educator. M.S., D.N.P.

WINTHROP UNIVERSITY
Rock Hill, South Carolina 29733
Web site: www.winthrop.edu

Founded 1886. Located 25 miles SW of Charlotte, North Carolina. State control. Semester system. Library: 638,000 volumes, 2706 subscriptions. Total University enrollment: 6400.

Annual tuition: full-time resident $4917, nonresident $9140; per semester hour resident $412, nonresident $763. On-campus housing available for married and single students; 54 married housing units. Average academic year housing costs: $5200 (including board) for single students; $6100 for married students. Contact Director, Residence Life, for housing information. Phone: (803)323-2260.

Graduate School

Enrollment: full-time 256, part-time 389. University faculty: full- and part-time 162. Degrees conferred: M.A., M.S., M.F.A., M.Mth., M.A.T., M.L.A., M.M., M.Ed., M.B.A., M.M.E., M.S.W., Ed.S., S.S.P.

ADMISSION REQUIREMENTS. Official transcripts from all postsecondary institutions attended, GMAT (business), GRE/ MAT, NTE/Class III Professional Teaching Certificate for certain programs required in support of application. TOEFL or ELS Language Center English proficiency level 109 required for international applicants. Accepts transfer applicants. Graduates of colleges not accredited by a regional accrediting agency must be approved by the Graduate Council. Apply to the Office of Graduate Studies; no specified closing date. Application fee $35, $50 for international applicants. Phone: (800)411-7041; (803)323-2204.

ADMISSION STANDARDS. Selective. Usual minimum average: 3.0 (A = 4).

FINANCIAL AID. Annual awards from institutional funds: scholarships, research assistantships, graduate assistantships, internships, Federal W/S, loans. Approved for VA benefits. Forms for assistantships available in Office of Graduate Services. Apply by February 15 to Financial Aid Office for all federal programs. Phone: (803)323-2189; fax: (803)323-2557. Use FAFSA and institutional FAF. Aid available for part-time students.

DEGREE REQUIREMENTS. For all master's: 30-60 semester hours minimum; M.A., M.S. thesis optional. For Ed.S., S.S.P.: 60–66 semester hours beyond the bachelor's.

FIELDS OF STUDY.

COLLEGE OF ARTS AND SCIENCES:
Biology. M.S.
English. M.A.
History. M.A.
Human Nutrition. M.S.
Liberal Arts. M.L.A.
Mathematics. M.Mth.
School Psychology. M.S., SSP.
Social Work. M.S.W.
Spanish. M.A.

COLLEGE OF BUSINESS ADMINISTRATION:
Business Administration. Includes accounting, finance, international software project management. M.B.A.

RICHARD W. RILEY COLLEGE OF EDUCATION:
Counseling and Development. Includes community/agency, school. M.Ed.
Curriculum and Instruction. Includes early childhood, educational technology, elementary, secondary. M.Ed.
Education. Includes art (K–12), biology, business/marketing, English, French, family and consumer sciences, mathematics, music (K–12), physical (K–12), social studies, Spanish, theater. M.A.T.
Educational Leadership. M.Ed.
Middle Level Education. M.Ed.
Physical Education. M.S.
Reading. M.Ed.
Special Education. M.Ed.

COLLEGE OF VISUAL AND PERFORMING ARTS:
Arts Administration. M.A.
Art and Design. M.F.A.
Art Education. M.A.
Conducting. M.M.
Music Education. M.M.E.
Performance. M.M.

MEDICAL COLLEGE OF WISCONSIN
Milwaukee, Wisconsin 53226-0509
Web site: www.mcw.edu

Founded 1913, became a freestanding school of medicine in 1967. CGS member. Coed. Public, formerly associated with Marquette University. Semester system. Special facilities: Bioinformatics Research Center, Biostatistics Consulting Center, Cancer Center, Cardiovascular Center, Center for AIDS Intervention Research, Center for Animal Research Imaging, Center for the Study of Bioethics, End of Life Physician Education Resource Center, Foley Center for Aging, Free Radical Research Center, Functional Imaging Research Center, General Clinical Research Center, Health Policy Institute, Human Molecular Genetics Center, Injury Research Center, National EST Center, MRI Center, Blood Research Institute. The College's NIH ranking is number 68th among all U.S. Institutions with 205 awards/grants valued at $84,030,609. According to The Center at University of Florida, the College is ranked number 93rd in receipt of Federal Research fund with $83,026,000. The Library: approximately 230,000 volumes, 1200 subscriptions. Total University enrollment: 1600.

No on-campus housing available. Total average costs for all other expenses beyond tuition: $12,000.

Graduate School of Biomedical Sciences

Annual tuition: full-time $11,340, per credit $630.

Enrollment: full-time 200. Faculty: full-time 160, part-time 46. Degrees conferred: M.A., M.P.H., M.S., Ph.D.

ADMISSION REQUIREMENTS. Transcripts, GRE, three letters of recommendation, personal statement, interview required in support of application. Online application available. TOEFL (minimum score 580) required of all foreign applicants. Accepts transfer applicants. Graduates of unaccredited colleges not considered. Apply to Office of Admissions June 1 (Fall), December 1 (Spring). Application fee $40. Phone: (414)456-8218; e-mail: gradschool@ mcw.edu.

ADMISSION STANDARDS. Competitive. Usual minimum average: 3.0 (A = 4).

FINANCIAL AID. Scholarships, stipends, research assistantships, fellowships, Federal W/S, loans. Apply to Director of Financial Aid by February 15. Phone: (414)456-8208. Use FAFSA. About 20% of students receive some aid from College and outside sources.

DEGREE REQUIREMENTS. For M.A.: 30 credit, full-time, two-year program; clinical practicum, teaching practicum; thesis. For M.P.H.: three- to four-year part-time program; research project. For M.S.: 30–36 semester hours minimum; foreign language requirement varies by department; comprehensive exam; thesis. For Ph.D.: six semesters in residence, at least two semesters in full-time study; qualifying exam; dissertation; final oral exam. For M.D.-Ph.D.: satisfactory completion of six- to seven-year program.

FIELDS OF STUDY.
Bioethics. Includes medical ethics and medical law. Ph.D.
Bioinformatics. Joint program with Marquette University. M.S.
Biomedical Sciences. Includes the following departments: biophysics, biochemistry, cell biology, neurobiology and anatomy, microbiology and molecular genetics, pharmacology and toxicology. Interdisciplinary. Ph.D.
Biophysics. M.S., Ph.D.
Biostatistics. Includes neuroscience research, Bayesian methods. Ph.D.
Epidemiology. M.S.
Functional Imaging. Joint program with Marquette University. M.S.
Healthcare Technologies Management. Joint program with Marquette University. M.S.
Medical Informatics. Joint degree programs with Milwaukee School of Engineering. M.S.
Neurosciences. Includes eleven basic and clinical science departments. Interdisciplinary. Ph.D.
Pharmacology and Toxicology. Includes cardiovascular pharmacology, molecular pharmacology, neuropharmacology, signal transduction. Ph.D.
Physiology. Interdisciplinary. M.S., Ph.D.
Public Health. M.P.H.

Medical School
Web site: www.mcw.edu

Founded 1893. NIH ranking is 68th among all U.S. institutions with 205 awards/grants worth $84,030,609.

Annual tuition: resident $32,400, nonresident $37,900. No on-campus housing available. Total average for all other expenses: $12,500.

Enrollment: first-year class 204, total 807 (men 53%, women 47%, minorities 23%, state residents 46%). Faculty: full-time 758, part-time 58. Degrees conferred: M.D., M.D.-Ph.D. (Medical Scientist Training Program).

ADMISSION REQUIREMENTS. AMCAS report, transcripts, MCAT, two letters of recommendation, personal interview required in support of application. Supplemental application required. Has EDP; apply between June 1 and August 1. Interview by invitation only. Preference given to state residents. Graduates of unaccredited colleges not considered. Apply to Committee on Admissions after June 1, before November 1. Application fee $60. Phone: (414)456-8246; fax: (414)456-6506.

ADMISSION STANDARDS. Very competitive for nonresidents, selective for residents. Accepts about 8% of all applicants. Number of applications 5645 (5093 out-of-state); number interviewed 701 (493 out-of-state); number of acceptance 475 (315 out-of-state); number enrolled 204 (108 out-of-state). Mean Composite MCAT 9.8, mean UGPA 3.72. *U.S. New & World Report* ranking is in the top 50 of all U.S. medical schools in primary care programs.

FINANCIAL AID. Scholarships, loans. Apply to Director of Financial Aid after acceptance, before April 24. Phone: (414) 456-8208. Use FAFSA. About 20% of students receive some aid from College and outside sources.

DEGREE REQUIREMENTS. For M.D.: satisfactory completion of four-year program; all students must pass USMLE Step 1 prior to entering third year; all students must take USMLE Step 2 and record a score. For M.D.-Ph.D.: satisfactory completion of six to seven-year program.

FIELDS OF GRADUATE STUDY.
Biochemistry. Ph.D.
Bioethics. M.A., M.S.
Bioinformatics. M.S.
Biomedical Science. Interdisciplinary. Ph.D.
Biophysics. Ph.D.
Biostatistics. Ph.D.
Cell Biology, Neurobiology and Anatomy. Ph.D.
Cellular and Integrative Physiology.
Epidemiology. M.S.
Functional Imaging. Ph.D.
Medical Informatics. M.S.
Microbiology and Molecular Genetics. Ph.D.
Neuroscience. Interdisciplinary. Ph.D.
Occupational Medicine. M.P.H.
Pharmacology and Toxicology. Ph.D.
Physiology. Ph.D.
Public Health. M.S., M.P.H.

UNIVERSITY OF WISCONSIN— EAU CLAIRE
Eau Claire, Wisconsin 54702-4004
Web site: www.uwec.edu

Founded 1916. Located 85 miles E of St. Paul, Minnesota. CGS member. Coed. State control. Semester system. Special facilities: Foster Art Gallery, Center for Communication Disorders, Human Development Center, Kate Gill Literary Research Center, S. W. Casey Observatory, James Newman Clark Bird Museum, Pigeon Lake Field Station, L. E. Phillips Planetarium. Library: 764,275 volumes, 3376 subscriptions. Total University enrollment: 10,500.

Annual fees: full-time resident $6223, nonresident $16,833; per credits resident $345, nonresident $935. On-campus housing for single graduate students, none for married students. Average academic year housing costs: $3850 (including board). Contact

Director of Housing for both on- and off-campus housing information. Phone: (715)836-3674. Day-care facilities available.

Graduate Studies

Graduate study since 1960. Enrollment: full-time 124, part-time 283. Graduate faculty: full-time 36, part-time 21. Degrees conferred: M.A., M.A.T., M.B.A., M.E., M.M., M.S., M.S.N., M.S.T., M.S.E.

ADMISSION REQUIREMENTS. Official transcripts, GRE/GMAT, interview required in support of application. TOEFL required for international applicants. Accepts transfer applicants. Apply to Director of Admissions at least 60 days prior to registration. Application fee $45. Phone: (715)836-5415; fax: (715) 836-2409.

ADMISSION STANDARDS. Relatively open. Usual minimum average for probationary admission: 2.25 (A = 4).

FINANCIAL AID. Annual awards from institutional funds: scholarships, fellowships, graduate assistantships, tuition waivers, Federal W/S, loans. Approved for VA benefits. Apply by March 1 to Director of Financial Aid. Phone: (715)836-3733, Fax: (715)836-2380. Use FAFSA. About 40% of full-time students receive aid other than loans from University and outside sources. Aid available for part-time students.

DEGREE REQUIREMENTS. For master's: 30-36 semester hours minimum, at least 21 in residence; thesis/nonthesis option/final paper; final written/oral comprehensive exam.

FIELDS OF STUDY.

COLLEGE OF ARTS AND SCIENCES:
Biology. M.S.
English. M.A.
History. M.A.
School Psychology. Ed.S.

COLLEGE OF BUSINESS:
Business Administration. M.B.A.

COLLEGE OF EDUCATION AND HUMAN SCIENCES:
Biology. M.A.T., M.S.T.
Communication Disorders. M.S.
Elementary Education. M.S.T.
English. M.A.T., M.S.T.
History. M.A.T., M.S.T.
History/Social Science. M.S.T.
Mathematics. M.A.T., M.S.T.
Nursing. M.S.N.
Professional Development. M.Ed.
Reading. M.A.T.
Special Education. M.S.Ed.

UNIVERSITY OF WISCONSIN— LA CROSSE

La Crosse, Wisconsin 54601-3742
Web site: www.uwlax.edu

Founded 1909. Located 125 miles W of Madison. CGS member. Coed. State control. Semester system. Special facilities: Bureau of Business and Economic Research, Center for Education Profession, Rhea Pederson Reading Center, River Studies Center. Library: over 673,000 volumes, 2200 subscriptions. Total University enrollment: 9400.

Annual fees: full-time resident (and Minnesota contract) $6223, nonresident $16,833. Limited on-campus housing for single grad-

uate students only. Average academic year housing costs: $4100 (including board). Contact Director of Campus Housing for both on- and off-campus housing information. Phone: (608)785-8075. Day-care facilities available.

Graduate Studies

Graduate study since 1956. Enrollment: full-time 366, part-time 898. University faculty teaching graduate students: full-time 119, part-time 55. Degrees conferred: M.B.A., M.E.P.D., M.P.H., M.S., M.S.Ed.

ADMISSION REQUIREMENTS. Transcript, GMAT (Business) required in support of application. TOEFL required for international applicants. Accepts transfer applicants. Graduates of unaccredited institutions not considered. Apply to Admissions Office at least one month prior to registration. Rolling admissions process. Application fee $45. Phone: (608)785-8939; fax: (608) 785-8940.

ADMISSION STANDARDS. Selective. Required minimum overall GPA of 2.85, or 3.0 (A = 4) in last 60 undergraduate credits.

FINANCIAL AID. Graduate assistantships, grants, tuition waivers, Federal W/S, loans. Approved for VA benefits. Apply by March 15 to Director of Financial Aid. Phone: (608)785-8604. Use FAFSA. About 50% of students receive aid from University and outside sources. Aid available for part-time students.

DEGREE REQUIREMENTS. For master's: 30-48 credit hours minimum, at least 24 in residence; thesis/final document; final oral/written exam.

FIELDS OF STUDY.

COLLEGE OF BUSINESS ADMINISTRATION:
Business Administration. M.B.A.

COLLEGE OF LIBERAL STUDIES:
Professional Development. Includes learning community. M.Ed.
Reading. Includes reading teacher, teacher reading specialist, classroom teacher. M.S.Ed.
School Psychology. Ed.S.
Special Education. M.S.Ed.
Student Affairs Administration in Higher Education. M.S.Ed.

COLLEGE OF SCIENCE AND HEALTH:
Biology. Includes concentrations in aquatic science, cellular biology, clinical microbiology, microbiology, nurse anesthesia, physiology. M.S.
Clinical Exercise Physiology. M.S.
Health Education. Includes community health education, school health education. M.S.
Human Performance. Includes athletic training. M.S.
Occupational Therapy. M.S.
Physical Education Teaching. Includes adapted physical education, adventure/outdoor pursuits, health as a lifestyle. M.S.
Physical Therapy. D.P.T.
Physician Assistant Studies. M.S.
Public Health in Community Health Education. M.P.H.
Recreation Management. M.S.
Software Engineering. M.S.E.
Sport Administration. M.S.
Therapeutic Recreation. M.S.

UNIVERSITY OF WISCONSIN

Madison, Wisconsin 53706-1380
Web site: www.wisc.edu

Founded 1848. CGS and AAU member. Coed. State control. Semester system. Special facilities: Aquatic Sciences Center, Sea

Grant Institute, Water Resources Institute, Institute on Aging, Biotechnology Center, Center for Demography and Ecology, Developmental and Molecular Toxicology Center, Educational Research and Development Center, Institute for Molecular Virology, Institute for Research in the Humanities, Industrial Relations Research Institute, Institute for Environmental Studies, Space Science and Engineering Center, McArdle Cancer Research Laboratory, Synchrotron Radiation Center, Waisman Center on Mental Retardation and Human Development, Wisconsin Regional Primate Center, Wisconsin Center for Applied Microelectronics, Wisconsin Clinical Cancer Center, Women's Studies Research Center. The University's NIH ranking is 20th among all U.S. institutions with 670 awards/grants valued at $257,144,598. According to The Center at University of Florida, the University is ranked 8th in receipt of Federal Research funds with $363,231,000 and it ranks 4th for total University research expenditures with $721,248,000. The University's endowment assets rank it 45th, with a value of $1,046,722,000. In 2004, the University awarded 628 doctorates which ranked it 7th among all U.S. institutions eligible to award that degree. Seventy-one of the University's faculty members have been elected to National Honor Academies and this ranks it 14th among all U.S. institutions. The Library: approximately 6,100,000 volumes, 66,000 subscriptions. Total University enrollment: 40,300.

Annual tuition: full-time resident: $7019.28, Minnesota compact students $7736.04, nonresident $18,471.84; Business: resident $8111.28, Minnesota Compact $17,869.32, nonresident $19,689.84. Limited on-campus housing available for graduate students. Average academic year housing costs: $6400 for single students, $8900 for married students. Contact Director of Residence Halls, Assignment Office of University Housing for both on- and off-campus housing information. Phone: (608)262-2522. Day-care facilities available.

Graduate School

Established 1904. Enrollment: full- and part-time 8620 (men 55%, women 45%). Faculty: full- and part-time about 2100. Degrees conferred: M.A., M.B.A., M.F.A., M.M., M.Acc., A.Mus.D., Ph.D.

ADMISSION REQUIREMENTS. Official transcripts required in support of School's application. GRE Subject Tests, GMAT required by many departments. Evidence of proficiency in English or TOEFL, or MELAB required for international students. Interview not required. Accepts transfer applicants. Graduates of unaccredited institutions not considered. Apply to Office of Graduate Admission at least six weeks prior to registration. Application fee $45. Phone: (608)262-2433; fax: (608)262-5134.

ADMISSION STANDARDS. Very selective for most departments, competitive for others. Usual minimum average: 3.0 (A = 4).

FINANCIAL AID. Scholarships, fellowships, teaching research/project assistantships, internships, grants, tuition waivers, Federal W/S, loans. Approved for VA benefits. Apply by January 15 to appropriate department with completed forms, transcripts, and GRE Subject Test. Phone: (608)262-3060. Use FAFSA. Aid available for part-time students.

DEGREE REQUIREMENTS. For master's: two semesters minimum, at least one in residence. In addition, each department has its own requirements regarding oral/written exams and thesis/nonthesis option. For M.F.A.: 4 semesters minimum, at least two in residence; final oral exam. For Ph.D.: six semesters minimum, at least three semesters in residence, and one year in full-time attendance; comprehensive preliminary exam; thesis; final oral exam. For A.Mus.D.: essentially the same as for the Ph.D.

FIELDS OF STUDY.
Accounting.
Actuarial Science.
African Studies.
Afro-American Studies.
Agricultural and Applied Economics.
Agricultural Engineering.
Agricultural Journalism.
Agroecology.
Agronomy.
Animal Sciences.
Anthropology.
Art.
Art Education.
Art History.
Arts Administration.
Astronomy.
Atmospheric and Oceanic Sciences.
Bacteriology.
Biochemistry.
Biological Systems Engineering.
Biomedical Engineering.
Biometry.
Biomolecular Chemistry.
Biophysics.
Biotechnology.
Botany.
Business.
Cancer Biology. Includes oncology.
Cartography and Geographic Information Systems.
Cellular and Molecular Biology.
Chemical Engineering.
Chemistry.
Chinese.
Civil and Environmental Engineering.
Classics.
Communication Arts.
Communicative Disorders.
Comparative Literature.
Computer Science.
Conservation Biology and Sustainable Development.
Consumer Behavior and Family Economics.
Continuing and Vocational Education.
Counseling.
Counseling Psychology.
Creative Writing.
Curriculum and Instruction.
Dairy Science.
Design Studies.
Development Studies.
Economics.
Education Administration.
Educational Leadership and Policy Analysis.
Educational Policy Studies.
Educational Psychology.
Electrical Engineering.
Endocrinology-Reproductive Physiology.
Engineering.
Engineering Mechanics.
English.
Entomology.
Environment and Resources.
Environmental Chemistry and Technology. Includes water chemistry.
Environmental Monitoring.
Finance, Investments, and Banking.
Food Science.
Forestry.
French.
French Studies.
Genetics.
Geography.
Geological Engineering.
Geology.
Geophysics.

German.
Greek.
Hebrew and Semitic Studies.
History.
History of Science.
Horticulture.
Human Ecology. Includes consumer behavior and family economics, design studies.
Industrial Engineering.
Information Systems.
International Public Affairs.
Italian.
Japanese.
Journalism and Mass Communication.
Kinesiology.
Land Resources.
Landscape Architecture.
Languages and Cultures of Asia.
Latin.
Latin American, Caribbean, and Iberian Studies.
Legal Institutions.
Library and Information Studies.
Life Sciences Communication.
Limnology and Marine Science.
Linguistics.
Manufacturing Systems Engineering.
Marketing.
Mass Communications.
Materials Science.
Mathematics.
Mechanical Engineering.
Medical Genetics.
Medical Microbiology and Immunology.
Medical Physics.
Metallurgical Engineering
Microbiology.
Molecular and Cellular Pharmacology.
Molecular and Environmental Toxicology.
Music. Includes education, ethnomusicology, history, performance, theory.
Neuroscience.
Nuclear Engineering and Engineering Physics.
Nursing.
Nutritional Sciences.
Occupational Therapy.
Operations and Technology Management.
Pharmaceutical Sciences.
Pharmacy.
Philosophy.
Physics.
Physiology.
Plant Breeding and Plant Genetics.
Plant Pathology.
Political Science.
Population Health.
Portuguese.
Psychology.
Public Affairs. Includes international public affairs.
Real Estate and Urban Land Economics.
Rehabilitation Psychology.
Risk Management and Insurance.
Rural Sociology.
Scandinavian Studies.
Science Education.
Second Language Acquisition.
Slavic Languages and Literature.
Social Welfare.
Social Work.
Social and Administrative Sciences in Pharmacy.
Sociology.
Soil Science.

Spanish.
Special Education.
Statistics.
Supply Chain Management.
Theatre and Drama.
Therapeutic Science.
Urban and Regional Planning.
Veterinary Science.
Water Chemistry.
Water Resources Management.
Wildlife Ecology.
Women's Studies.
Zoology.

Law School (53706-1399)
Web site: www.law.wisc.edu

Established 1868. Located on main campus. ABA approved since 1923. AALS charter member. Semester system. Full-time day study. Special facilities: Center for Patient Partnerships, East Asian Legal Studies Center, Frank J. Remington Center, Global Legal Studies Center, Great Lakes Indian Law Center, Institute for Legal Studies (ILS), Resource Center on Impaired Driving. Special programs: Criminal Justice Administration Program, Legal Assistance to Institutionalized Persons Program (LAIP); exchange programs with JLU-Giessen, Giessen, Germany; University of Groningen, The Netherlands; European University Institute, Florence, Italy; Diego Portales University, Santiago, Chile; Catholic University, Lima, Peru; University of the Witwatersrand, Johannesburg, South Africa; University of Sheffield, Sheffield, United Kingdom; University of Paris X, Nanterre, Paris, France; Pontifical Catholic University, Rio de Janeiro, Brazil; study abroad in Chile, Germany, Italy, the Netherlands, Peru, South Africa, United Kingdom. Law library: 553,997 volumes, 6173 subscriptions; has LEXIS, NEXIS, WESTLAW, DIALOG; has more than 300 network connections.

Annual tuition: resident for J. D. and graduate programs $12,653, nonresident for J.D. and graduate programs $30,816; part-time $1058 per credit. On-campus housing available for both single and married students. Contact Office of University Housing for on-campus housing information. Phone: (608)252-2522. Law students tend to live off-campus. Contact Campus Assistance Center for off-campus information. Phone: (608)262-2400. Contact the Family Housing Office for off-campus married housing information. Phone: (608)262-2789. Off-campus housing and personal expenses: approximately $13,650.

Enrollment: first-year class 270; total 817 (men 52%, women 48%, minorities 26%); limited part-time study. Faculty: full-time 55, part-time 40. Student to faculty ratio 13.1 to 1. Degrees conferred: J.D., J.D.-M.A. (Ibero-American Studies, Philosophy, Sociology, Urban and Regional Planning), J.D.-M.B.A., J.D.- M.L.I., J.D.-M.L.S., J.D.-M.P.A., J.D.-M.S. (Environmental Studies, Industrial Relation), J.D.-Ph.D. (Philosophy, Sociology), LL.M., S.J.D.

ADMISSION REQUIREMENTS. For J.D. program: LSDAS Law School report, bachelor's degree, transcripts, LSAT, personal statement, résumé, two letters of recommendation required in support of application. TOEFL required for international applicants. Interview not required. Accepts a few transfer applicants on space available basis only. Apply to Admissions Committee of School after October 1, before February 1. Fall admission only. Application fee $45. Phone: (608)262-5914.

ADMISSION REQUIREMENTS FOR TRANSFER APPLICANTS. Accepts transfers from other ABA-accredited schools. Admission limited to space available. At least one year of enrollment, Dean's letter indicating the applicant is in good standing, prefer applicants in the top 15% of first-year class, LSAT, LSDAS, personal statement regarding reason for transfer, undergraduate transcript, current law school transcript required in support of

School's application. Apply to Admission Office by July 1 (Fall). Preference given to Wisconsin residents. Admission decision made within one month of receipt of application. Application fee $45. Will consider visiting students.

ADMISSION REQUIREMENTS FOR LL.M., S.J.D. APPLICANTS. For LL.M.: all applicants must hold a J.D. or equivalent law degree. Official transcripts, three letters of recommendations, a plan of work (at least four double-spaced, typed pages, including a statement of objective, outline of proposed research and explanation of course/seminar needs), consent of a faculty member of the law school to act as the principal academic adviser required in support of LL.M. application. In addition, holders of law degrees from foreign countries must submit proof of completion of all academic work necessary for entering a law profession in the applicant's home country; TOEFL (minimum score 625) required for all international applicant whose native language is other than English. Apply by March 1 (Fall), October 1 (Spring) to Committee on Academic Program. Application fee $45. Phone: (608)262-9120.

For S.J.D.: all applicants must hold a J.D. or the equivalent law degree and usually a LL.M. from the University of Wisconsin. Official transcript, three letters of recommendation, LL.M. thesis or equivalent project, at least six double-spaced, typed pages outlining objective, methodology, required materials and timetable, consent of a faculty member of the law school faculty to act as the principal academic adviser required in support of S.J.D. application. In addition, holders of law degrees from foreign countries must submit proof of completion of all academic work necessary for entering the law profession in the applicant's home country; TOEFL (minimum score 625) required for all international applicant whose native language is other than English. Apply by March 1 (Fall), October 1 (Spring) to Committee on Graduate Program. Application fee $45. Phone: (608)262-9120.

ADMISSION STANDARDS. Selective. Accepts approximately 24% of all students. Number of applicants 3157; number of acceptance 743; number enrolled 270; LSAT (75% of students have a score at or above 158); GPA (75% of students have a GPA at or above 3.30). *U.S. News & World Report* ranking is in the top 31 of all U.S. law schools.

FINANCIAL AID. For J.D. program: scholarships, Federal W/S, loans. Apply by February 1 to Financial Aid Office. Phone: (608) 262-5914. Use FAFSA (School code: 003895). For graduate study: scholarships, research fellowships, teaching assistantships. Apply by March 1 to the Dean (attention: Research Committee). About 26% of students receive aid other than loans from School.

DEGREE REQUIREMENTS. For J.D.: 90-credit-hour program, at least final 30 credits in residence. For LL.M.: at least 24 credits beyond the J.D.; one year in residence; thesis/research project. For S.J.D.: one year minimum in residence; thesis. For master's and doctoral degrees: see Graduate School listing above.

School of Medicine and Public Health
Room #2138 HSLC
Web site: www.med.wisc.edu

Initiated a two-year program in 1907, expanded to four-years in 1924. Located at Health Science Learning Center. Special facilities: Biotechnology Center, Cardiovascular Research Center, Center for Global Health, Center for Neuroscience, Center for Tobacco Research and Intervention, Clinical Nutrition Center, Environmental Toxicology Center, Eye Research Institute, General Clinical Research Center, Institute on Aging, Population Health Institute, Primate Research Center, UW Comprehensive Cancer Center, Waisman Center on Mental Retardation and Human Development. NIH ranking is 20th among all U.S. institutions with 670 awards/grants worth $257,144,598. Library: 336,000 volumes, 3500 subscriptions.

Annual tuition: resident $22,264, nonresident $33,388. On-campus rooms and apartments available for both single and married students. Contact Assignments Office for both on- and off-campus housing information. Phone: (608)262-2522. Medical students tend to live off-campus. Off-campus annual housing and personal expenses: between $14,000 and $17,000.

Enrollment: first-year class 163, total 618 (men 48%, women 52%, minorities 18%, state residents 84%). Faculty: full-time 1031, part-time 190. Degrees conferred: M.D., M.D.-M.P.H., M.D.-M.S., M.D.-Ph.D. (M.S.T.P.).

ADMISSION REQUIREMENTS. Preference given to state residents, U.S. citizens, and permanent residents who have taken all their undergraduate work at an accredited U.S. or Canadian institution. Bachelor's degree from an accredited institution required. Has EDP for state residents only; applicants must apply through AMCAS (official transcripts sent by mid-May) between June 1 and August 1. Early applications are encouraged. Submit secondary/supplemental application, a personal statement, three recommendations to Office of Admission within two weeks of receipt of application. Interviews are by invitation only and generally for final selection. Notification normally begins October 15. All other applicants apply through AMCAS (file after June 1, before November 1), submit MCAT scores (will accept MCAT test results from the last three years), official transcripts for each school attended (should show at least 90 semester credits/135 quarter credits; submit transcripts by mid-May to AMCAS), service processing fee. Preference given to state residents. Submit an application fee of $45, a supplemental application, a personal statement, pre-professional committee evaluation, and three recommendations from science faculty to the Admission Committee within two to three weeks of receipt of supplemental materials, but no later than December 1. Interviews are by invitation only and generally for final selection. Accepts transfer applicants on a space available basis only. In addition, M.D.-Ph.D. integrated degree applicants must submit a supplemental application and there is a separate interview by invitation. GRE is required for fellowship consideration. Contact the Admissions Office or Student Services Coordinator for current information and any additional admissions requirements; phone: (608)265-6344; fax: (608)263-4925. First-year students admitted Fall only. Rolling admissions process, notification starts November 15 and is finished when class is filled.

ADMISSION STANDARDS. Very competitive for nonresidents, selective for residents. Accepts about 9% of all applicants. Number of applications 2602 (1965 out-of-state); number interviewed 630 (128 out-of-state); number of acceptance 277 (80 out-of-state); number enrolled 163 (24 out-of-state). Mean Composite MCAT 10.4, mean UGPA 3.74. *U.S. New & World Report* ranking is in the top 9 (research) and in the top 27 (primary care) of all U.S. medical schools.

FINANCIAL AID. Service Commitment Scholarship Program, grants, institutional loans, HEAL, alternative loan programs, NIH stipends, loans available. Assistantships/fellowships/stipends may be available for M.D.-Ph.D. degree candidates. Financial aid applications and information are generally available at the on-campus, by-invitation interview. All financial aid is based on proven need and generally is in the form of long-term loan programs. Apply by March 1. Contact the Financial Aid Office for current information. Phone: (608)262-3060. Use FAFSA (School code: 003895), also submit Financial Aid Transcript, Federal Income Tax forms. Approximately 85% of students receive some form of financial assistance.

DEGREE REQUIREMENTS. For M.D.: satisfactory completion of four-year program; all students must pass USMLE Step 1 prior to entering third year and must pass USMLE Step 2 prior to awarding of M.D. For M.D.-M.S.: generally a four-and-one-half-to five-and-one-half-year program. For M.D.-Ph.D.: generally a seven-year program.

FIELDS OF GRADUATE STUDY.
Biomolecular Chemistry.
Cellular and Molecular Biology.
Genetic Counseling. M.S.
History of Medicine.
Medical Genetics.
Medical Physics.
Microbiology.
Neuroscience.
Oncology.
Pathology and Laboratory Medicine.
Physiology.
Population Health Sciences. Includes Preventive Medicine.
Public Health. M.P.H.

College of Veterinary Medicine (53706-1102)
Web site: www.vetmed.wisc.edu

Founded 1983. Semester system. Special facility: Environmental Toxicology Center.

Annual tuition: residents $16,470, nonresidents $24,540. On-campus housing available. Estimated living expenses: $7910. Total all other expenses: $5720.

Enrollment: first-year class 103, total 420 (men 28%, women 72%, minorities 5%, residents 75%), 55 graduate students. Faculty: full- and part-time 80. Degrees conferred: D.V.M., D.V.M.-M.S., D.V.M.-Ph.D.

ADMISSION REQUIREMENTS. VMCAS report (nonresident), transcripts, GRE, 60 undergraduate credits minimum, three evaluation/recommendations, animal/veterinary experience support of application. Supplemental application required. Preference given to state residents. Accepts transfer applicants on a space-available basis only. Apply to Office of Academic Affairs after June 1, before October 1. Application fee $45. Phone: (608) 263-2525.

ADMISSION STANDARDS. Competitive. Accepts about 10–15% of all applicants. Number of applications 1145 (978 out-of-state); number interviewed n/a (n/a out-of-state); number of acceptance n/a (n/a out-of-state); number enrolled 80 (n/a out-of-state). Usual minimum UGPA: 2.80 (A = 4). GRE mean score (V + Q) 1211 resident, 1292 nonresident; mean UGPA 3.55 resident, 3.65 nonresident.

FINANCIAL AID. Scholarships, assistantships, Federal W/S, loans. Apply to Director of Student Financial Aid. Use FAFSA.

DEGREE REQUIREMENTS. For D.V.M.: satisfactory completion of four-year program. For joint degree programs: see Graduate School listing above.

FIELDS OF GRADUATE STUDY.
Cell and Molecular Biology.
Genomics.
Infectious Disease.
Immunology.
Neuroscience.
Oncology.
Pharmacology & Toxicology.
Physiology.

UNIVERSITY OF WISCONSIN—MILWAUKEE
Milwaukee, Wisconsin 53201-0340
Web site: www.uwm.edu

Founded 1956. CGS member. Coed. State control. Semester system. Special facilities; Center for Architecture and Urban Planning Research, Center for Business Competitiveness, Center for Great Lakes Studies/Great Lakes Research Facility, Center for Latin American, Center for Nursing Research and Evaluation, Center for 21st Century Studies, Field Station, Great Lakes Water Institute, Institute on Race and Ethnicity, Laboratory for Surface Studies, Management Research Center, Marine and Freshwater Biomedical Sciences Center, Center for Urban Initiatives and Research, Center for Urban Transportation Studies, Urban Research Center, Center for Women's Studies. Library: 1,300,000 volumes, 10,000 subscriptions. Total University enrollment: 27,500.

Annual tuition: full-time resident $9116, nonresident $23,482; per credit resident $585, nonresident $1483. Limited on-campus housing available for single students. Average academic year housing costs: $5200–$7600. Contact Director of Residence Life for both on- and off-campus housing information. Phone: (800)622-0287, (414)229-4065. Day-care facilities available.

Graduate School
Web site: www.uwm.edu/Dept/Grad_Sch

Graduate study since 1965. Enrollment: full-time 2000, part-time 2072. Faculty: full-time 735. Degrees conferred: M.A., M.S., M.Arch., M.B.A., M.F.A., M.I.L.R., M.M., M.L.I.S., M.P.A., M.S.W., M.U.P., Ph.D.

ADMISSION REQUIREMENTS. Official transcripts required in support of School's application. Online application available. GRE/GMAT/MAT recommended. Interview required for some programs. TOEFL required for international applicants. Accepts transfer applicants. Graduates of unaccredited institutions not considered. Apply to Graduate School by January 1 (Fall and Summer), September 1 (Spring). Rolling admission process. Application fee domestic $45, international applicants $75. Phone: (414) 229-4982; e-mail: gradschool@uwm.edu.

ADMISSION STANDARDS. Selective. Usual minimum average: 2.75 (A = 4).

FINANCIAL AID. Scholarships, fellowships, teaching assistantships, research assistantships, teaching assistantships, internships, tuition waivers, Federal W/S, loans. Approved for VA benefits. Apply by mid-January to the Graduate School Fellowship Office for fellowships; to appropriate department for assistantships; to Financial Aid Office by April 15 for all other programs. Phone: (414)229-4541; fax: (414)229-5689. Use FAFSA. Aid available for part-time students.

DEGREE REQUIREMENTS. For master's: 24-48 semester hours; thesis/nonthesis option for many majors; final written/oral exam for some majors. For Ph.D.: 54 credits minimum beyond the bachelor's; foreign language or research skill for most programs; dissertation; final oral defense.

FIELDS OF STUDY.
Administrative Leadership and Supervision in Education. M.S.
Anthropology. M.S., Ph.D.
Architecture. M.Arch., Ph.D.
Art. M.A., M.F.A.
Art Education. M.S.
Art History. M.A.
Biological Sciences. M.S., Ph.D.
Business Administration. M.B.A., E.M.B.A.
Chemistry. M.S., Ph.D.
Clinical Laboratory Sciences. M.S.
Communication. M.A., Ph.D.
Communications Sciences and Disorders. M.S.
Computer Science. M.S. Ph.D. offered through Engineering Department.
Criminal Justice. M.S.
Cultural Foundations of Education. M.S.
Curriculum and Instruction. M.S.

Economics. M.A., Ph.D.
Educational Psychology. M.S., Ph.D.
Engineering. M.S., Ph.D.
English. M.A., Ph.D.
Exceptional Education. M.S.
Foreign Language and Literature. M.A.
Geography. M.A., M.S., Ph.D.
Geosciences. M.S., Ph.D.
Health Care Informatics. M.S.
Health Sciences. Ph.D.
History. M.A.
Human Resources and Labor Relations. M.H.R.L.R.
Information Studies. Ph.D.
Kinesiology. M.L.S.
Liberal Studies. M.L.S.
Library and Information Science. M.L.I.S.
Management Science. Ph.D.
Mass Communication. M.A.
Mathematics. M.S., Ph.D.
Medical Informatics. Ph.D.
Music. M.M.
Nonprofit Management and Leadership. M.S.
Nursing. M.S., Ph.D.
Occupational Therapy. M.S.
Performing Arts. Includes dance, film, and theater. M.F.A.
Philosophy. M.A.
Physics. M.S., Ph.D.
Political Science. M.A., Ph.D.
Psychology. M.S., Ph.D.
Public Administration. M.P.A.
Social Work. M.S.W., Ph.D.
Sociology. M.A.
Urban Education. Ph.D.
Urban Planning. M.U.P.
Urban Studies. M.S., Ph.D.

UNIVERSITY OF WISCONSIN— OSHKOSH

Oshkosh, Wisconsin 54901-3551
Web site: www.uwosh.edu

Established 1871. Located 85 miles NW of Milwaukee. Coed. State control. Semester system. Library: 446,700 volumes, 5219 subscriptions.

Annual tuition/fees: full-time resident and Minnesota reciprocity $6924, $9638 (Business); nonresident $17,534, $20,274 (Business). On-campus housing for 50 graduate men, 50 graduate women; none for married students. Average academic year housing costs: $2570 (single room, two semesters). Apply to Director of Residence Life for both on- and off-campus housing information. Phone: (920)424-3212. Day-care facilities available.

Graduate School

Established 1963. Enrollment: full-time 190, part-time 1012 (men 35%, women 65%). University faculty teaching graduate students: full-time 245, part-time 17. Degrees conferred: M.S., M.S.N., M.S.Ed., M.B.A., M.P.A.

ADMISSION REQUIREMENTS. Official transcripts required in support of School's application. GMAT or GRE, interview required by some programs. Online application available. TOEFL required for international applicants. Accepts transfer applicants. Graduates of unaccredited institutions not considered. Apply to Dean of Graduate School at least three months prior to registration. International applicants at least 6 months prior to registration. Application fee domestic $45, international $75. Phone: (920) 424-1223; fax: (920)424-7317; e-mail: gradschool@uwosh.edu.

ADMISSION STANDARDS. Selective. Usual minimum average: 2.75 (A = 4). Some programs require 3.0 minimum.

FINANCIAL AID. Annual awards from institutional funds: academic scholarships, assistantships, advanced opportunity grants to minority students, internships, Federal W/S, loans. Approved for VA benefits. Apply by March 15 to Financial Aid Office. Phone: (920)424-3377. Use FAFSA. About 20% of students receive aid other than loans from University and outside sources. Aid sometimes available to part-time students.

DEGREE REQUIREMENTS. For master's: 30-48 semester hours minimum, at least 21 in residence; admission to candidacy; thesis/research paper; comprehensive oral/written exam.

FIELDS OF STUDY.
Biology/Microbiology. GRE for admission. M.S.
Business Administration. GMAT for admission. M.B.A.
Counselor Education. M.S.Ed.
Curriculum and Instruction. M.S.Ed.
Educational Leadership and Policy Analysis. Cooperative Program with University of Wisconsin, Madison. M.S.
Educational Leadership. M.S.
Elementary Education. M.S.Ed.
English. M.A.
Global Business Administration. G.M.B.A.
Information Systems. M.S.
Mathematics Education. M.S.
Nursing. M.S.N.
Physics. M.S.
Psychology. GRE for admission. Includes experimental, industrial/organizational. M.S.
Public Administration. M.P.A.
Reading. M.S.Ed.
Social Work. M.S.W.
Special Education. M.S.Ed.

UNIVERSITY OF WISCONSIN— PLATTEVILLE

Platteville, Wisconsin 53818-3099
Web site: www.uwplatt.edu

Founded 1866. Located 70 miles SW of Madison. Coed. State control. Semester system. Library: 422,000 volumes, 2100 subscriptions. Total University enrollment: 6400.

Annual tuition: full-time resident $6160, Minnesota resident $6548, nonresident $19,770; per credit resident $342, Minnesota resident $363, nonresident $931. On-campus housing for single graduate students. Average academic year housing costs: $2792 (room only). Average summer housing cost: $350–$450. Contact Director of Student Housing for both on- and off-campus housing information. Phone: (608)342-1845; e-mail: egley@uwplatt.edu. Day-care facilities available.

School of Graduate Studies

Graduate study since 1957. Enrollment: full-time 1021, part-time 386. Graduate faculty: full-time 5, part-time 90. Degrees conferred: M.S., M.S.Ed.

ADMISSION REQUIREMENTS. Official transcripts required in support of School's application. Online application available. TOEFL required for international applicants. Interview not required. Accepts transfer students. Apply to the School of Graduate Studies by July 1 (Fall), November 1 (Spring). Application fee $45. Phone: (800)362-5515, (608)342-1125; fax: (608)342-1122; E-mail: admit@uwplatt.edu.

ADMISSION STANDARDS. Selective. Usual minimum average: 2.75; 2.9 for last 60 credits (A = 4).

FINANCIAL AID. Assistantships, internships, grants, Federal W/S, loans. Approved for VA benefits. Apply by July 1 to Dean of the School of Graduate Studies. Phone: (608)342-1836; fax: (608)342-1122. Use FAFSA. About 20% of students receive aid other than loans from all sources. Aid available for part-time students.

DEGREE REQUIREMENTS. For master's: 30-36 semester hours minimum, at least 24 residence; thesis; oral exam/research paper; comprehensive exam.

FIELDS OF STUDY.
Adult Education. M.S.Ed.
Computer Science. M.S.
Counselor Education. M.S.Ed.
Elementary Education. M.S.Ed.
Industrial Technology Management. M.S
Middle School Education. M.S.Ed.
Secondary Education. M.S.Ed.
Vocational-Technical Education. M.S.Ed.

UNIVERSITY OF WISCONSIN— RIVER FALLS

River Falls, Wisconsin 54022-5013
Web site: www.uwrf.edu

Founded 1874. Located 30 miles SE of St. Paul, Minnesota. CGS member. Coed. State control. Semester system. Library: 448,000 volumes, 1660 subscriptions.

Annual tuition: full-time resident $7022, Minnesota resident $7408, nonresident $17,600; per credit resident $443, Minnesota resident $465, nonresident $1033. On-campus housing for single students, limited number of married students. Average annual housing cost: $3800 for single students. Apply to Housing Director. Day-care facilities available.

Outreach and Graduate Studies

Graduate study since 1962. Enrollment: full-time 142, part-time 205 (men 35%, women 65%). University faculty: full-time 243, part-time 5. Degrees conferred: M.S.Ed., M.M., M.S.

ADMISSION REQUIREMENTS. Official transcripts, bachelor's degree in support of application. Some programs require interview and letters of recommendation. GRE or MAT for counseling program. TOEFL required for international students. Accepts transfer students. Apply to the Office of Graduate study; deadlines vary by department. Application fee $45. Phone: (715)425-3843; fax: (715)425-3185.

ADMISSION STANDARDS. Relatively open. Minimum average: 2.75 (A = 4).

FINANCIAL AID. Annual awards from institutional funds: assistantships, internships, Federal W/S, loans. Approved for VA benefits. Apply to Dean of Graduate School. Phone: (715)425-3141. Use FAFSA (School code: 003923). Aid available for part-time students. About 40% of students receive aid from University and outside sources.

DEGREE REQUIREMENTS. For master's: 30-40 credit hours minimum (no more than 9 credits in transfer); thesis/final document; final oral/written exam.

FIELDS OF STUDY.
Agriculture Education. M.S.
Communicative Disorders. M.S.Ed., M.S.
Counseling. M.S.Ed.
Elementary Education. M.S.Ed.
Fine Arts. M.S.Ed.
Language, Communication, and Literature. M.S.Ed.
Management. M.M.
Mathematics. M.S.Ed.
Professional Development. M.S.Ed.
Reading. M.S.Ed.
School Psychology. M.S.Ed., Ed.S.
Science. M.S.Ed.
Social Science. M.S.Ed.

UNIVERSITY OF WISCONSIN— STEVENS POINT

Stevens Point, Wisconsin 54481-3897
Web site: www.uwsp.edu

Founded 1894. Coed. State control. Semester system. Special facilities: Center Wisconsin Environmental Field Station, Forest and Wildlife Research Station, Planetarium, Museum of Natural History. Library: 362,500 volumes, 1800 subscriptions. Total University enrollment: 8600.

Annual tuition: full-time resident $7022, Minnesota resident $7408, nonresident $17,600; per credit resident $443, Minnesota resident $465, nonresident $1033. On-campus housing for single students only. Average academic year housing costs: $4322 (including board). Contact Director of Student Housing for both on-and off-campus housing information. Phone: (715)346-3511. Day-care facilities available.

Graduate Studies

Enrollment: full-time 96, part-time 106. Full-time faculty teaching graduate students: 20. Degrees conferred: M.A., M.B.A., M.M., M.S.T., M.S., M.S.E., M.M.Ed.

ADMISSION REQUIREMENTS. Official transcripts, GRE required in support of application. TOEFL required for international applicants. Accepts transfer applicants. Graduates of unaccredited institutions not considered. Apply to Director of Admissions by May 1 (Fall), November 15 (Spring). Some graduate programs have earlier deadlines and may require additional application materials. Rolling admissions process. Application fee $45. Phone: (715)346-2441.

ADMISSION STANDARDS. Selective. Usual minimum average: 2.75 (A = 4). Individual graduate programs may require a higher G.P.A.

FINANCIAL AID. Research assistantships, graduate assistantships, internships, Federal W/S, loans. Approved for VA benefits. Apply May 1 to Dean of Graduate School for assistantships; to Director of Financial Aid for all other programs. Phone: (715) 346-4771. Use FAFSA. Aid sometimes available for part-time students.

DEGREE REQUIREMENTS. For master's: 30–36 credits minimum, including culminating experience, at least 24–30 in residence; admission to candidacy; thesis/nonthesis option; final written/oral exam for some programs.

FIELDS OF STUDY.
Audiology. Joint programs with University of Wisconsin, Madison. Au.D.
Business Administration. Cooperative program with University of Wisconsin, Oshkosh. M.B.A.

Communication. M.A.
Communicative Disorders. Includes speech-language pathology. M.S.
Education. M.S.Ed.
Educational Administration. Cooperative program with University of Wisconsin, Superior. M.S.Ed.
Elementary Education. M.S.Ed.
Guidance and Counseling. Cooperative program with University of Wisconsin, Oshkosh. M.S. Ed.
Human and Community Resources. M.S.
Music Education. M.M.Ed.
Natural Resources. M.S.
Nutritional Sciences. M.S.
Teaching. Includes biology, English, history, reading. M.S.

UNIVERSITY OF WISCONSIN—STOUT
Menomonie, Wisconsin 54751
Web site: www.uwstout.edu

Chartered 1893. Located 60 miles E of St. Paul. State control. Semester system. Special facilities: Design Research Center, Manufacturing Technology Transfer Center, Center for Innovation and Development, Center for Excellence in Advanced Technology, Center for Vocational, Technological and Adult Education, Center for Excellence in Tourism, Food and Tourism Industries, Social Science Research Center. Library: 229,900 volumes, 1600 subscriptions. Total University enrollment: 7900.

Tuition: per credit resident $331.62, Minnesota resident $308.35, nonresident $553. Off-campus housing only. Average academic year room and board costs: $5400 for married students, $4220 for single students. Contact Stout Student Affairs Office. Phone: (715)232-2100. Day-care facilities available.

Graduate School

Graduate study since 1935. Enrollment: full-time 303, part-time 262. Graduate faculty: full-time 194, part-time 0. Degrees conferred: M.S., M.S. Ed., Ed.S.

ADMISSION REQUIREMENTS. Official transcripts required in support of College's application. GRE required for Applied Psychology. Interview required for some programs. TOEFL required for international applicants. Accepts transfer applicants. Apply to Graduate Student Evaluator at least one month prior of registration. Application fee $45. Phone: (715)232-1322; fax: (715)232-2413.

ADMISSION STANDARDS. Selective in some departments, relatively open in others. Usual minimum average: 2.5 (A = 4).

FINANCIAL AID. Annual awards from institutional funds: scholarships, teaching/research assistantships, grants, tuition waivers, Federal W/S, loans. Approved for VA benefits. Apply by April 1 to Financial Aid Director. Phone: (715)232-1363; fax: (715)232-5246. Use FAFSA. About 50% of students receive aid other than loans from University and outside sources. Aid available for part-time students.

DEGREE REQUIREMENTS. For master's: 30–48 semester hours minimum, at least 6 in residence; thesis or final paper. For Ed.S.: 36 semester hours beyond the master's.

FIELDS OF STUDY.
Applied Psychology. Includes health psychology, industrial/organizational psychology, program evaluation. M.S.
Career and Technical Education. Includes administration, marketing education, local vocational education coordinator, special needs, teaching. M.S., Ed.S.

Education.
Family Studies and Human Development. M.S.
Food and Nutrition Sciences. Includes food science and technology, human nutritional science, food and nutrition management and marketing. M.S.
Home Economics. Include apparel, design manufacturing and retailing, early childhood, family and consumer education, family studies and human development. M.S.
Hospitality and Tourism. Includes global hospitality management (Online degree program). M.S.
Industrial Technology Education. M.S.
Information and Communication Technologies. M.S.
Manufacturing Engineering. M.S.
Marriage and Family Therapy. M.S.
Mental Health Counseling. Includes community mental health/agency counseling, clinical mental health counseling, alcohol and other drug abuse counseling, career counseling, child and adolescent counseling, eating disorders, gerontological counseling, health psychology counseling, M.S.
Risk Control. M.S.
School Counseling. M.S.
School Psychology. M.S.Ed., Ed.S.
Technology Management. Program is administered by Indiana State University and is offered through a consortium of seven universities across the U.S. Ph.D.
Training and Development. M.S.
Vocational Rehabilitation. Includes rehabilitation facility administration, rehabilitation counseling, school to work transition, vocation evaluation. M.S.
Vocational Rehabilitation.

UNIVERSITY OF WISCONSIN—SUPERIOR
Superior, Wisconsin 54880-2873
Web site: www.uwsuper.edu

Founded 1893. CGS member. Coed. State control. Semester system. Special facilities: Halden Fine and Applied Arts Center, Lake Superior Research Institute. Library: 285,000 volumes, 1600 subscriptions. Total University enrollment: 2800.

Annual tuition: full-time resident $7098, Minnesota resident $7486, nonresident $17,708; per credit resident $519, Minnesota resident $541, nonresident $1109. On-campus housing for single students only. Average academic year housing costs: $4576 (including board). Off-campus housing costs; $400–$600. Contact Resident Life Center for both on- and off-campus housing information. Phone: (715)394-8438. Day-care facilities available.

Graduate Division

Established 1949. Enrollment: full-time 99, part-time 277. University faculty: full-time 92; part-time 27. Degrees conferred: M.A., M.S.Ed., Ed.S.

ADMISSION REQUIREMENTS. Official transcripts required in support of application. GRE/GMAT required by some departments. Online application available. Interview required for Ed.S. program. TOEFL required for international applicants. Accepts transfer applicants. Apply to Dean of Graduate Division by April 1 (Fall), October 15 (Spring). Rolling admissions process. Application fee $45; $75 for international applicants. Phone: (715) 394-8295; fax: (715)394-8040.

ADMISSION STANDARDS. Selective. Usual minimum average: 2.5 (A = 4).

FINANCIAL AID. Annual awards from institutional funds: scholarships, assistantships, minority fellowships, internships, grants, tuition waivers, Federal W/S, loans. Apply by April 15 to Dean of Graduate Division for assistantships; to the Financial Aid Office for all other programs. Phone: (715)394-8200. Use FAFSA (School code: 003925). About 25% of students receive aid other than loans from School and outside sources. Aid available for part-time students.

DEGREE REQUIREMENTS. For M.A., M.S.Ed.: 30–36 credits minimum, at least 24 in residence; MAT for candidacy; thesis/final project; final written/oral exam. For Ed.S.: 30 credits minimum beyond the master's, final written/oral exams; internship may be required.

FIELDS OF STUDY.
Communicating Arts. M.A.
Counseling. Includes community, human relations, school. M.S.Ed.
Educational Administration. M.S.Ed., Ed.S.
Instruction. M.S.Ed.
Reading. M.S.Ed.
Special Education. M.S.Ed.
Visual Arts. M.A.

UNIVERSITY OF WISCONSIN—WHITEWATER

Whitewater, Wisconsin 53190-1790
Web site: www.uww.edu

Established 1868. Located 51 miles W of Milwaukee. CGS member. Coed. State control. Semester system. Library: 683,500 volumes, 2206 subscriptions. Total University enrollment: 10,750.

Annual tuition: full-time resident $6900, $7454 (Business), non-resident $17,510, $18,090 (Business); per credit resident $383.50, $414 (Business), nonresident $972, $1005 (Business). On-campus housing for single students only. Average academic year housing costs: $3600 (including board). Contact Office of Residential Life for both on- and off-campus housing information. Phone: (262) 472-1151. Day-care facilities available.

School of Graduate Studies

Enrollment: full- and part-time 1189. Faculty: 307. Degrees conferred: M.A.T., M.S.Ed., M.S., M.B.A., M.E.P.D., M.M.E.

ADMISSION REQUIREMENTS. Official transcripts required in support of School's application. Online application available. GMAT required for Business. TOEFL required for international applicants. Accepts transfer applicants. Graduates of unaccredited colleges not considered. Apply to School of Graduate Studies by July 15 (Fall), December 1 (Spring). Rolling admissions process. Application fee $45. Phone: (262)472-1006; fax: (262)472-5027.

ADMISSION STANDARDS. Relatively open. Usual minimum average: 2.5 (A = 4).

FINANCIAL AID. Assistantships, internships, fee waivers, Federal W/S, loans. Approved for VA benefits. Apply by March 15 to Dean, School of Graduate Studies, for assistantships; to the Financial Aid Office for all other programs. Use FAFSA. Aid available for part-time students.

DEGREE REQUIREMENTS. For all master's: 30–36 semester hours minimum; thesis/nonthesis option; internships for some programs; final written or oral comprehensive exam option.

FIELDS OF STUDY.

COLLEGE OF ARTS AND COMMUNICATION:
Communication. M.S.

COLLEGE OF BUSINESS AND ECONOMICS:
Accounting. M.P.A.
Business Administration. Includes accounting, decision support systems, finance management, managerial economics, marketing, international business. M.B.A.
Business and Marketing Education. M.S.
Computer Information Systems. M.S.
School Business Management. M.S.E.

COLLEGE OF EDUCATION:
Communicative Disorders. M.S.
Counseling. M.S.
Curriculum and Instruction. Includes art education, early childhood, gifted and talented, reading. M.S.
Educational Leadership and Policy Analysis. M.S.
Reading. M.S.E.
Safety. Includes occupational, school, traffic. M.S.
Special Education. Includes MR, EM, learning disabilities, early childhood, severely, profoundly handicapped, transitional needs; M.S.E.

COLLEGE OF LETTERS AND SCIENCE:
Public Administration.
School Psychology. M.S.E.

WORCESTER POLYTECHNIC INSTITUTE

Worcester, Massachusetts 01609-2247
Web site: www.wpi.edu

Founded 1865. Located 35 miles W of Boston. CGS member. Coed. Private control. Semester system. Special facilities: Alden Research Laboratories (fluid mechanics), Aluminum Casting Research Laboratory, Applied Bioengineering Center, Computational Electromagnetics and Ultrasonics Systems Design and Development, Center for Crystal Growth in Space, Center for Holographic Studies and Laser Technology, Catalytic Sciences Laboratory, Electron Microscopy Laboratory, Center for Inorganic Membrane Studies, Center for Intelligent Processing of Materials, Magnetic Imaging Center, Manufacturing Engineering Application Center, Nuclear Reactor (pool type), Powder Metallurgy Center, computation facility, Van de Graaff accelerator, Center for Wireless Information Networks Studies. Library: 340,500 volumes, 2700 subscriptions. Total Institute enrollment: 3900.

Tuition: per credit hour $977. No on-campus housing for single or married graduate students. Contact Residential Services Office for off-campus housing information. Phone: (508)831-5645.

Graduate Program

Enrollment: full-time 467, part-time 370. Graduate faculty: full-time 189, part-time 50. Degrees conferred: M.B.A., M.Eng., M.S., Ph.D.

ADMISSION REQUIREMENTS. Official transcripts, GRE/GMAT (for some departments), three letters of recommendation required in support of application. Online application available. GRE recommended. Interview not required. TOEFL required for international applicants. Accepts transfer applicants. Graduates of unaccredited institutions not considered. Apply by March 1 to Office of Graduate Studies and Enrollment. Application fee $70. Phone: (508)831-5301; fax: (508)831-5717; e-mail: gao@wpi.edu.

ADMISSION STANDARDS. Selective for most departments. Usual minimum average: 3.0 (A = 4).

FINANCIAL AID. Annual awards from institutional funds: fellowships, scholarships, teaching assistantships, assistantships, internships, grants, tuition waivers, loans. Approved for VA benefits. Apply by February 1 (for priority consideration) to Office of Graduate Admissions. Phone: (508)831-5469; fax: (508)831-5743. Use FAFSA and institutional FAF. About 47% of full-time students receive aid other than loans from Institute and outside sources.

DEGREE REQUIREMENTS. For M S., M.Eng.: 30–36 credit hours minimum, at least 20 in residence; thesis/nonthesis option. For M.B.A.: 45 credits, minimum, at least 30 in residence; computer proficiency. For Ph.D. minimum of three years or about 90 credits beyond the bachelor's, at least 30 credits of research; one year in full-time residence; dissertation; final oral exam.

FIELDS OF STUDY.
Applied Mathematics. M.S.
Applied Statistics. M.S.
Biochemistry. M.S.
Biology and Biotechnology. M.S.
Biomedical Engineering. M.E., M.S., Ph.D.
Biotechnology. Ph.D.
Chemical Engineering. M.S., Ph.D.
Chemistry. M.S., Ph.D.
Civil Engineering. M.E., M.S., Ph.D.
Clinical Engineering. M.E.
Computer Science. M.S., Ph.D.
Construction Project Management. M.S.
Electrical Engineering. M.S., Ph.D.
Environmental Engineering. M.S., Ph.D.
Financial Mathematics. M.S.
Fire Protection Engineering. M.S., Ph.D.
Impact Engineering. Interdisciplinary. M.S.
Industrial Mathematics. M.S.
Information Technology. M.S.
Manufacturing Engineering. M.S., Ph.D.
Manufacturing Engineering Management. Interdisciplinary. M.S.
Marketing and Technological Innovation. M.S.
Materials Process Engineering. M.S.
Materials Science and Engineering. M.S., Ph.D.
Mathematical Sciences. Ph.D.
Mathematics for Educator. M.M.E.
Mechanical Engineering. M.S., Ph.D.
Operations Design and Leadership. M.S.
Physics. M.S., Ph.D.
Power Systems Management. Interdisciplinary. M.S.
Social Science. Interdisciplinary. Ph.D.
Systems Dynamics. M.S.
Systems Engineering. Interdisciplinary. M.S.
System Modeling. Interdisciplinary. M.S.
Technology M.B.A. Includes concentration entrepreneurship, information security management, information technology, operations management, process design, supply chain management, technological innovation, technology marketing. M.B.A.

WORCESTER STATE COLLEGE
Worcester, Massachusetts 01602-2597
Web site: www.worcester.edu

Founded 1874. Located 30 miles W of Boston. Coed. State control. Semester system. Special facilities: Center for Effective Instruction, Center for Health Professions, Center for the Study of Human Rights, Center for Business and Industry, Latino Education Institute, Intergenerational Urban Institute. Library: 150,000 volumes, 1000 subscriptions. Total College enrollment: 5500.
Tuition: per credit, $150. No on-campus housing available.

Graduate School

Graduate study since 1947. Enrollment: full- and part-time 870. Faculty: full-time 43, part-time 26. Degrees conferred: M.S., M.Ed., Certification Programs.

ADMISSION REQUIREMENTS. Transcripts, two letters of recommendation, GRE or MAT, interview required in support of application. TOEFL required for international applicants. Accepts transfer applicants. Graduates of unaccredited institutions not considered. Apply to Admissions Office at least one month prior to projected date of entrance, except for Speech-Language Pathology and Occupational Therapy (contact department for deadlines). Application fee $30 state residents, $40 for nonresidents. Phone: (508)793-8120; fax (508)793-8100.

ADMISSION STANDARDS. Selective. Usual minimum average: 2.75 (A = 4).

FINANCIAL AID. Assistantships, internships, grants, Federal W/S, Federal and private loans. Approved for VA benefits. Apply to Financial Aid Office; no specified closing date. Phone: (508) 793-8056; fax: (508)793-8194. Use FAFSA.

DEGREE REQUIREMENTS. For master's: 33–36 semester hours minimum, at least 24 in residence; final written/oral exam.

FIELDS OF STUDY.
Biotechnology. M.S.
Community Health Nursing. M.S.
Early Childhood Education. M.Ed.
Elementary Education. M.Ed.
English. M.Ed.
History. M.Ed.
Health Education. M.Ed.
Health-Care Administration. M.S.
Human Services Management. MS.
Leadership and Administration. M.Ed.
Management. M.S.
Middle School Education. M.Ed.
Moderate Special Needs. M.Ed.
Nonprofit Management. M.S.
Occupational Therapy. M.S.
Reading. M.Ed.
Spanish. M.Ed.
Secondary Education. M.Ed.
Speech-Language Pathology. M.S.

WRIGHT STATE UNIVERSITY
Dayton, Ohio 45435
Web site: www.wright.edu

Became independent unit in 1967. CGS member. Coed. State control. Quarter system. Special facilities: Cox Institute, Center for Environmental Quality, Groundwater Management Center, NASA-Lewis Research Center, Intelligent Systems Applications Center, Kettering Research Laboratory, Center for Labor-Management Cooperation, Edison Materials Technology Center, Ohio Aerospace Institute, Center for Urban and Public Affairs. Library: 1,000,000 bound volumes, 5000 subscriptions. Total University enrollment: 15,400.
Tuition: full-time per quarter resident $3001, nonresident $5482; per quarter hour for less than 11.5 hours, resident $310, nonresident $507. On-campus housing available. Average academic year housing costs: $4400 (including board) for single students; $8500 for married students. Contact Office of Residence Services for both on- and off-campus housing information. Phone: (937)775-4172.

School of Graduate Studies
Web site: www.wright.edu/sogs

Graduate study since 1965. Enrollment: full- and part-time 3400. University faculty teaching graduate students: full-time

646, part-time 40. Degrees conferred: M.A., M.S., M.Ed., M.B.A., M.S.C.E., M.S.E., M.S.T., M.A.T., M.R.C., M.Hum., M.Mus., M.U.A., Ed.S., Psy.D., Ph.D.

ADMISSION REQUIREMENTS. Transcripts required in support of School's application. Online application available. TOEFL (minimum score 550), TSE required for international applicants. GRE required for M.S. in Economics, M.A. in Applied Behavioral Science, M.S.C.E. in computer engineering, M.S. in computer science, M.S. in human factors and industrial/organizational psychology, M.U.A. in urban administration and the Psy.D., Ph.D. programs. The GMAT is required for the M.B.A., M.Acc. GRE/MAT required for College of Education and Human Services programs. Accepts transfer applicants. Apply to Assistant Dean and Director of Graduate Admissions and Records at least one month prior to registration. Application fee $25. Phone: (937)775-2976; fax: (937)775-2453; e-mail: wsugrad@wright.edu.

ADMISSION STANDARDS. Selective. Usual minimum average: 2.7 (A = 4).

FINANCIAL AID. Annual awards from institutional funds: scholarships, research assistantships, teaching assistantships, graduate assistantships, internships, predoctoral and postdoctoral fellowships, Federal W/S, loans. Approved for VA benefits. Apply to School of Graduate Studies for assistantships, fellowships, internships; to Office of Financial Aid for all other programs. No specified closing date. Phone: (937)775-2321. Use FAFSA. About 50% of full-time students receive aid.

DEGREE REQUIREMENTS. For master's: 45 quarter hours minimum, at least 33 in residence; thesis for most M.A. and M.S. programs; comprehensive exam. For M.B.A.: 51 credit program. For Ph.D.: two-year minimum in residence beyond the master's; reading knowledge of one foreign language; written/oral exam; dissertation; final oral exam. For Psy.D.: essentially the same as for Ph.D., except a research tool in place of the one foreign language.

FIELDS OF STUDY.
Accountancy. M.Acc.
Aerospace Medicine. M.S.
Anatomy. M.S.
Applied Statistics. M.S.
Biochemistry and Molecular Biology. M.S.
Biological Sciences. Includes environmental sciences. M.S., Ph.D.
Business Administration. M.B.A.
Chemistry. M.S.
Classroom Teacher. M.A., M.Ed.
Computer Engineering. M.S.C.E.
Computer Science. M.S.
Computer Science and Engineering. Ph.D.
Criminal Justice and Social Problems. M.A.
Counseling. M.S., M.R.C., M.S.
Earth and Environmental Sciences. M.S.
Earth Science. M.S.T.
Educational Leadership. M.A., M.Ed.
Engineering. Includes biomedical, electrical, human factors, materials science and engineering, mechanical. M.S.Egr., Ph.D.
English. Literature, Composition and Rhetoric, TESOL. M.A.
Environmental Sciences. Ph.D.
History. M.A.
Human Factors and Industrial/Organizational Psychology. M.S.
Humanities. M.Hum.
Interdisciplinary Science and Mathematics. M.S.T.
International and Comparative Politics. M.A.
Logistics Management. Includes supply chain management. M.S.
Mathematics. Includes applied. M.S.
Microbiology and Immunology. M.S.
Music. Includes music education, performance. M.M.
Nursing. M.S.
Pharmacology and Toxicology. M.S.

Physics. Includes medical physics. M.S., M.S.T.
Physiology and Biophysics. M.S.
Psychology. M.S., Ph.D., Psy.D.
Public Administration. M.P.A.
Public Health. M.P.H.
Pupil Personnel Services. M.A., M.Ed.
Social and Applied Economics. M.S.

Boonshoft School of Medicine (P.O. Box 1751)
Web site: www.med.wright.edu

Established 1973. Quarter system. Special facilities: Comprehensive Neuroscience Center, Center for Genomics Research, Center for Global Health Systems, Management & Policy, Center for Healthy Communities, Homeland Emergency Learning & Preparedness Center, Center for Interventions, Treatment & Addictions Research, Lifespan Health Research Center. Library: 100,000 volumes, 1200 subscriptions.

Annual tuition: resident $24,834, nonresident $34,422. No on-campus housing available. Off-campus annual housing and personal expenses: between $10,000 and $12,000.

Enrollment: first-year class 100, total 402 (men 43%, women 57%, minorities 25%, state residents 90%). Faculty: full-time 333, part-time and volunteers 1251. Degrees conferred: M.D., M.D.-M.B.A., M.D.-M.P.H., M.D.-M.S., M.D.-Ph.D.

ADMISSION REQUIREMENTS. AMCAS report, transcripts, MCAT, recommendations required in support of application. Interview and supplementary application by invitation only. Preference given to state residents. Has EDP (Ohio residents only); apply between June 1 and August 1. Accepts transfer applicants. Apply to Office of Student Affairs/Admissions after June 1, before November 15. Application fee $40. Phone: (937)775-2934; fax: (937)775-3322.

ADMISSION STANDARDS. Selective. Accepts about 9% of all applicants. Number of applications 2710 (1760 out-of-state); number interviewed 541 (83 out-of-state); number of acceptance 225 (39 out-of-state); number enrolled 100 (14 out-of-state). Mean Composite MCAT 9.1, mean UGPA 3.57.

FINANCIAL AID. Limited scholarships, loans, grants. Apply after acceptance to Office of Student Affairs. Phone: (937)775-2934. Use FAFSA (School code: 003078). About 90% of students receive some aid from School.

DEGREE REQUIREMENTS: For M.D.: satisfactory completion of four-year program. For M.B.A., M.P.H., Ph.D.: see Graduate School listing above.

FIELDS OF GRADUATE STUDY.
Aerospace Medicine. M.S.
Anatomy. M.S.
Biochemistry and Molecular Biology. M.S.
Biomedical Sciences. Ph.D.
Environmental Sciences. Ph.D.
Microbiology and Immunology. M.S.
Pharmacology and Toxicology. M.S.
Physiology and Biophysics. M.S.
Public Health. M.P.H.

UNIVERSITY OF WYOMING
Laramie, Wyoming 82071-3108
Web site: www.uwyo.edu

Founded 1886. CGS member. State control. Semester system. Special facilities: American Heritage Center, Anthropology Museum, Center for Rural Health Research and Education, Elk

Mountain Observatory, Enhanced Oil Recovery Institute, Geological Museum, International Archive of Economic Geology, Institute of Business and Management Services, Mineral Research and Reclamation Center, National Park Service Research Center, Laramie Petroleum Research Center, Natural Resources Research Institute, Red Buttes Research Center, Rocky Mountain Herbarium, Small Business Development Center, Survey Research Center, Wyoming Geographic Information Science Center, Wyoming Statistical Analysis Center. Library: more than 1,000,000 volumes, 13,000 subscriptions; is a Federal Document Depository. Total University enrollment: 13,100.

Annual tuition: full-time resident $3720, nonresident $10,704; per credit, resident $155, nonresident $446. On-campus housing for 700 married students; limited for single graduate students. Average academic year housing costs: $4800 for married students, $6218 (including board) for single students. Contact Director of Housing for both on- and off-campus housing information. Phone: (307)766-3179. Day-care facilities available.

Graduate School

Web site: www.grad.uwyo.edu

Graduate study since 1897. Enrollment: full-time 817, part-time 917. University faculty teaching graduate students: full-time 500, part-time 52. Degrees conferred: M.A., M.S., M.A.E., M.A.T., M.M., M.S.E., M.S.T., M.B.A., M.P.A., M.F.A., M.P., I.M.A., I.M.S., Ed.S., Ed.D., Ph.D., Ph.D.E.

ADMISSION REQUIREMENTS. Transcripts, three letters of recommendation, GRE, GMAT (Business) required in support of School's application. Online application available. GRE Subject required by some departments. TOEFL (minimum score 525) required for international applicants. Interview generally not required. Accepts transfer applicants. Graduates of unaccredited institutions not considered. Apply to Admissions Office by June 1. Application fee $50. Phone: (307)766-2287; fax: (307)766-2374.

ADMISSION STANDARDS. Very selective for most departments, selective for the others. Usual minimum average: 3.0 (A = 4).

FINANCIAL AID. Annual awards from institutional funds: scholarships, grants, research fellowships, teaching assistantships, research assistantships, internships, traineeships, tuition waivers, Federal W/S, loans. Approved for VA benefits. Apply by February 15 to appropriate department chair for fellowships, assistantships; to Financial Aid Office for all other programs. Phone: (307)766-2116; fax: (307)766-3800. Use FAFSA. About 75% of students receive aid other than loans from School and outside sources. Aid available for part-time students.

DEGREE REQUIREMENTS. For master's: 30–52 semester hours minimum; thesis/nonthesis option in some departments; final oral/written exam. For Ed.S.: 30 hours minimum beyond the master's, at least two semesters in residence. For Ed.D.: three years minimum beyond the bachelor's, at least 78 semester hours residence including one and a half consecutive semesters; preliminary exam; final project; reading knowledge of one foreign language or competency in research tool often required; final oral/written exam. For Ph.D.: 72 semester hours minimum beyond the bachelor's, at least 18 semester hours in residence; preliminary exam; thesis; final oral/written exam.

FIELDS OF STUDY.

COLLEGE OF AGRICULTURE:
Agricultural Economics. M.S.
Agricultural Economics/Water Resources. Interdisciplinary. M.S.
Agronomy. M.S., Ph.D.
Animal and Veterinary Science. M.S., Ph.D.
Entomology. M.S., Ph.D.
Entomology/Water Resources. Interdisciplinary. M.S.

Family and Consumer Science. M.S. only.
Food Science and Human Nutrition. Interdisciplinary. M.S.
Molecular Biology. M.S., Ph.D.
Rangeland Ecology and Watershed Management. M.S., Ph.D.
Rangeland Ecology and Watershed Management/Water Resources. Interdisciplinary. M.S.
Reproductive Biology. Interdisciplinary. Ph.D.
Soils Science. M.S., Ph.D.
Soils Science/Water Resources. M.S.

COLLEGE OF ARTS AND SCIENCES:
American Studies. Interdepartmental. M.A. only.
Anthropology. M.A., Ph.D.
Botany. M.S., Ph.D.
Botany/Water Resources. Interdisciplinary. M.S.
Chemistry. M.S., M.S.T., Ph.D.
Community and Regional Planning. M.P. only.
Communication and Journalism. M.A. only.
English. Includes creative writing (M.F.A.). M.A., M.F.A.
French. M.A.
Geography. M.A., M.P., M.S.T.
Geography/Water Resources. Interdisciplinary. M.A.
Geology. M.S., Ph.D.
Geology/Water Resources. Interdisciplinary. M.S.
Geophysics. M.S., Ph.D.
Geophysics/Water Resources. Interdisciplinary. M.S.
German. M.A.
History. GRE Subject for admission; one language for M.A. M.A., M.S.T.
Interdisciplinary Masters. Self-designed master's with up to three curricula combined. I.M.A., I.M.S.
International Studies. Interdepartmental; one language, thesis for M.A. M.A. only.
Mathematics. M.A. M.A.T., M.S., M.S.T., Ph.D.
Molecular and Cellular Life Sciences. Ph.D.
Music. Includes applied music, music history and literature, theory and composition. M.A. only.
Natural Science. M.S., M.S.T.
Neurosciences. Ph.D.
Philosophy. M.A. only.
Physics. GRE Subject for admission. M.S., M.S.T., Ph.D.
Planning. M.P.
Political Science. M.A.
Psychology. Thesis for M.A. M.A., M.S., Ph.D.
Psychology/Early Childhood Development. M.A., M.S.
Public Administration. M.P.A.
Recreation and Park Administration. M.S. only.
Reproductive Biology. Interdisciplinary. M.S., Ph.D.
Sociology. Thesis for M.A.; M.A. only.
Spanish. M.A.
Statistics. M.S., Ph.D.
Zoology and Physiology. M.S., Ph.D.
Zoology and Physiology/Water Resources. M.S.

COLLEGE OF BUSINESS:
Accounting. M.S.
Business Administration. GMAT for admission. M.B.A.
E-Business. M.S.
Economics. M.S., Ph.D.
Economics Finance. M.S.
Finance. M.S.

COLLEGE OF EDUCATION:
Adult and Postsecondary Education. M.A., Ed.S., Ed.D.
Community Counseling. M.S.
Counselor Education. Includes counselor education and supervision (Ph.D.), school counseling (M.S.), student affairs in higher education (M.S.). M.S., Ph.D.
Curriculum and Instruction. M.A., Ed.D., Ph.D.
Educational Leadership. M.A., Ed.S., Ed.D., Ph.D.

Instructional Technology. M.S., Ed.D.
Special Education. M.A., Ed.S.

COLLEGE OF HEALTH SCIENCES:
Audiology. M.S.
Nursing. M.S.
Kinesiology and Health Education. M.S.
Social Work. M.S.W.
Speech-Language Pathology. M.S.

COLLEGE OF ENGINEERING:
Atmospheric Sciences. M.S., Ph.D.
Bioengineering. Interdisciplinary; thesis for M.S.
Chemical Engineering. Thesis for M.S. M.S. only.
Civil Engineering. M.S., Ph.D.
Computer Science. M.S., Ph.D.
Electrical Engineering. M.S., Ph.D.
Environmental Engineering. Interdisciplinary. M.S. only.
Mechanical Engineering. M.S., Ph.D.
Petroleum Engineering. M.S., Ph.D.

College of Law (82071-3035)

Web site: www.uwyo.edu/law

Established 1920. ABA approved since 1923. AALS member. Public control. Semester system. Law library: 285,827 volumes, 1852 subscriptions; has LEXIS, NEXIS, WESTLAW, INFOTRAC; has more than 150 network connections.

Annual tuition: resident $7635, nonresident $16,155. On-campus housing available. Apply to Director of Housing. Total average cost for all other expenses: $12,332.

Enrollment: first-year class 80; total 231 (men 56%, women 44%, minorities 8%). Faculty: full-time 12, part-time 6. Student to faculty ratio is 17.2 to 1. Degrees conferred: J.D., J.D.-M.B.A., J.D.-M.P.A.

ADMISSION REQUIREMENTS. LSDAS Law School report, bachelor's degree, transcripts, LSAT (no later than February) personal statement, résumé, personal essay, three letters of recommendation required in support of application. TOEFL required of international applicants. Preference given to state residents. Accepts transfer applicants. Graduates of unaccredited institutions not considered. Apply to Director of Admissions after September 1, before March 1. Rolling admission process. Fall admission only for beginning students. Application fee $50. Phone: (307)766-6416.

ADMISSION STANDARDS. Selective. Accepts approximately 26% of all students. Number of applicants 728; number of acceptance 188; number enrolled 80; LSAT (75% of students have a score at or above 149); GPA (75% of students have a GPA at or above 3.06). *U.S. News & World Report* ranking is in the third tier of all U.S. law schools.

FINANCIAL AID. Scholarships, fellowships, Federal W/S, loans. Apply to Director of Financial Aids by February 15. Phone: (307) 766-3214. Use FAFSA (School code: 003932). About 50% of students receive aid other than loans from College.

DEGREE REQUIREMENTS. For J.D.: satisfactory completion of three-year program, at least two years in residence; 88-semester-hour program.

XAVIER UNIVERSITY

Cincinnati, Ohio 45207-5311
Web site: www.xavier.edu

Founded 1831. Coed. Private control. Roman Catholic. Semester system. Library: 307,000 volumes, 2500 subscriptions. Total University enrollment: 6665.

Tuition: per credit $680 (M.B.A.), $555 (M.A., M.S., M.H.S.A.), $585 (M.Ed.), $640 (Occupational Therapy), $505 (Counseling), $320 (M.Ed.-Catholic School), $690 (Psy.D.). No on-campus housing, except on a space-available basis. Contact Director of Residence Life for off-campus housing information. Phone: (513) 745-4894.

Graduate School

Graduate study since 1946. Enrollment: full-time 775, part-time 2011. University faculty: full- and part-time 308. Degrees conferred: M.A., M.B.A., M.Ed., M.S., M.H.S.A., Psy.D.

ADMISSION REQUIREMENTS. Official transcripts required in support of School's application. Online application available. GRE/MAT/GMAT required for some departments. TOEFL required for international applicants. Accepts transfer applicants. Graduates of unaccredited institutions not considered. Apply to Graduate Services Office at least one month prior to registration. Application fee $35; $45 for M.B.A. applicants. Phone: (800) 344-4690, (513)745-4392; fax: (513)745-1048; M.B.A.: (513) 745-3527; e-mail: xugrad@xu.edu.

ADMISSION STANDARDS. Selective. Usual minimum average: 2.7 (A = 4), varies by program.

FINANCIAL AID. Annual awards from institutional funds: scholarships, assistantships, tuition waivers, internships, Federal W/S, loans. Approved for VA benefits. Apply by February 15 to Graduate Services Office for scholarships, assistantships; to Financial Aid Office for all other programs. Phone: (513)745-3142; fax: (513)745-2806. Use FAFSA. About 5% of students receive aid other than loans from University and outside sources. Aid available for part-time students.

DEGREE REQUIREMENTS. For M.A.: 30 semester hours minimum, at least 24 in residence; MAT for candidacy; reading knowledge of one foreign language in some programs; thesis; final oral exam. For M.B.A.: 36 semester hours minimum, at least 27 in residence; GMAT for candidacy. For M.Ed.: 30–42 semester hours minimum, at least 24–36 in residence; MAT for candidacy. For M.S.: 30 semester hours minimum, at least 24 in residence; MAT for candidacy; thesis/research paper; final oral/written exam. For M.H.S.A.: 60 semester hours minimum, at least 45 in residence; GMAT for candidacy; residency requirement. For Psy.D.: 80 credit minimum, full-time program; candidacy; clinical practicum; clinical competency exam; internship; dissertation.

FIELDS OF STUDY.
Administration. M.Ed.
Business Administration. M.B.A.
Community Counseling. M.A.
Criminal Justice. M.S.
Elementary Education. M.Ed.
English. M.A., M.Ed.
Experimental Psychology. M.A.
Health Services Administration. Includes long-term care. M.H.S.A.
Human Resource Development. M.Ed.
Industrial-Organizational Psychology. M.A.
Montessori Education. M.Ed.
Multicultural Literature for Children. M.Ed.
Nursing. Includes education, forensics, health care law, nursing administration, school nurse. M.S.
Occupational Therapy. M.O.T.
Psychology. Includes clinical child & adolescent, apply geropsychology, psychology of persons with severe mental disabilities. Psy.D.
Reading. M.Ed.
School Counseling. M.A.
Secondary Education. M.Ed.
Special Education.

Sport Administration. M.Ed.
Theology. M.A.

XAVIER UNIVERSITY OF LOUISIANA

New Orleans, Louisiana 70125-1098
Web site: www.xula.edu

Founded 1925. CGS member. Coed. Private control. Roman Catholic affiliation. Semester system. Library: 238,400 volumes, 2000 subscriptions. Total University enrollment: 4100.

Tuition: per credit $220. No on-campus housing for graduate students. Day-care facilities available.

Graduate School

Enrollment: full-time 185; part-time 50 (men 35%, women 65%). Graduate faculty: full-time 7, part-time 8. Degrees conferred: M.A., M.Th.

ADMISSION REQUIREMENTS. Transcripts, two letters of recommendation, GRE or MAT required in support of application. Online application available. TOEFL required for international applicants. Interview not required. Accepts transfer applicants. Graduates of unaccredited colleges not considered. Apply to Dean of School by July 1 (Fall), December 1 (Spring). Application fee $30. Phone: (504)483-7487; fax: (504)485-7921.

ADMISSION STANDARDS. Relatively open. Minimum average: 2.5, 3.0 in major field (A = 4).

FINANCIAL AID. Scholarships, internships, tuition waivers, Federal W/S, loans. Approved for VA benefits. Apply to Financial Aid Office; no specified closing date. Phone: (504)483-3517; fax: (504)482-6258. Use FAFSA. Aid available for part-time students.

DEGREE REQUIREMENTS. For master's: 33 credits minimum; thesis/nonthesis option.

FIELDS OF STUDY.
Counseling. Includes community counseling, school counseling. M.A.
Curriculum and Instruction. Includes early childhood education, elementary education, reading, secondary education, special education. M.A.
Educational Leadership. Includes administrative and supervision of instruction. M.A.
Elementary Education. M.A.T.
Pastoral Theology. M.P.T.
Secondary Education. M.A.T.
Special Education. Includes mild/moderate. M.A.T.
Theology. M.Th.

YALE UNIVERSITY

New Haven, Connecticut 06520
Web site: www.yale.edu

Founded 1701. Located 80 miles NE of New York City. CGS member. Coed. Private control. Semester system. Special facilities: Beinecke Rare Book and Manuscript Library; Peabody Museum of Natural History; Art Gallery; Paul Mellon Center for British Art and British Studies; observatory; computer center; Child Study Center, Kline Geology Laboratory; Kline Chemistry Research Laboratory; Josiah Willard Gibbs Research Laboratories for biology, physics, molecular biology, biophysics; Center for International and Area Study; Nuclear Structure Laboratory for "Emperor" tandem electrostatic Van de Graaff accelerator; Kline Biology Tower for research and graduate training in biological sciences; Electron and Heavy Ion Accelerator Laboratories; Becton Engineering and Applied Science Center; Institute of Sacred Music; Institute for Social and Policy Studies; Social Interaction Laboratory; Political Science Research Laboratory. The University's NIH ranking is 10th among all U.S. institutions with 334 awards/grants valued at $336,742,948. According to The Center at University of Florida, the University is ranked 18th in receipt of Federal Research funds with $296,713,000 and it ranks 28th for total University research expenditures with $387,644,000. The University's endowment assets rank it 2nd, with a value of $12,747,150,000. In 2004, the University awarded 340 doctorates which ranked it 36th among all U.S. institutions eligible to award that degree. One hundred one of the University's faculty members have been elected to National Honor Academies and this ranks it 5th among all U.S. institutions. The Library: approximately 10,500,000 volumes, 55,000 subscriptions. Total University enrollment: 11,500.

Annual tuition: full-time $30,500; modest continuing registration fee after the fourth year. On-campus housing for married students, graduate men and women. Average academic year housing costs: $17,610 single students, $26,676 married students. Contact University Housing Department for both on- and off-campus housing information. Phone: (203)432-2167.

Graduate School of Arts and Science

Graduate School organized in 1847, graduate study since 1732. Enrollment: full- and part-time 2150. University faculty teaching graduate courses: over 500. Degrees conferred: M.A., M.S., M.Phil., Ph.D. (M.A. as a terminal degree only in International and Developmental Economics, International Relations, African Studies, Afro-American Studies, American Studies, Archeological Studies, East Asian Studies, English, German, History, History of Medicine and Life Sciences, Medieval Studies, Music, Near Eastern Languages and Civilizations, Soviet and East European Studies, Slavic Languages and Literature, and Statistics. M.S. as a terminal degree only in Engineering and Applied Science, Mathematics, Molecular Biophysics and Biochemistry).

ADMISSION REQUIREMENTS. Transcripts, GRE, three letters of recommendation, personal statement of purpose required in support of application. Online application available. GRE Subject Test required by astronomy, biology, chemistry, computer science, economics, engineering and applied science, English language and literature, genetics, pharmacology, physics, physiology, statistics. Interview required in some cases. GMAT may be required for some programs. TOEFL, TSE (required for doctoral programs) required for international applicants. Accepts transfer applicants, usually for Ph.D. only. Apply to Coordinator, Graduate Admissions, P.O. Box 1504A, Yale Station, New Haven, Connecticut 06520, preferably one year prior to desired entrance but no later than December 7. Normally admits Fall only. Application fee $85. Phone: (203)432-2770.

APPLICATION STANDARDS. Competitive to very selective. Usual minimum average: 3.0 (A = 4).

FINANCIAL AID. Scholarships, fellowships, assistantships, Federal W/S, loans. Apply by January 2 to appropriate department chair for fellowships, assistantships; to Director of Financial Aid for all other programs. Phone: (203)432-2739. Use FAFSA. Support for Graduate School students while they are in residence at Yale comes from a great variety of sources. More than 95% of full-time candidates for the Ph.D. degree receive substantial aid from Yale or from other institutions and agencies interested in graduate education.

DEGREE REQUIREMENTS. For master's en route to Ph.D.: completion of first year of Ph.D. program; one academic year in full-time residence; recommendation by the appropriate department for the award of the degree, subject to final review by the Committee on Degrees. For terminal master's (full- and part-time programs): one or two academic years of full-time residence depending on the program; high-pass average with at least one term grade of Honors in one full-year graduate course or in two full-term graduate courses. foreign language requirements set by department; master's essay required by some departments. For M.Phil.: completion of all requirements for the Ph.D. except those relating directly to the dissertation. For Ph.D.: three academic years in residence; no more than four years to fulfill foreign language and course requirements as set by individual departments; grade of Honors in at least one full-year course or two full-term courses; qualifying written/oral exam; admission to candidacy; prospectus and dissertation; final oral exam.

FIELDS OF STUDY.

African Studies. Two-year M.A. program; proficiency in one African language.

African-American Studies. Ph.D.

American Studies. Reading knowledge of two languages or high level of proficiency in one language required. M.A., Ph.D.

Anthropology. Faculty decides with each student individually the particular requirements in respect to languages, statistics, or other research tools. M.A., Ph.D.

Applied Mathematics. GRE Subject Test encouraged. M.A., Ph.D.

Applied Physics. M.S., Ph.D.

Archaeological Studies. No foreign language required. M.A.

Astronomy. Working knowledge of at least two languages; one French, German, or Russian required. M.S., Ph.D.

Atmospheric Science. Interdepartmental.

Biological and Biomedical Sciences. GRE Subject Test recommended; MCAT can be substituted for some programs. Contact BBS department for application. Ph.D.

Biomedical Engineering. M.S., Ph.D.

Biostatistics. M.S.

Cell Biology. No foreign language requirement. Ph.D.

Cellular and Molecular Physiology. Apply through the BBS department. Ph.D.

Chemical Engineering. M.S., Ph.D.

Chemistry. GRE required, a foreign language not required. Ph.D.

Classics. Reading knowledge of French and German, good knowledge of Greek and Latin grammar and ability to read representative passages in both languages at sight required. Ph.D.

Comparative Literature. Reading knowledge of two modern languages plus Latin or Greek required. Ph.D.

Computer Science. No foreign language required. Ph.D.

East Asian Languages and Literature. One European language plus Chinese and Japanese required. Ph.D.

East Asian Studies. Two-year M.A. program; Chinese or Japanese plus French or German proficiency required. M.A.

Ecology and Evolutionary Biology. Ph.D.

Economics. No foreign language required unless connected with dissertation research. Ph.D.

Electrical Engineering. M.S., Ph.D.

English Language and Literature. Ability to read simple prose in three languages or demonstration of the same level of competence in one language and advanced competence in a second language required; one language must be Latin or Greek. Ph.D.

Epidemiology and Public Health. GRE Subject Test optional. Ph.D.

European and Russian Studies. M.A.

Experimental Pathology. GRE or MCAT for admission. Ph.D.

Film Studies. Ph.D.

Forest and Environmental Studies. GRE required for admission, GRE Subject optional. Ph.D.

French. Reading knowledge of a second Romance language; Latin and non-Romance language (usually German) required. Ph.D.

Genetics. No foreign language required. Ph.D.

Geology and Geophysics. No foreign language required, but students may be assigned foreign language literature in certain fields of specialization. Ph.D.

Germanic Languages and Literature. Reading knowledge of French and Latin as well as thorough preparation in German required. M.A., Ph.D.

History. Reading knowledge of one foreign language required. M.A., Ph.D.

History of Art. Reading knowledge of German and second language relevant to proposed specialty within the field of art history required. Ph.D.

History of Science and Medicine. M.S., Ph.D.

Immunobiology. Writing sample required; GRE recommended. Ph.D.

Immunology. Apply through BBS department. Ph.D.

International and Developmental Economics. M.A.

International Relations. Reading knowledge of one foreign language (usually French or German) required for admission; two-year M.A. program. M.A.

Investigation Medicine. Ph.D.

Italian Language and Literature. Reading knowledge of a second Romance language, Latin, and a non-Romance language (usually German) required. Ph.D.

Linguistics. Proficiency in French and German. Ph.D.

Management. Accepts either GRE or GMAT for admission. Ph.D.

Mathematics. GRE/Subject Test for admission; reading knowledge of two foreign languages required. M.S., Ph.D.

Mechanical Engineering. M.S., Ph.D.

Medieval Studies. Reading knowledge of simple Latin (medieval prose), French, and German required. M.A., Ph.D.

Microbiology. Apply through BBS department. Ph.D.

Molecular Biophysics and Biochemistry. No foreign language required. Apply through BBS department. Ph.D.

Molecular, Cellular, and Developmental Biology. Apply through BBS department. Ph.D.

Music. Reading knowledge of German and French or Italian required. M.A., Ph.D.

Near Eastern Languages and Civilizations. Includes Arabic and Islamic studies, archaeology of the ancient Near East, Assyriology, Egyptology, coptic, northwest Semitic studies. Reading knowledge of French and German required. M.A., Ph.D.

Neurobiology. No foreign language required. Ph.D.

Neuroscience. No foreign language required. Ph.D.

Nursing. Ph.D.

Pharmacology. Apply through BBS department. Ph.D.

Philosophy. Reading proficiency in French and German required. Ph.D.

Physical Chemistry. Proficiency in French, Russian, or preferably German required. Ph.D.

Physics. Proficiency in one foreign language required. Ph.D.

Political Science. Demonstration of competence in one foreign language required. Ph.D.

Psychology. No language requirement. Ph.D.

Religious Studies. Reading proficiency in French and German required. Ph.D.

Renaissance Studies. Reading exams in Latin prose, Italian, and a third language chosen from French, German, Greek, or Spanish. Ph.D.

Slavic Languages and Literature. Adequate command of the Russian language plus a reading knowledge of French and German required. M.A., Ph.D.

Sociology. Proficiency in statistics, methods, and theory; reading knowledge of French, German, or Russian required. Ph.D.

Spanish and Portuguese. Reading knowledge of a second Romance language, Latin, and a non-Romance language (usually German) required. M.A., Ph.D.

Statistics. M.S., Ph.D.

Urban Education Studies. M.A.

School of Architecture

Visual arts study since 1832. Library 151,300 volumes.

Annual tuition: $33,800, fees $810. On-campus housing available.

Enrollment: full-time 199. Faculty: full-time 15, part-time 37. Degrees conferred: M.Arch. I., M.Arch. II., M.E.D., M.Arch.-M.B.A., M.Arch-M.E.D.

ADMISSION REQUIREMENTS. Transcripts, GRE, portfolio, three letters of reference, personal history required in support of School's application. For M.E.D.: research topics and proposed program of study required. TOEFL required for international applicants. Graduates of unaccredited institutions not considered. Apply by January 4 for postprofessional program, by January 1 for others. Fall admission only. Application fee $85. Phone: (203)432-2291; fax: (203)432-7175.

ADMISSION STANDARDS. Very competitive. Usual minimum average: 3.5 (A = 4).

FINANCIAL AID. Annual awards from school funds: scholarships, fellowship, teaching assistantships, Federal W/S, loans. Approved for VA benefits. Apply by February 1 to appropriate department for scholarships, assistantship; to Financial Aid Office for all other programs. Phone: (203)432-2291. Use FAFSA. Some 65% of students receive aid from loan sources and the School.

DEGREE REQUIREMENTS. For M.Arch. I.: B.A. or B.S. required, completion of three-year, full-time program, two years in residence. For M.Arch. II.: a two-year, full-time postprofessional program; in final term an appropriate independent studies thesis may be approved. For M.E.D.: B.A., B.S., B.Arch. or M.Arch. required, completion of two-year program, three semesters in residence; thesis/independent project. For postprofessionals: B.Arch. or equivalent, two-year residence.

FIELDS OF STUDY.
Architecture.
Environmental Design.

School of Art

Tuition: full-time $27,300. Graduate enrollment: full-time 119. No part-time students. School faculty: full-time 11, part-time 74. Degree conferred: M.F.A.

ADMISSION REQUIREMENTS. Official transcripts, three letters of recommendation, slide or digital portfolio, one-page statement of intent required in support of School's application. No Online application available. TOEFL required for international applicants. Interview not required. Admits Fall only. Apply to Admissions Office by January 9. Rolling admissions process. Application fee $90. Phone: (203)432-2600; e-mail artschool.info @yale.edu.

ADMISSION STANDARDS. Selective. Selection based on talent and academic preparation.

FINANCIAL AID. Annual awards from institutional funds: scholarships, grants, assistantships, Federal W/S, loans. Apply by February 28 (priority deadline) to Office of Student Financial Services. Phone: (203)432-2700; fax: (203)432-7557. Use FAFSA (School code: 001426). About 50% of students receive some aid from School and outside sources.

DEGREE REQUIREMENTS. For M.F.A.: 60-credit, two-year program.

FIELDS OF STUDY.
Graphic Design.
Painting.
Painting/Printmaking.
Photography.
Printmaking.
Sculpture.

Divinity School

Yale College was founded in 1701 to train ministers; the religion programs separated from Yale College in 1822, and the Divinity School was established.

Tuition: full-time $18,400; per course $2300. Graduate enrollment: full-time 411 (men 50%, Women 50%). No part-time students. School faculty: full-time 33, part-time 10. Degrees conferred: M.A.R. (both a Comprehensive M.A.R. and a Concentrated M.A.R. are offered), M.Div., S.T.M. For doctoral study apply to Department of Religion, Graduate School of Arts and Sciences.

ADMISSION REQUIREMENTS. Official transcripts, three letters of recommendation, personal essays, five-page writing sample required in support of School's application. Online application available. TOEFL (minimum score 600) required for international applicants. Interview not required. Accepts transfer applicants. Apply to Admissions Office by January 15 (priority filing), February 1 (standard filing). Admits Fall only. Rolling admissions process. Application fee $75. Phone: (203)432-5360; fax: (203)432-7475.

ADMISSION STANDARDS. Selective.

FINANCIAL AID. Annual awards from institutional funds: renewable academic scholarships, internships, grants (need-based), Federal W/S, loans. Apply to Director of Admissions by March 1. Phone: (203)432-5026; fax: (203)432-7475. Use FAFSA and CSS Profile. About 75% of students receive some aid from School and outside sources.

DEGREE REQUIREMENTS. For M.Div.: 72 credit units in full-time residence. For M.A.R.: 48 credit units in full-time residence. For S.T.M.: 24 credit unit minimum in full-time residence; thesis. *Note:* Divinity School preschool available; none for infants, toddlers.

FIELDS OF STUDY.
Divinity. M.Div.
Religion. M.A.R.
Sacred Theology. S.T.M.

School of Drama

Graduate studies in drama since 1925. Annual tuition: $25,735. Graduate enrollment: 199. No part-time students. Limited number of Special Students for one year. School faculty: full- and part-time 69. Degrees conferred: M.F.A., D.F.A., Certificate in Drama, Technical Internship Certificate.

ADMISSION REQUIREMENTS. Transcripts, statement of purpose, résumé, official transcripts, three letters of recommendation required in support of application. Samples of work, GRE required in Dramaturgy and Dramatic Criticism, Stage Management, Technical Design and Production, and Theater Management. TOEFL required for international applicants. Apply to the School of Drama by January 1 for Acting and Directing; February 1 for all other departments; February 15 for financial aid applicants. Application fee $100, $50 for Technical Internship Certificate. Phone: (203)432-1507; fax: (203)432-9668.

ADMISSION STANDARDS. Selective to very competitive.

FINANCIAL AID. Scholarships, grants, internships, Federal W/S, loans. Apply by February 15 to Financial Aid Office. Phone: (203)432-1540. Use FAFSA and CSS Profile. About 87% of students receive aid other than loans from School and outside sources.

DEGREE REQUIREMENTS. For M.F.A. and Certificate in Drama: granted upon completion of three years' residency and successful completion of coursework. For D.F.A.: oral qualifying exam; approved written dissertation within two years after completing Yale M.F.A. For Internship Certificate; awarded upon completion with distinction of the one-year internship program.

FIELDS OF STUDY.

Acting. Audition and interview for admission. M.F.A., Certificate in Drama.

Design. Includes scene, costume, lighting; interview, portfolio for admission (no slides). M.F.A., Certificate in Drama.

Directing Session. Interview for admission.

Dramaturgy and Dramatic Criticism. Interview of qualified applicant for admission, two writing samples; GRE.

Playwriting. One original play. M.F.A., Certificate in Drama.

Sound Design. GRE, interview for admission. M.F.A., Certificate in Drama.

Stage Management. GRE, interview for admission. M.F.A.

Technical Design and Production. GRE, interview for admission. M.F.A., Certificate in Drama.

Technical Internship Program. GRE or SAT; interview for admission.

Theater Management. GRE, interview for admission. M.F.A.

School of Forestry and Environmental Studies

Established 1900. Special facilities: Center for Biodiversity and Conservation Science, Center for Coastal and Watershed Systems, Center for Environmental Law and Policy, Center for Industrial Ecology, Global Institute of Sustainable Forestry, Hixon Center for Urban Ecology, Tropical Resources Institute.

Annual tuition: full-time $27,300. Graduate enrollment: full-time 265, part-time 4. School faculty: full-time 28, part-time 4. Degrees conferred: M.F., M.F.S., M.E.S., D.F.E.S., M.E.M.-M.A. (Economics, International Relation), M.F.M.A. (Economics, International Relation), M.E.M-M.B.A., M.F-M.B.A., M.E.M.-J.D., M.F.-J.D., M.E.M.-M.P.H., M.F.-M.P.H. The Ph.D. is offered through the Graduate School.

ADMISSION REQUIREMENTS. Official transcripts, GRE/GMAT/LSAT, résumé, three letters of recommendation required in support of School's application. Online application available. TOEFL required for international applicants. Interview not required but encouraged. Graduates of unaccredited institutions not considered. Apply to Director of Admission by January 1. Application fee $90, $70 (online). Phone: master's (203)432-5106, doctoral applicants (203)432-5146; fax: (203)432-5942.

ADMISSION STANDARDS. Competitive. Usual minimum average: 3.0 (A = 4).

FINANCIAL AID. Scholarships, grants, teaching assistantships, loans. Approved for VA benefits. Apply to Director of Financial Aid by February 15 for M.F., M.F.S., M.E.S.; by January 1 for Ph.D., D.F.E.S. Phone: (203)432-6100. Use FAFSA (School code: 001426).

DEGREE REQUIREMENTS. For M.E.M.: two years full-time 48 credit program; selection of advanced study program. For M.E.S., M.F.S.: two-year full-time 48 credit program; thesis or major paper. For M.F. (one-year M.F. available for professionals with at least seven years full-time forestry experience); two-year 48 credit multidisciplinary program; internship. For Ph.D.: see Graduate School listing above. For D.F.E.S.: similar to Ph.D. program.

FIELDS OF STUDY.

Environmental Management. Includes ecology, ecosystems and biodiversity, forestry, forest science and the management of forests for conservation and development, global change and polity, health and environment, industrial environmental management, policy economics and law, the social ecology of conservation and development, urban ecology and environmental planning, design, and values, water science, policy and management.

Environmental Science.

Forest Science.

Forestry.

Note: School has special program with Peace Corps, which promotes volunteer service.

Law School (P.O. Box 208215)

Web site: www.law.yale.edu

Established 1801. ABA approved since 1923. AALS member. Semester system. Full-time day study. Special facilities: John M. Olin Center for Law, Economics and Public Policy, China Law Center, Center for Law and Philosophy, Center of International Law and Policy, Center for the Study of Corporate Law, Orville H. Schnell, Jr. Center for International Human Rights. Law library: 1,129,973 volumes, 11,103 subscriptions; has LEXIS, NEXIS, WESTLAW, DIALOG, OCLC; has more than 1000 network connections; is a Federal Government Depository.

Annual tuition: for J.D. $40,900; LL.M., M.S.L. $35,400; J.S.D. $6100 per term. On-campus housing available for both single and married students. Annual on-campus living expenses: $15,700. Housing deadline June 1. Contact Housing Department for both on- and off-campus housing information. Phone: (203)432-9756. Law students tend to live off-campus. Off-campus housing and personal expenses: approximately $15,000.

Enrollment: first-year class 201; total 576 (men 51%, women 49%, minorities 30%). Faculty: full-time 60, part-time 25. Student to faculty ratio is 7.8 to 1. Degrees conferred: J.D., J.D.-M.A., J.D.-M.B.A., J.D.-M.D., J.D.-M.Div., J.D.-M.E.S., J.D.-M.P.A., J.D.-M.P.P.M., J.D.-Ph.D. (American Studies, Economics, History, Philosophy, Political Science), LL.M. (generally open for those committed to law teaching as a career), LL.M. (for persons who have completed a basic legal education and received a university degree in law in another country), M.S.L. (Master's of Studies in Law, for nonlawyers), J.S.D. (open to LL.M. graduates from Yale only).

ADMISSION REQUIREMENTS. LSDAS Law School report, bachelor's degree, transcripts, two letters of recommendation, LSAT, 250-word essay required in support of application. Accepts transfer applicants. Graduates of unaccredited colleges not considered. Apply by February 1 to Office of Admission for J.D. program; to Graduate Committee for graduate programs. Joint degree applicants must apply to and be accepted by both programs. Beginning students admitted Fall only. Application fee $70. Phone: (203)432-4995.

ADMISSION REQUIREMENTS FOR TRANSFER APPLICANTS. Accepts about 10–12 transfers each year from other ABA-accredited schools. At least one year of enrollment, Dean's letter indicating the applicant is in good standing, applicants must have maintained a weighted B average, LSAT, LSDAS, personal statement regarding reason for transfer, essay, two letters of recommendation, undergraduate transcripts, current law school transcript required in support of School's application. Apply to Director of Admission after May 1, before July 20. Admission decision made by the first week of August. Application fee $70. Will consider visiting students.

ADMISSION REQUIREMENTS FOR LL.M. APPLICANTS. All applicants must have graduated from either an AALS member law school or an ABA-accredited law school with a high rank in class. If from another country, the applicant must have graduated with a high rank from a law school or law faculty with standards substantially equivalent to those of U.S. applicants. Official undergraduate college/university transcripts, official law school transcript, résumé, proposed study plan, personal statement, two letters of recommendation required in support of application. In addition, TOEFL is required for those whose native language is not English; all transcripts and recommendations must be in English or accompanied by an English translation.

Admits Fall only. Apply by December 15 to Graduate Programs Office. Application $75. Phone:(203)4332-1693; e-mail: coutrue@ mail.law.yale.edu.

ADMISSION STANDARDS. Selective. Accepts approximately 6% of all students. Number of applicants 235; number of acceptance 188; number enrolled 200; LSAT (75% of students have a score at or above 168); GPA (75% of students have a GPA at or above 3.79). *U.S. News & World Report* ranking is in the first tier among all U.S. law schools.

FINANCIAL AID. Scholarships, Federal W/S, loans; fellowships, assistantships for graduate law study. Apply to the Office of Financial Aid by March 15. Phone: (203)432-1688. Use FAFSA (School code: E00444). Apply to the Secretary of Graduate Financial Aid Committee for fellowships, assistantships, and certain scholarships. About 75% of students receive aid from School.

DEGREE REQUIREMENTS. For J.D.: 81 credit program, at least three years in full-time residence. For LL.M.: at least 24 credit hours beyond the J.D., two semesters minimum in full-time residence. For M.S.L.: one year in full-time residence. For J.S.D.: two semesters minimum beyond the J.D. in full-time residence; dissertation.

School of Management (P.O. Box 208200)
Web site: www.yale.edu/som

Established 1976 Accredited program: M.B.A. The Master in Public and Private Management degree was changed to M.B.A. on September 1, 1998, by vote of faculty; recognized Ph.D. Located on main campus. Special facilities: Chief Executive Leadership Institute, International Center for Finance, International Institute for Corporate Governance, the Partnership on Nonprofit Ventures.

Annual tuition: full-time M.B.A. $42,000; Ph.D. $27,300. On-campus rooms and apartments available for both single and married students. Average annual on-campus housing cost: $13,320. Contact Graduate Housing Office for both on- and off-campus housing information. Phone: (203)432-9756. Estimated annual M.B.A. budget for tuition, room and board, and personal expenses: approximately $69,100.

Enrollment: M.B.A. full-time 350. Faculty: full-time 47, part-time 49; all have Ph.D./D.B.A. Degrees conferred: M.B.A. (full-time only) joint degree programs can be arranged with the Schools of Architecture, Divinity, Drama, Epidemiology and Public Health, Forestry and Environmental Studies, Law, Nursing and the following programs from the Graduate School Arts and Science: East Asian Studies, International Development Economics, International Relations, Russian and East European Studies, Ph.D. (degree is offered through the Graduate School).

ADMISSION REQUIREMENTS. All applicants should have a bachelor's degree from a recognized institution of higher education and a strong mathematics background. Students are required to have their own personal computer. Contact School of Management at (203)432-5932 for application material and information. Online applications available. Applications for downloading are generally available in August; Adobe Acrobat Reader is required. Early applications are encouraged for both admission and financial aid consideration. Beginning students are admitted Fall only. Both U.S. citizens and international applicants apply by October 24 (round 1), January 9 (round 2), March 12 (round 3). Submit School of Management application, GMAT results (will accept GMAT test result from the last five years, latest acceptable date is March), official transcripts from each undergraduate/graduate school attended, three letters of recommendation, three essays, résumé (prefers at least four years of work experience), and an application fee of $180 to the Admission Office, School of Management. In addition, international students (whose native language is other than English) should submit a TOEFL or IELTS report (minimum score TOEFL 600; IELTS 7), certified transla-

tions and evaluations of all official transcripts, recommendations should be in English or with certified translations, proof of health/immunization certificate, and proof of sufficient financial resources for two years of academic study. For current information and/or modification in admission requirements, the international applicant's contact phone number is (203)432-2305. On-campus visits are encouraged. Interviews are by invitation only. Joint degree applicants must apply to and be accepted by both schools and programs; contact the Admissions Office for current information and specific admission requirements. Admission decisions are made in three rounds. Applications received by October 24 will be notified by January 18; applications received by January 9 will be notified by April 4; applications received by March 12 will be notified by May 9.

ADMISSION REQUIREMENTS FOR DOCTORAL APPLICANTS. Contact Ph.D. Office, School of Management at (203)432-6028 for application material and information. Application can be downloaded from Web site, Adobe Acrobat Reader is required. Beginning students are admitted Fall only. Both U.S. citizens and international applicants apply by January 2. Submit School of Management application, GMAT scores (will accept GMAT test results from the last five years), official transcript from each undergraduate/graduate school attended, three letters of recommendation, four or five essays, résumé, statement of goals and objectives, and application fee of $75 to the Admission Office. In addition, international students (whose native language is other than English) should submit a TOEFL report (minimum score 600), certified translations and evaluations of all official transcripts, recommendations should be in English or with certified translations, proof of health/immunization certificate. International students' contact: (203)432-2305. Interviews are encouraged. Notification is generally made by mid-April.

ADMISSION STANDARDS. Highly selective. For M.B.A.: mean GMAT: 701; mean GPA: 3.46 (A = 4). *U.S. News & World Report* ranking is in the top 14 of all U.S. business schools. *Business-Week* listed the School in the top 25 of all U.S. business schools.

FINANCIAL AID. Scholarships, minority scholarships, fellowships, graduate assistantships, Federal Perkins Loans, Stafford Subsidized and Unsubsidized Loans, Federal W/S available; Public Service Loan Forgiveness Program. Financial aid may be available for international students from the University; submit Financial Aid Application for Foreign Students. Assistantships, fellowships may be available for joint degree candidates. Financial aid applications and information are generally included with admission materials; apply by March 15. Request scholarship, fellowship, assistantships and all need-based financial aid information from the School of Management. Use FAFSA (School code: 001426), also submit Financial Aid Transcript, Federal Income Tax forms. Approximately 65% of students receive some form of financial assistance.

DEGREE REQUIREMENTS. For M.B.A.: 18-course, 54-credit full-time program, including 7 elective courses, two-year program; summer internships between first and second year; M.B.A. degree program must completed in two years. For M.B.A.-master's: generally the joint degree program reduces the time required for both degrees taken separately by approximately one year. For Ph.D.: three-to-five year program; general written/oral exam, dissertation proposal, oral defense; dissertation; final oral defense.

FIELDS OF STUDY.
Accounting. Ph.D.
Business Administration. Concentrations in finance, leadership, marketing, operation management, public management, strategy. M.B.A.
Finance. Ph.D.
Leadership in Healthcare. M.B.A.
Marketing. Ph.D.

School of Medicine (06510)
Web site: www.med.yale.edu/ysm

Established 1810. Located at the Medical Center. Semester system. NIH ranking is 10th among all U.S. institutions with 868 awards/grants worth $336,742,948. Library: 380,000 volumes, 2600 subscriptions.

Annual tuition: $40,720. On-campus rooms and apartments available for both single and married students at the Medical Center. Contact Housing Department for both on- and off-campus housing information. Phone: (203)432-9756. Housing and personal expenses: approximately $16,500

Enrollment: first-year class 100, total 440 (men 46%, women 54%, minorities 29%, state residents 8%). Faculty: full-time 999, part-time 39. Degrees conferred: M.D., M.D.-M.B.A., M.D.-J.D., M.D.-M.Div., M.D.-M.P.H., M.D.-Ph.D. (M.S.T.P.)

ADMISSION REQUIREMENTS. For M.D. program: AMCAS report, transcripts, two letters of recommendation, MCAT required in support of application. Interviews by invitation only. Supplemental application required. Applicants must have completed at least three years of college study. Transfer applicants seldom accepted. Has EDP; apply between June 1 and August 1. Graduates of unaccredited colleges not considered. Apply to Assistant Dean for Admissions after June 1, before October 15. Application fee $75. Phone: (203)785-2643; fax: (203)785-3234. For M.P.H. program: transcripts, GRE, three letters of recommendation required in support of application. Applicants must hold either (1) the degree of M.D., D.D.S., Ph.D., or D.V.M. or equivalent, or (2) master's or bachelor's in biological or social sciences plus professional academic qualifications or experience. Graduates of unaccredited colleges not considered. Apply to Department of Epidemiology and Public Health by March 1. Application fee $85. Phone: (203)784-2844.

ADMISSION STANDARDS. Very competitive. Accepts about 6% of all applicants. Number of applications 3708 (3503 out-of-state); number interviewed 767 (692 out-of-state); number of acceptance 220 (194 out-of-state); number enrolled 100 (80 out-of-state). Mean Composite MCAT 11.4, mean UGPA 3.75. *U.S. News & World Report* ranking is in the top 8 of all U.S. medical schools.

FINANCIAL AID. For M.D.: Scholarships, merit scholarships, minority scholarships, Service Commitment Scholarships, Grants-in-Aid, institutional loans, HEAL, NIH stipends, Federal Perkins Loans, Stafford Subsidized and Unsubsidized Loan Programs are available. Assistantships, fellowships, stipends may be available for M.D.-Ph.D., combined degree candidates. All financial aid is based on documented need. Financial aid applications and information are generally available at the on-campus, by-invitation interview or they will be sent out to all applicants in January. Contact Financial Aid Office for current information. Phone: (203)785-2645. Use FAFSA (School code: E00450), also submit NEED ACCESS application, Financial Aid Transcript, Federal Income Tax forms. Approximately 90% of students receive some form of financial assistance. For M.P.H.: scholarships, grants, loans. Apply by March 1 to Financial Aid Office. Use FAFSA (M.P.H. code: 001426).

DEGREE REQUIREMENTS. For M.D.: satisfactory completion of four-year program; thesis. All students must pass USMLE Step 1 prior to entering third year and USMLE Step 2 prior to awarding of M.D. For M.P.H.: two-year, 60 credit program, at least three terms are spent in full-time residence; internships; thesis. For M.D.-M.P.H.: generally a five- to five-and-one-half-year program. For M.D.-Ph.D., M.D.-J.D.: generally six- to seven-year programs.

FIELDS OF GRADUATE STUDY.
Biomedical Engineering.
Biostatistics. M.P.H.
Cell Biology.
Cellular and Molecular Physiology.
Chemistry.
Computer Science.
Chronic Disease Epidemiology. M.P.H.
Environmental Health Sciences. M.P.H.
Epidemiology of Microbial Diseases. M.P.H.
Experimental Pathology.
Genetics and Development.
Global Health. M.P.H.
Health Management. M.P.H.
Health Policy and Administration. M.P.H.
Immunobiology.
Immunology.
Microbiology.
Molecular Biophysics and Biochemistry.
Molecular, Cellular and Developmental Biology.
Neurobiology.
Neuroscience.
Pharmacologic Sciences and Molecular Medicine.
Pharmacology.
Translational Research. Includes genomics and proteonomics, clinical immunology.

School of Music

Tuition: $27,300. Graduate enrollment: full-time 214. School faculty; full-time 30, part-time 33. Degrees conferred: M.M., M.M.A., D.M.A. A Certificate program is offered for those who do not hold a bachelor's degree, and an Artist Diploma is offered for those who hold a master's degree.

ADMISSION REQUIREMENTS. Official transcripts, résumé, three letters of recommendation, prescreening recording required in support of School's application. Auditions/interviews by invitation and based on audition tape. Online application available. GRE exams required of composers, conductors, organists, and M.M.A. candidates. TOEFL (minimum score 550) required for international applicants. Apply to Director of Admissions by December 31. Application fee $100. Phone: (203)432-4151; fax: (203)432-7448.

ADMISSION STANDARDS. Highly selective.

FINANCIAL AID. Annual awards from institutional funds: scholarships, fellowships, Federal W/S, loans. Apply to Financial Aid Office by February 28. Phone: (253)432-1962. Use FAFSA (School code: 001426) and institutional FAF. About 90% of students receive aid other than loans from School and outside sources.

DEGREE REQUIREMENTS. For M.M.: 72 semester hours minimum, at least two years in full-time residence; reading knowledge of a modern European language; public presentation of recital/compositions each year of residency. For M.M.A.: 108 semester hours minimum, at least three years in full-time residence; public presentation of recitals/compositions every year; thesis; comprehensive written and oral examination. For A.D.: two-year full-time program; 14 credits per term; one solo recital/one major ensemble performance/one performance of a worked composed. For D.M.A.: awarded to candidates who have earned the M.M.A. at Yale and whose achievements in the music profession in the following two to five years have reached the level of distinction to merit granting the degree.

FIELDS OF STUDY.
Composition.
Conducting. Includes orchestral and choral.
Performance. Includes vocal and instrumental.

Sacred Music. Interdisciplinary; cooperative program with Divinity School.

School of Nursing

Established in, and graduate study since, 1923. Special facilities: Center for Excellence in Chronic Illness Care, Center for Health Policy and Ethics. Annual tuition: $27,910. On-campus housing available at the Medical Center/Hospital. Three programs of study available: master's program for applicants with R.N. licensure and baccalaureate degree in any discipline; or master's program for non-nurse college graduates.

Graduate enrollment: full-time 184, part-time 65. Teaching faculty: full-time 54, part-time 33. Members of other University faculties also give instruction. Degrees conferred: M.S.N., M.S.N.-M.B.A., M.S.N.-M.P.H., Ph.D. (offered through the Graduate School of Arts and Sciences).

ADMISSION REQUIREMENTS: Transcripts, three personal references, GRE, admission essay, personal interview required in support of School's application. Online application available. For the R.N. master's program, nursing experience desirable but not required. TOEFL required of international applicants. Interviews are by invitation only and are for final selection. Transfer applicants usually not accepted. Graduates of unaccredited institutions not considered. Apply to Student Affairs Office by November 15 for non-nurse program; January 15 for R.N. master's program; March 1 for D.N.Sc. program. For R.N. applicants there are three admission cycles: apply by January 15, notification is by April 15; apply by April 1, notification by June 15; apply by May 1, notification by July 15. Rolling admissions process. Full-time, scheduled part-time, and nonmatriculated study available. Fall admission only. Application fee $75. Phone: (203)785-2389; fax: (203)737-5409.

ADMISSION STANDARDS. Competitive. Usual minimum average: 3.0 (master's applicants), 3.2 (doctoral applicants) (A = 4).

FINANCIAL AID. Traineeships, scholarships, Federal W/S, loans. Approved for VA benefits. Apply by February 1 to School for traineeships, scholarships; to Financial Aid Office for all other programs. Phone: (203)785-2389; fax: (203)737-5409. Use FAFSA (School code: 001426). Doctoral students are awarded two years of tuition, health coverage, and stipend.

DEGREE REQUIREMENTS. For M.S.N.: 40 credits full-time program for R.N. master's program and three-year full-time program for graduate entry non-nurse program; scholarly inquiry praxis; final oral exam. For Ph.D.: see Graduate School of Arts and Sciences.

FIELDS OF STUDY.
Adult Advanced Practice Nursing. Includes acute care nurse practitioner, clinical nurse specialist, oncology nurse practitioner.
Adult, Family, Gerontological and Women's Health Primary Care Specialty. Includes adult nurse practitioner, adult and gerontological nurse practitioner, family nurse practitioner, gerontological nurse practitioner, women's health nurse practitioner.
Nurse-Midwifery Specialty.
Nursing Management, Policy and Leadership Specialty.
Pediatric Nurse Practitioner Specialty. Includes chronic illness.
Psychiatric-Mental Health Nursing. Includes psychiatric nurse practitioner; concentrations in adult, child/adolescent, primary care.
Note: Once a Clinical Specialty has been selected, the following concentrations are offered: Diabetes Care, Health Care Ethics.

FIELDS OF DOCTORAL STUDY.
Acute and Critical Care.
Children with Mental Health Disorders.
Chronic Illness. Includes cardiovascular disease, diabetes, cancer, HIV/AIDS.

End-of-Life and Palliative Care.
Environmental Health.
Gerontological and Long-Term Care.
Health Equity and Care of Vulnerable Populations.
Maternal and Child Health.
Policy and Politics of Health Care.
School and Community-Based Interventions.
Self and Family Management.

YESHIVA UNIVERSITY
New York, New York 10033-3201
Web site: www.yu.edu

Founded 1886. CGS member. Coed. Private control. Semester system. Special facilities: Yeshiva University Museum, research centers in various diseases, Center for Research in Cancer, Rose Fitzgerald Kennedy Center for Research in Mental Retardation and Human Development, Jack and Pearl Resnick Gerontology Center, Legal Services Clinic, Center for Psychological Intervention. The University's NIH ranking is 41st among all U.S. institutions with 642 awards/grants valued at $155,228,278. According to The Center at University of Florida, the University is ranked 60th in receipt of Federal Research funds with $128,894,000 and it ranks 80th for total University research expenditures with $177,236,000. The University's endowment assets rank it 46th, with a value of $1,003,024,000. In 2004, 6 of the University's faculty members have been elected to National Honor Academies and this ranks it 73rd among all U.S. institutions. The Library: approximately 1,100,000 volumes, 10,000 subscriptions. Total University enrollment: 6500.

No on-campus housing available.

Bernard Revel Graduate School

Established 1937. Semester system. Tuition: per credit $795.
Enrollment: full-time 8, part-time 88. Harry Fischel School for Higher Jewish Studies (established 1945) is Summer component. Summer enrollment: 21. Faculty: full-time 9, part-time 5. Degrees conferred: M.A., Ph.D.

ADMISSION REQUIREMENTS. Official transcripts, appropriate bachelor's degree, knowledge of Hebrew language, literature, and Judaic studies, GRE required in support of School's application. Interview and entrance exam sometimes required. TOEFL required for international applicants. Accepts transfer applicants. Apply to Office of Admissions at least three months prior to registration. Rolling admissions process. Application fee $25. Phone: (212)960-5254; fax: (212)960-5245.

ADMISSION STANDARDS. Selective. Usual minimum average: 3.0 (A = 4).

FINANCIAL AID. Scholarships, fellowships, tuition waivers, loans. Apply by February 15 to Dean of the Graduate School for scholarships, assistantships; to Financial Aid Office for all other programs. Phone: (212)960-5253. Use FAFSA (School code: 002903).

DEGREE REQUIREMENTS. For M.A.: 30 credits minimum; comprehensive exam; thesis/nonthesis option/research project. For Ph.D.: 42 credits beyond the M.A. in Jewish Studies; reading knowledge of Hebrew; qualifying exam; dissertation; final oral exam.

FIELDS OF STUDY.
Bible. M.A., Ph.D.
Jewish Philosophy. M.A.
Medieval Jewish History. M.A., Ph.D.

Modern Jewish Philosophy. M.A., Ph.D.
Talmudic Studies. M.A.

Azrieli Graduate School of Jewish Education and Administration

Established 1983. Semester system. Tuition: per credit $835.
Enrollment: full-time 1, part-time 226. School faculty; full-time 6, part-time 11. Degrees conferred: M.S., Specialist's Certificate, Ed.D.

ADMISSION REQUIREMENTS. Official transcripts, two letters of recommendation, GRE and writing sample, evidence of advanced background in Jewish Studies and competence in Hebrew required in support of School's application. For Specialist and Ed.D. applicants, at least two years of teaching experience in an accredited school is required. Online application available. TOEFL (minimum score 550) required for international students. Accepts transfer applicants. Graduates of unaccredited institutions not considered. Apply to the Office of the Dean at least three months prior to registration. Application fee $35. Phone: (212)960-0186.

ADMISSION STANDARDS. Selective. Usual minimum average: 2.75 (A = 4).

FINANCIAL AID. Scholarships, loans. Apply by April 1 to Office of Student Finances of the University. Phone: (212)960-5269. Use FAFSA (School code: 002903). Aid available for part-time students.

DEGREE REQUIREMENTS. For M.S.: 30 credit program; supervised student teaching; comprehensive written exam. For Specialist's: 30 credit program; supervised administration internships in Jewish education; comprehensive written exam. For Ed.D.: 65 credit program beyond master's; internship in administration and supervision in Jewish education; comprehensive written exam; dissertation; final oral defense.

FIELDS OF STUDY.
Jewish Administration and Supervision.
Jewish Education.

Benjamin N. Cardozo School of Law (10003-4391)
Web site: www.cardozo.yu.edu

Established 1976. Located at the foot of Fifth Avenue in historic Greenwich Village. ABA approved since 1978. AALS member. Private control. Semester system. Full-time, day study only. Special facilities: Jacob Burns Institute of Advanced Legal Studies, Samuel and Ronnie Heyman Center for Corporate Governance, Floersheimer Center for Constitutional Democracy. Law library: 515,715 volumes, 6389 subscriptions; has LEXIS, NEXIS, WESTLAW, OCLC.
Annual tuition: $37,270; LL.M. $31,800. No on-campus housing available. Law students may live off-campus in Cardozo Residence Hall. Contact Admissions Office for additional off-campus options. Off-campus housing and personal expenses: approximately $23,700.
Enrollment: first-year class full-time 247, part-time 117; total full- and part-time 952 (men 50%, women 50%, minorities 21%). Faculty: full-time 52, part-time 64. Student to faculty ratio is 15.8 to 1. Degrees conferred: J.D., J.D.-M.A. (Economics, Philosophy, Political Science, Sociology–New School University), J.D.-M.S. (Management–New School University), J.D.-M.S.W. (Yeshiva University), J.D.-LL.M., LL.M. (Comparative Legal Thought, General Studies, Intellectual Property Law).

ADMISSION REQUIREMENTS. LSDAS Law School report, bachelor's degree, transcripts, LSAT, two letters of recommendation, personal statement required in support of application. Ac-

cepts transfer applicants. Graduates of unaccredited colleges not considered. Apply by April 1 for priority consideration. Admits September (traditional program), January and May (Accelerated Entry Plan). LL.M. programs admit Fall and Spring. Application fee $65. Phone: (212)790-0274; fax: (212)790-0482.

ADMISSION STANDARDS. Selective. Accepts 43% of total annual applicants. Number of full-time applicants 4776, part-time 436; number of full-time acceptance 1124, part-time 184; number enrolled full-time 247, part-time 117; LSAT (75% of full-time class have a score at or above 162, part-time 156); GPA (75% of full-time class have a GPA at or above 3.19, part-time 3.27). *U.S. News & World Report* ranking is in the 52nd of all law schools.

FINANCIAL AID. Scholarships, assistantships, Federal W/S, loans. Apply to Financial Aid Office by April 15. Phone: (212) 790-0392. Use FAFSA (School code: 002903). Approximately 68% of students receive some form of aid.

DEGREE REQUIREMENTS. For J.D.: satisfactory completion of 84-credit program. For LL.M.: 24 credit program.

Albert Einstein College of Medicine—Sue Golding Graduate Division of Medical Sciences
1300 Morris Park Avenue
Bronx, New York 10461
Web site: www.aecom.yu.edu

Establish 1957. Special facilities: Chanin Institute for Cancer Research, Center for Synchrotron Biosciences, Center for Aids Research, Center for Reproductive Biology, Children's Evaluation and Rehabilitation Center, Comprehensive Bone Center, Diabetes Research and Training Center, Gruss Magnetic Resonance Research Center, Institute for Aging Research, Institute for Communicative Disorders, Institute for Community and Collaborative Health, Marion Bessin Liver Research Center, Neuropsychopharmacology Center, Resnick Gerontology Center, Rose Fitzgerald Kennedy Center for Research in Mental Retardation and Human Development, Seaver Foundation for Bioinformatics.
Annual tuition: $26,000. Housing facilities same as for College of Medicine.
Enrollment: full-time 217 (men 55%, women 45%). Faculty full-time 415; no part-time faculty. Degree conferred: Ph.D.

ADMISSION REQUIREMENTS. Transcripts, two or three letters of recommendation, GRE required in support of application. Online application available. TOEFL required for international applicants. Accepts transfer applicants. Graduates of unaccredited colleges not considered. Apply to Director of Admissions by January 15. Application fee $60. Phone (718)430-2345; fax: (718) 430-8655; e-mail: phd@aecom.yu.edu.

ADMISSION STANDARDS. Selective. Accepts about 12% of total annual applicants.

FINANCIAL AID. Tuition scholarships and fellowship stipends available in most departments. Apply to appropriate department chair by February 1; for all other aid, contact the Student Finance Officer. Phone: (718)430-2336. Use FAFSA (School code: 002903).

DEGREE REQUIREMENTS. For Ph.D.: three years minimum of full-time study totaling 90 credits, at least two years in residence; written/oral exam in a foreign language; qualifying exam; thesis; oral exam.

FIELDS OF STUDY.
Anatomy and Structural Biology.
Biochemistry.
Cell Biology.
Developmental and Molecular Biology.

Microbiology and Immunology.
Molecular Genetics.
Molecular Pharmacology.
Neuroscience.
Pathology.
Physiology and Biophysics.

Albert Einstein College of Medicine

Web site: www.aecom.yu.edu

Established 1955. Located at the Westchester Heights campus (Bronx, 10461), adjacent to Jacobi Medical Center. Semester system. Special facilities: Biodefense Proteomics Research Center, Chanin Institute for Cancer Research, Cardiovascular Research Center, Center for Reproductive Biology, Comprehensive Bone Center, Institute for Aging Research, Institute for Brain Disorders and Neural Regeneration, Institute for Communicative Disorders, Marion Bessin Liver Research Center. Special programs: International Health Fellowships and programs in Israel, Germany, France, Sweden, and Japan. NIH ranking is 41st among all U.S. institutions with 642 awards/grants worth $155,228,278. Library: 250,000 volumes, 2400 subscriptions.

Annual tuition: $41,700. The College operates two apartment complexes for both single and married students. Contact Housing Office for both on- and off-campus housing information. Phone: (718)430-3552. Housing and personal expenses: approximately $21,000.

Enrollment: first-year class 180 (15 in M.D.-Ph.D.), total 751 (men 46%, women 54%, minorities 33%, state residents 46). Faculty: full-time 2500, part-time and volunteers 450. Degrees conferred: M.D., M.D.-M.S., M.D.-Ph.D. (M.S.T.P.).

ADMISSION REQUIREMENTS. AMCAS report, transcripts, letters of recommendation, MCAT required in support of application. Supplemental application required. Has EDP; apply between June 1 and August 1. Interviews by invitation only. Applicants should have completed four years of college study; in exceptional cases, three years. Graduates of unaccredited colleges not considered. Apply after June 1, before November 1. Application fee $100. Phone: (718)430-2106; fax: (718)430-8825.

ADMISSION STANDARDS. Very competitive. Accepts about 8% of all applicants. Number of applications 6307 (4865 out-of-state); number interviewed 1368 (940 out-of-state); number of acceptance 552 (366 out-of-state); number enrolled 180 (100 out-of-state). Mean Composite MCAT 10.4, mean UGPA 3.70. *U.S. New & World Report* ranking is in the top 39 of all U.S. research medical schools, in top 18 for primary care.

FINANCIAL AID. Scholarships, merit scholarships, minority scholarships, Grants-in-Aid, institutional loans, HEAL, alternative loan programs, NIH stipends, Federal Perkins Loans, Stafford Subsidized and Unsubsidized Loans, Service Commitment Scholarship programs are available. M.S.T.P. carries a full tuition scholarship and a stipend. All financial aid is based on documented need. Financial aid applications and information are generally available at the on-campus, by-invitation interview. Contact the Student Finance Officer for current information. Phone: (718)430-2336. Use FAFSA (School code: G09895), also submit Financial Aid Transcript, Federal Income Tax forms. Approximately 80% of students receive some form of financial assistance.

DEGREE REQUIREMENTS. For M.D.: satisfactory completion of four-year program. All students must pass USMLE Step 1 prior to entering third year and USMLE Step 2 prior to awarding of M.D. For M.D.-Ph.D.: generally a six- to seven-year program.

FIELDS OF GRADUATE STUDY.
Anatomy and Structural Biology.
Biochemistry.
Cell Biology.

Developmental and Molecular Biology.
Microbiology and Immunology.
Molecular Genetics.
Molecular Pharmacology.
Neurosciences.
Pathology.
Physiology and Biophysics.

Ferkauf Graduate School of Psychology

Established 1965. Semester system. Annual tuition: $29,060, per credit $1320.

Enrollment: full-time 285, part-time 52 (men 20%, women 80%). School faculty: full-time 28, part-time 70. Degrees conferred: M.A., Psy.D., Ph.D.

ADMISSION REQUIREMENTS. Transcripts, two letters of recommendation, GRE required in support of School's application. GRE Subject Test recommended. Online application available. TOEFL (minimum score 550) required for international students. Accepts transfer applicants. Graduates of unaccredited institutions not considered. Apply to the Office of Admissions by January 15 (Psy.D., Ph.D.), February 15 (M.A.). Application fee $35. Phone: (718)430-3820; fax: (718)430-3252.

ADMISSION STANDARDS. Competitive for most departments. Usual minimum average: 3.0 (A = 4).

FINANCIAL AID. Scholarships, fellowships, assistantships for teaching/research, internships, grants, Federal W/S, loans. Apply by March 1 to Office of Student Finances of the University. Phone: (212)960-5269. Use FAFSA (School code: 002903). Aid available for part-time students.

DEGREE REQUIREMENTS. For M.A.: 36 credits; thesis/nonthesis option; comprehensive exam. For Psy.D., Ph.D.: 78 credits minimum; comprehensive exam, dissertation; final oral exam.

FIELDS OF STUDY.
Applied Psychology. M.A.
Clinical Health Psychology. Ph.D.
Clinical Psychology. Psy.D.
Developmental Psychology. Ph.D.
General Psychology. Includes experimental, developmental, social-personality. M.A.
School-Child Clinical Psychology. Psy.D.
School Psychology. M.S., Psy.D.

Wurzweiller School of Social Work

Established 1957. Graduate study only. Tuition: per credit $885 (M.S.W.); $1040 per credit (Ph.D.).

Enrollment: full-time 353, part-time 120. Faculty: full-time 24, part-time 36. Degrees conferred: M.S.W., Ph.D., Certificate in Jewish Communal Services.

ADMISSION REQUIREMENTS. Official transcripts, interview, three letters of recommendation, personal statement required in support of application. Two interviews required for doctoral applicants and an M.S.W. from an accredited college or university. Online application available. TOEFL (minimum score 550) required for non-English-speaking applicants. Accepts transfer applicants. Graduates of unaccredited colleges not considered. Fall admission only. Apply by May 1, April 15 (Ph.D. programs). Rolling admissions process. Application fee $50. Phone: (212)960-0810; (212)960-0840 (doctoral applicants); fax: (212)960-0822.

ADMISSION STANDARDS. Competitive. Usual minimum average: 3.0 (A = 4).

FINANCIAL AID. Scholarships, grants, fellowships, research assistantships, internships, Federal W/S, loans, stipends from private, national, and state agencies. Approved for VA benefits. Apply to School's Admissions Officer by March 15 for Block Plan, May 1 for all programs. Phone: (212)960-5269; fax: (212)960-0037. Use FAFSA (School code: 002903).

DEGREE REQUIREMENTS. For M.S.W.: 60 credits, including prescribed courses; 1200 hours of field instruction; written essay. For Ph.D.: three years beyond the M.S.W.; prescribed and elective seminars; comprehensive exams; field study; dissertation; final oral exam.

FIELDS OF STUDY.
Community Social Work.
Jewish Communal Services. Certificate only.
Social Casework/Clinical Social Work.
Social Group Work.
Social Welfare. Ph.D.
Note: The M.S.W. is offered in four formats: Concurrent, Plan for Employed Persons (P.E.P.), Block, Clergy.

YOUNGSTOWN STATE UNIVERSITY
Youngstown, Ohio 44555-0002
Web site: www.ysu.edu

Founded 1908. CGS member. Coed. State control. Semester system. Special facilities: Center for Historic Preservation, Center for International Studies and Programs, Ethics Center, Professional Communication Design and Production Center, Public Service Center. Library: 993,314 volumes, 6518 subscriptions.

Tuition: per credit, area resident $307, resident $315, nonresident $315. On-campus housing available for single students only. Average academic year housing costs: $6500 (including board). Contact Housing Office for both on and off-campus housing information. Phone: (330)941-3547. Day-care facilities available.

School of Graduate Studies

Graduate study since 1967. Enrollment: full-time 206, part-time 962 (men 40%, women 60%). Graduate faculty: full-time 246, part-time 41. Degrees conferred: M.A., M.B.A., M.M., M.P.T., M.P.H., M.S., M.S.E., M.S.Ed., Ed.D.

ADMISSION REQUIREMENTS. Official transcripts required in support of application. Online application available. GRE/MAT/GMAT, interview required for some programs. TOEFL (minimum score 550) required for international applicants. Accepts transfer applicants. Graduates of unaccredited institutions not considered. Apply to Graduate School Admissions Office at least two months prior to registration. Application fee $30, $75 for international applicants. Phone: (330)941-3091; fax: (330)941-1580.

ADMISSION STANDARDS. Selective in some departments, relatively open in others. Usual minimum average: 2.75 (A = 4).

FINANCIAL AID. Annual awards from institutional funds: scholarships, fellowships, research assistantships, teaching assistantships, internships, Federal W/S, loans. Approved for VA benefits. Apply by March 1 to Office of the Dean for fellowships, assistantships; to Financial Aid Office for all other programs. Use FAFSA. About 35% of students receive aid from University and outside sources. Aid available for part-time students.

DEGREE REQUIREMENTS. For master's: 30–45 semester hours minimum, at least 24–36 in residence; thesis/nonthesis option or final paper. For Ed.S.: 30 semester hours beyond the master's; special project. For Ed.D.: 90 semester hours minimum beyond the master's, at least two years in residence; qualifying exam; research tool; dissertation; final oral exam.

FIELDS OF STUDY.
American Studies. M.A.
Biology. M.S.
Business Administration. M.B.A., E.M.B.A.
Chemistry. M.S.
Civil and Environmental Engineering. M.S.E.
Clinical Nurse Specialist—Chronic Illness Care. M.S.N.
Clinical Nurse Specialist—School Nurse. M.S.N.
Computing and Information Systems. M.C.I.S.
Counseling. M.S.Ed.
Creative Writing. M.F.A.
Criminal Justice. M.S.
Economics. M.A.
Educational Administration. M.S.Ed.
Educational Technology. M.S.Ed.
Electrical and Computer Engineering. M.S.E.
English. M.A.
Environmental Studies. M.S.
Financial Economics. M.A.
Health and Human Services. M.H.H.S.
History. M.A.
Industrial and System Engineering. M.S.E.
Jazz Studies. M.M.
Master Teacher—Elementary. M.S.Ed.
Master Teacher—Secondary. M.S.Ed.
Mathematics. M.S.
Mechanical Engineering. M.S.E.
Music Education. M.M.
Music History and Literature. M.M.
Music Performance. M.M.
Music Theory and Composition. M.M.
Nurse Anesthetist. M.S.N.
Physical Therapy. M.P.T.
Public Health. M.P.H.
Social Work. M.S.W.
Special Education. M.S.Ed.

LOCATION OF INSTITUTIONS, BY STATE

Since the institutional entries in the main body of this book are arranged alphabetically without reference to locations, page numbers are not provided here.

Alabama
Alabama Agricultural and Mechanical
  University
Alabama State University
Alabama, University of
  Birmingham
  Huntsville
  Tuscaloosa
Auburn University
Auburn University (Montgomery)
Jacksonville State University
Montevallo, University of
North Alabama, University of
Samford University
South Alabama, University of
Troy University
Troy University (Dothan)
Troy University (Montgomery)
Tuskegee University
West Alabama, University of

Alaska
Alaska, University of

Arizona
Arizona State University
Arizona State University West
Arizona, The University of
Northern Arizona University
Phoenix, University of
Thunderbird, School of Global Management

Arkansas
Arkansas State University
Arkansas, University of
  Fayetteville
Central Arkansas, University of
Harding University
Henderson State University

California
Alliant International University
Antioch Los Angeles
Antioch Santa Barbara
Azusa Pacific University
California College of the Arts

California Institute of Technology
California Institute of the Arts
California Lutheran University
California Polytechnic State University,
  San Luis Obispo
California State Polytechnic University,
  Pomona
California State University
  Bakersfield
  Chico
  Dominguez Hills
  East Bay
  Fresno
  Fullerton
  Hayward
  Long Beach
  Los Angeles
  Northridge
  Sacramento
  San Bernardino
  San Marcos
  Stanislaus
California, University of
  Berkeley
  Davis
  Hastings College of the Law
  Irvine
  Los Angeles
  Riverside
  San Diego
  San Francisco
  Santa Barbara
  Santa Cruz
California Western School of Law
Chapman University
Claremont Graduate University
Dominican University of California
Golden Gate University
Health Sciences College of Osteopathic
  Medicine of the Pacific, University of
Holy Names University
Humboldt State University
La Verne, University of
Loma Linda University
Loyola Marymount University
Mills College
Monterey Institute of International Studies
Mount St. Mary's College
National University

Naval Postgraduate School
Notre Dame de Namur University
Pacific, University of
Pepperdine University
Pepperdine University—Culver City
Point Loma Nazarene University
Redlands, University of
San Diego State University
San Diego, University of
San Francisco Art Institute
San Francisco Conservatory of Music
San Francisco State University
San Francisco, University of
San Jose State University
Santa Clara University
Sonoma State University
Southern California College of
  Optometry
Southern California, University of
Southwestern University School
  of Law
Stanford University
Thomas Jefferson School of Law
Touro University College of Osteopathic
  Medicine
Western University of Health Sciences
Whittier College

Colorado
Adams State College
Colorado School of Mines
Colorado State University
Colorado, University of
  Boulder
  Colorado Springs
  Denver
  Health Sciences Center
Denver, University of
Northern Colorado, University of

Connecticut
Bridgeport, University of
Central Connecticut State University
Connecticut, The University of
  Storrs
  Health Center
Eastern Connecticut State University

Fairfield University
Hartford, University of
Health Center, University of
  Connecticut
New Haven, University of
Quinnipiac University
St. Joseph College
Southern Connecticut State University
Trinity College
Wesleyan University
Western Connecticut State University
Yale University

Delaware
Delaware, University of
Widener University

District of Columbia
American University, The
Catholic University of America, The
District of Columbia, University of
Gallaudet University
Georgetown University
George Washington University, The
Howard University

Florida
Barry University
Central Florida, University of
Florida Agricultural and Mechanical
  University
Florida Atlantic University
Florida Coastal School of Law
Florida Institute of Technology
Florida International University
Florida State University
Florida, University of
Jacksonville University
Miami, University of
North Florida, University of
Nova Southeastern University
Rollins College
St. Thomas University
South Florida, University of
Stetson University
West Florida, University of

Georgia
Armstrong Atlantic State University
Augusta State University
Berry College
Clark Atlanta University
Columbus State University
Emory University
Fort Valley State University
Georgia College and State
  University
Georgia Institute of Technology, The
Georgia Medical College of
Georgia Southern University
Georgia State University
Georgia, The University of
Kennesaw State University
La Grange College
Mercer University
Morehouse School of Medicine
Oglethorpe University
Valdosta State College
West Georgia, University of

Hawaii
Hawaii Pacific University
Hawaii, University of

Idaho
Boise State University
Idaho State University
Idaho, University of

Illinois
Art Institute of Chicago, The School of the
Bradley University
Chicago State University
Chicago, The University of
Concordia University Chicago
DePaul University
Dominican University
Eastern Illinois University
Governors State University
Illinois Institute of Technology
Illinois State University
Illinois, University at
  Chicago
  Springfield
  Urbana
John Marshall Law School
Loyola University Chicago
Midwestern University—Chicago College of
  Osteopathic Medicine
National Louis University
Northeastern Illinois University
Northern Illinois University
Northwestern University
Olivet Nazarene University
Rockford College
Roosevelt University
Rosalind Franklin University of Medicine and
  Science
Rush Medical College
St. Xavier University
Southern Illinois University
  Carbondale
  Edwardsville
Western Illinois University

Indiana
Ball State University
Butler University
Indiana State University
Indiana University
  Bloomington
  Indianapolis
Indianapolis, University of
Notre Dame, University of
Purdue University
  Calumet
  West Lafayette
Rose-Hulman Institute of Technology
St. Francis, University of
Valparaiso University

Iowa
Drake University
Dubuque, University of
Iowa State University of Science and
  Technology
Iowa, The University of
Loras College
Morningside College
Northern Iowa, University of
Osteopathic Medicine and Health Sciences,
  University of

Kansas
Emporia State University
Fort Hays State University
Kansas City University of Medicine and
  Bioscience
Kansas Medical Center, University of
Kansas State University
Kansas, University of
Pittsburg State University
Washburn University of Topeka
Wichita State University

Kentucky
Eastern Kentucky University
Georgetown College
Kentucky, University of

Louisville, University of
Morehead State University
Murray State University
Pikeville College School of Osteopathic
  Medicine
Salmon P. Chase College of Law of Northern
  Kentucky University
Spalding University
Union College
Western Kentucky University

Louisiana
Louisiana State University and Agricultural
  and Mechanical College
Louisiana State University Health Sciences
  Center
Louisiana State University in Shreveport
Louisiana Tech University
Louisiana at Lafayette, University of
Louisiana at Monroe, University of
Loyola University New Orleans
McNeese State University
New Orleans, University of
Northwestern State University of Louisiana
Southeastern Louisiana University
Southern University and Agricultural and
  Mechanical College
Tulane University
Xavier University of Louisiana

Maine
Maine, University of
Medicine, University of
New England College of Osteopathic
  Medicine, University of
Southern Maine, University of

Maryland
Baltimore, University of
Bowie State University
Frostburg State University
Goucher College
Hood College
Johns Hopkins University, The
Loyola College in Maryland
Maryland at Baltimore, University of
Maryland Institute College of Art
Maryland, University of
Maryland–Baltimore County, University of
McDaniel College
Morgan State University
Salisbury State University
Towson University
Uniformed Services University of the Health
  Sciences
Washington College

Massachusetts
Assumption College
Babson College
Bentley College
Boston College
Boston University
Brandeis University
Bridgewater State College
Clark University
Emerson College
Fitchburg State College
Framingham State College
Harvard University
Massachusetts College of Art
Massachusetts College of Pharmacy and
  Allied Health Sciences
Massachusetts Institute of Technology
Massachusetts, University of
  Amherst
  Boston
  Dartmouth
  Lowell
Mount Holyoke College

New England Conservatory of Music
New England School of Law
Northeastern University
Salem State College
Simmons College
Smith College
Springfield College
Suffolk University
Tufts University
Western New England College
Westfield State College
Wheelock College
Worcester Polytechnic Institute
Worcester State College

Michigan
Andrews University
Central Michigan University
Cranbrook Academy of Art
Detroit College of Law, Michigan State
Detroit Mercy, University of
Eastern Michigan University
Marygrove College
Michigan State University
Michigan Technological University
Michigan, The University of
Northern Michigan University
Oakland University
Saginaw Valley State University
Siena Heights University
Thomas M. Cooley Law School
Wayne State University
Western Michigan University

Minnesota
Bemidji State University
Hamline University
Mayo Medical School
Minnesota State University, Mankato
Minnesota, University of
Minnesota Duluth, University of
Minnesota State University, Moorhead
St. Cloud State University
St. John's University
St. Mary's University of Minnesota
St. Scholastica, College of
St. Thomas, University of
William Mitchell College of Law
Winona State University

Mississippi
Delta State University
Jackson State University
Mississippi College
Mississippi Medical Center, University of
Mississippi State University
Mississippi University for Women
Mississippi, The University of
Southern Mississippi, University of
William Carey College

Missouri
A.T. Still University
Central Missouri State University
Drury University
Health Sciences, University of
Kirksville College of Osteopathic Medicine
Lincoln University
Maryville University of St. Louis
Missouri University of Science and
    Technology
Missouri, University of
    Columbia
    Kansas City
    St. Louis
Northwest Missouri State University
Saint Louis University
Southeast Missouri State University
Southwest Missouri State University
Truman State University

Washington University
Webster University

Montana
Montana State University
    Billings
    Bozeman
Montana Tech of the University of Montana
Montana, University of

Nebraska
Chadron State College
Concordia University
Creighton University, The
Nebraska, University of
    Kearney
    Lincoln
    Medical Center
    Omaha
Wayne State College

Nevada
Nevada, University of
    Las Vegas
    Reno

New Hampshire
Antioch New England Graduate School
Dartmouth College
Franklin Pierce Law Center
New Hampshire, University of
Plymouth State College
Rivier College

New Jersey
Drew University
Fairleigh Dickinson University
    Madison
    Teaneck
Jersey City University
Kean University
Medicine and Dentistry of New Jersey,
    University of
Monmouth University
Montclair State University
New Jersey, College of
New Jersey Institute of Technology
Princeton University
Rider University
Rowan University
Rutgers University
    Camden
    Newark
    New Brunswick
Seton Hall University
Stevens Institute of Technology
William Paterson University of New Jersey

New Mexico
Eastern New Mexico University
New Mexico Highlands University
New Mexico Institute of Mining and
    Technology
New Mexico State University
New Mexico, The University of
Western New Mexico University

New York
Adelphi University
Albany, Law School of Union University
Albany Medical College
Albany, The University at
Alfred University
Bank Street College of Education
Brooklyn Law School
Buffalo, University at
Canisius College
City University of New York, The

Bernard M. Baruch College
Brooklyn College
City College, The
Graduate School and University Center
Herbert H. Lehman College
Hunter College
John Jay College of Criminal Justice
Queens College
Staten Island, The College of
Clarkson University
Columbia University
Cornell University
C. W. Post Center of Long Island University
Elmira College
Fordham University
Hofstra University
Iona College
Ithaca College
Juilliard School, The
Long Island University (Brooklyn)
Manhattan College
Manhattan School of Music
Manhattanville College
Mount Sinai School of Medicine
New Rochelle, College of
New School University
New York College of Osteopathic Medicine
New York Institute of Technology
New York Law School
New York Medical College
New York, State University of, at
    Binghamton
    Downstate Medical Center (Brooklyn)
    Upstate Medical University (Syracuse)
New York, State University of, College at
    Brockport
    Buffalo
    Cortland
    Environmental Science and Forestry at
        Syracuse
    Fredonia
    Geneseo
    New Paltz
    Oneonta
    Oswego
    Plattsburg
    Potsdam
New York, State University of, Institute of
    Technology at Utica/Rome
New York University
Niagara University
Pace University
Polytechnic University
Pratt Institute
Rensselaer Polytechnic Institute
Rochester Institute of Technology
Rochester, University of
Rockefeller University, The
Sage Colleges
St. Bonaventure University
St. John's University
Saint Rose, The College of
Sarah Lawrence College
Stony Brook University
Syracuse University
Touro College—School of Law
Union College
Wagner College
Yeshiva University

North Carolina
Appalachian State University
Campbell University
Duke University
East Carolina University
North Carolina Agricultural and Technical
    State University
North Carolina Central University
North Carolina State University at Raleigh
North Carolina, The University of
    Chapel Hill
    Charlotte

Greensboro
Wilmington
Wake Forest University
Western Carolina University

North Dakota
Minot State University
North Dakota State University
North Dakota, University of

Ohio
Air Force Institute of Technology
Akron, University of
Antioch University McGregor
Bowling Green State University
Capital University
Case Western Reserve University
Cincinnati, University of
Cleveland State University
Dayton, University of
John Carroll University
Kent State University
Medical College of Ohio at Toledo
Miami University
Northeastern Ohio University
Ohio Northern University
Ohio State University, The
Ohio University
Toledo, University of
Union Institute and University
Wright State University
Xavier University
Youngstown State University

Oklahoma
Central Oklahoma, University of
East Central University
Health Science Center, University of
  Oklahoma
Northeastern State University
Northwestern Oklahoma State University
Oklahoma City University
Oklahoma State University
  Center for Health Sciences
  Stillwater
  Tulsa
Oklahoma, University of
Oral Roberts University
Southeastern Oklahoma State University
Southern Nazarene University
Southwestern Oklahoma State University
Tulsa, The University of

Oregon
Eastern Oregon University
Lewis and Clark College
Oregon Health Sciences University
Oregon State University
Oregon, University of
Pacific University
Portland State University
Portland, University of
Southern Oregon University
Western Oregon University
Willamette University

Pennsylvania
Bloomsburg University of Pennsylvania
Bryn Mawr College
Bucknell University
California University of Pennsylvania
Carnegie Mellon University
Clarion University of Pennsylvania
Dickinson School of Law, The
Drexel University
Duquesne University
East Stroudsburg University of Pennsylvania
Edinboro University of Pennsylvania
Gannon College
Indiana University of Pennsylvania

Kutztown University of Pennsylvania
Lake Erie College of Osteopathic Medicine
Lehigh University
Mansfield University of Pennsylvania
Marywood University
Millersville University of Pennsylvania
Pennsylvania College of Optometry
Pennsylvania State University
  University Park
  Harrisburg
  Hershey Medical Center
Pennsylvania, University of
Philadelphia College of Osteopathic Medicine
Pittsburgh, University of
Robert Morris University
St. Francis University
St. Joseph's University
Scranton, University of
Shippensburg University of Pennsylvania
Slippery Rock University of Pennsylvania
Temple University
Thomas Jefferson University
University of the Arts
University of the Sciences in Philadelphia
Villanova University
West Chester University of Pennsylvania
Westminster College
Widener University
Wilkes University

Puerto Rico
Inter American University
Ponce School of Medicine
Pontifical Catholic University of Puerto
  Rico
Puerto Rico, University of
Puerto Rico Mayaguez, University of

Rhode Island
Brown University
Bryant University
Providence College
Rhode Island College
Rhode Island School of Design
Rhode Island, University of
Roger Williams University

South Carolina
Citadel, The Military College of South
  Carolina
Clemson University
Converse College
Furman University
South Carolina, Medical University of
South Carolina State University
South Carolina, University of
Winthrop University

South Dakota
Northern State University
South Dakota School of Mines and
  Technology
South Dakota State University
South Dakota, University of

Tennessee
Austin Peay State University
East Tennessee State University
Fisk University
Meharry Medical College
Memphis, University of
Middle Tennessee State University
South, University of the
Southern College of Optometry
Tennessee State University
Tennessee Technological University
Tennessee, University of
  Chattanooga
  Health Science Center
  Knoxville

Martin
Space Institute
Vanderbilt University

Texas
Abilene Christian University
Angelo State University
Baylor College of Dentistry
Baylor College of Medicine
Baylor University
Dallas, University of
Hardin-Simmons University
Houston, University of
  Houston
  Clear Lake
Incarnate Word, University, of the
Lamar University
Midwestern State University
North Texas, University of
Our Lady of the Lake University
Prairie View A&M University
Rice University
St. Edward's University
St. Mary's University
St. Thomas, University of
Sam Houston State University
Southern Methodist University
South Texas College of Law
Stephen F. Austin State University
Sul Ross State University
Tarleton State University
Texas A&M University
  College Station
  Commerce
  Corpus Christi
  Kingsville
Texas Christian University
Texas Southern University
Texas State University, San Marcos
Texas Tech University
Texas Wesleyan University
Texas Woman's University
Texas, The University of
  Arlington
  Austin
  Brownsville
  Dallas
  El Paso
  Health Science Center at Houston
  Health Science Center at San Antonio
  Medical Branch Galveston
  Pan American
  Permian Basin
  San Antonio
  Southwestern Health Science Center
  Tyler
Trinity University
West Texas A&M University

Utah
Brigham Young University
Utah State University
Utah, University of

Vermont
Bennington College
Goddard College
Middlebury College
St. Michael's College
Vermont Law School
Vermont, University of

Virginia
Eastern Virginia Medical School
George Mason University
Hampton University
Hollins College
James Madison University
Longwood University
Lynchburg College
Old Dominion University

Radford University
Regent University
Richmond, University of
Virginia Commonwealth University
Virginia Polytechnic Institute and State
    University
Virginia State University
Virginia, University of
Washington and Lee University
William and Mary, The College of

Washington

Antioch University Seattle
Central Washington University
Eastern Washington University
Gonzaga University
Pacific Lutheran University
Puget Sound, University of

Seattle Pacific University
Seattle University
Walla Walla College
Washington State University
Washington, University of
Western Washington University
Whitworth College

West Virginia

Marshall University
West Virginia School of Osteopathic
    Medicine
West Virginia University

Wisconsin

Cardinal Stritch College
Marquette University

Milwaukee School of Engineering
Wisconsin, Medical College of
Wisconsin, University of
    Eau Claire
    La Crosse
    Madison
    Milwaukee
    Oshkosh
    Platteville
    River Falls
    Stevens Point
    Stout
    Superior
    Whitewater

Wyoming

Wyoming, University of

INSTITUTIONAL ABBREVIATIONS

A.C.U. *Abilene Christian University*
Adams St. C. *Adams State College*
Adelphi U. *Adelphi University*
A.F. Inst. *Air Force Institute of Technology*
A.T. Still U. *A.T. Still University*
Ala. A&M U. *Alabama Agricultural and Mechanical University*
Ala. St. U. *Alabama State University*
Albany Law Sch. *Albany Law School*
Albany Med. C. *Albany Medical College*
Albany, U. *The University at Albany*
Alfred U. *Alfred University*
Alliant Intl. U. *Alliant International University*
Amer. U. *The American University*
Andrews U. *Andrews University*
Angelo St. U. *Angelo State University*
Antioch N. E. Grad. Sch. *Antioch New England Graduate School*
Antioch (L.A.) *Antioch Los Angeles*
Antioch (Santa Barbara) *Antioch Santa Barbara*
Antioch U. (McGregor) *Antioch University McGregor*
Antioch U. (Seattle) *Antioch University Seattle*
Appal. St. U. *Appalachian State University*
Ariz. St. U. *Arizona State University*
Ariz. St. U. (West) *Arizona State University–West*
Ark. St. U. *Arkansas State University*
Armstrong Atlantic St. U. *Armstrong Atlantic State University*
Sch. Art Inst. Chicago *The School of the Art Institute of Chicago*
Assump. C. *Assumption College*
Auburn U. *Auburn University*
Auburn U. (Montgomery) *Auburn University at Montgomery*
Augusta St. U. *Augusta State University*
Austin Peay St. U. *Austin Peay State University*
Azusa Pac. U. *Azusa Pacific University*
Babson C. *Babson College*
Ball St. U. *Ball State University*
Bank St. C. *Bank Street College of Education*
Barry U. *Barry University*
Baruch C. (C.U.N.Y.) *Bernard M. Baruch College of the City University of New York*
Baylor C. Dentistry *Baylor College of Dentistry*
Baylor C. Med. *Baylor College of Medicine*
Baylor U. *Baylor University*
Bemidji St. U. *Bemidji State University*
Bennington C. *Bennington College*
Bentley C. *Bentley College*
Berry C. *Berry College*
Bloomsburg U. *Bloomsburg University of Pennsylvania*
Boise St. U. *Boise State University*
Boston C. *Boston College*
Boston U. *Boston University*
Bowie St. U. *Bowie State University*
Bowl. Gr. St. U. *Bowling Green State University*
Bradley U. *Bradley University*

Brandeis U. *Brandeis University*
Bridgewater St. C. *Bridgewater State College*
Brooklyn C. (C.U.N.Y.) *Brooklyn College of the City University of New York*
Brooklyn Law *Brooklyn Law School*
Brown U. *Brown University*
Bryant U. *Bryant University*
Bryn Mawr C. *Bryn Mawr College*
Bucknell U. *Bucknell University*
Butler U. *Butler University*
B.Y.U. *Brigham Young University*
Cal. C. Arts *California College of the Arts*
Cal. Inst. Arts *California Insitute of the Arts*
Cal. Luth. U. *California Lutheran University*
Cal. Poly. St. U. (San Luis Obispo) *California Polytechnic State University at San Luis Obispo*
Cal. St. Poly. U. (Pomona) *California State Polytechnic University at Pomona*
Cal. St. U. (Bakersfield) *California State University at Bakersfield*
Cal. St. U. (Chico) *California State University at Chico*
Cal. St. U. (Dominguez Hills) *California State University at Dominguez Hills*
Cal. St. U. (E.B.) *California State University, East Bay*
Cal. St. U. (Fresno) *California State University at Fresno*
Cal. St. U. (Fullerton) *California State University at Fullerton*
Cal. St. U. (Humboldt) *Humboldt State University*
Cal. St. U. (Long Beach) *California State University at Long Beach*
Cal. St. U. (L.A.) *California State University at Los Angeles*
Cal. St. U. (Northridge) *California State University at Northridge*
Cal. St. U. (Sacramento) *California State University at Sacramento*
Cal. St. U. (San Bernardino) *California State University at San Bernardino*
Cal. St. U. (San Francisco) *San Francisco State University*
Cal. St. U. (San Jose) *San Jose State University*
Cal. St. U. (San Marcos) *California State University, San Marcos*
Cal. St. U. (Sonoma) *Sonoma State University*
Cal. St. U. (Stanislaus) *California State University at Stanislaus*
Cal. Tech. *California Institute of Technology*
Cal. U. (Pa.) *California University of Pennsylvania*
Cal. West. Sch. Law *California Western School of Law*
Campbell U. *Campbell University*
Canisius C. *Canisius College*
Capital U. *Capital University*
Card. Stritch C. *Cardinal Stritch College*
Carnegie Mellon U. *Carnegie Mellon University*
Case West. Res. U. *Case Western Reserve University*
Catholic U. *The Catholic University of America*
Catholic U. P.R. *Pontifical Catholic University of Puerto Rico*
C.C.N.Y. (C.U.N.Y.) *City College of the City University of New York*
Cent. Conn. St. U. *Central Connecticut State University*
Cent. Mich. U. *Central Michigan University*
Cent. Mo. St. U. *Central Missouri State University*

Cent. Wash. U.   *Central Washington University*
Chadron St. C.   *Chadron State College*
Chapman U.   *Chapman University*
Chase C. Law   *Salmon P. Chase College of Law of Northern Kentucky University*
Chicago St. U.   *Chicago State University*
Citadel   *The Citadel*
Claremont Grad. U.   *Claremont Graduate University*
Clarion U.   *Clarion University of Pennsylvania*
Clark Atl. U.   *Clark Atlanta University*
Clark U.   *Clark University*
Clarkson U.   *Clarkson University*
Clemson U. Clemson University
Cleve. St. U.   *Cleveland State University*
C. N. Rochelle   *College of New Rochelle*
Colo. Sch. Mines   *Colorado School of Mines*
Colo. St. U.   *Colorado State University*
Columbia U.   *Columbia University*
Columbus St. U.   *Columbus State University*
Concordia U. (Ill.)   *Concordia University*
Concordia U. (Nebr.)   *Concordia University*
Converse C.   *Converse College*
Cornell U.   *Cornell University*
Cranbrook Acad. Art   *Cranbrook Academy of Art*
Creighton U.   *The Creighton University*
C. St. Rose   *The College of Saint Rose*
C. St. Scholastica   *College of St. Scholastica*
C. Staten Island (C.U.N.Y.)   *The College of Staten Island of the City University of New York*
C.U.N.Y. (Grad. Ctr.)   *The City University of New York*
C. Wm. & Mary   *The College of William and Mary*
C.W. Post (L.I.U.)   *Long Island University, C. W. Post Campus*
Dartmouth C.   *Dartmouth College*
Delta St. U.   *Delta State University*
DePaul U.   *DePaul University*
Des Moines U.   *Des Moines University of Health Sciences*
Detroit C. Law   *Michigan State University—Detroit College of Law*
Dickinson Sch. Law   *The Dickinson School of Law*
Dominican U.   *Dominican University*
Dominican U. (Calif.)   *Dominican University of California*
Drake U.   *Drake University*
Drew U.   *Drew University*
Drexel U.   *Drexel University*
Drury U.   *Drury University*
Duke U.   *Duke University*
Duquesne U.   *Duquesne University*
East Car. U.   *East Carolina University*
East Cent. U.   *East Central University*
East. Conn. St. U.   *Eastern Connecticut State University*
East. Ill. U.   *Eastern Illinois University*
East. Ky. U.   *Eastern Kentucky University*
East. Mich. U.   *Eastern Michigan University*
East. N. Mex. U.   *Eastern New Mexico University*
East. Ore. U.   *Eastern Oregon University*
East Stroudsburg U.   *East Stroudsburg University of Pennsylvania*
East Tenn. St. U.   *East Tennessee State University*
East. Va. Med. Sch.   *Eastern Virginia Medical School of the Medical College of Hampton Roads*
East. Wash. U.   *Eastern Washington University*
Edinboro U.   *Edinboro University of Pennsylvania*
Elmira C.   *Elmira College*
Emerson C.   *Emerson College*
Emory U.   *Emory University*
Emporia St. U.   *Emporia State University*
Fairfield U.   *Fairfield University*
F.D.U. (Madison)   *Fairleigh Dickinson University*
F.D.U. (Teaneck)   *Fairleigh Dickinson University*
Finch U. Health Sci.   *Finch University of Health Sciences of the Chicago Medical School*
Fitchburg St. C.   *Fitchburg State College*
Fla. A&M U.   *Florida Agricultural and Mechanical University*
Fla. Atlantic U.   *Florida Atlantic University*
Fla. Coastal Sch. of Law   *Florida Coastal School of Law*
Fla. Inst. Tech.   *Florida Institute of Technology*
Fla. Int'l. U.   *Florida International University*
Fla. St. U.   *Florida State University*
Fordham U.   *Fordham University*
Fort Hays St. U.   *Fort Hays State University*
Fort Valley St. U.   *Fort Valley State University*

Framingham St. C.   *Framingham State College*
Franklin Pierce Law Ctr.   *Franklin Pierce Law Center*
Frostburg St. U.   *Frostburg State University*
Furman U.   *Furman University*
Gallaudet U.   *Gallaudet University*
Gannon U.   *Gannon University*
Geo. Mason U.   *George Mason University*
Georgetown C.   *Georgetown College*
Georgetown U.   *Georgetown University*
Geo. Wash. U.   *The George Washington University*
Georgia C. & St. U.   *Georgia College and State University*
Georgia Inst. Tech.   *The Georgia Institute of Technology*
Georgia So. U.   *Georgia Southern University*
Georgia St. U.   *Georgia State University*
Goddard C.   *Goddard College*
Golden Gate U.   *Golden Gate University*
Gonzaga U.   *Gonzaga University*
Goucher C.   *Goucher College*
Gov. St. U.   *Governors State University*
Hamline U.   *Hamline University*
Hampton U.   *Hampton University*
Hardin-Simmons U.   *Hardin-Simmons University*
Harding U.   *Harding University*
Harvard U.   *Harvard University*
Hastings C. Law   *University of California, Hastings College of the Law*
Hawaii Pac. U.   *Hawaii Pacific University*
Henderson St. U.   *Henderson State University*
Hofstra U.   *Hofstra University*
Hollins U.   *Hollins University*
Holy Names U.   *Holy Names University*
Hood C.   *Hood College*
Howard U.   *Howard University*
Hunter C. (C.U.N.Y.)   *Hunter College of the City University of New York*
Idaho St. U.   *Idaho State University*
Ill. Inst. Tech.   *Illinois Institute of Technology*
Ill. St. U.   *Illinois State University*
Ind. St. U.   *Indiana State University*
Ind. U.   *Indiana University*
I.U.P.U.I.   *Indiana University Purdue University Indianapolis*
Ind. U. Penn.   *Indiana University of Pennsylvania*
Inter American U.   *Inter American University*
Iona C.   *Iona College*
Iowa St. U.   *Iowa State University of Science and Technology*
Ithaca C.   *Ithaca College*
Jackson St. U.   *Jackson State University*
Jacksonville St. U.   *Jacksonville State University*
Jacksonville U.   *Jacksonville University*
James Madison U.   *James Madison University*
Jersey City St. U.   *Jersey City State University*
John Carroll U.   *John Carroll University*
John Jay C. (C.U.N.Y.)   *John Jay College of Criminal Justice of the City University of New York*
John Marshall Law Sch.   *John Marshall Law School*
Johns Hopkins U.   *The Johns Hopkins University*
Juilliard   *The Juilliard School*
Kans. City U. Med. & Bio.   *Kansas City University of Medicine and Bioscience*
Kans. St. U.   *Kansas State University*
Kean U.   *Kean University*
Kent St. U.   *Kent State University*
Kirksville C.   *Kirksville College of Osteopathic Medicine*
Kutztown U.   *Kutztown University of Pennsylvania*
Lake Erie C.   *Lake Erie College of Osteopathic Medicine*
Lamar U.   *Lamar University*
Lehigh U.   *Lehigh University*
Lehman C. (C.U.N.Y.)   *Herbert H. Lehman College of the City University of New York*
Lewis & Clark C.   *Lewis and Clark College*
Lincoln U.   *Lincoln University*
L.I.U.   *Long Island University, Brooklyn Campus*
L.I.U. (C.W. Post)   *Long Island University, C.W. Post Campus*
Loma Linda U.   *Loma Linda University*
Longwood U.   *Longwood University*
Loras C.   *Loras College*
Loyola C. (Md.)   *Loyola College (Maryland)*
Loyola Marymount U.   *Loyola Marymount University (Los Angeles)*
Loyola U. Chicago   *Loyola University Chicago*
Loyola U. (La.)   *Loyola University New Orleans*

L.S.U. *Louisiana State University and Agricultural and Mechanical College*
L.S.U. H.S.C. *Louisiana State University Health Sciences Center*
L.S.U. Shreveport *Louisiana State University in Shreveport*
La. Tech U. *Louisiana Tech University*
Lynchburg C. *Lynchburg College*
Manhattan C. *Manhattan College*
Manhattan Sch. Music *Manhattan School of Music*
Manhattanville C. *Manhattanville College*
Mansfield U. *Mansfield University of Pennsylvania*
Marquette U. *Marquette University*
Marshall U. *Marshall University*
Marygrove C. *Marygrove College*
Md. Inst. C. Art *Maryland Institute College of Art*
Maryville U. *Maryville University of Saint Louis*
Marywood U. *Marywood University*
Mass. C. Art *Massachusetts College of Art*
Mass. C. Pharmacy *Massachusetts College of Pharmacy and Allied Health Sciences*
Mayo Med. Sch. *Mayo Medical School*
McDaniel C. *McDaniel College*
McNeese St. U. *McNeese State University*
Med. C. Georgia *Medical College of Georgia*
Med. C. Ohio *Medical College of Ohio at Toledo*
Med. C. Penn. *Medical College of Pennsylvania and Hahnemann University*
Med. C. Wis. *Medical College of Wisconsin*
Med. U. So. Car. *Medical University of South Carolina*
Meharry Med. C. *Meharry Medical College*
Mercer U. *Mercer University*
Miami U. (Ohio) *Miami University (Ohio)*
Mich. St. U. *Michigan State University*
Mich. Tech. U. *Michigan Technological University*
Middlebury C. *Middlebury College*
Mid. Tenn. St. U. *Middle Tennessee State University*
Midwestern St. U. *Midwestern State University*
Midwest. U. *Midwestern University–Chicago College of Osteopathic Medicine*
Millersville U. *Millersville University of Pennsylvania*
Mills C. *Mills College*
Milwau. Sch. Eng. *Milwaukee School of Engineering*
Minn. St. U. (Mankato) *Minnesota State University Mankato*
Minn. St. U. (Moorhead) *Minnesota State University Moorhead*
Minot St. U. *Minot State University*
Miss. C. *Mississippi College*
Miss. St. U. *Mississippi State University*
Miss. St. U. Women *Mississippi University for Women*
M.I.T. *Massachusetts Institute of Technology*
Mo. U. Sci. & Tech. *Missouri University of Science and Technology*
Monmouth U. *Monmouth University*
Mont. St. U. *Montana State University*
Mont. Tech *Montana Tech of the University of Montana*
Montclair St. U. *Montclair State University*
Monterey Inst. *Monterey Institute of International Studies*
Morehead St. U. *Morehead State University*
Morehouse Sch. Med. *Morehouse School of Medicine*
Morgan St. U. *Morgan State University*
Morningside C. *Morningside College*
Mt. Sinai Sch. Med. *Mount Sinai School of Medicine*
Mt. St. Mary's C. *Mount St. Mary's College*
Murray St. U. *Murray State University*
Natl. Louis U. *National-Louis University*
Natl. U. *National University*
Naval P.G. Sch. *Naval Postgraduate School*
New Eng. Cons. Music *New England Conservatory of Music*
New Eng. Sch. Law *New England School of Law*
N.J.I.T. *New Jersey Institute of Technology*
N. Mex. Highlands U. *New Mexico Highlands University*
N. Mex. Inst. M&T *New Mexico Institute of Mining and Technology*
N. Mex. St. U. *New Mexico State University*
New Sch. U. *The New School University*
Niagara U. *Niagara University*
No. Ariz. U. *Northern Arizona University*
No. Car. A&T *North Carolina Agricultural and Technical State University*
No. Car. Cent. U. *North Carolina Central University*
No. Car. St. U. (Raleigh) *North Carolina State University at Raleigh*
No. Dak. St. U. *North Dakota State University*

Northeastern Ill. U. *Northeastern Illinois University*
No. E. Ohio U. *Northeastern Ohio Universities*
No. E. St. U. *Northeastern State University*
Northeastern U. *Northeastern University*
No. Ill. U. *Northern Illinois University*
No. Kent. U. *Northern Kentucky University*
No. Mich. U. *Northern Michigan University*
No. St. U. *Northern State University*
Northrop U. *Northrop University*
Northwestern U. *Northwestern University*
Notre Dame U. *Notre Dame de Namur University*
Nova S.E. U. *Nova Southeastern University*
No. W. Mo. St. U. *Northwest Missouri State University*
No. W. Okla. St. U. *Northwestern Oklahoma State University*
No. W. St. U. La. *Northwestern State University of Louisiana*
N.Y.I.T. *New York Institute of Technology*
N.Y. Law Sch. *New York Law School*
N.Y. Med. C. *New York Medical College*
N.Y.U. *New York University*
Oakland U. *Oakland University*
Ohio No. U. *Ohio Northern University*
Ohio St. U. *The Ohio State University*
Ohio U. *Ohio University*
Okla. City U. *Oklahoma City University*
Okla. St. U. *Oklahoma State University*
Okla. S. U. Health Sci. *Oklahoma State University Center for Health Sciences*
Okla. St. U. (Tulsa) *Oklahoma State University in Tulsa*
Old Dom. U. *Old Dominion University*
Olivet Naz. U. *Olivet Nazarene University*
Oral Roberts U. *Oral Roberts University*
Ore. Health & Sci. U. *Oregon Health and Science University*
Ore. St. U. *Oregon State University*
Our Lady Lake U. *Our Lady of the Lake University*
Pace U. *Pace University*
Pac. Luth. U. *Pacific Lutheran University*
Pac. U. *Pacific University*
Penn. C. Opt. *Pennsylvania College of Optometry*
Penn. St. U. *Pennsylvania State University*
Penn. St. U. Harrisburg *Pennsylvania State University at Harrisburg*
Penn. St. U. Med. Ctr. *Pennsylvania State University Milton S. Hershey Medical Center*
Pepperdine U. *Pepperdine University*
Pepperdine U. (Culver City) *Pepperdine University, Culver City*
Phila. C. Osteo. Med. *Philadelphia College of Osteopathic Medicine*
Pikeville C. *Pikeville College School of Osteopathic Medicine*
Pittsburg St. U. *Pittsburg State University*
Plymouth St. C. *Plymouth State College*
Point Loma Nazarene U. *Point Loma Nazarene University*
Poly. U. *Polytechnic University*
Ponce Sch. Med. *Ponce School of Medicine*
Pont. Cath. U. P.R. *Pontifical Catholic University of Puerto Rico*
Portland St. U. *Portland State University*
Prairie View A&M U. *Prairie View Agricultural and Mechanical University*
Pratt Inst. *Pratt Institute*
Princeton U. *Princeton University*
Providence C. *Providence College*
Purdue U. *Purdue University*
Purdue U. (Calumet) *Purdue University Calumet*
Queens C. (C.U.N.Y.) *Queens College of the City University of New York*
Quinnipiac U. *Quinnipiac University*
Radford U. *Radford University*
Regent U. *Regent University*
Rhode Island C. *Rhode Island College*
Rhode Island Sch. Design *Rhode Island School of Design*
Rice U. *Rice University*
Rider U. *Rider University*
R.I.T. *Rochester Institute of Technology*
Rivier C. *Rivier College*
Robert Morris U. *Robert Morris University*
Rockefeller U. *The Rockefeller University*
Rockford C. *Rockford College*
Roger Williams U. *Roger Williams University*
Rollins C. *Rollins College*
Roosevelt U. *Roosevelt University*
Rosalind Franklin U. Med. & Sci. *Rosalind Franklin University of Medicine and Sciences*

Rosary C.   *Rosary College*
Rose-Hulman Inst. Tech.   *Rose-Hulman Institute of Technology*
Rowan U.   *Rowan University*
R.P.I.   *Rensselaer Polytechnic Institute*
Rush Med. C.   *Rush Medical College of Rush University*
Rutgers U.   *Rutgers University*
Rutgers U. (Camden)   *Rutgers University Camden*
Rutgers U. (Newark)   *Rutgers University Newark*
Sage C.   *The Sage Colleges*
Sag. Val. St. U.   *Saginaw Valley State University*
Salem St. C.   *Salem State College*
Salisbury St. U.   *Salisbury State University*
Samford U.   *Samford University*
Sam Houston St. U.   *Sam Houston State University*
San Fran. Art Inst.   *San Francisco Art Institute*
San Fran. Conserv. Music   *San Francisco Conservatory of Music*
San Fran. St. U.   *San Francisco State University*
Santa Clara U.   *Santa Clara University*
Sarah Lawrence C.   *Sarah Lawrence College*
S.D.S.U.   *San Diego State University*
Seattle Pac. U.   *Seattle Pacific University*
Seattle U.   *Seattle University*
Seton Hall U.   *Seton Hall University*
S. F. Austin St. U.   *Stephen F. Austin State University*
Shippensburg U.   *Shippensburg University of Pennsylvania*
Siena Heights U.   *Siena Heights University*
Simmons C.   *Simmons College*
Slippery Rock U.   *Slippery Rock University of Pennsylvania*
Smith C.   *Smith College*
Southeastern La. U.   *Southeastern Louisiana University*
Southeastern Okla. St. U.   *Southeastern Oklahoma State University*
Southeast Mo. St. U.   *Southeast Missouri State University*
So. Cal. C. Optometry   *Southern California College of Optometry*
So. Car. St. U.   *South Carolina State University*
So. C. Optometry   *Southern College of Optometry*
So. Conn. St. U.   *Southern Connecticut State University*
So. Dak. Sch. M&T   *South Dakota School of Mines and Technology*
So. Dak. St. U.   *South Dakota State University*
So. Ill. U.   *Southern Illinois University*
So. Ill. U. (Edwardsville)   *Southern Illinois University at Edwardsville*
So. Meth. U.   *Southern Methodist University*
So. Nazarene U.   *Southern Nazarene University*
So. Ore. U.   *Southern Oregon University*
So. Tex. C. Law   *South Texas College of Law*
So. U. & A&M C.   *Southern University and Agricultural and Mechanical College*
Southwest Mo. St. U.   *Southwest Missouri State University*
Southwestern Okla. St. U.   *Southwestern Oklahoma State University*
Southwestern U. Law   *Southwestern University School of Law*
Spalding U.   *Spalding University*
Springfield C.   *Springfield College*
St. Bonaventure U.   *St. Bonaventure University*
St. Cloud St. U.   *St. Cloud State University*
St. Edward's U.   *St. Edward's University*
St. Francis U.   *St. Francis University*
St. John's U. (Minn.)   *St. John's University (Minnesota)*
St. John's U. (N.Y.)   *St. John's University (New York)*
St. Joseph C. (Conn.)   *St. Joseph College (Connecticut)*
St. Joseph's U. (Penn.)   *St. Joseph's University (Pennsylvania)*
St. Louis U.   *Saint Louis University*
St. Mary's U. (Minn.)   *St. Mary's University of Minnesota*
St. Mary's U.   *St. Mary's University*
St. Michael's C.   *St. Michael's College*
St. Thomas U.   *St. Thomas University*
St. Xavier U.   *St. Xavier University*
Stanford U.   *Stanford University*
Stetson U.   *Stetson University*
Stevens Inst. Tech.   *Stevens Institute of Technology*
Stony Brook U. (S.U.N.Y).   *Stony Brook University, State University of New York*
Suffolk U.   *Suffolk University*
Sul Ross St. U.   *Sul Ross State University*
S.U.N.Y. (Binghamton)   *State University of New York at Binghamton*
S.U.N.Y. (Oswego)   *State University of New York at Oswego*
S.U.N.Y.C. (Brockport)   *State University of New York College at Brockport*
S.U.N.Y.C. (Buffalo)   *State University of New York College at Buffalo*

S.U.N.Y.C. (Cortland)   *State University of New York College at Cortland*
S.U.N.Y.C. Environ. Sci. & For. (Syracuse)   *State University of New York College of Environmental Science and Forestry at Syracuse*
S.U.N.Y.C. (Fredonia)   *State University of New York College at Fredonia*
S.U.N.Y.C. (Geneseo)   *State University of New York College of Arts and Sciences at Geneseo*
S.U.N.Y.C. (New Paltz)   *State University of New York College at New Paltz*
S.U.N.Y.C. (Oneonta)   *State University of New York College at Oneonta*
S.U.N.Y.C. (Plattsburgh)   *State University of New York College at Plattsburgh*
S.U.N.Y.C. (Potsdam)   *State University of New York College at Potsdam*
S.U.N.Y. Downstate   *State University of New York Downstate Medical Center at Brooklyn*
S.U.N.Y. I.T.   *State University of New York Institute of Technology at Utica/Rome*
S.U.N.Y. Upstate   *State University of New York Upstate Medical University at Syracuse*
Syracuse U.   *Syracuse University*
Tarleton St. U.   *Tarleton State University*
Teachers C.   *Teachers College (Columbia University)*
Temple U.   *Temple University*
Tenn. St. U.   *Tennessee State University*
Tenn. Tech. U.   *Tennessee Technological University*
Tex. A&M U.   *Texas Agricultural and Mechanical University—College Station*
Tex. A&M U. (Commerce)   *Texas A&M University—Commerce*
Tex. A&M U. H.S.C.   *Texas A&M University System Health Science Center*
Tex. A&M U. (Corpus Christi)   *Texas Agricultural and Mechanical University, Corpus Christi*
Tex. A&M U. (Kingsville)   *Texas A&M University—Kingsville*
Tex. Christ. U.   *Texas Christian University*
Tex. So. U.   *Texas Southern University*
Tex. St. U. San Marcos   *Texas State University, San Marcos*
Tex. Tech U.   *Texas Tech University*
Tex. Tech U. H.S.C.   *Texas Tech University Health Sciences Center*
Tex. Wesleyan U.   *Texas Wesleyan University*
Tex. Woman's U.   *Texas Woman's University*
Thom. Cooley Law Sch.   *Thomas M. Cooley Law School*
Thom. Jefferson Sch. Law   *Thomas Jefferson School of Law*
Thom. Jefferson U.   *Thomas Jefferson University*
Thunderbird   *Thunderbird School of Global Management*
Touro C.   *Touro College*
Towson U.   *Towson University*
Trinity C.   *Trinity College*
Trinity U.   *Trinity University*
Troy U.   *Troy University*
Troy U. (Dothan)   *Troy University at Dothan*
Troy U. (Mont.)   *Troy University (Montgomery)*
Truman St. U.   *Truman State University*
Tufts U.   *Tufts University*
Tulane U.   *Tulane University*
Tuskegee U.   *Tuskegee University*
U. Akron   *University of Akron*
U. Ala.   *University of Alabama*
U. Ala. (Birm.)   *University of Alabama at Birmingham*
U. Ala. (Huntsville)   *University of Alabama at Huntsville*
U. Alaska   *University of Alaska*
U. Ariz.   *The University of Arizona*
U. Ark.   *University of Arkansas*
U. Arts   *The University of the Arts*
U. Balt.   *University of Baltimore*
U. Bridgeport   *University of Bridgeport*
U. Buffalo (S.U.N.Y.)   *University at Buffalo, State University of New York*
U. Cal. (Berkeley)   *University of California at Berkeley*
U. Cal. (Davis)   *University of California at Davis*
U. Cal. (Irvine)   *University of California at Irvine*
U. Cal. (Riverside)   *University of California at Riverside*
U. Cal. (San Diego)   *University of California at San Diego*
U. Cal. (San Fran.)   *University of California at San Francisco*
U. Cal. (Santa Barbara)   *University of California at Santa Barbara*
U. Cal. (Santa Cruz)   *University of California at Santa Cruz*
U. Cent. Ark.   *University of Central Arkansas*
U. Cent. Fla.   *University of Central Florida*

U. Cent. Okla.   *University of Central Oklahoma*
U. Chicago   *The University of Chicago*
U. Cincinnati   *University of Cincinnati*
U.C.L.A.   *University of California, Los Angeles*
U. Colo.   *University of Colorado, Boulder*
U. Colo. C.S.   *University of Colorado, Colorado Springs*
U. Colo. Denver   *University of Colorado, Denver*
U. Colo. Health Sci. Ctr.   *University of Colorado Health Science Center*
U. Conn.   *The University of Connecticut*
U. Conn. Health Ctr.   *University of Connecticut Health Center*
U. Dallas   *University of Dallas*
U. Dayton   *University of Dayton*
U. Del.   *University of Delaware*
U. Denver   *University of Denver*
U. Detroit Mercy   *University of Detroit Mercy*
U.D.C.   *University of the District of Columbia*
U. Dubuque   *University of Dubuque*
U. Fla.   *University of Florida*
U. Georgia   *The University of Georgia*
U. Hartford   *University of Hartford*
U. Hawaii   *University of Hawaii at Manoa*
U. Houston   *University of Houston*
U. Houston   (Clear Lake)   *University of Houston, Clear Lake*
U. Idaho   *University of Idaho*
U. Ill.   *University of Illinois*
U. Ill. (Chicago)   *University of Illinois at Chicago*
U. Incarnate Word   *University of the Incarnate Word*
U. Indianapolis   *University of Indianapolis*
U. Iowa   *The University of Iowa*
U. Kans.   *University of Kansas*
U. Kans. Med. Ctr.   *University of Kansas Medical Center*
U. Ky.   *University of Kentucky*
U. La Verne   *University of La Verne*
U. La. (Lafayette)   *University of Louisiana at Lafayette*
U. La. (Monroe)   *University of Louisiana at Monroe*
U. Louisville   *University of Louisville*
U. Maine   *University of Maine*
U. Maine (Portland-Gorham)   *University of Maine at Portland-Gorham*
U. Mass.   *University of Massachusetts*
U. Mass. (Boston)   *University of Massachusetts Boston*
U. Mass. (Dartmouth)   *University of Massachusetts Dartmouth*
U. Mass. (Lowell)   *University of Massachusetts Lowell*
U. Md.   *University of Maryland*
U. Md. (Baltimore)   *University of Maryland at Baltimore*
U. Md. (Baltimore Cnty.)   *University of Maryland Baltimore County*
U. Med. & Dent. N.J.   *University of Medicine and Dentistry of New Jersey*
U. Memphis   *University of Memphis*
U. Miami (Fla.)   *University of Miami*
U. Mich.   *The University of Michigan*
U. Minn.   *University of Minnesota*
U. Minn. (Duluth)   *University of Minnesota Duluth*
U. Miss.   *The University of Mississippi*
U. Miss. Med. Ctr.   *University of Mississippi Medical Center*
U. Mo. (Columbia)   *University of Missouri at Columbia*
U. Mo. (K.C.)   *University of Missouri at Kansas City*
U. Mo. (St. Louis)   *University of Missouri at St. Louis*
U. Mont.   *University of Montana*
U. Montevallo   *University of Montevallo*
U.N.H.   *University of New Hampshire*
U. N. Mex.   *The University of New Mexico*
U. N. Orleans   *University of New Orleans*
U. Neb.   *University of Nebraska*
U. Neb. (Kearney)   *University of Nebraska at Kearney*
U. Neb. (Med. Ctr.)   *University of Nebraska Medical Center*
U. Neb. (Omaha)   *University of Nebraska at Omaha*
U. Nev.   *University of Nevada, Reno*
U. Nev. (Las Vegas)   *University of Nevada, Las Vegas*
U. New Eng. C.O.M.   *University of New England College of Osteopathic Medicine*
U. New Haven   *University of New Haven*
U. No. Ala.   *University of North Alabama*
U. No. Car. (Chapel Hill)   *The University of North Carolina at Chapel Hill*
U. No. Car. (Charlotte)   *University of North Carolina at Charlotte*
U. No. Car. (Greensboro)   *The University of North Carolina at Greensboro*

U. No. Car. (Wilmington)   *University of North Carolina at Wilmington*
U. No. Col.   *University of Northern Colorado*
U. No. Dak.   *University of North Dakota*
U. No. Fla.   *University of North Florida*
U. No. Iowa   *University of Northern Iowa*
U. No. Tex.   *University of North Texas*
U. Notre Dame   *University of Notre Dame*
U. Okla.   *University of Oklahoma*
U. Okla. Health Sci. Ctr.   *University of Oklahoma Health Science Center*
U. Ore.   *University of Oregon*
U. Pac.   *University of the Pacific*
U. Penn.   *University of Pennsylvania*
U. Phoenix   *University of Phoenix*
U. Pitt.   *University of Pittsburgh*
U. Portland   *University of Portland*
U. Puerto Rico   *University of Puerto Rico*
U. Puerto Rico, Mayaguez   *University of Puerto Rico, Mayaguez*
U. Puget Sound   *University of Puget Sound*
U. Redlands   *University of Redlands*
U. Rhode Island   *University of Rhode Island*
U. Richmond   *University of Richmond*
U. Rochester   *University of Rochester*
U. San Diego   *University of San Diego*
U. San Fran.   *University of San Francisco*
U. Sci. Phila.   *University of the Sciences in Philadelphia*
U. Scranton   *University of Scranton*
U. So. Ala.   *University of South Alabama*
U. So. Cal.   *University of Southern California*
U. So. Car.   *University of South Carolina*
U. So. Dak.   *University of South Dakota*
U. So. Fla.   *University of South Florida*
U. So. Maine   *University of Southern Maine*
U. So. Miss.   *University of Southern Mississippi*
U. South   *University of the South*
U. St. Francis   *University of St. Francis*
U. St. Thomas   *University of St. Thomas*
U. St. Thomas (Minn.)   *University of St. Thomas*
U. St. Thomas (Tex.)   *University of St. Thomas*
U. Tenn.   *University of Tennessee*
U. Tenn. (Chattanooga)   *University of Tennessee at Chattanooga*
U. Tenn. H.S.C.   *University of Tennessee Health Science Center*
U. Tenn. (Martin)   *University of Tennessee at Martin*
U. Tenn. Space Inst.   *University of Tennessee Space Institute*
U. Tex. (Arlington)   *The University of Texas at Arlington*
U. Tex. (Austin)   *The University of Texas at Austin*
U. Tex. (Brownsville)   *The University of Texas at Brownsville*
U. Tex. (Dallas)   *The University of Texas at Dallas*
U. Tex. (El Paso)   *The University of Texas at El Paso*
U. Tex. Health Sci. Ctr. (Houston)   *The University of Texas Health Science Center at Houston*
U. Tex. Health Sci. Ctr. (San Antonio)   *University of Texas Health Science Center at San Antonio*
U. Tex. Med. Br. (Galveston)   *University of Texas Medical Branch at Galveston*
U. Tex. S.W. Med. Ctr. (Dallas)   *The University of Texas Southwestern Medical Center at Dallas*
U. Tex. Pan Amer.   *The University of Texas—Pan American*
U. Tex. Perm. Basin   *The University of Texas of the Permian Basin*
U. Tex. (San Antonio)   *The University of Texas at San Antonio*
U. Tex. (Tyler)   *The University of Texas at Tyler*
U. Toledo   *University of Toledo*
U. Tulsa   *The University of Tulsa*
U. Utah   *University of Utah*
U. Vt.   *University of Vermont*
U. Va.   *University of Virginia*
U. Wash.   *University of Washington*
U. West Ala.   *University of West Alabama*
U. West Ga.   *University of West Georgia*
U. Wis.   *University of Wisconsin*
U. Wis. (Eau Claire)   *University of Wisconsin Eau Claire*
U. Wis. (La Crosse)   *University of Wisconsin La Crosse*
U. Wis. (Milwaukee)   *University of Wisconsin Milwaukee*
U. Wis. (Oshkosh)   *University of Wisconsin Oshkosh*
U. Wis. (Platteville)   *University of Wisconsin Platteville*
U. Wis. (River Falls)   *University of Wisconsin River Falls*
U. Wis. (Stevens Point)   *University of Wisconsin Stevens Point*
U. Wis. (Stout)   *University of Wisconsin Stout*

U. Wis. (Superior) *University of Wisconsin Superior*
U. Wis. (Whitewater) *University of Wisconsin Whitewater*
U. Wyo. *University of Wyoming*
Uniformed Serv. U. Health Sci. *Uniformed Services University of the Health Sciences*
Union C. (Ky.) *Union College (Kentucky)*
Union C. (N.Y.) *Union College (New York)*
Union Inst. *The Union Institute and University*
Utah St. U. *Utah State University*
Va. Commonwealth U. *Virginia Commonwealth University*
Valdosta St. C. *Valdosta State College*
Valparaiso U. *Valparaiso University*
Vanderbilt U. *Vanderbilt University*
Va. Poly. Inst. *Virginia Polytechnic Institute and State University*
Va. St. U. *Virginia State University*
Villanova U. *Villanova University*
Vt. Law *Vermont Law School*
Wagner C. *Wagner College*
Wake Forest U. *Wake Forest University*
Walla Walla C. *Walla Walla College*
Washburn U. *Washburn University of Topeka*
Wash. & Lee U. *Washington and Lee University*
Wash. St. U. *Washington State University*
Wash. U. (Mo.) *Washington University*
Wayne St. C. *Wayne State College*
Wayne St. U. *Wayne State University*
Webster U. *Webster University*
Wesleyan U. *Wesleyan University*
West. Car. U. *Western Carolina University*
West Chester U. Pa. *West Chester University of Pennsylvania*
West. Conn. St. U. *Western Connecticut State University*
West Ga. St. U. *State University of West Georgia*
West. Ill. U. *Western Illinois University*

West. Ky. U. *Western Kentucky University*
West. Mich. U. *Western Michigan University*
West. New Eng. C. *Western New England College*
West. N. Mex. U. *Western New Mexico University*
West. Oregon U. *Western Oregon University*
West Tex. A&M U. *West Texas A&M University*
West. U. Health Sci. *Western University of Health Sciences*
West Va. Sch. Osteo. Med. *West Virginia School of Osteopathic Medicine*
West Va. U. *West Virginia University*
West. Wash. U. *Western Washington University*
Westfield St. C. *Westfield State College*
Westminster C. *Westminster College*
Wheelock C. *Wheelock College*
Whittier C. *Whittier College*
Whitworth C. *Whitworth College*
Wichita St. U. *Wichita State University*
Widener U. *Widener University*
Wilkes U. *Wilkes University*
Willamette U. *Willamette University*
Wm. Carey C. *William Carey College*
Wm. Mitchell C. Law *William Mitchell College of Law*
Wm. Paterson U. *William Paterson University of New Jersey*
Winona St. U. *Winona State University*
Winthrop U. *Winthrop University*
Worcester Poly. Inst. *Worcester Polytechnic Institute*
Worcester St. C. *Worcester State College*
Wright St. U. *Wright State University*
Xavier U. (La.) *Xavier University of Louisiana*
Xavier U. (Ohio) *Xavier University*
Yale U. *Yale University*
Yeshiva U. *Yeshiva University*
Youngstown St. U. *Youngstown State University*

INDEX TO FIELDS OF STUDY

American colleges and universities offer graduate and professional degree programs in a bewilderingly varied number of disciplines and areas of specialization. An indication of the scope of opportunities for advanced study is found in the index that follows, listing major fields of study and the institutions that provide them.

Before turning to the index, it is *very important* that the user read and understand the following explanatory notes. Without knowledge of these caveats, the reader may overlook available educational opportunities.

1. Major and subfields of study are listed under these headings:

Agriculture
(Typically includes Agribusiness,
    Agricultural Economics, Agricultural
    Education, Agricultural Engineering,
    Agronomy, Animal Behavior, Animal
    Sciences, Dairy Sciences, Entomology,
    Plant Molecular Biology, Plant Science,
    Plant Pathology, Plant Physiology, Poultry
    Science; may include Agricultural
    Extension, Botany, Crop Science, Soils
    Sciences)
Architecture (Includes Architectural History)
    Naval Architecture
Area Studies
    African/African-American Studies
    Asian/Asian American Studies
    Brazilian Studies
    Canada Area Studies
    Caribbean Studies
    Egyptology
    European Studies
    Hispanic/Iberian Studies
    Indo-European Studies
    Islamic Studies/Literature
    Jewish Studies
    Latin American Studies
    Mediterranean Studies
    Mexican-American Studies
    Native American Studies
    Near/Middle Eastern Studies
    New York Area Studies
    North American Studies
    Pacific Area Studies
    Russian/East European Studies
    Uralic Studies
Basic Medical Sciences
(Typically includes Anatomy, Microbiology,
Pathology, Pharmacology, Physiology; often
includes Endocrinology, Neurological Sci-
ences, Parasitology, Virology)
    Bacteriology
    Immunology
    Infectious Diseases
    Radiological Sciences
    Toxicology
Biological Sciences
(Typically includes Biology, Entomology,
Zoology)

Biochemistry
Bioethics
Bioinformatics
Biomathematics/Biostatistics
Biometry/Biometrics
Biophysics
Cancer Biology
Cardiovascular Sciences
Cell Biology
Computational Biology
Environmental Biology
Evolutionary Biology
Genetic Counseling
Genetics
Marine Biology
Molecular Biology
Molecular Genetics
Neurobiology
Reproductive Biology
Business/Business Administration,
Commerce/Management (Typically includes
Accounting, Finance, Marketing; often
includes Advertising, Industrial Adminis-
tration, Industrial and Labor Relations,
Operations Research, Public Relations;
majors in Economics are also common in
graduate schools of business as well as in
graduate schools of arts and science)
    Actuarial/Insurance Management
    Electronic Commerce
    Entrepreneurship
    Hotel/Hospitality Management
    *Human Resource and Development/Man-
        agement*
    Information Science/System/Studies
    International Business/Economics
    Management Information Systems
    Management of Technology
    Management Strategy and Policy
    Nonprofit Management
    Quantitative Analysis/Studies
    Supply Chain Management/Logistics
    Real Estate
    Taxation
Communications (Typically includes Mass
    Communication, Organizational
    Communication)
    Creative Writing/Writing

*Film/Television (Typical includes Broad-
    casting, Cinema, Motion Picture)*
Internet and Interactive Multimedia
Journalism
Technical Communication/Writing
Telecommunication
Computer Sciences (Typically includes
    Artificial Intelligence/Robotics, Computer
    Systems, Computer Information Systems,
    Human Computer Interaction,
    Management Systems)
Criminal Justice/Corrections/Criminology
    (May include Law Enforcement, national
    security studies, police science)
Dentistry
Education
(Typically includes Administration and Su-
pervision, Curriculum and Instruction, Ele-
mentary and Secondary Education,
Evaluation and Research, Foreign Language
Education, Foundations and Philosophy,
Guidance and Counseling, Health Educa-
tion, History and Philosophy of Education,
Physical Education, School Psychology,
Special Education; often includes Business
Education, Early Childhood Education, Ex-
tension Education, Middle School Educa-
tion, Speech Pathology and Audiology,
Student Personnel Services, Vocational/
Technology Education: offered by more than
500 institutions in all 50 states, so individual
institutions are not listed here)
    Adult Education (Typically includes Com-
        munity Education)
    Art Education
    *Bilingual/Multilingual/Multicultural Edu-
        cation*
    Community College Teaching
    Computers in Education
    *Drug and Alcohol/Substance Abuse Coun-
        seling*
    Education of the Gifted
    Education of the Multiple Handicapped
    Educational Media/Instructional Technology
    English as a Second Language
    Exercise/Sport Science
    Learning Disabilities
    Marriage and Family Counseling

Recreation/Recreational Administration
Safety Education
School Librarianship, Library Science, Library Media
Sports Management
Teaching of Emotionally Disturbed
Teaching of Mentally Retarded
Teaching of Physically Handicapped
Urban Education

Engineering and Technology
(Typically includes Applied Sciences, Chemical Engineering, Civil Engineering, Computer Science/Engineering, Construction Engineering, Electrical Engineering, Energy Engineering, Engineering and Applied Sciences, Industrial Engineering, Mechanical; often includes Aeronautical/Astronautical Engineering, Material Engineering/Science, Mechanics, Metallurgy/Metallurgical Engineering, Operations Research, Structural Engineering, Systems Engineering/Science)
Architectural Engineering
Bioengineering/Biomedical Engineering
Building Science
Ceramic Sciences/Engineering
Engineering Management
Environmental Engineering
Geological, Geosciences, Geotechnical Engineering
Manufacturing Engineering
Marine Science/Engineering, Ocean Engineering, Oceanography
Mineral/Mining Engineering/Technology
Ocean Engineering
Optical Sciences
Paper Engineering/Science/Technology
Petroleum Engineering
Photonics
Polymer Engineering/Science
Software Engineering
Systems Engineering
Textile Engineering/Science
Transportation/Traffic Engineering

Environmental Sciences
(Typically includes Ecology, Forestry, Forest Science, Wood Science/Technology)
Fish/Wildlife Management
Hydrology
Landscape Architecture
Meteorology/Atmospheric Sciences
Range Management/Science
Sustainable Development
Water Resources Administration

Fine Arts
(Typically includes Art History, Studio Arts; often includes Commercial Arts, Applied Arts, Crafts, Design, Graphic Design, Industrial Design)
Arts Management
Arts Therapy
Interior Design
Museum Training/Studies/Historic Preservation
Photography
Textile Design

Foreign Languages/Literatures
(Typically includes French, German, Spanish; often includes Italian, Portuguese, Romance Languages)
African Languages
Akkadian
Bengali
Caucasian
Celtic
Chinese/Japanese/Asian Languages
Greek
Hebrew/Arabic/Near and Middle Eastern Languages/Literatures
Hindi
Latin
Russian/Slavic Languages
Sanskrit
Scandinavian Languages/Literatures
Translation and Interpretation
Urdu

Home/Consumer Economics, Food Science, Food Service, Technology, Child and Family Life, Nutrition
Horticulture
Humanities
(Typically includes English and History: offered by nearly 400 institutions in all 50 states, so individual institutions are not listed here)
Classics
Comparative Literature
Folklore
Linguistics
Philosophy

Law
Liberal/Interdisciplinary/Multidisciplinary Studies
Library/Science/Information Studies
Medicine
Medical Illustration
Medical Technology
Physician Assistant Studies
Tropical Medicine

Music
(Typically includes Composition, Music Education, Music History, Musicology, Performance, Theory; may include Ethnomusicology)
Music Therapy

Nursing and Health Professions
Child Care/Pediatric Nursing
Family Nursing (Typically includes Adult, Geriatric, Maternity, Parent, Child)
Forensic Nursing
Gerontological Nursing
Health Care/Health Services/Hospital Administration/Management
Nurse Anesthesia
Nurse Midwifery
Nursing (Typically includes Advanced Practice Nursing, Administration, Education, Medical Surgical)
Occupational Therapy
Oncology Nursing
Physical Therapy
Prosthetics
Psychiatric Nursing
Public/Community Health Nursing
Rehabilitation Counseling/Services

Optometry/Vision Sciences

Osteopathic Medicine
Pharmacy
(Typically includes Pharmaceutical Chemistry, Pharmaceutical Science, Pharmacognosy; for Pharmacology, see Basic Medical Sciences listing above)
Physical Sciences
(Typically includes Chemistry, Mathematics and Physics; often includes Applied Mathematics; offered by nearly 400 institutions, so individual institutions are not listed)
Analytical Chemistry
Applied Physics
Astronomy/Planetary Sciences/Space Science
Chemical Physics
Geochemistry
Geology
Geophysics

Public Administration
(Typically includes Energy Management and Policy, Public Policy, Public Management, Public Affairs)
Public and Community Health
Environmental and Occupational Health
Epidemiology
International Health

Religion
(Typically includes Bible Studies, Religious Studies, Theology; often includes Religious Education)
Social Sciences
(Typically includes Economics, Political Science, Psychology, Sociology)
Anthropology
Archaeology
Geographic Information Systems
Geography
Medieval/Renaissance Studies
Peace Studies/Science, Conflict Resolution
Population Studies
Rural Sociology
Sports Psychology
Urban Studies
Women's/Feminists' Studies

Social Work
(Typically includes Human Services, Social Service, Social Welfare)
Theater/Drama/Theater Arts
(Typically includes Acting, Directing, Speech Arts; often includes Criticism, Theater/Costume Design, Technical Production)
Arts Administration
Dance
Dance Therapy
Media Studies
Music Theater
Playwriting
Theater for Deaf
Theater Management

Urban Design/City Planning
(Typically includes City Planning, Community Planning, Environmental Design, Urban and Regional Planning, Urban Design)
Veterinary Medicine
(Typically includes Veterinary Sciences)

2. Each major and subfield heading is followed by the abbreviated names of every institution offering study leading to a degree in even one of the subfields customarily associated with the larger area. Thus, if an institution offers *only* fisheries biology, for example, its name is nevertheless included under BIOLOGICAL SCIENCES. The major fields are complete in listing appropriate institutions as of the time of preparation of this manuscript. Inasmuch as the information presented here is only as accurate as that provided by the institutions, and inasmuch as changes occur rapidly in higher education, some programs may not have been properly credited, or may have been discontinued, modified, or added. It bears repeating that this *Guide* is intended only as a first source of information, and certainty in academic planning information can be assured only by contacting the institution in which one is interested.

3. Subfields listed under the major headings are those of special interest or those sufficiently unusual to justify special notice. The student should bear in mind that nomenclature and departmental organization vary substantially from institution

to institution. Using the BIOLOGICAL SCIENCES example again, a biology department may offer majors in botany, zoology, entomology, fisheries biology, cellular biology, and others, but this information may not have been made clear or available. Any one of these may have the status of separately constituted academic departments, so that a graduate school with a biology department offering study in botany may have another department, with a different faculty, in zoology. Entomology, a branch of zoology, may be available through still another department. College catalogs can be unilluminating on such points, and seemingly endless combinations can be constructed. The point is, the major listings can be assumed to be as accurate as possible, but the subfields cannot. A potential student should first determine whether the broad field of study in which he or she is interested is available at a particular institution, *then* look to the subfields for clarification, remembering that the latter may be incomplete.

4. At multidivisional universities, study in a particular field may be offered by two or more divisions. Biochemistry may be a program of the chemistry or biology departments of the graduate school of arts and science and also available in the medical school of the same university. Universities with several campuses may offer the same major at three or more different locations *and* divisions. All divisions of an institution must therefore be checked for a particular program.

5. Since names describing fields of study frequently differ, the most common variations parenthetically follow the labels used in this index. When appropriate, it is noted that certain majors are "typically" or "often" included under any given heading.

6. Historically, a number of areas of study have grown and split, the new parts coming under different jurisdictions within the same institution. The dividing lines often remain vague, however. Home economics and music are examples. Home economics might be offered by a school of agriculture, a school of home economics, and a school of education, all in the same university. For this index, some fields of study have been combined in recognition of this commonality. For instance, although there may be three separate departments providing study in musicology, performance, and music education, in practice it is relatively unusual for an institution to offer one and not the others.

7. The abbreviations used for the institutions are meant to be understandable as they stand. If they are not, the reader can refer to the explanatory table that precedes this index. As a final note, the slash mark means *only* "and/or" in this index, as throughout this book.

Agriculture

(Typically includes Agricultural Economics, Agribusiness, Agricultural Education, Agricultural Engineering, Agronomy, Animal Behavior, Animal Sciences, Dairy Science, Entomology, Plant Molecular Biology, Plant Science, Plant Pathology, Plant Physiology, Poultry Science; may include Agricultural Extension, Crop Science, Soils Sciences)

Ala. A&M U.
Angelo St. U.
Ariz. St. U.
U. Ariz.
Ark. St. U.
U. Ark.
Auburn U.
B.Y.U.
Cal. Poly. St. U. (San Luis Obispo)
Cal. St. Poly. U.(Pomona)
Cal. St. U. (Chico)
Cal. St. U. (Fresno)
U. Cal. (Berkeley)
U. Cal. (Davis)
U. Cal. (Riverside)
U. Cal. (Santa Barbara)
Cent. Mo. St. U.
Clemson U.
Colo. St. U.
U. Colo.
U. Conn.
Cornell U.
Corpus Christi St. U.
U. Del.
East. Ky. U.
Fla. A&M U.
Fla. St. U.
U. Fla.
U. Georgia
U. Hawaii
U. Idaho

Ill. St. U.
U. Ill.
Iowa St. U.
Kans. St. U.
U. Ky.
L.S.U.
U. Maine
U. Md.
M.I.T.
U. Mass.
Mich. St. U.
U. Minn.
U. Mo. (Columbia)
Miss. St. U.
Mont. St. U.
U. Mont.
Murray St. U.
U. Neb.
U. Nev. (Reno)
U. N.H.
S.U.N.Y.C. Environ. Sci. & For. (Syracuse)
N. Mex. St. U.
No. Car. A&T C.
No. Car. St. U. (Raleigh)
No. Dak. St. U.
Northwest Mo. St. U.
Ohio St. U.
Okla. St. U.
Ore. St. U.
Penn. St. U.
Prairie View A&M U.
U. Puerto Rico
Purdue U.
U. Rhode Island
Rutgers U.
Sam Houston St. U.
Santa Clara U.
S. F. Austin St. U.
So. Car. St. U.
So. Dak. St. U.
So. Ill. U. (Carbondale)
Southern U.
Sul Ross St. U.
Stanford U.
Tarleton St. U.
Tenn. St. U.

U. Tenn.
Tex. A&M U.
Tex. A&M U. Commerce)
Tex. A&M U. (Kingsville)
Tex. St. U.
Tex. Tech U.
U. Tex. (Austin)
Tuskegee Inst.
Utah St. U.
U. Vt.
Va. Poly. Inst.
Va. St. U.
Wash. St. U.
U. Wash.
Wayne St. U.
West Tex. A&M U.
W. Va. U.
West. Ill. U.
West. Ky. U.
U. Wis.
U. Wis. (River Falls)
U. Wyo.

Architecture

(Includes Architectural History)

Ariz. St. U.
U. Ariz.
Auburn U.
Ball St. U.
Buffalo U. (S.U.N.Y.)
Cal. Poly. St. U. (San Luis Obispo)
Cal. St. Poly. U.(Pomona)
U. Cal. (Berkeley)
U.C.L.A.
Carnegie Mellon U.
Catholic U.
C.C.N.Y. (C.U.N.Y.)
U. Cincinnati
Clemson U.
U. Colo. (Denver)
Columbia U.
Cornell U.
Cranbrook Acad. Art
Fla. A&M U.

U. Fla.
Georgia Inst. Tech.
Harvard U.
U. Hawaii
Howard U.
U. Houston
U. Idaho
Ill. Inst. Tech
U. Ill.
U. Ill. (Chicago)
Iowa St. U.
Kans. St. U.
U. Kans.
Kent St. U.
U. Kentucky
L.S.U.
U. Md.
M.I.T.
Miami U. (Ohio)
U. Miami (Fla.)
U. Mich.
U. Minn.
Miss. St. U.
Mont. St. U.
Morgan St. U.
U. Neb.
U. Nev.
N.J.I.T.
U. N. Mex.
N.Y.I.T.
No. Car. St. U. (Raleigh)
U. Notre Dame
Ohio St. U.
Okla. St. U.
U. Okla.
U. Ore.
Penn. St. U.
U. Penn.
Pratt Inst.
Princeton U.
U. Puerto Rico
Rhode Island Sh. D.
R.P.I.
Rice U.
U. So. Cal.
U. So. Fla.
Syracuse U.

U. No. Car. (Chapel Hill)
U. Notre Dame
N.Y.U.
Ohio St. U.
Ohio U.
U. Pac.
U. Pitt.
Princeton U.
Queens C. (C.U.N.Y.)
S.D.S.U.
So. Meth. U.
Stanford U.
U. Tex. (Austin)
Tulane U.
Vanderbilt U.
West Va. U.
U. Wis.

.MEDITERRANEAN
STUDIES
Brandeis U.

MEXICAN-AMERICAN
STUDIES
Cal. St. U. (L.A.)
Cal. St. U. (Northridge)
San Jose St. U.

NATIVE AMERICAN/
AMERICAN INDIAN
STUDIES
U. Ariz.
U. Ca. (Davis)
U.C.L.A.
U. Kans.
Mont. St. U.
U. Okla.

NEAR/MIDDLE EASTERN
STUDIES
U. Ariz.
Brandeis U.
Brown U.
B.Y.U.
U. Cal. (Berkeley)
U.C.L.A.
U. Chicago
Columbia U.
Cornell U.
Georgetown U.
Geo. Wash. U.
Harvard U.
Ind. U.
Johns Hopkins U.
U. Mich.
Monterey Inst.
N.Y.U.
Ohio St. U.
U. Penn.
Princeton U.
U. Tex. (Austin)
U. Utah
U. Va.
Wash. U.
U. Wash.
Wayne St. U.
Yeshiva U.

NEW YORK AREA
STUDIES
C.U.N.Y. (Grad. Ctr.)

NORTH AMERICAN
STUDIES
U. Ala.
U. Alaska
U. Ariz.
Appal. St. U.
Baylor U.
Boston C.
Boston U.

Bowl. Gr. St. U.
Brandeis U.
Buffalo U. (S.U.N.Y)
B.Y.U.
Brown U.
Cal. St. U. (Fullerton)
Cal. St. U. (L.A.)
Cal. St. U. (Northridge)
U. Cal. (Berkeley)
U.C.L.A.
Case West. Res. U.
Columbia U.
U. Del.
East Car. U.
East. Mich. U.
Emory U.
Fla. St. U.
Geo. Wash. U.
Harvard U.
U. Hawaii
Ind. U.
U. Iowa
Johns Hopkins U.
U. Kans.
U. Md.
U. Mass. (Boston)
Mich. St. U.
U. Mich.
U. Minn.
U. Miss.
N. Mex. Highlands U.
U. N. Mex.
S.U.N.Y.C. (Cortland)
N.Y.U.
No. East. St. U.
U. Notre Dame
Penn. St. U.
U. Penn.
Purdue U.
St. Louis
St. Mary's U.
S.D.S.U.
Seton Hall U.
U. So. Maine
Trinity C.
Utah St. U.
Wash. St. U.
C. Wm. & Mary
U. Wyo.
Yale U.

PACIFIC AREA STUDIES
Geo. Wash. U.
U. Hawaii

RUSSIAN/EAST
EUROPEAN STUDIES
American U.
Ariz. St. U.
Boston C.
Brown U.
U. Cal. (Davis)
U. Chicago
C.C.N.Y. (C.U.N.Y.)
Columbia U.
Cornell U.
Fla. St. U.
Georgetown U.
Geo. Wash. U.
Harvard U.
Hunter C. (C.U.N.Y.)
U. Ill.
U. Ill. (Chicago)
Ind. U.
U. Iowa
Johns Hopkins U.
U. Kans.
Mich. St. U.
U. Mich.
U. Minn.
Monterey Inst.
Ohio St. U.

Princeton U.
U. So. Cal.
Stanford U.
U. Tex. (Austin)
U. Va.
U. Wash.
Wayne St. U.
U. Wis.
Yale U.

URALIC STUDIES
Columbia U.
Ind. U.

Basic Medical Sciences

(Typically includes Anatomy, Microbiology, Pathology, Pharmacology, Physiology; often includes Endocrinology, Neurological Sciences, Parasitology, Virology)

U. Ala.
U. Ala. (Birm.)
Albany Med. C.
American U.
Angelo St. U.
Ariz. St. U.
U. Ariz.
Ark. St. U.
U. Ark.
Auburn U.
Ball St. U.
Baylor U.
Boston U.
Bowl. Green St. U.
Brandeis U.
B.Y.U.
Brooklyn C. (C.U.N.Y.)
Brown U.
Bryn Mawr C.
Bucknell
U. Buffalo (S.U.N.Y)
Butler U.
Cal. Inst. Tech.
Cal. St. U. (Fresno)
Cal. St. U. (Fullerton)
Cal. St. U. (Long Beach)
Cal. St. U. (L.A.)
U. Cal. (Berkeley)
U. Cal. (Davis)
U. Cal. (Irvine)
U.C.L.A.
U. Cal. (Riverside)
U. Cal. (San Diego)
U. Cal. (San Francisco)
Carnegie Mellon U.
Case West. Res. U.
Catholic U.
U. Cent. Fla.
U. Chicago
U. Cincinnati
C.C.N.Y. (C.U.N.Y.)
Clemson U.
Colo. St. U.
U. Colo.
U. Colo. Health Sci. Ctr.
U. Conn.
U. Conn. Health Ctr.
Columbia U.
Cornell U.
Creighton U.
Dartmouth C.
U. Dayton
U. Del.
DePaul U.
Drexel U.
Duke U.
Duquesne U.
East Car. U.
East Tenn. St. U.
Emory U.
F.D.U.

Fla. Inst. Tech.
Fla. St. U.
U. Fla.
Fordham U.
Geo. Mason U.
Georgetown U.
Geo. Wash. U.
Georgia Inst. Tech.
Med. C. Georgia
Georgia St. U.
U. Georgia
Harvard U.
U. Hawaii
U. Health Sci. (Chicago)
Howard U.
Hunter C. (C.U.N.Y.)
Idaho St. U.
U. Idaho
Ill. Inst. Tech.
Ill. St. U.
U. Ill. (Chicago)
Ind. St. U.
Ind. U.
Ind. U.P.U.I.
Iowa St. U.
U. Iowa
James Madison U.
Johns Hopkins U.
Kans. St. U.
U. Kans.
Kent St. U.
U. Ky.
Lehigh U.
Loma Linda U.
L.I.U.
L.S.U. H.S.C.
La. Tech. U.
U. La. (Lafayette)
U. Louisville
Loyola U. Chicago
U. Maine
Marquette U.
Mayo Grad. Sch.
U. Md.
U. Md. (Baltimore)
M.I.T.
U. Mass.
U. Mass. (Worcester)
McNeese St. U.
Meharry Med. C.
Miami U.
U. Miami
Mich. St. U.
Mich. Tech. U.
U. Mich.
U. Minn.
Miss. St. U.
U. Miss. Med. Ctr.
U. Mo. (Columbia)
U. Mo. (K.C.)
Mont. St. U.
U. Mont.
Morehead St. U.
Mt. Sinai Sch. Med.
U. Neb.
U. Neb. Med. Ctr.
U. Nev. (Reno)
U. N.H.
U. Med. & Dent. N.J.
N. Mex. St. U.
U. N. Mex.
U. N. Orleans (Med. Ctr.)
N.Y. Med. C.
S.U.N.Y.C. (Potsdam)
S.U.N.Y. Downstate
S.U.N.Y. Upstate
N.Y.U.
No. Car. Cent. U.
No. Car. St. U. (Raleigh)
U. No. Car. (Chapel Hill)
No. Dak. St. U.
U. No. Dak.
Northeastern U.

No. Ill. U.
U. No. Tex.
No. W. St. U. La.
Northwestern U.
U. Notre Dame
Nova U.
Med. C. Ohio
Ohio St. U.
Ohio U.
Okla. St. U.
U. Okla.
U. Okla. Health Sci. Ctr.
Old Dominion U.
Oregon Health & Sci. U.
Ore. St. U.
U. Ore.
U. Pac.
Penn. St. U.
U. Penn.
Phila. C. Pharm.
U. Pitt.
Princeton U.
U. Puerto Rico
Purdue U.
Queens C. (C.U.N.Y.)
R.P.I.
U. Rhode Island
Rice U.
U. Rochester
Rockefeller U.
Roosevelt U.
Rosalind Franklin U.
Rush U.
Rutgers U.
St. John's U. (N.Y.)
St. Louis U.
S.D.S.U.
San Fran. St. U.
San Jose St. U.
Seton Hall U.
U. So. Ala.
Med. U. So. Car.
So. Dak. St. U.
U. So. Dak.
U. So. Cal.
U. So. Car.
U. So. Fla.
So. Ill. U.
So. Meth. U.
Stanford U.
Stevens Inst. Tech.
Stony Brook U. (S.U.N.Y.)
Syracuse U.
Temple U.
Tenn. St. U.
U. Tenn. (Knoxville)
U. Tenn. (Memphis)
Tex. A&M U.
Tex. A&M U. H.S.C.
Tex. Christian U.
Tex. Tech U. H.S.C.
U. Tex. (Austin)
U. Tex. Health Sci. Ctr. (Houston)
U. Tex. Health Sci. Ctr. (San Antonio)
U. Tex. S.W. Med. Ctr. (Dallas)
U. Tex. Med. Branch (Galveston)
Thom. Jefferson U.
Tufts U.
Tulane U.
U. Tulsa
Uniformed Serv. U. Health Sci.
Utah St. U.
U. Utah
Vanderbilt U.
U. Vt.
Va. Commonwealth U.
Va. Poly. Inst.
Va. St. U.
U. Va.
Villanova U.
Wagner C.
Wake Forest U.

Wash. St. U.
Wash. U.
U. Wash.
Wayne St. U.
W. Va. U.
C. Wm. & Mary
Wayne St. U.
Med. C. Wis.
U. Wis.
Wright St. U.
U. Wyo.
Yale U.
Yeshiva U.

BACTERIOLOGY
U. Iowa
Purdue U.
U. Tenn. (Memphis)
U. Tex. Med. Br. (Galveston)
U. Va.
U. Wash.
U. Wis.
W. Va. U.

IMMUNOLOGY
Albany Med. C.
U. Ala.
U. Ariz.
U. Ark. Med Sci.
Baylor C. Med.
Boston U.
Brown U.
U. Buffalo (S.U.N.Y.)
Cal. Inst. Tech.
U. Cal. (Berkeley)
U. Cal. (Davis)
U.C.L.A.
U. Cal. (San Diego)
U. Cal. (San Fran.)
Case West. Res. U.
U. Cin.
U. Chicago
Colo. St. U.
U. Colo. Health Sci. Ctr.
U. Conn. Health Ctr.
Cornell U.
Creighton U.
Dartmouth C.
Drexel U.
Duke U.
East Car. U.
Emory U.
Fla. St. U.
U. Fla.
Georgetown U.
Geo. Wash. U.
Harvard U.
U. Ill. (Chicago)
Ind. U.
Iowa St. U.
U. Iowa
Johns Hopkins U.
Kans. St. U.
U. Kans.
U. Ky.
U. Louisville
L.S.U. H.S.C.
Loyola U. (Chicago)
Marquette U.
U. Md. (Baltimore)
M.I.T.
U. Mass. (Worcester)
Mayo Gr. Sch.
U. Med. & Dent. N.J.
U. Miami
Mich. St. U.
U. Mich.
U. Minn.
U. Mo. (Columbia)
U. Neb.
N.Y. Med. C.
N.Y.U.
No. Car. St. U.

U. No. Car. (Chapel Hill)
U. No. Dak.
U. No. Tex. Health Sci. Ctr.
Northwestern U.
Ohio St. U.
U. Okla. Health Sci. Ctr.
Oregon Health & Sci. U.
Penn. St. U.
U. Penn.
U. Pitt.
Purdue U.
U. Rochester
Rosalind Franklin U.
Rush U.
Rutgers U.
St. Louis U.
U. So. Ala.
U. So. Cal.
Med. U. So. Car.
U. So. Dak.
U. So. Fla.
U. So. Maine
Stanford U.
Stony Brook U. (S.U.N.Y.)
Temple U.
U. Tenn.
Tex. A&M U. H.S.C.
U. Tex. (Austin)
U. Tex. Health Sci. Ctr. (Houston)
U. Tex. Med. Br. (Galveston)
U. Tex. S.W. Med. Ctr. (Dallas)
Thom. Jefferson U.
Tufts U.
Tulane U.
Uniformed Serv. U. Health Sci.
Utah St. U.
U. Utah
Vanderbilt U.
Va. Commonwealth U.
U. Va.
Wake Forest U.
Wash. U.
U. Wash.
Wayne St. U.
W. Va. U.
U. Wis.
Wright St. U.
Yale U.
Yeshiva U.

INFECTIOUS DISEASES
U. Cal (Berkeley)
Cornell U.
U. Georgia
Georgetown U.
Geo. Wash. U.
Harvard U.
Loyola U. Chicago
U. Minn.
U. Pitt.
Purdue U.
U. Tex. Med. Br.
Uniformed Services U.
Yale U.

RADIOLOGICAL SCIENCES
U. Cal. (Irvine)
Colo. St. U.
Georgetown U.
Geo. Wash. U.
U. Iowa
U. Okla.
U. Tex. Health Sci. Ctr. (Houston)
U. Tex. S.W. Med. Ctr. (Dallas)

TOXICOLOGY
U. Ala. (Birmingham)
U. Albany (S.U.N.Y.)
American U.
A.T. Still U.

U. Ariz.
U. Ark.
Brown U.
U. Buffalo (S.U.N.Y.)
U. Cal. (Davis)
U. Cal. (Irvine)
U.C.L.A.
Case West. Res. U.
U. Cincinnati.
U. Colo. Health Sci. Ctr.
Columbia U.
U. Conn.
Cornell U.
Dartmouth C.
Duke U.
Duquesne U.
Fla. A&M U.
U. Fla.
Geo. Wash. U.
Med. C. Georgia
U. Ga.
U. Ill. (Chicago)
Ind. U.
Iowa St. U.
Johns Hopkins U.
U. Kans.
U. Ky.
L.I.U.
L.S.U. H.S.C.
U. Louisville
U. Md.
U. Md. (Baltimore)
M.I.T.
U. Mass. Med. Sch. (Worcester)
U. Med. & Dent. N.J.
Mich. St. U.
U. Mich.
U. Minn.
U. Minn. (Duluth)
U. Miss.
U. Miss. Med. Ctr.
U. Mo. (Columbia)
U. Mo. (Kansas City)
U. Neb.
U. N. Mex.
N.Y.U.
No. Car. St. U. (Raleigh)
U. No. Car. (Chapel Hill)
Northeastern U.
Northwestern U.
Ohio St. U.
Okla. St. U. Health Sci.
Oregon St. U.
U. Pitt.
U. Puerto Rico
Purdue U.
U. Rhode Island
U. Rochester
Rutgers U.
St. John's U. (N.Y.)
S.D.S.U.
U. Sci. Phila.
U. So. Cal.
Stony Brook U. (S.U.N.Y.)
U. Tenn.
Tex. A&M U.
Tex. A&M U. H.S.C.
Tex. Tech U.
U. Tex. Health Sci. Ctr. (Houston)
U. Tex. Med. Br. (Galveston)
Thom. Jeff. U.
Utah St. U.
U. Utah
Vanderbilt U.
Va. Commonwealth U.
Wash. St. U.
U. Wash.
Wayne St. U.
W. Va. U.
Med. C. Wis.
U. Wis.
Wright St. U.

Biological Sciences

(Typically includes Biology, Botany, Zoology/ Entomology; often includes Marine Biology, Fisheries Biology; see also *Basic Medical Sciences*)

A.C.U.
Adelphi U.
U. Akron
Ala. A&M U.
Ala. St. U.
U. Ala.
U. Ala. (Birm.)
U. Alaska
Albany Med. C.
U. Albany (S.U.N.Y.)
American U.
Andrews U.
Angelo St. U.
Appal. St. U.
Ariz. St. U.
U. Ariz.
Ark. St. U.
U. Ark.
Auburn U.
Austin Peay St. U.
Ball St. U.
Barry U.
Baylor U.
Bemidji St. U.
Bloomsburg U. Pa.
Boise St. U.
Boston C.
Boston U.
Bowl. Gr. St. U.
Bradley U.
Brandeis U.
U. Bridgeport
Bridgewater St. U.
Buffalo U. (S.U.N.Y.)
B.Y.U.
Brooklyn C. (C.U.N.Y.)
Brown U.
Bucknell U.
Cal. Inst. Tech.
Cal. Poly. St. U. (San Luis Obispo)
Cal. St. Poly. U.(Pomona)
Cal. St. U. (Chico)
Cal. St. U. (East Bay)
Cal. St. U. (Fresno)
Cal. St. U. (Fullerton)
Cal. St. U. (L.A.)
Cal. St. U. (Long Beach)
Cal. St. U. (Northridge)
Cal. St. U. (Sacramento)
Cal. St. U. (San Bernardino)
Cal. St. U. (San Marcos)
Cal. St. U. (Stanislaus)
U. Cal. (Berkeley)
U. Cal. (Davis)
U. Cal. (Irvine)
U.C.L.A.
U. Cal. (Riverside)
U. Cal. (San Diego)
U. Cal. (San Francisco)
U. Cal. (Santa Barbara)
U. Cal. (Santa Cruz)
Carnegie Mellon U.
Case West. Res. U.
Catholic U.
U. Cent. Ark.
U. Cent. Fla.
Cent. Mich. U.
Cent. Mo. St. U.
U. Cent. Okla.
Cent. Wash. U.
Chicago St. U.
U. Chicago
U. Cincinnati
C.C.N.Y. (C.U.N.Y)
Clarion U. Pa.
Clark Atlanta U.

Clark U.
Clemson U.
Cleve. St. U.
Colo. St. U.
U. Colo.
U. Colo. Health Sci. Ctr.
Columbia U.
U. Conn.
U. Conn. Health Ctr.
Cornell U.
Creighton U.
Dartmouth C.
U. Dayton
U. Del.
Del. St. U.
Delta St. U.
U. Denver
DePaul U.
U. Detroit Mercy
Drexel U.
Duke U.
Duquesne U.
East Car. U.
East Stroudsburg U. Pa.
East Tenn. St. U.
East. Ill. U.
East. Ky. U.
East. Mich. U.
East. N. Mex. U.
East Tenn. St. U.
East. Va. Med. Sch.
East. Wash. U.
Edinboro U. Pa.
Emory U.
Emporia St. U.
F.D.U. (Madison)
F.D.U. (Teaneck)
Finch U. Health Sci.
Fisk U.
Fla. A&M U.
Fla. Atlantic U.
Fla. Inst. Tech.
Fla. Int'l. U.
Fla. St. U.
U. Fla.
Fordham U.
Fort Hays St. U.
Frostburg St. U.
Geo. Mason U.
Georgetown U.
Geo. Wash. U.
Med. C. Georgia
Georgia C. St. U.
Georgia Inst. Tech.
Georgia So. U.
Georgia St. U.
U. Georgia
Hampton U.
U. Hartford
Harvard U.
U. Hawaii
Hofstra U.
U. Houston
Howard U.
Humboldt St. U.
Hunter C. (C.U.N.Y.)
Idaho St. U.
U. Idaho
Ill. Inst. Tech.
Ill. St. U.
U. Ill.
U. Ill. (Chicago)
Incarnate Word U.
U. Indianapolis
Ind. St. U.
Ind. U.
Ind. U. Penn.
I.U.P.U.I.
Iowa St. U.
U. Iowa
Jackson St. U.
Jacksonville St. U.
James Madison U.
John Carroll U.

Johns Hopkins U.
Kans. St. U.
U. Kans.
Kent St. U.
U. Ky.
Lamar U.
Lehigh U.
Lehman C. (C.U.N.Y.)
Loma Linda U.
L.I.U.
L.S.U.
L.S.U. H.S.C.
La. Tech U.
U La. (Lafayette)
U. La. (Monroe)
U. Louisville
Loyola U. Chicago
Loyola U. (La.)
U. Maine
Marquette U.
Marshall U.
U. Md. (Baltimore)
U. Md. (Baltimore Cnty.)
M.I.T.
U. Mass.
Mayo Grad. Sch.
McNeese St. U.
Meharry Med. C.
Miami U. (Ohio)
U. Miami (Fla.)
Mich. St. U.
Mich. Tech. U.
U. Mich.
Mid. Tenn. St. U.
Midwest St. U.
Midwest U.
Millersville U. Pa.
Minn. St. U. (Mankato)
U. Minn.
Miss. C.
Miss. St. U.
U. Miss.
U. Mo. (Columbia)
U. Mo. (K.C.)
U. Mo. (St. Louis)
Mont. St. U.
U. Mont.
Montclair U.
Morehead St. U.
Morehouse Sch. Med.
Morgan St. U.
Mt. Sinai Sch. Med.
Murray St. U.
N.J.I.T.
U. Neb. (Kearney)
U. Neb. (Omaha)
U. Nev.
U. Nev. (Reno)
U. N.H.
U. Med. & Dent. N.J.
N. Mex. Highlands U.
N. Mex. St. U.
U. N. Mex.
U. N. Orleans
U. N. Orleans (Med. Ctr.)
New Sch. U.
Pittsburgh St. U.
S.U.N.Y. (Binghamton)
S.U.N.Y.C. (Brockport)
S.U.N.Y.C. (Buffalo)
S.U.N.Y.C. (Cortland)
S.U.N.Y.C. (Fredonia)
S.U.N.Y.C. (Geneseo)
S.U.N.Y.C. (New Paltz)
S.U.N.Y.C. (Oneonta)
S.U.N.Y.C. (Plattsburgh)
S.U.N.Y.C. Environ. Sci. & For. (Syracuse)
N.Y. Inst. Tech.
N.Y. Med. C.
N.Y.U.
U. No. Ala.
No. Car. A&T St. U.
No. Car. Cent. U.

No. Car. St. U. (Raleigh)
U. No. Car. (Chapel Hill)
U.N.C. (Charlotte)
U. No. Car. (Greensboro)
U. No. Colo.
No. Dak. St. U.
U. No. Dak.
U. No. Fla.
U. No. Tex.
Northeastern U.
Northeastern Ill. U.
No. E. Mo. St. U.
No. Ariz. U.
U. No. Colo.
No. Ill. U.
U. No. Iowa
No. Mich. U.
Northwest Mo. St. U.
Northwestern U.
U. Notre Dame
Nova U.
Oakland U.
Med. C. Ohio
Ohio St. U.
Ohio U.
Okla. St. U. Health Sci.
U. Okla.
U. Okla. Health Sci. Ctr.
Old Dom. U.
Ore. Health & Sci. U.
Ore. St. U.
U. Ore.
U. Pac.
Med. C. Penn.
Penn. St. U.
U. Penn.
Pittsburg St. U.
U. Pitt.
Ponce Sch. Med.
Portland St. U.
Prairie View A&M U.
Princeton U.
U. Puerto Rico
Purdue U.
Purdue U. (Calumet)
Queens C. (C.U.N.Y.)
Quinnipiac C.
R.P.I.
Rhode Island C.
U. Rhode Island
Rice U.
U. Richmond
U. Rochester
Rockefeller U.
Rosalind Franklin U.
Rutgers U.
Rush U.
St. Cloud St. U.
St. Francis U.
St. John's U. (N.Y.)
St. Joseph C. (Conn.)
St. Louis U.
St. Mary's U.
Sam Houston St. U.
San Fran. St. U.
U. San Fran.
S.D.S.U.
San Jose St. U.
Seton Hall U.
Shippensburg U. Pa.
Smith C.
Sonoma St. U.
U. So. Ala.
Med. U. So. Car.
So. Car. St. U.
U. So. Car.
So. Dak. St. U.
U. So. Dak.
U. So. Fla.
So. Conn. St. U.
Southeast Mo. St. U.
Southeastern Mass. U.
U. So. Cal.
So. Conn. St. U.

So. Ill. U.
So. Ill. U. (Edwardsville)
So. Meth. U.
U. So. Miss.
So. U. A&M C.
Southwest Mo. St. U.
Stanford U.
S.F. Austin St. U.
Stevens Inst. Tech.
Stony Brook U. (S.U.N.Y.)
Sul Ross St. U.
Syracuse U.
Temple U.
Tenn. St. U.
Tenn. Tech. U.
U. Tenn.
U. Tenn. (Memphis)
Tex. A&M U.
Tex. A&M U. (Commerce)
Tex. A&M U. H.S.C.
Tex. Christ. U.
Tex. So. U.
Tex. St. U.
Tex. Tech U.
Tex. Tech U. H.S.C.
Tex. Woman's U.
U. Tex. (Arlington)
U. Tex. (Austin)
U. Tex. (Dallas)
U. Tex. (El Paso)
U. Tex. (San Antonio)
U. Tex. (Southwestern Med. Sch.
   Dallas)
U. Tex. (Tyler)
U. Tex. Health Sci. Ctr.
   (Houston)
U. Tex. Health Sci. Ctr. (San
   Antonio)
U. Tex. Med. Br. (Galveston)
Thom. Jeff. U.
U. Toledo
Touro C.
Towson U.
Tufts U.
Tulane U.
U. Tulsa
Tuskegee U.
Uniformed Services U.
Utah St. U.
U. Utah
U. Vt.
Vanderbilt U.
Villanova U.
Va. Commonwealth U.
Va. Poly. Inst.
Va. St. U.
U. Va.
Wake Forest U.
Walla Walla C.
Wash. St. U.
Wash. U. (Mo.)
U. Wash.
Wayne St. U.
Wesleyan U.
West Chester U. Pa.
U. West Fla.
West Tex. St. U.
W. Va. U.
West. Car. U.
West. Conn. St. U.
West. Ill. U.
West. Ky. U.
West. Mich. U.
West N. Mex. U.
West. Wash. U.
Wichita St. U.
Wilkes U.
C. Wm. & Mary
Wm. Patterson U.
Winona St. U.
Med. C. Wis.
U. Wis.
U. Wis. (Eau Claire)
U. Wis. (La Crosse)

U. Wis. (Milwaukee)
U. Wis. (Oshkosh)
U. Wis. (Platteville)
Worcester Poly. Inst.
Worcester St. C.
Wright St. U.
U. Wyo.
Yale U.
Yeshiva U.
Youngstown St. U.

BIOCHEMISTRY
U. Ala. (Birmingham)
U. Alaska
U. Albany (S.U.N.Y.)
U. Ak.
Albany Med. C.
Ariz. St. U.
U. Ariz.
U. Ark.
Baylor C. Med.
Boston C.
Boston U.
Brandeis U.
Buffalo U. (S.U.N.Y.)
B.Y.U.
Brown U.
Cal. Inst. Tech.
Cal. St. U. (Fullerton)
Cal. St. U. (Hayward)
Cal. St. U. (Long Beach)
Cal. St. U. (L.A.)
U. Cal. (Berkeley)
U. Cal. (Davis)
U. Cal. (Irvine)
U. C. L.A.
U. Cal. (Riverside)
U. Cal. (San Diego)
U. Cal. (San Fran.)
U. Cal. (Santa Barbara)
Carnegie Mellon U.
Case West. Res. U.
C.C.N.Y. (C.U.N.Y.)
U. Chicago
U. Cincinnati
Clemson U.
Colo. St. U.
U. Colo.
Columbia U.
U. Conn. Health Ctr.
Cornell U.
Creighton U.
Dartmouth C.
U. Del.
De Paul U.
Duke U.
Duquesne U.
East. Car. U.
East Tenn. St. U.
Emory U.
Fla. Int'l. U.
Fla. St. U.
U. Fla.
Georgetown U.
George Washington U.
Med. C. Georgia
Georgia Inst. Tech.
Georgia St. U.
U. Georgia
Harvard U.
U. Hawaii
U. Houston
Howard U.
Hunter C. (C.U.N.Y.)
U. Idaho
Ill. Inst. Tech.
U. Ill.
U. Ill. (Chicago)
Ind. U.
I.U.P.U.I.
Iowa St. U.
U. Iowa
Johns Hopkins U.
Kans. St. U.

U. Kans.
Kent St. U.
U. Ky.
Lehigh U.
Loma Linda U.
L.S.U. H.S.C.
U. Louisville
Loyola U. Chicago
U. Maine
U. Md.
U. Md. (Baltimore)
U. Md. (Baltimore County)
M.I.T.
U. Mass.
U. Mass. (Lowell)
U. Mass. (Med. C. Worcester)
Mayo Grad. Sch.
Meharry Med. C.
Miami U.
U. Miami
Mich. St. U.
U. Mich.
U. Minn.
U. Minn. (Duluth)
Miss. St. U.
U. Miss. Med. C.
U. Mo. (Columbia)
U. Mo. (K.C.)
U. Mo. (St. Louis)
Mont. St. U.
U. Mont.
Mt. Sinai Sch. Med.
U. Neb.
U. Neb. Med. Ctr.
U. Nev. (Reno)
U.N.H.
U. Med. & Dent. N.J.
N. Mex. Inst. M&T
N. Mex. St. U.
U. N. Mex.
S.U.N.Y. Downstate
S.U.N.Y. Upstate
New York Med. C.
N.Y.U.
No. Car. St. U.
U. No. Car. (Chapel Hill)
No. Dak. St. U.
U. N. Dak.
No. Ill. U.
U. No. Tex.
Northwestern U.
U. Notre Dame
Med. C. Ohio
Ohio St. U.
Ohio U.
Okla. St. U.
U. Okla. Health Sci. C.
Old Dom. U.
Ore. Health & Sci. U.
Ore. St. U.
U. Ore.
U. Pac.
Med. C. Penn.
Penn St. U.
U. Penn.
U. Pitt.
U. Puerto Rico
Purdue U.
Queens U. (C.U.N.Y.)
R.P.I.
U. Rhode Island
Rice U.
U. Rochester
Rosalind Franklin U.
Rush U.
Rutgers U.
St. Louis U.
U. San Fran.
San Jose St. U.
U. Scranton
Seton Hall U.
U. So. Ala.
U. So. Cal.
U. So. Car.

Med. U. So. Car.
So. Dak. St. U.
So. Ill. U.
U. So. Miss.
So. U. A&M.C.
Stanford U.
Stevens Inst. Tech.
Stony Brook (S.U.N.Y.)
Syracuse U.
Temple U.
U. Tenn.
U. Tenn. (Memphis)
Tex. A&M U.
Tex. A&M U. H.S.C.
Tex. Tech U. H.S.C.
U. Tex. (Austin)
U. Tex. Health Sci. Ctr. (Houston)
U. Tex. Health Sci. Ctr. (San
   Antonio)
U. Tex. Med. Branch (Galveston)
U. Tex. S.W. Med. Ctr. (Dallas)
Thom. Jefferson U.
U. Toledo
Tufts U.
Tulane U.
Uniformed Services U. Health Ctr.
Utah St. U.
U. Utah
Va. Commonwealth U.
Va. Poly. Inst.
U. Va.
Vanderbilt U.
Villanova U.
U. Vt.
Wake Forest U.
Wash. St. U.
Wash. U.
U. Wash.
Wayne St. U.
Wesleyan U.
W. Va. U.
Med. C. Wis.
U. Wis.
Wright St. U.
Yale U.
Yeshiva U.

BIOETHICS
Albany Med. C.
Boston U.
Case West. Res. U.
Cleveland St. U.
Drew U.
Duquesne U.
Loma Linda U.
Mich. St. U.
U. Penn.
U. Pitt.
Rush U.
St. Louis U.
U. Tenn.
U. Va.
Med. C. Wisc.

BIOINFORMATICS
U. Ark.
Boston U.
Cal U. (San Diego)
U. Cinn.
U. Colo.
Duke U.
Ga. Inst. Tech.
Geo. Mason U.
Geo. Wash. U.
U. Idaho
Ind. U.
Iowa St. U.
Johns Hopkins U.
Marquette U.
Miss. St. U.
Med U. N. J.
U. Mich.
No. Car. St. U.
Northeastern U.

Northwestern U.
Ore. St. U.
Penn St. U.
U. Pitt.
Poly U.
R.I.T.
U. So. Fla.
Stevens Inst. U.
Tex. Tech. U.
U. Tex. Med. Br.
Va. Commonwealth U.
Va. Poly Tech.
Vanderbilt U.
U. Wash.
Med. C. Wisc.
Yale U.

BIOMATHEMATICS/ BIOSTATISTICS

U. Ala. (Birmingham)
U. Albany
Ariz. St. U.
Boston U.
Brown U.
Buffalo U. (S.U.N.Y.)
Cal. St. U. (East Bay)
U. Cal. (Berkeley)
U. Cal. (Davis)
U.C.L.A.
Case West. Res. U.
U. Cinn.
Colo. Health Sci. C.
Columbia U.
Drexel U.
Emory U.
Fla. St. U.
U. Fla.
Geo. Mason U.
Georgetown U.
Geo. Wash. U.
Harvard U.
Iowa St. U.
Johns Hopkins U.
U. Ill. (Chicago)
U. Iowa
Loma Linda U.
U. Mass.
U. Mich.
U. Minn.
Mt. Sinai Sch. Med.
N.Y. Med. C.
N.Y.U.
No. Car. St. U. (Raleigh)
U. N.C. (Chapel Hill)
U. No. Tex.
Ohio St. U.
U. Okla. Health Sci. Ctr.
Ore. Health & Sci. U.
U. Penn.
U. Pitt.
Rice U.
U. Rochester
Rutgers U.
Stony Brook U. (S.U.N.Y.)
S.D.S.U.
Med. U. So. Car.
U. So. Cal.
U. So. Car.
U. So. Fla.
Tufts U.
Tulane U.
U. Utah
Vanderbilt U.
Va. Commonwealth U.
U. Vt.
West. Mich. U.
U. Wash.
Med. C. Wis.
Yale U.

BIOMETRY/BIOMETRICS

U. Ala. (Birmingham)
U. Albany (S.U.N.Y.)
U. Buffalo (S.U.N.Y.)

U.C.L.A.
Case West. Res. U.
U. Colo. Health Sci. Ctr.
Columbia U.
Cornell U.
L.S.U. H.S.C.
U. Minn.
Mt. Sinai Sch. Med.
U. Neb.
No. Car. St. U. (Raleigh)
U. N.C. (Chapel Hill)
Oregon St. U.
U. So. Cal.
Med. U. So. Car.
Temple U.
U. Tex. Health Sci. Ctr.
  (Houston)
Va. Commonwealth U.
U. Wis.

BIOPHYSICS

U. Ala. (Birmingham)
Ariz. St. U.
U. Ark.
Baylor C. Med.
Boston U.
Brandeis U.
U. Buffalo (S.U.N.Y.)
Cal. Inst. Tech.
Carnegie Mellon U.
Case West. Res. U.
U. Cal. (Berkeley)
U. Cal. (Davis)
U. Cal. (Irvine)
U. Cal. (San Diego)
U. Cal. (San Fran.)
U. Chicago
U. Cincinnati
Clemson U.
U. Colo.
Columbia U.
U. Conn.
Cornell U.
Duke U.
East Car. U.
East Tenn. St. U.
Emory U.
Fla. St. U.
Georgetown U.
Harvard U.
U. Hawaii
U. Houston
Howard U.
U. Ill.
U. Ill. (Chicago)
Ind. U.
I.U.P.U.I.
Iowa St. U.
U. Iowa
Johns Hopkins U.
U. Kans.
U. Ky.
U. Louisville
L.S.U. H.S.C.
U. Md. (Baltimore)
Mayo Grad. Sch.
U. Miami
Mich. St. U.
U. Mich.
M.I.T.
U. Minn.
U. Miss.
U. Mo. (Kansas City)
Mt. Sinai Sch. Med.
U. Neb.
U. Med. & Dent. N.J.
S.U.N.Y. Downstate
N.Y.U.
Northwestern U.
U. No. Car. (Chapel Hill)
U. Notre Dame
Med. C. Ohio
Ohio St. U.
U. Okla. Health Sci. Ctr.

Ore. St. U.
U. Penn.
U. Pitt.
Princeton U.
Purdue U.
R.P.I.
U. Rhode Island
U. Rochester
U. So. Cal.
U. So. Fla.
Stanford U.
Stony Brook U. (S.U.N.Y.)
Syracuse U.
U. Tenn. (Memphis)
Tex. A&M U.
U. Tex. (Arlington)
U. Tex. (Austin)
U. Tex. (Houston)
U. Tex. S.W. Med. Ctr. (Dallas)
U. Utah
U. Vt.
Va. Commonwealth U.
Va. Poly. Inst.
U. Va.
Vanderbilt U.
Wake Forest U.
Wash. St. U.
Wash. U.
U. Wash.
Wayne St. U.
Med. C. Wis.
U. Wis.
Wright St. U.

BIOTECHNOLOGY

U. Ala.
Brown U.
U. Buffalo (S.U.N.Y.)
B.Y.U.
U. Cal. (Irvine)
U. Conn.
Dartmouth C.
U. Del.
East Car. U.
Fla. Inst. Tech.
Harvard U.
Howard U.
Ill. Inst. Tech.
Ill. St. U.
Ill. U. (Chicago)
U. Mass.
U. Mass. (Worcester)
M. Md.
U. Minn.
U. Nev. (Reno)
No. Car. St. U.
U. No. Tex.
Northeastern U.
Northwestern U.
Okla. St. U.
U. Penn.
Purdue U.
So. Ill. U.
Tex. A&M U.
Tex Tech U.
U. Tex. (Dallas)
U. Tex. (San Antonio)
Thom. Jefferson U.
Tufts U.
U. Utah
U. Va.
U. Wash.
U. Wis.
Worcester Poly Inst.

CANCER BIOLOGY

U. Ariz.
Brown U.
U. Buffalo (S.U.N.Y.)
U. Cal. (San Diego)
U. Chicago
U. Colo.
Dartmouth C.
U. Del.

Drexel U.
Georgetown U.
Harvard U.
U. Mass. (Worcester)
Mayo Grad. Sch.
U. Miami
Med U. N. J.
U. Neb.
U. No. Car. (Chapel Hill)
Northwestern U.
N.Y.U.
U. Penn.
U. So. Fla.
Stanford U.
U. Tex. Health (Houston)
U. Utah
Vanderbilt U.
Wake Forest U.
Wayne St. U.
W. Va. U.
U. Wis.
Yale U.
Yeshiva U.

CARDIOVASCULAR SCIENCES

Albany Med. C.
Baylor C. Med.
U. Cal. (San Diego)
Dartmouth C.
Med. C. Ga.
U. Md.
Med. U. N. J.
Northeastern U.
Tex. A&M U.
U. Va.

CELL BIOLOGY

U. Ala.
Albany Med. C.
U. Albany (S.U.N.Y.)
Ariz. St. U.
U. Ariz.
U. Ark.
Baylor C. Med.
Boston U.
Brandeis U.
Brown U.
U. Buffalo (S.U.N.Y.)
Cal. Inst. Tech.
U. Cal. (Berkeley)
U. Cal. (Davis)
U. Cal. (Irvine)
U.C.L.A.
U. Cal. (San Diego)
U. Cal. (San Fran.)
U. Cal. (Santa Barbara)
Carnegie Mellon U.
Case West. Res. U.
Catholic U.
U. Chicago
U. Cincinnati
Colo. St. U.
U. Colo.
U. Colo. Health Sci. Ctr.
Columbia U.
U. Conn.
U. Conn. Health Ctr.
Cornell U.
Creighton U.
Dartmouth C.
U. Del.
Drexel U.
Duke U.
East Car. U.
East Tenn. St. U.
Emory U.
Emporia St. U.
Finch U. Health Sci.
Fla. St. U.
U. Fla.
Geo. Mason U.
Geo. Wash. U.
Georgetown U.

U. Rhode Island
U. Rochester
Rockefeller U.
Rutgers U.
U. So. Cal.
Med. U. So. Car.
Stanford U.
Stony Brook U. (S.U.N.Y.)
Temple U.
U. Tenn.
Tex. A&M U.
Tex. A&M U. H.S.C.
U. Tex. Health Sci. Ctr. (Houston)
U. Tex. Health Sci. Ctr. (San Antonio)
U. Tex. S.W. Med. Ctr. (Dallas)
Thom. Jefferson U.
Tufts U.
Tulane U.
U. Utah
U. Vt.
Va. Commonwealth U.
Va. Poly. Inst.
U. Va.
Wake Forest U.
Wash. St. U.
Wash. U.
U. Wash.
Wayne St. U.
W. Va. U.
Med. C. Wis.
Yale U.
Yeshiva U.

MARINE BIOLOGY/ SCIENCE
U. Alaska
Cal. St. U. (Stanislaus)
U. Cal. (San Diego)
U. Cal. (Santa Barbara)
U. Del.
Duke U.
East Car. U.
Fla. Inst. Tech.
Fla. St. U.
U. Hawaii
U. Houston
L.S.U.
U. Maine
U. Md.
U. Mass.
U. Miami
U. No. Car. (Wilmington)
Nova U.
Ore. St. U.
U. Ore.
U. Rhode Island
Rutgers U.
San Fran. St. U.
U. So. Cal.
U. So. Fla.
Stevens Tech. Inst.
U. Wash.
U. West Fla.

MOLECULAR BIOLOGY
U. Ala. (Birmingham)
Albany Med. C.
U. Albany (S.U.N.Y.)
Ariz. St. U.
U. Ariz.
U. Ark.
Baylor C. Med.
Boston U.
Brown U.
U. Buffalo (S.U.N.Y.)
B.Y.U.
Cal. Inst. Tech.
U. Cal. (Berkeley)
U. Cal. (Davis)
U. Cal. (Irvine)
U.C.L.A.
U. Cal. (San Diego)

U. Cal. (San Francisco)
U. Cal. (Santa Barbara)
Carnegie Mellon U.
Case West. Res. U.
U. Chicago
U. Cinn.
Colo. St. U.
U. Colo.
U. Colo. Health Sci. Ctr.
Columbia U.
U. Conn.
U. Conn. Health Ctr.
Cornell U.
Dartmouth C.
U. Del.
Drexel U.
Duke U.
East Car. U.
Emory U.
Fla. Inst. Tech.
Fla. St. U.
U. Fla.
Geo. Mason Univ.
Geo. Wash. Univ.
Georgetown U.
Med. C. Georgia
U. Georgia
Harvard U.
U. Hawaii
Howard U.
U. Idaho
Ill. Inst. Tech.
U. Ill.
U. Ill. (Chicago)
Ind. U.
I.U.P.U.I.
Iowa St. U.
U. Iowa
Johns Hopkins U.
Kans. St. U.
U. Kans.
Kent St. U.
Lehigh U.
L.S.U. H.S.C.
Loyola U. (Chicago)
U. Louisville
U. Maine
U. Md.
U. Md. (Baltimore)
Marquette U.
U. Mass.
U. Mass. Med. Sch. (Worcester)
Mayo Med. Sch.
U. Miami
Mich. St. U.
U. Mich.
U. Minn.
U. Minn. (Duluth)
Miss. St. U.
U. Mo. (K.C.)
Mt. Sinai Sch. Med.
U. Neb.
U. Nev. (Reno)
U. Med. & Dent. N.J.
N. Mex. St. U.
U. N. Mex.
S.U.N.Y. Downstate
S.U.N.Y. Upstate
N.Y. Med. C.
N.Y.U.
U. No. Car. (Chapel Hill)
U. No. Tex. Health Sci. Ctr.
Northwestern U.
U. Notre Dame
Med. C. Ohio
Ohio St. U.
Ohio U.
Okla. St. U.
U. Okla. Health Sci. C.
Ore. Health & Sci. U.
Ore. St. U.
U. Oregon
Penn. St. U.
U. Penn.

U. Pitt.
Princeton U.
Purdue U.
R.P.I.
U. Rhode Island
U. Rochester
Rutgers U.
St. Louis U.
S.D.S.U.
San Fran. St. U.
San Jose St. U.
Seton Hall U.
U. So. Ala.
U. So. Cal.
Med. U. So. Car.
U. So. Car.
So. Ill. U.
U. So. Miss.
Stanford U.
Stony Brook U. (S.U.N.Y.)
Temple U.
U. Tenn.
U. Tenn. (Memphis)
Tex. A&M U.
Tex. A&M U. H.S.C.
U. Tex. (Austin)
U. Tex. (Dallas)
U. Tex. (San Antonio)
U. Tex. Health Sci. Ctr. (Houston)
U. Tex. Health Sci. Ctr. (San Antonio)
U. Tex. Med. Br. (Galveston)
Tex. Woman's U.
Thom. Jeff. U.
Tufts U.
Tulane U.
Uniformed Serv. U. Health Sci.
Utah St. U.
U. Utah
Vanderbilt U.
U. Vt.
Va. Commonwealth U.
Va. Poly. Inst.
U. Va.
Wake Forest U.
Wash. St. U.
Washington U.
U. Wash.
Wayne St. U.
West Va. U.
U. Wis.
Wright St. U.
U. Wyo.
Yale U.
Yeshiva U.

MOLECULAR GENETICS
U. Ala.
U. Cal. (Irvine)
U.C.L.A.
U. Chicago
U. Cinn.
Duke U.
Emory U.
U. Fla.
Georgia St. U.
Harvard U.
U. Ill. (Chicago)
I.U.P.U.I.
U. Kans.
U. Md.
U. Mass. (Worcester)
Mich. St. U.
U. Med. N.J.
N.Y.U.
Ohio St. U.
Okla. St. U.
U. Pitt.
U. Rhode Island
Rutgers U.
Stony Brook U. (S.U.N.Y.)
Tex. Tech. U.
U. Tex. Health Center (Houston)
U. Va.

U. Vt.
Wake Forest U.
Wash. U. (St. Louis)
Med. C. Wisc.

NEUROBIOLOGY
U. Ala.
U. Albany (S.U.N.Y.)
U. Ark.
Boston U.
Brandeis U.
Cal. Inst. Tech.
U. Cal. (Irvine)
U.C.L.A.
U. Cal. (San Diego)
Carnegie Mellon U.
Case West. Res. U.
U. Chicago
Columbia U.
U. Conn.
Cornell U.
Duke U.
Georgia St. U.
Harvard U.
U. Ill. (Chicago)
I.U.I.P.U.
U. Iowa
U. Ky.
U. Louisville
L.S.U.H.S.C.
Loyola U. (Chicago)
U. Md.
Marquette U.
U. Mo. (Columbia)
U. No. Car. (Chapel Hill)
N.Y.U.
Northwestern U.
U. Penn.
U. Pitt.
Purdue U.
U. Rochester
Rutgers U.
U. So. Car.
U. Tenn.
U. Tex. (Austin)
U. Tex. (San Antonio)
U. Utah
U. Vt.
Wake Forest U.
U. Wash.
Wayne St. U.
U. Wisc.
Yale U.
Yeshiva U.

REPRODUCTIVE BIOLOGY
Cornell U.
East. Va. Med. Sch.
U. Hawaii
Northwestern U.
N.Y.U.
W. Va. U.
U. Wyo.

Business

(Business Administration, Commerce, Management: typically includes specializations in Accounting, Finance, Marketing; often includes Advertising, Industrial Administration, Industrial and Labor Relations, Insurance, Operations Research, Public Relations, Quality Control, Real Estate, Taxation; majors in Economics are also common in graduate schools of business as well as in graduate schools of arts and science)

A.C.U.
Adelphi U.

U. Akron
Ala. A&M U.
Ala. St. U.
U. Ala.
U. Ala. (Birm.)
U. Ala. (Huntsville)
U. Alaska
U. Albany (S.U.N.Y.)
Alfred U.
Alliant Intl. U.
American U.
Andrews U.
Angelo St. U.
Antioch N.E.
Antioch U. (L.A.)
Antioch U. (McGregor)
Appal. St. U.
Ariz. St. U.
Ariz. St. U. (West)
U. Ariz.
Ark. St. U.
U. Ark.
Assump. C.
Auburn U.
Auburn U. (Montgomery)
Augusta St. U.
Austin Peay St. U.
Azusa Pac. U.
Babson C.
Ball St. U.
U. Baltimore
Barry U.
Baruch C. (C.U.N.Y.)
Baylor U.
Bentley C.
Berry C.
Bloomsburg U. of Pa.
Boise St. U.
Boston C.
Boston U.
Bowie St. U.
Bowl. Gr. St. U.
Bradley U.
U. Bridgeport
Bridgewater St. C.
Bryant U.
U. Buffalo (S.U.N.Y.)
B.Y.U.
Brooklyn C. (C.U.N.Y.)
Bucknell U.
Butler U.
Cal. Luth. U.
Cal. Poly. St. U. (San Luis
  Obispo)
Cal. St. Poly. U. (Pomona)
Cal. St. U. (Bakersfield)
Cal. St. U. (Chico)
Cal. St. U. (Dominguez Hills)
Cal. St. U. (East Bay)
Cal. St. U. (Fresno)
Cal. St. U. (Fullerton)
Cal. St. U. (Long Beach)
Cal. St. U. (L.A.)
Cal. St. U. (Northridge)
Cal St. U. (Sacramento)
Cal. St. U. (San Bernardino)
Cal. St. U. (San Marcos)
Cal. U. (Pa.)
U. Cal. (Berkeley)
U. Cal. (Davis)
U. Cal. (Irvine)
U.C.L.A.
U. Cal. (Riverside)
Campbell U.
Canisius C.
Capital U.
Card. Stritch C.
Carnegie Mellon U.
Case West. Res. U.
Catholic U.
U. Cent. Ark.
Cent. Conn. St. U.
U. Cent. Fla.
Cent. Mich. U.

Cent. Mo. St. U.
U. Cent. Okla.
Cent. St. U.
Chadron St. U.
Chapman U.
U. Chicago
U. Cincinnati
Citadel
Claremont Grad. U.
Clarion U. of Pa.
Clark Atlanta U.
Clark U.
Clarkson U.
Clemson U.
Cleve. St. U.
Colo. St. U.
U. Colo.
Columbia U.
Columbus St. U.
U. Conn.
Cornell U.
Creighton U.
U. Dallas
Dartmouth C.
U. Dayton
U. Del.
Delta St. U.
U. Denver
DePaul U.
U. Detroit Mercy
Dominican U.
Dominican U. Calif.
Drake U.
Drexel U.
Drury U.
U. Dubuque
Duke U.
Duquesne U.
East Carolina U.
East Tenn. St. U.
East. Ill. U.
East. Ky. U.
East. Mich. U.
East. N. Mex. U.
East. Wash. U.
Emory U.
Emporia St. U.
Fairfield U.
F.D.U. (Madison)
F.D.U. (Teaneck)
Fitchburg St. C.
Fla. A&M U.
Fla. Atlantic. U.
Fla. Inst. Tech.
Fla. Int'l. U.
Fla. St. U.
U. Fla.
Fordham U.
Fort Hays St. U.
Framingham St. C.
Frostburg St. U.
Gannon U.
Geo. Mason U.
Georgetown U.
Geo. Wash. U.
Georgia C. St. U.
Georgia Inst. Tech.
Georgia So. C.
Georgia St. U.
U. Georgia
Golden Gate U.
Gonzaga U.
Gov. St. U.
Hamline U.
Hampton U.
Hardin-Simmons U.
U. Hartford
Harvard U.
Hawaii Pac. U.
U. Hawaii
Henderson St. U.
Hofstra U.
Holy Names U.
Hood C.

U. Houston
U. Houston (Clear Lake)
Howard U.
Humbolt St. U.
Idaho St. U.
U. Idaho
Ill. Inst. Tech.
Ill. St. U.
U. Ill.
U. Ill. (Chicago)
Incarnate Word U.
U. Indianapolis
Ind. St. U.
Ind. U.
I.U.P.U.I.
Ind. U. Penn.
Inter American U.
Iona C.
Iowa St. U.
U. Iowa
Ithaca C.
Jackson St. U.
Jacksonville St. U.
Jacksonville U.
James Madison U.
John Carroll U.
Johns Hopkins U.
Kans. St. U.
U. Kans.
Kent St. U.
Kutztown U. of Pa.
U. Ky.
U. La. (Lafayette)
U. La. (Monroe)
Lamar U.
U. LaVerne
Lehigh U.
Lincoln U.
L.I.U.
L.I.U. (C.W. Post)
L.S.U.
L.S.U. Shreveport
La. Tech. U.
U. Louisville
Loyola C. (Md.)
Loyola Marymount U.
Loyola U. (Chicago)
Loyola U. (La.)
Lynchburg C.
U. Maine
Manhattan C.
Marquette U.
Marshall U.
U. Md.
Marywood U.
M.I.T.
U. Mass.
U. Mass. (Boston)
U. Mass. (Dartmouth)
U. Mass. (Lowell)
McNeese St. U.
U. Memphis
Mercer U.
Miami U. (Ohio)
U. Miami (Fla.)
Mich. St. U.
Mich. Tech. U.
U. Mich.
Mid. Tenn. St. U.
Midwest St. U.
Minn. St. U. (Mankato)
Minn. St. U. (Moorhead)
U. Minn.
U. Minn. (Duluth)
Miss. C.
Miss. St. U.
U. Miss.
U. Mo. (Columbia)
U. Mo. (K.C.)
U. Mo. (St. Louis)
Monmouth U.
U. Mont.
Montclair U.
U. Mont.

Morehead St. U.
Morgan St. U.
Murray St. U.
Natl. U.
Natl. Louis U.
Naval P.G. Sch.
U. Neb. (Kearney)
U. Neb.
U. Neb. (Omaha)
U. Nev.
U. Nev. (Reno)
U. N.H.
U. New Haven
N.J.I.T.
N. Mex. Highlands U.
N. Mex. St. U.
U. N. Mex.
U. N. Orleans
C. New Rochelle
New Sch. U.
C.U.N.Y. (Grad. Ctr.)
S.U.N.Y. (Binghamton)
S.U.N.Y. (New Paltz)
S.U.N.Y. C. (Oneonta)
S.U.N.Y. (Oswego)
S.U.N.Y. I.T.
N.Y.I.T.
N.Y.U.
Niagara U.
U. No. Ala.
No. Car. Cent. U.
No. Car. St. U.
U. No. Car. (Chapel Hill)
U. No. Car. (Charlotte)
U. No. Car. (Greensboro)
U. No. Car. (Willmington)
No. Dak. St. U.
U. No. Dak.
U. No. Fla.
U. No. Iowa
U. No. Tex.
No. E. Ill. U.
No. E. St. U.
Northeastern U.
No. Ariz. U.
No. Ill. U.
No. Ky. U.
U. No. Iowa
No. W. Mo. St. U.
Northwestern U.
Notre Dame U.
U. Notre Dame
Nova U.
Oakland U.
Ohio St. U.
Ohio U.
Okla. City U.
Okla. St. U.
U. Okla.
Old Dom. U.
Olivet Naz. U.
Oral Roberts U.
Ore. St. U.
U. Ore.
Our Lady Lake U.
Pace U.
Pac. Luth. U.
U. Pac.
Penn. St. U.
U. Penn.
Pepperdine U. (Culver City)
U. Phoenix
Pittsburg St. U.
U. Pitt.
Plymouth St. C.
Point Loma Nazarene U.
Poly U. N.Y.
Pont. Cath. U. P.R.
Portland St. U.
U. Portland
Prairie View A&M U.
Providence C.
U. Puerto Rico
U. Puerto Rico (Mayaguez)

Purdue U.
Purdue U. (Calumet)
Queens C. (C.U.N.Y.)
Quinnipiac U.
Radford U.
U. Redlands
Regent U.
R.P.I.
U. Rhode Island
Rice U.
Rider U.
Rivier C.
U. Richmond
Robert Morris U.
Rochester Inst. Tech.
U. Rochester
Rockford C.
Rollins C.
Roosevelt U.
Rowan U.
Rutgers U.
Sage Grad. Sch.
Saginaw Val. St. U.
St. Bonaventure U.
St. Cloud St. U.
St. Edward's U.
St. Francis U.
U. St. Francis (Ind.)
St. John's U. (N.Y.)
St. Joseph's U.
St. Louis U.
St. Mary's U. (Minn.)
St. Mary's U. (Tex.)
C. St. Rose
C. St. Scholastica
U. St. Thomas
U. St. Thomas (Tex.)
St. Xavier U.
Salem St. U.
Salisbury St. U.
Samford U.
Sam Houston St. U.
S.D.S.U.
San Fran. St. U.
San Jose St. U.
U. San Diego
U. San Fran.
Santa Clara U.
U. Scranton
Seattle Pac. U.
Seattle U.
Seton Hall U.
Sonoma St. U.
U. So. Ala.
U. So. Cal.
So. Car. St. U.
U. So. Car.
U. So. Dak.
U. So. Fla.
So. East. Mo. St. U.
Southeastern Okla. St. U.
So. Ill. U.
So. Ill. U. (Edwardsville)
U. So. Maine
So. Meth. U.
U. So. Miss.
So. Nazarene U.
So. Ore. U.
So. U. & A&M C.
Southwest Mo. St. U.
Southwestern Okla. St. U.
Stanford U.
S. F. Austin St. U.
Stetson U.
Stevens Inst. Tech.
Stony Brook U. (S.U.N.Y.)
Suffolk U.
Sul Ross St. U.
Syracuse U
Tarleton St. U.
Temple U.
Tenn. St. U.
Tenn. Tech. U.

U. Tenn.
U. Tenn. (Chattanooga)
U. Tenn. (Martin)
Tex. A&M U.
Tex. A&M U. (Commerce)
Tex. A&M U. (Corpus Christi)
Tex. A&M U. (Kingsville)
Tex. Christ. U.
Tex. So. U.
Tex. St. U.
Tex. Tech U.
Tex. Woman's U.
U. Tex. (Arlington)
U. Tex. (Austin)
U. Tex. (Brownsville)
U. Tex. (Dallas)
U. Tex. (El Paso)
U. Tex. (San Antonio)
U. Tex. (Permian Basin)
U. Tex. (Tyler)
Thunderbird
U. Toledo
Towson U.
Trinity U.
Troy U.
Troy U. (Dorthan)
Troy U. (Montgomery)
Tulane U.
U. Tulsa
Union C.
Utah St. U.
U. Utah
Valdosta St. U.
Vanderbilt U.
U. Vt.
Villanova U.
Va. Commonwealth U.
Va. Poly. Inst.
Va. St. U.
U. Va.
Wagner C.
Wake Forest U.
Washburn U.
Wash. St. U.
Wash. U. (Mo.)
U. Wash.
Wayne St. C.
Wayne St. U.
Webster U.
West Chester U. Pa.
West Ga. U.
W. Va. U.
West. Car. U.
West. Conn. St. U.
West. Ill. U.
West. Ky. U.
West. Mich. U.
West. New Eng. C.
West. N. Mex. U.
West Tex. A&M U.
W. Va. U.
West. Wash. St. U.
Wichita St. U.
Widener U.
Wilkes U.
Williamette U.
C. Wm. & Mary
Wm. Carey C.
Wm. Paterson U.
Winthrop U.
U. Wis.
U. Wis. (Eau Claire)
U. Wis. (La Crosse)
U. Wis. (Milwaukee)
U. Wis. (Oshkosh)
U. Wis. (Stevens Point)
U. Wis. (Stout)
U. Wis. (Whitewater)
Worcester Poly. Inst.
Wright St. U.
U. Wyo.
Xavier U. (Ohio)
Yale U.

Youngstown St. U.

ACTUARIAL/INSURANCE SCIENCES

Ball St. U.
Boston U.
Cent. Conn. St. U.
U. Cent. Fla.
Georgia St. U.
U. Hartford
Ind. U.
U. Mich.
U. Minn.
U. Neb.
N.Y.U.
U. No. Tex.
Penn. St. U.
U. Penn.
Roosevelt U.
St. John's U.
Temple U.
Va. Commonwealth U.
U. Wis.
Youngstown St. U.

ELECTRONIC COMMERCE

Adelphi U.
U. Akron
American U.
Ark. St. U.
Boston U.
U. Buffalo (S.U.N.Y.)
Cal. St. U. (East Bay)
Carnegie Mellon U.
U. Cinn.
Clemson U.
Creighton U.
U. Denver
DePaul U.
East. Mich. U.
F.D.U.
Fla. Atlantic U.
Fla. Inst. Tech.
Ga. Inst. Tech.
Ill. Inst. Tech.
Johns Hopkins U.
U. Md.
Marywood U.
Ntl. U.
Northwestern U.
N.Y.I.T.
N.Y.U.
U. Phoenix
Regent U.
R.P.I.
U. San Fran.
St. Xavier U.
Stevens Inst. Tech.
Temple U.
West Chester U. Pa.
Xavier U.

ENTREPRENEURSHIP

U. Akron
American U.
Baruch C. (C.U.N.Y.)
Cal. Luth. U.
Cal. St. U. (East Bay)
Columbia U.
U. Dallas
U. Del.
DePaul U.
Fla. Atlantic U.
Fla. Inst. Tech.
U. Fla.
F.D.U.
F.D.U. (Madison)
Georgia St. U.
U. Hawaii
U. Houston
Ill. Inst. U.
U. Iowa

U. Louisville
U. Minn.
Northwestern U.
Penn St. U.
Regent U.
R.P.I.
S.D.S.U.
U. So. Fla.
Stevens Inst. Tech.
Tex. Tech. U.
Wilkes U.
U. Wisc.
Xavier U.

HOTEL/ HOSPITALITY MANAGEMENT

U. Ala.
U. Cent. Fla.
Cent. Mich. U.
Colo. St. U.
Cornell U.
U. Denver
East Stroudsburg U.
F.D.U. (Madison)
F.D.U. (Teaneck)
Fla. Int'l. U.
Geo. Wash. U.
Golden Gate U.
U. Hawaii
U. Houston
Iowa St. U.
Kans. St. U.
U. Ky.
U. Md.
U. Mass.
Mich. St. U.
U. Mo. (Columbia)
U. Nev.
U. New Haven
N.Y.U.
Ohio St. U.
Okla. St. U.
Penn. St. U.
Purdue U.
R.I.T.
Roosevelt U.
U. So. Cal.
U. So. Car.
Temple U.
U. Tenn.
Tex. Tech U.
Tex. Women's U.
Va. Poly. Inst.
U. Wisc. (Stout)

HUMAN RESOURCE DEVELOPMENT/ MANAGEMENT

(Typically includes Career Development/Management, Personnel Management, Industrial and Labor Relations)

A.C.U.
Adelphi U.
U. Akron
U. Ala.
U. Albany (S.U.N.Y.)
American U.
Antioch U. (L.A.)
Auburn U.
Auburn U. (Mont.)
Azusa Pac. U.
Barry U.
Baruch C. (C.U.N.Y.)
Boston C.
Boston U.
Bowie St. U.
U. Bridgeport
Cal. St. U. (East Bay)

Bryant U.
U. Buffalo (S.U.N.Y.)
B.Y.U.
Cal. St. Poly. U. (Pomona)
Cal. St. U. (East Bay)
Cal. St. U. (Sacramento)
U. Cal. (Berkeley)
Carnegie Mellon U.
Case West. Res. U.
U. Chicago
Clarkson U.
Colo. St. U.
U. Colo.
Columbia U.
U. Denver
DePaul U.
Duquesne U.
East Car. U.
F.D.U. (Teaneck)
Fla. A&M U.
Fla. Inst. U.
Fla. Int'l. U.
U. Fla.
Fordham U.
Geo. Wash. U.
Georgia St. U.
Golden Gate U.
U. Hartford
Hofstra U.
U. Houston
Ill. Inst. Tech.
Ill. St. U.
Ind. U.
Iona C.
Iowa St. U.
L.I.U. (C.W. Post)
Marywood U.
M.I.T.
Miami U.
Mich. St. U.
Middle Tenn. St. U.
Miss. St. U.
No. Car. St. U.
Northeastern U.
No. Ill. U.
Northwestern U.
Nova U.
N.Y.U.
Ohio St. U.
Okla. City U.
Okla. St. U.
U. Ore.
Pace U.
Penn St. U.
U. Penn.
U. Pitt.
Poly. U.
Purdue U.
R.P.I.
Robert Morris U.
Rutgers U.
St. Edward's U.
St. John's U. (N.Y.)
S.D.S.U.
U. San Diego

MANAGEMENT STRATEGY

Alliant Intl. U
U. Ariz.
Azusa Pac. U.
Baruch C. (C.U.N.Y.)
Cal. St. U. (East Bay)
Case West. Res. U.
Claremont Grad U.
Clemson U.
DePaul U.
Drexel U.
Geo. Wash. U.
Georgia St. U.
Ill. Inst. Tech.
U. Iowa
U. Minn.
U. N. Mex.

U. No. Car. (Chapel Hill)
U. No. Tex.
Northwestern U.
N.Y.I.T.
N.Y.U.
Pace U.
Purdue U.
Regent U.
Rutgers U.
Stevens Inst. Tech.
Syracuse U.
Temple U.
Towson U.
Tufts U.
U. Wis.

MANAGEMENT OF TECHNOLOGY

Air F. Inst. Tech.
U. Akron
U. Albany (S.U.N.Y.)
Alliant Intl. U.
Boston U.
Carnegie Mellon U.
Cent. Conn. St. U.
U. Cinn.
Colo. Sch. Mines
Columbia U.
U. Del.
U. Denver
East Car. U.
East. Mich. U.
Fairfield U.
Geo. Mason U.
Geo. Wash. U.
Harvard U.
Idaho St. U.
Ill. St. U.
U. Ill.
Ind. St. U.
Marquette U.
Marshall U.
U. Md.
Mercer U.
U. Miami
U. Minn.
Ntl. U.
N.J.I.T.
U.N.H.
U. N. Mex.
N.Y.I.T.
N.Y.U.
No. Car. A&T St. U.
No. Car. St. U.
No. Ky. U.
Okla. St. U.
U. Penn.
Pepperdine U.
U. Phoenix
Poly. U.
Portland St. U.
R.P.I.
So. Dak. Sch. Mines
Stevens Inst. Tech.
Stony Brook U. (S.U.N.Y.)
Tex. A&M U.
Tex. St. U.
U. Tulsa
Villanova U.
Wash. St. U.
U. Wash.
U. Wis.
U. Wis. (Stout)

NONPROFIT MANAGEMENT

Azusa Pac. U.
Boston U.
Case West Res. U.
U. Cent. Fla.
Cleveland St. U.
Columbia U.
U. Conn.
U. Del.

DePaul U.
F.D.U. (Teaneck)
Fla. Atlantic U.
Geo. Wash. U.
Georgia St. U.
U. Iowa
Ind. U.
I.U.P.U.I.
L.I.U. (C.W. Post)
U. Md.
U. Memphis
U. Mo. (St. Louis)
New Sch. U.
U. No. Car. (Greensboro)
U. Notre Dame
N.Y.U.
Pace U.
U. Pitt.
Regent U.
Robert Morris U.
U. San Diego
U. San Fran.
St. Cloud St. U.
St. Xavier U.
Seattle U.
Seton Hall U.
Suffolk U.
Tufts U.
Willamette U.

QUANTITATIVE ANALYSIS/STUDIES

Baruch C. (C.U.N.Y.)
Cal. St. U. (East Bay)
U. Cal. (Santa Barbara)
U. Cinn.
Clark Atl. U.
DePaul U.
Drexel U.
F.D.U. (Teaneck)
Hofstra U.
Lehigh U.
L.S.U.
La. Tech. U.
Loyola C.
U. Mo. (St. Louis)
Montclair U.
U. No. Car. (Chapel Hill)
N.Y.U.
U. Ore.
Purdue U.
R.P.I.
U. Rhode Island
Rutgers U.
St. John's U. (N.Y.)
St. Louis U.
Seton Hall U.
Syracuse U.
Tex. Tech U.
U. Tex. (Arlington)
Troy U. (Dothan)
Va. Commonwealth U.

REAL ESTATE

American U.
U. Ariz.
Bentley C.
U. Cal. (Berkeley)
U. Cinn.
Columbia U.
Cornell U.
U. Denver
Depaul U.
Fla. Atlantic U.
U. Fla.
Geo. Wash. U.
Georgia St. U.
U. Hawaii
L.I.U.
U. Memphis
N.Y.U.
U. No. Tex.
Northwestern U.
Penn. St. U.

U. Penn.
U. San Diego
U. So. Cal.
So. Meth. U.
Tex. A&M U.
U. Tex. (Arlington)
Va. Commonwealth U.
Webster U.
U. Wis.

SUPPLY CHAIN MANAGEMENT

Ariz. St. U.
Cal. St. U. (East Bay)
Case West. Res. U.
U. Dallas
East. Mich. U.
Howard U.
Lehigh U.
U. Memphis
U. Minn.
Mich. St. U.
U. Mo. (St. Louis)
No. Car. St. U.
U. No. Car. (Greensboro)
Rutgers U.
U. San Diego
Syracuse U.
U. Wis.
Wright St. U.

TAXATION

U. Akron
U. Ala.
Albany U. (S.U.N.Y.)
American U.
Ariz. St. U.
Baruch C. (C.U.N.Y.)
U. Baltimore
Bentley C.
Boston U.
Bryant U.
Cal. St. U. (East Bay)
Cal. St. U. (Fullerton)
Cal. St. U. (L.A.)
Capital U.
Case West. Res. U.
U. Cent. Fla.
Chapman U.
U. Cinn.
U. Colo.
U. Denver
DePaul U.
Drake U.
Drexel U.
Duquesne U.
Fairfield U.
F.D.U. (Madison)
F.D.U. (Teaneck)
Fla. Atlantic U.
Fla. Int'l. U.
Fla. St. U.
U. Fla.
Fordham U.
Georgetown U.
Geo. Wash. U.
Georgia St. U.
Golden Gate U.
U. Hartford
U. Hawaii
Hofstra U.
Ill. Inst. Tech.
Ind. U.
L.I.U.
L.I.U. (C.W. Post)
Loyola Marymount U.
L.S.U.
U. Memphis
U. Miami
U. Minn.
Miss. St. U.
U. Miss.
U. Mo. (Kansas City)
U. Mo. (St. Louis)

Ntl. U.
U. N. Haven
U. N. Mex.
U. N. Orleans
S.U.N.Y. (Albany)
N.Y.U.
U. No. Tex.
Northeastern U.
No. Ill. U.
Nova U.
U. Okla.
Pace U.
Regent U.
Robert Morris U.
Rutgers U.
St. John's U. (N.Y.)
St. Thomas U.
St. Xavier U.
U. San Diego
San Jose St. U.
Seton Hall U.
U. So. Cal.
U. So. Car.
So. Meth. U.
Suffolk U.
Temple U.
U. Tenn.
Tex. Tech U.
U. Tex. (Arlington)
U. Tex. (San Antonio)
U. Toledo
U. Tulsa
Va. Commonwealth U.
Villanova U.
Wash. St. U.
U. Wash.
Wayne St. U.
Widener U.

Communications

(Includes Mass Organizational
Communication)

A.C.U.
U. Akron
U. Ala.
U. Alaska
U. Albany (S.U.N.Y.)
American U.
Andrews U.
Angelo St. U.
Ariz. St. U.
U. Ariz.
Ark. St. U.
U. Ark. (Little Rock)
Art Inst. Chicago
Auburn U.
Austin Peay St. U.
Ball St. U.
U. Baltimore
Barry U.
Baylor U.
Bloomsburg U. Pa.
Boise St. U.
Boston U.
Bowie St. U.
Bowl. Gr. St. U.
B.Y.U.
Bridgewater St. U.
Brooklyn C. (C.U.N.Y.)
Brown U.
U. Buffalo (S.U.N.Y.)
Butler U.
Cal. Inst. Arts
Cal. St. U. (Chico)
Cal. St. U. (East Bay)
Cal. St. U. (Fresno)
Cal. St. U. (Fullerton)
Cal. St. U. (Long Beach)
Cal. St. U. (L.A.)
Cal. St. U. (Northridge)
Cal. St. U. (Sacramento)

U. Cal. (Berkeley)
U. Cal. (Davis)
U.C.L.A.
U. Cal. (San Diego)
U. Cal. (Santa Barbara)
Canisus C.
Carnegie Mellon U.
Catholic U.
Cent. Conn. St. U.
U. Cent. Fla.
Cent. Mich. U.
Cent. Mo. St. U.
Chapman U.
U. Chicago
U. Cinn.
Clarion U. Pa.
Clark U.
Clemson U.
Cleveland St. U.
Colo. St. U.
U. Colo.
U. Colo. C.S.
U. Colo. Denver
Columbia U.
U. Conn.
Cornell U.
U. Dayton
U. Del.
U. Denver
DePaul U.
Drake U.
Drexel U.
Drury U.
Duquesne U.
East. Mich. U.
East Tenn. St. U.
East. Wash. U.
Edinboro U. Pa.
Emerson C.
Emporia St. U.
F.D.U. (Teaneck)
Fla. Atlantic U.
Fla. Inst. Tech.
Fla. St. U.
U. Fla.
Fordham U.
Fort Hays Kans. St. U.
Gallaudet U.
Georgetown U.
Geo. Mason U.
Geo. Wash. U.
Georgia So. U.
Georgia St. U.
U. Georgia
Gov. St. U.
U. Hartford
Harvard U.
Hawaii Pac. U.
U. Hawaii
Howard U.
U. Houston
Idaho St. U.
Ill. Inst. Tech.
Ill. St. U.
U. Ill.
U. Ill. (Chicago)
U. Incarnate Word
Ind. St. U.
Ind. U.
I.U.P.U.I.
Iona C.
Iowa St. U.
U. Iowa
Ithaca C.
Jackson St. U.
Jacksonville St. U.
Kans. St. U.
U. Kans.
Kent St. U.
U. Ky.
U. La. (Lafayette)
U. La. (Monroe)
U. La Verne
Lehman C. (C.U.N.Y.)

L.S.U.
La. Tech U.
Loyola Marymount U.
Loyola U.
U. Maine
Marquette U.
Marshall U.
U. Md.
Marywood U.
U. Mass.
U. Memphis
Miami U. (Ohio)
U. Miami
Mich. St. U.
Mich. Tech. U.
U. Mich.
U. Minn.
Minn. St. U. (Mankato)
Minn. St. U. (Moorhead)
Miss. C.
Miss. St. U.
U. Miss.
U. Mo. (Columbia)
U. Mo. (K.C.)
Mont. St. U.
U. Mont.
Monmouth U.
Montclair U.
U. Montevallo
Morehead St. U.
Ntl. U.
N.J.I.T.
U. Neb. (Kearney)
U. Neb. (Lincoln)
U. Neb. (Omaha)
U. Nev. (Las Vegas)
N. Mex. St. U.
U. N. Mex.
U. N. Orleans
C. N. Rochelle
S.U.N.Y.C. (Brockport)
S.U.N.Y.C. (New Paltz)
New Sch. U.
N.Y.I.T.
N.Y.U.
No. Car. St. U.
U. No. Car. (Chapel Hill)
U. No. Car. (Charlotte)
U. No. Car. (Greensboro)
No. Dak. St. U.
U. No. Dak.
No. E. Ill. U.
Northeastern U.
U. No. Colo.
U. No. Iowa
U. No. Tex.
Northwestern U.
Notre Dame U.
U. Notre Dame
Ohio St. U.
Ohio U.
U. Okla.
U. Ore.
Pace U.
U. Pac.
Penn. St. U.
U. Penn.
Pepperdine U.
Pittsburg St. U.
U. Pitt.
Portland St. U.
U. Portland
U. Puerto Rico
Purdue U.
Purdue U. (Calumet)
Queens C. (C.U.N.Y.)
Quinnipiac U.
Regent U.
R.P.I.
Rhode Island Sch. Design
R.I.T.
Roosevelt U.
Rutgers U.
Sage Grad. U.

St. Cloud St. U.
St. John's U.
St. Louis U.
St. Mary's U.
S.D.S.U.
San Fran. Art Inst.
San Fran. St. U.
San Jose St. U.
Seton Hall U.
Shippensburg U. Pa.
Simmons C.
U. So. Cal.
U. So. Car.
So. Dak. St. U.
U. So. Dak.
U. So. Fla.
So. Ill. U.
So. Meth. U.
U. So. Fla.
U. So. Miss.
So. Nazarene U.
Southwest. Mo. St. U.
Stanford U.
S. F. Austin St. U.
Suffolk U.
Sul Ross St. U.
Syracuse U.
Teachers C. (Columbia U.)
Temple U.
U. Tenn.
Tex. A&M U.
Tex. Christ. U.
Tex. St. U.
Tex. Tech U.
Tex. Woman's U.
U. Tex. (Arlington)
U. Tex. (Austin)
U. Tex. (Dallas)
U. Tex. (El Paso)
U. Tex. (Pan American)
U. Tex. (Tyler)
Towson U.
Troy U.
Utah St. U.
U. Utah
U. Vt.
Villanova U.
Va. Poly. Tech.
U. Va.
Wake Forest U.
Wash. St. U.
Wash. U.
U. Wash.
Wayne St. C.
Wayne St. U.
Webster U.
W. Va. U.
West Chester U. Pa.
U. West. Fla.
West. Ill. U.
West. Ky. U.
West. Mich. U.
Wichita St. U.
Wm. Paterson U.
U. Wis.
U. Wis. (Milwaukee)
U. Wis. (Stevens Point)
U. Wis. (Superior)
U. Wis. (Whitewater)
U. Wyo.

CREATIVE WRITING/ WRITING

A.C.U.
U. Akron
U. Ala.
U. Alaska
American U.
Antioch U. (L.A.)
Antioch U. (McGregor)
Ariz. St. U.
U. Ariz.
U. Ark.
Ball St. U.

Bennington C.
Boise St. U.
Boston U.
Bowl. Gr. St. U.
Brooklyn C. (C.U.N.Y.)
Brown U.
Cal. C. Arts
Cal. St. U. (Chico)
Cal. St. U. (Fresno)
Cal. St. U. (Long Beach)
Cal. St. U. (Sacramento)
Cal. St. U. (San Marcos)
U. Cal. (Davis)
U. Cal. (Irvine)
Carnegie Mellon U.
U. Cent. Fla.
Cent. Mich. U.
U. Cent. Okla.
Chapman U.
U. Chicago
City C. (C.U.N.Y.)
Claremont Grad. U.
Clemson U.
Cleveland St. U.
Colo. St. U.
U. Colo.
Columbia U.
Cornell U.
U. Denver
DePaul U.
East. Ky. U.
East. Mich. U.
East. Wash. U.
Emerson C.
Fla. Int'l. U.
Fla. St. U.
Ga. St. U.
Geo. Mason U.
Goddard C.
Hofstra U.
Hollins U.
U. Houston
Hunter C. (C.U.N.Y.)
U. Idaho
Ill. St. U.
U. Ill. (Chicago)
Ind. U.
Ind. U. Pa.
U. Iowa
Johns Hopkins U.
Kent St. U.
L.I.U.
U. La. (Lafayette)
U. Louisville
Loyola Marymount U.
L.S.U.
Manhattanville C.
U. Mass.
U. Mass. (Dartmouth)
U. Md.
U. Memphis
Miami U.
U. Miami
Mich. St. U.
U. Mich.
Mills C.
Minn. St. U. (Mankato)
Minn. St. U. (Moorhead)
Miss. St. U.
U. Mo. (St. Louis)
U. Mont.
Murray St. U.
Natl. Louis U.
National U.
U. N.H.
U. Neb.
U. Nev.
N. Mex. St. U.
New Sch. U.
S.U.N.Y. (Binghamton)
N.Y.U.
No. Car. St. U.
U. No. Car. (Greensboro)

No. Ariz. U.
No. Mich. U.
Northeastern U.
Northwestern U.
U. Notre Dame
Okla. City U.
Okla. St. U.
U. Okla.
U. Ore.
Penn. St. U.
U. Penn.
Purdue U.
Queens C. (C.U.N.Y.)
R.P.I.
Roosevelt U.
Rowan U.
Rutgers U.
S.D.S.U.
San Fran. St. U.
U. San Fran.
Sarah Lawrence C.
Seton Hall U.
Sonoma St. U.
So. Ill. U.
So. Meth. U.
U. So. Cal.
U. So. Car.
Syracuse U.
Temple U.
U. Tenn.
Towson U.
Tex. St. U.
U. Tex. (Austin)
U. Tex. (El Paso)
Utah St. U.
U. Utah
U. Va.
Va. Commonwealth U.
Wash. U.
U. West Fla.
West. Ill. U.
West. Mich. U.
W. Va. U.
Wichita St. U.
Wright St. U.
U. Wyoming

FILM/TELEVISION

(Broadcasting, Cinema,
Criticism, Motion Pictures)

U. Ala.
American U.
Antioch U. (McGregor)
Art Inst. Chicago
Auburn U.
Boston U.
Brooklyn C. (C.U.N.Y.)
Butler U.
B.Y.U.
Cal. C. Arts
Cal. Inst. Arts
Cal. St. U. (Fullerton)
U.C.L.A.
Carnegie Mellon U.
Catholic U.
Cent. Mich. U.
Chapman U.
U. Cinn.
Claremont Grad. U.
U. Colo.
Columbia U.
U. Denver
DePaul U.
Emerson C.
Emory U.
Fla. St. U.
U. Fla.
Ga. St. U.
Geo. Mason U.
U. Ga.
Hollins U.

Howard U.
Ind. U.
U. Iowa
Kans. St. U.
U. Kans.
Loyola Marymount U.
Marquette U.
Marywood U.
Mass. C. Arts
U. Md.
U. Memphis
Miami U.
U. Miami (Fla.)
Mich. St. U.
U. Mich.
U. Minn.
Mont. St. U.
U. Mont.
Ntl. U.
N.Y.U.
U. No. Car.
  (Chapel Hill)
U. No. Car.
  (Greensboro)
U. No. Tex.
Northwestern U.
Ohio St. U.
Ohio U.
U. Okla.
U. Ore.
Penn. St. U.
U. Pitt.
Regent U.
Rhode Island Sch. Design
R.I.T.
S.D.S.U.
San Fran. Art. Inst.
San Fran. St. U.
San Jose St. U.
U. So. Cal.
So. Ill. U.
So. Meth. U.
Stanford U.
S. F. Austin St. U.
Syracuse U.
Temple U.
U. Tenn.
U. Tex. (Austin)
Tulane U.
U. Utah
U. Va.
U. Wash.
Wayne St. U.
W. Va. U.
U.Wis. (Milwaukee)

INTERNET/ INTERACTIVE MULTIMEDIA

Alfred U.
Brooklyn C. (C.U.N.Y.)
Duquesne U.
Fla. St. U.
U. Fla.
U. Ga.
Georgetown U.
Georgia Inst. Tech.
I.U.P.U.I.
L.I.U. (C.W. Post)
U. Miami
N.J.I.T.
N.Y.U.
Pratt Inst.
Quinnipiac U.
Robert Morris U.
R.I.T.
S.D.S.U.
U. San Fran.
U. So. Cal.
Syracuse U.
Towson U.
Va. Commonwealth U.
West. Ill. U.

JOURNALISM

U. Ala.
U. Alaska
American U.
Angelo St. U.
Ariz. St. U.
U. Ariz.
Ark. St. U.
U. Ark.
Auburn U.
Ball St. U.
Baylor U.
Boston U.
Cal. St. U.
  (Fresno)
Cal. St. U.
  (Fullerton)
Cal. St. U.
  (Northridge)
U. Cal. (Berkeley)
Cent. Mich. U.
U. Colo.
Columbia U.
Drexel U.
Emerson C.
U. Fla.
Georgia C. & St. U.
U. Georgia
Harvard U.
Hofstra U.
U. Ill.
Ind. U.
Iowa St. U.
U. Iowa
Kans. St. U.
U. Kans.
Kent St. U.
L.S.U.
U. Md.
Marquette U.
Marshall U.
U. Memphis
U. Miami (Fla.)
Mich. St. U.
U. Mich.
U. Miss.
U. Mo. (Columbia)
U. Mont.
Murray St. U.
N.Y.U.
U. Neb.
U. Nev. (Reno)
U. No. Car.
  (Chapel Hill)
U. No. Tex.
Northeastern U.
Northwestern U.
Ohio St. U.
Ohio U.
U. Okla.
U. Ore.
Penn. St. U.
U. Portland
Quinnipiac U.
Regent U.
Roosevelt U.
U. So. Cal.
U. So. Car.
So. Dak. St. U.
So. Ill. U.
Stanford U.
Syracuse U.
Temple U.
U. Tenn.
Tex. A&M U.
Tex. Christ U.
Tex. So. U.
U. Tex. (Austin)
Va. Com. U.
W. Va. U.
U. Wis.
U. Wis.
  (Milwaukee)

San Jose St. U.
Santa Clara U.
Shippensburg U.
So. Dak. Sch. M&T
U. So. Cal.
U. So. Car.
U. So. Dak.
So. Ill. U.
U. So. Fla.
U. So. Maine
So. Meth. U.
So. Ore. U.
Stanford U.
C. Staten Island (C.U.N.Y.)
S. F. Austin St. U.
Stevens Inst. Tech.
Stony Brook U. (S.U.N.Y.)
Suffolk U.
Syracuse U.
Temple U.
U. Tenn.
U. Tenn. (Chattanooga)
Tex. A&M U.
Tex. A&M U. (Commerce)
Tex. A&M U. (Corpus Christi)
Tex. A&M U. (Kingsville)
Tex. St. U.
Tex. Tech. U.
U. Tex. (Arlington)
U. Tex. (Austin)
U. Tex. (Dallas)
U. Tex. (El Paso)
U. Tex. (San Antonio)
U. Tex. (Tyler)
Troy U.
Troy U. (Dothan)
Tufts U.
Tulane U.
U. Tulsa
Union C.
Utah St. U.
U. Utah
Vanderbilt U.
U. Vt.
Villanova U.
Va. Commonwealth U.
Va. Poly. Inst.
U. Va.
Wake Forest U.
Wash. St. U.
Wash. U. (Mo.)
U. Wash.
Wayne St. U.
Webster U.
West Chester U. Pa.
W. Va. U.
West. Car. U.
West. Conn. U.
U. West Fla.
U. West Ga.
West. Ill. U.
West. Ky. U.
West. Mich. U.
West Va. U.
West. Wash. U.
Wichita St. U.
C. Wm. & Mary
U. Wis.
U. Wis. (Milwaukee)
Worcester Poly. Inst.
Wright St. U.
U. Wyo.
Yale U.

Criminal Justice/ Corrections/Criminology

(Includes Law Enforcement,
Police Science)

U. Ala.
U. Ala. (Birm.)
U. Alaska
U. Albany (S.U.N.Y.)

American U.
Ariz. St. U.
U. Ark.
Armstrong Atlantic St. U.
Auburn U. (Mont.)
U. Baltimore
Boise St. U.
Boston U.
Bowl. Gr. St. U.
U. Buffalo (S.U.N.Y.)
Cal. St. U. (Fresno)
Cal. St. U. (Long Beach)
Cal. St. U. (L.A.)
Cal. St. U. (Sacramento)
Cal. St. U. (San Bernardino)
U. Cal. (Irvine)
U. Cent. Fla.
U. Cent. Okla.
Cent. Conn. St. U.
Cent. Mich. U.
Cent. Mo. St. U.
Chapman U.
Chicago St. U.
U. Cincinnati
Clark Atl. U.
U. Colo. (Denver)
Columbus St. U.
U. Del.
Delta St. U.
DePaul U.
U. Detroit Mercy
East Car. U.
East Cent. U.
East. Ky. U.
East. Mich. U.
East Tenn. St. U.
Fitchburg St. U.
Fla. Int'l. U.
Fla. St. U.
U. Fla.
Fordham U.
Ga. St. U.
Geo. Wash. U.
Ill. St. U.
U. Ill. (Chicago)
Ind. St. U.
Ind. U.
Ind. U. Penn.
Iona C.
U. Iowa
I.U.P.U.I.
Jackson St. U.
Jacksonville St. U.
Jersey City St. U.
John Jay C. (C.U.N.Y.)
Kent St. U.
L.I.U. (C.W. Post)
U. La. (Monroe)
U. Louisville
L.S.U.
Loyola U. (Chicago)
Marshall U.
U. Md.
Marywood U.
U. Mass. (Lowell)
U. Memphis
Mich. St. U.
Mid. Tenn. St. U.
Minn. St. U. (Mankato)
U. Minn.
Minot St. U.
U. Mo. (K.C.)
U. Mo. (St. Louis)
Monmouth U.
U. Mont.
Natl. U.
U. Neb.
U. Nev.
U. N. Haven
N. Mex. St. U.
C.U.N.Y. (Grad. Ctr.)
S.U.N.Y.C. (Buffalo)
Niagara U.
No. Car. Cent. U.

U. No. Car. (Charlotte)
U. No. Dak.
U. No. Tex.
No. East. St. U.
Northeastern U.
Northwestern U.
No. Ariz. U.
Nova U.
Okla. City U.
Okla. St. U.
Penn. St. U.
U. Pitt.
Portland St. U.
Radford U.
R.I.T.
Rutgers U.
Saginaw Val. St. U.
St. Cloud St. U.
St. John's U.
St. Joseph U.
St. Mary's U. (Tex.)
Sam Houston St. U.
S.D.S.U.
San Jose St. U.
Seton Hall U.
Shippensburg U. Pa.
So. E. Mo. St. U.
U. So. Car.
U. So. Fla.
So. Ill. U.
U. So. Miss.
Southwest Tex. St. U.
Suffolk U.
Sul Ross St. U.
Temple U.
Tenn. St. U.
U. Tenn.
U. Tenn. (Chattanooga)
U. Tex. (Arlington)
U. Tex. (San Antonio)
U. Tex. (Tyler)
U. Toledo
Troy U.
Valdosta St. U.
Villanova U.
Va. Commonwealth U.
Wash. St. U.
Washburn U.
Wayne St. U.
Webster U.
West Chester U. Pa.
West Ill. U.
West. New Eng. C.
West. Ore. U.
Westfield St. U.
Wichita St. U.
Widener U.
U. Wis. (Milwaukee)
Wright St. U.
Xavier U. (Ohio)
Youngstown St. U.

Dentistry

U. Ala. (Birm.)
Boston U.
U. Buffalo (S.U.N.Y.)
U.C.L.A.
U. Cal. (San Francisco)
Case West. Res. U.
U. Colo. Health Sci. Ctr.
Columbia U.
U. Conn. Health Ctr.
Creighton U.
U. Detroit Mercy
U. Fla.
Med. C. Georgia
Harvard U.
Howard U.
U. Ill. (Chicago)
Ind. U.
U. Iowa
U. Ky.
Loma Linda U.

U. Louisville
L.S.U. H.S.C.
Marquette U.
U. Md. (Baltimore)
U. Med. & Dent. N.J.
Meharry Med. C.
U. Mich.
U. Minn.
U. Miss. Med. Ctr.
U. Mo. (K.C.)
U. Neb. Med. Ctr.
N.Y.U.
U. No. Car. (Chapel Hill)
Nova U.
Ohio St. U.
U. Okla. Health Sci. Ctr.
Oregon Health & Sci. U.
U. Pac.
U. Penn.
U. Pitt.
U. Puerto Rico
Med. U. So. Car.
U. So. Cal.
So. Ill. U. (Edwardsville)
Stony Brook U. (S.U.N.Y.)
Temple U.
U. Tenn. (Memphis)
Tex. A&M U. H.S.C. (Baylor C. Dent.)
U. Tex. Health Sci. Ctr. (Houston)
U. Tex. Health Sci. Ctr. (San Antonio)
Tufts U.
Va. Commonwealth U.
U. Wash.
W. Va. U.

Education

(Typically includes
Administration and Supervision,
Curriculum and Instruction, Ele-
mentary and Secondary Teach-
ing. Evaluation and Research,
Foreign Language Education,
Foundations and Philosophy of
Education, Guidance and Coun-
seling, Health/Physical Education,
History and Philosophy of Edu-
cation, Home Economics Educa-
tion, Reading Specialist,
Recreation, School Psychology,
Special Education, Speech
Pathology and Audiology, Voca-
tional/Distributive/Occupational
Education; often includes Busi-
ness Education, Early Childhood
Education, Extension Education,
Middle School Education, Student Personnel Services; offered
by more than 500 institutions in
all 50 states, so individual institutions are not listed here)

ADULT EDUCATION
(INCLUDES COMMUNITY
EDUCATION)
U. Ala.
U. Alaska
U. Ark.
Auburn U.
Ball St. U.
U. Buffalo (S.U.N.Y.)
Cal. St. U. (L.A.)
U. Cent. Okla.
Cent. Mo. St. U.
Cleve. St. U.
U. Conn.
Columbia U. (Teachers C.)
U. Denver
Drake U.
E. Car. U.
East. Wash. U.
Fla. A&M U.

DRUG AND ALCOHOL/
SUBSTANCE ABUSE
COUNSELING
Antioch N. E. Grad. Sch.
Gov. St. U.
L.I.U.
U. No. Fla.
Sage Grad. Sch.
Springfield C.

EDUCATION OF THE
GIFTED
U. Ala.
Ariz. St. U.
Ark. St. U.
U. Ark.
Barry U.
Cal. St. U. (L.A.)
Cal. St. U.
    (Northridge)
Cal. St. U.
    (Sacramento)
Chicago St. U.
Clark Atlanta U.
Cleveland St. U.
Columbia U.
    (Teachers C.)
U. Conn.
Converse C.
Drury U.
Emporia St. U.
Georgia C. & St. U.
U. Georgia
Hofstra U.
U. Houston
Hunter C. (C.U.N.Y.)
Ind. St. U.
Ind. U. Pa.
Jacksonville U.
U. Kans.
Kent St. U.
U. La. (Lafayette)
Mansfield U. Pa.
Millersville U. Pa.
Minn. St. U. (Mankato)
U. Minn.
U. Mo. (Columbia)
U. Neb. (Kearney)
C. N. Rochelle
U. No. Car. (Charlotte)
U. No. Colo.
U. No. Iowa
Northeast. Ill. U.
Nova U.
Ohio U.
Okla. City U.
Purdue U.
U. St. Thomas (Minn.)
U. So. Ala.
U. So. Miss.
U. So. Fla.
Stetson U.
Tex. A&M U.
W. Ky. U.
W. Va. U.
W. Wash. U.
C. Wm. & Mary
U. Wis. (Whitewater)
Whitworth C.
Wright St. U.
Xavier U.
Youngstown St. U.

EDUCATION OF THE
MULTIPLE
HANDICAPPED
U. Ark.
Ariz. St. U.
Cleveland St. U.
Columbia U.
    (Teachers C.)
Georgia C. St. U.
Minot St. U.

EDUCATIONAL MEDIA/
INSTRUCTIONAL
TECHNOLOGY
Adelphi U.
U. Alaska
U. Albany (S.U.N.Y.)
Alliant Int'l. U.
American U.
Appla. St. U.
Ariz. St. U.
U. Ark.
Auburn U.
Azusa Pac. U.
Barry U.
Bloomsburg U. Pa.
Boise St. U.
Boston U.
Bowl. Gr. St. U.
B.Y.U.
Cal. St. U. (Chico)
Cal. St. U. (East Bay)
Cal. St. U. (Fullerton)
Cal. St. U. (Los Angeles)
Cal. St. U. (San Bernardino)
U. Cent. Ark.
Cent. Conn. St. U.
U. Cent. Fla.
Cent. Mich. U.
Cleveland St. U.
U. Colo.
U. Conn.
U. Dayton
Drexel U.
Duquesne U.
East. Car. U.
East. Wash. U.
East Stroudsburg U.
East Tenn. St. U.
Emporia St. U.
Fairfield U.
F.D.U. (Teaneck)
Fla. Atlantic U.
Fla. Int'l. U.
Fla. St. U.
Frostburg St. U.
Gallaudet U.
Gannon U.
Geo. Mason U.
Geo. Wash. U.
Georgia St. U.
U. Ga.
U. Hartford
Harvard U.
U. Hawaii
Hofstra U.
U. Houston
Idaho St. U.
Ind. U.
Ind. U. Pa.
Iona C.
Iowa St. U.
Jackson St. U.
Jacksonville St. U.
Jacksonville U.
Kean U.
Kent St. U.
Kutztown St. U.
U. Ky.
L.I.U.
L.I.U. (C. W. Post)
U. Louisville
Loyola U. Chicago
L.S.U.
U. Maine
U. Mass.
McDaniel C.
McNeese St. U.
U. Md.
U. Memphis
Mich. St. U.
U. Mich.
Minn. St. U. (Mankato)
U. Minn.

Miss. St. U.
U. Mo. (Columbia)
Mont. St. U.
Montclair U.
Ntl. Louis U.
Ntl. U.
U. Neb.
U. Neb. (Omaha)
U. Nev.
N.J. City U.
U. N. Mex.
U. No. Car. (Charlotte)
U. No. Car. (Greensboro)
U. No. Car. (Wilmington)
U. No. Dak.
N.Y.I.T.
N.Y.U.
No. Ariz. U.
No. Car. A&T St. U.
No. Car. St. U.
No. Ill. U.
Northwestern U.
Notre Dame U.
Nova U.
Oakland U.
Ohio U.
Old. Dom. U.
Our Lady of Lake
Penn. St. U.
Pepperdine U.
U. Phoenix
Pittsburg St. U.
Portland St. U.
Purdue U.
Robert Morris U.
R.I.T.
Rowan U.
San Fran. St. U.
U. San Fran.
San Jose St. U.
S.D.S.U.
Seton Hall U.
U. So. Cal.
U. So. Car.
U. So. Dak.
U. So. Fla.
U. So. Ill.
St. Cloud St. U.
St. Joseph's U.
Stony Brook U. (S.U.N.Y.)
Syracuse U.
Teacher's C. (Columbia U.)
U. Tenn.
U. Tenn. (Chattanooga)
Tex A&M U.
Tex. So. U.
Tex. Tech. U.
U. Tex. (San Antonio)
U. Toledo
Towson U.
Utah St. U.
Valdosta St. U.
Va. Poly. Inst.
U. Wash.
Wayne St. U.
Webster U.
U. West. Fla.
West. Ill. U.
West. Ky. U.
West Tex A&M U.
Widener U.
Wilkes U
U. Wyo.

ENGLISH AS A SECOND
LANGUAGE
U. Ala.
U. Ariz.
Adelphi U.
Alliant Intl. U.
American U.
Ariz. St. U.
Azusa Pac. U.

Ball St. U.
Boston U.
U. Buffalo (S.U.N.Y.)
B.Y.U.
Cal. St. U. (Dominguez Hills)
Cal. St. U. (Fresno)
Cal. St. U. (Fullerton)
Cal St. U. (L.A.)
Cal. St. U. (Sacramento)
Cal St. U. (San Bernardino)
U.C.L.A.
Catholic U.
Cent. Conn. St. U.
U. Cent. Fla.
Cent. Mich. U.
Cent. Wash. U.
U. Cinn.
U. Colo.
U. Del.
Drexel U.
Duquesne U.
East. Mich. U.
East. Naz. C
Emporia St. U.
Fairfield U.
U. Fla.
Fordham U.
Gannon U.
Geo. Mason U.
Georgetown U.
Georgia St. U.
Gonzaga U.
U. Hawaii
Hofstra U.
U. Houston
Hunter C. (C.U.N.Y.)
U. Idaho
U. Ill.
U. Ill. (Chicago)
Ind. St. U.
Ind. U.
U. Ind. Pa.
I.U.P.U.I.
Kent St. U.
Lehman C. (C.U.N.Y.)
L.I.U.
U. Md.
U. Mass.
U. Miami
Mich. St. U.
U. Mich.
Mid. Tenn. St. U.
U. Minn.
Montclair U.
Mont. Inst. Intl. Studies
U. Neb.
U. Nev.
U. Nev. (Reno)
N.J. City U.
U. New Paltz (S.U.N.Y.)
No. Ariz. U.
U. No. Car. (Charlotte)
U. No. Car. (Greensboro)
U. No. Iowa
U. No. Va.
Nova U.
S.U.N.Y.C . (Cortland)
S.U.N.Y.C. (Fredonia)
N.Y.U.
Ohio U.
Okla. City U.
U. Penn.
U. Phoenix
U. Pitt.
Portland St. U.
Queens C. (C.U.N.Y.)
Regent U.
Rider U.
Rutgers U.
U. San Fran.
U. Scranton
St. Cloud St. U.
St. John's U. (N.Y.)

S.D.S.U.
San Fran. St. U.
San Jose St. U.
Seattle Pac. U.
Seattle U.
Simmons C.
U. So. Cal.
U. So. Car.
So. Ill. U.
Stony Brook U. (S.U.N.Y.)
Teachers C. (Columbia U.)
Temple U.
U. Tenn.
Tex. A&M U.
U. Tex. (Arlington)
U. Tex. (San Antonio)
U. Toledo
Wash. St. U.
U. Wash.
West Chester Pa.
W. Va. U.
Wright St. U.

EXERCISE/SPORTS SCIENCE
U. Akron
U. Ala.
American U.
Appl. St. U.
Ariz. St. U.
A.T. Still U.
Austin Peay St. U.
Ball St. U
Barry U.
Bloomsburg U. Pa.
Boise St. U.
U. Buffalo (S.U.N.Y.)
Brooklyn C. (C.U.N.Y.)
Cal St. U. (Fresno)
Cal. U. Pa.
U. Cal. (Davis)
U. Cent. Fla.
Cleveland St. U.
Colo. St. U.
U. Conn.
U. Dayton
U. Del.
East Car. U.
East. Mich. U.
Fla. Atlantic U.
Fla. Int'l. U.
Fla. St. U.
U. Fla.
Geo. Mason U.
Geo. Wash. U.
Howard U.
U. Houston
Ind. U.
Iowa St. U.
U. Iowa
Kent St. U.
U. Ky.
La. U. (Monroe)
L.I.U.
La. Tech. U.
Marshall U.
U. Memphis
Miami U.
U. Miami
U. Minn.
Miss. St. U.
U. Miss.
U. Mo. (Columbia)
U. Mont.
Montclair U.
S. U. N.Y. (Cortland)
U. Neb.
U. Nev.
U. No. Car. (Chapel Hill)
U. No. Car. (Charlotte)
U. No. Car. (Greensboro)
No. Dak. St. U.
Northeastern U.

Oakland U.
Ohio U.
U. Okla.
Ore. St. U.
Purdue U.
U. Rhode Island
St. Cloud St. U.
S.D.S.U.
U. So. Car.
Springfield C.
Syracuse U.
Tenn. St. U.
U. Tenn.
Tex. Tech. U.
Tex. Women's U.
U. Tex. (Arlington)
U. Tex. (El Paso)
U. Utah
Va. Commonwealth U.
Wake Forest U.
Wash. St. U.
Wayne St. U.
U. West. Fla.
Wichita St. U.
W. Va. U.

LEARNING DISABILITIES
(Includes Multiple Handicaps)
Ala. A&M U.
U. Ala.
U. Ala. (Birm.)
U. Ariz.
U. Ark.
Ball St. U.
Bank St. C.
Bloomsburg St. U.
Boston C.
Brooklyn C. (C.U.N.Y.)
Bowl. Gr. St. U.
Cal. St. U. (Chico)
Cal. U. Pa.
Card. Stritch C.
Cent. Mo. St. U.
Cent. St. U.
Chapman U.
Chicago St. U.
Clarke C.
Cleveland St. U.
Columbia U. (Teachers C.)
Columbus C.
DePaul U.
U. Detroit Mercy
East Cent. St. U.
East. Mont. C.
Gallaudet U.
Georgia C. St. U.
Georgia St. U.
U. Georgia
Hampton U.
Hunter C. (C.U.N.Y.)
U. Ill.
Iowa St. U.
James Madison U.
Kent St. U.
U. La Verne
Lehman C. (C.U.N.Y.)
U. Maine
U. Mass. (Lowell)
Memphis St. U.
Minn. St. U. (Mankato)
Minot St. U.
Mont. St. U.
Montclair U.
C. N. Rochelle
U. Neb. (Kearney)
U. Neb. (Omaha)
N.Y.U.
U. No. Car. (Chapel Hill)
Northeastern Ill. U.
Northwestern U.
U. Ore. C. Education
Our Lady Lake U.
U. Pitt.

Radford U.
U. Redlands
U. Richmond
Rockford C.
U. St. Francis (Ind.)
C. St. Rose
St. Xavier U.
U. Santa Clara
Seton Hall U.
U. So. Fla.
U. So. Conn.
Stetson U.
Valdosta St. U.
West. Oregon U.
W. Va. U.
Winona St. U.
U. Wis. (Superior)
Worcester St. U.
Xavier U.

LIBRARIANSHIP, LIBRARY SCIENCE, LIBRARY MEDIA
U. Ala.
Appal. St. U.
U. Ariz.
Azusa Pac. U.
Boston U.
U.C.L.A.
Catholic U.
Cent. Mich. U.
Cent. Mo. St. U.
Chicago St. U.
Clarion U. Pa.
Clark Atl. U.
Columbia U.
   (Teachers C.)
U. Denver
Drexel U.
East Car. U.
Emporia St. U.
Fla. St. U.
U. Hawaii
I.U.P.U.I.
Kent St. U.
Kutztown U. Pa.
U. Ill.
Ind. U.
U. Iowa
L.I.U. (C.W. Post)
L.S.U.
Marywood U.
McDaniel C.
U. Md.
U. Mo. (Columbia)
N. Car. Cent. U.
U. No. Car. (Greensboro)
U. No. Tex.
U. Okla.
U. Pitt.
Pratt Inst.
Queens C. (C.U.N.Y.)
U. Rhode Island
Rowan U.
Rutgers U.
St. John's U. (N.Y.)
Sam Houston St. U.
San Jose St. U.
Simmons C.
U. So. Car.
So. Conn. St. U.
U. So. Fla.
U. So. Miss.
Spalding U.
Syracuse U.
U. Tenn.
Tex. Woman's U.
U. Tex. (Austin)
U. Wash.
Wayne St. U.
U. Wis.
U. Wis. (Milwaukee)
Wright St. U.

MARRIAGE & FAMILY COUNSELING/THERAPY
A.C.U.
U. Akron
U. Ala. (Birmingham)
Alliant Intl. U.
Antioch N. E. Grad. Sch.
Azusa Pac. U.
Barry U.
B.Y.U.
U. Bridgeport
Cal. Luth. C.
Cal. St. U. (Dominguez Hills)
Cal. St. U. (Fresno)
Cal. St. U. (Northridge)
Cent. Conn. St. U.
Chapman U.
Drexel U.
East Car. U.
Fairfield U.
Fla. St. U.
U. Fla.
Golden Gate U.
Hofstra U.
Idaho St. U.
Ind. St. U.
Iona C.
Iowa St. U.
Kans. St. U.
U. La. (Monroe)
U. La Verne
Loma Linda U.
L.I.U. (C.W. Post)
Loyola Marymount U.
U. Md.
U. Mass.
Mich. St. U.
Minn. St. U. (Mankato)
Monclair St. U.
Nova U.
U. Phoenix
U. Pitt.
Purdue U.
U. San Diego
San Fran. St. U.
U. San Fran.
Santa Clara U.
San Fran. St. U.
Seattle Pac. U.
Seton Hall U.
Sonoma St. U.
U. So. Cal.
Stetson U.
Syracuse U.
Tex. Tech U.
Tex. Woman's U.
Utah St. U.
Va. Poly. Tech.
U. Wis. (Stout)

RECREATION/PARK/ RECREATIONAL ADMINISTRATION/ MANAGEMENT/ LEISURE STUDIES
U. Ala.
Ariz. St. U.
U. Ark.
Baylor U.
Boston U.
Bowl. Gr. St. U.
B.Y.U.
Cal. St. U. (Chico)
Cal. St. U. (Long Beach)
Cal. St. U. (Northridge)
Cal. St. U. (Sacramento)
Cent. Mich. U.
Cent. Wash. U.
Clemson U.
Cleveland St. U.
Colo. St. U.
U. Conn.
Delta St. U.

East Car. U.
East. Ky. U.
Fla. Int'l. U.
Fla. St. U.
U. Fla.
Fort Hays St. U.
Georgia So. U.
Georgia St. U.
U. Georgia
U. Hawaii
Howard U.
U. Idaho
U. Ill.
Ind. U.
U. Iowa
U. Kans.
Kent St. U.
U. La. (Monroe)
Lehman C. (C.U.N.Y.)
U. Memphis
Mich. St. U.
Mid. Tenn. St. U.
U. Minn.
U. Miss.
U. Mo. (Columbia)
U. Mont.
Morehead St. U.
Murray St. U.
U. Neb.
U. Neb. (Kearney)
U. Nev.
U. N. Mex.
S.U.N.Y.C. (Brockport)
S.U.N.Y.C. (Cortland)
N.Y.U.
No. Car. Cent. U.
No. Car. St. U.
No. Car. St. U. (Raleigh)
U. No. Car.
  (Chapel Hill)
U. No. Colo.
U. No. Ill.
U. No. Tex.
Ohio U.
Okla. St. U.
Penn. St. U.
U. Penn.
Purdue U.
Radford U.
U. Rhode Island
San Fran. St. U.
San Jose St. U.
Slippery Rock U. Pa.
So. Dak. St. U.
U. So. Cal.
U. So. Miss.
So. Conn. St. U.
So. Ill. U.
Springfield C.
Temple U.
Tenn. St. U.
U. Tenn.
Tex. A&M U.
Tex. St. U.
U. Toledo
Utah St. U.
U. Utah
Va. Commonwealth U.
Va. Poly. Inst.
Wayne St. U.
U. West Fla.
West. Ill. U.
West. Ky. U.
W. Va. U.
U. Wash.
U. Wis.
U. Wis. (La Crosse)
Wright St. U.

SAFETY EDUCATION
Cent. Mo. St. U.
N.Y.U.
U. Tenn.

SPORTS MANAGEMENT
U. Ala.
Barry U.
Boise St. U.
Bowl. Gr. St. U.
Brooklyn C. (C.U.N.Y.)
Canisius C.
U. Cent. Fla.
Citadel
Cleveland St. U.
East Stroudsburg U.
Fla. Atlantic U.
Fla. St. U.
Geo. Wash. U.
Georgia St. U.
Gonzaga U.
Howard U.
Ind. St. U.
Ind. U. Pa.
U. Iowa
Kent St. U.
Marshall U.
U. Mass.
U. Miami
U. Mich.
U. Minn.
Miss. St. U.
Mont. St. U.
U. Nev.
No. Car. St. U.
U. Car. U. (Chapel Hill)
U. No. Colo.
No. Dak. St. U.
No. Ill. U.
N.Y.U.
Ohio U.
U. Rhode Island
Robert Morris U.
U. San Fran.
St. Cloud St. U.
Seton Hall U.
U. So. Car.
Springfield C.
Temple U.
U. Tenn.
Troy U.
Valparaiso U.
Wash. St. U.
Wayne St. U.
West. Ill. U.
Wichita St. U.
W. Va. U.
Xavier U.

TEACHING OF EMOTIONALLY DISTURBED
Ala. A&M U.
U. Ala.
U. Albany (S.U.N.Y.)
U. Ariz.
Ball St. U.
Boston U.
Bowl. Gr. St. U.
Brooklyn C. (C.U.N.Y.)
Cal. U. (Pa.)
Cent. Mo. St. U.
Chicago St. U.
City C. (C.U.N.Y.)
Cleveland St. U.
Columbia U. (Teachers C.)
East. Mich. U.
Hampton U.
Hofstra U.
Kent St. U.
Lehman C. (C.U.N.Y.)
Mich. St. U.
Minn. St. U. (Mankato)
Minot St. U.
C. N. Rochelle
U. Neb. (Omaha)
Northeastern Ill. U.
U. Pitt.

Radford U.
U. St. Francis (Ind.)
Syracuse U.
C. St. Rose
U. So. Fla.
Va. Commonwealth U.
Valdosta St. U.
West Car. U.
U. Wis. (Superior)

TEACHING OF MENTALLY RETARDED
Ala. A&M U.
U. Ala.
Appal. St. U.
U. Ariz.
Ball St. U.
Bloomsburg St. U.
Boston U.
Bowl. Gr. St. U.
Brooklyn C. (C.U.N.Y.)
Cal. U. (Pa.)
Cal. St. U. (Dominguez Hills)
Chicago St. U.
City C. (C.U.N.Y.)
Cleveland St. U.
Columbia U. (Teachers C.)
Duquesne U.
East. Mich. U.
Fort Hays Kans. St. U.
Georgia C. St. U.
Hampton U.
Hofstra U.
Kent St. U.
Lehman C. (C.U.N.Y.)
Marygrove C.
Mich. St. U.
Minn. St. U. (Mankato)
Minot St. U.
U. Mo. (St. Louis)
U. Neb. (Omaha)
C. N. Rochelle
Northeastern U.
Northeastern Ill. U.
U. Pitt.
Radford U.
U. St. Francis (Ind.)
C. St. Rose
U. So. Fla.
Syracuse U.
Va. Commonwealth U.
Valdosta St. U.
West. Car. U.

TEACHING OF PHYSICALLY HANDICAPPED
U. Ala.
U. Ariz.
U. Ark.
Ball St. U.
Boston U.
Cal. U. (Pa.)
Cleveland St. U.
Columbia U. (Teachers C.)
Duquesne U.
East. Mich. U.
Hofstra U.
Kent St. U.
Lehman C. (C.U.N.Y.)
Minn. St. U. (Mankato)
Minot St. U.
U. Pitt.
Valdosta St. U.

URBAN EDUCATION
Cal. St. U. (L.A.)
U. Chicago
City C. (C.U.N.Y.)
Cleveland St. U.
Columbia U. (Teachers C.)
Harvard U.
Jersey City St. U.

Morgan St. U.
U. Mass. (Boston)
U. Neb. (Omaha)
Northeastern Ill. U.
Temple U.
Tex. So. U.
Va. Commonwealth U.
U. Wis. (Milwaukee)

Engineering and Technology

(Typically includes Applied Sciences, Chemical Engineering, Civil Engineering, Computer Science/Engineering, Construction Engineering, Electrical Engineering, Energy Engineering, Engineering and Applied Sciences, Industrial Engineering, Mechanical Engineering; often includes Aeronautical/Astronautical Engineering, Engineering, Materials Engineering/Science, Mechanics, Metallurgy/Metallurgical Engineering, Nuclear Engineering/Science, Operations Research, Structural Engineering, Systems Engineering/Science)

A.F. Inst.
U. Akron
Ala. A&M U.
U. Ala.
U. Ala. (Birm.)
U. Ala. (Huntsville)
U. Alaska
Alfred U.
Ariz. St. U.
U. Ariz.
U. Ark.
Auburn U.
Boston U.
Bradley U.
U. Bridgeport
Brown U.
Bucknell U.
U. Buffalo (S.U.N.Y.)
B.Y.U.
Cal. Inst. Tech.
Cal. Poly. St. U. (San Luis Obispo)
Cal. St. Poly U. (Pomona)
Cal. St. U. (Chico)
Cal. St. U. (Fresno)
Cal. St. U. (Fullerton)
Cal. St. U. (Long Beach)
Cal. St. U. (L.A.)
Cal. St. U. (Northridge)
Cal. St. U. (Sacramento)
U. Cal. (Berkeley)
U. Cal. (Davis)
U. Cal. (Irvine)
U.C.L.A.
U. Cal. (San Diego)
U. Cal. (Santa Barbara)
Cal. U. Pa.
Carnegie Mellon U.
Case West. Res. U.
Catholic U.
U. Cent. Fla.
Cent. Mo. St. U.
Cent. Wash. U.
U. Cincinnati
C.C.N.Y. (C.U.N.Y.)
Clarkson U.
Clemson U.
Cleveland St. U.
Colo. Sch. Mines
Colo. St. U.
U. Colo.
U. Colo. (Denver)
Columbia U.

U. Va.
U. Vt.
Wake Forest U.
Wash. U.
U. Wash.
U. Wisc.
Worcester Poly. Inst.
Wright St. U.
U. Wyo.

BUILDING SCIENCE
Ariz. St. U.
Auburn U.
U. Cal. (Berkeley)
Carnegie Mellon U.
Colo. St. U.
Cornell U.
U. Fla.
Georgia St. U.
U. So. Car.

CERAMIC SCIENCES/ ENGINEERING
Alfred U.
U. Cal. (Berkeley)
U.C.L.A.
Case West. Res. U.
U. Cincinnati
Clemson U.
U. Fla.
Georgia Inst. Tech.
U. Ill.
Mo. U. Sci. & Tech.
Penn. St. U.
R.P.I.
Rutgers U.

ENGINEERING MANAGEMENT
A.F. Inst.
U. Akron
U. Ala. (Huntsville)
U. Alaska
U. Buffalo (S.U.N.Y.)
B.Y.U.
Cal. Poly. St. U. (San Luis Obispo)
Cal. St. U. (Northridge)
U. Cal. (Berkeley)
Carnegie Mellon U.
Case West. Res. U.
U. Cent. Fla.
Clarkson U.
Colo. St. U.
U. Colo.
Cornell U.
Dartmouth C.
U. Dayton
U. Detroit Mercy
Drexel U.
Duke U.
Fla. Inst. Tech.
Geo. Wash. U.
Ga. Inst. Tech.
Kans. St. U.
U. Kans.
U. La. (Lafayette)
Lamar U.
Lehigh U.
L.S.U.
Loyola Marymount U.
Marquette U.
U. Md.
U. Md. (Baltimore Cnty.)
M.I.T.
U. Mass.
Mercer U.
Mich. St. U.
U. Mich.
Milwaukee Sch. Eng.
Mo. U. Sci. & Tech.
N.J.I.T.
Ntl. U
U. No. Car. (Charlotte)

Northeastern U.
Northwestern U.
Oakland U.
Okla. St. U.
Old Dom. U.
Penn St. U.
Portland St. U.
Poly. U.
R.I.T.
R.P.I.
Robert Morris U.
St. Mary's U. (Tex.)
Santa Clara U.
U. So. Cal.
U. So. Fla.
S. Meth. U.
Stanford U.
Stevens Inst. Tech.
Syracuse U.
U. Tenn. (Chattanooga)
U. Tenn (Space Institute)
Tex. A&M U.
Tex. Tech U.
Tufts U.
U. Tulsa
Union Grad. C.
U. Utah
Va. Poly. Inst.
Wash. St. U.
Wash. U.
Wayne St. U.
Webster U.
West. Mich. U.
Widener U.

ENVIRONMENTAL ENGINEERING
U. Ala.
U. Alaska
U. Ariz.
U. Ark.
Auburn U.
U. Buffalo (S.U.N.Y.)
Cal. Inst. Tech.
Cal. Poly. St. U. (San Luis Obispo)
U. Cal. (Berkeley)
U. Cal. (Davis)
U. Cal. (Irvine)
U.C.L.A.
Carnegie Mellon U.
Case West. Res. U.
Catholic U.
U. Cent. Fla.
U. Cincinnati
Clarkson U.
Clemson U.
Colo. Sch. Mines
Colo. St. U.
U. Colo.
Columbia U.
U. Conn.
Cornell U.
Dartmouth C.
U. Dayton
Drexel U.
Duke U.
Fla. Inst. Tech.
Fla. Int'l. U.
U. Fla.
Geo. Wash. U.
Georgia Inst. Tech.
U. Hawaii
U. Houston
Humboldt St. U.
Idaho St. U.
Ill. Inst. Tech.
U. Ill.
Iowa St. U.
U. Iowa
Johns Hopkins U.
U. Kans.
Lamar U.
Lehigh U.

L.S.U.
U. Louisville
Loyola Marymount U.
U. Maine
Manhattan C.
Marquette U.
U. Md.
M.I.T.
U. Mass.
U. Mass. (Lowell)
U. Memphis
Mich. St. U.
Mich. Tech. U.
U. Mich.
Milwaukee Sch. Eng.
U. Miss.
Mo. U. Sci. & Tech.
U. Mo. (Columbia)
Mont. St. U.
Mont. Tech
U. Neb.
U. Nev.
New Mex. Inst.
New Mex. St. U.
N.J.I.T.
S.U.N.Y.C. Environ. Sci. & For. (Syracuse)
N.Y.I.T.
U. N. Car. (Chapel Hill)
No. Dak. St. U.
U. No. Dakota
Northeastern U.
Northwestern U.
Ohio U.
Okla. St. U.
U. Okla.
Old Dom. U.
Ore. Health & Sci.
Ore. St. U.
Penn. St. U.
U. Penn.
U. Pitt.
Poly. U.
R.P.I.
U. Rhode Island
Rice U.
Rose-Hulman Inst. Tech.
Rutgers U.
San Jose St. U.
U. So. Cal.
So. Dak. St. U.
So. Meth. U.
Stanford U.
Stevens Inst. Tech.
Syracuse U.
U. Tenn.
Tex. A&M U.
Tex. A&M U. (Kingsville)
Tex. Tech U.
U. Tex. (Austin)
Tufts U.
Tulane U.
Utah St. U.
Vanderbilt U.
Va. Poly. Inst.
U. Va.
Villanova U.
Wash. St. U.
Wash. U.
U. Wash.
Wayne St. U.
W. Va. U.
U. Wis.
Worcester Poly.
U. Wyo.
Youngstown St. U.

GEOLOGICAL/ GEOSCIENCES/ GEOTECHNICAL ENGINEERING
U. Alaska
U Ariz.

Auburn U.
U. Cal. (Berkeley)
U.C.L.A.
Catholic U.
Colo. Sch. Mines
Colo. St. U.
U. Colo.
Cornell U.
U. Del.
U. Idaho
Ill. Inst. Tech.
U. Ill. (Chicago)
Iowa St. U.
L.S.U.
U. Maine
Marquette U.
Mich. St. U.
U. Minn.
M.I.T.
U. Mo. Sci. & Tech.
U. Mo. (Columbia)
Mont. Tech
U. Nev. (Reno)
N. Mex. Inst. M&T
Northwestern U.
U. Okla.
U. Rhode Island
R.P.I.
U. So. Cal.
So. Dak. Sch. M&T
Tex. A&M U.
U. Tex. (Austin)
Tufts U.
U. Utah
Wash. St. U.
U. Wash.

MANUFACTURING ENGINEERING
Ariz. St. U.
Boston U.
Bowl. Gr. St. U.
Bradley U.
Cal. Poly. St. U. (San Luis Obispo)
U.C.L.A.
Clemson U.
Colo. St. U.
U. Colo.
Cornell U.
Dartmouth U.
U. Detroit Mercy
Drexel U.
East Car. U.
East Tenn. St. U.
Fla. St. U.
Ill. Inst. Tech.
U. Iowa
Kans. St. U.
U. Ky.
Lehigh U.
La. Tech. U.
U. Md.
Marquette U.
U. Mass.
U. Mass. (Lowell)
U. Memphis
M.I.T.
Mich. St. U.
U. Mich.
Mo. U. Sci. & Tech.
Minn. St. U. (Mankato)
U. Mo. (Columbia)
U. Neb.
U. N. Mex.
N.J.I.T.
No. Car. St. U.
No. Dak. St. U.
Northeastern U.
Northwestern U.
Ohio U.
Ore. St. U.
Penn. St. U.
Poly. U.

U. Dayton
U. Del.
Ill. Inst. U.
Iowa St. U.
L.S.U.
Marquette U.
U. Memphis
M.I.T.
U. Mo. (Columbia)
Morgan St. U.
U. Nev.
N.J.I.T.
Northwestern U.
Ohio U.
Penn. St. U.
Poly. U.
Princeton U.
U. Rhode Island
R.P.I.
U. So. Cal.
Tex. A&M U.
Villanova U.
Wash. U. (St. Louis)
U. Wash.

Environmental Health/ Sciences/Studies

(Typically includes Ecology, Forestry, Forest Science, Wood Science/Technology)

Ala. A&M U.
U. Ala.
U. Alaska
U. Albany (S.U.N.Y.)
American U.
Antioch N.E.
U. Ariz.
Ark. St. U.
Baylor U.
Brown U.
U. Buffalo (S.U.N.Y.)
B.Y.U.
Cal. Inst. Tech.
Cal. Poly. St. U. (San Luis Obispo)
Cal. St. Poly. U. (Pomona)
Cal. St. U. (Fullerton)
U. Cal. (Berkeley)
U. Cal. (Davis)
U. Cal. (Irvine)
U.C.L.A.
U. Cal. (Santa Barbara)
U.C.L.A.
Case West. Res. U.
U. Chicago
U. Cincinnati
City C. (C.U.N.Y.)
Clarkson U.
Clemson U.
Colo. Sch. Mines
U. Colo. (Denver)
Columbia U.
U. Conn.
Cornell U.
Drexel U.
Duke U.
Duquesne U.
East Tenn. St. U.
Fla. Atlantic U.
Fla. Inst. Tech.
Fla. Int'l. U.
U. Fla.
Ga. Tech.
Geo. Mason U.
Geo. Wash. U.
U. Georgia
U. Hawaii
Harvard U.
Humbolt St. U.
Hunter C. (C.U.N.Y.)
Idaho St. U.
U. Idaho

U. Ill.
Ind. U.
Iowa St. U.
Jackson St. U.
Johns Hopkins U.
U. Kans.
U. Ky.
Lehigh U.
L.I.U. (C.W. Post)
L.S.U.
Loyola Marymount U.
U. Maine
Marshall U.
U. Md.
U. Md. (Baltimore Cnty.)
M.I.T.
U. Mass.
U. Mass. (Boston)
U. Mass. (Lowell)
McNeese St. U.
Miami U. (Ohio)
U. Miami (Fla.)
Mich. St. U.
Mich. Tech. U.
U. Mich.
Minn. St. U. (Mankato)
U. Minn.
Mont. St. U.
U. Mont.
Montclair U.
U. Neb.
U. Nev. (Reno)
U. N. Haven
N.J.I.T.
N. Mex. Inst. M&T
C.U.N.Y. (Grad Ctr.)
S.U.N.Y.C. Environ. Sci. & For. (Syracuse)
No. Car. St. U. (Raleigh)
U. No. Car. (Chapel Hill)
No. Ariz. U.
No. Dak. St. U.
U. No. Iowa
U. No. Tex.
Nova U.
Ohio St. U.
Ohio U.
Okla. St. U.
U. Okla.
Ore. Health & Sci. U.
Ore. St. U.
Penn. St. U.
U. Penn.
U. Pitt.
Poly. U.
Portland St. U.
Purdue U.
R.I.T.
R.P.I.
U. Rhode Island
Rice U.
Rutgers U.
Shippensburg U. Pa.
U. So. Car.
U. So. Conn.
So. Dak. St. U.
So. Ill. U.
So. Ill. U. (Edwardsville)
So. Meth. U.
S. F. Austin St. U.
Stony Brook U. (S.U.N.Y.)
Tenn. Tech. U.
U. Tenn.
Tex. A&M U. (Corpus Christi)
Tex. Christ. U.
Tex. Tech. U.
U. Tex. (Arlington)
U. Tex. (San Antonio)
Tufts U.
Tuskegee U.
Utah St. U.
U. Utah
Vanderbilt U.
Va. Poly. Inst.

U. Va.
Wash. St. U.
U. Wash.
U. West. Fla.
W. Va. U.
West. Tex. A&M U.
West. Wash. U.
Wichita St. U.
C. Wm. & Mary
U. Wis.
Wright St. U.
U. Wyo.
Yale U.

FISH/WILDLIFE MANAGEMENT

U. Alaska
U. Ariz.
Auburn U.
B.Y.U.
Clemson U.
Colo. St. U.
Cornell U.
U. Dela.
U. Fla.
Frostburg St. U.
Humboldt St. U.
U. Idaho
Iowa St. U.
L.S.U. A&M C.
U. Maine
U. Md.
U. Mass.
U. Miami (Fla.)
Mich St. U.
U. Minn.
Miss. St. U.
U. Mo. (Columbia)
Mont. St. U.
U. Mont.
U. Neb.
U. N.H.
N. Mex. St. U.
S.U.N.Y.C. Environ. Sci. & For. (Syracuse)
No. Car. St. U. (Raleigh)
U. No. Dak.
Ore St. U.
Penn. St. U.
Purdue U.
U. Rhode Island
So. Dak. St. U.
Sul Ross. St. U.
Tenn. Tech. U.
U. Tenn.
Tex. A&M U.
Tex. A&M U. (Kingsville)
Tex. St. U.
Tex. Tech U.
Utah St. U.
Va. Poly. Inst.
U. Vt.
U. Wash.
W. Va. U.

HYDROLOGY

U. Ariz.
Auburn U.
Cal. St. U. (Bakersfield)
Cal. St. U. (Chico)
U. Cal. (Davis)
U.C.L.A.
C. Envir. Sci. & Forestry (S.U.N.Y.)
Colo. St. U.
Cornell U.
Georgia Inst. Tech.
Georgia St. U.
Idaho St. U.
U. Idaho
Ill. St. U.
M.I.T.
Mo. U. Sci. & Tech.
U. Nev. (Reno)

N. Mex. Inst. M&T
U. N. H.
Tex. A&M U.
Wash. St. U.
U. Wash.
West Va. U.

LANDSCAPE ARCHITECTURE

Ariz. St. U.
U. Ariz.
Auburn U.
Ball St. U.
Cal. St. Poly U. (Pomona)
U. Cal. (Berkeley)
Clemson U.
Colo. St. U.
U. Colo.
Cornell U.
Fla. A&M U.
Fla. Int'l. U.
U. Fla.
U. Georgia
Harvard U.
U. Idaho
U. Ill.
Iowa St. U.
Kans. St. U.
L.S.U.
U. Mass.
Mich. St. U.
U. Mich.
U. Minn.
Miss. St. U.
Morgan St. U.
S.U.N.Y.C. Environ. Sci. & For. (Syracuse)
U. New Mex.
No. Car. St. U. (Raleigh)
Ohio St. U.
Okla. St. U.
U. Okla.
U. Ore.
Penn St. U.
U. Penn.
Rhode Island Sch. Design
U. So. Cal.
Tex A&M U.
Tex. Tech U.
U. Tex. (Arlington)
U. Tenn.
Utah St. U.
U. Va.
Va. Poly. Inst.
Wash. St. U.
U. Wash.
U. Wis.

METEOROLOGY/ ATMOSPHERE SCIENCES

U. Ala. (Huntsville)
U. Alaska
U. Albany (S.U.N.Y.)
U. Ariz.
U. Cal. (Davis)
U.C.L.A.
U. Chicago
City C. (C.U.N.Y.)
Clemson U.
Colo. St. U.
U. Colo.
Columbia U.
Cornell U.
Creighton U.
U. Del.
Drexel U.
Fla. Int'l. U.
Fla. St. U.
Georgia Inst. Tech.
U. Hawaii
U. Ill.
Iowa St. U.
Johns Hopkins U.
U. Kansas

U. Md.
M.I.T.
U. Miami
U. Mich.
U. Mo. (Columbia)
Mont. St. U.
Naval P.G. Sch.
U. Nev. (Reno)
U.N.H.
N. Mex. Inst. M&T
No. Car. St. U.
Ohio St. U.
U. Okla.
Ore. St. U.
Penn. St. U.
Princeton U.
Purdue U.
Rutgers U.
St. Louis U.
San Jose St. U.
So. Dak. Sch. M&T
So. Dak. St. U.
Stony Brook U. (S.U.N.Y.)
Tex. A&M U.
Tex. Tech U.
Utah St. U.
U. Utah
Wash. St. U.
U. Wash.
U. Wis.
U. Wyo.
Yale U.

RANGE MANAGEMENT/ SCIENCE
U. Ariz.
B.Y.U.
U. Cal. (Berkeley)
Colo. St. U.
U. Idaho
Kans. St. U.
Mont. St. U.
N. Mex. St. U.
No. Dak. St. U.
Okla. St. U.
Ore. St. U.
Sul Ross St. U.
Tex. A&M U.
Tex. Tech U.
Utah St. U.
U. Wyo.

SUSTAINABLE DEVELOPMENT
Brandeis U.
Carnegie Mellon U.
Clark U.
Columbia U.
U. Conn.
U. Ga.
Ill. Inst. Tech.
U. Md.
Mich. Tech. U.
Slippery Rock U. Pa.
U. Wash.
West. Ill. U.
U. Wis.

WATER RESOURCES/ ADMINISTRATION
U. Ariz.
U. Cal. (Berkeley)
U. Cal. (Davis)
Colo. St. U.
U. Del.
Duke U.
Fla. Inst. Tech.
U. Fla.
Geo. Wash. U.
U. Idaho
U. Ill.
Iowa St. U.
U. Kans.
U. Mich.

U. Minn.
Mo. U. Sci. & Tech.
Mont. Tech
U. Nev.
U. Nev. (Reno)
U. N.H.
U. N. Mex.
U. Okla.
S.U.N.Y.C. Environ. Sci. & For. (Syracuse)
Penn. St. U.
Princeton U.
Rutgers U.
So. Dak. Sch. Mines
So. Dak. St. U.
Tex. A&M U.
Utah St. U.
Villanova U.
U. Vt.
Wash. St. U.
U. Wis.
U. Wyo.

Fine Arts

(Typically includes Art History, Studio Arts; often includes Commercial Art, Applied Art, Crafts, Design, Graphic Design, Industrial Design)

Adams St. U.
Adelphi U.
U. Ala.
Albany (S.U.N.Y.)
Alfred U.
American U.
Ariz. St. U.
U. Ariz.
Ark. St. U.
U. Ark.
Art. Inst. Chicago
Auburn U.
Ball St. U.
Barry U.
Bennington C.
Bloomsburg U. Pa.
Boise St. U.
Boston U.
Bowl. Gr. St. U.
Bradley U.
B.Y.U.
Brooklyn C. (C.U.N.Y.)
Brown U.
Bryn Mawr C.
U. Buffalo (S.U.N.Y.)
Cal. C. Arts
Cal. Poly. St. U. (San Luis Obispo)
Cal. St. U. (Chico)
Cal. St. U. (Fresno)
Cal. St. U. (Fullerton)
Cal. St. U. (Long Beach)
Cal. St. U. (L.A.)
Cal. St. U. (Northridge)
Cal. St. U. (Sacramento)
U. Cal. (Berkeley)
U. Cal. (Davis)
U. Cal. (Irvine)
U.C.L.A.
U. Cal. (Riverside)
U. Cal. (San Diego)
U. Cal. (Santa Barbara)
Carnegie Mellon U.
Case West. Res. U.
Catholic U.
Cent. Conn. St. U.
U. Cent. Fla.
Cent. Mich. St. U.
Cent. Mo. St. U.
Cent. Wash. U.
U. Chicago
U. Cincinnati

C.C.N.Y. (C.U.N.Y.)
Claremont Grad. U.
Clemson U.
Cleveland St. U.
Colo. St. U.
U. Colo.
Columbia U.
U. Conn.
Cornell U.
Cranbrook Acad. Art
U. Dallas
U. Del.
U. Denver
Drake U.
Drexel U.
Duke U.
East Car. U.
East Tenn. St. U.
East Ill. U.
East. Mich. U.
East. Wash. U.
Edinboro U. Pa.
Emory U.
Fla. Atlantic U.
Fla. Int'l. U.
Fla. St. U.
U. Fla.
Fort Hays St. U.
Geo. Wash. U.
Georgia So. U.
Georgia St. U.
U. Georgia
Gov. St. U.
U. Hartford
Harvard U.
U. Hawaii
Hollins U.
U. Houston
Howard U.
Hunter C. (C.U.N.Y.)
Idaho St. U.
U. Idaho
Ill. Inst. Tech.
Ill. St. U.
U. Ill.
U. Ill. (Chicago)
Ind. St. U.
Ind. U.
Ind. U. Pa.
U. Indianapolis
Iowa St. U.
U. Iowa
Jacksonville U.
James Madison U.
Jersey City St. U.
Johns Hopkins U.
Kans. St. U.
U. Kans.
Kent St. U.
U. Ky.
Lamar U.
Lehman C. (C.U.N.Y.)
L.I.U. (C.W. Post)
L.S.U.
La. Tech. U.
U. Louisville
Marshall U.
Md. Inst. C. Art
U. Md.
U. Md. (Baltimore Cnty.)
Marywood U.
Mass. C. Art.
M.I.T.
U. Mass.
U. Mass. (Dartmouth)
McDaniel C.
U. Memphis
Miami U. (Ohio)
U. Miami (Fla.)
Mich. St. U.
U. Mich.
Mills C.
Minn. St. U. (Mankato)
Minn. St. U. (Moorhead)

U. Minn.
U. Minn. (Duluth)
Miss. C.
Miss. St. U.
U. Miss.
U. Mo. (Columbia)
U. Mo. (K.C.)
Mont. St. U.
U. Mont.
Montclair U.
Morehead St. U.
Ntl. U.
U. Neb.
U. Neb. (Kearney)
U. Nev.
N. Mex. St. U.
U.N.H.
U. N. Mex.
U. N. Orleans
C. New Rochelle
New School U. (Parsons Sch. Design)
C.U.N.Y. (Grad. Ctr.)
S.U.N.Y. (Binghamton)
S.U.N.Y.C. (New Paltz)
S.U.N.Y.C. (Oswego)
N.Y.U.
No. Car. St. U. (Raleigh)
U. No. Car. (Chapel Hill)
U. No. Car. (Greensboro)
U. No. Colo.
U. No. Dak.
U. No. Tex.
No. Ill. U.
U. No. Iowa
No. W. St. U. La.
Northwestern U.
U. Notre Dame
Ohio St. U.
Ohio U.
Okla. St. U.
U. Okla.
Old Dom. U.
U. Ore.
Otis Art Inst. L.A.
Penn. St. U.
U. Penn.
Pittsburg St. U.
U. Pitt.
Portland St. U.
Pratt Inst.
Princeton U.
Purdue U.
Queens C. (C.U.N.Y.)
Radford U.
Regent U.
Rhode Island C.
Rhode Island Sch. Design
Rice U.
R.I.T.
R.P.I.
U. Rochester
Rockford C.
Rutgers U.
St. Cloud St. U.
St. Louis U.
Sam Houston St. U.
S.D.S.U.
San Fran. Art. Inst.
San Fran. St. U.
San Jose St. U.
Seattle Pac. U.
Seton Hall U.
Smith C.
U. So. Cal.
U. So. Car.
So. Conn. St. U.
U. So. Dak.
U. So. Fla.
Southeast Mo. St. U.
So. Ill. U.
So. Ill. U. (Edwardsville)
So. Meth. U.
So. Ore. St. U.

Stanford U.
S. F. Austin St. U.
Stony Brook U. (S.U.N.Y.)
Sul Ross St. U.
Syracuse U.
Temple U.
U. Tenn.
Tex. A&M U. (Commerce)
Tex. A&M U. (Kingsville)
Tex. Christ. U.
Tex. Tech U.
Tex. Woman's U.
U. Tex. (Austin)
U. Tex. (El Paso)
U. Tex. (San Antonio)
U. Tex. (Tyler)
U. Arts
Towson U.
Tufts U.
Tulane U.
U. Tulsa
Union Inst.
Utah St. U.
U. Utah
Va. Commonwealth U.
U. Va.
Vanderbilt U.
Wash. St. U.
Wash. U. (Mo.)
U. Wash.
Wayne St. U.
Webster U.
West Tex. A&M U.
W. Va. U.
West. Ky. U.
West. Mich. U.
West. Wash. U.
Wichita St. U.
Wm. Paterson U.
U. Wis.
U. Wis. (Milwaukee)
U. Wis. (Superior)
U. Wyo.
Yale U.

ARTS MANAGEMENT
U. Akron
American U.
Boston U.
Cal. St. U. (Dominguez Hills)
Carnegie Mellon U.
U. Cincinnati
Columbia U. (Teachers C.)
Drexel U.
East. Mich. U.
Fla. St. U.
Golden Gate U.
Ill. St. U.
Ind. U.
Montclair U.
U. N. Orleans
New Sch. U. (Parsons Sch. Design)
S.U.N.Y. (Binghamton)
N.Y.U.
U. No. Car. (Charlotte)
Ohio St. U.
Okla. City U.
U. Ore.
Pratt Inst.
St. Mary's U. (Minn.)
Seton Hall U.
U. So. Cal.
So. Meth. U.
Syracuse U.
Temple U.
Tex. Tech U.
Va. Poly.
Webster U.
U. Wis.

ART THERAPY
Sch. Art Inst. Chicago
U. Arts

U. Bridgeport
Cal. St. U. (L.A.)
Drexel U.
Emporia St. U.
Geo. Wash. U.
Hofstra U.
U. Ill. (Chicago)
L.I.U. (C.W. Post)
U. Louisville
Loyola Marymount U.
Marywood U.
U. N. Mex.
C. N. Rochelle
S.U.N.Y.C. (Buffalo)
N.Y.U.
No. Ill. U.
Notre Dame U.
Pratt Inst.
Seton Hall U.
So. Ill. U. (Edwardsville)
Springfield C.
U. Wis. (Superior)

INTERIOR DESIGN
U. Ala.
Ariz. St. U.
Sch. Art Inst. Chicago
U. Cincinnati
Drexel U.
Fla. St. U.
U. Fla.
U. Houston
Ind. U.
Iowa St. U.
U. Kans.
U. Ky.
La. Tech U.
U. Mass. (Dartmouth)
Md. Inst. C. Art
U. Memphis
U. Minn.
New Sch. U. (Parsons Sch. Design)
U. No. Car. (Greensboro)
No. Ill. U.
U. No. Tex.
Ohio St. U.
U. Ore.
Pratt Inst.
Rhode Island Sch. Design
R.I.T.
Syracuse U.
Temple U.
Tex. Woman's U.
Utah St. U.
Va. Poly. Inst.
Wash. St. U.
Wayne St. U.
U. Wis.

MUSEUM TRAINING/ STUDIES HISTORIC PRESERVATION
Sch. Art Inst. Chicago
Bank St. C.
Baylor U.
Boston U.
Cal. St. U. (Fullerton)
Case West. Res. U.
U. Cent. Okla.
C.C.N.Y. (C.U.N.Y.)
Colo. St. U.
U. Colo.
Columbia U.
U. Del.
U. Denver
Duquesne U.
East. Mich. U.
Fla. St. U.
U. Fla.
Framingham St. C.
Geo. Wash. U.
Hampton U.
Harvard U.

U. Kans.
U. Mich.
Mid. Tenn. St. U.
U. Mo. (St. Louis)
U. Neb.
S.U.N.Y.C. (Buffalo)
S.U.N.Y.C. (Oneonta)
N.Y.U.
U. No. Car. (Greensboro)
U. Ore.
U. Penn.
Rutgers U.
San Fran. St. U.
Seton Hall U.
U. So. Cal.
U. So. Car.
So. Ill. U. (Edwardsville)
Syracuse U.
Tex. Tech U.
Tufts U.
Va. Commonwealth U.
U. Vt.
U. Wash.
Wayne St. U.
C. Wm. & Mary

PHOTOGRAPHY
U. Ala.
Sch. Art Inst. Chicago
Barry U.
Bradley U.
Brooklyn C. (C.U.N.Y.)
Cal. C. Arts
Cal. Inst. Arts
Cal. St. U. (Fullerton)
Cal. St. U. (L.A.)
U. Colo.
Columbia U.
Cornell U.
Cranbrook Acad. Art
U. Fla.
Geo. Wash. U.
Georgia St. U.
U. Houston
Ill. St. U.
U. Ill. (Chicago)
Ind. St. U.
Ind. U.
James Madison U.
L.S.U.
La. Tech U.
Md. Inst. C. Art
Mass. C. Art
U. Memphis
U. Miami
U. Mich.
Mills C.
U. Mo. (K.C.)
U. Mont.
U. N. Orleans
S.U.N.Y.C. (New Paltz)
New Sch. U.
U. No. Tex.
U. Notre Dame
Ohio U.
U. Okla.
Otis Sch. Art & Design
Pratt Inst.
Rhode Island Sch. Design
R.I.T.
San Fran. Art Inst.
San Jose St. U.
U. So. Car.
So. Meth. U.
Syracuse U.
Temple U.
U. Tenn.
Tex. Woman's U.
Utah St. U.
U. Utah
Va. Commonwealth U.
Wash. St. U.
Wash. U.
Yale U.

TEXTILE DESIGN
Cal. C. Arts
U. Cal. (Davis)
Cornell U.
Cranbrook Acad.
Ind. St. U.
Ind. U.
U. Kans.
Kent St. U.
Mass. C. Arts
U. Mass. (Dartmouth)
U. Minn.
U. No. Tex.
Rhode Island Sch. Design
So. Ill. U. (Edwardsville)
Syracuse U.
Temple U.
Tex. Woman's U.
U. Wis.

FOREIGN LANGUAGES/ LITERATURES

(Typically includes French, German, Spanish; often includes Italian, Portuguese, Romance, Russian/Slavic Languages)

U. Akron
U. Ala.
U. Albany (S.U.N.Y.)
American U.
Appal. St. U.
Ariz. St. U.
U. Ariz.
U. Ark.
Auburn U.
Ball St. U.
Bennington C.
Binghamton U.
Boston C.
Boston U.
Bowl. Gr. St. U.
Brooklyn C. (C.U.N.Y.)
Brown U.
Bryn Mawr C.
U. Buffalo (S.U.N.Y.)
B.Y.U.
Cal. St. U. (Fullerton)
Cal. St. U. (Long Beach)
Cal. St. U. (L.A.)
Cal. St. U. (Northridge)
Cal. St. U. (Sacramento)
U. Cal. (Berkeley)
U. Cal. (Davis)
U. Cal. (Irvine)
U.C.L.A.
U. Cal. (Riverside)
U. Cal. (San Diego)
U. Cal. (Santa Barbara)
Case West. Res U.
Catholic U.
Cent. Conn. St. U.
U. Chicago
U. Cincinnati.
C.C.N.Y. (C.U.N.Y.)
Colo. St. U.
U. Colo.
Columbia U.
U. Conn.
Cornell U.
U. Del.
U. Denver
Duke U.
Duquesne U.
East. Mich. U.
Emory U.
F.D.U. (Madison)
F.D.U. (Teaneck)
Fla. Atlantic U.
Fla. St. U.
U. Fla.
Fordham U.
Georgetown U.

Geo. Mason U.
Geo. Wash. U.
Georgia St. U.
U. Georgia
Harvard U.
U. Hawaii
U. Houston
Howard U.
Hunter C. (C.U.N.Y.)
U. Idaho
Ill. St. U.
U. Ill.
U. Ill. (Chicago)
Ind. St. U.
Ind. U.
Iona C.
U. Iowa
Johns Hopkins U.
Kans. St. U.
U. Kans.
Kent St. U.
U. Ky.
L.I.U.
L.S.U.
U. La. (Lafayette)
La. Tech U.
U. Louisville
U. Maine
Marquette U.
U. Md.
U. Mass.
U. Memphis
Miami U. (Ohio)
U. Miami (Fla.)
Mich. St. U.
U. Mich.
Middlebury C.
Millersville U. Pa.
Minn. St. U. (Mankato)
U. Minn.
Miss. St. U.
U. Miss.
U. Mo. (Columbia)
U. Mont.
Montclair U.
Monterey Inst.
U. Neb.
U. Nev.
U. Nev. (Reno)
N. Mex. St. U.
U. N. Mex.
C.U.N.Y. (Grad. Ctr.)
S.U.N.Y. (Binghamton)
N.Y.U.
No. Car. A&T St. U.
No. Car. Cent. U.
U. No. Car. (Chapel Hill)
U. No. Car. (Greensboro)
U. No. Colo.
No. Ill. U.
U. No. Iowa
U. No. Tex.
Northwestern U.
U. Notre Dame
Ohio St. U.
Ohio U.
U. Okla.
U. Ore.
Penn. St. U.
U. Penn.
U. Pitt.
Portland St. U.
Princeton U.
Purdue U.
Queens C. (C.U.N.Y.)
Rhode Island C.
U. Rhode Island
Rice U.
U. Rochester
Rutgers U.
St. John's U. (N.Y.)
St. Joseph's C. (Pa.)
St. Louis U.
S.D.S.U.

San Fran. St. U.
San Jose St. U.
Seton Hall U.
Simmons C.
Smith C.
So. Conn. St. U.
U. So. Fla.
U. So. Cal.
U. So. Car.
So. Ill. U.
Stanford U.
Stony Brook U. (S.U.N.Y.)
Syracuse U.
Temple U.
U. Tenn.
Tex. St. U.
Tex. Tech U.
U. Tex. (Austin)
U. Tex. (El Paso)
U. Tex. (San Antonio)
U. Tex. (Pan American)
U. Toledo
Tufts U.
Tulane U.
U. Utah
Vanderbilt U.
U. Vt.
Villanova U.
U. Va.
Wash. St. U.
Wash. U. (Mo.)
U. Wash.
Wayne St. U.
West Chester U. Pa.
W. Va. U.
West Ky. U.
West. Mich. U.
Wichita St. U.
Winthrop U.
U. Wis.
U. Wis. (Milwaukee)
U. Wyo.

AFRICAN LANGUAGES
U. Albany (S.U.N.Y.)
Boston U.
U.C.L.A.
Columbia U.
Cornell U.
Fla. Int'l. U.
Harvard U.
Howard U.
U. Ill.
Johns Hopkins U.
Mich. St. U.
N.Y.U.
Northwestern U.
Ohio St. U.
Ohio U.
St. John's U.
U. So. Fla.
U. Wis.
Yale U.

AKKADIAN
Catholic U.
Columbia U.
Harvard U.

BENGALI
U. Chicago

CAUCASIAN
Columbia U.

CELTIC
Harvard U.

CHINESE/JAPANESE/ ASIAN LANGUAGES
Boston C.
B.Y.U.
U. Cal. (Berkeley)
U. Cal. (Irvine)

U.C.L.A.
U. Cal.
  (Santa Barbara)
U. Chicago
U. Colo.
Columbia U.
Cornell U.
Fla. St. U.
Georgetown U.
Harvard U.
U. Hawaii
U. Ill.
Ind. U.
U. Iowa
U. Kans.
Kent St. U.
U. Mass.
U. Md.
Mich. St. U.
U. Mich.
Middlebury C.
U. Minn.
Monterey Inst.
N.Y.U.
U. No. Car. (Chapel Hill)
Northwestern U.
Ohio St. U.
U. Ore.
U. Pitt.
Portland St. U.
Princeton U.
St. John's (N.M.)
San Fran. St. U.
U. So. Cal.
Stanford U.
U. Tex. (Austin)
Wash. U. (Mo.)
U. Wash.
Wayne St. U.
U. Wis.
Yale U.

GREEK
Boston C.
Bryn Mawr C.
U. Cal. (Berkeley)
U.C.L.A.
Catholic U.
U. Chicago
Columbia U.
Fla. St. U.
U. Ill.
Ind. U.
U. Iowa
John Carroll U.
U. Mich.
U. Minn.
U. Miss.
N.Y.U.
Northwestern U.
Stanford U.
U. Tex. (Austin)
Tufts U.
U. Vt.

HEBREW/ARABIC/NEAR AND MIDDLE EASTERN LANGUAGES/ LITERATURES
U. Ariz.
Brandeis U.
Brown U.
B.Y.U.
U. Cal. (Berkeley)
U.C.L.A.
Catholic U.
U. Chicago
Columbia U.
Cornell U.
Drew U.
Emory U.
Georgetown U.
Harvard U.
Ind. U.

Johns Hopkins U.
U. Kans.
U. Mich.
Middlebury C.
U. Minn.
N.Y.U.
Ohio St. U.
U. Penn.
Princeton U.
U. Tex. (Austin)
U. Utah
U. Va.
U. Wash.
Wayne St. U.
U. Wis.
Yale U.

HINDI
U. Chicago

LATIN
Ariz. St. U.
U. Ariz.
Ball St. U.
Boston C.
Brown U.
Bryn Mawr C.
U. Cal. (Berkeley)
U.C.L.A.
U. Cal. (Santa Barbara)
Catholic U.
U. Chicago
Columbia U.
Duke U.
Fla. St. U.
Fordham U.
Harvard U.
Ill. St. U.
U. Ill.
Ind. U.
U. Iowa
John Carroll U.
U. Kans.
U. Ky.
U. Md.
U. Mich.
U. Minn.
U. Miss.
Northwestern U.
N.Y.U.
Ohio St. U.
Princeton U.
Stanford U.
U. Tex. (Austin)
Tufts U.
U. Vt.
West Chester U. Pa.

RUSSIAN/SLAVIC LANGUAGES
U. Albany (S.U.N.Y.)
U. Ariz.
American U.
Boston C.
Brown U.
Bryn Mawr. U.
U. Cal. (Berkeley)
U.C.L.A.
Columbia U.
Cornell U.
DePaul U.
Duke U.
Fla. St. U.
Harvard U.
Hofstra U.
U. Ill.
U. Ill. (Chicago)
Ind. U.
U. Iowa
U. Kans.
Kent St. U.
U. Md.
Mich. St. U.
U. Mich.

Middlebury C.
U. Minn.
Monterey Inst.
N.Y.U.
U. No. Car.
 (Chapel Hill)
Northwestern U.
Ohio St. U.
U. Ore.
Penn. St. U.
U. Pitt.
San Fran. St. U.
U. So. Cal.
Stanford U.
Stony Brook U. (S.U.N.Y.)
U. Tenn.
U. Tex. (Austin)
U. Va.
U. Wash.
Wayne St. U.
U. Wis.
U. Wis. (Milwaukee)
Yale U.

SANSKRIT
U. Chicago
Harvard U.

SCANDINAVIAN LANGUAGES/ LITERATURES
B.Y.U.
U. Cal. (Berkeley)
U.C.L.A.
U. Chicago
Columbia U.
Cornell U.
Harvard U.
U. Minn.
U. Wash.
U. Wis.

TRANSLATION AND INTERPRETATION
U. Albany (S.U.N.Y.)
American U.
U. Ark.
Binghamton U. (S.U.N.Y.)
Georgia St. U.
Gallaudet U.
U. Iowa
Kent St. U.
Montclair U.
Monterey Inst.
Rutgers U.

URDU
U. Chicago

Home/Consumer Economics, Food Science, Food Service, Technology, Child and Family Life, Nutrition

U. Akron
Ala. A&M U.
U. Ala.
Andrews U.
Appal. St. U.
Ariz. St. U.
U. Ariz.
U. Ark.
Auburn U.
Ball St. U.
Boston U.
Bowl. Gr. St. U.
U. Bridgeport
B.Y.U.
Brooklyn C. (C.U.N.Y)
U. Buffalo (S.U.N.Y.)
Cal. Poly. St. U. (San Luis
 Obispo)

Cal. St. Poly. U.(Pomona)
Cal. St. (Chico)
Cal. St. U. (Fresno)
Cal. St. U. (Long Beach)
Cal. St. U. (L.A.)
Cal. St. U. (Northridge)
U. Cal. (Berkeley)
U. Cal. (Davis)
U.C.L.A.
Case West. Res. U.
Cent. Mich. U.
Cent. Mo. St. U.
Cent. Wash. U.
Chapman U.
U. Chicago
U. Cinn.
Clemson U.
Colo. St. U.
Columbia U.
U. Conn.
Cornell U.
U. Del.
U. Denver
Drexel U.
East Car. U.
East. Ill. U.
East. Ky. U.
East. Mich. U.
East Tenn. St. U.
F.D.U. (Teaneck)
Fla. A&M U.
Fla. St. U.
U. Fla.
Framingham St. U.
Georgia C. & St. U.
Georgia So. U.
U. Georgia
Harvard U.
U. Hawaii
Hood C.
Howard U.
Hunter C. (C.U.N.Y.)
Idaho St. U.
U. Idaho
Ill. St. U.
U. Ill.
Incarnate Word U.
Ind. St. U.
Ind. U. Pa.
Iowa St. U.
Johns Hopkins U.
Kans. St. U.
U. Kans.
Kent St. U.
U. Ky.
U. La. (Lafayette)
Lamar U.
Lehman C. (C.U.N.Y)
Loma Linda U.
L.S.U.
La. Tech U.
U. Maine
Marshall U.
U. Md.
Marywood U.
U. Mass.
U. Memphis
Mercer U.
Miami U. (Ohio)
Mich. St. U.
Minn. St. U. (Mankato)
Minn. St. U. (Moorhead)
U. Minn.
Miss St. U.
U. Mo. (Columbia)
Montclair U.
U. Neb.
U. Nev. (Reno)
U. N.H.
N. Mex. St. U.
U. N. Mex.
N.Y.U.
No. Car. A&T St. U.

No. Car. St. U. (Raleigh)
U. No. Car. (Greensboro)
No. Dak. St. U.
Northeastern U.
No. Ill. U.
U. No. Tex.
Nova U.
Ohio St. U.
Ohio U.
Okla. St. U.
U. Okla.
Ore. St. U.
Penn. St. U.
U. Pitt.
U. Puerto Rico
Purdue U.
U. Rhode Island
Rutgers U.
Sage Grad. Sch.
S.D.S.U.
San Fran. St. U.
San Jose St. U.
U. So. Cal.
So. Car. St. U.
So. Dak. St. U.
So. East. Mo. St. U.
So. Ill. U.
U. So. Miss.
Southern U.
Stanford U.
Syracuse U.
Tenn. St. U.
U. Tenn.
U. Tenn. (Martin)
Texas A&M U.
Tex. So. U.
Tex. Tech U.
Tex. Woman's U.
U. Tex. (Austin)
U. Tex. (Dallas)
Tulane U.
Tuskegee U.
Utah St. U.
U. Utah
Va. Poly. Inst.
U. Vt.
Wash. St. U.
U. Wash.
Wayne St. U.
W. Va. U.
West. Car. U.
West Ky. U.
West. Mich. U.
Winthrop U.
U. Wis.
U. Wis. (Stevens Point)
U. Wis. (Stout)
U. Wyo.

Horticulture

U. Ark.
Auburn U.
B.Y.U.
U. Cal. (Davis)
Clemson U.
Colo. St. U.
Cornell U.
U. Del.
U. Fla.
U. Georgia
U. Hawaii
Iowa St. U.
Kans. St. U.
L.S.U.
U. Maine
U. Md.
Mich. St. U.
U. Minn.
Miss. St. U.
U. Mo. (Columbia)
U. Neb.
N. Mex. St. U.

No. Car. St. U.
 (Raleigh)
No. Dak. St. U.
Ohio St. U.
Okla. St. U.
Oregon St. U.
Penn. St. U.
U. Puerto Rico
Purdue U.
Rutgers U.
So. Ill. U.
U. Tenn.
Tex. A&M U.
Tex. Tech U.
Va. Poly. Inst.
Wash. St. U.
U. Wash.
W. Va. U.
U. Wis.

Humanities

(Typically includes
English and History; offered by
nearly 400 institutions in all 50
states, so individual institutions
are not listed here)

CLASSICS
U. Albany (S.U.N.Y.)
U. Ariz.
Ball St. U.
Boston C.
Boston U.
Brown U.
Bryn Mawr C.
U. Buffalo (S.U.N.Y.)
B.Y.U.
U. Cal. (Berkeley)
U. Cal. (Davis)
U. Cal. (Irvine)
U.C.L.A.
U. Cal. (Santa Barbara)
Catholic U.
U. Chicago
U. Cinn.
U. Colo.
Columbia U.
Conn. C.
U. Conn.
Cornell U.
Duke U.
Fla. St. U.
U. Fla.
Fordham U.
Georgia St. U.
U. Georgia
Harvard U.
U. Hawaii
Hunter C. (C.U.N.Y.)
U. Ill.
Ind. U.
U. Iowa
John Carroll U.
Johns Hopkins U.
U. Kans.
Kent St. U.
U. Ky.
Loyola U. (Chicago)
U. Md.
U. Mass.
U. Mich.
U. Minn.
U. Miss.
U. Mo. (Columbia)
U. Neb.
C.U.N.Y. (Grad. Ctr.)
N.Y.U.
U. No. Car. (Chapel Hill)
U. No. Car. (Greensboro)
Northwestern U.
Ohio St. U.
U. Ore.

U. Penn.
U. Pitt.
Princeton U.
Rutgers U.
San Fran. St. U.
U. So. Cal.
Stanford U.
Syracuse U.
U. Tex. (Austin)
Tufts U.
Tulane U.
Vanderbilt U.
Villanova U.
U. Va.
U. Vt.
Wash U. (Mo.)
U. Wash.
Wayne St. U.
U. Wis.
Yale U.

COMPARATIVE
LITERATURE
American U.
Ariz. St. U.
U. Ariz.
U. Ark.
B.Y.U.
Brown U.
U. Buffalo (S.U.N.Y.)
Cal. St. U. (Fullerton)
U. Cal. (Berkeley)
U. Cal. (Davis)
U. Cal. (Irvine)
U.C.L.A.
U. Cal. (Riverside)
U. Cal. (San Diego)
U. Cal. (Santa Barbara)
U. Cal. (Santa Cruz)
Carnegie Mellon U.
Case West. Res. U.
Catholic U.
U. Chicago
Claremont Grad. U.
U. Colo.
Columbia U.
U. Conn.
Cornell U.
U. Dallas
Dartmouth C.
Duke U.
Emory U.
F.D.U. (Teaneck)
Fla. Atlantic U.
U. Georgia
Harvard U.
Hofstra U.
U. Ill.
Ind. U.
U. Iowa
Kent St. U.
L.S.U.
U. Md.
U. Mass.
Mich. St. U.
U. Mich.
U. Minn.
U. Mo. (Columbia)
U. N. Mex.
C.U.N.Y. (Grad. Ctr.)
S.U.N.Y. (Binghamton)
N.Y.U.
U. No. Car. (Chapel Hill)
Northwestern U.
U. Notre Dame
Ohio St. U.
Okla. City U.
U. Ore.
Penn. St. U.
U. Penn.
Princeton U.
U. Puerto Rico
Purdue U.

U. Rochester
Rutgers U.
San Fran. St. U.
San Jose St. U.
U. So. Cal.
U. So. Car.
Stanford U.
Stony Brook U. (S.U.N.Y.)
Tex. A&M U.
Tex. Tech U.
U. Tex. (Austin)
U. Tex. (Dallas)
U. Utah
Vanderbilt U.
Wash. U. (Mo.)
U. Wash.
Wayne St. U.
West. Ky. U.
W. Va. U.
U. Wis.
U. Wis. (Milwaukee)
Yale U.

FOLKLORE
U. Cal. (Berkeley)
U.C.L.A.
Geo. Wash. U.
Ind. U.
U. La. (Lafayette)
U. No. Car. (Chapel Hill)
U. Ore.
U. Penn.
U. Tex. (Austin)
Utah St. U.
West. Ky. U.

LINGUISTICS
U. Ala.
U. Alaska
U. Albany (S.U.N.Y.)
Ariz. St. U.
U. Ariz.
Ball St. U.
Boston C.
Boston U.
B.Y.U.
Brown U.
U. Buffalo (S.U.N.Y.)
Cal. St. U. (Fresno)
Cal. St. U. (Fullerton)
Cal. St. U. (Long Beach)
Cal. St. U. (Northridge)
Cal. St. U. (San Bernar
dino)
U. Cal. (Berkeley)
U. Cal. (Davis)
U.C.L.A.
U. Cal. (San Diego)
U. Cal. (Santa Barbara)
U. Cal. (Santa Cruz)
Carnegie Mellon U.
U. Chicago
U. Colo.
U. Conn.
Cornell U.
U. Del.
East. Mich. U.
Fla. Atlantic U.
Fla. Int'l. U.
U. Fla.
Gallaudet U.
Geo. Mason U.
Georgetown U.
Ga. St. U.
U. Georgia
Harvard U.
U. Hawaii
Hofstra U.
U. Houston
U. Ill.
U. Ill. (Chicago)
Ind. St. U.
Ind. U.

U. Iowa
U. Kans.
U. Louisville
L.S.U.
U. Md.
U. Mass.
M.I.T.
Mich. St. U.
U. Mich.
U. Minn.
U. Mo. (Columbia)
U. Mont.
Montclair U.
U. N. Mex.
C.U.N.Y. (Grad. Ctr.)
N.Y.U.
U. No. Car. (Chapel Hill)
N. East. Ill. U.
U. No. Dak.
Northwestern U.
Oakland U.
Ohio St. U.
Ohio U.
U. Ore.
Penn. St. U.
U. Penn.
U. Pitt.
Purdue U.
U. Puerto Rico
Queens C. (C.U.N.Y.)
Rice U.
Rutgers U.
S.D.S.U.
San Fran. St. U.
San Jose St. U.
U. So. Cal.
U. So. Car.
U. So. Fla.
So. Ill. U.
Stanford U.
Stony Brook U.
Syracuse U.
Teachers C. (Columbia)
Temple U.
U. Tenn.
Tex. Tech U.
U. Tex. (Arlington)
U. Tex. (Austin)
U. Tex. (El Paso)
U. Utah
U. Va.
U. Wash.
Wayne St. U.
W. Va. U.
U. Wis.
Yale U.

PHILOSOPHY
U. Albany (S.U.N.Y.)
American U.
Ariz. St. U.
U. Ariz.
U. Ark.
Baylor U.
Boston C.
Boston U.
Bowl. Gr. St. U.
Brooklyn C. (C.U.N.Y.)
Brown U.
U. Buffalo (S.U.N.Y.)
Cal. St. U. (Long Beach)
Cal. St. U. (L.A.)
U. Cal. (Berkeley)
U. Cal. (Davis)
U. Cal. (Irvine)
U.C.L.A.
U. Cal. (Riverside)
U. Cal. (San Diego)
U. Cal. (Santa Barbara)
Carnegie Mellon U.
Catholic U.
Cent. Mich. U.
U. Chicago

U. Cincinnati
Claremont Grad. U.
Cleveland St. U.
Colgate U.
Colo. St. U.
U. Colo.
Columbia U.
U. Conn.
Cornell U.
U. Dallas
U. Denver
DePaul U.
Duke U.
Duquesne U.
Emory U.
Fla. St. U.
U. Fla.
Fordham U.
Georgetown U.
Geo. Wash. U.
Georgia St. U.
U. Georgia
Gonzaga U.
Harvard U.
U. Hawaii
U. Houston
Howard U.
U. Ill.
U. Ill. (Chicago)
Ind. U.
I.U.P.U.I.
U. Iowa
Johns Hopkins U.
U. Kans.
Kent St. U.
U. Ky.
L.S.U.
U. Louisville
Loyola U. (Chicago)
Marquette U.
U. Md.
M.I.T.
U. Mass.
U. Memphis
Miami U. (Ohio)
U. Miami (Fla.)
Mich. St. U.
U. Mich.
U. Minn.
U. Miss.
U. Mo. (Columbia)
U. Mo. (St. Louis)
Montclair U.
U. Mont.
U. Neb.
U. Nev. (Reno)
U. N. Mex.
New Sch. U.
C.U.N.Y. (Grad. Ctr.)
S.U.N.Y. (Binghamton)
S.U.N.Y.
N.Y.U.
U. No. Car. (Chapel Hill)
No. Ill. U.
Northwestern U.
U. Notre Dame
Ohio St. U.
Ohio U.
Okla. City U.
Okla. St. U.
U. Okla.
U. Ore.
Penn. St. U.
U. Penn.
U. Pitt.
Princeton U.
U. Puerto Rico
Purdue U.
R.P.I.
U. Rhode Island
Rice U.
U. Rochester
Rutgers U.

St. John's U.
St. Louis U.
St. Mary's U.
U. St. Thomas (Tex.)
S.D.S.U.
San Fran. St. U.
San Jose St. U.
U. So. Car.
U. So. Cal.
U. So. Fla.
So. Ill. U.
So. Ill. U. (Edwardsville)
U. So. Miss.
Stanford U.
Stony Brook U. (S.U.N.Y.)
Syracuse U.
Temple U.
U. Tenn.
Tex. A&M U.
Tex. Tech U.
U. Tex. (Austin)
U. Toledo
Tufts U.
Tulane U.
U. Utah
Vanderbilt U.
Villanova U.
Va. Poly.
U. Va.
Wash. St. U.
Wash. U. (Mo.)
U. Wash.
Wayne St. U.
West Chester U. Pa.
West. Mich. U.
U. Wis.
U. Wis. (Milwaukee)
U. Wyo.
Yale U.

Law

U. Akron
U. Ala.
Albany Law Sch.
American U.
Ariz. St. U.
U. Ariz.
U. Ark.
U. Ark. (Little Rock)
U. Balt.
Barry U.
Baylor U.
Boston C.
Boston U.
U. Buffalo (S.U.N.Y.)
B.Y.U.
Brooklyn Law Sch.
U. Cal. (Berkeley)
U. Cal. (Davis)
U.C.L.A.
Cal. West. Sch. Law (San Diego)
Campbell U.
Capital U.
Case West. Res. U.
Catholic U.
Chapman U.
Chase C. Law
U. Chicago
U. Cinn.
Cleveland St. U.
U. Colo.
Columbia U.
U. Conn.
Cornell U.
Creighton U.
U. Dayton
U. Denver
DePaul U.
U. Detroit Mercy
Dickinson Sch. Law
U. D.C.
Drake U.
Duke U.

Duquesne U.
Emory U.
Fla. Coastal Sch. Law
Fla. St. U.
U. Fla.
Fordham U.
Franklin Pierce Law Ctr.
Geo. Mason U.
Georgetown U.
Geo. Wash. U.
Georgia St. U.
U. Georgia
Golden Gate U.
Gonzaga U.
Hamline U.
Hastings C. Law (U. Cal.)
Harvard U.
U. Hawaii
Hofstra U.
U. Houston
Howard U.
U. Idaho
Ill. Inst. Tech.
U. Ill.
Ind. U.
I.U.P.U.I.
Inter American U.
U. Iowa
John Marshall Law Sch.
U. Kans.
U. Ky.
U. La Verne
Lewis & Clark C.
L.S.U.
U. Louisville
Loyola Marymount U.
Loyola U. (Chicago)
Loyola U. (La.)
Marquette U.
U. Md. (Baltimore)
U. Memphis
Mercer U.
U. Miami (Fla.)
Mich. St. U. (Detroit law)
U. Mich.
U. Minn.
Miss. C.
U. Miss.
U. Mo. (Columbia)
U. Mo. (K.C.)
U. Mont.
U. Neb.
U. Nev.
New Eng. Sch. Law
U. N. Mex.
N.Y. Law Sch.
N.Y.U.
No. Car. Cent. U.
U. No. Car. (Chapel Hill)
U. No. Dak.
Northeastern U.
No. Ill. U.
Northwestern U.
U. Notre Dame
Nova U.
Ohio No. U.
Ohio St. U.
Okla. City U.
U. Okla.
U. Ore.
Pace U.
U. Pac.
U. Penn.
Pepperdine U.
Pont. Cath. U. P.R.
U. Pitt.
U. Puerto Rico
Queens C. (C.U.N.Y).
Quinnipiac C.
Regent U.
U. Richmond
Roger Williams U.
Rutgers U. (Camden)
Rutgers U. (Newark)

St. John's U. (N.Y.)
St. Louis U.
St. Mary's U.
St. Thomas U.
U. St. Thomas (MN)
Samford U.
U. San Diego
U. San Fran.
Santa Clara U.
Seattle U.
Seton Hall U.
U. So. Cal.
U. So. Car.
U. So. Dak.
So. Ill. U. (Carbondale)
U. So. Maine
So. Meth. U.
So. Tex. C. Law
So. U. & A&M C.
Southwestern U. Law
Stanford U.
Stetson U.
Suffolk U.
Syracuse U.
Temple U.
U. Tenn.
Tex. So. U.
Tex. Tech U.
Tex. Wesleyan U.
U. Tex. (Austin)
Thom. M. Cooley Law Sch.
Thom. Jefferson Sch. Law
Touro C.
U. Toledo
Tulane U.
U. Tulsa
U. Utah
Valparaiso U.
Vanderbilt U.
Vermont Law Sch.
Villanova U.
U. Va.
Wake Forest U.
Washburn U. Topeka
Wash. & Lee U.
Wash. U. (Mo.)
U. Wash.
Wayne St. U.
West. New Eng. C.
W. Va. U.
Whittier C.
Widener U.
Willamette U.
C. Wm. & Mary
Wm. Mitchell C. Law
U. Wis.
U. Wyo.
Yale U.
Yeshiva U.

Liberal/ Interdisciplinary/ Multidisciplinary Studies

A.C.U.
U. Albany (S.U.N.Y.)
Antioch N. E. Grad Sch.
Auburn U.
Boise St. U.
Boston U.
Bradley U.
Brooklyn C. (C.U.N.Y.)
B.Y.U.
Cal. St. U. (Chico)
Cal. St. U. (Fullerton)
Cal. St. U. (Long Beach)
Cal. St. U. (San Bernardino)
U. Cal. (Irvine)
Card. Stritch U.
Cent. Wash. U.
Clark U.
Columbia U.
Creighton U.
Dartmouth C.

U. Del.
DePaul U.
U. Detroit Mercy
Drew U.
Duke U.
Duquesne U.
East Tenn. St. U.
East. Wash. U.
Emory U.
Fla. Int'l. U.
Fordham U.
Frostburg St. U.
Geo. Mason U.
Georgetown U.
Hamline U.
Harvard U.
Hofstra U.
Hollins U.
U. Idaho
Ind. U.
I.U.P.U.I.
Jacksonville St. U.
Johns Hopkins U.
Kean U.
Kent St. U.
L.S.U. (Shreveport)
U. Maine
Manhattanville C.
McDaniel C.
U. Memphis
U. Miami
Mills C.
Minn. St. U. (Moorhead)
Miss. C.
Monmouth U.
U. Mont.
N. Mex. St. U.
U. New Mex.
New Sch. U.
S.U.N.Y.C. (Brockport)
S.U.N.Y.C. (Buffalo)
S.U.N.Y.C. (Plattsburgh)
N.Y.U.
No. Ariz. U.
No. Car. St. U.
U. No. Car. U.
   (Charlotte)
U. No. Car. U. (Greensboro)
U. No. Colo.
Northwestern U.
Notre Dame U.
Ohio U.
Okla. City U.
U. Okla.
Old Dom. U.
U. Penn.
Queens C. (C.U.N.Y.)
Reed C.
U. Richmond
Rollins C.
Rutgers U.
St. John's U.
U. St. Thomas (Tex.)
S.D.S.U.
Simmons C.
U. So. Fla.
So. West. Tex. St. U.
Stony Brook U. (S.U.N.Y.)
Syracuse U.
Temple U.
Tex. Christ. U.
U. Tex. (Arlington)
U. Tex. (Dallas)
U. Tex. (El Paso)
U. Tex. (Pan American)
U. Tex. (Tyler)
U. Toledo
Towson U.
Tulane U.
Va. Commonwealth U.
Vanderbilt U.
Villanova U.
Wake Forest U.
Wesleyan U.

Cal. St. U. (Northridge)
Cal. St. U. (Sacramento)
U. Cal. (Berkeley)
U. Cal. (Davis)
U. Cal. (Irvine)
U.C.L.A.
U. Cal. (Riverside)
U. Cal. (San Diego)
U. Cal. (Santa Barbara)
U. Cal. (Santa Cruz)
Carnegie Mellon U.
Case West. Res. U.
Catholic U.
U. Cent. Ark.
Cent. Mich. U.
Cent. Mo. St. U.
U. Cent. Okla.
Cent. Wash. U.
U. Chicago
U. Cincinnati
C.C.N.Y. (C.U.N.Y.)
Claremont Grad. U.
Cleve. St. U.
Colo. St. U.
U. Colo.
Columbia U.
Concordia U. (Ill.)
U. Conn.
Converse C.
Cornell U.
U. Del.
U. Denver
DePaul U.
Drake U.
Duke U.
Duquesne U.
East Car. U.
East Ill. U.
East. Ky. U.
East. Mich. U.
East. N. Mex. U.
East. Wash. U.
Emory U.
Emporia St. U.
Fla. Atlantic U.
Fla. Int'l. U.
Fla. St. U.
U. Fla.
Geo. Mason U.
Georgia So. U.
Georgia St. U.
U. Georgia
Hardin-Simmons U.
U. Hartford
Harvard U.
U. Hawaii
Hollins U.
Holy Names U.
U. Houston
Howard U.
Hunter C. (C.U.N.Y.)
U. Idaho
Ill. St. U.
U. Ill.
Ind. St. U.
Ind. U.
I.U.P.U.I.
Ind. U. Pa.
U. Iowa
Ithaca C.
Jacksonville St. U.
Jacksonville U.
James Madison U.
Jersey City St. U.
Johns Hopkins U.
Juilliard Sch.
Kans. St. U.
U. Kans.
Kent St. U.
U. Ky.
Lamar U.
Lehman C. (C.U.N.Y.)
L.I.U. (C.W. Post)
L.S.U.

U. La. (Lafayette)
U. La. (Monroe)
U. Louisville
Loyola U. (La.)
U. Maine
Manhattan Sch. Music
Mansfield U. Pa.
Marshall U.
U. Md.
Marywood U.
U. Mass.
U. Mass. (Lowell)
McDaniels C.
McNeese St. U.
U. Memphis
Mercer U.
Miami U. (Ohio)
U. Miami (Fla.)
Mich. St. U.
U. Mich.
Mid. Tenn. St. U.
Mills C.
Minn. St. U. (Mankato)
Minn. St. U. (Moorhead)
U. Minn.
Minot St. U.
Miss. C.
U. Miss.
U. Mo. (Columbia)
U. Mo. (K.C.)
U. Mont.
Montclair U.
U. Montevallo
Morehead St. U.
Morgan St. U.
Murray St. U.
U. Neb.
U. Neb. (Kearney)
U. Neb. (Omaha)
U. Nev.
U. Nev. (Reno)
New Eng. Cons. Music
U. N.H.
N. Mex. St. U.
U. N. Mex.
U. N. Orleans
New Sch. U.
C.U.N.Y. (Grad. Ctr.)
S.U.N.Y. (Binghamton)
S.U.N.Y. (Fredonia)
S.U.N.Y.C. (Potsdam)
N.Y.U.
N. Car. Cent. U.
U. No. Car. (Chapel Hill)
U. No. Car. (Greensboro)
U. No. Colo.
No. Dak. St. U.
U. No. Dak.
U. No. Fla.
Northeastern Ill. U.
No. Ariz. U.
No. Ill. U.
U. No. Iowa
U. No. Tex.
No. Wash. U.
Northwestern St. U. La.
Northwestern U.
Notre Dame U.
U. Notre Dame
Oakland U.
Ohio St. U.
Ohio U.
Okla. City U.
Okla. St. U.
U. Okla.
U. Ore.
U. Pac.
Penn. St. U.
U. Penn.
Pittsburg St. U.
U. Pitt.
Portland St. U.
U. Portland
Prairie View A&M U.

Princeton U.
Queens C. (C.U.N.Y.)
Radford U.
U. Redlands
Rhode Island C.
U. Rhode Island
Rice U.
Rider U. (Westminister Choir
  Sch.)
U. Rochester
Roosevelt U.
Rowan U.
Rutgers U.
St. Cloud St. U.
St. John's U. (Minn.)
C. St. Rose
Salisbury St. U.
Samford U.
Sam Houston St. U.
S.D.S.U.
San Fran. Cons. Mus.
San Fran. St. U.
San Jose St. U.
Santa Clara U.
Smith C.
U. So. Cal.
U. So. Car.
U. So. Dak.
U. So. Fla.
Southeast Mo. St. U.
Southeastern La. U.
U. So. Cal.
So. Ill U.
So. Ill. U. (Edwardsville)
So. Meth. U.
U. So. Miss.
Southwestern Okla. St. U.
Stanford U.
Stony Brook U. (S.U.N.Y.)
S. F. Austin St. U.
Sul Ross St. U.
Syracuse U.
Temple U.
Tenn. St. U.
U. Tenn.
U. Tenn. (Chattanooga)
Tex. A&M U. (Kingsville)
Tex. Christ. U.
Tex. So. U.
Tex. St. U.
Tex. Tech U.
Tex. Woman's U.
U. Tex. (Austin)
U. Tex. (El Paso)
U. Tex. (San Antonio)
U. Tex. (Tyler)
U. Toledo
Towson U.
Truman St. U.
Tufts U.
Tulane U.
U. Tulsa
U. Utah
Valdosta St. U.
Valparaiso U.
Va. Commonwealth U.
U. Va.
Wash. St. U.
Wash. U. (Mo.)
U. Wash.
Wayne St. U.
Webster U.
Wesleyan U.
West Chester U. Pa.
West Car. U.
West. Ga. U.
West Tex. A&M U.
W. Va. U.
West. Ill. U.
West. Ky. U.
West. Mich. U.
W. Va. U.
West. Wash. St. U.
Wichita St. U.

Winthrop U.
U. Wis.
U. Wis. (Eau Claire)
U. Wis. (Milwaukee)
U. Wis. (Stevens Point)
U. Wis. (Whitewater)
Wright St. U.
U. Wyo.
Yale U.
Youngstown St. U.

MUSIC THERAPY

Fla. St. U.
Mich. St. U.
N.Y.U.
So. Meth. U.
Tex. Woman's U.

Nursing and Health Professions

CHILD-CARE/CHILD HEALTH/PEDIATRIC NURSING

Baylor U.
U. Buffalo (S.U.N.Y.)
Case West. Res. U.
Catholic U.
U. Cent. Fla.
U. Cinn.
Columbia U.
U. Del.
Duke U.
Georgia St. U.
U. Hawaii
Hunter C. (C.U.N.Y.)
U. Ill. (Chicago)
I.U.P.U.I.
Kent St. U.
Loma Linda U.
L.S.U.
U. Md.
Marquette U.
Mich. St. U.
U. Minn.
U. Mo. (K.C.)
U. Nev.
N.Y.U.
Northeastern U.
Ore. Health & Sci. U.
U. Penn.
U. San Diego
Seton Hall U.
U. So. Car.
Stony Brook U. (S.U.N.Y.)
Tex. Tech. U.
Tex. Women's U.
Va. Commonwealth U.
Vanderbilt U.
Villanova U.
Wayne St. U.
Wright St. U.

FAMILY NURSING

(Typically includes Adult, Geriatric, Maternity, Parent–Child)

Adelphi U.
Ariz. St. U.
Boston C.
U. Buffalo (S.U.N.Y.)
Cal. St. U. (Fresno)
Case West. Res. U.
Catholic U.
U. Colo. Health Sci. Ctr.
Columbia U.
Duke U.
Emory U.
Med. C. Georgia
U. Hawaii
Hunter C. (C.U.N.Y.)
U. Ill. (Chicago)
Ind. U.

Kent St. U.
Loma Linda U.
L.S.U. H.S.C.
Marquette U.
U. Md.
U. Mass.
U. Miami
U. Mo. (K.C.)
N.Y.U.
Ore. Health & Sci. U.
U. Penn.
U. Pitt.
Med. U. So. Car.
Seton Hall U.
Stony Brook U. (S.U.N.Y.)
U. Tenn. (Memphis)
U. Tex. Health Sci. Ctr.
  (Houston)
U. Tex. Health Sci. Ctr. (San
  Antonio)
U. Utah
Vanderbilt U.
Villanova U.
Va. Commonwealth U.
Wayne St. U.

FORENSIC NURSING
Cleveland St. U.
U. Colo.
Duquesne U.
Fitchburg U.
Quinnipiac U.
Vanderbilt U.

**HEALTH CARE/HEALTH
SERVICES/HOSPITAL
ADMINISTRATION/
MANAGEMENT**
U. Ala. (Birm.)
American U.
Ariz. St. U.
A.T. Still U.
U. Balt.
Barry U.
Baruch C. (C.U.N.Y.)
Baylor U.
Boston U.
Brandeis U.
Brooklyn C. (C.U.N.Y.)
U. Buffalo (S.U.N.Y.)
B.Y.U.
Cal. St. U. (Bakersfield)
Cal. St. U. (Chico)
Cal. St. U. (East Bay)
Cal. St. U. (Long Beach)
Cal. St. U. (Los Angeles)
Cal. St. U. (San Bernardino)
U.C.L.A.
Capital U.
Card. Stritch C.
Carnegie Mellon U.
Case West. Res. U.
Chapman U.
U. Cinn.
Clark U.
Cleveland St. U.
U. Colo.
Columbia U. (Teachers C.)
Columbus St. U.
U. Conn.
Cornell U.
U. Dallas
DePaul U.
Drexel U.
U. Detroit Mercy
Duke U.
Duquesne U.
Emory U.
Fairfield U.
Fla. Int'l. U.
U. Fla.
Framingham St. C.
Gannon U.
Geo. Wash. U.

Georgia St. U.
Golden Gate U.
Gov. St. U.
U. Hartford
U. Hawaii
Harvard U.
Hofstra U.
Hunter C. (C.U.N.Y.)
U. Ill. (Chicago)
Ind. U.
I.U.P.U.I.
Iona C.
U. Iowa
Johns Hopkins U.
U. Kans.
U. Ky.
Kent St. U.
U. La Verne
Loma Linda U.
L.I.U.
L.I.U. (C.W. Post)
Loyola U. (Chicago)
L.S.U. (Shreveport)
Marywood U.
U. Mass. (Lowell)
U. Md.
U. Memphis
Med. U. So. Car.
U. Miami
U. Mich.
U. Minn.
Miss. C.
U. Mo. (Columbia)
U. Mo. (K.C.)
U. Miss.
Mont. St. U.
Natl. U.
U. N. Haven
Northeastern U.
New Sch. U.
New York Med. C.
N.Y.U.
U. No. Car. (Charlotte)
U. No. Tex.
Northwestern U.
Nova U.
Ohio St. U.
Ohio U.
Okla. St. U.
U. Okla.
Ore. Health & Sci. U.
Ore. St. U.
Our Lady Lakes U.
Pace U.
Pac. Luth. U.
Penn. St. U.
U. Phoenix
U. Pitt.
Quinnipiac U.
R.I.T.
Rosalind Franklin U.
Rutgers U.
Sage Grad. Sch.
St. Joseph's U.
St. Louis U.
St. Mary's U. (Minn.)
St. Xavier U.
Seton Hall U.
Simmons C.
U. So. Cal.
U. So. Car.
U. So. Maine
Southeast Mo. St. U.
Southwest Tex. St. U.
Springfield C.
Stony Brook U. (S.U.N.Y.)
Suffolk U.
Syracuse U.
Temple U.
U. Tenn.
Tex. A&M U.
Tex. Tech. U.
Tex. Women's U.
Thunderbird

Towson U.
Trinity U.
Tulane U.
Union C.
Va. Commonwealth U.
Villanova U.
Wagner C.
U. Wash.
Wash. St. U.
Webster U.
Widener U.
Wilkes U.
Wright St. U.
Xavier U. (Ohio)
Youngstown U.

NURSE ANESTHESIA
U. Ala. (Birm.)
Albany Med. C.
Ark St. U.
Barry U.
Baylor C. Med.
Boston C.
U. Buffalo (S.U.N.Y.)
Cal. St. U. (Long Beach)
U.C.L.A.
Case West. Res. U.
U. Cinn.
Columbia U.
DePaul U.
U. Detroit Mercy
Drexel U.
Duke U.
Emory U.
Fairfield U.
Gannon U.
Med. C. Georgia
Gonzaga U.
U. Kans.
U. Mich.
U. Med. N.J.
U. Miami
U. Minn.
U. No. Car. (Greensboro)
Northeastern U.
Oakland U.
U. Penn.
U. Pitt.
Med. U. So. Car.
U. So. Ill.
  (Edwardsville)
U. Tenn.
  (Chattanooga)
T.C.U.
U. Tex Health Sci. Ctr.
  (Houston)
Va. Commonwealth U.
Villanova U.
Wayne St. U.
Webster U.
Xavier U. (La.)

NURSE MIDWIFERY
Boston U.
Case West. Res. U.
U. Cinn.
U. Colo. Health Sci. Ctr.
Emory U.
Ill. St. U.
U. Ill. Chicago
U. Kans.
U. Md.
Marquette U.
U. Miami
U. Med. N.J.
N.Y.U.
Ore. Health & Sci. U.
U. Penn.
Med. U. So. Car.
Stony Brook U. (S.U.N.Y.)
Teachers C. (Columbia U.)
U. Tex. (El Paso)
Va. Commonwealth U.
Vanderbilt U.

NURSING

(Typically includes Nurse Practitioner, Administration, Education, Medical Surgical)

A.C.U.
Adelphi U.
U. Akron
U. Ala. (Birm.)
U. Ala. (Hunt.)
U. Alaska
Andrews U.
Ariz. St. U.
U. Ariz.
Ark. St. U.
U. Ark.
Armstrong Atlantic St. U.
Auburn U. (Mont.)
Azusa Pac. U.
Ball St. U.
Barry U.
Baylor U.
Bloomsburg U. Pa.
Boston C.
Bowie St. U.
Bradley U.
U. Buffalo (S.U.N.Y.)
B.Y.U.
Cal. St. (Bakersfield)
Cal. St. U. (Chico)
Cal. St. U. (Dominguez Hills)
Cal. St. U. (Fresno)
Cal. St. U. (Long Beach)
Cal. St. U. (L.A.)
Cal. St. U. (Sacramento)
U.C.L.A.
U. Cal. (San Fran.)
Capital U.
Card. Stritch U.
Case West. Res. U.
Catholic U.
U. Cent. Ark.
U. Cincinnati
Clarion U. Pa.
Clemson U.
Cleveland St. U.
U. Colo. Health Sci. Ctr.
Columbia U. (Teacher C.)
U. Conn.
Creighton U.
U. Del.
DePaul U.
Delta St. U.
U. Detroit Mercy
Drake U.
Drexel U.
Duke U.
Duquesne U.
East Car. U.
East. Ky. U.
East. Tenn. St.
East. Wash. U.
Edinboro U. Pa.
Emory U.
Fairfield U.
F.D.U. (Teaneck)
Fla. Atlantic U.
Fla. Int'l. U.
Fla. St. U.
U. Fla.
Fort Hays St. U.
Gannon U.
Geo. Mason U.
Georgetown U.
Georgia C. St. U.
Med. C. Georgia
Georgia St. U.
Gonzaga U.
Gov. St. U.
Hampton U.
Hardin-Simmons U.
U. Hartford
U. Hawaii

Holy Names U.
Howard U.
Hunter C. (C.U.N.Y.)
Idaho St. U.
U. Ill. (Chicago)
Incarnate Word U.
Ind. St. U.
I.U.P.U.I.
Ind. U. Pa.
U. Iowa
Jacksonville St. U.
Jacksonville U.
Johns Hopkins U.
Kean U.
Kent St. U.
U. Kans. Med. Ctr.
U. Ky.
Lehman C. (C.U.N.Y.)
L.I.U.
Loma Linda U.
L.S.U. H.S.C.
U. Louisville
Loyola U. Chicago
U. Maine
Marquette U.
Marshall U.
U. Md.
U. Md. (Baltimore)
U. Mass.
U. Mass. (Boston)
U. Mass. (Dartmouth)
U. Mass. (Lowell)
Mercer U.
U. Miami
Mich. St. U.
U. Mich.
Midwest. St. U.
Minn. St. U. (Mankato)
Miss. St. U. Women
U. Minn.
U. Miss.
U. Mo. (Columbia)
U. Mo. (K.C.)
Monmouth U.
Mont. St. U.
Murray St. U.
U. Neb.
New Jersey City U.
U. Nev. (Las Vegas)
U. Nev. (Reno)
Niagara U.
U.N.H.
U. Med. & Dent. N.J.
N. Mex. St. U.
U. N. Mex.
U. N. Orleans Med. Ctr.
C. N. Rochelle
S.U.N.Y. (Binghamton)
S.U.N.Y.C. (New Paltz)
S.U.N.Y. Downstate
S.U.N.Y. Upstate
N.Y.U.
No. Ariz. U.
U. No. Car. (Chapel Hill)
U. No. Car. (Charlotte)
U. No. Car. (Greensboro)
U. No. Colo.
No. Dak. St. U.
U. No. Dak.
No. Ill. U.
No. Mich. U.
Northwestern St. U. La.
Nova U.
Oakland U.
Med. C. Ohio
Ohio St. U.
Okla. City. U.
U. Okla. Health Sci. Ctr.
Old Dom. U.
Ore. Health & Sci. U.
Pace U.
Pac. Luth. U.
Penn. St. U.
U. Penn.

U. Phoenix
Pittsburgh St. U.
U. Pitt.
Point Loma Naz. U.
U. Portland
Purdue U.
  (Calumet)
Radford U.
U. Rhode Island
Rivier C.
U. Rochester
Rush U.
Rutgers U.
Sage Grad. Sch.
St. Joseph's C.
St. Louis U.
C. St. Scholastica
St. Xavier U.
Salem St. C.
Salisbury St. U.
Sanford U.
S.D.S.U.
U. San Diego
San Fran. St. U.
U. San Fran.
San Jose St. U.
U. Scranton
Seattle Pac. U.
Seattle U.
Seton Hall U.
Simmons C.
Slippery Rock U. Pa.
Sonoma St. U.
Southeast Mo. St. U.
U. So. Ala.
U. So. Car.
Med. U. So. Car.
U. So. Cal.
So. Conn. St. U.
So. Dak. St. U.
U. So. Fla.
So. Ill. U.
  (Edwardsville)
U. So. Maine
Southwest Mo. St.
Spalding U.
Stony Brook U. (S.U.N.Y.)
Syracuse U.
Temple U.
Tenn. St. U.
U. Tenn.
U. Tenn. (Chattanooga)
U. Tenn. (Memphis)
Tex. A&M U. (Corpus
  Christi)
T.C.U.
Tex. Woman's U.
U. Tex. (Arlington)
U. Tex. (El Paso)
U. Tex. Health Sci. Ctr.
  (Houston)
U. Tex. Health Sci. Ctr. (San
  Antonio)
U. Tex. (Tyler)
Thom. Jefferson U.
U. Toledo
Towson U.
Troy U.
U. Tulsa
U. Utah
Valdosta St. U.
Valparaiso U.
Vanderbilt U.
Villanova U.
U. Va.
Va. Commonwealth U.
U. Vt.
Wagner C.
Wash. St. U.
U. Wash.
Wayne St. U.
Webster U.
West Tex. A&M U.
W. Va. U.

West Chester U. Pa.
West. Conn. St. U.
West. Ky. U.
West. U. Health Sci.
Wheelock C.
Wichita St.
Widener U.
Wilkes U.
Winona St. U.
U. Wis.
U. Wis. (Eau Claire)
U. Wis. (Milwaukee)
U. Wis. (Oshkosh)
Wright St. U.
U. Wyo.
Xavier U.
Xavier U. (La.)
Yale U.
Youngstown U.

OCCUPATIONAL THERAPY

U. Ala. (Birm.)
A.T . Still U.
Barry U.
Boston U.
U. Buffalo (S.U.N.Y.)
Cal St. U. (Sacramento)
U. Cal. (Davis)
U. Cent. Ark.
U. Cinn.
Cleveland St. U.
Colo. St. U.
Creighton U.
Duquesne U.
East. Ky. U.
East. Mich. U.
East. Wash. U.
Fla. Int'l. U.
U. Fla.
Gannon U.
Med. C. Georgia
U. Hawaii
Idaho St. U.
I.U.P.U.I.
U. Ill.
U. Ill. Chicago
James Madison U.
U. Kans. Med. Ctr.
Midwestern U.
U. Miss.
U. Mo. (Columbia)
U. Neb.
U. Nev. (Reno)
U.N.H.
U. N. Mex.
U. Med. N.J.
N.Y.I.T.
N.Y.U.
U. No. Car. (Chapel Hill)
U. No. Car. (Greensboro)
U. No. Dak.
Nova U.
Ohio St. U.
U. Okla. Health Sci. Ctr.
U. Pitt.
Quinnipiac U.
C. St. Scholastica
Sage Grad. Sch.
San Jose St. U.
Seton Hall U.
U. So. Ala.
U. So. Cal.
Med. U. So. Car.
U. So. Dak.
U. So. Maine
Springfield C.
St. Louis U.
Stony Brook U. (S.U.N.Y.)
Teachers C. (Columbia U.)
Temple U.
Tex. Tech. U.
  Health Sci. Ctr.
Tex. Women's U.

U. Tex. Health Sci. Ctr. (San
  Antonio)
U. Tex. Med. Br.
Thom. Jefferson U.
U. Toledo
Towson U.
Tufts U.
U. Utah
Va. Commonwealth U.
U. Vt.
Wash. U.
U. Wash.
Wayne St. U.
W. Va. U.
U. Wis. (Milwaukee)
Xavier U.

ONCOLOGY NURSING

Case West. Res. U.
Columbia U.
U. Del.
Duke U.
Emory U.
Loyola U. (Chicago)
U. Penn.

PHYSICAL THERAPY

Ala. St. U.
U. Ala. (Birm.)
Andrews U.
Armstrong Atlantic U.
Angelo St. U.
Ark. St. U.
A.T. Still U.
Azusa Pac. U.
Baylor U.
Boston U.
Bradley U.
Buffalo U. (S.U.N.Y.)
Cal. St. U. (Fresno)
Cal. St. U. (Long Beach)
Cal. St. U. (Northridge)
U. Cal. (San Francisco)
U. Cent. Ark.
U. Cent. Fla.
Cent. Mich. U.
Chapman U.
Cleveland St. U.
U. Colo.
U. Conn.
Creighton U.
U. Del.
Drexel U.
Duke U.
Duquesne U.
East Car. U.
East. Wash. U.
Emory U.
Fla. A&M U.
Fla. Int'l. U.
U. Fla.
Gannon U.
Geo. Wash. U.
Med. C. Georgia.
Georgia St. U.
Gov. St. U.
Hampton U.
U. Hartford
Humboldt St. U.
Hunter C. (C.U.N.Y.)
Idaho St. U.
U. Ill. Chicago
I.U.P.U.I.
U. Iowa
U. Kans.
U. Ky.
L.I.U.
Loma Linda U.
L.S.U. H.S.C.
U. Md.
Marquette U.
U. Mass. (Lowell)
U. Miami.
Midwestern U.

U. Tex. Health Sci. Ctr. (San Antonio)
U. Tex. S.W. Med. Ctr. (Dallas)
U. Toledo
U. Utah
Va. Commonwealth U.
Wash. St. U.
U. Wash.
Wayne St. U.
W. Va. U.
U. Wis.
Xavier U. (La.)

Physical Sciences

(Typically includes Chemistry, Mathematics, and Physics; offered by nearly 400 institutions, so individual institutions are not listed here; also often includes Statistics, Applied Mathematics)

ANALYTICAL CHEMISTRY
U. Akron
Binghamton U. (S.U.N.Y.)
Boston C.
B.Y.U.
Cal. St. U. (Fullerton)
Cal. St. U. (L.A.)
Case West. Res. U.
U. Cinn.
Clarkson U.
Cleveland St. U.
Cornell U.
Gov. St. U.
Fla. St. U.
U. Ga.
Geo. Wash. U.
Georgetown U.
U. Houston
Howard U.
Ill. Inst. Tech.
Ind. U.
Kans. St. U.
Kent St. U.
U. Louisville
Marquette U.
U. Md.
Miami U.
Mich. St. U.
U. Mich.
Miss. St. U.
U. Mo. (K.C.)
U. Mont.
U Neb.
Northeastern U.
Old Dom. U.
Ore. St. U.
Purdue U.
Rutgers U.
San Jose St. U.
Seton Hall U.
So. Dak. U.
U. So. Fla.
Stevens Inst. Tech.
U. Tenn.
U. Tex. (Austin)
U. Toledo
Tufts U.
Va. Commonwealth U.
Vanderbilt U.
Wake Forest U.
Wash. St. U.
W. Va. U.
U. Wis.

APPLIED PHYSICS
Ala. A&M U.
Appal. St. U.
U. Ariz.
U. Ark.
Binghamton U. (S.U.N.Y.)
Brooklyn C. (C.U.N.Y.)

U. Buffalo (S.U.N.Y.)
U. Cal. (San Diego)
U. Cent. Okla.
Colo. Sch. Mines
Columbia U.
Cornell U.
DePaul U.
Geo. Mason U.
Harvard U.
Iowa St. U.
Johns Hopkins U.
U. La. (Lafayette)
U. Mass. (Boston)
U. Md.
U. Mich.
U. Mo. (St. Louis)
N.J.I.T.
U. New Orleans
No. Ariz. U.
U. No. Car. (Charlotte)
Princeton U.
Rice U.
R.P.I.
Rutgers U.
U. So. Fla.
So Ill. U.
Stanford U.
Tex. A&M U.
Tex. Tech U.
Va. Commonwealth U.
Va. Poly. Inst.
U. Wash.
W. Va. U.
Yale U.

ASTRONOMY/ PLANETARY SCIENCES/ SPACE SCIENCES
U. Alaska
Ariz. St. U.
U. Ariz.
Boston U.
Bowl. Gr. St. U.
U. Buffalo (S.U.N.Y.)
B.Y.U.
Cal. Inst. Tech.
U. Cal. (Berkeley)
U.C.L.A.
U. Cal. (Santa Cruz)
Case West. Res. U.
U. Chicago
Clemson U.
U. Colo.
Columbia U.
Cornell U.
Creighton U.
Dartmouth C.
U. Del.
Fla. Inst. Tech.
U. Fla.
Georgia St. U.
U. Ga.
Harvard U.
U. Hawaii
U. Ill.
Ind. U.
Iowa St. U.
U. Iowa
Johns Hopkins U.
U. Kans.
U. Ky.
L.S.U.
U. Md.
M.I.T.
U. Mass.
Mich. St. U.
U. Mich.
Minn. St. U. (Mankato)
U. Minn.
U. Mo. (Columbia)
U. Neb.
N. Mex. St. U.
U. No. Car. (Chapel Hill)

Northwestern U.
Ohio St. U.
Ohio U.
Ore. St. U.
Penn. St. U.
U. Penn.
U. Pitt.
Princeton U.
Rice U.
U. Rochester
R.P.I.
S.D.S.U.
U. So. Car.
Stony Brook U. (S.U.N.Y.)
T.C.U.
Tex. Tech U.
U. Tex. (Austin)
Vanderbilt U.
U. Va.
U. Wash.
Wesleyan U.
U. Wis.
U. Wyo.
Yale U.

CHEMICAL PHYSICS
U. Colo.
Columbia U.
Cornell U.
Fla. St. U.
Georgetown U.
Harvard U.
Kent St. U.
U. Louisville
Marquette U.
U. Md.
Mich. St. U.
U. Nev. (Reno)
Ohio St. U.
Princeton U.
U. So. Car.
U. Tenn.
U. Utah
Va. Commonwealth U.
W. Va. U.

GEOCHEMISTRY
Cal. Inst. Tech.
Cal. St. U. (Fullerton)
U.C.L.A.
Colo. Sch. Mines.
Columbia U.
Cornell U.
Ga. Inst. Tech.
Geo. Wash. U.
U. Hawaii
U. Ill. (Chicago)
Ind. U.
M.I.T.
U. Mich.
Mont. Tech.
N. Mex. M&T
Mo. U. Sci. & Tech.
U. Nev. (Reno)
Ohio U.
Penn. St. U.
Purdue U.
R.P.I.
U. Tulsa
Wash. St. U.
Wash. U.
Yale U.

GEOLOGY
U. Akron
U. Ala.
U. Alaska
U. Albany (S.U.N.Y.)
Ariz. St. U.
U. Ark.
Auburn U.
Ball St. U.
Baylor U.
Boise St. U.

Boston C.
Bowl. Gr. St. U.
B.Y.U.
Brooklyn C. (C.U.N.Y.)
Bryn Mawr C.
U. Buffalo (S.U.N.Y.)
Cal. Inst. Tech.
Cal. St. U. (Bakersfield)
Cal. St. U. (Chico)
Cal. St. U. (East Bay)
Cal. St. U. (Fresno)
Cal. St. U. (Long Beach)
Cal. St. U. (L.A.)
Cal. St. U. (Northridge)
U. Cal. (Berkeley)
U. Cal. (Davis)
U.C.L.A.
U. Cal. (Riverside)
U. Cal. (Santa Barbara)
Case West. Res. U.
Cent. Mich. U.
Cent. Wash. U.
U. Cincinnati
C.C.N.Y. (C.U.N.Y.)
Colo. Sch. Mines
Colo. St. U.
U. Colo.
Columbia U.
U. Conn.
Cornell U.
U. Del.
Duke U.
East Car. U.
East. Ky. U.
East. Wash. U.
Fla. Atlantic U.
Fla. St. U.
U. Fla.
Fort Hays St. U.
Geo. Wash. U.
Georgia St. U.
U. Georgia
Harvard U.
U. Hawaii
U. Houston
Idaho St. U.
U. Idaho
U. Ill.
U. Ill. (Chicago C.)
Ind. St. U.
Ind. U.
I.U.P.U.I.
Iowa St. U.
U. Iowa
Johns Hopkins U.
Kans. St. U.
U. Kans.
Kent St. U.
U. Ky.
U. La. (Lafayette)
Lehigh U.
Loma Linda U.
L.S.U.
U. Maine
U. Md.
M.I.T.
U. Mass.
U. Memphis
Miami U. (Ohio)
U. Miami
Mich. St. U.
Mich. Tech. U.
U. Mich.
U. Minn.
U. Miss.
Mo. U. Sci. & Tech.
U. Mo. (Columbia)
U. Mo. (K.C.)
Mont. Tech
U. Mont.
U. Neb.
U. Nev. (Reno)
U. N.H.
N. Mex. Inst. M&T

Roosevelt U.
Rutgers U.
Sage Grad. Sch.
St. Edward's U.
St. Louis U.
St. Mary's U.
S.D.S.U.
San Fran. St. U.
U. San Fran.
San Jose St. U.
Seattle U.
Seton Hall U.
Shippensburg U. Pa.
Sonoma St. U.
U. So. Ala.
U. So. Cal.
U. So. Car.
U. So. Dak.
U. So. Fla.
Southeast Mo. St. U.
So. Ill. U.
U. So. Maine
So. Meth. U.
Southwest Mo. St. U.
Suffolk U.
Sul Ross St. U.
Syracuse U.
Tenn. St. U.
U. Tenn.
U. Tenn. (Chattanooga)
Tex. A&M U.
Tex. So. U.
Tex. St. U.
Tex. Tech U.
U. Tex. (Arlington)
U. Tex. (Austin)
U. Tex. (Dallas)
U. Tex. (Pan American)
U. Tex. (San Antonio)
U. Toledo
Troy U.
Tufts U.
Tulane U.
U. Utah
Valdosta St. U.
U. Vt.
Villanova U.
Va. Commonwealth U.
Va. Poly. Inst.
U. Va.
Wash. U.
U. Wash.
Wayne St. U.
Webster U.
West Chester U. Pa.
West. Car. U.
West. Ga. U.
West. Ky. U.
West. Mich. U.
W. Va. U.
Wichita St. U.
Widener U.
C. Wm. & Mary
U. Wis.
U. Wis. (Milwaukee)
U. Wis. (Oshkosh)
Wright St. U.
U. Wyo.

Public and Community Health

U. Ala. (Birm.)
U. Alaska
U. Albany (S.U.N.Y.)
Barry U.
Boston U.
Brooklyn C. (C.U.N.Y.)
U. Buffalo (S.U.N.Y.)
Cal. St. U. (Fresno)
Cal. St. U. (Fullerton)
Cal. St. U. (Long Beach)
Cal. St. U. (Northridge)

Cal. St. U. (Sacramento)
U. Cal. (Berkeley)
U.C.L.A.
Case West. Res. U.
Cleveland St. U.
U. Colo. Health Sci. Ctr.
Columbia U.
U. Conn.
U. Denver
Drexel U.
East Tenn. St. U.
Emory U.
Fla. Int'l. U.
U. Fla.
Geo. Wash. U.
Harvard U.
U. Hawaii
Hunter C. (C.U.N.Y.)
Idaho St. U.
U. Ill.
U. Ill. (Chicago)
Ind. U.
U. Iowa
Johns Hopkins U.
U. Kans.
U. Ky.
L.I.U.
Loma Linda U.
L.S.U.
U. Mass.
U. Md.
U. Med. & Dent. N.J.
Meharry Med. C.
U. Miami
Mich. St. U.
U. Mich.
Minn. St. U. (Mankato)
U. Minn.
U. Mo. (Columbia)
N.J.I.T.
U. Neb.
U. Nev.
U. Nev. (Reno)
U. N. Mex.
N.Y. Med. C.
N.Y.U.
U. No. Car. (Chapel Hill)
No. Ill. U.
U. No. Colo.
U. No. Tex.
Northwestern U.
Nova U.
Med. C. Ohio
Ohio St. U.
U. Okla. Health Sci. Ctr.
Old Dom. U.
Ore. St. U.
U. Ore.
U. Pitt.
U. Puerto Rico
Purdue U.
U. Rochester
Rutgers U.
Sage Grad. Sch.
St. Louis U.
S.D.S.U.
San Fran. St. U.
San Jose St. U.
U. So. Cal.
Med. U. So. Car.
U. So. Car.
U. So. Fla.
Stony Brook U. (S.U.N.Y.)
Temple U.
U. Tenn.
Tex. A&M U.
U. Tex. Health Sci. Ctr. (Houston)
U. Tex. Med. Br. (Galveston)
Thom. Jefferson U.
U. Toledo
Tufts U.
Tulane U.

U. Utah
Va. Commonwealth U.
U. Va.
Wash. St. U.
U. Wash.
Wayne St. U.
West. Ky. U.
W. Va. U.
Wichita St. U.
Med. C. Wis.
U. Wis.
U. Wis. (La Crosse)
Wright St. U.
Yale U.

ENVIRONMENTAL/ OCCUPATIONAL HEALTH

U. Ala. (Birm.)
U. Albany (S.U.N.Y.)
U. Ark. Med. Sci.
Binghamton U. (S.U.N.Y.)
Boston U.
Cal. St. U. (Fresno)
Cal. St. U. (Northridge)
U. Cal. (Berkeley)
U.C.L.A.
U. Cinn.
Colo. St. U.
Columbia U.
U. Conn.
Duke U.
East Car. U.
East. Ky. U.
East Tenn. St. U.
Emory U.
U. Fla.
Gannon U.
Geo. Wash. U.
U. Georgia
Harvard U.
Hunter C. (C.U.N.Y.)
U. Ill. Chicago
Ind. St. U.
Ind. U. Pa.
U. Iowa
Johns Hopkins U.
Loma Linda U.
Loyola U. Chicago
Meharry Med. C.
U. Miami
U. Mich.
U. Minn.
Montclair U.
Murray St. U.
U. Nev. (Reno)
U.N. Haven
N.J.I.T.
N. Y. Med. C.
U. No. Car. (Chapel Hill)
U. No. Tex. H.S.C.
Northwestern U.
N.Y.U.
Med. U. Ohio
U. Okla.
Old Dom. U.
Ore. St. U.
Penn. St. U.
U. Pitt.
Poly. U.
U. Puerto Rico
Purdue U.
S.D.S.U.
U. So. Car.
U. So. Fla.
Stony Brook U. (S.U.N.Y.)
Temple U.
Tex A&M U. H.S.C.
Towson U.
Tufts U.
Tulane U.
Va. Commonwealth U.
Wash. St. U.
U. Wash.

Wayne St. U.
West Chester U. Pa.
W. Va. U.
Med. C. Wis.
U. Wis. (Eau Claire)
Yale U.

EPIDEMIOLOGY

U. Ala. (Birm.)
U. Albany (S.U.N.Y.)
U. Ariz.
Boston U.
U. Buffalo (S.U.N.Y.)
Cal. St. U. (Long Beach)
U. Cal. (Berkeley)
U. Cal. (Davis)
U.C.L.A.
U. Cal. (San Diego)
Case West. Res. U.
U. Cinn.
U. Colo.
Columbia U.
Cornell U.
Duke U.
East Tenn. St. U.
Emory U.
U. Fla.
Georgetown U.
Geo. Wash. U.
Harvard U.
U. Hawaii
U. Ill. Chicago
U. Iowa
Johns Hopkins U.
Loma Linda U.
U. Louisville
U. Md. (Baltimore)
U. Mass.
U. Miami
Mich. St. U.
U. Mich.
Med. U. N.J.
N.Y. Med. C.
N.Y.U.
No. Car. St. U.
U. No. Car. (Chapel Hill)
U. No. Tex. H.S.C.
U. Okla.
Ore. Health & Sci. U.
U. Penn.
U. Pitt.
Purdue U.
U. Rochester
S.D.S.U.
U. So. Cal.
Med. U. So. Car.
U. So. Car.
U. So. Fla.
Stanford U.
Temple U.
Tex. A&M U.
U. Tex. Health Sci. Ctr. (Houston)
Tufts U.
Tulane U.
Va. Commonwealth U.
U. Va.
Wake Forest U.
U. Wash.
Med. C. Wis.

INTERNATIONAL HEALTH

Boston U.
Brandeis U.
Emory U.
Geo. Wash. U.
Harvard U.
Johns Hopkins U.
U. Mich.
U. So. Fla.
Tufts U.
Tulane U.

U. Wash.
Yale U.

Religion

(Typically includes Bible
Studies, Religious Studies,
Theology; often includes Reli-
gious Education)

A.C.U.
Andrews U.
Ariz. St. U.
Assumption C.
Azusa Pac. U.
Barry U.
Baylor U.
Boston C.
Boston U.
Brown U.
U. Cal. (Berkeley)
U. Cal. (Santa Barbara)
Card. Stritch C.
Catholic U.
U. Chicago
Claremont Grad. U.
Colgate U.
U. Colo
Columbia U.
Concordia U. (Ill.)
U. Dallas
U. Dayton
U. Denver
U. Detroit Mercy
Drew U.
Duke U.
Duquesne U.
Emory U.
Fla. Int'l. U.
Fla. St. U.
U. Fla.
Fordham U.
Gannon U.
Geo. Wash. U.
U. Georgia
Gonzaga U.
Hardin-Simmons U.
Harvard U.
U. Hawaii
Holy Names U.
U. Incarnate Word
Ind. U.
U. Iowa
John Carroll U.
U. Kans.
Loma Linda U.
Loyola U.
Loyola U. (Chicago)
Loyola U. (La.)
Marquette U.
Marygrove C.
Marywood U.
Miami U. (Ohio)
Mt. St. Mary's C.
N.Y.U.
U. No. Car. (Chapel Hill)
Northwestern U.
Notre Dame U.
U. Notre Dame
Okla. City U.
Olivet Naz. U.
Oral Roberts U.
U. Pac.
U. Penn.
Pepperdine U.
U. Pitt.
Point Loma U.
U. Portland
Princeton U.
Providence C.
Rice U.
St. Bonaventure U.
St. John's U. (Minn.)

St. John's U. (N.Y.)
St. Joseph C. (Conn.)
St. Louis U.
St. Mary's U.
St. Mary's U. (Minn.)
St. Michael's C.
U. St. Thomas (Tex.)
Samford U.
U. San Diego
U. San Fran.
Santa Clara U.
Seattle U.
Seton Hall. U.
Smith C.
U. So. Cal.
U. So. Car.
U. So. Fla.
So. Meth. U.
So. Naz. U.
Southwest Mo. St.
Spalding U.
Stanford U.
Syracuse U.
Temple U.
U. Tenn.
Tex. Christ. U.
Vanderbilt U.
Villanova U.
U. Va.
Wake Forest U.
Wash. U.
U. Wash.
Xavier U. (Ohio)
Yale U.
Yeshiva U.

Social Sciences

(Typically includes Economics,
Political Science, Psychology,
Sociology)

A.C.U.
Adelphi U.
U. Akron
Ala. A&M U.
U. Ala.
U. Ala. (Birm.)
U. Ala. (Huntsville)
U. Alaska
U. Albany (S.U.N.Y.)
Alfred U.
Alliant Intl. U.
American U.
Andrews U.
Angelo St. U.
Antioch N. E. Grad. Sch.
Antioch (L.A.)
Antioch U. (McGregor)
Antioch (Santa Barbara)
Antioch U. (Seattle)
Appal. St. U.
Ariz. St. U.
U. Ariz.
Ark. St. U.
U. Ark.
Assump. C.
Auburn U.
Auburn U. (Montgomery)
Augusta St. U.
Austin Peay St. U.
Azusa Pac. U.
Ball St. U.
U. Baltimore
Baruch C. (C.U.N.Y.)
Barry U.
Baylor U.
Bemidji St. U.
Boston C.
Boston U.
Bowl. Gr. St. U.
Brandeis U.
U. Bridgeport

Bridgewater St. C.
B.Y.U.
Brooklyn C. (C.U.N.Y.)
Brown U.
Bryn Mawr C.
Bucknell U.
U. Buffalo (S.U.N.Y.)
Cal. Inst. Tech.
Cal. Luth. U.
Cal. Poly St. U. (San Luis
   Obispo)
Cal. St. Poly U. (Pomona)
Cal. St. U. (Bakersfield)
Cal. St. U. (Chico)
Cal. St. U. (Dominguez Hills)
Cal. St. U. (East Bay)
Cal. St. U. (Fresno)
Cal. St. U. (Fullerton)
Cal. St. U. (Long Beach)
Cal. St. U. (L.A.)
Cal. St. U. (Northridge)
Cal. St. U. (Sacramento)
Cal. St. U. (San Bernardino)
Cal. St. U. (San Marcos)
Cal. St. U. (Stanislaus)
Cal. U. Pa.
U. Cal. (Berkeley)
U. Cal. (Davis)
U. Cal. (Irvine)
U.C.L.A.
U. Cal. (Riverside)
U. Cal. (San Diego)
U. Cal. (San Fran.)
U. Cal. (Santa Barbara)
U. Cal. (Santa Cruz)
Carnegie Mellon U.
Case West. Res. U.
Catholic U.
U. Cent. Ark.
Cent. Conn. St. U.
U. Cent. Fla.
Cent. Mich. U.
Cent. Mo. St. U.
U. Cent. Okla.
Cent. Wash. U.
Chapman U.
Chicago St. U.
U. Chicago
U. Cincinnati
Citadel
C.C.N.Y. (C.U.N.Y.)
Claremont Grad. U.
Clark U.
Clark Atlanta U.
Clemson U.
Cleveland St. U.
Colo. St. U.
U. Colo.
Columbia U.
Concordia U.
Conn. C.
U. Conn.
Cornell U.
U. Dallas
Dartmouth C.
U. Dayton
U. Del.
Delta St. U.
U. Denver
DePaul U.
U. Detroit Mercy
Dominican U. (Calif.)
Drake U.
Drew U.
Drexel U.
Duke U.
Duquesne U.
East Car. U.
East Stroudsburg U. Pa.
East Tenn. St. U.
East. Ill. U.
East. Ky. U.
East. Mich. U.

East. N. Mex. U.
East. Wash. U.
Edinboro U. Pa.
Emory U.
Emporia St. U.
Fairfield U.
F.D.U. (Madison)
F.D.U. (Teaneck)
Fla. A&M U.
Fla. Atlantic U.
Fla. Inst. Tech.
Fla. Int'l. U.
Fla. St. U.
U. Fla.
Fordham U.
Fort Hays St. U.
Framingham St. C.
Frostburg St. U.
Gallaudet U.
Geo. Mason U.
Geo. Wash. U.
Georgetown U.
Georgia C. St. U.
Georgia Inst. Tech.
Georgia So. U.
Georgia St. U.
U. Georgia
Goddard C.
Golden Gate U.
Gonzaga U.
Gov. St. U.
U. Hartford
Harvard U.
U. Hawaii
Henderson St. U.
Hofstra U.
Holy Names C.
Hollins U.
Hood C.
U. Houston
U. Houston (Clear Lake)
Howard U.
Humbolt St. U.
Hunter C. (C.U.N.Y.)
Idaho St. U.
U. Idaho
Ill. Inst. Tech.
Ill. St. U.
U. Ill.
U. Ill. (Chicago)
Ind. St. U.
Ind. U.
I.U.P.U.I.
Ind. U. Penn.
Inter American U.
Iona C.
Iowa St. U.
U. Iowa
Jackson St. U.
Jacksonville St. U.
James Madison U.
Jersey City St. U.
Johns Hopkins U.
John Jay C. (C.U.N.Y.)
Kans. St. U.
U. Kans.
Kean U.
Kent St. U.
U. Ky.
Lamar U.
Lehigh U.
Lewis and Clark C.
Lincoln U.
Loma Linda U.
L.I.U.
L.I.U. (C.W. Post)
Loras C.
L.S.U.
L.S.U. (Shreveport)
La. Tech U.
U. La. (Monroe)
U. Louisville
Loyola C.

Loyola Marymount U.
Loyola U. (Chicago)
U. Maine
Marquette U.
Marshall U.
U. Md.
U. Md. (Baltimore)
Marywood U.
M.I.T.
U. Mass.
U. Mass. (Boston)
McNeese St. U.
U. Memphis
Miami U. (Ohio)
U. Miami (Fla.)
Mich. St. U.
U. Mich.
Mid. Tenn. St. U.
Midwestern St. U.
Millersville U. Pa.
Minn. St. U. (Mankato)
Minn. St. U. (Moorhead)
U. Minn.
Miss. C.
Miss. St. U.
U. Miss.
U. Mo. (Columbia)
U. Mo. (K.C.)
U. Mo. (St. Louis)
Monmouth U.
Mont. St. U.
U. Mont.
Montclair St. U.
Morehead St. U.
Morgan St. U.
Mount Holyoke C.
Murray St. U.
Natl. Louis U.
Natl. U.
U. Neb.
U. Neb. (Omaha)
U. Nev.
U. Nev. (Reno)
U. N.H.
N. Mex. Highlands U.
N. Mex. St. U.
U. N. Mex.
U. N. Orleans
C. New Rochelle
New Sch. U.
C.U.N.Y. (Grad. Ctr.)
S.U.N.Y. (Binghamton)
S.U.N.Y.C. (Brockport)
S.U.N.Y.C. (New Paltz)
S.U.N.Y.C. (Oswego)
N.Y.U.
No. Car. Cent. U.
No. Car. St. U. (Raleigh)
U. No. Car. (Chapel Hill)
U. No. Car. (Charlotte)
U. No. Car. (Greensboro)
No. Dak. St. U.
U. No. Dak.
U. No. Fla.
Northeastern U.
No. Ill. U.
No. Ariz. U.
U. No. Colo.
No. Ill. U.
U. No. Iowa
U. No. Tex.
U. No. Tex. Health Sci. Ctr.
No. W. Mo. St. U.
No. W. Okla. St. U.
No. W. St. U. La.
Northwestern U.
Notre Dame U.
U. Notre Dame
Nova U.
Ohio St. U.
Ohio U.
Okla. St. U.
U. Okla.

U. Okla. Health Sci. Ctr.
Old Dom. U.
U. Ore.
Our Lady Lake U.
Pace U.
Pac. Luth. U.
Pac. U.
U. Pac.
Penn. St. U.
U. Penn.
Pepperdine U.
U. Phoenix
Pittsburg St. U.
U. Pitt.
Portland St. U.
Prairie View A&M U.
Princeton U.
U. Puerto Rico
Purdue U.
Purdue U. (Calumet)
Queens C. (C.U.N.Y.)
Radford U.
R.P.I.
Rhode Island C.
U. Rhode Island
Rice U.
U. Richmond
Rochester Inst. Tech.
U. Rochester
Rockford C.
Rollins C.
Roosevelt U.
Rowan U.
Rutgers U.
Sage Grad. Sch.
Saginaw Val. St. U.
St. Bonaventure U.
St. Cloud St. U.
U. St. Francis
St. John's U. (N.Y.)
St. Joseph's U. (Penn.)
St. Louis U.
St. Mary's U.
C. St. Rose
Salisbury St. U.
Sam Houston St. U.
S.D.S.U.
San Fran. St. U.
U. San Fran.
San Jose St. U.
U. Scranton
Seattle U.
Seton Hall
Shippensburg U. Pa.
Sonoma St. U.
U. So. Ala.
U. So. Cal.
U. So. Car.
So. Dak. St. U.
U. So. Dak.
U. So. Fla.
Southeastern La. U.
So. Conn. St. U.
So. Ill. U.
So. Ill. U. (Edwardsville)
So. Meth. U.
U. So. Miss.
So. Naz. U.
So. Ore. U.
So. U. & A&M C.
Southwest Mo. St.
Spalding U.
Stanford U.
S. F. Austin St. U.
Stony Brook U. (S.U.N.Y.)
Suffolk U.
Sul Ross St. U.
Syracuse U.
Temple U.
Tenn. St. U.
U. Tenn.
U. Tenn. (Chattanooga)
Tex. A&M U.

Tex. A&M U. (Commerce)
Tex. A&M U. (Corpus Christi)
Tex. A&M U. (Kingsville)
Tex. Christ. U.
Tex. So. U.
Tex. St. U.
Tex. Tech U.
Tex. Woman's U.
U. Tex. (Arlington)
U. Tex. (Austin)
U. Tex. (Brownsville)
U. Tex. (Dallas)
U. Tex. (El Paso)
U. Tex. (Permian Basin)
U. Tex. (Tyler)
U. Toledo
Towson U.
Trinity C.
Trinity U.
Tufts U.
Tulane U.
U. Tulsa
Union Inst.
Utah St. U.
U. Utah
Valdosta St. U.
Valparaiso U.
Vanderbilt U.
U. Vt.
Villanova U.
Va. Commonwealth U.
Va. Poly. Inst.
Va. St. U.
U. Va.
Wake Forest U.
Washburn U.
Wash. St. U.
Wash. U. (Mo.)
U. Wash.
Wayne St. U.
Webster U.
Wesleyan U.
West Chester U. Pa.
W. Va. U.
West. Car. U.
U. West Fla.
West. Ill. U.
West. Ky. U.
West. Mich. U.
West Tex. A&M U.
West. Wash. U.
Westfield St. C.
Wichita St. U.
Widener U.
C. Wm. & Mary
Winthrop U.
U. Wis.
U. Wis. (Eau Claire)
U. Wis. (La Crosse)
U. Wis. (Milwaukee)
U. Wis. (Oshkosh)
U. Wis. (River Falls)
U. Wis. (Superior)
U. Wis. (Whitewater)
Wright St. U.
U. Wyo.
Xavier U. (Ohio)
Yale U.
Yeshiva U.
Youngstown St. U.

ANTHROPOLOGY

U. Ala.
U. Ala. (Birmingham)
U. Alaska
U. Albany (S.U.N.Y.)
American U.
Ariz. St. U.
U. Ariz.
U. Ark.
Ball St. U.
Boston U.
Brandeis U.

U. Buffalo (S.U.N.Y.)
B.Y.U.
Brown U.
Cal. St. U. (Bakersfield)
Cal. St. U. (Chico)
Cal. St. U. (East Bay)
Cal. St. U. (Fullerton)
Cal. St. U. (Long Beach)
Cal. St. U. (L.A.)
Cal. St. U. (Northridge)
Cal. St. U. (Sacramento)
U. Cal. (Berkeley)
U. Cal. (Davis)
U. Cal. (Irvine)
U.C.L.A.
U. Cal. (Riverside)
U. Cal. (San Diego)
U. Cal. (San Fran.)
U. Cal. (Santa Barbara)
U. Cal. (Santa Cruz)
Case West. Res. U.
Catholic U.
U. Chicago
U. Cincinnati
Colo. St. U.
U. Colo.
Columbia U.
U. Conn.
Cornell U.
U. Denver
Duke U.
East Car. U.
East. N. Mex. U.
Emory U.
Fla. Atlantic U.
Fla. St. U.
U. Fla.
Geo. Wash. U.
Georgia St. U.
U. Georgia
Harvard U.
U. Hawaii
U. Houston
Hunter C. (C.U.N.Y.)
Idaho St. U.
U. Idaho
U. Ill.
U. Ill. (Chicago)
Ind. U.
Iowa St. U.
U. Iowa
Johns Hopkins U.
U. Kans.
Kent St. U.
U. Ky.
Lehigh U.
L.S.U.
U. Md.
Marshall U.
U. Mass.
U. Memphis
Mich. St. U.
U. Mich.
Minn. St. U. (Mankato)
U. Minn.
U. Miss.
U. Mo. (Columbia)
U. Mont.
Montclair U.
U. Neb.
U. Nev.
U. Nev. (Reno)
N. Mex. St. U.
U. N. Mex.
New Sch. U.
C.U.N.Y. (Grad. Ctr.)
S.U.N.Y. (Binghamton)
N.Y.U.
U. No. Car. (Chapel Hill)
No. Ariz. U.
No. Ill. U.
U. No. Tex.
Northwestern U.

Ohio St. U.
U. Okla.
Ore. St. U.
U. Ore.
Penn. St. U.
U. Penn.
U. Pitt.
Portland St. U.
Princeton U.
Purdue U.
Rice U.
Rutgers U.
S.D.S.U.
San Fran. St. U.
U. So. Cal.
U. So. Car.
U. So. Fla.
So. Ill. U.
So. Meth. U.
U. So. Miss.
Stanford U.
Stony Brook U. (S.U.N.Y.)
Syracuse U.
Temple U.
U. Tenn.
Tex. A&M U.
Tex. St. U.
Tex. Tech U.
U. Tex. (Arlington)
U. Tex. (Austin)
U. Tex. (San Antonio)
U. Toledo
Tulane U.
U. Tulsa
U. Utah
Vanderbilt U.
U. Va.
Wake Forest U.
Wash. St. U.
Wash. U. (Mo.)
U. Wash.
Wayne St. U.
West. Ky. U.
West. Mich. U.
West. Wash. U.
W. Va. U.
Wichita St. U.
C. Wm. & Mary
U. Wis.
U. Wis. (Milwaukee)
U. Wyo.
Yale U.

ARCHAEOLOGY
Ariz. St. U.
U. Ariz.
Boston U.
Brown U.
Bryn Mawr C.
U. Cal. (Berkeley)
U.C.L.A.
U. Chicago
Columbia U.
Cornell U.
Fla. St. U.
Geo. Mason U.
Harvard U.
Ill. St. U.
Ind. U.
U. Mass. (Boston)
U. Memphis
Mich. Tech. U.
U. Mich.
U. Minn.
U. Mo. (Columbia)
C.U.N.Y. (Grad. Ctr.)
N.Y.U.
No. Ariz. U.
U. No. Car. (Chapel Hill)
U. Penn.
Princeton U.
So. Meth. U.
U. Tenn.

U. Tex. (San Antonio)
Tufts U.
U. Va.
Wash. St. U.
Wash. U.
Yale U.

GEOGRAPHIC INFORMATION SYSTEMS
U. Akron
U. Albany U. (S.U.N.Y.)
Boston U.
U. Buffalo (S.U.N.Y.)
Clark U.
U. Cent. Ark
U. Colo.
U. Conn.
U. Denver
Ga. Inst. Tech.
Geo. Mason U.
Georgia St. U.
Hunter C. (C.U.N.Y.)
Idaho St. U.
U. Minn.
U. Mont.
No. Ariz. St. U.
No. Car. St. U.
U. No. Car. (Greensboro)
Penn. St. U.
U. Pitt.
St. Louis U.
Tex. St. U.
U. Tex. (Dallas)
U. Toledo
W. Va. U.
U. Wis.

GEOGRAPHY
U. Akron
U. Ala.
U. Albany (S.U.N.Y.)
Appal. St. U.
Ariz. St. U.
U. Ariz.
U. Ark.
Ball St. U.
Boston U.
U. Buffalo (S.U.N.Y.)
B.Y.U.
Cal. St. U. (Chico)
Cal. St. U. (East Bay)
Cal. St. U. (Fresno)
Cal. St. U. (Fullerton)
Cal. St. U. (Long Beach)
Cal. St. U. (L.A.)
Cal. St. U. (Northridge)
Cal. U. (Pa.)
U. Cal. (Berkeley)
U. Cal. (Davis)
U.C.L.A.
U. Cal. (Riverside)
U. Cal. (Santa Barbara)
Cent. Conn. St. U.
Chicago St. U.
U. Chicago
Clark U.
U. Colo.
U. Conn.
U. Del.
U. Denver
East Car. U.
East Tenn. St. U.
East. Ky. U.
East. Mich. U.
Fla. Atlantic U.
Fla. St. U.
U. Fla.
Geo. Mason U.
Geo. Wash. U.
Georgia St. U.
U. Georgia
U. Hawaii

Hunter C. (C.U.N.Y.)
U. Idaho
U. Ill.
U. Ill. (Chicago)
Ind. St. U.
Ind. U.
I.U.I.P.U.
Ind. U. Penn.
U. Iowa
Johns Hopkins U.
Kans. St. U.
U. Kans.
Kent St. U.
U. Ky.
L.S.U.
Marshall U.
U. Md.
U. Mass.
U. Memphis
Miami U. (Ohio)
U. Miami
Mich. St. U.
Minn. St. U. (Mankato)
U. Minn.
U. Mo. (Columbia)
U. Mont.
Murray St. U.
U. Neb.
U. Neb. (Omaha)
U. Nev. (Reno)
N. Mex. St. U.
U. N. Mex.
U. N. Orleans
S.U.N.Y. (Binghamton)
No. Ariz. U.
U. No. Car. (Chapel Hill)
U. No. Car. (Charlotte)
U. No. Car. (Greensboro)
U. No. Dak.
Northeastern Ill. U.
No. Ill. U.
U. No. Iowa
Northwestern U.
Ohio St. U.
Ohio U.
Okla St. U.
U. Okla.
Ore. St. U.
U. Ore.
Penn. St. U.
Portland St. U.
Rutgers U.
St. Cloud St. U.
S.D.S.U.
San Fran. St. U.
San Jose St. U.
U. So. Cal.
U. So Car.
So. Dak. St. U.
U. So. Fla.
So. Ill. U.
So. Ill. U. (Edwardsville)
U. So. Miss.
Syracuse U.
Temple U.
U. Tenn.
Tex. A&M U.
Tex. St. U.
U. Tex. (Austin)
U. Toledo
Towson U.
Utah St. U.
U. Utah
Va. Poly. Inst.
U. Vt.
U. Wash.
Wayne St. U.
West Chester U. Pa.
West. Ill. U.
West. Ky. U.
West. Mich. U.
West. Wash. U.
W. Va. U.

U. Wis.
U. Wis. (Milwaukee)
U. Wyo.

MEDIEVAL/ RENAISSANCE STUDIES
Ariz. St. U.
Boston C.
Catholic U.
U. Colo.
Columbia U.
U. Conn.
Cornell U.
Duke U.
Fordham U.
Harvard U.
Ind. U.
Marquette U.
U. Minn.
U. Mo. (Columbia)
C.U.N.Y. (Grad. Ctr.)
S.U.N.Y. (Binghamton)
U. Notre Dame
Rutgers U.
So. Meth. U.
West. Mich. U.
Yale U.

PEACE STUDIES/ SCIENCE/CONFLICT RESOLUTION
A.C.U.
American U.
Antioch U. (McGregor)
U. Baltimore
Brandeis U.
Cal. St. U. (Dominguez Hills)
Cornell U.
U. Denver
Duquesne U.
Geo. Mason U.
U. Hawaii
Johns Hopkins U.
U. Mass. (Boston)
U. Mo. (Columbia)
U. Mo. (St. Louis)
Montclair U.
U. No. Car. (Greensboro)
Nova U.
U. Notre Dame
U. Penn.
Pepperdine U.
Portland St. U.
U. San Diego
Tufts U.
Wayne St. U.

POPULATION STUDIES
Columbia U.
Georgetown U.
Harvard U.
Johns Hopkins U.
U. Mich.
Penn St. U.
U. Penn.
Princeton U.

RURAL SOCIOLOGY
Auburn U.
Cornell U.
Iowa St. U.
U. Mo. (Columbia)
U. Mont.
No. Car. St. U.
Ohio St. U.
Penn. St. U.
So. Dak. St. U.
U. Tenn.
U. Wis.

SPORT PSYCHOLOGY
Barry U.
Cal. St. U. (Fresno)

Cleveland St. U.
Fla. St. U.
U Fla.
U. Iowa
Purdue U.
So. Conn. St. U.
Springfield C.
W. Va. U.

URBAN STUDIES
U. Akron
Ala. A&M U.
U. Albany (S.U.N.Y.)
Boston U.
Brooklyn C. (C.U.N.Y.)
U. Cal. (Irvine)
U. Cent. Okla.
Cleveland St. U.
U. Del.
East Tenn. St. U.
Fla. St. U.
Georgia St. U.
Hunter C. (C.U.N.Y.)
Jersey City St. U.
L.I.U.
U. Louisville
M.I.T.
Mich. St. U.
Minn. St. U. (Mankato)
U. Mo. (K.C.)
Montclair U.
N.J.I.T.
U. N. Orleans
New Sch. U.
C.U.N.Y. (Grad. Ctr.)
N.Y.U.
Old Dom. U.
U. Penn.
Portland St. U.
Queens C. (C.U.N.Y.)
Rutgers U.
So. Conn. St. U.
St. Louis U.
Temple U.
Tex. A&M U.
U. Tex. (Arlington)
Trinity U.
Tufts U.
Va. Commonwealth U.
Va. Poly. Inst.
U. Wash.
U. Wis. (Milwaukee)
Wright St. U.

WOMEN'S/FEMINIST STUDIES
U. Ala.
U. Albany (S.U.N.Y.)
U. Ariz.
Brandeis U.
U. Buffalo (S.U.N.Y.)
U.C.L.A.
U. Cal. (Santa Barbara)
U. Cinn.
Claremont Grad. U.
Clark Atlantic U.
Cornell U.
DePaul U.
Drew U.
Duke U.
East. Mich. U.
Emory U.
U. Fla.
Geo. Wash. U.
U. Georgia
Georgia St. U.
Goddard C.
U. Iowa
U. Louisville
U. Mass. (Boston)
U. Md. (Baltimore)
U. Mich.
Minn. St. U. (Mankato)
U. Minn.

New. Sch. U.
C.U.N.Y. (Grad. Ctr.)
N.Y.U.
U. No. Car. (Greensboro)
No. Ill. U.
Ohio St. U.
U. Okla.
U. Pitt.
Roosevelt U.
Rutgers U.
San Fran. St. U.
Sarah Lawrence C.
S.D.S.U.
U. So. Car.
So. Conn. St. U.
U. So. Fla.
So. Ill. U. (Edwardsville)
St. Mary's U.
Stony Brook U. (S.U.N.Y.)
Tex. Women's U.
Towson U.
Wash. St. U.
U. Wash.

Social Work

(Includes Human Services, Social Service, Social Welfare)

Adelphi U.
U. Akron
Ala. A&M U.
U. Ala.
Albany U. (S.U.N.Y.)
Ariz. St. U.
U. Ark.
Barry U.
Baylor U.
Boise St. U.
Boston C.
Boston U.
Brandeis U.
B.Y.U.
Bryn Mawr C.
U. Buffalo (S.U.N.Y.)
Cal. St. U. (Bakersfield)
Cal. St. U. (Chico)
Cal. St. U. (Fresno)
Cal. St. U. (Long Beach)
Cal. St. U. (Sacramento)
Cal. St. U. (San Bernardino)
Cal. St. U. (Stanislaus)
U. Cal. (Berkeley)
U.C.L.A.
Case West. Res. U.
Catholic U.
U. Cent. Fla.
Cent. Mich. U.
U. Chicago
U. Cincinnati
Clark Atl. U.
Cleveland St. U.
Colo. St. U.
Columbia U.
Columbia U. (Teachers C.)
U. Conn.
U. Denver
East Car. U.
East. Mich. U.
East. Wash. U.
Fla. A&M U.
Fla. Int'l. U.
Fla. St. U.
Fordham U.
Gallaudet U.
Geo. Mason U.
Georgia St. U.
U. Georgia
Gov. St. U.
U. Hawaii
U. Houston
Howard U.
Hunter C. (C.U.N.Y.)
U. Ill.

U. Ill. (Chicago)
I.U.P.U.I.
U. Iowa
Jackson St. U.
U. Kans.
U. Ky.
L.S.U.
U. Louisville
Loma Linda U.
Loyola U. (Chicago)
U. Maine
U. Md.
U. Md. (Baltimore)
Marywood U.
U. Mass (Boston)
Mich. St. U.
U. Mich.
Minn. St. U. (Moorhead)
U. Minn.
U. Mo. (Columbia)
U. Mo. (St. Louis)
U. Neb. (Omaha)
U. Nev.
U. Nev. (Reno)
U. N.H.
N. Mex. Highlands U.
N. Mex. St. U.
C.U.N.Y. (Grad. Ctr.)
S.U.N.Y.C. (Brockport)
N.Y.U.
No. Car. A&T St. U.
U. No. Car. (Chapel Hill)
U. No. Car. (Charlotte)
U. No. Car. (Greensboro)
U. No. Dak.
Ohio St. U.
Okla. St. U.
U. Okla.
Our Lady Lake U.
U. Penn.
U. Pitt.
Portland St. U.
U. Puerto Rico
Radford U.
Rhode Island C.
Rutgers U.
St. Louis U.
Salem St. U.
S.D.S.U.
San Fran. St. U.
San Jose St. U.
S. F. Austin St. U.
Simmons C.
Smith C.
So. Conn. St. U.
U. So. Cal.
U. So. Car.
U. So. Fla.
So. Ill. U.
U. So. Miss.
Southwest Mo. St.
Spalding U.
Springfield C.
Stony Brook U. (S.U.N.Y.)
Syracuse U.
Temple U.
U. Tenn.
Tex. St. U.
U. Tex. (Arlington)
U. Tex. (Austin)
Tulane U.
U. Utah
Valdosta St. U.
Va. Commonwealth U.
U. Vt.
Walla Walla C.
Wash. U. (Mo.)
U. Wash.
Wayne St. U.
W. Va. U.
West. Mich. U.
Wichita St. U.
Widener U.
U. Wis.

U. Wis. (Milwaukee)
Yeshiva U.

Theater/Drama

(Speech/Drama, Speech Arts, Theater Arts; typically includes Acting, Directing; often includes Children's Theater, Criticism, Theater/Costume Design, Technical Production)

U. Akron
U. Ala.
U. Albany (S.U.N.Y.)
Ariz. St. U.
U. Ariz.
Ark. St. U.
U. Ark.
Baylor U.
Bennington C.
Boston U.
Bowl. Gr. St. U.
Brandeis U.
B.Y.U.
Brooklyn C. (C.U.N.Y.)
Brown U.
Butler U.
Cal. Inst. Arts
Cal. St. U. (Fullerton)
Cal. St. U. (Long Beach)
Cal. St. U. (L.A.)
Cal. St. U. (Northridge)
Cal. St. U. (Sacramento)
U. Cal. (Berkeley)
U. Cal. (Davis)
U. Cal. (Irvine)
U.C.L.A.
U. Cal. (San Diego)
U. Cal. (Santa Barbara)
U. Cal. (Santa Cruz)
Carnegie Mellon U.
Case West. Res. U.
Catholic U.
Cent. Mich. U.
Cent. Mo. St. U.
Cent. Wash. U.
U. Cincinnati
U. Colo.
Columbia U.
U. Conn.
Cornell U.
U. Del.
DePaul U.
East. Mich. U.
Emerson C.
Fla. Atlantic U.
Fla. St. U.
U. Fla.
Geo. Wash. U.
U. Georgia
U. Hawaii
U. Houston
Humboldt St. U.
Hunter C.
  (C.U.N.Y.)
Idaho St. U.
U. Idaho
Ill. St. U.
U. Ill.
U. Ill. (Chicago)
Ind. St. U.
Ind. U.
U. Iowa
Kans St. U.
U. Kans.
Kent St. U.
U. Ky.
U. La. (Monroe)
Lamar U.
L.I.U. (C.W. Post)
L.S.U.
U. Louisville
U. Maine

U. Md.
U. Mass.
U. Memphis
Miami U. (Ohio)
U. Miami (Fla.)
Mich. St. U.
U. Mich.
Minn. St. U. (Mankato)
U. Minn
U. Miss.
U. Mo. (Columbia)
U. Mo. (K.C.)
U. Mont.
Montclair U.
U. Neb.
U. Neb. (Omaha)
U. Nev.
U. N. Mex.
U. N. Orleans
New Sch. U.
C.U.N.Y. (Grad. Ctr.)
S.U.N.Y. (Binghamton)
N.Y.U.
U. No. Car. (Chapel Hill)
U. No. Car. (Greensboro)
No. Dak. St. U.
U. No. Dak.
U. No. Tex.
No. Ill. U.
Northwestern U.
Ohio St. U.
Ohio U.
Okla. City U.
Okla. St. U.
U. Okla.
U. Ore.
Penn. St. U.
Pittsburgh St. U.
U. Pitt.
Portland St. U.
U. Portland
Purdue U.
Regent U.
Rhode Island C.
Roosevelt U.
Rowan U.
Rutgers U.
St. John's U.
S.D.S.U.
U.S.D.
San Fran. St. U.
San Jose St. U.
Sarah Lawrence C.
Smith C.
U. So. Cal.
U. So. Car.
U. So. Dak.
U. So. Fla.
So. Ill. U.
So. Meth. U.
U. So. Miss.
Southwest Mo. St. U.
Southwest Tex. St. U.
Stanford U.
S. F. Austin St. U.
Stony Brook U. (S.U.N.Y.)
Sul Ross St. U.
Syracuse U.
Temple U.
U. Tenn.
Tex. A&M (Commerce)
Tex. Christ. U.
Tex. St. U.
Tex. Tech U.
Tex. Woman's U.
U. Tex. (Austin)
U. Tex. (El Paso)
U. Tex. (Pan American)
Tufts U.
Tulane U.
Utah St. U.
U. Utah
Villanova U.
Va. Commonwealth U.

Va. Poly. Inst.
U. Va.
Wash. St. U.
Wash. U.
U. Wash.
Wayne St. U.
W. Va. U.
West. Ill. U.
West. Wash. U.
U. Wis.
U. Wis. (Milwaukee)
U. Wis. (Superior)
Yale U.

ARTS ADMINSTRATION
U. Akron
American U.
Boston U.
Carnegie Mellon U.
U. Cinn.
Claremont Grad. U.
Drexel U.
East. Mich. U.
Fla. St. U.
Ind. U.
Montclair U.
U. New Orleans
U. No. Car. (Charlotte)
N.Y.U.
Ohio St. U.
U. Ore.
Pratt Inst.
Rhode Island C.
Sch. Art Inst. Chicago
Seton Hall U.
U. So. Cal.
Teachers C. (Columbia)
Temple U.
Va. Poly. Inst.
Webster U.
U. Wis.

DANCE
American U.
Ariz. St. U.
Bennington C.
B.Y.U.
Butler U.
Cal. St. U. (Fullerton)
Cal. St. U. (Long Beach)
U. Cal. (Irvine)
U.C.L.A.
U. Cal. (Riverside)
Case West. Res. U.
U. Cincinnati
U. Colo.
Columbia U. (Teachers C.)
Fla. St. U.
Geo. Mason U.
U. Hawaii
Hunter C. (C.U.N.Y.)
Idaho St. U.
U. Ill.
Ind. U.
U. Iowa
U. Md.
Mills C.
U. Mich.
U. Minn.
U. Neb.
U. Nev.
S.U.N.Y.C. (Brockport)
U. N. Mex.
N.Y.U.
U. No. Car. (Greensboro)
Ohio St. U.
U. Okla.
U. Ore.
Sam Houston St. U.
Sarah Lawrence C.
Smith C.
So. Meth. U.
Temple U.
Tex. Christ. U.

Tex. Woman's U.
U. Tex. (Austin)
Tulane U.
U. Utah
U. Wash.
U. Wis. (Milwaukee)

DANCE THERAPY
Hunter C. (C.U.N.Y.)

MEDIA STUDIES
U. Ala.
American U.
U. Ariz.
Ark. St. U.
Boston U.
U. Buffalo (S.U.N.Y.)
Cal. St. U. (Fullerton)
Carnegie Mellon U.
Cent. Mich. U.
City C. (C.U.N.Y.)
U. Colo.
U. Denver
Fla. St. U.
U. Fla.
Fordham U.
Howard U.
Hunter C. (C.U.N.Y.)
Ind. U.
U. Iowa
Kutztown U. Pa.
L.S.U.
Marquette U.
Marywood U.
U. Md.
M.I.T.
Mich. St. U.
U. Mich.
Ntl. U.
New Sch. U.
Northwestern U.
N.Y.U.
Ohio U.
R.I.T.
S.D.S.U.
San Fran. St. U.
C. Staten Island (C.U.N.Y.)
U. So. Cal.
U. So. Car.
So. Ill. U.
So. Ill. U. (Edwardsville)
Syracuse U.
Temple U.
U. Tenn.
Tex. So. U.
U. Tex. (Austin)
Wash. St. U
Wayne St. U.
Webster U.

MUSIC THEATER
Fla. St. U.
Ind. U.
U. Mich.
N.Y.U.

PLAYWRITING
Catholic U.
N.Y.U.
Temple U.

THEATER MANAGEMENT
Columbia U.
Emerson C.
U. Miami
N.Y.U.
Yale U.

Urban Design/City Planning
(Typically includes Community Planning, City Plan-

ning, Environmental Design, Urban and Regional Planning, Urban Design)

U. Akron
Ala. A&M U.
U. Albany (S.U.N.Y.)
American U.
Ariz. St. U.
U. Ariz.
Auburn U.
Ball St. U.
Boston U.
U. Buffalo (S.U.N.Y.)
Cal. Poly. St. U. (San Luis Obispo)
Cal. St. Poly. U. (Pomona)
Cal. St. U. (Chico)
U. Cal. (Berkeley)
U. Cal. (Davis)
U. Cal. (Irvine)
U.C.L.A.
Catholic U.
U. Cincinnati
Clemson U.
Cleveland St. U.
U. Colo.
Columbia U.
Cornell U.
East. Ky. U.
East. Wash. U.
Fla. Atlantic U.
Fla. St. U.
U. Fla.
Georgia Inst. Tech.
Harvard U.
U. Hawaii
Hunter C. (C.U.N.Y.)
Ill. Inst. Tech.
U. Ill.
U. Ill. (Chicago)
Ind. U.
I.U.P.U.I.
Iowa St. U.
U. Iowa
Jackson St. U.
Kans. St. U.
U. Kansas
U. La. (Lafayette)
U. Louisville
U. Md.
M.I.T.
U. Mass.
U. Memphis
U. Miami
Mich. St. U.
U. Mich.
Minn. St. U. (Mankato)
U. Minn.
Morgan St. U.
U. Neb.
U. N. Mex.
U. N. Orleans
N.Y.U.
U. No. Car. (Chapel Hill)
Northeastern Ill. U.
Ohio St. U.
U. Okla.
Old Dom. U.
U. Ore.
Penn. St. U.
U. Penn.
U. Pitt.
Portland St. U.
Pratt Inst.
Princeton U.
U. Puerto Rico
R.P.I.
Rice U.
Rutgers U.
S.D.S.U.
San Jose St. U.
U. So. Cal.

Temple U.
U. Tenn.
Tex. A&M U.
Tex. So. U.
Tex. Tech U.
U. Tex. (Arlington)
U. Tex. (Austin)
U. Toledo
Utah St. U.
U. Utah
Va. Commonwealth U.
Va. Poly. Inst.
U. Va.
Wash. St. U.

U. Wash.
Wash. U. (Mo.)
Wayne St. U.
West Chester U. Pa.
West. Ky. U.
U. Wis.
U. Wis. (Milwaukee)
U. Wyo.
Yale U.

Veterinary Medicine

Auburn U.
U. Cal. (Davis)

Colo. St. U.
Cornell U.
U. Fla.
U. Georgia
U. Ill.
Iowa St. U.
Kans. St. U.
L.S.U.
U. Md.
Mich. St. U.
U. Minn.
Miss. St. U.
U. Mo. (Columbia)
U. Neb.

No. Car. St. U. (Raleigh)
Ohio St. U.
Okla. St. U.
Ore. St. U.
U. Penn.
Purdue U.
U. Tenn. (Knoxville)
Tex. A&M U.
Tufts U.
Tuskegee U.
Va. Poly. Tech.
Wash. St. U.
U. Wis.